American Place Names of Long Ago

AMERICAN PLACE NAMES *of Long Ago*

A Republication of the Index to Cram's Unrivaled Atlas of the World as Based on the Census of 1890

Assembled, with an Introduction
by

Gilbert S. Bahn, Ph.D.

Excerpted and reprinted from the 1898 edition of
Cram's Unrivaled Atlas of the World
by Genealogical Publishing Co., Inc.
Baltimore, Maryland, 1998

Library of Congress Catalogue Card Number 97-78458
International Standard Book Number 0-8063-1557-1
Made in the United States of America

Table of Contents

States and Territories

Introduction

Urban and suburban development probably has been the greatest cause of the disappearance of American place names of the past from present atlases, road maps, telephone directories, and new census tabulations. There have been other man-made causes also, such as the flooding of land through the creation of reservoirs and lakes. Some deliberate name changes have been made without any attendant changes of landscape. For example, the site of the Long Island village where I attended high school assertively had been named Skunk's Misery before it became the village of Malverne, and one could scarcely be surprised that settlers were unhappy to continue use of the previous name. Truth or Consequences, New Mexico, adopted its name to profit from the publicity deriving from a radio program bearing those words from its title.

Thus there are a variety of reasons why a place name that served its purpose well enough long ago may not be found in a modern finding tool. When one is looking for persons—one's own ancestors or someone else's—the story behind the disappearance of a place name is immaterial. Just finding where on a map that place was, in order to search for records, is the objective. Moreover, as I believe always to be the case in American genealogy, the real test is to place the locality within the correct county where the appropriate records may be expected to reside—if they were indeed created and if they have survived over time.

When I became interested in genealogy, just by chance I possessed (via inheritance) what I consider to be a very valuable finding tool. It is a copy of an atlas published in 1898 by George F. Cram, who had offices in Chicago and New York. The title is *Cram's Unrivaled Atlas of the World.* This volume contains exactly 500 numbered pages, and the final 106 of them comprise a very detailed index, alphabetically by state, "of every county, city, town, village and post-office in the United States, and [it] shows the population of the same according to the Census of 1890." The brief explanation preceding the index states that there "are some small places whose population was taken together with the civil district in which they are located"; for these listings "X" is given in place of a count. This comment surely seems to say that it was the 1890 census that associated the names of these small places with their counties, and this connection makes the extent of the index especially valuable. These places were so small—inevitably, so rural—that the census taker did not find reason to list their counts separately. However, in knowing what particular little areas he was covering as he proceeded, the census taker included the place names on his tabulation pages. There may be no official record anywhere else because such places did not officially exist as separate entities. In using the census of 1850, I found a few examples of such cases even where the counting unit was the township.

It is the disappearance of place names since the end of the nineteenth century that makes present republication of the index of Cram's atlas a worthwhile endeavor. A sample of the index, based on three columns of names, 25 pages apart, showed about 45 percent of the names to bear the "X" instead of a count. Moreover, 35 percent of the places in this sample had counts of less than a hundred persons—one count was only 8, and another only 10. It is no wonder that such tiny localities may have vanished from notice rather than flourished from population influx.

Other than to prepare this Introduction, my effort has been a cut-and-paste procedure on photocopied pages of the index. The original pages have type in an area of about 9 1/2 x 13 inches, with six columns per page. The publisher chose a page size of 5 1/2 x 8 1/2 inches for this republication, with three columns per page and with top and bottom margins of 1/2 inch. This layout meant that only the top portion of the first column could match position, 1998 edition compared to 1898. The bottom portion of the first column, in the 1898 edition, became the top portion of the second column in the 1998 edition. There was no pattern to the cut-and-paste operation, simply an advancement piece by piece so as to fill up three columns with lengths of 7 1/2 inches, then proceed to the next new page, and cut into the next old page as required for more material. Because of this cutting, because the type used by Cram was so small, and also because lines were very closely spaced, tiny bits of letters (and of parentheses in particular) may have been severed when the cutting was made to end one new column and begin another. This work was done as carefully as possible, and probably only a forensic scientist would notice such imperfections; still, I confess that they exist for such an expert to discover.

On the other hand, there was at least one instance where the type was damaged before my copy of Cram's atlas was printed; this broken type made a bad impression for Riverside, Illinois. In some places, printer's ink seems to have smudged. In a few places, population counts are faint or not discernible. Modern photocopiers can do a good job (and they had to) to permit this republication. Although my copy of Cram's atlas had so deteriorated at the binding as to free the individual pages, they could not have been used directly even if they had been printed on only one side (and not needed to be cut up) or even if the republication were to be done full-sized at 9 1/2 x 13 inches plus margins. The original index pages were printed on quite inferior paper resembling the wood pulp paper used presently for newspapers. Over the intervening century this paper became rather badly discolored. The photocopies that I relied on to duplicate the pages for my cut-and-paste operation did quite a fine job of eliminating this darkening. Some of this discoloration may have survived in the white spaces between columns since there was no way to avoid it completely.

Relative to the condition of the original atlas, I feel it pertinent to remark that one is probably very unlikely to find a copy of Cram's atlas even in most libraries that have substantial holdings of antique atlases. Clearly it was rather cheaply produced, and thus copies were unlikely to have survived until finally recognized as worthy of preservation. The atlas was not intended as archival material; it was intended to support popular interest in world geography, with emphasis on that of the United States. There are 72 narrative pages dealing with the United States, and 48 pages dealing with the rest of the world. (When the atlas went to press, Hawaii had not yet been annexed to the United States; it thus occupies the last page preceding the index, at the end of the coverage of the rest of the world.)

Presumably, other atlases produced at about the same time for a scholarly rather than popular clientele have survived to satisfy the needs for someone today who is researching geography as known in 1898 rather than genealogy. However, a few comments must be said in behalf of Mr. Cram. The detail of his maps appears to be as fine as the detail of his index. It is only regarding the matter of material durability—the inferior paper stock being selected to allow for a popular selling price at the time—that his atlas may be deemed somewhat defective. Furthermore, he may have presented the finest representation of the then-current geography of present-day Oklahoma as has ever existed. It was then partly Indian Territory and partly Oklahoma Territory, and the two portions are in their respective alphabetical positions in the index. Likewise, Cram's detailed maps for about 40 United States cities may have vastly excelled their treatment in any competitive work, but that fact has no pertinence to genealogical pursuits.

It needs to be pointed out that only the continental United States is included in Cram's index, with no comparable treatment of the rest of the world. This fact reinforces the presumption that Cram had access to the 1890 census records and did not need to assemble the vast amount of information in the index bit by bit. It is fair to state that the gathering and processing of comparable data on place names and locations for the rest of the world would have been impossible in view of the technological limitations of the period. To do it only for the United States while starting from scratch would have been next to impossible for a commercial endeavor.

In using this republished version of Cram's index to find the county location of an obscure and obsolete place name, one must apply some caution. Very common names may have been used locally at a number of different places in a state; that is, in a number of different counties. For example, there are two Cow Creeks in Kansas and likewise in West Virginia. There are two Smithlands and also two Smiths in Iowa. Now if such similarities are true of the index, traditional genealogical accounts may apply to some other Cow Creek in Kansas or to some other Smithland in Iowa, that did not even get noticed as a minute separate locality by the census taker. As an example, I cite my own unsuccessful effort to locate Black Rock, Vermont. According to a traditional account, there was such a place—a stopover on a migration route for some years. However, I was fortunate to obtain an official modern disclaimer of the recognition of Black Rock as a Vermont place name of the past. Its use must have been very localized and of short duration as well. So might be the case with some Cow Creek, or the like, in a traditional account that one is endeavoring to follow to courthouse records somewhere. The finding of a place name in the index can assure that a place of that name did exist in the county stated, but, even so, it may not be the identical place that one is trying to pin down. Nevertheless, with well over a hundred thousand place names, Cram's index can lead to the correct courthouse in a great many difficult cases.

Reproduced on the following page is the header material that Cram placed at the top of his first index page. The layout first required photocopying the header material in enlarged form, then cutting and pasting each line to fit the present page size. Such pasting will explain the somewhat imperfect appearance insofar as alignment is concerned. Imperfections of type, of course, go back to the original. While this material deals with finding a location on one of Cram's maps—obviously irrelevant here per se—the significance is that the wording makes a point clear: Cram's index letters apply to the state, not to the county. The index leads one only to the county and affords no help as to where within the county was the locality of interest. Without this warning, a user might quite fairly presume that the index letters were intended to fill in for place names left off the maps (making them redundant as to place names appearing on the maps). Not so. The index letters are of no genealogical help; consider them to be extraneous information.

ALPHABETICAL LIST OF TOWNS AND COUNTIES.

The following is an alphabetical list, by states, of every county, city, town, village and post-office in the United States, and shows the population of the same according to the Census of 1890. There are some small places whose population was taken together with the civil district in which they are located, and the exact figure being unknown are marked thus—x. State capitals and large cities are in caps, thus—BOSTON. County towns are in full-faced type, thus—**Buffalo.** Post-offices are in Roman, thus—Hinsdale. Places not post-offices are in italic thus—*Ashby*. Express offices are indicated thus—•. The index letters refer to that portion of the state in which the several counties are located, as follows:— C................Central.

N...............Northern	E.................Eastern
S................Southern	W ....Western
N. E........North-Eastern	N. W.......North-Western
S. E.........South-Eastern	S. W........South-Western

To find any place, first find the county in which it is situated, using the index letters to ascertain its location. The county name being large is quickly seen, and the town will be readily found within its boundaries if on the map. Many small places have been left off the maps owing to lack of space to engrave them, but they will all be found in this list, and their locations can be readily determined by means of the index letters.

ALABAMA.

COUNTIES.	INDEX.	POP.
Autauga	C	13,330
Baldwin	SW	8,941
Barbour	SE	34,898
Bibb	C	13,824
Blount	N	21,927
Bullock	SE	27,063
Butler	S	21,641
Calhoun	NE	33,835
Chambers	E	26,319
Cherokee	NE	20,459
Chilton	C	14,549
Choctaw	SW	17,526
Clarke	SW	22,624
Clay	E	15,765
Cleburne	NE	13,218
Coffee	SE	12,170
Colbert	NW	20,189
Conecuh	S	14,594
Coosa	C	15,906
Covington	S	7,536
Crenshaw	S	15,425
Cullman	N	13,439
Dale	SE	17,225
Dallas	S	49,350
De Kalb	NE	21,106
Elmore	C	21,732
Escambia	S	8,666
Etowah	N	21,926
Fayette	NW	12,823
Franklin	NW	10,681
Geneva	SE	10,690
Greene	W	22,0 7
Hale	W	27,501
Henry	SE	24,847
Jackson	NE	28,026
Jefferson	C	88,501
Lamar	NW	14,187
Lauderdale	NW	23,739
Lawrence	NW	20,725
Lee	E	28,694
Limestone	N	21,201
Lowndes	S	31,550
Macon	E	18,439
Madison	N	38,119
Marengo	SW	33,095
Marion	NW	11,347
Marshall	N	18,935
Mobile	SW	51,587
Monroe	SW	18,990
Montgomery	SE	56,172
Morgan	N	24,089
Perry	C	29,332
Pickens	W	22,470
Pike	SE	24,423
Randolph	E	17,219
Russell	E	24,093
Saint Clair	N	17,353
Shelby	C	20,886
Sumter	W	29,574
Talladega	C	29,346
Tallapoosa	E	25,460
Tuscaloosa	W	30,352
Walker	NW	16,078
Washington	SW	7,935
Wilcox	S	30,816
Winston	NW	6,552
Total		1,513,017

TOWN. COUNTY.	INDEX.	POP.
Abbeville, Henry	SE	465
Abbott, Conecuh	S	×
Abel, Cleburne	NE	×
Abercrombie, Bibb	C	×
Abercrombie, Russell	E	×
Aberfoil, Bullock	SE	300
● *Abernant*, Tuscaloosa	W	×
Abernathy, Cleburne	NE	50
Abner, Clay	E	×
Achates, Talladega	C	×
Activity, Monroe	SW	×
● Ada, Montgomery	SE	300
Adams, Dallas	S	×
● Adamsville, Jefferson	C	×
Addison, Winston	NW	50
Adella, Calhoun	NE	×
Addville, Jefferson	C	×
● Adger, Jefferson	C	1,000
Adler, Perry	C	×
Adville, Blount	N	×
Aetna, Geneva	SE	×
Affonee, Bibb	C	10
Afton, Barbour	SE	×
Agricola, Tallapoosa	E	×
Al, Cleburne	NE	×
Aiken, Crenshaw	S	×
Aimwell, Marengo	SW	×
Air, Morgan	N	×
● Akron Junction, Hale	W	250
● *Alabama Rolling Mill*, Jefferson	C	×
Alamuchee, Sumter	W	×
Alanthus, Franklin	NW	×
● Alberta Station, Wilcox	S	×
Alberton, Coffee	SE	×
● Albertville, Marshall	N	200
Alco, Escambia	S	249
● Aldrich, Shelby	C	×
● Alexander City, Tallap'sa.	E	679
● Alexandria, Calhoun	NE	125
Alexis, Cherokee	NE	100
● *Alfretta*, Jefferson	C	×
Alfrede, Fayette	NW	×
● *Alfred's*, Pike	SE	×
● Alice, Jefferson	C	25
● *Allen*, DeKalb	NE	×
Allen's Factory, Marion	NW	×
● Allenton, Wilcox	S	200
Allhill, Marion	NW	×
Alliance, Macon	E	×
Allsborough, Colbert	NW	50
Allsup, Calhoun	NE	×
Allula, St. Clair	N	×
Alma, Clarke	SW	×
Almond, Randolph	E	30
Alonzo, Winston	NW	×
● Alpine, Talladega	C	75
● *Alta*, Fayette	NW	×
Alto, Jackson	NE	×
● *Alva*, Pike	SE	×
Amacus, Geneva	SE	×
Amber, Monroe	SW	×
Amberson's, Cherokee	NE	×
Ambrose, Montgomery	SE	×
Amity, Jefferson	C	×
Amos, Winston	NW	×
● **Andalusia**, Covington	S	270
Anderson Creek, L'dale	NW	20
Andersonville, Monroe	SW	×
Anderton, Blount	N	×
Andrews Inst., DeKalb	NE	×
● *Anita*, Bibb	C	×
Annette, Baldwin	SW	×
● Anniston, Calhoun	NE	9,998
Anro, Lamar	NW	50
Ansley, Pike	SE	×
Antioch, Pickens	W	×
Apple Grove, Morgan	N	50
Aquilla, Choctaw	SW	30
Arab, Marshall	N	50
Ararat, Choctaw	SW	×
Arbacoochee, Cleburne	NE	×
Arcola, Lamar	NW	50
Andrews' Chapel, Russell	E	×
● Argo, Jefferson	C	25
Ardell, Walker	NW	×
Argus, Crenshaw	S	×
Arguta, Dale	SE	×
● Ariosto, Dale	SE	×
Ark, Winston	NW	×
Arkadelphia, Blount	N	150
● Arlington, Wilcox	S	250
Arnold, Wilcox	S	×
Aroney, DeKalb	NE	×
Arthur, Lauderdale	NW	×
Asbury, Dale	SE	×
Ashby, Bibb	C	50
Ashford, Henry	SE	×
Ashland, Clay	E	635
Ashville, St. Clair	N	300
Aster, Limestone	N	×
● **Athens**, Limestone	N	940
● Atkeison, Clarke	SW	×
Atlas, Lauderdale	NW	×
● Attalla, Etowah	N	1,254
● Auburn, Lee	E	1,440
● *Auburn Station*, Lee	E	×
Augustin, Perry	C	×
Aurora, Etowah	N	50
Autaugaville, Autauga	C	200
Avoca, Lawrence	NW	25
● Avondale, Jefferson	C	1,642
Avrey, Etowah	N	×
Awin, Wilcox	S	×
Axle, Monroe	SW	×
Aycock, Chambers	E	×
Ayres, Jefferson	C	×
Ayrshire, Clay	E	×
Baggett, Wilcox	S	×
Bailey Springs, L'dale	NW	25
Baileyton, Cullman	N	100
Baker, Henry	SE	×
● *Baldwin*, Autauga	SW	×
Balkum, Henry	SE	×
Ballard, Fayette	NW	×
Ball Flat, Cherokee	NE	×
Ball Play, Etowah	N	×
Balm, Blount	N	×
Bamford, Shelby	C	×
Bana, Tallapoosa	E	×
● Bangor, Blount	N	50
Bankhead, DeKalb	NE	×
● Banks, Pike	SE	×
● Bankston, Fayette	NW	100
Barber, Chambers	E	×
● Barachias, Montgomery	SE	×
● *Barclay*, Talladega	C	×
Barlow Bend, Clarke	SW	×
● *Barnes' Cross Rd's*, Dale	SE	200
Barnesville, Marion	NW	×
Barr's Mill, Pike	SE	×
Bartlett, Marshall	N	×
● Barton, Colbert	NW	75
Bartonville, Walker	NW	×
Basham's Gap, Morgan	N	50
Bashi, Clarke	SW	100
● Bass Station, Jackson	NE	31
● Batesville, Barbour	SE	100
Battle Ground, Cullman	N	×
Battles, Baldwin	SW	400
● *Baugh's*, Jefferson	C	×
Baxter, Lamar	NW	×
● Baylor, Jefferson	C	×
● Bay Minette, Baldwin	SW	200
Bayou Labatre, Mobile	SW	×
● *Bayou Sara*, Mobile	SW	×
Beach Grove, Walker	NW	×
Bean Rock, Marshall	N	×
Bean's Gap, Cleburne	NE	×
● Bear Creek, Marion	NW	25
Beard, Pickens	W	×
Beason's Mill, Cleburne	NE	×
Beaver Creek, Dale	SE	600
● Beaver Meadow, Mobile	SW	130
● Beaverton, Lamar	NW	×
Beaver Valley, St. Clair	N	×
Beda, Covington	S	×
Bedford, Lamar	NW	×
Bedsole, Clarke	SW	12
Beecham, Cleburne	NE	×
Beechboro, Jackson	NE	×
Beeson, Colbert	NW	25
● Behrman, Clarke	SW	×
Belcher, Barbour	SE	×
Belew, Lauderdale	NW	×
Bel Green, Franklin	NW	300
Belknap, Dallas	S	×
Bell, Madison	N	8
Bellefonte, Jackson	NE	100
● Belle Mina, Limestone	N	75
Belle Sumter, Jefferson	C	×
Belleville, Conecuh	S	250
Bellevue, Dallas	S	25
● Bell Factory, Madison	N	100
Bell's Landing, Monroe	SW	200
Bell's Mills, Cleburne	NE	75
Belltown, Cleburne	NE	×
Belmont, Sumter	W	75
Benevola, Pickens	W	×
Benson, Chilton	C	50
Bennettsville, Etowah	N	25
Bentleyville, Coosa	C	×
● Benton, Lowndes	S	265
Bera, Calhoun	NE	×
Bergamot, Choctaw	SW	×
Berkley, Madison	N	25
● Berlin, Dallas	S	×
Berly, Lamar	NW	×
Bermuda, Conecuh	S	×
Berneys, Talladega	C	×
Berry's Store, Jackson	NE	×
● Berry Station, Fayette	NW	200
Bertha, Dale	SE	×
● Bessemer, Jefferson	C	4,544
Bessie Mines, Jefferson	C	×
Best, Crenshaw	S	×
Bethany, Pickens	W	50
Bethel, Wilcox	S	18
Bethlehem, Perry	C	×
Betts, Conecuh	S	×
Beulah, Lee	E	100
Bevill's Store, Choctaw	SW	60
Bexar, Marion	NW	200
● Bibbville, Bibb	C	100
Bienville, Mobile	SW	×
Bigbee, Washington	SW	×

Big Creek, Geneva.........SE 25
● *Big Springs*, Bibb........C ×
Bilbhead, Pickens.........W ×
Biler, Winston..........NW ×
Billingsley, Autauga........C ×
Bingham, Elmore............C ×
Binion's Creek, Tuscaloosa. W 50
Bird, Blount...............N ×
● *Birmile*, Wilcox......... S ×
● **BIRMINGHAM**, Jefferson..........C 26,178
● *Birmingham Junc.*, Sh'by. C ×
Bishop, Colbert...........NW 30
● *Biven*, Jefferson........ C ×
Blackburn, Limestone......N ×
Black Creek Falls, Etowah. N ×
Blackman, Chambers.........E ×
Black Oak, DeKalb....... NE 10
Blacksher, Baldwin ......SW ×
Blacks Bluff, Wilcox........S 200
Black's Store, Clay ....E ×
Blackwell, Madison ....N ×
Bladen Springs, Choctaw .SW 440
Blaine, Cherokee ....NE ×
Blake, DeKalb............NE ×
Blake's Ferry, Randolph...E 40
Blands, Dallas ....S ×
Bledsoe, Talladega.......... C ×
● Blocton, Bibb ....C 3,500
● *Blocton Junction*, Bibb...C ×
Bloomfield, Madison.........N 25
Bloomington, Jackson....NE ×
Blossburg, Jefferson ....C 692
● Blount Springs, Blount...N 300
Blountsville, Blount....N 288
Blowhorn, Lamar........ NW ×
Blue, Bullock ....SE ×
● *Blue Creek Junction*, Jeff. C ×
● *Blue Pond*, Cherokee....NE ×
Blue Rock, Marshall........N 50
Blue Spring, Morgan ....N ×
Bluff City, Morgan ....N ×
Bluff Spring, Clay...........E 100
Bluffton, Cherokee ...... .NE ×
Boaz, Marshall...............N 40
Bob, Pike ....SE ×
Boen, Marshall.............N ×
Bogue, Dallas ....S ×
● Boguechitto, Dallas..........S ×
Boiling Springs, Wilcox ....S 600
● Boligee, Greene..........W 300
● Boliver, Jackson........NE 33
● Bolling, Butler ....S 150
Bomar, Cherokee..........NE ×
Bonnette, Conecuh........... S ×
Bon Secour, Baldwin .....SW ×
Boom, Tuscaloosa..........W ×
● *Boothton*, Bibb ....C ×
Booth Town, Shelby ....C ×
Borden Springs, Cleburne NE ×
Bosenberg, Cullman..........N ×
Bosworth, Chambers ... .E ×
● *Bowens*, Cherokee......NE ×
Bowles, Conecuh............S ×
Box, Shelby .... C ×
Boyd, Barbour ....SE ×
Boyd, Walker............NW ×
● *Boyd's Tank*, Chambers..E ×
Boykin, Escambia...........S ×
● *Boyles*, Jefferson ....C 25
Bozeman, Autauga...........C 346
Brackin, Henry............SE 50
Bradford, Coosa ....C 30
● *Bradford*, Jefferson ......C ×
● Bradleyton, Crenshaw....S ×
Bragg's, Lowndes ....S 100
● *Brake's*, Jefferson ....C ×
Branchville, St. Clair ....N 150
● Brandon, DeKalb.......NE 50
Brannen, Coffee ....SE ×
Brantley, Crenshaw.........S ×
Braze, Conecuh ....S ×
Bremen, Cullman ....N 200
● **Brewton**, Escambia.....S 1,115
Brice, Etowah ....N ×
Brick, Lawrence ....NW 10
● *Brick Yard*, Dallas.........S ×
● *Brickyard Junc.*, JeffersonC ×
● Bridgeport, Jackson....NE 500
Bridgeport, Wilcox..........S 40
● Bridges, Dallas...........S 50
Bridgeton, Shelby...........C ×
Bridgeville, Pickens ....W ×
● Brierfield, Bibb ....C 1,000
Bright, Cullman ....N ×
Brightstar, Blount.........N ×
Briscoe, Morgan............N ×

● Brock's Gap, Jefferson....C 200
● *Broken Arrow*, St. Clair..N ×
Bromley, Baldwin ....SW ×
● Brompton, St. Clair ......N 25
Brooklyn, Conecuh..........S 100
● Brookside, Jefferson.......C 580
Brook's Store, Limestone...N 8
Brooksville, Blount ....N 100
Brookwood, Tuscaloosa .... W 200
Broomtown, Cherokee....NE ×
● Brown's, Dallas .... S 150
● Brownsborough, Madison. N 50
Brown's Creek, Winston. NW ×
Brownsville, Clay..........E 15
Bruceville, Bullock........SE 25
● Brundidge, Pike ....SE 350
Bruner, Calhoun ....NE 50
Brush Creek, Perry ....C 50
● Bryan Station, Jefferson..C ×
Bryant, Jackson .... NE ×
Buckeye, Clay .... E ×
Buck Horn, Pike ....SE ×
Buck Snort, Fayette......NW ×
Buena Vista, Monroe .....SW 100
● Buffalo, Chambers........E 100
Buford, Etowah. ....N ×
Bughall, Bullock ....SE ×
Bugville, Dallas .... S ×
Bulger's Mills, Tallapoosa...E 250
● *Bullard Shoals*, Jefferson.C ×
Bull Mountain, Marion..NW ×
Bullock, Crenshaw..........S 300
Burcham Mills, LauderdaleNW ×
Burkard, Cullman...........N ×
● Burkville, Lowndes.......S 300
Burleson, Franklin.......NW 75
● Burnsville, Dallas .... S 100
Burnt Corn, Monroe....... SW 50
Burton's Hill, Greene......W 50
Bush, Barbour.............SE ×
Butler, Choctaw ....SW 275
Butlers Mill, Montgomery. SE 25
Butler Springs, Butler ......S 100
Buttston, Tallapoosa........E ×
Buyck, Elmore...............C 50
Byars, Pickens .... W ×
● Bynum, Calhoun........NE ×
● *Cadle*, Bibb .... C ×
Cahaba, Dallas ....S 400
● Caldwell, St. Clair ....N 25
Caledonia, Wilcox...........S ×
● Calera, Shelby............C 753
● Calhoun, Lowndes........ S 100
Calhoun's Store, Bullock..SE ×
Callahan, Jackson ....NE ×
● *Calumet*, Walker.......NW ×
● Calvert, Washington....SW ×
Cambridge, Randolph.......E ×
Cambridge, Dallas ....S ×
Camden, Wilcox ....S 545
Campbell, Clarke ....SW ×
● Camp Hill, Tallapoosa ....E 866
Camp's Mills, Marion.....NW ×
Camp Smith, Colbert.....NW ×
Camp Spring, Lawrence. NW ×
Canaan, Lamar...........NW ×
Cane, Fayette ....NW ×
Cane Creek, Calhoun.......NE ×
● Canoe Station, Escambia..S ×
Canterbery, St. Clair.......N ×
Canton Bend, Wilcox........S 25
● Carbon Hill, Walker.....NW 568
● Cardiff, Jefferson ....NE 203
Cardin, Jackson......... NW ×
Carl, Cullman ....N ×
Carlisle, Monroe ....SW ×
Carlowville Dallas ....S 130
● *Carl's Station*, Sumter.. W ×
Carmichael, Madison ....N ×
● Carney, Baldwin.........SW 100
Carney's Bluff, Clarke....SW ×
Caro, Limestone............N ×
● *Carpenter*, Jackson .... NE ×
Carriger, Limestone ....N 5
Carrollton, Pickens.....W 450
● Carson, Washington ....SW ×
● Carthage, Hale..........W 200
Cartwright, Limestone .....N 6
● Castleberry, Conecuh .....S 100
Catalpa, Pike.............SE ×
● Catherine, Wilcox ....S ×
● *Catoctin*, Jefferson........C ×
● *Catoma*, Montgomery...SE ×
Caudle, Bibb...............C ×
Cave Spring, Fayette.....NW ×
● Cedar Bluff, Cherokee..NE 194
Cedar Crossing, Morgan ....N 30

Cedar Plains, Morgan ...... N 100
Cedar Ridge, Marshall......N ×
Cedar Springs, Cherokee..NE ×
Cedarville, Hale ....W 50
Center Point, Montgomery.SE ×
Central, Elmore............C 50
Central Mills, Dallas ....S 10
Centre, Cherokee........NE 847
Centre Hill, Limestone......N 18
Centre Line, Franklin....NW ×
Centre Ridge, Pike........SE ×
Centre Spring, Walker..NW ×
Centre Star, Lauderdale..NW 50
● **Centreville**, Bibb...... C 239
Chadwick, Perry...... .....C 75
Chalk Bluff, Marion......NW ×
Chalkville, Jefferson........C ×
Chambers, Montgomery...SE ×
● *Chamblee*, Tuscaloosa .... W ×
Chance, Cherokee........ NE ×
● Champion, Blount.........N ×
Chandler Sp'gs, Talladega...C ×
Channahatchee, Elmore ....C ×
Chapel Hill, Chambers......E ×
Chapman, Butler .... S ×
● *Chappell's Sp'gs*, Etowah. N ×
Charlton, Dale.............SE ×
● Chastang, Mobile ....SW ×
Chavies, DeKalb ....NE ×
Cheatwood, Cleburne .....NE ×
● *Chehaw*, Macon.......... E ×
● Chepultepec, Blount.......N 300
● Cherokee, Colbert......NW 400
Cherry, Clarke............SW ×
● Chesterfield, Cherokee..NE ×
Chestnut, Monroe.........SW ×
Chewacla, Lee...............E 25
Chickasaw, Walker ......NW ×
Chickasabogue, Mobile..... S ×
● Childersburgh, Talladega..C 777
Chilton, Chilton.............C ×
China Grove, Pike .... SE 200
● Choccolocco, Calhoun...NE 601
Choctaw Corner. Clarke...SW 200
Choctawhatchee, Henry.....SE ×
Christiana, Randolph ....E ×
● *Christine*, Covington......S ×
Chub Hill, Franklin.........NW 15
Chulafinnee, Cleburne.... NE 100
Chumley, DeKalb..........NE 10
● Chunchula, Mobile......SW 258
Church Hill, Tallapoosa .... W ×
Churubusco, Franklin... NW ×
Cicero, Cleburne ....NE ×
● Citronelle, Mobile.......SW 500
Claiborne, Monroe ....SW 700
● **Clanton**, Chilton........C 623
Clarence, Blount ....N ×
Clark's Mill, Autauga.......C ×
Clarkson, Cullman... ....N ×
Clay, Jefferson..............C 100
Clayhatchee, Dale..........SE ×
Clay Hill, Marengo.........SW ×
● *Clay's*, Autauga ....C ×
Claysville, Madison.........N ×
● **Clayton**, Barbour......SE 997
● Clear Creek, Chilton......C ×
Clear Spring, Etowah.......N ×
● Clement's Depot, Tus'sa.. W ×
Cleveland, Blount...........N 100
● *Cleveland*, Mobile.......SW ×
● *Clietts*, Macon ....E 50
Clifton, Wilcox ....S 150
Clifty, Cullman..............N ×
Clinton, Greene ....W 250
Clintonville, Coffee ....SE 75
● Clio, Barbour............SE 100
Clopton, Dale..............SE 100
● *Clough's Store*, Macon....E 20
Cloverdale, Lauderdale...NW ×
Cluttsville, Madison.........N 50
● Coalburgh, Jefferson......C 842
● Coal City, St. Clair........N 150
Coaldale, Jefferson..........C ×
Coal Fire, Pickens ....W ×
● Coaling, Tuscaloosa......W 200
Coal Valley Walker......NW ×
Coalville Shelby ....C ×
● Coatopa, Sumter ....W 75
Coats Bend, Etowah ....N 40
Cobb, Shelby...............C ×
● *Cobbville*, Clarke........SW ×
● Cochran, Barbour........SE 20
Coden, Mobile ....SW ×
Cody, Lamar ....NW ×
Coffee Springs, Geneva ....SE ×
Coffeeville, Clarke ....SW 100

Coffey's Store, Jackson....NE 8
Cohasset, Conecuh..........S ×
Cohort, Crenshaw..........S ×
Coker, Tuscaloosa..........W ×
Cokerville, Monroe........SW ×
● *Cold Creek*, Mobile.....SW ×
Cold Water, Cleburne.....NE ×
● *Coldwater*, Calhoun.... NE ×
Cole, Lawrence...........NW ×
Colefield, Walker.........NW ×
Coleman, Crenshaw..........S 75
Coleman's, Elmore..........C 75
Coleridge, Barbour........SE 100
Cole's Mill, Clay..........E ×
Coleta, Clay..................E ×
● *Collbran*, DeKalb.......NE 50
Colley, Elmore..............C 25
Collier, Marshall............N ×
● *Collins*, Jefferson.........C ×
● Collinsville, De Kalb....NE 367
Collirene, Lowndes..........S 100
Coloma, Cherokee..........NE ×
Colquitt, Montgomery.....SE ×
● Columbia, Henry........SE 960
● **Columbiana**, Shelby...C 654
● *Colvin*, Jefferson..........C ×
Colvin's Gap, Calhoun.....NE ×
Comer, Lauderdale.......NW ×
Commerce, Conecuh.........S ×
Como City, Jefferson........C ×
● Compton, Blount..........N ×
Concord, Lawrence.........NW ×
Concrete, Tallapoosa........E ×
Conde, Clarke.............SW ×
Conecuh River, Covington..S ×
● *Connellsville Junc*, Jeffer.C ×
Connellsville Mines, Jeffer..C ×
Conway, Lamar.... ......NW ×
● *Cook*, Talladega...........C ×
Cook's Springs, St. Clair....N 20
Cook's Stand, Crenshaw.....S ×
● **Cooper, Chilton**........C 600
● Coosada Station, Elmore..C 36
Coosa River, Elmore ....C ×
Coosa Valley, St. Clair......N 10
Coppensaw, Choctaw......SW ×
Copper Mines, Clay ....E ×
● Cordell, DeKalb..........NE 25
● Cordova, Walker.......NW 100
Cormick, Walker.........NW ×
● Cornelia, St. Clair........N 125
Corn House, Randolph........E ×
● Corona, Walker........NW 400
Cosby's Gap, St. Clair.......N ×
Cotaco, Morgan..............N ×
Cotnam, DeKalb..........NE ×
Cottage Hill, St. Clair.......N ×
Cottle's Mill, Covington.....S ×
● Cottondale, Tuscaloosa...W ×
Cottongin, Bibb..............C ×
Cotton Hill, Barbour......SE ×
Cotton's Store, Elmore......C 25
Cotton Valley, Macon.......E 100
Cottonville, Marshall.......N 25
Cottonwood, Henry........SE ×
Country, Blount............. N ×
County Line, Pike ....SE ×
● Courtland, Lawrence...NW 579
● *Cove Creek*, Etowah......N ×
● *Covin*, Fayette.........NW ×
Covington, Lauderdale...NW ×
Cowarts, Henry..........SE ×
Cowikee, Barbour......... SE 100
● Cowles' Station, Macon...E ×
Cowpens, Tallapoosa........E 60
● Cox, Mobile.............SW ×
● *Cox's*, Cherokee.........NE ×
Cox's Mill, Barbour........SE ×
Coy, Wilcox..................S ×
Craige, Blount...............N ×
Crane Hill, Cullman.........N ×
Crawford, Russell............E 50
● *Crawford*, Dallas..........S ×
Creek Stand, Macon..........E ×
Crenshaw, Dallas.............S ×
● Creola, Mobile..........SW ×
● Creswell Station, Shelby..C ×
Crete, Conecuh...............S ×
● Crew's Depot, Lamar...NW 175
Crewsville, Coosa...........C ×
Crittenden's Mills, Dale...SE ×
Crooked Creek, Cullman...N ×
● Cropwell, St. Clair........N 125
Crosby, Henry.............SE ×
Cross Keys, Macon..........E ×
Cross Trails, Coffee ....SE ×
Crossville, DeKalb.......NE 40

Crowton, Morgan...........N 20
Crudup, Etowah............N ×
Cruess, Perry ....C ×
Crump, Tuscaloosa.........W ×
Crumptonia, Dallas..........S ×
Crystal Lake, St. Clair......N ×
● Cuba Station, Sumter....W 300
● **Cullman**, Cullman.....N 1,017
Culpepper, Wilcox...........S ×
Cunningham, Clarke......SW ×
● *Cunningham*, Jefferson..C ×
Cureton's Bridge, Henry...SE ×
● Curl's Station, Sumter...W 50
Curry, Pike.................SE ×
● *Curry's*, Talladega........C ×
Curtis, Coffee...............SE ×
Cushing, Marshall..........N ×
● Cusseta, Chambers........E 250
● *Cypress*, Lauderdale...NW ×
Cyprian, Talladega...........C ×
● **Dadeville**, Tallapoosa. W 873
● *Dago*, Jefferson............C ×
● *Dahinda*, Jefferson.......C ×
Dailey, Franklin.........NW ×
Dailey's, Calhoun.........NE ×
● *Dailey's*, Cleburne......NE ×
Daisy, Butler..................S ×
Daleville, Dale............. SE 50
● *Daley's*, Bibb.............C ×
● Dallaston, Dallas...........S ×
Damascus, Coffee..........SE ×
Dan, Madison................N 10
Dannelly, Covington........S ×
Danville, Morgan............N 250
Daphne, Baldwin.........SE 549
Darlington, Marion.......NW 100
● *Darlington*, Franklin..NW 75
Data, Bibb....................C ×
Daugherty, Jackson.......NE ×
● *Davis*, Shelby.............C ×
Davenport, Montgomery..SE 50
● *Davis*, Shelby..............C ×
Davis Bluff, Clarke.......SW ×
Davis Creek, Fayette.....NW 500
Davis Cross Roads, Cher..NE 25
Daviston, Tallapoosa........E 141
Dawkins, Macon..............E ×
Dawson, DeKalb..........NE 25
Dawsons, Wilcox............S ×
● Day's Gap, Walker.....NW 421
Dayton, Marengo.........SW 412
Dead Level, Clarke ....SW 100
Dean, Clay ....E ×
● DeArmanville, Calhoun.NE 150
● Deatsville, Elmore ....C 100
DeBerniere, Jefferson.......C ×
● Decatur, Morgan ....N 2,765
● *Decatur Junction*, Lime's.N ×
● Deer Park, Washington.SW 125
● *Deer Range*, Conecuh.....S ×
Delcon, Pike...............SE ×
● Delmar, Winston ...... NW 200
Delta, Clay...................E 100
● Demopolis, Marengo....SW 1,898
Dennard, Monroe ....SW ×
Denton, Colbert..........NW ×
Denver, Tallapoosa ....E ×
● Deposit, Madison ....N 15
● *Dermid*, Montgomery ...SE ×
Desco Limestone .... N ×
DeSotoville, Choctaw .....SW 100
Detroit, Lamar ....NW 100
Devenport, Montgomery ..SE ×
Devonia, Geneva ....SE ×
Dexter, Elmore ....C ×
Diamond, Marshall ....N ×
● Dickinson, Clarke...... SW ×
● Dick's Creek, Macon.......E 25
● Dickson, Colbert ....NW 125
● *Dillards*, Dale..............SE ×
Dillburgh, Pickens.........W ×
Dingler, Randolph..........E ×
Dismal, Winston ....NW ×
● Dixie, Chilton .... C 150
Dixon's Mills, Marengo ...SW 300
Dodsonville, Jackson......NE 33
● Dogwood, Shelby ....C ×
Dollar, Coosa.................C ×
Dolomite, Jefferson.......... C ×
Doran's Cove, Jackson... NE ×
Dot, Coffee.................SE ×
● Dothen, Henry...........SE 247
Doublehead, Chambers......E 200
Double Springs, Wins NW 300
Douglasville, Escambia......S 150
Dove, Sumter............. W 75
Dover, Blount ....N ×

Downing, Escambia ....S ×
Dowly, Baldwin............SW ×
Dozier, Crenshaw ....S ×
Dreher, Cullman ....N ×
Driggers Mills, Barbour.. SE ×
Driver, Chambers...........E ×
Dry Cove, Jackson.........NE ×
Dry Creek, Fayette.......NW ×
Dublin, Fayette ....NW ×
● *Dubois*, Blount............N ×
Duck Springs, Etowah......N 30
● *Dudley*, Tuscaloosa ......W ×
Dudleyville, Tallapoosa .....E 50
Dug, Colbert..............NW 25
● Duke, Calhoun..........NE ×
Duke, Monroe ....SW ×
Duke's Switch, Chilton......C ×
● *Dunavan*, Shelby..........C ×
Dundee, Geneva...........SE ×
● *Duncan*, Jefferson........C ×
● Dunham, Butler ....S 200
Dunlap, Baldwin..........SW ×
Durrow, Pickens ....W ×
Dutton, Jackson ....NE ×
● *Dyas Creek*, Baldwin... SW 100
Eagle, Walker ....NW ×
Eagle Mills, Fayette.....NW ×
Earlton, Butler ....S ×
Earnest, Jefferson .... C ×
● *Earp*, Dallas ....S ×
Easonville, St. Clair.........N 100
Easta Boga, Talladega ...... C 150
● *Easta Boga*, Calhoun...NE ×
● *East and West Junction*, Calhoun .... NE ×
East Bend, Talladega........C ×
East Birmingham, Jeff'n...C 308
Eastep, Lauderdale ....NW ×
East Gadsden, Etowah.......N ×
East Lake, Jefferson........ C 1,500
Easton, Tallapoosa ....E ×
Eatonton, Franklin...... NW ×
Echo, Dale .... SE 200
Eclectic, Elmore ....C 100
● Eden, St. Clair.............N 200
Edgewood, Elmore..........C ×
Edgil, Walker ....NW ×
Edith, Perry ....C ×
Edmond, Lawrence ......NW ×
Edna, Cherokee............NE ×
● *Edwards Furnace*, Bibb..C ×
● **Edwardsville**, Cleb..NE 446
Ego, Cherokee ....NE ×
Ehren, Pickens.............W ×
● Elamville, Barbour......SE 20
● **Elba**, Coffee ....SE 285
● Eldridge, Walker ......NW ×
● Eleanor, Dallas..............S ×
● *Elgin*, Tuscaloosa........W ×
Elias, Clay ....E ×
Elizabeth, Coffee.............E ×
Elizabeth, Dallas..............S 60
Elk, Winston ....NW ×
● Elkmont, Limestone......N 238
Elk River Mills, Limestone..N ×
Ella, Butler ....S ×
Ellaville, Winston..........NW ×
● Elliott, Jefferson............C ×
Ellison, Marengo............SW ×
● Elmore, Elmore.............C 100
Elora, Jackson.............NE ×
Elton, Geneva.............SE 75
Ely, Hale .... W ×
● *Elyton*, Jefferson.........C 750
Emmitton, DeKalb.........NE ×
Emory, Choctaw...........SW ×
Emuckfaw, Tallapoosa .....E ×
Energy, Chilton ....C ×
● *Englewood*, Tuscaloosa..W ×
Enitachopco, Clay...........E ×
Enoch, Choctaw...........SW ×
Enon, Bullock ....SE 150
● Ensley, Jefferson............C 1,000
● *Ensley Furnaces*, Jeffer'n C ×
Enterprise, Coffee ....SE ×
● Epes Station, Sumter..... W 200
Equality, Coosa..............C 75
Erwin, Fayette...........NW ×
Escanaba Forks, Conecuh..S ×
● *Escambia Junc.*, Esc'bia..S ×
● Escatawpa, Wash'ton. ..SW 150
Estaville, Limestone ....N 10
Estill's Fork, Jackson.....NE 31
Etha, Cullman ....N 25
Etowahton, Etowah ....N ×
● Eufaula, Barbour.........SE 4,394
Eulaton, Calhoun ....NE ×
Eunola, Geneva.............SE ×

Eureka, Talladega..........C	×
Eustis, Clarke..............SW	×
● **Eutaw**, Greene.........W	1,115
Eva, Morgan.................N	×
● Evans, Hale...............W	×
● **Evergreen**, Conecuh...S	1,783
Ewell, Dale.................SE	×
Exie, Cherokee............NE	×
Ezellville, Pickens.........W	×
Ezra, Jefferson.............C	×
Ezzell, Franklin..........NW	×
Fabius, Jackson...........NE	34
● Fackler, Jackson.......NE	60
Fadette, Geneva...........SE	×
Fail, Choctaw.............SW	×
Fairfield, Covington.........S	400
Fairford, Washington ....SW	×
Fairoaks, Conecuh.........S	×
● Fairview, St. Clair........N	250
● Falkville, Morgan.........N	300
Fannie, Escambia...........S	×
● Farill, Cherokee.........NE	25
Farmer, Shelby C	×
Farmersville, Lowndes......S	75
Fatama, Wilcox.............S	×
● Faunsdale, Marengo....SW	211
● **Fayette, C. H.**, Fayette NW	900
Fayetteville, Talladega......C	300
● *Fearns*, Madison.........N	×
Felix, Perry.................C	50
Fenton, Etowah.............N	×
Ferguson, Washington ...SW	×
● **Fernbank, Lamar**......NW	150
Ferncliff, Jackson ....NE	10
● *Fernland*, Mobile ......SW	×
Finchburgh, Monroe......SW	×
Finley, Chambers...........E	×
Firestone, Cherokee......NE	×
Fish Pond, Tallapoosa ......E	×
Fish River, Mobile........SW	×
Fisk, Madison...............N	6
● Fitzpatrick's, Bullock...SE	357
Five Mile, Hale ....W	×
● Five Points, Chambers...E	×
Flat Rock, Clay..............E	×
Fleaming, Geneva.........SE	×
Fleetwood, Pike...........SE	×
● *Fleming*, Tuscaloosa...NW	×
Fleta, Escambia.............S	×
Fleta, Montgomery........SE	×
● Flint, Morgan ....N	200
Flint Factory, Madison....N	×
Flint Hill, Clay.............E	×
● Flomaton, Escambia......S	450
● Flora, Bullock...........SE	10
Florala, Covington ....S	200
● **Florence**, Lauderdale, NW	6,012
Floy, DeKalb ....NE	×
Folsom, Perry................C	×
Fordton, Franklin.......NW	×
Forest, Butler...............S	×
Forest Home, Butler........S	250
Forester's Chapel, Randolph, E	×
Fork, Monroe.............SW	×
Forkland, Greene..........W	250
Forney, Cherokee.........NE	×
Fort Bluff, Morgan.........N	×
Fort Browder, Barbour ...SE	75
Fort Davis, Macon..........E	×
● Fort Deposit, Lowndes....S	518
● Fort Mitchell, Russell....E	×
Fort Morgan, Mobile ....SW	×
● **Fort Payne**, DeKalb. NE	2,698
Fort Worth, Butler..........S	×
Fosheeton, Tallapoosa......E	×
Fossil, Jefferson............C	×
Fosters, Tuscaloosa ....W	50
● *Fowl River*, Mobile.....SW	25
Fox, Tuscaloosa.............W	×
Fox Creek, Randolph.......E	×
Francis, Calhoun ....NE	×
Francisco, Jackson ....NE	25
Franconia, Pickens ....W	×
Frankfort, Franklin.......NW	50
● *Franklin*, Macon.........E	×
Franklin, Henry...........SE	30
Frankville, Washington...SW	×
Fredonia, Chambers ....E	300
French Mills, Limestone....N	6
Fresco, Coffee ....SE	×
Friendship, Marshall.....NW	×
Frio, Coffee.................SE	×
Fullerton, Cherokee.......NE	×
Furman, Wilcox............S	195
Furnace, Bibb C	×

Gabbett, Macon,............E	×
Gad, DeKalb...............NE	×
● **Gadsden**, Etowah......N	2,901
Gainestown, Clarke.......SW	75
Gainesville, Sumter........W	1,017
Galatia, Conecuh............S	×
Gallant, Etowah ....N	×
● Gallion, Hale ....W	×
Galliton, Marshall..........N	×
Galloway, Walker........NW	×
● Gamble Mines, Walker.NW	×
Gandy's Cove, Morgan......N	×
Garden, Pickens ....W	75
● Garden City, Blount......N	100
Garfield, Fayette.........NW	×
● Garland, Butler...........S	300
Garrison Point, Blount.....N	25
Garth, Jackson ....NE	×
Gasque, Baldwin..........SW	×
Gaston, Sumter.............W	12
● Gastonburg, Wilcox.......S	×
● Gate City, Jefferson.......C	500
Gateswood, Baldwin......SW	×
Gay, Randolph...............E	×
Gaylesville, Cherokee.....NE	250
Gay's Landing, Marengo..SW	×
Geesbend, Wilcox...........S	×
Geneva, Geneva ....SE	637
Gentry, Lamar...........NW	×
● Georgiana, Butler.........S	456
Geraldine, DeKalb ....NE	×
Germania, Calhoun ....NE	100
Getup, Morgan.............N	×
Gibsonville, Clay............E	20
● *Giles*, Bibb................C	×
Gilbertsborough, Limestone. N	20
Gipson, DeKalb...........NE	×
Gipsy, Limestone...........N	×
● Girard, Russell ....E	3,000
Girard, Etowah............ N	×
Gladstone, Madison.........N	10
Glasgow, Butler..............S	×
Glee, Pike...................SE	×
● Glen Allen, Fayette....NW	100
Glendale, Monroe.........SW	×
● *Glenn's*, Etowah..........N	×
Glenville, Russell...........E	282
● *Glenwood*, Crenshaw..... S	×
Glick Store, Marengo.....SW	×
Glover, Clarke............SW	×
Gnatville, Cherokee.......NE	×
Goddard, Marion.........NW	25
Godwin, Dale...............SE	×
Goldbranch, Coosa..........C	×
● Gold Hill, Lee.............E	100
Gold Mine, Marion.......NW	25
Goldville, Tallapoosa........E	×
Golightly, Madison..........N	×
Good Hope, Elmore......... C	25
Good Springs, Limestone...N	12
● *Good Springs*, Franklin, NW	×
● Good Water, Coosa.........C	589
Good Way, Escambia.......S	×
Goosepond, Pickens ....W	×
Gopher Town, Pike.......SE	×
Gordo, Pickens ....W	×
● Gordon, Henry..........SE	200
Gordonsville, Lowndes......S	150
Goshen Hill, Pike.........SE	×
Gosport, Clarke...........SW	75
● *Gothite*, Tuscaloosa ......W	×
● *Grace*, Jefferson.......... C	×
● Grady, Montgomery.....SE	×
Grafton, Henry............SE	×
Graham, Randolph...........E	40
● Grand Bay, Mobile......SW	150
Granger, Henry.............SE	50
Grant, Marshall..............N	10
Grantley, Cleburne ....NE	×
Grantville, Cherokee......NE	×
Graphite, Clay...............E	×
Grassy, Marshall.............N	×
● Gravella, Conecuh.. ......S	100
● *Gravel Pit*, Escambia.....S	×
Gravelly Spring, L'Dale..NW	40
Gravleeton, Walker ......NW	×
● *Grays*, Calhoun......... NE	×
Gray's Chapel. Jackson....NE	13
Grayton, Calhoun ....NE	×
● *Greeley*, Tuscaloosa......W	×
Green Bay, Covington ......S	×
● Greenbrier, Limestone...N	500
Greene, Jefferson...........C	×
Greenfield, Madison........N	×
Green Grove, Madison .....N	25
Green Hill. Lauderdale...NW	50
● **Green Pond, Bibb**........C	800

● *Greens*, Jefferson C	×
● **Greensborough**, Hale W	1,759
Greensport, St. Clair........N	×
● **Greenville**, Butler.....S	2,806
● *Greenway*, Calhoun.....NE	×
Greenwood, Baldwin ......SE	×
Greenwood, Bullock........SE	×
Greerton, Jackson ....NE	×
Gregory, Pickens............W	×
Grenada, Lawrence.......NW	×
Greshamton, Clay .... E	×
Griffin, Tuscaloosa ....W	×
Grove Hill, Clarke.....SW	225
Grove Oak, DeKalb ....NE	×
Grover, Cherokee.........NE	×
Grubbs, Barbour ....SE	×
● Guerryton, Bullock......SE	100
● Guin, Marion...........NW	600
Guin, Fayette ....NW	×
● *Gulf Junction*, Dallas.....S	×
Gum Pond, Lawrence....NW	10
Gum Spring, Blount........N	30
● **Guntersville**, Marshall. N	471
Gurganus, Walker........NW	×
Gurley, Madison............N	570
● *Gurley*, Blount...........N	×
Gurley's Creek, Jefferson...C	×
Gurnee, Shelby..............C	291
● *Gurnee Junction*, Bibb... C	×
● *Gurnee Station*, Bibb..... C	×
Hackleburgh, Marion ....NW	25
Hackneyville, Tallapoosa....E	100
Haddock, Lauderdale ....NW	×
Haden, Madison ....N	30
● *Haftel*, Crenshaw.........S	×
Hagler, Tuscaloosa ....W	×
● Hairston, Greene.........W	50
Haleburgh, Henry ....SE	×
Haley's, Marion ....NW	100
● Haleysville, Winston...NW	1,000
Halford, DeKalb..........NE	×
Hall's Mills, Marion .....NW	×
Hallsville, Pike............SE	×
Hallton, Covington..........S	×
● Hamburgh, Perry..........C	125
Hamilton, Marion .... NW	500
● *Hamilton*, St. Clair.......N	×
Hammac, Escambia.........S	×
● *Hammocks*, Escambia ....S	×
Hamner, Sumter ....W	×
Hampden, Marengo.......SW	200
Hamptonville, Covington....S	×
Hanby's Mills, Blount.......N	50
● Hanceville, Blount ....N	400
Hancock, Cherokee.......NE	×
Handley, Randolph ....E	×
Handy, Fayette...........NW	×
Hanover, Coosa C	×
Happy Land, Chambers.....E	×
Hardswicksburgh, Henry..SE	20
Harkness, Blount ....N	×
Harlan, Clay ....E	×
Harmonious, Jackson ....NE	×
Harmony, Pike............SE	×
Harpersville, Shelby C	200
● Harrell, Dallas ....S	50
● Harris, Barbour ....SE	150
● *Harris*, Limestone........N	10
Harrisburgh, Bibb C	×
● Hartsell's, Morgan........N	596
● Hatchechubbee, Russell...E	100
● *Hatches*, Hale............W	×
Hatcher, Dale..............SE	×
Hatchers, Clay..............E	×
Hatchett Creek, Clay........E	×
Hatton, Lawrence ....NW	10
Havana, Hale..............W	350
Hawk, Morgan ....N	×
Hawkinsville, Barbour ....SE	350
Haworth, Etowah...........N	×
Haw Ridge, Dale............SE	100
Hayes, Tuscaloosa..........W	×
● *Hayesville*, Greene ...... W	50
Haymon, Coffee ....SE	×
Hayneville, Lowndes ....S	355
● *Hay's Mill*, Limestone ...N	×
Haysville, Greene ....W	50
Haywood, Randolph ....E	×
Hazel Green, Madison ......N	60
Hazen, Dallas ....S	×
Headland, Henry.......... SE	600
Healing Springs, Wash'n..SW	×
● Hebron, Calhoun........NE	30
Hector, Bullock............SE	10
● Heflin, Cleburne ....NE	383
● Helena, Shelby............C	350
● *Helena Coal Branch*, Jeff. C	×

Post Office	Pop.
Helicon, Crenshaw..........S	×
Henagar, DeKalb......... NE	25
Henderson, Pike ....SE	25
Hendrick, Blount ....N	25
Henry, Pickens..............W	×
● Henryellen, Jefferson C	459
Henryville, Marshall........N	50
Herbert, Conecuh ....S	×
Herndon, Baldwin ....SW	×
Hewitt, Walker ....NW	×
● *Hickman*, Talladega C	×
Hickman's, Tuscaloosa ....W	×
Hickory Flat, Chambers ....E	200
Hickory Grove, Lowndes....S	×
Hicks, Cleburne...........NE	×
Hicks, Pike.................SE	×
Higdon, Jackson ....NE	13
High Bluff, Geneva........SE	×
High Falls, Geneva........SE	×
Highland, Shelby.............C	×
Highland Home, Crenshaw..S	100
High Mound, Blount ....N	×
High Shoals, Randolph......E	100
Hightogy, Lamar.........NW	×
Hightower, Cleburne......NE	×
Hilaryton, Conecuh ....S	×
Hill, Etowah ....N	×
● *Hilldale*, Shelby C	×
Hillians' Store, Marshall....N	25
Hilliardsville, Henry ......SE	×
● *Hillman*, Jefferson........C	×
● Hillsboro, Lawrence....NW	300
Hilton, Covington ....S	×
Hinton, Choctaw...........SW	×
Hissop, Coosa C	×
Hodges, Marion ....NW	×
Hokes Bluff, Etowah ....N	50
Hollinger, Monroe ....SW	×
● Hollins, Clay..............E	422
Hollow Square, Hale.......W	250
Holly Spring, Fayette ...NW	×
Holly Tree, Jackson.......NE	40
Holly Pond, Cullman ....N	15
● Hollywood, Jackson....NW	21
Holmes, Clay.................E	×
● *Holmes Gap*, Cullman....N	×
Holtville, Elmore C	×
Honea, Madison.............N	×
Honoraville, Crenshaw......S	×
Hood, St. Clair..............N	×
Hooper Mills, Cleburne...NE	×
Hope, Marion..............NW	×
Hopeful, Talladega..........C	×
● Hope Hull, Montgomery SE	×
Hopewell, Cleburne ......NE	×
● *Horse Creek*, Walker...NW	1,500
Horton, Marshall ....N	×
Hospelaga, Lee ....E	×
Host, Crenshaw ....S	×
Hot Spur, Shelby.............C	×
Houston, Winston.........NW	200
Howard, Mobile ....SW	×
Howe, Barbour ....SE	20
Howel's Cross Roads, Cher. NE	30
Howelton, Etowah ....N	40
Hudson, Crenshaw ....S	×
● *Hudson*, Lamar ....NW	50
Huffman, Jefferson C	×
Huggins, Coffee ....SE	×
● *Hughe's Siding*, Jefferson.C	×
Hulaco, Morgan ....N	×
Huldah, Blount..............N	25
● Hull, Tuscaloosa..........W	433
Humphrey, Tuscaloosa.....W	×
Hunter, Colbert ....NW	15
Hunter, Dallas ....S	×
● **Huntsville**, Madison.. N	7,995
Hurley, Cherokee .... NE	×
● *Huron*, Jefferson C	×
Hurricane, Tuscaloosa.....W	×
● Hurricane Bayou, Bldw.SW	×
● Hurtsboro, Russell........E	435
Hyatt, Marshall..............N	×
● Hyde Park, Limestone....N	10
● *Hygeia Hotel*, Mobile...SW	×
Hyram, Russell ....E	×
Icy, Fayette..............NW	×
Idaho, Clay ....E	×
Iddo, Pike..................SE	×
Ider, DeKalb.................S	×
Igo, Monroe ....SW	×
Igoburgh, Franklin.......NW	×
Independence, Autauga.....C	25
Index, Jackson ....NE	×
Indian Branch, Pike......SE	×
Indian Creek, Bullock......SE	20
Indian Creek, Henry......SE	×

Post Office	Pop.
Indian Hill, Perry. C	×
Industry, Butler ....S	×
Ingate, Mobile.............SW	×
Ingleton, Colbert..........NW	200
Inman, St. Clair.............N	×
Intercourse, Sumter ....W	×
● Inverness, Bullock ......SE	100
Iola, Covington...............S	×
Ireland Hill, Marion......NW	×
Irma, Elmore C	×
● Ironaton, Talladega.......C	562
Iron Bridge, Cullman ......N	×
Iron City, Calhoun........NE	150
● Irondale, Jefferson........C	500
● *Irondale Station*, Jeffers..C	×
Iron Mountain, Calhoun..NE	×
Ironville, Perry..............C	25
● Isbell, Franklin.........NW	75
Ishkooda, Jefferson C	×
Isidore, Lawrence..........NW	×
Island Home, Tallapoosa....E	×
Isney, Choctaw ....SW	100
Iwana, Coosa................C	×
Jack's Springs, Escambia...S	×
● Jackson, Clarke ....SW	250
● Jacksonburg, Lauderd..NW	15
● Jackson's Gap, Tallapoosa.E	207
● *Jackson's Lake*, Elmore..C	×
● **Jacksonville**, Calh...NE	1,237
● James, Bullock..........SE	100
● *James*, DeKalb ....NE	×
● Jamestown, Cherokee.. NE	×
● **Jasper**, Walker.......NW	780
Jayvilla, Conecuh ....S	×
Jeddo, Franklin.............NW	×
Jeff, Madison ....N	10
Jefferson, Marengo ....SW	150
● Jemison, Chilton..........C	500
Jena, Tuscaloosa ....W	×
● Jenifer, Talladega..........C	323
Jenkins, Calhoun ....NE	×
Jennings, Lawrence.......NW	×
Jericho, Perry...............C	30
Jernigan, Russell. ....E	300
Jesseton, Lawrence...... NW	×
Jewell, Lamar.............NW	50
Jimhill, Walker............NW	×
Jink, Marshall...............N	×
● Johns, Jefferson C	×
Johnson, Crenshaw ....S	×
Johnson's Mill, Marion..NW	×
● *Johnson's Mill*, Tuscal.. W	×
● Jonesborough, Jefferson..C	150
Jones Chapel, Cullman .....N	10
Jones Mills, Monroe .....SW	×
Jones Switch, Autauga......C	×
Jonesville, Jefferson........C	×
Joppa, Cullman...............N	10
Jordan, Elmore................C	×
Josephine, Baldwin.........SW	×
Josie, Pike ....SE	×
Joy, Blount....................N	×
Judson, Chambers ....E	×
Jug, Walker...............NW	×
● Julian, Crenshaw ....S	×
Jumbo, Chilton...............C	×
Junction, Etowah ....N	×
○ *Junction*, Walker .....NW	×
● *Junction*, Lee..............E	×
Kansas, Walker ....NW	100
Kaolin, DeKalb ....NE	×
Keel, Marshall................N	×
○ Keener, Etowah............N	75
Kelly's Creek, St. Clair.....N	75
● Kellyton, Coosa............C	25
Kemp's Creek, Cleburne..NE	×
Kempsville, Monroe ......SW	30
Kendall's Cross Roads, Chs.E	×
Kendell, Lauderdale......NW	×
Kennamer Cove, Marshall..N	×
● Kennedy, Lamar ....NW	300
Kent, Elmore C	×
Kentuck, Talladega..........C	×
● *Kewahatchie*, Shelby......C	×
Key, Cherokee.............NE	×
● *Keyton's*, Montgomery .SE	×
Key's Mill, Madison........N	×
● Kimbrough's, Wilcox.....S	×
Kimo, Lawrence ....NW	×
Kimulga, Talladega.........C	25
Kincheon, Chilton C	×
King, Walker..........NW	×
King's Landing, Dallas......S	250
Kingston, Autauga..........C	×
Kingville, Lamar..........NW	75
Kinhaw, Macon..............E	×
Kinlock, Lawrence.......NW	×

Post Office	Pop.
Kinsey, Henry.............SE	×
Kinterbish, Sumter.......NE	×
Kirby's Creek, Jackson...NE	15
● Kirkland, Escambia.......S	×
Kirk's Grove, Cherokee...NE	25
Kitson, Talladega C	×
Kleg, Dale...................SE	×
Knowle, Marion ....NW	×
Knoxville, Greene..........W	75
● *Knoxville*, Pike...........SE	×
Koenton, Washington ....SW	×
Kolb, Etowah ....N	×
Koon, Pickens ....W	×
Kosh, Jackson ....NE	10
Kowaliga, Elmore...........C	50
● Kushla, Mobile...........SW	×
Kyles, Jackson.............NE	×
Kyleton, Morgan ....N	×
Kymulga, Talladega..........C	×
● *Lacey's*, Shelby...........C	×
Lacey's Spring, Morgan.....N	75
● Ladiga, Calhoun.........NE	30
Ladonia, Russell ....E	×
● **LaFayette**, Chambers..E	1,369
Lagerville, Etowah..........N	×
Lakeview, Covington........S	×
Lakeview, Jefferson..........C	×
Lamar, Randolph ....E	25
Lamberta, Baldwin.......SW	×
● Lamison, Wilcox...........S	×
Lamont, Butler.............S	×
● *Lancaster*, Talladega.......C	×
Landersville, Lawrence...NW	100
Lane's Mills, Winston....NW	×
Laneville, Hale..............W	25
● Laney, Calhoun..........NE	×
Langdon City, Cherokee.. NE	×
Langston, Jackson........NE	25
● Lapine, Crenshaw..........S	×
La Place, Macon ....E	50
Larkin's Fork, Jackson...NE	8
● Larkinsville, Jackson...NE	216
Larrisa, Winston.........NW	×
Latham, Baldwin..........SE	×
Lauderdale, Coosa...........C	×
Laurel, DeKalb ....NE	×
Lavender, Dale............SE	×
● Lawrence, Cherokee....NE	×
Lawrence Cove, Morgan....N	100
Lawrenceville, Henry......SE	200
Lax, Limestone..... ....N	×
Lay, Cherokee ....NE	×
Leander, Clay...............E	×
● *Leatherwood*, Calhoun..NE	×
Lebanon, DeKalb..........NE	300
Lee, Conecuh ....S	×
● Leeds, Jefferson C	250
● *Lee's*, Sumter........... W	×
● Leesburgh, Cherokee ...NE	×
● Leesdale, Morgan..........N	25
Legg, Fayette............ NW	×
● Legrand, Montgomery...SE	25
● Leighton, Colbert ....NW	350
Leith, Walker.............NW	×
● *Leland*, Walker.........NW	×
Leled Lane, Tuscaloosa.....W	×
Lenora, Choctaw ....SW	×
Lentzville, Limestone.......N	14
Leon, Crenshaw ....S	10
Leonard, Cherokee.........NE	×
Leslie, Clay....................E	×
● Letohatchee, Lowndes.....S	112
Level Plain, Dale..........SE	×
Level Road, Randolph......E	×
Leverett, Coffee............SE	×
Le Vert, Perry C	×
Lewis, Shelby C	×
● Lewisburg, Jefferson......C	×
Lewiston, Greene ....W	×
Lexington, Lauderdale ...NW	35
Liberty, Blount ....N	50
Lightwood, Elmore C	×
Lile, Lawrence ....NW	×
Lillian, Baldwin...........SW	×
Lily, Chilton..................C	8
Limestone, Madison ....N	3
● Lim Rock, Jackson .....NE	100
● Lincoln, Talladega C	100
Linden, Marengo ....SW	500
Lineburg, Pickens.........W	9
Lineville, Clay............. E	234
Linn's Crossing, Jefferson ..C	×
● *Linton*, Jefferson C	×
● Linwood, Pike...........SE	100
Little Oak, Pike............SE	×
Little River, Baldwin......SE	×

 Alabama Alabama

Little River, Cherokee ....NE ×
● *Littleton*, Etowah........N 40
Littlesville, Winston......NW ×
● Littleville, Colbert......NW 15
Little Warrior, Blount......N ×
● *Little Warrior*, Jefferson.C ×
● Live Oak, Crenshaw.......S ×
● **Livingston**, Sumter...W 850
● Loachapoka, Lee.........E 357
Loango, Covington ....S ×
Lochthree, St. Clair.........N ×
Lockville, Monroe ....SW ×
Lodi, Barbour ....SE ×
Loflin, Russell ....E ×
Lofty, Randolph ....E ×
Logan, Cullman..............N 100
● *Logan's*, Dallas ....S ×
● Lomax, Chilton ....C 50
London, Marengo ....SW ×
● Long Island, Jackson...NE ×
● Longview, Shelby ....W 250
Lookout, DeKalb..........NE ×
Looling, Colbert..........NW ×
Looxapalia, Lamar ......NW ×
Loretto, Cullman ....N ×
Loss Creek, Walker .....NW ×
Lot, Marshall ....N ×
Louina, Randolph...........E 250
● Louisville, Barbour......SE 288
Lovan, Monroe ....SW ×
Loveless, DeKalb..........NE ×
Lowe, Madison ....N ×
Lower Peach Tree, Wilcox..S 250
Lowery, Blount............N ×
Lowndesborough, Lowndes..S 450
● *Lowndesborough Station*,
● Lowndes..................S 260
Loyd, Cullman..............N 10
Lubbub, Pickens...........W ×
Lucas, Lamar............NW ×
Luckey, Walker..........NW ×
Lumber Mills, Butler........S ×
● *Lumberton*, Wash'gton.SW ×
Lumpkin, Marshall ....N ×
Luna, DeKalb.............NE ×
Lusk, Choctaw.............SW ×
Luther's Store, Marengo..SW ×
Luttrell, DeKalb ....NE ×
● Luverne, Crenshaw........S 451
Lydia, DeKalb............NE ×
Lynch, Shelby...............C ×
● Lynn, Winston ....NW 100
● *McAdory*, Jefferson ......C ×
McBee, Pickens............W ×
● McCalla, Jefferson ....C 50
McClanahan, Morgan ......N ×
● *McCombs*, Jefferson ......C ×
McConnell's, Tuscaloosa....W 25
● *McCoy*, Saint Clair.......N ×
● *McDonald*, Dallas ....S ×
● *McDonald's*, Limestone..N ×
● McDowell, Sumter.......W ×
● McElderry, Talladega.....C ×
McEntyre, Clarke..........SW ×
McFall, Talladega ....C ×
McFarlin, Conecuh.........S ×
● *McGeehes*, Montgomery.SE ×
● *McIntosh*, Washington.SW ×
McIntosh Bluff, Wash'ton.SW 150
McKinley, Marengo.......SW 300
McLarty, Blount............N ×
McLure, Pike...............SE ×
McNab, Cullman ....N ×
McNeill, Conecuh ....S ×
McRae, Henry ....SE ×
McSwains Mills, Dale.....SE 25
McVille, Marshall ....N ×
McWilliams, Jefferson ......C ×
Mack, Calhoun.............NE ×
Mackey, Cherokee ....NE ×
Macon, Calhoun ....NE ×
Mad Indian, Clay ....E ×
Maddox, Colbert.........NW ×
Madera, Autauga............C ×
Madison Cross Rds, Madison N 10
● Madison Station, Madison.N 555
● *Magazine Point*, Mobile SW ×
● *Magella*, Jefferson........C ×
Magic, Winston..........NW ×
Magnolia, Marengo........SW 5,000
Magnolia Springs, Bald'In. SW ×
Mahan, DeKalb ....NE ×
Maitland, Clay ....E ×
Malone Ferry, Randolph....E ×
● *Manack*, Lowndes ....S 50
Manasco, Walker.........NW ×

Manchester, Marshall.......N ×
Manningham, Butler........S 100
Mantua, Greene............W ×
Maple Grove, Cherokee...NE ×
● Maplesville, Chilton......C 800
Marble Valley, Coosa........C 50
Marchville, Mobile........SW ×
Marcoot, Chambers ....E ×
Marcumville, Tuscaloosa...W ×
Marcus, DeKalb ....NE ×
Mardisville, Talladega ......C ×
● Margerum, Colbert.....NW 25
● *Maricopa*, Crenshaw .....S ×
● Marietta, Walker.......NW 50
● **Marion**, Perry ....C 1,982
● *Marion Junction*, Dallas..S 50
● *Markle*, Crenshaw........S ×
Markton, Etowah............N ×
● *Mar's Hill*, Lauderdale.NW ×
Marl, Geneva ....SE ×
Marlow, Baldwin ....SW ×
Marshall, Marshall..........N 10
Martha, Geneva............SE 206
● Marthadell, Calhoun....NE ×
Martin's Cross Rds, Cal'n.NE ×
Martins Mill, Marshall......N 25
● Martin's Station, Dallas...S 150
Martling, Marshall..........N ×
Marvyn, Russell............E 250
Mary, Tallapoosa..........E ×
Marylee, Walker..........NW ×
Mason, Escambia............S ×
Massey, Morgan ....N ×
● Massillon, Dallas ....S 25
● Mathews, Montgomery ..SE 110
Matilda, Tallapoosa ....E ×
Mattie, Escambia ....S ×
Maud, Colbert............NW 10
● *Maury*, Jefferson.........C ×
● *Maxwell*, Tuscaloosa ....W ×
May Apple, Cullman ....N ×
● *Maylene*, Shelby ....C ×
Maynard's Cove, Jackson..NE 31
Maynor, Blount..............N ×
Maysville, Madison ....N 218
Meadows, Chambers ....E ×
Meadville, Montgomery ...SE ×
Mechanicsville, Lee ....E 150
Mellow Valley, Clay.........E ×
Mellville, Winston..........NW ×
Melton's Mill, Tallapoosa....E ×
Meltonsville, Marshall...... N 20
Melvin, Choctaw ....SW 75
Memphis, Pickens...........W 250
● *Menlow*, Jackson ....NE ×
Mentone, DeKalb ....NE 25
● *Mercury*, Madison.........N 8
Meridianville, Madison .....N 100
Merigold, Madison...........N ×
● Merrellton, Calhoun ....NE ×
Merritt, Pike................SE ×
Methlon, Cleburne..........NE ×
Micaville, Cleburne ....NE 25
Mid, Marshall ....N ×
● Midland City, Dale......SE ×
● Midway, Bullock........SE 612
● *Midway Station*, BullockSE 100
● Miles, Talladega...........C ×
● *Miles*, Escambia..........S ×
● *Milhous*, Dallas...........S ×
● Milldale, Tuscaloosa......W 300
● *Miller*, Greene...........W ×
Miller's Ferry, Wilcox......S ×
Millersville, Clay...........E 150
● Millport, Lamar........NW 244
Millry, Washington.......SW 500
Milltown, Chambers.........E 350
Millville, Geneva..........SE ×
Milner, Randolph............E ×
Milo, Pike..................SE 75
Milton, Autauga............C ×
Mims, Monroe ....SW ×
Minden, Calhoun ....NE ×
Minorville, Marshall.........N ×
● Minter, Dallas..............S 40
Mitchell's Mill, Elmore.....C ×
● Mitchell Station, Bull'k..SE 296
Mixon, Conecuh.............S ×
● **Mobile**, Mobile........SW 81,076
● *Mobile Jc.*, Jefferson......C ×
Molloy, Lamar ....NW ×
Mona, Fayette............NW ×
Mon Louis, Mobile........SW ×
Monroeville, Monroe..SW 250
Monrovia, Madison ....N 15
Mont Calm, Fayette......NW ×
Monterey, Butler............S 150

Monte Sano, Madison.......N ×
● Montevallo, Shelby........C 572
● **MONTGOMERY**, Montgomery...SE 21,883
Montgomery Hill, BaldwinSW 200
Monticello, Pike..........SE ×
Montrose, Baldwin.........SW ×
Moody, Jefferson ....C 50
Moody, Saint Clair..........N 50
Moorefield, Chambers ......E ×
Moore's Bridge, Tuscaloosa.W ×
Moore's Mill, Madison ......N ×
Mooresville, Limestone.....N 143
● *Morgan*, Jefferson....... C ×
Morgan Spring, Perry ......C ×
● Morganville, Lowndes ....S 56
Moriah, Coosa...............C ×
● Morris, Jefferson..........C 15
Morriston, Baldwin........SW ×
Morrisville, Calhoun......NE 100
Morrowville, Dallas ....S ×
Morton, Jefferson...........C ×
Morton Pond, Marshall....N ×
Morvin, Clarke............SW 25
Moscow, Lamar ....NW ×
Moseley, Clay...............E ×
Moshat, Cherokee...........N ×
● *Moseley's Mill*, CherokeeNE ×
Moss, Marengo ....SW ×
Motes, Winston...........NW 200
Motley, Tallapoosa.........E ×
● Mott's Mill, Lee ....E ×
Moulton, Lawrence....NW 500
Mounds, Jefferson..........C ×
Mountainboro, Etowah...... N ×
● Mountain Creek, Chilton..C 300
Mountain Home, Law'ce.NW ×
Mountain Meadow, Clay....E ×
Mountain Mills, Colbert..NW 100
Mount Alvis, Cullman.......N ×
Mount Andrew, Barbour..SE 15
Mount Carmel, Montg'ery.SE 150
Mount Hebron, Greene.....W 75
Mount Hilliard, Bullock...SE 195
Mount Hope, Lawrence ..NW 100
Mount Ida, Crenshaw ....S ×
Mount Level, Bullock......SE ×
● Mount Meigs, Mont'gry..SE 100
● *Mount Meigs Station*, Montgomery..............SE ×
Mount Olive, Coosa..........C ×
● Mount Pinson, Jefferson...C 75
Mount Pleasant, Monroe..SW 250
Mount Rozell, Limestone...N 15
Mount Sterling, Choctaw..SW 150
Mount Union, Conecuh.....S ×
● Mount Vernon, Mobile..SW 700
Mount Willing, Lowndes.....S 231
Mount Zion, DeKalb......NE ×
● *Moxley*, Talladega........C ×
● *Mud*, Dallas...............S ×
Mud Creek, Jackson......NE ×
Mulberry, Autauga ....C ×
● Munford, Talladega.........C 147
Murphree's Valley, Blount. N 200
● Muscadine, Cleburne....NE 100
Muscogee Mills, Baldwin SE ×
Museville, Perry ....C ×
Musgrove, DeKalb.........NE ×
● Myrtle, Montgomery....SE 50
Myrtlewood, Marengo....SW ×
Naches, Franklin........NW ×
● Naftel, Montgomery ....SE ×
Naheola, Choctaw........SW ×
Nanafalia, Marengo.......SW 50
Nances Creek, Calhoun...NE ×
Nanna Hubba, Mobile....SW ×
Narrows, Jackson.........NE ×
Nat, Jackson...............NE ×
Natches, Monroe..........SW ×
● Natural Bridge, Winston, NW ×
● Nauvoo, Walker ....NW ×
Neal's Mill, Pickens.......W ×
Nealton, Clarke..........SW ×
Nebo, Madison.............N 10
Necessity, Madison ....N ×
Nector, Blount.............N 130
Needmore, Cullman........N ×
Neel, Morgan..............N ×
Nellie, Wilcox..............S 200
Nelsonville, Franklin,....NW 97
Nero, Monroe.............SW ×
● *Nero*, Lauderdale......NW ×
Nesmith, Cullman..........N 120
Nettleboroough, Clarke.....E 800
● Newbern, Hale...........W 450

Newburgh, Franklin	NW	100
● New Castle, Jefferson	C	250
● New Decatur, Morgan	N	3,565
Newell, Randolph	E	×
New Goshen, Cherokee	NE	65
New Hope, Madison	N	150
New Lexington, Tuscaloosa	W	70
New Market, Madison	N	300
New Marrs, Bibb	C	62
New Moon, Cherokee	NE	77
● *New Orleans Jc.*, Dallas	S	×
New Providence, Crenshaw	S	30
New River, Fayette	NW	130
New Site, Tallapoosa	E	109
● Newton, Dale	SE	520
Newtonville, Fayette	NW	30
New Topia, Dale	E	×
Neymans Store, Cherokee	NE	10
Nichola, Clarke	SW	×
Nicholson's Gap, DeKalb	NE	130
Nicholsville, Marengo	SW	52
Nisi, Dale	SE	×
Nix, Etowah	N	25
Nixburgh, Coosa	C	100
Noah, Cherokee	NE	×
Noblin, Geneva	SE	27
Nobusiness, Morgan	N	×
Norman, Lamar	NW	×
North, Marshall	N	25
● *North Birmingham*, Jeff.	C	×
Northcutt, Lamar	NW	×
Northport, Tuscaloosa	W	413
Norton, Etowah	N	×
Norwood, Crenshaw	S	×
● Notasulga, Macon	E	332
● Nottingham, Talladega	C	×
Nunez, Lamar	NW	×
Oakbowery, Chambers	E	25
Oakfuskee, Cleburne	NE	137
Oak Grove, Mobile	SW	×
● *Oak Grove*, Montgomery	SE	40
Oak Grove, Perry	C	30
● *Oak Hill*, Etowah	N	×
Oakland, Lauderdale	NW	25
● *Oakland*, Walker	NW	×
Oak Lane, Cleburne	NE	50
Oak Level, Cleburne	NE	150
Oak Lone, Cleburne	NE	50
Oakmulgee, Perry	C	200
Oakville, Lawrence	NW	40
Oaky Streak, Butler	S	19
Oates, Henry	SE	×
Oateston, Barbour	SE	27
Octagon, Marengo	SW	50
Odenheim, Tuscaloosa	W	33
● *Oden's*, Talladega	C	×
Odenville, Saint Clair	N	97
Ofelia, Randolph	E	×
● Ohatchee, Calhoun	NE	13
Olaville, Limestone	N	×
Oldenham, Tuscaloosa	W	×
Oldfield, Talladega	C	×
● *Old Jonesborough*, Jeff'on.	C	65
Old Spring Hill, Marengo	SW	800
Old Town, Conecuh	S	20
Oleander, Marshall	N	150
Olivia, Conecuh	S	×
● Olmstead Sta., Tuscaloosa	W	65
Olney, Pickens	W	200
Olustee Creek, Pike	SE	75
Omaha, Randolph	E	40
Omega, Bullock	SE	×
O'Neal, Limestone	N	×
● Oneonta, Blount	N	250
Opal, Conecuh	S	×
● **Opelika**, Lee	E	3,703
Opine, Covington	S	65
Ora, Lawrence	NW	×
Oregon, Jefferson	C	97
Oregonia, Tuscaloosa	W	65
Orion, Pike	SE	300
Orr's Store, Dallas	S	×
● Orrville, Dallas	S	321
Osanippa, Chambers	E	130
Oswalt, Cleburne	NE	×
Oswichee, Russell	E	50
Otho, Henry	SE	50
● *Otis Mill*, Mobile	SW	×
Ottery, Calhoun	NE	75
Owen's Cross Rds., M'dson.	N	25
Owl, Winston	NW	×
● Oxanna, Calhoun	NE	748
● Oxford, Calhoun	NE	1,473
● Oxmoor, Jefferson	C	556
● **Ozark**, Dale	SE	1,195
Padgett, Jackson	NE	×
● Paint Rock, Jackson	NE	300

Alabama

● Palestine, Cleburne	NE	50
● *Palmers*, Jefferson	C	×
Palmetto, Pickens	W	25
Palo, Fayette	NW	97
Pansey, Henry	SE	×
Panther, Montgomery	SE	84
Paradise, Baldwin	SW	×
Paris, Wilcox	S	×
Parker, Coffee	SE	×
Parker, Elmore	C	×
Park's Store, Jackson	NE	65
● Parrish, Walker	NW	×
Partlow, Saint Clair	N	×
Partridge, Jefferson	C	12
● *Passing Track*, Jefferson	C	×
● Patsburg, Crenshaw	S	×
● Patton, Walker	NW	×
Payneville, Sumter	W	25
Peace, Blount	N	×
Peaceburgh, Calhoun	NE	100
Peachbloom, Conecuh	S	×
Peacock, Crenshaw	S	18
Pearce's Mills, Marion	NW	200
Pea Ridge, DeKalb	NE	×
Pea River, Barbour	SE	65
Pearl, Tuscaloosa	W	×
Pebble, Winston	NW	130
Peek's Hill, Calhoun	NE	100
Peerson, Limestone	N	×
Pegram, Colbert	NW	×
Pelham, Shelby	C	140
● Pell City, Saint Clair	N	100
Pendergrass, Marshall	N	30
Penn, Coffee	NE	×
Pennington, Choctaw	SW	×
Pentonville, Coosa	C	130
● Perdido Station, Bald'w.	SW	75
Perdue, Coffee	SE	×
Perdue Hill, Monroe	SW	282
Perote, Bullock	SE	195
● *Perry's Mill*, Montg'ery	SE	50
Perryville, Perry	C	100
Pevey, Washington	SW	×
Peters, Marshall	N	66
● Petrey, Crenshaw	S	×
Pettey, Limestone	N	8
Pettusville, Limestone	N	32
● *Phebe*, Crenshaw	S	×
● *Phelan's*, Cullman	N	×
● Phifer, Tuscaloosa	W	×
Phipps, Hale	W	60
● Phoenix City, Lee	E	3,700
Pickens Landing, Clarke	SW	200
Pickensville, Pickens	W	150
● Piedmont, Calhoun	NE	711
Pierce Mines, Jefferson	C	100
Pigeon Creek, Butler	S	130
● Pike Road, Montgomery	SE	100
Pikeville, Marion	NW	260
Pilgrim, Fayette	NW	25
Pinckneyville, Clay	E	50
● Pine Apple, Wilcox	S	520
Pineburr, Tallapoosa	E	×
Pine Forest, Saint Clair	N	10
Pine Grove, Bullock	SE	25
● *Pine Grove*, Coosa	C	×
● Pine Hill, Wilcox	S	130
Pine Level, Montgomery	SE	500
Pine Springs, Lamar	NW	100
Pine Tucky, Perry	C	70
Pine View, Talladega	C	×
Pine Ville, Monroe	SW	200
● *Piney Woods*, Bibb	C	×
Pinnacle, Cullman	N	75
Pisgah, Jackson	NE	21
Pitt, Lawrence	NW	×
Pitt, Russell	E	×
Pittman, Randolph	E	×
● Pittsboro, Russell	E	×
Plano, Cherokee	NE	32
● Plantersville, Dallas	S	100
● *Plateau*, Mobile	SW	×
Pleasant Gap, Cherokee	NE	×
Pleasant Grove, Pickens	W	50
Pleasant Hill, Dallas	S	250
● *Pleasant Hill Station*, D'l's	S	×
Pleasant Planes, Henry	SE	50
Pleasant Ridge, Greene	NW	300
Pleasant Site, Franklin	NW	100
Pleasant Valley, Wash'n.	SW	×
● Plevna, Madison	N	20
Plott, Pickens	W	×
Point Clear, Baldwin	SW	30
Polk, Dallas	S	×
● Pollard, Escambia	S	389
Pondville, Bibb	C	25
Pontus, Butler	S	65

Alabama

Pool, Lawrence	NW	×
Poplar Creek, Limestone	N	×
Poplar Ridge, Madison	N	50
Porter, Jefferson	C	20
● Portersville, DeKalb	NE	75
Portersville, Mobile	SW	200
Portland, Dallas	S	75
Posey, Franklin	NW	×
Postoak, Bullock	SE	×
Potash, Randolph	E	×
Pottersville, Pike	SE	65
● *Pouncey*, Clarke	SW	×
● Powderly, Jefferson	C	×
Powellville, Walker	NW	×
● Powers, Hale	W	×
Prairie Bluff, Wilcox	S	250
Pratt Mines, Jefferson	C	1,946
● **Prattville**, Autauga	C	724
Presley, Baldwin	SW	×
Preston, Marshall	N	15
● *Price*, DeKalb	NE	×
Priceville, Morgan	N	15
● Prichard, Mobile	SW	15
● Pride's Station, Col'rt.	NW	75
Princeton, Jackson	NE	10
Prince's Landing, Clarke	SW	×
Proctor, Saint Clair	N	×
Proctor, Coosa	C	×
Progress, Lawrence	NW	×
Pronto, Pike	SE	×
Propell, Shelby	C	×
● Prospect, Walker	NW	×
Providence, Pickens	W	20
● Pruitton, Lauderdale	NW	25
Pushmataha, Choctaw	SW	200
Putman, Marengo	SW	65
● Quid Nunc, Limestone	N	10
Quinsey, Coosa	C	×
● Quinton, Jefferson	C	×
Quito, Shelby	C	×
Rabbit Town, Calhoun	NE	65
● Ragan's, Talladega	C	×
● Ragland, St. Clair	N	300
Ragsdale, Marshall	N	20
Raif Branch, Montgomery	SE	97
Rains, DeKalb	NE	×
Raleigh, Pickens	W	69
● Ramer, Montgomery	SE	200
Ramsey, Sumter	W	100
Randall, Calhoun	NE	300
Randolph, Bibb	C	300
Range, Conecuh	S	40
Rat, Covington	S	32
Rawhide, Lauderdale	NW	20
Ray, Baldwin	SW	34
Rayner, Cherokee	NE	×
Razburgh, Jefferson	C	32
● *Raynes*, Cherokee	NE	×
● *Reader's*, Jefferson	C	×
● Read, Calhoun	NE	×
Reaves, Etowah	N	×
Red Apple, Marshall	N	36
Red Bay, Franklin	NW	×
● *Red Bud*, Washington	SW	52
Red Bud, Etowah	N	×
● Redding, Jefferson	C	474
● *Red Gap Junction*, Jeff.	C	×
Red Hill, Marshall	N	130
Red Level, Covington	S	150
Red Oak, Monroe	SW	×
Reedbrake, Marshall	N	25
Reeder's Mill, Barbour	SE	×
Reese, Marion	NW	64
Reese, Montgomery	SE	×
● *Reesville*, Etowah	N	×
Reform, Pickens	W	100
Refuge, Talladega	C	×
● *Reid's*, Blount	N	×
Rehoboth, Wilcox	S	150
Rembert, Marengo	SW	41
● Remlap, Blount	N	34
● Rendalia, Talladega	C	40
● Renfroe, Talladega	C	202
Rep, Madison	N	10
● Repton, Conecuh	S	76
Rescueville, Choctaw	SW	×
Reserve, Lauderdale	NW	×
Reuben, Tuscaloosa	W	65
Reynolds, Bullock	SE	10
Rhodesville, Lauderdale	NW	×
Richards, Lamar	NW	×
● *Richardson*, Wash'n	SW	×
Richmond, Dallas	S	150
Ricks, Cherokee	NE	65
Riddle Spring, Jefferson	C	×
Ridge, Fayette	NW	20

Place	Pop.
Ridge Grove, Lee............E	25
Riley, Monroe ....SW	240
● *Riley's* Russell............E	×
Ringgold, Cherokee ......NE	30
Ripley, Limestone ....N	10
Rising Fawn, Walker....NW	×
River Bend, Bibb C	32
River Falls, Covington......S	×
River Hill, Jackson ....NE	×
River Ridge, Monroe......SW	130
● Riverside, St. Clair ....N	300
● Riverton, Colbert ......NW	150
River View, Chambers......E	×
● Roanoke, Randolph...... E	631
Robbins' Cross Roads, Jeff..C	500
Roberts, Escambia ....S	32
Robinson, Escambia ....S	×
Robinson Springs, Elmore ..C	140
Robjohn, Choctaw ....SW	×
Rockaway, Limestone ......N	×
Rockbridge, DeKalb ......NE	×
Rock Creek, Colbert......NW	65
Rockdale, Randolph ....E	67
Rockett's Station, Jefferson.C	×
Rockeyhead, Dale. ....SE	×
Rockford, Coosa.........C	240
Rock Mills, Randolph.......E	385
Rock Run, Cherokee......NE	260
● Rock Run Stat'n,Ch'rok'eNE	×
● Rock Springs, Etowah....N	×
Rock West, Wilcox..........S	×
Rockwood, Franklin .....NW	×
Rocky Mount, Clay ....E	65
Rocky Ridge, Jefferson C	×
Rodentown, DeKalb.......NE	520
Rodney, Coffee ....SE	×
Rogers, DeKalb .... NE	×
Rogersville, Lauderdale ..NW	300
Rome, Covington............S	80
Romulus, Tuscaloosa ...... W	32
Rosalie, Jackson..........NE	×
Roscoe, Colbert ....NW	×
Rosebud, Wilcox ....S	65
Rose Hill, Covington ....S	89
Rosemary, Hale ....W	×
Rosewood, Cleburne ......NE	250
Rosinton, Baldwin ....SW	32
Rosser, Sumter .... W	140
● Round Mount'n,Ch'r'keeNE	30
Rowell, Wilcox..............S	35
● *Rowells*, Cleburne ......NE	×
● Rowland, Limestone......N	12
Roxana, Lee ....E	65
Royal, Blount ....N	×
Ruby, Cullman ....N	10
Ruddick, Chilton C	×
● *Ruffner*, Jefferson C	×
Runville, Butler..............S	×
● *Rural*, Clarke ....SW	65
● Russellville, Franklin..NW	920
Rutledge, Crenshaw ......S	314
Ryan Creek, Cullman ....N	×
Rye, Limestone .... N	×
● Safford Station, Dallas... S	×
● *Saginaw*, Covington....... S	×
● *Saint Clair*, Saint Clair... N	120
● Saint Clair, Lowndes ....S	260
Saint Clair Sp'gs, St.Clair..N	×
● Saint Elmo, Mobile....... SW	100
Saint Florian,Lauderdale.NW	200
Saint'sStore, Colbert..... NW	12
Saint Stephens,Wash'nSW	387
● Salem, Lee....................E	600
Salitpa, Clarke.............SW	65
Sallie, Wilcox .... S	×
Sal Soda, Crenshaw...........S	32
Salter, Coosa..................C	65
Saltmarsh, Dallas............S	65
Samantha, Tuscaloosa...... W	×
Sambo, Talladega............C	×
Sanders, Geneva .... SE	×
Sand Lake, Colbert....... NW	×
Sand Mountain, DeKalb.. NE	25
● *Sand Pit*, Washington. SW	×
Sand Rock, Cherokee..... NE	130
Sand Spring, Limestone.... N	6
Sand Tuck, Elmore C	30
Sandusky, Jefferson C	×
Sandy Creek, Chambers .... E	100
Sandy Ridge, Lowndes...... S	300
Sanford, Covington..........S	15
Santa, Jackson........... NE	70
● Saragossa, Walker..... NW	×
Sardis, Dallas .... S	×
● *Sardis*, Fayette........ NW	×
Sauty Mills, DeKalb ...... NE	65
Saville, Crenshaw.......... S	200

Place	Pop.
Savoy, Marion............NW	×
● Sawyerville, Hale........ W	130
Scott, DeKalb .... NE	×
● **Scottsboro,** Jackson..NE	959
● Scott's Station, Perry..... C	40
Scottsville, Bibb............ C	150
Scrap, Jefferson C	32
Seaborn, Etowah.......... N	25
● **Seale,** Russell........... E	299
● Searcy, Butler .... S	300
● *Searight*, Covington...... S	×
Sedan, Wilcox .... S	300
● Seddon, St. Clair......... N	×
Selfville, Blount............N	×
Sellers, Montgomery...... SE	×
● **Selma,** Dallas............S	7,622
Sepulga, Conecuh .... S	65
● *Seven Mile*, Montgomery.SE	×
Severe, Perry............... C	×
Sewell, Randolph............ E	90
Sewickley, Lawrence.... NW	×
Shackleville, Butler .... S	×
● *Shades Creek*, Jefferson...C	×
Shady Grove, Pike.........SE	×
Sharon, Chambers.......... E	260
● Sharon, Walker ....NW	1,500
Sharp, Pickens............ W	26
Shaw, Jackson............ NE	10
Shearman, Sumter .... W	250
● Sheffield, Colbert....... NW	2,731
Sheffield, Fayette......... NW	×
● Shelby, Shelby............. C	753
Shelby Springs, Shelby......C	50
Shell, Butler................ S	65
● *Shellhorn*, Pike......... SE	×
Shepherd, Fayette.........NW	×
Sherman, Sumter.......... W	130
Sherrer Hill, Dallas.........S	×
Shield's Mill, Dallas....... S	25
Shiloh, Marengo.......... SW	260
Shinbone, Clay...............E	120
Shirley, Covington........... S	98
Shoal Creek, Cleburne..... NE	195
Shoal Ford, Limestone .... N	×
Shopton, Bullock...........SE	×
Short Creek, Jefferson......C	×
● Shorter's Depot, Macon... E	150
Shorterville, Henry.........SE	200
Shottsville, Marion....... NW	25
Shoults, Chilton C	×
Sibley Mills, Baldwin.....SW	150
Sidney, Marshall.............N	97
Silas, Choctaw............ SW	32
● Siluria, Shelby.............. C	130
Silver Run, Talladega....... C	75
Simcoe, Cullman........... N	65
Simmons, Shelby........... C	×
Simpkinsville, Monroe....SW	200
Simpson, Morgan .... N	20
Sims Chapel, Washington.SW	×
Singleton, Clarke.......... SW	32
● *Singleton's*, Saint Clair...N	25
Sipsey Turnpike,Tuscal'sa..W	65
● *Sipsey*, Walker.........NW	×
● *Sipsey*, Fayette .... NW	×
Sipsy Mills, Pickens....... W	×
Sitzville, Morgan........... N	×
Six Mile, Bibb.............. C	300
Sizemoore, Lamar.........NW	×
Skelton, Jefferson C	×
Skelton, Tuscaloosa........ W	×
Skinnerton, Conecuh .... S	×
Skipperville, Dale.......... SE	300
Skirum, DeKalb........... NE	10
Sky, Escambia .... S	×
● Slackland, Cherokee....NE	77
● *Slada's*, Washington....SW	×
Slate, Saint Clair.......... N	8
Slate Hill, Randolph.........E	×
Slater's Landing,Choctaw SW	×
● *Slaughter's*, Tallapoosa... E	×
Slick, Bibb.................. C	25
Sloan, Blount.............. N	×
● Sloss, Jefferson........... C	265
● *Sloss' Quarry*, Jefferson..C	×
Smelley, Talladega C	41
Smithfield, Jefferson........C	×
Smithsonia, Lauderdale.. NW	15
● Smith's Station, Lee ...... E	75
Smithville, Henry......... SE	×
Snake Creek, DeKalb..... NE	×
Snead, Blount............. N	50
● Snowdoun, M'tgomery.. SE	26
● Snow Hill, Wilcox........ S	400
Soapstone, Dallas.......... S	×
Society Hill, Macon......... E	200

Place	Pop.
Solomon, Cleburne........NE	65
Solomon's Mills, Barbour. SE	×
Somerville, Morgan..... N	200
South Butler, Butler....... S	200
● South Calera, Shelby......C	×
● South Florence,Colb't. NW	30
South Hill, DeKalb....... NE	87
South Lowell, Walker....NW	75
Souwilpa, Choctaw........SW	87
● *Spalding Junction*, J'son.C	×
Sparkville, Cherokee......NE	×
● *Sparta*, Conecuh.......... S	130
Spaulding, Jefferson........ C	×
Speed, Coosa.................C	×
Speed, Pickens ....W	×
● *Speigener*, Elmore........ C	×
Spencer, Fayette......... NW	155
Spigner's Station, Elmore.. C	×
Spio, Barbour..............SE	×
Spradley, Shelby............ C	13
● *Sprague Junc.*, Mont'gy.SE	×
Spring Bluff, Baldwin ....SW	×
● Spring Garden,Cher'kee NE	250
● *Spring Hill*, Barbour....SE	150
● Spring Hill, Mobile..... SW	325
● *Springs Junc.*, Shelby....C	×
● Spring Valley, Colbert. NW	40
● Springville, Saint Clair...N	350
Sprott, Perry................C	65
Spruce Pine, Franklin....NW	25
Stafford, Pickens.......... W	25
○ *Standiford*, Tuscaloosa.. W	×
Stanfield, Etowah.......... N	×
Stanton, Chilton.............C	200
Star, Lamar.............. NW	25
Star Hill, Barbour.......... C	69
Starkville, Cherokee...... NE	×
Starling, Cherokee........NE	×
Starlington, Butler..........S	×
● *State Line*, Limestone.... N	15
● *State Line*,Washington. SW	×
Statesville, Autauga C	32
Steadham, Escambia......... S	37
● Steel's Depot, St. Clair....N	50
● Stemly, Talladega C	×
Step, Lawrence ....NW	×
● *Stephens*, Jefferson....... C	×
Stephens Mill, Pickens .... W	×
Sterling, Cherokee........ NE	160
● Sterrett, Shelby...........C	13
● Stevenson, Jackson .... NE	586
● Stewart's Station, Hale.. W	255
Stewartsville, Coosa.........C	30
Stidham, Marion .... NW	×
Stinson, Marion.......... NW	×
Stockton, Baldwin........ SW	238
Stoddard, Montgomery.... SE	19
Stone, Pickens............. W	150
Stone Hill, Cleburne..... NE	77
● *Stones*, Montgomery.... SE	×
● Stough, Fayette.........NW	×
● Strasburgh, Chilton.......C	50
● Strata, Montgomery..... SE	30
Strawberry, Blount .... N	32
Street, Marshall............ N	×
Strickland, Dale..........SE	50
Stringer, Morgan........... N	65
Stringfellow, Butler .... S	×
● Stroud, Chambers.........E	285
● Sturdevant, Tallapoosa....E	97
Sublett's Ferry, Jackson..NE	×
Sugar, Lauderdale.........NW	65
● Suggsville, Clarke...... SW	200
● Sulligent, Lamar....... NW	200
● Sullivan, Escambia.........S	×
Sullivan Mill, Escambia.... S	×
Sulphur Spring, Calhoun. NE	150
Sulphur Springs, DeKalb..NE	43
Summerfield, Dallas....... S	383
Summit, Blount............ N	75
● *Summit*, Franklin......NW	×
● *Sumter*, Jefferson.........C	×
Sumterville, Sumter........W	150
● *Sunflower*,Washington..SW	×
Sunshine, Hale............W	×
Sunnyside,Morgan...........N	40
● Sunny South, Wilcox..... S	×
Sunset, Jackson........... NE	×
Surles, Crenshaw............S	×
Susanna, Tallapoosa..........E	32
● Suspension, Bullock.....SE	10
Swamp, Macon..............E	19
Swan, Cullman .... N	×
Swancott, Limestone....... N	8
Swanhill, Randolph......... E	×
Swearengin, Marshall...... N	20
Sweet Water, Marengo....SW	65

Alabama

Place	Pop.
Swift, Baldwin............SW	36
● Sycamore, Talladega......C	20
Sykes' Mills, Elmore........C	50
● Sylacauga, Talladega......C	464
Sylvan, Tuscaloosa.........W	100
Tabanacle, Coffee..........SE	×
Tabitha, Covington..........S	×
Tabor, Etowah..............N	×
● *Tacoa*, Shelby............C	×
Taff, Cherokee.............NE	×
● **Talladega**, Talladega...C	2,063
Talladega Sp'gs., Talladega..C	×
Tallahatta Springs, Clarke.SW	150
Tallassahatchee, Calhoun.NE	×
Tallassee, Elmore...........C	1,413
Talley, Jackson............NE	×
Tallula, Fayette...........NW	50
Talmage, Perry.............C	69
Talucah, Morgan............N	×
● Tampa, Calhoun.........NE	×
Tankersly's Store, M't'ery..SE	25
● *Tannehill*, Tuscaloosa....W	26
Tappan, Blount.............N	×
Tasso, Dallas...............S	65
● *Tate*, Dallas.............S	×
Tattilaba, Clarke..........SW	×
Tavern, Winston...........NW	×
● *Tayloe's*, Perry...........C	65
Taylor, Geneva............SE	67
Taylorsburg, Saint Clair....N	×
● Tecumseh, Cherokee....NE	300
Tekoa, Monroe.............SW	×
Temple, Pickens............W	87
Ten Broeck, De Kalb.....NE	×
● Tennille, Pike............SE	×
● *Tensas*, Baldwin........SW	100
Tensaw, Baldwin..........SW	650
Terry, Dallas...............S	65
Texas, Marion............NW	50
Thaddeus, Tallapoosa.......E	83
● Tharin, Montgomery....SE	130
Tharp, Colbert............NW	×
Theo, Perry.................C	390
Theodore, Mobile..........SW	277
Theresa, Baldwin.........SW	325
Thirty-Nine, DeKalb.......NE	10
● Thomas, Jefferson........C	500
● Thomasville, Clarke....SW	291
● Thompson, Bullock.....SE	100
Thorn Hill, Marion........NW	72
● *Thorn Hill*, Talladega....C	×
Thornton, Tallapoosa........E	13
● Three Notch, Bullock...SE	50
Tickridge, Limestone.......N	×
Tidmore, Blount.............N	50
Tidwell, Blount.............N	×
Tilden, Dallas.............NE	25
Tiller's Cross Roads, Chambers.......E	15
Tinela, Monroe...........SW	×
Tioc, Choctaw...........SW	×
Tishabee, Greene...........W	24
Titus, Elmore...............C	×
Toad Vine, Jefferson........E	75
Tohopeka, Tallapoosa.......E	13
Tolbut, Randolph............E	×
Toledo, Fayette............NW	25
Toll Gate, Marion.........NW	×
Tombigbee, Marengo.....SW	13
Tompkinsville, Choctaw..SW	75
Tootoo, Madison............N	×
● Town Creek, Lawrence.NW	201
● Townly, Walker........NW	×
● *Trammels*, Talladega.....C	×
Traveller's Rest, Coosa......C	65
Treadway, Russell...........E	×
Trenton, Jackson...........NE	31
Triana, Madison.............N	200
Trickem, Cleburne.........NE	×
Trimble, Cullman...........N	×
● Trinity Station, Morgan..N	200
Trio, Bibb..................C	×
Trotter, Pike..............SE	×
● **Troy**, Pike.................SE	3,449
Truett, Tallapoosa..........E	×
● Trussville, Jefferson.......C	462
Tryan, Coffee..............SE	×
● Tuckersburgh, Chambers.E	130
Tuckers Store, M'tgomery.SE	50
● *Tullis*, Barbour..........SE	×
Tupelo, Jackson...........NE	32
Turkestan, Monroe.......SW	×
● Turkeytown, Etowah.....N	100
Turnbull, Monroe.........SW	150
● *Turner*, Bibb.............C	×
Turner, Talladega...........C	130
Tuscahoma, Choctaw......SW	32

Alabama

Place	Pop.
● **Tuscaloosa**, Tuscaloosa, W	4,215
● **Tuscumbia**, Colbert.NW	2,491
Tuskegee, Macon........E	1,803
Tyler, Dallas................S	×
Tyner, Tuscaloosa..........W	77
Uchee, Russell..............E	50
Uhland, Russell.............E	×
Umbria, Mobile...........SW	×
Union, Greene..............W	20
Union Grove, Marshall.....N	×
● **Union Springs**, Bul'k.SE	2,049
● Uniontown, Perry........C	854
Unity, Cullman.............N	×
University, Tuscaloosa.....W	×
Upshaw, Winston........NW	×
Upton, Etowah.............N	×
Urbanity, Butler............S	26
Valhermoso Springs, M'or'n.N	25
● Valley Head, De Kalb...NE	233
● Vance, Tuscaloosa.......W	100
Vanderbilt, Jefferson.......C	×
● Vandiver, Shelby.........C	×
● Van Dorn, Marengo....SW	100
Vashti, Clarke.............SW	32
Vaughanville, Geneva......SE	100
● Venetia, Mobile.........SW	65
Vera, Dale.................SE	×
Vera Cruz, Covington.......S	65
● Verbena, Chilton..........C	756
Vernon, Lamar.........NW	192
Veto, Limestone............N	15
Victoria, Coffey............SE	130
Vidette, Crenshaw..........S	65
Vienna, Pickens............W	125
● Village Springs, Blount...N	50
Vilula, Perry................C	×
● Vincent, Shelby...........C	×
● Vinegar Bend, Wash't'n.SW	×
Vinehill, Autauga...........C	×
Vineland, Marengo.......SW	×
Vines, Jefferson............C	×
Viola, Blount...............N	77
Volina, Conecuh............S	×
Waco, Franklin...........NW	69
Wacoochee, Lee.............E	100
Waddell, Jefferson..........C	×
● Wadsworth, Autauga.....C	224
● Wagar, Washington....SW	×
Waits Mill, Coosa...........C	×
Waldo, Talladega...........C	75
Waldrep, Randolph.........E	×
● Walker Springs, Clarke.SW	100
● Wallace, Escambia........S	500
Walling, Morgan............N	×
Wallston, Jackson.........NE	×
Walnut Bluff, Wilcox......S	275
Walnut Grove, Etowah.....N	300
Walnut Hill, Tallapoosa.....E	98
Walter, Cullman............N	×
Wanamaker, Shelby........C	×
Wannville, Jackson........NE	×
Ward, Chambers............E	×
Ware, Elmore...............C	25
● *Wares*, Jefferson..........C	×
● *Warners*, Cleburne.....NE	×
Warrenton, Marshall........N	200
● Warrior, Jefferson.........C	1,000
Warrior Stand, Macon......E	215
Warsaw, Sumter............W	125
Warwick, Geneva..........SE	65
Waterhouse, Cherokee.....NE	×
Waterloo, Lauderdale....NW	200
Water Oak, Pike..........SE	×
Watford, Geneva..........SE	×
Watsonia, Greene...........W	×
● Waverly, Lee..............E	150
Wayside, Fayette..........NW	130
Weatherford, Escambia.....S	×
● Weaver's Station, Calh'nNE	200
Webster, Lauderdale.....NW	×
Webster, Fayette..........NW	×
Wedowee, Randolph.....E	250
Wee Bee, Cleburne........NE	×
Weed, Dale................SE	×
● *Weems*, Jefferson.........C	×
Wehadkee, Randolph.......E	65
Wehoga, Cleburne........NE	×
Weldon, Shelby..............C	260
Welsh, Chambers...........E	×
Wem, Madison.............N	×
Woegufka, Coosa...........C	×
Weoka, Elmore..............C	50
Wesley, Henry.............SE	130
West, Randolph.............E	×
West Bend, Clarke........SW	×
West Calera, Shelby.......C	×
● *West End*, Jefferson......C	×

Alabama

Place	Pop.
West Greene, Greene.......W	97
Westmoreland, Limestone..N	25
Weston, Henry.............SE	15
● **Wetumpka**, Elmore...C	619
● *Wewoka*, Talladega.......C	×
Wharf Boat, Marshall......N	×
Wharton, Cherokee.......NE	×
● Whatley, Clarke.........SW	×
Wheat, Cullman............N	×
● Wheeler Station, L'rnceNW	100
Wheelerville, Clay..........E	65
● *Wheeling*, Jefferson.......C	65
● Whistler, Mobile.........SW	500
White Cloud, Talladega......C	260
● White Hall, Lowndes......S	50
● White Oak Springs, B'rb SE	75
White Plains, Calhoun....NE	202
White Pond, Henry........SE	×
Whitesburgh, Madison......N	50
Whitesville, Marshall.......N	×
Whitfield, Sumter..........W	×
● Whitney, Saint Clair......N	50
Whiton, DeKalb...........NE	50
Whitsitt, Hale...............W	×
Wicksburgh, Dale..........SE	260
Wiggins, Covington.........S	86
● *Wilcox*, Conecuh..........S	×
Wiley, Tuscaloosa..........W	×
● *Wilhite*, Morgan..........N	×
Williamsburgh, Marengo..SW	65
Williams' Mill, Covington..S	65
● Williams Station, Escm'biaS	25
Willow, Blount..............N	×
Wills, DeKalb.............NE	65
Wilmington, Walker.....NW	93
Wilson, Escambia...........S	309
Wilson Ridge, Calhoun....NE	×
● Wilsonville, Shelby........C	100
Windham, Baldwin.......SW	×
Windhams, Pickens........W	32
● Winfield, Marion........NW	300
Wingard, Pike.............SE	×
Wininger, Jackson.........NE	×
Winn, Clarke..............SW	32
Winston, Winston.......NW	100
● *Wirten's Gap*, CherokeeNE	×
Wise, Chambers.............E	×
Wolf, Walker.............NW	87
Wolf Branch, Coffee......SE	×
Wolf Creek, Saint Clair.....N	25
Womack Hill, Choctaw....SW	410
Wooddale, Morgan..........N	×
Woodland Mills, Morgan....N	20
● Woodlawn, Jefferson.....C	506
Woodley, Montgomery.....SE	65
Wood's Bluff, Clarke.....SW	820
● Woodstock, Bibb..........C	150
● Woodville, Jackson......NE	200
● Woodward, Jefferson.....C	795
● *Woodward Jc.*, Jefferson.C	×
Wooley Springs, Limestone.N	32
● *Woolfolk*, Pike...........SE	×
Wooten, Blount.............N	×
Worthy, Pike...............SE	×
Wright, Lauderdale......NW	×
Wylam, Jefferson...........C	×
● Wymond, Jefferson........C	×
● *Wynnette*, Talladega......C	×
Wynnville, Blount..........N	25
Yancey, Etowah............N	×
Yantley Creek, Choctaw..SW	40
Yates, Tallapoosa...........E	×
Yellow Bluff, Wilcox.........S	97
Yellow Pine, Washington.SW	×
● *Yolande*, Tuscaloosa.....W	×
● *Yonge's*, Lee.............E	×
● York Station, Sumter....W	415
Young, Marion..........NW	×
Zana, Tallapoosa...........E	204
Zeigler, Barbour..........SE	×
Zidonia, Cleburne.........NE	×
Zinn, Butler...............S	×
Zoe, Henry................SE	×
Zornville, Henry..........SE	100
Zuber, Talladega...........C	×

ALASKA.

DISTRICTS.	POP.
Arctic........................	3,222
Kodiak........................	6,112
Kuskokwim....................	5,424

Alaska

Place	Population
Nushagak	2,726
Southeastern	8,038
Unalaska	2,361
Yukon	3,912
Total	31,795
Afognac, Kodiak	409
Agivavik, Nushagak	30
Agowik, Yukon	51
Aguliagamute, Kuskokwim	94
Agulukpukmute, Nushagak	22
Agumak, Kuskokwim	41
Ahgomekhelanaghamute, Kuskokwim	15
Ahgulakhpaghamute, Kuskokwim	19
Ahguliagamute, Kuskokwim	106
Ahpokagamute, Kuskokwim	210
Ahquenach-khlugamute, Kuskokwim	6
Akakhpuk, Nushagak	9
Akeklehahamute, Yukon	75
Akgulurigiglak, Nushagak	61
Akiagamute, Kuskokwim	97
Akiakchagmute, Kuskokwim	43
Akutan, Unalaska	80
Alaganok, Kodiak	48
Alagnagmute, Yukon	68
Alitak, Kodiak	420
Andreievsky, Yukon	10
Angnovchamute, Nushagak	16
Ankahchagmute, Yukon	103
Annovokhamute, Kuskokwim	15
Anvik, Yukon	191
Apahiachamute, Kuskokwim	91
Askinaghamute, Kuskokwim	138
Atchalugumute, Kuskokwim	39
Atka, Unalaska	132
Atnik, Arctic	33
Attu, Unalaska	101
Auk Settlements, Southeastern	324
Avnuligmute, Yukon	38
Ayaktalik, Kodiak	106
Aziavigamute, Nushagak	96
Bartlett Bay, Southeastern	40
Belkofsky, Unalaska	180
Berners Bay, Southeastern	5
Bethel, Kuskokwim	20
Black River Settlements, Yukon	125
Borka, Unalaska	57
Boundary Camp, Yukon	18
Bradford, Nushagak	166
Bristol Bay	×
Burroughs Bay, Southeastern	134
Cape Douglas, Kodiak	85
Cape Fox	×
Cape Krusenstern, Arctic	45
Cape Lees	×
Cape Nome, Arctic	41
Cape Smythe, Arctic	246
Carmel, Nushagak	189
Chalitmute, Kuskokwim	358
Chechinamute, Kuskokwim	81
Chernovsky, Unalaska	78
Chican, Southeastern	88
Chignik Bay, Kodiak	193
Chilkaht Lake, Kodiak	34
Chilkat, Southeastern	153
Chilkoot Mission, Southeastern	106
Chimingyangamute, Kuskokwim	40
Chokfoktoleghagamute, Kuskokwim	18
Christangamute, Nushagak	83
Chuligmute, Kuskokwim	32
Chuligmute Upper, Kuskokwim	30
Coal Harbor, Unalaska	15
Cook's Inlet	×
Davids Camp, Yukon	66
Douglas, Southeastern	402
Dununuk, Kuskokwim	48
Eagle Harbor, Kodiak	77
East Point, No. 1, Kuskokwim	36
East Point, No. 2, Kuskokwim	41
Ekaluktalugumute, Kuskokwim	24
English Bay, Kodiak	107
Erkleetpaga, Arctic	20
Etohlugamute, Kuskokwim	25
Fish Bay, Southeastern	4
Flagatlokai, Yukon	16
Fort Tongas, Southeastern	50

Alaska

Place	Population
Fort Wrangel, Southeastern	316
Funter Bay, Southeastern	25
Gambier Bay, Southeastern	8
Gilakhamute, Kuskokwim	22
Golofnin Bay, Arctic	25
Gologamute, Nushagak	29
Golsova, Yukon	44
Hindasetukee, Southeastern	143
Holikitsak, Yukon	114
Hoochinoo, Southeastern	381
Hoonah, Southeastern	438
Howcan, Souteastern	×
Huckiung, Nushagak	32
Huseloft River	×
Icy Cape, Arctic	57
Igagik, Nushagak	60
Ighiak, Kodiak	94
Ighiakchaghamute, Kuskokwim	81
Igivachochamute, Nushagak	31
Ignalook, Arctic	85
Ignitok, Arctic	64
Ikaleaveagmute, Yukon	38
Ikalinkamute, Nushagak	60
Iko-agmute, Yukon	65
Ikogmute, Yukon	140
Iliamna, Kodiak	76
Ingahamute, Yukon	50
Ingamatsha, Kodiak	73
Ingeramute, Kuskokwim	35
Insiachamute, Nushagak	42
Isha, Kodiak	30
Itkarapaga, Arctic	8
Jackson, Southeastern	105
Juneau, Southeastern	1,253
Kaguiak, Kodiak	112
Kahlukhtughamute, Kuskokwim	29
Kahmute, Kuskokwim	40
Kailwigamute, Kuskokwim	157
Kakawaterka, Southeastern	70
Kakhonak, Nushagak	28
Kakwaltoo, Southeastern	77
Kakwok, Nushagak	45
Kalhonehagmute, Yukon	45
Kaltkagamute, Kuskokwim	29
Kanagamute, Kuskokwim	35
Kanagmute, Kuskokwim	41
Kanakanak, Nushagak	53
Kanatak, Kodiak	26
Kanegmute, Yukon	53
Kanikhluk, Kodiak	73
Kanulik, Nushagak	54
Karluk, Kodiak	1,123
Kashunahmute, Kuskokwim	232
Kaskanak, Nushagak	66
Kassan, Southeastern	47
Kassiachamute, Nushagak	50
Kassilof, Kodiak	117
Katmai, Kodiak	132
Kavalonah, Nushagak	13
Kaviaghamute, Kuskokwim	59
Keavyamute, Yukon	97
Kenai, Kodiak	264
Kengugmute, Yukon	54
Kennachananaghamute, Kuskokwim	181
Kichikan, Southeastern	40
Kikiktowrik, Yukon	23
Kikikhtagmute, Kuskokwim	119
Killisnoo, Southeastern	79
Killuda, Kodiak	22
Kinegnagamute, Kuskokwim	92
Kinegnagmute, Kuskokwim	76
Kingaghee, Arctic	488
Kinik, Kodiak	160
Kinuyak, Nushagak	51
Kivichakh, Nushagak	37
Klakwan, Southeastern	326
Klawock, Southeastern	287
Kl-changamute, Kuskokwim	49
Klinquan, Southeastern	27
Klukukhu, Southeastern	15
Klutagmute, Kuskokwim	21
Kochlogtogpagamute, Kuskokwim	20
Kodiak, Kodiak	495
Koeluk	×
Koggiung, Nushagak	133
Kohtokaket, Yukon	24
Kolmakovsky, Kuskokwim	26
Koot, Kuskokwim	117
Koot River Settlements, Kuskokwim	74
Korovinsky, Unalaska	41
Koshigin, Unalaska	46
Kotlik, Yukon	31
Kous Island	×

Alaska

Place	Population
Koyukuk River Settlements, Yukon	174
Kozerevsky, Yukon	131
Kuskohkagamute, Kuskokwim	115
Kustatan, Kodiak	45
Kwichampingagamute, Kuskokwim	25
Kwigamute, Kuskokwim	43
Kyktoltowtin, Yukon	23
Lagoon No. 1, Kuskokwim	30
Lagoon No. 2, Kuskokwim	36
Lake Bay, Southeastern	31
Lake Village, (*Chageluk River*) Yukon	3
Lake Village, (*Copper River*) Kodiak	136
Lomavigamute, Kuskokwim	53
Loring, Southeastern	200
Lowell, Kodiak	12
Makeymute, Yukon	50
Makushin, Unalaska	51
Meshik, Nushagak	74
Metlakahtla, Southeastern	823
Millerton, Nushagak	165
Mitchell, (*Yukon diggings*) Yukon	238
Mitrofania, Kodiak	49
Morzhovoi, Unalaska	68
Mumtrahamute, Kuskokwim	162
Mumtrekhlagamute, Koskokwim	33
Napaimute, Nushagak	11
Napaimute, Kuskokwim	23
Napaskeagamute, Kuskokwim	97
Newturit, Yukon	9
Nikhkak, Nushagak	42
Ninilchilik, Kodiak	81
Noghelingamute, Nushagak	16
Noh-chamute, Kuskokwim	28
Norkluk, Arctic	13
Norton Sound Settlements, Arctic	283
Notaloten, Yukon	15
Novokhtolahamute, Kuskokwim	55
Nowikakat, Yukon	77
Ntealeyta, Yukon	7
Nuchek, Kodiak	145
Nuklukayet, Yukon	120
Nulato, Yukon	118
Nulochtagamute, Nushagak	31
Nunachanaghamute, Kuskokwim	135
Nunavoknak-chlugamute, Kuskokwim	107
Nushagak, Nushagak	268
Odiak, Kodiak	273
Oh-hagamute, Kuskokwim	36
Old Harbor, Kodiak	86
Ozernoy, Unalaska	45
Paimute, Yukon	65
Pakwik, Nushagak	93
Pastolik, Yukon	113
Point Barrie, Southeastern	92
Point Barrow, Arctic	152
Boint Belcher, Arctic	114
Point Ellis, Southeatern	170
Point Hope, Arctic	301
Point Lay, Arctic	77
Popof Island, Unalaska	146
Porcupine River Settlements, Yukon	150
Port Clarence, Arctic	485
Pybus Bay, Southeastern	26
Pyramid Harbor, South'st'rn	77
Queakhpaghamute, Kuskokwim	75
Quelelochamute, Kuskokwim	112
Quiechlop-chamute, Kuskokwim	83
Quiechochlogamute, Kuskokwim	65
Quilochugamute, Kuskokwim	12
Quinhaghamute, Kuskokwim	10
Sahruyuk, Nushagak	32
Saint George, Unalaska	93
Saint Lawrence Island, Arctic	267
Saint Michael, Yukon	101
Saint Paul, Unalaska	244
Sakar, Southeastern	21
Sakataloden, Yukon	39
Salmon Bay, Suotheastern	42
Sand Point, ——	×
Sannak, Unalaska	132

Town, District	Pop.
Sea Horse Island, Yukon	15
Seldovia, Kodiak	99
Semenovsky, Unalaska	3
Senati, Yukon	40
Seymour Channel, South'tn.	9
Shacktolit, Yukon	38
Shinyagamute, Kuskokwim	7
Shovenaghamute, Kuskokwim	62
Singick, Arctic	12
SITKA, Southeastern	1,190
Sledge Island, Arctic	67
Steamer Arctic, Yukon	27
Stugarok, Nushagak	7
Sumdum, Southeastern	42
Summer Camp, Yukon	44
Sushetno, Kodiak	142
Swetlaya Retchka, Yukon	44
Takashki, Yukon	80
Tanana, (*Upper River Settlements*) Yukon	203
Tanyut, Yukon	37
Tapkak, Arctic	51
Tatitlak, Kodiak	90
Teeketnagmute, Yukon	27
Teenahotozna, Yukon	8
Tefaknaghamute, Kuskokwim	195
Thin Point, Unalaska	231
Tiengaghamute, Kuskokwim	60
Tlegochitnagmute, Yukon	60
Togiagamute, Nushagak	94
Togiak, Nushagak	14
Tolstoi Bay, Southeastern	17
Tongass Narrows	×
Topolnik, Yukon	42
Toyonok, Kodiak	115
Trinachamute, Nushagak	20
Tulukagnagamute, Kuskokwim	17
Tuluksagmute, Kuskokwim	62
Tunaghamute, Kuskokwim	71
Tvastonagamute, Yukon	33
Tzeeto-at, Yukon	22
Uganak, Kodiak	31
Ugashik, Nushagak	154
Ugavigamute, Kuskokwim	57
Ugokhamute, Kuskokwim	68
Ukevok, Arctic	200
Ulokagmute, Kuskokwim	27
Ulukuk, Yukon	25
Umnak, Unalaska	94
Unalaklik, Yukon	175
Unalaska, Unalaska	317
Unangashik, Nushagak	190
Unga, Unalaska	159
Uyak, Kodiak	246
Uzinkee, Kodiak	74
Vinisahle, Kuskokwim	140
Voznesensky, Unalaska	43
Wainwright Inlet, Arctic	72
Windham Bay, Southeastern	11
Wingham Island, Kodiak	150
Wokhlehoghamute, Kuskokwim	19
Wrangell, Southeastern	316
Wrangell Bay, Kodiak	62
Yakutat, Southeastern	308
Yekook, Nushagak	65
Yess Bay, Southeastern	85
Yukokakat, Yukon	39

ARIZONA.

COUNTY	INDEX.	POP.
Apache	NE	4,281
Cochise	SE	6,938
Coconino	N	×
Gila	SE	2,021
Graham	SE	5.670
Maricopa	C	10,986
Mohave	NW	1,444
Navajo Ind. Res	NE	×
Pima	S	12,673
Pinal	S	4,251
Yavapai	C	8,685
Yuma	SW	2,671
Total		59.620

Arizona

TOWN. COUNTY.	INDEX.	POP.
Abbyes Spring, Maricopa	C	×
● *Adonde*, Yuma	SW	×
Agency, Apache	NE	×
Agua Caliente, Maricopa	C	×
Agua Fria Valley, Yavapai	C	×
Alexandra, Yavapai	C	190
● *Allanstown*, Apache	NE	×
Allen, Pima	S	30
Alma, Maricopa	C	×
Alma, Pinal	S	×
Alpine, Apache	NE	90
American Flag, Pima	S	45
● *Angell*, Yavapai	C	×
Antelope Valley, Yavapai	C	35
● *Araby*, Yuma	SW	×
Arivaca, Pima	S	236
Armer, Gila	SE	×
● *Ash Fork*, Yavapai	C	5
Aubrey, Mohave	NW	×
● *Aubrey*, Yavapai	C	325
Aultman, Yavapai	C	10
Aztec, Pima	S	35
● Aztec, Yuma	SW	×
Babbits, Yavapai	C	×
Bakers Butte, Yavapai	C	×
● *Banghart*, Yavapai	C	×
Bayard, Yavapai	C	×
Beavers Head, Yavapai	C	×
● Bellemont, Coconino	N	×
● Benson, Cochise	SE	348
Big Bug, Yavapai	C	115
Big Sandy, Mohave	NW	×
● *Billings*, Apache	NE	30
Bisbee, Cochise	SE	1,535
Blind Tank, Yuma	SW	×
Bonita, Graham	SE	75
● *Bosque*, Maricopa	C	42
● *Bowie*, Cochise	SE	130
Brannock, Cochise	SE	×
Breon, Mohave	NW	×
Briggs, Yavapai	C	×
● *Brookline*, Cochise	SE	×
Bryce, Graham	SE	×
Buckeye, Maricopa	C	×
Bueno, Yavapai	C	65
Bumble Bee, Yavapai	C	×
Butte City, Pinal	S	195
● *Cachise*, Cochise	SE	×
Cababi, Pima	S	130
● Calabasas, Pima	S	130
Campbell, Mohave	NW	×
● *Campbell*, Yavapai	C	×
Camp Hualapai, Mohave	NW	×
Camp Verde, Yavapai	C	150
● *Canisteo*, Cochise	SE	×
● Canon Diablo, Coconino	N	90
● *Carrizo*, Apache	NE	×
● Casa Grande, Pinal	S	328
Castle Dome L'ding, Yuma	SW	×
Catalpa, Gila	SE	×
Cave Creek, Maricopa	C	×
Cave Dwellings, Apache	NE	×
Cedar Springs, Graham	SE	×
Centennial, Yuma	SW	×
Central, Graham	SE	×
Cerbat, Mohave	NW	×
Cerro Colorado, Pima	S	×
● *Challender*, Yavapai	C	130
Charleston, Cochise	SE	455
Cherry, Yavapai	C	×
Chino, Yavapai	C	33
● *Chino*, Yavapai	C	×
● Chrystoval, Yuma	SW	×
Cienega, Yavapai	C	80
Clarksvale, Yavapai	C	×
● *Clearwater*, Yavapai	C	×
Cliff Dwellings, Yavapai	C	×
● Clifton, Graham	SE	600
Clip, Yuma	SW	60
● *Colfred*, Yuma	SW	×
Concho, Apache	NE	×
Congress, Yavapai	C	242
● *Contention*, Cochise	SE	325
Copper Basin, Yavapai	C	×
Copperopolis, Pinal	S	×
Cordes, Yavapai	C	×
Cornville, Yavapai	C	×
● *Coronado*, Graham	SE	×
● *Cosnino*, Yavapai	C	×
Cottonwood, Pinal	S	×
Cottonwood, Yavapai	C	34
Cox, Yavapai	C	×
● Crittenden, Pima	S	75
● *Crookton*, Yavapai	C	×
Crown King, Yavapai	C	×
● *Dennison*, Yavapai	C	×
DeNoon, Pinal	S	×
Desert, Pima	S	×
Doanville, Yuma	SW	×
● *Donaldson's*, Yavapai	C	×
Dos Cabezos, Cochise	SE	300
● Dragoon, Cochise	SE	40
● *Drake*, Mohave	NW	×
Dripping Springs, Gila	SE	×
Dudleyville, Pinal	S	62
● Duncan, Graham	SE	86
Dunlap, Graham	SE	390
East Bridge, Mohave	NW	×
● *East Verde*, Gila	SE	×
Edith, Maricopa	C	×
Ehrenberg, Yuma	SW	290
● *Elgin*, Cochise	SE	×
El Paso, Pima	S	×
Empire Ranch, Pima	S	×
● *Estrella*, Maricopa	C	×
Eureka, Yuma	SW	×
Eureka Spring, Graham	SE	×
● Fairbank, Cochise	SE	478
● *Fairview*, Yavapai	C	×
● **Flagstaff**, Coconino	N	963
● **Florence**, Pinal	S	1,486
Fort Apache, Apache	NE	413
Fort Bowie, Cochise	SE	250
Fort Defiance, Navajo, Ind. Res	NE	130
Fort Grant, Graham	SE	498
Fort Huachuca, Cochise	SE	296
Fort Lowell, Pima	S	545
Fort McDowell, Maricopa	C	×
Fort Mohave, Mohave	NW	×
Fort Moroni, Yavapai	C	×
Fort San Carlos, Gila	SE	344
Fort Thomas, Graham	SE	300
Fort Verde, Yavapai	C	×
● *Fort Whipple*, Yavapai	C	×
● *Franconia*, Mohave	NW	×
Fulton, Yavapai	C	×
Galeyville, Cochise	SE	×
Ganado, Apache	NE	×
● *Garland*, Yavapai	C	×
Gatewood, Cochise	SE	×
● Gila Bend, Maricopa	C	135
● *Gila City*, Yuma	SW	×
Gillett, Yavapai	C	260
Glencoe, Cochise	SE	200
● **Globe**, Gila	SE	803
Gold Basin, Mohave	NW	×
Goodwin, Graham	SE	650
Graham, Graham	SE	×
Granite Water, Yuma	SW	×
Greaterville, Pima	S	260
● *Guthrie*, Graham	SE	×
Hackberry, Mohave	NW	260
● *Hackberry Station*, Moh	NW	×
Harcuvar, Maricopa	C	×
● *Hardy*, Apache	NE	×
Harqua Hala, Yuma	SW	×
Harrisburg, Yuma	SW	×
Harshaw, Pima	S	260
Harts Place, Yavapai	C	×
Hassayampa, Yavapai	C	×
Hatch Spring, Yuma	SW	×
● *Haulapai*, Mohave	NW	×
● *Heaton*, Pinal	S	×
Heber, Apache	NE	×
Hillside, Yavapai	C	×
● Holbrook, Apache	NE	306
Hot Springs, Yavapai	C	×
Houck's Tank, Apache	NE	65
Howells, Yavapai	C	115
● *Huachuca*, Cochise	SE	×
Hudson, Maricopa	C	×
Hulls Springs, Yavapai	C	×
Hunapai, Mohave	NW	×
● *Jaynes*, Pima	S	×
Jerome, Yavapai	C	250
Juniper, Yavapai	C	32
Keam's Canon, Apache	NE	32
Kear's District, Yavapai	C	×
Kenilworth, Pinal	S	×
Kennedy's Station, Maric	C	×
● **Kingman**, Mohave	NW	322
Kirby, Yavapai	C	×
● *Kyrene*, Maricopa	C	×
LaNoira, Pima	S	×
La Osa, Pima	S	×
Las Playos, Pima	S	×
Lee's Ferry, Coconino	N	32
Lehi, Maricopa	C	269
● *Ligurta*, Yuma	SW	×
Linden, Apache	NE	×
Little Giant, Gila	SE	×
Lochiel, Pima	S	×
Logan City, Pima	S	×
● *Longfellow*, Yavapai	C	×

Post Office, County	Index	Pop.
● *Long Meadow*, Yavapai	C	×
Lost Basin, Mohave	NW	32
● *Luzena*, Cochise	SE	×
Lynx Creek, Yavapai	C	×
McDowell, Maricopa	C	115
● *McLellan*, Yavapai	C	×
McMillen, Gila	SE	215
Mammoth, Pinal	S	×
Mammoth Spring, Yuma	SW	×
Manlyville, Pinal	S	65
● Maricopa, Pinal	S	240
Maxey, Graham	SE	×
Mayer, Yavapai	C	×
Mesa, Maricopa	C	600
Mesaville, Pinal	S	100
● *Mescal*, Pinal	S	63
● *Milton*, Yavapai	C	×
Mineral City, Yuma	SW	×
Mineral Park, Mohave	NW	200
Minnehaha Flat, Yavapai	C	×
Mishonginivi, Apache	NE	×
Mohave City, Mohave	NW	160
Mohawk, Yuma	SW	×
● *Mohawk Summit*, Yuma	SW	×
Moncopai, Yavapai	C	×
Monitor, Yuma	SW	×
● *Montezuma*, Maricopa	C	×
Monument, Pima	S	×
Monument, No. 1, Yuma	SW	×
Monument, No. 4, Yuma	SW	×
Monument, No. 6, Pima	S	×
Monument, No. 7, Pima	S	×
Monument, No. 9, Pima	S	×
Monument, No. 12, Pima	S	×
Morenci, Graham	SE	758
● *Mormon*, Yavapai	C	×
Mormonderry, Yavapai	C	×
Munn's Valley, Yavapai	C	×
● Navajo, Apache	NE	130
Nephi, Maricopa	C	×
New Water, Yuma	SW	×
● Nogales, Pima	S	1,194
Noonville, Pima	S	×
● *North Siding*, Graham	SE	×
Norton, Yuma	SW	65
Nugget, Gila	SE	130
Nutrioso, Apache	NE	×
● *Ochoa*, Cochise	SE	×
Ochoaville, Cochise	SE	65
● *Olga*, Cochise	SE	×
Olive, Pima	S	×
Oracle, Pinal	S	65
Oraibi, Apache	NE	×
Orizaba, Pinal	S	×
Oro, Graham	SE	×
Oro Blanco, Pima	S	130
Orreal Spring, Yavapai	C	×
Overton, Maricopa	C	×
● *Painted Rock*, Maricopa	C	×
Pajarito, Pima	S	×
Palomas, Yuma	SW	×
● Pantano, Pima	S	130
● *Papago*, Pima	S	×
Park, Apache	NE	×
Parker, Yuma	SW	50
Patagonia, Pima	S	×
Payson, Gila	SE	32
● Peach Springs, Mohave	NW	265
Peck Mine, Yavapai	C	×
Parrahatchopet Water, Yuma	SW	×
Peoria, Maricopa	C	×
● **PHOENIX**, Maricopa	C	3,152
● *Picacho*, Pinal	S	130
Pima, Graham	SE	195
Pinal, Pinal	S	1,125
Pine, Gila	SE	×
Pinedale, Apache	NE	×
Pine Spring, Yavapai	C	×
● *Pineveta*, Yavapai	C	×
Pioneer, Gila	SE	500
Pipe Springs, Yavapai	C	×
Pleasant Valley, Gila	SE	×
Pomoso, Yuma	SW	×
● *Point of Rocks*, Yavapai	C	×
Poso Bueno, Pima	S	×
Powell, Mohave	NW	97
Powers, Cochise	SE	×
Pratt, Maricopa	C	×
● **Prescott**, Yavapai	C	1,759
● *Prescott Junction*, Yavapai	C	×
Providence Wells, Pima	S	×
● *Puntney*, Yavapai	C	×
Quijotoa, Pima	S	25
● *Railroad Pass*, Cochise	SE	×
Redington, Pima	S	60
● *Red Rock*, Mohave	NW	×
Red Rock, Pinal	S	×
● *Reese's*, Yavapai	C	×
Reliable, Yavapai	C	×
Reno, Gila	SE	×
Reymert, Pinal	S	254
Richmond, Gila	SE	×
Riley Wells, Graham	SE	×
● *Rillito*, Pima	S	×
Riverside, Pinal	S	65
Rodes Ranch, Yuma	SW	×
● *Ross*, Yavapai	C	×
Rucker, Cochise	SE	×
Rye, Gila	SE	32
Sacaton, Pinal	S	32
● *Sacaton*, Pinal	S	×
Safford, Graham	SE	200
Sahuarito, Pima	S	19
Saint David, Cochise	SE	260
Saint John's, Apache	NE	482
● Saint Joseph, Apache	NE	130
Salero, Pima	S	130
Sample, Cochise	SE	×
San Carlos, Gila	SE	×
● *Sanders*, Apache	NE	×
Sanford, Pinal	S	130
● *San Fords*, Pima	S	×
San Jose, Graham	SE	×
San Pedro, Cochise	SE	×
San Rafael, Pima	S	×
● San Simon, Cochise	SE	×
San Xavier, Pima	S	×
Sassabi Flat, Pima	S	×
● Seligman, Yavapai	C	×
● Sentinel, Maricopa	C	65
Seymour, Maricopa	C	65
● *Sheldon*, Graham	SE	×
Shichoamari, Apache	NE	×
Shipaualuvi, Apache	NE	×
Shougapavi, Apache	NE	×
Show Low, Apache	NE	200
Signal, Mohave	NW	300
Silent, Yuma	SW	195
Silver King, Pinal	S	212
Simmons, Yavapai	C	195
Skull Valley, Yapavai	C	×
Smith's Mill, Maricopa	C	×
Snow Flake, Apache	NE	500
Solomonsville, Grah'm	SE	287
● *Sonoita*, Pinal	S	×
● *South Siding*, Graham	SE	×
Springerville, Apache	NE	443
Stanton, Gila	SE	×
Stanton, Yavapai	C	130
● *Stanwix*, Maricopa	C	×
Steels Station, Cochise	SE	×
Stockton, Mohave	NW	×
Stoddard, Yavapai	C	165
Stoneman Lake, Yavapai	C	×
Strawberry, Coconino	N	×
● *Sullivan*, Yavapai	C	×
Sunset, Apache	NE	200
Supai, Yavapai	C	×
● *Sweet Water*, Pinal	S	×
Sycamore Springs, Yavapai	C	×
Tacna, Yuma	SW	×
Tanque Verde, Pima	S	×
Taylor, Apache	NE	77
● Tempe, Maricopa	C	2,000
Tanajos Altos, Yuma	SW	×
● Teviston, Cochise	SE	130
Te-wa, Apache	NE	×
● *Texas Hill*, Yuma	SW	×
Thatcher, Graham	SE	×
Thomas, Graham	SE	195
Tip Top, Yavapai	C	65
● *Toltec*, Pinal	S	×
● **Tombstone**, Cochise	SE	1,875
Tonto, Gila	SE	165
Total Wreck, Pima	S	325
Tres Alamos, Cochise	SE	×
Trout Spring, Apache	NE	×
● *Traxton*, Mohave	NW	×
Tubac, Pima	S	520
Tuba City, Coconino	N	×
● **Tucson**, Pima	S	5,150
Turquoise, Cochise	SE	×
● *Vails*, Pima	S	×
● *Vanarman*, Cochise	SE	×
Vekol, Pinal	S	×
● *Verde*, Yavapai	C	×
● *Verde Bridge*, Yavapai	C	×
Vulture, Maricopa	C	350
Walker, Yavapai	C	200
● *Walnut*, Yavapai	C	×
Walnut Grove, Yavapai	C	×
Walpi, Apache	NE	×
Washington, Pima	S	195
Wheatfield, Maricopa	C	65
Whipple, Yavapai	C	338
White Rock Spring, Ap'che	NE	×
Wickenburg, Maricopa	C	135
Wilgus, Cochise	SE	×
● Willcox, Cochise	SE	396
● Williams, Coconino	N	199
● *Wilmot*, Pima	S	×
● *Windmill*, Yavapai	C	×
● Winslow, Apache	NE	363
Woodruff, Apache	NE	25
Woodside, Yavapai	C	25
● *Yampai*, Yavapai	C	×
● *Yorks*, Graham	SE	×
Young, Gila	SE	×
● *Yucca*, Mohave	NW	×
● **Yuma**, Yuma	SW	1,773

ARKANSAS.

COUNTY.	INDEX.	POP.
Arkansas	E	11,432
Ashley	SE	13,295
Baxter	N	8,527
Benton	NW	27,716
Boone	NW	15,816
Bradley	S	7,972
Calhoun	S	7,267
Carroll	NW	17,288
Chicot	SE	11,419
Clark	SW	20,997
Clay	NE	12,200
Cleburne	N	7,884
Cleveland	S	11,362
Columbia	SW	19,893
Conway	C	19,[illegible]
Craighead	NE	12,025
Crawford	NW	21,714
Crittenden	E	13,940
Cross	E	7,693
Dallas	S	9,296
Desha	SE	10,324
Drew	SE	17,352
Faulkner	C	18,342
Franklin	NW	19,934
Fulton	N	10,984
Garland	C	15,328
Grant	C	7,786
Greene	NE	12,908
Hempstead	SW	22,796
Hot Spring	C	11,603
Howard	SW	13,789
Independence	N	21,962
Izard	N	13,038
Jackson	NE	15,179
Jefferson	C	40,881
Johnson	NW	16,758
La Fayette	SW	7,700
Lawrence	NE	12,984
Lee	E	18,886
Lincoln	SE	10,255
Little River	SW	8,903
Logan	W	20,774
Lonoke	C	19,263
Madison	NW	17,402
Marion	N	10,390
Miller	SW	14,714
Mississippi	NE	11,635
Monroe	E	15,336
Montgomery	W	7,923
Nevada	SW	14,832
Newton	NW	9,950
Ouachita	S	17,033
Perry	C	5,538
Phillips	E	25,341
Pike	SW	8,537
Poinsett	NE	4,272
Polk	W	9,283
Pope	NW	19,458
Prairie	C	11,374
Pulaski	C	47,329
Randolph	NE	14,485
St. Francis	E	13,543
Saline	C	11,311
Scott	W	12,635
Searcy	N	9,664
Sebastian	W	33,200
Sevier	SW	10,072
Sharp	N	10,418
Stone	N	7,043
Union	S	14,977

Van Buren	N	8,567
Washington	NW	32,024
White	C	22,946
Woodruff	E	14,009
Yell	W	18,015
Total		1,128,179

TOWN. COUNTY.	INDEX.	POP.
Abilene, Saline	C	×
Accident, Montgomery	W	130
Actus, Sebastian	W	50
Ada, Conway	C	30
Adamsville, Bradley	S	65
Adler, Izard	N	1(
Adler, Johnson	NW	×
● *Adler*, Jackson	NE	×
Adona, Perry	C	57
● Afton, Fulton	N	20
Agnos, Fulton	N	10
Ain, Grant	C	130
Akin Farm, Saline	C	46
Akron, Independence	N	50
Alabam, Madison	NW	32
Albertha, Randolph	NE	100
Alco, Stone	N	32
Alderbrook, Independence	N	×
● Alexander, Pulaski	C	143
Alice, Drew	SE	35
● Alicia, Lawrence	NE	75
Allbrook, Howard	SW	32
Allegan, Pope	NW	×
Allen, Benton	NW	×
Allen's Landing, Phillips	E	×
Alligator Bluff, Ashley	SE	×
● Alma, Crawford	NW	486
Almond, Cleburne	N	150
● *Almont*, Crittenden	E	×
Almyra, Arkansas	E	5
Alpha, Yell	W	10
Alpine, Clark	SW	250
● *Alpine*, Faulkner	C	250
Alread, Van Buren	N	5
● Alston, Franklin	NW	15
Altharp, Saline	C	×
● Altheimer, Jefferson	C	150
● Altus, Franklin	NW	469
Alvis, Independence	N	[illegible]
Aly, Yell	W	33
● *Amberg*, Greene	NE	×
Amelia, Mississippi	NE	×
Amity, Clark	SW	211
Amos, Baxter	N	13
Amos, Clark	SW	10
Anderson, Izard	N	35
Andros, Crawford	NW	32
Anna, Crawford	NW	5
Annieville, Lawrence	NE	×
Annover, Cleveland	S	10
Anoloko, Union	S	×
Antimony, Howard	SW	40
Antioch, White	C	×
Antonie, Pike	SW	100
Anvil, Stone	N	×
Aplin, Perry	C	125
Appleton, Pope	NW	150
Arcadia, Hempstead	SW	×
Archey, Van Buren	N	×
Arel, Cleburne	N	×
● Argenta, Pulaski	C	3,000
● **Arkadelphia**, Clark	SW	1,455
● **Arkansas City**, D'sha	SE	500
Arkansas Post, Arkansas	E	50
Armada, Crawford	NW	65
Armstrong, Sharp	N	32
Armstrong Landing, Crit'dn	E	20
Armstrong Spring, White	C	25
Arnett, Washington	NW	33
Arp, Pike	SW	×
Arthur, Conway	C	×
Ashdown, Little River	SW	×
Ash Flat, Sharp	N	306
Ashford, Crittenden	E	30
Ashton, Clark	SW	18
Ashvale, Lonoke	C	×
Askew, Lee	E	19
● *Astor*, Jefferson	C	×
Atheistan, Mississippi	NE	×
● *Atkins*, Pulaski	C	×
● Atkins, Pope	NW	660
Atlanta, Columbia	SW	100
Attica, Randolph	NE	×
Atwood, Howard	SW	32
Auburn, Lincoln	SE	×
Auburn, Sebastian	W	×
Audley, Cleveland	S	×
Augsburg, Pope	NW	195
● **Augusta**, Woodruff	E	519
● *Augusta Station*, W'druff	E	×
Aurora, Madison	NW	100
● *Aurich*, Prairie	C	×
● Austin, Lonoke	C	100
Austin Station, Lonoke	C	150
Auvergne, Jackson	NE	25
Ava, Perry	C	×
Avery, Lincoln	SE	×
Avilla, Saline	C	46
● Avoca, Benton	NW	100
Baker, Polk	W	26
● Bald Knob, White	C	250
● *Baldwin*, Washington	NW	×
Balloon, Yell	W	20
Balls, Marion	N	×
Bankhead, Jefferson	C	550
Banner, Cleburne	N	40
Banty, Pulaski	C	×
Barber, Scott	W	200
Barcelona, Crawford	NW	×
Bard, Greene	NE	×
Bardstown, Mississippi	NE	×
Barfield, Mississippi	NE	57
Barham, Ouachita	S	25
● *Baring Cross*, Pulaski	C	×
Barkada, Drew	SE	20
Barker, Hempstead	SW	60
Barling, Sebastian	W	×
Barney, Faulkner	C	×
Barren Fork, Izard	N	290
Barrettsville, Prairie	C	97
Bartholomew, Ashley	SE	60
● Barton, Phillips	E	25
Barton Landing, Miss	SE	130
Baskins, Searcy	N	×
Bassville, Grant	C	×
Batavia, Boone	NW	20
● **Batesville**, Inde'dence	N	2,150
Batson, Johnson	NW	×
● *Baucum*, Pulaski	C	×
● Baxter, Drew	SE	200
Baxter, Johnson	NW	×
● Bay, Craighead	NE	100
Bay Bridge, Craighead	NE	×
Bayou Bartholomew, A'ly	SE	100
Bayou Meto, Arkansas	E	50
● *Bayou Meto*, Lonoke	C	15
Bay Village, Cross	E	50
Beall, Fulton	N	×
Bear, Montgomery	W	175
Bear Creek, Searcy	N	60
● Bearden, Ouachita	S	250
● *Beards*, Woodruff	E	×
Beaty, Benton	NW	10
● Beaver, Carroll	NW	100
Becker, Hot Spring	C	30
● *Becton*, Woodruff	E	×
Bedford, Sebastian	W	×
● Beebe, White	C	86
Bee Branch, VanBuren	N	35
Beech Bluffs, Dallas	S	×
Beech Creek, Ashley	SE	×
Beech Creek, Dallas	S	×
● Beirne, Clark	SW	200
Beith's Landing, Desha	SE	15
Belcher, Prairie	C	×
Belfast, Grant	C	20
Bellefonte, Boone	NW	100
Belleville, Yell	W	247
Belleville, Jefferson	C	×
Belles, Pike	SW	40
Bell's Store, Nevada	SW	×
Belmont, Crawford	NW	60
Belva, Scott	W	55
● *Bemis*, Woodruff	E	×
Bengay, Fulton	N	15
Bengay, Sharp	N	×
Ben Lomond, Sevier	SW	25
Bennett, Monroe	E	×
Bennett River, (see Beal)		×
Bennett's, Baxter	N	10
● **Benton**, Saline	C	647
● **Bentonville**, Benton	NW	1,677
Benyard, St. Francis	E	×
Berea, Ashley	SE	25
Berlin, Ashley	SE	×
● Berlin, Johnson	NW	79
Bermuda, Arkansas	E	65
Bernard, Chicot	SE	×
Berryville, Carroll	NW	549
● Bethel, Greene	NE	50
Bethesda, Independence	W	×
Beulah, Prairie	C	×
Beverly, Sebastian	W	60
Bexar, Fulton	N	20
Bidville, Crawford	NW	10
● *Bierne*, Clark	SW	200
● *Big Bay Siding*, C'head	NE	65
Big Bend, Polk	W	15
● *Big Creek*, Cleveland	S	×
● *Big Creek*, Crittenden	E	×
Big Flat, Baxter	N	150
Big Fork, Polk	W	13
Big Hill, Calhoun	S	×
Big Lake, (see Osceola)		×
Big North Fork, Baxter	N	×
Big Pond, (see Mountain Home		×
Bills, Pike	SW	30
Bingen, Hempstead	SW	125
Bingham Springs, Perry	C	×
Birdell, Randolph	NE	15
Birta, Yell	SW	19
Bishop, Little River	SW	×
Bismarck, Hot Spring	C	25
Biswell Springs, Sebastian	W	×
Bivens, Little River	SW	×
Blackburn, Washington	NW	×
Black Fish, (see Tyronza)		×
● *Blackfish*, St. Francis	E	×
Black Fork, Scott	W	12
Black Jack, Scott	W	×
● Black Rock, Lawrence	NE	761
Black Springs, Montgomery	W	200
Blackton, Monroe	E	×
● *Blackville*, Conway	C	130
Blaine, Logan	W	15
Blakemore, Lonoke	C	×
Blanchard Springs, Union	S	197
Blanchton, Bradley	S	45
Blanco, Searcy	N	75
Bland, Saline	C	28
Blansett, Scott	W	15
Blanville, Sharp	N	×
Bledsoe, Lee	E	30
Bliss, White	C	13
Blocher, Saline	C	325
Blocker, Logan	W	×
Bloomer, Sebastian	W	75
Bloomfield, Benton	NW	89
Bloomington, Benton	NW	×
Blue Ball, Scott	W	10
Blue Mountain, Stone	N	325
Blue's Point, (see Bledsoe)		×
Bluff City, Nevada	SW	25
Bluffton, Yell	W	25
Blytheville, Mississippi	NE	×
Board Camp, Polk	W	50
Bob, Saline	C	×
Bodcan, LaFayette	SW	195
Bodcaw, Nevada	SW	75
Bodman, Drew	SE	20
Boeuff River, Chicot	SE	×
Boggy, Miller	SW	×
Boles, Scott	W	50
Bombay, Drew	SE	20
● *Bonair*, St. Francis	E	×
Bon Air, Stone	N	×
● Bono, Craighead	NE	10
Boone, Boone	NW	15
Booneville, Logan	W	496
Boonsborough, Washt'n	NW	400
Boothe, Scott	W	100
Booty, Arkansas	E	×
Borum's L'd'g, (see Osceola)		×
Boston, Madison	NW	50
Boston Mountain, Newtn	NW	×
● Boughton, Nevada	SW	80
Bourlands' Store, Nevada	SW	136
Bowen, Pike	SW	×
Bowen's Bridge, (see Auvergne)		×
Box, Columbia	SW	×
Boxley, Newton	NW	10
Box Spring, Yell	W	×
Boyce, Logan	W	10
Boyd, Miller	SW	×
Boydsville, Clay	NE	100
Brad, White	C	×
● Bradford, White	C	200
Bradix, Prairie	C	×
● Bradley, LaFayette	SW	30
Bradley, Cleveland	S	10
Bradley Landing, (see Oldham)		×
Bragg, Yell	W	30
Brakeville, Lincoln	SE	×
Brawley, Scott	W	46
Brazils, Saline	C	66
Breckenridge, Conway	C	32
● Brentwood, Wash'n	NW	25
Briggsville, Yell	W	60
Bright's Place, Pulaski	C	10
Bright Star, Miller	SW	100
Brightwater, Benton	NW	150

Place	Region	Pop.
●Brinkley, Monroe	E	1,510
Brisbane, Nevada	SW	×
Brister, Columbia	SW	20
Bristol, Faulkner	C	50
British, Logan	W	×
Britton, Crawford	NW	5
Britts, Clark	SW	×
Brockett, Randolph	NE	20
Brocktown, Pike	SW	15
Brolaski, Mississippi	NE	260
●*Brookbans*, Greene	NE	×
●Brookland, Craighead	NE	100
Brooklyn, Baxter	N	21
Brooks, Grant	C	38
Brownstown, Sevier	SW	100
Brownsville, Lonoke	C	×
Bruno, Marion	N	15
Brushy Lake, Cross	E	×
Brushyville, Grant	C	250
●Bryant, Saline	C	150
Buck Horn, Stone	N	28
Buck Knob, Scott	W	63
●Buckner, Columbia	SW	312
●*Buckner's Grove*, Was'n	NW	×
Buckrange, Howard	SW	×
Buckville, Montgomery	W	75
Budge, La Fayette	SW	×
●*Buell*, Sebastian	W	×
●Buena Vista, Ouachita	S	150
●*Buffalo*, Greene	NE	×
Buffalo City, (see Yellville)		×
Buffalo Lick, Poinsett	NE	25
Buford, Baxter	N	15
Bulger, Polk	W	×
Burkesville, Franklin	NW	×
Burk, Saline	C	5
Burlington, Boone	NW	10
Burnett's Land'g, (see Red F'k		×
Burnville, Sebastian	W	15
Butlerville, Lonoke	C	75
Buttry, Benton	NW	×
Butt's Store, Johnson	NW	×
Byler, Izard	N	×
Byron, Fulton	N	×
●*Cabin Creek*, Johnson	NW	×
●Cabot, Lonoke	C	350
Cache, Craighead	NE	×
●*Cache*, Greene	NE	×
●*Cache River*, Monroe	E	×
Caddo Gap, Montgomery	W	50
Caglesville, Pope	NW	40
Calamine, Sharp	N	50
●Caldwell, St. Francis	E	×
Caledonia, Union	S	15
Calf Creek, (see Blanco)		×
Calhoun, Columbia	SW	65
Calico, Logan	W	40
Calico Rock, Izard	N	20
Calmer, Cleveland	S	×
●**Camden**, Ouachita	S	2,571
●*Cameron Mill*, Miller	SW	×
Camp, Fulton	N	10
●*Campbell*, Jackson	NE	×
Campbell, Searcy	N	15
Campbell's L'dg, (see Bledsoe)		×
●*Canaan*, Lee	E	×
Cane Creek, Faulkner	C	×
Cane Hill, (see Boonsboro)		×
Caney, Nevada	SW	200
●Canfield, LaFayette	SW	32
Cannon, Benton	NW	10
Canton, Sharp	N	97
Cany Fork, Pike	SW	45
Capark, Newton	NW	×
Carden's Bottom, Yell	W	20
Cardiff, Scott	W	×
●Carlisle, Lonoke	C	185
Carmel, Chicot	SE	28
Carolan, Logan	W	25
Carouse, Nevada	SW	×
Carriola, Chicot	SE	35
Carrollton, Carroll	NW	300
Carson's Lake, Mississippi	NE	×
Carter's Store, Wash'g'tn	NW	20
Casa, Perry	C	195
Cascade, Faulkner	C	50
Cash, Craighead	NE	13
Cass, Franklin	NW	10
Casscoe, Arkansas	E	25
Cassville, Newton	NW	20
Catcher, Crawford	NW	×
Cato, Faulkner	C	15
Caulksville, Logan	W	300
Cauthron, Scott	W	45
Cavanaugh, Sebastian	W	20
Cave Creek, Newton	NW	25
Cecil, Franklin	NW	32

Arkansas

Place	Region	Pop.
Cedar Creek, Scott	W	40
Cedar Glades, Montgomery	W	150
●*Cedars*, Sebastian	W	×
Cedar Hill, Nevada	SW	×
Cedar Hill, Yell	W	×
Cedar Point L'd'g, (see Conway)		×
Cedarville, Crawford	NW	80
Center, Sharp	N	57
Center Hill, White	C	200
Center Ridge, Conway	C	200
Centerville, Yell	W	×
Central, Sebastian	W	10
Centre Point, Howard	SW	297
Centre Prairie, Logan	W	×
Centreville, Montgomery	W	65
Centreville, (see Kenyon)		×
Cerro Gordo, Little River	SW	30
Chadwick, Faulkner	C	×
Chalk, Van Buren	N	×
Chalk Bluff, Clay	NE	97
Chambersville, Calhoun	S	100
Champagnolle, Union	S	100
Champion, Arkansas	E	×
Chaney, Pike	SW	×
Chapel Hill, Sevier	SW	75
Charleston, Franklin	NW	370
Charlotte, Independence	N	97
Cheek, Phillips	E	×
Cherokee Bay, Randolph	NE	×
Cherokee City, Benton	NW	100
Cherry Grove, Grant	C	50
●Cherry Valley, Cross	E	50
Chester, Desha	SE	200
●Chester, Crawford	NW	222
Chickalah, Yell	W	250
Chickasawba, Mississippi	NE	90
Chicot, (see Arkansas City)		×
●Chidester, Ouachita	S	50
Chip, Union	S	32
Chismville, Logan	W	150
Chocoville, Sebastian	W	×
Choctaw, Van Buren	N	46
Chula, Yell	W	×
●*Cicalla*, St. Francis	E	×
Cincinnati, Washington	NW	138
Cinda, Mississippi	NE	×
●**Clarendon**, Monroe	E	1,060
●Clarketon, Crittenden	E	100
Clarksburgh, Greene	NE	×
Clarkson, Sharp	N	×
●**Clarksville**, Johnson	NW	937
Claude, Van Buren	N	50
Claunch, Craighead	NE	×
Clay, White	E	15
Clayton, Nevada	SW	25
Clayville, Clay	NE	60
Clear Creek, Boone	NW	×
Clear Creek, (see Powell)		×
Clear Lake, Mississippi	NE	×
Clear Mount, Miller	SW	×
Clear Spring, Clark	**SW**	**25**
Clear Water, White	C	38
Cleburne, Cross	E	×
Clem, Perry	C	×
Clementine, Benton	NW	×
Cleveland, Conway	C	303
Cleveland, Washington	NW	250
●Clifton, Lee	E	15
Clifty, Madison	NW	20
Cline, Johnson	NW	32
Clinton, Van Buren	N	176
Clio, (see Kedron)		×
Clover Bend, Lawrence	NE	25
Clow, Hempstead	SW	×
Clyde, Washington	NW	150
●Coal Hill, Johnson	NW	802
●*Coal Mine*, Pope	NW	×
●*Coal Mines*, Sebastian	W	×
Coats, Sharp	N	×
●*Coats*, Woodruff	E	×
Cobbs, Lonoke	C	15
Cobbville, (see Eubanks Mills)		×
Coffee Creek, Phillips	E	10
Coffeyville, Jackson	NE	×
Coin, Carroll	NW	×
Cold Mountain, Newton	NW	×
Coldwater, Cross	E	×
Coleborough, Little River	SW	13
Coleman, Drew	SE	25
College Hill, Columbia	SW	50
Collegeville, Saline	C	200
Collier Hill, Pike	SW	×
●Collins, Drew	SE	250
Collins Bluff, Miller	SW	26
●Colona, Woodruff	W	25
●Colt, St. Francis	E	50

Arkansas

Place	Region	Pop.
Columbia, Chicot	SE	75
Columbus, Hempstead	SW	217
Colville, Benton	NW	50
●Combs, Madison	NW	200
Combs Station, Madison	NW	×
Como, Cleveland	S	83
Compton, Hempstead	SW	×
Compton, Newton	NW	×
Concord, Lawrence	NE	×
Concord, Union	S	×
Convenience, Independence	N	13
Converse, (see Spadra)		×
●**Conway**, Faulkner	C	1,207
Cook, Cleveland	S	13
Cooper, Grant	C	×
Cooper, St. Francis	E	×
Cooper's L'd'g, (see Swan Lake		×
Copeland, Van Buren	N	45
Coras, Cleburne	N	×
Cord, Independence	N	38
Corinth, Howard	SW	100
●*Cork Screw*, Jefferson	C	×
Corley, Logan	W	50
●Cornerstone, Jefferson	C	30
Cornerville, Lincoln	SE	125
Cornie, Union	S	×
●Corning Clay	NE	584
Corwin, Saline	C	×
Cossatot, Sevier	SW	×
Cotton Belt, Columbia	SW	×
Cotton Centre, Jefferson	C	65
●Cotton Plant, Woodruff	E	429
●*Couch*, Columbia	SW	×
Council Bend, (see Bledsoe)		×
Cove, Polk	W	150
Cove City, (see Lee's Creek)		×
Covington, (see Locust Bayou)		×
●*Cowan*, Monroe	E	×
Craig's Mill, Saline	C	5
Cravens, Franklin	NW	58
●Crawfordsville, Crit'nd'n	E	100
Creech, Benton	NW	32
Creole, (see Spielerville)		×
Crescent, Sebastian	W	×
Creswell, Cleveland	S	×
Crockett, Clay	NE	25
Crockett's Bluff, Arkansas	E	75
Cromwell, Jackson	NE	×
Croom Mill, (see Oxford)		×
●Crosses, Madison	NW	×
Cross Hollow, Benton	NW	×
Crossington, Garland	C	×
Cross Lanes, Crawford	NW	×
Cross Roads, Washington	NW	×
Crow, Scott	W	50
Crowley, Greene	NE	40
●*Crowleys*, Cross	E	80
Crowell's L'd'g, (see G'd'n Lake)		×
Crump, Benton	NW	10
Crystal Hill, Montgomery	W	×
Crystal Springs, M'tg'm'ry	W	×
Culberhouse, Craighead	NE	×
Culp, Baxter	N	×
●Cummins, Lincoln	SE	50
●*Cuneo*, Prairie	C	×
Curia, Independence	N	19
●Curtis, Clark	SW	100
●Cushman, Independence	N	50
Cut Off, La Fayette	SW	300
Cut Off, (see Park Place)		×
Cut Short, Calhoun	S	65
Cypert, Phillips	E	×
Cypress, Ashley	SE	50
Cypress Creek, Desha	SE	×
Cypress Fork, Columbia	SW	25
Cypress Valley, Faulkner	C	20
Dade, Grant	C	23
Dahoma, Franklin	NW	×
Daisy, Greene	NE	8
Dalark, Dallas	S	208
Dale, Johnson	NW	35
●Daleville, Clark	SW	200
Dallas, Polk	W	383
Dalton, Randolph	NE	40
Damascus, Faulkner	C	×
Damon, Yell	W	×
Danville, Yell	W	250
●**Dardanelle**, Yell	W	1,456
Darysaw, Grant	C	×
Davenport, White	C	×
Davis, Columbia	SW	65
Davis, Johnson	NW	×
Dayton, Sebastian	W	100
De Ann, Hempstead	SW	50
Deaslee, La Fayette	SW	×
Deble, Searcy	N	×
Decatur, Benton	NW	40

● Dee, Craighead..........NE. 20
DeKalb, Cleburne.......... N ×
● Delaney, Madison ......NW 200
● *Delaplaine*, Greene.....NE ×
Delaware, Logan ....W 40
Delaware, Yell............W 26
Delay, Grant................ C 40
Delta Cross................E 83
Delta, Nevada............SW 83
De Luce, Arkansas..........E ×
● *Dempsey*, Columbia.....SW 28
Denieville, Independence...N 100
Denmark, White........... C 25
Dennard, Van Buren........ N 32
Denton's Mill, Scott........W ×
Denver, Carroll...........NW 10
● Dermott, Chicot.........SE 200
DeRoche, Hot Spring....... C 150
Des Arc, Prairie.......... C 546
Desha, Independence.......N 65
Des Moines, Prairie.........C ×
De Sota, Marion............N 195
DeSoto, Searcy........... N ×
● **Devall's Bluff**, Prairie. C 380
DeView, Woodruff..........E 200
Devore, Washington......NW 340
DeWitt, Arkansas........ E 946
● *De Witt Sta.*, Arkansas...E ×
● Dexter, Jefferson......... C 50
Diamond, VanBuren ....N ×
● *Diaz*, Jackson........ NE ×
● *Diaz Junction*, Jackson. NE ×
Dickey, Pulaski.............C 10
Dickson, Benton..........NW 50
Dilolo, Union................S 35
Dinsmore, Newton.......NW 35
Divide, Conway.............C ×
Dixie, Perry................. C 83
Dob, Calhoun..................S ×
Dobyville, Clarke.......... SW 25
Dodd City, Marion..........N 50
Doe Branch, Pulaski..........C 85
Dogwood, Grant..............C 83
Don, Clay.................... NE ×
Donald, Franklin..........NW ×
● Donaldson, Hot Spring....C 175
Dora, Howard.............SW ×
Dora, Crawford........... NW 15
Dorcheat, Columbia...... SW ×
Dorea, Crawford.........NW ×
Dorietta, Franklin........NW 12
Doss, Pike..................SW ×
Dosy, Lawrence...........NE 32
Dota, Independence ....N ×
Double Wells, Jefferson.....C 165
● *Doubling Switch*, Independence......................N ×
Doughertys, Phillips........E ×
Douglas, Lincoln.............SE 50
Dovepark, Clark...........SW 65
Dovepark, Hot Spring...... C ×
Dover, Pope ....NW 528
● Dowling, Ouachita ....S 25
Downey's Spring, R'nd'ph NE ×
Doyle, Hempstead......... SW ×
Drake's Creek, Madison..NW 150
Driggs, Logan............... W 10
Dry Fork, Carroll.........NW 10
● Dry Run, Dallas......... S 200
Dublin, Logan...............W 60
Duckett, Howard......... SW 13
Duckville, (see Elmo) .... ×
Due West, Lee............. E ×
Duff, Searcy................ N 25
Dugger's Mills, Boone....NW 50
● **Dumas**, Desha......... SE 10
Dump, Washington...... NW 10
● *Duncan*, Monroe..........E 25
Dunham, (see Keo) .... ×
Dunn, Monroe................ E 45
Dunn's L'd'g, (see Park Place) ×
Durrell, Arkansas.......... E ×
● Durham, Washington.. NW 40
Dutchess Creek, Yell...... W ×
Dutch Mills, Washington.NW 100
Dutton, Madison..........NW 25
● Dyer, Crawford......... NW 50
Eads, Crawford.......... NW 10
Eagle Creek, (see Orlando)... ×
Eagle Hill, Polk............W 25
● Eagle Mills, Ouachita..... S 10
● Earl, Crittenden ....E ×
● *East Little Rock*, P'lski.. C ×
Fbb, Grant...................C ×
Echo, Scott .... W 82
Economy, Pope............ NW ×
Eden, Columbia .... SW 97

Arkansas

Eddy, Drew............... SE ×
Edge, VanBuren........... N ×
● Edmondson, Crittenden.. E 30
Edward, Independence..... N ×
Edwin, Sevier............ SW ×
Egbert, White .... C 15
Egger, Polk.................. W 50
Eglantine, VanBuren ...... N 57
Egypt, Craighead......... NE ×
● *Eighty Eight Mile Post*, Prairie .... C ×
Elders, Dallas .... S ×
El Dorado, Union......... S 455
Eldorado Landing, Union.. S 12
Eldridge, Howard .... SW 32
Eleyville, Hempstead..... SW 30
Eleven, Randolph .... NE ×
Elgin, Jackson............NE 10
Eli, Jackson................ NE ×
Elixir, Boone .... NW 50
Elizabeth, Fulton .... N 50
Elkhorn, Benton......... NW 25
● *Elkins*, Washington....NW ×
Eller, Baxter............... N 113
Elliott, Ouachita............ S ×
Ellsworth, Logan .... W 20
Elm, Clark .... SW ×
● *Elmo*, Crittenden.........E 25
Elmo, Independence........N 25
Elmore, Hot Spring.......SW ×
Elmot, Mississippi .... NE 20
Elm Springs, Washing'n. NW 150
Elm Store, Randolph......NE 50
Elmwood, Boone.......... NW 50
Elnora Mine, Montgomery W ×
Elon, Ashley..............SE 77
El Paso, White...............C 350
Emmet, Nevada .... SW 125
Enders, Faulkner.......... C 20
● England, Lonoke........ C 250
Engle, Izard................ N 20
● English, Jefferson....... C 350
Enola, Faulkner............ C 50
● *Ensign*, Pulaski.......... C ×
Enterprise, Sebastian...... W 20
Eola, Fulton................ N ×
Epsy, Yell...................W ×
Era, Miller..................SW ×
Erin, Grant.................. C ×
Eros, Marion............... N 60
Esau, Perry.................. C 65
Esculapia, Benton.......NW ×
Esther, Franklin.......... NW ×
Ethel, Arkansas............ E ×
Etna, Franklin............NW ×
● *Etta*, Hot Spring.......... C 52
Eubank's Mills, Johnson.. NW 10
Euclid, Howard...........SW ×
Eugene, Fulton........... N ×
Eunice, Hot Spring........ C ×
● *Eureka Springs*, Benton NW ×
● **Eureka Springs**, Carroll........................ NW 3,706
Eva, (see Floyd) .... ×
● *Evans*, Ouachita........... S ×
Evansville, Washington.. NW 250
Evening Shade, Sharp.. N 281
Evergreen, Washington.. NW ×
Ewing, Grant................C 19
Excelsior, Sebastian........W 100
Exchange L'd'g, (see Laconia) ×
Exter, Marion............. N 10
Eye, Calhoun ....S ×
Fagi, Phillips............... E ×
Fairchild, Garland.......... C ×
● Fairfield, Jefferson..........C 25
Fair Hill, (see Wing) .... ×
Fairmount, Prairie.........C 10
Fairplay, Saline............. C 32
Fairview, (see Osage)......... ×
Fairview, Dallas..............S 150
Fairview, (see Pleasant Plane) ×
● Faith, Jefferson.............C 97
● *Fakes*, Woodruff......... E ×
Falcon, Nevada........... SW 40
Falls L'd'g, (see Fulton, Tenn.,) ×
Fallsville, Newton.........NW 10
Fancher, Madison....... NW 15
Fancy Hill, Montgomery... W 45
Farmer, Scott................ W 12
Farmington, Washington. NW 150
Farribaville, Sevier....... SW 97
Faulkner Gap, Faulkner....C 150
Fawn, Searcy .... N ×
Fay, Hempstead........... SW 30
● *Fayette Junction*, Was'n NW ×

Arkansas

● **Fayetteville**, Was'n..NW 2,942
Featherston, Mississippi...NE ×
Felix, Washington........NW 15
● *Felton*, Lee ....E 15
Fenter, Grant .... C ×
Fergerson's Mill, Yell...... W ×
Fern, Franklin .... NW ×
Fifteen Mile Bayou, (see Marion) ×
Finch, Greene............NE 60
● *Finn*, Ouachita............S ×
● Fisher, Poinsett........ NE 25
Fisherville, Poinsett...... NE 35
● *Fitzgerald*, Jackson.... NE 5
Fitzpatrick,, Lee............E ×
Flat, Logan .... W ×
Flat Bayou, Jefferson...... C 92
Fletcher, Pulaski........... C ×
Flint, Benton............ NW ×
Flippin, Marion........... N 20
Flora, Fulton............. N 35
Floral, Independence ...... N 16
Florence, Drew........... SE 60
Flowery, Franklin........NW 15
Floyd, White .... C 75
Flynn, Woodruff.............E ×
Ford, Jackson............ NE ×
Ford's Land., (see Lake Port) ×
● Fordyce, Dallas.............S 980
Forley, Washington......NW ×
● **Forrest City**, St Fran.. E 1,021
Fort Douglas, Johnson... NW 40
Fort Logan, Howard...... SW ×
● **Fort Smith**, Sebastian. W 11,311
Fort Smith Crossing, P'ka..C ×
Fort Smith Junction, Seb'n W ×
Fortune, (see Walnut Bend) ×
Forum, Madison.........NW 20
Fouke, Miller..............N ×
Fountain Hill, Ashley ..... SE 50
● *Fourche*, Pulaski........ C ×
Fourche Dam, Pulaski.......C ×
Fouville, Mississippi...... NE 13
Francis, Boone........... NW 50
Franklin, Izard............. N 165
Fredonia, (see Surrounded Hill........................ ×
Freeman, Pope .... NW 26
Frenchman's Bayou, (see Golden Lake) .... ×
French Port, Ouachita...... S 13
Fresco, Ouachita............S ×
Friendship, Hot Spring...... C ×
Friley's Creek, Madison...NW ×
● Frisco, Crawford......... NW 50
Frisco Junc., Crawford.. NW ×
Fritz, Crittenden........... E 65
Frog Pond, Lincoln....... SE 15
Frog Valley, Crawford.. NW ×
Frost, Miller.............SW ×
Fuller, Scott................W 25
● Fulton, Hempstead.....SW 337
● *Fulton's*, Hempstead....SW ×
Gageville, Greene.........NE ×
Gaines Landing, Chicot....SE 20
● Gainesville, Greene.....NE 300
Gaither, Boone............NW ×
Galena, Howard...........SW 30
● *Galla*, Pope............NW 97
Gallatin, Benton.........NW ×
● Galloway, Pulaski.........C 100
Galloway's Farm, (see Akron) ×
Galveston, LaFayette......SW 200
Game Hill, Franklin......NW ×
Gammiel, Franklin.......NW 20
● Garfield, Benton........NW 100
Garfield, Conway...........C 100
● Garland, Miller..........SW 450
Garlandville, Hempstead..SW 83
● Garner, White...............C 13
Garnerville, (see Haynes) .... ×
Garnett, Lincoln...........SE 50
Garrettson's Landing, Jeff..C 75
● Garvey, Crittenden........E 35
● *Gaskins*, Carroll..........NW ×
Gassville, Baxter............N 100
Gaston's Mill, Montgomery W ×
Gate, Scott...................W ×
● *Gatlin*, Crawford.......NW ×
● *Gaulett*, Poinsett........NE ×
● Gavin, Crittenden.........E ×
Geesville, Pope............NW ×
● Genoa, Miller..............SW 260
● *Gentry*, Greene...........NE ×
Gentry, Pike................SW ×
George's Creek, Marion.....N 30
Georgetown, Pope........NW 122
Georgia, Pike..............SW ×

Arkansas
Arkansas

Place	Region	Pop.
●Germantown, Conway	C	50
Gibbons Landing, Faulkner	C	×
Gid, Izard	N	25
●Gifford, Hot Spring	C	50
●Gilkeson, Craighead	NE	25
Gilkey, Yell	W	70
Gillen's Landing, Phillips	E	×
●Gilmore, Crittenden	E	13
Gin, Cleburne	N	×
Gipson, Scott	W	50
Gladstone, Montgomery	W	×
Glasgow, LaFayette	SW	×
Glass Village, Conway	C	×
Glen, Carroll	NW	×
Glendale, Lincoln	SE	22
Glen Low, Desha	SE	×
Glenville, Nevada	SW	100
●*Glenwood*, Monroe	E	×
●*Gold Creek*, Faulkner	C	×
Golden City, Logan	W	×
Golden Hill, (see Violet)		×
Golden Lake, Mississippi	NE	50
Golden Mill, Miller	SW	×
●Goldman, Arkansas	E	168
Goodbar, Lonoke	C	×
Good Hope, Faulkner	C	×
Goodlett, Hempstead	SW	×
Good Luck, Desha	SE	×
●Goodwin, St. Francis	E	100
Goshen, Washington	NW	100
Gotha, Crawford	NW	×
Grace, Johnson	NW	38
●*Grace*, Jefferson	C	×
Graddy Landing, Desha	SE	32
●Grady, Lincoln	SE	50
Graham, Independence	N	10
Grandee, Crittenden	E	×
●Grand Glaise, Jackson	NE	25
Grand Lake, Chicot	SE	100
Grand Lake, Lee	E	×
Grange, Sharp	N	25
Grangeville, Izard	N	×
Grant, Madison	NW	20
Grapevine, Grant	C	700
Graphic, Crawford	NW	100
Gravelly Hill, Yell	W	300
Gravel Pit, Greene	NE	×
Gravel Ridge, Bradley	S	18
●Grays, Woodruff	E	100
Grayson, Crittenden	E	65
Graywood, Cleveland	S	26
Greasy Valley, VanBuren	N	×
Greely, Jefferson	C	40
Greenback, Jefferson	C	75
Greenbrier, Faulkner	C	300
●Greenfield, Poinsett	NE	195
●*Greenfield*, Monroe	E	×
Green Forest, Carroll	NW	100
Green Grove, Faulkner	C	×
●*Greenland*, Washington	NW	×
Green Mount, Lincoln	SE	×
Green Ridge, Scott	W	20
Greensborough, Craighead	NE	96
Greenville, Washington	NW	×
●Greenway, Clay	NE	31
●**Greenwood**, Sebastian	W	587
Greer, Jefferson	C	35
Gregory, Woodruff	E	×
Griffin, Clay	NE	×
Grove, Drew	SE	×
Groveland, Lonoke	C	13
Grubbs, Jackson	NE	×
Gubertown, Craighead	NE	32
●Guernsey, Hempstead	SW	25
Gulf Spring, Nevada	SW	15
Gum Log, Pope	NW	46
Gum Pond, Arkansas	E	×
●Gum Springs, Clark	SW	30
Gunter, (see Brentwood)		×
Gum Springs, Cleveland	S	130
●Gurdon, Clark	SW	802
Guy, Faulkner	C	×
●Hackett, Sebastian	W	458
Hackler, (see Fritz)		×
Hagarville, Johnson	NW	75
Hagler, Arkansas	E	×
Halcomb, Sevier	SW	×
Hale, Crawford	NW	×
Haleside, Lee	E	×
●Halley, Desha	SE	13
●Halliday, Greene	NE	327
Halstead, Pulaski	C	70
Halstedville, Phillips	E	×
Hamburgh, Ashley	SE	655
Hamilton, Lonoke	C	20
Hamlet, Faulkner	C	10
●Hamlin, Cross	E	×
Hamlin's Land., see Bledsoe)		×
Hammett, (see Greenway)		×
Hammonsville, White	C	32
Hampton, Calhoun	S	132
●*Handy Ran*, Phillips	E	×
Hanks, Van Buren	N	32
Hannaberry, Arkansas	E	32
Harbour, Calhoun	S	30
Hardages, Clark	SW	×
●Hardy, Sharp	N	150
●Harlow, Calhoun	S	200
Harman's Gap, Cleburne	N	×
Harmony, Johnson	NW	5
Harold, Montgomery	W	6
Haroldton, Crawford	NW	25
●Harris, Washington	W	10
●**Harrisburgh**, P'ns'tt	NE	482
Harrison, Boone	NW	1,438
Hartford, Sebastian	W	200
Hartley, Polk	W	32
●Hartman, Johnson	NW	200
Harwood Island, Chicot	SE	50
●*Hatchie Coon*, Poinsett	NE	×
Hattieville, Conway	C	100
Hatton, Polk	W	20
Havana, Randolph	NE	×
Haws, Garland	C	×
●Haynes, Lee	E	255
Hazel Grove, Independence	N	15
Hazel Valley, Wash'gton	NW	75
●Hazen, Prairie	C	458
Hearn, Clark	SW	15
Heber, Cleburne	N	1,000
Hebron, Clark	SW	×
Heckatoo, Lincoln	SE	175
Hector, Pope	NW	25
●**Helena**, Phillips	E	5,189
Helth, Madison	NW	32
Henderson, Baxter	N	15
Henderson, Woodruff	E	×
Henrico, Desha	SE	65
●Hensley, Saline	C	200
Hepsey, Marion	N	×
Herd, Benton	NW	20
Hermitage, Bradley	S	×
Herndon, Greene	NE	10
Hess Landing, (see Marcella)		×
Hickman, Mississippi	NE	×
Hickman's Bend, Miss'ppi	NE	260
Hickory Creek, Hempstead	SW	80
Hickory Plains, Prairie	C	30
●*Hickory Ridge*, Cross	E	×
Hickory Ridge, Phillips	E	×
Hickory Station, M'tgm'ry	W	91
Hickory Valley, Indep'd'ce	N	30
●*Hicks*, St. Francis	E	×
Hicksville, Phillips	E	20
Hico, Benton	NW	50
●Higginson, White	C	35
Highland, Sharp	N	83
Hight, Franklin	NW	25
High Tower, Greene	NE	×
Hillochee, Washington	NW	×
Hillsboro, Union	S	125
Hilton, Sharp	N	19
Hilltop, Boone	NW	32
Hillville, Chicot	SE	30
Hindsville, Madison	NW	200
Hiram, Cleburne	N	50
●*Hix*, Phillips	E	×
Hobart, Logan	W	77
Hockers, Jefferson	C	26
Holla Bend, Pope	NW	×
Holland, Faulkner	C	10
●*Holland*, Lonoke	C	×
Hollis, Perry	C	32
Holwell, Monroe	E	×
Holly Branch, Bradley	S	×
●Holly Grove, Monroe	E	353
Holly Springs, Dallas	S	175
Hollywood, Clark	SW	103
●Homan, Miller	SW	25
Honeaville, Nevada	SW	20
●Hood, Washington	NW	130
●Hope, Hempstead	SW	1,937
Hopedale, Desha	SE	10
●*Hopefield*, Crittenden	E	×
Hopeville, Calhoun	S	×
Hopper, Montgomery	W	20
Hopper Creek, Yell	W	×
Horace, Pulaski	C	×
Horsehead, Columbia	SW	35
Horsehead, Johnson	NW	×
Hortense, Franklin	NW	×
●**Hot Springs**, Garland	C	8,086
Hottentot, Carroll	NW	15
Houseville, Faulkner	C	×
Houston, Perry	C	13
Howard, Conway	C	×
Howard, Faulkner	C	×
●Howell, Woodruff	E	100
●Hoxie, Lawrence	NE	102
Hubard, Washington	NW	10
Huddleston, Pike	SW	×
Hudson, Ouachita	S	×
●Hudspeth, Chicot	SE	20
Huey, Pike	SW	×
Hughes, Crittenden	E	26
●*Hulburt*, Crittenden	E	×
●*Huma*, Phillips	E	×
●Humphrey, Arkansas	E	50
Hunt, Johnson	NW	12
●Hunter, Woodruff	E	32
Hunters Home, (see Spring Creek		× ×
●Huntington, Sebastian	W	896
Huntsville, Madison	NW	862
Hurlberts Station, (see West Memphis		×
Hurricane, Saline	C	20
Hurricane Hill, LaFayette	SW	×
●Hyde Park, Phillips	E	13
Hydrick, Cross	E	25
Hynum, Arkansas	E	130
Ico, Grant	C	15
Ida, Cleburne	N	×
Idaho, (see Golden Lake)		×
Idell, Logan	W	×
●Imboden, Lawrence	NE	157
Independence, Baxter	N	×
India, Newton	NW	×
Indian Bay, Monroe	E	140
Indian Creek, Carroll	NW	50
Ingalls, Bradley	S	20
Ingram, Randolph	N E	10
Ink, Polk	W	×
Ipava, (see Mansfield)		×
Ironton, Pulaski	C	×
●*Irwin*, Jackson	NE	×
Isabella, Pope	NW	×
Island, Sebastian	W	×
Iuka, Izard	N	40
Ivanhoe, Searcy	N	15
Ivesville, Pulaski	C	32
Ivington, Howard	SW	×
Ivy, Dallas	S	25
Jackson, Greene	NE	×
Jackson, Randolph	NE	421
Jacksonburgh, Carroll	NW	50
●Jacksonport, Jackson	NE	421
●Jacksonville, Pulaski	C	75
●*James*, Independence	N	×
James, Lee	E	×
James' Land'g, (See Oldham)		×
●*James Mill*, Crittenden	E	×
Jamestown, Grant	C	×
Jamestown, Independence	N	100
Jane's Store, (see Kingville)		×
Jasper, Newton	NW	300
Jay, Logan	W	125
●Jefferson, Jefferson	C	100
●*Jefferson Springs*, Jefferson	C	×
Jenkin's Ferry, Grant	C	×
Jennings Falls, Yell	W	×
●Jenny Lind, Sebastian	W	×
●Jenson, Sebastian	W	65
●Jericho, Crittenden	E	260
Jersey, Bradley	S	35
Jerusalem, Conway	C	×
Jessieville, Garland	C	×
Jewell, Benton	NW	×
Joan, Clark	SW	32
●Johnson, Washington	NW	10
Johnson's Landing, Randolph	NE	×
Johnsville, Bradley	S	100
●**Jonesborough**, Cr'gd	NE	2,065
●*Jones Island*, Monroe	E	×
Jones Landing, (see Grayson)		×
Jones' Mill, LaFayette	SW	×
Jonestown, Garland	C	25
Jordanbrook, Sevier	SW	32
Joslyn, Clark	SW	×
Judea, Madison	NW	10
●Judsonia, White	C	475
Julious, Crittenden	E	25
Jumbo, Izard	N	×
●*Junction*, Crittenden	E	×
●*Junction*, La Fayette	SW	×
●*Junction*, Monroe	E	×
Junet, Grant	C	18
Kearney, Jefferson	C	×
●Kedron, Cleveland	S	150

Place	Region	Pop.
● Keevil, Monroe	E	2
Keller, Little River	SW	×
Kellogg Mine, Pulaski	C	×
Kelt, Grant	C	32
Kendall, Faulkner	C	×
● Kensett, White	C	60
Kent Landing, (see Askew)		×
Kennan's Mills, (see Hinsville)		×
Kenyon, Jackson	NE	15
Kenzie, (see Centreville)		×
Keo, Lonoke	C	×
● Kerr's, Lonoke	C	97
Key, Benton	NW	10
Key, (see La Grange)		×
Keysville, (see Red Stone)		×
Keyton, Clark	SW	×
Killgore, Newton	NW	×
Kinard, Union	S	×
Kinderhook, Cleburne	N	50
King City, (see Mitchell)		×
● Kingsland, Cleveland	S	464
King's Mills, Sharp	N	15
Kingston, Madison	NW	100
Kingsville, Randolph	NE	25
Kirby, Pike	SW	35
Kirk, Saline	C	×
Kirtley, Carroll	NW	×
● Knobel, Clay	NE	100
Knowlton, Desha	SE	×
Knowlton's Landing, D'sha	SE	15
● Knoxville, Johnson	NW	250
● *Kutler*, Saline	C	×
La Anguille, Cross	E	×
La Belle, Saline	C	×
Lacey, Drew	SE	100
Lackland, Nevada	SW	20
Laconia, Desha	SE	150
La Crosse, Izard	N	125
Lafave, Scott	W	×
● La Grange, Lee	E	216
Lake City, Craighead	NE	40
● *Lake Dick*, Jefferson	C	×
Lake Farm, Jefferson	C	×
Lake Landing, Union	S	20
Lakeport, Chicot	SE	30
● *Lakes*, Crittenden	E	×
Lake Village, Chicot	SE	100
● *Lallie*, Sebastian	W	×
● Lamar, Johnson	NW	500
Lamartine, Columbia	SW	47
Lambert, Union	S	×
Lamberton, Monroe	E	10
Lambethville, Crittenden	E	10
Lamp, Van Buren	N	×
Lanark, Bradley	S	65
● Lancaster, Crawford	NW	10
Laneburgh, Nevada	SW	30
Langeal, Cross	E	×
Langley, Pike	SW	20
Lansing, Crittenden	E	×
Lapile, Union	S	20
Larissa, Lonoke	C	×
Larue, Benton	NW	15
Last Prairie, Miller	SW	×
Latham, Van Buren	N	×
● Latour, Phillips	E	20
Laughlin, Columbia	SW	×
Lauratown, Lawrence	NE	5
Laurel, Pope	NW	15
Lavaca, Sebastian	W	150
Lawrence, Garland	C	10
● *Lawrence*, Hot Spring	C	×
Lawrenceville, Monroe	E	×
Layton, Jackson	NE	10
Lead Hill, Boone	NW	833
Leander, Jefferson	C	×
Leard, Clark	SW	15
Lebanon, Searcy	N	×
Lebanon, Sevier	SW	×
Lebanon, Johnson	NW	5
Lecont, Pulaski	C	×
Lecroy, Hot Spring	C	×
Lee, Lee	E	82
Lee's Creek, Crawford	NW	100
Lee's Landing, LaFayette	SW	32
Lehi, Cleveland	S	195
Lemric, Sevier	SW	×
● *Lennetts*, Jefferson	C	×
Leon, Franklin	NW	66
Leonardsville, Crawford	NW	×
Leopold, (see Clarketon)		×
Leslie, Searcy	N	100
Leslie Centre, Arkansas	E	×
● Lester, Ouachita	S	30
Leverney, Montgomery	W	×
Levesque, Cross	E	10
● Lewisville, LaFayette	SW	255

Place	Region	Pop.
● Lexa, Phillips	E	20
Lexington, Van Buren	N	×
Liberty, Ouachita	S	15
Liberty Springs, Van Buren	N	32
Lick Branch, Benton	NW	10
Lick Mountain, Conway	C	60
Liddesdale, Columbia	SW	19
Lightle, Monroe	E	×
● Lilley, Ouachita	S	30
● *Lillie*, Crawford	NW	×
Lima, Randolph	NE	10
Limestone Valley, N'wt'n	NW	×
Lincoln, Washington	NW	10
Lincoln's Mills, Benton	NW	×
Linden, (see Millbrook)		×
Linder, Faulkner	C	×
Lindon, Pike	SW	×
● Lindsay, Lawrence	NE	50
Lindseyville, (see Albertha)		×
Linsley's Landing, Miss'pi	NE	32
Linville, Johnson	NW	×
Linwood, Lawrence	NE	100
● Linwood, Jefferson	C	100
Lisbon, Union	S	35
Lissie, Pike	SW	×
Litha, Lawrence	NE	×
● Little Bay, Calhoun	S	250
Little Fouche, Pulaski	C	×
Little Red, White	C	25
Little River, Little River	SW	98
● **LITTLE ROCK**, P'l'ki	C	25,874
Little Springs, (see Spring Valley)		×
Little Star, Carroll	NW	15
Lively, Hempstead	SW	20
Liverpool, (see Hartford)		×
Livingston, Stone	N	×
Lochinvar, LaFayette	SW	×
Lockesburgh, Sevier	SW	451
Locust Bayou, Calhoun	S	15
Locust Cottage, Jefferson	C	40
Lodi, Pike	SW	×
Logan, Benton	NW	25
Log Town, Crawford	NW	×
Lollie, Faulkner	C	×
Lonann, Ouachita	S	×
● London, Pope	NW	100
Lonelm, Franklin	NW	40
Lone Grove, Woodruff	E	×
Lone Rock, Baxter	N	100
Long Creek, Perry	C	×
Long Prairie, Drew	SE	×
Long Ridge, (see Carolan)		×
Long View, Ashley	SE	25
Lono, Hot Spring	C	50
● **Lonoke**, Lonoke	C	858
Loomis, Jefferson	C	8
Lorado, Greene	NE	8
● *Lost Swamp*, St. Francis	E	×
Louis, Columbia	SW	×
Louisiana Line, (see Jones, La)		×
Loulyma, Greene	NE	15
Love, Montgomery	W	×
Loveland, Cross	E	×
Lowann, Ouchita	S	×
Lowe, Jackson	NE	×
● Lowell, Benton	NW	50
Lowry, Boone	NW	20
Loyal, Sharp	N	25
Loyal Hill, Clay	NE	×
Lucky, Montgomery	W	×
Ludwig, Johnson	NW	8
Luella, Drew	SE	×
Lufra, Ouachita	S	13
Lulu, St. Francis	E	×
Lumber, Columbia	SW	×
Luna Landing, Chicot	SE	35
Lunenburg, Izard	N	25
Lunet, Ouachita	S	×
Lutherville, Johnson	NW	100
Lynn, Lawrence	NE	×
Lynn, Miller	SW	×
Lynnville, Hempstead	SW	×
● McAlmont, Pulaski	C	30
McBee Landing, Marion	N	15
McConnell's Landing, (see Grayson)		×
● *McCoy*, Cleveland	S	×
● *McCreanor's*, Lonoke	C	×
● *McCreary*, Jackson	NE	×
● McCrory, Woodruff	E	299
● McDaniels, St. Francis	E	×
● *McDonald*, Jackson	NE	×
McDonald's Store, (see Newport)		×
McGavock, Mississippi	NE	10
● McGehee, Desha	SE	15

Place	Region	Pop.
● *McGehee Jc*, Desha	SE	×
McKinney, Cleveland	S	45
● *McKinney*, Miller	SW	×
McKinney, (see Mount Ida)		×
McLain, Clark	SW	32
McLaughlin, Crittenden	E	×
McNeely's Ridge, Clark	SW	×
● McNeil, Columbia	SW	294
McPherson, Baxter	N	×
McRae, Sevier	SW	×
McRae, White	C	75
● Mabelvale, Pulaski	C	65
Macedonia, Columbia	SW	10
Macey, Craighead	NE	10
Mackville, Cleveland	S	×
● Macon, Jefferson	C	30
Madding, Jefferson	C	65
Maddry, Hot Spring	C	10
● Madison, St. Francis	E	100
Madrid, Pope	NW	×
Magazine, Logan	W	183
Magnet, Hot Spring	C	15
● **Magnolia**, Columbia	SW	1,486
Maguire's Store, W'sh'gt'n	NW	120
● **Malvern**, Hot Spring	C	1,520
● Mammoth Spring, Fulton	N	1,000
Manchester, Clark	SW	30
● *Mandeville*, Miller	SW	×
Manfred, Montgomery	W	32
Mangrum, Craighead	NE	×
Manifee, Conway	C	10
Mankins, Washington	NW	40
● Mansfield, Sebastian	W	243
Mantee, Madison	NW	×
Maple, Carroll	NW	20
Marble, Madison	NW	40
MarbleCity, (see Willcockson)		×
Marcella, Stone	N	20
Marche, Pulaski	C	82
● **Marianna**, Lee	E	1,126
● **Marion**, Crittenden	E	200
● Marked Tree, Poinsett	NE	25
Mark Twain, (see St. Thomas)		×
● Marmaduke, Greene	NE	100
Marsden, Bradley	S	×
Marshall, Searcy	N	278
Marshall Prairie, N'wt'n	NW	26
Mars Hill, La Fayette	SW	25
Martin Junction, Woodruff	E	×
Martin's Creek, Sharp	N	25
Martin's Store, (see Newport)		×
Martinville, Faulkner	C	125
● Marvell, Phillips	E	150
Marvinville, Yell	W	75
Mason, Washington	NW	×
Masona, Chicot	SE	13
Mason Valley, Benton	NW	30
Massard, Sebastian	W	19
Maumelle, Pulaski	C	×
Maxville, Sharp	N	15
May, Garland	C	65
Mayberry, Montgomery	W	×
Mayflower, Faulkner	C	50
Maynard, Randolph	NE	25
Maysville, Benton	NW	100
Mazarn, Montgomery	W	18
● Mead, St. Francis	E	×
Mebaneville, Cross	E	19
● Medford, Desha	SE	25
Melbourne, Izard	N	209
Melton, Lincoln	SE	×
Mendenhall, Nevada	SW	×
● Menifee, Conway	C	150
Mentor, Arkansas	E	×
● Meredith, Woodruff	E	25
Meyers, Garland	C	×
Micawber Station, Jeff	C	15
Middlebrook, Randolph	NE	100
Middle Settlement, VanB'rn	N	13
Midway, Drew	SE	20
Midway, Hot Spring	C	×
● *Midway*, Monroe	E	2
Milan, Yell	W	10
Mill Brook, St. Francis	E	77
Mill Creek, (see Elmwood)		×
● *Mill Creek*, Pope	NW	×
Millkin, Little River	SW	×
Milltown, Sebastian	W	13
Millville, Ouachita	S	26
Millwood, Little River	SW	×
● Milner, Columbia	SW	38
Milo, Ashley	SE	18
Milor, Sebastian	W	×
Mine Creek, Howard	SW	×
Mineral, Pulaski	E	13
Mineral Springs, Howard	SW	300
Minneola, Little River	SW	58

● Minturn, Lawrence.....NE 40
Mitchell, Fulton............N 25
● Moark, Clay...........NE 50
Mobley, Independence......N ×
Modoc, Phillips............E 83
Moffit, Washington.......NW ×
Moize Landing, Conway....C ×
Monarch, Marion...........N 15
Money, Logan..............W ×
Monroe, Monroe...........E ×
Montana, Johnson........NW 10
● **Monticello**, Drew ....SE 1,285
Montongo, Drew...........SE 150
● Montreal, Sebastian..... W ×
Montrose, Sebastian........W ×
Montsville, Bradley..........S ×
Moore, Faulkner.............C 26
● Moorefield, Independence N 30
Moore's Landing, (see Arkansas Post)...................... ×
Moore's Mills, Washt'n....NW 65
Moreland, Pope............NW 78
Morganton, Van Buren.....N ×
Moro, Lee..................E 100
Moro Bay, Bradley..........S 150
Morrell, Ashley...........SE 75
● **Morrilton**, Conway....C 1,644
Morris, Arkansas.........E ×
Morris, Craighead........NE ×
Morrison Bluff, Logan......W 100
Morrow, Washington .... NW 10
● Morton, Woodruff.......... E ×
Morton City, Franklin... NW ×
Mossville, Newton........NW ×
● Motz, Miller............. SW 20
Moulton, Columbia......... SW 15
Mound City, Crittenden.....E 25
Mount Adams, Arkansas....E 50
● Mountainburgh, Cr'f'd..NW 60
Mountain Fork, Polk...... W 50
Mountain Glen, Garland.... C 15
Mountain Home, BaxterN 242
Mountain Mill, Madison..NW ×
● *Mountain Springs*, B'neNW ×
Mountain Top, Franklin..NW ×
Mountain Valley, Garland..C 25
Mountain View, Stone..N 500
Mount Elba, Cleveland .... S ×
Mount Etna, Independence N ×
Mount Hayes, Wash'n... NW ×
Mount Hersey, Newton.. NW 20
Mount Holly, Union .... S 250
Mount Ida, Montgomery. W 400
Mount Judea, Newton....NW 20
Mount Levi, Johnson..... NW 82
Mount Moriah, Nevada....SW ×
Mount Nebo, Yell..........W ×
Mount Olive, Izard......... N 25
Mount Parthenon, NewtonNW 40
Mount Pisgah, White....... C 25
Mounts, Franklin........ NW ×
Mount Vernon, Faulkner ... C 250
Mount Saint Francis River, Phillips..................E 825
Muddy Fork, Howard .... SW 32
Mud Lake, (see Williamette). ×
● Mulberry, Franklin.... NW 321
Mundell, Carroll..........NW 10
Murfreesborough, Pike SW 159
Murillo, Van Buren........ N 13
Murray, Newton...........NW 390
● *Murta*, Lawrence ....NE 45
Myatt, Fulton.............. N 10
Myer's Landing, Sebastian..W ×
Myrtle, Boone.............NW ×
Nalls, Columbia.......... SW ×
Nashes, Miller .... SW ×
● Nashville, Howard ..... SW 810
Nathan, Pike............. SW 20
Natick, Jefferson............ C ×
National, Logan............ W 128
Natural Dam, Crawford.. NW 15
Natural Steps, Pulaski..... C ×
Neal, Sebastian .... W 32
Nebo, Benton ....NW 150
Nebraska, Scott.............. W 78
Neelly, Yell.................. W 10
Negro Hill, White.......... C 83
Nellie, Ashley.............. SE ×
Nelson, Drew...............SE 15
Nelson Landing, Conway... C ×
Netta Boc, Sevier .... SW ×
● Nettleton, Craighead ... NE 25
● Newark, Independence.. N 150
Newburgh, Izard............ N 150
Newcastle, St. Francis...... E 13
New Como, White........... C ×
New Edinburg, Cleveland...S 300
● New Gascony, Jefferson...C 25
New Haven L'nd'g, (see Osceola) ×
New Hope, Izard.............N ×
New Hope, Pike.......... SW 50
New Lewisville, LaF'y'tte. NW 500
New London, Union.........S 50
New Market, Sebastian.... W ×
New Moon, Howard ...... SW ×
● **Newport**, Jackson....NE 1,571
New Port Landing, Ou'ch'ta.S 12
New Troy, Polk........... W ×
Nichols, Polk.............. W ×
● *Niemeyer*, Pulaski........ C ×
Nimrod, Perry...............C ×
Nix, Dallas.................. S 50
Noah, Newton............NW ×
● Noble's Lake, Jefferson....C 75
Nodena, Mississippi........ NE 40
Noland, Randolph .... NE 32
● Nolton, Cross............. E 10
Norman, Calhoun.......... S ×
Normandy, Ashley........SE ×
Norphlet, Union............ S ×
North Creek, Phillips....... E 20
North Fork, Baxter......... N 15
North Little Rock, (see Argenta) ×
North Point, Pulaski.........C 25
Northwood, Pope........ NW ×
Norwoodville, Sevier......SW 50
Nubia, Jefferson............ C 32
Nuna, Saline................ C 66
Nyra, Saline................C ×
Oak Bluff, Clay........... NE 196
Oakdale, Monroe.......... E ×
● *Oak Dormick*, Poinsett. NE ×
Oak Flat, Van Buren........N ×
Oak Forest, Lee .... E 10
Oak Grove, Carroll .... NW 30
Oak Grove, Desha..........SE ×
Oak Hill, Carroll.......... NW 83
Oakland, (see Linwood)....... ×
Oakland, Marion.............N 20
Oakley, Arkansas...........E ×
Oakville, Jefferson.......... C ×
Oakwood, Drew........... SE ×
Oark, Johnson............ NW 10
● *O'Bear*, Poinsett .... NE ×
Obin, Grant................. C 13
Oden, Montgomery .... W 50
Ogden, Little River ....SW 20
Ogden, Montgomery .... W 50
Oil Trough, Independence.. N 50
Okay, Grant .... C 26
● O'Kean, Randolph...... NE 25
Okolona, Clark............SW 500
Ola, Yell.................... W 100
Oldham, Crittenden .... E 65
Old Hickory, Conway....... C 107
Old Smith L'nd'g, (see Greenb'k) ×
Old Town, (see Sunk Land) .. ×
Old Town, (see Red Stone)... ×
Olena, Arkansas............. E ×
Ollo, Scott.................. W 10
Olive Hill, Saline........... C ×
Oliver's Landing, Phillips... E 13
Olivar Woodyard, (see Sunflower Landing, Miss.,)..... ×
Olivet, Carroll.............NW ×
Olmstead, Pulaski.......... C ×
● Olyphant, Jackson.........NE 10
Oma, Hot Spring............C 20
Omaha, Boone ....NW 40
Omega, Carroll............. NW 15
Omega, Yell .... W ×
Onset, Marion.............. N 15
Onyx, Yell.................. W 32
Ophir, Montgomery.......... W ×
Oppelo, Conway .... C 40
Opposition, Lawrence..... NE 20
Ops, Hot Spring............. C 20
Optimus, Stone............ N ×
Oregon, Boone............ NW 32
O'Rear, Union .... S ×
Orion, Grant................. C 260
Orlando, Cleveland.......... S 10
Osage, Carroll............. NW 100
Osage Mills, Benton...... NW 75
Osceola, Mississippi..... NE 458
Otokana, Miller.............SW ×
Otto, Faulkner .... C 25
Overt, White.................. C ×
Owensville, Salin .... C 10
Owlet, Prairie .... C ×
Oxford, Izard .... N 100
● Ozan, Hempstead....... SW 91
● **Ozark**, Franklin......NW 862
Ozone, Johnson .... NW 15
Pacific Landing, Crit'd'n... E ×
Pacific Place, (see St.Thomas) ×
Pactolus, Benton .... NW 15
Pageville, Grant............ C ×
● Palarm, Faulkner......... C ×
Palatka, Clay .... NE ×
Palestine, Columbia...... SW ×
● Palestine, St. Francis .... E 163
● Palmer, Monroe........... E 45
Palmyra, Lincoln............SE 30
Pangburn, White.............C 32
Panola, Lonoke ....C ×
Pansy, Cleveland .... S ×
Paraclifta, Sevier ....SW 34
Paradise, Drew............SE ×
Paradise, Prairie.......... C ×
● **Paragould**, Greene.. NE 1,666
● *Parham*, Arkansas...... E ×
Paris, Logan............... W 547
● Parkdale, Ashley......... SE 300
Parker's Store, Pulaski..... C 130
● *Parkin*, Cross............ E ×
Park Place, Lee .... E 15
Parks, Scott................ W 40
● *Parma*, Lincoln........... SE ×
Parn, Benton .... NW ×
Parnell, Lonoke .... C ×
Parsonville, Lawrence.... NE 10
● *Paroquet*, Independence. N 65
● *Parmly*, Greene......... NE ×
Pastoria, Jefferson.......... C 75
Pates, Howard............ SW 15
Patrick, Madison..........NW 00
Patsie, Logan............... W ×
Patterson's Bluff, Logan... W 75
Pauline, Franklin......... NW 30
Paxson, White.............. C 30
Payton, Hempstead...... SW ×
Peace, White............... C ×
● Peach Orchard, Clay.... NE 60
Pearcy, Garland............ C ×
Pea Ridge, Benton........ NW 50
Pearl, Pope .... NW ×
Pearson, Cleburne..........N 30
Pecan Point, Mississippi.. NE 100
Pedlo, Boone .... NW ×
Peel, Marion................N 20
Pembina, Baxter........... N ×
Pendleton, Desha..........SE 482
Peoria, Sebastian .... W 57
● Perkins, Poinsett....... NE ×
Perryville, Perry........ C 310
Peru, Randolph........... NE 25
Peters, Lee................. E ×
Petersburgh, Ashley ...... SE 14
Peters Landing, Lee....... E ×
Petit Jean, Yell............W ×
Petteys, Mississippi....... NE ×
Pettigrew Mills, (see Silver Springs........................ ×
Pettus, Lonoke...............C 46
Petty, Sevier ....SW 32
Peytonsville, Little River..SW 25
Phelps, Jackson .... NE 10
Philadelphia, (see La Crosse). ×
Phillips Bayou, Lee........ E 100
Picayune, Howard........ SW 60
Pickler, Columbia .... SW 15
● **Piggott**, Clay...........NE 800
● Pillow, Phillips........... E 35
Pillows' Lane, (see Helena).. ×
Pilot Hill, (see Salem) .... ×
Pilot Knob, Polk........... W ×
Pinchback's Mills, Cleveland. S ×
Pinckney, Crittenden........ E 10
● **Pine Bluff**, Jefferson....C 9,952
Pinecastle, Bradley......... S ×
● *Pine City*, Monroe........ E 12
Pine Grove, Dallas.......... S 35
Pine Hill, Ashley............SE 57
Pineland, Pike..............SW 13
Pineville, Izard............. N 100
Piney, Pope............... NW 150
Piney, Carroll............. NW 83
Piney, (see Berlin)............. ×
Piney Grove, Jefferson......C ×
Pinnacle Springs, Faulkner. C 25
● Pitkin, Washington.... NW 35
Pitman, Clay .... NE 25
Pittsburgh, Johnson......NW ×
Plainfield, Columbia......SW ×
Planters, Phillips .... E 25
Plantersville, Drew.........SE 50
● *Plants*, White .... C 400

Place, County	Dir.	Pop.
Plata, Montgomery	W	×
Pleasant, Boone	NW	97
Pleasant Hill, Franklin	NW	108
Pleasant L'd'g, (see Williamette)		×
Pleasant Plains, Ind'p'ce	N	50
Pleasant Prairie, Prairie	C	×
Pleasant Ridge, Boone	NW	10
Pleasant Valley, (see Hight)		×
Plum Bayou, Jefferson	C	200
● Plummerville, Conway	C	214
Plymouth, Franklin	NW	×
Pocahontas, Randolph	NE	507
Poe, Cross	E	×
Poe, Grant	C	25
Poindexter, Crittenden	E	12
● *Poindexter*, Monroe	E	×
Point Cedar, Hot Spring	C	100
Point Peter, Searcy	N	20
Point Pleasant, Ashley	SE	×
Point Remove, Conway	C	×
Polk Bayou, Sharp	N	25
Pollard, Clay	NE	50
Polo, Carroll	NW	60
Pond, Benton	NW	×
Pontiac, Polk	W	×
● *Poping*, Franklin	NW	×
Poplar Bluff, (see Parkdale)		×
● Poplar Grove, Phillips	E	200
Porter, Crawford	NW	130
● Portia, Lawrence	NE	571
● Portland, Ashley	SE	500
Post Oak, Calhoun	S	×
Poteau, Scott	W	150
Potter, Polk	W	25
● Potts' Station, Pope	NW	75
Pott's Store, (see Bellefonte)		×
Poughkeepsie, Sharp	N	10
Powell, Marion	N	50
● *Powell*, Craighead	NE	100
Powell Station, (see Patrick)		×
Powers, Johnson	NW	×
Powhatan, Lawrence	NE	220
Poynter, Desha	SE	×
Prairie, Drew	SE	×
● *Prairie Cen.*, Prairie	C	13
Prairie Grove, Wash'n	NW	412
Prairie Landing, (see Champ'n		×
Prairie View, Logan	W	150
Prairieville, Arkansas	E	65
Prattsville, Grant	C	50
● **Prescott**, Nevada	SW	1,287
Preston's Bluff, Arkansas	E	×
● Preston, Faulkner	C	50
Princeton, Dallas	S	164
Proctor, Crittenden	E	×
Providence, Searcy	N	×
Puckett, Benton	NW	32
Pyleville, Marion	N	×
● *Quigley*, St. Francis	E	×
Quincy, Newton	NW	40
Quitman, Cleburne	N	327
Quito, Polk	W	32
Racine, (see Williamette)		×
Raiford, Calhoun	S	×
Rainey, Jefferson	C	33
Rally Hill, Boone	NW	100
Ralph, Izard	N	×
Ramsey, Carroll	NW	×
Ramsey, Dallas	S	13
Ranch, Montgomery	W	×
Randall, Cleveland	S	10
Ranger, Yell	W	×
Rankin, Little River	SW	×
Ransom, Polk	W	30
● Ravenden, Lawrence	NE	50
Ravenden Spr'gs, R'nd'lph	NE	25
Rawlison, St. Francis	E	×
● *Rawsey*, Arkansas	E	×
Raymond, Monroe	E	×
● Rector, Clay	NE	490
● *Red Bluff*, Jefferson	C	75
Redemption, Perry	C	×
● Redfield, Jefferson	C	400
Red Fork, Desha	SE	50
Red Land, Pike	SW	26
Red Rock, Newton	NW	20
Red Store, Phillips	E	5
Reed, Sharp	N	×
Reeder, Ouachita	S	40
Reed's Creek, Sharp	N	50
Reed's Landing, Pulaski	C	105
● Reedville, Desha	SE	10
Reever L'd'g, Crittenden	E	57
Reform, Saline	C	×
Register, Hempstead	SW	×
Relf's Bluff, Lincoln	SE	20
Remmel, Jackson	NE	×
Remond, Ouachita	S	×
Rene Landing, (see Park Pl.)		×
Revilee, Logan	W	13
Reyburn, Saline	C	13
Reyno, Randolph	NE	75
Rhea's Mills, Wash'n	NW	15
Rhode, Polk	N	19
Riceville, (see Edmondson)		×
● *Richardson*, Jefferson	C	×
Richland, Columbia	SW	×
Richmond, Little River	SW	307
Rich Mountain, Polk	W	×
Richwood, Lonoke	C	10
Rickert, Washington	NW	×
Ridge, Craighead	NE	×
Riley, Yell	W	40
Ringville, (see Clifton)		×
● *Rio Vista*, White	C	130
Ripley, Ashley	SE	15
Ripley, Cleveland	S	×
● Rison, Cleveland	S	200
● Riverside, Wooodruff	E	150
Rives, Drew	SE	35
Roberts, Miller	SW	×
Robinson, Benton	NW	50
● Rob Roy, Jefferson	C	150
Rock Creek, Pike	SW	60
Rockford, Izard	N	×
Rockhouse, Madison	NW	10
Rock Spring, Union	S	×
Rocky, Polk	W	15
Rocky Comfort, Little Riv.	SW	234
● Roe, Monroe	E	10
● Rogers, Benton	NW	1,265
Roland, Pulaski	C	10
Roller's Bluff, Benton	NW	×
Rolling Prairie, (see Val'y Sp'gs)		×
Romance, White	C	25
Rome, Clark	SW	57
Rome City, Benton	NW	25
Rondo, (see Cleveland)		×
Rondo, Miller	SW	×
Roots, Monroe	E	×
Rosadale, Howard	SW	41
Rosadale, Franklin	NW	×
Rosa Lee, (see Walnut Bend)		×
Roscoe, Boone	NW	32
Rose Bud, White	C	400
Rosedale, Pulaski	C	×
Rose Hill, Ouachita	S	×
Rosemary, (see Red Fork)		×
Roseville, Logan	W	103
Rosie, Independence	N	×
Ross, Pope	NW	×
Ross Creek, Scott	W	×
● *Rosser*, Woodruff	E	×
Rosslow, Marion	N	×
Rossmere, Chicot	SE	38
Rosston, Nevada	SW	36
Round Bottom, (see Mout'n View)		×
Round Hill, Dallas	S	×
Round Prairie, (see Bloomf'd)		×
Round Top, Benton	NW	15
Rover, Yell	W	250
Rowell, Cleveland	S	10
Roy, Pike	SW	×
Royston, Pike	SW	×
● *Rozell*, Woodruff	E	×
Rozelle, Mississippi	NE	×
● Rudy, Crawford	NW	10
Rufus, Jackson	NE	13
Rule, Carroll	NW	25
Rural, Grant	C	46
Ruray, Faulkner	C	32
Rush, Marion	N	15
Rushing, Stone	N	46
● Russell, White	C	150
● Russellville, Pope	NW	1,321
Ruth, Fulton	N	×
Ryker, Newton	NW	×
Sage, Izard	N	15
Saint Charles, Arkansas	E	200
Saint Clair, Crittenden	E	70
● Saint Francis, Clay	NE	356
Saint James, Stone	N	100
Saint James, Independence	N	×
Saint Joe, Searcy	N	50
Saint John, Cleveland	S	×
St. Louis Landing, Phillips	E	32
Saint Mary's Landing, Jefferson	C	25
● Saint Paul, Madison	NW	417
Saint Thomas, Crittenden	E	65
Saint Vincent, Conway	C	650
Salado, Independence	N	10
Salem, Fulton	N	300
Salem, Sebastian	W	117
Salem Springs, (see Sexton)		×
Saline, Dallas	S	130
● *Saline*, Bradley	S	×
Saline Mill, Howard	SW	×
Salvador, Phillips	E	65
● *Samples*, Jefferson	C	×
Samterville, (see Surr'd Hill)		×
Sanders, Hot Spring	C	15
Sand Hill, (see Newport)		×
Sand Point, Crawford	NW	165
Sandtown, Independence	N	13
Sandy Springs, Grant	C	13
Sanson, Faulkner	C	×
Sans Souci, Mississippi	NE	20
Santos, Pope	NW	50
Sara, Hot Spring	C	×
Sarassa, Lincoln	SE	25
Saratoga, Howard	SW	211
Saratoga, Johnson	NW	100
Sardis, Hempstead	SW	100
Sassafras, Arkansas	E	×
● *Saulsburg*, Monroe	E	×
● Sayre, Ouachita	S	25
Scanlan, Crittenden	E	32
Scates, Greene	NE	×
Scipio, Drew	SE	35
Scotland, Van Buren	N	13
● Scott, Lonoke	C	×
Scotts, Clark	SW	×
Scottsville, Pope	NW	75
● *Screeton*, Prairie	C	×
Searcy, White	C	1,203
Seay, Woodruff	E	×
Seba, Benton	NW	10
● Sedgwick, Lawrence	NE	125
Seelig, Lee	E	125
Selah, Ashley	SE	×
Selma, Drew	SE	100
Seminary, Ouachita	S	30
● *Sennett's*, Jefferson	C	300
Sentell's Landing, LaFay'te	SW	15
Senter, (see Buena Vista)		×
Serene, Randolph	NE	13
Settlement, Van Buren	N	×
Sevier, Perry	C	36
Sexton, Washington	NW	50
Sexton's L'nd'g, (see St. Thos.)		×
Seymour, Craighead	NE	×
Seyppel, Crittenden	E	×
Shamrock, Calhoun	S	13
Shark, Yell	W	57
Sharman, Columbia	SW	125
Sharpsburg, Cross	E	×
Sharp's Cross Roads, Ind.	N	26
Shaver, Boone	NW	15
Shaw, Saline	C	15
Shawnee, Mississippi	NE	×
Shelby, White	C	×
● *Sheppard*, Hempstead	SW	13
Sheridan, Grant	C	184
● Sherril, Jefferson	C	×
Shiloh, Cleburne	N	94
Shoal Creek, Logan	W	30
● *Shoffner*, Jackson	NE	×
Shoppach, Saline	C	×
Shotwell, Craighead	NE	×
Shover Spring, Hempstead	SW	×
Shuler, Union	S	32
● *Sibley*, Crittenden	E	×
● Sidell, Saline	C	32
Siding No. 1, (see Roe)		×
Sidney, Sharp	N	25
Silex, Pope	NW	10
Siloam Springs, Benton	NW	821
Silver City, Montgomery	W	50
Silver Hill, Sevier	SW	20
Silver Springs, Benton	NW	10
Simpson, Bradley	S	125
Sims, Montgomery	W	32
Sitka, Sharp	N	13
● *Sisemore*, Lonoke	C	×
Slate, Saline	C	×
Slatonville, Sebastian	W	×
Sleeth, Jefferson	C	×
Smackover, Union	S	40
Smart, Jefferson	C	45
Smeadley, Johnson	NW	40
Smithland, Columbia	SW	19
● Smithton, Clark	SW	100
Smithville, Lawrence	NE	25
Smyrna, Pope	NW	×
Snapp, Woodruff	E	77
Snowball, Searcy	N	75
Snow's Landing, (see Barfield)		×
Snyder, Ashley	SE	28
Social Hill, Hot Spring	C	175
Solgohachia, Conway	C	150

South Bend, Lincoln........SE 10
Southern Home, Yell........W 60
South Fork, Fulton........N 80
Southland, Phillips........E ×
● Spadra, Johnson........NW 100
Spavinaw, Benton........NW ×
Speir, Crawford........NW ×
● *Speiser*, Pulaski........C ×
Spencer, Crawford........NW ×
Spencerville, (see Newport)... ×
Spielerville, Logan........W 30
● *Spirit Lake*, La Fayette.SW ×
Spotville, Columbia........SW ×
Spring Creek, Lee........E 64
● Springdale, Washington NW 906
Springfield, Conway........C 240
Spring Garden, Garland....C ×
Spring Hill, (see Hope)........ ×
Springtown, Benton........NW 150
Spring Valley, Wash'n... NW 50
● Stamps, La Fayette........SW ×
Stanley, Arkansas........E 10
Star City, Lincoln........SE 204
Star of the West, Pike....SW 30
State Line, Columbia........SW 25
Stattler, Crawford........NW 10
● Staunton, Washington..NW 25
● Stephens, Ouachita........S 379
Sterling, Chicot........SE 80
Stirling, (see Mt, St.Fran's Riv.) ×
Stevens Creek, White........C 97
Stewarts Town, Marion....N ×
Stillwater, Montgomery... W 13
Stone, Marion........N 65
● Stonewall, Greene........NE 25
Stonewall Landing, Miss.. NE 260
Stop, Crawford........NW ×
Story, Montgomery........W 32
Stottsville, Craighead........NE 32
Stoutts Landing, (see Morril't'n) ×
Stover, Dallas........S ×
Strain, Washington........NW 32
Stranger's Home, Law.r.. NE 10
Strawberry, Lawrence....NE 40
Strickler, Washington....NW 15
Stuart, Cross........E ×
Sturgis, Bradley........S 20
● Stuttgart, Arkansas........E 1,165
Sub Rosa, Franklin........NW 25
Sugar C'k Cor., (see Bay Vil'ge) ×
Sugar Grove, Logan........W 20
Sugar Loaf, Sebastian........W 15
Sugar Loaf Mills, Marion..N ×
Sugar Loaf Spr'gs, Cleburne N 322
Suggs, Madison........NW 10
Sullivan, Scott........W ×
Sulphur, Garland........C 25
Sulphur City, Washington. NW 15
Sulphur Fork, Miller....SW ×
● Sulphur Rock, Ind'nce... N 387
● Sulphur Springs, Bent'n NW 400
Sulphur Springs, Faulkner C ×
Sulphur Springs, Garland..C 25
Summers, Washington... NW 15
Summerville, Calhoun........S 75
● *Summit*, Washington.. NW ×
● *Summit*, St. Francis........E ×
Summit Home, (see Winslow) ×
Sumpter, Bradley........S 82
Sunk Land, Craighead....NE ×
Sunny Side, Chicot........SE 80
Sunrise, White........C ×
Sunset, Howard........SW ×
Sunset, Washington........NW 10
Sunshine, (see Goldman)...... ×
Sunshine, Ashley........SE 30
Supply, Randolph........NE 25
● Surrounded Hill, Prairie..C 60
Susan, Jackson........NE ×
Sutton, Pike........SW 19
Swain, Newton........NW 25
● Swan Lake, Jefferson........C 75
● Sweet Home, Pulaski........C 130
Sweet Home, Sevier........SW ×
● Swifton, Jackson........NE 75
Sycamore, Boone........NW 15
Sylamore, Stone........N 58
Sylarsville, Lee........E 32
Sylva, Marion........N 35
Tackett, Montgomery........W ×
● *Tamo*, Jefferson........C ×
Tarrytown, Crawford....NW 32
Tate, Clark........SW ×
Tatumville, Saline........C 60
Taylor, Lawrence........NE ×
Taylor's Creek, (see Colt).... ×
Ten Mile, Fulton........N 60

Arkansas

Terry's Ferry, (see Bright's Pl.) ×
Tevis, White........C ×
● **Texarkana**, Miller... SW 3.528
The Narrows, (see Mount'b'g) ×
Thomasville, Prairie........C ×
● Thompson, Madison....NW 50
Thompsonville, Carroll..NW ×
● Thornton, Calhoun........S 406
Three Creeks, Union........S 160
Thurman, Clay........NE 10
Tichnor, Arkansas........E 35
● Tillar, Drew........SE 25
Tilmanville, Greene........NE 10
● *Tilton*, Cross........E 65
Timbo, Stone........N 50
Tina, Cleburne........N ×
Tipton, Izard........N ×
Toledo, Cleveland........N 75
Tollete, Howard........SW ×
● Toltec, Lonoke........C 50
Tolu, Washington........NW 50
Tomahawk, Searcy........N 12
Tomberlins, Lonoke........C 10
Tomlinson, (See Boothe).... ×
Tomlinson, Sebastian........W ×
Toney, Marion........N 26
● Toronto, Jefferson........C 10
Totten, Pulaski........C 80
Totter, (see Ashville)........ ×
Trafalgar, Ashley........SE ×
● Traskwood, Saline........C 150
Tremont, Ouachita........S 107
Trenton, Phillips........E 75
Trident, Benton........NW 10
Triggville, Miller........SW ×
● Trippe, Desha........SE 20
Troy, Columbia........SW ×
Troy, Drew........SE ×
Troy, Ouachita........S ×
Trust, Cleburne........N ×
● *Tucker*, Jefferson........C ×
● Tuckerman, Jackson....NE 100
Tulip, Dallas........S 100
Tull, Grant........C ×
● Tupelo, Jackson........NE 130
● *Tupelo Springs*, Clark..SW ×
Turin, Grant........C 25
Turkey Creek, Stone........N ×
Turner, Phillips........E 40
Turnip, White........C 19
Tyler, Cleburne........N ×
Tyner, Phillips........E ×
Tyro, Lincoln........SE 50
● Tyronza, Cross........E 10
Ulm, Prairie........C ×
Ultima Thule, Sevier........SW 50
Umpire, Howard........SW 25
Union, Fulton........N 50
Union City, Perry........C ×
Uniontown, Crawford....NW 150
Uno, Lawrence........NE 195
Ussery, Garland........C ×
Vaden, Clark........SW ×
Valley, Hot Spring........C 50
Valley Grove, Monroe........E ×
Valley Springs, Boone....NW 200
Vallier, Arkansas........E ×
● **Van Buren**, Crawf'd.NW 2,291
Vanden, Clark........SW ×
Van Duzer, Ouachita........S ×
● Vanndale, Cross........E 282
Van Winkle's Mills, (see Fay'v'le) ×
● Varner, Lincoln........SE 75
Vaucluse, Chicot........SE 10
Vesta, Franklin........NW 65
Victor, Independence........N ×
Victoria, Jefferson........C ×
Vidette, Fulton........N 13
Village, Columbia........SW 15
Vilonia, Faulkner........C 300
Vina, Fulton........N ×
Vinage, Hot Spring........C ×
Vincent, Crittenden........E ×
Vinehill, Boone........NW ×
Vineland, Franklin........NW 13
Vineyard, Bradley........S ×
Vineyard, Lee........E 25
Viney Grove, Wash'ton.. NW 56
Viola, Fulton........N 15
Violet, Arkansas........E 40
Violet Hill, Izard........N 75
● Wabbaseka, Jefferson....C 251
Waco, Cleburne........N 57
Waddell, Desha........SE ×
Wager, Benton........NW 25
● *Wagnor*, Monroe........E ×
Wake, Baxter........N ×

Arkansas

Walcott, Greene........NE 50
● Waldo, Columbia........SW 709
Waldron, Scott........W 487
Walker, White........C 10
Walkers, Crawford........NW 32
Walkers, Columbia........SW ×
Wallaceburgh, Hempstead, SW 100
Walnut, Newton........NW 10
Walnut Bend, Lee........E 50
Walnut Grove, Ind'dence...N 100
Walnut Hill, Lafayette....SW 100
● Walnut Lake, Desha........SE 55
● Walnut Ridge, Lawrence NE 457
Walnut Tree, Yell........N 75
Walter Chapel, Prairie........C 33
Wampoo, Pulaski........C 25
● Ward, Lonoke........C 50
Ward, Yell........W ×
Wardsdale, Craigshead... NE 40
Ware, Columbia........SW 18
War Eagle, Madison........NW ×
War Eagle Mills, Benton..NW 50
Warm Springs, Randolph. NE 25
● **Warren**, Bradley........S 492
Warrenton, Lincoln........SE ×
Warsaw, Pulaski........C ×
Washburn, Sebastian........W 15
● **Washington**, Hem'd.SW 519
Washita, Montgomery........W ×
Watalula, Franklin........NW 20
Water Creek, Marion........N ×
Water Valley, Randolph..NE ×
Waters, Montgomery........W 32
Watkins, Boone........NW 66
● *Watson*, Woodruff........E ×
Watson, Desha........SE 50
Wattensaw, Lonoke........C 25
Wattensaw, Prairie........C ×
Watts, Searcy........N 32
Waveland, Yell........W 10
Wayside, Hot Spring........C ×
Weatherly's Mill, (see Clifton) ×
Weaver's, Dallas........S ×
Webb City, Franklin........NW 300
Wedington, Washington..NW 75
Weedons, Lonoke........C ×
● Weiner, Poinsett........NE 25
Welch, Montgomery........W ×
Welcome, Columbia........SW ×
● Weldon, Jackson........NE 25
Wells Creek, Newton........SW 15
Wesley, Madison........NW 50
Wesson, Union........S ×
Western Grove, Newton..NW 250
● West Fork, Wash'n....NW 150
● *West Memphis*, Critt'n... E 375
Westover, Phillips........E 25
● West Point, White........C 300
West Pairie, (see Weiner)... ×
Westwood, St. Francis........E ×
Wharton, Madison........NW 10
Wheeler, Washington....NW 10
● Wheeling, Fulton........N 10
● Wheetley, St. Francis........E 250
● Whelen Springs, Clark..SW 25
Whitcomb, Carroll........NW 32
White, Woodruff........E ×
White Bluff, Jefferson........C ×
● White Hall, Poinsett....NE 120
Whitener, Madison........NW 75
White Oak, Cleveland........S 45
● *White Oak*, Franklin...NW ×
White River, Desha........SE 185
White Riv. Bridge, (see Beaver) ×
White Rock, Franklin....NW 15
White's Mills, Garland........C ×
White's Store, (see Red Store) ×
White Sulph. Sp'gs. Jeff'n..C 32
Whitfield, Conway........C ×
Whittington, Garland........C 60
Wideman, Izard........N 15
● *Wideners*, St. Francis....E ×
● *Wiener*, Poinsett........NE 25
Wiggs, Garland........C 32
Wilbern, Jackson........NE ×
Wild Cherry, Fulton........N 15
Wiley's Cove, Searcy........N 50
Wilks, Union........S ×
● *Wilkins*, Jefferson........C ×
Wilcockson, Newton........NW 25
Williamette, Jefferson........C 50
Williams, Clay........NE 10
● *Williamsburgh*, Lincoln.SE ×
● Williford, Sharp........N 100
Willisville, Nevada........SW 25
Willow, Dallas........S 55
Willowdale, Pulaski........C 19

Town, County	Index	Pop.
● Wilmar, Drew	SE	25
Wilmington, Union	S	×
Wilmington Land'g, Union	S	4
Wilson, Pike	SW	×
Wilsons, Monroe	E	×
Wilson's Cross Roads, H'd	SW	×
Wilton, Little River	SW	×
Wilton, Pike	SW	×
● Winchester, Drew	SE	50
Wine Hill, Franklin	NW	×
Winfield, Scott	W	50
Wing, Yell	W	×
Winninghaw, Poinsett	NE	×
Winona Springs, Carroll	NW	25
Winslow, Washington	NW	200
Winsted, Sharp	N	×
Wise, Columbia	SW	×
Witcherville, Sebastian	W	250
● Witherspoon, Hot Spring	C	75
Wittsburgh, Cross	E	21
Witt's Springs, Searcy	N	75
Wolf Bayou, Cleburne	N	75
Wolf Creek, Pike	SW	50
Womble, Hot Spring	C	×
Woodlawn, Nevada	SW	60
● Woodson, Saline	C	111
Wood View, Desha	SE	×
Woolley, Union	S	30
● *Woolsey's*, Washington	NW	35
Wooster, Faulkner	C	25
● Wrightsville, Pulaski	C	100
● *Wyandotte*, Hot Spring	C	×
Wylie, Prairie	C	×
Wyloe, Ouachita	S	15
● Wyman, Washington	NW	20
● Wynne, Cross	E	565
● *Wynne Junction*, Cross	E	×
Yardelle, Newton	NW	10
Yellville, Marion	N	263
Yocum, Carroll	NW	100
● *Yoder*, Arkansas	E	×
Yorktown, Lincoln	SE	97
Yorkville, Sevier	SW	40
Youngville, (see Weiner)		×
Yuba, Cleburne	N	×
Zadock, Johnson	NW	×
Zama, Nevada	SW	×
Zebra, Fulton	N	×
Zelkirk, Scott	W	×
Zenobia, Crawford	NW	×
Zion, Izard	N	32
Zuber, Saline	C	×

CALIFORNIA.

COUNTIES.	INDEX.	POP.
Alameda	W	93,864
Alpine	E	667
Amador	C	10,320
Butte	C	17,939
Calaveras	C	8,882
Colusa	C	14,640
Contra Costa	W	13,515
Del Norte	NW	2,592
El Dorado	C	9,232
Fresno	C	32,026
Glenn	W	×
Humboldt	NW	23,469
Inyo	E	3,544
Kern	S	9,808
Lake	W	7,101
Lassen	N	4,239
Los Angeles	S	101,454
Marin	W	13,072
Mariposa	C	3,787
Mendocino	W	17,612
Merced	C	8,085
Modoc	N	4,986
Mono	E	2,002
Monterey	W	18,637
Napa	W	16,411
Nevada	C	17,369
Orange	S	13,589
Placer	C	15,101
Plumas	N	4,933
Sacramento	C	40,339
San Benito	W	6,412
San Bernardino	SE	25,497
San Diego	SE	34,987
San Francisco	W	298,997
San Joaquin	C	28,629
San Luis Obispo	S	16,072
San Mateo	W	10,087
Santa Barbara	S	15,754
Santa Clara	W	48,005
Santa Cruz	W	19,270
Shasta	N	12,133
Sierra	E	5,051
Siskiyou	N	12,163
Solano	C	20,946
Sonoma	W	32,721
Stanislaus	C	10,040
Sutter	C	5,469
Tehama	N	9,916
Trinity	NW	3,719
Tulare	C	24,574
Tuolumne	C	6,082
Ventura	S	10,071
Yolo	C	12,684
Yuba	C	9,636
Total		1,208,130

TOWN. COUNTY.	INDEX.	POP.
● Acampo, San Joaquin	C	100
Acorn, Humboldt	NW	×
● Acton, Los Angeles	S	×
Addington, Lassen	W	×
Adelaida, San Luis Obispo	S	263
Adin, Modoc	N	500
Afton, Glenn	C	×
Aetna Springs, (see Lidell)		×
● *Agatha*, Merced	C	×
● Ager, Siskiyou	N	50
● Agnew, Santa Clara	W	65
● Agua Caliente, Sonoma	W	×
● Alameda, Alameda	W	11,165
Alamo, Contra Costa	W	50
Albertson, (see Roberts)		×
Albion, Mendocino	W	250
● Alcalde, Fresno	C	×
Alcatraz, San Francisco	W	280
Alderney, Marin	W	×
Alder Point, (see Blocksburg)		×
● Alessando, S. Ber'dino	SE	×
Alex'der Val'y, (see Healdsb'g)		×
● *Alexis*, San Bernardino	SE	×
Alfa, Shasta	N	×
Algerine, (see Jamestown)		×
● Alhambra, Los Angeles	S	808
● Alila, Tulare	C	×
● *Alingard*, Merced	C	×
Aliso, San Bernardino	SE	×
Alleghany, Sierra	E	150
● *Allendale*, Solano	C	82
Allen Springs, Lake	W	40
Allison, San Diego	SE	×
Alison's Ranch, (see Grass Val)		×
● Alma, Santa Clara	W	196
Almaden Cross'g, S'ta Clara	W	×
● *Almond*, Orange	S	×
Alosta, Los Angeles	S	×
● *Alpine*, Los Angeles	S	×
Alpine, San Diego	SE	×
● Alta, Placer	C	50
Altadena, Los Angelos	S	×
● Altamont, Alameda	W	40
Altaville, (see Angel's Camp)		×
● *Alto*, Marin	W	×
Alton, Humboldt	NW	×
Alturas, Modoc	N	550
Alum Rock, (see San Jose)		×
● Alvarado, Alameda	W	300
● Alviso, Santa Clara	W	500
● Alvord, Inyo	E	×
● *Alvord*, San Bernardino	SE	×
● *Amadee*, Lassen	N	×
Amador City, Amador	C	984
● *Amaranth*, Yolo	C	×
● *Amboy*, San Bernardino	SE	×
Amedee, Lassen	N	×
America, Sonoma	W	32
● *American Riv. Bridge*, Sac.	C	×
Amesport, (see Half Moon Bay)		×
● *Amsterdam*, Merced	C	×
● Anaheim, Orange	S	1,273
● Anderson, Shasta	N	588
Anderson Val., (see Boonville)		×
Angel Island, Marin	W	465
Angel's Camp, Calaveras	C	917
Angwin, Napa	W	×
● *Anito*, Butte	C	×
● *Annadel*, Sonoma	W	×
Annaly, (see Freestone)		×
Annette, Kern	S	×
● Antelope, Sacramento	C	182
Antelope, Sprs. Amador	C	×
Antelope Val. (see Coleville)		×
Anthony House, Nevada	C	×
● Antioch, Contra Costa	W	635
● Applegate, Placer	C	40
Apricot, Monterey	W	×
● Aptos, Santa Cruz	W	200
AqueductCity, (see PineGrove)		×
Arabella, Lake	W	×
● Arbuckle, Colusa	C	375
Arbuckle, (see Ono)		×
● *Arcade*, Sacramento	C	×
● Arcadia, Los Angeles	S	×
Arcata, Humboldt	NW	962
Arch Beach, Orange	S	×
● *Arena*, Merced	C	×
Argaville, Lassen	N	×
● *Arlington*, San Bernar'o.	SE	64
Arlington Place, San Bernardino	SE	×
Arlynda, (see Ferndale)		×
● Armona, Tulare	C	×
● Arno, Sacramento	C	×
● *Arnty Point*, Solano	C	×
● *Arrowhead*, San Bern'o.	SE	×
Arrow Head Springs, San Bernardino	SE	26
● Arroyo Grande, San Luis Obispo	S	466
Arroyo Park, Los Angeles	S	×
Artesia, Los Angeles	S	40
● *Ash Hill*, San Bernar'o.	SE	×
Ashland, (see Folsom)		×
Ashton, Lassen	N	×
● Asti, Sonoma	W	×
● *Asylum*, San Bernardino	SE	×
● *Athena*, Colusa	C	×
● Athlone, Merced	C	25
Atlanta, San Joaquin	C	80
● Atwater, Merced	C	57
Auberry, Fresno	C	130
● **Auburn**, Placer	C	1,595
Auburndale, (see S. Riverside)		×
Auckland, Tulare	C	×
● *Aurant*, Los Angeles	S	×
Avalon, Los Angeles	S	×
Avenal, San Luis Obispo	S	×
Avery, Calaveras	C	×
● *Avila*, San Luis Obispo	S	×
Avon, Butte	C	×
● *Avon*, Contra Costa	W	×
● Azusa, Los Angeles	S	250
Bachelor, Lake	W	65
● *Baden*, San Mateo	W	×
● Bagdad, San Bernardino	SE	×
Baird, Shasta	N	×
● **Bakersfield**, Kern	S	2,626
● *Baldwin*, Los Angeles	S	×
● *Bale*, Napa	W	×
Ballard, Santa Barbara	S	65
Ballena, San Diego	SE	400
Ballona, (see Palms)		×
● *Ballona Junc.*, Los Ang's.	S	×
Ball's Ferry, Shasta	N	40
Ball's Ranch, Siskiyou	N	×
● *Bandini*, Los Angeles	S	×
Bangor, Butte	C	300
Banner, San Diego	SE	×
● Banning, San Bernar'o.	SE	40
● Banta, San Joaquin	C	520
● *Bardins*, Monterey	W	×
Bardsdale, Ventura	S	×
● *Barro*, Napa	W	×
● Barstow, San Bernardino	SE	100
Bartlett Springs, Lake	W	130
Barzilla, San Mateo	W	×
● *Base Line*, San Bernard'o	SE	×
● Batavia, Solano	C	260
Bates, Fresno	C	×
Bath, Placer	C	100
Battle Cr., (see Ball's Ferry)		×
Baulines, Marin	W	×
Baville, Amador	C	×
Baxter, Mariposa	NW	×
Bay Farm Island, Alameda	W	×
● *Bay Junction*, Marin	W	×
● Bayles, Shasta	N	26
● *Bay Point*, Contra Costa	W	×
Bayside, Humboldt	NW	×
● *Bealville*, Kern	S	×
Bear Creek, (see Georgetown)		×
Bear Harbor, Mendocino	W	×
Bear River, Yuba	C	×
Bear Valley, (see Big Trees)		×
Bear Valley, Mariposa	C	200
Beatrice, Humboldt	NW	390
● Beaumont, San Bernard'o	SE	200

Beckwith, Plumas..........N 25
Beckwith Pass, (see Summit) X
● *Belle*, Napa............W X
Beellevlew, (see Hamptonville) X
Belleville, Tulare...........C 32
Bellota, San Joaquin........C 50
Bells Station, Napa ....W X
Bell's Station, Santa Clara..W 32
● Belmont, San Mateo......W 150
● *Benali*, Sacramento.......C X
Ben-Hur, Mariposa...........C X
● Benicia, Solano...........C 2,361
● Ben Lomond, Santa Cruz.W X
Bennet Val., (see Glen Ellen) X
Bennington, Los Angeles....S X
Benton, Mono...............E 120
● *Benton Station*, Mono....E X
Berdan, Butte..............C 85
● Berendo, Fresno...........C 110
● Berkeley, Alameda...... W 5,101
● Berlin, Colusa.............C 100
Bernabe, (see San Antonio).. X
● *Bernal*, Marin........... W X
Bernardo, San Diego.......SE 122
Berry Creek, Butte..........C 90
Berryessa, Santa Clara.....W X
● *Berryman*, Contra Costa.W X
Berryvale, (see Mott) X
Bertha, Lake...............W 48
Beswick, Siskiyou..........N 47
● Bethany, San Joaquin.....C 123
Bethlehem, Santa Clara.... W X
Bidwell's Bar, Butte........C 85
Bieber, Lassen..............N 100
Big Bar, Trinity..........NW 90
Bigbend, Butte............ C 120
Big Dry Creek, Fresno......C 25
Big Meadows, (see Prattville) X
● Biggs, Butte...............C 571
Big Oak Flat, Tuolumne.... C 150
Big Pine, Inyo.............. E 150
Big River, (see Mendocino) .. X
Big Trees, Calaveras....... C 55
Big Trees Sta., Santa Cruz. W X
Big Tree Sta., (see Wawona). X
Big Valley, (see Bieber)...... X
Bijou, El Dorado............C 50
Binghamton, Solano.........C 60
● *Binney Junction*, Yuba...C X
Birchville, (see Sweetland)... X
Bird's Landing, Solano......C 50
● Bishop, Inyo...............E 840
Bitter Spring, San Ber'dnoSE X
Bitter Water, San Benito...W 75
Bixby Canyon, (see Monterey) X
Black Bear, Siskiyou....... N 200
● *Black Butte Sum't*, Sisk'yuN X
Bl'k Diamond, Con. Costa..W 300
Bl'k Mountain, San Diego.SE X
Black Rock, (see Independ.). X
● Black's Station, Yolo......C 150
Blair, **(see Stella)** X
Blanco, Monterey.......... W 35
Blocksburgh, Humboldt. NW 150
Bloomfield, Sonoma........W 300
● Blue Canyon, Placer.......C 100
Blue Lake, Humboldt....NW 700
Blue Lake Park, (see Bertha) X
● Boca, Nevada.............C 266
Bodega, (see Smith's Ranch). X
Bodega Cor., (see Smith's R'h) X
● *Bodega Roads*, Sonoma..W X
Bodie, Mono................E 595
Bogus, Siskiyou............ N 155
Bolinas, Marin............. W 400
Bolinas Ridge, Marin......W X
● *Bolsa*, Orange............ S X
Bonds, Los Angeles.........S X
Bonita, San Diego .... SE X
Bonny Doon, Santa Cruz...W X
Bonsall, San Diego........ SE X
Boonville, Mendocino......W 100
● Borden, Fresno...........C 35
Borro, Napa...............W X
Borrough Val., (see Toll H'se) X
Boston Ranch, Amador.... C X
Boston Ranch, (see Hurleton) X
Boston Ravine, (see Grass Val.) X
● Boulder Creek, S'ta Cruz.W 489
Bouldin Island, San Joaquin.C 150
Boulevard, Los Angeles....S X
Bourne's L'dg, (see Gualala). X
● *Box Springs*, S'nBe'rdinoSE X
● *Bracks*, San Joaquin......C X
Bradford Mines, Lake.....W X
● Bradley, Monterey.......W 75

Brays, Alameda...........W X
● Brentwood, Contra Costa.W 150
Bricelard, Humboldt.....NW X
Bridgeport, Mono........E 250
Bridgeport, (see Cordelia) ... X
Bridgeville, Humboldt....NW 20
● *Brighton*, Sacramento....C X
● *Bristol*, San Bernardino.SE X
Bronco, (see Floriston) X
Brooklyn, Alameda........ W X
● Brooks, Yolo............ C 130
● *Brookshurst*, Orange......S X
● *Brookside*, San Be'rdino SE X
Brown's Valley, Yuba.......C 500
Brownsville, Yuba.......... C 260
Brown's Well, San Diego..SE X
Brush Creek, Butte......... C 130
Bryson, Monterey.......... W X
Buchanan, Fresno.......... C 15
Buckeye, (See Shingle Sprs.). X
Buckeye, Shasta............W 50
● *Buckhorn*, Ventura.......S X
Bucksport, Humboldt....NW X
Buck's Ranch, Plumas......N 67
● Buena, San Diego........ SE 20
● Buena Park, Orange......S X
Buena Vista, Amador.......C X
Buena V'ta, (seeKnight's Fy.) X
● *Buena Vista*, Nevada.... C X
● *Buena Vista*, Sonoma... W X
Bullard's Bar, Yuba.........C 15
Bull Creek, (see Coulterville) X
Buntingville, (see Janesville) X
● Burbank, Los Angeles.... S 250
Burckhalter, Nevada........C X
● *Burdells*, Marin .... W X
Burgess, Shasta............ N X
Burgettville, (see Swasey).... X
Burnett, (see Coyote)........ X
● *Burnett's*, Stanislaus......C X
Burney Valley, Shasta.......N 100
Burnold'sSta., (see Rohnerv'l.. X
Burnt Ranch, Trinity.....NW 97
Burrough, Fresno...........C X
Burrough Val., (see Toll Hou.) X
● Burson, Calaveras..........C 32
Burwood, San Joaquin.......C X
Butchers Ranch, Placer.....C 20
Butchertown, Alameda ....W X
● *Butler*, Fresno.............C X
Butte City, Glenn...........C 250
Butte Creek, Butte..........C X
Butte Meadows, Butte.......C X
Butte Valley, Plumas........N 160
Butteville, (see Edgwood)..... X
Buzzard's Roost, (see Round Mountain).................. X
Byersville, Stanislaus....... C X
Byrne's Ferry, Calaveras... C 15
● Byron, Contra Costa......W 100
Byron Hot Springs, C'ra Cl'aW X
● *Cabazon*, San Diego.....SE X
Cacheville, Yolo ....C X
● *Cactus*, San Diego.......SE 97
● *Cadanassa*, Yolo......... C X
Cadillac, Siskiyou.......... N X
● *Cadiz*, San Bernardino..SE X
Cahto, Mendocino.......... W 75
Cahuenga, Los Angeles......S X
Cahuilla, San Diego........SE X
● Cajon, San Bernardino..SE X
Cajon Heights, San Diego..SE X
Calabasas, Los Angeles.......S X
Calico, San Bernardino....SE 1,500
● Caliente, Kern............ S 455
● *Califa*, Fresno.............C X
● Calistoga, Napa.......... W 1,200
● *Calkin*, Santa Barbara....S X
Callahan's Ranch, Siskiyou.N 125
Calpella, Mendocino........ W 50
Camanche, Calaveras........C 195
Cambria, San Luis Obispo...S 288
● *Cameron*, Kern........... S X
Camp Badger, Tulare........C 85
● Campbell, Santa Clara....W X
Campbell's Hot Springs, Santa Clara.................... W X
Camp'l's Sprs, (see SierraVal.) X
Camp Capitola, (see Capitola) X
Camp Gaston, (see Hoopa Val.) X
Camp Grant, Humboldt..NW X
Camp Independence, Inyo..E X
Camp Lincoln, Del Norte.NW X
Campo, San Diego.........SE 50
Campo Seco, Calaveras......C 200
Campo Seco, (see Jamestown) X
● *Camp Taylor*, Marin.... W X

Camp Thirteen, (seeCharleston) X
Camptonville, Yuba.........C 350
● Camulos, Ventura........S X
● Cana, Butte...............C 260
Canby, Modoc.............. N 32
● *Cando*, Fresno............C X
● *Cannon*, Solano...........C X
Canon House, (see Monticello) X
● *Canon Siding*, San Diego.SE X
● *Cantara*, Siskiyou.........N X
Canton Mine, Inyo......... E X
Cantua, Fresno.............C X
● Capay, Yolo...............C 250
● *Cape Horn Mills*, Placer.C X
Capell, Napa...............W X
Capetown, Humboldt.....NW X
● Capistrano, Orange.......S 300
Capitola, Santa Cruz........W X
Carbon, Shasta..............N 82
● *Carbondale*, Amador..... C X
Carey, Mendocino..........W X
● Carlsbad, San Diego.....SE 100
Carlton, (see Clements) X
Carmenita, Los Angeles......S X
● *Carnadero*, Santa Clara..W 260
Carneross, (see Napa)........ X
● Carpenteria, Santa B'bara.S 100
● ***Carrigers***, **Sonoma**...... W X
Carrville, Trinity.........NW X
Carson Hill, (see Angel's C'mp) X
Carters, Tuolumne..........C X
● Caruthers, Fresno.........C X
● *Casa Blanca*, S'n B'rdinoSE X
● *Cascade*, Nevada......... C X
Cashin's Stn., (see Templeton) X
● *Cashmere*, Yolo.......... C X
Caspar, Mendocino.........W 206
Cassel, Shasta............. N X
● *Castiac*, Los Angeles......S X
● *Castle*, San Joaquin......C X
● *Castle Crag*, Shasta.......N X
● Castroville, Monterey.... W 641
Cathay, Mariposa...........C 32
Cat's Bar, Humboldt.... NW X
Cayton, Shasta..............N 32
Cayucos, San Luis Obispo... S 150
● Cazadero, Sonoma....... W X
Cecilville, Siskiyou......... N 65
Cedarville, Modoc.......... N 200
● Centinela, Los Angeles....S X
Central City, (see SantaMaria) X
Central Colony, Fresno.....C 510
Central House, Butte........C 130
Centre House, (seeNevadaCity) X
● Centreville, Alameda.....W 300
Centreville, (see John Adams) X
Centreville, (see King's River) X
Centreville, (see Shasta)...... X
Centreville, (see Linconville). X
Centro, (see Gladstone)...... X
● Ceres, Stanislaus..........C 150
● *Cerritos*, Los Angeles......S X
Cerro Gordo, Inyo.......... E 65
Chalkford, (see Bieber)....... X
● *Chandlers*, Sutter.........C X
Channel, Butte.............C X
Chaparral, Butte............C X
● *Chapman*, Los Angeles... S X
● *Charleston*, San Joaquin..C X
● Chat, Lassen..............N 38
Chatsworth, Los Angeles....S X
Cherokee, Butte........... C 700
Cherokee, (see Patterson).... X
Chester, (see Merced)....... X
● *Chestnut*, Siskiyou.......N X
● Chicago Park, Nevada....C X
● Chico, Butte.............. C 2,894
Chiles, Napa................W 13
Chili Gulch, (see Mokelumne Hill)..................... X
China Flat, Humboldt.... NW 65
China Flat, (see Downieville) X
Chinese Camp, Tuolumne...C 260
Chino, San Bernardino.... SE 195
Chipp's Island, Solano......C X
Chittendens, San Benito....W X
Cholame, San Luis Obispo...S 65
Chollas Valley, (see SanDiego) X
● *Cholone*, Monterey.......W X
Chowchilla, Mariposa.......C 130
Christine, Mendocino.......W 50
● *Chromite*, Shasta..........N X
● Chualar, Monterey.........N 100
Chula Vista, San Diego....SE 15
Churntown, (see Buckeye)... X
● *Cicero*, Sacramento....... C X

● *Cirnega*, Los Angeles..... S ×
● Cisco, Placer............C 25
● *Citrona*, Yolo............C ×
Citrus, Inyo................E ×
Citrus, (see Covina)......... ×
Clairville, (see Geyserville)... ×
Claremont, Alameda.......W 278
● Claremont, Los Angeles...S 130
Clarksburgh, Yolo..........C ×
Clarkson, Kern............S ×
● *Clark Summit*, Marin.... W ×
Clarksville, El Dorado...... C 455
Clay, Sacramento............C 25
Clay Station, Sacramento...C 25
Clayton, Contra Costa...... W 150
Clayton Hill, (see Hornitos).. ×
Clear Creek, Butte..........C ×
Clear Lake, Modoc..........N 130
Clearwater, Los Angeles.....S ×
● *Clement Junc.*, Los A'g'l's.S ×
● Clements, San Joaquin....C 333
Cleone, Mendocino......... W 50
Clifton, Fresno............C 260
Clinton, Amador...........W 400
Clinton, Mono..............E 130
Clinton, (see Truckee)....... ×
● Clipper Gap, Placer.......C 20
Clipper Mills, Butte.........C 200
Cloudman, Tuolumne........C 97
● Cloverdale, Sonoma.......W 768
Clover Swale, Modoc........ N ×
● *Clyde*, San Joaquin....... C ×
● Coalinga, Fresno..........C ×
Coarse Gold Gulch, Fresno..C 10
Coast, Santa Cruz.......... W ×
● *Coburn's*, Monterey......W ×
Cœur, Trinity...........NW 100
Cohassett, Butte............ C ×
Colby's Landing, (see Nord). ×
Colegrove, Los Angeles..... S ×
Coleman Val., (see Occid'nt'l) ×
Coleridge, Trinity........ NW ×
● Cole's, Siskiyou.......... N ×
Coleville, Mono............ E 100
● Colfax, Placer............C 670
College City, Colusa.........C 887
College Park, Santa Clara..W ×
Collegeville, San Joaquin... C 100
● *Collins*, Fresno.......... C ×
Collinsville, Solano..........C 100
● Colma Station, San Mateo W ×
Coloma, El Dorado..........C 200
● *Colorado*, San Diego..... SE ×
● Colton, San Bernardino.SE 1,315
Columbia, Tuolumne.........C 450
Col'mbia Flat, (see St. Law'nce) ×
Col'mbia Hill, (see N. Col'mbia) ×
Columbus House, (see Strawberry Valley)............ ×
● **Colusa**, Colusa.......... C 1,336
● Colusa Junction, Colusa.. C ×
Colyer, Tehama............ N ×
● Cometa, San Joaquin.....C ×
Comptche, Mendocino..... W ×
● Compton, Los Angeles.... S 636
Concord, Contra Costa..... W 878
Con Cow, Butte............. C 65
Confidence, (see Sugar Pine). ×
Congress Springs, Santa Clara W ×
Conley, Sacramento .... C 82
Conn Valley, (see Sacramento) ×
Cool, El Dorado.............C 82
● *Coomb's*, Yuba............C ×
● *Cooper's*, Monterey...... W 20
● Copley, Shasta............N ×
Copper City, (see Ydalpom).. ×
Copperopolis, Calaveras .... C 232
Copper Vale, Lassen ....N 32
○ Cordelia, Solano.......... C 300
Cornelian, Placer........... C ×
Cornell, Modoc.............. N 32
● Corning, Tehama......... N 210
● Cornwall, Contra Costa.. W 97
● Coronado, San Diego.... SE [illegible]
Coronado Heights, San Diego SE ×
Carral de Piedra, (see Steele's) ×
Corralitos, Santa Cruz ..... W 100
● *Corte Madera*, Marin.... W ×
Coso, Inyo...................E ×
Cosumne, Sacramento...... C [illegible]
Cota, San Diego.......... SE ×
● *Cotate*, Sonoma......... W ×
Cotopaxi Mine, Inyo...... E ×
Cottage Grove, Siskiyou....N ×
● *Cottonwood*, San B'rdino SE ×
● Cottonwood, Shasta...... N 269

Coulterville, Mariposa...... C 525
Courtland, Sacramento..... C 195
Coutolenc, Butte........... C ×
Covelo, Mendocino..........W 200
Coville, (see Easton)........ ×
Covina, Los Angeles........ S ×
Cowles, San Diego .... SE ×
Cox Bar, (see Big Bar)....... ×
● *Cox's Lane*, Butte........ C ×
● Coyote, Santa Clara....... W 300
Coyote Holes, (see Freeman). ×
Cozzens, Sonoma .... W 130
Craig, Modoc .... N ×
Cramer, Tulare............ C ×
Cranmore, Sutter........... C ×
Crescent City, DelNorte NW 907
Crescent Mills, Plumas..... N 202
● *Creston*, Napa........... W ×
Cressey, (see Livingston)..... ×
Creston, San Luis Obispo.... S 50
Crockett, Contra Costa .... W 301
Cromberg, Plumas.......... N 32
● *Cross Creek*, Tulare...... C 32
Crow City, San Bernardino SE ×
● Crow's Landing, Stanislaus C 32
Cruessville, Monterey......W ×
Crystal Creek, Siskiyou.... N ×
Cuba, (see Boca)............ ×
● Cucamonga, S'n B'nr'dio.SE 90
Cuffey's Cove, (see Elk)...... ×
Cummings, Mendocino .... W ×
Cupertino, Santa Clara..... W 65
● *Curtis*, Yolo.............. C ×
Cuyamaca, San Diego......SE ×
● *Cypress Park*, Monterey. W ×
● Daggett, San Bernardino SE 100
Dalces, Los Angeles......... S ×
Damascus, Placer .... C ×
Dana, Shasta...............N ×
● *Danby*, San Bernardino.SE ×
Danville, Contra Costa..... W 50
● *Danville*, Los Angeles .... S ×
Dark Canyon, (see Harris)... ×
Darrah, Mariposa........... C 260
Darwin, Inyo............... E 75
● *Dathol*, Fresno.......... C ×
● *Daultons*, Fresno .... C ×
Daunt, Tulare .... C ×
Davenport L'nd'g, (see Coast) ×
Davis Creek, Modoc........ N 170
Davis Ranch, (see Trinity Cn'tr) ×
● Davisville, Yolo .... C 547
Day, Modoc................ N ×
Daylor's R'nch, (see Cosumne) ×
Dayton, (see Grainland)...... ×
Deadwood, Trinity....... NW 286
De Camp, Los Angeles......S ×
● Declezville, S'n Bernard'o SE ×
● Decoto, Alameda .... W 100
Dedrick, Trinity.......... NW ×
Deer Creek, (see Delano)..... ×
Deer Flat, (see Shingletown) ×
Dehesa, San Diego.........SE ×
● Delano, Kern............. S 401
● *Delavan*, Colusa......... C ×
● *Delhi*, Merced .... C ×
Del Mar, San Diego.........SE 18
● *Del Monte*, Monterey.... W 83
● *Delta*, Shasta .... N 26
● De Luz, San Diego........SE 35
Del Sur, Los Angeles........S ×
Delta, (see Baylis)........... ×
Denny, Trinity........... NW ×
Denverton, Solano.......... C 10
Derbec Mines, Nevada......C ×
DeRedwood, (see Laurel)..... ×
Descanso, San Diego ...... SE 50
Deseret, Fresno............ C ×
Diamente, San Diego...... SE ×
● Diamond Spring, ElD'r'do C 100
● Dinuba, Tulare........... C 100
● *Divide*, Santa Barbara.... S ×
● Dixon, Solano .... C 1,082
Dobbins, Yuba.............. C 40
Dobbyns' Cr'k, (see Blocksb'g) ×
Dog Town, (see Magalia)..... ×
Dog Town, (see Angel's Camp) ×
Dog Town, (see Bolinas)..... ×
Dolde, Shasta .... N ×
● *Dominguez*, Los Angeles..S ×
● *Donahue*, Sonoma....... W ×
● Donner, Placer ....C 26
Dorris, Siskiyou...........N ×
Dorrisville, (see Alturas)...... ×
● *Dos Palmas*, San Diego..SE ×
Dos Palos, Merced.......... C ×
Dougherty Mills, Santa Cruz W ×

Dougherty's Station, A'm'da W 320
Douglas City, Trinity..... NW 175
Douglas Flat, Calaveras..... C 100
Dove, San Luis Obispo...... S ×
● Downey, Los Angeles..... S 1,000
Downieville, Sierra..... E 600
Dow's Prairie, Humboldt. NW ×
● *Doyle*, Lassen .... N ×
● *Drew*, San Bernardino.. SE ×
● *Drummond*, Sonoma.... W ×
Dry Camp, San Diego..... SE 260
● *Drylyn*, San Diego...... SE ×
Dry Slough, (see Grimes).... ×
Drytown, Amador......... C 120
Duarte, Los Angeles......... S 100
Dublin, Alameda .... W 250
Dudley, Tulare............C ×
● *Dugane*, El Dorado ..... C ×
Dulzura, San Diego .... SE ×
● Duncan's Mills, Sonoma. W 390
Dundee, Los Angeles.......S ×
Dunlap, Fresno............ C 130
● Dunnigan, Yolo...........C 125
● Dunsmuir, Siskiyou...... N 300
● Durham, Butte.......... C 130
● Dutch Flat, Placer........ C 682
Dutch Corners, (see Newman) ×
Dutton's Landing, Solano... C ×
Dyerville, Humboldt..... NW ×
Eagle Creek, Modoc........ N ×
Eagle Creek, (see Ono)....... ×
Eagle Lake, Modoc........ N ×
Eagleville, Modoc.......... N 100
Eal, Humboldt.......... NW ×
Earlham, (see El Modena)... ×
East Berkeley, (see Berkeley). ×
● *Eastberne*, San B'n'rd'o..SE ×
East Fork, (see Coleridge)... ×
● *East Highlands*, San Bernardino..............SE ×
East Hopland, (see Hopland). ×
● *East Oakland*, Alameda. W ×
Easton, Fresno..............C 80
● East Pasadena, Los A'g'l's.S ×
E. Petaluma, (see Petaluma) ×
● East Riverside, San Bernardino .... SE ×
● *East San Gabriel*, Los A'g'ls S ×
East San Jose, Santa Clara. W ×
E. Santa Cruz, (see Santa Cruz) ×
● Echo, El Dorado..........C ×
Eddy's Landing, Colusa ....C 25
Eden L'nd'g, (see Mt. Eden).. ×
● *Eden Vale*, Santa Clara.. W ×
● Edgwood, Siskiyou....... N 200
Edna, San Luis Obispo.......S ×
● *Edson*, San Bernardino..SE ×
● *Egan*, San Diego........ SE ×
El Cajon, San Diego.......SE 100
El Capitan, San Diego......SE ×
● El Casco, San Bernardino SE ×
El Dorado, Calaveras.......C 200
● El Dorado, El Dorado..... C 100
Elena, Shasta............. N ×
Elizabeth Lake, Los Angeles.S 130
Elk, Mendocino............. W 216
Elk Camp, Del Norte.... NW ×
Elk Creek, Glenn............C 60
● Elk Grove, Sacramento... C 202
● *Elkhorn*, Monterey...... W ×
Elklawn, Siskiyou......... N ×
Elk Mountain, (see Lakeport) ×
Elk River, Humboldt.....NW ×
Elliott, San Joaquin .... C 100
● *Ellis*, San Joaquin....... C ×
Elmer, Kern............... S ×
Elmhurst, Alameda........W ×
● Elmira, Solano.............C 317
● El Modena, Orange........S ×
El Monte, Los Angeles...... S 200
● *Elmore*, Trinity........NW ×
El Nido, San Diego........SE ×
● *El Robel*, Mendocino.....W ×
● Elsinore, San Diego......SE 600
● El Toro, Orange...........S ×
El Verano, Sonoma........ W ×
Elvina, (see Mulberry)....... ×
● *Elwood*, Santa Barbara... S ×
● *Ely*, Yolo............... C ×
Ely's, Lake...............W ×
● *Ely's*, Sonoma........... W ×
Ematon, Sacramento........ C ×
● *Emerald*, Stanislaus...... C ×
Emerald Bay, El Dorado....C ×
Emeryville, Alameda........W 228
● Emigrant Gap, Placer.....C 125
Emmett, San Benito........W 65

Empire Ranch, (see Smartsv.) ×
Encinal, (see Alameda) ×
● Encinitas, San Diego SE 100
Englewood, Humboldt NW 65
Enterprise, Butte C 90
Epperson, Colusa C 65
Erie, San Benito W 60
Escalante, (see Esparto) ×
● Escondido, San Diego SE 541
● *Escondido Junc.*, S Diego SE ×
Esmeralda, Calaveras C ×
● *Esparanza*, Yolo C ×
● Esparto, Yolo C 60
Esperanza, Tulare C ×
● *Essex*, Nevada C ×
Estrella, San Luis Obispo S ×
● Etiwanda, S. Bernardino SE 75
Etna Mills, Siskiyou N 271
Etna Springs, (see Lidell) ×
Etta, Sierra E 200
Eureka, Humboldt NW 4,858
Eureka Mills, Plumas N 350
Eureka South, Nevada C 400
Evergreen, Santa Clara W 130
● *Evergreen St.*, Los Angeles S ×
● *Ewings*, Nevada C ×
● Exeter, Tulare C ×
Fagan, Amador C ×
● *Fairfax*, Marin W ×
Fairfield, Solano C 505
Fairmont, Los Angeles S ×
● *Fair Oaks*, Los Angeles S ×
Fair Play, El Dorado C 65
Fariview, Orange S ×
● *Fairview*, Colusa C ×
● Fall Brook, San Diego SE 300
Fall River Mills, Shasta N 150
Fandango Val., (see Willow Ranch) ×
Farmersville, Tulare C 20
● Farmington, San Joaquin C 300
Fnyal, (see San Pedro) ×
Farquhar, Tehama N ×
● Felton, Santa Cruz W 259
● *Felton Jc.*, Santa Cruz W ×
● *Fenner*, San Bernardino SE ×
● *Fernando*, Los Angeles S ×
Ferndale, Humboldt NW 763
Fiddletown, (see Oleta) ×
Field's Landing, Humb'lt NW ×
● Fillmore, Ventura S ×
Fine Gold Gulch, Fresno C 5
● *Finnell*, Tehama N ×
Firebaugh, Fresno C 50
First Garrote, (see Groveland) ×
Fisherman's Bay, Sonoma W 142
Fisher's Bridge, (see Bolota) ×
FishRanch, (see Contra Costa) ×
Fish Ranch, Contra Costa W ×
Fish Ranch, (see Truckee) ×
Fish Rock, Mendocino W 65
Fish Spring, (see Big Pine) ×
Fisk's Mill, Sonoma W 130
Five Mile H'se, (see Watsonv'l) ×
Flea Valley, (see Con Cow) ×
Fleener, Modoc N ×
● Florence, Los Angeles S 750
Florentine, San Diego SE ×
Flores, (see San Emedios) ×
● Florin, Sacramento C 75
● Floriston, Nevada C 60
● *Flosden*, Solano C ×
● *Flowing Well*, S. Diego SE ×
Flume House, (see Volcano) ×
Flume House, (see Mokelumne Hill) ×
Folsom City, Sacramento C 699
Forbestown, Butte C 260
Forest City, Sierra E 238
Forest Hill, Placer C 650
Forest House, (see Yreka) ×
Forest Home, Amador C 77
● Forest Lake, S. Joaquin C ×
Forest Ranch, Butte C 32
● Forestville, Sonoma W 80
Forks of ElkRiver, (see Eureka) ×
Forks of Salmon, Siskiyou N 65
Forster, Orange S ×
Fort Bidwell, Modoc N 250
Fort Bragg, Mendocino W 945
Fort Crook, (see Burgettville) ×
Fort Jones, Siskiyou N 266
Fort Mason, San Francisco W ×
Fort Robinson, San Diego SE ×
Fort Ross, Sonoma W 50
● *Fortuna*, Fresno C ×
Fortuna, Humboldt NW 300

Fort Winfield Scott, S Fris. W ×
Fort Yuma, (see Yuma, Ariz.) ×
Foster Sta., Amador C ×
Foster's, San Diego SE ×
● *Fountain*, Mendocino W ×
Fouts Springs, Colusa C 30
● Fowler, Fresno C 100
Francis, Trinity NW 20
Franklin, Sacramento C 260
Frazier, Tulare C 40
Fredonia, Lassen N ×
Freedom, Santa Cruz W 120
Freeman, Kern S ×
Freeport, Sacramento C 150
● Freestone, Sonoma W 400
French Camp, San Joaquin C 300
French Corral, Nevada C 150
French Creek, Butte C ×
French Gulch, Shasta N 200
Freshwater, Humboldt NW 65
Fresno, Fresno C 10,818
Fresno Cross, (see Coarse Gold Gulch) ×
Fresno Flats, Fresno C 150
● *Frink's*, San Diego SE ×
Frohm, Santa Clara W ×
Frontier House, (see Petaluma) ×
Fruitland, Humboldt NW ×
Fruitland, San Diego SE ×
Fruitvale, (see Oakland) ×
Fruitvale, Fresno C 38
● Fruto, Glenn C ×
● Fullerton, Orange S 600
● Fulton, Sonoma W 350
● *Fulton Wells*, Los Angeles S 65
Fyffe, El Dorado C 19
Gains, Tulare C ×
Gaither's Cors. (see Yuba City) ×
● Galt, Sacramento C 700
Gans, Humboldt NW ×
Garberville, Humboldt NW 195
● *Garcia*, Marin W ×
Gardemeyer, (see Bakersfield) ×
Gardena, Los Angeles S ×
Garden Grove, Orange S 50
Garden Valley, El Dorado C 20
Garey, Santa Barbara S ×
Garfield, Fresno C ×
● Garvanza, Los Angeles S 411
Gas Point, Shasta N 65
Gasquet, Del Norte NW 32
Gaston's, Los Angeles S ×
Gate, (see Jackson's Gate) ×
Gatesville, (see Eureka) ×
● Gazelle, Siskiyou N 50
Genesee, Plumas N 15
● *Geneva*, Colusa C 100
George Creek, (see Lone Pine) ×
Georgetown, El Dorado C 320
Georgia Slide, (see Georgetown) ×
● Germantown, Glenn C 150
Gertrude, Fresno C 20
Geyser Springs, Sonoma W 65
● Geyserville, Sonoma W 100
Gibbs Oil Spring, Tulare C ×
● *Gibson*, Shasta N ×
Gibsonville, Sierra E 150
Gilmore, Colusa C 83
● Gilroy, Santa Clara W 1,694
Gilroy Hot Springs, S. Clara W 65
● *Girard*, Kern S ×
● *Girvan*, Shasta N ×
Gladstone, Los Angeles S 40
● *Gladysta*, San Bernar'o. SE ×
● *Glamis*, San Diego SE ×
Glazier, Siskiyou N ×
Gleasonville, (see Henleyville) ×
Glenbrook, Lake W 130
● *Glenbrook*, Nevada C ×
● *Glenburn*, Kern S ×
Glencoe, Calaveras C 65
Glendale, (see Blue Lake) ×
Glendale, Los Angeles S ×
Glendale Jc., Los Angeles S ×
● Glendora, Los Angeles S 300
● Glen Ellen, Sonoma W 60
Glennville, Kern S 130
● Glenwood, Santa Cruz W 50
Globe, Tulare C ×
● *Gloster*, Kern C 125
● *Goff's*, San Bernardino SE ×
Golden Gate, Alameda W 788
Golden Gate, Marin W ×
Golden Hill, San Diego SE ×
Gold Hill, Humboldt NW ×
● Gold Run, Placer C 211
● Goleta, Santa Barbara S 500

● Gonzales, Monterey W 359
Goodwin, San Luis Obispo S ×
● *Goodwins*, Sonoma W ×
Goodyear's, Solano C 325
Goodyear's Bar, Sierra E ×
Goodyear's Sta., (see Suis'n C'y) ×
Goose Lake, (see Wil'w Ranch) ×
Gorman's Station, Los Ang. S 195
● Goshen, Tulare C 10
Gottville, Siskiyou N ×
● *Graciosa*, Santa Barbara S ×
● Grafton, Yolo C 300
Grainland, Butte C 150
Grand Island, Colusa C 163
Grangeville, Tulare C 100
Granite Hill, El Dorado C ×
Graniteville, Nevada C 234
● *Grant's*, Sonoma W ×
Grant Springs, Mariposa C 26
Grapeland, San Bernar'o. SE ×
Grasshopper V., (see Merrrilv.) ×
● Grass Valley, Nevada C 4,032
Gravelly Valley, (see Hullville) ×
Grayson, Stanislaus C 331
Great West Mine, (see Midd'tn) ×
● *Green Brae*, Marin W ×
Green Valley, El Dorado C ×
Green Valley, (see Forestville and Occidental) ×
Green Valley, Sonoma W ×
Greenville, Plumas N 640
● Greenwich, Kern S 350
● *Greenwood*, Colusa C ×
Greenwood, El Dorado C 180
Greenwood Creek, (see Elk) ×
● *Grenada*, Siskiyou N ×
● Gridley, Butte C 686
Griffin's Marin W ×
Grimes, Colusa C 50
Grimes Landing, Colusa C ×
Grizzly Bear House, Placer C ×
Grizzly Bluff, Humboldt NW ×
Grizzly Flats, El Dorado C 125
Groveland, Tuolumne C 150
Grubgulch, Fresno C 46
Guadaloupe, Santa Barbara S 200
Gualala, Mendocino W 267
Gubserville, Santa Clara W 97
● Guerneville, Sonoma W 600
● Guinda, Yolo C ×
Gullion's Bar, (see Lincolnville) ×
● *Gustine*, Merced C ×
Guthries Station, Sac'm'to. C ×
Gypsum, Orange S ×
Hagginsville, Sacramento C ×
● *Halconera*, Colusa C ×
Half Moon Bay, San Mateo W 450
Half Way House, (see Hayw'ds) ×
Half Way House, (see Avery) ×
● Halleck, San Bernardino SE 130
Hamburgh, Siskiyou N 90
Haines, Monterey W ×
● *Hamlet*, Marin W 40
● *Hammil*, Mono E ×
Hamilton, (see Acampo) ×
● Hanford, Tulare C 942
Hangtown Cross, Sacram'to C ×
Hansen, Humboldt NW ×
Hansonville, Yuba C 65
Happy Camp, Siskiyou N 350
Happy Hollow, (see Port Wine) ×
Harbin Springs, Lake W ×
● *Hardwick*, Fresno C ×
Harold, Los Angeles S 200
● *Harper*, San Bernardino SE ×
● *Harrington*, Colusa C ×
Harris, Humboldt NW 97
● *Harris*, Santa Barbara S ×
Harrisburg, (see Warm Sprgs) ×
Harrison, San Mateo W ×
Hart, Shasta N ×
● *Hartley*, Solano C ×
● *Haslett*, San Berdardino SE ×
Hatchet Cr., (see Montg'y Cr.) ×
Hat Creek, (see Cassell) ×
Hausen, Lassen W ×
Havilah, Kern S 330
Hawkinsville, Siskiyou N 300
Hawk's Corner, (see Elliott) ×
Hawley, San Diego SE 13
Hayden Hill, Lassen N 260
Hay Fork, Trinity NW 250
● Haywards, Alameda W 1,419
● Hazel Creek, Shasta N 260
Hazel Green, (see Coulterville) ×
● Healdsburgh, Sonoma W 1,485
Hearst, Mendocino W ×

● *Heinlen*, Tulare..........C ×
Helena, Trinity..........NW ×
Helix, San Diego..........SE 32
● *Hemet*, San Diego.......SE ×
Hemlock, Mendocino......W ×
● Henley, Siskiyou..........N 90
Henleyville, Tehama.........N 32
Henry's, (see Timber Cove)... ×
● *Herbert*, Fresno..........C ×
Hermitage, Mendocino.....W 260
Hermosa, (see Pasadena)..... ×
● Herndon, Fresno..........C ×
Herrick's Crossing, Tulare..C ×
● Hesperia San Bernar'o. SE ×
Hetten, Trinity..........NW ×
● Hickman, Stanislaus......C ×
Hicksville, Sacramento......C ×
Highbridge, (see Gualala).... ×
Highland, Alameda........W ×
● *Highland*, San Bernar'o.SE ×
● *Highland Jc.*, San Ber'do SE ×
● *Highland Park*, Los Ang.S ×
Highland Springs, Lake.... W 32
● *Hilarita*, Marin..........W ×
Hildreth, Fresno............C ×
● *Hillgirt*, Sonoma.........W ×
● *Hills*, Sonoma............W ×
● Hillsdale, Santa Clara....W ×
Hill's Ferry, (see Newman).. ×
Hill Side, Napa............W ×
● *Hinckley*, San Bernar'o. SE ×
Hispanolia, Kern..........S ×
Hites Cove, (see Jerseydale) .. ×
● *Hoffman Avenue*, M't-rey W ×
Hog's Back Mine, Placer... C ×
● *Holden*, San Joaquin..... C ×
● **Hollister**, San Benito..W 1,234
Hollywood, (see Prospect Park & Colegrove).......... ×
Holmes' Corner, (see Madison) ×
● *Holms*, Nevada.......... C ×
● *Homer*, San Bernardino.SE ×
Homestead, San Joaquin....C 637
● *Honby*, Los Angeles...... S ×
● *Honcut Station*, Butte.... C 437
● Honcut, Yuba............ C 140
Honolulu, Siskiyou.........N 50
● Hooker, Tehama.......... N ×
Hoopa Valley, Humboldt.NW 130
Hooperville, Siskiyou.......N ×
Hopeton, Merced............C 260
● *Hopevale*, Santa Barbara..S ×
● Hopland, Mendocino..... W 523
Hopper Canyon, (see Piru City) ×
Hornbrook, Siskiyou....... N ×
Hornitos, Mariposa..........C 276
Horr's Ranch, Stanislaus....C 10
Hotaling, Placer............C 32
Hot Sigler Sp'gs, (see Sig'r Sp'gs) ×
Hot Springs, (see Bridgeport) ×
Hot Springs, Placer.........C ×
Hough Springs, Lake.......W 39
● *Howard*, Sonoma......... W ×
Howards R'ch, (see Sierra City) ×
Howard Springs, Lake.....W ×
Howard's Sta., (see Occid't'l) ×
Howe Creek, (see Alton)...... ×
Howe, San Diego.......... SE 32
Howlands Flat, Sierra......E 100
Hausna, San Luis Obispo....S ×
Hueneme, Ventura...........S 250
Huero Huero, (see Creston).. ×
Hullville, Lake...............W ×
Humboldt Bay, Humboldt NW ×
Humbug, (see Yreka)........ ×
Humbug Flat, (see Ophir) ... ×
Humbug Valley, (see Longdale) ×
Hunters, Tehama...........N ×
Hurleton, Butte.............C ×
● Huron, Fresno.............C 100
Hyampom, Trinity.........NW ×
● Hyde Park, Los Angeles..S ×
Hydesville, Humboldt....NW 400
Hyland, (see Laurel Grove).. ×
Iaqua, Humboldt..........NW 81
● *Ibex*, San Bernardino... SE ×
Idlewild, San Bernardino..SE ×
● Igerna, Siskiyou..........N ×
● *Ignacio*, Marin............W ×
Igo, Shasta..................N 200
Imusdale, Monterey.........W 130
Independence, Calaveras....C ×
Independence, Inyo.....E 250
● *Independence Stat'n*, Inyo.E ×
Indian C'k, (see Hooperville) ×
Indiana Ranch, (see Dobbins) ×
Indian Diggins, El Dorado.. C ×

California

Indian Gulch, Mariposa.....C 50
Indian Hill, Sierra..........E 60
Indian Spring, Inyo..........E ×
Indian Sp'gs, (see Rough and Ready)...................... ×
Indian Valley Mine, Plumas N ×
● Indio, San Diego..........S ×
Inglenook, Mendocino..... W 195
● *Inglewood*, Los Angeles...S ×
Inglewood, Napa...........W ×
● Ingomar, Merced..........C ×
Ingram's, (see Cazadero)..... ×
Inskip, Butte................C 97
Inwood, Shasta............N ×
Inyo, Inyo...................E ×
● Ione, Amador.............C 806
Iowa City, Placer............C 500
Iowa Hill, (see Iowa City) ... ×
● *Irrigosa*, Fresno...........C ×
● *Irvine*, Orange............S ×
● Irvington, Alameda.......W 250
● *Irvington*, San Bern'ino.SE ×
Islnnd, (see Ferndale)........ ×
Isleton, Sacramento.........C 75
Ivanhoe, Los Angeles.......S 332
Ivanpah, San Bernardino..SE 230
Iversen, Mendocino........W ×
● *Ivy*, Los Angeles..........S ×
Jacinto, Glenn..............C 50
Jackson, Amador.........C 1,100
Jackson's Gate, Amador....C ×
Jackson's Valley, (see Cahto). ×
Jacksonville, (see Chinese Camp) ×
● *Jamesan*, Fresno.........C ×
Jamesburgh, Monterey.....W ×
Jamestown, Tuolumne......C 272
Jamul, San Diego..........SE 65
Janesville, Lassen.........N 130
● *Java*, San Bernardino...SE ×
Jeffreys, Los Angeles........S ×
Jenny Lind, Calaveras.......C 100
Jensens, Monterey.........W ×
Jerseydale, Mariposa........C ×
Jersey Landing, Con. Costa W 32
Jesus Maria, Calaveras..... C ×
John Adams, Butte.......... C 65
Johnsonville, (see Franklin). ×
Johnstonville, Lassen.......N 200
Johnsville, Plumas.......... N 300
Johntown, (see Garden Val'y) ×
Jolon, Monterey............W 196
Jordan, Mono...............E ×
Judsonville, Contra Costa..W 200
Julian, San Diego .... SE 150
Junction, (see Roseville) ..... ×
● *Junction*, Sonoma....... W ×
Junction City, Trinity.... NW 260
Junction Station, (see Alton). ×
Junction Sta., (see La Grange) ×
Juniper, Lassen .... N ×
● Kaweah, Tulare .... C ×
● Keeler, Inyo.............. E 50
● *Keenbrook*, San Ber'do..SE ×
● Keene, Kern.............. S ×
Kelley Creek, El Dorado.... C ×
Kellogg, Sonoma .... W ×
Kelsey, El Dorado .... C 65
Kelseyville, Lake .... W 282
Kelso, Fresno .... C ×
● *Kenilworth*, Sonoma.... W ×
● Kennett, Shasta.......... N ×
Kenny, Mendocino .... W ×
Kent, Sutter............... C ×
Kenyon, Fresno .... C ×
Kernville, Kern............ S 500
● *Keys*, Stanislaus.......... C ×
● *Kid Creek Mills*, Sonoma W ×
● *Kimberlena*, Kern......... S ×
● King City, Monterey..... W 253
● Kingsburgh, Fresno...... C 291
King's River, Fresno....... C 100
King's Station, (see Bodie)... ×
● Kirkwood, Tehama...... N ×
Klamath, Humboldt.......NW ×
Klamath Bl'fs, (see Martin's F'y) ×
Klamath Mill, Siskiyou....N ×
Klamath Riv., (see Cres. City) ×
Kneeland, Humboldt .... NW ×
Klinknerville, (see Oakland). ×
Knibkerb'r Ranch, (see Gr'wd) ×
Knight's Ferry, Stanislaus.. C 250
● *Knights Landing*, Yolo...C 287
Knight's Valley, Sonoma..W ×
Knoxville, Napa........... W 390
Korbel, Humboldt........ NW ×
Korbels, Sonoma .... W 42

California

● *Kramer*, San Bernardino SE ×
● *Kress Summit*, Nevada...C ×
Kreyenhagen'r, (see Los Banos) ×
● *Kurand*, Colusa.......... C ×
La Canada, Los Angeles..... S 325
● *La Costa*, San Diego.... SE ×
La Crescenta, Los Angeles.. S ×
Laddville, (see Livermore) ... ×
● *Ladrillo*, San Diego..... SE ×
La Fayette, Contra Costa... W 100
Lagona Beach, Orange...... S ×
La Gaviota, (see Las Cruces). ×
La Grange, Stanislaus ...... C 125
La Guenada, Santa Barbara S ×
Laguna, (see Cleone) .... ×
Luguna, (see Elsinore) ...... ×
Lagunita, (see Darwin) ...... ×
● *Lagunitas*, Marin........W ×
La Honda, San Mateo......W 260
● *La Jolla*, San Diego.....SE ×
Lake Bigler, Placer........ C ×
Lake Chorbot, Alameda....W ×
Lake City, Modoc .... N 100
Lake City, Nevada.......... C 10
● *Lake Majella*, Monterey. W 100
Lakeport, Lake .... W 991
Lakeside, San Diego....... SE 161
Lake Tahoe, (see Tahoe) ..... ×
Lake Valley, El Dorado .... C ×
● *Lake View*, Placer .... C ×
● *Lake View*, Santa Barbara S ×
● Lakeville, Sonoma....... W 65
● Lamanda Park, Los An's.. S 100
La Mesa, San Diego.........SE ×
● Lancaster, Los Angeles....S 75
Lancha Plana, Amador..... C 200
● *Lander*, Placer........... C ×
Lane's Mineral Sprgs, Calav's C ×
● Lang, Los Angeles........ S 83
Langtown, (see Capay) ...... ×
La Panza, San Luis Obispo..S ×
● *La Patera*, Santa Barbara S ×
La Porte, Plumas .... N 214
La Presa, San Diego....... SE ×
La Punta, San Diego.......SE ×
● Largo, Mendocino........W ×
Laribee, Humboldt ...... NW ×
● Larkspur, Marin .... W 32
Las Cruces, Santa Barbara..S ×
● *Las Flores*, San Diego...SE ×
Lassen Cr., (see Willow Ranch) ×
Last, Fresno.............. C ×
● Lathrop, San Joaquin .... C 577
● Latrobe, El Dorado....... C 165
Latson, Shasta............ N ×
Laurel, Santa Cruz........ W 40
● *Laurel Creek*, San Mateo W ×
● *Lavic*, San Bernardino...SE ×
La Vina, Fresno............ C ×
Lawrence, Santa Clara..... W ×
Laws, Inyo.................E ×
Laytonville, Mendocino.... W 65
Leavitt's Sta., (see Bridgeport) ×
Lebright Sta., (see Mariposa).. ×
Leesville, Colusa............ C 40
● *Le Frances*, Santa Clara. W ×
Leighton, Shasta........... N ×
Leland, Shasta............. N ×
● *Lemon*, Los Angeles...... S ×
● Lemoore, Tulare.......... C 651
Leon, San Diego.......... SE ×
● *Lerdo*, Kern............ S ×
Letcher, Fresno............ C ×
● *Leucadia*, San Diego.... SE ×
Lewis, Mariposa .... C ×
Lewiston, Trinity .... NW 200
Lexington, (see Alma)........ ×
Lick Observatory, S'ta Clara W ×
Lidell, Napa........... .... W ×
● *Liegan*, Lassen.......... N ×
Likely, Modoc............. N 40
● Lillis, Fresno............ C ×
● *Lillis Station*, Fresno.... C ×
Lima, (see Hildreth)......... ×
Lime Kiln, Tulare .... C 25
Limerick, (see San Ramon)... ×
● Lincoln, Placer........... C 961
● *Lincoln Park*, Los Angeles S ×
Lincolnville, (see F'ks of Sal'n) ×
Lindale, Modoc .... N ×
● *Linda Rosa*, San Diego..SE ×
● Linda Vista, San Diego..SE ×
Linden, San Joaquin........ C 130
● Lindsay, Tulare.......... C ×
Linne, San Luis Obispo ..... S ×
Linn's Valley, (see Glenville). ×

Place	
● *Linora*, Merced C	×
Little Kimshew, Butte C	×
Little Lake Val., (see Willits).	×
Little River, Mendocino W	243
Little Shasta, Siskiyou N	200
Little Stony, (see Stony Ford).	×
● *Littons*, Sonoma W	×
● Live Oak, Sutter C	200
● Livermore, Alameda W	1,391
● Livingston, Merced C	75
Llanada, San Benito W	×
Llano, Los Angeles S	×
Lobetus Sta., (see Span'h T'n)	×
● Lockeford, San Joaquin C	472
Lockwood, Monterey W	×
Lodge, Fresno C	×
● Lodi, San Joaquin C	1,018
● *Logandale*, Colusa C	×
Loganville, Sierra E	×
● *Loma*, Sutter C	×
● *Loma Alto*, San Diego SE	×
Loma Prieta, Santa Cruz W	×
Loma Sta., (see Butte M'd'ws)	×
Lompoc, Santa Barbara S	1,015
Lompoc L'nd'g, (see Lompoc).	×
● Lone Pine, Inyo E	225
Lonestar, Fresno C	×
Longanoole, Colusa C	×
● Long Beach, Los Angeles S	564
Long Valley, Lassen N	130
Long Valley, (see Cahto)	×
Longville, Plumas N	260
Lonoak, Monterey W	×
Lookout, Inyo E	59
Lookout, Modoc N	×
● Loomis, Placer C	20
Lopez Sta., (see San Fernando)	×
● Lordsburg, Los Angeles S	100
● *Lorenzo*, Alameda W	250
Lorenzo, (see Boulder Creek)	×
Lorin, Alameda W	743
● Los Alamos, Santa Barbara S	500
● **LOS ANGELES**, Los Angeles SE	50,395
● *Los Angeles Junc.*, San Diego SE	×
● Los Banos, Merced C	25
● Los Berros, San Luis Ob'po. S	×
Los Casitas, Los Angeles S	×
Los Gatos, Santa Clara W	1,652
● *Los Guilicos*, Sonoma W	120
● Los Nietos, Los Angeles S	×
● Los Olivos, Santa Barbara S	×
Los Posen, (see Springville)	×
Lotus, El Dorado C	195
Lovejop Sta., (see Pilot Hill)	×
Lovelock, Butte C	50
Lowden's Ranch, Trinity NW	32
Lowell Hill, Nevada C	91
Lower Fruitvale, Alameda W	×
Lower Lake, Lake W	500
● *Lower Soda Springs*, Sh'ta N	×
Lowery's, Tehama N	×
Low Gap, Mendocino W	32
Loyalton, Sierra E	300
● *Ludlow*, San Bernardino SE	×
Lugonia, (see Redlands)	×
Lumber Dump, Shasta N	×
Lumpkin, Butte C	×
Lundy, Mono E	300
● *Lurline*, Colusa C	×
Lusardi, San Diego SE	×
● *Lyman*, Colusa C	×
● *Lynwood*, Los Angeles S	×
Lyonsville, Tehama N	65
McAdams Creek, Siskiyou N	×
● *McAvoy*, Contra Costa W	×
● *McCloud*, Siskiyou N	×
● *McConnells*, Sacramento C	×
McDonald, Mendocino W	×
McGees, San Diego SE	×
● *McGills*, Sonoma W	×
McKinney, Placer C	×
McLeansville, (see Hoopton).	×
● *McMullin*, Fresno C	×
● McPherson, Orange S	60
● Mabel, Shasta N	13
Machado, (see Palms)	×
Mackville, (see Clements)	×
● *Macy*, Colusa C	×
Madeline, Lassen N	×
● Madera, Fresno C	950
● Madison, Yolo C	250
Mad River, (see Blue Lake)	×
● Madrone, Santa Clara W	32
● *Madrone*, Sonoma W	×
Magallia, Butte C	100
Magnetic Sprgs, (see Glenw'd)	×
● *Mail Dock*, Solano C	×
Maine Prairie, Solano C	25
● Malago, Fresno C	×
Malakoff, Nevada C	×
● *Malton*, Tehama N	×
Mammoth Grove, Calaveras C	×
● *Mammoth Tank*, S'nD'go SE	×
Manchester, Mendocino W	100
Mandala, (see Kneeland)	×
Mansfield, Monterey W	×
Manton, Tehama N	×
● *Manzanito*, Marin W	×
● *Maple*, Napa W	×
Maple Creek, Humboldt NW	×
● Marcuse, Sutter C	×
Mare Island, Solano C	×
Marengo, Los Angeles S	×
Mariposa, Mariposa C	366
Markham, Sonoma W	×
Markleeville, Alpine E	149
● Mark West, Sonoma W	235
● *Marlboro*, Orange S	×
● Marshall, Marin W	260
● **Martinez**, Contra Costa W	1,600
Martin's, Monterey W	×
Martin's Ferry, Humboldt NW	×
Martin's Ranch, (see Sh'p Rh.)	×
Martinsville, (see Burnt Rh.).	×
● **Marysville**, Yuba C	3,991
Matakoff, Nevada C	×
Matilija, Ventura S	×
Mattole Valley, (see Petrolia)	×
Maxwell, Colusa C	500
May, Amador C	97
Maybert, Nevada C	×
● Mayfield, Santa Clara W	1,200
● Mayhews, Sacramento W	×
Maynard's, (see Del Sur)	×
Mayten, Siskiyou N	×
Mazeppa, (see Ferndale)	×
● *Meachams' Carrigers*, Sonoma W	×
Meadow Valley, Plumas N	65
Meadow View, (see Greenville)	×
Meineck's, (see Taylor's F'y).	×
● Melitta, Sonoma W	×
● Melrose, Alameda W	130
Mendocino, Mendocino W	806
Mendon, (see Indian Digg's).	×
● *Mendota*, Fresno C	×
Menifee, San Diego SE	×
● Menlo Park, San Mateo W	400
● Mentone, San Bernar'o SE	×
● *Merazo*, Napa W	×
● **Merced**, Merced C	2,009
Merced Falls, Merced C	260
Meridian, Sutter C	150
Merle, San Diego SE	×
Merrillville, Lassen N	195
Merrimac, Butte C	82
● *Merritt*, Yolo C	×
Merton, San Diego SE	×
● Mesa Grande, San Diego SE	130
Mescal, (see Manton)	×
Mesilla Val., (see Pence's Rh.)	×
● *Mesmer*, Los Angeles S	×
● *Mesquite*, San Diego SE	×
Messina, San Bernardino SE	100
● Metz, Monterey W	×
Myer's L'dg, (see Southport)	×
Michigan Bar, Sacramento C	60
Michigan Bluff, Placer C	377
Middle Bar, Amador C	×
● *Middle Creek*, Shasta N	40
Middlefork, Shasta N	×
Middletown, Lake W	327
● **Midway, Alameda** W	12
● *Miles*, San Luis Obispo S	130
Milford, Lassen N	225
● Millbrae, San Mateo W	243
Mill Creek, (see Pine Grove).	×
Mill Creek, (see Lundy)	×
Miller, Mendocino W	65
● *Millers*, Marin W	×
Miller Station, Amador C	×
● *Millerton*, Marin W	×
● *Mills*, Colusa C	×
Mill Station, Sacramento C	×
● Mills College, Alameda W	×
● *Millsholm*, Lake C	×
Mill Valley, Marin W	×
Millville, Shasta N	300
● *Mill Wood*, Marin W	×
Milo, Tulare C	×
● Milpitas, Santa Clara W	400
Milquatay, (see Campo)	×
● Milton, Calaveras C	250
Minersville, Trinity NW	150
Minneapolis, Los Angeles S	×
● *Minneola*, Fresno C	×
● Minturn, Fresno C	5
● *Miraflores*, Orange S	×
Miramonte, Kern S	×
Mission Junction, Los Ang. S	×
Mission San Jose, Alameda W	700
Mitchells, Los Angeles S	×
Modena, (see El Modena)	×
● **Modesto**, Stanislaus C	2,402
● *Modjeska*, Orange S	×
Modock, Inyo E	×
Mohawk, Plumas N	40
● Mojave, Kern S	260
Mokelumne Hill, Calaveras C	573
Mokelumne Sta., (see Lodi)	×
Moneta, Los Angeles S	×
Mono Lake, Mono E	×
Mono Mills, Mono E	97
Mono Road, (see Sugar Pine).	×
● Monrovia, Los Angeles S	907
Monserrate, San Diego SE	×
● Monson, Tulare C	×
● Montague, Siskiyou N	250
● Montalvo, Ventura S	×
● *Monte*, Los Angeles S	×
● Monterey, Monterey W	1.662
Montevista, (see Alameda)	×
Montevista, (see Sunland)	×
Montezuma, Tuolumne C	66
Montgomery Creek, Shasta N	77
Monticello, Napa W	100
● Monticeto, Santa Barbara S	×
● *Montpellier*, Stanislaus S	×
Moody's Gulch, Santa Clara S	×
Moon's Ranch, Tehama N	×
Moony Flat, Nevada C	×
Moore's Flat, Nevada C	15
Moore's Station, Butte C	437
Mooretown, Butte C	×
Moosa, San Diego SE	45
● *Morena*, San Diego SE	×
Moreno, San Bernardino SE	×
● *Morgan*, Los Angeles S	×
● *Morley*, Shasta N	×
Mormon Bar, (see Mariposa).	×
Mormon Island, Sacramento C	50
● *Morocojo*, Monterey W	×
● *Morrano*, San Joaquin C	×
Morro, San Luis Obispo S	50
● *Mortmere*, San Diego SE	×
● *Moscow*, Sonoma W	×
Moss Landing, Moterey W	×
Mott, Siskiyou N	250
Moulton's Landing, Colusa C	×
● *Mound City*, San Bern'o SE	×
Mount'n House, (see Brush C'k)	×
Mount'n House, (see Venado)	×
Mountain House, Mariposa C	×
Mountain House, Sierra E	×
Mountain Meadows, Lassen N	×
Mountain Ranch, Calaveras C	×
Mountain Spr's, (see Enterpr)	×
● Mountain View, S. Clara W	1,000
● *Mount Avenue*, San Ber'o SE	×
Mount Bullion, Mariposa C	55
Mt. Diablo, (see Walnut Cr.)	×
● Mount Eden, Alameda W	350
Mount Hamilton, S. Clara W	×
Hount Hebron, Siskiyou N	×
Mount Hope, San Diego SE	×
Mount Olivet, Sonoma W	×
Mt. Pleasant Ranch, Sierra E	×
Mt. Shasta, (see Little Shasta)	×
Mud Springs, (see El Dorado)	×
Mud Springs, Los Angeles S	×
Mugginsville, (see Orofino)	×
Mulberry, San Benito W	×
Mulfords Landing, Al'm'da W	×
● *Mullen*, Yolo C	×
Murphy, Santa Clara W	585
Murphy's, Calaveras C	570
● Murrietta, San Diego SE	150
● *Muscatel*, Fresno C	×
Musick, San Luis Obispo S	×
Musquito Gulch, (see Glencoe)	×
Myrtle, Los Angeles S	×
Mystic, Nevada C	×
● *Nadeau Park*, Los Ang'l's E	×
● *Nahant*, San Bernar'do SE	×
Nantan, San Bernardino SE	×
● **Napa**, Napa W	4,395
● Napa Junction, Napa W	130
Napa Soda Springs, Napa W	32
Naples, Santa Barbara S	×

Narbo, (see Coarse Gold G'ch) ×
Nashville, El Dorado........C 65
Nasimento, (see Veratina) ... ×
Nassau Valley, (see Milton).. ×
Natchez, (see Bangor) ...... ×
National City, San Diego..SE 1,358
Natividad, Monterey....... W 100
Natoma, Sacramento........C 32
● *Naud Junction*, Los Ang. S ×
Navarro, Mendocino....... W 202
● Needles, San Bernard'o..SE 500
Neenach, Los Angeles.......S ×
Nellie, San Diego.........SE 33
● Nelson, Butte............C 150
Nelson Point, Plumas...... N 50
Nestor, San Diego......... SE ×
Neubert, Yuba............C ×
● **Nevada City**, Nevada.. C 2,524
● New Almaden, S'nta Cl'ra W 65
● Newark, Alameda....... W 200
Newberry Sta., (see Berkeley) ×
● *Newberry*, San B'rd'no..SE ×
Newbert, Yuba.............C 32
Newburg, (see Slide)....... ×
Newbury Park, Ventura....S 97
● Newcastle, Placer.........C 335
● *New England Mills*, Pl'cr C ×
● Newhall, Los Angeles..... S 80
New Haven, (see Miller)..... ×
New Hope, San Joaquin .... C 65
New Idria, San Benito..... W 300
New Jerusalem, Ventura... S 75
● Newman, Stanislaus...... C 621
Newport, Orange..........S 50
Newport, Solano............C ×
Newport Beach, Orange....S ×
Newport Harbor, Orange... S ×
Newport L'nd'g, (see Newport) ×
New Republic, (see Santa Rita) ×
New River, (see Coeur) ...... ×
Newtown, El Dorado....... C 130
***Newtown*, (see Buckeye).....** ×
New Town L'nd'g, (see Rio Vista) ×
New York Flat, Sierra....... E ×
New York L'nd'g, (see Bl.Diam.) ×
Newville, Glenn .... C 100
Niagara, Shasta........... N ×
Nicasio, Marin............ W 225
Nicolaus, Sutter .... C 100
● Niles, Alameda.......... W 400
Nimshew, Butte............ C 65
Nine Mile House, (see Nev.City) ×
● Nipomo, San Luis Obispo.. S 215
Nojoqui, Santa Barbara..... S 65
● Nord, Butte .... C 200
Nordhoff, Ventura.......... S 244
● Norman, Glenn.......... C 20
North Amer. Ranch, Calav's C ×
● *Northan*, Los Angeles.... S ×
North Bloomfield, Nevada...C 497
North Branch, Calaveras....C 57
North Columbia, Nevada... C 200
North Cow Cr., (see Oak Run) ×
● North Cucamonga, San Bernardino.................SE ×
● *Northern Junction*, Yolo..C ×
North Fork, Fresno..........N ×
● *North Fork*, Humboldt NW ×
North Fork, (see Junc. City).. ×
N. Grass Valley, (see Gr.Val.) ×
● North Ontario, San Bernardino .... SE ×
● North Pomona, Los A'g'ls.S ×
● *North Rochester*, San Bernardino............ SE ×
● North San Diego, S'nD'go SE 32
North San Juan, Nevada....C 303
● North Temescal, Alameda W 1,000
● *North Vallejo*, Solano.... C ×
Nortonville, Contra Costa.. W 130
● Norwalk, Los Angeles.... S 150
● Novato, Marin....... W 300
Novelty, Siskiyou........ N ×
Noyo, Mendocino......... W 100
Nuevo, San Diego..........SE 32
Oak Bar, Siskiyou.......... N 25
Oak Bottom, Shasta......... N ×
● Oakdale, Stanislaus........C 1,012
Oak Grove, San Diego..... SE 20
● *Oak Grove*, San Mateo....W ×
Oak Grove, (see Mayfield).... ×
● *Oak Grove*, Sonoma......W ×
● *Oak Knoll*, Napa........ W ×
● **Oakland**, Alameda..... W 48,682
● *Oakland Pier*, Marin..... W ×
Oakland Pt., (see W. Oakl'd). ×
Oak Run, Shasta............N 19

Oak Valley, (see Camptonv.). ×
● Oakville, Napa .... W 300
Oakwood, Fresno..........N ×
Oasis, Mono .... E ×
Oat Hill, Napa........... W ×
● Occidental, Sonoma...... W 130
Ocean Beach, San Diego .. SE ×
● Oceanside, San Diego ... SE 600
● Ocean View, San F'nci'co. W 97
● Ogilby, San Diego........SE ×
O Jai, Ventura..............S ×
Olancho, Inyo .... E 65
● *Old Felton*, Santa Cruz.. W ×
Old Gilroy, (see Ysidro) ...... ×
Old Mission, (see El Monte). ×
Old Town, San Diego..... SE 32
Oleander, Fresno .... N 32
Olema, Marin.............. W 200
Oleta, Amador .... C 300
Olinda, Shasta............ N ×
Olive, Orange.............. S ×
Olivenhain, San Diego..... SE ×
● *Olivewood*, Los Angeles... S ×
Omega, Nevada............ C 25
Omo Ranch, El Dorado...... C ×
O'Neals, Fresno .... N ×
Oneonta, San Diego........SE 100
Onion Valley, Plumas...... N ×
Ono, Shasta................N 30
● Ontario, San Bernardino.SE 683
Onyx, Kern................ S 40
Ophir, Placer.............C 400
● Orange, Orange.......... S 866
Orangevale, Sacramento.... C ×
Orcutt, San Diego......... SE ×
Oregon Hill, (see Greenville.. ×
Oregon House, Yuba........ C 20
Orick, Humboldt .... NW ×
Oriental, Glenn............. C ×
Orinda Park, Contra Costa W ×
● Orland, Glenn............ C 440
Orleans, Humboldt...... NW 75
Ornes, Inyo............... E ×
Oro Fino, Siskiyou..........N 142
● *Oro Grande*, San B'r'd'no SE ×
Orolewa, (see Clipper Ms.) ... ×
Orosi, Tulare .... C ×
● **Oroville**, Butte......... C 1,787
Orr's, Mendocino.......... W ×
● *Ortega*, Santa Barbara.... S ×
Osgood, San Diego .... SE ×
● Otay, San Diego......... SE 175
Otey's Ranch, Siskiyou .... N ×
Owl Spring, San Ber'dino..SE ×
● *Oxalis*, Fresno........... C ×
Ozena, Ventura............ S ×
● *Pachappa*, San Bernardino SE ×
Pachecho, Contra Costa.... W 232
● *Pacheco*, Marin......... W ×
Pacific, El Dorado .... C ×
Pacific Beach, San Diego.. SE 200
● Pacific Grove, Monterey. W 1,336
Pacific Mills, Santa Cruz.. W ×
● *Pacoima*, Los Angeles.... S ×
● *Page's*, Sonoma..........W ×
Paicines, San Benito....... W 20
Painted Rock, San Luis Ob'po S ×
Painters, Los Angeles...... S ×
Painter's Landing, Colusa..C ×
● *Pajaro*, Santa Cruz...... W 100
Pala, San Diego............SE 65
● Palermo, Butte .... C ×
Palmdale, Los Angeles...... S 60
Palmdale, San Diego...... SE ×
● Palms, Los Angeles........ S 40
Palm Spring, San Diego... SE ×
Palo Alto, Santa Clara..... W ×
Palvadero, (see Huron)...... ×
● *Pampa*, Kern .... S ×
Panamint, Inyo............ E ×
Panoche, San Benito....... W 520
● Paperville, Marin........ W 195
Paradise, Butte............ C 261
Paraiso Springs, Monterey. W 325
Park, El Dorado........... C ×
Parkfield, Monterey.........W ×
Parkison, Colusa.......... C ×
● *Park Street*, Alameda....W ×
Parsons, Tuolumne......... C ×
Partzwick, (see Benton) ..... ×
● Pasadena, Los Angeles....S 4,882
Paskenta, Tehama..........N 25
Paso Flat, Kern........... S ×
● Paso Robles, San L. Ob'po.S 827
Patchin, Santa Clara....... W 100
Patterson, Nevada.......... C 50

Patterson Sta., (see Routier) ×
Pattiway, Kern............S ×
Paulinville, (see Hansonville). ×
Pauma, (see Pala) .... ×
Paynes Creek, Tehama..... N ×
Peachland, Sonoma........W ×
Peach Tree, Monterey......W 130
Pearson's Spr., (see Sara.Spr.) ×
Pebble, Siskiyou............N ×
Pennington, Sutter..........C 25
● Penn's Grove, Sonoma...W ×
● Penryn, Placer............C 219
Pentz, Butte............... C 280
Pepperwood, Humboldt..NW ×
Peralta, Alameda.......... W 774
● Perkins, Sacramento..... C ×
● Perris, San Diego.........SE 100
● *Perrys*, Santa Clara...... W 15
Pescadero, San Mateo...... W 221
● Petaluma, Sonoma.......W 3,692
● Peters, San Joaquin.......C 65
Petrolia, Humboldt.......NW 260
Phillipsville, Humboldt...NW 77
Philo, Mendocino.......... W ×
Picard, Siskiyou...........N ×
Pico Heights, Los Angeles.. S ×
Piedmont, Alameda.........W 634
Piedmont Springs, Alameda W ×
Pieto, Mendocino...........W ×
Pike City, Sierra........... E 175
Pillarcitos, (see Millbrae).... ×
Pilot Hill, El Dorado........C 300
● *Pilot Knob*, San Diego.. SE ×
Pinckney, (see Cottonwood).. ×
Pine City, Mariposa.........C ×
Pine Grove, Amador........C 100
Pine Gr., (see Clipper Ms.).... ×
Pine Ridge, (see Toll House).. ×
Pino (see Loomis) .... ×
Pinerock, San Benito.......W ×
● Pinole, Contra Costa..... W 340
● *Pioneer*, Santa Clara.....W ×
Pioneer Cr., (see Pine Grove) ×
● Piru City, Ventura........S ×
Pittsburg L'nd'g, (see Princ'n) ×
Pittsville, Lassen.......... N ×
Pittville, Shasta............ N 20
● Pixley, Tulare........... C ×
● **Placerville**, El Dorado.C 1,690
Plainfield, Yolo............ C 75
Plainsberg, Merced......... C 400
Plano, Tulare..............C 100
Plateau, Shasta............ N ×
Pleasant Grove, Sutter......C 130
● Pleasanton, Alameda..... W 812
Pleasant Valley, El Dorado..C 390
Pleasant View, (see Sunolglen) ×
Pleyto, Monterey...........W 20
Plumas Eureka Mine, Pl'm'sN ×
Plymouth, Amador.........C 768
Point Arena, Mendocino....W 709
● *Point Isabel*, Contra Costa W ×
● *Point of Rocks*, San Bernardino............ SE ×
Point Reyes, Marin.........W ×
● Point Reyes Stat'n, Marin W 50
Point Timber, Contra Costa W 65
Poker Flat, Sierra..........E 90
Pokegama, Siskiyou........N ×
Poland, (see Lockeford)..... ×
Pollaskey, Fresno...........C ×
Polovdeora, (see Huron) ..... ×
Pomegranate, Amador......C ×
Pomo, Mendocino...........W 130
● Pomona, Los Angeles......S 3,634
Pools Landing, (see Isleton). ×
Pope Valley, Napa......... W 400
Poplar, Tulare............ C ×
● *Port Ballona*, Los Ang....S ×
● Port Costa, Contra Costa. W 627
Port Delgada, Humboldt.NW ×
● Portersville, Tulare.......C 606
● Port Harford, San L.Ob'poS 65
Port Kenyon, Humboldt. NW 70
Portugee, Shasta...........N 100
Port Wine, Sierra...........E 120
Posa Chine, (see Huron)..... ×
● *Poso*, Kern...............S 32
Poso Creek, (see Bakersfield) ×
Posts, Monterey............W ×
Potrero, San Diego.........SE 75
Potter, Modoc..............N ×
Potter Valley, Mendocino..W 700
Poverty Hill, (see Jamestown) ×
Poway, San Diego..........SE 400
Powellton, Butte...........C 78

Place	Pop.
Powerville, (see Blue Lake)..	×
Pozo, San Luis Obispo.......S	185
Prattville, Plumas..........N	195
Presidio, San Francisco....W	×
● Preston, Sonoma.........W	×
Priest Valley, Monterey....W	32
Princeton, Glenn............C	150
Princeton, Mariposa........C	×
● Proberta, Tehama.........N	×
Prospect Park, Los Angeles S	×
● *Prosser Creek*, Nevada....C	×
Providence, San Ber'dino..SE	65
Providence City, Lassen..... N	×
● Puente, Los Angeles.......S	150
Punta Gorda, Ventura...... S	×
Purdy's, Sierra...............E	×
Purissama, San Mateo......W	130
Q. Ranch, Amador.............C	×
Quartz Jc., (see Coarse Gold Gulch)......................	×
Quartz M't'n, (see Jamestown)	×
Quartzville, (see Nashville)...	×
● *Queen*, Mono.................E	×
Quincy, Plumas.......... N	546
Radec, San Diego............SE	×
Rail Road Flat, Calaveras.. C	100
Rainbow, San Diego.......SE	×
Railsville, (see Bates)........	×
● *Ramirez*, Yuba...........C	×
Ramona, Los Angeles.......S	100
Romona, San Diego ....SE	100
Rancheria Creek, Amador..C	×
● *Ranchita*, San Diego.... SE	65
Randolph, (see Etta)........	×
Rattlesnake, (see Alabaster).	×
Rat'snakeCr., (seeBigOak Flat	×
● Ravenna, Los Angeles.......S	50
Ravenswood, San Mateo... W	×
● *Rawson*, Trinity........ NW	×
● Raymond, Fresno...........C	×
● *Raymond*, Los Angeles... S	×
Reclamation, Sonoma.......W	×
● **Red Bluff**, Tehama.....N	2,608
Red Clover, Plumas......... N	×
● **Redding**, Shasta.........N	1,821
Redlands, San Bernardino.SE	1,904
● *Redlands*, San Ber'dino..SE	×
● Redondo Beach, Los Ang..S	603
Red Point, (see Iowa Hill)...	×
Red Rock, Lassen............ N	×
Red Valley, (see Bishop Cr.)..	×
● **Redwood City**, San Mateo...........................W	1,572
● Reedley, Fresno............C	200
● *Reeds*, San Luis Obispo....S	×
● *Reeds*, Yuba.................. C	×
Regna, Del Norte.......... NW	×
Reiff, Lake......................W	×
Relief Hill, Nevada.........C	×
Requa, Del Norte............NW	×
Reservation, (see Bakersfield)	×
● Rialto, San Bernardino..SE	200
● *Richfield*, Tehama......... N	×
Rich Gulch, Calaveras....... C	×
Richland, San Diego.......SE	×
Riley, Tehama................N	×
● Rincon, San Bernardino.SE	500
Rio Dell, Humboldt.........NW	213
Rio Vista, Solano............C	648
● Ripon, San Joaquin.......C	150
● Rivera, Los Angeles.......S	150
Riverdale, Fresno............C	130
Riverside, (see Blue Lake)....	×
● Riverside, San Ber'dino.SE	4,683
Riverview, San Diego.......SE	×
Roaring Riv., (see Janesville)	×
Roberts, Shasta..............N	×
Roberts' Fy., (seeHorr'sRanch)	×
Robert's Lnd'g, (seeSanL'rnzo)	×
Robinson's Ferry, Calaveras C	120
Rochester, SanBernardino.SE	×
Rock Cr. Can., (seeGeorget'n)..	×
Rockland, Del Norte..... NW	97
● Rocklin, Placer...........C	1,056
Rockport, Mendocino.......W	×
Rock Ranch, (see Cottage Gr.)	×
Rock Ranch, (see OrleansBar)	×
Rockville, Solano........... C	65
Rocky Point, Sierra.........E	65
● *Rogers*, Kern............... S	×
Rohnerville, Humboldt...NW	700
● Root, San Luis Obispo.....S	130
● Rosamond, Kern............S	97
Rose Canyon, (see San Diego)	×
Rosedale, Kern...............S	×
Rose Sprs, (see Green Valley)	×

Place	Pop.
● Roseville, Placer...........C	345
● Ross, Marin.................W	×
Rossmoyne, Los Angeles....S	×
Rotterdam Colony, Merced..C	×
Rough and Ready, Nevada..C	90
Rough & Ready, (see EtnaMs.)	×
Round Mountain, Shasta....N	×
Roundtop, Amador.......... C	×
Round Top House, Napa...W	×
Round Valley, Inyo.........E	40
Round Valley, (see Covelo)..	×
● Routier Station, Sacra'to..C	38
● *Rowen*, Kern............... S	×
Rowland, (see Bijou)........	×
● Rumsey, Yolo............. C	×
● *Rupert*, Yuba.............. C	×
Russell, Sacramento.........C	×
RussellStation, (see Mt. Eden)	×
● *Russian River*, Sonoma..W	130
● Rutherford, Napa........W	×
● *Ruthven*, San Diego.....SE	×
● **SACRAMENTO**, Sacramento...........................C	26,386
Sage, San Diego........... SE	×
● Saint Helena, Napa.......W	1,705
St. James, (see Orange)......	×
Saint John, Glenn...........C	150
Saint Louis, Sierra.......... E	50
St. Louis, Sonoma..........W	×
St. Louis Ranch, Merced....C	×
● Salida, Stanislaus..........C	40
● **Salinas**, Monterey......W	2,339
Salinas Cross, (see Soledad)..	×
Salmon Creek, (see Beatrice).	×
Salmon Cr., (seeWhitesboro)	×
Salmon Falls, El Dorado....C	77
● *Salsbury*, Sacramento.... C	×
● *Salton*, San Diego........SE	×
Salt Pt., (see Fisk's Mill)	×
San Andreas, Calaveras.. C	462
● *San Andreas*, Santa Cruz. W	5
● *San Anselmo*, Marin.....W	×
San Antonio, (see King's City)	×
San Antonio, San Berna'do.SE	×
San Antonio Camp, (see Esmaralda)...................	×
● San Ardo, Monterey..... W	20
San Benito, San Benito.....W	293
San Barnabe, (see Kingleity).	×
● **San Bernardino**, San Bernardino................ SE	4,012
● San Bruno, San Mateo....W	65
● *San Buena Ventura*, Ve't'aS	2,320
● *San Clemente*, Marin.... W	×
● *Sand Cut*, Kern..........S	×
● *Sand Cut*, Monterey.....W	×
Sanders, Fresno.............C	×
● **SAN DIEGO**, S'n D'goSE	16,159
● San Dimas, Los Angeles.. S	×
Sand Mound, Contra CostaW	×
Sanel, (see Hopland)........	×
San Felipe, Santa Clara.....W	65
● San Fernando, Los Ang'ls.S	600
● **SAN FRANCISCO**, San Francisco................ W	297,997
● San Gabriel, Los Angeles..S	737
● Sanger, Fresno............C	428
● *San Geronimo*, Marin....W	65
San Gorgonio, (see Beaumont)	×
San Gregorio, San Mateo... W	50
San Ignatio, (see Jacinto)...	×
San Jacinto, San Bern'do..SE	×
● San Jacinto, San Diego..SE	661
San Joaquin Cy., (seeVernalis)	×
● **San Jose**, Santa Clara.. W	18,060
San Jose Valley, (see Pozo)..	×
● *San Juan*, Orange........ S	600
San Juan, San Benito.......W	463
San Juan Capistrano, (see Capistrano)..................	×
● San Leandro, Alameda...W	1,800
● San Lorenzo, Alameda...W	300
San Lorenzo, (see BoulderCr.)	×
● San Lucas, Monterey .... W	125
● **San Luis Obispo**, San Luis Obispo............... S	2,995
San Luis Rey, San Diego...SE	50
● San Marcos, San Diego... SE	30
SanMargarita, (see SanRafael)	×
● *San Martine*, Santa Clara.W	×
● San Mateo, San Mateo.... W	1,000
San Miguel, (see Ocean View)	×
● San Miguel, San Luis O'po.S	158
● *San Onofre*, San Diego.. SE	×
● San Pablo, Contra Costa..W	367
San Pasqual, San Diego....SE	×
● San Pedro, Los Angeles...S	1,240

Place	Pop.
● San Quentin, Marin.......W	390
● **San Rafael**, Marin......W	3,290
San Ramon, Contra Costa.. W	100
San Salvador, (San Ber'dino)	×
Sansevain, S. Bernardino..SE	×
San Simeon, S. Luis Obispo..S	40
● **Santa Ana**, Orange.....S	3,628
● Santa Anita, Los Angeles..S	×
● **Santa Barbara**, S.BbraSE	5,864
● Santa Clara, Santa Clara..W	2,891
● **Santa Cruz**, Santa CruzW	5,596
● *Santa Cruz Beach*, S.CruzW	×
Santa Clara Val., (see New Jerusalem)............	×
● Santa Fe Springs, L.A'gles.S	65
S'nta Margarita, (seeSanRaf'l)	×
● Santa Margarita, S.L'sO'po.S	×
● Santa Maria, S. Barbara. SE	1,000
● Santa Monica, Los AngelesS	1,580
● Santa Paula, Ventura..... S	1,047
Santa Rita, Monterey.......W	50
● **Santa Rosa**, Sonoma...W	5,220
Santa Ynez, Santa BarbaraSE	211
Santa Ysabel, San Diego...SE	×
Santee, San Diego......... SE	×
San Timoteo Canon, San Bernardino.................SE	×
San Ysidro, Santa Clara.....W	20
Saratoga Sprs. (see Bachelor)	×
Saratoga, Santa Clara...... W	600
● Sargent, Santa Clara..... W	130
● Saticoy, Ventura ....S	218
● *Satonis*, Shasta............S	×
Sattley, Sierra.................E	32
● *Saugus*, Los Angeles......S	×
● **Sausalito**, Marin...........W	1,334
● *Sauterne*, Yolo.............C	×
● Savannah, Los Angeles....S	130
Sawpit Flat, Plumas....... N	×
Sawyer's Bar, Siskiyou..... N	125
Scales, Sierra.................E	260
● *Schellville*, Sonoma.......W	×
School House Sta., (seeColoma)	×
Scotia, Humboldt.........NW	454
Scott River, Siskiyou...... N	300
Scott's Bar, Siskiyou ....N	300
Scottsville, (see Blue Lake)...	×
Scott Valley, (see Ft. Jones).	×
Scribner, Humboldt........NW	×
● *Seacliff*, Ventura.........S	×
● *Sear's Point*, Sonoma.....W	×
Searsville, San Mateo.......W	65
Seaside, Monterey..........W	×
Sea View, Sonoma..........W	130
● Sebastopol, Sonoma.......W	300
Seiad Valley, Siskiyou.......N	32
● Selby, Contra Costa...... W	×
Selby's Sw., (see Nelson's),....	×
● Selma, Fresno............C	1,150
● *Selwyn*, San Diego.......SE	×
● *Seminary Park*. AlamedaW	×
Sentinel, Fresno............ C	×
● *Sepulvedo*, Los Angeles...S	×
Sequoia, Tuolumne..........C	×
● Serena, Santa Barbara.....S	×
● *Sesma*, Trinity......... NW	×
● *Sespe*, Ventura...........S	×
Seven MileHouse, (see Merced)	×
● *Seven Palms*, San Diego.SE	×
● *Shady Run*, Placer....... C	×
Shandon, San Luis Obispo...S	×
Sharon Val., Yuba...........C	×
Shasta, Shasta.............N	500
Shaw's Flat, Tuolumne.....C	×
Sheep Ranch, Calaveras.....C	358
● *Shelbleys*, Nevada....... C	×
Sheldon, (see Elk Grove)......	×
● *Shell Mound*, Contra CostaW	×
Shellville, Sonoma..........W	×
● Sheridan, Placer.......... C	150
Sherwood, Mendocino.....W	130
● Shingle Springs, El DoradoC	195
Shingletown, Shasta........ N	40
● *Shorb*, Los Angeles....... S	×
Shumway, Lassen...........N	×
● *Siberia*, San Bernardino. SE	×
Siempreviva, San Diego... SE	×
Sierra Buttes Mine, (seeSierraCy.)	×
Sierra City, Sierra..........E	632
Sierra Madre, Los Angeles...S	400
Sierra Madra Villa, L.A'g'lsS	×
Sierra Nevada House, SierraE	×
Sierra Pt., (see Millbrae)....	×
Sierra Valley, Sierra........ E	200
Sierraville, (see Sierra Val.)..	×
Signal Port, Mendocino....N	×
● *Silsby*, Butte.............C	×

Place	Pop.
Silver Creek, Alpine.........E	32
Silver Lake, Amador........C	×
Silverville, Solano...........C	×
Simi, Ventura..................S	×
Simmler, San Luis Obispo...S	×
● *Sims*, Shasta...............N	×
Singley's Fy., (see Table Bluff)	×
Sis Quoc, Santa Barbara.....S	97
● Sisson, Siskiyou...........N	556
● Sites, Colusa................C	×
Skaggs Springs, Sonoma... W	×
Slack Canyon, Monterey....W	97
Slate Creek Sta., (see Delta)..	×
Sleighville House, (see Camptonville)	×
● *Slawson*, Los Angeles.....S	×
Slide, (see Fortuna)	×
Slippery Ford, El Dorado....C	132
Slough House, (see Consumne)	×
Smartville, Yuba...........C	350
Smith River, Del Norte...NW	250
Smith's Flat, El Dorado.....C	65
● Smithson, Shasta......... N	65
Smith's Ranch, Sonoma....W	175
Smithville, (see Little Stony).	×
Snelling, Merced............C	250
Snow Cr., (see Darrah).......	×
● *Snowdon*, Siskiyou.......N	×
Snyders, Los Angeles....... S	×
● *Sobrante*, Contra Costa...W	×
● *Sobra Vista*, Sonoma....W	×
Soda Rock, Sonoma........W	×
Soda Springs, (see Donner)..	×
● *Soda Springs*, Nevada.... C	36
Soda Springs, San Diego..SE	×
Solana, Humboldt...... NW	20
● Soldier's Home, L's Angeles S	×
● Soledad, Monterey...... W	217
Somersville, Contra Costa.. W	371
Somes Bar, Siskiyou........N	20
● Sonoma, Sonoma...........W	757
Sonoma L'n'd, (see St. Louis	×
● *Sonoma Mills*, Sonoma.. W	×
Sonora, Tuolumne.........C	1,441
● Soquel, Santa Cruz.......W	250
● Sorrento, San Diego.....SE	×
● *Soto*, Tehama.............N	×
Sotoville, (see Santa Rita)	×
Soulsbyville, Tuolumne..... C	300
South Bay, Humboldt....NW	×
S. Cucamonga, (see Cucamonga)	×
Southern Sta., (see Hazel Cr.)	×
South Fork, Modoc........ N	×
South Fork, Siskiyou.......N	×
S. Los Angeles, Los Angeles.S	×
South Los Guilicos, Sonoma W	261
S. Oeanside, (see Oceanside).	×
● South Pasadena, L. Ang'ls.S	623
● South Riverside, S. Bn'do SE	280
South San Diego, San Diego SE	50
● *South Side*, Los Angelos.. S	50
● *South Vallejo*, Solano.....C	500
● Spadra, Los Angeles.........S	25
Spanish Ranch, Plumas.....N	10
Spanish Dry Diggings, El Dorado ....E	×
Spanishtown, (see Half Moon Bay)..........................	×
● *Spences*, Monterey.......W	×
Spenceville, Nevada..........C	100
● Spottiswood, Kern........ S	32
Spring, San Bernardino...SE	×
Spring Garden Ranch, (see Oroville)	×
Spring Valley, (see Arbuckle)	×
Springville, (see Fortuna)....	×
Springville, Ventura.......... S	200
Spruce Gr., (see Blockbsburgh)	×
Squaw Creek, Shasta....... N	×
Squaw Rock, Mendocino...W	×
Squaw Valley, Fresno.........C	97
Stanfield Ranch, (see Oregon House)	×
Stanon's, Lake.............W	×
Starkey, (see Shandon)........	×
Starville, Fresno............C	×
Staten Island, Sacramento. C	×
State Prison, Sacramento... C	×
● *Steele's*, San Luis Obispo..S	×
Steele Swamp, Modoc...... N	×
● Stege, Contra Costa...... W	×
Stella, Shasta.............. N	46
Stewart's Point, Sonoma...W	×
Stewartville, Contra Costa..W	32
Stillwater, Shasta...........N	65
● **Stockton**, San Joaquin..C	14,424
● *Stockton Wharf*, San Joa. C	×

California

Place	Pop.
● ***Stock Yards*, Alameda...W**	×
Stony Ford, Colusa..........C	35
Stony Point, Sonoma.........W	61
Stowe, San Diego............SE	×
Strawberry Val., (see Glenw'd)	×
Strawb'ry Val., (see Berryvale)	×
Strawberry Valley, Yuba....C	65
● *Strong's Canyon*, Placer..C	×
Stuart, Santa Barbara...... S	×
● *Studebaker*, Los Angeles..S	×
Sturgeon, Merced...........C	×
Sugar Pine, Tuolumne..... C	×
● Suisun City, Solano........ C	499
Sullivan Creek, (see Sonora).	×
Sulphur Bank, Lake...... W	×
Sulphur Creek, Colusa......C	40
Sumac, San Diego.........SE	×
Summerhome, Santa Barbara S	×
Summerhome, Tulare.......C	×
Summerland, Santa Barbara S	×
Summerville, (see Carters)...	×
● *Summit*, Placer...........C	26
Summit, Plumas............N	25
Summit, Butte..............C	×
● *Summit*, San Bernardino SE	×
● *Summit*, San Luis Obispo.S	×
Sum't House, (see Bell's Sta.)	×
Sumner, Kern...............S	622
Sunbeam, El Dorado........C	×
Sunbeam, Placer............C	×
Sundale, Butte..............C	×
Sunland, Los Angeles........S	×
Sunny Side, San Diego.... SE	×
Sunny South, Placer.........C	×
● Sunolglen, Alameda......W	250
Sunset, (see Shandon)........	×
Sur, Monterey...............W	×
Surprise Val., (see Lake City)	×
Surrey, Los Angeles..........S	×
● *Surrey*, Yolo..............C	×
Susanville, Lassen........ N	882
Suscal, Napa...............W	×
● Sutter City, Yuba......... C	250
Sutter Creek, Amador...... C	1,351
Sutton H'se, (see Butte Mead's)	×
● *Swansea*, Inyo..............E	×
Swasey, Shasta.............N	×
Swauger, Humboldt......NW	×
Sweetland, Nevada........... C	175
Sweetwater, (see Dehesa).....	×
Sweetwater Dam, San Diego SE	×
Sweetwater Junc., San D'go SE	×
● *Swingle*, Yolo C	×
Sycamore, Colusa C	20[illegible]
Sycamore Grove, Los Angeles S	×
Sycamore Grove Park, Los Angeles........................ S	×
Table Bluff, Humboldt... NW	80
Table Rock, Sierra.......... N	651
Tache, Fresno..............C	50
● *Tagus*, Tulare.............C	×
Tahoe, Placer............... C	50
Taison, San Jaquin......... C	520
● *Talbot*, Fresno........... C	×
Tallac, El Dorado........... C	65
Talmage, Mendocino ...... W	×
● *Tamalpais*, Marin ...... W	×
● *Tamarack*, Nevada C	×
● *Tancred*, Yolo............C	130
Tates, Inyo................ E	400
● *Tawrusa*, Tulare...........C	×
Taylor Mine, El Dorado....C	×
Taylorsville, Plumas........ N	160
● *Taylorville*, Marin.......W	×
● *Teal*, Solano..............C	×
● *Tehachapi*, Kern.........S	255
Tehachapi Sum., (see Gr'nwich)	×
● Tehama, Tehama..........N	350
● *Tejunga*, Los Angeles......S	×
Telegraph City, Calaveras...C	150
● Temecula Sta., San Diego SE	35
Temescal, Alameda........ W	2,032
Temescal, San Bernardino.SE	150
● Templeton, San Luis Obispo S	308
Templeville, Sonoma.......W	×
● *Tennant*, Santa Clara....W	32
Tennant's, Santa Clara.....W	×
Terrabella, Tulare..........C	×
Terre Cotta, San Diego.... SE	×
● *Thenard*, Los Angeles.... S	×
● *The Needles*, San B'd'no. SE	325
● *The Palms*, Los Angeles..S	×
Thermal, Fresno.............C	×
● *Thermal*, San Diego.....SE	×
Thome's Creek, (see Paskenta)	×
● Thompson, Los Angeles...S	57

California

Place	Pop.
● *Thompson*, Napa........ W	×
Thorn, Humboldt........ NW	×
Three Mile H'se, Los Ang'l's S	×
Three Mile H'se, (see Turlock)	×
Three Rivers, Tulare........C	130
Tia Juana, San Diego...... SE	150
Tia Juana Heights, S'nD'go SE	×
Tia Juana Jc., San Diego.SE	×
● *Tibbetts*, Inyo............E	×
Tibbets, (see Oneonta).........	×
● Tiburon, Marin............W	×
Tiecate, (see Potrero).........	×
Timberville, Ventura........S	×
● Tipton, Tulare............ C	125
● *Tocalmo*, Marin...........W	195
Tocalmo, Marin..............W	×
Todd, Placer................ C	20
● *Tokay*, Tulare.............C	×
Tokoloma, Marin.......... W	×
Toland's Landing, Solano ..C	×
Toll House, Fresno...........C	75
Toll House, (see Calistoga)...	
Toll Road, (see Fresno)......	×
● Tomales, Marin.......... W	225
Topaz, Mono................E	20
Torney, Contra Costa.......W	×
● *Tortuga*, San Diego..... SE	×
Tower House, Shasta........ N	×
● Towle, Placer..............C	317
● *Town Talk Summit*, Nev. C	×
● Tracy, San Joaquin....... C	100
Traftons, Monterey........W	×
● Traver, Tulare............ C	438
● *Trego*, San Joaquin.......C	32
Trego, (see Harold)......... N	×
● Tremont, Solano...........C	32
Tremont Valley House, (see Jenny Lind).................	×
Trenton, Sonoma.......... W	×
● Tres Binos, San Benito... W	260
Trimmer, Fresno........... C	×
Trinidad, Humboldt......NW	140
Trinity, Trinity...........NW	×
Trinity Centre, Trinity... NW	260
● Tropico, Los Angeles.......S	×
● Truckee, Nevada..........C	1,350
Tuhunga, Los Angeles........S	65
● Tulare, Tulare............ C	2,697
● *Tunnel*, Los Angeles......S	×
● *Tunnel Thirteen*, Placer..C	×
Tuolumne, Tuolumne.........C	×
● Turlock, Stanislaus.........C	203
Tuscan Sprs. (see Red Bluff).	×
● Tustin City, Orange....... S	600
Tuttletown, Tuolumne......C	×
Twenty-six Mile House, Sta's C	65
Twenty-Eight Mile House, Stanislaus....................C	×
Twin Oaks, San Diego..... SE	×
Two Rocks, Sonoma.......W	×
● *Tyrone Mills*, Sonoma...W	45
● **Ukiah**, Mendocino......W	1,627
***Ulmer*, San Bernardino....SE**	×
Uncle Sam, (see Kelseyville)..	×
Undine, San Joaquin........C	36
Union, Merced...............C	130
Union City, (see Alvarado) W	×
● *Union Hill*, Nevada.......C	×
Union House, Sacramento..C	57
Uniontown, (see Lotus)......	×
● University, Los Angeles..S	×
Upper Fruitvale, Alameda. W	×
Upper Lake, Lake............W	296
Upper Mattole, Humboldt NW	30
● *Upper Soda Springs*, S'you N	×
Usal, Mendocino............ W	×
Voca Station, (see Elmira)...	×
● Vacaville, Solano......... C	725
● Vallejo, Solano............C	6,343
Vallejo Cross, (see Vallejo)..	×
● *Vallejo Jc.*, Contra Costa. W	×
Vallejo Mills, (see Niles).....	×
Valleton, Monterey ....W	×
Vallevista, San Diego......SE	×
Valley Center, San Diego..SE	100
● Valley Ford, Sonoma.....W	150
● Valley Springs, Calaveras.C	125
Vallicita, Calaveras..........C	200
Valona, Contra Costa......W	374
● *Vanden*, Solano.......... C	×
● *Vaucluse*, Yuba........... C	×
● *Vega*, Monterey.......... W	×
Venado, Colusa..............C	55
● **Ventura**, Ventura.......S	2,320
● *Verana*, Sonoma ....W	×
Veratina, Monterey......... W	×
● *Verde*, San Luis Opispo... S	×

Town, County, Index	Pop.
Verdugo, Los Angeles.......S	19
● Vernalis, San Joaquin.... C	×
Vernon, Stanislaus...........C	×
● Vernondale, Los Angeles. S	×
● *Vervain*, Los Angeles.....S	×
● Victor, San Bernardino. SE	×
● *Victoria*, San BernardinoSE	×
Viejas, San Diego..........SE	23
Villa Park, Orange..........S	×
● *Villa Verona*, Butte......C	×
● Vina, Tehama............ N	232
● *Vincent*, Los Angeles..... S	×
Vineland, Los Angeles......S	×
Vinelvnd Sta., Napa.......W	×
Vineyard, San Diego.......SE	45
● *Vineyard*, Sonoma...... W	×
● *Vinvale*, Los Angeles.....S	×
● *Violet*, Solano............C	×
Virginia, San Diego........SE	×
Virginia Bar, (see Honolulu)	×
● **Visalia**, Tulare..........C	2,885
● Vista, San Diego.........SE	35
Volcano, Amador........... C	358
● *Volcanó Springs*, S'n D'oSE	×
● Volta, Merced............ C	×
Voss Mills, (see Nevada City)	×
Waddell, Santa Cruz........W	×
Waddington, Humboldt..NW	×
● *Wade*, Kern.............. S	×
Wade, Modoc...............N	×
Wages Creek, (see Westport).	×
Wahoo. (see Port Wine)......	×
Wakefield, San Joaquin.....C	×
● *Waldo Point*, Marin..... W	×
Walker, Siskiyou...........N	×
Walker's Basin, Kern...... S	×
● Wallace, Calaveras....... W	200
Walnut Creek, Contra Costa.W	400
Walnut Grove, Sacramento. C	212
Walsh Station, Sacramento..C	50
● *Walters*, San Diego..... SE	×
● *Walthall*, San Joaquin....C	×
● *Wanda*, Orange.......... S	×
● *Warfield*, Sonoma....... W	×
● Warm Springs, Alameda.W	×
Warner, San Diego......... SE	×
● *Warren*, Kern............S	×
Warren Cr., Humboldt.. NW	×
Warthan, Fresno............C	40
Wash, Plumas.............. N	×
Washington, Yolo.......... C	400
Washington, Nevada......... C	225
Washington Colony, Fresno.C	929
Washington Cor., (see Irving)	×
● *Washington Street*, L's A's.S	×
Washoe House, (see Petaluma)	×
● Waterford, Stanislaus.....C	50
Waterloo, San Joaquin......C	×
● *Waterman*, San Berna'o.SE	32
● *Watriss*, Sonoma........ W	×
Watrous Gulch, (see Ono)....	×
● *Watsons*, Sonoma........W	×
Watsonville, Santa Cruz....W	2,149
● Waugh, Shasta..............N	40
Waukena, Tulare.............C	×
● *Waverly*, San Joaquin.... C	×
Wawona, Mariposa..........C	×
Weaverville, Trinity..NW	768
● *Webster*, Yolo........... C	×
Weed's Pt., (see Camptonv'le)	×
Weimar, Placer.............C	×
Weitchpec, Humboldt....NW	20
Weldon, Kern ....S	75
● West Berkeley, Alameda. W	500
West Branch, Butte.........C	×
West Butte, Sutter..........C	15
● *West End*, Alameda.....W	×
● *West End*, Marin........W	×
W. FallBrook, (see FallBrook)	×
● *West Glendale*, Los Ang'lesS	×
West Hopland, (see Sanel)...	×
● Westley, Stanislaus....... C	×
Westminster, Orange......... S	300
● West Oakland, Alameda. W	×
West Point, Calaveras.......C	266
Westport, Mendocino...... W	200
Westville, Placer............C	×
Wheatfield, Fresno..........C	×
Wheatland, Yuba........... C	630
Whippoorwill Mine, Inyo...E	×
Whiskey Dig'in's, (seeNew'rk)	×
Whiskey Hill, (see Freedom)	×
Whiskey Slide, Calaveras...C	×
Whiskeytown, (see Stella)...	×
Whitehall Sta., Mendocino.W	×
White River, Tulare.........C	50
● *White Rock*, Sacramento. C	×
White Rock, (see Eureka)....	×
White Rock, (see Coeur)......	×
Whitesboro, Mendocino.... W	100
White's Bridge, Fresno..... C	15
● *White's Hill*, Marin......W	×
White Sulphur Sprs, Napa..W	×
White Sulphur Spr'gs, So'a.W	×
● *White Water*, San Diego.SE	×
Whitmore, Shasta.......... N	×
● *Whitney's*, Placer........ C	×
● Whittier, Los Angeles.....S	585
Wick's Landing, Alameda. W	×
● *Wigmore*, Santa Barbara. S	×
● *Wildeson*, Los Angeles....S	×
Wild Flower, Fresno.........C	25
● Wildomar, San Diego....SE	150
● *Wildwood*, Sonoma......W	×
Wildwood, Trinity........NW	×
Wiley's Sta., (see Pine Gr.)..	×
● Williams, Colusa..........C	461
Williamsb'rg, (see Tehachapi)	×
Willits, Mendocino......... W	815
● **Willow**, Glenn...........C	1,176
Willow Cr., (see Merrillville)	×
Willow Cr., (see Ager).......	×
Willow Cr., (see Duncan's Ms.)	×
Willow Ranch, Modoc....... N	65
Willow Spring, San B'rd'o.SE	×
● Wilmington, Los Angeles. S	687
Wilmore, (see Long Beach)..	×
Wilson, Humboldt....... NW	×
● *Wilson*, Sutter............C	×
Wilson Wall, Inyo..........E	×
● Winchester, San Diego.. SE	×
● Windsor, Sonoma.......W	225
Wingate Bar, Del Norte.NW	×
● *Winsted*, Nevada..........C	×
● Winters, Yolo.............C	700
● *Winthrop*, Los Angeles....S	×
Wire Bridge, (seeDaylor'sR'nch)	×
● *Wiseburn*, Los Angeles... S	×
Wolf, Nevada...............C	×
● *Wolfskill*, Solano..........C	×
Wonder Mine, Inyo........ E	×
● Woodbridge, San Joaquin.C	288
Wooden Valley, Napa .....W	×
Woodford's Alpine...........E	65
● **Woodland**, Yolo....... C	3,069
Wood's Cross, (see Jamesto'n)	×
Woodside, San Mateo.......W	300
Wood's Sw., (see Acampo)....	×
Woodville, (see Bolinas)......	×
Woodville, Tulare...........S	50
Woody, Kern.................S	×
Workman's Mill, (seeElMonte)	×
Wrights, Santa Clara.......W	30
Wrights Fy., Sonoma.......W	×
Wright's Sta., (see Sisson)...	×
Wyandotte, Butte...........C	65
Wynema, (see Hueneme).....	×
Wynola, San Diego......... SE	×
Yager, Humboldt......... NW	32
Yankee Hill, Butte..........C	75
Yankee Hill, Tuolumne C	×
Yankee Jim's, Placer.......C	100
● *Yarmouth*, San Joaquin..C	×
Ydapom, Shasta ....N	×
Yocumville, Siskiyou........N	75
Yokohl, Tulare..............C	×
● Yolo, Yolo.................C	225
● Yorba, Orange.............S	×
Yorkville, Mendocino......W	97
Yo Semite, Mariposa........C	260
You Bet, Nevada............C	100
● Yountville, Napa.........W	231
● **Yreka**, Siskiyou.........N	1,100
● *Ysdora*, San Diego......SE	×
● **Yuba City**, Sutter......C	562
Yuba Dam, (see Marysville)..	×
Yuba Mine, (see Maybert)...	×
● *Yuba Pass*, Placer.......C	×
● *Yuleka*, Siskiyou.........N	×
● *Yulupa*, Sonoma........ W	×
Zaca, Santa Barbara........S	×
Zayante Cr., (see Felton)....	×
Zebra, Fresno...............C	×
Zem Zem, Napa........... W	132
Zinn, Shasta..............N	×
Zucker, San Bernardino...SE	×

COLORADO.

COUNTIES.	INDEX.	POP.
Arapahoe	C	132,135
Archuleta	SW	826
Baca	E	1,479
Bent	SE	1,313
Boulder	N	14,082
Chaffee	C	6,612
Cheyenne	E	534
Clear Creek	C	7,184
Conejos	S	7,193
Costilla	S	3,491
Custer	S	2,970
Delta	W	2,534
Dolores	SW	1,49[illegible]
Douglas	C	3,006
Eagle	C	3,725
Elbert	E	1,856
El Paso	C	21,239
Fremont	C	9,156
Garfield	NW	4,478
Gilpin	C	5,867
Grand	N	604
Gunnison	W	4,359
Hinsdale	SW	862
Huerfano	S	6,882
Jefferson	C	8,450
Kiowa	E	1,243
Kit Karson	E	2,472
Lake	C	14,663
La Plata	SW	5,509
Larimer	N	9,712
Las Animas	SE	17,208
Lincoln	E	689
Logan	NE	3,070
Mesa	W	4,260
Montezuma	SW	1,529
Montrose	W	3,980
Morgan	NE	1,601
Otero	E	4,192
Ouray	SW	6,510
Park	C	3,548
Phillips	E	2,642
Pitkin	W	8,929
Prowers	E	1,969
Pueblo	S	31,491
Rio Blanco	W	1,200
Rio Grande	S	3,451
Routt	NW	2,369
Saguache	S	3,313
San Juan	SW	1,572
San Miguel	SW	2,909
Sedgwick	NE	1,293
Summit	NW	1,906
Washington	E	2,301
Weld	NE	11,736
Yuma	E	2,596
Total		412,198

TOWN. COUNTY. INDEX.	POP.
Abbey, Pueblo.............. S	×
Abbott, Arapahoe........... C	10
● *Aberdeen*, Gunnison..... W	×
● *Aberdeen Junction*, G'n'nW	×
● Acequia, Douglas......... C	10
● *Adair*, Las Animas......SE	×
Adams, Larimer............ N	35
● *Adana*, Prowers..........E	×
● *Adobe*, Fremont.......... C	×
● Agate, Elbert............. E	10
Aguilar, Las Animas.......SE	200
● **Akron**, Washington.....E	559
● Alamosa, Conejos.........S	973
Albany, Prowers...........E	50
Alder, Saguache.............S	10
Alfalfa, Weld.............NE	×
Alford, Larimer.............N	32
● *Alicante*, Lake...........C	×
Allen, Gunnison........... W	19
● *Allenton*, Eagle C	×
● Alma, Park C	367
● Almont, Gunnison....... W	77
Alnwick, El Paso........... C	×
● Alpine, Chaffee...........C	75
● *Alpine Tunnel*, Chaffee .. C	13
Altona, Boulder .... N	50
Alvord, Larimer ....N	10
● *Americus*, Chaffee....... C	×
● Ames, San Miguel....... SW	15
● Amherst, Phillips.........E	25
Angora, Otero.............. E	×
Animas, La Plata...........SW	180
Animas Forks, San Juan.. SW	100

Place	Pop.
Antelope Park, Hinsdale. SW	25
Antelope Springs, Hins... SW	10
● Anthracite, Gunnison....W	×
Antlers, Garfield.........NW	26
● Antonito, Conejos........S	315
● *Apache*, Huerfano........S	10
● Apishapa, Las Animas...SE	100
● *Arapaho*, Cheyenne......E	×
Arboles, Archuleta.......SW	50
● Archer's, Jefferson.......C	10
● *Arena*, Chaffee..........C	×
● *Arena*, Cheyenne........E	×
● *Argentine*, Summit....NW	13
● Argo, Arapahoe..........C	300
● *Argo Junction*, Arapahoe..C	×
● *Argo Park*, Arapahoe....C	×
Arickaree, Arapahoe.......C	10
● Arkansas Junction, Lake..C	×
● Arkins, Larimer...........N	50
● Arlington, Kiowa.........E	100
Armour, Pueblo...........S	×
● Aroya, Cheyenne.........E	×
● Arriba, Lincoln..........E	50
● *Arthurs*, Park...........C	×
● Arvada, Jefferson.........C	120
● *Ascalon*, Cheyenne.......E	×
Ashcroft, Pitkin...........W	41
Ashland, Kit Carson........E	×
● **Aspen**, Pitkin..........W	5,108
● Aspen Junction, Eagle....C	200
● *Athol*, Weld............NE	×
Atlanta, Baca..............E	×
● *Atlantic*, Gunnison......W	×
● Atwood, Logan...........NE	25
Augusta, Custer...........S	×
Aurora, Arapahoe..........C	×
Austin, Garfield..........NW	×
Avendale, Kit Carson.......E	×
Avoca, Arapahoe...........C	×
● *Avon*, Eagle..............C	×
Axial, Routt..............NW	65
Ayr, Prowers..............E	×
Badger, Arapahoe..........C	10
Badito, Huerfano...........S	15
● *Bagdad*, Lincoln..........E	×
● Bailey, Park..............C	20
● *Baker's Summit*, Summit NW	×
● Bald Mountain, Gilpin....C	933
● Baldwin, Gunnison.......W	100
● *Baldy*, Costilla..........S	×
Balzac, Garfield..........NW	×
● Barela, Las Animas.....SE	25
Barlow, (see Glenwood Spr's)	×
● *Barnes*, Las Animas.....SE	×
● Barr, Arapahoe...........C	25
● *Bartholomews*, Summit NW	×
● *Bath*, Park..............C	×
● *Battista*, Montezuma...SW	×
● *Baxter*, Pueblo..........S	×
Bear Canon, Douglas.......C	25
● *Bear Creek*, Montezuma SW	×
Beaumont, El Paso.........C	×
● Beaver Brook, Jefferson..C	×
● Beaver Creek, Fremont..C	10
Bedrock, Montrose........W	×
● *Belden*, Eagle...........C	×
● *Belleview*, Chaffee.......C	×
● *Bellevue*, El Paso........C	×
● *Bellevue Junction*, L'r'm'r N	25
Bellvue, Larimer...........N	25
Beloit, Kit Carson..........E	150
● Bennet, Arapahoe........C	50
Bent Canyon, Las Animas..SE	25
● *Benton*, Otero...........E	10
Berkeley, Arapahoe........C	×
Berlin, Arapahoe...........C	×
● Berthoud, Larimer.......N	228
Berwind, Las Animas......SE	10
● *Beshoar*, Las Animas....SE	×
● *Bessemer Junction*, Pueblo S	3,317
● Bethune, Kit Carson......E	25
Beulah, Pueblo.............S	50
Biedell, Saguache..........S	10
● *Bierstadt*, El Paso.......C	×
● *Big Hill*, Jefferson.......C	×
Big Sandy, El Paso.........C	30
● Bijou Basin, El Paso......C	75
● *Birdseye*, Lake...........C	×
Birmingham, Huerfano.....S	×
● *Blackburn*, Custer........S	40
● Black Hawk, Gilpin......C	1,067
Black Lake, Ouray.......SW	×
Bland, Elbert...............E	83
● *Blanca*, Costilla..........S	150
● *Boaz*, Las Animas.......SE	×
● *Bocea*, LaPlata..........SW	×
Bonanza, Saguache..........S	96

Colorado

Place	Pop.
● *Bonita*, Gunnison........W	195
Book Cliff, Mesa...........W	×
● Boone, Pueblo............S	15
● *Boreas*, Park............C	×
● *Borst*, El Paso...........C	×
Boston, Baca...............E	10
● **Boulder**, Boulder......N	3,330
● *Boulder Junction*, Bo'lder N	×
● Bovina, Lincoln..........E	10
Bowen, Rio Grande.........S	65
Bowman, Chaffee...........C	25
Box Elder, Larimer........N	×
● *Boyds*, Weld............NE	×
● *Bo-ye-ro*, Lincoln.........E	10
● *Braddock*, Summit....NW	×
Bradford, Huerfano........S	×
● Brandon, Kiowa..........E	10
● **Breckenridge**, S'm't NW	800
● *Bridgeport*, Mesa........W	×
● *Bridge Three*, Fremont..C	×
● Brighton, Arapahoe......C	306
● *Bristol*, Larimer..........N	10
● Brookfield, Baca.........E	×
Brookvale, Clear Creek.....C	×
Brookside, Fremont.........C	150
● Broomfield, Boulder......N	10
● Brown, Montrose........W	100
● *Brown*, San Miguel....SW	×
● Brown's Canon, Chaffee..C	×
● Brush, Morgan..........NE	112
Bryant, Phillips............E	10
● *Buckingham*, Weld....NE	×
● **Buena Vista**, Chaffee...C	1,500
● Buffalo Creek, Jefferson..C	200
Buffalo Springs, Park.......C	50
● *Buffalo Tank*, Jefferson..C	×
Buford, Rio Blanco........W	×
Burdett, Washington.......E	10
● **Burlington**, Kit Carson E	146
● *Burnham*, Arapahoe......C	×
● *Burnito*, Fremont........C	×
● *Burns Junction*, Boulder N	×
Burro Bridge, San Juan..SW	×
● Busk, Lake...............C	×
Butler, Larimer............N	×
Butte City, Las Animas....SE	×
● *Butte's*, El Paso..........C	×
Butte Valley, Huerfano....S	×
● *Buxton*, Saguache........S	×
● Byers, Arapahoe..........C	50
● *Cabeza*, Mesa...........W	×
● *Cable Junction*, El Paso..C	×
● Caddoa, Bent............SE	50
● Calhan, El Paso..........C	50
● *Calumet*, Chaffee.........C	80
● *Cameo*, Mesa............W	×
● *Cameron*, Elbert.........E	×
Cameville, Montrose........W	25
Canadian, Larimer.........N	25
● Canfield, Boulder........N	150
● **Canon City**, Fremont..C	2,825
● *Canon Mine*, Boulder....N	×
Capitol City, Hinsdale....SW	50
Capulin, Conejos...........S	250
● Carbondale, Garfield...NW	166
● Cardiff, Garfield........NW	300
Caribou, Boulder...........N	100
Carlisle, Kit Carson........E	25
● *Carlisle*, Pueblo..........S	50
● Carlton, Prowers.........E	30
Carnero, Saguache..........S	250
Carpenter, Mesa...........W	×
● Carr, Weld..............NE	×
● *Carracas*, Archuleta...SW	×
Carriso, Baca...............E	×
Carson, Hinsdale.........SW	×
● *Carter's*, Pueblo..........S	×
● *Cascade*, Chaffee.........C	×
● Cascade, El Paso.........C	50
Cassells, Park..............C	10
● **Castle Rock**, Douglas..C	315
● *Castles*, Eagle............C	×
● Castleton, Gunnison......W	10
Catherin, Conejos..........S	×
● Catlin, Otero.............E	40
● *Cattle Creek*, Garfield..NW	×
● *Cebolla*, Gunnison.......W	×
● *Cedar Creek*, Montrose...W	×
● *Cedar Point*, Elbert......E	×
Cedar Valley, (see Amherst).	×
● **Central City**, Gilpin....C	2,480
● Centreville, Chaffee.......C	32
● *Cerro Summit*, Montrose.W	×
● *Chacra*, Garfield.......NW	×
● Chandler, Fremont.......C	100
Chapin, Kit Carson..........E	×
● *Chapman*, Boulder.......N	×

Colorado

Place	Pop.
Chapman, (see Newcastle)...	×
● *Chappell*, Las Animas....SE	×
● *Charcoal*, Chaffee........C	32
Chattanooga, San Juan....SW	200
● *Chemung*, Cheyenne......E	×
Chenoa, Logan............NE	×
● *Chester*, Saguache........S	×
● Cheyenne Wells, Ch'n'e...E	150
● *Chico*, Pueblo............S	×
● *Chicosa Junction*, Las Animas...SE	×
Chihuahua, Summit......NW	100
Chilcott, Pueblo............S	×
● *Chimney Gulch*, Jefferson.C	×
● *Chipeta*, Delta...........W	×
● Chivington, Kiowa........E	98
Chromo, Archuleta.......SW	×
● *Church's*, Jefferson......C.	×
● Cimarron, Montrose......W	100
● *Circle Crossing*, Arapahoe C	×
● Claremont, Kit Carson....E	50
Clark, Routt.............NW	×
Clay Spur, Jefferson........C	×
Claytonia, Saguache.........S	40
● *Clelland*, Fremont.........C	×
Clemmons, Elbert...........E	78
Cliff, Jefferson.............C	×
● *Cliff*, Jefferson...........C	300
● *Cliff Junction*, Fremont...C	×
● *Cliffs Spur*, Larimer......N	×
● *Cleora*, Chaffee...........C	250
● *Clifton*, Mesa............W	×
● Climax, Lake.............C	×
● *Coal Branch Junc.*, Park.C	×
● Coal Creek, Fremont.....C	1,150
Coaldale, Fremont..........C	100
● *Coal Mine*, Garfield....NW	×
Coal Park, Boulder.........N	×
● Coalridge, Garfield.....NW	×
● *Coal Tank*, Jefferson.....C	×
● *Coals Spur*, Park.........C	×
Cockrell, Conejos...........S	32
● *Cody*, Washington........E	×
● *Coke Oven*, Las Animas..SE	×
Collbran, Mesa............W	×
Colma, Ouray.............SW	×
● *Colona*, Montrose........W	×
● *Colorado Central Cut Off*, Arapahoe...C	×
● Colorado City, El Paso....C	1,788
● **Colorado Springs**, El Paso.....C	11,140
Colorow, Grand.............N	65
● *Colorow*, Montrose.......W	×
● Como, Park..............C	374
● *Concentrator*, Pitkin.....W	×
● *Conchito Junction*, Hu'f'no S	14
Condon, Arapahoe..........C	10
Conejos, Conejos..........S	500
Cooper, Eagle..............C	10
Cope, Arapahoe.............C	10
Corcoran, Arapahoe........C	×
● *Corkscrew*, Montezuma.SW	×
Corkscrew Gulch, Ouray..SW	×
Cornwall, (see Jasper)......	×
● Corona, Weld...........NE	10
● *Coronado*, Arapahoe......C	×
Cortez, Montezuma.....SW	332
Cortrite, Park..............C	×
Coryell, (see Stanley).......	×
Coryell, Garfield.........NW	×
Cosden, Gunnison..........W	10
● Cotopaxi, Fremont........C	200
Cotton Creek, Saguache.....S	35
● *Cottonwood*, Gilpin.......C	×
Cottonwood Springs, ChaffeeC	40
Coulter, Grand.............N	×
Craig, Routt..............NW	100
● *Crane Park*, Lake.......C	×
Crawford, Delta............W	×
● *Creech*, Lincoln..........E	×
● Creede, Saguache.......SW	800
Crescent, Grand............N	×
● Crested Butte, Gunnison.W	857
Crestone, Saguache.........S	125
Creswell, Jefferson..........C	150
● *Crevasse*, Mesa..........W	×
● Crisman, Boulder.........N	25
● Crook, Logan............NE	10
Crooks, Gunnison..........W	×
● *Crookton*, Gunnison......W	×
● *Crosson*, Jefferson........C	60
Crow, Pueblo...............S	×
Crystal, Gunnison..........W	50
● *Crystal Creek*, Montrose.W	×
Crystal Lake, Jefferson.....C	10
● *Crystal Lake*, Lake........C	26

● Cucharas, Huerfano....... S 20
Cuenin, Saguache........... S ×
● *Culver Siding*, El Paso.... C ×
● Cumbres, Conejos........ S ×
Currant Creek, Fremont.... C 10
● *Currecanti*, Gunnison.... W ×
● *Curtin*, Summit......... NW ×
Curtis, Washington......... E ×
● Dake, Park................ C 25
● Dallas, Ouray........... SW 541
● *Dallas Divide*, San Mig'l, SW ×
● *Davenport*, Saguache...... S ×
● Dawkins, Pueblo.......... S 40
● *Dawson's*, Jefferson...... C ×
Deansbury, Douglas......... C ×
● *Deansbury*, Jefferson..... C ×
De Beque, Mesa........... W 25
Decatur, Baca.............. E ×
● *Deep Creek*, San Miguel. SW ×
● *Deer Run*, Mesa.......... W ×
● Deer Trail, Arapahoe...... C 150
● *Delhi*, Las Animas....... SE ×
● **Del Norte**, **Rio Grande**.. **S** 736
● **Delta**, Delta............ W 470
● **DENVER**, Arapahoe... C 106,713
Denver Mills, Arapahoe..... C ×
● *Derby*, Arapahoe.......... C ×
● *Deuel*, Las Animas....... SE ×
● Deuel, Morgan.......... NE 150
● *Dick*, Weld.............. NE ×
● Dickey, Summit......... NW ×
● Dillon, Summit......... NW 133
● *Diston*, Kiowa............ E ×
● *Divide*, Chaffee........... C 165
● Divide, El Paso.......... C 10
Dix, LaPlata.............. SW ×
● *Dixon*, Weld............ NE ×
● *Dixon's Mill*, Boulder..... N ×
● Dolores, Montezuma.... SW 50
● *Dome Rock*, Jefferson..... C 20
● *Dominguez*, Delta........ W ×
● Dotsero, Eagle........... C 25
● *Douglas*, Douglas......... C 133
● *Dover*, Weld............ NE ×
Downing, Las Animas..... SE ×
● Doyleville, Gunnison..... W 25
● *Duff*, Arapahoe........... C 65
● Dumont, Clear Creek...... C 50
● *Duncan*, Delta........... W ×
● *Dundee*, Pueblo.......... S ×
● *Dune*, Saguache.......... S ×
● **Durango**, La Plata... SW 2,726
● *Dwyer*, Summit......... NW ×
● *Dyer*, El Paso........... C ×
● Eads, Kiowa.............. E 50
Eagalite, Mesa............ W ×
● Eagle, Eagle.............. C 10
● *Earl*, Las Animas....... SE ×
East Idaho Sprs, Clear C'k. C 323
● Eastonville, El Paso....... C 100
● Eaton, Weld............ NE 50
Ebert, Arapahoe........... C ×
● *Echo*, Fremont........... C ×
● Eckley, Yuma............. E 15
Eddy, Routt.............. NW ×
● *Eden*, Pueblo............ S ×
● Edgerton, El Paso........ C ×
Edwards, Eagle............ C 65
Egeria, Routt............ NW 100
● *Eilers*, Lake............. C ×
● Elbert, Elbert............. E 150
● *Eldredge*, Montrose...... W ×
● Elizabeth, Elbert......... E 200
● *Elk Creek*, Jefferson..... C ×
● *Elko*, Saguache.......... S ×
● *Elk Park*, San Juan.... SW ×
Elkton, Gunnison......... W ×
● El Moro, Las Animas.... SE 355
El Paso, El Paso........... C 20
● *Elsmere*, El Paso......... C ×
Emerson, Phillips.......... E ×
● Emma, Pitkin............ W 10
● Empire, Clear Creek..... C 134
● Engle, Las Animas...... SE 701
● *Engleville Junc.*, Las An. SE ×
● *English Gulch*, Lake...... C ×
● Erie, Weld.............. NE 662
● *Escalante*, Delta......... W ×
Escalante, Routt......... NW ×
● Estabrook, Park......... C 25
Estes Park, Larimar........ N 50
Eureka, San Juan......... SW 49
● Evans, Weld............. NE 306
Evergreen, Jefferson....... C 200
● *Fair Grounds*, Las An... SE ×
● **Fair Play**, Park........ C 301
Fairview, Custer........... S 32

● *Fairview*, Montrose...... W ×
● *Fairy Glen*, Fremont..... C ×
● Falcon, El Paso.......... C 25
● *Fall Creek*, San Miguel. SW ×
● *Fall River*, Clear Creek... C ×
● *Farmers*, Weld......... NE ×
● Farnham, Summit..... NW 50
● *Fergus*, Kiowa............ E ×
Ferguson, Garfield....... NW ×
● *First View*, Cheyenne.... E ×
● *Fisher*, Chaffee.......... C ×
● Flagler, Kit Carson....... E 25
● Fleming, Logan......... NE 25
Flora, Sedgwick.......... NE ×
● Florence, Fremont........ C 750
● *Florida*, La Plata....... SW ×
● Florissant, El Paso....... C 439
● *Floyd Hill*, Clear Creek... C ×
Forbes, Las Animas........ SE 350
● *Forbes Mine*, Las An'as. SE ×
● *Forbes Junc.*, Las An... SE ×
● Forks Creek, Jefferson.... C 10
● **Fort Collins**, Larimer. N 2,011
● *Fort Crawford*, Montrose W 50
● Fort Garland, Costilla..... S 100
● Fort Logan, Arapahoe.... C ×
● Fort Lupton, Weld...... NE 113
● **Fort Morgan**, M'gan. NE 488
● Fountain, El Paso........ C 100
Fowler, Otera............. E 20
Fox, Arapahoe............. C ×
● Franceville, El Paso....... S 100
● *Franceville Junc.*, El P'o.. S ×
Franktown, Douglas........ C 30
Fraser, Grand............. N 32
Freeland, Clear Creek....... C 500
● *Freeland*, Clear Creek.... C ×
● *Fremont Pass*, Lake...... C ×
● *French Gulch*, Lake...... C ×
Friend, Arapahoe........... C 75
● Frisco, Summit........ NW 25
● Fruita, Mesa............ W 100
Frying Pan, Eagle.......... C 10
● Galatea, Kiowa........... E 20
● *Galien*, Logan.......... NE ×
● *Garden of the Gods*, El P'o C ×
Gardner, Huerfano.......... S 100
● *Garfield*, Chaffee......... C 50
● *Garland*, Costilla.......... S 100
Garnett, Costilla............ S 150
● Garo, Park............... C 20
● Garrison, Costilla......... S 100
● *Gate View*, Gunnison.... W ×
● *Gaylor's Spur*, Jefferson.. C ×
Geneva Gulch, Park......... C 25
● **Georgetown**, Clear C'k. C 1,927
Gillespie, Jefferson......... C ×
Gilman, Eagle.............. C 442
● *Gilman*, Jefferson......... C ×
● *Gilson Gulch*, Clear Creek C ×
● *Glaciers*, Gunnison....... W ×
● *Glade*, Douglas........... C ×
Gladstone, San Juan...... SW ×
● *Glencoe*, Jefferson....... C ×
Glendale, Fremont.......... C 32
● *Glenwood*, Garfield..... NW ×
● **Glenwood Springs**, Garfield.................... NW 920
Globeville, Arapahoe........ C ×
● *Godfrey*, Elbert........... E ×
Goff, Kit Carson........... E ×
● **Golden**, Jefferson....... C 2,383
● Gold Hill, Boulder........ N 150
● *Gomers Mills*, Elbert..... E ×
● *Goodnight*, Pueblo........ S ×
● *Goodrich*, Morgan....... NE ×
● *Gorge*, Fremont.......... C ×
Gothic, Gunnison........... W 75
● *Govetown*, Custer......... S ×
● *Grabiola*, Gunnison...... W ×
● Granada, Prowers........ E 163
Grand Butte, (see N. Castle).. ×
● **Grand Junction**, Mesa W 2,030
Grand Lake, Grand......... N 75
● **Graneros, Pueblo**........ S 25
● Granite, Chaffee.......... C 150
● *Granite Spur*, Jefferson... C ×
● Grant, Park.............. C 56
● *Graymount*, Clear Creek. C ×
● *Grays*, Saguache.......... S ×
● **Greeley**, Weld......... NE 2,395
Greenhorn, Pueblo......... S 15
● Greenland, Douglas....... C 25
● Green Mountain Falls, El Paso........................ C 50
Greenwood, Custer.......... S 500-
● Grover, Weld........... NE 25

● *Gulf Junction*, Pueblo.... S ×
Gulnare, Las Animas...... SE ×
● **Gunnison**, Gunnison.. W 1,105
● *Gunnison Smelter*, Gun'n W ×
Guston, Ouray............ SW ×
● *Guy Gulch*, Jefferson..... C ×
Gwillimville, El Paso....... C ×
● Gypsum, Eagle............ C 25
● *Hagen*, Ouray.......... SW ×
● *Hagerman*, Pitkin....... W ×
Hahn's Peak, Routt...... NW 30
Hale, Arapahoe............ C ×
● *Half Way*, Park.......... C ×
Half Way House, El Paso.. C ×
● *Hall's*, Clear Creek...... C ×
Hall Valley, Park.......... C 50
Hamilton, Park............ C 20
● *Hancock*, Chaffee........ C 10
● *Hanging Bridge*, Fremont C ×
● Hardin, Weld........... NE 13
Harlow, Mesa............ W ×
Harman, Arapahoe......... C 743
● *Harman*, Washington.... E ×
● *Harps*, Chaffee........... C ×
Harris, Arapahoe........... C ×
● *Harris*, Jefferson......... C ×
Harrisburg, Arapahoe...... C 10
● Hartsel, Park............ C 82
Haskell, Kiowa............ E ×
Haskill, San Miguel....... SW ×
● Hastings, Las Animas.... SE 200
● *Hatchery*, Arapahoe...... C ×
● *Haswell*, Kiowa.......... E ×
● *Hathaways*, Summit... NW 25
● *Haver*, Park............. C ×
Haworth, Larimer.......... N ×
Hawxhurst, Mesa.......... W 10
● Haxtum, Phillips........ E 25
Hayden, Routt........... NW 97
● *Hayden*, Lake............ C ×
● *Hayes*, Costilla.......... S ×
● *Hay Ranch*, Park........ C ×
● *Haywood Springs*, Chaffee C 15
Hebron, Larimer........... N 42
● *Hecla Junction*, Chaffee.. C ×
● *Henderson*, Arapahoe..... C ×
● Henry, Conejos........... S 50
● *Hereford*, Weld......... NE ×
● Hermosa, La Plata...... SW 132
● *Herrick*, Pueblo.......... S ×
● *Hierro*, Gunnison....... W ×
Hesperus, La Plata....... SW 500
Higbee, Otero............. E 65
● Higgins, Chaffee......... C ×
● *Highland*, Boulder...... N ×
Highlandlake, Weld...... NE ×
Highlands, Arapahoe....... C 5,161
Highmore, Garfield...... NW ×
Higho, Larimer........... N ×
● *Hilldon*, Saguache........ S ×
Hillsboro, Weld........... NE 65
Hillside, Fremont......... C 25
● *Hillside Spur*, Ouray... SW 10
● Hill Top, Douglas......... C ×
● *Hilton*, Bent............ SE ×
● *Hinkles*, Gunnison....... W ×
● Hoehne, Las Animas.... SE 25
● Holly, Prowers.......... E 100
Holtwold, Elbert.......... E ×
Holy Cross, Eagle......... C 65
● **Holyoke**, Phillips...... E 649
Home, Larimer............ N 65
● *Home Ranch*, La Plata. SW ×
Honnold, Routt......... NW ×
● *Hoosier*, Park........... C ×
● *Hopkins*, Eagle.......... C ×
Horseshoe, Park.......... C 100
Hortense, Chaffee......... C ×
Hotchkiss, Delta.......... W 50
● *Hotchkiss*, Weld....... NE ×
● *Hot Springs*, Saguache... S ×
Hot Sulphur Springs, G'd N 50
● Howard, Fremont........ C 50
Howardsville, San Juan... SW 100
● Howbert, Park.......... C 50
Hoyt, Elbert............. E ×
● Hudson, Weld........... NE 10
● *Huerfano*, Huerfano...... S 10
● **Hugo**, Lincoln.......... E 200
● *Hulbert*, El Paso......... C ×
● Husted, El Paso.......... C 25
Hutchinson, Jefferson...... C 10
● Hyde, Washington....... E 25
Hydraulic, Montrose....... W ×
Hygiene, Boulder......... N 20
● *Hygiene*, Boulder........ N ×
Idaho Creek, Boulder...... N ×

Place	Pop.
● Idaho Springs, Clear Cr...C	1,338
Idalia, Arapahoe...C	50
● *Idlewild*, Park...C	×
● Ignacio, La Plata...SW	35
● Iliff, Logan...NE	25
● Illium, San Miguel...SW	10
Ilse, Custer...S	50
Independence, Arapahoe...C	×
Independence, (see Sparkill)..	×
Indianapolis, Arapahoe...C	×
● *Inman*, Kiowa...E	×
Interlaken, Lake...C	×
Inthe, Arapahoe...C	×
● Irondale, Arapahoe...C	×
● *Iron Springs*, Otero...E	×
● Ironton, Ouray...SW	400
Irwin, Gunnison...W	250
● Island Station, Arapahoe. C	63
● Ivanhoe, Pitkin...W	×
Ivywild, El Paso...C	×
● *Jack's Cabin*, Gunnison..W	×
Jackson, Gunnison...W	40
Jamestown, Boulder...N	212
Janeway, Pitkin...W	×
Jaroso, Las Animas...SE	×
Jasper, Rio Grande...S	10
● Jefferson, Park...C	100
● *Jerome Park*, Pitkin...W	×
● *Jersey*, Arapahoe...C	×
Johnstown, Arapahoe...C	×
● *Juanita*, Archuleta...SW	×
● **Julesburg**, Sedgwick. NE	202
Juniata, Pueblo...S	63
● *Kahnah*, Mesa...W	×
Kanorado, Cheyenne...E	×
● *Keeldar*, Lake...C	×
● *Keene*, Weld...NE	×
● *Kelker*, El Paso...C	×
● *Kenmuir*, El Paso...C	×
● Kenosha, Park...C	×
● *Kenwood*, Arapahoe...C	×
● *Keota*, Weld...NE	×
Kester, Park...C	50
Keystone, San Miguel...SW	×
● *Keystone*, Summit...NW	×
● Kezar, Gunnison...W	32
● *Kilburn*, Kiowa...E	×
● King, Park...C	×
Kiowa, Elbert...E	81
Kirk, Arapahoe...C	×
● Kit Carson, Cheyenne...E	50
● *Kohinoor*, Clear Creek...C	×
● Kokomo, Summit...NW	100
Kraft, Chaffee...C	×
Kremmling, Grand...N	10
Kuhn's Crossing, Elbert...E	65
● *La Boca*, La Plata...SW	×
Ladore, Routt...NW	×
● *Lady Murphy*, Chaffee...C	×
● Lafayette, Boulder...N	410
● LaGarita, Saguache...S	300
● Laird, Yuma...E	10
● La Jara, Conejos...S	150
● **La Junta**, Otero...E	1,439
● *Lake*, Lincoln...E	×
● **Lake City**, Hinsdale..SW	1,607
Lake George, Park...C	×
● *Lake Hughes*, Ouray...SW	×
● *Lake Junction*, Gunnison W	×
● **Lamar**, Prowers...E	566
Lamartine, Clear Creek...C	200
Lamb, Jefferson...C	×
Landsman, Kit Carson...E	×
● Langford, Boulder...N	233
Lansing, Arapahoe...C	35
● *La Plata Junc.*, La PlataSW	×
● La Porte, Larimer...N	50
● *Larimer*, Pueblo...S	×
● Larkspur, Douglas...C	100
● La Salle, Weld...NE	20
● **Las Animas**, Bent...SE	611
La Sauses, Conejos...S	×
Lavender, Dolores...SW	×
● La Veta, Huerfano...S	361
● Lawson, Clear Creek...C	250
Lay, Routt...NW	30
● **Leadville**, Lake...C	11,212
● *Leadville Junction*, Lake..C	×
● *Lebanon*, Clear Creek...C	×
● *Lee Siding*, Jefferson...C	×
● *Lehigh Coal Mine*, DouglasC	×
Lenado, Pitkin...W	×
● *Leon*, Garfield...NW	×
Leopard, San Miguel...SW	×
● *Leopard Creek*, San.Mig. SW	×
Le Roy, Logan...NE	10
● *Leschers*, Larimer...N	×

Place	Pop.
Leslie, Washington...E	10
● *Levisy*, Pueblo...S	×
Liberty, Rio Grande...S	×
● *Lidderdale*, Jefferson...C	×
Lily, Routt...NW	100
● *Lime Creek*, Pitkin...W	×
● Limon Station, Lincoln...E	50
Lincoln City, Summit...NW	100
Lindon, Arapahoe...C	50
● *Little Buttes*, El Paso...C	×
● *Little Mountain*, Sum't NW	×
● Littleton, Arapahoe...C	200
Livermore, Larimer...N	10
● *Lizard Head*, Dolores...SW	×
Lockett, Saguache...S	×
Logan, Arapahoe...C	×
● *Lolita*, Otero...E	×
● *London*, Park...C	33
Lone Dome, Montezuma..SW	×
● Longmont, Boulder...N	1,543
● *Long's Junction*, Las An..SE	×
● *Lord's Ranch*, Lake...C	×
Lord's Spur, Larimer...N	×
● *Loretto*, Arapache...C	×
● Los Cerritos, Conejos...S	50
Los Magotes, Saguache...S	10
● *Los Pinos*, Conejos...S	19
Los Pinos, La Plata...SW	25
Los Sauches, Conejos...S	20
● Louisville, Boulder...N	596
● Loveland, Larimer...N	698
● *Lowland*, Elbert...E	×
Ludlum, Yuma...E	×
● *Lupton*, Weld...NE	75
● Lyman, Arapahoe...C	45
● Lyons, Boulder...N	574
Lytle, El Paso...C	32
McCoy, Eagle...C	×
McFerran, El Paso...C	25
● *McGee's*, Chaffee...C	×
● *McGinty*, Costilla...S	×
● *Macon*, Fremont...C	×
Madrid, Las Animas...SE	10
● *Magnolia*, Arapahoe...N	65
Magnolia, Boulder...N	50
Maher, Montrose...W	25
● *Malaby's*, Larimer...N	×
Malachite, Huerfano...N	20
● Malta, Lake...C	109
Manassa, Conejos...S	642
● *Manassa Sta.*, Conejos...S	×
Mancos, Montezuma...SW	150
Manhattan, Larimer...N	10
● *Manitou Iron Spr'gs*, ElP.C	×
● *Manitou Junction*, El PasoC	×
Manitou Park, (see Wod'ld Pk.)	×
● Manitou Springs, El Paso.C	1,439
Marble, Gunnison...W	×
Marion, Garfield...NW	120
● *Marion*, Gunnison...W	×
● *Marsh*, Fremont...C	×
● *Marshall*, Boulder...N	200
Marshall Basin, San MiguelSW	300
● *Marshall Junction*, Boul. N	×
● *Marshall Pass*, Saguache..S	×
● *Martinsen*, Las Animas..SE	×
● *Masters*, Weld...NE	×
● Mattison, Elbert...E	×
Maxey, Baca...E	×
Maxwell, Las Animas...SE	217
Maybell, Routt...NW	25
● *Mayfield*, Jefferson...C	×
● *Mayo*, Summit...NW	×
● Maysville, Chaffee...C	78
● *Meadows*, Park...C	×
● *Meadows*, Pueblo...S	×
● *Mears Junction*, Chaffee..C	10
Meeker, Rio Blanco...W	260
● Melvin, Arapahoe...C	×
Menger, Las Animas...SE	×
● *Menoken*, Montrose...W	×
● Merino, Logan...NE	10
Mesa, Mesa...W	10
● *Mesa*, Pueblo...S	×
● *Metcalf*, Park...C	×
● *Michigan*, Park...C	×
Middleton, San Juan...SW	×
● *Midway*, Chaffee...C	×
● *Midway*, Gunnison...W	×
● *Military Junc.*, Arapahoe.C	×
● *Military Post*, Arapahoe..C	×
● *Miller Creek*, Pitkin...W	×
Millet, Washington...E	×
● *Mill Gulch*, Jefferson...C	×
Minaret, Gunnison...W	60
Miner, Larimer...N	×
Mineral Point, San Juan..SW	250

Place	Pop.
Minneapolis, Baca...E	50
Minnehaha, El Paso...C	×
● Minturn, Eagle...C	300
● *Mirage*, Lincoln...E	×
● *Mirage*, Saguache...S	×
● Mitchell, Eagle...C	250
● *Mitchell*, Weld...NE	×
● Moffat, Saguache...S	100
● Monarch, Chaffee...C	300
Montclair, Arapahoe...C	330
● *Montelores*, Dolores...SW	×
● Monte Vista, Rio Grande..S	1,625
Montezuma, Summit...NW	250
● **Montrose**, Montrose...W	1,330
Montville, Costilla...S	**60**
Monument, El Paso...C	177
● *Mooreville*, Arapahoe...C	×
Moraine, Larimer...N	78
Morgan, Montezuma...SW	×
● Morley, Las Animas...SE	×
Morland, El Paso...C	10
● *Morris*, Garfield...NW	×
● Morrison, Jefferson...C	254
Mosca, Costilla...S	50
● *Mound*, Gunnison...W	×
Mountaindale, Park...C	77
Mountain View, El Paso...C	×
Mount Carbon, Gunnison..W	×
● *Mount Carbon*, Jefferson.C	×
● Mount Princeton, Chaffee.C	10
Mount Sneffels, Ouray...SW	200
Mount Vernon, Jefferson..C	20
● *Mule Shoe*, Huerfano...S	×
Mulvane, Prowers...E	×
● *Namouna*, Cheyenne...E	×
● *Nantes*, Weld...NE	×
Nast, Pitkin...W	×
● Nathrop, Chaffee...C	50
Naturita, Montrose...W	40
Nederland, Boulder...N	10
● Needleton, La Plata...SW	×
● Nepesta, Pueblo...S	60
● *Nepesta*, Pueblo...S	×
Nevadaville, Gilpin...C	933
● New Castle, Garfield...NW	311
Newton, Arapahoe...C	44
● New Windsor, Weld...NE	173
● Ni Wot, Boulder...N	50
Noland, Boulder...N	500
● *Norrie*, Pitkin...W	×
● *Northrop*, Boulder...N	×
North Star, Gunnison...W	50
Norwood, San Miguel...SW	25
● *Numa*, Otero...E	×
● Nyburg, Pueblo...S	×
● *Oak Creek*, Fremont...C	250
● *Oak Creek Junction*, Fr'mtC	350
Oakes, Arapahoe...C	100
● *Ogle*, Eagle...C	×
● Ohio, Gunnison...W	50
● *Ojo*, Huerfano...S	×
● Olney, Otero...E	×
Ophir, San Miguel...SW	113
● Orchard, Weld...NE	10
● Ordway, Otero...E	25
● *Oredel*, Boulder...N	×
● *Orient*, Saguache...S	×
Oro City, Lake...C	222
● *Orr*, Weld...NE	×
Orsburn, Elbert...E	×
Orson, Mesa...W	20
Ortiz, Conejos...S	200
● Osier, Conejos...S	200
● Otis, Washington...E	129
● *Otto*, Chaffee...C	×
● **Ouray**, Ouray...SW	2,534
● *Ouray Junction*, Mt'rose. W	×
Overland Park, Arapahoe..C	×
Oversteg, Gunnison...W	×
Pagoda, Routt...NW	×
Pagosa Springs, Arch'taSW	250
● Palisades, Mesa...W	×
● Palmer Lake, El Paso...C	35
● Pando, Eagle...C	×
Pandora, San Miguel...SW	25
● *Paoli*, Phillips...E	×
Paonia, Delta...W	50
● Parachute, Garfield...NW	10
Paradox, Montrose...W	10
Park, Park...C	25
● Parkdale, Fremont...C	40
● Parker, Douglas...C	×
● Park Siding, Jefferson...C	×
● Parlin, Gunnison...W	25
● *Parma*, Rio Grande...S	×
Parrott, La Plata...SW	26
● *Paymaster*, Ouray...SW	×

● Peachblow, Eagle.........C X
Pearl, Larimer.............N X
Pella, (see Hygiene)........ X
Perry Park, Douglas....... C X
● Petersburgh, Arapahoe... C 100
Peyton, El Paso............ C 10
Pictou, Huerfano............S 100
● *Piedmont*, Ouray.......SW X
Piedra, Archuleta.........SW 46
● *Pike View*, El Paso...... C X
● *Pierce*, Weld...........NE X
● Pine, Jefferson...........C 400
● *Pine Creek*, Lake.........C X
● *Pine Grove*, Jefferson.....C 200
Pine River, La Plata......SW 30
Pinewood, Larimer.........N X
Pinkhamton, Larimer...... N 13
● Pinneo, Washington...... E X
● *Pinon*, Pueblo............ S 40
● *Pinon*, Pueblo............S X
● Pitkin, Gunnison..........W 371
Pittsburgh, Gunnison...... W 20
● *Placer*, Costilla...........S 50
● Placerville, San Miguel. SW 30
● *Plateau*, Douglas.........C X
Platoro, Conejos............S 400
● Platte Canon, Jefferson... C 30
● *Platte River*, Park.......C X
Platte Station, Park........ C 12
● Platteville, Weld........NE 213
● *Plumbs*, Weld.......... NE X
● *Pocono*, Saguache.........S X
● *Poncha Pass*, Saguache...S X
● Poncho Springs, Chaffee..C 101
Porter, La Plata..........SW X
● Portland, Ouray.........SW 116
Powderhorn, Gunnison.....W 97
Powell, Las Animas........SE 65
Pring, El Paso.............C X
Progress, Baca..............E X
Prospect, Gunnison ....W X
● Prowers, Bent...........SE X
● **Pueblo**, Pueblo..........S 28,128
Pullen, Larimer.............N X
● *Pultney*, Pueblo...........S X
● *Quartz*, Gunnison........W 15
Querida, Custer.............S 400
● *Ralston*, Jefferson........C X
● Ramah, El Paso............C 10
Rand, Larimer..............N X
Rangely, Rio Blanco........W 15
● *Raspberry*, Chaffee ....C X
● *Rathbone*, Pitkin........W X
Rathbone, Summit....... NW X
● Raymer, Weld..........NE 10
Recen, Summit...........NW 147
● **Red Cliff**, Eagle.........C 383
Red Elephant, Clear Creek. C 150
● *Red Hill*, Park............C X
● *Red Lion*, Logan.........NE 20
● Red Mountain, Ouray...SW 300
● *Reno*, Fremont............C X
● Resolis, Elbert............E X
Richan, Larimer...........N X
Rico, Dolores............SW 1,134
● Ridgway, Ouray........ SW 300
● Rifle, Garfield..........NW 25
Rio Aquilla, Eagle..........C 10
Rito Alto, Saguache.........S 35
● River Bend, Elbert.........E 50
● Riverside, Chaffee.........C 132
● *Riverside*, Jefferson.......C X
● *Roan*, Mesa...............W X
● Robb, Yuma...............E X
● Robinson, Summit.....NW 300
● *Robinson*, Bent..........SE X
● ***Rock Creek*, Eagle.........C** 10
Rock Creek, Summit.....NW 10
Rockford, Garfield....... NW 20
Rockland, Logan..........NE 25
Rock Ridge, Douglas........C 20
● *Rock Spur*, Jefferson..... C X
● Rockvale, Fremont....... C 750
● Rockwood, La Plata....SW 20
Rocky, Park................ C 10
● Rocky Ford, Otero........E 468
● Roggen, Weld..........NE 50
Rollinsville, Gilpin..........C 255
● Romley, Chaffee.......... C 50
Rosita, Custer............. S 304
Rosalias, Elbert............ E X
Roses Cabin, Hinsdale.... SW X
● Roswell, El Paso..........C 250
● *Rouarks*, Park.............C X
● *Roubideau*, Delta......... W X
● *Round Hill*, Saguache.....S X
● Rouse, Huerfano..........S 100

Colorado

● *Rouse's Junc.*, Huerfano..S X
Routt, Routt..............NW X
● *Ruby*, Mesa.............. W X
Ruction, (see Walden)........ X
● Ruedi, Eagle..............C X
Ruff, Baca...................E X
● Russell, Costilla........... S 25
Russell Gulch, Gilpin........C 673
Rye, Pueblo................. S 100
Saddle Horse, El Paso.......C X
Saguache, Saguache...... S 660
Saint Cloud, Larimer....... N X
● Saint Elmo, Chaffee.......C 450
Saint John's, Summit....NW 30
Saint Kevin, Lake...........C X
Saint Mary's, Huerfano...... S 15
St. Thomas, (see Sopris) X
● *Saint Vrains*, Weld.....NE X
● Salida, Chaffee............C 2,586
Salina, Boulder............ N 25
● Salt Creek, Pueblo........S 65
Sanborn, Lincoln............E 25
● *San Carlos*, Pueblo...... S X
● *Sands*, Garfield........ NW X
Sanford, Conejos............ S 200
San Isabel, Saguache........S X
San Juan, Hinsdale....... SW 325
San Luis, Costilla..........S 150
● **San Miguel**, San Mig'l SW 150
San Pedro, Costilla..........S 400
San Rafael, Conejos......... S X
● Santa Clara, Huerfano.... S X
● *Santa Clara Junc.*, Hu'f'no S X
● Sapinero, Gunnison...... W 25
● Sargents, Saguache........S 40
Satank, Garfield..........NW 10
Saxonia, Park............. C 75
● *Schwanders*, Chaffee......C X
Scissors, Huerfano...........S 65
Scofield, Gunnison...........W X
Scranton, Arapahoe.........C 50
● *Secor*, Boulder............N X
● Sedalia, Douglas...........C 100
● Sedgwick, Sedgwick.... NE 10
● Seibert, Kit Carson........E 50
Selak, Grand.............. N 50
● Sellar, Pitkin............ W X
Selkirk, Park............... C X
● Semper, Jefferson..........C X
● *Shale*, Mesa...............W X
Sharpsdale, Huerfano....... S X
● *Shawano*, Saguache.......S X
● *Sheridan Junction*, Arapa' C X
Sheridan Lake, Kiowa.. E 150
● Sherman, Eagle...........C 40
● *Sherwood*, Eagle..........C X
Shields, Arapahoe...........C X
● *Shirley*, Chaffee...........C 19
● *Shoshone*, Garfield.....NW X
● *Siding*, Kit Carson........E X
● *Sidney*, Elbert.............E X
Sidney, Routt.............NW X
Siebert, Kit Carson..........E 50
Siloam, Pueblo...............S X
Siloam Springs, Garfield. NW 350
● *Silt*, Garfield........... NW X
Silver Cliff, Custer.........S 546
● *Silver Lake*, Huerfano..... S X
● Silver Plume, Clear Cr'k..C 908
Silverton, San Juan.....SW 2,000
● *Silvia*, Las Animas...... SE X
● Slaghts, Park............. C 50
Slater, Routt..............NW 25
● *Sligo*, Weld............. NE X
● *Sloane*, Eagle.............C X
● *Smith Hill*, Gilpin.........C X
● Snowden, Lake.............C X
● Snyder, Morgan.........NE 25
Soda Springs, Lake..........C 90
● *Soda Springs*, Fremont...C X
● Sopris, Las Animas......SE 983
● *Sorrento*, Cheyenne.......E X
● *South Canon*, Garfield. NW X
South Denver, Arapahoe....C X
South Platte, Jefferson.......C 25
● *South Fork*, Rio Grande..S X
South Fork, San Miguel.. SW X
● *South Platte*, Jefferson... C 25
South Pueblo, Pueblo.......S X
Sparkill, Pitkin............ W 45
Spicer, Larimer..............N 40
● *Spike Buck*, Fremont......C X
● Spinney, Park............ C X
Springdale, Boulder......... N 50
Springfield, Baca..........E 90
Spring Gulch, Pitkin ...... W X
Stamford, Las Animas.....SE 65

Colorado

Stanley, Costilla.............S 18
● Starkville, Las Animas.. SE 928
● *State Line*, Prowers.......E X
Steamboat Spring, Routt. NW 150
● **Sterling**, Logan.......NE 540
● *Stevens Gulch*, Jefferson..C X
● Stewart, Kiowa............E 25
● *Stoneham*, Weld..........NE X
● *Stone Spur*, Jefferson......C X
Stonewall, Las Animas.....SE 50
Stonington, Baca............E 10
● Stout, Larimer.............N 25
● *Strasburg*, Arapahoe..... C X
Streator, Costilla.............S 50
Struby, Douglas.............C X
● *Stuart*, Kiowa.............E 25
Stunner Conejos............S 150
Sublette, Conejos............S X
● Sugar Loaf, Boulder......N 165
Sullivan, Arapahoe......... C X
Summit, El Paso.............C X
● *Summit*, San Juan......SW X
● Summit Park, El Paso....C 25
Summitville, Rio Grande...N 50
Sunflower, Conejos..........S X
Sunnyside, Hinsdale......SW X
● Sunset, Boulder............N 25
Sunshine, Boulder.......... N 25
Sunshine, Garfield....... NW 300
Sunview, El Paso........... C X
● *Suttons*, Summit.......NW X
● *Swallows*, Pueblo.......... S 65
Swan, Summit............NW 65
Swift, Prowers..............E 10
● *Swissvale*, Fremont...... C X
● *Sybl*, Otero............... E X
Symes, Jefferson............ C 25
Table Rock, El Paso........ C 200
Talpa, Huerfano .... S 10
● *Taylors*, Pueblo.......... S X
● Taylorville, Pueblo........S 65
● ***Teachout*, Gunnison......W** X
● **Telluride**, San Miguel SW 766
Tennessee Pass, Eagle ...... C 30
Texas Creek, Fremont...... C 65
● Thatcher, Las Animas .. SE X
● Thomasville, Pitkin.......W 250
● *Thompson's*, Las Animas SE X
● *Three Mile Tank*, Lake... C X
Thurman, Arapahoe......... C X
● Timnath, Larimer.......... N 80
● Timpas, Otero............. E X
Tinball, Jefferson .... C 50
Tin Cup, Gunnison.......... W 300
Tindale, Jefferson............C X
● *Tioga*, Huerfano .... W X
● *Tip Top*, El Paso......... C 50
Tiptop, Gilpin.............. C X
● *Toll Gate*, Fremont....... C X
● *Tomah*, Douglas...........C X
Tomichi, Gunnison .... W 50
● *Toluca*, Douglas.......... C X
Toponas, Routt......... NW X
Tourist City, (see Walsenb'gh) X
Tourtelotte, Pitkin .... W 614
● Towner, Kiowa .... E 10
Townsend, Arapahoe....... C X
● *Tower Junction*, Boulder N X
● *Trail City*, Bent .... SE 50
● Trimble, La Plata.......SW 25
● *Trinchera*, Costilla........S X
● Trinchera, Las Animas..SE 50
● **Trinidad**, Las Animas SE 5,523
Troublesome, Grand.........N 79
Trout Lake, San Miguel... SW 10
Troy, Las Animas......... SE X
Trull, Routt.............. NW 10
Truro, Park .... C X
● *Tuna*, Huerfano............ S X
● *Tunnel*, Mesa.............. W X
● *Tunnel Spur*, Pitkin .... W X
Tuttle, Kit Carson.......... E X
Twin Lakes, Lake............C 50
● *Twin Lakes*, Lake......... C 50
● *Tyrone*, Las Animas.... SE X
Ula, Custer....................S 30
● *Una*, Garfield............NW X
● *Unaweep*, Mesa.......... W 10
Uncompahgre, Montrose.. W 10
Undercliffe, Pueblo........ S 83
University Park, Arapahoe..C X
Urmston, Jefferson ....C X
● *Utah Junction*, Arapahoe. C X
● *Utah Line*, Mesa .... W X
Ute, Huerfano............... S X
● *Ute Park*, El Paso......... C 25
Valdai, Larimer............ N X

CONNECTICUT.*

Town, County, Index	Pop.
● *Valentine Spur*, Larimer N	×
● *Vallejo*, La Plata SW	×
● *Valley Spur*, Gunnison W	×
● *Vallie*, Fremont C	10
● Valmont, Boulder N	10
● Valverde, Arapahoe C	×
● *Vanderbilt*, Ouray SW	×
● *Vance Junc'n*, S'n Mig'l SW	×
Vega, Mesa W	×
● *Vegas*, Pueblo S	×
● *Venice*, Chaffee C	×
● *Veta Pass*, Huerfano S	×
● *Verde*, Pueblo S	×
Vermillion, Jefferson C	20
Veteran, Saguache S	×
Viceto, La Plata SW	×
● *Vidals Spur*, Gunnison W	×
Vilas, Baca E	43
● Villa Grove, Saguache S	200
Villa Park, Arapahoe C	×
Virginia Dale, Larimer N	×
Virginius, Ouray SW	150
● Vona, Kit Carson E	10
● Wagon Wheel Gap, Rio G. S	25
● *Wahatoya*, Huerfano S	×
Wakeman, Phillips E	×
Walden, Larimer N	64
Wallet, Kit Carson E	×
● **Walsenburgh**, H'f'ano S	928
Ward District, Boulder N	424
Washburn, Arapahoe C	×
● Watervale, Las Animas SE	25
Water Valley, Kiowa E	10
● Watkins, Arapahoe C	75
● Watson, Pitkin W	10
Waunita, Gunnison W	×
● Webster, Park C	100
Weir, Sedgwick NE	×
● *Weldon*, Morgan NE	×
● Wellsville, Fremont C	15
Wentz, Weld NE	×
● Westcliffe, Custer S	192
● *West Denver*, Arapahoe C	×
● *West Glenwood*, Gar'ld NW	×
Weston, Las Animas SE	50
● *Wests*, Las Animas SE	×
Wetmore, Custer S	25
● *Wheatland*, Jefferson C	×
● *Wheeler*, Garfield NW	×
● Wheeler, Summit NW	25
White Cross, Hinsdale SW	25
White Pine, Gunnison W	143
White River, Rio Blanco S	25
● *White Rock*, Boulder N	×
● Whitewater, Mesa W	10
● *Whitford*, Las Animas SE	×
Whitney, Kiowa E	×
● *Widefield*, El Paso C	98
● *Wier*, Sedgwick NE	×
● Wigwam, El Paso C	130
Wilde, Prowers E	100
● *Wilders*, Summit NW	×
● *Wilde's Spur*, Larimer N	×
● *Wild Horse*, Cheyenne E	×
● *Wild Horse*, Chaffee C	×
● Willard, Logan NE	×
● Williamsburgh, Fremont C	350
● *Wilson's*, Clear Creek C	×
● *Windsor*, Weld NE	×
Winfield, Chaffee C	75
Winona, Larimer N	×
● Wolcott, Eagle C	25
● *Wolhurst*, Douglas C	×
● Woodland Park, El Paso C	50
● *Woodruff*, Fremont C	×
● *Woodstock*, Gunnison W	×
● *Woody Creek*, Pitkin W	100
● *Wootton*, Las Animas SE	×
● Wray, Yuma E	125
● *Wynetka*, Arapahoe C	200
Yale, Kit Carson E	×
Yampa, Routt NW	65
● *Yankee Girl*, Ouray SW	×
Yorkville, Fremont C	15
● *Youman*, Gunnison W	×
● **Yuma**, Yuma E	241
Zapato, Costilla S	×
● *Zangs Spur*, Boulder N	×
Zuck, Prowers E	×

County	Index	Pop.
Fairfield	SW	150,081
Hartford	N	147,180
Litchfield	NW	53,542
Middlesex	S	39,524
New Haven	S	209,058
New London	SE	76,634
Tolland	N	25,081
Windham	NE	45,158
Total		746,258

*In many of the towns of the State the population given embraces the township.

TOWN. COUNTY. INDEX.	POP.
● Abington, Windham NE	250
Addison, Hartford N	×
● *Air Line Junction*, Win. NE	×
Allington Siding, New Haven S	×
● *Allyn's Point*, New Lond. SE	×
Almyville, Windham NE	×
● Andover, Tolland N	401
● Ansonia, New Haven S	10,342
● *Arnold's*, Middlesex S	×
Ashford, Windham NE	778
Ashwillet, New London SE	×
Aspetuck, Fairfield SW	50
Attawaugan, Fairfield SW	×
Attawangan, Windham NE	×
Atwoodville, Tolland N	×
● *Avery's*, New London SE	×
● Avon, Hartford N	1,182
Bakersville, Litchfield NW	142
Ballouville, Windham NE	×
Ball's Pond, Fairfield SW	×
● Baltic, New London SE	450
Bangall, Fairfield SW	×
● Bantam, Litchfield NW	400
Barkhamsted, Litchfield NW	1,130
Battie, New London SE	×
● Bayport, Fairfield SW	400
● Beacon Falls, New Haven S	505
Bean Hill, New London SE	250
● *Beckley*, Hartford N	×
Bennetts Bridge, Fairfield SW	×
Berkshire, (see Sandy Hook).	×
Berlin, Hartford N	2,600
● *Berlin Station*, Hartford N	×
Bethany, New Haven S	550
● Bethel, Fairfield SW	2,335
Bethlehem, Litchfield NW	543
Bill Hill, New London SE	×
● Birmingham, New Haven S	4,413
● Black Hall, New London SE	×
Black Rock, Fairfield SW	500
● Bloomfield, Hartford N	1,308
● Bolton, Tolland N	452
Bolton Notch, Tolland N	×
● *Boston Neck*, Hartford N	×
● Botsford, Fairfield SW	300
Bozrah, New London SE	1,005
Bozrahville, New London SE	500
Bradleyville, Litchfield NW	×
● *Branch Switch*, Hartford N	×
● Branchville, Fairfield SW	500
● Branfort, New Haven S	4,460
● **BRIDGEPORT**, Fairfield SW	48,866
Bridgewater, Litchfield NW	617
● Bristol, Hartford N	7,382
● Broad Brook, Hartford N	800
Brockway, New London SE	×
● Brookfield, Fairfield SW	989
Brookfield Centre, F'field SW	250
● *Brookfield Junction*, Fairfield SW	×
Brooklyn, Windham NE	2,628
Brook's Vale, New Haven S	×
Buckingham, Hartford N	300
● Buckland, Hartford N	300
Bull's Bridge, Litchfield NW	×
Burlington, Hartford N	1,302
● *Burlington Station*, H'ford N	×
● *Burnhams*, Hartford N	×
● Burnside, Hartford N	300
Burrville, Litchfield NW	195
Campbell's Mills, New Lon SE	×
● Campville, Litchfield NW	200
● Canaan, Litchfield NW	970
Canaan Valley, Litchfield NW	200
● Cannon, Fairfield SW	150
Canterbury, Windham NE	947
● *Canterbury Station*, Windham NE	×
● Canton, Hartford N	2,500
Canton Centre, Hartford N	150
● *Cedar Hill*, New Haven S	×
Cedarville, Middlesex S	×
● Central Village, W'h'm NE	700
● Centre Brook, Middlesex S	650
● *Centre Street*, New Haven S	×
Centre Groton, New Lon. SE	×
Centre Hill, Hartford N	×
● *Centreville*, New Haven S	×
● Chapinville, Litchfield NW	275
Chaplin, Windham NE	542
● *Chaplin*, Windham NE	65
● *Charter Oak*, Hartford N	×
● *Cherry Brook*, Hartford N	×
Cheshire, New Hampshire S	1,929
● *Cheshire Station*, N. Haven S	400
● *Cheshire Street*, New Haven S	×
● Chester, Middlesex S	1,301
Chesterfield, New London SE	100
Chestnut Hill, Tolland N	×
Chestnut Hill, Middlesex S	×
● Clark's Corner, W'dham NE	65
Clark's Falls, New London SE	100
● *Clayton*, Hartford N	×
● Clinton, Middlesex S	1,384
● Clintonville, New Haven S	200
● *Club House*, Tolland N	×
● Cobalt, Middlesex S	500
● Colchester, New London SE	2,988
Cold Spring, (see Botsford).	×
Colebrook, Litchfield NW	1,098
Colebrook River, Litchfi'd NW	300
● *Colebrook Station*, Litchfield NW	×
● Collinsville, Hartford N	1,957
Columbia, Tolland N	740
Comstock's Bridge, N.L'dn SE	195
● *Congamond*, Hartford N	×
● *Connecticut River*, N.L'dn SE	×
● *Cooks*, Hartford N	×
Copper Hill, Hartford N	×
Cornwall, Litchfield NW	547
● Cornwall Bridge, Lch'ld NW	250
Cornwall Centre, Litchfi'd NW	×
Cornwall Hollow, Litchfi'd NW	×
Cos Gob, (see Bayport)	×
● *Cos Cob Bridge*, Fairfi'd SW	400
● *Cottage Grove*, Hartford N	×
Coventry, Tolland N	1,875
Coventry Dpt., (see S. Cov'try)	×
● *Crescent Beach*, N.Ln'dn SE	×
● Cromwell, Middlesex S	1,987
Crystal Lake, Tolland N	×
● **Danbury**, Fairfield SW	16,552
● Danielsonville, Windham NE	2,700
● Darien, Fairfield SW	2,276
● *Dayville*, Windham NE	1,200
● Deep River, Middlesex S	1,100
● *Derby*, New Haven S	1,556
● *Dividend*, Hartford N	×
Doaneville, New London SE	×
Dodgeinville, Fairfield SW	×
● *Dublin Street*, N. Haven S	×
Duncan, Middlesex S	×
Durham, Middlesex S	856
Durham Centre, Middlesex S	×
● *Dyke*, Hartford N	×
● Eagleville, Tolland N	600
● East Berlin, Hartford N	426
E. Bridgeport, (see Bridgep'rt)	×
East Brooklyn, **Windham NE**	×
● East Canaan, Litchfield NW	350
East Cornwall, Litchfield NW	×
● *East Danbury*, Fairfield SW	×
● *East Farms*, New Haven S	×
Eastford, Windham NE	561
East Glastonbury, Hartford N	300
East Granby, Hartford N	661
East Haddam, Middlesex S	2,599
● East Hampton, Middlesex S	1,400
● East Hartford, Hartford N	4,455
East Hartford Meadow, H'rd N	×
East Hartland, Hartford N	300
● East Haven, New Haven S	955
East Kent, Litchfield NW	×
East Killingly, Windham NE	700
● East Litchfield, Litchfi'd NW	200
East Lyme, New London SE	2,048
● *East Lyme Stat'n*, N.L'dn SE	2,045
East Morris, Litchfield NW	×
● East Norwalk, Fairfield SW	1,000
Easton, Fairfield SW	1,001
East Plymouth, Litchfield NW	×
East Putnam, Windham NE	×
● East River, New Haven S	400
● East Thompson, W'dhm NE	×

Place	Pop.
● East Wallingford, N.H'vn.S	×
● East Willington, Tolland..N	100
● East Windsor, Hartford.. N	2,890
● East Windsor Hill, H'ford.N	825
● *East Winsted*, Litchf'dNW	×
East Woodstock, W'dhm..NE	200
Ekonk, Windham.........NE	×
● Ellington, Tolland........N	1,539
● Elliott, Windham.......NE	×
● *Ellithorpe*, Tolland.......N	×
Ellsworth, Litchfield..... NW	263
● Elmwood, Hartford.........N	6,756
Elys Ferry, New London..SE	×
Enfield, Hartford...........N	7,199
● *Enfield Bridge*, Hartford.N	×
Essex, Middlesex...........S	2,035
● *Essex Station*, Middlesex.S	700
● Fairfield, Fairfield......SW	3,868
● *Fair Grounds*, Fairfield.SW	×
Fair Grounds, Fairfield.. SW	×
● Fair Haven, New Haven.. S	1,520
Falls Village, Litchfield.. NW	500
● *Falls Village Station*,L'NW	×
Farmington, Hartford......N	3,179
Farms Village,(seeSimsbury)	×
● *Farmington Station*,H'frdN	×
● *Fernwick*, Middlesex..... S	×
● Fitchville, New London.SE	×
● *Fitchville Junc.*,NewL'n SE	×
● *Five Mile River*, F'field.SW	500
Flanders, New London....SE	100
Fluteville, Litchfield...... NW	×
Forestville, Hartford...... N	800
Fort Trumbull,New L'n.. SE	×
Franklin, New London ....SE	585
Gale's Ferry, New London.SE	125
Gardner's Lake, New L'n..SE	×
● Gaylordsville, Litchf'd. NW	300
● Georgetown, Fairfield.. SW	250
Gildersleeve, Middlesex..... S	1,100
Gilead, Tolland............. N	300
Glasgo, New London...... SE	200
Glastonbury, Hartford......N	3,457
● Glenbrook, Fairfield.....SW	250
Glenville, Fairfield........SW	550
● *Goodspeeds*, Middlesex....S	600
Goodspeeds Landing, M'd'x.S	500
Goshen, Litchfield........NW	972
Goshen, New London......SE	×
● Granby, Hartford.........N	1,251
Graniteville, New London. SE	×
Grantville, Litchfield.....NW	195
● *Gravel Pit*, New Haven....S	×
Greenfield Hill, Fairfield..SW	100
Green Manville,(seeMysticBr.)	×
● Green's Farms.Fairfield SW	583
● Greenville, New London SE	3,400
Greenwich, Fairfield......SW	10,131
● *Greenwich Stat'n*,F'fieldSW	×
● Greystone, Litchfield...NW	50
Griswold, New London.... SE	3,113
● Grosvenor Dale,Wind'm.NE	1,500
● Groton, New London....SE	5,539
Groton Centre, (see Groton).	×
● Grove Beach, Middlesex..S	×
● Guilford, New Haven.....S	2,780
Gurleyville, Tolland........ N	100
● **Haddam**, Middlesex.... S	2,095
Haddam Neck, Middlesex...S	455
Hadlyme, New London.... SE	300
● *Hadlyme Station*, Mid'x..S	×
Hamburgh, New London..SE	1,000
Hamden, New Haven...... S	3,882
Hammertown, Litchfield. NW	×
● Hampton, Windham....NE	632
● *Hancock*, Litchfield....NW	×
Hanover, New London.....SE	521
Harrisville, Windham.....NE	×
● **HARTFORD**, Hart'd..N	53,230
Hartland, Hartford.........N	565
Harwinton, Litchfield.....NW	943
Hattertown, Fairfield.....SW	×
● Hawleyville, Fairfield...SW	400
● *Hawleyville Junc.*, F'l'dSW	×
● *Haydens*, Hartford....... N	×
● Hazzardville, Hartford... N	800
Hebron, Tolland............ N	1,039
● Higganum, Middlesex.....S	550
● *Highland*, Middlesex.....S	×
Highland Park, Hartford... N	100
High Ridge, Fairfield..... SW	200
● *High Rock Grove*,New H'nS	×
Highwood, New Haven......S	200
Hitchcockville, (see Riverton)	×
● *Hobart*, Fairfield.......SW	×
Hockanum, Hartford....... N	425
Hope Valley, Tolland.......N	×

Connecticut

Place	Pop.
Hopeville, New Haven...... S	×
Hopeville, New London....SE	×
Hopewell, Litchfield......NW	×
● Hop River, Tolland.......N	×
Hoskins, Hartford..........N	×
Hotchkissville, Litchfield NW	700
Howard Valley, Windham.NE	×
Huntington, Fairfield.....SW	3,054
Huntsville, Litchfield.....NW	1,000
Hurlbutt, Fairfield........SW	×
Ivoryton, Middlesex.........S	600
● Jewett City, New L'd'n..SE	1,875
● *Jewett City Sta.*,N. L'd'n.SE	×
Johnsonville, Middlesex....S	180
● *Joyceville*, Litchfield... NW	×
● Judd's Bridge, L'chf'ld.NW	×
Kensington, Hartford.......N	700
● Kent, Litchfield........ NW	1,383
Kent Furnace, Litchfield.NW	×
Killingly, Windham.........NE	7,027
Killingly Centre,(seeDayville)	×
Killingworth, Middlesex.... S	582
● *Lake*, Litchfield........NW	×
● Lakeville, Litchfield....NW	800
● Lanesville, Litchfield....NW	100
Laurel Glen, New London..SE	30
Laysville, New London....SE	×
Lebanon, New London....SE	1,670
● *Lebanon*, New London..SE	×
Lebanon Valley, New L'n.SE	×
Ledyard, New London.....SE	1,183
Leesville, Middlesex.........S	150
● Leete Island, New Hav'n...S	205
Leffingwell, New London..SE	×
● Leonard Bridge,New L'nSE	×
Liberty Hill, New London. SE	450
● **Lime Rock, Litchfield..NW**	600
Lisbon, New London......SE	548
● **Litchfield**, Litchfield.NW	1,058
● *Litchfield*, Litchfield....NW	200
Little Haddam, Middlesex...S	×
Little River, Middlesex..... S	×
Lockwood, Fairfield...... SW	50
● Long Hill, Fairfield.....SW	350
Long Ridge, Fairfield.....SW	500
Long Society, New London SE	×
Lovett's Station, (see Lisbon).	×
● Lyme, New London.......SE	977
● *Lyman Viaduct*,New L'nSE	1,027
Lyons Plain, Fairfield.....SW	×
● Madison, New Haven..... S	1,429
Main Street, New Haven....S	×
● *Maltby's Siding*, L'ch'dNW	×
Manchester, Hartford.......N	8,222
● *Manchester*, Hartford.....N	×
Manchester Green, Hartf'd..N	800
Mansfield, Tolland..........N	1,911
Mansfield Centre, Tolland.. N	350
● Mansfield Depot, Tolland.N	100
Marble Dale, Litchfield...NW	200
Marion, Hartford...........N	200
Marlborough, Hartford......N	582
Marlborough Mills,HartfordN	×
● *Maromas*, Middlesex..... S	×
Mashapaug, Tolland........ N	150
● Massapeag, New London.SE	×
● Mechanicsville,W'dh'm. NE	800
● Melrose, Hartford........ N	300
● Meriden, New Haven......S	21,652
● Merrow, Tolland...........N	200
● *Merwinsville*, LitchfieldNW	300
Mianus, Fairfield..........SW	400
Middlebury, New Haven.....S	566
● Middlefield, Middlesex....S	1,002
● *Middlefield Centre*, Middlesex.........S	×
Middle Haddam, Middlesex. S	600
● Middletown, Middlesex ...S	9,013
● Milford, New Haven...... S	3,811
Mill Brook, Litchfield....NW	100
● Milldale, Hartford........N	300
Millington, Middlesex........S	×
● Mill Plain, Fairfield.....SW	350
Millstone Point, N'w L'nd.SE	200
Milton, Litchfield.........NW	200
Mine Hill, Litchfield..... NW	×
Minortown, Litchfield....NW	×
● Mohegan, New London..SE	×
Monroe, Fairfield......... SW	994
● *Monroe Station*,Fairf'ld SW	×
Montowese, New Haven .... S	300
Montville, New London....SE	2,344
● *Montville Station*, New London........ SE	900
Moodus, Middlesex.........S	1,200
Moose Meadow, Tolland.... N	×

Connecticut

Place	Pop.
Moosup, Windham........ NE	1,500
Morris, Litchfield .... NW	584
● *Morris*, Litchfield....... NW	×
Morris Cove, New Haven... S	×
● Mount Carmel,New Haven S	1,700
Mount Carmel Centre, New Haven .... S	×
Mount Hope, Tolland ...... N	50
● Mystic, New London.... SE	600
Mystic Bridge, NewLondonSE	1,500
Mystic Island,New LondonSE	×
Mystic River, New L'nd'n. SE	2,100
Naubuc, Hartford......... N	500
● Naugatuck, New Haven...S	4,780
● *Naugatuck Junction*, New Haven.......... S	×
Nepaug, Litchfield........NW	80
New Boston, Windham....NE	250
● New Britain, Hartford... N	19,007
● New Canaan, Fairfield..SW	2,701
New Fairfield, Fairfield.. SW	670
Newfield, Middlesex........ S	×
Newfield, Litchfield...... NW	×
Newhallville,New Haven....S	×
● New Hartford, Litchf'd NW	3,160
N.Hartford Cen.,(seeNepaug)	×
● **New Haven**,NewHavenS	87,298
● Newington, Hartford .... N	953
● Newington Junction, Hartford .... N	×
● **New London**,N Lond'nSE	13,757
● New Milford, Litchfield.NW	3,917
New Preston, Litchfield.. NW	400
● *New Preston*,Litchfield NW	×
New Saybrook, Middlesex.. S	×
● Newtown, Fairfield.....SW	3,539
● Niantic, New London... SE	1,000
Nichols, Fairfield......... SW	200
● Noank, New London.... SE	900
● Norfolk, Litchfield .... NW	1,546
● Noroton, Fairfield.......SW	700
Noroton Heights, FairfieldSW	×
North Ashford, Windham.NE	148
● North Bloomfield,H'tfd...N	×
North Branford,New Haven.S	825
● *North Bridgeport*,Ffd.. SW	×
North Canaan, (see Canaan).	×
North Canton, Hartford..... N	175
North Colebrook,Litchf'd NW	75
North Coventry, Tolland... N	200
● *North Cromwell*,M'ddles'xS	×
Northfield, Litchfield.... NW	550
Northford, New Haven..... S	700
● *Northford Station*, New Haven.......... S	200
● North Franklin, New London........ SE	×
North Glastonbury, Hartf'd N	×
North Granby, Hartford.... N	400
● North Grosvenor Dale, Windham......... NE	800
North Guilford, New Haven.S	500
● North Haven,New Haven. S	1,862
● North Kent, Litchfield..NW	×
North Lyme,New London. SE	×
North Madison, New Haven..S	200
North Norfolk, Litchfield NW	200
North Plain, Middlesex..S	×
North Somers, Tolland..... N	×
North Stamford, Fairfield SW	600
North Sterling,Windham..NE	150
North Stonington,N L'dn..SE	1,463
Northville, Litchfield .... NW	150
● North Westchester, New London........ SE	×
North Wilton, Fairfield .. SW	250
● North Windham, Windham.......... NE	150
North Woodbury,Litchf'd NW	555
North Woodstock, Wind'mNE	550
● Norwalk, Fairfield..... SW	17,747
Norwich Falls,N. London.SE	×
● **Norwich**,New London SE	16,156
● Norwich Town, New London......... SE	1,100
Oakdale, New London.....SE	×
● Oakville, Litchfield.... NW	300
Occum, New London ......SE	×
Old Lyme, (see Lyme)........	×
Old Mystic, New London.. SE	600
● Oneco, Windham........NE	350
● Orange, New Haven...... S	4,537
● Ore Hill, Litchfield..... NW	300
Oronoque, Fairfield ...... SW	×
● *Osborn*, Hartford .... N	×
Oxford, New Haven .... S	902
● *Osborntown*, New Haven..S	×

Oyster Point, New Haven...S ×
● Packerville, Windham..NE 125
● **Parkville, Hartford ...... N** 150
Pawcatuck, New London ..SE 2,800
Pegville, Hartford.......... N ×
Pendleton Hill, N. London..SE ×
● Pequabuck, Litchfield..NW 250
Phoenixville, Windham.. NE 127
● *Pines Bridge*, New Haven. S ×
● Pine Meadow, LitchfieldNW 600
● *Pine Orchard*, New HavenS ×
● Plainfield, Windham....NE 4,582
Plainfield Junction, W'n'dNE ×
● Plainville, Hartford...... N 1,993
● Plantsville, Hartford......N 1,500
Plattsville, Fairfield.......SW 100
Pleasant Valley, Litchhf'dNW 200
Plymouth, Litchfield.... NW 2,147
Polkville, Hartford.........N ×
Pomfret, Windham....... NE 1,471
● Pomfret Centre, W'hamNE ×
Pomfret Landing, W'ham. NE ×
● *Pomperang Valley*, New Haven .... S ×
Poquetanuck, New LondonSE 400
Poquonock, Hartford.......N 1,200
● Poquonock Bridge, N.L'nSE 500
● *Poquonnock Junc.*, N. L. SE ×
● Portland, Middlesex...... S 4,687
● *Powder Track*, Tolland...N ×
Preston, New London.....SE 2,555
Prospect, New Haven..... SE 455
● *Prospect*, New Haven......S ×
● Putnam, Windham..... NE 6,512
Putnam Heights, W'ham..NE ×
Quaddick, (see Thompson)... ×
Quaker Farms, New Haven..S ×
Quaker Hill, New London.SE ×
Quarryville, Tolland........N 200
● Quinebaug, Windham...NE 250
● *Quinnipiack*, New Haven..S ×
Rainbow, Hartford..........N 350
Rawson, Windham.........NE ×
● *Reading*, Fairfield......SW 400
Redding, Fairfield........ SW 1,546
Redding Ridge, Fairfield..SW 1,543
Reynolds Bridge, L'hfield.NW 300
Ridgebury, Fairfield...... SW 50
● Ridgefield, Fairfield.... SW 2,235
Riverbank, Fairfield.....SW ×
● Riverside, Fairfield.....SW ×
Riverside, New Haven...... S ×
Riverton, Litchfield.......NW 500
Robertsville, Litchfield...NW 125
● Rockfall, Middlesex.......S 310
Rockland, New Haven......S ×
● Rockville, Tolland.........N 7,772
● Rocky Hill, Hartford.....N 1,069
● Romford, Litchfield.....NW ×
Round Hill, Fairfield......SW 400
● Rowayton, Fairfield.... SW 500
Roxbury, Litchfield.......NW 936
● *Roxbury*, Litchfield.....NW 310
● *Roxbury Falls*, Lh'fieldNW ×
● Roxbury Stat'n, Lh'fieldNW 250
● *Sachem's Head*, N'w HavenS ×
● *Sadd's Mill*, Tolland.......N ×
Salem, New London.......SE 481
● Salisbury, Litchfield.... NW 3,420
● Sandy Hook, Fairfield.. SW 1,000
● Sanford, Fairfield........SW 375
● Saugatuck, Fairfield.....SW 500
Savin Rock, New Haven....S ×
● Saybrook, Middlesex ..... S 1,484
● *Saybrook Junction*, Md'sexS ×
● Saybrook Point, Middlesex.S 410
Scantic, Hartford............N 200
Scitico, Hartford............N 400
Scotland, Windham....... NE 506
● *Scotland Station*, W'dhmNE ×
Sea View House, N. Haven..S ×
● Seymour, New Haven.....S 3,300
Shailerville, Middlesex......S ×
Shaker Station, Hardford...N 210
Sharon, Litchfield......... NW 2,149
Sharon Valley, Litchfield.NW 100
Shelton, Fairfield......... SW 1,952
● *Shelton*, New Haven......S ×
● *Shepaug*, Litchfield.... NW 100
Sherman, Fairfield........SW 668
Shewville, New London... SE ×
Short Beach, New Haven... S ×
Silver Lane, Hartford.......N ×
Silver Mine, Fairfield.....SW ×
● Simsbury, Hartford...... N 1,874
● *Smith's*, Middlesex........S ×

Smith's Ridge, (see N. Canaan) ×
Somers, Tolland............ N 1,407
Somerville, Tolland.........N 400
● Sound Beach, Fairfield.SW ×
South Britain, New Haven.. S 600
Southbury, New Haven......S 1,089
South Canaan, Litchfield. NW 55
● South Canterbury, W'hmNE ×
South Coventry, Tolland....N 800
● *South Coventry*, Tolland..N 1,100
South Farms, (see Middleton) ×
● Southford, New Haven....S 400
South Glastonbury, H'ford. N 1,000
South Haven, (see East Haven) ×
● Southington, Hartford.... S 5,501
● *Southington Road*, N.H'v'nS ×
● South Kent, Litchfield.NW ×
South Killingly, Windam. NE 425
● South Lyme, N'w LondonSE 200
● South Manchester, H'ford N 4,300
South Meriden, New Haven.S ×
South Norfolk, Litchfield.NW ×
● South Norwalk, FairfieldSW 8,628
● Southport, Fairfield.... SW 1,500
● Southville, Litchfield....NW 50
● South Wethersfield, H'f'rdN ×
● Sou. Willington, Tolland, N ×
● South Wilton, Fairfield.SW 10
● *South Wilton Siding*, Fairfield......................SW ×
● Sou. Windham, Wind'm.NE 400
South Windsor, Hartford...N 1,736
● *South Windsor*, Hartford N ×
South Woodstock, Wind'mNE 200
● Springdale, Fairfield.....SW 200
Spring Hill, Tolland....... N ×
Square Pond, Tolland...... N 100
Stafford Tolland............N 2,182
● Stafford Springs, Tolland..N 2,353
Staffordville, Tolland ....N 4,535
● Stamford, Fairfield.... SW 15,700
Standish Hill, N. London. SE ×
Stanwich, Fairfield........SW 500
State Line, Litchfield.....NW ×
● *Steeles*, Tolland...........N ×
Stepney, Fairfield..........SW 400
● Stepney Depot, Fairfield SW 350
● Sterling, Windham......NE 1,051
● Stevenson, Fairfield.... SW ×
Stevenson, New Haven......S 100
Stillmanville, New Lond.. SE ×
● *Still River*, Litchfield...NW ×
● *Stock Yard*, New Haven..S ×
● Stonington, New LondonSE 7,184
● *Stonington Junction*, New London .... SE ×
● *Stonington Point*, N.Lon.SE ×
● Stony Creek, New Haven. S 1,000
● *Stony Hill Siding*, F'r'f'ldSW ×
Storrs, Tolland............. N ×
Straitsville, New Haven.....S ×
● Stratford, Fairfield.....SW 2,608
● *Stratton Brook*, HartfordN 350
● Suffield, Hartford........ N 3,169
● *Summit*, Litchfield.....NW ×
● ***Summit***, **Litchfield.... NW** ×
● ***Summit***, **New Haven......S** ×
● Taftville, New London...SE 2,500
● Talcottville, Tolland.......N 3,751
● *Talmage Hill*, Fairfield SW ×
● Tariffville, Hartford......N 340
Taunton, Fairfield........SW ×
Terryville, Litchfield......NW 1,200
● *Terryville Station*, L'ch.NW ×
● ***Thamesville***, **New Lon.. SE**
Thomaston, Litchfield....NW 985
● *Thomaston Stat'n*, L'chNW ×
Thompson, Windham...... NE 5,580
● *Thompson Station*, W'mNE ×
● Thompsonville, Harfford. N 4,000
Titicus, Fairfield..........SW 250
Tolland, Tolland..........N 1,037
● *Tolland*, Tolland.......... N 250
Torringford, Litchfield...NW ×
● Torrington, Litchfield..NW 4,283
Totoket, New Haven........S ×
● *Towantic*, New Haven....S ×
Tracy, New Haven..........S ×
Trioaks, Middlesex......... S ×
● Trumbull, Fairfield.....SW 1,453
Turnerville, Tolland........ N 500
Twin Lakes, Litchfield.. NW ×
● Tyler City, New Haven....S ×
● Tylerville, Middlesex......S 608
● Uncasville, New London .SE 750
Union, Tolland............ N 431

Union City, New Haven.....S 1,438
● *Union City Station*, N.H'n.S ×
● Unionville, Hartford..... N 1,676
● *Upper Switch*, New LondSE ×
● Vernon, Tolland..........N 1,026
Vernon Centre, Tolland.... N ×
● *Vernon Centre Stat'n*, Tol.N ×
Vernon Depot, Tolland.....N 400
Vernon Sta., (see Vernon)... ×
● Versailles, New London. SE 400
Vinton's Mills, Hartford....N ×
Voluntown, New London..SE 1,060
● Wallingford, New Haven..S 4,230
Wapping, Hartford......... N 200
Warehouse Point, Hartford.N 750
● *Warehouse Point Station*, Hartford....................N ×
Warren, Litchfield....... NW 477
Warrenville, Windham....NE 350
Washington, Litchfield...NW 1,633
● Wash'ton Depot, L'chf'dNW 175
● Waterbury, New Haven...S 28,646
Waterford, New London...SE 2,661
● *Waterford Station*, New London.................SE ×
● Watertown, Litchfield..NW 2,323
● Waterville, New Haven... S 700
● Wauregan, Windham... NE 1,100
Waverly Grove, New Haven.S ×
● Weatogue, Hartford......N 250
West Ashford, Windham..NE 110
West Avon, Hartford........N ×
● Westbrook, Middlesex.... S 874
West Brooklyn, (see Brooklyn) ×
● West Cheshire, New H'n.. S 400
Westchester, New London.SE 400
● *Westchester*, Litchfield. NW ×
● West Cornwall, Litchfield..S 250
● *West Cromwell*, MiddlesexS 225
● *Westfield*, Middlesex......S ×
Westford, Windham...... NE 300
West Goshen, Litchfield. NW 300
West Granby, Hartford......N 350
West Hartford, Hartford....N 1,930
West Hartland, Hartford... N ×
● West Haven, New Haven..S 2,500
● *West Haven Station*, New Haven.....................S ×
West Kinglingly, (see Danielv.) ×
West Meriden, (see Meriden). ×
Westminster, Windham...NE 400
● West Morris, Litchfield.NW ×
● West Mystic, New L'd'n.SE 584
● West Norfolk, Litchfl'dNW 200
West Norwalk, Fairfield..SW ×
Weston, Fairfield......... SW 772
Westport, Fairfield....... SW 3,715
● *Westport Station*, Fr'ld.SW 500
● West Redding, Fairfield.SW 400
● West Simsbury, Hartford. N 350
West Stafford, Tolland......N 500
West Stratford, Fairfield. SW ×
● *West Street Junc.*, Tol'n'd.N ×
West Suffield, Hartford.....N 100
West Thompson, W'dh'm..NE 200
● *West Thompson Station*, Windham..............NE ×
West Torrington, L'chf'd. NW ×
Westville, New Haven.......S 1,500
● West Willington, Tolland. N 250
● West Winsted, Litchf'd.NW 3,000
West Woodstock, W'dh'm.NE 150
● Wethersfield, Hartford... N 2,271
● *Wheaton's*, Litchfield..NW ×
Whigville, Hartford........ N ×
Whitneyville, New Haven...S 200
Wickebequock, New L'don.SE ×
Williamsville, Windham.NE ×
● Willimantic, Windham..NE 8,648
Willington, Tolland.........N 906
● *Wilsons*, Hartford.........N ×
● *Wilson's Point*, Fairf'ldSW ×
Wilsonville, Windham.... NE 400
● Wilton, Fairfield........ SW 1,722
Winchester, Litchfield....NW 1,237
Winchester Centre, L'h'd.NW 5,186
● *Windermere*, Tolland.... N ×
Windham, Windham......NE 1,384
● Windsor, Hartford.........N 2,954
● Windsor Locks, Hartford.N 2,758
Windsorville, Hartford..... N 200
● Winnipauk, Fairfield...SW 200
● Winsted, Litchfield.....NW 4,846
Winthrop, Middlesex........S 150
● *Winthrop*, New London.SE ×
Wolcott, New Haven........S 522

Town, County	Index	Pop.
Wolcottville, (see Torrington)		×
Woodbridge, New Haven	S	926
Woodbury, Litchfield	NW	1,815
● *Woodland*, Hartford	N	×
● Woodmont, New Haven	S	200
● *Woods*, Hartford	N	×
Woodstock, Windham	NE	2,309
Woodstock Valley, W'h'm.	NE	500
Woodtick, New Haven	S	×
Woodville, Litchfield	NW	85
Woodville, Tolland	N	×
● Yalesville, New Haven	S	400
● Yantic, New London	SE	350
Zoar Bridge, New Haven	S	100

DELAWARE.

TOWN.	COUNTIES.	POP.
Kent	C	32,664
New Castle	N	97,182
Sussex	S	38,647
Total		168,493

TOWN. COUNTY.	INDEX.	POP.
Adamsville, Kent	C	20
Andrewville, Kent	C	50
Angola, Sussex	S	[illegible]
Argo, Sussex	S	×
● *Armstrong*, New Castle	N	×
● Ashland, New Castle	N	150
● *Augustine*, New Castle	N	×
● *Bacon Mill Pond*, Sussex	S	×
Bayard, Sussex	S	50
Bayville, Sussex	S	25
● Bear, New Castle	N	50
Beaver Valley, New Castle	N	250
● Bellevue, New Castle	N	500
Bethel, Sussex	S	378
● *Bethesda*, Sussex	S	×
● *Bingham*, New Castle	N	×
● Blackbird, New Castle	N	342
Blackiston, Kent	C	×
Blackwater, Sussex	S	250
● *Bombay Hook*, Kent	C	85
Bowers, Kent	C	150
● *Brandywine Springs*, New Castle	N	×
Brenford, Kent	C	25
● Bridgeville, Sussex	S	576
● *Broad Creek*, Sussex	S	×
● *Broadkill*, Sussex	S	50
Brownsville, Kent	C	25
Bunting, Sussex	S	25
Camden, Kent	S	553
● *Canal*, New Castle	N	×
● Cannon, Sussex	S	25
Canterbury, Kent	C	160
● *Carey*, Sussex	S	×
● Carpenter, New Castle	N	×
● Carrcroft, New Castle	N	25
● *Casho's Switch*, N. Castle	N	×
● *Centre*, New Castle	N	×
Centreville, New Castle	N	110
● Cheswold, Kent	C	200
Choate, New Castle	N	20
Christiana, New Castle	N	318
● Claymont, New Castle	N	228
● Clayton, Kent	C	540
Columbia, Sussex	S	30
● *Concord*, New Castle	N	×
Concord, Sussex	S	296
● Cooch's Bridge, N. Castle	N	200
● Cool Spring, Sussex	S	200
● *Corbit*, New Castle	N	×
● *Cypress*, Sussex	S	×
Cowgill, Kent	C	30
● Dagsborough, Sussex	S	175
Deakyneville, New Castle	N	375
● Delaney's, New Castle	N	100
Delaware Breakwater, S's'x.	S	×
● Delaware City, N. Castle	N	969
● *Delaware Junc.*, N.Castle	N	×
● *Delaware River Pier*, New Castle	N	×
● Delmar, Sussex	S	360
Dinah's Corner, Kent	C	25
● *Dodd's*, Sussex	S	×
● **DOVER**, Kent	C	3,061
● *Dover Fair Grounds*, Kent	C	×
Down's Chapel, Kent	C	30
Draw Bridge, Sussex	S	140
● *Drawbridge Junction*, New Castle	N	×
Du Pont's Mills, New Castle	N	×
● *East Junction*, N. Castle	N	×
● Edgemoor, New Castle	N	822
Edgemoor Iron Works, New Castle	N	×
● Ellendale, Sussex	S	200
Elsmere, New Castle	N	×
● Farmington, Kent	C	468
● Farnhurst, New Castle	N	×
● Faukland, New Castle	N	300
● Felton, Kent	C	403
Fieldsboro, New Castle	N	60
Forest, New Castle	N	20
Fort Delaware, New Castle	N	×
● *Foster's Siding*, Kent	C	×
● Frankford, Sussex	S	519
Frederica, Kent	C	621
● **Georgetown**, Sussex	S	1,353
● *Ginn*, New Castle	N	×
● Glasgow, New Castle	N	130
● *Gordon Heights*, N. Castle	N	×
● Granogue, New Castle	N	40
● *Greenbank*, New Castle	N	×
Green Spring, New Castle	N	372
● Greenville, New Castle	N	200
● Greenwood, Sussex	S	254
Grubbs, New Castle	N	100
● *Grubbs Landing*, N.Castle	N	×
Gumborough, Sussex	S	100
Guyencourt, New Castle	N	20
● *Hagley*, New Castle	N	×
● Hareson, Sussex	S	50
Hare's Corner, New Castle	N	50
● *Harmony*, New Castle	N	×
● Harrington, Kent	C	1,400
● Hartly, Kent	C	60
● *Harvey*, New Castle	N	×
● *Hazel Dell Park*, N.Castle	N	×
Hazlettville, Kent	C	225
Henry Clay Factory, New Castle	N	829
Hickman, Kent	C	30
Highlands, New Castle	N	325
● Hockessin, New Castle	N	361
Hollandville, Kent	C	50
● Holly Oak, New Castle	N	100
Hollyville, Sussex	S	60
● Houston Station, Kent	C	250
● *Keeney*, New Castle	N	×
● *Kennett Road*, N.Castle	N	×
● Kentmere, New Castle	N	392
● Kenton, Kent	C	241
● *Kiamenski*, New Castle	N	×
● Kirkwood, New Castle	N	62
● *Landlith*, New Castle	N	×
● Laurel, Sussex	S	2,388
Lebanon, Kent	C	226
Leipsic, Kent	C	355
● Lewes, Sussex	S	1,700
● Lincoln, Sussex	S	318
Little Creek, Kent	C	285
Lowe's Cross Roads, Sussex	S	50
● *Lumbrook*, New Castle	N	×
McClellandsville, N. Castle	N	25
McDonough, New Castle	N	140
Magnolia, Kent	C	216
● Marshallton, New Castle	N	419
Masten, Kent	C	×
Mermaid, New Castle	N	50
● *Messick*, Sussex	S	×
Middleford, Sussex	S	100
● Middletown, New Castle	S	1,454
Midway, Sussex	S	25
● Milford, Kent	C	1,226
● *Mill Creek Jc.*, N. Castle	N	×
● Millsborough, Sussex	C	324
Millville, Sussex	S	200
Milton, Sussex	S	1,074
Mission, Sussex	S	50
● Montchanin, New Castle	N	50
● Mount Cuba, New Castle	N	50
● Mount Pleasant, N.Castle	N	200
● Nassau, Sussex	S	75
● Newark, New Castle	N	1,191
● *Newbridge*, New Castle	N	×
● New Castle, New Castle	N	4,010
● Newport, New Castle	N	711
Oakel, Sussex	S	25
● Oak Grove, Sussex	S	30
Ocean View, Sussex	S	160
Odessa, New Castle	N	640
Ogleton, New Castle	N	25
Omar, Sussex	S	30
Pearson's Corner, Kent	C	85
● *Pencader*, New Castle	N	×
Petersburgh, Kent	C	50
● *Pine Grove*, Kent	C	×
Pleasant Hill, New Castle	N	100
● Porters, New Castle	N	25
Port Penn, New Castle	N	310
● Redden, Sussex	S	50
Red Lion, New Castle	N	50
● Rehoboth, Sussex	S	259
● *Reybold*, New Castle	N	×
Rising Sun, Kent	C	125
● Robbins, Sussex	S	50
● Rockland, New Castle	N	410
Rodney, Sussex	S	30
● *Ross*, Sussex	S	×
Roxana, Sussex	S	500
● *Ruthby*, New Castle	N	×
Saint George's, New Castle	N	323
Sandtown, Kent	C	20
● Seaford, Sussex	S	1,462
● Selbyville, Sussex	S	254
● *Sharp's Hill*, Sussex	S	×
Shortly, Sussex	S	30
● *Shorts*, Kent	C	×
● Silverbrook, New Castle	N	×
● *Silver Slide*, New Castle	N	×
● Slaughter, Kent	C	25
Smith, Sussex	S	25
● Smyrna, Kent	C	2,455
South Milford, Sussex	S	1,339
● *Southwood*, New Castle	N	×
● Stanton, New Castle	N	279
● *Stanton Station*, N.Castle	N	×
● State Road, New Castle	N	100
● Stockley, Sussex	S	100
Summit Bridge, New Castle	N	150
Sycamore, Sussex	S	20
Talleyville, New Castle	N	100
Taylor's Bridge, New Castle	N	263
● Thompson, New Castle	N	290
Thompsonville, Kent	C	30
● Townsend, New Castle	N	387
Trinity, Sussex	S	30
● *Union Junc.*, New Castle	N	×
● *Vandyke*, New Castle	N	35
Vernon, Kent	C	40
● Viola, Kent	C	30
Waples, Sussex	S	30
Ward, Sussex	S	25
Warwick, Sussex	S	25
● *West Junc.*, New Castle	N	×
Whitesville, Sussex	S	60
Williamsville, Sussex	S	25
Willow Grove, Kent	C	110
● **WILMINGTON**, New Castle	N	61,431
● *Wilson*, New Castle	N	×
● *Winterthur*, New Castle	N	×
● Wooddale, New Castle	N	50
Woodland Sussex	S	211
● *Wood's Branch*, Sussex	S	×
● Woodside, Kent	C	100
● Wyoming, Kent	C	497
● Yorklyn, New Castle	N	150

Dist. of Columbia.

Town, County	Index	Pop.
Washington	W	230,932
● Anacostia, Washington	W	2,000
● *Anacostia Station*, Wash.	W	×
Benning, Washington	W	50
Boundary, Washington	W	×
Brightwood, Washington	W	1,000
Brookland, Washington	W	×
Brook's Station, Washt'n.	W	25
● *Deanwood*, Washington	W	×
East Capitol, Washington	W	×
Eckington, Washington	W	×
Fort Meyer, Washington	W	×
Garfield, Washington	W	×
Georgetown, Washington	W	14,046
Giesboro, Washington	W	×
Good Hope, (see Garfield)		×
● Ivy City, Washington	W	×
● *Lamond*, Washington	W	×
Le Droit Park, Washington	W	×
● *Metropolitan Junc.*, Wash	W	×
● *Mills*, Washington	W	×
Mount Pleasant, Wash't'n.	W	3,000
● *Navy Yard*, Washington	W	×
Oak Grove, (see Brightwood)		×

● *Potomac Junc.*, Wash'tn.W ×
● *Rives*, Washington....... W ×
Rosslyn, Washington...... W ×
Saint Albans, Washington. W ×
● *Shepherd*, Washington... W ×
South Washington, Wash... W ×
● *Scott's*, Washington...... W ×
Takoma Park, Washington . W ×
Tenallytown, Washington.. W 350
● Terra Cotta, Washington. W 70
Twining, Washington...... W ×
● *Union Stock Yards*, W'n W ×
● *Uniontown*, Washington. W 2,000
● *University Station*, W'n.. W ×
● **WASHINGTON**, W'n W 188,932
Washington Heights, W'n.. W ×
W. Washington, (see Georget.) ×
Winthrop Heights, W'ton... W ×

FLORIDA.

COUNTIES.	INDEX.	POP.
Alachua	N	22,934
Baker	N	3,333
Bradford	N	7,516
Brevard	S	3,401
Calhoun	NW	1,681
Citrus	S	2,394
Clay	N	5,154
Columbia	N	12,877
Dade	S	861
DeSoto	S	4,944
Duval	N	26,800
Escambia	NW	20,188
Franklin	NW	3,308
Gadsden	NW	11,894
Hamilton	N	8,507
Hernando	W	2,476
Hillsborough	C	14,941
Holmes	W	4,336
Jackson	NW	17,544
Jefferson	NW	15,757
La Fayette	N	3,686
Lake	C	8,034
Lee	S	1,414
Leon	NW	17,752
Levy	C	6,586
Liberty	NW	1,452
Madison	N	14,316
Manatee	S	2,895
Marion	C	20,796
Monroe	S	18,786
Nassau	N	8,294
Orange	C	12,584
Osceola	S	3,133
Pasco	S	4,249
Polk	C	7,905
Putnam	N	11,186
Saint John's	**N**	**8,712**
Santa Rosa	**NW**	**7,961**
Sumter	**C**	**5,368**
Suwannee	N	10,524
Taylor	C	2,122
Volusia	C	8,467
Wakulla	NW	3,117
Walton	NW	4,816
Washington	NW	6,426
Total		391,422

● Abbott, Pasco.............S 28
Aberdeen, Jackson.......NW ×
Abe's, Spring, Calhoun...NW 200
● Acme, Polk...............C ×
● *Acton*, Polk...............C 200
Add, Hernando.............W 28
● *Agnew*, Marion...........C ×
Alachua, Alachua..........N ×
Alafia, Hillsborough.........C 100
Alamo, Gadsden..........NW 240
Albion, Levy..................C ×
Alliance, Jackson........ NW ×
Alpine, Washington......NW ×
● *Altamont*, Orange.........C 200
● Altamonte Springs, Orange C ×
Alto, Sumter..................C ×
● Altoona, Lake..............C 120
Alva, Lee.....................S 15
Anastasia, Saint John's.....N ×
● Anclote, Hillsborough.... C 85
Anita, Citrus...............S ×
Ankona, Brevard............S ×
Anona, Hillsborough........C 120
● Anthony, Marion..........C 231
Apalachicola, Fr'kl'n.NW 2,727
● Apopka, Orange.......... C 490
● Arcadia, DeSoto...........S 400
● Archer, Alachua...........N 101
Argo, Pasco..................S ×
● Arglye, Walton..........NW 300
Arlington, Citrus............S 30
● *Arlington*, Duval......... N ×
● Armour, Hillsborough....C ×
● Armstrong, St. John's....N ×
● Arredonda, Alachua......N 100
Artesia, Brevard............S ×
Arthur, Lake.................C ×
Ashley, Pasco...............S ×
Ashton, Osceola............S ×
Astabula, Lake..............C 125
● Astor, Lake................C 50
● Astor Park, Lake......... C ×
Athens, Clay..................N ×
● *Athens*, Clay...............N ×
Atwater, Manatee...........S ×
● Auburndale, Polk..........C 125
● Aucilla, Jefferson...... NW 216
● Aurantia, Brevard........ S 50
● *Avenue*, Marion...........C ×
Averill, Brevard.............S ×
● Avoca, Hamilton...........N ×
Avon Park, De Soto..........S 18
● *Bache's Mill*, Suwannee..N ×
Bagdad, Santa Rosa...... NW 523
● *Bakersburg*, Volusia......C ×
● Baker's Mill, Hamilton....N 85
● *Bald Hill*, Suwannee.....N ×
● Baldwin, Duval.............N 250
● *Bamboo*, Sumter..........C 45
Banana, Putnam.............N ×
Bannerville, Putnam........N ×
● Barberville, Volusia...... C 125
Barco, Levy...................C ×
Barkers, Holmes.........NW ×
Barsville, Columbia........ N 25
● **Bartow**, Polk..............C 1,386
● Bartow Junction, Polk... C ×
Bartow Junction, Duval....N ×
Bascom, Jackson.........NW 150
Bass, Brevard................S ×
● Bayard, Duval..............N 30
● Bay City, Hernando......W 40
Bayhill, Sumter..............C ×
Bay Point, Santa Rosa...NW ×
Bay Port, Hernando.........W ×
Bay Ridge, Orange..........C ×
Bay View, Hillsborough.....C 160
Baywood, Putnam...........N ×
Beauclerc, Duval.............N 125
Beaufort, Taylor.............N ×
● *Belair*, Leon.................NW ×
● *Bella'reva*, Lake...........C ×
Bells Mill, Columbia........N ×
● Bellview, Marion............C 130
Bellville, Hamilton. ....N 75
Belmont, Hamilton...........N 75
Belmore, Clay.................N 85
Benedict, Marion.............C 75
Ben Haden, Wakulla.....NW ×
Benton, Columbia ....N 145
● *Bents*, Orange..............C ×
● Beresford, Volusia ....C 85
Berrydale, Santa Rosa....NW ×
Bethel, Walton...........NW 350
● *Big Cypress*, Pasco.........S ×
● *Big Cypress*, Orange..... C ×
Bilory, Santa Rosa ....NW ×
Bird Island, Saint John's...N ×
● *Birds*, Lake..................C ×
● *Bishop's Grove*, Marion...C ×
Blackman, Santa Rosa....NW ×
● *Black Point*, Duval.........N ×
Blackwater, (see Bagdad).... ×
Blanche, Polk 13
● Blanton, Pasco..............S ×
Blitchton, Marion............C ×
Bloomfield, Lake.............C 200
Bloomingdale, Hillsborough C 250
Blount's Ferry, Columbia...N 125
Blountstown, Calhoun NW ×
Bloxham, Leon.............NW ×
Blue Spring, Marion ....C ×
Blue Springs, Lake...........C ×
● Bluff Springs, Escambia NW 100
● Boardman, Marion..........C 18
Boggy Creek, Orange........C ×
● *Bohemia*, Escambia ....NW ×
● *Bohemia*, Santa Rosa...NW ×
● *Bond's Mill*, Volusia......C ×
● Bonifay, Holmes ....NW 200
● *Bonnie Burn*, Orange ....C ×
● *Bookers*, Hillsborough....C ×
● Bostwick, Putnam.........N 90
● Boulogne, Nassau ....N 130
● *Bowden*, Duval.............N ×
● Bowling Green, De Soto ..S 35
Boyd, Marion...................C ×
Bradfordville, Leon ......NW 20
Braiden Town, Manatee.S 200
● Brandon, Hillsborough ...C ×
● *Brandy Branch*, Nassau. N ×
● Branford, Suwannee......N 835
Brantley, Brevard............S ×
Bravaldo, Suwannee.........N ×
● Brent, Escambia ....NW ×
Bridge Creek, Jackson...NW ×
Bridgeport, Putnam.........N ×
● *Briggs*, Volusia ....C ×
Bristol, Liberty.........NW 50
● **Brinson**, Levy ....C 291
● Brooklyn, Clay ....N ×
Brooklyn, Duval...............N ×
● *Brooklyn Lake*, Clay .....N ×
● **Brooksville**, Hernando W 512
Broward, Duval ....N ×
Brown, Columbia..............N ×
● ***Bryansville***, **Polk.........C** **23**
Bryceville, Nassau.........N 150
Buckhorn, Calhoun...... NW ×
● *Bucki Junction*, Suwannee N ×
Buckinham, Lee............ S ×
Buda, Orange.................. C ×
Buena Esparanza. St. John's N ×
● *Buena Vista*, St. John's.. N ×
● Buffalo Bluff, Putham....N ×
Burlington, Suwannee......N ×
● *Burnside Beach*, Duval.. N ×
● Bushnell, Sumter..........C ×
● Callahan, Nassau......... N 100
● Calvinia, De Soto.......... S ×
Camden, Marion............C ×
Campbell, Osceola............S 15
Campbellton, Jackson....NW 250
Camp Pinckney, Nassau....N ×
● Campville, Alachua.......N 275
Canaveral, Brevard..........S 13
● Candler, Marion........... C 125
● Cantonment, Escambia. NW ×
Carlson, Sumter............ C ×
Carmell, Pasco................S ×
Carrabelle, Franklin..... NW 482
Carterville, Saint John's....N ×
● Caryville, Washington..NW 350
● Cason, Lake..................C ×
Cassia, Lake...................C 125
Castalia, De Soto.............S 40
● *Cedar Hammock*, Sumpter C ×
● Cedar Keys, Levy......... C 1,600
Cedarville, La Fayette......N ×
● Centre Hill, Sumter.......C 87
● *Centre Park*, Duval.......N ×
Centreville, Leon.......... NW 75
● **Cerro Gordo**, Holmes NW 360
Chaffin, (see Mullligan)....... ×
● Chaires, Leon............NW 20
Charleston, Suwannee.......N ×
● *Charlie Apopka*, De Soto..S ×
Charlotte Harbor, De Soto...S 200
Chaseville, Duval.............N ×
● Chattahoochee, Gads'n .NW 383
● *Chattahoochee River*, Jackson...........................NW ×
Cheevertown, Baker........N ×
Cherry Hill, Polk..............C 20
Cherry Lake, Madison......N 20
Chester, Nassau.............N 100
● *Chetwynd*, Lake...........C ×
Chicora, Polk.................C ×
Chiefland, Levy...............C ×
● Chipco, Pasco................S 100
● Chipley, Washington...NW 854
Chipley Sta., (see Chipley)... ×
Chipola, Calhoun..........NW 25
Chuluota, Orange........... C 120
Chumuckla, Santa Rosa..NW 60
Churchill, Marion............C ×
Cincinnati, Polk..............C ×
● Citra, Marion.............. C 387
● Citronelle Citrus.......... S ×
City Point, Brevard......... S 125
● Clarcona, Orange......... C ×
Clarksville, Marion......... C ×
● *Clarksville*, Saint John's..N ×
Clay Springs, Orange.........C ×
● Clear Water Harbor, Hillsborough............................C 600

● Clermont, Lake...C 125
● Cleveland, De Soto...S 40
Clifton, Brevard...S ×
Clifton, Orange...C ×
Clinch, Clay...N ×
● *Clydes*, Orange...C ×
Coatsville, Holmes...NW ×
Cocoa, Brevard...S 312
Cocoanut Grove, Dade...S 87
Coe's Mills, Liberty...NW ×
● *Colegrove*, Putnam...N 10
● Coleman, Sumter...C 48
Collina, Marion...C 85
● Columbia, Columbia...N ×
● *Columbus*, Suwannee...N ×
● *Como*, Putnam...N ×
● Conant, Lake...C 125
Concord, Gadsden...NW 100
● Cone, Putnam...N 100
Conner, Marion...C ×
Conway, Orange...C 30
Coquina, Brevard...S ×
Cora, Santa Rosa...NW ×
● *Cork*, Hillsborough...C 20
Corleys, Lake...C ×
Cortez, Manatee...S ×
Cosmo, Duval...N ×
● Cottondale, Jackson...NW 200
Cotton Plant, Marion...C 90
● *Couper*, Hernando...W ×
Courtney, Brevard...S ×
● *Cow Creek*, Volusia...C ×
Cow Pen Branch, St. John's N ×
Crandall, Nassau...N 60
● *Crawford*, Nassau...N 48
Crawfordville, Wak'la NW 200
● Crescent City, Putnam...N 554
● *Crescent City Landing*, Putnam...N ×
● Crestview, Walton...NW 200
Crewsville, DeSoto...S 20
Cromanton, Calhoun...NW ×
● *Cross Bayou*, Hillsbor'gh C ×
● Crown Point, Orange...C ×
● Crow's Bluff, Lake...C ×
● Crystal River, Citrus...S 208
● *Cummings*, Lake...C ×
● *Cunningham's*, Lake...C ×
Curtis Mills, Wakulla...N 52
Cutler, Dade...S 90
● Cypress, Jackson...N 20
Czar, Calhoun...N 45
● **Dade City**, Pasco...S 321
● *Dahoma*, Nassau...N 48
Dallas, Marion...C ×
Danceville, Suwannee...N ×
● Davenport, Polk...C 35
● *Dayerville*, Alachua...N ×
● Daytona, Volusia...C 771
Dead Man's Bay, LaFayette N 30
● *Dean*, Suwannee...N ×
● *Deerland*, Walton...NW ×
● **DeFuniakSprings**, Walton...MW 672
Dekle, Bradford...N ×
● DeLand, Volusia...C 1,113
● *DeLand Junction*, Volusia C ×
● *DeLand Landing*, Lake...C ×
● *Delaware*, Hernando...W ×
● DeLeon Springs, Volusia...C 235
Dellwood, Jackson...NW 35
Delphos, Hernando...W ×
Denaud, Lee...S ×
● Denver, Putnam...N ×
Derby, Marion...C ×
DeSoto, Hillborough...C 25
● *Dinner Island*, St. John's N ×
● Dinsmore, Duval...N ×
Diston, Pasco...S 25
Disston City, Hillsborough...C 15
Dixon, Santa Rosa...NW ×
● Dover, Hillsborough...C 100
● *Dragem Jc.*, Sumter...C 60
Drayton Island, Putnam...N 90
● *Drews*, Columbia...N ×
● Drexel, Pasco...S 15
● Drifton, Jefferson...NW 20
Drummond, Alachua...N ×
Duette, Manatee...S ×
Duke, St. John's...N ×
● Dunnedin, Hillsborough...C 200
● Dunnellon, Marion...C 532
Dunster, Marion...C ×
● *Durbin*, St. John's...N ×
● Dutton, Nassau...N 18
● Duval, Duval...N ×
● Dyall, Nassau...N ×

● Eagle Lake, Polk...C ×
● *Eagle Lake*, Sumter...C ×
Eagle Mines, Marion...C ×
Ealum, Walton...NW ×
Earlton, Alachua...N ×
Early Bird, Marion...C ×
Earnestville, Pasco...S 87
East Apopka, Orange...C ×
● *East Cove*, Hillsborough...C ×
East Jacksonville, Duval...N ×
● Eastlake, Marion...C 18
● *East Palatka*, Putnam...N ×
East Sharon, Clay...N ×
● *Eaton*, Duval...N ×
Eatonville, Orange...C ×
Eau Gallie, Brevard...S 88
Econfina, Washington...NW 35
Eden, Brevard...S 60
● *Edgewood*, Duval...N ×
Edwards, Gadsden...NW ×
Egleston, Duval...N ×
● Ehren, Pasco...S ×
● *Eichelberger*, Marion...C ×
Eldora, Volusia...C 48
● Eldorado, Lake...C ×
● Eldridge, Volusia...C ×
Electra, Marion...C ×
● Ellaville, Madison...N 800
Ellenton, Manatee...S 20
● Ellerslie, Pasco...S 32
Elliston, Citrus...S ×
● Ellzey, Levy...C 100
● *Ellsworth Jc.*, Lake...C ×
Elmwood, Marion...C ×
Emeralda, Lake...C ×
Emerson, Suwannee...N ×
● Emporia, Volusia...C 150
Englewood, Orange...C ×
Enos, Brevard...S ×
● **Enterprise**, Volusia...C 250
● *Enterprise Junc.*, Volusia C ×
Erie, Manatee...S ×
Escambia, Escambia...NW 100
● *Escambia*, Santa Rosa...NW 150
Estiffanulga, Liberty...NW ×
● Ethel, Lake...C ×
Ethel, Orange...C ×
Etoniah, Putnam...N 60
Euchee Anna, Walton...NW 125
Eureka, Marion...C 300
● Eustis, Lake...C 800
Evergreen, Nassau...N 17
● Evinston, Alachua...N 15
Exeter, Lake...C 70
● Fairbanks, Alachua...N 150
Fairfield, Duval...N ×
Fairmount, Citrus...S 20
Fair Oaks, Orange...C ×
Fairview, Marion...C ×
● *Fakes*, Marion...C ×
Fannin, Levy...C ×
Fantville, Marion...C 18
Farmdale, Calhoun...NW ×
● *Fatio*, Volusia...C ×
● Favorita, St. John's...N
Fayetteville, LaFayette...N ×
Federal Hill, Clay...N ×
Federal Point, Putnam...N 200
Fellowship, Marion...C 30
● **Fernandina**, Nassau...N 2,803
● *Ferrell*, Leon...NW ×
Ferry Pass, Escambia...NW 240
Fidelis, Santa Rosa...NW ×
Figulus, Dade...S ×
● *Finger's Mill*, Alachua...N ×
● *Fitzgerald*, Hernando...W ×
● Fitzhugh, Polk...C ×
Fitzville, Orange...C ×
Flagler, Suwannee...N ×
● *Fleming*, Clay...N ×
Flemington, Marion...C 100
Floral Bluff, Duval...N ×
Floral City, Citrus...S 50
Floraville, DeSoto...S ×
Florence, St. John's...N 300
Floridelphi, Hillsborough...C ×
Fogartyville, Manatee...S 100
Folsom, Jackson...NW 30
● Forest City, Orange...C 200
● Formosa, Orange...C ×
Forrest, LaFayette...N ×
Forshala, Leon...NW ×
Fort Barranca, Escambia NW ×
Fort Brook, Hillsborough...C 448
Fort Call, Bradford...N ×
Fort Clinch, Nassau...N ×
Fort Drum, Brevard...S ×

Fort Eagle, Suwannee...N 17
Fort Fanning, Levy...C 20
Fort Gadsden, Franklin...NW ×
Fort Gates, Putnam...N ×
Fort George, Duval...N 125
Fort Green, DeSoto...S 240
Fort Lauderdale, Dade...S ×
Fort McCoy, Marion...C ×
● Fort Mason, Lake...C 125
● Fort Meade, Polk...C 267
Fort Myers, Lee...S 575
● Fort Ogden, DeSoto...S 500
Fort Pierce, Brevard...S ×
Fort Reed, Orange...C 298
● Fort White, Columbia...N 376
Foster Park, Marion...C 50
● Francis, Putnam...N 200
Frankland, Alachua...N 40
● *Franklin's*, Lake...S ×
Freedman's Forest, Suwannee...N ×
Freeport, Walton...NW 200
Fruit Cove, St. John's...N 90
Fruitland Park, Lake...C ×
Fulton, Duval...N 200
Gabriella, Orange...C ×
● Gainesboro, Orange...C 60
● **Gainesville**, Alachua...N 2,790
Galter, Marion...C ×
● Galt, Santa Rosa...NW ×
Garden Park, Marion...C ×
Garfield, Volusia...C ×
Geneva, Orange...C 300
● Genoa, Hamilton...N ×
Georgetown, Putnam...N 300
Georgiana, Brevard...S 80
● Gilmore, Duval...N ×
Glen Alice, Sumter...C ×
● *Glencoe*, Volusia...C 100
● *Glendale*, Lake...C 225
● Glen Ethel, Orange...C ×
● *Glen Park*, Suwannee...N ×
● Glen St. Mary, Baker...N 125
● Glenwood, Volusia...C ×
Godwin, Pasco...S ×
Goldsborough, Orange...C ×
Golden Rod, Orange...C ×
Gomez, Dade...S ×
● *Gonzales*, Santa Rosa...NW ×
● *Good Range*, Santa Rosa NW ×
● *Gordon's*, Marion...C ×
● *Gordonsville*, Polk...C ×
● *Gore*, Levy...C 85
Goshen, Brevard...S ×
Gotha, Orange...S ×
Goulding, Escambia...NW ×
Graceville, Jackson...NW 65
Gracy, Alachua...N ×
Grahamsville, Marion...C 150
● *Granada*, Orange...C ×
● Grandin, Putnam...N ×
● Grand Island, Lake...C ×
Grand Ridge, Jackson...NW ×
● *Grand View*, Lake...C ×
● *Grange*, Brevard...S ×
Grant, Brevard...S ×
● Grasmere, Orange...C 120
● **Green Cove Springs**, Clay...N 1,196
● Greenland, Duval...N 60
● *Greenleaf*, Marion...C ×
Green Pond, Polk...C ×
● Greenville, Madison...N 360
Greenwood, Jackson...NW 350
Grove City, DeSoto...S ×
Grove Park, Alachua...N 70
Grover, Suwannee...N ×
Guilford, Bradford...N ×
Gulf Hammock, Levy...C 100
Gulf City, Hillsborough...C 90
Gulf Junction, Marion...C ×
Gulf Key, Pasco...S 22
Habana, Suwannee...N ×
● *Hagen*, Columbia...N ×
● Hague, Alachua...N 295
● Haines City, Polk...C 300
Halifax, Volusia...C ×
Hambro, Citrus...S ×
Hamburgh, Madison...N 55
Hamilton, Hamilton...N 15
● Hammock, Alachua...N ×
● *Hammond*, Volusia...C ×
● Hampton, Bradford...N 200
Hansontown, Duval...N ×
Harbor View, DeSoto...S ×
Hardeeville, Brevard...S ×
Harlem, Putnam...N ×

Harmony, Madison.........N	×
● *Harpersville*, Orange..... C	×
● *Harris Grove*, Marion.... C	×
Harrison, Washington....NW	×
Hartland, Brevard.......... S	×
● Hart's Road, Nassau......N	60
● *Hart's Road Jc.*, Nassau.N	×
Harvard, Marion............C	55
Harwood, Volusia...........C	15
Harwood Station, Volusia.. C	×
● Haskell, Polk.............C	18
● Hastings, St. John's...... N	×
Hatch's Bend, LaFayette...N	45
Hattysburg, Suwanne......N	×
● *Haulover*, Brevard........ S	120
Havana, Gadsden.........NW	×
Hawk's Park, Volusia.......C	140
● Hawthorn, Alachua.......N	500
● *Haye's*, Marion........... C	×
Haywood, Jackson....... NW	300
Heath, Brevard.............. S	×
Heidtville, Marion...........C	35
● *Helena*, Lake............ C	145
Helena, DeSoto............ S	×
Herlong, Columbia......... N	×
Hermitage, Gadsden......NW	×
Hernando, Citrus............S	60
Hibernia, Clay..............N	15
Higdon, Madison........... N	×
● *Higginbotham*, Nassau.. N	×
● Highland, Clay............N	258
Highland, Orange...........C	×
● Highland Park, Volusia...C	×
● High Springs, Alachua....N	100
Higley, Lake............... C	100
● Hilliard, Nassau.......... N	300
● *Hirtzel*, Osceola...........S	×
Hiwassee, Orange...........C	×
Hogarth's Land., St. John'sN	×
Holland, Leon............NW	×
● Hollister, Putnam.........N	200
● Holly Hill, Volusia........C	×
Holmes, Holmes..........NW	120
● Holt, Santa Rosa....... NW	40
● *Holy Branch*, St. John's..N	×
● Homeland, Polk.......... C	40
Homosassa, Citrus.......... S	30
Hooker's Prairie, Polk......C	×
Hopedale, Suwannee........N	×
Hope Sound, Dade.......... S	×
Horse Creek, (see Davenport)	×
Horsehead, Walton.......NW	×
Horti, Brevard...............S	×
Hoskins, Columbia......... N	×
● Houston, Suwannee.......N	50
Hudnal, Putnam............N	×
Hudson, Pasco.............. S	15
● *Hudson on the Suwannee*, Suwannee .... N	×
● Hull, DeSoto...............S	×
Hunters Hill, Hernando....W	×
Huntingdon, Putnam........N	×
● *Huntingdon*, Putnam.... N	300
● *Hutton's Mills*, Volusia...C	×
Hypoluxo, Dade..............S	×
Iamonia, Leon............NW	50
Idalia, Leon.............. NW	×
Iddo, Taylor.................N	×
Idlewild, Duval.............N	×
Irmi, Hamilton..............N	×
● *Indiana*, Sumter.......... C	×
Indian Mound, Duval..... N	×
Indianola, Brevard..........S	×
Indian Springs, Lake.........C	400
● Inglehame, Nassau........N	×
● Inter Lachen, Putnam....N	207
● *Intersection*, Orange......C	×
Inverness, Citrus............S	25
Inwood, Jackson.........NW	×
Iola, Calhoun.............NW	100
Ionia, Clay... ....N	50
Island, Osceola..............S	×
● Island Grove, Alachua....N	60
● Island Lake, Orange...... C	100
Istachatta, Hernando.......W	50
● *Italia*, Nassau............N	120
Ivanhoe, Leon..............N	×
Izagora, Holmes..........NW	50
Jack Mound, St. John's....N	×
● **Jacksonville**, Duval.. N	17,201
Jacksonville Junc., Duval..N	×
Jaffery, Volusia..............C	×
● *Jane Jay*, Polk...........C	×
Jasminola, Duval.......... N	×
● **Jasper**, Hamilton........N	300
Jennings, Hamilton........ N	30
Jennings, Suwannee........N	×

Florida

● *Jennings Sta.*, Hamilton..N	×
Jensen, Brevard............ S	×
Jessamine, Pasco............S	×
Jessup, Orange..............C	×
Jewell, Dade.................S	×
● *John's Branch*, Alachua. N	×
● Johnson, Putnam..........N	40
Johnson's Pond, Levy...... C	×
John's Pass, Hillsborough...C	100
Joiner's, Orange............ C	×
Jolly Bay, Walton........NW	×
Jonesville, Alachua..........N	45
Judson, Levy.................C	20
● *Juliette*, Marion........... C	×
● *Junction*, Clay............N	×
Juno, Dade...................S	×
Jupiter, Dade.................S	×
● Kanapaha, Alachua...... N	×
● Kathleen, Polk............C	25
Keaton, Taylor..............N	**×**
Keene, Hillsborough........C	×
Kelly, Osceola................S	×
Kelly, Duval.................N	×
Kendrick, Marion............C	×
● Keuka, Putnam.......... N	×
Keystone Hillsborough......C	15
Keystone Park, HillsboroughC	35
● *Keystone Park*, Pasco....S	×
Keysville, Hilsborough......C	30
Key West, Monroe........S	18,080
● Killarney, Orange.........C	×
Kings's Ferry, Nassau......N	260
Kingsley, Clay............. N	240
King's Road, Duval........N	×
● *Kingston*, Volusia.........C	×
Kinney, Putnam.............N	×
Kismet, Lake.............. C	50
● **Kissimmee**, Osceola....S	1,086
● *Knights*, Hillsborough....C	×
Knox Hill, Walton........NW	×
● Lacoochee, Pasco..........S	15
● LaCrosse, Alachua.........N	300
● Lady Lake, Lake..........C	250
● LaGrange, Brevard........S	85
Lake Ashby, Volusia........C	×
Lake Bird, Taylor...........N	18
● *Lake Brantley*, Orange... C	×
● **Lake Butler**, Bradford N	240
Lake Charm, Orange........C	×
● **Lake City**, Columbia...N	2,020
● *Lake City Jc.*, Columbia..N	×
● Lake Como, Putnam.......N	200
Lake George, Putnam.......N	200
● Lake Helen, Volusia...... C	90
Lake Howell, Orange....... C	×
Lake Iamonia, Leon..... NW	100
● *Lake Jessup*, Orange......C	120
Lake Joe, Taylor.............N	18
Lake Kerr, Marion...........C	50
Lake Kerr, Putnam......... N	75
● Lakeland, Polk........... C	552
● *Lake Loche*, Polk......... C	30
Lake Mable, Orange........ C	×
● Lake Maitland, Orange....C	400
● Lake Mary, Orange C	×
Lakemont, Orange...........C	×
Lake Newnan, Alachua.... N	×
● Lake Ogden, Columbia... N	×
Lakeside, Clay.............. N	120
● Lakeview, Clay............N	×
● Lakeville, Orange..........C	200
Lake Weir, Marion...........C	480
Lake Worth, Dade............S	100
Lamont, Jefferson........NW	100
Lamp, Calhoun............NW	×
● *Lancaster*, Lake.......... C	×
● Lane Park, Lake...........C	50
● Lanier, Lake..............C	100
● Largo, Hillsborough.......C	32
● *La Villa Junction*, Duval N	×
● *Lawrence*, Leon........NW	×
● Lawtey, Bradford.........N	200
Lebanon, Levy.............. C	×
Lecanto, Citrus..............S	200
● Lee, Madison............. N	50
● Leesburgh, Lake..........C	722
● Leitner, Marion............C	60
Leland, Madison............N	×
● *Lellman's* Hillsborough...C	×
● Lenard, Pasco..............S	20
Leno, Columbia............ N	14
Leroy, Marion.............. C	×
● Lesley, Hillsborough......C	×
Leton, Hamilton.............N	×
Levyville, Levy..............C	100
Light House, Brevard.......S	×

Florida

Limestone, Walton....... NW	120
● Limona, Hillsborough.....C	25
● Linden, Sumter...........C	×
● Lisbon, Lake..............C	125
Litesville, Bradford........ N	×
Littlé River, Suwannee..... N	90
● **Live Oak**, Suwannee...N	687
● Liverpool, DeSoto.........S	50
● Livingston, Orange........C	×
● Lloyd, Jefferson........NW	300
● Lochloosa, Alachua.......N	60
● *Lockhart's Mill*, Orange..C	×
Lockwood, Orange.......... C	900
● *Lofton*, Nassau........... N	×
Loland, Putnam.............N	×
Long Branch, Duval........N	×
Longview, Jackson.......NW	×
● Longwood, Orange........C	57
● *Lord's*, Orange............C	×
Louisville, Suwannee.......N	×
● Lowell, Marion........... C	×
Loyce, Pasco................ S	×
● Lulu, Columbia.......... N	×
● *Lundy*, Putnam..........N	×
Luraville, Suwannee........N	90
Lynne, Marion.............. C	150
McAlpin, Suwannee. ....N	15
● *McCain*, Marion..........C	×
● *McClenny*, Baker.........N	334
McCrab, LaFayette......... N	20
● McDavid, Escambia....NW	50
● *McDonald's*, Orange......C	×
● *McDonald's Saw Mill*, Marion........................ C	×
● McIntosh, Marion.........C	×
● *McKinnon*, Orange...... C	×
● McMeekin, Putnam...... N	120
McRae, Clay................N	200
● *McRea's Mill*, Alachua...N	×
● **Macclenny**, Baker.....N	334
Mackinnon, Orange.........C	×
● Macon, Pasco..............S	85
● **Madison**, Madison......N	781
Magdalene, Hillsborough....C	×
● *Magnolia Grove*, St. John'sN	×
● Magnolia Springs, Clay...N	×
● *Maitland*, Orange.........C	400
Malabar, Brevard........... S	90
Maltese, DeSoto.............S	30
Manatee, Manatee...........S	289
Mandarin, Duval............N	1,100
● Mango, Hillsborough......C	20
Mannfield, Citrus,........ S	30
● Manville, Putnam........ N	100
Marco, Lee..................S	15
Margaretta, Hamilton......N	×
● **Marianna**, Jackson..NW	926
● Marietta, Duval...........N	33
● Marion, Hamilton ....N	200
● Markham, Orange........ C	×
Marshville, Marion..........C	×
Martel, Marion..............C	×
● Martin, Marion........... C	25
Mary Esther, Santa Rosa. NW	75
Marysville, Calhoun...... NW	48
● Mascotte, Lake............C	×
● Massacre, Sumter.........C	60
Matanzas, St. John's........N	60
Maudville, LaFayette...... N	×
● *Maxville*, Duval..........N	×
Maxville, Washington.... NW	30
Mayo, LaFayette............N	40
● Mayport, Duval...........N	294
● *Maytown*, Volusia...... .C	×
Medulla, Polk............. C	300
Melbourne, Brevard.........S	99
Melrose, Alachua.......... N	267
Melvin, Hamilton.......... N	×
● *Mercers*, Suwannee...... N	×
● *Meredith's*, Levy..........C	×
● *Merrifield*, St. John's.....N	×
Merrimack, Orange.........C	45
Merritt, Brevard...........S	**120**
Messina, Lake...............C	×
● *Mexico*, Pasco........... S	×
Miakka, Manatee............S	150
Miami, Dade.............. S	125
● Micanopy, Alachua.......N	494
● *Micanopy Junc.*, AlachuaN	×
Micco, Brevard..............S	25
Miccosukee, Leon........ NW	100
Middleburgh, Clay..........N	217
● *Middleton*, St. John's.... N	×
Midland, Polk...............C	20
Midway, Gadsden.........NW	90
Mikesville, Columbia....... N	160

Place, County, Section	
Miller's Ferry, Wash'ton. NW	100
● *Miller's Mill*, Alachua.... N	×
Millerton, Hillsborough..... C	×
● *Millerton*, Orange......... C	×
● Milligan, Santa Rosa... NW	×
● Millview, Escambia.... NW	400
● **Milton**, Santa Rosa... NW	1,455
● *Milwood*, Marion.......... C	×
● Mims, Brevard........... S	×
● Minneola, Lake........... C	200
● *Minorville*, Orange....... C	×
● Mohawk, Lake........... N	×
● Molino, Escambia...... NW	100
● *Monroe*, Orange......... C	×
● Montague, Marion........ C	100
● Monclair, Lake........... C	250
Monte Vista, Lake......... C	×
● **Monticello**, Jefferson NW	1,218
● Montverde, Lake.......... C	×
● *Moody's Mill*, Levy....... C	×
● Moore, Polk.............. C	×
Morganton, Lee............ S	28
Morganville, Marion........ C	×
Mortonhurst, Brevard....... S	×
Moseley Hall, Madison...... N	×
Moss Bluff, Marion.......... C	50
● Mossy Head, Walton... NW	×
Motto, Dade............... S	×
Moultrie, St. John's......... N	300
● *Mount Carril*, Suwannee. N	×
● Mount Dora, Lake........ C	200
● *Mount Homer*, Lake...... C	×
Mount Lee, Citrus.......... S	×
Mounteocha, Alachua...... N	×
● Mt. Pleasant, Gadsden. NW	100
Mount Tabor, Columbia.... N	115
● *Mount Tabor*, Marion.... C	×
● *Muscogee*, Escambia... NW	200
Myers, Lee................. S	400
Mykka, DeSoto............. S	×
Naples, Lee .... S	×
Narcoossee, Osceola......... S	×
Narrows, Brevard........... S	50
Nashua, Putnam............ N	120
Natural Bridge, Walton.. NW	45
Neal's Landing, Jackson.. NW	125
Nebo, Bradford............. N	×
● Neoga, St. John's......... N	×
● Nesbitt, Duval............ N	×
New Augustine, St. John's.. N	553
New Berlin, Duval.......... N	175
Newburg, Clay............. N	×
● *New Branford*, Suwannee N	200
Newburn, Suwannee....... N	×
New Cadiz, Hillsborough... C	×
Newlan, Suwannee......... N	×
Newman's Lake, Alachua.. N	200
● Newnansville, Alachua... N	×
Newport, Wakulla .... NW	×
● New River, Bradford..... N	×
● New Smyrna, Volusia..... C	287
New Troy, LaFayette.... N	75
● *New Upsala*, Orange..... C	×
● Nocatee, DeSoto......... S	35
Nora, Santa Rosa......... NW	×
● *Norris Siding*, Volusia... C	×
● *N. Branch Jc.* St. John's N	×
North Citra, Duval........ N	×
Norvella, Clay.............. N	15
Norwalk, Putnam........... N	250
Norway, Gadsden........ NW	×
Nutter, Suwannee.......... N	×
Oakdale, Citrus............. S	25
Oak Grove, Santa Rosa... NW	50
Oak Hill, Volusia........... C	240
● Oakland, Orange.......... C	73
● Oak Lawn, Dade.......... S	×
● *Oakside*, Putnam......... N	×
Oak Villa, Putnam.......... N	60
● Obrine Station, Suwannee N	200
● **Ocala**, Marion........... C	2,904
Ocheesee, Calhoun....... NW	×
Ochesse, Jackson......... NW	50
● Ocklawaha, Marion....... C	150
Ocklocknee, Leon......... NW	×
Ocoee, Orange.............. C	360
Octahatchee, Hamilton..... N	×
● *Odessa*, Pasco............ S	×
● *Ogden*, Columbia......... N	×
● Okahumpka, Lake......... S	×
Old Town, LaFayette....... N	250
● Olive, Escambia........ NW	×
● *Oliver Park*, Alachua..... N	×
Olustee, Baker............. N	25
Oneco, Manatee............ S	×
● *Onoro*, Orange........... C	×
Orange, Liberty.......... NW	20
● Orange Bend, Lake....... C	800
Orange Bluff, Nassau....... N	×
● Orange City, Volusia...... C	500
● *Orange City Junc.*, Volusia C	×
Orange Dale, St. John's.... N	200
● Orange Heights, Alachua. N	100
Orange Hill, Washington. NW	×
● Orange Home, Sumter.... C	45
● Orange Lake, Marion...... C	100
Orange Mills, Putnam...... N	85
● Orange Park, Clay....... N	228
Orange Springs, Marion..... C	100
Orchid, Brevard............ S	×
Oriana, Volusia............ C	120
● *Orient*, Hillsborough...... C	×
● Oriole, Hernando......... W	50
● **Orlando**, Orange........ C	2,856
Orleans, Citrus............. S	12
● Ormond, Volusia.......... C	239
● *Ormond, Junction*, Volusia C	×
Oscar, Santa Rosa....... NW	×
Osceola, Alachua........... N	×
Osprey, Manatee............ S	60
● Osteen, Volusia.......... C	45
Otahite, Santa Rosa...... NW	×
● Otter Creek, Levy......... C	25
● Oviedo, Orange........... C	53
Owens, DeSoto............. S	90
● Owensboro, Pasco........ S	×
● *Owl City*, Suwannee...... N	×
● Oxford, Sumter........... C	200
● Ozona, Hillsborough...... C	200
● Pablo Beach, Duval...... N	237
Padlock, Suwannee.......... N	10
Paisley, Lake............... C	10
● **Palatka**, Putnam........ N	3,039
Palatka Heights, Putnam.. N	454
Palermo, St. John's........ N	×
Palestine, Bradford........ N	×
Palma Sola, Manatee........ S	300
Palm Beach, Dade.......... S	12
● Palmer, Alachua......... N	75
Palmetto, Manatee.......... S	224
● Palm Springs, Orange.... C	×
Panama Park, Duval....... N	×
● Panasoffkee, Sumter...... C	75
● Paola, Orange............ C	200
Paradise, Alachua.......... N	120
Parish, Manatee............ S	85
Parker, Washington...... NW	×
Parkersburg, Marion....... C	×
● *Park Place*, Citrus....... S	×
● Pasadena, Pasco.......... S	34
● *Pasco*, Pasco............ S	×
Patterson, Putnam......... N	×
● *Pattersonville*, Putnam.. N	×
Paxton, Hamilton.......... N	×
Payne, Columbia........... N	×
Pedrick, Pasco............. S	×
Pedro, Marion............ C	×
Pelot, Hillsborough......... C	×
● Pemberton, Sumter....... C	200
● *Pemberton's Ferry*, Hernando.................. W	10
● Penial, Putnam.......... N	×
Penn, Putnam.............. N	20
● **Pensacola**, Escambia NW	11,750
Pensacola Navy Yard, Escambia............... NW	×
● Peoria, Clay............. N	×
Perico, Manatee........... S	×
Perry, Taylor............ N	100
Peru, Hillsborough......... C	250
Pettway, Jackson........ NW	×
● *Pharr*, Polk............ C	×
● Phillips, Duval.......... N	565
Phoenix, Alachua......... N	40
Phosphate, DeSoto......... S	×
● Phosphoria, Polk......... C	×
● *Pickett*, Duval........... N	×
Picnic, Hillsborough....... C	×
Picolata, St. John's........ N	94
● *Piedmont*, Orange........ C	×
● Pierson, Volusia......... C	×
Pineaway, Walton........ NW	×
● Pine Barren, Escambia. NW	100
● Pinecastle, Orange....... C	250
● *Pine Crest*, Orange C	×
● **Pine Level**, DeSoto..... S	250
Pinellas, Hillsborough....... C	200
● Pinemount, Suwannee.... N	200
Pinesville, Alachua........ N	×
Pinhook, Jefferson....... NW	48
● Pittman, Lake........... C	120
● *Pittsburgh*, Duval........ N	×
● Plant City, Hillsborough.. C	349
● *Platt's*, Lake............. C	×
Plummer's, Duval.......... N	×
● Plymouth, Orange........ C	120
Point Washington, Wash. NW	50
Polish, Polk............... C	30
● *Polly's Mill*, Marion...... C	×
● Pomona, Putnam......... N	48
Ponceaunah, Lake......... C	×
● Ponce de Leon, Holmes NW	150
Ponce Park, Volusia........ C	45
Poplarhead, Calhoun..... NW	×
Port Jackson, Jackson... NW	×
Portland, Walton......... NW	600
Port Orange, Volusia........ C	400
Port Richey, Pasco......... S	×
● Port Tampa, Hillsborough C	278
Port Tampa City, Duval... N	×
Potolo, Holmes........... NW	×
● *Powells*, Duval.......... N	×
Powellton, (see Cantonment).	×
● *Prairie Creek*, Alachua.. N	×
President City, Putnam.... N	×
○ *Princeville*, Duval........ N	×
Providence, Bradford....... N	200
● Punta Gorda, DeSoto...... S	262
Punta Rassa, Lee........... S	25
● Putnam Hall, Putnam... N	40
● **Quincy**, Gadsden.... NW	681
● *Quinette*,, Santa Rosa.. NW	×
Racy Point, St. John's...... N	25
Raulerson, St. John's....... N	×
● *Ravenswood*, Lake........ C	250
Raymond, Polk............. C	×
Red Bay, Walton......... NW	25
● Reddick, Marion.......... C	100
Red Oak, Calhoun....... NW	×
● *Reed's*, Duval........... N	×
Register, Taylor............ C	×
Rhodes Store, Jefferson.. NW	×
● Richland, Pasco........... S	100
Richmond, Lake............ C	×
Ridgewood, Putnam........ N	120
Riverhead, Hillsborough.... C	×
● River Junc., Gadsden.. NW	100
● Riverland, Hernando.... W	×
Riverside, Putnam......... N	×
Riverview, Hillsborough.... C	×
Rixford, Suwannee......... N	240
Roberts, Escambia....... NW	×
● *Robinson*, DeSoto........ S	×
● Rochelle, Alachua........ N	200
Rock Bluff, Liberty....... NW	12
Rock Ledge, Brevard........ S	248
Rock Mines, Citrus......... S	×
Rock Springs, Marion....... C	128
Rockwell, Marion........... C	×
Rocky Hill, Suwannee...... N	×
Rollins College, Orange..... C	×
Romeo, Marion............ C	×
● *Rosefield*, Duval.......... N	×
Rosehill, Citrus............. S	15
Rose Hill, Orange.......... C	×
● Rosewood, Levy.......... C	150
● *Rowena*, Orange......... C	×
● *Roy*, St. John's.......... N	×
Royal, Sumter............. C	×
● *Runnymede*, Osceola..... S	×
Rural, Hernando.......... W	30
Rutland, Sumter........... C	25
Rutledge, Alachua......... N	×
● *Rutledge*, Orange........ C	×
Rye, Manatee.............. S	20
● *Sabin*, Polk............. C	×
● *Sadie*, Lake............. C	×
Safety Harbor, Hillsborough C	×
St. Andrew's Bay, Wash'n NW	357
● **St. Augustine**, St. John's N	4,742
● *St. Catharine*, Sumter.... C	×
St. Clair, Lake............ C	×
St. Cloud, Osceola......... C	×
St. Francis, Lake.......... C	×
St. James City, Lee......... S	25
● Saint Leo, Pasco.......... S	×
Saint Lucie, Brevard........ S	35
● Saint Mark's, Wakulla.. NW	150
Saint Nicholas, Duval....... N	350
● Saint Petersburg, Hillsb'h. C	271
● *Saint Petersburgh Wharf*, Hillsborough............ C	×
Saint Teresa, Franklin... NW	×
Saint Thomas, Pasco....... S	50
Salem, Taylor.............. N	120
Salt Marsh, (see Bluff Sprs.).	×
Sampala, Madison.......... N	×
Sampson, Bradford......... N	×
● *Sampson*, Jackson..... NW	×
● San Antonio, Pasco....... S	50
San Carlos, Suwannee..... N	×

● Sanderson, Baker........ N 100
Sand Hills, St. John's...... N ×
Sandy, Manatee............. S ×
● Sanford, Orange.......... C 2,01?
Sanibel, Lee................ S ×
San Mateo, Putnam.......... N 200
● *San Mateo Jc.*, Putnam.. N ×
● San Pablo, Duval.......... N ×
Santa Rosa P'k, Santa Rosa NW 6?
● Santos, Marion............ C 5?
● *Saranac*, Alachua......... N ×
Sarasota, Manatee........... S 20?
Satsuma, Putnam.......... N ×
● Satsuma Hights, Putnam. N ×
● Sauble, Putnam........... N 75
Scotland, Gadsden......... NW 60
● *Scotts*, DeSoto............. S ×
Scrub Hammock, Suwannee N ×
● Seaside, Hillsborough..... C ×
Sebastian, Brevard.......... S 105
● Seffner, Hillsborough..... C 100
● Seller's Lake, Lake....... C ×
Selman, Calhoun.......... NW ×
Seminole, Hillsborough..... C ×
Seneca, Lake............... C 480
Seven Oaks, Hillsborough... C ×
● Seville, Volusia........... C 600
Sewalls Point, Dade......... S 20
Shady Grove, Taylor........ C ×
● Sharon, Clay.............. N 120
Sharpes, Brevard............ S ×
Shell Creek, DeSoto......... S ×
● *Sheridan*, Lake........... C ×
Shiloh, Volusia.............. C 30
Shingle, Osceola............ S ×
Shingle Creek, Osceola...... S ×
● *Sidney*, Hillsborough...... C ×
Silver Lake, Orange......... C ×
Silver Pond, Putnam......... N ×
● Silver Springs, Marion.... C 54
Silver Spring Junc., Marion C ×
Silver Springs Park, Marion C 400
Sim's City, Columbia....... N ×
● Sisco, Putnam............. N 120
Sligh, Lake................. C ×
● *Smailes Creek*, Clay...... N ×
Smith Creek, Wakulla.... NW 35
Smithville, Putnam......... N ×
● Sneads, Jackson.......... NW 50
● *Snyders*, Gadsden....... NW ×
● *Soldier*, Orange........... C ×
Sopchoppy, Wakulla..... NW 175
● Sorrento, Lake............ C 200
South Beach, St. John's.... N ×
South Gulch, St. John's.... N ×
● South Jacksonville, Duval N 378
● South Lake Weir, Marion. C 300
● *Sparkman*, Hillsborough. C ×
● Sparr, Marion............ C 240
Springfield, Duval.......... N ×
Spring Garden, Volusia..... C 03
Spring Glen, Duval......... N ×
Spring Grove, Lake......... C 25
Spring Lake, Clay......... N ×
● *Spring Park*, Marion..... C 400
Spring Warrior, Taylor..... N 25
Stage Pond, Citrus.......... S 25
Stanley, DeSoto............ S ×
● Stanton, Marion.......... C 200
● Starke, Bradford......... N 669
Steinhatchee, LaFayette.... N 30
● *Statens*, Orange.......... C ×
Stephensville, Taylor....... N 50
Sterling, Walton.......... NW 30
Stewartville, Alachua....... N ×
Stockton, Marion.......... C 240
Stokes, Putnam............ N ×
● Stonewall, Duval......... N ×
Stratmore, Nassau......... N ×
● Summerfield, Marion..... C ×
Summerlin, DeSoto.......... S ×
● *Summerville*, Duval...... N 50
Summerville, Holmes...... W ×
● Summit, Marion.......... C 25
Sumner, Levy.............. C ×
● **Sumterville**, Sumter... C 214
● *Sumterville Junc.*, Sumter C ×
Sunny Hill, Leon.......... NW 50
● *Sunny Side*, Lake......... C ×
Sunnyside, Osceola......... S ×
Sunnyside, Taylor.......... N ×
● Sutherland, Hillsborough. C 50
● Suwannee, Suwannee..... N 10
Suwannee Shoals, Columbia. N 45
● *Suwannee Val.*, Columbia N ×
● *Sweetwater*, Duval....... N ×
Switzerland, St. John's..... N ×

Sycamore, Gadsden...... NW ×
Sydney, Hillsborough....... C ×
Sylvania, Sumter........... C ×
● Sylvan Lake, Orange...... C 240
Syracuse, Putnam.......... N 50
● *Tacony*, Pasco............ S ×
Tahiti, Dade................ S ×
● **TALAHASSEE**, L'n. NW 2,934
● *Talliferro's*, Bradford.... N ×
Tallulah, LaFayette......... N ×
● **Tampa**, Hillsborough.... C 5,532
Tangerine, Orange.......... C 200
● Tarpon Springs, Hillsb'gh. C 327
● *Tarrytown*, Sumter...... C ×
Tascawilla, Orange......... C ×
● **Tavares**, Lake........... C 500
● *Teasdale*, Putnam........ N ×
● *Tedderville*, Polk......... C ×
● Temple's Mills, Bradford. N 25
Terra Ceia, Manatee......... S ×
Terra Cotta, Hernando.... W 30
The Jetties, St. John's...... N ×
Theressa, Bradford.......... N ×
The Springs, Volusia........ C ×
Thompson, Lee.............. S 23
Thonotosassa, Hillsborough. C 20
● *Thurston*, Bradford....... N ×
● *Tildenville*, Orange....... C ×
Tillman, Brevard............ S ×
● *Tillson*, Lake............. C ×
Tisonia, Duval............. N ×
● **Titusville**, Brevard...... S 746
● *Titusville Wharf*, Brevard S ×
● Tocoi, St. John's.......... N ×
● *Tocoi Junction*, St. John's N ×
● *Tomoka*, Volusia.......... C ×
● *Toronto*, Orange.......... C ×
Townsend's Fy., Alachua.. N ×
Trenton, Alachua........... N 48
Tropic, Brevard............. S 120
● *Troy*, Orange.............. C 35
● *Turkey Creek*, Hillsborough C ×
Turnbull, Brevard........... S ×
● *Turnout*, Duval........... N ×
● *Tuscawilla*, Orange...... C ×
Twin Lakes, Pasco.......... S 25
Twin Lakes, Hernando .... W 25
● *Twin Lakes*, Orange...... C ×
Tyner, Hamilton............ N 120
● Umatilla, Lake............ C 125
Union, Columbia.......... N ×
Union, Walton............ NW ×
Upsala, Orange............. C ×
Valkaria, Brevard........... S ×
● Valrico, Hillsborough..... C ×
● *Varn's Crossing*, Lake.... C ×
● *Vaughan's Mills*, Lake... C ×
Venice, Manatee............ S ×
Vernon, Washington... NW 50
● Verona, Duval............ N ×
Viana, Citrus............... S ×
● Victoria, Lake............ C 90
● *Victoria*, Orange......... C ×
Villa City, Lake............ C ×
Villa Franca, Lee........... S ×
Villa Nova, Orange......... C ×
Viola, Lake................ C ×
● *Volusia*, Volusia.......... C 250
Wacissa, Jefferson........ NW ×
Waco, Orange.............. C ×
● Wahneta, Polk............ C 25
● *Wait's Junction*, Lake... C ×
● Wakulla, Wakulla ..... NW ×
Wakulla Sprs., Wakulla. NW ×
● Waldo, Alachua.......... N 580
● *Walkill*, Clay............ N ×
● Warnell, Sumter.......... C ×
Warrington, Escambia... NW 1,301
Watertown, Columbia...... N ×
● Wauchula, DeSoto........ S 30
Waukeenah, Jefferson..... NW 100
Waveland, Brevard.......... S ×
● *Waycross Junc.*, Duval.. N ×
● *Wayland*, Orange........ C ×
Waylonza, Taylor........... N ×
● Webster, Sumter.......... C ×
● Weir Park, Marion....... C ×
● Wekiva, Orange .... C ×
Welaka, Putnam........... N 150
● Wellborn, Suwannee..... N 200
● Welshton, Marion......... C 300
● West Apoka, Lake........ C 225
● *W. Branford*, LaFayette.. N 100
● *West De Land*, Volusia... C ×
● Westfarm, Madison....... N 155
Westlake, Hamilton........ N ×
West Side, Orange.......... C ×

● *West Tocoi*, Clay......... N 43
● Westville, Holmes...... NW 250
Wetappo, Washington.... NW ×
Wetumpka, Gadsden..... NW ×
Wewahitchka, Calhoun... NW 100
● *White House*, Duval...... N ×
White Pine, Calhoun..... NW ×
● White Springs, Hamilton. N 543
Whitfield, Walton........ NW ×
Whitney, Lake.............. C ×
● *Wilby*, Duval............. N ×
● *Wilcox*, Orange........... C 90
● *Wilderness*, Clay......... N 40
● Wildwood, Sumter........ C 419
Wilkerson's, Clay........... N ×
● *Willford*, Clay............ N ×
Williston, Levy............. C 100
Willow, Hillsborough....... C ×
● *Wilmott*, Polk............ C ×
Windermere, Orange........ C ×
● *Windermere*, St. John's.. N ×
Windsor, Alachua.......... N 400
Winfield, Columbia......... N ×
Winnemissett, Volusia...... C 45
Winnston, Polk............ C 14
Winsted, Lake.............. C ×
● *Winter Garden*, Orange.. C ×
● Winter Haven, Polk...... C 30
● Winter Park, Orange...... C 270
Wiscon, Hernando.......... W 25
Withlacoochee, Hernando.. W ×
Wood, Walton............ NW ×
● Woodbridge, Orange...... C ×
Woodville, Leon.......... NW ×
Worthington, Bradford..... N 33
● Wyman's, Alachua....... N ×
Wyoma, Marion............ C ×
Yallaha, Lake.............. S 101
● *Ybor City*, Hillsborough.. C 2,000
Yellow Bluff, (see Ozona).... ×
● *Yelvington*, St. John's.... N 60
Yneistra, Santa Rosa..... NW ×
York, Marion.............. C ×
Yulee, Alachua............ N ×
Yular, Alachua............ N ×
● *Zeigler's*, Marion......... C ×
● Zellwood, Orange......... C 360
Zif, Bradford............... N ×
Zion, Dade.................. S ×
● Zolfo, DeSoto............. S 23

GEORGIA.

COUNTIES.	INDEX.	POP.
Appling	SE	8,676
Baker	SW	6,140
Baldwin	C	14,608
Banks	NE	8,562
Bartow	NW	20,616
Berrien	S	10,694
Bibb	C	42,370
Brooks	S	13,979
Bryan	SE	5,520
Bulloch	E	13,712
Burke	E	28,501
Butts	C	10,565
Calhoun	SW	8,438
Camden	SE	6,178
Campbell	W	9,115
Carroll	W	22,301
Catoosa	NW	5,431
Charlton	SE	3,335
Chatham	SE	57,740
Chattahoochee	W	4,902
Chattooga	NW	11,202
Cherokee	N	15,412
Clarke	N	15,186
Clay	SW	7,817
Clayton	W	8,295
Clinch	S	6,652
Cobb	N	22,286
Coffee	S	10,483
Colquitt	S	4,794
Columbia	E	11,281
Coweta	W	22,354
Crawford	C	9,315
Dade	NW	5,707
Dawson	N	5,612
Decatur	SW	19,949
De Kalb	N	17,189
Dodge	C	11,452
Dooly	S	18,146
Dougherty	SW	12,206

County	Location	Population
Douglas	W	7,794
Early	SW	9,792
Echols	S	3,079
Effingham	E	5,599
Elbert	NE	15,376
Emanuel	E	14,703
Fannin	N	8,724
Fayette	W	8,728
Floyd	NW	28,391
Forsyth	N	11,155
Franklin	NE	14,670
Fulton	NW	84,655
Gilmer	N	9,074
Glascock	E	3,720
Glynn	SE	13,420
Gordon	NW	12,758
Greene	C	17,051
Gwinnett	N	19,899
Habersham	NE	11,573
Hall	N	18,047
Hancock	C	17,149
Haralson	W	11,316
Harris	W	16,797
Hart	NE	10,887
Heard	W	9,557
Henry	W	16,220
Houston	C	21,613
Irwin	S	6,316
Jackson	N	19,176
Jasper	C	13,879
Jefferson	E	17,213
Johnson	C	6,129
Jones	C	12,709
Laurens	C	13,747
Lee	SW	9,074
Liberty	SE	12,887
Lincoln	NE	6,146
Lowndes	S	15,102
Lumpkin	N	6,867
McDuffie	E	8,789
McIntosh	SE	6,470
Macon	W	13,183
Madison	NE	11,024
Marion	W	7,728
Meriwether	W	20,740
Miller	SW	4,275
Milton	NW	6,208
Mitchell	SW	10,906
Monroe	C	19,137
Montgomery	C	9,248
Morgan	C	16,041
Murray	NW	8,461
Muscogee	W	27,761
Newton	C	14,310
Oconee	N	7,713
Oglethorpe	NE	16,751
Paulding	NW	11,948
Pickens	N	8,182
Pierce	SE	6,379
Pike	W	16,300
Polk	NW	14,945
Pulaski	C	16,559
Putnam	C	14,842
Quitman	SW	4,471
Rabun	NE	5,606
Randolph	SW	15,267
Richmond	E	45,194
Rockdale	C	6,813
Schley	W	5,443
Screven	E	14,424
Spalding	W	13,117
Stewart	SW	15,682
Sumter	SW	22,107
Talbot	W	13,258
Taliaferro	C	7,291
Tattnall	SE	10,253
Taylor	W	8,666
Telfair	S	5,477
Terrell	SW	14,503
Thomas	SW	26,154
Towns	N	4,064
Troup	W	20,723
Twiggs	S	8,195
Union	N	7,749
Upson	W	12,188
Walker	NW	13,282
Walton	N	17,467
Ware	SE	8,811
Warren	E	10,957
Washington	C	25,237
Wayne	SE	7,485
Webster	SW	5,695
White	N	6,151
Whitfield	NW	12,916
Wilcox	S	7,980
Wilkes	NE	18,081
Wilkinson	C	10,781
Worth	S	10,048
Total		1,837,353

Place	Location	Population
Abba, Irwin	S	25
● **Abbeville**, Wilcox	S	657
Aberdeen, Emanuel	E	×
Absalom, Hall	N	50
Achords, Montgomery	C	×
● Acree, Worth	S	100
Acton, Harris	W	×
● Acworth, Cobb	N	815
Ada, Dooly	S	50
● Adairsville, Bartow	NW	531
● Adam, Richmond	E	585
● *Adams*, Lee	SW	40
● Adams Park, Twiggs	C	×
Adamsville, Fulton	NW	×
Adasburgh, Wilkes	NE	×
● Adel, Berrien	S	527
● Adgateville, Jasper	C	15
Adrian, Emanuel	E	×
● *Adventure*, Richmond	E	400
Aerial, Habersham	NE	200
Afton, Berrien	S	×
Agate, Floyd	NW	250
Agnes, Lincoln	NE	×
● Agricola, Glascock	E	20
Ahlberg, Appling	SE	260
Aikenton, Jasper	C	×
Ailey, Montgomery	C	75
Air Line, Hart	NE	200
Alaculsy, Murray	NW	130
Alamo, Montgomery	C	75
● *Alamo*, Telfair	S	×
● **Albany**, Dougherty	SW	4,008
Alcove, Burke	E	×
● *Alcovy*, Newton	C	×
Alexander, Burke	E	100
Alexanderville, Echols	S	50
Alford, Merriwether	W	×
Alfred, Rabun	NE	×
Algernon, Gwinnett	N	65
Alice, Pickens	N	60
● Allapaha, Berrien	S	449
● Allatoona, Bartow	NW	200
● Allen's, Richmond	E	30
Allen's Mills, Carroll	W	33
Allentown, Wilkinson	C	35
Alliance, Decatur	SW	×
Alliance, Jasper	C	×
Alligator, Telfair	S	26
● Almon, Newton	C	20
Alpharetta, Milton	N	256
● Alpine, Chattooga	W	15
Alps, Meriwether	W	×
Altamaha, Tatnall	SE	25
Alto Banks	NE	100
Amandaville, Hart	NE	42
Amason, Bibb	C	×
● **Americus**, Sumter	SW	6,398
Amicalola, Dawson	N	40
Amity, Lincoln	NE	×
● Amoskeag, Dodge	C	150
● *Anandale*, Habersham	NE	×
Anchor, Wayne	SE	×
● Andersonville, Sumter	SW	200
Andrews, Heard	W	×
Annie, Lowndes	S	32
Anon, Oglethorpe	NE	100
Antioch, Troup	W	150
● *Antioch*, Oglethorpe	NE	×
Anvil Block, (see Ellenwood)		×
Anvil Block, Henry	W	75
Aonia, Wilkes	NE	15
Apex, Mitchell	SW	31
Appalachee, Morgan	C	×
Appleton, Montgomery	C	50
Apple Valley, Jackson	N	50
Appling, Columbia	E	112
Aquavia, Hart	NE	25
● Arabi, Dooly	S	200
Arcadia, Liberty	SE	150
Arcola, Bulloch	E	130
● *Argyle*, Clinch	S	×
Arlen, Bulloch	E	×
● Arlington, Calhoun	SW	417
● Armena, Lee	SW	×
Armuchee, Floyd	NW	32
Arnold, Milton	N	38
Arp, Banks	NE	50
Arthur, Laurens	C	37
Artic, Warren	E	×
Asbury, Troup	W	60
Ascalon, Walker	NW	32
● Ashburn, Worth	S	403
Ashland, Franklin	NE	×
Ashley, Wilcox	S	25
Ashwood, Berrien	S	×
● Astor, Clayton	W	65
Asylum, Baldwin	C	×
● **Athens**, Clarke	N	8,639
● **Atkinson**, Wayne	SE	150
● **ATLANTA**, Fulton	NW	65,533
● *Atlanta Junc.*, Floyd	NW	×
● *Atlanta Shops*, Fulton	NW	×
Attapulgus, Decatur	SW	20
Atwood, Sumter	SW	×
Auboro, Gwinnett	N	×
Aubrey, Heard	W	×
Auburn, Gwinnett	N	30
Aucilla, Thomas	SW	50
● **Augusta**, Richmond	E	33,300
Auraria, Lumpkin	N	75
Aurum, Warren	E	×
● Austell, Cobb	N	582
Austin, Dade	NW	×
Austin, Morgan	C	×
Autney, McDuffie	E	40
Ava, Berrien	S	80
Avalon, Franklin	NE	60
Avant, Pierce	SE	×
● Avera, Jefferson	E	200
Avondale, McDuffie	E	25
● *Avondale*, Bibb	C	×
Axoka, Whitfield	NW	16
● Ayersville, Habersham	NE	100
Azalia, Screven	E	250
Babb, Henry	W	15
Bachlott, Charlton	SE	×
● Baconton, Mitchell	SW	175
Bahama, McIntosh	SE	×
Bailey's Mills, Camden	SE	300
● **Bainbridge**, Decatur	SW	1,668
● *Bainbridge Jc.*, Decatur	SW	50
● Bairdstown, Oglethorpe	NE	100
Bait, Miller	SW	×
Baldwinville, Talbot	W	×
Ball Ground, Cherokee	N	296
Balloon, Clinch	S	38
Ball's Church, Wilkinson	C	15
Bamah, Monroe	C	30
Bamboo, Wayne	SE	×
Bandanna, Montgomery	C	100
Banksville, Banks	NE	75
Banner, Liberty	SE	65
● Banning, Carroll	W	300
Barber's Creek, Jackson	N	100
Barnard, Taylor	W	×
Barnes, Meriwether	W	×
● Barnesville, Pike	W	1,839
● Barnett, Warren	E	73
Barretsville, Dawson	N	30
● *Barrons*, Jones	C	×
● *Barrons Lane*, Macon	W	×
● *Bartow*, Bartow	NW	×
● Bartow, Jefferson	E	437
Bascobel, Jackson	N	20
Bascom, Screven	E	10
Base, Butts	C	×
● *Bass Ferry*, Floyd	NW	×
Bastonville, Glascock	E	15
Batesville, Cherokee	N	25
Bath, Richmond	E	70
● *Bath Station*, Richmond	E	×
● *Battle Field*, Walker	NW	×
Battle Ground, Johnson	C	75
Baughville, Talbot	W	75
● **Baxley**, Appling	SE	337
Bay, Colquitt	S	×
Bayard, Harris	W	32
Bayboro, Colquitt	S	15
Bay Branch, Emanuel	E	33
Bay Creek, Gwinnett	N	65
● *Bay View*, (see Johnston Sta.)		×
Beach, Ware	SE	50
Beachs., Harris	W	×
Bealwood, Muscogee	W	×
Beards Creek, Liberty	SE	100
Beasley, Jefferson	E	×
Beathoney, Milton	N	×
Beatty's, Polk	NW	×
Beaverdale, Whitfield	NW	61
Beckham, Early	SW	×
Bede, Wilcox	S	×
Bee, Wilcox	S	20
Beech Hill, Wilkinson	C	15
Beehive, Dodge	C	×
Beeks, Pike	W	50
Beersheeba, Henry	W	×
Bela, Campbell	W	×

● Belair, Richmond	E	75
● Belknap, Bryan	SE	120
Belleville, McIntosh	SE	×
Belleview, Talbot	W	100
● Bellmont, Hall	N	25
● *Bell Springs*, Glascock	E	×
● Bellton, Hall	N	211
Bellville, Tatnall	SE	×
Bellvista, Glynn	SE	×
Bellwood, Fulton	NW	587
Bellwood, Muscogee	W	×
● *Belt Junction*, Fulton	NW	×
Beltwood, Burke	E	10
Ben, Dooly	S	×
Bender, Laurens	C	×
Benderburgh, Whitfield	NW	10
Benevolence, Randolph	SW	125
Ben Hill, Fulton	NW	50
● *Bennocks*, Richmond	E	×
Berkshire, Gwinnett	N	50
Berlin, Lowndes	S	82
Berrien, Tatnall	SE	×
Berrys, Polk	NW	×
● Berzelia, Columbia	E	100
Bessie, Wilkes	NE	×
● *Best's*, Bartow	NW	×
Bessielon, Washington	C	×
● Bethlehem, Walton	N	100
Beulah, Laurens	C	15
Bickley, Ware	SE	100
Big Creek, Forsyth	N	200
Big Sandy, Twiggs	C	×
Bill, Montgomery	C	150
Billarp, Douglas	W	40
Billow, Carroll	W	×
Bingen, Decatur	SW	260
Birdford, Tattnall	SE	10
● Bishop, Oconee	N	×
Black, Bulloch	E	100
Black Creek, Screven	E	115
● **Blackshear**, Pierce	SE	656
Blackville, Emanuel	E	60
● *Blackville*, Screven	E	×
Blackwells, Cobb	N	×
Bladen, Stewart	SW	100
Blaine, Pickens	N	×
Blairsville, Union	N	114
● **Blakely**, Early	SW	441
● *Blalock*, Fayette	W	×
Blalock, Rabun	NE	×
Blanton, Crawford	C	×
Bliss, Bulloch	E	82
Bitch, Bulloch	E	50
Bloodworth, Wilkinson	C	150
Bloomingdale, Chatham	SE	×
Blount, Monroe	C	100
Blountsville, Jones	C	150
Blowing Cave, Decatur	SW	×
Bloys, Bulloch	E	175
Blue Ridge, Fannin	N	264
● Blue Spring, Gordon	NW	52
Bluffton, Clay	SW	298
● Blythe, Richmond	E	200
Bobo, Gordon	NW	19
Boiling, Cherokee	N	×
Bold Spring, Franklin	NE	75
Bolen, Ware	SE	32
● Bolingbroke, Monroe	C	100
Boliver, Bartow	NW	×
● Bolton, Fulton	NW	100
● **Bonaire, Houston**	**C**	25
● Boneville, McDuffie	E	×
Booth, Jackson	N	×
● *Bostick*, Talbot	W	75
● Boston, Thomas	SW	646
Bostwick, Morgan	C	75
Botsford, Sumter	SW	75
Bowdon, Carroll	W	354
● Bowdre, Hall	N	25
Bowenville, Carroll	W	×
Bowers, Crawford	C	×
● Bowersville, Hart	NE	275
● Bowman, Elbert	NE	323
● Box Spring, Talbot	W	60
Boxwood, Wilkinson	C	40
Boyettville, Decatur	SW	20
Boyle, Marion	W	50
Boynton, Catoosa	NW	11
● Bradley, Jones	C	10
Brag, Bulloch	E	×
Braganza, Ware	SE	100
Bramblett, Rabun	NE	×
Branchville, Laurens	C	100
Brandon, Walton	N	75
Brannons, Cherokee	N	×
Brantley, Marion	W	200
Brass, Towns	N	300
● Brasswell, Paulding	NE	100
● Breman, Haralson	W	312
Brent, Monroe	C	×
Brentwood, Wayne	SE	100
● *Brewer*, Effingham	E	75
Brewton's Bridge, Tatnall	SE	200
● Briceville, Floyd	NW	50
● *Brick Yard*, Floyd	NW	×
Bridge, Emanuel	E	×
● Brinson, Decatur	SW	50
Brinsonville, Burke	E	100
Broad, Wilkes	NE	25
Brogdon, Fayette	W	25
Bronco, Walker	NW	15
● Bronwood, Terrell	SW	406
Brooker, Coffee	S	×
● Brookfield, Berrien	S	50
Brooklyn, Stewart	SW	×
● Brooks' Station, Fayette	W	100
● *Brown's*, Henry	W	×
Broughton Island, (see Darien)		×
Brown's Bridge, Forsyth	N	30
● Brown's Crossing, Baldwin	C	25
Brownsville, Paulding	NW	50
Broxton, Coffee	S	57
Bruce, Montgomery	C	×
● **Brunswick**, Glynn	SE	8,459
Brunswick & Western Junction, Dougherty	SW	×
Brushy, Spalding	W	50
Brutus, Laurens	C	×
● *Bruton*, Laurens	C	75
● *Bryant*, Gilmer	N	×
Bryan, Bryan	SE	×
Bryantville, Cobb	N	100
● **Buchanan**, Harrison	W	324
Buck Creek, Screven	E	300
● Buck Head, Morgan	C	30
Buck Horn, Laurens	C	65
Buck's Still, Wayne	SE	×
● **Buena Vista**, Marion	W	788
Buff, Gordon	NW	10
● Buford, Gwinnett	N	496
● Bullards, Twiggs	C	75
Bullochville, Meriwether	W	90
Bunkley, Camden	SE	26
Buren, Union	N	15
Burke, Lee	SW	32
Burketts, Bibb	C	15
Burns, Twiggs	C	25
Burnt Mountain, Pickens	N	60
● Burroughs, Chatham	SE	×
Burton, Rabun	NE	100
Burwell, Carroll	W	20
Bussey, Meriwether	W	30
● **Butler**, Taylor	W	712
Butler's Island, Glynn	SE	50
● Butts, Emanuel	E	×
Byrd, Floyd	NW	25
Byrdville, (see Hazlehurst)		×
Byromville, Dooly	S	25
● Byron, Houston	C	219
Cabaniss, Monroe	C	30
Cadiz, Franklin	NE	×
Cadley, Warren	E	×
Cains, Gwinnett	N	25
● Cairo, Thomas	NW	521
Caldwell, Union	N	26
● *Caldwell*, Floyd	NW	×
● **Calhoun**, Gordon	NW	680
Calvary, Decatur	SW	80
● Camak, Warren	E	110
Camden, Camden	SE	×
Cameron, Screven	E	150
● **Camilla**, Mitchell	SW	866
Camp, Chattooga	W	×
Campagne, Towns	N	50
Campbellton, Campbell	W	100
Camp Creek, Union	N	8
Camps, Telfair	S	×
● Campton, Walton	N	32
● Candler, Hall	N	100
● *Canoochee*, Emanuel	E	×
Canoochoe, Emanuel	E	75
Canton, Cherokee	N	659
Cap, Irwin	S	32
Captolo, Screven	E	150
Carbondale, Whitfield	NW	×
Cardville, Jones	C	65
● *Carey*, Greene	C	×
Carlisle, Gilmer	N	×
Carlton, Madison	NE	×
● *Carne*, Dodge	C	×
Carnesville, Franklin	NE	275
● **Carrollton**, Carroll	W	1,451
● Carr's Station, Hancock	C	25
Carsonville, Taylor	W	22
Cartecay, Gilmer	N	100
Carter's, Murray	NW	25
● **Cartersville**, Bartow	NW	3,171
Cary, Pulaski	C	65
Cash, Gordon	NW	8
Cason, Wilcox	S	100
Cassandra, Walker	NW	27
● Cass Station, Bartow	NW	50
Cassville, Bartow	NW	200
● Cataula, Harris	W	150
Cat Creek, Lowndes	S	100
Catie, Carroll	W	×
Catoosa, Catoosa	NW	×
Catoosa Spring, Catoosa	NW	100
Cave, Bartow	NW	×
Cave Spring, Floyd	NW	952
Cawthon, Hancock	C	50
● Cecil, Berrien	S	203
Cedar Grove, Walker	NW	99
Cedar Hill, Gwinnett	N	83
Cedar Ridge, Whitfield	NW	45
Cedar Springs, Early	SW	100
● **Cedartown**, Polk	NW	1,625
● Cement, Bartow	NW	300
Center, Decatur	SW	×
● *Center*, Jackson	N	×
Centerside, White	N	130
● *Central Junc.*, Chatham	SE	×
Centre Post, Walker	NW	25
Centreville, Gwinnett	N	150
Centreville, Wilkes	NE	30
● Ceres, Crawford	C	100
Cerlastae, Columbia	E	×
● Chalker, Washington	C	×
Chalybeate Springs, Meri'r.	W	85
● **Chamblee, DeKalb**	**N**	60
● *Chambliss*, Webster	SW	×
Chapel Hill, Douglas	W	100
Chastain, Thomas	SW	75
● *Chattahoochee*, Fulton	NW	×
● *Chattahoochee*, Muscogee	W	×
Chattahoochee River, Decatur	SW	×
Chattooga Creek, Walker	NW	65
Chattoogaville, Chattooga	NW	65
● Chauncy Dodge	C	633
Cheap, Banks	NE	65
Cheevertown, Baker	SW	150
Chelsea, Chattooga	NW	15
Chenubee, Webster	SW	15
Cherokee, Marion	W	10
Cherokee Mills, Cherokee	N	50
Cherry Log, Gilmer	N	100
Chestatee, Forsyth	N	56
● Chester, Dodge	C	×
Chestnut Flat, Walker	NW	5
Chestnut Gap, Fannin	N	10
Chestnut Mountain, Hall	N	×
Chet, Whitfield	NW	14
● Chickamauga, Walker	NW	150
China Hill, Telfair	S	200
● Chipley, Harris	W	500
Choestoe, Union	N	41
Chokee, Lee	SW	125
● *Chula*, Irwin	S	×
Chulio, Floyd	NW	32
Church Hill, Marion	W	100
Cisco, Murray	NW	97
Clara, Fulton	NW	×
Clark, Bulloch	E	×
● **Clarkesville**, Hab'm.	NE	396
Clark's Mill, Crawford	C	25
● Clarkston, DeKalb	N	271
Clarksboro, Jackson	N	×
Claud, Houston	C	×
Claude, Washington	C	×
Claxton, Tattnall	SE	×
Clay Hill, Lincoln	NE	25
Clayton, Rabun	NE	200
Clayville, Telfair	S	85
● Clem, Carroll	W	82
Clements, Catoosa	NW	×
● Cleola, Harris	W	25
Cleveland, White	N	200
● *Clifton*, DeKalb	N	250
● *Clifton*, Chatham	SE	×
Clifton, Tatnall	SE	×
● Climax, Decatur	SW	50
Clinch, Clinch	S	×
Clinch Haven, Clinch	S	65
Cling, Appling	SE	32
Clinton, Jones	C	200
Clito, Bulloch	E	×
Clopton, Putnam	C	100
Cloverdale, Dade	NW	10
Cluese, Columbia	E	50
Clyattville, Lowndes	S	30

 Georgia Georgia

Place, County	Region	Population
Clyde, Bryan	SE	200
Clyo, Effingham	E	×
Coal City, Dade	NW	360
Coal Mountain, Forsyth	N	75
● Cobb, Sumter	SW	20
Cobbtown, Tattnall	SE	100
Cobbville, Telfair	S	35
● Cochran, Pulaski	C	1,000
● *Cocke*, Terrell	SW	×
Coffee, Pierce	SE	125
● Cohutta, Whitfield	NW	268
Cohutta Springs, Murray	NW	55
Coker, Milton	N	×
Cold Water, Elbert	NE	32
● *Cole*, Terrell	SW	×
Cole City, Dade	NW	225
Colewan's, Worth	S	×
● Coleman, Randolph	SW	211
Cole's Crossing, Fannin	N	8
Coley's, Pulaski	C	×
Coley's Station, Pulaski	C	60
Colfax, Marion	W	×
Colima, Gordon	NW	32
● Collier, Monroe	C	15
● Collins, Tatnall	SE	×
Colquitt, Miller	SW	150
● **Columbus**, Muscogee	W	17,303
● *Comer*, Madison	NE	46
Commissioner, Wilkinson	C	40
Commodore, Tatnall	SE	150
● Concord, Pike	W	360
Concordia, Elbert	NE	26
Condor, Laurens	C	100
● *Condor Station*, Laurens	C	×
● Coney, Dooly	S	200
Conley, Clayton	W	75
● *Conley*, Tatnall	SE	×
Connesauga, Gilmer	N	50
Constantine, Jackson	N	10
● Constitution, DeKalb	N	25
● **Conyers**, Rockdale	C	1,349
Coogle's Mill, Macon	W	25
Cookstown, Wilcox	S	50
Cooksville, Heard	W	50
Cool Spring, Wilkinson	C	150
Cooper, Hart	NE	×
Cooper, (see Nicholson)		×
● Cooper Heights, Walker	NW	20
Coosa, Floyd	NW	200
Coosa Creek, Union	N	21
Coosawattee, Gordon	NW	42
Copeland, Dodge	C	100
● *Copeland*, Copeland	NW	32
Cora, Newton	C	30
Corbin, Bartow	NW	×
● Cordele, Dooly	S	1,578
Cordray, Calhoun	SW	15
Corinth, Heard	W	120
Cork, Butts	C	100
● Cornelia, Habersham	NE	175
Cornell, Fulton	NW	26
Cornucopia, Jones	C	25
Corsica, Tatnall	SE	×
Cost, Banks	NE	32
Cottage Mills, Chattahoochee	W	50
Cottondale, Terrell	SW	×
Cotton Hill, Clay	SW	150
● *Cotton Yard*, Bibb	C	×
County Line, Carroll	W	26
Cove City, Whitfield	NW	25
Covena, Emanuel	E	150
● **Covington**, Newton	C	1,823
Cowan, Morgan	C	×
Cowart, Bibb	C	25
● *Cowarts*, Early	SW	×
● *Cowards*, Emanuel	E	×
Cox, Dodge	C	50
Craig, Gwinnett	N	×
Cranberry, Harris	W	×
Crane-eater, Gordon	NW	24
● Crawford, Oglethorpe	NE	450
● **Crawfordville**, Tall'ro.	C	584
● *Crawley's*, Crawford	C	×
Craytonia, Fannin	N	6
Creighton, Cherokee	N	50
Crescent, McIntosh	SE	10
● Creswell, Spalding	W	75
Cribb, Emanuel	E	×
Crisp, Irwin	S	75
Crispin Island, Glynn	SE	×
Critic, Elbert	NE	32
Cromer's, Franklin	NE	25
● Cross Keys, De Kalb	N	32
Cross Plains, Carroll	W	×
Cross Roads, Terrell	SW	15
Crow, Whitfield	NW	×
Crowder, Troup	W	20
Crowsville, Paulding	NW	×
Crystal Springs, Floyd	NW	75
Cuba, Early	SW	×
● Culloden, Monroe	C	150
● Culverton, Hancock	C	100
Cumberland, Camden	SE	45
Cumming, Forsyth	N	356
● *Cunningham*, Floyd	NW	×
Curran, Marion	W	×
● *Cushingville*, Burke	E	×
● **Cusseta**, Chattahoochee	W	241
● *Cusseta Sta.*, Chattahoo'e	W	×
Cutcane, Fannin	N	20
● **Cuthbert**, Randolph	SW	2,328
● *Cuyler*, Bryan	SE	×
Cyclone, Screven	E	×
● *Cycloneta*, Irwin	S	×
Cypress, Pulaski	C	×
Dache, Gwinnett	N	×
Dahlonega, Lumpkin	N	896
Daisy, Bryan	SE	120
Daisy, Tatnall	SE	120
Dakota, Dooly	S	25
● *Dakota*, Worth	S	×
● Dale's Mill, Wayne	SE	200
● **Dallas**, Paulding	NW	455
● **Dalton**, Whitfield	NW	3,046
Damascus, Early	SW	200
● Dames Ferry, Monroe	C	100
Dames Mills, Clinch	S	×
Danburgh, Wilkes	NE	200
Daniell's Mills, Douglas	W	200
Daniels, Polk	NW	×
Danielsville, Madison	NE	149
Danton, Tattnall	SE	40
Darien, McIntosh	SE	1,491
Dariot, Liberty	SE	125
● Dasher, Lowndes	S	×
Daton, Echols	S	×
Davie, Hall	N	×
● *Davis*, Worth	S	×
● Davisborough, Wash'ton	C	224
Davis Mills, Wilcox	S	35
Davisville, Newton	C	10
● Davittes, Polk	NW	×
Dawnville, Whitfield	NW	8
● **Dawson**, Terrell	SW	2,284
● **Dawsonville**, Dawson	N	175
● *Days*, Oglethorpe	NE	100
● *Dearing*, McDuffie	E	130
● **Decatur**, DeDalb	N	1,013
Decora, Gordon	NW	6
Deepstep, Washington	C	25
Defaugh, Catoosa	NW	×
Dekel, Emanuel	E	97
Delano, Oconee	N	×
Delray, Upson	W	32
Delta, Macon	W	20
Delzel, Twiggs	C	×
● Demorest, Habersham	NE	208
● Dempsey, Dodge	C	175
Dennard, Houston	C	×
Dennis, Murray	NW	10
● *Dennis*, Putnam	C	50
Denton, Coffee	S	32
Deptford, Chatham	SE	×
Derby, Troup	W	×
Deseronto, Putnam	C	×
● Desoto, Sumter	SW	15
● Devereaux Station, Ha'ck	C	100
● *Dewey Rose*, Elbert	NE	×
Dewitt, Mitchell	SW	×
Dewsville, Baker	SW	×
Deweyrose, Elbert	NE	×
● Dexter, Laurens	C	10
Diadem, Elbert	NE	×
Dickey, Calhoun	SW	20
Dillon, Dade	NW	40
Dinsmore, Milton	N	32
● Dixie, Brooks	S	150
Dixon, Dowson	N	200
● *Dixon's*, Walker	NW	×
Doboy, McIntosh	SE	250
● *Dock Junction*, Glynn	SE	×
● Doctor Town, Wayne	SE	100
Dodges Boom, Telfair	S	×
Dodo, Laurens	C	20
Dodson, Coweta	W	×
Doles, Worth	S	32
Don, Harris	W	32
● *Don*, Polk	NW	×
Donaldson, Laurens	C	25
● Donaldsville, Decatur	SW	100
Doogan, Murray	NW	26
● *Donovan*, Johnson	C	15
Dooling, Dooly	S	×
Dora, Fannin	N	×
● Doraville, DeKalb	N	100
Dorchester, Liberty	SE	175
Dorminey's Mill, Irwin	S	100
● *Dorsey*, Morgan	C	×
Dot, Colquitt	S	×
Double Branches, Lincoln	NE	50
Doudy, Madison	NE	97
Dougherty, Dawson	N	20
Douglas, Coffee	S	400
● **Douglasville**, Douglas	W	863
Dovedale, Baldwin	C	25
● Dover, Screven	E	60
● Dove's Creek, Elbert	NE	10
Dowdy, Madison	NE	100
Dower, Troup	W	×
Downs, Washington	C	20
● Doyle, Marion	W	50
Draketown, Haralson	W	125
Dranesville, Marion	W	100
Drayton, Dooly	S	125
Drew, Forsyth	N	×
Drewryville, Spalding	W	75
Drone, Burke	E	120
Dry Branch, Bibb	C	20
Drypond, Jackson	N	×
● **Dublin**, Laurens	C	862
● Dubois, Dodge	C	275
Duck, Union	N	×
Duck Creek Walker	NW	32
● Ducker Station, Dou'ty	NW	150
Dudley, Laurens	C	×
● *Dug Down*, Polk	NW	×
● *Dugdown*, Haralson	W	×
Duke, Ware	SE	150
Dukesville, Heard	W	12
● Duluth, Gwinnett	N	319
● *Dunlap*, Oglethorpe	NE	×
Dunn, Murray	NW	10
● Dunwoody, DeKalb	N	75
● DuPont, Clinch	S	200
Durden, Emanuel	E	35
● *Durdenville*, Emanuel	E	×
Duval, Terrell	SW	25
Dwight, Washington	C	×
● *Dykes*, Floyd	NW	×
Dyson, Wilkes	NE	30
Eagle Cliff, Walker	NW	24
Eagle Grove, Hart	NE	25
Earl, Lee	SW	×
Earleys, Floyd	NW	×
Early, Floyd	NW	×
Earnest, Fayette	W	×
East Albany, Dougherty	SW	×
Eastanollee, Franklin	NE	50
East Atlanta, DeKalb	N	×
East Highlands, Decatur	SW	×
● **Eastman**, Dodge	C	1,082
Easton, Fulton	NW	×
● East Point, Fulton	NW	738
East Rome, Floyd	NW	514
Eastville, Oconee	N	×
Eastwood, Thomas	SW	26
● **Eatonton, Putnam**	C	1,682
Ebenezer, Chattooga	NW	40
Ebenezer, Liberty	SE	×
Echeconnee, Houston	C	40
Echols, Forsyth	N	50
● Eden, Effingham	E	150
Edge Cliff, Walker	NW	×
● Edgewood, DeKalb	N	250
Edison, Calhoun	SW	310
Edna, Wilcox	S	×
● Edwardsville, Fulton	NW	65
Eelbeck, Chattahoochee	W	×
Effie, Whitfield	NW	14
● Egypt, Effingham	E	180
● **Elberton**, Elbert	NE	1,572
Elder, Oconee	N	32
● *Eldorado*, Berrien	S	×
Eldorendo, Decatur	SW	32
● *Eleven Mile Turnout*, Glynn	SE	×
Elgin, Butts	C	50
● *Elizabeth*, Cobb	N	×
● Elko, Houston	C	15
● Ellabell, Bryan	SE	×
Ella Park, Camden	SE	×
● **Ellaville**, Schley	W	300
● Ellenwood, Clayton	W	100
● Ellerslie, Harris	W	75
● **Ellijay**, Gilmer	N	437
Elliott, Appling	SE	32
Ellis, Columbia	E	×
Elm, Colquitt	S	20
Elmer, Screven	E	×
Elmo, Coffee	S	×
Elmina, Telfair	S	×

Place, County	Section	Population
Elmwood, Twiggs	C	×
Elsie, Laurens	C	×
Elsie, Ware	SE	×
Elza, Tattnall	SE	30
Embry, Paulding	NW	50
● Emerson, Bartow	NW	100
Emet, Bulloch	E	×
Emily, Carroll	W	35
Emma, Dawson	N	25
● Emmaline, Emanuel	E	×
Empire, Dodge	C	100
Enal, Bulloch	E	60
Endicott, Bulloch	E	40
Enecks, Screven	E	325
English, Colquitt	S	32
English Eddy, Tattnall	SE	100
● Enigma, Berrien	S	100
Enon, Jasper	C	30
Enon Grove, Heard	W	60
● Enterprise, Lee	SW	50
Enville, Wayne	SE	115
Epping, Montgomery	C	×
Erastus, Banks	NE	75
Erick, Telfair	S	×
Erin, Meriwether	W	50
Erwin, Gordon	NW	15
● Esom Hill, Polk	NW	190
Essie, Richmond	E	×
● *Esqueline*, Muscogee	W	×
● Estelle, Walker	NW	9
Ethel, Johnson	C	×
Etna, Polk	NW	100
Etowah, Floyd	NW	20
Etta, Paulding	NW	×
Eubanks, Columbia	E	35
Eudora, Jasper	C	50
Euharlee, Bartow	NW	144
Eula, Jasper	C	50
Eunice, Dodge	C	×
Euphaupee, Bryan	SE	×
Eureka, Dooly	S	40
Eureka Mills, Elbert	NE	20
Eva, Houston	C	20
Evan's Mills, DeKalb	N	×
Evansville, Troup	W	100
Evelyn, Glynn	SE	250
Evens, Columbia	E	32
Everetts, Crawford	C	×
● Everett's Springs, Floyd	NW	75
● Everett's, Sta., Crawford	C	150
Evergreen, Irwin	S	150
● *Eves*, Floyd	NW	×
Ewell, Newton	C	50
Excelsior, Bulloch	E	100
● Exeter, Pierce	SE	50
Experiment, Spalding	W	×
Exposition Mills, Fulton	NW	601
Exum, Macon	W	×
● Faceville, Decatur	SW	150
● **Fairburn**, Campbell	W	695
Fairchild, Decatur	SW	32
Faircloth, Mitchell	SW	50
Fair Mount, Gordon	NW	150
Fair Play, Morgan	C	100
Fairview, Chattooga	NW	×
Fambros, Upson	W	×
Fancy Bluff, Glynn	SE	50
Farley, Harris	W	×
● Farmington, Oconee	N	65
Farmville, Gordon	NW	15
Farrar, Jasper	C	×
Faulk, Twiggs	C	25
Favors, Talbot	W	×
Fay, Henry	W	×
● **Fayetteville**, Fayette	W	380
Feagin, Houston	C	75
Felix, Colquitt	S	35
● Felton, Haralson	W	314
Fender, Clinch	S	100
Fenn, Dooly	S	×
Fentress, Telfair	S	×
Ferguson, Lee	SW	×
Feronia, Coffee	S	250
Ferry, Floyd	NW	130
● *Ficklin*, Wilkes	NE	×
Fickling, Taylor	W	25
Fidelle, Gordon	NW	15
Fido, Henry	W	25
Field's Cross Roads, Milton	N	50
Fillmore, Whitfield	NW	×
● Findlay, Dooly	S	25
● Fish, Polk	NW	25
Fishdam, Oglethorpe	NE	×
Fitts, Carroll	W	26
Fitzpatrick, Twiggs	C	×
Five Forks, Madison	NE	×
Five Points, Jones	C	×

Georgia

Place, County	Section	Population
Flake, DeKalb	N	45
Flanders, Emanuel	E	26
Flatbranch, Gilmer	N	33
Flat Creek, Fayette	W	×
● Flat Rock, Muscogee	W	×
Flat Shoals, Meriwether	W	100
Flatwoods Academy, Elbert	NE	130
● Fleming, Liberty	SE	200
Fleming, Glynn	SE	×
Flemington, Liberty	SE	200
Flint, Mitchell	SW	300
● Flintstone, Walker	NW	100
● Flippen, Henry	W	100
Flo, Floyd	NW	32
Flora, Monroe	C	×
Florence, Stewart	SW	200
● *Florence*, Morgan	C	×
Florence, Hall	N	×
● Flovilla, Butts	C	422
● Flowery Branch, Hall	N	350
Floyd Springs, Floyd	NW	50
Fly, Bulloch	E	×
Folks, Calhoun	SW	200
● Folkston, Charlton	SE	150
Folsom, Bartow	NW	50
● *Folsom*, Habersham	NE	×
Ford, Bartow	NW	×
Ford's Store, Hart	**NE**	**350**
● *Forest*, Clinch	S	×
● *Foresters*, Lee	SW	×
Forest Hall, Burke	E	57
● *Forest Station*, Clayton	W	15
Forrest, Catoosa	NW	25
● *Forrest*, Columbia	E	×
Forestville, Floyd	NW	771
● **Forsyth**, Monroe	C	920
Fort Buffington, Cherokee	N	25
● **Fort Gaines**, Clay	SW	1,097
Fort Lamar, Madison	NE	300
Fort Mountain, Murray	NW	35
● *Fort Mudge*, Pierce	SE	×
Fort Oglethorpe, Chatham	SE	×
Fort Pulaski, Chatham	SE	×
● Fortson, Muscogee	W	30
Fortsow's Crossing, M's'gee	W	×
● Fort Valley, Houston	S	1,752
Foster, Brooks	S	×
Foster's Mills, Floyd	NW	100
Foster's Store, Chattooga	NW	15
Fouche, Floyd	NW	26
Fountainville, Macon	W	50
Fowler, Jackson	N	×
● Fowlstown, Decatur	SW	100
Franklin, Heard	W	250
Franks, Jones	C	×
● Frankville, Monroe	C	×
Frazier, Pulaski	C	75
Fredrick, Oglethorpe	NE	×
Free, Meriwether	W	10
Free Homes, Cherokee	N	50
● *Freemans*, Floyd	NW	×
Freemansville, Milton	N	83
Friendship, Sumter	SW	200
Frolona, Heard	W	×
Fullington, Dooly	S	30
Fullwood Springs, Polk	NW	×
Fuqua, Dooly	S	×
Furnace, Walker	NW	×
● Gabbettville, Troup	W	100
Gaddistown, Union	N	10
● *Gaillard*, Crawford	C	×
● **Gainesville**, Hall	N	3,202
● *Galvan's*, Richmond	E	×
Garbutt, Emanuel	E	×
Garden Valley, Macon	W	250
Gardi, Wayne	SE	100
Garfield, Emanuel	E	200
Garland, Lumpkin	N	×
Garlandville, Franklin	NE	25
Garrant, Coffee	S	400
● *Gatewood*, Sumter	SW	×
Gay, Meriwether	W	50
Gays, Emanuel	E	×
Gem, Bulloch	E	200
● Geneva, Talbot	W	150
Gentry's Mills, Dawson	N	×
● **Georgetown**, Quitman	SW	348
Gerber, Walker	NW	20
Gertrude, Liberty	SE	260
Getup, Walker	NW	10
Gholston, Madison	NE	×
● **Gibson**, Glascock	E	197
Gilbert, Clay	SW	×
Giles, Chattahoochee	W	26
● Gillsville, Hall	N	100
● Gilmore, Cobb	N	×
Gip, Irwin	S	×

Georgia

Place, County	Section	Population
Girard, Burke	E	50
Girth, Burke	E	×
Gladesville, Jasper	C	20
Glee, Troup	W	×
● Glenalta, Marion	W	25
Glenloch, Heard	W	×
● Glenmore, Ware	SE	[illegible]
Glenn, Heard	W	[illegible]
Glennville, Tattnall	SE	×
● Glenwood, Montgomery	C	60
Glovers, Jones	C	20
● Godfrey, Morgan	C	×
● Godwinsville, Dodge	C	110
● Goggansville, Monroe	C	500
Golden Gate, Fulton	NW	32
Goldin, Haralson	W	×
Goldsborough, Pulaski	C	150
Goloid, Screven	E	325
Good Hope, Walton	N	100
● Goodman, Irwin	S	32
● *Goodman*, Wilcox	S	×
Goodwill, Franklin	NE	26
● *Goodwin's*, DeKalb	N	32
Gooseberry, Webster	SW	×
● Gordon, Wilkinson	C	400
Gordon Springs, Whitfield	NW	24
Gore, Chattooga	NW	10
Goshen, Lincoln	NE	54
Goss, Elbert	NE	97
Gough, Burke	E	×
Grace, Lumpkin	N	25
● Gracewood, Richmond	E	65
● Grady, Polk	NW	100
Grady, Lincoln	NE	×
● Graham, Appling	SE	300
Grange, Jefferson	E	100
Grangersville, Macon	W	100
Grants, Harris	W	×
● Grantville, Coweta	W	654
Grapevine, Gwinnett	N	65
Grassdale, Bartow	NW	32
Grassfield, Jasper	C	15
Gravel Springs, Forsyth	N	×
● Graves Station, Terrell	SW	100
● Gray, Jones	C	100
● *Grays*, Coffee	S	×
● Graysville, Catoosa	NW	306
Green, Bulloch	E	130
Greenbush, Walker	NW	24
● **Greeneville**, Meriwether	W	800
Green Hill, Stewart	SW	150
Green Hill, Chattahoochee	W	50
● **Greensborough**, Gr'ne	C	1,313
● Green's Cut, Burke	E	100
● *Green's Mill*, Macon	W	×
Greenville, Meriwether	W	800
Greenway, Polk	NW	25
● Greenwood, Henry	W	50
Greenwood, Oconee	N	×
● *Gresham*, Walton	N	75
Greshamville, Greene	C	100
● Gresston, Dodge	C	32
● **Griffin**, Spalding	W	4,503
Griffins Landing, Burke	E	×
Grimes, Harris	W	×
Grimsley, Laurens	[illegible]	×
Grindle, Lumpkin	N	×
Griselda, Decatur	SW	×
● Griswoldville, Jones	C	30
● Grovania, Houston	C	25
Grove Level, Branks	NE	25
Grove Point, Chatham	SE	×
Grover, Wilcox	S	40
● Grovetown, Columbia	E	350
● Guild, Walker	NW	10
Gully Branch, Coffee	S	227
Gum Branch, Liberty	SE	×
Gum Spring, Bartow	NW	×
● Guyton, Effingham	E	541
● *Haasville*, Fulton	NW	×
Hack Branch, Montgomery	C	30
● Haddock Station, Jones	C	100
Hagan, Tattnall	SE	×
● Hahira, Lowndes	S	25
Haides, Screven	E	65
Haines, Lowndes	S	65
● Halcyon Dale, Screven	E	500
Hales, Pike	W	×
Halfway, Lumpkin	N	×
***Halloca*, Chattahoochee**	**W**	[illegible]
● Hall's Mill, Bartow	NW	30
Hambyville, Troup	W	50
● **Hamilton**, Harris	W	500
● Hamlet, Polk	NW	100
● *Hammets*, Crawford	C	200
Hammond, Fulton	NW	200
● Hampton, Henry	W	422

Hancock, Burke E ×
Hancock's Landing, Burke E 32
Handy, Coweta W 65
Hannah, Douglas W ×
●Hapeville, Fulton NW 100
Haralson, Coweta W 114
●Hardaway, Dougherty SW 100
Hard Cash, Elbert NE ×
Hardeman, Harris W 65
Hardup, Baker SW ×
Hardy, Baker SW ×
Hargett, Harris W 40
Hargrave, Catoosa NW ×
●Harlem, Columbia E 647
Harmony, Forsyth N ×
●Harmony Grove, Jackson N 611
●*Harper*, Floyd NW ×
Harrell, Decatur SW ×
Harris, Meriwether W 25
Harrisburg, (see Augusta)...
●Harrisburg, Walker NW ×
Harris City, Meriwether W ×
●Harrison, Washington C 575
Harrisonville, Richmond E ×
Hart, Bibb C 15
Hartford, Cherokee N ×
Hartsfield, Colquitt S 30
●**Hartwell**, Hart NE 800
Harveys, Talbot W ×
Harville, Bulloch E 150
Hassler Mill, Murray NW 20
Hat, Irwin S 100
●Hatcher's Sta., Quitman SW 65
Hatoff, Laurens C 15
Hattie, Houston C ×
●**Hawkinsville**, Pulaski C 755
Hawpond, Tattnall SE 50
Hay, Paulding NW ×
Haynesville, Houston C 150
Haynie, Floyd NW 150
Hay's Mill, Lee SW 40
Haywood, Chattooga NW 14
Hazen, Columbia E ×
●Hazlehurst, Appling SE 290
Hazlehurst, Glynn SE ×
Head's Ferry, Habersham NE 65
Headstall, McDuffie E 55
Heard, Houston C ×
Heardmont, Elbert NE 25
Heath, Burke E 175
Hebron, Washington C 25
●Helena, Telfair S ×
Hell's Gate, Baker SW ×
Helena, (see Washington) .... ×
Hematite, Polk NW ×
Hemp, Fannin N 15
Hemphill, Fulton NW 100
Hempstead, Colquitt S 225
Henderson, Houston C 250
Hendricks, Upson W 25
Henry, Franklin NE 32
●*Henry's*, Walker NW ×
●Hephzibah, Richmond E 500
●Herndon, Burke E 250
Hiawassee, Towns N 150
●Hichitee, Chattahoochee W ×
Hickory Flat, Cherokee N 50
Hickory Grove, Crawford C 40
Hickory Level, Carroll W 32
Hico, Douglas W ×
Higdon's Store, Fannin N 50
Higgins, Monroe C ×
Higgston, Montgomery C 43
High Falls, Monroe C 90
●High Point, Walker NW 26
High Shoals, Oconee N 210
High Tower, Forsyth N 100
Hills, Burke E 100
●Hillman, Taliaferro C 50
Hills, Harris W ×
●Hillsborough, Jasper C 166
Hillsdale, Worth S ×
●Hilton Station, Early SW 100
Hinesville, Liberty SE 200
Hine's Tank, Harris W ×
Hinton, Pickens N 25
●Hiram, Paulding NW 100
Hix, Madison NE 40
Hobbs, Stewart SW 20
●Hoboken, Pierce SE 180
Hodo, Johnson C ×
●Hogansville, Troup W 518
Hoggard's Mill, Baker SW 100
Hoggs, Marion W 25
Hoke, Madison NE ×
Hoke, Gwinnett N ×
●*Holcombe*, Burke E 20

Holders, Floyd NW ×
Holland, Chattooga NW 11
Holland's Mills, Carroll W 25
Hollingsworth, Banks NE 75
Hollonville, Pike NW 65
Holly Creek, Murray NW 22
●Holly Springs, Cherokee NW 75
●Hollywood, Richmond E 100
Holmesville, Appling SE 100
Holt, Wilcox S 25
●Holton, Bibb C 175
●*Holts*, Dougherty SW ×
Homer, Banks NE 50
●**Homerville**, Clinch S 350
Hood, Union N ×
Hood's, Pickens N ×
●*Hook's Crossing*, Emanuel E ×
●Hooker, Dade NW ×
Hooper, Haralson W 20
Hootens, Meriwether W ×
Hope, Pike W 65
Hoppsville, Wayne SE ×
Horace, Emanuel E 150
Horkan, Colquitt S 30
Horn's Cross Roads, Meri'. SW 50
Hortense, Wayne SE 26
Horton, Dodge C 50
●Hoschton, Jackson N 207
Hot House, Fannin N 32
House Creek, Wilcox S 200
Houston, Heard W 100
●Howard, Taylor W 100
●*Howell*, Fulton NW ×
Howell's Mills, Fulton NW 65
Howelton, Paulding NW ×
Hoy's, Cobb N ×
Hudson, Sumter SW 75
Huff, Gwinnett N 50
Hughes, Murray NW 10
Hughes, Wilkinson C ×
●*Hull*, Clarke N ×
Hulmeville, Elbert NE 150
Humber, Stewart SW 25
Humming, Berrien S ×
Humphreys, Clinch S 247
Hunt, Towns N 500
Huntington, Sumter SW ×
Huntsville, Paulding NW 20
Hurricane, Appling SE 26
Huxford, Coffee S ×
Hybert, Clinch S ×
Ice, Pierce SE ×
●Idaverper, Chattahoochee W 10
Igo, Gordon NW 10
Ila, Madison NE 100
●*Inaha*, Irwin S ×
India, Walton N ×
Indian Springs, Butts C 500
Inglewood, Dodge C 15
Inman, Fayette W 130
Inverness, McIntosh SE ×
Irby, Irwin S ×
Irene, Washington C ×
Iric, Bulloch E 100
Iron City, Decatur SW 25
Iron Rock, Franklin NE 30
Ironville, Bartow NW ×
●*Irwin*, Stewart SW ×
Irwins Cross Roads, W'sh'tn C 25
Irwinton, Wilkinson C 300
Irwinville, Irwin S 100
Isabella, Worth S 300
●*Isabella Station*, Worth S ×
Island Shoals, Henry W ×
Isom, Brooks S ×
Ivanhoe, Bulloch E 42
●Ivey, Wilkinson C 50
Ivy Log, Union N 20
●**Jackson**, Butts C 922
Jacksonville, Telfair S 125
Jaeckel, Emanuel E ×
Jakin, Early SW ×
●Jamaica, Glynn SE 100
●James, Jones C 175
Jamestown, Chattahoochee W 20
Japanese, Marion W ×
Jarrett, Hall N ×
Jarriel, Tattnall SE ×
●**Jasper**, Pickens N 333
Jay, Lumpkin N 25
●**Jefferson**, Jackson N 540
Jeffersonton, Camden SE 50
Jeffersonville, Twiggs C 250
Jehue, Dodge C ×
●*Jenkins*, Columbia E ×
●Jenkinsburgh, Butts C 75
●*Jennings*, Webster SW ×

Jerome, Heard W ×
Jersey, Walton N 100
Jerusalem, Pickens N 45
Jester, Stewart SW 20
●**Jesup**, Wayne SE 907
Jewell's, Hancock C 500
Jewellville, Banks NE 25
Jimps, Bulloch E 97
Jincy, Wilcox S 50
Job, Sumter SW 32
Jockey, Pickens N ×
Joel, Carroll W 25
●*Johnson*, Dooly S ×
●*Johnson's*, Jefferson E ×
Johnsons, Emanuel E ×
●*Johns'n's Wareh'se*, Eman'l E ×
●Johnston Station, Liberty SE 150
Johnston, Sumter SW ×
●*Johnsonville*, Appling SE ×
Johntown, Pickens N 40
Johntown, Dawson N ×
●Jolly, Pike W 25
●*Jones*, Clay SW ×
●**Jonesborough**, Clayt'n C 503
Jones' Crossing, Muscogee W ×
Jones' Mill, Meriwether W 25
Jonesville, McIntosh SE ×
Jordan's Store, Pike W 65
Joseph, Fulton NW 26
●Josephine, Early SW ×
Josslyn, Liberty SE 50
Judson, Catoosa NW 10
Jug Tavern, Walton N 202
Jula, Wilcox S ×
●Juliette, Monroe C 75
●*Junction*, Randolph SW ×
●*Junction*, Clinch S ×
●*Junction*, Bibb C ×
Juniper, Marion W 125
●*Juniper*, Talbot W ×
Juno, Dawson N 130
●*Kalluiah Junc.*, Spalding W 75
Kartah, Chattooga NW 10
●Kathleen, Houston C 30
Kedron, Coweta W 75
Keeter, Cherokee N 75
Keith, Catoosa NW 50
Keithsburg, Cherokee N ×
Keller, Bryan SE ×
Kelper, Cherokee N ×
Kenna, Lincoln NE 32
●Kennesaw, Cobb N 168
●Kensington, Walker NW 100
Kent, Montgomery C ×
Key, Brooks S 200
●Keysville, Burke E ×
Kibbee, Montgomery C ×
●*Killens*, Clay SW ×
●*Kimbroughs*, Webster SW ×
Kincaid, Chattooga NW 10
●*Kinchefoanee*, Marion W ×
King's, Newton C ×
King's Bay, Camden SE ×
●*Kingsborough*, Harris W 77
Kings Crossing, Wilcox S 25
●Kingston, Bartow NW 559
Klok[illegible], Columbia E 40
●Kirkland, Coffee S 75
Kirkwood, DeKalb N ×
Kirkwood, Fulton NW ×
Kissemee, Berrien S 50
Kite, Johnson C 250
Kittrells, Appling SE ×
Kittrells, Johnson C ×
Kline, Randolph SW 50
Kno[illegible], Henry W ×
Knott, Morgan C ×
Knowles, Appling SE ×
●**Knoxville**, Crawford C 580
Koon, Thomas SW ×
●*Kramer*, Haralson W 200
Kyle, Fannin N 8
Laconte, Berrien S 50
●La Cross, Schley W 100
●*Ladds*, Bartow NW ×
●**La Fayette**, Walker NW 377
Laff, Tattnall SE ×
●**La Grange**, Troup W [illegible],090
Laidsborough, Carroll W ×
●Lake Creek, Polk NW ×
●Lake Park, Lowndes S 250
Lamar, Sumter SW 26
Lamars Mill, Upson W 150
Lamkins, Columbia E ×
Lamont, Jefferson E ×
Lamont, Monroe C 30
Lancaster, Wayne SE ×

Place	Region	Pop.
Land, Hall	N	75
Landers, Floyd	NW	×
Landrum, Dawson	N	×
Landsberg, Montgomery	C	65
Lang, Carroll	W	65
Langtry, Emanuel	E	195
Laredo, Cherokee	N	20
Laston, Bulloch	E	300
Laurens Hill, Laurens	C	130
● Lavender, Floyd	NW	×
Lavender, Wilkinson	C	50
La Villa, Houston	C	50
● Lavonia, Franklin	NE	283
● **Lawrenceville**, G'nn'tt	N	566
Lawson, Colquitt	S	97
● Lawtonville, Burke	E	112
Lax, Coffee	S	×
● Lays, Cherokee	N	×
Leah, Columbia	E	×
Leakton, Newton	C	50
● Leary's Calhoun	SW	267
Leathersville, Lincoln	NE	70
Leb, Thomas	SW	25
● *Lebanon*, Cheokee	N	×
Lee Pope, Crawford	C	×
● **Leesburgh**, Lee	W	442
Leguin, Newton	C	×
Leighton, Coffee	S	×
● Leliaton, Coffee	S	220
Lelon, Berrien	S	50
Leno, Habersham	NE	40
● Lenox, Berrien	S	×
Leo, White	N	×
Leonard, Bryan	SE	30
Leoron, Columbia	E	×
Leslie, Sumter	SW	77
Lester, Campbell	W	×
Leverett, Lincoln	NE	70
● *Leveretts*, Webster	SW	×
● Lewiston, Wilkinson	C	×
Lexington, Oglethorpe	NE	600
● *Lexington*, Oglethorpe	NE	×
Liberty, Greene	C	×
Liberty Hill, Pike	W	100
Lifsey, Pike	W	15
Lightfoot, Wilkinson	C	25
Ligon, Bartow	NW	×
Lilly Pond, Gordon	NW	31
● *Lime Branch*, Polk	NW	30
Lina, Wilkes	NE	×
Lincolnton, Lincoln	NE	220
Lindale, Floyd	NW	32
Lindsey, Washington	C	25
Linsay Creek, Muscogee	W	×
Linton, Hancock	C	176
Lisbon, Lincoln	NE	40
Lisbon, Walker	NW	×
Lithia Springs, Douglas	W	290
● Lithonia, DeKalb	N	1,182
Little Creek, Haralson	W	65
● *Littlejohn*, Sumter	SW	×
Little Rittle, Morgan	C	×
Little River, Cherokee	N	×
● *Little River*, Wilkes	NE	×
Little Row, Gordon	NW	15
Littleville, Clayton	W	32
Live Oak, Decatur	SW	×
Liverpool, Forsyth	N	×
Livingston, Floyd	NW	75
Lizella, Bibb	C	20
Lizzie, Cobb	N	×
Locketts, Dougherty	SW	×
Lockhart, Lincoln	NE	35
Loco, Lincoln	NE	×
● Locust Grove, Henry	W	255
● Lodi, Coweta	W	[illegible]
Lodrick, Randolph	SW	150
Loftin, Heard	W	×
Loganville, Walton	N	338
Lois, Berrien	S	×
● Lombardy, McDuffie	E	100
Lone Oak, Meriwether	W	×
● *Lone Oak*, Houston	C	×
Lone Oak, Troup	W	×
● *Long*, Polk	NW	×
● Long Branch, Tattnall	SE	100
Long Branch, Liberty	SE	150
Long Cane, Troup	W	100
Long Pond, Montgomery	C	200
Long Pond, Lowndes	S	×
Longs, Polk	NW	×
Longstreet, Pulaski	C	140
Long Swamp, (see Marble Hill)		×
● *Longview*, Banks	NE	×
● *Longview*, Emanuel	E	×
Long View, Dodge	C	200
Larone, Bibb	C	32

Place	Region	Pop.
Lost Mountain, Cobb	N	15
Lothair, Montgomery	C	120
Lott, (see Mt. Vernon)		×
Loudsville, White	N	20
Loughridge, Murray	NW	14
● **Louisville**, Jefferson	E	836
● Louvale, Stewart	SW	200
● *Louvale Jc.*, Stewart	SW	×
● Lovejoy's Station, Clayton	W	50
Lovelace, Troup		25
● Lovett, Laurens	C	150
Lowe, Macon	W	×
Lowell, Carroll	W	25
Lowery, Fayette	W	×
● *Lowry*, Spalding	W	×
Lucky, Wilcox	S	×
Ludville, Pickens	N	54
● Luella, Henry	W	20
Luke, Berrien	S	26
● Lula, Hall	N	100
● Lulaton, Wayne	SE	10
● Lumber City, Telfair	S	471
● **Lumpkin**, Stewart	SW	1,100
Luther, Warren	E	50
Luthersville, Meriwether	W	300
Lyncorn, Ware	SE	×
● Lyerly, Chattooga	NW	22
Lyneville, Taliaferro	C	50
● Lyons, Tattnall	SE	50
Lytle, DeKalb	N	×
Lytle, Walker	NW	6
McArthur, Montgomery	C	195
● McBean Depot, Richmond	E	200
McClellan's Mill, Worth	S	25
McClure, Milton	N	×
McConnell, Cherokee	N	46
● *McConnell*, Walker	NW	×
McCrary, Bibb	C	×
McCrary, Muscogee	W	×
McDade, Richmond	E	×
McDaniel, Pickens	N	×
● *McDaniels*, Gordon	NW	17
McDonald, Thomas	SW	200
● McDonald's Mill, Coffee	S	75
● **McDonough**, Henry	W	515
McElroy, Bibb	C	×
McElhannon, Jackson	N	50
● McGinnis, Bartow	NW	50
McGregor, Montgomery	C	×
● *McGriff's* Pulaski	C	×
● McHenry, Gordon	NW	17
● McIntosh, Liberty	SE	200
McIntosh, Butts	C	315
● *McIntyre*, Wilkinson	C	×
McIvor, Cobb	N	×
McKibben, Butts	C	50
McNutt, Oconee	N	40
● McPherson, Paulding	NW	50
● **McRae**, Telfair	S	400
McVille, Telfair	S	400
McWhorter, Douglas	W	25
Mabel, Cherokee	N	×
● Mableton, Cobb	N	128
Mabry, Carroll	W	32
● Machen, Jasper	C	228
● **Macon**, Bibb	C	22,746
Macon Junction, Bibb	C	×
Macopin, Paulding	NW	×
● *Maddox*, Sumter	SW	×
● **Madison**, Morgan	C	2,13[illegible]
Madison Springs, Madison	NE	44
Magdalena, Meriwether	W	57
Magnes, Lowndes	S	32
Magnolia, Mitchell	SW	×
Mahan, Miller	SW	25
Malbone, Bartow	NW	26
Malden Branch, Bryan	SE	27
Mallory, Morgan	C	×
Mallorysville, Wilkes	NE	50
Malven, Emanuel	E	50
● Manassas, Tattnall	SE	46
● **Mandeville, Carroll**	W	×
Manor, Ware	SE	150
● *Manta*, Chattahoochee	W	×
Maple, Morgan	C	60
Mapleford, Colquitt	S	×
Marble Hill, Pickens	N	×
Marble Switch, Whitfield	NW	×
● *Marco*, Jasper	C	×
Marcus, Jackson	N	25
● **Marietta**, Cobb	N	3,384
Marion, Lowndes	S	×
Marion, Worth	S	×
Markett, Sumter	SW	×
● Marlow, Effingham	E	175
Marquis, Decatur	SW	×
Mars, Lowndes	S	×

Place	Region	Pop.
● Marshallville, Macon	W	1,086
● Martin, Franklin	NE	75
● Martindale, Walker	NW	×
Martinez, Richmond	E	50
Marysville, Emanuel	E	32
Massey, Montgomery	C	×
● *Massey's* Muscogee	W	×
● *Massey Mill*, Bibb	C	×
Math, Emanuel	E	200
Matlock, Tattnall	SE	100
● Matthews, Jefferson	E	50
Mattie, Pulaski	C	20
Mattox, Sumter	SW	×
Mauda, Hancock	C	25
Maulden Branch, Bryan	SE	×
Mauldin's Mills, Hall	N	100
Max, Talbot	W	50
● Maxey's Oglethorpe	NE	250
Maxwell, Jasper	C	30
May, Colquitt	S	×
May Bluff, Camden	SE	150
Mayfield, Hancock	C	50
Mayhaw, Miller	SW	×
Maynard, Monroe	C	150
Maystown, Butts	C	30
● Maysville, Jackson	N	327
Mazeppa, Milton	N	100
● *Meadows*, Johnson	C	×
● Meansville, Pike	W	75
Mechanicsville, Jasper	C	15
Medicus, Madison	NE	×
Medoc, Emanuel	E	×
Meeks, Johnson	C	×
● Meigs Thomas	SW	100
● *Meldrum*, Chatham	SE	×
Meldrim, Effingham	E	×
Mellville, (see Lyerly)		×
● Melrose, Lowndes	S	150
Melson, Floyd	NW	32
Menlo, Chattooga	NW	22
Mercer's Mills, Worth	S	130
● Meriweather, Baldwin	C	100
Merritt, Emanuel	E	75
● Mesena, Warren	E	135
Metasville, Wilkes	NE	×
● Metcalf, Thomas	SW	156
Metter, Bulloch	E	25
Mica, Cherokee	N	10
Middlebrooks, Pike	W	×
Middle Ground, Screven	E	40
● Middleton, Elbert	NE	×
● Midland, Muscogee	W	×
● Midville, Burke	E	300
Midway, Meriwether	W	32
● Milan, Telfair	S	20
Milford, Baker	SW	100
● **Milledgeville**, Baldwin	C	3,322
● Millen, Screven	E	500
● *Miller's*, Gordon	NW	52
Miller's Station, Chatham	SE	×
Mill Haven, Screven	E	100
Mill Ray, Bulloch	E	200
Mills, Whitfield	NW	26
Millstone, Oglethorpe	NE	80
Milltown, Berrien	S	150
● Millwood, Ware	SE	100
● Milner, Pike	W	500
Milner's Store, Fayette	W	×
Mimosa, Walker	NW	×
Mimsville, Baker	SW	30
Mineata, Jasper	C	25
● Mineola, Lowndes	S	×
● Mineral Bluff, Fannin	N	76
Mineral Springs, Pickens	N	65
● Minneta, Jasper	C	25
Minnie, Irwin	S	50
Minton, Worth	S	40
Miriam, Decatur	SW	150
● Mission Ridge, Walker	NW	50
● Mitchell, Glascock	E	25
Mitchellton, Screven	E	100
Mize, Franklin	NE	×
Mizpah, Effingham	E	25
Mobley Pond, Screven	E	150
Modesto, Cherokee	N	×
Modoc, Emanuel	E	26
● Mogal, Berrien	S	×
● Molena, Pike	W	198
Monk, Campbell	W	×
● **Monroe**, Walton	N	983
● Monteith, Chatham	SE	130
Montevideo, Hart	NE	32
● Montezuma, Macon	W	706
Montgomery, Putnam	C	×
● **Monticello**, Jasper	C	849
Mont Lily, Whitfield	NW	×
● *Montpelier*, Crawford	C	×

Montrose, Wilkinson........C ×
Montrose, Laurens.........C ×
● *Moon's*, Walker........NW ×
Moore, Chattooga........NW ×
Moore, Laurens...........C ×
Moore's Mills, Cherokee....N 50
● *Moor's Mill*, Clayton.....W 77
Morel, Effingham..........E ×
● Moreland, Coweta.........W 100
Morgan, Calhoun ....SW 180
Morganton, Fannin .....N 170
● Morganville, Dade .....NW 19
Morrison, Bryan ....SE ×
Morrison, Dade ....NW ×
● Morris Station, QuitmanSW 100
● Morrow's Station,ClaytonW 40
Montimer, Forsyth.........N ×
● Morton, Jones.............C 15
Morven, Brooks.............S 75
Moss, Banks.............NE ×
Mossy Creek, White ....N 35
Moultrie, Colquitt ....S 100
Mountain Hill, Harris...... W 25
Mountain Scene, Towns......N 200
Mountaintown, Gilmer......N 200
● Mount Airy, HabershamNE 201
Mount Gilead, Muscogee...W ×
Mount Hope, Floyd ......NW ×
● Mount Pleasant, Wayne .SE 100
Mount Vernon, Montg'y C 707
Mountville, Troup..........W 100
Mount Zion, Carroll.........W 10
● Moxley, Jefferson..........E 100
Mozelle, Jackson. ....N ×
Mud Creek, Clinch ....S 60
Mudge, Pierce.............SE ×
● Mulberry Grove, Harris..W 50
● Munnerlyn, Burke.........E 150
● *Murchinsons*, Bartow..NW ×
Murray's Cross Roads, SchleyW 120
Murrayville, Hall...........N ×
● *Muscogee*, Muscogee.....W ×
● Musella, Crawford ....C ×
Myra, Appling..............SE 45
● Myrtle, Houston ....C 25
Nacoochee, White ....N 200
● **Nahunta, Wayne** ....SE 150
Nail's Creek, Banks.......NE 50
Nameless, Laurens..........C 50
● *Nances*, Muscogee ....W 70
Nankin, Brooks.............S 20
Nannie, Floyd............NW 75
Napoleon, Union............N 10
Nashville, Berrien........S 426
Nasworthy, Johnson........C ×
Natlance, Cobb............N ×
● Naylor, Lowndes..........S 200
● Neal, Pike.................W 20
Nebo, Paulding...........NW 40
● *Nebula*, Harris...........W ×
Needham, Ware............SE 50
Nellwood, Bulloch..........E 200
● Nelson, Pickens...........N 266
Netta, Gilmer ....N ×
Nettie, Forsyth.............N ×
New, Chattooga...........NW ×
Newborn, Newton ....C 230
New Bridge, Lumpkin......N 100
New England City, Dade.NW 201
● *New Holland Spring*,HallN ×
New Hope, Paulding .....NW 25
New Market, Monroe ....C 50
● **Newnan**, Coweta.......W 2,859
● *New Point*, Sumter.....SW ×
Newport, Fannin ....N 6
New Providence, Wilkinson C 15
New Rome, Floyd........NW ×
Newsville, Haralson........W 32
Newton, Baker ....SW 600
Newton Factory, Newton ...C 200
Newtown, Madison.........NE 150
Nicholls, Coffee.............S 150
● Nicholson, Jackson.......N 200
Nickville, Elbert..........NE 100
● Nicojack, Cobb............N 65
Nielly, Telfair...............S 60
Nil, Wilcox ....S 100
● *Ninety Eight Mile Post*, Coffee ....S 220
● Noah, Jefferson...........E 50
Noble, Walker............NW ×
Nolan, Morgan.............C ×
Nona, Putnam ....C ×
● Norcross, Gwinnett ......N 713
Normandale, Dodge........C 125
Norton, Whitfield........NW 10
Norway, Harris............W ×

Georgia

● Norwood, Warren ....E 332
Note, Putnam...............C ×
Novetta, Forsyth ....N ×
Nunez, Emanuel............E 32
Oak Bower, Hart...........NE 26
Oakdale, Fulton..........NW ×
● Oakfield, Worth..........S 32
Oak Grove, Fulton........NW ×
Oakgrove, Quitman.......SW 26
Oakland, Meriwether.......W 75
● *Oakland*, Terrell........SW ×
● *Oak Lawn*, Houston.......C 32
Oakley Mill, Cobb...........N 100
Oak Ridge, Meriwether.....W 20
Oakshade, Fulton.........NW ×
Oakwell, Camden...........SE 25
Oaky, Effingham............E ×
Oatts, Burke ....E 32
Obe, Colquitt ....S 80
● *Obrien*, Glynn...........SE ×
Ocala, Irwin.................S 27
Ocean Hotel, Glynn........SE ×
Ocee, Milton................N ×
● Ochillee, Chattahoochee..W ×
● *Ochillee*, Chattahoochee..W ×
● Ochlochnee, Thomas....SW 202
Ocilla, Irwin ....S 75
Ocmulgee, Telfair ....S ×
Ocmulgee Mills, Butts.......C 50
● Oconee, Washington......C 200
Oconee Mills, Hall ....N 32
● *Oconee Siding*, Baldwin...C ×
Odell, Forsyth...............N ×
● *Odells*, Hall................N ×
● Odessa, Wayne...........SE ×
Odessaville, Meriwether....W ×
Odomville, Emanuel ....E 250
● Odum, Wayne ....SE 97
● Offerman, Pierce......... SE 350
● Ogeechee, Screven.........E 50
● *Oglesby*, Elbert.........NE ×
Oglesby Hill, Emanuel......E ×
● **Oglethorpe**, Macon ...W 486
Ohoopee, Tattnall..........SE 140
Okapilco, Brooks............S 170
Okefenokee, Clinch ....S 31
Ola, Henry ....W 50
Old Town, Jefferson........E ×
● Oliver, Screven ....E 200
Omaha, Stewart...........SW 150
O'Neal's Mills, Troup.........W 80
● *One Hundred and Sixty Five Mile Post*, Dougherty. SW ×
Onida, Liberty.............SE ×
Ono, Campbell ....W ×
● Oostanaula, Gordon ....NW 21
Ophir, Cherokee ....N 55
Orange, Cherokee...........N 30
● Orchard Hill, Spalding ...W 100
Ore Bank, Polk ....NW ×
Ore Bed, (see Fish Creek).... ×
● Oreburg, Floyd...........NW ×
Oredell, Polk.............NW ×
Oreville, Polk.............NW ×
Orletta, Stewart..........SW 10
Orr, Gilmer.................N ×
Orrville, Jackson..........N ×
Orsman, Floyd...........NW 100
Osanda, Campbell ....W 25
Osborn, Towns..............N 50
Oscarville, Forsyth ....N ×
Osceola, Oconee............N 20
● *Ossahatchie*, Harris......W ×
● Oswald, Telfair.............S ×
Other, Paulding.......... NW 32
● Ousley, Lowndes..........S 100
● *Outland*, Screven.........E ×
Oval, Paulding ....NW 20
● *Overstreet*, Emanuel...... E ×
Overton, Elbert...........NE 50
Owensbyville, Heard ....W 125
Owen's Ferry, Camden ....SE 300
Owlden, Coffee ....S ×
Oxford, Newton.............C 791
Paceville, Coffee ....S ×
Page, Cherokee.............N 50
Palace, Appling ....SE 32
● Palmetto, Campbell......W 552
Palmour, Dawson...........N 50
● *Palmyra*, Lee..........SW ×
Panhan, Warren ....E ×
Panola, DeKalb.............N 225
Panthersville, DeKalb ......N 75
Paoli, Madison ....NE 200
● *Paramore Hill*, Screven..E ×
Paran, Monroe ....C 325
Paris, Coweta...............W 32
Parish, Bulloch..............E 20

Georgia

● *Parker's*, Sumter....... SW ×
Parker's Store, Hart ......NE 77
Parkerville, Worth..........S 100
Parkonia, Coffee............S ×
Park's White ....N ×
Park's Mills, Greene........C 50
Parnell, Columbia...........E 130
Parrish, Bulloch............E 20
● Parrott, Terrell. ....SW 75
Paschal, Talbot............W ×
Patesville, Dooly ....S 80
Patillo, Monroe ....C 15
Patten, Thomas...........SW 57
● Patterson, Pierce........SE 230
Paul, Echols.................S 26
Paxton, Liberty............SE ×
● *Paynes*, Crawford ....C ×
Pay Up, Hart..............NE 42
Peach Stone Shoals, Henry W 75
● Peachtree Park, Fulton.NW ×
Pearly, Laurens ....C 20
● Pearson, Coffee...........S 500
Pecan, Clay................SW 15
Peeksville, Henry ....W 40
● Pelham, Mitchell.........SW 385
Pelicanville, Glynn ....SE ×
● Pembroke, Bryan....... SE ×
● Pendarvis, Wayne ....SE 75
● Pendergrass, Jackson.....N 100
● *Pendlet'n'sCross'g*,Fult'nNW ×
Penfield, Greene ....C 300
● *Penia*, Dooly..............S ×
Pennick, Glynn............SE 32
Pennington, Morgan........C 15
Penns, Greene...............C ×
● Perkins Junction, Burke. E 200
● **Perry**, Houston..........C 665
Perry's Mills, Tattnall ......SE 175
Persimmon, Rabun........NE 26
Petermans, Mitchell ......SW ×
Petersburg, Gordon ......NW 14
Peterson, Montgomery......C ×
Peterson, Sumter ....SW ×
Peyton, Appling ....SE 32
● *Peyton*, Fulton.........NW ×
Pharr, Pickens..............N 32
● Phelps, Whitfield.......NW 8
Phidelta, Banks...........NE 40
Phillip's Mill, Coffee.........S 97
Philmon, Taylor.............W ×
Philomath, Oglethorpe....NE 50
● *Philomee*, Lee..........SW ×
Picciola, Laurens...........C 40
Pickren, Coffee..............S ×
● Piedmont, Pike ....W ×
Pierceville, Fannin ....N 19
Pike, Montgomery ....C 32
Pike's Peak, Twiggs.........C ×
Pinebloom, Coffee...........S 95
Pine City, Wilcox............S ×
● Pine Grove, Appling.....SE 200
● *Pinehurst*, Dooly..........S 20
Pine Log, Bartow.........NW 100
Pine Mountain, Rabun....NE 40
Pinetucky, Jefferson........E 20
Pineville, Chattahoochee ...W 75
Pineville, Marion...........W 100
Pinia, Dooly.................S 50
Pink, White ....N 20
Pinora, Effingham...........E ×
Pinson's Station, (see Nannie) ×
Pinta, Macon...............W ×
Pippin, Jones...............C 40
Pirkle, Gwinnett.........N ×
Pisgah, Gilmer ....N ×
Pistol, Wilkes ....NE 50
Pitts, Wilcox...............S 50
Pittsburgh, Fulton ....NW 684
● Plains, Sumter......... SW 100
● Plainville, Gordon......NW 100
Planter, Madison..........NE ×
Pleasant Grove, Fosryth....N 75
Pleasant Hill, Talbot........W 100
Pleasant Retreat, White ....N 200
Plenitude, Jones.......... C ×
Plowshare, Carroll..........W 26
Plug, Carroll.............W ×
Poindexter, Schley.........W 130
Point Peter, Oglethorpe...NE 60
Polk, Union ....N ×
Polksville, (see The Glades).. ×
Pomona, Spalding..........W 100
Ponce de Leon Sp'gs, F'ltn NW ×
● *Ponder*, Webster........SW ×
Pond Fork, Jackson.........N 65
Pond Spring, Walker.....NW 22
Pond Town, Miller ....SW 26

Post Office, County		Pop.
● Pooler, Chatham	SE	×
● *Popes*, Oglethorpe	NE	×
● Pope's Ferry, Monroe	C	260
Poplar Hill, Telfair	S	35
Poplar Springs, Haralson	W	65
Porter Mill, Habersham	NE	148
Porter's Landing, Screven	E	77
Porter Springs, Lumpkin	N	×
Posco, Polk	NW	×
Post Oak, Catoosa	NW	6
Pots Mountain, Dawson	N	130
● Poulan, Worth	S	250
Pound, Upson	W	×
Pounds, Muscogee	W	×
● Powder Springs, Cobb	N	262
● Powellville, Coweta	W	120
Powelton, Hancock	C	20
● Powersville, Houston	C	150
Prather, Habersham	NE	×
Prattsburgh, Talbot	W	100
Prentice, Wayne	SE	×
Prenticeville, Wayne	SE	65
● *Prentiss*, Appling	SE	125
Prescott, Echols	S	32
● **Preston**, Webster	SW	300
Price, Hall	N	32
Pringle, Washington	C	100
● Priors, Polk	NW	85
● *Proctor*, Laurens	C	×
Protection, Gilmer	N	×
Providence, Sumter	SW	150
Pruettville, Calhoun	SW	25
Pruit, Banks	NE	×
● *Psalmonda*, Chattahoochee	W	×
Pucketts, Coweta	W	×
Puckett Station, Coweta	W	45
Pulaski, Pulaski	C	45
● *Pulaski*, Wilkinson	C	×
Pumpkin, Paulding	NW	32
● Putnam, Marion	W	150
Pye, Wayne	SE	35
Pyles Marsh, Glynn	SE	×
Quantock, Screven	E	78
Quebec, Union	N	26
Queenland, Wilcox	S	×
Quilp, Berrien	S	40
Quince, Tattnall	SE	×
Quinsee, Lee	SW	×
● **Quitman**, Brooks	S	1,868
Rabun Gap, Rabun	NE	100
Rabun Gap J'c'n, (see Cornelia)		×
Raccoon Mills, Chattooga	NW	250
● Racepond, Charlton	SE	295
● Ragland, Troup	W	×
Raiford, Mitchell	SW	×
● Raleigh, Meriwether	W	50
Ralls, Lowndes	S	×
Ralph, Douglas	W	×
Ralterwood, Carroll	W	×
Ramsey, Murray	NW	10
Randa, Lumpkin	N	32
● *Randall*, Stewart	SW	×
Randel, Colquitt	S	35
Ranger, Gordon	NW	×
Rawlins, Dodge	C	×
Ray's Mills, Berrien	S	130
Raytown, Taliaferro	C	300
● Recovery, Decatur	SW	25
● Redan, DeKalb	N	58
Red Belt, Catoosa	NW	×
Red Bluff, Montgomery	C	200
Red Bud, Gordon	NW	100
Red Clay, Whitfield	NW	85
Red Hill, Franklin	NE	×
Red Level, Wilkinson	C	20
Red Oak, Campbell	W	70
Reed, Harris	W	×
Reed Creek, Hart	NE	45
Reedy Springs, Laurens	C	300
Reesburg, Floyd	NW	×
Reese, Morgan	C	100
Reeves, Gordon	NW	×
Reeves' Station, Gordon	NW	35
Regnant, Johnson	C	200
Rehoboth, Harris	W	×
Rehoboth, Morgan	C	25
● *Reids*, Bibb	C	×
● *Reids*, Pike	W	×
Reidsfield, Wilcox	S	×
Reidsville, Tattnall	SE	300
Remus, Paulding	NW	32
Renfroes, Chattahoochee	W	×
● Resaca, Gordon	NW	197
Resourse, Screven	E	×
Rett, Carroll	W	×
Rex, Clayton	W	70
● Reynolds, Taylor	W	283

Post Office, County		Pop.
● Rhine, Dodge	C	15
Rhodesville, Decatur	SW	10
Riceborough, Liberty	SE	100
Richardson, Rockdale	C	32
● Richland, Stewart	SW	457
● Richmond, Richmond	E	250
● Richwood, Dooly	S	50
Ricksville, Emanuel	E	325
Rico, Campbell	W	×
Riddleville, Washington	C	225
Ridge, Richmond	E	×
Ridgeville, McIntosh	SE	×
Ridgeway, Harris	W	×
Riggton, Tattnall	SE	20
Rincon, Effingham	E	×
Ring, Telfair	S	×
● **Ringgold**, Catoosa	NW	465
Rio, Oglethorpe	NE	×
Ripley, Madison	NE	×
● Rising Fawn, Dode	NW	927
Ritch, Wayne	SE	32
● Riverdale, Clayton	W	25
River Junction, Cherokee	N	×
Riverside, Berrien	S	50
Riverside, Heard	W	×
Rivertown, Campbell	W	20
Rixville, Emanuel	E	×
Roberta, Crawford	C	100
● *Roberts*, Jones	C	×
Robertsville, Jones	C	×
● *Robinson*, Floyd	NW	×
● *Robinson*, Greene	C	×
Robinson, Taliaferro	C	×
Robley, Crawford	C	25
● Rochelle, Wilcox	S	500
Rockalo, Heard	W	50
● *Rock Creek*, Walker	NW	×
Rock Fence, Elbert	NE	×
● Rock Mart, Polk	NW	411
Rockpile, Dawson	N	45
Rock Pond, Decatur	SW	20
● Rock Spring, Walker	NW	10
Rocky Creek, Gordon	NW	23
Rocky Face, Whitfield	NW	10
● Rocky Ford, Screven	E	450
Rocky Mount, Meriwether	W	100
Rocky Plains, Newton	C	20
Rogers, Burke	E	150
● *Rogers*, Bartow	NW	×
Rollins, Paulding	NW	57
● **Rome**, Floyd	NW	6,957
Roney, Sumter	SW	×
Roopville, Carroll	W	123
Rosa, Johnson	C	20
Roscoe, Coweta	W	200
Rose Hill, Union	N	×
● *Roseland*, Fulton	NW	×
Rosier, Burke	E	×
● Rossville, Walker	NW	200
● Roswell, Cobb	N	1,200
Roswell Juct'n, (see Chamblee)		×
Round Lake, Brooks	S	×
● Round Oak, Jones	C	75
Round Top, Gilmer	N	×
● *Rounsaville*, Floyd	NW	26
● Rountree, Emanuel	E	260
Routhwell, Chatham	SE	66
Rover, Spalding	W	32
Rowan, Berrien	S	×
Rowland, Upson	W	×
Roxana, Paulding	NW	130
Roy, Gilmer	N	40
● Royston, Franklin	NF	340
Ruark, Dougherty	SW	×
Ruby, Bartow	NW	×
Ruby, Irwin	S	26
Ruckersville, Elbert	NE	75
● *Ruffs*, Cobb	N	×
Rufus, Bulloch	E	×
Rural Vale, Whitfield	NW	11
Rush, Webster	SW	25
Russellville, Monroe	C	100
Ruth, Greene	C	26
● Rutland, Bibb	C	50
● Rutledge, Morgan	C	588
Ryley, Macon	W	×
● *Saffold*, Early	SW	×
Saint Charles Coweta	W	×
Saint Clair, Burke	E	×
Saint Marks, Meriwether	W	300
Saint Mary's, Camden	SE	575
Saint Simon's Mills, Glynn	SE	600
Salem, Oconee	N	32
● Salem, Walker	NW	10
Sallacoa, Cherokee	N	25
● *Salter*, Sumter	SW	×
● *Salt Springs*, Douglas	W	290

Post Office, County		Pop.
Salubrity, Franklin	NE	26
● **Sandersville**, Wash'ton	C	1,760
Sand Hill, Carroll	W	50
● *Sand Hill*, Wayne	SE	100
Sand Town, Campbell	W	39
Sandy Cross, Oglethorpe	NE	50
Sandy Point, Crawford	C	25
Sandy Ridge, Henry	W	25
Santa Luca, Gilmer	N	20
Sap, Thomas	SW	×
Sapello, McIntosh	SE	39
Sappville, Ware	SE	×
Sarah, Sumter	SW	×
Sardis, Burke	E	250
● *Sargents*, Coweta	W	×
Sasser, Terrell	SW	150
Satilla Bluff, Camden	SE	500
● Saussy, Clinch	S	120
● **Savannah**, Chatham	SE	43,189
● *Saw Dust*, Columbia	E	150
Saw Mill, Chatooga	NW	40
Scale Works, Floyd	NW	×
● Scarborough, Screven	E	75
Scarlett, Camden	SE	70
Scearcorn, Pickens	N	×
● *Schatulga*, Muscogee	W	×
● Schlatterville, Pierce	SE	30
Schley, Schley	W	15
● Scotland, Telfair	S	258
Scott, Habersham	NE	×
● *Scotts*, Taylor	W	×
● Screven, Wayne	SE	200
● *Sebastopol*, Burke	E	20
Seborn, Fulton	NW	×
Seed, Habersham	NE	32
● Selina, Clayton	W	32
Sellers, Appling	SE	10
● Seney, Polk	NW	250
● Senoia, Coweta	W	863
Sessoms, Appling	SE	×
Settendown, Forsyth	N	50
● *Seven Mile Siding*, Col'b'a	E	×
● Seville, Wilcox	S	291
Seward, Montgomery	C	75
● Shady Dale, Jasper	C	152
● Shady Grove, Carroll	W	20
● Shannon, Floyd	NW	150
● *Shanty Twenty Nine*, Clay	SW	×
● Sharon, Taliaferro	C	172
Sharpe, Walker	NW	×
● Sharpsburgh, Coweta	W	177
Sharp Top, Cherokee	N	×
Shaw, Walker	NW	×
Sheffield, Camden	SE	×
Shell Bluff, Burke	E	20
● Shellman, Randolph	SW	462
Sheltonville, Forsyth	N	105
Shepherd, Coffee	S	32
● Shiloh, Harris	W	150
Shoal Creek, Hart	NE	100
Shoals, Warren	E	75
Shot, Emanuel	E	26
Shoulder, Hancock	C	65
Sibble, Wilcox	S	25
Sibley, Dooly	S	×
Sidney, Emanuel	E	50
● *Sidney*, Clark	N	×
Signboard, Liberty	SE	195
Siko, Bulloch	E	×
Siloam, Greene	C	100
Silver City, Forsyth	N	362
● Silver Creek, Floyd	NW	75
Silver Hill, Chattooga	NW	10
Silver Shoal, Banks	NE	×
Silvey, Meriwether	W	×
Simeon, Dooly	S	40
Simpson, Heard	W	×
Sims, Lowndes	S	×
● *Simsville*, Emanuel	E	×
Sirrom, Emanuel	E	×
Sister's Ferry, Effingham	E	100
Siver, Carroll	W	×
Skeinah, Fannin	N	600
Skellies Sta. (see Oostanaula)		×
Skelton, Milton	N	100
● *Skidaway*, Chatham	SE	×
Sloqumb, Jones	C	×
● Smarr's Station, Monroe	C	100
Smiley, Liberty	SE	130
Smithborough, Jasper	C	20
Smithborough, Talbot	W	×
Smithonia, Oglethorpe	NE	50
Smith's Mills, Jasper	C	100
● Smithville, Lee	SW	500
● Smyrna, Cobb	N	416
Snapfinger, DeKalb	N	78
Snapping Shoals, Newton	C	200

Place, County	Region	Pop.
Sneads, Columbia	E	×
Snellville, Gwinnett	N	200
Snelson, Merriwether	W	26
Sniff, Berrien	S	150
Snow, Dooly	S	175
● Social Circle, Walton	N	737
● *Sofkee*, Bibb	C	20
Solo, Forsyth	N	×
Solomon, Twiggs	C	×
Sonoraville, Gordon	NW	50
Sophia, Bartow	NW	×
Soque, Habersham	NE	150
South Atlanta, Fulton	NW	×
● *South Millen*, Emanuel	E	×
South Brunswick, Glynn	SE	×
South Newport, McIntosh	SE	30
● *Southover Junc.* Chatham	SE	×
South Rome, Floyd	NW	×
Sowhatchee, Early	SW	32
Spann, Johnson	C	130
● Sparks, Berrien	S	307
● **Sparta**, Hancock	C	1,540
Spivey, Putnam	C	×
Spooner, Miller	SW	×
Spoonville, Houston	C	100
Spread, Jefferson	E	95
Springfield, Effingham	E	150
Springhaven, Laurens	C	×
Spring Hill, Montgomery	C	130
Spring Place, Murray	NW	194
● Springvale, Randolph	SW	225
Stamp Creek, Bartow	NW	25
Stamps, Upson	W	×
● *Standford Mill*, Harris	W	25
Standfordville, Putnam	C	75
Stansell, Elbert	NE	×
Stapleton, Jefferson	E	31
Stapleton, Johnson	C	×
● *Stapleton Sta.*, Jefferson	E	×
Stark, Butts	C	60
Starks, Whitfield	NW	×
Starrsville, Newton	C	215
● *State Line*, Fannin	N	130
State Line, Heard	W	200
● **Statenville**, Echols	S	350
Statesborough, Bulloch	E	425
Steam Mill, Decatur	SW	225
Stella, Berrien	S	25
● Stellaville, Jefferson	E	100
● Stephens, Oglethorpe	NE	100
● Stephens' Pottery, B'dwin.	C	200
Stephensville, Wilkinson	C	135
● Sterling Station, Glynn	SE	100
● *Stewart*, Sumter	SW	×
Stewart, Newton	C	×
Stewart's Mill, Schley	W	45
Stewarts Mill, Fulton	NW	×
● Stilesborough, Bartow	NW	200
● Stillmore, Emanuel	E	×
Stillwell, Effingham	E	180
● Stinson, Meriwether	W	130
Stirling, Montgomery	C	97
● Stockbridge, Henry	W	287
● Stockton, Clinch	S	329
Stokesville, Coffee	S	×
● Stone Mountain, DeKalb	N	929
Stono, Milton	N	×
Storeville, Forsyth	N	×
Story, Cobb	N	×
● *Strickland*, Spalding	W	×
Strouds, Monroe	C	32
Strumbay, Liberty	SE	×
Stubbs, Mitchell	SW	×
Subligna, Chattooga	NW	150
Suches, Union	N	32
Sugar Hill, Hall	N	26
● Sugar Valley, Gordon	NW	164
● Sulphur Springs, Dade	NW	10
Sumach, Murray	NW	22
● *Summerfield*, Bibb	C	×
● Summertown, Emanuel	E	65
● **Summerville**, Ch't'a	NW	560
Summerville, (see Augusta)		×
● Summit, Emanuel	E	65
● *Summit*, Harris	W	×
● Sumner, Worth	S	400
● Sumter, Sumter	SW	20
● Sun Hill, Washington	C	30
Sunnydale, Richmond	E	×
● Sunny Side, Spalding	W	200
● Surrency, Appling	SE	200
Susina, Thomas	SW	15
Sutallee, Cherokee	N	25
● Suwanee, Gwinnet	N	166
● **Swainsborough**, Em'l.	E	395
Swan, Irwin	S	×
● Sweetgum, Fannin	W	15
Sweet Water, Gwinnett	N	25
Swift Creek, Bibb	C	×
Swifton, Upson	W	82
● Sycamore, Irwin	S	100
● **Sylvania**, Screven	E	838
Synndale, Richmond	E	×
Sylvester, Worth	S	54
Tails Creek, Filmer	N	50
Talasse, Jackson	N	×
● **Talbotton**, Talbot	W	1,140
● Taliaferro, Chattooga	NW	50
Talking Rock, Pickens	N	141
● Tallapoosa, Haralson	W	1,699
Tallman, Decatur	SW	×
Tallokas, Brooks	S	250
● Tallulah Falls, Rabun	NE	149
Talona, Gilmer	N	50
Tanhan, Warren	E	×
Tanner, Coffee	S	×
Tarborough, Camden	SE	200
Tarver, Echols	S	50
● Tate, Pickens	N	500
Tatum, Forsyth	N	25
Tax, Henry	W	×
Taylor, Crawford	C	250
● *Taylors*, Dooly	S	×
Taylor's Creek, Liberty	SE	150
● Taylorsville, Bartow	NW	87
Tazewell, Marion	W	150
Teagle, Gwinnett	N	26
Tell, Campbell	W	×
Teloga, Chattooga	NW	×
Teloga Springs, Chatt'oga	NW	24
Temperance, Telfair	S	125
● Temple, Carroll	W	240
● Tennille, Washington	C	953
Tesnatee, White	N	32
Texas, Heard	W	25
Thad, Chattahoochee	W	260
Tharpe, Houston	C	×
The Glades, Hall	N	100
Thena, Washington	C	125
● The Rock, Upson	W	150
● *Thomas*, Burke	E	×
Thomas Mills, Floyd	NW	×
● **Thomaston**, Upson	W	1,181
● **Thomasville**, Tho's.	SW	5,514
Thompson, Harris	W	×
Thompson's Mills, Jackson	N	46
Thoms, Montgomery	C	×
● **Thomson**, McDuffie	E	836
Thorntonville, Marion	W	×
● Thrift, Emanuel	E	×
Thurman, Meriwether	W	10
Tickanetley, Gilmer	N	×
Tidings, Chattooga	NW	10
● Tifton, Berrien	S	800
Tiger, Rabun	NE	×
Tignall, Wilkes	NE	×
● Tilton, Whitfield	NW	182
Tippettville, Dooly	S	×
Tison, Tattnall	SE	100
● *Tivola*, Houston	C	×
Tobler, Upson	W	100
● Toccoa, Habersham	NE	1,120
Tolona, Gilmer	N	×
Tompkins, Camden	SE	50
● Toomsborough, Wilkinson	C	154
Toonigh, Cherokee	N	10
● *Topeka Junction*, Upson	W	120
Tosh, Montgomery	C	32
Towaliga, Butts	C	75
Town Creek, Gilmer	N	60
● Towns, Telfair	S	100
Toy, Houston	C	×
Track Rock, Union	N	26
Trader's Hill, Charlton	SE	75
Travisville, Clinch	S	×
Tray, Habersham	NE	32
● **Trenton**, Dade	NW	378
Trickum, Whitfield	NW	30
● Trion Factory, Chat'ga.	NW	807
Trip, Gwinnett	N	100
Triplett, Wilkes	NE	3[illegible]
Tropic, Sumter	SW	×
Troup Factory, Troup	W	300
Tuckahoe, Screven	E	35
Tucker, Sumter	SW	×
● Tugalo, Habersham	NE	50
Tulip, Chattooga	NW	×
Tump, Emanuel	E	×
Tunis, Henry	W	75
● Tunnell Hill, Whitfield	NW	860
● Turin, Coweta	W	161
Turkey, Laurens	C	65
Turkey Creek, Dooly	S	65
● Turnerville, Haber'am	NE	20
● *Turnout*, Chatham	SE	×
● *Turnout*, Lowndes	S	×
● *Turnout*, Mitchell	SW	×
● *Turnout* Pierce	SE	×
● *Turnout*, Thomas	SW	×
● *Turnout*, Ware	SE	×
● *Turnout*, Wayne	SE	×
Turnpike, Cherokee	N	×
● Tusculum, Effingham	E	75
Tuton, Mitchell	SW	25
Tweed, Laurens	C	250
Twiggsville, Twiggs	C	50
Twilight, Miller	SW	20
Two Run, Lumpkin	N	50
● Tybee, Chatham	SE	×
Tyre, Douglas	W	90
Tyrone, Wilkes	NE	×
● Ty Ty, Worth	S	358
● Unadilla, Dooly	S	25
Union, Stewart	SW	110
Union Blue, Screven	E	×
Union Island, McIntosh	SE	×
● Union Point, Greene	C	700
● *Union Station*, Stewart	SW	×
Unionville, Monroe	C	25
Unity, Harris	W	82
● Upatoie, Muscogee	W	50
Upshaw, Cobb	N	26
● *Uptonville*, Charlton	SE	125
Urena, Banks	NE	10
Valambrosa, Laurens	C	×
● **Valdosta**, Lowndes	S	2,854
Valentine, Echols	S	×
Valley, Elbert	W	30
Valley Store, Chattooga	NW	10
● *Van Burens*, Jones	C	×
Vanceville, Berrien	S	195
Vandiver, Rabun	NE	20
Van's Valley, Floyd	NW	32
Vanzant's Store, Fannin	N	57
Varn, Ware	SE	×
● Varnell's Stat'n, W'tf'd.	NW	81
● *Vaughn's*, Spalding	W	75
Veazey, Greene	W	58
● Verbena, Montgomery	C	×
Vernon, Troup	W	27
Vesta, Oglethorpe	NE	25
Vic, Irwin	S	26
Vickery's Creek, Forsyth	N	25
Victory, Carroll	W	100
● Vidalia, Montgomery	C	×
● **Vienna**, Dooly	S	536
Villanow, Walker	NW	64
● Villa Rica, Carroll	W	426
Vines Mills, Worth	S	45
● Vineyard, Spalding	W	65
● Vining Station, Cobb	N	100
Viola, Heard	W	×
Violet, Meriwether	W	32
● Virgil, Jackson	N	75
Visage, Towns	N	50
Vivian, Screven	E	32
● Waco, Haralson	W	857
Waddells, Polk	NW	900
● **Wadley, Jefferson**	E	[illegible]
Wahoo, Lumpkin	N	65
● Wainright, Charlton	SE	125
● Walden, Bibb	C	100
Walesca, Cherokee	N	50
Walkee, Laurens	C	×
● Walker Station, Coug'tys	SW	40
Walnut, Jackson	N	×
Walnut Grove, Walton	N	75
Walnut Hill, Franklin	NE	10
Waltertown, Ware	SE	450
● Walthourville, Liberty	SE	500
Walthrall, Polk	NW	×
Wano, Henry	W	65
● Waresborough, Ware	SE	500
● Waring, Whitfield	NW	×
● Warm Springs, M'wether	W	130
Warners, Polk	NW	×
Warnerville, Meriwether	W	25
● *Warren*, Walker	NW	×
● **Warrenton**, Warren	E	974
Warrior, Bibb	C	150
Warsaw, Milton	N	50
● Warthen, Washington	C	150
Warwick, Worth	S	25
War Woman, Rabun	NE	×
● **Washington**, Wilkes	NE	2,631
Waterville, Walker	NW	10
● *Waters*, Screven	E	20
● **Watkinsville**, Oconee	N	314
● Waverly Hall, Harris	W	200
● **Way Cross**, Ware	SE	3,364
● **Waynesborough**, B'ke	E	1,711

Town, County	Index	Pop.
● Waynesville, Wayne	SE	300
Waynmanville, Upson	W	50
● Wayside, Jones	C	25
● Way's Station, Bryan	SE	150
Weatherleys, Whitfield	NW	×
Weaver, Pike	W	32
Webb, Milton	N	50
Webster, Harris	W	×
Webster Place, Elbert	NE	25
Welborn's Mills, Houston	C	×
Welch, Towns	N	×
Welcome, Coweta	W	×
Wells, Murray	NW	10
● Wellston, Houston	C	15
● Wenona, Dooly	S	20
Wesley, Oconee	N	×
● *Wessboro*, Walker	NW	×
West Atlanta, Fulton	NW	×
● West Bowersville, F'klin	NE	80
Westbrook, Laurens	C	×
West End, Fulton	NW	1,445
● Westlake, Twiggs	C	125
● Weston, Webster	SW	215
● Westonia, Coffee	S	100
● West Point, Troup	W	1,254
● *Wheaton*, Appling	SE	85
Wheeler, Gordon	NW	35
● *Wheless*, Richmond	E	×
● Whigham, Decatur	SW	264
White, Bartow	NW	×
● White Hall, Clarke	N	×
White House, Henry	W	25
● Whitepath, Gilmer	N	20
White Plains, Greene	C	510
● *White Plains Jc.*, Greene	C	×
● Whitesburg, Carroll	W	294
● *White Springs*, Floyd	NW	×
White Sulphur Springs, Meriwether	W	150
● *White Sulphur Sp'gs*, Hall	N	25
Whitesville, Harris	W	85
Whitewater, Crawford	C	20
● *Whitfield*, Troup	W	×
● *Whiting*, Baldwin	C	×
Whitney, Walton	N	32
Whitsett, Lee	SW	20
Whittington, Worth	S	26
● Wicker, Washington	C	×
Wier, Dawson	N	50
● *Wiggins*, Emanuel	E	260
● *Wigginsville*, Marion	W	96
Wilcox, Coffee	S	×
Wildwood, Dade	NW	26
Williford, Dooly	S	×
● *Wilkerson's*, Dooly	S	×
Wilkins, Floyd	NW	×
● Willacoochee, Coffee	S	398
Willard, Putnam	C	×
● *Williams*, Butts	C	×
● Williamsburgh, Cal'hn	SW	172
● Williamson, Pike	W	150
● *Williamson*, Screven	E	×
Williamsville, (see Flat Shoals)		×
● *Willis*, Terrell	SW	×
Willow, Lumpkin	N	26
● Willingham, Worth	S	233
Wilson, Appling	SE	×
● *Wilsons*, Hancock	C	×
Wilsonville, Douglas	W	×
● Winchester, Macon	W	20
Windsor, Walton	N	40
Winfield, Hancock	C	200
Winfred, Jasper	C	80
Winn, Douglas	W	×
● *Winston*, Douglas	W	130
● Winterville, Oglethorpe	NE	400
Winton, Newton	C	50
Wiregrass, Clinch	S	100
Wisdom's Store, Harris	W	18
● *Wise*, Bibb	C	×
● Wishart, Wilcox	S	25
Withers, Clinch	S	75
Wolf Fork, Rabun	NE	×
Wood, Warren	E	×
● Woodbury, Meriwether	W	369
● Woodcliff, Screven	E	100
Woodhull, Decatur	SW	×
Woodlawn, Murray	NW	100
Wood's Mill, Heard	W	×
Wood Station, Catoosa	NW	6
● Woodstock, Cherokee	N	100
Woodstock, (see Philomath)		×
● *Woodstock Branch*, Polk	NW	×
● Woodville, Greene	C	500
Woodward, Fulton	NW	×
● *Wooley*, Bartow	NW	×
Woolley's Ford, Hall	N	65
● Woolsey, Fayette	N	65
Wootten's Mill, Telfair	S	50
Worth, Worth	S	50
Worthville, Butts	C	50
● Wrens, Jefferson	E	125
Wrightsboro, McDuffie	E	20
● **Wrightsville**, Johnson	C	910
Wye, Pike	W	×
Wych, Elbert	NE	×
Wylly, Laurens	C	60
Wynn's Mill, Henry	W	130
Wynnton, Muscogee	W	×
Xerxes, Meriwether	W	100
Yacht, Screven	E	45
Yanoola, Lumpkin	N	32
Yanceys, Floyd	NW	×
Yarborough, Floyd	NW	65
Yatesville, Upson	W	100
Yellow Creek, Dawson	N	25
Yellow Dirt, Heard	W	20
Yellow River, Gwinnett	N	200
Yeomans, Emanuel	E	32
York, Houston	C	50
Yorkville, Paulding	NW	160
Young Cane, Union	NW	32
Young Harris, Towns	N	50
● *Youngs*, Washington	C	50
● Youngs, Polk	NW	50
Younker, Dodge	C	×
Ypsilanti, Talbot	W	×
Zaidee, Montgomery	C	40
● **Zebulon**, Pike	W	315
● Zeigler, Screven	E	×
Zeland, Irwin	S	32
● *Zelobee*, Marion	W	×
● Zetella, Spalding	W	25
Zoar, Bulloch	C	20
Zula, Chattooga	NW	×

IDAHO.

COUNTIES.	INDEX.	POP.
Ada	W	8,368
Alturas	C	2,629
Bear Lake	SE	6,057
Bingham	SE	13,575
Boise	C	3,342
Cassia	S	3,143
Custer	C	2,176
Elmore	C	1,870
Idaho	C	2,955
Kootenai	N	4,108
Latah	N	9,173
Lemhi	C	1,915
Logan	S	4,169
Nez Perces	N	2,847
Oneida	S	6,819
Owyhee	S	2,021
Shoshone	N	5,382
Washington	C	3,836
Total		84,385

TOWN. COUNTY.	INDEX.	POP.
Ætna, (see Bay Horse)		×
Albany Falls, Kootenai	N	×
Albeni, Kootenai	N	×
Albion, Cassia	S	179
Alder, Custer	C	×
● *Algoma*, Kootenai	N	×
Almo, Cassia	S	60
Alpha, Boise	C	×
Alpine, Washington	C	×
● American Falls, Oneida	S	100
● *Anderson*, Kootenai	N	×
Antelope, Alturas	C	×
Arangee, Bingham	SE	×
Arco, Alturas	C	65
● *Arimo*, Bingham	SE	97
● *Athol*, Kootenai	N	×
Atlanta, Elmore	C	100
Avon, Latah	N	×
Badger, Bingham	SE	×
Bancroft, Bingham	SE	×
Ballard, Owyhee	S	×
Banner, Boise	C	100
Bannister, Lemhi	C	×
● Basalt, Bingham	SE	×
Basin, Cassia	S	65
Battle Creek, Oneida	S	65
Bay Horse, Custer	C	500
Bay Horse Jc. (see Bay Horse)		×
Bear Lake, (see Paris)		×
● Beaver, Bingham	SE	260
● Bellevue, Logan	S	892
Bennington, Bear Lake	SE	196
Berry, Bingham	SE	200
Birch Creek, Bingham	SE	×
● *Bisuka*, Ada	W	×
● **Blackfoot**, Bingham	SE	600
Blaine, Latah	N	×
● Bliss, Logan	S	50
Bloomington, Bear Lake	SE	400
● **Boise City**, Ada	W	2,311
Bolton, Alturas	C	×
Bonanza City, Custer	C	250
Bonner's Ferry, Kootenai	N	×
Boonville, (see Silver City)		×
Bortel, Bingham	SE	×
Boulder, Alturas	C	260
Boulder City, Kootenai	N	25
Boulder Cr., (see Ketchum)		×
Bradford, Logan	S	300
Brannan, Washington	C	×
Brickaville, Latah	N	×
Bridge, Cassia	S	65
Briggs, Logan	S	×
Brownlee, Washington	C	65
Bruneau Valley, Owyhee	S	97
Bullion, Alturas	C	500
● Burke, Shoshone	N	600
Butte, Cassia	S	×
● *Cabinet*, Kootenai	N	×
Cabinet L'nd'g, (see Sandy Pt)		×
Cady, Shoshone	N	×
● Caldwell, Ada	W	779
Caleb, Custer	C	32
● *Calvin*, Bingham	SE	×
● Camas, Bingham	SE	130
Camas Creek, Latah	N	×
Cameron, Nez Perces	N	150
● *Cannon*, Oneida	S	×
Carbon, Shoshone	N	×
Carbonate, Custer	C	×
● Card, Oneida	S	×
Carey, Logan	S	×
Carriboo, Bingham	SE	×
Caskell, Lemhi	C	×
Castle Creek, Owyhee	S	97
● *Cataldo*, Shoshone	N	×
Cedarville, Nez Perces	N	×
Center, Boise	C	×
Central, Owyhee	S	×
Centreville, Boise	C	255
Challis, Custer	C	356
Chambers, Latah	N	×
● *Chatcolet*, Kootenai	N	×
Cherry Creek, Oneida	S	×
Chesterfield, Bingham	SE	240
● *China Point*, Bingham	SE	×
Chloride, Kootenai	N	×
Clark's Fork, Kootenai	N	50
● *Clark's Fork*, Kootenai	N	50
Clayton, Custer	C	252
Clear Water, Idaho	C	×
● *Cleft*, Elmore	C	×
Cleveland, Bingham	SE	×
Cliff, Custer	C	×
Clifton, Oneida	S	375
Clyde, Bingham	SE	×
● *Cocolala*, Kootenai	N	×
● Coeur d'Alene, Kootenai	N	491
Cold Springs, Elmore	C	×
Colson, Bingham	SE	×
Conant, Cassia	S	×
Concordia, Custer	C	×
Conor, Cassia	S	×
Cornwall, Latah	N	150
Corral, Logan	S	×
Cottonwood, Nez Perces	N	25
Council Valley, Washington	C	77
Craig's M'nt'n, Nez Perces	N	25
Crane, Washington	C	×
● *Crater*, Bingham	SE	×
Crawford, Boise	C	×
Crichton, Logan	S	100
Crossport, Kootenai	N	200
Crystal City, (see Clayton)		×
Custer, Custer	C	260
Dairy, Owyhee	S	×
Dale, Washington	C	×
DeLamar, Owyhee	S	×
Delta, Shoshone	N	40
Desmet, Kootenai	N	×
Dickey, Custer	C	×
● Dingle, Bear Lake	SE	×
Doniphan, Logan	S	×
● *Downey*, Bingham	SE	×
● *Dry Creek*, Bingham	SE	×
Dubois, Ada	W	×
Eagle, Shoshone	N	50
● *Eagle Rock*, Bingham	SE	500

Earncliff, Cassia .... S ×
● *Eatonville*, Kootenai .... N 25
Edmunds, Bingham .... SE ×
Egin, Bingham .... SE ×
Elba, Cassia .... S 200
Elizabeth, Logan .... S ×
Elk City, Idaho .... C 25
Ellis, Custer .... C ×
Emmett, Ada .... W 125
Enaville, Shoshone .... N ×
Era, Alturas .... C ×
Ethels, (see Rocky Bar) .... ×
Eugene, Boise .... C ×
Evolution, Shoshone .... N 20
Fairview, Oneida .... S 65
Falk's Store, Ada .... W 50
Falls, Oneida .... S ×
Falls, Washington .... C ×
Fish Haven, Bear Lake .... SE 135
Fish Lake, Kootenai .... N ×
Flint, (see Silver City) .... ×
Florence, Idaho .... C 390
Fort Hall, Bingham .... SE 60
Fort Lapwai, Latah .... N ×
Fort Lemhi, Lemhi .... C ×
Fort Sherman, Kootenai ... N ×
● Franklin, Oneida .... S 600
Fraser, Shoshone .... N ×
Freedom, Idaho .... C 20
● *Frisco*, Shoshone .... N ×
Frost, Custer .... C ×
Fry, Kootenai .... N 100
Galena, Alturas .... C 520
Garden Valley, Boise .... C 250
● Garner, Oneida .... S ×
● Gem, Shoshone .... N 500
● Genesee, Latah .... N 282
Gentile Valley, Bingham .. SE 500
● Georgetown, Bear Lake. SE 212
Gibsonsville, Lemhi .... C 100
Gilman, Logan .... S 65
Glenn, Shoshone .... N 10
Glenn's Falls, Logan .... S ×
● Glenn's Ferry, Elmore .... C 333
Glenwood, Idaho .... C ×
Goldburg, Custer .... C ×
Goose, Cassia .... S ×
● *Grace*, Bingham .... SE ×
● *Granite*, Shoshone .... N ×
Graham, Boise .... C 250
Grand View, Owyhee .... S ×
Grangeville, Idaho .... C 540
Granville, Idaho .... C ×
Gray's, Bingham .... SE 100
Haden, Bingham .... SE ×
● **Hailey**, Alturas .... C 2,000
Halfway, Kootenai .... N ×
Harlo, Boise .... C ×
Harrison, Kootenai .... N 25
● Hauser, Kootenai .... N ×
● *Hawgood*, Bingham .... SE ×
Hays, Logan .... S ×
Helena, Washington .... C ×
Henderson, Owyhee .... S ×
Henry, Bingham .... SE ×
High, Boise .... C ×
● *High Bridge*, Bingham ... SE ×
Hoffman, Washington .... C ×
Hoodoo, Latah .... N ×
● Hope, Kootenai .... N 600
Horse Shoe Bend, Boise .... C ×
Houston, Custer .... C 100
Howe, Bingham .... SE 50
● *Howell*, Latah .... N ×
Humphrey's, Logan .... S 80
Hunter, Ada .... W ×
Idaho City, Boise .... C 750
● Idaho Falls, Bingham ... SE 500
Illville, Kootenai .... N ×
Independence, Bingham ... SE ×
Indian Valley, Washington .. C 130
● *Inkom*, Bingham .... SE ×
Iona, (see Idaho Falls) .... ×
Island, Cassia .... S ×
Jamestown, Latah .... N 75
Jessie, Cassia .... S ×
Joel, Latah .... N ×
John Days, Idaho .... C 5
Jordan Creek, Custer .... C ×
● Juliaetta, Latah .... N 100
Junction, Lemhi .... C 200
Kaintuck, Bingham .... SE 500
Karnai, Nez Perces .... N ×
● Kellogg, Shoshone .... N 50
Kelso, Cassia .... S ×
● Kendrick, Latah .... N 250
● Ketchum, Alturas .... C 450
Keuterville, Idaho .... C 14

Kilgore, Bingham .... SE ×
● *Kimama*, Logan .... S ×
● *King Hill*, Elmore .... C ×
● Kingston, Shoshone .... N 60
Kooskia, Idaho .... C ×
● Kootenai, Kootenai .... N 250
● *Kuna*, Ada .... W ×
Labelle, Bingham .... SE ×
Lago, Bingham .... SE ×
Lake, Bingham .... SE ×
Lakeview, Kootenai .... N ×
● Lane, Kootenai .... N ×
Laneville, Cassia .... S ×
Lapham, Bingham .... SE ×
Lapwai, Nez Perces .... N 50
Lardo, Boise .... C ×
Lava, Bingham .... SE ×
● *Lava*, Bingham .... SE 130
Lava Creek, Alturas .... C ×
Leduc, Logan .... S ×
Leesburgh, Lemhi .... C 32
Leland, Nez Perces .... N 25
Lemhi Agency, Lemhi .... C 130
Lenville, Latah .... N ×
● *Leon*, Nez Perces .... N ×
Leslie, Custer .... C ×
Lewiston, Nez Perces .... N 849
Lewisville, Bingham .... SE ×
Liberty, Bear Lake .... SE 65
Lidyville, Latah .... N ×
Lime Rock, Elmore .... C ×
Linden, Latah .... N ×
Little Camas, (see M'nt'nHome ×
Littlefield, Shoshone .... N 10
Lolo, Shoshone .... N ×
Long Valley, (see Vanwyck) ×
Lost River, Alturas .... C ×
● *Lovell*, Kootenai .... N ×
Lower Boise, Ada .... W ×
Lyman, (see Independence) ×
McAuley, Shoshone .... × ×
● McCammon, Bingham .. SE 65
Malad City, Oneida .... S 1,000
Malta, Cassia .... S 65
● *Manchester*, Shoshone ... N ×
● *Manson*, Bear Lake .... SE ×
Marion, Cassia .... S ×
● Market Lake, Bingham .. SE 125
Marsh, Boise .... C ×
Marshall, Kootenai .... N ×
Martin, Alturas .... C 65
Marysville, Bingham .... SE ×
Mason Nez Perces .... N 15
Mayfield, Elmore .... C ×
Meadows, Washington .... C 125
Medimont, Kootenai .... N 10
● *Medbury*, Elmore .... C ×
Menan, (see Platte) .... ×
● *Michaud*, Oneida .... S ×
Middleton, Ada .... W 190
Middle Valley, Washington .. C 65
Milo, (see Kellogg) .... ×
Mineral, Washington .... C ×
● Minidoka, Logan .... S ×
Mink, Oneida .... S ×
Mink Creek, Oneida .... S 360
● *Mission*, Kootenai .... N 25
● Montpelier, Bear Lake .. SE 1,174
● *Mora*, Ada .... W ×
Morgan, (see Oxford) .... ×
Morrell, Oneida .... S ×
Morse, Custer .... C ×
● **Moscow**, Latah .... N 2,000
Mountain Cove, Latah .... N ×
Mountain Home, Elmore .... C 233
Mount Idaho, Idaho .... C 190
Muldoon, Alturas .... C 65
● Mullan, Shoshone .... N 500
Murray, Shoshone .... N 250
Myrtle, Shoshone .... N 20
● *Nameko*, Ada .... W ×
● Nampa, Ada .... W 347
● *Napati*, Logan .... S ×
Naples, (see Shoshone) .... ×
Neely, Oneida .... S ×
Newport, Kootenai .... N 20
Niceolai, Lemhi .... C 350
Nine Mile, Bingham .... SE ×
Noonda, Logan .... S ×
● *Notus*, Ada .... W ×
Nounan, Bear Lake .... SE ×
● *Novene*, Bear Lake .... SE ×
● *Nupher*, Bear Lake. .... SE ×
Oakley, Cassia .... S 1,000
● *Oden*, Kootenai .... N ×
Ola, Boise .... C ×
● Old Mission, Kootenai .... N 25
Old's Ferry, Washington ... C ×

Omega, Bingham .... SE ×
● Oneida, Bingham .... SE 130
● *Onyx*, Bingham .... SE ×
Oreana, Owyhee .... S ×
● Osburn, Shoshone .... N 100
Oswego, Alturas .... C ×
Ovid, Bear Lake .... SE 190
● *Owinza*, Logan .... S ×
● *Owyhee*, Ada .... W ×
● Oxford, Bingham .... SE 900
● *Pack River*, Kootenai .... N ×
Pagari, Logan .... S ×
Paris, Bear Lake .... SE 893
● Parma, Ada .... W ×
● Payette, Ada .... W ×
Payette Store, Ada .... W ×
● *Payne*, Bingham .... SE ×
Paynes, Logan .... S ×
● *Pebble*, Bingham .... SE ×
● Pend d'Oreille, Kootenai. N ×
Pendleton, Bingham .... SE ×
● *Pescadero*, Bear Lake ... SE ×
● *Picabo*, Logan .... S ×
Pierce City, Shoshone .... N 60
Pine, Elmore .... C 150
Pine Grove, Elmore .... C 150
Pioneerville, Boise .... C 260
Pittsburg Landing, Idaho ... C 525
Placerville, Boise .... C 200
Platt, Bingham .... SE 300
● *Pleasant Valley*, Bing'm SE ×
● *Plummer*, Kootenai .... N ×
● Pocatello, Bingham .... SE 2,500
● *Port Neuf*, Bingham .... SE ×
● Post Falls, Kootenai .... N 500
Presto, Bingham .... SE ×
● Preston, Oneida .... S 300
Priest River, Kootenai .... N 25
Quartzburgh, Boise .... C 70
● *Ramsey*, Kootenai .... N ×
● **Rathdrum**, Kootenai .. N 218
Red Warrior, Elmore .... C ×
● *Reverse*, Elmore .... C ×
Rexburg, (see Kaintuck) .... ×
Reynolds, Owyhee .... S ×
Riblett, Cassia .... S ×
Rigby, Bingham .... SE ×
Riverdale, Oneida .... S 160
Riverside, Ada .... W 40
Robinsons Bar, Custer .... C ×
Rock Creek, Cassia .... S 65
Rockland, Oneida .... S ×
Rockville, Owyhee .... S ×
Rocky Bar, Elmore .... C 500
Rose, Washington .... C ×
Roseberry, Boise .... C ×
● Ross Fork, Bingham .... SE 150
Rustic, Idaho .... C 50
Ruthburg, Washington .... C 65
St. Anthony, Bingham .... SE ×
St. Charles, Bear Lake .... SE 400
St. Joe, Kootenai .... N ×
St. John's, Oneida .... S ×
St. Maries, Kootenai .... N 100
St. Paul, (see Riverside) .... ×
Salmon City, Lemhi .... C 500
Salmon Falls, Logan .... S ×
Salubria, Washington .... C 150
Samaria, Oneida .... S 500
● *Sand Point*, Kootenai .... N 150
Santa, Kootenai .... N ×
Sater, Washington .... C ×
Saw Tooth, Alturas .... C 390
Seneaguotteen, Kootenai ... N ×
Seven Devils, (see Helena) .... ×
Shafer, Boise .... C ×
Shealer's Ferry, Idaho .... C ×
Sherman, Kootenai .... N ×
Short, Elmore .... C ×
● **Shoshone**, Logan .... S 958
Shoshone Falls, Logan .... S ×
Shoup, Lemhi .... C 50
Silver City, Owyhee .... S 433
Sinker, Owyhee .... S ×
Slate Creek, Idaho .... C ×
Small, Bingham .... SE ×
Smoky, Alturas .... C 300
● Soda Springs, Bingham .. SE 350
Soldier, Logan .... S ×
South Mountain, Lemhi .... C ×
South Mountain, Owyhee ... S ×
Southwick, Nez Perces .... N ×
Spring, Washington .... C ×
Spring Hill, (see Montana) ... ×
Spring Mountain, Lemhi ... C 97
Springvail, Bingham .... SE ×
● *Squaw Creek*, Bingham. SE 67
Standrod, Cassia .... S ×

Stanton, Logan	S	×
Star, Ada	W	×
Starner, Latah	N	25
Stone Switch, Kootenai	N	×
Sublett, Cassia	S	260
● Swan Lake, Bingham	SE	×
Sweet, Boise	C	×
Tammany, Nez Perces	N	×
Taney, Latah	N	×
Taylor, Bingham	SE	×
Teton, Bingham	SE	×
● *Thatcher*, Bingham	SE	×
Thatcher, Cassia	S	×
Thomas Fork, Bear Lake	SE	×
● *Thornton*, Kootenai	N	×
Three Creek, Owyhee	S	×
Thurman's Mills, Ada	W	32
● *Ticeska*, Logan	S	×
● *Tikura*, Logan	S	×
● *Tilma*, Kootenai	N	×
● *Topaz*, Bingham	SE	×
● Toponis, Logan	S	50
Treesureton, Bingham	SE	65
Triumph, Alturas	C	×
● *Tunupa*, Logan	S	×
Union, Logan	S	×
Vanwyck, Boise	C	×
Vienna, Alturas	C	195
Viola, Latah	N	50
● Vollmer, Latah	N	250
Waha, Nez Perces	N	5
● Wallace, Shoshone	N	878
Walters, Ada	W	×
● *Wapi*, Logan	S	×
Ward, Cassia	S	×
● Wardner, Shoshone	N	1,500
● *Wardner Junc.*, Shoshone	N	100
Warm Springs, (see Warren)		×
Warren, Idaho	C	400
Warrior, Alturas	C	×
Washington, (see Warren)		×
● Washoe, Ada	W	200
● *Watts*, Kootenai	N	×
● *Waucanza*, Logan	S	×
Webber, Kootenai	N	×
Weippe, Shoshone	N	×
● **Weiser**, Washington	C	901
Weston, Oneida	S	500
White Bird, Idaho	C	25
Whitinger's Mts., Nez Perces	N	50
● Whitney, Oneida	S	×
Wilburus, Washington	C	×
Wilford, (see Berry)		×
Woodbine, Logan	S	65
Woodland, Lemhi	C	×
Wood River Dist., (see Ketch'm)		×
Yale, Cassia	S	×

ILLINOIS.

COUNTIES.	INDEX.	POP.
Adams	W	61,888
Alexander	S	16,563
Bond	S	14,550
Boone	N	12,203
Brown	W	11,951
Bureau	N	35,014
Calhoun	W	7,652
Carroll	NW	18,320
Cass	W	15,963
Champaign	E	42,159
Christian	C	30,531
Clark	E	21,899
Clay	S	16,772
Clinton	S	17,411
Coles	E	30,093
Cook	NE	1,191,922
Crawford	SE	17,283
Cumberland	E	15,443
DeKalb	N	27,066
DeWitt	C	17,011
Douglas	E	17,669
Du Page	NE	22,551
Edgar	E	26,787
Edwards	SE	9,444
Effingham	S	19,358
Fayette	S	23,367
Ford	E	17,035
Franklin	S	17,138
Fulton	W	43,110
Gallatin	SE	14,935
Greene	W	23,791
Grundy	N	21,024
Hamilton	S	17,800
Hancock	W	31,907
Hardin	SE	7,234
Henderson	W	9,876
Henry	NW	33,338
Iroquois	E	35,167
Jackson	S	27,809
Jasper	SE	18,188
Jefferson	S	22,590
Jersey	SW	14,810
Jo Daviess	NW	25,101
Johnson	S	15,013
Kane	N	65,061
Kankakee	E	28,732
Kendall	N	12,106
Knox	W	38,752
Lake	NE	24,235
La Salle	N	80,798
Lawrence	NE	14,693
Lee	N	26,187
Livingston	C	38,455
Logan	C	25,489
McDonough	W	27,467
McHenry	N	26,114
McLean	SW	63,036
Macon	S	38,083
Macoupin	C	40,380
Madison	C	51,535
Marion	S	24,341
Marshall	C	13,653
Mason	NW	16,067
Massac	SW	11,313
Menard	C	13,120
Mercer	NW	18,545
Monroe	SW	12,948
Montgomery	C	30,003
Morgan	W	32,636
Moultrie	C	14,481
Ogle	N	28,710
Peoria	C	70,378
Perry	S	17,529
Piatt	C	17,062
Pike	W	31,000
Pope	S	14,016
Pulaski	S	11,355
Putnam	N	4,730
Randolph	SW	25,049
Richland	SE	15,019
Rock Island	NW	41,917
Saint Clair	SW	66,571
Saline	S	19,342
Sangamon	C	61,195
Schuyler	W	16,013
Scott	W	10,304
Shelby	C	31,191
Stark	C	9,982
Stephenson	NW	31,338
Tazewell	C	29,556
Union	S	21,549
Vermilion	E	49,905
Wabash	SE	11,866
Warren	W	21,281
Washington	S	19,262
Wayne	SE	23,806
White	SE	25,005
Whiteside	NW	30,854
Will	NE	62,007
Williamson	S	22,226
Winnebago	N	39,938
Woodford	C	21,429
Total		**3,826,351**

*Population included in Chicago.

TOWN. COUNTY.	INDEX.	POP.
● Abingdon, Knox	W	1,321
● **Adair**, McDonough	W	169
Adams, Adams	W	125
Adams' Cors, (see Allendale)		×
● *Adams*, Livingston	C	×
● Addieville, Washington	S	117
● Addison, Dupage	NE	485
Addison Street, Cook	NE	×
● Adeline, Ogle	N	256
● Adrian, Hancock	W	150
● Advance, Jasper	SE	30
● Aetna, Coles	E	100
Afolkey, Stephenson	NW	75
● *Aiken*, Jo Daviess	NW	×
● Akin, Franklin	S	100
Akron, Peoria	C	32
● *Aladdin*, Pike	W	×
● Albany, Whiteside	NW	611
● **Albion**, Edwards	SE	937
● Alden, McHenry	N	100
● *Aldridge*, Union	S	×
● **Aledo**, Mercer	NW	1,601
● *Alexander*, Kane	N	×
● Alexander, Morgan	W	150
● Alexis, Warren	W	562
● Algonquin, McHenry	N	500
● Alhambra, Madison	C	250
● Allendale, Wabash	SE	400
Allen's Spring, Pope	S	6
Allentown, (see Farlow)		×
● Allentown, Tazewell	C	30
● *Allenville*, Moultrie	C	45
● *Allerton*, Piatt	C	×
● Allerton Vermilion	E	63
Allison, Lawrence	NE	7
● Alma, Marion	S	225
● *Alma*, Saint Clair	SW	165
● Almora, Kane	N	×
● Alpha, Henry	NW	200
● Alpine, Cook	NE	40
● Alsey, Scott	W	150
● Alta, Peoria	C	75
● Altamont, Effingham	S	1,044
● *Altenheim*, Cook	NE	×
● Alton, Madison	C	10,294
● Altona, Knox	W	654
● Alton Junction, Madison	C	195
● *Alton Summit*, Madison	C	×
● Alto Pass, Union	S	389
Altorf, (see Kankakee)		×
● Alvin, Vermilion	E	300
● *Alworth*, Winnebago	N	×
● Amboy, Lee	N	2,257
● America, Pulaski	S	40
Ames, Monroe	SW	13
Amity, Richland	SE	13
● Anchor, McLean	SW	200
● Ancona, Livingston	C	300
Andalusia, Rock Island	NW	281
● Anderson, Cass	W	×
● *Anderson*, Macoupin	C	×
Andover, Henry	NW	259
● Anna, Union	S	2,295
Annapolis, Crawford	SE	150
● Annawan, Henry	NW	387
● Antioch, Lake	NE	303
Antonius, Adams	W	26
● Apple River, JoDaviess	NW	572
● Appleton, Knox	W	10
● Aptakisic, Lake	NE	10
Arcadia, Morgan	W	100
Archie, Vermilion	E	50
● Arcola, Douglas	E	1,733
● *Arden*, Pike	W	×
● Arenzville, Cass	W	356
● Argenta, Macon	S	350
Argo, Carroll	NW	15
● Argyle, Winnebago	N	50
● Argyle Park, Cook	NE	*
● Arlington, Bureau	N	436
● Arlington Heights, Cook	NE	1,424
● Armington, Tazewell	C	241
● Armstrong, Vermilion	E	250
● Arnold, Morgan	W	×
● *Aroma*, Kankakee	E	×
● *Arrington*, Wayne	SE	50
● Arrowsmith, McLean	SW	320
● Arthur, Moultrie	C	586
● *Ashdale*, Carroll	NW	×
Ash Grove, Iroquois	E	[illegible]
● Ashkum, Iroquois	E	300
● Ashland, Cass	W	1,045
● Ashley, Washington	S	1,035
● Ashmore, Coles	E	446
● Ashton, Lee	N	680
Ashville, Schuyler	W	16
● Assumption, Christian	C	1,076
● Astoria, Fulton	W	1,357
● Athens, Menard	C	944
Athensville, Greene	W	150
● Atkinson, Henry	NW	534
● Atlanta, Logan	C	1,178
Atlas, Pike	W	30
● Atterberry, Menard	C	30
Attila, Williamson	S	25
Atwater, Macoupin	C	250
● Atwood, Piatt	C	530
● *Auburn*, Clark	E	×
● Auburn, Sangamon	C	874
● *Auburn Junction*, Cook	NE	×
● Auburn Park, Cook	NE	*
● Augusta, Hancock	W	1,077
● Aurora, Kane	N	19,688
● Austin, Cook	NE	4,051
Aux Sable, Grundy	N	×
● Ava, Jackson	S	807
● Avena, Fayette	S	100
Avery, JoDaviess	NW	×
● Aviston, Clinton	S	381
● Avon, Fulton	W	692

Place		
● Avondale, Cook	NE	*
Babylon, Fulton	W	50
Baden Baden, Bond	S	20
● Baders, Schuyler	W	150
● Baileyville, Ogle	N	187
● *Bainbridge*, Williamson	S	×
● Baker, LaSalle	N	×
● *Baker*, McLean	SW	×
● *Baker's Lane*, Crawford	SE	×
● Balcom, Union	S	×
Bald Mound, Kane	N	×
● *Baldwin*, Greene	W	390
● Baldwin, Randolph	SW	298
Ball, White	SE	×
Ballard, McLean	SW	×
Bandow, Cook	NE	*
Banner, Fulton	W	100
● *Bannister's*, Marion	S	×
Barclay, Ogle	N	×
● Barclay, Sangamon	C	250
● *Barco*, Madison	C	×
Barcoville, Madison	C	×
Bardolph, McDonough	W	447
Barnard, Adams	W	20
● Barnes McLean	SW	×
● Barnett, Montgomery	C	20
● Barnhill, Wayne	SE	100
● *Barr*, Cook	NE	×
Barreville, McHenry	N	40
● Barrington, Cook	NE	848
● Barrow, Greene	W	100
Barr's Store, Macoupin	C	50
● Barry, Pike	W	1,354
● Barstow, Rock Island	NW	25
● Bartelso, Clinton	S	×
● Bartlett, Cook	NE	263
● *Bartlett*, Peoria	C	×
● *Bartley*, Gallatin	SE	×
● Bartonville, Peoria	C	1,000
● *Barwells*, Perry	S	×
● **Basco, Hancock**	W	827
● Batavia, Kane	N	3,543
Batchtown, Calhoun	W	75
● Bates, Sangamon	C	50
● Bath, Mason	NW	384
Bauman, Adams	W	×
Bay, (see Mozier)		×
Bay City, Pope	S	50
● Bayle City, Fayette	S	25
● Baylis, Pike	W	368
Bay Station, (see McNoel)		×
● *Beach Bluff*, Wayne	SE	×
● Beardstown, Cass	W	4,226
● Bearsdale, Macon	S	25
● Beason, Logan	C	150
● Beaucoup, Washington	S	48
Beaver, Clinton	S	×
Beaver Creek, Bond	S	100
Beaverton, Boone	N	×
● Beaverville, Iroquois	E	300
● *Beckwith*, Vermilion	E	×
Bedford, Pike	W	20
● Beecher, Will	NE	342
● Beecher City, Effingham	S	300
● Beech Ridge, Alexander	S	65
Beechville, Calhoun	W	65
Bee Creek, Pike	W	10
● Belknap, Johnson	S	358
● *Bell*, Logan	C	×
Bell, Marion	S	26
Bell Air, Crawford	SE	100
● Belle Flower, McLean	SW	300
Belle Plain, Marshall	C	75
Belle Prairie, Hamilton	S	195
● Belle Rive, Jefferson	S	550
Belleview, Calhoun	W	100
● **Belleville**, St. Clair	SW	15,361
Belleville Junc. St Clair	SW	×
Bellmont, Wabash	SE	487
● *Bellewood*, Cook	NE	×
● *Belmont*, Cook	NE	×
● **Belvidere**, Boone	N	3,867
● *Beman*, Lawrence	NE	×
● Bement, Piatt	C	1,129
Benjaminsville, (see Holder)		×
● Bensenville, Du Page	NE	295
● Benson, Woodford	C	338
● Bentley, Hancock	W	144
● **Benton**, Franklin	S	939
● *Benton*, Lake	NE	×
Benville, Brown	W	15
● Berdan, Greene	W	150
● *Berger*, Cook	NE	×
Berlin, Sangamon	C	260
● *Berlin*, Sangamon	C	×
Bernadotte, Fulton	W	100
Bernice, Cook	NE	×

Place		
● *Berry*, Sangamon	C	78
Berryton, Cass	W	390
Berryville, Richland	SE	19
● Berwick, Warren	W	200
● Berwyn, Cook	NE	×
● Bethalto, Madison	C	879
● Bethany, Moultrie	C	688
Bethel, Morgan	W	50
● *Bethell*, Jackson	S	×
● *Betterton*, Bond	S	50
Beverly, Adams	W	200
● *Beverly Hill*, Cook	NE	×
Bible Grove, Clay	S	200
● *Big Bay*, Massac	SW	×
● *Big Cut*, Carroll	NW	×
Big Foot Prairie, McHen'ys	N	×
● Biggs, Mason	NW	×
● Biggsville, Henderson	W	487
Big Neck, Adams	W	15
● Big Rock, Kane	N	200
Big Sandy, Morgan	W	×
● Billett, Lawrence	NE	32
● Bingham, Fayette	S	178
● *Birchwood*, Cook	NE	×
● Birds, Lawrence	NE	300
● Bird's Bridge, Will	NE	40
● Birkbeck, DeWitt	C	10
● Birkner, Saint Clair	SW	200
Birmingham, Schuyler	W	50
● Bishop, Mason	NW	100
● Bishop Hill, Henry	NW	330
● *Bismark*, Peoria	C	×
● Bismarck, Vermilion	E	200
Bixby, Vermilion	E	25
Blackberry, Kane	N	×
Blackburn, Christian	C	25
● *Blacks*, Adams	W	×
● Blackstone, Livingston	C	150
Blaine, Boone	N	150
Blair, Randolph	SW	100
Blairsville, Williamson	S	15
● *Blakes*, La Salle	N	×
● *Blanding*, Jo Daviess	NW	×
Blanding, Jo Daviess	NW	×
Blandinsville, McDonough	W	877
Blank's Station, Du Page	NE	10
● *Blodgett*, Will	NE	×
● Bloomfield, Johnson	S	175
Bloomfield, Scott	W	×
Bloomingdale, Du Page	NE	463
● **Bloomington**, McL'n	SW	20,484
Blount, Vermilion	E	40
Blue Grass, Vermilion	E	100
● Blue Island, Cook	NE	2,521
Blue Island Junc't, Cook	NE	×
● Blue Mound, Macon	S	696
● Blue Point, Effingham	S	25
● Blue Ridge, Piatt	C	50
Bluff City, Schuyler	W	75
● *Bluff City*, Fayette	S	20
Bluff Dale, Greene	W	65
● *Bluff Hall*, Adams	W	×
● Bluffs, Scott	W	421
● Bluff Springs, Cass	W	30
● Bluford, Jefferson	S	100
Blyton, Fulton	W	19
Boaz, Massac	SW	×
Bogie, Lawrence	NE	×
Bogota, Jasper	SE	150
Bolivia, Christian	C	×
● Bolton, Stephenson	NW	×
● *Bond*, Sangamon	C	×
● Bondville, Champaign	E	100
● Bone Gap, Edwards	SE	150
● Bonfield, Kankakee	E	150
Bonus, Boone	N	100
● Boody, Macon	S	200
● Boos' Station, Jasper	SE	75
● *Booths*, Grundy	N	×
Borton, Edgar	E	15
● *Borton Junction*, Edgar	E	15
● Boskydell, Jackson	S	×
● Boulder, Clinton	S	20
Bourbon, Douglas	E	50
Bourbonnais Grove, K'n'kee	E	600
● Bowen, Hancock	W	376
Bowlesburg, (see Loding)		×
Bowlesville, Gallatin	SE	455
● *Bowman*, Edgar	E	×
Bowmanville, Cook	NE	*
Bowyer, Richland	SE	×
● Boyd, Jefferson	S	30
● Boyleston, Wayne	SE	×
Boynton, Tazewell	C	40
● Braceville, Grundy	N	2,150
● Bradbury, Cumberland	E	40
Braden, Hamilton	S	×

Place		
● Bradford, Stark	C	604
● Bradfordton, Sangamon	C	15
● Bradley, Tazewell	C	10
Bradshaw, Union	S	×
● **Braidwood**, Will	NE	4,641
● ***Brainerd***, **Cook**	NE	×
Branch, **Saint Clair**	SW	×
● *Branch Junction*, Marion	S	×
Brayfield, Franklin	S	50
● Breckenridge, Sangamon	C	100
● Breed's, Fulton	W	200
● Breese, Clinton	S	808
Bremen, Randolph	SW	50
Brewer, Vermilion	E	×
● *Brewster's*, Pike	W	×
● Briar Bluff, Henry	NW	150
● *Briar Hill*, Kane	N	×
● *Brickton*, La Salle	N	×
Bridge Junction, Madison	C	×
● *Bridge Junction*, Peoria	C	×
● *Bridge Junction*, Will	NE	×
● *Bridge Junct'n*, St. Clair	SW	×
● *Bridge Junction*, Alex'd'r	S	×
● *Bridgeport*, Cook	NE	×
● Bridgeport, Lawrence	NE	500
Bridgewater, Greene	W	×
Brighton, Jersey	SW	45
● Brighton, Macoupin	C	697
● *Brighton Park*, Cook	NE	*
● Brimfield, Peoria	C	719
● *Brisbane*, Will	NE	×
● *Briscoe*, Clark	E	×
● Bristol, Kendall	N	300
● Broadlands, Champaign	E	300
● Broadwell, Logan	C	231
● Brocton, Edgar	E	292
● *Brokaw*, McLean	SW	×
● *Brookdale*, Cook	NE	×
● Brookline Park, Cook	NE	*
● *Brooklyn*, Saline	S	×
● *Brooklyn*, Massac	SW	216
Brooklyn, St. Clair	SW	×
Brooklyn, Schuyler	W	225
Brooks, Madison	C	219
Brookville, Ogle	N	150
● Broughton, Hamilton	S	300
● Browning, Schuyler	W	380
● Browns, Edwards	SE	300
Brown's Mill, (see Irondale)		×
● Brownstown, Fayette	S	200
● Brownsville, White	SE	75
● Bruce, Moultrie	C	50
Brunkhorst L'ndg., Jackson	S	×
Brunswick, Shelby	C	×
Brushy Fork, Douglas	E	30
Brussels, Calhoun	W	228
● Bryant, Fulton	W	309
● *Bryden*, Jackson	S	×
Buchanan, (see Dunn)		×
Buckeye, Stephenson	NW	20
Buck Horn, Brown	W	50
Buck Horn Island, Pike	W	×
● Buckingham, Kankakee	E	158
● Buckley, Iroquois	E	433
● *Buckner*, Franklin	S	×
● Buda, Bureau	N	990
● Budd, Livingston	C	25
Buena Park, Cook	NE	×
● Buena Vista, Steph'son	NW	100
● Buffalo, Sangamon	C	500
Buffalo Grove, Lake	NE	80
● Buffalo Hart, Sangamon	C	700
Buffalo Prairie, R. Island	NW	20
Bumpus, Jefferson	S	40
Buncombe, Johnson	S	35
● Bunker Hill, Macoupin	C	1,269
● Bureau, Bureau	N	363
● Bureau Siding, Lee	N	×
Burksville, Monroe	SW	150
● *Burksville*, Monroe	SW	×
● *Burlingame*, Cass	W	×
● Burlington, Kane	N	100
● *Burlington Park*, DuP'e	NE	×
Burnham, Cook	NE	25
Burns, Henry	NW	×
● Burnside Crossing, C'k	NE	*
● Burnside, Hancock	W	280
Burnt Prairie, White	SE	250
● *Burr Oak*, Cook	NE	×
Burrowsville, Piatt	C	×
Burton, Adams	W	92
● Burton View, Logan	C	50
● Bushnell, McDonough	W	2,314
● Bushton, Coles	E	50
● Butler, Montgomery	C	311
● *Butts*, Kankakee	E	×
Buxton, Clinton	S	×

Place	Pop.
●*Bybee*, Fulton............W	13
Byerton, Calhoun...........W	20
●*Byrneville*, Du Page ....NE	×
●Byron, Ogle...............N	698
●Cabery, Ford...............E	342
●Cable, Mercer..........NW	1,276
Cadwell, Moultrie............C	×
●Cahokia, Saint Clair ....SW	100
●**Cairo,** Alexander.........S	10,324
●Caledonia, Boone...........N	184
●*Caledonia Junction*, B'ne N	×
●Calhoun, Richland.......SE	150
California Avenue, Cook..NE	×
Calumet, Cook..............NE	250
●*Calumet River*, Cook....NE	×
●*Calvary*, *Cook* ....NE	×
●Calvin, White............SE	×
●Camargo, Douglas ....E	500
●**Cambridge**, Henry.. NW	940
Camden, Schuyler...........W	400
Camden Mills, (see Milan)...	×
●Cameron, Warren........W	350
Campbell, Coles..............E	50
●Campbell Hill, Jackson ...S	280
Camp Grove, Stark C	300
●Camp Point, Adams......W	1,170
●Campus, Livingston.......C	250
●Canaville, Williamson.....S	×
●*Cantine*, Madison.........C	×
●Canton, Fulton...........W	5,604
●Cantrall, Sangamon.......C	150
●Capron, Boone............ N	436
Carber's Ridge, (see Karber's Ridge)	×
●Carbon Cliff, Rock I'sl. NW	300
●Carbondale, Jackson......S	2,382
●**Carlinville**, Macoupin..C	3,293
●Carlock, McLean..........SW	150
●Carlton, De Kalb.........N	×
●**Carlyle,** Clinton..........S	1,784
●Carman, Henderson......W	300
●**Carmi,** White..........SE	2,785
●*Carnahan*, Lee...........N	×
●Carpenter, Madison.......C	150
●Carpentersville, Kane....N	754
●Carrier's Mills, Saline.....S	350
Carroll, Carroll..........NW	×
●**Carrollton,** Greene....W	2,258
●Carrow, Kankakee.........E	30
●Carterville, Williamson ...S	969
●**Carthage,** Hancock....W	1,654
●*Carthage Junction*, H's'n W	×
●Cary Station, McHenry...N	430
●Casey, Clark ....E	844
●Caseyville, Saint Clair...SW	475
●Casner, Macon.............S	100
Caspar's, Washington ....S	30
●*Cass*, Cass................W	×
●Castleton, Stark...........C	200
●*Castleton*, Kankakee......E	×
Castor, Wayne..............SE	13
Catfish, Edgar..............E	×
●Catlin, Vermilion..........E	275
●*Caton*, Marshall C	×
●*Caton Farm*, Will.......NE	×
Cave in Rock, Hardin......SE	200
Cawthon, Williamson ....S	32
●**Cayuga, Livingston........C**	**200**
●Cazenovia, Woodford.......C	100
●*Cedar*, Whiteside.......NW	×
Cedar Bluff, Johnson........S	×
Cedar Mills, Greene........W	10
Cedarville, Stephenson...NW	325
●*Cement Works*, LaSalle ..N	×
Centennial, Stephenson..NW	32
●*Center*, Tazewell..........C	×
●*Centerville*, Grundy.......N	×
Central City, Grundy....... N	673
●Central City, Marion......S	304
●Centralia, Marion..........S	4,763
●Central Park, Cook.....NE	*
Centre, Schuyler...........W	×
●*Centre Point*, Knox......W	×
Centre Ridge, (see Swedona).	×
Centreville, Platt............C	100
Centerville, (see School)......	×
●Centreville Station,St.Cl'SW	200
●Cerro Gordo, Platt.........C	939
●Chadwick, Carroll......NW	250
Chalfin Bridge, Monroe...SW	20
●Challacombe, Macoupin..C	×
Chambersburgh, Pike......W	200
Chamness, Williamson......S	×
●Champaign, Champaign...E	5,839
Champlin, Livingston...... C	×
●Chana, Ogle...............N	250
●*Chandler*, Cook.........NE	×
●Chandlerville, Cass.......W	910
Channahon, Will..........NE	325
●Chapin, Morgan..........W	500
●Chapman, Montgomery...C	10
●*Chappell*, Cook..........NE	×
●Charity, Vermilion........E	25
●**Charleston,** Coles......E	4,135
●Charlotte, Livingston......C	20
●Charter Grove, DeKalb...N	10
Chase, Peoria...............C	×
●Chatham, Sangamon.......C	482
●Chatsworth, Livingston...C	827
●Chattan, Adams..........W	20
Chauncey, Lawrence......NE	100
●Chebanse, Iroquois........E	616
●Cheltenham, Cook......NE	*
●*Cheltenham Beach*, Cook NE	*
●Chemung, McHenry.......N	250
●Cheneysville, Vermilion..E	50
●Chenoa, McLean........SW	1,226
●*Cherry Hills*, Will.......NE	1,100
●Cherry Point, Edgar....... E	200
●Cherry Valley, Win'eb'go N	800
●**Chester,** Randolph....SW	2,708
●Chesterfield, Macoupin... C	374
●*Chestervale*, *Logan*........C	×
●Chesterville, Douglas.......E	50
Chestline, Adams...........W	×
●Chestnut, Logan...........C	100
●**CHICAGO,** Cook.... NE	1,099,850
●*Chicago & Evanston Junc.*, Cook ....NE	×
●Chicago Heights, Cook.. NE	35
●Chicago Lawn, Cook ....NE	*
●*Chickering*, Grundy ......N	×
Chili, Hancock ....W	100
●Chillicothe, Peoria C	1,632
Chowrow, (see Bee Creek)....	×
●Chrisman, Edgar...........E	820
●Christopher, Franklin.....S	[illegible]
●*Church*, Saint Clair.....SW	[illegible]
Cicero, (see Chicago)	×
Cincinnati, Pike............W	10
Cincinnati, (see Pin Oak)	×
Circleville, Tazewell.........C	100
●Cisco, Platt...............C	350
●Cisne, Wayne ....SE	300
●*Cissna Junc.*, Iroquois....E	×
●Cissna Park, Iroquois....E	400
●Civer, Fulton.............W	25
Claire Stat'n, (see Mid' Grove)	×
Clara, Coles.................E	40
●Clare, DeKalb ....N	50
●Claremont, Richland ....SE	212
Clarence, Ford..............E	100
●Clarendon Hills,DuPage NE	249
Clark, Jersey .... SW	×
Clark Centre, Clark.........E	140
●Clarkdale Junc., Cook.. NE	130
Clarke City, Kankakee......E	200
●*Clark's*, Cook.............NE	×
●Clarksdale, Christian......C	100
Clarkson, Wayne ....SE	×
●Clay City, Clay ....S	850
Clay's Prairie, Edgar........E	50
●Clayton, Adams ....W	1,033
●Claytonville, Iroquois.....E	400
Clear Creek, Putnam ....N	65
Cleone, Clark ....E	20
Cleveland, Henry.........NW	99
Cliffdale, Calhoun ....W	×
●*Clifton*, Cook ....NE	×
●Clifton, Iroquois ....E	474
●*Clifton Terrace*, Madison. C	×
●**Clinton,** DeWitt.........C	2,598
●*Clintonville*, Kane........N	500
●*Cliola*, Adams............W	×
●*Clores*, Randolph ....SW	×
●Cloverdale, DuPage.....NE	15
Cloverville, Shelby C	×
●*Clybourn Junction*, Cook NE	×
●Clyde, Cook..............NE	250
●*Clyde*, Macoupin..........C	×
●*CoalBranchJunc.*,Grundy N	×
●*Coal Chute*, Will.........NE	×
●Coal City, Grundy ....N	1,672
●*Coal Mines*, Will..........NE	×
●*Coal Shaft*, Sangamon....C	×
●*Coal Track*, LaSalle ......N	×
●Coal Valley, Rock Island NW	207
Coalville, Livingston C	300
●*Coalville Junc.*, Livingston C	×
●Coatsburgh, Adams ......W	308
●Cobden, Union ....S	994
Cockrell, Stephenson.....NW	×
●Coffeen, Montgomery C	518
Cohn, Clark ....E	80
●*Coke Ovens*, Jackson ......S	×
●Colchester, McDonough..W	1,643
Coldbrook, Warren.........W	×
Cole Dale, Mercer........NW	×
●Colehour, Cook ....NE	*
●*Coleman*, Kane...........N	×
●Coles, Moultrie............C	30
Coles, Clinton ....S	×
Coleta, Whiteside.........NW	300
●Colfax, McLean.........SW	600
●*Colliers*, Peoria C	×
●*Collinsburgh*, Johnson....S	×
●Collinsville, Madison.......C	3,498
●Colmar, McDonough ......W	40
●Colona Station, Henry..NW	250
Colorado, Pope...............S	×
●Columbia, Monroe......SW	1,267
●*Columbiana*, Greene......W	×
Columbus, Adams..........W	201
Columbers, (see Wool)	×
●Colusa, Hancock ....W	20
●*Colvin*, DeKalb............N	×
●Colvin Park, DeKalb .....N	10
●*Combs Switch*, Platt C	×
●Comer, Macoupin.........C	×
Commercial Point, Al'x'nder S	100
Como, Whiteside ....NW	20
Compromise, Champaign ...E	×
●Compton, Lee..............N	234
●*Comstock*, Madison C	×
●Conant, Perry..............S	20
●Concord, Morgan...........W	100
●***Cone*, Saint Clair........SW**	**×**
Conger, Woodford...........C	50
Congerville, Woodford C	50
●*Conleys*, Cook .... NE	×
Conlogue, Edgar ....E	60
●*Conover*, Mason ....NW	×
Conrad, Calhoun ....W	×
●*Constance*, Cook.........NE	×
Conway Park, Cook.......NE	×
Cook's Mills, Coles...........E	200
●Cooksville, McLean .....SW	50
●Cool Bank, Pike..........W	40
●Cooper, Tazewell..........C	20
Cooperstown, Brown........W	100
Coppers Creek Lock and Dam, (see Canton)...............	×
●*Cora*, Sangamon C	×
Coral, McHenry..............N	75
●Cordova, Rock Island ..NW	443
Corinth, Williamson.........S	100
●Cornell, Livingston C	437
●Cornland, Logan C	100
Cornwall, Henry ....NW	×
Corryville, (see Linn)..........	×
●*Corwith*, Cook ....NE	200
●*Coster*, Grundy ....N	×
Cottage Grove, Cook ....NE	*
Cottage Hill, Putnam ....N	32
Cottage Home, Williamson ..S	40
●*Cotter*, Madison............C	×
●Cotton Hill, Sangamon....C	60
Cottonwood, Gallatin ....SE	235
●Coultersville, Randolph.SW	598
Council Hill, Jo Daviess..NW	×
●Council Hill Sta., JoDa's NW	125
●Courtland, DeKalb ....N	313
●Covell, McLean ....SW	40
●Cowden, Shelby............C	702
●*Cowen*, Perry ....S	×
●Cowling, Wabash ....SE	75
●*Coyne*, McHenry ....N	×
●Coyne, Grundy ....N	×
●*Coynes*, Will ....NE	×
Crab Orchard, Williamson ..S	150
●Cragin, Cook ....NE	*
●Craig, Perry.................S	30
●*Craigs*, Edgar..............E	×
●Crainville, Williamson ....S	×
●Cramer, Peoria.............C	25
●*Crampton*, Henry ....NW	195
●Crandall, Tazewell........C	×
Crawford, Cook............NE	*
●Creal Springs, Williamson S	539
●Crescent City, Iroquois....E	500
●Creston, Ogle..............N	329
●Crete, Will ....NE	642
Crickett, Jasper ....SE	×
Crittendon, Franklin.........S	65
Croake, Cumberland ....E	25
●Cropsey, McLean.........SW	130
●*Cross*, Jersey ....SW	×
Cross Plains, Sangamon......C	26
Cross Roads, (see Simpson)..	×
●Crossville, White..........SE	250
●*Crown*, Saint Clair......SW	×
●Cruger, Woodford C	25

Place		
Crumpton, (see Healy)		×
● *Crumbaugh*, McLean	SW	×
Crystal Lake Cr'g., (see Crystal Lk.)		×
● Crystal Lake, McHenry	N	781
Crystal Lake Junction, McHenry	N	×
● Cuba, Fulton	W	1,114
● Cullom, Livingston	C	200
● Cummings, Cook	NE	2,000
● *Cummings Stat'n*, Cook	NE	*
● Curran, Sangamon	C	150
Currier's Mill, (see Carrier's Ms.)		×
● Curtis, Menard	C	×
Curtisville, (see Samsville)		×
● Cushman, Moultrie	C	30
● Custer, Sangamon	C	100
● Custer Park, Will	NE	100
● Cutler, Perry	S	150
● *Cuyler*, Cook	NE	×
Cypress Creek, Johnson	S	×
● *Cypress Junction*, Gallatin	SE	×
● Daggett, Carroll	NW	×
● Dahinda, Knox	W	25
● Dahlgren, Hamilton	S	801
Daisy, Calhoun	W	×
● Dakota, Stephenson	NW	283
● Dale, Hamilton	S	×
● Dallas City, Hancock	W	747
● Dalton City, Moultrie	C	331
Damascus, Stephenson	NW	150
● Damiansville, Clinton	S	100
● Dana, LaSalle	N	221
● Danforth, Iroquois	E	300
● Danvers, McLean	SW	506
● **Danville**, Vermilion	E	11,491
● *Danville Junction*, Verm'n	E	×
Danway, LaSalle	N	50
Darlington, (see McClusky)		×
● *Darmstadt*, Saint Clair	SW	×
Darmstadt, Saint Clair	SW	200
● Darwin, Clark	E	200
● Daum, Greene	W	×
● *Dauphin Park*, Cook	NE	×
● Davis, Stephenson	NW	455
● Davis Junction, Ogle	N	300
● *Dawes*, Perry	S	×
● Dawson, Sangamon	C	500
Daysville, Ogle	N	100
● Dayton, LaSalle	N	232
● **Decatur**, Macon	S	16,841
● Decorra, Henderson	W	25
Deeker, Cook	NE	×
● Deer Creek, Tazewell	C	125
● Deerfield, Lake	NE	250
Deerfield Prairie, (see Esmond)		×
● Deer Grove, Whiteside	NW	100
● *Deering*, Cook	NE	*
● Deer Park, La Salle	N	×
● Deer Park Glen, LaSalle	N	×
Deer Plain, Calhoun	W	20
● Deers, Champaign	E	30
Degognia, Jackson	S	×
● DeKalb, DeKalb	N	2,579
● Delafield, Hamilton	S	195
● Delana, McLean	SW	60
● Deland, Platt	C	400
● Delavan, Tazewell	C	1,176
● Delay, Macoupin	C	×
● Delhi, Jersey	SW	50
● *Dell Abbey*, Grundy	N	×
● De Long, Knox	W	10
● Del Rey, Iroquois	E	125
● *Dempster Street*, Cook	NE	*
Denmark, Perry	S	20
● Dennison, Clark	E	150
● *Dennison*, Williamson	S	175
● *Denny*, Perry	S	×
Denny, Warren	W	×
● Denrock, Whiteside	NW	×
● Denver, Hancock	W	150
● De Pue, Bureau	N	455
Derinda, Jo Daviess	NW	20
Derinda Center, Jo Dav's.	NW	20
Derry, Pike	W	250
Deselm, Kankakee	E	50
● De Soto, Jackson	S	376
● Des Plaines, Cook	NE	986
Detroit, Pike	W	161
Devona, Mercer	NW	×
● Dewey, Champaign	E	150
● De Witt, De Witt	C	265
● Dexter, Effingham	S	15
● Diamond, Grundy	N	100
Diamond Cross, **R'dolph.**	**SW**	**×**
Diamond Lake, Lake	NE	50
Diamond Mines, Vermilion	E	×
● Dickerson, Champaign	E	20
● *Dickey's*, Kankakee	E	25
● Dieterich, Effingham	S	100
Dillon, Tazewell	C	200
● Dillsburgh, Champaign	E	25
● Dimmick, La Salle	E	40
Diona, Coles	E	100
● Disco, Hancock	W	75
● Divernon, Sangamon	C	150
Divide, Jefferson	S	30
● *Divine*, Grundy	N	×
● Dix, Jefferson	S	175
● **Dixon**, Lee	N	5,161
Dixon's Sprs., (see Allen Sprs.)		×
Doddsville, McDonough	W	75
Doherty, Gallatin	SE	×
Dolson, Clark	E	25
Dolton Junction, Cook	NE	×
Dolton's Station, Cook	NE	1,110
Donald, Cook	NE	×
● Dongola, Union	S	733
● Donnellson, Montgomery	C	200
● *Donnellville*, Clark	E	×
● Donovan, Iroquois	E	250
● *Dorans Crossing*, Coles	E	×
● Dorchester, Macoupin	C	104
● Dorsey, Madison	C	50
● *Douglas*, Cook	NE	150
● Douglas, Knox	W	150
Douglas, St. Clair	SW	×
● *Douglas Park*, Cook	NE	×
Dover, Bureau	N	220
● Downer's Grove, Du P'e.	NE	960
● Downs, McLean	SW	350
Dozaville, Randolph	SW	×
● *Drake*, Greene	W	×
● *Dressor*, Fayette	S	×
● Drivers, Jefferson	S	50
● *Drummond*, Will	NE	×
Drury, Rock Island	NW	150
Dryden, Jefferson	S	×
Dublin, Montgomery	C	×
● Dubois, Washington	S	304
● Dudley, Edgar	E	147
Dudleyville, Bond	S	20
Dunbar, Stephenson	NW	10
● Duncan, Stark	C	100
● *Duncan's*, Gallatin	SE	×
Duncan's Mills, Fulton	W	65
● Duncanville, Crawford	SE	32
● Dundas, Richland	SE	300
● Dundee, Kane	N	2,500
Dumfermline, Fulton	W	150
● Dunkel, Christian	C	30
● Dunlap, Peoria	C	175
Dunleith, (see E. Dubuque)		×
Dunn, Moultrie	C	200
● Dunning, Cook	NE	100
Dupage, Will	NE	100
● *Dupont*, Cook	NE	×
● Duquoin, Perry	S	4,052
● Durand, Winnebago	N	489
Durham, Hancock	W	26
Durley, Bond	S	15
Dutch Hollow Mines, St.Cl'r	SW	×
● Dwight, Livingston	C	1,354
Eagle Lake, Will	NE	150
Eagle Point, Ogle	N	50
● Earlville, LaSalle	N	1,05[illegible]
Early Dawn, Lee	N	19
● Easburn, Iroquois	E	×
● *East Batavia*, Kane	N	×
East Burlington, Kane	N	150
● E. Cape Girardeau, Alex'r	S	×
● E. Carondelet, St. Clair.	SW	401
● *East Clinton*, Whiteside	NW	×
East Decatur, Macon	S	×
● E. Dubuque, Jo Daviess	NW	1,069
East Dundee, Kane	N	1,1[illegible]
● *East Grove*, Du Page	NE	6[illegible]
● *East Hannibal*, Pike	W	×
● *East Joliet*, Will	NE	×
East Louisiana, Pike	W	×
● East Lynn, Vermilion	E	25[illegible]
East Newbern, Jersey	SW	×
E. Northf'd, (see Shermerv'le)		×
● Easton, Mason	NW	300
East Paw Paw, DeKalb	N	150
● East Peoria, Tazewell	C	250
● East Plato, Kane	N	10
● *East Rockford*, W'nebago	N	×
East Roseland, Cook	NE	25
● East St. Louis, St. Clair	SW	15,169
East Wheatland, Will	NE	50
Eaton, Crawford	SE	100
Eberle, Effingham	S	×
Eddyville, Pope	S	212
● Edelstein, Peoria	C	50
● Eden, Peoria	C	50
● Edgar, Edgar	E	175
● Edgewater, Cook	NE	*
● Edgewood, Effingham	S	255
Edgington, Rock Island	NW	200
● Edinburgh, Christian	C	806
● Edison Park, Cook	NE	×
Edmunds, Hancock	W	×
● Edwards, Peoria	C	250
● **Edwardsville**, Madison	C	3,561
● *Edwardsville Crossing*, Madison	C	×
● *Edwardsv'e Junction*, Madison	C	×
● **Effingham**, Effingham	S	3,260
● Effner, Iroquois	E	25
● Egan City, Ogle	N	25
● *Eggers*, Cook	NE	×
● *Eggleston*, Cook	NE	×
Ela, Lake	NE	×
Elba, Gallatin	SE	50
Elbridge, Edgar	E	51
● Elburn, Kane	N	584
● Elco, Alexander	S	100
El Dara, Pike	W	241
● Eldena, Lee	N	103
● *Elders Siding*, McLean	SW	×
Elderville, Hancock	W	30
● El Dorado, Saline	S	900
● Eldred, Greene	W	×
Eldridge, Edgar	E	50
● Eleanor, Warren	W	50
● Eleroy, Stephenson	NW	150
● Elgin, Kane	N	17,82[illegible]
Elida, Winnebago	N	20
Eliza, Mercer	NW	50
● Elizabeth, Jo Daviess	NW	495
Elizabethtown, Hardin	SE	652
Elk Grove, Cook	NE	150
● Elkhart, Logan	C	414
Elkhorn, Washington	S	100
Elkhorn Grove, Carroll	NW	100
Elk Prairie, Jefferson	S	40
● Elkville, Jackson	S	145
● Ellery, Edwards	SE	75
Ellington, Adams	W	×
● Elliott, Ford	E	300
Elliotstown, Effingham	S	87
Ellis Grove, Randolph	SW	200
Ellis Mound, Hamilton	S	25
Ellison, Warren	W	150
Ellisville, Fulton	W	[illegible]55
● *Ellisville Station*, Fulton	W	×
● Ellsworth, McLean	SW	[illegible]00
Elm Branch, Wayne	SE	×
Elm Grove, Adams	W	13
● Elmhurst, Du Page	NE	1,050
Elmira, Stark	**C**	**200**
Elmore, Peoria	**C**	**186**
● Elmwood, Peoria	C	1,548
● El Paso, Woodford	C	1,353
● Elsah, Jersey	SW	27
● Elsdon, Cook	NE	*
● *Elsmere*, Cook	NE	25
● Elva Station, De Kalb	N	25
● Elvaston, Hancock	W	307
Elvira, Johnson	S	50
● Elwin, Macon	S	200
● Elwood, Will	NE	243
● *Embarrass Siding*, Coles	E	×
● Emden, Logan	C	208
Emerson, Whiteside	NW	100
● Emery, Macon	S	130
● Emington, Livingston	C	129
Emma, White	SE	×
● Empire, McLean	SW	10
Empire, (see Galt)		×
Endor, Will	NE	50
● Enfield, White	SE	870
● *Enfield Junction*, White	SE	×
● Englewood, Cook	NE	*
Englewood Heights, Cook	NE	×
English Prairie, McHenry	N	×
Enion, Fulton	W	10
● *Enos*, Macoupin	C	×
Enterprise, Wayne	SE	55
● Eola, Du Page	NE	20
● *Epperson*, McDonough	W	×
● Equality, Gallatin	SE	622
● Erie, Whiteside	NW	535
Ernest, Clark	E	8
● *Ernst*, Clark	E	×
Erwin, Cook	NE	×
Erwin, Schuyler	W	75
● Esmond, De Kalb	N	25
● Essex, Kankakee	E	266
● Etna, Coles	E	100
● Eubanks, Adams	W	30
● *Euclid Park*, Cook	NE	×
Eugene, Knox	W	130

 Illinois Illinois

Place	Pop.
● Eureka, Woodford C	1,481
● Evans, Marshall C	20
Evans Mill, Morgan ....W	×
● Evanston, Cook ....NE	4,000
Evansville, Randolph ......SW	407
● *Evarts*, Stephenson ....NW	×
● Evergreen Park, Cook..NE	×
● *Eversman*, Effingham.....S	×
Ewing, Franklin ....S	296
Ewington, Effingham.......E	10
Exchange, Marion..........S	×
Excelsior Mills, Jo Dav's.NW	×
Exeter, Scott...............W	244
● Exline, Kankakee ....E	30
● Eylar, Livingston C	50
● *Fairbanks*, Moultrie......C	×
● Fairbury, Livingston......C	2,324
● **Fairfield**, Wayne.....SE	1,881
● Fair Grange, Coles........E	50
Fair Haven, Carroll ......NW	25
● Fairland, Douglas.........E	400
● Fairman, Marion..........S	100
● Fairmount, Vermilion....E	619
Fairmount Park, Cook...NE	×
● Fairview, Fulton..........W	492
● *Fairview Park*, Cook...NE	×
Fair Weather, Adams ......W	200
● Fall Creek, Adams ....W	50
Falling Springs, St. Clair.SW	×
● Falmouth, Jasper........SE	30
● Fancher, Shelby C	30
Fancy Prairie, Menard.......C	30
Fandon, McDonough.......W	70
Faney, Woodford..........C	130
Fargo, Brown ....W	24
● Farina, Fayette ....S	618
● Farlow, Moultrie..........C	50
● Farmdale, Tazewell.......C	130
● Farmer City, De Witt.....C	1,367
● Farmersville, Montg'ry...C	100
● Farmingdale, Sangamon..C	50
● Farmington, Fulton......W	1,375
Farm Ridge, LaSalle........N	34
Farwell, Cook ....NE	×
● Fayette, Greene..........W	150
Fayetteville, St. Clair .....SW	312
● *Feehanville*, Cook ......NE	×
Felter, Greene..............W	25
● Fenton, Whiteside .....NW	70
Ferdinand, Rock Island..NW	×
● Fernwood, Cook.........NE	818
● Ferrell, Edgar ....E	50
● Ferris, Hancock..........W	305
● Flatt, Fulton.............W	30
● Ficklin, Douglas.........E	20
● Fidelity, Jersey ....SW	200
Fidelity, Champaign........E	×
● *Fielding*, DeKalb.......N	×
Fieldon, Jersey ....SW	291
Fifer, McLean..............SW	×
● Fillmore, Montgomery....C	200
● Filson, Douglas ....E	35
Findlay, Shelby C	×
● Finney, Jackson ....S	32
● Fisher, Champaign........E	500
● *Fishers*, Vermilion ......E	×
Fisher's L'd'g, (see Bee Creek)	×
Fish Hook, Pike............W	50
Fish Lake, St. Clair ......SW	×
Fithian, Vermilion..........E	300
Fitts Hill, Franklin..........S	60
Fitzgerrel, Jefferson ....S	75
● *Five Points*, Edgar........E	×
● Flagg, Ogle...............N	21
● *Flagg Centre*, Ogle.......N	327
● Flanagan, Livingston C	384
● Flat Rock, Crawford....SE	151
Flatville, Champion.........E	25
Flemington, Edgar ....E	10
● Fletcher, McLean........SW	10
Flint, Hamilton ....S	60
● Flora, Clay ....S	1,695
Floraville, St. Clair.........SW	150
Florence, Pike ....W	150
● Florence Station, St'ph'n NW	150
Florid, Putnam.............N	100
● Foosland, Champaign.....E	150
Fordham, Cook...........NE	×
● Forest City, Mason .....NW	300
● Forest Glen, Cook ......NE	*
● Forest Hill, Cook........NE	30
● *Forest Hill*, Cook.......NE	×
● *Forest Home*, Cook.....NE	×
● Formosa, Madison C	19
Forrest, Livingston C	1,021
● Forreston, Ogle...........N	1,118
● Forsyth, Macon...........S	125
Fort Charles, Randolph ..SW	×
Fort Hill, Lake ....NE	×
● *Fortieth St. Junct'n*, C'k NE	×
● *Fort List*, Jasper ....SE	×
Fort Sheridan, Lake........NE	451
Foster, Rock Island ......NW	25
Fosterburgh, Madison.......C	110
Foster Pond, Monroe .....SW	20
● Fountain Bluff, Jackson...S	30
Fountaindale, Ogle ....N	×
Fountain Green, Hancock..W	250
● *Four Mile Cros'g*, St.Cl'r SW	×
● Fowler, Adams ....W	200
● Fox, Kendall ....N	×
Fox Lake, Lake ....NE	50
● *Fox River Junction*, Kane N	×
● *Fox River Switch*, Kane ..N	×
Foxville, Marion ....S	100
● *France*, Vermilion ....E	×
Frankfort, Franklin ....S	[illegible]
Frankfort, Will.............NE	×
● Frankfort Station, Will. NE	700
● Franklin, Morgan.........W	578
● Franklin Grove, Lee .....N	736
Franklin Park, Hardin ....SE	30
Franks, DeKalb ....N	×
Fraser's, White ....SE	×
● Frederick, Schuyler......W	250
● Fredonia, Williamson.....S	130
● Freeburgh, St. Clair ....SW	848
Freedom, La Salle ....N	100
● *Freeman*, Kane ....N	×
● **Freeport**, Stephenson. NW	10,189
Fremont Centre, Lake ....NE	45
French Grove, Peoria.......C	30
● French Village, St. Clair SW	100
Friend Grove, Wabash.....SE	×
Friendsville, Wabash ......SE	300
Frogtown, Clinton...........S	50
● *Frontenac*, DuPage.....NE	×
● Fruit, Madison............C	×
Fullersburgh, DuPage .... NE	200
Fuller's Point, Coles ....E	25
● Fullerton, DeWitt.........C	13
● Fulton, Whiteside.......NW	2,099
● *Fulton Junc.*, Whiteside NW	×
● Funkouser, Effingham ....S	75
● *Funk's Grove*, McLean .SW	×
● *Furman's*, St. Clair ....SW	×
Gage's Lake, Lake ....NE	15
Galatia, Saline ....S	519
● **Galena**, Jo Daviess... NW	5,635
● *Galena Junc.*, Jo Dav's .NW	×
● **Galesburgh**, Knox.... W	15,264
● Galesville, Piatt...........C	60
● *Galewood*, Cook ....NE	×
Gallagher, Richland....... SE	×
● Gallatia, Saline............S	519
Galloway, La Salle..........N	×
● Galt, Whiteside ....NW	100
● Galton, Douglas...........E	20
● *Galum*, Perry ....S	×
● Galva, Henry..............NW	2,409
Gauntown, Johnson..........S	×
Gano, Cook ....NE	*
Gap Grove, Lee ....N	25
● Garber, Ford ....E	25
● Garden Plain, White'e ..NW	25
● Garden Prairie, Boone....N	194
● Gardner, Grundy..........N	1,094
● *Gardner's Park*, Cook..NE	×
Gard's Point, Wabash......SE	45
● Garfield, La Salle..........N	90
Garfield Park, Cook ......NE	*
Garland, Edgar ....E	10
● Garrett, Douglas ....E	200
● *Gartside*, Saint Clair....SW	×
● *Gary*, Cook ....NE	×
Gary, (see Leonore)	×
Gasville, Jackson.............S	×
● *Gatton*, Sangamon........C	×
● *Gaugers*, Will.............NE	×
● Gays, Moultrie C	99
● *Geff*, Wayne ....SE	×
● Geneseo, Henry ....NW	3,182
● *Genet*, Winnebago.........N	×
● **Geneva**, Kane ....N	1,692
● *Geneva Switch*, Kane.....N	×
● Genoa, DeKalb ....N	634
● Georgetown, Vermilion..E	662
● Gerlaw, Warren ....W	75
● *German Prairie*, Sang'n.. C	×
● Germantown, Clinton. ....S	537
Germantown, Vermilion ....S	1,178
German Town, Woodford ..C	×
● German Valley, Steph'n NW	150
● Gibson City, Ford.........E	1,803
● Gifford, Champaign.......E	400
Gila, Jasper..............SE	50
● Gilbert's Kane............N	250
● *Gilbirds*, Brown..........W	77
Gilchrist, Mercer ....NW	100
Gilead, Calhoun ....W	×
● Gillespie, Macoupin.......C	948
● *Gilletts*, Will ....NE	×
● Gillum, McLean ....SW	17
● Gilman, Iroquois..........E	1,112
Gilmer, Lake ....NE	50
● *Gilmore*, Effingham ......S	77
● Gilson, Knox ....W	200
● Girard, Macoupin C	1,524
● *Given*, Cook..............NE	×
● Gladstone, Henderson....W	500
● Glasford, Peoria...........C	268
Glasgow, Scott ....W	187
● *Glenahl*, Jackson ....S	×
● Glenarm, Sangamon C	100
Glenburn, Vermilion ....E	25
● Glen Carbon, Madison C	×
● Glencoe, Cook ....NE	569
Glendale, Pope ....S	15
● Glen Ellyn, DuPage.....NE	473
● Glenwood, Cook ....NE	200
● *Globe*, Cook.............NE	×
● Godfrey, Madison.........C	228
Godley, Will...............NE	296
Goeselville, Cook..........NE	50
Golconda, Pope............S	1,174
Golconda Island, Pope......S	×
● Golden, Adams............W	466
Golden Eagle, Calhoun .....W	19
● Golden Gate, Wayne.....SE	×
● Goodenow, Will..........NE	200
● Goodfield, Woodford.......C	×
● Good Hope, McDonough .W	368
Gooding's Grove, Will.....NE	50
● Goodrich, Kankakee ......E	20
● Goodwine, Iroquois ....E	50
Goose Island, Alexander ....S	30
Goose Island, Cook ....NE	*
● Gordon, Crawford ....SE	32
Goreville, Johnson ....S	50
● Gossett, White............SE	10
Gower, DuPage ....NE	25
Graceland, Cook..........NE	*
Grade Siding, Lake.........NE	×
● Grafton, Jersey ....SW	927
Grand Chain, Pulaski ......S	×
● Grand Crossing, Cook ..NE	*
Grand Detour, Ogle.........N	250
● Grand Ridge, La Salle ....N	328
● Grand Tower, Jackson....S	624
Grand View, Edgar ....E	177
● *Grange Hill*, Jackson .....S	×
● Granger, Du Page ......NE	×
● *Grant*, Kankakee.........NE	×
Grant, Williamson ....S	×
Grantfork, Madison..........C	300
● Grant Park, Kankakee ...E	340
● Grantsburgh, Johnson ....S	200
Grant Works, Cook.......NE	×
Granville, Putnam...........N	148
● Grape Creek, Vermilion ..E	778
Grass Lake, Lake..........NE	×
Grass Lake, McHenry ......N	×
● Grass Land, Saint Clair. SW	×
● *Gravel Pit*, Alexander ....S	×
● *Gravel Pit Siding*, DeWitt C	×
● *Grayland*, Cook ....NE	×
● Graymont, Livingston....C	100
● Gray's Lake, Lake ......NE	150
● Grayville, White .... SE	1,999
● *Grayville Junc.*, Edwards SE	×
Gray Willow, (see Wasco)....	×
Greenbush, Warren ....W	200
● *Greendale*, Marion ....S	×
● Greenfield, Greene.......W	1,131
Green Garden, Will.......NE	×
Green Oak, Bureau ....N	×
Green River, Henry ......NW	150
● *Green's Switch*, Macon....S	×
● Greenup, Cumberland ....E	858
● *Greenup Hill*, Cumberland E	×
Greenvale, Jo Daviess ....NW	25
● Green Valley, Tazewell ...C	250
● Greenview, Menard.......C	1,106
Greenville, Bond.........S	1,868
● *Greenwich*, Kankakee ....E	×
Greenwood, McHenry......N	150
● *Greggs*, DuPage.........NE	×
Gresham, Franklin..........S	×
● Gretna, DuPage ....NE	×
● Gridley, McLean........SW	474
Griffin, Mercer ....NW	30
● *Griffiths*, Clark............E	×
● Griggsville, Pike.........W	1,400
Griggsville L'd'g, (see Griggs'e)	×

Grinnell, Massac..........SW ×
Griswold, (see Walpole)...... ×
● Griswold, Livingston......C 50
Griswold Lake, Lake......NE ×
● *Griswold Place*, St. ClairSW ×
● *Gronso*, Kankakee........E ×
Grossdale, Cook ....NE ×
● *Gross Park*, Cook ......NE *
Grossville, Hardin.........SE ×
Grouse, Kane...............N ×
Grove, Boone ....N 232
● *Grove*, Tazewell..........C ×
Grove City, Christian........C 150
● Groveland, Tazewell ......C 200
Grover, Edgar ....E ×
● *Grover's Station*, Bureau.N ×
● Grubb, Jackson ....S 65
Guilford, Jo Daviess .....NW ×
● Gurnee, Lake ....NE 100
● *Gurney*, Cass.........W ×
● Guthrie, Ford..........E 30
● *Hadley*, Pike..........W ×
● Hagaman, Macoupin ......C 30
● Hagarstown, Fayette.. .S 100
● *Hagener*, Cass..........W 40
Hainesville, Lake ....NE 150
● *Hainesville*, Tazewell.....C 65
Hahnanan, Whiteside....NW ×
● Haldane, Ogle.............N 200
Half Day, Lake .... NE 150
Hallock, Peoria,............C 150
● *Halls*, Peoria ....C ×
Hallstown, (see Galatia)...... ×
● Hallsville, DeWitt.........C 100
Hamburgh, Calhoun........W 100
Hamel, Madison ....C 100
● Hamilton, Hancock......W 1,301
Hamlet, Mercer ....NW 100
Hamletsburgh, Pope ....S 150
Hammock, Hamilton........S ×
● Hammond, Platt..........C 300
● *Hammond Junc.*, Cook.NE ×
● Hampshire, Kane.........N 696
● *Hampton*, Will..........NE ×
● *Hampton*, Moultrie ....C ×
● Hampton, Rock Island. NW 341
Hampton Sta., (see Dunn).... ×
Hanaman, Whiteside ....NW ×
Hancock, (see Carthage)..... ×
Handy, Crawford..........SE ×
● Hanna City, Peoria ....C 65
Hanover, (see Germantown).. ×
Hanover, Jo Daviess.......NW 743
● *Hanover*, Saint Clair....SW ×
● *Hanover Station*, JoDa'sNW ×
● *Hanson*, Shelby..........C ×
Happy Hollow, Rock Isl'dNW ×
● *Happyville*, Greene ......W ×
Hardin, Calhoun ....W 311
Hardinsville, Crawford ....SE 40
Harker's Corners, Peoria....C 50
Harlem, Cook............NE ×
● Harlem, Winnebago......N 100
● Harmon, Lee ....N 132
Harmony, Saint Clair.....SW ×
Harmony, McHenry ....N 100
● Harper, Ogle..............N 40
Harperville, (see Fish Hook). ×
● Harpster, Ford............E 15
● *Harris*, Platt.............W 26
Harrisburg, (see Rose Hill) .. ×
● **Harrisburgh**, Saline....S 1,723
● *Harrison*, Jackson.........S ×
Harrison, Winnebago........N 200
Harrisonville, Monroe......SW 250
● Harristown, Macon........S 300
Hart, Knox ....W ×
Hartford, Saline.............S 38
● Hartland, McHenry.......N 65
● Hartsburgh, Logan........C 26[illegible]
Hartsville, Pope...........S 30
● Harvard, McHenry ....N 1,967
● *Harvard Junc.*, McH'nry.N ×
● Harvel, Montgomery......C 246
● Harvey, Cook ....NE 1,500
● *Harwood*, Champaign ....E ×
Haselwood, Adams.........W ×
Hastings, Calhoun ....W 32
Hastings, (see Chicago) ...... ×
Hastings, Vermilion ....E ×
Hatton, Clark..............E 65
● **Havana**, Mason ......NW 2,525
● Havelock, Cook..........NE *
Hawley, Henry ....NW 195
● *Hawley*, Tazewell.........C 32
● Hawahorn, White ....SE 30
● *Hawthorne*, Cook.......NE *
Haxville, Iroquois.........E 25
● Hayes, Douglas...........E 40
● *Hayford*, Cook..........NE 50
● Haynes, Jersey..........SW ×
● Hazel Dell, Cumberland ..E 150
● Hazelhurst, Carroll.....NW 50
Hazen, Adams..............W 10
Hazlitt, Rock Island......NW ×
● Healey, Livingston........C 25
Heathsville, Crawford .....SE 25
● Hebron, McHenry ....N 300
Hecker, Monroe...........SW 250
● Hegewisch, Cook ....NE *
Hellsburgh, Fayette ....S 20
● Henderson, Knox........W 163
● Henderson Station, Ford..E 75
● Hendrix, McLean.........SW 19
Hennepin, Putnam ......N 574
● Henning, Vermilion ......E 20
● *Henrietta*, DeKalb........N ×
● Henry, Marshall ....C 1,512
Henton, Shelby.............C 40
Herald, White.............SE 50
● Herbert, Boone...........N 50
● Herborn, Shelby ....C 20
● Hermon, Knox...........W 100
● Hermosa, Cook ....NE *
Herod Springs, Pope ....S ×
Heron, Hamilton............S ×
● Herrick, Shelby.............C 100
Harrin's Prairie, WilliamsonS 100
● Herscher, Kankakee......E 224
● Hersman, Brown...........W 150
Hervey City, (see Outten) .... ×
● Hettick, Macoupin ....C 50
● Heyworth, McLean......SW 566
● Hickman, Iroquois........E 30
Hickory, Lake ....NE 25
● *Hickory Grove*, Carroll.NW ×
Hickory Hill, Marion........S 10
Hickory Ridge, Hancock ...W 50
Hicks, Hardin ....SE ×
● Hidalgo, Jasper..........SE 100
● *Higgins*, Richland.........SE ×
Higginsville, Vermilion .....E 65
● Highland, Madison........C 1,857
● Highland Park, Lake....NE 2,163
● *Highlands*, DuPage.....NE ×
● *High Prairie*, St. Clair..SW ×
● High Ridge, Cook.........NE ×
High Switch, Saint Clair.. SW ×
Highwood, (see Ft. Sheridan) ×
● Hildreth, Edgar...........E 100
Hill, Effingham...............S 125
Hillerman, Massac ....SW ×
● Hillery, Vermilion........E 38
Hilliard, Tazewell ....C ×
● **Hillsborough**, Montg'yC 2,000
● Hillsdale, Rock Island..NW 100
Hill's Grove, McDonough ..W 20
Hillside, Cook.............NE ×
● *Hilton*, Tazewell ....C 325
● *Hilltop*, Menard...........C ×
● Hinckley, DeKalb ....N 496
● Hinesborough, Douglas ...E 288
● Hinsdale, DuPage........NE 1,584
● *Hinton*, Vermilion........E ×
Hissong, Fayette ....S ×
● *Hites*, Coles ....E 69
Hitt, Carroll.............NW 55
● *Hitt*, La Salle.............N ×
Hodge's Park, Alexander ...S 125
Hoeret, (see Grant Park) ..... ×
● Hoffman, Clinton ....S ×
● Holcomb, Ogle.............N 120
● Holder, McLean ....SW 50
● Holliday, Fayette..........S 150
● *Hollis Junction*, Peoria...C ×
Hollowayville, Bureau......N 150
Holly, (see Clare) .... ×
Holstead, Johnson ....S ×
Holstein, Kane.............N 50
● Holts, Perry...............S 90
● *Holts*, Perry...............S ×
Home, Wayne...............SE 30
● Homer, Champaign.......E 917
● Homewood, Cook ....NE 600
● Honey Bend, MontgomeryC 10
Honey Creek, Ogle..........N 75
● Hoodville, Hamilton .....S 20
● Hook, Jefferson ....S 20
● Hookdale, Bond...........S 10
● Hoopeston, Vermilion.....E 1,911
Hooppole, Henry ....NW 50
Hoosier Prairie, Clay ....S 30
Hope, Vermilion ....E 50
● Hopedale, Tazewell.........C 471
● *Hopkins*, Whiteside ....NW 10
● Hopkins Park, Kankakee.E 130
Hopper's Mills, Henderson. W 50
● Horace, Edgar ....E 100
Hord, Clay..................S 50
● Hornsby, Macoupin ....C 40
● *Horse Creek*, Will.......NE ×
Horse Prairie, Randolph. SW ×
● *Horse Shoe Lake*, Madison C ×
● Horton Station, Pike.....W 10
● Houston, Randolph .....SW 25
● Howard, Champaign......E 50
Howardsville, Stephenson NW ×
● *Howe*, Douglas...........E 20
● Hoyleton, Washington ....S 361
● *Hubbards*, Wayne ....SE ×
● Hudson, McLean........SW 273
● Huey, Clinton ....S 450
● *Hughes*, Douglas..........E ×
Hughes, Edgar..............E ×
Hugo, Douglas ....E 60
● Hull, Pike................W 300
● Humbodlt Park, Cook.. NE *
● Humbolt, Coles ....E 279
● Hume, Edgar ....E 433
Hume, Whiteside.........NW ×
● Humrick, Vermilion......E 55
Hunter, Boone..............N 15
● Huntley, McHenry........N 550
● Hunts City, Jasper.......SE 300
Huntsville, Schuyler.........W 196
● *Hurricane*, Greene.......W ×
Hurricane, Fayette..........S ×
Hurricane, Montgomery ....C 10
● *Huston's*, Richland......SE ×
● Hutsonville, Crawford...SE 582
Hutton, Coles ....E 50
● Hyde Park, Cook ....NE *
● Hyman, Cook...........NE ×
● *Ice Track Spur*, S'ngm'n. C ×
Ideal, Carroll..............NW ×
Idlewild, Alexander.........S 40
● *Idlewild*, Jefferson........S ×
Idlewood, Jefferson ....S 30
● Iles Junction, Sangamon..C 200
● Illiana, Edgar.............E 300
Illinois City, Rock Island. NW 150
● *Illinois Midland*, Macon..S ×
● Illiopolis, Sangamon ......C 689
● *Imbs*, St. Clair.........SW ×
Independence, (see Pittsfield) ×
● Indianola, Vermilion .....E 472
Industry, Cook ....NE ×
Industry, McDonough......W 432
● Ingalton, DuPage ....NE 50
Ingraham, Clay..............S 150
Inman, Gallatin ....SE 50
● Iola, Clay.................S 200
Ionia, Warren..............W 90
● *Iowa Junction*, Hends'n. W 350
● *Iowa Junction*, Peoria ...C ×
● Ipava, Fulton ....W 667
● Irene, Boone ....N ×
Iron, White.................SE 50
● *Irondale*, Cook ....NE *
● Iroquois, Iroquois.........E 393
● Irving, Montgomery ......C 630
● Irving Park, Cook.......NE *
● Irvington, Washington....S 200
● Irwin, Kankakee ....E 50
● Isabel, Edgar ....E 125
Island, Lawrence..........NE ×
● *Island Grove*, Sangamon..C ×
● Itasca, DuPage..........NE 400
● Iuka, Marion.............S 362
Ivanhoe, Lake..............NE 200
● Ivesdale, Champaign......E 323
Ivy Landing, Monroe......SW 30
● **Jacksonville**, Morgan. W 12,935
● *Jacksonville Junc.*, M'g'n W ×
Jalapa, Greene ....W ×
Jamestown, Clinton ....S 150
● Janesville, Coles ....E 217
● Jefferson, Cook ....NE *
Jefferson Corner, Whites'eNW ×
● Jeffersonville, Wayne....SE 256
Jersey Landing, (see Elsah).. ×
● **Jerseyville**, Jersey...SW 3,207
● Jewett, Cumberland .....E 335
Joetta, Hancock............W 40
Johannisburgh, Washington.S 50
Johnsburgh, McHenry......N 300
Johnsonville, Wayne.......SE 300
● *Johnstone*, Cook........NE *
Johnstown, Cumberland ....E 112
● **JOLIET**, Will........ NE 23,264
● **Jonesborough**, Union.S 1,000
● *Jonesville*, Winnebago....N ×
Joppa, Massac.............SW 50

Jordon, (see Hord)		×
Jordanville, Morgan	W	10
● Joslin, Rock Island	NW	100
● Joy, Mercer	NW	150
Jubilee, Peoria	C	260
● Judd, Cook	NE	*
● Jules, Cass	W	×
● ***Junction*, Macon**	S	×
● *Junction*, Pike	W	×
● *Junction*, Tazewell	C	×
Junction City, Gallatin	SE	×
● *Kampenville*, Randolph	SW	×
Kampsville, Calhoun	W	172
● Kane, Greene	W	551
Kaneville, Kane	N	300
● Kangley, La Salle	N	934
● **Kankakee**, Kankakee	E	9,025
● *Kankakee Junc.*, W'dford	C	×
● Kansas, Edgar	E	1,037
● Kappa, Woodford	C	250
Karber's Ridge, Hardin	SE	60
● Kasbeer, Bureau	N	50
Kaser, Greene	W	×
Kaskaskia, Randolph	SW	50
● Kaufman, Madison	C	32
Kedron, Gallatin	SE	×
Kedron, Saline	S	×
● *Keene's*, Wayne	SE	100
● Keensburgh, Wabash	SE	150
Keenville, Wayne	SE	50
● Keithsburgh, Mercer	NW	1,484
● *Keithburgh Junc.*, M'c'r	NW	×
● *Keller*, Peoria	C	×
Kellerville, Adams	W	100
● *Keisey*, Mason	NW	×
● *Kemp*, Douglas	E	×
● Kemper, Jersey	SW	50
● Kempton, Ford	E	201
● *Kempton Junc.*, Livi'gston	C	×
Kendall, Kendall	N	×
● Kenilworth, Cook	NE	×
● *Kenner's*, Clay	S	×
● Kenney, DeWitt	C	497
● Kensington, Cook	NE	*
● Kent, Stephenson	NW	100
● *Kenwood*, Cook	NE	×
Keokuk Junc., (see Golden)		×
● Kernan, La Salle	N	50
Kershaw Sprs., Morgan	W	×
● Kewanee, Henry	NW	4,569
● Keyesport, Clinton	S	200
Kibble, Crawford	SE	100
Kickapoo, Peoria	C	300
Kidd, Monroe	SW	×
Kidley, Edgar	E	25
● Kilbourn, Mason	NW	200
● Kinderhook, Pike	W	500
● *Kinder*, Madison	C	×
● Kingman, Shelby	C	×
● King's, Ogle	N	600
● *King's*, Perry	S	×
Kingsbury, Whiteside	NW	×
Kingston, (see Fair Weather)		×
● Kingston, DeKalb	N	295
Kingston Mines, Peoria	C	150
Kingston's, Cook	NE	×
● Kinmundy, Marion	S	1,045
● Kinsman, Grundy	N	129
● Kirkland, DeKalb	N	410
● *Kirks*, Ford	E	×
● Kirkwood, Warren	W	949
● *Kirwin*, Cook	NE	×
Kishwaukee, Winnebago	N	150
● *Kittredge*, Carroll	NW	×
● *Knights*, Macon	S	×
● *Knox*, Knox	W	×
● Knoxville, Knox	W	1,728
Kolze, Cook	NE	×
● *Koster*, Kankakee	E	×
Kramm, Peoria	C	250
● Kumler, McLean	SW	50
● Kyte River, Ogle	N	75
Lace, DuPage	NE	50
LaClair, DeKalb	N	32
● La Clede, Fayette	S	125
● **Lacon**, Marshall	C	1,649
● La Crosse, Hancock	W	50
● *Lacton*, DuPage	NE	×
● Ladd, Bureau	N	800
● La Fayette, Stark	C	250
● Lafox, Kane	N	150
● La Grange, Cook	NE	2,31[illegible]
La Grange, Brown	W	25
● La Harpe, Hancock	W	1,113
● La Hogue, Iroquois	E	100
● *Lake*, Saint Clair	SW	×
● Lake Bluff, Lake	NE	100
● Lake City, Moultrie	C	115
Lake Creek, Williamson	S	100
● Lake Forest, Lake	NE	1,203
● Lake Fork, Logan	C	30
● Lakeside, Cook	NE	×
Lake View, Cook	NE	*
● Lake Villa, Lake	NE	150
● Lakewood, Shelby	C	75
● Lake Zurich, Lake	NE	200
Lamb, Hardin	SE	×
● Lamoille, Bureau	N	516
● Lanark, Carroll	NW	1,295
Lancaster, Wabash	SE	200
● Lancasterville, Lake	NE	50
Landes, Crawford	SE	25
● Lane, DeWitt	C	150
● Lanesville, Sangamon	C	30
Lansing, Cook	NE	400
● La Place, Piatt	C	300
● La Prairie, Adams	W	194
La Prairie Centre, Marshall	C	35
● Larchland, Warren	W	100
● La Rose, Marshall	C	300
● La Salle, LaSalle	N	9,855
● Latham, Logan	C	265
● *Latham*, Winnebago	N	×
Latona, Jasper	SE	25
Laur, Jefferson	S	150
Laura, Peoria	C	25
● *Laura*, Peoria	C	×
● *Lauretta*, McLean	SW	×
● Lavergne, Cook	NE	*
● *Lawler*, Gallatin	SE	×
● Lawndale, Logan	C	25
Lawn Ridge, Marshall	C	300
● Lawrence, McHenry	N	300
● **Lawrenceville**, L'nce	NE	865
● *Lawrenceville Junc.*, Lawr'e	NE	×
● *Laws Siding*, Jo Davie's	NW	×
Lead Mine, Jo Daviess	NW	×
● *Lead Switch*, Jo Daviess	NW	×
● Leaf River, Ogle	N	339
● Leaman, Fulton	W	150
Leamington, Gallatin	SE	×
● Leasure, Douglas	E	×
● Lebanon, St. Clair	SW	1,636
● *Lebanon City*, St. Clair	SW	×
● *Leda*, Sangamon	C	50
● *Ledford*, Saline	S	×
● Lee, DeKalb	N	264
Lee Centre, Lee	N	250
● *Leeds*, LaSalle	N	×
Leeseburgh, Fulton	W	10
Legal, Stephenson	NW	×
● Leithton, Lake	NE	×
● Leland, LaSalle	N	554
● *Lementon*, St. Clair	SW	20
● Lemont, Cook	NE	4,000
● Lena, Stephenson	NW	1,270
Lenz, St. Clair	SW	×
● Lenzburgh, St. Clair	SW	266
Leon, Whiteside	NW	97
● Leonore, LaSalle	N	×
Leo Rock, Jackson	S	×
L'Erable, Iroquois	E	100
● Lerna, Coles	E	400
● Le Roy, McLean	SW	1,258
● *Leslie*, Tazewell	C	×
Lester, Marion	S	50
● Leverett, Champaign	E	32
● **Lewistown**, Fulton	W	2,166
● Lexington, McLean	SW	1,187
Liberty, Adams	W	245
Liberty Prairie, Madison	C	65
● Libertyville, Lake	NE	550
Lick Creek, Union	S	100
Light House, Ogle	N	×
● Lily, Tazewell	C	75
● Lily Lake, Kane	N	100
Lima, Adams	W	251
Limerick, Bureau	N	50
● **Lincoln**, Logan	C	6,725
Lincoln Green, Johnson	S	25
Lincoln Park, Cook	NE	*
● Linden Park, Cook	NE	×
● Lindenwood, Ogle	N	150
Linn, Wabash	SE	75
● Lintner, Piatt	C	25
Lis, Jasper	SE	×
Lisbon, Kendall	N	200
● Leslie, DuPage	NE	75
● Litchfield, Montgomery	C	5,811
● Literberry, Morgan	W	75
● Little Indian, Cass	W	30
Little Rock, Kendall	N	100
Littleton, Schuyler	W	100
● Little York, Warren	W	500
Lively Grove, Washington	S	40
Liverpool, Fulton	W	150
● *Livingston*, Knox	W	×
● *Llewellyn Park*, Cook	NE	×
● Loami, Sangamon	C	383
● Loceyville, Bureau	N	260
● *Locketts*, V[illegible]rmilion	E	×
● *Lock Haven*, Jersey	SW	×
● Lockport, W[illegible]	NF	2,449
Locust Grove, Franklin	S	130
● Loda, Iroquois	E	598
● Lodemia, Livingston	C	×
● Lodge, Piatt	C	100
Loding, Rock Island	NW	100
Logan, Edgar	E	25
Logansport, Hamilton	S	25
Logansville, Jefferson	S	40
● Lomax, Henderson	W	100
● Lombard, DuPage	NE	515
● Lombardville, Stark	C	200
● London Mills, F[illegible]ton	W	661
Long Tree, Bureau	N	40
Long Branch, Sali[illegible]	S	100
● Long Creek, M[illegible]	S	90
Long Grove, Lake	NE	100
Long Lake, [illegible]	C	75
Long Lake, La[illegible]	NE	×
● Long Point, L[illegible]vingston	C	300
Lo[illegible] Prairie, Wayne	SE	30
● Longview, [illegible]hampaign	E	300
● Longwoo[illegible], Cook	NE	×
Loogootee, Fayette	S	75
Loomis Avenue, Cook	NE	×
Loon Lake, Lak[illegible]	NE	×
● Lora[illegible] Ada[illegible]s	W	327
Lora[illegible] S[illegible]phenson	NW	100
● Lorenzo, Will	NE	10
● Lostant, La Salle	N	378
Louden City, Fayette	S	30
Louis, (see Hartville)		×
● **Louisville**, Clay	S	637
Lourds, Woodford	C	40
Lovejoy, St. Clair	SW	×
● Lovington, Moultrie	C	767
● Lowder, Sangamon	C	500
Lowell, La Salle	N	200
Lower Hills, Hamilton	S	19
● *Lower Peoria*, Peoria	C	×
● Low Point, Woodford	C	60
Lowry, Cook	NE	×
● Loxa, Coles	E	150
Loyd, Menard	C	195
● Ludlow, Champaign	E	29[illegible]
Lusk, Pope	S	32
● Lyndon, Whiteside	NW	461
● Lynn Centre, Henry	NW	100
Lynnville, Morgan	W	200
Lyons, Cook	NE	732
Lytleville, McLean	SW	36
● *McCaffrey*, Cook	NE	×
● *McCall*, Hancock	W	26
● *McClary*, Livingston	C	×
● *McClure*, Alexander	S	×
● McClusky, Jersey	SW	26
● McConnell, Stephenson	NW	65
McCook, Cook	NE	×
McCormick, Pope	S	×
● McDowell, Livingston	C	60
McFain's, Jersey	SW	×
McHenry, McHenry	N	979
● *McHenry*, McHenry	N	1,187
McKee, (see Kellerville)		×
McKeen, Clark	E	100
McKinstrys' [illegible]ors, Kankakee	E	20
● *McLanes*, Crawford	SE	×
● McLean, McLean	SW	500
● *McLeansborough Junction*, Hamilton	S	×
● **McLeansborough**, Hamilton	S	1,355
McNoel, Massac	SW	×
● McPherson, Coles	SW	×
McQueen, Kane	N	50
● McVey, Macoupin	C	50
● *Mc Williams*, Montgomery	C	×
Mac, (see Seatonville)		×
Macedonia, Hamilton	S	150
Mackey, Logan	C	×
● Mackinaw, Tazewell	C	545
● *Mackinaw Dells*, W'dford	C	×
Mackville, Piatt	C	×
● **Macomb**, McDonough	W	4,052
● Macon, Macon	S	819
● Macoupin, Macoupin	C	30
Madison, Madison	C	30
● Madison Street, Cook	NE	*
Madonnaville, Monroe	SW	30
Maeystown, Monroe	SW	100

● *Magnet*, Coles .... E ×
Magnolia, Putnam .... N 287
● Mahomet Champaign ..... E 473
Mainville, Cook .... NE 100
● Makanda, Jackson .... S 344
● Malden, Bureau .... N 319
Mallard, Hancock .... W 10
● Malta, DeKalb .... N 461
Malvern, Whiteside ...... NW 80
● Manchester, Scott .... W 408
Mandell, Cook .... NE 25
● Manhattan, Will .... NE 257
● Manheim, Cook .... NE 50
● Manito, Mason .... NW 444
● Manix, Madison .... C ×
Manley, Fulton .... W 10
Manlius, Bureau .... N 50
Mannon, Mercer .... NW 20
● Mansfield, Piatt .... C 533
● Manteno, Kankakee ...... E 627
● Manville, Livingston ...... C 100
Maple Grove, Edwards ..... SE 13
● *Maple Grove*, Bond .... S ×
● Maple Park, Kane .... N 382
Maple's Mill, Fulton .... W 30
● Mapleton, Peoria .... C 50
● Maplewood, Cook .... NE *
Maquon, Knox .... W 501
● Marble Head, Adams ..... W 90
Marbletown, Fulton .... W 15
Marcelline, Adams .... W 137
● *Marcus*, Carroll .... NW ×
● **Marengo, McHenry** .... N **1,445**
● Marietta, Fulton .... W 150
Marine, Madison .... C 637
● **Marion**, Williamson ..... S 1,338
● Marissa, Saint Clair ..... SW 876
● Markham, Morgan .... W ×
● *Marley*, Edgar .... E 65
● Marcey, Will .... NE 75
● Marlow, Jefferson .... S 30
● Maroa, Macon .... S 1,164
● Marseilles, LaSalle .... N 3,542
● **Marshall**, Clark .... E 1,900
● *Marshall Junction*, Clark . E ×
● Marshall's Ferry, Whit'de SE 7
Marston, Mercer .... NW 40
● Martha, Platt .... C ×
Martinsburgh, Pike .... W 50
Martin's Store, Hamilton .... S 20
● Martinsville, Clark .... E 779
● Martinton, Iroquois .... E 12
● *Marvin*, Cook .... NE ×
● Maryland, Ogle .... N 105
Marysville, Vermilion ...... E 186
● Mascoutah, Saint Clair .. SW 2,032
● Mason, Effingham .... S 425
● Mason City, Mason ...... NW 1,869
Massac Creek, Massac .... SW 195
Massbach, Jo Daviess ..... NW 15
Masters, Franklin .... S ×
● *Matanzas*, Mason ...... NW ×
● Mattison, Cook .... NE 338
● Mattoon, Coles .... E 6,833
● Maud, Wabash .... SE 65
● *Maxwell*, Peoria .... C ×
● Maxwell, Sangamon .... C ×
Mayberry, Wayne .... SE 10
● Mayfair, Cook .... NE *
● Mays Station, Edgar ...... E 40
● Maysville, Pike .... W 20
● Mayview, Champaign ..... E 25
● Maywood, Cook .... NE 1,500
● Mazon, Grundy .... N 300
● *Mazonia*, Grundy .... N ×
Meacham, DuPage .... NE 130
Mead, Williamson .... S ×
● Meadows, McLean .... SW 50
Mechanicsburg, Sangamon .. C 426
Media, Henderson .... W 150
● *Media Station*, Henderson W ×
● Medora, Macoupin .... C 470
● *Meharry*, McLean ...... SW ×
Melrose, Clark .... E 100
● *Melrose*, Cook .... NE ×
Melville, Madison .... C 50
● Melvin, Ford .... E 491
● *Melwood*, Edgar .... E ×
Menard, Randolph .... SW ×
● Mendon, Adams .... W 640
● Mendota, LaSalle .... N 3,542
● *Menert*, Tazewell .... C ×
● Menominee, Jo Daviess NW 57
Meppen, Calhoun .... W 50
● Meredosia, Morgan .... W 621
● Meriden, LaSalle .... N 56
● Merna, McLean .... SW 50

● Merriam, Wayne .... SE 100
Merrimac Point, Monroe .. SW 40
● Merritt, Scott .... W 100
● **Metamora**, Woodford .. C 758
● Metcalf, Edgar .... E 241
Meteer, Brown .... W ×
● **Metropolis City**, Massac SW 3,573
Middle Creek, Hancock .... W 30
● Middle Grove, Fulton .... W 100
● Middle Point, White ..... SE 10
● Middlesworth, Shelby ..... C 10
Middleton, (see Long Prairie) ×
Middletown, Logan .... C 30
Midland, Edgar .... E ×
Midland City, DeWitt ..... C 180
○ Midway, Edgar .... E 60
Mier, (see Lancaster) .... ×
● Milan, Rock Island .... NW 692
● Miles' Station, Macoupin .. C 165
● *Mile Thirty-Two*, Union .. S ×
Miles, Marion .... S 25
Miley, Clinton .... S ×
● Milford, Iroquois .... E 957
● Millard Avenue, Cook .. NE *
● Millbrig, Jo Daviess .... NW 25
● Millbrook, Kendall .... N 150
Millburn, Lake .... NE 100
● Mill Creek, Union .... S 200
● Milledgeville, Carroll ... NW 446
Miller, Ford .... E ×
● *Miller's*, Madison .... C ×
Millersburg, (see Baden Baden) ×
● Millersburgh, Mercer .. NW 300
● Millersville, Christian ..... C 50
Milliken, Hancock .... W ×
● Millington, Kendall .... N 301
● Millsdale, Will .... NE 50
● Mill Shoals, White .... SE 221
Mills' Prairie, Edwards .... SE 65
● Millstadt, Saint Clair .... SW 1,186
● *Millstadt Junc.*, Monroe SW ×
Millville, (see Marble Head) . ×
● Milmine, Piatt .... C 200
Milo, Bureau .... N 50
Milroy, Henderson .... W ×
Milton, Pike .... W 415
● *Milton Siding*, Logan ..... C ×
● Mineral, Bureau .... N 188
● Minier, Tazewell .... C 664
● Minonk, Woodford .... C 2,316
● Minooka, Grundy .... N 360
● *Mira*, Champaign .... E ×
● Missal, Livingston .... C 25
Mission Fields, Vermilion .. E ×
● *Mission Mines*, Vermilion E ×
● *Mitchell*, Madison .... C ×
Mitchellsville, Saline .... S 100
Mitchie, Monroe .... SW 130
● *Moawequa*, Shelby .... C 818
● Moccasin, Effingham .... S 100
● Mode, Shelby .... C 25
Modena, Stark .... C 100
● Modesto, Macoupin .... C 75
Modoc, Randolph .... SW 100
● *Moffatts*, Peoria .... C ×
● Mokena, Will .... NE 364
● Moline, Rock Island .... NW 12,000
● Momence, Kankakee ...... E 1,635
● *Momence Junc.*, Kan'kee . E ×
● Monarch, McLean .... SW 16
● Monee, Will .... NE 445
Money Creek, McLean .... SW 25
● Monica, Peoria .... C 200
● **Monmouth**, Warren ... W 5,936
● *Monroe*, Coles .... E ×
● Monroe Centre, Ogle ...... N 400
Monroe City, Monroe ..... SW 100
● Mont Clare, Cook .... NE *
Monterey, Fulton .... W 20
Montezuma, Pike .... W 40
● *Montgomery*, Coles .... E ×
● Montgomery, Kane .... N 263
● **Monticello**, Platt .... C 1,643
● *Montrose*, Cook .... NE 195
● Montrose, Effingham .... S 30
Moonshine, Clark .... E ×
Moore's Prairie, Jefferson ... S 30
Morea, Crawford .... SE 50
● Moreland, Cook .... NE *
Moreisville, (see Carrier's Mills)
● *Morgan*, Morgan .... W ×
● Morgan Park, Cook ..... NE 1,027
Morgansville, Christian ..... C ×
● **Moro, Madison** .... C 106
● *Morrell Park* Cook .... NE ×
Morrellville, Brown .... W 40

● **Morris**, Grundy .... N 3,653
Morris City, White .... SE 223
● **Morrison**, Whiteside . NW 2,088
● Morrisonville, Christian ... C 844
Morristown, Henry .... NW 40
● Mortimer, Edgar .... E 50
Morton, (see Morton Grove). ×
● Morton, Tazewell .... C 657
● Morton Grove, Cook .... NE 100
Morton Park, Cook .... NE 120
Moscow, Union .... S 30
● *Mosiers*, Kankakee .... E ×
● Mossville, Peoria .... C 90
● *Moulton*, Shelby .... C ×
● **Mound City**, Pulaski ... S 3,000
● Mounds Junction, Pulaski S ×
● Mound Station, Brown ... W 219
Mount Auburn, Christian .. C 222
● Mountain Glen, Union .... S 100
Mt. Carbon, (see Murphysboro) ×
Mount Carmel, Jackson .... S 528
● **Mount Carmel**, Wab'h SE 3,376
● **Mount Carroll**, C'r'l NW 1,836
Mount Erie, Wayne .... SE 266
● Mount Forest, Cook ..... NE 300
● Mount Greenw'd, Cook . NE 100
● *Mount Hope*, Cook ..... NE ×
● *Mount Joy*, Logan .... C ×
● Mount Morris, Ogle .... N 895
● Mount Olive, Macoupin ... C 1,986
● *Mount Olivet*, Cook ..... NE ×
Mount Palatine, Putnam ..... N 200
Mt. Pleasant, (see Mound Sta.) ×
● *Mount Pleasant*, Jackson S ×
Mount Pleasant, Union ...... S 50
● Mount Prospect, Cook .. NE 75
● Mount Pulaski, Logan .... C 1,357
● **Mount Sterling**, Br'n. W 1,655
● **Mount Vernon**, Jeff'n. S 3,233
● Mount Zion, Macon ..... NW 350
● Moweaqua, Shelby .... C 848
Mozier, Calhoun .... W 10
Muddy Valley, Jackson ...... S 150
● Mulberry Grove, Bond ..... S 500
● Mulkeytown, Franklin .... S 150
Muncie, Vermilion .... E 150
Munday's Cor., (see Marshall) ×
● Munster, LaSalle .... N 30
● Murdock, Douglas .... E 140
● **Murphysbor'h**, Jacks'n S 3,880
● Murrayville, Morgan ...... W 422
● Myrtle, Ogle .... N 100
Na-au-say, Kendall .... N ×
● Nachusa, Lee .... N 68
● Nameoki, Madison .... C 75
● Naperville, DuPage ..... NE 2,216
● Naples, Scott .... W 452
● **Nashville**, Washington. S 2,084
Nat'l Stock Yards, St. Clair SW 800
● Natrona, Mason .... NW 100
Nauvoo, Hancock .... W 1,208
Neadmore, Clark .... E 40
● Nebo, Pike .... W 453
● *Neeley*, Edgar .... E ×
● Neelyville, Morgan .... W 75
● Nekoma, Henry .... NW 200
● Nelson, Lee .... N 48
● *Nemo*, Warren .... W ×
● Neoga, Cumberland .... E 829
● Neponset, Bureau .... E 542
Nettle Creek, Grundy .... N ×
● Nevada, Livingston .... C 150
● Nevins, Edgar .... E 24
Newark, Kendall .... N 390
● New Athens, Saint Clair SW 624
● New Baden, Clinton .... S 250
New Bedford, Bureau .... N 100
● New Berlin, Sangamon ... C 494
● Newbern, Jersey .... SW 50
● New Boston, Mercer ... NW 445
New Brighton, St. Clair . SW 868
● New Burnside, Johnson .. S 596
● New Canton, Pike .... W 424
● New Castle, Saline .... S ×
● *New Chicago*, Cook ..... NE ×
New City, Sangamon .... C 25
New Columbia, Massac .... SW 50
● New Dennison, W'mson .. S ×
● New Design, Monroe ... SW 50
● New Douglas, Madison .... C 555
● Newell, Vermilion .... E 32
● *Newell*, Vermilion .... E ×
New Genesee, Whiteside. NW ×
● New Grand Chain, Pulaski S 200
● New Hanover, Monroe. SW 50
New Hartford, Pike .... W 110
New Haven, Gallatin ...... SE 336

Place	Pop.
New Hebron, Crawford...SE	50
● New Holland, Logan......C	250
New Jordan, Whiteside..NW	×
New Lebanon, DeKalb.......N	10
● New Lenox, Will.......NE	200
New Liberty, Pope..........S	100
● Newman, Douglas.......E	990
Newmansville, Cass........W	25
● New Memphis, Clinton....S	150
● New Milford, Winnebago.N	200
New Minden, Washington...S	217
● New Palestine, Rand'ph SW	65
● New Philadelphia, McDonough..................W	181
● *Newport*, Madison........C	×
● New Salem, Pike ....W	307
Newton, (see Adams)........	×
● **Newton**, Jasper ....SE	1,428
● New Windsor, Mercer..NW	477
Ney, DeKalb..................N	×
● Niantic, Macon............S	639
Niles, Cook ....NE	400
Niles Centre, Cook.........NE	400
● Nilwood, Macoupin.......C	300
● Niota, Hancock..........W	143
Nippersink, Lake.........NE	×
● Noble, Richland..........SE	424
● Nokomis, Montgomery...C	1,305
● Nora, JoDaviess.........NW	309
● Normal, McLean........SW	3,459
● *Normal Junc.* McLean.SW	×
● *Normal Park*, Cook....NE	*
● *Norman*, Livingston......C	×
● *Normantown*, Will.....NE	×
● Norris, Fulton...........W	300
● Norris City, White........SE	500
North Alton, Madison.......C	762
Northampton, Peoria........C	100
● North Aurora, Kane.......N	200
● *North Bellville*, St. ClairSW	×
● *North Cairo*, Alexander..S	×
North Cairo, Pulaski.......S	×
North Division, Cook.....NE	×
● *North Dixon*, Lee.........N	×
● *North Edgewater*, CookNE	1,043
● *North Evanston*, Cook.NE	600
● *North Glen Ellyn*, DuPage NE	×
● North Henderson, M'rc'rNE	275
North Northfield, Cook...NE	35
● *North Oswego*, Kendall..N	×
North Peoria, Peoria........C	1,086
North Plato, Kane...........N	25
● *North Roseland*, Cook..NE	×
North Springfield, Sang'on.C	1,043
North Utica, LaSalle........N	1,094
Northwest, Cook...........NE	×
Northville, LaSalle..........N	100
● *North Wayne*, DuPage.NE	×
Nortonville, Will..........NE	×
Norway, LaSalle.............N	95
Norwood, Mercer........NW	50
● Norwood Park, Cook...NE	700
Norris, White.............SE	×
● Nunda, McHenry.........N	438
Nursery, Carroll.........NW	×
Oak, Pope...................S	97
● *Oakdale*, Cook..........NE	*
● Oakdale, Washington......S	150
● Oakford, Menard..........C	200
● *Oak Forest*, Cook.......NE	×
● Oak Glen, Cook..........NE	300
● *Oak Glen*, Cook..........NE	×
Oak Grove, McLean........SW	65
● Oak Hill, Peoria..........C	75
● Oakland, Coles...........E	995
● *Oakland*, Cook..........NE	×
Oakland Park, Macon......S	×
● Oak Lawn, Cook.........NE	50
● Oakley, Macon............S	200
● *Oak Mound*, Fulton......W	10
● Oak Park, Cook........NE	4,771
Oak Point, Clark...........E	25
● Oaktown, Pulaski..........S	20
Oakville, Union.............S	×
● Oakwood, Vermilion......E	500
Obed, Shelby................C	×
● Oblong, Crawford.......SE	390
● Oconee, Shelby............C	332
● Ocoya, Livingston.........C	50
● Odell, Livingston..........C	800
● Odin, Marion..............S	817
● O'Fallon, Saint Clair....SW	865
● *O'Fallon Junc.* St. ClairSW	×
● Ogden, Champaign........E	334
Ogle Mercer..............NW	×
● *Ogles*, Saint Clair.......SW	×

Place	Pop.
● Oglesby, LaSalle..........N	1,000
● Ohio, Bureau.............N	364
● *Ohio & Mississippi Junc.* Gallatin...............SE	×
● Ohlman, Montgomery.....C	50
● Okawville, Washington....S	472
Old Duquoin, Perry.........S	25
Old Harmony, Saint Clair..SW	×
Old Ripley, Bond............S	25
Olena, Henderson..........W	100
Olga, Hamilton.............S	×
Olive Branch, Alexander....S	97
● Oliver, Edgar.............E	60
● Olmsted, Pulaski..........S	203
● **Olney**, Richland ....SE	3,831
● Omaha, Gallatin ....SE	428
Omega, Marion..............S	100
● Onarga, Iroquois.........E	994
Oneco, Stephenson........NW	20
● Oneida, Knox ....W	699
Ontario, Knox ....W	×
● Ontarioville, DuPage....NE	250
● Opdyke, Jefferson.........S	200
● Ophiem, Henry.........NW	100
Ophir, La Salle............N	25
● **Oquawka**, Henderson..W	802
● Ora, Jackson...............S	125
Orange, Clark...............E	26
Orange Prairie, Peoria......C	×
● Orangeville, StephensonNW	347
Oraville, Jackson............S	125
● Orchard Mines, Peoria....C	200
● Orchard Place, Cook....NE	125
Orchardville, Wayne.........SE	40
● Oreana, Macon ....S	200
● **Oregon**, Ogle ....N	1,566
Orio, (see Linn)	×
● Orion, Henry...........NW	624
● *Orison*, Cook..........NE	×
Orizaba, (see Long View)	×
Orland, Cook...............NE	150
● Orleans, Morgan..........W	80
● *Ormonde*, Warren.........W	20
Osage, Franklin ....S	50
● Osborn, Rock Island ...NW	65
Osceola, Stark..............C	80
● Osco, Henry............NW	80
Oskaloosa, Clay..............S	100
● Osman, McLean.........SW	50
Ospur, De Witt..............C	×
● Oswego, Kendall..........N	641
● **Ottawa**, La Salle ....N	9,985
● *Ottawa Springs*, La Salle .N	×
Otter, La Salle..............N	×
Otterville, Jersey..........SW	173
Otto, Fulton.................W	25
● *Otto Junction*, Kankakee. E	×
Ottsville, Bureau............N	50
● Outten, Macon ....S	60
Ovington, Cook ....NE	500
● Owaneco, Christian C	250
● Owen, Winnebago ....N	25
Ox Bow, Putnam ....N	50
Oxford, Henry............NW	×
Oxville, Scott...............W	130
Ozark, Johnson ....S	175
● Pacific, Cook............NE	*
Paderborn, Saint Clair....SW	×
● Padua, McLean ....SW	45
Paines Point, Ogle..........N	45
● Palatine, Cook...........NE	891
Palermo, Edgar..............E	100
● Palestine, Crawford .....SE	732
Palestine, Randolph ......SW	×
● Palmer, Christian.........C	432
● Palmyra, Macoupin C	505
Palo Alto, Hamilton.........S	40
● Paloma, Adams ....W	40
Palos, (see Orland)...........	×
Painter, Sangamon C	×
● Pana, Christian C	5,077
● Panola Station, Woodford.C	132
Panther, Sangamon.........C	×
● Papineau, Iroquois........E	141
Paradise, Coles..............E	102
● **Paris**, Edgar...............E	4,496
● Parker, Johnson ....S	15
● Parkersburgh, Richland.SE	196
● Park Manor, Cook......NE	*
● Park Ridge, Cook.......NE	987
● Parkside, Cook ....NE	*
Parkville, Champaign.......E	100
Parmer, (see Mills Prairie)...	×
● Parnell, DeWitt.......	×
● Parrish, Franklin	[illegible]
Pasfield, Sangamon C	×
Passport, Richland.........SE	65

Place	Pop.
Pastime Park, DeWitt......C	×
Pasturefield, Lawrence....NE	×
● Patoka, Marion............S	502
Patterson, Greene..........W	150
● *Patterson's*, Will ....NE	×
● Patton, Wabash ....SE	77
Pavilion, Kendall...........N	200
Pawnee, Sangamon C	400
● *Pawnee Junc.*, Sangamon C	×
● Paw Paw, Lee ....N	826
● **Paxton**, Ford ....E	2,187
Payne, Edgar ....E	×
Payson, Adams.............W	500
Pearl, Macon ....S	×
● Pearl, Pike................W	928
● Pecatonica, Winnebago...N	1,059
● **Pekin**, Tazewell..........C	6,347
● *Pekin Junction*, Tazewell C	101
Pellonia, Massac ....SW	150
● Pengeld, Champaign......E	300
Pennington Point, McDon..W	25
● *Pennock*, Cook..........NE	*
Penrose, Whiteside.......NW	50
● **PEORIA**, Peoria.......C	41,024
● Peotone, Will ....NE	717
● Percy, Randolph........SW	400
Perry, Pike.................W	705
● *Perry Springs*, Brown... W	20
Perry Springs, Pike ....W	20
● *Perrys*, Jackson...........S	×
Perryton, Mercer.........NW	×
● Perryville, Winnebago ...N	×
Persifer, Knox ....W	×
● Peru, LaSalle ....N	5,550
● Pesotum, Champaign..... E	300
● Peters, Madison...........C	32
Petersburg, (see Astoria)	×
● **Petersburgh**, Menard..C	2,342
Peters Creek, Hardin......SE	×
Petersville, Mercer.......NW	10
● Phelps, Warren ....W	10
● Philadelphia, Cass.........W	175
● *Phillips*, Fulton...........W	×
Phillipstown, White ....SE	150
● Philo, Champaign..........E	491
Phoenix, Douglas ....E	65
● Piasa, Macoupin...........C	100
● *Piasa Bluffs*, Jersey....SW	×
Pierceburgh, Crawford ....SE	×
Pierceville, DeKalb ....N	×
● Pierron, Bond..............S	50
● Pierson Station, Platt C	150
Pigeon, Jefferson............S	40
● Pike, Pike ....W	10
Pilot, Vermilion.............E	50
Pilot Knob, Washington ....S	×
● **Pickneyville**, Perry... S	1,298
Pine Creek, Ogle............N	10
Pine Rock, Ogle ....N	10
Pineville, (see Bayles)........	×
● Pingree Grove, Kane .....N	100
Pink Prairie, Henry......NW	×
● Pinkstaff, Lawrence ....NE	100
Pin Oak, Wayne ....SE	20
Piopolis, Hamilton ....S	97
● Piper City, Ford ....E	460
● Pisgah, Morgan ....W	10
Pitcherville, (see Stockton) ..	×
Pittsburgh, Fayette..........S	15
● *Pittsburgh*, Saint Clair..SW	×
● **Pittsfield**, Pike........W	2,295
● *Pittsfield Junction*, Pike. W	×
● Pittwood, Iroquois........E	100
● Plainfield, Will ....NE	852
● Plainview, Macoupin......C	100
Plainville, Adams ....W	200
Plano, Kendall..............N	1,825
Plato, Iroquois..............E	15
● Plato Centre, Kane ....N	25
Plattville, Kendall ....N	480
Pleak's Corner, Shelby......C	×
Pleasant Green, Stark C	×
Pleasant Hill, Jo Daviess NW	×
● Pleasant Hill, Pike.......W	310
Pleasant Mound, Bond......S	25
● Pleasant Plains, SangamonC	518
Pleasant Ridge, Madison ...C	×
Pleasant Valley, Jo Davi'sNW	25
Pleasant View, Schuyler....W	105
Plum, Scott................W	×
Plumfield, Franklin.........S	30
Plum Hill, Washington......S	75
Plum River, Jo Daviess ..NW	350
● Plymouth, Hancock......W	710
● Poag, Madison C	×
● Pocahontas, Bond.........S	372
Poco, Pope ....S	12

● *Pocock*, Montgomery.....C ×
● *Poe*, Monroe.........SW ×
● *Point Calumet*, Cook....NE ×
● *Poland*, Randolph......SW ×
● Polo, Ogle...........N 1,728
Polsgrove, (see Mt. Carroll).. ×
Pomeroy, Mercer.........NW 15
● Pomona, Jackson........S 150
● Ponemah, Warren.........W 10
● **Pontiac**, Livingston.....C 2,784
Pontiac Junction, L'vingst'nC ×
● Pontoosuc, Hancock.....W 249
● Poplar City, Mason.....NW 10
● Poplar Grove, Boone.....N 232
● *Portage Curve*, Jo D'vi'sNW ×
● PortByron, Rock Island NW 775
● *Port Byron Junction*, Rock Island.................N ×
Portersville, Jackson.........S ×
Port Jackson, Crawford...SE ×
Portland, Franklin..........S ×
Portland, Whiteside.....NW ×
Port Du Point, Saint Cl'r SW 97
● Posey, Clinton............S 75
● Potomac, Vermilion......E 500
● Pottstown, Peoria.........C 260
Powellton, Hancock........W 75
Prairie Centre, La Salle.....N 200
● Prairie City, McDonough W 812
● *Prairie Creek*, Will.....NE ×
Prairie du Pont, Saint Cl'rSW ×
Prairie du Rocher, R'nd'phSW 408
● Prairie Hall, Mason........S 25
Prairie Home, Shelby.......C 25
Prairie Town, Madison......C 150
Prairie View, Douglas......E ×
● Prairie View, Lake......NE 25
Prairieville, Lee.............N 30
Pratt, Whiteside..........NW 260
● Pre-emption, Mercer...NW 100
● Prentice, Morgan........W 40
Preston, Randolph.........SW 100
Prettyman, Tazewell........C 50
Price, Lawrence...........NE 19
Priceville, (see Downs)....... ×
● **Princeton**, Bureau.....N 3,396
● Princeville, Peoria........C 641
Proctor, Ford...............E 25
Progress, Union.............S ×
● Prophetstown, Whites'e NW 694
● *Prospect*, Champaign.....E ×
● *Prospect*, Sangamon......C ×
Prosperity, Franklin.........S ×
Providence, Bureau.........N 100
Proviso, Cook.............NE 50
Pujol, Randolph...........SW 57
● Pulaski, Pulaski...........S 100
Pulaski, Hancock..........W 50
Pulley's Mill, Williamson....S 30
● Pullman, Cook...........NE *
● *Purlington*, Cook.......NE ×
● *Put Creek*, Fulton.......W ×
● Putnam, Putnam.........N 280
● Pyatt, Perry...............S 20
Queen City, (see Schwer)..... ×
● *Queens Lake*, Clinton......S 65
Quigley, Shelby..............C 15
● **QUINCY**, Adams.......W 31,494
● *Quincy Junction*, Pike...W ×
Quiver, Mason............NW 26
Raccoon, Marion............S 20
Raddleville, Jackson........S ×
● Radford, Christian........C 65
● *Radley*, Lee..............N ×
● Radom, Washington.......S 100
● Rafetown, Jasper........SE ×
● *Raibs*, Saint Clair.......SW ×
● Raleigh, Saline............S 200
Rameyville, Peoria.........C 20
● Ramsey, Fayette...........S 598
Randall, Knox..............W 10
● Randolph, McLean......SW 20
Range, Jefferson............S ×
● *Rankin*, Saint Clair.....SW 350
● Rankin, Vermilion.........E 314
● Ransom, La Salle..........N 338
● **Rantoul, Champaign**......E 1,074
● Rapatee, Knox.............W 50
● Rapids City, Rock Isl'd.NW 288
● Rardin, Coles..............E 80
Raritan, Henderson........W 275
Raum, Pope..................S 12
● *Raven*, Edgar..............E ×
● Ravenswood, Cook......NE *
● Ravinia, Lake............NE 650
● *Rawalts*, Fulton.........W 40
● Ray, Schuyler.............W 150

● Raymond, Montgomery...C 841
● *Rayville*, Vermilion......E ×
● Reader, Macoupin........C 10
● Reading, Livingston.......C 100
Rectorville, (see Broughton).. ×
● Red Bud, Randolph.....SW 1,176
● Reddick, Kankakee.......E 160
Redhead, Richland........SE ×
● Redmon, Edgar............E 99
Red Oak, Stephenson.....NW 10
● *Red Oak Station*, Steph'nNW ×
Reeb's Station, Saint Clair.SW 100
Reed, Henderson.............W 10
● *Reeders*, Macoupin........C ×
● *Reed's Crossing*, Boone...N ×
● *Rees*, Franklin............S ×
Reevesville, Johnson.........S ×
Reform, Jefferson.............S ×
Regent, Johnson..............S ×
Reinhard, La Salle..........N 10
● *Relief Number One*, Tazewell.....................C ×
● *Relief Number Two*, Tazewell.....................C ×
Renault, Monroe..........SW 300
● Reno, Bond.................S 100
● Rentchler, Saint Clair...SW 75
● *Rexford*, Cook..........NE ×
● Reynolds, Rock Island. NW 300
● *Reynolds*, Union..........S ×
● Rhodes, Cook............NE ×
● *Richard*, La Salle.........N 45
● Richardson, Kane........N 40
Richfield, Adams............W 30
● Richland, Sangamon......C 50
Richland Grove, Rock Isl'dNW 77
● Richmond, McHenry.....N 415
● Richton, Cook...........NE 450
● Richview, Washington....S 465
Rich Woods, Crawford....SE ×
Rickel, Henry............NW ×
● Ridge Farm, Vermilion...E 757
● Ridgefield, McHenry......N 300
● *Ridgeland*, Cook.........NE 250
● Ridgely, Sangamon.......C 1,007
Ridge Prairie, Saint Clair. SW ×
● Ridgeville, Iroquois.......E 25
● Ridgway, Gallatin........SE 523
● Ridott, Stephenson.....NW 400
Riffle, Clay.................S ×
● Riggston, Scott............W 50
● Rileyville, Saline...........S 100
● Rinard, Wayne...........NE 125
● Ringwood, McHenry.....N 300
● Rio, Knox..................W 300
● Riola, Vermilion...........E 25
Ripley, Brown...............W 304
Risdon, Saint Clair.........SW 30
● Rising, Champaign.........E 50
● Risk, Livingston...........C 25
● Ritchey, Will..............NE 75
● Riverdale, Cook...........NE *
● *Riverdale*, Greene.........W ×
● *River Forrest*, Cook.....NE 150
● **River Grove**, Cook.......NE 287
● *River* [illegible], Saint Cl'rSW ×
● **Riverside**, Cook.........NE 900
Riverside Junction, Cook..NE ×
● **Riverton**, Sangamon......C 1,127
● *Roaches*, Jefferson.........S ×
● **Roanoke**, Woodford.......C 831
● **Roberts**, Ford..............E 325
● **Robinson**, Crawford.. SE 1,387
Robinson Creek, Shelby......C 32
Robinson's, Randolph....SW ×
● Rochelle, Ogle..............N 1,789
● Rochester, Sangamon.....C 300
Rochester, Wabash........SE ×
Rock, Pope..................S 30
● Rockbridge, Greene......W 336
● Rock City, Stephenson. NW 148
Rock Creek, Hardin.......SE 12
● Rockfeller, Lake.........NE 150
● Rock Falls, Whiteside..NW 1,900
● **Rockford**, Winnebago..N 23,584
Rock Grove, Stephenson. NW 200
● **Rock Island, R.I.**...NW 13,634
● *Rock Island Junction*, Whiteside............NW ×
● Rockport, Pike...........W 225
● Rockton, Winnebago.....N 892
Rockville, Kankakee.......E 20
Rockwood, Randolph.....SW 100
● Rodden, Jo Daviess.....NW ×
● Roger's Park, Cook.....NE 1,708
● Rohrer, Morgan..........W ×
● Roland, White...........SE 50

Rollins, Lake..............NE 50
● Rollo, DeKalb............N 100
● Rome, Peoria.............C 90
Rome, Jefferson............S 186
● *Romeo*, Will..............NE 26
● *Rondout*, Lake...........NE 100
● Roodhouse, Greene.......W 2,360
● *Roak's Creek*, Livingston..C ×
● *Rosalthe*, Livingston......C 10
● Rosborough, Randolph .SW 260
● Roscoe, Winnebago.......N 500
● *Roscoe Cros'g*, WinnebagoN ×
Rose, Iroquois..............E 32
Rose Bud, Pope..............S 59
Rosecrans, Lake...........NE 50
Rosedale, Jersey...........SW 40
● *Rose Hill*, Cook...........NE *
● Rose Hill, Jasper.........SE 150
Roseland, Cook............NE *
● Roselle, DuPage.........NE 200
● Rosemond, Christian......C 300
● Roseville, Warren........W 788
Rosewood, Jefferson........S ×
Rosiclare, Hardin.........SE 274
Roslyn, Cumberland........E ×
Ross Grove, DeKalb........N ×
● Rossville, Vermilion.......E 879
● Round Grove, WhitesideNW 120
● Round Knob, Massac......S 32
● Rowe, Livingston.........C 40
● Rowell, DeWitt...........C 25
Royal, Champaign............E 30
Rozetta, Henderson........W 100
Ruark, Lawrence...........NE 10
● *Ruby*, Winnebago........N ×
● Rugby, Livingston.........C 25
Ruma, Randolph..........SW 100
Rupe, Jefferson.............S ×
Rural, Rock Island.......NW 77
Rural Hill, Hamilton........S 35
Rush, Jo Daviess.........NW 30
● **Rushville**, Schuyler...W 2,500
● *Russell*, Clay..............S ×
● Russell, Lake............NE 80
Russellville, Lawrence....NE 284
● Rutland, La Salle..........N 500
● *Sabina*, McLean...........C 32
● *Sacramento*, Kankakee...E ×
● Sacramento, White......SE 20
● Sadorus, Champaign......E 277
● Sag Bridge, Cook.......NE 500
Saidora, Mason..............C **50**
Sailor Springs, Clay.........S 300
● Saint Anne, Kankakee....E 718
● Saint Augustine, Knox...W 255
● Saint Charles, Kane.......N 1,690
● Saint David, Fulton......W 300
● Saint Elmo, Fayette.......S 354
● *Sainte Maria*, Cook....NE ×
● SantFrancisv'e, Lawr'ce NE 432
Saint George, Kankakee....E 25
● Saint Jacob, Madison...SW 475
Saint James, Fayette........S 10
● Saint John, Perry..........S 200
● Saint Joseph, Champaign .E 552
Saint Libory, Saint Clair..SW 300
● Saint Marie, Jasper......SE 318
● *Saint Mary*, Iroquois.....E ×
Saint Mary's, Hancock....W 50
Saint Morgan, Madison...NW 13
Saint Patrick, (see Van Orin) ×
Saint Paul, Fayette..........S 50
Saint Rose, Clinton..........S 40
Saint Wendel, Clay.........S ×
● **Salem**, Marion...........S 1,493
Salina, Kankakee............E ×
Saline Mines, Gallatin.....SE 25
Salisbury, Sangamon.........C 300
● Salt Creek, DuPage.....NE 100
● *Salt Creek Siding*, DeWitt.C ×
● *Saluda*, Knox.............W ×
Samoth, Massac.............S 200
Samsville, Edwards........SE 75
Sanburn, Johnson............S 100
Sand Lake, Lake..........NE ×
● Sandoval, Marion..........S 834
Sand Prairie, (see Sands).... ×
● *Sand Ridge*, Grundy......N ×
● Sand Ridge, Jackson......S ×
● Sands, Tazewell.............C 10
● *Sands*, Whiteside......NW ×
● *Sand Spur*, Randolph..SW ×
● *Sands Prairie*, Tazewell..C 10
● Sandusky, Alexander.....S 100
● *Sandusky*, Vermilion.....E ×
● Sandwich, DeKalb........N 2,516
Sanfordville, Whiteside..NW ×

Place		Pop.
●Sangamon, Macon	C	30
●*Sangamon*, Sangamon	C	×
●*Sangamon Siding*, Sang'n.	C	×
●*Sanger*, Sangamon	C	×
●San Jose, Mason	C	307
Sante Fe, Alexander	S	50
Saratoga, Marshall	C	×
Sato, Jackson	S	×
●Saunemin, Livingston	C	366
●Savanna, Carroll	NW	3,097
●Savoy, Champaign	E	75
Saxon, Henry	NW	×
●Saybrook, McLean	C	851
●Scales Mound, Jo Davi's	NW	350
Schapville, Jo Daviess	NW	35
Schaumburg, Cook	NE	50
●*Schiller Park*, Cook	NE	×
School, White	SE	75
●*Schurman*, Saint Clair	SW	×
Schutz Mills, Greene	W	30
Schwer, Iroquois	E	40
●Sciota, McDonough	W	238
●*Sconce*, Vermilion	E	×
Scottdale, Saint Clair	SW	×
●Scott Land, Edgar	E	129
Scott Mill, Brown	W	×
●Scottsburgh, McDonough	W	40
Scott's Station, (see Wabash)		×
Scottsville, (see Wabash)		×
Scottville, Macoupin	SW	363
●Scovel, Livingston	C	15
Sears, Rock Island	NW	250
●Seaton, Mercer	NW	75
●Seatonville, Bureau	N	536
Sebastopol, Madison	SW	20
●Secor, Woodford	C	379
●Seehorn, Pike	W	10
Seester, Cook	NE	75
Sellers, Champaign	E	×
Sellinger, Saint Clair	SW	×
Selma, McLean	C	200
Seminary, Fayette	S	×
●Seneca, LaSalle	N	1,190
Sepo, Fulton	W	×
●Serena, La Salle	N	76
●Seville, Fulton	W	30
●Seward, Winnebago	N	60
Sexton, Shelby	C	20
●Seymour, Champaign	E	200
●Shabbona, DeKalb	N	502
Shabbona Grove, DeKalb	N	150
●Shannon, Carroll	NW	591
Sharon, Henry	NW	×
●Sharpsburgh, Christian	C	50
Sharps L'd'g, (see Sheldons Gr)		×
●Shattuc, Clinton	S	20
Shaumburgh, Cook	NE	65
●Shaw, Lee	N	40
●*Shawnee Junc.*, Hamilton	S	×
●**Shawneetown**, Gall'ln	SE	2,000
●*Sheep Pens*, Grundy	N	×
●Sheffield, Bureau	N	993
●**Shelbyville**, Shelby	E	3,162
●Sheldon, Iroquois	E	910
Sheldon's Grove, Schuyler	W	35
●Shepherd, Pike	W	25
Sherburnville, Kankakee	E	50
●Sheridan, La Salle	N	425
●*Sheridan Junc.*, La Salle	N	×
●Sherman, Sangamon	C	100
●Shermerville, Cook	NE	125
Shetlerville, Hardin	SE	100
Shield, Lake	NE	×
Shiloh, Saint Clair	SW	200
Shilo Center, Champaign	E	45
Shilo Hill, Randolph	SW	100
Shinkle, Shelby	C	30
●Shinn, Pike	W	10
●Shipman, Macoupin	C	410
●Shirland, Winnebago	N	100
●Shirley, McLean	SW	200
●Shobonier, Fayette	S	200
●*Sholl Siding*, Peoria	C	×
●*Shooting Park*, Cook	NE	×
●Shop Creek, Montgomery	C	×
●Shumway, Effingham	S	175
●Sibley, Ford	E	404
●Sidell, Vermilion	E	150
Siding, La Salle	N	×
●Sidney, Champaign	E	581
Siegert, Edwards	SE	×
●Sigel, Shelby	C	258
Iloam, Brown	W	100
Silver Creek, Calhoun	W	20
Silver Creek, Madison	C	×
Silverton, Jasper	SE	13
●Simons, Cook	NE	*
●Simpson, Johnson	S	300
●Sims, Wayne	SE	100
●Sinclair, Morgan	W	100
●Six Mile, Wayne	SE	100
Skates, Shelby	C	×
●Skelton, Logan	C	19
●Smithborough, Bond	S	393
●Smithdale, Livingston	C	15
●Smithfield, Fulton	W	300
●Smithshire, Warren	W	25
Smith L'd'g, (see Merrimac Pt.)		
Smithton, Saint Clair	SW	411
Smithville, Peoria	C	100
●Smothersville, Franklin	S	132
Snicarte, Mason	NW	50
Snider, Vermilion	E	10
Snowflake, Franklin	**S**	**×**
●*Soldiers Home*, Adams	W	×
●Sollitt, Kankakee	E	100
Soloman, DeWitt	C	20
Solon Mills, McHenry	N	50
Somerset, Saline	S	25
●Somonauk, DeKalb	N	468
Sonora, Hancock	W	40
●Sorento, Bond	S	538
●*South Addison*, DuPage	NE	×
South America, Saline	S	45
Southampton, (see Princev'e)		×
●*South Aurora*, Kane	N	×
●South Chicago, Cook	NE	*
South Chicago Shops, Cook	NE	×
●*South Chicago and Southern Junction*, Cook	NE	×
South Danville, Vermilion	E	799
South Division, Cook	NE	×
●South Elgin, Kane	N	505
●*South Elmhurst*, DuPage	NE	×
●South Englewood, Cook	NE	*
●*South Englewood Junction*, Cook	NE	×
●South Evanston, Cook	NE	3,000
●*South Freeport*, Step'n	NW	×
South Grove, DeKalb	N	×
South Harvey, Cook	NE	×
South Henderson, Hender'n	W	32
South Holland, Cook	NE	1,005
South Hume, Whiteside	NW	×
●*South Junc.*, Saint Clair	SW	×
●South Lynne, Cook	NE	*
South Mount Forest, Cook	NE	50
●*South Oak Park*, Cook	NE	×
South Okawville, Washington	S	650
●*South Ottawa*, La Salle	N	×
●*South Park*, Cook	NE	×
South Peoria, Peoria	C	1,638
Southport, Peoria	C	25
South Ridgeland, Cook	NE	×
●*South Roseland*, Cook	NE	×
●*South Shore*, Cook	NE	×
South Springfield, Sang'n	C	393
Southwest, Cook	NE	*
Spankey, Jersey	SW	×
Sparks, Clinton	S	65
Spark's Hill, Hardin	SE	130
●Sparland, Marshall	C	471
●Sparta, Randolph	SW	1,979
●*Spaulding*, Cook	NE	×
Spaulding, Sangamon	C	×
●Spencer, Will	NE	180
●Spring, Brown	W	20
Spring Bay, Woodford	C	147
●Spring Bluff, Lake	NE	10
Spring Creek, (see Del Rey)		×
●Springerton, White	SE	200
●**SPRINGFIELD**, Sa'g'n	C	24,963
●*Springfield Junc.*, Sanga'n	C	×
Spring Garden, Jefferson	S	181
Spring Grove, McHenry	N	80
Spring Hill, Whiteside	NW	125
Spring Lake, Mason	NW	×
Spring Station, Brown	W	30
Spring Valley, Adams	W	×
●Spring Valley, Bureau	N	3,837
●Springville, Union	S	100
●Staley, Champaign	E	75
●Stallings, Madison	C	32
●Stanford, McLean	SW	389
Stanton, Stephenson	NW	×
Star, Hancock	W	20
●Stark, Stark	C	100
Starks, (see Wayne)		×
●*Starnes*, Sangamon	C	×
State Line, Clark	E	×
●*State Line*, Cook	NE	×
●*State Line*, Vermilion	E	×
●Staunton, Macoupin	C	2,209
Stavanger, La Salle	N	×
●*Steele*, Will	NE	×
●Steeleville, Randolph	SW	401
●Sterling, Whiteside	NW	5,824
●Stevens, Stephenson	NW	×
●Steward, Lee	N	300
●Stewardson, Shelby	C	617
●*Stickney*, Cook	NE	×
●Stillman Valley, Ogle	N	410
●Stilwell, Hancock	W	100
Stirrup Grove, Macoupin	C	32
Stockland, Iroquois	E	×
●Stockton, Jo Daviess	NW	379
Stocks, Tazewell	C	32
●Stock Yards, Cook	NE	*
●*Stock Yards Junc.*, Cook	NE	×
●*Stoehrs* Tazewell	C	10
●Stokes, White	SE	10
●Stone, Lee	N	65
Stone Avenue, Cook	NE	×
Stone Church, Washington	S	25
●Stone Fort, Saline	S	464
Stone Prairie, Adams	W	390
●*Stone Quarry*, Saint Cl'r	SW	×
Stones Corners, McHenry	N	×
●Stonington, Christian	C	270
●Stookey, Saint Clair	SW	650
●*Stony Island*, Cook	NE	130
●Stoy, Crawford	SE	×
●Strasburgh, Shelby	C	258
●Stratford, Ogle	N	×
●*Straut*, Pike	W	×
●Strawn, Livingston	C	233
●Steator, La Salle	N	11,414
Streator Junc., La Salle	N	×
●*Streator Junc.*, W'dford	C	×
Stringtown, (see Pellonia)		×
Stringtown, Richland	SE	32
●Stronghurst, Henderson	W	300
●Strout, Pike	W	10
●Stubblefield, Bond	S	25
Sturgis, Cook	NE	×
●Sublette, Lee	N	300
Suez, Mercer	NW	40
Suffern, Macon	S	×
●*Sugar Creek*, Jackson	S	×
●Sugar Grove, Kane	N	100
●**Sullivan**, Moultrie	C	1,468
●Summerdale, Cook	NE	*
●Summerfield, Saint Clair	S	557
Summer Hill, Pike	W	150
●*Summers*, McLean	SW	×
●Summerson, Saint Clair	S	×
●Summit, Cook	NE	455
●*Summit*, Knox	W	195
Summit, Rock Island	NW	×
●*Summit*, Saint Clair	SW	×
●Summit, Will	NE	×
Summit Station, (see Vienna)		×
Summum, Fulton	W	200
●Sumner, Lawrence	NE	1,037
Sumpter, White	SE	×
Sunbeam, Mercer	NW	25
Sunbury, (see Dwight)		×
Sunfield, Perry	S	150
●Sunny Hill, Henry	NW	25
Sunrise, La Salle	N	×
●Sunset, Kane	N	32
●*Surrey*, Warren	W	×
Sutter, Hancock	W	80
●Swan Creek, Warren	W	125
●Swango, Edgar	E	65
●Swanwick, Perry	S	100
Swedona, Mercer	NW	159
●Sweet Water, Menard	C	200
Swisher, DeWitt	C	25
●*Switch D.*, Ford	E	×
●Swygert, Livingston	C	20
●**Sycamore**, DeKalb	N	2,987
●***Sycamore Junc.*, DeKalb**	**N**	**×**
Sylvan, Cass	W	×
●Symerton, Will	NE	100
●Table Grove, Fulton	W	400
●Tallula, Menard	C	445
●Tamalco, Bond	S	40
Tamarack, Will	NE	30
●Tamaroa, Perry	S	1,000
●Tampico, Whiteside	NW	429
●*Tansey*, Sangamon	C	×
Tansill, Pope	S	45
Taylor, Ogle	N	20
Taylor Hill, Franklin	S	20
●Taylor Ridge, Rock Isl'd	SW	25
●**Taylorville**, Christian	C	2,829
●*Tedens*, Du Page	NE	×
●Teheran, Mason	NW	56
Temple Hill, Pope	S	×
●Tennessee, McDonough	W	313
●Terra Cotta, McHenry	N	25
Terra Haute, Henderson	W	250

Place	Section	Population
● Teutopolis, Effingham	S	800
● Texas City, Saline	S	25
● Thackery, Hamilton	S	75
Thackery, Hamilton	S	×
● *Thatcher's Park*, Cook	NE	×
● Thawville, Iroquois	E	300
Thebes, Alexander	S	100
The Grove, Cook	NE	×
Thomas, Bureau	N	10
● Thomasborough, Ch'p'n	E	190
● Thomasville, Montgomery	C	10
● Thompsonville, Franklin	S	309
● Thomson, Carroll	NW	374
● Thornton, Cook	NE	374
● *Thornton Junc.*, Cook	NE	×
Three Mile Prairie, Wash'n	S	30
Thurman, Hamilton	S	×
● Tice, Menard	C	30
Ticona, La Salle	N	×
● Tilden, Randolph	SW	75
Tile Factory Switch, Verm'n	E	×
Tilford (see Bluford)		×
● *Tillman*, Saint Clair	SW	×
● *Tilton*, Vermillion	E	474
● *Timbuctoo*, Carroll	NW	×
Time, Pike	NW	146
Timothy Cumberland	E	15
● Tinley Park, Cook	NE	300
Tioga, Hancock	W	300
● Tiskilwa, Bureau	N	801
Todd's Point, Shelby	C	75
● **Toledo**, Cumberland	E	676
● Tolono, Champaign	E	902
Toluca, Marshall	C	10
● Tomlinson, Champaign	E	10
● Tonica, La Salle	N	473
● Tonti, Marion	S	150
● Topeka, Mason	NW	141
● **Toulon**, Stark	C	945
● Towanda, McLean	SW	402
● Tower Hill, Shelby	C	543
Tracy, Cook	NE	×
● *Tracy*, Kankakee	E	260
● Tremont, Tazewell	C	508
● Trenton, Clinton	S	1,384
Trigg's Mill, Effingham	E	×
● Trilla, Coles	E	90
● Trimble, Crawford	SE	50
● Triumph, La Salle	N	50
● Trivoli, Peoria	C	100
● *Trousdale*, Jo Daviess	NW	×
● Troutman, Macon	C	12
● Trowbridge, Shelby	C	40
● Troy, Madison	SW	826
Troy (see Joliet)		×
● Troy Grove, La Salle	N	283
● Trumbull, White	SE	15
Truro, Knox	W	10
● *Trutter*, Sangamon	C	×
Truxton, Bureau	N	×
Tryon's Grove, McHenry	N	×
● Tucker, Kankakee	E	80
● *Tucker*, Ogle	N	×
Tullamore, Tazewell	C	130
● Tunnel Hill, Johnson	S	200
● *Tunnel Switch*, Jersey	SW	×
● Turner, Du Page	NE	1,506
Turner Park, Cook	NE	650
● Turpin, Macon	C	×
● **Tuscola**, Douglas	E	1,897
Twin Bluffs, La Salle	N	×
● *Twin Grove*, McLean	C	×
Udina, Kane	N	100
● Ulah, Henry	NW	50
● *Ulery*, Moultrie	C	×
● Ullin, Pulaski	S	250
Ulrich, Moultrie	C	×
● *Union*, Clark	E	×
● *Union*, Mason	C	×
● Union, McHenry	N	300
Union Centre, Cumberland	E	50
● Union Grove, Whiteside	NW	195
● Union Hill, Kankakee	E	30
Union Point, Union	S	×
Union Stock Yards, Cook	NE	*
Unionville, Massac	S	×
Unity, Alexander	S	125
● Upper Alton, Madison	SW	1,803
Upper Alton Sta., Madison	SW	×
● **Urbana**, Champaign	E	3,511
● Ursa, Adams	W	125
Ustick, Whiteside	NW	50
Utah, Warren	W	50
Utica (see Banner)		×
● Utica, La Salle	N	1,700
Utopia, Du Page	NE	50
● Valley City, Pike	W	50
Van Buren, De Kalb	N	32

Illinois

Place	Section	Population
Vancils Point, Macoupin	SW	×
● **Vandalia**, Fayette	S	2,144
Vandercook, Vermillion	E	800
● Van Orin, Bureau	N	100
● *Van Steinberg Siding*, F'd	E	×
● Varna, Marshall	C	398
Venedy, Washington	S	193
● *Venedy Station*, Wash't'n	S	×
Veni, Effingham	S	30
● Venice, Madison	SW	932
● *Venice*, Saint Clair	SW	×
● *Venice & Carondelet Junc.*, Saint Clair	SW	×
● Vera, Fayette	S	100
● Vergennes, Jackson	S	275
● Vermillion Grove, Vermi'n	E	200
● Vermillion, Edgar	E	325
Vermillionville, La Salle	N	20
● Vermont, Fulton	W	1,158
Vernal, Vermillion	E	10
● Vernon, Marion	S	200
● Verona, Grundy	N	212
● Versailles, Brown	W	517
● Vevay Park, Cumberland	E	5
Viaduct Junction, Cook	NE	×
Victoria, Knox	W	308
● *Victoria*, Cass	W	×
● **Vienna**, Johnson	S	828
● Villa Grove, Douglas	E	100
● Villa Ridge, Pulaski	S	300
Villas, Crawford	SE	25
● *Vineland*, Union	S	×
● Viola, Mercer	NW	421
● Virden, Macoupin	SW	1,610
● **Virginia**, Cass	W	1,602
● *Virginia Junction*, Cass	W	×
Vishnew, McDonough	W	×
Volo, Lake	NE	150
● Voorhies, Piatt	C	12
● *Vulcan*, Monroe	SW	×
Wabash, Pike	**W**	×
Wabash, Wayne	NE	20
● *Wabash*, White	SE	7
● Waddam's Grove, St'h'n	NW	150
● Wadsworth, Lake	NE	100
● Wady Petra, Stark	C	30
● Waggoner, Montgomery	C	140
Wagners Landing, Jackson	S	×
Wakefield, Richland	SE	100
● *Walden*, Cook	NE	×
● *Waldheim Cemetery*, C'k	N1	×
● Waldron, Kankakee	E	308
Wales, Ogle	N	×
● Walker, Macon	C	40
● *Walker*, Will	NE	×
Walkerville, Greene	W	100
Wall, Jefferson	S	20
● Wallace, De Kalb	N	250
Wallace Sta., (see Rapatee)		×
Walla-Walla, Cumberland	E	×
Wallbaum, Henderson	W	100
Wallingford, Will	NE	70
● Walnut, Bureau	N	605
● Walnut Grove, M'Don'h	W	30
● Walnut Hill, Marion	S	125
● *Walnut Junction*, Bureau	N	×
● Walnut Prairie, Clark	E	55
Walpole, Hamilton	S	75
● Walshville, Montgomery	C	167
Waltersburgh, Pope	S	35
● Walton, Lee	N	12
Waltonborough, Gallatin	SE	8
Wanboro (see Albion)		×
● Wanda, Madison	SW	30
● *Wann*, Madison	SW	50
● Wapella, De Witt	C	371
● *Wards*, Saint Clair	SW	×
● *Ware*, Union	S	×
● Warner, Henry	NW	30
● Warren, Jo Daviess	NW	1,172
● *Warrenhurst*, DuPage	NE	×
● Warrensburg, Macon	C	500
● Warrenton, Edgar	E	20
● Warrenton Grove, Lake	NE	25
Warrenville, DuPage	NE	250
● *Warriners*, Alexander	S	×
● Warsaw, Hancock	W	2,721
Wartburg, Monroe	SW	65
● *Warrenhurst*, DuPage	NE	×
Wartrace, Johnson	S	×
● Wasco, Kane	N	25
● Washburn, Woodford	C	598
● Washington, Tazewell	C	1,301
● Wash'gt'n Heights, Cook	NE	2,283
Washington Park, Cook	NE	×
● Wataga, Knox	W	586
● *Watch Factory*, Kane	N	×

Illinois

Place	Section	Population
● Waterloo, Monroe	SW	1,860
● Waterman, DeKalb	N	351
● Watertown, Rock Isl'nd	NW	25
● **Watseka**, Iroquois	E	2,017
● Watson, Effingham	S	326
Wauconda, Lake	NE	368
● **Waukegan**, Lake	NE	4,915
● Wauponse, Grundy	N	50
● Waverly, Morgan	W	1,337
Wayland, Schuyler	W	10
● Wayne, DuPage	NE	175
Wayne, Jackson	S	×
● Wayne City, Wayne	NE	600
● Waynesville, DeWitt	C	368
● *Weaver Hill*, Union	S	×
● *Webbs*, Jefferson	S	×
Webb's Hill, Franklin	S	25
Webster, Hancock	W	125
● Wedron, La Salle	N	117
● Weedman, McLean	C	50
● *Weldon*, Cook	NE	×
● Weldon, De Witt	C	400
Welga, Randolph	SW	32
● Wellington, Iroquois	E	400
● Welton, Effingham	S	25
Wem, Kankakee	E	50
Wempletown, Winnebago	N	10
● Wenona, Marshall	C	1,053
● *Wentworth*, Cook	NE	×
● Wesley, Tazewell	C	100
● *West Belleville*, Saint Cl'r	SW	×
● West Brooklyn, Lee	N	250
West Division, Cook	NE	×
West Dundee, Kane	N	873
● *West Elgin*, Kane	N	×
● West End, Saline	S	35
Western Saratoga, Union	S	40
● Western Springs, Cook	NE	451
● Westfield, Clark	E	510
● *West Genoa*, DeKalb	N	×
West Hallock, Peoria	C	75
West Ham'd, (see Ham'd, Ind.		×
● *West Havanna*, Mason	NW	×
● *West Hinsdale*, DuPage	NE	×
West Jersey, Stark	C	125
● West Liberty, Jasper	SE	300
● West McHenry, McHenry	N	500
● *West Maywood*, Cook	NE	×
● *West Newell*, Vermillion	E	25
West Northfield, (see Oak Glen)		×
● Weston, McLean	C	200
● West Point, Hancock	W	300
Westport, Lawrence	NE	×
● West Ridge, Douglas	E	25
West Roseland, Cook	NE	1,407
● West Salem, Edwards	SE	476
West Springfield, Sangamon	C	668
● West Union, Clark	E	125
● Westville, Vermillion	E	45
● *Westv'e Cross'g*, Vermil'n	E	×
● West York, Crawford	SE	300
● Wetaug, Pulaski	S	100
Weathersfield, (see Kewanee)		×
● *Wetzel*, Edgar	E	10
Wheatland, Alexander	S	50
● **Wheaton**, DuPage	NE	1,622
● *Wheaton*, Randolph	SW	×
● Wheeler, Jasper	SE	250
● Wheeling, Cook	NE	811
Whitefield, Bureau	N	×
● White Hall, Greene	W	1,961
● White Heath, Piatt	C	100
White House, Union	S	×
White Oak, Montgomery	C	25
● *White Oak*, Saint Clair	SW	×
White Oak Point, Fayette	S	65
White Oak Springs, Brown	W	10
White Pigeon, Whiteside	NW	50
White Rock, Ogle	N	50
White Willow, Kendall	N	×
Whitley's Mts., (see Equality)		×
Wieman, (see German Valley)		×
Wilberton, Fayette	S	×
● Wilburn, Marshal	C	25
● *Wilderman*, Saint Clair	SW	×
● *Wildwood*, Cook	NE	32
Willard, Alexander	S	×
● *Willards*, Cook	NE	×
Willards Landing, Union	S	×
● Willey, Christian	C	30
● Williamsburgh, Moultrie	C	30
● Williamsfield, Knox	W	200
● Williamsville, Sangamon	C	444
● Willow, Jo Daviess	NW	60
● Willow Hill, Jasper	SE	450
● Willow Springs, Cook	NE	200
● Wilmette, Cook	NE	1,458

● Wilmington, Will	NE	1,576
● Wilsman, La Salle	N	×
● Wilson, Livingston	C	15
Wilsonburgh, Richland	SE	65
Wilson's, Randolph	SW	×
***Wilson's Switch*, Randolph**	**SW**	×
Wilton Center, Will	NE	200
● **Winchester**, Scott	W	1,542
Windom, Washington	S	×
● Windsor, Shelby	C	888
● Windsor Park, Cook	NE	*
Wine Hill, Randolph	SW	30
● Winfield, DuPage	NE	250
● Wing, Livingston	C	85
● Winnebago, Winnebago	N	464
● Winnetka, Cook	NE	1,079
● *Winslow*, Cumberland	E	×
● Winslow, Stephenson	NW	332
Winterrowd, Effingham	S	75
Winters, Jo Daviess	NW	20
● Wireton, Cook	NE	×
● Witt, Montgomery	C	50
Woburn, Bond	S	25
● Wolcott, Peoria	C	50
Wolf Creek, Williamson	S	25
● Wolf Lake, Union	S	×
● *Wolf's*, Kendall	N	×
Wolfs Crossing, [illegible]	NE	×
Wolrab Mills, Hardin	SE	50
● Womac, Macoupin	SW	×
● Woodbine, Jo Daviess	NW	10
Woodburn, Macoupin	SW	236
● Woodbury, Cumberland	E	×
● Woodford, Woodford	C	60
● Woodhull, Henry	NW	608
● Woodland, Iroquois	E	350
● Wood Lawn, Jefferson	S	350
● Woodlawn Park, Cook	NE	*
● *Woods*, Madison	SW	×
● Woodside, Sangamon	C	50
● Woodson, Morgan	W	200
● **Woodstock**, McHenry	N	1,683
● Woodville, Adams	W	30
Woodworth, Iroquois	E	40
Woody, Greene	W	65
● *Wood Yard*, Edgar	E	×
Wool, Pope	S	100
● Woosung, Ogle	N	200
● Worden, Madison	SW	522
● Worth, Cook	NE	275
Wrayville, Rock Island	NW	10
● *Wright*, Coles	E	×
Wrights Grove, Cook	NE	×
● Wrightsville, Greene	W	200
● Wyanet, Bureau	N	670
● *Wyckles*, Macon	C	×
Wynoose, Richland	NE	12
● Wyoming, Stark	C	1,116
● Xenia, Clay	S	878
● Yale, Jasper	SE	200
Yankee Hollow, Jo Davi's	NW	32
Yankeetown, Woodford	C	×
Yantisville, Shelby	C	20
● Yates City, Knox	W	687
Yates Landing, Pulaski	S	×
Yatesville, Morgan	W	×
● Yellow Creek, Stephens'n	NW	600
Yoch, Saint Clair	SW	×
York, Clark	E	294
Yorktown, Bureau	N	100
● **Yorkville**, Kendall	N	375
● *Youngblood*, Morgan	W	×
● Youngsdale, Kane	N	×
● Youngstown, Warren	W	60
Yuton, McLean	C	×
● *Zachary*, Clinton	S	×
● *Zanesville*, Montgomery	C	×
● *Zarleys*, Will	NE	×
Zenobia, Sangamon	C	18
Zif, Wayne	NE	15
Zion, Carroll	NW	×
Zion Station, (see Maud)		×
● Zulu, Warren	W	50
Zurna, Rock Island	NW	×

INDIANA.

COUNTIES.	INDEX.	POP.
Adams	NE	20,181
Allen	NE	66,689
Bartholomew	S	23,867
Benton	W	11,903
Blackford	E	10,461
Boone	C	26,572
Brown	S	10,308
Carroll	C	20,021
Cass	N	31,152
Clark	S	30,259
Clay	W	30,536
Clinton	C	27,370
Crawford	S	13,941
Daviess	SW	26,227
Dearborn	SE	23,364
Decatur	SE	19,277
DeKalb	NE	24,307
Delaware	E	30,131
Dubois	SW	20,253
Elkhart	N	39,201
Fayette	E	12,630
Floyd	S	29,458
Fountain	W	19,558
Franklin	E	18,366
Fulton	N	16,746
Gibson	SW	24,920
Grant	C	31,493
Greene	SW	24,379
Hamilton	C	26,123
Hancock	C	17,829
Harrison	S	20,786
Hendricks	C	21,498
Henry	E	23,879
Howard	C	26,186
Huntington	NE	27,644
Jackson	S	24,139
Jasper	NW	11,185
Jay	E	23,478
Jefferson	SE	24,507
Jennings	SE	14,608
Johnson	C	19,561
Knox	SW	28,044
Kosciusko	N	28,645
Lagrange	NE	15,615
Lake	NW	23,886
LaPorte	NW	34,445
Lawrence	S	19,792
Madison	C	36,487
Marion	C	141,156
Marshall	N	23,818
Martin	SW	13,973
Miami	N	25,823
Monroe	S	17,673
Montgomery	W	28,025
Morgan	C	18,643
Newton	NW	8,803
Noble	NE	23,359
Ohio	SE	4,955
Orange	S	14,678
Owen	W	15,040
Parke	W	20,296
Perry	S	18,240
Pike	SW	18,544
Porter	NW	18,052
Posey	SW	21,529
Pulaski	NW	11,233
Putnam	W	22,335
Randolph	E	28,085
Ripley	SE	19,350
Rush	E	19,034
St. Joseph	N	42,457
Scott	S	7,833
Shelby	**C**	**25,454**
Spencer	SW	22,060
Starke	NW	7,339
Steuben	NE	14,478
Sullivan	SW	21,877
Switzerland	SE	12,514
Tippecanoe	W	35,078
Tipton	C	18,157
Union	E	7,006
Vanderburgh	SW	59,809
Vermillion	W	13,154
Vigo	W	50,195
Wabash	N	27,126
Warren	W	10,955
Warrick	SW	21,161
Washington	S	18,619
Wayne	E	37,628
Wells	NE	21,514
White	NW	15,671
Whitley	NE	17,768
Total		2,192,404

TOWN. COUNTY.	INDEX.	POP.
Aaron, Switzerland	SE	25
Aberdeen (see Bacon)		×
Abington, Wayne	E	200
● Aboite, Allen	NE	60
● Abydel, Orange	S	×
● Academy, Allen	NE	25
● Acton, Marion	C	500
● *Adams*, Allen	NE	×
● Adams, Decatur	SE	400
● Adamsborough, Cass	N	150
Adel Owen	W	×
● Advance, Boone	C	100
Adeyeville, Perry	S	150
● Ainsworth, Lake	NW	20
● *Air Line Junc.*, Hamilton	C	×
● Akron, Fulton	N	700
Alamo, Montgomery	W	272
Alaska, Owen	W	200
● Albany, Delaware	E	571
● **Albion**, Noble	NE	1,229
● *Aldine*, Starke	NW	25
● Alert, Decatur	SE	112
● Alexandria, Madison	C	715
● Alfonte, Madison	C	70
Alfordsville, Daviess	SW	200
Algiers, Pike	SW	100
● Allda, LaPorte	NW	65
● Alldine, Starke	NW	25
Allen's Creek, Monroe	S	32
Allen's Sta., (see Springport)		×
Allensville, Randolph	E	×
Allensville, Switzerland	SE	68
Alliance, Marion	C	×
● *Alliance*, Madison	C	×
Allisonville, Marion	C	100
Alma, Whitley	NE	×
Alpha, Scott	S	48
● Alpine, Fayette	E	80
Alquina, Fayette	E	100
Alto, Howard	C	300
● Altoga, Dubois	SW	200
Alton, Crawford	S	277
Altona, DeKalb	NE	100
Alum Cave, Sullivan	SW	×
Alvarado, Steuben	NE	300
● Ambia, Benton	W	293
● Amboy, Miami	N	402
Americus, Tippecanoe	W	50
● Amity, Johnson	C	100
● Amo, Hendricks	C	300
Ample, Jay	E	15
● **Anderson**, Madison	C	10,741
Andersonville, Franklin	E	400
● Andrews, Huntington	NE	1,390
Angleton, Kosciusko	N	10
● **Angola**, Steuben	NE	1,840
Annapolis, Parke	W	470
● Anoka, Cass	N	100
Anthony, Delaware	E	10
● *Anthony's*, Pulaski	NW	×
Antioch, Jay	E	×
Antiville, Jay	E	50
Antrim, Marion	C	×
Apalona, Perry	S	×
Arba, Randolph	E	150
● Arcadia, Hamilton	C	670
Arcadia, (see Arthur)		×
Arcana, Grant	C	25
● Arcola, Allen	NE	250
● Argos, Marshall	N	1,101
● Ari, Allen	NE	50
● Arlington, Rush	E	500
Armiesburgh, Parke	W	100
● *Armstrong*, Lawrence	S	×
● Armstrong, Vand'rb'rgh	SW	20
Arney, Owen	W	25
● *Arnolds*, Whitley	NE	×
Aroma, Hamilton	C	115
Art, Clay	W	57
Arthur, Pike	SW	400
Artic, DeKalb	NE	20
● *Ascension*, Sullivan	SW	300
● Ashboro, Clay	W	200
● *Ashby's*, Montgomery	W	×
● Ashersville, Clay	W	100
● Ash Grove, Tippecanoe	W	×
● Ashland, Henry	E	100
Ashton, Ripley	SE	×
● *Asylum*, Tippecanoe	W	×
● Atherton, Vigo	W	50
● Atkinson, Benton	W	50
Atkinsonville, Owen	W	75
● Atlanta, Hamilton	C	500
● Attica, Fountain	W	2,320
● Atwood, Kosciusko	N	250
● **Auburn**, DeKalb	NE	2,415
● Auburn Junc., DeKalb	NE	150
● *Augusta*, Marion	C	300
Augusta, Pike	SW	250
● Aurora, Dearborn	SE	3,929
● Austin, Scott	S	400

Place	Pop.
Aventon, Dearborn........SE	×
● Avery, Clinton........... C	25
● Avilla, Noble............NE	576
● Avoca, Lawrence.........S	100
● Avon, Hendricks..........C	100
Avonburg, (see Jay)	×
Avondale, Delaware........ E	×
Axton, (see Lake & Richland)	×
Aydelott, Benton...........W	20
● Aylesworth, Fountain....W	25
● *Aylesworth*, Porter.... NW	×
● Ayrshire, Pike..........SW	×
● Azalia, Bartholomew......S	100
● B, Tippecanoe............W	25
● Babcock, Porter........NW	25
Badger, White............ NW	15
Baileytown, Porter.......NW	×
● Bainbridge, Putnam......W	473
Baker's Corner, Hamilton...C	60
Balbec, Jay.................E	100
Baldwin, Allen...........NE	50
● *Ball's*, Tippecanoe....... W	×
Ballstown, Ripley..........SE	25
Banquo, Huntington....... NE	75
Banta, Johnson.............C	25
Bar, Vanderburgh......... SW	×
Barber's Mills, Wells......NE	75
Barbersville, Jefferson.....SE	237
Bargersville, Johnson....... C	100
● Barnard, Putnam........ W	75
Barnes, Jennings.......... SE	82
Barren, (see Ramsey)........	×
● *Barrett*, Posey..........SW	×
Bartle, Washington......... S	×
Bartlettsville, Lawrence.....S	×
Bartonia, Randolph ....E	50
Bascom, Ohio...............SE	50
Bassett, Howard............C	×
Bateham, Sullivan........SW	×
● Batesville, Ripley........SE	1,169
Bath, Franklin..............E	65
● Battle Ground, Tip'canoe W	456
Beall, Knox...............SW	×
Bean Blossom, Brown.......S	227
Bear Branch, Ohio..........SE	100
Beard, Clinton.............. C	35
Beaver City, Newton...... NW	×
Beaver Dam, Kosciusko.... N	50
Beaver Timber, Newton...NW	195
● *Beck*, Gibson............SW	50
Beck's Grove, Brown....... S	35
Beck's Mills, Washington....S	10
Beckville, (see Orth)..........	×
● **Bedford**, Lawrence..... S	3,351
● *Bedford Junc.*, Lawrence. S	×
Beecamp, Jefferson..........SE	100
● Beech Grove, Marion...... C	×
Beech Grove, (see Burlington)	×
Beechy Mire, Union......... E	10
● *Beeson*, Wayne...........E	75
● *Beeville*, Tippecanoe......W	25
Belden, Wabash.............N	100
● *Belknap*, Vanderburgh. SW	×
Belle Fontaine, (see Hector).	×
Belle Union, Putnam........W	100
Belleview, Jefferson......... SE	50
● *Belleview*, St. Joseph..... N	×
Belleville, Hendricks.........C	300
Bellmore, Parke.............W	400
Belmont, Brown............. S	25
● *Belt Junction*, Marion....C	×
● *Belt Road*, Marion........C	×
● Ben Davis, Marion.........C	100
Bengal, Shelby..............C	30
Benham, Ripley........... SE	45
Benjamin, Vermillion.......W	200
● *Bennett's Crossing*, Rush. E	×
● Bennett's Switch, Miami..N	150
● Bennettsville, Clark.......S	26
Bennington, Switzerland.. SE	100
Bentley, Fayette............E	50
Benton, Elkhart.............N	250
● *Benton*, Lake.......... NW	×
● Bentonville, Fayette...... E	150
Benville, Jennings.........SE	25
Benwood, Clay............ W	100
Benz, Crawford............. S	×
● *Berkley*, Boone.......... C	×
● Berlingon, Marshall..... N	50
● Berne, Adams.......... NE	544
● *Bernice*, Lake.........NW	×
● *Berry Lake*, Lake...... NW	×
● *Bethany Park*, Morgan...C	×
Bethel, (see Stout)	×
Bethel, Wayne.............. E	124
Bethlehem, Clark............S	100
Bibler, Lake..............NW	25
● Bicknell, Knox..........SW	450
Big Creek, Jefferson.......SE	×
Bigfoot, Fulton.............N	10
Big Indian, Cass........... N	25
Big Spring, Boone.......... C	100
Billingsville, Union..... ... E	85
● Bingen, Adams.........NE	50
● Bippus, Huntington.....NE	300
● Birdseye, Dubois........SW	419
● Birmingham, Miami......N	75
● Blackburn Station, Pike.SW	×
Black Creek, Harrison...... S	×
Blackford, Jasper........ NW	50
● *Black Oak*, Daviess..... SW	65
● Blaine, Jay................E	65
Blairsville, Posey......... SW	110
Blanche, Monroe............S	10
Blankenship, Martin......SW	×
● Blocher, Scott............S	125
● *Blodgett*, Elkhart..........N	×
● **Bloomfield**, Greene....S	1,229
Bloomfield, (see Midway)	×
● Bloomingdale, Parke.... W	431
Blooming Grove, Franklin..E	90
Bloomingport, Randolph....E	150
Bloomingsburgh, Fulton....N	120
Blo'gsp't Sta., (see Carlos Ci'y)	×
● **Bloomington**, Monroe.S	4,018
Blossom, Monroe............S	×
Blountsville, Henry.........E	200
Blue, Ohio.................SE	10
Blue Creek, Franklin.......E	25
Blue Grass, Fulton......... N	300
Blue Lick, Clark............ S	35
Blue Ridge, Shelby.........C	135
Blue River, Washington.....S	20
Blue River Island (see Leavenworth)	×
Bluff Creek, Johnson....... C	60
Bluff Mills, Montgomery...W	×
Bluff Point, Jay............E	150
● **Bluffton**, Wells.......NE	3,589
Bly, Wells..................NE	10
● Bobo, Adams........... NE	50
● *Boehmer*, Huntington...NE	20
● Boggstown, Shelby........C	200
● Bolivar, Wabash..........N	15
Bono, Lawrence.............S	15
● Boone Grove, Porter...NW	1:5
Boonville, Warrick.... SW	1,881
● Borden, Clark.............S	400
● *Bossert*, Lawrence........ S	195
● *Boston*, Crawford.........S	×
Boston, Wayne..............E	146
Boston Station, (see Eckerty)	×
● Boswell, Benton......... W	558
Boundary, Jay..............E	200
● Bourbon, Marshall........N	1,064
Bovine, Gibson............SW	15
● Bowers, Montgomery....W	65
Bowling Green, Clay.......W	467
Bowman, Pike.............SW	10
Boxley, Hamilton...........C	200
Boyceton, Delaware.........E	×
● Boyleston, Clinton.........C	200
Bracken, Huntington..... NE	100
● *Bradbury*, Madison.......C	×
Bradford, Harrison..........S	200
Bradford (see Monon).......	×
Bradley's, Spencer........SW	×
● Brady, Shelby.............C	25
Bragg, Randolph............E	25
Bramble, Martin...........SW	10
● *Branch's*, Johnson....... C	×
Branchville, Perry..........S	25
Brand, Clay................W	10
● *Brandon*, Rush...........E	×
● *Braxtons*, Orange.........S	×
Brayton, Hendricks.........C	×
● **Brazil**, Clay.......... W	5,905
Breckenridge, Harrison.....S	20
● Bremen, Marshall........ N	1,076
● *Bretzville*, Dubois........SW	65
● Brewersville, Jennings..S E	150
Brey, Morgan...............C	×
● *Breyfogle*, Monroe.........S	×
● *Briant*, Jay...............E	250
● Brice, Jay............... E	100
Brick Chapel, Putnam..... W	75
● *Bridgeport*, Clark.........S	97
Bridgeport, Harrison........S	×
● Bridgeport, Marion........C	204
Bridgeton, Parke.......... W	200
Bright, Dearborn...........SE	100
Brighton, Lagrange....... NE	50
● **Brightwood, Marion...... C**	1,387
● Brimfield, Noble........NE	254
Brinckley,, Randolph.......E	25
● Bringhurst. Carroll....... C	400
● Bristol, Elkhart...... ... N	535
Bristow, Perry............. S	50
● Broad Ripple, Marion.... C	100
Bromer, Orange.. .... N	20
● *Brompton*, Hamilton..... C	×
● Brook, Newton........ NW	100
Brookfield, Shelby..........C	350
● Brooklyn, Morgan........C	545
Brooksburgh, Jefferson....SE	120
● Brookston, White...... NW	447
● **Brookville**, Franklin..E	2,028
● *Broom Hill*, Clark........S	65
● *Brownell*, Miami......... N	×
● Brownsburgh, Hendricks.C	623
Brown's Corners, Hunt'gt'n NE	60
Brownstown, (see Mt. Prospect)	×
● **Brownstown**, Jackson.S	1,422
● Brown's Valley, Montg'y. W	114
● Brownsville, Union........E	258
● Bruce's Lake, Fulton.....N	25
● Bruceville, Knox....... SW	350
● *Bruins*, Madison..........C	×
Brunswick, Lake..........NW	75
Brushy Prairie, Lagrange. NE	50
● Bryant, Jay...............E	250
Bryantsburgh, Jefferson...SE	129
Bryant's Creek, Monroe.....S	75
Bryantsville, Lawrence..... S	60
Buck, Switzerland..........SE	14
● *Buck Creek*, Greene....... SW	×
Buck Creek, Tippecanoe... W	250
● Buckeye, Huntington....NE	50
● Buckskin, Gibson...... SW	×
Bud, Johnson...............C	×
Buel City (see Cass)...........	×
Buena Vista, Monroe.........S	50
Buena Vista (see Rosewood).	×
Buena Vista (see Cerro Gordo)	×
Buffalo, White............NW	15
● Buffaloville, Spencer... SW	150
Bufkin, Posey............ SW	×
● Bunker Hill, Miami...... N	538
Burchard, Sullivan........SW	32
● Burdick, Porter.........NW	50
● Burket, Kosciusko....... N	300
Burlington, Carroll......... C	500
Burlington (see Arlington...	×
● Burnett, Vigo............W	50
● Burnett's Creek, White NW	479
● *Burnettsville*, White....NW	479
● Burney, Decatur......... SE	50
● *Burnham*, Lake....... NW	×
Burns, Elkhart............N	×
● Burn's City, Martin.....SW	75
Burnside, Clinton......... C	10
● *Burnside*, Shelby......... C	×
● Burnsville, Bartholomew..S	75
● Burr Oak, Marshall.......N	90
● Burrows, Carroll..........C	150
● *Burton*, Lawrence.........S	×
● Burton, Tippecanoe......W	83
● *Bushrod*, Greene....... SW	×
● *Busseron*, Knox.........SW	×
● Butler, DeKalb........... NE	2,521
Butler Switch, Jennings...SE	10
● Butlerville, Jennings.... SE	250
Bynum, Shelby..............C	25
Byrneville, Harrison....... S	15
Byron, Parke............... W	×
● Cahorn's, Posey..........SW	50
Cadiz, Henry................E	307
Calcium, Bartholomew..... S	×
Cale, Martin.............. SW	40
● *Calumet*, Lake..........NW	×
Calvertville, Greene....... SW	10
Calvin Sta., (see Stewarts V.)	×
● Cambria, Clinton.......... C	50
● Cambridge City, Wayne...E	1.782
Camby, Marion..............C	50
● Camden, Carroll.......... C	800
● Cammack, Delaware......E	200
● *Campbells*, Orange.........S	×
● Campbellsburgh, Wash'n. S	418
Cana, Jennings. .... SE	15
Canaan, Jefferson..........SE	100
Canal, Warrick.......... SW	150
● Cannelburgh, Daviess...SW	276
● **Cannelton**, Perry.......S	1,991
Canton, Washington.........S	300
Cape Sandy, Crawford.......S	10
● Carbon, Clay........... W	521
Carbondale, Warren.........W	50
● Cardonia, Clay.......... W	200
● Carlisle, Sullivan........SW	503
● Carlos City, Randolph.... E	100

Place	Section	Population
● Carmel, Hamilton	C	471
Carmel, Harrison	S	×
Carp, Owen	W	30
● Carpentersville, Putnam	W	175
Carroll, Carroll	C	75
● *Carroll's Craig*, Allen	NE	×
Carrollton (see Darwin)		×
● Carrollton, Hancock	C	300
Carr's Mill (see Temple)		×
● *Carr's Tank*, White	NW	×
● *Carter's*, Marion	C	×
● Cartersburgh, Hendricks	C	300
● Carthage, Rush	E	482
Cason, Boone	C	50
● *Cass*, Cass	N	×
● Cass, Sullivan	SW	300
● *Casselo*, Lake	NW	×
● Cassville, Howard	C	75
Castle, Randolph	E	25
● Castleton, Marion	C	100
Cataract, Owen	W	150
● Cates, Fountain	W	75
● Catlin, Parke	W	200
● Cayuga, Vermillion	W	400
● Cedar Beach, Kosciusko	N	25
● Cedar Creek, DeKalb	NE	55
● Cedar Grove, Franklin	E	300
● Cedar Lake, Lake	NW	50
Cedarville, Allen	NE	50
Cedar Wood, Harrison	S	30
Celestine, Dubois	SW	120
Celia, Allen	NE	10
Celina, Perry	S	30
● *Cement Mills*, Clark	S	×
● Cementville, Clark	S	550
Central, Harrison	S	40
Central Barren, Harrison	S	×
● Centre, Howard	C	250
Centre Point, Clay	W	517
Centre Square, Switzerland	SE	70
● Centreton, Morgan	C	300
Centre Valley, Hendricks	C	60
● Centreville, Wayne	E	864
Centreville, (see Lewis)		×
Centreville, (see Oakland)		×
● *Centreville Pike*, Wayne	E	30
Cerro Gordo, Randolph	E	50
● Ceylon, Adams	NE	100
● Chalmers, White	NW	200
Chamberlain, Allen	NE	20
Chambersburgh, Orange	S	110
Chamness, Henry	E	×
Champion, Jennings	SE	150
● Chandler, Warrick	SW	150
● Charlestown, Clark	S	888
● Charlottesville, Hancock	C	400
Charm, Elkhart	N	×
● Chase, Benton	W	60
Cheadle, Clinton	C	×
Chelsea, Jefferson	SE	30
● *Cherry Grove*, M'tgomery	W	×
Chester, Wayne	E	150
● Chesterfield, Madison	C	150
● Chesterton, Porter	NW	931
Chesterville, Dearborn	SE	100
Chestnut Crossing, (see Alton)		×
Chestnut Hill, Washington	S	25
● Chestnut Ridge, Jackson	S	100
Chetwynd, Morgan	C	×
Chicago, DeKalb	NE	10
Chicago Siding, (see Foster)		×
● Chili, Miami	N	250
China, Jefferson	SE	25
● Chrisney, Spencer	SW	500
Christian, (see Princeton)		×
Christiansburgh, Brown	S	×
● *Christman's*, Porter	NW	25
● Churubusco, Whitley	NE	869
● Cicero, Hamilton	C	631
Cincinnati, Greene	SW	75
● *Cincinnati, Richmond and Chicago Junction*, Wayne	E	×
● *Circleville*, Clinton	C	×
● *Clanricarde*, La Porte	NW	×
Clare, Hamilton	C	10
● *Clark*, Pike	SW	×
● Clarke, Randolph	E	×
● Clarke Station, Lake	NW	100
● *Clark's*, Daviess	SW	×
● *Clark's*, Pulaski	NW	×
Clarksburgh, Decatur	SE	500
● Clark's Hill, Tippecanoe	W	450
Clark's Prairie, (see Odon)		×
Clark's Sta., (see Cannelsburg)		×
Clarksville, Clark	S	1,692
Clarksville, Hamilton	C	200
● Clay City, Clay	W	1,004
Clay City, (see Buffalo)		×
● Claypool, Kosciusko	N	500
Claysville, Clark	S	×
Claysburg, (see Jeffersonville)		×
● *Claysville*, Huntington	NE	×
Claysville, Washington	S	10
● *Clay Switch*, Clay	W	×
● Clayton, Hendricks	C	500
● *Clear Creek*, Huntington	NE	×
○ Clear Creek, Monroe	S	100
Clear Lake, Steuben	NE	50
Clear Springs, Jackson	S	300
Cleona, Brown	S	25
● Clermont, Marion	C	300
● Cleveland, Hancock	C	130
● Clifford, Bartholomew	S	175
Clifton, Union	E	40
Clifty, Decatur	SE	300
● Clinton, Vermillion	W	1,365
Clinton Falls, Putnam	W	97
Clough, (see Highland)		×
● Cloverdale, Putnam	W	437
● Cloverland, Clay	W	150
Clunette, Kosciusko	N	100
Clyde, Owen	W	×
● Clymers, Cass	N	100
● Coal Bluff, Vigo	W	300
● Coal City, Owen	W	150
Coal Creek, Fountain	W	100
● Coatsville, Hendricks	C	450
● Coburgh, Porter	NW	50
● Cochran, Dearborn	SE	790
● Coesse, Whitley	NE	210
Coffee, Clay	W	70
● *Cohasset*, Hamilton	C	×
● Colburn, Tippecanoe	W	300
Cold Spring, Dearborn	SE	50
Cole's Cor., (see Bear Branch)		×
● Colfax, Clinton	C	730
● Collamer, Whitley	NE	300
● *College Corners*, Union	E	×
● Collett, Jay	E	150
Collingwood, Allen	NE	25
Collins, Whitley	NE	100
Collins Store, (see Deerfield)		×
Coloma, Parke	W	200
Colter Corner, Franklin	E	50
Columbia, Fayette	E	×
● **Columbia City**, Whit'y	NE	3,027
● **Columbus**, Bartholom'w	S	6,719
Combs, Clinton	C	×
● Commiskey, Jennings	SE	32
● Como, Jay	E	75
Concord, (see Maurice)		×
Concord, DeKalb	NE	50
Concord, Tippecanoe	W	60
● **Connersville**, Fayette	E	4,548
Conroe, Tippecanoe	W	65
Convenience, Harrison	S	15
● *Converse*, Miami	N	×
● *Cooleys*, Franklin	E	×
Cope, Morgan	C	40
● *Corinne*, Owen	W	×
Corkwell, Jay	E	25
Corner, Sullivan	SW	×
● *Cornbrook*, Bartholomew	S	×
Cornettsville, Daviess	SW	10
Correct, Ripley	SE	45
● Cortland, Jackson	S	200
● Corrunna, DeKalb	NE	350
● Cory, Clay	W	250
● **Corydon**, Harrison	S	880
● *Corydon Junction*, Har'on	S	65
Cosperville, Noble	NE	10
Cottage Grove, Union	E	50
● *County Line*, Vigo	W	×
● Courter, Miami	N	30
● **Covington**, Fountain	W	1,891
● Cowan, Delaware	E	200
● *Cox's*, Marshall	N	×
Cox's Mills, Wayne	E	50
● *Coxton*, Lawrence	S	×
● Coxville, Parke	W	601
Craig, Switzerland	SE	×
● Craigville, Wells	NE	90
● Crandall, Harrison	S	80
● **Crawfordsville**, M'g'ry	W	6,089
● *Crawfordsv'e Junc.*, M'g'y	W	×
Cresco, Whitley	NE	10
● Creston, Lake	NW	200
Creswell, Jefferson	SE	×
● Crete, Randolph	E	25
● Crisman, Porter	NW	25
Crisps' Cross Roads, Harrs'n	S	10
Crittenden, Cass	N	×
● Cromwell, Noble	NE	400
Crooked Creek, Steuben	NE	150
● *Crossley*, Madison	C	26
Cross Plains, Ripley	SE	150
Cross Roads, Delaware	E	20
Cross Roads, (see Cope)		×
● Crothersville, Jackson	S	599
Crown Center, Morgan	C	×
● **Crown Point**, Lake	NW	1,907
Crownville, (see Boonville)		×
Crozier, Dearborn	SE	×
● Crumtown, St. Joseph	N	100
Crystal, Dubois	SW	25
Cuba, Owen	W	75
● Culver, Tippecanoe	W	25
Cumback, Daviess	SW	65
● Cumberland, Marion	C	300
Curryville, (see Shelburn)		×
● Curryville, Wells	NE	120
● Curtisville, Tipton	C	145
Curveton, Cass	N	100
Cushman, (see Springer)		×
Custer, DeKalb	NE	25
Cutler, Carroll	C	125
● Cyclone, Clinton	C	40
● Cynthiana, Posey	SW	300
Cynthiana, (see Blue Ridge)		×
● **Cypress**, Vanderburgh	SW	400
● ***Cypress***, **Knox**	**SW**	×
● Daggett, Owen	W	65
● Dale, Spencer	SW	651
● Daleville, Delaware	E	250
Dalton, Wayne	E	100
● Dana, Vermillion	W	495
● **Danville**, Hendricks	C	1,569
Darcy, Carroll	C	97
● *Dark Hollow*, Lawrence	S	×
● Darlington, Montgomery	W	461
Darmstadt, (see Inglefield)		×
Darwin, Carroll	C	10
● *Darwin*, Putnam	W	×
● *Davis*, LaPorte	NW	×
Davis, Starke	NW	30
● Dawkins, Allen	NE	67
● *Dawson*, Warrick	SW	×
● Dayton, Tippecanoe	W	500
Deacon, Cass	N	10
● Deal, Lawrence	S	×
● **Decatur**, Adams	NE	3,142
● Decker, Knox	SW	125
● Deedsville, Miami	N	125
Deep River, Lake	NW	50
Deer Creek, Carroll	C	500
● *Deer Creek*, Carroll	C	×
Deerfield, Randolph	E	100
● *Deerfield Station*, Rand'ph	E	195
● De Forest, Warrick	SW	32
Dego, Cass	N	×
● De GoniaSpr'gs, Warrick	SW	20
● DeKalb, DeKalb	NE	60
Delaney's Creek, Wash'ton	S	10
Delaware, Ripley	SE	165
Delectable Hill, (see Algiers)		×
● De Long, Fulton	N	75
● **Delphi**, Carroll	C	1,923
Delta, Parke	W	×
Deming, Hamilton	C	125
● De Motte, Jasper	NW	100
● Denham, Pulaski	NW	40
Denmark, Owen	W	20
● Denver, Miami	N	900
● De Pauw, Harrison	S	125
● Deputy, Jefferson	SE	215
Derby, Perry	S	200
Dern, White	NW	×
Desolation, Fulton	N	×
● De Soto, Delaware	E	78
Dewberry, (see Friendship)		×
Dexter, Perry	S	130
Diamond, Parke	W	×
Dice, Newton	NW	×
● *Dickason*, Vermillion	W	×
Dickeyville, Warrick	SW	15
Dildaville, Grant	C	×
Dillman, Wells	NE	25
● Dillsborough, Dearborn	SE	439
● Disko, Wabash	N	296
Ditney, Warrick	SW	35
● Dixon, Greene	SW	67
● *Dock Siding*, Lake	NW	×
Dogwood, Harrison	S	×
Dolan, Monroe	S	×
Domestic, Wells	NE	20
● Donaldson, Marshall	N	150
Dongola, (see Oakland City)		×
Don Juan, Perry	S	98
● *Dooley*, Parke	W	×
Doolittle's Mills, Perry	S	25
Door Village, LaPorte	NW	75

Indiana
Indiana

Place	Section	Population
Dora, Wabash	N	100
● *Douglass*, Gibson	SW	×
Dover, Dearborn	SE	200
Dover, (see Webster)		×
Dover Hill, Martin	SW	125
● Dow, Cass	N	×
Downeyville, Decatur	SE	45
Drake, Grant	C	×
Draper, Miami	N	65
● Dresden, Greene	SW	100
Drewersburg, Franklin	E	28
● Dublin, Wayne	E	806
Dubois, Dubois	SW	100
Dudley, Monroe	S	10
Dudleytown, Jackson	S	200
● Duff, Dubois	SW	45
● Dugger, Sullivan	SW	600
Dukes, Allen	NE	10
Dumont, Marion	C	×
● Dundee, Madison	C	200
Dundee, (see Roll)		×
Dundee, (see Mohawk)		×
● *Dune Park*, Lake	NW	×
● Dunfee, Whitley	NE	41
● Dunkirk, Jay	E	1,024
● Dunlap's, Elkhart	N	10
Dunlapsville, Union	E	180
Dunnington, Benton	W	15
● *Dunn's*, Jasper	NW	×
● Dunreith, Henry	E	168
● *Dunville*, Jasper	NW	50
● Dupont, Jefferson	SE	200
● Durbin, Hamilton	C	×
● *Durham*, LaPorte	NW	65
● Dyer, Lake	NW	400
Eagle, Sullivan	SW	40
● Eagle Lake, Kosciusko	N	25
● Eaglesfield, Clay	W	25
● Eagletown, Hamilton	C	250
● *Eames*, Warrick	SW	×
● Earle, Vanderburgh	SW	40
● Earl Park, Benton	W	600
● East Chicago, Lake	NW	1,255
East Connersville, Fayette	E	458
East Enterprise, Swit'nd	SE	45
● *East Fowler*, Benton	W	×
● East Germant'n, Wayne	E	338
● *Easton*, Benton	W	×
Easton, (see Gale)		×
East Pleasanton, Kosciusko	N	×
● *East Shelbyville*, Shelby	C	15
● Eaton, Delaware	E	600
Eby, Warrick	SW	65
Eck, Marion	C	×
Eckerty, Crawford	S	200
● Eclipse, Jackson	S	×
Economy, Wayne	E	245
Eden, Hancock	C	100
● *Edgemoor*, Lake	NW	×
Edgerton, Allen	NE	175
● Edinburgh, Johnson	C	2,031
Edna Mills, Clinton	C	72
● Edwards, Vigo	W	50
● Edwardsport, Knox	SW	670
● Edwardsville, Floyd	S	100
Eel River, Allen	NE	×
● *Eel River*, Clay	W	130
Ege, Noble	NE	25
Egg Harbor, Gibson	SW	×
Egypt, (see Owasco)		×
● *Ehrlich*, Clay	W	×
Ekin, Tipton	C	100
● Elberfeld, Warrick	SW	250
El Dorado, Hamilton	C	50
Elizabeth, Harrison	S	267
Elizabeth, (see Dale)		×
● Elizabethtown, Bart'lm'w	S	430
Elizaville, Boone	C	100
● Elkhart, Elkhart	N	11,360
Elkinsville, Brown	S	50
● Ellettsville, Monroe	S	712
● *Elliott*, Vanderburgh	SW	×
Ellis, Steuben	NE	25
● Elliston, Greene	SW	×
● Ellsworth, Dubois	SW	50
● *Ellsworth*, Vigo	W	×
Elmdale, Montgomery	W	30
● Elnora, Daviess	**SW**	500
Elrod, Ripley	**SE**	100
Elston, Tippecanoe	W	10
● Elwood, Madison	C	2,284
Emdel, Tippecanoe	W	×
Eminence, Morgan	C	225
● Emison, Knox	SW	75
Emma, Lagrange	NE	65
Emmettsville, Randolph	E	30
Englewood, Montgomery	W	66
Emporia, Madison	C	×
● English, Crawford	S	423
● English Lake, Starke	NW	100
Enochsburgh, Franklin	E	85
Enterprise, Spencer	SW	50
Epsom, Daviess	SW	100
Erie, Lawrence	S	23
● *Erie*, Miami	N	32
● *Erskine*, Vanderburgh	SW	×
Ervin, Howard	C	50
● *Erwin*, Posey	SW	130
Ethel, Orange	S	×
● Etna Green, Kosciusko	N	411
Euclid, Daviess	SW	×
Eugene, Vermillion	W	350
Euphemia, Hendricks	C	×
● *Eureka*, Clay	W	×
Eureka, Spencer	SW	125
Evans' Landing, Harrison	S	12
Evanston, Spencer	SW	×
● Evanston, Spencer	SW	×
● Evansville, V'nd'rbg	SW	50,756
Everton, Fayette	E	200
Ewing, Jackson	S	300
● Ewington, Decatur	SE	200
Exchange, Morgan	C	78
Fairbanks, Sullivan	SW	100
● *Fairchilds*, Greene	SW	×
Fairfax, Monroe	S	31
Fairfield, Franklin	E	300
● *Fairfield*, Howard	C	150
Fairfield Centre, De Kalb	NE	60
● *Fair Grounds*, V'nd'rb'g	SW	×
● Fairland, Shelby	C	513
● Fairmount, Grant	C	1,462
● Fair Oaks, Jasper	NW	150
● *Fairplay*, Vanderburgh	SW	50
Fairview (see Groves)		×
● *Fairview*, Marion	C	×
Fairview, Randolph	E	25
Fairveiw (see Sugar Branch)		×
Fallen Timber, Randolph	E	×
● Falmouth, Rush	E	175
Fansler, Allen	NE	×
● Farabee, Washington	S	20
Fargo, Orange	S	×
● Farmer, Owen	W	150
● *Farmers*, Rush	E	×
● Farmersburgh, Sullivan	SW	301
Farmers Institute, Tp'nc'no	W	65
Farmers Retreat, D'rborn	SE	150
● Farmersville, Posey	SW	130
Farmerton, Rush	E	×
● *Farmington*, Rush	E	×
● Farmland, Randolph	E	770
● *Farm Siding*, Starke	NW	×
● Farnsworth, Sullivan	SW	40
● *Farrington*, Vigo	W	50
Farrville, Grant	C	20
Faulkner, Jefferson	SE	25
Fayette, Boone	C	100
Fayette, Marion	C	100
Fayetteville, Fayette	E	200
Fayetteville, Lawrence	S	100
● Fenn's, Shelby	C	50
● Fenton, Marion	C	×
Ferdinand, Dubois	SW	627
● *Ferdinand Station*, D'bs	SW	65
● *Ferguson's*, Allen	NE	32
● Fern, Putnam	W	65
Ferndale, Parke	W	15
Flat, Jay	E	25
● Fickle, Clinton	C	20
Fidelity, (see Otwell)		×
● *Fields*, Lake	NW	×
● Fillmore, Putnam	W	100
Fincastle, Putnam	W	150
Finck's, Ripley	SE	30
● *Fisher's*, Hamilton	C	×
Fishersburgh, Madison	C	250
● Fisher'sSwitch, H'm'lton	C	230
Fish Lake, Elkhart	N	20
● *Fish Lake*, LaPorte	NW	×
● *Five Mile*, Marion	C	×
Flackville, Marion	C	×
● Flat Rock, Shelby	C	200
Fleener, Monroe	S	×
● Fleming's, Jackson	S	×
● *Fleming's*, Lake	NW	×
Fletcher, Fulton	N	×
Flint, Steuben	NE	95
● Flora, Carroll	C	639
Florence, Switzerland	SE	300
● Florida, Madison	C	50
Floyd's Knobs, Floyd	S	200
Folsomville, Warrick	SW	410
● Foltz, Jefferson	SE	25
● Fontanet, Vigo	W	521
Foraker, Elkhart	N	×
Ford's Crossing, Cass	N	25
● Foresman, Newton	NW	100
Forest, Clinton	C	300
Forest City, Newton	NW	×
Foresters, LaPorte	NW	×
Forest Hill, Decatur	SE	124
● *Forest Hill*, Vigo	W	×
Forestville, Madison	C	×
Forney, White	NW	30
● *Forsyth*, Lake	NW	×
● Fort Branch, Gibson	SW	748
● Fort Ritner, Lawrence	S	100
● Fortville, Hancock	C	685
● FORT WAYNE, Allen	NE	35,393
● Foster, Warren	W	20
● Fountain, Fountain	W	100
● Fountain City, Wayne	E	492
● Fountaintown, Shelby	C	310
● Fowler, Benton	W	1,285
● *Fowler*, Greene	SW	×
● Fox, Grant	C	10
● Francesville, Pulaski	NW	403
● Francisco, Gibson	SW	300
● Frankfort, Clinton	C	5,919
● Franklin, Johnson	C	3,781
Franklin, Wayne	E	80
● *Franklin*, Whitney	NE	869
● Frankton, Madison	C	520
Fravel, Adams	NE	10
Fredericksburgh, Wash'ton	S	211
Fredonia, Crawford	S	50
● Freedom, Owen	W	285
Freelandville, Knox	SW	200
Freeman, Owen	W	×
● *Freeport*, Jackson	S	×
Freeport, Shelby	C	80
Freetown, Jackson	S	250
● Fremont, Steuben	NE	672
● *French*, Vermillion	W	×
● French Lick, Orange	S	100
● Frenchtown, Harrison	S	65
Friedheim, Adams	NE	20
Friendship, Ripley	SE	150
● Friendswood, Hendricks	C	100
Fruits, Montgomery	W	×
Fugard, Greene	SW	×
Fulda, Spencer	SW	150
Fulton, Fulton	N	200
Fuquay, Warrick	SW	30
● Furnessville, Porter	NW	100
Gabtown, (see Earl)		×
● Gadsden, Boone	C	×
Gaff, Ripley	SE	20
● Gale, Hendricks	C	25
Galena, Floyd	S	250
● *Gales*, Lake	NW	×
Galey's Land, (see Rono)		×
● Gallaudet, Marion	C	×
● Galveston, Cass	N	600
● Gar Creek, Allen	NE	25
Garfield, Montgomery	W	25
Garman, Allen	NE	×
● Garrett, DeKalb	NE	2,167
● *Garvin*, Vanderburgh	SW	×
Gasburgh, Morgan	C	50
● Gath, Adams	NE	10
Gaynorville, Decatur	SE	10
● *Gebhart*, Cass	N	×
Geetingsville, Clinton	C	50
● Gem, Hancock	C	100
● Geneva, Adams	NE	748
Geneva, Shelby	C	150
Genoda, Lawrence	S	×
Gent, Monroe	S	×
● Gentryville, Spencer	SW	300
Georgetown, Brown	S	135
Georgetown, Cass	N	20
● Georgetown, Floyd	S	256
● Georgia, Lawrence	S	25
German Ridge, Perry	S	50
Germantown, (see Galena)		×
Germantown, Marion	C	27
● *Germantown*, Wayne	E	338
● Germany, Fulton	N	10
● Gessie, Vermillion	W	150
● *Gibson's*, Lake	NW	195
Gilbert, Vigo	W	10
Gilboa, Benton	W	×
Gilead, Miami	N	20
● Gilman, Madison	C	100
● Ging's, Rush	E	125
Giro, Gibson	SW	×
Gladish, Pike	SW	25
● *Gleason's*, LaPorte	NW	×
Glen Dale, Daviess	SW	75
● *Glendale*, Vigo	W	×
● Glen Hall, Tippecanoe	W	65
● Glenn, Vigo	W	×

Glenn's Valley, Marion......C 50
● Glenwood, Rush.......... E 275
Glezen, Pike.............. SW 150
Goblesville, Huntington...NE 60
Godsey, Monroe.............S ×
Goeglein, Allen........... NE 15
● Goldsmith, Tipton.........C 200
● *Goldthwaite*, Pike...... SW ×
● Goodland, Newton..... NW 889
Goodview, Randolph........E 50
Goodwin's Corner, Union...E 50
● **Goshen**, Elkhart........ N 6,033
● Gosport, Owen........... W 720
● *Gosport Junction*, Owen. W ×
Goss Mill, Jackson..........S 32
Gowdy, Rush............. E ×
Grafton, Posey............SW 35
Graham, Jefferson.........SE 30
● *Graham, No.1*, Daviess..SW ×
● *Graham No.2*, Daviess..SW ×
● *Grand Calumet Heights*, Lake................NW ×
● *Grand Rapids & Indiana Junction*, Wayne....... E ×
Grand View, Spencer..... SW 694
● Granger, St. Joseph...... N 75
Grant, Fulton...............N 50
Grant City, Clay............W ×
● *Grant Crossing*, Vigo.... W 50
Grantsburgh, Crawford..... S 125
Granville, Delaware.........E 150
Grass, Spencer............SW ×
● Grasscreek, Fulton....... N 25
● *Grassmere*, Lake.......NW ×
Grass Valley, (see Valley City) ×
● *Gravel Hill*, Benton ...... W ×
● *Gravelotte*, Tippecanoe... W ×
● *Gravel Pit*, Knox.......SW ×
● *Gravel Pit*, Madison...... C ×
● *Gravel Pit*, Vigo......... W 300
Gravel Point, Harrison......S 40
● Gravelton, Kosciusko.....N 25
Gray, Hamilton..............C ×
● Grayford, Jennings......SE 20
Grayson, Lawrence..........S ×
Graysville, Sullivan....... SW 75
Green Brier, Orange......... S 260
● **Greencastle**, Putnam..W 4,390
● *Greencastle Junc.*, Putn'm W 50
Green Centre, Noble...... NE 20
Greendale, Dearborn...... SE 435
Greene, Jay................ E 100
● **Greenfield**, Hancock...C 3,100
Greenfield Mills, Lagrange. NE 25
Green Hill, Warren.........W 164
Green Oak, Fulton..........N 75
Greensborough, Henry......E 318
● **Greensburgh**, Decat'r SE 3,596
● Green's Fork, Wayne.....E 325
● Greentown, Howard...... C 721
Greenville, Floyd...........S 313
● Greenwood, Johnson......C 862
● *Greenwood*, Wells........NE ×
Gresham, (see New Salisbury) ×
● Griffin, Posey.......... NW 200
● *Griffin*, Rush..............E 12
● Griffith, Lake.......... NW ×
● *Grimwood*, Vanderb'h..SW 40
● *Grismore*, Noble........ NE ×
Groomsville, Tipton.........C 40
Groveland, Putnam........ W 100
● Grover Town, Starke...NW 150
Groves, Fayette.............E 75
● *Gudgel*, Gibson......... SW ×
● Guernsey, White....... NW 130
● Guilford, Dearborn...... SE 300
● Guion, Parke..............W 40
Guionsville, Dearborn...... SE 25
● Guthrie, Lawrence........ S 100
Guy, Howard................C ×
Gwaltneyville, (see Midway). ×
● Gwynneville, Shelby.......C 100
Hackleman, Grant.......... C 100
Hackman's Cr. Rds., (see Batesv'e) ×
● *Hadley*, Allen...........NE ×
● Hadley, Hendricks.........C 60
Hageman, Porter..........NW 641
● Hagerstown, Wayne...... E 873
Halbert's Bluff, (see Shoals).. ×
● *Haley*, Wayne............ E ×
Haley's Mills, (see Millport). ×
Halford, Madison........... C ×
Half-Way, (see Red Key) .... ×
Hall, Morgan................C 200
Hall's Corners, Allen......NE 100
Halo, Washington...........S ×
Hamburg, (see Sellersburg).. ×

Hamburgh, Franklin........E 300
Hamilton, Allen.......... NE ×
● *Hamilton*, Rush.......... E 25
Hamilton, Steuben..........NE 250
Hamilton, St. Joseph....... N 30
● Hamlet, Starke..........NW 300
● Hammond, Lake....... NW 5,428
● Hamrick, Putnam........W 15
Hancock, Harrison...........S 35
Haney's Corner, Ripley....SE 50
● Hanfield, Grant........... C 32
● Hanna, LaPorte.........NW 500
● *Hanna Station*, White. NW ×
Hanover, Jefferson........ SE 459
Hanover Centre, Lake....NW 100
Hansdale, **Clark**.............S ×
Hardensburg, Jennings ...SE 300
Hardinsburg, Washington...S 138
Hardy, Scott..................S 25
Hargan, Jefferson.......... SE ×
Harlan, Allen.............. NE 500
● *Harlans*, Marion..........C ×
Harlansburgh, Huntington NE 30
● *Harleys*, Carroll......... C ×
● Harmony, Clay...........W 1,020
● Harper, Decatur.........SE 25
Harrell, Jefferson..........SE 30
● *Harris*, Marshall........ .N ×
Harrisburgh, Fayette........ E 100
Harrisburg, Grant...........C 145
Harris City, Decatur........ SE 209
Harrison, (see Harrison, Ohio) ×
Harrison, Martin...........SW ×
Harrisonville, (see Trinity Sprs.) ×
● *Harris Switch*, Decatur. SE ×
● Harristown, Washington..S 60
Harrisville, Randolph........E 100
● Harrodsburgh, Monroe....S 400
● **Hartford City**, Bl'kf'd. E 2,287
Hartford, (see English) .... ×
● *Hartsdale*, Lake........NW ×
Hartsville, Bartholomew.... S 474
● *Hartsville Crossing*, Barth.S ×
Harveysburgh, Fountain... W 150
● *Haskell*, LaPorte.......NW ×
Hasting, Kosciusko.........N ×
● *Hastings*, Morgan........ C ×
Hatch's Mills, La Porte...NW 25
Hatfield, Spencer...........SW ×
● Haubstadt, Gibson...... SW 300
Haughville, Marion...........C 2,144
Hausertown, Owen.........W 140
Haussdale, Clark..............S ×
Haven, Ripley..............SE ×
● *Hawkins*, Daviess.......SW ×
Hawpatch, Lagrange.........NE 90
● Hayden, Jennings....... SE 300
Haymond, Franklin..........E 40
Haysville, Dubois......... SW 200
● *Hazelrigg*, Boone......... C 50
Hazelwood Hendricks........C 30
Hazelwood Sulphur Springs, (see English) ×
● Hazleton, Gibson....... SW 608
Headlee, White............NW 50
● *Heath*, Boone..............C ×
Heath, Tippecanoe......... W ×
Heaton, Greene...........SW ×
● Hebron, Porter..........NW 689
● Heckland, Vigo............W ×
Hecla, Whitley.............. NE 200
Hector, Jay.................. E 80
● *Hedden*, Pike.......... SW ×
● Hedrick, Warren..........W 75
Hege, Jennings.............SE 25
Heilman, Warrick......... SW 25
Helix, Orange............... S 15
Heller's Corners, Allen....NE 25
● Heltonville, Lawrence.....S 300
● Hemlock, Howard......... C 100
Henderson, Rush.............E 35
Hendricksville, Greene... SW ×
● Henryville, Clark.......... S 400
Henryville, (see St. Henry)... ×
● *Hepburn*, Posey......... SW ×
Herbemont, Morgan......... C 50
● Herbst, Grant...............C 25
Hesston, La Porte........ NW ×
● Hessville, Lake.......... NW 40
Heuser's St'e, (see New Salisb'y) ×
Hibbard, Marshall.......... N 25
Hickory Grove, Dubois....SW 25
Hicks, Jefferson............ SE 25
● Highland, Lake........ NW 15
● *Highland*, Vermillion.... W ×
Highland, Montgomery.... W 48
Hill Grove, Harrison........ S ×

Hillham, Dubois.......... SW 100
● Hillsburgh, Clinton...... C 250
● Hillsborough, Fountain.. W 400
Hillsboro, Clinton...........C 150
● Hillsdale, Vermillion.....W 200
Hindostan, (see Bryant's Cr.) ×
● Hitchcock, Washington... S 40
● Hoagland, Allen.........NE 150
● Hobart, Lake...........NW 1,010
Hobbieville, Greene.......SW 100
● Hobbs, Tipton..............C 150
Holland, Dubois............SW 300
Hollandsburgh, Parke......W 100
● *Hollister*, Hamilton.......C ×
Holman, Dearborn.........SE 120
● *Holman*, Scott............ S 125
● *Holmes*, Boone............C ×
Holmesville, La Porte....NW 25
● Holton, Ripley............SE 200
Home, Jefferson............ SE 65
● Homer, Rush...............E 130
Honduras, Adams..........NE 10
● Honey Creek, Henry.......E 175
Hooker, Washington........S ×
● Hoosierville, Clay........ W 100
● Hoover, Cass............ N 100
● *Hoover's*, Fulton.......... N 50
Hooversburgh, Miami....... N 65
● Hope, Bartholomew.......S 1,009
Hopewell, Ripley.......... SE 200
● Horace, Decatur..........SE 25
● *HorseShoeBend*, Lawrence S ×
● Hortonville, Hamilton.... C 200
● *Hosmer*, Pike.............SW ×
Houston, Jackson............ S 150
Hovey, Posey..............SW ×
How, Jefferson............. SE ×
Howard, Parke..............W 100
● *Howell*, Vanderburgh...SW 800
Howesville, Clay........... W 300
● Howlands, Marion......... C 50
● *Hubbell*, Owen..............W ×
Hubbell's Cor., (see Weisburg) ×
Hubbel Station, Greene.. SW ×
Hudnut, Parke................W ×
Hudson, Steuben.......... NE 300
Huff, Spencer.............. SW 65
Huffman, Spencer..........SW 20
● *Huff's*, Martin........... SW ×
Huffville, Greene.......... SW ×
● *Hulberts*, Porter.........NW 100
Hunt, (see Worthington) ..... ×
● *Hunter's*, Marion......... C ×
● Huntertown, Allen..... NE 250
Hunterville, Franklin........E 100
● Huntingburgh, Dubois..SW 3,167
● **Huntington**, Hunt'n. NE 7,328
● *Hunts Switch*, Vermillion W ×
Huntsville, Randolph....... E 157
● Hurlburt, Porter.........NW 100
● Huron, Lawrence......... S 200
Hursh, Allen................NE 25
Huth, Franklin...............E ×
Hutton, Vigo................W ×
● *Hyatts*, Knox............SW ×
Hyde, Jennings.............SE ×
● Hymera, Sullivan........SW 100
● Hyndsdale, Morgan....... C 20
● Idaville, White......... NW 500
Idem, (see Celestine)......... ×
Idlewild, Harrison............S 20
● *Iglehart*, Vanderburgh.SW ×
Ijamsville, Wabash...........N 163
Ilion, Marshall................N 200
● *Independence*, Fountain.. W 100
Independence, Madison..... C ×
● **Independence, Warren... W** 500
Indiana Mineral Springs, Warren..................... W 30
● **INDIANAPOLIS**, Marion..C 105,436
● Indian Springs, Martin..SW 35
● Inglefield, Vanderburgh SW 100
● *Inman's*, St. Joseph......N ×
● *Inverness*, DeKalb....... NE ×
● Inwood, Marshall....... N 400
Iola, Pike..................SW 8
Iona, Knox................ SW ×
Ireland, Dubois............ SW 250
Iris, Harrison............... S ×
● *Iron Bridge*, Pike.......SW 75
● *Ironton*, Martin...........SW ×
● Irvington, Marion.........C 650
● *Island City*, Greene.... SW ×
● Ivanhoe, Lake............NW ×
● Jackson, Tipton............C 100
Jacksonburgh, Wayne...... E 200

Indiana
Indiana

Place	Population
● *Jackson Hill*, Sullivan..SW	×
● *Jackson's*, Starke......NW	×
● *Jackson's Hill*, Wayne....E	×
● *Jacobs*, Daviess.........SW	×
Jadden, Grant..............C	40
Jalapa, Grant...............C	150
● Jamestown, Boone........C	616
Jamestown, (see New Lisbon)	×
Jamestown, St. Joseph..... N	×
Janesville, (see Laketon).....	×
Jasonville, Greene........ SW	100
● **Jasper**, Dubois.........SW	1,281
● *Jay*, Jay..................E	×
Jay, Switzerland..........SE	25
Jeff, Wells.................NE	×
● Jefferson, Clinton.........C	300
● **Jeffersonville**, Clark...S	10,666
Jerome, Howard............C	200
Jersey, Switzerland.........SE	×
● Jessup, Parke........... W	75
● Jewell, Howard...........C	50
● Johnsburgh, Dubois......SW	65
● Johnson, Randolph....... E	25
● Johnson's Crossing, Mad'n C	26
● Johnsonville, Warren.... W	75
● *Johnstown*, Greene.....SW	×
● *Joliet Pit*, Lake........ NW	×
● Jolietville, Hamilton......C	250
Jonesborough, Greene......SW	25
● Jonesborough, Grant......C	687
● Jonesville, Bartholomew..S	350
Joppa, Hendricks........... C	35
Jordan, Jay................ E	50
● *Jordan*, Daviess........ SW	×
Jordan Village, Owen...... W	100
● Judson, Parke........... W	200
● *Julian*, Newton........NW	25
Juliet, (see Yocky)...........	×
● Julietta, Marion...........C	45
● *Junction*, Allen.........NE	×
● *Junction*, Decatur.......SE	×
● *Junction*, Marion..........C	×
● *Junction*, Montgomery.. W	×
● *Junction*, Tippecanoe....W	×
● *Kankakee*, Starke..... NW	×
● *Kankakee*, St. Joseph.....N	×
● *Kankakee Pit*, St. JosephN	×
Kappa, Howard.............C	20
Kasson, Vanderburgh.....SW	150
Keck's Church, (see Burns City)	×
Keckville, (see Burns City)...	×
● *Kellers*, Wabash..........N	150
Kellerville, Dubois.........SW	30
Kelseyville, Allen..........NE	×
Kelso, Dearborn.......'.... SE	×
● Kempton, Tipton......... C	300
● Kendallville, Noble.....NE	2,960
● Kennard, Henry.......... E	300
Kennedy, Dearborn.........SE	25
● *Kennedy*, Spencer......SW	×
Keno, Gibson.............SW	×
Kent, Jefferson............SE	100
● **Kentland**, Newton...NW	918
● Kercheval, Spencer.....SW	150
● *Kesler*, Noble............NE	×
● Kewanna, Fulton..........N	647
● Keystone, Wells........ NE	125
● Kickapoo, Warren....... W	25
● Killmore, Clinton.........C	100
Kimball, Owen........... W	×
● Kimmell, Noble..........NE	10
Kinder, Johnson............ C	25
Kindles Landing, Harrison .S	×
● King, Gibson.............SW	100
● Kingman, Fountain......W	300
● Kingsbury, LaPorte.....NW	150
● *King's Cave Quarries*, Harrison.......... S	×
● Kingsland, Wells........NE	100
Kingsley Chapel, see Graysville).........	×
Kingston, Decatur .... SE	250
● Kinzie, Kosicusko .... N	25
● Kirklin, Clinton......... C	550
● Kirkpatrick, MontgomeryW	50
Kirksville, Monroe .... S	25
Kit, Jay .... E	10
Klaasville, Lake..........NW	40
Kleiner, Posey............ SW	15
Knechts, Franklin.......... E	×
● Knightstown, Henry..... E	1,867
● Knightsville, Clay........ W	1,148
● Kniman, Jasper........NW	20
● *Knowels*, Gibson....... SW	×
● **Knox**, Starke .... NW	790
Knoxville, (see Dubois)......	×
● **Kokomo**, Howard...... C	8,261
● *Kokomo Junc.*, Howard...C	×
● Koleen, Greene .... SW	250
Koro, Carroll C	25
● *Kosciusko*, Kosciusko....N	100
Kossuth, Washington........S	50
● Kouts, Porter.......... NW	500
Kreps, Wells............... NE	10
Kreuzburg, Lake........ NW	75
● Kurtz, Jackson .... S	25
● Kyana, Dubois.......... SW	125
Kyle, Dearborn .... SE	×
LaClair, Hendricks C	20
Laconia, Harrison.......... S	133
● Lacrosse, LaPorte......NW	75
● Ladoga, Montgomery.... W	857
● **LaFayette**, Tippecanoe W	16,243
● *LaFayette Junc*, Tip'c'noeW	×
● LaFountaine, Wabash.... N	600
● **Lagrange**, Lagrange..NE	1,784
● LaGro, Wabash...........N	549
Lake, Spencer............ SW	350
● Lake Cicott, Cass.........N	25
Lake Gage, Steuben.......NE	10
Lake Maxkinkuckee, Marsh'lN	×
Lake Mills, (see Rockport)...	×
● *Lakeside*, Lake......... NW	×
Lakeside. Pulaski........ NW	10
Lakeside Park, Kosciusko..N	×
● Lake Station, Lake .... NW	250
● Laketon, Wabash .... N	528
● *Laketon Junc.*, Wabash.. N	×
Lake Valley. Morgan........ C	50
Lake Village. Newton.... NW	50
● Lakeville, St. Joseph..... N	200
● Lamar, Spencer .... SW	×
Lamar Sta, (see Buffaloville).	×
Lamb, Switzerland .... SE	25
● *Lamberts*, Bartholomew.. S	×
Lamong, Hamilton...........C	10
Lancaster, (see Salamonio)..	×
Lancaster, (see River)	×
Lancaster, Jefferson...... SE	[illegible]
Lancaster, (see Leipsic)......	×
Lancaster, Owen...........W	×
● *Lancaster Branch*, Clay. W	×
● Landersdale, Morgan......C	25
● Landess, Grant.......... C	200
Lanesville, Harrison .... S	277
● Langdon, Jackson......... S	50
● *Lansing*, Lake.........NW	×
● LaOtto, Noble .... NE	250
● LaPaz, Marshall.......... N	300
● *LaPaz Junc.*, Marshall....N	×
● Lapel, Madison........... C	200
Lapland, Montgomery......W	25
● **LaPorte**, LaPorte..... NW	7,126
● *LaPorte Junc.*, LaPorte NW	×
● *Lardona*, Shelby......... C	×
● Larwill, Whitley........ NE	650
Lasher, Perry.............. S	×
Laud, Whitley .... NE	400
Laugherty, Ohio........... SE	300
● Laurel, Franklin..........E	1,000
Laraca, Randolph.......... E	×
Lawler, Washington .... S	15
● Lawrence, Marion........ C	400
● **Lawrenceburgh**, Dearborn............SE	4,284
● *Lawrenceburgh Junction*, Dearborn...........SE	×
Lawrenceport, (see River Vale)	×
Lawrenceville, Dearborn.. SE	100
● Layton, Fountain........ W	×
● Leatherwood, Parke....... W	75
Leavenworth, Crawford.S	792
● **Lebanon**, Boone........ C	3,682
● Lee, White............. NW	40
● Leesburgh, Kosciusko.... N	345
Leesville, Lawrence .... S	150
● Leipsic, Orange .... S	125
Leisure, Madison............C	20
● Leiter's Ford, Fulton .... N	150
Lemastersville, Pike........ SW	25
Lemons, Monroe.............S	×
● Lena, Parke .... W	340
● *Lennox*, Carroll C	40
Leo, Allen..................NE	500
Leopold, Perry............... S	200
Leota, Scott................. S	25
Leoti, (see Standale)...........	×
● LeRoy, Lake............ NW	75
● *Lester*, Greene...........SW	×
Lesterville, Washington..... S	10
● Letts Corner, Decatur... SE	200
Levi, Jefferson .... SE	25
● *Levings*, Fulton .... N	×
● *Lewis*, Sullivan.......... SW	×
Lewis, Vigo................. W	200
● Lewis Creek, Shelby.......C	90
Lewisburg, Cass........... N	×
● Lewisville, Henry......... E	420
Lewisville, (see Alaska)	×
● Lexington, Scott.......... S	450
Lexington (see Cutler)	×
Liber, Jay................... E	139
Liberal, Spencer.......... SW	×
● **Liberty**, Union...........E	1,314
● Liberty Centre, Wells... NE	300
● Liberty Mills, Wabash.... N	300
Libertyville, Vigo.......... W	25
Lick Creek, (see Abydel)	×
● Ligonier, Noble..........NE	2,195
Lilly Dale, Perry............ S	60
● Lima, Lagrange...........NE	578
● Limedale, Putnam....... W	50
Limestone, Lawrence........S	×
● *Lime Switch*, Cass........ N	25
● Lincoln, Cass.............. N	200
● *Lincoln*, Spencer........ SW	×
Lincolnville, (see Benham'sSt'e)	×
Lincolnville. Wabash........N	200
● Linden, Montgomery.....W	300
Linden Hill, Wayne.........E	×
● *Lineville*, Lake......... NW	×
Linkville, Marshall......... N	40
Linn Grove, Adams........ NE	200
Linnsburg, Montgomery... W	×
● Linton, Greene..........SW	958
● *Linton Road*, Greene...SW	×
● Linwood, Madison.........C	90
Linzey, Brown............... S	25
Lippe, Posey...............SW	×
● *Lisbon*, Henry............E	200
● *Lisbon*, Noble............NE	125
Little Point, Morgan........C	30
● Littles, Pike.............SW	10
Littleton, Pike.............. SW	10
Little York, Washington.... S	100
● *Liverpool*, Lake......... NW	×
Livonia, Washington....... S	194
● Lizton, Hendricks..........C	300
● Lochiel, Benton..........W	190
Locke, (see Nappanee)........	×
Lockman, Brown........... S	×
Lockport, Carroll.......... C	100
Lockport, (see Riley).........	×
Lock Spring, Ripley ....SE	195
Loco, Carroll..............C	×
Locust Point, Harrison......S	30
Logan, Dearborn............SE	80
● *Logan*, Lawrence......... S	×
● **Logansport**, Cass.......N	13,328
● London, Shelby............ C	100
Long Branch, (see Otwell)...	×
● *Long Cliff*, Cass .... N	×
● *Longneckers*, Dearborn. SE	×
Long Run, Switzerland....SE	×
● *Longs*, LaPorte........ NW	×
Longsdorf, Elkhart.........N	×
● *Long Siding*, Fountain...W	×
Longview, Montgomery.... W	110
● Longwood, Fayette....... E	50
● Loogootee, Martin...... SW	988
Lookout, Ripley........... SE	15
● *Loraine*, Hamilton........C	×
Lorane, Whitley...........NE	40
Loree, Miami............... N	25
● Losantville. Randolph.....E	300
Lost River, Martin........SW	17
● *Lost River*, Orange........S	×
● Lottaville, Lake........ NW	25
● Lotus, Union..............E	50
Lovely Dale (see Monroe City)	×
● Lovett, Jennings.........SE	858
● *Lowell*, Bartholomew.....S	×
● Lowell, Lake.......... NW	761
Lowry's Switch (see Orestes).	×
● Lucerne, Cass..............N	25
● *Luce Ranch*, Jasper....NW	×
Ludlow (see Kellerville)......	×
Luray, Henry............... E	55
Lusk's Springs, Parke......W	×
● Lyles, Gibson........... SW	12
● Lynn, Randolph...........E	518
Lynnville, Warrick.........SW	350
● Lyons, Greene.......... SW	200
● Lyon's, Station, Fayette...E	130
● *Lyonton*, Sullivan.......SW	300
McCameron, Martin.......SW	25
● McCool, Porter.........NW	60
McCordsville, Hancock......C	300
● *McCowans*, Delaware.... E	×
● McCoy, Decatur...... ....SE	×
● McClutchanville, Van'bgSW	32

Place	Pop.
● McGary, Gibson........SW	12
● *McGrain*, Harrison....... S	×
● McGrawsville, Miami...... N	50
McGregor, Jefferson.......SE	×
McKinley, Washington......S	×
McNatts, Wells............ NE	×
McVille, Greene.......... SW	**10**
● Mace, Montgomery...... W	300
Macedonia, Delaware.......E	130
● *Machler's*, LaPorte.... NW	×
● Mackey, Gibson.........SW	18
● Macksville, Vigo.........W	300
● Macy, Miami............ N	316
● **Madison**, Jefferson.... SE	8,936
● Madrid, Spencer........SW	8
● Magley, Adams..........NE	10
Magnolia, Crawford.........S	30
● Mahalasville, Morgan..... C	225
● *Main Street*, Miami...... N	×
Majenica, Huntington.....NE	300
Makin, Huntington....... NE	25
● *Malcolm*, Vigo..........W	×
● Malott Park, Marion......C	50
Manchester, Dearborn.... NE	300
● *Manchester Sta.*, Dearb'nSE	×
Manhattan, Putnam........W	100
● Manilla, Rush..............E	400
● Mansfield, Parke........ W	300
● Manson, Clinton.......... C	50
Manville, Jefferson......... SE	70
● *Maple Grove*, Putnam... W	×
● Maples, Allen...........NE	200
● Mapleton, Martin.......... C	300
Maple Valley, Henry.........E	50
Maplewood, Fayette........ E	659
● Maplewood, Hendricks... C	25
Marble Corner, Ripley.....SE	40
Marble Hill, Jefferson......SE	40
● Marco, Greene..........SW	250
● Mardenis, Huntington.. NE	20
● Marengo, Crawford........S	669
Mariah Hill, Spencer......SW	100
Marietta (see West Fork)....	×
Marietta, Shelby..............C	275
● **Marion**, Grant...........C	8,769
Marion (see Marco)..........	×
● *Marion*, Sullivan....... SW	×
Marion Mills, Owen....... W	200
Markland, Switzerland.... SE	250
Markle, Huntington........NE	670
● *Markle*, Wells........... NE	×
● *Markles*, Vigo............W	×
● Markleville, Madison..... C	175
● *Marlboro*, Jasper....... NW	×
Marmont, Marshall..........N	200
● Marshall, Parke..........W	325
● *Marshfield*, Scott.......... S	×
Marshfield, Warren.........W	300
Marshland (see De Long)....	×
● *Martin*, Vanderburgh...SW	25
Martinsburgh, Washington..C	85
Martin Sta. (see Glenzen)....	×
● **Martinsville**, Morgan..C	2,680
Martz, Clay.................W	185
● Marysville, Clark...........S	100
Mason, Wabash.............N	×
Matamoras, Greene...... SW	25
● *Mathew*, Morgan..........C	×
Mattsville, Hamilton........ C	10
Mauckport, Harrison....... S	272
Maumee, Jackson........... S	20
● Mauzy, Rush................E	12
● Max, Boone................C	100
● Maxams, Gibson..........SW	25
Maxinkuckee, Marshall.... N	75
Maxville, Randolph.........E	200
Maxville, Spencer........ SW	×
● Maxwell, Hancock.........C	180
● *Maynard*, Lake........NW	×
● Mays, Rush................E	50
● *Maysville*, Daviess......SW	×
● Maywood, Marion..........C	125
Mead, Brown.................S	×
● Mecca Mills, Parke...... W	×
Mechanicsburgh, Henry......E	200
Mechanicsville (see Zipp's)..	×
● Medaryville, Pulaski... NW	450
● Medora, Jackson..........S	600
Melissaville, Ripley.........SE	15
● Mellott, Fountain.........W	150
Meltzer, Shelby............. C	75
● Memphis, Clark............S	400
● Mentone, Kosciusko......N	780
● *Mentor*, Dubois.........SW	200
● Merom, Sullivan........SW	412
Merriam, Noble............NE	150
Merrillville, Lake........ NW	150

Indiana

Place	Pop.
Messena, Hendricks.........C	40
● Messick, Henry............E	50
● Metamora, Franklin......E	500
Metea, Cass.................. N	50
Metz, Steuben..............NE	300
● Mexico, Miami............N	500
● Miami, Miami............ N	300
● Michigan City, LaPorte NW	10,776
● Michigantown, Clinton....C	298
Middleberry (see Clay City)..	×
● Middlebury, Elkhart..... N	542
Middle Fork, Clinton........C	300
● *Middle Fork*, Jefferson. SE	×
● *Middletons*, Howard......C	200
● Middletown, Henry.......E	851
Middletown, (see Toga)......	×
Middletown (see Prairie Cr.).	×
Midland, Greene.........SW	25
Midway, Allen............NE	×
Midway, Spencer..........SW	75
● Mier, Grant...............C	200
Mifflin, Crawford............S	40
Milan, Ripley...............SE	318
Milford, Decatur.......... SE	231
● Milford, Kosciusko.......N	677
Milford, Warren.......... W	×
● *Milford Junc.*, Kosciusko. N	×
Mill Ark, Fulton........... N	40
● *Millbranch*, Clay........ W	×
● Mill Creek, LaPorte......NW	75
Milledgeville, Boone.........C	25
● Miller, Lake..............NW	100
● *Millers*, Bartholomew.... S	×
● *Millers*, Gibson.........SW	×
● *Millers*, Spencer........SW	×
Millersburg, Orange........ S	×
Millersburg (see Canal)......	×
● Millersburgh, Elkhart.... N	394
● *Millersburgh*, Lawrence...S	×
● *Millersport*, Dubois....SW	45
Millersville, Marion........C	60
● Millgrove, Blackford......E	92
Millhousen, Decatur....... SE	224
● Milligan, Parke.......... W	20
Millport, Washington....... S	35
Mills' Corners, Jay...........E	50
● Milltown, Crawford.......S	300
● Millville, Henry...........E	200
Millwood, Kosciusko....... N	200
● Millner'sCorners,HancockC	150
● Milo, Huntington....... NE	30
● Milroy, Rush...............E	750
Milton, (see Guionsville).....	×
● Milton, Wayne..............E	742
Mineral Beach, Kosciusko..N	×
● Mineral City, Greene....SW	100
Minshall (see Jessup).......	×
● Nishawaka, St. Joseph....N	3,371
● Mitchell, Lawrenee........S	1,583
● *Mitchellville*, Marion......C	×
Mixersville, Franklin........E	100
Moberly, Harrison...........S	×
● Modoc, Randolph..........E	600
● Mohawk, Hancock.........C	65
Mollie, Blackford........... E	15
Mongo, Lagrange...........NE	125
Monitor, Tippecanoe.......W	65
● Monmouth, Adams..... NE	60
● **Monon, White..........NW**	**1,064**
● Monroe, Adams.........NE	200
Monroe City, Knox.........SW	589
● Monroeville, Allen......NE	673
Monrovia, Morgan.......... C	300
● Montclair, Hendricks......C	60
● Monterey, Pulaski.......NW	226
● Montezuma, Parke.......W	658
● Montgomery, Daviess...SW	415
● **Monticello**, White...NW	1,518
● Montmorenci, TippecanoeW	300
● Montpelier, Blackford....E	808
MonumentCity,Huntingt'nNE	30
Mooney, Jackson............S	65
Moonsville, (see Anderson)...	×
● Moore, DeKalb..........NE	50
Moorefield, Switzerland... SE	115
● *Moorefield*, Marion....... C	×
● Mooreland, Henry........ E	210
Mooresburgh, Pulaski.....NW	32
● Moore's Hill, Dearborn..SE	469
Mooresville, (see Floyd's Knobs)	×
● *Mooresville*, DeKalb.... NE	50
● Mooresville, Morgan...... C	891
Moore's Vineyard, Barth'w..S	50
Mooretown, Lawrence...... S	×
Mooreville, Floyd........... S	×
Moral, Shelby............... C	200
● Moran, Clinton............C	200

Indiana

Place	Pop.
● *Morehouse*, Elkhart......N	×
● *Morgan*, LaPorte...... NW	×
Morgantown, Dearborn...SE	×
● Morgantown, Morgan.....C	600
● Morocco, Newton....... NW	397
● Morris, Ripley...........SE	400
● Morristown, Shelby.......C	561
Morton, Putnam........... W	50
Moscow, Rush...............E	100
Moten, Cass................N	×
● Mott, Harrison.............S	×
● *Mound City*, Warren.... W	×
Mountain Spring, Martin..SW	30
Mount Auburn, Shelby......C	144
Mount Auburn, Wayne......E	144
● Mount Ayr, Newton....NW	500
Mount Carmel, Franklin....E	142
Mount Carmel,(see Campb'b'g)	×
● Mount Comfort, Hancock.C	100
Mount Etna, Huntington..NE	262
Mount Healthy, Barthol'w..S	50
Mount Hope, DeKalb..... NE	15
Mount Jackson, Marion.... C	313
Mount Liberty, Brown...... S	30
Mount Meridan, Putnam.... W	100
Mount Moriah, Brown.......S	65
Mount Olive, Martin...... SW	×
Mount Olive, (see Ditney)....	×
Mount Pisgah, Lagrange.. NE	50
Mount Pleasant, Daviess.SW	×
Mount Pleasant, Perry...... S	25
Mount Prospect, Crawford..S	30
● Mounts, Gibson..........SW	10
Mount Sterling, Switzerl'd.SE	150
● Mount Summit, Henry....E	231
Mount Tabor, (see Stinesv'e)	×
Mount Vernon, (see Somerset)	×
● **Mount Vernon**, Pos'ySW	4,705
Mount Vernon,(see Red Key)	×
● *Mount Vernon Junction*, Gibson................SW	×
Mount Washington,PutnamW	×
Mount Zion, Wells........ NE	50
● Muddy Fork, Clark....... S	50
Mud Lick, Jefferson....... SE	50
● Mulberry, Clinton..........C	529
Mulberry, Tippecanoe......W	15
● **Muncie**, Delaware........E	11,345
● *Muncie Junction*, Allen. NE	×
● *Murray*, Daviess.........SW	×
● Murray, Wells.......... NE	100
● *Murray Road*, Wells... NE	×
Myers, Madison............ C	50
● *Myers*, Vanderburgh... SW	×
Myhart, Allen...............NE	25
Myler, St. Joseph...........N	174
● Nabb, Clark................S	100
Nabb, Scott................ S	110
Napoleon, Ripley..........SE	400
● Nappanee, Elkhart....... N	1,493
Narrows, Sullivan........ SW	×
● **Nashville**, Boone.........C	395
Nashville, (see Lovely Dale)..	×
Natchez, (see Shoals)..........	×
Nat'l Military Home, Grant.C	×
● *Nealis*, Boone C	×
● *Nebecker's*, Fountain.... W	×
● *Nebo*, Dearborn......... SE	×
● Nebraska, Jennings..... SE	150
● Needham, Johnson.........C	100
Needmore, Brown............S	100
Needmore, Owen...........W	20
● *Neels*,Wayne..............E	×
Neff, Randolph..............E	50
Neil's Creek, Jefferson.... SE	×
● Nelson, Vigo........... W	50
Nettle Creek, (see Dalton)....	×
● Nevada, Tipton........... C	75
Nevada Mills, Steuben.... NE	75
● Nevin, Harrison............S	20
● **New Albany**, Floyd....S	21,059
New Alsace, Dearborn.....SE	500
New Amsterdam, Harrison..S	172
Newark, Greene.......... SW	150
● New Augusta, Marion.....C	300
New Baltimore, Posey....SW	×
New Bellsville, Brown......S	150
Newbern, Bartholomew.....S	250
● Newberry, Greene......SW	400
New Bethel, Marion.........C	196
New Boston, (see Huff).......	×
● New Britton, Hamilton.... C	100
New Brunswick, Boone.....C	60
New Brunswick, Clay......W	×
● *Newburg*, Clay...........W	150
Newburg, Decatur.........SE	150
Newburgh, Warrick.......SW	1,046
New Burlington, Delaware..E	73

Indiana
Indiana

● New Carlisle, St. Joseph..N	607
● **New Castle**, Henry.....E	2,697
● *New Castle Junc.*,Henry. E	×
New Chicago, (see Blackford)	×
New Columbus, (see Ovid....	×
New Corner, Delaware......E	200
New Corydon, Jay........NW	150
New Cumberland, Grant....C	300
New Durham, LaPorte...NW	40
New Elizabeth, (see Lizton)..	×
● New Era, DeKalb.......NE	10
New Frankfort, Scott.......N	97
New Garden,(see Fountain City)	×
New Goshen, Vigo......... W	150
● New Harmony, Posey...SW	1,197
● New Haven, Allen...... NE	1,079
New Holland, Wabash......N	75
New Lancaster, Jay......NW	×
New Lancaster, Tipton......C	75
● New Lebanon, Sullivan. SW	100
● New Lisbon, Henry....... E	183
New London, Howard.......C	200
New Marion, Ripley........ SE	200
New Market, (see Oregon)...	×
● New Market, Montgom'y W	300
New Maysville, Putnam....W	102
New Middletown, Harrison..S	212
New Mount Pleasant, Jay NW	150
● New Palestine, Hancock..C	404
● New Paris, Elkhart.......N	400
New Philadelphia, Wash'ton S	100
New Pittsburgh, Randolph..E	100
● ***New Pittsburgh***, Sul'v'nSW	×
● *New Pittsburgh Junction*, Sullivan...............SW	×
● New Point, Decatur..... SE	500
● **Newport**, Vermillion... W	551
New Prospect,(see West Baden)	×
● New Providence, Clark... S	350
● New Richmond, Montg'y. W	150
● New Ross, Montgomery..W	270
New Salem, Rush........... E	200
New Salisbury, Harrison.... S	200
● *Newton*, Wabash......... N	×
Newton Stewart, Orange.... S	50
Newtonville, Spencer..... SW	200
Newtown, Fountain.........W	350
● *Newtown Junction*, D'b'n SE	×
● New Trenton. Franklin...E	120
Newville, DeKalb......... NE	200
New Washington, Clark.....S	285
● New Waverly, Cass.......N	300
New Winchester, Hend'ks.. C	50
● *Nickel*, Porter..........NW	×
● Nickel Plate, Starke....NW	31
Nine Mile, Allen.......... NE	25
Nineveh, Johnson..........C	400
● *NinnescahLakes*,L'g'n'e NE	×
● *Nixon*, Henry........... E	×
Noah, Shelby...............C	100
Noble, Howard.............C	×
● **Noblesville**, Hamilton. C	3,057
● Nora, Marion.............. C	50
Normal, Grant..............C	50
● *Norman*, Jackson..........S	50
Normanda, Tipton.......... C	150
Norman Station, Jackson...S	50
● *Norris*, Washington.........S	×
Norristown (see Winterroud)	×
● *North Bedford*, Monroe...S	×
● *North Delphi*, Carroll.....C	×
North Elkhart, Elkhart....N	×
Northfield, Boone...........C	25
● North Grove, Miami......N	150
● *North Howell*,V'nd'b'ghSW	×
● North Indianapolis,MarionC	1,479
● North Judson, Starke.. NW	572
● *North Kirtland*, Adams NE	×
North Liberty, St. Joseph...N	400
● North Madison, Jeff...... SE	500
● North Manchester, W'b'h N	2,384
● *North Marion*, Grant.....C	×
● North Salem, Hendricks..C	505
North's Landing, Ohio.....SE	200
● *North Tower*, Clark........S	×
● North Union, Montg'm'y W	97
● North Vernon, JenningsS E	2,012
North Webster, Kosciusko..N	200
Nortonburgh, Bartholomew S	15
● *Norton Creek*, VermillionW	×
Norway, White.......... NW	75
● Nortre Dame, St. Joseph. N	596
Nottingham, Wells........NE	104
Noxid, Pike...............SW	×
● Null's Mills, Fayette......E	50
Numa, Parke.............W	×
● Nutwood, St. Joseph..... N	20
● Nye, Marshall............ N	×
Nyesville, Parke......... ..W	100
● Oak, Pulaski........... NW	100
Oakalla, Putnam........... W	65
● *Oakdale*, Jennings........SE	79
● Oakdam, Vanderburgh. SW	×
● Oakford, Howard.........C	150
Oak Forest, Franklin.......E	250
● *Oakland*, Putnam........W	×
Oakland, Spencer.........SW	120
● Oakland City, Gibson...SW	1,524
● Oaklandon, Marion.......C	353
● *Oakley*, Hendricks.........C	60
● *Oakplain*, Hendricks......C	×
Oak Ridge, Martin.........SW	×
● *Oak Siding*, Lagrange.. NE	×
● Oaktown, Knox.........SW	300
● Oakville, Delaware........E	153
● Oakwood, LaPorte..... NW	×
Oard Spring, Scott.........S	32
Oatsville, Pike............ SW	50
● Ober, Starke............NW	30
Occident, Rush............E	50
● Ockley, Carroll........... C	25
Octagon, Tippecanoe....... W	15
Odd, Parke.................W	×
Odell, Tippecanoe.......... W	30
Odessa, Benton............W	20
● Odon, Daviess...........SW	192
Offiel, Montgomery.........W	×
Ogden, Henry................E	300
Ohio Falls, Clark............S	15
Oil Creek (see Alton).........	×
Oldenburgh, Franklin........E	690
Old Pekin (see Pekin)........	×
Oldtown, Jackson........... S	100
Olean, Ripley............. SE	75
Ollo, Hamilton..............C	40
Oliphant, Pike............SW	25
● Olive Hill, Wayne.........E	30
● Oliver, Posey............SW	30
● *Olivers*, St. Joseph.........N	×
Omega, Hamilton........... C	70
Ontario, Lagrange..........NE	200
Onward, Cass............... N	200
● *Onward Station*, Cass.... N	×
● *Opedee*, Vermillion.......W	×
● Ora, Starke.............NW	150
Orange, Fayette.............E	130
Orangeville, Orange......... S	100
Orchard Grove, Lake.....NW	25
Oregon, Clark...............S	58
● Orestes, Madison..........C	50
Organ Spring, Washington..S	×
Oriole, Perry................ S	25
● Orion, Kosciusko..........N	×
Orland, Steuben..........NE	500
● Orleans, Orange..........S	857
Ormas, Whitley........... NE	32
Orth, Montgomery......... W	100
Oscar, Decatur........... SE	×
● Osceola, St. Joseph....... N	500
● Osgood, Ripley........... SE	841
● Ossian, Wells............NE	700
Oswego, Kosciusko......... N	100
● *Otess*, Grant..............C	×
● Otis, LaPorte............NW	500
● Otisco, Clark...............S	200
● Otterbein, Benton.........S	300
● *Otter Creek Junction*, VigoW	×
Otto, Clark..................S	20
Otwell, Pike...............SW	200
Oufa, Steuben.............NE	25
● *Overholzer*, Clay..........W	×
Ovid, Madison..............C	50
● Owasco, Carroll...........C	25
Owen, Clark................S	57
● Owensburgh, Greene....SW	450
● Owensville, Gibson .... NW	759
Owl Prairie, (see Elnora)....	×
● Oxford, Benton........... W	808
● Packerton, Kosciusko.... N	250
Padora (see Wickliffe).......	×
● Paisley, Lake...........NW	50
Palestine, Kosciusko.......N	150
● Palmer, Lake............NW	50
● *Palmer*, St. Joseph.......N	×
● *Palmerston*, Fountain... W	×
Palmyra, Harrison.......... S	160
● *Panhandle Junction*,M'snC	×
● **Paoli**, Orange.............S	707
● *Paper Mill Siding*, WhiteNW	×
Paradise, Warrick......... SW	×
● **Paragon**, Morgan......... C	300
Paris, Jennings.......... SE	200
● Paris Crossing, Jennings.SE	150
Park, Greene.............SW	40
● Parker, Randolph.........E	500
Parkersburgh, Montgom'ry W	124
Parker's Settlement, Po'y.SW	10
Parkville, Parke...........W	×
● *Parkwood*, Floyd.........S	×
Parrett, Vanderburgh.... SW	×
● *Parry*, Wayne............E	×
Pashan, Lagrange........NE	25
● *Pashan Station*, Lagra'eNE	×
Pate, Ohio.................. SE	25
● Patoka, Gibson......... SW	729
Patricksburgh, Owen.......W	400
Patriot, Switzerland........SE	[illegible]
Patronville, Spencer...... SW	30
● Patton, Carroll............C	100
● Pawnee, Montgomery....W	×
● Paxton, Sullivan........SW	100
Payne, Monroe.............S	×
● *Paynes*, Clay............W	×
● Peabody, Whitley........NE	150
● Pecksburgh, Hendricks...C	75
Pegtown (see Mt. Prospects).	×
● Pekin, Washington........S	100
Pella (see Guilford)...........	×
● Pendleton, Madison.......C	996
Pennsylvaniaburg, Ripley.SE	25
Pennville, Jay...............E	697
Penville, Wayne............E	85
● Penobscot, Montgomery. W	×
Peoria, Franklin.............E	40
● *Peoria Junction*, Cass....N	×
Peppertown, Franklin...... E	200
● *PercyJunction*,Newton NW	×
● *Perigo*, Warrick........SW	×
Perkinsville, Madison.......C	300
Perrysburgh, Miami........ N	80
Perrysville, Vermillion......W	507
● *Perrysville Station*,Ver'n W	×
● Perth, Clay.................W	400
● **Peru**, Miami..............N	7,028
Peter Cooper, Brown........S	30
● **Petersburgh**, Pike...SW	1,494
● Peterson, Adams........NE	25
Petersville, Bartholomew....S	35
Pettit, Tippecanoe..........W	25
● Pettysville, Miami.........N	40
Phenix, Wells...............NE	10
● Philadelphia, Hancock....C	200
Philomath, Union.......... E	50
Phlox, Howard..............C	×
Pickard's Mill, Clinton C	269
● Pierceton, Kosciusko.....N	897
● Pierceville, Ripley.......SE	175
● Pigeon, Spencer.........SW	50
● *Pigeon Creek*, Vander'h SW	×
Pike's Crossing, Boone......C	×
Pike's Peak, Brown.........S	100
Pikeville, Pike.............SW	100
Pilot Knob, Crawford.......S	75
● Pimento, Vigo........... W	150
Pine, Cass...................N	×
● *Pine*, Lake............. NW	130
● Pine Village, Warren.... W	275
Pinkamink, Jasper.........NW	×
● Pittsborough, Hendricks..C	600
● Pittsburgh, Carroll....... C	327
Pittsburg, (see Hymera)	×
● Plainfield, Hendricks..... C	909
● Plainville, Daviess...... SW	400
Plano, Morgan.............. C	20
Plato, Lagrange.......... NE	10
Pleasant, Switzerland......SE	250
Pleasant Grove, Jasper...NW	50
Pleasant Hill, (see Oakville).	×
● *Pleasant Hill*, M'ntgom'y W	×
● Pleasant Lake, Steuben. NE	520
● Pleasant Mills, Adams.. NE	135
Pleasant Plain, Hunting'n. NE	100
● Pleasant Ridge, Jasper. NW	25
Pleasant View, Wabash.....N	100
Pleasantville, (see Spurgeon).	×
Pleasantville, Sullivan.... SW	225
Plevna, Howard.............C	100
● Plummer, Greene...... SW	×
Plum Tree, Huntington.... NE	125
● **Plymouth**, Marshall... N	2,723
Poe, Allen.................NE	100
● *Pogue*, Newton.........NW	150
Point Isabel, Grant.........C	150
Poland, Clay................W	160
Poling, Jay..................E	10
Polk Patch, (see Selvin)	×
Polk Run, (see Vesta)	×
Pond Creek Mills, Knox.. SW	×
● Poneto, Wells...........NE	220
● *Pontiac*, Boone........... C	×
Pony, Jay.................. E	×

Place	Dir.	Pop.
Popcorn, Lawrence	S	×
Poplar Grove, Howard	C	65
● Porter, Porter	NW	300
● *Porters*, Tippecanoe	W	83
Portersville, Dubois	SW	150
Porter Station, (see Hageman)		×
Port Fulton, Clark	S	1,104
Portland, (see Fountain)		×
● **Portland**, Jay	E	3,725
Portland Mills, Putnam	W	150
● *Posey*, Posey	SW	×
● Poseyville, Posey	SW	571
● Poston, Ripley	SE	100
Potato Creek, Montgomery	W	32
● *Potters*, Allen	NE	130
Potters, (see Ari)		×
● Powers, Jay	E	200
● *Prairie*, Vigo	W	×
● Prairie City, Clay	W	×
Prairie Creek, Vigo	W	300
● *Prairie Switch*, Allen	NE	×
Prairieton, Vigo	W	300
Prather, Clark	S	32
Prattsburgh, (see Melissaville)		×
● Preble, Adams	NE	75
● Prescott, Shelby	C	100
Priam, Blackford	E	×
● **Princeton**, Gibson	SW	3,076
● *Princeton Junction*, G'n	SW	×
Prince William, Carroll	C	20
Prosser Switch, (see Huron)		×
● *Providence*, Clark	S	350
Providence, Johnson	C	5
Pucker Brush, Wabash	N	25
Pulaski, Pulaski	NW	100
● Purcell's, Knox	SW	65
● Putnamville, Putnam	W	204
Pyrmont, Carroll	C	100
Quaker Hill, Vermillion	W	50
Quakertown, Union	E	50
● *Quarry*, Martin	SW	×
Queensville, Jennings	SE	100
Quercus Grove, Switzerl'd	SE	35
Quincy, (see Elwood)		×
● Quincy, Owen	W	300
Raber, Whitley	NE	30
● Raccoon, Putnam	W	80
● Radnor, Carroll	C	200
Raglesville, Daviess	SW	125
● *Railsback*, Marshall	N	×
● Rainstown, Hendricks	C	40
Rainsville, Warren	W	150
Raleigh, Rush	E	125
Ramelton, Brown	S	75
● Ramsey, Harrison	S	75
● Randolph, Randolph	E	100
Ranger, Perry	S	20
● *Range Road*, Fountain	W	×
● Raub, Benton	W	100
● *Raubs*, Tippecanoe	W	×
● Ray, Steuben	NE	150
● *Rays*, Wabash	N	×
● Ray's Crossing, Shelby	C	50
Raysville, Henry	E	225
Red Bridge, Wabash	N	25
Red Cloud, Knox	SW	40
● Reddington, Jackson	S	100
● *Redesdale*, Lake	NW	×
● Redkey, Jay	E	922
● *Redwood*, Warren	W	×
● Reed, Delaware	E	35
● *Reed*, Lawrence	S	×
● *Reeds*, Kosciusko	N	×
● *Reedville*, Hancock	C	300
● *Reinfurth's*, LaPorte	NW	×
● Reelsville, Putnam	W	200
Reese's Mill, Boone	C	116
Reeve, Martin	SW	×
Rego, Orange	S	6
Rehoboth, Harrison	S	18
Rei, (see Delaware Station)		×
Reiffsburgh, Wells	NE	35
● Remington, Jasper	NW	904
● *Renner*, Blackford	E	×
● Reno, Hendricks	C	100
● **Rensselaer**, Jasper	NW	1,455
Reserve, Miami	N	90
Retreat, Jackson	S	×
Rexville, Ripley	SE	150
● Reynolds, White	NW	348
● Riceville, Crawford	S	150
Richards, Brown	S	25
Richardson, St. Joseph	N	×
Richland, Rush	S	100
Richland, (see Lake)		×
Richland Centre, Fulton	N	25
● **Richmond**, Wayne	E	16,680

Place	Dir.	Pop.
● Rich Valley, Wabash	N	150
Richwoods, Delaware	E	16
Riddertown, Jay	E	×
Ridgeport, (see Newark)		×
● Ridgeville, Randolph	E	922
Ridgeway, Howard	C	10
Ridgon, Grant	C	203
● Riley, Vigo	W	550
● Rileysburgh, Vermillion	W	25
● *Rincon*, Greene	SW	×
● Ripley, Noble	NE	10
● *Ripley*, Pulaski	NW	×
Rising Sun, Ohio	SE	1,689
● *Rivare*, Adams	NE	×
River, Huntington	NE	130
● River Side, Fountain	W	40
● *Riverside*, LaPorte	NW	×
Riverton, Sullivan	SW	×
River Vale, Lawrence	S	20
● *Riverview*, Elkhart	N	×
● Roachdale, Putnam	W	428
● Roann, Wabash	N	582
● Roanoke, Huntington	NE	532
Roberts, Fountain	W	×
● Robison, Greene	SW	50
● Rob Roy, Fountain	W	50
Roby, Lake	NW	×
● **Rochester**, Fulton	N	2,467
Rock Creek, Huntington	NE	50
Rockdale, Franklin	E	15
● Rockfield, Carroll	C	300
● Rockford, Jackson	S	200
● *Rock Hill*, Spencer	SW	×
Rockland (see Moreland)		×
Rocklane, Johnson	C	81
● **Rockport**, Spencer	SW	2,314
● *Rockport Junction*, Sp'r	SW	150
● **Rockville**, Parke	W	1,689
● *Rock Wood*, Greene	SW	×
● Roeskes, LaPorte	NW	×
● *Rogers*, Daviess	SW	×
Rogers' Station, Pike	SW	×
Rogersville, Henry	E	25
Roll, Blackford	E	150
● Rolling Prairie, LaPorte	NW	500
Rome, Perry	S	300
● Rome City, Noble	NE	500
RomeringStation (see Abydel)		×
● Romney, Tippecanoe	W	200
● Romona, Owen	W	100
Rono, Perry	S	100
Root, Allen	NE	×
Rosamond, Dubois	SW	×
● *Rose Bank*, Dubois	SW	×
● Roseburgh, Grant	C	100
Roseburg, Union	E	25
● Rosedale, Parke	W	873
● *Rosedale*, Pulaski	NW	×
● Rose Hill, Wabash	N	50
● Rose Lawn, Newton	NW	300
Roseville, Parke	W	650
Rosewood, Harrison	S	14
● Ross, Lake	NW	25
● *Ross*, Vigo	W	×
● Rosston, Boone	C	100
● Rossville, Clinton	C	594
Round Grove, White	NW	×
● Royal Centre, Cass	N	527
Royalton, Boone	C	90
● Royerton, Delaware	E	300
● Rugby, Bartholomew	S	25
● *Rugby*, St. Joseph	N	×
Rumble, Pike	SW	×
● Rural, Randolph	E	75
Rush Creek Valley, Wash'n	S	100
● **Rushville**, Rush	E	3,475
Russell's Mills, Parke	W	25
● Russellville, Putnam	W	327
● Russiaville, Howard	C	603
Ruth, Wells	NE	10
● Rutland, Marshall	N	21
Ryman, Washington	S	×
● *Rynear*, Fountain	W	65
Sabine, Marion	C	×
● Saint Anthony, Dubois	SW	150
Saint Bernice, Vermillion	W	400
Saint Croix, Perry	S	100
● *Saint George*, Vanderb'h	SW	×
Saint Henry, Dubois	SW	40
● Saint James, Gibson	SW	40
● Saint Joe Station, DeKa'b	NE	500
● Saint John, Lake	NW	100
● *Saint Johns*, DeKalb	NE	60
Saint John's Switch, Sh'y	C	50
Saint Joseph, Vanderb'h	SW	50
● Saint Joseph's Hill, Clark	S	60
Saint Leon, Dearborn	SE	368

Place	Dir.	Pop.
● Saint Louis Crossing, Bar.	S	200
Saint Magdalene, Ripley	SE	45
● Saint Mary's, Vigo	W	150
Saint Maurice, Decatur	SE	100
Saint Meinrad, Spencer	SW	482
Saint Nicholas, (see Spade's)		×
Saint Omer, Decatur	SE	250
● Saint Paul, Decatur	SE	1,000
Saint Peter's, Franklin	E	70
● Saint Phillip, Posey	SW	15
Saint Vincent, Allen	NE	×
Saint Wendell's, Posey	SW	125
Salamonia, Jay	E	150
● **Salem**, Washington	S	1,975
Salem Centre, Steuben	NE	200
Salina, Fulton	N	25
● Saline City, Clay	W	350
Salt Creek, Porter	NW	20
● *Salters' Switch*, Fayette	E	×
● Saltilloville, Washington	S	200
Saluda, Jefferson	SE	25
● Samaria, Johnson	C	15
● Sandborn, Knox	SW	200
● *Sand Creek*, Parke	W	×
● **Sandford**, Vigo	W	200
● *Sand Pit*, Lawrence	S	×
● Sandusky, Decatur	SE	75
● *Sandy Hook*, Daviess	SW	×
San Jacinto, Jennings	SE	50
● San Pierre, Starke	NW	300
Santa Claus, Spencer	SW	100
Santa Fe, Miami	N	100
Santa Fe Town, (see Santa Claus)		×
● Saratoga, Randolph	E	150
● Sardinia, Decatur	SE	150
● *Sardinia Crossing*, D'tur	SE	83
Sargent, Martin	SW	×
Saturn, Whitley	NE	×
Saulsbury, (see New Salisbury)		×
● Saxony, Lake	NW	15
Scalesville, Warrick	SW	100
● Schererville, Lake	NW	125
● *Schimmels*, LaPorte	NW	×
Schnellville, Dubois	SW	200
Schooner, Brown	S	65
Schooner Point, Crawford	S	6
Scipio, (see Mount Carmel)		×
● Scipio, Jennings	SE	300
● Scircleville, Clinton	C	100
Scotland, Greene	SW	200
Scott, Lagrange	NE	100
● **Scottsburgh**, Scott	S	618
Scottsville, Floyd	S	40
● Seafield, White	NW	20
Seba, Washington	S	65
Sebastopol, Wayne	E	×
● Sedalia, Clinton	C	200
● Sedan, DeKalb	NE	100
● Sedley, Porter	NW	65
● Seeleyville, Vigo	W	100
● *Selby*, Kosciusko	N	×
● Sellersburgh, Clark	S	500
● Selma, Delaware	E	365
Selvin, Warrick	SW	300
● Servia, Wabash	N	450
Sevastopol, Kosciusko	N	150
● *Seven Mile*, Knox	SW	×
● Sexton, Rush	E	90
● Seybert, Lagrange	NE	10
● Seymour, Jackson	S	5,337
● Shadeland, Tippecanoe	W	25
● Shanghai, Howard	C	40
Shannondale, Montgomery	W	100
Sharp's Mills, Harrison	S	20
● Sharpsville, Tipton	C	277
Sharptown, Franklin	E	25
Shawnee Mound, Tip'canoe	W	25
Shawswick, Lawrence	S	×
● *Sheffield*, Lake	NW	×
● Shelburn, Sullivan	SW	378
● Shelby, Lake	NW	25
● *Shelby's*, Fountain	W	×
● **Shelbyville**, Shelby	C	5,451
● Sheldon, Allen	NE	150
Shepherd, Boone	C	×
● Sheridan, Hamilton	C	1,134
Sherman, Randolph	E	50
● Sherwood, Jennings	SE	25
● Shideler, Delaware	E	200
Shields, Jackson	S	35
● *Shipman*, Vermillion	W	×
● Shipshewana, Lagrange	NE	250
● Shirley, Hancock	C	×
● *Shirley*, Hancock	C	×
● **Shoals**, Martin	SW	738
Shoppell, Owen	W	×
Shore, Lagrange	NE	50

Short, Martin............. SW 50
Shrock, Lagrange......... NE 50
Siberia, Perry.............. S 20
Sidconger, Fulton.......... N 50
● Sidney, Kosciusko........ N 300
Silas, Blackford............. E 20
Silver Creek, (see Sellersburg). ×
● Silver Lake, Kosciusko... N 570
Silverville, Lawrence........ S 75
● Silverwood, Fountain.... W 25
Silverwood, Parke.......... W ×
● *Simons*, Lake............ NW ×
● Simpson, Huntington... NE 50
● Sims, Grant................ C 150
Sims Station, (see Short)..... ×
Sinks, Harrison.............. S 30
Sitka, White................ NW 50
Slabtown (see Rosston)....... ×
Slate, Jennings............ SE 65
● *Slate Cut*, Clark............ S ×
● Sleeth, Carroll............ C 37
Sligo, Marshall.............. N ×
● *Slinkard*, Greene........ SW ×
Smartsburgh, Montgomery. W 15
Smedley, Washington........ S 10
● *Smedley's*, Washington... S 10
Smelser's Ms, (see Rushville) ×
Smiley, Daviess........... SW ×
Smithfield, Wayne......... E ×
Smithland, Shelby.......... C 150
● *Smith's*, Floyd............ S ×
● *Smith's*, Knox........... SW ×
● *Smith's Crossing*, D'tur.. SE 100
● *Smith's Mines*, Clay...... W ×
● Smithson, White......... NW ×
Smith's Valley, Johnson.... C 75
● Smithville, Monroe........ S 116
Smyrna, Decatur........... SE 65
● *Smythe*, Vanderburgh.. SW ×
Snacks, Marion.............. C ×
Snoddy Mills (see Coal Creek) ×
● Snow Hill, Randolph...... E ×
Snyder, Henry............... E 150
Soaprille, (see Bennington).. ×
Soest, Allen................ NE ×
● *Soldier's Home*, Grant.... C ×
● *Soldier's Home Junc.*, Grant C ×
● Solitude, Posey.......... SW 8
Solon, Clark.................. S 10
Solsberry, Greene.......... SW 200
Somerset, Wabash.......... N 300
● Somerville, Greene........ S 100
Soonover, Gibson.......... SW 45
● **South Bend**, St. Joseph N 21,819
South Bethany, Bartm'w.... S 50
South Boston, Washington.. S 50
South Delphi, Carroll....... C 168
South Gate, Franklin....... E 20
South Granger, Monroe..... S 32
South Marion, Grant........ C ×
South Martin, Martin...... SW ×
South Milford, Lagrange.. NE 275
South Peru, Miami.......... N 253
● Southport, Marion......... C 324
● South Raub, Tippecanoe. W 97
South Union, see Victor)..... ×
● *South Vernon*, Jennings SE ×
● *South Vincennes*, Knox SW ×
South Wabash, Wabash..... N 507
● *South Wanatah*, L'rte.. NW ×
South Waveland, (see Waveland)................................ ×
South Wayne, Allen....... NE 1,107
South West, Elkhart........ N 40
● South Whitley, Whitley. NE 720
● Spades, Ripley........... SE 200
● Sparksville, Jackson...... S 155
Sparta, Dearborn.......... SE 75
Spartanburgh, Randolph.... E 225
Spearsville, Brown......... S 150
● *Speeds*, Clark.............. S ×
● *Speichers*, Wabash........ N 75
● **Spencer**, Owen......... W 1,868
Spencerville, DeKalb...... NE 350
● Spiceland, Henry......... E 637
● Spiker, Wabash........... N 75
Spraytown, Jackson.........S 40
● *Spriggsboro*, Porter.... NW ×
Springboro, White........ NW 15
● *Springcave*, Owen......... W ×
Spring Creek Mills, (see Logansport)................................ ×
Springdale, Ripley......... SE ×
● Springer, Bartholomew... S 25
Springerville, Fayette....... E 150
Springfield, Franklin....... E 30
● *Springfield*, Lagrange... NE ×

Indiana

Spring Fountain Park, Kosciusko........................ N ×
Spring Grove, Wayne....... E 99
Spring Hill, Decatur....... SE 32
● *Spring Hill*, Vigo........ W ×
● Springport, Henry........ E 150
Spring Station, (see Chrisney) ×
Springtown, (see Marengo)... ×
Springville, LaPorte...... NW ×
● Springville, Lawrence..... S 200
Spurgeon, Pike........... SW 150
● *Stacer*, Vanderburgh... SW 65
Staffordshire, Sullivan.... SW 50
Stamper's Creek, Orange.... S 80
Stanford, Monroe........... S 100
Stanley, Noble............ NE ×
Stanley, Warrick.......... SW ×
● Star City, Pulaski....... NW 250
● *State Line*, Lake........ NW ×
● *State Line*, Vanderburgh SW ×
● State Line, Warren....... W 201
● Staunton, Clay........... W 549
● *Stave Track*, Clay......... W ×
● Steam Corner, Fountain. W 25
Steele, Adams............. NE 50
Steel's, (see Glenwood)....... ×
Stendal, Pike.............. SW 250
● Stephenson, Warrick... SW 30
Stephensport, (see Scalesville) ×
Sterling, (see Veedersburgh). ×
● *Stevens*, Fountain........ W 25
Steven's Station (see Fuquay). ×
● *Stevenson*, Greene...... SW ×
Stewartsville, Posey....... SW 250
Stilesville, Hendricks....... C 400
● Stillwell, LaPorte....... NW 100
● Stinesville, Monroe........ S 405
Stip's Hill, Franklin........ E 200
Stockton, (see Coal City)...... ×
● Stockwell, Tippecanoe.... W 500
Stohler, Madison............ C ×
● *Stone*, Randolph........... E ×
● Stone Bluffs, Fountain... W 100
● *Stoners*, Allen.......... NE ×
Stone's Crossing, Johnson... C 75
Stone Station, Randolph.... E 80
● *Stone Switch*, Decatur... SE ×
Stony Point, Jefferson..... SE 65
Story, Brown................. S 60
Stout, Delaware............. E 50
● Stoutsberg, Jasper..... NW ×
● *Straight Line Junction*, Vanderburgh................ SW ×
● *Stratford*, Marion......... C ×
● *Strathmore*, Lake...... NW ×
● Straughn, Henry.......... E 200
Strawtown, Hamilton........ C 20
Strong's L'nd'g (see Rosewood) ×
● *Studebaker*, St Joseph.... N ×
Stumke's Corners, Ripley. SE 25
Sugan, Jefferson........... SE ×
Sugar Branch, Switzerland SE 63
● *Sugar Creek*, Lake....... NW ×
Sugar Grove, Tippecanoe.. W 100
Sugar Grove, Fulton....... N 10
● **Sullivan**, Sullivan.... SW 2,222
Sulphur Hill, Shelby........ C ×
● Sulphur Springs, Henry... E 251
Sulphur Wells, Crawford.... S ×
● Sumanville, Porter..... NW 25
● Summit, DeKalb.......... NE 75
● *Summit*, Clark............ S 18
● *Summit*, Gibson......... SW ×
● *Summit*, Greene......... SW ×
● *Summit*, Hendricks........ C ×
● *Summit*, Marshall......... N ×
● *Summit*, Tippecanoe...... W ×
● Summit Grove, V'rm'l'on W 100
● Summitville, Madison..... C 752
Sumner, (see Johnsonville),.. ×
Sumption Prairie, St.J's'ph. N 45
● *Sunnyside*, Marion....... C ×
● Sunman, Ripley.......... SE 500
● Surprise, Jackson......... S ×
● Surrey, Jasper.......... NW 50
● Survant, Pike........... SW 75
Swalls, Vigo................. W ×
● Swan, Noble............ NE 100
● Swanington, Benton..... W 50
Swanville, Jefferson....... SE 25
● Swayzee, Grant............ C 300
Swaze's Mill, (see Dover Hill) ×
● Sweet Home, St. Joseph.. N 40
● Sweetser's, Grant.......... C 300
● *Swift's*, LaPorte........ NW ×
● *Switch "C,"* Clinton....... C ×
● Switz City, Greene...... SW 250

Indiana

● Sycamore, Haward........ C 300
Sylvania, Parke............ W 200
Synton, (see Cass)............ ×
● Syracuse, Kosciusko...... N 518
Syria, Orange................ S 38
Tabor, Delaware............. E 25
● *Taggart's*, Morgan........ C ×
● Talbot, Benton........... W 125
● *Talbot*, Benton........... W ×
Talmage, White........... NW ×
Tampico, (see Centre)........ ×
Tampico, Jackson........... S 100
● Tangier, Parke............ W 300
Tanner, Greene........... SW ×
Tanglewood, Ripley....... SE ×
Tapp, Howard................ C 150
● *Tarkington*, Howard...... C ×
Tassinong, Porter........ NW 100
● Taswell, Crawford .... S 200
● *Taylor's*, Whitley........ NE 30
● Taylorsville, Bartholomew S 500
Taylorsville, (see Selvin)..... ×
Tecumseh, Vigo............. W 50
● Teegarden, Marshall...... N 100
● Tefft, Jasper............ NW 50
● Tell City, Perry........... S 2,094
● Temple, Crawford.......... S 13
● Templeton, Benton...... W 400
● Tennyson, Warrick..... SW 150
● Terhune, Boone............ C 150
● Terre Coupee, St. Joseph. N 50
● *Terre Hall*, Howard ...... C 100
● **TERRE HAUTE** V'go W 30,217
● Thayer, Newton.......... NW 30
● *Thomas*, Daviess......... SW ×
● *Thomas*, Warren.......... W 32
● *Thomaston*, LaPorte... NW 20
● *Thompsons*, Jasper.... NW ×
Thompson Sta., (see Brady Sta.) ×
● *Thornhope*, Pulaski.... NW 100
● Thorntown, Boone......... C 1,530
Thurman, Allen.......... ME ×
● Tilden, Hendricks.......... C 60
● *Tile Siding*, Montgomery W ×
● Tillman, Carroll........... C 50
Tinkerville, (see Crawfordsv'e) ×
● *Tioga*, White........... NW ×
● Tiosa, Fulton............... N 200
● *Tippecanoe*, Marshall..... N ×
Tippecanoetown, (see Ilion).. ×
● **Tipton**, Tipton............ C 2,697
Titusville, Ripley.......... SE 20
Tobinsport, Perry.......... S 100
● Tocsin, Wells............ NE 115
Todd, Monroe............... S 20
Toga, Shelby................ C 100
● Toleston, Lake......... NW 400
Tollgate, Hendricks......... C ×
Toney, Wells.............. NE ×
Toronto, Vermillion......... W 85
● Toto, Starke............ NW 50
Tower, Crawford............. S ×
Tracy, LaPorte........... NW 40
Trader's Point, Marion...... C 60
● Trafalgar, Johnson........ C 700
Trainor, Daviess.......... SW ×
Trask, Grant.................. C 57
● Treaty, Wabash............ N 100
Trenton, Randolph......... E ×
Trenton, Blackford......... E 100
Trinity Springs, Martin... SW 125
● *Troutmans*, Montgomery W ×
● *Troy*, DeKalb............. NE ×
● Troy, Perry................ S 554
Tulip, Greene............. SW ×
Tunker, Whitley.......... NE 25
● Tunnelton, Lawrence...... S 200
Turkey Creek, Steuben.... NE 25
Turner, Clay................ W 300
Turpie, Johnson............ C ×
Twelve Mile, Cass........... N 30
Twin Lakes, Lagrange.... NE ×
● Twin Lake, Marshall...... N ×
Tyler, Orange............... S ×
Tyler's Land'g, (see Fredonia) ×
● *Tyner*, Fayette .... E ×
Tyner City, Marshall........ N 200
● *Tyrone*, Vermillion...... W 200
● Underwood, Scott.......... S 30
● *Union*, Huntington..... NE ×
Union, Franklin............ E 125
● *Union*, Huntington..... NE 20
Union, Pike.............. SW 200
● Union Center, LaPorte. NW 30
● Union City, Randolph..... E 2,681
Uniondale, Wells.......... NE 225
Union Grove, Grant......... C 40

Indiana

● Union Mills, LaPorte...NW 500
Unionpor., Randolph....... E 125
Uniontown, Perry..........S 50
Uniontown, Jackson........S 10
Unionville, Monroe.........S 50
● Upland, Grant............ C 300
● Upton, Posey........... SW 10
● Urbana, Wabash..........N 200
● Urmeyville, Johnson......C 50
Utica, Clark...............S 400
Valeene, Orange............S 75
● Valentine, Lagrange.... NE 100
Valley City, Harrison........S 64
● Valley Mills, Marion.....C 150
● Vallonia, Jackson.........S 300
● **Valparaiso,** Porter.. NW 5,090
● VanBuren, Grant......... C 550
● *Vandalia*, Clay.......... W ×
Vandalia, Owen........... W 75
● *VanSycles*, Morgan.......C ×
● *Vaughan*, VanderburghSW 300
Vawter's Park, Kosciusko...N ×
● *Veale*, Daviess..........SW ×
● Vedder, Vigo.............W 10
Veedersburgh, Fountain... W 930
● *Velonia*, Jackson.........S ×
Velpen, Pike..............SW 250
Vera Cruz, Wells..........NE 233
● Vermont, Howard....... C 30
● **Vernon,** Jennings......SE 613
● *Verona*, Cass.............N ×
Versailles, Ripley.......SE 421
Vesta, Clark................S 25
Vevay, Switzerland.......SE 1,663
Victor, Monroe.............S 10
● Vienna, Scott............ S 200
Vigo, Vigo.................W 10
Vilas, Owen................W 50
● **Vincennes,** Knox .... SW 8,853
Vine Springs, Ripley...... SE 26
Vineyard, Switzerland.....SE ×
Viola, Noble.............. NE 10
Virgie, Jasper............NW ×
● Vistula, Elkhart..........N 200
Vivalia, Putnam............W 30
Vogel, Dearborn...........SE 20
Volga, Jefferson........... SE 20
Voorhees, Ripley.......... SE ×
● *Votaw*, Wayne............E ×
● *Wabash*, Carroll..........C ×
● **Wabash,** Wabash.......N 5,105
● *Wabash Cros'g*, LaPorteNW ×
● *Wabash Junction*, AllenNE ×
Waco, Daviess............ SW ×
● Wadena, Benton......... W 80
● Wadesville, Posey.......SW 200
● Wagoner, Miami..........N 100
● Waikel, Wells...........NE 150
● Wailesborough, B'rth'mewS 100
Wakarusa, Elkhart..........N 600
Wakeland, Morgan..........C 20
Wakeup, Brown.............S ×
● Waldron, Shelby..........C 400
● Walkerton, St. Joseph....N 885
Wall, Jay...................E 25
Wallace, Fountain..........W 150
● Wallen, Allen........... NE 175
● Walnut, Marshall.........N 190
Walnut Grove, Warren.....W 45
● *Walnut Hill*, M'tgomery W ×
● *Walnut Level*, Wayne.... E ×
● Walton, Cass..............N 469
Waltz, Wabash............ N 25
Wanamaker, Marion........C ×
● Wanatah, LaPorte......NW 500
Ward, Boone...............C ×
● Warren, Huntington....NE 1,120
Warren Station, (see Saratoga) ×
● *Warren*, St. Joseph.......N 120
Warrenton, Gibson.......SW 40
Warrington, Hancock.......C 175
● **Warsaw,** Kosciusko.....N 3,574
● *Warwick*, St. Joseph..... N ×
● **Washington,** Daviess. W 6,064
Washington, (see Greenfork) ×
Waterford, LaPorte...... NW 40
● Waterford Mills, Elkhart..N 150
● Waterloo, DeKalb.......NE 1,473
Waterman, Parke..........W 200
● *Water Valley*, Newton. NW 15
● Watson, Clark.............S 50
● *Watson*, Clay........... W ×
● *Watson*, Greene........SW ×
Waugh, Boone............. C ×
● Waveland, Montgomery..W 663
● *Waverly*, Cass...........N ×
Waverly, Morgan...........C 75
● Wawaka, Noble.........NE 350

Indiana

Wawpecong, Miami.........N 210
Wayback, Carroll.......... C ×
● Waymansville, B'tho'lmewS 110
Waynesburgh, Decatur.... SE 120
● Waynesville, BartholomewS 100
● Waynetown, M'tgomery..W 576
● Wea, Tippecanoe........W 13
Weaver, Grant............. C 45
Webster, Wayne........... E 150
● *Webster's*, St. Joseph.....N ×
Weirtown, Washington......S ×
● Weisburgh, Dearborn....SE 100
● Wellsboro, LaPorte.... NW 200
● *Welsh*, Greene..........SW ×
Weltes, Warrick.......... SW 40
● ***Wendel*, Posey**..........SW ×
● Wesley, Montgomery.... W ×
● West Baden, Orange.......S 100
West Brownst'n, (see Brownst'n) ×
Westchester, Jay...........E 60
West College Corner, Union. E 290
● Westfield, Hamilton...... C 815
West Fork, Crawford....... S 70
● *West Fort Wayne*, AllenNE ×
West Franklin, Posey.....SW 75
West Harrison, Dearborn. SE 320
West Indianapolis, Marion..C 3,527
West Lafayette, TippecanoeW 1,242
Westland, Hancock..........C 50
● West Lebanon, Warren... W 644
West Liberty, Howard.......C 75
West Madison, Jefferson.. SE 457
● West Middleton, Howard..C 200
● West Newton, Marion.....C 300
Westover, Ripley.......... SE ×
Weston, Jennings..........SE ×
● Westphalia, Knox...... SW 30
● *West Point*, Huntington NE 300
West Point, Tippecanoe.... W 300
West Point, Wabash........N ×
● Westport, Decatur.......SE 452
West Salem, (see Alaska) .... ×
● West Shoals, Martin.... SW ×
● *West Side*, Marion........ C ×
● West Union, Parke...... W 25
● *West Vernon*, Jennings..SE ×
● Westville, LaPorte......NW 522
● Wheatfield, Jasper..... NW 200
● Wheatland, Knox.......SW 400
● Wheaton, Putnam........W 25
Wheatonville, (see Elberfield) ×
● Wheeler, Porter........NW 75
Wheeler, White...........NW 50
Wheelers, Carroll...........C ×
Wheeling, Delaware.........E 125
● Whitaker, Morgan........ C 50
Whitcomb, Franklin........E 195
White Cloud, Harrison...... S 30
White Hall, Owen..........W 40
● Whiteland, Johnson.......C 212
White Lick, Boone..........C 195
White Oak, Pike.......... SW 17
● Whitestown, Boone....... C 800
● Whitesville, Montgomery W 250
White Water, Wayne........E 123
● Whiting, Lake..........NW 1,408
● *Whitings*, Lake........ NW 75
● *Whitman*, Pike.........SW 75
Whittington, Bartholomew..S ×
Wickliffe, Crawford......... S 15
● *Wiggs*, Bartholomew..... S ×
Wilbur, Morgan.............C 100
Wild Cat, Carroll............C 25
● Wilders Station, La P'te NE ×
Wiles, Tipton...............C 10
Wiley's L'ding, (see Florence) ×
Wilkey, Sullivan..........SW ×
● Wilkinson, Hancock...... C 165
● *Wilkinson's*, Warrick...SW 32
● *Williams*, Adams.......NE 50
● *Williams*, Clay...........W ×
● *Williams*, Elkhart.........N ×
● Williams, Lawrence.......S 40
Williamsburg, (see Nineveh) ×
Williamsburgh, Wayne......E 250
● *Williams Cr's'g*, Morgan..C ×
● **Williamsport,** WarrenSE 1,027
● Williamstown, Decatur..SE 15
Willis Grove, Knox....... SW 15
● Willow Branch, Hancock.C 124
● *Willow Creek*, Porter....W ×
● *Willow Valley*, Martin.SW ×
● Willvale, LaPorte...... NW 10
Wilmington, Dearborn.... SE 300
● *Wilmington*, DeKalb... NE ×
Wilmot, Noble............ NE 25
● *Wilson*, Daviess........ SW ×
● *Wilson*, Posey.......... SW ×

Indiana

Wilson, Shelby..............C ×
● *Wilson's*, Lake.........NW ×
● *Wilson's*, Clark..........S 40
● **Winamac,** Pulaski...NW 1,215
● **Winchester,** Randolph..E 3,014
● Windfall, Tipton.......... C 561
Windsor, Randolph......... E 250
Winfield, Lake............NW 25
● Wingate, Montgomery... W 400
● *Winkfield*, Henry.........E ×
Winona, Starke...........NW ×
Winship, Pulaski........ NW ×
● Winslow, Pike.......... SW 1,200
● *Winslow*, Porter.......NW ×
Winterroud, Shelby......... C 50
● Wintersville, Decatur....SE 97
● Winthrop, Warren...... W 100
● Wirt, Jefferson.......... SE 45
Witt, Dearborn............SE ×
● Wolcott, White.........NW 246
● Wolcottville, Lagrange..NE 600
Wolf Creek, Marshall.......N 50
Wolf Lake, Noble.........NE 200
● Woodburn, Allen....... NE 50
● Woodbury, Hancock......C 120
Woodland, St. Joseph.......N 100
Woodruff, Lagrange.......NE 50
Woodruff Place, Marion....C 161
● *Woods*, Randolph.........E ×
Woodside, Marion......... C ×
Woodville, (see Kennard).... ×
● *Woodville*, Carroll....... C 50
● Woodville, Porter......NW 40
● *Woodyard*, Monroe.......S ×
Woody's Corner, (see Tangier) ×
● Wooster, Kosciusko...... N 90
● *Worcester*, Elkhart.......N ×
Worth, Harrison........... S ×
● Worthington, Greene... SW 1,448
Wright, Greene.......... SW 7
Wright's Corners, D'rborn.SE 75
Wyandotte, Crawford....... S ×
Wynn, Franklin ....E 30
● Xenia, Miama.............N 921
Yaney, Adams............NE 10
Yankeetown, Warrick.... SW 50
● Yeddo, Fountain......... W 200
● *Yellowbank*, Franklin....E ×
Yellowstone, Monroe....... S ×
● Yeoman, Carroll...........C 40
● Yocky, Lawrence......... S 50
York, Elkhart.............N 15
● *York*, Noble............NE ×
York Centre, Steuben.....NE 65
● Yorktown, Delaware......E 450
Yorkville, Dearborn.......SE 100
Young America, Cass.......N 500
Young's Creek, Orange......S 200
● Youngstown, Vigo....... W 75
● Yountsville, MontgomeryW 125
Zanesville, Wells...........NE 300
● Zard, Jasper............NW 35
● Zelma, Lawrence..........S 12
Zenas, Jennings...........SE 100
● *Zigler*, St. Joseph.........N ×
● Zionsville, Boone..........C 825
Zipp's, Vanderburgh......SW 125
Zulu, Allen................NE 32

Indian Territory.

NATIONS AND RESERVATIONS.	INDEX.	POP.
Cherokee	NE	30,666
Cherokee Outlet	NW	×
Chickasaws	S	8,000
Choctaws	SE	24,000
Creek	E	1,866
Ottawa	NE	162
Peoria	NE	186
Quapaws	NE	80
Seminole	C	4,000
Seneca	NE	×
Shawnee	NE	×
Wyandotte	NE	378
Total		87,699

TOWN.	NATION.	INDEX.	POP.
Ada	Chickasaw N	S	×
● Adair	Cherokee N	NE	75
● Afton	Cherokee N	NE	200
● *Albia*	Cherokee N	NE	×

Indian Terr.

Place	
● Albion, Choctaw N......SE	×
● Alderson, Choctaw N...SE	×
Alex, Chickasaw N.........S	×
Alikchi, Choctaw N........ SE	×
Al-lu-we, Cherokee N......SE	25
Alma, Cherokee N........NE	×
● *Alston*, Cherokee Outlet NW	×
Alva, Cherokee Outlet....NW	×
Annette, Choctaw N.......SE	×
● Antlers, Choctaw N...... SE	×
Arbeka, Seminole N........ C	25
Arbuckle, Chickasaw N.....S	×
● Ardmore, Chickasaw N... S	1,000
● *Armstrong*, Choctaw N..SE	45
Arthur, Chickasaw N....... S	×
Atlee, Chickasaw N........ S	×
● **Atoka**, Choctaw N.....SE	800
Bacone, Creek N...........C	×
Baird, Choctaw N..........SE	×
Baldwin, Chickasaw N...... S	55
Baptist, Cherokee N...... NE	45
Bartlesville, Cherokee N..NE	×
Beef Creek, Chickasaw N...S	×
Bell, Choctaw N..........SE	×
● Bengal, Choctaw N......SE	×
Bennington, Choctaw N...SE	×
● Berwin, Chickasaw N.....S	×
● Big Cabin, Cherokee N..NE	×
Big Creek, (see Hudson)......	
● *Bird's Point*, Cher. Ou't NW	×
Blaine, Choctaw N..........SE	×
Blue, Choctaw N...........SE	×
● Bluejacket, Cherokee N. NE	25
Boggy Depot, Choctaw N..SE	25
Bokoshe, Choctaw N....... SE	×
Bolin, Cherokee N.........NE	×
Bolm's Ferry, Cherokee N NE	20
● *Bond*, Creek N...........C	×
Bon Ton, (see Eagletown)....	
Braden, Choctaw N........SE	×
Bradley, Chickasaw N.........S	75
● Braggs, Cherokee N.... NE	50
● Braidwood, Choctaw N..SE	10
Breedlove, Cherokee N....NE	×
Brazil Station, Choctaw N.SE	×
Briartown, Cherokee N... NE	10
Broken Arrow, Creek N.... C	25
Brooken, Choctaw N...... SE	32
Brownsville, Chickasaw.N..S	×
● Bryan, Choctaw N.......SE	×
Buckhorn, Chickasaw N.... S	×
Buffalo Spring, Cher.Ou'tNW	×
Buffalo Spring Stage Station, Cherokee Outlet........NW	×
Bunch, Cherokee N...... NW	×
Burgevin, Choctaw N......SE	×
Burneyville, Chickasaw N...S	75
Burt, Chickasaw N..........S	×
● *Bushyhead*, CherokeeN. NE	×
● Butler, Choctaw N...... SE	×
Byrd, Choctaw N..........SE	×
Cache, Choctaw N......... SE	×
● Caddo, Choctaw N.......SE	500
● Cale, Choctaw N.........SE	×
● Cameron, Choctaw N....SE	75
Campbell, Cherokee N.... NE	[illegible]00
Camp Creek, Cherokee N. NE	×
Camp Supply, Cher.Ou't. NW	[illegible]00
Canadaville, Cherokee N. NE	×
● Caney, Choctaw N.......SE	×
Cartersville, Choctaw N... SE	×
Caston, Choctaw N.........SE	×
● *Catale*, Cherokee N.....NE	×
● Catoosa, Cherokee N....NE	75
● Cavanal, Choctaw N.....SE	×
Cayuga, Seneca N.........NE	×
Cedar, Choctaw N........SE	×
● *Cedars*, Choctaw N....... S	×
Center, Chickasaw N.......S	×
● Checotah, Creek N........C	10
Cheek, Chicasaw N.........S	×
● Chelsea, Cherokee N....NE	[illegible]00
CherokeeJunc., CherokeeNNE	×
Cherokee Town, Chick. N...S	×
Childer'sCross, (see Muscogee)	×
Chili, Choctaw N.......... SE	×
● *Chilloco*, Cherokee Ou't NW	×
Childer's Sta., (see Sallisaw)..	×
Choska, Creek N............E	×
● Choteau, Cherokee N... NE	[illegible]50
● Claremore, CherokeeN .NE	[illegible]00
● *Clayton*, Choctaw N.....SE	×
Cliff, Chickasaw N.......... S	×
Coal Creek, (see Redoak).....	×
Coalgate, Choctaw N....... SE	×
● *Coal Mine No. 1*, Choctaw N SE	×

Indian Terr.

Place	
● *Coal Mine*, Choctaw N..SE	×
● Colbert, Chickasaw N.....S	[illegible]00
● *Compton*, Choctaw N....SE	×
Coody's Bluff, Cherokee N NE	×
Coo-y-yah, Cherokee N.... NE	13
Cornish, Chickasaw N........S	×
● *Correta*, Cherokee N....NE	×
Co-teh-se-tah, Cherokee N.NE	×
Cottonwood, Cherok..e N. NE	×
Courtney, Chickasaw N..... S	×
Cottonwood Grove, Cherokee Outlet..................NW	×
Coveda Mission, Creek N...C	×
Cowlington, Choctaw N....SE	×
● *Davenport*, Choctaw N..SE	20
Davis, Chickasaw N.........S	×
Dixie, Chickasaw N.........S	×
Doaksville, Choctaw N.....SE	97
● Dougherty, Chickasaw N. S	×
Dresden, Chickasaw N..... S	×
Duncan, Chickasaw N.......S	50
● Durant, Choctaw N........SE	32
Durwood, Chickasaw N.......S	×
Eagle, Cherokee N........NE	×
● *Eagle Chief*, Cherokee Outlet...........NW	×
Eagle Town, Choctaw N...SE	×
Eastman, Chickasaw N......S	×
Echo, Cherokee N.......... NE	×
Econtuchka, Seminole N....C	100
Eldridge, Cherokee N.... NE	×
Elk, Chickasaw N...........N	×
Elliott, Cherokee N.......NE	×
Elmore, Chickasaw N.......S	×
Emet, Chickasaw N......... S	10
● ***Enid***, **Cherokee Outlet.NW**	×
Enterprise, Choctaw N.... SE	×
Erin Springs, Chickasaw N..S	20
Etna, Choctaw N.......... SE	×
● Eufaula, Creek N......... C	500
Fairland, Cherokee N.....NE	×
● Fanshawe, Choctaw N...SE	×
Fawling, Cherokee N.......NE	×
Fishertown, Creek N.........C	26
Fleetwood, Chickasaw N....S	×
Flint, Cherokee N.........NE	130
● *Folsom*, Choctaw N..... SE	×
Fontana, Chickasaw N..... S	×
● Fort Gibson, Cherokee N NE	500
Fort Holmes, Creek N.......C	×
FortMcCollough, Chic'w N.SE	×
Fort Sprinkey (see Catoosa)..	×
Fort Supply, Chero'eeOut NW	100
Fort Wichita, Chickasaw N.S	×
Foster, Chickasaw N........ S	×
Fourmile, Peoria N.......NE	×
● Foyil, Cherokee N...... NE	25
Fred, Chickasaw N..........S	×
● *Frink*, Choctaw N.......SE	×
● *Gage*, Cherokee Outlet..NW	×
● *Gaines Creek*, Choctaw N SE	×
Gap, Chickasaw N...........S	×
Garfield, Cherokee N..... NE	10
Gary, Choctaw N......... SE	50
Gattis, Chickasaw N........S	×
Gertrude, Choctaw N......SE	×
● Gibson Station, Creek N.. C	26
Gilmore, Choctaw N.......SE	×
Glaze, Chickasaw N.........S	×
Going Snake, Cherokee N.NE	10
Golconda, Choctaw N.......SE	×
● Good Land, Choctow N..SE	×
● *Goodwin*, Cher. Outlet. NW	×
Grady, Chicasaw N..........S	×
Graham, Chickasaw N...... S	×
● Grand River, Wy'dote N.NE	97
● Grant, Choctaw N........SE	×
Green Hill, Choctaw N.... SE	×
Griffin, Cherokee Outlet..NW	×
Grove, Cherokee N.........NE	10
● *Hamden*, Choctaw N.... SE	×
● Hanson, Cherokee N.... NE	20
● *Hardon*, Cher. Outlet.. NW	×
Harland, Cherokee N..... NE	×
Harrison, Choctaw N.......SE	×
Hartshorne, Choctaw N....SE	×
Hayden, Cherokee N.......NE	×
Hoyt City, Cherokee N....NE	×
Healdton, Chickasaw N......S	×
Helliswa, Seminole N........ C	×
● *Heman*, Cher'e Outlet..NW	×
Hennepin, Chickasaw N....S	×
Hewitt, Chickasaw N........S	×
Hickory, Cherokee N...... NE	×
Hildebrand's Mills, Ch'eN NE	×
Hillabee, Creek N...........E	×
Holder, Chickasaw N........S	×

Indian Terr.

Place	
Hope, Chickasaw N..........S	×
Hoyt, Choctaw N.......... SE	×
Hudson, Cherokee N......NE	×
● *Illinois*, Cherokee N....NE	×
Indianola, Choctaw N..... SE	×
● *Inditerark*, Choctaw N...SE	×
● *Inola*, Cherokee N......NE	×
Inola, Creek N.............. E	10
Iron Bridge, Choctaw N... SE	×
Ittilallak, Chickasaw N..... S	×
Jimtown, Chickasaw N......S	×
Johnson, Chickasaw N......S	×
● *Kamama*, Cherokee N .NE	×
Kavanaugh, (see Kennedy)..	×
Kedron, Cherokee N......NE	×
Kee-too-wah, Cherokee N.NE	×
Keith, Chickasaw N.........S	×
● *Kelso*, Cherokee N......NE	×
Kema, Peoria N.......... NE	×
Kemp, Chickasaw N..........S	×
Kennady, s Choctaw N..... SE	×
Keys, Choctaw N.........NE	×
● Kiamichi, Choctaw N....SE	×
Kinnison, Cherokee N.... NE	×
● Kiowa, Choctaw N.......SE	77
Kolb, Choctaw N.......... SE	×
● Kosoma, Choctaw N.....SE	×
Krebs, Choctaw N......... SE	3,000
Kulli Inla, Choctaw N..... SE	×
Kully Chaha, Choctaw N...SE	45
● *LaFourcheMaline*, ChocNSE	×
● *Lapita*, Choctaw N......SE	×
Lark, Chickasaw N..........S	×
Leader, Choctaw N.........SE	×
Lebanon, Chickasaw N......S	150
Leeper, Chickasaw N........S	×
● Leflore, Choctaw N.......SE	×
● Lehigh, Choctaw N......SE	3,000
● *Leliaetta*, Creek N........C	×
● Lenapah, Cherokee N...NE	×
Leon, Chickasaw N..........S	97
Liddle, Choctaw N.........SE	×
● *Limestone Gap*, Cha'w N.SE	130
Linn, Chickasaw N..........S	×
Loco, Chickasaw N.......... S	×
Locust Grove, Cherokee N NE	20
Lone Grove, Chickasaw N...S	×
Long View, Choctaw N....SE	×
Lukfata, Choctaw N.........SE	×
● McAlester, Choctaw N.. SE	5,000
McGee, Chickasaw N.......S	×
McKey, Cherokee N...... NE	×
● *Mackey*, Cherokee N... NE	×
Manard, Cherokee N.......NE	×
Mannsville, Chickasaw N... S	×
Marietta, Chickasaw N......S	250
Marlowe, Chickasaw N.......S	×
Max, Peoria N............. NE	×
Maxey, (see Fanshaw).......	×
Mays, Cherokee N .... NE	75
● *Mazie*, Creek N..........C	×
Miami, Peoria N.......... NE	75
Mill Creek, Chickasaw N....S	[illegible]
Milton, Choctaw N......... SE	×
● Minco, Chickasaw N...... S	×
● *Mingo*, Cherokee N......NE	×
Monroe, Choctaw N.......SE	32
Morehead, Cherokee N. ..NE	×
Mountain, Choctaw N......SE	×
Moyer's Switch, ChoctawN SE	×
● Muldrow, Cherokee N.. NE	400
● Muscogee, Creek N.........C	2,000
Nail, Choctaw N .... SE	×
Naples, Chickasaw N.........S	×
Nebo, Chickasaw N......... S	×
Nelson, Choctaw N.......... SE	82
New SpringPlace, Cher.N.NE	×
● *Noel*, Cherokee Outlet..NW	×
● Nowata, Cherokee N....NE	×
Oakland, Chickasaw N...... S	100
Oak Lodge, Choctaw N.... SE	195
Oaks, Cherokee N.........NE	45
● *Oak-ta-ha*, Creek N.......C	×
Oil Springs, Chickasaw N...S	×
Okmulgee, Creek N......C	150
Okolona, Choctaw N....... SE	×
Okshwali, Choctaw N..... SE	×
Ola, Choctaw N .... SE	×
● Ooloogah, Cherokee N.. NE	20
Olympus, Cherokee N.....NE	20
Osage Sp'g, Ch'kee O'tl't.NW	×
● *Oseuma*, Cherokee N... NE	×
Ouray, Senaca N...........NE	×
● Overbrook, Chickasaw N..S	×
Paden, Cherokee N....... NE	15
Panther, Choctaw N.......SE	×
● Paoli, Chickasaw N....... S	×
Parr, Chickasaw N..........S	×

Town	Index	Pop.
● Paul's Valley, Chickasaw N	S	×
Pensee, Chickasaw N	S	40
Paw Paw, Cherokee N	NE	10
Pearl, Chickasaw N	S	×
Pecan, Cherokee N	NE	×
● *Peck*, Choctaw N	SE	×
Peery, Chickasaw N	S	×
Peoria, Peoria N	NE	×
Perry, Cherokee N	NE	×
Petersburg, Chickasaw N	S	×
Petuna, Chickasaw N	S	×
Pleasant Bluff, (see Tamaha).		×
Pleasant Ridge, Choctaw N	SE	×
Pocola, Chactaw N	SE	×
● *Pond Creek*, Cher. Outlet	NW	12
Pooler, Ottawa Res	NE	20
Porum, Choctaw N	SE	×
● Poteau, Choctaw N	SE	×
Prairie City, Cherokee N	NE	75
Price, Chickasaw N	S	×
Pryor Creek, Cherokee N	NE	100
● Purcell, Chickasaw N	S	2,000
Raysville, Chickasaw N	S	×
● *Reams*, Choctaw N	SE	×
Reck, Chickasaw N	S	×
● Red Fork, Creek N	E	25
Redland, Cherokee N	NE	10
Red Oak, Choctaw N	SE	225
Reichart, Choctaw N	SE	×
Remy, Cherokee N	NE	×
Rex, Chickasaw N	S	×
Richards Station, (see Caddo)		×
Ridge, Creek N	E	×
Ringo, Cherokee N	NE	×
Rio, (see Anadarko, Okl.)		×
Robberson, Chickasaw N	S	×
● Rodney, Choctaw N	SE	×
Roff, Chickasaw N	S	×
Rome, Cherokee N	NE	×
Rose, Cherokee N	NE	×
● *Ross*, Creek N	E	×
RushCreek, Chickasaw N	S	×
● *Russell Creek*, Ch'r'kee N	NE	×
Russelville, Choctaw N	SE	×
Ryan, Chickasaw N	S	×
● *Sageegah*, Cherokee N	NE	×
Salina, Cherokee N	NE	×
● Sallisaw, Cherokee N	NE	50
Sanders, Cherokee N	NE	13
Sandy, Chickasaw N	S	×
Sans Bois, Choctaw N	SE	130
● Sapulpa, Creek N	E	20
Sa-sak-wa, Seminole N	C	65
● Savanna, Choctaw N	SE	×
● *Seminole*, Cherokee N	NE	×
● *Sequoyah*, Cherokee N	NE	×
Se-quo-yah, Cherokee N	NE	10
● *Shattuck*, Ch'rekee O'tl't	NW	×
● *Shawnee*, Wyandotte N	NE	97
Shawnee Creek, Choctaw N	SE	×
Sheridan's Roost, Cherokee Outlet	NW	×
Short Mount'n, (see Cowling'n)		×
Silver City, Chickasaw N	S	×
Simon, Chickasaw N	S	×
Ski-a-took, Cherokee N	NE	10
● *Smallwood*, Choctaw N	SE	×
Smithville, Choctaw N	SE	×
● SouthCanadian, Ch't'w N	SE	300
● South M'Alester, Ch't'w N	SE	×
Spears, Cherokee N	NE	×
Spitlog's Ms., Cherokee N	NE	×
Springer, Chickasaw N	S	×
Springfield, Creek N	E	20
Spring Station, Choctaw N	SE	×
Springtown, Choctaw N	SE	50
● Standley, Choctaw N	SE	×
● *Stock Y'd*, Ch'r'kee O'tl't.	NW	×
Stonewall, Chickasaw N	S	100
● Stringtown, Choctaw N	SE	50
Summerfield, Choctaw N	SE	×
● *Summit*, Creek N	E	×
Swimmer, Cherokee N	NE	×
Talala, Cherokee N	NE	20
TAHLEQUAH, Cherokee N	NE	1,200
● Tallhina, Cboctaw N	SE	×
Tamaha, Choctaw N	SE	25
● *Taneha*, Creek N	E	×
Texanna, Cherokee N	NE	×
● Thackerville, Chickas'w. N	S	120
Thomas, Chickasaw N	S	×
Thurman, Choctaw N	SE	×
Tiawah, Cherokee N	NE	×
Tiger, Creek N	E	×
Tishomingo, Chickasaw N	S	100
Tucker, Chickasaw N	S	×
● *Tucker*, Cherokee Outlet	NW	×
● Tulsa, Creek N	E	200
● Tushka Homma, Ch't'w N	SE	×
Tussy, Chickasaw N	S	×
Ulm, Cherokee N	NW	×
Velma, Chickasaw N	S	×
● *Verdigris*, Cherokee N	NE	77
● Vian, Cherokee N	NE	×
● Vinita, Cherokee N	NE	1,160
Viola, Chickasaw N	S	×
Wadeville, Choctaw N	SE	×
● Wagoner, Creek N	E	250
Wallville, Chickasaw N	S	×
Wapanucka, Choctaw N	SE	×
● *Warren*, Cherokee O'tlet	NW	×
Warwick, Cherokee O'tlet.	NW	×
● Washita, Chickasaw N	S	×
Wau-hil-lau, Cherokee N	NE	260
● *Waukomis*, Ch'kee O'tl't	NW	×
● Wayne, Chickasaw N	S	×
● Waynoka, Ch'kee O'tl't.	NW	×
Wea-la-ka, Creek N	E	97
Webber's Falls, Ch'kee N	NE	200
Welch, Cherokee N	NE	×
● Wellington, Creek N	E	15
Wesley, Chickasaw N	S	×
Wetmore, Choctaw N	SE	×
We-tum-ka, Creek N	E	26
● **We-wo-ka**, Seminole N	C	100
● *Wharton*, Ch'kee Outl't.	NW	×
Wheelock, Choctaw N	SE	25
WhiteBead Hill, Ch'kas'w N	S	×
● *WhiteHead*, Ch'kee O'tl't	NW	×
Whitefield, Choctaw N	SE	×
● *White Oak*, Cherokee N	NE	×
White Water, Cherokee N	NE	×
Whiting, Quapaws N	NE	×
● Wilburton, Choctaw N	SE	×
● *WildHorse*, Ch'kee O'tl't	NW	×
Willis, Chickasaw N	S	×
● *Willow Springs*, Cherokee Outlet	NW	×
Wilson, Chickasaw N	S	×
Winchester, Cherokee N	NE	×
● *Winthrop*, Ch'kee O'tl't	NW	×
● Wistar, Choctaw N	SE	×
Woodford, Chickasaw N	S	25
Woodville, Chickasaw N	S	×
● *Woodward*, Ch'kee O'tl't	NW	100
Woolsey, Chickasaw N	S	×
Wybark, Creek N	E	10
● WynneWood, Chickasaw N	S	1,000
Yarnaby, Chickasaw N	S	×
Yellow Hills, Chickasaw N	S	×

IOWA.

COUNTIES.	INDEX.	POP.
Adair	SW	14,534
Adams	SW	12,292
Allamakee	NE	17,907
Appanoose	S	18,961
Audubon	W	12,412
Benton	E	24,178
Black Hawk	C	24,219
Boone	C	23,772
Bremer	NE	14,630
Buchanan	E	18,997
Buena Vista	NW	13,548
Butler	N	15,463
Calhoun	W	13,107
Carroll	W	18,828
Cass	SW	19,645
Cedar	E	18,253
Cerro Gordo	N	14,864
Cherokee	NW	15,659
Chickasaw	NE	15,019
Clarke	S	11,332
Clay	NW	9,309
Clayton	NE	26,733
Clinton	E	41,199
Crawford	W	18,894
Dallas	C	20,479
Davis	S	15,258
Decatur	S	15,643
Delaware	E	17,349
Des Moines	SE	35,324
Dickinson	NW	4,328
Dubuque	E	49,848
Emmet	NW	4,274
Fayette	NE	23,141
Floyd	N	15,424
Franklin	N	12,871
Fremont	SW	16,842
Greene	C	15,797
Grundy	C	13,215
Guthrie	W	17,380
Hamilton	C	15,319
Hancock	N	7,621
Hardin	C	19,003
Harrison	W	21,356
Henry	SE	18,895
Howard	NE	11,182
Humboldt	N	9,836
Ida	W	10,705
Iowa	E	18,270
Jackson	E	22,771
Jasper	C	24,943
Jefferson	SE	15,184
Johnson	E	23,082
Jones	E	20,233
Keokuk	SE	23,862
Kossuth	N	13,120
Lee	SE	37,715
Linn	E	45,303
Louisa	SE	11,873
Lucas	S	14,563
Lyon	NW	8,680
Madison	S	15,977
Mahaska	S	28,805
Marion	S	23,058
Marshall	C	25,842
Mills	SW	14,548
Mitchell	N	13,299
Monona	W	14,515
Monroe	S	13,666
Montgomery	SW	15,848
Muscatine	E	24,504
O'Brien	NW	13,060
Osceola	NW	5,574
Page	SW	21,341
Palo Alto	NW	9,318
Plymouth	NW	19,568
Pocahontas	NW	9,533
Polk	C	65,410
Pottawattamie	SW	47,430
Poweshiek	C	18,394
Ringgold	S	13,556
Sac	W	14,522
Scott	E	43,164
Shelby	W	17,611
Sioux	NW	18,370
Story	C	18,127
Tama	C	21,651
Taylor	SW	16,384
Union	S	16,9[illegible]0
VanBuren	SE	16,253
Wapello	S	30,426
Warren	S	18,269
Washington	SE	18,468
Wayne	S	15,670
Webster	C	21,582
Winnebago	N	7,325
Winneshiek	NE	22,528
Woodbury	W	55,632
Worth	N	9,247
Wright	N	12,057
Total		1,911,896

TOWN. COUNTY.	INDEX.	POP.
● Abbott, Hardin	C	75
Abbyville, Delaware	E	×
Abingdon, Jefferson	SE	300
● Ackley, Hardin	C	1,286
● Ackworth, Warren	S	120
Acme, Howard	NE	25
● Adair, Adair	SW	722
● Adams, Muscatine	E	15
Adamsonville, Jasper	C	×
Adaville, Plymouth	NW	×
Addison, Humboldt	N	×
● **Adel**, Dallas	C	995
● Adelphi, Polk	C	75
Advance, Guthrie	W	×
● **Afton**, Union	S	1,045
● *Afton Junction*, Union	S	×
● Agency, Wapello	S	442
● Ainsworth, Washington	SE	400
● Akron, Plymouth	NW	494
Albany, Davis	S	60
Albaton, Monona	W	50
● **Albia**, Monroe	S	2,359
● Albion, Marshall	C	384
● Alden, Hardin	W	512
Aldrich, Wright	N	×
● Alexander, Franklin	N	50
● *Alger*, Linn	E	×
● **Algona**, Kossuth	N	2,068
Allen's Grove, Scott	E	25
● Allerton, Wayne	S	807

Place	Pop.
Alice, Grundy..............C	×
Allison, Butler...........N	500
Almira, Delaware..........E	25
● Almont, Clinton.........E	75
● Almoral, Delaware.......E	100
Alpha, Fayette...........NE	73
● Alta, Buena Vista......NW	768
● Alta Vista, Chickasaw.. NE	13
● Alton, Sioux...........NW	708
● Altoona, Polk...........C	326
Alvord, Lyon............NW	50
Amador, Wapello..........S	×
● Amana, Iowa.............E	600
● Amber, Jones............E	100
● Ames, Story.............C	1,276
Amish, Johnson............E	60
Amity, (see College Springs)..	×
Amity, Scott..............E	20
Amityville, Des Moines.... SE	×
Amsterdam, (see Upper Grove)	×
Amund, Winnebago..........N	×
● **Anamosa, Jones**........E	2,078
● Anderson, Fremont.....SW	70
● Andover, Clinton.........E	15
Andrew, Jackson...........E	307
● Angus, Boone............C	704
● Anita, Cass.............SW	695
● Ankeny, Polk............C	35
Anna, Buena Vista.......NW	×
Annieville, Clay..........NW	×
● Anthon, Woodbury.......W	70
● Aplington, Butler.........N	427
Appanoose, Wapello.......S	×
Arbor Hill, Adair.........SW	50
● Arcadia, Carroll.........W	463
● Archer Grove, O'Brien. NW	25
Aredale, Butler............N	×
Argand, Jones.............E	57
● Argyle, Lee.............SE	75
● Arion, Crawford..........W	25
● Arispee, Union...........S	34
Armour, Pottawattamie...SW	25
Armstrong, Emmet......NW	300
● *Arnold*, Humboldt.......N	×
● *Arnold's Park*, Dick'son NW	×
Arquitt, Dubuque...........E	×
Arrow, Grundy............C	×
● Arthur, Ida..............W	125
Ashawa, Polk..............C	97
Ash Grove, Davis...........S	45
● Ashton, Osceola........NW	309
Ashland, Wapello..........S	×
● Aspinwall, Crawford.....W	180
● Astor, Crawford..........W	150
● Atalissa, Muscatine.......E	300
● Atkins, Benton............E	150
Atlantic, Buchanan.........E	×
● **Atlantic**, Cass.........SW	4,351
Attica, Marion..............S	300
● Atwood, Keokuk.........SE	×
Auburn, (see Douglas).......	×
Auburn, Mahaska...........S	×
● Auburn, Sac..............W	174
● **Audubon**, Audubon... W	1,310
Augusta, Des Moines......SE	150
● Aurelia, Cherokee.....NW	533
● Aurora, Buchanan........E	200
Aurora, Keokuk..........SE	57
● Avery, Monroe............S	300
● Avoca, Pottawattamie.. SW	1,700
● Avon, Polk...............C	20
Ayer's Corners, (see Wilton Jc.)	×
● Ayershire, Palo Alto... NW	200
Babcock, Linn.............E	×
Bach Grove, Wright.........N	×
● Badger, Webster..........C	100
● Bagley, Guthrie..........W	400
Bailey, Hancock...........N	×
● Bailey, Mitchell...........N	50
Baker, Jefferson...........SE	32
● Baldwin, Jackson.........E	227
● *Ballinger*, Lee...........SE	×
Balltown, Dubuque.........E	60
Balluff, Scott..............E	260
Ballyclough, Dubuque.......E	25
● Bancroft, Kossuth.........N	657
Bangor, Marshall............C	50
Bankston, Dubuque.........E	150
Barclay, Black Hawk.......C	×
● Bard, Louisa.............SE	25
● Barnes, Mahaska..........S	75
● Barney, Madison..........S	50
● Barnum, Webster.........C	100
Barryville, Delaware........E	×
● Bartlett, Fremont......SW	100
Barwood, Scott............E	×
● Bassett, Chickasaw..... NE	300
● Batavia, Jefferson....... SE	307
● Battle Creek, Ida.........W	387
Bauer, Marion..............S	20
● Baxter, Jasper............C	225
● Bayard, Guthrie...........W	348
● *Bayfield*, Muscatine.......E	×
● Beacon, Mahaska..........S	570
● Beaconsfield, Ringgold....S	50
● Beaman, Grundy..........C	262
Bear Grove, Guthrie....... W	75
● Beaver, Boone............C	40
● *Buck's*, Lee..............SE	×
● Beckwith, Jefferson.....SE	65
● **Bedford**, Taylor...... SW	1,643
Beebeetown, Harrison.....W	100
Beetrace, Appanoose.......S	×
● Belfast, Lee..............SE	75
Belgrove, Butler............N	×
Belinda, Lucas..............S	40
● Belknap, Davis............S	150
● Bell, Crawford............W	25
Bell Air, Johnson...........E	×
● Belle Plaine, Benton......E	2,623
Belleville, Jefferson........SE	57
● Bellevue, Jackson......... E	1,394
● Belmond, Wright..........N	803
● *Belmont Junc.*, Wright...N	×
● Beloit, Lyon.............NW	50
Belvidere, Monona......... W	100
Benan, Carroll.............. W	×
Benbow, Lee..............SE	×
● Bennett, Cedar.......... ...E	1,000
Bennettville, Dubuque... ..E	×
Benton, Mills............. SW	×
● Benton, Ringgold...........S	25
Benton City, Benton.........E	×
● Bentonsport, Van Buren SE	283
Benton Stat'n, (see Garrison).	×
● Bentonville, Wayne.......S	×
Bergen, Allamakee........NE	65
● Berkley, Boone........... C	40
● Berlin, Tama..............C	50
● Bernard, Dubuque.........E	85
● Bertram, Linn.............E	200
● Berwick, Polk.............C	15
● *Bethany Junc.*, Decatur.. S	50
Bethel City, Marion.........S	165
Bethlehem, Wayne...........S	75
● Beulah, Clayton..........NE	25
● *Beverly*, Linn.............E	×
● Bevington, Madison........S	175
● Bidwell, Wapello...........S	×
Big Mound, Lee.............SE	26
● Big Rock, Scott.............E	150
Big Spring, Wayne...........S	25
● Bingham, Page.......... SW	35
Birdwell, Wapello...........S	×
Binns, Page................SW	×
● Birmingham, VanBuren SE	545
● Bismarck, Clayton......NE	65
Blackmore, Ringgold.........S	10
Bladensburg, Wapello........S	100
Blaine, Buena Vista...... NW	19
● Blairsburgh, Hamilton.... C	100
● Blairstown, Benton........E	583
● Blakesburgh, Wapello......S	250
Blakeville, Black Hawk.....C	32
● Blanchard, Page........ SW	432
● Blencoe, Monona..........W	200
● Blockly, Decatur............S	100
● Blockton, Taylor.........SW	400
● **Bloomfield**, Davis.........S	1,913
● *Bloomfield Junction*, Davis S	×
● *Blue Grass*, Muscatine....E	×
Blue Grass, Scott.............E	250
Bluff Creek, Monroe......... S	25
Bluff Park, Lee............ SE	×
● *Bluffsiding*, Lee.......... SE	×
Bluffton, Winneshiek..... NE	125
● Bode, Humboldt............N	400
Bois D'Arc, Black Hawk....C	×
● Bolan, Worth...............N	40
Boltonville, Iowa.............E	×
Bon Accord, Johnson.......E	**57**
● Bonair, Howard.........NE	30
● Bonaparte, VanBuren...SE	762
● Bondurant, Polk...........C	25
● **Boone**, Boone...........C	6,520
Boonesborough, Boone......C	2,000
● Booneville, Dallas..........C	250
● Border Plains, Webster... C	20
Botna, Shelby............. W	35
● Bouton, Dallas.............C	25
Bovina, Tama...............C	×
Bowen, Jones............... E	145
Boxelder, Mills........... SW	×
Boxholm, Boone............ C	150
● Boyd, Chickasaw........NE	50
● Boyden, Sioux..........NW	277
Boyleston, Henry..........SE	18
● Braddyville, Page.........SW	175
Bradford, Chickasaw......NE	100
● Bradgate, Humboldt......N	85
● Brainard, Fayette.......NE	50
Brandon, Buchanan..........E	250
● Brayton, Audubon....... W	124
● Brazil, Appanoose.........S	476
● Breda, Carroll.............W	256
● Bremer, Bremer..........NE	25
● *Bridge*, Wapello............S	×
● *Bridgeport*, Wayne.........S	×
● Bridgewater, Adair..... SW	190
Bridgewater, Clay.........NW	×
● Brighton, Washington...SE	861
Briscoe, Adams...........SW	40
Bristol, Worth...............N	100
● Bristow, Butler............N	257
● Britt, Hancock............ N	818
Brodway, Linn...............E	×
● Bromley, Marshall.........C	100
● *Brompton*, Monroe........S	25
● Brooklyn, Poweshiek...... C	1,202
● Brooks, Adams......... SW	300
Brookville, Jefferson...... SE	75
Brough, Dallas.............. C	57
● Brown, Clinton............E	100
Browning, Carroll..........W	19
Browntown, (see Sherman) ..	×
Brownsville, Poweshiek.....C	83
Brownville, Mitchell........N	100
Bruce, Wright...............N	×
● *Brughier B'ge*, Woodbury. W	×
● *Brush*, Clarke.............S	×
● Brush Creek, Fayette... NE	593
Brushy, Webster............ C	25
● Bryant, Clinton............ E	91
● Bryantburg, Buchanan.... E	50
● Buchanan, Cedar.......... E	25
Buchanan, (see Siam)........	×
Buck Creek, Bremer......NE	20
Buckeye, (see Luzerne).......	×
● Buck Grove, Crawford...W	20
Buckingham, (see Traer).....	×
Buckland, Allamakee.....NE	30
Bucyrus, Lucas............. S	×
Bucyrus, Manaska.......... S	×
● *Buda*, Wayne............. S	50
Buena Vista, Clinton.........E	14
● *Buena Vista*, Lee....... SE	×
● *Buena Vista*, Clayton... NE	70
● Buffalo, Scott............. E	379
Buffalo Centre, Winnebago. N	×
Buffalo Fork, Kossuth..... N	130
Buffalo Grove, Buchanan... E	100
● *Bullards*, Lee.............SE	×
Bunch, Davis.................S	×
Buncombe, Dubuque...........E	35
● Burchinal, Cerro Gordo...N	25
● Burdette, Franklin.........N	25
Burgess, Clinton............E	5
Burk, Benton................E	×
○ **Burlington**, Des Mo's. SE	22,565
● *Burlington Junc.*, D.M's SE	×
● *Burnett*, Linn..............E	50
● Burnside, Webster..........C	50
Burrell, Decatur..............S	10
Burr Oak, Winneshiek....NE	200
Burt, Kossuth................N	200
Business Corners, Van Bu'n SE	50
● Bussey, Marion.............S	300
Bustt, Howard............ NE	57
● Butler, Keokuk.............SE	15
Butler Centre, Butler........N	200
Butlerville, Tama............ C	50
Byron, Humboldt........... N	×
● Cadda, Scott...............E	×
Cairo, Louisa................SE	125
● Calamus, Clinton...........E	216
Caledonia, Ringgold..........S	45
Calhoun, Appanoose......... S	15
Calhoun, Harrison.......... W	150
● California, Harrison.......W	50
Callanan, Hamilton........ C	×
● Callender, Webster........C	125
● Calliope, Sioux......... NW	623
● Calmar, Winneshiek.... NE	813
Caloma, Marion.............. S	50
● Calumet, O'Brien.......NW	50
● Camanche, Clinton.........E	753
● Cambria, Wayne........... S	100
● Cambridge, Story.......... C	432
● *Cameron*, Cerro Gordo....N	×
● *Cameron*, Dubuque...... E	×
Camp, Polk.................C	32

Place		Pop.
●Cainpbell, Polk	C	25
Campton, Delaware	E	×
Canby, Adair	SW	×
Canfield, Black Hawk	C	50
Canton, Jackson	E	200
●Cantril, Van Buren	SE	356
Capron, Marshall	C	15
●*Carbon*, Davis	S	×
Carbon, Adams	SW	200
Carbonado, Mahaska	S	×
●Carbon Junction, Webster	C	×
Cardiff, Mitchell	N	×
Carl, Adams	SW	100
●Carlisle, Warren	S	500
Carlton, (see Popejoy)		×
●Carnarvon, Sac	W	25
●Carnes, Sioux	NW	×
●Carnforth, Poweshiek	C	35
●Carpenter, Mitchell	N	116
●**Carroll**, Carroll	W	2,448
Carrollton, Carroll	W	25
Carrs Point, Montgomery	SW	×
Carrville, Floyd	N	52
●Carson, Pottawattamie	SW	391
Carterville, Mitchell	N	25
●*Casady*, Webster	C	13
●*Cascade*, DesMoines	SE	×
●Cascade, Dubuque	E	955
●Casey, Guthrie	W	452
●Castalia, Winneshiek	NE	200
●Castana, Monona	W	125
Castle Grove, Jones	E	30
Castleville, Buchanan	E	×
●*Cattese*, Dubuque	E	×
Cealville, Webster	C	×
●Cedar, Mahaska	S	20
Cedar Bluff, Cedar	E	150
●Cedar Falls, Black Hawk	C	3,459
Cedar Grove, Lucas	S	×
●Cedar Mines, Monroe	S	100
●**CEDAR RAPIDS**, Linn	E	18,020
Cedar Valley, Cedar	E	15
Cedar Valley Lime Kilns, Cedar	E	×
●Centerdale, Cedar	E	15
●**Centerville**, Appanoose	S	3,668
Central City, Linn	E	467
Centralia, Dubuque	E	40
Centre, Page	SW	×
●Centre Grove, Dubuque	E	16
●Centre Junction, Jones	E	210
●Centre Point, Linn	E	615
Ceres, Clayton	NE	65
Chancy, Clinton	E	1,039
●Chapin, Franklin	N	200
●**Chariton**, Lucas	S	3,122
●**Charles City**, Floyd	N	2,802
●Charleston, Lee	SE	150
●Charlotte, Clinton	E	231
●Charter Oak, Crawford	W	567
Chase, Johnson	E	13
●Chatsworth, Sioux	NW	×
●*Chautauqua*, Pot'wt'a'les	SW	×
●Chelsea, Tama	C	318
Chequest, Davis	S	15
●**Cherokee**, Cherokee	NW	3,441
●Chester, Howard	NE	50
Chester Centre, Poweshiek	C	50
Chesterfield, Polk	C	130
●Chickasaw, Chickasaw	NE	200
●*Chickasaw Siding*, Floyd	N	×
●Chillicothe, Wapello	S	214
●Chisholm, Monroe	S	20
●Churchville, Warren	S	100
●Churdan, Greene	C	377
●Cincinnati, Appanoose	S	432
Civil Point, Audubon	W	13
Clanton, Madison	S	32
●Clare, Webster	C	200
●Clarence, Cedar	E	629
Clarendon, (see Galva)		×
●**Clarinda**, Page	SW	3,262
●*Clarinda Junc.*, Mont'gy	SW	×
●**Clarion**, Wright	N	744
Clark, Clay	NW	×
●*Clark*, Mills	SW	×
●Clarkson, Warren	S	30
●Clarksville, Butler	N	735
●Clay, Washington	SE	200
Clayford, Jones	E	×
Clay Mills, Jones	E	40
Clay's Grove, Lee	SE	40
●Clayton, Clayton	NE	400
Clayton Centre, Clayton	NE	150
Clear Creek, Allamakee	NE	×
●Clearfield, Taylor	SW	452
Clearfield, Poweshiek	C	×

Iowa

Place		Pop.
●Clear Lake, Cerro Gordo	N	1,130
Cleghorn, Cherokee	NW	60
●*Cleghorn*, Plymouth	NW	×
●Clemons, Marshall	C	100
●Clermont, Fayette	NE	488
●*Cleveland*, Lucas	S	807
●Cleves, Hardin	C	50
●*Cliffland*, Wapello	S	×
Clifton, (see Cotter)		×
Climax, Montgomery	SW	10
Climbing Hill, Woodbury	W	50
●**Clinton**, Clinton	E	13,619
●Clio, Wayne	S	100
Clipper, Ringgold	S	25
●Clive, Polk	C	×
Cloud, Marion	S	10
Clutterville, Butler	N	×
Clyde, Jasper	C	50
Coal Creek, Keokuk	SE	50
●Coalfield, Monroe	S	200
●*Coalport*, Jefferson	SE	×
●*Coal Siding*, Jasper	C	×
●*Coal Siding*, Dallas	C	×
Coalton, Monroe	S	×
●Coalville, Webster	C	75
●Coburgh, Montgomery	SW	60
●Coggon, Linn	E	200
●Coin, Page	SW	425
Coldwater, Cerro Gordo	N	25
Coldville, Tama	C	×
Colesburgh, Delaware	E	400
●Colfax, Jasper	C	957
College Springs, Page	SW	491
○Collett, Jefferson	SE	25
●Collins, Story	C	250
●Colo, Story	C	261
Columbia, Marion	S	100
Columbus City, Louisa	SE	459
●Columbus Junc., Louisa	SE	935
●Commerce, Polk	C	150
Communia, Clayton	NE	20
Competine, Wapello	S	50
Concord, Hancock	N	130
Condit, Jones	E	×
●Conesville, Muscatine	E	300
Confidence, Wayne	S	50
Conger, (see Revington)		×
Conger, Wayne	S	×
Conkling, Audubon	W	×
●*Connables*, Lee	SE	×
Connell, Tama	C	×
●Conover, Winneshiek	NE	165
●Conrad Grove, Grundy	C	157
●Conroy, Iowa	E	12
●Conwa, Taylor	SW	379
●*ConwayCrossing*, Ta'l'rs	SW	×
Cool, Warren	S	30
Coon Creek, Crawford	W	×
●Coon Rapids, Carroll	W	73
●*Coon Siding*, Greene	C	×
●Cooper, Greene	C	35
Cooperville, Wapello	S	×
Copher, Osceola	NW	×
●Coppock, Henry	SE	52
Coralville, Johnson	E	173
●Cordova, Marion	S	×
●Corley, Shelby	W	25
●**Corning**, Adams	SW	1,682
Corn Valley, Sioux	NW	×
●Correctionville, W'db'ry	W	1,869
●Corwith, Hancock	N	334
Cory, Keokuk	SE	500
●**Corydon**, Wayne	S	962
Cosgrove, Johnson	E	25
Coster, Butler	N	50
Cottage, Hardin	C	30
Cottage Grove, Polk	C	×
Cottage Hill, Dubuque	E	50
Cotter, Louisa	SE	50
Cotton Grove, Henry	SE	32
Cottonville, Jackson	E	50
●Cottonwood, Lee	SE	25
Coulson, Cherokee	NW	×
COUNCIL BLUFFS, Pottawattamie	SW	21,474
Council Hill, Clayton	NE	×
County Line, Hamilton	C	×
●County Line, Jefferson	SE	40
●Covington, Linn	E	50
Crabb, Jackson	E	40
Crab Apple, Linn	E	×
Crathorne, Plymouth	NW	25
Crawford, Woodbury	W	×
●Crawfordsville, W's'gt'n	SE	300
Creamery, Cerro Gordo	N	×
Cream Hill, (see Hampton)		×
Creek, Dallas	C	×
Crescent, Pottawattamie	SW	200

Iowa

Place		Pop.
●**Cresco**, Howard	NE	2,018
●Creston, Union	S	7,200
Creswell, Keokuk	SE	×
●*Crippen*, Palo Alto	NW	×
●Crocker, Polk	C	50
●Cromwell, Union	S	269
Cromwell Centre, Clay	NW	×
●*Crosby*, Fremont	SW	×
●Croton, Lee	SE	96
Crowfoot, Buchanan	E	10
●Crown, Decatur	S	13
Crozier, Buena Vista	NW	18
Crystal, **Tama**	C	100
Crystal Lake, Hancock	N	×
●*Cuba*, Keokuk	SE	50
●Cumberland, Cass	SW	450
●Cumming, Warren	S	35
Cupid, Winneshiek	NE	×
●Curlew, Palo Alto	NW	50
●Cushing, Woodbury	W	150
○Cylinder, Palo Alton	NW	30
Dahlonego, Wapello	S	300
Dairy, Washington	SE	×
Dairyville, Grundy	C	25
●**Dakotah**, Humboldt	N	353
Dalby, Allamakee	NE	×
Dale, Guthrie	W	100
●*Dale*, Scott	E	×
Dallas, Marion	S	100
●Dallas Centre, Dallas	C	445
●Dalton, Plymouth	NW	×
●Dana, Greene	C	40
●Danbury, Woodbury	W	423
Danforth, Johnson	E	57
●Danville, Des Moines	SE	300
●*Darby*, Appanoose	S	×
Darbyville, Appanoose	S	×
Darwin, Page	SW	×
Dasie, Page	SW	×
●**Davenport**, Scott	E	26,872
David, Mitchell	N	×
●Davis City, Decatur	S	594
Davis Corners, Howard	NE	×
●Dawson, Dallas	C	25
Dawson, Jasper	C	×
●Dayton, Webster	C	669
Daytonville, (see Wellman)		×
●Dean, Appanoose	S	30
●Decatur, Decatur	S	215
●**Decorah**, Winneshiek	NE	801
●Dedham, Carroll	W	273
●Deep River, Poweshiek	C	291
Deer Creek, Worth	N	×
Deerfield, Chickasaw	NE	65
Deering, Winnebago	N	×
●Defiance, Shelby	W	323
●DeKalb, Decatur	S	15
Delano, Winnebago	N	×
●Delaware, Delaware	E	400
De Leon, Cherokee	NW	30
●Delhi, Delaware	E	400
●Delmar, Clinton	E	518
Deloit, Crawford	W	200
●Delphos, Ringgold	S	75
●Delta, Keokuk	SE	409
●**Denison**, Crawford	W	1,182
Denmark, Lee	SE	300
●*Dennis*, Appanoose	S	20
●Denova, Henry	SE	25
Denver, Bremer	NE	200
●Derby, Lucas	S	200
Derrinane, Dubuque	E	×
Derrough, Warren	S	×
●**DES MOINES**, Polk	C	50,093
●De Soto, Dallas	C	328
●Devon, Chickasaw	NE	×
●Dewar, Black Hawk	C	25
●De Witt, Clinton	E	1,359
●Dexter, Dallas	C	607
●Diagonal, Ringgold	S	100
Diamond, Appanoose	S	×
●Dickens, Clay	NW	50
Dickey, Bremer	NE	20
●Diff, Appanoose	S	12
●Dillon, Marshall	C	125
●Dinsdale Tama	C	20
●*Dixie*, Jasper	C	×
●Dixon, Scott	E	250
Dodgeville, Des Moines	SE	25
Dolliver, Emmet	NW	×
●Donahue, Scott	E	40
●Donnan, Fayette	NE	×
Donnan Junc., Fayette	NE	×
●Donnellson, Lee	SE	200
●*Donnelly*, Marion	S	×
●Doon, Lyon	NW	200
Doran, Mitchell	N	32
Dorchester, Allamakee	NE	100

● *Doubleday*, Floyd........N ×
● Doud's Station, V. Buren SE 150
Douglass, Fayette........NE 300
Dover, (see Ionia)........ ×
Dover, Lee........SE 40
Dover Mills, Fayette......NE ×
● Dow City, Crawford......W 451
● Downey, Cedar........E 100
Downersville, Jones........E ×
Downsville, (see Weston)..... ×
● Dows, Wright........N 600
● Drakesville, Davis........S 803
Draper, Jasper........C 15
Dresden, Chickasaw.......NE ×
● *Druid Station*, Hamilton. C ×
Dry Creek, Linn........E ×
Dryden, Tama........C ×
Dry Lake, Wright........N ×
Dublin, Washington........SE 75
● **DUBUQUE**, Dubuque..E 30,311
● *Dubuque Shops*, Dubuque E ×
● Dudley, Wapello........S 50
Duke, Dubuque........E 32
● Dumont, Butler........N 200
● Dunbar, Marshall........C 40
Duncan, Hancock........N ×
● Duncombe, Webster......C 200
● Dundee, Delaware........E 50
● Dunkerton, Black Hawk..C 100
● Dunlap, Harrison........W 1,088
● Dunreath, Marion........S 200
● Durango, Dubuque........E 50
● Durant, Cedar........E 505
● Durham, Marion........S 100
● Dyersville, Dubuque......E 1,272
● Dysart, Tama........C 775
● *Eads*, Calhoun........W 19
Edenville, Marshall........C ×
Eagle Centre, Black Hawk..C 50
Eagle City, Hardin........C ×
● Eagle Grove, Wright.....N 1,881
● *Eagle Point*, Dubuque....E ×
● Earlham, Madison........S 302
● Earling, Shelby........W 400
● Earlville, Delaware.......E 569
● Early, Sac........W 277
Earnest, Lyon........NW ×
● *East Clayton*, Clayton.. NE ×
● *East Cleveland*, Lucas.... S 950
● *East Creston*, Union........S ×
● *East Des Moines*, Polk... C ×
East Elkport, Clayton.....NE 250
East Melrose, (see Melrose).. ×
● East Nodoway, Adams..SW 260
East Peru, Madison........S 125
East Orange, Sioux.....NW ×
East Ottumwa, Wapello.... S ×
Eastport, Fremont........SW 195
● *East Rapids*, Linn........E ×
East Side, Polk........C ×
Eatonville, (see Chester)..... ×
● *Eckards*, Clayton.......NE ×
● Eddyville, Wapello........S 815
Eden, Fayette........NE 100
● Edgewood, Clayton..... NE 350
● *Edmore*, Dubuque........E ×
Edna, Lyon........NW ×
Edwards, Black Hawk......C ×
● Ehler, Delaware........E 14
● Elberon, Tama........C 150
Elcho, O'Brien........NW ×
● Eldon, Wapello........S 1,72[illegible]
● **Eldora**, Hardin........C 1,577
● **Eldora Junction, Hardin**..C ×
El Dorado, Fayette........NE 175
● Eldridge, Scott........E 125
● Elgin, Fayette........NE 369
Elida, (see Knoxville)....... ×
Elizabeth, Grundy........C ×
● **Elkader**, Clayton..... NE 745
Elk Creek, Worth........N ×
Elkhart, Polk........C 10
Elk Horn, Shelby........W 75
● Elkport, Clayton........NE 500
Elk River, (see Almont)...... ×
● *Elk River Junc.*, Clinton..E ×
Elk Run, Sac........W ×
Elkton, Buena Vista..... NW ×
Ellington, Hancock........N 60
● Elliott, Montgomery....SW 317
Elliott, (see Ladoga)........ ×
Ellis, Hardin........C 10
● Ellsworth, Hamilton......C 200
● Elma, Howard........NE 1,100
Elingrove, Calhoun........W 150
● *Elmira*, Johnson........E 195
● *Elmira Junc.*, Johnson...E ×

Elmo, Hancock........N ×
Elmont, Linn........E 20
Elm Springs, (see Green..... ×
Elon, Allamakee........NE 25
● Elrick, Louisa........SE 4
Elvira, Clinton........E 31
● Elwell, Story........C 50
● Elwood, Clinton........E 180
● Ely, Linn........E 300
Emeline, Jackson........E 35
● Emerson, Mills........SW 404
Emert, Black Hawk........C 25
● **Emmetsburgh**, Palo Alto NW 1,584
Empire, Wright........N ×
Enfield, (see Strawberry Pt.). ×
Enterprise, Black Hawk....C ×
Ephesus, Dallas........C 25
● Epworth, Dubuque....... E 348
Erastus, Guthrie........W ×
Ernie, Floyd........N ×
● *Essen*, Hancock........N ×
● Essex, Page........SW 564
● **Estherville**, Emmet. NW 1,475
Eugene, (see Tingley)........ ×
Eureka, Adams........SW 25
Eureka (see Haven)........ ×
Evans, Mahaska........S 609
● Evanston, Webster........C ×
Eveland, Mahaska........S 10
Evergreen, Tama........C ×
● Everly, Clay........NW 500
● Ewart, Poweshiek........C 150
● *Excelsior*, Mahaska........S 700
● Exira, Audubon........W 575
● Exline, Appanoose........S 76
Factoryville, Dubuque........E ×
● Fairbank, Buchanan......E 448
● Fairfax, Linn........E 250
● **Fairfield**, Jefferson... SE 3,391
● *Fair Ground*, Dubuque...E ×
Fairhaven, Tama........C 26
● Fairmount, Jasper........C 19
● Fairport, Muscatine.......E 200
Fairview, Jones........E 175
Fairwill, Palo Alto....... NW 25
Fanslers, Guthrie........W 40
● Farley, Dubuque........E 582
● Farlin, Greene........C 7
Farmer City, Fremont....SW 26
Farmers, Sioux........NW ×
● Farmersburg, Clayton.. NE 100
Farmer's Creek, Jackson....E ×
Farmersville, (see Metz)...... ×
● Farmington, Van Buren.SE 1,002
● Farnhamville, Calhoun...W 137
● Farragut, Fremont..... SW 406
● Faulkner, Franklin...... N 50
● Fayette, Fayette........ NE 1,062
Felix, Warren........S 45
Fenton, Kossuth........N 50
● Ferguson, Marshall....... C 150
Ferry, Mahaska........S 32
● *Ferry Switch*, Woodbury W ×
Fertile, Worth........N 100
Festina, Winneshiek...... NE [illegible]
Fielding, Cherokee........NW ×
Fierce, Decatur........S ×
● Fifield, Marion........S 10
Fifteen Mile, Tama........C 40
● Fillmore, Dubuque........ E 30
Finchford, Black Hawk.....C 50
Fiscus, Audubon........W 10
Fisk, Adair........SW ×
● *Fishville*, Mahaska........S ×
● Flagler's, Marion........S 500
Flemingville, Linn........E 20
Flint, Mahaska........S ×
Florenceville, Howard.... NE 50
● Floris, Davis........S 200
● Floyd, Floyd........N 400
● *Floyd Crossing*, Floyd....N ×
Floyd Valley, (see Le Mars). ×
Flugstad, Hamilton........C ×
● Folletts, Clinton........E 40
● Folsom, Mills........SW 25
● Fonda, Pocahontas.....NW 625
● Fontanelle, Adair.......SW 830
Foote, Iowa........E 50
Forbush, Appanoose........S ×
● Ford, Warren........S 50
Forest City, Winnebago..N 895
Forest Home, Poweshiek....C 50
Forest Mills, Allamakee...NE 20
Forestville, Delaware....... E 60
Forsyth, Palo Alto........NW ×
● Fort Atkinson, Win'iek NW 480

● **Fort Dodge**, Webster.. C 4,871
● *Fort Dodge Junc.*, Webster C ×
● **Fort Madison**, Lee...SE 7,901
Foster, Madison........S ×
● Foster, Monroe........S 30
Four Corners, Jefferson... SE 25
Fox, Iowa........E ×
Franklin, Decatur........S ×
● *Franklin*, Jasper........C ×
Franklin, Lee........SE 333
Franklin Mills, Des Moines SE ×
● Franklin Station, Lee....SE 400
Frank Pierce, Johnson......E 32
Frankville, Winneshiek...NE 150
Frederica, Bremer........NE 125
● Fredericksburgh, Ch'saw NE 321
● Fredonia, Louisa........SE 250
Fredric, Monroe........S 150
Fredsville, Grundy........C ×
Freedom, Lucas........S 10
Freeman, Cerro Gordo..... N ×
Freeport, Winneshiek......NE 200
● Fremont, Mahaska........S 500
French Creek, Allamakee. NE 20
● Froelich, Clayton....... NE 30
● Fruitland, Muscatine...... E 32
Fryburg, (see Rowan)........ ×
Frytown, (see Frank Pierce) ×
Fulton, Jackson........E 150
Fulton, (see Stockton)....... ×
Funk's Mills, (see Decatur C'y) ×
● Gainford, Mahaska........S 26
Gale, Woodbury........W ×
Galesburgh, Jasper........C 100
Gallon, Cass........SW 10
● Galland, Lee........SE 150
● Galt, Wright........N 100
● Galva, Ida........W 150
● **Galvin, Marshall**........C 25
Gambril, Scott........E 25
Garden, Boone........C ×
Garden Grove, Decatur..... S 554
● *Garfield*, Appanoose... S 12
Garley, Cass........SW ×
Garnavillo, Clayton....... NE 450
● Garner, Hancock........N 679
● Garrison, Benton........E 367
Garry Owen, Jackson.......E 50
Garvey, Pocahontas...... NW ×
● Garwin, Tama........C 150
Gatesville, Buchanan........E 25
● Gaza, O'Brien........NW 50
Gear, Madison........S ×
Gem, Clayton........NE ×
Geneseo, (see Rockwell)...... ×
Geneseo, Tama........C ×
● Geneva, Franklin........N 300
Genoa, Wayne........N 70
Genoa Bluff, Iowa........E 35
● George, Lyon........NW 250
Georgetown, (see Pin Oak)... ×
Georgetown, Monroe........S 25
German, Hancock........N ×
German City, Woodbury... W 40
German Valley, Kossuth....N ×
Germanville, Jefferson.... SE 35
Gessford, Cedar........E ×
● Girard, Clayton........NE 100
● Gifford, Hardin........C 175
● Gilbert, Scott........E 150
● Gilbert Station, Story..... C 80
Gilbertville, Black Hawk... C 500
Gillespie, Benton........E 12
Gillett, Clay........NW ×
● Gilman, Marshall........C 473
● Gilmore City, Pocah'tas NW 550
Gilpin, Madison........S 13
● Given, Mahaska........S 100
● Gladbrook, Tama........C 556
● Gladstone, Tama........C 50
Glasgow, Jefferson........SE 100
● Glendale, Jefferson........SE 40
● Glendon, Guthrie........W 100
● Glen Ellen, Woodbury... W ×
Glenroy, (see Lime Springs).. ×
● **Glenwood**, Mills......SW 1,890
● Glidden, Carroll........W 5[illegible]
● Golden, Delaware........E 60
● Goldfield, Wright........N 343
● Goodell, Hancock........N 130
● Goose Lake, Clinton......E 42
Gopher, Osceola........NW ×
● Gordon's Ferry, Jackson,.E ×
● *Goshen*, Ringgold........S 227
Gosport, Marion........S 50
● Gowrie, Webster........C 526
Grace Hill, Washington....SE 40

Place	Dir.	Pop.
Graceville, Guthrie	W	×
● Graettinger, Palo Alto	NW	100
● *Graf*, Dubuque	E	55
● Grafton, Worth	N	200
● *Graham*, Johnson	E	×
Grainville, (see Howard)		×
● Grand Junction, Greene	C	932
● Grand Mound, Clinton	E	247
● Grand River, Decatur	S	300
Grand View, Louisa	SE	450
● Granger, Dallas	C	18
● Granite, Lyon	NW	×
Grant, Montgomery	SW	100
● Grant Centre, Monona	W	×
Grant City, Sac	W	300
Granville, Mahaska	S	×
● Granville, Sioux	NW	300
● Gravity, Taylor	SW	210
● Gray, Audubon	W	110
● *Grayson*, Boone	C	×
● *Greasers*, Benton	E	×
Great Oak, Palo Alto	NW	×
● Greeley, Delaware	E	300
Greenbay, Clarke	S	×
Greencastle, Jasper	C	125
Green Centre, Iowa	E	50
● Greene, Butler	N	845
● **Greenfield**, Adair	SW	1,048
● Green Island, Jackson	E	123
● Green Mountain, Marshall	C	50
Green Tree, Scott	E	25
Greenvale, Dallas	C	×
Green Valley, Decatur	S	×
Greenville, Clay	NW	150
Greenville, Lucas	S	×
Greenwood, Chickasaw	NE	50
Greenwood Centre, Kos'th	N	×
Gregg, Johnson	E	19
Gresham, Black Hawk	C	19
Gri[?]nsville, Appanoose	S	12
● Grimes, Polk	C	100
● Grinnell, Poweshiek	C	3,332
● *Grinnell and Montezuma Junction*, Poweshiek	C	×
● Griswold, Cass	SW	752
Grosvenor, (see Granger)		×
Grove, Audubon	W	×
Grove, Humboldt	N	×
Grove City, Cass	SW	×
Grove Creek, Delaware	E	×
Grove Creek, (see Uniontown)		×
Grove Hill, Bremer	NE	×
● Groveland, Clarke	S	20
● **Grundy Centre**, Grundy	C	1,161
● Guernsey, Poweshiek	C	100
Guss, Taylor	SW	20
● **Guthrie Centre**, Gut'le	W	1,037
● Guttenburg, Clayton	NE	1,160
● *Hagerty*, Monroe	S	×
● Halbur, Carroll	W	80
● Hale, Jones	E	75
Hall, Davis	S	19
● Hamburgh, Fremont	SW	1,634
● *Hamill*, Lee	SE	64
● Hamilton, Marion	S	250
● Hamlin, Audubon	W	×
● **Hampton**, Franklin	N	2,067
● Hancock, Pottawat'mie	SW	167
● *Haney's*, Mills	SW	×
● Hanley, Madison	S	25
● *Hanna*, Kossuth	N	×
Hanover, Allamakee	NE	×
Hanover, Buena Vista	NW	×
● Hansell, Franklin	N	169
Happy Hollow, Wapello	S	×
● Harcourt, Webster	C	50
Hardin, Clayton	NE	200
● *Harding*, Polk	C	×
Harding, (see Pleasanton)		×
Hardy, Humboldt	N	75
● **Harlan**, Shelby	W	1,765
Harlan Junction, Pot'w't'e	SW	×
● Harper, Keokuk	SE	253
● Harper's Ferry, A'm'k'e	NE	150
● Harris, Osceola	NW	20
Hartford, Warren	S	300
Hartland, Marshall	C	×
Hartland, Worth	N	×
● Hartley, O'Brien	NW	519
Hartwick, Delaware	E	×
● Hartwick, Poweshiek	C	108
● Harvard, Wayne	S	150
● Harvey, Marion	S	150
● *Hastie*, Polk	C	×
● Hastings, Mills	SW	322
Hatch, Kossuth	N	×
Hauntown, (see Elk River)		×
● Havelock, Pocahontas	NW	225

Place	Dir.	Pop.
Haven, Tama	C	200
● Haverhill, Marshall	C	80
● **Havre, Washington**	SE	25
● Hawarden, Sioux	NW	744
● Hawk Eye, Fayette	NE	250
Hawleyville, Page	SW	100
● Hawthorn, Montgomery	SW	75
Hayes, Adams	SW	13
● Hayesville, Keokuk	SE	75
● Hayfield, Hancock	N	50
Hay Siding, Clay	NW	×
Hazard, (see Meriden)		×
Hazel, Dubuque	E	×
Hazel Green, Delaware	E	40
● Hazelton, Buchanan	E	500
Hebron, Adair	SW	200
Hedge, Iowa	E	×
● *Hedges Siding*, Woodbury	W	×
● Hedrick, Keokuk	SE	592
Helena, Tama	C	100
Hempstead, (see Fillmore)		×
● Henderson, Mills	SW	201
Henkeltown, (see Foote)		×
● *Henton's*, Mills	SW	25
● Hepburn, Page	SW	75
Herdland, Clay	NW	×
● Herndon, Guthrie	W	150
Hesper, Winneshiek	NE	300
● *Heytmans*, Allamakee	NE	×
Hibbsville, Appanoose	S	50
● Hickory, Monroe	S	40
Hickory Grove, Jackson	E	×
Higginsport, Jackson	E	×
● *High Bridge*, Dallas	C	×
Highbrier, Decatur	S	×
High Creek, Fremont	SW	×
High Lake, Emmet	NW	20
Highland, Clayton	NE	×
Highland Centre, Wapello	S	25
Highland Grove, Jones	E	×
Highlandville, Winneshiek	NE	50
High Point, Decatur	S	30
● Highview, Hamilton	C	×
● Hillsboro, Henry	SE	200
● Hillsdale, Mills	SW	193
● Hill's Sid'ng, Johnson	E	×
● Hilton, Monroe	S	80
● *Hinsdale*, Lee	SE	25
● Hinton, Plymouth	NW	100
Hirondelle, Worth	N	×
Hiteman, Monroe	S	×
Hitesville, Butler	N	25
● *Hobart*, Kossuth	N	×
Hodge, Wayne	S	25
Hohenzollern, Crawford	W	×
Holaday's, Adair	SW	×
Holbrook, Iowa	E	40
● Holland, Grundy	C	200
Holly Springs, Woodbury	W	75
● Holmes, Wright	N	20
● Holstein, Ida	W	539
Holt, Taylor	SW	100
Homan, Tama	C	×
Home, VanBuren	SE	×
Homer, Hamilton	C	100
● Homestead, Iowa	E	450
Honey Creek, P'ttaw't'mie	SW	25
Hopewell, Mahaska	S	×
Hopeville, Clarke	S	400
● Hopkinton, Delaware	E	668
Hoprig, Emmet	NW	×
Horace, Audubon	W	×
Horn, Jasper	C	×
● Hornick, Woodbury	W	50
Horton, Bremer	NE	75
Hoskins, Woodbury	W	×
● Hosper, Sioux	NW	200
● *Hotel Orleans*, Dick'son	NW	65
● Houghton, Lee	SE	20
Howard, Tama	C	×
Howard Centre, Howard	NE	×
● *Howell*, Marion	S	×
Hoyt, Adams	SW	×
● Hubbard, Hardin	C	452
● Hudson, Black Hawk	C	200
● Hughes, Hardin	C	×
● Hull, Sioux	NW	566
Hull, Boone	C	×
● Humboldt, Humboldt	N	1,075
● Humeston, Wayne	S	642
Hummaconna, Monroe	S	32
Hunters, Dickinson	NW	×
Huron, Des Moines	SE	40
Husam, Scott	E	×
● Hutchins, Hancock	N	10
● Huxley, Story	C	100
Hyde, Winneshiek	NE	13
Iconium, Appanoose	S	111

Place	Dir.	Pop.
● **Ida Grove**, Ida	W	1,563
Idaho, Hardin	C	32
Idlewild, Buchanan	E	×
Illyria, Fayette	NE	25
● Imogene, Fremont	SW	279
● **Independence**, B'ch'an	E	3,163
Indianapolis, Mahaska	S	300
● **Indianola**, Warren	S	2,254
● *Indianola Junc.*, Lucas	S	×
Ingart, Ringgold	S	65
● *Ingersoll*, Dallas	C	×
Inham, Franklin	N	×
● Inwood, Lyon	NW	300
Ioka, Keokuk	SE	125
Ion, Allamakee	NE	100
Ionia, Chickasaw	NE	300
● *Iona Station*, Chickasaw	NE	×
Iowa Centre, Story	C	300
● **Iowa City**, Johnson	E	7,016
● Iowa Falls, Hardin	C	1,796
● *Iowa Junc.*, Washington	SE	×
Iowa Lake, Emmet	NW	×
● *Iowa River*, Johnson	E	40
● Ira, Jasper	C	20
● Ireton, Sioux	NW	412
Iron Hills, Jackson	E	75
Irving, Benton	C	100
● Irvington, Kossuth	N	30
● Irwin, Shelby	W	500
Isabel, Jones	E	×
● *Isabel Park*, Pot'wat'les	W	×
Isted, Winneshiek	NE	×
Iveyville, Adams	SW	35
Ivy, Polk	C	32
Jackson, Adair	SW	32
Jackson Centre, Webster	C	×
● Jackson Junc., Winnes'k	NE	25
Jacksonville, Chickasaw	NE	65
Jacksonville, Clarke	S	10
● *Jacob Siding*, Black H'wk	C	×
● Jamaica, Guthrie	W	200
● James, Plymouth	NW	30
Jamestown, Scott	E	50
● Jamison, Clarke	S	50
● Janesville, Bremer	NE	300
Jasper City, (see Kellogg)		×
Jay, Clarke	S	10
Jeddo City, (see Logan)		×
● **Jefferson**, Greene	C	[illegible],875
Jeffriesville, Clayton	NE	50
Jerico, Chickasaw	NE	×
● Jerome, Appanoose	S	30
● Jesup, Buchanan	E	573
● Jewell, Hamilton	C	414
Jewell Junc., (see Jewell)		×
Jobes, Audubon	W	×
Johnson, Jones	E	×
Johnson's Mills, (see Alpha)		×
● Jolley, Calhoun	W	100
Jubilee, Black Hawk	C	25
● Judd, Webster	C	25
● *Julien*, Dubuque	E	×
● *Junction*, Cedar	E	×
● ***Junction*, Fayette**	NE	×
● *Junction Switch*, Jones	E	×
● *Kain*, Allamakee	NE	×
● Kalo, Webster	C	400
● *Kalo Junction*, Webster	C	×
● Kalona, Washington	SE	211
● Kamrar, Hamilton	C	60
Kasson, Madison	S	50
● Keb, Wapello	S	×
● Kellerton, Ringgold	S	277
● Kelley, Story	C	65
● Kellogg, Jasper	C	700
● *Kelsey*, Dallas	C	25
Kelsy, Polk	C	25
Kendallville, Winneshiek	NE	100
● *Kennebec*, Monona	W	×
● Kennedy, Dallas	C	10
● Kensett, Worth	N	120
● Kent, Union	S	120
Kentner, Carroll	W	×
● Kenwood, Crawford	W	8
Kenwood Park, Linn		136
● **KEOKUK**, Lee	SE	14,101
● **Keosauqua**, Van Bu'n	SE	831
● Keota, Keokuk	SE	777
Kerr, Scott	E	×
● Keswick, Keokuk	SE	300
● *Ketchams*, Henry	SE	20
● *Kew*, Ringgold	S	32
Key, Bremer	NE	25
● Keystone, Benton	E	200
Key West, Dubuque	E	50
● *Kidder*, Dubuque	E	×
Kier, Buchanan	E	×
● Kilbourn, VanBuren	SE	75

Iowa		
● Kilduff, Jasper	C	50
Kimballton, Audubon	W	50
King, Dubuque	E	32
Kingsbury, Grundy	C	32
● Kingsley, Plymouth	NW	649
● *Kingston*, Decatur	S	×
Kingston, DesMoines	SE	100
● Kinross, Keokuk	SE	200
● Kirkman, Shelby	W	200
Kirkville, Wapello	S	714
● *Kirkville Station*, Wapello	S	×
Kirkwood, Appanoose	S	×
Kiron, Crawford	W	25
Kissimmee, Calhoun	W	×
● Klemme, Hancock	N	50
Klinger, Bremer	NE	×
● Kniffin, Wayne	S	8
Knittel, Bremer	NE	25
● Knowlton, Ringgold	S	300
Knox, Fremont	SW	40
● **Knoxville**, Marion	S	2,632
Kossuth, DesMoines	SE	300
Kossuth Centre, Kossuth	N	65
Koszta, Iowa	E	100
● *Krum*, Jefferson	SE	×
Lacelle, Clarke	S	20
● Lacey, Mahaska	S	50
● Lacona, Warren	S	301
● LaCrew, Lee	SE	30
● Laddsdale, Davis	S	50
● Ladoga, Taylor	SW	10
● Ladora, Iowa	E	224
Lafayette, Linn	E	50
Lagrange, Lucas	S	×
● LaHoyt, Henry	SE	20
● *Lainesville*, Jackson	E	×
Lake Centre, Hamilton	C	19
● Lake City, Calhoun	W	1,160
Lakin's Grove, Hamilton	C	×
Lake Manawa, Pot'watt'e	SW	×
● Lake Mills, Winnebago	N	604
● *Lake Okoboji*, Dick'son	NW	100
Lake Park, Dickinson	NW	225
Lakeport, Woodbury	W	×
Lakeside, Emmet	NW	×
● Lake View, Sac	W	366
● Lamoille, Marshall	C	200
● Lamoni, Decatur	S	800
● Lamont, Buchanan	E	250
● LaMotte, Jackson	E	154
Lancaster, Keokuk	SE	300
Langfitt, Dallas	C	×
● Langworthy, Jones	E	150
● Lansing, Allamakee	NE	1,668
Lapage, Dubuque	E	×
● Laporte City, Black Hawk	C	1,052
Laporte, Clarke	S	×
● Larchwood, Lyon	NW	200
Lark, Worth	N	×
Larland, Audubon	W	×
● Larrabee, Cherokee	NW	100
Last Chance, Lucas	S	57
Latham, Webster	C	×
● Latimer, Franklin	N	70
Latrobe, Story	C	×
● Lattner's, Dubuque	E	55
● Latty, DesMoines	SE	32
● Laurel, Marshall	C	150
● Laurens, Pocahontas	NW	318
● Lawler, Chickasaw	NE	464
● Lawn Hill, Hardin	C	50
Lawrence, Mills	SW	27
Lawrenceburgh, Warren	S	×
Leando, Van Buren	SE	175
Lebanon, Van Buren	SE	100
LeClaire, Scott	E	906
● Ledyard, Kossuth	N	×
Lee, Union	S	×
● Leeds, Woodbury	W	×
● *Leeson*, Ringgold	S	32
● LeGrand, Marshall	C	425
● Lehigh, Webster	C	870
● Leighton, Mahaska	S	250
● Leland, Winnebago	N	100
● **LeMars**, Plymouth	NW	4,036
Lena, Wright	N	32
Lena, Webster	C	×
● Lenox, Taylor	SW	706
● **Leon**, Decatur	S	1,422
Leonard, Taylor	SW	30
Leota, Sac	W	×
LePage, Dubuque	E	×
● LeRoy, Decatur	S	75
● Lesan, Ringgold	S	32
● Leslie, Clarke	S	100
● Lester, Lyon	NW	25
Lester, (see Dunkerton)		×

Iowa		
● Letts, Louisa	SE	325
● Levey, Polk	C	32
● Lewis, Cass	SW	579
Lewisburgh, Wayne	S	40
Lexington, Washington	SE	75
Liberty, Clarke	S	50
Liberty Centre, Warren	S	150
● Libertyville, Jefferson	NE	250
● *Lida*, Warren	S	×
Likens, Benton	E	×
● Lima, Fayette	NE	30
Lime City, (see Munn)		×
● *Lime Kilns*, Cedar	E	×
● Lime Spring, Howard	NE	550
Lincoln, Grundy	C	150
● Linden, Dallas	C	200
● Lineville, Wayne	S	606
Linn, Dallas	C	×
● *Linn*, Linn	E	×
● Linn Grove, Buena Vista	NW	250
Linn Junction, Linn	E	×
● Linton, Des Moines	SE	25
Linwood, Scott	E	32
● Lisbon, Linn	E	1,079
● Liscomb, Marshall	C	313
Little Cedar, Mitchell	N	25
● Little Port, Clayton	NE	175
***Little River*, Decatur**	**S**	**×**
● Little Rock, Lyon	NW	100
Little Sioux, Harrison	W	400
Littleton, Buchanan	E	100
Little Turkey, Chickasaw	NE	25
● Livermore, Humboldt	N	459
Living Spring, Pottawat'e	SW	25
Livingston, Appanoose	S	60
Lizard, Pocahontas	NW	×
● Lockridge, Jefferson	SE	200
Locust, Winneshiek	NE	20
● **Logan**, Harrison	W	827
● Lohrville, Calhoun	W	435
● Lone Tree, Johnson	E	250
● Long Grove, Scott	E	100
● Long Point, Tama	C	×
● *Longview*, Van Buren	SE	×
● Lorah, Cass	SW	15
Lore, Dubuque	E	50
Loretto, Warren	S	×
● Lorimor, Union	S	300
Lossing, Monona	W	×
● Lost Nation, Clinton	E	213
● Lothrop, Warren	S	65
Lott's Creek, Kossuth	N	×
● *Louisa*, Linn	E	×
Lourdes, Howard	NE	25
● Loveland, Pottawatta'e	SW	100
● Lovilia, Monroe	S	300
● Lowden, Cedar	E	405
Lowell, Henry	SE	150
● *Lower Yard*, Benton	E	×
● Low Moor, Clinton	E	200
● *Lowther*, Howard	NE	10
Loy, (see Yorktown)		×
● Luana, Clayton	NE	200
Luca Grove, Marion	S	×
● Lucas, Lucas	S	1,320
Lucerne, Wayne	S	×
Lucky Valley, Woodbury	W	75
Ludlow, Allamakee	NE	×
Luni, Wright	N	×
● *Luray*, Marshall	C	×
● Luther, Boone	C	25
Lutra (see Elgin)		×
● Luton, Woodbury	W	25
● Luverne, Kossuth	N	425
Luxemburgh, Dubuque	E	30
● Luzerne, Benton	E	300
Lycurgus, Allamakee	NE	10
Lyman, Cass	SW	40
● Lynnville, Jasper	C	261
● *Lynnville Junction*, Jas'r.	C	×
● Lyons, Clinton	E	5,799
Lytle City, (see Parnell)		×
McBride, Madison	S	10
● McCallsburg, Story	C	75
● McCausland, Scott	E	100
● *McDill*, Clarke	S	×
● McGregor, Clayton	NE	1,160
● McIntire, Mitchell	N	75
● *McJunkin*, Washington	SE	×
McKnight, Humboldt	N	×
● McPaul, Fremont	SW	65
McPherson, Madison	S	26
McVeigh, Van Buren	SE	75
● Macedonia, Pottawatt'e	SW	300
Mackey, Boone	C	20
Macks, Carroll	W	×
Macksburgh, Madison	S	186

Iowa		
● *Macuta*, Lee	SE	×
Madison, (see Hayfield)		×
Madison, Jones	E	57
● *Madison Junc.*, Hancock	N	×
● Madrid, Boone	C	565
Magnolia, Harrison	W	300
● *Maine*, Appanoose	S	57
● Malcom, Poweshiek	C	372
● Mallard, Palo Alto	NW	180
Mallory, Shelby	W	×
● *Malmo*, Calhoun	W	×
● Malone, Clinton	E	50
● Maloy, Ringgold	S	200
● Malta, Marshall	C	×
● Malvern, Mills	SW	1,003
● **Manchester**, Delaware	E	2,344
Manhattan, Keokuk	SE	50
● Manilla, Crawford	W	526
● Manly, Worth	N	200
● Manning, Carroll	W	1,233
● Manson, Calhoun	W	822
Manteno, Shelby	W	50
Manti, Fremont	SW	×
Maple Grove, Madison	S	×
Maple Hill, Emmet	NW	×
Maple Landing, Monona	W	100
● Maple River, Carroll	W	75
● Mapleton, Monona	W	782
● **Maquoketa**, Jackson	E	3,077
● Marathon, Buena Vista	NW	300
● Marble Rock, Floyd	N	433
● Marcus, Cherokee	NW	671
Maremack, (see Deedsville)		×
Marena, Ringgold	S	5
● **Marengo**, Iowa	E	1,710
● Marietta, Marshall	C	32
● **Marion**, Linn	E	3,094
Mark, Davis	S	20
● Marne, Cass	SW	350
● Marsh, Louisa	SE	10
Marshall, (see Wayland)		×
● **Marshalltown**, Mars'l.	C	8,914
● Martelle, Jones	E	125
Marthon, (see Earling)		×
● *Martins*, Scott	E	×
● Martinsburgh, Keokuk	SE	322
Marysville, (see Urbana)		×
Marysville, Marion	S	348
● **Mason City**, Cerro Gor'o	N	4,007
● *Mason City Junction*, Cerro Gordo	N	×
● Masonville, Delaware	E	300
● Massena, Cass	SW	279
● *Massey*, Dubuque	E	×
● Massillion, Cedar	E	150
● Matlock, Sioux	NW	25
Mauch Chunk, Mahaska	S	125
● Maurice, Sioux	NW	500
Maxfield, Bremer	NE	100
● *Maxon*, Monroe	S	×
● Maxwell, Story	C	453
May City, Osceola	NW	×
● Maynard, Fayette	NE	371
Maysville, (see Reeve)		×
● Mechanicsville, Cedar	E	612
● Mederville, Clayton	NE	50
Medford, Warren	S	×
● Mediapolis, Des Moines	SE	489
Medora, Warren	S	50
● *Meirotto*, Lee	SE	×
● Melbourne, Marshall	C	150
Melleray, Dubuque	E	50
Melpine, Muscatine	E	×
Melrose, Grundy	C	×
Melrose, Monroe	S	450
● Meltonville, Worth	N	25
Melville, Audubon	W	40
● Menlo, Guthrie	W	389
Menoti, Buena Vista	NW	×
Mentor, Bremer	NE	×
● Meriden, Cherokee	NW	241
Meroa, Mitchell	N	150
● Merrill, Plymouth	NW	200
Merrimac, Jefferson	SE	30
● *Mertensville*, Lee	SE	×
● Meservey, Cerro Gordo	N	100
● Metz, Jasper	C	75
Middleburgh, Washington	SE	×
Middleburgh, Sioux	NW	15
Middlefield, Buchanan	**E**	**10**
● *Middle Lock*, Lee	SE	×
Middleport, Clarke	S	×
Middle River, Madison	S	46
● Middletown, Des Moines	SE	25
Midland, Tama	C	×
Midland, Hardin	C	×
● *Midland Junc.*, Clinton	E	×

● *Midway*, Johnson........ E ×
Midway, Woodbury........ W ×
● *Midways*, Boone.........C ×
Milan, Lucas...............S ×
● Miles, Jackson...........E 600
● Milford, Dickinson.....NW 450
Milford, (see Grant).......... ×
Milledgeville, Appanoose....S 19
Miller, Hancock............N ×
Millersburgh, Iowa..........E 300
Miller's Creek, Black Hawk.C ×
● *Millman*, Warren.........S ×
● *Mills*, Mills............SW ×
Mills Station, Pottawat'e..SW 25
● Millville, Clayton....... NE 40
● Milo, Warren.............S 318
● Milton, Van Buren...... SE 643
● Minburn, Dallas...........C 300
● Minden, Pottawattamie.SW 287
● Mineola, Mills.......... SW 300
Mineral Ridge, Boone.......C 110
● Minerva, Marshall.........C 50
● *Minerva Junc.*, Marshall. C ×
● Mingo, Jasper.............C 100
Minkler, Bremer..........NE ×
● Minnie, Dickinson...... NW 65
● Missouri Valley, HarrisonW 2,797
● Mitchell, Mitchell.........N 309
● Mitchellville, Polk........C 704
● Modale, Harrison........ W 288
● Moingona, Boone......... C 500
● Mona, Mitchell........... N 200
● Mondamin, Harrison.....W 257
● Monette, Union.......... S 10
● *Moningers*, Marshall......C 25
● Monmouth, Jackson......E 300
● Monoma, Clayton....... NE 460
● Monroe, Jasper........... C 952
● Montieth, Guthrie........W 25
Monterey, Davis.............S 150
● **Montezuma**, PoweshiekC 1,062
Monti, Buchanan............E 100
● Monticello, Jones.........E 1,938
● Montour, Tama........... C 409
● Montpelier, Muscatine.... E 120
● Montrose, Lee.......... SE 778
● Mooar, Lee.............. SE ×
Mooreville, Tama............C 35
Moorhead, Monona..........W 40
● Moorland, Webster....... C 40
● Moravia, Appanoose.......S 311
Morfordsville, Johnson......E 65
Morgan, Crawford......... W 25
Morgan Valley, Marion......S 300
● Morley, Jones..............E 35
● *Morning Side*, Woodbury. W ×
● Morning Sun, Louisa.....SE 881
● Morrison, Grundy.........C 165
● Morse, Johnson............E 150
Morsman, Page...........SW 10
Mortimer, Ringgold..........S 13
Morton, Pottawattamie...SW ×
Mortons Mills, Mt'gom'ry.SW 25
● Moscow, Muscatine....... E 300
Motor, Warren..............S ×
Moun City, (see Ash Grove).. ×
Mound Hope, Sac.......... W ×
● Moulton, Appanoose....... S 769
● Mount Auburn, Benton...E 300
● **Mount Ayr**, Ringgold.. S 1,265
Mount Carmel, Carroll..... W 50
● Mount Clara, Lee........ SE ×
Mount Etna, Adams...... SW 100
● Mount Hamill, Lee....... SE 64
Mount Hope, Black Hawk..C ×
● Mount Joy, Scott..........E 50
Mount Pisgah, Harrison.... W 60
● **MountPleasant**,HenrySE 3,997
● *Mount Pleasant Junction*, Henry................ SE ×
Mount St. Joseph, Dubuque E ×
● Mount Sterling, VanB'n.SE 200
● Mount Union, Henry ... SE 75
Mount Valley, Winnebago.. N 32
● Mount Vernon, Linn...... E 1,259
● Mount Zion, Van Buren SE 100
● Moville, Woodbury....... W 295
● Muchakinock, Mahaska...S 1,000
● *Muchakinock Yard*, M'k'aS ×
Muddy, Calhoun .... W ×
Munn, Cedar................E 50
Munterville, Monroe........S ×
Munterville, Wapello........S 100
● Murphy, Jasper............C ×
● Murray, Clarke............S 666
● *Murrows*, Polk.......... C ×
● **Muscatine**, Muscatine..E 11,454

Musquaka, Iowa........... E 100
Myron, Allamakee........ NE 30
● Mystic, Appanoose........ S 875
● Nanson, PottawattamiesSW ×
Nasheim, Winnebago.......N ×
● Nashua, Chickasaw..... NE 1,240
● *Nashville*, Lee..........SE ×
● Nashville, Jackson........E 50
● Nassau, Keokuk.........SE 200
Nasset, Winneshiek.......NE ×
National, Clayton.......... NE 150
Navan, Winneshiek.........N ×
● *Nebraska City Junction*, Fremont................SW ×
Necot, Linn................ E ×
Needmore, Harrison........ W 25
Nelson, Guthrie............ W 10
● *Neoga*, Pottawattamie..SW ×
● Neola, Pottawattamie...SW 917
Neptune, Plymouth...... NW 10
● **Nevada**, Story...........C 1,66[illegible]
Nevinville, Adams........ SW 30[illegible]
New Alba, Winneshiek....NE ×
● New Albin, Allamakee..NE 411
Newbern, Marion............S 300
● New Boston, Lee........ SE 59
New Buda, Decatur.........S ×
● Newburgh, Jasper......... C 200
● Newell, Buena Vista... NW 540
● Newhall, Benton............E 200
● **New Hampton**,Chi'wNE 1,314
● New Hartford, Butler.....N 300
New Haven, Mitchell....... N 18
New Hope, Union............S ×
New Jefferson, (see Jefferson) ×
Newkirk, Sioux........... NW 50
● New Liberty, Scott....... E 75
● New London, Henry......SE 580
● New Market, Taylor.... SW 320
New Oregon, (see Cresco).... ×
● Newport, Louisa.........SE 50
New Providence, Hardin....C 200
New Redding, Ringgold.....S 214
● New Sharon, Mahaska.... S 1,026
New Sweden, Jefferson....SE ×
● **Newton**, Jasper.........C 2,564
Newtonville, Buchanan..... E 25
New Vienna, Dubuque......E 350
● New Virginia, Warren.... S 250
New York, Wayne.......... S 150
● Nichol, Muscatine.........E 287
Niles, Floyd.................N 25
● Nira, Washington........SE 50
● Noble, Washington........ SE [illegible]
● ***Nobleton*, Polk**........... C ×
● *Nodaway*, Adams...... SW 200
● Noel, Scott..................E ×
Nora, Humboldt.............N ×
● *Nora Junction*, Floyd.....N 26
● Nora Springs, Floyd......N 846
Nordland, Worth............N 18
● Nordness, Winneshiek..NE 25
● Norman, Winnebago..... N 73
● *Norris*, Black Hawk......C ×
Norris, (see Liscomb)........ ×
North, Madison.............S ×
● *North Bellvue*, Jackson...E ×
● Northborough, Page....SW 105
North Branch, Guthrie.....W 50
● North Buena Vista,Cl't'nNE 70
North Des Moines, Polk....C ×
● North English, Iowa.......E 400
Northfield, Des Moines.... SE 50
● *North Junc.Switch*,Du'q'eE ×
North Liberty, Johnson......E 100
● North McGregor, Clayt'nNE 509
North Mills, Page........ SW ×
North River, Madison.......S ×
● *North Skunk*, Poweshiek.C ×
North Washington, Ch'aw.NE 100
● **Northwood**, Worth.... N 859
Norton, Clarke..............S ×
● Norwalk, Warren.......... S 250
● Norway, Benton.......... E 401
Norway Centre, Wright.... N ×
● Norwich, Page............SW 80
Norwood, Lucas..............S 25
● Nugent, Keokuk........ SE 25
Nugent, (see Coggon)........ ×
● Numa, Appanoose........S 125
Nyman, Page...............SW 25
Oakfield, Audubon......... W ×
● Oak Grove, Poweshiek...C 20
● Oakland, Pottawattamie. W 686
● Oakland Mills, Henry....SE 50
Oakland Valley, Franklin.. N 100
● Oakley, Lucas............ S 40

Oak Point, Van Buren.....SE ×
Oak Spring, Davis...........S ×
● *Oakton*, Scott.............E ×
● Oakville, Louisa......... SE 15
● Oasis, Johnson.............E 150
O'Brien, O'Brien......... NW ×
● Ocheyedan, Osceola.... NW 200
Odd, Woodbury............ W ×
● Odebolt, Sac.............W 1,122
● Oelwein, Fayette........NE 830
● Ogden, Boone......... ...C 689
Ohio, (see Peru)............. ×
● Okoboji, Dickinson.... NW 100
Ola, Lucas..................S ×
Olaf, Wright................N ×
Olden, (see Alden)........... ×
Oldfield, Polk.................C ×
Old Mission, Winneshiek..NE ×
● Olds, Henry..............SE 50
O'Leary, Plymouth.......NW ×
● Olin, Jones................E 519
Olio, Union.................S ×
● Olivet, Mahaska........... S 50
● Ollie, Keokuk........... SE 200
Olmitz, Lucas................S 35
Olympus, Harrison......... W ×
● **Onawa**, Monona......... W 1,358
● Oneida, Delaware.......... E 75
Ononwa, (see Lettsville)...... ×
● Onslow, Jones.............E 237
● Ontario, Story.............C 175
Ora Dell, (see Dunreath)..... ×
● *Oralabor*, Polk............C ×
Orange, Clinton..............E ×
● **Orange City**, Sioux..NW 1,246
● Orchard, Mitchell....... N 200
Ord, Madison................S 10
Orford, (see Montour)....... ×
● Orient, Adair........... SW 130
● Oriba, Warren.............S 22
Orleans, Appanoose.........S ×
Ormanville, Wapello........ S 100
Orono, Muscatine........ SW 10
● Ortonville, Dallas......... C 10
● **Osage**, Mitchell......... N 1,913
● Osborne, Clayton........NE 33
Osborne, Howard......... NE ×
● **Osceola**, Clarke......... S 2,120
● Osgood, Palo Alto......NW 25
● **Oskaloosa**, Mahaska....S ,558
Osprey, Monroe.............S ×
● Ossian, Winneshiek..... NE 609
● Osterdock, Clayton......NE 140
Oswalt, Jasper.............. C 100
● Otho, Webster............ C 30
● *Otis*, Linn................ E ×
Otisville, (see Dowes).......... ×
● Otley, Marion............ S 200
● Oto, Woodbury...........W 247
Otranto, Mitchell............ N 150
● Otranto Station, Mitchell. N ×
Otter Creek, Jackson....... E 175
Otterville, Buchanan........ E 100
● **Ottumwa**, Wapello .... S 14,001
● *OttumwaJunction*, WapelloS ×
Ovid, Wayne................S ×
● Owasa, Hardin............ C 100
Owen Centre, Cerro Gordo.. N ×
● Oxford, Johnson............E 515
● Oxford Junction, Jones...E 752
● Oxford Mills, Jones........E 250
● Ovens, Plymouth.......NW 100
Ozark, Jackson............. E 50
Pacific City, Mills.........SW 250
● Pacific Junction, Mills..SW 744
● Packwood, Jefferson.....SE 100
● Page, Page...............SW 50
Palermo, Grundy.......... C ×
● *Palisade*, Linn............E ×
Palmyra, Warren........... S 200
Palo, Linn.................. E 275
● Panama, Shelby........... W 379
● Panora, Guthrie.......... W 809
Panther, Dallas.............C 25
● *Paradise*, Jackson.........E ×
● Paralta, Linn............... E 20
● *Paris*, Davis................S ×
Paris, Linn....................E 120
Park, Cerro Gordo.......... N 25
● Parkersburgh, Butler.....N 760
Parks, Lyon............... NW ×
● Parnell, Iowa................ E 200
Parrish, Des Moines....... SE 35
Parvin, Pocahontas.......NW ×
Pas, Jackson................E 32
● *Passing Track*, BuchananE ×
● Paton, Greene.............C 245

Patriot, Decatur	S	×
● *Patterson*, Des Moines	SE	×
● Patterson, Madison	S	133
Paul, Benton	E	×
● Paulina, O'Brien	NW	510
● Payne, Fremont	SW	×
Peach, Buena Vista	NW	×
Pedee, Cedar	E	22
Peiro, Woodbury	W	50
● Pekin, Keokuk	SE	30
● Pella, Marion	S	2,408
Peoria, Mahaska	S	150
Peoria City, Polk	C	×
● Peosta, Dubuque	E	75
● Percival, Fremont	SW	300
● Percy, Marion	S	30
● Perkins, Sioux	NW	×
● Perlee, Jefferson	SE	100
● Perry, Dallas	C	2,880
● **Persia, Harrison**	W	400
● Peru, Madison	S	125
Petersburgh, Delaware	E	120
● Peterson, Clay	NW	371
Phillipsburg, Clarke	S	10
Phillipston, Bremer	NE	×
Philo, Sac	W	×
● Pickering, Marshall	C	×
Pierce, Jones	E	×
Pierceville, Van Buren	SE	40
● Pierson, Woodbury	W	100
Pigeon, Pottawattamie	SW	×
Pilotburg, Washington	SE	×
Pilot Grove, Lee	SE	75
● *Pilot Grove Station*, Lee	SE	×
● Pilot Mound, Boone	C	200
Pilot Rock, Cherokee	NW	10
Pine Mills, Muscatine	E	20
Pin Oak, Dubuque	E	×
● Pioneer, Humboldt	N	65
Pittsburgh, Van Buren	SE	125
Pitzer, Madison	S	×
● Plainfield, Bremer	NE	350
Plain View, Scott	E	25
● Plano, Appanoose	S	150
● Plato, Cedar	E	10
Platt, Clay	NW	×
Platteville, Taylor	SW	70
Pleasant, (see Decorah)		×
● *Pleasant Creek*, Jackson	E	×
Pleasant Grove, Des Moines	SE	125
● Pleasanton, Decatur	S	350
● Pleasant Plain, Jefferson	SE	225
Pleasant Prairie, Muscatine	E	25
Pleasant Valley, Scott	E	400
Pleasant View, Humb'ldt	N	×
Pleasant View, Madison	N	×
● Pleasantville, Marion	S	510
● Plover, Pocahontas	NW	200
Plum Hollow, Fremont	SW	×
● Plymouth, Cerro Gordo	N	246
● *Plymouth Junc.*, C'ro Gro	N	×
Plymouth Rock, Win'sh'k	NE	35
Pocahontas, Pocahontas	NW	200
Point Isabel, Wapello	S	×
Point Louisa, Louisa	SE	×
Point Pleasant, Hardin	C	×
Polen, Ringgold	S	×
● Polk, Polk	C	446
● *Polk City Junction*, Polk	C	×
● Polo Station, Worth	N	25
● Pomeroy, Calhoun	W	481
● Popejoy, Franklin	N	200
Poplar Grove, Hamilton	C	×
Pony, Bremer	NE	×
● *Port Allen*, Muscatine	E	40
● Portland, Cerro Gordo	N	100
Port Louisa, Louisa	SE	×
● Portsmouth, Shelby	W	250
● Postville, Allamakee	NE	884
Potosia, Plymouth	NW	×
● Potter, Tama	C	25
Powersville, Floyd	N	10
Powhatan, Pocahontas	NW	×
Poyneer, Ringgold	S	×
Prairieburgh, Linn	E	250
● Prairie City, Jasper	C	684
Prairie Creek, (see Bernard)		×
Prairie Grove, Clarke	S	27
Preparation, Monona	W	10
● Prescott, Adams	SW	300
● Preston, Jackson	E	489
Price, Audubon	W	×
Price, Madison	S	×
Primghar, O'Brien	NW	519
Primrose, Lee	SE	200
Princeton, Scott	E	398
● Prole, Warren	S	25
● Promise City, Wayne	S	300

Protivin, Howard	NE	50
● Pulaski, Davis	S	200
Putnam, Fayette	NE	×
Quandahl, Allamakee	NE	50
● Quarry, Marshall	C	150
Quasqueton, Buchanan	E	700
Queen City, Adams	SW	×
Queen's Point, Madison	S	×
Quick, Pottawattamie	SW	25
● Quigley, Clinton	E	15
● Quimby, Cherokee	NW	225
Quincy, Adams	SW	146
Racine, Buena Vista	NW	×
● Radcliffe, Hardin	C	350
Rahm, Kossuth	N	25
Rake, Winnebago	N	×
● *Ralston*, Carroll	W	×
Ramona, Tama	C	×
Ramsay, Kossuth	N	50
● Randalia, Fayette	NE	200
● Randall, Hamilton	C	175
● Randolph, Fremont	SW	276
● Rands, Calhoun	W	×
Rangall, Henry	SE	×
● *Rathton*, Hardin	C	20
● Ray, Appanoose	S	40
● Raymond, Black Hawk	C	150
Read, Clayton	NE	165
● Reasnor, Jasper	C	100
Reed's Ridge, Allamakee	NE	×
● Redding, Ringgold	S	250
● Redfield, Dallas	C	397
● **Red Oak**, Montgomery	SW	3,321
RedOakJunction, Montg'ry	SW	×
Red Rock, Marion	S	100
Reeder's Mills, Harrison	W	40
Reel's, Pottawattamie	SW	25
Reeve, Franklin	N	50
● Reinbeck, Grundy	C	731
● *Relay*, Appanoose	S	×
● Remsen, Plymouth	NW	580
Reno, Cass	SW	10
● Renwick, Humboldt	N	200
Republic, Chickasaw	NE	25
● Rhodes, Marshall	C	434
● Riceville, Mitchell	N	600
Richfield, Fayette	NE	×
● Richland, Keokuk	SE	531
Richmond, Washington	SE	275
Rickardsville, Dubuque	E	25
Rickord, Hardin	C	5
Ridgedale, Polk	C	×
Ridgeport, (see Mineral Rid'e)		×
● Ridgeway, Winneshiek	NE	300
● *Ridley*, Clayton	NE	×
● Riggs, Clinton	E	50
Riley, Ringgold	S	×
Ringgold, Ringgold	S	×
Ringsted, Emmet	NW	×
● Rippey, Greene	C	600
Rising Sun, Polk	C	200
● *Ritter*, O'Brien	NW	×
● River Junction, Johnson	E	40
● Riverside, Washington	SE	608
● River Sioux, Harrison	W	200
● Riverton, Fremont	SW	560
River View, Lyons	NW	×
● Robertson, Hardin	C	100
Robin, Benton	E	×
● Robins, Linn	E	25
Rochdale, (see Botna)		×
Rochester, Cedar	E	50
Rock, Cerro Gordo	N	×
Rock Branch, Woodbury	W	20
Rock Creek, Mitchell	N	13
Rock Dale, Dubuque	E	134
● Rock Falls, Cerro Gordo	N	122
● Rockford, Floyd	N	1,010
● **Rock Rapids**, Lyon	NW	1,394
Rockton, Marshall	C	×
● **Rock Valley, Sioux**	NW	542
Rockville, Delaware	E	135
● Rockwell, Cerro Gordo	N	381
● **Rockwell City**, Calh'n	W	516
● Rodman, Palo Alto	NW	50
● Rodney, Monona	S	100
● Roland, Story	C	400
Rolfe, Pocahontas	NW	529
● Rome, Henry	SE	200
● Root's Siding, Butler	N	10
● Roscoe, Des Moines	SE	25
Rose Grove, Hamilton	C	×
● Rose Hill, Mahaska	S	200
● *Rose Hill*, Polk	C	×
Roselle, Carroll	W	90
Rose Mountain, Warren	S	×
Rosendale, Hamilton	C	20

Roslea, Emmet	NW	×
● Ross, Audubon	W	50
Rossville, Allamakee	NE	75
Round Grove, Scott	E	32
● *Round House*, Clayton	NE	×
Rousseau, Marion	S	20
● Rowan, Wright	N	50
● Rowley, Buchan	E	100
Roxie, Bremer	NE	×
● *Rubens*, Pocahontas	NW	×
● Rudd, Floyd	N	300
● Runnells, Polk	C	296
Rural, Linn	E	×
● Russell, Lucas	S	443
● Ruthven, Palo Alto	NW	580
● Rutland, Humboldt	N	150
● *Rutledge*, Wappello	S	×
● Ryan, Delaware	E	25
● Sabula, Jackson	E	918
● *Sabula Junction*, Jackson	E	×
● *Sabula Siding*, Jackson	E	×
● **Sac City**, Sac	W	1,249
● *Sac City Y*, Sac	W	×
Sageville, Dubuque	E	×
● Saint Ansgar, Mitchell	N	609
● Saint Anthony, Marshall	C	150
Saint Charles, (see Charles C'y)		×
● Saint Charles, Madison	S	387
Saint Clair, Monona	W	×
Saint Donatus, Jackson	E	100
● *Saint Joe Junction*, Polk	C	×
Saint John, Harrison	W	×
Saint Joseph, Kossuth	N	×
Saint Lucas, Fayette	NE	150
● Saint Mary's, Warren	S	50
● Saint Olaf, Clayton	NE	100
● Saint Paul, Lee	SE	90
Saint Sebald, Clayton	NE	×
● Salem, Henry	SE	551
Salina, Jefferson	SE	200
● Salix, Woodbury	W	400
Samville, Wayne	S	×
● Sanborn, O'Brien	NW	1,075
● *Sand Pit*, Clinton	E	×
● *Sand Prairie*, Lee	SE	125
● Sand Spring, Delaware	E	150
● Sandusky, Lee	SE	100
Sandyville, Warren	S	100
● Santiago, Polk	C	25
Saratoga, Howard	NE	20
● *Sargent's Bluff*, Woodb'y	W	425
Saude, Chickasaw	NE	×
Savannah, Davis	S	150
● Sawyer, Lee	SE	×
Saxon, Wayne	S	×
● *Saylors*, Polk	C	×
Saylorsville, Polk	C	100
● Schaller, Sac	W	333
Schonberg, Warren	S	×
● *Schrunks*, Clayton	NE	×
Sciota, Montgomery	SW	25
● Scotch Grove, Jones	E	25
Scott, Floyd	N	26
Scott Centre, Fayette	NE	×
Scottswood, Pottawattamie	SW	×
● Scranton City, Greene	C	715
Sedgewick, Decatur	S	×
● Searsboro, Poweshiek	C	153
Seaton, Fayette	NE	×
● Secor, Hardin	C	32
● *Sedan*, Appanoose	S	12
Seigel, Bremer	NE	10
● Selection, Monroe	S	50
● Selma, Van Buren	SE	300
Selma, Wayne	S	×
Seneca, Kossuth	N	×
● Seney, Plymouth	NW	100
● Seargeant Bluff, Woodb'y	W	425
Sevastopol, (see Des Moines)		×
Sewal, Wayne	S	50
● Sexton, Kossuth	N	25
● Seymour, Wayne	S	1,058
Shabbona, O'Brien	NW	×
Shady Grove, Buchanan	E	10
● Shambaugh, Page	SW	150
● Shannon City, Union	S	100
● *Sharon*, Appanoose	S	×
Sharon, Warren	S	×
Sharon Center, Johnson	E	25
● Sharpsburg, Taylor	SW	100
● *Shawandasee*, Dubuque	E	×
Sheffield, Dubuque	E	×
● Sheffield, Franklin	N	610
● Shelby, Shelby	W	582
Shelbyville, Shelby	W	×
● Sheldahl, Polk	C	225
Sheldahl Cross'g, (see Slater)		×

●Sheldon, O'Brien.......NW 1,478
●Shell Rock, Butler........N 733
ShellRock Falls, (see Rock Fal) ×
Shellsburgh, Benton........ E 468
●Shenandoah, Page...... SW 2,440
●*Shepard*, Union...........S ×
Sheridan, Poweshiek........C 25
Sheridan, (see Boyden)...... ×
Sherman, Poweshiek........C 25
Sherrill, Dubuque...........E 75
Sherrill's Mound, Dubuque E ×
Shiloh, Cedar............. E ×
Shirley, Pocahontas...... NW 13
Shoo Fly, Johnson..........E ×
Showman, Keokuk..........SE ×
Shueyville, Johnson.........E 125
Siam, Taylor.............. SW 100
●**Sibley**, Osceola....... NW 1,090
●*Siding One Hundred and Fourteen*, Wayne........S ×
●*Siding One Hundred and Forty*, Wayne......... S ×
●**Sidney**, Fremont......SW 839
●**Sigourney**, Keokuk...SE 1,523
●Silver City, Mills..........SW 324
Silver Creek, Delaware..... E 35
Silver Lake, Worth..........N 13
Silver Station, Ringgold.....S ×
●Sioux Centre, Sioux.... NW 100
●**SIOUX CITY**, Woodbury W 37,806
SiouxCityStock Yds., Woodb'y W ×
●Sioux Rapids, Buena V. NW 650
●*Skunk Coal Mine*, Jasper. C 1,024
Slagle, Keokuk............SE 65
●Slater, Story..............C 400
●Sloan, Woodbury.........W 449
Smayville, (see Colo)......... ×
Smithland, Monona........W ×
●Smithland, Woodbury.... W 369
●*Smiths*, Jackson..........E ×
●*Smiths*, Decatur...........S 10
Smyrna, Clarke.............S ×
●*Sny Magill*, Clayton.....NE 26
Soldier, Monona............W 20
Solomon, Mills............SW 25
●**Solon, Johnson**...........E 353
Somber, Worth..............N ×
●*Somerset*, Warren.........S 300
●*Somerset Junc.*, Warren.. S ×
Sonora, Powesheick..........C 13
●South Amana, Iowa.......E 250
●*South Des Moines*, Polk..C ×
●South English, Keokuk..SE 500
South Flint, Des Moines...SE ×
●*South Jc. Switch*, Dubuque E ×
So. Keosauqua, (see Keosauq'a) ×
●*South Ottumwa*, Wapello..S ×
●Spaulding, Union...........S 70
●Spechts Ferry, Dubuque..E 15
●**Spencer**, Clay...........NW 1,813
●Sperry, Des Moines......SE 80
Spillville, Winneshiek.....NE 300
●**Spirit Lake**, D'ck'ns'n NW 782
Spragueville, Jackson....... E 130
Spring Brook, Jackson......E 150
Springdale, Cedar...........E 145
●*Springdale*, Woodbury...W ×
Springfield, Keokuk.......SE 100
●Spring Hill, Warren...... S 125
Springvale, (see Humboldt).. ×
Spring Valley, Decatur......S 25
●Springville, Lynn..........E 518
Springwater, Winneshiek..NE 50
Stacyville, Mitchell.........N 350
Stacyville, (see Georgetown).. ×
Stanford, Hardin.......... C ×
Stanford, Marshall..........C ×
●Stanhope, Hamilton.........C 50
●Stanley, Buchanan.........N 25
●Stanton, Montgomery...SW 399
●Stanwood, Cedar...........E 302
Stapleton, (see Lawler)....... ×
Star, Marion.................S 25
●*Stark*, Mahaska...........S ×
●State Centre, Marshall.... C 854
●*State Centre Junc.*, M'rsh'l C ×
●*State Line*, Taylor........SW ×
●Steamboat Rock, Hardin..C 367
Steele, (see Plano)......... ×
●Stennett, Montgomery..SW 25
Sterling, Jackson...........E 200
●*Steuben*, Davis............S ×
Stickley's Mts., (see Nodaway Ms. ×
Stiles, Davis................S 100
Stillwater, Mitchell.........N ×
Stilson, Hancock............N ×
●*Stimsons*, Calhoun....... W ×

●Stockport, Van Buren...SE 25
●Stockton, Muscatine......E 200
●*Stock Yards*, Clinton.....E ×
●Stone City, Jones.........E 200
●**Storm Lake**, Beuna V. NW 1,682
●Story City, Story..........C 536
●Strahan, Mills...........SW 25
Strand, Adams..............SW ×
●*Strange Siding*, W'db'ry. W ×
●Stratford, Hamilton.......C 400
●Strawberry Point, Cl'ton. NE 911
Stringtown, (see Traxler).... ×
●Struble, Plymouth..... NW ×
●Stuart, Guthrie...........W 2,052
Sugar Creek, Cedar.........E 26
●*Sugar Creek*, Lee.........SE ×
●Sully, Jasper.............C 150
●Sulphur Sp'gs, Beuna V. NW 50
Summer's, Benton..........E ×
●Summerset, Warren........S 100
●*Summit*, Fremont...... SW 25
●*Summit*, Muscatine........E 32
Summit, (see Mt. Zion)....... ×
●Summitville, Lee.........SE 200
●Sumner, Bremer.........NE 861
●Superior, Dickinson....NW 100
Surry, Greene..............C 32
●Sutherland, O'Brien....NW 490
●Swaledale, Cerro Gordo.. N 200
●Swan, Marion..............S 419
Swan Lake, Emmet...... NW 20
Swanton, Butler............N ×
Swea, Kossuth...............N 25
●Swedesburgh, Henry.... SE 100
Sweetland, Muscatine.......E 25
Sylva, Dubuque...........E ×
Syracuse, (see Plainfield) .... ×
●Tabor, Fremont.........SW 503
Tailor Hill, Grundy.........C ×
●Taintor, Mahaska.......... S 50
Tallahoma, Lucas.......... S ×
Talleyrand, Keokuk....... SE 100
●Talmage, Union............S 50
●Tama, Tama............. C 1,741
●*Tamworth*, Polk..........C 75
●Tara, Webster.............C 50
Tarkio, Page..............SW ×
Taylor, Pottawattamie.... SW 20
Taylorsville, Fayette......NE 25
●Teeds, Clinton........... E 60
Temple Hill, Jones..........E ×
●Templeton, Carroll.......W 269
Tenold, Worth............ N 25
Terre Haute, (see Burrell)... ×
Terry, (see Walford)......... ×
●Thayer, Union............S 125
Thomas, Ringgold..........S 50
Thompson, Winnebago......N ×
Thompson's Mills, Dubuque E 25
●Thor, Humboldt...........N 300
●Thornburgh, Keokuk....SE 350
●*Thornburgh Junc.*, Keo. SE ×
●Thornton, Cerro Gordo...N 100
●Thorpe, Delaware.........E 25
●Thoten, Winneshiek.... NE ×
●Thrall, Wright.............N 50
Thurman, Fremont.......SW 395
●Ticonic, Monona......... W ×
Tieville, Monona.......... W ×
●Tiffin, Johnson ....E 100
●*Tieville*, Madison.........S ×
●Tilton, Poweshiek........ C 25
●Tingley, Ringgold.........S 295
●Tioga, Mahaska............S 25
●**Tipton**, Cedar.......... E 1,599
Tipton Grove, Hardin....... C ×
Tivoli, Dubuque............E 42
●Toddville, Linn...........E 50
●**Toledo**, Tama........... C 1,836
Toolsborough, Louisa......SE 150
●Toronto, Clinton...........E 78
Towner, Polk..............C ×
●Tracy, Marion.............S 275
●Traer, Tama.............. C 1,014
●*Trask*, Appanoose........ S ×
Traxler, Henry........... SE ×
Tremaine, Hamilton......... C ×
●Trent, Polk...............C ×
●Trentham, Linn............E 50
Trenton, Henry............SE 200
Trimello, Clay.............NW ×
●Tripoli, Bremer..........NE 300
Troy, Davis.................S 500
Troy Mills, Linn...........E 100
●Truro, Madison............S 100
Tunnel, Hamilton..........C 25
Tunnel Siding, Polk........C ×

●Turin, Monona...........W 80
●Turkey River, Clayton.. NE 50
●*Turkey River Junction*, Clayton..............NE ×
●*Turnout*, Scott.......... E ×
●Tuskeega, Decatur........S 30
Tuttle Grove, Guthrie......W ×
Twin Lakes, Calhoun.......W ×
Twin Oak, Louis..........SE ×
Tyner, Polk...............C 35
●**Tyrone, Monroe**...........S 55
●*Udell*, Appanoose........ S ×
Ulster, Floyd...............N 25
●Underwood, Pottawat'e. SW 200
●Union, Hardin............ C 514
●*Union*, Union..............S ×
Unionburgh, Harrison..... W 8
Union Centre, Jackson......E ×
Union Hill, Ringgold...... S ×
Union Mills, Mahaska...... S 50
●*Union Pacific Transfer*, Pottawattamie........ SW ×
Union Prairie, Allamakee NE ×
Union Ridge, Franklin.....N ×
Uniontown, Delaware...... E ×
●Uniontown, Appanoose....S 212
Unique, Humboldt......... N ×
Unity, Johnson............ E ×
University Place, Polk..... C ×
Updegraff, Clayton........NE 100
Upland, Lyon..............NW ×
Upton, Van Buren.........SE 25
Urbana, Benton.............E 400
●Ute, Monona............ W 350
Utica, Van Buren..........SE 60
●Vail, Crawford........... W 538
●Valeria, Jasper...........C 100
Valley, Washington........SE 35
ValleyCity, (see Pleasant Val'.) ×
Valley Farm, Linn......... E ×
●Valley Junction, Polk.... C ×
Valley View, Harrison..... W 150
Van Buren, Jackson........ E 485
●Vancleve, Marshall....... C 100
Vandalia, Jasper........... C 300
●Van Horn, Benton........E 501
Van Meter, Dallas.......... C 467
●Van Wert, Decatur........S 300
Vega, Henry...............SE ×
●*Ventura*, Cerro Gordo....N ×
●Veo, Jefferson............SE 20
Verbeck, Humboldt........ N ×
●Verdi, Washington...... SE 57
Vernon, (see Luverne)....... ×
Vernon, Van Buren....... SE 400
●Victor, Iowa.............. E 616
●Viele, Lee................ SE 15
Village Creek, Allamakee NE 100
Villanova, Clinton..........E 32
●Villisca, Montgomery...SW 1,711
○Vincennes, Lee.......... SE 125
●Vincent, Webster.......... C 50
Vining, Tama............... C 200
Vino, Adair...............SW ×
●**Vinton**, Benton......... E 2,865
●Viola, Linn................ E 300
Viola Centre, Audubon..... W 50
Viona, Humboldt.......... N ×
Vista, Buchanan............E ×
Vogt, Plymouth...........NW ×
●Volga, Clayton.......... NE 400
Volney, Allamakee........NE 100
Voss, Emmet..............NW ×
Von, Humboldt............ N ×
●*Wabash Junction*, Polk.. C ×
Wacousta, Humboldt...... N ×
●Wadena, Fayette..........NE 150
Wagner, Clayton..........NE ×
Walden, Keokuk.......... SE ×
●*Walden*, Cedar........... E ×
Wales, Montgomery.......SW 10
●Walford, Benton...........E 50
●Walker, Linn............. E 500
Walkerville, Page..........SW 20
●Wallingford, Emmet... NW 20
○Wall Lake, Sac.............W 439
●Walnut, Pottawattamie. SW 811
Walnut City, Appanoose.....S 43
Walnut Fork, (see Olin)..... ×
Walsh, Appanoose...........S ×
Waltham, Tama.............C 58
Wanamaker, Ringgold.......S ×
●*Waneta*, O'Brien.......NW ×
●**Wapello**, Louisa.......SE 1,009
Wapsa, Linn..............E ×
Wapsie, Bremer...........NE 25
●*Warrack*, Carroll........W ×

Town, County	Index	Pop.
● Warren, Lee	SE	25
Warsaw, Wayne	S	100
● Washburn, Black Hawk	C	75
● **Washington**, Wash'n.	SE	3,235
● Washington Mills, D'buq'e	E	75
Washington Prairie, Win'k	NE	30
● Washta, Cherokee	NW	500
● **Waterloo**, Black Hawk	C	6,674
Waterman, Wright	N	77
● *Waterman Siding*, O'Br.	NW	×
● *Water Tank*, Lee	SE	×
Watertown, Floyd	N	×
● Waterville, Allamakee	NE	150
● Watkins, Benton	E	200
Watson, Clayton	NE	25
Waubeek, Linn	E	250
● Waucoma, Fayette	NE	406
● Waukee, Dallas	C	240
● **Waukon**, Allamakee	NE	1,610
● Waukon Junction Al'ke.	NE	25
● Waupeton, Dubuque	E	×
Waverly, Bremer	NE	2,346
● *Waverly Junction*, B'm'r	NE	×
Wax, Cass	SW	25
● Wayland, Henry	SE	350
● *Wayland Crossing*, W'sh	SE	×
● Wayne, Henry	SE	5
● Webster, Keokuk	SE	100
● **Webster City**, Hamilton	C	2,829
Wedesburgh, Henry	SE	×
Weidland, Woodbury	W	10
● Weldon, Decatur	S	510
Weller, Monroe	S	23
● Wellman, Washington	SE	600
Wells, Madison	S	10
● Wellsburgh, Grundy	C	160
● Welton, Clinton	E	80
Wendell, Cherokee	NW	×
Wentworth, Mitchell	N	×
● Wesley, Kossuth	N	440
West Albany, Fayette	NE	×
● West Bend, Palo Alto	NW	325
● West Branch, Cedar	E	474
● West Burlington, D's M's	SE	836
● West Chester, Wash'ton.	SE	125
West Dayton, (see Dayton)		×
West Decorah, Winneshiek	NE	447
West Dubuque, Dubuque	E	×
Western College, Linn	E	150
Westerville, Decatur	S	90
● Westfield, Plymouth	NW	21
● West Gate, Fayette	NE	125
● West Grove, Davis	S	250
West Exira, (see Exira)		×
● *West Keithsburg*, Louisa.	SE	×
● West Liberty, Muscatine	E	1,268
West McGregor, Clayton	NE	74
West Mitchell, Mitchell	N	232
● Weston, Pottawattamie	SW	100
Westphalia, Shelby	W	50
West Pilot, Iowa	E	130
● West Point, Lee	SE	498
West Prairie, Linn	E	×
● *West Rapids*, Linn	E	×
West Scott, Buena Vista	NW	×
● Westside, Crawford	W	448
West Troy, Iowa	E	×
● **West Union**, Fayette	NE	1,676
● Wever, Lee	SE	60
Wexford, Allamakee	NE	×
● What Cheer, Keokuk	SE	3,246
● Wheatland, Clinton	E	569
Wheeler, Pottawattamie	SW	75
Wheeler, Mitchell	N	×
● *Wheeler*, Boone	C	×
Whipple, Pottawattamie	SW	40
White Ash, Washington	SE	90
● *White Breast*, Lucas	S	×
White Cloud, Mills	SW	27
White Oak, Mahaska	S	25
White Pigeon, Keokuk	SE	25
Whitesborough, Harrison	W	×
White Sulphur, Scott	E	×
● *Whitfield*, Jefferson	SE	×
● Whitling, Monona	W	4[illegible]
Whitman, (see Luverne)		×
● Whittemore, Kossuth	N	57[illegible]
● Whitten, Hardin	C	19[illegible]
Wichita, Guthrie	W	20
● Wick, Warren	S	20
Willard, Wapello	S	×
Willey, Carroll	W	25
● Williams, Hamilton	C	300
● Williamsburgh, Iowa	E	635
Williamstown, Chickasaw	NE	50
Willida, Lyon	NW	×
Willingford, Emmet	NW	×

Town, County	Index	Pop.
● Willits, Van Buren	SE	20
Willoughby, Butler	N	×
Willow Creek, Clay	NW	×
Wilson, Jasper	C	×
● *Wilson's Junc.*, Black H'k	C	×
Wilsonville, Van Buren	SE	150
● *Wilton*, Muscatine	E	×
● Wilton Junction, Mu'cati'e	E	1,212
Winchester, Van Buren	SE	100
Windham, Johnson	E	33
Windsor, Fayette	NE	×
● Winfield, Henry	SE	461
● Winslow, Black Hawk	C	50
● **Winterset**, Madison	S	2,281
● Winthrop, Buchanan	E	370
● Wiota, Cass	SW	168
● Wirt, Ringgold	S	200
Woden, Winnebago	N	×
● Wolcott, Scott	E	355
Wolf Creek, Tama	C	×
Wolf Dale, Woodbury	W	×
Wood, Clayton	NE	30
● Woodbine, Harrison	W	815
Woodbridge, Cedar	E	×
● Woodburn, Clark	S	336
Woodland, Decatur	S	75
● *Woodley's Siding*, W'db'y	W	×
Woodside, Winneshiek	NE	×
Woodville, Winneshiek	NE	×
● Woodward, Dallas	C	328
● Woolson, Jefferson	SE	25
● Woolstock, Wright	N	250
Wooster, Jefferson	SE	10
Worth, Boone	C	×
● Worthington, Dubuque	E	300
● Wright, Mahaska	S	25
Writer, Keokuk	SE	×
● Wyman, Louisa	SE	20
● Wyoming, Jones	E	704
● Yale, Guthrie	W	50
Yalton, Washington	SE	×
Yankee, Clay	NW	×
● Yarmouth, Des Moines	SE	50
Yatton, Washinghton	SE	100
● *Yellow River*, Allamakee	NE	×
York Center, Iowa	E	×
● Yorkshire, Harrison	W	25
● Yorktown, Page	SW	100
Yough, (see Ogden Station)		×
Youngstown, Polk	C	×
● *Zachary*, Jasper	C	×
Zalia, Union	S	×
● Zearing, Story	C	212
Zenorsville, Boone	C	300
Zero, Lucas	S	50
● *Zollicoffer Lake*, Dubuque	E	×
● Zwingle, Dubuque	E	150

KANSAS.

COUNTIES.	INDEX.	POP.
Allen	SE	13,509
Anderson	E	14,203
Atchison	NE	26,758
Barber	S	7,973
Barton	C	13,172
Bourbon	SE	28,575
Brown	NE	20,319
Butler	SE	24,055
Chase	E	8,233
Chautauqua	SE	12,297
Cherokee	SE	27,770
Cheyenne	NW	4,401
Clark	SW	2,357
Clay	N	16,146
Cloud	N	19,295
Coffey	E	15,856
Comanche	S	2,549
Cowley	SE	34,478
Crawford	SE	30,286
Decatur	NW	8,414
Dickinson	C	22,273
Doniphan	NE	13,535
Douglas	E	23,961
Edwards	S	3,600
Elk	SE	12,216
Ellis	C	7,942
Ellsworth	C	9,272
Finney	SW	3,350
Ford	SW	5,308
Franklin	E	20,271
Garfield	SW	881
Geary	E	10,423

County	Index	Pop.
Gove	W	2,994
Graham	NW	5,029
Grant	SW	1,308
Gray	SW	2,415
Greeley	W	1,264
Greenwood	SE	16,309
Hamilton	W	2,027
Harper	S	13,266
Harvey	C	17,601
Haskell	SW	1,077
Hodgeman	W	2,395
Jackson	NE	14,626
Jefferson	NE	16,620
Jewell	N	19,349
Johnson	E	17,385
Kearney	SW	1,571
Kingman	S	11,823
Kiowa	SW	2,873
Labette	SE	27,586
Lane	W	2,060
Leavenworth	NE	38,485
Lincoln	C	9,709
Linn	E	17,215
Logan	W	3,384
Lyon	E	23,196
McPherson	C	21,614
Marion	C	20,532
Marshall	NE	23,912
Meade	SW	2,542
Miami	E	19,614
Mitchell	N	15,037
Montgomery	SE	23,104
Morris	E	11,381
Morton	SW	724
Nemaha	NE	19,249
Neosho	SE	18,561
Ness	W	4,944
Norton	NW	10,617
Osage	E	25,062
Osborne	N	12,083
Ottawa	N	12,581
Pawnee	C	5,204
Phillips	N	13,661
Pottawatomie	NE	17,722
Pratt	S	8,118
Rawlins	NW	6,756
Reno	S	27,079
Republic	N	19,002
Rice	C	14,451
Riley	NE	13,183
Rooks	N	8,018
Rush	C	5,204
Russell	C	7,333
Saline	C	17,442
Scott	W	1,262
Sedgwick	S	43,626
Seward	SW	1,503
Shawnee	E	49,172
Sheridan	NW	3,733
Sherman	NW	5,261
Smith	N	15,613
Stafford	S	8,520
Stanton	SW	1,031
Stevens	SW	1,418
Sumner	S	30,271
Thomas	NW	5,538
Trego	W	2,535
Wabaunsee	E	11,720
Wallace	W	2,468
Washington	N	22,894
Wichita	W	1,827
Wilson	SE	15,286
Woodson	SE	9,021
Wyandotte	NE	54,407
Total		1,427,096

TOWN. COUNTY.	INDEX.	POP.
● Abbyville, Reno	S	200
● **Abilene**, Dickinson	C	3,547
Achilles, Rawlins	NW	35
● Ackerland, Leavenworth	NE	20
Acme, Geary	E	35
● Ada, Ottawa	N	100
● *Adams*, Kingman	S	×
Adamson, Rooks	N	32
Adell, Sheridan	NW	25
Admire, Lyon	E	200
● *Admire*, Lyon	E	×
Adrian, Jackson	NE	39
Aetna, Barber	S	50
Afton, Sedgwick	S	32
● Agenda, Republic	N	50
Agnes City, Lyon	E	40
● Agra, Phillips	N	150
● Agricola, Coffey	E	30

Place, County	Section	Pop.
Ainsworth, Wichita	W	×
Air, Lyon	E	42
Akron, Cowley	SE	100
● *Alameda*, Kingman	S	100
● Alamota, Lane	W	38
Alanthus, Gove	W	50
● Albert, Barton	C	65
Albia, Washington	N	150
● Albion, Harper	S	25
Alburtis, Morris	E	60
Alcona, Rooks	N	32
Alcyone, Sheridan	NW	45
● Alden, Rice	C	150
Aleppo, Sedgwick	S	×
● Alexander, Rush	C	75
Alfred, Douglas	E	45
● Aliceville, Coffey	E	100
● Allida, Geary	E	5
Allamead, Lincoln	C	10
Allegan, Rice	C	3
Allen, Lyon	E	150
● *Allen Station*, Lyon	E	×
Alliance, Ellsworth	C	60
Allison, Decatur	NW	×
● **Alma**, Wabaunsee	E	1,125
● Almena, Norton	NW	366
Alpha, McPherson	C	40
● Alta, Harvey	C	11
● *Altair*, Thomas	NW	×
● Altamont, Labette	SE	454
● Alta Vista, Wabaunsee	E	200
● Alton, Osborne	N	338
● Altoona, Wilson	SE	265
Amador, Butler	SE	50
Amber, Barber	S	×
Amboy, Rooks	N	46
America City, Nemaha	NE	50
● Americus, Lyon	E	393
● Ames, Cloud	N	111
● *Amiot*, Anderson	E	×
● Andale, Sedgwick	S	250
Anderson, Smith	N	46
● Andover, Butler	SE	150
● Angola, Labette	SE	15
● Annelly, Harvey	C	120
● Anness, Sedgwick	S	50
● Anson, Sumner	S	16
● Antelope, Marion	C	45
● **Anthony**, Harper	S	1,806
Antrim, Stafford	S	119
Appanoose, Douglas	E	13
Appleton, Clark	SW	×
Appomattox, Grant	SW	34
Aral, Butler	SE	40
● Arcadia, Crawford	SE	557
● *Arcola*, Ellsworth	C	×
● Argentine, Wyandotte	NE	4,732
● Argonia, Sumner	S	376
Arispie, Pottawattomie	NE	20
● Arkalon, Seward	SW	100
● Arkansas City, Cowley	SE	8,347
● Arlington, Reno	S	400
Arma, Crawford	SE	25
Armistead, Pratt	S	45
Armourdale, (see Kansas City)		×
● *Armstrong*, Wyandotte	NE	250
Arnold, Labette	SE	83
Aroma, Dickinson	C	65
● Arrington, Atchinson	NE	100
Arthur, Hodgeman	W	40
Arvonia, Osage	E	150
● Asherville, Mitchell	N	100
● **Ashland**, Clark	SW	459
Ashmead, Ellsworth	C	50
● Ashton, Sumner	S	×
Ash Valley, Pawnee	C	107
● Assaria, Saline	C	130
● Astor, Greeley	W	10
● **ATCHISON**, Atchison	NE	13,963
● *Atchison and Nebraska Junction*, Doniphan	NE	×
Athelstane, Clay	N	65
Athens, Jewell	N	10
● Athol, Smith	N	40
● Atlanta, Cowley	SE	325
● Attica, Harper	S	553
Atwater, Meade	SW	10
● **Atwood**, Rawlins	NW	450
Aubrey, Johnson	E	200
Auburn, Shawnee	E	50
● Augusta, Butler	SE	1,343
Augustine Springs, Logan	W	×
● Aulne, Marion	C	25
Aurora, (see Olivet)		×
● Aurora, Cloud	N	200
Aurora, Osage	E	10
Austin, Neosho	SE	50
Avery, Reno	S	26

Place, County	Section	Pop.
Avilla, Comanche	S	34
Avoca, Jackson	NE	20
Avon, Coffey	E	46
● Axtell, Marshall	NE	645
● *Axtell Junction*, Nemaha	NE	×
● *Azua*, Bourbon	SE	×
Bacon, Lincoln	C	65
Baden, Douglas	E	×
Badger Creek, Lyon	E	70
Bagley, Montgomery	SE	×
● Baileyville, Nemaha	NE	125
● Baker, Brown	NE	300
● Bala, Riley	NE	125
● Baldwin, Douglas	E	935
Ballard's Falls, Wash'gton	N	65
● Bancroft, Nemaha	NE	10
● *Bangor*, Miami	E	×
Banks, Osborne	N	40
● *Banner*, Harper	S	×
● Banner, Trego	W	35
Banner City, (see Elmo)		×
● Barclay, Osage	E	150
● Barnard, Lincoln	C	200
Barnard, (see Boicourt)		×
● *Barnard*, Sumner	S	×
● Barnes, Washington	N	400
Barnesville, Bourbon	SE	25
● Barrett, Marshall	NE	100
Barry, Coffey	E	150
Bartholdi, Barton	C	50
● Bartlett, Labette	SE	90
Bartondale, Russell	C	47
● Basehor, Leavenworth	NE	×
Basel, (see Bern)		×
Bashan, Lincoln	C	40
Bassettville, Decatur	NW	65
Bateham, Clay	N	65
Bates, Pratt	S	32
● *Batesville*, Woodson	SE	×
● *Bath*, Reno	S	×
Battle Hill, McPherson	C	40
● Bavaria, Saline	C	150
● Baxter Springs, Cherokee	SE	1,248
● Bayard, Allen	NE	25
Bayne, Russell	C	32
Bayne, Lincoln	C	6
● Bayneville, Sedgwick	S	10
● Bazaar, Chase	E	60
● Bazine, Ness	W	100
● Beagle, Miami	E	40
● Beardsley, Rawlins	NW	×
● Beattie, Marshall	NE	648
● Beaumont, Butler	SE	157
Beaver, Sheridan	NW	×
Beaverton, Rawlins	NW	32
Bee, Montgomery	SE	65
● Bedford, Stafford	S	×
● Beeler, Ness	W	25
Belfield, Rush	C	45
Belgica, Greeley	W	×
Belknap, Elk	SE	32
● Bellaire, Smith	N	50
● Bellefont, Ford	SW	12
● Belle Plaine, Sumner	S	659
Belle Springs, Dickinson	C	36
● **Belleville**, Republic	N	1,868
● Belmont, Kingman	S	30
● **Beloit**, Mitchell	N	2,455
● Belpre, Edwards	S	45
● Belvidere, Kiowa	SW	50
● Belvoir, Douglas	E	50
● Belvue, Pottawatomie	NE	60
Beman, Morris	E	100
● Bendena, Doniphan	NE	10
● Benedict, Wilson	SE	150
● *Benedict Junc.*, Wilson	SE	×
● *Bennett*, Lyon	E	×
● Bennington, Ottawa	N	390
Ben's Ranch, Ellsworth	C	47
● Bentley, Sedgwick	S	100
● Benton, Butler	SE	250
● Ben Wade, Pawnee	C	50
Berlin, Bourbon	SE	78
● Bern, Nemaha	NE	200
Bernal, Reno	S	×
● Berryton, Shawnee	E	×
Bertie, Graham	NW	×
● Berwick, Nemaha	NE	5
● Bethel, Wyandotte	NE	×
● Beulah, Crawford	SE	210
● *Berard*, Jackson	NE	×
● Beverly, Lincoln	C	150
Biays, Russell	C	×
Big Bend, Phillips	N	127
● Bigelow, Marshall	NE	217
● *Big Hill*, Labette	SE	×
Big Springs, Douglas	E	51

Place, County	Section	Pop.
● *Big Stranger*, L'venw'th	NE	50
Bingham, Greenwood	SE	×
● *Birch*, Anderson	E	×
Birch, Sedgwick	S	48
● Bird City, Cheyenne	NW	145
Bird Nest, Pawnee	C	45
Birley, Chase	E	40
● Birmingham, Jackson	NE	30
Bishop, Jewell	N	47
Bismarck, (see Halifax)		×
● *Bismarck Grove*, Douglas	E	×
Bitter Creek, Sumner	S	49
Bittertown, (see Olpe)		×
● *Blackburn*, Harper	S	×
Black Jack, Douglas	E	80
Blackstone, Sumner	S	25
● Black Wolf, Ellsworth	C	40
● Blaine, Pottawatomie	NE	125
● *Blair*, Doniphan	NE	312
● Blakeman, Rawlins	NW	200
Blanchard, Kingman	S	19
Block, Miami	E	11
● *Bloom*, Ford	SW	50
Bloomfield, Phillips	N	37
● Bloomington, Osborne	N	30
Blue Hill, Mitchell	N	45
● Blue Mound, Linn	E	689
● Blue Rapids, Marshall	NE	905
Blue Stem, Russell	C	32
● Bluff City, Harper	C	194
Bluffton, Coffey	E	×
● Bogue, Graham	NW	125
● Boicourt, Linn	E	97
● Boling, Leavenworth	NE	32
● Bolton, Montgomery	SE	50
Bonaccord, Dickinson	C	×
Bonasa, Wichita	W	×
Bond, Douglas	E	33
Bone Springs, Reno	S	40
● Bonita, Johnson	E	30
● Bonner Springs, Wyand'e	NE	225
Bonnie Doon, Ness	W	50
Boon, Sumner	S	40
● Booth, Reno	S	×
Border, Stanton	SW	×
Bosna, Trego	W	26
Boston Mills, Cherokee	SE	50
Bow Creek, Phillips	N	13
Bower, Norton	NW	42
Box, Cowley	SE	10
● *Boyd*, Barton	C	×
● Boyle, Jefferson	NE	10
● *Braddock*, Harvey	C	×
Braid, Ottawa	N	×
● Bradford, Wabaunsee	E	×
Bradley, Chautauqua	SE	×
● Brainerd, Butler	SE	180
Braman Hill, Wyandotte	NE	47
Brandley, Seward	SW	×
Branch, Jewell	N	×
Brantford, Washington	N	12
● Brazilton, Crawford	SE	100
● Bremen, Marshall	NE	24
● Brenham, Kiowa	SW	×
● Brenner, Doniphan	NE	25
Brett, Norton	NW	44
● *Brewer*, Ottawa	N	×
● Brewster, Thomas	NW	70
● Bridgeport, Saline	C	250
Briggs, Geary	E	42
Brigham, Greenwood	SE	×
Brighton, Kingman	S	65
● *Bristol*, Coffey	E	×
Bristow, Osborne	N	10
● *Brittsville Sta.*, Mitchell	N	390
Broderick, Pottawatmie	NE	×
● Bronson, Bourbon	SE	352
Brooklyn, Barton	C	260
● Brooks, Wilson	SE	×
● Brookville, Saline	C	345
Bross, Kingman	S	600
Brotherton, Clay	N	40
● Broughton, Clay	N	40
● Brownell, Ness	W	150
Brown's Grove, (see Burdett)		×
Brownsville, Chautauqua	SE	15
● Bucklin, Ford	SW	150
Buckner, Hodgeman	W	×
● Bucyrus, Miami	E	3
Buda, Ness	W	15
Buel, Mitchell	N	65
Buena Vista, Barton	C	65
Buffalo, Reno	S	×
● Buffalo, Wilson	SE	500
● Buffalo Park, Gove	W	200
● Buhler, Reno	S	×
● Bunker Hill, Russell	C	157
● Burden, Cowley	SE	508

Place	Pop.
● Burdett, Pawnee C	75
Budgeville, Wilson SE	46
● Burdick, Morris E	×
● *Burgess*, Butler SE	×
Burick Rooks N	×
Burkton, Franklin E	×
● Burlingame, Osage E	1,472
● **Burlington**, Coffee E	2,239
● *BurlingtonJunc.*, Franklin E	×
● Burns, Marion C	200
Burntwood, Rawlins NW	×
● Burr Oak, Jewell N	597
● Burrton, Harvey C	695
Burt, Woodson SE	77
● *Burton*, Ellsworth C	×
Busby, Elk SE	40
● *Bush City*, Anderson E	×
● Bushong, Lyon E	×
● Bushton, Rice C	136
Butte, Logan W	×
● Buxton, Wilson SE	15
Byers, Meade SW	25
Byron, Woodson SE	32
Cabbell, Logan W	40
Cactus, Norton NW	39
Cadell, Rooks N	×
Cadmus, Linn E	30
Cage, Butler SE	×
Cahola, Morris E	40
● Cain, Rice C	83
● Cairo, Pratt S	40
● Caldwell, Sumner S	1,642
● *Cale*, Cowley SE	×
Calhoun, Cheyenne NW	×
● Calista, Kingman S	13
● *Calorific*, Wyandotte NE	×
Calvert, Norton NW	×
Calvin, (see Englevale)	×
● Cambridge, Cowley SE	100
● *Cameron City*, Cowley SE	×
● Canada, Marion C	75
Candlish, Ness W	130
Canema, Barber S	50
○ Caney, Montgomery SE	542
● Canton, McPherson C	420
Capioma, Nemaha NE	20
● Carbondale, Osage E	847
Carbon Hill, Osage E	×
Cariboo, Butler SE	32
● *Carll*, Graham NW	×
● *Carlos*, Dickinson C	40
Carlton, Dickinson C	121
● Carlyle, Allen SE	50
Carmel, Cloud N	×
● *Carmi*, Pratt S	32
● Carneiro, Ellsworth C	50
● *Carney*, Marshall NE	×
Carntyne, Kingman S	98
Carrol, Greenwood SE	×
Carson, Brown NE	19
Carthage, Meade SW	97
Carwood, Wichita W	×
Cascade, Chautauqua SE	66
Cash City, Clark SW	×
Cassady, Stafford S	20
● Castleton, Reno S	25
Catalpa, Gove W	×
Catharine, Ellis C	45
Cato, Crawford SE	150
Caven, Pratt S	×
Cave Springs, Elk SE	50
● Cawker City, Mitchell N	898
Cecil, Labette SE	13
● Cedar Bluffs, Decatur NW	200
Cedar Ford, Butler SE	41
● *Cedar Grove*, Chase E	141
● Cedar Junction, Johnson E	200
Cedar Point Chase E	180
● Cedar Vale, Chautauqua SE	640
● Cedarville, Smith N	200
Cedron, Lincoln C	40
Central City, Anderson E	66
● Centralia, Nemaha NE	534
Centre, Chautauqua SE	57
Centre Ridge, Woodson SE	25
● Centreville, Linn E	500
Centropolis, Franklin E	150
Cess, Morton SW	×
Chalk Mound, Wabaunsee E	50
● Challacombe, Ness W	×
Chandler, Rooks N	46
Chantilly, Kearney SW	46
● Chanute, Neosho SE	2,826
Chaplin, Elk SE	×
● Chapman, Dickinson C	435
Chard, Neosho SE	65
Chardon, Rawlins NW	×
Charity, Clay N	57

Place	Pop.
Charlotte, Sherman NW	×
Charleston, Greenwood SE	×
● *Charleston*, Gray SW	×
Chase, Rice C	358
● Chautauqua, Chautauqua SE	350
Chelsea, Butler SE	50
● Cheney, Sedgwick S	304
Chepstow, Washington N	5
● Cherokee, Crawford SE	1,087
Cherry, Cherokee SE	45
● Cherry Vale, Montgomery SE	2,104
Cheshire, Morris E	130
Chester, Jefferson NE	46
● Chetopa, Labette SE	2,265
Cheyenne, Osborne N	135
Chicago, Sheridan NW	66
● Chico, Saline C	140
● Chicopee, Crawford SE	409
● Chiles, Miami E	×
Chillico, Cowley SE	×
● Chouteau, Johnson E	×
● *Christie*, Cloud N	32
Christopher, Reno S	39
Churchill, Ottawa N	300
● Cicero, Sumner S	10
Cimarron, Gray SW	**500**
***Cincinnati*, Grant SW**	**520**
● **Circleville, Jackson NE**	215
Cisna, Sumner S	×
● Claflin, Barton C	200
Claim, Kingman S	40
Clara, Washington N	×
Clarence, Stevens SW	×
● *Clarendon*, Rice C	×
● Clarksburgh, Bourbon SE	50
Clarkson, Riley NE	20
Claude, Woodson SE	×
Clawson, Garfield SW	×
● **Clay Centre**, Clay N	2,802
● Clayton, Norton NW	20
Clear Creek, Nemaha NE	30
Clear Dale, Sumner S	20
Clearfield, Douglas E	×
Clear Water, Sedgwick S	408
● Cleburne, Riley NE	50
● Clements, Chase E	200
Cleo, Brown NE	37
● Cleveland, Kingman S	71
Clifford, Smith N	40
Clift, Haskell SW	×
● Clifton, Washington N	622
● Climax, Greenwood SE	90
● Clinton, Douglas E	50
● *Clinton Station*, Douglas E	×
Cloverdale, Chautauqua SE	100
Clugh, Cheyenne NW	×
● Clyde, Cloud N	1,137
Coalburgh, Linn E	32
● Coalvale, Crawford SE	50
● Coats, Pratt S	×
Cocayne, (see Augustine Springs)	×
● Codell, Rooks N	50
● Coffeyville, Montgomery SE	2,282
Cohvich, Sedgwick S	212
Colbert, Lincoln C	7
● **Colby**, Thomas NW	516
● **Coldwater**, Comanche S	480
● Colfax, Chautauqua SE	×
● *College Green*, Sedgwick W	×
● Collyer, Trego W	50
Colokan, Greeley W	×
Coloma, Woodson SE	60
Colono, Trego W	60
Colony, Anderson E	474
● **Columbus**, Cherokee SE	2,160
Colusa, Haskell SW	×
● Colwich, Sedgwick S	212
Comanche, Comanche S	10
Comet, Brown NE	10
● Comiskey, Morris E	×
Concord, Sumner S	36
● **Concordia**, Cloud N	3,184
Conductor, Grant SW	25
Conkling, Pawnee C	25
● Connor, Wyandotte NE	25
Conquest, Wichita W	×
Constant, Cowley SE	45
● Conway, McPherson C	250
● Conway Springs, Sumner S	681
Cookville, Woodson SE	50
Cool, Cloud N	66
● Coolidge, Hamilton W	472
Coonsville, Linn E	×
Coopersburgh, Rice C	65
Cope, Jackson NE	83
Copeland, Thomas NW	×
Cora, Smith N	50
● Corbin, Sumner S	174

Place	Pop.
Corbitt, Ford SW	32
● *Cordley*, Wilson SE	×
Corinth, Osborne N	×
● *Cornell*, Crawford SE	×
● Corning, Nemaha NE	291
● Coronado, Wichita W	100
Corvallis, Smith N	36
● Corwin, Harper S	25
Coss, Brown NE	26
● Costello, Montgomery SE	4
● **Cottonwood Falls**, Chase E	770
● *CouncilBluffsJc.*, Atch'n NE	×
● **Council Grove**, Morris E	2,211
Coursen's Grove, Mitchell N	50
● Courtland, Republic N	267
Covert, Osborne N	60
Covington, Smith N	57
Cowboy, Ness W	37
○ *Cow Creek*, Ellsworth C	×
● *Cow Creek*, Crawford SE	×
● Coyville, Wilson SE	200
Crainville, Republic N	47
● Crandall, Coffey E	20
● Crane, Montgomery SE	15
● Crawford, Rice C	15
Creola, Garfield SW	75
Cresco, Anderson E	×
Cresson, Rooks N	26
● Crestline, Cherokee SE	100
Creswell, Marion C	19
● Crisfield, Harper S	25
● Critzer, Linn E	30
Croft, Pratt S	×
Crook, Thomas NW	×
Crosby, (see Selkirk)	×
● Crotty, Coffey E	100
Crow, Phillips N	46
Crown Point, Saline C	25
Crystal Lake, Lane W	×
Crystal Plains, Smith N	64
● Crystal Springs, Harper S	15
● Cuba, Republic N	415
● *Cuba Station*, Republic N	×
● Cullison, Pratt S	80
● Culver, Ottawa N	50
Cumberland, Thomas NW	58
● Cummings, Atchison NE	50
Cundiff, Morton SW	×
● Cunningham, Kingman S	195
Custer, Smith N	32
Cutts, Lane W	585
Cuyler, Garfield SW	40
Cyrus, Trego W	13
● *Dacey*, Rice C	×
Dafer, Leavenworth NE	×
● *Dalby*, Atchison NE	×
Dalesville, Marshall NE	×
● Dalton, Sumner S	10
● *Damar*, Rooks N	×
Damorris, Morris E	×
● Dana, Phillips N	×
Danby, Ness W	64
● Danville, Harper S	215
● *Danville*, Mitchell N	×
● *Dartmouth*, Barton C	×
Darwin, Doniphan NE	36
David, Morton SW	×
Davidson's, Cowley SE	×
● *Davidson*, Sedgwick S	×
● Day, Washington N	5
● Dearing, Montgomery SE	×
● *Deavers*, Osage E	×
Decatur, Decatur NW	100
Deep Hole, Clark SW	57
● Deerfield, Kearney SW	10
Deerhead, Barber S	10
● *Deering Junc.*, Mont'ry SE	×
● De Graff, Butler SE	25
Deland, Thomas NW	×
● Delavan, Morris E	100
Delhi, Osborne N	77
Delight, Ellsworth C	32
Dell, Lyon E	×
● Dellvale, Norton NW	×
Delmore, McPherson C	×
● Delphos, Ottawa N	561
Delta, Jewell N	45
***De Munn*, Thomas NW**	**×**
● Denison, Jackson NE	125
Denmark, Lincoln C	35
● Dennis, Labette SE	200
● Densmore, Norton NW	30
● *Denton*, Doniphan NE	×
Dentonia, Jewell N	4
Dentonville, Doniphan NE	100
● Derby, Sedgwick S	256
Dermot, Stevens SW	12
● *Derry*, Greenwood SE	×

 Kansas Kansas

Place, County	Region	Population
Derry, Greenwood	SE	25
● De Soto, Johnson	E	350
● Detroit, Dickinson	C	100
Devizes, Norton	NW	50
● Devon, Bourbon	SE	100
Dewey, Washington	N	×
De Witt, Washington	N	57
● Dexter, Cowley	SE	371
Dial, Osborne	N	32
● Diamond Springs, Morris	E	50
Dickeyville, Phillips	N	60
Digby, Saline	C	×
● **Dighton**, Lane	W	304
● *Dill*, Wilson	SE	×
Dillon, Dickinson	C	50
● *Dillwyn*, Stafford	S	×
Dispatch, Smith	N	×
Dixon, (see De Graff)		×
● *Dobson*, Johnson	E	×
● **Dodge City**, Ford	SW	1,763
● Doniphan, Doniphan	NE	347
● Dorrance, Russell	C	200
● Doster, Sumner	S	10
● *Double*, Doniphan	NE	×
● Douglass, Butler	SE	737
Dover, Shawnee	E	75
Dowell, (see Wellsford)		×
● *Downing*, Morris	E	20
● Downs, Osborne	N	938
● *Doyle*, Harvey	C	×
Dragoon, Osage	E	40
● *Drake*, Jackson	NE	×
Drake, Ness	W	60
Dresden, Kingman	S	×
● Dresden, Decatur	NW	100
● *Drum*, Montgomery	SE	×
● Drury, Sumner	S	23
Dry Creek, Saline	C	10
● *Drywood*, Crawford	SE	×
Dublin, Sumner	S	65
Dubuque, Russell	C	10
Duckworth, Comanche	S	10
● *Dudley*, Neosho	SE	×
● Dun, Wilson	SE	35
● Dunavant, Jefferson	NE	65
● *Dunaway*, Greenwood	SE	×
● *Duncan*, Miami	E	×
● Dundee, Barton	C	10
● Dunlap, Morris	E	408
● Dupont, Lane	W	10
Duquoin, Harper	S	59
Durachen, Butler	SE	60
● Durham, Marion	C	100
Dwight, Morris	E	200
Eagle, Barber	S	×
Eagle Rapids, Smith	N	60
Eagle Springs, Doniphan	NE	×
● Earleton, Neosho	SE	200
Earnest, Rooks	N	36
Easdale, Ellis	C	41
● *Eastern Junc.*, Neosho	SE	×
East Geuda Springs, Cowley	SE	169
● East Norway, Doniphan	NE	10
Easton, Leavenworth	NE	50
East Wolf, Russell	C	10
● *Eaton*, Cowley	SE	×
Eatonville, Cowley	SE	×
Echo, Douglas	E	10
Eden, Atchison	NE	25
Edgecombe, Butler	SE	32
● Edgerton, Johnson	E	321
Edith, Logan	W	×
● *Edmister*, Leavenworth	NE	×
● Edmond, Norton	NW	150
● Edna, Labette	SE	321
● Edson, Sherman	NW	×
● Edwardsville, Wyandotte	NE	200
Edwin, Stanton	SW	75
● Effingham, Atchison	NE	361
Ego, Gray	SW	5
● Elbing, Butler	SE	100
● *Elbon*, Russell	C	×
Elco, Lyon	E	36
● **El Dorado**, Butler	SE	3,339
Eldred, Barber	S	×
Eleanor, Harvey	C	38
● Elgin, Chautauqua	SE	300
Eli, Cowley	SE	19
Elinor, Chase	E	×
Elivon, (see Hesston)		×
● *Elizabeth*, Johnson	E	×
Elk, Chase	E	10
Elkader, Logan	W	×
● Elk City, Montgomery	SE	796
● Elk Falls, Elk	SE	350
● *Elkhorn*, Montgomery	SE	×
● *Ellinor*, Chase	E	×
Ellinwood, Barton	C	684
Elliott, Sheridan	NW	×
● Ellis, Ellis	C	1,107
Ellsworth, Ellsworth	C	1,620
● Elm City, Labette	SE	15
Elm Creek, Marshall	NE	57
● Elmdale, Chase	E	300
● *Elmer*, Reno	S	×
Elmira, Mitchell	N	77
Elm Mills, Barber	S	50
● Elmo, Dickinson	C	100
● Elmont, Shawnee	E	×
Elm Valley, Rush	C	36
● Elsmore, Allen	SE	150
● Elwood, Doniphan	NE	377
● Elyria, McPherson	C	57
Embry, Harper	S	×
Emerald, Anderson	E	41
Emerson, Stafford	S	×
Eminence, Garfield	SW	100
Emmet, Wyandotte	NE	×
● Emmons, Washington	N	65
Emory, Kearney	SW	×
Empire City, Cherokee	SE	923
● **Emporia**, Lyon	E	7,551
● *Emporia Junction*, Lyon	E	×
Enfield, Rooks	N	×
● Englevale, Crawford	SE	13
● Englewood, Clark	SW	175
Enne, Rawlins	NW	32
Enon, Barber	S	26
Enosdale, Washington	N	×
Ensign, Gray	SW	30
Ensign Station, Gray	SW	×
● Enterprise, Dickinson	C	804
Equity, Anderson	E	120
● **Erie**, Neosho	SE	1,176
● Esbon, Jewell	N	100
● Eskridge, Wabaunsee	E	548
Essex, Garfield	SW	5
Esther, Shawnee	E	×
● Eudora, Douglas	E	618
Eugene, Ford	SW	×
● **Eureka**, Greenwood	SE	2,259
● *Eureka Lake*, Riley	NE	×
● *Evans*, Chase	E	×
Evansville, Comanche	S	45
● Everest, Brown	NE	478
Everett, (see Vernon)		×
● Ewell, Sumner	S	10
Ewing, Lyon	E	60
Example, Haskell	SW	×
Excelsior, Mitchell	N	32
Exeter, Clay	N	46
● *Ezbon*, Jewell	N	×
Fact, Clay	N	32
Fairdale, Wyandotte	NE	×
● Fairfield, Wabaunsee	E	20
Fair Haven, Norton	NW	60
● *Fairholme*, Leavenworth	NE	×
● Fairmount, Leavenworth	NE	100
Fairplay, Ness	W	37
Fairport, Russell	C	47
● Fairview, Brown	NE	250
Fall Leaf, Leavenworth	NE	46
Fall River, Greenwood	SE	454
● *Falls*, Sumner	S	×
● Falun, Saline	C	25
Fame, Greenwood	SE	52
Fancy Creek, Clay	N	65
● Fanning, Doniphan	NE	25
Fargo, Graham	NW	40
Farisville, Ellsworth	C	×
Farland, McPherson	C	26
● Farlington, Crawford	SE	200
Farlinville, Linn	E	100
Farmersburgh, Chautauqua	SE	13
● Farmington, Atchison	NE	150
Farms, McPherson	C	35
Farnsworth, Lane	W	10
Far West, Morris	E	65
● Faulkner, Cherokee	SE	11
Fawn, Montgomery	SE	35
Fay, Russell	C	×
Federal, Hamilton	W	×
Fellsburgh, Edwards	S	48
Fenton, Rush	C	26
● *Fernie*, Reno	S	×
● Flat, Elk	SE	10
Fidelity, Brown	NE	×
Field, Morris	E	38
Fillmore, Lane	W	×
Findley, Linn	E	25
Fingal, Rush	C	×
Finney, Woodson	SE	42
Firmis, Graham	NW	38
Fisher, Stanton	SW	×
Flavius, Rush	C	45
● *Fleming*, Crawford	SE	×
Fleta, Morris	E	36
Fletcher, Stanton	SW	×
Flint Ridge, Greenwood	SE	48
● Floral, Cowley	SE	97
● *Florena*, Marshall	NE	×
● Florence, Marion	C	1,229
● *Folsom*, Cherokee	SE	×
Folsom, Haskell	SW	×
Fonda, Ford	SW	×
● Fontana, Miami	E	256
● Ford, Ford	SW	148
Forest Hill, Russell	C	46
● Formoso, Jewell	N	150
Forrester, Ness	W	46
● Fort Leavenworth, L'th.	NE	×
● Fort Riley, Geary	E	20
● **Fort Scott**, Bourbon	SE	1,946
● Fostoria, Pottawatomie	NE	53
Fountain, Osage	E	×
● Fowler, Meade	SW	100
Fox, Harper	S	×
Fox Creek, Chase	E	×
Francis, Ness	W	60
● Frankfort, Marshall	NE	1,053
Franklinville, Ness	W	×
Fred, Marion	C	41
● Frederic, Rice	C	123
● **Fredonia**, Wilson	SE	1,515
Freedom, Butler	SE	40
Freeman, Stafford	S	×
● *Freemont*, McPherson	C	×
● Freeport, Harper	S	138
Free Will, Osborne	N	×
Friend, Scott	W	×
Friendship, Cherokee	SE	×
Frisco, Morton	SW	240
Frisco Crossing, Harper	S	×
Front, Allen	SE	×
● Frontenac, Crawford	SE	600
● *Fruitland*, Leavenworth	NE	×
Fullerton, Hodgeman	W	×
Fullerton, (see Hamilton)		×
● Fulton, Bourbon	SE	506
● Furley, Sedgwick	S	50
Galatia, Barton	C	40
● Galena, Cherokee	SE	2,496
Galesburgh, Neosho	SE	200
Gallagher, Comanche	S	×
● Galt, Rice	C	×
● Galva, McPherson	C	255
Gandy, Sherman	NW	32
● **Garden City**, Finney	SW	1,490
● Garden Plain, Sedgwick	S	250
● Gardner, Johnson	E	515
● Garfield, Pawnee	C	160
● Garland, Bourbon	SE	250
Garlington, Franklin	E	×
● **Garnett**, Anderson	E	2,191
● Garrison, Pottawatomie	NE	50
● *Garrison Crossing*, Riley	NE	×
Gaskill, Washington	N	×
● *Gatesville*, Clay	N	×
● Gaylord, Smith	N	314
Geary, Doniphan	NE	10
● Gem, Thomas	NW	×
● Geneseo, Rice	C	399
● Geneva, Allen	SE	50
George, Pawnee	C	36
Gere, Barton	C	48
Germania, Sedgwick	S	50
Germantown, Smith	N	32
Gettysburg, (see Penokee)		×
● Geuda Springs, Cowley	SE	355
Gibson, Trego	W	6
Gideon, Douglas	E	37
● *Gilbert*, Mitchell	N	×
Gilfillan, Bourbon	SE	40
Girard, Crawford	SE	2,541
● *Gladstone*, Chase	E	×
Gladstone, Rawlins	NW	456
● *Gladys*, Sedgwick	S	5
● Glasco, Cloud	N	461
Glendale, Bourbon	SE	×
● *Glendale*, Douglas	E	×
● Glen Elder, Mitchell	N	407
Glen Grouse, Cowley	SE	32
● Glenloch, Anderson	E	31
Glenn, Johnson	E	46
Glen Sharrald, Rice	C	45
Glenwood, Leavenworth	NE	32
Globe, Douglas	E	10
● Goddard, Sedgwick	S	210
● Godfrey, Bourbon	SE	65
● Goff's, Nemaha	NE	277
Gognac, Stanton	SW	×

Golden, Grant............SW	15
Goode, Phillips..........N	45
Good Intent, Atchison.....NE	40
● **Goodland**, Sherman..NW	1,027
● Goodrich, Linn..........E	100
Goodwater, Gove..........W	×
● Gordon, Butler..........SE	100
● Gorham, Russell.........C	25
Goshen, Graham..........NW	40
● *Goss*, Harper..........S	×
Gove, Gove...........W	118
Grace, Sherman.........NW	×
Grafton, Chautauqua......SE	42
● Grainfield, Gove.......W	99
Granada, Nemaha.......NE	20
Grand Centre, Osborne.....N	68
Grand Haven Shawnee.....E	109
Grand Prairie, Brown....NE	13
● Grand Summit, Cowley..SE	130
Grand View, Morris......E	×
Grand View, Ford.......SW	×
Granger, Comanche.......S	103
● *Grant*, Harper..........S	×
Grant, Riley..............NE	65
● Grantville, Jefferson....NE	100
Graves, Cloud............N	41
● *Gray*, Hodgeman.........W	×
● **Great Bend**, Barton.... C	2,450
● Greeley, Anderson........E	514
● Green, Clay..............N	160
Greenbush, Crawford......SE	40
Green Elm, Crawford......SE	40
● Greenleaf, Washington... N	916
Green Ridge, Stafford......S	32
● **Greensburgh**, Kiowa SW	515
Greenvale, Russell........C	65
● Greenwich, Sedgwick.....S	97
● *Greenwood*, Greenwood. SE	32
Gregory, Jewell...........N	10
● Grenola, Elk..............SE	608
Gretna, Phillips...........N	×
● Gridley, Coffey...........E	250
Griffin, Woodson..........SE	×
● Grigsby, Scott............W	10
Grimm, Wabaunsee.........E	×
● Grinnell, Gove...........W	25
Grinter, Wyandotte.......NE	×
Griswold, Sherman.......NW	×
● *Groom*, Linn.............E	26
● Groveland, McPherson....C	×
● Grover, Douglas..........E	25
Guelph, Sumner............S	40
● Guilford, Wilson.........SE	40
Guittard Station, Marshall NE	65
Gurney, Cheyenne........NW	×
Guy, Sheridan............NW	×
Gypsum, Saline............C	530
Hackberry, Gove..........W	32
● *Hackney*, Cowley.......SE	×
● Haddam, Washington.....N	419
Hadley, Crawford..........SE	51
● Halcyon, Wichita........W	×
Hale, Chautauqua..........SE	61
Half Way, Cloud...........N	42
● Halifax, Wabaunsee......E	×
● Hallowell, Cherokee.....SE	200
● Hall's Summit, Coffey.....E	25
● *Hallville*, Saline..........C	×
● Halstead, Harvey.........C	1,071
● *Hamburg*, Pawnee.........C	×
● Hamilton, Greenwood...SE	206
● Hamlin, Brown..........NE	216
● Hammond, Bourbon.....SE	50
Hampton, Rush.............C	5
Hanback, Norton.........NW	13
Hancock, Lane............W	×
Hanover, Washington.......N	903
● *Hanston*, Hodgeman.....W	×
Happy, Graham.......... NW	60
Hardilee, Smith............N	38
● Harding, Bourbon.......SE	20
Hardtner, Barber...........S	×
Hargrave, Rush.............C	×
Harkness, Leavenworth...NE	×
● Harlan, Smith............N	109
Harma, Gray..............SW	×
Harmony, Pawnee..........C	46
Harold, Ness..............W	75
● Harper, Harper...........S	1,579
Harper Junction, Kingman.S	×
● Harris, Anderson.........E	230
Harrison, Jewell...........N	65
● Hartford, Lyon...........E	441
● Hartland, Kearney.......SW	193
● Harveyville, Wabaunsee..E	150
● Haskell, Anderson........E	38
Hatfield, Finney..........SW	×
Hatton, Hamilton..........W	×

● Havana, Montgomery...SE	114
● Haven, Reno..............S	250
● Havensville, Pot'wato'le NE	276
● Haverhill, Butler........SE	19
● Haviland, Kiowa.........SW	85
Hawkeye, Decatur........NW	60
Hawley, Russell............C	45
● Haworth, Republic........N	×
● Hawthorn, Atchison.....NE	×
● *Hayden*, Labette........SE	×
Haynesville, Pratt.........S	32
● **Hays City**, Ellis.........C	1,242
Haysville, Sedgwick.........S	130
● Hazleton, Barber..........S	319
● Healey, Lane..............W	25
Heber, Cloud...............N	45
● *Hecla*, Anderson..........E	×
Hedgewood, Norton......NW	260
● Heizer, Barton............C	×
● Helmick, Morris...........E	×
Helvetia, Meade..........SW	×
Hendricks, Finney........SW	×
Henry, Sheridan..........NW	×
● Hepler, Crawford........SE	269
● Herington, Dickinson.....C	1,353
● Herkimer, Marshall.... NE	200
Herman, Lincoln............C	32
● Herndon, Rawlins......NW	140
● Hertha, Neosho..........SE	14
Hesper, Douglas............E	40
Hess, Gray..............SW	32
● Hesston, Harvey..........C	75
Hewins, Chautauqua.......SE	50
● *Hewins*, Chautauqua....SE	×
● Hiattville, Bourbon......SE	20
● **Hiawatha**, Brown.....NE	2,486
Hickman, Greenwood.....SE	×
High Bridge, Atchison....NE	×
Highhill, Rooks...........N	26
Highland, Doniphan.......NE	493
● Highland Sta., DoniphanNE	75
Highpoint, Ness...........W	60
● Hill City, Graham......NW	545
● Hillsboro, Marion........C	555
● Hillsdale, Miami..........E	250
Hillside, Phillips...........N	46
● Hilltop, Greenwood.......SE	43
● *Hilton*, McPherson.......C	×
Hink, Crawford............SE	×
Hodgeman, Hodgeman.....W	40
● *Hog Back*, Ellis..........C	×
● Hoge, Leavenworth.....NE	×
● Hoisington, Barton.......C	416
Holbrook, Hodgeman......W	×
Holland, Dickinson.........C	×
● Hollenberg, Washington..N	166
● Holliday, Johnson.........E	150
Holling, Douglas............E	26
● Hollis, Cloud..............N	38
● Hollyrood, Ellsworth.....C	150
Holmes, Wallace...........W	×
● **Holton**, Jackson......NE	2,727
Holy Cross, Pottawatomie.NE	42
● Home, Marshall.........NE	134
● *Homer*, Russell...........C	45
Homestead, Chase..........E	40
● Homewood, Franklin.....E	20
Hooker, Decatur..........NW	32
● Hooser, Cowley..........SE	24
● Hope, Dickinson..........C	632
Hopewell, Washington......N	39
● Horace, Greeley..........W	150
● Horanif, Wyandotte.....NE	40
● *Horners*, Marion.........C	×
● Horton, Brown..........NE	3,316
● Hortonburgh, Lyon.......E	40
Hosford, Montgomery.....SE	41
Hoskins, Rooks............N	45
Houston, Graham........NW	45
● **Howard**, Elk..........SE	1,015
● *Howell*, Ford............SW	×
● **Hoxie**, Sheridan......NW	245
● Hoyt, Jackson...........NE	170
● Hudson, Stafford..........S	40
Hugoton, Stevens......SW	136
● Hukle, Sedgwick...........S	×
● Hull, Marshall...........NE	×
● Humboldt, Allen.........SE	1,367
● Hund's Station, Leven'th NE	100
● Hunnewell, Sumner........S	168
Huntsville, Reno...........S	52
● Huron, Atchison.......NE	200
Hurst Crossing, (see Corbin).	×
● **Hutchinson**, Reno.....S	8,682
● *Hutchinson's Wye*, Mar'l NE	×
Hutton, Rush..............C	39
● Hymer, Chase.............E	49

● Idana, Clay..............N	100
Idell, Crawford...........SE	65
● Idenbro, Labette........SE	×
Igo, Rooks................N	60
Ilion, Rawlins...........NW	×
● Imes, Franklin...........E	50
● Imperial, Garfield......SW	×
● **Independence**, M'tg'y SE	3,127
Indianola, Butler..........SE	60
● *India*, Douglas..........E	×
Industry, Clay.............N	200
● Ingalls, Gray............SW	200
Ingalls, (see Bayne)........	×
● Inman, McPherson.......C	90
Invermay, Atchison.......NE	×
Inyo, Harper................S	40
● **Iola**, Allen..............SE	1,706
Ionia, Jewell...............N	100
● Iowa Point, Doniphan..NE	200
Iowaville, Sedgwick.........S	15
● *Irene*, Hamilton..........W	×
Irene, (see Cairo)............	×
● Irving, Marshall........NE	375
● Isabel, Barber.............S	×
Island, Neosho.............SE	65
Itasca, Sherman.........NW	×
● **Iuka**, Pratt...............S	110
● *Ivanuar*, Osborne.........N	×
Ivanhoe, Haskell.........SW	40
Ivanpah, Greenwood.......SE	5
Ivy, Lyon...................E	40
Iwacura, Clay..............N	38
Jack, Russell..............C	32
Jackson, Decatur.........NW	60
Jacksonburgh, Smith.......N	10
Jacksonville, Neosho......SE	65
● *Jaggard*, Wyandotte....NE	×
Jaggard, Leavenworth....NE	×
Jalma, Meade..............SW	×
● Jamestown, Cloud........N	372
Jaqua, Cheyenne.........NW	×
● Jarbalo, Leavenworth...NE	50
Jasper, Meade...........SW	75
● Jefferson, Montgomery..SE	15
Jenkins, Comanche.........S	×
● Jennings, Decatur......NW	200
Jerome, Gove...............W	30
Jetmore, Hodgeman.....W	324
● Jewell, Jewell............N	702
● *Jewett*, Linn..............E	×
Jimtown, Phillips...........N	32
Jingo, Miami................E	40
Joash, Meade..............SW	65
Johnson, Stanton.........SW	143
● Johnstown, McPherson...C	10
Jonesburgh, Chautauqua...SE	50
Jordon Springs, (see Langdon)	×
Judson, Smith..............N	60
Julia, Kingman.............S	×
● *Junction*, Bourbon......SE	×
● *Junction*, Sedgwick.......S	×
● *Junction*, Wyandotte...NE	×
● **Junction City**, Geary..E	4,502
Jurett, Wilson............SE	32
Juse, Woodson.............SE	×
● Kackley, Republic.........N	×
● *Kalloch*, Montgomery...SE	×
● *Kalula*, Graham.......NW	×
Kalvesta, Garfield.........SW	8
● Kanona, Decatur.......NW	40
● Kanopolis, Ellsworth.....C	272
● *Kanorado*, Sherman...NW	×
Kansada, Ness..............W	32
● *Kansas Cen.Jc.*..JeffersonNE	×
Kansas Centre, Rice.......C	97
● **Kansas City**, Wyan'e.NE	38,316
● *Kansas Falls*, Geary.....E	×
Kearney, Kearney.........SW	5
● Keats, Riley.............NE	25
Kebar, Graham..........NW	32
● Kechi, Sedgwick...........S	×
Keelville, Cherokee........SE	30
Keene, Wabaunsee..........E	65
● Keighley, Butler.........SE	40
Kellogg, Cowley...........SE	20
● Kelly, Nemaha...........NE	10
● Kelso, Morris..............E	20
● Kendall, Hamilton.......W	67
Kenilworth, Stafford........S	46
Kennebec, Russell..........C	60
Kennedy, Dickinson.........C	×
Kennekuk, Atchison......NE	100
● Kensington, Smith........N	200
● Kent, Reno.................S	10
Kepple, Wichita.............W	×
Keysville, Pawnee..........C	×
● Kickapoo City, Leaven'h NE	100
Kidderville, Hodgeman....W	60

Kansas		
Kill Creek, Osborne	N	25
● Kilmer, Shawnee	E	×
● Kimbal, Neosho	SE	200
Kimeo, Washington	N	7
● Kincaid, Anderson	E	284
● *King*, Montgomery	SE	×
Kingman, Kingman	S	2,390
Kingsdown, Ford	SW	100
Kingston, (see Edna)		×
● Kingsville, Shawnee	E	65
● *Kinneys*, Osage	E	525
● **Kinsley**, Edwards	S	771
● Kiowa, Barber	S	893
● Kipp, Saline	C	×
Kirkfield, Edwards	S	×
● Kirwin, Phillips	N	689
Kismet, Seward	SW	×
Klink, Sherman	NW	×
Knauston, Finney	SW	×
Knox, Sumner	S	×
Koloko, Washington	N	103
Konantz, Stanton	SW	×
Kong, Coffey	E	×
Kuhnbrook, Marion	C	×
Kuka, Thomas	NW	×
● *Kyle*, Coffey	E	×
Kyle, Morton	SW	×
● Labette, Labette	SE	250
La Blanche, Sherman	NW	×
● *Lackmans*, Johnson	E	×
Laclede, Pottawattomie	NE	75
● **La Crosse**, Rush	C	513
● La Cygne, Linn	E	1,135
● Ladore, Neosho	SE	100
Lafayette, Stevens	SW	50
● La Fontaine, Wilson	SE	125
La Grand, (see Springfield)		×
La Grange, Marshall	NE	26
● La Harpe, Allen	SE	40
● *Laird*, Ness	W	×
Lake City, Barber	S	125
Lakeland, Meade	**SW**	×
Lakeside, Bourbon	SE	3
● *Lake View*, Douglas	E	27
● *Lake View*, McPherson	C	37
● Lakin, Kearney	SW	258
Lamar, Ottawa	N	35
Lamasco, Graham	NW	×
Lamborn, Sherman	NW	100
Lamon, Montgomery	SE	×
Lamont, Greenwood	SE	×
La Mont's Hill, Osage	E	60
● Lancaster, Atchison	NE	50
Landrum, Clark	SW	×
● Lane, Franklin	E	500
● Laneville, Labette	SE	12
● *Lang*, Lyon	E	×
● Langdon, Reno	S	25
● Langley, Ellsworth	C	15
● *Lanham*, Washington	N	×
● Lansing, Leavenworth	NE	1,468
Lapeer, Douglas	E	65
Lapland, Greenwood	SE	40
Laporte, Grant	SW	×
Larimer, Montgomery	SE	50
● Larkin, Jackson	NE	140
● **Larned**, Pawnee	C	1,861
Lashmet, Kingman	S	×
Lasker, Ford	SW	×
● Latham, Butler	SE	268
Latimer, Morris	E	×
Laton, Rooks	N	46
Laurel, Hodgeman	W	×
Lava, Sherman	NW	×
Lawndale, Pratt	S	40
Lawnridge, Cheyenne	NW	×
Lawrence, Douglas	E	9,997
● Lawrenceburgh, Cloud	N	45
● *Lawrence Junction*, Jeff	NE	×
● *Lawrence & Emporia Junc.*, Jefferson	NE	×
Lawson, Grant	SW	×
● Lay, Montgomery	SE	40
Leanna, Allen	SE	×
LEAVENWORTH, Leavenworth	NE	19,768
● *Leavenworth Junc.*, Leavenworth	NE	×
● Lebanon, Smith	N	301
● Lebo, Coffey	E	538
● Lecompton, Douglas	E	450
● *Lee*, Jefferson	NE	×
Leeds, Chautauqua	SE	60
Leesburgh, Stafford	S	32
● Lehigh, Marion	C	275
Leland, Graham	NW	60
● Le Loup, Franklin	E	35

Kansas

Kansas		
● Lenape, Leavenworth	NE	100
Lena Valley, Lyon	E	36
● Lenexa, Johnson	E	230
● Lenora, Norton	NW	231
● Leon, Butler	SE	456
● Leona, Doniphan	NE	171
● Leonardville, Riley	NE	410
Leoranda, Graham	NW	×
● Leoti, Wichita	W	341
Lerado, Reno	S	30
● LeRoy, Coffey	E	893
● *LeRoy Junction*, Coffey	E	×
Leslie, Reno	S	34
Letitia, Clark	SW	40
Levant, Thomas	NW	×
Levy, Sumner	S	32
● Lewis, Edwards	S	200
Lexington, Clark	SW	25
● Liberal, Seward	SW	372
● Liberty, Montgomery	SE	344
Lida, Chase	E	40
Liebenthal, Rush	C	100
Lily, Morris	E	40
Lima, Elk	SE	44
● **Lincoln**, Lincoln	C	1,100
● Lincolnville, Marion	C	275
Linda, Rawlins	NW	×
● Lindsborg, McPherson	C	968
● Lindsey, Ottawa	N	10
● Linn, Washington	N	222
Lindale, Rush	C	×
● Linwood, Leavenworth	NE	306
Lisbon, Gove	W	×
● *Lisbon*, Logan	W	×
Lister, Wallace	W	×
Litchfield, Crawford	SE	888
● *Litchfield Junction*, Craw	SE	×
● Little River, Rice	C	340
Little Valley, McPherson	C	38
Livingston, Stafford	S	49
Liverpool, Stanton	SW	5
Lockport, Haskell	SW	×
Loco, Haskell	SW	×
Locust Grove, Atchison	NE	32
Lodi, Barber	S	38
● Logan, Phillips	N	390
Logansport, Logan	W	×
● *Lomax*, Osage	E	×
London, (see Belle Plain)		×
● Lone Elm, Anderson	E	125
Lonelake, Gray	SW	×
● *Lone Oak*, Crawford	SE	13
Lone Tree, McPherson	C	38
Lone Walnut, Lincoln	C	47
Longford, Clay	N	60
● *Longford Station*, Clay	N	×
● Long Island, Phillips	N	400
● Longton, Elk	SE	624
● Lorena, Butler	SE	60
Lorenz, Garfield	SW	×
● Loring, Wyandotte	NE	15
● Lorraine, Ellsworth	C	115
● Lost Springs, Marion	C	150
Lotta, Kingman	S	32
● Louisburgh, Miami	E	760
Louisville, Pottawatomie	NE	382
● *Lovewell*, Jewell	N	15
Lovewell, Republic	N	×
Lovewell Station, Jewell	N	25
● Lowe, Chautauqua	SE	25
Lowell, Cherokee	SE	260
● Lowemont, Leavenworth	NE	×
● Lowell Station, Cherokee	SE	×
Loyal, Garfield	SW	46
● Lucas, Russell	C	150
Lucerne, Sheridan	NW	15
Luctor, Phillips	N	150
● Ludell, Rawlins	NW	100
Ludwick, Pratt	S	×
● Luray, Russell	C	150
Luther, Morris	E	48
Lydia, Kearney	SW	×
Lyle, Decatur	NW	65
● **Lyndon**, Osage	E	935
Lyon, Dickinson	C	40
● **Lyons**, Rice	C	1,754
● McAllaster, Logan	W	20
● McCracken, Rush	C	281
● McCune, Crawford	SE	700
● McDonald, Rawlins	NW	100
● McFarland, Wabaunsee	E	100
McHale, Rooks	N	60
● *McIntosh*, Jefferson	NE	×
● McLain, Harvey	C	×
● McLouth, Jefferson	NE	311
● **McPherson**, McPherson	C	3,172
● *McPherson College*, McPherson	C	×

Kansas

Kansas		
Mabel, Seward	SW	×
Macgraw, Sheridan	NW	×
● Macksville, Stafford	S	156
Macomb, Gray	SW	×
Macon, Wallace	W	×
● **Macyville, Cloud**	**N**	**66**
Madeline, Wichita	W	×
● Madison, Greenwood	SE	623
● *Madison Junc.*, Gre'nw'd	SE	×
Magda, Lyon	E	×
Magic, Riley	NE	36
Magnolia, Sedgwick	S	200
● Mahaska, Washington	N	50
● Maherville, Barton	C	10
● Maize, Sedgwick	S	150
Majella, Bourbon	SE	×
● Manchester, Dickinson	C	125
● **Manhattan**, Riley	NE	3,004
● **Mankato**, Jewell	N	800
Manley, Marshall	NE	×
● *Manning*, Clark	SW	×
● Manning, Scott	W	×
● *Mansfield*, Finney	SW	45
Mansfield, Wabaunsee	E	45
Manteno, Ness	W	36
● *Manville*, Brown	NE	×
Maple City, Cowley	SE	130
● Maple Hill, Wabaunsee	E	150
● Mapleton, Bourbon	SE	175
● Marena, Hodgeman	W	25
Margaret, Lincoln	C	41
Maria, Leavenworth	NE	40
Mariadahl, Pottawatomie	NE	98
● Marietta, Marshall	NE	×
Marietta, Reno	S	46
● **Marion**, Marion	C	2,047
● Marmaton, Bourbon	SE	25
Marney, Cheyenne	NW	×
● Marquette, McPherson	C	367
Marshall, Pawnee	C	45
Martin, Ellis	C	46
● Marvin, Phillips	N	150
Marydel, Saline	C	520
● **Marysville**, Marshall	NE	1,913
Masmer, Ellsworth	C	×
Matanzas, Chautauqua	SE	40
Matfield Green, Chase	E	150
● Mathewson, Labette	SE	10
Matsonville, Kiowa	SW	×
Matteson, Phillips	N	60
Maud, Morton	SW	×
Maxson, Osage	E	60
May Day, Riley	NE	12
● *Mayetta*, Jackson	NE	50
● Mayfield, Sumner	S	138
● *Mayline*, Hamilton	W	×
Mayo, Comanche	S	×
Mayview, Jewell	N	7
● Maywood, Wyandotte	NE	98
● **Meade**, Meade	SW	457
Meadow Brook, Johnson	E	41
Media, Douglas	E	150
● **Medicine Lodge**, B'ber	S	1,095
● Medina, Jefferson	NE	25
● Medora, Reno	S	×
● *Medway*, Hamilton	W	×
Melior, Barber	S	×
Mell, Wallace	W	×
Melrose, Cherokee	SE	40
● Melvern, Osage	E	461
Melville, Ottawa	N	60
Menager, Wyandotte	NE	×
Mendota, Ellis	C	41
● Menlo, Thomas	NW	×
● Menoken, Shawnee	E	3
● Mentor, Saline	C	25
Meredith, Cloud	N	97
● Meriden, Jefferson	NE	400
● *Meriden Junc.*, Jefferson	NE	×
● Merriam, Johnson	E	50
Meitilla, Meade	SW	10
Messer, Cherokee	SE	25
● *Metcalf*, Sumner	S	×
Metz, Chautauqua	SE	32
● Miami, Linn	E	40
● Michigan Valley, Osage	E	20
Middle Branch, Hodgeman	W	65
Middletown, Wilson	SE	10
● *Midland*, Jefferson	NE	×
Midlothian, (see Freeport)		×
● Midway, Crawford	SE	246
● *Midway*, Ellsworth	C	×
● Milan, Sumner	S	229
Milford, Geary	E	220
● *Milford*, Geary	E	×
Millard, Barton	C	45
Millbrook, Graham	NW	×
● Miller, Lyon	E	×

Place		
● Millerton, Sumner	S	75
● *Mills*, Rush	C	×
Millwood, Leavenworth	NE	50
● Milo, Lincoln	C	20
Milroy, Hodgeman	W	×
● Milton, Sumner	S	30
● Miltonvale, Cloud	N	591
Milwaukee, Stafford	S	38
● Mina, Marshall	NE	×
● *Mineola*, Shawnee	E	×
Minera Point, Anderson	E	22
Minersville, Cloud	N	10
Minerva, Labette	SE	60
Mingona, Barber	S	50
● **Minneapolis**, Ottawa	N	1,840
Minneha, Sedgwick	S	×
Minneola, Clark	SW	100
● *Miocene*, Leavenworth	NE	×
Mirage, Rawlins	NW	×
● *Mission*, Harvey	C	×
● Mitchell, Rice	C	50
Mitchellville, Stanton	SW	50
● Modoc, Scott	W	×
● Moline, Elk	SE	527
Mono, Reno	S	32
● Monett, Chautauqua	SE	25
Monitor, McPherson	C	25
Mabel, Kingman	S	×
● Monmouth, Crawford	SE	250
Monon, Station	SW	×
● *Monotony*, Wallace	W	×
Monroe, Lincoln	C	130
● Monrovia, Atchinson	NE	20
Montana, Labette	SE	150
Monterey, Riley	NE	15
Montezuma, Gray	SW	32
Monticello, Johnson	E	175
● Mont Ida, Anderson	E	200
● Montrose, Jewell	N	67
● Monument, Logan	W	50
● *Moody*, Coffey	E	×
Moodyville, Pottawatimie	NE	15
Moonlight, Stevens	SW	×
● *Moore's*, Leavenworth	NE	40
● Morantown, Allen	SE	463
● Morehead, Neosho	SE	75
Morgan, Chase	E	130
● Morganville, Clay	N	233
Morland, Graham	NW	80
● Morrill, Brown	NE	308
● *Morris*, Wyandotte	NE	×
● Morrow Station, Washing'n	N	100
● Morse, Johnson	E	50
Mortimer, Labette	SE	30
Morton, Montgomery	SE	×
Morton, Morton	SW	260
Moscow, Stevens	SW	30
Moss Springs, Geary	E	32
Motor, (see Codell)		
● **Mound City**, Linn	E	888
Mound Creek, Miami	E	32
● Moundridge, McPherson	C	443
● Mornd Valley, Labette	SE	545
Mount Ayr, Osborne	N	×
Mount Carmel, Crawford	SE	38
● Mount Hope, Sedgwick	S	241
Mount Ida. (see Mont Ida)		×
Mount Nebo, Pratt	S	64
Mount Olivet, Leavenw'rth	NE	38
● Mount Pleasant, Atchison	NE	10
● *Mount Zion*, Ellsworth	C	×
Mullberry, Saline	C	102
● Mulberry Grove, Crawf'd	SE	350
Muldrow, Sherman	NW	×
Mule Creek, Ellsworth	C	×
● Mullinville, Kiowa	SW	79
● Mulvane, Sumner	S	724
Mumford, Barber	S	40
● Muncie, Wyandotte	NE	130
● Munden, Republic	N	50
Munjor, Ellis	C	60
Murdock, Butler	SE	31
● *Murdock*, Kingman	S	41
● Muscotah, Atchison	NE	524
Museum, Sheridan	NW	41
Myers Valley, Pottawa'mie	NE	25
Myra, Woodson	SE	25
Myrtle, Phillips	N	32
Nadeau, Jackson	NE	×
Nance, Phillips	N	48
● Narka, Republic	N	100
Naron, Pratt	S	37
Nasby, Saline	C	32
● Nashville, Kingman	S	45
Nathan, Barton	C	60
National Military Home, Leavenworth	NE	×

Kansas

Place		
Natoma, Osborne	N	×
● *Natrona*, Pratt	S	×
Nauvoo, Comanche	S	×
● Navarre, Dickinson	C	45
● Neal, Greenwood	SE	144
● *Nearman*, Wyandotte	NE	×
● Neely, Leavenworth	NE	×
● Nekoma, Rush	C	×
Nellans, Butler	SE	44
Nelson, Cloud	N	65
● Neodesha, Wilson	SE	1,528
● Neola, Stafford	S	40
● Neosho Falls, Woodson	SE	606
● Neosho Rapids, Lyon	E	308
Nescatunga, Comanche	S	46
● **Ness City**, Ness	W	869
● Netawaka, Jackson	NE	241
● *Nettleton*, Edwards	S	×
Neuchatel, Nemaha	NE	10
● Neutral, Cherokee	SE	75
Neville, Sherman	NW	×
Nevada, Ness	W	×
● New Albany, Wilson	SE	250
New Almelo, Norton	NW	×
Newark, Wilson	SE	78
New Basel, Dickinson	C	80
Newber, Dickinson	C	47
Newbury, Wabaunsee	E	75
● New Cambria, Saline	C	100
New Chillicothe, Dickinson	C	45
● *New Elgin*, Chautauqua	SE	130
New Haven, Reno	S	47
Newhope, Smith	N	10
Newington, Johnson	E	×
New Kiowa, (see Kiowa)		×
New Kirk, Ford	SW	×
New Lancaster, Miami	E	100
● Newman, Jefferson	NE	10
● New Murdock, Kingman	S	200
● New Salem, Cowley	SE	175
New Tabor, Republic	N	40
● **Newton**, Harvey	C	5,605
New Windsor, Cherokee	SE	32
Niagara, Stevens	SW	×
● *Nichols*, Jefferson	NE	×
Nickel, Kiowa	SW	×
● Nickerson, Reno	S	1,662
Nicodemus, Graham	NW	50
● Niles, Ottawa	N	65
Nilesville, Ottawa	N	65
Nimrod, Lincoln	C	57
Ninnescha, (see Cunningham)		×
● Niotaze, Chautauqua	SE	125
Nixon, Pawnee	C	45
● Noble, Rice	C	32
Noland, Ford	SW	×
Nonchalanta, Ness	W	14
Nora, Pratt	S	65
● Norcatur, Decatur	NW	300
Norfolk, Ellis	C	×
North Branch, Jewell	N	25
North Bend, Finney	SW	×
● *North Cedar*, Jackson	NE	10
North Cedar, Jefferson	NE	×
Northcott, Anderson	E	50
Northfield, Sherman	NW	×
● *North Lawrence*, Douglas	E	×
● *North Ottawa*, Franklin	E	×
● North Topeka, Shawnee	E	×
● North Wichita, Sedgwick	S	×
● **Norton**, Norton	NW	1,074
● Nortonville, Jefferson	NE	669
● *Norway*, Doniphan	NE	57
● Norway, Republic	N	20
● Norwich, Kingman	S	301
● Norwood, Franklin	E	45
Numa, Butler	SE	×
Nyra, Rooks	N	53
Oak, Jefferson	NE	×
Oak, Seward	SW	×
● Oak Hill, Clay	N	70
Oakland, Shawnee	E	×
Oakland, Wyandotte	NE	300
● Oakley, Logan	W	176
● Oak Mills, Atchison	NE	25
● Oak Valley, Elk	SE	202
● Oakwood, Linn	E	10
Oanica, Kearney	SW	×
Oasis, Smith	N	×
● Oatville, Sedgwick	S	60
● **Oberlin**, Decatur	NW	976
● *O'Brien*, Miami	E	×
● Ocheltree, Johnson	E	55
Odee, Meade	SW	59
Odense, Neosho	SE	97
Odessa, Jewell	N	32
Odin, Barton	C	65

Kansas

Place		
● Offerle, Edwards	S	85
● Ogallah, Trego	W	25
● Ogden, Riley	NE	173
Ogdensburg, (see Ransom)		×
Ohio, Smith	N	77
Ohio Centre, Sedgwick	S	40
Okaw, Kingman	S	32
● Oketo, Marshall	NE	334
Oklahomo, Kingman	S	57
● **Olathe**, Johnson	E	3,294
● *Olathe Park*, Johnson	E	×
● Olcott, Reno	S	60
● *Olds*, Miami	E	×
Oliver, Haskell	SW	×
Olivet, Osage	E	20
● *Olivet Station*, Osage	E	×
● Olmitz, Barton	C	25
Olney, Rush	C	45
● Olpe, Lyon	E	300
Olsburg, Pottawatomie	NE	185
Omio, Jewell	N	227
● Onaga, Pottawatomie	NE	423
● Oneida, Nemaha	NE	311
● Oneonta, Cloud	N	×
Ontario, Jackson	NE	57
● *Ontario Station*, Nemaha	NE	×
Ophir, Butler	SE	×
● Opolis, Crawford	SE	178
Orange, Norton	NW	×
Orbitello, Lincoln	C	57
Orchard, Linn	E	32
Orie, Sumner	S	32
Orlando, Cheyenne	NW	×
● Oronoque, Norton	NW	100
Orwell, Hodgeman	W	90
Orworth, Lincoln	C	45
● Osage City, Osage	E	3,469
● Osage Mission, Neosho	SE	1,097
● Osawatomie, Miami	E	2,662
● **Osborne**, Osborne	N	1,174
Oskaloosa, Jefferson	NE	773
Osro, Chautauqua	SE	×
Ost, Reno	S	40
● **Oswego**, Labette	SE	2,571
● Otego, Jewell	N	78
● Otis, Rush	C	100
● **Ottawa**, Franklin	E	6,248
Otterbourne, Thomas	NW	57
Otto, Cowley	SE	40
Ottumwa, Coffey	E	100
● *Oursler*, Marion	C	×
● Overbrook, Osage	E	172
Oro, Butler	SE	45
● Oxford, Sumner	S	665
Oxide, Ellsworth	C	45
● Ozawkie, Jefferson	NE	200
Ozro, Chautauqua	SE	10
● Padonia, Brown	NE	25
● Page, Logan	W	×
Pageton, Trego	W	8
Painter, Scott	W	×
Palacky, Ellsworth	C	25
Palatine, Ellis	C	×
● Palco, Rooks	N	20
Palermo, Doniphan	NE	10
● Palmer, Washington	N	203
Palmyra, Butler	SE	45
Paola, Miami	E	2,943
Palo, Rooks	N	×
Paradise, Russell	C	65
Parallel, Washington	N	65
Pardee, Atchison	NE	160
Paris, Lincoln	C	32
● Parker, Linn	E	200
Parker, Montgomery	SE	3
● Parkersville, Morris	E	202
● Parnell, Atchison	NE	7,245
● Parsons, Labette	SE	6,736
● Partridge, Reno	S	200
Passaic, Kearney	SW	×
Patmos, Coffey	E	×
● Patterson, Harvey	C	×
● Pauline, Shawnee	E	32
● Pavillion, Wabaunsee	E	40
● Pawnee Rock, Barton	C	204
● Pawnee Station, Bourbon	SE	150
Pawnee Valley, Hodgeman	W	59
Paw Paw, Elk	SE	65
● Paxico, Wabaunsee	E	200
Paxson, Pratt	S	×
● Peabody, Marion	C	1,474
Peace Creek, Reno	S	77
● Pearl, Dickinson	C	32
● Peck, Sedgwick	S	×
Pearlett, Meade	SW	13
Pegg, Clark	SW	×
Pelton, Stafford	S	×

Kansas

Place	
● Penalosa, Kingman....... S	25
Pence, Scott........ W	10
● *Pen Dennis*, Lane........W	×
● Pendleton, Miami.........E	32
● *Penfield*, Labette........ SE	10
Penfield, (see Olivet)	×
Penokee, Graham........ NW	290
Penquite, Ottawa........... N	×
Pentheka, Rawlins....... NW	×
Peoria, Franklin............ E	160
Peotone, Sedgwick.......... S	30
Perkins, Montgomery..... SE	×
● Perry, Jefferson.......... NE	500
Perrysburg, (see Oakwood)..	×
● Perth, Sumner........... S	150
● Peru, Chautauqua......... SE	200
Peru Junction, Chautauqua SE	×
Peters, Kingman............ S	28
Petersburgh, Lane......... W	×
● Peterton, Osage........... E	100
Pfeifer, Ellis............... C	×
Phelps, Sheridan......... NW	×
Phila, Johnson.............. E	×
● **Phillipsburg**, Phillips. N	992
● *Phipps*, Ellsworth........ C	×
● Piedmont, Greenwood...SE	300
● Pierce Junction, Brown NE	×
● Pierceville, Finney......SW	50
Pine Grove, Butler.........SE	40
Pinon, Lincoln..............C	40
Pioneer, Rush...............C	45
Pipe Creek, Ottawa......... N	59
● Piper, Wyandotte....... NE	25
● Piqua, Woodson......... SE	100
● Pittsburgh, Crawford....SE	6,697
● *Pixley*, Barber............ S	×
Plainville, Rooks............N	347
Plano, Stafford..............S	×
Pleasant Dale, Rush.......... C	65
Pleasant Green, Phillips.... N	77
Pleasant Grove, Douglas.... E	100
● Pleasanton, Linn..........E	1,139
Pleasant Plain, Osborne.... N	57
● Pleasant Ridge, Leav'w'h NE	×
Pleasant Valley, Lincoln.... C	4
Pleasant View, Cherokee.. SE	32
● Plevna, Reno..............S	40
Pliny, Saline................C	×
Plumb, Lyon..................E	97
Plum Grove, Butler........SE	130
Plummer, Scott........... W	×
Plymell, Finney...........SW	10
● Plymouth, Lyon.......... E	97
Plymouth, Dickinson....... C	×
Poe, Ottawa..................N	10
Poheta, Saline...............C	40
Point View, Pawnee.........C	57
● Pollard, Rice..............C	×
● Pomeroy, Wyandotte... NE	100
● Pomona, Franklin........ E	466
● Pontiac, Butler.......... SE	28
Pop Corn, Osage............ E	32
● Pope, Leavenworth..... NE	×
Poplar Hill, Dickinson......C	32
Poppleton, Comanche...... S	32
Portage, Rooks............. N	×
Porterville, Bourbon.......SE	20
● Portis, Osborne.......... N	150
● Portland, Sumner......... S	50
● *Port Williams*, Atchison NE	×
Post Creek, Wabaunsee......E	32
Pottawatomie, Coffey........E	45
● Potter, Atchison........ NE	50
Pottersburgh, Lincoln...... C	32
Potterville, Osborne....... N	52
● Potwin, Butler.......... SE	123
Powell, Phillips............N	57
● Powhattan, Brown......NE	150
Prairie Centre, Johnson.....E	25
● Prairie View, Phillips .... N	75
● **Pratt**, Pratt.............S	1,418
Prattburgh, Stafford.........S	65
● Prescott, Linn.............E	241
Presley, Sherman........ NW	×
● Preston, Pratt.............S	150
● Pretty Prairie, Reno...... S	25
● *Price*, Nemaha......... NE	×
● Princeton, Franklin...... E	300
Proof, Wichita............ W	×
Prosper, Ellsworth..........C	65
● Protection, Comanche.....S	100
Providence, Butler....... SE	20
● Purcell, Doniphan.......NE	25
Purdyville, **Hodgeman..... W**	57
Purity, Reno.............. S	18
● Putnam, Harvey.......... C	×
Pyramid, Gove........... W	×

Kansas

Place	
Quakerville, Cherokee.....SE	×
● Quarry, Marion..........C	×
● Quenemo, Osage..........E	643
Quickville, Thomas...... NW	45
● Quincy, Greenwood..... SE	65
● Quindaro, Wyandotte... NE	300
● Quinter, Gove........... W	100
Quinton Heights, Shawnee..E	×
Quivera, Wyandotte.......NE	10
Radical, Montgomery.......SE	50
● Rago, Kingman.........S	60
Rainbelt, Meade..........SW	65
● *Ramapo*, Wyandotte....NE	×
● Ramona, Marion..........C	×
Rancho, Elk...............SE	×
● Randall, Jewell.........N	239
● Randolph, Riley........ NE	303
Range, Ellsworth.......... C	45
● Ransom, Ness.......... W	50
● Ransomville, Franklin....E	150
● Rantoul, Franklin........ E	97
● *Rapp*, Osage.............E	×
Rapture, Jewell............N	×
Ratcliff, Gray............ SW	13
Rattlesnake, Stafford........S	32
Ravanna, Garfield.........SW	100
Rawlins, Rawlins........ NW	130
● Ray, Pawnee..............C	×
● Raymond, Rice............C	137
Rayville, Norton.........NW	40
● Reading, Lyon.............E	200
Reamsville, Smith........... N	60
Red Bud, Cowley.........SE	5
Red Clover, Johnson..........E	77
● Redfield, Bourbon.......SE	162
Red Stone, Cloud.......... N	64
● *Redwing*, Barton.......... C	×
● Reece, Greenwood.......SE	179
Reeder, Kiowa............ SW	65
Reedsville, Marshall...... NE	×
Reeve, Anderson.............E	×
● Reno, Leavenworth.....NE	75
Republic, Republic......... N	228
● *Republic City*, Republic.. N	×
● Reserve, Brown..........NE	25
● Rest, Wilson...........SE	32
Rex, (see Blackstone).......	×
● Rexford, Thomas.........NW	×
Reynold, Kiowa..........SW	×
Rhoades, Dickinson......... C	35
● Rice, Cloud................N	25
Richfield, Morton.........SW	164
● Richland, Shawnee........E	130
● *Richland*, Kingman.......S	×
● Richmond, Franklin......E	300
● Richter, Franklin.........E	×
● Ridgeway, Osage..........E	50
● *Riley Centre*, Riley......NE	130
Riley, Riley............. NE	180
Ripon, Labette...........SE	65
● Riverdale, Sumner........ S	15
Riverside, Ness.............W	50
● *Riverside*, Leavenworth. NE	×
Riverton, Reno...............S	46
Riverview, (see Kansas City)..	×
Roanoke, Stanton..........SW	×
● Robinson, Brown....... NE	380
● Rochester, Kingman...... S	46
● Rock, Cowley.............SE	75
● Rock Creek, Jefferson.. NE	60
● *Rockeby*, Coffey...........E	×
Rockford, Bourbon.........SE	17
● Rockland, Chase...........E	×
Rocklow, Allen............. SE	26
Rockport, Rooks........... N	130
Rockville, Miami.............E	65
Rockwell City, Norton....NW	45
● Rogers, Chautauqua.....SE	×
Rollin, Neosho..............SE	×
● Rome, Sumner.............S	50
● *Ronald*, Bourbon.........SE	×
Rooks Centre, Rooks........ N	12
● Roper, Wilson............SE	6
● Rosalia, Butler............SE	50
Roscoe, Graham...........NW	97
● Rose, Woodson.......... SE	×
Rose Bank, Dickinson...... C	60
Rosedale, Wyandotte.......NE	2,276
● Rose Hill, Butler......... SE	75
● Rosemont, Osage......... E	×
Rosette, Lincoln..............C	12
Rosevale, (see Broughton) ...	×
● Rossville, Shawnee.........E	420
Rotate, Rawlins.......... NW	×
Rotterdam, Osborne........N	5
Round Mound, Osborne.....N	5
Roundup, Barber.............S	×

Kansas

Place	
Rowland, Rush............. C	45
Roxbury, McPherson........C	10
● *Rozel*, Pawnee........... C	×
Rubens, Jewell............ N	25
Ruble, Leavenworth...... NE	×
Ruby, Sedgwick............S	×
● Ruella, Harper........... S	32
● Ruleton, Sherman......NW	×
Runnymede, Harper........ S	200
Rural, Jefferson........... NE	×
● Rush Centre, Rush.......C	214
● **Russell**, Russell..........C	961
Russell Springs, Logan......E	117
● *Rust*, Crawford.........SE	×
Rutland, Montgomery..... SE	10
Ruweda, Greenwood.......SE	×
Ryan, Rush..................C	60
● *Ryan's*, Doniphan..... NE	×
● Sabetha, Nemaha....... NE	1,368
● Saffordville, Chase........ E	50
● *Sage*, Pawnee............C	×
Saint Benedict, Nemaha.. NE	50
Saint Bridget, Marshall... NE	32
Saint Clere, Pottawattomie NE	50
● **Saint Francis**, Chey'e NW	400
● Saint George, Pott'wat'le NE	50
● **Saint John**, Stafford....S	865
Saint Joseph, Cloud..........N	100
Saint Mark, Sedgwick.......S	40
● Saint Mary's, Pott'wato'e NE	1,174
Saint Peter, Cloud..........N	×
Saint Theresa, Wichita.....W	×
Salem, Jewell...............N	50
Salemsburgh, Saline........ C	10
● **Salina**, Saline...........C	6,149
Sallee, Kingman.............S	×
Salt City, (see Geuda Springs)	×
Salt Creek Val., Leavenw'h NE	×
Saltville, Mitchell.......... N	130
Sandago, Stafford.............S	47
Santa Fe, Haskell.......... SW	166
Sappaton, (see Chardon).....	×
● Saratoga, Pratt............S	25
Sarcoxie, Jefferson.........NE	×
Saunders, Rush............. C	×
● *Savannah*, Pottawato'ie NE	×
● Savonburgh, Allen.......SE	40
● Sawyer, Pratt.............S	59
● Saxman, Rice..............C	×
● Scammon, Cherokee.....SE	748
● Scandia, Republic.........N	653
Schoharie, Ness............ W	×
● Schroyer, Marshall......NE	×
Scio, Rawlins.............NW	60
● Scipio, Anderson..........E	65
● **Scott**, Scott............. W	229
● *Scott Junc.*, Bourbon....SE	×
● Scottsvile, Mitchell....... N	117
● **Scranton, Osage...........E**	**1,572**
Seabrook, Shawnee......... E	×
Seaman, Linn.................E	×
Section, Coffey.............. E	35
● **Sedan**, Chautauqua.....SE	970
● Sedgwick, Harvey.........C	652
● *Sedgwick Junction*, Harvey C	×
Sedowa, Sedgwick.............S	×
● Seeley, Cowley............SE	12
Sego, Reno..................	65
● Seguin, Sheridan........N W	×
● Selden, Sheridan......N W	100
● Selkirk, Wichita.......... W	45
● Selma, Anderson.........E	17
● **Seneca**, Nemaha.....N E	2,032
Seopo, Republic............N	100
Seth, Morton.............S W	×
Severance, Doniphan....N E	377
Severn, (see Bellaire)........	×
● Severy, Greenwood.....S E	382
● Seward, Stafford.......... S	60
Sexton, Barber............ S	45
● *Sexton*, Wilson.......... SE	×
● Shady Bend, Lincoln......C	40
Shaffer, Rush................C	×
● Shannon, Atchison......NE	26
● Sharon, Barber............S	80
● Sharon Springs, Wallace.. W	178
● Sharpe, Coffey............. E	×
Sharp's Creek, McPherson.. C	40
● Shaw, Neosho.............SE	50
Shawnee, Johnson............E	400
Sheffield, Decatur.........NW	33
Sheldon, Harvey........... C	×
Shep, Comanche.............S	×
● Sherdahl, Republic.......N	×
Sheridan, (see Selden).......	×
● *Sherlock*, Finney.........SW	35
Sherman Centre, Sherman NW	260

Kansas

Sherman City, Cherokee...SE	50
Shermanville, Sherman...NW	60
● Sherwin Junction, Ch'keeSE	100
Sherwood, Smith...N	27
Shibboleth, Decatur...NW	69
● Shields, Lane...W	7
Shiloh, Hamilton...W	×
● Shipton, Saline...C	×
Shockey, Grant...SW	27
Shorey, Shawnee...E	×
Short Creek, Cherokee...SE	×
● Sibley, Douglas...E	25
Sidell, (see Roper)...	×
Sidney, Ness...W	50
● Sigel, Douglas...E	×
Silicia, Phillips...N	×
● *Silkville*, Franklin...E	×
Silverdale, Cowley...SE	32
● *Silverdale*, Cowley...SE	×
● Silver Lake, Shawnee...E	256
Silverly, Garfield...SW	×
● *Silverton*, Pratt...S	×
● Simpson, Mitchell...N	100
● *Sitka*, Clark...SW	×
● *SixCorners*, Leavenw'rth NE	×
Skelton, Sheridan...NW	×
● Skiddy, Morris...E	150
Slate, Rooks...N	45
Smith Centre, Smith...N	767
Smoky Hill, McPherson...C	×
● Smolan, Saline...C	25
Snokomo, Wabaunsee...E	×
Snyder, Ford...SW	×
● Soldier, Jackson...NE	193
● *Soldiers Home*, L'ven'th. NE	×
● Solomon City, Dickinson..C	839
● Solomon Rapids, Mitchell N	97
Somerset, Miami...E	100
Soudan, Kingman...S	32
Soule, Gray...SW	×
Sou. Belle Plaine, Sumner..S	×
South Bend, Morris...E	35
South Cedar, Jackson...NE	65
● *South Dodge*, Ford...SW	×
● South Haven, Sumner...S	465
South Hutchinson, Reno...S	321
● *South Lawrence*, Douglas.E	×
● *Sou. Leavenworth*, Leavenworth...NE	×
● South Mound, Neosho...SE	30
South Orinoco, Norton...NW	×
South Park, Johnson...E	250
● *South Topeka*, Shawnee..E	×
Southwell, Ness...W	5
● *South Wichita*, Sedgwick.S	×
● *South Winfield*, Cowley.SE	×
Sparta, McPherson...C	×
● Spearville, Ford...SW	300
● *Spencer*, Shawnee...E	×
● *Spences*, Washington...N	×
● *Spica*, Thomas...NW	×
● Spivey, Kingman...S	205
● *Spring*, Harper...S	×
Spring Creek, Chautauqua.SE	77
Springdale, Leavenworth..NE	100
Springfield, Seward...SW	500
● Spring Hill, Johnson...E	573
Spring Lake, Meade...SW	68
Springside, Pottawattomie NE	40
● Springvale, Pratt...S	40
Spring Valley, McPherson..C	95
Spurgeon, Grant...SW	×
● Stafford, Stafford...S	640
● *Standish*, Leavenworth. NE	×
● Stanley, Johnson...E	150
Stanton, Miami...E	50
Staples, Kiowa...SW	×
Star, Greenwood...SE	×
● Stark, Neosho...SE	135
State Valley, Cherokee...SE	32
State Center, Barton...C	30
● *State Line*, Harper...S	×
Stella, Reno...S	×
Stephenson, Republic...N	×
● Sterling, Rice...C	1,641
Sternerton, Montgomery..SE	26
● *Sterry*, Lyon...E	×
Steuben, Jewell...N	×
● Stillwell, Johnson...E	200
Stitt, Dickinson...C	46
● Stockdale, Riley...NE	20
Stockholm, Wallace...W	×
Stockrange, Ellis...C	80
● **Stockton**, Rooks...N	880
Stolzenbach, Marshall...NE	×
Stormont, Osage...E	×
Stotler, Lyon...E	35

Kansas

Stover, Labette...SE	19
Stowe, (see Lockport)...	×
Stowell, Hamilton...W	×
● Straight Creek, Jackson. NE	×
Stranger, Leavenworth...NE	×
Strawberry, Washington...N	120
Strawn, Coffey...E	25
● Strong, Chase...E	976
Stuart, Smith...N	32
● Stuttgart, Phillips...N	×
Stuyvesant, Osborne...N	×
Success, Russell...C	650
Sugar, Miami...E	×
Sugar Loaf, Rooks...N	45
Sugar Valley, Anderson...E	40
● *Sugar Works*, Shawnee...E	×
● Sulphur Springs, Cloud...N	83
● Summerfield, Marshall..NE	102
● *Summit*, Butler...SE	×
● Summerville, Ottawa...N	8
Sun City, Barber...S	75
Sunny Dale, Sedgwick...S	20
Sunnyside, Dickinson...C	40
***Sunset*, Sumner...S**	45
Superior, (see Inman)...	×
Surprise, Grant...SW	65
Surrey, Rooks...N	35
Sutphen's Mill, Dickinson...C	50
Sutton, Lane...W	×
● *Swayne*, Dickinson...C	×
Swede Creek, Marshall...NE	×
Sweet Home, Smith...N	65
● *Swissvale*, Osage...E	×
● *Sycamore*, Montgomery.SE	×
Sycamore Springs, Butler..SE	40
● Sylvan Grove, Lincoln...C	200
● *Sylvan Park*, Morris...E	×
● Sylvia, Reno...S	205
● **Syracuse**, Hamilton...W	324
Tabor, Clay...N	45
● Talmage, Dickinson...C	×
Taloga, Morton...SW	25
● Talmo, Republic...N	20
● Tampa, Marion...C	×
Tannehill, Cowley...SE	65
● *Tasco*, Sheridan...NW	×
● *Taussig*, Cowley...SE	×
Taw, Haskell...SW	×
Taylor, Nemaha...NE	32
● Tecumseh, Shawnee...E	20
Tehama, Cherokee...SE	130
Tell, Dickinson...C	×
Templin, Wabaunsee...E	×
● Terre Cotta, Ellsworth...C	57
Terryton, Finney...SW	10
● Tescot, Ottawa...N	209
● Tevis, Shawnee...E	×
● Thayer, Neosho...SE	544
● *Thomas*, Ellsworth...C	8
Thompsonville, Jefferson..NE	86
Thornton, Rawlins...NW	×
Thrall, Greenwood...SE	×
Throop, Washington...N	×
Thurford, Thomas...NW	×
Thurman, Chase...E	57
Tiago, Republic...N	45
Tidy, Stafford...S	×
Tiffany, Gove...W	×
● Timken, Rush...C	×
Tipton, Mitchell...N	106
● Tisdale, Cowley...SE	15
Toledo, Chase...E	20
Tolerville, Sedgwick...S	×
Tonganoxie, Leavenworth.NE	673
● Tonovay, Greenwood...SE	6
Toogana, Lane...W	×
● **TOPEKA**, Shawnee...E	31,007
Topland, Sherman...NW	×
Topsy, Lincoln...C	130
● Toronto, Woodson...SE	552
● Torrance, Cowley...SE	50
● *Toulon*, Ellis...C	×
● Towanda, Butler...SE	156
Tower Spring, Lincoln...C	32
Townsend, Cowley...SE	×
Trading Post, Linn...E	200
● Traer, Decatur...NW	40
Trail, Lyon...E	×
Tregola, Trego...W	×
● Trenton, Saline...C	25
● *Tresham*, Cowley...SE	×
● **Tribune**, Greeley...W	90
Trivoli, Ellsworth...C	15
Troublesome, Smith...N	45
● **Troy**, Doniphan...NE	730
● *TroyJunction*, DoniphanNE	×
Tully, Rawlins...NW	77

Kansas

Tully, Pratt...S	85
Turck, Cherokee...SE	×
Turkey Creek, Wallace...W	×
Turkville, Ellis...C	40
● Turner, Wyandotte...NE	200
● Turon, Reno...S	250
Twelve Mile, Smith...N	77
Twin Creek, Osborne...N	5
Twin Falls, Greenwood...SE	57
Twin Mound, Douglas...E	50
Tyner, Smith...N	10
● *Tyro*, Montgomery...SE	×
Tyrone, Seward...SW	×
● Udall, Cowley...SE	338
Uhl, Smith...N	×
Ulysses, Grant...SW	198
Underwood, Greeley...W	×
Union, Osage...E	32
Union Centre, Elk...SE	77
● Uniontown, Bourbon...SE	344
Union Valley, Lincoln...C	45
● Upola, Elk...SE	×
Upton, Phillips...N	×
● Urbana, Neosho...SE	50
Ursula, Kiowa...SW	×
● *Usher*, Leavenworth...NE	×
● *Ushers*, Franklin...E	×
Ute, Sheridan...NW	×
● Utica, Ness...W	50
● Utopia, Greenwood...SE	32
Valdore, Graham...NW	×
● Valeda, Labette...SE	150
● Valencia, Shawnee...E	65
● Valentine, Harvey...C	×
Valley Brook, Osage...E	×
● Valley Centre, Sedgwick..S	167
● Valley Falls, Jefferson..NE	1,180
Valparaiso, Stevens...SW	×
● Vance, Wyandotte...NE	×
● *Vance*, Linn...E	×
Vanhem, Clark...SW	50
Vansburgh, Ness...W	77
Varck, Cherokee...SE	150
● Vassar, Osage...E	15
Vaughn, Rawlins...NW	×
Vega, Wallace...W	×
Venango, Ellsworth...C	40
Venice, Sedgwick...S	25
● Vera, Wabaunsee...E	×
Verbeck, Barton...C	32
● Verdi, Ottawa...N	20
Verdigris, Lyon...E	59
● Vermillion, Marshall...NE	300
● *Verner*, Thomas...NW	×
● Vernon, Woodson...SE	25
● Vesper, Lincoln...C	10
Vesta, Clark...SW	19
Veteran, Stanton...SW	×
Victor, Mitchell...N	45
● Victoria, Ellis...C	100
Vidette, Shawnee...E	40
Vietsburgh, Neosho...SE	90
Vilas, Wilson...SE	50
Vincent, Osborne...N	45
● Vine Creek, Ottawa...N	23
● Vining, Clay...N	241
● Vinland, Douglas...E	25
● Vinton, Cowley...SE	×
Vinton, Riley...NE	32
Viola, Sedgwick...S	×
Violenta, Sheridan...NW	×
● Virgil, Greenwood...SE	200
Viroqua, Morton...SW	×
● Vliets, Marshall...NE	12
Volland, Wabaunsee...E	×
Voltaire, Sherman...NW	40
Von, Comanche...S	×
Voorhees, Stevens...SW	×
Vosburgh, Stafford...S	57
Wabash, Gray...SW	×
● Wabaunsee, Wabaunsee...E	50
Waco, Sedgwick...S	65
● *Wade*, Leavenworth...NE	×
Wagnerville, Phillips...N	57
Wade, Miami...E	32
***Wagram*, Dickinson...C**	×
● Wagstaff, Miami...E	25
● *Wakarusa*, Douglas...E	×
● Wakarusa, Shawnee...E	25
Wa Keeney, Trego...W	439
● Wakefield, Clay...N	241
Wakeman, Norton...NW	795
● Waldeck, Marion...C	×
● Waldo, Russell...C	100
● Walker, Ellis...C	200
● Walkertown, Bourbon...SE	26
● Wallace, Wallace...W	220

Kansas		
Wall Street, [illegible]an	E	35
● Wallula, Wyandotte	NE	×
● Walnut, Crawford	SE	539
Walnut Grove, Mitchell	N	×
Walsburg, Riley	NE	×
● Walton, Harvey	C	249
Wamego, Pottawatomie	NE	1,473
Wanamaker, Shawnee	E	×
Wannersburgh, Allen	SE	32
Ward, Wilson	SE	910
● Waring, Ness	W	×
Warnerton, (see Hall Summit)		×
Warren, Sherman	NW	×
Warrendale, Grant	SW	×
● Warwick, Republic	N	80
Washburn, Wichita	W	×
Washington, Washington	N	1,613
● *Washington*, Douglas	E	×
Waterford, Stevens	SW	×
Waterloo, Kingman	S	130
● Waterville, Marshall	NE	557
● Wathena, Doniphan	NE	694
Watson, Shawnee	E	25
● Wauneta, Chautauqua	SE	100
Waushara, Lyon	E	40
Waveland, Shawnee	E	65
● Waverly, Coffey	E	548
Wayland, Stanton	SW	65
● Wayne, Republic	N	60
● Wayside, Montgomery	SE	×
Wea, Miami	E	150
● Weaver, Douglas	E	×
Weaver, Osage	E	77
Webb, Barton	C	15
● Webber, Jewell	N	20
Webster, Rooks	N	200
Weeks, Lyon	E	85
Weir, Cherokee	SE	2,138
● *Wier City Junc.*, Cherokee	SE	×
● *Welborn*, Wyandotte	NE	×
Welcome, Geary	E	×
● Welda, Anderson	E	200
Welland, Cherokee	SE	×
Wellington, Sumner	S	4,391
● *Wellington Junc.*, Sumner	S	×
Wellmanville, Ness	W	32
● *Wells*, Ottawa	N	×
● Wellsford, Kiowa	SW	125
● Wellsville, Franklin	E	392
Weltbote, Washington	N	40
Wendall, Edwards	S	130
● Weskan, Wallace	W	×
Wesley, Dickinson	C	×
● *West Argentine*, Wy'n'e	NE	×
West Asher, Mitchell	N	45
West Cedar, Phillips	N	45
Western Park, Elk	SE	45
Westfield, McPherson	C	32
Westgate, Geary	E	40
Westmoreland, Pott'ie	NE	478
Westola, Morton	SW	×
Weston, Geary	E	100
● Westphalia, Anderson	E	375
● West Plains, Meade	SW	62
West Point, Rush	C	26
● *West Wichita*, Sedgwick	S	×
● Wetmore, Nemaha	NE	522
● Wheatland, McPherson	C	59
● Wheaton, Pottawattomie	NE	150
● Wheeler, Cheyenne	NW	×
● Wherry, Rice	C	×
Whitaker, Miami	E	×
● *White*, Butler	SE	×
● White Church, Wyandotte	SE	150
● White City, Morris	E	391
● White Cloud, Doniphan	NE	699
● *Whitelaw*, Greeley	W	×
White Hall, Cherokee	SE	57
White Rock, Republic	N	5
● White Water, Butler	SE	184
Whitfield, Graham	NW	25
● Whiting, Jackson	NE	381
Whitman, Sumner	S	×
Whitsau, Finney	SW	25
● **Wichita**, Sedgwick	S	23,853
● Wichita Heights, Sedgwick	S	×
Widerange, Ottawa	N	18
● *Wiggam*, Lyon	E	×
● *Wilbur*, Greenwood	SE	×
Wilburn, Ford	SW	75
Wild Cat, (see Keats)		×
● Wilder, Johnson	E	80
Wild Horse, Graham	NW	10
Wilkinson, Logan	W	×
● Willard, Shawnee	E	×
Willcox, Trego	W	35
● Williamsburgh, Franklin	E	502

Kansas		
● Williamstown, Jefferson	NE	75
● Willis, Brown	NE	200
Willow Springs, Douglas	E	77
Wilmington, Wabaunsee	E	25
● Wilmore, Comanche	S	50
● Wilmot, Cowley	SE	50
● *Wilroads*, Ford	SW	×
Wilsey, Morris	E	200
● Wilson, Ellsworth	C	770
● Wilsonton, Labettte	SE	×
● Winchester, Jefferson	NE	429
● Windom, McPherson	C	165
Windsor, Ottawa	N	5
Winfield, Cowley	SE	5,184
● *Winfield Junc.*, Cowley	SE	×
● *Wingate*, Butler	SE	×
Winkle's Mills, Riley	NE	35
● *Winkler's Mills*, Riley	NE	×
Winnesheik, McPherson	C	40
Winona, Logan	W	150
Winterset, Russell	C	40
● *Winton*, Montgomery	SE	×
Wise, Allen	SE	32
Wittrup, Hodgeman	W	57
● *Wolf Creek Tank*, Brown	NE	×
Womer, Smith	N	19
● Wonderly, Saline	C	×
Wonsevu, Chase		
Woodberry, Reno	[illegible]	[illegible]
● Woodbine, Dickinson	C	100
Woodey, Lincoln	C	45
Woodland, Bourbon	SE	×
Woodlawn, Nemaha	NE	60
● Woodruff, Phillips	N	150
Woodsdale, Stevens	SW	68
Woodstock, Jefferson	NE	130
● Woodston, Rooks	N	150
Woodville, Russell	C	40
Worden, Douglas	E	32
Worth, Butler	SE	×
Wortley, Woodson	SE	×
● Wreford, Geary	E	75
● Wright, Ford	SW	31
● *Wyandotte*, Wyandotte	E	×
● Wyckoff, Lyon	E	10
Wyoming, Marshall	NE	32
Xenia, Bourbon	SE	150
Yate, Ottawa	N	65
● **Yates Center**, Woodson	SE	1,305
● Yoder, Reno	S	20
Yordy, **Ellsworth**	**C**	**40**
York, Saline	C	×
● *York*, Sedgwick	S	×
● *Yoro*, Linn	E	×
Youngtown, Marion	C	65
● *Younts Quarry*, Cowley	SE	×
Yoxall, Osborne	N	59
● *Yuma*, Cloud	N	130
Zamora, Hamilton	W	30
● Zarah, Johnson	E	×
● Zcandale, Riley	NE	15
Zella, Stevens	SW	×
Zenobia, Scott	W	×
Zenith, (see Sylvia)		×
Zionville, Grant	SW	15
Zoe, Russell	C	×
Zoro, Linn	E	×
● Zurich, Rooks	N	×
● Zyba, Sumner	S	11

KENTUCKY.

COUNTIES.	INDEX.	POP.
Adair	S	13,721
Allen	S	13,692
Anderson	C	10,610
Ballard	SW	8,390
Barren	S	21,490
Bath	NE	12,813
Bell	SE	10,312
Boone	N	12,246
Bourbon	N	16,976
Boyd	NE	14,033
Boyle	C	12,948
Bracken	N	12,369
Breathitt	E	8,705
Breckinridge	W	18,976
Bullitt	N	8,291
Butler	W	13,956
Caldwell	SW	13,186
Calloway	SW	14,675
Campbell	N	44,208
Carlisle	SW	7,612
Carroll	N	9,266
Carter	NE	17,204
Casey	C	11,848
Christian	SW	34,118
Clark	C	15,434
Clay	SE	12,447
Clinton	S	7,047
Crittenden	W	13,119
Cumberland	S	8,452
Daviess	W	33,120
Edmonson	W	8,005
Elliott	NE	9,214
Estill	C	10,836
Fayette	C	35,698
Fleming	NE	16,078
Floyd	E	11,256
Franklin	N	21,267
Fulton	SW	10,005
Gallatin	N	4,611
Garrard	C	11,138
Grant	N	12,671
Graves	SW	28,534
Grayson	W	18,688
Green	C	11,463
Greenup	NE	11,911
Hancock	W	9,214
Hardin	C	21,304
Harlan	SE	6,197
Harrison	N	16,914
Hart	C	16,439
Henderson	W	29,536
Henry	N	14,164
Hickman	SW	11,637
Hopkins	W	23,505
Jackson	C	8,261
Jefferson	N	188,598
Jessamine	C	11,248
Johnson	E	11,027
Kenton	N	54,161
Knott	E	5,438
Knox	SE	13,762
La Rue	C	9,433
Laurel	SE	12,747
Lawrence	NE	17,702
Lee	E	6,205
Leslie	SE	3,964
Letcher	SE	6,920
Lewis	NE	14,803
Lincoln	C	15,962
Livingston	W	9,474
Logan	SW	23,812
Lyon	SW	7,628
McCracken	SW	21,051
McLean	W	9,887
Madison	C	24,348
Magoffin	E	9,196
Marion	C	15,648
Marshall	SW	11,287
Martin	E	4,209
Mason	NE	20,773
Meade	W	9,484
Menifee	E	4,666
Mercer	C	15,034
Metcalfe	S	9,871
Monroe	S	10,989
Montgomery	C	12,367
Morgan	E	11,249
Muhlenberg	W	17,955
Nelson	C	16,417
Nicholas	N	10,764
Ohio	W	22,946
Oldham	N	6,754
Owen	N	17,676
Owsley	E	5,975
Pendleton	N	16,346
Perry	SE	6,331
Pike	E	17,378
Powell	C	4,698
Pulaski	S	25,731
Robertson	N	4,684
Rock Castle	C	9,841
Rowan	NE	6,129
Russell	S	8,136
Scott	N	16,546
Shelby	N	16,521
Simpson	SW	10,878
Spencer	C	6,760
Taylor	C	9,353
Todd	SW	16,814
[illegible]gg	SW	13,902
[illegible]mble	N	7,140
Union	W	18,229
Warren	SW	30,158
Washington	C	13,622
Wayne	S	12,852
Webster	W	17,196
Whitley	SE	17,590

County	Index	Pop.
Wolfe	E	7,180
Woodford	C	12,380
Total		1,858,635

TOWN. COUNTY.	INDEX.	POP.
Aaron, Letcher	SE	×
Aaron's Run, (see Side View)		×
Abbott, Trimble	N	33
Aberdeen, Butler	W	10
Abes Shop, Christian	SW	×
Abigail, Robertson	N	25
Abner, Nicholas	N	25
Absher, Adair	S	42
Adaburg, Ohio	W	8
● Adairville, Logan	SW	600
Adams, Lawrence	NE	25
Add, Laurel	SE	77
● Addison, Breckinridge	W	100
● *Aden*, Carter	NE	25
Adolphus, Allen	S	86
● Aetnaville, Ohio	W	10
Agnew, (see Rankin)		×
Akersville, Monroe	S	100
Albany, Clinton	S	300
Albany Landing, Cumb'r'l'd	S	25
Albia, Pulaski		×
Albott's Creek, Floyd	E	×
Albrittain, (see Penrod)		×
Alcorn, Jackson	C	100
Alex, Wayne	S	20
Alexander, (see Adolphus)		×
● *Alexander*, Fulton	SW	×
Alexandria, Campbell	N	800
Alford, Mercer	C	×
Alger, Estill	C	×
● Aliceton, Boyle	C	40
● *Allegham*, Fayette	C	×
Allegre, Todd	SW	10
Allendale, Green	C	1,000
Allen Springs, Warren	SW	100
● Allensville, Todd	SW	426
Allensville, Clark	C	90
Alliance, Floyd	E	×
● *Alms House*, Jefferson	N	×
Alone, Metcalfe	S	32
Alonzo, Allen	S	32
Alpha, Clinton	S	75
● Alpine, Pulaski	S	260
Alsile, Whitley	SE	×
Alphoretta, Floyd	E	100
Alstott, Casey	C	×
● Altamont, Laurel	SE	215
Alton, Anderson	C	250
● Alton Station, Anderson	C	×
Alumbaugh, Estill	C	×
Alum Springs, Boyle	C	53
Alvaton, Warren	SW	50
Alzey, Henderson	W	10
Amandaville, Cumberland	S	35
Ambrose, Jessamine	C	100
● America, Lee	E	30
Amity, Hardin	C	×
Ammie, Clay	SE	100
Amoret, McLean	W	97
Amphias, (see Tolu)		×
● Anchorage, Jefferson	N	300
Anderson, Logan	SW	×
● *Anderson*, Kenton	N	×
● *Anderson*, Todd	SW	×
Anderson City, (see Orr)		×
Andersonville, (see Guston)		×
Andrews, Laurel	SE	32
Andy, Martin	E	×
Andyville, Meade	W	20
● Anglin, Carter	NE	25
● *Anita Springs*, Oldham	N	×
Anneta, Grayson	W	35
Annville, Jackson	C	75
● *Annora*, Crittenden	W	×
Ansel, Pulaski	S	50
Anthoston, Henderson	W	16
Antioch, Washington	C	15
Antioch Mills, Harrison	N	25
Anytime, Graves	SW	×
Apple Grove, (see Nobob)		×
Apple Tree, Breathitt	E	40
Arab, Lincoln	C	25
ArcadiaSprings, (see Dawson)		×
Arch, Letcher	SE	×
Argentum, Greenup	NE	25
● Argillite, Greenup	NE	30
● *Argyle*, Powell	C	25
Ariadne, Clinton	S	65
● *Arigo City*, Boyd	NE	×
Arlen, Clark	S	25
● Arlington, Carlisle	SW	574
Arnetville, Marshall	SW	×
Arnold, Ohio	W	13
Aron, Bourbon	N	25
● Artemus, Knox	SE	150
Arthur, Letcher	SE	26
Ashbrook, Anderson	C	20
● *Ashbys*, Jefferson	N	×
Ashbysburgh, Hopkins	W	100
Ash Camp, Pike	E	25
● Ashland, Boyd	NE	4,195
Ashland Junction, Boyd	NE	×
● *Askins*, Grayson	W	×
Aspen Grove, (see PeachGrove)		×
● *Asphalt*, Grayson	W	×
Athens, Fayette	C	173
Athertonville, LaRue	C	400
● *Athol*, Breathitt	E	×
Atoka, Boyle	C	×
Attention, (see Wesleyville)		×
Atterson, Casey	C	20
Attilla, LaRue	C	18
Atwells, Meade	W	×
Atwood, Kenton	N	×
● Auburn, Logan	SW	613
Audubon, Henderson	W	693
● Augusta, Bracken	N	1,447
Aulick, Pendleton	N	15
Aurora, Marshall	SW	200
● Austerlitz, Bourbon	N	25
Austin, Barren	S	20
Austinburgh, Kenton	N	×
Avena, Harrison	N	10
● Avenstoke, Anderson	C	6
Avery, Owen	N	×
● Avon, Fayette	C	×
Avoy, (see Crab Orchard)		×
Axtel, Breckinridge	W	×
Ayre's Land'g, (see Hawesv'e)		×
Babbage, (see Hardinsburg)		×
Bac, Mercer	C	15
Back Bone, Elliott	NE	25
Backusburgh, Calloway	SW	10
Bacon Creek, (see Bonnieville)		×
● Bagdad, Shelby	N	200
Bailey, Harlan	SE	100
● *Bailey*, Rowan	NE	×
Bailey's Switch, Knox	SE	×
Bainbridge, Christian	SW	15
Baker, Letcher	SE	125
● Bakersport, Hopkins	W	10
Bakerton, Cumberland	S	×
Bald Eagle, (see Sharpsburg)		×
Bald Hill, (see Barterville)		×
Baldock, Casey	C	×
Bald Rock, Laurel	SE	26
Baldwin, Madison	C	×
Ballardsville, Oldham	N	60
● *Balls*, Campbell	N	×
Ball's Fork, Knott	E	×
Balls Landing, Owen	N	13
Balltown, Nelson	C	50
Baltimore, Hickman	SW	10
Bandana, Ballard	SW	148
Bangor, Morgan	E	25
● Bank Lick, Kenton	N	25
● *Banks*, Kenton	N	×
Banocks, Wayne	S	×
Baptist, Harrison	N	25
● **Barboursville**, Knox	SE	1,162
● **Bardstown**, Nelson	C	1,524
Bardstown Junction, Bul't't.	N	150
● **Bardwell**, Carlisle	SW	578
Barefoot, Nicholas	N	10
Bark Camp Mills, Whitley	SE	19
Barlow City, Ballard	SW	104
Barnetts, Lincoln	C	×
Barnetts, Ohio	W	×
Barnett's Creek, Johnson	E	10
Barnsley, Hopkins	W	60
Barrallton, Bullitt	N	26
Barren, Warren	SW	×
Barren, (see Godfrey)		×
● *Barren Fork*, Pulaski	S	×
Barretts Ferry, Ohio	W	×
Bart, Wayne	S	×
Barterville, Nicholas	N	100
Barton, (see Stone)		×
● *Bashaws*, Jefferson	N	×
● Baskett, Henderson	W	15
Bass, Pike	E	25
Bath Furnace, Bath	NE	×
Battletown, Meade	W	×
● Baugh, Logan	SW	32
Baxter, Harlan	SE	25
Bayou Mills, Livingston	W	25
Bays Fork, Warren	SW	75
Bazo Blade, Letcher	SE	×
● *Beachland*, Jefferson	N	×
Beachville, Metcalf	S	25
● Beams, Nelson	C	30
● Beard, Oldham	N	100
Bearfoot, Nicholas	N	10
Bear Wallow, Barren	S	75
● **Beattyville, Lee**	E	600
Beaver Floyd	E	10
Beaver, Knott	E	25
● Beaver Dam, Ohio	W	274
Beaver Lick, Boone	N	34
Beckboro, Harrison	N	×
Becknerville, Clark	C	30
Beckton, Barren	S	8
Beda, Ohio	W	54
● *Bedford*, Bourbon	N	×
Bedford, Trimble	N	250
Beech, Shelby	N	×
Beech Grove, McLean	W	400
Beechland, Washington	C	30
● *Beechwood*, Jefferson	N	×
● Beechwood, Owen	N	20
Beefhide, Pike	E	25
Beelerton, Hickman	SW	15
Bee Lick, Rock Castle	C	×
Bee Lick, Pulaski	S	50
Bee Spring, Edmonson	W	30
Belcourt Bracken	N	×
● *Bell*, Christian	SW	10
Bell City, (see Boydsville)		×
● *Bellfonte*, Boyd	NE	×
Bellefonte, Greenup	NE	×
Bellefont Furnace, (seeCoalt'n)		×
Belle Point, Franklin	N	457
Belleville, Webster	W	×
Belleview, Christian	SW	50
● *Bellevue*, Boone	N	140
Bellevue, Campbell	N	3,163
● *Bells*, Jefferson	N	×
Bell's Trace, (see Willard)		×
● Belmont, Bullitt	N	50
● *Belmont*, Campbell	N	50
● *Belton*, Muhlenberg	W	19
Belton Store, (see Casey Creek)		×
Benge, Clay	SE	70
Bennett's Fork Junc., Bell	SE	×
Bennettstown, Christian	SW	60
● Benson, Franklin	N	50
Benson, (see Linton)		×
Bent Branch, Pike	E	30
Benton, Marshall	SW	344
● *Benton*, Kenton	N	97
● Berea, Madison	C	600
● *Berkeley*, Carlisle	SW	77
Berkshire, Boone	N	20
Berlin, Bracken	N	100
Bernard, Mason	NE	25
Bernstadt, Laurel	SE	500
Berry, Custer	NE	×
● Berry, Harrison	N	268
Berry's Lick, Butler	W	78
● *Berryville*, Powell	C	×
Berryville, (see Alex)		×
Bertram, Muhlenberg	W	13
Bessie, Martin	E	×
Bestonia, Mercer	C	×
Bet, Carter	NE	25
Bethany, Owen	N	20
Bethatra, (see Hobbitt)		×
Bethel, Bath	NE	100
● *Bethel Grove*, Kenton	N	×
Bethelridge, Casey	C	×
Bethlehem, Henry	N	100
● *Bethlehem*, Hardin	C	×
Betram, (see Greenville)		×
Beverly, Christian	SW	20
● Bevier, Muhlenberg	W	299
Bevinsville, (see Clifty)		×
● Bewleyville, Breckinridge	W	200
Biddle, Scott	N	20
Bigbone, Boone	N	×
● Big Clifty, Grayson	W	350
Big Creek, Clay	SE	30
Big Eagle, (see Stonewall)		×
Big Hill, Madison	C	50
Big Reedy, Edmonson	W	30
Big Renox, Cumberland	S	20
Big South Rolling Fork, (see Power's Store)		×
Big Spring, Breckinridge	W	250
Big Spring, (see Townsville)		×
Big Springs (see Hobbs)		×
Big Wilson, Lee	E	×
Bilvia, Letcher	SE	300
Bingham, Bell	SE	26
Birdie, Anderson	C	40
Birdsville, Livingston	W	100
Birk's City, Daviess	W	200

Kentucky

Place		
Birmingham, Marshall	SW	273
● *Bishop*, Jefferson	N	×
Bishopton, (see Faulkner)		×
Blackberry, Pike	E	×
Blackburn, Union	W	8
Black Creek, Powell	C	×
● Blackford, Webster	W	250
Black Jack, (see Weston)		×
Black Rock, Grayson	W	15
Black's Ferry, Monroe	S	75
Blackwater, (see Ezel)		×
Blackwell, Henry	N	×
Bladeston, Bracken	N	40
Blaine, Lawrence	NE	300
Blair's Mills, Morgan	E	26
● Blanchett, Grant	N	50
● *Blanken Bakers*, Jefferson	N	×
● **Blandville**, Ballard	SW	372
BlankenshipFerry, (seeCreelsboro)		×
Blincoe, Washington	C	10
Blood, Calloway	SW	10
Bloom, Graves	SW	×
● Bloomfield, Nelson	C	750
Bloomington (see Anthorston)		×
Bloomington, Magoffin	E	10
Bloss, Rock Castle	C	×
Bluebank, Estill	C	10
● *Blue Cut*, Logan	SW	×
Blue Cut, (see Lewisburg)		×
Blue Eagle Mills, Grant	N	×
Blue Grass Landing, B'k'ge	W	15
Blue Lick Springs, Nicholas	N	40
Blue Spring Grove, (see Hiseville)		×
Bluff City, Henderson	W	15
● Boaz, Graves	SW	40
Bobtown, Madison	C	10
Boddie, Christian	SW	×
Bogie Mills, (see Ruthton)		×
Bogus, **Madison**	**C**	8
Bohon, Mercer	C	75
Boles, Monroe	S	8
Bolt's Fork, Boyd	NE	15
Bonanza, Floyd	E	25
Bonayr, Barren	S	×
Bond, Mercer	C	×
● *Bond's*, McCracken	W	×
Bond's Mills, (see Ripyville)		×
● Bondville, Mercer	C	×
● *Bonita*, Woodford	C	×
● Bonnieville, Hart	C	200
Bonny, Morgan	E	25
● Booker, Washington	C	×
Boone, Madison	C	×
Boone, Menifee	E	×
Boone's Gap, Garrard	C	×
● **Booneville**, Owsley	E	350
Boonsboro, (see Ford)		×
Boon's Camp, Johnson	E	195
Boon's Creek, Garrard	C	×
● Boothe, Hardin	C	3
Booth's Landing, Woodford	C	×
Borah's Ferry, (see Select)		×
Bordley, Union	W	175
Boreing, Laurel	SE	8
Bossdale, Jefferson	N	×
Boston, (see Long Run)		×
Boston, (see Lot)		×
● Boston, Nelson	C	114
● Boston Station, Pendleton	N	114
Botland, Nelson	C	60
Bottom, Russell	S	×
BourbonStock Yards, Jefferson	N	×
Bourne, Garrard	C	×
● Bowen, Powell	C	25
Bowling Green, Wa'n.	SW	8,803
Bowman, Breathitt	E	25
Bowmansville, Johnson	E	×
Boxville, Union	W	250
● Boyd, Harrison	N	150
● *Boyd's Mills*, Casey	C	×
Boydsville, Graves	SW	75
● *Bracht*, Kenton	N	32
● Bradford, Bracken	N	25
Bradford's Store, Knox	SE	×
Bradfordsville, Marion	C	179
● *Bradshaw*, Todd	SW	×
Bradshaw's, (see Roseville)		×
● *Brady's*, Rowan	NE	×
Brafford's Store, (see Gray's)		×
Bramblett, Nicholas	N	10
Branch, Harrison	N	25
● **Brandenburgh**, Meade	W	495
Brandon Mill, (see Murray)		×
● *Branham*, Lawrence	NE	40
Branhan, Pike	E	×
● Brannon, Jessamine	C	30
Brashearsville, (see Hazard)		×
Brasher, Gallatin	N	130
Bratton, Robertson	N	80
Braxton, Mercer	C	×
Brayville, Campbell	N	25
Breck, Owen	N	25
Breckinridge, Harrison	N	25
Breeding's, Adair	S	40
Bremen, Muhlenberg	W	200
Brent, Campbell	N	×
Brentwood, Green	C	×
Brewer's Mills, Marshall	SW	150
Bridge Junc., Ballard	SW	×
Bridgeport, Franklin	N	60
Bridgeport, Mason	NE	×
Bridgeville, Robertson	N	×
Bridgeville, (see Germantown)		×
Briensburgh, Marshall	SW	87
● *Brier Creek*, Whitley	SE	×
Bright, Casey	C	32
Brightshade, Clay	SE	30
Bristow, Rowan	NE	105
● Bristow, Warren	SW	100
Broadwell, Harrison	N	50
● Brodhead, Rock Castle	C	277
Bromley, Kenton	N	×
Bromley, Owen	N	15
Bronston, Pulaski	S	150
Brooklyn, Mercer	C	×
Brooklyn, Butler	W	75
● Brooks, Bullitt	N	75
Brookville, Bracken	N	330
● *Broshears*, Mason	NE	×
Brownhampton, (seeCleopatra)		×
Browning, Daviess	W	×
Brownsborough, Oldham	N	156
Brown's Cross Roads, Cl't'n	S	20
Brown's Station, Daviess	W	×
● Brown's Valley, Daviess	W	×
Brownsville, Edmonson	W	113
Bruce, Barren	SW	30
Brucetown, (see Lexington)		×
Bruin, Elliott	NE	50
● Brumfield, Boyle	C	32
● Brummett's Sta., W'tl'y	SE	×
Brush Creek, (see Artemus)		×
● *Brush Creek*, Rock Castle	C	×
Brushy, Taylor	C	65
Brushy, Pike	E	×
● *Bryant*, Fayette	C	×
Bryant'sStation, (seeBrannon)		×
Bryant's Store, Knox	SE	40
Bryantsville, Garrard	C	266
● Buchanan, Lawrence	NE	100
Buchanan Mills, (see Greensburg)		×
Buck, Knott	E	26
Buck Creek, Owsley	E	50
Buckeye, Garrard	C	50
Buck Horn, (see Beda)		×
● Buckner, Oldham	N	50
Bucksville, (see Auburn)		×
● Budtown, Bourbon	N	40
Buechel, Jefferson	N	10
Buel, McLean	W	15
Buena, Calloway	SW	×
Buena Vista, Garrard	C	30
Buena Vista, Graves	SW	130
Buena VistaSprings, (see Russellville)		×
● *Buena VistaStation*, Lewis	NE	×
Buffalo, LaRue	C	214
Buffalo, Floyd	E	×
Buffalo City, (see Caseyville)		×
Buffalo Furnace, Greenup	NE	×
Buffalo Landing, (see New Concord)		×
BuffaloTrace, (seeBartervillc)		×
Buford, Ohio	W	100
Buford Store, see Rocky Hill Station)		×
Bugg, Hickman	SW	32
Bulah, Hickman	SW	×
● *Bullitt's*, Jefferson	N	×
Bullittsville, Boone	N	30
Bull's Run, (see Hampton)		×
Buncombe, Knott	E	10
Buras, Breckinridge	W	30
Burdick, Taylor	C	19
● *Burgess*, Boyd	NE	×
● Burgin, Mercer	C	303
Burika, Robertson	N	25
Burkesville, Cumberland	S	950
● Burkley, Carlisle	SW	77
Burlington, Boone	N	400
Burnet, Hopkins	W	×
Burnetta, Pulaski	S	32
Burnetta, Casey	C	×
Burning Springs, Clay	SE	30
● Burnside, Pulaski	S	420
Burnsville, (see Sims' Store)		×
Burtonville, Lewis	**NE**	150
Bushong, (see Sulphur Lick)		×
Bush's Store, Wolfe	E	×
Bush's Store, Laurel	SE	250
Bushy Knob, Madison	C	×
Busseyville, Lawrence	NE	25
● Butler, Pendleton	N	560
● *Butlers*, Logan	SW	×
Butlersville, (see Trammel)		×
Butlersville, Greene	C	32
Bubeetown, Madison	C	40
Byron, Clay	SE	×
Byrns' Land'g, (see Monterey)		×
Cabell, Wayne	S	25
Cabin Creek, Lewis	NE	65
● Caddo, Pendleton	N	25
● *Cadentown*, Fayette	C	60
Cadiz, Trigg	SW	890
Cain's Store, Pulaski	S	73
Cairo, Henderson	W	209
Caldwell's Crossing, Lincoln	W	65
Caledonia, Trigg	SW	57
Calf Creek, Martin	E	100
Calhoun, McLean	W	637
● California, Campbell	N	816
● *Callahan's*, Jefferson	N	×
Callaway, Bell	SE	75
Callinsville, (see Morgan)		75
● Calvary, Marion	C	130
● Calvert City, Marshall	SW	142
Camargo, Montgomery	C	150
● Camden, Oldham	N	25
Camdenville, (see Orr)		×
● Campbellsburgh, Henry	N	342
● **Campbellsville**, Taylor	C	1,018
Camp Ground, (see Boring)		×
Camp Ground, Lawrence	NE	×
Camp Knox, Greene	C	50
Camp Nelson, Jessamine	C	20
Camp Springs, Campbell	N	10
Campton, Wolfe	E	317
Canada, Pike	E	20
Canby, Owen	N	35
Cane Creek, Laurel	SE	×
Cane Creek, Mercer	C	×
Cane Ridge, Bourbon	N	100
● Cane Spring, Bullitt	N	50
Cane Valley, Adair	S	75
Caney, Morgan	E	20
Caney Creek, Green	C	×
Caney Creek, Hopkins	W	×
Caney Fork, (see PetersCreek)		×
● Caneyville, Grayson	W	273
Canmer, Hart	C	350
Cannonsburgh, Boyd	NE	100
Canoe Fork, Breathitt	E	×
Canton, Trigg	SW	309
Cardonee, Scott	N	×
Cardwell, Washington	C	10
Carlinburgh, Henderson	W	50
● **Carlisle**, Nicholas	N	1,081
Carlow, (see Dixon)		×
Carmack, Lyon	SW	×
Carmel, Trimble	N	×
● Carntown, Pendleton	N	25
Carneytown, Grayson	W	273
Carpenter, Whitley	SE	40
Carrington, Menifee	E	×
Carrollton, Carroll	N	1,720
● Carr's, Lewis	NE	30
Carrs Fork, (see Sassafras)		×
Carrsville, Livingston	W	240
Carrsville Sta., (see Ripyville)		×
Carson, Knott	E	25
Carter's, Bell	E	×
Cartersville, Garrard	C	×
Carthage, Campbell	N	275
Cartwright, Clinton	S	19
Cary's Lan'g, (seeCloyd's Lan'g)		×
Cases Station, (see Olympia)		×
Caseville, (see Paynesville)		×
Casey Creek, Adair	S	75
Casey Creek, Casey	C	×
Caseyville, Union	W	301
Cash, Hardin	C	×
● Cask, Christian	SW	350
Cassaday, Warren	SW	15
Cat, Lawrence	NE	32
○ *Catalpa*, Lawrence	NE	×
● Catawba, Pendleton	N	25
● Cat Creek, Powell	C	20
● *Cathecassa*, Clark	C	×

● **Catlettsburgh**, Boyd NE 1,374
● *Catnip*, Jessamine........ C ×
● Cave City, Barren......... S 362
Cave Hill, Warren.......... SW 40
Caverna, (see Horse Cave).... ×
● Cave Spring, Logan..... SW 50
● *Cayce*, Hancock.......... W ×
● Cayce, Fulton........... SW 150
Cayce Station, (see Lewisport) ×
● Cecilian, Hardin........... C 200
Cedar Bluff Mills, Edmond. W 40
Cedar Grove, Boyle.......... C 32
Cedar Grove, (see Weeden)... ×
Cedar Grove, Menifee......... E 10
● *Cedar Grove*, Pulaski..... S ×
Cedar Springs, Allen......... S 57
Cedarville, Rock Castle...... C ×
Celery, Hart.................. C ×
● Central City, Muhlenberg W 1,144
Central Covington, Kent'n.. N 981
Centralville, Madison........ C ×
Centre, Metcalfe............. S 60
Centre Point, Monroe........ S 75
Centretown, Ohio.......... W 150
● Centreville, Bourbon..... N 150
Ceralvo, Ohio................ W 75
● Cerulean Springs, Trigg. SW 150
● *Chaffe*, Boyd............ NE ×
Chalybeate Spri'gs, Edm'son W ×
Chambers, Hancock......... W 12
Chambers, Menifee.......... E 75
Chapel Gap, Lincoln......... C ×
Chapel Hill, Allen........... S 15
Chapeze, Sta., (see Trunnelton) ×
Chaplin, Nelson............ C 155
Chaplin Pike, (see Smileyt'n) ×
Chaplintown, Barren......... S ×
● *Chapman*, Union......... W ×
Chapman's L'd'g, La'renceNE 32
Charleston, (see Dawson).... ×
Charley, Lawrence......... NE 175
Charlotte Furnace, Carter. NE 100
Chatham, Bracken......... NE 25
● *Chattaroi*, Boyd......... NE ×
Chavies, Perry.............. SE 30
Cheap Store Valley, (see Enoch) ×
Check, Grayson............ W ×
Chelsea, Hopkins............ W ×
Chenault, Breckinridge.... W ×
● *Chenowee*, Breathitt...... E ×
Cherokee, Lawrence...... NE 35
Cherry, Calloway.......... SW ×
Cherry Grove, Grant....... N ×
Cherry Hill, (see Caledonia).. ×
● Chester, Mason.......... NE 1,000
Chestnut Grove, Shelby..... N 40
Chestnut Hill, Letcher..... SE ×
Chewning, Trigg........... SW 10
● Chicago, Marion.......... C 225
● Chilesburgh, Fayette...... C 50
Chinquapin Rough, JacksonC 520
Christiansburgh, Shelby.... N 125
Church Hill, Christian..... SW 8
Cicero, Woodford........... C 150
Cisney, Muhlenberg........ W 110
Clabe, Green............... C ×
● Clardy, Christian......... SW ×
Clarence, Pulaski........... S ×
● *Clark*, Mason........... NE ×
Clark's Creek, Grant....... N ×
Clark's Ferry, (see Aberdeen) ×
● Clarkson, Grayson........ W 50
Clark's Salt Works, (seeM'nc'r) ×
● Clark Station, Jefferson.. N ×
Claryville, Campbell......... N 25
Clate, Knox................. SE ×
● Claxton, Caldwell....... SW 26
● *Clay*, Bourbon............ N ×
Clay, Webster.............. W 323
● Clay City, Powell......... C 1,065
Clay Ferry, (see Cleveland).. ×
Clay Lick, Menifee.......... E ×
Clay Lick Fork, Metcalf.... S ×
Claymour, Todd............ SW 25
Claypool, Warren.......... SW 50
Claypool Mill, Allen........ S 15
Claysville, Bourbon......... N 433
Claysville, Harrison......... N 95
Clay Village, Shelby........ N 100
Clay's Ferry, Madison...... C ×
Clear Fork, Bell............ SE 40
Clear Point, (see Seymour) .. ×
Clear Springs, Graves..... SW 50
Clementsville, Casey....... C ×
Cleopatra, McLean.......... W 12
● Clermont, Bullitt......... N 100
Cleveland, Fayette.......... C 77

Clifford, Lawrence........ NE 50
● *Cliffside*, Boyd.......... NE ×
● Clifton, Jefferson......... N 135
Clifton Mills, Breckinridge. W 60
Clifton Springs, (see Marion) ×
Clifty, Todd................ SW 75
Clifty, Muhlenberg......... W ×
Climax, Rock Castle........ C ×
● **Clinton**, Hickman.... SW 1,347
Clinton Station, (see Oakton) ×
Clintonville, Bourbon........ N 300
Clio, (see Bronson)......... ×
Cloud, Edmonson.......... W ×
Clover Bottom, Jackson..... C 40
Clover Bottom, Woodford... C 32
Clover Fork, Harlan....... SE 45
● Cloverport, Breckinridge W 1,527
Cloyd's Landing, CumberlandS 15
Clyde, Wayne................ S 40
Coakley, Green............... C ×
Coal Run, Pike.............. E 19
● Coalton, Boyd............ NE 100
● Cobb, Caldwell.......... SW 30
Coburn, Knott.............. E ×
Coeburg, (see Tampico) ...... ×
Cogswell, Rowan.......... NE 10
Coke, (see Tyrone)............ ×
Colby, Clark............... C ×
Colby Station, Clark........ C ×
Cold Spring, Campbell...... N 300
Coldwater, Calloway...... SW 100
Coldwater, Martin......... E ×
Coleman, Pike.............. E 20
Colemansville, (see Berry).... ×
● Colesburgh, Hardin....... C 140
Colesville, (see Doddy)....... ×
College Hill, Madison....... C 200
Collingsworth, Jackson...... C 10
Colly, Letcher.............. SE 25
Collierville, McCracken... SW ×
Colrosa, Spencer............ C ×
Columbia, Adair.............. S 800
● Columbus, Hickman.... SW 873
Colville, Harrison........... N 25
Colyer, Madison............. C ×
Combs, Madison............. C 25
Comb's Ferry, (see Pine Grove) ×
Commerce Landing (see Parkersville)................... ×
Commercial Point, Union.. W 145
Commercial Summit, (see Pine Knot)...................... ×
Conant, Bell................ SE 25
● Concord, Lewis........... NE 188
Concord, Fleming......... NE ×
Concordia, Meade........... W 151
● *Coney Island*, Campbell.. N 25
Confederate, Lyon......... SW 32
Confluence, Leslie......... SE ×
Congleton, McLean.......... W 10
Conkling, Owsley........... E 20
Connelly, Fulton........... SW ×
Connersville, Harrison...... N 150
● Conniff, Green............ C 26
● *Consolation*, Shelby...... N ×
Constance, Boone........... N 50
Constantine, Breckinridge.. W 25
● Conway, Rock Castle...... C 150
● *Cooks*, Rock Castle....... C ×
Cooksburgh, Rock Castle.... C ×
● Coolidge, Pulaski......... S 100
Coon Creek, Leslie......... SE ×
Coon Hollow, Nelson........ C 50
Coon's, Montgomery........ C ×
● *Cooper's*, Rowan......... NE ×
Cooper's Mills, Pulaski...... S 32
Coopersville, Wayne......... S 40
Copebranch, Breathitt...... E 25
Copley, (see Inez) .... ×
Cora, Anderson.............. C 6
Coral Hill, Barren........... S 60
● Corbin, Whitley.......... SE 75
● *Corey*, Carter........... NE ×
Cordova, Grant.............. N 40
Corena, Daviess............ W ×
● Corinth, Grant............ N 400
Corinth, Logan........... SW ×
Corn Creek, Trimble......... N 100
Cornelia, Magoffin.......... E ×
● *Cornetts*, Montgomery.... C ×
Cornishville, Mercer........ C 125
Cornwell, Menifee.......... E 150
Correll, Wayne.............. S 15
● Corydon, Henderson..... W 777
Costelow, Logan........... SW 10
Cottageville, Lewis........ NE 200
Cottonburgh, Madison....... C 32

Count's Cross R'ds, Carter NE 100
Country Store (see Pon)...... ×
Cove Dale, Lewis.......... NE 10
● **COVINGTON**, Kenton N 37,371
● Cowan, Fleming......... NE 100
Cox's Creek, Nelson......... C 30
Coxville, (see Vanderburg)... ×
Coy, Marshall............. SW 15
Crab Orchard, Rock Castle.. C ×
● Crab Orchard, Lincoln.... C 453
Craftsville, Letcher........ SE 25
Craig, Daviess............. W ×
Craigs, Bath............... NE 10
Crailhope, Green............ C 45
Crains, Fleming............ NE 25
Crandell, (see Wrightsburg).. ×
Crane Nest, Knox.......... SE 32
Crawford, Laurel........... SE 25
● *Crawfordville*, Breck'r'geW ×
Craycraft, Adair............. S 10
● Crayneville, Crittenden.. W 50
Crayton, Nicholas.......... N 40
Creech, Harlan............. SE 50
Creelsborough, Russell...... S 100
● Crescent, Boone........... N 26
● Crescent Hill, Jefferson... N 50
Crescent Springs, Kenton.. N ×
Creswell, Caldwell........ SW 10
● Crider, Caldwell......... SW 30
Crider, Cumberland......... S ×
Crigger, Pike................ E ×
● Crittenden, Grant......... N 440
Crittenden Springs, Crit'n.. W ×
● *Croakes*, Nelson.......... C ×
Crockettsville, Breathitt.... E 20
Crocus, Adair................ S 10
● Crofton, Christian....... SW 428
Cromwell, Ohio............. W 185
Crooked Creek, Rock Castle. C ×
● Crooks, Bath............. NE 25
Crookville, Madison......... C ×
● Cropper, Shelby.......... N 150
Crossland, Calloway....... SW 150
Cross Plains, (see Niagara) .. ×
Cross Roads, (see Custer) .... ×
Cross Roads, (see Summerville) ×
Cross Roads, (see Allensville) ×
Cross Roads, (see Waverly) .. ×
Cross Roads, Laurel........ SE 19
● *Crow-Hickman*, Daviess. W ×
Crowsville, (see Inroad) ...... ×
Cruceville, (see Marion) ...... ×
Crum, Lewis.............. NE 20
Cruseton, Daviess.......... W 10
● Crutchfield, Fulton..... SW 30
Cuba, Graves.............. SW 50
Cubage, Bell............... SE 30
Cub Run, Hart.............. C 75
Culbertson, Boyd........... NE 25
● *Culbertson*, Kenton....... N ×
Cullen, Union............... W 40
Cumberland, Harlan....... SE ×
Cumberland, (see Monticello) ×
Cumberland, Whitley...... SE 32
Cumberland City, Clinton... S 195
● *Cumberland Falls*, PulaskiS ×
Cumberland Falls, Whitley SE 40
Cumberland Gap, (seeCumberland Gap, Tenn.)......... ×
● *Cumberland River*, LyonSW 19
Cummins, Whitley........ SE 65
Cunningham, Carlisle..... SW 8
● *Cunningham*, Bourbon... N 40
Cupio, Bullitt.............. N 20
Curdsville, Daviess........ W 341
● *Curdsville*, Mercer........ C 255
● *Curnutt*, Lawrence..... NE 10
● *Curry*, Mercer........... C ×
Curry's Run, (see Robinson's Station)..................... ×
Custer, Breckinridge....... W 75
Cutch, Floyd................ E ×
Cutshin, Leslie............. SE 30
Cyclone, Monroe............ S ×
● **Cynthiana**, Harrison... N 3,016
Cypress Hickman......... SW 60
Cypress Creek, McLean..... W ×
Dabney, Pulaski............ S 15
Daiseyville, Pulaski......... S 10
Daisydell, Breathitt......... E 25
Dale, Campbell.............. N 32
Dallam's Creek, Logan.... SW 36
Dallas, Pulaski.............. S 30
Dallisburg, Owen.......... N 50
Dalton, Hopkins............ W 75
Dalton, Lincoln............ C 32
Daniels Creek, Johnson..... E ×

Danleyton, Greenup.......NE 25
● Dant, Marion.............C 15
● **Danville**, Boyle.........C 3,766
Danville Junction, (see Junction City)................ ×
Darby, Warren...........SW 19
Davenport, Butler..........W 15
Davidson, Nicholas.........N 25
Davis, Scott...............N 70
Davistown Camp, Garrard..C ×
● Dawson, Hopkins........ W 525
Daysborough, Wolfe........ E 25
Daysville, Todd...........SW 75
● Dayton, Campbell........ N 4,264
Deadwood, Casey........... C ×
Deane, Letcher............SE ×
● *Dean Field*, Ohio....... W ×
● Deatsville, Nelson........ C 60
● De Bard, Carter..........NE 100
● *Decourcy*, Kenton........N ×
Deer Creek, Carter........ NE 40
Deerlick, Logan...........SW ×
Defiance, Floyd............E ×
Defoe, Henry...............N 25
● Defries, Hart..............C ×
● De Kovan, Union........ W 800
Delaware, Daviess..........W 100
Della, Grant...............N ×
● *De Moss*, Campbell.......N ×
● De Mossville, Pendleton..N 116
● *Dempster*, Ohio.......... W ×
Denison, Hart..............C ×
Denmark, Russell...........S 13
Denney, Wayne..............S ×
● *Dennis*, Logan.......... SW 32
● Denton, Carter...........NE 432
Denver, Johnson............E 25
Deposit, Jefferson.........N 35
Depoy, Muhlenberg........ W 10
Derifield, Lawrence....... NE 32
Deskin, Pike...............E 30
● Dexter, Calloway........SW ×
Dexter, (see Maysville)....... ×
Dexterville, Butler......... W 37
Dezarn, Green..............C 15
Diamond Isl'd Be'd, Hend'nW 10
Diana, Laurel............ SE 32
Dick, Pike................E ×
Dickey's Mills, Edmonson..W 50
Dick Robinson, Garrard.... C ×
● *Dickson*, Rowan........ NE ×
Dillingham, Adair...........S 77
Dillon, Laurel.............SE ×
Dingus, Morgan.............E 25
Dishman, Whitley.......... SE 25
Disputanta, Rock Castle.....C 10
● *Dividing Ridge*, Hart..... C ×
Dividing Ridge, Pendleton..N 40
Dixie, Henderson.......... W 150
● *Dixon*, Boone........... N ×
Dixon, Webster...........W 546
Dixville, (see Nevada)........ ×
Doctor's Fork, Boyle....... C ×
Doddy, Allen...............S 26
● Dodge, Clark..............C 60
Doe Run, (see Weeden)...... ×
Dog Creek, Hart............C 60
Donaldson, Clark.......... C 25
Donaldson, (see Maple Grove) ×
Donansburg, Green.......... C 26
Donelton, Greenup........NE 25
● Donerail, Fayette.........C 16
Donnelly, Lee..............E ×
Doorway, Owsley............E 32
Dorrett's Run, Hardin.......C 8
Dorton, Pike...............E ×
Dory, Clay................SE 25
Dot, Logan................SW 13
Dotson, Floyd...............E ×
Doubling Springs Landing, (see Bowling Green).......... ×
Doudton, Pendleton......... N 15
Doughty's Cr., (see Smith'sGr) ×
Douglas, Casey............. C 12
● *Douglas*, Christian......SW ×
Doups Point, (see Sapony)... ×
● Dover, Mason...........NE 515
Dow, Knox................SE ×
Downingsville, Grant.......N 130
Doylesville, Madison........ C 25
● Drakesboro, Muhlenberg.W 400
Drake's Grove, (see Eberly).. ×
Drake's Mills, Wolfe........E ×
● *Drake's Mills*, Hopkins..W ×
● *Dravo*, Jefferson......... N ×
Drennon Land., (see Springf'd) ×
Drennon Springs, Henry....N 10

Dripping Springs, (see Crab). ×
Drip Rock, Jackson.........C 50
Drownville, (see Waco)...... ×
Dryden, Wayne.............S 12
Dry Fork, Barren...........S 10
● Dry Ridge, Grant.........N 130
● Dry Run, Scott...........N 50
Dublin, Graves............SW 120
● Duckers, Woodford.......C 40
Duck Run, Whitley........SE ×
Duff, Grayson............. W 13
Dukedon, (see Dunkedom, Tenn. ×
● Dulaney, Caldwell.......SW 30
Dunbarton, Daviess........ W 32
Duncan, Mercer.............C 50
Duncan, (see Kingsville).... ×
Duncan, Lincoln............C ×
● *Duncannon*, Madison.....C ×
Duncan's Store, (see Dixon).. ×
● *Dundee*, Powell...........C ×
Dungansville, (see Tolu)..... ×
● Dunmor, Muhlenberg.... W 82
Dunnville, Casey........... C 136
Dupont, (see Nelson)......... ×
Durham, Christian........SW 195
Durham, Pulaski...........S ×
● *Duvall*, Scott.............N ×
Duvall's Landing, GreenupNE 10
Duvall's Mills, Trimble.....N 10
Dwale, Floyd...............E 25
Dwarf, Perry..............SE 25
Dycusburgh, Crittenden....W 100
Dyer, Lewis...............NE ×
Dykes, Pulaski..............S 40
● Eadston, Rowan.........NE 10
Eadsville, Wayne...........S ×
Eagle Hill, Owen...........N 10
● Eagle Station, Carroll.....N 100
Earle's, Muhlenberg........W 35
● Earlington, Hopkins..... W 748
Earnestville, Owsley........ E ×
East Bend Landing, Boone. N 69
● East Bernstadt, Laurel...SE 600
● *East Cairo*, Ballard.....SW 348
East Eagle, Owen.......... N 20
Easterday, Carroll......... N ×
East Fork, Metcalfe.........S 60
East Hickman, Fayette......C 12
● *Eastern Kentucky Junc.*, Carter............NE 57
● *East Louisville*, Jefferson N ×
East Point, Johnson.........E 40
East Union, Nicholas.......N 25
● East View, Hardin........ C 200
● Eastwood, Jefferson...... N 30
Easy Gap, Hardin..........C ×
Eberly, Union.............W 10
● Echols, Ohio..............W 32
Eclipse Mills, (see Pee Dee).. ×
● **Eddyville**, Lyon......SW 680
● Eden, Jefferson...........N 15
Eden, Martin.............. E 309
Edenton, Madison..........C 20
Edgarton, Pike..............E 20
Edgehill, Calloway........SW ×
● *Edgehill*, Shelby.........N ×
Edmonton, Metcalfe......S 300
● Edwards, Logan.........SW 25
Egs, Grayson...............W ×
Eighty Eight, Barren........S 50
Egypt, (see Pond Fork)....... ×
● *Egypt*, Rowan.......... NE 65
● Ekron, Meade............W 14
Elamton, Morgan...........E 25
Elba, McLean..............W 10
Elder, Morgan............. E ×
Eldorado, (see McAfee)....... ×
● Elihu, Pulaski............S 12
● Elizabeth, Bourbon.......N 6
● **Elizabethtown**, HardinC 2,260
Elizabethville, Pendleton...N 20
Elizaville, Fleming.........NE 164
● Elkatawa, Breathitt.......E 25
● *Elk Chester*, Fayette......C ×
Elk Creek, Spencer........ C 25
Elk Creek Mills, Pulaski....S ×
Elk Fork, Morgan...........E 25
Elk Horn, Taylor............C 100
Elkhorn, Letcher..........SE ×
● *Elkhorn*, Franklin.........N ×
Elkhorn, (see South Elkhorn) ×
● Elkin, Clark..............C 30
● **Elkton**, Todd.......... SW 1,158
● *Elkton & Guthrie Junction*, Todd..............SW ×
Elliottville, Rowan........ NE 105
Ellisburgh, Casey............C 65

● Elliston, Grant............N 150
Elliston, (see Waco)........ ×
Ellisville, Nicholas..........N 10
Ellisville, (see Powers Store). ×
Ellwood, Webster....... ...W 10
Elm Grove, Bracken........N 25
Elm Lick, (see Horton)....... ×
Elmo, Christian.......... SW 200
Elm Spring, Washington... C ×
Elmville, Franklin..........N 300
Elmwood Wayne............S ×
● *Elmwood*, Webster........W 10
Elon, (see Brush Creek)..... ×
Elroy, Adair................S 20
● Elva, Marshall..........SW ×
Elvira, Clay..............SE 25
Elvira, Laurel.............SE ×
Elwood, Muhlenberg.......W ×
Elza, Breckinridge.........W ×
● Emanuel, Knox..........SE 50
Emberton, Monroe..........S 13
● Eminence, Henry.........N 2,002
Emma, (see Fallsburg)....... ×
Emma, Magoffin............E ×
● *Emmons*, Fleming..... NE ×
● Empire, Christian.......SW 216
Emporia, Ohio.............W ×
Empire Iron W'ks, (see Rinaldo) ×
Engle, Estill................C 15
● English, Carroll...........N 50
Enoch, Taylor..............C 10
Enola, Ohio...............W ×
Enon, Caldwell...........SW 10
Ensor, Daviess.............W 25
● *Enterprise*, Carter...... NE 32
Enterprise, (see Bowling Green) ×
Eolia, Letcher............ SE ×
Ep, Owen................. N 10
● *Epley*, Logan.......... SW ×
Epley Station, Logan......SW ×
Epperson, McCracken.... SW ×
Era, Christian............SW 10
● Erlanger, Kenton.........N 700
Esculapia Springs, Lewis..NE 3[illegible]
Estesburgh, Pulaski.........S 10
Esto, Russell...............S 10
Ethal, Clay................SE ×
Ethridge, Gallatin..........N 20
Etoile, Barren...............S 8
● Eubank, Pulaski..........S 10[illegible]
Eubanks' Store, (see Mud Lick) ×
Euclid, (see Forest Cottage)... ×
● Eureka, Lyon............SW 10
Evans, Letcher............ SE ×
Evans, (see Laco)........... ×
Evans' Landing, (see Tennessee Rolling Works)........ ×
Evanston, Greenup....... NE 25
Evarts, Bell..............SE ×
Evarts, Harlan ....**SE** **25**
Eveleigh, Grayson..........W 15
Evena, Harrison...........N 25
Eversole, Owsley............E 24
Evona, Casey...............C ×
Ewell, Lincoln............. C ×
● Ewing, Fleming.........NE 150
Ewingford, Trimble........ N 40
● Ewington, Montgomery...C ×
Exie, Green.................C ×
Ezel, Morgan...............E 124
● *Factories*, Jefferson...... N ×
Factory, Butler.............W 10
Fainville, Estill............ C ×
Fair Dealing, Marshall....SW 12
Fairfield, Nelson...........C 200
● *Fair Grounds*, Daviess... W ×
Fair Grounds, (see Crescent Hill) ×
● *Fair Grounds*, Mason....NE ×
● *Fairlee*, Clark.............C 65
Fairmount, Jefferson.......N 100
Fairplay, Adair..............S ×
Fairport, Breckinridge.... W ×
Fairthorn, Hart.............C 10
Fairview, Todd.............SW 183
Fairview, (see Oakwoods)..... ×
Fairview, (see Briensburg)... ×
● *Fairview*, Lewis......... NE ×
Faith, McLean..............W 10
Falcon, Magoffin............E 25
● *Falcon*, Hancock........ W ×
Fallsburg, Lawrence...... NE 50
Falkner, Whitley..........SE ×
Falls of Blaine, (see Louisa). ×
● Falls of Rough, Grayson. W 200
● **Falmouth**, Pendleton..N 1,146
Fancy Farm, Graves......SW 86
● Fariston, Laurel.........SE 70

Post Office, County	Dir.	Pop.
Farmdale, Franklin	N	370
● Farmers, Rowan	NE	367
Farmerville, (see Rufus)		×
Farmington, Graves	SW	89
Farnsworth Mills, (see PeeDee)		×
Faubush, Pulaski	S	75
● Faulconer, Boyle	C	10
Faulkner, Livingston	W	×
Fawnburgh, Owen	N	×
Faywood, Woodford	C	65
Fearis, Lewis	NE	77
Fed, Floyd	E	10
Feliciana, Graves	SW	×
Fenton, Trigg	SW	×
Fenwick, Washington	C	10
● Ferguson, Logan	SW	75
Fern Creek, Jefferson	N	350
Fern Leaf, Mason	NE	50
Ferrell, Pike	E	×
Fielden, Elliott	NE	50
Figg, Shelby	N	×
● *Fillmore*, Ballard	SW	×
● *Filson*, Powell	C	25
Fincastle, Lee	E	×
● *Fincastle*, Wolfe	E	×
● Finchville, Shelby	N	75
Finley, Taylor	C	×
Finnell, Scott	N	25
Fireclay, Carter	NE	25
● Fisherville, Jefferson	N	50
Fishing, Pulaski	S	×
Fish Point, (see Livingston)		×
Fish Trap, Pike	E	25
Fiskburgh, Kenton	N	250
Fitchburgh, (see Furnace)		×
Fitz, Johnson	E	×
Fix Landing, (see Wise L'd'g)		×
Flagfork, Franklin	N	40
Flagg Spring, Campbell	N	65
Flaherty, Meade	W	20
Flanagan, Clark	C	25
Flatcreek, Bath	NE	25
Flat Gap, Johnson	E	93
● Flat Lick, Knox	SE	300
● Flat Rock, Pulaski	S	300
Flat Springs, Wayne	S	×
Flatwood, Garrard	C	32
Fleenerville, Butler	W	×
● **Flemingsburgh**, Fleming	NE	1,172
Flener, (see Aberdeen)		×
Fletcher, Laurel	SE	×
Flingsville, Grant	N	25
Flint, Calloway	SW	×
Flippen, Monroe	S	256
Floral, Hancock	W	×
Flora's Store, (see Linton)		×
Florence, Boone	N	375
Florence Station, McCrac'n	SW	50
● *Florida Heights*, Jefferson	N	×
● Flournoy, Union	W	15
● *Floyds*, Pulaski	S	×
Floydsburgh, Oldham	N	50
Floyd's Fork, Jefferson	N	65
Folsomdale, Graves	SW	32
Fontana, Carter	NE	×
Fonthill, Russell	S	10
Foot of Stewart Island, (see Birdsville)		×
● *Forbes*, Lawrence	NE	×
Ford, Fleming	NE	×
● Ford, Clark	C	381
Ford, Madison	C	×
Ford's Ferry, Crittenden	W	75
● Fordsville, Ohio	W	281
Fordyce, Warren	SW	×
● *Forest*, Jefferson	N	×
Forest Cottage, Clinton	S	30
Forest Home, Woodford	C	×
Foreston, (see Kuttawa)		×
Forestville, Hart	C	20
Forgyville, (see Quality Val'y)		×
Forkland, Boyle	C	×
Forks Cuney of Buck Creek, (see Buck Creek)		×
Forks of Corn Creek, (see Corn Creek)		×
Forks of Elkhorn, Franklin	N	60
Forks of Locust, (see Locust)		×
Forkton, Monroe	S	×
Formans Springs, Lewis	NE	25
● *Fort Estill*, Madison	C	15
● *Fort Estill Junc.*, Madison	C	×
Fort Garrett, Woodford	C	×
Fort Heinman, Calloway	SW	×
● Fort Jefferson, Ballard	SW	×
Fort Luckett, (see Milton)		×
Fort Pennington, Monroe	S	×

Kentucky

Post Office, County	Dir.	Pop.
Fort Spring, Fayette	C	26
● *Fort Thomas*, Campbell	N	×
Forty-Two Mile House, (see Mason)		×
● Foster, Bracken	N	300
Fountain Run, Monroe	S	300
Four Mile Creek, Bell	SE	×
Four Oaks, Pendleton	N	×
Fox, Estill	C	×
Fox Creek, Anderson	C	30
Foxport, Fleming	NE	10
Foxsprings, Fleming	NE	×
Fox Town, Jackson	C	×
Foy, (see Unity, Tenn)		×
Fraley, Rowan	NE	26
Frances, Crittenden	W	10
Francisville, (see Hebron)		×
● **FRANKFORT**, Fran'n	N	7,892
● **Franklin**, Simpson	SW	2,324
Franklin Cross Rds., Hardin	C	15
Franklin's Mills, Fleming	NE	×
Franklinton, Henry	N	60
Franks, Breckinridge	W	×
Fraser, Wayne	S	10
Frederick, Madison	C	×
Fredericksburg, (see Fredericktown)		×
Fredericktown, Washington	C	72
● Fredonia, Caldwell	SW	249
Freedom, Barren	S	50
● *Freestone*, Lewis	NE	×
Freestone, Rowan	NE	27
Free Union, Webster	W	32
Frenchburgh, Menifee	E	222
Frenchtown, Livingston	W	×
Fren, Johnson	E	130
Frew, Johnson	E	30
Friedland, Lyon	SW	×
Friendship, Caldwell	SW	20
Fritz, Whitley	SE	40
Frost, Greenup	NE	25
Frostburgh, Hopkins	W	×
Frozen Creek, Breathitt	E	25
Fruit Hill, Christian	SW	20
Fry, Calloway	SW	×
Fry, Green	C	40
Fuget, Johnson	E	25
● *Fullers*, Lawrence	NE	×
● Fulton, Fulton	SW	1,818
● *Fulton's*, Jefferson	N	×
Fulton's Landing, Greenup	NE	65
Fultz, Carter	NE	×
Furnace, Estill	C	15
Furnace, Menifee	E	×
Futrell's Landing, (see Linton)		×
Gabbard, Owsley	E	×
Gadberry, Adair	S	15
Gainesville, (see Wooley's)		×
Gainesville, Allen	S	150
Galen, Johnson	E	25
Galena, Livingston	W	×
Galloway's Mills, Warren	SW	10
● Gallup, Lawrence	NE	50
Galveston, Floyd	E	×
Gamaliel, Monroe	S	60
Gano, Boyle	C	×
● *Gap*, Madison	C	×
Gap Creek, Wayne	S	80
Gapville, Magoffin	E	×
Garden Cottage (see Bronston)		×
Gardnersville, Pendleton	N	40
● Garfield, Breckinridge	W	40
● *Garland*, Lewis	NE	×
Garner, Boyd	NE	15
● *Garnet*, Harrison	N	×
Garnettsville, Meade	W	200
Garnettsville, (see Dalton)		×
Garrett, Meade	W	50
Garrettsburgh, Christian	SW	70
● Garrison, Lewis	NE	30
Gasper, Logan	SW	×
● *Gates*, Rowan	NE	10
Gatewood, Daviess	W	20
Gatewood, Hancock	W	×
Gatewoods, Montgomery	C	×
Gaw, Daviess	W	10
Gay's Creek, Perry	SE	×
● *Geiger's Lane*, Boyd	NE	×
Geigersville, (see Kilgore's)		×
Geneva, Henderson	W	50
Gentry's Mill, Adair	S	×
George's Creek, Lawrence	NE	35
● **Georgetown**, Scott	N	3,000
● Germantown, Mason	NE	229
Germantown, Bracken	N	229
Gertrude, Bracken	N	×
Gest, Henry	N	150
● Gethsemane, Nelson	C	40

Kentucky

Post Office, County	Dir.	Pop.
Ghent, Carroll	N	525
Gibson, LaRue	C	×
● Gilbert's Creek, Lincoln	C	25
● Gilbertsville, Marshall	SW	60
Gillmore, Wolfe	E	19
Gilman's Point, (see St. Mathews)		×
Gilpin, Casey	C	30
Gimlet, Elliott	NE	20
Girdler, Knox	SE	75
Girkin, Warren	SW	13
Gishton, Muhlenberg	W	50
Gittings, Cumberland	S	32
● Glade, Marshall	SW	×
Glades, (see Walnut Grove)		×
Gladie, Menifee	E	35
Gladstone, Marshall	SW	×
● **Glasgow**, Barren	S	2,051
● Glasgow Junction, Barren	S	217
Gleanings, LaRue	C	57
● *Glenarvon*, Clark	C	×
● *Glencairn*, Powell	C	×
● Glencoe, Gallatin	N	300
● Glendale, Hardin	C	100
● Glendeane, Breckinridge	W	100
Glendora, Boyd	NE	×
● *Glenn*, Lewis	NE	×
Glen's Fork, Adair	S	120
Glen Springs, Lewis	NE	×
● Glenview, Jefferson	N	×
Glenville, McLean	W	100
Glenville, (see Bloomfield)		×
Glenwood, Lawrence	NE	40
Glover's Creek, (see Summer Shade)		×
Goble, Carter	NE	25
Godfrey, Allen	S	×
Godman, Muhlenberg	W	×
Goff, Edmonson	W	97
Goff's Crossing, (see Leach)		×
Goforth, Pendleton	N	20
Goggins' Landing, (see Albany Landing)		×
Gold City, Simpson	SW	57
Golden Creek, (see Carpenter)		×
Golden Pond, Trigg	SW	75
Golds Webster	W	×
Goochland, Rock Castle	C	15
Goodloe, Floyd	E	32
Goodnight, Barren	S	×
Goose Creek, (see Dunnville)		×
● *Goose Creek*, Jefferson	N	×
Goose Rock, Clay	SE	×
● *Gordon*, Muhlenberg	W	×
Gordon Station (see Depoy)		×
Gordonsville, Logan	SW	350
Gordonsville, Hopkins	W	×
Gore's, (see Junction City)		×
Goresburg, (see Junction City)		×
Gose, Wayne	S	×
Goshen, Oldham	N	52
Gosport, (see Cromwell)		×
Gott's Store, Warren	SW	×
Gough, (see Cross Roads)		×
Gover, (see Elihu)		×
● Gracey, Christian	SW	40
Gradyville, Adair	S	200
Graefenberg, Shelby	N	100
Grahamton, Meade	W	275
Grahamville, McCracken	SW	×
● *Grahns*, Carter	NE	×
Grahamville, (see Maxan's Mills)		×
Graingertown, (see Commercial Point)		×
● *GrandAvenueCave*, Barren	S	×
Grand Crossing, Bracken	N	38
● Grand Rivers, Livingston	W	900
● *Grand View*, Kenton	N	10
Grand View, (see Marion)		×
Grand View, Hardin	C	10
Grange City, Fleming	NE	131
Grange Store, Pike	E	50
Grangetown, (see Rocky Hill)		×
● Grant, Boone	N	26
● ***Grant*, Carter**	NE	×
● Grant's Bend, Kenton	N	26
Grant's Lick, Campbell	N	60
Grapevine, Perry	SE	25
Grassland, Boyd	NE	32
Grassy Creek, Morgan	E	25
Grassy Lick, Montgomery	C	100
Gratz, Owen	N	205
● *Gravel Switch*, Lincoln	C	×
● *Gravel Switch*, Livingston	W	×
● Gravel Switch, Marion	C	50
Graves, Knox	SE	×
Graves Shoal (see Richardson)		×
● Gray, Knox	SE	100

Gray Hawk, Jackson........C ×
● *Gray's Branch*, Greenup NE ×
● **Grayson,** Carter.......NE 433
Grayson Springs, Grayson.. W 83
● *Grayson Spring Station*, Grayson.................W 50
Graysville, (see Guthrie) ..... ×
Great Crossings, Scott...... N 355
Greek, Johnson............ E ×
Green Briar Springs, (see Crab Orchard)....... ×
Green Castle, Warren..... SW 50
● Greendale, Fayette........C 355
Green Grove, Cumberland.. S 13
Green Hall, Jackson........ C 40
Green Hill, Warren....... SW 50
Greenleaf, (see Beaver)....... ×
Green Mount, Laurel...... SE 20
Green River, Lincoln........ C 8
Green River Bridge, (see Campbellville)....... ×
● **Greensburgh,** Green.. C 552
Green's Ferry, (see Smithland) ×
● **Greenup,** Greenup.... NE 669
Greenup Lime Works, G'n'p NE 50
● **Greenville**, Muhlenburg W 968
● Greenwood, Pulaski.......S 300
Greenwood, Warren.......SW ×
Greenwood Lake, (see Erlanger) ×
Gregory, Wayne..............S 20
Gresham, Green...............C 40
Gresham's Store, (see Parkersville)...................... ×
Grider, Cumberland..........S ×
Griffin, Bullitt...............N ×
Grissom's Landing, Daviess W 175
Grooms, Montgomery.......C ×
Ground Squirrel Spring, (see Upton).............. ×
● Grove Centre, Union.....W 25
Groverdale, Magoffin.........E ×
Goverton, (see Salt River) .... ×
● *Grubb's*, Boone............N ×
Grubridge, (see Harper's Ferry) ×
Grundy, Pulaski..............S 75
Gubser, Campbell............N 25
Gudesville, (see Penrod)...... ×
Gulnare, Pike................ E 10
Gum Grove, Union............W ×
● Gum Sulphur, Rock Castle C 75
Gunpowder, Boone......... N 25
● Guston, Meade.............W 75
Guthrie, Todd..............SW 449
Gypsy, Magoffin..............E 10
Habit, Daviess...............W 25
Hadden, Montgomery.......C ×
● Hadensville, Todd.......SW 200
Hadley, Warren............SW 20
Hager, Magoffin..............E 40
Hagersville, (see Pearl) ...... ×
Haginsville, Breathitt....... E 26
Hahntown, Nelson...........C ×
Hall, Pulaski.................S ×
Haleburgh, Hancock........ W 65
Haley's Mill, Christian.... SW 10
Half Way, Allen..............S 75
Halifax, Allen................S 32
Hall, Knott...................E 25
Hallam, Owen.................N 25
Hall's Gap, (see Maywood)... ×
Halsell, Warren.............SW 32
Halstore's, (see Veals Store) . ×
Hamby's Station, Hopkins..W 15
Hamilton, Boone.............N 50
● *Hamilton*, Fayette..........C ×
● *Hamilton Station*, Ohio..W 302
Hamlet, Marshall.......... SW 38
Hamlin, Calloway..........SW 18
Hammack, Garrard..........C 26
Hammels, Trimble............N ×
Hammond, Trimble......... N ×
Hammonville, Hart.......... C 111
Hampton, Livingston.......W 112
● *Hampton*, Boyd..........NE 425
Hanly, Jessamine.. ....C 50
Hansborough Sta., (see Shelbv'e) ×
Hansford, Rock Castle.... C ×
● Hanson, Hopkins.........W 376
● *Harding*, Union............W ×
● *Happy Hollow*, Pulaski... S 260
Harcourt, Marion............C ×
Hardcastle, Warren.........SW ×
Hardin, Marshall...........SW ×
● **Hardinsburgh,** B'k'r'e W 681
Hardin Springs, Hardin......C 50
Hardinsville, (see Graefenb'g) ×
Hardmoney, McCracken..SW 36
Hardscrabble, (see Cherry Gro.) ×
Hardyville, Hart.............C 200
Hargis, Breathitt........... E ×
Harlan, Harlin............SE 361
Harmony, Owen............ N 50
Harmony Landing, Oldham N ×
● Harned, Breckinridge.... W ×
● Harold, Crittenden.......W 15
Harp, Franklin..............N 60
Harper's Ferry, Henry....... N 40
Harp's Head, Webster......W ×
Harreldsville, Butler....... W 15
● Harris, Madison...........C 15
Harrisburgh, (see Harris Gro.) ×
Harrisburgh, Owen......... N 25
Harris' Ferry, (see College Hill) ×
Harris Grove, Calloway... SW 50
Harrison Station, (see Hanson) ×
Harrisonville, Shelby....... N 100
● **Harrodsburgh,** Mercer C 3,230
● Harrod's Creek, Jefferson N 75
Hartford, Ohio...........W 740
Harvieland, Franklin.......N 130
Harvy, Marshall............SW 20
Haskinsville, (see Camp Knox) ×
Hatfield, Pike...............E ×
Hathaway, Boone............N ×
● Hatton, Shelby ....N 70
Havilandsville, Harrison....N 50
● **Hawesville,** Hancock. W 1,013
Hawthorne, Campbell........N 20
Hayesville, (see Andersonville) ×
● *Hayne's*, Daviess..........W ×
Haynesville, Ohio...........W 25
Hays, Warren...............SW 15
Hays Spring, (see Fair Mount) ×
Haystack, Powell........... C ×
Haysville, Marion.......... C 57
Haysville, (see White Mills... ×
Hazard, Perry..............SE 200
● Hazel, Calloway.........SW ×
Hazel Green, Wolfe.........E 218
● Hazle Patch, Laurel..... SE 258
Hazlewood, Ballard....... SW 8
Head of Grassy, Lewis.....NE 25
Head Quarters, Nicholas ...N 90
Hearin, Webster.............W 20
Hebbardsville, Henderson..W 800
Hebron, Boone............. N 40
● Hedges, Clark..............C 289
Hedger, Menifee............ E ×
Hedgeville, Boyle........... C ×
Heekin, Grant.............. N 20
Hegira, Cumberland..........S 20
● *Heilman*, Rowan..........NE ×
● Helena, Mason.........NE 130
Helena, (see Barterville)..... ×
● Helena Station, Mason.. NE 100
Helfer's Mill, (see Lewisburg) ×
HellGateShoals, (see Paintsv'e) ×
Helton, Leslie...............SE 25
● Hempridge, Shelby......... N 35
● **Henderson,** Henderson W 8,835
Hendricks, Magoffin........ E 50
Hendricks, (see Goodman).... ×
Henry, Morgan..............E 30
Henryville, (see Lewisburg).. ×
● Henshaw, Union.......... W 30
Herbert, Montgomery.......C ×
Herman, Union ....W 15
● *Herman*, Todd..........SW ×
● Herndon, Christian..... SW 75
● *Herndon*, Scott...........N ×
Herrings Land'g, (see Eureka) ×
Heselton, Lewis.............NE ×
Hesler, Owen................ N 50
Hestand, Monroe.............S ×
Hettie, Anderson............C ×
Hibbardsville, Henderson.. W ×
Hibernia, La Rue............C 32
● **Hickman,** Fulton.... SW 1,652
Hickory Flat, Simpson....SW 35
Hickory Grove, (see Abbott) . ×
● Hickory Grove, Graves..SW 145
Hico, Calloway............SW 40
Higdon, Grayson............ W 15
Higgason, (see Osceola)...... ×
● *Higginsport Station*, B'k'n N ×
Highbaugh's Mill, (see Bonnlev'e) ×
● High Bridge, Jessamie....C 150
High Bridge, Mercer........C ×
High Grove, Nelson.........C 50
High Knob, Clay...........SE 125
Highland, (see Hico)......... ×
Highland, Lincoln............C 80
● *Highland*, Kenton........N ×
Highland, (see Aurora)...... ×
● *Highland*, Henderson....W ×
Hightower, Pendleton......N ×
Hightower's Store, (see Williamst'n ×
Hike's Point, Jefferson..... N 15
Hilda, Lewis............... NE 25
● *Hillenmeyer*, Fayette..... C ×
Hill Grove, Meade..........W 40
Hillsborough, (see Coldwater) ×
● Hillsborough, Fleming..NE 212
Hillsdale, Bracken..........N ×
Hillside, Pulaski............S ×
● Hill Spring, Henry....... N 57
Hilltop, (see Summerville)... ×
Hilton, Monroe.............S 12
Hindman, Knott.......... E 150
Hinesdale, Hart..............C ×
Hines' Mills, (see Sulphur Sprs.) ×
Hink, Barren.................S ×
Hinkleville, Ballard.......SW 75
Hinsleytown, Christian....SW 40
● Hinton, Scott.............N 75
Hiseville, Barren............S 194
Hites Run, Breckenridge...W ×
Hitesville, Union...........W 100
● Hobbs, Bullitt.............N 20
● **Hodgensville,** LaRue..C 542
Hoertz, Jefferson............N ×
Hogg, Letcher...............SE ×
Hog's Falls, (see Smallhous) ×
Holbrook, Grant............N 40
Holland, Allen...............S 70
Holloway, Ballard........SW ×
Holly Hill, Whitley......... SE 40
● Holt, Breckinridge.......W 19
Holy Cross, Marion..........C 40
Home, Pike...................E 25
Homer, Logan...............SW 25
Homestead, Jefferson ...... N ×
Home Valley, (see Gudesville) ×
Honaker's F'ry, (see Bowl'gGr'n) ×
Honaker's L'd'g, (see Deskin). ×
Honesty, Kenton............ N 10
Honey Cut, (see Rossville).... ×
Honeysuckle, Franklin.....N ×
● *Honshell*, Boyd.......... NE ×
Hood's Run, Greenup..... NE 30
Hooktown, Nicholas.........N 75
Hooppole, Anderson........ C 10
Hope, Montgomery...........C 25
● Hopewell, Greenup..... NE 25
Hopewell, (see Fordsville).... ×
● **Hopkinsville,** Chr't'n SW 5,833
Hopper, Knox...............SE ×
Hopson, Caldwell.......... SW 32
Horace, Anderson...........C ×
Hornbeck's Mills, Grayson.. W 8
Horn's Store, (see Horntown) ×
Horntown, Grayson........ W 10
● Horse Branch, Ohio...... W 50
● Horse Cave, Hart..........C 598
Horse Shoe Bottom, Russell .S 28
● Horton, Ohio..............W 150
Hoskinston, Leslie.........SE 25
House's Store, (see Benge)... ×
Houston L'd'g, (see Corn Creek) ×
● *Howard*, Hardin...........C ×
Howard, Mason........... NE 25
Howard's Mills, Montgomery C 25
Howard's Mills, (see Lunar). ×
● Howel, Christian........SW 10
Howesburg, Jefferson.......N 57
Howe's Valley, Hardin...... C 40
Hubble, Lincoln..............C 57
● *Huddleston*, Whitley.... SE 32
Hudgins, Greene.............C 20
Hudson, Breckinridge......W 25
Hueysville, Floyd............E ×
Huff, Edmonson.............W 18
Hughes' Mill, (see Sonora).. ×
Human Valley, (see Boxville) ×
Hume Store, Boone.........N ×
Humphrey, Casey............ C 33
● Hunnewell, Greenup....NE 97
Hunt, Clark.................. C 50
● Hunters Depot, Nelson....C 15
Huntersville, Clinton........S ×
Huntsville, Butler..........W 90
Huntsville, Pendleton....... N ×
Hurricane, (see Tolu)........ ×
Hustonville, Lincoln........ C 435
Hutcherson's Mills, (see Bedford) ×
● Hutchinson's, Bourbon...N 200
Huxley, Laurel.............SE 6
Hyattsville, Garrard.........C 30
Hyden, Leslie............SE 80
Hydro, Warren............SW ×
Ibex, Elliott.................NE 10
Ida, Clinton..................S ×

Illwill, Clinton.............S ×
● Isley, Hopkins.............W ×
● Independence, Kenton...N 804
Indian Bottom, Letcher....SE 25
Indian Creek, Knox.......SE 30
● Indian Fields, Clark,......C 50
Indian Run, Bullitt.........N ×
Inez, Martin.................E 180
● *Ingalls Park*, Campbell..N ×
Ingram, Bell..................SE 20
Inroad, Adair...............S ×
● *Inverness*, Breathitt......E ×
Inwood, Adair..............S ×
● *Iola*, Marshall..............SW ×
Irad, Lawrence............NE 10
Irma, Crittenden...........W 20
Ironbridge, Warren.......SW ×
Iron Hill, Crittenden.......W ×
Iron Mound, Estill..........C ×
Ironton, Trigg...............SW ×
● **Irvine**, Estill.............C 400
● *Irving*, Pendleton........N ×
● Irvington, Breckinridge..W 140
Irvin's Store, Russell........S 32
● *Irvinsville*, (see Head Quarter) ×
Isaac, (see Lot)............... ×
Isaacs, Pulaski..............S ×
● Island, McLean...........W 40
Island City, Owsley.........E 30
Isonville, Elliott...........NE 25
Iuka, Livingston............W 50
Ivyton, Magoffin............E 15
Jabez, Russell...............S 25
● **Jackson**, Breathitt......E 450
Jackson, (see Ryle).............. ×
Jackson's Store, (see Dixon) . ×
Jacksonville, (see Bagdad).... ×
Jacksonville, Henry........N ×
Jacksonville, Bourbon.......N 10
Jackstown, Bourbon........N 130
Jacobs, Carter..............NE 50
Jamboree, Pike..............E 25
Jamestown, Russell......S 154
● Jamison, Carter...........NE 25
Jarrett, (see Edwards) ...... ×
Jarvis' Store, Knox........SE 32
Jasper, (see Yosemite)....... ×
Jasper, Clark.................C ×
Jay, Russell..................S ×
● Jeffersontown, Jefferson..N 348
Jeffersonville, Montgomery.C 150
Jellico, (see Jellico, Tenn.)... ×
Jenkensville, Washington...C ×
Jensonton, Washington......C 65
Jeptha, (see Hindman)....... ×
Jeremiah, Letcher...........SE 20
● Jericho, Henry............N 250
Jersey City, (see Paducah) .... ×
● Jessamine, Jessamine.....C 390
Jesse, Perry.................SE 25
● Jett, Franklin...............N 25
Jett's Creek, Breathitt.......E 25
Jimtown, (see Fountain Run) ×
Jim Wood, Boyd...........NE ×
Jobe, Lawrence...........NE ×
Joe, Pike.....................E 10
John, Pike....................E 10
John's Creek, Pike..........E 25
Johns Hill, Campbell........N ×
Johnson, Scott...............N ×
● Johnson Junction, F'm'g NE 30
Johnson's, Christian.......SW 25
Johnsons, Montgomery.....C ×
Johnsonville, (see Stinnett)... ×
Johnsville, Bracken..........N 150
Jolly, Daviess...............W ×
● *Jolly*, Breckinridge......W ×
● *Jones*, Whitley...........SE ×
Jonesburgh, Harlan........SE 25
● Jones Station, Ohio.......W ×
Jonesville, (see Jarvis' Store) . ×
Jonesville, Owen............N 40
Joppa, (see Shumla).......... ×
● Jordan, Fulton............SW 100
Josephine, Scott............N 25
Joshua, (see Flag Fork)...... ×
Joshua, Owsley...............E ×
Joyce, Casey..................C ×
Judson, Garrard.............C ×
Judy's, Montgomery.........C 25
● Julian, Christian.........SW 30
● *Junction*, Breckinridge..W ×
Junction, (see Reynoldsville). ×
● *Junction*, Franklin........N ×
● Junction City, Boyle.......C 648
Juno, Pulaski..................S ×
Justice, Logan.............SW ×

Justice Grange, Pike........E 32
Kaler, Graves...............SW 15
Kane, Campbell..............N 55
Kansas, Graves.............SW 40
● *Katy*, Carter.............NE ×
Keavy, Laurel...............SE 40
Keel, Logan.................SW 13
Keene, Jessamine............C 500
Keefer, Grant.................N 25
Kelat, Harrison..............N 50
● *Keller*, Harrison..........N ×
● Kelly, Christian...........SW 100
Kellyville, (see Cane Valley) . ×
Kelsey, Caldwell...........SW ×
Keltner, Adair................S 32
Kendall, Russell..............S ×
Kennard, Mason.............NE ×
● Kennedy, Christian.....SW 25
● *Kenney*, Bourbon.........N ×
Kenny, Scott.................N ×
Kensee, Whitney............SE 400
● *Kensington*, Boone.......N ×
● Kenton, Kenton...........N 100
● *Kenton Heights*, Kenton. N ×
Kenton Furnace, Greenup NE ×
Kentontown, Robertson....N 50
Kerby Knob, Jackson.......C ×
Kerntz Landing, Gallatin..N 32
Kessinger, Hart..............C ×
Kettle, Cumberland.........S 15
Keysburgh, Logan.........SW 200
● *Key's Creek*, Boyd......NE ×
Keysers, (see Leitchfield)..... ×
● *Keyser's Creek*, Boyd...NE ×
● Key West, Kenton.........N 25
Kezer, Knott..................E 25
Kidd's Store, Casey.........C 150
Kidder, Wayne...............S ×
Kiddville, Clark..............C 150
Kiefer, Grant................N 10
Kilgore, Boyd...............NE 100
● Kilgore, Carter...........NE 25
Kimble, Russell...............S 20
Kimper, Pike.................E ×
King Bee, (see Burdick)..... ×
King's Creek, Letcher.....SE 30
King's Landing, (see Richardson's Landing)................ ×
King's Mills, Henderson.....W 40
● *King's Mountain*, Lincoln C 400
King's Store, Garrard.......C 32
Kingston, Madison...........C 150
● Kingsville, Lincoln.........C 400
Kinkead, Pendleton.........N 32
● *Kinkaid*, Scott.............N 10
Kinner, Lawrence..........NE ×
● *Kinross*, Clark.............C ×
Kinsey, Pulaski...............S ×
Kirbyton, Carlisle..........SW 50
● Kirk, Breckinridge.......W ×
Kirkland, Washington.......C ×
Kirklevington, Fayette......C ×
Kirkmansville, Todd.......SW 103
Kirksey, Calloway.........SW 75
Kirksville, Madison..........C 150
Kirkwood, Mercer...........C ×
● Kiserton, Bourbon.........N 25
Kissie, Estill..................C ×
● *Knapps Siding*, Jefferson N ×
Knifley, Adair.................S ×
Knob Creek, (see Cupio)...... ×
Knob Lick, Metcalfe.........S 100
● *Knob Lick*, Lincoln.......C ×
Knob Lick, Webster.........W 15
Knottsville, Daviess........W 215
Knowlton, Powell............C ×
Knoxford, Knox.............SE ×
Knoxville, Pendleton........N 250
Knuckles, Bell...............SE 13
● *Kriegers*, Oldham........N ×
● Kuttawa, Lyon............SW 587
● *Kuttawa Mills*, Lyon...SW ×
Labascus, Casey..............C 19
Lacey Creek, Wolfe.........E ×
Lackey, Floyd.................E 25
● Lacy, Rowan...............NE ×
La Fayette, Christian......SW 215
La Fayette, (see Centre) ..... ×
Laffoon, Daviess.............W 5
● **La Grange**, Oldham....N 670
● Lair, Harrison..............N 150
Lairsville, (see Rowena)...... ×
● Lakeland, Jefferson.......N ×
● Laketon, Carlisle.........SW 13
Lamasco, Lyon..............SW 186
● *Lamb*, Kenton.............N ×
● **Lancaster**, Garrard.....C 1,850
Lane, Wolfe...................E 10

● Langford, Rock Castle....C 40
Langley, Floyd...............E 25
Langnan, Laurel............SE 15
● *Lanham*, Boyd............NE ×
Larkin, Christian..........SW ×
Larue, Clay..................SE 65
● Laso, Whitley.............SE 40
Laura Furnace, Trigg.....SW 66
Laurel Bluff, Muhlenberg..W ×
Laurel Bridge, (see Lily)..... ×
Laurel Creek, Clay.........SE 100
Laurel Station, (see Argillitte) ×
● **Lawrenceburgh**, A'd'n C 1,382
Lawrenceville, Grant.......N 150
Lawson's Point, (see Clay)... ×
● Lawton, Carter...........NE 168
● *Lawton's Bluff*, McC'ken SW ×
Laxton, (see Hamlin) .... ×
Laynesville, Floyd...........E 10
Laytonville, Christian.....SW ×
Leach, Grayson...............W 25
Leadford, Harlan...........SE ×
Leadingham, Elliott.......NE 10
● *Leamington*, Fayette.......C ×
Leather's Store, Henderson..C 50
● **Lebanon**, Marion.........C 2,816
● Lebanon Junction, Bullitt N 250
Lee, Butler...................W 15
Lee City, Wolfe..............E 20
Leepert, Trimble.............N ×
Leesburgh, Harrison.........N 101
Lee's Landing, (see Corn Cr.) ×
Lee's Mills, (see New Columbia) ×
Leeslick, Harrison...........N 57
Leitchfield, Grayson.....W 421
Lemon, McLean..............W ×
Leniton, Grant...............N ×
Lenore, Nelson...............C 13
● Lenoxburgh, Carter.....NE 10
● *Leon*, Carter..............NE ×
Leonard, Harlan............SE 20
Leonville, Calloway.......SW 32
Leotonia, Lawrence.......NE 25
Le Roy, Pulaski................S ×
Leslie, Cumberland...........S 106
Levee, Montgomery..........C 100
Level Green, Rock Castle....C 25
Levias, Crittenden...........W 40
● Levingood, Pendleton....N 25
Lewellen, Lee..................E ×
● *Lewis*, Daviess.............W 300
● Lewisburgh, Logan......SW 224
Lewisburgh, (see Covington). ×
Lewisburg, McCracken....SW 20
Lewisburg, Mason.........NE 200
Lewisburgh, Muhlenberg..W ×
Lewis' Creek, Letcher......SE ×
Lewis Mills, (see Zion)........ ×
● Lewisport, Hancock.......W 435
● **LEXINGTON**, Fayette C 21,567
Liberty, (see Dycusburg)..... ×
Liberty, Casey...............C 136
Liberty Hall, (see Mattingly). ×
Liberty Station, (see Sanders) ×
Lick Branch, (see Albany Landing)..... ×
Lickburgh, Magoffin.........E 25
● *Licking*, Bath.............NE ×
Licking, Nicholas............N 15
Lick Skillett, (see Olmstead).. ×
Liletown, Green..............C 75
● Lily, Laurel.................SE 250
Limaburgh, Boone...........N 24
Limestone, Carter..........NE 83
● Limeville, Greenup.......NE ×
Limp, Hardin..................C 20
Lincoln, Pulaski...............S ×
Line Creek, Pulaski...........S 75
Linefork, Letcher............SE ×
Line's Mill, Hart.............C ×
Linn Grove, (see Harris Grove) ×
Linton, Trigg.................SW 29
Linwood, Hart.................C 15
Lisman, Webster..............W 10
Little, Greenup..............NE ×
Little Barren (see Osceola)... ×
Little Cake, Adair.............S ×
Little Creek, Pike............E ×
● Little Cypress, Marshall.SW 61
Little Eagle, (see Sadieville).. ×
Little Hickman, Jessamine..C 75
Little Kentucky River, (see Ewingford)........................ ×
Little Mount, Spencer.......C 60
Little Prairie, (see White Plains).......................... ×
Littlerock, Bourbon.........N 200
Little Sandy, Elliott.......NE 20

Kentucky
Kentucky

● *Littleton*, Carter ... NE ×
Little Union, (see Morganfield) ×
Little York, (see Brandenburg) ×
● Livermore, McLean ... W 622
● Livia, McLean ... W 75
● *Livingstone*, Crittenden ... W ×
● *Livingstone*, Caldwell ... SW ×
● Livingston, Rock Castle ... C 200
Lloyd, Lewis ... NE ×
Load, Greenup ... NE ×
Lobb, Green ... C ×
Lochland, Jefferson ... N ×
Lock, Bell ... SE 40
Lockport, Henry ... N 152
● *Lockwoods*, Boyd ... NE ×
Locust, Carroll ... N [illegible]
Locust Branch, Estill ... C 18
Locust Grove, (see Rosine) ... ×
○ Lodiburgh, Breckenridge W 10
Logana, Jessamine ... C ×
Logansport, Butler ... W 20
Logan, Shelby ... N ×
Loglick, Clark ... C 25
Lola, Livingston ... W 75
● **London**, Laurel ... SE 1,200
Lonesome, Menifee ... E 32
Lone Star, Taylor ... C 20
Long Branch, Martin ... E 10
● Long Branch, Meade ... W ×
Long Creek, (see Robertson Cr.) ×
LongFallsCreek, (see Glennville) ×
Long Fork, Pike ... E 26
● Long Grove, Hardin ... C 40
Long Lick, Scott ... N 100
● Long Run, Jefferson ... N 100
Longview, Christian ... SW 75
● *Longview*, Jefferson ... N ×
Lookout, Pike ... E 20
Loradale, Fayette ... C 10
● Loretto, Marion ... C 175
Lost Creek, Breathitt ... E 15
Lost Run, Breckinridge ... W 65
Lot, Whitley ... SE 150
● **Louisa**, Lawrence ... NE 834
● **LOUISVILLE**, Jeff ... N 61,129
● *Louisville Southern Park*, Shelby ... N ×
Lovelaceville, Ballard ... SW 169
● *Lovell*, Knox ... SE ×
Lovesville, Spencer ... C ×
● Lowell, Garrard ... C 25
Lowell's Mills, Mason ... NE 25
Lowes, Graves ... SW 112
Lomansville, Lawrence ... NE 35
Lucas, Barren ... S ×
● Ludlow, Kenton ... N 2,469
Lula, Russell ... S ×
Lulaton, Leslie ... SE 40
● *Lumber Point*, Lee ... E ×
Lunar, Nelson ... C ×
Lusby's Mill, Owen ... N 50
Luterton, Marshall ... SW 43
Lykins, Magoffin ... E 25
Lynchburgh, Garrard ... C ×
● Lyndon, Jefferson ... N 50
● *Lyne*, Jessamine ... C ×
Lynn, Greenup ... NE 10
● *Lynn*, Nelson ... C 100
Lynn Camp, Laurel ... SE 97
Lynnville, Graves ... SW 100
Lyonia, Hancock ... W 50
Lyons Station, La Rue ... SE ×
Lytle Fork, Scott ... N 130
● McAfee, Mercer ... C 100
McBath's Landing, (see Cumberland) ×
● McBrayer, Anderson ... C 40
McBreath's Landing, WayneS 32
● *McClain*, Henderson ... W ×
McConnel, Letcher ... SE ×
McCown's Ferry, (see Mortonsville) ×
McCreary, Garrard ... C 32
McDaniel's, Breckinridge ... W 50
McDonald'sLanding, Henderson W ×
McDowell, Floyd ... E 40
McGinnis, Warren ... SW ×
McGlone, Carter ... NE 200
● McGowan, Caldwell ... SW ×
● McHenry, Ohio ... W 463
● *McHugh's*, Boyd ... NE ×
McKee, Jackson ... C 75
McKenzie, Lewis ... NE ×
● McKinney, Lincoln ... C 226
McKinneysburg, Pendleton N ×
McLeod's Station, Logan ... SW 40
McLoney, Harrison ... N ×
McMillan's Landing, (see Tompkinsville) ×
● McNary, Muhlenberg ... W 50
McNary, Hopkins ... W 25
● *McNew's*, Rock Castle ... C ×
McQuady, Breckinridge ... W 55
McReynold's Mill, (see Russellville) ×
McWhorter, Laurel ... SE 75
Macedonia, Christian ... SW 40
Mackoy, Greenup ... NE 32
Mackville, Washington ... C 250
Macoville, Boone ... N 25
Maddog, Leslie ... SE ×
Madison Mills, Warren ... SW 32
● **Madisonville**, H'pk'ns W 2,212
Madline, Pulaski ... S ×
Magan, Ohio ... W 75
Maggard, Letcher ... SE 25
Magness, Marshall ... SW ×
Magnolia, La Rue ... C 80
● *Mahan*, Whitley ... SE 40
Mahon, Marshall ... SW ×
Mains, Pendleton ... N 100
● *Major*, Henderson ... W ×
Malcom, Clay ... SE ×
Mallorys, Owen ... N 65
Mallory's Mill, (see NewColumb's) ×
Maloneton, Greenup ... NE 26
Mallott, Jefferson ... N 30
Maltaton, Pike ... E ×
● Mammoth Cave, Edm's'n W 30
Manchester, Clay ... SE 300
● *Manchester Sta.*, Lewis ... NE ×
Mandrake, Letcher ... SE 85
● Manitou, Hopkins ... W 70
● Mannington, Christian ... SW 100
Mannsville, Taylor ... C 83
Manse, Garrard ... C ×
Manton, (see Loretto) ... ×
Maple, Taylor ... C ×
Maple Grove, Trigg ... SW 100
Maplesville, Laurel ... SE ×
Marcellus, Edmonson ... W ×
Marcus, Pendleton ... N ×
● Maretburgh, Rock Castle ... C 100
Margoda, (see Monterey) ... ×
Mariba, Menifee ... E 50
● **Marion**, Crittenden ... W 840
Marksbury, Garrard ... C 30
Marrowbone, Cumberland ... S 100
Marshall, Bath ... NE 30
● *Marshall*, Mason ... NE ×
Marsh Creek, Whitley ... SE 25
Martha, Lawrence ... NE 50
Martha's Mill, (see Tilton) ... ×
Martin, Lewis ... NE ×
Martinsburg, Elliott ... NE 151
Martinsburgh, Monroe ... S 30
Martinsville, Barren ... S ×
Mary, Magoffin ... E ×
Marydell, Laurel ... NE 40
● *Mary Mines*, Carter ... NE ×
● Mason, Grant ... N 50
Mason's Creek, (see Beech Gro.) ×
Mason's Mills, (see Dot) ... ×
Masonville, Daviess ... W 75
Massack, McCracken ... SW 15
Massey's Mills, Warren ... SW ×
Matthews, Breckinridge ... W 40
● *Mattingly*, Daviess ... W ×
Mattingly, Breckinridge ... W 70
Mattoon, Crittenden ... W ×
Maud, Washington ... C 75
Maulden, Jackson ... C 25
Maupin, Clinton ... S ×
● *Maurice*, Kenton ... N ×
Mavity, Boyd ... NE 10
Maxon's Mills, McCrackenSW 100
Maxwell Spr., (see Alum Sprs.) ×
● *May*, Boyd ... NE ×
● *Mayde*, Madison ... C ×
● **Mayfield**, Graves ... SW 2,909
Maynard, Lawrence ... NE ×
Mayo, Mercer ... C 15
Mayo Park, (see Caneyville) ... ×
May's Lick, Mason ... NE 352
● **Maysville**, Mason ... NE 5,358
Maytown, Morgan ... E [illegible]
● Maywood, Lincoln ... C [illegible]
● *Meade Springs*, Meade ... W [illegible]
Meadeville, (see Hill Grove) ... ×
Meador, Allen ... S ×
Meadorsville, Whitley ... SE 10
Meadow Creek, Whitley ... SE 30
● *Meadow Lawn*, Jefferson ... N ×
● *Meads*, Boyd ... NE ×
● *Meeks*, Boyd ... NE ×
Meeting Creek, Hardin ... C 25
Melber, McCracken ... SW [illegible]
● Melbourne, Campbell ... N 25
Melrose, Hardin ... C ×
Melrose, Marshall ... SW ×
● MemphisJunc., Warren ... SW 267
Mentor, Campbell ... N ×
● Mercer Station Muhlenb. W 140
Merino, (see Irvington) ... ×
Merrill, (see Cat Creek) ... ×
Merrimac, Taylor ... C 75
Merritt, Clark ... C 25
Mershon's Cr. Rds., Laurel SE 30
Meshack, Monroe ... S 26
Messer, Knox ... SE ×
● Middleburgh, Casey ... C 145
Middle Fork, Jackson ... C 13
Middlepoint, Knox ... SE ×
Middleton, Logan ... SW ×
◐ Middlesborough, Bell ... SE 3,271
Middleton, (see Stowers) ... ×
Middletown, Jefferson ... N 302
Midland, Bath ... NE ×
● *Midland*, Fayette ... C ×
Midlothian, Warren ... SW ×
● Midway, Woodford ... C 1,185
Mike, (see Hueysville) ... ×
Milan, McCracken ... SW ×
Milburn, Carlisle ... SW 297
Milby, Green ... C ×
Miles, (see Jordan) ... ×
Milford, Bracken ... N 200
Mill Creek, (see Red Hill) ... ×
● Mill Creek, Mason ... NE 30
● Milldale, Kenton ... N 1,003
Milledgeville, Lincoln ... C 250
● Millersburgh, Bourbon ... N 850
Millers Creek, Estill ... C 20
Millerstown, Grayson ... W 133
Millersville, (see Glens Fork) ×
Milliken's Store, Simpson ... SW 65
Million, Madison ... C 397
Mills, Knox ... SE ×
Mill Springs, Wayne ... S 45
Millstone, Letcher ... SE 25
Milltown, Adair ... S 75
Millville, Woodford ... C 100
Millwood, Bullitt ... N 20
● Millwood, Grayson ... W 125
Millwood, Mason ... NE 32
Milton, Trimble ... N 458
Minerva, Mason ... NE 200
Minfoville, Casey ... C ×
Mingo, (see Climax) ... ×
Mining City, Butler ... W 237
Minnie, Floyd ... E 20
Minnie, (see Laso) ... ×
Minoma, Jefferson ... N ×
Minor, Rowan ... NE ×
Minorsville, Scott ... N 50
Minta, Graves ... SW ×
Minton Landing, (see Geneva) ×
Mintonville, Casey ... C 40
Miranda, Nicholas ... N 25
● *Mitchell*, Boyd ... NE ×
◐ Mitchellsburgh, Boyle ... C 230
Mitchell's Mills, Robertson ... N 32
Mize, Morgan ... E 26
Moberly, Madison ... C ×
Monica, Lee ... E ×
Monroe, Hart ... C 130
Monterey, Owen ... N 312
Montezuma, Webster ... W ×
Montfort, Washington ... C 10
Montgomery, Trigg ... SW 95
Montgomery, (see Hazlewood) ×
● *Montgomerys*, Caldwell ... SW 26
Monticello, Wayne ... S 413
Montpelier, Adair ... S 18
● *Montrose*, Fayette ... C ×
Moody, (see New Buffalo) ... ×
Mooleyville, Breckinridge ... W 125
◐ *Moore*, Jefferson ... N ×
Moorefield, Nicholas ... N 150
Moore's Creek, Jackson ... C 50
Moore's Ferry, Bath ... NE 26
Moore's Mill, (see Claysville) ×
Moore's Sta., (see Guthrie) ... ×
● Mooresville, Washington ... C 40
Moor's Mill, (see Claypool Mills) ×
Moranburgh, Mason ... NE 32
● **Morehead**, Rowan ... NE 491
● Moreland, Lincoln ... C 50
● *Morgan*, Hardin ... C ×
● Morgan, Pendleton ... N 50
● **Morganfield**, Union ... W 1,094

Morgansville, Kenton.......N ×
Morgantown, Butler....W 250
Morning Glory, Nicholas....N 20
● Morning View, Kenton...N 195
Morrill, Jackson...........C 25
● Mortimer, Logan ....SW 25
● Morton's Gap, Hopkins .W 548
Mortonsville, Woodford.....C 200
○ Moscow, Hickman......SW 315
● *Moscow Sta.*, Pendleton..N ×
Moseleyville, Daviess ......W 30
Motier, (see Carntown) ...... ×
Motley, Warren..........SW ×
Mount Aerial, Allen.........S 60
Mount Aetna, Ohio........W ×
● *Mountain Top*, Carter..NE ×
Mount Auburn, Pendleton..N 30
Mount Carmel, Fleming..NE 175
Mount Eden, (see Hawesville) ×
Mount Eden, Spencer.......C 193
● *MountFreedom*, JessamineC ×
Mount Gilead, Mason.....NE 25
Mount Guthrie, (see Maretb'h) ×
Mount Hermon, Monroe....S 40
Mount Hor, Bracken.........N 60
Mount Lebanon, Jessamine. C 32
Mount Olive, Union.........W ×
Mount Olivet, Robertson N 327
Mount Pisgah, Wayne.......S 30
Mount Pleasant, (see Harlan) ×
Mount Pleasant, (see Bedford) ×
Mount Salem, Lincoln......C 18
● Mount Savage, Carter...NE 400
Mount Sherman, LaRue.....C 100
● **Mount Sterling**, Montgomery.......C 3,629
● **Mount Vernon**, Rock Castle..........C 500
Mount Washington, Bullitt..N 327
Mount Zion, Grant..........N 25
Mount Zion, Union........W ×
Mouth Card, Pike..........E 22
Mouth of Abbott, Floyd.....E 10
Mouth of Bear Creek, (see Dickey's Ms.)........ ×
Mouth of Beaver, (see Beaver) ×
Mouth of Big Creek, (see Big Creek)........ ×
Mouth of Cow, Floyd..........E 10
Mouth of Elkhorn, (see Swallowfield)....... ×
Mouth of Greasy, (see Ward City)....... ×
Mouth of Greasy Creek, (see Horseshoe Bottom)..... ×
Mouth of Hickman, (see Tolu) ×
Mouth of Laurel, Lewis....NE 10
Mouth of Middle Creek, (see Prestonburg)........ ×
Mouth of Miller's Creek, (see Miller's Creek) .... ×
Mouth of Meed, (see Laynesv'l) ×
Mouth of Pond, Pike.........E 100
Mouth of Pond Creek, (see People's) .... ×
Mouth of Prater, Floyd.....E 10
Mouth of Stone Coal, Pike..E 20
Mouth of Wolf Creek, (see Jamestown) .... ×
Moxley, Owen..............N 50
Moxley's Landing, L'v'gst'n W ×
Mud Camp, (see Marrowbone) ×
Muddy Fork, Scott.........N ×
Mud Lick, Monroe...........S 12
● Mud River, Muhlenberg..W 130
● *Muhlenberg*, Muhlenberg W ×
● Muir, Fayette.............C 70
Mulberry Grove, Webster..W ×
● Muldraugh, Meade.......W 58
Mulford, Union...........W 213
Mullikin, Livingston........W ×
Mullin's, (see East Bernstadt) ×
● *Mullins*, Rock Castle......C ×
Mullin's Station, Kenton....N 200
Mullis, Whitney.............SE ×
● **Munfordville**, Hart....C 350
Munson, Rowan............NE 25
Murphy, Anderson..........C ×
Murphysville, Mason......NE 75
Murray, Clark..............C 25
Murray, Calloway.......SW 518
Muse's Mills, Fleming.....NE 35
● Music, Carter........... NE ×
● Myers, Nicholas.......... N 30
● Myrtle, Johnson.......... E 250
Nailton, Hardin.............C ×
Nancy, Pulaski..............S 26

Kentucky

Napoleon, Gallatin..........N 100
Narrows, Daviess.........W ×
● *Narrows*, Clay...........SE 33
Nash, Edmonson...........W 13
Nathanton, Jackson.........C 32
● *Natural Bridge*, Powell..C ×
● Nazareth, Nelson.........C ×
Nealton, (see Nicholasville).. ×
Neave, Bracken............N 25
● Nebo, Hopkins............W 183
Nebo Station, (see East View) ×
Ned, Breathitt.............E 20
Needmore, Floyd...........E 130
Needmore, (see Liberty)...... ×
Needmore, (see Ogden's Landing) ×
Neetsville, (see Watson)...... ×
Nehemiah, Magoffin.........E 30
Nell, Adair..................S ×
● *Nelson*, Clark.............C ×
● Nelson, Muhlenberg.......W 25
● Nelsonville, Nelson.....NE 1 0
● Nepton, Fleming.........NE 212
Nesbit, Johnson............E ×
● *Netherlands*, Fayette.....C ×
Nevada, Mercer.............C 101
● Nevins, Mercer...........C ×
Newby, Madison...........C ×
New Castle, Henry.......N 485
● New Chapel, Hancock... W ×
New Columbus, Owen......N 146
Newcombe, Elliott.........NE 25
Newcomb's Ford, (see Caseyville)........ ×
New Concord, Calloway...SW 80
New Eagle Mills, Grant.....N 100
● Newell, Pulaski...........S 19
● *New Forest*, Bourbon....N ×
Newfoundland, Elliott.....NE 56
New Fruit, Hardin.........C 40
New Hampshire Furnace, Greenup...........NE ×
● New Haven, Nelson.......C 389
● New Hope, Nelson.........C 322
New Liberty, Owen.........N 400
Newman, Daviess.........W 15
New Market, Marion........C 100
● **NEWPORT**, Campbell.N 24,918
New Providence, Calloway SW 50
● *New Richmond*, Campbell N ×
New Roe, Allen.............S 100
● Newstead, Christian.... SW 50
● Newtown, Scott...........N 60
Newville, Daviess.........W 40
New York, Allen...........S 30
New York Landing, (see Alzy) 40
Niagara, Henderson........W 60
● **Nicholasville**, Jessam'e C 2,154
Nicholson, Kenton.........N ×
Nick, Marshall............SW 40
Nickells, (see Green River).. ×
Nina, Garrard...............C 32
Nipp, Rock Castle..........C ×
Noah, Lewis...............NE 25
Nobob, Barren..............S 175
● Nolin, Hardin.............C 150
Nonchalanta, Greenup....NE ×
Nonesuch, Woodford........C 40
● Normal Boyd.............NE 150
● Normandy, Spencer.......C 30
Norman's Landing, (see Rankin) ×
Normansville, Boone.......N 25
North Benson, Shelby......N ×
● *North Fork*, Boyle........C 40
North Fork, Bracken.......N 100
● North Fork, Mason.....NE ×
North Middletown, B'rb'n..N 496
North Pleasureville, Henry.N 194
● *Northup*, Lawrence.....NE 50
● *North Siding*, McLean...W ×
North Tower, (see High Bridge) ×
● *Norton*, Boyd...........NE ×
● Nortonville, Hopkins.....W 70
● Norwood, Pulaski..........S 65
Nugent, (see Wallace Station) ×
● Nunn, Crittenden........W ×
Oakford, (see Loopee)......... ×
● Oak Grove, Christian .. SW 35
● *Oak Hill*, Daviess........ W ×
Oak Hill, Whitley..........SE ×
Oakland, (see Sharp)......... ×
● *Oakland*, Boyd..........NE ×
● Oakland, Warren.......SW 300
Oakland Mills, Nicholas....N 50
● *Oak Lawn*, Kenton......N ×
Oak Level, Marshall.......SW 18
Oakley, Bath..............NE 40
Oakley, Laurel.............SE ×
Oak Mills, (see Liletown).... ×

Kentucky

Oak Ridge, Livingston......W ×
Oaks, McCracken.........SW ×
Oaks, (see Huntersville),...... ×
● *Oaks*, Ohio...............W ×
● Oakton, Hickman.......SW 180
● Oakville, Logan.........SW 35
Oak Woods, Fleming......NE 75
○ O'Bannon, Jefferson......N 300
Oberlie's Station, Spencer...C ×
Obion Creek, Hickman....SW ×
○ *O'Donnell*, Daviess.......W ×
Odds, Knox................SE ×
Oddville, Harrison.........N 75
Odessa, Bath..............NE 25
Ogden, Ballard............SW 300
Oggs, Montgomery..........C ×
Oil Centre, Pulaski..........S ×
● Oil City, Barren...........S ×
Oil Springs, Johnson........E 30
Oil Springs, Clark..........C ×
O. K., Lincoln...............C 32
Okolona, Jefferson..........N ×
Olaton, Ohio................W ×
Old Beaver Furnace, M'n'fe E ×
Old Cane Creek Furnace, Bath NE ×
● *Old Deposit*, Jefferson....N ×
Old Fort, Hopkins..........W ×
Oldham, Oldham............N 6
Oldhamsburg, (see Goshen).. ×
Old Hickman, (see Hickman . ×
Old Smithland, Livingston.W ×
Oldtown, Greenup........NE 65
Olloville, Lawrence.......NE 20
Olive, Marshall............SW 60
● Olive Hill, Carter.......NE 186
● Olmstead, Logan.........SW 100
● Olympia, Bath...........NE 303
Olympian Springs, Bath..NE ×
Omega, (see Conner)......... ×
Omer, Morgan..............E 25
● Oneonta, Campbell.......N ×
Onton, Webster............W 16
Ophir, Morgan..............E 50
Orangeburgh, Mason......NE 120
Orchard, Magoffin...........E 32
Ordinary, Elliott...........NE 45
Oregon, (see Salvisa)......... ×
Oreknob, Pike...............E 26
Orell, Jefferson............N 30
Oriska, (see Hodgensville).... ×
● Orlando, Rock Castle .....C 18
● *Ormsbys*, Jefferson.......N ×
Orr, Anderson..............C 150
Oscar, Ballard............SW ×
Osceola, Green.............C 120
Osceola, (see Pineville)....... ×
Ossipee, Pendleton..........N ×
Otho, Fleming.............NE ×
Ottenheim, Lincoln.........C 47
Otter, LaRue................C 25
Otter Creek, (see Powersburg) ×
● *Otter Creek*, Hardin.......C ×
● *Otter Pond*, Caldwell....SW ×
Oval, Jefferson..............N ×
Oven Fork, Letcher........SE 50
Owens Landing, Ballard..SW ×
● **Owensborough**, Dav's W 9,837
Owensboro Jc., (see Central Jc.) ×
Owenton, Owen..........N 847
Owingsville, Bath.....NE 763
Oxford, Scott...............N 83
Pace's, (see Summer Shade). ×
Paceton, Muhlenberg......W ×
● Pactolus, Carter........NE 50
● **Paducah**, McCracken SW 12,797
Page, (see Bakerton)........ ×
Pageville, Barren............S 25
Paineston, (see Nelson)...... ×
Painter, Pulaski.............S ×
● Paint Lick, Garrard........C 300
Paintsville, Johnson......E 506
Paisley, Wayne..............S 65
Palatka, Jefferson..........N 32
Palma, Marshall...........SW 48
Palmyra, (see Rapids)....... ×
Palmyra, (see Winona)....... ×
Palo, Ohio..................W ×
Panola, Madison............C ×
Pancone, Clay..............SE 25
Panther, Daviess..........W 20
Paradise, Muhlenberg......W 150
Paragon, Morgan............E 20
Parina, Bracken...........N 58
● **Paris**, Bourbon..........N 4,218
● *Paris Junction*, Bourbon N ×
Park, Barren.................S 25
Parkersburgh, McCracken SW 8
Parker's Grove, LaRue......C 10

Kentucky

Parker's Lake, Pulaski......S ×
Parkland, Jefferson.........N 78
Parkland, (see Louisville)... ×
Parkersville, (see Lamasco).. ×
● *Park's Mill*, Nicholas.... N ×
Parksville, Boyle...........C 160
Parmleysville, Wayne....... S 20
Parnell, Wayne..............S 50
Paroquet Springs, Bullitt...N ×
Partridge, Letcher.........SE 25
Pascal, Hart...............C ×
● *Pates*, Daviess...........W 32
Patesville, Hancock........ W 162
Patsey, Estill..............C 250
Patsey, Powell.............C ×
Patterson Creek, Whitley..SE 40
Pattertown, (see Murray).... ×
Pattonia, Johnson.......... C 650
Pattyville, Ohio........... W ×
Paw Paw, Pike...............E 10
Paxton, Breathitt...........E ×
● Payne's Depot, Scott......N 100
● *Payne's Farm*, Fayette...C ×
Payneville, Meade..........W 100
Peach Grove, Pendleton....N 15
● Peach Orchard, Lawr'ce NE 450
Peacock, (see Pittsburg)..... ×
● *Peak's*, Scott.............N ×
Peak's Mill, Franklin.......N ×
Pearl, Bracken..............N 27
Peartree, Breathitt.........E ×
Pebworth, Lee...............E 19
Peckenpaugh, Meade........W 19
● *Peck's*, Lawrence.......NE ×
Peed, Mason...............NE 10
PeeDee, Christian........SW 75
Pekin, (see Wilmore)........ ×
Pekin, Rowan..............NE ×
● *Pelham*, Fayette..........C 119
Pellville, Hancock..........W 119
Pellyton, Adair.............S 80
Pelo, (see Clinton)............ ×
● Pembroke, Christian... SW 66
● *Pence*, Lewis............NE ×
● Pendleton, Henry......... N 50
● Penick, Marion........... C 20
Pennebaker, Meade........ W 25
● Penrod, Muhlenberg..... W 72
Penshurst, Pendleton.......N ×
Peonia, Grayson............W 32
Peoples, Jackson............C ×
Percal, Elliott.............NE 25
Perkins, Madison............C 50
● *Perkins*, Lincoln..........C ×
Perrington Sta., (see Farmdale) ×
Perryville, Boyle............C 436
Persimmon, Monroe......... S ×
● Peru, Oldham............. N 150
Peter, (see Jamboree)......... ×
Peterborough Ave., Bell...SE ×
Peter Cave, Martin..........E ×
Petersburgh, Boone.........N 525
Petersburg, (see Sebree)...... ×
Petersburg, (see Mannington) ×
Petersburgh, Nelson........C ×
Peters Creek, Barren........S 19
Petersville, Lewis......... NE 100
Petra, Bracken..............N 45
● Petri Station, Hancock...W ×
Petroleum, Allen............S 45
Petro's Quarry, Warren.. SW ×
● Pettit, Daviess............W ×
Petty, Anderson.............C ×
● Pewee Valley, Oldham....N 435
Peytona, Shelby.............N 15
Peytonsburgh, Cumberland .S 10
Phalen, Warren...........SW 20
Phelps, Pike................E ×
Phil, Casey..................C 00
● Phillipsburgh, Marion.....C 32
● Philpot, Daviess..........W 25
Pierce, Breckinridge ...... W ×
Pierce, Green.............. C 65
Pierce Bretwood, (see Bretwood) ×
Pig, Edmonson..............W 10
Pigeon Roost, Clay.........SE 10
Pigeon Roost, Ohio.........W ×
● *Pike Crossing*, Boyd....NE ×
Pike View, Hart..............C ×
Pikeville, Pike...........E 71
Pilgrim, Martin..............E ×
Pilot Knob, Simpson.......SW ×
Pilot Oak, Graves.........SW 35
Pilot View, Clark...........C 10
Pina, Webster..............W 16
Pinchem, Todd.............SW 25
Pinckard, Woodford.........C 40
Pinckneyville, Livingston...W 572

Kentucky

Pine Creek, Edmonson..... W ×
● Pine Grove, Clark........ C 40
● Pine Hill, Rock Castle.... C 200
● Pine Knot, Whitley......SE 150
Piner, Kenton.............. N ×
Pine Springs, Rowan...... NE 32
Pine Top, Knott.............E 25
● **Pineville**, Bell......... SE 2,500
Piney, Crittenden.......... W ×
Pink, Jessamine.............C 130
Pinsonfork, Pike............E ×
Piqua, Robertson...........N 10
● Pisgah, Woodford.........C ×
Pitman, (see Pittsburg)...... ×
Pitman, Taylor..............C 18
Pitman Creek, (see Somerset) ×
● Pittsburgh, Laurel.......SE 511
Pitt's Point, Bullitt.........N 80
Plains, Breckinridge....... W ×
Planter's Hall, Breckinridge W 10
Plato, Pulaski...............S 97
Plattsburg, (see Petersburgh) ×
Pleasant, Martin............. E 36
Pleasant Grove, (see Boydsv'e) ×
Pleasant Hill, Mercer....... C 125
Pleasant Home, Owen......N 50
Pleasant Point, Lincoln.....C ×
Pleasant Ridge, Daviess.... W 30
Pleasant Val., Rock Castle.C 26
● Pleasant Valley Mills, Nicholas.......................N 50
● Pleasant View, Whitley .SE 200
● Pleasure Ridge Park, Je'n N 100
● Pleasureville, Henry......N 202
Plugtown, Mason..........NE ×
Plumbville, Mason........ NE 32
Plum Lick, Bourbon.........N 200
Plummer's Landing, Fle'ng NE 100
Plummers Mill, Fleming..NE 100
● Poindexter, Harrison.....N 25
Point Burnside, (see Burnsi'e) ×
Pointer, Pulaski..............S ×
Point Isabel, (see Burnside).. ×
Point Halleck, Carlisle.....W ×
● Point Leavell, Garrard....C 10
Point Pleasant, Ohio........W 28
Polin Washington............C 25
Polkville, Warren.........SW 20
Polleyton, Whitley.........SE 26
Polsgrove, Franklin........ N 75
Pomeroyton, Menifee.......E 35
Pomp, Morgan...............E ×
Pon, Christian.............SW 18
Pond Branch, (see Monterey) ×
Ponder, Clay...............SE 32
Pond Fork, (see Welchburg). ×
Pongo, Rock Castle......... C ×
Pony, Crittenden.......... W ×
Poole's Mill, Webster...... W 200
Pool's Creek, Campbell.....N ×
Poor Fork, Harlan .... SE 25
Poplar Creek, (see Laso)...... ×
Poplar Flat, Lewis..........NE 80
Poplar Grove, McLean..... W 12
Poplar Grove, Owen.........N 100
Poplar Hill, Casey...........C 30
Poplar Neck, (see Balltown). ×
● Poplar Plains, Fleming. NE 229
Porter, Scott................N 50
● *Porters*, Bourbon ....N ×
Portlando, (see Louisville)... ×
Portland, Pendleton.........N ×
Portridge, Letcher.........SE 10
Port Royal, Henry...........N 220
● *Posey*, Henderson.........W ×
● Potters, Lawrence.......NE ×
Potters Fork, Letcher.......SE ×
Pottertown, Calloway..... SW 65
Pottsville, Graves.......... SW 25
Pottsville, (see Texas)........ ×
Powar's Store, Casey........C 75
Powderly, Muhlenberg.....W ×
Powder Mills, Hart.........C 100
Powell's Mills, Pike........ E 50
● *Power's*, Daviess..........W ×
Powersburgh, Wayne....... S 40
Powers Station, Daviess....W 25
Power's Store, Casey ....C 75
Powersville, Bracken........N 75
Praise, Pike..................E 50
Balltown, Fayette.......... C ×
Preachersville, Lincoln......C 75
Prentiss, Ohio...............W 20
Preston, Breckinridge.......W 22
● *Preston*, Bath............NE ×
Prestonburg, Floyd..... E 305
● *Prestonia*, Jefferson.......N ×
● *Preston Iron Mine*, Bath NE ×

Kentucky

Prestonville, (see Wideawake) ×
● *Prewitt*, Montgomery.....C ×
● *Price's*, Barren............S ×
Price's Mill, Simpson......SW 40
Priceville, Hart.............C 250
Priceville, (see Garfield)..... ×
● Princess, Boyd...........NE 10
● **Princeton**, Caldwell..SW 1,857
Pritchard, Graves.........SW 45
Proctor, Lee................ E 277
Profitt, Letcher.............SE ×
Prospect, (see Wickliffe) .... ×
● Prospect, Jefferson.......N 12
Prosperity, Lawrence..... NE 25
Providence, (see Murray)..... ×
● Providence, Webster......W 522
Providence, (see Hammond) . ×
Pruett, Kenton..............N 25
● Pryorsburgh, Graves....SW 227
Pugh, Lewis................NE ×
Pueblo, Wayne...............S ×
● Pulaski, Pulaski............S 25
Pulltight, (see Bremen)...... ×
Puncheon, Magoffin........ E ×
Puncheon Camp, (see Barren) ×
Purdy, Adair.................S 25
Pyles, Livingston...........W ×
Quail, Rock Castle .... C 32
Quality Valley, Butler......W 50
Quarry Switch, (see Clermo't) ×
● *Quesenberry*, Clark....... C ×
Quicksand, Breathitt........ E ×
Quick Sand Mills, Breathitt E ×
Quick's Cross Roads, (see Hebron) ×
Quincey, (see Murray)......... ×
● Quincy, Lewis............NE 279
Quod, Magoffin...............E 33
Rabbit Hash, Boone.........N 40
Raccoon, (see Mike)........... ×
Raccoon Bend, Laurel......SE 57
Raccoon Furnace, Gr'nup NE ×
Radical, Lee..................E 32
Ragland, McCracken......SW ×
Ragsdale, Graves..........SW 33
● *Railey*, Woodford..........C ×
Raleigh, Union..............W 60
Ralston's Mills, (see Bruce) .. ×
Ramsey, McCracken......SW ×
Ramsey Store, (see Monticello) ×
Randolph, Metcalfe..........S 60
● *Randolphs*, Jefferson.....N ×
Randville, Lewis............NE 25
● *Rankin*, Henderson......W ×
Rankin, Wayne...............S 75
● *Rankins*, Clark............C ×
Rapids, Simpson............SW 40
Raspberry, Rock Castle......C ×
Ratcliff, Lawrence........ NE 25
Raven, Knott.................E 25
● Rawhide, Logan.........SW 19
Ray, Logan..................SW 25
Raywick, Marion.............C 175
● Read, Henderson..........W ×
Ready, Grayson..............W 42
Rectorville, Mason.........NE 50
Redash, Whitley............SE 600
Red Bird, (see Knuckols) .... ×
Red Bud, Pike...............E ×
Redbush, Johnson............E 25
Red Fox, Knott..............E 130
● Red Hill, Hardin............C 75
● Red House, Madison...... C 18
Red Lick, Metcalfe...........S 10
Red Oak, Grayson...........W 26
● *Red Oak*, Logan..........SW ×
● *Red River Station*, Logan SW ×
Redwine, Morgan.............E 25
Reedsville, Carter...........NE 195
Reedville, (see Conway) ...... ×
Reedyville, Butler...........W 75
Regina, Green................C ×
Relief, Morgan...............E 25
Renaker, Harrison...........N 25
Renfrow, Ohio...............W 12
● *Renick*, Clark..............C ×
● Repton, Crittenden.......W 20
Republican, Knott...........E 25
Resort, Carter...............NE ×
Retta, Pulaski................S ×
Reynolds Station, Daviess..W 20
● Reynold's Station, Ohio.. W ×
Reynoldsville, Bath....... NE 50
Rhea, Calloway.............SW ×
Rhoda, Edmonson...........W ×
Rhodelia, Meade............ W 65
Ricedale, (see Drakesboro)... ×
● *Rice's Crossing*, Boone...N ×
Rice Station, Estill...........C ×

Riceville, Johnson.......... E ×
● *Rich*, Christian......... SW ×
● Richardson, Lawrence.. NE 25
Richardson's Landing, Me'de W 25
Richardsville, Warren.... SW 75
Richland, Daviess.......... W ×
Richland, Harrison.......... N 32
Richland Mills, Warren.. SW ×
Rich Lieu, Logan.......... SW 40
● **Richmond**, Madison.... C 4,753
Richmond Jc., (see Stanford) . ×
● Rich Pond, Warren..... SW 119
● Richwood, Boone......... N 20
Riddle, Elliott.......... NE 26
Ridgeway, (see Persimmonv'e) ×
Riggs, (see Willow Shade)..... ×
Rightangle, Clark.......... C 30
Rightsville, (see Pennebaker) ×
● Riley, Marion.......... C 150
Rinaldo, Lyon.......... SW 10
● Rineyville, Hardin......... C 65
Ringo's Mills, Fleming.... NE 25
Rio, Hart.......... C 57
Ripyville, Anderson.......... C 75
Ritner, Wayne.......... S ×
River, Johnson.......... E 25
● *Riverside*, Clark.......... C 30
Riverside, Jefferson.......... N ×
Riverside, Warren......... SW ×
Riversville, (see Clifty)....... ×
Riverton Junc., Greenup. NE 125
● River View, Jefferson.... N 150
● *Riverview*, Jefferson...... N 65
Roachville, Green.......... C ×
Roanoke, LaRue.......... C 32
Roaring Spring, Trigg..... SW 75
● Robard, Henderson....... W 682
● Robertson, Harrison...... N 30
● *Robinson*, Harrison........ N ×
Robinson Creek, Pike....... E 50
Robinson Mines, (see Island) ×
Robinsonville, Union....... W ×
Rochester, Butler.......... W 510
Rock, Graves.......... SW ×
Rock Bridge, Monroe....... S 100
Rockbridge, Shelby.......... N ×
Rock Castle, Trigg......... SW 101
● *Rockcastle River*, R.Castle. C ×
Rockcastle Springs, Pulaski. S 75
Rock Dale, Owen.......... N 20
● Rockfield, Warren...... SW 150
Rock Gap, Lee.......... E 32
● Rock Haven, Meade...... W 50
● Rockhold's, Whitley..... SE 75
Rockhouse, Letcher....... SE 65
Rockland, Warren........ SW ×
Rockland Mills, Metcalfe... S 26
Rock Lick, Breckinridge... W 43
● Rockport, Ohio.......... W 435
Rockport Coal Mines, Ohio W ×
● *Rock Quarry*, Jessamine . C ×
Rocksprings, Bracken...... N 46
Rock Springs, (see Cairo) .... ×
● Rockvale, Breckinridge.. W 75
● *Rockville*, Lawrence.... NE ×
Rocky Hill, Barren.......... S 200
● Rocky Hill Station, Ed'n. W 200
Rocky Point, Monroe....... S ×
Rodbourn, Rowan........ NE 32
Rodemer, Allen .... S ×
Rodgersville, (see Terrill) .... ×
Roff, (see Stephensport)....... ×
● Rogers Gap, Scott......... N 50
Rolling Fork, Casey........ C 168
Rollings, Casey.......... C 18
Rollington, (see Pewee Vall'y) ×
Rome, Daviess.......... W 10
● *Rome*, Lewis.......... NE ×
● Roost, Bell.......... SE 40
Roscoe, (see Lewe's) .... ×
Rosedale, Carter.......... NE 25
Rosedale, Letcher.......... SE 57
Rose Hill, (see Gishton)...... ×
Rose Hill, Mercer.......... C 50
Rosetta, Breckinridge....... W 50
Roseville, Barren.......... S 75
Roseville, (see Lyonia)....... ×
Rosewood, (see Cisney)....... ×
● Rosine, Ohio.......... W 160
● Ross, Campbell.......... N 40
Rossington, McCracken.. SW ×
Ross Settlement, Carter... NE ×
● *Rosslyn*, Powell.......... C 20
● Rothwell, Menifee......... E 27
Rough and Ready, (see Alton ×
Rough Creek, Allen......... S 32
Round Hill, (see Kirksville) . ×
Round Stone, (see Uptonville) ×
● Round Stone, Rock Castle C ×
Rousseau, Breathitt......... E 15
Rowena, Russell.......... S 75
● Rowland, Lincoln.......... C 512
● Rowlett's, Hart.......... C 250
Roxana, Letcher.......... SE 25
Roy, (see Calloway .... ×
Royalton, Russell.......... S 195
Ruckerville, Clark.......... C 80
Rudd, Carlisle.......... W 10
Ruddel's Mills, Bourbon.... N 240
● *Rudd's*, Jefferson.......... N ×
Rufus, Caldwell.......... SW 25
Rugless, Lewis.......... NE ×
Rule, Rock Castle.......... C ×
Rumsey, McLean.......... W 207
Runnyan, Pike.......... E ×
Rural, Pike.......... E ×
● Rush, Boyd.......... NE 25
Rush Branch, Marion....... C 18
● Russel, Greenup......... NE 323
Russell Cave, Fayette....... C 132
Russell Springs, (see Esto)... ×
● **Russellville**, Logan.. SW 2,253
● Ruth, Breckinridge...... W ×
● *Ruth*, Grayson.......... W ×
Ruthton, Madison.......... C 10
Rutland, Harrison.......... N 175
Ryan, Fleming.......... NE ×
● *Rylands*, Kenton.......... N 40
Ryle, Gallatin.......... N 25
Sacramento, McLean....... W 297
● Sadieville, Scott.......... N 170
Saffron Hill, (see McDaniels) ×
● Saint Charles, Hopkins... W 449
Saint Cloud, Knott.......... E ×
Saint Elmo, (see Elmo)...... ×
● Saint Helens, Lee.......... E 200
● Saint John, Hardin......... C 20
● SaintJohn'sAsylum, Kenton N 260
Saint Joseph, Daviess........ W 18
Saint Lawrence, Daviess.... W ×
● Saint Mary's, Marion...... C 200
● Saint Mathew's, Jefferson N 100
● Saint Vincent, Union..... W ×
Salem, Livingston.......... W 200
Salineburgh, Trigg......... SW 25
Saloma, Taylor.......... C 88
Salt Creek, Perry.......... SE 100
● Salt Lick, Bath.......... NE 150
● Salt River, Bullitt......... N 26
Salt Trace, Harlan......... SE ×
Salt Works, Pulaski......... S ×
Saltwell, Nicholas.......... N 25
● Salvisa, Mercer.......... C 400
● *Salvisa Station*, Mercer... C ×
Salyersville, Magoffin.... E 339
Sample, Breckinridge...... W ×
Sams, Estill.......... C 20
● Samuel's Depot, Nelson... C 110
● Sanders, Carroll.......... N 277
● *Sandersville*, Fayette..... C ×
Sandford, Fleming......... NE 10
Sandfordtown, (see Honesty). ×
Sand Hill, Warren.......... SW ×
Sand Hill, Greenup........ NE ×
Sand Hill, Lewis.......... NE 40
Sand Spring, Jackson....... C ×
Sandy City, Boyd.......... NE 10
Sandy Fork, Leslie.......... SE 30
Sandy Hook, Elliott.... NE ×
Santafe, Bracken.......... N 50
Sapony, Jefferson.......... N 75
Sapp, Fleming.......... NE 10
Sardis, Mason.......... NE 255
Sassafras, Knott.......... E 25
● Saulsbury, Carter........ NE 10
Savage, Clinton.......... S 32
● *Savage Branch*, Boyd... NE 25
Savoyard, Metcalfe.......... S ×
Sawyer, Pulaski.......... S ×
Sax, Jefferson.......... N ×
Saxony, Jefferson.......... N ×
● Saxton, Whitley.......... SE ×
Sayers' Depot, (see Deatsville) ×
Scale, Marshall.......... SW 50
Schochoh, Logan.......... SW 200
Schollsville, Clark.......... C 300
Schuler, Pendleton.......... N ×
Schultz, Greenup.......... NE ×
● Science Hill, Pulaski...... S 300
Scott, Kenton.......... N 100
● Scottsburgh, Caldwell.... SW 40
● Scott's Station, Shelby.... N 20
● **Scottsville**, Allen....... S 575
Scrabble, Shelby.......... N 15
Scuffletown, Henderson.... W 50
Seatonville, (see Malott)...... ×
Seaville, Washington........ C 40
Sebastian, Owsley.......... E ×
● Sebree, Webster.......... W 959
Sedalia, Graves.......... SW 100
See, Powell.......... C 25
Seeley's Mines, (see Cromwell) ×
Select, Ohio.......... W 100
Sellars, Morgan.......... E 35
Selma, Harrison.......... N ×
Semiway, McLean.......... W ×
Sentinel, Menifee.......... E ×
Sergent, Letcher.......... SE ×
Setser, Floyd.......... E 10
Settle, Allen.......... S ×
Seven Guns, Union.......... W 10
Seventy Seven, Metcalfe.... S ×
Seventy Six, Clinton......... S 50
Sexton's Creek, Clay....... SE 168
Seymour, Hart.......... C 20
● *Shackleford*, Bath...... NE ×
Shackleford Station, (see Gilpen) ×
Shady Grove, Crittenden... W 79
Shady Nook, Harrison...... N 75
ShakertownStation, (see Pleasant Hill ×
Shakerville, (see South Union ×
Shandy, Hart.......... C 59
Shannon, Mason.......... NE 55
● *Sharon*, Fayette.......... C ×
Sharon Grove, Todd...... SW 100
Sharp, Marshall.......... SW 50
Sharpsburgh, Bath.......... NE 516
Sharpsville, Washington..... C 35
● Shawhan, Bourbon....... N 140
● *Shawnee*, Powell.......... C ×
● *Shearer*, Madison.......... C ×
Shearer Valley, Wayne...... S 50
● Shelby City, Boyle......... C 325
● **Shelbyville**, Shelby.... N 2,679
● **Shepherdsville**, Bullitt N 251
Sherburne, Fleming...... NE 194
Sheridan, Crittenden....... W ×
● *Sherleys*, Jefferson....... N ×
● Sherman, Grant.......... N 25
Shermanville, Pulaski....... S 25
Shiloh, Calloway.......... SW 49
Shiloh, (see Liberty).......... ×
Shippingport, Jefferson.... N ×
Shoal, Leslie.......... SE ×
Shockey, Wolfe.......... E 32
Shopville, Pulaski.......... S 25
Short Creek, Grayson...... W 75
● *Shorts*, Daviess.......... W ×
Shotwell's Mines, (see Dekoven) ×
Shoulder Blade, Breathitt... E ×
Shreve, Ohio.......... W 26
Shrewsbury, Grayson....... W 150
Shumla, Floyd.......... E 10
Sidell, Clay.......... SE 25
Side View, Montgomery..... C 50
Sidney, (see McBrayer) ..... ×
Sikes, Breathitt.......... E 32
Silent Run, Hopkins....... W 20
● *Siloam*, Greenup......... NE ×
Silome, Whitley.......... SE ×
Silva, LaRue.......... C ×
● Silver Creek, Madison..... C 90
● *Silver Grove*, Campbell... N ×
● Simpsonville, Shelby..... N 290
Sims Store, Caldwell...... SW ×
Sinai, Anderson.......... C 30
Sinking Creek, Breckinridge. W ×
Sinking Fork, Christian... SW 10
● *Sinks*, Rock Castle......... C ×
Sip, Johnson.......... E 25
Sirocco, Meade.......... W ×
Skaggs, Lawrence.......... NE ×
Skidmore, Clay.......... SE 10
Skilesville, Muhlenberg.... W 25
● Skillman, Hancock....... W ×
Skinnersburgh, Scott....... N 50
Skinner Shop, Fayette...... C 26
Skinner's Mill, Clark....... C ×
Skip, Pulaski.......... S ×
Skylight, Oldham.......... N 10
Slack, Mason.......... NE ×
● *Slade*, Powell.......... C 20
Slades, Wolfe.......... E 20
● *Slate Lick*, Madison....... C ×
Slater, Ballard.......... SW 32
Slaughters, Webster........ W ×
● Slaughterville, Webster.. W 493
Slavans, Wayne.......... S ×
Slick Rock, Barren.......... S 35
● Sloans Valley, Pulaski.... S 140

Kentucky

Slow Go, (see Akersville).....	×
Slusher's Mill, Bell.........SE	25
Small, Pulaski..............S	×
Smallhous, Ohio.............W	16
Smallwood, Clay.......... SE	×
Smileytown, (see Wakefield).	×
Smith Branch, Breathitt....E	×
●Smithfield, Henry........ N	147
Smithland, Livingston...W	541
Smith's Creek, Carter...... NE	20
Smith'sCrossRoads,Metcalfe S	30
●Smith's Grove, Warren. SW	550
Smith's Hotel, Owen........N	×
Smith's Mills, Henderson.. W	75
Smithville, Bullitt.......... N	50
Smithville, (see Cairo)........	×
Smitsonville, Harrison......N	75
Smoky Valley, Carter..... NE	45
Smoot Creek, Letcher..... SE	×
Smyrna, Jefferson.......... N	65
Snider, Rock Castle......... C	12
Snowville, Barren..........S	19
●*Snyder's*, Lewis......... NE	×
●Soldier, Carter........... NE	150
Solitude, Bullitt............ N	26
●**Somerset**, Pulaski.......S	2,625
●Sonora, Hardin..............C	228
Sorgho, Daviess............ W	125
South, Grayson..............W	×
SouthCarrollton, M'hl'burg. W	525
South Columbus, HickmanSW	×
South Covington, Kenton...N	520
South Elkhorn, Fayette..... C	50
●*South Erlanger*, Kenton. N	×
●*South Fork*, Lincoln...... C	32
South Fork, Owsley.........E	×
South Hill, Butler..........W	20
●South Louisville, Jeffers'nN	1,782
South New Hope,(seeNew Hope)	×
●South Park, Jefferson.... N	70
●*South Portsmouth*,Gr'n'pNE	377
●*South Ripley*, Mason......NE	×
South Sherburne, Nicholas.. NE	×
●South Union, Logan.... SW	150
Southville, Shelby......... N	8
Spa, Logan...............SW	20
Sparksville, Adair..........S	30
Sparrow, Anderson......... C	30
●Sparta, Gallatin...........N	200
Spears, Jessamine..........C	40
Speedwell, Madison......... C	75
Spence Branch, Martin..... E	30
●Spencer, Montgomery.....C	50
Spokane, Logan...........SW	×
Spoon, Calloway.......... SW	18
Spoonville, Garrard......... C	25
●Spottsville, Henderson... W	513
Spout Spring, (see Furnace)..	×
Spradling, Wolfe............E	130
Spraggens' Store,(see Power'sSt'e)	×
Sprey Creek, (see Milton).....	×
Spring, Woodford...........C	30
Spring Creek, Clay.........SE	30
Springdale, Mason......... NE	50
●**Springfield**,Washingt'nC	1,000
Spring Grove, Union....... W	75
Spring Hill, Hickman.....SW	15
●Spring Hill, BreckinridgeNE	15
Spring Hill, (see Turner's)...	×
●Spring Lick, Grayson.... W	150
Springport, Henry...........N	25
●Spring Station, Woodford C	65
●Springville, Greenup....NE	377
Sprout, Nicholas............N	40
Spruceburgh, Whitley..... SE	39
●Spurlington, Taylor.......C	75
Squiresville, Owen..........N	100
●Stacy, Perry..............SE	10
Staffordsburg, Kenton.......N	50
Staley, Boyd...............NE	20
Stamping Ground, Scott....N	311
Standing Rock, Lee.........E	×
Stanfield Mines, (see SpringGrove)	×
●**Stanford**, Lincoln.......C	1,385
Stanley, Daviess............W	30
●**Stanton**, Powell..........C	200
Staple, Johnson............E	×
Star, (see Union Star)........	×
Star Furnace, Carter..... NE	40
Star Lime Works, Lyon...SW	35
Stark, Elliott..............NE	10
Star Mills, (see Long Grove).	×
●State Line, Fulton......SW	×
State Line, Allen............ S	20
Station Camp, Estill.........C	40
Steadmansville,(see Frankf'rt)	×
Steele, Morgan..............E	32

Kentucky

Stephens, Owen............N	×
Stephens, Elliott.......... NE	×
●Stephensburgh, Hardin... C	40
●Stephensport, Breckinri'eW	262
●Stepstone, Montgomery...C	100
Steuben Lick, (see Madisonv'e)	×
Steubenville, Wayne.........S	35
Stewart, Mercer.............C	40
Stewartsville, (see Select)	×
Stewartsville, Grant........ N	80
Stick, Knott................ E	×
Stillwater, Wolfe............E	30
●*Stine*, Jefferson...........N	×
Stinnett, Anderson..........C	75
●Stithton, Hardin..........C	48
Stivers' Mills, Shelby.......N	20
Stockholm, Edmonson..... W	37
Stokes, Russell..............S	×
Stone, Crittenden...........W	20
●Stone, Garrard............C	20
●*Stone City*, Lewis.........NE	25
Stonewall, Scott.............N	10
Stony Fork, Bell.......... SE	×
Stony Point, Bourbon...... N	40
Stouts Cross Roads, Todd. SW	19
Stout's Landing, Lewis....NE	57
Stowers, Simpson......... SW	100
Straight Fork, (see Davis)...	×
●*Strait Creek Mines*,Cart NE	30
Stratton, Pike...............E	×
●*Strawberry*, Jefferson....N	×
Stringtown, Fleming.......NE	×
Stringtown, Marshall......SW	×
Stringtown, (see Bardstown).	×
Strongville, Breathitt.......E	×
●*Stroud*, McLean...........W	×
Stroud's, (seeCentral City)....	×
Strunk's Lane,(see PineKnot)	×
Stubblefield, Graves.......SW	57
Sturgeon, Owsley........... E	18
●Sturgis, Union........... W	327
Sugar Creek, Gallatin......N	16
Sugar Grove, Butler........W	15
Sullinger's Store, (see Tolu)..	×
●Sullivan, Union.......... W	20
●Sulphur, Henry............N	823
Sulphur Creek, (see Burksv'e)	×
●Sulphur Lick, Monroe....N	75
Sulphur Springs, Ohio......W	75
Sulphur Well, Metcalfe......S	137
Summer Shade, Metcalfe.....S	210
Summersville, Green........C	40
●*Summit*, Boyd.......... NE	×
●*Summit*, Mason.........NE	×
●*Summit*, Lawrence......NE	×
●Summit, Hardin.............C	57
●*Summit*, Franklin.........N	×
Sumner, Whitley.......... SE	×
Sumpter, Wayne.............S	26
Sunfish, Edmonson.........W	×
Sunnybrook, Wayne..........S	×
Sunny Lane, Butler......... W	×
Sunnyside, Warren........ SW	×
Sunrise, Harrison...........N	100
Sunset, Fleming...........NE	25
Susie, Wayne................S	×
Suterville, Scott............N	25
●Sutherland, Daviess......W	×
Sutherland Land., HarrisonW	×
Sutton, Ohio................W	×
Suttons Mill, Whitley..... SE	×
Swallowfield, Franklin......N	10
Swampton, Magoffin.........E	50
Swan, Graves..............SW	×
Swan Creek, Whitley......SE	×
SweetHome,(see North Pleasurev'e	×
Sweet Owen, Owen...........N	25
Switzer, Franklin...........N	32
Sword, Pike................E	×
Sycamore, Clark.............C	5
Sylvan Dell, Harrison.......N	15
Symsonia, Graves.........SW	10
Tablow, Mercer............. C	×
Tackitt, Pike................E	10
Tackitts Mill, Owen.......... N	×
Tadella, Pike.................E	×
●*Talbot*, Bourbon......... N	×
●*Tallega*, Lee...............E	30
Talmage, Mercer.............C	25
Tampico, Adair............. C	3
Tandy, Carroll...............N	5
Tangletown, Mason.......NE	×
Tanker, Clay.............. SE	25
Tanksley, Clay............SE	×
Tannery, Lewis..............NE	×
Tarfork, Breckinridge...... W	×
●*Tar Springs*, Breck'ridgeW	×

Kentucky

●*Tates*, Daviess............W	×
Tates Creek, (see Perkins) ...	×
●Tateville, Pulaski......... S	52
Tattleton, (see Salvisa)......	×
Taulbee, Breathitt.......... E	25
Taylor Station, (see Eastwood)	×
●Taylor Mines, Ohio.......W	353
Taylorsport, Boone.........N	32
●*Taylor's Switch*, Ohio....W	×
●**Taylorsville**, Spencer..C	619
Teatersville, Garrard........C	×
●*Tebbs*, Clark...............C	×
Teges, Clay...............SE	25
Temperance, Simpson.... SW	32
Temple Hill, Barren.........S	75
Ten Mile, Campbell.........N	×
Tennessee Rolling Works,(see Rinaldo)................	×
Terrill, Madison............C	20
Terry, Christian.........SW	×
Texas, Washington..........C	100
Tharp, Lewis...............NE	×
The Glades, Laurel........ SE	×
The Ridge, Elliott.........NE	195
The Square, Christian.....SW	×
Thomas, Floyd..............E	×
Thompkins, Christian.....SW	×
Thompson Sta., (see Flournoy)	×
Thompsonville, Pulaski.....S	×
●Thomson, Clark............C	22
●*Thomson*, Lewis........ NE	×
Thornburg, (see Dixon)......	×
Three Forks, Warren..... SW	50
●*Three Forks City*, Lee....E	×
Three Mile House,(seeHenders'n	×
Three Springs, Hart.........C	100
●Thurston, Daviess.........W	15
Thurlow, Green.............C	25
Tice, Graves..............SW	×
●*Tichenor*, McLean....... W	×
Tidal Wave, Whitley.......SE	19
Tietzville, (see Rock Springs)	×
Tilden, Webster............W	50
Tilden, Clark...............C	19
Tilton, Fleming............NE	96
Tinker, Clay...............SE	25
Tioga, Franklin.............N	15
●*Tipple*, McCracken.....SW	×
●Tip Top, Hardin.......... C	100
Todd's Point, Shelby........N	20
Toddville,(see Bryantsville) ..	×
Toledo, Pulaski..............S	×
Tolesborough, Lewis...... NE	200
Tolu, Crittenden............W	50
Toliver, Wolfe.............. E	×
Tom, Mercer................C	75
Tompkinsville,Monroe..S	500
●Tonieville, LaRue..........C	12
Topeka, Union..............W	×
Topton, Laurel............ SE	×
●Torrent, Wolfe..............E	25
Torr's Store, (see Shelbyville)	×
Totten's L'd'g,(seeCorn Creek)	×
Tourgee, Warren......... SW	×
Tousey, Grayson............W	20
Townsville, Butler..........W	×
Trace, Campbell............N	×
Tracy, Barren...............S	60
Tradewater, Crittenden.... W	32
Tradewater Bridge,(seeDawson)	×
Trammel, Allen..............S	75
●*Transylvania*, Jefferson..N	×
Traveller's Rest, Owsley.....E	35
Treadway, Clay.............SE	×
Trench, Elliott.............NE	25
●Trenton, Todd.......... SW	455
Trevor, (see Spring Hill).....	×
Trickum,(see Rutland Mts.)..	×
Trunnelton, (seeBradst'n Jc.)	×
Trigg Furnace, Trigg..... SW	32
Trimble, Pulaski............S	26
●Triplet, Rowan...........NE	25
Trisler, Ohio...............W	×
Trotter, Lewis.............NE	×
Troublesome, Perry........SE	30
Trout, Trimble..............N	×
Trout's Cr's Ro's,(see Elkton)	×
Troy, Woodford.............C	75
Truesville, Owen............N	30
Trunnelton, (see Bardstown)	×
Tryer's Hill, Jefferson......N	×
Tuckahoe, Mason.......... NE	15
●*Tucker*, Jefferson......... N	×
Tucker's Store, (see Linmore)	×
Tulip, Clark.................C	×
●*Tunnel*, Lawrence........NE	×
Tunnel City, (see King'sMts.)	×
●Tunnel Hill, Hardin.......C	8

Tunnel Hill, Knott.........E	×
Tunnel Hill, (see Antioch)...	×
Turk, Adair...................S	×
Turkeyfoot, (see Roger's Gap)	×
Turner, Ballard......... ..SW	×
● Turner's Station, Henry.. N	195
Turnersville, (see McKinneys)	×
Tuttle, Laurel..............SE	40
Twin Oaks, Graves....... SW	26
● *Twin Tunnels*, Mu'lenb'rgW	×
● *Tygart*, Carter..........NE	168
Tygart's Switch, (see Limest'e)	×
Tygart's Valley, Greenup..NE	100
Tyner, Jackson..............C	75
Tyrone, Anderson...........C	474
Ulysses, Lawrence.........NE	20
● *Uma*, Pendleton..........N	×
Underwood Fur., Livi'gstonW	×
UnderwoodSta., (see Madisonv'e)	×
Union, Boone...............N	300
Union City, Madison........ C	50
Union Hall, Estill........... C	×
Union Mills, Jessamine......C	40
Union Point, (see Levias)	×
Union Star, Breckinridge.. W	140
● Uniontown, Union........ W	1,037
Unison, Pike............. E	×
Unity, Muhlenberg.........W	×
Uno, Hart...................C	25
● *Upland*, Pulaski.......... S	×
Upper Tygart, Lewis......NE	45
● Uptonville, Hardin........C	300
Utica, Daviess..............W	200
Utility, (see Gatewood).......	×
Utzinger, Boone............ N	25
● *Vadens*, Oldham.......... N	×
Vail, (see Salt Lick Sta.,)	×
Vail, Trimble............. NE	×
Valley, Lewis .... NE	45
● Valley Hill, Washington.. C	32
Valley Oak, Pulaski.........S	20
● Valley Station, Jefferson. N	40
Valley View, Madison.......C	×
Valley View, (see Halsell)....	×
● Vanersdell, Mercer....... C	×
Vanburen, Anderson........C	30
Vance, Bell................SE	×
● **Vanceburgh**, Lewis..NE	1,110
Vance's Mills, (see Franklin)	×
Vanderburgh, Webster.....W	200
Vandyke, Anderson.........C	×
Van Fleet, (see Princeville) .	×
● *Van Metre*, Fayette...... C	×
Vaughan, Christian...... SW	×
Vaughn's Mill, Estill........ C	40
Veals Store, (see Sedalia).....	×
Veazey, Hopkins........... W	75
● *Veech*, Spencer........... C	×
Veechdale, Shelby..........N	×
Veechton, (see Millwood)	×
Vegaburgh, Wayne......... S	×
Venters, Pike...............E	10
Venus, Harrison............ N	65
● Verona, Boone........... N	245
● **Versailles**, Woodford...C	2,500
Vertrus, Hardin.............C	30
Vessie, Lawrence ....NE	×
Vest, Knott................. E	25
Vicksburg, Livingston......W	×
● Victoria, Hancock........ W	186
Vienna, (see Log Lick).......	×
View, Crittenden...........W	×
● *Vileys*, Fayette.......... C	×
● Vine Grove, Hardin.......C	397
Viola, Graves..............SW	20
Viper, Perry...............SE	32
● *Virden*, Powell............C	×
Virgie, Pike.................E	×
● Visalia, Kenton...........N	300
Vox, Laurel ....SE	×
Vulton Creek, Graves.....SW	8
Wabd, (see Mt. Vernon)	×
Waco, Madison.............C	250
● Waddy, Shelby...........N	75
Wadesboro, Calloway..... SW	75
Wade's Gap, Clinton........S	×
Wade's Mill, Clark.......... C	878
Wagersville, Estill.......... C	×
● Wakefield, Spencer....... C	100
● Walbridge, Lawrence...NE	32
Walker's, Knox.......... SE	×
● *Walker's*, Montgomery...C	×
Walkerville, Lewis........NE	×
Wallace, Woodford......... C	40
● Wallace Station, WoodfordC	15
Walllaceton, Madison.......C	15
Waller, Ohio...............W	32
Wallingford, Fleming......NE	30
Wallin's Creek, Harlin.....SE	25
Wallonia, Trigg........... SW	300
Walnut Bottom, (see Alzey).	×
Walnut Flat, Johnson.......C	×
● *Walnut Grove*, CaldwellSW	30
Walnut Grove, Morgan..... E	42
Walnut Grove, Pulaski......S	×
● Walnut Hill, Fayette......C	×
Walnut Lick, (see Ryle)	×
Waltersville, Powell.........C	10
● Walton, Boone...........N	484
Walton's Lick, (see Willisburg)	×
Wampum, Pendleton.......N	×
Wanamaker, Webster......W	×
Warburg, (see Blood)	×
Ward City, Johnson.........E	25
Wardsville, (see Sparrow) ...	×
Warfield, Martin....... .E	150
Warnock, Greenup........NE	×
Warsaw, Gallatin..........N	676
Warwick, Mercer...........C	×
Washington, Daviess.......W	×
Washington, Mason....... NE	529
● *Wasioto*, Bell........... SE	×
● *Watauga*, Clark..........C	×
Waterford, Spencer......... C	58
Waterloo, Pulaski...........S	50
Waterloo, Boone...........N	26
● Water Valley, Graves...SW	115
Waterview, Cumberland.....S	10
● *Watkin's Glen*, Casey.....C	×
● Watson, Adair.............S	50
Watts, Taylor C	×
● Waverly, Union..........W	241
Wax, Grayson..............W	×
● Waynesburgh, Lincoln....C	40
Wayside, Shelby............N	32
Wayside, Spencer........... C	×
Weaver City, (see Cullen)	×
Weavertown, (see Mill Springs)	×
● *Weaverton*, Henderson...W	×
Webbs, Green...............C	10
Webb's Cross Roads, Russell S	30
Webbville, Lawrence......NE	10
Webster, Breckinridge..... W	53
Weeden, Estill..............C	15
● *Welborn*, Muhlenberg....W	×
Welchburg, Jackson.........C	100
Welch's Creek, Butler......W	×
Weldon's, Crittenden...... W	26
Weldon, Meade.............W	×
Wellington, Menifee.........E	50
Wells, Martin................E	25
● *Wells*, Scott.............N	×
● *Wellsburg*, Bracken......N	×
Wesley, Hickman.........SW	25
Wesley, Russell.............S	×
Wesleyville, Carter.........NE	200
● West Bend, Powell........C	25
West Clifty, Grayson....... W	15
West Covington, Kenton....N	1,757
Westerfield, Ohio......... .W	×
West Fork, Christian......SW	15
West Liberty, Morgan... E	234
West Louisville, Daviess....W	250
West Louisville, Jefferson.. N	×
Weston, Crittenden.........W	158
Weston, (see Carlisle)	×
West Pineville, (see Pineville)	×
West Plains, Graves.......SW	75
● West Point, Hardin....... C	300
Westport, Oldham.......... N	181
West Union, Owen.........N	40
West View, Breckinridge.. W	40
Whalen, Daviess............W	×
Wheatley, Owen............ N	100
Wheeler's Mill, Grayson....W	18
Whippoorwill, (see Ferguson)	×
Whitakersville, Magoffin....E	40
Whitby, Boyd............. NE	40
Whitehall, (see View)........	×
White Hall, Madison.........C	50
White House, (see Myrtle) ...	×
White Mills, Hardin.........C	115
White Oak, Morgan.........E	30
White Oak Gap, Pulaski.....S	50
White Plains, Christian.. SW	×
● White Plains, Hopkins... W	59
White Post, Pike............E	75
● White Run, Ohio......... W	20
Whitesburg, Letcher...SE	300
● White's Station, Madison..C	20
White Stone Quarry, WarrenSW	×
● White Sulphur, CaldwellSW	×
White Sulphur, Scott........N	20
White Sulphur Springs, (see Boxville)	×
Whitesville, Daviess........ W	398
● *Whitewood*, Green........C	×
● *Whitley*, Pulaski.......... S	35
Whitt, Carter..............NE	25
● *Whitts*, Lawrence...... NE	×
● Whynot, Lee.............. E	75
● **Wickliffe**, Ballard....SW	959
Wickliffe Landing, (see Trout)	×
Wide-awake, Carroll.. ......N	150
Wilbur, Lawrence.........NE	10
Wild Cat, Whitley..........SE	20
Wilcox, (see Enterprise).....	×
● *Wilders*, Campbell........N	×
● Wildie, Rock Castle.......C	100
Wilkins, LaRue.............C	×
● Willard, Carter......... NE	431
Willett's Quarry, Bell..... SE	×
● *Williams*, Boyd.........NE	×
Williams, (see Mannington)..	×
● **Williamsburgh**, W'tl'ySE	1,376
● *Williams Creek Tunnel Carter*.................NE	×
● *Williamsons*, Jefferson...N	×
Williamsport, Webster..... W	×
● **Williamstown**, Grant N	573
Willisburgh, Washington....C	130
Willow Church, Bracken...N	45
Willow Grove, Bracken.....N	45
Willowtown, Taylor......... C	32
Willow Shade, Metcalfe......S	16
● Wilmore, Jessamine...... C	200
● *Wilson*, Lewis............SE	30
● Wilson Station, H'd'rs'n..W	18
Wilson Gap, Bell.......... SE	
Wilsonville, (see Falls of Rough)	×
Wilsonville, Spencer........ C	150
● **Winchester**, Clark.....C	4,519
Windom, (see Brannon)......	×
Winesap, Hart..............C	×
● Wingo, Graves..........SW	451
Winona, Trimble............N	30
Winston, Estill............ C	100
Wisemantown, (see Irvine) ..	×
Wise's Landing, (see Corn Creek)	×
● Withers, Rock Castle......C	25
Wolf Creek, Meade......... W	58
● *Wolf Lick*, Logan.......SW	×
Wolford, Pike............. E	×
Wolf's Landing, (see Fair Dealing)..........	×
● Woodbine, Whitley...... SE	150
● Woodburn, Warren.....SW	350
Woodbury, Butler..........W	94
Woodford, Pike............E	×
Woodford Landing, (see Clifton)	×
Woodlake, Franklin........ N	100
Woodland, Meade...........W	26
● *Woodlawn*, Jefferson.... N	×
● Woodlawn, Nelson........ C	40
● *Woodside*, Jefferson......N	×
● *Woodside*, Kenton........N	×
Woodsonville, Hart..........C	300
Woodstock, Pulaski.........S	50
Woodville, McCracken....SW	200
Woodward's Creek, (see Sam's)	×
Wooten Creek, Leslie...... SE	25
Worth, Oldham............. N	20
Worthington, Jefferson..... N	30
Worthington, Ohio........W	×
● *Worthington*, HendersonW	×
● Worthville, Carroll....... N	203
Wright, Letcher........... SE	40
● *Wrights*, Bourbon........N	×
● *Wrights*, Boyd..........NE	×
● *Wrights*, Lawrence..... NE	×
Wrights, Taylor............C	×
Wrightsburg, McLean...... W	25
Wright's Store, (see Hustonville)	×
Wring, Trigg..............SW	×
● Wurtland, Greenup.....NE	50
● *Wyandotte*, Fayette...... C	×
Wyett, Elliot..............NE	×
Wyoming, Bath........... NE	97
Yancey, Washington........ C	×
● Yarnallton, Fayette.......C	25
Yatesville, (see Dixon)	×
Yellow Creek, Bell.........SE	65
Yellow Hill, Perry.........SE	×
Yelvington, Daviess........ W	800
Yocum, Morgan.............E	30
● *Yoder*, Spencer.......... C	×
York, Greenup............NE	×
● Yosemite, Casey..........C	397
● Yost, Muhlenberg........W	20
Yostville, (see South Union)..	×
● *Youell*, Boone............N	×
Young's Creek, Whitley... SE	30
● *Young's High Bridge*, A'n C	×

Town, County	Index	Pop.
Youngs Springs, Bath	NE	25
Young's Store, (see Monroe)		×
Zachariah, Lee	E	75
Zatto, Pike	E	×
Zebulon, Pike	E	25
Zero, Hart	C	×
Zilpah, Shelby	N	×
Zion, Henderson	W	250
Zion, Greenup	NE	×
● Zion Station, Gran	NE	50
● *Zion Station*, (see Frost)		×
Ziza, Whitley	SE	×
Zoneton, Bullitt	N	25

LOUISIANA.

COUNTIES.	INDEX.	POP.
Acadia	C	13,231
Ascension	SE	19,545
Assumption	S	19,629
Avoyelles	C	25,112
Bienville	NW	14,108
Bossier	NW	20,330
Caddo	NW	31,555
Calcasieu	SW	20,176
Caldwell	N	5,814
Cameron	SW	2,828
Catahoula	C	12,802
Claiborne	NW	23,312
Concordia	C	14,871
DeSoto	NW	18,860
East Baton Rouge	C	25,922
East Carroll	NE	12,362
East Feliciana	C	17,903
Franklin	NE	6,900
Grant	C	8,270
Iberia	S	20,997
Iberville	S	21,848
Jackson	N	7,453
Jefferson	SE	13,221
LaFayette	S	15,966
LaFourche	SE	22,095
Lincoln	N	14,753
Livingston	E	5,769
Madison	NE	14,135
Morehouse	NE	16,786
Natchitoches	NW	25,836
Orleans	SE	242,039
Ouachita	N	17,985
Plaquemines	SE	12,541
Pointe Coupee	C	19,613
Rapides	C	27,642
Red River	NW	11,318
Richland	NE	10,230
Sabine	W	9,390
Saint Bernard	SE	4,326
Saint Charles	SE	7,737
Saint Helena	E	8,062
Saint James	SE	15,715
Saint John Baptist	SE	11,359
Saint Landry	C	40,250
Saint Martin	S	14,881
Saint Mary's	S	22,416
Saint Tammany	E	10,160
Tangipahoa	E	12,655
Tensas	NE	16,647
Terre Bonne	SE	20,167
Union	N	17,304
Vermillion	S	14,234
Vernon	W	5,903
Washington	E	6,700
Webster	NW	12,466
West Baton Rouge	C	8,363
West Carroll	NE	3,748
West Feliciana	C	15,062
Winn	N	7,0 2
Total		1,118,587

TOWN. COUNTY.	INDEX.	POP.
Abbattoir, Orleans	S E	.
Abbeville, Vermillion	S	635
● Abita Springs, Saint Tam'y	E	100
Acme, Concordia	C	100
Ada, Grant	C	100
Adaline, Vernon	W	×
Afton, Tensas	N E	×
Aimwell, Catahoula	C	×
Alabama Church, Lincoln	N	35
Alabama Landing, Union	N	25
Albemarle, Assumption	S	150

Town, County	Index	Pop.
● *Alden Bridge*, Bossier	NW	×
Alden's Bridge, Bossier	NW	×
● **Alexandria**, Rapides	C	2,861
● Algiers, Orleans	SE	4,700
Algedon, Madison	NE	×
● *Allen Greene*, Lincoln	N	×
● Allemand's, Saint Charles	SE	100
Allen, Natchitoches	NW	300
Allentown Saw Mill's, Bossier	NW	×
Alliance, Plaquemines	SE	×
● *Alligator*, Tangipahoa	E	×
Almadane, Vernon	W	40
Alpha, Natchitoches	NW	500
Alsatia L'd'g, East Carroll	NE	25
Alto, Richland	NE	250
Alto Landing, Pointe Coupee	C	×
● Altoona, Madison	NE	35
Ama, Saint Charles	SE	×
Ambrosia, (see Zachary)		×
● Amelia, Saint Mary's	S	20
● Amesville, Jefferson	SE	30
● **Amite City**, Tangipahoa	E	1,510
Amite River, Livingston	E	100
Anacoco, Vernon	W	×
Anchor, Pointe Coupee	C	100
Anchorage, West Baton R'ge	C	×
Andora, Red River	NW	×
Angola, West Feliciana	C	250
Ansel, Bossier	NW	100
Antioch, Claiborne	NW	×
Arabi, Saint Bernard	SE	1,500
Arbroth, West Baton Rouge	C	60
Arcadia, Bienville	NW	862
Archibald, Richland	NE	×
● Arcola, Tangipahoa	E	233
Ariel, La Fourche	SE	82
Arizonia, Claiborne	NW	148
● Arkana, Bossier	NW	×
Armistead, Bienville	NW	×
Armstrong, Saint Bernard	SE	×
Arnaudville, Saint Landry	C	300
Asher, Rapides	C	×
Ashland Pl'tat'n, Concordia	C	×
Ashland Plantation, Red River	NW	25
Ashley's, Concordia	C	×
Ashly, Madison	NE	20
Ash Point, Bossier	NW	25
Ashton, East Carroll	NE	50
Ashton Plantation, Rapides	C	25
Ashwood, Tensas	NE	×
Athens, Claiborne	NW	78
Atherton, Madison	NE	×
● *Athlone*, Concordia	C	×
Atkins' Landing, Bossier	NW	50
Atlanta, Winn	N	60
Auburn, Orleans	SE	×
● *Averit*, Lincoln	N	15
Avery, Iberia	S	×
Aycock, Claiborne	NW	35
Babb's Bridge, Rapides	C	60
Bagdad, Rapides	C	15
Bailey, Tangipahoa	E	30
● Baker, East Baton Rouge	C	80
● Baldwin, Saint Mary's	S	500
Balltown, Washington	E	.8
Bank, Saint Bernard	SE	×
Barataria, Jefferson	SE	×
Barbin's Landing, Avoyelles	C	45
● Barbreck, Saint Landry	C	60
Barehead, Calcasieu	SW	×
● Barnes, Madison	NE	×
Barrett, Grant	C	×
● Bartels, Saint Mary's	S	20
Basile, Acadia	C	×
Baskinton, Franklin	NE	85
Bass Landing, East Carroll	NE	.
Bassville, Grant	C	25
● **Bastrop**, Morehouse	NE	1,200
● **BATON ROUGE**, East Baton Rouge	C	10,478
Baton Rouge Barracks, East Baton Rouge	C	×
● *Baton Rouge Junc.*, West Baton Rouge	C	×
Bay, Calcasieu	SW	50
Bayou Barbary, Livingston	E	30
Bayou Black, Terre Bonne	SE	120
Bayou Boeuf, Saint Mary's	S	20
Bayou Chene, Saint Martin	S	20
Bayou Chicot, Saint Landry	C	160
Bayou Choupique, Avoyelles	C	120
Bayou Current, Saint Landry	C	32
Bayou Des Allemands, (see Allemand's)		×
Bayou DuLarge, (see Houma)		×
● Bayou Goula, Iberville	S	769

Louisiana

Town, County	Index	Pop.
Bayou Goula Landing, East Bayou Rouge	C	×
Bayou Grosse Tete, Pointe Coupee	C	70
Bayou La Chute, Caddo	NW	45
Bayou Lacomb, Saint Tam'y	E	100
Bayou Lethsworth, (see Smithl'd		×
Bayou Macon, Franklin	NE	40
● *Bayou Natchez*, N'toches	NW	×
Bayou Paul L'd'g, Iberville	S	15
Bayou Pierre, Natchitoch	NW	×
Bayou Poydras, West Baton Rouge	C	40
Bayou Ramos, Saint Mary's	S	200
● *Bayou Sale*, Saint Mary's	S	60
Bayou Sale Sta., (see Foster)		×
● **Bayou Sara**, West Felici	C	608
Bayou Scie, Sabine	W	10
Bayou Tigre, Vermillion	S	250
Bayou Tunica, West Feliciana	C	75
Bayou Vermillion, V'million	C	20
Beach, Caddo	NW	×
Bear, Calcasieu	SW	×
Beard's Landing, (see Glade)		×
Beaver, Saint Landry	C	69
Becks, Caddo	NW	×
Beckworth, Calcasieu	SW	×
Bedford, Red River	NW	×
Bedford Landing, Madison	NE	×
● *Bee Bayou*, Richland	NE	×
Beeler's Landing, Tensas	NE	40
● *Beggs*, Saint Landry	C	10
Beiler's Landing, Tensas	NE	40
Belair, Plaquemines	SE	405
Bellair Cove, Saint Landry	C	×
Belle Chase, Plaquemine	S	×
● Belle Hellene, Ascension	SE	200
Belle Place, Iberia	S	25
Belle Rose, Assumption	S	240
● *Belleview*, Saint Landry	C	×
Bellevue, Bossier	NW	212
Belle Vue, Plaquemines	SE	×
● Bell's Store, East Feliciana	C	30
Bellwood, Natchitoches	NW	50
Belmont, Sabine	W	45
Benham, East Carroll	NE	500
Bennettville, Rapides	C	25
● **Benton**, Bossier	NW	75
● *Benton*, Saint Tammany	E	×
Benton's Ferry, Livingston	E	63
Bermuda, Natchitoches	NW	250
Bertie, Assumption	S	60
Bertrand, Winn	N	×
Bertrand, Pointe Coupee	C	×
Bertrandville, Plaquemines	SE	205
● Berwick, Saint Mary's	S	769
Bethany, Caddo	NW	25
Bethlehem, Claiborne	NW	×
Bienville, Bienville	NW	×
Big Bend, Avoyelles	C	200
Big Cane, Saint Landry	C	100
Bisland's L'd'g, (see Montegut)		×
Bismark, Rapides	C	×
Black Bayou, Caddo	NW	45
Blackburn, Claiborne	NW	20
Black Creek, Grant	C	18
Black Hawk, Concordia	C	323
● *Black River*, Concordia	C	30
Blair's L'd'g, Red River	NW	×
Blair Sta., Calcasieu	SW	×
Blairstown, East Feliciana	C	×
Blanchard, DeSoto	NW	×
Blankston, Caldwell	N	×
Blind River, (see Maurepas)		×
Blume, Bienville	NW	20
Bodcau, Bossier	NW	×
Bodoc, Avoyelles	C	25
● *Boeuf*, Assumption	S	×
Boeuf River, Caldwell	N	×
Bohemia, Plaquemines	SE	×
Bondurant L'd'g, Tensas	NE	×
Bonfouca, Saint Tammany	E	400
● Bonita, Morehouse	NE	150
Bonnet Carre, Sai't John B'p't	SE	850
Bordelonville, Avoyelles	C	150
Boreta, Saint Landry	C	×
● *Bosco*, Ouachita	N	×
Boscobel, (see Cuba)		×
Bossier City, Bossier	NW	202
Bourgere, Concordia	C	×
Boughton, Richland	NE	×
● Boutte, Saint Charles	SE	100
Bowie's Point, Concordia	C	15
Bowman's Landing, Tensas	NE	35
● Boyce, Rapides	C	301
Breaux Bridge, Saint Martin	S	654
Breland, Tangipahoa	E	×
● *Breville*, Natchitoches	NW	×

Briarfield Landing, Caddo NW ×
Brice, Bienville.......... NW ×
Brilliant Point, Saint James SE ×
Broadwell's Store, Natchi. NW 100
Brodnax, Morehouse...... NE 50
Brooklyn, Jackson......... N ×
● Broussard, LaFayette..... S 75
Brown, Bienville......... NW 20
Brownlee, Bossier......... NW ×
Brown's Landing, Tensas. NE ×
Brunett, East Carroll....... NE 30
● Brusly Landing, W. BatR... C 315
Bryan City, Franklin..... NE ×
Buck Eye Landing, Grant. . C ×
Buckhorn, Webster...... NW 20
Buck Ridge L'd'g, Tensas. NE 100
Bulah, Bienville.......... NW 25
Bullitts Bayou, Concordia.... C 50
Bunch's Bend, East Carroll NE 120
● Bunkie, Avoyelles....... C 299
Buras, Plaquemines........ SE 250
Burbridge, Plaquemines . . SE ×
Burissa, Calcasieu........ SW 32
Burke Station, Iberia........ S 20
Burk Place, Bienville.... NW 25
Burkville, E. Baton Rouge. . C ×
● Burnside, Ascension..... SE 25
● *Burnt Bridge*, Concordia. C ×
Burr's Ferry, Vernon....... W 60
● *Burtville*, East Baton Rouge C ×
Butler, De Soto........... NW 60
Butler, Plaquemines....... SE ×
Butler's L'd'g, (see Natchitoches) ×
Cabin Teele L'd'g, Madison NE ×
● Cades, Saint Martin....... S 30
Cadeville, Ouachita......... N 40
Calcasieu, Calcasieu........ SW 70
Calhoun, Ouachita.......... N 50
● *California*, Madison.... NE 15
Callahan's Bluff, Cameron SW 100
Callaway, Richland......... NE ×
Cameron, Cameron..... SW 100
Camindaville, Jefferson... SE ×
Camp Harney, E. Baton Ro'e C ×
Camp Parapet, Jefferson. . SE 744
Campti, Natchitoches..... NW 310
Canal, Acadia............... C ×
Cane Ridge, Claiborne.... NW ×
Cane River, Natchitoches NW 10
Caney, Vernon............. W ×
Cannon Store, Iberville..... S 80
Canton, Calcasieu......... SW ×
Cardure, East Baton Rouge. C ×
● Carencro, La Fayette..... S 289
● *Carlin*, Ouachita......... N ×
Carlyle's Landing, Madison NE ×
Carmel, De Soto... ...... NW ×
Carnarvon, Saint Bernard. SE ×
● *Carpenter's*, Richland. . NE ×
Carr's, Concordia........... C 15
Carrollton, Jefferson....... SE 3,000
Carter's, East Feliciana..... C ×
Carter's Landing, Catahoula C 8
Carterville, Bossier....... NW 25
Carthage, Winn............. N ×
Cartville, Acadia............ C 25
Casonville, Morehouse.... NE 35
Cassandra, Avoyelles...... C 60
Castor's Landing, Caldwell. N 50
Castor Sulphur Springs, Catahoula............ C 10
Catfish L'd'g, Pointe Coupee C ×
Causey, Morehouse........ NE 45
Cedar Grove, Plaquemines SE ×
Cedar Grove, Sabine .... W ×
Cedar Ota, Livingston...... E 10
Cedarton, Lincoln.......... N ×
Center Point, Avoyelles..... C ×
Centerville, Livingston...... E ×
● Central, Saint James.... SE 65
● *Central*, Terre Bonne... SE 40
Centreville, Saint Mary's.... S 414
● Chacahoula, Terre Bonne SE 100
Chalmette, Orleans........ SE ×
Chappeau Pela, Tangipahoa. E 100
Charenton, Saint Mary's..... S 500
Charlieville, Richland..... NE 20
Chatalgnier, Saint Landry... C 300
● *Chef Menteur*, Orleans. . SE ×
Chenal, Pointe Coupee..... C 100
● Cheneyville, Rapides...... C 200
● *Cheniere*, Ouachita........ N 70
Chenier Perdue, Cameron SW 25
Chenierre Camenada, Jeffe'n SE ×
Cherry Ridge, Union....... N 20
Chestnut, Natchitoches... NW ×
● *Chevy Chase*, Concordia. . C ×

China, Calcasieu.......... SW 25
Chinchuba, Saint Tammany. E ×
Chipola, Saint Helena....... E 50
● *Chloe*, Calcasieu........ SW ×
Chloie, Red River......... NW ×
● Chopin, Natchitoches... NW 50
● Choudrant, Lincoln....... N ×
Church Point, Acadia........ C 40
Cinclaire, West Baton Rouge C 18
City Point, Plaquemines. . SE ×
City Price, Plaquemines... SE 22
● *Claiborne*, Saint Tammany E ×
Clarence, Natchitoches... NW ×
Clayborne, Iberville......... S ×
● *Clayton*, Concordia....... C ×
Clayton, Union.............. N ×
● *Cleola*, Morehouse...... NE ×
● **Clinton**, East Feliciana. C 974
Clio, Livingston.............. E 100
Cloutierville, Natchitoches NW 150
Cofield, Ascension.......... SE 20
Cold Water, Winn.......... N 30
Cole's Store, Caddo....... NW 30
Colfax, Grant.............. C 161
Collins, Morehouse........ NE 80
Collinsburgh, Bossier..... NW 100
Colson's, Union............. N ×
Columbia, Caldwell...... N 852
Columbus, Sabine......... W 20
Colyell, Livingston........ E 25
Como, Franklin........... NE 18
Como, West Feliciana....... C ×
Concession, Plaquemines. . SE 50
● *Concordia*, Concordia..... C ×
Contreas, Plaquemines.... SE ×
● **Convent**, Saint James. . SE 1,000
Converse, West Feliciana.... C ×
Conway, Union.............. N ×
Cook, DeSoto............... W 50
Cook's Landing, Po'te C'pee C 120
● *Copeland*, Catahoula...... C ×
Copenhagen, Caldwell........ N 50
Corleyville, Sabine......... W ×
Cora, Vernon................ W ×
● *Corey*, Caldwell.......... N ×
Corinne, Orleans............ SE ×
● *Cote Blanche*, Saint Mary's S ×
Cote Gelle, LaFayette........ S 15
Cotile, (see Boyce)............ ×
Cottonburg, Grant.......... C ×
Cotton Plant, Caldwell..... N 15
Cottonport, Avoyelles........ C 500
Cottonport, (see West Monroe) ×
Cotton Valley, Webster... NW 22
Cottonville, (see Baker)...... ×
Cottonwood, Vernon....... W ×
Cottonwood Store, (see New Carthage)................... ×
Couley, Winn................. N ×
Coulie Croche, Saint Landry C 20
Coushatta, Red River. . NW 619
● **Covington**, Saint Tamma'y E 976
Cow Island, Cameron..... SW 15
Crane, Rapides.............. C 38
Creedmore, Plaquemines. . SE ×
Creole, Cameron........... SW 20
● *Crescent*, Terre Bonne... SE ×
● *Crew Lake*, Richland.... NE ×
Cross, Concordia........... C 20
● *Cross Bayou*, Concordia. . C ×
● **Crowley**, Acadia...... NE 420
Crown Point, Calcasieu. . SW ×
Crowville, Franklin......... NE 65
Cuba, Ouachita.............. N 25
Curtis, Bossier............. NW ×
Cut Off, La Fourche........ SE 20
● Cypre-mort, Saint Mary's. S 300
● *Cypremort*, Saint Mary's. . S 20
● Cypress, Natchitoches. . NW 25
● *Cypress City*, Concordia. . C ×
Daisy, Plaquemines......... SE 500
Dalcour, Plaquemines....... SE 500
Dalkeith, Madison........ NE ×
● Dallas, Madison.......... NE ×
Dalley, Jackson............ N 25
Danville, Caddo........... NW ×
D'Arbonne, Union........... N 40
Darcyville, East Baton Rouge C ×
Darlington, Saint Helena..... E 50
Darnell's Gin, Sabine....... W 20
Darrow, Ascension........ SE 399
Davis, Catahoula............ C ×
● *Davis*, Saint Charles..... SE 15
Davis Mills, Vernon......... W ×
Deer Range, Plaquemines. SE ×
De la Croix, Orleans........ SE ×
● *De Lacroix*, Saint Martin. S ×
● Delhi, Richland......... NE 620

● *Delogny*, Saint James... SE ×
Delph, Saint Tammany .... ×
● Delta, Madison .... NE 320
● *Deneg'ee*, Franklin..... NE ×
Dennis Mills, Saint Helena. . E ×
Derbonne Station, (see Derry) ×
Derby's Place, Saint Cha's. SE 20
Derouen, Iberia............. S 22
● Derry, Natchitoches.... NW 45
● *DeSair*, Saint John Baptist SE ×
De Siard, Ouachita.......... N 30
● *Des Allemand's*, S't Cha's SE ×
Devall, West Baton Rouge. . C 100
Devil's Flats, Plaquemines SE ×
Diamond, Plaquemines.... SE 250
Diceville, Richland....... NE ×
Dickard, Tensas........... NE ×
Dickson's Cross Roads, Bossier.................. NW ×
Dido, Vernon................ W 18
Dime, Plaquemines........ SE 25
Dixie, Bossier............. NW 30
● **Donaldsonville**, Ascension................... SE 3,121
Dooley, Caddo............ NW ×
Dorcheat, Webster......... NW 30
Dorcyville, Iberville......... S 505
● Doss, Morehouse........ NE ×
Dossman, Saint Landry...... C 30
Douglas, Lincoln............. N 30
Downsville, Union.......... N 100
● Doyline, Webster...... NW 300
Dreyfus, Iberville............ S ×
Dry Creek, Calcasieu...... SW 25
● Dubberly, Webster..... NW ×
● *Dubuisson*, Saint Landry. . C 40
● *Duchamp*, St. Martin..... S 18
Duck Port, Madison........ NE 50
Ducro's Station, S'nt Ber'd SE 6
● *Dugan*, Saint Charles.... SE ×
Dulac, Terre Bonne......... SE 90
Durand's Landing, Nat'es NW 50
● Duson, LaFayette......... S 15
Dutch Town, Ascension.... SE 32
Dyer, Rapides............... C ×
Dykesville, Claiborne..... NW 60
East Pendleton, Sabine..... W 30
East Point, Red River.... NW 75
Ebenezer, Acadia........... C ×
Echo, Acadia................ C ×
Eden, Catahoula............. C 20
Edgard, St. John Baptist SE 650
● Edgerley, Calcasieu..... SW 60
Edna, Bienville........... NW ×
Egg Bend, Avoyelles......... C 40
Egypt, Natchitoches....... NW 18
Elba, Saint Landry.......... C 25
Eldorado, Madison........ NW ×
Elkhorn Landing, Jefferson SE ×
Elkinsville, Saint Charles. . SE 220
● Ellendale, Terre Bonne. . SE 65
Ellis, Ascension............. SE 60
Elmer, Rapides.............. C 22
Elmwood, Vernon........... W 50
Elysian Field's Street, O's. SE ×
Empire, Plaquemines...... SE 50
Empire Mill, Plaquem'es. . SE 80
● English Look Out, St. T... E 30
English Turn, Plaquem's. . SE 350
Enterprise, Catahoula..... . C 30
● Eola, Avoyelles............. C 227
Eppa, East Carroll........ NE ×
Erwin, Orleans.............. SE ×
Erwin, Caddo.............. NW ×
Esperanza, Red River.... NW ×
Esterly, Calcasieu......... SW 28
● Esterwood, Acadia......... C 24
● Ethel, East Feliciana...... C 40
Ettingham, Tensas......... NE ×
Eugenia, St. John Baptist. SE ×
Eureka, Caldwell........... N 50
Eva, Concordia............... C 15
Evangeline, Acadia.......... C ×
● *Evangeline*, Calcasieu. . SW ×
Evergreen, Avoyelles....... C 500
● *Ewing*, LaFourche........ SE ×
Exposition, Plaquemines. . SE ×
Fabacher, Acadia........... C 250
Fairmount, Grant........... C 25
Fairview, Concordia........ C 125
Fairview, Plaquemines.... SE ×
● *Fallon*, Saint Charles... SE ×
Fanny, Plaquemines...... SE ×
Farmerville, Union..... N 472
Fausse Point, (see Loreauville) ×
Favret, Plaquemines...... SE ×
Felixville, East Feliciana... C ×

Louisiana

Louisiana

Place, Parish	Section	Population
Fishville, Grant	C	25
Flat Bayou, Red River	NW	×
Flat Creek, Winn	N	40
Flaggville, Saint Charles	SE	338
● *Fletcher's*, Concordia	C	×
Flete Landing, (see New Texas)		×
Florence, Catahoula	C	×
● Florenville, Saint Tammany	E	×
Florrisant, Plaquemines	SE	×
Flournoy, Caddo	NW	30
Flowery Mound, Concordia	C	25
Floyd, West Carroll	NE	144
● Fordoche, Pointe Coupee	C	65
Foreman, East Baton Rouge	C	×
Forest, West Carroll	NE	30
● Forksville, Ouachita	N	78
Forlorn Hope, Iberville	S	600
● *Forstall*, Saint James	E	×
Fort Jackson, Plaquemines	SE	×
Fort Jesup, Sabine	W	25
Fort Livingston, Jefferson	SE	×
Fort Necessity, Franklin	NE	20
Fort Pike, Orleans	SE	30
Fortson's, (see Murrell's L'ding)		×
● Foster, Saint Mary's	S	50
Foster's Hedge, E. Baton Rouge	C	×
● Fouche, Ouachita	N	75
● **Franklin**, Saint Mary's	S	2,127
Franklinton, Washington	E	97
Fredericksburg, Caldwell	N	×
Freetown, Saint Charles	SE	403
French Settlement, Liv'gst'n	E	300
● Frenier, St. John Baptist	SE	60
Friendship, Bienville	NW	55
Frierson's Mill, DeSoto	NW	50
Frog Level, Caddo	NW	30
● Frogmore, Concordia	C	25
Frozard, Saint Landry	C	×
Funny Louis, (see Summerv'e)		×
Gaar's Mills, Winn	N	15
Gallion, Morehouse	NE	×
Galvez, Ascension	SE	240
Gansville, Winn	N	75
● *Gardere*, East Baton Rouge	C	125
Garfield, Caddo	NW	30
● Garland, Saint Landry	C	15
Ga senville, Saint Charles	SE	274
Gassies, West Baton Rouge	C	×
Gay, Calcasieu	SW	×
Gayden, East Feliciana	C	200
● *Geary*, Ascension	SE	×
Geismar, Ascension	SE	28
● *Generally*, Saint Tammany	E	×
● *Gentilly*, Orleans	SE	×
Germania Store, E. Baton Rouge)		×
Gheens, LaFourche	SE	18
● Gibsland, Bienville	NW	400
● Gibson, Terre Bonne	SE	200
Gibson's Landing, Concordia	C	50
Gilbert, Franklin	NE	25
● Girard, Richland	NE	150
Glade, Catahoula	C	15
● Glencoe, Saint Mary's	S	25
Glen Ella, Caldwell	N	×
● Gloster, DeSoto	NW	375
Godwin, Rapides	C	20
Goldman, Tensas	NE	30
Gold Point, (see Plaquemines)		×
● *Goldsboro*, Orleans	SE	×
Gonzales, Ascension	SE	45
Good Hope La'd'g, Concordia	C	90
Goodrich L'd'g, East Carroll	NE	250
Gordon, Claiborne	NW	35
Gordon, Ouachita	N	90
Gorman, Washington	E	24
Gorum, Natchitoches	NW	×
Goshen, Richland	NE	15
Gouldsboro, Jefferson	SE	30
Grace, DeSoto	NW	×
Grand Caillou, Terre Bonne	SE	×
Grand Bayou, Plaquemines	SE	×
● Grand Cane, DeSoto	NW	85
Grand Chenier, Cameron	SW	1,200
Grand Cote, Iberia	S	18
● Grand Coteau, Saint Landry	C	333
Grand Ecore, Natchitoches	NW	50
Grand Grosseille, Calcasieu	SW	65
Grand Isle, Jefferson	SE	55
Grand Lake, Cameron	SW	×
Grand Point, Saint Martin	S	×
Grand Prairie, Plaquemines	SE	25
Grangeville, Saint Helena	E	100
Grappe's Bluff, Natchit'es	NW	72
Grayson, Caldwell	N	×
Greene, Concordia	C	×
Greens, West Feliciana	C	×
Greensburgh, Saint Helena	E	280
Green Store, Avoyelles	C	×
Greenville, Catahoula	C	×
● Greenwood, Caddo	NW	133
Greenwood, Plaquemines	SE	×
Greenwood Plantation, (see Bayou Sara)		×
Gregg, Vermillion	S	36
● **Gretna**, Jefferson	SE	3,332
Griffin, Madison	NE	30
Grissby, Bienville	NW	×
● *Grosse Tete*, Iberville	S	×
Guichard, Orleans	SE	×
Guidry's, La Fourche	SE	×
● *Guilletts*, Tangipahoa	E	48
Gum, Rapids	C	15
Gum Swamp, Morehouse	NE	25
● *Gusman*, Saint Tammany	E	×
Guthrie, Saint Tammany	E	×
Guy, Grant	C	×
● Hansville, Avoyelles	C	75
Hackberry, Cameron	SW	45
Hadnot, Grant	C	×
● **Hahnville**, Saint Char's	SE	447
Hale, Caddo	NW	×
Halloo, (see Pearl River)		×
Hamburg, Avoyelles	C	60
● Hammond, Tangipahoa	E	692
● Hank's Mill, Bossier	NW	×
Happy Jack, Plaquemines	SE	125
Happy Point, Plaquemines	SE	×
Hard Scrabble L'd'g, Tensas	NE	×
Hardshell, Vernon	W	12
Hard Times, (see Magnolia)		×
Hard Times La'd'g, Tensas	NE	400
Harlem, Plaquemines	SE	×
Harris, Natchitoches	NW	×
Harrisonburgh, Catahoula	C	359
Harvell's Mills, Saint Helena	E	×
Harvey, Jefferson	SE	150
● *Harvey's Canal*, Jefferson	SE	×
Hatcher, Sabine	W	28
● Haughton, Bossier	NW	305
Haynesville, Claiborne	NW	200
Head, Ouachita	N	×
Head of Island, Livingston	E	35
Head of Passes, Plaquem's	SE	×
Hearn, Webster	NW	×
Hebron, Jackson	N	×
● *Helena*, Concordia	C	×
Hemphill, Rapides	C	×
Henderson, East Carroll	NE	30
Henry, Vermillion	S	×
Herbert, Plaquemines	SE	×
Herbert's Bluff, Cameron	S	100
Hermitage, W. Baton Rouge	C	200
Hester, Saint James	SE	18
Hickory Branch, Calcasieu	SW	20
Hickory Valley, Winn	N	×
Hicks, Vernon	W	10
Hico, Lincoln	N	10
Highland, Tensas	NE	30
Highland, W. Baton Rouge	C	×
Hill's Springs, Livingston	E	25
Hineston, Rapides	C	100
Hogan's Landing, Caldwell	N	25
Hogan's Landing, Madison	NE	30
● Hohen Solms, Ascension	SE	100
Holloway, Rapides	C	×
Holly Grove, Franklin	NE	10
● *Holly Ridge*, Richland	NE	×
Holly Springs, Claiborne	NW	25
Holywood, East Baton Rouge	C	×
Holum, Caldwell	N	35
Home Place, Plaquemines	SE	40
Home Place, Concordia	C	×
Homer, Claiborne	NW	1,132
Hood's Mills, Jackson	N	20
Hopedale, Saint Bernard	SE	100
Hope Villa, East Baton Rouge	C	50
● **Houma**, Terre Bonne	SE	1,280
Howard, Red River	NW	×
Hubertville, Iberia	S	45
● *Hughes*, Bossier	NW	×
Hughes Spur, Bossier	NW	×
Hurricane, Winn	N	×
Husser Mill, Tangipahoa	E	×
Iatt, Grant	C	15
Illawara, East Carroll	NE	300
Illyria, Plaquemines	SE	×
● Independence, Tangipahoa	E	50
Independence L'd'g, Bossier	NW	×
Indian Bayot, Vermillion	S	80
Indian Mound, E. Bat. Rouge	C	20
● *Indian Village*, Iberville	S	×
Indian Village, Ouachita	N	30
Iola, Calcasieu	SW	15
● Iowa, Calcasieu	SW	18
Iowa Point Landing, West Feliciana	C	×
Irene, East Baton Rouge	C	20
Irish Bend, Saint Mary's	S	25
Ironton, Plaquemines	SE	×
Island, Iberville	S	40
Ivan, Bossier	NW	×
Iverson, Red River	NW	30
Jack, Catahoula	C	×
Jackson, East Feliciana	C	1,276
● Jacksonville, Calcasieu	SW	100
Jamba, Natchitoches	NW	×
Jamestown Landing, St. J's	SE	25
● Jeanerette, Iberia	S	1,309
● *Jefferson*, Jefferson	SE	50
Jena, Catahoula	C	50
● Jennings, Calcasieu	SW	412
Jesuit's Bend, Plaquemines	SE	243
● Jewella, Caddo	NW	30
Johnson, Calcasieu	SW	×
Johnson, Saint John Baptist	SE	×
Johnson's Bayou, Cameron	SW	60
Jones, Morehouse	NE	28
Jonesville, Catahoula	C	172
Jump, Plaquemines	SE	25
● *Junction*, Bossier	NW	×
Junior, Plaquemines	SE	50
Kaney, Calcasieu	SW	×
Katie, Tangipahoa	E	×
● Keatchie, DeSoto	NW	526
● Keithville, Caddo	NW	20
● *Kellers*, Morehouse	NE	×
● *Kelleys*, Richland	NE	×
Kellogg's Landing, Madison	NE	50
Kemp's, Tensas	NE	×
Kenilworth, Plaquemines	SE	×
● Kenner, Jefferson	SE	175
Kent's Mill, Tangipahoa	E	×
Kent's Store, East Feliciana	C	25
● Kentwood, Tangipahoa	E	20
Kilbourne, West Carroll	NE	60
Killainer's Plantation, Madison	NE	×
Killian, Livingston	E	×
Killona, Saint Charles	SE	×
Kinder, Calcasieu	SW	×
King, Madison	NE	85
● *King's*, Ouachita	N	×
Kingston, DeSoto	NW	25
Kirk's Ferry, Catahoula	C	18
Kisatchie, Natchitoches	N	30
Klotzville, Assumption	S	20
Knowles, Lincoln	N	18
Knowlton, Iberville	S	×
Knox, Concordia	C	×
Knox Point, Bossier	NW	×
Labadieville, Assumption	S	408
● *La Branch*, Saint Charles	SE	×
La Cache, Terre Bonne	SE	×
Lacasine, Calcasieu	SW	25
● *Lacasine Sta.*, Calcasieu	SW	×
La Croix, La Fourche	SE	×
● **La Fayette**, La Fayette	S	2,106
● *La Fourche*, Richland	NE	×
● Lafourche, Crossing, La Fourche	SE	500
Lake Arthur, Calcasieu	SW	30
Lake Arthur, Vermillion	S	×
● *Lake Catherine*, Orleans	SE	×
Lake Charles, Calcasieu	SW	3,442
● *Lake Charles Sta.*, Calc'eu	SW	×
Lake Concordia, Concordia	C	×
Lake End, Red River	NW	×
Lakeland, Pointe Coupee	C	50
● *Lake One*, Madison	NE	×
Lake Providence, East Carroll	NE	642
Lake Saint John, Concordia	C	12
● *Lake Shore*, Orleans	SE	×
Lakeside, Cameron	SW	×
Lake Village, Natchitoches	NW	458
Lamar, Franklin	NE	15
Lamarque, Concordia	C	30
Lamothe, Rapides	C	65
● Lamourie Bridge, Rapides	C	80
Lane, (see Southwood)		×
● Lanesville, Webster	NW	200
Langston, Claiborne	NW	×
Lapine, Ouachita	N	12
La Place, Saint Martin	S	150
La Place Sta., (see Eugenia)		×
L'Argent, Tensas	NE	60
La Rewsite, Plaquemines	SE	×
● *Larosen*, Caddo	NW	×
Lassiter, (see Oxford)		×
Last Chance, Plaquemines	SE	×
Latanache, Pointe Coupee	C	40
Latex, Caddo	NW	×

Place	Loc.	Pop.
Lauderdale, Saint James	SE	×
● Laurel Hill, West Feliciana	C	30
Lavacca, Catahoula	C	15
● *Lavonia*, Pointe Coupee	C	×
Lawrence, Plaquemines	SE	30
Leaville, East Feliciana	C	×
Lecompte, Rapides	C	125
Ledoux, Calcasieu	SW	×
● Lee, Orleans	SE	60
● *Lee Bayou*, Concordia	C	×
Leesburg, (see Cameron)		×
Lee's Creek, Washington	E	12
Lee's Landing, Tensas	NE	×
Leesville, Vernon	W	1,000
Legonier, Pointe Coupee	C	15
Lehman, Concordia	C	200
Leland, Catahoula	C	30
● *Lena*, Rapides	C	100
Lena Station, Rapides	C	×
Leola, (see Robeline)		×
Leonville, Saint Landry	C	400
● *LeSassierStar*, SaintChar's	SE	×
Lettsworth, Pointe Coupee	C	×
Levert, West Baton Rouge	C	×
Liberty Hill, Bienville	NW	50
Lidon's Ferry, La Fayette	S	×
Lind Grove, (see Bonita)		×
● Lindsay, East Feliciana	C	25
Line, Morehouse	NE	×
Linwood, Plaquemines	SE	×
Lisbon, Claiborne	NW	100
Lismore, Concordia	C	45
Little Caillou, (see Houma)		×
Little Rock, Plaquemines	SE	15
● *Little Woods*, Orleans	SE	15
Live Oak, Livingston	E	10
Liverpool, Saint Helena	E	20
Livonia, Pointe Coupee	C	75
Lobdell, West Baton Rouge	C	15
Locharbor, Ouachita	N	25
Lockport, La Fourche	SE	300
Logan Landing, (see Luling)		×
● Logansport, DeSoto	NW	281
Log Town, Ouachita	N	150
Longstreet, DeSoto	NW	45
Longueville, LaFourche	SE	228
Longwood, Caddo	NW	50
Longwood L'd'g, East Carroll	NE	15
Lookout, Saint Helena	E	20
● *Lookout*, Saint Tammany	E	30
Loretta, Calcasieu	SW	18
Loreauville, Iberia	S	350
● Louisa, Saint Mary's	S	20
● *Louise*, Saint Charles	SE	×
Love's Lake, Red River	NW	10
Love's Mill, Bossier	NW	×
Loyd, Rapides	C	70
Lucy, Saint John Baptist	SE	200
Lula, DeSoto	NW	200
Luling, Saint Charles	SE	200
● *Lum's*, Madison	NE	×
Lutcher, Saint James	SE	×
● McCall, Ascension	SE	60
McDonoughville, Jefferson	SE	2,235
McGinty, Webster	NW	×
McRae, Pointe Coupee	C	×
McShan, Sabine	W	×
Macedonia, Jackson	C	×
Macks Bayou, Bossier	NW	×
Madisonville, Saint Charles	SE	469
Madisonville, Saint Tammany	E	574
Magee, Washington	E	×
Magnolia, East Baton Rouge	C	20
Magnolia, Plaquemine	SE	×
Magnolia, Saint Bernard	SE	×
Malagay, La Fourche	SE	25
Mallett, Natchitoches	NW	×
Mamon, Saint Landry	C	×
Mammoth Prairie, Acadia	C	300
● *Manchac*, Tangipahoa	E	180
Manchac, East Baton Rouge	C	125
Mandeville, Saint Tammany	E	1,012
Mangham, Richland	NE	×
Manifest, Catahoula	C	20
● **Mansfield**, Desoto	NW	908
Mansura, Avoyelles	C	144
Many, Sabine	W	133
Marcy Cut-off, Natchitoche	NW	×
● *Marincouin*, Iberville	S	×
Marion, Union	N	400
Marksville, Avoyelles	C	540
Marsalis, Claiborne	NW	×
Marston, Nachitoches	NW	30
Martin, Plaquemines	SE	32
Marthaville, Nachitoches	NW	382
Mary, Plaquemines	SE	×
Mascot, Plaquemines	SE	×
Maud, Caldwell	N	24
Maurepas, Livingston	E	16
Mayer, Saint Helena	E	15
Meadow, (see Merryville)		×
Medora, Iberville	S	×
Melbourne, East Carroll	NE	25
Melder, Rapides	C	38
Meilleur L'd'g, Saint Mary's	S	×
Melrose, Nachitoches	NW	×
● Melville, Saint Landry	C	361
● **Mermenton**, Acadia	C	100
Merrick, Pointe Coupee	C	45
Merrit, Saint Bernard	SE	×
Mer Rouge, Morehouse	NE	150
Merryville, Calcasieu	SW	40
Meyersville, Avoyelles	C	35
M. G. Canal, Saint Bernard	SE	×
● *Micheaud*, Orleans	SE	×
Midkiff, Sabine	W	×
Midway, Avoyelles	C	25
Midway, Bossier	NW	40
● *Milburn*, Avoyelles	C	×
Miles, West Feliciana	C	×
Milford, Rapides	C	20
Millandon, Saint Bernard	SE	×
Milliburn, Avoyelles	C	25
Mill Creek, Sabine	W	15
Miller, Acadia	C	×
Millersville, Acadia	C	67
Millerton, Claiborne	NW	×
● Mill Haven, Ouachita	N	90
Milliken's Bend, Madison	NE	300
Millsborough, Winn	N	24
● *Milneburg*, (see New Orleans)		×
Milton, Vermillion	S	×
Minden, Webster	NW	1,298
Minorca, Concordia	C	×
Missionary, Caddo	NW	×
Mitchell, Sabine	W	×
Moanona, Orleans	SE	×
Mon Plaisir, Plaquemines	SE	×
MONROE, Ouachita	N	3,256
Monsecour, Plaquemine	SE	×
Montana, Natchitoches	NW	30
Montcalm, Bienville	NW	50
Montegut, Terre Bonne	SE	×
Monterey, Concordia	C	×
Montgomery, Grant	C	144
Monticello, Plaquemines	SE	×
Moore's Landing, Madison	NE	×
Mooringsport, Caddo	NW	65
Moorland, Rapides	C	60
Mora, Natchitoches	NW	30
Moran, Plaquemines	SE	×
Moreauville, Avoyelles	C	250
● *Moreland*, Rapides	C	60
● Morgan City, Saint Mary's	S	2,291
● *Morgan's Landing*, Or's	SE	×
Morganza, Pointe Coupee	C	30
● *Moro*, Concordia	C	×
● Morrow, Saint Landry	C	60
● *Morton*, Concordia	C	×
Morville, Concordia	C	×
Mosely's Bluff, Union	N	40
● Mound, Madison	NE	100
● Mount Airy, Saint John Baptist	SE	25
Mount Herman, Washington	E	×
Mount Lebanon, Bienville	NW	200
Mount Pelier, Saint Helena	E	40
Mount Pleasant, Caldwell	N	40
Mount Pleasant, E. B. R'ge	C	10
Mount Point, Washington	E	×
Mount Zion, Winn	N	×
Mouth of Cane River, Ne's	NW	75
Mulberry, Bienville	NW	24
Murdock, Tangipahoa	E	×
Murrell's Landing, Red River	NW	×
Murrell's Point, Webster	NW	×
● *Murtagh*, Jefferson	SE	×
Musson, Iberville	S	25
Myatt, Ouachita	N	×
Myles, Washington	E	×
Myrtle Grove, Avoyelles	C	×
Myrtle Grove, Plaquemine	SE	50
Mystic, Calcasieu	SW	25
Naborton, De Soto	NW	×
Nairn, Plaquemines	SE	×
Napoleonville, Assumption	S	722
Nash, Jackson	N	×
● **Natchitoches**, Nat'es	NW	1,820
National, Iberville	S	×
NebraskaLanding, Madison	NE	50
Negreet, Sabine	W	25
Neptune, Plaquemines	SE	20
Nero, Plaquemines	SE	27
New Carrollton, Jefferson	SE	20
New Carthage, Tensas	NE	35
Newell's Ridge, Tensas	NE	60
Newellton, Tensas	NE	125
New Era, Concordia	C	60
● **New Iberia**, Iberia	S	3,447
New Light, Tensas	NE	10
● **NEW ORLEANS**, Orleans	SE	242,039
New Poland, (see Poland)		×
Newport, Winn	N	40
New River, (see Belle Helene)		×
New Roads, Pointe Coupee	E	600
New St. Louis, E. B. Rouge	C	50
New Texas, Pointe Coupee	C	300
Newton, Natchitoches	NW	×
Newtown, Terre Bonne	SE	411
Niblett's Bluff, Calcassieu	SW	30
Nicholls, Plaquemines	SE	×
NormandyLanding, Concordia	C	15
● Norwood, East Feliciana	C	60
Notleyville, Saint Landry	C	40
Nutmeg, Bienville	NW	30
Oak Grove, West Carroll	NE	75
Oak Hill Bossier	NW	×
Oakland, Union	N	75
Oakley, Franklin	NE	16
Oakley Landing, Madison	NE	×
Oaklin Spring, Calcasieu	SW	45
Oak Point, Plaquemines	SE	×
● Oak Ridge, Morehouse	NE	296
● *Oak Ridge*, Saint Tammany	E	200
Oakville, Plaquemines	SE	390
Oberlin, Calcasieu	SW	×
Oction, Grant	C	30
Odenburg, Avoyelles	C	20
Okaloosa, Ouachita	N	30
O. K. Landing, (see Bermuda)		×
Old Field, Livingston	E	20
Olga Jump, Plaquemines	SE	15
Oliphant, (see Timon)		×
Olive Branch, East Feliciana	C	25
● Olivier, Iberia	S	25
Olympic Plantation, Catahoula	C	×
Omega, Madison	NE	80
● **Opelousas**, St Landry	C	1,572
Orange City, La Fourche	SE	×
Orange Farm, Plaquemines	SE	×
● *Orange Grove*, Plaquemines	SE	×
Orono, Claiborne	NW	×
Orville, East Feliciana	C	80
● *Overt*, Saint John Baptist	SE	×
Ott's Mills, Livingston	E	25
Ouachita City, Union	N	100
Oubre, Saint James	SE	×
Owens, Claiborne	NW	×
● Oxford, DeSoto	NW	72
Paincourtville, Assumption	S	350
Palestine, Washington	E	12
● Palmetto, Saint Landry	C	60
Palo Alto, Iberville	S	×
Parham's, Catahoula	C	20
Pass Manchac, Tangipahoa	E	25
Patin, Saint Martin	S	×
Patoutville, Iberia	S	60
● Patterson, Saint Mary's	S	1,414
Paulina, Saint James	SE	×
Peace Grove, Tangipahoa	E	23
Peach Grove, Saint Charles	SE	×
Pearceville, Saint Landry	C	×
Pearl, Calcasieu	SW	17
Pearl River, Saint Tammany	E	50
● *Pearl River*, Saint Tammany	E	×
Peariville, Saint Tammany	E	30
Pecan, Natchitoches	NW	18
● *Pecan Grove*, Orleans	SE	×
● *Peck*, Catahoula	C	×
Peignour, Vermillion	S	×
● Pelican, DeSoto	NW	×
Perry, Vermillion	S	27
Petite Anse Island, Iberia	S	300
Phillip's Bluff, Calcasieu	SW	20
Pickett, Bossier	NW	24
Pickett, Calcasieu	SW	24
Pilcher's Point, East Carroll	NE	100
Pilot Town, Plaquemines	SE	×
Pinchburg, Calcasieu	SW	×
Pine Bluff, Caldwell	N	10
Pine Grove, (see Iowa)		×
Pine Grove, Saint Helena	E	20
Pine Hill, Calcasieu	SW	32
Pine Ridge, Winn	N	×
Pineville, Rapides	C	540
● Plain Dealing, Bossier	NW	×
Plain Store, East Baton Rouge	C	40
Plain View, Livingston	E	20
Plaisance, Saint Landry	C	250
Planchville, Avoyelles	C	40

Place	Pop.
Plantersville, Morehouse..NE	25
● **Plaquemine**, Iberville..S	3,222
Plaquemine Brulee, Acadia. C	50
Plattenville, Assumption....S	150
Plancheville, Avoyelles.......C	40
● Pleasant Hill, Sabine.....W	150
Pleasanton, Webster......NW	×
Pointeala Hache, Plaquemines..................SE	1,500
Point, Union...............N	×
● *Point Aux Herbes*, Or'n. SE	×
Point Celeste, Plaquemines SE	×
PointeCoupee, PointeCoupee C	350
Point Lookout, EastCarroll NE	×
Point Michel, Plaquemine. SE	40
Point Pleasant, Tensas.... NE	75
Poirier La'd'g, Saint JamesSE	×
Poland, Rapides............C	125
● Ponchatoula, Tangipahoa. E	459
Ponchartrain Jc., Orleans. SE	×
Popeville, Washington......E	×
● **Port Allen**, W.B. RougeC	200
Port Barre, Saint Landry....C	350
Port Barrow, Ascension...SE	500
Port Eads, Plaquemines... SE	250
Port Hickey, E. B. Rouge...C	50
Port Houmans, Ascension SE	×
Port Hudson, E. B. Rouge.. C	250
Port Vincent, Livingston....E	300
Potash, Plaquemines........ SE	×
Pot Cove, Saint Landry......C	×
Pottsville, De Soto....... NW	×
Poupperille, Saint Landry.. C	×
● *Powell*, Jefferson.........SE	×
Poydras, Saint Bernard....SE	75
Poydras Junc., SaintBernardSE	×
Prairie Home, Grant.........C	×
Prairie Landing, FranklinNE	×
Prairie Mer Rouge, (see Mer Rouge)	×
Prairieville, Ascension.....SE	30
Pratt's Mill, Morehouse..NE	×
Preston, Point Coupee......C	×
● *Preston*, Caddo........ NW	×
Pride, East Baton Rouge....C	18
Prohibition, Catahoula......C	×
Prospect, Sabine.......... W	×
● Provencal, NatchitochesNW	482
Prudhomme, Natchito's..NW	25
● Prudhomme, Acadia......C	150
Pugh, LaFourche.......... SE	48
Quadrate, Rapides..........C	×
Quarantine, Plaquemines..SE	10
● *Quebec*, Madison.........NE	×
Quirk, Sabine............. W	×
Raccourci, Pointe Coupee...C	250
● Raceland, La Fourche...SE	750
Radford, Cameron........SW	×
● Ramos, Saint Mary's......S	×
Ramsey, Vermillion.........S	20
● Rapides, Rapides.........C	28
Ratcliff, West Feliciana.....C	20
Ratea, Ascension..........SE	×
Raven Camp, Grant.........C	25
● *Ravenwood*, PointeCoupeeC	×
Raymond, Calcasieu...... SW	×
● Rayne, Acadia............C	569
Rayville, Richland.......NE	366
● *Rebecca*, Terre Bonne... SE	×
Red Fish, Avoyelles.........C	×
Red Hill, Winn...............N	20
Red Land, Bossier........NW	160
Red Mouth, Richland..... NE	36
Red River Landing, P'te C'e.C	250
Redtop, Acadia............ C	×
Redwine, Jackson...........S	25
Regan, Acadia.............C	×
Regina, Iberville...........S	25
Reggio, Plaquemines......SE	×
Reids, Livingston...........E	×
● Reisor, Caddo.......... NW	10
Relief, Claiborne..........NW	×
● *Remy's*, Saint James.... SE	×
Rhinehart, Catahoula....... C	25
● Rhoda, Saint Mary's.......S	23
Richardville, NatchitochesNW	×
Richland, Madison........NE	×
● *Ricohoc*, Saint Mary's.....S	×
Ridge, LaFayette............S	28
● Rigolets, Orleans........SE	×
Ringgold, Bienville.........NW	100
Rivers Landing, Concordia..C	×
● *River Switch*, Saint Tammany E	×
● *Riverton*, Caldwell..........N	×
Roane, Lincoln..............N	65
● Robeline, Natchitoches. NW	676
Robertdale, East Carroll...NE	30
Robertson, Washington.....E	×
Robertsville, Natchitoches NW	289
Robson, Caddo...........N W	100
Rochester, Jackson........N	×
Rock Point, Caddo....... N W	100
Rocky Mount, Bossier....N W	60
Rodolph, Caldwell..........N	×
Rolly, Sabine..............W	×
● Rosa, Saint Landry........C	22
Rose Bluff, (see Calcasieu)....	×
Rosebud, Vernon...........W	×
Rosedale, Iberville..........S	400
Rosefield, Catahoula.........C	200
Rose Hill, Caddo......... NW	40
Rose Hill Landing, W.B'n R'geC	60
Roseland, Tangipahoa.......E	281
Roseland Store, (see Sarpy)..	×
Rosenthal, Concordia.........C	×
● *Rousseau*, La Fourche....SE	×
Routon, Catahoula..........C	×
Row Landing, West FelicianaC	60
Roy, Natchitoches........NW	×
Royalty, Sabine..............W	×
Roysville, LaFayette........S	×
Ruddock, Saint John Baptist SE	×
Rush Point, Caddo........N W	36
● **Ruston**, Lincoln.......... N	767
● *Sabine*, Calcasieu.........SW	20
Saint Amant, Ascension...SE	18
Saint Ann, Plaquemines.. SE	×
Saint Bernard, St.Ber'dSE	2[illegible]
● *Saint Charles*, St.CharlesSE	200
Saint Clair, Plaquemines..SE	×
Saint Francisville, WestFelicianaC	950
● Saint Gabriel, Iberville....S	1,000
Saint James, Saint James..SE	500
Saint James Landing, OrleansSE	×
SaintJoeSwitch, SaintTammany. E	×
● *SaintJohn*, St.JohnBaptistSE	100
Saint Joseph, Tensas...NE	473
● *Saint Louis, Arkansas and Texas Junc.*, Bossier. NW	×
● Saint Martinville, St.M',n. S	1,814
Saint Mary's Plantation, (see Brusly Landing)..........	×
Saint Maurice, Winn.........N	85
Saint Maurice Landing, Pointe Coupee..........C	×
Saint Patrick's, Saint JamesSE	150
● *Saint Peter's*, St. JohnBap.SE	×
Saint Rosalie, PlaqueminesSE	×
Saint Sophie, Plaquemine...SE	566
Saline, (see Blair Station)....	×
Saline, Bienville..........NW	15
● *Salt Mine*, Iberia......... S	×
Salt Works, Plaquemines..SE	212
Sandtree, Bienville........ NW	30
Sandy Creek, Vernon.......W	18
San Patricio, Sabine........W	75
Sarepta, Webster.......... NW	30
Sarpy, Saint Charles....... SE	32
● *Sarpus*, Saint Charles... SE	×
Savories, Plaquemines.....SE	25
● *Sauver*, Jefferson..........SE	×
Saxonholm, Saint Bernard SE	×
Scally, Saint Mary's.........S	25
Scarsdale Plantation, Plaquemines.........SE	25
● Shriever, Terre Bonne...SE	150
Science Hill, Saint Landry...C	30
Scotland, East Baton Rouge C	×
● Scott, La Fayette..........S	50
Sebastopol, Plaquemines.. SE	×
Sebastopol, West Feliciana..C	×
Security, Catahoula..........C	30
Seeleyville, Saint Landry....C	25
● *Segura*, Ibera...............S	×
Serena, Concordia............C	×
Serpent, Calcasieu........ SW	×
Seymourville, Iberville.......S	×
Shady Grove, Washington...E	10
Shady Side Plantation, Saint Mary's.................S	250
Shaw, Grant..................C	×
Shelburn, East Carroll.... NE	×
Shell Bank, Cameron..... SW	25
Shell Beach, Vermillion......S	×
Shell Beach, Saint Bernard SE	180
Shiloh, Union...............N	250
Ship BayouLanding, Ten'sNE	×
Shongaloo, Webster...... NW	×
● **Shreveport**, Caddo...NW	11,979
● *Shreveport Junc.*, CaddoNW	×
Shulteston, Saint Landry....C	30
Sibley, Lincoln..............N	30
● *Sibley*, Webster......... NW	×
● *Sicard*, Ouachita..........N	×
Sicily Island, Catahoula..... C	250
Sikes Ferry, Webster.....NW	×
Sills, Winn.................N	18
Simmesport, Avoyelles......C	125
Simmons, Calcasieu.......SW	×
Simpson, Vernon...........W	×
● Simsboro, Lincoln......... N	248
Sinope, Caldwell...........N	25
Slab Town, Vernon.........W	38
● Slaughter, East Feliciana..C	58
● *Slayton*, Concordia....... C	×
● Slidell, Saint Tammany...E	364
Smithland, Pointe Coupee.. C	50
Smithville, Vernon.........W	×
Smoke Bend, Ascension...SE	×
Socolo, Plaquemines........SE	×
● *SocolaJunc.*, PlaqueminesSE	×
● *Sodas*, Sabine.......... W	150
Solleau, Calcasieu......... SW	30
Solar, Grant................C	18
Sordelet, Plaquemines..... SE	×
● *Sorrel*, Saint Mary's.......S	100
Soulouque, Iberville.........S	35
● *Southdown*, Terre BonneSE	×
Southport, Jefferson.......SE	12
● *Southport Jc.*, Orleans.. SE	×
South West Pass, Plaqu'nesSE	150
Southwood, Ascension.....SE	202
Spanish Fort, Orleans.....SE	×
Sparta, Bienville.......NW	300
Spearsville, Union..........N	100
Speicher, Sabine...........W	×
S. P. Landing, NatchitochesNW	70
Springfield, Livingston......E	600
Springfield L'd'g, (see Irene) .	×
● *Spring Hill*, Ouachita.... N	×
Spring Ridge, Caddo..... NW	50
Springville, Livingston.. E	60
● *Stacy*, Concordia..........C	×
Stafford Point, Catahoula....C	×
Starlight, Natchitoches...NW	×
Starns, Livingston..........E	15
Starts Landing, Catahoula..C	55
State Line, Claiborne.....NW	×
Stein's Bluff, Union........ N	50
Stella, Tensas........... NE	50
Stella, Plaquemines....... SE	×
Stella Plantation, Pl'q'nes SE	×
● Stonewall, DeSoto.......NW	100
Stony Point, E. Baton RougeC	100
Story, Orleans.............SE	×
Sugar Creek, Claiborne...NW	12
Sugartown, Calcasieu..... SW	300
● Sulphur City, Calcasieu. SW	80
● *Sulphur Mine*, CalcasieuSW	80
Summerfield, Claiborne.. NW	100
Summerville, Catahoula.....C	25
Sumpter, Lincoln...........N	×
Sun, Saint Tammany........E	25
Sunny Hill, Washington......E	12
Sunny South, DeSoto.... NW	60
Sunrise, Plaquemines......SE	50
Sunset, Saint Landry........C	20
● *Sun Set*, Saint Landry.....C	333
Sunshine, Iberville..........S	200
● *Sycamore*, Concordia..... C	×
● *Tacony*, Concordia......... C	×
Talisheck, Saint Tammany..E	×
Tallien, Assumption.........S	100
● **Tallula**, Madison........NE	300
● Tangipahoa, Tangipahoa...E	400
● Taylor, Bienville........ NW	50
Taylorville, East Feliciana..C	35
● *Tendal*, Madison.........NE	×
Tenmile, Calcasieu.........SW	×
Terre Aux Boef, Saint Bernard SE	350
Terre Bonne, (see Schriever)	×
Terre Haute, Saint John Baptist...............SE	×
Terre Promise, Plaquem'esSE	×
The Bay, Calcasieu........SW	80
Theoda, (see Cheneyville)....	×
Theriot, Terre Bonne......SE	×
Thibaut, Plaquemines.....SE	×
● *Thibodeaux Jc.*, LaFourcheSE	×
● **Thibodeaux**, LaFourcheSE	2,078
Thomas, East Baton Rouge. C	×
● Thomastown, Madison.. NE	15
Thompson, Calcasieu......SW	×
Thrailkill, Acadia...........C	×
● Tickfaw, Tangipahoa..... E	50
Tiger Bend, (see Haasville)...	×
Tiger Island, NachitochesNW	36
Tigerville, (see Gibson).......	×
Tillou, Morehouse.........NE	×
Tilden, Avoyelles..........C	50
Tilly, Vernon..............W	×
Timon, Natchitoches..... NW	25
Timothea, Webster....... NW	30

Tipton, (see Cansey) .... ×
Tobiasville, Ascension.....SE ×
Toca, Saint Bernard.......SE ×
Toledo, Vernon............ W 80
Tooley's, Catahoula..........C 20
Toro, Sabine...................W 30
Tortue, Vermillion..........S ×
Tramway L'd'g, Rapides....C 160
Trenton, Ouachita.......... N 300
Trichell, Nachitoches.....NW 15
Trinidad, Madison.........NE 20
Trinity, Catahoula...........C 160
Trinity L'd'g, (see Killona)... ×
Triva, Concordia.............. C 18
Troyville, (see Jonesville).... ×
Tunica, Winn..................N ×
Tunisburg, Orleans.......SE ×
Turpin, Morehouse ....NE ×
● *Turtle Lake*, Concordia...C ×
● *Twenty-six Mile Siding*, Madison .... NE ×
Tyne, Sabine............... W ×
Union, Saint James.........SE 35
Union Plant'n, Saint JamesSE ×
Union Point, Concordia.... C 14
Unionville, Lincoln.........N ×
Utility, Catahoula............C 50
● Vacherie, Saint James...SE 200
Valentine Landing, C'tah'la C 50
Valenzuela L'd'g, Assumpt'nS 85
● *Vallier*, Saint Charles...SE ×
● Vanceville, Bossier.... NW ×
Ventress, Pointe Coupee....C ×
Verduville, Saint Mary's.... S 100
Verline, Bossier...........NW ×
Vermilionville, (see LaFayette) ×
Vernon, Jackson..............N 200
Versailles, Orleans........ SE ×
Vickner Bayou, Ascension SE 60
Victoria, Nachitoches.... NW 422
● **Vidalia**, Concordia......C 821
Vienna, Lincoln .... N 50
Vilas, Grant...................C ×
Villa Vista, East Carroll...NE 75
Ville Platte, Saint Landry...C 250
Villere, Orleans............SE ×
Vincent, Calcasieu......... SW 50
Vining Mills, Lincoln....... N 30
Vinton, Calcasieu.......... SW 35
Violet, Saint Bernard.......SE ×
Violin, Saint Tammany..... E 12
Viva Pointe, Coupee......... C ×
Vowell's Mill, N'chito'hey NW ×
Waddill, DeSoto......... NW ×
Wadeville, Lincoln...........N ×
● Waggaman, Jefferson....SE 50
Walker, Livingston......... E ×
Wallace, Saint John BaptistSE 200
Walls, Winn................ N ×
Walnut Hill, Vernon....... W 50
Walnut Lane, Union.........N 50
Ward's Creek, E. Baton RougeC ×
Ward's Mills, Claiborne.. NW 60
Warsaw, Franklin........NE 72
● Washington, Saint LandryC 1,064
Waterloo, Pointe Coupee....C 650
Water Proof, Tensas...... NE 350
Watson L'd'g, Pointe CoupeeC ×
Wattsville, Winn............N ×
● Waverly, Madison........NE 54
Waverly L'd'g, Pointe CoupeeC ×
Weaver, Nachitoches.....NW ×
Weil, Rapides................ C 25
Welchton, Rapides.......... C 48
● Welcome, Saint James.. SE 600
Weldon, Union... .... N ×
● Welsh, Calcasieu.........SW 200
West End, Orleans......... SE ×
● Westlake, Calcasieu.....SW 750
West Melville, (see Melville).. ×
● West Monroe, Ouachita...N 447
Weston, Jackson..............N ×
● *West Pointe a la Hache*, Plaquemines............SE ×
● *West Pontchartrain Junction*, Orleans...........SE ×
● *Westwego*, Jefferson.....SE ×
Wheelock, Iberville..........S 20
White Castle, Iberville......S 603
Whitehall, Livingston.........E 35
● *Whitehall*, Saint James..SE 65
White Sulphur Springs, Catahoula...................C 65
● Whiteville, Saint Landry..C 60
Whittington, Washington.. E ×
Wild Lucia, Caddo.........NW ×
Wild Wood, Catahoula...... C 30

Williams, Red River......NW 30
Williamsport, Pointe Coupee C 70
Willow, Natchitoches.......NW 150
Willow Chute, Bossier....NW 15
● Wilson, East Feliciana....C 281
Wilson's Point, East CarrollNE 120
Wilton, Madison..........NE ×
Wilton L'd'g, East Carroll. NE 25
● *Winchester*, Saint James SE 600
Winnfield, Winn.........N 150
Winnsborough, F'klinNE 200
Winsted, Saint Mary's.......S ×
Woodland, East Feliciana...C 24
Woodland, Plaquemines.. SE ×
Wood Park, Plaquemines..SE ×
Woodville, Lincoln..........N 28
Youngsville, LaFayette.......S 200
● *Youngs*, East Feliciana...C ×
Young's Point, Madison..NE ×
Yscloskey, Plaquemines....SE ×
Zachary, East Baton Rouge. C 250
● *Zibilich*, Plaquemines....SE 50
Zona, Washington.... ......E 25

MAINE.*

COUNTIES.	INDEX.	POP.
Androscoggin	SW	48,968
Aroostook	NE	49,589
Cumberland	SW	90,949
Franklin	W	17,053
Hancock	S	37,312
Kennebec	SW	57,012
Knox	S	31,473
Lincoln	S	21,996
Oxford	SW	30,586
Penobscot	C	72,865
Piscataquis	C	16,134
Sagadahoc	SW	19,452
Somerset	W	32,627
Waldo	S	27,759
Washington	E	44,482
York	SW	62,829
Total		661,086

*In many of the towns of the state the population given embraces the township.

TOWN. COUNTY. INDEX. POP.

Abbott, Piscataquis..........C 622
● Abbot Village, Pis'taquis. C 140
Acadia, Aroostook........ NE ×
Acton, York.............. SW 878
Addison, Washington.......E ×
Addison Point, Washington. E 1,022
● *Agamenticus*, York.....SW ×
Albany, Oxford............ SW 645
Albion, Kennebec.........SW 1,042
Alexander, Washington.....E 337
● **Alfred**, York..........SW 1,030
Allamoosook Hancock......S ×
Allen's Mills, Franklin.....W ×
Alna, Lincoln................S 512
● Alton, Penobscot...........C 348
Amherst, Hancock..........S 375
Amity, Aroostook..........NE 420
Andover, Oxford...........SW 740
Andover Corners, (see Andover) ×
● *Annabessacook*, K'n'b'c SW ×
● Anson, Somerset.........W 1,444
Appleton, Knox..............S 1,080
● *Areys*, Kennebec.........SW ×
Argyle, Penobscot...........C 263
Arnold, Penobscot...........C ×
Arrowsic, Sagadahoc......SW 177
● *Arundel*, York..........SW ×
Ashdale, Sagadahoc.......SW ×
Ashland, Aroostook.......NE 568
Ash Point, Knox............ S ×
Ashville, Hancock............S ×
● *Askwith*, Somerset....... W ×
Asticon, Hancock..............S ×
Athens, Somerset.......... W 1,072
Atkinson, Piscataquis....... C 605
Atlantic, Hancock............S ×
● **Auburn**, And'scoggin.SW 11,250
Auburn Plains, AndroscogginSW ×
● **AUGUSTA**, KennebecSW 10,527
Aurora, Hancock..............S 175
Avon, Franklin .... W 439

Baggett's, Aroostook..... NE ×
Bailey Island, Cumberland SW ×
Baileyville, Washington.....E 226
Baileyville Station, Washington E ×
Baldwin, Cumberland.... SW 932
Barnard Plantation, Pis't'isC ×
● Bancroft, Aroostook.....NE 264
● **Bangor**, Penobscot......C 19,103
● *Bangs Siding*, Somerset. W ×
Bar Harbor, Hancock.......S 2,000
● Baring, Washington.......E 273
Bar Mills, York...........SW 119
● *Basin Mills*, Penobscot... C ×
Bass Harbor, (see Tremont) . ×
● **Bath**, Sagadahoc.......SW 8,213
Bay Point, Sagadahoc.....SW ×
Bay View, York........... SW ×
Bean's Corners, Franklin.. W ×
● *Bearce Road*, Oxford...SW ×
● *Beattie*, Franklin........ W ×
Beddington, Washington.....E 184
● *Bedells Crossing*, York. SW ×
● **Belfast**, Waldo.......... S 5,294
● Belgrade, Kennebec.... SW 1,090
Belgrade Mills, Kennebec.SW 144
Belmont, Waldo.............S 475
Bemis, Franklin...........W ×
Benedicta, Aroostook....NE 317
Benton, Kennebec........ SW 1,136
Benton Falls, Kennebec...SW 130
○ Benton Station, KennebecSW ×
Berry's Mill, Franklin..... W ×
Berwick, York.............SW 2,294
Berwick Branch, York....SW ×
● Bethel, Oxford...........SW 783
● Biddeford, York........SW 14,443
Biddeford Pool, York.....SW 828
● Bingham, Somerset...... W 757
Birch Harbor, Hancock......S ×
● *Bismarck*, Penobscot..... C ×
Blaine, Aroostook.........NE 784
Blake's, Cumberland..... SW ×
● Blanchard, Piscataquis....C 213
Blue Hill, Hancock..........S 1,980
Blue Hill Falls, Hancock.....S ×
Bolster's Mills, CumberlandSW ×
Bonny Eagle, Cumberland SW ×
● *Boggy Brook*, CumberlandSW ×
Boothbay, Lincoln.............S 1,718
Booth Bay Harbor, Lincoln. S 1,699
● *Boundary*, Franklin.....W ×
Bowdoin, Sagadahoc...... SW 940
Bowdoin Centre, SagadahocSW ×
● Bowdoinham, SagadahocSW 1,508
Bowery Beach, CumberlandSW ×
Boyd Lake, Piscataquis..... C ×
Bradford, Penobscot....... C 1,215
Bradford Centre, Penobscot.C 120
Bradley, Penobscot............C 823
● *Bradstreets*, Kennebec..SW ×
Branch, Somerset.......... W ×
Branch Mills, (see Palermo). ×
Bremen, Lincoln..............S 719
Brewer, Penobscot..........C 4,193
● *Brewer Village*, PenobscotC ×
Bridgewater, Aroostook.. NE 9.3
Bridgewater Center, Ar's'kNE ×
● Bridgton, Cumberland..SW 2,605
● *Bridgton Junction*, OxfordSW ×
Brighton, Somerset.........W 434
Bristol, Lincoln...............S 2,821
Britton's Mills, (see Livermore) ×
Broad Bay, Lincoln............S ×
Broad Cove, Lincoln........ S ×
Brockway's Mills, PiscataquisC ×
Brooklin, Hancock..........S 1,046
● Brooks, Waldo............ S 730
Brooksville, Hancock....... S 1,310
Brookton, Washington......E 429
● Brownfield, Oxford.....SW 1,134
Brownfield Centre PiscataquisC ×
● Brownville, Piscataquis...C 1,074
● *BrownvilleJunc.*, PiscataquisC ×
● Brunswick, CumberlandSW 6,012
● Bryant's Pond, Oxford..SW 250
● Buckfield, Oxford.......SW 1,200
Buck's Harbor, Washington E ×
Buck's Mills, Hancock...... S ×
● Bucksport, Hancock...... S 2,921
● Bucksport Centre, HancockS 1,500
Bunker Hill, Lincoln.........S ×
Burdin, Piscataquis.........C ×
Burkettville, Knox...........S ×
Burlington, Penobscot...... C 460
● Burnham Village, Waldo..S 846
● *Butlers Siding*, York...SW ×
Buxton, York.............SW 2,036

● Buxton Centre, York...SW 2,000
Byron, Oxford............SW 180
● **Calais**, Washington......E 7,290
Cambridge, Somerset.......W 425
Camden, Knox -...........S 4,621
● *Camp Benson*, Penobscot.C ×
Camp Caribou, Oxford....SW ×
Camp Ellis, York.........SW ×
Camp Ground, Waldo.......S ×
Canaan, Somerset.......... W 1,130
● Canton, Oxford.........SW 1,303
Canton Mills, (see Canton)... ×
Canton Point, Oxford.....SW ×
Cape Elizabeth, Cumber'l'dSW 5,459
● *Cape Elizabeth*, Cu'be'l'dSW ×
Cape Elizabeth Depot, Cumberland..............SW 100
Cape Neddick, York......SW ×
Capen's, Piscataquis.... ....C ×
Cape Porpoise, York......SW ×
Cape Rozier, Hancock.......S ×
Cardville, Penobscot ....C 800
● Caribou, Aroostook.....NE 4,087
● Carmel, Penobscot.........C 1,066
● *Carratunk Falls*, Som'set W ×
Carritunk, Somerset....... W 192
Carroll, Penobscot.......... C 546
Carthage, Franklin.........W 390
Cary Plantation, Aroostook NE 390
Casco, Cumberland....... SW 844
Cashs Corner, Cumberland NE ×
Castine, Hancock............S 987
Castle Hill, Aroostook.....NE 537
Caswell, Aroostook..........NE 350
Caswell Plantation, Ar'k. NE 212
● *Cathance*, Sagadahoc... SW ×
● *Cedar Grove*, Hancock....S ×
Cedar Grove, Lincoln........S ×
Center Lebanon, York....SW ×
Center Lovell, Oxford.....SW ×
Centraltown, Androsco'ginSW 1,150
Centre, Hancock............S ×
● *Centre*, Penobscot.........C ×
Centre Belmont, Waldo.....S ×
Centre Lincolnville, Waldo .S ×
Centre Montville, Waldo.... S ×
Centre Sidney, Kennebec. SW ×
● *Centre Waterboro*, York SW ×
● *Chadbourne's*, Cumb'l'd SW ×
● *Chamberlains*, Penobscot. C ×
Charleston, Penobscot...... C 971
Charlotte, Washington ....E 381
● *Chases*, Cumberland.....SW ×
Chase's Mills, Andr'sc'g'n.SW ×
Chebeague Isl'd, Cumb'l'dSW ×
● Chelsea, Kennebec......SW 2,356
● *Cherokee*, Aroostook....NE ×
Cherryfield, Washington....E 1,787
● *Chester*, Penobscot.........C 368
Chesterville, Franklin......W 770
Chicopee, York ....SW ×
China, Kennebec...........SW 1,423
● *Chipman's*, Hancock......S ×
● City Point, Waldo ....S ×
Clark Island, Knox......... S ×
Clark's Mill, York.......... SW ×
Cliffstone, Sagadahoc..... SW ×
Clifton, Penobscot...........C 284
● Clinton, Kennebec.......SW 1,518
Columbia, Washington...... E 587
Columbia Falls, Washington E 698
Concord, Somerset......... W 345
● *Conway Junction*, York SW ×
● *Cooks*, Cumberland......SW ×
Cooper, Washington......... E 264
Cooper's Mills, Lincoln......S ×
Coral, Aroostook ....NE ×
● Corinna, Penobscot......... C 1,207
Corinna Centre, Penobscot..C 350
Corinth, Penobscot...........C 1,154
● *Cornish*, Cumberland... SW 1,200
Cornish, York............... SW 1,118
Cornville, Somerset........ W 785
● Costigan, Penobscot...........C ×
Cousins Isl'd, Cumberland SW ×
Cranberry Isles, Hancock....S 330
Crawford, Washington......E 140
Crescent Surf, York........SW ×
Cross Hill, Kennebec.......SW ×
● *Crossuntic*, Penobscot.... C ×
● *Crowley Junc.*, A'd'sc'g'n SW ×
Crystal, Aroostook.........NE 297
● Cumberland, Cumb'rl'nd SW 1,487
● Cumberland Centre, C'l'd SW ×
● Cumberland Mills, Cu'l'd SW 2,700
Cundy's Harbor, Cumb'l'd SW ×
● Curtis' Corners, An'dr'n SW ×

Maine

Cushing, Knox.............. S 688
Cutler, Washington......... E 662
● *Daggett's*, Aroostook... NE ×
Damariscotta, Lincoln.......S 1,012
● *Damariscotta*, Lincoln....S ×
● Damariscotta Mills, L'nc'n S 100
● Damascus, Penobscot........C ×
● Danforth, Washington.... E 1,063
● Dannville, Androsc'g'n SW ×
● *Days Crossing*, Piscataqu'sC ×
● *Days Siding*, York..... SW ×
Dayton, York ....SW 500
Dead River, Somerset...... W 104
Dead River Mills, Hancock. S ×
Deblois, Washington........ E 76
Dedham, Hancock .... S 366
● *Deep Cut*, Sagadahoc... SW ×
Deering, Cumberland....... SW 5,353
Deering Centre, Cumb'land SW ×
● *Deering Stat'n*, Cumberl'dSW ×
Deer Isle, Hancock..........S 3,422
Denmark, Oxford...........SW 755
Dennysville, Washington... E 452
● Detroit, Somerset........ W 590
● Dexter, Penobscot........C 2,732
Dickvale, Oxford......... SW ×
Dixfield, Oxford........... SW 988
Dixfield Centre, Oxford...SW 925
Dixmont, Penobscot.......... C 919
Dixmont Centre, Penobscot. C ×
● **Dover**, Piscataquis...... C 1,942
Dover South Mills, P'sc't'q's. C 620
Dresden, Lincoln............S 1,043
● *Dresden*, Sagadahoc.... SW ×
Dresden Mills, Lincoln........S ×
Drew Plantation, Penobscot C 110
● *Driving Park*, Oxford.. SW ×
Dry Mills, Cumberland....SW ×
Duck Pond, Cumberland..SW ×
● *Dudley's*, Washington.... E ×
Durham, Androscoggin... SW 1,111
Dyer Brook, Aroostook... NE 221
Eagle Lake, Aroostook....NE 313
East Athens, Somerset..... W ×
East Auburn, Andr'sc'gn. SW ×
● East Baldwin, Cumb'l'd SW ×
East Bangor, Penobscot.....C ×
East Belmont, Waldo.......S ×
East Benton, Kennebec...SW ×
East Bethel, Oxford ...... SW ×
East Blue Hill, Hancock.... S ×
East Boothbay, Lincoln.......S 1,500
● East Bowdoinham, S'g'c SW ×
East Bradford, Penobscot...C ×
Eastbrook, Hancock...........S 246
East Brownfield, Oxford...SW ×
East Bucksport, Hancock...S ×
East Caribou, Aroostook..NE ×
East Corinna, Penobscot....C ×
East Corinth, Penobscot... C ×
East Dedham, Hancock..... S ×
● East Deering, Cumberl'dSW ×
East Denmark, Oxford...SW ×
East Dixfield, Franklin.....W ×
East Dixmont, Penobscot...C ×
● East Dover, Piscataquis...C 122
East Eddington, Penobscot..C ×
East Edgecomb, Lincoln.....S 125
East Exeter, Penobscot.......C 90
East Fairfield, Somerset....W ×
East Franklin, Hancock.....S ×
East Friendship, Knox.......S ×
East Fryeburgh, Oxford.. SW ×
East Gray, Cumberland.. SW ×
East Hampden, Penobscot.. C ×
East Harpswell, Cumberl'dSW ×
● *East Hebron*, Oxford...SW ×
East Hebron, Oxford......SW ×
● East Hiram, Oxford..... SW ×
East Holden, Penobscot.....C ×
East Jackson, Waldo..........S ×
East Jefferson, Lincoln......S ×
East Knox, Waldo ....S ×
East La Grange, Penobscot. C ×
East Lamoine, Hancock.....S ×
● East Lebanon, York.... SW ×
East Limington, York .... SW ×
East Lincoln, Penobscot.... C ×
● **East Livermore, And'c'n SW** 1,506
East Livermore Mills, And'n SW ×
East Lowell, Penobscot.......C ×
● *East Lyndon*, Aroostook NE ×
East Machias, Washington.. E 1,637
East Madison, Somerset.... W ×
East Madrid, Franklin..... W ×
East Mercer, Somerset.... SW ×
East Monmouth, Kennebec SW ×
East Mount Vernon, Ken'c SW ×

Maine

East New Castle, Lincoln....S ×
● East Newport, Penobscot. C ×
East New Portland, Somer'tW 65
East New Sharon, Franklin W ×
East Northport, Waldo......S ×
● East North Yarmouth, Cumberland.............. SW ×
Easton, Aroostook........ NE 978
East Orland, Hancock.........S ×
East Orrington, Penobscot.. C 225
East Otisfield, Cumberland SW ×
East Outlet, Piscataquis.... C ×
East Palermo, Waldo........S ×
East Parsonfield, York....SW ×
East Perham, Aroostook. NE ×
● East Peru, Oxford...... SW ×
East Pittston, Kennebec.. SW ×
● East Poland, An'scog'n..SW ×
Eastport, Washington.......E 4,908
East Raymond, Cumberl'dSW ×
● East Rumford, Oxford..SW ×
East Sangerville, Piscataquis C ×
East Searsmont, Waldo......S ×
East Sebago, Cumberland. SW ×
East Steuben, Washington.. E ×
East Stoneham, Oxford...SW ×
East Sullivan, Hancock......S 375
● East Sumner, Oxford... SW 66
East Surry, Hancock........ S ×
East Thorndike, Waldo......S ×
East Troy, Waldo ....S ×
East Turner, Androscoggin SW ×
● *East Turnout*, Kennebec SW ×
East Union, Knox...........S ×
East Vassalborough, K'bec SW 225
● *East Waldoboro*, Knox...S ×
East Wales, Androscoggin SW ×
East Washburn, Aroosto'k NE ×
● East Waterboro, York.. SW ×
East Waterford, Oxford.. SW ×
● East Wilton, Franklin... W 325
East Winn, Penobscot.......C ×
East Winthrop, Kennebec SW ×
● Eaton, Washington........E 374
Eddington, Penobscot.......C 729
Eden, Hancock...............S 1,916
Edes' Falls, Cumberland..SW ×
Edgecomb, Lincoln...........S 749
● *Egerys Mill*, Hancock.....S ×
Egypt, Hancock...............S ×
● Eliot, York.............. SW 1,463
Ellingwood's Corner, Waldo S ×
● **Ellsworth**, Hancock....S 4,804
○ Ellsworth Falls, Hancock. S 240
Elmwood, Knox...............S ×
● Embden, Somerset.......W 579
Embden Centre, Somerset.. W ×
Emery's Mills, York......SW ×
● *Empire Road*, Androsc'n SW ×
● Enfield, Penobscot...........C 769
Epping, Washington.........E ×
● Etna, Penobscot.............C 646
Etna Centre, Penobscot.....C ×
Eureka, Kennebec...........SW ×
Eustis, Franklin..............W 321
Exeter, Penobscot..............C 939
Exeter Mills, Penobscot.......C 30
Fairbanks, Franklin......... W ×
● Fairfield, Somerset...... W 3,510
Fairfield Centre, Somerset. W 120
● *Fair Grounds*, Andr'sc'n SW ×
● Falmouth, Cumberland. SW 1,580
Falmouth Foreside, Cu'b'l'd SW ×
● *Falmouth Sta.*, C'berl'd SW ×
● *Farmingdale*, Kennebec SW 821
● **Farmington**, Franklin W 1,243
Farmington Falls, Franklin W 200
Fayette, Kennebec...........SW 649
Fayette Corner, Kenebec. SW ×
Ferry Village, Cumberl'd SW 1,179
● *Fishers*, Penobscot....... C ×
Five Islands, Sagadahoc.. SW ×
Flagstaff, Somerset.........W 87
Flagstaff Junc., Somerset..W ×
● *Fobes*, Waldo.............. S ×
Forest City, Washington.... E 287
● Forest Station, Wash'ton. E ×
● Fort Fairfield, Ar'stook NE 3,526
Fort Kent, Aroostook.....NE 1,829
Fort Point, Waldo..........S ×
Fort Popham, (see Phippsb'g) ×
Fortune Rock, York.......SW ×
● *Foss Siding*, Penobscot...C ×
● Foxcroft, Piscataquis.....C 1,726
Frankfort, Waldo............S 1,099
Franklin, Hancock............S 1,264
● *Franklin Road*, Hancock.S ×
Freedom, Waldo............ S 510

Freeman, Franklin.........W	464
● Freeport, Cumberland..SW	2,482
Frenchville, Aroostook... NE	2,560
Friendship, Knox..........S	877
Frye, Oxford..............SW	×
● Fryeburgh, Oxford..... SW	495
Fryeburgh Centre, Oxford SW	68
● *Fuller Road*, Oxford...SW	×
● Gardiner, Kennebec.... SW	5,491
Garland, Penobscot......... C	973
● *George's River*, Knox......S	×
Georgetown, Sagadahoc...SW	849
● Gilbertville, Oxford.....SW	×
● Gilead, Oxford...........SW	336
Gilman, Piscataquis.......SW	×
Glenburn, Penobscot........C	583
Glenwood, Aroostook..... NE	183
Globe, Knox...............S	×
Golden Ridge, Aroostook. NE	×
● *Golders*, Androscoggin..SN	×
Goodale's Corner, PenobscotC	×
Good Will Farm, Kenneb'cSW	×
Goodwin's Mills, York....SW	200
● Gorham, Cumberland...SW	2,888
Gouldsborough, Hancock....S	1,709
Grafton, Oxford...........SW	98
GrandLakeStream, W'h'gt'nE	404
Grange, Waldo..............S	×
Granite, Hancock...........S	×
● *Granite Siding*, KenebecSW	×
Grant Isle, Aroostook.....NE	964
● *Gravel Pit*, CumberlandSW	×
● Gray, Cumberland......SW	1,517
Gray Corner, CumberlandSW	×
Great Chebeague Island, (see Cumberland)	×
Great Pond, Hancock.......S	×
● Great Works, Penobscot..C	×
● Greenbush, Penobscot.... C	659
● Greene, Androscoggin..SW	885
GreeneCorner, A'droscog'nSW	×
Greenfield, Penobscot.......C	231
● Green Lake, Hancock.....S	×
Green's Landing, Hancock..S	185
Green Vale, Franklin...... W	52
● Greenville, Piscataquis....C	781
Greenville Junc., Pisc'taquisC	×
Greenwood, Oxford.......SW	727
● *Grove Station*, York....SW	×
Groveville, York..........SW	×
● Guilford, Piscataquis......C	1,023
● *Hackett's Siding*, Penobs'tC	×
Haines Landing, Franklin..W	×
Haines Meadow, York.... SW	×
Haley, Lincoln..............S	×
● *Half Way*, Somerset.....W	×
Halldale, Waldo.............S	
● *Halletts*, Cumberland...SW	×
● Hallowell, Kennebec....SW	3,181
● *Hall's*, Penobscot..........C	×
Hamlin, Aroostook.........NE	612
Hamlin Plantation, Ar't'kNE	484
*Hammond Plantat'n*P'bscotC	×
Hampden, Penobscot........C	2,484
Hampden Centre, Penobscot C	390
Hampden Corner, Penobscot C	450
● Hancock, Hancock........S	1,190
Hancock Point, Hancock....S	×
Hanover, Oxford..........SW	21[illegible]
Harbor, Oxford......... ..SW	×
Harborside, (see Castine)	×
● Harding, Cumberland...SW	×
● *Harmons*, Cumberland. SW	×
Harmony, Somerset........ W	704
Harpswell Centre, Cumb'dSW	1,766
Harrington, Washington.... E	1,150
Harrison, Cumberland.... SW	1,071
● Hartford, Oxford....... SW	689
● Hartland, Somerset...... W	974
● *Harwards*, Sagadahoc.. SW	×
Hastings, Oxford..........SW	×
Haynesville, Aroostook... NE	280
Head Tide, Lincoln..........S	×
Hebron, Oxford............SW	600
● Hebron Station, Oxford.SW	×
Henderson, Piscataquis..... C	×
Hermon, Penobscot.........C	1,282
● Hermon Centre, Penobs'otE	×
● Hermon Pond, Penobscot C	×
● Hersey, Arookstook.....NE	151
● *Highland*, Penobscot..... E	×
● *Hillside*, Cumberland...SW	×
Hillside, Franklin...........W	×
● *Hink's L'd'g*, Penobscot.. C	×
● Hiram, Oxford..........SW	1,063
Hodgdon, Aroostook......NE	1,113
● Holden, Penobscot........C	609
● Holeb, Somerset..........W	27
Hollis, York...............SW	[illegible],278
● Hollis Centre, York.....SW	55
Holt's Mills, Penobscot......C	×
Hope, Knox.................S	641
● **Houlton**, Aroostook..NE	4,015
● *Houstons*, Penobscot......C	×
Howard, Piscataquis........ C	285
● *Howard's Siding*, Pisca'qisC	×
Howes Corner, Androscog'nSW	×
Howland, Penobscot.........C	171
● *Hoxie's Siding*, Somerset. W	×
● *Hoyt's*, Kennebec.......SW	×
Hudson, Penobscot..........C	510
Hull's Cove, Hancock....... S	×
Hunnewell's Pt., (seePhippsb'g)	×
● *Hurds*, Aroostook...... NE	×
Hurricane Island, Knox.....S	266
● Iceboro, Sagadahoc..... SW	×
● *Icepond*, Oxford........SW	×
Indian Point, Hancock......S	×
Indian River, Washington..E	88
Indian Rock, Franklin.....W	×
Industry, Franklin........ W	545
● *Ingalls Road*, Oxford.. SW	×
Intervale, Cumberland....SW	×
Island Falls, Aroostook... NE	223
Isle au Haut, Hancock.......S	206
Ilesboro, Waldo..............S	1,006
Islesford, Hancock..........S	×
● *Jackman*, Somerset......W	×
Jackmantown, Somerset... W	217
● *Jacks*, Sagadahoc.......SW	×
Jackson, Waldo..............S	522
● Jay, Franklin............ W	1,541
Jefferson, Lincoln...........S	1,391
Jemtland, Aroostook......NE	×
Jerusalem Plant'n, Franklin W	18
Joice, Lincoln................S	×
Jonesborough, Washington. E	624
Jonesport, Washington.... .E	1,917
● Katahdin Iron Works, Piscataquis..................... C	76
Keen's Mills, And'coggin. SW	×
Kenduskeag, Penobscot.....C	566
Kennebago Lake, Franklin W	×
● Kennebunk, York......SW	3,172
● Kennebunk Beach, YorkSW	×
● Kennebunk Port, York.SW	2,196
Kent's Hill, Kennebec.....SW	×
Kezar Falls, (see Porter)....	×
Kezar Falls, York ....SW	125
Kineo, Piscataquis..........C	×
Kingfield, Franklin........ W	601
● Kingman, Penobscot......C	671
Kingsbury, Piscataquis......C	205
Kittery, York..............SW	2,864
● Kittery Depot, York....SW	×
Kittery Foreside, (see Kittery)	×
● *Kittery Junction*, York.SW	×
● Kittery Point, York.....SW	210
Knightsville, Cumberland.SW	700
Knox, Waldo................. S	657
● *Knox*, Waldo............ S	×
Knox Center, Waldo........S	×
● Knox Station, Waldo......S	×
Kossuth, Washington....... E	×
● LaGrange, Penobscot..... C	721
● *Laings*, Penobscot.........C	×
● *Lake Anasagunticook*, Oxford.....................SW	×
● *Lake House*, Hancock .....S	×
Lakeshore, Kennebec..... SW	×
● Lakeside, Kennebec.... SW	×
● Lake View, Piscataquis...C	×
● Lambert Lake, Washingt'nE	152
Lambs Corner, Kennebec.SW	×
Lamoine, Hancock...........S	726
Lamoine Beach, Hancock...S	×
Larone, Somerset.......... W	×
Larrabee, Washington...... E	×
● *Lawrence's Mills*, Kene'cSW	×
Lebanon, York............SW	1,263
Lee, Penobscot..............C	929
● Leeds, Androscoggin....SW	999
● *Leeds Cross'g*, Androsc'nSW	×
● Leeds Junc., Androsc'n.SW	×
Levant, Penobscot...........C	880
● Lewiston, AndroscogginSW	21,701
● Lewiston Junc., Andru'nSW	×
Lexington, Somerset........W	199
● *Libby's*, Androscoggin..SW	×
Liberty, Waldo..............S	835
Lily Bay, Piscataquis........C	11
Limerick, York............SW	966
Limestone, Aroostook.....NE	933
Limington, York..........SW	1,092
● Lincoln, Penobscot.........C	1,756
● Lincoln Centre, Penobscot C	210
Lincoln Plantation, OxfordSW	59
Lincolnville, Waldo..........S	1,361
Linekin, Lincoln.............S	×
Linneus, Aroostook....... NE	965
● Lisbon, Androscoggin...SW	1,585
LisbonCentre, AndroscogginSW	×
● LisbonFalls, AndroscogginSW	3,120
Litchfield, Kennebec...... SW	1,126
LitchfieldCorners, KennebecSW	×
Litchfield Plains, KennebecSW	×
● *Littleboro*, AndroscogginSW	×
Little Chebeague Island, (see Cumberland)	×
● *Littlefields*, Waldo.........S	×
● *LittleRiver*, AndroscogginSW	3,120
Littleton, Aroostook...... NE	924
Livermore, Androscoggin.SW	1,151
Livermore Centre, An'sgnSW	×
● LivermoreFalls, An'sgn. SW	1,500
● Locke's Mills, Oxford...SW	124
Logan, Aroostook..........NE	×
● *Long Beach*, York......SW	×
Long Island, Cumberland.SW	×
● *Long Pond*, Somerset....W	53
Long Village, York...... SW	×
Lovell, Oxford............SW	853
Lowell, Penobscot............C	439
● Lowelltown, Franklin....W	49
LowerGrantIsle, AroostookNE	×
● *Low's Bridge*, Piscataquis C	×
Lubec, Washington.......... E	2,069
Ludlow, Aroostook....... NE	375
● *Lygonia*, Cumberland..SW	×
Lyman, York..............SW	854
Lynchville, Oxford.........SW	×
Lyndon, Aroostook....... NE	×
● *McKenzie's*, Hancock.....S	×
Machias, Washington.....E	2,035
● Machias Port, WashingtonE	1,437
● *Mackamp*, Somerset.....W	×
Macwahoc, Aroostook.....NE	216
Madawaska, Aroostook.. NE	1,[illegible]51
● Madison, Somerset....... W	1,[illegible]15
Madison Bridge, (see Madison)	×
Madison Centre, Somerset..W	181
Madrid, Franklin...........W	441
Magolloway Plantation, Oxford.......................SW	79
Mainstream, Somerset..... W	×
Mallison Falls, CumberlandSW	×
Maloy, Aroostook.........NE	×
Manchester, Kennebec....SW	612
Mansur's Mills, Aroostook NE	×
Maple, Piscataquis..........C	×
Maple Grove, Aroostook..NE	×
Mapleton, Aroostook......NE	832
Maplewood, York.........SW	×
● Maranacook, Kennebec.SW	×
Mariaville, Hancock.........S	271
Marion, Washington........ E	90
Marlboro, Hancock.......... S	×
● *Marshall's*, AndroscogginSW	×
Marshfield, Washington.. SW	299
Mars Hill, Aroostook......NE	837
Martinsville, Knox...........S	600
● *Maryland Ridge*, York.SW	×
Masardis, Aroostook......NE	250
Mason, Oxford.............SW	80
Matinicus, Knox..............S	196
● Mattawamkeag, PenobscotC	633
● *Mattocks*, Cumberland. SW	×
Maxfield, Penobscot C	134
Mayfield, Somerset..........W	74
Maysville Centre, AroostookNE	×
● *Meadow Brook*, Penobscot C	×
● Mechanic Falls, Androscoggin...................... SW	2,500
Meddybemps, Washington.. E	156
Medford, Piscataquis.........C	306
Medford Centre, PiscataquisC	×
Medomak, Lincoln...........S	×
Medway, Penobscot..........C	653
Mercer, Somerset...........W	584
● *Merrill's*, Androscoggin SW	×
● *Messalonskee*, Kennebec SW	×
Mexico, Oxford........... SW	355
Middle Dam, Oxford......SW	×
● *Middletown*, Penobscot...C	×
● Milford, Penobscot.........C	835
Millbridge, Washington......E	1,963
● *Mill Creek*, Penobscot.... C	×
● *Mill Road*, Cumberland SW	×
● Milltown, Washington.... E	×
● *Mill Village*, Franklin... W	×
● Milo, Piscataquis..........C	1,029

Place	
● *Milo Junction*, PiscataquisC	×
Milton Plantation, Oxford SW	211
● *Mine Meadow*, Androscoggin.....SW	×
Minot, Androscoggin....SW	1,355
● *Moluncas*, Aroostook...NE	77
Monarda, Aroostook.......NE	×
Monhegan, Lincoln.........S	90
● Monmouth, Kennebec..SW	1,362
Monroe, Waldo.............S	1,079
Monroe Centre, Waldo......S	×
● Monson, Piscataquis...... C	1,237
● *Monson Junc.*, PiscataquisC	×
● Montague, Penobscot.....C	×
Monticello, Aroostook.... NE	1,132
Montsweag, Sagadahoc....SW	×
Montville, Waldo............S	1,049
● *Moody's*, Penobscot...... C	×
● Moosehead, Piscataquis...C	×
Moose River, Somerset.....W	170
Moro, Aroostook.......... NE	199
Morrill, Waldo.............S	460
Morrisons Corner, KennebecSW	×
Moscow, Somerset..........W	422
Mount Abram, Franklin...W	×
Mount Abram Junc, Franklin.......W	×
Mount Chase, Penobscot....C	284
Mount Desert, Hancock.....S	1,355
● Mount Desert Ferry, Hancock.............S	×
● *Mount Hope*, Penobscot..C	×
Mount Vernon, Kennebec SW	940
Mousam Pond, York.......SW	×
Mouse Island, Lincoln.......S	×
Murray, Aroostook........NE	×
Muscongus, Lincoln.........S	123
● *Muscongus Bay*, Lincoln. S	×
Myra, Penobscot........... C	×
Naples, Cumberland......SW	846
Nealy's Corner, Penobscot..C	846
Neazie, Penobscot.......... C	×
● *Nequasset*, Sagadahoc..SW	×
Newburgh, Penobscot.......C	867
NewburghCentre, PenobscotC	×
Newburgh Village, PenobscotC	×
● New Castle, Lincoln.......S	1,282
Newfield, York............SW	796
● New Gloucester, Cumberland....................SW	1,234
● *Newhall*, Cumberland..SW	×
New Harbor, Lincoln.......S	×
New Limerick, Aroostook NE	567
● Newport, Penobscot.......C	1,188
New Portland, Somerset....W	1,034
Newry, Oxford............SW	343
New Sharon, Franklin.....W	1,064
New Sweden, Aroostook..NE	707
New Vineyard, Franklin...W	660
● Nobleborough, Lincoln....S	947
● *Norlands*, AndroscogginSW	×
● Norridgewock, Somerset. W	1,656
North Amity, Aroostook..NE	×
● North Anson, Somerset..W	1,454
North Appleton, Knox......S	×
North Auburn, And'sc'g'nSW	×
North Baldwin, C'mb'rl'd SW	×
North Bangor, Penobscot...C	×
North Bath, Sagadahoc....SW	×
● North Belgrade, K'n'becSW	×
● North Berwick, York...SW	1,803
North Blue Hill, Hancock...S	×
North Boothbay, (see Boothbay)	×
North Bradford, Penobscot. C	×
North Bradford Sta., Penobscot........................C	×
North Brewer, Penobscot...C	×
NorthBridgton, CumberlandSW	300
North Brooklin, Hancock...S	×
North Brooksville, Hancock.S	×
● *North Brownville*, Pisca's C	×
North Buckfield, Oxford..SW	×
● NorthBucksport, Hancock S	×
North Carmel, Penobscot...C	×
North Castine, Hancock.....S	×
NorthChesterville, Franklin W	×
North Cornville, Somerset. W	×
North Cushing, Knox.......S	×
North Cutler, Washington..E	×
North Deer Isle, Hancock...S	×
North Dexter, Penobscot...C	×
North Dixmont, Penobscot. C	×
North East Carry, Piscata's. C	19
Northeast Harbor, Hancock.S	×
North Edgecomb, Lincoln...S	×
North Ellsworth, Hancock..S	×
North Fairfield, Somerset..W	×
North Falmouth, Cumb'd SW	×
North Fayette, Kennebec.SW	×
Northfield, Washington.....E	143
North Freeman, Franklin..W	×
North Fryeburgh, Oxford SW	×
North Garland, (see Garland)	×
North Gorham, CumberlandSW	×
North Gray, Cumberland. SW	×
NorthGreene, AndroscogginSW	×
North Guilford, Piscataquis C	×
● North Hancock, Hancock.S	×
North Harpswell, Cumb'd.SW	×
North Haven, Knox.........S	552
North Hermon, Penobscot..C	×
North Hollis, York........SW	×
North Hope, Knox.........S	×
North Isleborough, Waldo..S	×
● North Jay, Franklin.....W	32
North Kennebunk, York. SW	×
North Lamoine, Hancock...S	×
North Lebanon, York.....SW	×
North Lee, Penobscot.......C	×
● North Leeds, Andros'n. SW	×
North Limington, York.. SW	×
● North Lincoln, Penobscot C	×
North Linneus, (see Linneus)	×
North Livermore, Andr'n SW	×
North Lovell, Oxford.....SW	×
North Lubec, Washington.. E	×
North Lyndon, Aroostook NE	×
North Madison, Somerset..W	×
North Mariaville, Hancock.S	×
NorthMonmouth, KennebecSW	×
North Monroe, Waldo.......S	×
North Newburgh, PenobscotC	×
North New Castle, Lincoln..S	200
North Newport, Penobscot. C	×
NorthNewPortland, SomersetW	303
North Newry, Oxford.... SW	×
North Nobleboro, Lincoln...S	×
North Norway, Oxford... SW	×
North Orland, Hancock.....S	×
● NorthOrrington, PenobscotC	×
North Palermo, Waldo......S	×
North Paris, Oxford...... SW	110
North Parsonfield, York..SW	×
North Penobscot, Hancock. S	×
North Perham, Aroostook NE	×
North Perry, Washington...E	×
North Pittston, Kennebec SW	×
Northport, Waldo...........S	691
Northport Camp Ground, Waldo......................S	×
North Pownal, Cumberl'd SW	×
North Raymond, Cumb'l'dSW	×
North Rumford, Oxford..SW	×
North Scarborough, C'm'l'dSW	×
North Searsmont, Waldo....S	×
North Searsport, Waldo.....S	×
North Sebago, Cumberla'dSW	×
North Sedgwick, Hancock..S	×
North Shapleigh, York....SW	275
NorthSidney, Kennebec..SW	×
● *North Street*, Kennebec.SW	×
North Troy, Waldo..........S	×
North Turner, Androsc'ginSW	×
North Turner Bridge, Androscoggin ....SW	×
North Union, Knox.........S	×
North Vassalboro, Ken'b'cSW	1,000
North Vienna, Kennebec. SW	×
North Waldoborough, Lin'lnS	×
North Warren, Knox........S	×
North Waterborough, Yo'kSW	×
North Waterford, Oxford.SW	110
North Wayne, Kennebec..SW	200
North West Harbor, (seeOrland)	×
North Whitefield, Lincoln...S	360
North Windham, Cumbl'dSW	×
North Windsor, KennebecSW	×
North Winterport, Waldo...S	×
North Woodstock, Oxford SW	×
North Woodville, Penobs't..C	×
North Yarmouth, C'mb'l'dSW	709
● *North Yarmouth*, Cumberland ....SW	827
Norton, Piscataquis........C	827
● Norway, Oxford.........SW	928
Norway Lake, Oxford.....SW	×
Notch, Franklin..............W	×
Number One, Aroostook..NE	×
Number Fourteen Plantat'n, Washington...............E	112
Oakfield, Aroostook.......NE	720
● Oakland, Kennebec......SW	2,044
● *Oakland Farm*, York...SW	×
Oak Point, Hancock..........S	×
● Ocean Park, York......SW	×
Ocean Point, Lincoln........S	×
Oceanville, Hancock........S	×
Ogunquit, York...........SW	×
● Olamon, Penobscot.......C	×
● Old Orchard, York......SW	877
● Old Town, Penobscot......C	5,312
● *Onawa*, Piscataquis.......C	×
Oraomo, Penobscot..........C	×
Orff's Corner, Lincoln.......S	×
Orient, Aroostook..........NE	244
Orland, Hancock............S	1,390
Orland Station, Hancock...S	×
● Orneville, Piscataquis.....C	492
● Orono, Penobscot..........C	2,790
● Orrington, Penobscot......C	1,406
Orrington Centre, PenobscotC	1,600
Orr's Island, Cumberland.SW	300
Otis, Hancock...............S	239
Otisfield, Cumberland.....SW	838
● *Otis Falls*, Franklin......W	×
Otisfield Gore, Ch'mberl'd SW	×
Otter Creek, Hancock.......S	×
Owl's Head, Knox...........S	×
Oxbow, Aroostook........NE	×
OxBow Plantat'n, Aro'st'kNE	94
● Oxford, Oxford.........SW	1,455
● *Packard Road*, Oxford.SW	×
Palermo, Waldo.............S	887
Palermo Centre, Waldo......S	×
● *Palmers*, Penobscot.......C	×
● Palmyra, Somerset........W	1,004
Paris, Oxford............SW	266
Parker's Head, Sagadahoc SW	×
● *Parkhurst's*, Aroostook NE	×
Parkman, Piscataquis.......C	813
Parlin Pond, Somerset......W	30
Parsonsfield, York........SW	1,398
● *Parsons*, York..........SW	×
● Passadumkeag, PenobscotC	343
Pattagumpus, Penobscot....C	×
Patten, Penobscot............C	936
● Pea Cove, Penobscot......C	×
Peak's Island, Cumberla'dSW	×
● *Pejepscot*, Sagadahoc....SW	×
Pemaquid, Lincoln...........S	×
Pemaquid Beach, Lincoln...S	×
Pembroke, Washington.....E	1,514
● *Penney's*, Cumberland . SW	×
Penobscot, Hancock.........S	1,313
● *Penobscot Junc.*, Penobs'tC	×
Perham, Aroostook....... NE	438
● *Perley's Mills*, Cu'berl'dSW	×
Perry, Washington..........E	945
● Peru, Oxford............SW	692
Phillips, Franklin...........W	1,394
Phipsburgh, Sagadahoc... SW	1,396
● *Pierce's*, Penobscot.......C	×
● Pine Point, CumberlandSW	×
● *PinePointBeach*, C'mb'dSW	×
Piscataquis Falls, (seeEnfield)	×
● Pishon's Ferry, Ken'becSW	×
● Pittsfield, Somerset...... W	2,503
Pittson, Kennebec.........SW	1,2.1
Plantation No 14, Washingt'nE	184
● Pleasantdale, Cumberl'dSW	300
Pleasant Point, Knox........S	×
Pleasantville, Knox.........S	×
Plymouth, Penobscot....... C	689
Poland, Androscoggin.... SW	2,472
● *Pollard Brook*, PenobscotC	×
Poor's Mills, Waldo.........S	×
Popham Beach, Sag d'hoc SW	×
Portage, Aroostook....... NE	×
Portage Lake Plantation, Aroostook..............NE	140
Port Clyde, Knox............S	300
Porter, Oxford.............SW	1,015
● **PORTLAND**, Cumb'dSW	36,425
Pownal, Cumberland......SW	[illegible]
● *Pownal*, Cumberland...SW	×
● Presque Isle, Aroostook. NE	3,046
Prentiss, Penobscot.........C	401
PresumpscotFalls, (seeFalmouth)	×
Pretty Marsh, Hancock..... S	×
Pride'sCorner, CumberlandSW	6,600
Princeton, Washington......E	1,027
Prospect, Waldo.............S	697
Prospect Ferry, Waldo......S	×
Prospect Harbor, Hancock..S	275
Prout's Neck, Cumberl'ndSW	×
Pulpit Harbor, Knox.........S	×
Quinn's Mills, Piscataquis...C	×
● Randolph, Kennebec... SW	1,281
Rangeley, Franklin........ W	616
● *Rankins Mill*, Oxford.. SW	×
Raymond, Cumberland... SW	927

Razorville, Knox............S ×
Readfield, Kennebec.......SW 1,176
● Readfield Depot, K'neb'cSW ×
Red Beach, Washington.... E ×
Redington, Franklin....... W ×
Redington Mills, Franklin. W 28
Reed Plantation, Aro'st'k. NE 202
● *Reed's Pond*, Hancock....S ×
Revere, Somerset.......... W ×
● Richmond, Sagadahoc.. SW 3,082
Richmond Camp Ground, Sagadahoc.............SW ×
Richmond Corners, S'g'd'cSW ×
● *Richville*, Cumberland..SW ×
Riggsville, Sagadahoc.....SW ×
Riley, Oxford..............SW 40
Ripley, Somerset........... W 478
● Riverside, Kennebec.....SW ×
● *River Switch*, Penobscot..C ×
Roach River, Piscataquis....S ×
Robbinston, Washington....E 787
● *Roberts*, Aroostook..... NE ×
Robie, Aroostook......... NE ×
● **Rockland**, Knox........S 8,174
Rockport, Knox.............S 2,150
Rockville, Knox.............S ×
Rome, Kennebec..........SW 500
Roque Bluff, Washington....E 154
Ross' Corners, York...... SW ×
Round Pond, Lincoln....... S ×
● *Rowe's* Androscoggin...SW ×
Roxbury, Oxford......... SW 222
Roxie, Aroostook.......... NE ×
Rumford, Oxford......... SW 898
Rumford Centre, Oxford..SW ×
Rumford Point, Oxford...SW ×
● Sabattus, Androscoggin.SW ×
SabbathdayLake, Cumb'l'dSW ×
Saccarappa, Cumberland..SW 6,800
● **Saco**, York............SW 6,075
● *Saco River*, York.......SW ×
Saint Albans, Somerset.... W 1,206
Saint David, Aroostook.... NE ×
Saint Francis, Aroostook. NE 461
Saint George, Knox.........S 2,491
Saint John, Aroostook....NE 226
Salem, Franklin............W 218
Salisbury Cove, Hancock....S ×
● *Sand Hills*, Piscataquis...C ×
● *Sand Pit*, Cumberland..SW ×
Sandy Bay, Somerset...... W ×
● *SandyCreek*,CumberlandSW 200
Sandy Point, Waldo........ S ×
Sanford, York............ SW 4,201
● Sangerville, Piscataquis...C 1,236
● *SangervilleSta.*,PiscataquisC ×
● *Sargent's*, Waldo.........S ×
Sargentville, Hancock...... S ×
● Scarborough, Cumb'la'dSW 1,794
● *ScarboroughCrossing*, Cumberland..................SW ×
● *Scates*, Aroostook.......NE ×
● *Seabury*, York...........SW ×
Seal Cove, Hancock..........S ×
Seal Harbor, Hancock.......S ×
Searsmont, Waldo............S 1,[illegible]44
Searsport, Waldo...............S 1,60[illegible]
Seawall, Hancock.............S ×
● Sebago, Cumberland....SW [illegible]61
● SebagoLake, CumberlandSW [illegible]2
Sebec, Piscataquis............C [illegible]
● Sebec Station, Piscataquis.C [illegible]
● Seboois, Penobscot..........C [illegible]
Sedgwick, Hancock ....S [illegible]
● *Sewall's Tank*, Cu'berl'dSW ×
Shapleigh, York. ....SW [illegible]68
● Shawmut, Somerset......W ×
Sheepscott Bridge, Lincoln..S 200
Sherman, Aroostook.......NE 909
Sherman Mills Aroostook NE 175
● *Shirley*, Piscataquis.......C 291
Shirley Mills, Piscataquis... C 303
● *Shuy*, Androscoggin......SW ×
Sidney, Kennebec.........SW 1,334
Sidney Centre, (see Sidney) .. ×
Silver Ridge Plantation, Aroostook................NE 195
● Silver's Mills Penobscot..C ×
Simpson's Corner, PenobscotC ×
Six Mile Falls, Penobscot... C ×
● **Skowhegan**, Somerset W 5,068
● *Sligo*, Cumberland.......SW ×
Small Point, Sagadahoc...SW ×
Smithfield, Somerset....... W 479
● *Smith's*, Penobscot....... C ×
Smithton, Waldo............ S ×
Smyrna, Aroostook....... NE 303
Smyrna Mills, Aroostook..NE ×
Snow Corner, Penobscot.... C ×
Snow's Falls, Oxford......SW ×
● Solon, Somerset............W 977
Somerville, Lincoln..........S 453
Sorrento, Hancock...........S ×
Sound, Hancock..............S ×
South Acton. York........SW ×
South Addison, Washington E ×
South Albion, Kennebec..SW ×
South Andover, Oxford...SW ×
South Atkinson, PiscataquisC ×
● *SouthAuburn*,A'drosc'nSW ×
South Bancroft,Aroostook NE ×
South Beddington,W'sh'ton.E ×
● South Berwick, York...SW 3,434
● SouthBerwickJunc.,Y'kSW ×
South Bethel, Oxford..... SW ×
South Blue Hill, Hancock...S ×
● South Brewer, Penobscot.C ×
South Bridgton, Cum'land SW 308
South Bristol, Lincoln........S ×
South Brooks, Waldo........S ×
South Brooksville, Hancock S ×
South Buxton, York.......SW ×
South Carthage, Franklin.. W ×
South Casco, Cumberland.SW ×
South Chesterville, Fr'kl'n. W ×
South China, Kennebec...SW ×
South Corinth, Penobscot...C ×
South Cushing, Knox........S ×
South Danville, An'drosc'nSW ×
South Deer Isle, Hancock...S 207
South Dover, Piscataquis....C ×
South Dresden, Lincoln..... S ×
South Durham, A'dsrosc'nSW ×
South Eliot, York...........SW ×
● *South End*, Penobscot....C ×
South Etna, Penobscot...... C ×
South Exeter, Penobscot.... C 35
South Freeport,Cm'b'rla'dSW ×
● South Gardiner,Ken'becSW ×
South Gouldsborough, H'n'kS ×
South Hancock, Hancock... S ×
South Harpswell,Cum'l'ndSW ×
South Hiram, Oxford..... SW ×
South Hodgdon, (see Hodgdon) ×
South Hollis, York........SW ×
South Hope, Knox.......... S ×
South Hudson, Penobscot...C ×
South Jefferson, Lincoln.... S ×
● SouthLaGrange,PenobscotC ×
South Leeds, AndroscogginSW ×
South Levant, Penobscot....C ×
● South Lewiston, A'dro'n SW ×
South Liberty, Waldo....... S ×
South Limington, York...SW ×
● South Lincoln, Penobscot. C ×
SouthLitchfield,Kennebec SW ×
SouthLiverpool,AndroscogginSW ×
South Lubec, Washington...E ×
SouthMoluncus,Aroostook NE ×
SouthMonmouth,KennebecSW ×
South Montville,Waldo.......S ×
● SouthNewburgh,PenobscotC ×
● South New Castle, LincolnS ×
South Norridgewock,S'm't. W ×
● SouthOrrington,PenobscotC 325
South Otisfield,Cumberland.SW ×
● South Paris, Oxford.... SW 1,164
South Parsonfield, York.. SW ×
South Penobscot, Hancock.. S ×
South Poland, AndroscogginSW ×
Southport, Lincoln........... S 533
South Portland,Cumberland SW ×
South Presque Isle, Ar'st'kNE ×
South Robbinston, WashingtonE ×
South Rumford, Oxford.. SW ×
South Sanford, York......SW ×
● South Sebec, Piscataquis. E ×
● *South Sebec Sta.*,PiscataquisC 220
South Smithfield, Somerset W ×
South Solon, Somerset......W ×
South Somerville, Lincoln.. S ×
South Springfield,PenobscotC ×
South Stetson, Penobscot... C ×
South Strong, Franklin....W ×
South Surry, Hancock.......S ×
South Thomaston, Knox..... S 1,534
South Turner,Androscoggin SW ×
South Union, Knox......... S ×
South Vassalborough, Kennebec...................SW ×
South Waldborough, Lin'n.. S ×
● South Warren, Knox......S ×
● *South Waterboro*,York.SW ×
South Waterford,Oxford..SW 120
South West Harbor, HancockS ×
South Weston, (see Weston).. ×
● South Windham,Cumberl'dSW ×
South Windsor, Kennebec SW ×
South Woodstock, Oxford SW ×
● *Spokane*, Penobscot...... C ×
Sprague's Falls,WashingtonE ×
Sprague's Mill, Aroostook NE ×
Springfield, Penobscot...... C 677
● Springvale, York........SW 4,164
Spruce Head, Knox..........S ×
Squirrel Island, Lincoln......S ×
Staceyville, Penobscot........C 250
Standish, Cumberland.... SW 1,841
Stark, Somerset..............W 766
● Steep Falls,CumberlandSW 239
Stetson, Penobscot...........C 618
Steuben, Washington........E 982
● *Stevens*, Aroostook..... NE ×
Stevens Plains AroostookNE ×
Stickney Corner, Knox.......S ×
● *Stickney River*, C'mbe'dSW ×
Stockton Springs, Waldo....S 1,149
Stoneham, Oxford........ SW 322
Stow, Oxford..............SW 291
● *Stowells*, Androscoggin.SW ×
Stratton, Franklin..........W ×
● Stockland's Ferry, Androscoggin.......................SW ×
Strong, Franklin........... W 627
● Stroudwater, Cumberl'dSW ×
Sullivan, Hancock...........S 1,379
Summit, Franklin..........W ×
Summit, Hancock............S ×
● *Summit*, Penobscot.......C ×
Summit, Piscataquis........ C ×
Sumner, Oxford............SW 901
Sunset, Hancock.............S ×
Surry, Hancock..............S 986
Swan's Island, Hancock.....S 632
Swanville, Waldo............S 689
Sweden, Oxford.......... ..SW 338
Temple, Franklin..........W ×
Temple, Franklin........... W 470
Tenant's Harbor, Knox......S 625
● *The Bridge*, Franklin.....W ×
● *The Elms*, York.........SW ×
● *The Falls*, Hancock.......S ×
The Forks, Somerset.......W 195
● *The Pond*, Waldo.........S ×
● Thomaston, Knox...........S 3,009
Thompson Lake,C'mberl'dSW ×
● *Thompson's Point*, Cumberland.....................SW ×
● Thorndike, Waldo.........S 589
Tilden, Hancock............S ×
Titcomb, Aroostook........NE ×
● *Todd's Farm*, WashingtonE ×
● Togus, Kennebec........ SW ×
● *Tomah*, Washington......E ×
Topsfield, Washington...... E 375
● Topsham, Sagadahoc....SW 1,394
Township, Penobscot........C ×
Township, Piscataquis......C 6
Township, Hancock.........S ×
Tremont, Hancock...........S 2,036
Trenton, Hancock............S 528
Trescott, Washington....... E 485
Trevett, Lincoln..............S ×
Troy, Waldo...............S 868
Turner, Androscoggin.... SW 2,01[illegible]
Turner Centre, Androsc'n.SW 35[illegible]
Union, Knox................ S 1,436
● Unity, Waldo...............S 922
Upper Dam, Oxford......SW ×
Upper Frenchville, Ar'st'kNE ×
Upper Gloucester, C'mbl'dSW ×
Upper Madawaska, Aroo'kNE ×
● Upper Stillwater,Penobsc'tC 875
Upton, Oxford........... SW 232
Van Buren, Aroostook.....NE 1,168
● Vanceborough, Washi'g'nE 870
● Vassalborough, Ken'bec SW 2,052
● Veazie, Penobscot.........C 650
Vienna, Kennebec.......... SW 495
Vinal Haven, Knox...........S 2,617
Waite, Washington...........E 159
● Waldo, Waldo..............S 581
● Waldoboro, Lincoln........S 3,505
Waldo Centre, (see Waldo)... ×
Waldo Station. Waldo.......S ×
Wales, Androscoggin......SW 45[illegible]
Wallagrass, Aroostook.... NE 595
● *Walnut Hill*, Cumberl'dSW ×
Walpole, Lincoln ....S 296
Waltham, Hancock...........S 242
● Warren, Knox...............S 2,03[illegible]

● *Warren Road*, Oxford..SW ×
Washburn, Aroostook.....NE 1,091
Washington, Knox..........S 1,230
● Waterborough, York...SW 1,357
Waterborough Centre, YorkSW ×
Waterford, Oxford.........SW 1,001
● Waterville, Kennebec...SW 7,107
Wayne, Kennebec..........SW 775
Webb, Franklin..............W ×
Webb's Mills, CumberlandSW ×
Webster, Androscoggin...SW 951
● *Webster*, Penobscot.........C 135
Week's Mills, Kennebec.. SW ×
Welchville, Oxford........SW 250
Weld, Franklin...............W 885
Wellington, Piscataquis.....C 584
● *Wells*, York............SW 2,029
● Wells, York...............SW ×
● Wells Branch, York....SW ×
● Wells Depot, York......SW ×
● *Wescustogo*, Cumberla'dSW ×
Wesley, Washington........E 227
West Appleton, Knox.........S ×
West Athens, Somerset.... W ×
West Auburn, Androscr'n SW ×
● West Baldwin, Cumber'dSW ×
West Bangor, Penobscot.... C ×
West Bath, Sagadahoc....SW 307
● West Bethel, Oxford....SW ×
● *West Biddeford*, York..SW ×
West Bowdoin, Sagadahoc SW ×
West Bridgton, Cumberl'dSW ×
West Bristol, Lincoln.........S ×
Westbrook, Cumberland..SW 6,632
● *Westbrook Junc.*, Cumb'dSW ×
West Brooklin, Hancock....S ×
West Brooksville, Hancock.S ×
West Brownfield, Oxford. SW ×
West Buxton, York.......SW ×
West Camden, (see Camden). ×
West Charleston, Penobscot C ×
West Corinth, Penobscot....C ×
West Cumberland, Cumb'dSW ×
West Denmark, Oxford...SW ×
● *West Dover*, Piscataquis.. C ×
West Dresden, Lincoln.......S ×
West Durham, Androsco'nSW 118
West Eden, Hancock.........S ×
West Ellsworth, Hancock... S ×
West Enfield, Penobscot.....C ×
West Falmouth, Cumber'dSW ×
West Farmingdale, Kenn'cSW ×
● WestFarmington, F'ank'nW ×
Westfield, Aroostook......NE 10.
West Forks, Somerset......W ×
West Forks Plant'n, Som'tW 146
West Frankfort, (seeFrankf't) ×
West Franklin, Hancock...S ×
West Freeman, Franklin...W ×
West Fryeburgh, Oxford. SW ×
West Gardiner, Kennebec.SW 858
West Garland, Penobscot....C 318
West Gorham, CumberlandSW ×
West Gouldsborough, Hanc'kS 275
West Gray, Cumberland...SW ×
West Hampden, Penobscot..C ×
West Hancock, Hancock....S ×
West Harpswell, Cumber'dSW ×
West Harrington, Washing'nE ×
West Hollis, York..........SW ×
West Holden, Penobscot....C ×
West Jonesport, Washingt'nE ×
● West Kennebunk, York SW ×
West Lebanon, York...... SW 91
West Leeds, AndroscogginSW ×
West Levant, Penobscot....C ×
West Lubec, Washington....E ×
West Madison, Somerset... W ×
● West Minot, Androscog'nSW 210
West Mount Vernon, Ken'cSW ×
West Newfield, York..... SW ×
West Oldtown, Penobscot...C ×
Weston, Aroostook..........NE 404
West Palmyra, Somerset... W ×
● West Paris, Oxford..... SW 232
West Pembroke, Washingt'nE ×
West Penobscot, Hancock...S ×
● West Peru, Oxford......SW ×
West Pittsfield, Somerset.. W ×
West Poland, Androscog'nSW ×
Westport, Lincoln...........S 451
● *Westport*, Sagadahoc... SW ×
● West Pownal, Cumb'la'dSW ×
West Ripley, Somerset.....W ×
West Rockport, Knox.......S ×
● West Scarborough, C'ml'dSW ×
West Searsmont, Waldo.....S ×

West Sidney, Kennebec...SW ×
West's Mills, Franklin... . W ×
West Southport, Lincoln.....S ×
West Sullivan, Hancock.....S ×
West Sumner, Oxford.... SW ×
West Tremont, Hancock....S ×
West Trenton, Hancock.....S ×
West Troy, Waldo...........S ×
● *Westville*, Franklin...... W ×
West Waldoborough, LincolnS ×
West Warren, Knox.........S ×
West Washington, Knox.....S ×
West Windsor, Kennebec. SW ×
West Winterport, Waldo.... S ×
West Woolwich, Sagad'hocSW ×
Whidden's Farm, Washing'nE ×
Whitefield, Lincoln...........S 1,215
● White Rock, Cumberl'd SW ×
● *White's*, Kennebec.......SW ×
White's Corner, Waldo......S ×
Whiting, Washington........ E 393
Whitneyville, Washington...E 413
Wigginsville, Penobscot.... C ×
Willard, Cumberland...... SW ×
Willimantic, Piscataquis.... C 446
● *Willis Crossing*, FranklinW ×
Wilson's Mills, Oxford....SW ×
● Wilton, Franklin......... W 1,622
Windham, Cumberland.. SW 2,216
Windham Centre, Cumbe'dSW 94
Windsor, Kennebec.......SW 852
● Winn, Penobscot...........C 936
● Winnecook, Waldo.........S ×
Winnegance, Sagadahoc...SW ×
● Winslow, Kennebec.....SW 1,814
● Winslow's Mills, Lincoln...S 2,006
Winter Harbor, Hancock....S 1,800
Winterport, Waldo...........S 1,926
● *Winterport Ferry*, Hanc'kS ×
● Winthrop, Kennebec....SW 2,111
Winthrop Centre, Kenne'cSW ×
● Wiscasset, Lincoln.........S 1,733
● Woodford's, Cumberla'dSW ×
Woodland, Aroostook.....NE 885
● *Woods*, Kennebec...... SW ×
Woodstock, Oxford....... SW 859
Woodville, Penobscot....... C 242
● Woolwich, Sagadahoc...SW 1,007
● *Wright's Siding*, Saga'ocSW ×
● Wytopitlock, Aroostook NE ×
● Yarmouth, Cumberland SW 2,098
● Yarmouthville, Cumbe'dSW ×
● York, York... ....SW 2,444
● York Beach, York......SW ×
York Corner, York.......SW ×
York Village, York.......SW ×

MARYLAND.

COUNTIES.	INDEX.	POP.
Allegany	NW	41,571
Anne Arundel	C	34,094
Baltimore	N	72,909
Calvert	S	9,860
Caroline	E	13,903
Carroll	N	32,376
Cecil	NE	25,851
Charles	S	15,191
City of Baltimore	N	434,439
Dorchester	SE	24,843
Frederick	NW	49,512
Garrett	NW	14,213
Harford	N	28,993
Howard	C	16,269
Kent	NE	17,471
Montgomery	C	27,185
Prince George's	C	26,080
Queen Anne's	E	18,461
St. Mary's	S	15,819
Somerset	SE	24,155
Talbot	E	19,736
Washington	NW	39,782
Wicomico	SE	19,930
Worcester	SE	19,747
Total		1,042,390

TOWN. COUNTY. INDEX. POP.

Abell's Wharf, (see Leonardtown)............ ×
● Aberdeen, Hartford...... N 448
● *Aberdeen Station*, Harford N ×
Abingdon, Harford......... N 200
Academy, Garrett........ NW ×
Accident, Garrett........ NW 100
Accokeek, Prince George's. C 210
● Adamstown, Frederick NW 100
Adelina, Calvert.............S ×
Agner Caroline..............E 15
Agricultural College, (see College Park)............ ×
● Aikin, Cecil............NE 30
● Airey's, Dorcester.......SE 40
● Alberton, Howard........ C 562
Alderton, Allegany........NW ×
Aldino, Harford.............N ×
● Alesia, Carroll..............N 50
● *Alexander Junction*, Prince George's...............C ×
Allen, Wicomico............SE 125
Allen's Fresh, Charles.......S 45
Allibone, Harford...........N 48
Alpha, Howard..............C ×
● Altamont, Garrett......NW 25
American Corners, Caroline E 30
● Ammendale, Prince George'sC ×
Anderson, (see Hanoverville). ×
Andersontown, Caroline.... E 20
● ANNAPOLIS, Anne Arundel.............C 7,604
● Annapolis Junc., Howard..C 86
● *Annapolis Road*, BaltimoreN ×
Anthony, Caroline...........E 30
● *Antietam*, Washington. NW 1,200
Antietam, Washington... NW ×
Appleton, Cecil.............NE 30
Aquasco, Prince George's...C 100
● Araby, Frederick...... NW 24
● Arbutus, Baltimore...... N ×
● *Arcadia*, Baltimore...... N ×
Arden, Somerset............SE 30
● Arlington, Baltimore..... N 300
Armiger, Anne Arundel..... C 12
● Arnold, Anne Arundel....C 10
● *Arrow City*, Anne Arundel C ×
● *Arundel*, Prince George's.C ×
● *Ardwick*, Prince George's C ×
Asbury, Anne Arundel......C 6
Ash, Washington.........NW ×
● Ashland, Baltimore........N 300
● *Ashland*, Queen Anne's...E 15
Ashton, Montgomery........C 25
● Athel, Wicomico.........SE 30
● *Avalon*, Baltimore....... N ×
Avenel, Montgomery........C 67
Avilton, Garrett..........NW 15
● Avondale, Carroll..........N 60
Avondale, (see Level) .... ×
Bachman's Mills, Carroll....N 60
● *Back River*, Baltimore... N ×
● *Bacon Hill*, Cecil.........NE ×
● *Bailey's*, Baltimore.......N ×
Bakersville, Washington. NW 25
● *Bald Friar*, Cecil.........NE ×
Baldwin, Baltimore.......N 175
● *Baldwin*, Cecil. ....NE ×
● *Balls Cross Roads*, Washington..................NW ×
● BALTIMORE, City of Baltimore.................N 434,439
Bank, Cecil..................NE 100
● Barclay, Queen Anne's... E 200
Bark Hill, Carroll...........N ×
● *Barksdale*, Cecil.........NE ×
Barksdale, Cecil............NE 20
● Barnesville, Montgomery. C 40
Barrellville, Allegany... NW ×
● Barren Creek Springs, Wicomico..................SE 250
● *Barrick*, Carroll..........N ×
Barritt, (see Winston)...... ×
Barry, (see Brunswick)...... ×
● Bartholows, Frederick. NW ×
● *Bartholows*, Washingt'n NW ×
Barton, Allegany..........NW 1,850
Bartonsville, Frederick.. NW ×
● *Basket*, Worcester.......SE ×
Battle, Calvert..............S 30
Bayard, Anne Arundel......C ×
Baynesville, Baltimore......N 30
● Bay Ridge, Anne Arundel C 30
Bay View, Cecil..........NE 50
● *Bay View*, Baltimore.....N ×
Beallsville, Montgomery.... C 20
Beal's Mill, Montgomery....C ×
Beane, Montgomery......... C ×
Beaver Creek, Washington NW 125
Beaver Dam, Baltimore.... N 241

Place	Pop.
Beckleysville, Baltimore...N	800
● *Beechfield*, Baltimore.....N	×
● *Beeler's Summit*, Wash'n NW	×
Beggs, Carroll.......N	15
● **Bel Air**, Harford.......N	1,416
Bel Air Road, (see Gardenv'e)	×
● Bel Alton, Charles.........S	75
Belcamp, Harford..........N	×
Belfast, Baltimore..........N	150
Bellevue, Talbot.............E	30
Belmont, Somerset........SE	×
Bells Mills, (see Beane)........	×
● Beltsville, Prince George's C	60
● *Belvidere*, Cecil.......... NE	×
Benedict, Charles............ S	126
Benevola, Washington.....NW	100
Benfield, Anne Arundel.....C	24
● Bengies, Baltimore........N	×
Benson, Hartford............N	×
● Bentley's Springs, B'tim're N	50
Berean, Baltimore..........N	24
Berkeleyville, (see Conowingo)	×
● Berlin, Worcester....... SE	974
Berrett, Carroll............W	60
Bertha, Calvert..............S	×
Bestpitch, Dorchester.......SE	20
● *Best Pitches Landing*, Dorchester.......SE	30
● *Best's Gate*, Anne Arundel C	×
Bethesda, Montgomery.......C	50
● Bethlehem, Caroline.......E	50
Betterton, Kent...........NE	30
● Beulah, Dorchester.......SE	50
Bier, Allegany..............NW	×
● *Bigg's*, Queen Anne's......E	×
● *Big Gunpowder*, Baltimo'e N	×
Bird Hill, Carroll...........N	35
Birdsville, (see South River)..	×
Bishop, Worcester......... SE	30
Bishop's Head, Dorchester. SE	200
Bishopville, Worchester.....SE	275
Bittinger, Garrett........ NW	12
Bivalve, Wicomico.........SE	50
Bixler, Carroll.............N	44
Black Horse, Harford........N	25
● *Black Oak*, Allegany...NW	×
Black Rock, Baltimore..... N	180
● Black's, Kent.......... NE	30
● Bladensburgh, Pr'ce Geo's C	503
Blakistone, (see St. Clement's Bay)	×
Bloom, Carroll..............N	36
● *Bloomfield*, Talbot.........E	×
● Bloomington, Garrett..NW	295
● *Bloomsbury*, Baltimore.. N	×
● *Blue Mount*, Baltimore.. N	×
● Blue Mountain, Wash'n NW	×
Blue Mountain House, Was'n NW	×
Blythedale, Cecil.........NE	150
Bolivar, Frederick.........NW	75
Bond's Wharf, (see Sotterly)	×
● *Boones*, Anne Arundel....C	×
Boonsborough, Washingt'n NW	766
Boothby Hill, Harford...... N	30
● *Borden Shaft*, Allegany NW	×
● Boring, Baltimore.........N	100
Bosley, Baltimore.......... N	×
Botte..ll, Howard...........C	×
Bottle Run, Allegany.......NW	90
Bowens, Calvert........... S	×
● Bowie, Prince George's...C	100
Boxiron, Worcester.........SE	30
● Boyd's, Montgomery C	10
Bozman, Talbot.............E	95
Braddock, Frederick.....NW	×
Bradenbaugh, Harford........N	×
Bradshaw, Baltimore....... N	100
● *Bradshaw*, Baltimore.... N	×
● *Brady*, Allegany........NW	50
● Branchville, Prince Geor's S	10
● Brandywine, Prince Geor's C	60
● Breathedsville, Washi'n NW	100
Brentland, (see McConchie).	×
Brent's Wharf, (see McConchie)	×
Brick Church Sta., (see Leeland)	×
● *Bridewell*, Howard....... C	×
Bridgeport, Frederick....NW	×
Bridgeport, (see Sharpsburg)..	×
Bridgetown, Caroline.......E	50
Brighton, Montgomery......C	500
Brightseat, Prince George's.C	30
● *Brightside*, Baltimore....N	×
Bristol, Anne Arundel....... C	150
Broadfording, Washingt'n NW	24
Broad Run, Frederick....NW	25
Broadwater, (see Sudley)...	×
Broadway, (see Brooklandv'e)	×
Brookeville, Montgomery...C	175

Place	Pop.
● Brooklandville, Baltimore N	15
● Brooklyn, Anne Arundel..C	700
Brookview, Dorchester.... SE	60
Broome's Island, Calvert....S	40
Broome's Wharf, (see Saint Mary's City)........	×
● *Brownings*, Garrett....NW	×
Browningsville, Montgome'y C	40
● Brownsville, Washing'n NW	75
● Bruceville, Carroll........N	100
Brummel, Carroll.......... N	×
● Brunswick, Frederick..NW	250
Bryantown, Charles..........S	100
● Buckeysto'n, Frederick NW	800
● Buck Lodge, Montgomery C	×
Bucktown, Dorchester.....SE	1,100
Budd's Creek, St. Mary's....S	25
Buena Vista, Calvert........S	×
Buena Vista Springs, Washington........NW	×
Burch, Calvert............ S	×
Burdette, Montgomery......C	×
Burkittsville, Frederick..NW	273
Burnt Mills, Montgomery...C	10
Burrisville, Queen Anne's.. E	×
Burrsville, Caroline.........E	100
● *Burtner's*, Washington NW	×
Burtonsville, Montgomery.. C	25
● *Busey's*, Baltimore.......N	×
○ Bush River, Harford..... N	×
Butler, Baltimore...........N	50
Butler's Tavern, (see Obligation)	×
● *Buxton's*, Prince George's C	30
● *Buzzard Rock*, Baltimore N	×
Bynum, Harford...........N	×
● *Bynum*, Harford........ N	×
Cabin Creek, Dorchester...SE	30
Cabin John, Montgomery... C	120
Cabin Run, Allegany.... NW	×
California, St. Mary's........S	50
Calvary, Harford...........N	100
Calvert, Cecil...............NE	100
● *Calverton*, City of Baltim'e N	1,000
● *Cambria*, Harford....... N	×
● **Cambridge**, Dorches'r SE	4,192
● *Camden Junc.*, Baltimore N	×
● *Camden Station*, Baltim'e N	×
Campbell, Worcester...... SE	20
● *Camp Parole*, Anne Arun'l C	×
Campbelltown, Worcester. SE	24
Camp Springs, Prince Geor's C	24
● *Canal*, Cecil............ NE	×
Canal Tunnel, Allegany..NW	15
● *Canton*, City of Baltimore N	×
Capitola, Wicomico........SE	50
● *Capital View Park*, M't'g'y C	×
Carlos, Allegany.........NW	×
Carmichael, Queen Anne's..E	75
Carny, Baltimore........... N	200
● Carroll, Carroll...........N	3,500
● *Carroll*, City of Baltimore N	×
● **Carrollton**, Carroll.........N	200
Carrsville, (see St. Dennis)...	×
Carsin's Run, Hartford.......N	150
● *Carville*, Queen Anne's... E	×
Castleton, Hartford..........N	50
Cathcart, (see Madonna).....	×
Catlin, Queen Anne's.........E	15
● *Catoctin*, Frederick.... NW	60
Catoctin Furnace, Frede'k NW	100
● Catonsville, Baltimore....N	2,115
● Cavetown, Washington. NW	287
Cayot's Corner, Cecil....... NE	30
Cearfoss, Washington.....NW	50
Cecilton, Cecil...............NE	485
Cedar Grove, Montgomery..C	120
Cedar Point, (see Newburg).	×
Cedartown, Worcester.....SE	20
Cedarville, Prince George's. C	×
Cedarville, Prince George's. C	×
● *Centre*, Baltimore........ N	×
Centreville, (see La Plata).. N	500
● **Centreville**, Q. Anne's. E	1,309
Centreville, (see Jarboesville) .	×
Ceresville, Frederick..... NW	×
Chance, Somerset.........SE	30
Chaneyville, Calvert.........S	10
● *Chapel*, Talbot............E	×
Chapel Point, (see Cox's Station)	×
Chaptico, St. Mary's.........S	70
● Charlestown, Cecil......NE	228
Charlesville, Frederick...NW	×
● *Charlton*, Prince George's C	10
Charlotte Hall, St. Mary's... S	150
Charlton Heights, P. Geo's..C	×
● Chase, Baltimore......... N	500
● Chatoolance, Baltimore.. N	×

Place	Pop.
Cheltenham, Prince George's C	100
Chemsonville, Frederick. NW	×
Cherry Hill, Cecil......... NE	400
Chesapeake City, Cecil.... NE	1,155
Chester, Queen Anne's......E	800
Chesterfield, Anne Arundel. C	25
● **Chestertown**, Kent...NE	2,632
Chesterville, Kent.........NE	100
Chestnut Hill, Harford......N	50
● Chewsville, Washington NW	150
● Childs, Cecil........... NE	200
Choptank, Caroline.......... E	40
Chrispin, Charles...........S	×
Chrome Hill, Harford...... N	50
Church Creek, Dorchester. SE	396
Church Hill, Queen Anne's..E	596
Churchton, Anne Arundel.. C	×
Churchville, Harford....... N	175
● *Claggett's*, Washington. NW	×
Claggettsville, (see Damascus).	×
○ *Claiborne*, Talbot......... E	×
● *Claremont*, Baltimore....N	×
Clarksburgh, Montgomery..C	70
Clarkson, Howard...........C	25
Clarksville, Howard..........C	75
Clarysville, Allegany..... NW	×
● Clayton, Harford......... N	75
Clear Spring, Washington NW	800
Clemsonville, Frederick....N	×
Clermont Mills, Harford.....N	20
● *Clifford's*, Baltimore....... N	×
Clifton Factory, (see Great Mills)	×
Clinton, Prince George's.... C	20
Clipper, Baltimore..........N	×
● Cloppers, Montgomery.....C	×
● *Cloud Cap*, Baltimore....N	×
● Cockeysville, Baltimore.. N	400
Cokeland, Dorcester........SE	50
Colburne, Worcester........SE	20
Cold Springs, (see Gavanstown)	×
Cole, Harford............... N	×
● *Colegate Creek*, Baltimore N	×
Coleman, Kent.............. C	50
Colesville, Montgomery..... C	15
● College Park, Prince George's C	30
● College of St. James, Washington..........NW	24
● Collington, Prince George's. C	20
Collin's Wharf, Wicomico. SE	20
○ Colora, Cecil............ NE	250
Colton's Wharf, (see Milestown)	×
Columbia, Howard......... C	10
Compt Mills, (see Finksburg)	×
Compton, St. Mary's.........S	50
Comus, Montgomery..........C	15
Conaway's, Anne Arundel.. C	30
Concord, Caroline...........E	50
Conococheague, Washington NW	40
● Conowingo, Cecil.........NE	200
● *Contee's*, Prince George's. C	×
Cooksey, Charles............S	×
Cooksville, Howard........ C	60
Cooper, Harford............N	×
Coopstown, Harford......... N	80
Copperville, Carroll........N	24
● Corbett, Baltimore.........N	30
Corbin, Worcester.......... SE	20
● Cordova, Talbot...........E	150
Cornersville, Dorcester.... SE	40
Cornfield, (see Point Lookout)	×
● Corriganville, Alleghany NW	20
Costa, Baltimore...........N	×
● *Costen*, Somerset.........SE	×
Cove, (see Fair Haven).......	×
Cove Point, Calvert.......... S	40
● *Coventon*, Baltimore.....N	×
Cowentown, Cecil.......... NE	30
● *Cowpens*, Baltimore......N	×
● *Cox*, Charles.............S	75
Cox's Station, (see Bel Alton)	×
● *Crabster*, Carroll........ N	×
● *Crabtree*, Garrett.......NW	×
Cranberry, Carroll...........N	5
● *Cranberry*, Carroll........N	×
Crapo, Dorcester...........SE	100
Creagerstown, Frederick NW	100
● Cresaptown, Alleghany. NW	50
Cresswell, Harford............N	100
● Crisfield, Somerset....... SE	1,565
● *Crisps*, Howard.......... C	×
● *Cromley's Mountain*, C'il NE	×
● *Cromwell*, Anne Arundel. C	×
Croom, Prince George's.....C	24
● Croom Station, Pr'ceGeo's C	20
Cropley, Montgomery.......C	×
Crosby, Kent..............NE	30
Cross Roads, Charles........S	5

Place	Pop.
● Crownsville, Anne Ar'del. C	86
Crumpton, Queen Anne's E	317
Crystal Falls, Washington NW	×
Cub Hill, Baltimore N	100
Cumberland & Pennsylvania Junction, Allegany N	×
● **Cumberland**, Allegany N	12,729
Cumberstone, Anne Arundel C	×
● *Curtis Bay*, Anne Ar'del. C	×
● *Curtis Bay Junc.*, Baltim'e N	×
Dailsville, Dorcester SE	15
Daisy, Howard C	15
Damascus, Montgomery C	200
Dames Quarter, Somerset SE	1,000
Daniel, Carroll N	68
Dar, Baltimore N	×
● *Darby's*, Montgomery C	×
Dares Wharf, Calvert S	×
Darlington, Hartford N	239
Darnall, Anne Arundel C	48
Darnestown, Montgomery C	75
Davidsonville, Anne Ar'del. C	60
● Dawson, Allegany N	×
Dawsonville, Montgomery C	41
Day, Carroll N	48
Daysville, Frederick NW	×
Dayton, Howard C	25
Deal's Island, Somerset SE	1,800
Deer Creek, Harford N	24
● *Deerfield*, Frederick NW	30
● Deer Park, Garrett NW	179
Delight, Baltimore N	×
Della, Frederick NW	50
Denning's, Carroll N	150
Denton, Caroline E	641
Dentsville, Charles S	38
● Derwood, Montgomery C	60
Dickerson, Montgomery C	50
● *Diggs*, Baltimore N	×
Dills Wharf, (see Wayside)	×
Doncaster, Charles S	50
● Dorsey, Howard C	15
● *Dorsey's Run*, Howard C	×
Double Pipe Creek, Carroll N	125
● Doubs, Frederick NW	40
Doub's Switch, (see Doubs)	×
Doughoregan, Howard C	30
● *Douglas*, Dorchester SE	×
Dover, Baltimore N	×
Downsville, Washington NW	120
Draw Bridge, Dorchester SE	46
Drawbridge, Baltimore N	×
● *Druid*, Baltimore N	×
Drumcliff, St. Mary's S	×
Drum Point, Calvert S	×
Dry Branch, Harford N	×
Dublin, Harford N	200
● *Dublin*, Somerset SE	×
● *Duffield*, Charles S	×
Dulaney's Valley, Baltimore N	×
Dunkirk, Calvert S	25
Dynard, (see St. Clement's Bay)	×
● Eakle's Mills, Washington NW	30
● Earleigh Heights, Anne Arundel C	×
Earleville, Cecil NE	50
East Creek, Somerset SE	60
● *East Garden*, Baltimore N	×
● East New Market, Dor'rS. E	700
● **Easton**, Talbot E	2,939
Eastport, Anne Arundel C	×
Eastview, Carroll N	×
● *Ebbvale*, Carroll N	48
Eckhart Mines, Allegany NW	811
● Eden, Somerset SE	75
● *Eder*, Cecil NE	×
Edesville, Kent NE	75
● Edgemont, Washington NW	40
● Edgewood Harford N	40
Ednor, Montgomery C	32
Edwards Ferry, Mo'tgomery C	10
Edwin, Somerset SE	×
Eklo, Baltimore N	100
Elder, Garrett NW	×
Eldersburgh, Carroll N	150
Eldorado, Dorchester SE	100
Elk Neck, Cecil NE	75
● Elk Ridge, Howard C	702
● **Elkton**, Cecil NE	2,318
● Ellerslie, Allegany NW	260
Ellerton, Frederick NW	100
● **Ellicott City**, Howard C	1,488
Elliott, Dorchester SE	60
Elmer, Montgomery C	×
● Elvaton, Anne Arundel C	×
Elwood, Dorchester SE	30

Maryland

Place	Pop.
● Embla, Baltimore N	×
● Emmitsburg, Frederick NW	844
Emmorton, Hartford N	25
● *Emory Grove*, Baltimore N	×
● *Empire Mills*, Garrett NW	×
Engle's Mills, Garrett NW	100
● Ennalls, Dorchester SE	40
Enterprise, (see Dennings)	×
Erickson, Howard C	×
Ernstville, Washington NW	200
Etchison, Montgomery C	×
Euclid, Washington NW	×
● *Eudowood*, Baltimore N	×
Evna, Baltimore N	24
Ewell, Somerset SE	100
Eylar, Frederick NW	×
Fair Haven, Anne Arundel C	25
Fair Hill, Cecil NE	125
Fairland, Montgomery C	100
Fairlee, Kent NE	100
Fairmount, Somerset SE	250
Fair Play, Washington NW	100
Fairview, Washington NW	40
Fairview, (see Frederick)	×
● *Fairview*, Baltimore N	30
Falls Road, (see Woodberry)	×
● Fallston, Harford N	150
● *Farm*, Baltimore N	×
Farm Creek, Dorchester SE	24
Farmington, Cecil NE	75
Faulkner, Charles S	×
Feagaville, Frederick NW	×
● *Federal*, Baltimore N	×
Federal Hill, Harford N	15
● Federalsburgh, Caroline E	543
Fell's Point, Baltimore N	×
Fenby, Carroll N	×
● *Fenwick*, Montgomery C	×
● *Fern Cliffs*, Harford N	×
Ferry Landing, (see Dunkirk)	×
● *Fiery's Siding*, Washi'ton NW	×
Finchville, Dorchester SE	30
Finksburg, Allegany NW	×
Finksburgh, Carroll N	125
Fishel, (see Harkins)	×
Fishing Creek, Dorchester SE	300
Fishing Point, St. Mary's S	25
Flint Stone, Allegany NW	1,439
Flintville, Harford N	×
Florence, Howard C	25
● Floyd, Garrett NW	36
Ford's Store, Queen Anne's E	1,000
Fords Wharf, Somerset SE	30
● Forest Glen, Montgomery C	45
● Forest Hill, Harford N	200
Forestville, Prince George's C	125
Forest Wharf, (see Oakville)	×
Fork, Baltimore N	75
Fort Foote, Prince George's C	30
Fort McHenry, Baltimore N	×
Fort Pendleton, Garrett NW	×
Fort Washington, Pr. Georg's C	56
Fountain Green, Hartford N	60
Fountain Mills, Frederick NW	25
● *Fountain Rock*, Fred'k NW	×
Four Locks, Washington NW	25
● Fowblesburgh, Baltimore N	×
Fowling Creek, Caroline E	10
Foxville, Frederick NW	150
● *Foy's Hill*, Cecil NE	×
Franklintown, Baltimore N	×
Franklinville, Baltimore N	208
Franklinville, (see Taylorsville)	×
● *Franklinville*, Garrett NW	36
Frazier, Calvert S	×
● **FREDERICK**, Fra'n NW	8,193
● *Frederick Junc.*, F'der'k NW	×
● *Frederick Junc.*, Carroll N	×
● *Frederick Road*, Baltimore N	×
Fredericktown, Cecil NE	48
Freedom, Carroll N	35
● Freeland, Baltimore N	50
● *Frenchtown*, Cecil NE	30
Friendly, Prince George's C	×
Friendship, Anne Arundel C	60
● *Friendship*, Worcester SE	×
● Friendsville, Garrett NW	100
Frizellburgh, Carroll N	200
● *Frost*, Anne Arundel C	×
Frostburgh, Allegany NW	3,804
● Fruitland, Wicomico SE	300
Fullerton, Baltimore N	180
Fulton, Howard C	8
● *Fulton Junc.*, City of Bal'e N	×
● Funkstown, Washi'gton NW	500
Furnace, Harford N	×
● Gaither's, Carroll N	×

Maryland

Place	Pop.
● Gaithersburgh, Montgo'ery C	75
Galena, Kent NE	266
Gales Town, Dorchester SE	275
Galesville, (see Galloway's)	×
Gallant Green, Charles S	108
Galloway's, Anne Arundel C	250
● *Galt*, Carroll N	×
Gamber, Carroll N	100
● *Gambrill's*, Washington NW	×
● Gambrill's, Anne Arundel C	130
● Gapland, Washington NW	×
● *Gap Siding*, Frederick NW	×
Gardenville, Baltimore N	324
Garfield, Frederick NW	40
Garland, Harford N	×
● *Garrett's Mill*, Wash'g'n NW	×
● Garrett Park, Montgomery C	×
Garrison, Baltimore N	×
● *Garrison Forest*, Baltim'e N	×
● *Geddings*, Anne Arundel C	×
Gemmills, Baltimore N	×
George's Great Junc., Allegany NW	×
Georgetown, (see Walkersv'e)	×
Georgetown, Kent NE	50
● Germantown, Mo'tgomery C	70
● *Gerstell*, Allegany NW	×
● *Ginrich's*, Baltimore N	×
● Girdletree, Worcester SE	200
Gist, Carroll N	24
Gittings, Baltimore N	×
Glen, Montgomery C	×
● Glen Arm, Baltimore N	×
● Glenburnie, Anne Aru'del C	×
● Glencoe, Baltimore N	300
Glen Cove, Harford N	150
Glen Echo, Montgomery C	×
Glenelg, Howard C	80
● Glen Falls, Baltimore N	30
Glen Morris, Baltimore W	30
Glenn Dale, Prince George's C	×
Glenville, Harford N	200
Glenwood, Howard C	40
Glymont, Charles S	75
● Glyndon, Baltimore N	311
Golden Hill, Dorchester SE	500
● Golden Ring, Baltimore N	×
● Goldsboro, Caroline E	100
● Golts, Kent NE	65
Goodhope, Frederick NW	×
Goodwill, Worcester SE	30
Gorman, Washington NW	×
● *Gorman*, Garrett NW	400
● *Gorsuch*, Carroll N	×
Gorsuch's Mills, Baltimore N	50
● *Gorsuch Road*, Carroll N	24
Goshen, Montgomery C	80
Govanstown, Baltimore N	900
Governor Run, Calvert S	10
● Graceham, Frederick NW	225
Graceton, Harford N	×
Grafton, (see Forest Hill)	×
Granite, Baltimore N	678
Grantsville, Garrett NW	200
Grave Run Mills, Baltimore N	50
Gray's, (see Ellicott City)	×
● *Gray's*, Howard C	×
Great Falls, Montgomery C	60
Great Mills, St. Mary's S	60
Green, Baltimore N	×
Greenfield Ms., (see Della)	×
Green Hill, Somerset SE	48
● Greenmount, Carroll N	×
Greenock, Anne Arundel C	×
Green Point, (see Cumberland)	×
● Greensborough, Caroline E	902
● Green Spring Furnace, Washington NW	48
● *Green Springs Junc.*, Baltimore N	×
Greenstone, Harford N	60
Greenwood, Baltimore N	60
● *Greenwood*, Baltimore N	×
Griffin, Caroline E	25
Grifton, Montgomery C	×
● Grimes, Washington NW	×
Gross, Allegany NW	×
Grove, Caroline E	20
Guilford, Howard C	200
● *Gunpowder*, Baltimore N	×
● *Gunpowder*, Carroll N	×
Guys, Queen Anne's E	75
Gwinn, Baltimore N	×
Gwynbrook, Baltimore N	×
● *Gwynn's Falls*, Baltimore N	×
Habnab, Somerset SE	30
● **Hagerstown**, Wa's't'n NW	10,118

● *Hagerstown Junction*, Washington ..... N W ×
Haight, Carroll ..... N ×
● *Halethrope*, Baltimore... N ×
Halfway, Washington ..... N W ×
Halls, Prince George's .... C 10
● *Halpine*, Montgomery.... C ×
Hambleton, Talbot ..... E 75
Hammettsville, (see Jarboesv'e) ×
● Hampden, City of Baltim'n'e N 2,500
● Hampstead, Carroll ..... N 521
Hancock, Washington ..... N W 815
Hanesville, Kent ..... N E 100
Hanover Switch, (see Hanoverv'e) ×
● Hanoverville, Howard ..... C 120
Hansonville, Frederick ... N W 50
● *Harewood Park*, Baltimore N ×
● *Harford*, Harford ..... N ×
Harford Furnace, Harford .. N 151
Harford Road, (see Parkville) ×
Harkins, Harford ..... N ×
● *Harleigh*, Baltimore ..... N ×
Harmans, Anne Arundel .... C 72
Harmony, Frederick ..... N W 150
● Harmony Grove, Fred'k N W 20
Harney, Carroll ..... N 125
● *Harper*, Talbot ..... E ×
● *Harrington*, Garrett .... N W ×
Harris Lot, Charles ..... S 35
Harrison, Dorchester ..... SE 20
Harrisonville, Baltimore .... N 60
● *Hartmann's*, Frederick N W ×
● Havre DeGrace, Harford .. N 3,244
● Hayden, Queen Anne's .... E 15
Hazen, Allegany ..... N W 200
Hebbville, Baltimore ..... N ×
Hebron, Wicomico ..... SE 30
● *Hebron*, Wicomico ..... SE ×
Heinsville, Allegany ..... N W ×
Hellen, Calvert ..... S 24
● *Hellman*, Baltimore ..... N ×
● *Hematite*, Caroline ..... E ×
● Henderson, Caroline ..... E 200
● Henryton, Carroll ..... E 24
Hereford, Baltimore ..... N 200
● *Herring Run*, Baltimore. N ×
Hernwood, Baltimore ..... N ×
Hickory, Hartford ..... N 43
Hick's Mill, Prince George's C 20
Highfield, Washington ..... N W 100
High Knob, Frederick .... N W ×
Highland, Howard ..... C 31
Highland, (see Street) ..... ×
● *Highlands*, Prince George's C ×
High Point, Harford ..... N ×
● *Highlandtown Junc.*, Baltimore ..... N 1,200
● *Hillen Station*, Prince Ge's C ×
● *Hills*, Prince George's .... C ×
Hillsborough, Caroline ..... E 171
Hill's Point, Dorchester .... SE 25
Hill Top, Charles ..... S 15
Hobbs, Caroline ..... E 20
● *Hoffman*, Carroll ..... N ×
Hoffmanville, Baltimore .... N 75
Holland's Cor., (see Sandy Spr.) ×
Holland's Island, Dorchest'r SE 30
● *Hollins*, Baltimore ..... N ×
● *Hollofield's*, Baltimore .... N ×
Hollywood, St. Mary's ..... S 15
● Homeland, Baltimore ..... N ×
Homestead, C. of Baltimore. N 900
House's Cut, Allegany .... N W ×
● Hood's Mills, Carroll ..... N 20
Hoopersville, Dorchester .. SE 600
Hoopstown, (see Arlington).. ×
Hope, Queen Anne's ..... E 10
Hopeland, Frederick ..... N W 100
● Hopewell, Somerset ..... SE 100
Hopewell Cross Roads, (see Level) ..... ×
Horn Point, (see Annapolis). ×
Horse Head, Prince George's C 40
Houcksville, Carroll ..... N 31
● Howardsville, Baltimore. N ×
Hoyes, Garrett ..... N W 42
Hudson, Dorchester ..... SE ×
Hughesville, Charles ..... S 25
Hullsville, Baltimore ..... N 486
Hunting Hill, Montgomery .. C 10
Huntingtown, Calvert ..... S 60
● Hurlock, Dorchester ..... SE 75
● *Hursley*, Worcester ..... SE 250
● Hutton, Garrett ..... N W 10
Huyett, Washington ..... N W ×
Hyattstown, Montgomery ... C 150

Maryland

● Hyattsville, Prince Georg's C 1,509
● Hydes, Baltimore ..... N ×
Hynson, Caroline ..... E 20
● *Iglehart's*, Anne Arundel. C ×
● Ijamsville, Frederick .. N W 75
● Ilchester, Howard ..... C 300
Index, Washington ..... N W ×
Indian Springs, Washing'n N W 15
Ingleside, Queen Anne's .... E 1,200
● Ironhill, Cecil ..... N E 25
● Ironshire, Worchester ... SE 60
● *Irving Park*, Howard .... C ×
● *Isaacs*, Howard ..... C ×
Island Creek, Calvert ..... S 30
Issue, Charles ..... S ×
Ivory, Howard ..... C ×
● Jackson, Cecil ..... N E 50
Jackson Mines, (see Lonaconi'g) ×
Jacksonville, Baltimore ..... N ×
Jacobsville, (see Armiger).... ×
James, Dorchester ..... SE 30
Jarboesville, St. Mary's ..... S 78
Jarrettsville, Hartford ..... N 120
Jefferson, Frederick ..... N W 320
Jerusalem Mills, Harford ... N 100
● *Jessop*, Baltimore ..... N ×
Jessup's, Anne Arundel ..... C 20
● *Jessup's Cut*, Howard ..... C 50
Jessup's Station, Howard ... C ×
Jewell, Anne Arundel ..... C 5
Johnsville, Frederick ..... N W 300
Jones, Worcester ..... SE 20
Jones Cross Roads, (see Lappans) ×
● Joppa, Hartford ..... N 75
Kalmia, Hartford ..... N ×
Kearney, Garrett ..... N W 18
● Keedysville, Washington N W 420
● Keep Tryst, Washington N W 350
● *Kellers*, Frederick ..... N W ×
Kemptown, Frederick .... N W 100
● Kennedyville, Kent .... N E 125
● Kensington, Montgomery. C ×
Kent Island, Queen Anne's.. E 1,500
● *Kenwood*, Baltimore ..... N ×
● Keyser, Garrett ..... N W ×
Keysville, Carroll ..... N 32
● *King's Creek*, Somerset .. SE ×
● Kingston, Somerset ..... SE 100
King's Valley, Montgomery. C 18
Kingsville, Baltimore ..... N 75
Kirby's Wharf, Talbot ..... E ×
● Kirkham, Talbot ..... E 20
Kirkwood, (see Prospect).... ×
Kitzmillersville, Garrett.. N W 74
Klej Grange, Worcester .... SE 50
Knoebel, Baltimore ..... N ×
● *Knowles*, Montgomery .... C 6
● Knoxville, Frederick ... N W 319
Kump, Carroll ..... N ×
● Ladiesburgh, Frederick N W 100
● *Lafayette*, Baltimore ..... N ×
● *Lake*, Baltimore ..... N 60
Lakeland, Prince George's.. C ×
● Lake Roland, Baltimore... N ×
Lake Shore, Anne Arundel.. C 6
Lakesville, Dorcester ..... SE 100
● *Lake Youghiogheny*, Garrett ..... N W ×
● *Lampson's*, Kent ..... N E ×
Lamotte, Carroll ..... N ×
Lancaster, (see Sudley) ..... ×
Lancaster Wharf, (see Rock Point) ..... ×
● Lander, Frederick ..... N W 60
● Landover, Prince George's C ×
● Landsdowne, Baltimore .. N ×
Lanhams, Prince George's.. C 60
Lankford, Kent ..... N E 30
● Lantz, Frederick ..... N W 30
Lapidum, Harford ..... N 75
La Plata, Charles ..... S 200
Lappans, Washington ..... N W ×
Lauraville, Baltimore ..... N 180
● Laurel, Prince George's ... C 1,984
Laurel Grove, St. Mary's.... S 50
Lauver, Carroll ..... N ×
Lavender Hill, (see Parkville) ×
Layhill, Montgomery ..... C 42
Laytonsville, Montgomery.. C 100
Leeds, Cecil ..... N E 175
● Leeland, Prince George's.. C 60
Lee's, Howard ..... C ×
Leitersburgh, Washington N W 350
Leon, Anne Arundel ..... C ×
Leonardtown, St. Mary's S 521
● Leslie, Cecil ..... N E 80
Level, Harford ..... N 400

Maryland

Lewistown, Frederick .... N W 270
● Liberty Grove, Cecil .... N E 175
Libertytown, Frederick .. N W 589
● Licksville, Frederick ... N W 40
● Lime Kiln, Frederick .. N W 175
Linchester, Caroline ..... E 20
● *Linden*, Prince George's .. C 60
● Linden, Montgomery ..... C 20
● Lineboro, Carroll ..... N 30
Line Bridge, Harford ..... N 20
Linganore, Frederick ..... N W 60
● Linkwood, Dorchester ... SE 300
● *Linthicum*, Anne Arundel C ×
Linwood, Carroll ..... N 50
Lisbon, Howard ..... C 120
Liverpool Point, Charles.... S ×
Little Orleans, Allegany .. N W 50
● *Little Seneca*, Montgomery C ×
Liverpool Point, (see Nanjemoy) ×
● *Llandaff*, Talbot ..... E ×
Lloyds, Dorcester ..... SE [illegible]
● *Lloyds*, Garrett ..... N W ×
Lochearn, Baltimore ..... N 240
● *Lochiel Mills*, Garrett .. N W ×
Lock No. 27, (see Potomac)... ×
Lock 53, Washington ..... N W ×
● *Lock No. 56*, Washington N W ×
● Lock Raven, Baltimore ... N ×
Locust Grove, Kent ..... N E 75
● *Locust Point*, Baltimore .. N ×
Lodi, Dorchester ..... SE 60
Lombard, Cecil ..... N E 30
Lonaconing, Allegany .... N W 4,595
Long Corner, Howard ..... C 40
● Long Green, Baltimore ... N 25
● *Long Siding*, Carroll ..... N ×
Long Ridge, Worcester .... SE ×
Longville, Carroll ..... N ×
Longwoods, Talbot ..... E 40
Loreley, Baltimore ..... N ×
● Loretto, Somerset ..... SE 20
Lothian, Anne Arundel ..... C 200
● *London Park*, City of Baltimore ..... N ×
Louisville, Carroll ..... N 60
Loveville, St. Mary's ..... S ×
Lower Marlborough, Calvert. S 75
Lower Ocean, Allegany ... N W ×
● *Lowndes*, Allegany .... N W ×
Lowrey, Baltimore ..... N ×
● Loy's, Frederick ..... N W 25
Ludwig, Harford ..... N ×
Luke, Allegany ..... N W ×
Lusby's, Calvert ..... S 90
● Lutherville, Baltimore .... N 663
Lydia, Washington ..... N W ×
● Lynch, Kent ..... N E 30
● *McAleer*, Frederick .... N W ×
McConchie, Charles ..... S ×
McDanieltown, Talbot ..... E 100
McDonough, Baltimore .... N ×
● *McGaw*, Harford ..... N ×
McGinnes, Queen Anne's... E 50
McHenry, Garrett ..... N W 50
● McIntyre, Harford ..... N ×
McKendree, Anne Arundel. C 42
● *McKinzie*, Allegany .... N W ×
McKinstry's Mills, Carroll.. N 75
McMaster, Worcester ..... SE 20
Mackall, Calvert ..... S 36
Macton, Harford ..... N ×
Madison, Dorcester ..... SE 145
Madonna, Harford ..... N 100
● Magnolia, Harford ..... N 75
Malcolm, Charles ..... S 30
● *Mallory's*, Howard ..... C ×
Manassas, Talbot ..... E 25
Mulladien Mills, Queen Anne's E 25
Manchester, Carroll ..... N 273
Manokin, Somerset ..... SE 20
Manor, Baltimore ..... N ×
Manor Lands, Garrett ... N W ×
Mantua Mills, Baltimore ... N ×
● Maple Grove, Carroll ..... N 25
Mapleville, Washington .. N W 24
● Marion Station, Somerset SE 150
● *Marlboro*, Prince George's. C 700
● Marley, Anne Arundel .... C 10
● Marriottsville, Howard .... C 72
Marshall Hall, Charles ..... S 120
Marston, Carroll ..... N 90
Martinsburgh, Montgomery. C 140
Marumsco, Somerset ..... SE 30
● Marydell, Caroline ..... E 200
Maryland Line, Baltimore .. N 100
Mason's Springs, Charles .... S ×
● Massey, Kent ..... N E 125

Mattapony, St. Marys.......S 12
Mattapex, Queen Anne's....E 25
Mattawoman, Charles.......S 10
Matthews, Talbot..........E 30
● Maugansville, Washington. NW 125
Mayberry, Carroll.......... N 150
Maynard Anne Arundel....C ×
Mayo, Anne Arundel........C ×
● Mechanicstown, Fred'k NW 930
Mechanic's Valley, Cecil.. NE 70
Mechanicsville, (see Louisville) ×
Mechanicsville, (see Hickory) ×
Mechanicsville, (see Olney)... ×
Mechanicsville, St. Mary's...S 200
Medford, Carroll...........N 48
Melitota, Kent............NE 60
● Melrose, Carroll.........N 86
● Melvale, Baltimore.......N 60
Mexico, (see Brummel)...... ×
Michaelsville, Harford......N 40
Middlebrook, Montgomery..C ×
● Middleburg, Carroll......N 200
Middle Point, Frederick..NW ×
● *Middle River*, Baltimore. N ×
Middletown, Frederick...NW 667
Midland Junction, Alle'y NW ×
Midland Mines, (see Ocean).. ×
Milestown, St. Mary's.......S 60
● Miller's, Carroll..........N ×
● Millersville, Anne ArundelC 30
● *Millersville*, Baltimore....N ×
Mill Green, Harford........N 40
● Millington, Kent........NE 485
Mills, Washington.........NW ×
Millstone, Washington....NW 100
MillstoneLand'g, (see Jarboesville)...... ×
● *Mill Switch*, WashingtonNW ×
● *Minefield*, Harford.........N ×
Mineral Spring, Garrett.. NW 30
● *Mistletoe Spring*, Prince George's............C ×
● Mitchellville, PrinceGeorge'sC 80
Millwood, (see Upper Marlboro) ×
Mondel, Washington..... NW ×
Monie, Somerset...........SE 70
● Monkton, Baltimore......N 40
● Monocacy, Montgomery.. C ×
● Monrovia, Frederick... NW 100
Montrose, Montgomery..... C 60
● *Morantown*, Allegany..NW ×
● Morgan, Carroll......... N 120
Morganza, St. Mary's........S 10
Moscow Mills, Allegany.. NW 218
Motter's, Frederick...... NW 25
● Mountain Lake Park, Garrett.................. NW 42
Mountain Lock, Washin'n NW ×
● *Mountain Siding*, Wash' NW ×
● Mount Airy, Carroll...... N 450
Mount Carmel, Baltimore.. N 45
● *Mount Clare*, Baltimore.. N ×
● *MountClareJunc.*, BaltimoreN ×
Mount Ephraim, Montgo'eryC 20
Mount Harmony, Calvert....S ×
● Mount Hope, Baltimore.. N ×
Mount Pleasant, (see Beggs) ×
Mount Pleasant, Frederi'kNW 130
Mount Pleas't, (see Maplevi'e) ×
MountSaint Mary's, Fred. NW ×
Mount Savage, Allegany..NW 2,000
● *Mount Savage Junction*, Allegany.........NW 20
Mount Vernon, Somerset..SE 40
Mount Vernon, (see Marston) ×
Mount Vernon Factory, (see Hampden) ×
● Mount Washington, Baltimore.................N 600
Mount Wilson, Baltimore...N ×
● Mount Winans, BaltimoreN 861
Mount Zion, (see Smithsburg) ×
Muddy Branch, (see Darnest'n) ×
Muirkirk, Prince George's..C 90
Mudge, Baltimore.......... N ×
Mullan, Allegany.........NW ×
● *Mullikin*, Prince George's.C 80
Mullinix, Montgomery.....C ×
Murley's Brook, (see Rush).. ×
Muttontown, (see Union Bridge) ×
Mutual, Calvert............S ×
Myersville, Frederick.... NW 150
Nanjemoy, Charles..........S 30
Nanticoke, Wicomico......SE 300
Neavitt, Talbot............E 20
Necker, Baltimore..........N ×
● Newark, Worcester......SE 200
Newburgh, Charles..........S 40
New Germany, Garrett...NW ×
● New Hope, Wicomico....SE 30
New London, Frederick..NW 100
New Market, (see MarylandLine) ×
New Market, Frederick..NW 423
● New Midway, Frederi'kNW 40
Newport, Charles............S 75
● New Windsor, Carroll.... N 414
● *New York Junc.*, Baltim'eN ×
Nichols, Caroline...........E 30
Noble's Mills, (see Darlington) ×
Norbeck, Montgomery......C 50
Norrisville, Harford........ N 102
North Branch, Baltimore...N 100
North Branch, Allegany.NW ×
● North East, Cecil.........NE 1,249
● *North East Quarry*, CecilNE ×
North Keys, Prince George'sC 40
North Point, Baltimore.....N ×
Norwood, Montgomery..... C ×
● *Notch Cliff*, Baltimore.... N ×
● *Notre Dame*, Baltimore.. N ×
Nottingham, Prince George'sC 40
Nutwell, Anne Arundel.... C ×
Nutwell, Charles............S ×
Oak Bluff, (see Mattawoman) ×
Oak Crest, Prince George's .C ×
Oakdale, Montgomery...... C ×
● *Oakington*, Harford...... N ×
● **Oakland**, Garrett.... NW 1,046
Oakland Mills, Howard......C 135
Oaklawn, (see Wheaton).... ×
Oakley, St. Mary's...........S ×
Oak Orchard, Frederick..NW 50
Oaks, St. Mary's...........S ×
Oak Springs, (see Nanjemoy) ×
Oakville, St. Mary's.........S 50
Oakwood, Cecil............NE 20
Obligation, Anne Arundel...C ×
Ocean, Allegany..........NW 600
● Ocean City, Worcester...SE 85
● *Octoraro Junction*, CecilNE ×
● Odenton, Anne Arundel...C 40
● Oella, Baltimore..........N 516
● *Offutt's*, Garrett........NW ×
Offut's Cr. Rds., (see Potomac) ×
Okonoko, Allegany.......NW ×
Oldtown, Allegany....... NW 500
Olive, Frederick..........NW ×
Olney, Montgomery.........C 187
● *Orange Grove*, Baltimore. N ×
Orangeville, Baltimore......N 200
Orangeville, Baltimore......N ×
Oregon, Baltimore..........N 360
Oresaptown, Allegany....NW ×
Oriole, Somerset...........SE 40
Orleans, (see Little Orleans).. ×
● *Osborne*, Harford..........N ×
Overton, Kent........... NE ×
● Owing's Mills, Baltimore. N 212
Oxen Hill, Prince George's..C ×
Oxford, (see Waverly)........ ×
● Oxford, Talbot...........E 1,135
● *Outre Park*, Montgomery.C ×
● *Paint Branch*, Pri'ce Ge'sC ×
Paradise, Harford..........N ×
● *Paradise*, Baltimore.... N ×
Parkersburg, Allegany....NW 297
Park Hall, St. Mary's........S 25
Park Mills, Frederick....NW 72
● Parkton, Baltimore.......N 300
Parkville, Baltimore.......N 120
● Parole, Anne Arundel.... C 30
Parran, Calvert..............S ×
● Parsonsburgh, WicomicoSE 150
Patapsco, Carroll.......... N 75
● *Patapsco*, Howard........C ×
● *Patapsco Neck*, (seeNorthPoint) ×
● *Patapsco June.*, Howard.C ×
Patterson's, Allegany.... NW ×
● Patuxent, Anne Arundel..C 72
● *Patuxent*, Anne Arundel .C 75
Patuxent City, (see Hughesv'e) ×
Pearl, Frederick......... NW ×
Pekin, Allegany...........NW 424
● Peninsula Junc., Somers'tSE 25
Penmar Park, Washing'nNW ×
Penwood Park, Baltimore. N ×
Percy Siding, Allegany.. NW ×
Perry Hall, Baltimore...... N 60
● Perryman, Harford.....NW 271
● Perryville, Cecil..........NE 344
Petersville, Frederick....NW 135
● *Pfiels*, Howard...........C ×
● *Philips*, Baltimore........ N ×
Philo, Washington........NW ×
● Philopolis, Baltimore.....N 30
● Phoenix, Baltimore.......N 150
Pikesville, Baltimore...... N 250
Pimlico, (see Mt. Washington) ×
Pindell, Anne Arundel......C ×
Pine Orchard, Howard......C 45
Pinesburgh, Washington. NW ×
● Piney Creek, Carroll......N 50
Piney Grove, Allegany... NW 36
Piney Point, St. Mary's......S 90
Pints, Allegany............W ×
Piscataway, Prince George's.C 72
Pisgah, Charles.............S 15
Pittsville, Wicomico.......SE 350
Pivot Branch, Cecil.......NE ×
● Plane No. 4, Frederick..NW 25
Pleasant Hill, Cecil........NE 30
Pleasant Valley, Carroll.... N 110
Pleasantville, Harford...... N 100
Pleasant Walk, Frederick. NW 40
Plum Point, Calvert.........S 20
Plyer, Montgomery......... C ×
● Pocomoke City, Worces'rSE 1,866
Point Lookout, St. Mary's...S ×
● Point of Rocks, FrederickN 364
Pomfret, Charles............S ×
Pomona, Kent..............N 50
Pomonkey, Charles..........S 50
Pompey Smash, (see ValeSummit) ×
Poolesville, Montgomery....C 250
● Pope's Creek, Charles.....S 60
● *Poplar*, Baltimore.........N ×
Poplar Springs, Howard.....C 45
● Port Deposit, Cecil......NE 1,908
Porter's, Carroll........... N 24
Port Republic, Calvert...... S 50
Port Tobacco, Charles....S 132
● *Potomac*, Allegany.....NW ×
Potomac, Montgomery.......C 15
Powellville, Wicomico.....SE 200
Powhatan, Baltimore....... N 310
Preston, Caroline...........E 350
● Price's Station, Q'nAnne's E 20
● *Primrose*, Baltimore..... N ×
Princeville, Baltimore...... N ×
Prince Fredericktown, Calvert..................S 456
● *Princepio*, Cecil.........NE ×
● **Princess Anne**, Sum'tSE 865
Principio, Cecil........... NE 40
Principio Furnace, Cecil...NE 175
Proctor, Baltimore.........N ×
Prospect, Harford.......... N 50
Prospect Hill, (see W. Friendship) ×
Protection, Garrett.......NW ×
Providence Mills, Cecil... NE 400
● Pumphrey, Anne Arundel C 10
Puncheon Land., Summit.SE 36
Purdum, Montgomery.......C ×
● *Putney& Riddle*, Howard.C ×
● Pylesville, Harford....... N 38
Quantico, Wicomico....... SE 300
● *Quarantine*, Baltimore...N ×
● QueenAnne, Queen Anne'sC 100
Queenstown, Queen Anne's. C 350
● *Queponco*, Worcester....SE ×
Quince Orchard, Montgo'eryC ×
● *Raisins*, Anne Arundel...C ×
Randallstown, Baltimore... N 200
● Randolph, Montgomery .. C ×
Raspeburg, (see Gardenville) ×
● Rawlings, Allegany.... NW 50
● *Ray's Quarry*, Mont'y.... C ×
Rayville, Baltimore.........N 35
Reckford, Baltimore........N 210
Redland, Montgomery.......C 15
● *Red Oak*, Worcester.....SE ×
● *Reel's Mill*, Frederick..NW ×
Rehobeth, Somerset....... SE 50
● *Reese's*, Baltimore........N ×
Reiffs, Washington........ NW ×
Reisterstown, Baltimore.... N 660
Relay Station, Baltimore...N 419
Reliance, Dorchester.......SE 85
● *Retreat Grove*, Freder'k NW ×
● *Revells*, Anne Arundel....C ×
Rhode River. (see Mayl)..... ×
● Rhodesdale, Dorchester. SE ×
● Rider, Baltimore......... N 5
Ridge, St. Mary's...........S ×
● Ridgely, Caroline.........E 215
Ridgeville, Frederick.... NW 25
Ringgold, Washington.....NW 170
● Rising Sun, Cecil.........NE 384
● Riverdale, Prince Geo's.. C ×
Riverside, Baltimore........N ×
Riverside, Charles...........S 42

● *Riverside*, Talbot.........E ×
River Springs, St. Mary's....S ×
Riverton, Wicomico....... SE 100
Riverview, Anne Arundel.. C ×
● *Robert's*, Allegany..... NW ×
Roberts, Queen Anne's.....E 50
● Robinson, Anne Arundel. C ×
● Rockawalking, Wicomico SE 30
Rock Creek, Montgomery... C ×
● *Rock Church*, Cecil..... NE ×
Rockdale, Baltimore........N 60
● *Rockdale*, Baltimore..... N ×
Rock Hall, Kent.......... NE 75
● *Rockland*, Baltimore.....N ×
Rock Point, Charles........S 50
● *Rock Run*, Cecil......... NE ×
Rock Springs, Cecil....... NE 50
● **Rockville**, Montgomery. C 1,568
● Rocky Ridge, Freder'k. NW 53
Rocky Spring, (see Huyett) .. ×
● *Rodger's*, Frederick....NW ×
Roe, Queen Anne's.........E 15
● *Rogers*, Baltimore........N ×
● Rohrersville, Washing'n NW 100
Roller, Carroll..............N ×
Rolphs, Queen Anne's.......E 25
● Rosaryville, Prince Geo's..C 60
● Rosedale, Baltimore...... N 30
● Rossville, Baltimore ....N 240
● *Round Bay*, Anne Ar'del. C ×
Rowlandsville, Cecil ...... NE 309
Roxbury Mills, Howard..... C 35
● Royal Oak, Talbot........ E 125
Rush, Allegany...........NW ×
Ruthsburgh, Queen Anne's..E 25
Rutland, Anne Arundel..... C 20
● *Ruxton*, Baltimore .... N ×
● Sabillasville, Frederick NW 200
St. Augustine, Cecil........ NE 50
St. Clement's Bay, St. Mary's.S 75
● St. Denis, Baltimore......N 419
● St. George, Baltimore.... N 24
St. George's Island, (see Piney Point .... ×
St. Inigoes, St. Mary's....... S 40
St. James, (see Monkton).... ×
● *St. James*, Washington. NW ×
St. Joseph, Baltimore ...... N 60
St. Leonard's, Calvert....... S 50
St. Margaret's, Anne Ar'd'l..C 30
● St. Martin's, Worcester..SE 40
St. Mary's City, St. Mary's.. S 60
● St. Michael's, Talbot...... E 1,329
● *St. Paul's*, Baltimore .... N ×
St. Peter's, Somerset...... SE ×
Salem, Dorchester .... SE 20
● **Salisbury**, Wicomico..SE 2,905
Sam's Creek, Carroll.........N 30
Sand Gates, St. Mary's ...... S ×
● *Sandy Hook*, Wash'ton. NW 350
Sandy Point, (see Pr. Fred'kt'n) ×
Sandy Spring, Montgomery..C 60
Sandyville, Carroll...........N ×
Sang Run, Garrett........NW 150
Sassafras, Kent............NE 210
Sassafras and Oak (see Hollywood) .... ×
Savage, Howard.............. C 637
● *Savage*, Howard.......... C ×
● *Savage Factory*, Howard. C ×
Scagg's Sta., (see Branchville) ×
● *Scarboro*, Worcester..... SE ×
Scarboro, Harford .... N ×
● *Schley's*, Frederick.... NW ×
Scotland, St. Mary's .... S 24
Scott's Level, Baltimore....N ×
Scrabbletown, (see So. River) ×
● Seabrook, Prince George's C ×
Seat Pleasant, Prince Geo's.C ×
Secretary, Dorchester..... SE 30
Secretary Creek, Dorchester SE 72
Seiss Grove, Allegany..... NW ×
● Selbysport, Garrett.....NW 40
Sellman, Montgomery ...... C 30
Seneca, Montgomery..........C 60
● Severn, Anne Arundel....C 31
Sewell, Harford............. N ×
Shady Side, Anne Arundel..C ×
Shamburgh, Baltimore....... N 100
● *Sharman's*, Washingt'n NW ×
Shane, Baltimore........... N 30
● Sharon, Harford........... N ×
● Sharpsburgh, Wash'ton. NW 1,163
Sharptown, Wicomico..... SE 427
● *Sharret's*, Carroll........ N ×
Shawan, Baltimore.......... N 50
Shawsville, Harford .... N 55

Shelltown, Somerset ...... SE 25
● Shepperd, Baltimore...... N ×
Sheridan's Point, Calvert... S ×
Sherwood, Talbot........... E 30
● *Sherwood*, Baltimore..... N 120
Shiloh, Carroll .... N ×
Shipley, Carroll .... N ×
● *Shipley's*, Anne Arundel..C ×
Shirktown, Queene Anne's.E ×
● *Short Lane*, Harford......N ×
● Showell, Worcester...... SE 25
Shure's Landing, Harford.. N 90
Silver Hill, Prince George's C ×
Silver Run, Carroll.......... N 200
● *Silver Spring*, Montgom'y.C ×
Simpsonville, Howard.......C 75
Sims' Corner, (see Burtonsville) ×
Singer, Harford .... N ×
● Singerly, Cecil.......... NE 30
● Skipnish, Garrett....... NW 25
Skipton, Talbot............. E 50
Slack Water, (see Bakersville) ×
Slidell, Montgomery........ C ×
Sliders, Allegany......... NW ×
Sligo, Montgomery.......... C 75
Smallwood, Carroll.......... N 60
● Smithsburgh, Wash'ton NW 487
Smith's Corners, Q. Anne's.E 24
Smith's Point, (see Cross Roads) ×
Smithville, (see Dunkirk) .... ×
Smithville, Caroline.........E 50
Smoketown, Washington. NW 30
● **Snow Hill**, Worcester.SE 1,483
Snufftown, Allegany......NW ×
Snydersburgh, Carroll...... N 50
Soldiers Delight, Baltimore.N 48
Sollers, Calvert..............S ×
Sollers, Baltimore............ N ×
Solleyville, (see Marley) ...... ×
Solomon's, Calvert.......... S 350
● *Sorrento*, Baltimore.......N ×
Sotterly, St. Mary's..........S 30
South Baltimore, An. Ar'del.C ×
South River, Anne Arundel.C 15
● *South Salisbury*, Wico'co SE ×
● *Sparks*, Baltimore........N 30
Sparrow's Point, Baltimore.N 2,507
● *Sparrow's Point Junction*, Baltimore .... N ×
● *Spears Wharf*, Baltimore N ×
Spence, Worcester .... SE 40
Spencerville, Montgomery.. C 100
Spickler, Washington..... NW ×
Spielmans, (see Fairplay) .... ×
Spielman's Mill, (see Mineral Spring .... ×
Springfield, Prince George's C 30
Springfield Mills, (see Berean) ×
Spring Grove, Wicomico.. SE 24
Spring Hill, Charles......... S ×
● *Spring Mills*, Carroll.....N ×
Spry's Gate, Kent.........NE ×
Stablersville, Baltimore .... N 60
Stafford, Harford........... N 80
Stag, Baltimore............ N ×
Starr, Queen Anne's........ E 30
Starr's Cor., (see Gunpowder) ×
● *State Asylum*, Baltimore . N ×
● *State Line*, Allegany.....NW ×
● *Stemmer's Run*, Baltim're E ×
● *Steinman's*, Baltimore....N ×
● Stepney, Harford........... N ×
● Stevenson, Baltimore.....N 60
Steelton, (see Sparrow's Point) ×
Stevensville, Queen Anne's..E 187
● Still Pond, Kent......... NE 268
● Stockton, Worcester.... SE 400
● *Stonebraker's*, Wash'ton NW ×
● *Stone House Cove*, Howard C ×
Stones Wharf, St. Mary's... S 30
● *Stony Run*, Howard...... C ×
● *Stoyer*, Garrett.........NW ×
Street, Harford.............N ×
Sudbrook Park, Baltimore. N ×
● Sudlersville, Queen Anne's.E 125
Sudley, Anne Arundel...... C 144
Sugarland, (see Poolesville).. ×
● *Sugar Loaf*, Frederick. NW ×
Suitland, Prince George's...C 100
Suitsville, Prince George's.. C 15
● Summerfield, Baltimore..N 35
Summit, Allegany........NW ×
Sunderland, Calvert......... S 10
Sunny Brook, Baltimore....N 5
● *Sunnyside*, Prince George's C ×
Sunnyside, Garrett....... NW ×
Sunshine, (see Unity)......... ×

● *Swan Creek*, Harford.....N 24
● Swanton, Garrett.......NW 50
Sweet Air, Baltimore........N 150
● Sykesville, Carroll........N 686
Sylmar, Cecil...............NE 30
Tall Pine, St. Mary's.........S 24
● Taneytown, Carroll....... N 566
● *Tank*, Carroll.............N 60
Tannery, Carroll............N 60
Tan Yard, Caroline.........E 30
Taylor, Harford.............N 60
Taylor's Island, Dorchester SE 1,000
Taylorsville, (see River View) ×
Taylorsville, Carroll........ N 50
T. B., Prince George's.......C 80
Temples, (see Oxen Hill)...... ×
Templeville, Queen Anne's. E 100
Ten Mile, on the Registertown Pike, (see Tobins)........ ×
● Texas, Baltimore.......... N 500
The Oaks, (see Allen's Fresh) ×
Theodore, Cecil........... NE 75
● The Rocks, Harford.....NE 60
Thirteen Mile Switch, (see Triumph).................. ×
Thomas Run, Harford..... NE 20
Thompson, (see Slidell) ...... ×
● *Three Mile Water Station*, Allegany..............NW ×
Thrift, Prince George's..... C 60
Thurston, Frederick......NW 30
Tilghman, Talbot............E 30
● *Timber Grove*, Baltimore. N ×
Timonium, Baltimore...... N 325
Tobins, (see Garrison)....... ×
Toddville, Dorchester......SE 30
Toddstown, Dorchester....SE ×
● Tolchester Beach, Kent. NE 5
● *Toliver*, Garrett........NW ×
Tomkinsville, (see Issue)..... ×
Town Creek, Allegany....NW ×
Town Point, Cecil......... NE 20
Townshend, Prince George's C ×
● **Towson**, Baltimore...... N 459
Tracy's Landing, Anne Arundel........................ C 40
● *Tracey*, Carroll...........N ×
Trappe, Talbot............. E 251
● *Trappe*, Talbot........... E ×
Trappe Road, Baltimore... N ×
Travilah, Montgomery...... C 20
● *Tredavon*, Talbot..........E ×
Trego, Washington....... NW ×
Trent Hall, (see Mechanicsville) ×
Trenton, Baltimore..........N 80
Trevanion, Carroll.......... N 56
Triadelphia, Howard........ C 30
Triumph, (see Bengies)...... ×
Troutville, Frederick.....NW ×
Truitt, Wicomico.......... SE 25
Trump, Baltimore............N ×
● *Tuckahoe*, Talbot..........E ×
Tull's Corner, Somerset....SE 50
Tunis Mills, Talbot..........E 150
Turner, Baltimore........... N ×
● *Turners*, Talbot.......... E ×
● *Turnpike*, Baltimore.....N ×
● *Tuscarora*, Frederick.. NW 40
Twilley, Wicomico.......... E 30
● *Twenty First*, Allegany NW ×
Two Johns, Caroline......... E 20
Two Locks, (see Four Locks). ×
Tyaskin, Wicomico.......... SE 250
Tyrone, Carroll............. N 30
Unicorn Mills, Queen Anne's E 75
● Union Bridge, Carroll.... N 743
Union Mills, Carroll........ N 200
Union Factory, (see Oella)... ×
Union Meeting House, (see Eklo)........................ ×
Uniontown, Carroll....... ..N 309
Unionville, (see Long Green). ×
Unionville, Frederick.... NW 200
Unionville, Talbot.......... E 24
Unity, Montgomery..........C 50
● Upperco, Baltimore....... N 100
Upper Cross Roads, Harf'd. N 30
Upper Fairmount, Som'rs't S E 15
Upper Falls, Baltimore..... N 100
● **Upper Marlborough**, Prince George's......... C 439
Upper Ocean, Allegany... NW ×
Upper Trappe, Wicomico. SE 60
Urbana, Frederick........ NW 256
Utica Mills, Frederick.... NW 200
Vale, Harford................N 20
Vale Summit, Allegany.. NW 135

Place	Pop.
Valley Lee, St. Mary's.......S	30
● Van Bibber, Harford.....N	10
Victor, Somerset............SE	20
Verona, Baltimore..........N	×
● Vienna, Dorchester......SE	424
● *Vinegar Hill*, Baltimore..N	×
● *Vineyard*, Baltimore.....N	×
● Wakefield, Carroll........N	50
● Waldorf, Charles...........S	75
● Walker'sSwitch, BaltimoreN	60
● Walkersville, FrederickNW	255
Wallville, Calvert............ S	30
Walnut Landing, Dorch'terSE	20
Walston, Wicomico....... SE	50
Wanamaker, Wicomico....SE	30
Wango, Wicomico.......... SE	30
● *Ward*, Montgomery...... C	×
Wareheim, (see Maple Grove)	×
Warfieldburgh, Carroll..... N	50
● *Waring*, Montgomery....C	×
Warren, Baltimore..........N	600
Warwick, Cecil..............NE	287
● *Washington*, WashingtonNW	×
● Washington Grove, Montgomery..................C	×
● *Washington Junction*, Frederick............NW	×
Washington Road, (see Mt. Winans)..................	×
● Waterbury, Anne Aru'del.C	35
Waters' Shop, (see McConchie)	×
● Watersville, Carroll.......N	50
● *Watervale*, Harford...... N	×
Watkins, Montgomery...... C	×
Waverly, City of Baltimore.N	1,000
Wayside, Charles.............S	×
Webster, Harford............N	275
Weisesburgh, Baltimore.... N	15
Welbourne, Worcester.....SE	20
● Wellham's Cross Roads, Anne Arundel...........C	×
Wenona, Somerset.........SE	40
Wentz, Carroll..............N	54
● Wesley, Worcester.......SE	20
West, Somerset.............SE	30
WestBeaverCreek, W'sh'nNW	×
● Western Port, AlleganyNW	1,526
Western Run, Baltimore... N	×
West Falls, Frederick....NW	30
West Friendship, Howard...C	60
● **Westminster**, Carroll..N	2,903
● Westover, Somerset..... SE	75
Westphalia, Prince George'sC	×
● *Westport*, Baltimore..... N	×
West River, Anne Arundel..C	100
Westwood, PrinceGeorge's.. C	30
Wetheredville, Baltimore...N	804
● Weverton, Washington.NW	200
● Whaleysville, Worcester.SE	150
Whayland, Wicomico...... SE	50
Wheaton, Montgomery......C	40
Wheel, Harford..............N	×
● *Whitaker*, Cecil.........NE	×
Whiteburgh, Worcester....SE	15
Whiteford, Harford........ N	×
● White Hall, Baltimore....N	100
White Hall, Harford........N	25
Whitehaven, Wicomico.... SE	175
Whiteleysburgh, Caroline... E	75
● White Marsh, Baltimore..N	×
● *White Oak*, Queen Anne's E	×
White Plains, Charles........S	50
White's Ferry, MontgomeryC	×
Whites Landing, (seeNottingh'm)	×
Whiton, Wicomico.........SE	25
Wicomico, Charles.......... S	60
Widgeon, Somerset........SE	70
● *Wilkins*, Baltimore.......N	×
● Williamsburgh, Dorch'ter SE	200
● *Williams*, Wicomico.... SE	×
● Williamsport, Washing'nNW	1,277
● *Williamsport Station*, Washington.................. NW	×
Williston, Caroline.......... E	90
Willoughby, Queen Anne's..E	25
Willows, Calvert.............S	60
Wilmoth's Switch, AlleganyNW	×
Wilna, Hartford............ N	90
● *Wilson's*, Garrett...... NW	36
Wimbledon, Harford....... N	×
● *Winans*, Baltimore.......N	×
● *Winan's Depot*, BaltimoreN	×
● *Winchester*, Anne Arun'elC	×
Winchester Road, Alleg'yNW	×
● *Windhams*, Montgomery.C	×
Winfield, Carroll............N	150
Wingate, Dorchester...... SE	×

Place	Pop.
Winston, Garrett......... NW	200
Wittman, Talbot............ E	60
Wolfsville, Frederick.... NW	200
● Woodberry, City of Balti'reN	1,000
● Woodbine, Carroll........N	60
● *Woodbrook*, Baltimore...N	×
● Woodensburgh, BaltimoreN	70
Woodfield, Montgomery.....C	10
● Woodland, Talbot.........E	100
Woodlawn, Cecil.......... NE	150
Woodmore, Prince George's.C	×
● Woodsborough, Fred'ckNW	350
● *Wood Siding*, Howard....C	×
● Woodstock, Howard...... C	208
Woodville, Frederick.....NW	10
Woodville, (see Aquasco).....	×
Woodville, Charles.......... S	×
Woodville, Worchester.... SE	10
● Woodwardville, AnneArundelC	75
Woolford, Dorchester......SE	200
Worthington L'd'g, (seeDarling'n	×
● Worton, Kent............NE	120
● *Wright's*, Caroline........E	×
Wright's Mills, Baltimore..N	×
Wye Mills, Talbot...........E	100
Wynne, St. Mary's.......... S	×
Yellow Springs, FrederickNW	×
Yeoho, Baltimore.......... N	×
● York Road, Carroll.......N	100
York Road, (see Waverly)...	×
● Zion, Cecil.............. NE	150

Massachusetts.*

COUNTIES.	INDEX.	POP.
Barnstable	**SE**	**29,172**
Berkshire	**W**	**81,108**
Bristol	SE	186,465
Dukes	SE	4,369
Essex	NE	299,995
Franklin	NW	38,610
Hampden	SW	135,713
Hampshire	W	51,859
Middlesex	E	431,167
Nantucket	SE	3,268
Norfolk	E	118,950
Plymouth	SE	92,700
Suffolk	E	484,780
Worcester	C	280,787
Total		2,238,943

*In many of the towns of the State the population given embraces the township.

TOWN. COUNTY. INDEX.	POP.
● Abington, Plymouth.....SE	4,260
Acton, Middlesex........... E	1,897
● *Acton*, Middlesex......... E	×
● Acushnet, Bristol........SE	1,027
● Adams, Berkshire........W	9,213
● Adamsdale, Bristol......SE	×
Adamsville, Franklin.... NW	×
Agawam, Hampden.......SW	2,352
Alandar, Berkshire..........W	70
Alford, Berkshire.......... W	297
● Allston, Suffolk .... R	×
● *Alm's House*, Middlesex.. E	×
Alton, (see Easton)...........	×
● Amesbury, Essex. ... NE	9,798
● Amherst, Hampshire .... W	4,512
● Andover, Essex......... NE	6,142
Annisquam, Essex........ NE	×
Apponegansett, Bristol.... SE	500
● Arlington, Middlesex..... E	5,629
● Arlington Heights, M'ds'x E	×
● *Armory*, Hampden..... SW	×
Artichoke, Essex.......... NE	×
Asbury Grove, Essex......NE	×
● Ashburnham, Worcester..C	2,074
Ashburnham Depot, (see Ashburnham)	×
● *Ashburnham Junc.*, W'c'strC	×
Ashby, Middlesex........... E	825
● Ashcroft, Norfolk........ E	×
Ashfield, Franklin.........NW	1,025
● Ashland, Middlesex ...... E	2,532
● Ashley Falls, Berkshire.. W	400
● *Ashmont*, Suffolk.........E	×
Ashleyville, Hampden.... SW	×
● *Assonet*, Bristol..... . SE	1,417
● Asylum Station, Essex..NE	×
● *Atherton*, Middlesex......E	×

Place	Pop.
● Athol, Worcester......... C	6,319
Athol Centre, Worcester.... C	2,642
● *Athol Junc.*, Hampden. SW	×
● *Atlantic*, Essex......... NE	×
● Atlantic, Norfolk.......... E	1,470
● Attleborough, Bristol....SE	7,577
● Attleborough Falls, B'st'l SE	×
● Auburn, Worcester........C	1,532
● Auburndale, Middlesex...E	×
● Avon, Norfolk.............E	1,384
● Ayer, Middlesex.......... E	2,148
Ayers Village, Essex..... NE	×
Back Bay, Suffolk.......... E	×
● *Baker's Bridge*, Middlesex E	×
● Baldwinsville, Worcester. C	×
● Ballard Vale, Essex.....NE	1,050
● Bancroft, Berkshire......W	205
● *Barbers Crossing*, W'c'st'r C	×
● Bardwell's Ferry, F'kl'nNW	×
● **Barnstable**, B'rnst'ble SE	4,023
Barre, Worcester........... C	2,239
● *Barre*, Worcester........ C	×
● Barre Plains, Worcester.. C	250
● *Barretts Junc.*, H'mpsh'reW	×
● Barrowsville, Bristol.... SE	×
Bay State, Hampshire......W	×
Bay View, Essex.......... NE	800
● Beach Bluff, Essex......NE	×
● *Beachmont*, Suffolk...... E	×
Beacon Park, Suffolk.......E	×
● *Bearcroft*, Bristol........SE	×
● *Beaver Brook*, Middlesex E	×
● Becket, Berkshire........W	946
Becket Centre, Berkshire.. W	50
● Bedford, Middlesex ...... E	1,092
● Bedford Spg's, Middlesex. E	×
Beechwood, Norfolk........E	×
● *Beechwood Sta.*, Suffolk.. E	×
● Belchertown, Hampshire. W	2,120
● Bellingham, Norfolk..... E	1,384
● *Bell Rock*, Middlesex..... E	×
● Belmont, Middlesex...... E	2,098
● Bemis, Middlesex .... E	×
Berkley, Bristol........... SE	894
● *Berkley Station*, Bristol. SE	×
● Berkshire, Berkshire.... W	200
● Berlin, Worcester.........C	884
● *Berlin Station*, Worcester.C	×
● Bernardston, Franklin. NW	770
● Beverly, Essex...........NE	10,821
● Beverly Farms, Essex...NE	×
● Billerica, Middlesex...... E	2,380
● *Bird Street*, Suffolk.......E	×
● Blackinton, Berkshire... W	1,000
● Blackstone, Worcester....C	6,138
● *Blackstone Jc.*, Worcester.C	×
Blandford, Hampden..... SW	871
● *Bleachery*, Middlesex.....E	×
Blue Hill, Norfolk..........E	×
Bolton, Worcester C	827
● *Bolton*, Worcester........ C	×
● Bond's Village, Hamp'enSW	1,000
● **BOSTON**, Suffolk.......E	448,477
Boston Highland, Suffolk...E	×
● Bourne, Barnstable......SE	1,442
● Bournedale, Barnstable..SE	195
● *Bowenville*, Bristol...... SE	×
● *Boxborough*, Middlesex.. E	325
Boxford, Essex............NE	865
● *Boxford Station*, Essex.NE	×
● *Boylston*, Suffolk......... E	×
● Boyleston, Worcester..... C	770
Boylston Centre, Worcester.C	115
● Bradford, Essex.........NE	3,720
● Braggville, Middlesex.....E	×
● Braintree, Norfolk........E	4,848
● *Bradley's*, Bristol....... SE	×
Brant Rock, Plymouth....SE	×
● *Brattles*, Middlesex.......E	×
● *Brayton*, Bristol.........SE	×
● *Braytonville*, Berkshire..W	×
Brewster, Barnstable......SE	1,003
● *Brewster Sta.*, B'rnstableSE	×
● Bridgewater, Plymouth. SE	4,249
Briggs' Corner, Bristol..... SE	30
Briggsville, Berkshire......W	250
● Brighton, Suffolk......... E	13,000
● Brightwood, Hampden..SW	×
Brimfield, Hampden......SW	1,096
● Brittania, Bristol........SE	×
● *Broadway*, Middlesex.....E	×
● Breckton, Plymouth.....SE	27,294
● Brookfield, Worcester.... C	3,352
● Brookline, Norfolk........E	12,103
● *Brookline Junc.*, Suffolk. E	×
● Brooks Station, WorcesterC	×
● *Brookside*, Middlesex.....E	×

Brookville, Norfolk........E ×
● *Brown's*, Plymouth..... SE ×
Bryantville, Plymouth.....SE 150
Buckland, Franklin......NW 1,570
● *BucklandSta.*, FranklinNW ×
Bunker Hill, Suffolk........E ×
Burlington, Middlesex..... E 617
● *Burtts*, Middlesex.........E ×
● Buzzard's Bay, Barnst'bleSE ×
● Byfield, Essex. ....NE 354
● **Cambridge** Middlesex.E 70,028
Cambridgeport, Middlesex.. E ×
● Campello, Plymouth.......SE ×
Camp MeetingGrounds, D'sSE ×
Cannonville, Plymouth......E ×
● Canton, Norfolk ....E 4,538
● Canton Junction, Norfolk E ×
Carlisle, Middlesex..........E 481
● *Carlisle*, Middlesex........E ,500
● *Cartonville*, Essex...... NE ×
Carver, Plymouth............SE 994
● *Carry Cut*, Suffolk.........E ×
● Caryville, Norfolk.........E ×
● Cataumet, Barnstable ...SE 42
● *Cedar Grove*, Suffolk.... E ×
● *Central*, Suffolk.......... E ×
● *Central Avenue*, Suffolk..E ×
● *Central Shaft*, Berkshire W ×
● *Central Square*, Middles'xE ×
Central Village, Bristol....SE ×
Centralville, (see Lowell)..... ×
● Centre Marshfield, Ply'thSE ×
Centreville, Barnstable.... SE 466
● *Chaces*, Bristol.......... SE ×
● *Chapins*, Worcester.......C ×
● *Chapel*, Norfolk...........E ×
Chapinville, Worcester......C ×
Chappaquiddic, Dukes.... SE ×
● Charlemont, Franklin..NW 972
● Charles River Village, Norfolk .... E ×
● Charlestown, Suffolk......E ×
Charlton, Worcester.........C 1,847
Charlton City, Worcester....C ×
● Charlton Depot, WorcesterC ×
● Chartley, Bristol..........SE ×
● Chatham, Barnstable.....SE 1,954
Chatham Port, Barnstable..SE 152
● *Cheapside*, Franklin... NW ×
● Chelmsford, Middlesex... E 2,695
Chelsea, Suffolk............ E 27,909
● *Chelsea Station*, Suffolk.. E ×
● *Chemistry*, Middlesex.....E ×
● *Cherry Brook*, Middlesex. E ×
● *Cherry Street*, Suffolk.... E ×
Cherry Valley, Worcester... C 872
● Cheshire, Berkshire......W 1,308
● *Cheshire Harbor*, Berk'ireW ×
● Chester, Hampden......SW 1,295
Chester Centre, Hampden.SW ×
Chesterfield, Hampshire.....W 608
● Chestnut Hill, Middlesex.. E ×
● *Chickering*, Suffolk.......E ×
● Chicopee, Hampden.....SW 14,050
Chicopee Centre, HampdenSW ×
● Chicopee Falls, HampdenSW 4,000
● *Chicopee Junc.*, HampdenSW ×
Chilmark, Dukes.......... SE 353
Chiltonville, Plymouth.......SE 770
● *City Farm*, Middlesex.... E ×
● City Mills, Norfolk.........E ×
● Clarendon Hill, Norfolk.. E ×
Clarksburg, Berkshire..... W 884
Clayton, Berkshire......... W 200
● *Clematis Brook*, Midd'sexW ×
Clifford, Bristol...........SE ×
● Clifton, Essex...........NE ×
● Cliftondale, Essex.......NE 900
Clifton Heights, Essex.... NE ×
● Clinton, Worcester........C 10,424
● Cochesett, Plymouth.... SE ×
Cochituate, Middlesex.......C 1,391
● Cohasset, Norfolk.........E 2,448
● Coldbrook Springs, Worc'rC ×
● Coldspring, Middlesex.... E ×
Cold Spring, Berkshire.... W ×
Colerain, Franklin.........NW 1,671
● *Cole's*, Bristol.......... SE ×
● *Cole's Switch*, Berkshire. W ×
● *College Hill*, Middlesex...E ×
● *Collins*, Hampden...... SW ×
● *Collins Street*, Middlesex. E ×
Collinsville, Middlesex.......E ×
Collinsville, Hampden.... SW ×
Colony, Norfolk...........E ×
● *Coltsville*, Berkshire..... W 75
● Concord, Middlesex.......E 4,427

Massachusetts

● Concord Junc., Middlesex E ×
● *Conomo*, Essex........ NE ×
● Conway, Franklin......NW 1,451
● *Conway Junc.*, Frank'nNW ×
● *Cook Street*, Middlesex.... E ×
Cooleyville, Franklin.....NW 79
● Cordaville, Worcester.....C 300
● Cottage City, Dukes...... SE 1,080
● *Cottage Farm*, Suffolk....E ×
Cottage Hill, Suffolk........E ×
Cotuit, Barnstable.........SE ×
Craigville, Barnstable......SE ×
● *Crane's*, Bristol.......... SE ×
● *Creamery*, Worcester.....C ×
● *Crescent Avenue*, Suffolk. E ×
● *Crescent Beach*, Suffolk.. E ×
● *Crystal Springs*, Bristol.SE ×
● *Cumberland Mills*, BristolSE ×
Cummingsville, Middlesex.. E ×
Cummington, Hampshire... W 787
● *Curtis Cross'g*, PlymouthSE ×
● *Curtis Street Jc.*, Essex.. NE ×
Curtisville, Berkshire...... W 200
Cuttyhunk, Dukes...........SE ×
● *Cypress Street*, Norfolk... E ×
● Dalton, Berkshire........W 2,885
Dana, Worcester............C 700
● Danvers, Essex......... NE 7,454
Danvers Centre, Essex.... NE ×
● *Danvers Junction*, EssexNE ×
● Danversport, Essex..... NE ×
Dartmouth, Bristol........SE 3,122
Davis, Franklin.......... NW ×
● *Dawsons*, Worcester.......C ×
● **Dedham**, Norfolk...... E 7,123
● *Dedham Junction*, NorfolkE ×
● Deerfield, Franklin.... NW 2,910
Deerfield, Franklin.........NW ×
Dell, Franklin........... NW ×
Dennis, Barnstable........ SE 2,829
Dennis Port, Barnstable .. SE ×
Dennyville, Worcester..... C ×
● *Devereux*, Essex........ NE ×
● Dighton, Bristol.......... SE 1,889
● Dodgeville, Bristol...... SE ×
● Dorchester, Suffolk ...... E ×
● Douglass, Worcester...... C 1,908
● Dover, Norfolk............ E 727
Dracut, Middlesex.......... E 1,996
Duckville, (see Bond's Village) ×
Dudley, Worcester.......... C 2,944
Dudley Hill, Worcester..... C ×
● *Dudley Street*, Suffolk.... E ×
● Dunstable, Middlesex..... E 416
● Duxbury, Plymouth .... SE 1,908
● Dwight, Hampshire...... W 32
● East Acton, Middlesex.... E ×
● East Billerica, Middlesex. E ×
● East Blackstone, Worc'r.. C ×
● East Boston, Suffolk...... E ×
● East Boxford, Essex..... NE ×
● East Braintree, Norfolk.. E ×
● East Brewster, Barnsta..SE ×
● East Bridgewater, Plym..SE 2,911
East Brimfield, Hampden.SW 175
● East Brookfield, Worc'r.. C ×
● East Cambridge, Mid'sex. E ×
East Carver, Plymouth.... SE ×
● East Charlemont, Fr'nk NW ×
East Chop, Dukes......... SE ×
● East Deerfield, Franklin NW ×
East Dennis, Barnstable... SE 488
East Douglass, Worcester... C ×
● *East Douglass Sta.*, Wor..C ×
● *East Everett*, Middlesex..E ×
East Falmouth, Barnstable SE 240
● *East Fitchburg*, WorcesterC ×
● East Foxborough, Norf'k..E ×
East Freetown, Bristol.... SE ×
● *East Freetown Sta.*, B'l SE ×
East Gloucester, (see Glo'c'r). ×
East Granville, Hampden. SW 250
● *East Groton*, Middlesex.. E ×
● Eastham, Barnstable.... SE 602
● Easthampton, Hampshire.W 4,395
East Harwich, Barnstable..SE ×
East Haverhill, Essex..... NE ×
● East Holliston, Middlesex.E ×
East Hubbardston, Worc'r... C ×
● *East Junction*, Bristol.. SE ×
East Lee, Berkshire........ W 200
● East Lexington, Mid'sex.. E 3,000
● *East Littleton*, Middlesex.E ×
● East Long Meadow, Hampden......................SW 1,608
● *East Lynn*, Middlesex.... E ×
East Mansfield, Bristol.... SE ×

Massachusetts

● *East Marshfield*, Plym.. SE ×
East Mattapoisett, Plym'th SE ×
● East Milton, Norfolk..... E ×
East Northfield, Franklin NW ×
● East Norton, Bristol.... SE ×
● Easton, Bristol......... SE 4,493
Eastondale, Bristol........ SE ×
● *Easton Turnpike*, BristolSE ×
East Orleans, Barnstable.. SE ×
East Otis, Berkshire....... W ×
East Pembroke, Plymouth. SE ×
● East Pepperell, Middlesex. E ×
East Phillipston, Worcester.C ×
● *East Portal*, Berkshire... W ×
East Princeton, Worcester.. C ×
East Providence Centre, B'l SE ×
● East Sandwich, Barnsta. SE 307
● East Saugus, Essex......NE 3,636
East Sharon, Norfolk....... E ×
East Sheffield, (see Clayton).. ×
East Shelburne, Franklin NW ×
East Somerville, Middlesex.E ×
East Stoughton, (see Sto'ghtn) ×
● *East Sudbury*, Middlesex E ×
● East Taunton, Bristol... SE ×
East Templeton, Worcester. C ×
● East Walpole, Norfolk ... E ×
● East Wareham, Plym ... SE ×
● *East Watertown*, Mid'les .E ×
● East Weymouth, Norfolk..E ×
● East Whately, Franklin NW ×
East Windsor, Berkshire... W 75
East Woburn, Middlesex... E ×
Eddyville, Plymouth ...... SE ×
● **Edgartown**, Dukes... SE 1,156
● *Edgeworth*, Middlesex....E ×
Egremont, Berkshire...... W 845
Egremont Plain, Berkshire W ×
● Egyyt, Plymouth........ SE ×
● *Eliot*, Middlesex.......... E ×
● Ellis, Norfolk .... E ×
Elm Grove, Franklin.... NW ×
● Elmwood, Plymouth.... SE 450
● Endicott, Norfolk........ E ×
● Enfield, Hampshire...... W 952
● Erving, Franklin....... NW 972
● Essex, Essex........... NE 1,713
● *Essex Falls*, Essex......NE ×
● Everett, Middlesex........E 11,068
● *Everett Junc.*, Middlesex.E ×
Fairfield, Hampden....... SW 350
● *Fairfield Station*, H'den SW ×
● Fairhaven, Bristol....... SE 2,919
● Fall River, Bristol.......SE 74,398
● *Falls Village*, Bristol... SE ×
● Falmouth, Barnstable... SE 2,567
Falmouth Heights, B'able.. SE ×
● *Faneuil*, Suffolk..........E ×
● Farley, Franklin....... NW ×
● *Farmers*, Bristol........ SE ×
● *Farm Hill*, Middlesex.... E ×
● *Farm Street*, Norfolk.... E ×
● *Farnum's*, Berkshire.... W ×
● Farnumsville, Worcester. C 650
● *Faulkner*, Middlesex .... E ×
● Fayville, Worcester....... C 450
Feeding Hills, Hampden.. SW 750
Felchville, (see Natick) ...... ×
● Fells, Middlesex.......... E ×
● *Fields Corner*, Suffolk.... E ×
Fisherville, Worcester ......C ×
Fiskdale, Worcester.......... C ×
● **Fitchburg**, Worcester..C 22,037
● *Flint Village*, Bristol... SE ×
● Florence, Hampshire .... W 2,789
Florida, Berkshire......... W 437
● *Forbes*, Suffolk.......... E ×
● *Forest Avenue*, Suffolk... E ×
Forestdale, Barnstable.... SE ×
● *Forest Hill*, Suffolk ...... E ×
● *Forest Lake*, Hampden SW ×
● *Forest River*, Essex.... NE ×
● Forge Village, Middlesex.E 300
Fort Independence, Suffolk.E ×
Fort Winthrop, Suffolk.....E ×
● Foxborough, Norfolk .... E 2,933
● Foxvale, Norfolk .... E ×
● Framingham, Middlesex..E 9,239
● *Farmingham Junc.* Mid's'xE ×
● Franklin, Norfolk......... E 4,831
● Franklin Park, Suffolk... E ×
Freetown, Bristol .... SE 1,417
● *Fresh Pond*, Middlesex...E ×
● Furnace, Worcester ...... C 97
● Gardner, Worcester ...... C 8,424
● *Gates Crossing*, Worcester C ×
Gay Head, Dukes.......... SE 139

 Massachusetts Massachusetts

Place	Population
● Georgetown, Essex......NE	2,117
● *Gibbs*, Hampden........SW	×
● Gilbertville, Worcester... C	1,230
Gill, Franklin.......... NW	960
● Glendale, Berkshire...... W	400
● *Glenwood*, Middlesex .... E	×
Globe Village, Worcester... C	×
● Gloucester, Essex ...... NE	24,651
● *Golden Cove*, Middlesex .. E	×
Goshen, Hampshire........ W	297
Gosnold, Dukes..........SE	135
Goulding's Village, Wor'st'r C	×
● Grafton, Worcester....... C	5,002
Granby, Hampshire........ W	765
● *Granite Bridge*, Suffolk...E	×
Graniteville, Middlesex.... E	900
Granville, Hampden...... SW	1,061
● Great Barrington, Berk'e W	4,612
Great Head, Suffolk......... E	×
Greenbush, Plymouth......SE	363
Greendale, Worcester.......C	×
Greenfield, Franklin...NW	5,252
Green Harbor, Plymouth..SE	×
● Greenwich, Hampshire.. W	526
● Greenwich Village, H'p're W	×
● Greenwood, Middlesex... E	×
● *Greylock*, Berkshire......W	×
Griswoldville, Franklin.. NW	×
● Groton, Middlesex........E	2,057
● **Groveland, Essex**....... NE	2,191
● Hadley, Hampshire.......W	1,669
● *Haggett's*, Essex.........NE	×
Halifax, Plymouth..........SE	562
● *Halifax Station*, Plym'th SE	×
● Hamilton, Essex......... NE	961
● *Hammond Street*, Middlesex E	×
Hampden, Hampden........SW	831
Hancock, Berkshire.........W	506
● Hanover, Plymouth.......SE	2,093
Hanson, Plymouth..........SE	1,267
● *Harbor View*, Suffolk.... E	×
Hardwick, Worcester....... C	2,922
● *Hardwick*, Worcester.....C	×
Harris, Bristol..............SE	×
● *Harrison Square*, Essex NE	×
Harrison's Square, Suffolk..E	×
Hartsville, Berkshire.......W	100
● Harvard, Worcester.......C	1,095
● *Harvard Street*, Suffolk.. E	×
● Harwich, Barnstable.....SE	2,734
● *Harwich Centre*, B'stable SE	×
Harwich Port, Barnstable. SE	×
● *Harwoods*, Worcester.... C	×
● *Hastings*, Middlesex......E	×
Hatchville, Barnstable.....SE	×
Hatfield, Hampshire........W	1,246
● *Hatfield Station*, H'mp're W	×
Hatherly, Plymouth....... SE	×
● Haverhill, Essex......... NE	27,412
● *Haverhill Bridge*, Essex NE	×
Hawley, Franklin........... NW	515
● Hayden Row, Middlesex. .E	×
● Haydenville, Hampshire. W	800
● *Hazelwood*, Norfolk........E	×
Head of the River, Bristol. SE	×
Heald Village, Worcester...C	×
Heath, Franklin...........NW	503
● *Heath*, Norfolk............E	×
● Hebronville, Bristol..... SE	×
● *Hemlock*, Bristol......... SE	×
● *Heywood's*, Worcester..... C	×
● *Hicksville*, Bristol....... SE	×
● *Highland*, Suffolk......... E	×
Highland Lake, Norfolk....E	×
Highland Light, Barnst'le.SE	×
● *Highlands*, Middlesex..... E	×
● Highlandville, Norfolk.... E	×
● *Hill Crossing*, Middlesex. E	×
● Hingham, Plymouth.......SE	4,564
Hingham Centre, Plym'th. SE	×
● Hinsdale, Berkshire.......W	1,739
● Holbrook, Norfolk.........E	2,474
● Holden, Worcester........C	2,623
Holland, Hampden.........SW	201
● Holliston, Middlesex......E	2,619
● Holyoke, Hampden.........W	35,637
● *Hoosac Tunnel*, Berkshire W	95
● Hopedale, Worcester..... C	1,176
● Hopkinton, Middlesex.... E	4,088
Hortonville, Bristol.........SE	×
● *Hospital Station*, Worc'r. C	×
Hough's Neck, Norfolk.....E	×
● Housatonic, Berkshire... W	1,200
House of Correction, Suff'k.E	×
● *Howarth's*, Worcester.... C	×
● *Howe's*, Essex........... NE	×
● *Howlands*, Plymouth....SE	×

Place	Population
● Hubbardston, Worcester..C	1,346
● Hudson, Middlesex....... E	4,670
● Hull, Plymouth...........SE	989
● Huntington, Hampshire..W	1,385
● Hyannis, Barnstable..... SE	1,510
Hyannis Port, Barnstable..SE	143
● Hyde Park, Norfolk...... E	10,193
Ice Houses, Middlesex..... E	×
● Indian Orchard, Ham'n. SW	1,800
● *Ingalls*, Suffolk...........E	×
● *Ingalls Crossing*, Essex. NE	×
● *Ingleside*, Hampden.... SW	×
● Ipswich, Essex..........NE	4,439
● *Iron Stone*, Worcester....C	×
● Island Creek, Plymouth.SE	×
● Islington, Norfolk......... E	×
● Jamaica Plain, Suffolk....E	×
● *Jamesville*, Worcester.... C	×
● Jefferson, Worcester.......C	×
Jenksville, (see Ludlow)......	×
● *Junction*, Berkshire..... W	×
● *Junction*, Essex.........NE	×
Katama, Dukes............ SE	×
● Kendal Green, Middlesex. E	×
● Kingston, Plymouth.....SE	1,659
● *King Street*, Norfolk..... E	×
● *Knight's Crossing*, Essex NE	×
● *Lake Crossing*, Worcester C	×
● LakePleasant, Franklin NW	×
● *Lake Shore*, Worcester....C	×
● *Lake Street*, Middlesex... E	×
● *Lake View*, Middlesex.... E	×
● Lake View, Worcester.....C	×
● Lakeville, Plymouth.....SE	935
Lamb City, Worcester........C	×
● Lancaster, Worcester..... C	2,201
Lanesborough, Berkshire.. W	1,018
Lanesville, Essex..........NE	200
● **Lawrence**, Essex...... NE	44,654
● *Lawrence Junc.*, Middlesex E	×
● Lee, Berkshire........... W	3,785
● Leeds, Hampshire........ W	1,000
Leicester, Worcester......... C	3,120
Lenox, Berkshire........... W	2,889
● *Lenox*, Berkshire........ W	×
● Lenox Dale, Berkshire... W	500
● Leominster, Worcester....C	7,269
● Leverett, Franklin..... NW	702
● Lexington, Middlesex.....E	3,197
Leyden, Franklin.........NW	407
Lincoln, Middlesex..........E	987
● *Lincoln Square*, Worcester C	×
● *Lincoln Station*, Middlesex E	×
● Linden, Middlesex....... E	500
● *Lindenwood*, Middlesex...E	×
Line, Franklin...............NW	75
● Littleton, Middlesex...... E	1,025
Littleton Common, Middl'x.E	×
Littleville, Hampden......SW	60
Lock's Village, Franklin. NW	×
● Long Meadow, Hamp'n. SW	2,183
Long Plain, Bristol........ SE	×
● *Long Siding*, Essex...... NE	×
● *Longwood*, Norfolk.......E	×
Loudville, Hampshire...... W	57
● **LOWELL**, Middlesex.. E	77,696
● *Lowell Junction*, Essex. NE	×
● Ludlow, Hampden........SW	1,939
Ludlow Centre, Hampden.SW	×
Ludlow City, Hampden... SW	×
Lunenburgh, Worcester..... C	1,146
Lunenburg, Worcester......C	×
● **LYNN**, Essex..........NE	55,727
● *Lynn Common*, Essex.. NE	×
● Lynnfield, Essex..........NE	787
● Lynnfield Centre, Essex. NE	430
● Magnolia, Essex..........NE	232
● Malden, Middlesex.........E	23,031
● *Malden*, Middlesex........ E	×
Manchaug, Worcester.......C	1,300
● Manchester, Essex...... NE	1,789
Manomet, Plymouth.......SE	×
● Mansfield, Bristol.........SE	3,432
● *Maple Grove*, Berkshire. W	×
● *Maplewood*, Middlesex... E	1,500
● Marblehead, Essex......NE	8,202
● *Marble Ridge*, Essex.... NE	×
Marion, Plymouth......... SE	871
● *Marion Station*, Plymouth SE	×
● Marlborough, Middlesex.. E	13,805
● *Marlboro Junc.*, Middle'x E	×
● **Marshfield, Plymouth**... SE	1,713
● *Marshfield Centre*, Plymouth SE	×
● Marshfield Hills, Plymouth SE	×
Marston's Mills, Barnstable SE	×
Martha's Vineyard, Dukes SE	×
Mashpee, Barnstable.......SE	298

Place	Population
● Matfield, Plymouth......SE	555
● Mattapan, Suffolk.........E	×
● Mattapoisett, Plymouth. SE	1,148
● *Mayflower Park*, Norfolk E	×
● Maynard, Middlesex...... E	2,700
● Medfield, Norfolk..........E	1,493
● *Medfield Junction*, Norfolk E	×
● Medford, Middlesex....... E	11,079
● *Medford Hillside*, Midd'sex E	×
● *Medford Junc.*, Middlesex E	×
● Medway, Norfork.........E	2,985
● Melrose, Middlesex....... E	8,519
● Melrose Highlands, M'd'ex E	×
Menauhant, Barnstable....SE	×
Mendon, Worcester......... C	919
Merrick, Hampden....... SW	×
● Merrimac, Essex........ NE	2,633
Merrimacport, Essex......NE	×
● *Messers*, Essex...........NE	×
Metcalf, Middlesex..........E	×
● *Metcalf*, Middlesex....... E	×
● Methuen, Essex.........NE	4,814
● Middleborough, Plym'th SE	6,065
Middlefield, Hampshire.... W	455
● *Middlesex Sta.*, Berkshire W	×
● *Middlesex Junc.*, Midd'sex E	×
● Middlesex Village, Mid'sex E	×
● Middleton, Essex.........NE	924
● Milford, Worcester........C	8,780
Millbrook, Plymouth...... SE	×
● Millbury, Worcester...... C	4,428
● *Millbury Junc.*, Worcester C	×
● Miller's Falls, Franklin NW	900
Millington, Franklin..... NW	62
● Millis, Norfolk............E	786
Mill River, Berkshire...... W	250
● Millville, Worcester..... W	6,095
● Milton, Norfolk...........E	4,278
● *Mirror Lake*, Middlesex..E	×
● *Mishawum*, Middlesex... E	×
Mittineague, Hampden....SW	1,000
Monroe, Franklin........ NW	282
Monroe Bridge, Franklin NW	×
● Monson, Hampden.......SW	3,650
Montague, Franklin......NW	6,296
● Montague City, Franklin NW	50
● *Montague Sta.*, Fra'k'n NW	×
● *Montello*, Plymouth.....SE	×
Monterey, Berkshire....... W	495
Montgomery, Hampden...SW	266
● Montrose, Middlesex......E	×
● *Montserrat*, Essex......NE	×
● Montvale, Middlesex..... E	×
Montville, Berkshire....... W	110
● Monument Beach, Barn'e SE	×
Moore's Corner, Franklin NW	×
● Mount Auburn, Middlesex E	×
Mount Blue, Plymouth.... SE	×
● *Mount Bowdoin*, Suffolk .E	×
● Mount Hermon, Fr'nk'n NW	×
Mount Holyoke, Hampshire W	×
● *Mount Hope*, Suffolk......E	×
● *Mount Pleasant*, Bristol SE	×
● *Mount Toby*, Franklin NW	×
● Mount Tom, Hampshire. W	×
Mount Wachusett, Worch'ter C	×
Mount Washington, Berk're W	148
● Munroes, Middlesex...... E	×
● *Muschopauge*, Worcester. C	×
● Myrick's, Bristol......... SE	×
● *Mystic*, Middlesex........E	×
● *Mystic Junction*, Middle'x E	×
Nahant, Essex..............NE	880
Nanepashemet, Essex.....NE	×
● Nantasket, Norfolk........E	×
Nantasket Beach, (see Hull).	×
Nantucket, Nantucket..SE	3,268
● Nashoba, Middlesex...... E	8,500
● Natick, Middlesex........ E	9,118
● Needham, Norfolk.........E	3,025
● *Neponset*, Suffolk.........E	×
New Ashford, Berkshire... W	125
● **NEW BEDFORD**, Bristol...SE	40,733
New Boston, Berkshire.... W	350
● New Braintree, Worcester C	573
● *New Braintree*, Worcester C	×
Newbury, Essex...........NE	1,427
● **Newburyport**, Essex NE	13,947
● *Newhall*, Essex..........NE	×
● New Lenox, Berkshire... W	200
New Marlborough, Berks'e W	1,305
New Salem, Franklin.... NW	856
● *New Salem Sta.*, Worch'er C	×
● Newton, Middlesex.......E	24,379
● Newton Centre, Middlesex E	×
● Newton Highlands, Mid'ex E	1,500

Massachusetts

Place	Pop.
● Newton Lower Falls, Mid'x E	1,400
● Newton Upper Falls, Mid'x E	1,200
● Newtonville, Middlesex...E	3,000
Nichewaug, Worcester......C	×
● Nobscot, Middlesex.......E	×
Nonquitt, Bristol..........SE	30
● Norfolk, Norfolk.........E	913
● North Abington, Plymo'hSE	240
● North Acton, Middlesex..E	×
● North Adams, Berkshire. W	16,074
● North Amherst, Hamps'reW	600
● **Northampton**, Hamp'eW	14,990
North Andover, Essex.... NE	3,742
● North Andover Depot, Essex NE	×
● North Ashburnham, Wor'rC	×
● North Attleborough, Bristol SE	6,727
North Becket, (see Becket) ..	×
● North Bellingham, Norf'lkE ..	×
North Bernardston, (see Bernardston)................	×
● *North Beverly*, Essex...NE	×
● North Billerica, MiddlesexE	×
North Blandford, HampdenW	200
● Northborough, Worcester C	1,952
North Brewster, Barnsta'leSE	×
● Northbridge, Worcester...C	4,603
Northbridge Centre, Worce'rC	×
● North Brookfield, Worces'rC	3,871
● North Cambridge, Middl'xE	9,000
North Carver, Plymouth...SE	×
North Chatham, Barnstab'sSE	190
● North Chelmsford, Mid'sexE	×
North Chester, Hampden. SW	×
North Cohasset, (see Cohassett)	×
● North Dana, Worcester....C	300
North Dartmouth, Bristol..SE	×
● *North Dartmouth Station*, Bristol.................SE	×
North Dennis, Barnstable.SE	×
● North Dighton, Bristol.. SE	×
North Duxbury, Plymouth SE	×
● North Eastham, Barnst'eSE	×
● North Easton, Bristol....SE	1,300
North Egremont, BerkshireW	175
● North Falmouth, Barnst'eSE	130
● Northfield, Franklin... NW	1,869
● Northfield Farms, Fra'nNW	375
● NorthFoxborough, NorfolkE	×
● *North Framingham*, Middlesex .... E	×
● North Grafton, Worcester C	×
North Hadley, Hampshire.. W	700
North Hanover, Plymouth.SE	×
● North Hanson, PlymouthSE	×
● North Harwich, Barnsta'eSE	×
● North Hatfield, Hampshi'eW	300
North Heath, Franklin...NW	×
● *North Lakeville*, Plymou'hE	×
● *North Lawrence*, Essex.NE	×
North Lee, (see Lee)..........	×
● North Leominster, Worc'rC	×
North Leverett, Franklin NW	×
● *North Lexington*, Mid'sexE	×
● *North Littleton*, MiddlesexE	×
North Marshfield, PlymouthSE	×
North Middleborough, Plym'h SE	×
● *North Monson*, HamptonSW	×
North Natick, Middlesex... E	×
North NewSalem, Fra'k'nNW	×
North Orange, Franklin..NW	500
● North Oxford, Worcester.C	×
● *North Oxford Mills*, W'ct'rC	×
North Pembroke, Ply'outhSE	×
● North Plymouth, Ply'u'hSE	×
North Prescott, Hampshire W	×
● North Raynham, Bristol.SE	×
● North Reading, Middl'sexE	874
North Rehoboth, Bristol...SE	×
North Rochester, Ply'outh.SE	×
North Rutland, Worcester..C	×
North Sandwich, Barn'bleSE	×
● North Scituate, Ply'outh.SE	1,100
North Scituate Beach, Plymouth.......................SE	×
● *North Somerville*, Mid'sexE	×
● North Stoughton, NorfolkE	259
● North Sudbury, Midd'sex.E	×
North Swansea, Bristol....SE	×
North Tisbury, Dukes.....SE	×
● North Truro, Barnstable.SE	×
North Uxbridge, Worcester.C	×
● *North Village*, Worcester.C	×
North Webster, Worcester..C	×
● North Westport, Bristol.SE	×

Massachusetts

Place	Pop.
North Weymouth, Norfolk.E	×
● *North Weymouth Station*, Norfolk.....................E	×
● North Wilbraham, Hampden...........................W	700
● North Wilmington, Midd'xE	×
● *North Woburn*, Mid'sex..E	1,225
● *North Woburn Junction*, Middlesex..................E	×
● *North Woods*, Worcester.C	×
● *North Worcester*, Wor't'r C	×
Norton, Bristol............SE	1,785
● *Norton*, Bristol...........SE	×
● Norton Furnace, Bristol SE	×
Norwell, Plymouth........ SE	1,635
Norwich Hampshire........W	300
● Norwood, Norfolk........E	3,733
● *Norwood Centre*, Nor'f'lkE	×
Oak Bluffs, Dukes.........SE	×
● Oakdale, Worcester.......C	×
● *Oak Grove*, Middlesex.....E	×
Oakham, Worcester.........C	738
● *Oak Island*, Suffolk......E	×
Oakland, Bristol...........SE	×
Oakland, Middlesex........E	×
● *Ocean Spray*, Suffolk.....E	×
● *Old Colony House* N'folk.E	×
● *Old Furnace*, Worcester..C	×
Onset, Plymouth...........SE	×
● *Onset Bay*, Barnstable...SE	×
● Orange, Franklin ......NW	4,568
● Orleans, Barnstable......SE	1,219
Osterville, Barnstable..... SE	×
Otis, Berkshire............W	583
● Otter River, Worcester... C	×
● Oxford, Worcester........C	2,616
Oxford, Bristol...........SE	×
● Palmer, Hampden......SW	6,520
● *Pansy Park*, Hampshire.W	×
● *Paper Mills*, Plymouth..SE	×
Parker Mills, Essex......NE	×
● *Park Street*, Middlesex... E	×
Paxton, Worcester..........C	445
● Peabody, Essex ....NE	10,158
● *Pecowsic*, Hampden....SW	×
Pelham, Hampshire.........W	486
● *Pemberton*, Plymouth...SE	989
Pembroke, Plymouth......SE	1,320
Pepperell, Middlesex........E	3,127
● *Pepperell Station*, Med'sexE	×
Perrys, Worcester..........C	×
Peru, Berkshire............W	305
Petersham, Worcester.......C	1,050
● *Phelp's Mills*, Essex......NE	×
● *Phillips Beach*, Essex...NE	×
Phillipston, Worcester......C	502
● *Phillipston*, Worcester....C	×
● *Pierce's Bridge*, MiddlesexE	×
Pigeon Cove, Essex.......NE	×
● **Pittsfield**, Berkshire...W	17,281
Plainfield, Hampshire......W	435
Plainville, Bristol..........SE	×
● Plainville, Norfolk........E	×
● *Pleasant Hill*, Essex.....NE	×
● Pleasant Lake, BarnstableSE	×
● *Pleasant Street*, Suffolk..E	×
● *Pleasantview*, Bristol.....SE	×
● **Plymouth**, Plymouth..SE	7,314
Plympton, Plymouth...... SE	597
● *Plympton*, Plymouth....SE	×
● Pocasset, Barnstable......SE	525
● *Point of Pines*, Suffolk...E	×
Point Shirley, Suffolk...... E	×
● Pondville, Norfolk........E	×
Ponkapog, Norfolk..........E	×
Pontoosuc, Berkshire...... W	×
● *Pope's Hill*, Suffolk.......E	×
Pottersville, Bristol........ SE	×
● Pratt's Junc., Worcester..C	×
Prattville, Plymouth...... SE	×
Prattville, Suffolk.......... E	×
Prescott, Hampshire....... W	376
● Pride's Crossing, Essex..NE	×
Princeton, Worcester........C	982
● Princeton, Depot, Worc'st'rC	×
● *Proctors*, Essex.........NE	×
● *Prospect Hill*, Middlesex.E	×
● Provincetown, B'rnst'bleSE	4,642
Pumping Station, Suffolk..E	×
● *Putnamville*, Essex.....NE	×
Quaise, Nantucket..........SE	×
● Quinapoxet, Worcester....C	300
● Quincy, Norfolk..........E	16,723
● *Quincy Adams*, Norfolk..E	×
Quincy Point, Norfolk......E	×
Quinsigamond, Worcester...C	×
Quisset, Barnstable........SE	105
● *Raddins*, Essex.........NE	×

Massachusetts

Place	Pop.
● Randolph, Norfolk.......E	3,946
Raynham, Bristol..........SE	1,340
● *Raynham*, Bristol.......SE	×
● Reading, Middlesex.......E	4,088
● *Reading Highlands*, Mid'xE	×
Readville, Norfolk..........E	×
● *Red Bridge*, Hampden..SW	×
Rehoboth, Bristol..........SE	1,786
● *Renfrew*, Berkshire.....W	×
● *Reservoir*, Norfolk...... E	×
● Revere, Suffolk...........E	5,668
Revere Beach, Suffolk.....E	×
● Richmond, Berkshire....W	796
● Richmond Furnace, B'ks'rW	300
Rider Village, Worcester...C	×
● Ridge Hill, Plymouth...SE	×
Ringville, Hampshire......W	×
Riverside, Franklin......NW	300
● *Riverside*, Hampden....SW	×
● *Riverside*, Norfolk.......E	×
● *Riverside Press*, MiddlesexE	×
● *Riverview*, Middlesex.....E	×
● *River Street*, Suffolk.....E	×
● *Roberts*, Middlesex.......E	×
● Rochdale, Worcester......C	400
Rochester, Plymouth......SE	1,012
● Rock, Plymouth..........SE	×
● Rock Bottom, Middlesex.E	×
● *Rockdale*, Norfolk........E	×
Rock Dale Mills, Berkshire W	100
● Rockland, Plymouth.....SE	5,213
● Rockport, Essex.........NE	4,087
Rockville, Norfolk..........E	×
● Roslindale, Suffolk.......E	×
Rowe, Franklin...........NW	541
● Rowley, Essex.......... NE	1,248
● Roxbury, Suffolk.........E	×
Royalston, Worcester.......C	1,030
● *Royalston*, Worcester.....C	×
● Russell, Hampden......SW	879
Russell's Mills, Bristol....SE	×
● Rutland, Worcester.......C	980
● *Rutland Summit*, W'cest'rC	×
● Sagamore, Barnstable...SE	300
● **SALEM**, Essex.........NE	30,801
● *Salem Junc.*, Middlesex..E	×
● Salisbury, Essex.........NE	1,316
Salisbury Beach, Essex....NE	×
● Salisbury point, Essex....NE	×
● *Sanderdale*, Worcester....C	×
Sandisfield, Berkshire......W	807
● Sandwich, Barnstable.....SE	1,819
● *Sandy Pond*, Middlesex..E	×
● *Satucket*, Plymouth......SE	×
● Saugus, Essex............NE	3,673
Saugus Centre, Essex.....NE	×
● *Saugus River Junc.*.E'xNE	×
● Saundersville, Worcester. C	600
● *Savin Hill*, Suffolk.......C	×
Savoy, Berkshire............W	569
Savoy Centre, Berkshire...W	×
● Saxonville, Middlesex.....E	2,000
Scituate, Plymouth...... .. SE	2,318
Scituate Centre, Plymouth SE	400
Scotland, Plymouth....... SE	×
● *Seaside Sta.*, Plymouth..SE	×
● Sea View, Plymouth......SE	×
Seekonk, Bristol...........SE	1,317
Segreganset, Bristol...... SE	×
● *Sequassett*, Bristol...... SE	×
Shaker Village, (see West Pittsfield)	×
● Sharon, Norfolk......... E	1,634
● *Sharon Heights*, Norfolk. E	×
Shattuckville, Franklin.. NW	×
● Shawmut, Bristol.........SE	×
● Sheffield, Berkshire ..... W	1,954
Shelburne, Franklin...... NW	1,553
● Shelburne Falls, Frank.NW	2,500
Sheldonville, Norfolk ..... E	400
● Sherborn, Middlesex...... E	1,381
Shirley, Middlesex.......... E	1,191
● *Shirley*, Suffolk...........E	×
Shirley Village, Middlesex.. E	124
● *Shore Line Junction*, M'x.E	×
● Shrewsbury, Worcester... C	1,449
Shutesbury, Franklin.....NW	453
Siasconset, Nantucket .... SE	131
● *Silver Hill*, Middlesex.... E	×
● *Silver Lake*, Middlesex... E	×
● Silver Lake, Plymouth... SE	×
Sixteen Acres, Hampshire..W	×
● Smith's Ferry, Hamp'lre..W	×
● *Smith's*, Hampshire..... W	×
Smith's Mills, Bristol......SE	×
Smithville, Worcester....... C	139
● Somerset, Bristol......... SE	2,106

● Somerville, Middlesex.... E 40,152
● *Somerville Junction*, M'd'x E ×
● *Somerville Highlands*, M'x E ×
● *Somerville Station*, M'd'x. E ×
● South Abington Station, Plymouth .... SE 4,529
● South Acton, Middlesex.. E 500
South Adams, (see Adams)... ×
● South Amherst, Ham'he.. W ×
● Southampton, Hampsh'e. W 1,017
● South Ashburnham, Worc'r C ×
South Ashfield, Franklin. NW 250
● South Athol, Worcester... C ×
South Attleborough, Bris'l SE 2,500
South Beach, Dukes ...... SE ×
● South Bellingham, Nor'k E ×
South Berlin, Worcester..... C ×
● South Billerica, Mid'sex.. E ×
● *South Bolton*, Worcester . C ×
● Southborough, Worcester. C 2,114
● South Boston, Suffolk.... E ×
● South Braintree, Norfolk E ×
● South Brewster, B'nst'le SE ×
● Southbridge, Worcester... C 7,655
South Byfield, Essex...... NE 243
South Carver, Plymouth... SE ×
● South Chatham, B'nst'le SE 400
● South Chelmsford, M'd'x. E ×
● *South Clinton*, Worcest.r. C ×
South Dartmouth, Bristol.. SE ×
● South Deerfield, Fr'k'n NW 1,600
● South Dennis, B'nst'ble.. SE 650
● South Duxbury, P'm'th. SE ×
● South Easton, Bristol.... SE 247
South Egremont, B'kshire.. W 450
South End, Suffolk............ E ×
South Essex, Essex .... NE ×
Southfield, Berkshire ...... W 160
● South Fitchburg, Worc'er. C ×
● South Framingham, M'd'x E ×
● South Franklin, Norfolk.. E ×
South Gardner, Worces'r... C ×
● *South Georgetown*, Essex NE ×
South Groveland, Essex... NE ×
South Hadley, Hampshire.. W 4,261
South Hadley Falls, H'p're.. W 2,800
● South Hanover, Plym'th SE ×
● South Hanson, Plym'th.. SE ×
● South Harwich, B'n'ble.. SE ×
South Hingham, Plym'th.. SE ×
South Hyannis, Barnstable SE ×
● South Lancaster, W'ester. C ×
● *South Lawrence*, Essex. NE ×
● South Lee, Berkshire .... W 200
● South Lincoln, Mid'sex... E ×
South Lynnfield, Essex... NE ×
● South Middleborough, Plymouth................ SE ×
● South Milford, Worcester. C ×
● *South Monson*, Ha'pden SW ×
South Natick, Middlesex.... E ×
South Orleans, Barnstable. SE ×
South Peabody, Essex .... NE 900
South Quincy, Norfolk..... E ×
South Rehoboth, Bristol... SE ×
● South Royalston, Wor'ter. C ×
South Sandisfield, B'kshire. W 75
South Sandwich, B'nst'le.. SE ×
South Scituate, Plymouth. SE ×
● South Sherborn, Mid'sex. E 32
● *South Spencer*, Worcester C ×
● South Sudbury, Mid'sex.. E 237
South Swansea, Bristol.... SE ×
● South Truro, Barnstable SE ×
● Southville, Worcester..... C 40
● South Walpole, Norfolk.. E ×
● South Wareham, Pl'm'th SE ×
● South Wellfleet, B'nst'ble SE ×
South Westminster, W'cest'r C ×
South Westport, Bristol... SE ×
● South Weymouth, Norf'k.. E ×
● Southwick, Hampden... SW [illegible]
South Williamstown, B'ksh'e W [illegible]
● *South Wilmington*, M'ds'x E ×
● *South Worcester*, W'rc'st'r C ×
South Worthington, H'psh'e W 200
South Wrentham, (see Wr't'm) ×
South Yarmouth, B'nst'ble. SE 925
● *South Yarmouth*, B'rnst'le SE ×
● Spencer, Worcester....... C 8,747
● *Springdale*, Norfolk........ E ×
● **SPRINGFIELD**, Hampden.............. SW 44,179
Spring Hill, Barnstable.... SE 396
● *Spring Street*, Suffolk.... E ×
Spruce Corner, Franklin. NW ×
Squibnocket, Dukes....... SE ×

Massachusetts

● State Farm, Plymouth.. SE ×
● State Line, Berkshire.... W 250
● *State Line*, Hampden... SW ×
● *State Line*, Worcester .... C ×
Stearnsville, Berkshire..... W 200
● Steep Brook, Bristol.... SE ×
● Sterling, Worcester ...... C 1,244
● Sterling Junc., Worcester. C ×
● *Stevens*, Essex.......... NE ×
● Still River, Worcester..... C 200
● Stockbridge, Berkshire... W 2,132
● *Stockbridge Iron Works*, Berkshire............. W ×
● *Stock Yards*, Norfolk.... E ×
● Stoneham, Middlesex..... E 6,115
● *Stone Haven*, Suffolk..... E ×
● *Stony Brook*, Middlesex.. E ×
● Stoughton, Norfolk....... E 4,852
Stow, Middlesex............ E 903
Sturbridge, Worcester...... C 2,074
● Sudbury, Middlesex...... E 1,197
● *Summit*, Worcester....... C ×
● *Summit Siding*, Worc'ster. C ×
Sunderland, Franklin..... NW 663
Sutton, Worcester .... C 3,180
● Swampscott, Essex..... NE 3,198
● Swansea, Bristol .... SE 1,456
Swansea Centre, Bristol... SE ×
Sweet's Corners, Berkshire W ×
Swift River, Hampshire.... W ×
● Tapleyville, Essex....... NE ×
Tarpaulin Cove, Dukes..... SE ×
● **Taunton**, Bristol...... SE 25,448
Teaticket, Barnstable...... SE ×
● Templeton, Worcester.... C 2,999
Tenneville, Hampden..... SW 100
● Tewksbury, Middlesex... E 2,515
● *Tewksbury Junc.*, M'd's'x E ×
● *Texas*, Worcester .... C ×
● Thorndike, Hampden... SW 1,100
● *Thornton*, Suffolk......... E ×
● Three Rivers, Hampden SW 1,300
● *Tilton's*, Norfolk......... E ×
Tisbury, Dukes............ SE 1,506
● *Tilicut*, Plymouth....... SE ×
Tolland, Hampden........ SW 393
● Topsfield, Essex........ NE 1,022
● *Tower Hill*, Middlesex.... E ×
Town Cove, Barnstable.... SE ×
● Townsend, Middlesex .... E 1,750
● Townsend Harbor, Mid'sx E 305
● *Tremont*, Plymouth..... SE ×
Truro, Barnstable......... SE 919
● *Truro Station*, Barnstable SE ×
● Tuft's College, Middlesex. E ×
Tully, Franklin.......... NW ×
● Turner's Fall's, Franklin NW 4,000
● *Turner's Falls Junction*, Franklin .... NW ×
● *Turnpike*, Middlesex..... E ×
● *Turnpike*, Plymouth.... SE ×
● Tyngsborough, Middlesex. E 662
Tyringham, Berkshire...... W 412
● *Union Market*, Middlesex E ×
● *Union Square*, Middlesex E ×
● Unionville, Norfolk....... E ×
● *Upper Falls*, Middlesex.. E ×
Upton, Worcester........... C 1,878
● Uxbridge, Worcester..... C 3,408
● Van Deusen, Berkshire.. W 55
Vineyard Haven, Dukes... SE 1,560
● Waban, Middlesex........ E ×
● *Wachusett*, Worcester.... C ×
● *Wadsworth*, Norfolk..... E ×
● Wakefield, Middlesex...... E 6,982
● *Wakefield Junc.*, Midd'sex E ×
Wales, Hampden........... SW 700
Walker, Bristol............ SE 32
● *Walnut Hill*, Middlesex.. E ×
● Walnut Hill, Norfolk...... E ×
● Walpole, Norfolk......... E 2,604
● Waltham, Middlesex...... E 18,707
Wamesit, Middlesex........ E ×
● *Wamesit Station*, Middlesex E ×
● *Wampum*, Norfolk....... E ×
Waquoit, Barnstable....... SE 250
● Ward Hill, Essex....... NE ×
● Ware, Hampshire......... W 7,329
● *Ware*, Hampshire......... W ×
● Wareham, Plymouth.... SE 3,451
● Warren, Worcester........ C 4,681
Warwick, Franklin...... NW 565
● *Washacum*, Worcester... C ×
● Washington, Berkshire... W 434
Waterford, (see Blackstone). ×
● Watertown, Middlesex.... E 7,073
● Waterville, Worcester.... C 500

Massachusetts

Wauwinet, Nantucket.... SE ×
● Waverly, Middlesex...... E 350
● Wayland, Middlesex...... E 2,060
● *Wayside Inn*, Middlesex. E ×
● Webster, Worcester....... C 7,031
● *Webster Junc.*, Worcester C ×
● *Webster Mills*, Worcester. C ×
● *Webster Place*, Plymouth SE ×
● *Weir Junction*, Bristol.. SE ×
● Wellesley, Norfolk........ E 3,600
● *Wellesley Farms*, Norfolk E ×
● Wellesley Hills, Norfolk.. E ×
● Wellfleet, Barnstable.... SE 1,291
● Wellington, Middlesex.... E ×
● *Wenaumet*, Barnstable.. SE ×
Wendell, Franklin........ NW 505
● Wendell Depot, Fr'nklin NW 340
Wenham, Essex.......... NE 886
● Wenham Depot, Essex.. NE ×
● West Acton, Middlesex... E 450
● *West Andover*, Essex... NE ×
● West Auburn, Worcester. C ×
● West Barnstable, B'nst'e SE ×
West Becket, Berkshire.... W 100
● *West Bedford*, Middlesex. E ×
● West Berlin, Worcester... C ×
● Westborough, Worcester.. C 5,195
West Boxford, Essex...... NE 350
● West Boylston, Worcester C 3,019
West Brewster, Barnstable. SE ×
● West Bridgewater, P'm'h. SE 1,917
● *West Brimfield*, H'pden. SW ×
● West Brookfield, W'rc'ter C 1,592
● *West Cambridge*, M'dlesex E ×
● West Chatham, B'nst'ble SE 225
● West Chelmsford, M'lessex E 90
West Chesterfield, Ha'psh'e. W 188
Westchester Highlands, Middlesex.............. E ×
West Chop, Dukes......... SE ×
West Cummington, H'psh'e W 250
Westdale, Plymouth....... SE ×
West Danvers, (see Danvers). ×
West Danvers Junction, Essex NE ×
West Dedham, Norfolk..... E ×
● West Deerfield, Franklin NW ×
West Dennis, Barnstable.. SE 800
West Dighton, Bristol..... SE ×
● West Dudley, Worcester.. C 240
West Duxbury, Plymouth. SE ×
● *West Everett*, Middlesex. E ×
● West Falmouth, B'nsta'e SE 400
West Farms, Hampshire.... W ×
● Westfield, Hampden.... SW 9,805
● West Fitchburg, W'rc'r... C ×
Westford, Middlesex....... E 2,250
● *Westford*, Middlesex...... E ×
● *Westford Station*, M'd'sex E ×
West Foxborough, Norfolk. E ×
West Gardner, Worcester... C ×
West Gloucester, Essex... NE 91
● *West Gloucester Station*, Essex.............. NE ×
West Granville, Hampden. SW 500
● West Groton, Middlesex.. E 300
Westhampton, Hampshire.. W 477
● West Hanover, Plymouth SE ×
West Harwich, Barnstable. SE ×
● West Hatfield, Hampshire W 150
West Hawley, Franklin.. NW ×
● West Hingham, Plymo'th SE ×
● *West Leominster*, Worc'ter C ×
West Leyden, Franklin... NW ×
● *West Lynn*, Middlesex.... E ×
● *West Manchester*, Essex NE ×
● West Mansfield, Bristol.. SE ×
● West Medford, Middlesex. E ×
● West Medway, Norfolk... E ×
West Millbury, Worcester... C ×
Westminster, Worcester..... C 1,688
● Westminster Depot, Wor'r C ×
West Newbury, Essex..... NE 1,796
● West Newton, Middlesex. E ×
West Northfield, Franklin NW 150
● Weston, Middlesex....... E 1,664
West Otis, Berkshire....... W ×
● *West Oxford*, Worcester.. C ×
● West Peabody Essex.... NE 10,200
West Pelham, Hampshire.. W ×
● West Pittsfield, Berkshire W 200
● ***West Portal***, **Berkshire.. W** ×
Westport, Bristol.......... SE 2,599
● *Westport Factory*, Brist'l SE ×
Westport Harbor, Bristol.. SE ×
Westport Point, Bristol... SE ×
● *West Quincy*, Norfolk.... E ×
● West Roxbury, Suffolk... E ×

Town, County	Index	Pop.
West Rutland, Worcester	C	×
● *West Rutland Station*, Worcester	C	×
West Scituate, Plymouth	SE	×
● *West Somerville*, Mid'ex	E	×
● WestSpringfield, Ham'n	SW	5,077
West Sterling, Worcester	C	×
● West Stockbridge, Berks'e	W	1,492
West Stockbridge Centre, Berkshire	W	×
● West Stoughton, Norfolk	E	×
● *West Street*, Middlesex	E	×
West Sutton, Worcester	C	×
West Tisbury, Dukes	SE	×
● West Townsend, Middlesex	E	1,739
● West Upton, Worcester	C	×
● Westvale, Middlesex	E	×
● *West Walpole*, Norfolk	E	×
● *West Ware*, Hampshire	W	×
● West Wareham, Plymo'h	SE	×
● West Warren, Worcester	C	×
West Whately, (see Whately)		×
West Worthington, Hamps'e	W	100
● *West Wrentham*, Norfolk	E	160
West Yarmouth, Barnstable	SE	360
● Weymouth, Norfolk	E	10,866
Weymouth Centre, Norfolk	E	×
Weymouth Depot, Norfolk	E	×
Weymouth Heights, Norfolk	E	×
● Whately, Franklin	NW	779
● *Whately*, Franklin	NW	×
● *Whipples*, Hampden	SW	×
● *Whitins*, Worcester	C	×
Whitinsville, Worcester	C	4,600
Whitman, Plymouth	SE	4,441
● *Whitman*, Plymouth	SE	4,520
● *Whitman Crossing*, Mid'x	E	×
● *Whitney's*, Middlesex	E	×
● *Whittenton*, Bristol	SE	×
Wianno, Barnstable	SE	×
Wilbraham, Hampden	SW	1,814
● Wilkinsonville, Worcester	C	×
● Williamsburgh, H'psh're	W	2,057
Williamstown, Berkshire	W	4,221
● Williamstown Sta., B'ksh'r	W	600
● Williamsville, Worcester	C	×
● Willimansett, Hampden	SW	×
● Wilmington, Middlesex	E	1,213
● *Wilmington Junc.*, Mid'x	E	×
● Winchendon, Worcester	C	4,390
Winchendon Sp'gs, Worc'st'r	C	×
● Winchester, Middlesex	E	4,861
● *Winchester Highlands*, Middlesex	E	×
Windsor, Berkshire	W	612
● *Winslow's*, Norfolk	E	×
● *Winslow's Crossing*, Plym	SE	×
● *Winter Hill*, Middlesex	E	×
Winthrop, Suffolk	E	2,726
● *Winthrop Beach*, Suffolk	E	×
● *Winthrop Centre*, Suffolk	E	×
Winthrop H'gl'nds, Suffolk	E	×
● *Winthrop Junc.*, Suffolk	E	×
● Woburn, Middlesex	E	13,499
● *Woburn H'hl'nds*, Mid'sex	E	×
● Wollaston, Norfolk	E	2,000
● *Woodbury*, Essex	NE	×
● *Wooland*, Middlesex	E	×
● Wood's Holl, Barnstable	SE	500
● *Wood Island*, Suffolk	E	×
Woodville, Middlesex	E	×
● *Woonsocket Junc.*, W'c's'r	C	×
● **WORCESTER**, W'c's'r	C	84,655
Worthington, Hampshire	W	714
● Wrentham, Norfolk	E	2,566
● *Wyoming*, Middlesex	E	×
Yarmouth, Barnstable	SE	1,760
● Yarmouth Farms, B'n'st	SE	×
Yarmouth Port, Barnstable	SE	1,800
● *Yarmouth Sta.*, B'rnst'ble	SE	×
● Zoar, Franklin	NW	200
● Zylonite, Berkshire	W	350

MICHIGAN.

COUNTIES.	INDEX.	POP.
Alcona	NE	5,409
Alger	NW	1,238
Allegan	SW	38,961
Alpena	NE	15,581
Antrim	N	10,413
Arenac	C	5,683
Baraga	NW	3,036
Barry	SW	23,783
Bay	C	56,412
Benzie	NW	5,237
Berrien	SW	41,285
Branch	S	26,791
Calhoun	S	43,501
Cass	SW	20,953
Charlevoix	N	9,686
Cheboygan	N	11,986
Chippewa	N	12,019
Clare	C	7,558
Clinton	C	26,509
Crawford	N	2,962
Delta	NW	15,330
* Dickinson	NW	×
Eaton	S	32,094
Emmet	N	8,756
Genesee	C	39,430
Gladwin	C	4,208
Gogebic	NW	13,166
Grand Traverse	NW	13,355
Gratiot	C	28,668
Hillsdale	S	30,660
Houghton	NW	35,389
Huron	E	28,545
Ingham	S	37,666
Ionia	C	32,801
Iosco	NE	15,224
Iron	NE	4,432
Isabella	C	18,784
Isle Royale	NW	135
Jackson	S	45,031
Kalamazoo	SW	39,273
Kalkaska	N	5,160
Kent	W	109,922
Keweenaw	NW	2,894
Lake	W	6,505
Lapeer	E	29,213
Leelanaw	NW	7,944
Lenawee	S	48,448
Livingston	S	20,858
Luce	N	2,455
Mackinac	N	7,830
Macomb	SE	31,813
Manistee	NW	24,230
Manitou	NW	860
Marquette	NW	39,521
Mason	W	16,385
Mecosta	C	19,697
Menominee	NW	33,639
Midland	C	10,657
Missaukee	N	5,048
Monroe	SE	32,337
Montcalm	C	32,637
Montmorency	N	1,487
Muskegon	W	40,013
Newaygo	W	20,476
Oakland	SE	41,245
Oceana	W	15,698
Ogemaw	N	5,583
Ontonagon	NW	3,756
Osceola	C	14,630
Oscoda	NE	1,904
Otsego	N	4,272
Ottawa	W	35,358
Presque Isle	N	4,687
Roscommon	N	2,033
Saginaw	C	82,273
Saint Clair	E	52,105
Saint Joseph	SW	25,356
Sanilac	E	32,589
Schoolcraft	NW	5,818
Shiawassee	C	30,952
Tuscola	E	32,508
Van Buren	SW	30,541
Washtenaw	SE	42,210
Wayne	SE	257,114
Wexford	NW	11,278
Total		2,093,889

* New county formed since census was taken. Population unknown.

TOWN. COUNTY.	INDEX	POP.
Aarwood, Kalkaska	N	×
Abbott, Mason	W	×
● *Abbotsford*, Saint Clair	E	×
● *Abitosse*, Gogebic	NW	×
● Abronia, Allegan	SW	32
Abscota, Calhoun	S	50
Achill, Roscommon	N	×
Acme, Grand Traverse	NW	175
Acton, Iosco	NE	×
● Ada, Kent	W	350
● Adair, Saint Clair	E	60
Adam's Corners, (see Ruth)		×
Adamsville, Cass	SW	200
● Addison, Lenawee	S	425
● *Addison Junc.*, Lenawee	S	×
● **Adrian**, Lenawee	S	8,756
Advance, Charlevoix	N	60
Ætna, Newaygo	W	40
Afton, Charlevoix	N	×
Agate Harbor, Keweenaw	NW	×
● Agnew, Ottawa	W	60
Agricultural College, Ingh'm	S	×
● Ainger, Eaton	S	×
● Akron, Tuscola	E	500
Alabaster, Iosco	NE	300
● Alamando, Midland	C	×
● Alamo, Kalamazoo	SW	90
● Alanson, Emmet	N	200
Alaska, Kent	W	300
● Alba, Antrim	N	750
● Albion, Calhoun	S	3,763
Alcona, Alcona	NE	100
● *Alecto*, Delta	NW	×
Alembic, Isabella	C	130
● *Alexander*, Chippewa	N	×
Algansee, Branch	S	35
● Alger, Arenac	C	150
Algodon, Ionia	C	32
Algoma, (see Rockford)		×
Algonac, Saint Clair	E	840
Alice, Oceana	W	×
● **Allegan**, Allegan	SW	2,669
Allen, Hillsdale	S	530
Allen Creek, Oceana	W	200
Allendale, Ottawa	W	150
● *Allen Station*, Hillside	S	×
● *Alleyton*, Newaygo	W	300
Allis, Presque Isle	N	×
● Allouez, Keweenaw	NW	2,000
● Alma, Gratiot	C	1,655
Almena, Van Buren	SW	100
Almer, Tuscola	E	×
Almira, Benzie	NW	30
Almont, Lapeer	E	717
● **Alpena**, Alpena	NE	11,283
● Alpine, Kent	W	150
● Alto, Kent	W	×
Alton, Kent	W	80
Altona, Mecosta	C	200
Alverson, Ingham	S	35
● Amadore, Sanilac	E	150
● Amasa, Iron	NE	500
● Amber, Mason	W	×
● Amble, Montcalm	C	×
Amboy, Hillsdale	S	20
Amity, Kalkaska	N	×
Amleith, Bay	C	×
Ammon, (see River Rouge)		×
Amsden, Montcalm	C	100
● Amy, Oakland	SE	180
Anchorville, Saint Clair	E	420
● Anderson, Livingston	S	×
Anderson Sta., (see Applegate)		×
● **Ann Arbor**, Washte'w	SE	9,431
● *Anthony*, Houghton	NW	×
● *Antoine*, Dickinson	NW	×
● *Antrim*, Antrim	N	480
Antrim, (see Glass River)		×
Appenzell, Crawford	N	×
● Applegate, Sanilac	E	350
Appleton, Emmet	N	×
Aral, Benzie	NW	100
Arbela, Tuscola	E	50
Arcadia, Manistee	NW	200
Archie, Grand Traverse	NW	75
Arenac, Arenac	**C**	**150**
Arendal, Manistee	NW	150
● *Argenta*, Allegan	SW	×
Argentine, Genesee	C	150
Argyle, Sanilac	E	60
Arkdale, Lapeer	E	×
Arkona, Antrim	N	×
Arland, Jackson	S	20
Arlington, Van Buren	SW	25
● Armada, Macomb	SE	638
● *Armstrong*, Iron	NE	×
● *Arn*, Iosco	NE	×
● *Arnold Lake*, Clare	C	×
● Arthur, Saginaw	C	39
Arthur Bay, Menominee	NW	45
Arvon, Baraga	NW	150
● Ashland, Newaygo	W	350
Ashland Centrê, Newaygo	W	97
● Ashley, Gratiot	C	711
Ashley, Kent	W	×
● Ashton, Osceola	C	200
Assyria, Barry	SW	100

Place	Region	Population
● Athens, Calhoun	S	441
Athlone, Monroe	SE	20
● Atkins, Saint Clair	E	100
● *Atkinson*, Iron	NE	×
Atlanta, Montgomery	N	100
Atlantic Mine, Houghton	NW	1,600
Atlas, Genesee	C	150
● Attica, Lapeer	E	353
Atwood, Antrim	N	350
● *Atwood's Landing*, Clare	C	×
● Auburn, Bay	C	300
● *Auburn*, Oakland	SE	100
Au Gres, Arenac	C	300
● Augusta, Kalamazoo	SW	[illegible]
Aurelius, Ingham	S	250
● Au Sable, Iosco	NE	4,328
Ausable, Oscoda	NE	×
Austerlitz, Kent	W	100
Austin, Oakland	SE	150
● *Austin Lake*, Kalamazoo	SW	×
Austin Mill, Sanilac	E	×
● **Au Train**, Alger	NW	300
● Averill, Midland	C	100
Avery, Berrien	SW	80
Averyville, (see Wyman)		×
● Avoca, Saint Clair	E	50
Avondale, Osceola	C	150
Ayr, Emmet	N	100
● Azalia, Monroe	SE	200
Bachelor, Mason	W	50
● **Bad Axe**, Huron	E	842
Badeaux Mills, (see Holton)		×
● *Bagdad*, Marquette	NW	×
● Bagley, Menominee	NW	200
● *Bagley*, Otsego	N	×
● Bailey, Muskegon	W	400
● *Bailies*, Newaygo	W	×
Bainbridge, Berrien	SW	30
Baker's Corners, (see Berville)		×
Bakertown, Berrien	SW	×
● **Baldwin**, Lake	W	429
Baldwins, (see Horton)		×
Ball, Cheboygan	N	32
Ball Creek (see Tyrone Sta.)		×
Ballards, Kent	W	×
Ballentine, Ontonagon	NW	×
Bamfields, Alcona	NE	×
● Bancroft, Shiawassee	C	642
Bandola, Wexford	NW	60
Banfield, Barry	SW	100
● Bangor, Van Buren	SW	904
● Bankers, Hillsdale	S	25
Banking Ground, Iosco	NE	×
● *Banks*, Bay	C	×
Banner, Sanilac	E	×
● Bannister, Gratiot	C	250
● Baraga, Baraga	NW	600
Barbeau, Chippewa	N	×
Barker Creek, Kalkaska	N	50
● Barkville, Delta	NW	700
Barnard, Charlevoix	N	×
● Barroda, Berrien	SW	×
● Barron Lake, Cass	SW	175
● *Barry*, Mecosta	C	30
Barryville, Barry	SW	25
Bartlett, Grand Traverse	NW	30
Barton, Newaygo	W	×
Bass Lake, (see Birkett)		×
● Bass River, Ottawa	W	50
● Batavia, Branch	S	100
● *Batcheller*, Mason	W	×
Bates, Grand Traverse	NW	×
Bates, (see Ashton)		×
● Bath, Clinton	C	300
● *Bath Mill*, Jackson	S	×
● Battle Creek, Calhoun	S	13,197
Batton's Crossing, Iosco	NE	×
Bauer, Ottawa	W	×
● **BAY CITY**, Bay	C	27,839
● *Bay City Junc.*, Wayne	SE	×
● *Bay City Road*, Midland	C	×
Bay de Noquette, Delta	NW	260
Bay Mill, Muskegon	W	×
Bay Mills, Chippewa	N	500
● *Bay Mills Sta.*, Chippewa	N	×
● Bay Port, Huron	E	150
● *Bay Port Junction*, Huron	E	×
● *Bay Siding*, Delta	NW	×
Bay Springs, Charlevoix	N	200
● Bay View, Emmet	N	50
Beacon, Marquette	NW	2,000
Beadles, Iosco	NE	×
● *Bear Creek*, Manistee	NW	×
● *Beardsleys*, Bay	C	×
Beaver, Newaygo	W	×
Bear Lake, Manistee	NW	432
Bear Lake Sta., (see Berlamont)		×
Beaser, Ontonagon	NW	×
● *Beaufait Station*, Wayne	SE	×
● *Beaufort Sta.*, Baraga	NW	×
● *Beaver*, Delta	NW	×
● Beaver Dam, Ottawa	W	70
Beaver Island, (see St. James)		×
● Beaver Lake, Ogemaw	N	100
Beaverton, Gladwin	C	300
Beckett, (see Valley Centre)		×
Beddow, Oakland	SE	×
Bedell, Bay	C	200
Bedford, Calhoun	S	300
Beebe, Gratiot	C	50
Beebe's Corners, (see Richmond)		×
● Beech, Wayne	SE	350
Beechville, (see N. Branch)		×
● Beechwood, Iron	NE	×
● *Beitner*, G'd Traverse	NW	×
● Belden, Wayne	SE	200
● Belding, Ionia	C	1,730
● *Belford*, Genesee	C	×
Belknap, Allegan	SW	×
Belknap, (see Crawford's Cor.)		×
Bell, Presque Isle	N	100
● **Bellaire**, Antrim	N	500
Bell Branch, Wayne	SE	75
Belle Oak, (see Locke)		×
Belle River, Saint Clair	E	65
Belle River, (see Columbus)		×
● Belleville, Wayne	SE	367
● Bellevue, Eaton	S	914
● *Bellows Siding*, Benzie	NW	×
● Belmont, Kent	W	40
● *Belsey*, Genesee	C	×
● *Belt Line Junc.*, Wayne	SE	×
Belvidere, Montcalm	C	195
● *Bendon*, Benzie	NW	×
Benee Cross'g, Ontonagon	NW	50
Bengal, Clinton	C	×
Benjamin Mills, Me'nee	NW	×
● Bennett, Lake	W	×
● Bennington, Shiawassee	C	365
Benona, Oceana	W	300
Benson, Wexford	NW	28
Bently, Bay	C	×
Benton, Washtenaw	SE	×
● Benton Harbor, Berrien	SW	3,692
● **Benzonia**, Benzie	NW	250
Berkshire, Sanilac	E	51
Berlamont, Van Buren	SW	100
● Berlin, Ottawa	W	400
Berlin, (see Belle River)		×
● Berne, Huron	E	150
● *Berne Junction*, Huron	E	×
● Berrien Centre, Berrien	SW	150
● **Berrien Springs**, B'n	SW	745
Berryville, Charlevoix	N	130
● Bertrand, Berrien	SW	200
● Berville, Saint Clair	E	350
● **Bessemer**, Gogebic	NW	2,566
● *Bessemer Junc.*, Gogebic	NW	×
Bethel, Branch	S	50
Betzer, Hillsdale	S	15
Big Beaver, Oakland	SE	250
Biggs, Oscoda	NE	×
Big Prairie, Newaygo	W	60
● **Big Rapids**, Mecosta	C	5,303
● *Big Rapids Junc.* Mus'gn.	W	×
Big River, Delta	NW	×
Big Rock, Montmorency	N	20
Big Spring, Ottawa	W	100
Bingham, Leelanaw	NW	250
● *Birch Creek*, Meno'inee	NW	×
● Birch Run, Saginaw	C	200
Bird, Oceana	W	45
Birkett, Washtenaw	SE	60
● Birmingham, Oakland	SE	899
Bismarck, Eaton	S	200
● Biteley, Newaygo	W	×
Blackberry Ridge, (see Sammon's Landing)		×
● Black Lake, Muskegon	W	×
● Blackmar, Saginaw	C	55
● *Blackmarr*, Oceana	W	×
● Black River, Alcona	NE	525
Black River Sta., (see Irondale)		
Black's Corners, (see Imlay)		×
● Blaine, St. Clair	E	300
Blair, Berry	SW	30
● Blanchard, Isabella	C	219
● *Blemers*, Gogebic	NW	×
Blendon, Ottawa	W	×
Bliss, Emmet	N	26
● Blissfield, Lenawee	S	1,132
Blodgett, Missaukee	N	×
Bloomer, Montcalm	C	30
● Bloomingdale, Van Bu'n.	SW	380
Blooming Valley, Oceana	W	×
Bluffton, Muskegon	W	600
Blumfield, Saginaw	C	150
Bodell's Mills, (see Ashland)		×
Bohemian, Ontonagon	NW	×
Bois Blanc, Mackinac	N	×
Bolton, Alpena	NE	×
Bonanza, (see Lake Odessa)		×
Bonney, Lenawee	S	×
● Boon, Wexford	NW	150
Borculo, Ottawa	W	200
Borland, Mecosta	C	×
● *Boston*, Houghton	NW	×
Boston, (see Saranac)		×
Boston, (see Pavilion)		×
Bostwick, Kent	W	35
● *Bowen*, Kent	W	×
Bowen Siding, (see Holton)		×
Bowen's Mills, Barry	SW	70
Bowne, Kent	W	100
Boyne, Charlevoix	N	46
● Boyne Falls, Charlevoix	N	300
Bradford, Midland	C	130
● Bradley, Allegan	SW	300
Brady, Saginaw	C	×
Brady, (see Vicksburg)		×
Bradley's Sta., (see Eastwood)		×
● Brampton, Delta	NW	200
● Branch, Mason	W	20
Brandon, Oakland	SE	×
Branagan's Corners, (see Roseburg)		×
Brant, Saginaw	C	80
● Bravo, Allegan	SW	200
● Breckenridge, Gratiot	C	500
● Breedsville, Van Buren	SW	212
● Brent Creek, Genesee	C	×
Brest, Monroe	SE	50
Brevort, Mackinac	N	×
Brice, Gratiot	C	×
● Bridgehamton, Sanilac	E	×
● Bridgeport, Saginaw	C	600
Bridgeport Centre, (see Bridg'pt)		×
Bridgeton, Newaygo	W	100
Bridgeville, Gratiot	C	200
● Bridgewater, Washtenaw	SE	100
● Bridgman, Berrien	SW	200
● Brighton, Livingston	S	741
Briley, Montgomery	N	40
Brinton, Isabella	C	50
Bristol, Lake	W	100
Bristol, Iosco	NE	×
● Britton, Lenawee	S	400
Brockway, Saint Clair	E	375
Brockway Centre, (see Yale)		×
Brockway Sta., (see Charlesworth)		×
● Bronson, Branch	S	875
Brookfield, Eaton	S	150
● *Brookfield*, Manistee	NW	195
● Brookings, Newaygo	W	100
Brooklin, (see Davis)		×
● Brooklyn, Jackson	S	596
Brooks, Newaygo	W	35
● *Brooks*, Saginaw	C	500
Brookside, Newaygo	W	×
Broomfield, Isabella	C	20
Brotherton, Houghton	NW	×
● Brouard, Barry	SW	20
Brown, Manistee	NW	×
● Brown City, Sanilac	E	352
● *Brownwells*, Kalamazoo	SW	×
Browns Dale, Otsego	N	×
● *Brown's Mills*, Van B'n	SW	×
● *Brown's Siding*, Calhoun	S	×
Brown's Sid'g, Marquette	NW	×
Brown's Sta., (see Sawyer)		×
Brownstown, (see Flat Rock)		×
Brownstown, (see Torch Lake)		×
Brownsville, Cass	SW	100
● Bruce Cross'g, Onto'g'n	NW	×
● *Brule*, Iron	NW	×
● Brutus, Emmet	N	100
Bryan, Monroe	SE	×
Bryants, Iosco	NE	×
● *Bryar Hill*, Monroe	SE	×
● Buchanan, Berrien	SW	1,994
Buchtel, (see Loomis)		×
Buckhorn, Cheboygan	N	26
Buckhorn, (see Rose)		×
Buel, Sanilac	E	32
● Buena Vista, Saginaw	C	175
● *Buffalo Mine*, Marquette	NW	×
Bunker Hill, Ingham	S	100
Burdickville, Leelanaw	NW	50
Burgess, Charlevoix	N	50
Burlington, Calhoun	S	304

Place	Pop.
Burlington, (see N'th Branch)	×
● *Burlington Sta.*, Calhoun. S	×
Burnham, Manistee...... NW	250
● *Burnham*, Isabella....... C	×
Burnip's Corners, Allegan SW	150
● *Burns*, Saint Clair........ E	×
Burns, Shiawassee.......... C	75
Burnside, Lapeer........... E	125
● *Burns Spur*, Delta..... NW	×
● Burr Oak, Saint Joseph SW	687
● Burt, Saginaw........... C	70
Burt Lake, Cheboygan..... N	×
● Burton, Shiawassee....... C	100
● *Bushville*, Cheboygan.... N	×
Buss, Leelanaw.......... NW	×
Butler, Branch.............. S	75
Butman, Gladwin........... C	×
● Butternut, Montcalm..... C	×
Buttersville, Mason........ W	×
● Byers, Mecosta........... C	25
● Byron, Shiawassee........ C	413
● Byron Centre, Kent...... W	300
● **Cadillac**, Wexford... NW	4,461
● Cadmus, Lenawee .... S	30
Cady, Macomb.............. SE	400
Cady's Corners, (see Cady)...	×
Cahoon, Isabella........... C	×
Cairns, Clare............... C	×
Caldwell, Isabella.......... C	60
Caledonia, (see La Barge)....	×
● Caledonia Station, Kent.. W	438
California, Branch.......... S	150
● Calkinsville, Isabella...... C	45
Calos, Calhoun......... .... S	×
● Calumet, Houghton.... NW	1,159
● *Calumet Mine*, Iron.... NE	×
Calvin, Cass............... SW	30
Cambria, Hillsdale......... S	350
Cambridge, Lenawee........ S	150
Camden, Hillsdale .... S	425
Campbell, Ionia............. C	250
● *Campbell*, Delta.......... NW	×
Campbell's Corn's, Ogemaw N	50
Camp Douglas, Manistee. NW	200
Canada Corners, Muskegon. W	20
Canandaigua, Lenawee...... S	150
Canboro, Huron .... E	25
Canby, Emmet............. N	×
Cannonsburgh, Kent....... W	250
● Canton, Wayne.......... SE	68
● Capac, St. Clair.......... E	600
● Carbondale, Menominee NW	50
● *Carey*, Lake.............. W	×
● Carland, Shiawassee C	60
● Carleton, Monroe........ SE	386
Carlisle, Eaton............. S	100
Carlton Centre, Barry..... SW	140
● *Carlisle*, Kent........... W	×
● Carney, Menominee.... NW	50
● **Caro**, Tuscola........... E	1,701
● *Caro Junction*, Tuscola... E	×
Carp, Marquette......... NW	×
Carpenter, Emmet .... N	30
● *Carpenters*, Lapeer....... E	75
● Carp Lake, Emmet....... N	15
● *Carp Lake*, Leelanaw.. NW	×
● Carrollton, Saginaw....... C	1,074
● *Carruther's Spur*, Mackl'c N	×
● Carson City, Montcalm.... C	921
● Carsonville, Sanilac....... E	600
Cascade, Kent.............. W	300
● *Cascade unction*, Marq. NW	×
Casco, (see W.st Casco)......	×
Casco, St. Clair............ E	400
● Caseville, Huron.......... E	508
Cash, Sanilac .... E	100
● Casnovia, Muskegon...... W	275
Cass Bridge, Saginaw....... C	40
● Cass City, Tuscola .... E	813
● **Cassopolis**, Cass...... SW	1,369
Cato, Montcalm............ C	125
Cat Head Village, Leel'naw NW	×
● *Cedar*, Menominee..... NW	×
Caywood, (see Gowen)......	×
Cedar, (see Gladwin)....... C	×
Cedar Bank, Jackson........ S	×
Cedar Creek, Barry....... SW	300
● Cedar Dale, Sanilac....... E	75
● *Cedar Grand Forks* Glad'n C	×
● Cedar Lake, Montcalm.... C	375
Cedar River, Menominee. NW	307
Cedar Run, Benzie....... NW	×
● Cedar Springs, Kent...... W	1,035
Cedarville, Menominee .. NW	×
Cedarville, Mackinac....... N	×
● Central Lake, Antrim.... N	245
Central Mine, Keweenaw.. NW	1,300

Place	Pop.
Centre, (see Hoytville)	×
Centre Harbor, (see Sand B'ch)	×
● Centre Line, Macomb.... SE	200
● **Centreville**, St. Jos .. SW	775
Centreville Sta'ion, Delta. NW	×
● Ceresco, Calhoun .... S	500
Ceylon, Barry.............. SW	40
● Chadwick, Ionia.......... C	130
● *Chamberlain's*, St. Jos... SW	×
● Champion, Marquette.. NW	1,200
● *Champion Junc.*, Marq. NW	×
Chandler, Ionia............ C	46
● *Chandler*, Clinton........ C	×
● *Chandler*, Wayne........ SE	×
Chapel, Kent.............. W	×
Chapin, Saginaw........... C	45
Chapin's Station, (see Eden)..	×
Charleston, Sanilac......... E	50
● Charlesworth, Eaton...... S	15
● Charlevoix, Charlevoix .. N	1,496
● **Charlotte**, Eaton....... S	3,867
Charlotteville, (see Bridg'm'n)	×
● Chase, Lake.............. W	388
● *Chase's*, Lenawee......... S	×
● Chassell, Houghton.... NW	×
Chauncey, Kent........... W	130
● **Cheboygan**, Cheboygan N	6,235
● *Cheboyganing*, Bay........ C	×
● Chelsea, Washtenaw..... SE	1,356
Chenaux, Mackinac........ N	50
● *Cheney*, Crawford........ N	100
Cherry Hill, Wayne....... SE	×
● *Cherry Valley*, School'ft NW	×
● Chesaning, Saginaw C	1,056
Cheshire, Allegan......... SW	150
Cheshire Mine, Marquette NW	×
● Chester, Eaton............ S	210
● Chesterfield, Macomb... SE	50
Chestonia, Antrim.......... N	×
Cherries Crossing, Alcona NE	×
● Chief, Manistee........ NW	×
● *Childs Mill*, Kent........ W	00
● Chilson, Livingston........ S	70
China, St. Clair............ E	×
● Chippewa Lake, Mecosta.. C	500
● Chippewa Station, Osceola. C	75
● *Chocolay*, Marquette... NW	×
Chubb's Corners, Livingston. S	×
Churchill, Ogemaw......... N	75
Church's Corners, Hillsdale.. S	60
Churchville, Chippewa...... N	×
● *Cisco*, Mackinac.......... N	×
Clareview, Wayne......... SE	×
Clam Lake, Antrim .... N	100
Clam River, (see Clam Lake).	×
Clam Union, (see Vogel C'tre)	×
● Clare, Clare.............. C	1,174
Clarence, (see Duck Lake)....	×
Clarenceville, (see Plank R'd)	×
● Clarendon, Calhoun....... S	150
● Clarion, Charlevoix ...... N	200
Clark, Lake............... W	×
Clark, Houghton......... NW	570
● *Clarks*, Huron............ E	×
● Clarksburg, Marqu'te.. NW	2[illegible]
Clarks Lake, Jackson....... S	×
● *Clarkson Station*, Oakl'd SE	×
● Clarkston, Oakland...... SE	387
● Clarksville, Ionia......... C	200
Clarksville, (see Rea).......	×
Clawson, Oakland......... SE	×
Clay Bank, Oceana .... W	45
● Clayton, Lenawee......... S	700
Clear Water, Kalkaska..... N	200
Clement, Gladwin C	200
Clement, Manistee........ NW	×
Clement Junction, Mason. W	×
Cleon, Manistee .... NW	×
Cleon, Wexford.......... NW	×
● Clifford, Lapeer........... E	306
Clifton, Keweenaw....... NW	350
Clifton Mine, Keweenaw NW	×
Clifton, (see Phœnix)	×
● Climax, Kalamazoo...... SW	369
● Clinton, Lenawee........ S	960
Clintonville, (see Dr'yt'n Pl's)	×
● Clio, Genesee............. C	577
● Cloverdale, Barry....... SW	×
● *Cloverville*, Muskegon.... W	×
● *Clowry*, Marquette..... NW	×
● Clyde, Oakland.......... SE	400
Clyde Station, (see Sterling)..	×
Clytie, Menominee....... NW	×
Coat's Grove, Barry...... SW	40
Cob Moo Sa, Oceana .... W	×
Codyville, (see Corinth)	×
Coe, Isabella......... C	×

Place	Pop.
● Cohoctah, Livingston...... S	100
● Colby, Montcalm........... C	125
Colden, Midland........... C	×
● *Cold Stream Siding*, Kalamazoo................ SW	×
● **Coldwater**, Branch..... S	5,247
● Cole, Oakland............ SE	×
● *Coleman*, Menominee.. NW	×
● Coleman, Midland........ C	510
Colerain, Oakland......... SE	×
Colfax, Wexford......... NW	50
● Collins, Ionia............ C	90
Collison, Benzie .... NW	×
● Coloma, Berrien......... SW	500
● Colon, Saint Joseph .... SW	489
● *Colon Junction*, St. Jos'h SW	×
Columbia, Jackson......... S	150
Columbia, Tuscola......... E	150
● *Columbia*, Van Buren.. SW	×
● Columbiaville, Lapeer.... E	578
Columbus, Saint Clair...... E	×
Colwell, Montcalm......... C	×
Colwood, Tuscola.......... E	100
Comins, Oscoda........... C	×
Commerce, Oakland....... SE	200
● Comstock, Kalamazoo.. SW	393
● Concord, Jackson........ S	580
● *Condit*, Calhoun.......... S	×
● Cone, Monroe.......... SE	75
Conger, Montcalm......... C	×
● *Conger*, Manistee...... NW	×
● Conklin, Ottawa.......... W	100
Conner's Creek, Wayne.... SE	500
● Constantine, St. Joseph. SW	1,346
Convis Centre, Calhoun..... S	×
● Conway, Emmet.......... N	157
● Cooks, Schoolcraft..... NW	100
Cook's Corners, (see Otisco)..	×
Cooks Station, Newaygo.... W	×
Cooley, Huron............ E	×
● Cooper, Kalamazoo.... SW	20[illegible]
● Coopersville, Ottawa..... W	790
● Copemish, Manistee.... NW	×
Copley, Lake............. W	300
Copper Falls Mine, Keweenaw.................. NW	1,000
Copper Harbor, Keween'w NW	150
● Coral, Montcalm.......... C	335
● *Corbus*, Lenawee.......... S	×
● Corey, Cass.............. SW	100
● *Corfu*, Manistee........ NW	×
● *Corinne*, Mackinac....... N	×
Corinth, Kent............. W	150
Cornell, (see Sebewa).........	×
Corning, Allegan.......... SW	32
Corrigan, Ogemaw.......... N	×
Cortland Centre, Kent...... W	57
● **Corunna**, Shiawassee... C	1,382
Corwin, Van Buren...... SW	×
Cottage Grove, Wayne..... SE	275
● *Cottage Park Spur*, C'pp'wa N	×
Cotton Lake, (see Mayfield)..	×
● *County House*, Wayne.. SE	×
● County Line, Saginaw..... C	150
● *County Line*, Muskegon. W	280
● Covert, Van Buren..... SW	325
Cracow, Huron............ E	×
Craig, Houghton.......... NW	325
Cranston, Oceana.......... W	×
● Crapo, Mecosta........... C	60
● *Crapo Farm*, Genesee.... C	×
Crawford, Isabella.......... C	40
Crawford, Crawford........ N	×
Crawford's Quarry, Presque Isle.................. N	200
Creel, (see Owendale)........	×
● *Creens*, Saginaw.......... C	×
● *Creery Siding*, Huron..... E	×
● *Creighton*, Schoolcraft. NW	×
Cressey, Barry........... SW	200
Creswell, Antrim........... N	33
● Crofton, Kalkaska........ N	130
● Crooked Lake, Clare....... C	100
Crooked Lake, (see Conway)..	×
● Crosby, Kent............. W	100
Crosby's Mills, Montcalm... C	×
Crossman, Tuscola......... E	650
Cross Village, Emmet....... N	480
Crossville, Montcalm........ C	×
● Croswell, Sanilac.......... E	504
Croton, Newaygo........... W	125
● Crow Island, Saginaw..... C	200
● *Crozer*, Gogebic.......... NW	×
Crozier's Mills, Ontonagon NW	×
Crystal, Montcalm......... C	200
● *Crystal City*, Benzie... NW	×
● **Crystal Falls**, Iron.. NE	1,240

Michigan
Michigan

Place	Population
● Crystal Lake, Houghton NW	×
Crystal Lake (see Crystal)...	×
Crystal Valley, Oceana..... W	175
● *Culver*, Arenac..........C	65
Cumber, Sanilac..........E	80
Curran, Alcona..........NE	×
Curtis, Alcona..........NE	400
Cushing, Cass.......... SW	30
● Custer, Mason..........W	400
Cutcheon, Missaukee.......N	×
● *Cyr*, Marquette.........NW	×
Dafter, Chippewa..........N	×
● Daggett, Menominee... NW	500
● Dailey, Cass..........SW	100
Dallas, (see Fowler)..........	×
Dalliba, Marquette.......NW	×
● Dalton, Muskegon........W	25
Damon, Ogemaw..........N	77
Danby, Ionia..........C	32
● *Daniels Siding*, Lake.... W	×
Dansville, Ingham..........S	366
● Dash, Muskegon..........W	280
Davis, Macomb..........SE	150
● Davisburgh, Oakland.... SE	300
Davison, (see Davison Station)	×
● Davison Station, Genesee..C	456
Davisville, (see Crosswell)....	×
Day, Cass..........SW	60
● Dayton, Berrien........SW	300
Dean's Mills, Montcalm.... C	×
Deanville, Lapeer..........E	150
● Dearborn, Wayne..........SE	700
● Decatur, Van Buren....SW	1,109
Deciple, Mecosta..........C	25
● Deckerville, Sanilac.......E	350
● Deep River, Arenac.......C	200
Deer Creek, Livingston.......S	100
● Deerfield, Lenawee.........S	421
Deerfield Centre, (see Madison)	×
● Deer Lake, Lake.......... W	371
Deer Park, Luce..........N	×
● *Deerton*, Alger.........NW	×
Defiance, Delta.......... NW	150
● Deford, Tuscola..........E	100
DelawareMine, K'ween'w.NW	25
Delhi Centre, (see Holt)......	×
● Delhi Mills, Washtenaw. SE	75
Dellwood, Eaton..........S	×
DeLoughary, Menominee.NW	600
● Delray, Wayne..........SE	600
● Delta, Eaton..........S	300
● *Delta Junc.*,SchoolcraftNW	×
● *Delta Switch*, Wayne.... SE	×
● Delton, Barry..........SW	32
● Delwin, Isabella.......... C	×
Denmark, Tuscola..........E	50
● *Denmark Junc.*, Tuscola..E	×
● Dennison, Ottawa..........W	50
● Denton, Wayne..........SE	250
Denver, Isabella..........C	×
Denver, Newaygo..........W	100
● *Depews Siding*, Macomb.SE	130
● Derby, Berrien..........SW	×
Detour, Chippewa..........N	500
● **DETROIT**, Wayne....SE	205,876
Detroit Junction, (see Grand Trunk Junction)..........	×
● Devereaux, Jackson.......S	100
Devil River, (see Osseneke)...	×
● Devil's Lake, Lenawee.....S	25
Dewing's Siding, Osceola....C	×
DeWitt, Clinton..........C	450
● Dexter, Washtenaw......SE	879
Diamond Lake, (see Cassopolis)	×
● Diamond Lake, Newaygo W	250
Diamond Springs, Allegan SW	300
Dickinson, Newaygo....... W	×
Dighton, Osceola.......... C	100
● Dimondale, Eaton..........S	320
● *Diorite*, Marquette..... NW	×
Disco, Macomb..........SE	300
● *Dishno*, Marquette.....NW	×
Dixboro, Washtenaw...... SE	×
Dodge, Clare..........C	311
Dollar Bay, Houghton.... NW	578
● Dollarville, Luce..........N	350
Dolsonville, (see Bay City)...	×
Donaldson, Chippewa.......N	25
● Dorr, Allegan..........SW	350
● *Dorr*, Midland..........C	×
● *Doster*, Barry..........SW	20
Doty, Allegan..........SW	×
● *Dougherty*, Menominee NW	×
Douglas, Allegan..........SW	404
Dover, Clare..........C	50
● Dowagiac, Cass..........SW	2,806
Dowling, Barry.......... SW	100
● Downington, Sanilac......E	375
● *Doyle*, Gratiot..........C	×
● Doyle, Saint Clair.........E	32
Drake, Lapeer..........E	×
● Drayton Plains, Oakland SE	120
Drenthe, Ottawa..........W	300
Driggs, Schoolcraft...... NW	×
● *Drissel*, Saginaw..........C	×
Drummond, Chippewa......N	250
● *Dryads*, Menominee... NW	×
● Dryden, Lapeer..........E	32[illegible]
Duck Lake, Calhoun..........S	100
Duck Lake, Muskegon......W	×
● Duffield, Genesee......... C	50
Dunbarville, (see Williamsburg)	×
Duncan, Cheboygan........ N	×
● Dundee, Monroe.........SE	1,166
● *Dunham*, Arenac..........C	×
Dunham Station, (see Sterling)	×
● *Dunleith*, Mackinac....... N	×
● Dunningville, Allegan.. SW	280
● Dunn Mine, Iron..........NE	×
Du Plain, Clinton..........C	250
● Durand, Shiawassee.......C	255
Dushville, Isabella..........C	250
● Dutton, Kent..........W	100
Dwight, Charlevoix..........N	×
● Eagle, Clinton..........C	141
Eagle Harbor, Keweenaw NW	280
● *Eagle Mills*, Kent..........W	×
● Eagle Mills, Marquette. NW	150
Eagle River, Keweenaw NW	400
● Eames, Oakland......... SE	25
Eardly, Kent..........W	×
East Bay, Grand Traverse NW	45
● *East Branch*, Luce.......N	×
East China, Saint Clair......E	×
East Cohoctah, Livingston...S	×
● *East Cooper*, Kalamazoo SW	×
East Dayton Tuscola........E	75
East Fremont, Sanilac.......E	×
East Gilead, Branch.........S	100
● *East Golden*, Oceana......W	108
East Greenwood, Saint Clair. E	50
East Holland, Ottawa...... W	×
East Jordon, Charlevoix....N	731
● Eastlake, Manistee..... NW	1,856
● *Eastlake*, Schoolcraft..NW	×
● East Le Roy, Calhoun.....S	×
● *Eastman*, Newaygo..... W	×
Eastmanville, Ottawa.......W	450
East Nankin, (see Nankin)	×
East Mosherville, Hillsdale. S	10
Easton, Shiawassee..........C	×
East Ovid, (see Ovid)..........	×
● East Paris, Kent......... W	×
Eastport, Antrim.......... N	150
East Riverton, Mason.......W	45
● *East Saginaw*, Saginaw.. C	*
● East Saugatuck, Allegan SW	100
East Side, Alpena..........NE	×
East Springport, Jackson.....S	×
● East Tawas, Iosco.......NE	2,226
East Thetford, Genesee......C	200
East Traverse Bay, (see East Bay)	×
East Windsor, (see Windsor).	×
● Eastwood, Saginaw.......C	200
● *Easy*, Tuscola..........E	65
● Eaton Rapids, Eaton...... S	1,970
● Eau Claire, Berrien..... SW	400
Echo, Antrim..........N	100
● Eckerman, Chippewa.... N	×
● Eckford, Calhoun..........S	75
● Ecorse, Wayne..........SE	450
● Eden, Ingham..........S	100
Edenville, Midland..........C	100
Edgel, Van Buren..........SW	×
● Edgerton, Kent.......... W	300
Edgewater, Benzie.........NW	×
Edgewood, Gratiot.......... C	60
● Edmore, Montcalm.........C	735
Edna, Roscommon..........N	×
Edson Corners, Missaukee..N	×
● Edwardsburgh, Cass.... SW	600
● *Eighty Foot Grade*, St.Clair E	×
● *Eight Mile Siding*, Wayne SE	×
● Elba, Lapeer..........E	150
Elbridge, Oceana..........W	50
● Eldred, Jackson..........S	×
Elgin, Ottawa..........W	×
Elk, Genesee..........C	150
Elk, Saginaw..........C	×
Elkland, Tuscola.......... E	×
Elk Rapids, Antrim..........N	1,200
● Elkton, Huron..........E	×
Ellington, Tuscola..........E	50
Elliott, Saint Clair.......... E	×
Ellis, Calhoun..........S	25
Ellisville, Isabella..........C	×
● Ellsworth, Antrim.........N	×
Ellsworth, Lake..........W	×
● Elm, Wayne..........SE	50
Elm Creek, Huron..........E	×
● Elmdale, Ionia..........C	25
Elmer, Sanilac..........E	100
Elm Hall, Gratiot..........C	350
● Elmira, Otsego..........N	500
Elm Rock, Leelanaw.....NW	×
Elmwood, Leelanaw......NW	×
Elmwood, Tuscola..........E	50
● *Elmwood*, Iron......... NE	×
Elmwood Station, (see Elm)..	×
● Elsie, Clinton..........C	396
Elva, Tuscola..........E	25
● Elwell, Gratiot..........C	200
Ely, Emmet..........N	×
Embo, Charlevoix..........N	×
● *Emens*, Muskegon....... W	×
Emerson, Chippewa.........N	80
● Emery, Washtenaw......SE	25
Emmet, (see White's Station).	×
● *Emery Junction*, Iosco. NE	×
● Emmet, Saint Clair....... E	350
Empire, Leelanaw......NW	200
Encampment, Chippewa....N	×
● *Engadine*, Mackinac.....N	×
● English, Menominee... NW	130
● Englishville, Kent.......W	200
Ennis, Luce..........N	×
● Ensign, Delta.......... NW	×
Ensley, Newaygo..........W	150
Entrican, Montcalm..........C	50
Epoufette, Mackinac.........N	75
Epsilon, Emmet..........N	50
Erie, Monroe..........SE	[illegible]0
● **Escanaba**, Delta..... NW	6,[illegible]8
Esmond, Iosco..........NE	×
Essexville, Bay..........C	1,545
Estella, (see Sumner).......	×
Eureka, Clinton..........C	250
● *Eureka Place*, Montcalm.C	×
● Eustis, Menominee.....NW	×
● Evans, Kent..........W	57
Evans Lake, Lenawee.......S	25
● Evart, Osceola..........C	1,269
Eveline, Charlevoix..........N	×
Evergreen, Saint Clair.......E	×
● Ewen Sta., Ontonagon..NW	350
Excelsior, Kalkaska..........N	×
Exeter, Monroe..........SE	10
● *Exposition Switch*, Wa'ne SE	×
● *Eyke*, Clare..........C	×
● Fabius, Saint Joseph....SW	×
● Factoryville, Saint Jose'h SW	25
Fairfax, Saint Joseph...... SW	40
● Fairfield, Lenawee........ S	350
● *Fair Ground*, Ingham.... S	×
● Fair Grove, Tuscola........E	400
Fair Haven, Saint Clair.......E	600
● Fairland, Berrien.......SW	×
Fairport, Lenawee.......... S	×
Fair Plains, (see Amsden)...	×
Fairview, Mason..........W	×
Fairview, Oscoda..........NE	100
Falcon, Sanilac..........E	300
Fallassburgh, Kent..........W	100
● Falmouth, Missaukee.....N	120
False Presque Isle, P'q'e Isle N	25
Fargo, Saint Clair..........E	175
Farmers Creek, Lapeer......E	100
Farmington, Oakland.......SE	320
● *Farnham*, Menominee. NW	×
● *Farnham*, Houghton...NW	40
Farnsworth, Wexford.... NW	25
Farowe, Ottawa..........W	×
Farrandville, Genesee......C	×
● Farwell, Clare..........C	584
● *Faunds*, Menominee...NW	×
Fawn River, Saint Joseph SW	50
Fawn River Sta., St.Joes'h SW	×
Fay, Saginaw..........C	×
Fayette, Delta..........NW	500
● *Federman*, Monroe.....SE	×
Fenn's Mills, (see Fennville)	×
● Fennville, Allegan.......SW	360
● Fenton, Genesee.......... C	2,[illegible]82
● Fenwick, Montcalm.......C	175
● Fergus, Saginaw..........C	200
Fern, Mason..........W	25
Ferris, Montcalm..........C	100
Ferry, Oceana..........W	275
● Ferrysburgh, Ottawa.... W	450
Ferryville, (see Custer)......	×

* Population included in Saginaw.

Place, County	Dir.	Pop.
● Fields, Newaygo	W	200
● Fife Lake, Grand Trav'e	NW	394
Filer City, Manistee	NW	700
● Filion, Huron	E	65
● Fillmore Centre, Allegan	SW	250
Fillmore, (see Freeport)		×
● Findley, Saint Joseph	SW	15
Finkton, Antrim	N	50
Fisher, Presque Isle	N	×
● Fishers Station, Kent	W	60
Fishville, Montcalm	C	×
● *Fisherville*, Bay	C	×
● *Fisk*, Allegan	SW	50
Fitchburgh, Ingham	S	150
Fitchville, Antrim	N	×
Fitzgerald, (see Maple Valley)		×
Five Lakes, Lapeer	E	250
Five Lakes, Otsego	N	×
Flanders, Alpena	NE	×
● *Flat Rock*, Delta	NW	×
Flat Rock, Alcona	NE	×
● *Flat Rock*, Wayne	SE	377
Fleming, Livingston	S	125
Fletcher, Kalkaska	N	32
● **Flint**, Genesee	C	9,803
● *Flint River Jc.*, Genesee	C	×
● Floodwood, Dickinson	NW	×
● Florence, St. Joseph	SW	400
Flower Creek, Oceana	W	100
● Flowerfield, St. Joseph	SW	125
Floyd, Isabella	C	×
● Flushing, Genesee	C	965
Ford River, Delta	NW	500
● *Ford River Sta.*, Delta	NW	×
● *Ford Siding*, Dickinson	NW	×
Forest City, Muskegon	W	×
Forester, Sanilac	E	100
Forest Grove, Ottawa	W	75
● *Forest Hall*, Cass	SW	×
Forest Hill, Gratiot	C	32
● *Forest Hill Sta.*, Gratiot	C	×
Forest Sta., (see Fredericville)		×
Forestville, Sanilac	E	400
Fork, Mecosta	C	×
● Forman, Lake	W	20
● Forsyth, Marquette	NW	150
Fort Gratiot, Saint Clair	E	2,000
● *Fort Howard*, Ottawa	W	×
● *Fort Wayne Jc.*, H'lsd'le	S	×
● *Ft. Wayne Switch*, Jacks'n	S	×
● Forest City, Dickinson	NW	75
● Fosters, Saginaw	C	100
● Fostoria, Tuscola	E	300
Fountain, Mason	W	100
Four Towns, Oakland	SE	57
● Fowler, Clinton	C	346
● Fowlerville, Livingston	S	945
● Francisco, Jackson	S	120
Frankenlust, Bay	C	×
Frankenmuth, Saginaw	C	350
● *Frankenmuth Sta.*, Sag'w	C	×
● *Frankentrost (or Trostville)* Saginaw	C	×
● Frankfort, Benzie	NW	1,175
● *Franklin*, Houghton	NW	×
Franklin, Oakland	SE	200
● Fraser, Macomb	SE	220
● Frederic, Crawford	N	150
Fredonia, Washtenaw	SE	130
● *Freedom*, Cheyboygan	N	×
● Freeland, Saginaw	C	350
● Freeport, Barry	SW	300
● Free Soil, Mason	W	306
Free Soil Mills, Mason	W	×
Freiburgers, Sanilac	E	25
● Fremont, Newaygo	W	1,097
● *Frenchtown*, Monroe	SE	×
Frielingville, Osceola	C	×
Frontier, Hillsdale	S	150
● *Frost*, Clare	C	×
Frost, Saginaw	C	50
● *Frost's*, Montcalm	C	×
● Fruitport, Muskegon	W	300
● *FruitportJunc.*, M'sk'gn	W	×
Fruit Ridge, Lenawee	S	40
Fuller's Mills, (see Liberty)		×
Fulton, Kalamazoo	SW	150
Fyfe Lake, (see Fife Lake)		×
● Gagetown, Tuscola	E	237
● Gaines Station, Genesee	C	301
● Galesburgh, Kalamazoo	SW	702
● Galien, Berrien	SW	492
Galloway, Saginaw	C	×
Galt, Missaukee	N	×
Ganges, Allegan	SW	100
Garden, Delta	NW	458
Garden Bay, Delta	NW	×

Place, County	Dir.	Pop.
Garden Dale, St. Clair	E	×
Garden River, Chippewa	N	×
● *Garfield*, Saginaw	C	150
Gaskill, Barry	SW	×
Gatesville, Chippewa	N	32
● **Gaylord**, Otsego	N	661
● *Gay's Spur*, Menominee	NW	×
Geary, Clinton	C	×
● *Geddes*, Washtenaw	SE	75
Geer, Washtenaw	SE	×
Genesee Village, Genesee	C	150
Geneva, Lenawee	S	100
Georgetown, Ottawa	W	32
Gerkey, Barry	SW	×
Gerrish, Missaukee	N	×
Germania, Sanilac	E	40
Germfask, Schoolcraft	NW	×
Geyerville, Cheboygan	N	×
● Gibraltar, Wayne	SE	350
Gibson, Allegan	SW	×
Giddings, Baraga	NW	×
Gilbert, Wexford	NW	250
● *Gilberts*, Newaygo	W	×
● *Gilchrist*, Mackinac	N	×
Gilead, Branch	S	250
● Gilford, Tuscola	E	100
Gilmore, Isabella	C	×
Gill's Pier, Leelanaw	NW	120
Girard, Branch	S	300
Gitchel, Ottawa	W	×
● Gladstone, Delta	NW	1,337
● **Gladwin**, Gladwin	C	903
Glass River, Shiawassee	C	59
Glen Arbor, Leelanaw	NW	400
Glendale, Van Buren	SW	125
● Glendora, Berrien	SW	53
Glen Haven, Leelanaw	NW	65
● Glen Lord, Berrien	SW	32
Glenn, Allegan	SW	80
Glennie Station, Alcona	NE	×
● Glenwood, Cass	SW	200
Gobleville, Van Buren	SW	500
Godfrey, Allegan	SW	×
Godfrey, Alpena	NE	×
Gogarnville, Alger	NW	×
● Gogebic Sta., Gogebic	NW	×
Golding, Oceana	W	×
Gold Spring, Kalkaska	N	×
● Goodell's, Saint Clair	E	200
Good Harbor, Leelanaw	S	200
Good Hart, Emmet	N	300
● Gooding, Kent	W	×
● Goodison, Oakland	SE	40
Goodland, Lapeer	E	×
● *Goodman*, Huron	E	×
Goodrich, Genesee	C	400
● *Goose Lake*, Marquette	NW	×
● *Gordon*, Marquette	NW	×
Gorton, Branch	S	10
● Gould City, Mackinac	N	×
Gowen, Montcalm	C	300
Graafschap, Allegan	SW	300
Graffville, (see Edmore)		×
Grace, Benzie	NW	×
● Grafton, Monroe	SE	20
● *Grahams*, Saginaw	C	×
Grams Crossing, Alcona	NE	×
● Grand Blanc, Genesee	C	250
● **Grand Haven**, Ottawa	W	5,023
● Grand Junc., Van Buren	SW	300
● Grand Ledge, Eaton	S	1,606
Grand Maire, Berrien	SW	×
Grand Marais, Alger	NW	300
Grand Pointe, Saint Clair	E	×
● **GRAND RAPIDS**, Kent	W	60,278
● *Grand Trunk Jc.*, St. Clair	E	×
Grand View, Oceana	W	×
● *Grand View*, Marquette	NW	×
● Grandville, Kent	W	800
● *Granite*, Marquette	NW	×
● Granite Bluff, Dickinson	NW	×
Grant, Kent	W	×
● *Grant*, Newaygo	W	×
Grant Centre, (see Blaine)		×
Grape, Monroe	SE	×
● Grass Lake, Jackson	S	617
● Grassmere, Huron	E	×
● *Gratiot Centre*, Saint Clair	E	×
● *Gratiot Road*, Wayne	SE	×
● Grattan, Kent	W	300
Grant, Gladwin	C	×
● *Gravel Pit*, Lenawee	S	×
● *Gravel Pit*, St. Joseph	S	×
● Grawn, Grand Traverse	NW	×
● **Grayling**, Crawford	N	700
Greenbush, Alcona	NE	500
Greenbush, (see Eureka)		×

Place, County	Dir.	Pop.
Green Creek, Muskegon	W	×
Green Dell, (see Chase)		×
● Greenfield, Wayne	SE	100
● *Green Lake*, G'd Trav'se	NW	×
Greenland, Ontonagon	NW	500
● Greenland Sta., Onta'on	NW	125
Greenleaf, Sanilac	E	25
● Green Oak, Livingston	S	40
● Greenville, Montcalm	C	3,056
Greenwood, Marquette	NW	×
● Greenwood, Ogemaw	N	30
Greenwood Centre, St. Clair	E	×
● Gregory, Livingston	S	140
Gresham, Eaton	S	75
● *Greylock*, Mackinac	N	×
Grind Stone City, Huron	E	462
Griswold, Kent	W	50
● *Groesbeck*, Ontonagon	NW	×
● Grosse Ile, Wayne	SE	900
Grosse Point, Wayne	SE	298
● *Grosvenor*, Lenawee	S	×
Grouleau, Alcona	NE	×
Grove, Newaygo	W	250
Groveland, Oakland	SE	×
Groverton, (see South Lake Linden)		×
● *Grover*, Houghton	NW	×
● Groverville, Calhoun	S	×
● *Groverton*, Saginaw	C	×
Gull Corners, (see Richland)		×
● Gulliver, Schoolcraft	NW	25
Gull Lake, Barry	SW	50
Gun Lake, Barry	SW	30
Gun Marsh, Allegan	SW	65
Gun Plains, (see Plainwell)		×
Gunnisonville, Clinton	C	×
Gurnee, (see Free Soil)		×
● Gustin, Alcona	NE	×
Hadley, Lapeer	E	256
● Hagar, Berrien	SW	40
Hagemnn, Hillsdale	S	10
Hagensville, Presque Isle	N	50
● *Haines*, Mecosta	C	×
● Haire, Wexford	NW	100
● Hale, Iosco	NE	×
● *Hale Lake*, Iosco	NE	×
Half Moon Lake, (see Cansovia)		×
● *Halls*, Muskegon	W	×
● Hallston, Alger	NW	×
Hamblen, Bay	C	×
● Hamburgh, Livingston	S	200
● *Hamburgh Junc.*, Liv'gst'n	S	×
● Hamilton, Allegan	SW	380
Hamilton, (see Swartz Creek)		×
Hammond, (see Dutton)		×
Hammonds Bay, Presque Isle	N	×
Hamtramck, (see Detroit)		×
● Hancock, Houghton	NW	1,172
● Hand Station, Wayne	SE	120
● *Handy*, Alcona	NE	×
Hanley, Ottawa	W	30
Hannah, Grand Traverse	NW	×
● Hanover, Jackson	S	363
Hansen, Oceana	W	×
● *Hanson's Spur*, Mn'nee	NW	×
● Harbert, Berrien	SW	×
● **Harbor Spr'gs**, Emmet	N	1,052
Harbor Spr'gs Jc., Emmet	N	×
Hardwood, Dickinson	NW	×
● *Haring*, Wexford	NW	130
● Harlan, Manistee	NW	×
Harlows, Marquette	NW	×
Harmon, Oscoda	NE	×
● *Harrietta*, Wexford	NW	335
Harrington, Ottawa	W	×
Harris, Ingham	S	×
● *Harris*, Menominee	NW	×
● Harrisburg, Ottawa	W	20
Harris Creek, (see Bowne)		×
● **Harrison**, Clare	C	752
● *Harrison*, Van Buren	SW	×
Harrisville, Alcona	NE	987
● *Harroun*, Newaygo	W	×
Harsen's Island, St. Clair	E	×
● **Hart**, Oceana	W	757
● Hartford, Van Buren	SW	1,044
Hartland, Livingston	S	400
● *Hartleys*, Gogebic	NW	×
● Hartman, Berrien	SW	200
● Hartsuff, Saint Clair	E	25
Hartwellville, Shiawassee	C	445
Hartwick, Osceola	C	100
● Harvard, Kent	W	×
Harvey, Marquette	NW	126
● *Harvey*, Marquette	NW	×
● *Haslemere*, Mackinac	N	×
● Haslett Park, Ingham	S	100

Place		Pop.
Hassler, (see Elba)	N	×
● **Hastings**, Barry	SW	2,972
Hasty, Gratiot	C	50
Hatmaker, Branch	S	10
● Hatton, Clare	C	130
Havana, (see Westwood)		×
● *Hawes Bridge*, Gladwin	C	×
Hawkhead, Allegan	SW	75
Hawkins, Newaygo	W	×
Hayes, Huron	E	100
Hazel Grove, Oceana	W	×
Hazelton, Shiawassee	C	150
Headland, Osceola	C	×
He-go-mic, Emmet	N	×
● Helena, Huron	E	×
Helena, Antrim	N	×
● *Helena*, Marquette	NW	×
● *Hemlock*, Saginaw	C	×
● Hemlock City, Saginaw	C	250
● *Hemlock Road*, Iosco	NE	×
● Henderson, Shiawassee	C	150
● *Hendrie*, Chippewa	N	×
● *Hendrie Pit*, Chippewa	N	×
● *Henry*, Alcona	NE	×
Henrietta, Jackson	S	200
● *Henrietta Station*, Jackson	S	×
● Hermansville, M'n'm'e.	NW	652
Herring Lake, Benzie	NW	×
Herrington, Ottawa	W	40
● **Hersey**, Osceola	C	328
Hesperia, Newaygo	W	506
Hessel, Mackinac	N	300
Hetherton, Otsego	N	×
Hickory Corners, Barry	SW	150
● High Bridge, Manistee	NW	×
Highland, Livingston	S	×
Highland, Oakland	SE	130
Highland Park, Wayne	SE	1,000
● Highland Station, Oakl'd	SE	300
● *Highway*, Houghton	NW	×
Highwood, Gladwin	C	×
Hill Creek, Houghton	NW	×
● Hillard's, Allegan	SW	50
Hillman, Montgomery	N	200
Hills Corners, (see Glendora)		×
● **Hillsdale**, Hillsdale	S	3,915
Hinchman, Berrien	SW	×
● *Hinkles*, Montcalm	C	×
● Hobart, Wexford	NW	100
Hodge, Grand Traverse	NW	×
Hodunk, Branch	S	25
Hoffman, Oceana	W	×
Holbrook, Sanilac	E	×
● *Holden Road*, Wayne	SE	×
● Holland, Ottawa	W	3,945
● *Hollister*, Iron	NE	×
● Holloway, Lenawee	S	75
● Holly, Oakland	SE	1,266
Hollywood, Berrien	SW	×
Holstein, Oceana	W	40
Holt, Ingham	S	300
● Holton, Muskegon	W	275
Home, Newaygo	W	×
● Homer, Calhoun	S	1,063
● Homestead, Benzie	NW	165
● *Hoopers*, Allegan	SW	×
Hoovertown, (see Rifle River)		×
Hope, Midland	C	97
Hopkins, Allegan	SW	450
● Hopkins Station, All'g'n	SW	700
Hopkins Road, Lapeer	E	×
Horr, Isabella	C	×
● Hoppertown, Allegan	SW	×
● *Horsehead Lake*, Mecosta	C	×
Horseshoe, Allegan	SW	×
● Horton, Jackson	S	400
● Horton's Bay, Charlevoix	N	75
● **Houghton**, Houghton	NW	2,062
Houghton Lake, Roscom'on	N	390
● *Houles*, Menominee	NW	×
Houseman, Oceana	W	×
● Howard City, Montcalm	C	1,137
Howard Station, (see **Bailey**)		×
Howardsville, St. Joseph	SW	30
● **Howell**, Livingston	S	2,387
● *Howell Junction*, Livingston	S	×
● *Howrys*, Gladwin	C	×
Howlandsburg, Kal'mazoo	SW	30
Hoxeyville, Wexford	NW	×
Hoytville, Eaton	S	350
Hubbard Lake, Alpena	NE	×
Hubbardstown, Ionia	C	360
● *Hubbell Junc.*, Mackinac	N	×
● Hudson, Lenawee	S	2,178
● Hudsonville, Ottawa	W	250
Hugart, Emmet	N	×
Hulburt, Chippewa	N	×

Michigan

Place		Pop.
● Humboldt, Marquette	NW	1,000
● Hungerford, Newaygo	W	200
Hunt, Ogemaw	N	100
● Hunter's Creek, Lapeer	E	200
● Hunt Spur, Mackinac	N	×
Hurd's Corners, (see E. Day'n)		×
Huron, Huron	E	125
Huron Bay, Baraga	NW	×
Huronia Beach, Saint Clair	E	×
Hyde, Delta	NW	×
● *Hylas*, Menominee	NW	×
● Ida, Monroe	SE	300
Idlewild, Montmorency	N	×
Imlay, Lapeer	E	100
● Imlay City, Lapeer	E	1,251
● Index, Lapeer	E	×
● *Indian Field*, Kalamazoo	SW	×
Indian Lake, Oscoda	NE	32
Indian Lake Sta. (see Pavilion)		×
● Indian River, Cheboygan	N	250
● *Indian Town*, Me'nee.	NW	×
● Ingalls, Menominee	NW	250
Ingersoll, Clinton	C	50
● Inkster, Wayne	SE	200
Inland, Benzie	NW	50
● *Inland Station*, Benzie	NW	×
Interior, Ontonagon	NW	1,000
Interior Junction, O'gon	NW	×
● Interlochen, G'd Trav'e	NW	100
Intermediate, Charlevoix	N	32
Inverness, (see Cheboygan)		×
Inwood, Charlevoix	N	75
● **Ionia**, Ionia	C	4,482
Iosco, Livingston	S	1,000
Iron City, Marquette	NW	×
Irondale, (see Ramsay)		×
● **Iron Mountain**, Dickinson	NW	8,599
● Iron River, Iron	NE	1,117
Iron River, Ontonagon	NW	×
● *Irons*, Lake	W	×
Ironton, Charlevoix	N	500
● Ironwood, Gogebic	NW	7,745
Iroquois, Chippewa	N	×
● Irving, Barry	SW	100
Isabella, (see Fowler Station)		×
● Isabella, Delta	NW	300
● *Isabella*, Isabella	C	×
● Ishpeming, Marquette	NW	11,197
● *Island Lake*, Livingston	S	×
● **Ithaca**, Gratiot	C	1,627
● *Ithaca Branch Junction*, Gratiot	C	×
Ivan, Kalkaska	N	150
Jack Pine, Crawford	N	40
● **Jackson**, Jackson	S	20,798
Jackson Furnace, Delta	NW	×
● *Jackson Junction*, Jackson	S	×
Jacobsville, Houghton	NW	×
Jacob City, (see Moran)		×
Jamestown, (see Penn)		×
Jamestown, Ottawa	W	500
● Jasper, Lenawee	S	275
● Jeddo, Saint Clair	E	400
● *Jefferson*, Cass	SW	×
Jefferson, Hillsdale	S	35
Jenison, Ottawa	W	500
Jenney, Tuscola	E	25
● Jennings, Missaukee	N	480
Jensen, Newaygo	W	×
Jericho, Newaygo	W	×
● Jerome, Hillsdale	S	200
Jerome, (see Edenville)		×
Jeromeville Station, (see Shingleton)		×
Jersey, Oakland	SE	×
● *Jessieville*, Gogebic	NW	100
Johnson, Jackson	S	×
● *Johnson's Spur*, Me'nee	NW	×
Johnstown, (see Banfield)		×
● Jones, Cass	SW	250
Jones' Mills, (see Cassopolis)		×
● Jonesville, Hillsdale	S	1,288
Joppa, Calhoun	S	×
Jordan, Antrim	N	×
● *Jordan*, Isabella	C	30
Joy, Charlevoix	N	×
Joyfield, Benzie	NW	100
Judd's Corners, Shiawassee	C	150
Judge, Crawford	N	×
Juhl, Sanilac	E	×
● *Junction*, Barry	SW	×
● *Junction*, Houghton	NW	×
● Juniata, Tuscola	E	200
● **Kalamazoo**, Kala'zoo	SW	17,853
Kalamo, Eaton	S	175
● **Kalkaska**, Kalkaska	N	1,161

Michigan

Place		Pop.
Kasson, Leelanaw	NW	×
● Kawkawlin, Bay	C	300
Kaywood, (see Gowen)		×
Kearney, Antrim	N	×
● *Kearsarge*, Houghton	NW	×
Kearsarge, Keweenaw	NW	×
Kearsley, (see Flint)		×
Keelersville, Van Buren	SW	300
Keene, Ionia	C	×
● *Ke-go-mic*, Emmet	N	×
Kellar, (see Logan)		×
● *Kelleys Corners*, Lenawee	S	195
● Kellogg, Allegan	SW	50
Kellsville, Menominee	NW	×
● Kendall, Van Buren	SW	200
Kendallville, Montcalm	C	×
Kennedy, Mackinac	N	×
Keno, Newaygo	W	150
Kenockee, Saint Clair	E	150
Kensington, Oakland	SE	65
● Kent City, Kent	W	400
● Kenton, Houghton	NW	×
Kentville, Benzie	NW	×
Kerby, Shiawassee	C	×
Keswick, Leelanaw	NW	×
Kewadin, Antrim	N	100
● Keystone, Grand Trav'se	NW	40
● Kibbie, Van Buren	SW	50
● Kiddville, Ionia	C	100
Kilkenny, Huron	E	×
Killmaster, Alcona	NE	200
Kilmanagh, Huron	E	150
● Kimball, Saint Clair	E	×
● Kinde, Huron	E	50
Kinderhook, Branch	S	100
● Kingsland, Eaton	S	×
● Kingsley, Grand Trave'e	NW	350
● King's Mill, Lapeer	E	100
● Kingston, Tuscola	E	300
● Kinney, Kent	W	×
● *Kinney*, Newaygo	W	×
Kinneyville, (see Winfield)		×
Kinross, Chippewa	N	×
Kintner, Tuscola	E	100
● *Kipling*, Delta	NW	×
Kirk, Newaygo	W	×
● *Kirk's Junction*, Ottawa	W	×
Kissington, (see Union)		×
● Kitchi, Houghton	NW	×
Klingensmith, Otsego	N	25
● Klinger's Lake, Saint Jo'n	SW	20
Kloman, (see English)		×
● Kneffs, Montcalm	C	×
Koehler, Cheboygan	N	40
● *Komoko*, Missaukee	N	×
Kulmbach, Saginaw	C	×
Labarge, Kent	W	75
Lacey, Barry	SW	75
● Lacota, Van Buren	SW	200
Lac View Deserts, Iron	NE	×
La Fayette, Gratiot	C	150
La Grange, Cass	SW	200
Laidlawville, Iosco	NE	×
● Laingsburgh, Shiawassee	C	654
Laird, Houghton	NW	×
● *Lake*, Clare	C	100
Lake, Mecosta	C	391
● Lake, Newaygo	W	100
● Lake Ann, Benzie	NW	×
Lake Brewster, G.Trav'se	NW	×
● **Lake City**, Missaukee	N	663
● Lake Cora, Van Buren	SW	×
● Lake George, Clare	C	40
● *Lake Gogebic*, Onto'gon	NW	×
Lake Harbor, Muskegon	W	300
● *Lake Junction*, Lake	W	×
● Lake Linden, Houghton	NW	1,851
● Lake Odessa, Ionia	C	635
Lake Pleasant, Washtenaw	SE	×
Lakeport, Saint Clair	E	150
Lake Ridge, Lenawee	S	25
Lake Side, Berrien	SW	200
Lakeside, (see Muskegon)		×
Lake Superior Iron Works, Houghton	NW	×
Laketon, (see Bridgman)		×
● Lakeview, Montcalm	C	1,024
Lakeville, Oakland	SE	150
● Lamb, Saint Clair	E	200
Lambertville, Monroe	SE	150
Lamont, Ottawa	W	260
Lamotte, Sanilac	E	100
Lane, Ogemaw	N	×
Langston, Montcalm	C	300
● **L'Anse**, Baraga	NW	655
● **LANSING**, Ingham	S	13,102
● *Lansing Siding*, Clare	C	×

● **Lapeer**, Lapeer......... E 2,753
Laphamville, (see Rockford). ×
● La Salle, Monroe.........SE 25
● Lathrop, Delta..........NW 150
Laurel, Sanilac...........E ×
Lawndale, Saginaw.........C ×
● Lawrence, Van Buren..SW 564
● Lawton, Van Buren....SW 788
Layton Corners, (see Henrietta) ×
Layton Corners, Saginaw....C 25
● Leaton, Isabella..........C 150
Leathem, (see Arthur Bay).... ×
Leavitt, Oceana............W ×
Lebanon, Clinton..........C ×
● Lee, Allegan...........SW 60
● Leesburgh, Saint Joseph.SW 80
Lee's Corner, Midland.......C 80
Leesville, Wayne..........SE 200
● Leetsville, Kalkaska......N 100
Leitch, Sanilac.............E ×
Leland, Leelanaw.......NW 400
● *Leland*, Isabella..........C ×
● *Lelands*, Washtenaw.....SE 25
● *Lemon Lake*, Manistee.NW ×
● Lenawee Junc., Lenawee..E 32
● Lennon, Shiawassee.......C 100
● Lenox, Macomb.........SE ×
Leon, Gratiot.............C ×
● Leonard, Oakland.......SE 300
● Leoni, Jackson...........S 300
Leonidas, Saint Joseph.....SW 250
● Le Roy, Osceola..........C 452
Le Roy Sta., (see Webberville) ×
● Leslie, Ingham............S 1,058
Lester, Branch............S 25
Letson, (see Brinton)......... ×
Leutz, Saginaw............C 50
● *Levington Siding*, Clare...C ×
● Levering, Emmet.........N 35
● *Lewis*, Mackinac.........N ×
Lexington, Sanilac..........E 712
Liberty, Jackson...........S 100
Lickley's Corners, Hillsdale.S 15
● Lilley, Newaygo..........W 200
Lima, Washtenaw..........SE 75
Lime Island, Chippewa......N ×
● *Lime Siding*, Calhoun.....S ×
Lincoln, Mason...........W 125
● *Lincoln Lake*, Kent......W ×
● Linden, Genesee..........C 552
● Linwood, Bay.............C 100
Linwood, Houghton......NW ×
Lisbon, Kent..............W 136
● Litchfield, Hillsdale......S 601
● *Little Falls*, OntonagonNW ×
Littlefield, Emmet..........N 32
Little Harbor, SchoolcraftNW ×
● *Little Lake*, Marquette.NW 150
Little Prairie Ronde, Cass.SW 200
Little River, Menominee.NW 40
Little Traverse, (see H'b'r Sprs) ×
Livingston, Berrien.......SW ×
Livonia, Wayne............SE 50
Locke, Ingham.............S 200
Lockport, Saint Joseph....SW ×
Lockwood, Kent............W 200
Lodi, Kalkaska............N 100
Logan, Kent..............W 65
London, Monroe...........SE 15
Long Lake, Grand TraverseNW ×
● *Long Lake*, Iosco.......NE ×
Long Rapids, Alpena......NE 200
● Loomis, Isabella..........C 300
● Lorenzo, Kent............W ×
● *Loudon*, Kent............W ×
● Lowell, Kent.............W 1,829
Lower Big Rapids, (see Big Rapids)........ ×
● Lucas, Missaukee.........N ×
Luce, Saginaw.............C ×
● **Ludington**, Mason....W 7,517
Lulu, Monroe.............SE 36
● Lum, Lapeer..............E ×
● *Lumberton*, Newaygo....W 130
● Luther, Lake............W 1,084
Luzerne, Oscoda..........NE 50
Lynn, Saint Clair..........E 130
Lyons, Ionia...............C 612
● *Lyons Station*, Ionia......C ×
● McBain, Missaukee.......N 50
● McBride's, Montcalm.....C 333
McClure, Gladwin..........C ×
● *McClure*, Saginaw........C ×
● McCords, Kent...........W ×
● McDonald, VanBuren..SW 20
● *McFarland*, MarquetteNW ×
● McIvor, Iosco...........NE ×

Michigan

McKann's Cor's, (see Pavilion) ×
McKinley, Oscoda.........NE 508
McKissicksville, (see Union). ×
McLane, Newaygo.........W ×
● *McManus*, Charlevoix...N ×
● McMillan, Luce..........N 50
McSorley, Alpena.........NE ×
● *Macatawa Jc.*, Ottawa...W ×
Mack City, Oscoda........C 35
Mackinac Island, Mackinac.N 750
● Mackinaw City, Cheb'yg'nN 333
● *Mack Road*, Wayne.....SE ×
Macomb, Macomb.........SE 150
Macon, Lenawee............S 250
Madison, Livingston........S 125
Malton, Delta...........NW ×
● Mancelona, Antrim......N 1,205
● Manchester, Washtenaw.SE 1,191
● *Manchester Jc.*, Wash'n'wSE ×
● **Manistee**, Manistee..NW 12,812
Manistee Junction, Mason..W ×
● *Manistee Cross*. Man'teeNW ×
● **Manistique**, Schoolc'tNW 2,940
● Manitou Beach, Lenawee.S 25
Manlius, (see Richmond).... ×
Manning, Cheyboygan......N ×
● *Mann Siding*, Clare.....C ×
● Mansfield, Iron.........NE ×
● Manton Wexford......NW 661
Maple, Ionia..............C ×
Maple City, Leelanaw.....NW 100
Maple Grove, Barry.......SW 100
● Maple Hill, Montcalm.....C 100
Maple Rapids, Clinton......C 533
Maple Ridge, Arenac........C 180
● *Maple Ridge*, Delta.....NW 32
Mapleton, (see Duplain).... ×
● Mapleton, G'd Traverse NW 400
● Maple Valley, Montcalm..C 650
Marathon, (see Columbiaville) ×
Marble, Mason............W 200
● *Marble*, Ottawa..........W ×
● Marcellus, Cass.........SW 830
● Marenisco, Gogebic......NW 100
● Marengo, Calhoun.........S 150
Marilla, Manistee.........NW 250
Marine City, St. Clair.......E 3,268
● Marion, Osceola..........C 700
● *Mark*, Clare..............C ×
Markell, Tuscola...........E ×
● Marlette, Sanilac..........E 700
● **Marquette**, MarquetteNW 9,093
Marshall, Calhoun........S 3,968
● *Marshfield*, Mecosta......C ×
Marshville, Oceana.........W 200
● Martin, Allegan.........SW 250
Martiney, Mecosta..........C ×
● *Martiney Station*, MecostaC ×
Martinsville, Wayne.......SE 150
Martyn's Cor., (see Eureka) ×
Marysville, St. Clair........E 300
● **Mason**, Ingham..........S 1,875
● Masonville, Delta........NW 25
Mastodon, Iron...........NE ×
● Mastodon Mine, Iron......NE 200
● Matchwood, OntonagonNW 100
Matherton, Ionia............C 350
Mathew's Cor., (see Richfield) ×
● Mattawan, Van Buren..SW 250
Mattison, Branch...........S 50
● Maybee, Monroe.........SE 300
Maybury, Wayne.........SE ×
● Mayfield, G'd Traverse.NW 200
● *Maynard's*, Mecosta......C ×
● Mayville, Tuscola.........E 728
Meade, Macomb...........SE 20
Meadville, (see Morgan)..... ×
Meadville, (see Port Austin). ×
Meadville, (see Dansville)...... ×
● Mears, Oceana...........W 350
Meauwataka, Wexford...NW ×
● Mecosta, Mecosta.........C 472
Medina, Lenawee...........S 225
Melaine's Cor., (see Lapeer). ×
● *Melbourne*, Saginaw......C ×
Melita, Arenac.............C ×
● Melvin, Salinac...........E 130
● Memphis, Macomb......SE 588
● Mendon, Saint Joseph..SW 808
● **Menominee**, M'mineeNW 10,630
● *Menominee River*, Men.NW ×
● Meredith, Clare..........C 500
● Meridian, Ingham.........S 200
● Merrill, Saginaw..........C 412
Merrillsville, Saint Clair....E ×
● *Merriman*, Dickinson..NW ×
● *Mershon*, Saginaw........C ×

Michigan

Mesick, Wexford.........NW 50
● Metamora, Lapeer........E 314
Methodist Mission, BaragaNW ×
● Metropolitan, DickinsonNW 400
Meyer, Menominee.......NW ×
● Michie, Bay..............C 125
● Michigamme, Ma'quetteNW 1,200
● Michigan Centre, Jackson.S 130
● Middleton, Gratiot........C ×
Middle Village, (see Goodhart) ×
● Middleville, Barry......SW 678
● **Midland**, Midland......C 2,277
● *Midway*, Marquette....NW ×
● Mikado, Alcona.........NE 125
● Milan, Washtenaw.......SE 917
Milburn, Osceola..........C 25
● Milford, Oakland........SE 1,138
Milita, (see Sterling)......... ×
● Millbrook, Mecosta.......C 400
Millbrook Station, Mecosta. C ×
Millburgh, Berrien........SW 113
● Mill Creek, Kent.........W 50
● Miller, Montcalm.........C ×
Miller Hill, Leelanaw....NW ×
Miller Settlement, (see Swartz Cr.) ×
● Millersville, Wexford...NW 50
● Millet, Eaton.............S 100
● Mill Grove, Allegan.....SW 200
● Millington, Tuscola.......E 454
Mills, Sanilac..............E 15
Mills, Houghton..........NW ×
● *Mills*, Iosco.............NE ×
Millville, (see Lapeer)........ ×
● Milo, Barry.............SW 45
Milo, Saginaw..............C ×
● Milton, Macomb.........SE 200
● *Milton Junction*, Osceola.C ×
● *Milwaukee Junc.*, WayneSE ×
Minard, Jackson............S ×
● Minden City, Sanilac......E 394
Mint, Saint Joseph........SW ×
Mio, Oscoda..............NE 150
Miriam, Ionia...............C 10
● *Missaukee Junc.*, WexfordNW ×
Mitchell, Antrim............N 32
Moddersville, Missaukee....N ×
Model City, (see Glenwood).. ×
● *Moffatt*, Arenac...........C ×
● Moline, Allegan.........SW 150
● *Monitor*, Bay.............C ×
● *Mono Lake*, Muskegon...W ×
● **Monroe**, Monroe.......SE 5,258
Monroe Centre, Gr. Trav..NW 200
● *Monroe Junc.*, Monroe..SE ×
● Montague, Muskegon....W 1,623
● Monteith, Allegan.......SW 25
Monterey, Allegan........SW 250
● Montgomery, Hillsdale....S 375
Montgomery, (see Moon).... ×
● *Montreal*, Gogebic.....NW ×
● Montrose, Genesee........C 300
Moon, Muskegon...........W 100
● Moorepark, Saint JosephSW 90
Mooreville, (see York)....... ×
Moore's Junction, Arenac...C ×
● *Moores Siding*, Clare......C ×
● Moorestown, Missaukee..N ×
● Moorland, Muskegon.....W 25
● Moran, Mackinac.........N 300
● Morenci, Lenawee.........S 1,218
Morey, Missaukee..........N ×
● Morgan, Barry...........SW 175
● *Morgan*, Marquette....NW ×
Morgan Station, (see WhiteCloud) ×
● Morley, Mecosta..........C 485
Morocco, Monroe..........SE 10
● Morrice, Shiawassee.......C 422
Morris Station, (see Bridgman) ×
● Moscow, Hillsdale.........S 250
● Mosherville, Hillsdale.....S 100
Mossback, Kalkaska........N ×
Mottville, Saint Joseph....SW 75
Mount Bliss, Antrim.......N ×
● **Mount Clemens**, Macomb SE 4,748
● Mount Forest, Bay........C 150
● Mount Morris, Genesee...C 351
● *Mount Olivet*, Macomb..SE ×
● **Mount Pleasant**, Isabella C 2,701
Mount Salem, Saint Clair...E ×
Mount Vernon, Macomb...SE 165
Mud Lake, Alcona.........NE ×
● *Mud Lake Junc.*, AlconaNE ×
● Muir, Ionia...............C 490
● Mullet Lake, Cheboygan..N 100
● Mulliken, Eaton...........S 200

Place	Pop.
Mundy, Genesee.............C	48
● Munger, Bay.............C	90
● Munising, Alger........NW	150
Munith, Jackson............S	300
● Munson, Lenawee.........S	50
Murphy, Baraga.........NW	×
Murray, Sanilac............E	×
● **Muskegon**, Muskegon. W	22,702
Muskegon Heights, Muskegon W	×
● *Muskegon Junction*, Kent W	×
● Nadeau, Menominee....NW	200
Nahma, Delta............NW	200
● *Nallville*, Wayne........SE	×
Nankin, Wayne...........SE	150
Naomi, Berrien..........SW	×
● Napoleon, Jackson........S	334
● *Narenta*, Delta........ NW	×
● Nashville, Barry........SW	1,029
● *Nason's*, Newaygo........W	×
National Mine, Marquette NW	900
Naubinway, Mackinac......N	578
● *Naubinway Jc.*, Mackinac N	×
Navan, Genesee............C	×
Neal, Grand Traverse.... NW	×
Neebish, Chippewa......... N	100
Needmere, (see Roxana).......	×
● Negaunee, Marquette.. NW	6,078
Nelson, Saginaw........... C	100
Nelson, (see Spencer's Mts.)..	×
Nelsonville, (see South Arm).	×
Neno, Isabella.............. C	×
● Nessen City, Benzie....NW	×
● Nestoria, Baraga.......NW	×
Newark, Gratiot.......... C	10
● **Newaygo**, Newaygo.... W	1,330
New Baltimore, Macomb..SE	865
New Baltimore, (see New Haven)	×
● Newberry, Luce..........N	1,115
Newberry, Wayne......... SE	×
New Boston, (see Pavilion) ..	×
● New Boston, Wayne.....SE	218
● New Buffalo, Berrien...SW	553
● *Newburg*, Cass..........SW	×
Newburgh, Lenawee.......... S	×
Newburgh, (see Nankin).....	×
New Casco, (see Glenn)	×
● New Era, Oceana.........W	100
New Groningen, Ottawa... W	100
● *Newhall*, Delta........ NW	×
● New Haven, Macomb....SE	606
New Haven Centre, Gratiot. C	50
New Holland, Ottawa.......W	150
New Home, Houghton....NW	×
● New Hudson, Oakland...SE	350
New Lothrop, Shiawassee...C	300
New Mission, (see Omena)...	×
Newport, Monroe..........SE	450
● New Richmond, Allegan SW	100
● *New River*, Huron........E	×
New Salem, Allegan....... SW	40
Newton, Calhoun.......... S	×
● Newtonville, Baraga... NW	100
New Troy, Berrien........SW	300
New York, Saginaw........ C	×
● *Nichols*, Calhoun..........S	×
Nicholsville, (see Little Prairie Ronde)	×
● Niles, Berrien...........SW	4,197
● *Nine Mile*, Bay...........C	×
● *Nipissing*, Lapeer.........E	×
● Nirvana, Lake........... W	200
Nixon, Missaukee.......... N	×
Noble, Branch...............S	15
Nolan, Roscommon..........N	×
Nonesuch, Ontonagon....NW	×
Noordeloos, Ottawa....... W	200
Norrisville, Leelanaw.... NW	100
● North Adams, Hillsdale...S	504
North Aurelius, Ingham.....S	75
North Batavia, Branch..... S	×
North Brownsville, (see Alaska)	×
● North Bradley, Midland...C	200
● North Branch, Lapeer.... E	705
North Burns, Huron........E	×
● North Detroit, Wayne...SE	×
North Dorr, Allegan...... SW	125
North Eagle, Clinton.......C	×
● *North Escanaba*, Delta NW	×
North Farmington, Oakla'd SE	50
North Grand Rapids, Kent. W	×
● *North Holland*, Ottawa..W	×
North Irving, Barry.......SW	×
● *North Lansing*, Ingham.. S	3,000
North Linden, (see Linden)..	×
North Manitou Island, Manitou NW	100
● North Morenci, Lenawee..S	25

Place	Pop.
North Muskegon, Muskegon W	1,590
North Newberg, Shiawassee.C	70
Northport, Leelanaw..... NW	302
● *North Saginaw*, Saginaw..C	*
● North Star, Gratiot....... C	150
● North Street, Saint Clair..E	×
North Unity, Leelanaw...NW	130
● Northville, Wayne.......SE	1,573
North Williams, Bay........C	×
● Norvell, Jackson...........S	150
Norwalk, (see Onekama).....	×
● Norway, Dickinson.... NW	3,000
Norway Hall, Lake..........W	×
Norway Mills, Menominee NW	×
Norwich, (see Stittsville).....	×
Norwood, Charlevoix........N	150
● Nottawa, Saint Joseph.. SW	400
Nova Scotia, (see Winfield)..	×
Novesta, Tuscola............E	65
● Novi, Oakland...........SE	250
● Nunica, Ottawa.......... W	350
● *Oa-at-ka Beach*, Bay...... C	×
● Oak, Wayne.............SE	150
● Oakdale Park, Kent.......W	×
Oakfield Centre, Kent......W	75
Oakfield, Kent............ W	×
● Oak Grove, Livingston......S	100
Oak Hill, Manistee.......NW	×
Oakland, Allegan......... SW	×
● *Oakland*, Berrien.......SW	×
● Oakley, Saginaw.......... C	299
Oakville, Monroe.......... SE	75
Oakwood, Oakland.........SE	200
Oakwood Park, Wayne.... SE	×
● O'Brien, Ontonagon....NW	50
Oceana, Oceana........... W	×
Oceola Centre, Livingston...S	×
Ocqueoc, Presque Isle......N	×
● Oden, Emmet............ N	50
Odessa, Oscoda............NE	×
O'Donnell, Barry...........SW	×
● Ogden, Lenawee..........S	35
Ogden Centre, Lenawee.....S	125
Ogemaw, Iosco............NE	×
● Ogemaw Springs, Ogemaw N	150
Ogontz, Delta.............NW	150
● Okemos, Ingham..........S	400
● Ola, Gratiot.............. C	150
Old Mission, G. Traverse. NW	70
Olds, Branch........... .... S	25
● *Olga*, Osceola...... C	×
Olga, Wexford........... NW	×
Olive Center, Ottawa....... W	260
Oliver Station, Huron.......E	×
Olivet, Eaton.............. S	790
● *Olivet Station*, Eaton......S	×
Olney, Shiawassee C	×
Omard, Sanilac.... ....E	32
Omena, Leelanaw........ NW	200
Omer, Arenac.......... C	150
Onaway, Presque Isle.......N	28
● Onekama, Manistee..... NW	700
● *Onekama Junction*, M'tee NW	×
● Onondago, Ingham........S	350
● Onota, Alger........... NW	100
● Onsted, Lenawee......... S	150
Ontario, Lenawee............S	15
● **Ontonagon**, Ont'gon. NW	1,500
● Opechee, Houghton..... NW	1,700
Oral, Clinton...............C	×
Ora Labor, (see Bayport).....	×
Orange, Ionia.............. C	75
Orange Hill, Alpena........NE	×
Orangeville, (see Hodunk)....	×
Orangeville Mills, Barry.. SW	300
Oray, Sanilac............. E	×
● Orchard Lake, Oakland..SE	130
● Oregon, Lapeer.......... E	75
● Orion, Oakland..........SE	522
● Orleans, Ionia.............C	200
● Orono, Osceola............C	150
Ortonville, Oakland.........SE	313
Orville, Mackinac...........N	100
● *Orville*, Saginaw........ C	×
Osborn, Benzie...........NW	×
● *Osborn's*, Calhoun.........S	×
● *Osceola*, Houghton..... NW	1,413
● *Osceola Junction*, W'x'd NW	×
Osceola Mills, Houghton. NW	566
● Oscoda, Iosco............NE	3,593
● Oshtemo, Kalamazoo... SW	300
Oskar, Houghton.........NW	×
● Osseo, Hillsdale.......... S	300
● Ossineke, Alpena.........NE	150
● Otia, Newaygo.............W	300
Otisco, Ionia.............. C	300
● Otisville, Genesee......... C	277

Place	Pop.
● Otsego, Allegan.........SW	1,626
● *Otsego Lake*, Otsego...... N	360
● Ottawa Beach, Ottawa....W	×
● Ottawa Lake, Monroe....SE	200
Ottawa Station, Ottawa..... W	150
● Otterburn, Genesee.......C	×
Otter Creek, Jackson.........S	150
● Otter Lake, Lapeer....... E	243
Overisel, Allegan..........SW	150
Oviatt, Leelanaw..........NW	75
● Ovid, Clinton........... C	1,423
Owens, (see McBain).........	×
● Owendale, Huron...........E	20
● Owosso, Shiawassee.......C	6,561
● *Owosso Junction*, Shi'ssee. C	×
Ox Bow, Oakland..........SE	100
● Oxford, Oakland......... SE	1,128
Oyer's Corners, (see Springport)	×
● Ozark, Mackinac......... N	×
● *Packard*, Van Buren....SW	×
● *Packard*, Ingham.........S	×
● *Page*, Emmet............ N	×
Paggeottown, (see Stronach).	×
● Paines, Saginaw...........C	150
● *Paines*, Iron............ NE	×
Paint Creek, (see Newcomb).	×
● Paint River, Iron....... NE	25
Palmer, (see Orleans)........	×
● Palmer, Marquette.....NW	1,011
● *Palms*, Mackinac......... N	×
● Palm Station, Sanilac..... E	60
● Palmyra, Lenawee........ S	250
Palo, Ionia................. C	300
Pangburn's Cors, Newaygo W	×
● *Panola*, Iron............ NE	×
● *Paradise*, (see Kingsley)...	×
● Paris, Mecosta............ C	500
Paris Mills, Huron.........E	×
Parisville, Huron........... E	75
● *Park City*, Newaygo.....W	×
● Parkinson, Gratiot........C	×
● Park Lake, Osceola....... C	75
Parks, Newaygo............W	×
Parkville, St Joseph......SW	225
● Parma, Jackson............S	490
● Parmelee, Barry.........SW	53
Parnell, Kent............. W	×
Parshallburg, (see Oakley)...	×
Parshallville, Livingston.... S	200
Parsons' Corners, (see Texas)	×
Partello, Calhoun...........S	100
● *Partridge*, Marquette..NW	×
Pascoe Mine, Marquette..NW	×
● *Patterson's*, Newaygo... W	×
Patterson's Ms., (see Belding)	×
● Pavillion Kalamazoo... SW	50
● **Paw Paw**, Van Buren SW	1,391
Paynesville, Ontonagon.. NW	×
Peach Belt, Allegan.......SW	130
● Pearl, Allegan.......... SW	70
Pearline, Ottawa........... W	×
Peck, Sanilac.............. E	350
● Pellston, Emmet...........E	50
Pembina, Menominee.... NW	×
Penasa, Osceola.............. C	×
Peninsula Mine, Hough'n NW	×
● Penn, Cass.............. SW	250
Penn Mine, Keweenaw.. NW	×
● *Pennocks*, Clare...........C	×
Penobscot, Muskegon... .. W	×
Pentecost, Lenawee......... S	16
● Pent Water, Oceana......W	1,510
Pequaming, Baraga....... NW	560
● *Perch*, Houghton...... NW	×
● Pere Cheney, Crawford... N	100
● *Perkins*, Delta.......... NW	×
● *Perrin*, Saint Joseph...SW	×
Perrinsville, Wayne....... SE	100
● Perrington, Gratiot....... C	349
● Perry, Shiawassee.........C	440
● *Peters*, Lake............ W	×
Peters, St. Clair............E	×
● Petersburgh, Monroe....SE	408
● Petoskey, Emmet......... N	2,872
● Pettysville, Livingston.... S	75
Pewabic, Houghton...... NW	×
● Pewamo, Ionia............C	384
Phelpstown, (see Webberville)	×
Phillips, Saginaw............C	×
Phoenix, Keweenaw......NW	1,000
● *Pickands Junc.*, Muske'n W	×
Pickford, Chippewa........ N	100
Pier Cove, (see Ganges).......	×
Pierport, Manistee.........NW	220
● Pierson, Montcalm.........C	215
Piersonville, (see Columbiaville)	×
● Pigeon, Huron......... . E	103

Michigan

Place	Pop.
Pigeon, (see West Olive)	×
● *Pike Lake*, Mackinac..... N	×
Pikes Peak, Wayne..........SE	200
● **Pinckney**, **Livingston**......S	449
● Pinconning, Bay..........C	885
Pine Creek, (see Otsego)......	×
Pine Creek, Calhoun........ S	150
● Pine Grove Mills, V B'n. SW	150
Pine Hill, Sanilac...........E	×
Pine Lake, (see Advance)	×
Pine Lake, (see Haslett Park)	×
Pine Lake, (see Cedar Sp'gs).	×
● *Pine Ridge*, Delta...... NW	×
Pine River, (see Arenac).....	×
Pine River, (see Charlevoix).	×
Pine Run, Genesee..........C	300
● Pines, Mackinac..........N	×
Pinnebog, Huron........... E	250
Pinora, (see Deer Lake)	×
Pioneer, Missaukee..........N	×
● *Piper*, Ogemaw......... N	125
Pipestone, Berrien......... SW	40
Pipestone Sta., (see Hartman)	×
Pittsburgh, Shiawassee......C	200
● Pittsfield, Washtenaw... SE	25
● Pittsford, Hillsdale........ S	400
Plainfield, Livingston....... S	300
Plainfield, (see Austerlitz)...	×
● *Plains*, Marquette......NW	×
● Plainwell, Allegan...... SW	1,414
Plank Road, Wayne....... SE	200
● *Plank's Tavern*, Ber'n. SW	×
Platte, Benzie............ NW	200
Pleasant, Kent........... W	×
Pleasant City, (see Sutt's Bay)	×
Pleasant Lake, (see Henrietta)	×
Pleasant Valley, Midland....C	57
Pleasant Valley, (see Pip'stc)	×
Pleasanton, Manistee....NW	×
Pleasant Valley, Midland....C	75
Pleasant View, Emmet..... N	57
● Plymouth, Wayne...... SE	1,172
● *Plymouth Junc.*, Wayne. SE	×
Plum's Mills, (see Mill Creek)	×
Podunk, (see Hastings)	×
Point au Frene, Chippewa. N	×
Pointe aux Pins, Mackinac..N	×
Point Lookout, Arenac..... C	×
Point Richards, Montcalm..C	×
● *Point Saint Ignace*, Mack N	×
Point Sable, Mason......... C	×
● Pokagon, Cass........... SW	300
● Pomona, Manistee..... NW	×
Pompei, Gratiot............. C	150
● **Pontiac**, Oakland...... SE	6,200
Pool, Lapeer.............. E	×
Popple, Huron.............. E	20
● Pori, Houghton......... NW	100
Portage, Manistee....... NW	150
● Portage, Kalamazoo.... SW	50
Portage Entry, Houghton NW	×
● *Portage Lake*, Saint Jos SW	×
● Port Austin, Huron....... E	571
Port Crescent, Huron....... E	500
Porter, Midland.............C	×
● *Porters*, Saginaw......... C	×
Port Hope, Huron .... E	393
● **Port Huron**, St. Clair..E	12,543
● Portland, Ionia.............C	1,678
Port Oneida, Leelanaw.....NW	×
Port Sanilac, Sanilac........ E	700
Port Sheldon, Ottawa...... W	×
Port Sherman, Muskegon..W	150
● Portsmouth, Bay...........C	100
Posen, Presque Isle......... N	100
Potter's, Saginaw.......... C	×
Pottersburg, (see Jeddo)	×
● Potterville, Eaton..........S	505
Poulsen, Mason............ W	×
● Powers, Menominee.... NW	300
Praha, Antrim............. N	×
Prairieville, Barry......... SW	300
Pratt Lake, Kent.......... W	×
● Prattville, Hillsdale....... S	125
Prentis' Bay, Mackinac.....N	75
● Prescott, Ogemaw......... N	75
Presque Isle, Presque Isle..N	×
Prestel, Clare............... C	×
Price, Clinton............... C	×
● *Prison Siding*, Ionia......C	×
Pritchardville, Barry.......SW	70
Prospect Lake, Van Buren SW	260
Provemont, Leelanaw.... NW	200
Prudenville, Roscommon... N	50
Puddleford, Jackson.........S	×
● Pulaski, Jackson.........S	200
● *Pulaski*, Jackson......... S	×

Michigan

Place	Pop.
Pullen's Corners, (see Rom'ls)	×
Purchase, Hillsdale..........S	×
Quaker, Lenawee............S	20
Quanicassee City, Tuscola... E	×
● *Quarry*, Huron.......... E	×
Quarry Spur, Delta......NW	×
● Quimby, Barry...........SW	100
● Quincy, Branch.......... S	1,250
● *Quincy Mine*, Houghton NW	×
● Quinnesec, Dickinson.. NW	322
● *Quinns*, Arenac.......... C	×
Rabbit River, (see Hamilton)	×
Raber, Chippewa........... N	×
● *Radford's Spur*, Men'm'ee NW	×
Raiguel, Lake............. W	×
● Raisin Centre, Lenawee...S	25
● Raisinville, Monroe......SE	50
● Ramsay, Gogebic...... NW	×
Randall, Saginaw...........C	×
Randolph, Osceola..........C	×
● Randville, Iron......... NE	×
Rankin, Genesee........... C	40
● *Rankin*, Oceana.......... N	×
Rann's Mill, Shiawassee.... C	×
● *Ransom*, Calhoun......... S	×
Ransom, Hillsdale........... S	150
● Rapid River, Delta..... NW	100
Rapids, Menominee...... NW	×
Rapinville, Mackinac....... N	×
Rapson, Huron..............E	×
● *Rapson's Siding*, Huron.. E	×
Rathbone, Gratiot......... C	×
Rattle Run, Saint Clair......E	135
Ratville, (see Hazelton)........	×
● Ravenna, Muskegon......W	250
Rawsonville, Wayne....... SE	100
Ray Centre, Macomb...... SE	80
Raymond, Charlevoix...... N	×
Raynold, (see Reynolds)	×
● Rea, Monroe............ SE	15
● Reading, Hillsdale........ S	1,000
Readmond, Emmet......... N	×
Rebel's Corners, Washtenaw SE	×
Recor's Point, St. Clair..... E	×
Redfield, Cass............. SW	20
Redford, Wayne ....SE	200
● Red Jacket, Houghton..NW	3,073
Redman, Huron .... E	×
Red Oak, Oscoda...........NE	×
Red Run Cor's, (see Cady) ...	×
Redruth, Baraga..........NW	×
Reed, (see Ferry)	×
● Reed City, Osceola.......... C	1,776
Reeder, (see Lake City).......	×
● Reeds, Kent.............W	×
● Reese, Tuscola........... E	500
● *Reeves*, Newaygo .... W	×
Relay Station, Menominee NW	×
Remick, Isabella.......... C	50
Remington, Montmorency..N	×
● Remus, Mecosta.......... C	200
● Reno, Ottawa............ W	×
● *Renton*, Calhoun..........S	×
● Republic, Marquette... NW	2,500
Rescue, Huron...............E	×
● **Resort Junction**, **Ottawa**. W	×
Rew, Clinton...............C	×
● *Rexford*, Chippewa....... N	×
● Reynold, Montcalm.........C	×
● Rhodes, Gladwin...........C	×
● Ribble, Huron............. E	40
Rice Creek, Calhoun......... S	250
Richfield, Genesee C	100
● Richland, Kalamazoo... SW	293
● *Richland Junction*, B'rry SW	×
Richmond, Macomb.........SE	.074
Richmondville, Sanilac...... E	35
● Richville, [illegible].......... E	250
Rickland, (see Cedar Lake)...	×
● *Ridge*, Alger..............NW	×
● Ridgeway, Lenawee....... S	300
Rienzi, Mecosta............ C	×
Rifle River, (see Omer).......	×
● Riga, Lenawee............. S	200
Riggsville, Cheboygan..... N	40
Riley, Clinton............... C	20
Riley Centre, Saint Clair.... E	500
Riley's Cor's, (see Pine Creek)	×
● *Ripley*, Houghton...... NW	×
River Bend, Clinton C	×
● Riverdale, Gratiot......... C	300
● River Raisin, Washtenaw SE	97
● River Rouge, Wayne.... SE	×
Riverside, (see Springwells) ..	×
● Riverside, Berrien...... SW	20
Riverton, Mason........... W	×
● *Riverview*, Berrien..... SW	×

Michigan

Place	Pop.
● Rives Junction, Jackson.. S	150
Roberts' Landing, Saint Clair E	90
Robbins, Ontonagon......NW	×
Robinson, Ottawa.......... W	150
● Rochester, Oakland......SE	900
● *Rochester Junc.*, Oakland SE	×
● Rock, Delta........... NW	82
Rock Elm, Charlevoix...... N	175
Rockery, Antrim........... N	×
Rock Falls, Huron..........E	×
● Rockford, Kent.......... W	900
● Rockland, Ontonagon.. NW	386
● Rock River, Alger..... NW	120
● Rockwood, Wayne.........SE	430
Rodington, Wexford.....NW	×
● Rodney, Mecosta............C	199
● *Roe Lake*, Alcona..........NE	×
Rogers City, Presque Isle N	431
● Rogersville, Genesee......C	100
● Rollin, Lenawee.......... S	150
● Rollo, Tuscola............ E	65
Rome, Lenawee...............S	100
● Romeo, Macomb.........SE	1,687
● Romulus, Wayne.........SE	100
● Rondo, Cheboygan....... N	150
Rookery, Antrim.......... N	×
● *Rooney*, Menominee....NW	×
● Roots, Jackson............S	×
● *Rootville*, Antrim.........N	×
● **Roscommon**, Roscom'n N	511
● Rose, Oakland...........SE	60
Roseburgh, Sanilac..........E	50
● *Rosebush*, Isabella........C	100
Rosedale, Chippewa......... N	×
Roseville, Macomb......... SE	500
Rosina, Ionia................C	×
● Ross, Kent.................W	40
● Rothbury, Oceana........W	60
Rougeville, Wayne..........SE	×
● *Round Lake*, Missaukee..N	×
Rowland, Isabella............C	65
Roxana, Eaton............. S	100
● Roy, Alcona............. NE	×
● Royal Oak, Oakland.....SE	500
Royalton, Berrien..........SW	210
Royce, Oscoda............. NE	×
Ruby, Saint Clair.............E	300
● Rudyard, Chippewa....... N	×
● *Rural*, Lapeer .... E	×
● Rushton, Livingston...... S	×
● Russell, Isabella.......... C	×
Russell's Mills, (see Chase)..	×
Rustford, Mecosta......... C	25
● Ruth, Huron...............E	150
Rutland, (see Kodunk)	×
Ryerson, Muskegon........W	×
● *Ryerson*, Newaygo........W	×
Ryno, Oscoda...............NE	125
Sac Bay, Delta.............NW	×
Saddle River, Mason.......W	×
Saganing, (see Worth).......	×
● *Sage*, Chippewa.......... N	×
● *Sage*, Luce................N	×
Sagerville, Shiawassee...... C	×
● *Saginaw Bay Jc.*, Saginaw C	×
● Saginaw, E. Side, Saginaw C	*
● *Saginaw Junc.*, Saginaw..C	×
● **Saginaw**, W. Side, Sag'aw C	46,322
● Sagola, Dickinson.......NW	400
Sailor's Encampment Island, (see Sault de Ste. Marie).	×
● Saint Charles, Saginaw...C	900
● Saint Clair, Saint Clair....E	2,353
Saint Clair Springs, S't. Clair E	×
● *Saint Collins*, Onton'g'n NW	×
Saint Elmo, Midland........C	×
Saint Helen, Roscommon.. N	1,006
Saint Helena, Mackinac....N	×
● **Saint Ignace**, Mackinac N	2,7[illegible]
Saint James, Manitou. NW	40[illegible]
● **Saint John's**, Clinton..C	3,127
● Saint Joseph, Berrien...SW	3,732
● *St. Lawrence*, Marquette NW	×
● *Saint Louis*, Gratiot...... C	[illegible],246
St. Mary's, (see Emmet).....	×
● Salem, Washtenaw...... SE	200
Salina, (see Saginaw, E. Side)	×
● Saline, Washtenaw.......SE	706
Salt River, (see Shepherd).....	×
● Salzburgh, Bay............C	×
● Samaria, Monroe..........SE	100
Sammons' Landing, Oceana W	150
● Sand Beach, Huron.......E	1,046
● Sand Creek, Lenawee..... S	100
Sanders, Manistee........NW	×

* Population included in Saginaw.

Place		Pop.
Sand Hill, Wayne	SE	77
● Sand Lake, Kent	W	386
● *Sand Lake*, Lenawee	S	×
● Sand River, Alger	NW	×
● Sands, Marquette	NW	25
● Sandstone, Jackson	S	160
Sandusky, (see Sanilac Centre)		×
Sandy, Montcalm	C	×
● Sanford, Midland	C	100
Sanilac Centre, Sanilac	E	403
● Saranac, Ionia	C	790
Satterlee's Mills, (see Rustford)		×
Saugatuck, Allegan	SW	779
SAULTE DE SAINT MARIE, Chippewa	N	5,760
● Saunders, Iron	NE	×
Sawersville, Osceola	C	×
● Sawyer, Berrien	SW	100
Scammon, Chippewa	N	154
Schaffer, Delta	NW	×
Schoeffen's Dock, (see Trenton)		×
● Schoolcraft, Kalamazoo	SW	836
● Scio, Washtenaw	SE	200
Scipio, Hillsdale	S	×
● Scofield, Monroe	SE	50
● Scotts, Kalamazoo	SW	100
● Scottville, Mason	W	147
● Sears, Osceola	C	250
Sebastopol, (see W. Windsor)		
Sebewa, Ionia	C	200
● Sebewaing, Huron	E	7[illegible]
Sedan, Charlevoix	N	×
● *Seeley's*, Mecosta	C	×
Selkirk, Ogemaw	N	×
● Seneca, Lenawee	S	25
● Seney, Schoolcraft	NW	200
Sethton, Gratiot	C	70
Seul Croix, Schoolcraft	NW	×
Seven Mile Hill, Iosco	NE	×
Seymour Lake, Oakland	SE	200
Shabbona, Sanilac	E	100
● Shaftsburg, Shiawassee	C	150
Sharon, Kalkaska	N	×
Sharon Hollow, Wash'naw	SE	×
Sharonville, Washtenaw	SE	×
Sharp's Corners, Lapeer	E	×
Sharpville, (see Sharp's Cor's)		×
Shattuckville, Saginaw	C	×
Shaw, (see Onaway)		×
Shaytown, Eaton	S	75
● *Shearer*, Ogemaw	N	×
● Shearer, Arenac	C	×
● *Shebeon*, Huron	E	×
● Sheffield, Kent	W	200
● *Shelby*, Macomb	SE	×
● Shelby, Oceana	W	994
● Shelbyville, Allegan	SW	250
Sheldon, (see Canton)		×
● Shepardsville, Clinton	C	200
● Shepherd, Isabella	C	469
● Sheridan, Montcalm	C	800
Sherman, Wexford	NW	750
Sherman City, Isabella	C	200
● *Sherman's Mill*, Grand Traverse	NW	×
Sherman Station, (see Bravo)		×
● Sherwood, Branch	S	447
Shetland, Leelanaw	NW	11
Shiawassee, Shiawassee	C	100
● Shiloh, Ionia	C	100
Shingleton, Alger	NW	×
● Shoup, Oakland	SE	×
● Shultz, Barry	SW	×
● *Sibleys*, Wayne	SE	×
Sickels, Gratiot	C	250
Siddons, Mason	W	×
● Sidnaw, Houghton	NW	×
Sidney, Montcalm	C	150
● *Siemans*, Gogebic	NW	×
Sigel, Huron	E	10
Siloam, Iosco	NE	×
● Silver Creek, Allegan	SW	175
● Simons, Antrim	N	50
Sischo's Cors., (see Brockway Centre)		×
● *Sisson*, Newaygo	W	×
● *Sissons*, Lenawee	S	×
Sister Lakes, Van Buren	SW	50
Sitka, Newaygo	W	×
Silver City, Gogebic	NW	×
Six Corners, Ottawa	W	150
Six Mile Creek, (see W. Haven)		×
● Six Lakes, Montcalm	C	250
Sixteen, (see Edenville)		×
Skanee, Baraga	NW	150
Sleeping Bear, (see Glen Arbor)		×
● *Slights*, Grand Traverse	NW	×

Michigan

Place		Pop.
Slocum Junction, Wayne	SE	×
● Slocum's Grove, Musk'g'n	W	40
● Smith, St. Clair	E	150
Smith's Corners, Oceana	W	87
Smith's Cor., (see W. Berlin)		×
● Smith's Creek, St. Clair	E	300
● Smith's Crossing, Midland	C	×
Smithville, (see Belden)		×
Smyrna, Ionia	C	300
● Snowflake, Antrim	N	170
● Snyder, Jackson	S	×
● Sodus, Berrien	SW	50
Solon, (see Cedar Springs)		×
Solon, Leelanaw	NW	40
● Somerset, Hillsdale	S	50
Somerset Centre, Hillsdale	S	200
● Sondma, Calhoun	S	75
Soo Junction, Luce	N	×
Soule, Huron	E	75
South Allen, Hillsdale	S	150
South Arm, Charlevoix	N	200
● *South Bay City*, Bay	C	×
South Blendon, Ottawa	W	35
● South Boardman, Kalkas.	N	350
South Butler, Branch	S	25
South Camden, Hillsdale	S	10
South Cass, Ionia	C	100
South Climax, (see Climax)		×
South Fairfield, Lenawee	S	25
Southfield, Oakland	SE	300
South Fox Island, (see St. James)		×
● South Frankfort, Benzie	NW	425
South Ganges, (see Ganges)		×
● South Grand Blanc, Oakl'd	SE	×
● South Grand Rapids, Kent	W	×
South Harrisville, Alcona	NE	×
South Haven, Van Buren	SW	1,924
South Jackson, Jackson	S	×
● South Lake Linden, Ho'ton	NW	2,000
● *South Lansing*, Ingham	S	×
● South Lyon, Oakland	SE	707
● South Manistique, Sch'c't	NW	388
South Manitou, Manitou	NW	128
South Milton, Antrim	N	×
South Monterey, Allegan	SW	×
South Riley, Clinton	C	250
● South Rockwood, Monroe	SE	200
● South Saginaw, Saginaw	C	×
● *South Shore Jc.*, Chippewa	N	×
Sova, Cheboygan	N	×
● Spalding, Menominee	NW	475
● Sparta, Kent	W	904
Speaker, Sanilac	E	200
Spencer Creek, Antrim	N	100
Spencer's Mill, Kent	W	120
Spicerville, Eaton	S	150
Spinks Corners, Berrien	SW	100
Spoonville, Ottawa	W	×
● Spring Arbor, Jackson	S	200
Spring Brook, Gratiot	C	25
Spring Brook, Kalamazoo	W	×
Spring Creek, Oceana	W	×
Springdale, Wexford	NW	450
Springfield, Oakland	SE	70
Spring Grove, Allegan	SW	1[illegible]
Spring Harbor, Charlevoix	N	×
● Spring Lake, Ottawa	W	1,168
● Springport, Jackson	S	407
Springtown, Livingston	S	×
Spring Vale, Charlevoix	N	×
● *Springville*, Wexford	NW	×
Springville, Lenawee	S	125
Springwells, (see Detroit)		×
Spurr Mountain, Baraga	NW	150
● *Staats Spur*, Mackinac	N	×
Stacy, Grand Traverse	NW	×
● *Stager*, Iron	NE	×
Stalwart, Chippewa	N	150
● Stambaugh, Iron	NE	600
● Standish, Arenac	C	611
● *Stanley Pit*, Lapeer	E	×
● **Stanton**, Montcalm	C	1,352
● *Stanton Junction*, Ionia	C	×
● Stanwood, Mecosta	C	265
Star City, Missaukee	N	×
Star Island, Saint Clair	E	×
● Stark, Wayne	SE	50
Starrville, Saint Clair	E	50
● *State Line*, Gogebic	NW	×
● *State Road*, Bay	C	×
● *State Road*, Manistee	NW	×
● *State Road*, Saginaw	C	×
Statzland, (see Zeeland)		×
Stearns, Midland	C	25
● *Stearns*, Lake	W	×
Stearns' Sta., (see Branch)		×
Stebbinsville, (see Collins)		×

Michigan

Place		Pop.
● Steiner, Monroe	SE	20
Stella, Gratiot	C	65
Stephens, Lapeer	E	75
● Stephenson, Menominee	NW	456
● Sterling, Arenac	C	200
Stetson, Oceana	W	×
● Stevensburgh, Chippewa	N	400
● Stevensville, Berrien	SW	400
Stiles, Newaygo	W	×
Stinson, Mecosta	C	×
● *Stimson Junction*, Mecosta	C	×
Stirlingville, Chippewa	N	×
Stittsville, Missaukee	N	20
● Stockbridge, Ingham	S	497
● *Stock Yards*, Wayne	SE	×
Stone Ledge, (see Hobart)		×
● *Stoneville*, Marquette	NW	×
● *Stony Creek*, Monroe	SE	×
Stony Creek, Oakland	SE	×
Stony Creek, (see Benona)		×
Stony Creek, Washtenaw	SE	60
● *Stony Island*, Wayne	SE	×
● Stony Point, Jackson	S	85
Storer, Antrim	N	60
● Strasburgh, Monroe	SE	50
Strickland, Isabella	C	125
● Stronach, Manistee	NW	500
Strongville, Chippewa	N	×
Stump, (see White River)		×
● *Sturgeon*, Baraga	NW	×
● Sturgeon River, Delta	NW	×
● Sturgis, Saint Joseph	SW	2,489
Sugar Grove, Mason	W	×
Sugar Island, Chippewa	N	400
● Sullivan, Muskegon	W	×
Summerfield, Clare	C	×
Summerton, Gratiot	C	150
Summerville, Cass	SW	150
● *Summerville*, Montcalm	C	×
● *Summit*, Baraga	NW	×
● *Summit*, Livingston	S	×
● *Summit*, Dickinson	NW	×
● *Summit*, Ogemaw	N	×
Summit, (see Salem)		×
● Summit City, Gr. Trav'e	NW	275
Summitville, Lake	W	30
Sumner, Gratiot	C	550
Sumter, (see New Boston)		×
Sun, Newaygo	W	×
● Sunfield, Eaton	S	100
● *Sunnyside*, Wayne	SE	×
Superior, Chippewa	N	309
● *Sutliff's*, Osceola	C	×
● Sutton, Lenawee	S	×
Sutton's Bay, Leelanaw	NW	250
● *Swain's*, Newaygo	W	×
Swan Creek, Allegan	SW	×
● *Swan Creek*, Saginaw	C	×
Swan Creek, (see Fair Haven)		×
● Swanzy, Marquette	NW	×
Swartzburg, (see Nankin)		×
Swartz Creek, Genesee	C	300
● *Swedetown*, Houghton	NW	×
● *Sweet's*, Muskegon	W	×
Sylvan, Washtenaw	SE	80
Sylvester, Mecosta	C	125
Talbot, Menominee	NW	×
● *Taft*, Iosco	NE	×
Tallmadge, Ottawa	W	75
Tallman, Mason	W	200
● *Tamarack*, Houghton	NW	×
Tamarack Mine, Houghton	NW	768
● Tanner, Manistee	NW	×
Tarry, Huron	E	×
● **Tawas City**, Iosco	NE	1,544
● *Taylor*, Baraga	NW	×
Taylor Centre, Wayne	SE	150
Taymouth, Saginaw	C	70
● Tecumseh, Lenawee	S	2,319
● Tekonska, Calhoun	S	5[illegible]
● Temperance, Monroe	SE	25
● Temple, Clare	C	×
Terry Station, Bay	C	×
Tews Mills, Montcalm	C	×
Texas, Kalamazoo	SW	125
● *Thayer*, Gogebic	NW	×
Thayer, Oakland	SE	×
Thetford Centre, (see E. Thetford)		×
● *Thomas*, Van Buren	SW	×
● Thomas, Oakland	SE	205
● Thomaston, Gogebic	NW	200
● *Thompson*, Ogemaw	N	×
Thompson, Schoolcraft	NW	325
Thompson's Cors., (see Kilmanagh)		×
● Thompsonville, Benzie	NW	500
● *Thorn Apple*, Barry	SW	×
Thornton, Saint Clair	E	110
Thornville, Lapeer	E	350

Thorp, Wexford..........NW ×
Three Lakes, Baraga.....NW ×
● Three Oaks, Berrien....SW 885
● Three Rivers, St. JosephSW 3,131
Thumb Lake, Charlevoix...N 30
Thurman, Eaton..........S 100
● *Tibbets*, Newaygo........W ×
Tietsort's, (see Model City) ... ×
Tigris, Oceana.............W ×
● Tipton, Lenawee..........S 50
Tittabawassee, (see Jay) ..... ×
Tittabawassee Sta., (seePaines) ×
Tompkins, Jackson.........S 100
Tonkin, Clare.............C ×
Tonguish, Wayne..........SE ×
● Topinabee, Cheboygan....N 45
Toquin, Van Buren........SW ×
Torch Lake, Antrim........N 100
● *Torch LakeJc.*, HoughtonNW ×
● *Totten*, Lake............W ×
Town House, Lenawee......S ×
● *Town Line*, Montcalm....C ×
Town Line Station, (see Union Pier) ...... ×
Town Line Station, (see Yew) ×
Towns, Branch..............S ×
● **Traverse City**, G'dT'eNW 4,353
● *Travis*, Kalamazoo.....SW ×
Travis Road, (see Woodville) ×
Tremaine's Cor., (see Orange) ×
● Trent, Muskegon.........W 150
● Trenton, Wayne.........SE 789
Trist, Jackson..............S ×
Trostville, (or *Frankentrost*) Saginaw ....C 50
● Trout Creek, Ont'agon.NW ×
● Trout Lake, Chippewa....N ×
● Trowbridge, Cheboygan..N ×
● *Trowbridge*, Ingham......S ×
TrowbridgePoint, (seeAlpena) ×
Troy, Oakland ....SE 100
Troy Station, (see Sawyer)... ×
Troutdale, Charlevoix......N ×
● Trufant, Montcalm....... C 500
Truitts, Cass.............SW ×
Trumbulls, Jackson........S 160
● *Tula*, Gogebic......... NW ×
● Turin, Marquette.........NW 150
● *Turnbulls*, Newaygo.....W ×
Turner, Arenac............C ×
Turtle Lake, Benzie......NW ×
Tuscola, Tuscola...........E 400
● Tustin, Osceola........... C 400
Twelve Corners, Berrien..SW ×
● Twin Lake, Muskegon....W 125
Tyner, Saginaw............C ×
● Tyre, Sanilac.............E 250
Tyrone, Livingston.........S 30
Tyrone Sta., (see Kent City) ×
Tyrrell, Oscoda.............NE ×
● Ubly, Huron...............E 400
● Ula, Kent..................W ×
Unadilla, Livingston........S 150
Undine, Charlevoix.........N 75
Union, Cass...............SW 150
● Union City, Branch ....S 1,156
Union Cor., (see Indian Lake) ×
Union Home, Clinton....... C 200
● Union Pier, Berrien.....SW 100
● Unionville, Tuscola.......E 414
● *Upper Big Rapids*, Mec's'taC ×
● *Upper Paris*, Mecosta ....C ×
Upton, Clare...............C ×
● *Uptons*, Saint Clair.......E ×
Upton Works, St. Clair.....E 165
Urania, Washtenaw........SE ×
Urban, Sanilac.............E ×
● *Urbanrest*, Oakland.....SE ×
● Utica, Macomb..........SE 563
Utica Plank, (see Fraser).... ×
● Valley Centre, Sanilac....E 200
● Vandalia, Cass..........SW 423
Van Decar, Isabella.........C 200
● Vanderbilt, Otsego........N 370
● *Vanhorns*, Jackson.......S ×
Van's Harbor, Delta......NW ×
● Van Winkle, Delta.......NW ×
Vanzile, (see Kitchi)......... ×
● Vassar, Tuscola...........E 1,682
Vaugh's, Alcona..........NE ×
Veenfliets, Saginaw.........C ×
Velzy, Kent...............W ×
Venice, Shiawassee.........C 38
Ventura, Ottawa...........W 200
Vergennes, (see Fallassburg) ×
● *Vermilac*, Baraga......NW ×

Michigan

● Vermontville, Eaton......S 730
Verne, Saginaw............C ×
● Vernon, Shiawassee.......C 585
Verona Mills, Huron........E 75
● Vestaburgh, Montcalm .. C 500
● Vickeryville, Montcalm...C 75
● Vicksburgh, KalamazooSW 921
Victor, Clinton.............C 150
Victorsville, Lenawee.......S ×
Victory, Mason............ W 130
Vienna, (see Meade).......... ×
● *Vienna*, Monroe.........SE ×
Vienna, Montgomery........N 520
Vincent, Menominee.....NW ×
Vine, Iosco................NE ×
● *Vineland*, Berrien......SW ×
● Viola, Mackinac..........N ×
Viola, Wexford..........NW ×
Vogle Centre, Missaukee... N 300
Volinia, Cass..............SW 100
Volinia Sta., (see Wakelee).. ×
Volney, Newaygo.......... W 100
Vosburg, (see Mill Gr.)...... ×
Vriesland, Ottawa.........W 200
● *Vriesland Sta.*, Ottawa.. W 70
● Vulcan, Dickinson..... NW 1,500
● *Wabash Junction*, W'e..SE ×
● *Wabick*, Marquette.... NW ×
Wacousta, Clinton.......... C 300
● Wadham's, Saint Clair....E 75
● Wadsworth, Huron........E 95
● Wahjamega, Tuscola......E 125
Waiske, (seeSault deSte. Marie) ×
Wariner, Monroe.........SE ×
● Wakefield, Gogebic.... NW 300
● Wakelee, Cass.......... SW 200
Wakeshma, (see Fulton)..... ×
Waldenburgh, Macomb.....SE 200
● Waldron, Hillsdale.........S 365
○ Wales, St. Clair........... E 150
Walkerville, Oceana........W ×
Walkley, Benzie.........NW ×
● Wallace, Menominee...NW 300
Wallaceville, Wayne.......SE 80
● Walled Lake, Oakland...SE 400
Walloon, Charlevoix.......N ×
Walnut, Oakland...........SE ×
● Walton, G'd Traverse..NW 200
● Waltz, Wayne...........SE 300
● *Warner*, Monroe........SE ×
● Warren, Macomb..........SE 200
● Wasepi, Saint Joseph... SW 125
Washington, (see E.Wash't'n) ×
● Washington, Macomb ...SE 350
● Waterford, Oakland.....SE 500
Waterford, Wayne.........SE 150
Waterloo, Jackson.......... S 125
● Waters, Otsego.......... N 200
○ Watersmeet, Gogebic.. NW 250
● *Water Street Jc.*, Bay.... C ×
Watertown, Tuscola.........E ×
● Watervliet, Berrien.....SW 500
Watkins, Washtenaw.......SE ×
● Watrousville, Tuscola..... E 300
● Watson, Allegan.........SW 50
● Waucedah, Dickinson.. NW 300
Waverly, VanBuren......SW 60
● Wayland, Allegan.......SW 523
● Wayne, Wayne.......... SE 1,226
● *Wayne Junction*, WayneSE ×
● *Webber's*, Ionia..........C ×
● Webberville, Ingham..... S 404
Webster, Washtenaw......SE ×
Weesaw, (see Hill's Corners). ×
Weinsburg, Washtenaw... SE ×
● *Welch*, Ogemaw..........N ×
Weldon, Benzie.......... NW ×
● *Weldon Bridge*, BenzieNW ×
● *Weldon Centre*, Benzie. NW ×
● Weldon Creek, Mason.... W 200
Wellington, Crawford...... N ×
● *Wellington*, Gogebic...NW ×
Wells, Bay..................C ×
Wells, Delta..............NW 65
● Wellsburg, Chippewa......N ×
Wellsburgh, Delta.........NW ×
● Wellsville, Lenawee.......S 15
● *Wenona Beach*, Bay......C ×
● We-que-ton Sing, Emmet N ×
● *West Au Train*, Alger. NW ×
● West Bay City, Bay....... C 12,981
West Berlin, St. Clair.......E ×
● **West Branch**, Oge'aw. N 1,302
West Campbell, Ionia.......C 300
● West Carlisle, Kent...... W ×
West Casco, Allegan....... SW 175
West Chester Sta., (seeConklin) ×

Michigan

West China, St. Clair.......E ×
● *West Detroit*, Wayne....SE ×
West End, Wayne..........SE ×
West Geneva, (see Geneva) ... ×
● *West Gladstone*, Delta. NW ×
West Greenbush, Alcona..NE ×
● West Harrisville, Alcona.NE 593
West Haven, Shiawassee.... C 300
West Ishpeming, Marqu'teNW ×
West Le Roy, Calhoun......S 80
● West Milbrook, Mecosta..C ×
● *Westminster*, G.Trvav'seNW ×
West Novi, (see Novi)........ ×
● West Olive, Ottawa.......W 75
● Weston, Lenawee......... S 200
West Owosso, (see Owosso)... ×
Westphalia, Clinton.........C 350
● *West Point*, SchoolcraftNW ×
West Sebewa, Ionia. ....C 250
West Sumpter, Wayne.... SE 125
West's Mill, Saginaw........C 20
● West Troy, Newaygo..... W 75
Westville, Montcalm .... C 300
West Watson, (see Abronia). ×
West Windsor, Eaton........S 250
● Westwood, Kalkaska...... N 200
● Wetzell, Antrim.......... N 200
Wexford, Wexford..........NW 75
● Wheatfield, Calhoun...... S 30
Wheatland, Hillsdale........ S 30
Wheatland, Wexford.... NW ×
Wheatland Centre, (see Remus) ×
● Wheeler, Gratiot..........C 300
● *Wheelerton*, Jackson......S 200
● *Whipple*, Gr. Traverse. NW ×
Whitbeck, Marquette .... NW ×
White, Hillsdale............. S 30
● White Cloud, Newaygo .. W 743
● White Dale, Schoolcraft NW ×
● *White Feather*, Bay...... C ×
White Fish, Delta........ NW ×
Whitefish Point, Chippewa..N 110
Whiteford Centre, Monroe..SE 150
● Whitehall, Muskegon.... W 1,903
White Lake, (see Whitehall).. ×
White Lake, Oakland...... SE 75
White Lake Cen., (see Ox Bow) ×
White Oak, Ingham.........S 150
● White Pigeon, St. Jos... SW 961
White Rock, Huron.........E 300
● *White's Kilns*, Allegan.SW ×
Whitesburg, Genesee........ C ×
White Stone Point, Arenac..C ×
White Swan, Kent..........W ×
Whiteville, Isabella..........C 40
White's Sta., (see Wheatfield). ×
Whiting, Arenac............ C 301
Whiting, Lapeer.............E 60
● Whitmore Lake, Wash'w SE 100
● *Whitmore Lake Station*, Livingston .... S ×
Whitmanville, (see La Grange) ×
Whitney, Arenac............C 301
● Whitney, Menominee .. NW 100
Whitneyville, Kent.........W 100
○ Whittaker, Washtenaw..SE 125
● Whittemore, Iosco....... NE 350
Wickware, Sanilac.......... E 40
Whitewater, Gr.Traverse. NW ×
Wilber, Iosco..............NE ×
● Wilderville, Calhoun...... S ×
Wild Fowl Bay, (see Bay Port) ×
Wildwood, Cheboygan...... N ×
Wiley, Mason............. W ×
Wilkinson, (seeLake Side)... ×
Willard, Bay................ C 250
Williams, (see Skinner) ...... ×
● Williams, Kalamazoo... SW 40
Williamsburgh,G. Trav'se NW 240
● Williamston, Ingham..... S 1,139
Williamsville, Cass......... SW 150
● Willis, Washtenaw...... SE ×
Willow Island, (see Saginaw, E. Side) .... ×
Willville, Lake............. W ×
● Wilmot, Tuscola......... E 75
Wilson, (see Deer Lake)...... ×
Wilson, (see Eastport) .... ×
○ Wilson, Menominee.... NW 200
○ *Wilsons*, Jackson ....S ×
Wilson's Landing, (see Sault de Ste. Marie) .... ×
Windom, Lenawee.......... S ×
Winfield, Ingham........... S 200
● *Wingleton*, Lake.......... W 200
● *Wings Junction*, Osceola. C ×

Town, County	Index	Pop.
Winn, (see Dushville)		×
● *Winsor*, Huron	E	×
Winterfield, Clare	C	×
Winters, Alger	NW	×
● *Winthrop Junc.*, Marq'tte	NW	×
● *Wise*, Isabella	C	×
Wisner, Tuscola	E	300
● *Witbeck*, Marquette	NW	×
● Withey, Houghton	NW	×
Withington, Jackson	S	×
● Wixom, Oakland	SE	150
Wolf Creek, Lenawee	S	×
● *Wolf Lake*, Lake	W	×
Wolf's Mill, Kent	W	×
Wolfton, Huron	E	×
● Wolverine, Cheboygan	N	462
● *Wood*, Lenawee	S	×
● *Woodbridge*, Lenawee	S	×
Woodburn, Oceana	W	100
● Woodbury, Eaton	S	50
● Wood Lake, Montcalm	C	250
● Woodland, Barry	SW	500
● Woodmere, Wayne	SE	300
● Wood's Corners, Ionia	C	75
● *Woodside*, Houghton	NW	×
● Woodstock, Lenawee	S	100
● Woodville, Newaygo	W	600
● *Wooster Hill*, Newaygo	W	×
● Worden, Washtenaw	SE	×
● Worth, Arenac	C	25
Worth, (see Tuscola)		×
Wright, Ottawa	W	×
Wright's Bridge, Midland	C	×
Wright's Lake, Otsego	N	×
● Wyandotte, Wayne	SE	3,817
● Wyman, Montcalm	C	150
● Yale, Saint Clair	E	937
Yankee Spring, Barry	SW	60
Yargerville, Monroe	SE	×
● *Yates*, Macomb	SE	×
Yates, Manistee	NW	40
Yew, Wayne	SE	×
York, Washtenaw	SE	150
● Yorkville, Kalamazoo	SW	200
● Ypsilanti, Washtenaw	SE	6,129
Yuba, Grand Traverse	W	139
● Zeeland, Ottawa	W	785
Zieglerburg, (see Redford)		×
● Zilwaukee, Saginaw	C	900
● Zion, Saint Clair	E	30
Zutphen, Ottawa	W	30

MINNESOTA.

COUNTIES.	INDEX.	POP.
Aitkin	E	2,462
Anoka	E	9,884
Becker	W	9,401
Beltrami	NW	812
Benton	C	6,284
Big Stone	W	5,722
Blue Earth	S	29,210
Brown	S	15,817
Carlton	E	5,272
Carver	C	16,532
Cass	N	1,247
Chippewa	SW	8,555
Chisago	E	10,359
Clay	W	11,517
Cook	NE	[illegible]
Cottonwood	SW	7,412
Crow Wing	C	8,852
Dakota	E	20,240
Dodge	SE	10,864
Douglas	W	14,606
Faribault	S	16,708
Fillmore	SE	25,966
Freeborn	S	17,962
Goodhue	SE	28,806
Grant	W	6,875
Hennepin	**C**	**185,294**
Houston	SE	14,653
Hubbard	N	1,412
Isanti	E	7,607
Itasca	N	743
Jackson	SW	8,924
Kanabec	E	1,579
Kandiyohi	C	13,997
Kittson	NW	5,387
Lac-qui-parle	SW	10,382
Lake	NE	1,299
Le Sueur	S	19,057
Lincoln	SW	5,691
Lyon	SW	9,501
McLeod	C	17,026
Marshall	NW	9,130
Martin	S	9,403
Meeker	C	15,456
Mille Lacs	C	2,845
Morrison	C	13,325
Mower	SE	18,019
Murray	SW	6,692
Nicollet	S	13,382
Nobles	SW	7,958
Norman	NW	10,618
Olmsted	SE	19,806
Otter Tail	W	34,232
Pine	E	4,052
Pipe Stone	SW	5,132
Polk	NW	30,192
Pope	W	10,032
Ramsey	E	139,796
Redwood	SW	9,386
Renville	SW	17,099
Rice	S	23,968
Rock	SW	6,817
St. Louis	NE	44,862
Scott	S	13,831
Sherburne	C	5,908
Sibley	S	15,199
Stearns	C	34,844
Steele	S	13,232
Stevens	W	5,251
Swift	W	10,161
Todd	C	12,930
Traverse	W	4,516
Wabasha	SE	16,972
Wadena	C	4,053
Waseca	S	13,313
Washington	E	25,992
Watonwan	S	7,746
Wilkin	W	4,346
Winona	SE	33,797
Wright	C	24,164
Yellow Medicine	SW	9,854
Total		1,301,826

TOWN. COUNTY.	INDEX.	POP.
Aabye, Norman	NW	25
Aastad, Otter Tail	W	50
● **Ada**, Norman	NW	622
Adair, Freeborn	S	×
● Adams, Mower	SE	216
Adelaide, Big Stone	W	32
● Adrian, Nobles	SW	671
● Afton, Washington	E	350
Agate Bay, St. Louis	NE	×
● Airlie, Pipe Stone	SW	38
● **Aitkin**, Aitkin	E	737
Akeley, (see La Prairie)		×
● Albany, Stearns	C	500
Alberta, Benton	C	20
● **Albert Lea**, Freeborn	S	3,305
Alba, (see Chester, Iowa)		×
Albin, Brown	S	×
Albion, Wright	C	57
Aldal, Polk	NW	15
● Alden, Freeborn	S	276
● Aldrich, Wadena	C	69
● **Alexandria**, Douglas	W	2,118
● *Allen*, St. Louis	NE	×
Alice, Kittson	NW	20
● *Allison*, Pope	W	×
Alma City, Waseca	S	200
Almelund, Chisago	E	×
Almon, Winona	SE	×
Alta Vista, Lincoln	SW	×
Alton, Faribault	S	32
● *Altoona*, Pipe Stone	SW	×
● Altura, Winona	SE	×
Amador, Chisago	E	32
● Amboy, Blue Earth	S	215
Amboy, Cottonwood	SW	×
● *Amboy*, Otter Tail	W	×
Ames, Hubbard	N	×
Amherst, Fillmore	SE	100
● Amiret, Lyon	SW	35
Amo, Cottonwood	SW	×
Amor, Otter Tail	W	32
Anderson, Pope	W	×
● Angus, Pold	NW	50
● Annandale, Wright	C	211
● **Anoka**, Anoka	E	4,252
Antrim, Watonwan	S	×
● Appleton, Swift	W	994
Arctander, Kandiyohi	C	24
Arendahl, Fillmore	SE	65
Argo, Winona	SE	×
● Argyle, Marshall	NW	306
● Arlington, Sibley	S	417
● Armstrong, Freeborn	S	30
● *Armstrong*, Hennepin	C	32
● *Arthur*, St. Louis	NE	×
Artichoke Lake, Big Stone	W	×
Ash, Grant	W	×
● Ashby, Grant	W	231
● Ash Creek, Rock	SW	25
Ashford, Redwood	SW	×
Ash Grove, Rock	SW	×
○ *Ashley*, Stearns	C	×
Ashton, Winona	SE	×
Aspelund, Goodhue	SE	40
Assumption, Carver	C	10
Athens, Isanti	E	20
Atherton, Wilkin	W	×
● *Atlantic Junc.*, Hennepin	C	×
Attica, Aitkin	E	×
● Atwater, Kandiyohi	C	429
● *Auburn*, Dakota	E	75
● Audubon, Becker	W	159
● Augusta, Carver	C	35
Aurdale, (see Fergus Falls)		×
● Aurora, Steele	S	40
● **Austin**, Mower	SE	3,901
● *Averill*, Clay	W	×
● Avoca, Murray	SW	170
● Avon, Stearns	C	250
Ayr, Goodhue	SE	22
Badger, Kittson	NW	15
Badger, Polk	NW	×
● *Bailey*, Sherburne	C	×
Bainbridge, Cottonwood	SW	×
● *Baker*, Clay	W	×
Bakerville, Meeker	C	×
● Balaton, Lyon	SW	175
● *Bald Eagle Lake*, Ramsey	E	30
● *Bald Eagle Junc.*, Ramsey	E	30
Balmoral, Otter Tail	W	×
Bandon, Renville	SW	×
Bangor, Otter Tail	W	×
Banks, Faribault	S	48
Barber, Faribault	S	×
● *Barden*, Scott	S	×
● *Barker*, Carlton	E	×
Barker, Traverse	W	×
● Barnesville, Clay	W	1,069
Barnsville, Dakota	E	×
● **Barnum**, Carlton	E	417
● Barrett, Grant	W	150
● Barry, Big Stone	W	50
● *Bassett Lake*, St. Louis	NE	×
● *Bass Lake*, Hennepin	C	×
Batavia, Todd	C	×
● *Batavia*, Big Stone	W	30
Bath, Freeborn	S	×
● Battle Lake, Otter Tail	W	250
● *Baxter*, Crow Wing	C	×
Baytown, (see South Stillwater)		×
● *Bear Creek*, Winona	SE	×
Beardsley, Big Stone	W	200
● *Beardsley Sta.*, Big Stone	W	×
Bear Valley, Wabasha	SE	132
Beaudry, Polk	NW	32
Beauford, Blue Earth	S	25
Beauleau, Norman	NW	×
Beaver, Winona	SE	300
Beaver Bay, Lake	NE	20
● Beaver Creek, Rock	SW	232
Beaver Falls, Renville	SW	500
Bechyn, Renville	SW	×
● Becker, Sherburne	C	40
Bee, Houston	SE	×
● Belgrade, Stearns	C	306
Belle Chester, Wabasha	SE	80
● *Belle Creek*, Goodhue	SE	×
● Belle Plaine, Morrison	C	814
Belle River, Douglas	W	20
Belleview, Blue Earth	S	×
● Bellingham, Lac-qui-parle	SW	166
Belmont, Jackson	SW	32
● *Belt Line Junction*, Anoka	E	×
● *Beltrami*, Polk	NW	165
Belvidere Mills, Goodhue	SE	40
● Belview, Redwood	SW	×
Belwood, Dakota	E	×
Ben Franklin, Murray	SW	12
Bennington, Mower	SE	×
● *Benoit*, Polk	NW	×
● **Benson**, Swift	W	877
● *Benton Junction*, Carver	C	39
Berg, Rice	S	×
Bergen, (see Lester Prairie)		×
Bergen, Jackson	SW	×
Berlin, Steele	S	57

Bernadotte, Nicollet.........S 12
Berne, Dodge..............SE 100
Bertha, Todd...............C 25
● Bethany, Winona........SE 25
Bethel, Anoka............. E 5
Big Bend, (see Hagen)........ ×
Big Bend, Cottonwood.... SW 32
● Bigelow, Nobles.........SW 50
● Big Lake, Sherburne......C 200
Big Spring, Fillmore.......SE ×
Big Stone, Big Stone....... W 278
Big Woods, Marshall..... NW ×
● Bingham Lake, Co'nw'd SW 100
Birch Cooley, Renville.... SW 255
● Birch Lake, Todd.........C 50
● Bird Island, Renville....SW 441
● Biscay, McLeod...........C ×
Bismarck, Sibley............S 350
Bixby, Steele...............S ×
Blackberry, Itasca........ N ×
Black Hammer, Houston.. SE 32
Black Oak, Goodhue.......SE 40
Blacksville, Brown..........S ×
Blaine, Blue Earth.......... S 32
● Blakeley, Scott............S 200
Blenheim, Lac-qui-parle...SW ×
Blomford, Isanti............E ×
Bloomfield, Hennepin.......C ×
Blooming Grove, (see Waseca) ×
● Blooming Prairie, Steele..S 308
Bloomington, Hennepin.... C ×
Bloomington Ferry, H'n'pin.C ×
● **Blue Earth City**, F'r'b'tS 1,569
Blue Mounds, Pope.......... W 22
● *Bluff Switch*, Jackson.. SW ×
● Bluffton, Otter Tail...... W 40
Bock, Mille Lacs............C ×
● Bongard, Carver...........C ×
Bonniwell's Mills, Meeker.. C 20
Boon Lake, Renville......SW ×
● *Borup*, Norman........ SW ×
● Boyd, Lac-qui-parle.....SW 75
Bradford, Isanti............ E 25
● *Bradley's*, Le Sueur.......S ×
Braham, Isanti..............E ×
● **Brainerd**, Cross Wing.. C 5,703
● Brandon, Douglas........W 225
Bratsberg, Fillmore....... SE 50
Bray, Polk.............. NW ×
● **Breckenridge**, Wilkin W 655
● *Breda*, St. Louis........ NE ×
Breese, Marshall......... NW ×
● *Breezy Point*, Hennepin.. C ×
Bremen, Wabasha.........SE 97
Brenner, Lyon............ SW 25
● Brewster, Nobles....... SW ×
● *Bridgeman*, Mille Lacs....C 260
● *Bridgewater*, Rice..........S 25
Brighton, Nicollet...........S 101
● *Brighton Junc.*, Anoka....E ×
● *Brights*, Wabasha........S ×
Bristol, Fillmore...........SE 65
Brockway, Stearns..........C 77
● *Bromling*, Blue Earth.....S ×
Bronson, Kanabec........... E 15
Brooklyn Centre, Hennepin.C 40
Brooks, Polk..............NW ×
● Brooten, Stearns..........C 100
Browerville, Todd...........C 86
Brownsburgh, Jackson... SW 50
● Brownsdale, Mower..... SE 282
● *Brown's Hill*, Pine........ E ×
● **Brown's Valley**, Traverse W 498
● Brownsville, Houston.... SE 471
● Brownton, McLeod....... C 384
● Bruce, Rock.............. SW ×
● *Brunson*, Kanabec........E ×
Brunswick, Kanabec.........E 75
Buckeye, Freeborn...........S ×
Buckman, Morrison..........C 25
Buck's Mills, Becker.......W 8
● **Buffalo**, Wright.........C 606
● Buffalo Lake, Renville..SW 50
● Buffington, Polk....... NW ×
Bullan, Polk..............NW ×
Burau, Wilkin............. W ×
Burbank, Kandiyohi........ C 16
● Burchard, Lyon.........SW 25
Burnesville, Anoka......... E ×
Burnhamsville, (see Pillsbury) ×
Burns, Anoka............... E 101
Burn's Station, (see Springfield) ×
Burschville, Hennepin...... C 50
Burtrum, Todd..............C ×
● *Burwell*, Polk.............NW ×
● Butterfield, Watonwan....S 200
Butternut Valley, (see Lake Crystal)................. ×

● Byron, Olmsted..........SE 29
● *Cable*, Sherburne......... C ×
● **Caledonia**, Houston...SE 92
Caledonia Junc., (see Reno).. ×
Cambridge, Isanti........E 258
Camden, Lyon..............SW 50
● Camden Place, Hennepin. C 150
Camp, Renville............SW 165
● Campbell, Wilkin........ W 300
Camp Ground, Washington. E ×
● Canby, Yellow Medicine SW 470
Cannon City, Rice...........S 72
● Cannon Falls, Goodhue. .SE 1,078
● *Cannon Falls Sta.*, Dak. SE ×
● *Cannon Junction*, Good'e SE ×
Cannon Valley, (see Cannon Falls)................... ×
Canosia, St. Louis......... NE ×
● Canton, Fillmore........SE 281
● *Cardigan Junction*, Ram'y E ×
Carlmona, Fillmore........SE 75
● Carlisle, Otter Tail........ W 65
Carlson, Swift.............. W ×
● **Carlton**, Carlton....... E 700
● Carman, Polk.......... NW 250
Caroline, Le Sueur.......... S 65
Carrollsville, Olmsted......SE 65
Carson, (see Osage)......... ×
● *Carthage*, Polk........NW ×
● *Carthage Junc.*, Polk..NW ×
● Carver, Carver.............C 625
● Cascade, Goodhue....... SE 50
Cassell, Wright..............C ×
● *Castle*, Washington........E ×
● Castle Rock, Dakota...... E 20
Catlin, St. Louis.......... NE ×
● Cazenovia, Pipe Stone.. SW ×
● *Cedar Lake*, Crow Wing.. C ×
Cedar Lake, Scott.......... S 10
Cedar Mills, Meeker........ C 25
Cedarville, Martin............S 59
● *Cement Works*, Blue Earth S ×
Centre Chain, Martin.........S 25
● **Centre City**, Chisago... E 100
Centreville, Anoka.......... C 200
● *Centreville*, Washington... E 12
Centreville, (see Witoka)..... ×
Centreville Sta., (see Hugo).. ×
Cereal, Wantonwan...........S 33
Ceresco, Blue Earth..........S ×
Ceresco, Lyon..............SW ×
CerroGordo, Lac-qui-parle SW 44
Chain City, Martin.........S 25
Champion Mills, Blue Earth S 20
Champlin, Hennepin....... C 325
● Chandler, Murray.......SW 15
● Chanhassen, Carver....... C 50
Chapin, Becker............ W ×
Charlesville, (see Vasa)....... ×
● **Chaska**, Carver......... C 2,210
● Chatfield, Fillmore......SE 1,335
● *Chatfield Junc.*, Olmsted SE ×
Chatham, Wright........... C 20
Chechalis, Le Sueur......... S 15
● *Chelsea Siding*, Wash'ton. E ×
Cheney, Dodge............SE 10
Cherry Grove, Fillmore... SE 32
● Chester, Olmsted........ SE 75
● Childs, Wilkin.......... W ×
Chippewa Agency, Becker.. W 200
Chippewa Village, Belt'l. NW ×
● Chisago City, Chisago..... E 200
Chisago Lake, (see Centre City) ×
Choice, Fillmore...........SE 25
● Chokio, Stevens.......... W ×
Chowen, Hennepin...........C 32
Christiana, Dakota......... W 40
Chubb Lake, (see Christiana). ×
● Clara City, Chippewa.....SW 150
● Claremont Dodge....... SE 300
● Clarissa, Todd.............C 300
● Clarkfield, Yellow Med'e. SW 178
Clark's Grove, Freeborn.... S 12
Clarksville, Big Stone..... W ×
Clauson, Pipe Stone.......SW 10
● Claybank, Goodhue......SE ×
● *Claymont*, Ramsey........ E ×
Clayton, Faribault...........S 130
● Clear Lake, Sherburne.... C 200
● Clear Water, Wright....... C 248
● *Clearwater Junc.*, Wright. C 150
Cleveland, Le Sueur.........S 132
Clifford, Becker............ W ×
● *Clifton*, St. Louis......... NE ×
Climax, Polk............ NW ×
● Clinton, Big Stone....... W 30
Clinton Falls, Steele..........S 50

● Clitherall, Otter Tail...... W 200
● Clontarf, Swift............ W 25
● Cloquet, Carlton........... E 2,530
● *Cloquet River*, St. Louis. NE 25
Clotho, Todd................. C 3
Clyde, Winona............ SE ×
Cobb River, Waseca......... S ×
● Cobden, Brown............S 25
Coburg, (see Amiret)........ ×
Cochran's Mills, Wright.... C 32
● *Cogel*, Todd............... C ×
● Cokato, Wright............ C 363
● Cold Spring, Stearns...... C 700
Colenso, Norman......... NW 32
Colfax, Kandiyohi............C 26
● Collegeville, Stearns...... C 100
Collingwood Lake, Meeker.. C 20
Collins, McLeod............ C ×
Collis, Traverse............. S 10
Cologne, Carver............. C 193
Columbia, Polk........... NW ×
Columbus, Anoka.......... E ×
● Combs, Washington...... E 120
Comfrey, Brown............ S 196
Compton, Itasca............ N ×
● *Comstock*, Clay.......... W ×
Concord, Dodge...........SE 75
● *Coney Island*, Carver..... C ×
Converse, Pipe Stone......SW ×
Cook's Valley, Wabasha... SE 10
Cooleysville, Steele...........S ×
● Coon Creek, Anoka.........E 32
Corcoran, Hennepin........ C 75
Cordova, LeSueur........... S 200
Corinna, Wright............ C 12
● Cork, Grant.............. W 30
Cormorant, Becker........ W 50
Cornet, Faribault............S 75
● *Corona*, Carlton.......... E 97
Corra, Olmsted............ SE ×
● Correll, Big Stone....... W 65
Cosmos, Meeker........... C 12
Cottage Grove, Washington.. E 100
Cottage Park, (see White Bear Lake) ×
● *Cottagewood*, Hennepin.. C ×
Cottonwood, Brown .... S ×
● Cottonwood, Lyon...... SW 150
● Courtland, Nicollet.........S 250
Credit River, Scott.......... S 50
● Cromwell, Carlton........ E 150
● **Crookston**, Polk..... NW 3,457
Crown, Isanti................ E ×
Crow River, Meeker........ C 28
● Crow Wing, Crow Wing.. C 50
● Crystal, Hennepin..........C 1,074
● *Cummings*, Polk....... NW ×
Current Lake, Murray.... SW 65
Currie, Murray............SW 300
● *Curry*, Washington....... E ×
● *Curtis*, Morrison.......... C ×
● Cushing, Morrison......... C ×
Custer, Big Stone .... W 20
● Cyrus, Pope............... W 80
Daggett Brook, Crow Wing.. C ×
● *Dahlgren*, Carver......... C 360
● Dakota, Winona......... SE 150
Dalbo, Isanti................ E 16
Dale, Cottonwood.......... SW ×
Dalstrop, Chisago........... E 300
● Dalton, Otter Tail....... W 100
Dane Prairie, Otter Tail.... W ×
Danewood, Chisago...........E 25
Dania, Otter Tail.......... W ×
● *Danvers*, Swift.......... W ×
Danville, Blue Earth........ S 65
● *Darling*, Morrison........ C ×
Darmstadt, Isanti.......... E ×
● Darwin, Meeker.......... C 38
● Dassel, Meeker............C 552
Davidson Mill, Norman.. NW ×
Davies, Otter Tail......... W ×
● Dawson, Lac-qui-parle.. SW 418
Daylight, Todd.............. C ×
Dayton, Hennepin........... C 75
● *Dayton Bluff*, Ramsey.... E ×
Dead Lake, Otter Tail...... W ×
Dean, Rice.................. S ×
● Deer Creek, Otter Tail... W 100
Deerfield, Steele............S 32
● Deer Wood, Crow Wing...C 125
Deer Wood, Kittson...... NW ×
Deet, Polk................NW 10
De Forest, (see Kinbrae)..... ×
● De Graff, Swift.......... W 100
● Delano, Wright........... C 889
● Delavan, Fairbault........S 252

Minnesota

● Delhi, Redwood .... SW 25
Dell, Faribault.............. S 200
● *Dellwood*, Ramsey........ E ×
Delton, Cottonwood ...... SW ×
Denmark, Washington....... E 200
● Dennison, Goodhue ..... SE 50
Denver, Rock.............. SW 40
Derynane, (see Hubertus).... ×
● *Desnoyer Park*, Anoka... E ×
● **Detroit City**, Becker.. W 1,510
● Dexter, Mower.......... SE 150
Dibley, Wilkin............... W ×
Dickson, Meeker............. C ×
● *Dilworth*, Clay........... W ×
Ditter, Hennepin.............. C ×
● Dodge Centre, Dodge.... SE 633
Dodge Cit , Steele .... S 32
● Donaldson, Kittson .... NW 30
● *Donald Switch*, Fillmore.SE ×
● Donnely, Stevens......... W 80
Dora, Otter Tail............. W 50
● *Doran*, Wilkin............ W ×
● *Doty*, Olmsted .... SE ×
● Douglas, Olmsted........ SE 50
● Dover, Olmsted.......... SE 400
● *Dower Lake*, Todd....... C 100
● Downer, Clay............ W ×
● Doyle, Le Sueur........... S 15
● Dresbach, Winona....... SE 300
Dresselville, LeSueur........ S 32
Duelm, Benton................ C 15
● Dugdale, Polk.......... NW 26
● **Duluth**, St. Louis..... NE 33,115
● *Duluth Junction*, Wash'g'n E ×
● Dumont, Traverse......... W 10
● Dundas, Rice............... S 554
● Dundee, Nobles......... SW 35
Dunnell, Martin.............. S 12
Dupont, Hennepin.......... C 60
● Eagle Bend, Todd .... C 306
● Eagle Lake, Blue Earth... S 350
Eagle Mills, (see Eggleston).. ×
Eagle Valley, (see Concord).. ×
Earl, Martin .... S ×
East Castle Rock, Dakota... E ×
East Chain Lakes, Martin.... S 40
East Des Moines, Murray. SW ×
● East Grand Forks, Polk NW 795
East Granite Falls, Ch'p'a SW 200
● *East Hastings*, Dakota... E ×
East Havana, (see Havana).. ×
● *East Henderson*, LeSueur. S ×
East Meriden, (see Meriden). ×
● *East Minneapolis*, H'n'p n C ×
● Easton, Faribault......... S 180
● *Ea t St. Cloud*, Benton... C 600
● *East St. Paul*, Ramsey.... E ×
● *East Spring Lake*, L'Su'ur S ×
East Union, Carver.......... C 30
● *East Wabasha*, Wabash. SE 40
● Echo, Yellow Medicine. SW 40
Eddsville, Renville........ SW 15
● *Eddys*, Hennepin.......... C ×
● *Eden*, Dodge............. SE ×
● Eden Prairie, Hennepin.. C 100
● Eden Valley, Meeker..... C 327
Eder, Pipe Stone.......... SW ×
● Edgerton, Pipe Stone... SW 178
Edgewood, Blue Earth...... S 32
Edina Mills, Hennepin....... C 531
● Edna, Polk .... NW 531
Edward, Otter Tail... ..... W ×
Edwards, Kandiyohi......... C ×
Edwardsville, (see Ortonville) ×
Effington, Otter Tail .... W 15
● Eggleston, Goodhue..... SE 20
Eidsvold, Goodhue......... SE 22
Eitzen, Houston............ SE 100
Elba, Winona............... SE 100
● **Elbow Lake**, Grant... W 267
● *Elevator Bay*, Washington E ×
● Elgin, Wabasha.......... SE 400
● Elizabeth, Otter Tail..... W 135
Elk Creek, Nobles........ SW ×
Elk Lake, Grant.............. W 15
● **Elk River**, Sherburne.. C 679
● *Elk River Jc.*, Sherburne. C ×
Elkton, Carleton............. E ×
● Elkton, Mower.......... SE 15
Ellington, Dodge............ SE 32
● *Elliott*, Wilkin............. W ×
Ellis, Cass.................... N ×
Ellsville, (see Skyberg) ...... ×
Ellsworth, Meeker.......... C ×
● Ellsworth, Nobles....... SW 258
Elm Dale, Morrison........... C 20
● *Elmer*, Clay.............. W ×

Minnesota

Elmer, Pipe Stone........ SW ×
● Elmore, Faribault......... S 488
● Ely, St. Louis........... NE 901
● Elysian, LeSueur.......... S 348
Emard, Polk .... NW 32
● *Embarras River*, St. Louis NE ×
Emerald, Faribault........... S 25
Emmons, Freeborn........... S 35
● Empire City, Dakota..... E 20
Enderly, Redwood......... SW 10
● *Endion*, St. Louis....... NE ×
Englund, Marshall....... NW ×
Enterprise, Winona........ SE 40
● *Erdahl*, Grant........... W 30
● Erhard, Otter Tail....... W 20
Erickson, Pope............... W 15
Erie, Becker.................. W 16
● *Erin*, Rice................. S ×
● Erskine, Polk.......... NW 60
Essex, Otter Tail.......... SE ×
● Essig, Brown............... S 25
Estes Brook, Mille Lacs..... C 83
● Esteville, Benton.......... C ×
● Etna, Fillmore.......... SE 25
● Etter, Dakota.............. E 78
● Euclid, Polk........... NW 50
● Evan, Brown............... S 20
● *Evans*, Faribault......... S ×
● Evansville, Douglas...... W 452
● *Everdell*, Wilkin......... W ×
Excel, Marshall.......... NW ×
● Excelsior, Hennepin...... C 619
● Eyota, Olmsted.......... SE 377
● Fairfax, Renville....... SW 351
Fairfield, Swift.............. W 17
Fair Haven, Stearns......... C 400
● **Fairmont**, Martin...... S 437
Fair Point, Goodhue....... SE 30
● *Fairview*, Hennepin...... C ×
● Fairview, Kittson....... NW ×
***Fairview*, Murray**........ SW ×
Fairwater, Winona........ SE 25
Faith, Norman.......... NW 25
Faly, Todd.................. C ×
● **Faribault**, Rice......... C 6,520
Farm Hill, Olmsted........ SE 65
Farming, Stearns........... C 12
● Farmington, Dakota...... E 657
Farnham, Wadena.......... C ×
● Farwell, Pope........... W 100
Faxon, Sibley............... S 35
Fay, Todd.................... C ×
● Felton, Clay............. W 25
● **Fergus Falls**, Otter Tail W 3,772
● Fertile, Polk........... NW 273
Fillmore, Fillmore........ SE 300
● *Finkle*, Clay............ W ×
● Finlayson, Pine............ E 121
Fir, Marshall............. NW 14
● Fisher, Polk............ NW 481
Fish Lake, (see Stark) .... ×
Fish Trap Lake, Morrison.... C 10
Floodwood, St. Louis...... NE ×
● Florence, Lyon.... ..... SW 8
Florence, St. Louis........ NE ×
Florita, Renville........... SW ×
● *Flynn*, Morrison........... C ×
Fodyang, Marshall....... NW ×
Foldal, Marshall........... NW 14
● Foley, Benton............. C 30
Folkedahl, Norman....... NW ×
● Fond du Lac, St. Louis.. NE 525
Fordenskjold, (see St. Oloff). ×
Forest City, Meeker......... C 160
● Forest Lake, Washington. E 50
● Forest Mills, Goodhue... SE 40
Forest Mound, Wabasha.. SE ×
● Foreston, Mille Lacs..... C 287
Forestville, Fillmore...... SE 287
Fort Ridgely, Nicollet...... S 16
● Fort Ripley, Crow Wing.. C 100
● Fort Snelling, Hennepin.. C 550
● Fosston, Polk.......... NW 207
Fossum, Norman......... NW 35
Foster, Big Stone.......... W 20
● Fountain, Fillmore...... SE 248
● *Four Lakes*, Washington. E ×
Fowlds, Pope................ W ×
Fox, Kittson.............. NW ×
● *Foxboro*, Carlton......... E ×
● Franconia, Chisago....... E 252
Frankford, Mower......... SE 32
Frank Hill, Winona....... SE 97
● Franklin, Renville...... SW 284
● Frazee City, Becker...... W 100
Freeborn, Freeborn.......... S 89
● Freeburgh, Houston..... SE 50

Minnesota

Freedom, Waseca........... S 10
Freeland, Lac-qui-Parle... SW ×
● *Freeman*, Polk........ NW ×
● Freeport, Stearns......... C 40
Fremont, Winona......... SE 50
● French, Otter Tail........ W ×
French Lake, Wright........ C 40
French Rapids, Crow Wing C ×
Friberg, Otter Tail.......... W 10
● Fridley, Anoka............ E 250
Friedham, Grant............ W 45
Frog Point, Polk.......... NW ×
Fron, Pope.................. W 14
● Frontenac, Goodhue..... SE 300
● Fulda, Murray.......... SW 348
● *Funk*, Wabasha......... SE ×
Gakadina, Lake........... NE ×
● Garden City, Blue Earth.. S 300
● Garfield, Douglas......... W 125
Garrison, Crow Wing....... C ×
Garvin, Lyon............. SW ×
● Gary, Norman......... NW 50
Gates, Stearns............... C ×
● Gaylord, Sibley............ S 387
Geneva, Freeborn............ S 75
● *Geneva Beach*, Douglas.. W ×
Genoa, Olmsted............ SE 160
Gentilly, Polk............ NW 50
George Lake, Stearns........ C ×
Georgetown, Clay........... W 128
● Georgeville, Stearns....... C 15
Germania, Mower......... SE ×
Getty, Stearns............... C ×
● Ghent, Lyon............ SW 40
● Gibbon, Sibley............ S 282
Gilbert, Morrison............ C ×
Gilchrist, Pope............... W 20
Gilfillan, Redwood....... SW ×
● Gilman, Benton............ C 40
Gladstone, Cass............. N ×
● Gladstone, Ramsey....... E 300
● *Glasgow*, Wabasha....... SE 25
● **Glencoe**, McLeod....... C 1 649
● Glenville, Freeborn........ S 250
● **Glenwood**, Pope......... W 627
Glitner, Chippewa........ SW ×
● Glyndon, Clay............ W 275
Golden Gate, Brown.......... S 100
Golden Valley, Hennepin... C 509
Goldleaf, Jackson........ SW ×
Goldner, Norman........ NW ×
● Goodhue, Goodhue...... SE 25
● Good Thunder, Blue Earth S 300
Goodwin, Hennepin.......... C 50
Goodwin, Wright............ C 50
Goose Lake, Washington.... E ×
Goose Prairie, Clay......... W ×
● Gordonsville, Freeborn.... S 45
Gossen, Polk............ NW ×
Gotha, Carver................ C 15
● Graceville, Big Stone.... W 508
Grafton, Sibley.............. S ×
● *Grainwood*, Scott.......... S ×
● Granada, Martin........... S 50
Grand Marais, Cook... NE 250
● Grand Meadow, Mower. SE 373
Grand Portage, Cook....... NE 360
Grand Rapids, Itasca......... N 900
Grand View, (see Marshall).. ×
Granger, Fillmore......... SE 110
● **Granite Falls**, Yellow Medicine.............. SW 800
● *Granite Falls*, Chippewa SW ×
Granite Lake, Wright........ C ×
● Grant, Washington........ E ×
Granville, Polk.......... NW ×
Grapeland, Faribault......... S ×
Grass Lake, Kanabec........ E 100
Gratzek, Marshall....... NW ×
Gravelville, Morrison....... C 125
● *Greeley*, Carlton.......... E ×
Greeley, Pine................ E ×
● Green Isle, Sibley.......... S 219
● Green Lake, Kandiyohi... C 15
● Greenland, Le Sueur...... S 15
Greenleaf, Meeker........... C 125
Greenleafton, Fillmore.... SE 125
Green Prairie, Morrison.... C 15
● Green Valley, Lyon..... SW 30
● *Gregory*, Morrison......... C ×
Gresham, Otter Tail.......... W 32
● Grey Eagle, Todd.......... C 200
● Grogan, Watonwan......... S ×
Groesbeck, Olmstead...... SE 20
● Ground House, Kanabec.. E ×
● Grove City, Meeker........ C 349
Grove Lake, Pope.......... W 20

Groveland Park, Hennepin. C ×
Grover, Winona.......... SE 25
● Grue, Kandiyohi.......... C ×
Gull Lake, Cass.......... N ×
● Gull River, Cass.......... N 439
Hackensack, Cass.......... N ×
Hader, Goodhue.......... SE 75
● Hadley, Murray.......... SW 50
Hagan, Chippewa.......... SW 50
Hale, McLeod.......... C ×
● **Hallock**, Kittson.......... NW 302
● Halstad, Norman.......... NW 50
● Hamburgh, Carver.......... C 50
● Hamel, Hennepin.......... C ×
Hamilton, Fillmore.......... SE 250
● Hamilton Station, Scott.......... S 200
● *Hamline*, Ramsey.......... E 2,000
● Hammond, Wabasha.......... SE 200
● Hampton, Dakota.......... E 15
● Hancock, Stevens.......... W 218
● *Handy*, Martin.......... S ×
Hanley, Yellow Medicine. SW ×
● Hanley Falls, Yel'w Med'e SW 150
Hanover, Wright.......... C 100
● *Hansen*, Todd.......... C ×
Hanska, Brown.......... S ×
Hanson, Olmsted.......... SE 15
Hansville, Polk.......... NW ×
● Hardwick, Rock.......... SW ×
● Harmony, Fillmore.......... SE 100
● Harris, Chisago.......... E 504
Harrison, Kandiyohi.......... C 15
Hart, Winona.......... SE 32
Hartford, Todd.......... C 500
● Hartland, Freeborn.......... S 60
Hartshorn, Wadena.......... C 20
Hassan, Hennepin.......... C 18
● **Hastings**, Dakota.......... E 3,705
● Hasty, Wright.......... C 50
● Hatfield, Pipe Stone.......... SW 25
Hauson, (see Burtrum) .... ×
● Havana, Steele.......... S 15
Havelock, Chippewa.......... SW ×
● *Haven*, Sherburne.......... C ×
Haverhill, Olmsted.......... SE ×
● Hawick, Kandiyohi.......... C 50
Hawkins, Blue Earth.......... S ×
● Hawley, Clay.......... W 270
● Hay Creek, Goodhue.......... SE 40
● *Hayden*, Todd.......... C ×
Hayes, Martin.......... S ×
● Hayfield, Dodge.......... SE 82
● Hayward, Freeborn.......... S 25
● *Hazel Park*, Ramsey.......... E ×
● Hazel Run, Yel'w Medi'e SW 25
● *Hazeltine*, Carver.......... C ×
Hazelwood, Rice.......... S 25
Heath, Pipe Stone.......... SW 32
● *Heckman*, Lyon.......... SW ×
● Hector, Renville.......... SW 354
Hegbert, Swift.......... W 10
● Heiberg, Norman.......... NW 50
Heidelberg, LeSueur.......... S 160
Helen, McLeod.......... C ×
● Helena, Scott.......... S 15
Hellem, Marshall.......... NW ×
● **Henderson**, Sibley.......... S 909
Hendricks, Lincoln.......... SW ×
Hendrum, Norman.......... NW 200
● Henning, Otter Tail.......... W 254
Henryville, Renville.......... SW 65
Henrytown, Fillmore.......... SE ×
● Hereford, Grant.......... W 16
● Herman, Grant.......... W 322
Hermantown, St. Louis.......... NE ×
● Heron Lake, Jackson.......... SW 496
Hersey, (see Brewster).......... ×
Herzhorn, Renville.......... SW ×
● *Hewitt*, Todd.......... C 20
Hickory, Aitkin.......... E ×
High Forest, Olmsted.......... SE 163
Highland, Fillmore.......... SE 20
● *Highland*, St. Louis.......... NE ×
Highland Grove, Clay.......... W ×
Highwater, Cottonwood.......... SW ×
● *Highwood*, Washington.......... E ×
Hildrethsburg, (see Marshall) ×
Hill, Chippewa.......... SW 32
● Hills, Rock.......... SW 46
● *Hillsdale*, Clay.......... W ×
● *Hilltop*, Polk.......... NW ×
● *Hill Track*, Blue Earth.......... S ×
● Hinckley, Pine.......... E 173
● *Hinsdale*, St. Louis.......... NE ×
● Hitterdal, Clay.......... W 25
● *Hixon*, Polk.......... NW ×
Hoff, Otter Tail.......... W 12

● Hoffman, Grant.......... W 75
● Hokah, Houston.......... SE 582
Holden, Goodhue.......... SE 57
Holding's Ford, Stearns.......... C 75
● Holland, Pipe Stone.......... SW ×
● Holloway, Swift.......... W 27
Hollywood, Carver.......... C 50
● *Holmes*, Polk.......... NW ×
Holmes City, Douglas.......... W 700
Holt, Marshall.......... NW ×
Holum, Kandiyohi.......... C ×
● *Holyoke*, Carlton.......... E 50
Home, Brown.......... S 32
Homedahl, Faribault.......... S ×
● Homer, Winona.......... SE 100
Hopatcong, Wadena.......... C ×
Hope, Blue Earth.......... S ×
● Hopkins, Hennepin.......... C 300
Horicon, Martin.......... S ×
Horton, Olmsted.......... SE ×
● Houston, Houston.......... SE 536
Hoverud, Pope.......... W ×
Hovland, Cook.......... NE ×
● Howard, Wright.......... C 610
● *Howell*, Carlton.......... E ×
Hubbard, Hubbard.......... N 300
Hudson, Douglas.......... W ×
Huff, Morrison.......... C 15
● Hugo, Washington.......... E 32
● *Hull's Corners*, Kandiyohi C ×
Humboldt, Marshall.......... NW 10
● *Humboldt*, Kittson.......... NW ×
Huntington, Cottonwood. SW 15
● Huntley, Faribault.......... S 40
Huntsville, (see Crookston).......... ×
Huot, Polk.......... NW 38
Hurdal, (see Ostrander).......... ×
● Hutchinson, McLeod.......... C 1,414
● *Hutchinson Junc.*, Hen'pin C ×
Iberia, Brown.......... S 25
Ibsen, Murray.......... SW ×
● *Iceland*, Blue Earth.......... S ×
Ida Mills, Douglas.......... W ×
Idlewild, Lincoln.......... SW 25
● Ihlen, Pipe Stone.......... SW ×
Independence, St. Louis.. NE ×
Indian Village, St. Louis. NE ×
Ingalls, Marshall.......... NW ×
Inman, Otter Tail.......... W ×
Inver, Traverse.......... W ×
● Invergrove, Dakota.......... E 200
● Iona, Murray.......... SW 100
Iron Lake, Murray.......... SW ×
Irving, Kandiyohi.......... C 32
Isanti, Isanti.......... E 100
● Isinour's, Fillmore.......... SE 13
Island, St. Louis.......... NE ×
Island Lake, Lyon.......... SW ×
● *Itasca*, Anoka.......... E ×
● *Ives*, Polk.......... NW ×
Jack Creek, Nobles.......... SW ×
● **Jackson**, Jackson.......... SW 720
Jadis, Kittson.......... NW 25
● Janesville, Waseca.......... E 921
● Jarrett's, Wabasha.......... SE 25
Jarvis, Becker.......... W ×
● Jasper, Big Stone.......... W 372
Jefferson, Le Sueur.......... S ×
Jeannettville, Renville.......... SW ×
Jesseland, Sibley.......... S ×
Johnsburg, Mower.......... SE ×
● Johnson, Big Stone.......... W 200
Johnson Siding, (see Detroit City).......... ×
● *Jonesville*, Crow Wing.......... C ×
● Jordan, Scott.......... S 1,233
Joy, Douglas.......... W 32
Judd, Dakota.......... E 32
Judson, Blue Earth.......... S 32
● *Junction*, Clay.......... W ×
● *Junction*, Dodge.......... SE ×
● *Junction*, Polk.......... NW ×
● *Junction*, Stevens.......... W ×
Junction Switch, Big Stone W ×
Kalmer, Norman.......... NW ×
● Kanarawzi, Rock.......... SW 25
● Kandiyohi Station, Kandiyohi C 100
● Kasota, Le Sueur.......... S 655
● Kasson, Dodge.......... SE 992
Kedron, Fillmore.......... SE 30
Keegan, Wabasha.......... SE 25
Keeville, Stevens.......... W ×
● Kellogg, Wabasha.......... SE 200
Kelso, Sibley.......... S 32
Keml, Cottonwood.......... SW ×
Kennebec, Stearns.......... C ×
● Kennedy, Kittson.......... NW 100

● Kensington, Douglas.......... W 200
● *Kent*, Lyon.......... SW ×
● Kent, Wilkin.......... W 25
● *Kenwood*, Hennepin.......... C ×
● Kenyon, Goodhue.......... SE 666
● Kerkhoven, Swift.......... W 250
● Kerrick, Pine.......... E ×
● Kettle River, Pine.......... E 40
● *Keyes*, Winona.......... SE ×
● *Keystone*, Polk.......... NW ×
Keystone, Wright.......... C 40
Kiester, Faribault.......... S ×
● Kilkenny, Le Sueur.......... S 200
● Kimball, Stearns.......... C 100
● Kimberly, Aitkin.......... E 15
● Kinbrae, Nobles.......... SW 50
King, (see McIntosh).......... ×
● *King's Cooley*, Wabasha SE ×
Kingston, Meeker.......... C 50
● *Kittson*, Polk.......... NW ×
Knife Falls, (see Cloquet).......... ×
● *Knife River*, St. Louis.. NE ×
Kost, Chisago.......... E 50
Kragero, (see Milan).......... ×
● Kragnes, Clay.......... W 15
Kron, Douglas.......... W 10
Kurtz, Clay.......... W ×
Lac-qui-parle, Lac-qui-p'r SW 150
● La Crescent, Houston.......... SE 200
● *Lafond*, Morrison.......... C 30
● Laird, Olmsted.......... SE 25
Lake, St. Louis.......... NE ×
Lake Addie, McLeod.......... C ×
Lake Amelia, Pope.......... W ×
Lake Andrew, Kandiyohi... C 26
Lake Belt, Martin.......... S 30
● **Lake Benton**, Lincoln SW 513
● Lake City, Wabasha.......... SE 2,128
● Lake Crystal, Blue Earth.. S 824
Lake Elizabeth, Kandiyohi.. C 12
● Lake Elmo, Washington.. E 75
Lake Eunice, Becker.......... W 25
● Lakefield, Jackson.......... SW 275
Lake Fremont, Sherburne.. C 32
Lake Henry, Stearns.......... C 40
Lake Jefferson, Le Sueur.......... S ×
Lake Johanna, Pope.......... W 36
● Lakeland, Washington.......... E 523
● *Lakeland Junction*, Washn E ×
Lake Lillian, Kandiyohi.......... C 100
● Lake Park, Becker.......... W 349
● *Lake Park Hotel*, Hennepin C ×
● *Lakeshore*, Ramsey.......... E ×
Lakeside, Renville.......... SW 300
Lakeside, St. Louis.......... NE 897
Lake Stay, Lincoln.......... SW 32
Lake Sybil, Otter Tail.......... W 65
Laketown, (see Augusta).......... ×
Lake Todd, McLeod.......... C ×
Lake Traverse, Traverse... W ×
● Lakeview, St. Louis.......... NE ×
Lake View, Traverse.......... W ×
● Lakeville, Dakota.......... E 258
Lake Washington, Le Sueur. S 35
● Lake Wilson, Murray... SW 100
● Lakey, Wabasha.......... SE ×
Lalone, Carlton.......... E ×
Lambert, Polk.......... NW 25
● Lamberton, Redwood... SW 202
● Lamoille, Winona.......... SE 65
● Lanesboro, Fillmore.......... SE 898
● Langdon, Washington.......... E 100
Langhei, Pope.......... W 20
● Lansing, Mower.......... SE 100
La Prairie, Itasca.......... N 225
Larson, Stevens.......... W ×
● *Lawndale*, Wilkin.......... W ×
Lawndale, Wilkin.......... W ×
Lawrence, Mille Lacs.......... C ×
Leaf Mountain, Otter Tail.. W 36
● *Leaf River*, Wadena.......... C ×
Leaf Valley, Douglas.......... W 78
Leavenworth, Brown.......... S 90
Ledoux, Morrison.......... C 25
Leech Lake, Cass.......... N 1,600
Leedston, Stearns.......... C 100
Leedston, (see St. Martin).......... ×
Lemond, Steele.......... S 10
● *Lena*, Goodhue.......... SE 10
Lenora, Fillmore.......... SE 76
● *Lenox*, Crow Wing.......... C ×
Leo, Lyon.......... SW 45
Lerdal, Freeborn.......... S ×
● Le Roy, Mower.......... SE 523
Lester, Rice.......... S 26
● *Lester Park*, St. Louis.. NE 100
● Lester Prairie, McLeod.... C 189

● Le Sueur, Le Sueur........S 1,763
Le Sueur Centre, LeSueurS 169
● Lewiston, Winona....... SE 324
Lexington, Le Sueur........ S 60
Libby, Aitkin.............. E ×
Lida, Otter Tail............W ×
Lillemon, Grant........... W 32
Lillian, (see Stanton)........ ×
Lilly Pond, Wright......... C ×
● *Lime*, Blue Earth.......... S ×
● Lime Creek, Murray....SW ×
● Lincoln, Morrison.........C ×
Lincoln, Kittson..........NW 32
Lincoln Station, Watonwan. S ×
● *Lincoln Park*, Hennepin. .C ×
Linden, Brown............. S 65
Lindsay, Polk.............. NW 25
● Lindstrom, Chisago....... E 125
Linnell, Becker............ W ×
● Lintonville, Kandiyohi....C 15
Linwood, Anoka............ E 65
Lisbon, (see Granite Falls) ... ×
● **Litchfield**, Meeker.....C 1,899
● *Little Canada*, Ramsey.... E ×
Little Cobb, Blue Earth.... S ×
● **Little Falls**, Morrison..C 2,354
● Little Rock, Nobles.....SW 32
● Little Sauk, Todd......... C 30
Little Valley, Olmsted..... SE 12
Livonia, Sherburne..........C 32
● Lockhart, Norman..... NW 8
Logan, Redwood.......... SW ×
Logering, Meeker..........C 10
Lohmansville, (see Lake Elmo) ×
Loken, Lac-qui-parle...... SW ×
London, Freeborn.............S 32
● *London*, St. Louis....... NE ×
Lone Cedar, (see Fairmont).. ×
Lonesome, Lyon............SW 25
Lone Tree, Chippewa...... SW ×
Lonetree Lake, Brown....... S 32
Long Hill, Stearns......... C ×
● Long Lake, Hennepin...... C 300
● **Long Prairie**, Todd....C 700
● *Long's Siding*, Mille Lacs.C ×
Loon Lake, Jackson....... SW ×
● Loretto, Hennepin......... C ×
Lortz, Blue Earth........... S ×
Louisa, (see Little River) .... ×
● Louisburg, Lac-qui-p'le..SW 50
Louriston, Chippewa....... SW 30
LowerSiouxAgency, Re'wd SW ×
● Lowry, Pope............. W 115
Lowville, Murray........... SW 25
● Luce, Otter Tail.......... W 50
Ludemann, Wright...........C ×
Lukens, Wadena............ C ×
Lutsen, Cook............... NE ×
● **Luverne**, Rock....... SW 1,466
Luxemburgh, Stearns....... C 35
Lydia, Scott................ S 100
● Lyle, Mower............ SE 306
● *Lyman*, Stearns......... C ×
● Lynd, Lyon.............. SW 25
Lyons, (see Thielmanton) .... ×
McCauleyville, Wilkin....... W 30
● *McCracken*, Wabasha... SE ×
McDonaldsville, (see Crook'tn) ×
● McGregor, Aitkin.......... E 15
● McHugh, Becker......... W ×
● McIntosh, Polk.......... NW 300
McVey, Pipe Stone.........SW 38
● *Maases*, Hennepin........C ×
● Mabel, Fillmore.......... SE 273
● *Macalester*, Ramsey...... E ×
● Madelia, Watonwan ...... S 852
● Madison, Lac-qui-parle..SW 625
Madison, Mower........... SE ×
● Madison Lake, Blue Earth.S 300
● Magnolia, Rock.......... SW 23
● *Mahtomedi*, Washington.. E ×
● Mah-to-wa, Carlton....... E 40
Maine, Otter Tail.......... W 10
Maine Prairie, Stearns...... C 500
● Mallory, Polk............ NW 50
Malmo, Aitkin.............. E ×
Manannah, Meeker......... C 120
● Manchester, Freeborn.... S 25
Manderson, Morrison........C ×
● **Mankato**, Blue Earth... S 8,838
● *Mankato Junction*, B'e E'hS ×
● Manley, Rock.......... SW 60
Manomin, Anoka.......... E ×
Mansfield, Freeborn........ S ×
● *Mansfield*, Pine......... E ×
Manston, Wilkin........... W ×
Manter, (see Hubbard) ...... ×

● *Mantor Junction*, Dodge SE ×
Mantorville, Dodge.... SE 460
Maple Bay, Polk..........NW 20
● Maple Glen, Scott......... S 65
Maple Grove, Hennepin.....C ×
● Maple Island, Washington E ×
● *Maple Lake*, Wright...... C 65
Maple Lake, Wright..........C 258
● Maple Plain, Hennepin....C 200
Maple Ridge, Isanti......... E 32
● Mapleton, Blue Earth..... S 607
● Marietta, Lac-qui-parle..SW 150
● *Marin*, Polk............NW ×
● Marine Mills, Washington. E 679
● Marion, Olmstead........ SE 25
Marion Lake, Otter Tail.... W ×
Markville, Hennepin........ C ×
Marmion, Hennepin........ C ×
Marshall, Lyon .... SW 1,203
Marsh River, Norman.... NW ×
Martin, Stearns............ C ×
● *Martin's Spur*, Chisago.. E ×
Maryland, Swift........... W ×
Marysburgh, Le Sueur...... S 15
Marystown, Scott........... S 50
● Masaba, St. Louis....... NE ×
Mason, Murray............SW ×
Matson, Kittson............NW ×
Maud, Big Stone............W 20
Maudada, Traverse........ W ×
May, Martin .... S 57
● Mayer, Carver .... C 150
● Maynard, Chippewa.... SW 45
Maywood, Benton .... C 200
● Mazeppa, Wabasha..... SE 1,000
Meadow, Rock............ SW 32
● Medford, Steele.......... S 350
Medina, Stevens............W ×
Medo, Blue Earth........... S 10
Meire's Grove, Stearns...... C 55
● Melby, Douglas........... W 19
● Melrose, Stearns.......... C 780
Melvin, Polk.............. NW ×
● Menahga, Wadena........ C ×
● Mendota, Dakota..........E 248
● Mentor, Polk .... NW 350
● Meriden, Steele........... S 50
● Merriam, Scott........... S 60
● Merriam Park, Ramsey .. E 2,500
● *Merrill*, Polk.......... NW ×
Merton, Steele............. S 45
● *Mesaba*, St. Louis ...... NE ×
Metz, Yellow Medicine....SW ×
Middleville, Wright......... C 25
● *Midland Junc.*, Wabasha SE ×
● *Midvale*, Washington.... E ×
Midway, St. Louis .... NE ×
Miesville, Dakota ....E 25
Milaca, Mille Lacs .... C 404
● *Milaca Junction*, MilleL'csC ×
● Milan, Chippewa........ SW 150
● Milford, Brown.......... S 40
Milford Station, (see Doyle). ×
Mille Lacs Lake, (see Mora). ×
● *Miller*, Pine............. E ×
Millersburgh, Rice.......... S 50
Millerville, Douglas........ W 65
● Mill Park, Otter Tail..... W 16
● Millville, Wabasha ...... SE 200
Miltona, Douglas .... W ×
● **Minneapolis**, Hene'pin.C 164,738
● *Minneapolis Junc.*, Hen'In C ×
Minneapolis Park, Hennepin C ×
● *Minnehaha*, Hennepin... C ×
● Minneiska, Wabasha .... SE 325
● *Minneopa*, Blue Earth.... S ×
● Minneota, Lyon......... SW 325
● Minnesota City, Winona. SE 400
● *Minnesota Falls*, Chi'e'aSW 125
● Minnesota Lake, Farib'ult.S 340
● *Minnesota Park*, Anoka.. E ×
Minnesota Point, (see Duluth) ×
Minnesota Transfer, (see St. Paul) .... ×
● Minnetonka, Hennepin....C 200
● Minnetonka Beach, H'pin.C 26
● *Minnetonka Mills*, H'pin.C ×
Minnetrista, Hennepin..... C ×
● Mission Creek, Pine...... E 107
Moe, (see Alexandria)........ ×
Moland, Rice............... S 10
Moltke, Sibley............. S 46
Money Creek, Houston.... SE 100
● *Money Creek*, Houston.. SE 130
Monitor, Otter Tail .... W 10
Monroe, (see Mabel) .... ×
Monroe, Martin............ S ×

● **Montivideo**, ChippewaSW 1,437
● Montgomery, Le Sueur.... S 1,086
● Monticello, Wright........C 503
● Montrose, Wright.........C 214
● **Moorhead**, Clay....... W 2,088
● Moose Island, Stevens..... W ×
● Moose Lake, Carlton...... E 169
● **Mora**, Kanabec.......... E 400
Moran, Todd............... C 32
Moran Brook, Todd........ C ×
● Morgan, Redwood...... SW 301
Morrill, Morrison.......... C ×
Mortizius, Wright .... C 161
● **Morris**, Stevens........ W 1,266
● Morristown, Rice.......... S 517
● *Morton*, Renville.........SW 453
Moscow, Freeborn.......... S 47
● Motley, Morrison .... C 525
Mound City, Hennepin...... C 130
● Mound Prairie, Houston.SE 20
● Mountain Lake, C'nw'd. SW 323
Mount Vernon, Winona... SE ×
Mountville, Sibley .... S 57
Mower City, (see Brownsdale)
● *Mulford's*, LeSueur ...... S
Mulligan, Brown........... S 32
Munich, (see New Munich) .. ×
● Murdock, Swift.......... W 130
● *Murray Hill*, Ramsey.... E ×
● Muskoda, Clay........... W 50
● *Myers*, Chippewa........SW 15
Myrna, Blue Earth.......... S 19
Myrtle, Freeborn............S ×
Nagonab, St. Louis....... NE ×
Namsos, Jackson........ SW 12
Nash, Stevens..............W 25
● *Nashua*, Wilkin............W ×
Nashville, (see E. G'd Forks) ×
Nashville Center, Martin.... S 50
● Nassau, Lac-qui-parle...SW 30
Naustdal, Stearns............C 10
Nealville, Itasca............N ×
Nebo, Todd................. C 32
Neby, Polk................NW 15
Neilsville, Polk............NW 10
● Nelson, Douglas .... W 40
● Nerstrand, Rice.............S 100
● *Nesbit*, Polk............ NW ×
Nerado, Mower.............SE ×
New Auburn, Sibley..........S 300
New Avon, Redwood. ....SW ×
● New Brighton, Ramsey...E 355
Newburgh, Fillmore.......SE 40
New Canada, Ramsey........E ×
● New Duluth, St. Louis..NE 600
● *New Germany*, Carver....C ×
New Grove, Lincoln......SW ×
New Hartford, Winona....SE 50
New Haven, Olmsted......SE ×
● Newhouse, Houston..... SE 10
New Hope, Meeker........ C ×
New Lisbon, Renville..... SW 10
● New London, Kandiyohi..C 211
New London, (see Lakeside). ×
New Market, Scott..........S 125
New Munich, Stearns........C 50
New Paynesville, Stearns...C ×
● Newport Washington.....E 300
● New Prague, Scott.........S 955
New Prairie, Pope...........W ×
● New Richland, Waseca....S 423
New Rome, Sibley.......... S 50
Newry, Freeborn........... S 5
New Sweden, Nicollet.......S 10
New Trier, Dakota...........E 129
● **New Ulm**, Brown.......S 3,741
● New York Mills, Otter Tail W 260
Nichols, Aitkin.............E 300
Nicholson, Crow Wing.......C 15
● Nicollet, Nicollet......... E 263
● *Nichols*, Dakota ....E ×
Nile, Brown................S ×
Nielsville, Polk............NW 10
Nimrod, Wadena............C ×
Nittedal, Houston...........SE 15
Nora, Pope..................W 65
● Norcross, Grant...........W 60
Norfolk, Renville...........SW ×
Norland, (see Minnesota).... ×
Norman, Lac-qui-parle...SW ×
Normand, (see French Lake) ×
Norman Sta., Norman...NW ×
Norseland, Nicollet..........S 30
● North Branch, Chisago ...E 685
● Northcote, Kittson..... NW 30
● Northfield, Rice.............S 2,659
North Fork, Stearns........C 200

Place	
● *N. Minneapolis*, Hennepin C	×
● Northome, Hennepin C	57
North Prairie, Morrison....C	75
North Renwood, RenwoodSW	25
● North Saint Paul, Ramsey, E	1,099
N. Sioux Falls, Pipe Stone SW	×
North Star, Martin.........S	130
Northtown, Hennepin C	×
● *Northtown Jc.*, Anoka... E	×
Norway, Goodhue......... SE	30
● *Norway*, St. Louis......NE	×
Norway Lake, Kandiyohi ...C	38
Norwegian Grove, Otter Tail W	20
● Norwood, Carver..........C	385
N. P. Junction, Carlton......E	612
Nunda, (see Twin Lakes)...	×
Oak Centre, Wabasha......SE	20
Oakdale, Washington........E	120
● *Oakdale Sta.*, Washington. E	120
Oaks, Stearns.............C	×
Oak Grove, Anoka..........E	32
Oak Hill, Todd..............C	45
● Oakland, Freeborn.........S	40
Oakland, Washington.......E	×
● Oak Park, Benton C	10
Oak Park, Washington......E	390
Oak Ridge, Winona........SE	25
Oak Springs, Anoka........ E	×
Oakwood, Washington......E	×
Oberle's Corners, Carver C	×
● *O'Brien*, Stearns..........C	×
O'Briens, Hennepin C	×
Odell, Cottonwood........SW	×
● Odessa, Big Stone........ W	100
Odin, Watonwan.............S	400
● *Okabena*, Jackson........SW	32
Okanan, Waseca............S	×
Oke's Station, (see Freeport).	×
Olga, Polk...............NW	×
● Olivia, Renville.......... SW	263
● *Olmsted*, Olmsted........SE	57
● Oneota, St Louis........NE	200
Opole, Stearns............ C	×
Opstead, Mille Lacs.......... C	×
● *Org*, Nobles..............SW	×
Oriole, Redwood...........SW	×
Orono, (see Elk River).......	×
● Oronoco, Olmsted....... SE	250
Orr, Jackson..............SW	32
Orrock, Sherburne...........C	100
● **Ortonville**, Big Stone. W	768
Osage, Becker...............W	150
● Osakis, Douglas...........W	472
Oscar, Otter Tail............W	×
Oscar Lake, Douglas ....W	12
● Oshawa, Nicollet.......... S	10
Oslo, Dodge................SE	25
● Osseo, Hennepin..........C	353
Ostrander, Fillmore ....SE	50
● *Ostrander*, Fillmore......SE	×
Othello, Olmsted.......... SE	×
● Otisco, Waseca............S	×
● Otisville, Washington.....E	20
Otsego, Wright..............C	18
● Ottawa, LeSueur..........S	200
● *Otter Creek*, Carlton...... E	×
Otter Tail City, Otter Tail.. W	15
Otto, (see St. Lawrence)......	×
Otto, Pope..................W	25
Ouisburgh, Lac-qui-parles.. W	×
Ovetia, Polk...............NW	×
● *Owasso*, Ramsey...........E	×
● **Owatonna**, Steele...... S	3,849
Owen, Houston...........SE	×
Oxford, Isanti..............E	130
Paddock, Otter Tail.........W	10
● *Palmer*, Waseca.......... S	8
Panola, Chisago............E	×
● Parent, Benton........... C	10
Park, (see Madison Lake)....	×
● *Parkdale*, Otter Tail.......W	57
Parker, (see Robbinsdale)...	×
Parker's Lake, Hennepin....C	×
Parker's Prairie, Otter Tail. W	150
● *Park Junc.*, Hennepin....C	×
● **Park Rapids**, Hubbard N	250
● *Parkton*, Otter Tail.......E	×
● Partridge, Pine.............E	
Passaic, Wadena..........C	
● Paynesville, Stearns...... C	352
Pelan, Kittson.............NW	×
Pelican Lake, Crow Wing.. C	×
Pelican Lake, Otter Tail....W	15
● Pelican Rapids, Otter Tail W	624
Pennock, Kandiyohi........ C	40
Peoria, Todd...............C	×
Perch, Watonwan...........S	×

Place	
Percy, Kittson............NW	×
● Perham, Otter Tail.......W	761
● Perley, Norman........ NW	100
Petersburgh, Jackson.....SW	32
● Peterson, Fillmore...... SE	150
Phelps, Otter Tail.......... W	×
● Philbrook, Todd..........C	30
Phillips, Big Stone.........W	14
Pickwick, Winona.........SE	100
● *Piedmont*, Winona......SE	×
Pikop, Grant...............W	×
● Pillager, Cass.............N	20
Pillsbury, Todd............ C	800
Pilot Grove, Faribault......S	×
Pilot Mound, Fillmore.....SE	75
Pine Bend, Dakota..........E	26
● **Pine City**, Pine..........E	535
● *Pine Grove*, Carlton...... E	547
● Pine Island, Goodhue....SE	548
Pine River, Cass............N	32
● **Pipe Stone**, Pipe Stone SW	1,232
Pixley, Martin...............S	30
● Plainview, Wabasha..... SE	1,000
● *Plainville Jc.*, Olmsted.. SE	×
● *Planks Crossing*, Olmsted SE	×
Plano, Nicollet............ S	×
● Plato, McLeod............ C	130
Pleasant Grove, Olmsted...SE	150
Pleasant Hill, Traverse....W	×
Pleasant Lake, (see Fairmont)	×
Pleasant Mounds, Blue Earth S	30
Pleasant Prairie, Martin.... S	×
Plum Creek, Scott..........S	18
Plymouth, Hennepin.........C	×
● Point Douglas, Washingt'n E	100
● *Pokegama*, Pine..........E	×
Pomme de Terre, Grant.... W	45
Popple, Beltrami.............NW	×
Portage, Aitkin.............E	×
● Porter, Yellow Medicine SW	30
Potsdam, Olmsted......... SE	100
Powell, Todd................C	×
Prague, (see New Prague)...	×
● Prairie Junc., Jackson..SW	50
Prairie Lake, Otter Tail....W	×
Prairie Mound, (see Kelso)..	×
Prairie Queen, Fillmore...SE	×
Prairieville, Rice............S	×
● Pratt, Steele...............S	25
Preble, Fillmore...........SE	32
Predmore, Olmsted........SE	×
Presto, Todd.............. C	585
● **Preston**, Fillmore..... SE	1,200
● **Princeton**, Mille Lacs.. C	816
Prinsburgh, Kandiyohi C	×
● Prior's Lake, Scott.........S	150
● *Prospect Park*, Ramsey.. E	×
● Prosper, Fillmore ....SE	50
Providence, Lac-qui-parle. SW	40
● *Pullman Ave.*, Washingt'n E	×
Purity, Carver..............C	45
● *Quamba*, Kanabec........E	×
Quincy, Olmsted...........SE	25
Racine, Mower.............SE	32
Rail Prairie, Morrison......C	×
Ramsdell, Otter Tail ....W	×
● *Ramsey*, Mower.........SE	×
Ramstad, Grant............W	16
● Randall, Morrison.........C	150
● Randolph, Dakota......... E	50
● Rapidan, Blue Earth......S	40
Rapidan Mills, Blue Earth.. S	×
Rapids, Blue Earth ....S	×
Raven Stream, Scott.........S	20
● Raymond, Kandiyohi..... C	10
Raymond, Stearns..........C	×
● *Reads Junc.*, Wabasha...SE	446
Red Lake, Beltrami...... NW	65
● Red Lake Falls, Polk... NW	774
Redinger, Cook.......... NE	×
Red Rock, Cottonwood......S	38
● *Red Rock*, Washington... E	×
Red Rock Lake, Douglas...W	50
Red Side, Redwood....... SW	×
● **Red Wing**, Goodhue..SE	6,294
● *Redwood*, Redwood.....SW	×
● **Redwood Falls**, R'w'd SW	1,238
● *Redwood Junction*, Brown S	×
● Reed's Landing, Wabasha SE	500
● *Regan*, Dakota.......... E	×
Reholt, Polk.............NW	×
● Reno, Houston.......... SE	100
Reno, Pope.................W	×
● *Reno*, St. Louis......... NE	×
● Renova, Mower..........SE	×
● Renville, Renville.......SW	413
Republic, Anoka............E	×

Place	
● *Revere*, Redwood....... SW	×
● Rice, Benton..............C	225
● *Rice*, Goodhue.......... SE	×
Rice City, Norman....... NW	20
Rice Creek, Anoka......... E	15
Riceford, Houston.........SE	85
Rice Lake, Dodge..........SE	26
● *Rice's Point*, St. Louis..NE	×
Richfield, Hennepin.........C	130
● *Richland*, Otter Tail..... W	×
Richland, Rice..............S	130
● *Richmond*, Stearns....... C	500
● Richmond, Winona......SE	25
Rich Prairie, Morrison......C	200
● Rich Valley, Dakota......W	25
Richwood, Becker..........W	50
Ridge, Pipe Stone.........SW	×
● Ridge, Polk............ NW	×
Ridgeville, Swift...........W	×
Ridgeway, Winona.........SE	10
● *Ridgewood Park*, Ramsey E	×
Rindal, Norman...........NW	35
Ringbo, Marshall.........NW	×
Ringvile, Kandiyohi........C	×
Rip, Dodge............... SE	×
Ripon, Lyon............. SW	10
Riverdale, Watonwan....... S	×
● *River Falls Junction*, Washington..............E	×
● *River Junction*, Houston SE	×
River Point, Steele.......... S	32
Riverside, (see Philbrook)....	×
● Robbinsdale, Hennepin... C	400
● *Robinson's Lake*, St. Lo'is NE	×
● **Rochester**, Olmsted...SE	5,321
Rock, Redwood...........SW	×
Rock, Pipe Stone.........SW	×
● Rock Creek, Pine..........E	200
Rock Dell, Olmsted........SE	50
Rockey, Norman.........NW	×
● Rockford, Wright.........C	340
Rock Lake, (see Marshall)....	×
● Rockville, Stearns....... C	70
● *Rock Wood*, Polk.......NW	×
Rocky Run, McLeod........C	×
● Rogers, Hennepin.........C	×
● *Rolette*, Norman....... NW	×
Rollag, Clay............... W	150
Rolling Fork, Pope........ W	×
Rolling Prairie, (see Belview)	×
● Rolling Stone, Winona.. SE	200
Roscoe, Goodhue...........SE	25
● *Roscoe*, Stearns.......... C	×
● *Rose*, Ramsey............E	×
● Rose Creek, Mower......SE	400
Rose Hill, Cottonwood....SW	×
Rose Lake, (see Fairmont)..	×
Roseland, Kandiyohi........ C	×
● Rosemount, Dakota.......E	198
Rosendale, Meeker..........C	×
Roseville, Kandiyohi........ C	8
Ross, Kittson.............NW	×
● *Ross*, Waseca.............S	×
● *Rossburg*, Aitkin..........E	×
Rosslyn, Chippewa........SW	20
● Rothsay, Wilkin...........W	174
● *Rothwell*, Morrison....... C	×
Round Grove, McLeod...... C	×
● Round Lake, Nobles....SW	25
● Round Prairie, Todd......C	10
Roussians Trading Post, St. Louis..................NE	×
Rowland, Hennepin.......NE	×
Royalton, Morrison........ C	582
Rudolph, (see Henderson)	×
Rumsey, Otter Tail.........W	×
Runeberg, Becker..........W	×
● Rush City, Chisago.......E	707
● Rushford, Fillmore......SE	968
Rush Lake, (see Rush City) ..	×
Rush Lake, (see Perham)	×
● Rushmore, Nobles.......SW	100
Rush Point, Chisago........E	200
Rush River, Sibley..........S	×
● Russell, Lyon...........SW	135
● *Russia*, Polk............NW	×
● Ruthton, Pipe Stone.... SW	43
Rutland, (see Fairmont)......	×
Ryan, Goodhue............ SE	20
● Sabin, Clay...............W	50
● Sacred Heart, Renville..SW	327
Saginaw, Itasca............ N	×
● *St. Albans*, Hennepin......C	×
St. Anna, Stearns........... C	15
St. Anthony, (see Minneapolis)	×
● *St. Anthony Park*, Ramsey E	1,000

Minnesota Minnesota

●St. Augusta, Stearns.......C 75
St. Benedict, Scott..........S ×
St. Bonifacius, Hennepin....C 32
●St. Charles, Winona.....SE 661
St. Clair, Blue Earth........S 300
●**St. Cloud**, Stearns.......C 7,686
●*St. Cloud Junc.*, Stearns..C ×
●*St. Croix Junc.*, Dakota..E ×
St. Francis, Anoka..........E 100
●*St. Francis*, Benton......C ×
St. Henry, Le Sueur........S 77
●St. Hilaire, Polk........NW 193
St. Hubertus, LeSueur......S 65
●**St. James**, Watonwan...S 939
St. John's College, Stearns..C ×
●St. Joseph, Stearns.........C 503
St. Lawrence, Otter Tail....W ×
●*St. Lawrence*, Scott.......S ×
St. Leo, Yellow Medicine..SW 10
●St. Louis Park, Hennepin.C 499
●*St. Louis River*, St.Louis NE ×
St. Martin, Stearns..........C 100
St. Mary, Waseca...........S ×
St. Mathais, Crow Wing.....C ×
St. Michael, Wright..........C 55
●St. Michael Station, W't...C 10
St. Nicholas, Stearns........C 35
St. Oloff, Otter Tail.........W 50
St. Patrick, Scott............S 12
●**ST. PAUL**, Ramsey....E 133,156
●*St. Paul Junc.*, Hennepin.C ×
St. Paul Park, Washington..E 1,173
●**St. Peter**, Nicollet.......S 3,671
●*St. Peter Junc.*, Winona.SE ×
St. Thomas, LeSueur........S ×
●St Vincent, Kittson....NW 450
St. Wendall, Stearns........C ×
●*Salida*, Sherburne........C ×
●Sanborn, Redwood......SW 300
Sanborn, Redwood.......SW ×
●Sandstone, Pine...........E 517
●*Sandstone Junc.*, Pine....E ×
Sanngren, Chippewa.....SW ×
Santiago, Sherburne.........C 20
Saratoga, Winona...........SE 75
Sardis, Big Stone...........W 7
●Sargeant, Mower.........SE 46
●Sauk Centre, Stearns......C 1,695
●**Sauk Rapids**, Benton..C 1,185
●Sawyer, Carlton...........E ×
Scrambler, Otter Tail......W ×
Scandia, Washington.......E 50
Schultzville, Kandiyohi.....C ×
Scovell, Murray...........SW ×
Scriven, Douglas...........W 12
●Sebeka, Wadena..........C 20
Seefield, (see Garvin)..........
Seely, Faribault............S 32
Selma, Cottonwood.......SW 10
●Shafer, Chisago............E 15
Shagawa, St. Louis......NE ×
●**Shakopee**, Scott.........S 1,757
●*Shakopee Shops*, Scott....S ×
Sham Lake, Lyon..........SW ×
Sharon, LeSueur............S 25
Shelburne, (see Buchard).... ×
Sheldon, Houston..........SE 150
Shell City, Wadena..........C 50
Shell Lake, Becker.........W ×
●Sherburne, Martin.........S 316
Sherman, Blue Earth........S 32
Shieldsville, Rice............S 70
●*Shirley*, Polk.............NW ×
●*Shoreham*, Hennepin.....C ×
Short Line Junc., Hennepin C ×
●*Short Line Park*, St.LouisNE ×
Silver Creek, Wright.........C 70
●*Silver Creek Siding*, Sh'ne.C ×
●Silver Lake, McLeod......C 180
●Simpson, Olmstead.......SE 30
Sioux Agency, Y'l'wM'd'neSW ×
●*Sioux Falls Junc.*, Nobles SW ×
Sioux Valley, Jackson....SW 32
Six Oaks, Olmsted.........SE 32
Skyberg, Goodhue..........SE 50
●**Slayton**, Murray......SW 380
●**Sleepy Eye**, Brown........S 1,518
Slettin, Polk..............NW 25
Smithfield, Wabasha.......SE 20
●Smith Lake, Wright.......C 100
●Smith's Mill, Waseca.......S 80
●Smithville, St. Louis....NE 18
Smithville Sta., Blue Earth..S 18
Snake, Marshall..........NW ×
Soland, Fillmore...........SE 25
●*Solberg's Point*, HennepinC ×
Somerset, (see Pratt)......... ×

●*Soo Line Junc.*, Ramsey..E ×
Sorllen's Mill, Yel'wMed'e.SW 20
●Soudan, St. Louis.......NE ×
●*Soule's Siding*, Mille Lacs.C ×
South Bend, Blue Earth.....S 132
South Branch, Watonwan...S 36
●*South Euclid*, Polk.... NW ×
●South Haven, Wright.....C 80
●*South Minneapolis*, Hei'in C ×
●South Park, Dakota.......E 200
●South Saint Paul, Dakota.E 2,242
●South Stillwater, Wash'n..E 1,304
South Troy, Wabasha......SE 25
●*South Western Junc.*, WinonaSE ×
Spangelo, Becker..........W 46
●Spaulding, Todd...........C ×
Spencer Brook, Isanti........E 50
Sperry, Martin...............S ×
●Spicer, Kandiyohi..........C 80
Spirit Lake, Otter Tail......W 20
●*Spirit Lake*, St. Louis...NE ×
Spring Creek, Goodhue....SE 40
Spring Creek, (see Pelican Lake) ×
●Springfield, Brown.........S 716
●Spring Grove, Houston..SE 394
Spring Hill, Stearns.........C 60
Spring Lake, Isanti..........E 10
●*Spring Park*, Hennepin..C ×
Spring Point, Marshall...NW 20
Spring Vale, Isanti..........E 20
●Spring Valley, Fillmore..SE 1,381
Spring Water, Rock......SW ×
Spruce Hill, Douglas.......W 100
●Stacy, Chisago............E 55
●*Staffordsville*, Hennepin..C ×
Stanchfield, Isanti..........E 200
Stanford, Isanti.............E 40
●*Stanley*, YellowMedicineSW ×
●Stanton, Goodhue........SE 40
●Staples, Todd..............C 1,500
●Starbuck, Pope...........W 224
Stark, Chisago.............E 25
Stately, Brown.............S 32
Stavanger, YellowMed'ne..SW 60
Steele Centre, Steele........S 32
●Steen, Rock.............SW ×
●Stephen, Marshall......NW 265
Sterling Centre, Blue Earth.S 50
●Stewart, McLeod..........C 166
Stewartville, Olmsted......SE 400
●**Stillwater**, Washington E 11,260
Stillwater Junc., WashingtonE ×
●Stockton, Winona.......SE 250
●*Stockwood*, Clay.........W ×
Stod, Otter Tail............W 20
Stoney Brook, St. Louis...NE ×
Stony Brook, (see Fergus Falls) ×
Stony Run, Yellow Med'neSW ×
Storden, Cottonwood......SW 65
Strand, Norman..........NW 75
Straus, Nicollet............S 50
Streeter, Hubbard.........N ×
Stroman, Morrison.........C ×
●Sturgeon Lake, Pine.....E 100
Suel, Scott.................S 32
●*Sullivans*, Polk.........NW ×
Summit, (see Tracy)......... ×
●*Summit*, Scott............S ×
●*Summit*, Washington.....E ×
●Sumter, McLeod...........C 20
Sunburgh, Kandiyohi.......C 10
Sundahl, Norman........NW 45
Sunrise City, Chisago.......E 250
Sutton, Mower.............SE ×
Svea, Kandiyohi............C ×
Sverdrup, Lyon..........SW 20
Swan Lake, Todd..........C ×
Swan River, Itasca.........N 25
Swan River, (see Le Deoux).. ×
●Swanville, Morrison.......C 50
Swenoda, Swift.............W 32
Swift Falls, Swift...........W 55
●*Sylvan Lake*, Cass........N ×
Syre, Norman............NW ×
Tabor, Polk...............NW ×
●*Tamarack*, Aitkin........E ×
Tamarac, (see Stephen)...... ×
Tensem, Clay...............W ×
●Taopi, Mower............SE 400
●Taunton, Lyon...........SW 10
●Taylor's Falls, Chisago....E 567
Tegneer, Becker............W ×
Teien, Kittson............NW ×
Tenhassen, Martin..........S 35
●Tenney, Wilkin..........W 60
●*Tenny*, Clay..............W ×
Terrace, Pope..............W 75

Terrebonne, Polk.........NW 48
Territtin, Traverse........W ×
Terry, Ly[illegible]...............SW 25
Thief River Falls, Polk...NW 191
●Thielmanton, Wabasha..SE 100
●Thomson, Carlton..........E 400
●*Thomson Junction*, Carl'n E ×
●Thorsborg, Grant.........W ×
●*Thorson*, Pope...........W 15
●*Thresher Works*, Hen'pin C ×
Thunderford, (see Good Th'd'r) ×
Thurs[illegible]y, Stearns..........C ×
●Tild[illegible], Polk..............NW 10
Till, Polk..................NW ×
●Tintah, Traverse..........W 50
●*Tintah Junction*, Wilkin W ×
Tivoli, Blue Earth...........S 60
●*Topeka*, Morrison........C ×
●Torah, Stearns.............C 500
Tordenskjold, Otter Tail....W ×
●*Tosca*, Mille Lacs.........C ×
●Tower, St. Louis..........NE 1,110
●*Tower Junction*, St.LouisNE ×
Town Site, Otter Tail.......C ×
Toziers Camp, Pine.........E ×
●Tracy, Lyon...............SW 1,400
Tracy, (see Lakey)......... ×
Trading Post, Mille Lacs...C ×
Transit, Sibley..............S 32
●*Traverse*, Nicollet.........S ×
Traverse des Sioux, Nicollet.S ×
Trenton, Carlton............E ×
Trenton, Freeborn..........S 40
Triumph, Martin.............S 32
Trondjem, Rice..............S ×
●Trosky, Pipe Stone.....SW 70
Trout Brook, Goodhue....SE ×
●*Trout Brook Junc.*, Rams'y E ×
Troy, Winona..............SE 25
Tremuli, (see Dalton)........ ×
Turtle Lake, (see Underwood) ×
Tweet, Polk................NW 10
●Twin Lakes, Freeborn.....S 150
●Twin Valley, Norman..NW 200
●Two Harbors, Lake.....NE 1,200
Two Rivers, Morrison.......C 100
●Tyler, Lincoln............SW 137
Tyrol, Stearns...............C 22
●Ulen, Clay..................W 150
●Underwood, Otter Tail...W 40
Union Centre, Le Sueur.....S ×
Union Hill, Le Sueur........S 28
Union Park, (see Merriam Pk) ×
Upsala, Morrison............C 200
Upshur, Todd...............C ×
Upton, Blue Earth...........S ×
Urness, Douglas.............W 104
●Utica, Winona.............SE 200
Vaaler, Lac-qui-parle.....SW ×
●*Vadnais Park*, Ramsey..E ×
Valley, Polk................NW 15
Valley Creek, Washington..E 350
Van, Douglas...............W ×
●*Varco*, Mower...........SE 32
Vasa, Goodhue.............SE 100
Verdal, Jackson..........SW 32
●Verdi, Lincoln...........SW 40
●Vermillion, Dakota........E 110
●Verndale, Wadena.........C 635
Vernon, Dodge............SE 50
●Vernon Centre, Blue Earth S 250
Veseli, Rice.................S 182
Vesta, Redwood...........SW ×
Vicksburgh, Renville.....SW 57
Victor, Wright...............C 32
●Victoria, Carver...........C 20
Viking, Marshall.........NW ×
Villard, Pope...............W 203
Vineland, Mille Lacs.........C ×
●Vining, Otter Tail.........W 200
●Viola, Olmsted..........SE 25
●*Virginia*, Rock..........SW ×
Vivian, Waseca..............S 32
●**Wabasha**, Wabasha....SE 2,487
●Waconia, Carver...........C 441
●Waconta, Goodhue.......SE ×
●**Wadena**, Wadena.......C 95
●*Wadena Junc.*, Otter Tail W ×
Wadsworth, Renville.....SW ×
Wakefield, Stearns.........C 16
●Walcott, Rice...............S ×
●*Waldo*, Lake.............NE ×
●Wallace, Dakota...........E 25
●Wall Lake, Otter Tail.....W 15
Walnut Grove, Martin......S 155
●Walnut Grove, Redwood SW 127
Walters, Blue Earth........S ×

Town, County	Index	Pop.
● Waltham, Mower	SE	100
Wamborg, (see Hoffman)		×
Wanamingo, Goodhue	SE	100
Wangs, Goodhue	SE	120
● *Wareham*, Pine	E	×
Warner, Kandiyohi	C	25
● *Warner*, Rock	SW	×
Warren, Marshall	NW	648
Warren, Winona	SE	×
● *Warrendale*, Ramsey	E	×
● Warsaw, Rice	S	100
Warwick, Hennepin	C	×
● **Waseca**, Waseca	S	2,482
Washburn, Hennepin	C	65
Washington, Fillmore	S	150
● Wasioja, Dodge	SE	250
Wastedo, Goodhue	SE	25
● Watab, Benton	C	×
● Waterford, Dakota	E	150
Watertown, Carver	C	362
● Waterville, Le Sueur	S	937
● Watkins, Meeker	C	40
● *Watosco*, Wilkin	W	×
● Watson, Chippewa	SW	150
Watson Creek, Fillmore	SE	30
Watters, Blue Earth	S	×
● Waverly Mills, Wright	C	370
Wawina, Itasca	N	×
Wayzata, Hennepin	C	273
● Weaver, Wabasha	SE	200
Webster, Rice	S	32
● Wegdahl, Chippewa	SW	30
● Welch, Goodhue	SE	15
● Welcome, Martin	S	140
Wellington, Renville	SW	×
● Wells, Faribault	S	1,208
● *Wells Junc.*, Blue Earth	S	×
● Wendell, Grant	W	100
Wesely, Rice	S	200
West Brainerd, (see Brainerd)		×
Westbrook, Cottonwood	SW	57
● West Concord, Dodge	SE	200
● *Westcott*, Dakota	E	×
● West Duluth, St. Louis	NE	3,368
● *West End*, St. Louis	NE	×
● *West End Junc.*, St. Louis	NE	×
Western, Otter Tail	W	65
Westfield Centre, Dodge	SE	32
Westford, Martin	S	32
West Lake, Kandiyohi	C	10
Westline, Redwood	SW	×
● *West Minneapolis*, Hennepin	C	×
● *West Minneapolis Transfer*, Hennepin	C	×
West Newton, Nicollet	S	40
● Westport, Pope	W	65
● *West Saint Paul*, Dakota	E	1,596
● *West Spring Lake*, Le Sueur	S	×
● *West Superior Junction*, St. Louis	NE	×
● *West Two Rivers*, St. Lo'is	NE	×
● West Union, Todd	C	50
West Valley, Marshall	NW	×
● Whalan, Fillmore	SE	98
● Wheatland, Rice	S	70
● Wheaton, Traverse	W	383
● *Wheeler*, Stevens	W	35
Wheeling, Rice	S	20
● *Wheelock*, Cass	N	×
● *White Bear Beach*, Ram'y	E	×
White Bear Centre, (see Starbuck)		×
● White Bear Lake, Ramsey	E	1,356
White Earth, Becker	W	260
White Fish Lake, Crow W'g	C	×
White Rock, Goodhue	SE	60
● *White Rock*, Traverse	W	×
Whitewater Falls, Winona	SE	25
● *Whitman*, Winona	SE	×
White Willow, Goodhue	SE	32
Wig, Polk	NW	×
● Wilder, Jackson	SW	100
Wild Rice, Norman	NW	25
Willewater, Polk	NW	×
Williamsville, Benton	C	×
● *Willington Grove*, H'n'sn	S	×
● **Willmar**, Kandiyohi	C	1,825
Willow Creek, Blue Earth	S	10
Willow Lake, Redwood	SW	×
● Willow River, Pine	E	30
Wilmington, Houston	SE	32
Wilno, Lincoln	SW	26
● *Wilson*, Ramsey	E	×
Wilson, Winona	SE	50
Wilton, Waseca	S	×
● **Windom**, Cottonwood	SW	835
Winfield, Renville	SW	
Winger, Polk	N	18
Winnebago Agency, (see St. Clair)		×
● Winnebago City, Faribault	S	1,108
Winnebago Val'y., Houston	SE	25
● Winnipeg Junction, Clay	W	25
● **Winona**, Winona	SE	18,208
Winsted, McLeod	C	267
● Winthrop, Sibley	S	438
Wiscoy, Winona	SE	100
● Withrow, Washington	E	×
Witoka, Winona	SE	100
Wolcott, Rice	S	12
● Wolverton, Wilkin	W	15
Woodbury, Washington	E	75
● Wood Lake, Yel'w M'd'e.	SW	100
● ***Woodland*, Hennepin**	C	×
Woodland, Wabasha	SE	×
Woodland, Otter Tail	W	×
Woodlawn, Winona	SE	×
Woodside, Polk	NW	15
● Woodstock, Pipe Stone	SW	250
● **Worthington**, Nobles	SW	1,161
Wren, Chippewa	SW	20
● *Wrenshall*, Carlton	E	×
● *Wright*, Carlton	E	×
Wrightstown, Otter Tail	W	50
Wrodahl, Clay	W	×
Wyanett, Isanti	E	×
Wyattville, Winona	SE	25
Wykeham, Todd	C	×
● Wykoff, Fillmore	SE	335
● Wylie, Polk	NW	18
● Wyoming, Chisago	E	100
Yellow Bank, Lac-qui-p'e.	SW	×
Yellow Medicine, Yel. Med.	SW	32
York, Fillmore	SE	100
York, Lake	NE	×
● Young America, Carver	C	287
Yucatan, Houston	SE	25
● *Zimmerman*, Sherburne	C	×
Zions, Stearns	C	32
● Zumbra Heights, Hennepin	C	×
● Zumbro Falls, Wabasha	SE	300
● Zumbrota, Goodhue	SE	867
● *Zumbrota Junc.*, Olmsted	SE	×

MISSISSIPPI.

COUNTIES.	INDEX.	POP
Adams	SW	26,031
Alcorn	NE	13,115
Amite	SW	18,198
Attala	C	22,213
Benton	N	10,585
Bolivar	W	29,980
Calhoun	N	14,688
Carroll	C	18,773
Chickasaw	N	19,891
Choctaw	C	10,847
Claiborne	SW	14,516
Clarke	E	15,826
Clay	E	18,607
Coahoma	NW	18,342
Copiah	SW	30,233
Covington	S	8,299
DeSoto	N	24,183
Franklin	SW	10,424
Greene	SE	3,906
Grenada	N	14,974
Hancock	S	8,318
Harrison	SE	12,481
Hinds	W	39,279
Holmes	C	30,970
Issaquena	W	12,318
Itawamba	NE	11,708
Jackson	SE	11,251
Jasper	E	14,785
Jefferson	SW	18,947
Jones	SE	8,333
Kemper	E	17,961
LaFayette	N	20,553
Lauderdale	E	29,661
Lawrence	S	12,318
Leake	C	14,803
Lee	NE	20,040
Le Flore	C	16,869
Lincoln	SW	17,912
Lowndes	E	27,047
Madison	C	27,321
Marion	S	9,532
Marshall	N	26,043
Monroe	NE	30,730
Montgomery	C	14,459
Neshoba	E	11,146
Newton	E	16,625
Noxubee	E	27,338
Oktibbeha	E	17,694
Pa[illegible]a	N	26,977
Pearl River	S	2,957
Perry	SE	6,494
Pike	S	21,203
Pontotoc	[illegible]	14,940
Prentiss	NE	13,679
Quitman	NW	3,286
Rankin	C	17,922
Scott	C	11,740
Sharkey	W	8,382
Simpson	S	10,138
Smith	C	10,635
Sun Flower	W	9,384
Tallahatchie	NW	14,361
Tate	N	19,253
Tippah	N	12,951
Tishomingo	NE	9,302
Tunica	NW	12,158
Union	N	15,606
Warren	W	33,164
Washington	W	40,414
Wayne	SE	9,817
Webster	C	12,060
Wilkinson	SW	17,592
Winston	E	12,089
Yalobusha	N	16,629
Yazoo	W	36,394
Total		1,289,600

TOWN. COUNTY.	INDEX.	POP.
Abbeville, La Fayette	N	200
● *Abbott*, Holmes	C	×
Abbott, Clay	E	100
● **Aberdeen**, Monroe	NE	3,449
Aberdeen Junction, Mon'e	NE	×
Abney, Itawamba	NE	2,000
● *Acher*, Monroe	NE	×
● Ackerman, Choctaw	C	600
Acme, Jasper	E	×
Acona, Holmes	C	100
● Adams Station, Hinds	W	75
Adams Landing, Warren	W	×
Adamsville, Greene	SE	×
Aden, Neshoba	E	×
Advance, Marion	S	×
Agricultural College, Ok'b'a	E	×
Ainsworth, Copiah	SW	20
Airey, Harrison	SE	×
Air Mount, Yalobusha	N	50
Alban Landing, (see Hood)		×
Albemarle, Issaquena	W	16
● *Alcorn*, Alcorn	NE	×
Alcorn City, Tishomingo	NE	×
Alden Station, (see Horn Lake)		×
Alesville, La Fayette	N	×
Alexander Landing, Warr'n	W	50
Alexis, Tunica	NW	×
Algoma, Pontotoc	N	25
Alice, Neshoba	E	
Allen, Copiah	SW	20
● *Allen*, Warren	W	×
Allendale, Attala	C	×
Allen's Store, Tishomingo	NE	25
Allen's Store, Itawamba	NE	125
Allen's Store, (see Tynes		×
Allgood's Mill, (see Brooksville)		×
Alliance, Noxubee	E	×
● Alligator, Bolivar	W	30
Alloway, Adams	SW	20
Alpika, DeSoto	N	10
Alpine, Union	N	×
Altitude, Prentiss	NE	×
Alto, Jasper	E	×
Alva, Montgomery	C	10
Alva, Webster	C	10
Amer, Hancock	S	×
Americus, Jackson	SE	20
Amitie, Pontotoc	N	×
Amory, Monroe	NE	739
Amy, Jones	SE	10
Anchorage, Coahoma	NW	35
Anderson, Madison	C	20
● Anding, Yazoo	W	125
Andover, Smith	C	×
● Anguilla, Sharkey	W	125
Anner, Hancock	S	×
Antioch, Prentiss	NE	25
Appleton, Harrison	SE	×
Arcadia, Issaquena	W	28
● Arcola, Washington	W	175

Post Office		
Ariel, Amite	SW	×
Arkabutla, Tate	N	148
● Armistead, Rankin	C	20
Armory, Monroe	NE	739
Arnot Adams	SW	80
● Artesia, Lowndes	E	313
Artonish, Wilkinson	SW	100
Ashland, Benton	N	138
Ashley, Copiah	SW	×
Ashwood Landing, LeFlore	C	×
● Ashwood Sta., Wilk'son	SW	25
Askew's Bluff, Panola	N	×
● *Asylum*, Hinds	W	×
Athens, Monroe	NE	×
Atlanta, Chickasaw	N	100
Auburn, Lincoln	SW	20
Augusta, Perry	SE	150
Austerlitz, Benton	N	×
Austin, Tunica	NW	400
Australia, Bolivar	W	30
Auter, Sharkey	W	25
Avaras, Greene	SE	×
Avera, Greene	SE	50
● *Avon*, Washington	W	70
Avondale, Bolivar	W	20
Ayres, Attala	C	25
Bachelor's Bend, Washin'n.	W	×
Baconville, Madison	C	20
Bailey, Lauderdale	E	50
Bailey's Sta., (see Hernando)		×
● Baird, Sun Flower	W	32
Baker, Union	N	25
● Baldwyn, Lee	NE	710
Baleshed, Issaquena	W	20
Ballard Mills, Itawamba	NE	50
Ballardsville, Itawamba	NE	×
Ballardsville, Lee	NE	×
Baloil, DeSoto	N	10
Banesville, Marshall	N	30
Bankston, Choctaw	C	10
Banner, Calhoun	N	200
Barksdale, Attala	C	20
Barlow, Copiah	SW	25
Barnes Land'g, Washington	W	10
● Barnett, Clarke	E	50
Barrs, Clay	E	×
Barton, Marshall	N	×
Barttahatchie, Monroe	NE	×
Basin, Jackson	SE	×
Bates Mill, Amite	SW	200
● Batesville, Panola	N	705
Batson, Perry	SE	×
Battlefield, Newton	E	×
Bay Spring, (see Tynes)		×
● **Bay St. Louis**, Hancock	S	1,974
Beach, Scott	C	×
Bear Creek, Hinds	W	18
Beardsville, Marion	S	×
Beasley, Clay	E	×
● *Beatty*, Carroll	C	×
● Beauregard, Copiah	SW	400
● Beauvoir, Harrison	SE	30
Beaver Creek, Amite	SW	150
Beech, Scott	C	250
Beech Grove, Copiah	SW	40
Beech Springs, Neshoba	E	100
Beeks, Monroe	NE	25
● Beelake, Holmes	C	20
Belen, Quitman	NW	184
Belle, Clay	E	100
Bellefontaine, Webster	C	15
● *Bellefontaine*, Jackson	SE	×
Belle Prairie, Yazoo	W	300
Bellevue, Bolivar	W	100
● *Bell's*, Lee	NE	×
● *Belmont*, Bolivar	W	×
Belmont, Bolivar	W	×
Belmont, Tishomingo	NE	25
Belton, Jasper	E	×
● Belzona, Washington	W	100
Benbell, Pontotoc	N	×
Benela, Calhoun	N	50
Ben Lomond, Issaquena	W	150
Bennet's Land., (seeRobs'nv'l)		×
● Benoit, Bolivar	W	×
Bently, Calhoun	N	100
Benton, Yazoo	W	800
● Bentonia, Yazoo	W	123
Berryville, Yazoo	W	×
Berwick, Amite	SW	×
Best, Montgomery	C	×
Bethany, Lee	NE	40
Betheden, Winston	E	×
Bethel, Jones	SE	×
Bethlehem, Marshall	N	20
● Beulah, Bolivar	W	60
Beulah, Union	N	20

Mississippi

Post Office		
Beverly Store, Adams	SW	15
Bewelcome, Amite	SW	×
Bezer, Smith	C	150
Bibbs, Bolivar	W	×
● Bigbee, Monroe	NE	200
Bigbee Valley, Noxubee	E	200
Bigby Fork, Itawamba	NE	30
Big Creek, Cal[illegible]		75
Big Oak, [illegible]	E	×
Big Springs, Clay	E	125
● Biloxi, Harrison	SE	3,234
Binford, Monroe	NE	×
Binnsville, Kemper	E	500
Birmingham, Lee	NE	85
Bishop, Scott	C	×
Bismark, Lawrence	S	20
Black Bayou, (see MinterCity)		×
Black Hawk, Carroll	C	300
Black Jack, (see Canaan)		×
Blackland, Prentiss	NE	×
Blackmonton, Carroll	C	10
Bland's, LaFayette	N	×
● *Blakely*, Warren	W	×
● Blanton, Sharkey	W	25
● *Blanton's Gap*, Choctaw	C	×
Blountville, Lawrence	S	300
Blue, Calhoun	N	×
● Blue Mountain, Tippah	N	250
● Blue Springs, Union	N	100
Bluff Creek, Jackson	SE	300
Bluff Springs, Jackson	SE	100
Bluff Springs, (see Pleasant Grove)		×
Blythe, DeSoto	N	×
Blythe's Land., (see Graball)		×
● Bobo, Coahoma	NW	25
● *Bogue*, Washington	W	×
● Bogue Chitto, Lincoln	SW	300
Boland's, Itawamba	NE	×
Bolivar, Bolivar	W	102
● Bolton, Hinds	W	1,000
Bon Eagle, Washington	W	×
● **Booneville**, Prentiss	NE	748
Border Springs, Lowndes	E	×
Borland's, Itawamba	NE	5
Bouge Station, (see Stoneville)		
Bournham, Lawrence	S	18
● Bovina, Warren	W	50
Bowdre, Tunica	NW	×
Bowen, Itawamba	NE	×
Bowers, (see Grenada)		×
Bowerton, Copiah	SW	20
Bowles, Chickasaw	N	×
Bowling Green, Holmes	C	45
Bowman, Tate	N	×
● Boyce, Wayne	SE	×
Boyce, Clay	E	35
Boyd, Lawrence	S	×
Boykins, Smith	C	22
● Bradley, Oktibbeha	E	25
Brame, Pontotoc	N	30
● **Brandon**, Rankin	C	835
Brandywine, Claiborne	SW	20
Braxton, Simpson	S	150
Brazelia, Noxubee	E	×
Brevet, Jasper	E	×
Bridgeport, Simpson	S	×
Bridges, Oktibbeha	E	×
Brierfield, Warren	W	×
Bright, DeSoto	N	×
Bright's Cor's, (see Carrollton)		×
Brit, Smith	C	×
Brock, Carroll	C	10
● **Brookhaven**, Lincoln	SW	2142
Brookville, Noxubee	E	424
Brown Place, (see Lula)		×
Brown's Creek, Prentiss	NE	5
Brown's Land'g, (see Ch'ston)		×
Brownsville, (see Stafford)		×
Brownsville, Hinds	W	75
Brown's Wells, Copiah	SW	25
Bruce, (see Pontotoc)		×
Brunswick, Warren	W	25
Brushy Creek, Jones	SE	×
● Bucatunna, Wayne	SE	150
Buck Creek, Greene	SE	26
● *Buckner's*, Washington	W	×
Buck Ridge L'd'g, (see Bolivar)		×
Buena Vista, Chickasaw	N	300
Buford, Marion	S	20
Bullock, Tippah	N	×
Bunche's Bend, (see Bl'k H'k)		×
Bunckley, Franklin	SW	18
Buncombe, Union	N	×
Bunker Hill, Smith	C	75
Bunnie, Lauderdale	E	×
Burdeaux Island, Tunica,	NW	×

Mississippi

Post Office		
● Burdett, Washington	W	25
Burketon, Grenada	N	×
Burketsville, Attala	C	38
Burk's Landing, Coahoma	NW	10
Burleigh, Issaquena	W	50
Burnham's Mill, Simpson	S	15
Burns, Smith	C	25
● Burnsville, Tishomingo,	NW	318
Burnt Mills, Tishomingo	NE	50
Burrow, Alcorn	NE	×
Burton's, Tishomingo	NE	40
Burton's Prentiss	NE	40
Burtonton, (see Carpenter)	SW	×
Busby, Tunica	NW	×
Butler, Warren	W	250
Buttern'kSp'gs, (see Thaxton)		×
● Byhalia, Marshall	N	474
● Byram, Hinds	W	100
Byrd's Store, Pike	S	18
Bywy, Choctaw	C	×
Cadaretta, Webster	C	15
Cairo, Clay	E	100
Caledonia, Lowndes	E	175
● Calhoun, Madison	C	50
Callao, Washington	W	×
Calmar, Warren	W	30
Calooga, Webster	C	×
Calvert, Kemper	E	100
Camden, Madison	C	125
Cameron, Madison	C	18
Campbell's Bridge, Marion	S	×
Campbellsville, Yazoo	W	20
Canaan, Benton	N	11
● Cannonsburgh, Jeffer'n.	SW	30
● **Canton**, Madison	C	2,131
Caraway, Simpson	S	25
● *Cardiff*, Warren	W	×
Cardsville, Itawamba	NE	17
Carley, Marion	S	50
● Carlisle, Claiborne	SW	100
Carmichael, Clarke	E	×
Carnesville, Tunica	NW	×
Carolina, Washington	W	50
● Carpenter, Copiah	SW	50
● *Carriere*, Hancock	S	×
● **Carrollton**, Carroll	C	488
Carson's L'd'g, (see Concordia)		×
Cartersville, Tishomingo	NE	30
Carthage, Leake	C	322
● Cary, Sharkey	W	75
Cascilla, Tallahatchie	NW	20
Caseyville, Lincoln	SW	220
Cash, Scott	C	41
Castilian Springs, Holmes	C	10
Caswell, LaFayette	N	50
Catchings, Sharkey	W	×
Catfish Point, Bolivar	W	30
Cato, Rankin	C	100
Caulfield, Wilkinson	SW	×
Cayce, Marshall	N	30
Cayuga, Hinds	W	20
● Cedar Bluff, Clay	E	×
Cedar Grove, Pontotoc	N	18
Cedarview, DeSoto	N	60
Central Academy, Panola	N	10
Central Grove, Monroe	NE	×
Centre, Attala	C	50
Centre Hill, (see Collierville, Tenn.)		
Centre Point, Tallahatchie	NW	×
● Centreville, Wilkinson	SW	250
● *Centreville*, Newton	E	150
Centreville, (see Wilcox)		×
Chadwell Mills, (see Ch'l'ston)		×
Chalybeate, Tippah	N	×
Chapel, Oktibbeha	E	×
Chapel Hill, Hinds	W	25
Chapeltown, Panola	N	×
Chapman, Rankin	C	×
Charleston, Talla'tchie	NW	412
● Chatawa, Pike	S	150
Chatham, Washington	W	150
Chautauqua, Harrison	SE	×
Cherokee, Lowndes	E	×
Cherry, Rankin	C	×
● Cherry Creek, Pontotoc	N	100
Cherry Hill, Calhoun	N	50
Chester, Choctaw	C	100
Chesterville, Pontotoc	N	100
Chewalla Mills, (see H'y S'pgs)		×
Chew's Landing, Holmes	C	260
Chickasahay, Kemper	E	×
China Grove, Pike	S	65
Chinquepin, Pearl River	S	×
Chita, Attala	C	30
Chiwapa, Pontotoc	N	×
Choccuma (see Grenada)		×
Choctaw Agency, Oktibbeha	E	40

Chotard, Issaquena........W 100
Christmas, Holmes........C ×
Chulahoma, Marshall.......N 175
● Chunkey's Station, N'w'tnE 30
Church Hill, Jefferson.... SW 150
Clack, (see Robinsonville).... ×
Claiborne, Jasper.......... E 300
● ***Claiborne*, Hancock.......S** ×
● *Clarksburgh*, Scott........C ×
Clarksburgh, Rankin........C 200
● Clarksdale, Coahoma...NW 781
Clark's Mill, Carroll........ C ×
Clarkson, Webster.......... C ×
Clarysville, Tippah.......... N ×
Clay, Pearl River............ S 20
Claysville, Union........... N ×
● Clayton, Tunica........ NW 10
● Cleveland, Bolivar........W 60
Cliff, Itawamba........... NE ×
Clifton, Jefferson......... SW 25
Cliftonville, Noxubee....... E 100
● Clinton, Hinds............W 500
● Clover Hill, Coahoma...NW 50
● Coahoma, Coahoma.... NW 100
Coatesville, Greene........ SE 25
● Cobb Switch, Lowndes.... E 90
Cobbville, Madison............C 23
Cockerham, Amite........SW ×
Cockrum, DeSoto............N 40
Coffadeliah, Neshoba........E 100
Coffee's Store, (see Caswell).. ×
● **Coffeeville**, Yalobusha.N 465
Colia, Carroll................ C 10
Colah, Leake............... C ×
Colbert, Marshall............ N 10
Cold Springs, (see Doloroso). ×
● Coldwater, Tate..............N 518
Coleman, Marshall............N 25
Cole's Creek, Calhoun........N 50
Coleville, Chickasaw........N 100
Cole's Hill, Calhoun........ N ×
● College Hill, LaFayette...N 50
Collier, Benton........... N ×
Collinsville, Lauderdale..... E 100
Columbia, Marion........ S 275
● **Columbus**, Lowndes....E 4,559
Coman's Bluff, Tippah........N ×
Commerce, Tunica........NW 50
● Como Depot, Panola......N 178
Complete, Lauderdale.......E ×
Concordia, Bolivar..........W 10
Conehatta, Newton..........E 27
Conlyville, Attala.............C 60
Congress, Chickasaw.........N ×
Conrad, Marshall............N ×
Conway, Leake................C 15
● *Conway*, Copiah........ SW ×
Cook's Landing, Tish'go..NE ×
Cooksville, Noxubee..........E 25
Coonewar, Lee............ NE 20
Cooper, Monroe............NE 25
Cooper's Wells, Hinds......W 30
Cooperville, Scott............ C ×
Coopwood, Winston...........E 100
Coosa, Leake................. C 85
● *Corinne*, Lauderdale......E ×
● **Corinth**, Alcorn.......NE 2,111
Cornersville, Marshall....... N 40
Cornersville, Union..........N 40
Cornwell, Winston............E 25
Corrona, Lee.................NE 20
Cotton Gin Port, (see Amory) ×
○ Cotton Plant, Tippah......N 30
Cotton Valley, Calhoun.....N ×
County Line, Newton.........E ×
County Line, Quitman... NW ×
Couparle City, Madison......C 50
● Courtland, Panola........ N 300
● *Cox*, Jones...............SE ×
Coxburgh, Holmes........... C 30
Craig, Yazoo.................W 50
● Crawford, Lowndes........E 225
Crevi, Tallahatchie....... NW 10
Crews, Tunica.............NW ×
Cripple Deer, Tishomingo.NE ×
Cross Roads, Jackson.......SE 700
Crowley, Webster............C ×
● Cruger, Holmes........... C 23
Crump, Yazoo................W ×
● Crystal Springs, Copiah. SW 997
Cuba, Alcorn...............NE ×
Cuba, Attala................ C 150
Cublake, DeSoto..............N ×
Cumberland, Webster.......C 150
Currie, Smith................C ×
Curry Creek, Covington.....S ×
Curtis, Jones...............SE 30

Cushtusa, Neshoba.........E ×
Cydonia, Panola............N ×
● Cynthia, Hinds........... W 18
Cypress, Tate................N ×
Cypress Grove, Jefferson..SW 100
Cypress Precinct, Oktibbeha E ×
● Dahomy, Bolivar.........W 5
Daisy, Jackson.............SE ×
Dale, Marion.................S ×
Daleville, Lauderdale....... E 500
Dallas, La Fayette...........N 50
Damascus, Scott.............C 25
Daniel, Smith.................C 75
Danville, Alcorn...........NE 50
Darden, Union................N 37
Darrington, Wilkinson....SW 22
● *Davis*, Madison............ C ×
● *Davis Mills No.1*, PearlR'v'rS ×
Davis' Store, (see Hillside).... ×
Daviston, Pearl River....... S ×
Davisville, Jasper............E ×
Days, DeSoto................N 5
Dayton, La Fayette.........N ×
● Dayton, Amite...........SW 18
Dead Man's Bend, AdamsSW ×
Deasonville, Yazoo.......... W 75
Decatur, Newton......... E 150
Deen, Covington.............S ×
Deerbrook, Noxubee.........E 200
Deer Creek, Sharkey.........W 200
Deer Creek, Washington....W 200
● *Deeson*, Boliver...........W ×
DeKalb, Kemper........ E 240
DeLay, La Fayette...........N 50
De Lisle, Harrison.........SE 25
Delo, Simpson..............S 25
Delta, Coahoma........ NW 50
Denham, Wayne........SE ×
Denman, Tallahatchie....NW ×
Denmark, La Fayette.........N 26
Dennis L'd'g, (see Australia).. ×
Dent, Holmes.................C ×
● Deovolente, Le Flore.......C ×
● *Derby*, Pearl River.........S 20
● DeSoto, Clarke..............E 500
DeSoto Front, DeSoto........N 10
Dexter, Marion...............S ×
Diamond, Warren............W ×
Dick, Yazoo.................W ×
● Dickerson, Coahoma...NW ×
Dickey, Amite..............SW 25
● *Dickson*, Yalobusha...... N ×
Dido, Choctaw...............C ×
Dillon, Pike..................S 200
Dinan, Pike..................S 20
● *Ditchley*, Washington.... W ×
Dixie, (see Horn Lake)....... ×
Dixie, La Fayette.............N ×
Dixie, Clay...................E ×
Dixon, Neshoba...............E 50
Dio, Simpson.................S 47
Dobson, Rankin..............C ×
Dobsonville, Smith...........C 30
Dogwood, Sharkey............W ×
Dogwood Ridge, (see HornLake) ×
Doloroso, Wilkinson...... SW 15
● *Donore*, Hinds............W ×
Dormantown, Newton......E 30
Dorsey's Store, (see Fredonia) ×
Dossville, Leake...............C 60
Dot, Franklin...............SW ×
Double Springs, Oktibbeha..E 125
Dover, Yazoo................W 98
Dow, Lowndes...............E ×
Dowd's Landing, (see Crews). ×
Dowdville, (see Watkinsville) ×
Dry Grove, Hinds............W 150
Dry Run, Prentiss.........NE 5
Dubbs, Tunica..............NW 30
● Dublin, Coahoma........NW 200
● Duck Hill, Montgomery...C 332
Dumas, Tippah................N 40
Dunbar, Lowndes.............E ×
Dunbarton, Issaquena.......W 110
● Duncan, Bolivar............W 100
Duncansby, Isaquena........W 150
Dundee, Tunica...........NW ×
Dunham, Wayne.........SE ×
Dun's Store, (see Thornton).. ×
● *Dupre*, Clay.................E ×
Durango L'ding, JeffersonSW ×
● Durant, Holmes............C 1,259
Duval's Landing, IssaquenaW 15
Dyer's Landing, Bolivar... W ×
Eades, Attala.................C ×
● Eagle, Alcorn..............NE 10
○ Eagle Nest, Coahoma...NW 10

Early Grove, Marshall......N 75
● Earnest, Coahoma......NW ×
● *Eastabuchie*, Jones......SE 100
Eastfork, Amite.......... SW 50
Eastman, Itawamba.......NE ×
Easton's L'd'g, (seeMoundL'd'g) ×
East Pascagoula, Jackson.SE ×
Eastville, Lauderdale....... E ×
Ebenezer, Holmes...........C 127
Echo, Amite..............SW ×
Eckles, Tate..................N 10
Ecru, Pontotoc..............N 100
● Eden, Yazoo..............W 28
Edinburgh, Leake............C 123
Edney, Wayne.............SE 30
● Edwards Hinds............W 400
Eggville, Lee..............NE ×
● Egremont, Sharkey...... W 30
● Egypt, Chickasaw.........N 100
Elba, Perry..................SE ×
Elberon, Harrison.........SE ×
Elena Planta'n, WashingtonW ×
Eley, Scott.................. C ×
Elise, Chickasaw............N ×
● Elizabeth, Washington...W ×
Ellena, Oktibbeha.......... E ×
Ellenton L'd'g, (see Bolivar). ×
● Elliott, Grenada........... N ×
Elliot's Mills, Panola........N 20
Ellistown, Union.............N 50
● Ellisville Depot, Jones...SE 961
Ellzey, Calhoun..............N ×
Elma, Prentiss.............NE ×
Elvadale, (see Satartia) ...... ×
Elzy, Calhoun...............N ×
Embry, Webster............ C 25
Emmaville, (see Sunny Side). ×
Emory, Holmes..............C 89
Energy, Clarke..............E 25
Engine, Neshoba.............E ×
Ennis, Kemper...............E ×
Ennis, Oktibbeha............E ×
Enola, Yazoo...............W 120
Enon, Perry................SE ×
Enondale, Kemper...........E ×
● Enterprise, Clarke........E 1,300
Eolia, (see Harrison Station). ×
● Erata, Jones............. SE 38
Ervin, Calhoun..............N ×
Erwin, Washington..........W 30
● *Erwins*, Washington..... W ×
Erwinsville, Lincoln......SW ×
Escatawpa, Jackson........ SE ×
● *Eskridge*, Montgomery... C ×
Esperanza, Pontotoc.........N 34
● Estabutchie, Jones.......SE 400
Estesmill, Leake.............C 40
● Estill, Washington......... W 20
Etchehonia, Jasper......... E ×
● Ethel, Attala...............C 50
Etta, Union...................N ×
Eucutta, Wayne............SE 50
Eudora, De Soto............. N 106
Eulogy, Holmes..............C 15
● Eupora, Webster............C 432
Eureka, (see Nettleton)...... ×
Eureka, (see Indianola)....... ×
Eureka, Yazoo..............W 60
Eureka Springs, Panola.... N 100
Eutaw, Bolivar............. W 10
Evans, Yazoo.................W 30
Evansville, (see Strayhorn)... ×
● Evansville, Tunica......NW 25
Everett, Simpson.............S ×
Evergreen, Itawamba.......NE ×
Everston, Bolivar............ W ×
Evina, Sharkey.............W ×
Ezra, Le Flore................C ×
Fagin, Tippah................N ×
Fairdale, Simpson............S ×
Fairfield, (see Ellistown)..... ×
Fairley, Jackson........... SE 25
Fairport, Noxubee............E ×
Fair River, Lincoln....... SW 55
Fairview, Union..............N ×
Falsonia, Sun Flower........W 40
● Falkner, Tippah............N 100
Famosa, Holmes............C 240
Fancher, Attala..............C ×
Fannin, Rankin...............C 200
Farmington, Alcorn......NE ×
Faroe, Smith..................C ×
Fay, Webster................C 5
● **Fayette**, Jefferson.....SW 400
Fearn's Springs, Winston... E 60
Felix, Grenada..............N ×
● Fentress, Choctaw........C 5

Place	Pop.
Fernwood, Pike..........S	×
● *Fish Lake*, Washington..W	×
Finger, Tippah..........N	10
Fitler's Landing, Issaquena W	×
Flatwood, Noxubee..........E	×
Flint Creek, Harrison......SE	36
● Flora, Madison..........C	228
Florence, Chickasaw........N	30
● *Flowers*, Issaquena....... W	×
Flowers Station, Warren..W	20
Flower Hill, Warren....... W	20
Flowers Place, Smith....... C	15
Floyd, Benton.......... N	×
Flynt, Covington..........S	×
● *Foltz*, Carroll..........C	×
Fondi, Wayne..........SE	×
Fordsville, Marion..........S	×
Fordyke, Yazoo..........W	×
Forest, Scott..........C	547
Forest Home, Warren......W	×
Fort Adams, Wilkinson...SW	400
Fort Bayou, Jackson..........SE	50
Fort Logan, Le Flore.......C	×
● *Fort Loring*, Le Flore.... C	×
Fort Stephens, Kemper..... E	50
● *Foster's*, Adams........SW	×
● *Fox Landing*, Warren... W	×
Fox Trap, Noxubee........ E	75
Franklin, Holmes.......... C	90
Frederic's Mill, (see Tillatoba)	×
Fredonia, Union.......... N	×
Freeny, Leake..........C	×
Free Run, Yazoo..........W	250
Freetown, Warren......... W	×
Freetrade, **Leake**..........C	28
French Camps, Choctaw.... C	267
● **Friar's Point**, C'homa. NW	674
Friendship, Lincoln...... SW	×
Friendship, Chickasaw..... N	×
Frost Bridge, Wayne...... SE	×
Fulcher, Choctaw..........C	5
Fulton, Itawamba...... NE	450
Furman, Jasper..........E	×
Furrs, Pontotoc.......... N	×
Fusky, Neshoba..........E	×
Futheyville, (see Grenada)...	×
Gaines Mills, Winston...... E	×
Gainesville, Hancock..........S	500
Galena, Marshall..........N	×
Gallatin, Copiah..........SW	D
● Gallman, Copiah........SW	180
Gallway, Union..........N	×
Garden City, Franklin..... SW	200
Garlandville, Jasper.........E	120
● Garner, Yalobusha........N	124
Garvin's Landing, (see Indianola)	×
Gatesville, see Crystal Springs)	×
● Gattman, Monroe.......NE	×
Gaylesville, Bolivar.......... W	×
Geeville, Prentiss.......... NE	10
George's Camp, Jones..... SE	500
Georgetown, Copiah......SW	180
● *Georgia Pacific Junction*, Washington.......... W	×
Gerenton, Carroll.......... C	×
Gerson's Landing, (see Roebuck Lake)..........	×
Gholson, Noxubee.......... E	100
Gibson, Monroe.......... NE	×
Gift, Alcorn..........NE	10
Gilbert, Scott..........C	36
Giles, Kemper.......... E	×
Gillsburgh, Amite..........SW	95
Gitano, Jones..........SE	20
Gladstone, Bolivar.......... W	10
Glasgow, Simpson..........S	×
● Glass, Warren.......... W	15
Gleaner, Neshoba..........E	×
Glen Allan, Washington.... W	50
Gencoe, (see Mound Landing)	×
● Glendale, Tunica.........NW	×
Glendora, Tallahatchie......NW	×
● *Glendoro*, Tallahatchie. NW	×
Glenloro, Washington...... W	250
● *Glen's*, Alcorn.......... NE	×
Glenville, Panola.......... N	30
Glenwood, Bolivar..........W	×
Gloster, Amite.......... SW	1,142
Glover, DeSoto.......... N	×
Golding, (see Blue Springs)...	×
● *Good Hope*, Holmes.......C	×
Good Hope, Leake..........C	75
● Goodman, Holmes.......... C	354
Goodwater, Clarke.......... E	×
Goodwater, Oktibbeha...... E	×
Gordon Sta., (see Port Gibson)	×
Goshen Springs, Rankin.... C	120

Place	Pop.
Goss, Marion.......... S	×
Graball, Tallahatchie..... NW	60
● Grace, Issaquena.........W	×
● Grady, Webster..........C	×
Graham, Union..........N	10
● *Graham*, Lauderdale..... E	×
Grand Gulf, Claiborne.... SW	200
Grange, Lawrence..........S	17
● *Gravel Siding*, T'sho'ngo NE	×
Graves, Benton..........N	×
Gray's Mill, (see Owens).....	×
Graysport, Grenada..........N	100
Greenbrier, Monroe........NE	×
Greene Crossing, Hinds.... W	22
Greenfield, Rankin.......... C	×
● Greengrove, Coahoma..NW	×
Green Hill, (see Craig)........	×
Greenleaf, De Soto..........N	×
● *Greens*, Rankin..........C	×
Greensborough, Webster....C	35
Green's Crossing, Hinds.... W	22
Green's Store, Copiah..... SW	1
● **Greenville**, Wash'gt'n. W	6,658
● **Greenwood**, LeFlore...C	1,055
Greer, Leake.......... C	36
Grenada, Grenada..........N	2,416
● *Grenada Junc.*, Grenada. N	×
Griffin, Perry..........SE	30
Griffith, Clay..........E	×
Grimesburgh, Rankin........C	×
Grimmtown, (see Lamont)...	×
Grubb Springs, Monroe...NE	×
Gulfport, Harrison.......... SE	38
● Gulf View, Hancock......S	×
Gum Branch, Winston..........E	×
Gum Grove, (see Thornton)...	×
Gum Grove Landing, Holmes C	50
Gum Ridge, Jefferson.....SW	100
Gumwood, Sun Flower.....W	18
Gunn, Smith..........C	28
● *Gunnison*, Bolivar....... W	175
Gunnison, Bolivar..........W	×
● Guntown, Lee..........NE	300
● Guyton, Tippah..........N	36
Gwinville, Lawrence. ...... S	78
Habalochelto, Hancock..... S	60
Haggard, Winston.......... E	×
Halsseyville, Warren....... W	18
Halifax, Yazoo.......... W	18
● *Halpins*, Sharkey.......... W	32
Hambrick, Montgomery.... C	×
● Hamburgh, Franklin... SW	75
Hamilton, Monroe......... NE	75
Hamlet, Jasper.......... E	×
● Hampton, Washington... W	20
Hanby, Noxubee..........E	×
Handle, Winston..........E	×
Handsborough, Harrison.. SE	1,021
Harbetts Landing, (see O. K.)	×
● Hardy Station, Grenada.. N	100
Harkinsville, (see St. Anns)..	×
Harlan, Noxubee..........E	60
Harmontown, La Fayette.. N	50
Harpersville, Scott..........C	138
Harrell's, DeSoto..........N	×
HarrisonSta, Tallahatchie NW	250
● Harrison, Jefferson.....SW	500
Harrisville, Simpson.......... S	200
Hashuqua, Noxubee......... E	150
Hassie, Oktibbeha.......... E	×
Hatchie, Tippah.......... N	×
● Hattiesburgh, Perry.....SE	1,172
Hatton, Yalobusha..........N	×
Havre, Panola.......... N	×
● *Hayes*, Jefferson..........SW	25
● Haynes Bluff, Warren.... W	50
Hays, Scott..........C	×
Hays City, Jefferson..........SW	36
Hays Landing, Issaquena.. W	50
Hays' Mill, (see Glenville)...	×
Hazel Dell, Prentiss..........NE	12
● **Hazelhurst**, Copiah..SW	1,800
Heathman, Sun Flower.... W	×
Heath's Store, (see Her'nville)	×
Heathville, Tippah..........N	×
Heathville, Benton..........N	×
Hebron, Lawrence..........S	300
● Heidelberg, Jasper........E	216
● Helm, Washington..........W	25
Hemingway, Carroll..........C	30
Henderson, Wayne..........SE	30
● *Henderson Point*, H'r's'n SE	×
He-No, Harrison..........SE	×
Henryville, Clay.......... E	×
Herbert, Kemper.......... E	×
● Hermanville, Claiborne. SW	50
● **Hernando**, DeSoto..... N	402

Place	Pop.
Hesterville, Attala.......... C	18
● Hickory, Newton.......... E	300
● Hickory Flat, Benton..... N	293
Hickory Grove, Oktibbeha..E	48
Hickory Plains, Prentiss..NE	30
Hidi Landing, (see Pluto)....	×
Higdon, Copiah.......... SW	32
High Hill, Leake..........C	20
Highland, Tishomingo.....NE	40
Highland Station, Hancock.S	10
Hightown, Alcorn..........NE	72
● Hillhouse, Coahoma....NW	×
Hillsborough, Scott.......... C	112
● Hillsdale, Pearl River.....S	25
Hillside, Tishomingo......NE	×
Hilton, Yazoo.......... W	18
Hinkle, Alcorn..........NE	10
Hinton, Perry..........SE	×
Hinze, Winston..........E	×
Hohenlinden, Webster......C	10
Holder, LaFayette..........N	×
Holladay Chickasaw..........N	×
● Hollandale, Washington..W	[illegible]
Hollands, Sharkey.........W	[illegible]
Hollands Landing, Sharkey W	240
Hollingworth Store, C'p'h.SW	30
Hollis, Calhoun..........N	×
Holly Grove, (see Indianola)..	×
Holly Ridge, Sun Flower... W	×
● *Holly Ridge*, Washington W	×
● **Holly Springs**, M'shall N	2,24[illegible]
● Hollywood, Tunica.....NW	50
Holmesville, Pike..........S	150
● Home Park, Yazoo.......W	50
Homestead, Scott..........C	×
Homewood, Scott.......... C	50
Homochitto, Franklin....SW	48
Hood, (see Webb)..........	×
Hoods Station, Washington W	20
Hooker, Lawrence..........S	200
Hookston, Lauderdale..........E	36
Hope, Neshoba..........E	×
Hopewell, Calhoun..........N	30
Horaceville, Scott..........C	×
Hordville, Smith..........C	×
● Horn Lake, DeSoto.......N	50
Horns, Leake..........C	40
Houlka, Chickasaw.......... N	99
House, Neshoba..........E	36
Houston, Chickasaw......N	89[illegible]
Howard, Holmes..........C	20
Howell, Jackson..........SE	×
Hudeyville, Wilkinson....SW	×
Hudson Dam, Tunica....NW	×
● Hudsonville, Marshall....N	7[illegible]
Hulberton, Coahoma.....NW	×
Humphreys, Claiborne....SW	1[illegible]
● Huntington, Bolivar......W	[illegible]5[illegible]
● *Huntington Junc.*, Wash. W	×
Huntsville, Montgomery....C	50
Huntsfield Landing, Le Fl'e C	24
Huron, Amite..........SW	×
Hurricane, DeSoto.......... N	×
Hurricane, Warren.......... W	175
Hurricane Creek, Laud'rd'e E	×
Hurst, Amite..........SW	22
Husapuckena, Bolivar..... W	[illegible]
Hutchins, Adams..........SW	120
Idlewild, Le Flore..........C	×
Independence, Tate..........N	7[illegible]
Indian Bayou, (see Indianola)	×
Indian Creek, (see R'b'n'ville)	×
● **Indianola**, Sun Flower W	249
● Ingleside, Claiborne.....SW	1[illegible]
Ingomar, Issaquena.......W	×
● *Ingomar* Pontotoc..........N	×
Ingomar, Union.......... N	×
Ingraham, Itawamba..... NE	×
Ingram's Mill, DeSoto......N	2[illegible]
Irwin, Tate..........N	×
Ita, Itawamba..........NE	×
● Itta Bena, Le Flore.......C	×
Ituma, Holmes..........C	1[illegible]
● **Iuka**, Tishomingo..... NE	1,01[illegible]
Jacinto, Alcorn.......... NE	100
● **Jackson**, Hinds.......W	5,920
Jackson Point, Adams....SW	×
Jacksonville, Kemper.......E	15
Jaketown, Washington.....W	×
James, Washington........ W	15
Java, Neshoba.......... E	×
Jaynesville, Simpson.......S	10[illegible]
Jeannette, Adams........ SW	×
Jefferson, Carroll.......... C	[illegible]0
Jerico, Itawamba......... NE	×
Jessamine, Jefferson......SW	1[illegible]
Jewell's Hill, Jasper........ E	3[illegible]

Johns, Rankin..............C ×
Johnson Station, Linc'nSW 12
Johnston's Station, Pike.... S 8
Johnsonville, Sun Flower..W 10
Joiner, Noxubee............E ×
Jones Bayou, (see Shaw's St'n) ×
Jonesborough, Tippah......N 1
● Jonestown, Coahoma...NW 28
Jonesville, Hinds...........W ×
Jordan River Bay, (see Kiln) ×
Juliet, Alcorn..............NE 1
Jupiter, Simpson............ 1
Juniper Grove, Pearl River. S ×
Kahnville, Amite.........SW 30
Katzenmier, Warren.......W ×
Kearney, Yazoo............W ×
Keen, (see French Camps)... ×
● Keirn, Holmes............C ×
Kellis' Store, Kemper.......E 60
Kellum, Alcorn...........NE ×
Kelly, DeSoto...............N 15
Kelly's Store, Attala.......C ×
Kemper Springs, Kemper..E ×
Kemperton, Kemper........E ×
Kenaga, Choctaw...........C 10
Kendrick, Alcorn..........NE ×
Kennedy'sStore, (seeRaraAvis) ×
Kennollia, Franklin.......SW 36
Kentuctah, Madison........C ×
Kentucky Bend, Wash'gt'n W ×
KentuckyLand'g, (seeBolivar) ×
● Kenwood, Washington...W ×
Keownville, Union..........N 25
● Kewanee, Lauderdale.....E ×
Kibberville, Franklin......SW ×
Kienstra, Adams..........SW 20
Kienstra's Store, Adams..SW ×
Kilgore, LaFayette.........N ×
● Kilmichael, Montgomery. C 60
Kiln, Hancock.............. S ×
Kimball's Store, Hancock.. S ×
King, Rankin...............C 15
Kingston, Adams.........SW 20
Kinion, Amite............SW ×
Kinlock, Sun Flower...... W ×
Kinsale, Sharkey...........W 35
Kirby, Webster............. C ×
Kirksy, Panola.............. N ×
Kirkville, Itawamba......NE ×
Kirksville, Lauderdale......E ×
Kirkwood, Madison..........C 68
Kittrell, Greene............ SE ×
Knight's Ferry, (see Courtl'd) ×
Knight's Mills, Jones......SE ×
● Knoxville, Franklin.... SW 91
● **Kosciusko**, Attala......C 394
Kosciusko Junction, H'm's.C ×
Kossuth, Alcorn...........NE 63
Kuhns, Bolivar..............W ×
● Lacey, Hancock .... S 30
Lackie, Monroe...........NE ×
LaFayette Springs, LaF'y'e. N 100
La Grange, Choctaw.........C 5
● Lake, Scott................C 250
Lake Beulah, Bolivar......W ×
Lake Burnside, Neshoba....E 36
LakeCharles, (seeMalone'sL'nd'g) ×
Lake City, Yazoo............W 25
Lake Como, Jasper.........E 150
● *Lake Cormorant*, DeSoto. N 60
Lake Creswell, Panola......N ×
● Lake View, DeSoto.......N ×
● Lake Washington, Wash'n W 300
● Lamar, Benton............N 50
Lambkin's Store, (seeCharlest'n) ×
Lamb's Land., (seeDeSotoFront) ×
Lamb's Mill, Copiah......SW ×
Lameta, Leake..............C ×
● Lamont, Bolivar......... W 40
Lancelot, Simpson...........S 35
Langside, Wilkinson......SW ×
La Place, Lauderdale.......E ×
● Lauderdale Sta., LauderdaleE 322
● Laurel, Jones.............SE 150
Laurel Hill, Neshoba........E 75
● Lawrence, Newton........E 135
Law's Hill, Marshall........ N 25
Leaf, Greene................SE 50
Leakesville, Greene....SE 60
● Learned, Hinds............W 119
Leatherman's Landing, (see ×
Othello) .... ×
Leaton, Amite............... SW 40
Lebanon, (see Waterford).... ×
Leconte, Tippah............ N ×
● Lee, Jefferson............SW 60
Leesburg, Rankin...........C 80
Leesburg, Washington......W ×
● Le Flore, Grenada.........N ×
Lehrton, Sun Flower.......W 25
Leighton, Lee..........NE ×
● Leland, Washington......W 55
Lena, Leake.................C 50
Lenox, Union...............N 30
Leo, Warren................W 275
Leonia, Jasper...............E ×
Leota Landing, Washington. W 200
Lespideza, Panola.......... N ×
Leverett, Tallahatchie....NW 48
Lewis, Jackson.............SE ×
Lewisburgh, De Soto........N 15
● **Lexington**, Holmes.... C 1,075
Liberty, Amite............SW 350
Liberty Hill, La Fayette.... N 10
Liddell, Montgomery....... C ×
Lightville, Marion...........S ×
Lilian, Scott..................C 500
Linden, Holmes.............C 60
Linden, Copiah............SW 120
Line Church, Jackson.....SE ×
Line Creek, (see Cumberland) ×
Linden Landing, Yazoo.... W 48
Linton, Clarke...............E ×
Linwood, (see Senatobia)..... ×
● *Lisk*, Lauderdale..........E ×
Little Black, Webster.......C ×
● Little, Bolivar............W ×
Little Springs, Franklin.. SW 189
Live Oak, Pike............. S ×
● Livingston, Madison...... C 150
Lizard Creek, (see Delay) .... ×
Lizelia, Lauderdale..........E 30
Loakfoma, Winston.........E ×
● Lobdell, Bolivar..........W ×
Loch Leven, (see Artonish)... ×
● Lockhart, Lauderdale.....E 150
Lodi, Montgomery.......... C 160
Logtown, Hancock..........S 353
Lonestar, Tippah........... N 48
● Long Beach, Harrison... SE 35
Longtown, Panola..........N 50
● Longview, Oktibbeha.....E ×
Longville, Lee.............NE ×
● Longwood, Washington..W 180
Lonoke, Benton............ N ×
Looxahoma, Tate...........N 97
Lorenzen, Sharkey......... W 30
● *Lost Gap*, Lauderdale.....E ×
Lottville, Madison...........C 18
Louisville, Winston......E 484
● Love's Station, De Soto...N 35
Lowrey, Tippah.............N ×
Loyd, Calhoun..............N 90
Lucern, Newton............ E ×
Lucile, Lauderdale..........E ×
Lucknow, Rankin...........C 23
Ludlow, Scott................C 150
● Lula, Coahoma .... NW ×
● *Lula*, Tunica...........NW ×
● Lumberton, Pearl River..S 500
Luxapelia, Lowndes.........E ×
Luxembourg, Issaquena....W 28
Lyle's Store, Lauderdale....E ×
Lynchburg, (see Horn Lake). ×
Lynn Creek, Noxubee...... E ×
Lynnwood, Rankin..........C 38
● Lyon, Coahoma......... NW 200
McAdams, Attala........... C ×
● *McAnerney*, Carroll...... C ×
McBride, Jefferson........SW 30
● McCaleb, Claiborne.....SW 6
McCall Creek, Franklin...SW 68
● McCarley, Carroll.........C ×
● McClure, Pearl River.....S ×
● McComb, Pike............S 2,383
McCondy, Chickasaw....... N 250
● McCool, Attala............C 246
McCormick Store, (seeHeld'b'g)
McCown, Lowndes..........E ×
McDonald's Mills, Perry.. SE ×
McDonald's Store, Jasper...E ×
● *McGee's*, Holmes..........C ×
McGehee L'nd'g., (see Terrene) ×
● *McIntyre*, Lowndes...... E ×
McKinney, (see Days) .... ×
McLemore, Coahoma.... NW ×
● McNair, Jefferson...... SW 75
● *McNeil*, LeFlore......... C ×
McNeill, Pearl River........S ×
● McNutt, LeFlore..........C 50
● *McRaven*, Hinds.........W 15
McVille, Attala...............C 58
McWhorter's, (see RedLand).. ×
Mabel, Jasper...............E 30
● Maben, Oktibbeha.........E ×
Macedonia, (see Sherman)... ×
Macedonia, Noxubee...... .E ×
Macksmith, Lawrence...... S ×
● **Macon**, Noxubee........E 1,565
Madden, Leake..............C 25
● Madison Station, Madison. C 100
Magee, Simpson.............S 35
● *Magenta*, Washington....W ×
Magna Vista, Issaquena...W ×
Magnolia, Coahoma......NW 72
● **Magnolia**, Pike.........S 676
Maharris, Copiah..........SW 25
● Mahon, Marshall..........N ×
● *Malone*, Marshall.........N ×
Malone's L'nd'g, CoahomaNW 20
Mana Vista, Issaquena....W ×
Manning, Tippah.......... N ×
Mannsdale, Madison....... C ×
Mantachie, Itawamba.....NE ×
Many Plantation, IssaquenaW ×
Maple Springs, LaFayette..N ×
Marcella, Holmes.......... C 16
Marianna, Marshall.........N ×
Marietta, Prentiss........ NE 100
● **Marion Sta., Lauderdale**..E 300
Marksville, Holmes......... C 30
Marshall Institute, (see Rossville, Tenn.).............. × ×
● Martin, Claiborne.......SW 76
● Martinsville, Copiah.... SW 125
Marydell, Leake.............C 12
● *Marye*, LeFlore ....C ×
● *Maryland*, LeFlore.......C ×
Masengale, Jasper...........E ×
Mashulavile, Noxubee.......E 100
Mason's L'nd'g, Washingt'nW ×
Masonton, Bolivar..........W 20
Mastodon, Panola.......... N 20
● *Matagordia*, Coahoma. NW ×
Matherville, Wayne....... SE ×
● Mathiston, Webster.......C 5
Matilda, Alcorn.......... NE ×
Matthews, Calhoun.........N ×
Matthews' Bend, Wash'gt'n. W ×
Mattie, Quitman..........NW ×
● Maxime, Bolivar.........W ×
Maxwell, Benton...........N ×
Mayersville, Issaquena. W 300
Mayfield, Montgomery......C 30
● Mayhew's Sta., Lowndes..E 106
Meadows Mills, Perry.....SE ×
Meadville, Franklin... SW 150
Mechanicsburgh, Yazoo....W 100
Medlar, Alcorn........... NE 96
● *Melrose*, Jones..........SE ×
Melrose, (see Stormville).... ×
Melrose, Panola............ N ×
Meridian, Lauderdale....E 10,624
● Merigold, Bolivar........ W 20
Merora, Tishomingo...... NE 25
Merwin, Amite............SW 125
Methena, Holmes...........C ×
Mhoon's L'n'd'g, Tunica..NW 120
● Mhoon's Valley, Clay..... E ×
● Michigan City, Benton....N 129
Mico, Jones.................SE ×
● Midway, Hinds...........W 125
● Mileston, Holmes......... C 28
Milesville, Holmes.......... C ×
Milldale, Neshoba...........E 50
● Miller, De Soto...........N 12
Millican, Prentiss.........NE ×
Millsaps, Copiah.......... SW ×
Millville, Madison...........C 50
Milton, Hancock............ S ×
Minerva, Montgomery...... C ×
● Minter City, Le Flore......C 50
Missionary, Jasper.........E ×
● **Mississippi City**, Harrison......................SE 534
Misterton, Grenada.........N ×
Miston, Itawamba.........NE 44
● *Mitchell*, Hancock........ S ×
Mitchell, Tippah............N ×
Mitchell's Mills, Attala.....C ×
Mitchell'sCr.Rds., (see Crevi). ×
Mize, Smith.................C 36
Modoc, Washington........W 25
Mogul, Pike..................S ×
Molino, Union..............N 30
Money, Carroll..............C 10
Money, Yalobusha..........N ×
Monroe, Perry..............SE 25
Monterey, Rankin...........C 42
Monte Vista, Webster.......C ×

● Montgomery, Lincoln...SW 100
Monticello, Lawrence.... S 600
Montochie, Itawamba.....NE 500
Montpelier, Clay...........E ×
Montrose, Jasper...........E 25
● *Moore's*, Bolivar.........W ×
Moore's Mills, Newton......E ×
Mooretown, DeSoto.........N ×
Mooreville, Lee...........NE 70
● Moorhead, Sun Flower...W ×
● *Moreno*, Coahoma......NW ×
● *Morey*, Yazoo............W ×
Morgan, (see Senatobia)..... ×
Morgan's Fork, Franklin SW 300
Morganville, La Fayette....N ×
Morriston, Perry.......... SE ×
Morrow, Lauderdale........ E ×
● Morton, Scott............ C 200
Mortondale, (see Sims)...... ×
Moscos, Covington.......... S ×
Moscow, Kemper........... E 100
● Moselle, Jones...........SE 50
Moss Point, Jackson.......SE 2,500
Mosstown, Hinds...........W ×
Mound Bayou, Bolivar......W 25
Mound City, Bolivar........W 15
Mound Landing, Bolivar... W 30
Mound Plant'n, Jefferson SW 120
Mount Carmel, Covington...S 225
Mount Hope, Copiah......SW ×
Mount Nebo, Kemper.......E 10
Mount Nebo, (see Hatton)....
Mount Olive, Covington.....S 200
Mount Pleasant, Marshall... N 110
Mount Vernon, Newton....E ×
Mount Zion, Pike........... S 65
Mount Zion, Simpson........S 35
Mud Creek, Pontotoc....... N ×
Mulberry, Marion...........S ×
● Muldon, Monroe........ NE 50
● Muldrow Station, Okitibb'a E ×
Murphreesborough, Tallahatchie.................NW ×
Murphy, Washington.......W ×
Murry, Tate..................N ×
● Myles, Copiah..........SW 25
Myrick, Jones.............. SE ×
Myrleville, Yazoo.......... W ×
● Myrtle, Union............ N 100
Nanachehaw, Warren...... W 10
Napoleon, Hancock.........S ×
● Narkeeta, Kemper........E 200
● **Natchez**, Adams......SW 10,101
Nations, Montgomery...... C ×
Neals, Chickasaw...........N ×
Neblett's L'd'g, (see Lobdell Sta.) ×
● Nesbitt, De Soto..........N 152
● Nettleton, Lee.......... NE 500
Nevada, Hinds..............W 50
● **New Albany**, Union...N 548
Newbell, Warren............W 25
New Era, Sharkey.........W ×
New Harmony, (see Nesbitt). ×
New Hope, Lowndes.........E ×
New Hope, (see Malone's L'd'g) ×
New Ireland, Newton ......E ×
Newman, Hinds............W 100
● *Newman's* Warren.......W ×
New Port, Attala............C 52
New Prospect, Choctaw.....C 150
New Site, Prentiss......... NE 20
● Newton, Newton..........E 400
Newtonville, Attala.......... C 62
New Town L'd'g, Warren.. W 300
Nibletts, Washington........W ×
● Nicholson, Hancock.......S 100
Nicksville, Marshall........ N ×
● *Nine Mile Cross.*, Adams SW ×
Nitta Yuma, Sharkey.......W 100
● *Nittayuma*, Washington. W ×
Noah, La Fayette...........N ×
Norfield, Lincoln.......... SW ×
Norfolk, De Soto............N 30
Norfolk Landing, De Soto..N 12
Norris, Scott................C ×
North Bend, Neshoba.......E ×
North Bogue Chitto, Neshoba E ×
North Mt. Pleasant, (see Mt. Pleasant).................. ×
Norton, Claiborne........ SW 60
Noxapater, Winston........ E ×
Nunnery, Amite.......... SW 30
Oak Grove, (see Collierv'e, Tenn.) ×
Oak Grove, Kemper........ E 47
Oak Hill, (see Bruce).......... ×
● Oakland, Yalobusha...... N 327
● Oak Lawn, Claiborne... SW 25

● Oakley, Hinds............ W 100
Oakohay, Covington.........S 12
Oak Ridge, Warren.........W 200
Oak Ridge, Leake...........C ×
Oaks, Madison............. C ×
Oak Vale, Lawrence.........S ×
Oak Wood, Bolivar.........W ×
● Ocean Springs, Jackson. SE 1,148
Ocobla, Neshoba............E ×
Ofahoma, Leake.............C 30
Offutt, Washington.........W 28
O. K., Tunica.............NW 20
Okachickama, (see Coffeeville) ×
● *Okahola*, Marion...........S ×
● *Okatibbee*, Lauderdale.... E ×
● Okolona, Chickasaw......N 2,099
Oktibbeha, Kemper.........E ×
Oktoc, Oktibbeha........... E 50
Old Cairo, Prentiss........NE ×
Old Franklin, Simpson......S 50
Old Hickory, Simpson....... S 63
Old Salem, Carroll.......... C ×
Olio, Amite.............. SW 25
● Olive Branch, De Soto....N 199
Olney, Neshoba............. E ×
O'Neal's, Amite.............SW ×
Ophelia, Marion............ S 15
Ora, Covington..............S 28
● Orange Grove, Jackson..SE 50
Orienta, Union..............N ×
Orion, Marshall.............N 10
Orizaba, Tippah.............N 30
● Orvisburgh, Pearl River...S 50
Orwood, La Fayette..........N 25
● Osborn, Oktibbeha........E ×
Osceola, Warren.............W ×
● Osyka, Pike................ S 742
Othello, (see Robinsonville) .. ×
Otho, Jasper................ E ×
● Overbey, Simpson.......... S ×
Overbey Station, Simpson...S 72
Overton, Alcorn.......... NE ×
Owen, Tunica..............NW ×
● Owens, Holmes........... C 200
Owensville, De Soto.........N ×
Oxberry, Grenada............ N ×
● **Oxford**, La Fayette..... N 1,546
Pace, Perry.................SE ×
● Pachuta, Clarke........... E 50
Palalta, (see Minter City)..... ×
Palestine, Hinds..............W ×
Palestine, (see Coldwater) ... ×
Palmer's Mill, (see Pittsboro) ×
● Palmetto Home, Yazoo.. W 100
Palmyra, Warren.............W 20
Palo Alto, Clay...............E 50
Palona, Leake................C 25
● Panther Burn, Sharkey.. W 50
Paris, La Fayette........... N 150
Parker, Clay.................E ×
● *Parkers*, Prentiss.......NE ×
Parker's, Yazoo..............W 50
Parksplace, Panola.......... N ×
Parmitchie, Alcorn........ NE ×
Parole Landing, Holmes.... C ×
● *Parsons*, Grenada..........N ×
Pascagoula, Jackson.......SE 350
Pass Bridge, (see Lula)....... ×
● Pass Christian, Harrison. SE 1,705
Passmore, Madison......... C 18
Passonia, Madison........... C 18
Patterson, Coahoma.......NW 18
Paulding, Jasper.........E 300
Paulette, Noxubee...........E ×
Paynes, Tallahatchie..... NW ×
Peach Creek, Panola.........N ×
Pearce, Yazoo...............W 22
Pearceville, (see Montochie).. ×
Pea Ridge, Kemper.........E ×
● *Pearl*, Hinds...............W ×
Pearl, Simpson...............S 25
Pearlington, Hancock.......S 1,000
● Pearson, Rankin...........C 75
Peden, Kemper.............E 100
● Peete, Grenada............N ×
Pegram, Benton.............N ×
Peeler's Landing, Warren..W 30
● Pelahatchee, Rankin......C 139
● *Pelahatchee Depot*, Rankin C 300
Penn, Lowndes..............E ×
● Penton, De Soto...........N 120
● Percy, Washington.......W 75
Perkinston, Harrison.......SE 25
Perkinsville, Winston.......E 50
Perryville, Winston..........N ×
Perth, Jefferson...........SW 100
● Perthshire, Bolivar...... W ×

● Pettit, Washington.......W 80
Phalia, Bolivar..............W 15
● Pheba, Clay................E ×
Philadelphia, Neshoba..E 100
Phœnix, Yazoo...............W 60
● Picayune, Hancock....... S 22
Picayune Springs, Harrison SE 10
● Pickens, Holmes...........C 500
Pickwick, Marion............S ×
Piketon, Scott...............C ×
Pinckneyville, Wilkinson.SW 68
Pine Bluff, Clay..............E 50
Pine Bluff, Copiah........ SW 72
Pine Grove, Benton......... N 30
Pine Grove, Simpson........ S 25
Pine Mountain, (see Holly Springs)..................... ×
Pine Ridge, Greene........SE 25
Pine Ridge, Copiah....... SW 25
Pine Spring, Lee............NE ×
Pine Valley, Yalobusha.....N 25
Pineville, Smith.............C 60
Pink, Rankin................ C ×
Pinnellville, Jones.........SE 36
Pinos, Jones................SE ×
Pinto, Choctaw..............C 5
● Piotona, Marion...........S 50
Pitts, Calhoun...............N ×
Pittsboro, Calhoun.......N 400
P. K., Jasper................E ×
● Plantersville, Lee........NE 12
Plattsburgh, Winston.......E 500
Pleasant Grove, Panola.....N 40
Pleasant Hill, De Soto...... N 250
Pleasant Mound, Panola...N ×
Pleasanton, Itawamba....N ×
Pleasant Ridge, Itawamba NE 60
Pleasant Springs, Kemper. E ×
Plenatude, (see Fairview).... ×
Plum Bluff, Jackson...... SE ×
Plum Point, De Soto........N ×
Pluto, Holmes...............C 80
Plymouth, Pontotoc........ N ×
Poagville, Tate............. N ×
● Pocahontas, Hinds....... W 70
Point Chicot, Washington..W ×
● *Pointevant*, Marion.......S ×
Pokal, Simpson.............. S ×
Polk's Landing, (see Robinsonville).................... ×
Polkville, Smith.............C 183
Ponta, Lauderdale............E ×
Pontocola, Pontotoc.........N ×
Pontotoc, Pontotoc.......N 535
Poolville, Union.............N ×
● Pope's Depot, Panola.....N 200
Poplar, Tate.................N ×
Poplar Corner, De Soto.....N 10
Poplar Creek, Montgomery. C 50
Poplar Springs, Union...... N 50
Poplar Springs, Pontotoc.. N ×
● **Poplarville**, Pearl River S 232
Porterton, La Fayette....... N ×
Porterville, Kemper........ E ×
● **Port Gibson**, Claiborne SW 1,524
Post Oak, Yalobusha....... N ×
● Potts Camp, Marshall.... N ×
Prairie Point, Noxubee..... E 75
● Prairie Station, Monroe. NE 90
Prattsville, De Soto........ N ×
Prattville, Madison..........C 18
Preston, Kemper............ E ×
Primmton, Wilkinson.... SW 20
Primrose, (see Pontotoc)..... ×
Prince, Kemper.............E 30
Prismatic, Kemper.......... E 30
Progression Wayne........ SE 30
Prospect, Newton.......... NE ×
Providence, Grenada....... N 18
Provine's Store, (see Cole's Creek)................... ×
Public Pond, Wilkinson.. SW ×
Prudeville, Pontotoc........N ×
Puckett, Rankin .... C ×
Pueblo, Pontotoc........... N ×
Pugh, Winston...............E 30
Pulaski, Scott................C ×
● *Purnell*, Le Flore...........C ×
● Purvis, Marion.............S 287
Pushmataha, Coahoma... NW ×
● Quincy, Monroe.........NE 40
● *Quinn's Switch*, Pike......S ×
● **Quitman**, Clarke....... E 395
Quiver, Sun Flower.........W ×
Rabbit Harbor, Jefferson. SW ×
Raburnville, Itawamba... NE ×

Raggio's Landing, (see Australia) ×
Rainer's, Newton..........E ×
Rainey, Tate..........N ×
Raleigh, Smith..........C 350
Ramsay, Harrison..........SE 33
Randall's Bluff, Winston....E ×
● *Rankin*, Rankin..........C ×
Randolph, Pontotoc..........N 50
Raper, Lee..........NE ×
Rara Avis, Itawamba.....NE ×
Ratliff, Itawamba..........NE ×
Rayburn, Hinds..........W ×
● **Raymond**, Hinds......W 000
Reagan, Calhoun..........N ×
● Red Banks, Marshall.....N 50
Red Creek, Jackson..........SE ×
Red Cross, (see Minter City). ×
Redding, Grenada..........N ×
Redding, Webster..........C ×
Reddoch, Covington..........S 25
Red Land, Pontotoc..........N 50
● Red Lick, Jefferson.....SW 50
Redmondville, Yazoo......W 50
Redstar, Lincoln..........SW ×
Redtop, Pearl River..........S ×
● Redwood, Warren..........W 25
Rees Store, Monroe.......NE ×
Reform, Choctaw..........C 5
Refuge, Washington..........W 30
Reganton, Claiborne......SW ×
Reid, Calhoun..........N 24
Renfroe, Leake..........C 30
Reno, Monroe..........NE ×
Renovo, Bolivar..........W ×
Rescue, Coahoma..........NW ×
Revive, Madison..........C 15
Rex, Oktibbeha..........E ×
● *Reynolds*, Monroe......NE ×
Reynolds, Panola..........N 32
Rials, Simpson..........S 25
Riceville, Pearl River.......S ×
Rich, Coahoma..........NW 120
● Richardson, Hancock.....S ×
● Richburgh, Marion..........S 20
Richland, Holmes..........C 100
Richmond, Covington.......S 18
Richmondlee, Lee..........NE 25
Ridge, Chickasaw..........N 30
Ridgeville, Tippah..........N ×
● Rienzi, Alcorn..........NE 350
Riggins, Monroe..........NE ×
Riley, Attala..........C ×
Rio, Kemper..........E 200
● **Ripley**, Tippah..........N 574
● Rising Sun, Le Flore......C ×
Riverside, Quitman......NW ×
● *Riverside Junction*, Sh'r'y W ×
Riversville, Newton..........E ×
Riverton, Bolivar..........W 10
● *Rixwood*, Le Flore..........C ×
Robertson, Clay..........E ×
Robertsonville, Coahoma. NW ×
● *Robinsons*, Tallahatchie NW ×
Robinson Springs, Madison. C ×
● Robinsonville, Tunica.. NW 50
Rockport, Copiah..........SW 100
Rocky Ford, (see Walton)..... ×
Rocky Springs, Claiborne. SW 50
Rodney, Jefferson..........SW 702
Roebuck, Le Flore..........C ×
Rokeby, Yazoo..........W 120
● **Rolling Fork**, Sharkey W 200
Rome, Winston..........E 30
Roscoe, Newton..........E ×
Rosebloom, Tallahatchie. NW ×
Rose Bower, De Soto.....N ×
● **Rosedale**, Bolivar......W 376
Rose Hill, Amite..........SW 200
Rose Hill, Jasper..........E ×
Roseneath, Yazoo..........W 69
● *Rosetta*, Amite..........SW ×
Rosetta, Wilkinson..........SW ×
Ross Mill, (see Cascilla)...... ×
● *Round Lake*, Bolivar.... W ×
Roundlake, Bolivar..........W ×
Rotten Bayou, (see Kiln).... ×
● Roxie, Franklin..........SW 30
Roy, Clarke..........E ×
Royal, Smith..........C ×
Ruckersville, Tippah..........N 30
● *Runneymead*, Le Flore...C ×
Rural, Montgomery..........C 36
Rural Hill, Winston..........E ×
Rushing's Store, Lauderdale E 48
Rushville, Kemper..........E ×
Russell, Lauderdale..........E ×
Russellville, Warren.......W 15

Mississippi

● Russum, Claiborne.....SW 15
Ruth, Lincoln..........SW ×
Ryan, Franklin..........SW 12
Sabougla, Calhoun..........N 10
Saint Anns, Leake..........C 20
St. Catherine's Bend, Ada's NE ×
● Saint Elmo, Claiborne.. SW 50
Saints Rest, Sun Flower....W 15
Salem, Benton..........N 25
● Sallis, Attala..........C 156
● Saltillo, Lee..........NE 400
● Sandersville, Jones......SE 300
Sandpoint, Smith..........C 22
Santee, Covington..........S 120
● Sapa, Webster..........C 5
● **Sardis**, Panola..........N 1,044
Sarepta, Calhoun..........N 300
Sartin's Store, Pike..........S 50
Sartinville, Pike..........S 50
Satartia, Yazoo..........W 75
Saulsbury, Lawrence..........S 32
● *Sawyers*, Montgomery....C ×
● Scooba, Kemper..........E 350
● *Scott*, Bolivar..........W ×
● **Scranton**, Jackson.... SE 1,353
Searcy, Marshall..........N ×
Sebastopol, Scott..........C ×
Selden, Tippah..........N 10
● **Senatobia**, Tate..........N 1,077
Sera, Amite..........SW ×
Sessumsville, Oktibbeha.....E 10
Seven Pines, Carroll..........C ×
Sevier, Lee..........NE 36
● *Shackelford*, Holmes......C ×
Shackelford's Lake, (see Falsonia ×
Shady Grove, Jasper..........E 36
● Shannon, Lee..........NE 329
Shannondale, (see Emmavi'e) ×
Sharkey, Tallahatchie....NW 90
Sharkey Station, Sharkey..W 42
Sharon, Madison..........C 100
Sharpsburgh, Madison......C 60
● Shaw, Bolivar..........W 201
Shawnee, Benton..........N ×
Shaw's Store, Jefferson...SW 30
Shealey, Newton..........E ×
Shelby Creek, Tippah..........N ×
● *Shelby*, Bolivar..........W ×
● Shell Mound, Le Flore....C 150
Shelton, Jefferson..........SW ×
● Sheppardtown, Le Flore.. C 30
● Sherard, Coahoma..... NW ×
● Sherman, Pontotoc..........N 79
Shiloh Landing, Issaquena. W 100
Ship, Webster..........C ×
Shipland, Issaquena..........W 20
Shivers, Simpson..........S 15
Shoccoe, Madison..........C ×
Shongelo, Smith..........C 50
Short, Tishomingo..........NE ×
Show Creek, Benton..........N 78
Shrock, Attala..........C 50
● Shubuta, Clarke..........E 589
● Shuqualak, Noxubee..........E 601
Siberia, (see Itta Bena)...... ×
● Siding, Lauderdale..........E 200
● Sidon, Le Flore..........C 119
Sierra, Neshoba..........E ×
Silent Shade, Holmes..........C 48
Siloam, Clay..........E 75
Silver City, Yazoo..........W 200
Silver Creek, Lawrence..........S 250
Silver Springs, Tippah......N 10
Similo, Lincoln..........SW ×
Simpson, Quitman..........NW ×
Simpsonville, (see Courtland) ×
Sims, Attala..........C 38
Singleton, Winston..........E 100
Skipwith's L'd'g, Issaquena W 250
Slabtown, (see Dubb's)....... ×
Slate Spring, Calhoun......N 300
Slayden's Crossing, Marshall N ×
● Smedes, Sharkey..........W 16
Smith, Neshoba..........E ×
Smithburgh, Pike..........S 15
Smithdale, Amite..........SW 22
Smith's Crossing, De Soto..N 24
Smith's Mills, Carroll..........C 10
● Smith's Station, Hinds.... W 50
Smithville, Monroe..........NE 200
Smyrna, Attala..........C 25
Snowville, Choctaw..........C ×
Sonora, Chickasaw..........N ×
Soso, Jones..........SE ×
● *Soudan*, Lincoln..........SW ×
Southland, Prentiss..........NE 36

Mississippi

Spanish Moss Bend, Wash'n W ×
Sparta, Chickasaw..........N 500
Spay, Choctaw..........C 24
Spencer, Copiah..........SW ×
Spinks, Kemper..........E ×
Spivey, Newton..........E ×
Splunge, Monroe..........NE ×
Sporine, Bolivar..........W ×
Spring Cottage, Marion......S 32
Spring Creek, Webster..........C ×
● *Spring Dale*, La Fayette. N ×
Springfield, Scott..........C ×
Spring Hill, Benton..........N ×
Springport, Panola..........N ×
Spring Valley, Webster.....C 25
Spurlock, Amite..........SW 13
Stafford, Bolivar..........W 15
Stalling's Ferry, Pike..... S ×
Stamper, Newton..........E ×
● Stampley, Jefferson.....SW 24
Stamp's Landing, Wilkin'n SW 100
Standing Pine, Leake....... C 30
● Stanton, Adams..........SW 30
● **Starkville**, Oktibbeha..E 1,725
Starnes, Webster..........C ×
Star L'd'g, (see De Soto Front) ×
Star Place, Panola..........N 20
● State Line, Greene..........SE 300
Station Creek, Covington....S 78
Steel, Scott..........C ×
Steen Creek, Rankin..........C 100
Steenston, Lowndes..........E ×
Steep Bank, Rankin..........C 50
Steephill, Marion..........S 60
Stegall, (see Troy).......... ×
● *Stewart*, Webster..........C ×
Stewart, Montgomery..........C ×
Stix, Perry..........SE ×
Stockdale, Hancock..........S ×
● Stoneville, Washington... W 650
Stonewall, Harrison....... SE 200
Stonewall Landing, Holmes. C 10
Stonewall's L'd'g, (see Shell Mound) ×
● Stonewall Station, Clarke. E ×
● Stonington, Jefferson... SW 22
Stop Land., (see Mound L'd'g) ×
Stormville, Bolivar.......W 10
● Stovall, Coahoma...... NW ×
Strayhorn, Tate..........N 100
● Strongs, Monroe..........NE ×
Stump's L'd'g, Wilkinson. SW ×
● *Sturdivants*, Tallahatchie NW ×
● Sturgis, Oktibbeha..........E 203
● Sucarnoochee, Kemper... E 150
Sugg, Calhoun..........N ×
● *Sulligent*, Monroe...... NE ×
Sulphur Springs, Madison...C 85
● Summit, Pike..........S 1,587
Sumner, Tallahatchie.....NW ×
Sunflower L'd'g, Coahoma NW 30
Sunny Side, Le Flore..........C 20
Sutton, Lincoln..........SW ×
● Swain, Washington..........W 38
● Swan Lake, Tall'h'tchie NW 20
Swanzy, Lowndes..........E 60
Swayze's Ferry, Adams..SW ×
Sweatman, Montgomery.....C 48
Sweet Home, (see Grenada).. ×
● Swiftwater, Washington..W 20
Sycamore, Chickasaw...... N ×
● *Sykes*, Monroe..........NE ×
Sylvarena, Smith..........C 60
Tabbville, Chickasaw..........N ×
Tacaleeche, Benton..........N ×
● Talawah, Marion..........S 100
● *Tallahatchie*, Panola.....N ×
Tallahoma, Jones..........SE ×
Talledora, Bolivar..........W ×
Tallula, Issaquena..........W 120
Talovah, Marion..........S ×
● *Tamola*, Kemper..........E ×
Tampico, Clay..........E 30
Tarbert, Wilkinson.......SW 25
Tate's Ridge, Amite......SW ×
Tatum, Grenada..........N 10
Tatum's Store, Grenada....N 42
● Taylor, LaFayette..........N 200
Taylorsville, Smith..........C 50
● Tchula, Holmes..........C 300
● *Tchula Junction*, Holmes C ×
Teasdale, Tallahatchie....NW ×
Temperance Hill, Monroe. NE ×
Temple, Lauderdale..........E 240
Temple Union, (see Blue Sprs) ×
Teoc, Carroll..........C 10
Terrene, Bolivar..........W 10
● Terry, Hinds..........W 250

Mississippi

Place	Index	Pop.
Terza, Panola	N	×
Texas, Kemper	E	×
Thaxton, Pontotoc	N	×
Theadville, Clarke	E	×
The Gums, Panola	N	5
Theo, Alcorn	NE	×
Thomastown, Leake	C	75
Thomasville, Rankin	C	18
Thompson, Amite	SW	×
Thompson's Store, Amite	SW	10
Thompsonville, Hinds	W	20
Thornton, Holmes	C	125
Thrailkill, Montgomery	C	120
Thrasher, Prentiss	NE	×
Three Rivers, Jackson	SE	33
Thyatira, Tate	N	60
● Tibbee Station, Clay	E	75
Tilden, Itawamba	NE	36
● Tillatoba, Yalobusha	N	40
● Tillman Station, Cl'bor'e	SW	×
Tilton, Lawrence	S	18
● Tiplersville, Tippah	N	30
Tippah, Benton	N	×
Toccopola, Pontotoc	N	190
Toccopola, LaFayette	N	×
Tokio, Wayne	SE	×
Tolerville, Holmes	C	25
Tolerton, Attala	C	25
● Tomnolen, Webster	C	10
● Toomsuba, Lauderdale	E	200
Topisaw, Pike	S	20
● Topton, Lauderdale	E	×
● Torrance, Yalobusha	N	50
Torrence Station, Yalob'sha	N	90
● Tougaloo, Hinds	W	150
Travis, Amite	SW	×
Tremont, Itawamba	NE	25
Trenton, Smith	C	200
Trimcane, Oktibbeha	E	×
Trinity, Lowndes	E	×
Triune, Yazoo	W	×
Trotter's Landing, (see Busby)		×
● *Trotter's Point*, C'homa	NW	×
Troy, Pontotoc	N	175
Tryus, Lawrence	S	50
Tubbs, Monroe	NE	×
Tubby, Itawamba	NE	×
● Tucker, Neshoba	E	×
Tugaloo, Hinds	W	×
Tula, La Fayette	N	×
Tulwiler, Tallahatchie	NW	×
● Tunica, Tunica	NW	198
● **Tupelo**, Lee	NE	1,477
● *Turnbull*, Wilkinson	W	×
Turnbull's Depot, W'k'son	SW	125
Turner, Tunica	NW	×
Turner's Store, Jackson	SE	×
Turnerville, Jasper	E	60
Turnetta, Madison	C	×
● *Tuscanola*, Jones	SE	25
Tuscola, Leake	C	25
● *Tutwiler*, Tallahatchie	NW	×
Twistwood, Jasper	E	350
Tyler Town, Pike	S	100
Tyner, Jackson	SE	×
Tynes, Tishomingo	NE	×
Tyro, Tate	N	125
Udora, Lincoln	SW	×
Una, Clay	E	×
Union, Newton	E	1,000
Union Church, Jefferson	SW	150
Union Mills, Tippah	N	×
University, LaFayette	N	×
Ursino, Warren	W	60
● Utica, Hinds	W	370
● Vaiden, Carroll	C	533
● Valley, Yazoo	W	15
● *Valley Hill*, Carroll	C	×
Valley Home, (see Teasdale)		
● Valley Park, Issaquena	W	28
Valley View, (see Carrollton)		×
Vance, Newton	E	×
Vancleave, Jackson	SE	×
Van Eaton, Perry	SE	×
Vann's Mill, (see Coffeeville)		×
Van Vleet, Chickasaw	N	×
● *Van Winkle*, Hinds	W	×
● Vaughan, Yazoo	W	250
Velma, Yalobusha	N	×
Verlilia, Madison	C	×
Vernal, Greene	SE	50
Vernon, Madison	C	×
● Verona, Lee	NE	465
Veto, Franklin	SW	75
● **VICKSBURG**, Warren	W	13,373
Vickland Landing, Shar'y	W	125
● Victoria, Marshall	N	10
Victoria, Bolivar	W	24
Villa Nova, Warren	W	×
Vimville, Lauderdale	E	×
Vinton, Clay	E	×
Viola, Jasper	E	×
Virgil, Rankin	C	15
● Vosburgh, Jasper	E	300
Vowell, Winston	E	×
Waco, (see Marianna)		×
● Wahalak, Kemper	E	500
Walker, Montgomery	C	×
Walker's Bridge, Pike	S	62
● *Walker's Switch*, Tis'm'o	NE	×
Wall, Newton	E	×
Wallace, Panola	N	×
● Wallerville, Union	N	30
Wall Hill, Marshall	N	150
● *Walls*, DeSoto	N	×
● Walnut, Tippah	N	30
Walnut Grove, Leake	C	166
Walthall, Webster	C	122
Walton, LaFayette	N	48
Walton, Union	N	×
Walton's Crossing, (see Lula)		×
Wamba, Attala	C	×
Wanamaker, Tunica	NW	×
Wardwell, Calhoun	N	×
● Warrenton, Warren	W	100
● *Warsaw*, Washington	W	78
Washington, Adams	SW	175
● Waterford, Marshall	N	150
Waterhole, Marion	S	22
● Water Valley, Yalobusha	N	2,832
Watkinsville, Neshoba	E	500
Watson, Marshall	N	30
Watsonia, Sharkey	W	26
Watt's Landing, (see C'nc'rd'a)		×
● *Wautublee*, Clarke	E	×
● Waveland, Hancock	S	328
● Waverly, Clay	E	30
● **Waynesborough**, Wayne	SE	458
● Way's Bluff, Madison	C	18
● Wayside, Washington	W	25
● Webb, Tallahatchie	NW	×
Webster, Winston	E	50
Weems, Jasper	E	×
● **Weir, Choctaw**	C	30
Welch, Covington	S	×
Welcome, Scott	C	×
Wellman, Lincoln	SW	×
Wells, Attala	C	50
Wenasoga, Alcorn	NE	50
● Wesson, Copiah	SW	3,168
● West, Holmes	C	250
● *Westburgh*, Washington	W	78
West Fork, Lawrence	S	×
West Jackson, Hinds	W	×
● *West Pascagoula*, J'k'n	SE	25
● **West Point**, Clay	E	2,762
West's, Holmes	C	×
West Station, Holmes	C	250
Westside, Claiborne	SW	15
Westville, Simpson	S	600
● Wheeler, Prentiss	NE	×
Wheelerville, Jones	SE	×
Wheelerville, Covington	S	48
Whistler, Wayne	SE	×
Whitaker, Wilkinson	SW	18
White, Hinds	W	×
Whiteapple, Franklin	SW	10
White Hall Sta., (see Mound L'd'g)		
White Oak, Greene	SE	×
● *Whites*, Clay	E	×
Whites, Rankin	C	×
Whitesand, Lawrence	S	×
Whynot, Lauderdale	E	×
Wilcox, (see French Camps)		×
● Wilczinski, Washington	W	26
Wildwood, Marion	S	×
Wilkesburgh, Covington	S	55
Wilkinson, Wilkinson	SW	15
Williamsburg, Covington	S	200
Williamsville, Grenada	N	10
Willis Mills, (see Graysport)		×
Williston, Leake	C	×
Willow Spring, Harrison	SE	30
● Winchester, Wayne	SE	200
● **Winona**, Montgomery	C	1,648
Winterville, Washington	W	25
Wolf, Harrison	SE	471
Wolf River, Harrison	SE	400
Woodbine, Yazoo	W	×
Woodburn, Sun Flower	W	×
Woodland, Chickasaw	N	×
Woodson, Monroe	NE	×
● **Woodville**, Wilkinson	SW	950
Wool Market, Harrison	SE	20
Wright, Bolivar	W	10
Yale, Itawamba	NE	×
Yamacran, Hancock	S	×
● **Yazoo City**, Yazoo	W	3,286
● *Yazoo Pass*, Coahoma	NW	×
Yeagers, Adams	SW	×
Yeagersville, Grenada	N	×
Yellow Creek, Tishomingo	NE	×
Yellow Rabbit, Benton	N	×
Yocony, Itawamba	NE	×
● Yokena, Warren	W	10
Yorka, Leake	C	24
Yota, Calhoun	N	×
Youngs, Grenada	N	×
Zebulon, Attala	C	30
Zeiglerville, Yazoo	W	100
Zephyr, Copiah	SW	×
Zero, Lauderdale	E	×
Zilpha, Attala	C	23
Zion Hill, Amite	SW	2,000
Zion Seminary, Covington	S	×
Zoyd, Itawamba	NE	×

MISSOURI.

COUNTIES.	INDEX.	POP.
Adair	N	17.417
Andrew	NW	16,000
Atchison	NW	15.533
Audrain	C	22.074
Barry	SW	22.943
Barton	SW	18.504
Bates	W	32.223
Benton	C	14,973
Bollinger	SE	13,121
Boone	C	26,043
Buchanan	NW	70,100
Butler	SE	10,164
Caldwell	NW	15.152
Callaway	C	25,131
Camden	C	10,040
Cape Girardeau	SE	22,060
Carroll	N	25.742
Carter	SE	4,659
Cass	W	23,301
Cedar	W	15,620
Chariton	N	26,254
Christian	S	14,017
City of St. Louis	E	451,770
Clark	NE	15,126
Clay	NW	19,856
Clinton	NW	17,138
Cole	C	17,281
Cooper	C	22,707
Crawford	C	11.961
Dade	SW	17,526
Dallas	C	12,647
Daviess	NW	20,456
DeKalb	NW	14,539
Dent	S	12,149
Douglas	S	14,111
Dunklin	SE	15.085
Franklin	E	28,056
Gasconade	E	11.706
Gentry	NW	19,018
Greene	SW	48,616
Grundy	N	17,876
Harrison	NW	21,033
Henry	W	28,235
Hickory	C	9,453
Holt	NW	15,469
Howard	C	17,371
Howell	S	18,618
Iron	SE	9,119
Jackson	W	160,510
Jasper	SW	50,500
Jefferson	E	22,484
Johnson	W	28,132
Knox	NE	13,501
Laclede	C	14,701
LaFayette	W	30,184
Lawrence	SW	26,228
Lewis	NE	15,935
Lincoln	E	18,346
Linn	N	24,121
Livingston	N	20,668
McDonald	SW	11,283
Macon	N	30,575
Madison	SE	9,268
Maries	C	8,600
Marion	NE	26,233

Mercer	N	14,581
Miller	C	14,162
Mississippi	SE	10,134
Moniteau	C	15,630
Monroe	NE	20,790
Montgomery	E	16,850
Morgan	C	12,311
New Madrid	SE	9,317
Newton	SW	22,108
Nodaway	NW	30,914
Oregon	S	10,467
Osage	C	13,080
Ozark	S	9,795
Pemiscot	SE	5,975
Perry	SE	13,237
Pettis	C	31,151
Phelps	C	12,636
Pike	NE	26,321
Platte	NW	16,248
Polk	SW	20,339
Pulaski	C	9,387
Putnam	N	15,365
Ralls	NE	12,294
Randolph	N	24,893
Ray	NW	24,215
Reynolds	SE	6,803
Ripley	SE	8,512
Saint Charles	E	22,977
Saint Clair	W	16,747
Sainte Genevieve	E	9,883
Saint Francois	E	17,347
Saint Louis	E	36,307
Saline	C	33,762
Schuyler	N	11,249
Scotland	NE	12,674
Scott	SE	11,228
Shannon	S	8,898
Shelby	NE	15,642
Stoddard	SE	17,327
Stone	SW	7,090
Sullivan	N	19,000
Taney	S	7,973
Texas	S	19,406
Vernon	W	31,505
Warren	E	9,913
Washington	E	13,153
Wayne	SE	11,927
Webster	S	15,177
Worth	NW	8,738
Wright	S	14,484
Total		2,679,184

TOWN. COUNTY	INDEX.	POP.
Abatis, Warren	E	19
Aberdeen, Pike	NE	10
Abo, Laclede	C	15
Acasto, Clark	NE	30
Acme, Clay	NW	10
Acorn Ridge, Stoddard	SE	32
Adair, Adair	N	30
Adams, Buchanan	NW	×
● *Adams*, Jackson	W	×
Adams Mill, Jasper	SW	×
Adel, Mercer	N	10
Adox, (see Mercer)		×
● Adrian, Bates	W	613
● Advance, Stoddard	SE	200
Affton, Saint Louis	E	40
● Agency, Buchanan	NW	200
Aisle, Christian	S	×
Akard, Cedar	W	25
Akers, Shannon	S	20
● Akinsville, Morgan	C	50
Akron, Harrison	NW	45
Alamode, Reynolds	SE	32
Alanthus Grove, Gentry	NW	100
Alba, Jasper	SW	150
● **Albany**, Gentry	NW	1,334
Alberta, Henry	W	10
● *Alderney*, Saint Louis	E	×
● Aldrich, Polk	SW	100
Alexandria, Clark	NE	536
Alice, Texas	S	10
Allendale, Worth	NW	300
● Allenton, Saint Louis	E	125
● Allenville, Cape Girardeau	SE	173
Alley, Shannon	S	15
Alliance, Bollinger	NE	×
Allison, Nodaway	NW	10
● Alma, LaFayette	W	179
Almartha, Ozark	S	15
Almon, Hickory	C	40
Alpha, Grundy	N	50
● Altamont, Daviess	NW	20
Alta Vista, Daviess	NW	25
Altenburgh, Perry	SE	183
Altheim, Saint Louis	E	20
Althorpe, Linn	N	25
Alton, Oregon	S	400
Altona, Bates	W	75
● Alvord, Mercer	N	10
● Amazonia, Andrew	NW	282
Ambrose, Ozark	S	15
Americus, Montgomery	E	100
● Amity, DeKalb	NW	150
Amoret, Bates	W	650
● *Amory*, Clay	NW	×
Amsterdam, (see Burrows)		×
Amy, Howell	S	×
● Anabel, Macon	N	25
Anderson, McDonald	SW	20
● Andover, Harrison	NW	50
Andrae, Jefferson	E	×
● Annada, Pike	NE	25
● Annapolis, Iron	SE	690
Annie, Buchanan	NW	×
Anson, Clark	NE	10
Anthonie's Mill, Crawford	C	10
Antioch, Clark	NE	10
Antler, Wright	S	×
Antonia, Jefferson	E	100
Antrim, Wright	S	12
Anutt, Dent	S	50
● Apex, Lincoln	E	25
Apple Creek L'nd'g, Perry	SE	×
Applegate, Webster	S	×
Appleton, Cape Girardeau	SE	96
● Appleton City, St. Clair	W	1,081
Aptus, Washington	E	×
● Arbela, Scotland	NE	122
Arbor, Cape Girardeau	SE	32
● Arcadia, Iron	SE	408
● Archie, Cass	W	278
Arcola, Dade	SW	100
Arden, Douglas	S	25
● Ardeola, Stoddard	SE	100
Ardmore, Macon	N	300
Argentville, Lincoln	E	×
Argo, Crawford	C	20
Argola, Lewis	NE	12
● Arkoe, Nodaway	NW	50
● Arlington, Phelps	C	40
● *Arloe*, City of Saint Louis	E	×
● Armstrong, Howard	C	248
Arnica, Cedar	W	30
Arno, Douglas	S	40
Arnoldsville, Buchanan	NW	25
Arnsberg, Cape Girardeau	SE	100
Arrow Rock, Saline	C	850
Art, Newton	SW	×
Artesian Springs, Platte	NW	×
● Arthur, Vernon	W	40
Ascot, Douglas	S	×
Ash, Monroe	NE	20
● Ashburn, Pike	NE	45
Asherville, Stoddard	SE	100
● Ash Grove, Greene	SW	1,350
● Ash Hill, Butler	SE	300
Ashland, Boone	C	373
Ashley, Pike	NE	360
● Ashton, Clark	NE	75
Asper, Carroll	N	20
Astoria, Wright	S	15
● Atchison Junc., Platte	NW	65
● Athelstan, Worth	NW	150
Athens, Clark	NE	200
Atherton, Jackson	W	50
● *Atherton*, Saint Louis	E	×
● ***Atherton***, **Jackson**	W	×
● *Athol*, Bates	W	×
● Atlanta, Macon	W	200
● *Atlas*, Dent	S	×
Atoka, Laclede	C	×
Attie, Oregon	S	10
Aubrey, Johnson	W	32
Auburn, Lincoln	E	60
Aud, Osage	C	×
Augusta, (see Thayer)		×
Augusta, Saint Charles	E	291
● Aullville, LaFayette	W	300
Ault, Carroll	N	×
● Aurora, Lawrence	SW	3,482
● Aurora Springs, Miller	C	421
Austin, Cass	W	130
Austin, (see Goss)		×
● Auxvasse, Callaway	SE	305
Ava, Douglas	S	221
Avalon, Livingston	N	444
Avenue City, Andrew	NW	50
● Avert, Stoddard	SE	×
● *Avery*, Dent	S	130
Avery, Hickory	C	×
Avilla, Jasper	SW	200
Avoca, Jefferson		185
Avon, Sainte Genevieve	E	40
Avon, Cass	W	×
● *Avon*, Clay	NW	×
Azen, Scotland	NE	20
Babbtown, Osage	C	22
Bachelor, Callaway	C	26
Bacon, Moniteau	C	×
● *Baden*, Saint Louis	E	×
Bado, Texas	S	20
● Bagnell, Miller	C	30
Bahner, Pettis	C	12
Bailey, Pulaski	C	15
● *Bailey*, Jefferson	E	×
Bailey's Creek, Osage	C	40
Bainbridge, Cape Girardeau	SE	×
Bainbridge, Clinton	NW	30
Bairdstown, Sullivan	N	×
Baker, Saint Clair	W	×
Bakersfield, Ozark	S	150
Baladan, (see Indian Sprs)		×
Baldridge, Pulaski	C	77
Ballard, Bates	W	50
Ballwin, Saint Louis	E	150
Balm, Cedar	W	40
Bals, Lincoln	E	10
Bancroft, Daviess	NW	101
Bandyville, Oregon	S	×
Banty, Jasper	SW	2
● Barfield, Ripley	SE	100
● Baring, Knox	SW	266
Barkersville, Callaway	C	50
● *Barkley*, Marion	NE	×
● *Barlow*, Wayne	SE	×
● Barnard, Nodaway	NW	427
Barnesville, Macon	N	10
Barnett, Morgan	C	30
Barney, Dent	S	26
Barnumton, Camden	C	26
● *Barracks*, Saint Louis	E	×
Barren, Carter	SE	×
● Barrett Station, St. Louis	E	×
Barr's Mills, (see Hester)		×
Barry, Clay	NW	100
Barryville, Macon	N	10
● Bartlett, Shannon	S	50
Bartold, Saint Louis	E	25
Bass, Cole	C	×
Bass Mills, Greene	SW	15
● Bates City, LaFayette	W	100
Bath, Laclede	C	×
Battsville, Carroll	N	108
Bauff, Taney	S	10
Baum's Mill, (see Carrollton)		×
Baur, Gasconade	E	×
Baxter, Stone	SW	15
Bay, Gasconade	E	75
Bayfield, DeKalb	NW	15
● Beaman, Pettis	C	30
● *Bean Lake*, Platte	NW	×
Bear Branch, Linn	N	40
Bear Creek, Cedar	W	50
● *Bear Creek*, Ralls	NE	×
● *Beasley*, Pike	NE	×
Beaufort, Franklin	E	150
Beaver, Douglas	S	20
● *Beaver*, Phelps	C	10
Bebra, Morgan	C	40
● *Becker*, Franklin	E	×
● Bedford, Livingston	N	60
Bedford, Bates	W	×
● *Bedford Station*, Livi'g'n	N	×
● Bedison, Nodaway	NW	25
Bee, Cape Girardeau	SE	10
● ***Bee Creek Junction***, Buchanan	NW	×
Bee Fork, Reynolds	SE	65
Beemont, Franklin	E	50
Bee Ridge, (see Knox City)		×
Beersheba, Montgomery	E	×
Belcher, Butler	SE	×
Belew's Creek, Jefferson	E	26
● Belfast, Newton	SW	×
Belgique, Perry	SE	×
Belgrade, Washington	E	100
Bell Air, Cooper	C	35
Bellamy, Vernon	W	20
Bell City, Stoddard	SE	×
Belle, Maries	C	10
Bellefontaine, Saint Louis	E	40
Bellefonte, Pulaski	C	32
Belleview, Iron	SE	150
Belleview Springs, Jackson	W	×
Belleville, Montgomery	E	32

Place	Pop.
● *Belleville Branch*, Jasper SW	×
Bellflower, Montgomery.... E	×
Bellville Mines, Jasper....SW	1,174
● Belmont, Mississippi.... SE	250
Belt Junction, Jackson.... W	×
● *Beloit*, Barton...........SW	50
● Belton, Cass..............W	988
● *Belvidere*, Jackson.......W	×
Bem, Gasconade............ E	10
● *Bement*, Clay...........NW	×
Bembow, Marion..........NE	40
Benjamin, Lewis...........NE	50
Bennett, Ripley............SE	20
● **Benton**, Scott...........SE	2?2
● *Benton*, Saint Louis.......E	×
● Benton City, Audrain.....C	109
Bentonville, Benton.........C	×
● Berger, Franklin.........E	200
Berlin, Gentry............NW	75
● Bernie, Stoddard..........SE	×
Berryman, Crawford........C	×
● *Berryman*, Iron..........SE	65
Berthaville, Randolph......N	10
● Bertrand, Mississippi.... SE	221
● *Berwick*, Newton....... SW	10
● Bessville, Bollinger......SE	25
Best Bottom, Montgomery..E	46
● **Bethany**, Harrison... NW	1,105
Bethel, Shelby............ NE	200
Bethlehem, Montgomery....E	10
Bethpage, McDonald......SW	15
Beulah, Phelps.............C	10
Beverly, (see Anabel)........	×
● Beverly Station, Platte. NW	20
● Bevier, Macon............N	876
Bible Grove, Scotland.....NE	30
Biehle, Perry.............SE	100
● *Big Blue Junction*, Jack'n W	×
Big Creek, Texas...........S	50
● Bigelow, Holt...........NW	150
Big Lick, **Howell............S**	**×**
Big Piney, Pulaski.......... C	26
Big River Mills, St. Fran'ois. E	50
Big Spring, Montgomery....E	75
● Billings, Christian..........S	464
● Billingsville, Cooper...... C	×
Billmore, Oregon.............S	10
● Birch Tree, Shannon....... S	535
● *Bird's Mill*, Mississppi.. SE	×
● Bird's Point, Mississippi. SE	400
● Birmingham, Clay......NW	401
Bishop, Greene............SW	10
Bishops, Christian...........S	10
● Bismarck, Saint Francois. E	837
Black, Reynolds........... SE	10
Blackbird, Putnam..........N	×
Black Bridge, Saint. Charles E	×
● Blackburn, Saline.........C	372
Black Jack, Saint Louis......E	200
Blackmer, Miller........... C	×
Black Oak, Caldwell.......NW	57
Black Walnut, Saint Charles. E	25
● Blackwater, Cooper........C	50
● Blackwell, Saint Francois. E	75
● *Blackwell*, Macon........ N	×
Blaine, Benton............. W	25
● Blairstown, Henry....... W	450
Bland, Gasconade...........E	40
Blende City, (see Lehigh).....	×
Blendsville, Jasper....... SW	1,500
● Blodgett, Scott............SE	50
Bloekow, Adair..............N	405
Bloomfield, Stoddard...SE	500
Blooming Rose, Phelps......C	15
Bloomington, Macon.........N	100
Bloomsdale, Ste. Genevieve. E	75
Blosser, Saline...............C	×
Blue Eye, Stone...........SW	130
Blue Lick, Saline............C	×
Blue Mill, Jackson...........W	25
Blue Mound, Livingston....N	20
Blue Ridge, Harrison......NW	160
Blue Springs, (see Inlow).....	×
● Blue Springs, Jackson... W	506
Bluffton, Montgomery...... E	10
● *Blum*, Wayne........... SE	×
Bly, Howell..................S	×
● Blythedale, Harrison... NW	160
● *Boaz*, Crawford...........C	×
Bobring, Saint Louis.........E	20
Boeger's Store, Osage....... C	100
Boeschenville, Benton....... C	40
Boeuf Breek, Franklin..... E	100
● Bogard, Carroll............N	3 0
Bois Brule, Perry...........SE	30
● Bois D'Arc, Greene.....SW	100
● Bolckow, Andrew......NW	405

Missouri

Place	Pop.
● Boles, Franklin..........E	60
● **Bolivar**, Polk..........SW	1,485
Bollinger's Mill, (see Zalania)	×
Bolton, Harrison......... NW	25
Bonanza, Caldwell........NW	25
● Bonfil's Station, St. Louis. E	75
Bohomme, Saint Louis......E	30
Bonner, Saint Louis.........E	×
Bonne Terre, Saint Francois E	3,719
● *Bonnot's Mill*, Osage......C	200
Boomer, Linn...............N	20
Boonesborough, Howard....C	75
● **Boonville**, Cooper......C	4,141
● *Booth*, Pike..............NE	65
Boschert Town, St. Charles. E	100
● *Boscobel*, Dent............S	×
● Boston, Barton..........SW	50
Boston, Christian............S	40
● Bosworth, Carroll........ N	650
Bounds, Wayne.............SE	×
● Bourbon, Crawford.......C	100
Bower's Mills, Lawrence..SW	190
● **Bowling Green**, Pike NE	1,564
● *Bowman*, Harrison.....NW	×
Boxford, DeKalb.........NW	20
Boyd, Dallas................C	65
Boyden, Newton...........SW	×
Boydsville, (see Carrington)..	×
Boyer, Wright...............S	12
Boyers, Cape Girardeau....SE	×
Boyler's Mill, Morgan.......C	40
● Boynton, Sullivan......... N	30
Bracken, Webster............S	32
Bradfield, Stone...........SW	×
Bradley, Carroll........... N	26
Bradleyville, Taney..........S	30
Braggadocio, Pemiscot.... SE	65
● Brandsville, Howell....... S	10
Branson, Taney..............S	20
● *Brant*, Moniteau..........C	×
Brantford, Ralls.......... NE	10
● Brashear, Adair.......... N	316
Brauersville, Benton........C	30
Brawley, Oregon............ S	×
● Braymer, Caldwell..... NW	599
Brazeau, Perry............ SE	25
Brazil, Washington......... E	×
Brazito, Cole.............. C	25
● Breckenridge, Caldwell NW	763
Breeze, Jasper............ SW	7
Bremen, Saint Louis........ E	×
● *Brentwood*, Saint Louis... E	×
Brest, Jasper..............SW	15
● Brevator, Lincoln..........E	25
Brewer, Perry............. SE	57
Brewersville, Perry........ SE	50
Briar Creek, Ripley........SE	26
Bridgeport, Warren..........E	50
● Bridgeton, Saint Louis....E	237
Brighton, Polk.............SW	237
● Briscoe, Lincoln........... E	30
Bristol, Jackson............W	×
Brock, Scotland............NE	50
Brockman, Miller............C	×
● Bronaugh, Vernon.......W	148
● Brookfield, Linn..........N	4,547
● Brookline Station, Gr'ne SW	200
Brocklyn, Harrison...... NW	20
Brosley, Cass...............W	30
Brotherton, Saint Louis.....E	×
Brown Branch, Taney.......S	10
● Browning, Linn.......... N	410
Browning, Sullivan..........N	117
Brownsdale, Daviess...... NW	×
● Brownington, Henry.......W	329
● *Brown's Springs*, Pettis . C	×
● Brown's Station, Boone...C	50
Brown's Switch, McDonald SW	×
● Brownwood, Stoddard...SE	100
Brumley, Miller............C	75
● *Brumund*, Stoddard.....SE	97
Brunot, Wayne............ SE	75
● Brunswick, Chariton..... N	1,748
● *Brush Creek*, Laclede.....C	×
Brussells, Lincoln............E	30
● *Bryan's*, Callaway........ C	×
Bryant, Douglas.............S	10
Buchanan, Bollinger.......SE	77
Buckhart, Douglas.......... S	32
Buckhorn, (see Alton)........	×
● Buckley, Greene........SW	100
● Bucklin, Linn............ N	711
● Buckner, Jackson.........W	164
Bud, Warren.................E	25
● *Buena Vista*, Clark.....NE	×
Buffalo, Dallas............ C	861
● Buffington, Stoddard.... SE	150

Missouri

Place	Pop.
Bula, (see Browning)........	×
● Bullion, Adair............N	10
● Bunceton, Cooper.........C	493
Buncombe, (see Beaman).....	×
Bunker Hill, Lewis....... NE	10
Burbois, Gasconade........ E	**40**
Burdett, Bates..............W	50
Burfordville, CapeG'rdeau. SE	50
Burke, Howell.............. S	40
Burlington, Boone...........C	65
● Burlington Junc., N'way NW	1,707
Burnham, Howell........... S	30
Burns, Polk...............SW	10
Burr Oak Valley, Lincoln...E	30
Burrows, Bates..............W	50
● *Burrows*, Mercer......... N	×
● Burton, Howard.......... C	100
● Busch, Pike.............NE	32
● Bushberg, Jefferson...... E	50
Bushnell, Barton..........SW	×
● **Butler**, Bates...........W	2,812
Butler, Wayne.............SE	×
● Butterfield, Barry...... SW	50
Buttsville, Grundy...........N	32
Byberry, Cooper........... C	×
Bynumville, Chariton.......N	50
● *Byrd Island*, CapeGir'd'u SE	×
Byrnesville, Jefferson.......E	30
Byron, Osage................C	25
● *Cabanne*, St. Louis........E	×
● Cabool, Texas..............S	359
Caddo, Webster............. S	×
● Cadet, Washington........E	50
● Cainesville, Harrison... NW	418
● Cairo, Randolph......... N	200
Caldwell, Callaway.......... C	75
Caledonia, Washington......E	200
● Calhoun, Henry........... W	698
● **California**, Moniteau...C	1,772
● Callao, Macon............ N	371
Callaway, Callaway..........C	×
Calumet, Pike...............NE	10
● *Cavalry Cemetery*, St. L'uis E	×
Calvy, Franklin..............E	32
Calwood, Callaway.......... C	75
● *Cama*, Clark.............NE	×
● Cambridge, Saline..........C	5
● Camden, Ray.............NW	650
● Camden Point, Platte.. NW	177
● Cameron, Clinton...... NW	2,917
Cameron Junc., Clinton.. NW	×
● *Camp*, Randolph......... N	×
● *Campbell*, Clay...........NW	×
● Campbell, Dunkin.......SE	200
● *Campbells*, Greene......SW	×
Campbellton, Franklin.......E	20
● Camp Branch, Pettis......C	×
Canaan, Gasconade...........E	25
Canaan Station, Dunklin..SE	×
Canal, Crawford.............C	×
Cane Creek, Butler......... SE	×
Caney, Ozark................S	10
● *Caney Creek*, Scott...... SE	32
Cane Hill, Cedar............W	75
Caneyville, Scott...........SE	×
● Canton, Lewis............NE	2,241
Cape Fair, Stone.......... SW	×
Cape Galena, Morgan....... C	30
● Cape Girardeau, Cape Girardeau...........SE	4,297
Caplinger's Mills, Cedar.... W	50
Cappeln, Saint Charles......E	40
Capp's Landing, Miller.....C	×
Caput, Barton.............SW	32
● *Carbon*, Macon........... N	×
● Carbon Centre, Vernon.. W	60
Carleton, Barton..........SW	50
● Carl Junction, Jasper...SW	699
● Carlow, Daviess........ NW	50
Carola, Butler............. SE	20
● *Carondelet*, Saint Louis...E	×
Carpenter's Store, Clinton NW	20
Carr, Stone............ .. NW	15
● Carrington, Callaway......C	50
● **Carrollton**, Carroll.... N	3,878
Carrsville, (see Petersburg)..	×
Carsonville, Saint Louis.....E	×
Carter's Mills, (see Piedmont)	×
Carterville, Jasper .... SW	2,884
● **Carthage**, Jasper.....SW	7,981
Caruth, Dunklin...........SE	75
Caruthersville, Pemiscot...SE	230
● Carytown, Jasper.......SW	75
Casco, Franklin..............E	50
● Cassidy, Christian.......... S	20
Cassville, Barry.........SW	626
Castello, Saint Louis........ E	×

Post Office	Pop.
● *Castle*, Sullivan .... N	375
● *Castlewood*, Saint Louis ... E	40
Castor, Bollinger .... SE	40
Catawba, Caldwell .... NW	20
● Catawissa, Franklin ...... E	125
Catherine, Saint Clair ...... W	×
Cavendish, Livingston ...... N	5
Cave Pump, Camden C	45
Caverna, McDonald .... SW	26
Cave Spring, Greene ...... SW	75
● Cawood, Andrew .... NW	50
● *Cecil*, Jackson .... W	×
● Cedar City, Callaway C	150
Cedar Creek, Taney .... S	20
Cedar Fork, Franklin .... E	165
● Cedar Gap, Wright .... S	100
Cedar Grove, Shannon .... S	20
Cedar Hill, Jefferson .... E	50
Cedar Valley, Taney .... S	25
Cedarville, Dade .... SW	50
Celina, Dent .... S	19
Celt, Dallas C	20
● Centaur Sta., Saint Louis. E	×
● *Centerton*, Saint Louis .... E	×
● Central, Saint Louis .... E	500
Central City, Putnam .... N	15
● Centralia, Boone C	1,275
Centre, Ralls .... NE	155
● Centre Town, Cole C	200
● Center View, Johnson .... W	400
Centreville, Reynolds ... SE	200
Centreville, (see Orearville) ..	×
● Centropolis, Jackson ..... W	25
● Chadwick, Christian .... S	100
Chain of Rocks, Lincoln .... E	100
Chalk Level, Saint Clair .... W	50
Chambersburgh, Clark .... NE	30
Chambersville, Dade ...... SW	35
● Chamois, Osage C	769
Champion City, Franklin .... E	40
● Chandler, Clay .... NW	30
Chantilly, Lincoln .... E	50
Chaonia, Wayne .... SE	50
Chapel Hill, La Fayette ..... W	65
● Chapin, Howell .... S	10
● Chapman, Benton C	×
Chariton, Putnam .... N	10
● *Chariton*, Macon .... N	×
Charity, Dallas C	30
● **Charleston**, Mississippi SE	1,381
Charleytown, (see St. Elizabeth)	×
Charlotte, Gasconade .... E	×
Chauncey, Camden C	12
● *Cheltenham*, Saint Louis .. E	300
Cherry Box, Shelby .... NE	15
Cherry Dell, Marion .... NE	15
Cherryville, Crawford C	30
Chesapeake, Lawrence .... SW	40
Chester, Nodaway .... NW	×
Chester Landing, Perry ... SE	×
● *Chicago Junc.*, Jackson .. W	×
● *Chicopee*, Carter .... SE	×
Chilhowee, Johnson .... W	100
● **Chillicothe**, Livingston N	5,717
● Chilton, Carter .... SE	×
Chouteau, Cooper C	×
Chraneville, Chariton .... N	27
Christopher, Newton ...... SW	10
Christy, Howell .... S	×
● Chula, Livingston .... N	50
Cincinnati, Ralls .... NE	20
Cisco, Livingston .... N	×
Civil Bend, Daviess .... NW	50
● *Clair*, Buchanan .... NW	×
● Clapper, Monroe .... NE	30
Clara, Callaway C	×
Clardy, Sainte Genevieve ... E	130
● Clarence, Shelby .... NE	1,078
● Clark, Randolph .... N	194
● Clarke City, Clark .... NE	30
● Clarksburgh, Moniteau C	350
● Clarksdale, De Kalb .... NW	145
Clark's Fork, Cooper C	25
Clarkson, Lawrence .... SW	10
● Clarksville, Pike .... NE	1,186
Clarkton, Dunklin .... SE	300
Claryville, Perry .... SE	100
● *Clay*, Clay .... NW	×
● *Clay City*, Clay .... NW	×
Claysville, Boone C	30
● **Clayton**, Saint Louis .... E	402
● *Clayton*, Vernon .... W	102
● *Clayton Road*, Saint Louis E	×
Claytonville, Clay .... NW	10
Clear Creek, Washington ... E	×
● *Clear Fork*, Johnson ..... W	×
● Clearmont, Nodaway ... NW	246

Missouri

Post Office	Pop.
Clear Springs, Texas .... S	15
Clearwater, Wayne .... SE	75
Cleavesville, Gasconade ..... E	30
Clementine, Phelps C	×
Cleopatra, Mercer .... N	40
Cleveland, Cass .... W	×
Cliff, Sainte Genevieve ..... E	10
● *Cliff Cave*, Saint Louis .... E	×
Clifton, Schuyler .... N	20
Clifton, (see Thayer)	×
● Clifton City, Cooper C	135
● *Clifton Heights*, Saint Louis E	×
● Clifton Hill, Randolph .... N	200
Climax Springs, Camden C	75
● **Clinton**, Henry .... W	4,737
Clintonville, Cedar .... W	75
Clio, Saline C	×
Clones, Iron .... SE	×
Clover Bottom, Franklin .... E	25
● *Club House*, Carter ...... SE	×
Clyde, Nodaway .... NW	259
Coalsburgh, Henry .... W	29
● Coatesville, Schuyler ..... N	100
Cobalt, Howell .... S	30
Cobb, Saint Clair .... W	15
Coburg, Saint Clair .... W	10
Cockrell, Jackson .... W	50
Cockrun, Dunklin .... SE	×
Coelleda, Camden C	×
Coffeysburgh, Daviess .... NW	250
● *Coffeyton*, Crawford C	12
Coffman, Sainte Genevieve .. E	30
● *Cohick*, Saint Louis .... E	×
Cold Spring, Douglas .... S	30
Cold Water, Wayne .... SE	40
● *Cole*, Cole C	×
● Cole Camp, Benton C	450
● Coleman, Cass .... W	20
College Mound, Macon ...... N	200
● *College View*, Saint Louis. E	×
● Collins, Saint Clair .... W	300
● *Colman*, Saint Louis ...... E	×
Coloma, Carroll .... N	125
Colony, Knox .... NE	100
● **Columbia**, Boone C	4,000
Columbus, Johnson .... W	150
Commerce, Scott .... SE	500
● *Como*, New Madrid ...... SE	30
Competition, Laclede C	70
Compton, Webster .... S	19
● Conception, Nodaway .. NW	100
Concord, Callaway C	98
Concord Hill, Warren .... E	×
● Concordia, La Fayette .... W	715
Coudray, Dent .... S	25
Confusion, Montgomery .... E	×
Conklin, Webster .... S	42
Connelly, (see Fairhaven Sprs.)	×
Conner, Taney .... S	30
● *Connett*, Buchanan ..... NW	×
Consville, (see Brownington).	×
● Converse, Clinton ...... NW	25
● Conway, Laclede C	217
Cook Station, Crawford C	25
Cookseyville, Grundy .... N	10
Cookville, Pulaski C	32
● *Cooley's Lake*, Clay .... NW	×
● *Cooper*, Miller C	98
Cooper's Hill, Osage C	100
Cooter, Pemiscot .... SE	60
Copeland, Saint Clair .... W	×
● Cora, Sullivan .... N	60
● Corder, La Fayette .... W	1,145
● Cordz, Howell .... S	100
Corks Hill, Saint Charles ... E	×
Cornelia, Johnson .... W	25
Cornersville, Hickory C	32
● Corning, Holt .... NW	176
● Cornland, Bates .... W	10
● Cornwall, Madison ...... SE	×
Corry, Dade .... SW	30
Corsicana, Barry .... SW	72
Corso, Lincoln .... E	25
● Cosby, Andrew .... NW	130
Cote Brilliant, Saint Louis. E	×
Cote, Sans Dessieu, Cal'w'y. C	20
Cottage, Macon .... N	×
Cottage, Saint Louis .... E	×
Cottbus, Howell .... S	48
Cottleville, Saint Charles ... E	300
Cottleville Station, St. Chas. E	×
Cotton Plant, Dunklin ..... SE	100
Cottonwood, (see Stahl)	×
Cottonwood Point, Pem't. SE	150
Couch, Oregon .... S	10
Coulstone, Dent .... S	15
● Courtney, Jackson .... W	35

Missouri

Post Office	Pop.
Courtois, Washington .... E	37
● *Cousinville*, Cape Gir'd'us SE	×
Cove, (see Olean)	×
Cove City, Bates .... W	10
Covington, Pemiscot ...... SE	195
● Cowgill, Caldwell ...... NW	865
Cox, Macon .... N	10
Coy, McDonald .... SW	15
Crab Orchard, Ray .... NW	50
● Craig, Holt .... NW	508
Crane, Stone .... SW	20
Crawford Station, Scotla'd NE	30
Cream Ridge, Livingston ... N	30
● *Cream Ridge*, Livingston .. N	65
Crebston, (see Stahl)	×
● Creighton, Cass .... W	308
● Crescent, Saint Louis ..... E	48
Cretcher, Saline C	×
● Creve Coeur, Saint Louis .. E	200
● *Crisp*, Jackson .... W	×
Crittenden, Morgan C	57
● Crocker, Pulaski C	175
● Crosno, Mississippi ...... SE	×
Cross Keys, Saint Louis ..... E	26
Cross Roads, (see Everton) ..	×
Cross Timbers, Hickory C	250
Crosstown, Perry .... SE	40
Cruise, Washington .... E	30
Crump, Cape Girardeau .... SE	65
Crystal City, Jefferson ...... E	1,104
● Cuba, Crawford C	497
● *Cumings*, Carter .... SE	×
Cunningham, Chariton ..... N	**196**
Cureall, Howell .... S	20
Curran, Stone .... SW	40
● Curryville, Pike .... NE	302
● Curzon, Holt .... NW	15
Custer, Dent .... S	10
● *Cutoff*, New Madrid ..... SE	×
Cyclone, McDonald .... SW	20
Cynthia, Reynolds .... SE	32
● Cyrene, Pike .... NE	250
Czar, Crawford C	×
Dadeville, Dade .... SW	200
Daisy, Cape Girardeau ..... SE	×
Dallas, Jackson .... W	50
● Dalton, Chariton .... N	332
● Dameron, Lincoln .... E	35
Damsel, Camden C	25
Dana, Bates .... W	50
Danby, Jefferson .... E	32
● Danforth, Adair .... N	200
Danville, Montgomery ... E	380
● Dardenne, Saint Charles .. E	25
Darien, Dent .... S	10
Darksville, Randolph .... N	100
● Darlington, Gentry ..... NW	242
● *Daugherty*, Cass .... W	19
● Dauphine, Osage C	200
Davenport, Dade .... SW	76
● Davis, Lincoln .... E	15
Davis, Saint Louis .... E	×
Davisville, Crawford C	20
● Dawn, Livingston .... N	350
● Dawson, Nodaway ...... NW	75
Day, Taney .... S	×
● *Day*, Stoddard .... SE	×
Dayton, Cass .... W	100
● *Dayton*, Newton .... SW	195
Dederick, Oregon .... S	32
● Dean, Andrew .... NW	10
● *Dean Lake*, Chariton ..... N	×
● Dearborn, Platte .... NW	239
De Bruin, Pulaski C	19
Decatur, Cole C	50
Decaturville, Camden C	45
Deeherd, Saint Clair .... W	×
● Deepwater, Henry .... W	1,102
● Deerfield, Vernon .... W	239
Deer Park, Boone C	10
Deer Ridge, Lewis .... NE	30
Defiance, Worth .... NW	65
Deguire, Madison .... SE	×
De Hodiamont, Saint Louis. W	×
● DeKalb, Buchanan ..... NW	300
● DeLassus, Saint Francois .. F	75
Delavan, Jackson .... W	×
Delaware Town, (see Billings)	×
Delhi, Crawford C	65
Dell Delight, Benton C	32
Dellia, Ozark .... S	×
Delpha, Putnam .... N	10
● *Delta*, Cape Girardeau ... SE	40
Demo, Laclede C	30
Denver, Worth .... NW	295
● *Derry*, Franklin .... E	×
Derrahs, Lewis .... NE	×

Place		
● Des Arc, Iron	SE	413
● De Soto, Jefferson	E	3,960
Des Peres, Saint Louis	E	100
Detmold, (see Boeuf Creek)		×
● *Dewey*, Franklin	E	×
● De Witt, Carroll	N	633
● Dexter, Stoddard	SE	792
Diagonal, Buchanan	NW	×
● *Diamond*, Jackson	W	×
Diamond, Newton	SW	15
Dicks, Cooper	C	×
● Diehlstadt, Scott	SE	20
● *Diggins*, Webster	S	×
Diiedo, Chariton	N	19
Dillard, Crawford	C	×
● *Dillon*, Phelps	C	×
Dimple, Jasper	SW	×
Dinsmore, Mercer	N	×
Dit, Ozark	S	10
Dittmer's Store, Jefferson	E	60
Dix, Dent	S	10
● Dixon, Pulaski	C	404
Dockery, Ray	NW	25
● *Docks*, Saint Louis	E	×
● Dodson, Jackson	W	×
Doe Run, Saint Francois	E	956
Dogwood, Douglas	S	19
Dolle's Mills, Bollinger	SE	32
● **Doniphan**, Ripley	SE	609
Dora, Ozark	S	15
● *Doran*, Johnson	W	×
● Dorchester, Green	SW	25
Doss, Dent	S	×
Dotham, Atchison	NW	10
Dottie, Saint Clair	W	×
Dougherty, Cass	W	×
Douglas, Gentry	NW	×
● Dover, LaFayette	W	150
● Downing, Schuyler	N	406
● *Dozier*, Saint Louis	E	×
● *Drake*, Saint Louis	E	×
Drake, Gasconade	E	100
● Dresden, Pettis	C	200
● *Drew*, Saint Louis	E	×
Drexel, Cass	W	200
Dripping Spring, Boone	C	20
Dripping Spring, Saint Louis	E	20
● Dry Branch, Franklin	E	50
Dry Creek, Crawford	C	30
Dryden, Ripley	SE	×
Dry Glaize, Laclede	C	15
Drynob, Laclede	C	15
Dry Springs, Ripley	SE	50
Dublin, Barton	SW	75
Dudenville, Jasper	SW	65
● Dudley, Stoddard	SE	65
Dugan, Vernon	W	×
Duggan, Wright	S	×
Dugginsville, Ozark	S	×
● *Dug Hill*, Buchanan	NW	×
● Dumas, Clark	NE	60
● Dumpville, Pettis	C	12
Duncan, Webster	S	25
Duncan, Clay	NW	×
Duncan's Bridge, Monroe	NE	100
● Dundee, Franklin	E	50
Dunksburg, Pettis	C	75
● Dunlap, Grundy	N	40
● Dunnegan, Polk	SW	×
Dupont, Nodaway	NW	15
Durgen's Creek, Lewis	NE	32
● Durham, Lewis	NE	150
Duroc, Benton	C	40
● Dutchtown, Cape Gir'd'n	SE	50
Dutzow, Warren	E	25
Duval, Barton	SW	×
Dwyer, Saint Louis	E	×
Dye, Platte	NW	10
● *Dyke*, City of Saint Louis	E	×
Dykes, Texas	S	25
Eagle Rock, Barry	SW	15
Eagleville, Harrison	NW	305
Earl, Callaway	C	×
Early, Lincoln	E	30
● East Atchison, Buch'n.	NW	300
East Bonne Terre, St. Fr's.	E	×
Easterville, Caldwell	NW	×
● East Joplin, Jasper	SW	×
● *East Leavenworth*, Platte	NW	120
● East Lynne, Cass	W	500
● Easton, Buchanan	NW	200
● East Prairie, Mississippi	SE	200
East Sedalia, Pettis	C	×
● *East St. Joseph*, Buch'n	NW	×
East Washburn, Barry	SW	250
Eaton's Mill, Ripley	SE	×
Eaudevie, Christian	S	20

Missouri

Place		
Ebenezer, Greene	SW	35
Ebro, Barry	SW	40
Eckelkamp, Warren	E	×
Economy, Macon	N	50
Eden, Dent	S	50
● *Eden*, Saint Louis	E	×
Edgar Springs, Phelps	C	75
● *Edgebrook*, Saint Louis	E	25
Edge Hill, Reynolds	SE	15
● Edgerton, Platte	NW	482
● *Edgerton Junc.*, Platte	NW	65
● Edgewood, Pike	NE	75
● **Edina**, Knox	NE	1,456
Edinburgh, Grundy	N	182
Edmonson, Benton	C	19
Edwards, Benton	C	18
● *Edwards*, LaFayette	W	10
● *Edwin*, Jasper	SW	×
Effie, Callaway	C	×
Eggleston, Ozark	S	×
Eglinton, Taney	S	40
Egypt Mills, Cape Girardeau	SE	100
● Eight Mile, Cass	W	35
Einstine Silver Mine, Mad'n.	SE	97
● Eldon, Miller	C	300
El Dorado Springs, Cedar	W	1,543
Eldridge, Laclede	C	10
● *Electric Works*, Newton	SW	×
Elgin, Shelby	NE	10
● *Elgin*, Sullivan	N	43
Elk Creek, Texas	S	25
Elk Dale, Atchison	NW	×
Elk Grove, Caldwell	NW	19
Elkhart, Bates	W	×
Elkhead, Christian	S	26
Elkhorn, Ray	NW	77
Elkland, Webster	S	30
Elk Lick Springs, Pike	NE	15
Elk Mills, McDonald	SW	65
Elko, Putnam	N	30
Elk Prairie, Phelps	C	45
Elkton, Hickory	C	60
Elleardsville, Saint Louis	E	×
● *Ellendale*, Saint Louis	E	×
Ellenorah, Gentry	NW	45
Ellington, Gentry	NW	75
● Elliott, Randolph	N	250
● Ellis, Vernon	W	195
Ellis Prairie, Texas	S	15
Ellisville, Saint Louis	E	20
Ellsinore, Carter	SE	150
Ellsworth, (see Barton City)		×
Elm, Johnson	W	10
● Elmer, Macon	N	150
● Elm Grove, Holt	NW	75
● Elmira, Ray	NW	40
● Elmo, Nodaway	NW	250
Elmont, Franklin	E	×
● *Elm Park*, Jackson	W	×
● *Elm Point*, Saint Charles	E	×
● Elm Wood, Saline	C	100
● *Elmwood Park*, St. Louis	E	×
Elrod, Andrew	NW	×
● Elsberry, Lincoln	E	390
● Elston, Cole	C	100
● Ely, Marion	NE	30
Embree, Texas	S	×
Emden, Shelby	NE	10
Emerson, Marion	NE	100
● *Emerson*, Saint Louis	E	200
Emerson Sta., (see Excello)		×
Eminence, Shannon	S	150
Emma, Saline	C	×
● Emmet, Dade	SW	100
Empire, (see Blendsville)		×
Empire Mills, Butler	SE	×
Empire Prairie, Andrew	NW	130
Energy, Schuyler	N	25
Enoch, Vernon	W	×
● Enon, Moniteau	C	15
● *Enon*, Saint Charles	E	×
Enterprise, Shelby	NE	10
Enyart, Gentry	NW	20
● Eolia, Pike	NE	125
Epworth, Shelby	NE	10
Ergo, Newton	SW	10
Erie, McDonald	SW	35
Ernest, Dade	SW	10
Esrom, Barton	SW	25
● Essex, Stoddard	SE	100
Estes, Pike	NE	25
● Estill, Howard	C	25
● Ethel, Macon	N	300
● Etlah, Franklin	E	20
Etna, Scotland	NE	30
● *Eugenia*, Crawford	C	×
Eunice, Texas	S	×

Missouri

Place		
Eureka, Perry	SE	×
● Eureka, Saint Louis	E	150
Eureka L'nd'g., (see Wilton)		×
● *Evanston*, Jackson	W	×
● Evansville, Monroe	NE	50
● Eve, Vernon	W	50
Evelyn, Macon	N	10
Everett, Cass	W	50
Eversonville, Linn	N	125
● Everton, Dade	SW	600
● Evona, Gentry	NW	100
● *Ewings*, Cole	C	×
● Excello, Macon	N	150
Excelsior, Morgan	C	25
● Excelsior Springs, Clay	NW	2,034
Exchange, Reynolds	SE	×
● Exeter, Barry	SW	244
● *Faiiers*, Benton	C	×
Fairbanks, Newton	SW	×
Fair Dealing, Ripley	SE	×
● Fairfax, Atchinson	NW	329
Fairfax, Adair	N	329
Fairfield, Benton	C	110
Fair Grove, Greene	SW	100
Fairhaven, Vernon	W	100
● *Fair Junction*, Clay	NW	×
Fairmont, Clark	NE	200
● Fair Play, Polk	SW	400
Fairport, DeKalb	SW	125
Fairview, Lincoln	E	19
● *Fairview*, Saint Louis	E	×
Fairville, Saline	C	75
Falling Springs, Douglas	S	×
● Famous, Lincoln	E	10
● *Fanita*, Saint Louis	E	×
Fanning, Crawford	C	150
● Farber, Audrain	C	272
Farley, Platte	NW	50
Farmer, Pike	NE	20
Farmersville, Livingston	N	75
Farmington, St. Francois	E	1,394
● Faucett, Buchanan	NW	×
● **Fayette**, Howard	C	2,247
Fayetteville, Johnson	W	200
Fearless, Camden	C	×
● *Fee Fee*, Saint Louis	E	×
● *Feely*, Bates	E	×
Femme Osage, St. Charles	E	50
Fenton, Saint Louis	E	100
● Ferguson, Saint Louis	E	100
Ferguson, Crawford	C	×
Fernnook, Ripley	SE	40
Fern Ridge, Saint Louis	E	30
Fertile, Washington	E	×
Festus, Jefferson	E	1,335
Feuersville, Osage	C	20
Fidelity, Jasper	SW	82
Filley, Cedar	W	150
Fillmore, Adair	W	261
Fillmore, Andrew	NW	261
Finey, Henry	W	×
Firth, Randolph	N	40
Fisher, Pemiscot	SE	150
Fisk, Stoddard	SE	×
Flag Springs, Andrew	NW	50
Flat Creek, Barry	SW	30
Flat River, Saint Francois	E	32
Flatwood, Miller	C	×
● Fleming, Ray	NW	200
● *Flint*, Gentry	NW	50
Flint, McDonald	SW	×
Flint's Hill, Saint Charles	E	×
Flora, Osage	C	×
Florence, Morgan	C	45
Florida, Monroe	NE	124
Florilla, Douglas	S	32
Florisant, Saint Louis	E	800
● *Floyd*, Ray	NW	×
Flucom, Jefferson	E	×
● Foley, Lincoln	E	75
Folsom, Callaway	C	×
Fontainbleau, Andrew	NW	25
Foote, Iron	SE	×
● *Forbes*, Holt	NW	×
● Ford, Gentry	NW	25
● Fordland, Webster	S	100
● *Fords*, Pike	NE	×
● *Forest City*, Saint Louis	E	×
● Forest City, Holt	NW	428
● Forest Green, Chariton	N	40
Forest Home, Lawrence	SW	10
● Foristell, Saint Charles	E	300
● *Forest Park*, Saint Louis	E	×
Forest Springs, Knox	NE	97
● *Forker*, Linn	N	40
Forkner's Hill, Webster	S	10
Forsyth, Taney	S	200

● *ForsytheJunction*, St. Louis E ×
● Fortescue, Holt NW 30
Fort Lyon, Benton C 15
● Fortuna, Moniteau C 200
● Foster, Bates W 513
● Fountain Grove, Linn N 40
Fourche a'Renault, Wash'n. E 30
Four Mile, (see Campbell) ×
Fowler, Texas S ×
Fox, Ray NW 20
Fox Creek, Saint Louis E 150
Francis, Pulaski C ×
Frankberg, Osage C ×
● Frankford, Pike NE 662
● Franklin, Howard C 132
● *Franks*, Pulaski C ×
● *Fray*, Franklin E ×
● Frazer, Buchanan NW 25
Fredericksburgh, Gasconade E 25
● **Fredericktown,** M'd'n SE 917
Freedom, Osage C ×
Freeland, Carter SE 500
● Freeman, Cass W 279
Freistatt, Lawrence SW 15
French Mills, Madison SE ×
French Village, Saint Fran's E 40
Friedheim, Cape Girardeau SE ×
● *Frisco Heights*, Franklin E ×
Frohna, Perry SE 200
Fruitland, Cape Girardeau SE ×
Frumet, Jefferson E 75
● *Fugett*, Mississippi SE ×
Fulkerson, Johnson W ×
● **Fulton,** Callaway C 4,314
Furr, (see Fayette) ×
Fuson, Wright S ×
Fyan, Laclede C 20
● *Gads Hill*, Wayne SE 130
Gage, Wright S ×
● Gailey, Pettis C 25
Gaines, Henry W 19
Gainesville, Ozark S 175
Galena, Stone SW 200
Galesburgh, Jasper SW 100
● **Gallatin,** Daviess NW 1,489
● Galloway, Greene SW 10
Galmey, Hickory C ×
● Galt, Grundy N 653
Gambleton, Saint Louis E ×
Gamburg, Ripley SE 25
Gamma, Montgomery E 30
Gant, Audrain C 25
Gara, Gentry NW 150
● Garden City, Cass W 227
● *Gardner*, Harrison NW ×
Garfield, Oregon S 50
● Garland, Henry W 28
Garrettsburg, Buchanan NW 25
Garrison, Christian S 15
Gartin, Clay NW ×
● Gasconade, Gasconade E 30
● Gates, Greene SW 10
Gatewood, Ripley SE 71
● *Gault*, Grundy N 150
Gaydon, Polk SW ×
Gaynor City, Nodaway NW 25
Gayoso, Pemiscot SE 137
Gay's Ridge, Stoddard SE ×
Gazette, Pike NE 32
Gebler, Gasconade E ×
● *Gedney*, Henry W ×
Gehm, Putnam N ×
Genova, Livingston N ×
Gentryville, Gentry NW 203
● Georgetown, Pettis C 25
Georgeville, Ray NW 30
Georgia City, Jasper SW 100
Gerard, Cass W ×
Germania, Schuyler N 12
Ghermanville, Iron SE ×
● Gibbs, Adair N 150
Gibson, Benton C 65
Gibson, Dunklin SE ×
● *Gibson*, Lincoln E ×
Gila, Dent S ×
Gilead, Lewis NE 20
Gill, Atchison NW ×
Gillett, Nodaway NW ×
● Gilliam, Saline C 321
Gilman, Dade SW ×
● Gilmore, Saint Charles E 50
Girdner, Douglas S ×
Gladden, Dent S 65
Glade Chapel, Jefferson E ×
Gladstone, Morgan C ×
Glaize, Camden C ×
● Glasgow, Howard C 1,781
● Glen Allen, Bollinger SE 30
● Glencoe, Saint Louis E 50
● *Glendale*, Jackson W ×
Glendale, Putnam N ×
● *Glendale*, Saint Louis E ×
Glendale, Schuyler N 10
● *Glenn Arbor*, Clay NW ×
● *Glen Park*, Jefferson E ×
● Glensted, Morgan C 20
● Glenwood, Schuyler N 451
● *Glenwood Junc.*, Schuyler N ×
● Glover, Iron SE ×
Gnatz, Saint Charles E ×
Golden Barry SW 70
● Golden City, Barton SW 773
Goldsberry, Macon N 25
Gooch's Mill, Cooper C 100
Goodland, Iron SE ×
Goodnight, Polk SW 45
Goodrick, (see Veve) ×
Goodson, Polk SW 40
Good Water, Iron SE 20
● Gordonville, Cape Girardeau SE 95
● Gorin, Scotland NE 386
Goshen, Mercer N 40
● Goss, Monroe NE 25
Gould Farm, Caldwell NW 30
● *Gowdy*, Cass W ×
● Gower, Clinton NW 328
Grab, Texas S ×
Grabeel, Ozark S 10
Graham, Nodaway NW 353
● *Graham's*, Saint Louis E ×
● Grain Valley, Jackson W 193
Granby, Newton SW 1,400
● *Granby City*, Newton SW ×
● *Grand Canyon*, Saint Louis E ×
Grand Centre, Randolph N ×
Grand Eddy, (see Crosstown) ×
● Grandin, Carter SE 579
Grand Pass, (see Napoleon) ×
● Grand Pass, Saline C 281
● Grand View, Jackson W ×
● Granger, Scotland NE 275
Grangeville, Newton SW 20
● *Granite Bend*, Wayne SE 250
● Graniteville, Iron SE 721
● **Grant City,** Worth NW 1,186
● *Grant's*, Saint Louis E ×
Granville, Monroe NE 100
Grapevine, Saint Clair W ×
● *Gratiot*, Saint Louis E ×
Gravel Hill, Cape Girardeau SE 25
Gravel Point, Texas S 25
Gravelton, Wayne SE 60
Graves Switch, McDonald SW ×
Gravois Mills, Morgan C 75
● Graydon Springs, Polk SW 50
● Gray Ridge, Stoddard SE 260
● Grayson, Clinton NW 25
● Gray's Summit, Franklin E 100
Graysville, Putnam N 25
Greasy, Dallas C ×
Greeley, Reynolds SE 150
● Greenbrier, Bollinger SE ×
● Green Castle, Sullivan N 267
● Green City, Sullivan N 318
● *Green Cox*, CapeGir'rdeau SE ×
Greendoor, Johnson W ×
Greene Springs, Vernon W 125
Greenfield, Dade SW 998
Greenfield L'd'g, Mississippi SE ×
Greenlawn, Ralls NE 5
● Green Ridge, Pettis C 300
Greensburg, Knox NE 60
Greenton, La Fayette W 50
● Green Top, Schuyler N 238
Greenville, Wayne SE 50
● Greenwood, Jackson W 296
Greer, Oregon S 20
● Gregory Landing, Clark NE 50
Gresham, Polk SW 10
Grey's Point, Lawrence SW 10
Griffin, Christian S ×
● *Grindstone Cr'k*, DeKalb NW ×
Griswold, Oregon S 20
Grove Dale, Maries C 25
Grover, Saint Louis E ×
Grover, Johnson W ×
● *Groves*, Saint Charles E ×
Grove Spring, Wright S 100
Grubbtown, Grundy N ×
Grubville, Jefferson E 100
● Guilford, Nodaway NW 150
Guinn, Christian S ×
● *Guinns*, Schuyler N ×
● Gulf, Polk SW 15
● Gumbo, Saint Louis E ×
● Gun City, Cass W 198
Gunter, Camden C 25
Guthridge Mills, Chariton N 75
● Guthrie, Callaway C 100
Guy, Atchison NW ×
Hackney, Greene SW ×
Hager's Grove, Shelby NE 70
Hailey, Barry SW 40
● Hainley'sSwitch, Missis'pi SE ×
● *Halberts*, Crawford C ×
● Hale, Carroll N 530
Haley City, (see Humphrey's) ×
Half Rock, Mercer N 100
Half Way, Polk SW 25
Halifax, Saint Francois E ×
● *Hallard*, Ray NW 57
Halleck, Buchanan NW 100
Halloran, Butler SE ×
● *Hall's*, La Fayette W ×
● *Hall's*, Buchanan NW 30
● *Hall's*, Cass W ×
● Hallsville, Boone C 92
Hall Town, Lawrence SW 50
Hamburgh, Saint Charles E 150
Hamden, Chariton N 5
● Hamilton, Caldwell NW 1,641
Hamilton, Saint Louis E ×
Hampton, Platte NW 20
Ham's Prairie, Callaway C 25
● Hancock, Pulaski C 25
Hanley, Mississippi SE ×
● **HANNIBAL,** Marion NE 12,857
● Hannon, Barton SW 100
Hanover, Jefferson E ×
Happy Valley, Harrison NW 10
Hardeman, Saline C ×
● Hardin, Ray NW 656
● *Hardin*, Lewis NE 360
● Harlem, Clay NW 150
● Harold, Greene SW 25
Harper, McDonald SW 50
Harper, Saint Clair W ×
● *Harrelson*, Cass W ×
● Harris, Sullivan N 50
● *Harris*, Ralls NE ×
Harrisburgh, Boone C 135
● **Harrisonville,** Cass W 1,645
● Harriston, Cooper C 20
● *Hart*, Butler SE 12
Hart, McDonald SW 15
● *Hart*, Macon N ×
Hartford, Putnam N 50
● *Hartman*, Ralls NE ×
Hartsburg, (see Bridgeton) ×
Hartville, Wright S 500
● Hartwell, Henry W 100
Harvester, Saint Charles E 50
● Harviell, Cutler SE 111
● Harwood, Vernon W 240
Haseville, Linn N 10
● Hassard, Ralls NE 50
Hastain, Benton C 19
Hatch, Ralls NE 15
Hatfield, Harrison NW 30
Hattie, Texas S ×
Hatton, Callaway C 35
Haw, Mercer N ×
Haw Creek, Pike NE 10
Hawkeye, Pulaski C ×
Hawkins, Monroe NE 32
Hawk Point, Lincoln E 25
Hawley, Wright S 32
Hayworth, Taney S ×
Hayden, Maries C ×
Haydenville, De Kalb NW ×
Hayward, Pemiscot SE 100
Hazel Run, Saint Francois E 130
Hazelton, Texas S 10
Hazelville, Scotland NE 25
Hazen, Webster S 20
Hazle Green, Laclede C 40
● *Headquarters*, Bollinger SE ×
Heartshorn, Texas S ×
Heatonville, Lawrence SW 10
Hebron, Livingston N ×
Hedge City, Knox NE 30
Hedrick, Dent S 65
● *Heights*, Saint Louis E ×
● *Heims*, Jackson W ×
● Helena, Andrew NW 125
● *Helton*, Marion NE ×
● Hematite, Jefferson E 100
Hemker, Franklin E ×
● Hemple, Clinton NW 25

Rockbridge, Ozark.......... S 15
Rock Creek, Jefferson...... E ×
● *Rock Creek*, Jackson..... W ×
Rock Hill, Saint Louis...... E 100
Rockingham, Ray........ NW 10
● *Rock Levee*, Cape Gir'u.. SE ×
Rock Prairie, (see Everton) .. ×
Rockport, Atchison.... NW 934
Rock Springs, Saint Louis.. E ×
Rock Spring, Washington... E 45
● Rockville, Bates.......... W 551
Rocky Comfort, McDonald SW 200
Rocky Mount, Miller........ C 40
Rodney, Linn.............. N 10
● *Rodney's*, Mississippi.... SE ×
● Rogersville, Webster...... S 150
Roland, McDonald........ SW 10
● **Rolla**, Phelps............ C 1,592
Rolling Home, Randolph... N 40
Romance, Ozark............ S 10
Rome, Douglas.............. S 40
Rondo, Polk .... SW 25
Roney, Hickory............ C 19
Rookins, Saint Clair........ W ×
Roscoe, Saint Clair......... W 159
● *Roseberry*, Nodaway....NW 12
● *Rosedale*, Saint Louis.....E ×
● *Rose Hill*, Saint Louis .... E ×
● Rosendale, Andrew .... NW 288
Rosier, Bates.............. W 150
● *Roswell*, Crawford........ C ×
● Rothville, Chariton........N 200
Roubidoux, Texas........... S 20
Round Grove, Lawrence.. SW 50
Round Spring, Shannon..... S 32
Rowena, Audrain...........C 19
Rowletta, Pettis............ C 19
Roxie, Butler.............. SE ×
Roy, Douglas.............. S 15
● *Rucker*, Bates........... W ×
Rucker, Boone.............. C ×
Rum Branch, C. Girardeau SE ×
Rural, Boone.............. C ×
● Rush, Andrew.......... NW 50
● Rush Hill, Audrain........C 210
Rush Tower, Jefferson...... E 30
● Rushville, Buchanan....NW 200
Russ, Laclede...............C ×
Russell, Howard........... C ×
Russell, Shannon............ S 45
● Russellville, Cole .... C 200
Russellville, (see Fox) .... ×
Ruth, Stone................SW ×
Rutledge, Scotland........ NE 150
● *Rutledge*, Knox.......... NE ×
Rutledge, McDonald...... SW ×
● Sabula, Iron..............SE 30
Sackville, Cedar .... W ×
Sackville, Greene .... SW 25
Safe, Maries.............. C ×
Saginaw, Newton..........SW 10
Sagrada, Camden........... C ×
● Saint Albans, Franklin....E ×
Saint Annie, Pulaski .... C 26
● Saint Aubert's, Callaway.. C 25
● *Saint Aubert*, Osage....... C ×
● Saint Catherine, Linn..... N 250
● **Saint Charles**, St. Ch'es E 6,161
● Saint Clair, Franklin......E 208
Saint Clement, Pike....... NE 25
● *Saint Cloud Springs*, Ray NW 6
Sainte Genevieve, Sainte Genevieve.... .... E 1,586
Saint Elizabeth, Miller ...... C 70
Saint Ferdinand, Saint Louis E 769
Saint Francisville, Clark...NE 100
Saint Francois, (see Farm't'n) ×
Saint George, Wright........ S 15
● Saint James, Phelps....... C 467
Saint Joe Lead Mines, (see Bonne Terre)............... ×
Saint John, Putnam .... N 30
Saint John's Store, Franklin E ×
● **SAINT JOSEPH**, Buchanan................ NW 52,324
● *Saint Joseph Junc.*, D'y's NW ×
Saint Leger, (see Udall)....... ×
● **SAINT LOUIS**, City of Saint Louis..... E 451,770
Saint Martin's, Morgan...... C 20
Saint Mary's, Ste. Genevieve E 446
Saint Patrick, Clark........ NE 30
Saint Paul, Saint Charles.... E 75
● *Saint Paul*, Saint Louis....E ×
● Saint Peter's, Saint Charles E 500
Saint Thomas, Cole......... C 200
Safe, Maries............ C ×

Missouri

Sagrada, Camden..........C ×
● **Salem**, Dent............S 1,315
Salem, Daviess..........NW ×
● Saline, Mercer...........N 10
Saline City, Saline.........C 130
Saling, Audrain .... C ×
● Salisbury, Chariton.......N 1,672
● *Salt River*, Ralls........NE ×
Salt Springs, Saline......... C 25
Samoa, Texas................S 15
● *Samos*, Mississippi...... SE ×
● Sampsell Station, Liv'g'n. N 40
San Antonio, Buchanan.. NW 32
Sandals, Ray..............NW 15
Sand Hill, Scotland........NE 60
Sandrock, Laclede.......... C ×
Sand Rock, Osage..........C ×
● *Sands*, Saint Louis........E ×
Sandstone, Vernon......... W 10
Sandy, Douglas............ S ×
Sandy Bridge, Jefferson....E 15
● *Sankey*, Crawford.........C ×
Santa Fe, Monroe........ NE 125
Santa Rosa, DeKalb...... NW 30
Sappington, Saint Louis.....E 150
Saratoga, McDonald.......SW 100
● Sarcoxie, Jasper........SW 1,172
● Sargent, Texas............ S 50
Sarvis Point, Webster....... S 20
● **Savannah**, Andrew..NW 1,288
● Saverton, Ralls..........NE 100
● Saxton, Buchanan......NW 80
Schall's, Perry..............SE 19
● Scearces, Clinton.......NW ×
● Schell City, Vernon...... W 847
Scheperville, Bollinger.... SE 32
Scheve, Jefferson.......... E ×
Schluersburgh, Saint CharlesE 75
Schofield, Polk...........SW 15
Scholten, Barry.......... SW 25
School, Stone............. SW ×
Scopus, Bollinger..........SE ×
Scotia, Crawford........... C 15
Scotland, Jasper.......... SW 50
● Scott's Station, Cole.......C 25
Scottsville, Sullivan.........N 50
● Scruggs, Cole............ C 12
Search, Morgan............ C ×
Sebree, Howard............ C 30
Seckman, Jefferson.........E ×
● **Sedalia**, Pettis........ C 14,068
Sedan, Douglas..............S ×
Sedgewickville, Bollinger..SE 70
Sedgwick, Linn............. N 32
Segin, Ripley.............. SE ×
Self, Stone................ SW ×
● Seligman, Barry........ SW 242
Selkirk, Laclede........... C ×
Sellers, Lewis............ NE ×
● *Selma*, Saint Louis........E ×
Senate Grove, Franklin.....E ×
Senath, Dunklin........... SE 65
● Seneca, Newton.........SW 1,101
Seney, Macon.............. N 32
Sentinel Prairie, Polk.....SW 20
Sereno, Perry..............SE ×
Service, Crawford...........C ×
Settle's Station, Platte....NW 20
Setz, Saint Francois......... E ×
Seventy Six, Perry.........SE 12
Seybert, Dade.............. SW 15
● Seymour, Webster........ S 388
● Shackleford, Saline....... C 75
Shady Grove, Polk.........SW 100
● *Shady Side*, Saint Louis...E ×
Shamrock, Callaway......... C 30
● Shannondale, Chariton....N 45
Sharon, Saline..............C 12
● *Sharon*, Polk............SW ×
Sharp, Ozark................S ×
Sharpsburg, (see Monroe City) ×
Sharer, (see Mount View).... ×
Shawnee, Shannon...........S ×
Shawnee Mound, Henry.... W 30
Shawneetown, CapeGi'r'u.. SE 100
● *Sheffield*, Butler..........SE ×
● Sheffield, Jackson......... W 500
● Shelbina, Shelby........ NE 1,691
Shelby, Linn................N 20
Shelbyville, Shelby.... NE 486
● Sheldon, Vernon......... W 396
Shell Knob, Barry....... SW 15
Shelter, Saint Louis........ E ×
● Sheridan, Worth........ NW 250
● Sherman, Saint Louis..... E 40
Sherrill, Texas..............S 10
Sherwood, Clark..........NE ×

Missouri

Shibley's Point, Adair...... N 43
Shiloh, Butler..............SE 15
Shipman, Grundy...........N 40
Shoal Creek, Barry........SW 25
Shoalsburg, Newton......SW ×
Shobe, Bates...............W 100
Shootman, Carroll..........N 40
● *Short*, Carter.............SE ×
Shott, Grundy..............N 40
Shotwell, Franklin......... E 30
Shrewsbury, Saint Louis.... E ×
● Sibley, Jackson...........W ×
Sibley, Ralls...............NE ×
● Sidney, Putnam.......... N 100
● Sikeston, Scott...........SE 636
● Silex, Lincoln............. E 151
● Silica, Jefferson...........E 20
Siloam Springs, Howell..... S 75
Silver Lake, Perry......... SE 50
Silverton, Douglas..........S 10
Simmons, Texas............S ×
Simpson, Johnson.......... W ×
Sinclair, Stone...........SW 26
Sinkin, Shannon........... S 19
Sisk, Ray.................NW 20
● Skidmore, Nodaway....SW 400
● *Skinker Road*, Saint LouisE ×
Skrainka, Madison.........SE 32
Slagle, Holk...............SW 25
● Slater, Saline..............C 2,400
Sledd, Pike...............NE ×
● Sleeper, Laclede.........C 10
● Sligo, Dent................S 486
● *Sligo*, Crawford...........C ×
Sloan, Adair................N ×
Smallett, Douglas...........S 10
Smileyville, Murion..........NE 10
Smith, Webster............S 20
● Smithfield, Jasper.......SW 100
● *Smith*, Lincoln............E ×
● *Smith Mines*, Phelps......C ×
Smith's Mills, Pike....... NE ×
● Smithton, Pettis...........C 369
● *Smithton*, Mississippi....SE ×
Smithville, Clay.......... NW 372
Snapp Chariton............ N 10
Sni Mills, Jackson.......... W 25
● Snyder, Chariton......... N ×
Soleville, Cooper........... C ×
Somerset, (see Cleopatra).... ×
Somerset, Ozark.............S 10
Sonttag, Dunklin..........SE ×
South Broadway, City of Saint Louis....................NE ×
South Carrollton, Carroll...N 117
South Fork, Howell..........S 20
● South Greenfield, Dade.SW 430
● *South Iatan*, Platte....NW ×
● *South Kirkwood*, St. LouisE ×
● *South Orongo*, Jasper...SW ×
● *South Point*, Franklin....E 162
● **South Saint Louis, City of St. Louis** ....E ×
● *South Side*, Saint Louis...E ×
South West City, McDonaldSW 707
Spalding, Ralls.............NE 40
Spanish Lake, Saint Louis...E 65
● Sparta, Christian..........S 100
● *Speed*, Cooper............C ×
Spencer, Lawrence.........SW 50
Specnerburgh, Pike........NE 150
Sperry, Adair...............N 10
● Spickardsville, Grundy...N 481
Spira, Ozark...............S 32
Splitlog, McDonald........SW 50
Splitlog Junc., McDonald.SW ×
● Sprague, Bates...........W 267
● *Spraul*, Clark...........NE ×
Spring Bluff, Franklin....NE 25
Spring City, St. Clair ......W ×
Spring Creek, Phelps....... C 85
Springer's Mill, Dent.......S ×
● **Springfield**, Greene..SW 21,850
● *Spring Fork*, Pettis...... C ×
Spring Garden, Miller.......C 85
Spring Grove, Dallas........C 26
Spring Hill, Livingston..... N 90
● *Spring Park*, St. Louis...E ×
Spring Rose, (see Dunnegan Springs)................ ×
Spring Valley, Camden..... C 16
Spruce, Bates..............W 50
Spurgeon, Newton .... SW 26
Squires, Douglas............ S 10
● Stahl, Adair.............. N 100
Staley, Cass................W ×

 Missouri Missouri

Place	Region	Population
●Stanberry, Gentry	NW	2,035
Stancil, Pemiscot	SE	X
●Standish, Carroll	N	X
Stanford, Texas	S	40
●Stanhope, Saline	C	X
Stanley, Buchanan	NW	25
●Stanton, Franklin	E	20
Star, Barry	SW	130
Starfield, Clinton	NW	15
Stark, Pike	NE	10
Starkenburg, Montgomery	E	X
Starlight, Grundy	N	X
Star Ridge, Polk	SW	15
Star's Mill, Texas	S	X
Steadman, Macon	N	X
●**Steelville**, Crawford	C	591
Steen Prairie, Maries	C	30
Steffenville, Lewis	NE	75
Steinhagen, Warren	E	X
●Steinmetz, Howard	C	15
Stella, Nelson	SW	20
●*Stephens*, Boone	C	X
Stephen's Store, Callaway	C	75
●Sterling, Howell	S	10
Stet, Carroll	N	X
●*Stevens*, Saint Louis	E	X
Stewart, Pemiscot	SE	65
●Stewartsville, DeKalb	NW	557
Sticklerville, Sullivan	N	25
●Stillings, Platte	NW	50
●*Stillwell*, Pike	NE	X
●Stockbridge, Buchanan	NW	X
Stockton, Cedar	W	508
●*Stock Yards*, Pike	NE	X
Stokley, Pettis	C	X
Stolpe, Gasconade	E	X
Stone Hill, Dent	S	15
Stono, Saint Francois	E	X
Stony Hill, Gasconade	E	25
●Stoutland, Camden	C	170
●Stoutsville, Monroe	NE	253
Stover, Morgan	C	15
●Stafford, Greene	SW	40
●Strasburg, Cass	W	200
Stratmann, Saint Louis	E	32
Stringtown, (see Lohman)		X
Stringtown, (see Hannibal)		X
Strodersville, C. Girardeau	SE	50
Strother, Monroe	NE	20
Stuart City, (see Drexel)		X
Stultz, Texas	S	X
Sturdivant, Bollinger	SE	X
●Sturgeon, Boone	C	713
●Sturges, Livingston	N	X
●Sublett, Adair	N	81
Success, Texas	S	25
Sue City, Macon	N	100
Suel, Scott	SE	X
●*Sugar Creek*, Stoddard	SE	X
●Sugar Lake, Platte	NW	40
Sugartree, Carroll	N	15
●Sullivan, Franklin	E	300
●Sulphur Springs Landing, Jefferson	E	100
Sumach, Dunklin	SE	X
Summersville, Texas	S	100
Summit, (see Bevier)		X
●Summit, Washington	E	40
Summi ville, Washington	E	40
●Sumner, Chariton	N	286
Sunlight, Washington	E	X
Sunnyside, Wright	S	10
Sunset, Polk	SW	10
Sunshine, Ray	NW	X
Sutter, Saint Louis	E	X
●*Sutton*, Saint Louis	E	X
Swan, Taney	S	35
Swan Lake, (see Barryville)		X
●Swanwick, Ray	NW	20
●Swedeborg, Pulaski	C	50
Sweet Home, Ottawa	NW	30
●Sweet Springs, Saline	C	1,137
Swiss, Gasconade	E	50
Switzler, Boone	C	X
Sycamore, Ozark	S	X
Syenite, Saint Francois	E	200
Sylvania, Dade	SW	97
●Syracuse, Morgan	C	187
Taberville, Saint Clair	W	150
Tabo, LaFayette	W	12
Tackner, Benton	C	X
Taggart, Harrison	NW	90
Taitsville, Ray	NW	90
Taladego, Dent	S	45
●*Talbot*, Howard	C	X
●Talmage, Newton	SW	15
Taney City, Taney	S	10
Tanglefoot, Jefferson	E	600
Taos, Cole	C	65
●Targio, Atchison	NW	1,156
Tarsney, Jackson	W	X
●Taskee Station, Wayne	SE	X
Tavern, Maries	C	12
●Taylor, Marion	NE	25
●*Taylor*, Ralls	NE	X
Taylor Roads, Saint Louis	E	X
Taylorwick, Saint Louis	E	X
Teagues, Webster	S	50
Teal, Cole	C	15
Tedieville, Pettis	C	X
Temple, Vernon	W	20
Ten Mile, Macon	N	10
●*Terra Cotta*, Jackson	W	X
Terre Haute, Putnam	N	20
Terry, Saint Clair	W	X
●Thayer, Oregon	S	1,143
Theodosia, Ozark	S	10
Theresa, (see Williamsville)		X
Thomas, Harrison	NW	10
Thomas Hill, Randolph	N	50
Thomasville, Oregon	S	50
●Thompson, Audrain	C	50
Thompson's L'd'g, Mississippi	SE	X
●*Thoms*, Jasper	SW	X
Thornfield, Ozark	S	10
Thornleigh, Pettis	C	20
●Thornton, Clay	NW	X
Thorpe, Dallas	C	97
Thrush, Henry	W	X
Thurman, Newton	SW	30
Thurman's Switch, Newton	SW	X
Tidwell, Taney	S	10
Tiff City, McDonald	SW	75
Tiffin, Saint Clair	W	35
Tilden, Dallas	C	X
Tilman, Stoddard	SE	12
Tilsit, Cape Girardeau	SE	32
●Tina, Carroll	N	400
●Tindall, Grundy	N	20
Tinney's Grove, Ray	NW	77
●Tipton, Moniteau	C	1,253
●Tipton Ford, Newton	SW	20
●*Tip Top*, Iron	SE	X
Titus, Phelps	C	12
Todd, Morgan	C	X
Toledo, Callaway	C	X
●Tolona, Lewis	NE	30
Topsy, Mercer	N	1
Toronto, Camden	C	25
●*Tower Grove*, Saint Louis	E	X
Trace Creek, Madison	SE	19
Tracy, Platte	NW	250
Trail, Ozark	S	20
Traverse, Barry	SW	X
●Tremont, Polk	SW	10
●**Trenton**, Grundy	N	5,039
Tribulation, McDonald	SW	26
Tribune, Pulaski	C	32
●Triplett, Chariton	N	313
●*Troutman*, Cape Girardeau	SE	X
Troutt, Washington	E	X
●**Troy**, Lincoln	E	971
●Truesdail, Warren	E	100
Truxton, Lincoln	E	150
Tuckahoe, Jasper	SW	X
Tucker, Ripley	SE	X
Tulip, Monroe	NE	20
Tullvania, Macon	N	X
Tuque, Warren	E	26
Turley, Texas	S	10
Turnback, Dade	SW	40
●Turner's, Greene	SW	25
●Turney's Station, Clinton	NW	163
Turpin, Pike	NE	10
Tuscumbia, Miller	C	238
●*Tuxedo Park*, Saint Louis	E	X
Twane, Dent	S	95
Twelve Mile, Madison	SE	26
Twin Springs, McDonald	SW	50
Tyler, Pemiscot	SE	X
Tyrone, Texas	S	X
Udall, Ozark	S	20
Ulam, Sainte Genevieve	E	12
Ulman's Ridge, Miller	C	13
Umpire, Wright	S	12
Undine, Washington	E	X
●**Union**, Franklin	E	610
Union Depot, Jackson	W	X
Union Grove, Gentry	NW	20
●Union Star, DeKalb	NW	272
Uniontown, Perry	SE	150
●**Unionville**, Putnam	N	1,118
Unity, Scotland	NE	10
Upalika, Wayne	SE	X
Upton, Scotland	NE	X
Urbana, Dallas	C	150
●Urich, Henry	W	312
Useful, Osage	C	45
●Utica, Livingston	N	657
Utter, Ralls	NE	50
Vale, Douglas	S	X
Valentine, (see Bedison)		X
Valle's Mines, Jefferson	E	200
Valley City, Johnson	W	30
●*Valley Forge*, Saint Louis	E	X
Valley Forge, St. Francois	E	X
●Valley Park, Saint Louis	E	75
Valley Ridge, Dunklin	SE	12
Van Buren, Carter	SE	100
Vancleve, Maries	C	12
●Vandalia, Audrain	C	979
●Varner, Ripley	SE	150
Varvel, Texas	S	X
Vastus, Butler	SE	X
Vattle, Ray	NW	X
Velors, Christian	S	15
Venable, Texas	S	15
Vera Cruz, Douglas	S	15
Verdella, Barton	SW	40
●Vermont, Cooper	C	35
●Verona, Lawrence	SW	600
●**Versailles**, Morgan	C	1,211
Vest, Phelps	C	10
Veve, Vernon	W	10
●Vibbard, Ray	NW	127
Vichey, Maries	C	10
Victor, Monroe	NE	50
●Victoria, Jefferson	E	200
Vienna, (see Economy)		X
Vienna, Maries	C	105
Viessman, Maries	C	X
Vigus, Saint Louis	E	X
Vilander, Crawford	C	32
●Villa Ridge, Franklin	E	X
Vincit, Dunklin	SE	25
●Vineland, Jefferson	E	30
Vinemont, Bollinger	SE	X
Vinitia, Schuyler	N	10
Vinton, Bates	W	40
Viola, Stone	SW	10
Virgil City, Cedar	W	100
Virginia, Bates	W	100
●Vista, Saint Clair	W	X
Vogel, (see Jackson)		X
Vogel's Switch, Mississippi	SE	X
Voice, Vernon	W	X
●*Von Schraders*, Saint Louis	E	X
Voris, Buchanan	NW	X
Voyage, Gentry	NW	10
●*Vulcan*, Iron	SE	X
●Waco, Jasper	SW	75
Waddill, Newton	SW	65
Wade, McDonald	SW	10
Wagoner, Cedar	W	X
●Wakenda, Carroll	N	206
Waldo, Webster	C	100
Waldo Park, Jackson	W	X
Waldock, Andrew	NW	40
●Waldron, Platte	NW	50
●*Wales*, Vernon	W	X
●Walker, Vernon	W	594
Walkersville, Shelby	NE	X
Wall, Newton	SW	10
●Wallace, Buchanan	NW	190
Walnut, Macon	N	80
Walnut City, (see Foster)		X
●Walnut Grove, Greene	SW	300
Walnut Shade, Taney	S	30
Wanamaker, Saline	C	X
Wanda, Newton	SW	10
Wappapello, Wayne	SE	X
●*Ward*, Bates	W	X
Wards, Saint Charles	E	X
Wardsville, Cole	C	65
Ware, Jefferson	E	20
Warnerville, (see Kerbyville)		X
Warren, Marion	NE	100
●**Warrenburgh**, J'h's'n	W	4,706
Warren's Store, Reynolds	SE	12
●**Warrenton**, Warren	E	664
●**Warsaw**, Benton	C	700
Warwick, Johnson	W	X
●Washburn, Barry	SW	250
●Washington, Franklin	E	2,725
Washington Centre, Hr's'n	NW	25
Wataga, Mercer	N	10
●Waterloo, LaFayette	W	26
Waterville, (see Bakersfield)		X
●*Water Works*, B'ch'an.	NW	455
Watkins, (see So. Greenfield)		X
●Watson, Atchison	NW	238

● *Watson*, Pike.......... NE ×
Wattsville, (see Rogersville). ×
● Waverly, LaFayette...... W 826
● Wayland, Clark .... NE 150
● *Wayne*, Jackson .... W ×
Waynesville, Pulaski... C 150
● Weatherby, DeKalb.... NW 134
Weaubleau, Hickory........ C 160
● Webb City, Jasper...... SW 5,043
Weber, Lewis............. NE 25
Webster, Webster........... S ×
● Webster Groves, SaintLouisE 1,783
Weingarten, Ste.GenevieveSE ×
Welch, Monroe............NE 20
Welcome, Osage............ C 30
Weldon, Maries............ C 40
Weldon Sp'g, Saint Charles . E 100
● Wellington, LaFayette... W 446
Wellston, Saint Louis....... E ×
● Wellsville, Montgomery.. E 1,138
● Wentworth, Newton.... SW 100
● Wentzville, Saint Charles E 457
● Westboro, Atchison.... NW 216
West Cabanne, Saint Louis. E ×
West Eldorado, Cedar..... W ×
West Ely, Marion......... NE 75
West Fork, Reynolds......SE 10
● *West Glasgow*, Saline.... C ×
West Hartford, Ralls......NE 40
● *West Joplin*, Jasper....SW ×
West Kansas City, Jackson W ×
West Liberty, Putnam......N ×
● West Line, Cass.......... W 178
● Weston, Platte.......... NW 1,134
Westphalia, Osage.......... C 200
● **West Plains**, Powell... S 2,091
● *West Platte*, Platte.... NW ×
West Point, (see Dana) ...... ×
Westport, Jackson.......... W 1,000
● *West Quincy*, Marion... NE 260
West Saint Louis, City of Saint Louis.................... E ×
West Union, Cass.......... W 20
Westville, Chariton .... N 75
Wet Glaize, Camden........ C 65
Wheatland, Hickory........ C 500
Wheeler, Pulaski........... C ×
● Wheeling, Livingston.... N 250
Whitcomb, Jackson .... W ×
White Church, Howell...... S 15
White Cloud, Nodaway.. NW ×
White Hare, Cedar........ W 10
● *White House*, Saint Louis E ×
White Ledge, Marion.....NE ×
White Oak, Dunklin.......SE 10
White Oak Grove, Greene SW ×
● *White Rock*, Pine.......NE ×
White Rock, (see Miami Sta.) ×
White Rock Prairie, (see Caverna) .... ×
● *White's*, Pettis........... C 25
Whiteside, Lincoln.......... E 25
White's Store, Howard......C ×
Whitesville, Andrew..... NW 200
● Whitewater, C'peGir'd'u SE 68
Whiting, Mississippi....... SE 300
● *Whitten*, Gentry........ NW 32
Wichern's Landing, (see Wittenberg) .... ×
Wickes, Jefferson .... E ×
● *Wickes*, Saint Louis...... E ×
Wien, Chariton............. N 50
● Wilcox, Nodaway...... NW 30
Wilderness, Oregon.......... S 25
● *Wilkinson*, Saint Louis... E ×
● Willard, Greene........ SW 30
Williamsburgh, Callaway... C 100
Williamstown, Lewis......NE 179
● Williamsville, Wayne....SE 435
Wilmathsville, Adair....... N 87
● Willow Brook, Buchanan NW 25
● Willow Springs, Howell.. S 1,535
Wilmot, Ray............ NW 97
Wilson, Adair.............. N 10
Wilson, Crawford .... C ×
Wilson's, Wayne.......... SE ×
Wilson Mills, Crawford..... C 50
Wilton, Boone............. C 20
Winchester, Clark......... NE 200
Windom, Saint Louis....... E ×
● Windsor, Henry.......... W ..,427
● *Windsor*, Jefferson....... E ×
● *Windsor Spring*, SaintLo'sE ×
● Winfield, Lincoln.......... E 300
Winigan, Sullivan........... N 100
Winner, Clay..............NW ×
● Winona, Shannon......... S 602

Winslow, DeKalb..........NW 30
● Winston, Daviess.......NW 470
Wintersville, Sullivan........N 40
● *Winthrop*, Buchanan...NW 496
● *Winthrop Jc.*, Buchanan NW ×
● Wishart, De Kalb.........NW 35
● Wither's Mills, Marion..NE 15
Wittenberg, Perry......... SE 133
Wolfe, Vernon............. W 3
Wolf Island, Mississippi.....S 20
● *Wommack*, Lincoln....... E ×
Woodhill, Dallas............C 20
● Woodland, Marion........NE 50
● *Woodland*, Saint Louis... E ×
Woodlandville, Boone.......C 35
Woodlawn, Monroe........ NE 150
● *Woodlawn*, Saint Louis... E ×
● Woodruff, Platte....... NW 10
Woodside, Oregon...........S 10
Woodson, Saline............ C 12
● *Woodstock*, Saint Louis...E ×
Woodville, Macon...........N 30
Woollam, Gasconade.........E 40
Worcester, Audrain.........C 15
● Worland, Bates...........W 100
Worsham, Wright...........S ×
● Wright City, Warren......E 383
Wrightville, Dunklin.......SE ×
● Wyaconda, Clark........NE 400
Wyandotte, Grundy......... N ×
Wyreka, (see Ayersville)..... ×
● Xenia, Putnam............ N 10
Xerxes, Polk..............SW ×
Yancy Mills, Phelps.........C 80
● Yates, Randolph..........N 25
Yeakley, Greene...........SW 32
● *Yeatman*, Saint Louis.....E ×
Yingst, Lawrence.........SW 10
York, Atchison............NW 25
Younger's, Boone.......... C 40
Young's Creek, Audrain.... C 12
Yount, Perry............. SE 25
Zadock, Stoddard..........SE ×
Zalma, Bollinger...........SE 100
Zebra, Camden..............C ×
● Zeitonia, Wayne......... SE 50
Zell, Saint Genevieve........ E 130
Zig, Adair................. N 19
Zincite, Jasper............SW 1,500
Zion, Madison.............SE 19
Zodiac, Vernon.............W 27
Zola, Schuyler............ N 10
Zora, Benton............... C 16

MONTANA.

COUNTIES.	INDEX.	POP
Beaver Head	SW	4,655
Cascade	C	8,755
Choteau	N	4,741
Custer	SE	5,308
Dawson	NE	2,056
Deer Lodge	W	15,155
Fergus	C	3,514
Gallatin	S	6,246
Indian Reservation	S	×
Jefferson	C	6,026
Lewis & Clarke	C	19,145
Madison	SW	4,692
Meagher	C	4,794
Missoula	NW	14,427
Park	S	6,881
Silver Bow	SW	23,744
Yellowstone	S	2,065
Total		132,159

TOWN. COUNTY. INDEX. POP.

Ada, Custer................SE ×
Adobetown, Madison......SW 15
● *Ainslie*, Custer......... SE ×
Alamo, Beaver Head......SW ×
Albright, Custer.......... SE 19
Alger, Fergus...............C ×
● Alhambra, Jefferson......C 50
Allard, Dawson...........NE ×
Allerdice, Beaver Head....SW 200
● *Allen*, Cascade.......... C ×
Aliston's, Custer...........SE ×
Alpine, Fergus..............C ×
Alta, Jefferson..............C ×
Alzada, Custer..............SE 75

● *Amazon*, Jefferson........C ×
Amesville, Beaver Head..SW ×
● Anaconda, Deer Lodge...W 3,975
Andersonville, Fergus......C ×
Antelope Sta., Yellowstone..S ×
Antoine Ferry, Missoula..NW ×
● *Apex*, Beaver Head.....SW ×
Argenta, Beaver Head.....SW 140
● Arlee, Missoula..........NW 75
Armells, Fergus.............C ×
● Armington, Cascade ......C 25
● *Ashfield*, Dawson....... NE ×
Ashland, Custer.............SE 15
Ashley, Missoula...........NW 100
● *Assiniboine*, Choteau..... N 625
Augusta, Lewis & Clarke....C 150
● *Austin*, Choteau...........N ×
● Avon, Deer Lodge........W 25
Baker, Gallatin.............. S ×
Bald Butte, Deer Lodge.... W ×
● *Ballic*, Choteau............N ×
Bannock City, B'ver Head.SW 200
● *Barker*, Meagher......... C 150
Barott, Bergus...............C 15
● *Barratts*, Beaver Head.SW ×
Bar Rock, (see Demersville). ×
● Basin, Jefferson...........C 100
Basinski, Custer............SE ×
Baxendale, Lewis & Clarke.C ×
● *Bayliss*, Lewis & Clarke..C ×
● *Beach*, Dawson.......... NE ×
● *Bear Gulch*, Lewis&ClarkeC ×
● Bear's Mouth, DeerLodge W 10
Beartown, Deer Lodge ..... W 520
● *Beaver*, Missoula.......NW ×
Beaver Head Rock, B'r H'dSW ×
● *Beaver Hill*, Dawson....NE ×
● *Beaverton*, Dawson.....NE ×
● Bedford, Jefferson........C 25
Beebe, Custer..............SE ×
● *Beef Straight*, Jefferson.. C ×
● Belgrade, Gallatin.........S 50
Belknap, Choteau.......... N ×
● *Belknap*, Missoula......NW ×
Belleview, Choteau.........N ×
Belmont, Lewis & Clarke...C 15
● Belt, Cascade............. C 30
Beltane, Cascade............C ×
Benson's Landing, Gallatin. S 19
● *Benton*, Choteau.......... N 1,000
Bercail, Fergus............ C 10
● Bernice, Jefferson........ C 50
● *Beulah*, Cascade.......... C ×
Big Elk, Meagher............ C 5
● *Big Horn*, Ind. Reserva'n S ×
● Big Sandy, Choteau.......N 10
● Big Timber, Park..........S 265
● **Billings**, Yellowstone...S 1,575
● *Birdseye*, Lewis & Clarke.C ×
Birney, Custer............ .SE ×
● *Bitter Root*, Missoula.. NW ×
● *Blackfoot*, Choteau.......N ×
Blackfoot City, Deer Lodge W 50
Blackhawk, Meagher....... C ×
Black Pine, Deer Lodge....W 244
● *Blair*, Dawson..........NE ×
Blakeley, Indian ReservationS ×
● Blatchford, Custer...... SE ×
● Blossburg, Deer Lodge...W 75
● *Bluebird*, Silver Bow...SW ×
● *Boice*, Dawson...........NE ×
● Bonita, Missoula.......NW 50
● Bonner, Missoula.......NW 250
● *Borax*, Missoula........NW ×
● *Boulder*, Jefferson........C 1,000
Boulder Sta., (see Stone Sta.) ×
● **Boulder Valley**, J'ff'snC 195
Bowdoin, Dawson......... NE ×
Bowen, Beaver Head...... SW ×
Bower, Beaver Head..... SW ×
Bower's Ranch, Custer....SE ×
● Box Elder, Choteau...... N 150
● *Boyd*, Deer Lodge........W ×
● **Bozeman**, Gallatin......S 3,675
Bradford, Lewis & Clark....C ×
● *Bradley*, Deer Lodge......W ×
Brandenberg, Custer........SE 10
Brassey, Fergus.......... SW ×
Bremer, Choteau...........N ×
Brighton, Choteau......... N ×
● *Briggs*, Missoula....... NW ×
● *Brisbin*, Park............S ×
● *Brockton*, Dawson.......NE ×
Bruckman, Yellowstone.... S ×
Buell, Custer............. SE ×
Buffalo, Fergus..............C ×
● *Bull Mountain*, Ind. Res..S ×

● *Burnham*, Choteau.......N ×
Burlington, Silver Bow... SW 344
Burnt Pine, Beaver Head SW ×
● Butler, Lewis & Clarke... C ×
● **Butte City**, Silver Bow SW 17,393
Buxton, Silver Bow.......SW ×
Bynum, Choteau...........N 10
Cable, Deer Lodge.........W 100
● *Cairo*, Choteau.......... N ×
● *Calais*, Dawson......... NE ×
● *Calvin*, Jefferson..........C ×
● *Camde*, Choteau..........N ×
Cameron, Madison........ SW ×
Cameron's Ferry, Missoula NW 6
Campbell's, Ind'n Reserv'n..S ×
Campbell's, Dawson...... NE ×
Camp Alarm, Custer......SE ×
Canton, Meagher............C 25
Cantonment, Dawson.......NE ×
Canyon, Yellowstone.......S ×
● Canyon Creek, Lewis & Clarke C ×
Canyon Ferry, Meagher.....C 25
Capitol, Custer............SE ×
Carasco, Choteau........... N ×
● *Carlin*, Deer Lodge...... W ×
● *Carlow*, Choteau..........N ×
● Carlton, Missoula...... NW ×
Carroll, Fergus............ C ×
Carroll, Deer Lodge........ W 549
Carter, Missoula.. ......NW ×
Cartersville, Lewis & Clarke C 50
● Cascade, Cascade..........C 200
Castle, Meagher.............C 383
● *Cataract*, Jefferson.........C ×
Cavendish, Beaver Head.. SW ×
Cavetown, (see Canyon Ferry) ×
Cecil, Lewis & Clarke.......C ×
Centennial, Madison...... SW ×
● Central Park, Gallatin.... S 55
Centreville, Meagher......... C 200
Centreville, (see Butte City).. ×
Champion, Deer Lodge.....W 300
● *Chelsea*, Dawson.........NE ×
Cherry Creek Mine, Gallatin S ×
● *Chester*, Choteau.......... N ×
Chestnut, Cascade...........C 130
● *Chestnut*, Gallatin..........S ×
Cheyenne Agency, Custer. SE ×
Chico, Park................... S 10
● *Chicory*, Gallatin..........S ×
● *Childs*, Jefferson...........C ×
● Chinook, Choteau.........N 300
Choteau, Choteau...........N 200
Chrame, Dawson..........NE ×
Christian, Fergus...........SW ×
● *Cinnabar*, Park...........S 25
Cisero, Madison...........SW ×
● Clancey, Jefferson........ C 75
Clarence, Meagher..........C ×
Clark City, Gallatin.........S ×
Clark's Canon, Beaver H'd SW ×
Clark's Sta., Deer Lodge... W ×
Clarkston, Lewis & Clarke..C ×
● *Clasoil*, Jefferson......... C ×
Clearwater, Deer Lodge.... W ×
Clendenin, Meagher.........C 100
Cleora, Park..................S ×
● *Clermont*, Indian Reserv'n S ×
Clifford, Missoula........ NW ×
● *Clinton*, Choteau......... N ×
● *Clinton*, Missoula....... NW ×
● *Clough Junction*, Lewis & Clarke.............. C ×
Clyde Park, Park.............S ×
Coal Banks, Lewis & Clarke C ×
● *Coal Spur*, Park........... S ×
Cokedale, Park...............S 284
● *Colburn*, Choteau..........N ×
Cold Spring, Jefferson...... C ×
● *Colgate*, Dawson........NE ×
● *Collins*, Choteau..........N ×
● *Colo Gulch*, Lewis & Clarke C ×
● Columbia Falls, Missoula NW ×
Comet, Jefferson..............C 50
Como, Missoula...........NW 60
Confederate Gulch Mine, Meagher............C ×
● *Conlin*, Dawson.........NE ×
● *Conrad*, Choteau......... N 100
Cooke, Park...................S 200
Conway, Indian Reservations S ×
● *Cooper*, Missoula........NW ×
Copperopolis, Meagher......C ×
Cora, Cascade................C 15
● Corbin, Jefferson..........C 100
Corvallis, Missoula......... NW 450
Cottonwood, Fergus.........C 200

Coulson, (see Billings) .... ×
Courts, Gallatin..............S ×
● *Crabtree*, Beaver Head..SW ×
● Craig, Lewis & Clarke.... C 35
Crescent, Jefferson..........C ×
Crittenden, Dawson.......NE ×
Crow Agency, Indian Reser'n S 100
Crow Creek, Jefferson.......C 45
● *Cruse*, Lewis & Clarke.... C ×
● Culbertson, Dawson.... NE ×
● *Custer*, Yellowstone.......S 25
Cultay, Choteau.............N ×
● *Cutbank*, Choteau.........N ×
Cutler, Custer.............. SE 10
Cypress, Choteau........... N 6
● *Dailey's*, Gallatin.......... S ×
● *Daly's*, Beaver Head....SW ×
Darby, Missoula.......... NW 20
Darling, Beaver Head.... SW ×
Davidson, Choteau......... N ×
● *Dayton*, Choteau.......... N ×
Dearborn, Lewis & Clarke... C 75
De Borgia, Missoula..... NW ×
Deepdale, Meagher...........C ×
Deerfield, Fergus............ C ×
● **Deer Lodge City**, Deer Lodge.................. W 1,463
● Dell, Beaver Head...... SW ×
Demersville, Missoula....NW 1,500
● *Dempsey*, Deer Lodge.... W ×
Denton, Fergus.............. C ×
● *De Smet*, Missoula......NW 25
Devee, Meagher.............C 10
● *Dewey*, Custer............SE ×
Deway's, Beaver Head.... SW 50
Diamond, Dawson........ NE ×
Diamond City, Meagher.....C 50
Diamond Springs, Lewis & Clarke................. C ×
● **Dillon**, Beaver Head..SW 1,012
Dilworth, Park............. S ×
● Divide, Silver Bow......SW ×
● *Dixon*, Custer..............SE ×
Dixon's Ferry, Missoula. NW 5
Dodge, Lewis & Clarke.....C 10
● *Dodson*, Choteau......... N ×
● *Dorsey*, Missoula........NW ×
● Drummond, Deer Lodge. W 40
● *Dry Fork*, Choteau.......N ×
Dudley, Fergus............. C ×
● *Duffy's*, Lewis & Clarke.. C ×
● *Dunbar's*, Missoula.... NW ×
Duncan, Gallatin............S ×
● *Duncan*, Missoula.......NW ×
Dunkleberg, Deer Lodge... W ×
Dupuyer, Choteau........... N 50
● *Durham*, Choteau........N ×
● *Dyers*, Silver Bow...... SW ×
● *Earle*, Madison.........SW ×
● *East Butte*, Silver Bow.SW ×
East Gallatin, Gallatin.......S ×
● East Helena, Lewis & Clarke C 800
Eberhart's, Missoula.....NW ×
● *Eddy*, Missoula........ NW ×
Egan, Missoula........... NW 100
Ekalaka, Custer..............SE 5
Eldorado, Meagher.........C ×
● Elkhorn, Jefferson..........C 500
● Elk Park, Jefferson..........C 25
● Elliston, Deer Lodge......W 200
Elso, Fergus..................C ×
● *Elton*, Gallatin..............S ×
● *Emigrant*, Park............ S ×
Emmetsburg, Deer Lodge..W ×
Emigrant Gulch Mine, Park S ×
Empire, Lewis & Clarke.....C 200
Ennis, Madison........... SW 55
Enterprise, Missoula.....NW ×
Ericson, Custer............SE ×
Etchetah, Custer............SE 10
Etna, Custer..................SE ×
● *Eureka*, Choteau............N ×
Evans, Cascade.................C ×
● *Evaro*, Missoula....... NW ×
● *Exeter*, Choteau............N ×
Fairview, Beaver Head... SW ×
● Fallon, Custer..............SE ×
● Feeley, Silver Bow........SW ×
● *Ferry*, Missoula........NW ×
Ferry Point, Meagher...... C ×
● *Field*, Cascade.............. C ×
● Fin, Jefferson..............C ×
Fish Creek, Jefferson........ C 15
Fish Creek, Missoula..... NW 20
Flat Creek, Missoula..... NW 150
Flat Head Agency, Mos'la NW 10
Flatwillow, Fergus..........C 20

● Flint, Deer Lodge........W ×
Flintown, Missoula...... NW 10
Florence, Lewis & Clarke.. C 130
● Florence, Missoula.....NW 40
● Flowerree, Choteau...... N ×
Foley, Custer..............SE ×
Folsom, Fergus............. C ×
Forest City, Missoula.... NW 10
● Forsyth, Custer...........SE 308
● Fort Assinaboine, Choteau N 660
● **Fort Benton**, Choteau. N 624
Fort Browning, Choteau... N ×
Fort C. F. Smith, I'n Res'on S ×
Fort Custer, Indian Res .. SE 582
Fort Hawley, Choteau..... N ×
● Fort Keogh, Custer..... SE 1,500
Fort Logan, Meagher........ C 27
Fort Maginnis, Fergus......C 250
Fort Missoula, Missoula..NW 271
Fort Owen, Missoula .... NW ×
Fort Peck, Dawson.......NE ×
Fort Shaw, Cascade.........C 275
● *Foster*, Yellowstone....... S ×
Four Mile, Missoula...... NW 10
Fox, Beaver Head........SW ×
Franklin, Custer.......... SE ×
Freemans, Custer.......... SE ×
French Bar, Meagher...... C ×
French Gulch, Beaver H'd SW ×
French Gulch, Deer Lodge W ×
● Frenchtown, Missoula..NW 400
Fridley, Park............... S 10
Fulton, Lewis & Clarke.....C 10
Gaffney, Madison......... SW ×
Galem, Meagher............ C ×
● *Gallatin*, Gallatin.........S 25
Gallatin City, Gallatin......S ×
Gallop, Gallatin.............S ×
● *Galt*, Choteau............ N ×
Garden Land, Fergus...... C ×
Gardiner, Park............. S 50
Garland, Custer........... SE ×
● Garrison, Deer Lodge.... W 300
Georgetown, Deer Lodge...W ×
German Gulch, Silver Bow SW ×
● Glasgow, Dawson....... NE 338
● *Gleason*, Lewis & Clarke..C ×
● *Glen*, Beaver Head..... SW ×
Glendale, Beaver Head....SW 371
● **Glendive**, Dawson....NE 1,500
Glenrock, Custer........... SE ×
Gloster, Lewis & Clarke.... C 20
● *Gold Bar*, Lewis & Clarke C ×
● Gold Creek, Deer Lodge. W 20
Gold Dust, Jefferson....... C ×
Goodman Coulee, Cascade.. C 10
● *Gordon*, Gallatin .... S ×
Gorham, Cascade........... C 28
Gorman, Meagher........... C 28
Gould, Lewis & Clarke......C ×
Grace, Jefferson............ C 20
Grafton, Cascade............ C 25
Granite, Deer Lodge....... W 1,310
● Grantsdale, Missoula .. NW 500
Grassrange, Fergus......... C 20
● Grass Valley, Missoula. NW 30
● *Grayling*, Beaver Head SW ×
● **Great Falls**, Cascade...C 3,979
Gregory, (see Wickes)......... ×
● *Gregson's*, Deer Lodge.... W ×
Greson's Springs, Silv'r Bow SW 25
● Grey Cliff, Park.......... S ×
Gunderson, Silver Bow... SW 500
Gwendale, Deer Lodge .... W ×
Hackney, Silver Bow .... SW ×
Halbert, Fergus............ C ×
● *Halford's*, Jefferson...... C ×
● *Hall*, Park.................S ×
Halpin, Missoula .... NW ×
● Hamilton, Missoula.... NW 50
● Hardy, Cascade .... C ×
● Harlem, Choteau...........N 5
Harlow, Meagher.......... C ×
Harris, Custer.............. SE ×
Harrisburgh, Deer Lodge..W ×
● Harrison, Madison..... SW 20
● *Hartwell*, Jefferson ...... C ×
● *Haskell*, Deer Lodge..... W ×
Hasmarck, (see Phillipsb'g). ×
● Hathaway, Custer...... SE ×
● Havre, Choteau........... N ×
Hayden, Gallatin........... S ×
Hecla, Beaver Head...... SW 300
● **HELENA**, Lewis & Cl'ke C 15,657
Hell Gate, Missoula...... NW ×
Helmville, Deer Lodge..... W 25
Henderson, Deer Lodge.... W ×

● Heron, Missoula........NW 125
Highfield, Fergus.......... C ×
● *Highview*, Silver Bow..SW ×
Highwood, Choteau .... N ×
Hilgersville, Lewis & Clarke C ×
Hill, Missoula........... NW ×
Hillsdale, Gallatin .... S 10
● *Hingham*, Choteau ...... N ×
● *Hinsdale*, Dawson...... NE 15
Hockett's, Custer..........SE ×
● *Hodges*, Dawson........NE ×
● *Hodson*, Jefferson........ C ×
Hogan, Lewis & Clarke..... C ×
Holt, Missoula........... NW ×
Holts, Custer.............. SE ×
Home Park, Madison.....SW ×
● *Homestake*, Silver Bow SW ×
Hope, Jefferson .... C ×
Hope, Missoula .... NW ×
● *Hopper*, Park .... S ×
Hord's, Custer .... SE ×
Horr, Park..................S 150
● *Horse Plains*, Missoula NW ×
Horse Prairie, Beaver H'd SW ×
● Horton, Custer.........SE ×
Hotchkiss, Custer......... SE ×
Hotel Broadway, Lewis & Clarke.............. C ×
Hot Spring, Beaver Head.SW 50
● *Hot Springs*, Jefferson... C ×
Hot Springs, Lewis & Clarke C ×
● Howard, Custer.......... SE ×
Howes, Custer .... SE ×
● *Hoyt*, Dawson.......... NE 50
Hughesville, Meagher.......C 97
Hunter's Hot Springs, Park.S 50
● Huntley, Yellowstone.... S 65
Hurst, Meagher........... C ×
● *Huson*, Missoula.......NW ×
Hutton, Custer............. SE ×
Hyde, Custer.............. SE ×
Ida, Cascade.............. C ×
● *Iron*, Lewis & Clarke.... C ×
● Iron Mountain, Missoula NW ×
Iron Rod, Madison.......SW ×
Isabel, Deer Lodge .... W ×
Jay Gould, Lewis & Clarke.. C 500
● Jefferson City, Jefferson..C 200
Jefferson Island, Madison SW ×
● *Jefferson Island Station*, Madison............. SW ×
● Jocko, Missoula........ NW ×
Johnstown, Choteau........ N 75
Judith, Fergus.............. C 25
Junction, Yellowstone...... S 250
Junction, Madison........ SW 25
● Kalispell, Missoula...... NW 4,000
Keene, Deer Lodge......... W ×
● *Kesslers*, Lewis & Clarke.C ×
Kibbey, Cascade............ C 15
● *Kilva*, Dawson.......... NE ×
● *Kintyre*, Dawson .... NE ×
● *Kirkendall*, Jefferson.... C ×
● *Kohrs*, Deer Lodge...... W ×
Kootensay Trading Post, Missoula.............NW ×
Lacy, Choteau.............. N ×
Lake City, Missoula...... NW ×
● *Lake Wilder*, Jefferson... C ×
Lambetts, Dawson........ NE ×
Lame Deer, Custer........ SE ×
● *Lanark*, Dawson........ NE ×
● *Laredo*, Choteau........ N ×
● Laurel, Yellowstone...... S 15
Laurin, Madison........... SW 200
Lavina, Fergus............ C 25
Lee, Custer................ SE ×
Lee Mountain, Lewis & Clarke C 50
● *Lenox*, Dawson.......... NE ×
Lerengood, Deer Lodge.... W ×
Lewis, Madison........... SW ×
Lewistown, Fergus...... C 700
Libby, Missoula.......... NW 10
● Lima, Beaver Head.....SW 358
Lime Spur, Jefferson....... C ×
● *Lincoln*, Cascade.........C ×
Lincoln, Deer Lodge....... W ×
Linsdale, Dawson .... NE ×
Lion City, Beaver Head...SW 30
● **Livingston**, Park...... S 2,850
● *Lloyd*, Deer Lodge....... W ×
Lloyd, Choteau............. N ×
Lockhart, Jefferson.........C ×
● Logan, Gallatin........... S ×
● *Logging Creek*, Cascade...C 10
● Lo-Lo, Missoula........NW ×
● *Lookout*, Missoula......NW ×

Loraine, Madison......... SW ×
● *Lothrop*, Missoula...... NW ×
Louisville, Missoula...... NW ×
Lucille, Choteau........... N ×
Lyon City, Beaver Head.. SW 30
Lyon, Madison........... SW ×
McCarthyville, Missoula. NW ×
● *McClains*, Missoula.... NW ×
● *McClellan*, Dawson.....NE ×
McClintocks, Custer.......SE ×
● *McKeen*, Missoula..... NW ×
McLain's, Custer.......... SE ×
● *McLaughlins*, Missoula NW ×
● *McLeod*, Missoula......NW ×
McLeod, Park................ S ×
● *McMillan's*, Missoula..NW ×
● *Macon*, Dawson........ NE ×
Magnolia, Meagher.........C ×
● *Magpie*, Jefferson........ C ×
Maiden, Fergus............ C 400
● Malta, Dawson.......... NE 10
Mammoth, Madison.........SW ×
Mammoth Hot Springs, Yellowstone............... S ×
● Manhattan, Gallatin...... S ×
Mann, Cascade..............C 10
Margana, Madison....... SW ×
● *Marias*, Choteau......... N ×
Marie, Silver Bow........SW ×
Martina, Missoula........ NW 50
Martinsdale, Meagher.......C 100
● Marysville, Lewis & Clark C 1,489
Marysville Junc., Lewis & Clarke ×
● Mason, Indian ReservationsS ×
Mason's, Missoula........ NW ×
Meaderville, Silver Bow.. SW 1,075
Meadow Creek, Madison.. SW 15
Medicine Lodge, Dawson..NE ×
Medhurst, Deer Lodge..... W ×
● Melrose, Silver Bow.... SW 350
Melville, Park............... S 15
Merino, Meagher............C ×
● Merrill, Yellowstone......S ×
● *Merritt*, Indian Reservat'nS ×
Meyersburg, Park...........S ×
● Mid Canon, Cascade...... C ×
● *Midvale*, Choteau.........N ×
Mikado, Fergus.............C ×
● *Miles*, Missoula........NW ×
● **Miles City**, Custer.....SE 2,000
● *Milk River*, Dawson.... NE ×
● *Mill Creek*, Deer Lodge.. W ×
Millegan, Cascade............C ×
Mineral, Missoula........NW ×
● Mingusville, Dawson....NE 25
● *Minnehaha*, Lewis & Clark.C ×
● *Mission*, Gallatin......... S ×
Mission, Custer............SE ×
● **Missoula**, Missoula.. NW 3,426
Missoula, Missoula........ NW ×
● *Mitchell's*, Lewis & ClarkeC ×
Monaco, (see Columbia Falls) ×
● Monarch, Cascade......... C ×
● *Monida*, Madison.......SW ×
● *Montana City*, Jefferson..C 29
Moore's, Custer............SE ×
Moorhead, Custer...........SE ×
● *Moose Creek*, Lewis & C'k.C ×
Moose Creek, Silver Bow..SW ×
Mountain House, Missoula NW ×
● *Mountain Side*, Gallatin.. S 10
Mount Horeb, Silver Bow SW ×
Muddy, Custer..............SE 18
● *Muir*, Gallatin............ S ×
Musselshell, Yellowstone....S 50
● *Myers*, Indian Reservat'n.S ×
● *Nabb's*, Deer Lodge......W ×
● Nashua, Dawson........ NE 25
Neihart, Meagher...........C 800
Nelsonville, Fergus......... C ×
Nevada City, Madison.... SW 20
● New Chicago, Deer LodgeW 150
Newlon, Dawson...........NE ×
New York, Meagher........ C ×
Nine Mile, Missoula...... NW 15
Nobbs, Deer Lodge..........W ×
● Norris, Madison......... SW ×
● *North Fork*, Choteau.... N ×
North Great Falls, Cascade..C 150
Norwood, Silver Bow.....SW ×
● Noxon, Missoula....... NW 50
Nye, Park..................... S 10
Oka, Meagher................C 20
Old Crow Agency, Indian Reservation............ S ×
Olden, Meagher............ C ×
Old Silver Bow, Silver B'w SW 10

Old Town, Custer......... SE ×
● *Olive*, Missoula......... NW ×
Oliver, Beaver Head...... SW ×
Onge, Silver Bow.......... SW ×
Onondago, Meagher........ C ×
● *Oswego*, Dawson........ NE 15
Ovando, Deer Lodge........W ×
Overland, Fergus........... C ×
● *Painted Rock*, Choteau... N ×
● *Painted Rock*, Jefferson.. C ×
● *Paradise*, Missoula.....NW 15
Paradise, Park..............S ×
Pardee, Missoula......... NW ×
● **Park City, Yellowstone... S** 150
Pearmond, Dawson....... NE ×
Pease's Bottom, Custer....SE ×
● *Peigan*, Choteau..........N ×
● *Perma*, Missoula..........NW ×
Perrysburgh, Choteau......N ×
Philbrook, Fergus.......... C 50
● Phillipsburgh, D'r Lodge. W 1,058
Piedmont, Park.............S ×
Piegan, Choteau............ N 10
Pike's Peak, Deer Lodge.. W ×
Pioneer, Deer Lodge....... W 50
Pipe Stone Springs, Jefferson C 26
● Placer, Jefferson..........C 35
Placer, Silver Bow....... SW ×
● Plains, Missoula.......... NW 250
● *Pleasant Valley*, Missoula NW ×
Poindexter, Beaver Head. SW ×
● *Pompey's Pillar*, Indian Reservation............S ×
● Pony, Madison...........SW 150
● Poplar Creek Agency, Dawson................... NE 34
● *Portage*, Choteau.........N ×
● *Portal*, Jefferson......... C ×
Potomac, Missoula........ NW 100
Powder River, (see Glendive) ×
Powderville, Custer........SE 10
Powers, Lewis & Clarke.... C 35
Prickley Pear, Jefferson....C 19
● *Prickley Pear Junction*, Jefferson.........................C ×
Primus, Gallatin............S ×
Princeton, Deer Lodge.....W ×
Profile, Fergus..............C ×
Puller Springs, Madison..SW ×
Purtle's Spur, Missoula.. NW 25
Pyrenees, Deer Lodge......W ×
Pyretees, Missoula....... NW ×
● Quartz, Missoula......... NW 25
● Race Track, Deer Lodge..W 15
Radersburgh, Jefferson. C 150
Ralston, Silver Bow...... SW ×
Ramington, Cascade....... C 25
Rancher, Custer........... SE ×
● *Rapids*, Yellowstone......S ×
Ravalli, Missoula......... NW 15
Ravalli, Missoula.........NW 10
Raymond, Choteau.......... N ×
Red Bluff, Madison....... SW 75
● Red Lodge, Park...........S 624
Red Mountain, Silv'r B'w.SW 5
● *Red Mountain Junc.*, Lewis & Clarke............... C 5
● *Red Rock*, Jefferson...... C 65
● Red Rock, Beaver Head SW 50
Reed's Fort, Meagher.......C 200
● *Reedpoint*, Yellowstone...S ×
● *Reserve*, Indian ReservationS ×
Revenue, Madison.........SW 100
Reynolds, Indian ReservationS ×
● *Rhoebaugh*, Jefferson.... C ×
● Riceville, Cascade........ C ×
Richland, Park.............S ×
Ridgelawn, Dawson.......NE ×
● Rimini, Lewis & Clarke.. C 100
● Riverside, Missoula.... NW 50
● *Rivulet*, Missoula...... NW ×
Robare, Choteau............ N 10
Robinson, Meagher..........C 25
Rochester, Madison....... SW ×
Rochester, Deer Lodge.....W ×
Rock Creek, Missoula.... NW ×
Rocker, Silver Bow....... SW 100
Rockey Point, Choteau..... N 12
● *Rocky Spring*, Choteau... N ×
Rohner, Lewis & Clarke.... C ×
● *Rohrbaugh*, Jefferson.... C ×
● Rosebud, Custer.......... SE 25
● *Ross*, Silver Bow........SW ×
Roundup, Yellowstone.......S 10
● Rumsey, Deer Lodge.....W 300
Ryan, Indian Reservation...S ×
Ryan's Junction, (see Watson's) ×

Town, County	Index	Pop.
Sabra, Custer	SE	×
● *Saco*, Dawson	NE	×
Sadie, Custer	SE	×
Sahara, Fergus	C	×
Saint Clair, Cascade	C	50
Saint Ignatius, Missoula	NW	30
Saint Louis, Jefferson	C	50
Saint Paul's, Choteau	N	×
Saint Peter, Cascade	C	×
● *Saint Regis*, Missoula	NW	×
Saint Xavier, Custer	SE	×
Salesville, Gallatin	S	40
Salisbury, Madison	SW	32
● *Saltese*, Missoula	NW	×
● Sandcoulee, Cascade	C	500
● *Sanders*, Custer	SE	×
● *Sappington*, Gallatin	S	×
● *Savoy*, Choteau	N	×
Sedan, Gallatin	S	×
Selish, Missoula	NW	60
Seven Mile, Lewis & Clarke	C	10
Shambow, Madison	SW	×
Shawmut, Meagher	C	×
● *Shelby Junction*, Choteau	N	15
Sheep Creek, Meagher	C	×
Sheldon, Missoula	NW	40
Shepard, Choteau	N	×
Sheridan, Madison	SW	207
Shields, Gallatin	S	×
● *Shirley*, Custer	SE	×
Shonkin, Choteau	N	×
Sidney, Dawson	NE	×
● *Sidney*, Choteau	N	×
Sifton, Fergus	C	×
● *Silver*, Lewis & Clarke	C	100
Silver Bow, Silver Bow	SW	200
Silver Creek, Lewis & Clarke	C	×
Silver Junc., Lewis & Clarke	C	10
Silver Star, Madison	SW	100
● *Silverthorn*, Missoula	NW	×
Sixteen, Meagher	C	×
Skalkoho, Missoula	NW	×
Smead, Missoula	NW	×
Smelter, Cascade	C	10
● South Butte, Silver Bow	SW	801
● *Sphinx*, Gallatin	S	×
Spokane, Jefferson	C	48
Spotted Horse, Fergus	C	×
Spring, Beaver Head	SW	×
● Springdale, Park	S	16
● *Spring Gulch*, Missoula	NW	×
Spring Hill, Gallatin	S	30
Stacey, Custer	SE	×
Stanford, Fergus	C	200
Stark, Missoula	NW	×
Stearns, Lewis & Clarke	C	×
● Steele, Choteau	N	×
Stemple, Lewis & Clarke	C	15
Sterling, Madison	SW	×
● Stevensville, Missoula	NW	400
Stickney, Cascade	C	×
● Stillwater, Yellowstone	S	100
● *Stockholm*, Dawson	NE	×
● Stone Station, Deer Lodge	W	30
● *Storey*, Gallatin	S	×
Strader Ranch, Custer	SE	×
● Stuart, Deer Lodge	W	50
Sula, Missoula	NW	×
Summit, Choteau	N	10
Sunnyside, Gallatin	S	×
Sun River, Cascade	C	75
Sunset, Deer Lodge	W	7
Superior, Missoula	NW	200
Sweet Grass, Park	S	×
● *Swift*, Cascade	C	×
● *Tampico*, Dawson	NE	×
Tampa, Dawson	NE	×
Terra Firma, Deer Lodge	W	×
● Terry, Custer	SE	25
● *Teton*, Choteau	N	×
● *Thermal Springs*, Lewis & Clarke	C	×
● *Thistle*, Jefferson	C	×
● Thompson, Missoula	NW	339
Three Forks, Gallatin	S	50
● *ThreeForkStation*, Gallatin	S	×
Thurza, Yellowstone	S	×
Timberhill, Gallatin	S	15
● Timberline, Gallatin	S	100
Tobacco Plains, Missoula	NW	×
Tokna, Dawson	NE	×
● *Toledo*, Choteau	N	×
TongueRiverAgency, Custer	SE	15
● *Toohy*, Deer Lodge	W	×
● Toston, Meagher	C	200
● Townsend, Meagher	C	245
TradingPostFerry, Mi's'la	NW	×
● *Trail Creek*, Gallatin	S	×
● *Trask*, Jefferson	C	×
Trout Creek, Fergus	C	×
● Trout Creek, Missoula	NW	10
Truly, Cascade	C	×
● *Tunis*, Choteau	N	×
● *Tuscor*, Missoula	NW	×
Twin Bridges, Madison	SW	200
Ubet, Fergus	C	50
Ulida, Lewis & Clarke	C	×
● *Ulm*, Cascade	C	×
Unionville, Lewis & Clarke	C	125
Unity, Meagher	C	×
Utica, Fergus	C	50
Valleux, Choteau	N	×
● *Vandalia*, Dawson	NE	×
Vaters, Park	S	×
Vaughan, Lewis & Clarke	C	10
Vermillion, Missoula	NW	25
● *Verona*, Choteau	N	×
Vestel, Deer Lodge	W	×
● Victor, Missoula	NW	200
Vipond, Beaver Head	SW	×
Virginia City, Madison	SW	675
● *Vose*, Jefferson	C	×
● *Wades*, Lewis & Clarke	C	×
● *Wagner*, Choteau	N	×
Walkerville, Silver Bow	SW	1,743
● Wallace, Missoula	NW	×
● WarmSprings, DeerL'dge	W	150
Warren Spr'gs, L'wis&Cl'rke	C	35
Warrick, Choteau	N	×
Washington Bar, Madison	SW	×
Wash'gt'nGulch, Deer L'dge	W	×
Watseka, Madison	SW	×
Watson, Beaver Head	SW	×
● *Watson*, Cascade	C	×
● *Wayne*, Choteau	N	×
Weber, Jefferson	C	×
● *Weeksville*, Missoula	NW	50
● *West End*, Gallatin	S	×
● *Whately*, Dawson	NE	×
● *Whitefish*, Missoula	NW	×
○ Whitehall, Jefferson	C	45
White's, Meagher	C	×
● *White Pine*, Missoula	NW	×
White Sulphur Springs, Meagher	C	640
● *Wibaux*, Dawson	NE	×
● Wickes, Jefferson	C	600
Wilder, Fergus	C	×
Williams, Gallatin	S	×
● *Williams*, Beaver Head	SW	×
Willis, Beaver Head	SW	×
● Willow Creek, Gallatin	S	25
Willowglen, Deer Lodge	W	×
● *Willows*, Dawson	NE	×
● *Wilsey*, Indian Reservation	S	×
Winnecook, Meagher	C	×
Wisdom, Beaver Head	SW	×
● Wolf Creek, Lewis & Clarke	C	30
Wolfdene, Meagher	C	×
● Wolfpoint, Dawson	NE	×
Wolsey, Meagher	C	×
Woodin, Silver Bow	SW	×
● *Woodlin*, Missoula	NW	×
Woodside, Missoula	NW	×
● *Wood Siding*, Lewis & Cl'ke	C	×
● Woodville, Jefferson	C	50
Woodworth, Deer Lodge	W	×
Yale, Fergus	C	×
● Yantic, Choteau	N	5
● *Yates*, Dawson	N	×
Yellowstone, Yellowstone	S	×
Yogo, Meagher	C	×
York, Meagher	C	×
Younger, Custer	SE	×
Yreka, Deer Lodge	W	×
● *Zenith*, Jefferson	C	×
● *Zurich*, Choteau	N	×

NEBRASKA.

Counties.	Index.	Pop.
Adams	S	24,303
Antelope	N	10,399
Arthur	NW	91
Banner	W	2,435
Blaine	C	1,146
Boone	C	8,683
Boxbutte	NW	5,494
Boyd	N	695
Brown	N	4,359
Buffalo	C	22,162
Burt	NE	11,069
Butler	E	15,454
Cass	SE	24,080
Cedar	NE	7,028
Chase	NW	4,807
Cherry	N	6,428
Cheyenne	W	5,693
Clay	S	16,310
Colfax	E	10,453
Cuming	NE	12,265
Custer	C	21,677
Dakota	NE	5,386
Dawes	NW	9,722
Dawson	C	10,129
Deuel	W	2,893
Dixon	NE	8,084
Dodge	E	19,260
Douglas	E	158,008
Dundy	SW	4,012
Fillmore	SE	16,022
Franklin	S	7,693
Frontier	SW	8,497
Furnas	S	9,840
Gage	SE	33,344
Garfield	C	1,659
Gosper	S	4,816
Grant	NW	458
Greeley	C	4,869
Hall	C	16,513
Hamilton	C	14,096
Harlan	S	8,158
Hayes	SW	3,953
Hitchcock	SW	5,797
Holt	N	13,672
Hooker	NW	426
Howard	C	9,430
Jefferson	SE	14,850
Johnson	SE	10,333
Kearney	S	9,061
Keith	W	2,554
Keya Paha	N	3,920
Kimball	W	959
Knox	N	8,582
Lancaster	SE	76,395
Lincoln	W	10,441
Logan	C	1,378
Loup	C	1,662
McPherson	NW	401
Madison	NE	13,669
Merrick	C	8,758
Nance	C	5,773
Nemaha	SE	12,930
Nuckolls	S	11,417
Otoe	SE	25,403
Pawnee	SE	10,340
Perkins	SW	4,364
Phelps	S	9,869
Pierce	NE	4,864
Platte	E	15,437
Polk	C	10,817
Red Willow	SW	8,837
Richardson	SE	17,574
Rock	N	3,083
Saline	SE	20,097
Sarpy	E	6,875
Saunders	E	21,577
Scott's Bluff	W	1,888
Seward	SE	16,140
Sheridan	NW	8,687
Sherman	C	6,399
Sioux	NW	2,452
Stanton	NE	4,619
Thayer	SE	12,738
Thomas	NW	517
Thurston	NE	3,176
Todd	N	×
Valley	C	7,092
Washington	E	11,869
Wayne	NE	6,169
Webster	S	11,210
Wheeler	N	1,683
York	SE	17,279
Total		1,058,910

Town. County.	Index.	Pop.
● Abbott, Hall	C	25
Abby, Hooker	NW	50
● Able, Butler	E	50
Abington, Colfax	E	32
Acme, Greeley	C	26
● Adams, Gage	SE	250
● *Adams*, Kimball	W	×
Adaton, Sheridan	NW	10
● *Addis*, Sioux	NW	×

Place	Section	Population
Addison, Knox	N	12
Adellah, Sioux	NW	×
Admah, Washington	E	25
Adrian, Keya Pasha	N	8
Afton, Frontier	SW	60
Agee, Holt	N	10
● Agnew, Lancaster	SE	×
● **Ainsworth**, Brown	N	733
Akron, Boone	C	25
Albany, Sheridan	NW	10
● **Albion**, Boone	C	926
Albright, Sarpy	E	×
Alcove, Sheridan	NW	32
Alda, Hall	C	25
Alder Grove, Burt	NE	32
● Alexandria, Thayer	SE	450
Algernon, Custer	C	130
Allen, Dixon	NE	50
● *Allen*, Dixon	NE	×
Allendale, Chase	SW	32
● Alliance, Boxbutte	NW	829
Allston, Dundy	SW	15
● **Alma**, Harlan	S	905
Alma Junction, Clay	S	×
Almeria, Loup	C	50
Alpine, Franklin	S	12
Alvin, Hamilton	C	32
● Alvo, Cass	SE	100
● *Amboy*, Webster	S	35
Amelia, Holt	N	20
● Ames, Dodge	E	50
Amherst, Buffalo	C	100
Amity, Merrick	C	57
Andrew, Cedar	NE	12
● *Andrews*, Sioux	NW	×
Andrewsville, Cass	SE	15
● Angus, Nuckolls	S	25
● Anselmo, Custer	C	150
● Ansley, Custer	C	400
● Antioch, Sheridan	NW	×
Apple Creek, (see Dorsey)		×
Appleton, Sheridan	NW	×
● *Apex*, Wayne	NE	×
● *Arabia*, Cherry	N	10
Arago, Richardson	SE	100
Arando, Custer	C	×
● Arapahoe, Furnas	S	734
Arborville, York	SE	75
Arbuta, Gosper	S	×
● Arcadia, Valley	C	429
● Archer, Merrick	C	25
Arden, Boone	C	26
Argile, Custer	C	×
Argo, Burt	NE	10
Arizona, Burt	NE	10
● Arlington, Washington	E	412
● Armour, Pawnee	SE	×
Armstrong, Knox	N	10
Arnold, Custer	C	100
Arthur, Knox	N	26
Ashby, Grant	NW	×
Ashford, Banner	W	8
Ash Grove, Franklin	S	×
● Ashland, Saunders	E	1,601
● Ashton, Sherman	C	100
Aspinwall, Nemaha	SE	10
Asylum, Lancaster	SE	×
Aten, Cedar	NE	50
Athens, Lancaster	SE	×
● Atkinson, Holt	N	701
● Atlanta, Phelps	S	100
Atlee, Franklin	S	×
Auburn, Nemaha	SE	1,537
● *Auburn*, Nemaha	SE	×
Augustus, Logan	C	×
● **Aurora**, Hamilton	C	1,862
Austin, Sherman	C	26
Avery, Sarpy	E	×
● *Averys*, Douglas	E	×
● Avoca, Cass	SE	166
Avondale, Otoe	SE	×
● Axtell, Kearney	S	262
● Ayr, Adams	S	173
Badger, Holt	N	79
Bainbridge, Harlan	S	×
Bainesville, Holt	N	×
Baker, Boyd	N	×
Ballagh, Garfield	C	×
Balsora, Sherman	C	×
● Bancroft, Cuming	NE	344
Bang, Dodge	E	×
Banksville, Red Willow	SW	×
Banner, Banner	W	8
Barada, Richardson	SE	100
Barbor, Antelope	N	×
Barkey, Gage	SE	×
● *Barney*, Otoe	SE	×
● Barnston, Gage	SE	300
Bartlett, Wheeler	N	150
● Bartley, Red Willow	SW	220
● *Barton*, Deuel	W	×
Basin, Boyd	N	×
● **Bassett**, Rock	N	500
Batin, Webster	S	40
Battlebend, Custer	C	18
● Battle Creek, Madison	NE	352
Bayard, Cheyenne	W	×
● *Bay State*, Dodge	E	×
Bazile Mills, Knox	N	150
● **Beatrice**, Gage	SE	13,836
● **Beaver City**, Furnas	S	763
● Beaver Crossing, Seward	SE	100
● Bee, Seward	SE	200
Beechville, Custer	C	165
● Beemer, Cuming	NE	350
Bega, Stanton	NE	77
● Belden, Cedar	NE	100
● *Belfast*, Greeley	C	×
● Belgrade, Nance	C	40
Belknap, Holt	N	×
● Bellevue, Sarpy	E	209
● Bellwood, Butler	E	413
Belmont, Cass	SE	18
● Belmont, Dawes	NW	×
● Belvidere, Thayer	SE	359
● Benedict, York	SE	250
● **Benkleman**, Dundy	SW	357
● Bennet, Lancaster	SE	474
● Bennington, Douglas	E	75
Benson, Douglas	E	×
Benton, (see Richland)		×
● *Benton*, Colfax	E	×
Bentora, Sherman	C	×
● Berea, Boxbutte	NW	10
● *Berks*, Lancaster	SE	×
● Berlin, Otoe	SE	175
Bertha, Burt	NE	×
● Bertrand, Phelps	S	265
Berwick, Hall	C	13
● Berwyn, Custer	C	25
Bethany, Lancaster	SE	150
Beulah, Polk	C	×
Beulah, Nuckolls	S	6
● Beverly, Hitchcock	SW	×
● **Big Spring**, Deuel	W	75
● Bingham, Sheridan	NW	×
Birch, Pierce	NE	12
Birdwood, Lincoln	W	×
Bishop, Pierce	NE	10
Bismarck, Cuming	NE	12
Blackbird, Holt	N	40
Blackwood, Hitchcock	SW	40
● Bladen, Webster	S	100
Blaineville, Kearney	S	12
● **Blair**, Washington	E	2,069
Blakely, Madison	NE	×
Blanche, Chase	SW	×
Bliss, Holt	N	12
● Bloomfield, Knox	N	150
● **Bloomington**, Frank'n	S	464
● Blue Hill, Webster	S	796
● *Blue Hill Junction*, Web'r	S	×
● Blue Springs, Gage	SE	963
● *Blue Springs Junc.*, Gage	SE	×
Blue Valley, York	SE	32
Bluffton, Sherman	C	32
Blyville, Knox	N	×
Bodarc, Sioux	NW	×
● Boelus, Howard	C	250
Boheet, Platte	E	12
Boiling Spring, Cherry	N	×
Bole, Webster	S	32
Bondville, Red Willow	SW	12
● Bookwalter, Pawnee	SE	×
● Boone, Boone	C	10
● Bordeaux, Dawes	NW	130
● *Bosler*, Keith	W	×
● *Bostwick*, Nuckolls	S	50
● *Bowen*, Washington	E	×
Bower, Jefferson	SE	15
Bow Valley, Cedar	NE	25
Boxbutte, Boxbutte	NW	15
Box Elder, Red Willow	SW	5
Boyer, Cheyenne	W	×
● Bradish, Boone	C	25
● Bradshaw, York	SE	431
● Brady Island, Lincoln	W	25
● *Brady's Cross.*, Dakota	NE	×
● Brainard, Butler	E	306
Branch, Cedar	NE	65
● Brandon, Perkins	SW	×
Bratton, Nemaha	SE	50
● Brayton, Greeley	C	50
Brewer, Keya Paha	N	20
● **Brewster**, Blaine	C	50
● *Brickton*, Adams	S	×
● *Briggs*, Douglas	E	×
Bristow, Todd	N	×
● Brock, Nemaha	SE	348
● Broken Bow, Custer	C	1 647
● Bromfield, Hamilton	C	195
● Bronson, Cheyenne	W	10
Brownlee, Cherry	N	×
● Brownville, Nemaha	SE	980
● Brule, Keith	W	8
● Bruning, Thayer	SE	50
● Bruno, Butler	E	228
● Brunswick, Antelope	N	80
Buchanan, Lincoln	W	×
● Buda, Buffalo	C	25
Buffalo, Wheeler	N	12
Burbank, Boxbutte	NW	×
● Burchard, Pawnee	SE	201
Burlingame, Merrick	C	×
Burnett, Madison	NE	400
● Burress, Fillmore	SE	25
● Burr, Otoe	SE	100
Burrough, Sheridan	NW	×
● *Burrows*, Platte	E	×
Burton, Keya Paha	N	10
● Burwell, Garfield	C	378
Bushbury, Cass	SE	26
● *Bushnell*, Kimball	W	×
Butka, Loup	C	10
Butler, Buffalo	C	32
Butte, Boyd	N	150
Butterfly, Stanton	NE	×
● Byron, Thayer	SE	150
● *Cadams*, Nuckolls	S	×
● Cairo, Hall	C	150
Calamus, Valley	C	65
Caldwell, Scott's Bluff	W	×
● *Calhoun*, Washington	E	×
Callaway, Custer	C	300
Calvert, Dundy	SW	×
● Cambridge, Furnas	S	510
Camden, Seward	SE	40
Cameron, Hall	C	5
● Campbell, Franklin	S	200
Camp Clarke, Cheyenne	W	10
Cannonville, Harlan	S	×
Cantella, Dawson	C	26
Canton, Boxbutte	NW	×
Capay, Rock	N	×
Carisbrook, Furnas	S	32
● Carleton, Thayer	SE	458
Carlisle, Fillmore	SE	×
Carns, Keya Paha	N	10
Carpenter, Boxbutte	NW	×
Carrico, Hayes	SW	15
● Carroll, Wayne	NE	68
● *Carter*, Harlan	S	×
Cartney, Buffalo	C	×
Case, Hamilton	C	57
Catalapa, Holt	N	32
Catherine, Chase	SW	×
Catherton, Webster	S	22
● *Cayote*, Dawson	C	×
● Cedar Bluffs, Saunders	N	181
● *Cedar City*, Wheeler	N	×
● Cedar Creek, Cass	SE	150
***Cedar Hill*, Saunders**	E	6
● Cedar Rapids, Boone	C	484
Celia, Holt	N	12
● **Central City**, Merrick	C	1,368
Centre Valley, Cass	SE	×
● Ceresco, Saunders	E	211
Ceryl, Gosper	S	5
● **Chadron**, Dawes	NW	1,867
● Chalco, Sarpy	E	150
Chamber, Holt	N	50
Champion, Chase	SW	150
● Chapman, Merrick	C	200
Chappell, Deuel	W	75
● Charleston, York	SE	25
Chase, Chase	SW	15
Chase, Greeley	C	×
Chelsea, Holt	N	32
● Cheney, Lancaster	SE	50
Cherry Creek, Buffalo	C	65
● Chester, Thayer	SE	407
Chloe, Madison	NE	12
Christena, Kearney	S	×
Cincinnati, Pawnee	SE	×
● Claramont, Cedar	NE	25
Clarion, Madison	NE	×
● Clarks, Merrick	C	700
● Clarkson, Colfax	E	147
● **Clay Center**, Clay	S	390
● Clearwater, Antelope	N	215
Clement, Cherry	N	×

Nebraska
Nebraska

Place, County	Section	Pop.
Cleveland, Holt	N	32
Cleoria, Sherman	C	32
Cliff, Custer	C	×
Clifton, Nehama	SE	×
Clifton, Holt	N	40
● Clinton, Sheridan	NW	6
Closter, Boone	C	12
Cloverton, Webster	S	65
Clyde, Banner	W	×
Coburgh, Custer	C	×
● *Coburn*, Dakota	NE	×
● Cody, Cherry	N	35
● *Coffman*, Douglas	E	×
Coffman, Washington	E	×
Coker, Knox	N	×
Colberg, Chase	SW	×
Colbergen, Pierce	NE	5
Coldwater, Furnas	S	12
● Coleridge, Cedar	NE	315
College View, Lancaster	SE	200
Collins, Scott's Bluff	W	×
● Colon, Saunders	E	50
● Colton, Cheyenne	W	10
● **Columbus**, Platte	E	3,134
Compton, Cherry	N	×
● Concord, Dixon	NE	130
Congdon, (see Eddyville)	...	×
Conquest, Cherry	N	×
Conley, Holt	N	35
Constance, Cedar	NE	×
● Cook, Johnson	SE	100
Cooleyton, Loup	C	×
Coon Prairie, Boone	C	10
Corbin, Boxbutte	NW	×
● Cordova, Seward	SE	200
Cornell, Hitchcock	SW	25
● Cornlea, Platte	E	65
● Cortland, Gage	SE	509
Cotesfield, Howard	C	65
Cottonwood, Butler	E	65
Cottonwood Springs, Lin'cn	W	20
● *Covington*, Dakota	NE	364
● Cowles, Webster	S	150
Coxville, Dawes	NW	×
● Cozad, Dawson	C	542
● Crab Orchard, Johnson	SE	229
● Craig, Burt	NE	290
● Crawford, Dawes	NW	571
● Creighton, Knox	N	822
● Creston, Platte	E	200
Creswell, York	SE	×
Crete, Saline	SE	2,310
● *Crete Junction*, Saline	SE	×
Crockett, Knox	N	×
● Crookston, Cherry	N	20
Cropsey, Gage	SE	57
Crounse, Lancaster	SE	34
● Crowell, Dodge	E	50
Crystal Lake, Pierce	NE	×
Cuba, Rock	N	×
● **Culbertson**, Hitchcock	SW	460
Cullom, Cass	SE	×
Cumminsville, Wheeler	N	25
Cumro, Custer	C	×
Cupid, Frontier	SW	35
Curry, Colfax	E	×
● Curtis, Frontier	SW	378
● Cushing, Howard	C	100
Custer, Custer	C	130
Cyrus, Cheyenne	W	×
Daily Branch, Dixon	NE	×
● Dakota, Dakota	NE	400
● *Dakota Junc.*, Dawes	NW	×
Dale, Custer	C	25
Dale, Seward	SE	32
Dana, York	SE	×
● Danbury, Red Willow	SW	125
Danby, York	SE	×
Dannebrog, Howard	C	280
Dannevirke, Howard	C	×
Darnall, Keya Paha	N	10
● Davenport, Thayer	SE	513
● Davey, Lancaster	SE	62
● **David City**, Butler	E	2,028
Daviesville, Gosper	S	65
Davis, Clay	S	18
● Dawson, Richardson	SE	153
Day, Deuel	W	×
● Daykin, Jefferson	SE	100
● *DeBolt Place*, Douglas	E	×
Decatur, Burt	NE	593
● *Deerfield*, Douglas	E	×
Delay, Lincoln	W	5
Deloit, Holt	N	260
Delta, Otoe	SE	40
Denison, Boone	C	×
● Denton, Lancaster	SE	25

Place, County	Section	Pop.
● Deshler, Thayer	SE	75
● De Soto, Washington	E	10
● Deweese, Clay	S	×
● De Witt, Saline	SE	751
● *De Witt Junc.*, Saline	SE	×
● *Dexter*, Lincoln	W	×
● Dickens, Lincoln	W	5
● Dike, Hitchcock	SW	×
● Diller, Jefferson	SE	126
Divide, Sherman	C	×
● Dix, Kimball	W	5
● Dixon, Dixon	NE	60
● Dodge, Dodge	E	338
● *Dodge Street*, Douglas	E	×
● Doniphan, Hall	C	437
● Dorchester, Saline	SE	540
Dorp, Logan	C	165
Dorrington, Scott's Bluff	W	×
Dorsey, Holt	N	15
Doss, Dawson	C	15
Doty, Boyd	N	×
● Douglas, Otoe	SE	200
Douglas Grove, Custer	C	32
Dover, Otoe	SE	×
Dressen, Knox	N	65
Dresden, Otoe	SE	50
Driftwood, Hitchcock	SW	×
● *Druid Hill*, Douglas	E	×
Dry Creek, Madison	NE	×
Dublin, Boone	C	5
● Du Bois, Pawnee	SE	316
Dudley, Fillmore	SE	×
Duff, Rock	N	×
Dukeville, Knox	N	18
● Dunbar, Otoe	SE	50
● Duncan, Platte	E	10
● *Dundee Place*, Douglas	E	×
Dunlap, Dawes	NW	25
● Dunning, Blaine	C	50
Dustin, Holt	N	25
● Dwight, Butler	E	20
● Eagle, Cass	SE	205
Earl, Frontier	SW	×
● *East Strang Jc.*, Fillmore	SE	×
Eddy, Hayes	SW	×
Eddyville, Dawson	C	25
Edenburg, Saunders	E	×
● Edgar, Clay	S	1,105
● *Edholm*, Butler	E	×
● Edison, Furnas	S	50
Edith, Blaine	C	130
Eight Mile Grove, Cass	SE	40
● Elba, Howard	C	300
● Eldorado, Clay	S	×
Eldridge, Chase	SW	×
● Elgin, Antelope	N	200
● *Eli*, Cherry	N	×
Elizabeth, Lincoln	W	×
Elk City, Douglas	E	50
● Elk Creek, Johnson	SE	216
● Elkhorn, Douglas	E	325
● *Elkhorn Junction*, Douglas	E	825
Elkton, Nuckolls	S	12
Elk Valley, Dakota	NE	12
Elting, Sherman	C	12
● Ellis, Gage	SE	75
Elliston, Keith	W	×
● *Ellsworth*, Sheridan	NW	×
● Elm Creek, Buffalo	C	357
Elmer, Hayes	SW	10
● Elmwood, Cass	SE	303
Elora, Nuckolls	S	15
● Elsie, Perkins	SW	150
Elton, Custer	C	26
● Elwood, Gosper	S	373
● Elyria, Valley	C	10
● Emerald, Lancaster	SE	100
Emerick, Madison	NE	10
● Emerson, Dixon	NE	375
Emmet, Holt	N	32
● Emporia, Holt	N	×
Enders, Chase	SW	×
● Endicott, Jefferson	SE	256
Enfield, Greeley	C	12
Enterprise, Keya Paha	N	12
Equality, Frontier	SW	×
● Ericson, Wheeler	N	20
Erina, Garfield	C	12
Estell, Hayes	SW	10
Esther, Dawes	NW	×
Etna, Custer	C	×
Eudell, Custer	C	12
Eureka, Hayes	SW	×
● *Eureka*, York	SE	12
● Eustis, Frontier	SW	145
Eva, Harlan	S	12
Everett, Dodge	E	25

Place, County	Section	Pop.
● *Everson*, Harlan	S	×
● Ewing, Holt	N	348
● Exeter, Fillmore	SE	754
Factoryville, Cass	SE	5
● **Fairbury**, Jefferson	SE	2,630
Faires, Otoe	SE	×
● Fairfield, Clay	S	1,200
● Fairmont, Fillmore	SE	1,029
● *Fairmount Jc.*, Fillmore	SE	×
Fairview, Lincoln	W	5
● **Falls City**, Richardson	SE	2,102
Fandon, Frontier	SW	×
Farmers Valley, Hamilton	C	32
● Farnam, Dawson	C	100
● Farwell, Howard	C	×
Febing, Nemaha	SE	200
Fern, Sherman	C	12
Ferndale, Holt	N	12
● Filley, Gage	SE	301
● Firth, Lancaster	SE	259
Fleming, Boxbutte	NW	×
Fletcher, Washington	E	15
Flint, Perkins	SW	×
● Florence, Douglas	E	500
Floss, Greeley	C	×
● Flournoy, Thurston	NE	×
Folsomdale, Kearney	S	×
Fontanelle, Washington	E	75
Forest City, Sarpy	E	26
● Fort Calhoun, Washington	E	350
Fort Kearney, Kearney	S	×
Fort Niobrara, Cherry	N	600
● Fort Omaha, Douglas	E	700
● Fort Robinson, Dawes	NW	500
● Foster, Pierce	NE	15
Fowler, Douglas	E	×
Fox Creek, Lincoln	W	36
Francis, Wheeler	N	40
● Franklin, Franklin	S	556
Fraser, Phelps	S	45
Fredericksburg, Kearney	S	680
Freedom, Frontier	SW	×
● *Freeling*, Richardson	SE	×
Freeman, Gage	SE	45
Freeport, Banner	W	10
Freewater, Harlan	S	57
● **Fremont**, Dodge	E	6,747
Frenchtown, Antelope	N	100
Friedensau, Thayer	SE	260
● Friend, Saline	SE	1,347
Froid, Deuel	W	5
● **Fullerton**, Nance	C	1,200
Fulton, Colfax	E	32
Funk, Phelps	S	×
Galena, Hayes	SW	5
Gallop, Cherry	N	×
Gandy, Logan	C	300
● *Gannett*, Lincoln	W	×
● *Gardiner*, Platte	E	26
Garfield, Lincoln	W	40
Garman, Cheyenne	W	×
● Garrison, Butler	E	200
Gaslin, Lincoln	W	32
Gates, Custer	C	10
● *Gates*, Sarpy	E	×
Geer, Richardson	SE	18
Genet, Custer	C	×
● **Geneva**, Fillmore	SE	1,580
Genoa, Nance	C	793
Georgetown, Custer	C	15
● *Georgia*, Cherry	SW	15
Geranium, Valley	C	97
Gering, Scott's Bluff	W	200
● Germantown, Seward	SE	142
● Gibbon, Buffalo	C	646
● *Gibson*, Douglas	E	×
● Gilead, Thayer	SE	50
Gilchrist, Sioux	NW	×
● Gilmore, Sarpy	E	25
Girard, Saline	SE	12
● *Girard*, Boxbutte	NW	×
● Gladstone, Jefferson	SE	25
Glen, Sioux	NW	×
Glenalpin, Antelope	N	×
Glencoe, Dodge	E	10
Glendale, Antelope	N	32
● Glen Rock, Nemaha	SE	100
● Glenville, Clay	S	180
Glenwood, Nance	C	12
● Goehner, Seward	SE	50
Golden Spring, Burt	NE	32
Good Streak, Cheyenne	W	×
● Gordon, Sheridan	NW	500
● **Gothenburg**, Dawson	C	835
Gouldale, Keya Paya	N	10
Grace, Brown	N	×
● Graf, Johnson	SE	×

Place	Pop.
●Grafton, Fillmore.......SE	600
Grammercy, Sioux.......NW	×
Grand Island, Hall......C	7,036
Grand Rapids, Holt.........N	57
Granger, Scott's Bluff......W	10
●**Grant**, Perkins........SW	500
Granville, Platte............E	×
Gray, Wayne..............NE	×
Grayson, Sheridan.......NW	×
Greeley, Greeley..........S	65
●*Greeley Center*, Greeley...C	492
Green, Custer...............C	×
Greendale, (see Amhurst)....	×
●Greenwood, Cass........SE	495
Gregg, Boxbutte.........NW	×
●Gresham, York..........SE	350
●Gretna, Sarpy.............E	255
Grover, Seward............SE	32
Guernsey, Dawson..........C	6
●Guide Rock, Webster......S	336
●*Gunderson's Cross*, D'uglasE	×
●Hadar, Pierce............NE	45
●Haigler, Dundee.........SW	150
Hainesville Holt............N	32
Hale, Madison............NE	5
Halestown, Knox...........N	10
Halloran, Adams...........S	×
●Halsey, Blaine.............C	×
Halsted, Brown.............N	×
Hamburg, Red Willow....SW	10
●Hamilton, Osage........SE	×
Hamilton, Chase.........SW	×
Hammond, Rock............N	×
●Hampton, Hamilton......C	430
Hampton, Cheyenne.......W	×
Hancock, Dundy...........SW	×
●*Hanlon*, Lancaster......SE	10
Hanover, Gage.............SE	×
●Hansen, Adams...........S	100
●Harbine, Jefferson.......SE	125
Hardy, Nuckolls............S	343
Harlan, Custer.............C	40
Harmony, Kearney..........S	×
Harold, Holt................N	×
Harrisburg, Banner.....W	75
●Harrison, Sioux.........NW	11[?]
●**Harrington**, Cedar...NE	800
Hartford, Scott's Bluff ...	×
Hartman, Deuel............W	4
●Hartwell, Kearney........S	150
●Harvard, Clay.............S	1,076
●**Hastings**, Adams.......S	13,584
●Havelock, Lancaster.....SE	200
Havens, Cedar.............NE	26
●*Havens*, Merrick..........C	×
Hawley, Blaine.............C	×
Haydon, Phelps.............S	15
Hayes, Douglas............E	32
Hayes Centre, Hayes..SW	150
Hayestown, Sherman.......C	26
Haymow, Stanton.........NE	×
●Hay Springs, Sheridan. NW	378
●Hazard, Sherman.........C	25
Hazel Dell, Adams.........S	32
●*Heartwell*, Kearney.......S	100
Heath, Banner..............W	×
●**Hebron**, Thayer.........S	1,502
●*Hecla*, Hooker...........NW	×
Helena, Johnson..........SE	26
●Hemingford, Boxbutte.NW	150
●Henderson, York........SE	100
●Hendley, Furnas..........S	50
●Herman, Washington.....E	319
Herrick, Knox..............N	10
Herring Mills, Antelope....N	8
●Hershey, Lincoln.........W	×
Heun, Colfax................E	10
Hiawatha, Dundy.........SW	25
●Hickman, Lancaster.....SE	341
Higgins, Cheyenne.........W	×
Highland, Hayes..........SW	×
High, Custer...............C	32
●*Hiland*, Washington.....E	×
●Hildreth, Franklin.........S	141
Hillsdale, Nemaha........SE	50
●*Hillside*, Washington.....E	×
Hilton, Dawson.............C	×
●*Hindrey*, Lincoln........W	×
●Hoag, Gage..............SE	25
●Holbrook, Furnas.........S	×
●**Holdrege**, Phelps......S	2,601
●*Holdrege Junc.*, Phelps...S	×
Holland, Lancaster........SE	30
Hollman, Holt...............N	×
Holly, Sheridan...........NW	×
●Holmesville, Gage.......SE	220
●Holstein, Adams..........S	118
Homer, Dakota...........NE	251
●Hooper, Dodge............E	670
Hope, Hayes..............SW	×
●*Hope*, Madison..........NE	×
Hopewell, Frontier........SW	×
●Horace, Greeley...........C	×
●Hoskins, Wayne.........SE	75
Hough, Dawes............NW	×
●Houston, York...........SE	5
Howard City, Howard......C	150
●Howe, Nemaha...........SE	75
●Howell, Colfax.............E	197
●Hubbard, Dakota.........E	97
●Hubbell, Thayer...........E	330
Hudson, Hayes............SW	10
Hughes, Dawes..........NW	×
Hull, Banner................W	15
●Humboldt, Richardson..SE	1,114
Humpback, Dawson........C	20
●Humphrey, Platte........E	691
●Huntley, Harlan...........S	×
Hutchinson, Deuel..........W	×
Huxley, Custer..............C	31
●**Hyannis**, Grant......NW	50
Ickes, Cheyenne............W	×
Imperial, Chase........SW	159
●Inavale, Webster..........S	75
Indian Creek, York.......SE	12
●**Indianola**, Red Willow SW	579
Inez, Holt...................N	×
Ingallston, Rock............N	×
●*Ingham*, Lincoln..........W	×
Ingomar, Sheridan.......NW	32
●Inland, Clay................S	50
●Inman, Holt...............N	35
Ionia, Dixon...............NE	65
Ira, Boone...................C	10
Irvine, Keith...............W	×
Irvington, Douglas..........E	200
Irwin, Cherry...............N	×
Isla, Saunders..............E	12
●Ithaca, Saunders..........E	50
Ivanhoe, Lancaster........SE	×
●Ives, Dundy..............SW	10
●Jackson, Dakota.........NE	308
Jacobs, Dundy............SW	×
●*Jamaica*, Lancaster.....SE	20
Jamestown, Dodge..........E	32
Janesville, Custer..........C	×
●Janson, Jefferson........SE	150
Jefferson, Custer...........C	26
Jericho, Sherman..........C	26
Jess, Sheridan.............NW	×
Jessup, Antelope...........N	12
Jewell, Dawson............C	5
●Johnson, Nemaha.......SE	284
●Johnstown, Brown.......N	150
Jordan, Garfield............C	×
●*Josselyn*, Dawson.........C	×
Joy, Holt....................N	10
●Julian, Nemaha.........SE	50
●*Junction*, Adams..........S	×
●*Junction*, Dodge..........E	×
●*Junction*, Phelps..........S	×
●Juniata, Adams...........S	528
Kalamazoo, Madison......NE	×
●**Kearney**, Buffalo.......C	8,074
Keeler, Lincoln............W	32
●Keene, Kearney...........S	65
Kelso, Howard...............C	195
Kamma, Knox...............N	12
Kendall, Dawes...........NW	×
●Kenesaw, Adams..........S	500
●*Kenesaw Junc.*, Adams...S	×
●Kennard, Washington.....E	150
Kennedy, Cherry...........N	×
Kent, Loup..................C	50
●*Kent*, Nance...............C	×
Keota, Custer...............C	12
●*Kesterson*, Jefferson.....SE	×
●Kewanee, Cherry.........N	×
Keya Paha, Holt...........N	65
Keystone, Keith.............W	×
Kilgore, Cherry..............N	×
Kilmer, Lincoln.............W	×
●**Kimball**, Kimball.....W	193
Kingston, Custer............C	×
Kingston, Adams...........S	32
Kiowa, Thayer.............SE	10
Kirk, Banner................W	×
Kirkwood, Rock.............N	10
Knowles, Frontier........SW	×
Knoxville, Knox............N	10
Kowanda, Deuel............W	×
●Kramer, Lancaster......SE	×
Laclede, Polk...............C	×
Ladora, Blaine.............C	×
Laird, Frontier...........SW	×
Lake, Phelps...............S	26
Lake City, Holt............N	20
●Lakeside, Sheridan.....NW	10
Lamar, Chase.............SW	100
Lambert, Holt..............N	×
●Lancaster, Lancaster....SE	×
●Lanham, Gage...........SE	150
La Peer, Cheyenne.........W	×
●La Platte, Sarpy..........E	100
Largo, McPherson.......NW	×
Larissa, Scott's Bluff.......W	×
Lattin, Keya Paha..........N	32
Laura, Holt.................N	×
Lavaca, Cherry..............N	×
Lavinia, Holt..............N	40
Lawn, Boxbutte..........NW	10
Lawn, Douglas..............E	×
●Lawrence, Nuckolls.......S	150
●Lebanon, Red Willow...SW	150
Lee Park, Custer............C	10
●Leigh, Colfax..............E	249
Lemley, McPherson......NW	×
Lena, McPherson.........NW	×
Lenox, Chase..............SW	×
Leonard, Dawes...........NW	32
Leonie, Holt.................N	12
Leo Valley, Greeley.........C	×
●LeRoy, Adams.............S	25
Level, Dawson...............C	40
Lewellen, Deuel............W	×
Lewisburgh, Harlan........S	×
●Lewiston, Pawnee.......SE	100
●Lexington, Dawson.......C	1,392
Libby, Boxbutte...........NW	×
●Liberty, Gage.............SE	469
Lilac, McPherson.........NW	×
Lillian, Custer...............C	×
Limegrove, Dixon..........NE	25
●**LINCOLN**, Lancaster.SE	55,154
●Lindsay, Platte............E	125
●Linscott, Blaine............C	×
●Linwood, Butler...........E	309
●*Lisbon*, Perkins.........SW	×
●Litchfield, Sherman.......C	150
Little, Holt..................N	12
Littlejohn, Gage...........SE	×
●*Little Salt*, Lancaster....SE	×
Livingston, Banner.........W	×
Llewellen, Keith............W	×
Lloyd, Knox.................N	32
●*Lockwood*, Merrick.......C	26
Locust, Franklin............S	12
●Lodge Pole, Cheyenne....W	100
Lodi, Custer.................C	12
Logan, Logan..............C	45
Logan Grove, Dixon.......NE	12
Lomax, Custer...............C	×
Lomo, Keya Paha.........N	38
London, Nemaha..........SE	32
Lone Tree, Nance..........C	×
Long, Frontier...........SW	40
●Long Pine, Brown........N	562
Longwood, Custer..........C	×
Looking Glass, Platte.......E	12
●Loomis, Phelps............S	150
Loraine, Banner............W	×
Loretto, Boone..............C	10
Lost Creek, Platte..........E	60
●Louisville, Cass..........SE	653
●**Loup City**, Sherman....C	671
●Lowell, Kearney...........S	60
Loyal Hill, Lancaster......SE	12
Loyola, Hall.................C	12
Luce, Buffalo...............C	5
Lucile, Hayes..............SW	×
Luella, Sheridan..........NW	×
Luray, Frontier...........SW	40
●Lushton, York............SE	125
Lutes, Keya Paha...........N	40
Lyman, Fillmore...........SE	×
Lynch, Boyd.................N	10
●Lyons, Burt..............NE	532
●*McAlpine*, Sherman.......C	×
McCann, Cherry............N	12
McClean, Keya Paha........N	12
●McCook, Red Willow...SW	2,346
●McCool Junction, York.SE	204
McPherson, McPherson..NW	×
Mabelo, Brown..............N	97
Macon, Franklin.............S	25
Madison, Madison.......NE	930
●Madrid, Perkins.........SW	178
●*Magoon*, Custer...........C	32
Mahlla, Buffalo..............C	10
Maineland, Cass...........SE	32
Majors, Buffalo..............C	×

Place	Region	Pop.
● Malcolm, Lancaster	SE	75
Malinda, Boxbutte	NW	×
● Malmo, Saunders	E	25
Manchester, Custer	C	32
Manderson, Valley	C	8
Mankato, Boyd	N	×
● Manley, Cass	SE	50
Manning, Knox	N	×
Maple Creek, Dodge	E	32
Mapleville, Dodge	E	95
Marengo, Hayes	SW	×
Mariaville, Rock	N	12
Marlbank, Keya Paha	N	12
Marmora, Cherry	N	×
● Marquette, Hamilton	C	261
Mars, Knox	N	10
● Marsland, Dawes	NW	25
Martin, Chase	SW	10
Martinsburgh, Dixon	NE	100
● Martland, Fillmore	SE	15
Marysville, Seward	SE	25
● *Mascot*, Harlan	S	10
● *Mascot*, Douglas	E	×
● Mason City, Custer	C	250
Matthews, Holt	N	×
Matson, Platte	E	×
● Max, Dundy	SW	30
● Maxwell, Lincoln	W	12
May, Kearney	S	130
Mayberry, Pawnee	SE	5
Mayflower, Adams	S	12
● Maywood, Frontier	SW	75
Maze, Wayne	NE	×
● Mead, Saunders	E	324
● Meadow Grove, Madison	NE	75
Meadville, Keya Paha	N	15
Medicine, Lincoln	W	×
Meek, Gosper	S	×
Mellroy, Gage	SE	×
Memphis, Saunders	E	20
Menominee, Cedar	NE	50
Mentorville, Antelope	N	12
Mentzer, Merrick	C	32
● *Mercer*, Douglas	E	×
● *Merchiston*, Nance	C	×
Meriden, Dawson	C	×
● Merna, Custer	C	250
Merom, Dawson	C	×
Merrick, Merrick	C	40
Merrill, Holt	N	65
● Merriman, Cherry	N	10
Meserveville, Gage	SE	18
Middle Branch, Holt	N	12
Middleburgh, Richardson	SE	57
Middleport, Wheeler	N	12
Midvale, Brown	N	32
Midway, Cheyenne	W	10
Milburn, Custer	C	×
● Milford, Seward	SE	555
● Millard, Douglas	E	328
Milldale, Custer	C	25
Miller, Buffalo	C	200
Millerborough, Knox	N	65
● *Millers*, Douglas	E	×
● Millerton, Butler	E	25
● Milligan, Fillmore	SE	181
Mills, Keya Paha	N	12
● *Mills*, Washington	E	×
Milton, Gosper	S	10
Milton, Saunders	E	12
Minatare, Scott's Bluff	W	15
● **Minden**, Kearney	S	1,380
Mineola, Holt	N	10
● *Minnersville*, Otoe	SE	10
Mingo, Scott's Bluff	W	8
Mira Creek, Valley	C	157
Mirage, Sheridan	NW	10
Miram City, Hamilton	C	×
Mission Creek, Pawnee	SE	75
Mitchell, Scott's Bluff	W	8
● *Mocks Crossing*, Douglas	E	×
Moline, Franklin	S	25
Momence, Fillmore	SE	40
● Monroe, Platte	E	6
Monterey, Cuming	NE	32
Montrose, Sioux	NW	×
Moomaw, Sheridan	NW	×
Moore, Holt	N	32
● Moorefield, Frontier	SW	75
Moran, Wheeler	N	15
Morgan, Knox	N	×
Morrillville, Knox	N	12
● Morse Bluff, Saunders	E	×
Morseville, Adams	S	60
Mosser, Sheridan	NW	×
Mosside, Boone	C	18
● Moulton, Loup	C	×

Place	Region	Pop.
Mound, Howard	C	12
● Mount Clare, Nuckolls	S	38
Mount Pleasant, Cass	SE	×
● Mullen, Hooker	NW	×
Munt, Keya Paha	N	12
● Murdoch, Cass	SE	50
● Murray, Cass	SE	50
Myers, Dawson	C	5
Myrtle, Lincoln	W	×
● Nantasket, Buffalo	C	25
● Naponee, Franklin	S	50
Nasby, Sarpy	E	12
● *Natick*, Thomas	NW	×
Neapolis, Buffalo	C	32
Neboville, Platte	E	×
● **Nebraska City**, Otoe	SE	11,494
● *Nebraska City Junction*, Nemaha	SE	×
● *Nebraska Junction*, L'nc'ster	SE	×
Negunda, Webster	S	32
○ Nehawka, Cass	SE	150
● **Neligh**, Antelope	N	1,209
● **Nelson**, Nuckolls	S	913
● Nemaha City, Nemaha	SE	450
● Nenzel, Cherry	N	8
Neoma, Boone	C	32
Nesbit, Keya Paha	N	20
Nesbit, Logan	C	×
● Newark, Kearney	S	50
New Calloway, Custer	C	×
Newcastle, Dixon	NE	75
New Helena, Custer	C	25
● Newman Grove, Madison	NE	330
● Newport, Rock	N	75
● *New Rockford*, Gage	SE	×
Newton, Saunders	E	28
Newton, Burt	NE	32
● *Nichols*, Lincoln	W	33
● Nickerson, Dodge	E	100
● Nimberg, Butler	E	×
Niobrara, Knox	N	633
Niota, York	SE	×
Noblesville, (see Hyersville)		×
Noel, Custer	C	32
Nohart, Richardson	SE	25
Nonpareil, Boxbutte	NW	50
● Nora, Nuckolls	S	50
Norden, Keya Paha	N	85
● Norfolk, Madison	NE	3,038
● *Norfolk Junc.*, Madison	NE	×
● Norman, Kearney	S	×
Norris, (see Elm City)		×
● North Bend, Dodge	E	1,000
North Branch, Otoe	SE	65
North Cedar, Cuming	NE	×
North Loup, Valley	C	386
North Omaha, Douglas	E	×
● **North Platte**, Lincoln	W	3,055
Northside, Wayne	NE	26
Norval, Seward	SE	50
● *Norway*, Thomas	NW	×
● *Nunda*, Loup	C	32
Nysted, Howard	C	65
● Oak, Nuckolls	S	50
● *Oakchatham*, Douglas	E	×
● Oakdale, Antelope	N	630
● Oakland, Burt	NE	807
Oasis, Cherry	N	×
Obi, Custer	C	65
● Oconee, Platte	E	25
O'Connor, Greeley	C	30
Oconto, Custer	C	15
● Octavia, Butler	E	300
● Odell, Gage	SE	500
● *Odell Junction*, Gage	SE	×
● Odessa, Buffalo	C	25
● *O'Fallon*, Lincoln	W	8
● **Ogallala**, Keith	W	494
Ogan, Dodge	E	32
● Ohiowa, Fillmore	SE	369
Okay, Platte	E	×
● *Oketo*, Gage	SE	×
Olean, Colfax	E	65
Olive, Nance	C	65
Olive Branch, Lancaster	SE	65
Olnes, Boone	C	12
● **OMAHA**, Douglas	E	140,450
Omaha Agency, Thurston	NE	42
● *Omaha Heights*, Douglas	E	×
● *Omaha Junction*, Washington	E	×
Omega, McPherson	NW	×
Omro, Nance	C	26
● **O'Neill**, Holt	N	1,200
● Ong, Clay	S	75
Ono, Wheeler	N	12
Orafino, Frontier	SW	15
Oran, Furnas	S	12

Place	Region	Pop.
Orange, Franklin	S	57
● Orchard, Antelope	N	100
● **Ord**, Valley	C	1,208
● *Oreapolis*, Cass	SE	×
Orient, Knox	N	32
Orlando, Deuel	W	×
● Orleans, Harlan	S	812
Orleans Junction, Harlan	S	×
Ortello, Custer	C	40
Orton, Seward	SE	×
Orum, Washington	E	10
Osage, Otoe	SE	12
Osburn, Frontier	SW	12
Oscar, Phelps	S	×
● **Osceola**, Polk	C	947
Osco, Kearney	S	×
Oshkosh, Deuel	W	10
● Osmond, Pierce	NE	150
Otis, Hamilton	C	×
Otto, Webster	S	26
Ough, Dundy	SW	25
Over, Custer	C	67
● Overton, Dawson	C	150
Ox Bow, Nuckolls	S	97
● Oxford, Furnas	S	428
● *Oxford Junction*, Harlan	S	×
● Paddock, Holt	N	10
● *Paddock*, Merrick	C	×
● Page, Holt	N	100
Palestine, Platte	E	40
● Palisade, Hitchcock	SW	126
● Palmer, Merrick	C	200
● Palmyra, Otoe	SE	300
Palo, York	SE	40
● Panama, Lancaster	SE	75
● **Papillion**, Sarpy	E	600
Papillion Junction, Sarpy	E	×
Paragon City, Cedar	NE	×
Paris, Sherman	C	×
Parker, Holt	N	12
Parnell, Greeley	C	×
● Paul, Otoe	SE	26
● Pauline, Adams	S	75
Pawlet, Deuel	W	×
● **Pawnee City**, Pawnee	SE	1,550
● Paxton, Keith	W	50
Peake, Buffalo	C	40
Pearl, Chase	SW	×
Pebble, Dodge	E	5
Peckham, Lincoln	W	18
● *Peck's Grove*, Lancaster	SE	×
Pekin, Keya Paha	N	×
Pella, Lancaster	SE	12
Penbrook, Cherry	N	×
● Pender, Thurston	NE	429
Peoria, Knox	N	26
Perch, Rock	N	×
Perkins, Perkins	SW	8
● *Perry*, Red Willow	SW	×
● Peru, Nemaha	SE	624
● Petersburg, Boone	C	200
Peterson, Cuming	NE	13
Phase, Saunders	E	46
Phebe, Perkins	SW	8
Phelps, Phelps	S	5
Phillipsburgh, Custer	C	2
● Phillips Station, Hamilton	C	200
Pheonix, Holt	N	×
Pickard, Keith	W	×
● Pickrell, Gage	SE	100
● **Pierce**, Pierce	NE	563
● Pilger, Stanton	NE	162
Pilot, Custer	C	×
Pinecamp, Keya Paha	N	19
Pineglen, Brown	N	101
Pishelville, Knox	N	15
● Plainview, Pierce	NE	375
Plasi, Saunders	E	40
Plato, Saline	SE	40
● Platte Centre, Platte	E	302
● *Platte River*, Dodge	E	×
● **Plattsmouth**, Cass	SE	8,392
● Pleasant Dale, Seward	SE	25
Pleasant Hill, Saline	SE	200
Pleasant Home, York	SE	12
● Pleasanton, Buffalo	C	×
Pleasant Ridge, Harlan	S	×
Pleasant Valley, Dodge	E	12
Plum Valley, Knox	N	14
Plymouth, Jefferson	SE	10
Polander, Howard	C	×
● **Ponca**, Dixon	NE	1,009
● Portal, Sarpy	E	25
Postville, Platte	E	32
● Potter, Cheyenne	W	75
● Powell, Jefferson	SE	300
● Prague, Saunders	E	185

Nebraska

Nebraska

Place	Section	Population
Praha, Colfax	E	×
Prairie Centre, Buffalo	C	15
● Prairie Home, Lancaster	SE	97
Precept, Furnas	S	10
President, Platte	E	12
● Preston, Richardson	SE	150
Prime, Loup	C	×
● Princeton, Lancaster	SE	85
● Prosser, Adams	S	×
Pullman, Cherry	N	×
Purdam, Thomas	NW	5
Purple Cane, Dodge	E	×
● *Putnam*, Gage	SE	×
Putnam, Cherry	N	×
Quick, Frontier	SW	×
Quinton, Thurston	NE	×
● Ragan, Harlan	S	150
Ramsay, Deuel	W	×
Ranch, Boyd	N	×
Randal, Cheyenne	W	×
● Randolph, Cedar	NE	374
● Ravenna, Buffalo	C	628
● *Rawhide*, Dodge	E	×
Ray, Holt	N	65
● Raymond, Lancaster	SE	250
Red Bird, Holt	N	32
● **Red Cloud**, Webster	S	1,839
Redfern, Custer	C	45
Redington, Cheyenne	W	5
Redlion, York	SE	26
Red Willow, Red Willow	SW	105
Red Wing, Nance	C	32
Reed, Boxbutte	NW	×
● *Remington*, Dawes	NW	×
● Reno, Sheridan	NW	×
Repose, Saline	SE	×
● Republican City, Harlan	S	428
● *Republican Junc.*, Harlan	S	×
Rescue, Saunders	E	×
Rest, Custer	C	×
Rexford, Furnas	S	×
● Reynolds, Jefferson	SE	271
● Richfield, Sarpy	E	×
● Richland, Colfax	E	35
Richling, Knox	N	×
Richmond, Holt	N	65
● *Ridge*, Dixon	NE	×
Ridgeley, Dodge	E	32
Riege, Cherry	N	×
Riggs, Sheridan	NW	×
Rill, Hitchcock	SW	×
Ringold, Dawson	C	32
Rimmer, Frontier	SW	×
● Rising City, Butler	E	610
Riverdale, Buffalo	C	×
● *Rivers*, Hall	C	×
Riverside, Holt	N	68
● Riverton, Franklin	S	389
● Roca, Franklin	SE	191
Rock Bluff, Cass	SE	100
Rock Falls, Phelps	S	7
● Rockford, Gauge	SE	15
Rockton, Furnas	S	×
● Rockville, Sherman	C	25
● Rogers, Colfax	E	75
Rome, Holt	N	×
Romeyn, Phelps	S	×
● *Rosa*, Nuckolls	S	×
● *Roscoe*, Keith	W	×
Rosecrans, Sheridan	NW	×
● Roseland, Adams	S	250
Roselma, Boone	C	32
● Rosemont, Webster	S	×
Roten, Custer	C	32
Round Grove, Custer	O	65
Round Valley, Custer	C	×
Royville, Sioux	NW	×
● Ruby, Seward	SE	50
● Rulo, Richardson	SE	786
Rush, Franklin	S	12
● **Rushville**, Sheridan	NW	484
● Ruskin, Nuckolls	S	75
Russell, Frontier	SW	12
● *Rutland*, Dawes	NW	×
Ryno, Custer	C	40
● Sacramento, Phelps	S	195
St. Bernard, Platte	E	35
St. Charles, Cuming	NE	×
St. Clair, Antelope	N	×
St. Deroin, Nemaha	SE	50
● St. Edward, Boone	C	293
St. Helena, Cedar	NE	189
St. James, Cedar	NE	150
St. Joe, Hamilton	C	130
● St. Libory, Howard	C	25
St. Mary, Platte	E	5
● St. Michael, Buffalo	C	25
● **St. Paul**, Howard	O	1,263
St. Peter, Cedar	NE	25
St. Stephen, Nuckolls	S	155
● Salem, Richardson	SE	504
● *Salem Junc.*, Richardson	SE	×
● Saltillo, Lancaster	SE	25
● *Sanberg*, Dodge	E	×
Sandalia, Boone	C	×
Sand Creek, Saunders	E	57
Sandoz, Sheridan	NW	26
● *Sand Pit*, Dodge	E	×
Sandwich, Dundy	SW	×
Sandy, Wheeler	N	×
Sanford, Keya Paha	N	40
Sangco, Colfax	E	33
Santee Agency, Knox	N	300
Sappa, Harlan	S	×
Saratogo, Holt	N	32
● Sargent, Custer	C	150
● Sarles, Dawes	NW	×
● Saronville, Clay	S	100
Sartoria, Buffalo	C	75
● Savage, Antelope	N	10
● Sawyer, Fillmore	SE	×
Saxon, Saline	SE	57
Scandinavia, Harlan	S	97
● **Schuyler**, Colfax	F	2,160
Schwedt, Stanton	NE	×
● *Scio*, Otoe	SE	×
● Scotia, Greeley	C	418
● *Scotia Junc.*, Greeley	C	×
Scott, Webster	S	12
Scottville, Holt	N	10
● Scribner, Dodge	E	664
Seaton, Hamilton	C	30
Sedan, Scott's Bluff	W	×
Sedlov, Valley	C	×
● Seneca, Thomas	NW	15
Sett, Furnas	S	×
● **Seward**, Seward	SE	2,108
● *Seymour Park*, Douglas	E	×
Shamrock, Holt	N	×
Sharon, Buffalo	C	32
● Shelby, Polk	C	333
Shell Creek, Colfax	E	×
● Shelton, Buffalo	C	706
Sheridan, Garfield	C	12
Sherman, Furnas	S	×
Sherwood, Franklin	S	10
● Shickley, Fillmore	SE	307
Shiloh, Hamilton	C	32
● Shubert Richardson	SE	200
Sicily, Gage	SE	130
● *Siding Number Three*, Sioux	NW	×
● **Sidney**, Cheyenne	W	1,200
Silas, Lincoln	W	×
● Silver Creek, Merrick	C	250
Silver Lake, Adams	S	40
Silver Ridge, Dixon	NE	26
Silverthorn, Cheyenne	W	×
Simeon, Cherry	N	10
● *Simonds*, Dawson	C	×
● *Simon*, Dakota	NE	×
Simpson, Keya Paha	N	×
Sioux Valley, Fillmore	SE	×
Sioux, Sheridan	NW	26
Sireden, Knox	N	×
Sizer, Holt	N	40
Slocum, Holt	N	10
● Smartville, Johnson	SE	50
● Smithfield, Gosper	S	25
Smithland, (see Paragon)		×
● Smyrna, Nuckolls	S	×
● Snyder, Dodge	E	100
Somerford, Custer	C	×
● Somerset, Lincoln	W	×
● South Auburn, Nemaha	SE	600
● South Bend, Cass	SE	132
● *South Blair*, Washington	E	×
● *South Cut*, Douglas	E	×
South Loup, Buffalo	×C	×
● South Omaha, Douglas	E	8,062
● *South Omaha Junction*, Douglas	E	×
Southside, Holt	N	×
● South Sioux City, Dakota	NE	603
Spannuth, Lincoln	W	40
Sparks, Cherry	N	15
Sparta, Knox	N	10
Spaulding, Greeley	C	100
Spencer, Boyd	N	×
Spiker, Washington	E	10
Spragg, Rock	N	×
Sportville, Adams	S	32
● Sprague, Lancaster	SE	×
Spring Bank, Dixon	NE	32
Spring Creek, Johnson	SE	15
● Springfield, Sarpy	E	500
Spring Green, Furnas	S	10
● Spring Ranch, Clay	S	15
Springview, Keya Paha	N	200
Springville, Custer	C	×
● *Spur*, Butler	E	×
● Stafford, Holt	N	10
● Stamford, Harlan	S	00
Stanley, Buffalo	C	25
Stanton, Dakota	NE	200
● **Stanton**, Stanton	NE	857
● Staplehurst, Seward	SE	350
Star, Holt	N	10
Stark, Hamilton	C	10
● *State Line*, Nuckolls	S	×
Steele City, Jefferson	SE	380
● Steinauer, Pawnee	SE	100
● Stella, Richardson	SE	399
Stephenson, Keya Paha	N	4
● Sterling, Johnson	SE	800
Steuben, Frontier	SW	26
● *Stevenson*, Buffalo	C	×
● Stockham, Hamilton	C	211
Stockville, Frontier	SW	227
● Stoddard, Thayer	SE	50
Stop, Custer	C	57
Story, Sioux	NW	×
Stoughton, Red Willow	SW	×
Stowe, Frontier	SW	65
● Strang, Fillmore	SE	269
● Stratton, Hitchcock	SW	326
Strickland, Hayes	SW	×
Strohl, Loup	C	12
● Stromsburg, Polk	C	1,400
● Stuart, Holt	N	245
Sullivan, Hayes	SW	×
● Sumner, Dawson	C	75
Summer Hill, Douglas	E	15
Summit, Greeley	C	97
● *Summit*, Otoe	SE	×
● *Sumter*, Valley	C	×
Sunflower, Scott's Bluff	W	×
Sunlight, Cass	SE	×
Sunshine, Lincoln	W	×
● Superior, Nuckolls	S	1,614
● *Superior Junc.*, Nuckolls	S	×
● Surprise, Butler	E	300
Sutherland, Lincoln	W	×
● Sutton, Clay	S	1,541
Swaburgh, Dodge	E	×
Swan, Holt	N	×
● Swanton, Saline	SE	184
● Swedeburgh, Saunders	E	50
Swedehome, Polk	C	15
Sweetwater, Buffalo	C	10
Swift, Otoe	SE	×
Sylvia, Todd	N	×
● Syracuse, Otoe	SE	728
● Table Rock, Pawnee	SE	673
Tabor, Cheyenne	W	32
Talbott, Knox	N	40
Tallin, Custer	C	32
● Talmage, Otoe	SE	429
● Tamora, Seward	SE	184
Tarnov, Platte	E	×
● Tate, Pawnee	SE	×
Taylor, Loup	C	200
● **Tecumseh**, Johnson	SE	1,654
● *Tecumseh Junc.*, Johnson	SE	×
● **Tekamah**, Burt	NE	1,244
Tekonsha, Nance	C	×
Telbasta, Washington	E	×
● *Thacher*, Cherry	N	12
● Thayer, York	SE	75
● Thedford, Thomas	NW	100
Thomasville, Webster	S	×
Thompson, (see Mitchell)		×
Thompson, Holt	N	×
● Thompson, Jefferson	SE	×
Thornburg, Frontier	SW	8
Thornton, Polk	C	×
Thurman, Rock	N	×
● *Thummel*, Merrick	C	×
● *Thurston*, Douglas	E	×
● Tilden, Madison	NE	×
● Tobias, Saline	SE	539
● *Touhy's Spur*, Saunders	E	×
Townsend, Gage	SE	26
Tracyville, Gosper	S	×
● Trenton, Hitchcock	SW	267
Triumph, Custer	C	20
Trocnov, Buffalo	C	×
Troy, Greeley	C	12
● Trumbull, Clay	S	50
Tuckerville, Custer	C	×
Tufford, Custer	C	12

Town, County	Index	Pop.
Turkey Creek, Fillmore	SE	10
● Turlington, Otoe	SE	32
Turner, Holt	N	15
Twing, Holt	N	57
Tyghe, Keith	W	32
Tynerville, Howard	C	40
Tyrone, Red Willow	SW	19
● Ulysses, Butler	E	621
● Unadilla, Otoe	SE	195
Underwood, Hall	C	32
● Union, Cass	SE	200
Union Ridge, Gosper	S	12
University Place, Lancaster	SE	571
● Upland, Franklin	S	75
● Upton, Custer	C	×
Urbana, Phelps	S	12
● Utica, Seward	SE	466
Vacoma, Washington	E	20
Vailton, Red Willow	SW	12
● **Valentine**, Cherry	N	400
Val Grange, Red Willow	SW	×
● Valley, Douglas	E	378
● Valparaiso, Saunders	E	515
Van, (see Green Island)		×
Van Wyck, Lincoln	W	×
Varna, Saline	SE	×
Veda, Saunders	E	26
Velte, Dawson	C	32
● Venango, Perkins	SW	75
Venus, Knox	N	32
● Verdigris, Knox	N	207
● Verdon, Richardson	SE	253
Verdurette, Sherman	C	12
● Verona, Clay	S	75
● Vesta, Johnson	SE	100
Vick, Merrick	C	12
Vickory, Antelope	N	×
Victoria, Cass	SE	×
Vilas, Antelope	N	×
Vim, Antelope	N	×
Vincent, Furnas	S	5
Vinton, Valley	C	12
● Violet, Pawnee	SE	20
● Virginia, Gage	SE	150
● Vroman, Lincoln	W	×
● Wabash, Cass	SE	150
● Waco, York	SE	278
● **Wahoo**, Saunders	E	2,006
● Wakefield, Dixon	NE	700
● Wallace, Lincoln	W	250
Walnut Grove, Knox	N	15
● *Walnut Hill*, Douglas	E	300
● *Walters*, Fillmore	SE	×
Waltham, Buffalo	C	33
● Walton, Lancaster	SE	33
Walworth, Custer	C	10
Wanatah, Dawes	NW	×
Wanneta, Chase	SW	×
Warbonnet, Sioux	NW	×
● Warnerville, Madison	NE	50
Warsaw, Howard	C	×
Warren, Madison	NW	×
● Washington, Washington	E	50
● Waterbury, Dixon	NE	×
● Waterloo, Douglas	E	272
Water, Buffalo	C	×
Watertown, Buffalo	C	5
Watson, Knox	N	×
Watts, Lincoln	W	×
Wauneta, Chase	SW	75
● Wausa, Knox	N	100
● Waverly, Lancaster	SE	400
Wayland, Polk	C	57
● **Wayne**, Wayne	NE	1,178
● *Wayside*, Dawes	NW	×
Webster, Dodge	E	×
● **Weeping Water, Cass**	SE	1,350
Weigand, Knox	N	40
● *Weir*, Hooker	NW	×
Welch, Knox	N	×
● Wellfleet, Lincoln	W	10
Wellsville, Cheyenne	W	15
Wescott, Custer	C	50
● Western, Saline	SE	397
West Branch, Pawnee	SE	×
Westerville, Custer	C	18
Westgard, Nance	C	6
West Hill, Platte	E	×
● *West Lawn*, Douglas	E	×
● West Lincoln, Lancaster	SE	443
Westmark, Phelps	S	×
● Weston, Saunders	E	341
● **West Point**, Cuming	NE	1,842
West Salem, Franklin	S	×
● *West Side*, Douglas	E	×
● *West Strang Jc.*, Fil'm're	SE	×
West Union, Custer	C	75
Weyerts, Cheyenne	W	×
Wheatland, Webster	S	150
Wheeler, Wheeler	N	×
White Rabbit, Dawson	C	12
● Whitman, Grant	NW	10
● Whitney, Dawes	NW	100
Whitney, Red Willow	SW	×
Whittier, Lincoln	W	8
● **Wilber**, Saline	SE	1,226
● Wilcox, Kearney	S	250
Willard, Lincoln	W	×
Willford, Scott's Bluff	W	×
Williamsburgh, Phelps	S	20
Willow Creek, Saunders	E	×
Willowdale, Antelope	N	52
● Willow Island, Dawson	C	5
Willow Springs, Garfield	C	20
Wilson, Colfax	E	×
● Wilsonville, Furnas	S	300
Winchester, Chase	SW	×
Winfield, Brown	N	×
Winnebago, Thurston	NE	×
● Winneton, Knox	N	×
● Winside, Wayne	NE	130
Wirt, Custer	C	×
● Wisner, Cuming	NE	610
Wolbach, Greeley	C	30
● *Wolbach*, Howard	C	×
Woodburn, Platte	E	26
● Wood Lake, Cherry	N	50
● Woodlawn, Lancaster	SE	20
● Wood River, Hall	C	481
● Woodville, Platte	E	×
Wright, Brown	N	×
Wright, Scott's Bluff	W	×
Wrightsville, Buffalo	C	×
● Wymore, Gage	SE	2,420
● Wyoming, Otoe	SE	25
Xenia, Sarpy	E	26
Yale, Valley	C	33
Yankee, Perkins	SW	×
● **York**, York	SE	3,405
Yucca, Custer	C	32
● Yutan, Saunders	E	168
Zimmer, Frontier	SW	×
Zyba, Kearney	S	32

NEVADA.

COUNTIES.	INDEX.	POP.
Churchill	W	703
Douglas	W	1,551
Elko	NE	4,794
Esmeralda	SW	2,148
Eureka	C	3,275
Humboldt	NW	3,434
Lander	C	2,266
Lincoln	SE	2,466
Lyon	W	1,987
Nye	S	1,290
Ormsby	W	4,883
Storey	W	8,806
Washoe	W	6,437
White Pine	E	1,721
Total		45,761

TOWN. COUNTY.	INDEX.	POP.
Agency, Esmeralda	SW	×
Alabama City, Elko	NE	×
Alhambra, White Pine	E	×
● *Alpha*, Eureka	C	60
Amador, Landor	C	×
American Flat, (see Gold Hill)		×
Amos, Humboldt	NW	×
● *Anderson's*, Washoe	W	×
● *Argenta*, Lander	C	×
Arthur, Elko	NE	48
● Aurora, Esmeralda	SW	225
Aurum, White Pine	E	54
● **Austin**, Lander	C	1,215
● *Austin Junction*, Lander	C	×
Babel, Elko	NE	×
● *Bailey's*, Lander	C	30
● *Baltic*, Lyon	W	×
Barberville, Humboldt	NW	×
Barrett, Nye	S	×
● *Basalt*, Esmeralda	SW	×
● Battle Mountain, Lander	C	360
● Belleville, Esmeralda	SW	456
Belmont, Nye	S	250
● Beowawe, Eureka	C	50
Bernice, Churchill	W	60
Big Blue Spring, Nye	S	×
Birch Creek Station, Lander	C	×
● *Bishops*, Elko	NE	36
● *Blackburns*, Eureka	C	×
Blaine, Elko	NE	36
Blanco, Lander	C	×
Blue Eagle Spring, Nye	S	×
Bolivia, Churchill	W	×
Borax City, (see St. Clair)		×
● *Box Springs*, Eureka	C	×
● *Bridges*, Lander	C	×
Bristol, Lincoln	SE	×
● *Brown*, Humboldt	NW	30
● *Brown's*, Washoe	W	×
● *Brunswick*, Ormsby	W	×
Buffalo Meadows, Washoe	W	×
Buffalo Spring, Humboldt	NW	×
Bullion, Elko	NE	120
Bullion, Humboldt	NW	×
Bullion M'n'g Dist., Eureka	C	×
● *Bullionville*, Lincoln	SE	198
Bullionville, Douglas	W	×
Bullwhacker Spring, Nye	S	×
Bunkerville, Lincoln	SE	189
Butterfield Spring, Nye	S	×
Buttons, Humboldt	NW	×
Camp Thirty-Seven, Washoe	W	×
● Candelaria, Esmeralda	SW	345
Cannon City, Lander	C	×
● *Canyon*, Lander	C	×
Cape Horn Station, Lander	C	×
● Carlin, Elko	NE	413
● **CARSON CITY**, Ormsby	W	3,950
Carson Valley, Douglas	W	×
● *Caton's*, Lander	C	×
Cave Creek, Elko	NE	×
● ***Cedar*, Eureka**	C	×
● *Cedar*, Elko	NE	×
Cherry Creek, White Pine	E	600
Clan Alpine, (see Healy)		×
● Clarks, Washoe	W	×
● *Clark's*, Lander	C	×
● *Cleaver*, Lyon	W	×
Cleveland, White Pine	E	×
Clifton, Lander	C	×
● *Clifton*, Lyon	W	×
Clinton, (see Mason Valley)		×
Cloverdale, Nye	S	×
● *Clover Valley*, Lincoln	SE	41
● *Cluro*, Eureka	C	×
● *Coin*, Humboldt	NW	×
Cold Creek, White Pine	E	×
Columbia, Elko	NE	95
● Columbus, Esmeralda	SW	120
Como, (see Dayton)		×
Cooper, White Pine	E	×
Coryville, Esmeralda	SW	×
Cortez, Lander	C	×
● *Cosgrave*, Humboldt	NW	×
Cottonwood, Churchill	W	×
Cradleburg, Douglas	W	×
Crane Springs, Humboldt	NW	×
● *Cressid*, Churchill	W	×
Crow's Nest, Nye	S	×
Crystal Spring, Lincoln	SE	×
Cumberland, Humboldt	NW	×
Currant, Nye	S	×
● *Curtis*, Lander	C	×
Dalzell Sta., (see Sweetwater)		×
Danville, Nye	S	×
Dayton, Elko	NE	×
● **Dayton**, Lyon	W	576
● Deeth, Elko	NE	180
● *Desert*, Churchill	W	×
Diamond City, (see Eureka)		×
● *Diamond Station*, Eureka	C	×
● *Dillon*, Lander	C	×
Dolly Varden, Elko	NE	×
Downeyville, Nye	S	30
Duckwater, Nye	S	43
Dun Glen, Humboldt	NW	56
Dyer, Esmeralda	SW	×
Eagle Salt Works, Churchill	W	30
Eagleville, Churchill	W	×
East Belmont, (see Belmont)		×
Eberhardt, White Pine	E	122
Eight-Mile House, Lincoln	SE	×
Elbow Ranch, (see Aurora)		×
El Dorado Canyon, Lincoln	SE	195
● **Elko**, Elko	NE	600
Ellsworth, Nye	S	91
● Ely, White Pine	E	203

Place	Region	Pop.
Emigrant Spring, Nye	S	×
● Empire City, Ormsby	W	327
Essex, (see Verdi)		×
● **Eureka**, Eureka	C	1,609
● Eureka, Lyon	W	×
● Evans, Eureka	C	×
Fairlawn, Elko	NE	×
Fair Play, Elko	NE	×
Fairview, Douglas	W	×
● Fenelon, Elko	NE	×
Fish Lake, (see Columbus)		×
Flag Spring, Nye	S	×
Fletcher, Esmeralda	SW	×
● Fort Churchill, Lyon	W	104
Fort Halleck, Elko	NE	150
Fort McDermitt, (see McDermitt)		×
Fourteen Mile Sta., (see Ham't'n)		×
● Franktown, Washoe	W	100
Frisbie, Lander	C	180
Fryberg, Lincoln	SE	×
Furber, Elko	NE	×
Galena, Lander	C	460
● Garden Pass, Eureka	C	×
Gardnerville, Douglas	W	80
Garfield, (see Sodaville)		×
● Gartney, Elko	NE	×
Geddes, Eureka	C	120
Gemville, Humboldt	NW	×
● **Genoa**, Douglas	W	434
Gerald, (see Beowawe)		×
Geyser, Lincoln	SE	×
● Gillis, Esmeralda	SW	×
Glenbrook, Douglas	W	223
Glenco, White Pine	E	×
Glendale, (see Reno)		×
● Golconda, Humboldt	NW	25
● Gold Hill, Storey	W	4,531
Gold Mountain, Esmeralda	SW	180
● Grant's Point, Humboldt	NW	×
Grantville, Nye	S	55
Greenfield, (see Mason Valley)		×
● Hafed, Washoe	W	×
● Halleck, Elko	NE	60
● **Hamilton**, White Pine	E	260
● **Hawthorne**, Esm'alda	SW	337
● Hays Ranch, Eureka	C	×
● Haywards, Lyon	W	×
Healy, Churchill	W	36
● Helena, Lander	C	×
Heply, Washoe	W	×
Hickneytown, Elko	NE	×
Hiko, Lincoln	SE	90
Hill, Churchill	W	×
Hines' Hot Spring, Douglas	W	×
Hobart, Douglas	W	×
● Holborn, Elko	NE	×
Holbrook, Douglas	W	60
Hot Creek, Nye	S	×
Hot Spring, Churchill	W	×
Hot Spring, Elko	S	×
● Hot Springs, Humboldt	NW	32
Hot Sulphur Springs, Elko	NE	×
● Huffakers, Washoe	W	36
Humboldt City, Humboldt	NW	×
● Humboldt House, Humb't	NW	43
Huntington, Elko	NE	56
Incline, Washoe	W	120
Indian Queen, Esmeralda	SW	×
Indian Spring, White Pine	E	×
Ione City, Nye	S	×
● Iron Point, Humboldt	NW	×
Jacobsville, Lander	C	×
Jasper, (see Sprucemont)		×
Jefferson, Nye	S	×
Jett, Nye	S	×
● Junction, Nye	S	17
Kiernan, Lincoln	SE	×
Kingston, Lander	C	30
● Kinkead, Esmeralda	SW	×
Kinsley, White Pine	E	×
Lake Bigler, (see Glenbrook)		×
● Lake View, Ormsby	W	50
Lamoille, Elko	NE	×
Lander, Lander	C	×
● Lawton, Washoe	W	×
Ledli., (see Battle Mountain)		×
Lee, Elko	NE	120
Lewis, Lander	C	250
● Lewis Junction, Lander	C	×
Lida, Esmeralda	SW	244
Logan, Lincoln	SE	×
● Lookout, Ormsby	W	×
● Lorey, Elko	NE	44
● Lovelock's, Humboldt	NW	552
Lower Pyramid, Washoe	W	×
Lower Town, (see Winnemucca)		
● Luning, Esmeralda	SW	110

Place	Region	Pop.
McDermitt, Humboldt	NW	186
McGill, White Pine	E	×
Manse, Nye	S	×
Marmol, Washoe	W	×
● Mason, Lyon	W	×
Mason Valley, Lyon	W	557
Meadow Valley, Lincoln	SE	×
● Merrimac, Ormsby	W	×
Metallic, (see Candelaria)		×
Midas, Nye	S	210
● Mill City, Humboldt	NW	120
Miller's, Humboldt	NW	×
● Mill Station, Washoe	W	×
● Mineral, Eureka	C	×
Mineral City, White Pine	E	179
Mineral Hill Eureka	C	100
● Mirage, Churchill	W	42
Moapa, Lincoln	SE	×
● Molcen, Elko	NE	45
● Montello, Elko	NE	38
Montgomery, Nye	S	×
Moodyville, Lincoln	SE	×
● Moors, Elko	NE	60
Morey, Nye	S	18
Morton, Elko	NE	×
● Mound House, Lyon	W	×
Mound Valley, Elko	NE	×
Mountain City, Elko	NE	100
Muncy, White Pine	E	×
Napias, (see Eureka)		×
● Natches, Elko	NE	×
Newark, White Pine	E	×
● New Boston, Esmeralda	SW	×
Newtown, (see Ruby Hill)		×
Nickle, Churchill	W	×
North Fork, Elko	NE	×
North's Ranch, Humboldt	NW	×
● Oak, Eureka	C	×
Oneida Mill, Churchill	W	×
Ophir, Washoe	W	×
Ophir Canon, Nye	S	×
● Oreano, Humboldt	NW	66
Oriental, Esmeralda	SW	×
Osceola, White Pine	E	275
● Osino, Elko	NE	×
Overton, Lincoln	SE	×
Owyhee, Elko	NE	×
Pahrump, Nye	S	×
● Palisade, Eureka	C	65
Palmetto, Esmeralda	SW	×
Panaca, Lincoln	SE	334
Paradise Hill, (see Par'd'se V'l'y)		
● Paradise Val., H'mboldt	NW	143
Park Canon, (see Junction)		×
Patterson, Lincoln	SE	×
Peavine, Nye	S	×
Pedro, Lander	C	×
● Peko, Elko	NE	×
● Pezuop, Elko	NE	37
Pigeon Sprgs., (see Palmetto)		×
Pine Grove, Esmeralda	SW	360
● Pine Station, Eureka	C	×
Pinto, White Pine	E	×
Pinto Mills, Eureka	C	×
● **Pioche**, Lincoln	SE	676
Pittsburg, Lander	C	×
● Piute, Lander	C	×
Pony Spring, Lincoln	SE	×
Pyramid, Washoe	W	99
Queen City, Humboldt	NW	×
Ragtown, (see St. Clair)		×
● Raines, Eureka	C	×
● Ravenswood, Lander	C	×
Rebel Creek, (see Winnemucca)		×
● **Reno**, Washoe	W	5,000
Reveille, Nye	S	120
● Rhodes, Esmeralda	SW	×
Rioville, Lincoln	SE	30
● Rio Vista, Esmeralda	SW	×
Roberts Station, Eureka	C	×
Robinson Canyon, W'te Pine	E	×
Rockland, (see Pine Grove)		×
● Rose Creek, Humboldt	NW	×
Round Sprs., (see Hamilton)		×
Royal City, (see Pioche)		×
Ruby Hill, Eureka	C	1,500
Ruby Valley, Elko	NE	120
● Rye Patch, Humboldt	NW	78
Safford, (see Beowawa)		×
St. Clair, Churchill	W	189
St. Joseph, Lincoln	SE	254
St. Thomas, Lincoln	SE	×
Salt Springs Sta., Churchill	W	×
Salt Wells, Churchill	W	×
● Salvia, Washoe	W	×
San Antonio, (see Belmont)		×

Place	Region	Pop.
● Sanborn, Humboldt	NW	×
Santiago, Lyon	W	×
● Scales, Storey	W	×
Schellbourne, White Pine	E	103
● Schurz, Esmeralda	SW	×
Scottsville, (see Rye Patch)		×
● Seligman, White Pine	E	×
Shackle's Ranch, (see H'mil't'n)		×
Scheckell's Sta., (see Hamilton)		×
Shela Mills, Humboldt	NW	×
Sheephead, Washoe	W	43
Sheridan, Douglas	W	127
Shoshone, Eureka	C	×
Silver Canyon, (see Aurum)		×
● Silver City, Lyon	W	342
● Silver Creek, Lander	C	×
Silver Peak, Esmeralda	SW	30
Silver Sring Sta., Lincoln	SE	30
Skelton, Elko	NE	80
Slough Station, (see Hill)		×
● Soda Spr'gs. Esmeralda	SW	×
● Sodaville, Esmeralda	SW	×
South Fork, Elko	NE	×
Spanish Camp, (see H'wth'rne)		×
Spooner Sta., (see Glenbrook)		×
Spring City, Humboldt	NW	149
Sprucemont, Elko	NE	41
Star City, Humboldt	NW	×
Star King, Elko	NE	×
● Steamboat, Washoe	W	24
Stevens Sta., (see Hawthorne)		×
Stillwater, Churchill	W	254
Stofiel, Elko	NE	×
● Stone House, Humboldt	NW	38
Sulphur Spr'gs, (see S'etwater)		×
● Summit, Esmeralda	SW	×
● Summit, Eureka	C	×
Summit, Ormsby	W	×
Summit Spr'gs, Humboldt	NW	×
Sunnyside, Nye	S	×
Sutro, Lyon	W	430
● Sweetwater, Esmeralda	SW	60
Swift's Sta., (see Carson City)		×
● Taylor, White Pine	E	180
● Tecoma, Elko	NE	100
Tem-pah-ute, Lincoln	SE	×
Ten Mile, Humboldt	NW	×
● Thisbe, Lyon	W	×
Tippecanoe, Lyon	W	×
● Toana, Elko	NE	151
Toll House, Humboldt	NW	×
● Tulasco, Elko	NE	32
● Tule, Humboldt	NW	×
Tuley Canon, (see Palmetto)		×
● Tuscarora, Elko	NE	1,156
Twelve-Mile House, Douglas	W	×
Twenty-one-Mile H'se, Linc'n	SE	×
Twin River, Nye	S	30
Two-Mile Sta., Washoe	W	×
Tybo, Nye	S	20
● Ullin, Elko	NE	×
Union, Eureka	C	×
Unionville, Humboldt	NW	50
Upper Pyramid, Washoe	W	×
Upper Town, Humboldt	NW	×
Vanderbilt, Eureka	C	×
Vandewater, Humboldt	NW	×
● Vaughlin's, Lander	C	×
● **Verdi**, Washoe	W	100
● **Virginia City**, Storey	W	8,551
● Vista, Washoe	W	31
● Wabuska, Lyon	W	×
● Wadsworth, Washoe	W	537
Walker River, (see Wellington)		
● Walters, Lander	C	×
Warm Sprgs, (see Carson City)		×
Washington, Nye	S	×
Washington, Storey	W	×
● Washoe City, Washoe	W	109
● Watts, Lander	C	×
● Wellington, Lyon	W	108
● Wells, Elko	NE	254
White, Eureka	C	×
● White Plains, Churchill	W	33
White River, Nye	S	×
White Rock, Elko	NE	210
White Rose, Elko	NE	×
Willow Creek, Humboldt	NW	90
Willow Point, Humboldt	NW	30
Willow Spring, Nye	S	×
● **Winnemucca**, H'b't.	NW	1,037
Woodruff, Esmeralda	SW	×
● Woolsey, Humboldt	NW	×
Zelda, Churchill	W	×

New Hampshire.*

COUNTIES.	INDEX.	POP.
Belknap	C	20,321
Carroll	C	18,124
Cheshire	SW	29,579
Coos	N	23,211
Grafton	C	37,217
Hillsborough	S	93,247
Merrimack	S	49,435
Rockingham	SE	49,650
Strafford	SE	38,442
Sullivan	SW	17,804
Total		376,530

*In many of the towns of the State the population given embraces the township.

TOWN. COUNTY.	INDEX.	POP.
Acworth, Sullivan	SW	717
Albany, Carroll	C	377
● Alder Brook, Grafton	C	90
Alexandria, Grafton	C	679
● Allenstown, Merrimack	S	1,475
Alstead, Cheshire	SW	870
Alstead Centre, Cheshire	SW	×
● Alton, Belknap	C	1,372
● Alton Bay, Belknap	C	×
Amherst, Hillsborough	S	1,053
● Amherst Station, Hillsb'h.	S	47
● Amoskeag, Hillsborough	S	×
● Andover, Merrimack	S	1,090
● *Andover Plains*, Merrimack	S	×
● Antrim, Hillsborough	S	1,248
● Apthorp, Grafton	C	×
● Ashland, Grafton	C	1,193
● Ashuelot, Cheshire	SW	58
Atkinson, Rockingham	SE	483
● Atkinson Depot, Rock'm	SE	×
● Auburn, Rockingham	SE	631
● Avalanche, Carroll	C	×
● *Bagleys*, Merrimack	S	×
Bank Village, Hillsborough	S	×
Barnstead, Belknap	C	1,264
● *Barnstead*, Belknap	C	1,264
● *Barnstead Parade*, Belk'p	C	×
Barrington, Strafford	SE	1,408
● *Barrington*, Strafford	SE	×
● Bartlett, Carroll	C	1,247
● Bath, Grafton	C	935
● *Bayside*, Rockingham	SE	×
● *Bear Camp*, Carroll	C	×
● *Beatties*, Coos	N	×
Bedford, Hillsborough	S	1,102
● *Bedford Station*, Hillsb'h.	S	×
● *Belknap Point*, Belknap	C	×
● Belmont, Belknap	C	1,142
● *Belmont Junction*, Belknap	C	×
● Bemis, Carroll	C	×
● *Bennett Road*, Strafford	SE	×
● Bennington, Hillsborough	S	542
Benton, Grafton	C	244
Berkehaven, Sullivan	SW	×
Berlin, Coos	N	×
● Berlin Falls, Coos	N	3,729
Berlin Mills, Coos	N	×
● Bethlehem, Grafton	C	1,267
● *Bethlehem Junc.*, Grafton	C	120
● Blair, Grafton	C	×
● *Bloods*, Hillsborough	S	×
Boar's Head, Rockingham	S	×
● Boscawen, Merrimack	S	1,487
Bow, Merrimack	S	725
● *Bow Junction*, Merrimack	S	×
Bow Mills, Merrimack	S	×
● Bradford, Merrimack	S	819
Breezy Point, Grafton	C	×
Brentwood, Rockingham	SE	967
Brentwood Corner, R'k'm.	SE	×
Bridgewater, Grafton	C	332
● *Bridgewater*, Grafton	C	×
● Bristol, Grafton	C	1,524
Brookfield, Carroll	C	349
Brookline, Hillsborough	S	548
Burkehaven, Sullivan	SW	×
Cambridge, Coos	N	31
Campton, Grafton	C	982
● Campton Village, Grafton	C	300
● Canaan, Grafton	C	1,417
Canaan Centre, Grafton	C	×
Canaan Street, Grafton	C	×
● Candia, Rockingham	SE	1,108
Candia Village, R'kingh'm	SE	135

New Hampshire

TOWN. COUNTY.	INDEX.	POP.
● Canobie Lake, R'kingh'm	SE	×
Canterbury, Merrimack	S	964
● Canterbury Depot, M'r'm'k	S	×
Carroll, Coos	N	813
Carterville, Rockingham	S	×
● *Cavender's*, Hillsborough	S	×
● Center Conway, Carroll	C	120
● Centre Barnstead, Belk'p.	C	140
Centre Bartlett, Carroll	C	×
● *Centre Conway*, Carroll	C	120
Centre Effingham, Carroll	C	175
● Centre Harbor, Belknap	C	479
● Centre Ossipee, Carroll	C	195
Centre Sandwich, Carroll	C	275
Centre Strafford, Strafford	SE	×
Centre Tuftonborough C'l.	C	×
Centreville, Carroll	C	52
Chandlers, Coos	N	813
● *Chandler's Mills*, Sul'van	SW	×
● Charlestown, Sullivan	SW	1,466
Chatham, Carroll	C	329
● *Cherry Mountain*, Coos	N	×
Cheever, Grafton	C	×
● Chesham, Cheshire	SW	×
Cheshire Mills, Cheshire	SW	×
Chester, Rockingham	SE	958
Chesterfield, Cheshire	SW	1,046
Chesterfield Lake, Ches're.	SW	×
Chesterfield Factory, C'h'e	SW	300
Chichester, Merrimack	S	661
● *Chichester*, Merrimack	S	120
Chocorua, Carroll	C	×
Cilleyville, (see Andover)		×
● Claremont, Sullivan	SW	5,565
● Claremont Junc., Sul'an	SW	×
Clarksville, Coos	N	325
Clinton Grove, Hillsb'ough	S	×
● *Cold River*, Cheshire	SW	×
● *Cold Spring*, Belknap	C	×
Colebrook, Coos	N	1,736
● Columbia, Coos	N	605
● *Columbia Bridge*, Coos	N	×
● *Columbia Valley*, Coos	N	×
● **CONCORD**, Mer'mack.	S	17,004
Connecticut Lake, Coos	N	×
● Contoocook, Merrimack	S	350
● Conway, Carroll	C	2,331
● *Conway Centre*, Carroll	C	120
Conway Corner, Carroll	C	×
● Coos, Coos	N	300
● *Copperville*, Coos	N	×
Cornish, Sullivan	SW	954
Cornish Centre, Sullivan	SW	×
Cornish Flat, Sullivan	SW	145
Cotton Valley, Carroll	C	×
● Crawford House, Coos	N	28
Croydon, Sullivan	SW	512
Croydon Flat, Sullivan	SW	90
● Crystal, Coos	N	×
Dalton, Coos	N	596
● *Dalton Station*, Coos	N	×
● Danbury, Merrimack	SE	683
Danville, Rockingham	SE	666
Dartmouth, (see Jefferson)		×
Davis, Strafford	SE	×
Davisville, Merrimack	SE	×
Deerfield, Rockingham	SE	1,220
Deerfield Centre, R'k'ham.	SE	118
Deering, Hillsborough	S	531
Derry, Rockingham	SE	2,604
● Derry Depot, R'k'gham.	SE	500
Dexter, Strafford	SE	×
● *Diamonds Corner*, Merrimac	S	×
Dixville, Coos	N	11
Dorchester, Grafton	C	379
Dover, Strafford	SE	12,790
● *Dover Junction*, Rockingham	SE	×
● Dover Point, Strafford	SE	×
Drewsville, Cheshire	SW	105
Dublin, Cheshire	SW	582
Dummer, Coos	N	455
Dunbarton, Merrimack	S	524
● Durham, Strafford	SE	871
East Acworth, Sullivan	SW	40
East Alstead, Cheshire	SW	90
● East Andover, Mer'mack	S	220
● East Barrington, St'f'd.	SE	×
East Brentwood, R'k'ham.	SE	×
● East Candia, Rock'ham.	SE	×
East Canterbury, Mer'ack	S	×
East Chester, Rock'ham	SE	×
● East Concord, Merr'ack	S	318
East Deering, Hillsborough	S	×
East Derry, Rockingham	SE	145
● East Epping, Rock'ham.	SE	×
East Freedom, Carroll	C	×
East Grafton, Grafton	C	×

New Hampshire

TOWN. COUNTY.	INDEX.	POP.
East Hampstead, Roc'ham.	SE	×
● East Harrisville, Che're.	SW	×
● East Haverhill, Grafton	C	×
East Hebron, Grafton	C	×
● East Jaffrey, Cheshire	SW	1,465
● East Kingston, Rock'm.	SE	461
East Landaff, (see Landaff)		×
● East Lebanon, Grafton	C	×
East Lempster, Sullivan	SW	52
East Madison, Carroll	C	×
● *East Milford*, Hills'ough	S	×
East Nottingham, Roc'ham	SE	×
Easton Grafton	C	248
East Pembroke, Mer'mack	S	90
East Plainfield, Sullivan	SW	30
East Rindge, Cheshire	SW	120
● East Rochester, Straff'd.	SE	310
East Springfield, Sullivan	SW	×
East Sullivan, Cheshire	SW	×
East Swanzey, Cheshire	SW	215
● East Tilton, Belknap	C	90
East Unity, Sullivan	SW	×
East Wakefield, Carroll	C	90
● East Wakefield Depot, C'l.	C	×
East Washington, Sul'van	SW	123
● East Weare, Hills'bough	S	135
● East Westmoreland, C'e	SW	105
East Wolfborough, Carroll	C	×
Eaton, Carroll	C	514
Eaton Centre, Carroll	C	200
Effingham, Carroll	C	720
Effingham Falls, Carroll	C	129
● Elmwood, Hillsborough	S	×
Ellsworth, Grafton	C	150
● Enfield, Grafton	C	1,439
Enfield Centre, Grafton	C	190
● Epping, Rockingham	SE	1,721
Epsom, Merrimack	S	815
● *Epsom*, Merrimack	S	×
Errol, Coos	N	178
Etna, Grafton	C	×
● *Everett*, Hillsborugh	S	×
● **Exeter**, Rockingham	SE	4,284
● Fabyan House, Coos	N	×
● Farmington, Strafford	SE	3,064
● *Fernalds*, Carroll	C	×
Fitzwilliam, Cheshire	SW	1,122
● Fitzwilliam Depot, Ch'e.	SW	240
Flume House, Grafton	C	×
● *Foundry Station*, Straff'd	SE	×
Francestown, Hillsborough	S	837
● *Frankenstein*, Carroll	C	×
Franconia, Grafton	C	594
● Franklin, Merrimack	S	4,085
● Franklin Falls, Merrimack	S	4,064
● *Franklin Junc.*, Mer'mack	S	×
Freedom, Carroll	C	630
● Fremont, Rockingham	SE	726
Frost Point, Rockingham	SE	×
Gaza, Belknap	C	×
● *George's*, Coos	N	×
George's Mills, Sullivan	SW	120
● Gilford Village, Belknap	C	3,585
Gilmanton, Belknap	C	1,211
Gilmanton Iron W'ks, Bel'p.	C	300
Gilsum, Cheshire	SW	643
● *Glen*, Carroll	C	×
Glen House, Coos	N	×
● *Glen House*, Coos	N	×
● Goff's Falls, Hillsborough	S	×
● Goffstown, Hillsborough	S	1,981
● Goffstown Centre, Hillsb'h	S	212
● Gonic, Strafford	SE	300
● Gorham, Coos	N	1,710
● *Gorham Junction*, Coos	N	×
Goshen, Sullivan	SW	384
● Gossville, Merrimack	S	×
● Grafton, Grafton	C	787
● Grafton Centre, Grafton	C	40
Grange, Coos	N	×
Granite, Carroll	C	×
Grantham, Sullivan	SW	424
● Great Falls, Strafford	SE	6,207
● Greenfield, Hillsborough	S	607
● Greenland, Rockingham	SE	647
● Greenland Depot, R'k'm	SE	×
● Greenville, Hillsborough	S	1,255
Groton, Grafton	C	464
● Groveton, Coos	N	510
● *Groveton Junction*, Coos	N	×
● Guild, Sullivan	SW	×
● *Hallsville*, Hillsborough	S	×
Hampstead, Rockingham	SE	860
● *Hampstead Sta.*, Rock'h'm	SE	×
● Hampton, Rockingham	SE	1,330
● Hampton Falls, Rocx'm.	SE	622
● Hancock, Hillsborough	S	637

New Hampshire New Hampshire

Place	Pop.
● *Hancock Junction*, Hillsb'h S	×
● Hanover, Grafton C	1,817
Hanover Centre, Grafton C	×
● Harrisville, Cheshire SW	748
Hart's Location, Carroll C	187
● **Haverhill**, Grafton C	545
● *Haye's*, Strafford SE	×
● Hazen Junction, Coos N	×
Hebron, Grafton C	245
● Henniker, Merrimack S	1,385
● Hill, Merrimack S	548
Hillsborough, Hillsborough S	2,120
● Hillsborough, Bridge, Hill'hS	700
Hillsborough Centre, Hillsb'hS	40
Hillsborough Upper Village, Hillsborough S	×
● Hinsdale, Cheshire SW	2,258
Holderness, Grafton C	595
Hollis, Hillsborough S	1,000
● Hollis Depot, HillsboroughS	×
● *Holton's*, Hillsborough S	×
● Hookset, Merrimack S	1,893
Hopkinton, Merrimack S	1,817
Horn's Mills, Carroll C	×
● Hubbard, Rockingham SE	×
Hudson, Hillsborough S	1,092
● Hudson Centre, Hillsbo'h S	×
● Intervale, Carroll C	58
Isle of Shoals, RockinghamSE	12
Jackson, Carroll C	579
Jaffrey, Cheshire SW	1,43
Jefferson, Coos N	1,062
● Jefferson Highland, Coos N	×
● *Jefferson Station*, Coos N	×
● *Jones*, Carroll C	×
Kearsarge, Carroll C	×
● **Keene**, Cheshire SW	7,446
● *Kelleyville*, Sullivan SW	×
Kensington, Rockingham SE	547
Keyes, Sullivan SW	50
Kilkenny, Coos N	×
Kingston, Rockingham SE	1,120
● **Laconia**, Belknap C	6,143
● Lakeport, Belknap C	3,585
Lake Shore Park, Belknap C	×
Lakeside, Coos N	×
● *Lake Sunapee*, MerrimackS	×
Lake View, Carroll C	×
● *Lake Village*, Belknap C	3,585
● **Lancaster**, Coos N	3,373
Landaff, Grafton C	499
Langdon, Sullivan SW	305
Leavitt's Hill, RockinghamSE	×
● Lebanon, Grafton C	3,763
Lee, Strafford SE	606
● *Lee* Strafford SE	×
Leighton's Corners, Carroll C	×
Lempster, Sullivan SW	519
● Libbey's, Coos N	×
● *Lily Pond*, Belknap C	×
Lincoln, Grafton C	110
● Lisbon, Grafton C	2,060
Litchfield, Hillsborough S	252
Little Boar's Head, Rock'mSE	×
● *Littlefield's*, RockinghemSE	×
● *Little's*, Hillsborough S	×
● Littleton, Grafton C	3,365
● Livermore, Grafton C	155
● *Livermore Falls*, Grafton C	×
Lockehaven, Grafton C	×
Londonderry, Rockingham SE	1,220
● *Londonderry Station*, R'mSE	×
Long Island, Carroll C	×
● *Loon Cove*, Belknap C	×
Loudon, Merrimack S	1,000
Loudon Centre, Merrimack S	×
Loudon Ridge, Merrimack S	35
Lower Bartlett, Carroll C	45
Lower Gilmanton, Belknap C	90
Lyman, Grafton C	543
Lyme, Grafton C	1,151
Lyme Centre, Grafton C	×
Lyndeborough, Hillsb'rough S	657
● *McDonald's*, Hillsborough S	×
● Madbury, Strafford SE	367
● Madison, Carroll C	554
● **MANCHESTER**, H'ls'b S	44,126
● Maplewood, Grafton C	×
● Marlborough, Cheshire SW	1,695
● Marlborough Depot, Chs SW	120
Marlow, Cheshire SW	584
● Martin, Merrimack S	×
Mascoma, Grafton C	×
● Mason, Hillsborough S	629
● *Mason's*, Coos N	×
● Massabesic, Hillsborough S	×
● Mast Yard, Merrimack S	×
Meadows, Coos N	×
● Melvin Mills, Merrimack S	×
Melvin Village, Carroll C	120
Meredith, Belknap C	1,642
Meredith Centre, Belknap C	×
● Meredith, Belknap C	1,000
Meriden, Sullivan SW	115
Merrill, Strafford SE	×
● Merrimack, Hillsborough S	951
Messer's Crossing, (see Salem)	×
Middleton, Strafford SE	207
Milan, Coos N	1,029
● Milford, Hillsborough S	3,01
Millsfield, Coos N	62
Mill Village, Sullivan SW	×
● *Mill Village*, Carroll C	×
● Milton, Strafford SE	1,640
Milton Mills, Strafford SE	410
Mirror Lake, Carroll C	×
Monroe, Grafton C	478
Montcalm, Grafton C	×
Moultonborough, Carroll C	1,034
Moultonville, Carroll C	200
Mount Delight, (see Deerfield)	×
● *Mount Major*, Belknap C	×
● Mt. Pleasant House, Coos N	×
● Mt. Sunapee, Merrimack S	×
Mt. Vernon, Hillsborough S	479
● Mt. Washington, Coos N	×
● *Mount Willard*, Coos N	×
Munsonville, Cheshire SW	135
● *Nahor's*, Hillsborough S	×
● **NASHUA**, Hillsborough S	19,311
● *Nashua Junc.*, Hillsb'ro S	×
Nelson, Cheshire SW	832
New Alstead, (see Alstead)	×
New Boston, Hillsborough S	1,067
● Newbury, Merrimack S	487
New Castle, Rockingham SE	488
● New Durham, Strafford SE	579
● New Hampton, Belknap C	935
● Newington, Rockingham SE	401
New Ipswich, Hillsborough S	969
New London, Merrimack S	799
● NewMarket, RockinghamSE	2,742
● *New Market Junction*, Rockingham SE	×
● **Newport**, Sullivan SW	2,623
● Newton, Rockingham SE	1,064
● Newton Junction, R'ckm SE	500
North Barnstead, Belknap C	×
North Barrington, Straff'd SE	×
● North Boscawen, Merrim'kS	×
North Bow, Merrimack S	×
North Branch, Hillsborough S	90
● Nor. Charlestown, Sul'vn SW	52
North Chatham, Carroll C	×
● **North Chichester, Merrm'kS**	120
● *North Concord*, MerrimackS	×
● North Conway, Carroll C	603
North Danville, Rocking'm SE	×
North Dorchester, Grafton C	×
North Dunbarton, Merrim'k S	×
North Epping, Rockingham SE	×
● NorthfieldDepot, Merr'mk S	1,115
North Grantham, Sullivan SW	×
North Groton, Grafton C	×
● North Hampton, Rock'm SE	804
● North Haverhill, Grafton C	240
North Hinsdale, Cheshire SW	×
North Holderness, Grafton C	×
● North Lisbon, Grafton C	×
North Littleton, Grafton C	×
● North Londonderry, Rockingham SE	250
North Lyndeborough, Hillsb' S	×
North Monroe, Grafton C	×
North Newport, Sullivan SW	125
North Nottingham, R'm SE	×
North Richmond, Chesh'e SW	200
● North Rochester, Straff'd SE	×
North Salem, Rockingham SE	250
North Sanbornton, Belknap C	×
North Sandwich, Carroll C	91
North Strafford, Strafford SE	×
● *North Stratford*, Coos N	300
North Sutton, Merrimack S	99
● Northumberland, Coos N	1,356
Northumberland Mills, (see Northumberland)	×
● *Northville*, Sullivan SW	×
● North Wakefield, Carroll C	55
North Walpole, Cheshire SW	×
● North Weare, Hillsbor'gh S	200
North Wolfboro, Carroll C	55
Northwood, Rockingham SE	1,478
Northwood Centre, R'ck'm SE	120
Northwood Narrows, R'k'mSE	50
Northwood Ridge, Ro'k'm SE	115
● North Woodstock, Grafton C	×
Nottingham, Rockingham SE	988
● Oil Mill Village, Hillsb'h S	70
● *Orange Turnout*, Grafton C	245
Orford, Grafton C	916
Orfordville, Grafton C	×
● **Ossipee**, Carroll C	1,630
Ossipee Centre, (see Ossipee)	×
Ossipee Valley Carroll C	90
● *Parker's*, Hillsborough S	×
Parkhill, Cheshire SW	120
Pattenville, Grafton C	×
Pelham, Hillsborough S	791
Pembroke, Merrimack S	3,172
● Penacook, Merrimack S	×
Pequaket, Carroll C	×
● Percy, Coos N	×
● Peterborough, Hillsboro S	2,507
● *Pickerings*, Strafford SE	×
● Pierce's Bridge, Grafton C	120
Piermont, Grafton C	709
Pike Station, Grafton C	90
● *Pikes*, Carroll C	×
● *Pine Valley*, Hillsborough S	×
Pinkham, Coos N	8
Piper Hill, Coos N	×
Pittsburg, Coos N	669
● Pittsfield, Merrimack S	2,605
● *Place's*, Strafford SE	×
Plainfield, Sullivan SW	1,143
● Plaistow, Rockingham SE	1,085
● **Plymouth**, Grafton C	1,852
● **Portsmouth**, Rock'm SE	9,827
● Potter Place, Merrimack S	810
● *Powwow River*, R'k'ham SE	×
● Pratt's, Hillsborough S	N
● Profile House, Grafton C	×
Quaker City, Sullivan SW	×
● *Quebec Junction*, Coos N	×
● Quincy, Grafton C	×
● Randolph, Roos N	137
● Raymond, Rockingham SE	1,131
Red Hill, (see Moultonboro)	×
○ Redstone, Carroll C	×
● Reed's Ferry, Hillsb'ough S	200
● *Richardson's*, Hillsb'ough S	×
Richmond, Cheshire SW	476
Rindge, Cheshire SW	996
● *Riverside*, Cheshire SW	×
● *Riverside*, Strafford SE	×
● Riverton, Coos N	13
● *Robinson's*, Merrimack S	×
● Roby's Corner, Merrimack S	133
● Rochester, Strafford SE	7,396
● *Rollinsford*, Strafford SE	2,003
Roxbury, Cheshire SW	129
Rumney, Grafton C	947
● Rumney Depot, Grafton C	105
● *Russell's*, Hillsborough S	×
Rye, Rockingham SE	978
Rye Beach, Rockingham SE	×
Salem, Rockingham SE	1,805
● Salem Depot, Rock'ham SE	×
Salisbury, Merrimack S	655
SalisburyHeights, MerrimackS	105
● Salmon Falls, Strafford SE	2,003
● *Sanborn's*, Grafton C	×
Sanbornton, Belknap C	1,027
● Sandown, Rockingham SE	475
Sandwich, Carroll C	1,303
● *Sawyer's*, Strafford SE	×
● *Sawyer's River*, Grafton C	155
● Scott, Coos N	×
Scytheville, Merrimack S	120
● Seabrook, Rockingham SE	1,672
Sea View House, Rocking'mSE	×
● *Severance's*, RockinghamSE	×
Sharon, Hillsborough S	137
● Shelburne, Coos N	336
● *Shirley*, Hillsborough S	×
● Short Falls, Merrimack S	90
● *Side Track*, Merrimack S	×
Silver Lake, Carroll C	×
Snowville, Carroll C	×
● *Somersworth*, Strafford SE	6,207
South Acworth, Sullivan SW	218
South Albany, Carroll C	×
South Alexandria, Grafton C	×
South Barnstead, Belknap C	×
South Barrington, StraffordSE	×
● *South Bennington*, Hill'ghS	×
● South Charlestown, Sul'nSW	120
South Chatham, Carroll C	×
● South Columbia, Coos N	×
South Cornish, Sullivan SW	30

● South Danbury, Merrim,kS ×
South Deerfield, Rock'h'mSE 120
South Effingham, Carroll....C 120
South Hampton, Rock'hamSE 370
● South Keene, Cheshire..SW ×
South Kingston, Rock'hamSE ×
● South Lancaster, Coos....N ×
● South Lee, Strafford.....SE ×
● *South Littleton*, Grafton..C ×
● South Lyndeborough, Hillsborough.........S 200
● South Merrimack, Hillsb'hS 90
South Milton, (see Milton)... ×
South Newbury, MerrimackS ×
● South New Market, Rockingham..................SE 855
● South New Market Junction, Rockingham...........SE ×
● *South Penacook*, Merrim'kS ×
South Pittsfield, Merrimack.S ×
South Seabrook, Rock'g'mSE 120
South Stoddard, Cheshire.SW 110
South Sutton, Merrimack...S 15
South Tamworth, Carroll....C 120
South Wakefield, Carroll....C ×
South Weare, Hillsborough..S ×
South Windham, Rockin'mSE ×
South Wolfborough, Carroll.C 90
Springfield, Sullivan.......SW 540
● *Springfield Station*, Sul'nSW ×
● *Spring Haven*, Belknap..C ×
Stark, Coos.................N 703
● State Line, Cheshire....SW ×
Stewartstown, Coos...........N 1,002
Stoddard, Cheshire........SW 400
Strafford, Strafford.........SE 1,304
Strafford, Blue Hills, Strafford..................SE ×
Strafford Corner, StraffordSE ×
● Stratford, Coos............N 1,128
Stratham, Rockingham....SE 680
● *Stratham Station*, R'ck'mSE ×
Success, Coos...............N ×
Sugar Hill, Grafton..........C 120
Sullivan, Cheshire.........SW 337
● *Summit*, Cheshire.........SW ×
● *Summit Turnout*, GraftonC ×
Sunapee, Sullivan.........SW 900
● *Sunapee Station*, Sul'vanSW ×
● Suncook, Merrimack......S 3,163
Surry, Cheshire.............SW 270
Sutton, Merrimack..........S 849
Swanzey, Cheshire.........SW 1,600
Swiftwater, Grafton..........C 80
Tamworth, Carroll..........C 1,025
● *Tarbell's*, Hillsborough...S ×
Temple, Hillsborough........S 342
● *Tenth Section*, CheshireSW ×
● *The Narrows*, Coos.......N ×
The Weirs, Belknap..........C ×
Thompson Falls, Grafton..C ×
● Thornton, Grafton........C 632
● Thornton's Ferry, Hill'gh.S 127
● Tilton, Belknap...........C 1,521
● Troy, Cheshire..........SW 999
Tuftonborough, Carroll.....C 767
Tuftonborough Centre, (see Tuftonborough)........ ×
● Twin Mountain, Coos.....N 60
● *Tyler's*, Merrimack.......S ×
● Union, Carroll.............C 350
Unity, Sullivan...... .....SW 653
Uplands, Merrimack........S 60
Upper Bartlett, (see Bartlett) ×
Wadley's Falls, Strafford..SE ×
● Wakefield, Carroll........C 1,528
● Walpole, Cheshire.......SW 2,163
Ware's Ferry, Cheshire...SW ×
● Warner, Merrimack.......S 1,383
● Warren, Grafton..........C 875
● Warren Summit, Grafton.C 90
Washington, Sullivan.....SW 569
● Waterloo, Merrimack.....S ×
Water Village, Carroll.......C 53
Waterville, Grafton.........C 39
Weare, Hillsborough........S 1,550
Webster, Merrimack.........S 564
● *Websters Mills*, MerrimackS ×
● *Weirs*, Belknap............C ×
● Wentworth, Grafton......C 698
Wentworth's Location, Coos.N 25
● West Alton, Belknap.....C ×
● West Andover, Mer'mack.S 95
West Barrington, StraffordSE ×
West Brentwood, Rock'hmSE ×
West Campton, Grafton.....C 90
● West Canaan, Grafton....C 120
West Chesterfield, Ches'ireSW 90
West Claremont, Sullivan.SW 200
● West Concord, MerrimackS 1,025
● West Deering, HillsboroughS 90
● West Epping, Rockin'hmSE 175
West Goffstown, Hillsbor'gh.S ×
West Hampstead, Rock'h'mSE 135
● West Henniker, Merrim'kS 120
● West Hopkinton, Mer'm'kS 50
West Kingston, R'kingh'mSE ×
● West Lebanon, Grafton...C 570
● West Milan, Coos.........E 76
Westmoreland, Cheshire..SW 830
● Westmoreland Depot, Cheshire..........................SW ×
West Nottingham, Rockingham.......................SE 90
● West Ossipee, Carroll.....C 120
West Peterborough, Hillsb'hS 130
West Plymouth, Grafton....C ×
● Westport, Cheshire......SW 145
● West Rindge, Cheshire..SW 250
● *West Rochester*, StraffordSE ×
● West Rumney, Grafton...C 62
West Rye, Rockingham....SE ×
West Salisbury, Merrimack.S 90
West Springfield, Sullivan.SW 95
● West Stewartstown, Coos.N 250
● West Swanzey, CheshireSW 480
● West Thornton, Grafton..C 120
● Westville, Rockingham..SE ×
West Wilton, Hillsborough..S 95
● West Windham, Rock'm.SE ×
Whipples, Coos.............N ×
Whitcherville, Grafton.....C ×
● Whitefield, Coos...........N 2,041
Whitefield Village, Coos....N ×
● *White Mountain House*, Coos.........................N ×
● *White Mountain Transfer*, Grafton......................C ×
Wildwood, Grafton..........C ×
● *Willey's*, Hillsborough.....S ×
● *Willey House*, Carroll....C ×
● Willowdale, Grafton......C ×
Wilmot, Merrimack..........S 840
Wilmot Flat, Merrimack....S 250
● Wilson's Crossing, Rockingham.......................SE ×
● Wilton, Hillsborough.......S 1,850
● Winchester, Cheshire...SW 2,584
Windham, Rockingham...SE 632
● Windham Depot, R'kh'm SE ×
Windsor, Hillsborough......S 62
● Wing Road, Grafton......C ×
Wolfboro, Falls, Carroll....C ×
● Wolfboro Junc., Carroll..C 225
● Wolfborough, Carroll.....C 3,020
● Wolfborough Centre, Carroll C ×
Woodman's, Carroll.........C 90
● Woodstock, Grafton......C 341
● Woodsville, Grafton......C 1,000
● Zealand, Coos.............N ×
● *Zealand Junction*, Coos..N ×
Zealand Notch, Grafton....C ×

NEW JERSEY.

COUNTIES.	INDEX.	POP.
Atlantic	S	28,836
Bergen	NE	47,226
Burlington	C	58,528
Camden	SW	87,687
Cape May	S	11,268
Cumberland	S	45,438
Essex	NE	256,098
Gloucester	NW	28,649
Hudson	NE	275,126
Hunterdon	NW	35,355
Mercer	C	79,978
Middlesex	C	6,1754
Monmouth	C	69,128
Morris	N	54,101
Ocean	C	15,974
Passaic	N	105,046
Salem	SW	25,151
Somerset	C	28,311
Sussex	NW	22,259
Union	NE	72,467
Warren	NW	36,553
Total		1,444,933

● Absecon, Atlantic.........S 501
● *Ackerman Switch*, Sus'x NW ×
● *Acton*, Salem............SW ×
Aetna Mills, (see Medford).. ×
Afton, Morris...............N 350
● *Albion*, Camden.........SW ×
Aldine, Salem..............SW ×
● *Alexauken*, Hunterdon NW ×
● Allaire, Monmouth.......C 125
● Allamuchy, Warren....NW 760
● Allendale, Bergen.......NE 100
Allentown, Monmouth......C 1,050
● Allenwood, Monmouth...C 50
Alliance, Salem............SW 600
● Alloway, Salem..........SW 1,000
Almonesson, Gloucester...SW 100
Alpine, Bergen..............NE 106
Amwell, Hunterdon.....NW 30
● Ancora, Camden.........SW 200
Anderson, Warren........NW 105
● Andover, Sussex.......NW 300
Andover Furnace, WarrenNW ×
Andover Junction, SussexNW ×
● *Andrews*, Camden......SW ×
● Anglesea, Cape May.......S 161
● *Anglesea Junc.*, Cape MayS ×
● Annandale, Hunterdon.NW 500
Anthony, Hunterdon.....NW 100
Apger's Corner, H'tderdonNW 50
Applegarth, Middlesex......C ×
● *Appollonia*, Ocean........C ×
Arcola, (see Rochelle Park).. ×
Ardena, Monmouth.........C ×
Arlington, Hudson.........NE 1,000
● *Arlington Ave.*, Essex..NE ×
Armstrong's, Sussex.....NW ×
Arney's Mount, (see Juliust'n) ×
Asbury, Warren............NW 500
● *Asbury*, Gloucester.....SW ×
● Asbury Park, Monmouth.C 3,223
● *Asbury Sta.*, HunterdonNW ×
● *Ash Brook*, Middlesex....C ×
● Ashland, Camden.......SW 50
● *Asyla*, Camden.........SW 50
● *Asylum*, Mercer..........C ×
● Acto, Camden..........SW 200
● Athenia, Passaic..........N 90
● Atlantic City, Atlantic....S 13,055
● Atlantic Highlands, M'nth.C 945
● Atsion, Burlington........C 75
Auburn, Salem..............NW 200
● Audubon, Camden.......SW ×
● Augusta, Sussex.........NW 60
● Avalon, Cape May..........S ×
● *Avenal*, Middlesex.........C ×
● *Avenue B*, Monmouth....C ×
Avon-by-the-Sea, MonmouthC ×
● Avondale, Essex..........NE 200
● *Bacon's Neck*, CumberlandS ×
● Bakersville, Atlantic......S 450
● Baleville, Sussex.........SW 150
● Bamber, Ocean..............C 25
Babtistown, Hunterdon..NW 145
Barbertown, Hunterdon. NW ×
Bargaintown, Atlantic.......S 200
Barley Sheaf, Hunterdon.NW 10
● *Barnard*, Atlantic.........S ×
● Barnegat, Ocean...........C 1,000
● Barnegat City, Ocean.....C 57
● *Barnegat City Jc.*, Ocean. C ×
● Barnegat Park, Ocean....C 160
● *Barnegat Pier*, Ocean....C ×
● Barnsborough, Glo'cesterSW 200
● *Barrington*, Camden.....S ×
● Bartley, Morris............N 100
● Basking Ridge, Somerset.C 500
Bassett, Gloucester........SW ×
Bass River, (see New Gretna) ×
Batsto, Burlington..........C 50
● *Bay Draw*, Hudson.....NE ×
● Bayhead, Ocean............C 200
● *Bay Head Junc.*, Ocean...C ×
● Bayonne, Hudson.........NE 19,003
● *Bay Side*, Cumberland...S ×
● *Bay View*, Monmouth....C ×
Bayville, Ocean ....C 25
● *Bayway*, Union..........NE ×
● Beach Haven, Ocean......C 250
● *Beach View*, Ocean.......C ×
Beatyestown, Warren....NW 350
Beaver Run, Sussex......NW 64
Bedminster, Somerset ......C 120
Beemerville, Sussex......NW 200
Beesley's Point, Cape May..S 250
● *Beideman's*, Camden....SW ×
● Bellemawr, Camden....SW ×
● Belle Mead, Somerset.....C 56

Place	Population
● Belle Plain, Cape May.....S	150
● Belleville, Essex........NE	3,487
Belford, Monmouth........C	×
● Belmar, Monmouth.......C	359
Belmont, Hudson.........NE	×
● **Belvidere**, Warren...NW	1,768
● *Bennett*, Cape May........S	×
Bennett Mills, Ocean..........C	228
Bennett's Sta.,(seeCold Spr'g)	×
Bergen, Hudson...........NE	×
● Bergenfield, Bergen.... NE	300
● *Bergen Hill*, Middlesex...C	×
Bergen Square, (see Jer. City)	×
● *Bergen Point*, Hudson..NE	×
● *Berkeley*, Ocean..........C	60
Berkeley Arms, Ocean...... C	×
● Berkeley Heights,Union NE	360
Berkley, (see Clarksboro).....	×
Berkshire Valley, Morris...N	60
● Berlin, Camden.........SW	750
● Bernardsville, Somerset..C	200
● *Bethel*, Atlantic..........S	×
Bevans, Sussex...........NW	200
● Beverly, Burlington......C	1,957
Billingsport,(seePaulsborough)	
● Birmingham, Burlington.C	300
Bivalve, Cumberland........S	×
Black's Mills, Monmouth....C	125
Blackwell's Mills, Somerset.C	150
● Blackwood, Camden....SW	600
Blair, Sussex............NW	×
● Blairstown, Warren....NW	1,644
Blawenburgh, Somerset.....C	200
● *Blenheim*, Camden......SW	×
● Bloomfield, Essex.......NE	7,860
● *Bloomfield*, Middlesex.... C	×
● *Bloomfield Avenue*, EssexNE	×
● *Bloomfield Junc.*, Essex.NE	×
● *Bloomfield Station*,EssexNE	×
● Bloomingdale, Passaic.... N	1,000
Bloomington, Somerset.....C	801
● Bloomsbury, HunterdonNW	850
● Blue Anchor, Camden..SW	100
● *Bogota*, Bergen......... NE	×
Boiling Spr.,(see Rutherford)	×
● Boonton, Morris.........N	2,981
● Bordentown, Burlington..C	4,232
Bougher, Burlington........C	×
● Boundbrook, Somerset....C	1,462
● *Bound Brook Cr* ,SomersetC	×
● *Bowentown*, Cumberland. S	×
● *Bowne*, Hunterdon.....NW	30
● *Braddock*,Camden......SW	×
● Bradevelt, Monmouth.... C	×
Bradley Beach, Monmouth..C	×
● *Bradway*, Salem.......SW	×
Brainards, Warren........NW	110
Branchburg,(seeLong Branch)	×
● *Branch Port*, Monmouth.C	×
● Branchville, Sussex.... NW	600
● *Branchville Jc* ,Sussex.NW	×
Bricksburg, (see Lakewood) .	×
● *Bricksboro*, Cumberland..S	×
Bridgeboro, Burlington...S	×
Bridgeborough, Burlington..C	500
● Bridgeport, Gloucester..SW	600
● **Bridgeton**, CumberlandS	11,424
● *Bridgeton Jc.*,CumberlandS	×
● Bridgeville, Warren....NW	100
● Brielle, Monmouth.......C	×
Brigantine, Atlantic.........S	100
● *Brigantine Beach*,AtlanticS	×
● *Brighton Avenue*, EssexNE	×
● *Brills Junction*, Essex..NE	×
Broad Street, Essex.......NE	×
● Broadway, Warren.....NW	300
Brookdale, Essex..........NE	200
● Brookside, Morris.........N	270
Brook Valley, Morris.......N	30
● Brown's Mills, BurlingtonC	220
Brown's MillsJc.,BurlingtonC	×
● *Buckingham*, Ocean.......C	×
Budd Lake, Morris..........N	200
Budd Town, Burlington.....C	200
Buena, Atlantic.............S	100
● *Buena Vista*, Atlantic.... S	×
Bull's Ferry, Hudson.....NE	650
● *Bull's Island*, HunterdonNW	200
● Burleigh, Cape May.......S	150
● Burlington. Burlington...C	7,264
● *Burlington Junc.*, Burl'onC	×
Burrsville, Ocean............C	150
Bustleton, Burlington.......C	50
● Butler, Morris............N	500
● Buttzville, Warren.......NW	100
● *Byram*, Hunterdon.... NW	×
● Caldwell, Essex.........NE	2.432

New Jersey

Place	Population
● Californ, Hunterdon....NW	500
Calno, Warren.............NW	120
● *Cambridge*, Burlington...C	×
● **Camden**, Camden.....SW	58,313
● *Campgaw*, Bergen......NE	100
Canton, Salem............SW	150
Cape Island, (see Cape May).	×
● Cape May, Cape May...... S	2,136
● **Cape May,C. H.**,C. MayS	600
Cape May Point, Cape May..S	167
● Carlistadt, Bergen...... NE	1,200
● Carlton Hill, Bergen....NE	×
Carmel, Cumberland..........S	700
Carpenter's L'd'g,(seeMantua)	×
● Carpentersville, WarrenNW	200
● Carteret, Middlesex.......C	600
● *Cary's*, Morris............N	×
Cassville, Ocean.............C	405
Cecil, Gloucester..........SW	80
Cedar Bridge, (see Burrsville)	×
Cedar Brook, Camden.... SW	100
● *Cedar Brook*, Camden..SW	×
● *Cedar Creek*, Ocean.......C	150
● Cedar Grove, Essex...... NE	400
● Cedar Lake, Atlantic......S	25
● Cedar Run, Ocean.........C	100
● Cedarville, Cumberland...S	1,500
● *Central Avenue*, Cape MayS	×
● *Central Square*,Gl'cest'rSW	×
● *Central Street*, Essex... NE	×
Centreton, Salem..........SW	250
Centreville, (see Camden)	×
Centreville, Hunterdon...NW	130
● *Centreville*, Cumberland.. S	×
● *Centreville*, Hudson.....NE	×
Centreville, Monmouth.......C	×
Centreville, (see Knowlton)...	×
● Chadwick, Ocean......... C	25
Chambersburg, (see Trenton)	×
● Changewater, Warren..NW	200
● Chapel Hill, Monmouth...C	50
● Charlotteburgh, Passaic.. N	20
● *Charlottesburgh Jc.*, Pas'cN	×
● Chatham, Morris.......... N	713
● *Chelsea*, Atlantic..........S	×
● *Chelsea Ave.*, Monmouth. C	×
Cherry Hill, Bergen........NE	×
● *Cherry Hill*, Bergen.... NE	×
Cherryville, Hunterdon.. NW	150
Chesilhurst, Camden......SW	550
● Chester, Morris............N	713
Chesterfield, Burlington.....C	400
● *Chester Furnace*, Morris.N	×
● *Chester Junction*, Morris.N	×
● *Chestnut Hill*, Essex....NE	×
● *Chestnut Station*, EssexNE	×
● *Chewroad*, Camden......SW	×
Chew's Landing, Camden..SW	346
● *Church Street*,Glouces'rSW	×
Cinnaminson, Burlington... C	1,000
Claremont, (see Jersey City) .	×
Clarendon, Hudson....... NE	×
● Clarksborough,Glouc'terSW	310
Clarksburgh, Monmouth.....C	220
Clarksville,(see Glen Gardner)	×
● Clayton, Gloucester.....SW	1,807
● *Clayville*, Cumberland.....S	×
Clementon, Camden...... SW	300
Clermont, Cape May.........S	200
● Cliffwood, Monmouth.....C	40
● Clifton, Passaic........... N	400
● Clinton, Hunterdon.......N	1,975
Clinton Station,(seeAnnandale)	×
Clinton Place, Essex......NE	×
● Closter, Bergen......... NE	800
Clore, Sussex...........NW	×
● *Cloverdale*, Camden......SW	×
Clover Hill, Hunterdon.. NW	100
● *Clyde*, Somerset...........C	×
Cohansey, Salem...........SW	150
Cokesbury Hunterdon... NW	100
Cold Spring, Cape May...... S	300
Colesville, Sussex.........NW	200
Collier's Mill, Ocean.........C	227
● Collingswood, Camden..SW	539
● *Cologne*, Atlantic..........S	×
Colt's Neck, Monmouth.... C	200
● Columbia, Warren.......NW	200
● *Columbia Jc.*,Warren..NW	×
● Columbus, Burlington.... C	700
● *Colwell*, Atlantic..........S	×
● *Communipaw*, Hudson. NE	×
● *Como*, Monmouth..........C	×
Constable's Hook,(see Bayonne)	×
Convent Station, Morris.......N	32
● Cookstown, Burlington... C	300
Cooksville, Warren.......NW	150

New Jersey

Place	Population
● Cooper, Passaic...........N	×
● *Cooper's*, Gloucester....SW	×
● *Cooper Creek*, Camden..SW	×
Cooper's Point, (see Camden)	×
● Copper Hill, HunterdonNW	100
Corona, (seeHasbrouckHeights)	×
● *Carson's Inlet*,Cape May..S	×
● *Court House*, Cape May. .S	600
Court House, Essex.......NE	×
● *County Line*, Huterdon NW	×
● *Cox Station*, Ocean....... C	×
Coytesville, (see Fort Lee)...	×
Cramer's Hill, Camden....SW	**1,000**
Cranbury, Middlesex........C	1,569
● Cranbury Station, Mid'e'x C	60
Crane's Station, (see Iona)...	×
● Cranford, Union.......NE	1,200
● Cream Ridge, Monmouth C	250
● Cresskill, Bergen....... NE	150
Cropwell, Camden.. ..... SW	×
Cross Keys, Gloucester....SW	300
Cross Roads, (see Medford)..	×
Crosswicks, Burlington..... C	800
Croton, Hunterdon.......NW	100
● *Crystal Lake*, Bergen...NE	×
Culver, Ocean. C	×
● *Cut-off Junction*,SussexNW	×
● *Da Costa*, Atlantic........S	75
● Danville, Warren.......NW	100
● *Dare Street*, Gloucester.SW	×
● Daretown, Salem........SW	200
Darlington, Bergen......NW	×
● *Davenport*, Ocean..........C	×
Davidson's Mills, MiddlesexC	×
● Davis, Monmouth..........C	60
● Dayton, Middlesex.........C	400
● *Deacon's*, Burlington.....C	×
Deal, Monmouth............ C	200
● Deal Beach, Monmouth...C	100
● Dean's, Middlsex......... C	250
● Deckertown, Sussex....NW	821
● Decosta, Atlantic..........S	30
Deerfield Street, Cumb'erl'd. S	100
● *De Kays*, Sussex...... NW	×
● Delair, Camden.........SW	100
● Delanco, Burlington...... C	500
● Delaware, Warren.......NW	165
● Delaware Gap, Warren.NW	65
Delmont, Cumberland.......S	100
Delta, Bergen.............NE	×
● Demarest, Bergen.......NE	150
Dennisville, Cape May...... S	900
● Denville, Morris..........N	120
Dias Creek, Cape May.......S	200
Dividing Creek, CumberlandS	400
● *Dividing Creek*, Cumberl'dS	×
Dobbins, Burlington........ C	×
● *Dobb's*, Camden......... SW	×
● Dorchester, Cumberland..S	300
● *Dorell*, Camden..........SW	×
● *Doughty's*, Atlantic.......S	×
● Dover, Morris............ N	3,250
● Downer, Gloucester.....SW	100
Drakestown, Morris.........N	200
● *Drakesville*, Morris.......N	×
● Drakesville, Morris.......N	200
● *Drawbridge*, Atlantic.... S	×
● *Dudley*, Camden........SW	×
● *Dundee*, Passaic..........N	×
● Dundee Lake, Bergen...NE	200
● Dunellen, Middlesex....... C	1,060
● *Dunnfield*, Warren.....NW	×
Dupont, Monmouth..........C	×
Dutch Neck, Mercer........ C	200
● *East Bridgeton*,Cumberl'dS	×
East Creek, Cape May.......S	250
● *East Dover Jc.*, Morris...N	×
● *East End*, Hudson..... NE	×
● *East Ferry Street*, EssexNE	×
● *East Freehold*, MonmouthC	×
● *East Gloucester*,CamdenSW	×
● *East Long Branch*,Mon'thC	×
● East Millstone, Somerset..C	500
● *East Moorestown*, Burl'onC	×
● *East Newark Sta.*,Hud'nNE	×
● East Orange, Sussex .... NE	13,161
● *East Orange Sta.*,Essex NE	×
East Vineland, (see Vineland)	×
● Eatontown, Monmouth... C	1,000
Eayerstown, (see Mt. Holly).	×
Echo Lake, Passaic......... N	26
Edenburg, Monmouth...... C	×
● *Edgar's*, Middlesex.......C	×
Edgewater, Bergen........NE	350
● Edgewater Park,Burling'nC	400
Edinburgh, Mercer..........C	150
Edison, Sussex.......... NW	×

Place	Pop.
● Egg Harbor City, Atlantic..S	1,439
● Elberon, Monmouth.......C	30
● **Elizabeth**, Union.....NE	37,764
● *Elizabethport*, Union....NE	×
Ellisburgh, Camden.......SW	150
Ellisdale, Monmouth........C	300
● Elm, Camden...........SW	125
● Elmer, Salem...........SW	1,200
● *Elmora*, Union..........NE	×
● *Elmwood Road*, Burling'nC	×
● *Elsmere*, Gloucester....SW	×
Elton, Monmouth...........C	×
● Elwood, Atlantic.........S	475
Ely, Monmouth..............C	×
● *Emmett Street*, Essex...NE	×
● Englewood, Bergen.....NE	4,429
English Creek, Atlantic......S	×
● English Creek, Atlantic...S	300
● Englishtown, Monmouth..C	600
● *Ernston*, Middlesex.......C	×
● Erskine, Passaic.........N	×
● *Essex*, Essex............NE	×
Estelville, Atlantic.......... S	150
● Etna, Bergen .... NE	200
Etra, Mercer................ C	250
Everittstown, Hunterdon.NW	150
Evesboro, Burlington....... C	500
● *Evona*, Union.......... NE	×
Ewan's Mills, Gloucester..SW	250
● *Ewansville*, Burlington...C	×
● Ewingville, Mercer........C	125
Fairfield, Essex............NE	250
● *Fairfield*, Monmouth.....C	150
Fair Haven, Monmouth.......C	150
Fair House, Camden.......SW	×
● Fairlawn, Bergen....... NE	145
● *Fairmount*, Bergen....NE	×
Fair Mount, Hunterdon...NW	200
● Fairton, Cumberland.......S	400
● Fairview, Bergen....... NE	250
Fairview, Burlington.......C	25
Faitoute, Union.......... NE	×
● Fanwood, Union.........NE	600
● Far Hills, Somerset.......C	×
● Farmingdale, Monmouth. C	800
● *Farmington*, Atlantic.....S	×
Fellowship, Burlington..... C	200
● *Fenwick*, Salem.........SW	×
Ferrell, Gloucester.........SW	20
● *Ferremont Junc.*, Morris. N	×
Ferromonte, Morris........ N	×
● *Ferry Road*, Camden...SW	×
● *Ferry Street*, Essex..... NE	×
● Fieldsborough, BurlingtonC	800
● Finderne, Somerset.......C	120
Finesville, Warren........NW	300
● Finley Station, CumberlandS	200
● Fish House, Camden....SW	100
Fishing Creek, Cape May....S	150
Fisterville, (see Clayton)	×
Five Points, Gloucester... SW	150
○ *Flagtown*, Somerset...... C	120
● Flanders, Morris...........N	500
Flatbrookville, Sussex....NW	200
● *Flax Mill*, Hunterdon..NW	×
● **Flemington**, Hunte'nNW	2,000
● *Flemington Jc.*, Hunt'nNW	×
● Florence, Burlington..... C	1,000
● *Florence*, Camden......SW	×
● Folsom, Atlantic...........S	500
● *Ford*, Sussex...........NW	×
● Fords, Middlesex.........C	×
Ford's Corners, Middlesex..C	×
● **Forest Grove, GloucesterSW**	200
○ *Forest Hill*, Essex.......NE	×
● Forked River, Ocean......C	700
Fort Lee, Bergen..........NE	450
● *Fourteenth St.*, Cape May.S	×
● Frankfort, Somerset......C	120
● *Franklin*, Essex.........NE	2,018
● Franklin Furnace, SussexNW	500
● *Franklin Junc.*, SussexNW	628
Franklin Park, Middlesex.. C	350
● *Franklin ParkSta.*, Mid'exC	350
● Franklinville, GloucesterSW	400
Fredon, Sussex...........NW	25
● **Freehold**, Monmouth...C	2,932
Freiburgh, Bergen........NE	×
● *Freman*, Camden.......SW	×
● Frenchtown, Hunterd'n NW	1,023
Freneau, Monmouth........C	×
Friesburg, Salem.........SW	×
● *Fruit Grower's Union*, Atlantic .... S	×
● *Galilee*, Monmouth........ C	×
● *Garden Lake*, Camden..SW	×
● Garfield, Bergen........ NE	409
Georgetown, Burlington.... C	150
● *Germania*, Atlantic....... S	×
● *Germania*, Ocean......... C	×
● German Valley, Morris.. N	389
Gibbsborough, Camden... SW	175
● Gibbstown, Gloucester.. SW	300
● Gillette, Morris...........N	×
● Gladstone, Somerset...... C	×
● Glassborough, Glouc'r.. SW	2,800
Glendale, (see Kirkwood)	×
Glendola, Monmouth........C	×
● Glen Gardner, H'ter'n.. NW	500
● Glen Moore, Mercer...... C	50
● Glen Ridge, Essex...... NE	55
● Glenview, Morris........ N	50
Glenwood, Essex ....NE	×
Glenwood, Sussex......... NW	400
● Gloucester City, Camden SW	6,564
● *Gloucester Jc.*, Camden SW	×
Goshen, Cape May.......... S	400
Gouldtown, Cumberland.... S	160
Graham, Ocean C	×
● *Grandin*, Hunterdon .. NW	×
● *Grant Avenue*, Hudson. NE	×
● *Grant Avenue*, Union .. NE	×
● *Granton*, Hudson........NE	×
● *Grassy Sound*, Cape May..S	×
● *Great Island*, Union....NE	×
● *Great Meadows*, W'ren. NW	100
● *Great Notch*, Essex..... NE	×
Green Bank, Burlington.... C	180
Green Creek, Cape May..... S	360
● *Green Grove Avenue*, Mo'thC	×
Green Lake, Morris......... N	×
Greenland, Camden.........SW	32
● *Green Pond Junc.*, PassaicN	×
Greenport, Sussex........ NW	×
Green Village, Morris...... N	100
● Greenville, Hudson...... NE	100
○ Greenwich, Cumberland.. S	600
Greenwood Lake, Passaic...N	×
Grenloch, Camden........ SW	150
Griggstown, Somerset.......C	300
Grover, Hunterdon ...... NW	125
Groville, (see Yardville)......	×
Guttenberg, Hudson......... NE	1,947
● **Hackensack**, Bergen. NE	6,004
● Hackettstown, Warren. NW	2,417
● *Haddon Avenue*, CamdenSW	×
● Haddonfield, Camden...SW	2,502
● *Haddon Heights*, CamdenSW	×
● Hainesburgh, Warren.. NW	350
● *Hainesburgh Junc.*, W'rnNW	×
● Hainesport, Burlington... C	500
Hainesville, Sussex ...... NW	500
Halberton, Cumberland..... S	×
Haledon, Passaic............N	×
● *Halfway House*, Atlantic. S	×
Haleyville, Cumberland..... S	200
● Halsey, Sussex..........NW	×
● Hamburgh, Sussex..... NW	600
● Hamden, Hunterdon... NW	30
● Hamilton, Monmouth C	120
Hamilton Square, Mercer.... C	650
● Hammonton, Atlantic.... S	3,833
● *Hampton*, Hunterdon..NW	400
Hampton Junc., (see Junc.)..	×
Hancock's Bridge, Salem..SW	250
Hanover, Morris............ N	100
● *Hanover*, Burlington..... C	×
Hanover Neck, Morris......N	26
Harbourton, Mercer C	30
● *Harding*, Gloucester... SW	120
Hardingville, Gloucester.. SW	35
Hardwick, Warren........NW	583
● Harlingen, Somerset...... C	100
Harmersville, Salem...... SW	100
Harmony, Warren....... NW	210
● *Harmony Sta.*, Warren NW	×
● Harrington, Bergen.....NE	×
● *Harris*, Burlington........ C	×
Harrissia, Burlington....... C	100
● *Harrison*, Essex........ NE	×
● Harrison, Hudson ...... NE	8,338
○ *Harrison*, Sussex....... NW	×
● *Harrison Street*, Passaic..N	×
● Harrisonville, Glou'ter..SW	300
● Hartford, Burlington..... C	200
Hartford Station, Burl'gton C	200
● Harvey Cedars, Ocean.... C	25
● Hasbrouck Heights, B'gn NE	125
● Haworth, Bergen........ NE	×
● Hawthorne, Passaic...... N	55
Hazen, Warren............ NW	175
● Hazlet, Monmouth........ C	150
● Heislerville, Cumberland. C	425
● Helmetta, Middlesex.....C	200
● *Hendrickson*, Monmouth.C	×
Herbertsville, Ocean........ C	80
● *Hereford*, Cape May...... S	×
● *Heritage*, Gloucester....SW	×
● Hewitt, Passaic........... N	300
Hibernia, Morris.............. N	1,385
● *Hibernia Junc.*, Morris...N	×
● High Bridge, HunterdonNW	1,500
● Highlands, Monmouth.... C	100
● Hightstown, Mercer...... C	1,875
● Highwood, Bergen..... NE	40
Hillcrest, Mercer............C	×
● *Hillsboro*, Somerset...... C	×
Hillsborough, Somerset..... C	30
● Hillsdale, Bergen........NE	50
Hilton, Essex...............NE	45
● **HOBOKEN**, Hudson.NE	43,648
● *Hoffman's*, Middlesex.....C	×
● *Hoffman'sSiding*, H'tdonNW	×
● Hohokus, Bergen........NE	2,920
● Holland, Hunterdon...NW	100
● Holly Beach, Cape May....S	217
● *Hollywood*, Monmouth... C	×
Holmdel, Monmouth.........C	300
● *Homestead*, Hudson.... NE	180
Hopatcong, Morris .... N	40
● *Hopatcong Junc.*, Morris N	×
Hope, Warren............ NW	400
● Hopewell, Mercer C	400
● *Hopping*, Monmouth..... C	×
● *Hopping Junc.*, MonmouthC	×
● Hornerstown, Monmouth .C	150
● *Horton*, Morris........... N	×
Hotel Breslin, Burlington .. C	×
Houses, Sussex...........NW	30
● *Houtenville*, Middlesex... C	×
Howard, Warren.......... NW	40
● Howell, Monmouth.......... C	×
Hudson City, Hudson..... NE	×
Hulsetown, Monmouth......C	×
Huntley, (see Summit).......	×
Huntsburgh, Sussex...... NW	75
Hunts Mills, Sussex......NW	63
Huntsville, Sussex........ NW	36
● *Hurd*, Morris............. N	25
Hurdtown, Morris.......... N	25
Hurffville, Gloucester .... SW	300
● *Husted*, Cumberland......S	32
● *Hutchinsons*, Warren..NW	×
Idell, Hunterdon..........NW	50
● Imlaystown, Monmouth.. C	400
Indian Mills, Burlington.....C	50
● *Interlaken*, Monmouth.... C	×
● Iona, Gloucester........ SW	180
● Ironia, Morris............. N	100
Irving Place, Essex ...... NE	2,390
Irvington, Essex..........NE	2,390
● Iselin, Middlesex..........C	120
Island Heights, Ocean........ C	300
● *Island Heights Sta.*, Ocean C	×
● *Jackson Avenue*, Ca'den SW	×
Jackson's Mills, Ocean...... C	251
Jacksonville, Burlington.... C	75
Jacksonville, Middlesex... C	×
Jacobstown, Burlington C	400
● Jamesburgh, Middlesex.. C	1,429
Janvier, Gloucester....... SW	100
Jeffers, (see Scullville)........	×
● Jefferson, Gloucester.... SW	200
● **JERSEY CITY**, H'ds'nNE	163,003
Jersey City Heights, Huds'nNE	×
Jersey City Waterworks, Bergen.....................NE	×
Jerseyville, Monmouth......C	20
● Jobstown, Burlington.....C	200
Johnsonburgh, Warren...NW	250
● Juliustown, Burlington...C	400
● Junction, Hunterdon...NW	1,200
● Jutland, Hunterdon....NW	400
Kaighn's Point, (see Camden)	×
Karrsville, Warren.......NW	200
Kays, Sussex............NW	×
● Keansburgh, Monmouth..C	350
Kearney, (see Harrison).......	×
● *Kennedy*, Warren......NW	×
● Kenvil, Morris...........N	120
Kettle Creek, (see Osbornville)	×
Key East, Monmouth......C	325
● Key Port, Monmouth......C	3,411
● Kingsland, Bergen......NE	400
● Kingston, Somerset.......C	300
● Kingwood, Hunterdon.NW	50
● Kinkora, Burlington......C	100
● Kirkwood, Camden.....SW	340
● *Knickerbocker Row*, Burlington.................C	×
Knowlton, Warren....... NW	85

Place	Pop.
Kresson, Camden......... SW	250
● *Lacy*, Ocean.............. C	×
● LaFayette, Sussex..... NW	300
● *Lafayette*, Hudson...... NE	×
Lake Como, Monmouth.....C	O
Lake Denmark, Morris. ..N	×
● *Lake Grinnell*, Sussex..NW	×
● Lake Hopatcong, Morris. N	×
● *Lakeside*, Camden...... SW	×
● Lake View, Passaic.......N	110
● Lakewood, Ocean.........C	1,200
● *Lamberton*, Mercer.......C	×
● Lambertville, Hunt'rd'nNW	4,142
● *Lamb's Road*,GloucesterSW	×
Lamington, Somerset.......C	240
Landing, Morris............N	×
● Landisville, Atlantic......S	150
● Lanoka, Ocean............C	150
● *Lansdown*, Hunterdon.NW	100
● Laurel Springs, CamdenSW	100
● Lavallette, Ocean.........C	40
● *Lawnside*, Camden.....SW	×
● Lawrence Station, MercerC	250
Lawrenceville, Mercer......C	550
Layton, Sussex........... NW	300
● Lebanon, Hunterdon...NW	800
● Ledgewood, Morris.......N	200
Leeds Point, Atlantic........S	200
Leedsville, Monmonth.......C	300
● Leesburgh, Cumberland...S	600
● *Lehigh Junc.*, Warren..NW	×
● *Lennig*, Atlantic..........S	×
● *Leonards*, Gloucester...SW	×
Leonardville, Monmouth....C	110
● Leonia, Bergen......... NE	90
● *Lewisburg*, Sussex..... NW	×
● Lewistown, Burlington... C	200
● Liberty Corner, Somerset.C	200
Libertyville, Sussex.......NW	90
● *LimestoneSwitch*,Suss'xNW	×
Lincoln, Sussex.......... NW	×
● Lincoln Park, Morris.....N	80
Lincroft, Monmouth........C	×
● Linden, Union............NE	400
● Lindenwold, Camden... SW	175
Linvale, Hunterdon......NW	25
● Linwood, Atlantic.........S	526
LittleEggHarbor,BurlingtonC	×
● Little Falls, Passaic... ...N	1,404
● *LittleFallsStation*,PassaicN	×
● Little Ferry, Bergen....NE	100
● *LittleFerryJunc.*,H'dsonNE	×
● Little Silver, Monmouth.. C	150
Littleton, Morris............N	100
Little York, Hunterdon.. NW	500
Livingston, Essex......... NE	1,206
● *Llewellyn*, Essex........NE	×
Llewellyn Park, Essex....NE	×
Locktown, Hunterdon....NW	50
● *Locust Grove*, Camden..SW	×
● Lodi, Bergen.............NE	900
● *Lodi*, Burlington..........C	×
● *Lodi Junction*, Bergen..NE	×
Logansville, Morris... .....N	×
Longacoming, (see Berlin)...	×
● *Long Beach City*, Ocean..C	×
● *Long Beach Club*, Ocean..C	×
● Long Branch, Monmouth.C	7,231
Long Branch City, M'nm'th.C	×
● *Long Bridge*, Warren.. NW	×
Long Hill, Morris............N	40
● Longport, Atlantic........S	10
● *Long Reach*, Cumberland.S	×
● *Lapatcong*, Warren....NW	×
● *Lorillard*, Monmouth.....C	×
Lower Bank, Burlington....C	100
● *Lower Jamesburg*, Middlesex.........................C	×
Lower Squankum,Monmo'thC	105
Lower Valley, (see Califon)..	×
● *Low Moor*, Monmouth....C	×
Lumberton, Burlington.....C	575
Lyndhurst, Bergen........NE	120
● Lyons, Somerset..........C	82
● Lyons Farms, Union....NE	100
● McAfee Valley, Sussex.NW	50
● *McCainsville*, Morris.....N	240
McKee City, Atlantic........S	×
● *Macopin Lake Jc.*, MorrisN	×
● Madison, Morris...........N	1,761
● Magnolia, Camden......SW	250
● *Magnolia*, Salem.......SW	×
● Mahwah, Bergen.........NE	100
● Maine Avenue, Cumber'd.S	50
● Malaga, Gloucester..... SW	300
● Manahawkin, Ocean...... C	800
Manalapan, Monmouth......C	350

New Jersey

Place	Pop.
● Manasquan, Monmouth...C	7,506
Manasquan Station, Mon'thC	×
● Manchester, Ocean........C	700
Manhattan Park, Essex...NE	×
● Mantoloking, Ocean.......C	150
Mantua, Gloucester........SW	550
● Manumuskin, Cumb'land. S	150
● *ManunkaChunk*,War'nNW	×
Maple, Burlington.......... C	×
● *Maple Grange*, Sussex. NW	×
● Maple Shade, Burlington. C	50
Maplewood, Essex........ NE	×
Marcella, Morris............N	×
● *Marconnier*, Middlesex...C	×
● *Marion*, Hudson........NE	×
● Marksborough, Warren.NE	200
● Marlboro, Monmouth.....C	300
● Marlton, Burlington......C	800
Marmora, Cape May......... S	150
Marshall, (see Pennington)..	×
Marshalltown, Salem.....SW	60
● *Martins*, Sussex........NW	×
● *Martin's*, Ocean..........C	×
● *Martins Creek Station*, Warren..................NW	×
Martinsville, Somerset......C	250
● Masonville, Burlington... C	75
● Matawan, Monmouth.....C	1.455
● Maurer, Middlesex........C	×
Maurice River, Cumberland.S	×
● Mauricetown, Cumberl'ndS	500
● *Mauricetown*, Cumberl'ndS	×
● *MaxsonJunction*,Mon'uthC	×
● Mayetta, Ocean........... C	200
● **May'sLanding**,AtlanticS	[illegible],200
● Maywood, Bergen...... NE	95
● *Meadows*, Hudson......NE	×
● *Meadow's Junc.*,HudsonNE	×
Mechanicsville, Monmouth..C	25
● *Medford*, Camden...... SW	×
● Medford, Burlington......C	[illegible],200
● *Melfort*, Middlesex........C	×
● *Melrose*, Burlington...... C	×
● *Menantico*, Cumberland.. S	×
Mendham, Morris............N	200
● Menlo Park, Middlesex... C	187
Mercerville, Mercer.........C	×
● Merchantville, Camden.SW	1,225
● Metuchen, Middlesex.....C	2,000
● Mickleton, Gloucester..SW	75
● *Middle Branch*, Ocean....C	×
● Middlebush, Somerset.... C	100
● *Middle Thoro*, Cape May..S	×
● Middletown, Monmouth.. C	150
● Middle Valley, Morris.... N	75
Middleville, Sussex....... NW	200
● Midland Park, Bergen.. NE	100
● Midvale, Passaic..........N	60
Midvale, (see Jutlan)	×
● Milford, Hunterdon.... NW	800
Millbrook, Warren........NW	50
● Millburn, Essex..........NE	2,442
Millham, (see Trenton)	×
● Millington, Morris........N	60
Millstone, Somerset......... C	1,000
● *Millstone Junction*,Som't.C	×
● Milltown, Middlesex...... C	100
● Millville, Cumberland.....S	10,002
Millville Depot, Cumberland S	×
Milton, Morris.............. N	500
● *Mine Brook*, Somerset....C	×
● Mine Hill, Morris.........N	900
● *Minnisink*, Morris........N	×
● *Monks*, Passaic........... N	×
● *Monmouth Beach*, Mon'th C	×
● Monmouth Junc., M'd'sex.C	200
● *Monmouth Park Junction*, Monmouth............. C	×
Monroe, Morris .... N	×
● Monroe, Sussex........ NW	150
● *Monroe*, Sussex.........NW	×
Monroe Corners, Sussex..NW	150
Monroe Station, Sussex..NW	×
● Monroeville, Salem..... SW	360
Montague, Sussex........ NW	200
Montana, Warren........ NW	200
● Mont Clair, Essex ...... NE	8,611
● *Montclair Heights*, Es'x NE	×
● *Montclair Station*, Es'x. NE	×
Montgomery, Somerset..... C	60
Montrose, Essex.......... NE	×
● Montvale, Bergen....... NE	25
● Montville, Morris .... N	200
● *Moores*, Mercer........... C	×
● Moorestown, Burlington.. C	2,500
● *Morgan*, Middlesex....... C	×
● Morganville, Monmouth.. C	400

New Jersey

Place	Pop.
● *Morris*, Camden........SW	×
● *Morris Avenue*, Union..NE	×
● *Morris County Junction*, Morris.................. N	×
● Morris Plains, Morris.....N	45
● **Morristown**, Morris... N	8,156
Morrisville, Monmouth......C	100
● Mountain View, Passaic.. N	25
Mountainville, Hunt'don.NW	300
● Mount Airy,Hunterdon NW	50
Mount Arlington, Morris... N	30
Mount Bethel, Somerset.... C	×
● Mount Ephraim,CamdenSW	200
Mount Freedom, Morris....N	120
Mount Hermon, Warren..NW	30
● **Mount Holly**, Burl'g'n.C	5,500
● *Mount Holly Junc.*,Burn'nC	×
● Mount Hope, Morris......N	120
Mount Laurel, Burlington...C	200
Mount Olive, Morris........ N	130
● *Mount Pleasant*,Cape MayS	×
Mount Pleasant,(see Five P'ts)	×
Mount Pleasant,H'r'don.. NW	200
Mount Pleasant, Morris....N	×
● *Mount Pleasant*, Monm'h C	75
Mount Rose, Mercer........ C	30
● *Mount Royal*, Gloucest'rSW	×
Mount Salem, Sussex.....NW	45
Mount Tabor, Morris...... N	×
● *Muirhead's*, Hunterdon NW	×
● *Mulford*, Sussex........NW	×
● Mullica Hill,Gloucester. SW	1,000
● *Mullica Hill Road*,Gl'c'rSW	×
● Murray Hill, Union..... NE	30
● *Muskee*, Cumberland..... S	×
Mutual Junction, Morris .. N	×
● Naughright, Morris...... N	50
Navesink, Monmouth....... C	500
● *Nevesink Beach*,Monm'th C	×
Nelsonville, Monmouth C	×
Neptune City, Monmouth .. C	×
Nesco, Atlantic..............S	25
Neshanic, Somerset......... C	130
● Neshanic Station,Somer't.C	×
Netcong, Morris............ N	×
● Netherwood, Union .... NE	90
● **NEWARK**, Essex....NE	181,830
Newark Junction, Passaic..N	×
Newark Water-Mills,B'g'nNE	×
New Bedford, Monmonth... C	200
New Branch, Monmouth....C	50
New Bridge, Bergen...... NE	200
New Brooklyn, Middlesex.. C	200
● **New Brunswick**,Middlesex........................ C	18,603
● New Durham, Hudson.. NE	700
● New Egypt, Ocean........ C	800
Newell, Monmouth..........C	75
● Newfield, Gloucester....SW	500
● Newfoundland, Morris... N	600
● New Germantown,H't'nNW	400
New Gretna, Burlington.... C	200
● New Hampton, H'ter'n NW	400
● *Newkirk*, Salem........ SW	×
● New Lisbon, Burlington.. C	400
● **New Market, Middlesex** .. C	250
● New Milford, Bergen....NE	100
New Monmouth, Monmouth C	100
● Newport, Cumberland.... S	400
● New Providence, Union NE	120
● New Sharon, Monmouth.. C	50
● **Newton**, Sussex...... NW	3,003
● *Newton Junc.*, Sussex..NW	×
● *Newtonville*, Atlantic..... S	×
● *Newtown*, Mercer C	400
New Vernon, Morris....... N	75
New Village, Warren .... NW	50
New York, Susquehanna and Western Jc., Sussex..NW	×
Nolan's Point, Morris......N	×
● Nordhoff, Bergen....... NE	100
Norma, Salem .... SW	25
● *Normandie*, Monmouth...C	×
Normanock, Sussex......NW	×
● *North Asbury Park*,M'th C	×
North Atlantic City, (see Brigantine)	×
● *North Beach Haven*,OceanC	×
North Branch, Somerset.... C	150
● North Branch Depot,S'm't.C	60
● *North Cedarville*, Cumb'd.S	×
North Cramers Hill,C'm'n SW	×
● *North Elizabeth*, Union NE	×
● North Long Branch, M'th.C	120
● *Northmont*, Camden....SW	×
● *North Newark*, Essex...NE	×
North Orange, (see Orange).	×

● *North Patterson*, Passaic N	×
● *North Pemberton*, Burl'g'n C	×
North Roselle, Union..... NE	×
● *Northrups*, Sussex .... NW	×
● Northvale, Bergen....... NE	100
● North Vineland, Cumb'd..S	150
● *North Woodbury*, Gl'c'r SW	×
Norton, Hunterdon...... NW	100
● Norwood, Bergen....... NE	300
● Nutley, Essex .... NE	×
● Oak Dale, Hunterdon.. NW	10
Oak Grove, Hunterdon... NW	30
● *Oak Island*, Union..... NE	×
● Oakland, Bergen........NE	350
● *Oakland*, Camden...... SW	×
● *Oakland*, Salem......... SW	×
● Oak Ridge, Passaic....... N	60
● *Ocean Beach*, Monmouth..C	400
● Ocean City, Cape May..... S	452
● Ocean Grove, Monmouth..C	2,754
Oceanic, Monmouth C	300
Ocean Park, Monmouth.... C	×
● Ocean Port, Monmouth... C	500
● Ocean View, Cape May.... S	200
● Oceanville, Atlantic....... S	400
Oceanville, Monmouth...... C	100
● *Ogden*, Sussex.......... NW	×
● *Ogdens*, Gloucester......SW	×
● Ogdensburgh, Sussex...NW	700
● Old Bridge, Middlesex.... C	400
● Oradell, Bergen .... NE	200
● Orange, Essex .... NE	13,844
● *Orange Junction*, Essex NE	×
● Orange Valley, Essex... NE	1,550
● *Orchard Street*, Essex...NE	×
Oriental, Burlington........ C	×
● Orstrom, Camden ...... SW	×
Orston, Camden .... SW	×
● Ortley, Ocean.............. C	25
Osbornsville, Ocean......... C	200
Ostrander, Middlesex....... C	×
● *Ostrom* Ocean...........SW	×
● Owen, Sussex...........NW	×
● Oxford, Warren......... NW	400
● Palatine, Salem.......... SW	100
Palermo, Cape May...........S	150
● Palisades Park, Bergen. NE	×
● Palmyra, Burlington......C	1,800
Pamerapo, (see Bayonne)....	×
Pancoastville, (see Landisville)	×
● Papakating, Sussex.... NW	30
● *Paradise*, Gloucester...SW	×
● *Paramus*, Bergen......NE	×
● *Parkdale*, Camden.....SW	×
Parker, Morris..............S	35
● Park Ridge, Bergen.....NE	300
Parkville, Gloucester .....SW	60
Parry, Burlington...........C	100
Parsippany, Morris.......... N	300
● *Pascack*, Bergen........NE	300
● Passaic, Passaic...........N	13,028
● Passaic Bridge, Passaic...N	40
● *Passaic Junc.*, Bergen. NE	×
● *Passaic and Delaware Junction*, Union............NE	×
● **PATERSON**, Passaic..N	78,347
● Pattenburgh, Hunterdon NW	500
● *Paulding*, Salem.........SW	×
● Paulina, Warren....... NW	90
● Paulsborough, Glo'ster. NW	1,200
Pavonia, Hudson.......... NE	×
● *Pavonia*, Camden...... SW	600
● *Payway*, Union..........NE	×
● *Peahalo*, Ocean............C	×
● Peapack, Somerset.........C	250
● *Peapack Station*, Somerset C	×
● Pedricktown, Salem....SW	500
● *Pellettown*, Sussex.....NW	×
● Pemberton, Burlington...C	834
● *Penbryn*, Camden......SW	×
● Pennington, Mercer......C	1,000
● Penn's Grove, Salem....SW	1,200
Pennsville, (see Palmyra)....	×
Pennsville, Salem..........SW	250
○ Pensauken, Camden....SW	×
● *Penton*, Salem...........SW	×
Penwell, Warren..........NW	40
● Pequanac, Morris..........N	100
● *Pequest*, Warren.......NW	×
● *Perkins*, Burlington.......C	×
● *Perkintown*, Salem......SW	×
Perrineville, Monmouth.... C	150
● Perth Amboy, Middlesex. C	9,512
● *Perth Amboy Jc.*, Mid'sex.C	×
● *Perth Junc.*, Middlesex...C	×
Petersburg, Morris.......... N	×
Petersburgh, Cape May......S	400

New Jersey

Peters Valley, Sussex.....NW	40
● Phillipsburgh, Warren.NW	8,644
Phillipsburgh Depot, W'r'n NW	×
Piccatinny, Morris ....N	×
● *Picton*, Union.......... NE	×
Pine Brook, Morris..........N	120
● *Pine Brook*, Monmouth.. C	×
Pine Grove, (see Gloucester).	×
● *Pine View*, Ocean C	×
Piscataway, Middlesex C	50
● Pitman Grove, Glo'ster..SW	450
Pitt's Grove, Salem........SW	250
Pittstown, Hunterdon....NW	150
Pittstown, (see Elmer).......	×
● Plainfield, Union. ...... NE	11,267
● *Plains*, Sussex.........NW	×
● Plainsborough, Middlesex.C	500
Plainville, Somerset.........C	50
Plattsburg, (see Sykesville)...	×
Pleasantdale, Essex.......NE	×
Pleasant Grove, Morris.....N	113
Pleasant Mills, Atlantic..... S	200
Pleasant Run, Hunterdon NW	100
● *Pleasant Valley*, Bergen NE	×
Pleasant Valley, Sussex. NW	150
● Pleasantville, Atlantic.....S	1,800
Pleasure Bay, Monmouth.. C	100
Pluckemin, Somerset....... C	250
● *Point Airy*, Salem......SW	×
● Point Pleasant, Ocean.....C	800
Pointville, Burlington.......C	**850**
● *Pole Tavern*, (see Pitt's Grove)	×
Polkville, Warren.........NW	50
● Pomerania, Atlantic.... . S	10
● Pompton, Passaic.........N	400
● *Pompton Junc.*, Passaic..N	×
Pompton Lakes, Passaic....N	×
● Pompton Plains, Morris..N	50
Pontiac, Hudson...........NE	×
Poor House, Union.......NE	×
Porchtown, Gloucester ...SW	100
Port Colden, Warren..... NW	200
● Port Elizabeth, Cumb'rl'd.S	600
Port Johnson, Hudson....NE	×
Port Mercer, Mercer........C	35
● Port Monmouth, Monm'th C	400
Port Monmouth Jc., Mon'th C	×
Port Monmouth Shore, Monmouth.........................C	×
● Port Morris, Morris...... N	125
● Port Murry, Warren...NW	250
● *Port Norris*, Cumberland.S	×
● Port Norris, Cumberland. S	1,400
● Port Oram, Morris........N	756
Port Republic, Atlantic.....S	300
● *Port Washington*, War'n NW	×
Potterstown, Hunterdon. NW	45
● Pottersville, Hunterdon NW	200
Powerville, (see Boonton)....	×
● Princeton, Mercer........ C	3,422
● Princeton Junc., Mercer..C	59
● *Prospect*, Gloucester....SW	×
● Prospect Plains, Mid'sex..C	150
● *Prospect Street*, Cape May S	×
● *Prospect Street*, Passaic..N	×
Prospect St. Depot, Passaic N	×
Prospertown, Ocean........ C	50
Quakertown, Hunterdon. NW	200
● Quarryville, Sussex.....NW	90
● Quinton, Salem.........SW	500
● *Radix*, Gloucester...... SW	×
● Rahway, Union.........NE	7,105
● *Raleigh*, Camden....... SW	×
Rallstonville, Morris....... N	×
● Ramsey's, Bergen.......NE	450
Ramsey's Station, Bergen NE	450
Rancocas, Burlington.......C	350
Randolphville, Middlesex...C	175
● Raritan, Somerset........ C	2,556
● Raven Rock, Hunterd'n NW	200
Readington, Hunterdon....W	250
Reaville, Hunterdon......NW	250
Recklesstown, (see Chesterfi'ld)	×
● Red Bank, Monmouth.... C	4,145
● Red Lion, Burlington.....C	100
Red Mills, Bergen.........NE	50
Red Valley, Monmouth......C	150
● *Repauno*, Gloucester... SW	×
● Repaupo, Gloucester....SW	100
● *Ricefield*, Somerset....... C	65
Richfield, Passaic...........N	90
● Richland, Atlantic........S	150
● Richwood, Gloucester.. SW	100
● *Riddleton*, Salem....... SW	×
● Ridgefield, Bergen......NE	200
● Ridgefield Park, Bergen. NE	100
● Ridgewood, Bergen.....NE	500

New Jersey

● *Ridgewood Jc.*, Bergen. NE	×
Riegelsville, Warren..... NW	500
Rileyville, Warren........NW	100
● Ringoes, Hunterdon....HW	500
● Ringwood, Passaic....... N	255
● *Ringwood Junc.*, Passaic. N	×
● Rio Grande, Cape May.... S	200
● Riverdale, Morris........ N	×
● River Edge, Bergen.... NE	150
● *Riverside*, Essex........ NE	×
● Riverside, Burlington.....C	1,800
● *Riverside*, Hunterdon.. NW	×
● *Riverside*, Passiac........ N	×
● *Riverside*, Sussex.......NW	×
● Riverton, Burlington......C	600
River Vale, Bergen.........NE	300
Road Hall, Middlesex.......C	900
Roadstown, Cumberland.... S	400
● *Robanna*, Gloucester... SW	×
● *Robbins*, Monmouth......C	×
● Robbinsville, Mercer......C	200
● *Roberts*, Middlesex....... C	×
● *Robinvale*, Middlesex.....C	×
● Rochelle Park, Bergen. NE	150
● Rockaway, Morris.........N	1,270
Rockaway Valley, Morris..N	×
Rock Mills, Somerset....... C	×
● *Rockport Siding*, W'r'n NW	×
● Rocksburgh, Warren...NW	200
● Rocky Hill, Somerset..... C	400
Rosedale, Camden........ SW	×
Rosedale, Atlantic...........S	×
Roseland, Essex...........NE	851
● Roselle, Union...........NE	600
Rosemont, Hunterdon....NW	69
● Rosenhayn, Cumberland.. S	300
Roseville, Essex...........NE	×
Rowland Mills, H'terdon. NW	44
Roxburg, Warren........ NW	75
Roycefield, Somerset........C	65
● *Roys*, Sussex...........NW	×
● *Rulon's Road*, Gl'cester SW	×
● *Rumson Beach*, M'm'th.. C	×
● *Runnemede*, Camden...SW	×
Rustic, (see Drakesville)	×
● Rutherford, Bergen.....NE	2,293
● *Rutherford Junc.*, Ber'n NE	×
● *Rutherford Station*, B'n NE	250
● Saddle River, Bergen... NE	250
● **Salem**, Salem..........SW	5,516
Salem, Union............. NE	×
Salina, Gloucester......... SW	50
○ *Saltersville*, Hudson.....NE	×
Sand Brook, Hunterdon..NW	60
● *Sand Hill*, (see Yardville)..	×
● *Sandy Hook*, Monmouth..C	75
Sarepta, Warren......... NW	×
Sayreville, Middlesex C	3,509
Schalk's, Middlesex.........C	×
Schooley's Mountain, Mor's.N	300
● Schraalenburgh, Berg'n NE	200
○ *Schuetzen Park*, Hudson NE	×
Scobeyville, Monmouth..... C	50
Scotch Plains, Union ..... NE	500
Scudder's, Mercer..........C	×
Scullville, Atlantic.......... S	400
● Sea Bright, Monmouth....C	660
● *Sea Girt*, Monmouth...... C	43
Sea Grove, (see Cape May Point)	×
● Sea Isle City, Cape May... S	766
Sea Isle Junc., Cape May... S	×
Sea Plain, Monmouth...... C	200
● Seaside Park, Ocean...... C	350
● *Seaview*, Atlantic..........S	60
Seaville, Cape May.......... S	265
● *Seaville*, Cape May........ S	200
Sea Warren, Middlesex.....C	×
● Secaucus, Hudson.......NE	225
● *Seacaucus Station*, Hud'n NE	×
Seeley, Cumberland......... S	200
Sergeantsville, Hun'don.. NW	250
● Sewaren, Middlesex.......C	125
● Sewell, Gloucester...... SW	200
Sewell's Point, Cape May....S	×
Shadyside, Bergen........ NE	30
● Shamong, Burlington.....C	100
● *Shark River*, Monmouth..C	75
● *Sharon*, Monmouth.......C	50
Sharptown, Salem.........SW	850
Shelltown, (see Ellisdale).....	×
● *Sheppard's Mills*, C'm'l'nd S	×
● *Sherwin*, Gloucester....SW	×
Shiloh, Cumberland.........S	**1,004**
Shimers, Warren......... NW	225
Shippingport, Morris.......N	×
Shirley, Salem.............SW	150
Short Hills, Essex.........NE	200

New Jersey

Place	Pop.
● Shrewsbury, Monmouth.. C	300
● Sicklerville, Camden....SW	200
● Sidney, Hunterdon..... NW	100
● *Silver Lake*, Essex...... NE	×
Silverton, Ocean.......... C	50
● Singac, Passaic........... N	25
● Skillman, Somerset.......C	350
Smithburgh, Monmouth.... C	150
● Smith's Landing, Atlantic..S	400
Smith's Mills, Passaic.......N	90
● Smithville, Burlington.....C	550
● *Soho*, Essex............NE	×
● *Somerset*, Essex.........NE	×
● *Somerset*, Mercer......... C	×
● Somer's Point, Atlantic... S	500
● **Somerville**, Somerset.. C	3,861
● South Amboy, Middlesex..C	4,330
South Amboy Junc., MiddlesexC	×
Southard, Monmouth....... C	300
● South Atlantic City, Atl'nticC	150
South Bergen, (see Jersey City)	×
South Boundbrook, SomersetC	801
South Branch, Somerset.... C	150
● *South Camden*, Camden SW	×
South Dennis, Cape May.... S	300
● *South Elizabeth*, Union. NE	×
South Elizabeth Sta., Union NE	×
● *South Glassborough*, Gloucester............... SW	×
● *SouthGloucester*, C'mdenSW	×
● *SouthOgdensburgh*, S's'xNW	×
● South Orange, Essex....NE	3,106
South Park, Burlington.......C	200
● *South Paterson*, Passaic..N	×
South Pemberton, Bur'l't'n..C	834
South Penn's Grove, (see Helm's Cove)............	×
● South Plainfield, M'dles'x C	250
● South River, Middlesex...C	300
● South Seaville, Cape May..S	400
● *South Somerville*, S'mersetC	×
● *South Trenton*, Mercer...C	×
● South Vineland, C'mb'land S	300
Sparta, Sussex............NW	300
Sparta Depot, Middlesex....C	×
● *Sparta Junc.*, Sussex.. NW	×
● *Sparta Station*, Sussex. NW	×
● *Spa Spring*, Middlesex....C	×
● Spotswood, Middlesex....C	500
● *Springdale*, Camden....SW	×
Springfield, Union........ NE	959
Spring Garden, Middlesex...C	50
● SpringLakeBeach, M'nm'thC	80
● *Spring Mills*, (see Grenloch)	×
● *Spring Street*, Union....NE	×
● *Spring Tank*, Bergen...NE	×
● Springtown, Warren... NW	110
● *Spring Valley*, Bergen..NE	100
Spruce Run, (see Glen Gardner)	×
Squankum, Monmouth..... C	50
● Staffordville, Ocean.......C	50
● Stanhope, Sussex........NW	1,000
Stanley, Morris............ N	50
● Stanton, Hunterdon....NW	200
● Stanwick, Burlington.....C	150
State Insane Asylum, MorrisN	×
Steelmanville, Atlantic......S	50
● Stelton, Middlesex........C	40
Stephensburgh, Morris......N	120
Stephensville, (see Van Hiseville)........	×
Sterling, Morris............N	250
● *Sterling Forest*, Passaic..N	×
● Stevens, Burlington.......C	100
● Stewartsville, Warren..NW	500
● Stillwater, Sussex...... NW	100
● Stirling, Morris...........N	250
● Stockholm, Sussex.....NW	400
● Stockton, Hunterdon...NW	650
● Stoutsburgh, Somerset....C	120
● *Stratford*, Camden......SW	×
● Succasunna, Morris......N	400
● Summit, Union......... NE	3,000
● *Summit*, Sussex.........NW	×
● *Summit Switch*, Sussex NW	×
● Sunny Side, Hunterdon NW	60
● *Swain*, Cape May......... S	×
Swartswood, Sussex.......NW	200
● *Swartswood Junc.* S'sexNW	×
● *SwartswoodSta.* Sussex NW	×
● Swedesborough, G'c'ter. SW	2,053
Swinefield Bridge, Essex..NE	×
Sykesville, Burlington...... C	300
Tabernacle, Burlington...... C	50
Tabor, Morris..............N	×
● *Tatems*, Gloucester.....SW	×
Taylor, Burlington.........C	×

New Jersey

Place	Pop.
● *Teaneck*, Bergen.......NE	×
Telephone, (see Bordentown).	×
● Tenafly, Bergen.........NE	1,100
● Tennent, Monmouth......C	129
● *Thirtieth Street*, Cape MayS	×
● *Thirty-fourth Street*, CMayS	×
● Thorofare, Gloucester.. SW	150
● Three Bridges, H'nt'd'nNW	200
Three Turns, Burlington... C	40
Tinton Falls, Monmouth.... C	80
● Titusville, Mercer......... C	1,000
● *Toll Gate Road*, CamdenSW	×
● *Tomlin's*, Gloucester... SW	×
● **Tom's River**, Ocean....C	1,800
Town of Union, Hudson.. NE	10,643
● Townsbury, Warren....NW	100
Townsend Inlet, Cape May.. S	200
● *Tracy's*, Middlesex....... C	×
● Tranquility, Sussex.....NW	25
● Tremley, Union.........NE	200
● **TRENTON**, Mercer.... C	57,458
● Trenton Junction, Mercer C	25
Troy Hills, Morris.......... N	×
● Tuckahoe, Cape May......S	1,000
● Tuckerton, Ocean.........C	1,500
● Tumble, Hunterdon.... NW	25
Turkey, Monmouth.......... C	800
● *Turner's Road*, GloucesterSW	×
Turnersville, Gloucester.. SW	300
Tuttle's Corner, Sussex.. NW	×
● *Two Bridges*, Sussex...NW	×
● *Tyler Park*, Hudson....NE	×
● *Uncle Tom's*, Atlantic.... S	×
● *Undercliffe*, Bergen.....NE	×
Union, Union............. NE	250
Union, (see Belleville)	×
● *Union Hill*, (seeTown of Union)	×
Union Town, Middlesex....C	100
Union Valley, Passaic......N	30
Union Village, Somerset....C	×
● Unionville, Gloucester..SW	250
Unionville, Morris..........N	×
Upper Hibernia, Morris.... N	×
Upper Macopin, Passaic....N	50
● Upper Mt. Clair, Essex..NE	200
● Vail, Warren..............NW	75
Vailsburgh, Essex..........NE	120
● Valley, Hunterdon.......NW	300
● *Van Buskirks*, Hudson. NE	×
Vanderburgh, Monmouth...C	33
Vanderveer's Mills, Som'rs'tC	×
Vandeventers, Middlesex...C	×
Van Hiseville, Ocean........C	316
Van Liew's Cr., (see Wertsv'e)	×
● *Van Sickles*, Sussex....NW	×
● Ventnor, Atlantic......... S	×
● Vernon, Sussex..........NW	250
● *Vernoy*, Hunterdon....NW	×
Verona, Essex..............NE	500
Victoria, Gloucester.......SW	×
Vienna, Warren..........NW	150
Villa Park, Monmouth......C	×
● Vincentown, Burlington..C	3,822
● Vineland, Cumberland....S	3,822
● *Voorhees*, Somerset.......C	×
● *Vreeland Avenue*, PassaicN	×
Wading River, Burlington.. C	40
● Waldwick, Bergen.......NE	200
Wallpack Centre, Sussex. NW	150
Walnford, Monmouth.......C	41
Walnut Grove, Morris......N	100
Walnut Valley, Warren...NW	100
Walton, Bergen...........NE	×
● *Wanaque*, Passaic........N	50
● Waretown, Ocean.........C	300
Warren Paper Mills, Hunterdon..................NW	150
● *Warren Point*, Bergen..NE	×
● *Warren Street*, Mercer... C	×
Warrenville, Somerset...... C	200
● Warrington, Warren... NW	50
Washington, (seeSouth River)	×
● Washington, Warren...NW	2,834
● *WashingtonCross.*, MercerC	×
Washington Valley, MorrisN	×
Washingtonville, Somerset. C	50
● *Washingtonville*, Sus'exNW	×
● *Watchung*, Essex.......NE	×
● Waterford Works, Cam'nSW	500
● Waterloo, Sussex.......NW	100
● *Watsessing*, Hudson....NE	×
● *Watsessing Jc.*, Essex..NE	×
Watson's Corners, Salem. SW	200
● *Waverly*, Essex.........NE	75
Waverly Fair Grounds, EssexNE	×
Waverly Park, Essex......NE	×
Wawayanda, Sussex.....NW	120

New Jersey

Place	Pop.
● *Wayne*, Passaic..........N	50
Wayside, Monmouth.........C	×
● Weehawken, Hudson.....NE	1,923
● Weldon, Morris...........N	×
● *Wellwood*, Camden..... SW	×
● Wenonah, Gloucester...SW	300
Wertsville, Hunterdon....NW	50
● *West Arlington*, HudsonNE	×
West Asbury, (see Asbury Park)	×
West Bergen, (see Jersey City)	×
West Cape May, Cape May. S	757
● *West Collinswood*, Cam'nSW	×
● *Westcott's*, Cumberland...S	×
West Creek, (see East Creek).	×
● West Creek, Ocean.......C	400
● *West End*, Hudson......NE	×
● West End, Monmouth.....C	30
● *West End*, Gloucester..SW	×
● *West Englewood*, BergenNE	×
● Westfield, Union.........NE	2,500
West Freehold, Monmouth..C	100
West Grove, (see Asbury Park)	×
● West Hoboken, Hudson. NE	11,646
West Long Branch, Monm'thC	×
West Milford, Passaic.......N	200
● Westmont, Camden.....SW	300
● *Westmoretown*, BurlingtonC	1,500
● *West Neshanic*, Somerset. C	×
West Newark, Essex..... NE	×
● *West Newark Jc.*, EssexNE	×
West New York, Hudson. NE	1,000
● *West Norwood*, Bergen. NE	×
● Weston, Somerset.........C	120
● West Orange, Essex.....NE	×
● *West Palmyra*, BurlingtonC	×
● *West Paterson*, Passaic.. N	×
West Point Pleasant, Ocean. C	200
● *West Portal*, HunterdonNW	×
West Rutherford, (seeCarltonHill)	×
● *West Side Ave.*, Hudson NE	×
● West Summit, Union....NE	×
● Westville, Gloucester...SW	350
● Westwood, Bergen......NE	500
● Weymouth, Atlantic.......S	40
● Wheatland, Ocean.........C	100
● *Wheat Road*, Atlantic......S	×
Whiglane, Salem..........SW	50
Whippany, Morris.......... N	400
Whitehall, (see Glen Garden)	×
● *Whitehill*, Burlington.....C	800
White Horse, (see Kirkwood)	×
● White House, Hunterd'nNW	300
● White House Sta. Hut'nNW	400
● Whitesville, Ocean........C	240
● Whiting, Ocean............C	150
● Whickatunk, Monmouth..C	25
Wilburtha, Mercer..........C	300
● Wildwood, Cape May......S	×
● *Willett*, Camden.........SW	×
● Williamstown, Glo'cesterSW	600
● *Williamstown Junc.*, Camden..................... SW	×
Williamsville, (see Vernon)..	×
Willow Grove, Cumberland. S	100
● *Wilson*, Burlington.......C	×
● Wilton, Camden......... SW	250
● Windsor, Mercer..........C	250
● Winslow, Camden........SW	500
● *Winslow Jc.*, Camden.. SW	×
● *Wolferts*, Gloucester....SW	×
● Woodbine, Cape May......S	×
● Woodbridge, Middlesex .. C	4,227
● *Woodbridge Jc.*, MiddlesexC	×
● **Woodbury**, Glouces'erSW	3,911
● Woodcliff, Bergen.......NE	300
● *Woodfern*, Hunterdon. NW	×
Woodglen, Hunterdon....NW	60
● *Woodland*, Atlantic.......S	×
● Woodmansie, Burlington. C	50
Woodport, Morris............N	60
● Woodridge, Bergen..... NE	100
● Woodruff, Cumberland....S	48
● *Woodruff's Gap*, Sussex NW	×
● *Woodside*, Essex........NE	×
● Woodstown, Salem......SW	556
Woodsville, Mercer..........C	400
● *Woodville*, Somerset......C	×
● Wortendyke, Bergen....NE	1,000
● Wrightstown, Burlington. C	400
Wrightsville, (see Camden) ..	×
● Wyckoff, Bergen........NE	40
Wykertown, Sussex.......NW	90
Wyoming, Essex..........NE	×
● Yardville, Mercer.........C	600
● *Yellowbrook*, Monmouth. C	×
● Yorktown, Salem.......SW	200
Zingsem, Bergen......... NE	×

NEW MEXICO.

COUNTIES.	INDEX.	POP.
Bernalillo	C	20,913
Chaves	SE	×
Colfax	NE	7,974
Dona Ana	S	9,191
Eddy	SE	×
Grant	SW	9,657
Guadaloupe	E	×
Lincoln	SE	7,087
Mora	NE	10,618
Rio Arriba	NW	11,534
San Juan	NW	1,890
San Miguel	E	24,204
Santa Fe	C	13,562
Sierra	SW	3,630
Socorro	W	9,595
Taos	NW	9,868
Valencia	W	13,876
Total		153,593

TOWN. COUNTY.	INDEX.	POP.
Abbott, Colfax	NE	×
Abiquiu, Rio Arriba	NW	500
Acoma, Valencia	W	91
Acomita, Valencia	W	×
● *Aden*, Dona Ana	S	×
● *Afton*, Dona Ana	S	×
Agua Dulce, Mora	NE	×
Agua Negra, Mora	NE	×
● Alameda, Bernalillo	C	200
● *Alamillo*, Socorro	W	×
Alamosa, Sierra	SW	×
Alamosto, Sierra	SW	×
Alamo Viejo, Grant	SW	×
Albert, Mora	NE	100
● **Albuquerque**, Bernalillo	C	3,785
● Alcalde, Rio Arriba	NW	×
● *Aleman*, Sierra	SW	×
● *Algodones*, Bernalillo	C	140
Alhambra, Grant	SW	×
Alma, Socorro	W	200
● *Alps*, Colfax	NE	×
Altamont, Rio Arriba	NW	×
Altos, Grant	SW	×
Alumina, Grant	SW	×
● Amargo, Rio Arriba	NW	30
Amoles, Dona Ana	S	×
Angostura, Dona Ana	S	×
Angostura, Bernalillo	C	×
Ansonio, Grant	SW	×
Antelope, Valencia	W	×
● Anthony, Dona Ana	S	20
Anton Chico, Guadaloupe	E	500
Apache Spring, Socorro	W	×
Aqua-de-Lobo, Taos	NW	×
Archuleta, Bernalillo	C	×
Arms, Colfax	NE	×
Armijo, Bernalillo	C	×
● *Army*, Socorro	W	×
Arragan, San Miguel	E	375
Arroyo Honde, Taos	NW	500
Arroyo Seco, Taos	NW	500
● *Atlantic and Pacific Junction*, Bernalillo	C	×
● Azotea, Rio Arriba	NW	125
Aztec, San Suan	NW	15
● *Azul*, San Miguel	E	×
Baca, Mora	NE	10
Bacas Ranch, Valencia	W	×
Baldy, Colfax	NE	×
● *Barr*, Bernalillo	C	×
● *Barranca*, Taos	NW	×
Beaver, Socorro	W	×
Beenham, Mora	NE	25
● Belen, Valencia	W	1,500
Bell, Colfax	N	×
Bell Ranch, San Miguel	E	×
● Bernal, San Miguel	E	×
● Bernalillo, Bernalillo	C	400
● *Bernalillo Sta.*, Bernalillo	C	×
● *Bighorn*, Rio Arriba	NW	×
● *Billings*, Socorro	W	×
Black Hawk, Grant	SW	100
Black Rock Tank, Dona Ana	S	×
● *Blanchard*, San Miguel	E	×
● *Bletchers*, Colfax	NE	×
Bloomfield, San Juan	NW	120
● Blossburg, Colfax	NE	829
● *Blue Water*, Valencia	W	25
Bonanza, Santa Fe	C	40
Bonito Lincoln	SE	25
Bosquecito, Socorro	W	×
● *Bridge Street*, San Miguel	E	×
Brockman's Mills, Grant	SW	×
● *Brunswick*, Dona Ana	S	×
Buena Vista, Colfax	NE	555
Cabezon, Bernalillo	C	25
Cabra Spring, San Miguel	E	20
● *Caliente*, Taos	NW	×
● *Cambray*, Dona Ana	S	×
Camberino, Dona Ana	S	×
Canada Ranch, Sierra	SW	×
Cangillon, Rio Arriba	NW	×
● *Cannon Diablo*, Santa Fe	C	×
Canon, San Miguel	E	×
● *Canoncito*, Santa Fe	C	×
Canon City, Bernalillo	C	×
Canones, Rio Arriba	NW	×
Carbonaterille, Santa Fe	C	30
Carizello, Grant	SW	×
Carizello Mines, Grant	SW	×
Carlisle, Grant	SW	150
● *Carracas*, Rio Arriba	NW	×
● Carthage, Socorro	W	257
Casa Colorado, Socorro	W	×
Casa Salaza, Bernalillo	C	×
Caseta, Rio Arriba	NW	×
Cass, Lincoln	SE	×
Catalpa, Colfax	NE	×
Catierres, Bernalillo	C	×
● Catskill, Colfax	NE	300
Cebolla, San Miguel	E	100
Cebolles, Taos	NW	×
Cebolletta, Valencia	SW	×
Central, Grant	SW	257
● Cerrillos, Santa Fe	C	446
Cerro, Taos	NW	470
● Chama, Rio Arriba	NW	50
● Chamita, Rio Arriba	NW	100
Chapaderos, Socorro	W	×
Chaperito, San Miguel	E	×
Chappels Ranch, San Miguel	E	×
Charez Claim, Colfax	NE	×
● Chaves, Bernalillo	C	×
Cherry Valley, Mora	NE	10
Cherryville, Socorro	W	×
Chico Springs, Colfax	NE	×
Chilili, Bernalillo	C	300
Chloride, Sierra	SW	150
Chuchilla, Rio Arriba	NW	×
Chupadero, Mora	NE	×
Chupadero Ranch, Socorro	W	×
Chupadro Spring, Valencia	W	×
Cibolla, Rio Arriba	NW	×
Cienega, Valencia	W	×
Cienegdilla, Santa Fe	C	×
Cieneguilla, Taos	NW	×
Cimarron, Colfax	NE	200
Cimilorio, Colfax	NE	×
Clapham, Mora	NE	×
● Clayton, Colfax	NE	250
● *Clemow*, Socorro	W	×
● *Coleman*, Grant	SW	×
Collier's Ranch, Mora	NE	×
Colmor, Colfax	NE	100
Colorado, Dona Ana	S	400
Colorado, Taos	NW	×
Colorado, Valencia	W	×
Columbus, Grant	SW	×
Conchas, San Miguel	E	×
● *Connell*, Taos	NW	×
● *Conrad*, Grant	SW	×
Conturatis, Socorro	W	×
Cooks, Grant	SW	×
● Coolidge, Bernalillo	C	200
Cooney, Socorro	W	×
Copelands Ranch, Lincoln	SE	×
Copper, Bernalillo	C	400
Copper Mines, Rio Arriba	NW	×
Cordoras, Taos	NW	×
Corrales, Bernalillo	C	×
Costilla, Taos	NW	×
Council Rock, Socorro	W	×
● *Coxo*, Rio Arriba	NW	×
Coyote, Rio Arriba	NW	25
● *Crawford*, Grant	SW	×
● *Cresco*, Rio Arriba	NW	×
Cribbenville, Rio Arriba	NW	×
● *Crocker*, Sierra	SW	×
Cuba, Bernalillo	C	×
Cubero, Valencia	W	200
Cubero, Valencia	W	×
Cuchillo, Sierra	SW	150
● *Cumbres*, Rio Arriba	NW	×
● *Cutter*, Sierra	SW	×
Datil, Socorro	W	33
● *Defiance*, Bernalillo	C	50
● Deming, Grant	SW	1,136
Deserted Village, Rio Ar'ba	NW	×
● *Des Moines*, Colfax	NE	×
● *Detroit*, Dona Ana	S	×
● *Dillon*, Colfax	NE	×
Dolores, Santa Fe	C	×
● *Dona Ana*, Dona Ana	S	450
Donahoe's Ranch, Sierra	SW	×
● Dorsey, Colfax	NE	×
● *Dover*, Colfax	NE	×
Dowins Mill, Lincoln	SE	×
● Dulce, Rio Arriba	NW	×
Duran, Bernalillo	C	×
Durazno, Rio Arriba	NW	×
● Earlham, Dona Ana	S	50
East Las Vegas, San Miguel	E	2,312
Eastview, Valencia	W	×
Eddy, Eddy	SE	278
Eden, Guadaloupe	E	×
El Cuervo, San Miguel	E	100
Elizabethtown, Colfax	NE	100
El Joya, Rio Arriba	NW	×
Elkins, Colfax	NE	×
Elkins Ranch, San Miguel	E	×
● *Elota*, Bernalillo	C	×
El Pueblo, San Miguel	E	×
El Rito, Rio Arriba	NW	600
● *El Rito*, Valencia	W	200
● Embudo, Rio Arriba	NW	300
Emery, Bernalillo	C	×
● *Emery Gap*, Colfax	NE	×
Encierre, San Miguel	NE	×
Encinal, Valencia	W	×
Endee, Guadaloupe	E	×
● Engle, Sierra	SW	30
Ensenada, Rio Arriba	NW	×
● Espanola, Santa Fe	NW	200
Eureka, Colfax	NE	×
Eureka Mines, Grant	SW	×
Evansville, Grant	SW	600
Exter, Colfax	NE	×
Fair View, Sierra	SW	150
Farmington, San Juan	NW	50
Fernandez De Taos, (see Taos)		
Fisher's Park, Colfax	NE	×
Fleming, Grant	SW	20
Flora Vista, San Juan	NW	×
● *Florida*, Dona Ana	S	×
● Folsom, Colfax	NE	250
Fort Bayard, Grant	SW	509
Fort Craig, Socorro	W	×
Fort Cummings, Grant	SW	×
Fort Stanton, Lincoln	SE	253
Fort Sumner, Guadaloupe	E	100
Fort Union, Mora	NE	229
Fort Wingate, Bernalillo	C	480
● *Fraley*, Socorro	W	×
Francis, Eddy	SE	×
Franklin, Colfax	NE	×
Frisco, Socorro	W	×
Fruitland, San Juan	NW	×
● Fulton, San Miguel	E	×
● *Gage*, Grant	SW	100
Galena, Lincoln	SE	×
Galisteo, Santa Fe	C	100
Gallina, Rio Arriba	NW	×
Gallinas, Mora	NE	×
Gallinas Spring, San Miguel	E	×
● Gallup, Bernalillo	C	950
Garcia Ranch, Valencia	W	×
Gavilan, Rio Arriba	NW	×
Genova, San Miguel	E	×
Georgetown, Grant	SW	800
Gibson, Bernalillo	C	×
Gila, Grant	SW	×
Gladstone, Colfax	NE	50
● Glorieta, Santa Fe	C	200
Golden, Santa Fe	C	100
Gold Hill, Grant	SW	20
Golondrinos, Mora	NE	×
Grafton, Sierra	SW	25
Grahoria, Grant	SW	×
● *Grama*, Dona Ana	S	×
● *Grande*, Colfax	NE	×
Granite House, Colfax	NE	×
● Grant, Valencia	W	200
● Grenville, Colfax	NE	20
Guadalupita, Mora	NE	200
Gusano, San Miguel	E	×
Hachita, Grant	SW	40
Hadley, Grant	SW	×
Hall's Peak, Mora	NE	25
Halls, Grant	SW	×
Hanover, Grant	SW	×
● Hatch, Dona Ana	S	×
Hatches Range, San Miguel	E	×
Hermosa, Sierra	SW	75
Hillsborough, Sierra	SW	600

Place	Location	Pop.
● *Hillside*, Colfax	NE	×
Hilton, Dona Ana	S	×
Holts, Eddy	SE	×
Hope, Colfax	NE	×
Hope, Eddy	SE	×
Horn's Ranch, Sierra	SW	×
Horse Springs, Socorro	W	×
● *Hot Springs*, San Miguel	E	300
● Hudson, Grant	SW	20
● Isleta, Bernalillo	C	×
● *Jacona*, Santa Fe	C	×
Jarita Spring, Rio Arriba	NW	×
Jaroso, Mora	NE	×
Jemes, Bernalillo	C	2,500
Jemes Hot Springs, (see Archuleta)		×
Jewett, San Juan	NW	×
Johnson, San Miguel	E	50
Joseph, Socorro	W	×
Joyalaria, San Miguel	E	×
● *Juanita*, Rio Arriba	NW	×
Juan Tafoya, Valencia	W	×
Junction City, San Juan	NW	×
● *Kelleyville*, Colfax	NE	×
Kelly, Socorro	W	×
Kennedy, Lincoln	SE	×
Kettle Spring, Dona Ana	S	×
Kingston, Sierra	SW	633
Kiowa, Colfax	NE	×
● *Kroenig*, San Miguel	E	×
La Bajada, Bernalillo	C	×
La Canada, Santa Fe	C	×
La Cinta, (see El Cuervo)		×
La Concepcion, San Miguel	E	×
La Costilla, Taos	NW	100
La Cuesta, San Miguel	E	25
La Cueva, Mora	NE	200
Ladd, Colfax	NE	×
Lagona, Sierra	SW	×
● Laguna, Valencia	W	234
La Gusva, Bernalillo	C	×
La Jolla, Rio Arriba	NW	×
● La Joya, Socorro	W	500
La Joyita, Socorro	W	×
La Junta, (see Watrous)		×
Lake, Mora	NE	×
Lake Beds, Mora	NE	×
● Lake Valley, Sierra	SW	400
La Lacha, Grant	SW	×
La Liendre, San Miguel	E	×
La Luz, Dona Ana	S	×
La Medara, Bernalillo	C	×
La Mesa, (see Victoria)		×
La Mora Spring, Lincoln	SE	×
● Lamy, Santa Fe	C	50
● *Lanark*, Dona Ana	S	×
La Plata, San Juan	NW	15
Largo, San Juan	NW	500
Las Canadinas, San Miguel	E	×
Las Colonias, Guadaloupe	E	100
Las Corralles, Bernalillo	C	20
● **Las Cruces**, Dona Ana	S	2,300
Las Nutrias, Socorro	W	×
Las Nutritas, Rio Arriba	NW	×
Las Palomas, Sierra	SW	70
Las Tabias, Rio Arriba	NW	×
Las Tampas, Taos	NW	×
● **Las Vegas**, San Miguel	E	2,385
● Las Vegas Hot Springs, San Miguel	E	?00
La Union, Dona Ana	S	×
● *Lara*, Rio Arriba	NW	×
● Lava, Socorro	W	50
● Leasburg, Dona Ana	S	200
Leighton, Colfax	NE	×
Leitendorfs Well, Grant	SW	×
Lemitar, Socorro	W	500
Lesperance, San Miguel	E	×
● *Levy*, Mora	NE	×
Liberty, San Miguel	E	×
Lincoln, Lincoln	SE	400
● *Lisbon*, Grant	SW	×
● *Lobato*, Rio Arriba	NW	×
Loma Parda, Mora	NE	35
Lomitas, Valencia	W	×
Lone Mountain, Grant	SW	×
Lookout, Eddy	SE	300
● Lordsburg, Grant	SW	228
Lorenzo, Rio Arriba	NW	×
Los Alamos, San Miguel	E	300
Los Balen Buelos, Socorro	W	×
Los Brazos, Rio Arriba	NW	×
● *Los Cerrillo*, Santa Fe	C	250
Los Espinoses, Rio Arriba	NW	×
Los Gallinas, San Miguel	E	×
● **Los Lunas**, Valencia	W	1,000
Los Machos, San Miguel	E	×

Place	Location	Pop.
Los Montes, Taos	NW	×
Los Ojitos, San Miguel	E	×
Los Ojos, (see Park View)		×
Lower Penasco, Lincoln	SE	10
Los Penos, Valencia	W	×
Lower Plaza, Socorro	W	×
Lucero, Mora	NE	280
Luceros, Rio Arriba	NW	×
Luera Spring, Socorro	W	×
● *Luna*, Valencia	W	×
Luna, Socorro	W	200
Lyndon, Nona Ana	S	×
● Lynn, Colfax	NE	×
● *McAlpine*, Colfax	NE	×
● McCarty, Valencia	W	×
McKnight's, Grant	SW	×
Madison, Colfax	NE	20
● Magdalena, Socorro	NW	100
Magruders, Grant	SW	×
● *Malaga*, Eddy	SE	×
Malone, Grant	SW	×
Malpais Spring, Socorro	W	×
● Manuelito, Benralillo	C	150
Mazano, Valencia	W	200
Marguerita, San Miguel	E	×
Mariana, Rio Arriba	NW	×
Martinez, Colfax	NE	×
Mason's Ranch, Dona Ana	S	×
● Maxwell City, Colfax	NE	25
Mescalero, Dona Ana	N	×
● Mesilla, Dona Ana	S	1,500
● *Mesquite*, Dona Ana	S	×
Mestenito, Valencia	W	×
Miera, Moro	NE	10
Mimbres, Grant	SW	×
Mineral City, San Miguel	E	×
Mogollon, Socorro	W	×
● Monero, Rio Arriba	NW	100
Monica, Socorro	W	×
Montecillo, Sierra	SW	50
Moquine, Valencia	W	×
Mora, Mora	NE	600
Mora Park, Mora	NE	×
● *Mount Dora*, Colfax	NE	×
Mumes Spring, Lincoln	SE	×
Myer's Ranch, Moro	NE	×
Nambe, Santa Fe	C	×
Naranjos, Mora	NE	×
● *Navajo*, Rio Arriba	NW	×
Navajo, San Juan	NW	×
Navajo Church, Bernalillo	C	×
Negro, Sierra	SW	×
● *No Agua*, Taos	NW	×
Nogal, Lincoln	SE	54
Nutria, Valencia	W	232
Nutrias, Rio Arriba	NW	×
● *Nutt*, Dona Anna	S	×
Nutt Station, Sierra	SW	10
Oakwood Springs, San Miguel	E	×
Ocate, Mora	NE	300
Ojo Blanco, Grant	NW	×
Ojo Calente, Sierra	SW	50
Ojo Caliente, Taos	NW	50
Ojo Caliente, Valencia	W	×
Ojo de Barrenga, Bernalillo	C	×
Ojo de Colla, Bernalillo	C	×
Ojo de Gall, Valencia	W	×
Ojo del Anil, San Miguel	E	×
Ojo de la Parida, Socorro	W	×
Ojo de la Vac, Sante Fe	C	×
Ojo de los Cazos, Bernalillo	C	×
Ojo de Oso, Bernalillo	C	×
Ojo de Vermejo, Mora	NE	×
Ojo Gaudalupe, Bernalillo	C	×
Ojo Negro, Bernalillo	C	×
Ojo Sarco, Rio Arriba	NW	×
Ojo Sedillo, Bernalillo	C	×
Ojo Yrisarri, Bernalillo	C	×
Old Albuquerque, Bernalillo	C	1,733
Old Camp Mimbres, Grant	SW	×
Old Camp Sherman, Socorro	W	×
Old Camp Vincent, Socorro	W	×
Old Fort McLane, Grant	SW	×
Old Fort Wingate, Valencia	W	×
Old Las Nutrias, Socorro	W	×
Old Stone Tower, Rio Arriba	NW	×
Old Zuni, Valencia	W	×
Ollo, San Juan	NW	25
● *Onava*, San Miguel	E	×
Organ, Dona Ana	S	30
● *Ortiz*, Santa Fe	C	×
● *Osceola*, Sierra	SW	×
Otero, Colfax	NE	×
Pacific Mine, Grant	SW	×
Pajarito, Bernalillo	C	100
● *Palermo*, Eddy	SE	×
● *Palmilla*, Taos	NW	×

Place	Location	Pop.
Palo Amarillo, Taos	NW	×
Palomitas, Sierra	SW	×
Paquate Spring, Valencia	W	×
Paraje, Socorro	W	600
Parias Ranch, Socorro	W	×
Park City, Socorro	W	600
Park View, Rio Arriba	NW	20
Parsons, Lincoln	SE	×
Parton, Colfax	NE	×
Pashal, **Grant**	**SW**	×
Patricio, Lincoln	SE	×
Patterson, Socorro	W	×
Paytons, Chaves	SE	×
Peacock Ranch, Colfax	NE	×
● *Pecos*, San Miguel	E	×
● *Pels*, Colfax	NE	×
Pena Blanca, Bernalillo	C	×
Pena Flor, Colfax	NE	×
Penasco, Taos	NW	300
Peralto, Valencia	W	600
Pereas Ranch, Rio Arriba	NW	×
Pescado, Valencia	W	261
Petaca, Rio Arriba	NW	×
Picacho, Lincoln	SE	×
Pine Spring, Lincoln	SE	×
Pinos, Valencia	W	×
Pinos Altos, Grant	SW	870
Pinos Wells, Valencia	W	25
Placeres, Sierra	SW	×
Placidita, San Miguel	E	×
● *Placita*, San Miguel	E	×
Placita, Valencia	W	×
Playas Valley, Grant	SW	×
Plaza, Bernalillo	C	×
Plaza, Mora	NE	×
Plaza, San Miguel	E	×
Plaza de Alcade, Rio Ar'ba	NW	50
Plaza Media, Rio Arriba	NW	×
Pleasanton, Socorro	W	×
Pojuaque, Santa Fe	C	300
Polvadero, Colfax	NE	300
Ponil, Colfax	NE	×
● *Pope*, Socorro	W	×
Presidio, Dona Anna	S	×
Pueblito, Valencia	W	×
Pueblo Blanco Ruins, L'n.	SE	×
Pueblo Dolores, Santa Fe	C	×
Puerto de Luna, Guadaloupe	E	×
Puetocito, Lincoln	SE	×
Punta de Agua, Valencia	W	100
● Pyramid, Grant	SW	20
Quemado, Socorro	W	×
Questa, Taos	NW	×
Ramah, Valencia	W	50
Ranch, San Miguel	E	×
Ranch, Eddy	SE	×
Ranches of Taos, Taos	NW	2,000
● *Randall*, Dona Ana	S	×
● Raton, Colfax	NE	1,255
● *Red Bluff*, Eddy	SE	×
Red Canon, Socorro	W	×
Red Cloud, Lincoln	SE	×
Ricolite, Grant	SW	×
Ricomeda, Valencia	W	×
● Rincon, Dona Ana	S	200
Rinconada, Rio Arriba	NW	200
Rio Colorado, Taos	NW	450
Rio Puerco, Valencia	W	×
Rociada, San Miguel	E	20
● *Rogers*, Dona Ana	S	×
● *Romero*, San Miguel	E	×
Rosa, Rio Arriba	NW	350
● *Rosario*, Bernalillo	C	×
Roswell, Chaves	SE	343
Round Rock, Bernalillo	C	×
● Rowe, San Miguel	E	20
● *Royce*, Colfax	NE	×
Ruidoso, Lincoln	SE	×
Ruins, Valencia	W	×
Ruins, San Juan	NW	×
Ryado, Colfax	NE	50
● Sabinal, Socorro	W	300
Sabine Spring, San Miguel	E	×
Sabolleta, Bernalillo	C	×
Salado, Socorro	W	300
Salt Spring, Valencia	W	×
San Acacia, Socorro	W	300
San Antonia, Bernalillo	C	×
San Antonia, Bernalillo	C	×
● San Antonio, Socorro	W	700
San Augustine, Dona Ana	S	20
San Augustine Spring, Dona Ana	S	×
San Cristobal, Taos	NW	×
● *Sands*, San Miguel	E	×
San Felipe, Bernalillo	C	×
San Felipe, Mora	NE	×

Town, County	Index	Pop.
San Francisco, Socorro	W	×
San Geronimo, San Miguel	E	×
San Ignacio, Bernalillo	C	×
San Ignatio, San Miguel	C	×
● *San Idle Fonso*, Santa Fe	C	×
San Isidro, Socorro	W	×
San Jos, San Miguel	E	×
San Josa, San Miguel	E	×
San Jose, Chaves	SE	×
San Jose, Grant	SW	×
San Jose, Sierra	SW	×
● *San Jose*, Valencia	W	×
San Juan, Valencia	W	×
San Juan, Rio Arriba	NW	600
San Lorenzo, Grant	SW	50
● San Marcial, Socorro	W	1,000
San Mateo, Valencia	W	300
San Miguel, Dona Ana	S	×
● San Miguel, San Miguel	E	400
San Mill, Grant	SW	×
San Pablo, Rio Arriba	NW	×
San Pedro, Santa Fe	C	400
San Pedro, Socorro	W	800
San Rafael, Valencia	W	×
Santa Ana, Bernalillo	C	×
Santa Barbara, Dona Ana	S	×
● *Santa Clara*, Santa Fe	C	300
Santa Cruz, Santa Fe	NW	300
Santa Domingo, Bernalillo	C	×
● **SANTA FE**, Santa Fe	C	6,185
Santa Rita, Grant	SW	10
Santa Rosa, Guadaloupe	E	×
Santa Tonino, Mora	NE	×
San Ysidor, Bernalillo	C	×
Sapello, San Miguel	E	200
Savoia, Valencia	W	×
Seboyeta, Valencia	W	×
Sedillo, Bernalillo	C	×
● *Sellers*, Dona Ana	S	×
● Separ, Grant	SW	40
Servilleta, Rio Arriba	NW	×
● *Servilleta*, Taos	NW	×
Settlement, San Miguel	E	×
Settlement, Grant	SW	×
● Seven Rivers, Eddy	SE	150
Shakespeare, Grant	SW	50
Sharp's Claim, Colfax	NE	×
Shaws, Socorro	W	×
Sheep Spring, Valencia	W	×
● *Shoemaker*, Mora	NE	10
● *Silbert's*, Eddy	SE	×
● **Silver City**, Grant	SW	2,102
Slaagter's Ranch, Eddy	SE	20
Slocum's Government Agency, Dona Ana	S	×
Snake Ranche, Socorro	W	×
● **Socorro**, Socorro	W	4,200
Soldier's Farewell, Grant	SW	×
South Fork, Dona Ana	S	50
South Spring River, Linc'n	SE	20
● **Springer**, Colfax	NE	700
Spring Hill, Colfax	NE	×
● Stein's Pass, Grant	SW	100
● *Stewart Junction*, Taos	NW	×
Stockton, Colfax	NE	×
● *Strauss*, Dona Ana	S	×
● *Sublette*, Rio Arriba	NW	×
● *Sulzbache*, San Miguel	E	×
● *Summit*, Grant	SW	×
Sunnyside, San Miguel	E	×
Swarts, Grant	SW	×
Sweet Water, Colfax	NE	×
Tajique, Valencia	W	100
Tajon, San Miguel	E	×
Taos, Taos	NW	2,000
Taos Pueblo, Taos	NW	×
● Tecolote, San Miguel	E	50
Tecolotenos, San Miguel	E	×
Tejon, Bernalillo	C	×
Tesuque, Santa Fe	C	×
Thompsons, Grant	SW	×
Tierra Amarilla, Rio Arriba	NW	1,500
Tierra Blanca, Sierra	SW	×
Tijeras, Bernalillo	C	100
● *Tipton*, Mora	NE	×
Tiptonville, Mora	NE	25
● *Toltec*, Rio Arriba	NW	×
Tome, Valencia	W	×
● *Tonuco*, Dona Ana	S	×
Torreon, Valencia	W	×
Towne, Dona Ana	S	×
Tramperas, Mora	NE	25
Tres Alamos, Valencia	W	×
● Tres Piedras, Taos	NW	300
Tres Piedras, Rio Arriba	NW	×
Trinchera, Colfax	NE	×
Truchas, Rio Arriba	NW	×
Tularosa, Dona Ana	S	400
Tulerosa, Socorro	W	×
● *Tunis*, Grant	SW	×
Turquesa, Santa Fe	C	×
Turqui, Mora	NE	×
Unade Gato, Bernalillo	C	×
Una de Gato, Colfax	NE	×
Union, Dona Ana	S	20
● *Upham*, Sierra	SW	×
Upper Cangillon, Rio Ar'a	NW	×
● *Upper Las Vegas*, S. Mig'l	E	×
Upper Penasco, Lincoln	SE	30
Upper Tecolot, Mora	NE	×
Ute Creek, Colfax	NE	150
Valencia, Valencia	W	100
Vallecitos, Rio Arriba	NW	×
Valleto, Rio Arriba	NW	×
Valverde, Socorro	W	×
Vandoritos, Mora	NE	×
● *Vasquez*, Colfax	NE	×
Vaur, Mora	NE	150
Veda, Colfax	NE	×
Velarde, Rio Arriba	NW	600
Victoria, Dona Ana	S	100
Village, San Miguel	E	×
Village, Bernalillo	C	×
Villanueva, San Miguel	E	×
● *Volcano*, Taos	NW	×
● Wagon Mound, Mora	NE	175
● *Waldo*, Bernalillo	C	×
● Wallace, Bernalillo	C	50
Wallace, San Juan	NW	×
Warren, Grant	SW	×
● *Water Canon*, Socorro	W	×
● Watrous, Mora	NE	250
● *Watson*, Dona Ana	S	×
Weed, Lincoln	SE	50
White Oaks, Lincoln	SE	385
● *White Rock Canon*, S'a Fe	C	×
● Whitewater, Grant	SW	×
Whitfield, Socorro	W	×
● *Whitney*, Grant	SW	×
● *Williamson* [illegible]*nr*, Val'la	W	×
● *Willow Creek*, Rio Ar'a	NW	×
● *Wilna*, Grant	SW	×
● *Wingate*, Bernalillo	C	×
Zampta, Sierra	SW	×
Zia, Bernalillo	C	×
● *Zuni*, Dona Ana	S	×
Zuni, Valencia	W	×

NEW YORK.

COUNTIES.	INDEX.	POP.
Albany	E	164,555
Allegany	SW	43,240
Broome	S	62,973
Cattaraugus	SW	60,866
Cayuga	C	65,302
Chautauqua	SW	75,202
Chemung	S	48,265
Chenango	C	37,776
Clinton	NE	46,437
Columbia	SE	46,172
Cortland	C	28,657
Delaware	SE	45,496
Dutchess	SE	77,879
Erie	W	322,981
Essex	NE	33,052
Franklin	NE	38,110
Fulton	E	37,650
Genesee	W	33,265
Greene	SE	31,[illegible]8
Hamilton	NE	4,762
Herkimer	N	45,608
Jefferson	N	68,806
Kings	SE	838,[illegible]47
Lewis	N	29,806
Livingston	W	37,801
Madison	C	42,892
Monroe	W	189,5[illegible]
Montgomery	E	45,[illegible]
New York	SE	1,515,301
Niagara	W	62,491
Oneida	C	122,922
Onondaga	C	146,24
Ontario	W	48,45[illegible]
Orange	SE	97,[illegible]5
Orleans	W	30,803
Oswego	C	71,883
Otsego	C	50,8[illegible]1
Putnam	SE	14,849
Queens	SE	128,059
Rensselaer	E	124,511
Richmond	SE	51,693
Rockland	SE	35,162
St. Lawrence	N	85,048
Saratoga	E	57,663
Schenectady	E	29,797
Schoharie	E	29,164
Schuyler	SW	16,711
Seneca	C	28,227
Steuben	SW	81,473
Suffolk	SE	62,491
Sullivan	SE	31,031
Tioga	S	29,935
Tompkins	S	32,923
Ulster	SE	87,062
Warren	NE	27,866
Washington	E	45,690
Wayne	W	49,729
Westchester	SE	14[illegible],772
Wyoming	W	31,[illegible]3
Yates	W	21,001
Total		5,997,853

TOWNS. COUNTIES.	INDEX.	POP.
Abbotts, Cattaraugus	SW	150
Abbotts Cors, (see Armor)		×
● *Abbotts Road*, Erie	W	200
Abrams Landing, Suffolk	SE	×
● *Academy*, Essex	NE	4,000
Academy, Ontario	W	100
Accord, Ulster	SE	550
Acidalia, Sullivan	SE	×
Acra, Greene	SE	100
● Adams, Jefferson	N	1,360
● Adams' Basin, Monroe	W	274
● Adams Centre, Jefferson	N	600
● Adams Corners, Putnam	SE	50
Adams' Station, (see Delmar)		×
Adams Switch, Cattar'gus	SW	×
Adamsville, (see Delmar)		×
Adamsville, Washington	E	75
● Addison, Steuben	SW	2,166
Addison Hill, Steuben	SW	35
● Addison Junction, Essex	NE	×
Aden Lair, (Olmstedville)		×
Adirondack, Warren	NE	175
● Adrian, Steuben	SW	250
Adriance, (see Hopewell Jc.)		×
● Afton, Chenango	C	683
● *Akin*, Montgomery	E	150
● Akron, Erie	W	1,492
Alabama, Genesee	W	200
● *Alabama Sta.*, Genesee	W	×
● **ALBANY**, Albany	E	94,923
● *Albertson's* Queens	SE	×
Albia, (see Troy)		×
● **Albion**, Orleans	W	4,586
● *Albion*, Oswego	C	511
Alburgh, Franklin	NE	100
Alcove, Albany	E	×
● Alden, Erie	W	533
Alden Centre, Erie	W	150
Alder Bend, Clinton	NE	50
Alder Brook, Franklin	NE	100
● Alder Creek, Oneida	C	200
● Alexander, Genesee	W	300
Alexandria Bay, Jefferson	N	1,123
● Alfred, Allegany	SW	150
Alfred Centre, Allegany	SW	786
Algonquin, Franklin	NE	×
● Allaben, Ulster	SE	60
● Allegany, Cattaraugus	SW	1,400
Allen, Allegany	SW	×
Allendale, Jefferson	N	100
● *Allensborough*, Wash'ton	E	225
Allens Falls, St. Lawrence	N	×
Allen's Hill, Ontario	W	100
● Allentown, Allegany	SW	400
Alligerville, Ulster	SE	350
Alloway, Wayne	W	100
Alma, Allegany	SW	100
Alma, Orleans	W	×
● Almond, Allegany	SW	800
● Alpine, Schuyler	SW	230
Alplaus, Schenectady	E	20
Alps, Rensselaer	E	150
● Altamont, Albany	E	550
Altay, Schuyler	SW	100
● Alton, Wayne	W	300
● Altona, Clinton	NE	800
● *Alverson's*, Jefferson	N	×
Amagansett, Suffolk	SE	200
● Amawalk, Westchester	SE	75

Amber, Onondaga..........C 156
● Amboy, Onondaga........C ×
Amboy Centre, Oswego....C 100
● Amenia, Dutchess.......SE 700
Amenia City, Dutchess....SE ×
Amenia Union, Dutchess..SE 200
Ameniaville, (see Amenia)... ×
Ames, Montgomery..........E 500
● *Ames Street Junc.*.MonroeW 100
Amesville, (see Ulster Park).. ×
Amity, Orange...........SE 400
● Amityville, Suffolk..... NE 2,293
Ampersand, Franklin.....NE ×
● Amsterdam, MontgomeryE 17,336
● Ancram, Columbia..... SE 300
Ancram Centre, (see Ancram Lead Mines).............. ×
● Ancram Lead Mines, Columbia..........SE 200
Anderson's Cors., (see West Copake).................. ×
Andes, Delaware..........SE 416
● Andover, Allegany......SW 800
Andrusville, (see Burke)..... ×
○ **Angelica**, Allegany..SW 953
● Angola, Erie............W 650
● *Angola Siding*, Erie.....W ×
● *Angus*, Yates..........W ×
○ *Annandale*, Richmond..SE 125
Annandale, Dutchess...... SE 300
Anoka, Broome.............S ×
● Antwerp, Jefferson........N 912
● *Anybodys*, Cattaraugus.SW ×
○ Apalachin, Tioga..........S 475
● Apex, Delaware.........SE 100
Appleys, Sullivan.........SE ×
● Apulia, Onondaga......... C 100
Aquebogne, Suffolk....... SE 300
● *Aqueduct*, Queens.......SE ×
● *Aqueduct*, Schenectady...E ×
Aquetuck, Albany...........E 150
● Arcade, Wyoming........W 900
● Arcadia, Wayne..........W 800
● *Archdale*, Washington....E ×
Arctic, Chenango............C ×
● Arden, Orange...........SE ×
Ardonia, Ulster........... SE ×
○ Ardsley, Westchester....SE 380
Arena, Delaware..........SE 100
Argusville, Schoharie.......E 150
Argyle, Washington........ E 158
Arietta, Hamilton.......... N 125
Aristotle, Allegany....... SW ×
Ark, Yates..................W ×
● Arkport, Steuben.......SW 300
● Arkville, Delaware........SE 100
Arkwright, Chautauqua.. SW 35
Arkwright Sum'it,(see Arkw't) ×
Arlington, Dutchess....... SE 100
● *Arlington*, Richmond...SE ×
Armonk, Westchester.....SE 400
● Armor, Erie............ W 400
Arnot, Chemung............S ×
● *Arrochar*, Richmond....SE ×
Arthamomogue, Suffolk...SE ×
Arthur, Oswego.............C ×
● Arthursburgh, Dutchess.SE 50
Arverne, Queens......... SE ×
Asbury, Tompkins..........S ×
● *Ashantee*, Livingston.....W ×
Ashford, Cattaraugus......SW 150
● *Ashford*, Cattaraugus...SW 150
Ashland, Greene...........SE 300
Ashton, (see Wells)......... ×
Ashton, Ulster.............SE ×
● *Ashville*, Chautauqua... SW 50
Astoria, Queens......... SE ×
Athens, Greene............NE 2,024
● *Athens Junc.*,SchenectadyE ×
Athol, Warren..............NE 200
● Athol Springs, Erie......W 25
● Atlanta, Steuben........SW 525
Atlantic Park, Queens.... SE ×
Atlanticville, (see E. Inogue) ×
● Attica, Wyoming.........W 1,994
● Attlebury, Duchess......SE 50
● Atwater, Cayuga...........C 50
● **Auburn**, Cayuga.........C 25,858
Augusta, Madison..........O ×
Augusta, Oneida.............C 300
Aurelius, Cayuga............C 75
● Aurelius Station, Cayuga. C 75
● Auriesville, Montgomery. E 200
● Aurora, Cayuga...........C 555
Au Sable, Clinton.........NE 306
● Au Sable Chasm, Clinton NE 300
Au Sable Forks, Essex.... NE 757

Austerlitz, Columbia.......SE 150
● *Austin*, Cattaraugus.... SW ×
Austin, Cayuga..............C ×
Ava, Oneida.................C 100
Averill Park, Rensselaer... E 450
● Avoca, Steuben..........SW 953
● Avon, Livingston..........W 1,653
Avon Springs, (see Avon)...... ×
Axton, Franklin...........NE ×
Ayre, Otsego.................C ×
Babcock Hill, Oneida........C 50
● Babylon, Suffolk........ SE 2,500
Bacon Hill, Saratoga........E 600
Bailey's Four Corners, (see Hensonville).............. ×
Bainbridge, Chenango.......C 1,049
Baiting Hollow, Suffolk....SE 300
● *Baiting Hollow*, Suffolk.SE ×
Baker's Basin, Washington E ×
Bakers Mills, Warren.......NE 100
Balcom, Chautauqua..... SW ×
Bald Mountain, WashingtonE 60
● *Baldwin*, Essex...........NE ×
● Baldwin, Queens........ SE 210
● Baldwin Place, Westch'sterSE 150
● Baldwinsville, Onondaga..C 3,040
● **Ballston Spa**, Saratoga E 3,527
Ballston Centre, Saratoga..E ×
● Ballston Lake, Saratoga.. E 200
● Bangall, Dutchess....... SE 400
● *Bangor*, Franklin...... NE 800
Bangor, Franklin.........NE 800
Banks, Cattaraugus.......SW ×
Banksville, Westchester.. SE 450
Barberville, (see Poestenkill) ×
Barbourville, Delaware....SE 100
● Bardonia, Rockland.....SE ×
Bardons Sta., (see Bardonia) ×
Baretown, Oneida.......... C ×
Barker, Broome.............S ×
● Barker's, Niagara........ W 100
Barkersville, Saratoga......E 200
● Barnard's Crossing, MonroeW ×
Barnerville, Schoharie.......E 125
Barnes, Yates...............W ×
Barnes' Corner, Lewis......N 50
○ *Barnum's*, Sullivan......SE ×
● *Barnum's Island*, QueensSE ×
● *Barracks*, Clinton....... NE ×
Barre Centre, Orleans......W 200
Barrington, Yates...........W 200
● Barrytown, Dutchess....SE 150
Barryville, Sullivan.......SE 300
● Bartlett, Oneida.......... C 350
● Barton, Tioga............ S 200
Bartow-on-the-Sound, Westchester...................SE 500
Bartow Sta., Westchester..SE 500
● Basom, Genesee..........W ×
● **Batavia**, Genesee...... W 7,221
Batchellerville, Saratoga....E 150
Bates, Schoharie............E 400
○ *Bath*, Rensselaer..........E ×
● **Bath**, Steuben.........SW 3,261
● Bath Beach, Kings...... SE 1,619
Bath Junction, Kings.....SE ×
Bath-on-the-Hudson, Rens'erE 2,399
Battenville, Washington.... E 150
● Baychester, Westchester SE ×
● Bay Port, Suffolk.........SE 400
● Bay Ridge, King's.......SE 1,858
● Bay Shore, Suffolk.......SE 2,290
● Bay Side, Queens........SE 500
Bay State, Cattaraugus...SW ×
● *Bay View*, Chautauqua.SW ×
● *Bay View*, Erie..........W ×
Bay View, Ontario.........W ×
Bayville, Queens...........SE ×
● *Bayville Station*, QueensSE ×
● *Beach Channel*, Queens.SE ×
Beaches Corner, Greene...SE ×
Beach Landing, Lewis......N ×
● Beach Ridge, Niagara....W 25
● Bealsburgh, Monroe .....W ×
Beard's Hollow, Schoharie..E 150
Bearsville, Ulster..........SE 100
Bearytown, (see Fayette)..... ×
Beatysburgh, Sullivan.....SE ×
Beaver Brook, Sullivan.....SE ×
○ *Beaver Dam*, Orange....SE ×
● Beaver Dams, Schuyler.SW 250
Beaver Falls, Lewis.........N 500
Beaver Kill, Sullivan...... SE ×
Beaver Meadow, Chenango..C 200
Beaver River, Lewis.........N ×
Becker's Corners, Albany...E 250
Bedelltown, Queens.......SE ×

Bedford, Westchester......SE 500
○ *Bedford Park*, West'ster.SE ×
● Bedford Station, West'r. SE 500
● *Bedford Station*, Kings..SE ×
Beech Wood, Sullivan......SE 75
Beede's, Essex.............NE 150
○ Beekman, Dutchess......SE 120
Beekmantown, Clinton....NE 107
Beekmantown Sta.,ClintonNE 300
● Beerston, Delaware......SE 50
Belcher, Washington........E 63
● Belden, Broome...........S 60
● Belfast, Allegany.........SW 600
Belfort, Lewis................N 400
Belgium, Onondaga.........C 300
Belleayre, Ulster...........SE ×
Belle Isle, Onondaga.......C 200
● *Belle Isle*, Onondaga......C ×
● *Belleview*, Chautauqua..SW ×
Belleville, Jefferson....... N 452
● Bellmore, Queens....... SE 150
Bellona, Yates..............W 300
● *Bellona Station*, Yates...W ×
Bellport, Suffolk...........SE 500
○ *Bellport Station*, Suffolk SE ×
Bellvale, Orange........... SE 300
Bellwood, Lewis............N ×
● **Belmont**, Allegany....SW 950
Belmont, (see New York).... ×
Belmont Centre, Franklin NE 100
● *Belmont Junction*, Suf'k SE ×
● Belvidere, Allegany.... SW 250
Bemus Heights, Saratoga... E 175
● Bemus Point, Chaut'qua SW 150
Benedict, Fulton............E 100
● Bennett, Allegany....... SW ×
● *Bennett's*, Ontario....... W ×
Bennettsburgh, Schuyler..SW 150
Bennett's Cors.,(see Glovers'lle) ×
Bennett's Corners, Madison.C 25
Bennett's Creek, Steuben. SW 25
Bennettsville, Chenango.....C 125
Bennington, Wyoming......W 200
Benson, Hamilton........ NE ×
Benson Centre, Hamilton. NE 200
● Bensonhurst, Kings......SE ×
Benson Mines, St. Law'ce...N 100
Bentley's Corners, Jefferson N ×
● Benton Centre, Yates.... W 150
● *Berea*, Orange.......... SE ×
● Bergen, Genesee......... W 623
Bergen Landing, Queens.. SE ×
Bergholtz, Niagara........ W 180
● Berkshire, Tioga..........S 500
● Berlin, Rensselaer........ E 718
Berlin Centre, (see Centre Berlin)............................ ×
Berlin Village, Queens.... SE ×
Berne, Albany...............E 1,500
● Bernhard's Bay, Oswego.. C 222
Berryville, Montgomery.....E 100
● Besemer, Tompkins ...... S 50
Best, Rensselaer........... E ×
Bethany, Genesee.......... W 100
Bethel, Sullivan .... SE 200
Bethel Corners, Cayuga..... C 50
● Bethel Station, Dutches..SE ×
Bethlehem, (see Beth'lm Centre) ×
Bethlehem Center, Albany..E 125
● *Bethpage*, Queens....... SE ×
● *Bethpage Junc.*, Queens SE ×
Beulah, Ontario .... W ×
Big Brook, Oneida........... C 50
Big Creek, Steuben....... SW 25
Bigelow, St. Lawrence.......N ×
● Big Flats, Chemung......S 500
Big Hollow, Greene....... SE 75
● Big Indian, Ulster....... SE 100
● *Big Island*, Orange......SE ×
Biglow, St. Lawrence ...... N ×
● *Big Stream*, Yates........W ×
● Big Tree, Erie............W 200
● Billings, Dutchess....... SE 100
● Billsborough, Ontario.... W ×
Binghams Mills, Columbia SE 127
Bingham's Mills, (see Reniffe) ×
● **Binghamton**, Broome. S 35,005
● *Bingley*, Madison......... C ×
● Binnewater, Ulster....... SE 250
Birchton, Saratoga.......... E 50
Bird, Cattaraugus......... SW 50
Bird Nest Rock, Orange... SE ×
Birdsall, Allegany .... SW 100
Birmingham, (see Au Sable Ch'm) ×
Bishop Street, Jefferson.... N 200
Bishopville, Allegany...... SW ×
Black Brook, Clinton.... NE 100

 New York New York

Name	Pop.
● Black Creek, Allegany. SW	200
Black Lake, St. Lawrence.. N	×
Black Point, Ontario...... W	×
● Black River, Jefferson ... N	600
● Black Rock, Erie.......... W	×
Blaine, Montgomery........ E	50
● Blasdell, Erie........... W	×
● Blauvelt, Rockland......SE	500
Bleach, Westchester ...... SE	×
Blecker, Fulton............ E	300
Blenheim,(see N. Blenheim).	×
Bliss, Wyoming... W	400
○ *Bliss Summit*, Wyoming. W	×
Blissville,(see Long Isl. City).	×
Blockville, Chautauqua... SW	100
● Blodgett Mills, Cortland...C	100
● *Blood's Depot*, Steuben. SW	525
● Bloomingburg, S'l'van.. SE	400
● Bloomingdale, Essex....NE	600
● Blooming Grove, Orange SE	100
Blooming Grove,(see Defreestville)	×
● Bloomville, Delaware....SE	350
Blossom, Erie............. W	172
● Blossvale, Oneida......... C	300
Blue Mountain Lake, Hamilton .... NE	400
Blue Point, Suffolk........SE	×
Blue Ridge, Essex .... NE	150
Blue Stores, Columbia..... SE	150
● *Bluff Point*, Clinton.....NE	×
Bluff Point, Yates.......... W	150
● Blythebourne, Kings.... SE	×
Bohemia, Suffolk.......... SE	×
Boice, St. Lawrence........ N	×
● Boiceville, Ulster.........SE	75
● Bolivar, Allegany....... SW	1,500
Bolivar, Madison............C	20
Bolton, Warren............ NE	300
Bolton Basin, Orange......SE	×
Bolton Landing, Warren.. NE	×
Bombay, Franklin........ NE	200
● *Bombay Junc.*, Franklin NE	×
● Boomertown, Chau'qua. SW	50
● Boonville, Oneida......... C	1,613
Boquet, Essex............ NE	75
Borden, Steuben.......... SW	25
Boreas River, Essex...... NE	75
Borodino, Onondaga........ C	160
Boston, Erie .... W	300
Boston Centre, Erie........ W	100
● Boston Corner, C'l'mbia. SE	100
● Bouckville, Madison...... C	300
Boultonville, Westchester. SE	125
Bovina, Delaware..........SE	100
Bovina's Centre, Delaware. SE	200
Bowen, Cattaraugus...... SW	×
Bowen's Corners, Oswego...C	25
Bowery Bay Beach, (see North Beach)	×
● *Bowlers*, Allegany....... SW	×
● Bowmansville, Erie...... W	150
Boyd, Lewis................ N	×
Boyds, Steuben........... SW	×
Boylston Centre, Oswego....C	80
Boyntonville, Rensselaer....E	150
Braddock's Rapid, Oswego..C	×
Bradford, Steuben.......... SW	350
Brainard, Rensselaer .... E	125
● Brainard Station, Re's'la'r. E	175
Brainardsville, Franklin.. NE	150
Braman Corners, Sch'n't'dy. E	96
Branch, (see South Ballston).	×
Branch, Ulster............ SE	×
Branchport, Yates......... W	273
Brandon, Franklin.........NE	755
● *Brandy Brook*, Clinton. NE	×
Brant, Erie.................W	100
Brantingham, Lewis........N	×
Brant Lake, Warren...... NE	×
● *Brasher*, St. Lawrence... N	×
Brasher Falls, St. L'r'nce....N	570
Brasher Iron Wks, St. L'r'nce N	200
Brasie Corners, St. L'wr'nce N	×
Brayton, Warren .... NE	×
Breakabeen, Schoharie..... E	350
● Breesport, Chemung...... S	500
Brent Settlement, Lewis ....N	×
● Brentwood, Suffolk..... SE	100
● *Breslau*, Suffolk .... SE	974
Brevoort, Kings........... SE	×
● Brewerton, Onondaga.... C	336
● Brewster, Putnam ...... SE	1,500
Breezy Point, Queens..... SE	×
● *Brick Church*, Cayuga.... C	×
● Bridgehampton, Suffolk.SE	1,391
Bridgeport, Madison........ C	212
Bridgeport, Queens........SE	×
Bridgeville, Sullivan ...... SE	150
● Bridgewater, Oneida......C	224
● Brier Hill, St. Lawrence..N	200
● Brighton, Monroe........ W	705
● *Brighton Beach*, Kings..SE	×
● *Brills*, Dutchess......... SE	×
● *Brimmer Brook*, Alle'ny SW	×
● Brinckerhoff, Dutchess..SE	43
● *Brinker Place*, Monroe.. W	×
● Brisben, Chenango........C	250
Briscoe, Sullivan...........SE	100
Bristol, Ontario............W	410
Bristol Centre, Ontario.....W	75
Bristol Springs, Ontario....W	100
Broadalbin, Fulton..........E	708
● *Broad Channel*, Queens.SE	×
● *Broadway*, Queens......SE	×
Broadway, Rockland.......SE	×
Brockett's Br.,(see Dolgevi'e)	×
● Brockport, Monroe...... W	3,742
Brockville, Orleans.........W	×
● Brocton, Chautauqua... SW	812
● Brodhead, Ulster........ SE	50
Brodhead's Brick Kiln, UlsterSE	×
● Broken Straw, Chaut'ua SW	100
Bronxdale, Westchester...SE	×
● Bronxville, Westchester.SE	275
Brookdale, St. Lawrence....N	**200**
Brookfield, Madison.........C	561
● Brook Haven, Suffolk....SE	500
● *Brook Haven Sta.*, SuffolkSE	×
● **BROOKLYN**, Kings..SE	806,343
Brookmere, Monroe........W	×
Brook's Cross.,(see Brown's Sta.)	×
Brooks' Grove, Livingston..W	×
● Brookton, Tompkins......S	300
Brook Vale, Broome........S	×
Brookville, (see East Norwick)	×
Broome Centre, Schoharie...E	150
Brown Haven, Sullivan....SE	×
● Brown's Station, Ulster..SE	20
Brownsville, Kings.........SE	×
● Brownville, Jefferson......N	660
● *Brownville*, Sullivan.....SE	×
Bruceville, (see High Falls) ..	×
Brushland, (see Bovina Centre)	×
Brush's Mill, (see Brushton).	×
● Brushton, Franklin.....NE	598
Bruyans Basin, Ulster....SE	×
Bruynswick, Ulster.........SE	75
○ *Bryn Mawr Park*, W'tc'rSE	×
Buchanan, Westchester....SE	×
Buck's Bridge, St. LawrenceN	250
Buckton, St. Lawrence......N	×
● *Bucktooth*, Cattaraugus .SW	495
Buel, Montgomery..........E	100
Buellsville, Onondaga........C	60
Buena Vista, Steuben.....SW	50
● **BUFFALO**, Erie.......W	255,664
● *Buffalo Creek*, Erie...... W	×
● *Buffalo Creek Junc.*, ErieW	×
Buffalo Plains, (see Buffalo).	×
Bull Run, Ulster...........SE	200
Bull's Head, Dutchess.....SE	150
Bull's Head, Richmond.....SE	150
● Bullville, Orange..........SE	100
Bundy's Corners, (see Flat Creek)	×
● Bundy's Crossing, OswegoC	×
Burbanks, Richmond......SE	×
Burden, Columbia......... SE	300
Burdett, Schuyler..........SW	250
● *Burdicks*, Essex..........NE	150
● *Burgoyne*, Saratoga...... E	×
● Burke, Franklin...........NE	350
Burkes Hollow, (see Burke)..	×
Burlingham, Sullivan.......SE	300
● *Burlington*, Erie..........W	×
Burlington, Otsego..........C	125
Burlington Flats, Otsego....C	150
Burnhams, Chautauqua...SW	100
Burns', Allegany...........SW	×
Burns' Station, (see Burns)..	×
● Burns, Steuben......... SW	100
○ Burnside, Orange.........SE	600
Burnt Hills, Saratoga.........E	180
Burrell's Corners, HerkimerN	×
Burr's Mills, Jefferson......N	84
Burrville, Jefferson..........N	×
Burtonsville, Montgomery..E	130
Bushes Landing, Lewis......N	×
Bushnell's Basin, Monroe... W	171
Bushnellsville, Greene.....SE	100
Bushville, Sullivan.........SE	50
● *Bushwick*, Kings..........SE	×
● *Bushwick Junc.*, QueensSE	×
● *Bushkirk's*, Rensselaer ...E	100
Buskirk's Bridge, Washing'nE	300
Busti, Chautauqua..........SW	500
Butler Centre, Wayne......W	150
Butler's Falls, Orange.....SE	×
Butterfly, Oswego..........C	×
Buttermilk Falls, Sullivan SE	×
● Butternut Grove, Delaw'eSE	200
Butternuts, (see Gilbertsville)	×
Byersville, Livingston......W	150
● Byron, Genesee.......... W	300
● *Byron*, Genesee.......... W	400
Cabin Hill, Delaware.......SE	100
Cadiz, Cattaraugus.......SW	200
● Cadosia, Delaware.......SE	×
Cadosia Sum't, Delaware..SE	100
● *Cady*, Genesee........... W	×
● Cadyville, Clinton.......NE	150
● Cairo, Greene............SE	573
○ *Cairo Junction*, Greene..SE	×
● *Caldwell Station*, WarrenNE	500
● Caledonia, Livingston.... W	1,100
● *Caledonia*, St. Lawrence..N	×
Callanan's Corners, Albany..E	150
Callicoon, Sullivan.........SE	400
○ Callicoon Depot, Sullivan SE	400
● Calverton, Suffolk.......SE	×
Cambria, Niagara.......... W	300
○ Cambridge, Washington.. E	1,958
Camby, Dutchess..........SE	×
○ Camden, Oneida...........C	1,902
Camden Depot, Oneida......C	×
● Camelot, Dutchess.......SE	×
● Cameron, Steuben.......SW	300
● Cameron Mills, Steuben.SW	100
● Camillus, Onondaga.......C	487
● Campbell, Steuben.......SW	400
● Campbell Hall, Orange.. SE	275
● *Campbell Hall Jc.*, OrangeSE	×
Camp Ground, Wyoming.. W	×
Camp' M [illegible], Jefferson.... N	×
Campville, Tioga............ S	200
Camroden, Oneida.......... C	×
Canaan, Columbia.......... SE	120
Canaan Centre, Columbia..SE	50
Canaan Four Corners, Col'aSE	400
Canadice, Ontario.......... W	200
● Canajoharie, Montgomery E	2,089
● *Canal Branch*, Oneida......C	×
● **Canandaigua**, OntarioW	5,868
● Canarsie, Kings..........SE	2,452
Canarise Landing, KingsSE	×
● Canaseraga, Allegany...SW	659
● *Canaseraga*, Madison.....C	75
● Canastota, Madison....... C	2,774
● Candor, Tioga.............S	1,500
● Caneadea, Allegany.....SW	450
Canisteo, Steuben.........SW	×
● Canisteo, Steuben.......SW	2,071
Cannonsville, Delaware....SE	400
Canoe Place, Suffolk...... SE	×
Canoga, Seneca..............C	200
Canton, Onondaga..........C	×
● **Canton**, St. Lawrence...N	2,580
● Cape Vincent, Jefferson.. N	1,324
Capron, Oneida............. C	×
Cardiff, Onondaga...........C	250
Carlisle, Schoharie..........E	350
Carlton, Orleans............W	100
● Carlton Station, Orleans. W	×
● Carlyon, Orleans......... W	75
Carmansville, New York..SE	×
● **Carmel**, Putnam.......SE	600
Caroline, Tompkins......... S	×
Caroline Centre, Tompkins..S	100
● Caroline Depot, Tompkins S	50
Carpenter's Point, Orange.SE	×
● *Carroll*, Allegany........SW	×
● *Carrolls Switch*, Saratoga.E	×
● Carrollton, Cattaraugus.SW	600
● *Carr's Creek*, Delaware..SE	100
Carter's Landing, Lewis....N	×
Cartersville, Monroe....... W	×
Carterville, Oswego......... C	25
● Carthage, Jefferson.......N	2,278
Carthage Land., DutchessSE	300
● *Casanova*, New York....SE	×
● Cascade, Cayuga..........C	×
● *Cascade Mills*, Yates.....W	×
Cascade Valley, Broome.....S	100
Cascadeville, Essex........NE	50
● **Cases, Allegany........SW**	**×**
● Cassadaga, Chautauqua. SW	400
● Cassville, Oneida..........C	350
● Castile, Wyoming........ W	1,146
Castle Creek, Broome....... S	200
● Castleton, Rensselaer.....E	1,127
Castleton Corners, Richm'dS E	300

●Castorland, Lewis.........N 150
Catamount, Westchester...SE ×
●Catatonk, Tioga..........S 100
Catawba, Steuben.........SW 70
Catfish, Oswego............C ×
Catherine, Schuyler.......SW 100
Catlin, Chemung............S 75
●Cato, Cayuga...............C 550
Caton, Steuben.............SW 210
●**Catskill**, Greene........SE 4,920
Catskill Landing, Greene..SE 50
●CatskillStation,Columbia SE 20
●Cattaraugus,Cattaraug's SW 878
●*Cattatonk*, Tioga...........S 100
Cat Town, (see Oaksville).... ×
●Caughdenoy, Oswego.......C 300
●*Cauterskill*, Greene.......SE 90
●Cayuga, Cayuga.............C 511
●*Cayuga Junction*,Cayuga.C ×
●Cayuta, Schuyler..........SW 200
Cayutaville, Schuyler......SW 100
●Cazenovia, Madison........C 1,987
Cedar Beach, Steuben.....SW ×
●*Cedar Bluffs*, Saratoga...E ×
Cedar Hill, Albany..........E 400
Cedarhurst, Queens.........SE ×
Cedar Lake, Herkimer......N 200
Cedar River, (see Indian Lake) ×
Cedar Swamp, (see Glen Head) ×
Cedarvale, Onondaga.........C 150
Cedarville, Herkimer.......N 450
●*Cedarville*, Herkimer....N ×
●*Cemetery*, Albany..........E ×
Center, Herkimer............N 200
●*Center Park*, Monroe....W ×
●Central Bridge, Schoharie E 35
Centralia, Chautauqua....SW 150
●Central Islip, Suffolk....SE 100
●Central Park, Queens....SE 500
●Central Square, Oswego...C 550
Central Valley, Orange....SE 175
Centre, Herkimer............N 200
●Centre Berlin, Rensselaer E 200
Centre Brunswick, Rens'er. E 200
Centre Cambridge, Wash'on E 300
Centrefield, Ontario........W 100
Centre Lisle, Broome.........S 225
Centre Moriches, Suffolk..SE 500
Centreport, Cayuga..........C 50
Centreport, Suffolk.........SE 175
Centre Valley, Otsego.......C 75
●Centre Village, Broome...S 150
Centreville, Allegany.....SW 100
Centreville, (see Mooers Forks) ×
Centreville, Onondaga.......C ×
Centreville, Ulster..........SE ×
●Centreville Station,Sul'n SE 100
Centre WhiteCreek,Wash'n.E 800
●Ceres, Allegany...........SW 400
●*Chases*, Wyoming.........W ×
Chadwick Mills, Oneida.....C 850
●Chafee, Erie...............W ×
●Chambers, Chemung.......S 25
Champion, Jefferson........N 200
●Champlain, Clinton......NE 1,275
Channingsville, (see Wappinger's Falls) ×
Chapelsburg, Cattaraugus.SW 100
●Chapinville, Ontario.......W 200
●Chappaqua, Westchester.SE 735
Charleston, Montgomery....E 125
Charleston Four Corners, Montgomery...........E 175
●Charlotte, Monroe........W 930
Charlotte Centre, Chau'qua.SW 100
Charlotteville, Schoharie....E 100
Charlton, Saratoga..........E 175
Chase, Otsego...............C ×
Chase's Lake, Lewis.........N 300
Chase's Mills, St. Lawrence. N 200
Chaseville, Otsego...........C 85
Chasm Falls, Franklin....NE 100
●Chateaugay, Franklin...NE 1,172
Chateaugay Lake, Frank'nNE 500
●Chatham, Columbia.......SE 1,912
●Chatham Centre, Col'bia.SE 400
Chatham Four Corners, (see Chatham)............... ×
●Chaumont, Jefferson.....N 623
●Chauncey, Westchester..SE 100
●Chautauqua, Chaut'qua.SW 300
●Chazy, Clinton..........NE 1,000
●*Chazy Junc.*, Clinton...NE ×
●*Chazy Lake*, Clinton....NE ×
●Cheektowaga, Erie.......W 200
Cheever, Essex............NE 50
Chelsea, Richmond.........SE ×

●Chemung, Chemung.......S 375
Chemung Centre, Chemung.S ×
●Chenango Bridge, BroomeS 50
●Chenango Forks, Broome.S 450
Chenango Lake, Chenango..C ×
Cheningo, Cortland..........C 200
●Chepachet, Herkimer....N 50
●Cherry Creek, Chau'qua SW 676
●Cherry Valley, Otsego.....C 685
●*Cherubusco*, Clinton....NE 300
Cheshire, Ontario...........W 250
●Chester, Orange.........SE 800
Chester, (see Chestertown)... ×
Chesterfield, Essex........NE 75
Chestertown, Warren.....NE 800
Chesterville, (see Westerlo)... ×
Chestnut Ridge, Dutchess. SE 30
Cheviot, Columbia...........SE ×
●*Chicago*, Cortland.........C ×
●*Chichesters*, Ulster.......SE 350
Childwold, St. Lawrence....N ×
●*ChildwoldSta.*,Franklin NE ×
●Chili, Monroe..............W 100
Chili Junc., Monroe........W ×
●Chili Station, Monroe....W ×
Chiloway, Delaware........SE 35
China, Delaware.............SE ×
Chippewa Bay, St.Lawrence N 100
Chipmunk, Cattaraugus.. SW ×
●Chittenango, Madison.....C 792
●Chittenango Falls, Madi'n C 150
●Chittenango Sta.,Madison.C 200
Chittenden's Falls,(see Stockport)............... ×
Choconut Centre, Broome...S 150
Christian Hook, (see Rockville Centre)........... ×
●*Chubbs Dock*,Washington E 400
Churchtown, Columbia....SE 200
●Churchville, Monroe.....W 493
●*ChurchvilleJunc.*,MonroeW ×
●Churubusco,Clinton.....NE 300
Cicero, Onondaga...........C 275
Cicero Centre, Monroe.....W ×
●Cigarville, Onondaga.......C 50
Cincinnatus, Cortland.......C 650
Cinconia, Yates..............W ×
●Circleville, Orange.......SE 210
City, (see Smithfield).......... ×
City Island, Westchester...SE 1,206
Clare, St. Lawrence.........N ×
●*ClaremontPark*,New York SE ×
●Clarence, Erie.............W 500
●Clarence Centre, Erie....W 848
***Clarenceville*, (see Richmond Hill)..................** ×
Clarendon, Orleans.........W 300
Clarksborough,St Lawrence N 75
Clarksburgh, Erie...........W 200
Clark's Corners, (seeGansevoort) ×
●Clark's Mills, Oneida......C 393
Clarks Mills, Washington...E 50
Clarkson, Monroe...........W 319
Clarksville, Albany..........E 600
Clarksville, Allegany......SW ×
Clarksville, (see Middlefield). ×
Claryville, Sullivan.........SE 175
●Claverack, Columbia....SE 350
●*Clay*, Onondaga............C 300
Clayburgh, Clinton.........NE 50
●Clayton, Jefferson.........N 1,748
Clayton Center, Jefferson...N 50
●Clayville, Oneida...........C 843
Clear Creek, Chautauqua. SW 400
Clear Pond, Franklin.....NE ×
●Clear View, Cayuga.........C 400
Cleaver, Delaware..........SE ×
Clermont, Columbia.........SE 200
●Cleveland, Oswego..........C 839
Cleverdale, Warren........NE ×
Clifford, Oswego.............C ×
●*Clifton*, Chautauqua....SW ×
Clifton, Monroe.............W 150
Clifton, Niagara............W ×
●*Clifton*, Richmond........SE 1,700
Clifton Mines, St. Lawrence N ×
Clifton Park, Saratoga......E 225
●Clifton Springs, Ontario..W 1,297
●Clinton, Oneida.............C 1,269
●Clinton Corners,Dutch's.SE 300
●Clintondale, Ulster......SE 600
Clinton Hollow, Dutchess..SE 400
●Clinton Mills, Clinton...NE 100
Clinton Point, Dutchess...SE 50
●Clintonville, Clinton....NE 306
●Clockville, Madison.......C 200
Clove, Dutchess.............SE ×

●Clove BranchJunc.,Dut'sSE ×
Clove Church, Ulster......SE ×
Clovesville, Delaware......SE 85
●Clove Valley, Dutchess..SE 250
Club House, Orange........SE ×
Clums Corners, (see Cropseyville)..................... ×
●Clyde, Wayne.............W 2,638
●Clymer, Chautauqua.....SW 600
●Cobleskill, Schoharie.....E 1,822
Cobleskill Centre, (see Mineral Spring)................. ×
●Cochecton, Sullivan......SE 200
Cochecton Centre, SullivanSE 50
●Cockburn, Ulster.........SE ×
Coeymans, Albany..........E 1,200
Coeymans Hollow, Albany..E 300
●Coeymans Junction,Alb'y.E 100
Coeyman's Landing,(see Coeymans)................ ×
Coffin's Summit,(see Oak Summit)................... ×
●Cohocton, Steuben......SW 1,200
●Cohoes, Albany...........E 22,509
Cohoes Depot, Albany.......E ×
Colla, Washington...........E 180
Cokertown, Dutchess......SE 65
Colchester, Delaware......SE 75
●*Colchester Station*, Del'e.SE ×
Cold Brook, Herkimer......N 350
●*Cold Brook*, Ulster......SE ×
●Colden, Erie...............W 300
Coldenham, Orange..........SE 200
●*Cold Spring*,CattaraugusSW ×
Cold Spring, Onondaga.....C ×
●Cold Spring, Putnam....SE 3,500
●*Cold Spring*, Queens.....SE ×
Cold Spring Harbor, Suff'kSE 1,000
●*Cold Springs*, Steuben..SW ×
●Cold Water, Water.......W ×
Colemans, Oneida............C ×
●Coleman Station, Dutch'sSE 40
Coles Basin, Ulster.........SE ×
Cole's Mills, Putnam.......SE ×
Colesville, Broome..........S 528
Collamer, Onondaga.........C 100
●College Point, Queens...SE 6,127
●Colliersville, Otsego.......C 200
Collingwood, Onondaga.....C 100
●Collins, Erie...............W ×
Collins Centre, Erie........W 300
Collinsville, Lewis..........N 100
Colman's Mills, Oneida.....C 100
Colosse, Oswego..............C 150
Colton, St. Lawrence........N 635
Columbia, Herkimer.........N 100
Columbia, (see East Poestenkill)......................... ×
Columbia Sprs., (seeStottville) ×
Columbia Sprs., Herkimer. N ×
Columbiaville, Columbia.. SE ×
Columbus, Chenango........C 200
Columbusville, Queens.....SE ×
Commack, Suffolk..........SE 300
Como, Cayuga................C ×
●Comstock's, Washington..E 150
Concord, Erie................W ×
Concord, Richmond........SE 175
Conesus, Livingston........W 300
●Conesus Centre, Liv'ston.W 500
●*Conesus Lake Junction*, Livingston...............W ×
Conesville, Schoharie.......E 57
Conewango, Cattaraugus..SW 500
●Conewango Valley, Chautauqua................SW 450
●Coney Island, Kings.....SE 3,313
●Congers, Rockland.......SE ×
●Conklin Centre, Broome... 300
Conkling Forks, Broome....S ×
Conklingville, Saratoga.....E 300
●Conklin Station, Broome..S 300
Connecticut, Tioga..........S ×
Connelly, Ulster............SE 800
Conquest, Cayuga...........C 100
Constable, Franklin........NE 200
Constableville, Lewis.......N 800
●Constantia, Oswego.......C 241
Constantia Centre, Oswego..C ×
Cooks, Ontario..............W ×
●*Cooks*, Steuben.........SW ×
Cooksburg, Albany...........E 100
Cook's Corners, Franklin. NE 200
●*Cook's Falls*, Delaware..SE 100
Cook's Point, Ontario......W ×
Cooley's Basin, Monroe....W ×
Coomer, Niagara.............W 100

Coomer Station, Niagara... W ×
Coonrod, Oneida... C ×
● *Coons*, Saratoga... E ×
Cooper's Falls, St. Lawrence N 60
● Cooper's Plains, Steuben SW 300
● **Cooperstown**, Otsego.. C 2,657
● *Cooperstown Junc.*, Otsego C 50
● Coopersville, Clinton.... NE 250
● Copake, Columbia... SE 300
Copake, (see Copake)... ×
Copake Depot, (see Copake Iron Works)... ×
Copake Flats, (see Copake).. ×
● Copake Iron W'ks, Col'a. SE 450
Copenhagen, Lewis... N 777
Coram, Suffolk... SE 180
Corbettsville, Broome... S 150
● Corfu, Genesee... W 398
● Corinth, Saratoga... E 1,222
● Cornell, Westchester.... SE 150
Cornell Landing, Queens.. SE ×
● **Corning**, Steuben..... SW 8,550
Cornwall, Orange... SE 1,000
● *Cornwall*, Orange... SE ×
● Cornwall Landing, Or'ge. SE ×
● Cornwall-on-the-Hudson, Orange... SE 760
Cornwallville, Greene..... SE 100
● Corona, Queens... SE 2,862
Corona Park, Queens..... SE ×
● **Cortland**, Cortland.... C 8,590
● *Cortland Junction*, Cort'd C ×
Cossayuna, Washington..... E 200
Cottage, Cattaraugus..... SW 100
Cottekill, Ulster... SE 100
● Cotton's Madison... C ×
Countrymans, Herkimer... N ×
● *County House*, Steuben. SW ×
County Line, Niagara... W 50
● *County Line*, Orleans.... W 250
County Line, Sullivan..... SE ×
Couse, Rensselaer... E 40
Cove Neck, Queens... SE ×
Coventry, Chenango... C 300
● *Coventry*, Chenango... C 150
Coventryville, Chenango.... C 150
● Covert, Seneca... C 200
Coveville, Saratoga... E 70
Covington, Wyoming... W 300
● *Cowenhaven Lane*, Kings SE ×
Cowlesville, Wyoming..... W 300
● *Coxsackie*, Greene... SE 1,000
● Coxsackie, Greene... SE 1,611
● Coxsackie Sta., Columbia SE 75
Cox's Landing, (see St. Johnsville)... ×
Crab Meadow, Suffolk..... SE ×
● Craft's, Putnam... SE 100
● *Craigs*, Livingston... W ×
● Craigsville, Orange... SE 150
● *Crains Mills*, Cortland.... C 25
● Cranberry Creek, Fulton.. E 350
Cranberry Lake, St. Lawrence N ×
Crandell's Corners, Wash'n. E 100
● Cranesville, Montgomery. E 100
● *Cranston's* Orange... SE 2,237
Crary's Mills, St. Lawrence. N 150
● Craryville, Columbia.... SE 75
Crawford, Ulster... SE 50
● *Crawford Junction*, Or'ge SE ×
Cream Street, Dutchess.... SE ×
● Creedmoor, Queens... SE ×
Creek Centre, Warren.... NE 200
Creek Locks, Ulster... SE 150
● *Crescent*, Albany... E ×
Crescent, Saratoga... E 300
● Crittenden, Erie... W 150
Croghan, Lewis... N 445
Cronomer's Valley, Orange SE ×
Cropseyville, Rensselaer.... E 150
Crosby, Yates... W 25
Cross Lake, Onondaga... C ×
Cross River, Westchester.. SE 250
● *Crosstown Junction*, Erie W ×
Croton, Delaware... SE 400
● *Croton*, Putnam... SE ×
● Croton Falls, Westchest'r SE 300
● Croton Lake, Westchst'r. SE ×
● Croton-on-Hudson, Westch'r SE 700
Crouse's Store, Dutchess.. SE 80
● *Crowner's*, Allegany.... SW ×
● Crown Point, Essex.... NE 1,000
Crown Point Centre, Essex NE 550
● Crugers, Westchester.... SE 150
Crum Creek, Fulton... E ×
Crum Elbow, Dutchess... SE 50
Crumhorn, Otsego... C ×

Crystal Dale, Lewis... N ×
● Crystal Run, Orange.... SE ×
Crystal Spring, Yates... W 50
● Cuba, Allegany... SW 1,386
● *Cuddeback's*, Ontario.... W ×
● Cuddebackville, Orange.. SE 300
Cullen, Herkimer... N 75
● *Cummings*, Essex... NE ×
● *Curriers*, Wyoming..... W 100
Curry's, Sullivan... SE ×
Currytown, Montgomery... E 50
● Curtis, Steuben... SW 35
● Cutchogue, Suffolk..... SE 600
Cutler's Basin, Ulster..... SE ×
Cutting, Chautauqua..... SW 100
● Cuyler, Cortland... C 450
● Cuylerville, Livingston... W 300
● *Cuylerville*, Livingston.... W ×
● *Cypress Avenue*, Kings.. SE ×
Cypress Hills, Kings..... SE ×
Dairyland, Ulster... SE ×
Daisy, Ulster... SE 50
● Dale, Wyoming... W 150
● Dalton, Livingston... W 500
Danby, Tompkins... S 300
Dannatberg, Lewis... N ×
● Dannemora, Clinton.... NE 500
● Dansville, Livingstown.. W 3,758
● Danube, Herkimer... N 200
● Darien, Genesee... W 200
Darien Centre, Genesee.... W 200
Dashville, (see Rifton Glen).. ×
Davenport, Delaware... SE 500
● Davenport C'ntre, D'lw'e SE 200
Davids Island, Westches'r. SE ×
Davis, Sullivan... SE ×
● *Davis Crossing*, Chenango C ×
Daws, Genesee... W ×
Day, Saratoga... E 150
Day Centre, (see Day)... ×
● Daysville, Oswego... C 50
● Dayton, Cattaraugus.... SW 500
Dean's Corners, Saratoga... E 150
● Deansville, Oneida... C 200
De Bruce, Sullivan... SE 250
Decatur, Otsego... C 700
Deck, Herkimer... N 150
Deckers, Ulster... SE ×
Decker's Dock, Sullivan.... SE ×
Deerfield, Oneida... C 691
Deer Lick, Cattaraugus... SW ×
● Deer Park, Suffolk..... SE 100
● Deer River, Lewis... N 200
Defreestville, Rensselaer... E 100
De Grasse, St. Lawrence.... N ×
De Groff, Cayuga... C ×
De Kalb, St. Lawrence..... N 300
● De Kalb Junc., St. L'rence N 300
● De Lancey, Delaware.... SE 150
● *Delano*, Essex... NE ×
● *Delevan*, Erie... W ×
● *Delaware*, Erie... W ×
Delaware Acqueduct, Sul'n SE 75
Delaware Bridge, (see Tusten) ×
● **Delhi**, Delaware... SE 1,564
● Delmar, Albany... E 200
● *Delphi*, Madison... C ×
Delphi, Onondaga... C 300
Delta, Oneida... C 186
De Mott, Seneca... C ×
Demster, Oswego... C ×
Dempster's, Herkimer..... N ×
Denison, Herkimer... N ×
Denmark, Lewis... N 200
Denning, Ulster... SE 100
Dennisons Cors, (see Mohawk) ×
● *Denniston's*, Orange.... SE ×
Denton's Cors. (see Osb'n B'dge) ×
Denver, Delaware... SE ×
Depauville, Jefferson... N 400
De Peyster, St. Lawrence... N 250
● **Deposit**, Broome... S 1,530
● Derby, Erie... W ×
● De Ruyter, Madison... C 667
● *De Sono*, Onondaga... C ×
● Devereux Sta., Catta'gus SW ×
Deveraux, (see Stratford).... ×
De Witt, Onondaga... C 200
● *De Witt*, Onondaga... C 2,231
● De Witt Centre, Onondaga C 50
● De Wittville, Chauta'qua SW 300
Dexter, Jefferson... N 737
Dexterville, (see Jamestown). ×
Dexterville, Oswego... C 25
Dey's Landing, Seneca... C ×
Diamond, Herkimer... N ×

Diamond, Jefferson... N ×
● Diana, Lewis... N ×
Diana Station, Lewis... N ×
Dickerson, Cattaraugus.. SW ×
Dickerson's Eddy, Sullivan SE ×
Dickinson, Franklin..... NE 800
● Dickinson Centre, Fr'ln. NE 1,500
Dinehart's, Steuben... SW ×
Disco, Clinton... NE ×
Divine's Corners, Sullivan.. SE 100
● Dix, Oneida... C ×
● Dobbs Ferry, West'ster.. SE 2,083
Dolgeville, Herkimer... N 800
● Dongan Hills, Richmond SE 150
Doraville, Broome... S 65
Dormansville, Albany..... E 150
Dosoris, Queens... SE ×
● *Dougals*, Cayuga... C ×
● Douglass, Essex... NE ×
● Douglaston, Queens.... SE ×
Dover, (see Dover Plains).... ×
● Dover Furnace, Dutchess SE 100
● Dover Plains, Dutchess.. SE 662
● *Downing*, Montgomery.. E ×
Downsville, Delaware..... SE 550
Doyle, Erie... W ×
● Dresden, Yates... W 348
● Dresden Centre, Wash'ton E 400
● Dresden Sta., Wash'gton.. E [illegible]
Dresserville, Cayuga... C [illegible]
● *Driving Park*, Monroe.. W [illegible]
Dry Brook, Ulster... SE 400
● Dryden, Tompkins... S 663
Dryden Springs, Tompkins. S ×
Duane, Franklin... NE 285
● Duanesburgh, Schenectady E 150
Dugway, Oswego... C 100
Dunbarton, Oneida... C ×
● Dundee, Yates... W 1,200
Dundee Depot, Yates..... W ×
Dunham Hollow, Rensselaer E ×
● Dunham's Basin, Wash'tn E ×
● Dunkirk, Chautauqua.. SW 9,416
Dunn Brook, Oneida... C 100
Dunnings, Yates... W ×
Dunnsville, Albany... E 100
Dunraven, Delaware... SE 30
● *Dunsbeck Ferry*, Albany.. E ×
Dunton, Queens... SE ×
● *Dunwoodie*, Westchester SE ×
Durham, Greene... SE 300
● Durhamville, Oneida..... C 730
● Dutchess Junc., Dut'ess.. SE 100
Dutch Kills, (see Long Island City)... ×
Dutch Settlement, Herkimer N ×
Dwaar Kill, Ulster... SE 200
● *Dyke*, Allegany... SW ×
Dyke, Steuben... SW 21
● Dykeman's, Putnam..... SE 50
Dysinger, Niagara... W ×
● Eagle, Wyoming... W 200
● Eagle Bridge, Rensselaer.. E 450
Eagle Harbor, Orleans..... W 500
● *Eagle Harbor Sta.*, Orl'ns W ×
Eagle Mills, Rensselaer..... E 406
● *Eagle Valley*, Rockland SE ×
Eaglevillage, Onondaga.... C 60
● Earl, Yates... W ×
● *Earl's*, Wyoming... W ×
● Earlville, Madison... C 536
● *East Albany*, Rensselaer. E ×
● *East Alexander*, Genesee W ×
East Amherst, Erie... W ×
East Arcade, Wyoming.... W ×
East Arcadia, Wayne..... W ×
East Ashford, Cattaraugus SW 40
● East Aurora, Erie... W 1,582
East Avon, Livingston..... W 200
● East Beekmantown, Clin'n NE 300
East Berne, Albany... E 100
● East Bethany, Genesee... W 200
● East Bloomfield, Ontario. W 1,000
● East Bloomfield Sta., On'to W ×
● East Boston, Madison..... C 150
● East Branch, Delaware.. SE 258
East Brook, Delaware..... SE 258
East Brunswick, (see Cropseyv'e) ×
● East Buffalo, Erie... W ×
● *East Buffalo Junc.*, Erie. W ×
● *East Buskirk's*, Erie..... W ×
East Camp, (see Germanto'n) ×
East Campbell, Steuben... SW 75
● East Carlton, Orleans.... W ×
East Cayuga Villa'e, Ontario W ×
● East Chatham, Columbia SE 400
East Chazy, (see Chazy)..... ×

New York
New York

Place	Population
East Chester, Westchester.SE	300
● *East Chester*, Orange....SE	×
● East Clarence, Erie.......W	50
East Clarkson, (see Clarkson)	×
East Cobleskill, Schoharie.. E	×
East Coldenham, Orange.. SE	×
● East Concord, Erie.......W	200
East Constable, Franklin..NE	×
● East Corning, Steuben..SW	×
● East Creek, Herkimer....N	50
East Davenport, (seeDavenport)	×
East Dickinson, Franklin. NE	300
East Durham, Greene......SE	200
East Eden, Erie.............W	100
East Elba, Genesee.........W	×
East Elma, Erie............ W	125
East Elmira, Chemung......S	×
East Evans, Erie.......... W	×
East Fishkill, Dutchess.... SE	150
East Florence, Oneida.......C	100
East Floyd, Oneida..........E	×
East Frankfort, (see Frankfo't)	×
East Freetown, Cortland....C	×
East Gaines, Orleans........W	30
East Galway, Saratoga...... E	200
East Genoa, Cayuga..........C	×
East German, Chenango.... C	×
● EastGlenville, Schenect'dyE	65
East Grafton, (see Grafton)..	×
East Granger, Allegany...SW	×
East Greenbush, Rensselaer. E	96
East Greenwich, WashingtonE	500
East Groveland, Livingston W	80
● East Guilford, Chenango.. C	150
● *East Hamburg*, Erie.....W	×
East Hamilton, Madison.....C	100
● East Hamlin, Monroe.... W	50
East Hampton, Suffolk.... SE	500
East Hartford, Washington. E	75
● *East Hinsdale*, Queens..SE	200
● East Homer, Cortland.....C	75
East Houndsfield, Jefferson. N	75
East Hunter, (seeTannersvi'e)	×
East Islip, Suffolk..........SE	1,000
East Java, Wyoming........W	150
East Jewett, Greene........ SE	50
East Junius, (see Junius)....	×
● East Kendall, Orleans....W	120
East Kingston, Ulster......SE	×
East Koy, Wyoming.........W	100
● *East Lancaster*, Erie.....W	×
East Lansing, Tompkins.....S	50
East Leon, Cattaraugus... SW	×
East Lexington, (seeJewettCentre)	×
● East Line, Saratoga.......E	150
East Lockport, Niagara....W	×
East McDonough, Chenango C	50
East Maine, Boone..........S	×
East Marion, Suffolk.......SE	400
● East Martinsburgh, Lewis N	60
East Masonville, Delaware.SE	50
East Mendon, (see Mendon).	×
East Melrose, (seeNew York)	×
East Meredith, Delaware.. SE	500
East Moriches, Suffolk....SE	375
East Morrisania, (seeNewYork)	×
East Mount Vernon, Westchester .... SE	×
East Nassau, Rensselaer.... E	300
East Newark, Wayne......W	×
● *East New York*, Kings.NE	×
East Nichols, Tioga..........S	×
East Norwich, Queens.....SE	400
East Oakfield, Genesee..... W	80
Easton, Washington .... E	200
● *Easton*, Washington......E	×
East Oneonta, (see Oneonta).	×
East Onondaga, Onondaga.. C	300
● *East Oswego*, Oswego.....C	×
East Otto, Cattaraugus.... SW	300
East Palermo, Oswego...... C	100
● East Palmyra, Wayne.... W	100
East Park, Dutchess....... SE	280
East Patchogue, Suffolk...SE	×
● East Pembroke, Genesee. W	300
East Penfield, Monroe......W	50
East Pharsalia, Chenango...C	275
East Pitcairn, St. Lawrence.N	×
East Poestenkill, Rensselaer. E	100
● Eastport, Suffolk........ SE	150
East Port Chester, (see Port Chester)...............	×
● *Eastport Junction*, Suffolk....................SE	×
East Poughkeepsie, (see Arlington)............	×
East Quogue, Suffolk...... SE	100
East Randolph, C'ttaraugusSW	700
East Richfield, (see Richfield Springs)....................	×
● East River, Cortland......C	35
● *East Rochester*, Monroe..W	×
● East Rockaway, Queens.SE	1,250
East Rodman, Jefferson.....N	150
East Rush, Monroe.........W	400
East Salem, Washington.....E	150
● *EastSaratogaJunc.*,S'togaE	×
● *East Schaghticoke*,R'ss'l'rE	1,258
East Schodack, Rensselaer..E	300
● East Schuyler, Herkimer.N	100
East Scott, Cortland.........C	×
East Seneca, Erie...........W	70
East Setauket, Suffolk.....SE	×
East Shelby, Orleans....... W	150
East Sidney, Delaware.....SE	100
East Smithville, Chenango..C	25
East Springfield, Otsego.....C	300
East Steamburgh,SchuylerSW	82
● East Steuben, Oneida.....C	×
EastStockholm,St.LawrenceN	250
East Taghkanick, (see Taghkanick)	×
East Tarrytown, W'stch'st'rSE	×
East Troupsburgh, Steub'nSW	×
East Unadilla, (see Wells' Bridge)..................	×
● *East Utica*, Oneida.......C	×
East Varick, Seneca.........C	100
East Venice, Cayuga......... C	50
East Victor, (see Victor)....	×
● Eastview, Westchester.. SE	×
East Virgil, Cortland.......C	75
● *East Walden*, Orange...SE	×
East Watertown, Jefferson. N	×
East Williamsburg, QueensSE	×
● *East Waverly*, Tioga.....S	400
East Williamson, Wayne...W	×
● East Williston, Queens...SE	200
East Wilson, Niagara.......W	×
East Windham, Greene....SE	15
● East Windsor, Broome....S	×
● *East Winfield*, Herkimer. N	150
Eastwood, Onondaga........C	×
● East Worcester, Otsego...C	500
● Eaton, Madison.......... C	750
Eatonville, Herkimer.......N	100
● Ebenezer, Erie..........W	106
Echo, Suffolk..............SE	×
● Eddytown, Yates.........W	150
Eddyville, Cattaraugus....SW	552
Eddyville, Ulster..........SE	500
● Eden, Erie.............. W	500
Eden Centre, (see Eden)......	×
Edenton, St. Lawrence.....N	×
● Eden Valley, Erie........W	150
Edenville, Orange..........SE	150
Edgewater, Richmond.....SE	14,265
● Edgewood, Greene.......SE	250
● *Edgewood Siding*, MonroeW	×
Edicks, Herkimer.......... N	50
Edinburgh, Saratoga....... E	150
● Edmeston, Otsego.........C	500
Edmeston Centre, (see Edmeston)......................	×
Edson, Broome.............S	×
Edwards, St. Lawrence.... N	345
Edwardsville, St. Lawrence. N	200
Eggertsville, Erie..........W	100
Egypt, Monroe............ W	151
Eighmyville, Dutchess.....SE	×
● Elba, Genesee...........W	428
Elbow, Warren............NE	200
Elbridge, Onondaga.........C	693
Eldred, Sullivan.......... SE	150
● *Eldridge Park*, Chemung.S	×
Elgin, Cattaraugus........ SW	25
Elizabethtown, Essex.NE	573
● Elizaville, Columbia.....SE	86
● *Elk*, Cattaraugus....... SW	×
Elk Creek, Otsego...........C	120
Elkdale, Cattaraugus......SW	×
Elkhorn, Onondaga......... C	×
Elko, Cattaraugus........ SW	×
Ellenburgh, Clinton.......NE	500
Ellenburgh Centre, ClintonNE	500
Ellenburg Corners, (see Ellenburg)..................	×
● EllenburghDepot,Clint'nNE	400
● Ellenville, Ulster.........SE	2,881
● *Ellerslie*, Columbia......SE	×
Ellery, Chautauqua........SW	150
Ellicott, Erie..............W	25
● Ellicottsville, C'taraug's.SW	852
Ellington, Chautauqua ....SW	350
Ellis, Tompkins............S	×
Ellisburgh, Jefferson.......N	336
Ellsworth, Cayuga..........C	×
Elma, Erie.................W	200
● Elma Centre, Erie........W	×
Elmdale, St. Lawrence......N	×
● **Elmira**, Chemung.......S	30,893
Elmon, (see Chapachet)......	×
Elmont, Queens............SE	200
Elmore, (see Esopus).........	×
● *Elm Park*, Richmond...SE	175
● Elmsford, Westchester...SE	250
● Elm Valley. Allegany...SW	×
Elmwood Park, Onondaga..C	×
Elpis, Oneida...............C	×
Elsinore, (see Cadyville)......	×
● *Eltingville*, Richmond...SE	75
● Elton, Cattaraugus......SW	100
Elwood, Suffolk............SE	100
Emerson, Cayuga...........C	×
Eminence, Schoharie........E	150
Emmonsburg, Fulton........E	100
Emmonsville, Sullivan.....SE	×
Empyville, Oneida..........C	×
Enfield, Tompkins..........S	200
Enfield Centre, Tompkins...S	200
Enfield Falls, Tompkins.....S	40
English Brook, Cattar'ua.SW	×
● *Ennerdale*, Ontario......W	250
Eno, Dutchess.............SE	×
Enos, Oneida...............C	×
● Ensenore, Cayuga.........C	×
Enterprise, Dutchess ......SE	×
Ephratah, Fulton............E	400
● *Erastina*, Richmond....SE	2,000
● Erieville, Madison C	200
● Erin, Chemung............S	200
● Erwin, Steuben..........SW	25
● Esopus, Ulster............SE	300
● Esperance, Schoharie.....E	274
Essex, Essex...............NE	600
● *Essex Station*, Essex....NE	×
● Etna, Tompkins..........S	400
Euclid, Onondaga...........C	300
Eureka, Sullivan...........SE	500
Evans, Erie.................W	400
Evans Creamery, Broome..S	×
● Evans' Mills, Jefferson.....N	578
Evansville, Washington.....E	×
Evergreen, Queens.........SE	200
Everton, Franklin.........NE	×
Exeter, Otsego..............C	50
Fabius, Onondaga...........C	312
Factoryville, Richmond...SE	×
Factoryville, (see Waverly)..	×
Fairchilds, Steuben.......SW	×
Fair Dale, Oswego...........C	50
Fairfield, Herkimer.........N	300
Fairground, Suffolk........SE	×
● *Fair Ground*, Monroe ... W	×
● Fair Haven, Cayuga.......C	738
Fair Haven, Orleans.......C	50
Fair Mount, New York...SE	×
● Fair Mount, Onondaga....C	75
● Fair Oaks, Orange.......SE	×
● Fairport, Monroe.........W	2,552
● Fairview, Cattaraugus...SW	50
● *Fairview*, Wyoming......W	×
● Fairville, Wayne........ W	100
● Falconer, Chautauqua...SW	574
● *Falconer Ju'ction*, C'q'aSW	×
● *Falkirk*, Erie.............W	×
● *Falls*, Tompkins..........S	×
● Fallsburgh, Sullivan.....SE	150
● *Fallsburgh Sta.*, SullivanSE	50
● *Falls Junction*, Niagara..W	×
Falls Mill, Sullivan.........SE	50
● Fargo, Genesee............W	×
● Farlin, Albany...........E	190
Farmers Mills, Putnam....SE	100
Farmersville, Cattaraugus.SW	109
● FarmersvilleSta.Cat'g's..SW	200
● Farmer Village, Seneca...C	660
● Farmingdale, Queens....SE	575
Farmingdale, Orange.....SE	×
Farmington, Ontario.......W	150
● Farnham, Erie...........W	250
● Far Rockaway, Queens..SE	2,288
Fawns, Ulster...............SE	100
Fayette, Seneca............C	400
● *Fayette Siding*, Seneca...C	×
● Fayetteville, Onondaga....C	1,410
Federal Stores, (see Chatham)	×
● Felt's Mills, Jefferson.....N	300
Fenner, Madison............C	75
Fenner's Grove, Herkimer..N	×
● Fentonville, ChautauquaSW	300

Place	Section	Population
● Highlands Sta., Putnam	SE	490
High Market, Lewis	N	200
Highmount, Ulster	SE	30
Highup, Steuben	SW	×
Highview, Sullivan	SE	×
High Woods, Ulster	SE	500
● Hillburn, Rockland	SE	150
Hills, Ontario	W	×
● Hillsdale, Columbia	SE	350
Hillside, Columbia	SE	×
Hillside, Oneida	C	100
Hill Siding, Tompkins	S	×
Hill View, Warren	NE	125
Hiltonville, Alleghany	SW	60
● Himrods, Yates	W	325
Himrod's Junction, Yates	W	×
Hinckley, Herkimer	N	75
Hindsburgh, Orleans	W	300
Hinmansville, Oswego	C	100
● Hinsdale, Cattaraugus	SW	200
Hinsdale, (see East Hinsdale)		×
Hoag's Corners, Rensselaer	E	241
● Hobart, Delaware	SE	561
Hobokenville, Madison	C	×
● *Hodgeville*, Niagara	W	×
● *Hoffman*, Niagara	W	×
● Hoffman's, Schenectady	E	150
Hoffman's Gate, (see Martindale Depot)		×
Hogansburgh, Franklin	NE	250
Holbrook, Suffolk	SE	100
● Holland, Erie	W	582
● Holland Patent, Oneida	C	406
Hollands, Queens	SE	×
● Holley, Orleans	W	1,381
● Hollis, Queens	SE	×
Hollowville, Columbia	SE	150
Hollywood, St. Lawrence	N	×
● Holmes, Dutchess	SE	50
Holmes Mill, (see Stockholm Centre)		×
● Holmesville, Chenango	C	150
● *Homesville*, Oswego	C	150
● Holtsville, Suffolk	SE	×
● Homer, Courtland	C	2,500
Homestead, St. Lawrence	N	×
● *Homowack*, Ulster	SE	100
Honeoye, Ontario	W	300
● Honeoye Falls, Monroe	W	1,128
● *Honeoye Junc.*, Livingst'n	W	×
Honesville, Orange	SE	×
Honnedaga, Herkimer	N	×
Hooker, Lewis	N	×
● Hooper, Broome	S	150
Hooper's Valley, Tioga	S	100
● Hoosick, Rensselaer	E	300
Hoosick Corners, (see Hoosick)		×
Hoosick Falls, Rensselaer	E	7,014
● *Hoosick Junc.*, Rensselaer	E	50
Hope, Hamilton	NE	200
Hope Centre, (see Hope)		×
Hope Falls, Hamilton	NE	50
Hope's Hill, St. Lawrence	N	×
● *Hopeton*, Yates	W	50
● Hopewell Ontario	W	250
Hopewell Centre, Ontario	W	50
● Hopewell Junc., D'tchess	SE	250
Hopkinton, St. Lawrence	N	400
Hornbeck's Bridge, Ulster	SE	×
Hornbeck's Culvert, Orange	SE	×
Hornby, Steuben	SW	150
● Hornellsville, Steuben	SW	10,996
Hornellsville Junction, Steuben	SW	×
● Horseheads, Chemung	S	1,716
Horseshoe Siding, Catt's	SW	×
Horton, Delaware	SE	60
Hortons, Delaware	SE	×
Hortonville, Sullivan	SE	100
Hotel Champlain, Clinton	NE	30
● Houghton, Allegany	SW	200
● *Houton Farm*, Orange	SE	×
Houndsfield, (see East Houndsfield)		×
House Creek, Lewis	N	×
Houseville, Lewis	N	100
Howard, Steuben	SW	500
● *Howard's*, Essex	NE	×
● *Howard's Mill*, Wyoming	W	×
Howardville, Oswego	C	×
● Howell's Depot, Orange	SE	250
● Howe's Cave, Schoharie	E	150
Howlet Hill, Onondaga	C	×
● *Howlett's*, Cattaraugus	SW	×
● Hubbardsville, Madison	C	350
Hubbs, Saratoga	E	×
● **Hudson**, Columbia	SE	9,970
● *Hudson Junc.*, Orange	SE	×
Hudson River State Hospital, Dutchess	SE	×
Hughsonville, Dutchess	SE	200
● Huguenot, Orange	SE	350
● *Huguenot*, Richmond	SE	100
Hulbert's Mill, Lewis	N	×
Hulberton, Orleans	W	350
Hulett's Landing, Wash'gt'n	E	×
Hull's Mills, Dutchess	SE	60
● *Humaston*, Oneida	C	×
Hume, Allegany	SW	450
Humphrey, Cattaraugus	SW	25
Humphrey Centre, Catt's	SW	300
Humphreysville, Columbia	SE	65
Humphreys, Cattaraugus	SW	×
● Hunter, Greene	SE	699
Hunter's Land, Schoharie	E	300
Hunter's Point, (see Long Island City)		×
● *Huntington*, Suffolk	SE	×
Huntington, Suffolk	SE	3,028
● Hunt's, Livingston	W	300
Hunt's Corners, Cortland	C	175
● *Hunter's Point*, New York	SE	×
Huntsville, (see West Day)		×
Hurd, Sullivan	SE	×
Hurlberts, Chautauqua	SW	×
Hurley, Ulster	SE	800
● Hurleyville, Sullivan	SE	100
Huron, Wayne	W	200
Hurstville, Albany	E	×
● Husteds, Dutchess	SE	×
● Hyde Park, Dutchess	SE	700
● *Hyde Park*, Queens	SE	250
● Hyndsville, Schoharie	E	500
Ice Pond Putnam	SE	×
Ida Hill, (see Troy)		×
● Idlewild, Orange	SE	×
Idlewild, Yates	W	×
● *Idlewood*, Erie	W	×
Igerna, Warren	NE	×
● Ilion, Herkimer	N	4,057
Illingworth Landing, Lewis	W	×
Inavale, Allegany	SW	×
Independence, Allegany	SW	75
Independence Creek, Lewis	N	×
● *Indian Castle*, Herkimer	N	30
Indian Falls, Genesee	W	250
Indian Fields, Albany	E	300
Indian Lake, Hamilton	NE	300
Indian River, Lewis	N	×
Indian Spring, Sullivan	SE	×
Ingalls' Crossing, Oswego	C	25
Ingham's Mills, Herkimer	N	125
Ingleside, Steuben	SW	50
Ingraham, Clinton, Clinton	NE	80
Inland, Erie	W	×
● Inman, Franklin	NE	×
● *International Junc.*, N.Y.	SE	×
Inwood, New York	SE	×
Inwood, Queens	SE	1,277
Ionia, (see Memphis)		×
● *Iona Island*, Rockland	SE	×
Ira, Cayuga	C	250
● Ira Station, Cayuga	C	×
Ira Village, Cayuga	C	×
Ireland Cors., (see Loudonville)		×
Ireland Cors., (see Modena)		×
Ireland's Mills, Chhenango	C	×
● Irona, Clinton	NE	100
Iron Bridge, Herkimer	N	×
Irondale, (see Petersburg)		×
Irondale, Dutchess	SE	×
Irondequoit, Monroe	W	300
Iron Junc., (see Millerton)		×
Ironville, Essex	NE	200
● *Iron Works*, Rensselaer	E	×
Irvine Mills, Cattaraugus	SW	×
● *Irving*, Cattaraugus	SW	×
● Irving, Chautauqua	SW	300
● *Irving Siding*, Chautau'a	SW	×
● Irvington, Westchester	SE	2,299
● Ischua, Cattaraugus	SW	300
Island Cottage, Otsego	C	×
Isle of Wight, (see Lawrence Station)		×
● Islip, Suffolk	SE	2,000
Italy, Yates	W	200
Italy Hill, Yates	W	100
Itaska, Broome	S	×
● **Ithaca**, Tompkins	S	11,079
● *Ithaca Junction*, Cayuga	C	×
● *Ithaca Junction*, Cortland	C	×
Ivanhoe, Delaware	SE	×
Jackson, Tompkins	S	×
● *Jacksonburgh*, Herkimer	N	150
● Jackson Corners, D'hess	SE	75
● *Jackson's*, Cayuga	SW	×
Jacksonville, (see Urlton)		×
Jacksonville, (see Mt. Vision)		×
Jacksonville, Tompkins	S	250
Jack's Reef, Onondaga	C	125
● **Jamaica**, Queens	SE	5,361
● Jamesport, Suffolk	SE	500
● Jamestown, Chautauqua	SW	16,038
● Jamesville, Onondaga	C	353
Jamesville, (see Middle Grove)		×
● Jamison Road, Erie	W	×
Jasper, Steuben	SW	350
● Java, Wyoming	W	100
● Java Centre, Wyoming	W	125
● *Java Lake*, Wyoming	W	×
Java Village, Wyoming	W	300
Jay, Essex	NE	600
Jaynes, Yates	W	×
● Jayville, St. Lawrence	N	×
Jeddo, Orleans	W	150
Jefferson, Schoharie	E	225
Jefferson Valley, Westch'r	SE	150
Jeffersonville, Sullivan	SE	300
Jenksville, Tioga	S	100
Jerden Falls, Lewis	N	×
Jericho, Queens	SE	450
Jericho Landing, Suffolk	SE	×
Jerome Park, Westchester	SE	×
Jerry, Oswego	C	×
Jerusalem, Albany	E	×
Jerusalem, Queens	SE	×
● *Jessups Landing*, Saratoga	E	1,222
Jewett, Greene	SE	250
Jewett Centre, Greene	SE	100
● Jewettville Erie	W	×
Johnsburgh, Warren	NE	900
Johnson's, Cattaraugus	SW	×
● Johnson's, Orange	SE	500
● Johnsonsburgh, Wyoming	W	300
Johnson's Creek, Niagara	W	300
Johnsontown, Rockland	SE	50
● Johnsonville, Rensselaer	E	700
● **Johnstown**, Fulton	W	7,768
Johnsville, Dutchess	SE	125
Jonesburg, Columbia	SE	50
Jonespoint, Rockland	SE	75
● Jonesville, Saratoga	E	150
● Jordan, Onondaga	C	1,271
Jordon Falls, Lewis	N	300
Jordanville, Herkimer	N	150
Joshua's Rock, Warren	NE	×
Joy, Wayne	W	310
● *Junction*, Cattaraugus	SW	×
● *Junction*, Chautauqua	SW	×
Junction, Chemung	S	×
● *Junction*, Genesee	W	×
● *Junction*, New York	SE	×
Junction, (see Melrose)		×
● *Junction Kilns*, Clinton	NE	×
Junius, Seneca	C	200
● Kaaterskill, Greene	SE	150
● *Kaaterskill Junc.*, Greene	SE	×
● Kanona, Steuben	SW	200
● Karner, Albany	E	40
Karrdale, Allegany	SW	×
● Kasoag, Oswego	C	100
● Katonah, Westchester	SE	524
Katrine, Ulster	SE	400
Katsbaan, Ulster	SE	100
Kattelville, Broome	S	240
Kattskill Bay, Warren	NE	100
Keck's Centre, Fulton	E	100
Keefer's Corners, Albany	E	×
Keeler's Hol'w, (see Chittenango)		×
Keene, Essex	NE	250
● *Keene*, St. Lawrence	N	×
Keene Flats, Essex	NE	×
Keene Valley, Essex	NE	60
Keeneville, (see Spragueville)		×
Keeney's Settlement, Cortla'd	C	50
Keerys, Delaware	SE	×
Keeryville, (see Fisher's Eddy)		×
Keeseville, Essex	NE	1,103
● *Keeleys*, Schenectady	E	×
Kelloggsville, Cayuga	C	200
● Kelly's Cor., Delaware	SE	50
Kelley's Cut, Ontario	W	×
Kelly's Station, Schenectady	E	15
Kelsey, Delaware	SE	×
Kendaia, Seneca	C	100
● **Kendall**, Orleans	W	350
Kendall Mills, Orleans	W	250
● *Kendall*, Chemung	S	25
Kenmore, Erie	W	×

New York
New York

Place	Pop.
● Kennedy, Chautauqua.. SW	514
Kenoza Lake, Sullivan.....SE	200
Kensico, Westchester......SE	250
● *Kensico*, Westchester....SE	×
● *Kensington*, Erie........W	×
Kent, Saratoga..............E	100
Kent Cliffs, Putnam.......SE	100
Kent, Chautauqua........SW	×
● Kenwood, Madison..........C	750
● *Kenwood Junc.*, Albany..E	×
Kenyonville, Orleans.......W	200
Kerhonkson, Ulster........SE	500
Ketchum, Otsego.........C	28
● Ketchum's Cor., Saratoga.E	300
Ketchumville, Tioga.........S	50
Keuka, Steuben...........SW	50
Keuka College, Yates...... W	300
● *Keuka Mills*, Yates......W	×
Keuka Vineyard, SteubenSW	50
Keyserite, Ulster.........SE	×
Kiantone, Chautauqua.... SW	100
Kidder's Ferry, Seneca......C	25
Kiersteds, Delaware.......SE	×
Kilkare, Yates.............W	×
● Killawog, Broome..........S	300
● Kill Buck, Cattaraugus. SW	400
Kinderhook, Columbia.... SE	963
● *Kings*, Saratoga...........E	220
● *Kingsboro*, Fulton.........E	×
● Kingsbridge, New York. SE	×
Kingsbury, Washington.....E	77
King's Ferry, Cayuga....... C	400
● *Kings Ferry Sta.*, Cayuga. C	×
● *Kings Highway*, Kings. SE	×
● King's Park, Suffolk.... SE	×
Kings Settlement, Chenango. C	40
● King's Station, Saratoga..E	×
● **Kingston**, Ulster..... SE	21,261
Kinney's Four Cor., Oswego C	×
Kinslers, Cayuga............C	×
● *Kipps*, Orange............SE	×
Kirk, Chenango..............C	×
● Kirkland, Oneida..........C	132
● Kirkville, Onondaga....... C	926
● Kirkwood, Broome........S	157
Kirkwood Centre, Broome..S	×
Kirschnerville, Lewis.......N	25
Kiskatom, Greene......... SE	200
● *Kitchawan*, WestchesterSE	150
Kline, Montgomery.........E	100
● *Knapps*, St. Kawrence... N	200
● Knapp's Creek, Cattar's. SW	350
Knappville, Wayne......... W	×
Knight's Cr., (see Allentown)	×
Knightsville, Allegany....SW	×
Knowelhurst, Warren.....NE	250
Knowersville, (see Altamont)	×
Knowlesville, Orleans...... W	400
● *Knowlesville Sta.*, OrleansW	×
Knox, Albany...............E	200
Knoxboro, Oneida...........C	200
Knox Corners, (see Knoxboro)	×
● *Knox Station*, Albany....E	×
Knoxville, (see Stockbridge).	×
Kokomo, St. Lawrence....N	×
Kortright, Delaware.......SE	×
● *Kossuth*, Allegany......SW	×
● *Kowenhovens*, Kings....SE	×
Kreischerville, Richmond. SE	125
Kripple Bush, Ulster...... SE	100
Krumville, Ulster......... SE	100
Kuckville, Orleans......... W	70
Kyserike, Ulster...........SE	×
Lacawack, Ulster.......... SE	200
Lackawanna & Pittsburg Jc., Genesee............ W	×
● Lacona, Oswego........... C	333
Ladentown, Rockland......SE	×
● La Fargeville, Jefferson.. N	425
● La Fayette, Onondaga.....C	146
La Fayetteville, Dutchess.. SE	50
La Grange, Wyoming........ W	125
● La Grangeville, DutchessSE	200
Laidlaw, Cattaraugus......SW	×
Lairdsville, Oneida..........C	100
● *Lake*, Orange............SE	×
Lake Beach, Monroe....... W	×
● *Lake Bonaparte*, Lewis.. N	×
Lake Delaware, Delaware..SE	50
● **Lake George**, Warren NE	500
LakeGeorgeAssembly, War'nNE	×
Lake Grove, Suffolk........SE	200
Lake Hill, Ulster.......... SE	200
Lake Katrine, Ulster......SE	200
● Lakeland Onondago......C	×
Lakeland, Suffolk......... SE	150
● *Lake Mahopac*, Putnam. SE	500

Place	Pop.
Lake Mohegan, (see Mohegan)	×
Lake Pleasant, Fulton.......E	×
Lake Pleasant, (see Sageville)	×
Lakeport, Madison..........C	250
● Lake Ridge, Tompkins....S	100
Lake Road, Niagara........W	×
● *Lake ShoreStation*, WayneW	×
Lake Side, Wayne.......... W	300
● *Lakeside*, Onondaga.......C	×
● Lake View, Erie...........W	25
● *Lake View*, Madison......C	×
● Lakeville, Livingston.....W	400
● *Lakeville*, Orange.........SE	×
Lake Waccubuc, Westche'rSE	×
● Lakewood, Chautauqua. SW	×
Lamberton, Chautauqua.. SW	×
Lamont, Wyoming.......... W	200
● Lamson's Onondaga....... C	100
● Lancaster, Erie...........W	1,692
Landing, Seneca...........C	×
Lanesburgh, Lewis..........N	×
● Lanesville, Greene.........SE	450
Langdon, Broome...........S	×
Langford, Erie.............W	200
Lansing, Oswego...........C	×
● Lansingburgh, RensselaerE	10,550
Lansing's Sta., (see Stillwater)	×
Lansingville, (see De Lancey).	×
Lansingville, Tompkins..... S	125
● Laona, Chautauqua.......SW	400
Lapeer, (see Hunt's Corners)..	×
● Lapham, Clinton........NE	300
● Larchmont, Westchester. SE	700
● La Salle, Niagara.........W	250
Lassellsville, Fulton..........E	400
● *Latham's Cor.*, Chenango.. C	×
● *Latimer*, Onondaga....... C	×
Lattingtown, Queens...... SE	×
Laurel Hill, Queens........SE	500
● *Laurel House Sta.*, GreeneSE	×
Laurelton, (see Cold Spr. Har.)	×
Laurens, Otsego............ C	255
Lava, Sullivan............. SE	×
● *Lawrence*, St. Lawrence.. N	×
Lawrence, Schuyler....... SW	50
● Lawrence Sta., Queens.. SE	626
● *Lawrenceville*, Greene....SE	×
Lawrenceville, St. Lawrence. N	300
Lawrenceville, (see Rosendale)	×
● Lawton, Orange........ SE	×
Lawton Station, Erie....... W	50
Lawyersville, Schoharie .... E	175
● Lebanon, Madison......... C	250
Lebanon Lake, Sullivan.... SE	×
● Lebanon Springs, C'lmba. SE	700
Lebonef's, Franklin....... NE	×
Ledyard, Cayuga........... C	100
Lee, Oneida............... C	125
Lee Centre, Oneida.........C	320
Lee Corners, (see Stokes).....	×
● Leeds, Greene.......... SE	400
Leedsville, Dutchess....... SE	75
Leek, Cattaraugus....... SW	×
● *Lees*, Washington........ E	×
Leesville, Schoharie........ E	100
Leibhardt, Ulster.......... SE	200
● *Lehigh Junction*, Monroe W	×
● *Leicester*, Livingston..... W	×
Leila, Oneida.............. C	×
Leipzig, Herkimer..........N	×
Lena, Otsego............... C	142
Lenig, Lewis............. N	×
Lenox, Madison.......... C	250
Lenox Basin, (see Wampsville)	×
Lenox Furnace, (see Clockville)	×
Lent, Dutchess .... SE	75
Lentsville, Otsego.......... C	70
Leon, Cattaraugus........ SW	300
Leonardsville, Madison......C	236
Leptondale, Orange.........SE	×
Le Raysville, Jefferson.......N	150
● Le Roy, Genesee........ W	2,743
Le Roy's Mills, (see Frost Mills)	×
Leslie, Niagara........... W	×
Lester, Broome........... S	×
● Lester Shire, Broome.... S	×
● Levanna, Cayuga.........C	150
Lewbeach, Sullivan........ SE	50
Lewis, Essex............... NE	400
● *Lewis*, Livingston........ W	×
● *Lewis*, Ontario........... W	×
Lewisborough, Westchest'r SE	150
● *Lewis Siding*, Erie...... WS	×
● Lewiston, Niagara......... W	633
● *Lewiston Junction*, Niag'a W	×
Lexington, Greene......... SE	500
Leyden, Lewis............. N	250

Place	Pop.
● Leyden Station, Lewis.... N	×
● Liberty, Sullivan...... SE	735
● Liberty Falls, Sullivan .. SE	100
Libertyville, Ulster........ SE	100
● Lilly Dale, Chautauqua. SW	×
Lima, Livingston .... W	1,003
● *Lime*, Genesee.......... W	×
● Limerick, Jefferson...... N	300
● *Lime Rock*, Genesee..... W	×
● Limestone, Cattaraugus. SW	900
Limestreet, Greene......... SE	×
Lincklaen, Chenango........C	250
Lincklaen Centre, Chenango C	×
Lincoln, Wayne............. W	50
● Lincoln Park, Monroe... W	×
● Linden, Genesee.......... W	200
● Lindenhurst, Suffolk .... SE	350
Linkinson, (see Regis Falls)..	×
● Linlithgo, Columbia..... SE	200
Linoleumville, Richmond. SE	666
● Linwood, Livingston...... W	5[illegible]
Lisbon, St. Lawrence...... N	×
● Lisbon Centre, St. Law'ce. N	200
Lisha's Kill, Albany......... E	700
● Lisle, Broome............. S	421
Litchfield, Herkimer....... N	25
● *Litchfield*, Tioga......... S	×
Lithgow, Dutchess .... SE	150
Little Britain, Orange..... SE	×
● Little Falls, Herkimer... N	8,783
Little France, Oswego C	225
● Little Genesee, Allegany SW	75
Little Neck, Queens....... SE	1,000
● *Little Neck Station*, Qu'nsSE	×
Little Rapids, Lewis.........N	×
Little Rest, Dutchess.......SE	150
● Little River, St. Lawrence N	×
Little Sprite, (see Middle Sprite)	×
Little Utica, Onondaga...... C	58
● **Little Valley**, Cattara'SW	698
● Little York, Cortland..... C	75
Little York, (see Fowler)	×
● Liverpool, Onondaga..... C	1,284
Livingston, Columbia...... SE	200
● *Livingston*, Richmond.. SE	×
● Livingston Manor, S'l'van SE	350
Livingston Sta., (see Linlithgo)	×
Livingstonville, Schoharie.. E	600
Livonia, Livingston......... W	300
● Livonia Sta., Livingston.. W	738
Loch Muller, Essex....... NE	×
Loch Sheldrake, Sullivan.. SE	100
Loch Berlin, Wayne........W	150
● Locke, Cayuga............ C	400
● **Lockport**, Niagara .... W	16,038
● *Lockport Junc.*, Niagara. W	×
● Lockwood, Tioga..........S	173
● *Locust Avenue*, Queens..SE	×
Locust Grove, Lewis.......N	75
● *Locust Grove*, Monroe... W	×
● Locust Valley, Queens.. SE	600
Lodi, Seneca............... C	600
Lodi Centre, Seneca........C	100
Logan, Schuyler .... SW	75
Lombard, Chautauqua.... SW	×
● Long Beach, Queens .... SE	×
● *Long Branch*, Monroe... W	×
● *Long Bridge*, Onondaga.. [illegible]	×
● Long Eddy, Sullivan..... SE	50
● Long Island City, Queens. SE	30,50[illegible]
Long Lake, Hamilton....... NE	27[illegible]
● *Long Point*, Chautauqua SW	×
● *Long Point*, Yates....... W	×
● Long Year, Ulster....... SE	×
Loomis, Delaware..........SE	20[illegible]
● Looneyville, Erie .... W	2[illegible]
Loon Lake, Franklin........NE	250
● *Loon Lake*, Franklin.....NE	×
● Lordville, Delaware......SE	30[illegible]
Loretta, Erie .... W	×
● *Lorings*, Cortland.........C	×
Lorraine, Jefferson........ N	14[illegible]
Lotville, Fulton............ E	×
Loudonville, Albany......... E	30[illegible]
Louisville, St. Lawrence..... N	20[illegible]
Louisville Landing, St. L'ce. N	100
● Lounsberry, Tioga........ S	150
Lowell, Oneida............ C	150
Lower Beaver Meadow, (see Beaver Meadow)	×
Lower Cincinnatus, (see Cin's)	×
● *Lower Switch*, Tompkins..S	×
● *Lowerre*, Westchester... SE	×
Low Hampton, Washington. E	200
● Lowman, Chemung........ S	150
● *Low Point*, Dutchess.... SE	300
● **Lowville**, Lewis........N	2,511

Loxea, (see Jacksonville)	×
Loyd, Ulster.............. SE	200
● *Loyd Station*, Ulster.... SE	×
Ludingtonville, Putnam.... SE	35
● *Ludlow*, Westchester.... SE	×
Ludlows Landing, Suffolk.SE	×
Ludlowville, Tompkins..... S	400
Lumberville, (see Arena)	×
Lummisville, Wayne....... W	×
Luther, Rensselaer.......... E	×
Luzerne, Warren.......... NE	868
● Lycoming, Oswego.......... C	×
Lyker's, Montgomery ...... E	50
● Lyndonville, Orleans..... W	700
Lynn, Steuben............ SW	×
● Lyon Mountain, Clinton. NE	300
● **Lyons**, Wayne.......... W	4,475
Lyonsdale, Lewis............ N	250
● Lyon's Falls, Lewis......... N	150
Lyonsville, Ulster.......... SE	50
Lysander, Onondaga........ C	245
McClelland, (see Alburg)	×
● **McClure Settlem't, BroomeS**	100
● **McConnellsville, Oneida.. C**	807
McDonough, Chenango..... C	600
McGowan, Herkimer........ N	150
McGrawville, Cortland...... C	733
● McIntyre, Dutchess...... SE	100
McKinley, Montgomery.... E	×
● *McKinney's*, Tompkins.. S	×
McKownville, Albany....... E	125
● McLean, Tompkins....... S	600
● *McNair*, Livingston..... W	150
McNalls, Niagara.......... W	×
● *McQueens*, Livingston... W	×
Mabbettsville, Dutchess.... SE	180
MacDougall's, Seneca....... C	75
● Macedon, Wayne......... W	533
Macedon Centre, Wayne.... W	150
● Machias, Cattaraugus... SW	500
Mackey, Schoharie.......... E	50
Mackey's Cors, (see Mackey).	×
Macomb, St. Lawrence..... N	200
Madalin, Dutchess......... SE	800
Madawaska, Franklin.... NE	×
Madison, Madison.......... C	390
Madrid, St. Lawrence....... N	605
● *Madrid*, St. Lawrence.... N	×
Madrid Springs, St. Lawr'ce. N	200
Magee's Corners, Seneca.... C	50
Mahoning Point, Ch't'quaSW	×
● Mahopac, Putnam....... SE	×
● Mahopac Falls, Putnam. SE	75
● Mahopac Mines, PutnamSE	×
● *Maiden Lane*, Albany.... E	×
Maine, Broome............. S	400
● *Maine*, Cattaraugnas ... SW	×
Malcom, Seneca............ C	×
● Malden, Ulster.......... SE	[illegible]
Malden Bridge, Columbia.. SE	100
Malden Centre, (see Malden).	×
● Mallory, Oswego.......... C	350
● *Malloryville*, Tompkins... S	×
● **Malone**, Franklin..... NE	4,[illegible]6
Malta, Saratoga............ E	200
Maltaville, Saratoga........ E	90
● Mamaroneck, Westches'r SE	1,600
Manchester, Ontario........ W	300
Manchester Bridge, Dut'ss. SE	400
Manchester Centre, OntarioW	100
Mandana, Onondaga........ C	×
Manhanset House, Suffolk. SE	×
Manhasset, Queens......... SE	45[illegible]
● *Manhattan Beach*, KingsSE	×
● *Manhattan Beach Junction*, Kings................ SE	×
● Manlius, Onondaga....... C	942
● Manlius Centre, Onondaga. C	150
● Manlius Station, OnondagaC	200
Manning, Orleans.......... W	65
● Mannsville, Jefferson..... N	389
Manor Kill, Schoharie...... E	35
Manorton, Columbia....... SE	100
● Manorville, Suffolk....... SE	200
Mapes, Allegany.......... SW	×
● *Maple Bay*, Onondaga.... C	×
Maple Beach, Livingston... W	×
Maple Grove, Otsego........ C	60
● *Maple Grove*, Queens.... SE	×
Maple Hill, (see Williamstown)	×
● Maple Springs, Cha'qua. SW	×
Maple Street, Niagara...... W	×
● Mapleton, Cayuga......... C	×
● Mapleton Station, Nia'ra. W	×
Maple Valley, Otsego........ C	100
● *Maplewood*, Monroe ..... W	×
Maplewood Sullivan....... SE	×

● Marathon, Cortland....... C	1,198
Marbletown, Ulster........ SE	200
Marcellus, Onondaga........ C	563
● Marcellus Falls, On'daga.. C	200
● Marcy, Oneida............ C	1,200
Marengo, Wayne........... W	110
Margaretville, Delaware... SE	616
Mariaville, Schenectady..... E	150
Marietta, Onondaga......... C	147
Marilla, Erie................ W	400
● *Marilla*, Erie .... W	×
Marine Cock, Queens...... SE	×
● Mariner's Harbor, R'm'd. SE	2,000
Marion, Wayne............ W	800
Marionville, Onondaga...... C	50
Mariposa, Chenango........ C	×
● Markham, Cattaraugus. SW	×
● Marlborough, Ulster..... SE	870
Marshall, Alleghany....... SW	×
● *Marshall*, Oneida......... C	160
Marshall's Steuben....... SW	100
Marshfield, Erie............ W	×
Marshland, Tioga........... S	×
Marshville, Montgomery.... E	40
Marshville, St. Lawrence... N	×
● Martindale Depot, C'mbiaSE	100
Martinsburgh, Lewis........ N	285
● *Martinsburgh*, Lewis..... N	60
● Martinsville, Niagara.... W	5[illegible]0
● Martville, Cayuga......... C	140
Marvin, Chautauqua...... SW	300
● Maryland, Otsego......... C	150
Masonville, Delaware...... SE	400
● Maspeth, Queens........ SE	500
● *Massapequa*, Queens.... SE	503
● Massena, St. Lawrence ... N	1,049
Massena Centre, St. L'wr'ce N	50
Massena Springs, St. L'wr'ceN	500
● Matteawan, Dutchess.... SE	4,278
● Mattituck, Suffolk....... SE	500
● *Maxwells Crossing*, L'tonW	×
● Maybrook, Orange ...... SE	×
● *Maybrook Junc.*, OrangeSE	×
● Mayfield, Fulton.......... E	425
Maynard, Oneida........... C	275
● May's Mill, Yates........ W	×
● **Mayville**, Chautauqua SW	1,164
Meacham, Franklin....... NE	×
Meadowbrook, Orange..... SE	×
● *MeadowCrossover*, Q'eensSE	×
● Meadowdale, Albany...... E	75
● Mechanicstown, Orange.. SE	×
● Mechanicsville, Saratoga.. E	2,679
Mecklenburgh, Schuyler.. SW	700
● Medford Station, SuffolkSE	×
● Medina, Orleans.......... W	4,492
Medusa, Albany............ E	300
Medway, Greene........... SE	350
● Mellenville, Columbia... SE	564
● *Melrose*, New York...... SE	×
● Melrose, Rensselaer....... E	300
Melville, Suffolk.......... SE	×
Melvina, Queens.......... SE	×
● Memphis, Onondaga C	228
● *Menands*, Albany........ E	×
Mendon, Monroe .... W	204
Mendon Centre, Monroe.... W	80
Merchantville, (see Thurston)	×
Meredith, Delaware........ SE	100
Meredith Hollow, Del'w're.. SE	150
Meridian, Cayuga........... C	600
● Merrick, Queens......... SE	200
● Merrickville, Delaware.. SE	50
Merrifield, Cayuga.......... C	×
Merrill, Clinton............ NE	350
Merrillsville, (see Loon Lake)	×
Merrillsville, Madison C	×
● Merritt's Corners, W'c'terSE	×
● Mertensia, Ontario....... W	×
● Messengerville, Cortland. C	100
Metropolitan, Queens...... SE	×
Mettacahonts, Ulster ...... SE	250
Mexico, Herkimer.......... N	×
● Mexico, Oswego.......... C	1,315
● **Middleburgh, Schoharie.. E**	1,139
Middle Falls, Washington... E	450
Middlefield, Otsego.......... C	250
Middlefield Centre, Otsego.. C	200
● Middle Granville, Washn. E	500
Middle Grove, Saratoga..... E	200
Middle Hope, Orange...... SE	200
Middle Island, Suffolk..... SE	100
● Middleport, Niagara...... W	1,217
Middleport, (see Kerhonkson)	×
Middlesex, Yates........... W	350
Middle Sprite, Fulton .... E	100

● Middletown, Orange..... SE	11,977
Middle Village, Queens.... SE	504
● Middleville, Herkimer.... N	900
Midway, Tompkins.......... S	×
Milan, Dutchess........... SE	50
Mileses, Sullivan.......... SE	×
Mile Strip, Madison......... C	25
● Milford, Otsego........... C	800
Milford Centre, (see Milford)	×
Military Corners, JeffersonN	50
Millards, Niagara.......... W	×
● Millbrook, Dutches...... SE	693
Millbrook, (see Adirondack).	×
Millburn, Queens.......... SE	×
Miller's Bay, (see River View)	×
Millers, Franklin.......... NE	×
Millers, Ontario........... W	×
● Millers, Orleans.......... W	250
Miller Corners, Ontario.. W	200
Miller's Cor's, (see No. Nassua)	×
Miller's Landing, Suffolk. SE	×
Miller's Mills, Herkimer..... N	175
Miller's Place, Suffolk..... SE	×
Millersport, Erie.......... W	×
Millers Tank Creamery, B'meS	×
○ Millerton, Dutchess...... SE	638
Millin, (see Highland)........	×
● Mill Grove, Erie.......... W	200
Mill Point, Montgomery..... E	175
● Mill Port, Chemung....... S	700
Mills, Cattaraugus......... SW	×
Mills' Corners, Fulton....... E	20
Mills' Mills, Allegany..... SW	75
Millville, Orleans.......... W	150
● Milo Centre, Yates....... W	110
● *Milo Mills*, Yates........ W	×
● Milton, Ulster.......... SE	531
Milton Centre, Saratoga..... E	1
Mina, Chautauqua......... SW	200
Minaville, Montgomery..... E	500
Minden, Montgomery....... E	50
● *Mindenville*, Montgomery. E	100
● Mineola, Queens......... SE	200
Mineral Springs, Schoharie. E	75
Minerva, Essex............ NE	200
● Minetto, Oswego.......... S	150
● *Minetto*, Oswego......... C	×
Mineville, Essex.......... NE	1,844
Minisink, Orange.......... SE	150
Minnehaha, Herkimer...... N	×
Minnewaska, Ulster....... SE	×
● *Mitchell's*, Ontario....... W	×
Mitchellsville, Steuben.... SW	100
Mitchie, Sullivan.......... SE	×
● Modena, Ulster.......... SE	200
Moffitt's Store, (see W. Leb'on)	×
Moffittsville, Clinton...... NE	×
● Mohawk, Herkimer...... N	1,806
● *Mohawk*, Schenectady... E	×
Mohawk Hill, Lewis......... N	65
Mohawkville, (see Schenec'dy)	×
Mohegan, Westchester..... SE	100
Mohonk Lake, Ulster...... SE	×
● Moira, Franklin......... NE	400
Moline, (see Orwell)	×
Mombaccus, Ulster........ SE	×
Monclova, (see PrestonHollow)	×
Mongaup, Sullivan....... SE	350
Mongaup Valley, Sullivan. SE	500
● Monroe, Orange.......... SE	630
Monroe Works, (see S'thfield)	×
● Monsey, Rockland....... SE	200
Montague, Lewis........... N	150
● *Montauk Junc.*, Kings.. SE	×
Montela, Ulster........... SE	100
Monterey, (see De Grass)	×
Monterey, Schuyler....... SW	125
Montezuma, Cayuga........ C	307
Montezuma Sta., Cayuga... C	50
● Montgomery, Orange.... SE	1,024
● **Monticello**, Sullivan.. SE	1,016
Mont Moor, Rockland..... SE	×
● Montrose, Westchester.. SE	250
● *Monument*, Saratoga..... E	×
Moodna, Orange........... SE	275
Moody, Franklin.......... NE	50
Mooers, Clinton........... NE	1,000
Mooers Forks, Clinton.... NE	300
Mooers Junc., (see Mooers)..	×
● Moons, Chautauqua..... SW	100
Moore's Mill, Dutchess.... SE	250
Moose River, Lewis......... N	75
● Moravia, Cayuga.......... C	1,486
Morehouse, Yates.......... W	×
Morehouseville, Hamilton. NE	181
Moreland, Schuyler....... SW	50
Moreland Sta., Schuyler.. SW	25

 New York New York

Moresville, (see Grand Gorge) ×
Moreton Farm, Monroe.... W ×
● *Morgan*, Allegany......SW ×
Morganville, Genesee...... W 200
Moriah, Essex............NE 500
Moriah Centre, Essex .... NE 600
Moriah Four Cors., (seeM'r'ah) ×
● Moriches, Suffolk.......... SE 300
Morley, St. Lawrence.......N 350
Morris, Otsego............. C 601
● Morrisania, New York..SE ×
Morris Dock, (see New York) ×
● *Morris Heights*, NewYorkSE ×
● Morrisonville, Clinton.. NE 300
● *Morris Park*, Queens....SE ×
● Morristown, St.Lawrence. N 472
Morrisville, Madison.... C 726
● Morrisville Sta., Madison. C ×
Morse, Oswego.............. C ×
Morseville, (see Jefferson) ... ×
Mortimer, Monroe......... W ×
Morton's Corners, Erie..... W 150
● Moscow, Livingston..... W 275
Moses Kill, Washington.....E 110
Mosherville, Saratoga.......E 50
● *Mosholu*, New York....SE ×
● *Mott Haven*, New York.SE ×
Mottville, Onondago........C 551
Mountain Brook, Ulster.. SE ×
● Mountain Dale, Sullivan. SE 300
● *Mountain House Station*, Greene............... SE ×
● Mountainville, Orange.. SE 100
Mount Eden, New York..SE ×
Mount Hope, New York..SE ×
Mount Hope, Orange........ SE 200
● *Mount Hope*, WestchesterSE ×
● Mount Ivy, Rockland....SE ×
Mount Jefferson, Delaware SE ×
● Mount Kisko, Westc'esterSE 1,095
Mount Lebanon, Columbia SE 300
● Mount McGregor, SaratogaE ×
● *Mount Marion*, Ulster..SE ×
● Mount Morris, Livingston W 2,286
Mount Pleasant, Oswego....C ×
Mt. Pleasant, (see Greenfield Center)................ ×
● *Mount Pleasant*, Ulster.SE ×
● Mount Read, Monroe.... W 50
● Mount Riga, Dutchess.... SE 100
Mount Roderick, Cortland. C ×
● Mount Ross, Dutchess... SE 15
● *Mt.St. Vincent*, Westch'erSE ×
Mount Sinai, Suffolk.......SE 100
● Mount Upton, Chenango. C 350
● MountVernon, W'stch'st'rSE 10,830
Mount Vision, Otsego....... C 300
Mud Lock, Onondago....... C ×
Multzeskill, Rensselae......E 175
● *Mulhollon*, Steuben.... SW ×
● Mumford, Monroe....... W 455
Mundale, Delaware........SE 30
● Munnsville, Madison.......C 400
Munsonville, Fulton........ E 25
Murray, Orleans...........W 100
● *Murray*, Orleans........ W ×
Murray Hill, Queens......SE ×
Mycenæ, Onondaga..........C ×
● *Myers*, Cayuga...........C ×
Myers, Tompkins............S ×
Nanticoke, Broome........ S 150
● Nanuet, Rockland.......SE 1,500
● *Nanuet Junc.*, RocklandSE ×
Napanoch, Ulster..........SE 500
Napiers, Cattaraugus.....SW ×
Naples, Ontario............ W 1,266
Naples Landing, Ontario.. W ×
Napoli, Cattaraugus........SW 100
● Narrowsburgh, Sullivan.SE 485
Nashville, Chautauqua....SW 75
Nassua, Rensselaer......... E 356
● Natural Bridge, Jefferson. N 500
Natural Dam, St.Lawrence. N ×
Naumburgh, Lewis.......... N ×
Navarino, Onondaga........C 150
Nealville, Greene..........SE ×
● *Neck Road*, Kings.......SE ×
Negro Hills,, (see WhitePlains) ×
● *Neely Town*, Orange....SE ×
Neil's Creek, Steuben.....SW ×
Neilsville, Greene......... SE ×
Nelliston, Montgomery..... E 721
Nelson, Madison............ C 150
● *Nelson*, Steuben........SW ×
Nelson Flats, (see Nelson) .. ×
● *Nelson Switch*, Oswego... C ×
Nelsonvile, Putnam....... SE 800

● Neperan, Westchester...SE 50
● Nepera Park, WestchesterSE ×
● *Nepperhan*, Weschester SE ×
Neptune, Queens..........SE ×
Netherwood, Dutchess..... SE ×
Neversink, Sullivan....... SE 350
Neversink Aqueduct, O'ngeSE ×
Nevis, Columbia...........SE 65
New Albion, Cattaraugus. SW 200
● Newark, Wayne..........W 2,824
● Newark Valley, Tioga.....S 875
New Baltimore, Greene....SE 734
● New Baltimore Sta., Gr'eSE ×
● New Berlin, Chenango....C 979
● New Berlin Centre, Che'o. C ×
● *New Berlin Junc.*, Chn'go. C 150
New Boston, Lewis.........N ×
New Boston Land., Madison C ×
New Bremen, Lewis........N 100
New Bridge, Onondaga .....C 25
New Bridge, (see Belmore) .. ×
● NewBrighton, Richmond.SE 16.423
● **Newburgh**, Orange...SE 23,087
● *Newburgh Junc.*, OrangeSE ×
New Castle, Westchester.. SE 400
New Centreville, Oswego... C 100
● **New City**, Rockland. SE 400
New City Junc., Rockland.SE ×
Newcomb, Essex..........NE 300
New Concord, Columbia...SE 100
● New Dorp, Richmond... SE 50
Newfane, Niagara..........W 500
● Newfane Station, NiagaraW ×
Newfield, Tompkins.........S 500
● *Newfield Sta.*, Tompkins. S 500
New Hackensack, Dut'essS. E 200
● New Hamburgh, Dut'ess SE 500
● New Hampton, Orange..SE 300
● New Hartford, Oneida....C 912
● New Haven, Oswego.......C 200
● *New Hempstead*, Rock'dSE ×
New Hope, Cayuga..........C 600
New Hudson, Allegany.... SW ×
● New Hurley, Ulster.... SE 100
● New Hyde Park, Queens.SE 250
New Kingston, Delaware.. SE 90
Newkirk Mills, Fulton.......E 60
● New Lebanon, Columbia SE 400
● New Lebanon Centre, Columbia..........SE 150
New Lebanon Flats, (see West Lebanon).................. ×
New Lebanon Springs, (see Lebanon Springs)......... ×
New Lisbon, Otsego.........C 100
New London, Oneida.......C 450
● *New Lots*, Kings........ SE ×
Newman, Essex...........NE 200
● New Milford, Orange....SE 300
● *New Northport*, Suffolk.SE ×
New Ohio, (see Tunnel) ...... ×
New Oregon, Erie.......... W 300
● New Paltz, Ulster....... SE 935
New Paltz Landing, (see Highland) .... ×
● Newport, Herkimer......N 659
New Road, (see North Walton) ×
● New Rochelle, West'ter. SE 8,217
● *New RochelleJunc.*, W'tr SE ×
New Russia, Essex.......NE 100
New Salem, Albany.........E 700
● New Scotland, Albany.... E 100
New Springville, Rich'ond SE 875
New Suffolk, Suffolk...... SE ×
Newstead, Erie...........W 50
Newton Creek, (see Brooklyn) ×
Newtons, Chautauqua.... SW ×
Newton's Corners, H'm'tn NE 50
Newtonville, Albany.........E 100
● Newtown, Queens....... SE 1,000
New Utretch, (see Van Pelt Manor) .... ×
Newville, Herkimer........ N 100
● New Windsor, Orange...SE 614
● New Woodstock, Madison. C 450
● **NEW YORK**, N.Y...SE 1,515,301
New York Arsenal, N. Y'kSE ×
New York Mills, Oneida.... C 2,552
● Niagara Falls, Niagara... W 5,502
Niagara University, NiagaraW ×
Nice, Erie...............W ×
● *Nichols*, Steuben....... SW ×
● Nichols, Tioga............S 600
Nichols Landing, Steuben SW ×
Nicholville, St. Lawrence... N 500
Nile, Allegany........... SW 130
Niles, Cayuga............. S 100

● Nina, Tompkins.......... S ×
Nine Mile Creek, Onondaga. C ×
Nine Mile Point, Monroe.. W ×
● Nineveh, Broome......... S 450
● Niskayuna, Schenectady.. E 65
Nissaquay, Suffolk....... SE ×
● Niverville, Columbia.... SE 350
Noblesville, (see New Lisbon) ×
Norfolk, St. Lawrence.......N 600
Norman's Kill, (see Slingerland's) ×
Normansville, Albany...... E 100
North Albany, (see Albany) . ×
Northampton, Fulton.........E 200
North Argyle, Washington..E 208
North Babylon, Suffolk... SE ×
● **North Bangor, Franklin NE** 450
North Barton, Tioga.........S 50
● North Bay, Oneida........C 350
North Beach, Queens......SE ×
North Bergen, Genesee.....W 100
North Blenheim, Schoharie. E 600
North Bloomfield, Ontario. W 200
North Bolton, Warren.... NE 25
North Boston, Erie .... W 250
North Boylston, Oswego.... C ×
North Branch, Sullivan....SE 100
North Bridgewater, Oneida. C ×
North Broadalbin, Fulton.. E 100
● North Brookfield, Madison C
North Brookfield Sta., (see North Brookfield)........ ×
● *North Buffalo*, Erie...... W ×
North Burke, Franklin... NE 250
Northbush, Fulton........ E 20
North Cambridge, WashingtonE 25
North Cameron, Steuben..SW 25
● *North Candor*, Tioga..... S ×
North Castle, Westchester. SE ×
North Chatham, Columbia. SE 200
North Chemung, Chemung.. S 150
North Chili, Monroe...... W 200
North Clove, Dutchess......SE 50
● North Clymer, Chauta'uaSW ×
North Cohocton, Steuben. SW 450
North Colesville, Broome... S 100
● North Collins, Erie.......W 60
North Constantia, Oswego.. C ×
North Copake, (see Craryville) ×
● North Creek, Warren...NE 450
● *North Croghan*, JeffersonN ×
North Cuba, Allegany.....SW 100
North Deer Park, Suffolk.SE ×
NorthEastCentre, (seeMillerton) ×
North Easton, Washington..E 200
North Edmeston, Otsego.... C 180
North Elba, Essex........ NE 450
● *North Elmira*, Chemung. S 1,716
● North Evans, Erie....... W 200
● North Fair Haven, Cayuga C ×
North Fenton, Broome......S 150
North Franklin, Delaware. SE 75
North Fulton, Oswego.....C ×
North Gage, Oneida.........C 100
North Galway, Saratoga.....E 100
North Germantown, Co'biaSE 350
North Granville, WashingtonE 300
North Greece, Monroe..... W 200
North Greenbush, Rensse'er E ×
North Greenfield, Saratoga. E 55
North Greenwich, Washington E 350
North Hamden, Delaware. SE 25
North Hamlin, Monroe.... W 50
North Hammond, St.Law'ce N ×
● North Hannibal, Oswego..C 100
North Harpersfield, Del're. SE 100
North Hartland, Niagara.. W ×
North Hebron, Washington. E 200
● North Hector, Schuyler SW 35
North Hillsdale, Columbia SE 75
● North Hoosick, Rensselaer E 275
North Hudson, Essex..... NE 250
North Huron, Wayne.......W 100
North Jasper, Steuben....SW 25
● North Java, Wyoming.... W 300
North Kortright, DelawareSE 200
North Lansing, Tompkins...S 200
● North Lawrence, St.La'ce N 550
North Lincklaen, (seeLincklaen) ×
North Litchfield, Herkimer. N 250
North Manlius, Onondaga...C 200
North Milton, Saratoga..... E 150
North Nassau, Rensselaer... E 200
NorthNewYork, (seeNewYork) ×
● North Norwich, ChenangoC 175
North Otselic, (see Otselic)... ×
● North Parma, Monroe... W 487
North Pembroke, Genesee. W 100

● North Petersburgh, Ren'r E 200
North Pharsalia, Chenango. C 250
North Pitcher, Chenango... C 150
● Northport, Suffolk...... SE 600
● *Northport Junc.*, SuffolkSE ×
North Reading, Schuyler. SW ×
North Ridge, Niagara...... W 200
North Ridgeway, Orleans.. W ×
North River, Warren..... NE 400
Northrops, Yates.......... W ×
● North Rose, Wayne...... W 275
● North Rush, Monroe..... W 50
North Russell, St. LawrenceN 200
North Salem, Westchester.SE 400
North Sanford, Broome.....S 200
North Scriba, Oswego.......C ×
North Sea, Suffolk........ SE ×
● North Sparta, Livingston. W 150
● North Spencer, Tioga .... S 29
● North Stephentown, R's'r E ×
North Sterling, Cayuga..... C ×
● North Stockholm, St. Lawrence.................N 200
North Syracuse, Onondaga..C 200
● North Tarrytown, West'rSE 3,179
● *North Tonawanda*, Ni'raW 4,793
Northumberland, Saratoga..E 150
North Urbana, Steuben...SW ×
North Victory, Cayuga......C 100
● Northville, Fulton........ E 792
Northville, Suffolk........ SE ×
North Volney, Oswego...... C 25
● North Walton, Delaware SE 300
North Western, Oneida.......C 183
North West Point, Queens SE ×
North Wilna, Jefferson..... N 300
North Winfield, Herkimer..N 50
North Wolcott, Wayne..... W 100
Northwood, Herkimer......N 75
Norton Hill, Greene........ SE 60
● *Nortons*, Chautauqua...SW ×
● *Nortons* Tompkins........S 25
● *Norton Summit*, AlleganySW ×
Norway, Herkimer........ N 125
● **Norwich**, Chenango.... C 5,212
Norwich Corners, HerkimerN ×
Norwood, Queens......... SE ×
● Norwood, St. Lawrence...N 1,463
Noxon, Dutchess.......... SE ×
Number Four, Lewis....... N ×
● Nunda, Livingston....... W 1,010
● *Nunda*, Livingston.......W ×
● *Nunda Junc.*, LivingstonW ×
● Nyack, Rockland.........SE 4,111
● *Nypenn*, Chautauqua...SW ×
Oak Brook, Sullivan...... SE ×
● Oakdale Station, Suffolk.SE ×
Oakes, Ulster...............SE 150
Oakesville, Otsego...........C 150
● Oakfield, Genesee........W 578
Oak Hill, Columbia........ SE ×
Oak Hill, Greene.......... SE 375
● Oakland, Livingston......W 100
● Oakland Valley, Sullivan SE 250
Oak Lodge, Yates.......... W ×
Oak Orchard, Orleans......W 100
Oak Orchard, Oswego.......C ×
Oak Point, St. Lawrence....N ×
Oak Ridge, Montgomery....E ×
● Oak's Corners, Ontario...W 50
● Oak Summit, Dutchess.. SE 75
Oakville, Suffolk..........SE ×
Oakwood, Cayuga...........C ×
● *Oakwoods*, Richmond... SE ×
Oatka, Wyoming............ W ×
Obernburgh, Sullivan......SE ×
Obi, Allegany...............SW ×
● ***Ocean Park*, Richmond. SE** ×
● *Ocean Point*, Queens.....SE ×
● Oceanus, Queens......... SE ×
Oceanville, Queens.........SE ×
Odessa, Schuyler..........SW 400
Ogden, Monroe..............W 150
● Ogdensburg, St. LawrenceN 11,662
Ogoyago, Yates............ W ×
Ohio, Herkimer.............N 50
Ohioville, Ulster............SE 300
Olcott, Niagara..............W 500
● Old Chatham, Columbia. SE 150
Old Forge, Herkimer....... N 50
● *Old Northport*, Suffolk..SE 2,011
Old Westbury, Queens......SE 500
● Olean, Cattaraugus......SW 7,358
● Olive, Ulster..............SE 150
Olive Bridge, Ulster........SE 500
Oliverea, Ulster............SE ×
Olmstedville, Essex....... NE 100

Olympic, Suffolk.......... SE ×
Omar, Jefferson............N 150
Omro, Cayuga...............C ×
● *Onativia*, Onondaga.......C 146
● Oneida, Madison.......... C 6,083
● Oneida Castle, Oneida.....C 317
Oneida Lake, Madison.......C 100
● Oneida Valley, Madison...C 300
● Oneonta, Otsego...........C 6,272
Onondaga, Onondaga........C ×
Onondaga Castle, Onondaga. C 125
Onondago Hill, Onondaga...C 250
Onondaga Hol'w, (see Onondaga Va) ×
Onondaga Valley, Onondaga C 194
● Onoville, Cattaraugus...SW 150
● Ontario, Wayne......... W 1,000
● *Ontario Beach*, Monroe..W ×
Ontario Centre, Wayne.....W 100
Opening, Oneida........... C ×
Open Meadows, ChautauquaSW ×
Oppenheim, Fulton......... E 900
● *Oquaga*, Broome..........S 100
Oquaga Lake, Broome........S ×
● Oramel, Allegany.......SW 200
● Oran, Onondaga.......... C 100
● Orangeburgh, Rockland. SE 100
● *Orange Farm*, Orange...SE ×
Orange Lake, Orange......SE ×
Orangeport, Niagara....... W 75
Orangeville, Wyoming..... W 35
● Orchard Park, Erie...... W 500
Oregon, Putnam...........SE 100
Oregon, Warren............NE 200
Orient, Suffolk.............SE 808
Orient Point, Suffolk...... SE ×
Orient Works, Suffolk......SE ×
● Oriskany, Oneida.........C 860
● Oriskany Falls, Oneida....C 625
● Orleans, Ontario......... W 450
● Orleans Four Corners, Jefferson.................N 50
● Orr's Mills, Orange ....SE ×
Orville, (see De Witt)........ ×
Orville Feeder, Onondaga... C ×
Orwell, Oswego............. C 350
● *Osborne Hollow*, Broome..S 200
Osborneville, St. Lawrence.N ×
Osborn's Bridge, Fulton....E 100
● Oscawana, Westchester..SE 100
Osceola, Lewis..............N 200
Osceola, Oneida........... C ×
Ossian, Livingston.........W 300
Oswegatchie, St. Lawrence. N ×
● *Oswegatchie*, St. LawrenceN ×
Oswegatchie Lake, Lewis... N ×
● **Oswego**, Oswego....... C 21,842
Oswego Centre, Oswego..... C ×
● Oswego Falls, Oswego.....C 1,821
Oswego Junction, OnondagaC ×
Oswego Junction, Oswego.. C ×
● Otego, Otsego............ C 1,000
● *Otis*, Monroe............. W ×
Otisco, Onondaga...........C 175
Otisco Centre, (see Otisco).... ×
Otisco Valley, Onondaga..... C 25
● Otisville, Orange.........SE 300
Otsdawa, Otsego.............C 200
Otsego Lake, Otsego........C 50
Otselic, Chenango...........C 150
Otselic Centre, Chenango....C 50
Otter, Orange..............SE ×
Otter Creek, Lewis.........N ×
● *Otterkill*, Orange........ SE ×
Otto, Cattaraugus......... SW 400
Ouaquaga, Broome..........S 100
Oulcout, Delaware..........SE ×
● *Outlet*, Ontario.......... W ×
Outterson, Lewis........... N ×
Overlook, Dutchess.........SE ×
● **Ovid**, Seneca............C 641
● Ovid Centre, Seneca.......C 250
Owasco, Cayuga............ C 250
● Owasco Lake, Cayuga.....C ×
● **Owego**, Tioga...........S 6,000
Owen's Mills, Chemung...... S 100
Oxbow, Jefferson........... N 212
Ox Creek, Oswego.......... C ×
● Oxford, Chenango........ C 1,477
● Oxford Depot, Orange...SE 75
● Oyster Bay, Queens......SE 1,100
Ozone Park, Queens........ SE 539
● Padelford's, Ontario......W ×
Page Brook, Chenango......C 50
Page's Corners, (see Cullen). ×
Paine's Hollow, Herkimer..W 100
● Painted Post, Steuben.. SW 688
● Palatine Bridge, Montgo'y E 500
Palaukunk, Ulster........ SE 75

Palatine Church, Montgom'yE 75
● Palenville, Greene........SE 558
Palermo, Oswego............C 175
Palisades, Rockland.......SE 100
Palmer, Saratoga........... E 100
● Palmyra, Wayne......... W 2,131
● *Pamelia*, Jefferson........N ×
Pamelia Four Cors., Jeffers'nN 110
Panama, Chautauqua..... SW 379
● *Panama*, Chautauqua.. SW ×
Panther Brook, Sullivan..SE ×
● Paradise, Orange........SE ×
Paradox, Essex............NE 100
Pardee, Monroe............W ×
Paris, Oneida................C 450
● Paris Station, Oneida......C ×
● Parish, Oswego.............C 541
Parishville, St. Lawrence...N 578
Parishville Centre, St. Lawr'eN 75
● Park, Chemung...........S 25
Parker's, Lewis..............N ×
● *Park Hill*, Westchester.SE ×
Parkston, Sullivan..........SE ×
● Parksville, Sullivan..... SE 150
● Par'ville, Kings.........SE 831
Parlimans, Sullivan.......SE ×
Parma, Monroe..............W 146
● *Parma*, Monroe.......... W 487
Parma Centre, Monroe.....W 250
Pataukunk, Ulster.........SE ×
Patchin, Erie...............W ×
● Patchogue, Suffolk...... SE 2,800
Patria, Schoharie............E 100
Patten's Mills, Washington..E 502
● Patterson, Putnam.......SE 800
● Pattersonville, Schenect'y. E 300
Paul's Bridge, Herkimer...N ×
Paul Smith's, Franklin....NE ×
● *Paul Smith's*, Franklin. NE 755
Paul's Rock, Clinton......NE ×
Pavement, Erie.............W ×
● **Pavilion, Genesee.........W** 275
● Pavilion Centre, Genesee. W 25
● Pawling, Dutchess....... SE 630
Pawling Station, (see Pa'ling) ×
Peach Orchard, Schuyler. SW ×
Peaks Creek, Delaware.....SE ×
● Peakville, Delaware.....SE 86
● Pearl Creek, Wyoming... W 250
Pearl Point, Washington...E ×
● Pearl River, Rockland...SE 500
● Pearsall's, Queens.......SE 550
Peasleeville, Clinton.......NE ×
● *Pecksport*, Madison.......C 25
● Peconic, Suffolk.........SE 300
● Peekskill, Westchester..SE 9,676
Pekin, Niagara..............W 500
Pelham, Westchester ......SE 25
Pelham Bridge, Westch't'rSE ×
● Pelham Manor, W'stch'rSE 25
● Pelhamville, Westchest'rSE 200
● Pembroke, Genesee......W 300
Penataquit, (see Bayshore).... ×
Pendleton, Niagara.........W 225
● Pendleton Centre, Niag'a W ×
Penelope, Broome............S ×
● Penfield, Monroe........ W 394
Penfield Centre, Monroe.... W 50
● Pennellville, Oswego...... C 250
● **Penn Yan**, Yates........W 4,254
● *Penny Bridge*, Queens..SE ×
Penny's Basin, Ulster....SE ×
Penville, Cattaraugus.....SW ×
Peoria, Wyoming...........W 100
Pepacton, Delaware.........SE 100
Perch River, Jefferson......N 100
● Perkinsville, Steuben...SW 400
● Perry, Wyoming......... W 1,528
Perry Centre, Wyoming.... W 250
Perry City, Schuyler......SW 50
● *Perrys*, Wyoming..........W ×
● Perrysburgh, Cattar'g's.SW 350
Perry's Mills, Clinton..... NE 250
● Perryville, Madison........C 800
● Persia, Cattaraugus .....SW ×
Perth, Fulton................ E 150
Perth Centre, (see Perth)..... ×
● Peru, Clinton..............NE 375
Peru, (see Jack's Reefs)....... ×
● Peruville, Tompkins...... S 100
Peterborough, Madison......C 260
Petersburg, (see Clayburg)... ×
● Petersburgh, Rensselaer.. E 400
● *Petersburgh Junc.*, Rensl'rE ×
Peter Scott Creek, Oswego.. C ×
● Petrolia, Allegany....... SW 50
Pharsalia, Chenango........ C 75

● Phelps, Ontario.......... W 1,336
● *Phelps Junction*, Ontario W ×
● Philadelphia, Jefferson.... N 783
Phillip's Creek, Allegany.. SW 100
Phillips Lock, (see A'sterd'm) ×
● *Phillip's Mills*, Chaut'qua SW ×
● Phillipsport, Sullivan.... SE 350
● Philmont, Columbia..... SE 1,818
● Phoenicia, Ulster........ SE 200
● Phoenix, Oswego.......... C 1,466
● Phoenix Mills, Otsego..... C 100
Pickardsville, Niagara..... W ×
Pierces, Monroe........... W 50
Piercevillc, Madison........ C 75
● Piermont, Rockland..... SE 1,219
Pierrepont, St. Lawrence... N ×
Pierrepont Centre, St. L'nce N 175
● Pierrepont Manor, Jeff's'n N 225
○ *Piersons*, Genesee........ W ×
● Piffard, Livingston........ W 200
Pike, Wyoming.............. W 483
Pike, Wyoming............. W ×
Pike Village, Allegany.... SW ×
Pikeville, Allegany........ SW ×
Pillar Point, Jefferson...... N 200
Pinckney, Lewis............ N 150
Pine, Delaware............ SE ×
Pine Bank, Ontario........ W ×
● Pine Bush, Orange...... SE 350
Pine City, Chemung......... S 418
Pine Cottage, Yates........ W ×
● Pine Hill, Ulster......... SE 550
● Pine Island, Orange..... SE ×
Pine Island Junc, Orange SE ×
Pine Lake, Fulton.......... E 150
● Pine Plains, Dutchess.... SE 500
● *Pine Plains Sta.*, Dutch's SE ×
Pine Tree, Erie........... W ×
Pine Tree Siding, Erie..... W ×
● Pine Valley, Chemung .... S 200
● *Pine Valley*, Cattaraugus SW 500
Pineville, (see Spring Lake).. ×
Pine Woods, Madison........ C 75
Pine Woods, Orange....... SE ×
Pinnacle, Fulton........... E 150
Piseco, Hamilton.......... NE 80
Pitcairn, St. Lawrence...... N 125
Pitcher, Chenango.......... C 200
Pitcher Springs, Chenango.. C ×
Pitkins, Wyoming......... W ×
Pill Lock, Wayne.......... W ×
● Pittsfield, Otsego.......... C 65
● Pittsford, Monroe......... W 852
Pittstown, Rensselaer....... E 200
Plainfield Centre, Otsego.... C ×
Plains, Oneida............. C ×
Plainview, Queens......... SE ×
Plainville, Onondaga........ C 200
Plank Road, (see No. Syr'c'se) ×
Plato, Cattaraugus........ SW ×
Platt Cove, Greene......... SE 25
Plattekill, Ulster.......... SE 350
● **Plattsburgh**, Clinton NE 7,010
Plattsburgh Barracks, Cl'n NE ×
● *Pleasant Beach*, Onondaga C ×
Pleasant Brook, Otsego...... C 400
Pleasant Plains, Dutchess.. SE 200
● *Pleasant Plains*, R'hm'd SE 175
Pleasant Ridge, (see Cr'se's St.) ×
● Pleasant Valley, Duchess SE 438
● *Pleasant Valley*, Steub'n. SW ×
● Pleasantville, Westch't'r. SE 1,000
Pleasantville Sta., Westch'r SE ×
Plessis, Jefferson.......... N 325
○ *Plumadore*, Franklin... NE ×
Plutarch, Ulster........... SE 25
Plymouth, Chenango........ C 144
● Pocantico Hills, Westc't'r SE 250
Podunk, (see Centerville).... ×
Poestenkill, Rensselaer..... E 330
Point Au Rock, Clinton... NE 100
Point Breeze, Orleans....... W ×
● Point Chautauqua, C't'q'a SW ×
Point Peninsula, Jefferson.. N 75
Point Rock, Onedia......... C 150
Point Vivian, (see Alexandria) ×
Point Whiteside, Chau'q'a. SW ×
● Poland, Herkimer......... N 505
Poland Centre, Chautauq'a SW 10
Polkville, Onondaga........ C 134
● *Pomfret*, Chautauqua... SW ×
● Pomona, Rockland..... SE 200
Pompey, Onondaga.......... C ×
Pompey Centre, Onondaga.. C 75
Pompey Hill, Onondaga.... C 300
○ Pond Eddy, Sullivan..... SE 150
Poney Hollow, Tompkins.... S ×

New York

Ponquoque, Suffolk........ SE ×
Pontiac, Erie.............. W 100
Pool's Brook, Onondaga.... C ×
● Poolville, Madison........ C 165
Pope's Mills, St. Lawrence.. N 200
Poplar Ridge, Cayuga .... C 350
● **Portageville, Wyoming... W 600**
Port Benjamin, (see W'w'rs'g) ×
● Port Byron, Cayuga....... C 1,105
● Port Chester, Westches'r SE 5,274
● *Port Clinton*, Orange.... SE ×
● Port Crane, Broome....... S 250
Port Dickinson, Broome.... S 345
Port Douglass, Essex..... NE 40
Porter's Corners, Saratoga.. E 200
Porterville, Erie........... W ×
Port Eaton, Suffolk....... SE ×
Port Ewen, Ulster......... SE 1,211
Port Gibson, Ontario....... W 400
● *Port Gibson*, Wayne...... W ×
Port Glasgow, Wayne...... W ×
● Port Henry, Essex....... NE 2,436
Port Hixson, Ulster....... SE 25
Port Jackson, (see Valcour). ×
Port Jackson, (see Ams'rd'm) ×
Port Jackson, (see Accord).. ×
● Port Jefferson, Suffolk.. SE 2,026
● Port Jervis, Orange...... SE 9,327
● Port Kent, Essex........ NE 200
Portland, Chautauqua..... SW 350
● Portlandville, Otsego..... C 209
● Port Leyden, Lewis....... N 462
● *Port Morris*, New York. SE ×
Port Ontario, Oswego....... C 150
● *Port Orange*, Sullivan... SE ×
Port Orleans, (see Fisher's Landing)................ ×
● Port Richmond, Rich'nd. SE 6,290
Port Schuyler, (see West Troy) ×
● Portville, Cattaraugus.. SW 800
Port Washington, Queens.. SE 1,500
Port Woodhull, Oneida..... C ×
● Post Creek, Chemung...... S 100
● Potsdam, St. Lawrence... N 3,961
Potsdam Jc., (see Norwood). ×
Potter, Yates.............. W 150
Potter Hill, Rensselaer...... E 150
Potter's Hollow, Albany.... E 300
Pottersville, Warren....... NE 300
● **Poughkeepsie**, Dut's SE 22,206
Poughquag, Dutchess...... SE 125
● *PoughquagSta.*, Dutc'ess SE ×
Poundridge, Westchester.. SE 150
Prattham, Oswego.......... C 60
Prattsburgh, Steuben..... SW 607
Pratt's Falls, (see Pompey).. ×
● Pratt's Hollow, Madison.. C 300
Prattsville, Greene........ SE 384
Preble, Cortland........... C 227
Prentiss, Greene.......... SE 35
● Presho, Steuben........ SW 100
Preston, Chenango.......... C 75
Preston Hollow, Albany..... E 350
● Primrose, Westchester.. SE ×
● Prince's Bay, Richmond. SE 850
● Princetown, Schenectady. E 100
Produce Exchange, N. Y'k SE ×
Promised Land, Suffolk... SE ×
Prospect, Oneida........... C 326
Prospect Hill, (see Sharon Springs).................. ×
Prospect, Ulster.......... SE 100
● *Prospect Park*, Kings... SE ×
● Prospect Sta., Chau'qua SW ×
● *Prospect Station*, Oneida. C ×
● Protection, Erie.......... W 200
Providence, Saratoga...... E 15
Prussian Settlement, Lewis. N ×
● Pulaski, Oswego.......... C 1,517
Pull Hair, Delaware....... SE ×
Pulteney, Steuben......... SW 300
Pultneyville, Wayne........ W 450
● Pulver's, Columbia...... SE 30
Pulver's Corners, Dutchess SE 20
Purchase, Westchester..... SE 50
Purdy Creek, Steuben.... SW 50
● *Purdy's* Orange......... SE ×
● Purdy's Sta., Westchester SE 500
Putnam, Washington....... E 600
● Putnam Sta., Washington. E ×
Putnam Valley, Putnam... SE 250
Pyramid Lake, Essex..... NE 30
Quacken Kill, Rensselaer... E 250
● *Quaker Bridge*, Ca'rau's SW 50
Quaker Hill, Dutchess..... SE 50
Quaker Springs, Saratoga... E 400
● Quaker Street, Schn'tady. E 650

New York

Quality Hill, (see Lenox)..... ×
Quarantine, Richmond.... SE ×
Quarryville, Ulster........ SE 225
● Queens, Queens.......... SE 600
Queensbury, Warren...... NE 150
● Quogue, Suffolk......... SE 250
Raceville, Washington...... E 65
Racket River, St. Lawrence. N 30
Rainbow, Franklin........ NE 30
● *Rainbow*, Franklin..... NE ×
Ralph's, Clinton.......... NE ×
● Ramapo, Rockland....... SE 500
● Randall, Montgomery..... E 50
Randall Road, Niagara..... W 100
Randall's Island, N. York SE ×
● Randallsville, Madison.... C 100
● Randolph, Cattaraugus. SW 1,201
● Ransomville, Niagara.... W 300
● *Rapids*, Monroe......... W ×
Rapids, Niagara........... W 200
Raquette Lake, Hamilton. NE 150
● Rathboneville, Steuben. SW 400
Rathbunville, (see New Lond'n) ×
Ravenswood, Queens...... SE ×
Rawson, Cattaraugus..... SW 50
● *Rawson's*, Cattaraugus. SW ×
Ray, Genesee.............. W ×
Raybrook, Essex.......... NE ×
Raymertown, Rensselaer... E 150
Raymond, Niagara......... W ×
Raymondville, St. Lawrence N 250
● Rayville, Columbia...... SE 225
Read, Chenango............ C ×
● Reading Centre, Schuyler SW 100
Read's Creek, Delaware... SE 400
Reber, Essex............. NE ×
Rector, Lewis............. NE ×
● *Red Creek*, Monroe....... W ×
● Red Creek, Wayne....... W 492
Red Falls, Greene.......... SE 100
Redfield, Oswego.......... C 350
Redford, Clinton......... NE 700
● *Red Hill Switch*, Sullivan SE ×
● Red Hook, Dutchess.... SE 935
● Red House, Cattaraugus SW 500
Redman's Corners, (see Cl'k'n) ×
Red Rock, Columbia....... SE 150
● *Red Rock Siding*, Ulster. SE ×
● Redwood, Jefferson...... N 650
Reed's Corners, (see Mt. Read) ×
Reed's Corners, Ontario.... W 75
Reidsville, Albany......... E 100
Remington, Cattaraugus.. SW ×
● *Remington's*, Jefferson... N ×
● Remsen, Oneida.......... C 358
Renchan's Mills, Steuben. SW ×
Reniff, Tioga.............. S 150
● Rensselaer Falls, St. L'wr'e N 450
Rensselaerville, Albany..... E 400
Reserve, Erie............. W 500
Result, Greene............ SE 200
Retsof, Livingston......... W ×
Reuchens, Steuben....... SW ×
Rexford Flats, Saratoga..... E 150
Rexford's Falls, Chenango.. C ×
Rexville, Steuben......... SW 250
Reynale's Basin, Niagara... W 50
● **Reynolds, Rensselaer..... E ×**
● *Reynoldsville*, Dutchess. SE 50
● Reynoldsville, Schuyler. SW 300
● Rheims, Steuben........ SW 50
● Rhinebeck, Dutchess.... SE 1,649
● *Rhinebeck Upper*, D'tch'ss SE ×
● Rhinecliff, Dutchess..... SE 500
Ricard, Oswego............ C ×
● Rice's Jefferson.......... N ×
● *Riceville*, Cattaraugus.. SW ×
Riceville, (see Mayfield)..... ×
Richburgh, Allegany...... SW 374
Riches Corners, Orleans.... W ×
Richfield, Otsego.......... C 300
● *Richfield Junc.*, Oneida... C 350
● Richfield Springs, Otsego. C 1,623
● Richford, Tioga.......... S 400
● Richland, Oswego......... C 100
Richmond, Richmond.. SE 225
● Richmond Hill, Queens.. SE 626
Richmond Mills, Ontario... W 150
● *Richmond Valley*, Rich'd SE 100
● Richmondville, Schoharie. E 663
● *Richville*, Oswego......... C ×
● Richville, St. Lawrence... N 336
Rider's Mills, Columbia.... SE 100
Rider's Mills Sta., (see Rider's Mills)................ ×
Ridge, Livingston......... W 25
Ridgebury, Orange.... ...SE 300

New York

Place	Pop.
Ridgeland, Monroe.........W	50
Ridge Mills, Oneida..........C	200
Ridge Road, Niagara........W	50
Ridgeway, Orleans..........W	106
Ridgewood, Kings.........SE	×
● *Ridgewood*, Queens......SE	200
● *Rifle Range*, Monroe.....W	×
Rifton Glen, Ulster.........SE	500
Riga, Monroe..........W	50
Riker's Hollow, (see Ingleside)	×
Rio, Orange............SE	×
● Riparius, Warren.......NE	100
● Ripley, Chautauqua.....SW	800
● *Ripley Crossing*, Ch't'q'a SW	×
● *Rippleton*, Madison.......C	×
Risingville, Steuben ...... SW	40
Rivensbury, Madison....... C	×
● Riverdale, New York....SE	×
● **Riverhead**, Suffolk... SE	2,000
Riverside, Broome.......... S	×
● *Riverside*, Warren...... NE	30
● *Riverside Park*, Cattar's SW	×
● *River View*, Albany....... E	×
Riverview, Jefferson........N	100
Riverview, Niagara......... W	×
Roanoke, Genesee..........W	100
● *Roberts Dock Jc.*, Monroe W	×
Robertsonville, (see White Sulphur Springs)	×
Robbin's Island, Suffolk...SE	×
Robbin's Lane, Queens.... SE	×
● **ROCHESTER**, M'nroe W	133,896
Rochester, (see Accord)	×
Rockaway Beach, Queens..SE	1,502
● *Rockaway Junc.*, QueensSE	×
● *Rockaway Park*, QueensS E	×
● *Rock City*, Cattaraugus. SW	×
● *Rock City*, Cattaraugus..SW	×
Rock City, Dutchess....... SE	125
Rock City, (see Amsterdam) .	×
Rock City Falls, Saratoga.. E	500
● *RockCut Switch*, OnondagaC	×
● Rockdale, Chenango....... C	185
● Rock Glen, Wyoming.... W	×
● *Rock Glen Sta.*, Wyoming W	×
Rock Hill, Sullivan........ SE	50
● Rockland, Sullivan...... SE	600
Rockland Lake, Rockland..SE	525
● *RocklandPark*, RocklandSE	×
● Rocklet, Orange .... SE	×
Rock Lock, (see LeFever Falls)	×
● Rock Rift, Delaware .... SE	100
● Rock Stream, Yates.......W	200
● *Rock Stream*, Yates......W	×
● *Rock Tavern*, Orange... SE	×
Rockton, Montgomery..... E	50
Rock Valley, Delaware.... SE	50
Rock View, Cattaraugus.. SW	50
● Rockville, Allegany.....SW	×
Rockville, (see Sharon Springs)	×
● Rockville Centre, Queens SE	575
● Rockwell's Mills, Che'n'go C	100
Rockwood, Fulton.......... E	254
Rocky Point, Suffolk...... SE	100
Rocky PointLanding, S'ff'kSE	×
Rodman, Jefferson......... N	228
● Rogers Rock, Essex.... NE	×
● *Rogersville*, Steuben.... SW	75
● Rome, Oneida........... C	14,991
● Romulus, Seneca..........C	500
● Rondout, Ulster..........SE	×
● Ronkonkoma, Suffolk...SE	×
Root, (see Rural Grove)......	×
Roscoe, Sullivan............SE	200
Rose, Steuben.............SW	×
Rose, Wayne.............. W	800
● *Rose*, Wayne............. W	275
● Rosebank, Richmond....SE	×
Roseboom, Otsego C	600
Rose Hill, Onondaga......... C	×
Roselawn, (see Mamaroneck)	×
● Rosendale, Ulster........SE	1,706
● *Rose Point*, Orange...... SE	×
● Roseton, Orange .... SE	×
Rose Valley, Wayne.........W	×
Rosevelt, Oswego............C	×
● Rosiere, Jefferson......... N	50
● Roslyn, Queens...........SE	1,251
● Rossburgh, Allegany....SW	1,200
Rossie, St. Lawrence....... N	275
● Ross Mills, Chautauqua. SW	25
Rossville, Richmond ...... SE	800
● *Rotterdam*, Schenectady..E	150
● Rotterdam Junc., Schen'y E	300
Round Isl. Park, (see Clayton)	×
● Round Lake, Saratoga.... E	200
● *Round Pond*, Franklin NE	×

New York

Place	Pop.
Round Top, (see Palenville).	×
● Rouse's Point, Clinton..NE	1,856
Rowland, Dutchess........ SE	×
● Roxbury, Delaware......SE	500
Royalton, Niagara .... W	100
Rudeston, Hamilton....... NE	200
Rural Grove, Montgomery.. E	150
Rural Hill, Jefferson........N	45
Rush, Monroe............. W	400
● *Rush*, Monroe........... W	300
● Rushford, Allegany..... SW	600
Rushville, Yates............W	450
Ruskey, Dutchess..........SE	×
Russell, St. Lawrence.......N	350
● *Russell's*, Dutchess......SE	×
Russells, Cattaraugus .... SW	×
● *Russia*, Clinton......... NE	×
Russia, Herkimer .... N	200
Rutland, Jefferson..........N	100
Rutledge, Cattaraugus.... SW	×
Rutsonville, Ulster........ SE	25
● Rye, Westchester.........SE	1,200
Ryne's Corners, Schenec'y.. E	30
Sabbath DayPoint, Warren NE	×
Sacandaga Park, Fulton.... E	×
● Sacket's Harbor, Jefferson N	787
Sagaponack, Suffolk....... SE	200
Sage's Corners, (see New Ber'n)	×
Sage's Corners, Otsego......C	×
Sageville, Hamilton.... NE	125
● Sag Harbor, Suffolk..... SE	3,000
Saginaw, Franklin.........NE	×
● ***Sailor's Snug Har.***, **R'chm'dSE**	×
● Saint Andrew, Orange...... SE	×
● *Saint Elmo*, Ulster..... SE	×
● *Saint George*, Richmond.SE	×
● Saint James, Suffolk.... SE	×
● *Saint Johnland*, Suffolk.SE	×
Saint Johns, Rockland.....SE	50
Saint Johnsburgh, Niagara. W	550
● Saint Johnsville, Montg'y. E	1,263
Saint Lawrence, Jefferson .. N	120
● Saint Regis Falls, Fr'k'n NE	1,210
Saint Regis Lake, FranklinNE	75
Saint Remy, Ulster.........SE	75
● Salamanca, Cattaraugus.SW	3,692
● Salem, Washington....... E	1,400
Salem Centre, Westchester.SE	200
● *Salina*, Onondaga C	×
Salisbury, Herkimer.........N	170
Salisbury Centre, Herkimer N	250
● Salisbury Mills, Orange.. SE	350
● *Salmon River*, Clinton..NE	×
Salmon River, Oswego...... C	75
● Salt Point, Dutchess..... SE	250
Salt Springville, Otsego..... C	150
● Salt Vale, Wyoming......W	×
● Sammonsville, Fulton.... E	180
Samsonville, Ulster........SE	75
● Sanborn, Niagara........ W	287
● Sand Bank, Oswego.......C	551
● *Sand Hill*, Oswego.......C	50
Sand Lake, Rensselaer..... E	400
Sand's Point, Queens.....SE	×
● Sandusky, Cattaraugus..SW	400
Sandy Creek, Oswego....... C	723
● *Sandy Creek*, Oswego..... C	333
● Sandy Hill, Washington.. E	2,895
Sanford, Broome............S	100
● Sanford's Corners, Jeffer'nN	75
● Sangerfield, Oneida C	300
Sangerfield Cen., (see Sangf'd)	×
● Sanitaria Springs, Broome S	200
Santa Clara, Franklin.....NE	150
Saranac, Clinton.......... NE	550
Saranac Inn, Franklin.... NE	×
● Saranac Lake, Franklin NE	768
● *Saratoga Lake*, Saratoga.. E	×
● Saratoga Springs, Sarat'a.. E	11,975
Sardinia, Erie............ W	500
● Saugerties, Ulster........SE	4,237
● Sauquoit, Oneida..........C	504
● Savannah, Wayne......... W	505
Savilton, Orange............SE	×
● Savona, Steuben......... SW	569
Sawens, Genesee.......... W	×
Sawkill, Ulster.............SE	100
Sawmill River, (see Tarrytown)	×
Sawyer, Orleans............ W	×
● *Sawyer's*, Allegany...... SW	×
● *Sawyer's Creek*, Niagara. W	×
Saxton, Ulster.............SE	50
● Sayville, Suffolk........ SE	1,500
● Scarborough, Westch'r..SE	×
● Scarsdale, Westchester.. SE	250
● Schaghticoke, Rensselaer. E	1,258
● **Schenectady**, Schenec'y E	19,902

New York

Place	Pop.
● Schenevus, Otsego........ C	665
Schodack, (see Schodack L'dg)	×
SchodackCentre, Rensselaer E	100
● Schodack Depot, Rens'r.. E	200
● Schodack Landing, Rens'r. E	400
● **Schoharie**, Schoharie.. E	1,028
Schoonmakers, CattaraugusSW	×
Schroon Lake, Essex...... NE	400
Schroon River, Essex..... NE	150
Schultzville, Dutchess..... SE	260
Schuyler, (see East or West Schuyler)	×
Schuyler, Saratoga......... E	150
● *Schuyler Junc.*, Saratoga. E	×
Schuyler's Falls, Clinton.. NE	200
Schuyler's Lake, Otsego....C	500
● Schuylersville, Saratoga.. E	1,387
● Scio, Allegany ....SW	600
Sciota, Clinton............ NE	200
Scipio, Cayuga.............C	490
Scipioville, Cayuga..........C	500
Scotch Bush, Montgomery.. E	300
Scotchtown, Orange.........SE	125
● Scotia, Schenectady.......E	250
Scott, Cortland C	450
Scott Corners, WestchesterSE	×
Scottsburgh, Livingston.... W	150
Scott's Bush, Montgomery..E	×
● Scottsville, Monroe.......W	800
● *Scottsville*, Monroe.......W	×
● *Scottsville Crossing*, Liv'nW	×
Scriba, Oswego...............C	200
● *Scriba*, Oswego.............C	×
● *Sea Breeze*, Monroe.......W	×
Sea Cliff, Queens............SE	1,250
Sea Cliff Station, Queens..SE	×
● Seaford, Queens..........SE	503
Seager, Ulster..............SE	×
Searsburgh, Schuyler......SW	25
Searsville, Orange..........SE	×
Seaside, Queens........... SE	×
Sea Side, Richmond........ SE	125
Second Milo, Yates.........W	50
● Seely Creek, Chemung.... S	150
Selden, Suffolk ....SE	100
● Selkirk, Albany............E	50
Sempronius, Cayuga........ C	200
Seneca, Ontario............ W	50
● Seneca Castle, Ontario.... W	200
● Seneca Falls, Seneca.......C	6,116
● *Seneca Hill*, Oswego...... C	25
● *Seneca Mills*, Yates......W	×
Seneca Point, Ontario......W	×
● *Seneca River*, Cayuga.....C	×
● Sennett, Cayuga............C	400
Setauket, Suffolk.......... SE	1,000
● *Setauket Station*, SuffolkSE	×
● *Severance*, Monroe.......W	×
Sevey, St. Lawrence........ N	×
● Seward, Schoharie........ E	500
Seward Valley, Schoharie...E	300
● *Shaker Crossing*, Liv'gst'nW	×
Shakers, Albany.............E	300
Shamrock, Onondaga.........C	×
● Shandaken, Ulster.......SE	500
Shanley, Franklin ....NE	125
Sharon, Schoharie.......... E	300
Sharon Centre, Schoharie....E	200
● Sharon Springs, S'hoh'aie. E	622
● Sharon Station, DutchessSE	75
Shavertown, Delaware......SE	200
Shawangunk, (see Walkill)..	×
Shawnee, Niagara.......... W	90
● Shed's Corners, Madison..C	100
Sheenwater, Erie............W	×
● Sheepshead Bay, Kings..SE	600
● Shekomeko, Dutchess ...SE	60
Shelby, Orleans..............W	300
Shelby Basin, Orleans......W	×
Sheldon, Wyoming......... W	350
Sheldon Corners, (see Sh'ld'n)	×
Sheldons Cors., Chaut'qua SW	×
Sheldrake, Seneca...........C	150
● *Sheldrake Sta.*, Seneca....C	×
Shelter Island, Suffolk.....SE	150
ShelterIslandHeights, Suff'kSE	×
Shelving Rock, Washington. E	×
Shenandoah, Dutchess......SE	50
● Sherburne, Chenango..... C	960
● Sherburne Four Corners, Chenango C	×
Sherell, Madison C	×
● Sheridan, Chautauqua ..SW	400
● *Sheridan*, Chautauqua..SW	×
● **Sherman, Chautauqua** ..SW	785
Sherrill, Oneida..............C	×
Sherruck, Delaware........SE	100

Sherwood, Cayuga C 400
Shingle Creek, (seeKeenev'l'e) ×
Shinhopple, Delaware SE 50
● Shinnecock Hills, Suffolk SE ×
Shirley, Erie W 60
● Shokan, Ulster SE 400
Shongo, Allegany SW 200
Shongo, Cattaraugus SW ×
● *Short's Switch*, Madison C ×
● Shortsville, Ontario W 900
Short Tract, Allegany SW 500
Shrub Oak, Westchester SE 375
Shumla, Chautauqua SW ×
● Shunpike, Dutchess SE 25
● Shushan, Washington E 500
Shutter's Corners, Schoharie E 70
● Sidney, Delaware SE 1,358
● Sidney Centre, Delaware SE 600
Sidney Plains, (see Sidney) ×
● *Sierks*, Wyoming W ×
Siloam, Madison C 150
Silver Bay, Warren NE ×
● Silver Creek, Cha't'qua SW 1,678
Silver Hill, St. Lawrence N ×
Silver Lake, (see Bl'k Brook) ×
● *Silver Lake*, Wyoming W ×
● Silver Lake Assembly, Wyoming W ×
● *Silver Lake Junc.* Wy'ing W ×
● Silvernails, Columbia SE 50
● Silver Springs, Wyoming W 500
Simpsonville, Delaware SE ×
● Sinclairville, Chau'qua SW 510
● Sing Sing, Westchester SE 9,352
● *Sissons*, St. Lawrence N ×
● Skaneateles, Onondaga C 1,559
● Skaneateles Falls, On'daga C 150
● *Skaneateles Junc.* On'daga C 350
● *Skaneateles Sta.* Onondaga C ×
Skerry, Franklin NE 50
Skinnerville, St. Lawrence N 150
● Slate Hill, Orange SE 400
Slaterville Springs, Tompkins S 200
Sleightsburg, (see Kingston) ×
● *Sleepy Hollow*, W'ch'ster SE 3,739
Slide Mountain, Ulster SE 150
● Slingerland's, Albany E 500
Sliters, Rensselaer E 50
Sloan, Erie W ×
Sloansville, Schoharie E 300
● Sloatsburgh, Rockland SE 200
Slyborough, Washington E ×
Smithfield, Dutchess SE 50
Smithfield, (see Peterboro) ×
● Smith's Basin, Washington E 350
● Smithsborough, Tioga S 500
Smith's Corners, (see Medusa) ×
Smith's Landing, Greene SE 100
● Smith's Mills, Chau'qua SW 200
Smith's Mills, St. Lawrence N ×
Smith's Valley, (see R'd'lsville) ×
● Smithtown, Suffolk SE 800
Smithtown Branch, Suffolk SE 700
Smith Valley, Schuyler SW ×
● *Smithville*, Genesee SE 150
Smithville, Jefferson N 250
Smithville Flats, Chenango C 275
Smithville South, Queens SE 300
Smoky Hollow, (see H'll'wv'e) ×
● Smyrna, Chenango C 325
Snedekers, Chemung S ×
Snowdon, Otsego C 25
Snyder, Erie W 75
● *Snyder's*, Tompkins S ×
Snyders Corners, Rensselaer E 40
Snydertown, (see Hollowville) ×
Snyderville, Columbia SE 25
● Sodus, Wayne W 1,028
● Sodus Centre, Wayne W 400
● Sodus Point, Wayne W 500
Solon, Cortland C 150
● Solsville, Madison C 75
● Solway, Onondaga C 563
Somers, Westchester SE 400
● Somers Centre, West'h'r SE 200
Somerset, Niagara W 400
● *Somerset*, Niagara W 25
Somerville, St. Lawrence N 175
Sonora, Steuben SW 100
● Sonyea, Livingston W ×
South Addison, Steuben SW 100
● South Alabama, Genesee W 150
South Albion, Oswego C ×
South Alma, Cattaraugus SW ×
South Amenia, Dutchess SE 150
● Southampton, Suffolk SE 1,800

New York

South Apalachin, Tioga S ×
South Argyle, Washington E 200
● South Avon, Livingston W 100
● *South Ballston*, Saratoga E 200
South Bangor, (see Bangor) ×
South Barre, Orleans W 150
● South Bay, Madison C ×
South Bay, (see Cicero) ×
● *South Bay*, Washington E ×
South Beach, Richmond SE ×
● South Berlin, Rensselaer E 200
South Berne, Albany E 125
● South Bethlehem, Albany E 150
South Bloomfield, Ontario W 50
South Bolivar, Allegany SW ×
South Bombay, Franklin NE 200
South Bradford, Steuben SW 25
South Bristol, Ontario W 200
South Brookfield, Madison C 185
● *South Buffalo*, Erie W ×
South Butler, Wayne W 480
● South Byron, Genesee W 400
● South Cairo, Greene SE 100
● South Cambridge, Wash'n E 200
South Canisteo, Steuben SW ×
South Canton, (seeCrary's M's) ×
● *South Carrollton*, Catt's SW ×
South Centreville, Orange SE ×
South Champion, Jefferson N ×
South Chili, (see Clifton) ×
South Colton, St. Lawrence N 250
● South Columbia, Herk'er N 100
● South Corinth, Saratoga E 200
South Corners, (see Vienna) ×
● South Cortland, Cortland C 100
South Cuyler, Cortland C ×
South Danby, Tompkins S 50
South Dansville, Steuben SW 150
● South Dayton, Cattar's SW 500
● South Dover, Dutchess SE 125
South Durham, Greene SE 500
South Easton, Washington E 150
South Edmeston, Otsego C 150
South Edwards, St. Law'nce N 60
South Ellenburgh, Clinton NE ×
South Ellenville, (seeEllenv'e. ×
South Erin, Chemung S ×
● South Fallsburgh, Sull'n SE 50
● Southfields, Orange SE 300
South Fordham, New York SE ×
● South Gilboa, Schoharie E 95
South Glens Falls, Saratoga E 1,606
● South Granby, Oswego C ×
South Granville, Washington E 50
● South Greece, Monroe W 100
● *South Greenfield*, Kings SE 150
● South Greenfield, Saratoga E 40
South Hamilton, Madison C 50
● South Hammond, St. La'ce N 125
South Hannibal, Oswego C 125
South Hartford, Washington E 126
South Hartwick, Otsego C 75
South Haven, Suffolk SE ×
South Horicon, Warren NE 124
South Howard, Steuben SW 40
South Jamaica, Queens SE ×
South Jefferson, Schoharie E 50
● South Kortright, Del're SE ×
South Lansing, Tompkins S 150
● South Lima, Livingston W 26
● South Livonia, Livingston W 100
South Melrose, (see N. York) ×
South Millbrook, Dutchess SE 75
South Mt. Vernon, Westc'r SE 2,500
● South New Berlin, Che'go C 650
South New Haven, Oswego C ×
South Newstead, Erie W ×
● *South Nyack*, Rockland SE 1,496
● Southold, Suffolk SE 1,000
South Onondaga, Onondaga C 250
South Otselic, Chenango C 400
South Owego, Tioga S ×
● South Oxford, Chenango C 75
South Oyster Bay, Queens SE ×
South Petersburg, (see Pe'b'g) ×
● South Plattsburgh, C'ton NE ×
South Plymouth, Chenango C 150
● Southport, Chemung S 109
South Pultney, Steuben SW 75
● South Richland, Oswego C 150
South Ripley, Chautauqua SW ×
South Rondout, (seeKingston) ×
South Russell, St. Lawr'ce N ×
South Rutland, Jefferson N 120
South Salem, Westchester SE 500
South Sand Lake, Rensselaer E 125

New York

● South Schenectady, Sch'dy E 200
● South Schodack, Rens'er E 150
South Schroon, Essex NE 200
South Scriba, Oswego C ×
South Setauket, Suffolk SE ×
South Sodus, Wayne W 250
South Somerset, Niagara W ×
South Spafford, Onondaga C ×
South Stephentown, (seeSte'n) ×
South Stockholm, St. Law'e N 50
South Stockton, Chautau'a SW 200
South Syracuse, Onondaga C 200
South Trenton, Oneida C 134
South Troupsburgh, Ste'b'n SW 25
South Valley, Otsego C 500
● *South Vandalia*, Catt'us SW ×
Southville, St. Lawrence N 100
● South Wales, Erie W 80
South Westerlo, Albany E 300
South West Oswego, Oswego C 50
South Williamsburgh, Qu's SE ×
South Wilson, Niagara W ×
South Worcester, Otsego C 100
South Yonkers, Westches'r SE ×
Spafford, Onondaga C 150
● Sparkill, Rockland SE 816
● Sparrow Bush, Orange SE 300
Speedsville, Tompkins S 200
● Spencer, Tioga S 810
● Spencerport, Monroe W 695
● *Spencer Summit*, Tioga S 29
Spencertown, Columbia SE 450
● Speonk, Suffolk SE 200
Spinnerville, Herkimer N 40
Split Rock, Onondaga C ×
● Spragueville, St. Lawrence N 250
● Sprakers, Montgomery E 200
Spring Brook, Erie W 350
● *Spring Brook*, Erie W ×
Spring Cove, Franklin NE 75
Springfield, Otsego C 100
Springfield Centre, Otsego C 275
● *Springfield Sta.*, Queens SE 300
● *Springfield Store*, Queens SE 300
● *Spring Glen*, Ulster SE 100
● *Spring House*, Orange SE ×
Spring Lake, Cayuga C 100
● *Spring Lake*, Dutchess SE 175
● Springland, Queens SE 300
Spring Mills, Allegany SW 250
● *Spring Park*, Westchester SE ×
Springs, Suffolk SE ×
● *Spring Side*, Orange SE ×
● Springtown, Ulster SE ×
● Spring Valley, Rockland SE 1,028
● Springville, Erie W 1,883
Springville, Suffolk SE ×
● Springwater, Livingston W 500
Sprout Brook, Montgomery E 100
Spruceton, Greene SE 200
● *Spuyten Duyvil*, N. York SE ×
Squiretown, Suffolk SE ×
● Staatsburgh, Dutchess SE 496
● Stafford, Genesee W 200
Stalbird, St. Lawrence N ×
● Stamford, Delaware SE 819
Stanard's Corners, Allegany SW 150
Stanbro, Chenango C ×
● Standish, Clinton NE 200
● Stanfordville, Dutchess SE 450
● Stanley, Ontario W 400
Stanton Hill, Greene SE 95
Stanwix, Oneida C 109
● Stapleton, Richmond SE 4,000
● *Star Farm*, Chautauqua SW ×
Stark, St. Lawrence N ×
● Starkey, Yates W 450
Starkville, Herkimer N 300
● *Star Lake*, St. Lawrence N ×
Starlight, Sullivan SE ×
● State Bridge, Oneida C 300
State Dam, Franklin NE ×
● State Line, Broome S ×
State Line, Cattaraugus S ×
● *State Line*, Dutchess SE ×
Stateroad, Allegany SW ×
● Steamburgh, Cattaraugus SW 300
Steam Hill, St. Lawrence N ×
Stedman, Chautauqua SW 50
Steinway, (seeLongIslandCity) ×
Stella, Broome S ×
Stephens' Mill, Steuben SW 150
Stephensville, (see Alcove) ×
● Stephentown, Rensselaer E 250
Stephentown Centre, Rens'l'r E 250
Sterling, Cayuga C 500

Sterling Bush, Lewis........N 100
Sterling Forest, Orange...SE ×
● *Sterling Furnace*, OrangeSE ×
● Sterling Station, Cayuga..C ×
● Sterlington, Rockland...SE ×
Sterling Valley, Cayuga..... C 300
● *Sterling Val. Sta.*, Cayuga C ×
● Sterlingville, Jefferson... N 100
Stetsonville, (see New Lisbon) ×
Steuben, Oneida...........C 100
Steuben Valley, Oneida.....C ×
Stevens, Cattaraugus......SW ×
Stevensville, Sullivan......SE 200
Stewart, Schoharie..........E ×
● Stiles Station, Onondaga..C ×
Stillwater, Lewis............N ×
Stillwater, Saratoga..........E 747
● *Stillwater Centre*, SaratogaE ×
● Stissing, Dutchess....... SE 100
Stittville, Oneida............C 184
● Stockbridge, Madison.....C 275
Stockholm, St. Lawrence...N ×
Stockholm Centre, St. Law'ce N 100
● Stockport, Columbia....SE 1,980
● Stockport Sta., DelawareSE 75
Stockton, Chautauqua.... SW 700
Stockwell, Oneida.......... C ×
Stokes, Oneida............. C 60
Stone Arabia, Montgomery. E 75
● *Stone Bridge*, Orange....SE ×
Stone Church, Genesee.....W 100
Stoneco, Dutchess..........SE 250
Stone Dam, Allegany......SW ×
● Stonehouse, Dutchess....SE 50
Stone Mills, Jefferson........N 100
Stone Quarry, (see New Haven) ×
Stone Ridge, Ulster........SE 450
● Stony Brook, Suffolk....SE 506
Stony Brook Glen, SteubenSW 19
● *Stony Clove*, Greene.....SE ×
● *Stony Creek*, Warren....NE ×
● Stony Ford, Orange..... SE ×
● Stony Hollow, Ulster....SE 50
● Stony Point, Rockland...SE 514
● Storm King, Dutchess...SE 250
● Stormville, Dutchess.... SE 100
● Stottville, Columbia..... SE 675
Stow, Chautauqua.........SW 30
Strait's Corners, Tioga.......S 40
Stratford, Fulton........... E 114
Stratton, Tompkins.........S ×
● *Strattons Siding*, Steub'n SW ×
Street Road, Essex.........NE 300
● *Stroughs*, Jefferson.......N ×
Strykersville, Wyoming....W 500
● Stuyvesant, Columbia... SE 1,225
Stuyvesant Falls, ColumbiaSE 875
Suckertown, Clinton....... NE 50
Sucker Brook, St. Lawrence N ×
● Suffern, Rockland........SE 500
Sugar Hill, Schuyler.......SW ×
● Sugar Loaf, Orange......SE 150
Sullivanville, Chemung.......S 100
● SummerDale, ChatauquaSW 40
Summer Hill, Cayuga....... C 100
Summerville Beach, MonroeW ×
● *Summit*, Allegany...... SW ×
● *Summit*, Allegheny.....SW ×
● *Summit*, Cattaraugus... SW ×
● *Summit*, Chautauqua.... SW ×
● *Summit*, Chenango....... C ×
Summit, Schoharie...........E 300
● *Summit*, Saratoga.........E ×
● *Summit*, Tompkins........ S ×
● *Summit*, Washington..... E 200
Summit Mountain, Ulster. SE ×
Summit Park, Rockland.. SE ×
Summit Station, Onondaga..C ×
● Summitville, Sullivan... SE 200
Sun, Franklin.............NE ×
Sundown, Ulster...........SE 100
Sunken Meadow, Suffolk..SE ×
Sunnyside, Queens......... SE ×
Surprise, Greene...........SE 150
● Suspension Bridge, Niag'ra W 4,405
Suydam, Columbia.........SE ×
● Swain, Allegany.......... SW 183
Swale, Steuben............SW ×
● Swamp Mills, Sullivan...SE ×
● *Swamp Siding*, Tioga..... S ×
● Swartwood, Chemung.....S 50
Sweden Centre, Monroe....W 100
Sweden, Monroe.......... W ×
● Swormville, Erie........W 400
Sylva, Ulster..............SE ×
● *Sylvan*, Oneida.............C ×
● Sylvan Beach, Oneida.....C 200
● *Sylvan Junction*, Oneida. C ×
● Sylvan Lake, Dutchess...SE 100
● Syossett, Queens.........SE 150
● **SYRACUSE**, Onondaga.C 88,143
Tabasco, Ulster............ SE 50
Taberg, Oneida.............C 2,331
● *Taberg*, Oneida.......... C 300
Tacoma, Delaware.........SE ×
Taghkanick, Columbia.....SE 60
Tahawus, Essex...........NE ×
Talcottville, (see Booneville). ×
Talcville, St. Lawrence......N ×
Tallette, Chenango..........C ×
● Tallman, Rockland.......SE 400
Tamarac, (see Cropseyville).. ×
Tanghanic, Tompkins...... S ×
● *Tanners*, Columbia..... SE ×
● Tannersville, Greene.... SE 500
● Tappan, Rockland........SE 100
Tarrettsville, (see New Berlin) ×
● Tarrytown, Westchester.SE 3,562
● *Taughannock*, Tompkins.S ×
● TaughannockFalls, T'mk'sS ×
Taylor, Cortland............C 125
Taylor Centre, Cortland.....C ×
Taylor's on Schroon, War'nNE ×
Taylor Valley, Cortland.....C ×
Teals, Seneca.............. C ×
Teedville, (see Trout Creek).. ×
● *Terminal*, Monroe....... W ×
● *Terrace*, Erie.......... W ×
Terryville, Suffolk........ SE ×
Terwilligers, Ulster....... SE ×
Texas, Oswego..............C 150
Texas Valley, Cortland......C 150
Thayer's Corners, (see Westerlo) ×
Thayer's Corners, FranklinNE 100
The Abbey, (see Albany) ..... ×
The Corner, Ulster.........SE 100
● The Glen, Warren.........NE 75
The Narrows, Washington. E ×
The Raunt, Queens........SE ×
● Theresa, Jefferson........N 1,028
● *Theresa Junc.*, Jefferson. N ×
● Thiells, Rockland........SE 75
● Thomaston, Queens......SE ×
● *ThompsonHouse*, Put'amSE ×
● Thompson Ridge, OrangeSE ×
Thompson's Lake, Albany.. E ×
Thompson's Landing, (see De-Witt Center) .... ×
● *Thompsons*, Ontario..... W ×
Thompsons Switch, SuffolkSE ×
Thompsonville, Sullivan...SE 150
Thomson's Mills, Washing'n. E 100
Thorn Hill, Onondaga.......C ×
Thousand Is'd Park, JeffersonN ×
Three Mile Bay, Jefferson.. N 900
● *Three Mile BaySta.*, Jeff'nN ×
Three Mile Point, Otsego...C ×
● Three River Pt., OnondagaC ×
Throggs Neck, WestchesterSE ×
Throop, Cayuga.............C ×
Throopsville, Cayuga........C 400
Thurman, Warren.........NE 350
● *Thurman Sta.*, Warren. NE ×
Thurso, Jefferson.......... N ×
Thurston, Steuben......... SW 100
● Tiashoke, Rensselaer..... E 100
● Ticonderoga, Essex..... NE 2,267
● *Ticonderoga Jc.*, Essex. NE ×
● Tilly Foster, Putnam....SE ×
● Tioga Centre, Tioga....... S 350
● *Tip Top*, Allegany......SW ×
Titus, Franklin...........NE ×
Titusville, Franklin.......NE ×
● Tivoli, Dutchess......... SE 1,350
Toddsville, Otsego..........C 300
Tomhannock, Rensselaer....E 150
● Tomkins Cove, Rockland SE 200
Tompkins Corners, PutnamSE ×
● Tompkinsville, RichmondSE 1,400
● Tonawanda, Erie......... W 7,145
● Tottenville, Richmond...SE 1,500
Tower Hill, Richmond.... SE ×
Towlesville, Steuben...... SW 180
● Towner's, Putnam.......SE 400
● Town Line, Erie.........W 300
Townsend, Schuyler.......SW 150
Townsendville, Seneca...... C 100
Township, (see West Township) ×
Tracy Creek, Broome........S 350
● *Transit*, Erie.......... W 400
Transit Bridge, Allegany..SW 25
Travisville, Richmond.....SE 100
Tremaine's Corners, JeffersonN ×
● Tremont, New York.... SE ×
● Trenton, Oneida.......... C 284
● Trenton Falls, Oneida.....C 138
Trevett, Saratoga.......... E ×
Triangle, Broome........... S 210
● Tribes Hill, Montgomery..E 300
Tri States, Orange.......... SE ×
Troupsburgh, Steuben.... SW 350
Trout Brook, Delaware....SE 75
● *Trout Brook*, Delaware..SE 86
Trout Creek, Delaware.... SE 100
Trout River, Franklin.....NE 250
● **TROY**, Rensselaer........E 60,956
● Trumansburgh, TompkinsS 1,211
Trumbull Corners, TompkinsS 100
Truthville, Washington..... E 200
● Truxton, Cortland.........C 350
Tuckahoe, Suffolk..........SE ×
● Tuckahoe, Westchester..SE 1,000
● Tully, Onondaga.......... C 434
Tully Lake Park, Onondaga. C ×
Tully Valley, Onondaga.... C 498
● Tunesassa, Cattaraugus. SW 50
● Tunnel, Broome...........S 100
Tupper Lake, Franklin.... NE 250
Turin, Lewis................N 359
Turnbull, Schenectady..... E ×
● Turner's, Orange........SE ×
Turnwood, Ulster..........SE 200
● *Tuscarora*, Broome...... S ×
● Tuscarora, Livingston....W 225
Tusten, Sullivan.......... SE 75
● *Tusten Station*, Sullivan SE ×
● *Tuthill Station*, Sullivan SE ×
● Tuxedo Park, Orange... SE ×
● *Twin Ponds*, Franklin. NE ×
Tyner, Chenango............C 75
Tyre, Seneca............... C 150
Tyrone, Schuyler..........SW 350
Ulster Heights, Ulster..... SE ×
Ulster Landing, Dutchess. SE ×
● Ulster Park, Ulster.......SE 150
Ulsterville, Ulster..........SE 50
● Unadilla, Otsego.......... C 1,157
Unadilla Centre, Otsego.....C 100
Unadilla Forks, Otsego......C 500
● *Unadilla ForksSta.*, On'idaC ×
Underwood, Essex........ NE ×
● Union, Broome...........S 821
● *Union*, Rockland.........SE ×
Union Centre, Broome......S 250
Union Church, Albany......E 60
Union Corners, (see Elizaville) ×
Union Corners, (see East Park) ×
● *Union Course*, Queens...SE ×
Union Falls, Clinton...... NE ×
Union Grove, Delaware... SE 300
Union Hill, Monroe......... W 50
Union Mills, Fulton.........E 75
Union Place, Suffolk......SE ×
Union Society, Greene......SE 25
● Union Springs, Cayuga....C 1,066
● Union Square, Oswego....C 150
Union Valley, Cortland......C 125
● *Unionville*, Kings........SE 150
● Unionville, Orange.......SE 316
Unionville, (see Fruit Valley) ×
● *Unionville*, Westchester. SE ×
Upper Jay, Essex.......... NE 400
Upper Lisle, Broome........S 250
Upper Nyack, Rockland...SE 668
Upper Piermont, (see Sparkill) ×
● Upper Red Hook, Dutch'sSE 175
Upper Saranac Lake, Franklin..........NE 200
● *Upper Switch*, Tompkins..S ×
Urbana, Steuben..........SW ×
Urlton, Greene.............SE 150
● Ushers, Saratoga..........E 50
● **UTICA**, Oneida...........C 44,007
Utopia, Allegany..........SW ×
● Vail's Gate, Orange.......SE ×
● *Vail's GateJunc.*, Orange SE ×
Vail's Mills, Fulton......... E 200
Valatie, Columbia..........SE 1,437
● Valcour, Clinton.........NE 50
● Valhalla, Westchester...SE ×
● ValleyCottage, Rockland SE ×
● Valley Falls, Rensselaer.. E 1,200
● Valley Mills, Madison.....C 75
● Valley Stream, Queens.. SE 350
Valley Stream Junc., QueensSE ×
Vallonia Springs, Broome...S ×
Van Brunt, Kings.......... SE ×
● *Van Buren*, ChautauquaSW ×
● Van Buren, Onondaga.....C ×
● *Van Cortlandt*, New YorkSE ×

● *Van Cortlandt Park Junction*, New York........SE ×
● Vandalia, Cattaraugus..SW 1,200
● Van Ettenville, Chemung. S 567
● *Van Hoesen*, Rensselaer..E ×
Van Hornesville, Herkimer. N 300
● *Van Keuren's*, Orange..SE ×
● *Van Nest*, Westchester..SE ×
● Van Pelt Manor, Kings..SE ×
Van Vechten, see Pattersonville) .... ×
● *Van Vleets*, Steuben....SW ×
Van Vranken's Corners, (see Newtonville) .... ×
● Van Wagner, Dutchess..SE 80
● *Van Wicklens*, Kings...SE ×
Varick, Seneca..........C 50
● Varna, Tompkins.........S 175
● Varysburgh, Wyoming...W 200
Vaughns, Washington.......E ×
Vebber, (see Pierrepont)..... ×
Venice, Cayuga.............C 150
● Venice Centre, Cayuga....C 250
● Verbank, Dutchess.......SE 200
Verbank Village, Dutchess SE 150
Vermillion, Oswego.........E 100
● *Vermontville*, Franklin NE ×
● Vernon, Oneida...........C 377
Vernon Centre, Oneida......C 212
Verona, Oneida..............C 300
Verona Beach, Oneida......C ×
Verona Mills, Oneida........C ×
● Verona Station, Oneida...C ×
Verplanck, Westchester...SE 1,515
Versailles, Cattaraugus...SW 208
Vesper, Onondaga...........C 150
● Vestal, Broome...........S 150
Vestal Centre, Broome......S 200
● Victor, Ontario..........W 778
Victory, Cayuga.............C 400
● Victory Mills, Saratoga...E 822
● Vienna, Oneida............C 225
● *Villa Park*, Erie..........W ×
Villenova, Chautauqua....SW 200
Vincent, Ontario............W 100
Vine Valley, Yates..........W 50
Vintonton, Schoharie.......E 200
Viola, Rockland............SE 75
Virgil, Cortland.............C 250
Vischer's Ferry, Saratoga...E 206
Vista, Westchester.........SE 50
Voak, Yates................W 25
Volney, Oswego.............C 100
Volusia, Chautauqua......SW 100
● *Voorheesville*, Albany.... E 190
● *Vosburg*, Allegany..... SW ×
Waddington, St. Lawrence..N 910
● Wadhams Mills, Essex...NE 160
Wading River, Suffolk.....SE 100
Wadsworth, Livingston.... W ×
Wakefield, Westchester... SE ×
● Walden, Orange.........SE 2,132
Wales, Erie..................W 75
Wales Centre, Erie......... W 250
Walesville, Oneida.........C 70
Walker Valley, Ulster..... SE 200
● Walkill, Ulster.......... SE 450
● Wallace, Steuben....... SW 250
Walleys, Suffolk.........SE ×
● Wallington, Wayne.......W 50
● Walloomsack, Rensselaer. E 150
● Walton, Delaware....... SE 2,299
Walworth, Wayne............W 640
● *Walworth Station*, W'ne W ×
● Wampsville, Madison..... C 00
Wango, Chautauqua....... SW ×
● Wantagh, Queens........SE 200
Wappinger'sFalls, Dutchess SE 3,718
Wardner's, Franklin..... NE ×
● Warner's, Onondaga...... C 150
Warnerville, Schoharie......E 100
Warren, Herkimer...........N 140
Warrensburgh, Warren... NE 893
Warren's Corners, Niagara. W ×
● **Warsaw**, Wyoming.... W 3,120
Warsaw, Yates............ W ×
● Warwick, Orange........ SE 1,537
Warwick Woodlands, Orange SE ×
● *Washburn*, Chautauqua SW ×
Washington, (see South Millbrook) ×
Washington Hollow, Du'ss. SE 380
● Washington Mills, Oneida. C 1,195
Washington Square, Que'sSE ×
● Washingtonville, Orange SE 691
● *Washingtonville*, Westchester SE ×
● Wassaic, Dutchess...... SE 275
● *Waterboro*, Chautauqua SW ×

Waterburgh, Tompkins..... S 150
● Waterford, Saratoga......E 4,500
● *Waterford Junction* Sa'ga E ×
● **Waterloo**, Seneca.......C 4,350
● Water Mill, Suffolk......SE 200
● Waterport, Orleans...... W 300
● **Watertown**, Jefferson. N 14,725
● *Watertown Junction*, Je'n N ×
Watervale, Onondaga....... C 100
● Water Valley, Erie........W 75
● Waterville, Oneida.........C 2,024
Watervliet, (see West Troy).. ×
Watervliet Centre, Albany..E 300
● **Watkins**, Schuyler.....SW 2,600
● *Watkins Glen*, Schuyler SW ×
● *Watkins Station*, Sch'r. SW ×
Watson, Lewis..............N 100
Watts Mill, Cattaraugus..SW ×
● Watts Flats, Chau'qua..SW 300
Wautagh, (see Ridgewood).. ×
● *Waverly*, Suffolk........SE ×
● Waverly, Tioga............S 4,123
Wawarsing, Ulster.........SE 1,000
Wawbeek, Franklin...... NE 100
Wayland, Steuben........ SW 679
Wayne, Schuyler..........SW ×
Wayne, Steuben......... SW 350
Wayne Centre, Wayne...... W 200
Wayne Four Corners, St'nSW 350
● *Wayneport*, Wayne.......W ×
● Wayville, Saratoga........E 40
Weavertown, Saratoga......E ×
Webatuck, Dutchess.......SE 100
● Webb's Mills, Chemung...S 400
● Webster, Monroe........ W 634
Webster's Corners, Erie....W ×
● Webster's Crossing, Liv'n W 80
● Webster Station, Madison. C 75
● Wedgwood, Schuyler...SW ×
Weed Mines, Columbia....SE 100
● Weedsport, Cayuga....... C 1,580
Wegatchie, St. Lawrence...N 175
Welcome, Otsego............C ×
Wells, Hamilton.......... NE 1,200
● *Wells*, Chemung ....S 400
● Wells' Bridge, Otsego.....C 300
● Wellsburgh, Chemung...... S 850
● Wellsville, Allegany.... SW 3,435
Wellwood, Otsego...........C ×
Weltonville, Tioga...........S 75
● Wemple, Albany............E ×
● *Wende*, Erie...............W 200
Wendelville, Niagara.......W 75
Wesley, Cattaraugus......SW ×
● West, Cattaraugus.......SW 150
● West Albany, Albany.....E ×
West Alden, Erie............W 150
● *West Alden Sta.*, Erie.....W ×
West Allen, Allegany...... SW ×
West Almond, Allegany.. SW 80
West Amboy, Oswego....... C 200
● *West Athens*, Greene.....SE ×
West Bainbridge, Chenango. C ×
West Bangor, Franklin... NE 400
West Barre, Orleans.........W 250
● West Batavia, Genesee....W ×
West Beach, Monroe.......W ×
West Beekmantown, Ct'n. NE 40
● West Bergen, Genesee... W 100
West Berlin, (see Berlin)..... ×
West Berne, Albany.........E 200
West Bethany, Genesee.... W 40
● West Bloomfield, Ontario W 500
West Branch, Oneida........C 200
West Brighton, Monroe.....W 300
● *West Brighton*, Richm'd SE 6,000
● *West Brighton Beach*, Kings SE ×
West Brook, Delaware.....SE 100
● West Brooklyn, Kings...SE ×
● West Brookville, Sul'v'n. SE 250
West Burlington, Otsego....C 100
Westbury, Cayuga............C 150
● Westbury Station, Qu's..SE 200
● West Cambridge, Washing'n E 150
● West Camden, Oneida.....C 200
● West Camp, Ulster.......SE 50
● West Candor, Tioga........S 100
West Carthage, Jefferson...N 932
West Caton, Steuben....... SW 25
West Charlton, Saratoga....E 100
● West Chazy, Clinton.....NE 350
West Chenango, Broome....S ×
● West Chester, Westche'r. SE 10,029
West Clarksville, Allegany SW 200
West Colesville, Broome.... S 150
West Conesville, Schoharie..E 100
West Constable, Franklin. NE 400

West Copake, Columbia....SE 150
● West Cornwall, Orange..SE ×
● West Coxsackie, Greene. SE 1,000
● *West Craigville*, Orange. SE ×
● *West Crossing*, Orange..SE ×
● West Danby, Tompkins... S 100
● West Davenport, Del'w'e SE 150
West Day, Saratoga.......... E 102
West Dresden, (see Dresden). ×
● West Dryden, Tompkins..S 125
West Eaton, Madison....... C 500
West Edmeston, Otsego..... C 100
West End, Broome.......... S ×
Westerlo, Albany .... E 200
Westernville, Oneida....... C 250
West Exeter, Otsego........ C 150
● West Falls, Erie.........W 500
● *West Farms*, New York. SE ×
● West Fayette, Seneca..... C 100
● ***West Fayette Sta.***, Seneca C ×
● Westfield, Chautauqua..SW 1,983
Westfield Flats, (see R'ck'd). ×
Westford, Otsego............C 250
West Fort Ann, Washington. E 450
West Fulton, Schoharie..... E 225
West Galway, Fulton....... E 300
West Ghent, Columbia .... SE 25
West Granville Corners, Washington .... E 200
West Greece, Monroe...... W 200
West Greenfield, (see Mid'eGr.) ×
West Groton, Tompkins.....S 100
West Hadley, (see Conk'ville). ×
● West Hampton, Suffolk..SE 350
West Hampton Beach, S'f'k SE ×
● *West Haverstraw*, R'kl'd SE 180
West Hebron, Washington.. E 254
● West Henrietta, Monroe..W 130
West Hoosick, Rensselaer... E 175
● West Hurley, Ulster..... SE 250
West Italy, Yates...........W 75
● West Junius, Ontario.....W 25
West Kendall, Orleans..... W 150
West Kill, Greene..........SE 150
West Kingston, (see Kingston) ×
West Kortright, Delaware..SE 40
West Laurens, Otsego....... C 300
● West Lebanon, Columbia SE 400
West Leyden, Lewis......... N 150
West Lockport, Niagara... W ×
West Lowville, Lewis....... N 20
West Martinsburgh, Lewis..N 155
West Meredith, Delaware. SE 25
West Milton, Saratoga...... E 200
Westminster Pk., Jefferson N ×
● West Monroe, Oswego.... C 150
● Westmoreland, Oneida.....C 403
West Morrisania, (see N.Y'k) ×
West Mt. Vernon, Westch'r SE ×
West Newark, Tioga........ S ×
● West New Brighton, Richmond......................SE 6,000
● *West Newburgh*, Orange SE ×
West Nunda, Livingston.. W 1,010
● *West Nyack*, Rockland. SE ×
Weston, Schuyler..........SW 100
West Oneonta, Otsego.......C 250
West Onondaga Valley, Onondaga.......................C ×
● *Weston's*, St. Lawrence.. N ×
● Weston's Mills, Cattara'g'sSW 100
West Parishville, St. Law'nce N ×
● West Park, Ulster.......SE ×
● West Patterson, Putnam SE ×
West Perrysburg, Catta'gus SW ×
● *West Pawling*, Dutchess. SE 50
West Perth, Fulton..........E 25
West Pierpont, St. Lawrence N 200
West Plattsburgh, Clinton NE 150
● West Point, Orange..... SE 1,300
● Westport, Essex........ NE 563
West Potsdam, St. Lawrence N 125
West Providence, Saratoga..E 20
West Rathbone, Steuben. SW ×
West Richmondville, Sch'rie E 150
West River, Yates..........W ×
● West Rush, Monroe...... W 300
● West Salamanca, C't'r'g'sSW 495
West Sand Lake, Rensselaer. E 300
● *West Saratoga Jc.*, Saratoga E ×
West Saugerties, Ulster... SE 150
West Sayville, Suffolk..... SE 100
West Schuyler, Herkimer...N 250
● West Seneca, Erie........W 100
West Shelby, Orleans.......W 50
West Shokan, Ulster...... SE 125
● West Somers, Westches'r SE 150

Place	Index	Pop.
West Somerset, Niagara	W	50
● *West Sparta*, Livingston	W	×
West Stephentown, Rens'laer	E	350
West Stockholm, St. Law'ce	N	800
West Stony Creek, Warren	NE	75
West Taghkanick, Columbia	SE	100
● West Town, Orange	SE	200
West Township, Albany	E	100
● West Troy, Albany	E	12,967
West Union, Steuben	SW	×
West Utica, (see Utica)		×
● West Valley, Cattaraugus	SW	350
● *West Valley Falls*, R'ssel'r	E	×
● West Vienna, Oneida	C	138
Westville, Otsego	C	90
Westville Center, Franklin	NE	150
West Walworth, Wayne	W	210
● *West Waterford*, Saratoga	E	×
West Webster, Monroe	W	250
West Windsor, Broome	S	85
● West Winfield, Herkimer	N	741
Westwood, Erie	W	×
West Yorkshore, C'ttar'g's	SW	40
Wethersfield, Wyoming	W	100
Wethersfield Springs, Wy'g	W	300
Wevertown, Warren	NE	250
● Whallonsburgh, Essex	NE	250
Wheatly, Queens	SE	×
Wheatville, Genesee	W	100
● Wheeler, Steuben	SW	180
Wheelers, Hamilton	NE	×
● *Wheeler's*, Ontario	W	×
● *Wheeler's*, Oswego	C	100
Wheelertown, Herkimer	N	×
Whippleville, Franklin	NE	125
● White Church, Tompkins	S	×
White Creek, Washington	E	200
Whitefield, Ulster	SE	×
● Whitehall, Washington	E	4,434
● *Whitehouse*, Chautauqua	SW	×
● *White House*, Cat'r'ugus	SW	×
White Lake, Sullivan	SE	500
White Lake Corners, Oneida	C	×
Whitelaw, Madison	C	×
● **White Plains**, W'tch'r	SE	4,042
● Whiteport, Ulster	SE	200
● *Whites*, Monroe	W	×
● Whitesboro, Oneida	C	1,663
● *Whiteside*, Chautauqua	SW	×
● White's Store, Chenango	C	50
● Whitestone, Queens	SE	2,808
● *Whitestone Junc.* Queens	SE	×
● *Whitestone Landing*, Q'ns	SE	×
White Sulphur Spr's, Sul'v'n	SE	90
Whitesville, Allegany	SW	425
Whitfield, Ulster	SE	40
Whitman, Delaware	SE	×
● *Whitney's*, St. Lawrence	N	×
● Whitney's Crossings, A'g'y	SW	100
● Whitneys's Point, Broome	S	542
● Whitson, Westchester	SE	×
Wicks Cors. (see Paine's H'l'w)		×
● *Wicopee Junc.* Dutchess	SE	×
● *Wilber Switch*, Chenango	C	×
Wilbur, Ulster	SE	775
Wilber Basin, Saratoga	E	50
Wiley Corners, Steuben	SW	×
Wileysville, Steuben	SW	50
● Wilhelm, Erie	W	×
● Willard, Seneca	C	300
● *Willards*, Chenango	C	×
Willet, Cortland	C	160
Willets Point, Queens	SE	×
● *Willetts*, Cayuga	C	×
● Williams Bridge, W'tch'r	SE	1,685
Williamsburgh, Kings	SE	×
● Williamson, Wayne	W	600
● Williamstown, Oswego	C	550
Williamsville, Erie	W	900
Willink, Erie	W	2,000
● *Willis*, Queens	SE	200
Williston, Erie	**W**	**100**
● Willow Brook, Dutchess	SE	75
● Willow Creek, Tompkins	S	×
Willowemoc, Sullivan	SE	200
● *Willow Glen*, Onondaga	C	×
● Willow Glen, Saratoga	E	75
● Willow Point, Broome	S	×
● *Willow Vale*, Oneida	C	185
● Willsborough, Essex	NE	350
Willsborough Point, Essex	NE	×
● Willseyville, Tioga	S	100
Wilmington, Essex	NE	500
Wilmurt, Herkimer	N	50
Wilna, Jefferson	N	150
● Wilson, Niagara	W	683

Place	Index	Pop.
Wilson Creek, Tioga	S	×
Wilton, Saratoga	E	175
● Winchells, Dutchess	SE	×
Winchester, Erie	W	×
Windecker, Lewis	N	×
Windham, Greene	SE	425
Windom, Erie	W	×
● Windsor, Broome	S	524
● *Windsor Beach*, Monroe	W	×
Windsor Terrace, Kings	SE	1,645
● Winfield, Herkimer	N	150
● Winfield Junc., Queens	SE	819
● Wing's Station, Dutchess	SE	×
Winona, Jefferson	N	×
● Winterton, Sullivan	SE	200
● Winthrop, St. Lawrence	N	350
● Wirt Centre, Allegany	SW	×
Wiscoy, Allegany	SW	250
Wisner, Orange	SE	×
Witherbee, Essex	NE	300
Withey, Allegany	SW	×
● Wolcott, Wayne	W	902
Wolcottsburgh, Erie	W	150
Wolcottsville, Niagara	W	1,000
Wolf Hill, Albany	E	×
● *Wolf Pond*, Franklin	NE	×
● *Wolf Run*, Cattaraugus	SW	×
● Woodard, Onondaga	C	×
Woodbourne, Sullivan	SE	150
● Woodbury, Queens	SE	200
● Woodbury Falls, Orange	SE	×
● *Wood Creek*, Oneida	C	×
Woodford, Delaware	SE	300
● Woodhaven, Queens	SE	800
● *Woodhaven Junc.* Queens	SE	×
Woodhull, Steuben	SW	800
Woodland, Ulster	SE	40
● *Woodlands*, Westchester	SE	×
● Woodlawn, Kings	SE	×
● *Woodlawn*, New York	SE	×
● *Woodlawn Junc.*, N. Y.	SE	×
● *Woods*, Cayuga	C	×
Woods, Jefferson	N	×
● *Woodsburgh*, Queens	SE	150
● Wood's Falls, Clinton	NE	×
● Woodside, Queens	SE	710
● *Wood's Switch*, Chenango	C	×
Woodstock, (see New W'ds'k)		×
Woodstock, Ulster	SE	300
Woodville, Jefferson	N	175
Woodville, Ontario	W	50
Woodville, Suffolk	SE	×
● Wooglin, Chautauqua	SW	×
● Worcester, Otsego	C	1,300
Worksburg, Chautauqua	SW	×
Worth Centre, Jefferson	N	60
Worthville, Jefferson	N	100
● *Wrights*, Washington	E	×
Wright's Corners, Niagara	W	75
Wrightson, Oswego	C	×
Wrightsville, Clinton	NE	×
Wurtemburgh, Dutchess	SE	75
● Wurtsboro, Sullivan	SE	490
Wyandale, Erie	W	50
● Wyandance, Suffolk	SE	75
● *Wyckoff's*, Cayuga	C	×
Wynantskill, Rensselaer	E	160
● Wyoming, Wyoming	W	525
Yaleville, Chenango	C	40
Yaphank, Suffolk	SE	517
Yates, Orleans	W	300
● *Yates Dock*, Monroe	W	×
Yatesville, Yates	W	×
Yeagers, Cattaraugus	SW	×
● Yonkers, Westchester	SE	32,033
● York, Livingston	W	350
Yorkshire, Cattaraugus	SW	400
● Yorkshire Centre, C't'g's	SW	511
Yorktown, Westchester	SE	×
● Yorktown Heights, W'tc'r	SE	100
Yorkville, Oneida	C	1,500
● *Yosts*, Montgomery	E	×
Young, Onondaga	C	×
Young Hickory, Steuben	SW	24
Youngport, Suffolk	SE	×
● Youngs, Delaware	SE	100
Young's Corners, (see Rossie)		×
Youngstown, Niagara	W	490
Youngsville, Sullivan	SE	100
Yulan, Sullivan	SE	×
Zeliffs, Cattaraugus	SW	×
Zena, Ulster	SE	100
Zoar, Erie,	W	×
Zoar, Jefferson	N	60
● Zurich, Wayne	W	50

North Carolina.

COUNTIES.	INDEX.	POP.
Alamance	N	18,271
Alexander	W	9,430
Alleghany	NW	6,523
Anson	S	20,027
Ashe	NW	15,628
Beaufort	E	21,072
Bertie	NE	19,176
Bladen	S	16,763
Brunswick	S	10,900
Buncombe	W	35,266
Burke	W	14,939
Cabarrus	SW	18,142
Caldwell	W	12,298
Camden	NE	5,667
Carteret	E	10,825
Caswell	N	16,028
Catawba	W	18,689
Chatham	C	25,413
Cherokee	SW	9,976
Chowan	NE	9,167
Clay	SW	4,197
Cleveland	SW	20,394
Columbus	S	17,856
Craven	E	20,533
Cumberland	C	27,321
Currituck	NE	6,747
Dare	E	3,768
Davidson	C	21,70
Davie	W	11,621
Duplin	C	18,690
Durham	N	18,041
Edgecombe	NE	24,113
Forsyth	F	28,434
Franklin	N	21,090
Gaston	SW	17,764
Gates	NE	10,252
Graham	SW	3,313
Granville	N	24,484
Greene	E	10,039
Guilford	N	28,052
Halifax	NE	28,908
Harnett	**C**	**13,700**
Haywood	SW	13,346
Henderson	SW	12,589
Hertford	NE	13,851
Hyde	E	8,903
Iredell	W	25,462
Jackson	W	9,512
Johnston	C	27,239
Jones	E	7,403
Lenoir	E	14,879
Lincoln	SW	12,586
McDowell	W	10,939
Macon	SW	10,102
Madison	W	17,805
Martin	NE	15,221
Mecklenburgh	SW	42,673
Mitchell	W	12,807
Montgomery	C	11,239
Moore	C	20,479
Nash	N	20,707
New Hanover	SE	24,026
Northampton	NE	21,242
Onslow	SE	10,303
Orange	N	14,948
Pamlico	E	7,146
Pasquotank	NE	10,748
Pender	SE	12,514
Perquimans	NE	9,293
Person	N	15,151
Pitt	E	25,519
Polk	SW	5,902
Randolph	C	25,195
Richmond	S	23,948
Robeson	S	31,483
Rockingham	N	25,363
Rowan	W	24,123
Rutherford	SW	18,770
Sampson	C	25,096
Stanly	C	12,136
Stokes	N	17,199
Surry	NW	19,281
Swain	SW	6,577
Transylvania	SW	5,881
Tyrrell	E	4,225
Union	S	21,259
Vance	N	17,581
Wake	C	49,208
Warren	N	19,360
Washington	E	10,200
Watauga	NW	10,611
Wayne	C	26,100
Wilkes	NW	22,675
Wilson	C	18,644

Yadkin	NW	13,790
Yancey	W	9,490
Total		1,617,947

TOWN. COUNTY.	INDEX.	POP.
Aaron, (see Montezuma)		×
Abbeyville, Person	N	×
● Abbottsburgh, Bladen	S	300
Abbott's Creek, Davidson	C	25
Abbells, Johnson	C	24
● Aberdeen, Moore	C	227
Abernethy, Iredell	W	24
Abshers, Wilkes	NW	30
Accommodate, Rutherford	SW	×
Aconite, Randolph	C	×
Acresville, Beaufort	E	18
Acton, Buncombe	W	×
Adams Mills, (see Monroe)		×
● Addie, Jackson	W	10
Adelaide, Rockingham	N	18
Adley, Wilkes	NW	×
Adoir, Gates	NE	×
Adoniram, Granville	N	30
● Advance, Davie	W	75
Affinity, Robeson	S	×
● *Affordsville*, Robeson	S	×
Afton, Warren	N	32
Agreeta, Cherokee	SW	×
Aho, Watauga	NW	×
Ahoskie, Hertford	NE	×
Al, Person	N	×
Airlie, Halifax	NE	37
Airbellows, Alleghany	NW	×
● *Air Line Junc.*, Mecklenburgh	SW	×
Alasco, Harnett	C	×
Albemarle, Stanly	C	248
● *Albemarle & Raleigh Junc.*, Martin	NE	×
Albertson, Duplin	C	12
Albin, Granville	N	×
Albright, Alamance	N	×
Alco, Montgomery	C	×
Alderman, Cumberland	C	24
● Alexander, Buncombe	W	72
Alexandriana, (see Croft)		×
● Alfordsville, Robeson	S	20
Alfred, Robeson	S	×
Algiers, Ashe	NW	×
Algood, Yadkin	NW	×
Alice, Buncombe	W	×
Alleghany, Madison	W	×
Allemance, Guilford	N	30
Allensville, Person	N	×
● Allenton, Robeson	S	17
Allenton Ferry, Montgom'y	C	×
● All Healing, Gaston	SW	50
Alliance, Pamlico	E	×
Allison, Caswell	N	×
Allreds, Montgomery	C	32
Alma, Robeson	S	15
Alpha, Rowan	W	×
Alpine, Surry	NW	120
● *Alspaugh*, Forsyth	N	×
Altamahaw, Alamance	N	×
Altamont, Mitchell	W	75
Altan, Union	S	×
Alto, Buncombe	W	12
Aman's Store, Onslow	SE	12
Amantha, Watauga	NW	×
Amboy, Chowan	NE	20
Amelia, Alleghany	NW	×
● Ames, Union	S	24
Amherst, Lenoir	E	×
Amity Hill, Iredell	W	36
Ammon, Bladen	S	12
Anderson, Caswell	N	40
Andrews, Cherokee	SW	×
Angeline, Henderson	SW	×
Angle, Wayne	C	×
Angola, Onslow	SE	36
Anna, Alleghany	NW	×
● *Annandale*, Pender	SE	×
Anneta, Hertford	NE	×
Ansonville, Anson	S	100
Antioch, Robeson	S	40
Antler, Moore	C	×
Antonia, Cumberland	C	×
Antro, Cleveland	SW	×
● Apex, Wake	C	269
Apple Grove, Ashe	NW	42
Appletree, Greene	E	×
Applewhite, Columbus	S	×
Aquone, Macon	SW	36
Araphoe, Pamlico	E	×

North Carolina

TOWN. COUNTY.	INDEX.	POP.
● *Ararat*, Surry	NW	20
Arcadia, Davidson	C	25
Archdale, Randolph	C	224
Archer Lodge, Johnston	C	15
Arcola, Warren	N	30
● Arden, Buncombe	W	229
Argo, Nash	N	×
Argyle, Cumberland	C	16
Arlington, Mecklenburgh	SW	24
Armfield, Iredell	W	245
● Armour, Columbus	S	×
Armstrong, McDowell	W	×
Arnold, Davidson	C	×
Arnt, Catawba	W	×
Arolina, Richmond	S	×
Asbury, Montgomery	C	×
● *Asbury*, Wake	C	×
Ascend, Chatham	C	×
Ash, Brunswick	S	×
● **Ashborough**, Randolph	C	510
Ashcrafts Mills, (see Beaver Dam)		×
● **Asheville**, Buncombe	W	10,235
Ashford, McDowell	W	6
Ash Hill, Surry	NW	×
Ashland, Caswell	N	78
Ashley, Ashe	NW	×
Ashpole, Robeson	S	30
Ashton, Pender	SE	12
Aspen Grove, Rockingham	N	40
Assurance, Beaufort	E	×
Athens, Robeson	S	×
Athlone, Yancey	W	×
● Atkinson, Pender	SE	×
● Atlantic, Carteret	E	80
● *Atlantic*, Carteret	E	×
Atlee, Rockingham	N	×
● Auburn, Wake	C	50
Augusta, Davie	W	×
Aulander, Bertie	NE	163
Auman's Hill, (see Asbury)		×
Aurelian Springs, Halifax	NE	50
Aurora, Beaufort	E	251
Austin, Wilkes	NW	×
Autro, Cleveland	SW	24
● Autryville, Sampson	C	20
Averasboro, Harnett	C	50
Avery, Mitchell	W	12
Avery's Creek, Buncombe	W	30
Avilla, Alexander	W	×
Avoca, Bertie	NE	20
Avon, Dare	E	353
Ayden, Pitt	E	20
Ayersville, Stokes	N	30
● Ayr, Rutherford	SW	24
● *Azalea*, Buncombe	W	×
Bachelor, Craven	E	×
Bagley, Johnston	C	50
Bahama, Durham	N	12
Bailey, Davie	W	×
Bain, Davidson	C	20
Baird Mill, (see Bethel Hill)		×
Baird's Creek, Pamlico	E	300
Bakersville, Mitchell	W	700
Baird Creek, Yancey	W	60
Baldwin, Ashe	NW	12
Ballentine's Mills, Wake	C	18
Ballew, Cherokee	SW	×
● Balsam, Jackson	W	×
Balsam Grove, Transylvania	SW	42
Balston, Durham	N	×
Bamboo, Watauga	NW	24
Bandana, Mitchell	W	×
Bandy, Catawba	W	18
Bangor, Wake	C	×
Banks, Wake	C	6
Bannermans, Pender	SE	30
Banner's Elk, Watauga	NW	5
Bannockburn, Cumberland	C	×
Barclaysville, Harnett	C	35
Barium Springs, Iredell	W	×
Barker, Jackson	W	×
Barker's Cut, (see Lumberton)		×
● Barnard, Madison	W	24
Barnardsville, Buncombe	W	24
Barnes Cross Roads, (see Black Creek)		×
Barnes' Store, Wilson	C	18
Barnesville, Robeson	S	30
Barnitz, Chowan	NE	30
Barrett's Mountains, Alexander	W	×
Bason, Rockingham	N	×
Bass, Sampson	C	12
Bat Cave, Henderson	SW	90
Bath, Beaufort	E	50
Baton, Caldwell	W	12
● Battleboro, Nash	N	300

North Carolina

TOWN. COUNTY.	INDEX.	POP.
● Battle Ground, Guilford	N	×
Bancoms, Union	S	×
Baxter, Henderson	SW	×
Bay, Tyrrell	E	25
Bayboro, Pamlico	E	252
● *Baymead*, New Hanover	SE	×
Bayside, Beaufort	E	×
Beaman's Cross Roads, Samson	C	25
Beam's Mills, Cleveland	SW	24
Bean Shoals, Yadkin	NW	×
Beaver Creek, (see Trenton)		×
Bear Poplar, Rowan	W	15
Bear Wallow, Henderson	SW	18
Beatties Ford, (see Denver)		×
Beaufort, Carteret	E	2,007
Beaumont, Chatham	C	150
Beaver Creek, Ashe	NW	60
Beaver Creek, (see Trenton)		×
● Beaver Dam, Union	S	65
● *Beaver Island*, Rockingham	N	×
Beck, Wake	C	24
Bee Bald, Madison	W	×
Beech, Buncome	W	32
Beech Creek, Watauga	NW	24
Bee Log, Yancey	W	20
Begonia, Gaston	SW	48
● Belcross, Camden	NE	60
● Belew Creek Mills, Forsyth	N	25
Belfast, Davidson	C	×
Belhaven, Macon	SW	×
Bell, Buncombe	W	20
Bellair, Craven	E	×
● Belleport, Beaufort	E	×
Bellevoir, Chatham	C	36
Bell's Ferry, (see Grifton)		×
Bell Town, (see Oxford)		×
● Belmont, Gaston	SW	150
Belo, Surry	NW	×
Belvidere, Perquimans	NE	200
Belwood, Cleveland	SW	30
● Benaja, Rockingham	N	12
Benham, Wilkes	NW	×
Benjamin, Stokes	N	×
Benneham, (see Dutchville)		×
Bennett, Anson	S	×
● *Bennett*, Anson	S	×
Bensalem, Moore	C	150
● Benson, Johnston	C	191
Bentley, Alexander	W	×
Bentonville, Johnston	C	100
Berea, Granville	N	100
Berlin, Ashe	NW	×
Bernice, Ashe	NW	150
Berry, Rockingham	N	×
Bessemer City, Gaston	SW	×
Beston, Wayne	C	100
Beta, Jackson	W	10
● Bethania, Forsyth	N	300
Bethany, Davidson	C	10
Bethany Church, (see Statesville)		×
● Bethel, Pitt	E	377
Bethel Cross Roads, (see Yeopin)		×
Bethel Hill, Person	N	40
Bethesda, Gaston	SW	×
Bethlehem, Hertford	NE	25
Beulah, (see Bagley)		×
Beulaville, Duplin	C	51
● Beverly, Anson	S	30
● *Beverly*, Bertie	NE	×
Biddle University, (see Charlotte)		×
Biddleville, **Mecklenburgh**	SW	×
Big Creek, Stokes	N	24
Big Falls, Alamance	N	50
Big Laurel, Madison	W	24
Big Lick, Stanly	C	69
Big Oak, Moore	C	5
Big Pine, Madison	W	24
Big Ridge, Jackson	W	18
Big Rock, Granville	N	30
● *Big Sandy Run*, Pender	SE	×
Big Swamp, Bladen	S	×
Bilesville, Stanly	C	317
● Biltmore, Buncombe	W	×
Bines, Robeson	S	×
● *Bingham School*, Orange	N	300
● *Birch*, Surry	NW	×
Birdtown, Swain	SW	×
Bishop, New Hanover	SE	×
Bismarck, Johnston	C	×
Bizzell, Wayne	C	×
Blackburn, Catawba	W	×
● Black Creek, Wilson	C	191
Black Jack, Pitt	E	×
Blackman's Mills, Sampson	C	25
Blackmer, Rowan	SW	24

North Carolina

● Black Mountain, B'nc'mbe W 100
Blackstone, Caldwell W ×
Blackwells, Caswell N 10
Blackwood, Orange N 15
● Bladenborough, Bladen S 50
Bladen Springs, (see Green) ×
Blaine, Montgomery C 12
Blanch, Caswell N ×
Bland, Sampson C ×
Blevins, Ashe NW ×
● Bliss, Surry NW 20
Blocker's, (see Stedman) ×
Bloomington, Stanley C 12
Blount's Creek, Beaufort E 24
Blowing Rock, Watauga NW 35
Blue Ridge, Henderson SW 25
Blues, Moore C ×
Blue Wing, Granville N 70
Bluff, Madison W 150
Bly, Ashe NW ×
Boaz, Chatham C ×
Bobbitt, Vance N ×
Bogue, Carteret E 10
● *Bogue*, Columbus S 90
Boiling Springs, Cleveland SW 24
Bo lston, Henderson SW 42
● *Bolling*, Halifax NE ×
● Bolton, Columbus S 25
Bombay, Randolph C ×
Bonus, Jones E ×
Boomer, Wilkes NW 30
Boone, Watauga NW 144
Roone'sCrossR'ds, (seeJ'cks'n ×
Boonville, Yadkin NW 100
Border, Orange N 24
Bosley, Gates NE ×
● Bostic, Rutherford SW 200
Bostick's Mills, Richmond S 30
Bost's Mills, Cabarrus SW 48
Bowdinot, Chatham C ×
Bowden's, Duplin C 24
Bowie's Creek, Harnett C 24
Bowles, Wilkes NW ×
Bowling, Person N ×
Bowling's Store, (see Luster) ×
Bowman's Bluff, Hen'son SW 30
Bowmore, Robeson S ×
Boyd, Rockingham N ×
Boyd's Ferry, (seeGrimesl'nd) ×
Boyd's Neck, (seeElizabethCity) ×
Boyden, Surry NW ×
Boyett, Wilson C ×
Bradham's Store, (seeWallace) ×
Bradley's Store, Harnett C 72
Bradshaw, Orange N 24
Brady's Cross Roads, (see New Sterling) ×
Bragg, Richmond S ×
Branch's Store, Duplin C 24
● Branchville, Robeson S 24
● *Brassfield*, Durham N ×
Braswell's Store, (seeWhitak'r's) ×
Brasstown, Clay SW 30
Brayville, Chatham C ×
Breeze, Buncombe W ×
Brevard, Transylvania W 327
Brevard Sta., (see StanleyCr. ×
Brick Church, Guilford N 20
Brick Yard, Forsyth N ×
Bridge, (see Jubilee) ×
Bridgeport, Stanley C 20
Bridgersville, Wilson C ×
● Bridgewater, Burke W 20
Brief, Union S ×
Brier Creek, Wilkes NW 24
Briggsville, Madison W 24
Brighton, Mitchell W 24
Bright's Creek, Polk SW 36
Brindletown, Burke W 20
Bringle's, Davidson C 24
Brinkland, Bladen S 36
● *Brinkley's*, Brunswick S ×
Brinkleyville, Halifax NE 82
Bristow, Mecklenburgh SW ×
Bristow, Macon SW ×
Brittain, Rutherford SW 30
Britts, (see La Grange) ×
Britts, Robeson S ×
Broad River, McDowell W ×
Broad Shoals, Alexander W 24
Broadway, Moore C 60
Brodie, Warren N 19
Brompton, Bladen S ×
Brooklyn, Robeson S ×
Brooks, Alleghany NW ×
Brooks, Buncombe W 24
Brookston, Vance N 30

North Carolina

Brower's Mills, Randolph C 45
Brown Creek, Union S 24
Brown Mountain, Stokes N 19
Brown's Cross Roads, R'lph C 24
Brown's Store, Randolph C 24
● Brown's Summit, Guilford N 50
Brownsville, Granville N 30
Bruce, Cumberland C ×
Brummett's Creek, Mitchell W 48
Brunswick, Randolph C 24
Brunt, Cumberland C ×
Brush Creek, Chatham C 30
Brushy Mountain, Wilkes NW 18
Bryant, Chatham C ×
● **Bryson City**, Swain SW 250
Buchanan, Granville N 17
Bucher, Surry NW ×
Buck Forest, Transylvania SW ×
Buckhorn, Cumberland C ×
Buckland, Gates NE 90
Buckner, Chatham C ×
Buck Shoal, Yadkin NW 42
Buckvale, Watauga NW ×
Bueis, Robeson S ×
● Buena Vista, Buncombe C ×
Buffalo City, Dare E ×
Buffalo Cove, Caldwell W 24
Buffalo Ford, Randolph C 42
Buffalo Mills, see YadkinVal.) ×
Buffalo PaperMill, Clevel'd W 120
Bug Hill, Columbus S 6
Bulla, Randolph C 18
Bull Head, Greene E 24
● Bullock, Granville N ×
Bunch, Randolph C ×
Bunn's Level, Harnett C 50
Bunyon, Beaufort E 24
Burcham, Wilkes NW 12
Burden Mills, (see Lewiston) ×
Burdett, Mecklenburg SW 12
● **Burgaw**, Pender SE 366
Burgess, Perquimans NE ×
● Burlington, Alamance N 1,716
Burlow, Moore C ×
Burnington, Macon SW 24
Burnsville, Yancy W 200
● Busbee, Buncombe W 24
Bush Hill, (see Archdale) ×
Bushy Fork, Person N 20
● *Busick*, Guilford N 30
Butcher, Surry NW ×
Butler, Rutherford SW 48
Butler's Pond, Montgomery C ×
Buxton, Dare E 42
Byarsville, Cleveland SW 24
Bynum's, Chatham C 180
Byrd, Wilkes NW 24
● Byrdsville, Columbia S 6
Cabintown, Haywood SW ×
Cagle's Mills, (see Wanamaker) ×
● *Cahill's*, Stokes N ×
Cairo, Anson S 48
Calabash, Brunswick S 108
Calahaln, Davie W 50
Caldwell Institute, Orange N 20
● Caldwell's, Mecklenburgh SW 10
Caledonia, Moore C 30
Calhoun, Transylvania SW 25
Calico, Pitt E 19
California Creek, Madison W 24
Calvert, (see Jeptha) ×
Calvin, Burke W ×
● **Camden**, Camden NE 150
● Cameron, Moore C 236
Campbell, Stokes N 24
Camp Call, Cleveland SW 32
Camp Creek, Burke W 5
Cana, Davie W 100
Canary, Jones E ×
Candler, Buncombe W ×
Candor, Montgomery C ×
Cane Creek, Chatham C 24
Cane River, Yancey W 180
Canto, Buncombe W 30
Cape, Randolph C 30
Cape Hatteras, Dare E ×
Capel's Mills, Richmond S 30
Capps, Henderson SW ×
Caraway, Randolph C 12
Carbonton, Moore C 42
Carlisle, Davidson C ×
Carlos, Cumberland C 24
Carlton, Vance N ×
Carmel, Montgomery C 12
Carmichael, Cumberland C ×
Carney, Alamance N ×

North Carolina

Caroline Cen. Jc., Meckle'g SW ×
Carpenter, Gaston SW 12
Carrier's Springs, Buncombe W ×
Carson's Creek, Transylv'a SW 24
● *Carter's*, Rockingham N ×
Carter's Mills, Moore C 20
● **Carthage**, Moore C 485
● Cary, Wake C 423
Casar, Cleveland SW 48
Cases, Rockingham N 12
Cashiers, Jackson W 50
Castalia, Nash N 59
● Castle Hayne, NewHa'v'r SE 50
Castoria, Greene E 30
● *Caswell*, Jones E ×
Cataloochee, Haywood SW 24
● Catawba, Catawba W 196
Catfish, Catawba W 12
Catherine Lake, Onslow SE 50
Cathey, Jackson W 24
Catoosa, Buncombe W ×
Caudills, Johnson C ×
Cavanaugh, Duplin W 24
Cedar, Bladen S 24
Cedar Cliff, Alamance N 24
Cedar Creek, Cumberland C 45
Cedar Falls, Randolph C 255
Cedar Grove, Orange N 100
Cedar Hill, Anson S 90
Cedar Landing, (see Windsor) ×
● *Cedarhurst*, Onslow SE ×
Cedar Mountain, Trans'lv'a SW 6
Cedar Point, Carteret E 120
Cedar Rock, Franklin N 30
Cedar Run, Alexander W 48
Cedar Valley, Caldwell W 15
Ceffo, Person N 20
Celo, Yancey W 12
Centreville, Pitt E ×
Central Falls, Randolph C 120
Centre, Guilford N 15
Centre, Yadkin NW ×
Centre Bluff, (see Falkland) ×
Centre Grove, Person N 10
Centreville, Franklin N 50
● Cerro Gordo, Columbus S 129
● Chadbourn, Columbus S 156
Chaflu, Harnett C ×
Chalk, Gaston SW 19
Chalk Level, Harnett C 50
Chambers, Burke W 19
Chance, Sampson C ×
Chandler's Grove, Montgo'ry C 6
● Chapanoke, Perquimans NE 100
Chapel Hill, Orange N 1,017
Chapels Mills, Northamp'n NE ×
Charity, Yadkin NW 24
Charles, Onslow SE ×
Charleston, (see Bryson City) ×
● **Charlotte**, Mecklinb'h SW 11,557
Charm, Robeson S ×
Chase, Ashe NW ×
Cheeks, Randolph C 24
Cherokee, Swain SW 30
Cherryfield, Transylvania SW 20
Cherry Grove, Caswell N 24
Cherry Lane, Alleghany NW 24
Cherry Point, Craven E ×
● *Cherry's*, Beaufort E ×
● Cherryville, Gaston SW 200
Chester, (see Manndale) ×
Chesterfield, Burke W ×
Chestnut, Catawba W ×
Chestnut Ridge, Yadkin NW 12
Chiloe, Moore C ×
Chimney Rock, Rutherford SW 65
● China Grove, Rowan W 174
Chinquapin, Duplin C 295
Chocowinity, Beaufort E 96
Choga, Jackson W ×
Chowan, Chowan NE 30
Chronicle, Catawba W 20
Chublake, Person N 15
Churchill, Warren N 24
Cid, Davidson C 48
Clara, Stokes N ×
● Clarendon, Columbus S 24
Clarendon, Chatham C ×
● *Clarke's*, Craven E ×
Clark's Mills, Moore C 24
Clarksville, Davie W ×
● Clarkton, Bladen S 50
● Clay, Granville N 100
Claybrooks, Rockingham N ×
Clay Fork, Cumberland C 25
● Clayton, Johnson C 478
Clear Creek, Cabarrus SW 12

Place	Dir.	Pop.
Clear Run, Sampson	C	36
Clement, Sampson	C	×
Clemmonsville, Forsyth	N	100
Cleone, Union	S	×
● Cleveland, Rowan	W	150
Cleveland Mills, Cleveland	SW	308
Cleveland Sprs., (see Shelby)		×
Cliffdale, Rutherford	SW	×
Clifford, Rutherford	SW	×
Clifton, Ashe	NW	48
Climax, Guilford	N	48
Clingman, Wilkes	NW	30
● **Clinton**, Sampson	C	839
Clio, Iredell	W	30
Closs, Lenoir	S	×
Clotho, Transylvania	SW	×
Cloudland, Mitchell	W	15
Clover, Polk	SW	×
Clover Orchard, Alamance	N	60
Clybornville, Robeson	S	×
● Clyde, Haywood	SW	90
Coahoma, Lenoir	E	×
Coakley, Edgecombe	SE	×
Coalville, Cherokee	SW	×
Cobbs, Cherokee	SW	6
Cobton, (see Fort Barnwell)		×
Coburn's Store, Union	S	24
Cochrum, Yadkin	NW	×
Cockrells, Nash	N	×
Coddle Creek, Cabarrus	SW	30
Cody, Surry	NW	×
Coffer, Moore	C	×
Cofield, Cherokee	SW	×
Cogdell, Wayne	C	×
Coharie, Sampson	C	24
Cohooque, Craven	E	×
Coinjock, Currituck	NE	20
Cokesbury, Harnett	C	×
Coleman, (see Green River)		×
Colerain, Bertie	NE	250
Coleridge, Randolph	C	100
Cole's Store, Randolph	C	48
Colesville, (see Campbell)		×
Colfax, Guilford	N	100
Collington, Dare	E	×
Collettsville, Caldwell	W	22
Collier, Person	N	×
Collinsville, Polk	SW	24
Colly, Bladen	S	×
Colon, Chatham	C	×
Columbia, Tyrrell	E	209
Columbia Factory, (see Ramseur)		×
Columbus, Polk	SW	75
● *Colvard*, Cherokee	SW	×
Comet, Ashe	NW	24
Comfort, Jones	E	60
Como, Hertford	NE	54
Company Mills, Guilford	N	30
Company's Shops, (see Burling'n)		×
Concert, Ashe	NW	60
Conclave, Richmond	S	×
● **Concord**, Cabarrus	SW	4,339
● Conetoe, Edgecombe	NE	88
● Connelly's Springs, Burke	W	50
Connor, Wilson	C	×
● Conoho, Martin	NE	50
● Conoyer, Catawba	W	337
Conrads, Yadkin	NW	15
● *Conrad's*, Davison	C	×
Contenues, Wilson	C	×
● Contentnea, Greene	E	12
● Conway, Northampton	NE	×
Cool Spring, Iredell	W	20
Cool Spring, Surry	NW	×
Cooly Mills, Pender	SE	×
● *Cooper's*, Buncombe	W	60
Cooper's Gap, (see Poplar Grove)		×
Copal Grove, Stanly	C	18
● Copeland, Surry	NW	25
Corapeake, Gates	NE	×
Corbett, Caswell	N	24
● *Core Creek*, Craven	E	×
Corinth, Chatham	C	×
Cornelia, Cumberland	C	×
● Cornatzer, Davie	W	×
Costner, Gaston	SW	×
Cottonville, Stanly	C	30
Cottonwood, Mecklenburgh	SW	×
Council, Watauga	NW	×
● Councils Station, Bladen	S	20
County Line, Davie	W	24
● Cove, Craven	E	31
Cove Creek, Haywood	SW	×
Covington, Richmond	S	25
Cowan's Ford, Meckl'nb'h	SW	6
Cowarts, Jackson	W	×
Cowees, Macon	SW	×
Coxville, Pitt	E	24
● Cozart, Granville	N	×
Crab Creek, Henderson	SW	×
Crab Tree, Haywood	SW	25
Crab Tree Creek, (see Raleigh)		×
Craig, McDowell	W	×
Crain's Creek, (see Villanow)		×
Cranberry, Mitchell	W	×
● *Cranberry*, Mitchell	W	×
Crater's, Forsyth	N	×
Craven, Rowan	W	12
Crawford, Macon	SW	×
● Creedmore, Granville	N	×
Creek, Warren	N	30
Creeksville, Northampton	NE	24
Creston, Ashe	NW	100
● Creswell, Washington	E	202
Cricket, Wilkes	NW	×
● Croatan, Craven	E	24
● Croft, Mecklenburgh	SW	×
● Cronly, Columbus	S	122
Crooms, Columbus	S	60
Cross, Gates	NE	×
● Crossing, Catawba	W	60
Crossnore, Mitchell	W	12
Cross Roads, (see Jacksonville)		×
Cross Roads, (see Cottonville)		×
Cross Roads Church, Yd'n	NW	31
Cross Rock, Madison	W	24
Crossville, Gates	NE	×
● Crouse, Lincoln	SW	30
● *Crouse*, Gaston	SW	36
● Crowder's Creek, Gaston	SW	24
Crowder's Mountain, (see Dallas)		×
Crowell's, Halifax	NE	×
Crumpler, Ashe	NW	×
Cruso, Haywood	SW	×
Crutchfield, Surry	NW	×
Crystal, Guilford	N	30
Cuba, Rutherford	SW	35
Culberson, Cherokee	SW	75
Cullakanee, Clay	SW	×
Cullasaja, Macon	SW	30
Culler, Stokes	N	500
Cullowhee, Jackson	W	20
Cumberland, Cumberland	C	242
● Cunningham, Person	N	40
● Currie, Pender	SE	×
Curriersville, Moore	C	20
Currituck, Currituck	NE	100
Curtis' Mills, Alamance	N	90
Cypress Creek, Bladen	S	30
● *Cypress Lake*, Pender	SE	×
Cyrus, Onslow	SE	×
● Dabney, Vance	N	74
Daisy, Forsyth	N	×
Daisy, McDowell	W	×
● **Dallas**, Gaston	SW	441
● Dalton, Stokes	N	150
Dana, Henderson	SW	×
Danburry, Stokes	N	200
● *Dan River*, Stokes	N	×
Danville, Guilford	N	×
Darby, Wilkes	NW	×
Dardens, Martin	NE	×
Dark Ridge, Watauga	NW	12
Darlington, Rutherford	SW	×
Darly, Wilkes	NW	×
Davenport, Mecklenburgh	SW	×
● Davidson, Mecklenburgh	SW	481
Davidson's River, Transylv'a	SW	120
Davis, Carteret	E	24
Dawson's Cross Roads, Halif'x	NE	50
Dawson's Landing, Bladen	S	120
Day Book, Yancey	W	10
Daysville, Person	N	10
Dayton, Durham	N	36
Dealville, Alexander	W	×
Dean, Granville	N	×
Deaver's, (see Puella)		×
Debruhl's, Craven	E	×
Deep Creek, Anson	S	12
Deep River, Guilford	N	26
Deep Run, Lenoir	E	6
Deerfield, Watauga	NW	×
Defiance, Randolph	C	×
Dehart, Wilkes	NW	×
Delight, Cleveland	SW	×
Delk, Stokes	N	×
Dellaplane, Wilkes	NW	30
Delmont, Henderson	SW	24
Delphi, Allegany	NW	25
Delta, Sampson	C	25
Demia, Buncombe	W	×
Democrat, Buncombe	W	50
● *Dendron*, Burke	W	50
Denmark, Buncombe	W	×
● *Dennis*, Forsyth	N	×
Dennis, Gates	NE	×
Dennysville, Guilford	N	×
Denton, Davidson	C	25
Denver, Lincoln	SW	185
Depot, Haywood	SW	18
● Derita, Mecklenburgh	SW	12
Derr, Lincoln	SW	12
Devotion, Surry	NW	×
Dewdrop, Pender	SE	×
De Witt, Henderson	SW	×
Dexter, Granville	N	×
Dial, Cumberland	C	6
Diamond Hill, Anson	S	25
Dickinson, Harnett	C	×
Dicksboro, Pitt	E	×
● *Dickson*, Caldwell	W	×
Dico, Stokes	N	×
Dike, Polk	SW	×
Dillard, Stokes	N	18
Dillingham, Buncombe	W	×
Dills, McDowell	W	×
● Dillsboro, Jackson	W	×
Dimsdale, Polk	SW	36
Dismal, Sampson	C	90
Dixie, Mecklenburgh	SW	12
Dobag, Yancey	W	18
Dobbersville, Wayne	C	×
Dobbinsville, (see Lisbon)		×
Dobson, Surry	NW	225
Dockery, Wilkes	NW	50
Dockery's Store, Richmond	S	×
Doehead, Edgecombe	NE	×
Dogwood, Burke	W	×
● *Donaha*, Surry	NW	×
● Donnoha, Forsyth	N	25
Doolie, Iredell	W	24
Dora, (see Red Springs)		×
Dorado, Stokes	N	×
Dorsey, Swain	SW	×
Dort, Gates	NE	24
Dosier, Forsyth	N	×
Dothan, Columbus	S	×
Double Shoal, Cleveland	SW	120
Douglas, Rockingham	N	18
● Dover, Craven	E	80
Dowd, Stanly	C	12
Downingville, Bladen	S	18
Downsville, Caldwell	W	30
Draco, Caldwell	W	×
Dresden, Ashe	NW	×
Drew, Bertie	NE	×
● *Drexel*, Burke	W	×
Drumhill, Gates	NE	×
Drumsville, Catawba	W	12
Dry Creek, Montgomery	C	18
Dry's Mill, Cabarrus	SW	45
Drywells, Nash	N	×
Duck Creek, Onslow	SE	78
● Dudley, Wayne	C	75
Dudo, Richmond	S	12
Duffey, Robeson	S	×
Dukes, Nash	N	×
Dulins, Davie	W	×
Duncan, Rutherford	SW	30
● Dunn, Harnett	C	419
Dunsmore, Buncombe	W	×
Dupont, Wake	C	×
Duplin Cross Roads, (see Wallace)		×
Durant's Neck, Perquim	NE	35
Durbro, Cleveland	SW	24
● **Durham**, Durham	N	5,485
Duplin Road, Duplin	C	119
Durham's Creek, Beaufort	E	50
Dutch Cove, Haywood	SW	24
Dutchville, Granville	N	32
Dyer's Brook, Madison	W	×
● Dymond City, Martin	NE	100
Dysortville, McDowell	W	40
Eagle Mills, Iredell	W	125
Eagle Rock, Wake	C	25
Egletown, Northampton	NE	18
Eagle Springs, Moore	C	×
Earleys, Hertford	NE	×
● Earl Station, Cleveland	SW	×
Early's, Bertie	NE	×
Earpsborough, Johnston	C	40
Easons, Nash	N	×
East Bend, Yadkin	NW	125
● East Durham, Durham	N	×
Eastfield, Mecklenburgh	SW	48
East Fork, Transylvania	SW	36
East Lake, Dare	E	60
Eastland, Caswell	N	×
East Laport, Jackson	W	90
Eatmon, Nash	N	×
Ebenezer, Chatham	C	×

Echo, Robeson.............S ×
Eden, Randolph.............C 48
Edenboro', Montgomery....C ×
Edenton, Chowan......NE 2,205
Edgar, Randolph............C ×
Edge, Bladen...............S ×
● *Edgecombe*, Pender.....SE ×
Edgewood, Robeson..........S 60
Edgewood, Chatham........C ×
Edinborough, Montgomery..C 30
Edith, Catawba.............W ×
Edmiston, Rowan............W ×
Edmonds, Alleghany.....NW 24
Edneyville, Henderson....SW 50
Edonia, Cumberland........C 30
Edwards Cross Roads, Al'y NW 6
Edwards Mill, Beaufort.....E 62
Edwardsville, Surry......NW 24
Effie, Jackson.............W ×
● Efland, Orange............N ×
Efird's Mills, Stanly.......C 24
Egypt, (see Egypt Depot).... ×
● Egypt Depot, Chatham....C 125
● *Egypt Junction*, Chatham C ×
● *Eighty Nine Mile Siding*, Richmond..............S ×
Elam's, Warren.............N ×
Elbaville, Davie............W ×
Elbethel, Cleveland.......SW 6
Eldorado, Montgomery......C 100
Eldridge, Burke............W ×
Eleazer, Randolph..........C 18
● *Elebee*, Wake.............C ×
Elevation, Johnston.........C 150
Elf, Clay...................SW 24
Eli, Rowan..................W ×
● **Elizabeth City**, Pasquotank......................NE 3,251
Elizabethtown, Bladen..S 160
Elk Creek, Alleghany....NW 60
Elk CrossRoads, Watauga NW 10
Elkin, Surry...............NW 288
● *Elkinsville*, Bladen.......S 72
Elkin Valley, Surry......NW ×
Elko, Stokes................N 36
● Elk Park, Mitchell.......W 313
Elk Shoals, Alexander......W 48
Elkton, Bladen..............S ×
Elkville, Wilkes...........NW 24
● Ellenboro, Rutherford..SW 20
Ellendale, Alexander.......W 30
Ellerbe Springs, Richmond..S 24
Elle.'s Store, Watauga...NW ×
Ellijay, Macon..............SW ×
Ellington, Wake............C 24
● Elliot, Sampson...........C ×
Ellis, Bladen................S ×
● *Elisboro*, Rockingham...N ×
● Elm City, Wilson.........C 482
Elmer, Yancey..............W 12
Elm Grove, Chatham........C 90
● Elmwood, Iredell.........W 75
● Elon College, Alamance..N 50
El Paso, Brunswick..........S 12
Elroy, Wayne.................C ×
Elsie, Mitchell..............W 95
Emanuel, Caldwell..........W 24
Embro, Warren..............N ×
Emerson, Columbus........S ×
Emerson, Bladen............S ×
Emit, Johnston..............C ×
● Emma, Buncombe.........W 24
Empire, Randolph...........C 6
Endicott, Montgomery......C ×
Endor, Chatham............C ×
Energy, Chatham...........C ×
● Enfield, Halifax..........NE 568
England's Point, (see Ranger) ×
Englehard, Hyde..............E 140
Ennice, Alleghany.........NW ×
Enno, Wake..................C 30
Enochville, Rowan.........W 300
Enola, Burke................W 42
Enterprise, Davidson.......C 80
Eoka, Columbus.............S ×
Ephesus, Davie..............W ×
Epps Springs, Swain.....SW ×
Epsom, Vance...............N ×
Erastus, Jackson...........W ×
Erect, Randolph.............C 36
Erie Mills, Montgomery.....C 50
Ernul, Craven................E 30
Erwinsville, Cleveland....SW 26
Essex, Halifax..............NE ×
Estatoe, Mitchell...........W ×
Estelle, Caswell.............N 20
Etanis, Warren.............N ×

Ether, Montgomery.........C 50
Etna, Macon...............SW 12
Eugenia, Mitchell..........W ×
Eupeptic Springs, Iredell..W ×
Euphronia, Moore...........C ×
● Eure, Gates...............NE ×
Eureka, Wayne...............C 150
Euto, Union..................S 6
Eva, Perquimans...........NE ×
Evalin, Iredell...............W 12
Evans, Chatham.............C 24
● Everetts, Martin.........NE 100
Evergreen, Columbus.......S 48
Eves, Perquimans.........NE ×
Ewart, Mitchell.............W ×
Ewart, Buncombe...........W ×
Ewing, Wake..................C ×
Excelsior, Brunswick.......S 15
Exter, Bertie.................NE ×
Exum, Brunswick............S ×
Eye, Ashe....................NW ×
Eye, (see Star)................ ×
Ezra, Johnston..............C 12
Facerock, Buncombe.......W ×
Factory, Rutherford.......SW 48
● Fair Bluff, Columbus.....S 243
Fairfax, Swain..............SW 6
Fairfield, Hyde...............E 200
Fair Grove, Davidson.......C 24
Fair Haven, Moore..........C 75
Fairly's, Richmond..........S ×
Fairmont, Davidson.........C 60
● *Fairntosh*, Durham.......N ×
Fairplain, Wilkes..........NW ×
Fairplay, Stokes............N 24
Fairport, (see Kittrell)...... ×
Fairview, Buncombe........W 40
● Faison, Duplin.............C 256
Faith, Rowan................W ×
Falkland, Pitt.................E 61
Fall Cliff, Jackson..........W ×
Fall Creek, Chatham........C 24
● Falling Creek, Lenoir......E 40
Falls, Wake...................C 100
Fallston, Cleveland........SW 164
Fancy, Cleveland...........SW 30
Fancy Hill, Iredell..........W 36
Tar Creek, (see Englehard).. ×
Farm, Catawba..............W 43
● Farmers, Randolph.........C 24
Farmer's Turnout, Col'mbus S ×
Farmington, Davie..........W 200
Farmville, Pitt................E 140
Faro, Wayne..................C ×
Faucett, Orange..............N 30
Faust, Madison..............W ×
● **Fayetteville**, C'mb'rl'd C 4,222
Federal, New Hanover....SE ×
Feedmore, Granville........N ×
Felix, Davie..................W ×
Felts, Wilkes................NW 12
Fennimore, Mecklenburgh SW ×
Fentress, (see Pleasant Gard'n) ×
Ferguson, Haywood........SW ×
Ferndale, Rockingham.....N ×
Fernhurst, Jackson.........W ×
Ferrells, Nash...............N ×
Ferry, Rutherford..........SW 24
Fidelity, Jackson............W ×
Fields, Lenoir.................E 24
Fieldboro, Greene...........E 30
Fig, Ashe....................NW ×
Filo, Montgomery...........C ×
Finch, Nash..................N 108
Flue's Creek, Haywood...SW 24
Finger, Stanly................C ×
Finneywood, Meck'nburgh SW ×
First Broad, Rutherford..SW 60
Fish Dam, Durham..........N 70
Fisher, Mecklenburgh....SW ×
Fish Top, Polk..............SW ×
Fitch's Store, Caswell......N 24
Five Forks, Stokes..........N 48
Flaggtown, Montgomery....C 24
Flag Run, (see Lewiston).... ×
Flat Creek, Buncombe......W 24
Flat River, Durham..........N 25
● Flat Rock, Henderson..SW 491
Flat Rock, Surry..........NW ×
Flat Rock, Mitchell.........W ×
Flats, Macon................SW ×
Flat Shoal, Surry.........NW 30
Flemmings, Catawba.......W 12
● Fletcher, Henderson...SW ×
Flint, Wake...................C ×
Flinty Branch, Yancey.....W 24
Flora, Randolph..............C 36
● Floral College, Robeson...S 150

Florence, Pamlico...........E ×
Flower Hill, Randolph......C 24
Flows, Cabarrus...........SW 48
Flox, Onslow...............SE ×
Floyd, Cumberland..........C ×
Fly, Montgomery.............C ×
Flynn, Moore.................C ×
● *Folkstone*, Onslow......SE ×
Folsom, Bladen...............S ×
Fonta Flora, Burke.........W 20
Fontcol, Richmond...........S ×
Footville, Yadkin..........NW 30
Forbush, Yadkin...........NW 48
Ford, Stanly...................C 24
● Forest City, Rutherford SW 419
● Forestville, Wake..........C 250
● Forge, Surry.............NW 26
Fork, Pamlico.................E 19
Forkade, Moore..............C ×
Fork Church, Davie.........W 235
Fork Creek, Randolph.......C 6
Forks of Pigeon, Hayward.SW 36
Forney's Creek, Swain....SW 24
Fort Barnwell, Craven.......E ×
Fort Defiance, Caldwell....W ×
Fort Landing, Tyrrell.......E 25
Foscoe, Watauga..........NW ×
Foster, Person...............N ×
Fountain Hill, Greene......E 120
● Four Oaks, Johnston......C 62
Foust's Mills, Randolph.....C 120
Fowle, Jones..................E 24
Foxville, Buncombe........W 12
Francisco, Stokes............N 30
Frank, Mitchell..............W 12
Franklin, Macon........SW 251
Franklin, Rowan............W ×
● Franklinton, Franklin....N 583
Franklinville, Randolph....C 350
● Freeman, Columbus.......S 5
Freeman's Mills, Guilford..N 120
● Fremont, Wayne............C 377
Friedburgh, (see Hulon)...N ×
● Friendship, Guilford......N 60
Friezeland, Madison........W ×
Fruitland, Henderson......SW 36
Fuller's, Randolph...........C ×
Fulmore, Robeson............S 20
● *Fulp*, Stokes...............N ×
Fulton, Davie.................W ×
Furches, Ashe..............NW 30
Furrs, Cabarrus............SW 24
Gaddysville, Robeson.......S 10
Gage, Madison...............W ×
Gaither, McDowell..........W ×
Gale, Moore...................C ×
Galloway, Transylvania...SW ×
Galveston, Durham..........N ×
Gamble's Store, R'th'rf'rd SW 20
Gamewell, Caldwell.........W 10
Gannaway, Caswell..........N ×
Gant's Rockingham..........N ×
Gap Creek, Ashe...........NW 30
Garden City, McDowell.....W ×
Garden Creek, Haywood..SW 18
● *Gardins* McDowell.......W ×
Garfield, Rowan.............W 12
Garibaldi, (see Belmont) .... ×
● Garland, Sampson.........C ×
● Garner, Wake...............C 150
Garnett, Rutherford.......SW 32
● Garysburgh, North'pton NE 200
● *Gaston*, Halifax..........NE 50
● Gastonia, Gaston.........SW 1,033
● *Gates*, Gates..............NE ×
Gatesville, Gates........NE 232
Gatewood, Caswell..........N 30
Gath, Orange.................N 48
Gatlington, Gates..........NE 10
Gavin, Duplin.................C ×
Gaylord, Beaufort............E ×
Gem, Buncombe..............W ×
Geneva, (see South Mills) .... ×
Geneva, Rockingham........N 36
Gentry, Rockingham........N ×
Georgetown, Jackson.......W 24
Georgeville, Cabarrus.....SW ×
● Germantown, Stokes......N 200
● Ghio, Richmond.............S 12
● *Ghrist's Station*, Colum'us S ×
Gibbs, Burke..................W 12
● *Gibbs Cross Roads*, Cu'and C 6
Gibralter, Union..............S 12
Gibson's Mills, Richmond...S 25
● Gibson's Station, Richm'd..S 300
● Gibsonville, Guilford.....N 100
Giddensville, Sampson......C 40
Gift, Johnston...............C ×

Gilbert, Moore C ×
Gilead, Beaufort E ×
Giles' Mills, Sampson C 36
Gillburg, Vance N ×
Gillisville, Cumberland C ×
Gilmer's Store, Guilford N 12
Gilreath, Wilkes NW ×
Glade Creek, Alleghany NW 30
Gladesboro, Randolph C 24
Gladstone, Stanly C ×
Glady, Buncombe W 18
Glass, Wilkes NW ×
● *Glass's*, Cabarrus SW ×
Glass Siding, Rowan W ×
Glenaloon, Chatham C ×
● Glen Alpine, Burke W 252
Glen Ayre, Mitchell W 60
Glen Brook, Montgomery C 24
Glenburnie, Caldwell W 24
Glencoe, Buncombe W ×
Glendale, Alamance N 30
Glenfield, Greene E ×
Glen Inglis, Buncombe W 60
Glenmore, Johnston C 24
Glenn, Mitchell W ×
Glenola, Randolph C 6
● *Glenoe*, Pender SE ×
Glenview, Halifax NE ×
Glenville, Jackson W 48
Glenwood, Johnston C 120
● *Glenwood*, McDowell W ×
Gliden, Chowan NE 30
Globe, Caldwell W 20
Glover, Nash N ×
● Godwin, Cumberland C 25
Godwin's Harnett C ×
Godwin's, (see Benson) ×
Goff, Chatham C 30
Gold Creek, Nash N ×
Golden, Rutherford SW 18
● *Golden Valley*, Ruth'rf'd SW ×
Gold Hill, Rowan W 335
Gold Rock, Nash N ×
● **Goldsborough**, Wayne C 4,01
● Goldston, Chatham C 25
Good, Chatham C ×
Goodman, Anson S 114
Good Spring, Surry NW 24
Goodwill, Forsyth N 32
Goose Creek Island, Pamlico E 30
● *Goose Nest*, Martin NE ×
Gordon, (see Wilkesboro) ×
Gordonton, Person N 24
Gorman, Durham N ×
Goshen, Wilkes NW 36
Gould, Gaston SW ×
Governor's Island, Swain SW ×
Grace, Buncombe W ×
Grade, Alexander W 24
Grady, Robeson S ×
Gragg, Caldwell W ×
● **Graham**, Alamance N 991
Grandfather, Watauga NW ×
Grange, Transylvania SW 48
Granite, (see Brookston) ×
● Granite Falls, Caldwell W 207
● Granite Hill, Iredell W 60
● *Granite Quarry*, Rowan W ×
Grantham's Store, Wayne C 30
Grant's, Rockingham N ×
● *Grant's*, Wayne C ×
Grantsborough, Pamlico E 150
Grant's Landing, (see Jackson) ×
Grantville, Buncombe W 84
Grape Creek, Cherokee SW 24
Grapevine, Madison W 30
Grassy Creek, Ashe NW 30
Grassy Knob, Rutherford SW 12
Gravel Hill, Bladen S 30
Gravel Spring, Chatham C ×
Gray, Alleghany NW 30
Gray's Chapel, Randolph C 48
Gray's Creek, Cumberland C 25
Grayson, Ashe NW 48
Graywood, (see Newbern) 48
Great Falls, Richmond S 240
Green, (see Register) ×
Greenback, Warren N 12
Green Hill, Rutherford SW 90
Green Hill, (see Mount Airy) ×
Green Leaf, Wayne C ×
● Greenlee's, McDowell W 6
Green Level, Wake C 30
Green Mountain, Yancey W 60
Green Park, Watauga NW ×
● *Green River*, Henderson SW 10
Green River, Polk SW ×

● *Greens*, Granville N ×
● **Greensborough**, Guil'd N 3,317
● **Greenville**, Pitt E 1,937
Greenwood, Moore C 48
● Gregory, Currituck NE ×
● *Grenola*, Randolph C ×
Gretna, Greene NE ×
● Greystone, Vance N ×
● Griffith, Mecklenburgh SW 24
● Grifton, Pitt E 121
Grimesland, Pitt E 12
Grimsley, Ashe NW ×
Grindool, Pitt E 5
Grissom, Granville N 24
Grists, Columbus S 50
Grogansville, Rockingham N ×
Grove, Chatham C 40
Grove Hill, Warren N 48
Grover, Cleveland SW 126
Gudger, Tyrell E ×
Gudger's Mills, Buncombe W ×
Guilford College, Guilford N 20
● Gulf, Chatham C 75
Gulley's Mill, Wake C 15
Gunberry, Northampton NE ×
Gum Branch, Onslow SE 30
Gum Neck, Tyrrell E 70
Gunberry, Northampton NE ×
Gunpowder, Caldwell W ×
Guss, Iredell W ×
Gypsy, Henderson SW 30
Hackney, Chatham C 30
Haddock, Columbus S ×
Hadley Mills, Chatham C 25
Hagers, Lincoln SW ×
Hair's Landing, (see Grey's Creek) ×
Hale, Mitchell W ×
Hale Wood, Madison W 24
● **Halifax**, Halifax NE 361
● *Hall*, Jackson W ×
Hallsboro, Columbus S 145
Hall's Ferry, Davie W 24
Hall's Mills, Wilkes NW 24
Hallsville, Duplin C 24
Ham, Bladen S 12
Hamburg, (see Glenville) ×
Hamer, Caswell N 24
Hamilton, Martin NE 781
● Hamlet, Richmond S 100
Hammocks, New Hanover SE ×
Hampton, Granville N 24
Hampton, Sampson C ×
Hamptonville, Yadkin NW 100
Hambric, Rutherford SW 12
Handy, Davidson C ×
Hanes, Wilkes NW ×
Hanging Dog, Cherokee SW 24
Hannersville, Davidson C 10
Hanrahan, (see Pullett) ×
● *Happy Home*, Burke W 170
Harbinger, Currituck NE ×
Hardbank, Stokes N ×
● Harden, Gaston SW 36
Hare's Store, Johnston C 24
Hargrove, Granville N ×
Harlowe, Craven E 300
Harman, Watauga NW ×
Harman's Cr. Rds, (see Alex'r) ×
Harmony, Iredell W 30
Harper's, Johnston C 12
Harper's Cross Roads, Ch'm C 10
Harrells Sta., (see Tarboro) ×
Harrell's Store, Sampson C 200
Harrellsville, Hertford NE 110
Harrington, Harnett C 180
● Harrisburg, Cabarrus SW 100
Harris Mine, Jackson W ×
● Harrison, Mecklenburgh SW ×
Harrison Creek, Pender SE 24
Harrison's Depot, Caswell N ×
Harrisville, Montgomery C 8
Hartland Caldwell W 44
Harts, Rowan W 90
● *Hartsborough*, Edgec'mbe NE 30
Hartshorn, Alamance N 75
Hartsville, Wake C 6
Harvey, Lincoln SW ×
Haslin, Beaufort E 90
● Hassell, Martin NE ×
Hastings, Ashe NW ×
Hastings Cor., (see Camden) ×
Hasty, Richmond S 75
Hatteras, Dare E 48
Hattie, Watauga NW ×
● Havelock, Craven E 24
Hawfield, Alamance N 30

Hawley's Store, Sampson C 72
● Haw River, Alamance N 317
Hayes, Halifax NE ×
Hayes Store, Wake C ×
Hayesville, Clay SW 250
Hay Meadow, Wilkes NW 36
Hayne, Sampson C ×
Hay Stack, Surry NW 24
Haywood, Chatham C 195
Hazel, (see West Asheville) ×
Hazen, Pasquotank NE ×
Healing Springs, Davidson C 48
● *Healing Springs*, Gaston SW ×
Heathsville, Halifax NE 24
● Hebron, Mecklenburgh SW 12
Hedrick, Alexander W 24
Heflin, Nash N ×
Heilig's Mill, Rowan W 25
Helton, Ashe NW 25
Helton Iron Works, Ashe NW ×
Hemlock, Transylvania SW ×
● **Henderson**, Vance N 4,191
Henderson's Tanyard, (see Hadley's Mills) ×
● **Hendersonville**, Henderson SW 1,216
Hendrix, Wilkes NW 24
● Henrietta, Rutherford SW ×
Henry, Lincoln SW ×
Hensley, Yancey W ×
Hera, Transylvania SW ×
Hermitage, Ashe NW ×
Herrells, Mitchells W 48
Herring, Sampson C ×
● **Hertford**, Perquimans NE 733
Hester, Granville N ×
Hester's Store, Person N 100
● Hewitt's, Swain SW ×
Hexlena, Bertie NE ×
Hibriten, Caldwell W ×
● Hickory, Catawba W 2,023
Hickory Grove, Wake C 48
Hickstown, Durham N 100
Hicksville, Rutherford SW 30
● Hiddenite, Alexander W 75
Higgins, Yancey W ×
High Knob, Buncombe W 24
Highlands, Macon SW 233
● High Point, Guilford N 2,000
Hightowers, Caswell N 20
● Hillgirt, Henderson SW ×
Hilliardstown, Nash N 200
● **Hillsborough**, Orange N 662
Hillsdale, Guilford N 36
Hill's Store, Randolph C 12
● *Hilton*, New Hanover SE ×
Hilltop, Stokes N ×
Hinton, Guilford N 60
Hives, Sampson C 12
Hiwassee, Cherokee SW ×
Hobbs, Gates NE ×
Hobbsville, Gates NE ×
● Hobgood, Halifax NE ×
Hobton, Sampson C 15
Hobucken, Pamlico E ×
Hocut, Bladen S ×
Hodge, Cleveland SW ×
● Hoffman, Richmond S 20
Hogan, Rockingham N 25
Hogback Valley, Transy'a SW 30
Hollands, Wake C ×
Hollands, Pitt E ×
Hollis, Rutherford SW ×
● *Holloway*, Durham N ×
Holloway's, Person N 20
Hollow Poplar, Mitchell W 12
Holly, Rutherford SW ×
Holly Bush, Cleveland SW 130
Holly Grove, (see Corapeake) ×
Holly Springs, Wake C 218
Hollywood, Carteret E 60
Holman's, Davie W 30
Holman's Mills, Alamance N 180
Holsclaw, Alexander W ×
Holt, Guilford N ×
● *Holtsbury*, Davidson C ×
● *Holt's Mill*, Johnston C ×
● Hominy Creek, Bunc'be W 120
Hoods, Mecklenburgh SW 60
Hooker, Alleghaney NW 12
Hookerton, Greene E 173
Hoosier, Jackson W ×
Hoover Hill, Randolph C 25
Hope, Union S 6
● Hope Mills, Cumberland C 773
Hopewell, Mecklenburgh SW 6
Hopkins, Davidson C ×

Place	Region	Pop.
Horner's, Moore	C	×
Hornet, Mecklenburgh	SW	30
Hornyhead, Jackson	W	12
Horse Cove, Macon	SW	24
Horse Shoe, (see Elkinsville)		×
Horse Shoe, Henderson	SW	24
Horton, Watauga	NW	60
● Hothouse, Cherokee	SW	24
● Hot Springs, Madison	W	695
Houck, Caldwell	W	×
● House, Pitt	E	×
Houstonville, Iredell	W	36
Howard, Bertie	NE	36
Howellsville, Robeson	S	24
Hoyle, Randolph	C	×
Hub, Columbus	S	×
Hubert, Onslow	SE	×
● Hudson, Caldwell	W	10
Hudson, (see Jug Town)		×
Hugo, Lenoir	E	×
Hull's Cross Roads, Lincoln	SW	60
Hulon, Forsyth	N	10
Humphrey, Duplin	C	18
Hunkadora, Durham	N	12
Hunsucker's Store, (see Star)		×
Hunter's Bridge, Beaufort	E	48
Hunter's Lodge, Beaufort	E	×
● Huntersville, Mecklen'h	SW	431
Hunting Creek, Wilkes	NW	42
Huntley, Sampson	C	36
Hunt's, Nash	N	32
● *Huntsboro*, Granville	N	×
Huntsville, Yadkin	NW	50
Hurdle's Mills, Herson	N	40
Hurricane, Haywood	SW	×
Husk, Ashe	SW	×
Hutchinson's Store, Wake	C	48
Hyatt, Anson	S	×
Hycotee, Caswell	N	30
Idaho, Cumberland	C	8
Idalia, Beaufort	E	65
Idlewild, Ashe	NW	×
Idol's Mill, Ashe	NW	18
Ilex, Davidson	C	20
● *Ilion*, Columbus	S	×
Immer, Montgomery	C	×
Inanda, Buncombe	W	×
Independence, (see Blackwell's)		×
Indian Creek, Currituck	NE	×
Indian Town, Camden	NE	48
● Indian Trail, Union	S	12
Inez, Warren	N	×
Ingalls, Mitchell	W	×
Ingleside, Franklin	N	×
Ingold, Sampson	C	78
Ingram, Northampton	NE	24
Ink, Wilkes	NW	×
Inland, Moore	C	×
Institute, Lenoir	E	60
Inverness, Cumberland	C	12
Iola, Alamance	N	18
Ionia, Robeson	S	48
Ira, Wilkes	NW	×
● Iredell, Brunswick	S	36
Iredell, (see Fancy Hill)		×
Irena, Clay	SW	12
Iron Duff, Haywood	SW	×
Iron Hill, Columbus	S	24
● Iron Station, Lincoln	SW	100
Irvin, Transylvania	SW	×
Island Creek, (see Uwharie)		×
Island Ford, Rutherford	SW	×
Ita, Halifax	NE	×
Itasca, Johnston	C	×
Itiner, Johnston	C	×
Itom, Rutherford	SW	×
Ivanhoe, Sampson	C	×
Ivy, Madison	W	30
Jackson, Northampton	NE	750
Jackson Hill, Davidson	C	60
Jackson's Creek, Randolph	C	60
Jackson Springs, Moore	C	30
Jacksonville, Onslow	SE	170
Jacob's Fork, Catawba	W	145
James City, Craven	E	1,237
● Jamestown, Guilford	N	1,500
● Jamesville, Martin	NE	316
Janeiro, Pamlico	E	×
● Jarretts, Swain	SW	18
Jarvis, Bladen	S	×
Jarvisburg, Currituck	NE	24
Jason, Greene	E	×
Jasper, Craven	E	×
Jefferson, Ashe	NW	413
Jennings' Mills, Iredell	W	30
Jeptha, Transylvania	SW	×
Jernigan, Duplin	C	×
Jerome, Bladen	S	×
● *Jerome*, Johnson	C	×
Jerusalem, Davie	W	1,000
Jessup Landing, Bladen	S	×
Jesup, Moore	C	×
Jewell, Stokes	N	21
● Jimes, Davidson	C	36
Job, (see Ferndale)		×
Joford, Duplin	C	×
Johnson, Graham	SW	×
Johnson's Mills, Pitt	E	25
● John Station, Richmond	S	×
Jolliet, Forsyth	N	×
Jonas Ridge, Burke	W	24
Jonathan's Creek, Hayward	SW	130
Jonesboro, (see Hallsboro)		×
● Jonesborough, Moore	C	541
Jones' Creek, Anson	S	84
Jones Mine, Davidson	C	×
Jonesville, Yadkin	NW	55
Joppa, Orange	N	×
Jordans Grove, Orange	N	×
Joseph, Wayne	C	×
Joshua, Lenoir	E	×
Joy, Burke	W	12
● Joynes, Wilkes	NW	×
Juanita, Surry	NW	×
Jubilee, Davidson	C	×
Judesville, Surry	NW	×
Judkins, (see Macon)		×
Judson, Swain	SW	×
Jug Town, Catawba	W	155
● Julian, Guilford	N	300
Jumbo, Caldwell	W	×
Junaluska, Swain	SW	30
● *Junction*, Mecklenburgh	SW	×
Juno, Buncombe	W	×
Jupiter, Buncombe	W	×
Justice, Franklin	N	×
Kappa, Davie	W	×
Kapp's Mill, Surry	NW	40
Katesville, Franklin	N	×
Keelsville, Pitt	E	15
Keener, Sampson	C	×
Keeversville, (see Plateau)		×
Keith, Pender	SE	×
Kelford, Bertie	NE	×
Kellys, Bladen	S	30
Kelleysville, Mecklenburgh	SW	×
Kelsy, Watauga	NW	×
Kelvin Grove, Wake	C	30
Kemp's Mills, Randolph	C	50
Kenansville, Duplin	C	291
● Kenly, Johnston	C	137
● Kernersville, Forsyth	N	900
● Kerr, Sampson	C	×
Kershaw, Pamlico	E	30
Key, Harnett	C	×
● Keyser, Moore	C	295
Kidsville, Lincoln	SW	30
Kiger, Stokes	N	×
Kilby, Alexander	W	30
Kildee, Randolph	C	×
Kilkenny, (see Alligator)		×
● *Killmans*, Lincoln	SW	×
Killquish, Edgecombe	NE	×
Kimbolton, Chatham	C	36
Kimesville, Guilford	N	×
● *Kingsborough*, Edgec'be	NE	15
King's Cabins, Stokes	N	×
King's Creek, Caldwell	W	36
● King's Mountain, Cleve'd	SW	429
Kingville, Columbus	S	×
Kingwood, Mecklenburgh	SW	36
Kinlaw, Robeson	S	×
Kinsey, Cherokee	SW	150
● **Kinston**, Lenoir	E	1,726
Kirby, (see Conway)		×
Kirby's Crossing, (see Wilson)		×
● *Kirkland*, New Hanover	SE	×
● Kittrell, Vance	N	317
Kittrell's Cr. Rds., (see Berea)		×
Kitty Hawk, Currituck	NE	24
Klutts, Cabarrus	SW	×
Knap of Reeds, Granville	N	75
Knight, (see Brinkleyville)		×
Knights, Henderson	SW	×
Knob Creek, Cleveland	SW	48
Knoll, Macon	SW	×
Knott's Island, Currituck	NE	120
Knott's Store, Anson	S	12
Knottville, Wilkes	NW	×
● *Kollock Sta.*, Richmond	S	×
Kyle's Landing, Cumberland	C	12
Lacey, Alamance	N	24
Lackey, Alexander	W	×
Lacrosse, Guilford	N	×
● *Ladford*, Rockingham	N	×
Ladonia, Surry	NW	×
● La Grange, Lenoir	E	775
Lake Comfort, Hyde	E	50
Lake Landing, Hyde	E	75
● Lake Wacamaw, Columbus	S	150
Lamar, Alleghany	NW	×
Lambsville, Chatham	C	25
Lamont, Guilford	N	×
Lane's Creek, Union	S	35
Langdon, Rockingham	N	×
Langly, (see Greenville)		×
Lanier, Onslow	SE	36
Lansing, Ashe	NW	48
Lark, Cleveland	SW	18
Lasker, Northampton	NE	24
Lassiter's Mills, Randolph	C	45
Lassiter's Store, (see White House)		×
Latham's, Beaufort	E	48
● Lattimore, Cleveland	SW	×
Laurel, Franklin	N	100
Laurel Bluff, Surry	NW	×
Laurel Branch, Alleghany	NW	12
● Laurel Hill, Richmond	S	100
Laurel Springs, Alleghany	NW	×
● Laurinburgh, Richmond	S	1,357
Lavina, Haywood	SW	×
Lawrence, Edgecombe	NE	×
Laws, Orange	N	24
Lawsonville, Rockingham	N	30
Layton, Rockingham	N	×
Leachburgh, Johnston	C	15
Lead, Henderson	SW	×
Leaflet, Harnett	C	×
● Leaksville, Rockingham	N	726
Leaksville Cotton Mills, Rockingham	N	315
Leander, Watauga	NW	×
Leasburgh, Caswell	N	300
Leatherman, Macon	SW	×
Lebanon, Columbus	S	24
Ledford, Clay	SW	×
Ledger, Mitchell	W	30
Lee, Madison	W	30
Leechville, Beaufort	**E**	**67**
Lee's Mills, (see Roper)		×
Leesville, Robeson	S	48
Leewood, Chatham	C	12
Leggett, Edgecombe	NE	×
Leicester, Buncombe	W	150
Lemay, Wake	C	12
● Lemon Springs, Moor	C	36
● **Lenoir**, Caldwell	W	673
Lenoir Institute, (see Institute)		×
Lenox Castle, Rockingham	N	10
Lenton, Rockingham	N	×
Lentz, Rowan	W	×
Leo, Stanly	C	24
Leon, Duplin	C	18
Leonard, Madison	W	×
Leota, Chatham	C	×
Letha, Franklin	N	×
Letitia, Cherokee	SW	×
Level Cross, Randolph	C	18
Level Plains, Randolph	C	48
Levi, Davidson		
● *Lewis*, Granville	N	×
Lewis Fork, Wilkes	NW	×
● Lewiston, Bertie	NE	373
Lewisville, Forsyth	N	439
● **Lexington**, Davidson	C	1,440
● *Liberty*, Forsyth	N	×
● Liberty, Randolph	C	366
Liberty Hill, Iredell	W	300
Liberty Store, Guilford	N	24
Lick Creek, (see Cid)		×
Light, Davidson	C	×
● Lilesville, Anson	S	222
Lillington, Harnett	C	200
Lillington, Pender	SE	80
Lily, Camden	NE	10
Lima, Craven	E	×
Lime Rock, Stokes	N	5
Limestone, Buncombe	W	×
● **Lincolnton**, Lincoln	SW	957
Linden, Moore	C	×
Lindsay, Orange	N	×
Line, Rutherford	SW	30
Lineback, Mitchell	W	24
Linney, Ashe	NW	×
● Linville, Mitchell	W	×
Linville Cove, Mitchell	W	×
Linville's Store, Burke	W	×
● Linwood, Davidson	C	50
Lipe, Rowan	W	×
Lisbon, Sampson	C	25
Lisk, Rowan	W	×

Litaker, Rowan............ W ×
Litttle Creek, Madison..... W 24
Littlefield, Pitt............E ×
Little Pine Creek, Madison. W 48
Little Richmond, (see Rusk) . ×
Little River, Alexander.... W 15
Little River, Transylvania SW ×
Little River Academy, Cum'd C 200
Little Rock Creek, Mitchell W 24
Little's Mills, Montgomery..C ×
Little's Mills, Richmond.......S 40
Little Sugar Loaf, Bladen... S 30
● Littleton, Halifax.......NE 534
Lizzie, Greene.............. E ×
Lobdell, Chatham........... C ×
Lockville, Chatham......... C 150
Loco, Onslow.............SE ×
Locust Hill, Caswell......... N 75
Locust Level, Stanly........ C 42
● Lodo, Mecklenburgh....SW 30
Logan's Store, Rutherford SW 25
Loggy, Mitchell............ W 30
Lomax, Wilkes...........NW ×
Lonely, Moore...............C ×
Long Acre, Beaufort........E ×
Long Creek, Pender.......SE 200
Longford, Iredell.......... W ×
Long Island, Catawba......W ×
Longleaf, Moore............ C ×
Long Pine, Anson...........S 30
Long Ridge, Washington....E ×
Long's, Buncombe.......... W ×
Long's Store, Union...........S ×
Long Street, (see Osgood) .... ×
Long Time, Anson.......... S ×
Longtown, Yadkin....... NW 50
Longview, Guilford.........N ×
Look Out, (see Lilesville)..... ×
Lotta, Hertford............ NE ×
● **Louisburg**, Franklin.. N 667
Louise, Catawba...........W ×
Lousville, Columbus.........S 72
Lovelace, Wilkes......... NW 30
Loveland, (see Willis Cr.).... ×
● *Lovelady*, Caldwell....... W 36
Love's Level, Union........S 12
Lowder, Stanly.............C ×
Lowe, Robeson..............C ×
● Lowell, Gaston..........SW 300
Lowesville, Lincoln....... SW 50
Low Gap, Surry.......... NW ×
Loyd, Lincoln.............SW ×
Loy's Shop, Alamance...... N 30
● Lucama, Wilson.............C 250
Lucia, Gaston............ SW 35
Lucile, Wilkes.............NW ×
Lufty, Gaston..............SW ×
Lul, Wake.................. C ×
● Lumber Bridge, Robeson. S 80
● **Lumberton**, Robeson.. S 584
Lunsford, Johnston..........C ×
Luster, Durham.............N 48
Luther, Buncombe.........W ×
Lydia, Sampson............. C ×
Lyman, Duplin.............C 24
Lynch, Madison............ W 24
Lyndover, Durham......... N 12
● Lynn, Polk.............. SW ×
● Lyon's, Granville.........N ×
Lyon's Landing, Bladen.....S ×
Lytch, Richmond..............S 24
Lytton, Randolph...........C ×
McAdensville, Gaston.....SW 180
McArthurs, Robeson.........S ×
McCain's, Union............ S ×
McClamny, Wayne.........C ×
McCown, Durham.......... N 30
McCray, Alamance......... N 60
McCurdy, Iredell........... W 24
● McFarlan, Anson.......... S 125
McKeithan's Store, (see Town Creek)............... ×
McKee, Davidson........... C 60
McKoy, Sampson........... C ×
● McLeansville, Guilford... N 100
McNair, Richmond......... S ×
● McNatt, Robeson......... S 25
McNeely, Rockingham.....N ×
Mabry, Stanly...............C ×
Macedonia, Montgomery...C ×
Machpelah, Lincoln....... SW 24
Mack, Gates............... NE ×
Mack, Rutherford......... SW ×
● Mackey's Ferry, Was'ton. E 30
Macomber's Store, (see Wilmington)................ ×
● Macon, Warren............N 200

Madge, Mecklenburgh....SW ×
Madison, Rockingham.......N 450
Madra, (see Wadesboro)..... ×
● *Magessa*, Martin........ NE ×
Magnetic City, Mitchell.... W ×
● Magnolia, Duplin.......... C 460
Magruder, Bladen............S 30
Mahone, Ashe............NW ×
● Maiden, Catawba........ W 264
Maitland, Sampson.......... C ×
● *Majolica*, Rowan........ W ×
Makatoka, Brunswick......S ×
Makelyville, Hyde.......... F 25
Malee, Richmond........... S 12
Malmo, Brunswick......... S ×
Mamie, Cherokee.........SW ×
Mana, Yadkin.............. NW 24
● Manchester, Cumberland. C 50
Mangum, Richmond........ S 25
● Manly, Moore...............C 192
Manndale, Chatham.........C ×
Manning, Row[illegible]n..............W ×
Mann's Harbor, Dare........ E 24
● Manson, Warren...........N 80
Manteo, Da[illegible]...............E 20
Mapel Cypress, Craven. .....E 10
Mapel Hill, Pender...... ..SE 72
Maple Spr[illegible]gs, [illegible]kes.. .NW 24
Mapleton, [illegible]erc[illegible] .. ..NE 35
Maplev[illegible]e, [illegible] .. ....N 24
● Mar[illegible] .. ..SW 30
● Marg[illegible] NE 33
Maribel, Pa[illegible]...... ..E 8
Marines, On[illegible]ow........ .. SE 24
● **Marion**, McDowel ..... W 799
Marlborough, Pitt......... .. E 92
Marler, Yadkin.... ..... NW ×
Marley's Mills, Randolph....C 30
● Marlville, Bladen..........S 24
Marsh, Davidson... .... C 90
● **Marshall**, Madison ... W 203
Marshallberg, Carteret...... E ×
Mars Hill, Madison.........W 61
Martin, Yadkin........... NW ×
Martindale, MecklenburghSW 24
Martin's Mill, Montgomery. C 24
Mascot, Buncombe.........W ×
Mashburn's Store, (see Angola) ×
Mashoes, Dare.............E ×
Masonboro, New Hanover. SE ×
Masey, Wake................C 24
Mast, Watauga...........NW ×
Matawa, Randolph.........C ×
Matrimony, Rockingham...N 24
● Matthews, Mecklenburgh SW 335
Maud, Randolph........... C ×
Maximo, Cabarrus........ SW ×
● Maxton, Robeson.......... S 694
Maxwell, Henderson.......SW 30
● *Maxwell's Sta.*, Columbus. S 25
May, Harnett...............C 50
Mayfield, Rockingham..... N 42
Mayhew, Iredell............W ×
Mayo, Rockingham..........N 12
Maysville, Jones............ E 24
Maywood, Alamance....... N ×
Meadow Hill, Caldwell..... W 24
Meadows, Stokes.......... N ×
● *Meare's Bluff*, N. HanoverSE 100
Meat Camp, Watauga.... NW ×
● Mebane, Alamance........N 250
Mechanic, Randolph........ C 24
Medlin, Swain.............SW ×
Medoc, Halifax...............NE ×
Meherrin, (see Severn)....... ×
Meeksville, Wilson........... C ×
Melrose, Robeson........... S 42
● *Melrose*, Polk........... SW ×
Melville, Alamance..........N 136
Melvin Hill, Polk.......... SW 7
Memory, Rutherford.......SW 12
Menola, Hertford..........NE ×
Merchant Mills, Gates.....NE 20
Meredith, Orange.......... N ×
Merritts, Columbus......... S ×
Merrimon, Carteret..........E ×
Merry Hill, (see Avoca)...... ×
Merry Mount, Warren.........N 30
● Merry Oaks, Chatham.... C 75
Mesic, Pamlico...............E 30
Metalla, Warren.............N ×
● Method, Wake............C ×
Miami, Northampton.....NE ×
Mica, Mitchell.............W 12
Micaville, Yancy............W 36
Michael, Davidson......... C 42
Micro, Johnston........... C ×

● Middleburgh, Vance......N 75
Middle Cane, Wautauga.. NW 24
Middletown, Hyde..........E 75
Midland, Forsyth.............N ×
Midway, (see Dabney)....... ×
Midway, Davidson.......... C 36
Milburnie, Wake............C ×
● Mildred, Edgecombe....NE 81
Milesville, Caswell...........N 24
● Millboro, Randolph.........C ×
Mill Bridge, Rowan.........W 24
● Mill Brook, Wake........ C ×
Mill Creek, Person..........N 20
Milledgeville, Montgomery..C 70
Miller, Iredell...............W 30
Miller's Creek, Wilkes.... NW 48
Millertown, Rowan.........W 35
Mill Hill, Cabarrus.........SW 50
Milligan, Cleveland ....SW ×
● *Mill Point*, Guilford..... N ×
Mill Point, (see Elon College) ×
Millport, Chatham...........C ×
Millprong, Robeson......... S 20
Mills River, Henderson ...SW 40
Mills' Spring, Polk......... SW 200
Millwood, Chatham ....C 10
● *Millwood*, Rutherford..SW ×
Milo, Johnston..............C 24
● Milton, Caswell...........N 705
Milwaukee, Northampton NE ×
Mineola, Beaufort.......... E ×
● *Mineral Springs*, PenderSE ×
Mingo, Sampson............C ×
Mint Hill, Mecklenburgh. SW 36
Mintonsville, Gates.......NE ×
Miranda, Rowan ....W ×
Mission, Stanly..............C ×
Mitchell, Buncombe.........W 12
Mitchellstown, (see Nashville) ×
Mitchiner, Franklin........N ×
Mitford, Rowan............W ×
Mix, Sampson...............C ×
● Mizpah, Stokes ....N 24
Mocksville, Davie.......W 400
Moffit's Mills, Randolph.....C 20
Mohawk, Harnett...........C ×
Mollie, Columbus.......... S ×
Mombo, Catawba .... W 100
● Moncure, Chatham....... C 25
Money, Henderson.........SW ×
● **Monroe**, Union.............S 1,866
Monroeton, Rockingham... N 24
Montague, Pender.........SE ×
Monteith, Mecklenburgh. SW 36
Montezuma, Mitchell........W 36
Montford, McDowell....... W 18
Montgomery, Montgomery. C ×
Monticello, Washington.....E 60
Montpelier, Richmond........S 30
Montrose, Cumberland .....C ×
Montrose Landing, Cho'n NE ×
Montvale, Transylvania...SW ×
Moonstone, Swain........ SW ×
● Mooresboro, Cleveland. SW 197
Moore's Creek, Pender....SE 72
Moore's Mills, (see Wakefield) ×
● Mooresville, Iredell......W 886
Mooshaunee, Moore.........C 6
Moratock, Montgomery.....C ×
Moravian Falls, Wilkes...NW 120
● *Morehead*, Guilford......N ×
● **Moorehead City, Carteret**. E 1,064
● *MooreheadDepot*, CarteretE ×
Moretz Mills, Watauga...NW 42
Morgan Hill, Buncombe....W 15
Morgan's Mills, Union......S 15
● **Morganton**, Burke.... W 1,557
Moriah, Person..............N 24
Morristown, Moore.........C ×
● Morrisville, Wake.........C 149
Morrosenean, Robeson......S 24
Morton's Store, Alamance..N 42
● Morven, Anson............S 00
Moser, Surry.............. NW ×
Mosley, Surry............ NW 30
● Moss Neck, Robeson......S 75
Moulton, Franklin.........N ×
Mountain Creek, Catawba..W 24
Mountain Island, Gaston..SW 376
Mountain Road, Halifax. NE ×
Mountain View, Warren....N 25
● Mount Airy, Surry..... NW 1,768
Mount Bethel, Alexander.. W 24
Mount Carmel, Moore.......C 24
Mount Energy, Granville...N 50
Mount Gilead, Montgomery. C 106
Mount Gould, Bertie......NE 30

 North Carolina North Carolina

● Mount Holly, Gaston....SW 472
Mount Hope, Perquimans NE ×
● Mount Mourne, Iredell...W 75
Mount Nebo, Yadkin.....NW 60
● Mount Olive, Wayne......C 393
Mount Pisgah, Alexander..W 30
Mount Pleasant, Cabarrus SW 375
Mount Prospect, Union.....S ×
Mount Sterling, Haywood.SW ×
● Mount Tabor, Columbus...S 50
Mount Tirzah, Person.......N 40
Mount Ulla, Rowan........W 24
Mount Vernon, Rowan.....W 42
Mount Vernon Springs, Chatham.......................C 102
Mount View, Warren.......N ×
Mount Zion, Wilkes......NW 12
● Moyock, Currituck.....NE 25
Moyton, Wilson.............C ×
Mud Lick, Chatham.........C 35
Mulberry, Wilkes.........NW 120
Mullgrove, Catawba........W 25
● *Munn's Station*, Moore...C ×
Murfreesboro, Hertford...NE 674
● **Murphy**, Cherokee...SW 803
● *Murphy Junction*, B'n'o.W ×
Muscadine, Alexander......W 24
Muttenz, Caldwell..........W ×
Mutual Love, Meckl'nb'h.SW ×
Myatt's Mills, Wake.........C ×
Myra, Chowan............NE ×
Myrtle, Rutherford......SW 30
Nags Head, Dare............E 300
Nalls, Montgomery..........C 24
Nance, Rockingham........N 24
Nansemond, (see Eliz'b'hCity) ×
Nanothall, Graham.......SW ×
● Nantehala, Swain.......SW 48
Narrows, Pender..........SE ×
● **Nashville**, Nash.........N 401
Nathan's Creek, Ashe....NW 30
Nat Moore, Bladen..........S 20
● *Navassa*, Brunswick.......S ×
Neal, Halifax..............NE ×
● Nealsville, McDowell....W ×
Neatman, Stokes...........N 6
● Nebo, McDowell..........W 12
Needmore, Swain.........SW ×
Negrohead, Union..........S ×
● Nelson, Durham..........C ×
Nero, Chatham.............C ×
Nestor, Davie..............W ×
Neta, Davie...............W ×
Nettle Knob, Ashe.......NW 30
● Neuse, Wake..............C 100
Nevin, Mecklenburgh.....SW ×
● **Newbern**, Craven.......E 7,841
New Canal Bridge, (see South Mills)..................... ×
New Castle, Wilkes.......NW 11
● Newell, Mecklenburgh..SW 6
New Found, Buncombe....W 30
● *New Garden*, Guilford....N 30
New Hill, Wake.............C 75
New Hope, Iredell..........W 60
New Hope, (seeDurant'sNeck) ×
New House, Cleveland....SW 24
Newkirk's Bridge, (see Harrell's Store).............. ×
New Light, Wake...........C 50
● New London, Stanly......● 317
New Market, Randolph....C 40
● Newport, Carteret........E 218
New River, Alleghany....NW 48
New Salem, Randolph.......C 150
New Stirling, Iredell.......W 48
New Supply, Brunswick.....S 25
● **Newton**, Catawba.......W 1,038
Newton Grove, Sampson....C 63
Nicanor, Perquimans.....NE ×
Nicholson's, Alamance......N 6
Nicholson's Mills, Iredell...W 24
Nicholsonville, Cleveland.SW 30
Nimrod, Mecklenburgh...SW ×
Nina, Cherokee............SW ×
Nixonton, Pasquotank....NE 20
Noblin, Granville...........N ×
Noise, Moore................C ×
Nonah, Macon.............SW 12
Norfleet, Halifax..........NE 24
Norfolk, Iredell............W ×
Norman, Alleghany.......NW 24
Norris, Watauga..........NW 46
North Brook, Lincoln.....SW 60
North Catawba, Caldwell...W 30
North Cove, McDowell.....W 10
North Creek, (see Yeatesville) ×

Northside, Granville........N ×
● *North West Station*, Col'sS ×
North Wilkesboro, WilkesNW 100
Norton, Jackson...........W 12
Norval, Harnett.............C ×
Norwood, Stanley...........C 159
Nottla, Cherokee..........SW 24
Nolin, Alleghany........NW ×
Nussman, Cabarrus.......SW ×
Nye, Robeson...............S ×
Oakdale, Alamance.........N 48
Oakdale, Chatham.........C ×
Oak Forest, Iredell.........W 24
Oak Grove, Union...........S 24
Oak Hill, Granville.........N 30
Oakland, Nash..............N 38
Oak Ridge, Guilford.........N 40
Oaks, Orange...............N 45
Oaks Mills, Cumberland....C ×
Oak Spring, Rutherford..SW 30
Oak Summit, Forsyth.......N 12
Oakville, Warren...........N 15
Oberlin, Wade..............C ×
Obids, Ashe..............NW 24
Ocean, Carteret...........E ×
● *Ocean View*, Pender.....SE ×
Ocona Lufty, Swain.......SW 78
Ocracoke, Hyde.............E 20
Odessa, Pender............SE ×
Odom, Richmond............S ×
● *Ogburn*, Forsyth.........N ×
Oglesby, Carteret...........E ×
Ogreeta, Cherokee........SW 24
Oine, (see Ridgeway)......... ×
Okay, Forsyth...............N ×
Okeewemee, Montgomery..C ×
● **Okisko, Pasquotank.....NE** 2..
Ola, Cleveland............SW ×
Old Dock, Columbus.........S 42
Old Fields, Mitchell.........W ×
● Old Fort, McDowell......W 249
Old Ferry, (see Fayetteville). ×
Old Furnace, Gaston.......SW 30
● Old Hundred, Richmond..S 48
Old Red, (see Conway)......... ×
Old Richmond, Forsyth.....N 24
Old Sparta, Edgecombe....NE 200
Old Stores, Moore..........C ×
Old Town, (see Winston)..... ×
Old Trap, Camden........NE ×
Olin, Iredell................W 81
Olive Branch, Union........S 75
Olive Hill, Person...........N 48
● *Olivers*, Johnston........C ×
● Oliver's, Jones.............E ×
● *Olivette*, Buncombe......W ×
Olympia, Pamlico...........E ×
Omega, Rowan..............W ×
Onion, Brunswick...........S 42
Onvil, Montgomery.........C 42
Onward, Montgomery.......C ×
Ophir, Montgomery.........C 200
Ora, Sampson...............C ×
Orange Factory, Durham..N 50
Oregon, Rockingham.......N 60
Oregon Mills,(seeSouthCreek) ×
● Ore Hill, Chatham.........C 150
Ore Knob, Ashe..........NW 350
Organ Church, Rowan......W ×
Oriental, Pamlico..........E 300
Orinoco, Davidson..........C ×
Orleans, Lincoln.........SW 10
Ormondsville, Greene.......E 48
Ormorvan, Anson...........S ×
Orrum, Robeson.............S ×
Orton, Columbus............S 30
Orton Plantation,BrunswickS ×
● Osborne, Richmond.......S ×
Osbornville, Wilkes.......NW 15
Oscar, Jackson.............W ×
● Osgood, Chatham..........C 50
Osmond, Caswell...........N 15
Otis, Yadkin..............NW ×
Otter Creek, Rutherford..SW 35
Otto, Macon...............SW 30
Outlaw's Bridge, Duplin....C 12
Outlook, Madison...........W 18
Owenby, Buncombe.........W 30
Owenville, Sampson.........C 30
● **Oxford**, Granville.......N 2,907
Oxford's Ford, Catawba....W 10
Ozark, Wilkes.............NW 12
Pactolus, Pitt...............E 75
Page, Pender..............SE ×
Painter, Jackson...........W ×
Paint Fork, Madison.......W 24
Paint Gap, Yancey.........W 24

● Paint Rock, Madison....W ×
Paint Town, Swain.......SW ×
Palestine, Stanly...........W ×
Palm, Haywood...........SW ×
Palmerville, Stanly..........C 317
Palmyra, Halifax..........NE 114
Palo Alto, Onslow.........SE 60
Pamlico, Pamlico...........E 90
Panacea Springs, Halifax..NE 84
Pant, Haywood............SW 18
● Pantego, Beaufort........E 151
Panther Creek, Yadkin..NW 80
● Paris, Anson...............S ×
● Parkersburg, Sampson...C 50
Parkewood, Moore..........C 150
Parks, Wilkes.............NW 24
Parks Springs, (see Purley).. ×
Parlier, Wilkes..........NW ×
Parmele, Martin..........NE ×
Parsonville, Wilkes......NW ×
Partee, Alexander.........W ×
● *Pasquotank*, PasquotankNE ×
Paschal, Chatham...........C ×
Pastook, Davidson..........C ×
● Pates, Robeson.............S 10
Patmos, Chatham...........C ×
Patrick, Cherokee........SW ×
Patterson, Caldwell........W 100
Patterson's Bridge, Moore..C 7
● *Patterson*, Cleveland...SW ×
Patterson's Mill,(seeDurham) ×
Patton's Home, RutherfordSW 24
● Paw Creek, Mecklenb'g.SW 48
Peace, Macon.............SW ×
● Peachland, Anson..........S 58
● Peach Tree, Cherokee..SW 24
Peacock's Store, Columbus..S 48
Peanut, Onslow............SE 24
Pearl, Cleveland..........SW ×
Pearson, Burke.............W 30
Peden, Alleghany........NW ×
Pedlar's Hill, Chatham......C 24
● Pee Dee, Anson............S 48
Peek, Madison..............W 36
Pegues, Richmond..........S 12
Pekin, Montgomery.........C 30
Peletier's Mills, Carteret....E 60
● Pelham, Caswell..........N 50
● Pendleton, NorthamptonNE ×
● Penelo, Edgecombe.....NE 15
Penelope, Burke............W ×
Penland, Mitchell...........W 60
Penley, Watauga.........NW ×
Pennington, Stanly.........C ×
Penny, Johnston............C 32
Penny Hill, Pitt............E 50
Penrose, Transylvania....SW ×
Pensacola, Yancey..........W 48
Peoples, Chathoam..........C 24
Perfection, Craven..........E ×
Perin, Montgomery.........C ×
Perkinsville, Burke........W 42
Pernell, Wake...............C 60
Perry, Gaston.............SW 18
Perryville, Bladen...........S ×
Persimmon Creek,Cher'keeSW 12
Perth, Iredell...............W ×
Peru, Haywood............SW 24
● *Pescud*, Rutherford....SW ×
Petra Mills, Caldwell.......W 24
Pfafftown, Forsyth..........N 100
Pharsala, Moore............C ×
Phi, Rowan................W 6
Philadelphus, Robeson.......S 20
Phoebus, (see Elizabethtown) ×
● Phoenix, Brunswick......S 100
Piedmont, Rockingham.....N ×
Piedmont, Stokes...........N ×
Piedmont Springs, Burke..W 12
Pigeon River, Haywood...SW 236
Pigeon Valley, (see Clyde)... ×
Pike, Cumberland..........C 24
● Pikeville, Wayne..........C 122
Pilot, (see Delk)............. ×
● Pilot Mountain, Surry..NW 100
Pinckton, Ashe..........NW 24
● Pine Bluff, Moore.........C 25
Pine Grove,(seeRidge'sCreek) ×
Pine Hall, Stokes...........N ×
● Pine Level, Johnston.....C 264
Pine Ridge, Surry........NW 24
Pine View, (see Spring Hope) ×
● Pineville, MecklenburghSW 400
Piney Creek, Alleghany..NW 90
Pink Bed, Henderson.....SW 24
Pink Hill, Lenoir...........E 25
Pinkney, Wayne............C ×
Pinnacle, Buncombe.......W 60

● *Pinnacle*, Stokes......... N ×
Pino, Davie.................. W ×
Pinson, Randolph............ C ×
Pioneer Mills, Cabarrus... SW 20
Pireway, Columbus......... S 133
Pisgah, Randolph............ C ×
Pitch Landing, (see Bethle'm) ×
Pittard, (see Bullock)......... ×
● **Pittsborough**, Chatham C 600
Pittsburgh, Rowan......... W ×
Pitts Cross R'ds, Edgec'be. NE 25
Plain, Guilford............. N 30
● *Plainview*, Robeson....... S 24
Planters, Randolph......... C 24
Plateau, Catawba........... W 120
● Pleasant Garden, Guilford N 24
Pleasant Grove, Alamance. N 90
● Pleasant Hill, North't'n. NE 50
Pleasant Lodge, Alamance.. N 24
Pleasant Mount, (see Greenv'le) ×
● Pleasant Ridge, Gaston.. SW 40
Pleasantville, Rockingham. N 24
Plott, Haywood........... SW ×
● *Plotts*, Iredel........... W ×
Pluck, Chatham............ C 24
Plummerville, Robeson..... S 34
Plumtree, Mitchell......... W 90
Plyler, Stanly............. C 24
● **Plymouth**, Washington E 1,212
Pocket, Moore.............. C 6
Pocomoke, Franklin........ N ×
Pocosin, Columbus.......... S ×
Poe's, Harnett.............. C ×
Poindexter, Yadkin...... NW ×
Point, Cleveland.......... SW 6
Point Caswell, Pender..... SE 127
● *Point Peter*, NewHanov'r SE ×
Polenta, Johnston.... ..... C 30
Polk, Harnett............... C ×
● Polkton, Anson........... S 247
Polkville, Cleveland...... SW 72
Pollard, Onslow........... SE ×
Pool Springs, Iredell...... W ×
Pollocksville, Jones......... E 143
Polycarp, Alexander....... W ×
Pomona, Guilford.......... N ×
Pond, (see Stocksdale)....... ×
Pool, Rowan.............. W 25
Pool Springs, Iredell...... W ×
Poor's Ford, Polk......... SW 6
Poor's Knob, Wilkes..... NW ×
Poortith, Union............ S 24
Poplar Branch, Carrituck. NE 30
Poplar Grove, Polk....... SW 7
Poplar Hill, Anson.......... S 6
Pore's Knob, Wilkes..... NW ×
● *Porters*, Stanly.......... C ×
Portsmouth, Carteret....... E 60
Postell, Cherokee......... SW ×
● Potecasi, Northampton. NE 100
● Potter's, Union............ S ×
Powell's Mills, (see Warrent'n) ×
Powell's Point, Carrituck. NE 48
Powellsville, Bertie....... NE 200
Powelton, Richmond........ S 12
Prather's Creek, Allaghy. NW 30
Pratt, Johnston............ C 30
Pressly, Iredell........... W ×
Presstonvile, Stokes........ N 50
Price, Rockingham.......... N 20
Price's Creek, Yancey..... W ×
Price's Mill, Union.......... S 24
Prim, Randolph............. C ×
● Princeton, Johnston...... C 248
Princeville, Edgecombe... NE 428
Pritchett, Rockingham..... N ×
Proctor, Swain......... ...SW ×
Progress, Randolph......... C 10
Prong, Columbus............ S ×
Prospect Hall, Bladen...... S ×
Prospect Hill, Caswell...... N 100
Prosperity, Moore........... C 24
Providence, Chatham....... C 50
● *Providence*, Granville.... N 50
● *Providence*, Mecklenb'h SW ×
Proviso, Buncombe........ W ×
Puello, Transylvania...... SW 8
Pughs, Franklin............. N 12
Pullett, Pitt................ E 5
Pume, Henderson........ SW ×
Pump, Henderson........ SW 24
Pungo, Beaufort............ E 24
Purcepolis, Robeson......... S 20
Purlear, Wilkes.......... NW 12
Purley, Caswell............. N 35
Purnell, Granville.......... N ×
Quaker Gap, Stokes........ N 6

North Carolina

Qualla, Swain............ SW ×
Quallatown, Jackson....... W 90
● *Quarry*, Wilkes........ NW ×
Queen, Montgomery........ C ×
Queensdale, Robeson........ S 30
Query's, Mecklenburgh... SW 30
Quewhiffle, (see Keyser) ...... ×
Quiet, Moore............... C 48
Quinine, Randolph.......... C ×
Rachel, Randolph........... C ×
Raeford, Cumberland........ C 24
● **RALEIGH**, Wake...... C 12,678
Ralph, Randolph............ C ×
Ramoth, Buncombe........ W ×
Ramsaytown, Yancey...... W 20
● Ramseur, Randolph...... C ×
Ramseyville, Madison...... W 18
Ranaleburgh, Mecklenb'rg SW 48
Randalsville, Robeson....... S ×
● Randleman, Randolph.... C 1,754
Randolph, Randolph........ C ×
Rand's Mills, Wake......... C ×
Ranger, Cherokee......... SW 15
Rankin, Mecklenburgh... SW ×
Ransom's Bridge, Franklin. N 100
Ransomville, Beaufort...... E 100
Ray, Madison.............. W 30
Raymouth, Buncombe..... W ×
Raywood, Union............. S 24
Ready Branch, Wilkes.... NW 48
Reamston, Granville........ N ×
Record, Columbus........... S ×
Redallia, Pitt............... E ×
● Red Banks, Robeson....... S 20
Reddle's River, Wilkes... NW 30
Red Hill, Mitchell.......... W 31
Redland, Davie............ W ×
Red Mountain, Durham.... N 60
Red Oak, Nash............. N 12
Red Plains, (see Shore) ...... ×
Red Shoals, Stokes.......... N 24
● Red Springs, Robeson..... S 500
● *Red Spring Sta.*, Robeson. S ×
Reed's, Forsyth............ N 12
Reedy Creek, Davidson...... C 24
Reelsboro, Pamlico......... E ×
Reese, Watauga.......... NW ×
Reepsville, Lincoln........ SW 50
Register, Bladen............ S ×
● *Register's*, Brunswick .... S ×
Rehoboth, Northampton.. NE ×
Rehoboth, Lincoln........ SW ×
● Reidsville, Rockingham.. N 2,969
Reinhardt, Lincoln........ SW ×
Relief, Mitchell........... W ×
Rely, Watauga............ NW ×
Rena, Yadkin............ NW ×
Renston, Pitt................ E ×
Repose, Lenoir.............. E ×
Republic, Yadkin......... NW ×
Resaca, Duplin.............. C 24
Resort, Transylvania...... SW ×
Rest, Stanly................ C 10
Resthaven, Buncombe..... W ×
Retreat, Haywood......... SW ×
Reuben, Union............... S ×
Reynoldson, Gates........ NE 70
Rhine, Pender............ SE ×
Rhodes, Cumberland........ C 24
● *Rhodo*, Cherokee....... SW ×
Rialto, Chatham............ C 20
Riceville, Buncombe....... W 12
Richardson, Bladen......... S 10
Richardson's Creek, Union.. S 48
Richlands, Onslow........ SE 198
● Richmond, Chatham...... C 50
Richmond Hill, Yadkin.. NW 24
Rich Mountain, Jackson.... W 30
Rich Square, Northampt'n NE 643
● *Rich Square*, Northamp'n NE 310
Rickford, Surry.......... NW ×
Riddicksville, Hertford... NE 75
Ridge's Creek, Montgomery. C 15
Ridge Spring, Greene....... E 50
Ridgeville, Caswell......... N 24
● Ridgeway, Warren........ N 250
Riggsbee's Store, Chatham.. C 35
Riley's Cross Roads, Franklin N 34
Riley's Store, Randolph..... C 25
Rimer, Cabarrus.......... SW ×
Ringwood, Halifax........ NE 92
Rippetoe, Caldwell......... W ×
Risden, Caldwell........... W 18
Rise, Moore................. C ×
Ritchie, Stanley............ C 60
Ritchies Mills, Stanly...... C ×
● Riverdale, Craven........ E 24

North Carolina

River Hill, Iredell......... W 42
Riverpoint, Chatham........ C ×
River Side, Ashe......... NW 30
River View, Mecklenburgh SW 26
Rives Chapel, Chatham...... C ×
Roane's Mill, Macon....... SW 24
● *Roanoke & Southern Junc.*, Stokes.......... N ×
Roaring Gap, Wilkes..... NW 15
Roaring River, Wilkes... NW 72
Robbinsville, Graham. SW 40
Roberdell, Richmond........ S 120
● Robersonville, Martin... NE 228
Robeson, Columbus......... S 25
Robin Hill, Cumberland..... C 60
● *Robson*, Orange.......... N ×
Rochdale, Pitt............ E ×
Rochester, Robeson.......... S ×
Rock, Rowan............... W 74
● *Rock Branch*, Harnett.... C ×
Rock Creek, Alamance..... N 30
● Rock Cut, Iredell........ W 30
● Rockford, Surry........ NW 35
Rock Hole, Stanly.......... C 36
● **Rockingham**, R'hmond S 1,500
Rock Level, Rockingham... N 24
Rock Rest, Union............ S ×
Rock Spring, Orange........ N 30
Rockview, Buncombe...... W ×
Rockwell, Rowan........... W 24
Rockyhock, Chowan...... NE 20
● RockyMount, Ed'cumbe NE 816
Rocky Pass, McDowell...... W 30
● Rocky Point, Pender.... SE 25
● RockySprings, Rock'gham N 48
Rodanthe, Dare............. E 120
Roe, Carteret................ E 24
● Rogers Store, Wake....... C ×
Rolen, Ashe.............. NW ×
Rolesville, Wake............ C 150
● Rollins, Burke........... W 43
Rome, Johnston.............. C 20
Romola, Halifax... ...... NE ×
Ronda, Wilkes............ NW 24
Roper, Washington......... E 423
Roscoe, Chatham............ C ×
● *Rose*, Wayne.............. C ×
Rose Bay, (see Swan Quarter) ×
● Roseboro, Sampson........ C ×
Rose Dale, Pasquotank.... NE 50
● Rose Hill, Duplin.......... C 100
Roseman, Catawba......... W ×
Rosemead, Bertie......... NE ×
Roseville, Person.......... N 15
Rosinburg, Wake........... C 70
● Rosindale, Bladen......... S 10
Roslin, Cumberland......... C 25
Roten, Ashe.............. NW ×
● Rougemont, Durham..... N ×
● Round Knob, McDowell. W 36
Round Mountain, Wilkes. NW 42
Round Peak, Surry....... NW 30
Rountree, Pitt.............. E 5
Roverdell, Richmond....... S ×
Rowan, Rowan............. W ×
● Rowland, Robeson......... S 72
● **Roxborough**, Person.. N 421
● Roxobel, Bertie......... NE 140
Royal, Franklin............. N 10
Rozier, Robeson............. S ×
Rubicon, Moore............. C ×
Rudasill, Gaston.......... SW ×
● Ruffin, Rockingham...... N 100
● *Roggles*, Halifax........ NE ×
● Rural Hall, Forsyth....... N 40
● *Rush*, Randolph.......... C ×
Rushfork, Haywood...... SW ×
Rushing, Union............. S ×
● Rusk, Surry............ NW 25
Russell, Rowan............ W ×
Ruth, Forsyth.............. N 24
Rutherford College, Burke. W 200
● **Rutherfordton**, Rutherford .... SW 550
Rutherwood, Watauga.... NW 24
Ryan, Robeson.............. S 15
Ryland, Chowan......... NE ×
Saddle Tree, Robeson....... S ×
Safe, Duplin................ C ×
Sago, Mecklenburgh...... SW ×
Sains, Lincoln............ SW ×
Saint Elmo, Nash.......... N 36
Saint John, Hertford...... NE 50
Saint Jude, Watauga..... NW 24
Saint Lawrence, Chatham... C 60
Saint Lewis, Edgecombe.. NE ×
Saint Paul's, Robeson....... S 35

Saint Phillip, Brunswick....S ×
●Salem, Forsyth....N 2,711
●Salem Chapel, Forsyth....N 48
Salem Church, Randolph....C 40
●*Salem Junction*, Guilford. N 60
●**Salisbury**, Rowan......W 4,418
●Saluda, Polk....SW 300
Sand Bluff, Bladen....S 18
Sanders' Cr. Rds., (see Hester) ×
Sander's Store, Carteret.....E 10
Sandifer, Mecklenburgh..SW 30
Sands, Watauga....NW 100
●Sandy Bottom, Madison..W ×
Sandy Creek, Franklin.....N ×
Sandy Cross, Gates....NE 20
Sandy Grove, Chatham......C 42
Sandy Mush, Buncombe....W 10
Sandy Ridge, Stokes....N 5
Sandy Springs, Polk......SW 12
●Sanford, Moore....C 367
Sans Souci, Bertie....NE 12
Sapona, Davidson....C 12
Saratoga, Wilson....C 102
Sardis, Mecklenburgh....SW 24
Sarecta, Duplin....C 25
Sarem, Gates....NE ×
○*Sassafras Fork*, Granville N 180
Sasspan, Columbus....S ×
Satterwhite, Granville......N ×
Saulston, Wayne....C ×
Saunders, Cabarrus.......SW ×
Saw, Rowan.... W ×
●*Saw Mills*, Caldwell..... W ×
Sawyers Creek, (see Camden) ×
Sawyersville, Randolph..... C 30
Saxapahaw, Alamance......N 200
Saxon, Stokes.... N ×
Scalesville, Guilford........N 24
Scaly, Macon....SW 30
Scarboro, (see Mt. Gilead) ... ×
Scheneks, Cleveland ......SW ×
Science Hill, Randolph......C 30
Scism, Madison ....W ×
●Scotland Neck, Halifax. NE 778
Scott's Creek, Jackson.....W 60
●Scott's Cross Road's I'dell W 12
●Scott's Hill, Pender .....SE 24
Scottville, Ashe....NW 200
Scranton, Hyde....NW 200
Scull's Store, Nort'mpton NE ×
Scuppernong, Washington..E 50
Sea, Carteret....E ×
●Seaboard, Northampton NE 201
Seagle, Lincoln....SW ×
Sebern, Northampton.....NE ×
Sedges Garden, Forsyth.... N 24
●Selma, Johnston....C 527
●Semora, Caswell....N 24
Senia, Mitchell....W ×
Seth, Granville.... N ×
Settle, Iredell.... W 24
●*Setzer*, Catawba....W 30
Seven Springs, Wayne..... C 100
●Severn, Northampton.. NE ×
Sexton, Madison .... W ×
●*Sextons*, Martin.... NE ×
Shallotte, Brunswick....S 186
Shallow Ford, Alamance... N ×
Shamrock, Mecklenburgh.SW 12
Shankle, Stanly.... C ×
●Shannon, Robeson.... S 50
Sharon, Cleveland.....SW 12
Sharp, Rockingham....N 12
●Sharpsburgh, Nash.......N 65
Shatter, Warren.... N 18
Shawboro, Currituck......NE 200
Shawnee, Catawba.... W ×
Shaw's Mills, Guilford.......N 100
●**Shelby**, Cleveland.....SW 1,394
Shelton, Surry....NW ×
Shepard, Sampson.... C 50
●*Shepherd's*, Iredell....W ×
Sherford, Catawba.... W ×
Sherrill's Ford, Catawba...W 20
Sherwood, Cumberland.... C 24
Sheva, Mecklenburgh.....SW ×
Shiloh, Camden.... NE 150
Shine, Greene....E 48
Shinsville, Iredell.... W ×
●*Shoals*, Yadkin....NW ×
Shoals, Surry....NW ×
Shocco, Warren.... N ×
Shoe Heel, (see Maxton)...... ×
Shooting Creek, Clay......SW 36
Shope, Buncombe.........W 37
Shore, Yadkin....NW 96
Short Off, Macon....SW 6

Shotwell, Wake....C 60
Shoup's Ford, Burke.......W 48
Shull's Mills, Watauga... NW 30
Sidney, Beaufort....E 24
Sidney, (see Lebanon)........ ×
Siegle's Store, Lincoln.... SW ×
Sigma, Iredell....W ×
Sigmondsburg, (see Glen Alpin Station).... ×
Silas Creek, Ashe....NW 24
●Siler City, Chatham....C 254
Silk Hope, Chatham....C 72
●Siloam, Surry....NW 25
Silver, Stanly....C 30
Silver Dale, Onslow....SE 24
Silver Hill, Davidson....C 75
Silverlake, Madison....W ×
●*Silver Springs*, Buncombe W 36
Sim, Robeson....S ×
Simmon Grove, Chatham....C 24
Simpson's Store, Rock'gh'm N 30
Sincerity, Union....S ×
Sioux, Yancey....W ×
Sitton, Henderson.... SW ×
Sixforks, Wake.... C ×
Six Runs, Sampson.... C ×
Sixty Four Mile Siding Surry.... NW ×
Skinnersville, Washington..E ×
Skill, Moore....C ×
●Skyland, Buncombe.....W 75
●*Slack House*, Madison....W ×
Sladesville, Hyde....E 75
Slate, Stokes....N 12
Sleepy Creek, Wayne.... C 18
Sligo, (see Currituck). .... ×
●Sloan, Duplin.... C 30
Sloop Point, Pender.. .... SE 31
Smith, Stokes....N 60
●**Smithfield**, Johnston...C 550
Smith Grove, Davie........ W 174
Smith Mine, (see Lexington). ×
Smith's Creek, Pamlico.....E ×
Smiths 'Ford, Cabarrus... SW 24
Smithville, (see Southport)... ×
Smyrna, Carteret....E 120
Snapp, Gaston....SW 24
Snead's Ferry, Onslow.....SE 24
Sneedsboro, (see McFarlan).. ×
Snow Camp, Alamance..... N 100
Snow Creek, Iredell........W 48
●Snowden, Currituck.... NE 12
Snow Hill, Greene....E 283
Soapstone Mount, Randolph C 30
Soda Hill, Watauga.......NW ×
Solitude, Ashe....NW 8
Solo, Watauga....NW ×
Somerset, Chowan........ NE ×
Sonoma, Haywood........ SW 24
Sophia, Randolph....C ×
South Creek, Beaufort.......E 250
South Fork, Ashe....NW ×
●Southern Pines, Moore....C 1,500
●South Gaston, Halifax...NE 50
South Lowell, Orange.......N 30
South Mills, Camden.......NE 223
South Point, Gaston.......SW 30
Southport, Brunswick....S 1,207
South River, Rowan........W 75
South Toe, Yancey....W 42
●South Washington, P'der SE 30
●*Spach's* Stokes....N ×
Sparkling Catawba Springs, Catawba....W 24
Sparkman, Onslow........ SE ×
Sparta, Allegheny.......NW 95
Spear, Mitchell.... W 48
Speight's Bridge, Greene....E 15
Spencer, Moore.... C ×
Spero, Randolph.... C ×
Spiceland, Yancey....W ×
Spillman, Yadkin........ NW ×
Spilona, Johnston.... C 24
Splashy, (see Leaksville)..... ×
Splendor, Henderson......SW ×
Split Mountain, Haywood.SW ×
●Spout Springs, Harnett... C 30
Spray, Rockingham........ N ×
Spring Creek, Madison.....W 15
Springdale, Haywood.......SW 24
Springer, Onslow....SE ×
Springfield, Wilkes.......NW 24
●Spring Hill, Halifax.....NE 50
Spring Hope, Nash....N 248
SpringsCreek, (see Vandemere) ×
Springsville, Cabarrus.....SW 90
Spruce Pine, Mitchell...... W ×

Spurrier, Mecklenburgh..SW ×
●*Stacey*, Rockingham.....N ×
●Stackhouse, Madison.....W 24
Stagville, Durham....N 30
Stainback, Alamance....... N 10
●Staley, Randolph....C 18
Stallings, Franklin....N ×
Stanbury, Stokes....N ×
Stanhope, Nash....N 40
●Stanley's Creek, Gaston. SW 100
Stantonsburg, Wilson.......C 60
Star, Montgomery....C 25
Starsburg, Cumberland......C 12
Startown, Catawba....W 30
●*State Line*, Cherokee....SW ×
State Road, Surry....NW 15
Statestone, Beaufort........E ×
●**Statesville**, Iredell.... W 2,318
Stecoach, Graham....SW 30
●Stedman, Cumberland.... C 25
Steedsville, Vance.... N 18
Steel Creek, Mecklenburgh SW 24
●*Steel Creek Station*, Mecklenburgh....SW ×
Stella, Carteret....E 78
●Stem, Granville.... N 150
Sterling, Robeson....S 40
Stevens, Union....S 12
Stewart's Academy, Harnett C 24
Stice's Shoal, Cleveland... SW 24
Stocksville, Buncombe..... W 15
Stokesburg, (see Walnut Gove) ×
●Stokesdale, Guilford....N 200
Stone Mountain, McDowell W 120
Stone's-Bay-on-New-River, Onslow.... SE ×
●Stoneville, Rockingham.. N 115
Stonewall, Pamlico....E 190
Stonewall Station, (see Croft). ×
Stoney Knot, (see Copeland) . ×
Stony Creek, Caswell....... N 25
Stony Fork, Watauga.....NW 40
Stony Hill, Wilkes....NW 32
Stony Mill Church, Surry NW ×
●Stony Point, Alexander.. W 40
Stony Ridge, Surry.......NW 30
●Stout, Union....S 36
●Stovall, Granville....N 200
Strabane, Lenoir....E ×
Straits, Carteret....E 24
Straw, Wilkes.... NW ×
Strieby, Randolph.... C ×
Stubbs, Cleveland.... SW ×
●*Stultzs*, Stokes....N ×
Stump Sound, Onslow..... SE 12
Stumpy Point, Dare....... E ×
Sturgill's, Ashe....NW ×
Success, Buncombe........ W ×
Sugar Grove, Watauga... NW 10
Sugar Hill, McDowell...... W 10
Suit, Cherokee.... SW ×
●Sulphur Springs, M'tg'ry..C 5
●*Sulphur Springs*, Bunco'be W ×
●Summerfield, Guilford....N 75
Summerville, Harnett...... C ×
●*Summit*, Halifax....NE ×
Summit, Wilkes....NW ×
Sumner, Guilford .... N 24
●*Sumner*, Rowan.... W ×
Sunbury, Gates.... NE 150
Sunny, Tyrrell....E ×
Sunshine, Rutherford .... SW ×
Supply, Brunswick....S 25
Suri, Person.... N 10
Sussex, Ashe....NW ×
Sutherland's, Ashe....NW 30
Sutphin, Alamance....N 30
Sutton, Franklin....N 24
●Swain, Swain.... SW ×
Swan Creek, Yadkin......NW ×
●Swangs, Cleveland.... SW 6
●Swannanoa, Buncombe.. W 120
●*Swannanoa Tunnell*, McDowell....W ×
Swanner, Alexander....W 12
●Swann's Station, Moore.. C 50
Swan Quarter, Hyde.... E 125
Swansborough, Onslow.... SE 233
Sweet Home, Iredell....... W 150
Sweet Water, Watauga....NW 90
Swepsonville, Alamance.... N 326
Swift Island, Montgomery.. C 24
Swinton, Moore.... C ×
Switchback, New Hanover.SE ×
Sycamore, Halifax....NE 30
●Sylva, Jackson.... W 50
Sylvester, Chatham.... C ×

Place	Location	Pop.
Tabernacle, Guilford	N	60
Table Rock, Burke	W	10
Tablet, Chatham	C	×
Tabor, Robeson	S	×
Talbot, Wilson	C	×
Tally Ho, (see Stern)		×
Tampa, Mecklenburgh	SW	×
Tapatamee, Madison	W	×
● **Tarborough**, Edgec'e	NE	1,924
● Tarheel, Bladen	S	50
Tar Landing, Onslow	SE	15
● Tar River, Granville	N	100
Taylor, Wilson	C	12
Taylor's Bridge, Sampson	C	12
● **Taylorsville**, Alex'der	W	500
Taylor's Wharf, (see Harrellsville)		×
● Teachey's, Duplin	C	52
Teague, Haywood	SW	88
Teer, Orange	N	39
Telephone, Person	N	10
Temple, Wake	C	×
Tempting, Moore	C	×
Tennyson, Davie	W	×
Terrapin Point, Halifax	NE	×
● *Terrell*, McDowell	W	×
Tesenta, Macon	SW	×
Thagardville, Moore	C	×
Thaxton, Ashe	NW	×
Thermal City, Rutherford	SW	×
Theta, Madison	W	×
Third Creek, (see Cleveland)		×
Thomas, Northampton	NE	×
● Thomasville, Davidson	C	590
Thompsonville, Rock'gham	N	×
Three Forks, Yancey	W	24
Thurman, Craven	E	24
Thurston, Alexander	W	×
Tiger, Rutherford	SW	×
Tilden, Yadkin	NW	×
● Tillery, Halifax	NE	150
Timberlake, Person	N	10
Timothy, Sampson	C	×
Tippecanoe, Sampson	C	×
Tiptop, Transylvania	SW	×
● *Tise*, Forsyth	N	×
Tito, Haywood	SW	18
● Tobaccoville, Forsyth	N	30
Toisnot, Wilson	C	482
Tolarsville, Robeson	S	15
Toledo, Transylvania	SW	×
Toler's, Orange	N	×
Toluca, Cleveland	SW	×
● **Tomahawk, Sampson**	**C**	×
● Tomotla, Cherokee	SW	[illegible]
Tom's Creek, McDowell	W	×
Tony, Caswell	N	×
Topia, Alleghany	NW	12
Topsail Sound, Pender	SE	24
Topton, Cherokee	SW	×
Tory, Caswell	N	×
Town Creek, Brunswick	S	50
Townesville, Vance	N	75
Tracadia, Yadkin	NW	×
Tracy, Watauga	NW	×
Trading Ford, Rowan	W	×
Trail Branch, Madison	W	24
Transon, Ashe	NW	×
Trap Hill, Wilkes	NW	50
Treetop, Ashe	NW	×
Trent Creek, (see Stonewall)		×
Trenton, Jones	E	207
Triangle, Lincoln	SW	75
● *Trinity*, Guilford	N	×
Trinity College, Randolph	C	380
Trio, Rutherford	SW	×
Tripplett, Watauga	NW	42
● Troutman's, Iredell	W	109
Troy, Montgomery	C	200
Troy's Store, (see Liberty)		×
Troyville, Harnett	C	24
True, Randolph	C	×
● *Truitts*, Northampton	NE	×
Truth, Chatham	C	×
Trurine, Wayne	C	×
● Tryon, Polk	SW	500
Tuckahoe, Jones	E	72
Tuckaseege, Graham	SW	72
Tuckaseigee, Jackson	W	20
Tulin, Cabarrus	SW	6
Tulip, Stokes	W	×
Tulls, Currituck	NE	24
Tunis, Hertford	NE	250
Turkey, Sampson	C	×
Turlington, Harnett	C	30
Turners, Polk	SW	12
Turnersburgh, Iredell	W	80

Place	Location	Pop.
Turner's Mountain, Surry	NW	×
Turnout, Brunswick	S	×
● Turnpike, Buncombe	W	90
Turnpike, Washington	E	×
Turtletown, Cherokee	SW	24
● Tuscarora, Craven	E	30
Tuscola, Haywood	SW	12
Tuskeega, Graham	SW	×
Tusquitee, Clay	SW	42
Tweed, Buncombe	W	30
Twine, Clay	SW	×
Twitty, Rutherford	SW	24
Tyner, Chowan	NE	30
Tyra, Moore	C	24
Tyro Shops, Davidson	C	30
Tysar's Mills, Chatham	C	12
Tyson's March, (see Snow Hill)		×
Ugonda, Wake	C	×
Ulah, Randolph	C	×
Umbra, Durham	N	×
Unaka, Cherokee	SW	×
Union, Hertford	NE	102
● *Union*, Rutherford	SW	×
Union Chapel, (see Moss Neck)		×
Union Church, Moore	C	36
Union Hope, Nash	N	30
Union Ridge, Alamance	N	24
Unionville, Union	S	×
Unity, Mecklenburgh	SW	×
● University Station, Oran'e	N	30
Upton, Caldwell	W	24
Upward, Henderson	SW	×
Uree, Rutherford	SW	11
Uwharie, Montgomery	C	18
Valle Cruces, Watauga	NW	25
Valley Spring, Rutherford	SW	12
● *Valley Town*, Cherokee	SW	24
Vance, Iredell	W	60
Vanceboro, Craven	E	350
Vanceville, Buncombe	W	24
Vandalia, Guilford	N	12
Vandemere, Pamlico	E	90
Vander, Cumberland	C	×
Vannoy, Wilkes	NW	×
Vanteen, Wake	C	×
Variety Grove, Harnett	C	24
Varina, Wake	C	2[illegible]
Vashti, Alexander	W	×
● Vaughan, Warren	N	90
Vega, Sampson	C	×
● Vein Mountain, McDowell	W	×
Venable, Surry	NW	6
Veni, Halifax	NE	×
Verble, Rowan	W	24
Vest's Cherokee	SW	24
Viands, Wilkes	NW	×
Victor, Moore	C	×
Vienna, Forsyth	N	50
Vilas, Watauga	NW	18
Villa Franca, Rowan	W	×
Villanow, Moore	C	×
Vincent, Alamance	N	×
● Vineland, Columbus	S	400
Viola, Pender	SE	24
Virgil, Watauga	NW	×
Voliers, Robeson	N	×
Vox, Wilkes	NW	×
● Waco, Cleveland	SW	105
Waccamaw, Columbus	S	12
Waddell's Rockingham	N	×
Waddell's Ferry, (see El'zb'ht'n)		×
● Wade, Cumberland	C	×
● **Wadesborough**, A's'n	S	1,198
Wadeville, Montgomery	C	20
Wagoner, Ashe	NW	×
● *Wagoner's*, Forsyth	N	×
Wakefield, Wake	C	60
● Wake Forest, Wake	C	853
● Walkulla, Robeson	S	30
Walden, Brunswick	S	15
Walke, Bertie	NE	×
Walker, Forsyth	N	×
Walkersville, Union	S	30
Walkertown, Forsyth	N	25
Walkup, Union	S	30
● Wallace, Duplin	C	125
● Walnut Cove, Stokes	N	3[illegible]0
Walnut Hill, Ashe	NW	×
Walnut Run, Madison	W	12
● Walter, Wayne	C	30
Wampler, Yancey	W	30
Wanamaker, Montgomery	C	50
Wanchese, Dare	E	×
Ward's Mill, Onslow	SE	24
Ward's Store, (see Al'dsv'l'e)		×
Wardville, Chowan	NE	25
Warlick's Mills, Burke	W	24

Place	Location	Pop.
Warm Spr'gs, (see Hot Spr's)		×
Warne, Clay	SW	×
● Warren Plains, Warren	N	740
Warrenton, Warren	N	740
● Warsaw, Duplin	C	401
Washburn, Rutherford	SW	×
● **Washington**, Beausort	E	3,545
Watauga Falls, Watauga	NW	36
Waterloo, Union	S	×
● Watkins, Vance	N	×
Watkins, Granville	N	×
Watkinsville, Stokes	N	120
Watsonville, Rowan	W	30
Watts, Iredell	W	×
Waugh, Iredell	W	×
Waughton, Forsyth	N	424
Waverly, Cleveland	SW	12
● Waxhaw, Union	S	150
Way, Union	**S**	×
Waycross, Sampson	C	25
● **Waynesville**, Hayw'd	SW	455
Wayside, Swain	SW	30
Wearsville, Robeson	S	×
Weasel, Ashe	SW	30
● *Weaver's*, Rutherford	SW	×
Weaversford, Ashe	NW	48
Weaversville, Buncombe	W	216
Webb's Ford, (see Ellenboro)		×
Webster, Jackson	W	209
Weeksville, Pasquotank	NE	25
Wehutty, Cherokee	SW	×
Weisner, Iredell	W	×
Welch, Graham	SW	24
Welcome, Davidson	C	10
● Weldon, Halifax	NE	1,286
Weldon Bridge, N't'mpt'n	NE	×
Wendall, Wake	C	×
Wentworth, Rockingh'm	N	500
West, Columbus	S	×
● West Asheville, Buncombe	W	×
Westbrook, Bladen	S	24
West End, Moore	C	50
Western, Haywood	SW	×
Westfield, Surry	NW	10
Westminister, Guilford	N	×
West Ridge, Chatham	C	×
West's Mill, Macon	SW	30
● Westville, Harnett	C	30
Wharf, Anson	S	×
Wheatmore, Randolph	C	×
Wheeler, Ashe	NW	42
Whetstone, Granville	N	25
Whichard, Pitt	E	×
● Whitakers, Edgecombe	NE	800
White Hall, Bladen	S	25
Whitehead, Alleghany	NW	18
White House, Randolph	C	24
Whiteley, Stanly	C	×
White Oak, (see Winnie		×
White Oak Cr. Rds. (see M'ysv'e)		×
White Plains, Surry	NW	30
White Road, Forsyth	N	18
White Rock, Franklin	N	×
White Rock, Madison	W	24
Whiteside Cove, Jackson	W	60
White's, Bertie	NE	×
White's Store, Anson	S	25
Whiteville, Columbus	S	372
● *Whiteville Station*, C'l'mb's	S	×
Whitley, Stanly	C	12
● Whittier, Swain	SW	200
Whittington, Wilkes	NW	×
Why Not, Randolph	C	15
Wicker, Cumberland	C	×
Wiggins Cross Roads, Gates	NE	10
Wikle's Store, Macon	SW	30
Wilbar, Wilkes	NW	30
● Wildwood, Carteret	E	×
Wiles, Wilkes	NW	24
Wilhite, Yancey	W	X
● **Wilkesborough**, Ws	NW	336
● Wilkins, Granville	N	250
● *Wilkins*, Durham	N	×
Wilksville, Robeson	S	×
● Willard, Pender	SE	34
Willardville, Durham	N	50
Willeyton, Gates	NE	20
Williamsborough, Vance	N	134
Williamsburgh, Iredell	W	24
William's Forge, Catawba	W	×
Williams Mills, Chatham	C	12
● **Williamston**, Martin	NE	751
Willis Creek, Bladen	S	150
Willow Branch, Gates	NE	×
Willow Green, Greene	E	15
● **Wilmington**, NewH'n	SE	20,056
● Wilmot, Jackson	W	×

● **Wilson**, Wilson	C	2,126
● Wilson's Mills, Johnston	C	200
Wilson's Store, Stokes	N	25
● *Wilsonville*, Martin	NE	×
Wilton, Granville	N	100
Winchester, Union	S	30
● Winder, Moore	C	100
Windom, Yancey	W	×
Windsor, Bertie	NE	522
● Winfall, Perquimans	NE	100
Winnabow, Brunswick	S	24
Winnie, Bladen	S	×
● *Winona*, Onslow	SE	×
Winona, Richmond	S	×
Winslow, Harnett	C	12
Winstead, Person	N	15
● **Winston**, Forsyth	N	8,018
Winterville, Pitt	E	×
Winthrop, Carteret	E	×
Winton, Hertford	NE	419
Wise, Warren	N	×
Wit, Carteret	E	×
Withers, Stokes	N	30
Wittenberg, Alexander	W	60
Wolf Creek, Cherokee	SW	24
Wolf Mountain, Jackson	W	6
Wolf Pit, Onslow	SE	×
Wolf Pond, Union	S	×
● *Wolf's*, Mecklenburgh	SW	×
Wolfsville, Union	S	18
Womble, Chatham	C	×
Woodburn, Person	N	15
Woodford, Randolph	C	×
● Woodland, Northampton	NE	247
Woodleaf, Rowan	W	10
Woodley, Chowan	NE	×
● Woodsdale, Person	N	20
Woods, (see Benson)		×
Woodside, Rowan	W	×
Woodville, Perquimans	NE	200
Woodworth, Vance	N	60
Wooten, Columbus	S	×
Worry, Burke	W	×
Worthington, Gaston	SW	×
Worthville, Randolph	C	328
Wortman, Burke	W	30
Wrendale, Edgecombe	NE	×
● *Wrightsboro*, New H'ov'r	SE	×
● Wrightsville, New H'ov'er	SE	50
● Wyatt, Wake	C	×
Wyo, Yadkin	NW	×
Wythe, Harnett	C	×
Xenia, Duplin	C	×
Yadkin, (see Advance)		×
Yadkin College, Davidson	C	220
Yadkin Falls, Stanly	C	×
Yadkin Valley, Caldwell	W	24
Yadkinville, Yadkin	NW	175
Yanceyville, Caswell	N	450
Yarbro, Caswell	N	×
● *Yates*, Rockingham	N	×
Yeatesville, Beaufort	E	150
Yellow Creek, Graham	SW	24
Yellow Hill, Wilkes	NW	24
● *Yeopim*, Perquimans	NE	24
Yokley, Davidson	C	24
York Collegiate Institute, Alexander	W	70
Yorkville, (see Richardson)		×
Young's Cr. Rds., (see Adoniram)		×
● Youngsville, Franklin	N	205
Yount's Mills, (see Conover)		×
Yuma, Watauga	NW	×
Zachary's, Transylvania	SW	24
Zeb, Rowan	W	12
Zimmerman, Wilkes	NW	24
Zion, Yadkin	NW	24
Zionville, Watauga	NW	30
Zirconia, Henderson	SW	10
Zoar, Union	S	24
Zorah, Craven	E	×

NORTH DAKOTA.

COUNTIES.	INDEX.	POP.
Allred	NW	×
Barnes	SE	7,045
Benson	NE	2,460
Billings	SW	170
Boreman	S	×
Bottineau	N	2,893
Bowman	SW	6
Buford	NW	803
Burleigh	C	4,247
Cass	SE	19,613
Cavalier	NE	6,471
Church	C	74
Dickey	S	5,573
Dunn	W	159
Eddy	E	1,377
Emmons	S	1,971
Flannery	NW	72
Foster	E	1,210
Garfield	W	33
Grand Forks	E	18,357
Griggs	E	2,817
Hettinger	SW	81
Kidder	C	1,211
La Moure	SE	3,187
Logan	S	597
McHenry	N	1,584
McIntosh	S	3,248
McKenzie	W	3
McLean	C	860
Mercer	W	428
Morton	SW	4,728
Mountraille	NW	122
Nelson	NE	4,293
Oliver	C	464
Pembina	NE	14,334
Pierce	N	905
Ramsey	NE	4,418
Ransom	SE	5,393
Renville	N	99
Richland	SE	10 751
Rolette	N	2,427
Sargent	SE	5,076
Sheridan	C	5
Stark	SW	2,304
Steele	E	3,777
Stevens	C	16
Stutsman	S	5,266
Towner	N	1,450
Traill	E	10,217
Unorganized Territory		511
Wallace	W	24
Walsh	NE	16,587
Ward	N	1,681
Wells	C	1,212
Williams	W	109
Total		182,719

TOWN. COUNTY.	INDEX.	POP.
Abbottsford, Benson	NE	20
● *Abercrombie*, Richland	SE	×
● Absaraka, Cass	SE	32
Acton, Walsh	NE	25
Adams, Walsh	NE	×
● Addison, Cass	SE	20
Adler, Nelson	NE	×
● Adrian, La Moure	SE	25
Akra, Pembina	NE	×
Albert, Benson	NE	×
Albion, Stutsman	S	×
Alderman, Barnes	SE	120
Algeo, Barnes	SE	×
Alhalstead, Traill	E	×
● *Alicia*, Sargent	SE	×
Alma, Cavalier	NE	×
● *Almont*, Morton	SW	×
● *Alta*, Barnes	SE	×
● *Alton*, Traill	E	×
● Amenia, Cass	SE	50
● *Andrews*, Billings	SW	×
Aneta, Nelson	NE	16
● Anselm, Ransom	SE	×
● Antelope, Stark	SW	40
● *Apple Creek*, Burleigh	C	×
● Ardoch, Walsh	NE	214
● Argusville, Cass	SE	25
Armstrong, Emmons	S	32
Arrowwood, Stutsman	S	×
● Arthur, Cass	SE	60
● Arvilla, Grand Forks	E	100
Ashley, McIntosh	S	100
Ashtabula, Barnes	SE	×
Atwill, Stutsman	S	32
● Auburn, Walsh	NE	150
● *Avoca*, Buford	NW	×
● Ayr, Cass	SE	25
● *Babcock*, Sargent	SE	×
Bac, Cavalier	NE	×
Backoo, Pembina	NE	×
Baconville, Nelson	NE	×
Barker, Emmons	S	×
● Barlow, Foster	E	50
Barnes, Barnes	SE	40
● *Barney*, Richland	SE	×
Barrie, Richland	SE	33
● Bartlett, Ramsey	NE	50
● *Barton*, Pierce	N	×
● Bathgate, Pembina	NE	377
Bay Center, Pembina	NE	97
● *Bayne*, Richland	SE	×
● *Beach*, Billings	SW	×
● *Bean*, Grand Forks	E	×
Beaulieu, Cavalier	NE	35
Belcourt, Rolette	N	×
● Belfield, Stark	SW	200
● *Belle Plaine*, Sargent	SE	×
Belleville, Grand Forks	E	×
Bellevyria, Steele	E	×
Bellmont, Traill	E	14
Benoit, Rolette	N	100
Benzoin, Ramsey	NE	×
● *Berea*, Barnes	SE	×
● *Berlin*, La Moure	SE	×
● *Berthold*, Ward	N	×
● Berwick, McHenry	N	×
● Bisbee, Towner	N	100
● **BISMARCK**, Burleigh	C	2,186
Black, McHenry	N	130
● Blanchard, Traill	E	50
● *Bloom*, Stutsman	S	×
● *Blue Grass*, Morton	SW	×
Bollinger, Rolette	N	×
Bonnersville, Ransom	SE	×
● **Bottineau**, Bottineau	N	450
● Bowesmont, Pembina	NE	25
Boydton, (see Rolla)		×
● *Boynton*, Dickey	S	×
● Brampton, Sargent	SE	×
Brenner, Eddy	E	×
● *Brinsmade*, Benson	NE	25
Broncho, Williams	W	×
● Brookland, Sargent	SE	×
Bruce, Pembina	NE	×
Buchanan, Emmons	S	65
● *Buchanan*, Stutsman	S	×
Bue, Nelson	NE	×
● Buffalo, Cass	SE	177
● *Buford*, Buford	NW	×
● *Burleigh*, Burleigh	C	25
Burlington, Ward	N	15
● Buttzville, Ransom	SE	25
● Buxton, Traill	E	200
Byron, Cavalier	NE	×
Cable, Grand Forks	E	×
Caledonia, Traill	E	267
● **Cando**, Towner	N	200
● *Canfield*, Cass	SE	×
Cannon Ball, Morton	SW	20
Canton, Pembina	NE	32
Carder, McHenry	N	×
Carlisle, Pembina	NE	25
● **Carrington**, Foster	E	425
● Cashel, Walsh	NE	×
Casselman, Emmons	S	×
● Casselton, Cass	SE	840
Causey, Mercer	W	38
Cavalier, Pembina	NE	100
● Cayuga, Sargent	SE	35
Cecil, Towner	N	100
● *Chama*, Billings	SW	×
● Christine, Richland	SE	40
● Church's Ferry, Ramsey	NE	400
Clarena, Towner	N	×
● Clement, Dickey	S	×
● *Cleveland*, Stutsman	S	×
● Clifford, Traill	E	50
Coal Harbor, McLean	C	50
● Coburn, Ransom	SE	×
● Cogswell, Sargent	SE	200
Coldwater, McIntosh	S	×
● Colfax, Richland	SE	40
● Colgate, Steele	E	35
Conger, Burleigh	C	×
Conkling, McLean	C	32
Conoho, Martin	SW	×
● Conway, Walsh	NE	100
Coolin, Towner	N	×
● **Cooperstown**, Griggs	E	368
Corinne, Stutsman	S	20
● *Cotter's*, Cass	SE	×
Cowan, Cass	SE	×
● Crary, Ramsey	NE	75
● *Crescent Hill*, Dickey	S	×
Crofte, Burleigh	C	×
Cromwell, Burleigh	C	38
Crosier, Nelson	NE	×
● Crystal, Pembina	NE	35
● Crystal Springs, Kidder	S	65
● *Cuba*, Barnes	SE	×
● Cumings, Traill	E	25

Place, County	Region	Pop.
●*Curlew*, Morton	SW	×
Daily, Barnes	SE	50
Dakem, Emmons	S	×
Dale, Emmons	S	×
●*Dalrymple*, Cass	SE	×
Danbury, Emmons	S	×
Daniels, Cavalier	NE	×
Dash, Towner	N	×
●Davenport, Cass	SE	100
●Dawson, Kidder	C	300
●Dazey, Barnes	SE	300
Deapolis, Mercer	W	×
Deehr, Nelson	NE	×
De Groat, Ramsey	NE	50
●De Lamere, Sargent	SE	18
●*Delta*, Mountraille	NW	×
De Morris, Kidder	C	12
●*Denbigh*, McHenry	N	×
●Denney, Pierce	N	×
●Des Lacs, Ward	N	×
●De Villo, Richland	SE	×
●**Devil's Lake**, Ramsey	NE	846
●Dickey, La Moure	SE	35
●**Dickinson**, Stark	SW	2,500
Dillingham, Church	C	×
Dogden, Church	C	×
●*Downing*, Richland	SE	×
●Drayton, Pembina	NE	318
●*Driscoll*, Burleigh	C	×
●*Duane*, Dickey	S	×
Dunbar, Sargent	SE	×
Dundee, Walsh	NE	25
Dunseith, Rolette	N	100
●Durbin, Cass	SE	75
●Dwight, Richland	SE	150
●*Eagle's Nest*, Morton	SW	25
Easby, Cavalier	NE	25
Eaton, Dickey	S	35
Echo, Ward	N	×
●Eckelson, Barnes	SE	28
Edberg, Burleigh	C	32
●Edgeley, La Moure	SE	200
●Edinburgh, Walsh	NE	150
●Edmunds, Stutsman	S	25
●*Eland*, Stark	SW	×
Eldred, Cass	SE	×
Eldridge, Stutsman	S	25
●*Elgin*, Cavalier	NE	×
Elkwood, Cavalier	NE	12
●**Ellendale**, Dickey	S	761
Ellerton, Cavalier	NE	×
●Elliott, Ransom	SE	15
Ellsbury, Barnes	SE	33
●*Elton*, Mountraille	NW	×
Ely, McHenry	N	×
Embden, Cass	SE	×
●Emerado, Grand Forks	E	200
Emmonsburg, Emmons	S	32
●Enderlin, Ransom	SE	×
England, Ransom	SE	15
●Englevale, Ransom	SE	×
Erickson, McLean	C	32
●Erie, Cass	SE	30
Ernest, Pembina	NE	25
Esler, Stutsman	S	×
●Everest, Cass	SE	200
Ewen, Foster	E	×
Exeter, Emmons	S	65
Eyford, Pembina	NE	×
●Fairmount, Richland	SE	91
●*Fairview*, Richland	SE	×
●*FairviewJunction*, Richl'd	SE	×
Falconer, McLean	C	×
●**Fargo**, Cass	SE	5,664
●Farmington, Richland	SE	20
●Fingal, Barnes	SE	×
●*Fleming*, Cass	SE	×
Fletcher, (see Moselle)		×
●Forest River, Walsh	NE	60
●**Forman**, Sargent	SE	178
Forsby Sargent	SE	×
●Fort Abercrombie, Ric'd.	SE	200
Fort Abra'm Lincoln, Mo'n	SW	35
Fort Berthold, Garfield	W	60
●Fort Buford, Buford	NW	42
Fort Pembina, Pembina	NE	150
Fort Ransom, Ransom	SE	75
Fort Rice, Morton	SW	×
Fort Stevenson, Stevens	C	×
Fort Totten, Benson	NE	206
Fort Yates, Boreman	S	×
Fox Lake, Ramsey	NE	×
Freeborn, Eddy	E	×
●*Fryburg*, Billings	SW	×
●Fullerton, Dickey	S	50
Galchutt, Richland	SE	×
●Galesburg, Traill	E	40

Place, County	Region	Pop.
Gallatin, Griggs	E	32
Gardar, Pembina	NE	45
●Gardner, Cass	SE	25
Garfield, Walsh	NE	×
Gayton, Emmons	S	×
●Geneseo, Sargent	SE	15
●*Geneva*, Kidder	C	×
Gertrude, Cavalier	NE	20
Gledt, McIntosh	S	×
●Gilby, Grand Forks	E	400
Gill, Cass	SE	×
●Gladstone, Stark	SW	250
Glascock, Burleigh	C	40
●Glasston, Pembina	NE	20
Glencoe, Emmons	S	15
Glenfield, Foster	E	×
●Glen Ullin, Morton	SW	200
●**Glover, Dickey**	S	10
Golden Lake, Steele	E	×
●**Grafton**, Walsh	NE	1,594
Graham's Island, Benson	NE	×
●**Grand Forks**, G'd F'ks	E	4,979
●*GrandForksJunc.*, G'd F'ks	E	×
●Grand Harbor, Ramsey	NE	50
●Grandin, Cass	SE	150
●Grand Rapids, La Moure	SE	150
●Granville, McHenry	N	×
Gray, Stutsman	S	×
●Great Bend, Richland	SE	×
●*Greene*, Cass	SE	×
●*Greenfield*, Traill	E	×
Griffin, (see Moorcton)		×
Grinnell, Flannery	NW	69
Griswold, LaMoure	SE	20
Groat, Hettinger	SW	×
●Guelph, Dickey	S	27
Hackett, Barnes	SE	65
●*Haggard*, Cass	SE	×
Hague, Traill	E	90
Halison, Pembina	NE	30
●Hamilton, Pembina	NE	257
Hamlin, Sargent	SE	×
Hampton, Emmons	S	×
Hancock, McLean	C	78
●Hankinson, Richland	SE	300
●Hannaford, Griggs	E	25
Hannah, Cavalier	NE	30
Hannover, Oliver	C	×
●*Hansom*, Towner	N	×
●Harlem, Sargent	SE	106
Harmon, Morton	SW	57
Harrisburgh, Nelson	NE	35
●Harwood, Cass	SE	40
Hastings, Barnes	SE	×
●Hatton, Traill	E	150
●Havana, Sargent	SE	50
Hazelbrock, Kidder	C	×
Hazen, Mercer	W	86
●Hebron, Morton	SW	50
Helena, Griggs	E	×
Hensel, Pembina	NE	32
Hensler, Oliver	C	20
●Hickson, Cass	SE	45
●Hillsboro, Traill	E	715
●Hillsdale, Dickey	S	32
●*Hobart*, Barnes	SE	×
Holmes, Grand Forks	E	32
●Hoople, Walsh	NE	×
●Hope, Steele	E	238
●Horace, Cass	SE	35
Horn, Stutsman	S	×
Hoskins, (see Ashley)		×
●*Howe's*, Cass	SE	×
●*Hubbard Pitt*, Traill	E	×
Hull, Emmons	S	×
●Hunter, Cass	SE	194
Huron City, Pembina	NE	25
Hurricane Lake, Pierce	N	×
Hyde Park, Pembina	NE	32
Ingersoll, McLean	C	×
●Inkster, Grand Forks	E	211
Iola, Ramsey	NE	×
Island Lake, Rolette	N	20
Jackson, Ramsey	NE	25
●**Jamestown**, Stutsman	S	2,296
Jerusalem, Ramsey	NE	×
Jessie, Griggs	E	×
Jewell, McIntosh	S	32
●Johnstown, Grand Forks	E	25
●Jollette, Pembina	NE	×
Joslyn, Renville	N	×
●*Judson*, Morton	SW	×
●*Junction*, Traill	E	×
Kandiotta, Sargent	SE	40
Karlopolis, Stutsman	S	50
●Kelly's, Grand Forks	E	×
●Kelso, Traill	E	32

Place, County	Region	Pop.
●Kempton, Grand Forks	E	15
Kensington, (see Park River)		×
Keystone City, (see Monango)		×
●*Kilbernie*, Dickey	S	×
Kildahl, Ramsey	NE	20
●Kindred, Cass	SE	150
Kiner, Wells	C	×
King, Logan	S	×
Kinloss, Walsh	NE	195
Kirk, Bottineau	N	×
Klein, Oliver	C	×
Kloeppel, Richland	SE	×
●*Knife River*, Morton	SW	20
●*Knowlton*, Stark	SW	×
●Knox, Benson	SE	×
Kongsburg, Richland	SE	×
Krem, Mercer	W	×
●*Kurtz*, Morton	SW	×
●**Lakota**, Nelson	NE	227
Lake Ibsen, Benson	NE	×
Lakeview, LaMoure	SE	×
●*Lallie*, Benson	NE	×
Lambert, Walsh	NE	32
●**LaMoure**, LaMoure	SE	309
●**Langdon**, Cavalier	NE	291
Langedahl, Kidder	C	×
●Lanona, Barnes	SE	×
●Larimore, Grand Forks	E	553
Larose, Benson	NE	20
Larrabee, Foster	E	65
Latona, Walsh	NE	×
Laureat, Rolette	N	130
●*Ledgerwood*, Richland	SE	×
Lee, Nelson	NE	20
●Leeds, Benson	NE	100
Lemon, Cavalier	NE	40
●*Lehigh*, Richland	SE	×
●*Lehigh*, Stark	SW	×
●Leonard, Cass	SE	50
Leroy, Pembina	NE	100
●*Levant*, Grand Forks	E	×
Liberal, Nelson	NE	×
●Lidgerwood, Richland	SE	150
●**Lisbon**, Ransom	SE	935
Litchville, LaMoure	SE	32
●*Little Missouri*, Billings	SW	×
Livona, Emmons	S	97
Locke, Ramsey	NE	×
Logan, Ward	N	×
●*Lone Tree*, Ward	N	×
Lordsburg, Bottineau	N	40
Lorraine, Dickey	S	×
Lowell, McIntosh	S	×
●Lucca, Barnes	SE	5
●Ludden, Dickey	S	250
●*McArthur*, Pembina	NE	×
●McCanna, Grand Forks	E	40
Mcguire, Kidder	C	32
●McKenzie, Burleigh	C	×
McKinney, Renville	N	×
McLean, Cavalier	NE	×
McVille, Nelson	NE	82
●*Magnolia*, Cass	SE	×
Malda, Cavalier	NE	×
●**Mandan**, Morton	SW	3,000
●*Manitou*, Mountraille	NW	×
●*Mantador*, Richland	SW	×
●Manvel, Grand Forks	E	200
●Mapes, Nelson	SE	40
●Mapleton, Cass	SE	119
Mardell, Steele	E	63
●*Marmot*, Morton	SW	×
●*Marshall*, Ransom	SE	15
Matthews Range, Rolette	N	18
●Mayville, Traill	E	657
●*Meckinock*, Grand Forks	E	100
●Medbery, LaMoure	SE	32
Medford, Walsh	NE	200
●Medina, Stutsman	S	×
●**Medora**, Billings	SW	75
●**Mekinock, Grand Forks**	E	×
Melby, Foster	E	×
Melville, Foster	E	25
●Menoken, Burleigh	C	32
Mercer, Mercer	W	×
Merricourt, Dickey	S	32
●*Merricourt Sta.*, Dickey	S	×
Merrifield, Grand Forks	E	15
●Michigan, Nelson	NE	200
Michigan City, Nelson	NE	200
●Milnor, Sargent	SE	279
●Milton, Cavalier	NE	202
●**Minnewaukon**, Ben'n	NE	450
Minnie Lake, Barnes	SE	×
●Minot, Ward	N	575
●Minto, Walsh	N	467
Mona, Cavalier	NE	×

North Dakota

Place	Location	Pop.
● Monango, Dickey	S	125
● Montpelier, Stutsman	S	20
● Mooreton, Richland	SE	40
Morris, Eddy	SE	22
● Moselle, Richland	SE	×
Mountain, Pembina	NE	100
Mount Carmel, Cavalier	NE	×
Mouse River, McHenry	N	15
Mugford, Pembina	NE	32
● *Murray*, Traill	N	×
Napoleon, Logan	S	10
Nash, Walsh	NE	×
Nebo, Steele	E	×
● Neche, Pembina	NE	314
Nesson, Flannery	NW	32
Newbre, Ramsey	NE	×
Newburg, LaMoure	SE	×
New EnglandCity, Het'gr	SW	10
New Minneapolis, (see Eldridge)		×
● **New Rockford**, Eddy	E	200
New Saint Joseph, Pem'a	NE	100
● New Salem, Morton	SW	200
● Niagara, Grand Forks	E	100
● Nicholson, Sargent	SE	40
Noble, Cass	SE	57
Norman, Cass	SE	12
North Viking, Benson	NE	×
● Northwood, Grand Forks	E	268
Norton, Walsh	NE	30
Norton Station, (see Thompson)		×
Norwegian, McIntosh	S	×
● *Norwich*, McHenry	N	×
Nova, Walsh	NE	×
Nowesta, Pembina	NE	32
Oakdale, Dunn	W	×
● Oakes, Dickey	S	700
Oakville, Barnes	SE	×
● *Oatland*, Cass	SE	×
● Oberon, Benson	NE	50
● Odell, Barnes	SE	27
● Ojata, Grand Forks	E	100
Olga, Cavalier	NE	250
Omemee, Bottineau	N	×
Omio, Emmons	S	20
Ontario, Wells	C	×
● Oriska, Barnes	SE	150
● Orr, Grand Forks	E	50
Osago, Nelson	NE	×
Oshkosh, Wells	C	×
● Osnabrock, Cavalier	NE	10
● *Oswald*, Richland	SE	×
Ottawa, Griggs	E	30
Ottenton, (see Neche)		×
Ottofy, Nelson	NE	25
Owego, Ransom	SE	×
● Page, Cass	SE	200
Painted Woods, Burleigh	C	25
● *Parkhurst*, Stutsman	S	×
● Park River, Walsh	NE	534
● *Park River Junc.*, G.F'ks	E	×
● **Pembina**, Pembina	NE	670
Pendroy, McHenry	N	×
● Penn, Ramsey	NE	25
● *Perry*, Sargent	SE	×
● Perth, Towner	N	×
Peters, Kidder	C	×
● Petersburg, Nelson	NE	30
Petersen, Cass	SE	×
Pickert, Steele	E	×
Picton, Towner	N	×
Pilot, Grand Forks	E	×
● Pingree, Stutsman	S	30
● Pisek, Walsh	NE	40
● Pittsburgh, Pembina	NE	×
● Pleasant Lake, Benson	NE	×
Plymouth, Ransom	SE	40
● *Port Emma*, Dickey	S	×
● Portland, Traill	E	367
Power, Richland	SE	32
Praha, Walsh	NE	20
Prattford, Pembina	NE	×
Quay, Rolette	N	×
Quincy, Traill	E	40
Rand, Dunn	W	×
● Ransom, Sargent	SE	50
● *Ray*, Flannery	NW	×
● Reynolds, Grand Forks	E	100
● Richardton, Stark	SW	50
Richville Logan	S	×
Ridgefield, Cavalier	NE	×
● Rio, Stutsman	S	×
Ripley, Sargent	SE	×
● Ripon, Cass	SE	25
● *Riverdale*, Dickey	S	×
Rogers, Ramsey	NE	×
● Rolla, Rolette	N	255
Romfo, Cavalier	NE	40
Romness, Griggs	E	32
Roop, Emmons	S	×
● *Roseville*, Traill	E	25
● *Ross*, Mountraille	NW	×
● *Ross*, Wells	C	×
Ruby, Nelson	NE	×
● Rugby, Pierce	E	200
Russell, LaMoure	SE	33
● Rutland, Sargent	SE	150
Rutten, Ramsey	NE	×
Saint Andrew, Walsh	NE	40
● *Saint Andrew's Station*, Walsh	NE	×
Saint Carl, Ward	N	×
Saint Carl, Stevens	C	32
Saint George, (see Edgeley)		×
● **St. John's**, Rolette	N	100
Saint Thomas, Pembina	NE	477
Saint Vant, Pembina	NE	18
● Sanborn, Barnes	SE	227
● *Sandoun*, Ransom	SE	×
Sanger, Olive	C	×
Sansahville, Bottineau	N	×
● *Saunder's*, Cass	SE	×
● *Schurmeir*, Grand Forks	E	×
Sargent, (see Cogswell)		×
● *Scoria*, Billings	SW	×
Scovill, Ransom	SE	98
● *Sedalia*, Morton	SW	×
● Sentinel Butte, Billings	SW	32
● *Sewall*, Richland	SE	91
● Seymour, Richland	SE	100
● Sharlow, Stutsman	S	×
Sharon, Steele	E	×
● *Shawnee*, Grand Forks	E	×
● Sheldon, Ransom	SE	253
● *Sheldon Junc.*, Ransom	SE	×
Shepard, Pembina	NE	×
Sherbrooke, Steele	E	[illegible]5
● Sheyenne, Eddy	E	40
● *Sidney*, Cass	SE	×
Sidney, Towner	N	×
Silverleaf, Dickey	S	10
Silvista, Walsh	NE	×
● **Sims**, Morton	SW	150
Slaton, Mercer	W	14
Slaughter, Burleigh	C	32
Snyder, Towner	N	32
Sodhouse, Rolette	N	×
Sogn, Nelson	NE	×
● *Sonora*, Richland	SE	×
Soper, Cavalier	NE	×
● South Heart, Stark	SW	65
● Spiritwood, Stutsman	S	30
● *Sprague Lake*, Sargent	SE	10
● *Spring Brook*, Flannery	NW	×
Standingrock, Ransom	SE	×
● *Stanley*, Mountraille	NW	×
Stanton, Mercer	W	50
Starkweather, Ramsey	NE	32
● **Steele**, Kidder	C	133
Steidl, Logan	S	×
● Sterling, Burleigh	C	100
● *Stevensons*, Richland	SE	×
Stewartsdale, Burleigh	C	×
● *Stiles*, Richland	SE	12
Stillwell, Cavalier	NE	×
Stokesville, Pembina	NE	32
Strabane, Grand Forks	E	14
● Straubville, Sargent	SE	18
● *Sully Springs*, Billings	SW	×
● *Sunny Side*, Morton	SW	×
Svea, Barnes	SE	×
Svenby, Barnes	SE	×
● Sweet Briar, Morton	SW	32
Sydna, Ransom	SE	10
● **Sykeston**, Wells	C	100
● Tappen, Kidder	C	28
Tara, Steele	E	×
Tarsus, Bottineau	N	10
● Taylor, Stark	SW	32
Tewaukon, Sargent	SE	32
Theed, Billings	SW	×
Thexton, Pembina	NE	×
● Thompson, Grand Forks	E	150
Tiffany, Eddy	E	12
● *Tioga*, Mountraille	NW	×
Tomey, Walsh	NE	25
Tomlinson, Eddy	E	17
● *Towanda*, Sargent	SE	×
Tower City, Cass	SE	309
● Towner, McHenry	N	211
● *Trenton*, Buford	NW	×
Trieste, (see Mooreton)		×
Trysil, Cass	SE	45
Turtle Lake, McLean	C	×
Turtle River, Grand Forks	E	100
Twala, Rolette	N	×
● Tyler, Richland	SE	×
Tyner, Pembina	NE	×
Union, Cavalier	NE	×
● University, Grand Forks	E	×
● *Urbana*, Barnes	SE	×
Uxbridge, Barnes	SE	×
Valhall, Wells	C	×
● **Valley City**, Barnes	SE	1,089
● *Valley Junc.*, LaMoure	SE	×
Valmont, Cavalier	NE	×
Vang, Cavalier	NE	15
Venlo, Ransom	SE	×
Verner, Sargent	SE	32
● Verona, La Moure	SE	16
Vesleyville, Walsh	NE	×
Vesley, Walsh	NE	×
Vesta, Walsh	NE	10
Victoria, McLean	C	24
Viking, Benson	NE	20
Villard, McHenry	N	57
● Voss, Walsh	NE	×
● **Wahpeton**, Richland	SE	1,510
● Walcott, Richland	SE	53
Wales, Burleigh	C	32
Walhalla, Pembina	NE	200
● *Wallace*, Ward	N	150
Walle, Grand Forks	E	×
Walshville, Walsh	NE	×
Wamdusky, (see Lakota)		×
Warren, Cass	SE	×
Washburn, McLean	C	100
Watson, Cass	SE	490
Weber, Sargent	SE	15
● Weible, Traill	E	×
Welford, Pembina	NE	×
Weller, McLean	C	40
Wells, Wells	C	×
Westboro, Dickey	S	14
Westfield, Emmons	S	×
● Wheatland, Cass	SE	500
● *Wheelock*, Flannery	NW	×
Whitby, Wells	C	×
● White Earth, M'traille	NW	×
● Wild Rice, Cass	SE	20
Wildo, Towner	N	×
Williamsport, Emmons	S	24
● Williston, Buford	NW	29[illegible]
Willow City, Bottineau	N	150
Willows, Griggs	E	40
Winchester, Emmons	S	40
● Windsor, Stutsman	S	20
Wines, McHenry	N	×
Winona, Emmons	S	200
Wogansport, Burleigh	C	×
● *Woodhull*, Richland	SE	×
Wotwode, Richland	SE	13
Woodbridge, Cavalier	NE	125
● Woods, Cass	SE	×
Worthington, (see Valley City)		×
Wright, Dickey	S	×
● Wyndmere, Richland	SE	60
● York, Benson	NE	50
● Yorktown, Dickey	S	15
Young, Pembina	NE	22
Youngstown, McIntosh	S	32
● Ypsilanti, Stutsman	S	26
Yule, Billings	SW	×
Zion, Cass	SE	×

OHIO.

COUNTIES.	INDEX.	POP.
Adams	S	26,093
Allen	NW	40,644
Ashland	N	22,223
Ashtabula	NE	43,655
Athens	SE	35,194
Auglaize	W	28,100
Belmont	E	57,413
Brown	SW	29,899
Butler	SW	48,597
Carroll	E	17,566
Champaign	W	26,980
Clarke	W	52,277
Clermont	SW	33,553
Clinton	SW	24,240
Columbiana	NE	59,029
Coshocton	C	26,703
Crawford	N	31,927
Cuyahoga	NE	309,970

County		Pop.
Darke	W	42,961
Defiance	NW	25,769
Delaware	C	27,189
Erie	E	35,462
Fairfield	C	33,939
Fayette	S	32,309
Franklin	C	124,087
Fulton	NW	22,023
Gallia	S	27,005
Geauga	NE	13,489
Greene	W	29,820
Guernsey	E	28,645
Hamilton	**SW**	**374,573**
Hancock	NW	42,563
Hardin	W	28,939
Harrison	E	20,830
Henry	NW	25,080
Highland	S	29,048
Hocking	S	22,658
Holmes	C	21,139
Huron	N	31,949
Jackson	S	28,408
Jefferson	E	39,415
Knox	C	27,600
Lake	NE	13,235
Lawrence	S	39,556
Licking	C	43,279
Logan	W	27,386
Lorain	N	40,295
Lucas	NW	102,296
Madison	C	20,057
Mahoning	NE	55,979
Marion	C	24,727
Medina	N	21,742
Meigs	SE	29,813
Mercer	W	27,220
Miami	W	39,754
Monroe	E	25,175
Montgomery	W	100,852
Morgan	SE	19,143
Morrow	C	18,120
Muskingum	C	51,210
Noble	E	20,753
Ottawa	N	21,974
Paulding	NW	25,932
Perry	C	31,151
Pickaway	C	26,959
Pike	S	17,482
Portage	NW	27,868
Preble	W	23,421
Putnam	NW	30,188
Richland	N	38,072
Ross	S	39,454
Sandusky	N	30,617
Scioto	S	35,377
Seneca	N	40,869
Shelby	W	24,707
Stark	NE	84,170
Summit	NE	54,089
Trumbull	NE	42,373
Tuscarawas	E	46,618
Union	C	22,860
Van Wert	NW	29,671
Vinton	S	16,045
Warren	SW	25,468
Washington	SE	42,380
Wayne	N	39,005
Williams	NW	24,897
Wood	NW	44,392
Wyandot	N	21,725
Total		3,672,316

TOWN. COUNTY.	INDEX.	POP.
● Abanaka, Van Wert	NW	60
Abashai, Scioto	S	25
Abbeyville, Medina	N	100
Aberdeen, Brown	SW	874
Achor, Columbiana	NE	50
● *Ackerman*, Franklin	C	×
Acme, Medina	N	75
● *Acton*, Marion	C	×
● Ada, Hardin	W	2,079
● *Adair*, Monroe	E	×
Adam, Jackson	S	×
● Adams Mills, Muskingum	C	100
Adam's Mills, Meigs	SE	25
Adams Ridge, Defiance	NW	50
Adamsville, Muskingum	C	335
Adario, Richland	N	100
Addison, Champaign	W	513
● Addison, Gallia	S	90
● Addyston, Hamilton	SW	50
Adelaide, Marion	C	75
Adelphi, Ross	S	489
Adelphi Station, Pickaway	C	×
● Adena, Jefferson	E	40
Agate Farm, Allen	W	×
● Adrian, Seneca	N	250
● *Adrian*, Noble	E	×
● *Aetnaville*, Belmont	E	×
Africa, Delaware	C	20
● Afton, Clermont	SW	50
Agins, Monroe	E	25
● Agosta, Marion	C	384
Ai, Fulton	NW	150
Aid, Lawrence	S	×
Ainger, Williams	NW	30
● Air Hill, Montgomery	W	25
● Air Line Junc., Lucas	NW	40
Aitch, Monroe	E	20
● **Akron**, Summit	NE	27,601
● *Akron Junction*, Summit	NE	×
Alaska, Van Wert	NW	×
● *Albany*, Athens	SE	471
Albany, Tuscarawas	E	30
Alberta, Meigs	SE	50
Albion, Ashland	N	75
Alcony, Miami	W	100
Alden, Washington	SE	2
Alert, Butler	SW	12
● *Alexanders*, Cuyahoga	NE	×
Alexandersville, M'tg'm'y	W	250
● Alexandria, Licking	C	296
● *Alexis*, Lucas	NW	×
Alexis, Monroe	E	×
Alfred, Meigs	SE	40
● Alger, Hardin	W	300
Algonquin, Carroll	E	50
● Alice, Gallia	S	40
○ Alikanna, Jefferson	E	×
● *Allandale*, Hamilton	SW	×
● Alledonia, Belmont	E	×
Allensburg, (see Lynchburg)		×
Allensville, Vinton	S	150
Allentown, Allen	NW	125
● *Allentown*, Fayette	S	15
● Alliance, Stark	NE	7,607
● *Alliance Junction*, M'h'g	NE	×
Alma, Ross	S	75
● *Alnora*, Putnam	NW	×
● Alpha, Greene	W	300
● Alta, Richland	N	30
Altitude, Monroe	E	×
● Alton, Franklin	C	100
Alum Creek, Delaware	C	25
● *Alum Creek Junc.* Fr'k'ln	C	×
● Alvada, Seneca	N	100
Alvesta, Lucas	NW	10
● Alvordton, William	NW	400
● Amanda, Fairfield	C	469
● *Amanda*, Butler	SW	300
● Ambler, Belmont	E	×
● Amboy, Ashtabula	NE	300
Ambrose, Fulton	NW	50
● Amelia, Clermont	SW	400
American, Scioto	S	25
● Amesville, Athens	SE	200
Amherst, Lorain	N	1,750
Amity, (see Democracy)		×
Amity, Montgomery	W	70
Amity, (see West Canaan)		×
Amoy, Richmond	N	×
● Amsden, Seneca	N	150
● *Amsden*, Williams	NW	×
Amsterdam, Jefferson	E	100
Amwell, (see Sterling)		×
● Anderson, Ross	S	40
● Anderson's Ferry, H'ilt'n	SW	×
Andersonville, Ross	S	100
Andis, Lawrence	S	25
● Andover, Ashtabula	NE	733
Andrews, Morrow	E	×
Angola, Gallia	S	×
● Angus, Seneca	N	50
● Ankenytown, Knox	C	75
Anlo, Clarke	W	×
● Anna, Shelby	W	527
Annapolis, (see Sulphur Sp's)		×
Annapolis, Jefferson	E	139
● Ansonia, Darke	W	676
Anthony, Athens	SE	15
Antietam, Trumbull	NE	×
Antioch, (see New Antioch)		×
Antioch, Monroe	E	300
Antiquity, Meigs	SE	200
Antonis, Ross	S	×
Antone, Athens	SE	30
Antrim, Guernsey	E	300
● Antwerp, Paulding	NW	1,331
Apalachin, Stark	NE	×
Apple, Hocking	S	×
● Apple Creek, Wayne	N	428
Apple Grove, Meigs	SE	75
Appleton, Licking	C	110
Arabia, Lawrence	S	150
Arbaugh, Vinton	S	×
Arbela, Union	C	×
● Arcadia, Hancock	NW	490
● Arcanum, Darke	W	1,134
● Archbold, Fulton	NW	780
Archer, Harrison	E	75
Archer's Fork, Washingt'n	SE	30
● *Arden*, Hamilton	SW	×
● Arion, Scioto	S	25
Arkoe, Pike	S	20
Arkona, (see Pittman)		×
Arlington, (see Lockland)		×
● Arlington, Hancock	NW	600
● Arlington Heights, Ha'n	SW	222
● Armadale, Athens	SE	25
Armenia, Washington	SE	80
Armstrong, Allen	NW	30
● Armstrong's Mills, Belm't	E	50
Arnheim, Brown	SW	98
● *Arnold's Spur*, Jefferson	E	×
Arthur, Paulding	N	10
Asbury, Hamilton	SW	×
Ash, Licking	C	50
Ashbrook, Licking	C	×
● **Ashland**, Ashland	N	3,566
● Ashley, Delaware	C	628
Ashmont, Erie	N	×
Ash Ridge, Brown	SW	×
● Ashtabula, Ashtabula	NE	8,338
Ashtabula Harbor, (see H'b'r)		×
Ashton, Noble	E	10
● Ashville, Pickaway	C	430
● *Ashwood*, Defiance	NW	×
Athalia, Lawrence	S	199
● **Athens**, Athens	SE	2,620
Atherton, Licking	C	25
● *Athlone*, Butler	SW	×
● Atlanta, Pickaway	C	25
● *Atlanta Siding*, Cayu'ga	NE	×
Atlas, Belmont	E	150
Attica, Seneca	N	682
● *Attica*, Seneca	N	×
● Atwater, Portage	NE	300
Atwater Centre, Portage	NE	×
● Atwood, Carroll	E	×
Auburn, Geauga	NE	150
● Auburndale, Lucas	NW	1,609
● *Auglaize*, Allen	NW	×
● *Auglaize*, Van Wert	NW	×
● *Auglaize River*, Allen	NW	×
● Augusta, Carroll	E	210
Ault, Jefferson	E	×
Aultman, Stark	NE	25
Aurelius, (see Macksburg)		×
Aurora, Portage	NE	750
● Aurora Station, Portage	NE	×
● Austin, Ross	S	20
● Austinburgh, Ashtabula	NE	400
● Austintown, Mahoning	NE	275
● Ava, Noble	E	100
● Avenue, Franklin	C	75
● Avery, Erie	N	40
● *Avis*, Putnam	NW	×
Avlon, Perry	C	25
● Avon, Lorain	N	500
● Avondale, Coshocton	C	130
● *Avondale*, Hamilton	SW	4,473
● *Avondale*, Licking	C	×
Avon Lake, Lorain	N	×
● *Axlines*, Perry	C	×
Axtel, Erie	N	75
Ayersville, Defiance	NW	25
Azelda, Columbiana	NE	×
● Bachman, Montgomery	W	100
Bacon, Coshocton	C	50
Baconsburg, (see Cortland)		×
Baddow Pass, Holmes	C	×
● *Baileys*, Lucas	NW	25
● *Bailey*, Lucas	NW	25
● Bailey's Mills, Belmont	E	100
Bainbridge, Geauga	NE	90
● Bainbridge, Ross	S	1,000
● *Baird's Furnace*, Perry	C	×
● Bairdstown, Wood	NW	347
Baker, Darke	W	20
● *Baker's Junction*, Ross	S	×
Baker's Stone Mine, Richl'd	N	×
Baker's Store, Darke	W	40
Bakersville, Coshocton	SW	300
● Baldwin, Clermont	SW	10
● *Ballou*, Miami	W	×
● *Ballou*, Muskingum	C	×
Ballou, Shelby	W	20
● *Ballous*, Muskingham	C	×

Place, County		Pop.
Ballville, Sandusky	N	×
● Baltic, Tuscarawas	E	400
● Baltimore, Fairfield	C	505
● *Baltimore*, Montgomery	W	×
Bangor, Richland	N	25
Bangorville, Richland	N	24
● Bangs, Knox	C	500
Banner, Jackson	S	50
● Bannock, Belmont	E	20
Bantam, Clermont	SW	300
● Barberton, Summit	NE	2,500
Barclay, Trumbull	NE	200
Baresville, (see Hannibal)		×
Bargar, Harrison	E	×
Barlow, Washington	SE	125
Barnes, Richland	N	50
Barnesburgh, Hamilton	SW	600
● Barnesville, Belmont	E	3,207
● *Barnetts*, Preble	W	×
Barnhill, Tuscarawas	E	969
Barren Hill, (see Versailles)		×
Barrett's Mills, Highland	S	20
● Barr's Mills, Tuscarawas	E	100
BarrsMillsSta., (seeBeachCity)		×
Barry, Cuyahoga	NE	125
Barryville, Stark	NE	150
● *Bartles Junc.*, Lawrence	S	×
● *Bartlets Sta.*, Lawrence	S	30
Bartlett, Washington	SE	300
● *Bartlow*, Henry	NW	×
● Barton, Belmont	E	×
Bartramville, Lawrence	S	35
● Bascom, Seneca	N	250
Bashan, Meigs	SE	×
● Basil, Fairfield	C	406
● **Batavia**, Clermont	SW	953
● *BataviaJunc.*, Hamilton	SW	×
● Batford, Fulton	NW	×
Batesville, Noble	E	327
Bath, Summit	NE	75
Batson, Paulding	NW	10
● Bayard, Columbiana	NE	75
● Bays, Wood	NW	25
Bay's Bottom, (see Crown City)		×
Baywood, Clermont	SW	25
Bazetta, (see Cortland)		×
● Beach City, Stark	NE	400
● Beallsville, Monroe	E	512
Beamsville, Darke	W	150
Bear Creek, Scioto	S	30
Beasley's Fork, Adams	S	×
● Beatty, Clarke	W	×
● Beaver, Pike	S	200
● Beaver Dam, Allen	NW	397
● Beaver Pond, Adams	S	100
Beavertown, Montgomery	W	200
Beaver Sta., (see Xenia)		×
● *Beckers*, Montgomery	W	×
● *Becket*, Belmont	E	×
● Becketts, Washington	SE	×
Beck's Mills, Holmes	C	25
● Bedford, Cuyahoga	NE	1,043
Bedford, (see Burlingham)		×
● *Bedford Siding*, Cuyah'a	NE	×
Bee, Vinton	S	25
Beebe, Athens	SE	20
Beebetown, Medina	N	×
Beech, Licking	C	150
Beecher, Ross	S	×
● *Beech Hollow*, Coshocton	C	×
Beach Town, (see Frankfort)		×
● *Beechwood*, Clermont	SW	×
Beidler, Tuscarawas	E	50
● Belden, Lorain	N	100
Belfast, Clermont	SW	50
Belfast, Highland	S	150
Bell, Highland	S	120
● Bellaire, Belmont	E	9,934
Bellbrook, Greene	W	350
● Belle Centre, Logan	W	927
● **Bellefontaine**, Logan	W	4,245
Belle Point, Delaware	C	102
● Belle Valley, Noble	E	150
Belle Vernon, Wyandot	N	175
● Bellevue, Huron	N	3,052
Bellville, Richland	N	941
● Belmont, Belmont	E	384
● *BelmontAvenue*, Hamilton	SW	×
● Belmore, Putnam	NW	414
● Beloit, Mahoning	NE	240
● Belpre, Washington	SE	1,007
Bement, Cuyahoga	NE	300
Bennett's Corners, Medina	N	400
Bennington, Morrow	C	150
● *Bentley*, Trumbull	NE	×
Benton, Crawford	N	173
● *Benton*, Hancock	NW	×
Benton, Holmes	C	250
Benton Ridge, Hancock	NW	250
Bentonville, Adams	S	400
Benwood, Monroe	E	30
● Berea, Cuyahoga	NE	2,533
● *Berea WestSwitch*, Cuy'a	NE	×
● Bergholz, Jefferson	E	200
Berkey, Lucas	NW	50
Berkshire, Delaware	C	225
● *Berlin*, Delaware	C	×
Berlin, Holmes	C	150
Berlin, (see Berlin X Roads)		×
Berlin, (see Loramie's)		×
● Berlin Centre, Mahon'g	NE	300
● Berlin Cross Roads, Ja'k'n	S	275
Berlin Heights, Erie	N	517
● *Berlin Heights Sta.*, Erie	N	×
Berlin Station, (see Ceylon)		×
Berlinville, Erie	N	300
● Bernard, Brown	SW	×
Berne, Noble	E	150
Berne Station, Fairfield	C	50
Berrysville, Highland	S	67
Berton, Brown	SW	×
Berwick, Marion	C	500
● Berwick, Seneca	N	250
Berwyn, Tuscarawas	E	×
Bessemer, (see Buchtel)		×
● *Bests*, Mahoning	NE	×
● *Besuden*, Hamilton	SW	×
Beta, Fulton	NW	×
Bethany, Butler	SW	129
● *Bethel*, Belmont	E	×
● Bethel, Clermont	SW	625
● Bethesda, Belmont	SW	200
Bethesda, (see Buckskin)		×
Bethlehem, Richland	N	60
Bethlehem, (see Navarre)		×
● Bettsville, Seneca	N	513
● Beverly, Washington	SE	795
Bevis, Hamilton	SW	86
Biddle, Crawford	N	×
Big Island, Marion	C	50
Big Plain, Madison	C	150
● Big Prairie, Wayne	N	200
● Big Run, Athens	SE	275
Big Run Sta., (see Wakefield)		×
● Big Springs, Logan	W	100
● *Big Walnut*, Franklin	C	×
Billings, Noble	E	×
Bingham, Monroe	E	×
Binola, Cuyahoga	NE	×
● Bird's Run, Guernsey	E	40
Birmingham, Erie	N	300
Birmingham, (seeMilnersville)		×
● Bishopville, Morgan	SE	50
Bismarck, Huron	N	25
Bissell's, Geauga	NE	×
Blachleyville, Wayne	N	150
● *Black Ash*, Henry	NW	125
● Blackband, Tuscarawas	E	40
Blackberry, Ottawa	N	50
● *Black Creek*, Holmes	C	125
● *Black Dog Sid'g*, Summit	NE	×
● *Black Hand*, Licking	C	×
Blackhand Sta., Muskingum	C	59
Black Jack, Hocking	S	30
● Black Lick, Franklin	C	85
Black River, (see Lorain)		×
● Black Run, Muskingum	C	10
● *BlackSandSwitch*, Sum't	NE	×
Bladen, Gallia	S	100
Bladensburg, Gallia	S	100
Bladensburgh, Knox	C	300
● Blaine, Belmont	E	50
Blairville, Clermont	SW	150
Blake, Medina	N	×
● Blakeslee, Williams	NW	250
Blakes Mills, Tuscarawas	E	390
● *Blanchard*, Hardin	W	×
● Blanchester, Clinton	SW	1,196
Blanco, Mahoning	NE	10
● *Blancs*, Gallia	S	×
Blatchford, Hocking	S	×
Blendon, Franklin	C	×
● *Blessings*, Fayette	S	×
Bliss, Pickaway	C	×
● Blissfield, Coshocton	C	50
● *Bloom*, Scioto	S	100
Bloom Centre, Logan	W	100
● Bloomdale, Wood	NW	560
● Bloomer, Miami	W	75
Bloomfield, (see Clark's)		×
Bloomfield, (seeBloomingdale)		×
Bloomfield, Morrow	C	60
Bloomfield, (see Sago)		×
● *Bloomfield*, Jefferson	E	173
Bloomfield, (see Flints Mts.)		×
● Bloomingburgh, Fayette	S	638
Bloomingdale, Jefferson	E	200
BloomingdaleSta., (seeFairPlay)		×
Blooming Grove, Morrow	C	500
Bloomington, Clinton	SW	162
Bloomingville, Erie	N	75
● Bloom Switch, Scioto	S	200
Bloomingville, Hocking	S	100
● Bloomville, Seneca	N	758
Blowville, Clermont	SW	25
● Blue Ash, Hamilton	SW	60
Blue Ball, Warren	SW	100
● Blue Bell, Guernsey	E	25
Blue Creek, Adams	S	150
● Blue Rock, Muskingum	C	75
Bluestone, Cuyahoga	NE	100
● Bluffton, Allen	NW	1,290
Blume Rose, (seeDe La Palma)		×
Boardman, Mahoning	NE	100
● *Bodman*, Brown	SW	×
Boden, Guernsey	E	×
Bogart, Erie	N	250
Boggs, Gallia	S	×
● *Bogus Road*, Fayette	S	×
Boke's Creek, Union	C	×
Bolin's Mills, Vinton	S	20
● Bolivar, Tuscarawas	E	675
Bond, Guernsey	E	10
● Bond Hill, Hamilton	SW	400
Bonn, (see Whipple)		×
Bookwalter, Fayette	S	450
Booth, Tuscarawas	E	×
● *Booths*, Trumbull	NE	×
Borer's Corners, Franklin	C	20
Bosterville, Lawrence	S	×
Boston, (see Atlas)		×
Boston, Clermont	SW	292
● Boston, Summit	NE	100
Boston, Highland	S	56
Bostwick, Geauga	NE	60
Boswell, Mahoning	NE	50
● *Bosworth*, Summit	NE	×
● Botkins, Shelby	W	450
● *Botzum*, Summit	NE	×
Boughtonville, Huron	N	×
Bourneville, Ross	S	205
● Bowerston, Harrison	E	500
Bowersville, Greene	W	300
Bowler, Gallia	S	100
Bowling Green, (see Town Fork)		×
● **Bowling Green**, Wood	NW	3,467
● Bowlusville, Clarke	W	200
Bowmanville, (see Delightful)		×
Bowsher, Pickaway	C	25
Boyd, Miami	W	×
Boyd's Mills, (see Avondale)		×
● Braceville, Trumbull	NE	30
● *Brachmann's*, Hamilton	SW	×
Bradbury, Meigs	SE	×
● Bradford, Miami	W	1,338
● Bradner, Wood	NW	800
Bradrick, Lawrence	S	150
Brady, Guernsey	E	25
● *Brady's Lake*, Portage	NE	×
Bradyville, Adams	S	100
Brainerd's Mills, (seeUhrichsv'e)		×
● Branch Hill, Clermont	SW	100
Brandon, Knox	C	300
Brandt, Miami	W	241
Brandywine, Crawford	N	×
● Brashears, Hocking	S	500
● Brazier, Clermont	SW	25
Breakman, Lake	NE	×
● Brecksville, Cuyahoga	NE	250
● Brecon, Hamilton	SW	100
Brehm, Mercer	W	10
● Bremen, Fairfield	C	244
Brewster'sCoalBed, (seeAkron)		×
● Brier Hill, Mahoning	NE	×
● Brice, Franklin	C	35
● Briceton, Paulding	NW	200
Brickner, Putnam	NW	10
● Bridgeport, Belmont	E	3,369
Bridges, Highland	S	×
Bridgeville, (see Bird's Run)		×
Bridgeville, Muskingum	C	50
Bridgewater, Williams	NW	20
● *Bridge Works*, Lucas	NW	×
● Brier Hill, Mahoning	NE	×
● Briggs, Washington	SE	250
● Briggsdale, Franklin	C	40
● Brighton, (see Cincinnati) Hamilton	SW	×
● *Brighton*, Clarke	W	100
● Brighton, Lorain	N	50
Brighton, (see So. Brooklyn)		×
● Brilliant, Jefferson	E	944

Place	Pop.
Brimfield, Portage........NE	1,200
● *Brimfield*, Portage......NE	×
● *Brinkman's*, Putnam..NW	×
● Brink Haven, Knox.......C	300
● Brinley, Preble.......... W	60
● Brister, Monroe......... E	×
Bristol, Morgan............SE	10
● *Bristol*, Perry............C	25
Bristol, (see Marshallville)...	×
Bristolville, Trumbull.....NE	350
● *Bristolville Sta.*, TrumbullNE	×
Brittain, Summit...........NE	100
● *Broad Ave*, Hancock...NW	×
● Broadway, Union.........C	400
● *Broadway*, Cuyahoga...NE	×
● *Broadwell*, Hamilton...SW	×
Brock, Darke............. W	50
Brockway, Trumbull......NE	×
Broken Sword, Crawford..N	100
● *Bronson's*, Franklin......C	×
● Brookfield, Trumbull...NE	300
● Brooklyn, Cuyahoga....NE	4,585
Brooklyn Vil'ge, CuyahogaNE	4,948
● Brookville, Montgomery.W	618
● Broughton, Paulding...NW	100
Brownhelm, Lorain.........N	75
● Brownhelm Station, Lor'in N	100
● *Brown's*, Miami..........W	25
● *Brown's*, Jefferson....... E	50
Brown's Mill, (see Leavet'v'le)	×
Brown's Mills, Wash'gton..SE	50
Brownson Sta., (see W.Hayden)	×
Brown's Station, (see Jeddo).	×
Brownsville, Licking........C	380
Brownsville, Clermont....SW	100
Brownsville, Knox.........C	150
Brownsville, (see Jolly)......	×
Browntown, Brown.......SW	50
● *Bruce*, Belmont..........E	20
● *Bruners*, Sandusky.......N	×
Brunersburgh, Defiance..NW	150
Brunswick, Medina.........N	200
● *Bruxon*, Putnam........NW	×
● *Brush Creek*, Muskingum.C	200
● *Brush Fork Junc.*, Hoc'ng S	×
● *Brush Lake*, Champaign.W	×
Bruss, Darke..............W	25
● **Bryan**, Williams......NW	3,068
● *Bryson*, Greene.......... W	×
Buchanan, Monroe........ E	×
Buchanan, Pike............ S	40
● Buchtel, Athens......... SE	1,500
● *Buckeye*, Muskingum.... C	×
Buckeye, Summit........ NE	×
Buckeye City, Knox........ C	215
● Buckeye Cottage, Perry...C	×
● *Buckingham*, Perry....... C	200
● Buckland, Auglaize...... W	250
Buck Run, Adams.......... S	×
Bucks, Columbiana........ NE	75
● *Buck's Crossing*, Columb'aNE	×
● **Bucyrus**, Crawford.....N	5,974
Bud, Jackson...............S	30
Buell Lowell, Washington. SE	441
Buena Vista, Fayette.......S	150
Buena Vista, Scioto..........S	461
Buena Vista, (see Baltic)....	×
Buffalo, Guernsey...........E	150
Buford, Highland........... S	150
Bulah, Ashtabulah........ NE	×
Bulaville, Gallia............ S	25
Bulgoe, Crawford...........N	100
● Bundysburg, Geauga....NE	300
Bunkerhill, Butler........ SW	50
● Burkank, Wayne......... N	331
● Burgh Hill, Trumbull...NE	350
● Burgoon, Sandusky.......N	200
● *Burkets*, Perry.......... C	×
● Burkettsville, Darke.....W	250
● Burkhart, Monroe........E	50
Burlingham, Meigs........SE	125
● *Burlington*, Belmont.....E	×
Burlington, Lawrence.......S	250
● Burris, Jackson............S	25
● Burr Oak, Athens........ SE	25
Burr's Mills, (see Burr's Sta.)	×
Burr's Station, (see Pugh)...	×
Burton, Geauga.............NE	633
● *Burton*, Belmont.........E	×
● Burton City, Wayne...... N	300
● *Burton's*, Stark.........NE	×
● Burton Station, Geauga. NE	75
Burtonville, Clinton...... SW	70
Burt's, Franklin............C	35
● *Busenbarks*, Butler.... SW	×
Bushnell, Ashtabula...... NE	100
Bushong, Putnam........NW	×
Bush's Mill, Gallia..........S	110
Businessburgh, Belmont....E	100
● Butler, Richland......... N	700
● *Butler*, Harrison..........E	100
Butlerville, Warren.......SW	125
● Byer, Jackson.............S	200
● *Byers Junction*, Jackson..S	×
● Byesville, Guernsey.......E	789
Byhalia, Union..............C	200
Byington, Pike..............S	56
Byron, Greene..............W	53
● Cable, Champaign.........W	300
● *Cable Crossing*, Jefferson.E	×
● *Cackler's Cross.*, PortageNE	×
● **Cadiz**, Harrison......... E	1,716
● *Cadiz Junc.*, Harrison....E	70
Cadmus, Gallia..............S	×
Cadwallader, Tuscarawas... E	250
● *Cairo*, Allen...........NW	×
Cairo, Stark...............NE	100
Calais, Monroe..............E	135
Calcutta, Columbiana.....NE	100
● **Caldwell**, Noble........E	1,248
● Caledonia, Marion.........C	757
● *California*, Hamilton...SW	×
California, Brown........SW	100
California, Pike.............S	400
California, Hamilton......SW	376
Callhan, Guernsey.........E	×
● Calla, Mahoning........NE	50
Calm, Geauga.............NE	×
● Calumet, Jefferson........E	350
Calvary, Morgan...........SE	20
● Calvin, Hancock....... NW	×
● Camba, Jackson...........S	25
● **Cambridge**, Guernsey..E	4,361
● *Cambridge Mines*, Guern'yE	×
● Camden, Preble...........W	846
Cameron, Monroe..........E	250
Camp, Pike.................S	×
● Campbell, Lawrence......N	×
Campbells, Butler........ SW	×
● *Campbells*, Guernsey......E	150
● Campbellsport, Portage. NE	60
● Campbellstown, Preble.. W	100
Camp Chase, Franklin......C	58
● Camp Dennison, Ham't'nSW	292
● Camp Hagerman, W'r'n.SW	×
Camp Washington, Ham'tnSW	×
Canaan, Wayne............N	250
● Canaanville, Athens.....SE	40
● Canal Dover, Tuscarawas.E	3,470
● Canal Fulton, Stark.....NE	1,173
Canal Lewisville, Coshocton.C	300
● Canal Winchester, FranklinC	633
● Canfield, Mahoning.....NE	675
● *Canfield Road*, Wash'gt'nSE	×
● *Cannel Spur*, Coshocton..C	×
● *Cannelville*, Muskingum..C	177
Cannons Creek, Lawrence.. S	×
Cannonsburg, (see Dell Roy)	×
Cannonsburgh, Hancock. NW	50
● *Cannon's Cr'k. Jc.*, Law'ceS	×
Cannon's Mill, Columbia..NE	25
● **Canton**, Stark.........NE	26,189
Captina, Belmont.......... E	100
● *Captina*, Belmont........ E	×
Caraghar, Fulton..........SW	30
Carbondale, Athens........SE	150
● Carbon Hill, Hocking.....S	650
● Cardington, Morrow......C	1,428
● Carey, Wyandot..........N	1,605
Careytown, Highland....... S	×
Carlisle, Brown.........SW	150
Carlisle, (see Walnut Creek).	×
● Carlisle, Warren........SW	275
Carlisle, (see Berne).........	×
● Carlwick, Muskingum....C	10
Carmel, Highland......... S	115
Caroline, (see Attica)........	×
● Carpenter, Meigs........SE	10
Carrie, Ross................S	×
● Carrington, Perry.........C	×
● Carroll, Fairfield...........C	293
Carrollton, Carroll....... E	1,228
● *Carrollton*, Montgomery. W	400
● *Carrollton Sta.*, Montg'ryW	50
● Carrothers, Seneca.......N	100
Carr's Mills, Fayette.........S	150
Cars Run, Pike..............S	×
● Carthage, Hamilton.....SW	2,257
Carthagena, Mercer.......... W	100
Carthon, Perry..............C	30
Carysville, Champaign..... W	150
● Cascade, Putnam........NW	×
● *Case Avenue*, Cuyahoga. NE	×
Cassella, Mercer............W	100
● *Cassells*, Guernsey........E	10
Casstown, Miami...........W	292
Cassville, Harrison........E	25
● Castalia, Erie.............N	500
● Castine, Darke............W	250
● *Catawba*, Champaign....W	75
Catawba, Clarke............W	272
Catawba Island, Ottawa.....N	800
● Cavett, Van Wert.......NW	60
● Caywood, Washington...SE	37
● Cecil, Paulding.........NW	348
● *Cedar Grove*, Muskingum.C	×
Cedar Grove, Hocking.......S	×
Cedar Hill, Fairfield.........C	75
Cedar Mills, Adams.........S	100
● Cedar Point, Hamilton..SW	25
● Cedar Run, Muskingum.. C	25
Cedar Springs, Preble......W	21
Cedar Valley, Wayne.......N	50
● Cedarville, Greene....... W	1,355
Cedron, Clermont.........SW	100
● **Celina**, Mercer......... W	2,702
● *Centerton*, Huron.........N	200
Central Middle Branch, (see Oval City)...............	×
Central College, Franklin...C	87
● *Centre*, Lawrence..........S	×
Centre, Montgomery........W	250
● Centre Belpre, Wash'ton.SE	10
Centre Bend, Morgan.......SE	10
● Centreburgh, Knox....... C	588
Centre Canaan, (see Canaan).	×
Centrefield, Highland........S	100
Centre Point, Gallia.........S	40
● *Centre Road*, Geauga....NE	×
● Centreton, Huron.........N	200
Centre View, Monroe........E	75
Centre Village, Delaware....C	150
Centreville, (see Demos)......	×
Centreville, Gallia.......... S	215
Centreville, Clinton........SW	150
Centreville, (see Midway).....	×
Centreville, Montgomery...W	252
Centreville, (see Moscow Mills)	×
● Ceylon, Erie..............N	200
Chaffee, Cuyahoga........ NE	×
Chaffin's Mills Scioto........S	25
● Chagrin Falls, Cuyahoga. NE	1,243
Chalfant's, Perry.......... C	27
● Chalmar, Wood.......... NW	125
● *Chamberlain*, Medina.... N	×
Chamberlain's Crossing, Summit...................NE	×
Chambersburg, (see New Chambersburg)...........	×
Chambersburgh, M'tgom'y. W	69
Chambersburgh, Gallia......S	193
● Champion, Trumbull....NE	30
● Chandlersville, Mus'gum..C	250
Chapel, Ashtabula.........NE	120
Chapel Hill, Perry...........C	200
● Chapman, Jackson.........S	25
Chapman, Stark........... NE	10
Chapman's Mills, Gallia.......S	×
● **Chardon**, Geauga.....NE	1,084
Charity, Gallia...............S	×
● Charlestown, Portage...NE	650
Charloe, Paulding........ NW	80
Charm, Holmes........... C	50
● *Chase*, Hancock..........NW	×
Chase, Athens............ SE	50
Chasetown, Brown.......SW	25
Chaseville, Noble.............E	10
Chatfield, Crawford.........N	400
● *Chatfield*, Crawford...... N	×
Chatham, Licking............C	50
Chatham Centre, Medina....N	250
Chattanooga, Mercer....... W	80
● Chauncey, Athens........ SE	300
Chenoweth, Madison........ C	20
Cherry Fork, Adams.........S	350
● Cherry Grove, HamiltonSW	60
Cherry Valley, Ashtabula. NE	1,000
Cherryville, Lawrence.......S	10
Cheshire, Delaware..........C	150
● Cheshire, Gallia........... S	200
Chester, (see Chester Cr. Roads)	×
Chester, Meigs..............SE	146
Chester Cross Roads, G'u'a. NE	200
Chesterfield, (see Chester Hill)	×
● Chester Hill, Morgan.... SE	487
● *Chester Park*, HamiltonSW	×
Chesterville, Morrow........C	268
Chestnut Grove, Gallia...... S	25
● *Chestnut Ridge*, Trum'llNE	×
Cheviot, Hamilton........ SW	1,200
● Chicago, Huron............N	1,299

Place	Pop.
Chicago Junc., (see Chicago).	×
● *Chicago & Erie Pit.*, Hardin W	×
● Chickasaw, Mercer W	200
● *Children's Home*, Belm't. E	×
● Chili, Coshocton C	75
● **Chillicothe**, Ross S	11,288
Chilo, Clermont SW	219
● *Chippewa*, Summit NE	400
● Chippewa Lake, Medina N	200
Christiansburg, Champaign W	×
● Church Hill, Trumbull NE	400
Churchtown, Washington SE	10
Cicero, Defiance NW	20
● **CINCINNATI**, Hamilton SW	296,908
● *Cincinnati & Springfield Junction*, Hamilton SW	×
Circlegreen, Jefferson E	×
● **Circleville**, Pickaway C	6,556
● Claiborne, Union C	100
Claribel, Cuyahoga NE	×
Claridon, Geauga NE	50
Claridon, Marion C	40
Clarington, Monroe E	762
Clark's Coshocton C	300
● *Clark's*, Darke W	×
● *Clark's*, Geauga NE	×
Clarksburgh, Ross S	378
Clark's Corners, Ashtabula NE	50
● Clarksfield, Huron N	700
Clarkson, Columbiana NE	165
Clark's Station, (see Martin's Ferry)	×
● Clarksville, Clinton SW	339
Clarksville, Defiance NW	50
Clawson, Butler SW	50
● Clay, Jackson S	125
● *Claybank*, Perry C	25
Clay Centre, Ottawa N	35
● Clay Lick, Licking C	112
● *Claypools*, Muskingum C	×
Claysville, Guernsey E	100
Clayton, (see Bentonville)	×
Clayton, Montgomery W	350
Claytona, Noble E	×
● Clear Creek, Fairfield C	200
Clear Port, Fairfield C	350
Clemma, Gallia S	×
● *Clemons*, Licking C	×
● *Cleneay*, Hamilton SW	×
Clendening, Harrison E	×
Clermontville, Clermont SW	100
● **CLEVELAND**, Cy'a. NE	261,353
● *Clevenger*, Belmont E	×
● Cleves, Hamilton SW	1,227
Cliff Mines, (see Coal Run)	×
● Clifford, Scioto S	25
Cliffyville, Noble E	×
Clifton, Greene W	270
Cliftons, (see Agosta)	×
● Climax, Morrow C	63
● *Clinton*, Clinton SW	×
Clinton, Huron N	163
● Clinton, Summit NE	400
Clinton Station, (see Shreve).	×
Clinton Furnace, (see Wheelersburg)	×
Clinton Valley, Clinton SW	328
Clintonville, Franklin C	68
Clio, Guernsey E	6
Clipper Mills, Gallia S	25
Cloud, Morgan SE	10
● *Clough Pike*, Hamilton SW	77
Clover, Clermont SW	×
Cloverdale, Wood NW	×
Cluff, Hamilton SW	75
● Clyde, Sandusky N	2,327
● Coalburgh, Trumbull NE	400
Coal City, Hamilton SW	100
● *Coal Chutes*, Fayette S	×
● Coaldale, Muskingum C	×
Coaldale, (see Hemlock)	×
● *Coal Docks*, Cuyahoga NE	×
● Coal Grove, Lawrence S	150
Coal Hill, Muskingum C	25
Coalport, (see Pomeroy)	×
Coal Run, Washington SE	300
● Coalton, Jackson S	1,459
● Coats, Monroe E	5
● *Cochran's*, Highland S	×
Cochranton, Marion [illegible]	[illegible]
Cochransville, (see Centre View)	×
Coe Ridge, Cuyahoga NE	70
Coe's Station, Scioto S	×
● *Coffman*, Highland S	×
● *Cohoon*, Clermont SW	×

Place	Pop.
● *Coits*, Cuyahoga NE	×
Coitsville, Mahoning NE	100
● Colby, Sandusky N	25
● Cold Springs Clarke W	×
● Cold Water, Mercer W	490
Colebrook, Ashtabula NE	100
● Coleman, Columbiana NE	20
Colerain, Belmont E	50
Coletown, (see Mt. Heron)	×
Colfax, Fairfield C	50
Collamer, (see E. Cleveland).	×
● College Corner, Butler SW	591
● *College Hill*, Athens SE	×
● College Hill, Hamilton SW	1,109
● *College Hill Junc.*, H'lt'n SW	×
● Collins, Huron N	800
● Collinsville, Butler SW	200
● Collinwood, Cuyahoga NE	1,700
Colorado, (see Middle Creek)	×
● Colton, Henry NW	150
● *Columbia*, Hamilton SW	×
Columbia, Warren SW	×
Columbia, (see Nettle Lake).	×
Columbia Centre, Licking C	300
● Columbiana, Columbiana NE	1,112
● Columbia Station, Lorain N	75
● **COLUMBUS**, Franklin C	88,150
● Columbus Grove, P'tn'm NW	1,677
Comet, Summit NE	×
Comly, Perry C	×
Commercial Point, Pickaway C	265
Compher, Belmont E	×
Comstock, Scioto S	35
● Conant, Allen NW	25
● Concord, Lake NE	500
Concord, (see New Concord).	×
● *Conden*, Richland N	×
● Condit, Delaware C	300
● Conesville, Coshocton C	130
Congo, Perry C	×
Congress, Wayne N	229
● *Congress Lake*, Stark NE	×
● *Conine*, Hancock NW	×
● Conneaut, Ashtabula NE	3,241
● *Connelsville*, Mercer W	×
● Conotton, Harrison E	120
● Conover, Miami W	400
Constantia, Delaware C	×
● Constitution, Washington SE	100
● Continental, Putnam NW	895
Centreras, Butler SW	50
● Convenience, Fayette S	25
Converse, Van Wert NW	15
● Convoy, Van Wert NW	500
● Cook, Fayette S	30
Cook's, Athens SE	10
● *Cook's Crossing*, Summit NE	×
Cooksey, Licking C	25
Cookton, Richland N	50
● Coolville, Athens SE	330
Cooney, Williams NW	10
● Cooperdale, Coshocton C	26
Coopersville, Pike S	300
Coopersville, (see Harris Sta.)	×
Cope, Belmont E	100
● Copley, Summit NE	241
Copopa, Lorain N	50
Cora, Gallia S	75
● Cordelia, Hancock NW	50
Corinth, Trumbull NE	×
Cork, Ashtabula NE	50
● *Corlett*, Cuyahoga NE	×
Cornelian, Trumbull NE	100
Corner, Washington SE	×
Cornersburgh, Mahoning NE	125
Cornerville, Washington SE	40
● Corning, Perry C	1,551
Corryville, Hamilton SW	×
Corsica, Morrow C	×
● Cortland, Trumbull NE	697
Corwin, Preble W	25
Cory, Hancock NW	300
● **Coshocton**, Coshocton C	3,672
Cosmos, Darke W	25
Cottage Hill, Muskingum C	50
● *Country Club*, Hamilton SW	×
● *County Line*, Miami W	×
● *County Line*, Brown SW	×
● Cove, Jackson S	40
Coverdale, Hamilton SW	×
Coventry, (see Akron)	×
● Covington, Miami W	1,778
Cow Run, Washington W	100
Cox, Vinton S	20
● Cozaddale, Warren SW	143
● Crab Apple, Belmont E	10
Crabtree, Scioto S	10

Place	Pop.
Craft Station, Hocking S	100
Craig, Guernsey E	×
Cranberry, Allen NW	75
Cranberry Prairie, Mercer W	50
Crandall, Lorain N	25
Crane Nest, Monroe E	×
Craver, Clermont SW	×
● Crawfis College, Putnam NW	×
● Crawford, Wyandot N	35
Crayon, Champaign W	40
Creedville, Hamilton SW	25
Creighton, Guernsey E	55
● Creola Vinton S	70
● *Crescent*, Belmont E	×
● *Crescent*, Hamilton SW	×
● Crescentville, Butler SW	100
● Crestline, Crawford N	2,911
Crestone, Hamilton SW	×
● Creston, Wayne N	584
● Crestvue, Hamilton SW	×
● Creswell, Jefferson E	10
Creuzet, Gallia S	20
● Cridersville, Auglaize W	465
● Cromer's Seneca N	20
Crone, Scioto S	25
Crooked Tree, Noble E	40
● Crooksville, Perry C	250
Crossenville, Perry C	60
● *Crossing*, Darke W	×
● Crossing, Stark NE	×
Cross Keys, (see East Union)	×
● *Cross Roads*, Jackson S	125
Cross Roads, (see Midway)	×
Crosstown, Brown SW	50
● *Croswell*, Putnam NW	×
● Croton, Licking C	600
● *Crow*, Belmont E	×
Crown City, Gallia S	235
Croxton, Jefferson E	125
Cruzett, Gallia S	20
● Crystal Sprins, Stark NE	75
● Cuba, Clinton SW	148
● Culbertson, Lawrence S	500
● *Cullom's*, Hamilton SW	×
● Cumberland, Guernsey E	601
● *Cumberland Junc.*, Noble E	×
● Cummings, Wood NW	50
● Cumminsville, Hom'lt'n SW	×
● Curtellis, Hancock NW	50
● Curtice, Ottawa N	300
Curtisville, Wood NW	×
● *Cussac*, Muskingum C	×
● Custar, Wood NW	329
● Cutler, Washington SE	50
● Cuyahoga Falls, Summit NE	2,614
● Cyclone, Portage NE	100
● Cygnet, Wood NW	670
Cynthiana, (see Marathon)	×
Cynthiana, Pike S	300
● Dague, Paulding NW	75
Dairy, Monroe E	×
Daleyville, Pike S	100
Dallas, Highland S	100
Dalton, Wayne N	610
Dalzell, Washington SE	50
Damascoville, (see Damascus)	×
● *Damascus*, Mahoning NE	400
Damascus, Columbiana NE	400
● Danbury, Ottawa N	50
● Danford, Guernsey E	100
● *Danville Pike*, Highland S	170
Danville, Meigs SE	50
● Danville, Knox C	292
Danville, (see Range)	×
Darbyville, Pickaway C	257
● *Dare*, Washington SE	×
Darke, Darke W	25
● *Darlington*, Muskingum C	×
Darlington, Richland N	300
Darrowville, Summit NE	100
Darrtown, Butler SW	300
Dasie, Van Wert NW	75
Daugherty, Perry C	×
Davis, Richland N	75
● *Davis*, Clermont SW	×
● *Davis*, Scioto S	×
● *Davis Road*, Portage NE	×
Dawes, Washington SE	×
Dawkin's Mills, Jackson S	×
● Dawn, Darke W	300
● Dawson, Shelby NE	25
● **Dayton**, Montgomery W	61,220
● *Dean*, Lawrence S	25
Dean, Montgomery W	17
● *Dean's*, Athens SE	30
Deardoff, (see Black Band)	×
Dearing, Lawrence S	25

Place	Region	Pop.
Deavertown, Morgan	SE	200
Decatur, Brown	SW	300
Decaturville, Washington	SE	×
● De Cliff, Marion	C	79
● *Deep Run*, Jefferson	E	×
Deer Creek, Pickaway	C	15
● Deerfield, Portage	NE	150
Deer Lick, Williams	NW	30
● *Deer Park*, Hamilton	SW	25
Deersville, Harrison	E	290
● *Deffenbaugh*, Muskingum	C	×
● **Defiance**, Defiance	NW	7,694
● *Defiance Junction*, De'e	NW	100
● De Graff, Logan	W	1,074
● *De Kalb*, (see Tiro)		×
● **Delaware**, Delaware	C	8,224
● *Delaware Bend*, Defi'ce	NW	100
● *Del Carbo*, Muskingum	C	100
● Delhi, Hamilton	SW	531
Delightful, Trumbull	NE	60
● De Lisle, Darke	W	100
Dell, Washington	SE	25
● Dell Roy, Carroll	E	511
● Delmount, Fairfield	C	×
● Delphos, Allen	NW	4,546
● Delta, Fulton	NW	1,132
● *Delta Station*, Hamilton	SW	×
Delvin, Darke	W	25
Democracy, Knox	C	200
Demos, Belmont	E	175
Denmark, Morrow	C	80
Denmark, Ashtabula	NE	150
Dennis, Scioto	S	×
Dennison, (see Sherman)		×
● Dennison, Tuscarawas	E	2,925
Dent, Hamilton	SW	500
● Denver, Ross	S	50
Denver, Wood	NW	100
Depew, Shelby	W	×
● Derby, Pickaway	C	175
Derthick, Athens	SE	×
● Deshler, Henry	NW	1,114
● *Deshler Junc.*, Henry	NW	×
Deucher, Washington	SE	30
● Dunquat, Wyandot	N	200
● *Devol*, Washington	SE	×
Devol's Dam, Washington	SE	×
● Dewey, Trumbull	NE	×
● Deweyville, Hancock	NW	85
● Dexter, Meigs	SE	50
● Dexter City, Noble	E	217
Dialton, Clarke	W	100
Diamond, Portage	NE	150
Dickman, Putnam	NW	15
● Dicksonton, Perry	C	100
Diffen, Scioto	S	×
Digby, Wood	NW	10
Dille's Bottom, Belmont	E	50
Dilley, Lawrence	S	×
● Dillon, Muskingum	C	100
● *Dillon's Falls*, Musk'gum	C	×
Dillonvale, Jefferson	E	400
● *Dills*, Ross	S	×
Dilworth, Trumbull	NE	×
Dinsmore, (see Botkin Sta.)		×
Divide, Gurnsey	E	×
● Dixon, Van Wert	NW	170
Dixon Station, Perry	C	100
Dobbston, Lawrence	S	100
● Dodd's, Warren	SW	100
Dodgeville, Ashtabula	NE	×
Dodo, Clarke	W	24
● Dodson, Montgomery	W	150
Dodsonville, Highland	S	75
● Doherty, Monroe	E	5
Domino, Gallia	S	×
Don, Belmont	E	30
● *Doney's*, Franklin	C	×
Donnelsville, Clarke	W	243
Dora, Belmont	E	25
● *Dorninton*, Putnam	NW	×
● Dorset, Ashtabula	NE	150
Dorsey, Belmont	E	×
● *DoughtonJunc.*, Tr'mb'll	NE	×
● *Doughton*, Trumbull	NE	×
● Douglas, Putnam	NW	10
● *Douglass*, Wyandot	N	×
● Dove, Pike	S	50
● *Dover*, Union	C	112
● *Dover*, Cuyahoga	NE	×
Dover, Cuyahoga	NE	250
● Dowling, Wood	NW	300
● *Downards*, Perry	C	×
Downard, (see Riverton)		×
Downington, Meigs	SE	130
● Doylestown, Wayne	N	1,131
● *Drake*, Defiance	NW	×

Place	Region	Pop.
● *Drakes*, Perry	C	×
Drakesburg, Portage	NE	×
● Dresden, Muskingum	C	1,247
Dresden Junc., (see Trinway)		×
Drill, Belmont	E	347
Drinkle, Fairfield	C	×
● Drusilla, Putnam	NW	15
Dry Run, Scioto	S	50
● *Dry Run*, Columbiana	NE	×
Dublin, Franklin	C	296
Ducat, Wood	NW	25
Duck Creek, (see Caldwell)		×
● *Dudley*, Hardin	W	36
● Dudley, Noble	E	25
Duffy, Monroe	E	25
Dugan's Store, (see New'tv'le)		×
● *Dukay*, Wood	NW	25
● Dull, Van Wert	NW	25
Dumontville, Fairfield	C	40
● **Dunbar**, Washington	SE	25
Dunbarton, Adams	S	130
● Dunbridge, Wood	NW	350
Duncan's Falls, Muskingum	C	222
● Dundas, Vinton	S	150
● Dundee, Tuscarawas	E	200
● *Dunfee*, Belmont	E	×
Dungannon, Columbiana	NE	150
Dungannon, (see Ridge)		×
Dunham, Washington	SE	25
Dunkinsville, Adams	S	200
● Dunkirk, Hardin	W	1,220
Dunlap, Hamilton	SW	25
Dunlevy, Warren	SW	50
● Dupont, Putnam	NW	531
Durant, Morgan	SE	×
● *Durant Station*, Morgan	SE	×
● *Durbin*, Clarke	W	×
Durbin, Mercer	SE	×
Durgan, Gallia	S	×
● Duvall, Pickaway	C	25
● *Duvall*, Noble	E	×
Dye, Washington	SE	25
● Dyesville, Meigs	SE	100
● Dyson's, Guernsey	E	295
● *Eagle*, Vinton	S	×
Eagle City, Clarke	W	150
● *Eagle Creek*, Hancock	NW	×
Eagle Furnace, Vinton	S	25
● *Eagle Hill*, Tuscarawas	E	×
Eagle Mills, Vinton	S	50
● Eagleport, Morgan	SE	100
● Eagleville, Ashtabula	NE	200
● Earley, Mercer	W	25
● Earlville, Portage	NE	25
Early, Mercer	W	×
● *East Akron*, Summit	NE	×
East Canton, (see Canton)		×
East Carmel, Columbiana	NE	25
● East Claridon, Geauga	NE	400
● East Cleveland, Cuyah'a	NE	1,000
● *East Cummingsville*, Hamilton	SW	×
● *East Danville*, Highland	S	×
● *East End*, Clarke	W	×
● *East End*, Columbiana	NE	×
● East End, Cuyahoga	NE	×
East Fairfield, Columbi'na	NE	175
● *East Fremont*, Sandusky	N	×
East Greenville, Stark	NE	100
East Greenwood, Musk'g'm	C	10
● *East Hamersville*, Brown	SW	×
East Lewistown, Mahon'g	NE	75
East Liberty, Logan	W	300
East Liberty Sum. (see Sum't)		×
● East Liverpool, Col'mb'a	NE	10.956
● *East Loveland*, Clermont	SW	×
● *East Madisonville*, Hamilton	SW	×
● *Eastman's Switch*, Muskingum	C	×
● East Monroe, Highland	S	150
● *East Newark*, Licking	C	×
East Norwalk, Huron	N	300
● *EastNorwood*, Hamilton	SW	×
● Easton, Wayne	N	300
● East Orwell, Ashtabula	NE	×
● East Palestine, Colu'b'a	NE	1,816
East Plainfield, (see Plainf'd)		×
● East Plymouth, Ashtab'la	NE	100
East Richland, Belmont	E	100
East Ringgold, Pickaway	C	200
● East Rochester, Columbia	NE	200
East Rushville, (see Rushville)		×
East Springfield, Jefferson	E	197
● *East Toledo*, Lucas	NW	×
East Townsend, Huron	N	300
East Trumbull, Ashtabula	NE	150

Place	Region	Pop.
● *East Union*, Wayne	N	25
East Union, Wayne	N	25
East Union, Coshocton	C	100
East Union, (see McCleary)		×
East Walnut Hills, Hamil'n	SW	×
East Williamsfield, (see Wil'mf'd)		×
● Eastwood, Brown	SW	25
● **Eaton**, Preble	W	2,934
Ebenezer, Preble	W	25
Eber, Fayette	S	×
Eberly, Wood	NW	×
Echo, Meigs	SE	25
● *Echo*, Belmont	E	×
● *Eckerts Siding*, Fairfield	C	×
Eckley, Carroll	E	35
Eckmansville, Adams	S	300
● *Eden*, Delaware	C	150
Eden Station, Delaware	C	100
● *Eden Park*, Hamilton	SW	×
Edenton, Clermont	SW	250
Edenville, (see Nevada)		×
● Edgefield, Fayette	S	100
● *Edgemont*, Hamilton	SW	25
● Edgerton, Williams	NW	967
● *Edgewood*, Butler	SW	×
● Edinburgh, Portage	NE	150
● Edison, Morrow	C	345
Edith, Monroe	E	×
Edna, Gallia	S	×
Edon, Williams	NW	601
● Edward, Franklin	C	48
Edwardsville, Warren	SW	100
Edwina, Monroe	E	×
Ego, Vinton	S	×
Egypt, Belmont	E	×
● *Eharte*, Medina	N	×
Elfort, Scioto	S	10
● Elba, Washington	SE	155
● *Eldean*, Miami	W	×
● El Dorado, Preble	W	365
Elenor, Clermont	SW	30
● Elery, Henry	NW	100
● Elgin, Van Wert	NW	90
Eli, Fayette	S	100
● Elida, Allen	NW	399
● Elizabethtown, Hamilton	SW	200
Elizabethtown, (see Perryton)		×
Eliza Furnace, (see Wellston)		×
Elk, Noble	E	10
Elko, (see Union Station)		×
● Elkton, Columbiana	NE	150
● *Elleman's* Miami	W	×
Ellerton, Montgomery	W	150
Elliot, Morgan	SE	50
● *Elliottsville*, Jefferson	E	350
● Ellis, Muskingum	C	25
● *Ellison*, Lawrence	S	×
Elliston, Ottawa	N	200
Ellsberry, Brown	SW	50
● Ellsworth, Mahoning	NE	200
Ellsworth Stat'n, Mahoning	NE	×
● Elm Centre, Putnam	NW	50
Elm Grove, Pike	S	25
Elmira, Fulton	NW	75
● Elmore, Ottawa	N	1,198
Elmville, Highland	S	40
● Elmwood, Franklin	C	25
● *Elmwood*, Pickaway	C	×
● *Elmwood*, Hamilton	SW	×
● Elmwood Place, Hamil'n	SW	2,000
● *El Rose*, Hancock	NW	×
● Elroy, Darke	W	35
● *Elsmere*, Hamilton	SW	25
Elton, Stark	NE	100
● **Elyria**, Lorain	N	5,611
Emerald, Adams	S	30
● *Emerald*, Paulding	NW	60
Emerson, Jefferson	E	100
Emery, Fulton	NW	×
● *Emery Chapel*, Clarke	W	×
● Emmett, Paulding	NW	60
● Empire, Jefferson	E	441
Enfield, Harrison	E	10
Ennis, (see Chapman Sta.)		×
Eno, Gallia	S	175
Enoch, Noble	E	20
● Enon, Clarke	W	331
● *Enon*, Clarke	W	×
Ensee, Lawrence	S	×
Enterprise, Van Wert	NW	666
● Enterprise, Hocking	S	100
Enterprise L'd'g, (see Pomeroy)		×
● *Epworth Heights*, Clerm't	SW	×
Epworth, Richland	N	×
Equity, Washington	SE	×
Equity Station, Washingt'n	SE	×
Erastus, Mercer	W	90

Entry	Pop.
● Hiram, Portage......... NE	500
Hiram Rapids, Portage... NE	×
● Hiramsburgh, Noble..... E	70
Hixon, Athens............ SE	25
Hoadley, Gallia.......... S	25
Hoaglin, Van Wert....... NW	10
● Hobart, Wood.......... NW	15
Hockingport, Athens...... SE	150
● *Hofer*, Belmont......... E	×
Hohman, Washington..... SE	10
Holcomb, Gallia........... S	25
● *Holcombe*, Paulding.... NW	×
● Holgate, Henry......... NW	1,134
● Holland, Lucas......... NW	125
Hollansburgh, Darke....... W	400
Hollister, Athens......... SE	200
● Holloway, Belmont....... E	×
Hollowtown, Highland...... S	50
● *Holly*, Columbiana...... NE	×
Holly, Tuscarawas......... E	×
Holmes Mills, (see Fernwood)	×
● Holmesville, Holmes...... C	400
Holt, Jefferson............ E	15
Home, Highland........... S	10
● *Home Avenue Junc.*, Montgomery............ W	×
● Home City, Hamilton... SW	797
Homer, Licking............ C	300
Homer, (see Mountsville).....	×
● Homerville, Medina...... N	150
● Homeworth, Columbiana NE	250
Hood, Preble.............. W	30
● Hooker, Fairfield........ C	200
Hooksburgh, Morgan...... SE	15
Hopedale, Harrison......... E	424
● *Hope Furnace*, Vinton.... S	100
Hope Station, Vinton...... S	150
● *Hopetown*, Ross.......... S	25
Hopewell, Muskinghum.... C	200
● *Hopkins Avenue*, H'm't'n SW	×
Hopkinsville, Warren..... SW	40
● Horatio, Darke........... W	70
● Horr's, Champaign....... W	75
Hoskinsville, Noble......... E	40
Hostetters, Richland........ N	×
Houcktown, Hancock.... NW	175
● Houston, Shelby......... W	300
Howard, Knox............. C	350
Howell, Lawrence.......... S	25
● Howenstine, Stark...... NE	50
Howland Springs, (see Niles)	×
Hoyt's Corners, (see Hoytville).	×
● Hoytville, Wood........ NW	895
● Hubbard, Trumbull..... NE	1,498
● Huckleberry, Trumbull. NE	×
● Hudson, Summit........ NE	1,143
Hudsonville, (see Silver Creek)	×
Hue, Vivion................ S	×
Huffman's, Morgan........ SE	×
● Hughes, Butler......... SW	100
● Hulington, Clermont... SW	250
● Hull Prairie, Wood..... NW	140
Hull's, Athens............ SE	32
● Humboldt, Ross.......... S	25
● Hume, Allen........... NW	75
Hunchberger's, (see Union City, Ind.)...........	×
● Hunt, Knox.............. C	50
Hunter, Belmont............ E	70
● *Hunter*, Noble............ E	×
Huntersville, Miami........ W	760
Hunterville, (see Irondale)...	×
● Huntington, Lorain...... N	100
Huntsburgh, Geauga...... NE	250
● *Hunts Grove*, Hamilton. SW	×
● Huntstown, Putnam.... NW	100
Huntsville, Butler......... SW	×
● Huntsville, Logan........ W	500
Hurd's Corners, (see Akron).	×
● Hurford, Harrison........ E	×
● Huron, Erie.............. N	1,380
● *Hursh*, Stark........... NE	×
● Hustead, Clarke......... W	10
● *Hutchinson*, Monroe...... E	×
● Hyattville, Delaware...... C	100
Iberia, Morrow............. C	250
Ida, Lawrence.............. S	×
Idaho, Pike................ S	200
● Idlewild, Hamilton...... SW	200
● Iler, Seneca.............. N	50
Ilesboro, Hocking.......... S	80
● Independence, Cuyahoga NE	300
Independence, (see Wade).....	×
Independence, Richland.... N	266
● *Independence Road*, Cuyahoga NE	×
Indian Camp, Guernsey..... E	80
Industrial Home, Delaware. C	25
● *Infirmary*, Franklin...... C	×
● *Infirmary Switch*, Cuya'ga NE	×
● *Ingham*, Vinton.......... S	×
● Ingomar, Preble......... W	50
Inland, Summit.......... NE	×
Inverness, Columbiana.... NE	50
● Ira, Summit............ NE	150
Irene, Summit........... NE	×
● Irondale, Jefferson....... E	694
Iron Furnace, (see S. Webster)	×
● **Ironton**, Lawrence...... S	10,939
● *Ironton Junc.*, Jackson.. S	×
● Ironville, Lucas........ NW	400
Irville, Muskingum......... C	150
● Irvington, Adams......... S	×
● *Irwin*, Belmont.......... E	×
● Irwin, Union............. C	100
Irwin's Station, (see Camba).	×
Island Creek, Jefferson...... E	15
Isle Saint George, Ottawa.. N	×
Islesborough, Hocking...... S	30
Isleta, Coshocton........... C	50
Ithaca, Darke............. W	135
● Ivanhoe, Hamilton...... SW	100
● Ivorydale, Hamilton.... SW	200
● *Ixworth*, Butler......... SW	×
● **Jackson**, Jackson....... S	4,320
Jacksonboro, Butler...... SW	79
Jackson Centre, Shelby.... W	300
Jacksontown, Licking...... C	250
● Jacksonville, Athens.... SE	727
Jacksonville, (see Versailles).	×
Jackstown, (see Commerc'l Pt.)	×
● Jacobsburgh, Belmont.... E	150
Jacobsport, (see Plainfield)...	×
Jagger, (see Preston).........	×
● Jamestown, Greene...... W	1,104
● Jamton, Montgomery.... W	400
Jasper, Pike................ S	250
● *Jasper*, Fayette.......... S	×
● *Jasper Mills*, Fayette...... S	75
Java, Lucas.............. NW	300
● Jaybird, Adams........... S	25
● Jaysville, Darke.......... W	50
● Jeddo, Jefferson.......... E	50
● **Jefferson**, Ashtabula. NE	1,346
Jefferson, (see Germano).....	×
● *Jefferson*, Jefferson....... E	×
Jefferson, (see Plain).........	×
● Jeffersonville, Fayette..... S	800
Jelloway, Knox............ C	130
● Jenera, Hancock.......... C	300
Jeries, Monroe.............. E	×
Jerome, Union............. C	25
Jeromesville, Ashland...... N	301
Jerry City, Wood......... NW	530
Jersey, Licking............. C	158
● Jerusalem, Monroe....... E	112
Jerusalem, (see Zanesfield)...	×
● *Jerusalem*, Clermont.... SW	×
● Jesse, Portage.......... NE	×
● *Jethro*, Columbiana..... NE	×
● Jewell, Defiance........ NW	50
● Jewett, Harrison.......... E	506
Jimes, Jackson............. S	100
● *Jobes*, Harrison.......... E	×
● Jobs, Hocking............ S	×
Joe, Hocking............... S	×
John's Creek, Lawrence.... S	×
● *Johnson's*, Fayette........ S	×
● *Johnson's*, Montgomery. W	×
● *Johnson's*, Trumbull... NE	×
Johnson's Corners, Summit NE	150
Johnson's Cors., (see Sterling)	×
Johnson's Siding, (see Creola)	×
Johnson's Station, (see Dawn)	×
Johnsonville, Trumbull... NE	150
● Johnstown, Licking....... C	424
Johnstown, (see Ada)........	×
Johnsville, Montgomery... W	225
Johnsville, Morrow......... C	300
Jolly, Monroe............... E	105
● *Jones*, Butler.......... SW	100
Jones' Corners, Holmes..... C	25
Jones' Mills, (see Rush)......	×
● *Jonestown*, Van Wert.. NW	20
Joppa, Meigs............. SE	×
● *Jordan's*, Miami......... W	×
Jordon, Jackson............ S	60
● *Jordon*, Noble............ E	×
Joy, Morgan.............. SE	100
● *Judds*, Clermont....... SW	×
Judson, Athens........... SE	×
Jumbo, Hardin............ W	30
Junction, Paulding....... NW	200
● *Junction*, Fairfield........ C	×
● *Junction*, Stark......... NE	×
● *Junction*, Trumbull.... NE	×
● Junction City, Perry...... C	894
● *Junction Switch*, Belmont E	×
Junior Landing, (see Franklin Furnace).............	×
● Justus, Stark........... NE	200
Kalida, Putnam.......... NW	444
Kamms, Cuyahoga........ NE	50
● Kansas, Seneca........... N	350
Karle, Williams.......... NW	50
Karr, Hamilton......... SW	×
● *Keans*, Portage......... NE	×
Keene, Coshocton.......... C	200
Keifer, Muskingum........ C	25
Keith's, Noble.............. E	25
Kelly's Island, Erie......... N	889
Kelly's Mills, Lawrence..... S	18
Kelloggsville, Ashtabula.. NE	250
● *Kelly's*, Jefferson......... E	×
● Kelsey, Belmont.......... E	×
● *Kemery*, Stark.......... NE	×
● Kempton, Allen........ NW	25
Kenilworth, Trumbull.... NE	300
● Kennard, Champaign.... W	150
● Kennedy, Hamilton..... SW	150
Kennon, Belmont........... E	100
Kennonsburg, Noble........ E	75
Keno, Meigs.............. SE	25
● Kensington, Columbiana NE	250
● Kent, Portage........... NE	3,501
● **Kenton**, Hardin........ W	5,557
● Kerr, Gallia............... S	25
● *Kerr*, Monroe............ E	×
● Kessler, Miami........... W	75
Kettlersville, Shelby....... W	100
● Key, Belmont............. E	×
Keystone, Jackson.......... S	70
● *Keystone*, Jackson........ S	×
● *Kibbler's Siding*, Licking.. C	×
● Kidd, Belmont........... E	×
Kidd's Mines, (see Shields')..	×
● Kieferville, Putnam.... NW	100
Kilbourne, Delaware........ C	150
Kilgore, Carroll............ E	200
● *Kilgour*, Hamilton..... SW	×
● Killbuck, Holmes......... C	250
Kilmer, Noble.............. E	×
Kilvert, Athens........... SE	×
Kimball, Erie.............. N	75
● *Kimball*, Erie............ N	×
● Kimbolton, Guernsey..... E	261
● Kinderhook, Pickaway.... C	100
● *Kingfred*, Fayette........ S	×
● Kings, Athens.......... SE	50
Kingsbury, Meigs......... SE	×
● King's Creek, Champaign W	200
● Kings Mills, Warren.... SW	300
● Kingston, Ross........... S	751
Kingston Center, Delaware. C	×
Kingston Sta., Champaign. W	300
● Kingsville, Ashtabula... NE	600
● Kingsway, Sandusky..... N	20
● Kinnikinnick, Ross....... S	70
● Kinsey, Montgomery..... W	60
Kinsman, Trumbull...... NE	300
● *Kinsman*, Trumbull.... NE	200
Klousville, Madison........ C	75
● Kipton, Lorain........... N	300
● Kirby, Wyandot.......... N	300
Kirbyville, (see Marathon)....	×
Kirkersville, Licking........ C	500
● *Kirkerville*, Licking...... C	×
Kirkpatrick, Marion........ C	100
Kirksville, Shelby.......... S	25
● Kirkwood, Shelby........ W	100
● *Kirkwood*, Belmont...... E	×
Kirtland, Lake........... NE	250
● *Kishman's*, Lorain....... N	×
● Kitchen, Jackson......... S	50
Kittaning, Hocking......... S	×
Kitts Hill, Lawrence........ S	×
● *Kneisleys*, Greene....... W	×
Knight, Muskingum........ C	×
Knowlton, Ashland......... N	×
Knox, Vinton.............. S	20
● Knoxdale, Paulding.... NW	10
Knoxville, Jefferson........ E	300
Koch's, Wayne............. N	150
Koogle's Cors, Richland.... N	×
Koran, Sciota............... S	×
Kossuth, Auglaize......... W	125
● Krumroy, Summit...... NE	15
Kuhn, Monroe.............. E	×
● Kunkle, Williams...... NW	450
Kyger, Gallia............... S	125
Kygersville, Gallia.......... S	×
● Kyle's, Butler.......... SW	125
Kyle's Corners, Mahon'g.. NE	200

Place	Pop.
Labelle, Lawrence...S	35
● LaCarne, Ottawa...N	75
Laceyville, Harrison...E	50
● *La Fayette*, Allen...NW	350
La Fayette, (see Red Shaw)..	×
● *La Fayette*, Medina...N	90
La Fayette, Madison...C	250
● Lafetty, Belmont...E	×
● *LaGonda*, Clarke...W	×
La Grange, (see Brilliant)....	×
● *LaGrange*, Lawrence...S	50
● LaGrange, Lorain...N	551
Laing's, Monroe...E	30
Lake, Stark...NE	300
Lake Breeze, Lorain...N	20
Lake Fork, Ashland...N	150
Lakelet, Trumbull...NE	×
● *Lake Park*, Stark...NE	×
● *Lakeside*, Fairfield...C	25
● Lakeside, Ottawa...N	300
● *Lakeville*, Holmes...C	100
Lakeview, Logan...W	250
Lakewood, Cuyahoga...NE	×
Lamartine, Carroll...E	130
● Lamira, Belmont...E	35
● **Lancaster**, Fairfield...C	7,555
● Landeck, Allen...NW	20
● Lane, Lake...NE	×
Lane's Stores, (see W. Canaan)	×
● Langsville, Meigs...SE	150
Lanier, Preble...W	75
Lanier Station, (see Ingomar)	×
LaPorte, Lorain...N	100
● Larue, Marion...C	948
● *Lashley*, Belmont...E	×
● Latchie, Wood...NW	50
Latham, Pike...S	125
● Latimer, Trumbull...NE	40
Latimer's Crossing, T'mb'l NE	20
Latrobe, Athens...SE	30
LatrobeFurnace, (see Wells'n)	×
Lattas, Ross...S	50
Lattsburgh, Wayne...N	150
Lattasville, (see Lattas)...	×
● Latty, Paulding...NW	594
● *Laughlin Mills*, Belmont. E	×
● Laura, Miami...W	110
Laurel, Clermont...SW	138
● Laurelton, Jefferson...E	×
Laurelville, Hocking...S	266
● *Lawrence*, Lawrence...S	×
Lawrence, Washington...SE	10
● *Lawrence*, Stark...NE	841
Lawrence, Wood...NW	×
Lawrenceville, Clark...W	82
Layhigh, Butler...SW	×
● Layland, Coshocton...C	60
Layman, Washington...SE	15
Leach, Jackson...S	×
Leaper, Gallia...S	20
Leatherwood, (see Quaker City)	×
● Leavittsburgh, Trumb'l. NE	400
Leavittsville, Carroll...E	80
Lebanon, (see Masterton)....	×
● **Lebanon**, Warren...SW	3,050
● *Lebanon Junc.*, M'tg'm'y W	×
● Lee, Athens...SE	500
● Leelan, Warren...SW	100
Leesburg, Carroll...E	873
● Leesburgh, Highland...S	617
Leeper, Gallia...S	50
Lee's Creek, Clinton...SW	×
● *Lee's Siding*, Perry...C	×
● Leesville, Carroll...E	373
Leesville Cross Roads, C'wf'd N	203
● *Leesville*, Crawford...N	×
Leetonia, Columbiana...NE	2,826
● Leipsic, Putnam...NW	1,353
● *Leipsic Junc.*, Putnam..NW	50
Leistville, Pickaway...C	25
Leith, Washington...SE	×
Lelandville, Sandusky...N	×
● Lemert, Crawford...N	40
● Lemon, Butler...SW	×
● Le Moyne, Wood...NW	150
Lena, Miami...W	150
Lenox, Ashtabula...NE	100
Leo, Jackson...S	70
Leon, Ashtabula...NE	65
● Leonardsburgh, Delaware. C	150
Lerado, Clermont...SW	25
Le Roy, Medina...N	100
Le Sueur, Henry...NW	40
Leslie, Van Wert...NW	15
Le Sourdsville, Butler...SW	75
● *Lester*, Hamilton...SW	×
Letart Falls, Meigs...SE	500
Levanna, Brown...SW	294
● Level, Warren...SW	100
Levering, Knox...C	100
● *Lewis*, Muskingum...C	×
● Lewis, Morgan...SE	×
● Lewisburgh, Preble...W	486
○ Lewis Centre, Delaware...C	300
Lewis Hill, Richland...N	×
● *Lewis Mills*, Belmont...E	35
Lewistown, Logan...W	200
Lewisville, Monroe...E	150
Lewisville, (see Andersonville)	×
○ Lexington, Richland...N	432
Lexington Sta., (see New Lexington)...	×
Liberty, Montgomery...W	250
● Liberty Centre, Henry..NW	500
Liberty Corners, Crawford..N	100
Liberty Village, (see Kimb'l'n)	×
Lick Creek Landing, L'wr'e. S	200
● Licking Valley, Musk'g'm. C	38
● *Lick Run*, Hamilton...SW	×
● *Lick Run*, Athens...SE	50
● *Lick Run*, Tuscarawas...E	×
Liggett, Van Wert...NW	×
Lightsville, Darke...W	100
● Lilly, Scioto...S	50
● Lilly Chapel, Madison...C	125
● **Lima**, Allen...NW	15,981
Limaville, Stark...NE	200
Limburg, Washington...SE	×
● Lime City, Wood...NW	30
Limerick, Jackson...S	25
● Limestone, Ottawa...N	50
Lincoln, Gallia...S	25
Lincoln Centre, (see Fulton)..	×
Lindale, Clermont...SW	250
● *Linden*, Seneca...N	×
Lindenville, Ashtabula...NE	75
● *Lindenwald*, Butler...SW	×
● Lindsey, Sandusky...N	458
Link, Paulding...NW	10
Linn, Pike...S	×
● *Linndale*, Cuyahoga...NE	60
● *Linndale Station*, Cuyahoga...NE	×
Linnvale, Licking...C	100
Linscott's, Athens...SE	×
● *Linson*, Wood...NW	×
● Linton, Jefferson...E	50
Linton Mills, Coshocton...C	90
● Linwood, Hamilton...SW	1,291
● *Lippincotts*, Champaign..W	×
● Litchfield, Medina...N	300
Lithopolis, Fairfield...C	369
Little Etna Furnace, L'wr'e S	×
● Little Hocking, Wash'g'n SE	500
Little Mountain, Lake...NE	50
Little New York, Wyandot. N	40
Little Sandusky, Wyandot..N	75
Littleton, Highland...S	×
Little Wyandot, (see Bucyrus)	×
Little York, (see Updegraff's)	×
Little York, Montgomery..W	150
Little York, Wyandot...N	40
Liverpool, (see Rosedale)...	×
Liverpool, Medina...N	240
Liverpool, (see Rosedale)...	×
Lloyd, Portage...NE	60
Lock, Knox...C	25
● Lockbourne, Franklin...C	875
Lockington, Shelby...W	170
● Lockland, Hamilton...SW	2,474
● *Lockport*, Licking...C	×
Lockport, (see New Philadelphia)...	×
● *Locks*, Hocking...S	×
● Lock Seventeen, Tus'c'r's. E	100
● Lockville, Fairfield...C	80
Locust Corner, Clermont..SW	50
Locust Grove, Adams...S	150
● *Locust Grove*, Clarke...W	×
● *Locust Grove*, Licking...C	×
Locust Point, Ottawa...N	200
Locust Ridge, Brown...SW	100
● Lodi, Medina...N	568
● *Logan*, Marion...C	×
● **Logan**, Hocking...S	3,119
Logan's Gap, Brown...SW	40
Loganville, Logan...W	200
Log Cabin, (see Mountville)..	×
Logton, Columbiana...NE	×
Logtown, Clermont...SW	00
Lois, Scioto...S	25
Lombardville, Scioto...S	75
● **London**, Madison...C	3,313
Londonderry, Guernsey...E	100
Londonderry, Ross...S	250
Londonderry Station, Ross..S	125
Lone Star, Vinton...S	50
Long, Darke...W	×
Long Bottom, Meigs...SE	250
● *Long Hollow*, Lawrence...S	×
Long Lake, (see Akron)...	×
● Longley, Wood...NW	25
● *Long Run*, Jefferson...E	×
Long Run, Licking...C	5
● *Longs*, Columbiana...NE	×
● *Long Siding*, Montgomery W	×
● Longstreth, Hocking...S	50
● *Longview*, Hamilton...SW	×
● Longville, Marion...C	40
Lookout, Champaign...W	×
● Lorain, Lorain...N	4,863
Loramie's, Shelby...W	457
Lordstown, Trumbull...NE	50
● *Lordstown Station*, T'm'l NE	×
● Lore City, Guernsey...E	150
Lottridge, Athens...SE	×
Loudon, Adams...S	25
Loudonville, Ashland...N	1,444
Louis, Scioto...S	25
● Louisville, Stark...NE	1,323
● *Lounsberry*, Clermont..SW	×
● Loveland, Clermont...SW	761
Loveland, Hamilton...SW	392
Loveland Station, (see Calla).	×
● Lovell, Wyandot...N	65
Lovett's Adams...S	25
Lowell, Seneca...N	40
● *Lowell*, Mahoning...NE	×
Lowell, Washington...SE	450
● *Lowell Station*, Wash'ton SE	×
● Lowellville, Mahoning...NE	762
● *Lowell Gravel Hill*, Belm't E	×
Lower Newport, Wash'gton SE	60
Lower Salem, Washington. SE	250
Loyal Oak, Summit...NE	350
Loydsville, Belmont...E	175
● *Lucas*, Muskingum...C	×
Lucas, Richland...N	347
● Lucasville, Scioto...S	300
● Luckey, Wood...NW	400
● *Ludington*, Perry...C	×
Ludlow, (see Wingett Run)...	×
● Ludlow Falls, Miami...W	200
● Ludlow Grove, Ham't'n. SW	1,600
Ludwick, Highland...S	×
● Luke Chute, Washington. SE	×
Lumberton, Clinton...SW	150
Lundville, Washington...SE	×
Lyda, Athens...SE	×
● Lykens, Crawford...N	100
Lyme, Huron...N	80
● *Lyme*, Erie...N	×
● Lynchburgh, Highland...S	763
● *Lyndchester*, Hamilton..SW	×
● Lyndon, Ross...S	175
Lynx, Adams...S	30
Lyons, Fulton...NW	300
● Lyonsdale, Perry...C	10
Lyra, Scioto...S	×
Lysander, Athens...SE	×
Lytle, Warren...SW	150
● **McArthur**, Vinton...S	888
● *McArthur Junc.*, Vinton. S	150
● *McAvans*, Washington..SE	×
McClainville, Belmont...E	×
McCartyville, Shelby...W	100
McCleary, Noble...E	200
● *McClintocksburgh*, Por'e NE	×
● McClure, Henry...NW	332
● McComb, Hancock...NW	1,030
McConnelsville, Mor'n SE	1,771
McCoy's Station, (see Empire)	×
● *McCracken's Crossing*, Cuyahoga...NE	×
● *McCrea Park*, Muskingum C	×
● *McCulloch*, Scioto...S	×
McCullough, Adams...S	×
● *McCullough's*, Hamilton SW	×
● *McCulloughs*, Hamilton SW	×
● McCuneville, Perry...C	100
McCurdy, (see Stone Station)	×
● McCutchenville, Wyandot N	300
McDaniel's, Gallia...S	50
● *McDonald*, Butler...SW	×
McDonald, Muskingum...C	×
McDonaldsville, Stark...NE	100
● *McElroy*, Perry...C	×
● *McGarry*, Columbiana..NE	×
McGill, Paulding...NW	25
McGillsville, (see Lowellsville)	×
● McGonigle, Butler...SW	75

● McGuffey, Hardin........W	100
McKay, Ashland...........N	40
McKay Station, Clinton...SW	25
McKinley, Cuyahoga...... NE	×
McLean, Fayette........... S	30
● McLuney, Perry.......... C	69
McQuaid, Wayne............N	×
● *McVitty's* Hardin........W	×
McZena, Ashland........... N	30
Mabee's, Jackson...........S	40
Macedon, Mercer...........W	86
● Macedonia Depot, Sum'tNE	150
Mack, Hamilton...........SW	×
● Macksburgh, WashingtonSE	533
Macocheek, Logan..........W	20
Maddox, Adams.............S	25
● Maderia, Hamilton......SW	300
● Madison, Lake.......... NE	738
● *Madison*, Richland........N	×
● *Madison*, Jackson........ S	×
Madisonburgh, Wayne......N	100
Madison City, Butler.....SW	200
Madison Mills, Fayette......S	150
● Madisonville, Hamilton.SW	2,214
Madriver, Clarke...........W	100
Magnetic Springs, Union....C	257
Magnolia, Stark...........NE	300
● *Magnolia*, Carroll........E	×
● Maholm, Perry............C	200
● Mahoning, Portage......NE	30
Maineville, Warren....... SW	256
● *Maitland*, Williams.... NW	×
Malaby, Gallia...............S	×
Malaga, Monroe.............E	150
● Malinta, Henry.........NW	130
● Mallet Creek, Medina.... N	250
● Malta, Morgan...........SE	865
● Malvern, Carroll...........E	638
Manahan, Allen......... NW	10
Manara, Fayette.............S	×
Manchester, Adams......... S	1,965
Manchester, Summit......NE	200
Mandale, Paulding........NW	×
● *Manhattan*, Allen..... NW	×
Manhattan, (see Toledo).....	×
Manhattan, Lawrence.......S	×
● *ManhattanJunc.*, LucasNW	×
● Manning, Holmes.........C	125
Mansfield, Richland .....N	13,473
Mantua, (see Creighton).....	×
Mantua, Portage..........NE	800
Mantua Corners, (see Mantua)	×
● Mantua Station, PortageNE	676
Maple, Brown........... SW	×
Maple Grove, Seneca....... N	25
● Mapleton, Stark........ NE	100
● *Mapleton*, Belmont.......E	×
Maplewood, Shelby.........W	125
● *Maplewood*, Hamilton..SW	50
Marathon, Clermount.....SW	144
● Marble Cliff, Franklin....C	100
● Marblehead, Ottawa......N	800
● *MarbleheadJunc.*, Ott'w'aN	×
● *Marbletown*, Belmont....E	×
Marchland, Stark......... NE	50
Marcy, Fairfield............C	50
● Marengo, Morrow.........C	276
● Maria Stein, Mercer......W	205
Marice City, Putnam.....NW	895
● **Marietta**, Washington.SE	8,273
Marion, Lawrence..........S	120
● *Marion*, Hancock......NW	×
● **Marion**, Marion.........C	8,327
● *Marion Junc.*, Marion....C	×
Marit's, Morrow........... C	100
● Mark Centre, Defiance.NW	125
● Markle, Jefferson.........E	×
● *Marks*, Stark..........NE	×
Marlborough, Stark.......NE	271
Marquand, Muskingum.....C	50
● *Marlows*, Clinton.......SW	×
Marr, Monroe...............E	×
Marseilles, Wyandot........N	213
Marshall, Highland..........S	100
● *Marshall*, Trumbull....NE	×
● Marshallville, Wayne.....N	366
● Marshfield, Athens......SE	200
● *Marshs*, Hardin..........W	×
● Martel, Marion...........W	200
● Martin, Ottawa...........N	300
Martinsburg, Knox.......... C	257
● Martins Ferry, Belmont..E	6,250
Martinsville, (see Martins F'y)	×
● Martinsville, Clinton....SW	336
● **Marysville**, Union C	2,810
Mason, Warren........... SW	564
Masseyville, (see Waller).....	×

Massie, Scioto...............S	50
● Massillon, Stark ....NE	10,092
Mastersville, (see Conotton).	×
Masterton, Monroe..........E	150
Matamoras, (see NewM't'm's)	×
Mattville, Pickaway.........C	25
● Maud's, Butler..........SW	150
● Maumee, Lucas........ NW	1,645
● Maximo, Stark......... NE	200
Maxtown, Delaware C	×
Maxville, Perry.............C	100
Mayfield, Cuyahoga.......NE	500
May Hill, Adams............S	25
● Maynard, Belmont........E	400
Maysville, Wayne.......... N	100
Maysville, (see Kensington)..	×
Meade, Pickaway C	×
Meander, Trumbull.......NE	200
● Means, Harrison ....E	132
● *Means Cross*, Summit..NE	×
Mecca, Trumbull..........NE	150
Mechanicsburgh, Cha'paign. W	1,459
● Mechanicstown, Carroll...E	250
Mechanicsville, Ashtabula NE	100
● *Media*, Belmont..........E	100
● **Medina**, Medina........N	2,100
Medway, Clarke............W	400
● *Meeker*, Darke...........W	×
Meigs' Creek, Morgan.....SE	20
Meigsville, Morgan........ SE	50
● Melbern, Williams..... NW	125
Melgen, Licking..... C	×
Melmore, Seneca........... N	250
● Melrose, Paulding.......NW	430
● Melvin, Clinton.........SW	30
Memphis, Clinton.........SW	20
● Mendon, Mercer ....W	400
● Mentor, Lake...........NE	502
● Mercer, Mercer.......... W	300
Mercer, (see Rudolph)	×
Mercerville, Gallia.......... S	40
● Mermill, Wood.........NW	50
● *Mero*, Monroe............ E	20
Merriam, Muskingum......C	×
● *Mertz*, Belmont..........E	×
Mesopotamia, Trumbull ..NE	500
● *MessengerJunc.* SummitNE	×
Metamora, Fulton........NW	300
● Methan, Coshocton........C	20
● Metz, Summit.......... NE	100
Mexico, Wyandot...........N	50
Miami, Hamilton..........SW	300
● *Miami*, Lucas..........NW	×
Miami City, Miami.........W	125
● *Miami City*, MontgomeryW	×
● *Miami Crossing*, FranklinC	×
● Miamisburgh, M'tgom'ryW	2,952
● *Miami Siding*, Miami....W	×
Miamitown, Hamilton....SW	275
● Miamiville, Clermont...SW	203
Middle Bass, Ottawa........N	250
Middleboro, (seeEdwardsville)	×
Middlebourne, Guernsey....E	165
● Middle Branch, Stark...NE	250
Middleburg, Noble..........E	76
● Middlebury, Summit....NE	×
Middle Creek, Noble........E	100
● Middlefield, Geauga.....NE	400
Middle Fork, Hocking...... S	50
● Middle Point, VanWertNW	432
● Middleport, Meigs.......SE	3,211
Middleton, (see New W't'rf'd)	×
● Middletown, Butler.....SW	7,681
Middletown, (see M'dl'b'rne)	×
Middletown, (see Mt. Hope) .	×
● *Middletown Sta.* Butler SW	×
Middletown, Champaign...W	75
Middletown, (see Hancock)N	×
● Midland City, Clinton...SW	328
● *Midway*, Defiance .....NW	×
Midway, Guernsey.......... E	75
Midway, Madison...........C	200
Mifflin, Ashland........... N	300
Mifflinville, Franklin........C	25
● Milan, Erie.............. N	627
● Milford, Clermont......SW	995
● Milford Centre, Union.... C	718
● *Milford Sta.*, Hamilton.SW	×
Milfordton, Knox..........C	×
Mill Brook, Wayne.........N	×
● *Millbrook*, Wayne........N	×
Millbury, Wood.......... NW	546
Mill Creek, Hamilton.....SW	×
● *Milldale*, Hamilton..... SW	30
Milledgeville, Fayette.......S	250
● Miller City, Putnam....NW	150
Miller's, Lawrence..........S	×

● *Millers*, Guernsey........ E	×
● **Millersburgh**, HolmesC	1,923
● Millersport, Fairfield..... C	259
Millersport, Lawrence...... S	281
● Miller's Station, Harrison. E	50
Miller's Switch, (see Cave)...	×
Millerstown, Champaign...W	200
Millerstown, (see Corning) ..	×
● Millersville, Sandusky....N	55
● Millfield, Athens ....SE	100
Mill Grove, Morgan........SE	50
● Millport, Columbiana...NE	100
● *Millport*, Stark.........NE	75
● Mill Rock, Columbiana. NE	20
Millsport, (see Ashville)	×
● *Mills*, Gallia............. S	×
Milltown, Brown.........SW	×
Millville, Butler...........SW	275
Millville, Delaware..........C	150
● *Millville*, Hocking.........S	240
Millwood, (see Quaker City).	×
Milwood, Knox C	400
Milnersville, Guernsey......E	250
● *Milltomson*, Warren.... SW	×
Milton, Mahoning.........NE	20
● *Milton*, Ashland..........N	×
Milton, (see Wilmot).........	×
● Milton Centre, Wood...NW	334
Miltonsburgh, Monroe......E	123
Milton Station, (see Rittman)	×
Miltonville, Butler........SW	165
● *Minahan's Bend*, Ross....S	×
● Mineral, Athens.........SE	200
Mineral City, Tuscarawas.. E	893
● Mineral Point, TuscarawasE	1,200
● Mineral Ridge, TrumbullNE	851
● *Mineral Siding*, GuernseyE	×
Mineral Springs, Adams.....S	100
● *Mineral Springs*, Adams..S	100
Minersville, Meigs.........SE	980
● Minerton, Vinton..........S	100
● Minerva, Stark..........NE	1,139
● *Mines*, Muskingum.......C	×
● *Mine Twenty One*, Perry. C	×
● Mingo, Champaign.......W	300
● Mingo Junc., Jefferson... E	2,200
● Minster, Auglaize........W	1,126
Mio, Preble................ W	×
● Mishler, Portage........NE	100
Mitchaw, Lucas.......... NW	×
Moats, Defiance.......... NW	25
Modest, Clermont.........SW	×
● *Moffits*, Hancock.......NW	×
● Mogadore, Summit..... NE	400
Mohawk Village, Coshocton.C	75
Mohican, Ashland.......... N	140
Momeneetown, Lucas.... NW	×
● Monclova, Lucas....... NW	100
● Monday, Hocking......... S	400
● *Monday Creek Jc.*, HockingS	×
Monroe, Butler............SW	375
● *Monroe*, Jackson .... S	×
Monroe, Highland...........S	150
Monroe Centre, Ashtabula. NE	300
Monroe Centre, (seeMillersb'g)	×
Monroefield, Monroe........E	×
Monroe Furnace, Jackson..S	50
Monroe Mills, Knox.........C	40
● *Monroe Siding*, Greene..W	×
Monroe Station, Butler...SW	80
● Monroeville, Huron.......N	1,600
Monroeville, (see Croxton)...	×
Monterey, Clermont...... SW	100
Monterey, Mercer..........W	25
● Montezuma, Mercer......W	185
● Montgomery, Hamilton.SW	450
● *Montgomery's*, Licking...C	×
● Monticello, Van Wert..NW	100
● Montpelier, Williams...NW	1,298
Montra, Shelby............W	500
Montrose, Summit........ NE	75
Montville, Geauga.........NE	200
Moody, Gallia...............S	100
Moons, Fayette..............S	100
● *Moonville*, Vinton.........S	×
Moore, Adams............. S	×
Moorefield, Harrison........E	185
Moorefield, Clarke......... W	×
Moore's Fork, Clermont..SW	25
● *Moore's Junc.*, Wash'gt'nSE	×
Moore's Salt Works, Jeffers'nE	15
Moorland, Wayne...........N	60
● *Moran's Switch*, Marion..C	×
● *Morefield*, Clarke........ W	×
Morgan, (see Rock Creek) ...	×
Morgan Centre, Knox.......C	×
● Morgan Junc., Guernsey..E	10

Morgans, Pickaway.........C 100
● *Morgan's Run*, CoshoctonC ×
Morgans, Pickaway.........C 100
Morgansville, Morgan..... SE 50
Morgantown, Pike.......... S 200
Morges, (see Waynesburg)... ×
Morning Sun, Preble.......W 140
Mornington, Hamilton... SW ×
Morning View, Belmont....E ×
● Morrell, Marion..........C 151
● Morris, Seneca...........N 27
● *Morris*, Washington.....SE ×
Morrison, Paulding.......NW ×
● *Morrison Mine*, Noble....E ×
Morristown, Belmont.......E 371
Morrisville, Clinton.......SW 100
● Morrow, Warren..........SW 842
● Mortimer, Hancock.... NW 150
Morton, Monroe........... E 10
● *Morton's Cors.*,(seePagetown) ×
● *Mortonville*, Athens.....SE 10
Moscow, Clermont.........SW 591
Moscow Mills, Morgan.....SE 10
Mosk, Columbiana.........NE 100
● *Mosketo*, Trumbull..... NE ×
Moss Run, Washington....SE 25
● *Mott Town*, Portage....NE ×
Moulton, Auglaize..........W 150
● Moultrie, Columbiana...NE 50
Mound, Coshocton.......... C ×
● *Mounds*, Franklin.........C ×
Mount Adams, Hamilton.SW ×
Mount Airy, Hamilton.... SW 600
● *Mount Airy Station*, Hamilton...SW ×
Mount Auburn, (see Chauncey) ×
Mount Auburn, Butler.....SW ×
● Mount Blancha'd.Han'kNW 421
Mount Blanco, Meigs......SE ×
● Mount Carmel,ClermontSW 200
Mount Carrick, Monroe.....E 10
● Mount Cory, Hancock..NW 334
Mount Eaton, Wayne.......N 278
● Mount Ephraim, Noble...E 200
● **Mount Gilead**, MorrowC 1,329
● Mount Healthy,Ham'tonSW 1,145
Mount Heron, Darke.......W 100
Mount Holly, Clermont...SW 180
Mount Holly, (seeSpringVal.) ×
Mount Holly, (see Gann)..... ×
Mount Holly, Warren.... SW ×
Mount Hope, Holmes....... C 150
Mount Joy, Scioto...........S 60
● Mount Liberty, Knox.....C 200
Mount Lookout, (seeCincinn'i) ×
Mount Moral, (see Morral).. ×
Mount Olive, Clermont... SW 30
● Mount Orab, Brown.....SW 336
● Mount Perry, Perry.......C 125
Mount Pisgah, Clermont..SW 100
Mount Pleasant, Jefferson.. E 644
● *MountPleasantSta.*,Jeff'nE ×
Mount Pleasant,HamiltonSW 871
Mount Pleasant, (see Swan). ×
Mount Repose, Clermont..SW 50
Mount Saint Joseph,Hamil'nSW ×
● Mount Sterling, Madison..C 752
Mount Sterling, (seeHopewell) ×
● Mount Summit,Ham'tonSW ×
Mount Union, Stark......NE 800
● **Mount Vernon**, Knox.C 6,027
● *Mount Vernon*, LawrenceS 100
● Mount Victory, Hardin...W 689
Mountville, Morgan........SE 100
● MountWashing'n,Ham'tnSW 900
Mount Zion, Noble..........E ×
Mouth of Rush Run,(seeRushRun) ×
Mowery's Cors., Ashland...N ×
Mowrystown, Highland..... S 175
● Moxahala, Perry..........C 408
● *Muhlhauser*, Butler....SW ×
Mulberry, Clermont.......SW 100
Mulberry Corners, Geauga NE 200
Mummaville,(seeStillwaterJc.) ×
● Mungen, Wood......... SW 250
● Munroe Falls, Summit..NE 25
Munson, Medina............N ×
Munson Centre,(seeFowler'sMills) ×
● *Munson Hill*, Ashtabula NE 100
Muntanna, Putnam.........NW 10
Murdock, Warren.........SW 50
Murphy, Washington......SE ×
● *Murphy's Siding*,Hanc'kNW ×
● Murry, Hocking..........S 2,518
Museville, Muskingum......C 50
● *Muskingum*, Muskingum C ×
● *Muskingum*, Muskingum C ×
Muskingum, Washington..SE ×
● Musselman, Ross.........S 10
Mutton Jerk, (see Kingston). ×
Mutual, Champaign........ W 174
● Myers, Stark............NE 10
● *Myers*, Madison..........C ×
Myersville, Summit....... NE 50
Myrtle, Scioto..............S 10
Nairn, Scioto...............S 150
Nancy, Hocking.............S ×
● Nankin, Ashland..........N 50
● *Napier*, Washington.....SE ×
● **Napoleon**, Henry....NW 2,764
Napoleon, (see Black Creek) ×
● Nashport, Muskingum....C 150
Nashville, (see Darke)....... ×
Nashville, Holmes..........C 300
● National Military Home, Montgomery........... W 4,468
● *National Road*, Licking..C ×
● *National RoadSta.*,Mont'yW 100
● Navarre, Stark...........NE 1,010
● Neapolis, Lucas........ NW 100
Nebo, Defiance...........NW ×
Nebo, (see Bergholz)......... ×
● *Nebo*, Mahoning........ NE 25
Nebraska, Pickaway........ C 30
Needful, Highland...........S 25
Neel, Brown............. SW 30
Neelysville, Morgan....... SE 50
● *Neffs Siding*, Belmont...E ×
● Negley, Columbiana.... NE 300
● *Nelson*, Morgan......... SE ×
Nelson, Portage...........NE 150
Nelson Ledge, Portage....NE ×
● *Nelson'sCrossing*,PortageNE 150
● Nelsonville, Athens......SE 4,558
● Neowash, Lucas........NW 10
Neptune, Mercer...........W 150
Nero, (see New Philadelphia) ×
Nettle Lake, Williams....NW 75
Nettleton, Champaign......W 36
● Nevada, Wyandot.........N 802
Neville, Clermont.........SW 340
Nevin, Highland........... S ×
New Albany, Franklin......C 223
New Albany, Mahoning...NE 30
New Alexander,Columbi'aNE 60
● New Alexandria,JeffersonE 122
New Antioch, Clinton.... SW 180
● **Newark**, Licking........C 14,270
New Athens, Harrison.......E 420
New Baltimore, Stark.....NE 155
New Baltimore, Hamilton SW 100
● New Bavaria, Henry...NW 125
New Bedford, Coshocton....C 400
● New Berlin, Stark...... NE 463
N. Berlin Sta.,(seeMarchand) ×
Newberry, (see Mulberry).... ×
New Birmingham, (see Milnersville) .... ×
New Bloomington, Marion..C 600
New Boston, Scioto.........S ×
New Boston, (see Owensville) ×
● New Bremen, Auglaize.. W 1,239
New Buffalo, Mahoning...NE 100
Newburgh, Jefferson.......E ×
● Newburgh, Cuyahoga...NE ×
● *Newburgh*, Hamilton...NW ×
New Burlington, Clinton..SW 400
New Burlington,Hamilt'nSW ×
Newbury, (seeSouthNewbury) ×
Newbury, Clermont...... SW 100
New California, Union......C 50
● New Carlisle, Clark......W 958
New Castle, Coshocton......C 250
New Castle, (see Pilcher) .... ×
New Castle, (see Laings)..... ×
New Castle, (see Neeleysville) ×
New Chambersburgh,Col'aNE 50
● New Comerstown,Tus'wasE 1,251
● New Concord, MuskingumC 719
● New Corwin, Highland....S 30
● New Cumberland, Tus'as.E 150
● New Dover, Union........C 112
Newell's Run, Washington SE 40
New England, Athens..... SE 100
Newfain, Pike..............S ×
● New Franklin, Stark.....NN 106
New Garden, Columbiana.NE 200
New Gottingen, Guernsey.. E 50
New Guilford, Coshoction.. C 75
● New Hagerstown, Carroll...E 200
New Hampshire, Auglaize. W 200
New Harmony, Brown... SW 100
New Harrisburgh, Carroll.. E 100
New Harrison, (seeGettysb'g) ×
● New Haven, Huron.......N 400
New Haven, Hamilton....SW 250
New Hazleon, Stark...... NE ×
● New Holland, Pickaway..C 683
● *New Hope*, Preble........W 200
New Hope, Brown........SW 200
Newingburgh, Ross.........S 10
● New Jasper, Greene .....W 60
New Jefferson, (see Germana) ×
New Jerusalem, Logan.....W 20
New Knoxville, Auglaise...W 550
New Lebanon, MontgomeryW 149
New Lexington, Highland...S 210
● **New Lexington**,PerryC 1,470
New Lexington, Preble.... W 100
● **New Lisbon**,Col'mb'naNE 2,278
New London,(seePaddy's Run) ×
● New London, Huron.....N 1,096
● New Lyme, Ashtabula.. NE 1,000
● New Lyme Sta,AshtabulaNE ×
New Madison, Dark........W 478
● Newman, Stark. ....NE ×
New Market, (see Scio) ...... ×
New Market, Highland......S 125
New Martinsburgh, Fayette.S 200
New Matamoras, Wash'ton SE 590
New Middletown,Mahoning NE 200
New Milford, Portage.....NE 75
● New Moorefield, Clarke..W 874
New Moscow, Coshocton....C 100
New Palestine, Clermont..SW 100
New Palestine, (see Tawawa) ×
● New Paris, Preble....... W 842
New Petersburgh,Highl'n...S 232
● **New Philadelphia**,Tuscarawas.........E 4,456
● *New Pittsburgh*,Hocking.S ×
New Pittsburgh, Wayne....N 200
● New Plymouth, Vinton...S 180
Newport, Adams............S 130
● *Newport*, Tuscarawas.....E ×
Newport, (see Walnut Run).. ×
Newport, Washington.....SE 300
Newport, Shelby...........W 300
● New Portage, Summit..NE 200
New Princeton,(seeSpringMt.) ×
New Richland, Lawrence...S 50
● New Richland, Logan....W 140
● New Richmond,Cler'm'tSW 2,379
● New Riegel, Seneca......N 393
● *New River*, Butler......SW ×
New Rochester, Wood....SW 30
New Rumley, Harrison.... E 176
● New Salem, Fairfield.....C 189
● *New Salem Siding*, Ross..S ×
● *New Salisbury*,Columb'aNE ×
New Somerset, Jefferson... E 77
New Springfield,MahoningNE 400
New Stark, Hancock......NW 90
New Stark, Hardin.........W 25
● New Straitsville, Perry....C 2,782
Newton, Muskingum.........C 10
Newton, (see Pleasant Hill).. ×
Newton, (see Raymond's).... ×
● *Newton*, Athens.........SE 25
● Newton Falls,Trumbull.NE 698
● *NewtonJunction*,Athens.SE ×
● *Newton's*, Wood....... NW ×
Newtonsville, Clermont....SW 160
Newtonville,(seeWhite Cot'ge) ×
● Newtown, Hamilton....SW 552
Newtown, (see Peoli) .... ×
● New Vienna, Clinton...SW 871
Newville, Richland........N 100
● New Washington,Crawf'rdN 704
● New Waterford,Col'mb'aNE 275
Newway, Licking..........C 75
● New Weston, Darke..... W 75
New Westville, Preble...... W 150
New Westville Sta.,Preble. W ×
● New Winchester,Crawf'd.N 95
● Ney, Defiance.........NW 60
Nichols, Fayette............S ×
● *Nicholson*, Guernsey..... E ×
Nicholsville, Clermont....SW 100
Nickel Plate, Lorain....... N ×
● Niles, Trumbull.........NE 4,289
● *Niles*, Gallia..............S 40
Niles, (see Akron)............ ×
Nimisila, Summit.........NE ×
● Nine Mile, Clermont....SW 25
Nioga, Madison............C ×
Ningen, Ross................S 25
● Noble, Cuyahoga.........NE 25
Nobleville, Noble..........E 20
● *Norris*, Wood......... NW ×
● *Norris Mines*, Guernsey..E ×

Norristown, Carroll.........E 50
● North Amherst, Lorain.. N 1,648
● North Auburn, Crawford N 100
● North Baltimore, Wood NW 2,857
North Bass Island, Ottawa. N ×
● North Bend, Hamilton..SW 300
● North Benton, Mahoning NE 125
● North Berne, Fairfield....C 50
● North Bloomfield, Trum. NE 800
● *North Bloomfield Station*, Trumbull.............NE ×
● North Bristol, Trumbull NE 250
● *North Bristol Sta.*, Trum. NE ×
North Clayton, Miami...... W 25
North Columbus, Franklin..C ×
● North Creek, Putnam..NW 50
● North Dover, Cuyahoga. NE 20
● North Eaton, Lorain.....N 50
North Fairfield, Huron.....N 700
● *North Freesburgh*, Brown SW ×
Northfield, Summit.......NE 500
● *North Findlay*, Hancock NW ×
● North Georgetown, C'lm'NE 200
North Greenfield, Logan... W 50
● *North Hamilton*, Butler SW ×
North Hampton, Clarke....W 400
● North Industry, Stark.. NE 200
● North Jackson, Mahoning NE 400
North Kenova, Lawrence....S ×
North Kingsville, Asht'bla NE 850
● North Lawrence, Stark. NE 337
● North Lewisburgh, Cham. W 866
North Liberty, Adams.......S 300
North Liberty, Knox.........C 200
● *North Lima*, Allen.....NW ×
North Lima, Mahoning... NE 300
● North Linndale, C'yahoga NE 60
North Madison, Lake.......NE 60
North Monroeville, Huron..N 100
● *North Neff's*, Belmont....E ×
North Olmsted, Cuyahoga. NE ×
North Perry, (see Glenford). ×
North Richmond, Asht'b'la NE 250
North Ridgeville, Lorain....N 250
● North Robinson, Crawford N 257
North Royalton, Cuyahoga NE 200
North Salem, Guernsey..... E 100
North Sheffield, Ashtabula NE 200
North Solon, Cuyahoga....NE 100
North Springfield, Summit. NE 150
North Star, Darke.........W 100
North Toledo, (see Toledo)... ×
North Uniontown, Highland S 75
Northup, Gallia.............S 41
Northville, Champaign..... W 25
● North Washington, H'rd'n. W 265
North West, Williams.... NW 10
Northwood, Logan......... W 25
Norton, Delaware..........C 135
Norton, (see Johnson's Cors.) ×
Norton Centre, (see Johnson's Cors.)..................... ×
● **Norwalk**, Huron........N 7,195
● *Norwalk Junction*, Huron N ×
● *Norwich*, Muskingum....C ×
Norwich, Muskingum.......C 234
● Norwood, Hamilton.....SW 3,000
○ *Norwood Heights*, H'mlt'SW ×
● Nottingham, Cuyahoga..NE 300
● Nova, Ashland............N 200
Nutwood, Trumbull...... NE ×
Oak, Monroe...............E 50
Oakdale, Belmont...........E 10
Oakdale, Athens...........SE 25
● *Oakdale*, Putnam...... NW ×
Oakfield, (see Moxahala)...... ×
Oakfield, Trumbull........NE 200
Oak Grove, Guernsey........E ×
● *Oak Grove*, Muskingum...C ×
● Oak Harbor, Ottawa......N 1,681
● Oak Hill, Jackson......... S 657
Oakland, Butler.......... SW ×
Oakland, Clinton..........SW 32
Oakland, Muskingum.......C ×
● *Oakland*, Mercer......... W ×
Oakland, Fairfield..........C 165
● Oakley, Hamilton.......SW 600
● *Oakley Grove*, Hamilton SW ×
Oak Shade, Fulton....... NW 10
Oakwood, Paulding........NW 378
Oatville, Licking........... C 60
Obal, Gallia.................S ×
Obanon, Clermont.........SW ×
● Oberlin, Lorain.... ......N 4,376
O'Brienville, Hamilton....SW ×
Oceola, Crawford........... N 300
● Octa, Fayette............. S 150
● Odbert, Tuscarawas.......E 200
Odell, Guernsey............E 25
● Ogden, Clinton..........SW 50
● *Ogleton*, Butler......... SW ×
Ogontz, Erie...............N ×
Ohio, (see Bladensburg)...... ×
Ohio Furnace, (see Haverhill) ×
● Ohio City, Van Wert... NW 666
● Ohlstown, Mahoning....NE ×
Ohl's Town, Trumbull.... NE 25
● Oil Centre, Wood.......NW 25
Okeana, Butler...........SW 200
Okey, Lawrence.............S ×
● Okolona, Henry........ NW 150
Olbers, Athens............SE ×
● Old Fort, Seneca..........N 100
Oldham, Guernsey.......... E 10
● Old Town, Greene........W 75
● *Old Portage*, Summit...NE ×
Olena, Huron...............N 300
● Olentangy, Franklin......C 25
Olga, Washington..........SE ×
● *Olive*, Noble..............E ×
● Olive Branch, Clermont. SW 250
● Olive Furnace, Lawrence..S 300
Olive Green, Delaware.......C 110
Olive Green, Noble.........E 25
Olivesburgh, Richland...... N 140
Olivett, Belmont...........E ×
Olmsted, (see Olmsted Falls). ×
● Olmsted Falls, Cuyah'ga NE 342
Omar, Seneca...............N 80
● Omega, Pike............. S 280
● Oneida Mills, Carroll.......E 95
● *One Hundred and Six Mile Siding*, Stark..........NE ×
● Ontario, Richland........ N 200
Opera, Perry................C 25
Oran, Shelby.............. W 40
Orange, (see Nankin)........ ×
Orange, (see Austintown).... ×
Orange, Cuyahoga........ NE ×
● Orangeville, Trumbull..NE 400
● Orbiston, Hocking........ S 110
Orchard, Clarke............W ×
● *Ore Docks*, Cuyahoga... NE ×
● ***Oregon***, Mercer.......... W 25
● Oregonia, Warren...... SW 111
● Oreton, Vinton............S 100
Oreville, Hocking............S 50
● Orient, Pickaway..........C ×
● Orland, Vinton............S 15
Ormiston, Washington.....SE ×
● *Orphan's Home*, Greene. W ×
Orpheus, Jackson...........S ×
● Orrville, Wayne.......... N 1,765
Ort, Lawrence..............S 100
● Orwell, Ashtabula...... NE 1,000
Osage, Jefferson........... E ×
● Osborn, Greene.......... W 713
● Osgood, Darke............ W 242
Osman's, Adams.............S 10
● Osnaburg, Stark........ NE 800
● Ostrander, Delaware......C 357
Otho, Morgan............. SE 24
Otsego, Muskingum.........C 200
● **Ottawa**, Putnam......NW 1,717
Ottokee, Fulton.......... NW 100
Ottoville, Putnam........ NW 350
● Otway, Scioto............ S 1,612
Otwell's Mills, (see F't Jeffr'n) ×
Outhwaite, Hocking........ S 10
● Outville, Licking..........C 100
Oval City, Stark...........NE 125
● Overpeck, Butler....... SW 25
Overton, Wayne........... N ×
Ovid, Franklin..............C ×
● Owen, Marion.............C 50
Owensville, Clermont.....SW 692
● Oxford, Butler...........SW 1,922
Oxford, (see Killbuck)....... ×
● *Oxford*, Coshocton.........C ×
● *Oxtobys*, Clarke..........W ×
● Ozark, Monroe............E 100
Padanaram, Ashtabula....NE 200
Paddy's Run, Butler......SW 250
Padua, Mercer..............W 50
Pagetown, Morrow..........C 40
Pageville, Meigs..........SE 100
● **Painesville**, Lake....NE 4,755
Paint, Highland............S 791
Painter Creek, Darke..... W 100
Paintersville, Greene.......W 150
Paint Valley, Holmes........C 25
Palermo, Carroll............E ×
Palestine, (see East Palestine) ×
Palestine, (see Locust Grove) ×
Palestine, (see New Palestine) ×
Palestine, Darke........... W 260
○ Palestine, Pickaway.......C 150
Palestine, (see new Palestine) ×
Palmyra, Portage......... NE 250
● *Palmyra*, Portage...... NE ×
Palo Alto, Seneca...........N 25
Pancoastburgh, Fayette.....S 200
● Pandora, Putnam...... NW 150
Pansy, Clinton............SW ×
Paradise Hill, Ashland......N ×
Paragon, Wood...........NW 10
● Paris, Stark.............NE 219
Parisville, Portage........NE 300
Park, Columbiana..........NE 10
● *Park*, Warren.......... SW ×
Parkman, Geauga..........NE 300
● *Park Place*, Hamilton..SW ×
Park's Mills, Franklin......C ×
Parma, Cuyahoga.........NE 50
● Parrott, Fayette...........S 25
● *Pasco*, Belmont..........E ×
● Pataskala, Licking........C 568
Patmos, Mahoning........NE 50
Patriot, Gallia..............S 200
Patten Mills, Washington..SE 25
● Patterson, Hardin........W 247
Pattersonville, Carroll......E ×
Patton's Mills, Washington SE 25
● *Patton's Run*, Belmont..E ×
● **Paulding**, Paulding..NW 1,879
● *Pauls*, Stark............NE ×
● Pavonia, Richland........ N 50
Pawnee, Medina............N 200
Payne, Paulding...........NW 1,146
Payne's Corners, Trumbull NE 50
Peachton, Ottawa.......... N 25
● Pearl, Coshocton.........C 19
Pearson, Fayette.............S 25
Pedro, Lawrence............S 25
● Peebles, Adams............S 358
Peebles, Miami.............W ×
● Peerless Delaware........C 15
Pekin, Warren............SW 200
● *Pekin*, Carroll........... E 100
● *Pekin*, Stark............NE ×
● Pemberton, Shelby.......W 800
● Pemberville, Wood.....NW 843
● *Pendleton*, Hamilton... SW ×
Penfield, Lorain........... N 100
Peniel, Gallia...............S 25
● Peninsula, Summit.......NE 562
Pennsville, Morgan........SE 347
○ *Pen Twyn*, Coschocton...C ×
Penza, Trumbull..........NE 200
Peoli, Tuscarawas..........E 200
● Peoria, Union.............C 200
Peppers, Ross...............S ×
Perin's Mills, Clermont...SW 50
Perintown, Clermont .....SW 50
Perkins, Mahoning.........NE 300
● *Perkins*, Erie.............N ×
● Perry, Lake..............NE 250
● Perryopolis, Noble.........E 10
● Perrysburgh, Wood....NW 1,747
● Perrysville, Ashland.......N 522
Perryton, Licking...........C 150
Peru, Huron.................N 50
Petersburg, (see New P't'rsb'g) ×
● *Petersburg*, Lawrence.....S 506
Petersburg, (see Coal Grove) ×
Petersburgh, Mahoning...NE 700
● *Peterson's*, Miami....... W ×
● Pettisville, Fulton......NW 300
● Pfeiffer, Hardin...........W 75
● Phalanx, Trumbull .....NE 25
Phalanx Station, Trumbull NE ×
Pharisburg, Union..........C 300
Pherson, Pickaway..........C 25
● *Philadelphia Road*, H'r'on E ×
Philanthropy, Butler......SW 25
● *Phillipsburg*, Athens....SE 25
Phillipsburg, (see Brilliant).. ×
● *Phillipsburg*, Tuscarawas. E 215
Phillipsburg, Montgomery. W 270
Phillip's Farm, Allen....NW ×
Philo, Muskingum..........C 631
● Philothea, Mercer........W 25
Phoenix, Ashtabula.......NE 25
● Piccolo, Ottaw...........N 10
● Pickerington, Fairfield... C 290
Pickrelltown, Logan....... W 100
● Piedmont, Harrison...... E 235
● Pierce, Stark............NE 300
● *Pierce*, Muskingum.......C ×
● *Pierce*, Muskingum.......C ×
Pierpont, Ashtabula...... NE 350

Pigeon Run, Stark	NE	75
Pike, Pike	S	25
Pike, (see Creston)		×
Pike Run, (see Barnhill)		×
Pike Run, Vinton	S	×
● Piketon, Pike	S	1,022
● Pikeville, Darke	W	90
Pilcher, Belmont	E	100
Pine Grove, Gallia	S	×
PineGroveFurnace, L'wre'ce	S	×
Pine Valley, Jefferson	E	×
Pioneer, Williams	NW	596
Pioneer, Scioto	S	100
● *Pipe Creek*, Belmont	E	×
Pipesville, Knox	C	20
● Piqua, Miami	W	9,090
● *Piqua Crossing*, Miami	W	×
● *Piqua Junc.*, Miami	W	×
Pisgah, Butler	SW	250
Pitt, (see Harpster)		×
Pitchin, Clarke	W	100
● Pitsburgh, Darke	W	50
Pittsfield, Lorain	N	25
Plain, Wayne	N	60
● Plain City, Madison	C	1,245
Plainfield, Coshocton	C	234
● Plainville, Hamilton	SW	200
Plankton, Crawford	N	75
Plants, Meigs	SE	100
Plantsville, Morgan	SE	431
Platform, Lawrence	S	50
● Plattsburgh, Clarke	W	150
Platt's Fork, Athens	SE	25
Plattston, Fulton	NW	10
Plattsville, Shelby	W	150
● Pleasant Bend, Henry	NW	100
● Pleasant Corners, Fr'klin	C	50
Pleasant Grove, Belmont	E	80
Pleasant Hill, (see Pleasanton)		×
● Pleasant Hill, Miami	W	521
● *Pleasant Hill*, Clermont	SW	×
Pleasant Home, Wayne	N	60
Pleasanton, Athens	SE	115
● Pleasant Plain, Warren	SW	150
● Pleasant Ridge, H'milt'n	SW	1,027
Pleasant Run, Hamilton	SW	25
Pleasant Valley, (see L'k'g V'y)		×
Pleasant Valley, (see B'dg'p't)		×
Pleasant Valley, (see Pl'n C'y)		×
Pleasant Valley, (see Swazer)		×
Pleasant Valley, (see Joy)		×
Pleasant Valley, Athens	SE	100
Pleasant View, Fayette	S	110
Pleasant View, (see Jamest'n)		×
Pleasantville, Fairfield	C	521
● Plimpton, Holmes	C	300
Plumb'sCrossRoads, P'd'g	NW	60
● *Plum Run*, Adams	S	×
● Plymouth, Richland	N	1,133
● *Plymouth*, Ashtabula	NE	×
Plymouth (see Bartlett)		×
● Poast Town, Butler	SW	150
Poe, Medina	N	×
Poetown, Brown	SW	25
Point Isabel, Clermont	SW	125
Point Pleasant, Clermont	SW	125
● *Point Pleasant*, Gallia	S	×
● *Point Pleasant*, Guernsey	E	295
Point Rock, Meigs	SE	25
Poland, Mahoning	NE	391
● Polk, Ashland	N	264
Polkadotte, Lawrence	S	30
Polo, Miami	W	×
● **Pomery**, Meigs	SE	4,726
Pond Run, Scioto	S	50
● *Pontiac*, Huron	N	×
Poplar, Crawford	N	150
Poplar Grove, Pike	S	25
Poplar Ridge, Darke	W	25
● Portage, Wood	NW	438
Portage Center, Hancock	NW	×
● **Port Clinton**, Ottawa	N	2,049
● *Porter*, Gallia	S	20
● *Porterfield*, Washington	SE	25
● Portersville, Perry	C	50
● Port Homer, Jefferson	E	20
Port Huron, Jefferson	E	×
Port Jefferson, Shelby	W	397
Portland, (see Oak Hill)		×
Portland, Meigs	SE	300
● Portland Station, Jeff'son	E	300
● **Portsmouth**, Scioto	S	12,394
● *Portsmouth Junc.* Scioto	S	×
● Port Union, Butler	SW	77
Port Washington, Tusc'was	E	487
Port William, Clinton	SW	196
● Post Boy, Tuscarawas	E	100
Potsdam, Miami	W	300
Potter, Delaware	C	25
● Pottersburgh, Union	C	50
Poulton, Monroe	E	4
● Powell, Delaware	C	300
● *Powell*, Muskingum	C	×
Powellsville, Scioto	S	100
Powhattan, Champaign	W	×
Powhattan Point, Belmont	E	300
● Prairie Depot, Wood	NW	400
Prairie View, (see Mutton J'k)		×
Prall, Brown	SW	×
Pratt, (see Port Jefferson)		×
● *Pratt's*, Hancock	NW	×
Pratt's Fork, Athens	SE	50
Prattsville, (see Lone Star)		×
● *Prentice*, Wood	NW	×
● Presque Isle, Lucas	NW	×
Preston, Hardin	W	300
Preston, Hamilton	SW	250
Preston, (see Adams' Mills)		×
Price Hill, Hamilton	SW	×
Pricetown, Highland	S	152
Pride, Ross	S	×
Primrose, Williams	NW	10
Princetown, (see Clawson)		×
● *Pritchard's*, Portage	NE	×
Proctorville, Lawrence	S	480
Prohibition, Guernsey	E	×
● Prospect, Marion	C	830
● Prout, Erie	N	300
Providence, (see G'd Rapids)		×
● *Pryor*, Monroe	E	50
● Pugh, Belmont	E	100
● Pulaski, Williams	NW	140
Pulaskiville, Morrow	C	60
Pulse, Highland	S	10
Purity, Licking	C	50
Pursell, Hocking	NW	×
Put-in-Bay, Ottawa	N	282
● *Putnam*, Muskingum	C	×
Pyrmont, Montgomery	W	200
Quaker Bottom, (see Proct'v'le)		×
● Quaker City, Guernsey	E	845
● Qualey, Washington	SE	×
Quarry, Monroe	E	5
● *Quarry Siding*, Erie	N	×
● Quincy, Logan	W	488
Quincy Station, (see Shields)		×
Raab, Lucas	NW	×
Raccoon Island, Gallia	S	×
Racine, Meigs	SE	453
● Radcliff, Vinton	S	200
● Radnor, Delaware	C	600
Rado, Noble	E	10
Ragersville, Tuscarawas	E	350
Rainbow, Washington	SE	2
● *Rainey's*, Belmont	E	×
Rainsborough, Highland	S	239
Ramage, Belmont	E	25
Ramey, Ashland	N	×
● Randall, Cuyahoga	NE	200
Randolph, Portage	NE	200
Range, Madison	C	100
Rankin's L'nd'g, (see Cr'n City)		×
Rapids, Portage	NE	250
Rappsburgh, Lawrence	S	500
● Rarden, Scioto	S	296
Ratcliffburgh, Vinton	S	×
● Rattlesnake, Fayette	S	×
● **Ravenna**, Portage	NE	41[illegible]
● Rawson, Hancock	NW	458
Rawsonville, (see Grafton)		×
● **Raymond's, Union**	C	250
Ray City, (see Climax)		×
● Ray's, Jackson	S	54
Reading, (see Homeworth)		×
● Reading, Hamilton	SW	2,68[illegible]
Rea's Run, (see Wade)		×
● Red Bank, Hamilton	SW	100
● Redfield, Perry	C	300
Red Haw, Ashland	N	150
Redington, Perry	C	×
Red Lion, Warren	SW	125
Red Oak, Brown	SW	100
Red River, Darke	W	50
● *Reece*, Williams	NW	×
● *Reed*, Perry	C	250
● *Reeds*, Carroll	E	×
Reedsburgh, Wayne	N	150
Reed's Mills, Jefferson	E	×
● *Reed's Run*, Tuscarawas	E	×
Reedsville, Meigs	SE	200
Reedtown, Seneca	N	75
● Reese's, Franklin	C	75
● Reeseville, Clinton	SW	245
Reform, Fairfield	C	×
Reform, Licking	C	×
Rehoboth, Perry	C	200
Reid's, Paulding	NW	60
Reiley, Butler	SW	190
Reinersville, Morgan	SE	100
● *Relief*, Huron	N	×
● Relief, Washington	SE	×
● Remington, Hamilton	SW	100
● Rempel, Jackson	S	×
Remson's Corners, Medina	N	100
● *Rendcomb Junction*, Hamilton	SW	×
● Rendville, Perry	C	859
Reno, Washington	SE	5
Renrock, Noble	E	35
● Republic, Seneca	N	584
Resaca, Madison	C	25
Reservoir, Perry	C	×
● *Reservoir*, Mercer	W	×
Reservoir, Logan	W	×
Reservoir, Summit	NE	×
Rest, Darke	W	×
Revenge, Fairfield	C	10
● Rex, Miami	W	25
● *Rexford*, Harrison	E	×
● *Reynolds*, Lake	NE	×
Reynoldsburgh, Franklin	C	393
● Rialto, Butler	SW	150
● *Riblet*, Richland	N	×
Rice, Putnam	NW	100
● Richards, Lucas	NW	50
● *Richard's Branch*, Stark	NE	×
● *Richey*, Van Wert	NW	×
Richfield, Summit	NE	50
Richfield Centre, Lucas	NW	100
● Rich Hill, Knox	C	200
● *Richland*, Clinton	SW	×
● *Richland*, Logan	W	×
● *Richland*, Richland	N	×
● Richland, Vinton	S	100
Richmond, (see Leon)		×
Richmond, Jefferson	E	444
Richmond, Lake	NE	250
Richmond Centre, Ash'ula	NE	100
● Richmond Dale, Ross	S	300
● *Richmond Junction*, Hamilton	SW	×
Rich Valley, Noble	E	1[illegible]
● Richville, Stark	NE	101
● Richwood, Union	C	1,415
● *Riddle's Run*, Jefferson	E	×
Ridge, Noble	E	1[illegible]
● *Ridge*, Hancock	NW	×
Ridgeland, Henry	NW	1[illegible]
Ridgeville, (see Sardis)		×
Ridgeville, Warren	SW	10[illegible]
Ridgeville Corners, Henry	NW	15[illegible]
● Ridgeway, Hardin	W	321
Riggs, Ashtabula	NE	×
● Rimer, Putnam	NW	10
Rinard's Mills, Monroe	E	25
Ringgold, Morgan	SE	50
Ring's Mills, (see Jolly)		×
Rio Grande, Gallia	S	125
● Riota, Preble	W	25
Ripley, Brown	SW	2,483
● *Ripley*, Huron	N	×
Ripleyville, Huron	N	100
● Rising Sun, Wood	NW	485
● Ritters, Fulton	NW	10
● Rittman, Wayne	N	150
● *River Bank*, Cuyahoga	NE	×
● *River Bridge*, Hancock	NW	×
Riverdale, Pike	S	25
● Riverside, Hamilton	SW	1,171
River Styx, Medina	N	100
Riverton, Jackson	S	25
Rives, Richland	N	×
Rix's Mills, Muskingum	C	100
● Roachton, Wood	NW	20
● *Robbins*, Pike	S	50
● Robertsville, Stark	NE	200
Robins, Guernsey	E	300
● *Robinson*, Crawford	N	×
Robinson, Logan	W	25
● *Roby's Siding*, Huron	N	×
● Rochester, Lorain	N	218
Rochester, (see Navarre)		×
Rochester, (see Morrow)		×
Rock, Tuscarawas	E	25
● Rockaway, Seneca	N	25
● Rockbridge, Hocking	S	×
Rock Camp, Lawrence	S	200
Rock Creek, Ashtabula	NE	448
● Rock Creek Sta., Ashtab'a	NE	×
● *Rock Cut*, Muskingum	C	×
● *Rockdale*, Butler	SW	×

Place	Pop.
● Rockford, Mercer....... W	1,150
Rockhill, (see Kennon)	×
Rock House, Hocking......S	×
Rockland, Washington.... SE	150
Rock Mills, Fayette......... S	75
● Rockport, Cuyahoga.... NE	1,101
● *Rockport Sta.*, Cuyahoga NE	×
● *Rock Run*, Coshocton C	×
Rock Springs, (see Pomeroy).	×
Rockville, Adams........... S	150
● *Rockville*, Meigs.........SE	×
Rockville, (see Rural Dale)...	×
● *Rockwell*, Wood........NW	×
Rockwood, Lawrence....... S	100
● *Rocky Ford*, Clermont..SW	×
Rocky Fork, Licking....... C	25
Rocky Hill, Jackson........ S	25
● Rocky Ridge, Ottawa.....N	463
Rocky River, Cuyahoga... NE	300
Rodney, Gallia............ S	50
● Rogers, Columbiana.... NE	100
Rogersville, (see East Carmel)	×
Rogersville, (see Ragersville).	×
Rokeby Lock, Morgan...... SE	18
Rollersville, Sandusky......N	120
● Rome, Ashtabula........NE	150
Rome, Adams............... S	300
Rome, Franklin............C	84
Rootstown, Portage.......NE	200
● *Rootstown*, Portage.....NE	×
Roscoe, Coshocton..........C	800
Rosebud, Gallia............S	100
Rosedale, Gallia............S	100
Rosedale, Madison.......... C	200
Rosedale, Montgomery.....W	×
Rose Farm, Morgan....... SE	×
Rose Hill, Drake.......... W	70
● Rosemont, Mahoning... NE	200
● **Roseville, Muskingum** ...C	**714**
Ross, Butler..............SW	400
Rosseau, Morgan.......... SE	50
Ross Lake, Hamilton.......SW	×
● Rossmoyne, Hamilton.. SW	×
● *Rossville*, Darke..........W	254
Roughtonville, Huron...... N	×
Round Bottom, Monroe.....E	10
Roundhead, Hardin........ W	275
Rowenton, Ashtabula.......NE	×
Roweville, (see Baltic)........	×
Rowland, Morgan..........SE	10
Rowlesville, Gallia........ S	15
Rows, Ashland.............N	250
● Roxabell, Ross.............S	100
● Roxanna, Greene........ W	×
● Roxbury, Morgan....... SE	25
Royal, Vinton..............S	×
● *Royal*, Tuscarawas..........E	×
● *Royal Siding*, Clarke.... W	×
Royalton, (see North Royalton)	×
Royalton, Fairfield.......C	163
● *Royersville*, Lawrence......S	×
Rudden, Fairfield..........C	×
Rudolph, Wood..........NW	50
● Rue, Vinton...............S	×
Ruggles, Ashland...........N	100
● *Ruggles Station*, Ashland. N	×
Rumley, (see New Rumley) ..	×
Rural, (see Smith's Landing).	×
Rural Dale, Muskingum.....C	100
Rush, Tuscarawas...........E	10
Rush Creek, Union..........C	100
● Rushmore, Putnam.... NW	180
● *Rush Road*, Lake.......NE	×
● Rush Run, Jefferson...... E	100
● *Rush's*, Darke.......... W	×
● Rushsylvania, Logan..... W	497
● Rushtown, Scioto.......... S	25
● Rushville, Fairfield....... C	291
Russell, Geauga..........NE	500
● Russell, Highland........ S	200
Russell, (see Amwell)........	×
Russell's Place, Lawrence...S	100
Russellville, Brown.......SW	324
● Russia, Shelby.......... W	100
Ruth, Marion..............C	×
Ruthven, Jefferson.........E	×
● Rutland, Meigs.......... SE	300
Ryansville, Lawrence........S	25
Ryon, Scioto...............S	25
● Sabina, Clinton........ SW	1,080
● *Sage*, Hardin............W	×
Sago, Muskingum...........C	150
Saint Bernard, Hamilton. SW	1,779
Saint Charles, Butler......SW	×
Saint Clair, Columbiana...NE	150
● *Saint Clair*, Muskingum..C	×
● **St. Clairsville**, Belmont E	1,191
● *St. Clairsville Jc.*, Belmont E	×
Saint Clairsville Jc., Belmont E	×
● Saint Henry's, Mercer.... W	700
● Saint James, Morrow..... C	300
Saint John's, Auglaize......W	350
Saint Joseph's, Perry....... C	50
● *Saint Joseph's*, Hamilton SW	×
● Saint Louisville, Licking..C	264
Saint Martin's, Brown.... SW	160
● Saint Mary's, Auglaize... W	3,000
Saint Nicholas, (see Berwick)	×
● Saint Paris, Champaign.. W	1,145
Saint Paul's, Pickaway......C	15
Saint Peters, Mercer....... W	10
Saint Rosa, Mercer........ W	50
● Saint Stephen, Seneca.... N	25
● Salem, Columbiana..... NE	5,780
Salem, (see Annapolis).......	×
Salem, (see Lower Salem)....	×
Salem, Montgomery...... ..W	400
Salem Centre, Meigs.........SE	50
● *Salem Pike*, Montgomery W	×
● Salesville, Guernsey...... E	296
● Salina, Athens............ SE	120
● Salineville, Columbiana. NE	2,369
Salt Air, Clermont........SW	20
Saltillo, Holmes.............C	50
● *Saltillo*, Perry............C	150
Saltpetre, Washington..... SE	50
● *Salt Run*, Jefferson.......E	×
Samantha, Highland.........S	250
Sample, Mahoning......... NE	10
● Samsonville, Jackson......S	30
● *Sand Bank*, Hamilton.. SW	×
Sand Fork, Gallia........... S	30
Sand Hill, Erie.............N	50
Sand Hollow, Morgan..... SE	10
● Sandrun, Hocking..........S	100
● *Sandrun Junc.*, Hocking. S	×
● *Sandstone*, Fairfield......C	×
● **Sandusky**, Erie.......... N	18,471
● *Sandusky River*, Wyandot N	×
● Sandyville, Tuscarawas... E	300
● *Sanitarium*, Hamilton..SW	×
Sant, Vinton...............S	50
Santa Fe, Logan............W	25
● Sarahsville, Noble........ E	306
● Sardinia, Brown......... SW	600
Sardis, Monroe...............E	400
● *Sargents*, Pike.............S	25
Sater, Hamilton...........SW	×
Saundersville, Gallia....... S	100
Savannah, Ashland......... N	325
Savannah, (see Guysville) ..	×
● *Savona*, Darke............W	×
Saxon, Meigs...............SE	30
● Saybrook, Ashtabula....NE	350
● Sayre, Perry............. C	×
● *Schenck*, Butler.........SW	15
● Schooley, Ross.............. S	15
● Schumm, Van Wert....NW	25
● Scio, Harrison............ E	616
Scioto, Scioto...............S	200
● Scioto Furnace, Scioto.... S	100
● Sciotoville, Scioto......... S	986
● *Sciotoville Junc.*, Scioto....S	×
● Scipio Siding, Seneca..... N	25
Scipio, (see Philanthropy)......	×
Scofield, Brown............SW	×
Scotch Ridge, Wood......NW	200
● Scott, Van Wert.........NW	733
● *Scott*, Carroll.............. E	×
● *Scott*, Noble.............. E	×
● Scott's Crossing, Allen.NW	12
● *Scotts Lan'g*, Washingt'n SE	×
● *Scott's Mines*, Guernsey... E	100
Scott Town, Lawrence.......S	100
Scott Town, Marion.........C	120
Scott Town, (see Wingett Run)	×
● Scroggsfield, Carroll......E	25
Scrub, Adams...............S	×
Scudder, Mercer...........W	10
Seal, Wyandot............. N	×
● *Sealover*, Muskingum.....C	×
● *Seaman*, Adams...........S	30
● *Seawright*, Muskingum...C	×
Sebastain, Mercer.......... W	10
Sedalia, Madison............ C	225
● Sedamsville, Hamilton..SW	×
Sedan, Scioto...............S	35
Sedgwick, Lawrence.........S	×
Seeceder's Cors., Trumbull NE	×
Seelyville, (see Wood Grove).	×
● *Segars*, Hancock.......NW	×
Sego, Perry..................C	40
● Sekitan, Hamilton......SW	723
● Selden, Fayette.......... S	200
Selig, Adams................S	25
● Selma, Clarke...........W	255
● Seman, Adams............S	80
● *Semple*, Lorain........... N	×
● *Seneca*, Seneca........... N	×
● Senecaville, Guernsey.... E	461
Sentinel, Ashtabula....... NE	59
Seth, Clarke................W	25
● Seven Mile, Butler......SW	288
● *Seven Mile Siding*, Franklin C	×
● Seville, Midina............N	599
Seward, Fulton...........NW	85
Sewellsville, Belmont....... E	538
● Shackelton, Highland..... S	25
Shade, Athens............. SE	100
Shade River, Meigs........SE	×
Shadeville, Franklin.........C	200
Shady Grove, Fayette........S	20
● *Shady Side*, Belmont.....E	×
● *Shafers Siding*, Richland.N	×
● *Shaffer's*, Mercer......... W	×
Shaler's Mills, Knox........C	200
Shalersville, Portage......NW	200
Shane Crossing, Mercer.....W	993
Shanghai, (see McCoy's Sta).	×
Shanesville, Tuscarawas.....E	600
Shannon, Coshocton........ C	×
● *Shannon's Run*, Jefferson E	×
Sharon, (see Oakland)	×
Sharon, Noble...............E	275
● Sharon Centre, Medina...N	300
Sharonville, Pike.............S	100
● Sharonville, Hamilton.. SW	713
● Sharpsburgh, Athens.... SE	30
● *Sharpsburgh Junc.*, At'ns SE	×
Sharpsville, (see Willettville).	×
● Shasta, Van Wert...... NW	10
Shattuc, Clarke........... W	×
Shauck's, Morrow...........C	300
● Shawnee, Perry............C	3,266
● *Shawnee*, Allen........ NW	×
● *Shawnee Junc.*, Morgan.SE	×
● Shawtown, Hancock... NW	160
● *Shawville*, Lorain.........N	50
● *Sheatenhelms*, Seneca.... N	×
Sheep Run, Brown........SW	20
Sheffield, (see North Sheffield)	×
● Sheffield, Lorain..........N	25
Sheimersburg, (see New Prospect)	×
● Shelby, Richland.......... N	1,977
● *Shelby Junc.*, Richland.. N	×
Sheldon, Vinton............S	×
● *Sheley's*, Adams.......... S	×
Shell, Adams...............S	15
Shenandoah, Richland......N	60
Shenbarger's, Ashland......N	×
● Shepard, Franklin........ C	50
Shepherdstown, Belmont... E	40
● *Sheppard's Ridge*, Muskin'm C	×
Sheridan, Putnam.........NW	20
Sheridan Coal Works, La'ce..S	200
Sherman, Ashtabula......NE	×
● Sherman, Summit....... NE	100
● Sherodsville, Carroll...... E	893
Sherritt's, Lawrence..........S	20
● Sherwood, Defiance.... NW	541
● Shields, Belmont..........E	300
● Shiloh, Richland...........N	644
● Shinrock, Erie............N	75
Ship, Ashtabula............NE	×
Short Creek, Harrison...... E	200
● *Shoup's*, Greene..........W	10
● Shreve, Wayne.......... N	1,012
Shrimp, Adams............. S	×
Shyville, Pike............... S	25
● Siam, Seneca............. N	200
Sicily, Highland.............. S	20
● *Sicily Station*, Highland.. S	×
● *Siding Forty-Eight*, St'k NE	×
● *Siding Seventy*, Stark....NE	×
● *Siding Ten*, Cuyahoga.. NE	×
● *Siding Twenty-Eight*, Portage.............NE	×
● **Sidney**, Shelby......... W	4,850
● Signal, Columbiana..... NE	25
● Silver Creek, Hardin.....W	150
● *Silver Creek*, Medina..... N	×
Silver Hill, Wayne..........N	×
● *Silver Lake*, Logan........W	×
● Silverton, Hamilton......SW	150
Silverwood, Hancock.....NW	10
● Simons, Ashtabula.....NE	100
Simonsons, Hamilton......SW	×
● *Simpsons*, Jackson........S	×
Siney, Fulton..............NW	10
Sinking Spring, Highland...S	300
Sioux, Pike.................S	10

● Sippo, Stark ... NE 15
Sites, Hamilton ... SW ×
Sitka, Washington ... SE 100
Siverly, Vinton ... S 30
Six Points, Wood ... NW 25
● *Sixteen Mile Siding*, Crawford ... N ×
Sixteen Mile Stand, H'm'n SW 35
Skeel's Cross Roads, Mercer W 25
● *Skelley's*, Jefferson ... E 10
Skullfork, Guernsey ... E ×
● Slate Mills, Ross ... S 35
Slater, Gallia ... S ×
● *Slick*, Marion ... C ×
Sligo, (see Ogden) ... ×
Sligo, Guernsey ... E ×
Sloan's Station, (see Toronto) ×
● *Slocum's*, Scioto ... S ×
Slope, Trumbull ... NE ×
Slough, Fairfield ... C 25
Smalles, Morrow ... C ×
● *Smart's Spur*, Sandusky. N ×
Smeltzer's Mills, (see Wigner) ×
Smiley, Paulding ... NW 125
Smithfield, Jefferson ... E 639
Smithfield Station, (see Beloit) ×
Smith, Butler ... SW ×
Smith Road, Medina ... N 25
Smith's Landing, Clermont SW 90
● *Smiths*, Muskingum ... SW ×
● Smithville, Wayne ... N 482
Smithville, Wayne ... N ×
Smock, Hocking ... S ×
Smyrna, Harrison ... E 125
● *Sniders*, Fairfield ... C ×
● Snodes, Mahoning ... NE 10
● *Snow Fork Junc.*, Ath's. SE ×
Snowville, Meigs ... SE 25
Snyder, Hamilton ... SW ×
● *Snyders*, Clarke ... W 10
● *Snyders*, Wyandot ... N ×
● Socialville, Warren ... SW 75
Sodaville, (see Mineral Springs) ×
Sodom, Trumbull ... NE 150
● *Soldier's Home*, Erie ... N ×
● *Soldiers' Home Junc.*, Montgomery ... W 4,468
● Solon, Cuyahoga ... NE 300
● Somerdale, Tuscarawas ... E 250
Somerford, Madison ... C 282
Somers, Hancock ... NW ×
● Somerset, Perry ... C 1,127
Somersville, Union ... C 140
Somerton, Belmont ... E 250
● Somerville, Butler ... SW 330
● Sonora, Muskingum ... C 200
South Arlington, (see Vorhees) ×
● *South Akron*, Summit ... NE ×
South Belmont, (see Bellaire) ×
● *South Bantam*, Clerm't SW ×
South Bloomfield, Pick'ay.. C 272
South Bloomingville, Hock'g S 200
South Brooklyn, Cuyahoga. NE 900
● South Charleston, Clarke. W 1,041
***South Cleveland*, Cuyahoga NE** ×
● *South Cummingsville*, Hamilton ... SW ×
● *South Depot*, Franklin ... C ×
South Elmwood, Pickaway. C ×
South Euclid, Cuyahoga ... NE 300
● South Fincastle, Brown SW 50
Southington, Trumbull ... NE 100
South Kirtland, Lake ... NE 470
● South Lebanon, Warren SW 500
South Mantun Corner, Portage ... NE ×
● *South Milford*, Clermont SW ×
● *South Newark*, Licking ... C ×
South Newbury, Geauga.. NE 150
South New Lyme, Asht'la. NE 1,000
South Norwood, Hamilton SW ×
● South Olive, Noble ... E 150
South Park, Cuyahoga ... NE ×
South Perry, Hocking ... S 200
South Plymouth, (see Milledgeville) ... ×
South Point, Lawrence ... S 300
South Ridge, Ashtabula ... NE 200
South Salem, Ross ... S 263
● *Southside*, Hamilton ... SW ×
● South Solon, Madison ... C 345
South Thompson, Geauga. NE 90
South Toledo, (see Maumee). ×
South Warsaw, Allen ... NW 50
● South Webster, Scioto ... S 323
South Woodbury, (see Benning'n) ×
● Southworth, Allen ... NW 50

● South Zanesville, Musk'vm C ×
● *Spafford*, Shelby ... W ×
Spanker, Montgomery ... W 150
Spann, Clermont ... SW ×
Sparta, Morrow ... C 216
● *Sparta*, Stark ... NE 200
● *Spaulding's*, Jefferson ... E ×
Spear's Land, (see Houston). ×
Specht, Carroll ... E ×
● Spencer, Medina ... N 200
Spencer Mills, (see Spencer).. ×
● *Spencer*, Lucas ... NW ×
● Spencer's Sta., Guernsey.. E 60
Spencer Sta., (see Cozaddale). ×
● Spencerville, Allen ... NW 1,266
● Spokane, Trumbull ... NE ×
● Spore, Crawford ... N ×
● *Spout Spring*, Ross ... S ×
Sprague, Monroe ... E 10
● Spratt, Muskingum ... C 25
Springborough, Warren.. SW 413
Spring Dale, Hamilton ... SW 400
Spring Dale, Washington.. SE 10
Springer, Jackson ... S ×
● **Springfield**, Clarke ... W 31,895
● *Springfield Sta.*, Clarke.. W ×
Spring Grove, (see Winton Pl.) ×
Spring Hill, Franklin ... C ×
Spring Hills, Champaign ... W 158
Spring Lake, Williams ... NW 30
Spring Mills, Richland ... N 60
Spring Mountain, Cosho'n.. C 100
● Spring Valley, Greene ... W 538
Springville, Wayne ... N 100
Sprinklers Mills, Gallia ... S 25
Sprucevale, Columbiana ... NE 35
Stafford, Monroe ... E 350
● *Standing Stone*, Monroe.. E ×
Stanhope, Ashtabula ... NE ×
● *Stanhope*, Trumbull ... NE ×
● *Stanley*, Henry ... NW 50
Stanley, Putnam ... NW 10
● Stanleyville, Wash'ton ... SE 60
Stantontown, Morrow ... C 50
● *Starch Factory*, Franklin. C ×
● *Starkey*, Monroe ... E ×
● Starr, Hocking ... S 100
Startle, Jefferson ... E ×
● *State Fair Grounds*, Fr'k'n C ×
● *State Line*, Trumbull ... NE ×
● State Road, Trumbull ... NE ×
State Soldiers' Home, Erie.. N ×
● Station B, Cuyahoga ... NE ×
● Station 15, Harrison ... E 66
Staunton, Fayette ... S 200
Steamburgh, Ashtabula ... NE 100
Steam Corners, Morrow ... C 50
● *Steamtown*, Noble ... E ×
Steamtown, (see Woodworth) ×
Stedeke, Mercer ... W ×
● Steece, Lawrence ... S 25
Steel, Belmont ... E 25
Steel Run, Washington ... SE 4
Stella, Vinton ... S 25
● *Steinmans*, Mercer ... W ×
Steinsberger, Champaign ... W ×
● Stelvideo, Darke ... W 75
Stephens, Adams ... S 30
● Sterling, Wayne ... N 300
Steuben, Huron ... N 900
● **Steubenville**, Jefferson E 13,394
Stevens, Allen ... NW ×
● *Steward*, Allen ... NW 10
● Stewart, Athens ... SE 200
● *Stewart Junction*, Athens SE ×
● *Stewart's Furnace*, Tr'm'l NE ×
● Stewartsville, Belmont ... E 200
● Still Water, Tuscarawas ... E 15
● *Stillwater Junc.*, Mont'y. W 50
Stilwell, Holmes ... C 50
● *Stiles*, Hamilton ... SW ×
● Stockport, Morgan ... SE 416
● Stockton, Butler ... SW 50
Stockwells, Wood ... NW 50
● *Stock Yards*, Hamilton. SW ×
● *Stokes*, Warren ... SW ×
● *Stone*, Muskingum ... C 200
● Stone Creek, Tuscarawas.. E 200
Stone Lick, Clermont ... SW 150
● *Stone Track*, Delaware ... C ×
● Stony Ridge, Wood ... NW 150
● Storms, Ross ... S 25
● *Storrs*, Hamilton ... SW ×
Stout's, Adams ... S ×
● Stoutsville, Fairfield ... C 282
● Stovertown, Muskingum.. C 75
Stow Corners, Summit ... NE 100
● *Strakers*, Darke ... W ×

● Strasburgh, Tuscarawas ... E 225
Strasburg, (see Mowrystown) ×
Strasburg, (see Maximo) ... ×
Stratford, Delaware ... C 100
● *Streetsboro*, Portage ... NW ×
Streetsborough, Portage. NW 200
Stringtown, Brown ... SW 10
String Town, Pickaway ... C 100
Strongsville, Cuyahoga ... NE 250
● Struthers, Mahoning ... NE 250
● Stryker, Williams ... NW 1,017
● *Stuartsville*, Hancock.. NW 15
Success, Meigs ... SE ×
Suffield, Portage ... NW 150
○ *Suffield Station*, Portage NW ×
● Sugar Creek, Tuscarawas.. E 150
● Sugar Grove, Fairfield ... C 275
● *Sugar Grove*, Miami ... W ×
● Sugar Ridge, Wood ... NW 150
Sugartree, Guernsey ... E 50
Sugar Tree Ridge, Highl'd ... S 200
Suiter, Lawrence ... S 25
● Sullivan, Ashland ... N 100
● *Sullivants*, Franklin ... C ×
Sulphur Grove, Montg'y ... W 100
Sulphur Lick, Ross ... S ×
Sulphur Springs, Crawford.. N 500
● Summerfield, Noble ... E 582
Summerford, Madison ... C 500
● Summerside, Clermont. SW ×
● *Summit*, Clermont ... SW ×
Summit, Summit ... NE 100
○ *Summit*, Medina ... N ×
● *Summit*, Miami ... W ×
● Summit Hill, Ross ... S 25
● *Summit Grove*, Hamil'n. SW 200
● *Summit Grade Siding*, C's'n C ×
● Summit Station, Licking.. C ×
● *Summit Siding*, Hocking.. S 20
● *Summit Siding*, Holmes.. C ×
● *Summit Switch*, Franklin C ×
● *Summit Switch*, Jackson.. S ×
● Summitville, Columbi'a. NE 50
Sumner, Meigs ... SE 125
● Sunbury, Delaware ... C 475
Sunbury, (see Germantown). ×
● Sun Dale, Muskingum ... C 50
● *Sunfish*, Monroe ... E ×
Sunside, Trumbull ... NE ×
Sunfish Lot No. 6, (see Fr'k'n) ×
Sunshine, Brown ... SW ×
Superior, Trumbull ... NE ×
● *Superior Mine*, Athens.. SE ×
Surprise, Morrow ... C 20
Surryville, Brown ... SW 40
Sutton, Guernsey ... E 25
● *Swain's Siding*, Vinton.. S 125
Swan, Hocking ... S 125
Swan Creek, Gallia ... S 25
● *Swander*, Seneca ... N 27
● Swander's Cross'g, Shelby. W 100
● Swanton, Fulton ... NW 508
Swartz, Hocking ... S ×
Swazey, Monroe ... E ×
Sweden, Ashtabula ... NE 1,844
Sweet Wine, Hamilton ... SW 40
● Swifts, Washington ... SE 18
Swiftsville, (see Leo) ... ×
● *Swings*, Clermont ... SW ×
Swissheim, Highland ... S ×
Switzer, Monroe ... E 15
Sybene, Lawrence ... S ×
● Sycamore, Wyandot ... N 722
Sycamore Valley, Monroe.. E 10
Sylvania, (see Fredonia) ... ×
● Sylvania, Lucas ... NW 545
Sylvia, (see Patterson) ... ×
● Symmes, Hamilton ... SW 100
● Symmes' Corner, Butler. SW 100
Symmes' Creek, (see Roc'wd).. ×
Syracuse, Meigs ... SE 1,256
Tabor, Carroll ... E ×
Tacoma, Belmont ... E 150
● Tadmor, Montgomery ... W 170
Talaho, (see McCuneville)... ×
● Tallmadge, Summit ... NE 400
● Tamah, Mercer ... W 53
Tappan, Harrison ... E 150
Tariff, (see Okeana) ... ×
Tarlton, Pickaway ... C 448
Tawawa, Shelby ... W 200
Taylor, Geauga ... NE ×
● *Taylors*, Franklin ... C 80
Taylorsburgh, Montgomery W 25
Taylor's Creek, Hamilton. SW 25
● *Taylorsville*, Highland ... S 75
Taylorsville, (see Tadmore).. ×

Place	Pop.
Taylorskille, Muskingum...C	631
● Tecumseh, Darke........ W	50
Ted, Wood...............NW	100
Tedrow, Fulton...........NW	200
● Teegarden, Columbiana. NE	50
Teemes, Sandusky.......... N	10
Temperanceville, Belmont.. E	100
Temple, Lake.............NE	×
● *Terra Alta*, Hamilton.. SW	×
● Terrace Park, Hamilton SW	200
Terre Haute, Champaign...W	125
● *Texas*, Crawford......... N	×
Texas, Henry............NW	160
Texas, Monroe.............E	20
Texas Hollow, Lawrence....S	10
Thatcher, Pickaway.........C	×
● The Bend, Defiance..... NW	100
● *The Cabin*, Belmont...... E	×
● *Thirty Five Mile Siding*, Seneca.................. N	×
Thivener, Gallia............S	125
Thomastown, Summit.....NE	350
Thompson, Geauga.........NE	175
Thompson, (see West Lodi)...	×
● *Thornburgh*, Cuyahoga. NE	×
Thorndyke, Portage.......NW	×
● *Thorn Hill*, Mahoning..NE	109
● Thornport, Perry......... C	50
Thornville, Perry............C	405
● *Thorps*, Clarke...........W	×
● *Three Locks*, Ross........ S	×
● *Thrifton*, Ross............S	×
Thrifton, Highland..........S	25
● Thrifton, Ross.............S	×
Thurman, Gallia.............S	300
● Thurston, Fairfield........C	213
● **Tiffin**, Seneca............N	10,801
Tiger, Mahoning...........NE	×
Tileton, Shelby............W	100
● Tiltonsville, Jefferson.....E	300
Timberville, Paulding....NW	10
● *Tinker's Creek*, Cuyah'gaNE	×
Tinney, Sandusky............N	25
● Tippecanoe, Harrison.....E	300
● Tippecanoe City, Miami..W	1,465
● *Tippecanoe Shaft*, MahoningNE	×
Tipton, Paulding......... NW	10
● Tiro, Crawford........... N	400
TivertonCentre, (seeYankeeRdge)	×
● Tobasco, Clermont......SW	130
● *Tobasco Junc.*, ClermontSW	×
● Tobasco, Licking..........C	75
● *Tod Branch Jc.*, SummitNE	×
Todd's, Morgan............SE	10
● Tokio, Van Wert.......NW	25
● **TOLEDO**, Lucas.......NW	81,434
● *Toledo Junc.*, Richland.. N	×
● Tontogany, Wood........NW	175
Tope's Mills, (see Algonquin).	×
● Torch, Athens............SE	150
● Toronto, Jefferson.........E	3,500
Townfork, Jefferson.........E	25
Townline, Wood...........NW	×
● *Tower Hill*, Hamilton.. SW	×
● Townsend, Sandusky..... N	10
● Townwood, Putnam.....NW	12
● *Tracey*, Brown......... SW	×
● Tracy, Tuscarawas........ E	158
Tradersville, Madison.......C	100
Trail, Holmes...............C	25
Trail Run, Monroe......... E	25
Tranquilty, Adams.......... S	25
Transit, Hamilton..........SW	50
● *Trautman's*, Hamilton. SW	65
● Trebien's, Greene.......... W	50
Tremainsville, Lucas.....NW	×
● *Tremont*, Clarke..........W	279
Tremont City, Clarke.......W	279
● Trenton, Butler.........SW	360
Trenton, (see Tuscarawas)...	×
● *Trenton Pike*, Butler...SW	×
● Triadelphia, Morgan.....SE	50
● Trimble, Athens.........SE	440
Trimble's Bridge, (seeWaverly)	×
● Trinway, Muskingum.....C	300
Trio City, (see Junction City).	×
Triumph, Trumbull.......NE	×
● Trombley, Wood........ NW	75
● Trotwood, Montgomery..W	200
● Trowbridge, Ottawa...... N	75
Troy, (see Nova)............	×
Troy, (see Welchfield)	×
● **Troy**, Miami............ W	4,494
Trumbull, Ashtabula......NE	100
● Truro, Franklin...........C	×
Tubbsville, Henry........ NW	10
Tucson, Ross...............S	×

Place	Pop.
Tuel's Landing, (see Fly).....	×
Tully, Van Wert..........NW	×
Tunget Station, Allen.....NW	×
● Tunnel, Washington.....SE	25
● Tunnel Hill, Coshocton....C	50
TunnelHill, (seeMitchell'sSaltWks)	×
● *Tunnel Hill*, Monroe..... E	×
● *Tunnel Number One*, Lawrence.................. S	×
● *Tunnel NumberOne*, PerryC	×
● *TunnelNumberTwo*, PerryC	×
● *Tunnel Siding*, Perry.....C	×
Tunnelson, Vinton..........S	×
● *Tunnel Switch*, TuscarawasE	×
Tupper's Plains, Meigs.....SE	100
Turkey, (see Home)..........	×
Turkey, Highland............S	×
● *Turkey FootJc.*, SummitNE	×
● *Turner*, Tuscarawas...... E	200
Turner's Mills, Lorain..... N	×
● *Turtle Creek*, Warren...SW	206
● Tuscarawas, Tuscarawas. E	391
● *Tuscarawas*, Tuscarawas.E	×
● *Tusculum*, Hamilton... SW	×
Twenty Mile Stand, WarrenSW	50
Twilight, Monroe............E	×
Twin, Preble............. W	×
● Twinsburgh, Summit...NW	200
Tycoon, Gallia..............S	25
Tylerstown, (see Lake Fork).	×
Tylersville, Butler........ SW	×
Tymochtee, Wyandotte.....N	×
● Tyner, Guernsey..........E	×
Tyrone, Coshocton...........C	×
● Tyrrell Hill, Trumbull.. NE	75
● Uhrichsville, Tuscarawas. E	3,842
● Union, Montgomery......W	350
● *Union City*, Darke........W	1,293
Unionndale, (see Cadiz).......	×
● Union Furnace, Hocking. .S	200
Union Landing, (seeGrandview)	×
Union Plains, Brown......SW	100
● Unionport, Jefferson..... E	200
● Union Station, Licking....C	50
Uniontown, Belmont.........E	250
Uniontown, (see Fultonham).	×
Uniontown, (see Lake).......	×
● Union Vale, Harrison .... E	×
Union Village, Warren....SW	200
● Unionville, Lake.........NE	500
Unionville, (see Meigsville)...	×
● Unionville Centre, Union. C	231
Uniopolis, Auglaize........ W	170
Unity, Columbiana........NE	108
Uno, Shelby..................W	×
Updegraff, Jefferson..........E	25
● *UpperGravelHill*, BelmontE	×
● **UpperSandusky**, Wy'd'tN	3,572
Upshur, Preble............ W	×
Ural, Vinton...............S	25
● **Urbana**, Champaign....W	6,510
● Utica, Licking............C	763
● Utley, Athens........... SE	300
Utopia, Clermont......... SW	50
Vale's Mills, Vinton.........S	87
Valley, Columbiana........NE	25
● *Valley Crossing*, FranklinC	×
● *Valley Crossing*, Stark. NE	×
Valley Ford, Meigs........ SE	30
● *Valley House*, Preble....W	×
● *Valley Junc.*, Hamilton SW	×
● *Valley Junc.*, Tuscarawas E	100
● *Valley Mill*, Mahoning. NE	×
● *Valley Mills*, Greene.... W	×
● Vallonia, Belmont.........E	×
● Vanatta, Licking..........C	150
● Van Buren, Hancock...NW	268
Vanceton, Gallia............ S	25
Vandalia, Montgomery.....W	265
Vanderhoof, Athens.......SE	25
● Vanlue, Hancock...... NW	352
Van's Valley, Delaware..... C	35
Vanville, Logan.............W	10
● **Van Wert**, Van Wert NW	5,512
● *Vance's*, Ross ....S	×
● *Vaughn's*, Jackson ....S	50
● Vaughnsville, Putnam..NW	100
● Venedocia, Van Wert....W	200
● Venice, Erie..... ....N	180
Venice, Butler...............SW	350
● *Venice Switch*, Erie......N	×
Vera Cruz, Brown ....SW	60
● Vermillion, Erie..........N	1,200
● *Vermillion Station*, Erie.N	×
Vernon, Richland.......... N	60
Vernon, Trumbull.......... NE	300
● Vernon Junc. Richland...N	250

Place	Pop.
Verona, (see West Baltimore)	×
● Versailles, Darke........ W	1,385
Vester, Summit...........NE	×
● Vesuvius, Lawrence.......S	100
Veto, Washington......... SE	25
● Vickery, Sandusky ....N	50
Victor, Mahoning..........NE	200
Victor, Scioto................S	×
Victoria, Mercer ....W	25
● *Vienna*, Clinton......... SW	878
● Vienna, Trumbull ....NE	800
Vienna Cross Roads, ClarkeW	250
● Vigo, Ross................S	120
Villa, Clarke...............W	×
● Vincent, Washington....SE	100
Vine, Darke.................W	50
● *Vins Cliff*, Jefferson.......E	×
Vineyard Hill, Adams.......S	125
● Vinton, Gallia.............S	318
VintonFurnace, (seeV't'nSta)	×
● Vinton Station, Vinton....S	60
Violet, Mercer............ W	25
● *Violet*, Ottawa............N	×
Virgin, Washington ....SE	×
Vorhees, Montgomery..... W	150
● *Vorhies*, Noble...........E	×
Wabash, Mercer............W	75
Waco, Stark.............. NE	×
Wade, Washington.........SE	50
● *Wades*, Hamilton.......SW	×
● Wadsworth, Medina......N	1,574
Waggoner's Ripple, Adams. .S	25
● *Wagon Works*, Lucas..NW	×
● *Wagon Works Junction*, Lucas...............NW	×
Wagram, Licking........... C	35
● Wait's, Scioto ....S	25
Wakatomika, Coshocton.... C	75
● Wakefield, Pike...........S	100
● Wakeman, Huron.........N	700
Wakeup, Athens............SE	10
● Walbridge, Wood...... NW	250
Waldo, Marion..............C	151
Wales, Gallia.................S	60
Walhonding, Coshocton.....C	150
Walker's, Columbiana.... NE	50
Wallace Mills, Scioto........S	40
Waller, Ross................ S	250
Wallsburgh, Brown.......SW	30
Walnut, Pickaway...........C	×
Walnut Creek, Holmes.......C	150
Walnut Grove, Logan...... W	50
● Walnut Hills, Hamilton.SW	×
Walnut Run, Madison.......C	200
● *Walsen's Curve*, Perry....C	×
Walton, Fayette............S	×
Wamsley, Adams ....S	100
Wanamaker, Monroe.......E	×
● **Wapakoneta**, AuglaizeW	3,616
Ward, Washington.........SE	25
● *Wardens*, Ottawa ....N	×
● *Ward's*, Putnam.........NW	×
● *Ward' Crossing*, C'h'ga. NE	×
Warfel, Harrison........... E	×
Warmington, (see Massillon)	×
● Warner, Washington......SE	100
● Warnock, Belmont ....E	150
● **Warren**, Trumbull....NE	5,973
Warrensburgh, Delaware... C	30
Warrensville, Cuyahoga...NE	×
Warrenton, Jefferson.......E	300
● Warsaw, Coshocton.......C	376
● *Warwick*, Summit.........NE	×
Washington, (seeWash't'nv'e)	×
Washington, Guernsey......E	546
● **WashingtonC.H.**, F'y'eS	5,742
● *Washington*, Hardin.....W	×
● *Washington*, Jackson.....S	×
● Washingtonville, Col'na NE	1,500
Wassie, Trumbull...........NE	×
Waterford, (see Levering)....	×
● Waterford, Washington.SE	120
Waterloo, Lawrence.........S	125
Waterloo, Fairfield.........C	146
Waterloo, Fayette...........S	250
Watertown, Washington...SE	250
● Waterville, Lucas....... NW	586
● *Watheys*, Carroll.........E	×
Watkins, Union.............C	70
● Watson, Seneca...........N	25
Watt Farm, Allen........NW	×
Wattsville, Carroll.......... E	40
● *Wattsville Station*, CarrollE	×
● **Wauseon**, Fulton....NW	2,060
● **Waverly**, Pike.........S	1,567
Way, Monroe...............E	20
Wayne, (see Lindenville)	×

● Wayne, Wayne............N 100
● Waynesburgh, Stark....NE 510
Waynesfield, Auglaize......W 480
Waynesville, Warren......SW 704
● *Waynesville Sta.* War'nSW ×
● *Wayton*, Hancock......NW ×
Weaver's Corners, Huron....N 50
Weaver'sCors.(seeA'stint'wn) ×
● Weaver's Station, Darke. W 150
● Webb, Wood........NW 75
● Webb Summit, Hocking.. S 25
Weber, Jackson..........S 25
Webster, Darke.........W 500
Webster's (see Cannelsville).. ×
Webster, Scioto...........S 350
Wegee, Belmont..........E 100
● *Wegee Station*, Belmont..E ×
● Weilersville, Wayne......N 50
Welcome, Holmes..........C 75
Weldon, Trumbull.......NE ×
● *Welker*, Wood.........NW 100
● *Wellans*, Perry.........C ×
● Wellington, Lorain.......N 2,069
Wells Corners,(seeVermilion) ×
● Wellston, Jackson ....S 4,377
● Wellsville, Columbiana. NE 5,247
Welshfield, Geauga.......NE 200
Wendelin, Mercer.........W 15
● Wengerlawn, Montgomery W 75
West, Washington..........SE 30
● West Alexandria, Preble. W 575
West Andover, Ashtabula. NE 500
● West Austintown, M'h'gNE 210
● West Baltimore, Mo't'g'yW 350
West Beaver, Columbiana. NE 300
West Bedford, Coshocton...C 100
West Berlin, Delaware........C 100
● Westborough, Clinton.. SW 300
West Brookfield, Stark....NE 175
● West Cairo, Allen......NW 325
West Canaan, Madison......C 250
West Carlisle, Coshocton....C 300
● West Carrollton, Montg'yW 360
West Charleston, Miami....W 120
● West Chester, Butler....SW 259
WestChester,(seeCadwallader) ×
West Clarksfield, Huron....N 100
● West Cleveland, Cuy'ga. NE 4,117
● *West Dayton*, Montgo'ry W ×
West Dover, Cuyahoga....NE 25
West Elkton, Preble ....W 216
● *West End*, Clarke ....W ×
Western Star, Medina.....N 77
Western Star, Summit.....NE 88
● Westerville, Franklin.....C 1,329
● West Farmington, Tr'll. NE 400
Westfield, Morrow..........C 200
● West Hayden, Franklin...C 50
West Hope, Henry.......NW 50
West Independence, H'ckNW 200
● West Jefferson, Madison..C 778
● *West Junction*, Vinton... S ×
● West LaFayette, Coshoct'nC 500
West Lancaster, Fayette.... S 200
Westland, Morgan.........SE 16
West Lebanon, Wayne......N 150
● West Leipsic, Putnam..NW 502
● West Liberty, Logan..... W 1,250
West Lodi, Seneca..........N 300
● West Manchester, Preble W 400
West Mansfield, Logan..... W 431
West Mecca, Trumbull....NE 100
West Mentor, Lake........NE ×
West Middleburg, Logan... W 345
West Mill Grove, Wood.. NW 207
● West Milton, Miami......W 796
Westminster, Allen...... NW 350
● *Westminster*, Allen......NW ×
West Newton, Allen......NW 100
West Norwood, Hamilton SW 612
● Weston, Wood...........NW 845
West Point, Columbiana.. NE 25
West Point, Morrow........C 175
West Richfield, Summit.. NE 900
West Rushville, Fairfield....C 195
● West Salem, Wayne...... N 756
West Side, Cuyahoga......NE ×
● West Sonora, Preble....... W 200
● *West Springfield*, Clarke. W ×
● West Toledo, Lucas.... NW ×
West Union, Adams.......S 825
● West Unity, Williams.. NW 872
● West View, Cuyahoga...NE 200
● Westville, Champaign....W 300
Westville, (see Beloit)........ ×
West Walnut Hills, Ha'n.SW ×
● West Wheeling, Belmont. E 574

● West Williamsfield, Ashtabula..............NE 930
Westwood, Hamilton......SW 1,050
West Woodville, Clermont. SW 50
● *West Zanesville*, MuskingumC ×
● Wetmore, Pike...........S 25
Wetsel, Van Wert........NW 25
● *Weybourn*, Hamilton...SW ×
Weymouth, Medina.........N 250
● Wharton, Wyandot.......N 800
● *Wharton*, Scioto..........S ×
Wheat Ridge, Adams........ S 65
Wheeler, Lake..............NE ×
● Wheelersburgh, Scioto.... S 301
Wheeling, (see Guernsey).... ×
● *Wheeling Creek*, Belmont E ×
Wheeling Valley, (seeSt.Clairsville)...................... ×
Wheelock, Summit.........NE ×
Wheldon, Jackson.......... S 200
Whetstone, Morrow..........C 675
● *Whetstone*, Franklin......C ×
● Whigville, Noble..........E 75
● Whipple, Washington... SE 75
● *Whiskey Switch*, Pick'w'yC ×
Whisler, Pickaway..........C 10
Whitacres, Carroll.........E ×
● WhiteCottage, MuskingumC 250
● *WhiteEyesPlains*,CoshoctonC 50
Whitefox, Huron........... N 50
● White House, Lucas.... NW 507
● White Oak, Brown......SW 19
White Oak, (see Mt. Sterling) ×
● *WhiteOak Valley*,BrownSW ×
● White Sulphur, Delaware. C 25
White Water, Hamilton...SW 25
● *Whitmans*, Jackson.......S 15
Whitfield, Montgomery....W ×
● Whitmore, Sandusky.....N 10
Whitney, Belmont.......... E 25
Whittlesey, Medina.........N 150
Whitwell, Lawrence......... S ×
Whynot, Guernsey......... E ×
Wick, Ashtabula..........NE ×
Wickliffe, Lake........... NE 250
● *Wickliffe*, Lake......... NE ×
Widowville, Ashland.........N 20
Wiggonsville, Clermont...SW 41
Wights, Wood............NW ×
Wigner, Gallia.............. S 25
Wilberforce, Greene........ W 200
● *Wilberforce Sta.*, Greene W ×
Wildare, Trumbull........NE 5
● *Wild Wood Park*,MedinaN ×
● Wiley, Darke.............W 40
Wilgus, Lawrence............ S 10
● *Wilhelms*, Muskingum... C ×
Wilkesville, Vinton......... S 262
Wilkins' Run, Licking....... C 150
Willard, Cuyahoga........ NE ×
Willettville, Highland........ S 50
● *Williams*, Putnam.....NW ×
● Williamsburgh,ClermontSW 828
Williams Centre, W'iams. NW 100
● *Williamsdale*, HamiltonSW ×
Williamsfield, Ashtabula..NE 300
● *Williamsfield*,Ashtabula NE 175
Williamsport, (see Clarkson) ×
Williamsport, Morrow...... C 100
● Williamsport, Pickaway.. C 368
Williamston, Mahoning.. NE ×
● Williamstown,Hancock NW 50
● Williston, Ottawa..........N 125
● Willoughby, Lake......NW 1,219
● Willow, Cuyahoga...... NE ×
Willow Brook, Coshocton...C 25
● *Willow Creek*, HancockNW ×
Willow Dell, Darke........ W 100
● *Willowville*, Clermont..SW ×
Willow Wood, Lawrence.... S 30
Will's Creek, Coshocton.... C 100
● Willshire, Van Wert... NW 566
● **Wilmington**, ClintonSW 3,079
Wilmot, Stark............ NE 500
● Wilson, Adams............S 125
● *Wilson Avenue*, C'y'h'goNE ×
Wilson's Mills, Cuyahoga..NE 150
● *Wiltsee*, Clermont...... SW ×
Winameg, Fulton......... NW 10
● Winchester, Adams........ S 1,804
Winchester, (see Homeworth) ×
● *Winchester*, Franklin.....C 840
Winchester, (see Brown)..... ×
Winchester, (see Rocky Hill) ×
● *Winchester*, Preble...... W 389
Windfall, Medina...........N ×

● Windham, Portage.....NW 400
Windsor, (see Stockport) .... ×
Windsor, Ashtabula.......NE 800
Windsor Mills, Ashtabula. NE 200
Windsor Sta., (see Pavonia).. ×
● Wineland, Hancock....NW 40
Winesburg, Holmes.........C 300
Winfield, Tuscarawas.......E 129
Winfred, Washington..... SE ×
Wingert's Co'rs., (see Broken Sword)............. ×
Wingett Run, Washington.SE 50
Wingston, Wood..........NW 40
● Winkle, Highland..........S 25
Winona, Columbiana.......NE 160
● Winona Furnace, HockingS 125
● *WinslowPark*,HamiltonSW ×
Winterset, Guernsey........ E 250
Wintersville, Jefferson......E 100
● Winton Place, Hamilton SW 380
Wise, Van Wert..........NW 10
● *Wise*, Monroe............ E ×
Wiseman, Clarke...........W ×
Wisterman, Putnam.......NW 75
Withamsville, Clermont....SW 200
Wittens, Monroe............E ×
● Wolf, Tuscarawas.........E 101
Wolfdale, Van Wert.......NW 20
Wolf Creek, Washington.. SE ×
● Wood, Butler............SW 25
Woodberry, (see Woodview) ×
Woodford, Huron.......... N ×
● *Woodford*, Hamilton... SW ×
Wood Grove, Morgan.......SE 39
● Woodington, Darke...... W 300
Woodland, (see Willow Dell) ×
● Woodland, Union......... C 300
● *Woodland*, Mahoning.. NE ×
Woodland, Cuyahoga..... NE ×
Woodland, (see Willow Dell) ×
● Woodlawn, Hamilton...SW 25
Woodlyn, Pickaway.........C 25
● Woodsdale, Butler...... SW 100
● *Woodsdale Park*,ButlerSW ×
● *Woodsdale Sta.*, Butler SW ×
● **Woodsfield**, Monroe...E 1,031
● *Woodside*, Wood....... NW 25
● Woodstock, Champaign..W 310
Woodview, Morrow.........C 120
● Woodville, Sandusky..... N 600
Woodworth, Mahoning....NE 100
Woodyards, Athens.........SE 70
● **Wooster**, Wayne........N 5,901
WoosterSummit,(seeSmithville) ×
● Worstville, Paulding... NW 300
Worthington, Franklin..... C 341
● *WorthingtonSta*., FranklinC ×
Wren, Van Wert...........NW 150
● *Wright's Siding*,Hocking. S ×
Wrightstown, (see Calvary).. ×
Wrightsville, Madison.......C 100
Wyandot, Wyandot.........N 150
Wynant, Shelby............ W ×
Wyoming, Hamilton...... SW 1,454
● **Xenia**, Greene..........W 7,301
● *Xenia Junc.*, Greene....W ×
Yale, Portage.............NW 75
Yankeeburg, Washington..SE 25
Yankee Ridge, Coshocton...C 65
● *Yankeetown*, Brown....SW ×
Yankeetown,(see Pancoastb'g) ×
Yarico, Lawrence...........S ×
Yatesville, Fayette..........S 200
Yellow Bird, Pickaway..... C 49
Yellow Bud, Ross.......... S 175
Yellow Creek, (see Akron)... ×
● *Yellow Creek*, Jefferson.. E ×
Yellow Springs, Greene....W 1,375
Yellowtown, (see Thivener).. ×
Yelrah, Fairfield............C 25
● Yelverton, Hardin....... W 185
Yoder, Allen..............NW 10
Yono, Gallia..................S 85
● *York*, Sandusky..........N ×
● *York*, Sandusky..........N ×
York, (see Updegraff's)..... ×
York, Union..................C 100
● *York*, Medina............ N 250
● Yorkshier, Darke......... W 200
● *Yorktown*, Tuscarawas...E ×
Yorkville, (see Elgin)....... ×
● Yorkille, Jefferson........E 50
● *Yost*, Perry...............C ×
Youba, Athens..............SE ×
Young, (see Frederickdale).. ×
● Young, Scioto............ S 50
Young Hickory, MuskingumC 50

Town, County	Index	Pop.
Young's Mills, (see Irish Ridge)		×
● **Youngstown**, Mahon'g	NE	33,220
Youngsville, Adams	S	100
● Zaleski, Vinton	S	862
Zanesfield, Logan	W	318
● **Zanesville**, Muskingum	C	21,009
● *Zartman's*, Licking	C	×
Zeal, Meigs	SE	×
Zellner, Richland	N	×
Zeno, Muskingum	C	40
Zimmer, Franklin	C	×
● Zimmerman, Greene	W	150
Ziontown, Perry	C	×
● Zoar, Tuscarawas	E	325
Zoar, Warren	SW	×
● Zoar Station, Tuscarawas	E	100
Zone, Fulton	NW	×
Zuck, Knox	C	50

OKLAHOMA.

Counties.	Index.	Pop.
A	E	×
B	SE	×
Beaver	NW	2,674
C	N	×
Canadian	C	7,158
Cheyennes and Arapahoes	W	×
Cleveland	S	6,605
D	N	×
E	NW	×
F	W	×
G	W	×
H	W	×
I	C	×
Kansas	NE	×
Kingfisher	N	8,332
Kiowas, Comanches and Apaches	S	×
Logan	N	12,770
Oklahoma	C	11,742
Osages	NE	×
Otoes and Missourias	NE	×
Pawnee	NE	×
Payne	NE	7,215
Poncas	NE	×
Tonkawas	NE	×
Unassigned Land	SW	5,338
Total		61,834

Town. County.	Index.	Pop.
Aaron, Unassigned Land	SW	×
Adell, B	SE	×
Alfred, (see Mullhall)		×
Alpine, Beaver	NW	15
Alsford, Unassigned Land	SW	×
Altus, Unassigned Land	SW	×
Anadarko, Kiowas, Com. & Apaches	S	×
Anderson, B	SE	×
Antelope, Logan	N	×
Arapahoe, G	W	×
Arcadia, Oklahoma	C	×
Baker, A	E	×
Ball, Oklahoma	C	×
Beaver, Beaver	NW	150
Benton, Beaver	NW	×
Blue Grass, Beaver	NW	×
Bowman, Logan	N	×
Boyd, Beaver	NW	×
● Britton, Oklahoma	C	25
Buffalo, Beaver	NW	×
Burnett, B	SE	×
Burwick, Logan	N	×
Canadian, Canadian	C	×
Cantonment, D	N	×
Caple, Beaver	NW	×
Case, Cleveland	S	×
Cavett, Oklahoma	C	×
Center, Oklahoma	C	×
● Chaddick, Oklahoma	C	×
Chandler, A	E	×
Cheyenne, F	W	×
● Choctaw City, Oklahoma	C	50
Cimarron, Payne	NE	15
Clarkson, Payne	NE	15
Clayton, Payne	NE	15
Clear Lake, Beaver	NW	×
Clermont, Canadian	C	50
Clifton, A	E	×
Cloud Chief, H	W	×
Columbia, Kingfisher	N	×
Council Grove, Oklahoma	C	×
Crescent, Logan	N	45
Cushing, Payne	NE	×
Custer, Beaver	NW	×
● Darlington, Canadian	C	×
Davenport, A	E	×
Dial, Unassigned Land	SW	×
● Dover, Kingfisher	N	50
Downs, Kingfisher	N	50
Duke, Unassigned Land	SW	×
Dunbar, Unassigned Land	SW	×
Eagle Centre, Oklahoma	C	×
East Guthrie, Logan	N	2,141
Eda, Canadian	C	10
● Edmond, Oklahoma	C	294
El Dorado, Unassigned L'd	SW	×
Elmwood, Beaver	NW	×
● **Elreno**, Canadian	C	285
● *Elreno Station*, Canadian	C	×
Embree, Osages	NE	×
Erie, Kingfisher	N	×
Erie, Unassigned Land	SW	×
Eubank, Beaver	NW	×
Eva, Unassigned Land	SW	×
Ewing, Oklahoma	C	×
Fairview, Beaver	NW	×
Fairview, Logan	N	×
Falls, Cleveland	S	10
Florence, (see Kenton)		×
Fort Cobb, I	C	×
Fort Reno, Canadian	C	260
● Fort Sill, Kiowa, Com. and Apaches	S	326
Frazer, Unassigned Land	SW	300
Frisco, Canadian	C	327
Fulton, Beaver	NW	×
Gallienas, Beaver	NW	×
Garland, Beaver	NW	×
Garnettville, Oklahoma	C	×
Garrett, Beaver	NW	×
Gate City, Beaver	NW	×
Grand Valley, Beaver	NW	×
Gray Horse, Osages	NE	×
Greer, Unassigned Land	SW	×
Greysons, Osages	NE	×
● **GUTHRIE**, Logan	N	2,788
Hall, Cleveland	S	×
Hamton, Unassigned Land	SW	×
Hardesty, Beaver	NW	20
Harvey, A	E	×
● Hennessey, Kingfisher	N	300
Hereford, Beaver	NW	×
Herron, Canadian	C	×
Hess, Unassigned Land	SW	×
Hominy, Osages	NE	×
Horace, A	E	×
Idelah, Oklahoma	C	×
Indian Village, H	W	×
Ingalls, Payne	NE	26
Ingram, A	E	×
Island, E	NW	×
Ivanhoe, Beaver	NW	×
Jackson, Logan	N	×
Jester, Unassigned Land	SW	×
Johnesborough, Cleveland	S	×
Kaw Agency, Kansas	NE	×
Kenton, Beaver	NW	×
Keokuk Falls, B	SE	×
Kickapoo Station, A	E	×
King, B	SE	×
● **Kingfisher**, Kingfisher	N	1,134
Kinman, C	N	×
Kokomo, Beaver	NW	×
Lacey, Kingfisher	N	×
Lakeview, Logan	N	×
Langston, Logan	N	100
Lansing, Beaver	NW	×
Lavrock, Beaver	NW	×
● Lawrie, Logan	N	×
Lexington, Cleveland	S	223
Liberty, Canadian	C	×
Lima, Logan	N	×
Lincoln, Kingfisher	N	20
Lisbon, (see Kingfisher)		×
Lock, Unassigned Land	SW	×
Lockwood, Beaver	NW	×
Logan, Beaver	NW	×
Louis, Unassigned Land	SW	25
Lowrie, Logan	N	×
Magnolia, Otteo & Missourias	NE	×
Mangum, Un'signed Land	W	2[illegible]
Marena, Payne	NE	[illegible]
Marshall, Logan	N	5[illegible]
Martha, Unassigned Land	W	×
Martin, Logan	N	×
Mathewson, Canadian	C	×
Meridian, Beaver	NW	×
Milan, Cleveland	S	×
Miller, Oklahoma	C	12
● *Minco*, I	C	×
Mineral City, Beaver	NW	×
Mitchell, Beaver	NW	×
Momet, B	SE	×
● Moore, Cleveland	S	75
Morris, Unassigned Land	SW	×
Mount Walsh, Un'sign'd L'd	SW	×
● Mulhall, Logan	N	350
Murdock, Beaver	NW	×
Myrtle, Kingfisher	N	×
Navajoe, Unassigned Land	SW	50
Negro Settlement, Cleveland	S	×
● Noble, Cleveland	S	300
● Norman, Cleveland	S	787
● Okarche, Canadian	C	×
● **Oklahoma**, Oklahoma	C	4,151
Old Camp Auger, Kiowa, Comanche, and Apaches	S	×
Omer, Kingfisher	N	×
Optima, Beaver	NW	×
● Orlando, Logan	N	300
Osmit, B	SE	×
Otoe, Otoe & Missourias	NE	×
Paladora, Beaver	NW	×
Paris, Kingfisher	N	×
Partridge, A	E	×
Pawhuska, Osages	NE	50
Pawnee Agency, Pawnees	NE	923
Payne, Oklahoma	C	10
Peoria, Beaver	NW	×
Perkins, Oklahoma	C	275
Plumb, Payne	NE	×
Poe, Unassigned Land	SW	×
● *Polona*, Canadian	C	×
Ponca, Poncas	NE	175
● *Ponca Station*, Poncas	NE	×
Quartz, Unassigned Land	SW	×
Quincy, Cleveland	S	×
Ravens Spring, C	N	×
Red Fork, Kingfisher	N	×
● *Red Rock Station*, Oteo & Missourias	NE	×
Reno, Canadian	C	234
Riverside, Beaver	NW	×
Rosedale, Oklahoma	C	×
Rothwell, Beaver	NW	×
Sac and Fox Agency, A	E	32
Sacred Heart, B	SE	26
● Seward, Logan	N	10
Seymour, Oklahoma	C	×
Shade, Beaver	NW	×
Shawnee, B	SE	×
● *Shawneetown*, B	SE	25
Sheridan, Kingfisher	N	12
Silver, Oklakoma	C	×
Snyder, Kingfisher	N	×
Speer, A	E	×
Springvale, Logan	N	×
Standard, Logan	N	×
Stillwater, Payne	NE	480
Taloga, D	N	×
Tecumseh, B	SE	450
Thurston, Canadian	C	35
Tohee, Logan	N	25
Tum, B	SE	×
Tyrone, Beaver	NW	×
Union, Canadian	C	75
● *Union City*, Canadian	C	×
Union City, Kiowas, Comanches & Apaches	S	×
Vici, Unassigned Land	SW	×
Wagoza, B	SE	×
Wahtiaucah, Osages	NE	×
● *Walker*, Cleveland	S	×
Wanamaker, Kingfisher	N	20
Wandel, Kingfisher	N	×
Wantonga, C	N	×
Warren, Unassigned Land	SW	×
Waterloo, Logan	N	×
Wellston, A	E	×
West Guthrie, Logan	N	404
Willowvale, Unassigned L'd	SW	×
Windom, Payne	NE	×
Yates, Payne	NE	×
Yeldell, Unassigned Land	SW	×
Yukon, Canadian	C	300
Zion, Kingfisher	N	×

OREGON.

COUNTIES.	INDEX.	POP.
Baker	E	6,764
Benton	W	8,650
Clackamas	NW	15,233
Clatsop	NW	10,016
Columbia	NW	5,191
Coos	SW	8,874
Crook	C	3,244
Curry	SW	1,709
Douglas	SW	11,864
Gilliam	N	3,600
Grant	E	5,080
Harney	SE	2,559
Jackson	SW	11,455
Josephine	SW	4,878
Klamath	S	2,444
Lake	S	2,604
Lane	W	15,198
Linn	W	16,265
Malheur	SE	2,601
Marion	NW	22,934
Morrow	N	4,205
Multnomah	NW	74,884
Polk	NW	7,858
Sherman	N	1,792
Tillamook	NW	2,932
Umatilla	N	13 381
Union	NE	12,044
Wallowa	NE	3,661
Wasco	N	9,183
Washington	NW	11,972
Yam Hill	NW	10,692
Total		813,767

TOWN. COUNTY.	INDEX.	POP.
Acme, Lane	W	70
Acton, Morrow	N	120
● Adams, Umatilla	N	200
Agency, Crook	C	×
Aims, Clackamas	NW	×
● Airlie, Polk	NW	53
Ajax, Gilliam	N	4
Alba, Umatilla	N	120
● **Albany**, Linn	W	3,079
● *Albany Junction*, Linn	W	×
● *Albina*, Multnomah	NW	5,129
Alder, Wallowa	NE	30
Alderbrook, Clatsop	NW	442
● Ale, Marion	NW	20
● Alicel, Union	NE	×
Alkali, (see Arlington)		×
Allentown, (see Cornucopia).		×
Alma, Lane	W	×
Aloysius, Josephine	SW	×
Alpha, Lane	W	×
Alpine, Morrow	N	16
Alsea, Benton	W	340
Althouse, Josephine	SW	30
● Amity, Yam Hill	NW	450
Anderson, Josephine	SW	×
Andrews, Harney	SE	190
Angora, Coos	SW	8
Ankeny, Marion	NW	×
Antelope, Wasco	N	60
Antler, Lake	S	×
Apiary, Columbia	NW	×
Applegate, Jackson	SW	84
Arago, Coos	SW	×
Arcadia, Wallowa	NE	×
Argenti, Marion	NW	×
● Arlington, Gilliam	N	356
● *Armstrong*, Yam Hill	NW	×
Arthur, Multnomah	NW	×
● Ashland, Jackson	SW	1,784
Astoria, Clatsop	NW	6,184
● Athena, Umatilla	N	495
Atwood, Umatilla	N	60
Auburn, Baker	E	100
Auburn Station, Baker	E	×
Aukeny, Marion	NW	×
● Aumsville, Marion	NW	50
● Aurora Mills, Marion	NW	200
Austin, Grant	E	5
Averill, (see Bandon)		×
Axtell, Benton	W	×
Badger, Sherman	N	×
Bake Oven, Wasco	N	7
● **Baker City**, Baker	E	2,604
● Ballston, Polk	NW	110
Bancroft, Coos	SW	×
Bandon, Coos	SW	219
Bar, Malheur	SE	×

TOWN. COUNTY.	INDEX.	POP.
● Barlow, Clackamas	NW	×
Barnegat, Tillamook	NW	×
● *Barnhart*, Umatilla	N	×
● *Baron's Mill*, Marion	NW	×
Barron, Jackson	SW	×
Bateman, (see Fir)		×
● *Bates*, Linn	W	×
● *Bates*, Umatilla	N	×
Bay City, Tillamook	NW	200
Beagle, Jackson	SW	×
Beaver, Tillamook	NW	×
Beaver Glen, (see Whitaker).		×
● Beaverton, Washington	NW	250
Bedfield, Klamath	S	×
Bellevue, Yam Hill	NW	30
Belknap Springs, Lane	W	×
Bend, Crook	C	×
● *Bertha*, Washington	NW	×
Bethany, Washington	NW	30
Beulah, Malheur	SE	60
Bewley, (see Nehalem)		×
Big Butte, Jackson	SW	90
● Biggs, Sherman	N	50
Big Prairie, Lane	W	×
Blaine, Curry	SW	×
● Blalock, Gilliam	N	20
Blanton, Grant	E	×
Blitzen, Harney	SE	×
● Blodgett, Benton	W	×
● *Blue Mountain*, Umatilla	N	×
Blue River, Lane	W	×
Bly, Klamath	S	50
Bolt, Jackson	SW	12
Bonanza, Klamath	S	100
● *Bonneville*, Wasco	N	×
● *Boulder*, Linn	W	×
Bowdens, Malheur	SE	×
Boyd, Wasco	N	40
Bradbury, Columbia	NW	240
Braden, Umatilla	N	×
Braunsport, Columbia	NW	×
● Bridal Veil, Multnomah	NW	400
Bridgeport, Baker	E	61
● *Briedwell*, Yam Hill	NW	×
Britten, Baker	E	15
● *Broadmeals*, Yam Hill	NW	×
Brockway, Douglas	SW	×
● Brooks, Marion	NW	100
Brower, Multnomah	NW	×
Brownsborough Jackson	SW	16
● *Brown's Mill*, Linn	W	×
● Brownsville, Linn	W	580
Browntown, Josephine	SW	100
Bryant's, Multnomah	NW	×
Buena Vista, Polk	NW	200
Bully, (see Westfall)		×
Burns, Harney	SE	264
Burnt Ranch, Crook	C	31
Butte Creek, (see Marquam)		×
Butteville, Marion	NW	103
Buxton, Washington	NW	10
Caleb, Grant	E	25
Caledonia, (see Toledo)		×
Camas Prairie, (see Alba)		×
Camas Valley, Douglas	SW	30
Cameron, Lane	W	×
Camp Creek, Lane	W	×
Camp Harney, (see Harney)		×
Camp Polk, (see Sisters)		×
Camp Watson, Grant	E	48
● Canby, Clackamas	NW	150
● *Canemah*, Clackamas	NW	×
Cannon Beach, Clatsop	NW	×
Canon, Umatilla	N	×
Canyon City, Grant	E	304
Canyonville, Douglas	SW	250
Carico, Columbia	NW	×
Carll Douglas	SW	×
● Carlton, Yam Hill	NW	125
Cartwright's, Lane	W	×
Carus, Clackamas	NW	×
● Cascade Locks, Wasco	N	275
● Castle Rock, Morrow	N	20
Cathlamet, Clatsop	NW	×
● *Cayuse*, Umatilla	N	×
● *Cecil*, Morrow	N	×
Cedar Landing, (see Rainier)		×
Cedar Mill, Washington	NW	13
● Celilo, Wasco	N	20
Cemetery, Multnomah	NW	×
Centerville, (see Athena)		×
Centerville, Washington	NW	50
● Central Point, Jackson	SW	534
Chadwell, Clatsop	NW	49
● Champoeg, Marion	NW	72
Chehalem Gap, Yam Hill	NW	×
● Chemawa, Marion	NW	×

TOWN. COUNTY.	INDEX.	POP.
Cherry Creek, Crook	C	×
Cherryville, Clackamas	NW	35
Chetco, Curry	SW	48
Chewaucan Lake	S	×
● Chitwood, Benton	W	20
Christman, Lane	W	×
Civil Bend, Douglas	SW	×
● Clackamas, Clackamas	NW	350
Clarkes, Clackamas	NW	×
● Clarnie, Multnomah	NW	×
Clatskanie, Columbia	NW	212
● *Clawson*, Jackson	SW	×
Clem, Gilliam	N	30
● Cleone, Multnomah	NW	100
Cleveland, Douglas	SW	8
Clifton, Clatsop	NW	35
Clymax, Jackson	SW	×
Clymer, Marion	NW	×
Coaledo, Coos	SW	×
● Coburg, Lane	W	200
● *Cochrane*, Polk	NW	×
Coe, Marion	NW	×
Coes, Linn	W	×
● *Cold Springs*, Umatilla	N	×
● Colestin, Jackson	SW	×
Coles Valley, Douglas	SW	×
Collins, (see Lutgens)		×
● Columbia City, Col'bia	NW	50
● Comstock, Douglas	SW	20
Condon, Gilliam	N	73
Conemah, Clackamas	NW	×
Connor Creek, Baker	E	50
Contention, Gilliam	N	×
Coquille, Coos	SW	494
● Cornelius, Washington	NW	180
Cornucopia, Union	NE	150
● **Corvallis**, Benton	W	1,527
● Cottage Grove, Lane	W	500
Cove, Union	NE	223
● *Coyote*, Morrow	N	×
● *Crabtree*, Linn	W	×
Cracker, Baker	E	×
● *Cranor*, Linn	W	×
Crawfordsville, Linn	W	100
Crescent, Crook	C	×
● Creswell, Lane	W	100
Crook, Crook	C	×
Cross Hollows, Wasco	N	48
Cross Keys, Crook	C	×
Croston, Marion	NW	36
Crow, Lane	W	12
● Crowley, Polk	NW	×
Crown Rock, Gilliam	N	×
Croy, Sherman	N	×
Currinsville, Clackamas	NW	200
Dairy, Klamath	S	12
Daryville, (see Hardman)		×
Dale, Umatilla	N	×
● **Dallas**, Polk	NW	848
● *Dallas*, Wasco	N	×
Damascus, Clackamas	NW	35
Danby, Columbia	NW	×
Day's Creek, Douglas	SW	60
Dayton, Yam Hill	NW	304
● *Dayton Junc.*, Yam Hill	NW	×
● *Dayton Sta.*, Yam Hill	NW	×
Dayville, Grant	E	120
Deadwood, Lane	W	×
Dechutes, Sherman	N	20
● Deer Island, Columbia	NW	×
Delena, Columbia	NW	×
Dell, Malheur	SE	×
DemocratGulch, (see Aloysius)		×
De Moss Springs, Sherman	N	40
Dencer, Marion	NW	×
Denmark, Curry	SW	24
Derby, Jackson	SW	×
● *Derry*, Polk	NW	50
● *Des Chutes*, Sherman	N	60
Desert, Crook	C	×
Deskins, (see Prospect)		×
Detroit, Marion	NW	×
Dexter, Lane	W	35
Diamond, Harney	SE	×
● Dillard, Douglas	SW	70
● Dilley, Washington	NW	100
● *Divide*, Lane	W	×
Divide, Wallowa	NE	×
Dixie, Washington	NW	120
● *Dodson's*, Multnomah	NW	×
Dolph, Tillamook	NW	34
Dora, Coos	SW	×
Dotyville, Linn	W	19
● Douglas, Morrow	N	×
Dover, Clackamas	NW	×
● *Downing*, Umatilla	N	×
● *Downs*, Marion	NW	×

● Drain, Douglas SW 500
Draper, Jackson SW 60
Drewsey, Harney SE 30
Dryden, Josephine SW ×
Dufur, Wasco N 200
● Dundee Junc., Yam Hill NW 50
● *Durkee*, Baker E ×
Eagle Creek, Clackamas NW 73
Eagle Point SW 125
Eagle Valley, (see New B'dge) ×
● *Eastland*, Umatilla N ×
East Marshfield, Coos SW ×
● *East Portland*, Multn'h NW 10,532
● *East Side Junc.*, Marion NW ×
● Echo, Umatilla N 100
Eckley, Curry SW ×
Eddyville, Benton W 25
Egan, (see Burns) ×
Eightmile, Morrow N 36
● Elgin, Union NE 227
● Elk City, Benton W 20
Elk Creek, Union NE ×
Elk Flat, Union NE ×
Elk Head, Douglas SW ×
Elkhorn, Marion NW ×
Elk Rock, Multnomah NW ×
Elkton, Douglas SW 30
Ella, Morrow N 30
Ellensburg, (see Gold Beach) ×
Elliott, Coos SW ×
Elmira, Lane W 40
Ely, Clackamas NW ×
Emigrant Springs, Sherman N ×
Empire City, Coos SW 252
Encampment, (see Meacham) ×
Enchanted Prairie, (see Angora) ×
Enterprise, (see Hunters) ×
Enterprise, Wallowa NE 242
Eola, Polk NW 87
Erskineville, Sherman N 35
Etelka, Coos SW ×
Etna, Jackson SW ×
○ **Eugene**, Lane W 4,000
Evergreen, Harney SE ×
Everts, Umatilla N 28
Express, Baker E ×
Fairdale, Yam Hill NW 40
Fairfield, Marion NW 25
● Fair Grounds, Marion NW ×
Fairmount, Lane W ×
Fairview, Coos SW ×
Fairview, Marion NW ×
● *Fairview*, Multnomah NW ×
Fall Creek, Lane W 15
Falls City, Polk NW 200
Farmington, Washington NW 36
Ferry, Curry SW ×
Fife, Crook C ×
Fillmore, (see Mt. Angel) ×
Fir, Washington NW ×
Fishhawk, Columbia NW ×
Fletts, Gilliam N ×
Flora, Wallowa NE ×
Florence, Lane W 250
● *Foise*, Marion NW ×
Foley Springs, Lane W ×
Folley, Tillamook NW ×
● Forest Grove, Washing'n NW 668
Fort Klamath, Klamath S 10
Fort Stevens, Clatsop NW ×
Fossil, Gilliam N 153
Foster, Linn W ×
● *Foster*, Umatilla N 40
Fox, Grant E ×
Fox Valley, Linn W 210
Franklin, Lane W 30
Freewater, Umatilla N 150
● *French Prairie*, Marion NW ×
● *Froman*, Linn W ×
Fruita, Wallowa NE ×
● *Fry*, Linn W ×
Fulton, Multnomah NW 150
● *Fulton*, Umatilla N ×
Gale, Klamath S ×
Gales Creek, Washington NW 90
Galesville, Douglas SW 73
Galice, Josephine SW ×
Galloway, Morrow N ×
Garden Home, Washington NW 80
Gardiner, Douglas SW 229
Garibaldi, Tillamook NW 100
● Gaston, Washington NW 70
Gate Creek, Lane W ×
Gates, Linn W ×
Gates, Marion NW ×
George, Clackamas NW 30
● Gervais, Marion NW 400
Gibbon, Umatilla N ×
● Gillton, Columbia NW 42
Gladstone, Clackamas NW 150
Glenada, Lane W 56
Glencoe, Washington NW 75
● Glendale, Douglas SW 75
Glenn, Malheur SE 120
Glentena, Lane W ×
Glenwood, Washington NW ×
Glide, Douglas SW ×
Goble, Columbia NW ×
Gold Beach, Curry SW 300
● Gold Hill, Jackson SW 110
● *Goltra*, Linn W ×
Gooseberry, Morrow N 72
● Goshen, Lane W 25
Grand Ronde, Polk NW 75
● *Grand View*, Umatilla N ×
Granger, Benton W ×
Granite, Grant E 54
● Grant, Sherman N 100
● **Grant's Pass**, Josephine SW 1,432
Grant's Station, Wasco N ×
Grass Valley, Sherman N 100
Grave Creek, (see Leland) ×
Gravel Ford, Coos SW ×
● *Gravel Pit*, Josephine SW ×
Gray, Curry SW 31
Green Basin, Marion NW ×
Greens, Douglas SW ×
Greenville, Washington NW 32
● *Gregory*, Jackson SW ×
Gresham, Multnomah NW 75
Grizzly, Crook C ×
Grove City, Malheur SE 3
Grover, Sherman N ×
Hadleyville, Lane W ×
● Haines, Baker E 136
Hale, Lane W ×
Halfway, Union NE 15
● Halsey, Linn W 270
Halsted, (see Green Basin) ×
Hamilton, Grant E ×
Hardin, Crook C ×
Hardman, Morrow N 100
Hare, Clatsop NW ×
Harlan, Benton W ×
Harney, Harney SE 240
Harris, Benton W 300
● Harrisburgh, Linn W 413
● *Harrison*, Yam Hill NW ×
● *Havana*, Umatilla N ×
Hay Creek, Crook C 80
Haynesville, Klamath S ×
Haystack, Crook C ×
Hayward, Washington NW ×
Hazeldell, Lane W ×
Hebo, Tillamook NW 240
Heceta, Lane W ×
● Helix, Umatilla N 150
Hembree, Tillamook NW ×
Henness, (see Rock Creek) ×
● **Heppner**, Morrow N 675
Hereford, Baker E ×
Herling, Jackson SW ×
Hermann, Lane W ×
Highland, Clackamas NW 167
Hildebrand, Klamath S 100
● Hilgard, Union NE 429
Hill, Lane W 31
● **Hillsboro**, Washington NW 1,100
Hillsdale, Multnomah NW 60
● *Hillsdale*, Umatilla N ×
Hill's Mills, (see Dexter) ×
Hobsonville, Tillamook NW 50
Hillside, Douglas SW ×
Hogan, (see Melrose) ×
● Holbrook, Multnomah NW ×
Holly, Linn W 15
Homer, Grant E ×
● Hood River, Wasco N 201
Hopkins, Clatsop NW ×
Hoskins, Benton W 50
● Hot Lake, Union NE 30
Houlton, Columbia NW ×
Howard, Crook C ×
Howell, Marion NW ×
● Hubbard, Marion NW 117
Hudson, Douglas SW ×
Hullt, Marion NW ×
● Hunters, Columbia NW 75
● Huntington, Baker E 321
Idea, Gilliam N ×
Idol, Harney SE ×
Igo, Gilliam N ×
Imbler, Union NE 25
Imnaha, Wallowa NE ×
Independence, (see Granite) ×
● Independence, Polk NW 1,000
Ingles, (see Centerville) ×
● Ione, Morrow N 10
Irondale, Multnomah NW ×
Ironside, Malheur SE ×
Irving, Lane W 73
○ *Irving*, Lane W ×
● *Irvinville*, Linn W ×
Isabel, Lane W 68
● Island City, Union NE 150
Isthmus, Coos SW 50
Izee, Grant E ×
Jacksonville, Jackson SW 743
● Jasper, Lane W 30
● Jefferson, Marion NW 307
Jewell, Clatsop NW 55
John Day, Grant E 211
● *John Day's*, Sherman N ×
● *Johnson's Mills*, Marion NW 24
Jordan, Linn W 33
Jordan Valley, Malheur SE 225
Joseph, Wallowa NE 249
Joy, Wallowa NE ×
● *Junction*, Umatilla N ×
○ Junction City, Lane W 700
Juniper, Umatilla N 33
● *Juniper*, Umatilla N ×
Juntura, Malheur SE ×
● Kamela, Union NE 50
Keasey, Columbia NW ×
Keating, Union NE ×
Kellogg, Douglas SW 36
Keno, Klamath S 45
Kent, Sherman N ×
Kerby, Josephine SW 56
Kilchis, Tillamook NW 70
Killgaver, Multnomah NW ×
King's, Linn W ×
King, Marion SW ×
Kingsley, Wasco N 50
Kingston, Linn W ×
King's Valley, Benton W 20
Klamath Agency, Klamath S 120
Klamath Falls, Klamath S 364
Knappa, Clatsop NW 75
Knight, Marion NW ×
Kubli, Jackson SW ×
Lacomb, Linn W 30
Lacy, Clackamas NW ×
● La Fayette, Yam Hill NW 365
● La Grande, Union NE 2,583
Lake, Coos SW ×
● *Laka*, Union NE ×
Lake Creek, Jackson SW 15
Lakeview, Lake S 1,000
La Mu, Harney SE ×
Langell's Valley, Klamath S 96
Langlois, Curry SW 30
Larant, Douglas SW ×
Larch, Yam Hill NW ×
● *Latham*, Lane W 30
● Latourell Falls, Mult'h NW 60
Laurel, Washington NW 6
Lawen, Harney SE ×
Lawn Arbor, Polk NW ×
Leaburgh, Lane W 120
● Lebanon, Linn W 829
Lee, Coos SW ×
Leeds, Jackson SW ×
Leland, Josephine SW 130
● *Leland Station*, Josep'e SW ×
Lena, Morrow N ×
Lents, Multnomah NW ×
● *Lewisburg*, Benton W ×
Lewisburg, Marion NW ×
Lewisville, Polk NW 87
Lexington, (see Skipanon) ×
● Lexington, Morrow N 150
Libby, Coos SW 400
Liberty, Crook C ×
Lightner, Marion NW ×
Lincoln, Polk NW 50
Lincoln, (see Tillamook) ×
● *Linn*, Linn W ×
● Linnton, Multnomah NW 200
Little Elk, (see Eddyville) ×
Llano, Malheur SE ×
Llewellyn, Lane W ×
Lobster, Benton W ×
Logan, Clackamas NW ×
Lone Rock, Gilliam N 60
Lone Creek, Grant E 60
Long Tom, Lane W 90
Lookingglass, Douglas SW 52
Lorane, Lane W ×
Lostine, Wallowa NE 30

Oregon

Post Office	Pop.
Lost Prairie, Wallowa.....NE	×
Lost Valley, Gilliam........N	×
Louis, Douglas.............SE	×
Lowell, Lane...............W	25
Lower Cornucopia, (see Cor'pia)	×
● *Lowson*, Linn ....W	×
● *Luckiamute*, Polk......NW	×
Lucky Queen, Josephine..SW	48
Lutgens, Benton............W	14
● Lyons, Linn...............W	75
McAllister, (see Merlin)......	×
● McCoy, Polk...........NW	75
McEwensville, Baker.......E	×
McGraw's Landing, (see Br'db'y)	×
● McKee, Marion..........NW	×
McKinzie Bridge, Lane.....W	60
● **McMinnville**, Y'mH'lNW	1,368
Mabel, Linn................W	15
Macken, Polk..............NW	×
Macksburgh, Clackamas..NW	30
● Macleay, Marion.......NW	40
Malheur, Malheur..........SE	75
Manning, Washington....NW	×
Maple Dell, Multnomah..NW	×
● Marion, Marion.........NW	50
Marmot, Clackmas.......NW	×
Marquam, Clackamas....NW	50
Marshfield, Coos..........SW	1,461
Marshland, Columbia....NW	60
Mason, Malheur...........SE	×
Material Yard, Linn......W	×
Matney, Gilliam............N	×
Matoles, Crook..............C	×
Maxwell, Linn...............W	×
● *Maxwell*, Umatilla.......N	×
Mayger, Columbia..........NW	×
Mayville, Gilliam............N	30
Meacham, Umatilla.........M	50
● *Meacham*, Union.......NE	×
Meadow, Lane ....W	×
Meadow Brook, Clackamas NW	×
Meadows, (see Spikenard) ...	×
Meda, Tillamook..........NW	×
● Medford, Jackson......SW	967
Medical Springs, Union...NE	×
Medley, Clatsop..........NW	×
Mehama, Marion..........NW	100
Melrose, Douglas..........SW	×
Melville, Clatsop..........NW	×
● Merlin, Josephine......SW	100
● Middleton, Washington NW	150
● *Mikecha*, Umatilla......N	×
Mill City, Marion..........NW	150
● Millers, Linn..............W	60
Mill No 4, Benton.........W	×
Millwood, Douglas........SW	35
● *Milton*, Columbia......NW	×
● Milton, Umatilla.......N	544
● Milwaukee, Clackamas.NW	489
Minam, Union.............NE	×
Minerva, Lane.............W	×
Mink, Clackamas.........NW	×
Minto, Marion.............NW	×
Mishawaka, Clatsop......NW	×
● *Mission*, Umatilla........N	×
Mist, Columbia............NW	100
Mitchell, Crook............C	50
Mohawk, Lane..............W	30
Molalla, Clackamas......NW	50
Monitor, (see Mt. Angel)	×
Monkland, Sherman........N	50
● Monmouth, Polk.......NW	800
Monroe, Benton............W	75
Montavilla, Multnomah..NW	×
Monument, Grant...........E	×
Moore's Valley, Yam HillNW	×
Mooresville, Columbia...NW	×
Moro, Sherman............N	100
Morton, Klamath............S	×
● Mosier, Wasco..........N	75
Mountain Dale, Wash'ton.NW	84
Mountain Home, Lane.....W	×
● Mount Angel, Marion..NW	300
Mount Coffin, Columbia..NW	×
Mount Hood, Wasco........N	×
Mount Pleasant, Linn.....W	×
Mount Scott, Douglas.....SW	36
Mount Tabor, Multnomah NW	1,000
Mount Tabor Villa, Mult'hNW	×
Mount Vernon, Grant......E	30
Mowry, Crook...............C	×
● *Muddy*, Linn.............W	24
Mulino, Clackamas.........NW	20
● *Multnomah's Falls* Ml'hNW	×
Munkers, Linn............W	×
Murphy, Josephine.......SW	×
● Myrtle Creek, Douglas..SW	150

Oregon

Post Office	Pop.
Myrtle Point, Coos........SW	354
Nansene, Wasco............N	×
Narrows, Harney..........SE	×
Nashville, Benton..........W	×
Natal, Columbia.........NW	×
● Natron, Lane............W	30
Naylox, Klamath............S	32
Needy, Clackamas........NW	50
Neer, Columbia............NW	32
Nehalem, Tillamook .....NW	150
Neskowin, Tillamook....NW	×
Nestocton, Tillamook....NW	24
Nestucco Bay, Tillamook NW	×
Netarts, Tillamook.......NW	48
Newberg, Yam Hill.......NW	514
New Bridge, Union ....NE	275
Newellsville, (see Champoeg)	×
● New Era, Clackamas...NW	50
New Lake, (see Bandon).....	×
New Pine Creek, Lake......S	45
Newport, Benton..........W	121
Newport, Coos............SW	312
● *Newton*, Washington..NW	×
Niagora, Marion..........NW	75
● *Nichols*, Douglas.......SW	×
● Nolin, Umatilla...........N	50
Nonpareil, (see Oakland)....	×
Norfolk, Douglas.........SW	90
North Bend, Coos.........SW	400
North Canyonville, Doug'sSW	200
● *North Fork*, Umatilla....N	×
● North Powder, Union..NE	185
● *North Santiam*, Linn....E	×
● North Yam Hill, Y'm Hill NW	200
● *Norton*, Baker...........E	×
Norton's, Benton..........W	×
Norway, Coos..............SW	30
Nye, Umatilla...............N	68
● Nyssa, Malheur..........SE	×
Oak, Coos..................NW	×
Oak Creek, Douglas.......SW	24
● Oakland, Douglas.......SW	339
Oakley, Harney............SE	×
Oak Point, Columbia.....NW	×
Oakville, Linn...............W	×
Oasis, Gilliam...............N	32
Ocean View, Benton.......W	×
Ocheco, (see Prineville)......	×
Olalla, Douglas............SW	40
Olene, Klamath..............S	×
Olex, Gilliam................N	12
Olney, Clatsop............NW	48
Ona, Benton.................W	×
Oneatta, Benton...........W	50
● *Oneonta*, Multnomah...NW	18
Onion Peak, Tillamook...NW	90
● Ontario, Malheur........SE	175
Ophir, Curry................SW	×
● **Oregon City**, Clacka's NW	3,062
Oregon City Locks, Clack's NW	×
Oretown, Tillamook.......NW	120
Oro Dell, Union............NE	42
● Oswego, Clackamas....NW	544
Owyhee, Malheur..........SE	×
Paisley Lake.................S	94
Palatine Hill, Multnomah NW	×
Palestine, Multnomah....NW	×
● *Paper Mill*, Clackamas NW	×
Paradise, Wallowa.......NE	×
● Parker's Polk...........NW	×
Parkersburgh, Coos.......SW	75
Parkersville, Marion.....NW	20
Park Place, Clackamas...NW	×
Patterson's Mills, Dougl'sSW	×
Paulina, Crook..............C	15
Paynesville, Clackamas..NW	×
Pebble, Columbia.........NW	×
Peel, Douglas..............SW	×
● **Pendleton**, Umatilla...N	2,506
● *Pendleton Junc.*, Umatilla N	×
Peninsular, Multnomah..NW	×
Peoria, Linn................W	50
Perdue, Douglas..........SW	×
Peris, Columbia..........NW	×
Perham, Crook............C	×
Perry, Union...............NE	200
● Perrydale, Polk.........NW	50
Pettysville, Morrow.......N	×
Philomath, Benton........W	400
● Phoenix, Jackson.......SW	300
Pilot Rock, Umatilla.......N	130
Pine, Linn..................W	×
Pine City, (see Galloway).....	×
Pine, Union.................NE	35
Pittsburg, Columbia......NW	30
● Plainview, Linn..........W	×
Pleasant Hill, Lane........W	50
Pleasant Home, Mult'ah..NW	200

Oregon

Post Office	Pop.
● Pleasant Valley, Baker...E	×
Plevna, Klamath...........S	32
Plush, Lake..................S	×
Pocahontas, Baker.........E	×
Point Terrace, Lane........W	×
● *Polk*, Polk................NW	×
Port Black Lock, (see Den'k)	×
Porter, Coos...............SW	100
Poor Man's Cr., Jackson.SW	×
● **PORTLAND**, Mult'hNW	46,385
Port Orford, Curry........SW	75
Post, Crook..................C	×
Powell's Valley, Multn'h.NW	120
Prairie City, Grant..........E	222
Prairie Creek, Wallowa...NE	30
Price, Crook..................C	×
● *Priceboro*, Linn..........W	×
Prineville, Crook.........C	460
Progress, Washington....NW	×
Prospect, Jackson........SW	×
Prudy, Umatilla............N	31
Pyburn, Benton............W	×
● *Queonta*, Multnomah..NW	×
Quinn, Columbia...........NW	20
● *Quinn's*, Gilliam..........N	×
Rainier, Columbia.........NW	238
Raleigh, Washington.....NW	×
Randolph, Coos...........SW	36
Raun, Grant................E	×
● *Ray's Landing*, Y'm H'l NW	×
Redland, Clackamas......NW	×
● Reedville, Washington.NW	24
Remote, Coos.............SW	8
Rest, Harney..............SE	×
Reston, Douglas...........SW	×
Reuben, Columbia.........NW	×
● *Rice Hill*, Douglas......SW	×
● Rickreall, Polk..........NW	30
● Riddles, Douglas........SW	50
Ridge, Umatilla..............N	20
Ridgeway Wasco............N	×
Riley, Harney...............SE	×
Ritter, Grant.................E	18
Riverdale, Multnomah....NW	×
Riverside, (see Mist).........	×
Riverside, Malheur........SE	×
Riverside, Multnomah....NW	×
Riverton, Coos.............SW	×
Roberts, Yam Hill.........NW	×
Rock Point, Jackson......SW	25
Rockville, Gilliam..........N	54
Rockwood, Multnomah...NW	25
● *Rooster Rock*, Multn'h.NW	25
● **Roseburgh**, Douglas.SW	1,472
● *Rowena*, Wasco..........N	×
Rowe's, Douglas..........SW	50
● Rowland, Linn............W	10
Roy, (see Mount Angel)......	×
Royal, Lane..................W	×
● *Ruckles*, Douglas.......SW	×
● Ruddock, Umatilla........N	×
Rufus, Sherman.............N	30
Rural, Coos.................SW	×
Russellville, Multnomah.NW	×
Rutledge, Sherman..........N	×
Rye Valley, Baker..........E	50
Sailor Diggings, (see Waldo).	×
Saint Helen, Columbia NW	220
Saint John's, Multnomah.NW	310
● *Saint Joseph*, Yam Hill NW	29
Saint Louis, Marion.....NW	30
● Saint Paul, Marion.....NW	150
Salado, Benton.............W	×
● **SALEM**, Marion.....NW	10,422
Salmon, Clackamas......NW	×
Sam's Valley, Jackson....SW	20
Sandstone, Curry.........SW	×
Sandy, Clackamas........NW	30
Sanger, Union.............NE	100
Santiam, Linn...............W	×
Sauvies, Multnomah......NW	30
● *Sa[illegible]*, Umatilla..........NW	×
● Scappoose, Columbia...NW	75
Scholl's Ferry, Washing'n NW	16
Scio, Linn...................W	253
● *Scio Junction*, Linn......W	×
Scottsburgh, Douglas......SW	80
Scott's Mills, Marion.....NW	25
Seaforth, Curry...........SW	×
Seal Rock, Benton..........W	×
Seaside, Clatsop..........NW	300
Seaton, Lane................W	×
Sellwood, Multnomah....NW	600
Shake, Jackson...........SW	×
Shattuck, Multnomah....NW	×
● *Shaw*, Marion...........NW	×
Sheaville, Malheur.........SE	×

Town, County	Index	Pop.
● Shedd's, Linn	W	355
Shelburn, Linn	W	50
Shelby, Gilliam	N	×
Sherar Bridge, Wasco	N	30
● Sheridan, Yam Hill	NW	299
● *Sheridan Junction*, Polk	NW	×
Sherwood, Washington	NW	×
Shirk, Harney	SE	×
Siletz, Benton	W	×
Silver Lake, Lake	S	25
● Silverton, Marion	NW	511
Silvies, Harney	SE	×
● *Simpson*, Polk	NW	×
● *Siskiyou*, Jackson	SW	50
Sisters, Crook	C	×
Sitkum, Coos	SW	×
Siuslaw, Lane	W	×
Skipanon, Clatsop	NW	150
● *Smithfield*, Polk	NW	×
Smiths, Jackson	SW	×
● *Smockville*, Washington	NW	×
Soda Springs, Jackson	SW	38
Sodaville, Linn	W	66
South Beach, Benton	W	×
● *Southern Portland*, Multnomah	NW	×
Spanish Gulch, (see Camp Watson)		×
Sparta, Union	NE	125
● Spicer, Linn	W	60
Spikenard, Jackson	SW	×
● *Spofford*, Umatilla	N	×
Sprague River, (see Blythe)		×
● Springfield, Lane	W	871
Springwater, Clackamas	NW	×
● *Squally Hook*, Sherman	N	×
Stafford, Clackamas	NW	×
● *Stanton*, Umatilla	N	×
Star, Lane	W	×
Starkey, Union	NE	×
Starvout, Douglas	SW	×
Stayton, Marion	NW	381
Steamboat, Jackson	SW	×
● Steinman, Jackson	SW	×
Stephens, Douglas	SW	×
Sterlingville, Jackson	SW	×
Stewart, Crook	C	×
● *Stockes*, Umatilla	N	×
Stone, Malheur	SE	×
Straightsburg, Wasco	N	×
Sublimity, Marion	NW	80
Sulphur Springs, Douglas	SW	×
Summer Lake, Lake	S	25
Summerville, Union	NE	280
Summit, Benton	W	25
● *Summit*, Wasco	N	×
Sumner, Coos	SW	100
Sumpter, Baker	E	200
Sunnyside, Clackamas	NW	×
Sunnyview, Multnomah	NW	×
Susanville, Grant	E	×
● Suver, Polk	NW	38
Sweet Home, Linn	W	80
● Switzerland, Marion	NW	5
Sycamore, Multnomah	NW	×
Sylvan, Multnomah	NW	×
Syracuse, (see Falls City)		×
Table Rock, Jackson	SW	×
● Talent, Jackson	SW	80
● Tallman, Linn	W	10
● Tangent, Linn	W	129
Tay, (see Fall Creek)		×
Taylor, Multnomah	NW	×
● Telocaset, Union	NE	27
Ten Mile, Douglas	SW	×
● **The Dalles**, Wasco	N	3,800
● *Thomas Fork*, Linn	W	×
Thomas Mill, Jackson	SW	×
Thomson, Lane	W	×
Thurston, Lane	W	×
Tidewater, Benton	W	82
Tigardville, Washington	NW	75
Tillamook, Tillamook	NW	1,000
Tioga, Douglas	SW	×
Toledo, Benton	W	200
Tolo, Jackson	SW	50
● *Townsend*, Marion	N	×
Trask, Tillamook	NW	×
Trent, Lane	W	×
Troutdale, Multnomah	NW	300
● *Troutdale*, Multnomah	NW	×
Tryon, Columbia	NW	60
● Tualitin, Washington	NW	150
Tucker, Wasco	N	×
● Turner, Marion	NW	208
Turn Table, Multnomah	NW	×
● *Twin Buttes*, Linn	W	×

Town, County	Index	Pop.
Tygh Valley, Wasco	N	35
Ukiah, Umatilla	N	31
● Umatilla, Umatilla	N	75
Umqua Ferry, Douglas	SW	175
● **Union**, Union	NE	604
Union Mills, Clackamas	NW	17
Uniontown, Jackson	SW	20
● Unity, Baker	E	10
University Park, Multnomah	NW	×
Upper Astoria, Clatsop	NW	501
Utter City, (see Coos City)		×
Vale, Malheur	SE	131
Van, Harney	SE	×
Varien, Lane	W	40
Vernonia, Columbia	NW	200
Vesper, Clatsop	NW	×
● *Viento*, Wasco	N	×
Villard, (see Grant)		×
● *Vincents*, Yam Hill	NW	×
Vinemaple, Clatsop	NW	×
Vinson, Umatilla	N	17
Viola, Clackamas	NW	50
Vistillas, Klamath	S	×
Wagner, Grant	E	50
Wagner Creek, (see Talent)		×
Waldo, Josephine	SW	50
Waldport, Benton	W	70
Waldron, Benton	W	×
Waldron, Crook	C	96
● Walker, Lane	W	×
● Wallace, Lane	W	×
Wallace Sta., (see Rufus)		×
Wallowa, Wallowa	NE	9
Walterville, Lane	W	×
Walton, Lane	W	×
Wamic, Wasco	N	30
● *Wapato*, Yam Hill	NW	18
Wapinitia, Wasco	N	20
Wardton, Douglas	SW	×
Warm Springs, Crook	C	80
Warner Lake, Lake	S	×
● *Warren*, Columbia	NW	42
● Warren, Umatilla	N	×
Warrendale, Multnomah	NW	×
Warrenton, Clatsop	NW	50
Wasco, Sherman	N	90
Waterford, Columbia	NW	×
Waterloo, Linn	W	45
● Waterman, Grant	E	×
● Weatherby, Baker	E	25
Wellen, Jackson	SW	×
● Wells, Benton	W	25
West Albany, Benton	W	×
West Chehalem, Yam Hill	NW	66
Westfall, Malheur	SE	16
● *West Fork*, Douglas	SW	×
● Weston, Umatilla	N	568
Westport, Clatsop	NW	200
West Portland, Mult'mah.	NW	×
● *West Scio*, Linn	W	×
West Stayton, Marion	NW	×
West Union, Washington	NW	60
Wheatland, Yam Hill	NW	75
Wheeler, Crook	C	×
Whelpley, Jackson	SW	×
Whitcomb, Linn	W	10
Whiteaker, Marion	NW	20
● *White Point*, Jackson	SW	×
● Whiteson, Yam Hill	NW	×
● Wilbur, Douglas	SW	150
● *Wilbur*, Umatilla	N	120
Wilderville, Josephine	SW	25
Wildwood, Lane	W	×
Wilhoit, Clackamas	NW	75
● *Wilkins*, Lane	W	×
Willamette Forks, (see Coburg)		×
Willamette Slough, Mult'h	NW	×
Willamina, Polk	NW	150
Willard, Marion	NW	×
Williams, Josephine	SW	7
● *Willow Junction*, Morrow	N	×
● *Willows*, Gilliam	N	×
Willow Springs, Jackson	SW	×
Willow Springs, (see Ridge)		×
● Willsburgh, Multnomah	NW	100
Wilsonville, Clackamas	NW	×
Wimer, Jackson	SW	×
Winchester, Douglas	SW	50
Wingville, Baker	E	×
Winlock, Grant	E	×
Winniford, Douglas	SW	×
● Wolf Creek, Josephine	SW	30
● Woodburn, Marion	NW	405
Woodlawn, Multnomah	NW	×
Woods, Tillamook	NW	55
● *Woodstock*, Washington	NW	×
Woodstock, Multnomah	NW	×

Town, County	Index	Pop.
● Woodville, Jackson	SW	150
Wren, Benton	W	85
Wright, Jackson	SW	×
Wright's Ridge, Clackamas	NW	×
● *Wyeth*, Wasco	N	×
● Yaquina, Benton	W	500
Yaquina Bay, Benton	W	×
● *Yoakum*, Umatilla	N	×
● Yoncalla, Douglas	SW	30
Zena, Polk	NW	27
Zion, (see Currinsville)		×

PENNSYLVANIA.

COUNTIES.	INDEX.	POP.
Adams	S	33,486
Allegheny	SW	551,959
Armstrong	W	46,747
Beaver	W	50,077
Bedford	S	38,644
Berks	SE	137,327
Blair	C	70,866
Bradford	N	59,233
Bucks	SE	70,615
Butler	W	55,339
Cambria	C	66,375
Cameron	N	7,238
Carbon	E	38,624
Centre	C	43,269
Chester	SE	89,377
Clarion	W	36,802
Clearfield	C	69,565
Clinton	N	28,685
Columbia	C	36,822
Crawford	NW	65,324
Cumberland	S	47,271
Dauphin	C	96,977
Delaware	SE	74,683
Elk	N	22,239
Erie	NW	86,074
Fayette	SW	80,006
Forest	NW	8,482
Franklin	S	51,433
Fulton	S	10,137
Greene	SW	28,935
Huntingdon	C	35,751
Indiana	W	42,175
Jefferson	W	44,005
Juniata	C	16,655
Lackawanna	NE	142,088
Lancaster	SE	149,095
Lawrence	W	37,517
Lebanon	SE	48,131
Lehigh	E	76,631
Luzerne	E	201,203
Lycoming	N	70,579
McKean	N	46,863
Mercer	W	55,744
Mifflin	C	19,996
Monroe	E	20,111
Montgomery	SE	123,290
Montour	C	15,645
Northampton	E	84,220
Northumberland	C	74,698
Perry	C	26,276
Philadelphia	SE	1,046,964
Pike	NE	9,412
Potter	N	22,778
Schuylkill	E	154,163
Snyder	C	17,651
Somerset	SW	37,317
Sullivan	N	11,620
Susquehanna	NE	40,093
Tioga	N	52,313
Union	C	17,820
Venango	NW	46,640
Warren	NW	37,585
Washington	SW	71,155
Wayne	NE	31,010
Westmoreland	SW	112,819
Wyoming	NE	15,891
York	S	99,489
Total		5,258,014

TOWN. COUNTY.	INDEX.	POP.
Aaronsburgh, Centre	C	350
Abattoir Dove Yards, Phil'a	SE	×
Abbottsford, (see Philadelphia)		×
● Abbottstown, Adams	S	400
Abdera, Clinton	N	×
Aberdeen, Dauphin	C	25

● *Aberdeen Sta.*, Lancaster SE ×
Abington, Montgomery SE 200
● Abrams, Montgomery SE 150
Academia, Juniata C 250
● *Academy*, Delaware SE ×
Academy, Montgomery SE 400
● Academy Corners, Tioga N 125
Acker, Ferry C 50
Ackermanville, North'mp'tn E 850
● Ackley Station, Warren NW 100
● *Ackworth*, Chester SE ×
Acme, Westmoreland SW 25
● *Acorn*, Montgomery SW ×
Adah, Fayette SW 10
Adams, Armstrong W 25
● *Adams*, Schuylkill E ×
● *Adamsburg*, Snyder C 375
Adamsburgh, Westmorel'd SW 223
Adamsdale, Schuylkill E ×
Adamstown, Lancaster SE 603
● Adamsville, Crawford NW 150
Adava Station, (see Duff's) ×
Addingham, Delaware SE ×
Addison, Somerset SW 35
Adrian, Armstrong W 100
● *Adrian Mines*, Jefferson W ×
Advance, Indiana W 65
Ætna, (see Etna) ×
Afarata, Mifflin C ×
Agna, Schuylkill E ×
● Agnew, Beaver W 10
● *Agnew*, Allegheny SW ×
● Aiken, McKean N 250
Ailston, York S ×
● *Aineyville*, Lehigh E 639
Airville, York S 400
Airy Dale, Huntington C 150
Aitch, Huntingdon C 50
Akersville, Fulton S 100
● Akron, Lancaster SE 606
● *Aladdin*, Armstrong W ×
Alamanda, Northampton E 40
● *Alaska*, Northumberland C ×
● Alba, Bradford N 163
● Albany, Berks S 150
● Albion, Erie NW 366
● *Albion Station*, Erie NW ×
Albrightsville, Carbon E 200
● Alburtis, Lehigh E 500
● *Alcott's*, Somerset SW ×
Alden Station, Luzerne E 1,300
Aldenville, Wayne NE 100
● Alderson, Luzerne E ×
● Aldham, Chester SE ×
Aleppo, Greene SW 25
Alexander, McKean N ×
Alexandria, Huntingdon C 438
Alexandria, (see Vanderbilt) ×
Alfarata, Mifflin C ×
● Alford, Susquehanna NE 100
Alga, Cumberland S 50
Alice Hollow, (see Allis Hollow) ×
Alinda, Perry C 250
Aline, Snyder C 50
● **ALLEGHENY**, All'y SW 105,287
● *Allegheny Furnace*, Blair C 260
● *Allegrippus*, Blair C ×
Alleman's, Clearfield C ×
Allen, Cumberland S 600
● *Allen*, Susquehanna NE ×
● *Allen Lane*, Philadelphia SE ×
● Allenport, Washington SW 300
Allen's Mills, Jefferson W 200
Allensville, Mifflin C 300
● **Allentown**, Lehigh E 25,228
● *Allentown*, Allegheny SW ×
● Allenwood, Union C 275
Alliquippa, Beaver W ×
Alliquippa, Bedford S 30
Allis Hollow, Bradford N 40
● *Allison*, Schuylkill E ×
Allison Hill, (see Harrisburg) ×
Allison Sta., (see McGovern) ×
● Allport, Clearfield C ×
Almedia, Columbia C 500
● *Alnwick Grove*, Montg'ry SE ×
Alpine, York S 100
● *Alpsville*, Allegheny SW 130
Alsace, Berks SE ×
● Altenwald, Franklin S 50
● *Altodale*, Franklin S ×
● *Alton*, McKean N 600
● Altona, Blair C 30,337
Altus, Bradford N 32
Alum Bank, Bedford S 375
Alum Rock, Clarion W 50
Aluta, Northampton E 75
● Alverton, Westmoreland SW 700

Alvira, Union C 100
Amasa, Lackawanna NE ×
● *Amasa*, Mercer W ×
Amberson's Valley, Franklin S 300
● Ambler, Montgomery SE 1,073
● Ambleside, Fayette SW ×
Ambrose, Indiana W 40
Amesville, Clearfield C ×
● *Amieville*, Westmoreland SW ×
Amity, Washington SW 250
Amityville, (see Douglassville) ×
● Amsbry, Cambria C 100
Amsterdam, (see New Holland) ×
● Analomink, Monroe E 150
● Anandale, Butler W 60
Anchor Station, Warren NW ×
● Andalusia, Bucks SE 875
● *Anderson*, Mifflin C ×
● *Anderson*, Washington SW ×
Andersonburgh, Perry C 260
Andersontown, York S 100
Andesville, (see Loysville) ×
● *Andreas*, Schuylkill E ×
Andrew's Bridge, (see Octoraro) ×
Andrews Settlement, Potter N 50
Angelica, Berks SE 97
Angelica, (see Baldwin) ×
Angels, Wayne NE 25
Angora, Indiana W ×
● *Angora*, Philadelphia SE ×
Anise, Montgomery SE ×
Anita, Jefferson W ×
Annin Creek, McKean N 155
Annisville, (see Shira) ×
● Annville, Lebanon SE 1,283
● Anselma, Chester SE 300
● *Ansonia*, Tioga N 65
Ansonville, Clearfield C 50
Anstead, Somerset SW ×
Antes Fort, Lycoming N 650
Antestown, (see Bellwood) ×
● *Anthracite Tipple*, Alle'y SW ×
● Antrim, Tioga N 1,500
Apollo, Armstrong W 2,156
● *Apollo Sta.*, Westmorel'd SW 50
Appenzell, Monroe E 175
Applebachville, Bucks SE 240
Apple Grove, (see Winterstown) ×
● *Aqua*, Centre C ×
Aquashicola, Carbon E 350
● *Aqueduct*, Perry C 20
Aquetong, Bucks SE 100
Ararat, Susquehanna NE 100
Arbor, York S 30
Arbuckle, Erie NW 300
● *Arcadia*, Lancaster SE ×
● Archbald, Lackawanna NE 4,032
Arch Spring, Blair C 100
● Arcola, Montgomery SE 50
● *Ardara*, Westmoreland SW 5
● Arden, Washington SW 32
● *Ardenheim*, Huntingdon C ×
● Ardmore, Montgomery SE 2,205
Arendtsville, Adams S 300
Argenda, Warren NE ×
Argentine, Butler W 260
Argus, Bucks SE 60
Argyle, (see Petrolia) ×
Ariel, Wayne NE 300
Ariosa, Adams S ×
Arlington, Wayne NE 70
Arlington, Allegheny SW 50
Armagh, Indiana W 162
● Armbrust, Westmoreland SW 50
Armstrong, (see Shelocta) ×
Arndts, Northampton E ×
● *Arnold*, Westmoreland SW ×
Arnold, Armstrong W 10
● Arnot, Tioga N 644
Arona, (see Madison) ×
Arroyo, Elk N 35
● *Arters*, Northumberland C ×
● Arthurs, Clarion W 70
Artz, Schuylkill E 268
Asaph, Tioga N 25
Asbury, Columbia C ×
Ash, Chester SE 30
Ashbaugh, (see Leechburg) ×
● Ashbourne, Montgomery SE 700
● *Ashcom*, Bedford S ×
● Ashcroft, Clearfield C 786
Asherton, Northumberland C ×
Ashfield, Carbon E 75
● *Ashurst*, Lycoming N ×
● Ashland, Schuylkill E 7,346
Ashland Furnace, (see Chest Spr.) ×
● Ashley, Luzerne E 3,192

● *Ashman*, Fayette SW ×
● *Ashton*, Philadelphia SE ×
Ash Tree, Greene SW 5
● Ashville, Cambria C 2[illegible]
Askam, Luzerne E 70
Aspers, Adams S 50
● *Aspinwall*, Allegheny SW ×
Aspinwall, Bradford N 35
Aston Mills, Delaware SE 40
Astoria, Wayne NE 200
Asylum, Bradford N 600
● *Asylum Road*, Dauphin C ×
Atchison, Washington SW 50
Atco, Wayne NE 120
● Atglen, Chester SE 397
● Athens, Bradford N 3,274
Athensville, (see Ardmore) ×
Athol, Berks SE 302
Atkinson's Mills, Mifflin C 120
● Atlantic, Crawford NW 150
Attleboro, (see Langhorne) ×
Atwood, Armstrong W 185
● Auburn, Schuylkill E 880
Auburn Centre, Susqu'hna NE 300
Auburn Four Corners, Sus' NE 140
Auchey's, Schuylkill E ×
● Audenried, Carbon E 1,902
● *Aughanbaugh*, Clinton N ×
● Aughwick Mills, Hunt'don C 75
Augustaville, Northumb'l'd C 700
● *Auguston*, Forest NW ×
Aurora, Bradford N ×
● Austin, Potter N 1,679
Austinburgh, Tioga N 50
Austinville, Bradford N 160
Autumn Leaves, Wayne NE 25
● Avalon, Allegheny SW 1,000
Avata, Lancaster SE ×
Avella, Washington SW ×
● Avenue, Allegheny SW 1,453
● Avery, Wyoming NE ×
● Avoca, Luzerne E 3,031
● Avon, Lebanon SE 250
● Avondale, Chester SE 600
● Avonia, Erie NW 200
Avonmore, Westmoreland SW ×
● *Avonmore*, Indiana W 50
Avoy, Wayne NE ×
● Axemann, Centre C ×
Ayers, (see Brady) ×
Ayer's Hill, Potter N 32
Ayr, Fulton S 20
● *Babcock*, McKean N ×
● *Babcock's Mills*, McKean N 32
Bachmanville, Dauphin C 100
● Bacton, Chester SE 100
● Baden, Beaver W 390
● *Bagdad*, Westmoreland SW ×
Baidland, Washington SW ×
● *Bailey*, Perry C ×
● Bainbridge, Lancaster SE 652
● *Bair*, York S ×
● *Baird*, Washington SW ×
Bairdstown, (see Knight) ×
● *Baker*, Washington SW ×
● *Baker*, Somerset SW ×
● *Baker's*, Chester SE ×
● *Bakers*, Westmoreland SW ×
Bakers Bank, (see Rock Point) ×
Baker's Landing, Beaver W 24
Baker's Summit, Bedford S 120
Bakerstown, Allegheny SW 400
● *Bakerstown*, Allegheny SW ×
Bakerstown Landing, (see Webster) ×
Bakersville, Somerset SW 250
● Bala, Montgomery SE 270
Bald Eagle, York S 160
● *Bald Eagle*, Blair C 300
● *Bald Eagle Junc.*, Clinton N ×
Bald Hill, Greene SW 35
Bald Mount, Lackawanna NE 150
Bald Ridge, Butler W 800
● *Baldwin*, Allegheny SW ×
Baldwin, Butler W 350
Baldwin Sta., (see Steelton) ×
Balfour, Cumberland S 120
● *Ballast Siding*, Adams S ×
Ballibay, Bradford N 120
Balliett, Venango NW 40
● *Balliett*, Carbon E ×
Ballicttsville, Lehigh E 300
Balltown, Forest NW 150
Bally, Berkes SE 359
Balm, Mercer W 100
Balsam, Tioga N ×
Balsinger, Fayette SW ×

Place	Pop.
● *Bamford*, Washington.. SW	×
Banardtown, (see Beaver Falls)	×
Bancroft, Washington.... SW	×
Bandanna, York............ S	50
Bangor, Northampton...... E	2,509
● *BangorJunc.*, NorthamptonE	×
● *Banian Junc.*, Clearfield. C	×
Banksville, Allegheny.... SW	1,000
Bannerville, Snyder........C	85
● Banning, Fayette.......SW	×
● *Barber*, Union...........C	×
Barbour's Mills, Lycoming..N	227
● Barclay, Bradford........ N	829
● *Barclay Junc.*, Bradford. N	×
● Bard, Bedford............ S	100
Bardwell, Wyoming.......NE	32
Barfeldon, (see Liberty)	×
● Bareville, Lancaster..... SE	350
● Barker, Delaware....... SE	25
Barkeyville, Venango.... NW	150
Barlow, Adams..............S	20
Barnard's, Armstrong......W	30
● Barnes, Warren........NW	300
● Barneston, Chester...... SE	200
● Barnesville, Schuylkill... E	125
● Barnitz, Cumberland..... S	175
● Barnsley, Chester....... SE	75
Barr, Mifflin.............. C	25
● Barre Forge, Huntingdon. C	25
Barren Hill, (see Lafay'teHill)	×
Barren Hill, Philadelphia. SE	×
● *Barrett*, Clearfield........ C	×
Barrisville, Beaver........ W	10
Barronvale, Somerset.... SW	50
Barry, Schuylkill........... E	500
● *Barry Junction*, SchuylkillE	×
● *Barry Station*, Schuylkill. E	×
Bart, Lancaster........... SE	300
Bartholdi, Washington ... SW	10
Bartonsville, Monroe....... E	125
● Barto's, Berks........... SE	200
Bartville, Lancaster....... SE	50
Bascobel, Erie............NW	×
Basket, Berks............ SE	×
Baskinsville, Perry..........C	514
Bast, Schuylkill .... E	×
Bastress, Lycoming......... N	25
● Bath, Northampton ...... E	723
Baughmansville, (see E.Ber'n)	×
● *Baum*, Venango....... NW	×
● *Baumgardner*, L'ncastersSE	×
● Baumstown, Berks ..... SE	130
Bausman, Lancaster....... SE	50
Bavington, Washington... SW	100
Baxter, Jefferson.......... W	100
Bayne, Allegheny.........SW	×
● Beachdale, Somerset....SW	20
● Beach Haven, Luzerne.... E	300
● *Beach Haven Ferry*, L'zer'eE	×
Beach Pond, Wayne....... NE	200
Beadling, Allegheny...... SW	×
Beallsville, Washington... SW	360
Beamville, Allegheny..... SW	10
Bean, Bucks ....SE	35
Bean's Cove, Bedford....... S	25
Bear Creek, (see Bruin)......	×
● Bear Creek, Luzerne....... E	250
● *Bear Creek Junc.*, Luzerne E	×
Beardleys, McKean .... N	×
Bear Gap, Northumberland. C	300
● Bear Lake, Warren.....NW	313
● *Bear Loop*, Cambria...... C	×
● *Bear Run*, Fayette..... SW	×
● Beartown, Lancaster.... SE	150
Bear Valley, Northumberl'd C	×
● Beatty, Westmoreland.. SW	90
Beaumont, Wyoming...... NE	150
● *Beaupland*, Luzerne..... E	×
Beautiful, Franklin......... S	×
● **Beaver**, Beaver.........W	1,552
● *Beaver*, Chester......... SE	×
● *Beaver*, Huntingdon...... C	250
● *Beaver*, Dauphin..........C	×
Beaver Centre, Crawford. NW	150
Beaver City, Clarion....... W	200
Beaver Dam Mills, (see Atkinson's Mills)	×
● Beaver Falls, Beaver.....W	9,735
● Beaver Meadows, Carbon. E	600
● Beaver Springs, Snyder...C	375
● Beavertown, Snyder...... C	450
● Beaver Valley, Columbia..C	100
● Bechtelsville, Berks..... SE	93
Beckersville, Berks.........SE	50
● *Beck's*, Schuylkill.........E	50
● *Beck's Cut*, Somerset... SW	×
● *Beck's Mills*, Schuylkill...E	50
Beck's Mills, Washington. SW	50
● *Beck's Run*, Allegheny. SW	×
● **Bedford**, Bedford.......S	2,242
Bedford Springs, Bedford.. S	×
Bedminster, Bucks.......SE	170
Beech Cliff, Allegheny.... SW	300
Beech Creek, Clinton....... N	437
Beech Creek Station, Clinton N	×
● *Beech Glen*, Sullivan.......N	×
Beechmont, Allegheny....SW	×
● Beechtree, Jefferson..... W	500
● *Beech Tree Junc.*, Jeff's'n W	×
● Beechwood, Cameron.... N	100
Beers, Allegheny.......... SW	65
● *Beersville*, Huntingdon... C	×
Beersville, Northampton....E	×
● *Beeson*, Fayette.........SW	×
● *Beeson Mills*, Fayette.. SW	×
Beham, Washington...... SW	×
Bela, Clarion............... W	×
● Belbend, Luzerne......... E	331
Belden, Bedford............ S	50
Belfast, Northampton ...... E	375
● *Belford*, Clearfield........ C	150
● Belfry, Montgomery.....SE	150
Belknap, Armstrong........W	25
● *Bell*, Jefferson........... W	×
● Bellaire, Lancaster...... SE	50
Bellasylva, Wyoming...... NE	32
Belle Bridge, Allegheny.. SW	×
● **Bellefonte**, Centre..... C	3,946
Belle Grove, Lebanon......SE	150
Bellemonte, Lancaster.....SE	20
● Belle Valley, Erie...... NW	39
● Belle Vernon, Fayette.. SW	1,147
● *Belle Vernon Junc.* A'g'ySW	×
● *Belle View*, Allegheny..SW	×
Belleville, Mifflin.......... C	400
● Bellevue, Allegheny.... SW	1,418
● *Bellevue*, Lackawanna.. NE	×
Bellevue, (see Gap)	×
● *Bellevue*, Philadelphia... SE	×
Bellowsville, Beaver........ W	300
● *Bell Road*, Philadelphia. SE	×
● *Bell's*, Westmoreland... SW	×
● *Bell's Camp*, McKean.... N	32
Bells Landing, Clearfield.... C	100
Bell's Mills, (see Bl'k LickSta.)	×
● Bell's Mills, Jefferson.... W	50
Bell's Mills, (seeWest Newton)	×
Bells Run, McKean......... N	50
Bellton, Beaver........... W	×
● Bellwood, Blair.......... C	1,146
● *Belmont*, Philadelphia.. SE	×
Belmont, Wayne.......... NE	×
Belmont, (see Port Carbon)..	×
Belsano, Cambria.......... C	50
● Belsena Mills, Clearfield.. C	×
Beltzhoover, Allegheny... SW	2,009
Beltzville, Carbon .... E	50
Belview, (see Stanton).......	×
Belzaine, (see Allenport).....	×
Ben Avon, Allegheny..... SW	×
● *Benders Jc.*, Northampton E	×
Bendersville, Adams........ S	370
● *Bendersville Sta.*, Adams..S	×
● Benezett, Elk.............N	300
● *Benfer*, Snyder............C	166
Ben Franklin, N'thumb'l'd. C	×
● Ben Gully, Tioga..........N	×
Benjamin, Bucks.......... SE	300
● Bennett, Allegheny..... SW	4,500
● *Bennett*, Luzerne......... E	×
● Bennington Furnace, Bl'ir C	1,000
● Benore, Centre........... C	200
Bensalem, Bucks..........SE	25
● *Ben's Creek*, Cambria.....C	50
Bentley Creek, Bradford... N	160
Bentleyville, Washington. SW	229
● Benton, Columbia........ C	500
● *Benton*, Lancaster....... SE	50
Bentzel, York..............S	×
Benvenue, Dauphin........ C	175
● *Ben Venue*, Allegheny..SW	×
● Benzinger, Elk........... N	×
Berganot, Elk.............. N	×
Bergey, Montgomery...... SE	50
Berlinger, Indiana......... W	50
Berkeley, Somerset....... SW	×
● *Berkley*, Berks.......... SE	100
● Berks, Berks............. SE	2,200
Berlin, (see East Berlin)......	×
● Berlin, Somerset........SW	912
● *Berlin Junc.*, Adams.....S	×
Berlinsville, Northampton.. E	250
Bermudian, Adams .... S	504
● Berne, Berks............ SE	200
● *Bernhart*, Berks........ SE	×
● Bernice, Sullivan......... N	600
Bernville, Berks........... SE	365
● *Berry's Bridge*, Tioga.... N	×
Berrysburgh, Dauphin...... C	426
Berrytown, Bradford....... N	20
Berwick, Adams............ S	381
● Berwick, Columbia....... C	2,701
● Berwinsdale, Clearfield... C	32
● Berwyn, Chester .... SE	300
Bessemer, Lawrence....... W	100
● *Bessemer*, Allegheny....SW	×
● Best, Lehigh.............. E	275
Bethania, (see Kinzer's)......	×
Bethany, Wayne........... NE	134
● *Bethany*, Westmoreland SW	×
● Bethayres, Montgomery.SE	×
● Bethel, Berks ....SE	800
Bethel, (see Booth's Corner) .	×
Bethel, (see Fulton House)..	×
○ *Bethel*, Mercer...........W	81
● *Bethel*, Somerset........SW	75
Bethesda, Lancaster.......SE	75
● Bethlehem, Northampton E	6,762
● *Bethlehem Iron Works* Northampton......... E	×
● *BethlehemJunc.* N'th'mt'nE	×
● *Betzwood*, Montgomery. SE	×
● *Beuchler*, Schuylkill... ..E	×
Bevan, Montgomery.......SE	25
● *Beverly*, Lancaster...... SE	×
● *Biddle*, Westmoreland..SW	×
● *Bidwell*, Fayette........SW	10
● *Biehl*, Union.............C	50
● *Bierer*, Westmoreland..SW	×
Big Bend, (see Mercer).......	×
Big Bend, Venango...... NW	50
Big Cove Tannery, Fulton...S	67
Bigdam, York.............. S	×
● *Bigler*, Clearfield......... C	200
● Biglerville Adams........S	150
● *Big Mine Run Jc.* SchuylkillE	×
Bigmount, York............ S	30
Big Pond, Bradford........ N	50
Big Ridge, Clinton.......... N	×
● Big Run, Jefferson.......W	731
● *Big Run*, Lawrence.......W	×
● Big Shanty, McKean.....N	200
Big Spring, Cumberland.... S	100
Big Tree, Greene.......... SW	×
Bills, Somerset............ SW	20
● Bingen, Northampton....E	180
Bingham, Potter........... N	×
Bingham Centre, Potter.... N	50
Binkley's Bridge, LancasterSE	300
Birchardville, Susqueh'na. NE	150
● *Birdch Island*, Clinton...N	×
Birchrunville, Chester.....SE	125
Birdell, Chester...........SE	×
● Bird in Hand, Lancaster.SE	450
● *Birdsboro*, Berks........SE	130
● Birdsboro, Berks........SE	2,261
● *Birmingham*, AlleghenySW	×
● Birmingham, HuntingdonC	225
● *Birmingham Park*, Ch'sterC	×
Birney, Bradford...........N	30
Bismarck, Lebanon.........SE	575
● *Bissell*, Allegheny....... SW	×
Bissell, Washington.......SW	30
● *Bittenbender*, Berks.....SE	×
Bittersville, York..........S	150
Bitumen, Clinton...........N	×
Bixler, Perry..............C	50
Black, Bradford............N	195
Black Ash, Crawford.....NW	130
Blackburn, WestmorelandSW	40
● *Black Creek*, Luzerne.... E	×
● *BlackCreekJunction* C'b'nE	×
● *Black Diamond*, Wash'nSW	×
Black Forest, Potter.......N	×
Black Hawk, Beaver........W	75
Black Horse, Chester......SE	50
Black Horse, (see LeamanPl.)	×
Black Lick, (see Ebensburg) .	×
Black Lick, (seeBl'k Lick Sta.)	×
● Black Lick Station, Ind'a W	300
Blacklog, Juniata..........C	200
Blacklog, Huntingdon...... C	50
● *Black Ridge*, Luzerne....E	65
● Black Rock, York........S	300
● *Black's* Clarion......... W	×
Black's Gap, Franklin......S	140
Black's Run, Allegheny..SW	×
● Black Walnut, WyomingNE	260
● *Blackwell's*, Tioga........N	140
● Blackwood, Schuylkill....E	×
Blain, Perry............... C	249

Place	Pop.
● *Blain City*, Clearfield.....C	534
Blainsport, Lancaster......SE	100
● *Blair Furnace*, Blair.....C	×
● Blair's Corners, Clarion..W	150
Blair's Mills, Huntingdon...C	100
● Blair Station, AlleghenySW	×
● Blairsville, Indiana........W	3,126
● *BlairsvilleInt.* W'stm'l'dSW	100
Blakely, Lackawanna.....NE	2,552
● *Blake's*, Luzerne ....E	×
Blakeslee, Monroe..........E	100
● Blanchard, Centre........C	400
Blanco, Armstrong.... ....W	10
● Blandon, Berks.......... SE	200
Blanket Hill, Armstrong...W	20
Blindtown, Luzerne........ E	×
Bloody Run, (see Everett) ...	×
● *Bloom Ferry*, Columbia..C	×
Bloomfield, (see Pittsburg)..	×
Bloomfield, Crawford.... NW	50
Bloomfield, Perry...........C	737
Bloomingdale, Luzerne.....E	130
Blooming Glen, Bucks.....SE	300
Blooming Grove, Pike.....NE	150
Bloomington, Clearfield.....C	85
Blooming Valley, Crawf'dNW	206
● **Bloomsburgh**, Col'bia.C	4,635
Bloserville, Cumberland.... S	100
● Blossburgh, Tioga........ N	2,568
Blue Ball, Lancaster.......SE	250
● *Blue Ball*, Clearfield......C	50
Blue Bell, Montgomery....SE	100
● *Blue Grass*, PhiladelphiaSE	×
Blue Knob, Blair............C	110
Blue Ridge Summit, Fr'klinS	100
● Blue Rock, Chester......SE	210
● *Blue Rock*, Jefferson ....W	×
● *Blue Run*, Tioga ....N	×
● *BluestoneQuarry*, Fay'teSW	×
Bluff, Greene............. SW	×
● Blythedale, Allegheny.. SW	600
Boalsburgh, Centre........C	360
Bocktown, (see Seventy-Six).	×
● Bodines, Lycoming.......N	125
Boggs, Allegheny...........SW	×
Boggsville, Armstrong.....W	×
● Boiling Springs, Cumb'l'd.S	1,000
● Bolivar, Westmoreland.SW	410
Bomberger, Lebanon...... SE	×
● *Bonair*, Bucks.......... SE	×
● *Bonnaffon*, Philadelphia SE	×
Bonneauville, Adams.......S	200
Bonnie Brook, (see Butler) ..	×
● *Bonny Brook*, Cumberla'dS	×
Bonview, Lancaster ....SE	×
Booher Mine, Huntingdon..C	×
Boone, Somerset..........SW	75
● *Boone*, Delaware........SE	×
● Booneville, Clinton........N	1 0
Booth Corner, Delaware...SE	4 0
● Boothwyn, Delaware ....SE	25
Boquet, Westmoreland....SW	50
● Borard, Butler ....W	50
Bordell City, (see Southard) .	×
● *Border*, Cambria..........C	×
Borie, Potter................N	65
● *Borie's*, Bucks.......... SE	×
Boscobel, Erie...........NW	×
Bossardsville, Monroe.......E	90
● *Bossler*, Blair.............C	×
● Boston, Allegheny...... SW	400
Boston Mines, Luzerne.....E	×
Boston Run, Schuylkill.....E	×
Bottsville, Westmoreland.SW	15
Boucher, Westmoreland.. SW	100
● *Boughton*, Venango....NW	×
● *Bouquet*, Allegheny.... SW	×
Bousson, Crawford.......NW	30
● *Bovard*, Butler...........W	50
● *Bow*, Indiana............ W	×
Bower, Clearfield........... C	125
● *Bower Hill*, Allegheny..SW	45
Bower Hill, Washington..SW	25
● Bower's Station, Berks..SE	175
● *Bowman*, Somerset.....SW	20
● *Bowman's*, Carbon.......E	×
● *Bowman's*, Forest.......NW	×
Bowman Creek, Wyoming NE	195
● Bowmansdale, Cumb'land S	150
Bowmanstown, (see Prince).	×
Bowmansville, Lancaster..SE	250
● *Boyce*, Mercer...........W	×
Boyce's, (see Harriottsville)..	×
● Boyce Station, AlleghenySW	50
● *Boyd*, Northumberland ..C	×
● *Boyd*, Dauphin..... C	×
Boyd's, Adams..............S	18

Place	Pop.
Boyd's Mills, Wayne..... NE	×
● *Boyer Run Intersection* Westmoreland.........SW	×
Boyers, Butler............. W	50
Boyers Mill, (see Rural V'y)	×
● Boyertown, Berks.......SE	1,436
Boyle, Westmoreland.......SW	100
● Boynton, Somerset .....SW	59
● *Boynton*, Centre..........C	×
● *Brackenridge*, Alleghe'ySW	×
Brackney, Susquehanna.. NE	100
● *Bracker*, Somerset......SW	×
● Braddock, Allegheny... SW	8,561
● *Braddock*, Washington.SW	×
Braddock's Field, (see Braddock).........................	×
● Bradenville, W'tmorel'dSW	500
● Bradford, McKean.......N	10,514
● *Bradford Hills*, Chester.SE	×
● *Bradley*, Cambria.........C	×
● Bradleytown, Venango.NW	50
Brady, Clarion.............W	1,500
● *Brady*, Cumberland.......S	366
Brady, Indiana..............W	500
● *Brady*, Northumberland..C	×
● Brady's Bend, ArmstrongW	400
Brady's Run, (see Fallston)..	×
● *Braeburn*, Westmorel'dSW	40
Bragtown, (see Bermudian)..	×
● *Bralliers Siding*, Bedford.S	×
Braman, Wayne...........NE	50
● *Bramcote*, Montgomery.SE	×
● *Branch*, Mercer..........W	×
● Branch Dale, Schuylkill...E	1,000
● *Branch Intersection*, D'p'nC	×
● Branch Junc., West'landSW	100
● Branchton, Butler.........W	65
Branchtown, (see Philadel'a)	×
Branchville, (see McKean)...	×
● Brandamore, Chester....SE	10
● *Brandon*, Venango.....NW	×
● Brandonville, Schuylkill..E	150
● Brandt, Susquehanna...NE	500
● Brandtsville, Cumberland.S	25
Brandy Camp, Elk...........N	82
Brandywine Manor, Ches'rSE	500
● Brandywine Summit, Delaware..................SE	350
● *Brattonville*, Armstrong. W	100
Brave, Greene............SW	×
● Breadysville, Bucks..... SE	100
● *Breaker Number Ten*, Schuylkill...............E	×
Breakneck, (see Evans City)..	×
● Breinigsville, Lehigh.......E	175
● Breneman, Washington.SW	×
● Briar Creek, Columbia....C	×
Brick Church, Armstrong..W	×
Brickerville, Lancaster.... SE	250
Brick Tavern, Bucks...... SE	50
● *Bridesburgh*, Phila'phia.SE	×
● *Bridge*, Clarion.......... W	×
● *Bridge No. 28*, Luzerne...E	×
● *Bridge Junction*, LuzerneE	×
● *Bridgeport*, Cumberland..S	300
Bridgeport, Fayette.......SW	1,039
Bridgeport, WestmorelandSW	1,000
Bridgeton, (see Upper Black Eddy)........................	×
● Bridgeton, York.......... S	150
Bridge Valley, Bucks......SE	300
● Bridgeville, Allegheny..SW	600
Bridgewater, Beaver.......W	1,177
● Bridgewater, Bucks.....SE	75
● *Bridgewater*, Delaware.. W	×
Briggsville, Luzerne......... E	25
● *Bright*, Northumberland..S	×
● Brillhart, York............S	100
● *Brinker*, Butler...........W	×
● *Brinker Run Intersection*, Westmoreland........ SW	×
Brinkerton, Clarion........W	20
Brink Hill, Bradford........N	×
● Brinton, Allegheny.....SW	400
● *Brinton's Bridge*, ChesterSE	×
● Brisbin, Clearfield....... C	1,508
● Bristol, Bucks............SE	6,553
● *Bristol Road*, Bucks.....SE	×
Bristoria, Greene..........SW	100
Broad Axe, Montgomery.. SE	150
● Broad Ford, Fayette....SW	800
● Broad Mountain, Sch'kill.E	50
● *Broad Run*, Chester.....SE	×
Broad Top, Huntingdon.....C	240
Broadway, Luzerne........ E	×
Brock, Greene.............SW	25
● Brockport, Elk.......... N	300

Place	Pop.
● *Brockville*, Schuylkill.....E	×
● Brockwayville, Jefferson. W	929
● Brodbeck's, York.........S	100
Broder, McKean............N	×
Brodhead, (see Crafton)......	×
● Brodhead, Northampton..E	175
Brodheadsville, Monroe.....E	554
● *Brogueville*, York.........S	25
Brogueville, York...........S	150
● *Broken Rock*, Clarion....W	×
Brookdale, Susquehanna..NE	245
● *Brookfield*, Allegheny...SW	×
● *Brookfield*, Chester......SE	×
Brookfield, Tioga...........N	150
Brookland, Potter..........N	75
● *Brooklyn*, Chester.......SE	×
Brooklyn, Susquehanna...NE	300
● *Brookside*, Franklin.......S	×
Brookside, Lycoming.......N	42
● *Brookside*, Schuylkill.....E	×
● *Brook Siding*, SomersetSW	×
● *Brook's Mills*, Blair.......C	×
● Brookston, Forest......NW	300
● *Brook Tunnell*, Som'setSW	×
● **Brookville**, Jefferson..W	2,478
● *Brookwood*, Huntingdon..C	×
Broomall, Delaware....... SE	100
Broughton, Allegheny.... SW	×
Brower, Berks..............SE	100
● Brownfield, Fayette.....SW	300
Brown Hill, Crawford....NW	50
Brown Hollow, Lackaw'naNE	195
Brownington,(see West Lib'ty	×
Brownlee, Tioga............ N	10
● *Brown's*, Allegheny.... SW	×
Brown's, Beaver............W	50
● *Brown's*, Beaver......... W	×
● *Brown's* Clinton.......... N	100
Brownsburgh, Bucks......SE	100
Brownsdale, Butler.........W	100
Brown's Mills, Forest....NW	×
Brown's Mills,(see Kauffman)	×
● *Brownstone*, Dauphin.... C	×
Brownstown, Cambria...... C	550
Brownstown, (see Pittsburg).	×
Brownstown,(see West Earl).	×
Brownsville,(see Feasterville)	×
● Brownsville, Fayette....SW	1,417
● *Brownsville*, Schuylkill...E	×
Brownsville,(see Sandy Lake)	×
Browntown, (see Wyalusing)	×
● *Browntown*, Luzerne.....E	×
● *Brubaker Junction*, Cl'fi'dC	×
● *Bruce*, York............. S	×
● *Bruckarts*, Lancaster....SE	300
● Bruin, Butler............ W	225
Brumfieldville, Berks......SE	100
Brunnerville, Lancaster....SE	100
Brush Creek, Beaver........W	200
● *Brush Run*, Adams.......S	×
● Brushton, Allegheny... SW	×
Brushtown, (see Huntsdale)..	×
Brush Valley, Indiana.......W	225
Brushville, Bradford........N	89
Brushville, (see Susquehanna)	×
Bryan, Armstrong..........W	20
Bryan Mill, Lycoming......N	×
● Bryansville, York.........S	120
● Bryn Mawr, MontgomerySE	1,000
Brysonia, Adams............S	10
● *Buchanan*, Crawford.. NW	×
● *Buchanan's Road*, Ch'erSE	×
Buck, Lancaster............SE	150
● *Buckeye*, WestmorelandSW	×
Buckhorn, Columbia........C	175
● Buckingham, Bucks.....SE	500
Buckingham Valley, BucksSE	×
● *Buck Lock*, Dauphin......C	×
Buckmanville, Bucks.......SE	140
● Buck Mountain, SchuylkillE	45
Buck Run, Chester..........SE	50
Buck's Mills, (see Loretto)...	×
Bucktown, Somerset......SW	100
Bucksville, Bucks..........SE	50
Buck Valley, Fulton.........S	35
● *Buckville*, Schuylkill......E	×
● Buckwalter, Cameron.... N	500
Buell, Crawford...........NW	×
● Buena Vista, Allegheny.SW	672
Buena Vista, Butler....... W	200
Buffalo, Washington...... SW	59
● *Buffalo Bridge*, SomersetSW	×
● Buffalo Cross Roads, UnionC	50
Buffalo Mills, (see Worth'ton)	×
● Buffalo Mills, Bedford.....S	250
● Buffalo Run, Centre.......C	200
Buffington, Indiana........ W	×

Place	Pop.
● Bulger, Washington.... SW	150
Bullion, Venango.........NW	1,300
● *Bullis Mills*, McKean.... N	×
Bull Town, (see Banksville)..	×
Bumpville, Bradford........ N	50
● Bunker Hill, Lebanon...SE	20
BunkerHill, WestmorelandSW	897
● Bunola, Allegheny......SW	526
Burdette, Greene.........SW	×
● Burgettstown, Wash'tonSW	929
● *Burkett*, Blair............C	×
● *Burkholder*, Somerset..SW	×
Burlingame, Lycoming.....N	×
Burlington, Bradford......N	166
● Burmont, Delaware.....SE	200
BurnettStation,(seeHilliard's)	×
Burnham, Mifflin........... C	×
Burning Bush, Bedford......S	20
Burning Well, McKean.....N	130
● *Burn's Ford*, Fayette.. SW	×
Burnside, Clearfield.........C	292
Burnsville, (see West Finley)	×
Burnt Cabins, Fulton........S	150
● Burnwood, SusquehannaNE	400
● Burrell, Westmoreland.SW	50
● Burrows, McKean........N	200
Bursonville, Bucks.........SE	160
● Burtville, Potter..........N	100
Bushkill, Pike............ NE	150
Bushkill Centre, No'hamptonE	50
Bushkill Station, N'hamptonE	×
Bushman, Blair.............. C	15
● Bustleton, Philadelphia..SE	1,200
● *Bute*, Fayette...........SW	×
● **Butler**, Butler..........W	8,734
Butler, Schuylkill...........E	×
● *Butler Junction*, Butler. W	×
● *Butler's*, Potter.......... N	×
● *Butler Street*, AlleghenySW	×
Butment, Clearfield.........C	×
Buttercup, Butler..........W	25
Buttonwood, Lycoming.....N	**25**
● *Butts*, Centre............. C	×
● *Buttsville*, McKean.......N	600
● *Butzbach*, Luzerne........E	×
● Butztown, Northampton..E	150
Buyerstown, Lancaster.... SE	100
Buzz, Greene.............SW	×
Byberry, Philadelphia..... SE	50
● *Byberry Road*, Montg'erySE	×
● *Bycot*, Bucks............SE	×
● *Byers*, Chester...........SE	250
Byrom Centre, Venango..NW	100
● Byromtown, Forest.... NW	200
Cabbane, York.............. S	200
● *Cabeens Branch*, Lan'sterSE	×
● Cabel, Northumberland...C	32
Cabinet, (see Ardmore)	×
Cabin Run, Columbia....... C	×
Cacoosing, Berks...........SE	32
Cadis, Bradford.............N	25
Cain's, Lancaster...........SE	400
Calamity, (see West Elizabeth)	×
Calcium, Berks............ SE	32
Caldwell, Clinton............N	32
Caledonia, Elk..............N	200
● *California*, Luzerne.......E	×
California, Montour.........C	×
● California, Washington. SW	1,024
Calkins, Wayne........... NE	20
Callensburgh, Clarion...... W	2,164
● Callery, Butler........... W	200
Calls, Greene..............SW	×
● Caln, Chester............SE	130
● Calumet, WestmorelandSW	300
Calvin, Huntingdon.........C	100
Calvin'sCorners, CrawfordNW	32
Camargo, Lancaster...... SE	125
Cambra, Luzerne............E	200
CambriaSta., (see Anselma)..	×
Cambria, (see Johnstown)....	×
Cambria Mills, (seeFallenTimber)	×
Cambridge, Lancaster ..... SE	450
Cambridge, (seeCambridgeboro)	×
● Cambridgeboro, Craw'rdNW	912
● Camden, Allegheny.....SW	300
● Cameron, Cameron.......N	400
● *Cameron*, Northumbe'landC	×
● Cammal, Lycoming.......N	65
Cammal Junc., Lycoming..N	×
● *Campbell*, York...........S	×
Campbell'sFarm, (see Petrolia)	×
Campbelltown, Lebanon...SE	350
Campbellville, Sullivan..... N	40
● Camp Ground, Delaware SE	50
Camp Hill, Cumberland.....S	191
● *Camp Hill*, Montgomery SE	×
Camp Run, (see Lily).........	×

Place	Pop.
Camp Run, Jefferson.... ..W	×
Camp Siding, Cumberland..S	×
Camptown, Bradford........N	200
Canadensis, Monroe........E	200
Canal, Venango.......... NW	27
● *Canan*, Blair..............C	×
Canby, Columbia............C	65
Candor, Washington......SW	100
● Cannelton, Beaver........W	150
● Cannonsburgh, Washi'onSW	2,113
● Canoe Camp, Tioga...... N	100
● Canoe Creek, Blair........C	0
● *Canoe* [illegible] Jefferson.. W	×
Canoe Ridge, (see Flora)	×
● Canton, Bradford........ N	1,393
Capoosa, Lackawanna.....NE	×
Carbon, Carbon..............E	150
● *Carbon*, (see Dudley)	×
● *Carbon*, Lawrence......NE	1
● *Carbon*, Mercer..........W	×
● Carbon Black, Butler....W	90
● Carbon Center, Butler...W	
● Carbondale, LackawannaNE	10,833
Carbon Run, (see Barclay)...	×
Cardington, Delaware..... SE	50
Cardville, (see Burgettstown)	×
Carley Brook, Wayne.... NE	100
● **Carlisle**, Cumberland...S	4,620
● *Carlisle Junc.*, Cumberl'ndS	×
Carlisle Springs, CumberlandS	275
● *Carlsons*, Elk............N	×
● Carlton, Mercer...........W	50
● *Carman*, Elk.............N	100
● *Carman Interchange*, ElkN	×
● *Carman Station*, Elk.... N	×
● *Carman Transfer*, Elk...N	×
Carmichael's, Greene.....SW	445
● *Carney*, Westmoreland. SW	×
Carney, Wyoming.........NE	×
[illegible]rnot, Allegheny...... SW	×
Carothers, Lawrence.......W	×
● Carpenter, Lycoming.... N	25
Carpenters, (see Irwin)	×
● *Carpenter*, Philadelphia.SE	×
Carperstown, (see Annville).	×
Carrick, Allegheny........SW	1,000
Carrick Furnace, (see Metal)	×
● Carrier, Jefferson.........W	100
Carroll, Clinton.............N	100
Carrollton, (seeMongah'l'aCity)	×
Carrollton, Cambria..........C	634
Carsonvile, Dauphin........ C	100
Carter Camp, Potter.........N	32
Carter Hill, Erie......... NW	40
Cartwright, Elk.............N	500
Carversville, Bucks........SE	212
Carverton, Luzerne.........E	65
Cashtown, Adams...........S	175
● Cassandra, Cambria.......C	300
● Casselman, Somerset....SW	100
Cassville, Huntingdon.......C	185
Castanea, Clinton..........N	×
Castile, Greene............SW	10
● Castle Fin, York...........S	350
● Castle Shannon, Allegh'ySW	500
● Cataract, Clearfield....... C	×
● Catasauqua, Lehigh.......E	3,704
Catasauqua, Northampton.E	998
● Catawissa, Columbia......C	1,809
● *Catawissa, Jc.*, Columbia.C	×
● Catfish, Clarion.......... W	150
Cato, Center............... C	×
Caylor's Ferry, Beaver.....W	×
Cease's Mills, Lucerne...... E	65
Cecil, Washington.........SW	40
Cedar Grove, (seePhiladelphia)	×
Cedar Hill, Philadelphia.. SE	×
● *Cedar Hollow*, Chester.. SE	×
● Cedar Knowl, Chester...SE	200
● Cedar Lane, Lancaster.. SE	100
Cedar Rock, Huntingdon....C	×
● Cedar Run, Lycoming....N	40
Cedar Run, (see Centre).....	×
Cedars, Montgomery........SE	50
Cedar Springs, Clinton......N	150
Cedarville, Chester........ SE	200
Celia, Beaver...............W	×
Cementon, Lehigh...........E	300
● *Cemetery Siding*, CambriaC	×
Centennial, Adams..........C	150
Centerville, Cumberland....S	174
● Central, Columbia........ C	425
● Centralia, Columbia.......C	2,761
Centre, Perry.............. C	200
Centre Bridge, Bucks......SE	140
● Centre Hall, Centre....... C	441
Centre Hill, Armstrong.... W	10
Centre Hill, Centre..........C	50

Place	Pop.
Centre Mills, Centre.........C	65
● *Centre Mills Sta.*, Adams..S	×
Centre Moreland, Wyom'gNE	350
Centre Point, (see Worcester)	×
Centreport, Berks.........SE	**133**
● Centre Road Sta, Crawt'dNW	260
Centre Square, (see WestEarl)	×
Centre Square, Montg'm'rySE	100
Centretown, Mercer........W	50
Centre Val., Armstrong....W	40
● Centre Valley, Lehigh.... E	250
Centreview, Dauphin....... C	25
Centreville, (see Ridgeburg)..	×
Centreville, (see Deanville)...	×
Centreville, (seeBuckingham)	×
Centreville, (see Cumb'l'dVal.)	×
Centreville, (see Garfield)	×
Centreville, (seeNewFlorence)	×
Centreville, (see MiltonGrove)	×
Centreville, (see Liverpool)...	×
Centreville, (see E, Bethleh'm)	×
Centreville, Butler..........W	448
● *Centreville*, Chester......SE	150
● Centreville, Crawford..NW	274
● *Centreville*, Elk.......... N	×
Centreville, York........... S	×
Ceres, (see Ceres, N Y.)......	×
● Cessna, Bedford...........S	200
Cetronia, Lehigh............E	250
Ceylon, Greene............SW	136
● Chadd's Ford, Delaware.SE	150
● Chadd's Ford Jc., ChesterSE	×
Chaffee, Elk................ N	150
● Chain Dam, NorthamptonE	×
● Chalfont, Bucks.......... SE	500
Chalk Hill, (see Fayette Spr.)	×
Challenge, Elk..............N	100
● *Chambers*, Westmorela'dSW	×
● **Chambersburgh**, Franklin.............S	7,863
Chambersville, Indiana.....W	50
Champion, Fayette........SW	25
● *Chamouni*, Lycoming.....N	127
Chanceford, York.......... S	75
Chandlersburg, (see Elk Run)	×
Chandler's Valley, WarrenNW	400
Chandlerville, (see Landenburg)	×
Chaneysville, Bedford.......S	200
Chapel, Berks..............SE	75
Chapinville, Crawford....NW	65
● *Chapman*, Lehigh........ E	×
Chapman, Snyder........... C	280
● Chapman Quarries, North'nE	392
Chapman's Run, Bedford...S	50
● Charleroi, Washington..SW	2,500
● *CharleroiSta.*, Westm'ndSW	×
Charleston, (see Hill)	×
Charleston, Tioga...........N	130
Charlesville, Bedford........S	100
● Chartiers, Allegheny....SW	2,983
Chase's Mills, Tioga........ N	50
● Chatham, Chester....... SE	300
Chatham Run, Clinton.......N	300
Chatham Valley, Tioga......N	75
Chauncy, Luzerne...........E	×
Cheat Haven, Fayette.....SW	×
Cheerful, Clarion...........W	20
Chelsea, Delaware........ SE	286
● Cheltenham, Montgome'ySE	300
● *Chelten Hills*, Montgom'ySE	×
Chemung, Lycoming....... N	×
Chenango, Lawrence.......W	26
Cherry Flats, Tioga..........N	125
● *Cherry Ford*, Lehigh..... E	×
Cherry Grove, Warren... NW	300
Cherry Hill, Erie.........NW	100
Cherry Mills, Sullivan.......N	40
Cherry Ridge, Wayne..... NE	60
● Cherry Run, Union........C	100
Cherry Spring, Potter.......N	19
Cherry Tree, Venango.....NW	75
Cherry Tree, Indiana....... W	324
Cherryville, Northampton.. E	225
● Chester, Delaware.......SE	20,226
● Chester Heights, Delaw'reSE	50
Chester Hill, Clearfield......C	563
● Chester Springs, Chester.SE	340
● Chester Valley, Chester..SE	200
● *Chester Valley Intersection*, Chester................ SE	×
Chesterville, Chester.......SE	100
Chestnut Grove, (seeElizabetht'n)	×
● Chestnut Hill, Philadelp'aSE	2,300
Chestnut Level, Lancaster. SE	50
Chest Springs, Cambria..... C	255
● Cheswick, Allegheny....SW	17
● Chewton, Lawrence...... W	160
● Cheyney, Delaware...... SE	250

● Chickies, Lancaster......S E 300
● Chicora, Butler.......... W 1,162
● *Childs*, Erie............ NW ×
Chillisquaque, Northumb'l'dC 100
● Chinchilla, Lackawanna. NE 300
● *Chiques*, Lancaster.......SE 300
Choconut, Susquehanna...NE 400
● Christiana, Lancaster....SE 800
Christler's L'd'g, (seeShippingsp't) ×
● Christy Park, AlleghenySW 600
Chrome, Chester...........SE 75
Chrystal, Potter............N 195
● Chulasky, Northumberl'ndC 100
● Church, Clarion............W 50
● Church Hill, Bucks......SE 100
Churchtown, (see Allen) ..... ×
Churchtown, Lancaster....SE 840
● *ChurchtownRd.*, Lances'rSE ×
Churchville, (see Bally)....... ×
● Churchville, Bucks...... SE 100
Churchville, Dauphin....... C 603
Circleville, Westmoreland SW 300
Cisna Run, Perry............C 25
● *City Farm*, Allegheny.. SW 260
Clara, Potter...............N 260
● *Clermont*, Allegheny....SW ×
Clarence, Centre............ C 100
● Clarendon, Warren......NW 1,297
● Claridge, Westmoreland SW 200
Clarington, Forest.........NW 400
● **Clarion**, Clarion.........W 1,183
● *Clarion*, Elk...............N ×
● *Clarion Junc.*, Clarion....W ×
● *Clarion Junc.*, Elk....... N ×
● *Clarks*, Centre............C ×
● Clark, Mercer............W 300
● *Clark*, Mercer............W 200
Clarkestown, Lycoming.....N 93
Clarksburgh, Indiana...... W 100
● *Clarks Cross.*, Westmorel'dSW ×
● *Clark's Ferry*, Dauphin...C ×
Clarks Green, LackawannaNE 300
● Clark's Mills, Mercer.... W 200
● *Clark's Siding*, Cambria.. C ×
● Clark's Summit, Lacka'aNE 122
Clarkstown, Lycoming..... N 93
● *Clarks Valley*, Dauphin.. C ×
Clarksville, Greene....... SW 850
● *Clarksville*, Mercer...... W ×
Clarktown, (see Ten Mile) ... ×
Clarmont, (see Hoboken).... ×
Claussville, Lehigh.......... E 100
Clay, Lancaaster............SE 75
Clay Hill, Franklin..........S 25
Clay Lick, Franklin.......... S 42
Claysburgh, Blair............C 250
● Claysville, Washington..SW 1,041
Clayton, Berks..............SE 200
Clayville, Jefferson......... W 1 042
● **Clearfield**, Clearfield....C 2 248
Clearfield Bridge, Clearfield.C ×
● *Clearfield Junc.*, ClearfieldC ×
Clear Ridge, Fulton.......... S 41
Clear Spring, York...........S 175
Clearview, Lawrence.......W [illegible]
Clearville, Bedford..........S [illegible]
● *Clement*, NorthumberlandC ×
● Clemo, Wayne.......... NE 150
● Cleona, Lebanon.........SE ×
● Clermont, McKean........ N 450
● Cleversburgh, CumberlandS 200
● Cliff Mine, Allegheny...SW 10
Clifford, Susquehanna.....NE 400
● *Cliff's*, Bedford............S ×
● *Clifton*, Allegheny......S W ×
● *Clifton*, Dauphin..........C ×
Clifton, Lackawanna...... NE 250
● Clifton Heights, DelawareSE 1,820
Climax, Clarion............ W ×
● *Clingan*, Berks...........SE ×
Clinton, Allegheny........SW 250
Clinton, (see Kelly's Station). ×
● *Clinton*, Beaver..........W ×
● *Clinton*, Fayette.........SW ×
● *Clinton*, Potter........... N ×
Clintondale, Clinton........ N 175
Clintonville, Venango.....NW 253
Cloe, Jefferson.............. W ×
● Clokey, Washington.... SW 75
● *Clokeyville Jc.*, Washi'onSW ×
● *Clonmell*, Chester........SE 32
Cloud, Chester.............SE 50
Clover Creek, Blair.........C 169
Clover Hill, (seeEastBethleh'm ×
Clyde, Indiana..............W 30
● *Clyde*, Northampton.......E ×
● Coal Bluff, Washington. SW 300

● Coal Centre, WashingtonSW 569
Coal City, Venango..........SW 14
● *Coaldale*, Allegheny....SW ×
Coaldale, Bedford............S 272
● Coaldale, Schuylkill.......E 1,849
● Coal Glen, Jefferson......W 300
Coal Hill, Venango....... NW 30
● Coalmont, Huntingdon....C 219
● *Coal Pit*, WestmorelandSW ×
● *Coalport*, Carbon......... E ×
● Coalport, Clearfield....... C 855
● *CoalRun Junc.*, Clearfield. C ×
● *Coal Siding*, Somerset.. SW ×
● *Coal Siding*, York.........S ×
● Coaltown, Butler.........W 200
● *Coaltown Junc.*, Butler.. W ×
● Coal Valley, Allegheny..SW 300
● *Coal Works*, Allegheny.SW ×
● Coatesville, Chester......SE 3,680
● Cobham, Warren..... .NW 60
● Coburn, Centre.......... C 200
Cocalico, Lancaster.........SE 75
● *Cochran*, Allegheny.... SW 700
● *Cochran*, Fayette.........SW ×
● *Cochran Mine*, SomersetSW ×
● *Cochran's Mills*, Allegh'ySW 100
Cochran's Mills, ArmstrongW 100
● Cochranton, Crawford. NW 655
Cochranville, Chester......SE 350
Cocolamus, Juniata ....C 200
● Codorus, York.............S 500
● *Coffee Run*, Mckean.......N ×
Coffee Run, (see Entriken)... ×
● *Coffey'sCrossing*, Wash'nSW ×
Coffeetown, Northampton..E ×
Cogan House, Lycoming....N 75
● Cogan Station, Lycoming. N 150
Cogan Valley, (see Cogan)... ×
Coheva, Lebanon ....SE 800
● Cohn, Union..............C ×
● Cokeville, Westmorel'ndSW 664
Cold Creek, Bradford.......N 32
● *Cold Point*, MontgomerySE ×
● *Cold Run*, Berks..........SE ×
● *ColdSpring*, Bucks.......SE ×
● *Cold Spring*, Lebanon...SE 65
● *Cold Spring*, Lebanon...SE ×
Cold Spring, Wayne.......NE 30
● *Cold Spring*, York..........S ×
● Colebrook, Lebanon...... SE 100
Colebrookdale, Berks.......SE 800
● *Colebrookdale*, Berks....SE ×
● Colegrove, McKean ......N 40
Coleman, Allegheny.......SW ×
● *Coleman*, McKean.........N ×
● Coleman, Somerset .....SW 50
Colemanville, Lancaster...SE 250
Colerain, Lancaster.........SE 60
● *Cole's*, Huntingdon ....C 100
Colesburgh, Potter..........N 160
● Cole's Creek, Columbia...C 100
● Cole'sSummit, HuntingdonC 10
Coleville, Centre............C 592
Coleville, McKean...........N 75
● *Colfax*, Allegheny........ SW ×
Colfax, Huntingdon.........C 25
● *Colgrove*, Warren.......NW ×
Collamer, Chester ....SE 200
● *College*, Beaver ....W ×
● Collegeville, MontgomerySE 900
Colley, Sullivan ....N 350
● *Collier*, Blair..............C ×
● *Colliers*, Washington ...SW ×
● Collingdalle, Delaware ..SE 300
Collins, Lancaster..........SE 30
● *Collins*, Lancaster.......SE ×
Collins, Venango.........NW ×
Collinsville, (see Chanceford) ×
Collomsville, Lycoming.....N 350
● Colmar, Montgomery....SE 200
● *Colorado*, Schuylkill.......E ×
● Columbia, Lancaster.....SE 10,599
● ColumbiaCrossRds. Br'df'dN 75
● *Columbia*, Venango....NW ×
Columbia, (see Wesco)........ ×
● Columbus, Warren......NW 292
Colts, Erie.................NW ×
Colwyn, Delaware..........SE ×
Commettsburg, Beaver .... W 15
● *Comfort Run*, Clearfield..C ×
Comly, Montour ....C 25
Como, Wayne....... .....NE ×
Compassville, Chester .....SE 100
Conashaugh, Pike..........NE 50
● *Concord*, Erie.......... NW ×
Concord, Franklin ....S 165
Concord, (see Gordonville)... ×

● Concordville, Deleware..SE 450
● *Condron*, Cambria.........C ×
● Conemaugh, Cambria.....C 3,498
● *ConemaughFur.* W'm'l'dSW 20
● *Conestoge*, Chester...... SE 780
Conestoga, Lancaster......SE 600
● *Conestoga Fur.* L'ncasterSE ×
● Conewago, Lancaster....SW 65
● Confluence, Somerset...SW 444
Congo, Montgomery.......SE 60
Congruity, Westmoreland.SW 40
● *Conneaut Lake*, Cr'wf'dNW ×
● Conneautville, Cr'wf'rdNW 757
● *ConneautvilleSta.* C'wf'dNW ×
● Connellsville, Fayette.. SW 5,629
Conner, Somerset..........SW 100
Conner Colliery, Schuylkill.E ×
● *Connors*, Elk..... ......N ×
● *Connor's* Schuylkill ......E 513
● *Conococheaque*, Franklin.S ×
Conoquenessing, Butler....W 100
● Conoy, Lancaster..........SE ×
Conrad, Potter............ N ×
● Conshohocken, M'tg'm'ySE 5,470
Constitution, York..........S 200
Content, Jefferson......... W ×
● *Conway*, Beaver ....W 25
Conyngham, Luzerne....... E 375
Cookport, Indiana..........W 200
Cooks, Huntingdon.........C ×
Cook's, (see Arden) .... ×
Cooksburg, Forest.........NW 150
● *Cook's Ferry*, Beaver.... W ×
● Cook's Mills, Bedford......S 100
Cook's Mills, (see Tippecanoe) ×
● *Cook's Run*, Clinton......N ×
Cookstown, (see Fayette City) ×
● *Cool*, Susquehanna.......NE ×
Coolbaugh's Monroe ....E 22
Cool Spring, Jefferson......W 50
Cool Spring, (see Otter Creek) ×
● CoonIsland, WashingtonSW 50
Coon's Corners, CrawfordNW 25
● *Co-operativeMine*, S'mesetSW ×
Cooperdale, Cambria.......C 619
● Coopersbaugh, Lehigh.... E 454
Cooperstown, (see Glade Mills) ×
Cooperstown, Venango...NW 290
Cooper Tract, Forest.....NW 100
Cooperville, (see Smyrna).... ×
● *Copeland*, Allegheny....SW 1,349
Copella, Northampton...... E 100
● *Copenheffer*, Loncaster..SE ×
● Coplay, Lehigh............E 880
Cora, Huntingdon...........C 25
● *Cora Mines*, Fayette....SW ×
● Coraopolis, Allegheny.. SW 962
Corbindale, Delaware......SE ×
● Cordelia, Lancaster......SE 300
Corduroy, Elk...............N 250
Coreze, Delaware...........SE 100
Corinne, Chester...........SE 50
Cork Run, (seeMcKee'sRocks) ×
Cornell, Bucks............NE 50
● *Cornen*, Warren..........NW ×
● Corning, Lehigh.......... E 100
● *Cornog*, Chester.........SE ×
Cornplanter, Warren.....NW 80
Cornpropst's Mills, Hunt'd'nC 50
● Cornwall, Lebanon......SE 325
● *Cornwells*, Bucks ....SE 100
● Corry, Erie..............NW 5,677
● *Corry Junction*, Erie..NW ×
Corsica, Jefferson..........W 338
● *Corson's*, Montgomery..SE ×
● Corydon, Warren........ NW 400
● *CorydonSiding*, Warren NW ×
● Coryville, McKean ....N 300
Cosgrove, Allegheny......SW ×
Cosmus, Armstrong.........W ×
● Cossart, Chester.........SE ×
● Costello, Potter...........N 600
● *Cotrills*, Susquehanna.. NE 400
Cottage, Huntingdon........C 30
● **Coudersport**, Potter ..N 1,530
● Coulson, Mercer...........W ×
Coulter'sCorner, (seeBartville) ×
● *Coultersville*, Allegheny SW 921
● *Council Ridge*, Luzerne..E ×
County Farm, Allegheny.SW ×
● *County Home*, Westm'dSW ×
● *County Line*, Bucks.....SE ×
County Line, (see Telford)... ×
● County Line, Northum'd..C 25
● *Coursin*, Fayette........SW ×
● Courtney, Washington..SW 500
Covalt, Fulton...............S 50

● *Cove*, Perry.................. ×
Cove Forge, Blair...........C 75
● *Cove Forge*, Perry........C ×
Coventryville, Chester.....SE 30
Covert, Bradford.............N 30
● *Covert's Mill*, Lawrence..W ×
● *Cove Station*, Huntingdon C 31
● Covington, Tioga.........N 496
Covode, Indiana.............W 100
Cowen, Union..................C 100
● Cowanesque, Tioga.......N 150
Cowanesque Valley, Tioga. N 150
Cowansburg, (see Blackburg) ×
Cowanshannoc, (see Gosford) ×
Cowan's Station, (see Library) ×
Cowansville, Armstrong ... W 100
Coxton, Luzerne............E ×
Coxtown, see Fleetwood)..... ×
● *Cowley*, Bradford........ N 100
Coyleville, Butler.......... W 50
Crab Tree, Westmoreland SW 514
● Crafton, Allegheny..... SW 1,200
● *Craig*, Columbia..........C ×
Craig, Lackawanna....... NE 40
Craighead, Cumberland.....S 100
● *Craighead* Summit, Cumb'dS ×
Craigsville, Armstrong..... W 150
Craley, York.....................S 800
● *Cramer*, Jefferson....... W ×
Cramer, Indiana...............W 25
● *Cranberry*, Luzerne......E ×
Cranberry, Venango......NW 150
Cranberry Mines, VenangoNW ×
● *Crane*, Lehigh............ E 195
● *Crane Siding*, CumberlandS ×
Cranesville, Erie......... NW 150
Cranston, Allegheny......SW ×
Crates, Clarion...............W ×
Crawford, (see Carlisle)....... ×
Crawford, Huntingdon.....C ×
Crawford Cor's., VenangoNW 200
● *Crawford Junc.*, McKean N ×
● *Crayton*, Erie..........NW ×
Creamery, Montgomery....SE 100
● *Creasy*, Columbia.........C ×
Creekside, Indiana...........W 50
● Creighton, Allegheny...SW 800
● *Crellin Junction*, LuzerneE ×
Crenshaw, Jefferson........ W 200
● Crescentville, Philadel'a.SE 175
● Cresco, Monroe...........E 60
Cressman, Bucks..........SE ×
● Cresson, Cambria...........C 100
● Cressona, Schuylkill......E 1,481
Cresson Springs, Cambria.. C ×
Creswell, Lancaster........SE 225
● *Creswell*, Lancaster......SE ×
Creswell City, Armstrong..W ×
Crete, Indiana...................W 50
Cribb's, Westmoreland... SW 20
● *Cricket*, Philadelphia....SE ×
● *Crifts*, Bedford.......... S ×
Croft, Indiana..................W ×
● *Cromby*, Chester......... SE ×
● *Cromer*, Franklin.........S ×
Crooked Creek, Tioga.......N 200
Crooked Bridge, Bradford..N ×
Crooked Hill, (see Sanotoga). ×
● *Crosby*, McKean..........N ×
Cross Creek Village, Wash.SW 175
Cross Cut, (see Mahoningt'n) ×
Cross Fork, Potter............N 260
Crossgrove, Snyder..........C ×
● *Crossing*, Cumberland.... S ×
Crossingville, Crawford..NW 100
Cross Kill Mills, Berks....SE 300
Cross Roads, (seeElizabethv'e) ×
Cross Roads, York ....S 400
Crothers, Washington.....SW 200
Croton, Lawrence.............W ×
● *Crouches*, Washington..SW ×
Crowl, Northumberland.... C ×
● Crown, Clarion...........W 12
Crow's Mills, Greene......SW 25
Crowther, Lawrence....... W 40
Crumb, Somerset.........SW 25
● Crum Lynne, Delaware..SE 800
Crystal, Potter..............N ×
Crystal Spring, Fulton...... S 10
Crystal Spring, HuntingdonC ×
Culbertson, Franklin.........S 150
● **Cully, Lancaster.........SE** ×
Culmerville, Allegheny... SW 30
Culp, Blair........................C 50
Cumberland Valley, BedfordS 134
● Cumbola, Schuylkill......E 25
Cumiskey, Bradford........N ×

Pennsylvania

● *Cumming*, McKean...... N ×
Cummins, (see Waynesburg). ×
Cumru, Berks..................SE 130
● *Cunningham Sid'g*, Fayette NW ×
● Cupola, Chester..........SE 25
● *Cupp's*, Somerset.......SW ×
Curfew, Fayette.......... SW ×
Curley's Mills, (see Chalfant) ×
Curllsville, Clarion..........W 154
● *Curry*, Allegheny.......SW 57
Curry Run, Clearfield ......C 60
● Curryville, Blair.........C 100
● *Curtin*, Centre............C ×
● Curtin, Dauphin..........D 25
● Curwensville, Clearfield...C 1,664
Cush Creek, Indiana....... W ×
● *Cush Creek Jc.*, Clearfield.C ×
Custard's, Crawford......NW 200
● *Custer*, Lehigh............E ×
● *Custer*, Montgomery ....SE ×
● Custer City, McKean.....N 400
Cyclone, McKean...........N ×
● Cynwyd, Montgomery...SE 100
● Cypher, Bedford ....S 25
Dado, Lancaster............SE ×
Dagget's Mills, Tioga....... N 100
● Daguscahonda, Elk.......N 300
● Dagus Mines, Elk.........N 1,500
● Dahoga, Elk..................N 70
Dakin, Luzerne.............E ×
Dale, Berks.................SE 780
Dale City, (see Meyersdale)... ×
● *Dale Summit*, Centre.....C ×
Daleville, Lackawanna....NE 250
● Daley, Somerset......... SW 50
● *Dallas*, Allegheny......SW ×
● Dallas, Luzerne...........E 415
● Dallas City, McKean......N 260
● Dallastown, York..........S 779
● Dalmatia, Northumberl'd.C 400
● Dalton, Lackawanna..... SE 500
Damascus, Wayne..........NE 200
● *Dampman*, Chester..... SE 30
Danborough, Bucks........ SE 150
● Danielsville, NorthamptonE 125
● **Danville**, Montour.....C 7,998
● *Danville Sta.*, N'umberl'dC ×
● Darby, Delaware......... SE 2,972
Darby Center, Delaware...SE ×
● *Darkwater*, Schuylkill ...E ×
● Darling, Delaware.........SE 25
Darlings, McKean......... N ×
● Darlington, Beaver...... W 254
● *Darlington*, Westmorel'dSW ×
● Dauberville, Berks.......SE ×
● Dauphin, Dauphin........C 740
Davidge, Potter............ N ×
Davidsburgh, York............S 250
● *Davidson*, Fayette......SW 25
Davidson's Ferry, Fayette SW ×
Davidsville, (see Trade City). ×
● Davidsville, Somerset...SW 100
Davis, Indiana..................W 25
● *Davis*, Tioga.............N 50
● *Davis*, McKean...........N 25
Davis Grove, Montgomery.SE 100
Davis' Mills, (see IndianHead) ×
Davistown, Greene.........SW 100
Davisville, Bucks...........SE 125
● Dawson, Fayette........SW 668
● *Dawson*, Cambria........ C ×
● *Dawson*, Forest.......... NW ×
Day, Clarion....................W 20
● *Daylesford*, Chester.....SE ×
Day's Store, (see Nineveh)... ×
Dayton, Armstrong........ W 372
● *Dayton*, Dauphin.........C ×
Deal, Somerset..........SW 50
● Dean, Cambria..............C 20
● *Deans*, Somerset........SW ×
Deanville, Armstrong......W 50
Dearmin, Cambria.......... C ×
Dearth, Fayette...........SW ×
Decatur, Mifflin...............C 50
Deckard, Crawford..........NW 77
Decker's Point, Indiana.... W 75
Decorum, Huntington........C 25
Dee, Armstrong ....W 25
Deemston, Washington ...SW 40
Deep Valley, Greene......SW 50
Deer Creek, (see Harmarville) ×
● Deer Lick, Greene........SW 10
Defiance, Bedford ....S 200
● De Golia, McKean......... N ×
De Haven, Allegheny......SW 200
Delbertsville, Lehigh.......E 150
● Delblers, NorthumberlandC 19

Pennsylvania

● Delabole, Northampton...E 150
De Lancey, Jefferson.......W 58
De Laney, Cambria......... C ×
● Delano, Schuylkill........E 1,362
● *Delano*, Butler...........W 50
● *Delano Junction*, Sch'kill E ×
Delaware, Pike............NE 35
● Delaware Water Gap, Monroe.......................E 467
Delhil, Erie.................NW ×
Delight, Greene...........SW 10
Dellville, Perry................C 22
Delmar, Tioga................ N 50
Delmont, Westmoreland..SW 500
De Long, Berks............SE ×
Delongs, Lycoming.........N ×
Delps, Northampton.........E 260
Delphi, Montgomery.......SE 50
● Delta, York....................S 565
● Demmler, Allegheny....SW 700
● *Dempseys*, Northampton .E ×
Dempseytown, Venango..NW 115
Denglers, Berks........... SE ×
Denison, Westmoreland...SW 20
● *Denny*, Allegheny...... SW ×
● Denny, Butler...............W 50
Denny's Mills, (see Denny)... ×
Dent, Greene.................SW 50
Denton, Indiana..............W ×
Dent's Run, Elk............ N 150
● Denver, Lancaster.......SE 400
Deodate, Dauphin............ C 175
● *Der[illegible] J[illegible]tion*, ClearfieldC ×
● *Dering[illegible]*, Luzerne.........E ×
● Derrick City, McKean....N 500
Derr, Columbia...............C 75
● *Derry*, Dauphin.............C 150
● *Derry*, Montour............C ×
● *Derry*, Westmoreland.. SW ×
● Derry Church, Dauphin...C 250
● Derry-Station, W'tm'el'dSW 1,968
● *Derstines*, Bucks.........SE ×
De Turksville, Schuylkill... E 300
● Devault, Chester...........SE 50
● Devon, Chester.......... SE 100
Devon Inn, Chester........SE ×
● Dewart, Northumberland.C 300
● *Dew Drop*, Warren.... NW ×
Dexter, (see Oak Ridge)...... ×
De Young's, Elk............N 200
Diamond, Venango.......NW 100
● *Diamond*, Westmoreland.C ×
Diamondsville, (see Mitchell's Mills)....................... ×
Dibertsville, (see Stanton's Mills)........................ ×
● **Dick, Westmoreland......C** 50
● Dickerson Run, Fayette.SW ×
Dickey, Somerset......... SW ×
● *Dickey's*, Franklin........S ×
Dickey's Mountain, Fulton..S 20
Dickinson, Cumberland.....S 700
Dicksonburgh, Crawford.NW 75
● Dickson City, Lackawanna.................NE 3,110
● *Dieffenback*, Montour.....C ×
● Digel, McKean............ N ×
● *Dilks*, Butler................W ×
● *Dillerville*, Lancaster....SE ×
Dilliner, Greene.......... SW 10
● Dillinger, Lehigh...........E 100
● Dillingersville, Lehigh....E 230
● Dillsburgh, York...........S 587
● *Dillsburgh Junc.*, Cumb'ldS ×
Dilltown, Indiana......... W ×
Dilworthtown, Chester.....SE 100
Dime, Armstrong.......... W 20
Dimmsville, Juniata........ C 50
● Dimock, Susquehanna.. NE 200
Dimpsey, (see Wall)........... ×
Dingman's Ferry, Pike....NE 180
● Dinsmore, Washington..SW 25
Disston, Lancaster..........SE ×
Dividing Ridge, Somerset.SW 50
● *Dix*, Blair.....................C ×
● Dixmont, Allegheny....SW ×
Dixon, Wyoming..........NE 60
Dixonville, Indiana.........W 80
● *Dock Junction*, Erie....NW ×
● *Docklow*, Dauphin........ C ×
● *Dock Run Junc.*, Law'rceW ×
● Doe Run, Chester.......SE 150
Dolington, Bucks..........SE 120
● *Donaghmore*, Lebanon..SE ×
● *Donahoe*, Westmorela'dSW ×
● Donaldson, Schuylkill....E 958
● *Donaldson*, Warren....NW ×

Donation, Huntingdon...... C 50
Donegal, Westmoreland...SW 163
Donegal Spring, (see Maytown).................... ×
● *Doner's*, Cumberland..... S ×
Donley, Washington...... SW ×
Donnally's Mills, Perry......C 100
○ *Donohoe*, WestmorelandSW ×
Doolin, Venango......... NW ×
Dora, Jefferson............W ×
● *Dorlan*, Chester......... SE 50
Dormantown, Mifflin..........C 128
● *Dormer's*, Schuylkill.......E ×
● Dornsife, Northumber'nd.C 25
Dorrance, Luzerne..........E 100
Dorranceton, Luzerne.......E 586
● *Dorset*, Schuylkill..........E ×
● *Dorsey's*, Lancaster......SE 250
Dorseyville, Allegheny.... SW 50
Dot, Fulton...............S ×
● *Dotter*, Venango........NW ×
Dottysburg, (see Waynesburg) ×
● *Dougal*, Northumberland.C ×
Douglass, (see Sassamansville) ×
● *Douglass*, Allegheny....SW ×
● Douglassville, Berks......SE 200
● *Doutyville*, Northumber'dC ×
Dover, York .... S 465
● Dow, Schuylkill...........E 33
● *Dowlin*, Chester......... SE ×
Downey, Somerset........SW 30
● *Downeyville*, Butler......W ×
● Downingtown, Chester..SW 1,920
Doylesburgh, Franklin......S 100
Doyle's Mills, Juniata....... C 190
Doyle's Mill, McKean...... N ×
● **Doylestown**, Bucks...SE 2,519
Drab, Blair..................C 100
Draco, York.................S 50
● *Drake's Creek*, Carbon....E ×
Drake's Mills, Crawford..NW 112
● *Drake's Point*, Carbon....E ×
● Draketown, Somerset...SW 75
● *DraketownJunc.*, Some'tSW ×
Draper, Tioga...............N 20
● Dravosburgh, AlleghenySW 1,089
● Drehersville, Schuylkill...E 380
● Dreibelbis, Berks.........SE ×
● Drennen, WestmorelandSW 40
● *Dresher*, Lehigh.......... E ×
Dreshertown, MontgomerySE 300
● Drifton, Luzerne..........E 2,800
● *Drifton Junc.*, Luzerne...E ×
● Driftwood, Cameron........N 628
Drinker, Lackawanna.....NE 396
● *Drisher*, Montgomery.... SE ×
Drovers Home, Monroe.....E 115
● *Drove Yard*, PhiladelphiaSE ×
● Drumore, Lancaster.....SE 50
Drum's Luzerne..............E 350
Dryland, Northampton......E 75
● *Dryland Sta.*, Northam'tnE ×
Dry Run, Franklin..........S 250
● Dry Sawmill, Elk..........N 143
Dry Valley Cr'ss R'ds, UnionC 32
Dryville, Berks............ SE 100
Dry Wells, (see Quarryville). ×
Dublin, Bucks.............SE 300
Dublin Mills, Fulton....... S 100
● Du Bois, Clearfield.........C 6,149
Duboistown, Lycoming..... N 697
● Dudley, Huntingdon......C 281
● *Dudley*, Butler...........W ×
Duffield, Franklin...........S 20
● Duffryn Mawr, Chester..SE 139
Duffs, Allegheny..........SW ×
● Duffs, Westmoreland....SW 50
Dugall, Warren..........NW ×
● Duhring, Forest........NW ×
● Duke Centre, McKean....N 924
● *Dulls*, Somerset........SW ×
Dumas, Somerset......... SW 15
● Dunbar, Fayette........ SW 1,381
● *Dunbar Furnace*, Fay'teSW ×
● Duncan, Allegheny.....SW 500
● Duncannon, Perry........C 1,074
Duncan's Island, (see Ben Venue).................. ×
Duncansville, (see Widnoon). ×
● Duncansville, Blair.......C 1,277
Dundaff, Susquehanna.....NE 157
Dundore, Snyder............C 82
● *Dungarvin*, Huntingdon..C ×
● *Dunhams Mill*, Warren NW ×
Dunkard, Greene.......... SW 150
● *Dunkelbergers*, Northumberland..................C ×

Dunkle, Jefferson..........W ×
● *Dunlap*, Bucks..........SE ×
Dunlo, Cambria............C ×
● Dunmore, Lackawanna.NE 8,315
Dunnings, Bradford....... N 25
● *Dunnings*, Lackawanna.NE 443
Dunningsville, WashingtonSW 150
● *Dunn's Eddy*, Warren.NW ×
● Dunn's Sta., WashingtonSW 65
Dunsfort, Washington.....SW 27
Dunnstown, Clinton........N ×
Dupont, Luzerne...........E ×
Duquesne, Allegheny......SW 3,800
Durbin, Greene...........SW ×
Durell, Bradford.......... N 200
Durham, Bucks............SE 250
Durlach, Lancaster......... SE 175
● *Durward*, Juniata........ C ×
● Duryea, Luzerne......... E 2,000
● Dushore, Sullivan........ N 783
Dutch Hill, Clarion........ W ×
***Dutton*, Huntingdon........ C** 19
Dyberry, Wayne.......... NE 60
Dyerstown, Bucks......... SE 25
● Dysart, Cambria.......... C 50
Eagle, Warren............NW ×
Eagle Foundry, Huntingdon C 32
Eagle Hill, Schuylkill...... E ×
● *Eagle Mines Junc.*, F'te SW ×
Eagle Point, Berks......... SE 50
● Eagle Rock, Venango.. NW 150
Eagle's Mere, Sullivan...... N 50
Eagleton, (see Farrandsville). ×
Eagleton, Lycoming.........N ×
Eagleville, Montgomery... SE 150
● *Eagleville*, Centre.........C 400
Eakin's Corners, Venango NW ×
Earlington, Montgomery.. SE 100
Earlville, Berks............SE 100
● *Earnest*, Montgomery.. SE ×
East Allentown, Lehigh.... E 599
● East Bangor, Northamp'n E 804
East Barre, (see Saulsburg).. ×
East Benton, Lackawanna.NE 150
● East Berkley, Berks..... SE 100
● East Berlin, Adams....... S 595
East Bethlehem, Wash'g'n SW 200
● East Brady, Clarion....... W 1,228
East Branch, Warren.....NW 200
● *East Branch*, Warren..NW ×
East Bridgewater, Susq'na.NE 50
East Broadtop, Huntingdon.C 50
● East Brook, Lawrence... W 150
East Burlington, (see Burl'gn) ×
East Canton, Bradford......N 150
East Charleston, Tioga...... N 100
East Chatham, Tioga....... N 350
East Conemaugh, Cambria..C 1,158
East Coventry, Chester.....SE 50
East Downington, Chester.SE ×
● East Earl, Lancaster.....SE ×
● *East Elizabeth*, Alleg'y SW ×
East Emporium, Cameron.N
East Fallowsfield, (see Ercildoun)................... ×
East Falls, Schuylkill...... E ×
East Finley, Washington.. SW 40
● *East Franklin*, Schuylkill E ×
East Freedom, Blair........ C 260
East Greene, Erie.........NW 34
● *East Greensburgh*, W't'dSW ×
● East Greenville, Montgo'ySE 539
East Hanover, Lebanon.... SE 450
East Hebron, Potter........ N 130
East Hempfield, (see E. Peter'bg) ×
East Hickory, Forest..... NW 200
East Hollidaysburg, Blair.. C 136
Eastland, (see Kirk's Mills).. ×
East Lemon, Wyoming....NE 400
● East Liberty, Allegheny.SW ×
East Liberty, (see Vanderb't) ×
● *East Mahanoy Junc.*, Sc'llE ×
East Mahanoy Tunnel, Sc'llE ×
● *East Mansfield*, Allegh'y SW ×
● East Mauch Chunk, Car'n.E 2,772
● *East Middletown*, DauphinC ×
Eastmont, York........ S 40
East Moravia, Lawrence.... W 300
East Nantmeal, Chester... SE 50
East New Castle, Lawrence W ×
East New Milford, Susq'na NE 50
● **Easton**, Northampton.. E 14,481
East Parker, Clarion.......W ×
East Penn, Carbon......... E 325
● *East Pennsylvania Junc.*, Lehigh..........E ×
● East Petersburgh, Lan'r. SE 558

East Pike Run, (see ColeCentre) ×
East Point, Tioga......... N 100
East Prospect, York........ S 261
East Riverside, Fayette... SW 65
East Run, (see Purch'e Line) ×
East Rush, Susquehanna.. NE 30
East Salem, Juniata......... C 150
● *EastSalisbury*, SomersetSW ×
East Sandy, Venango..... NW 65
● *East Sandy*, Venango. NW ×
● *East Scranton*, L'kaw'na NE ×
East Sharon, Potter..........N 65
East Sharpsburgh, Blair .... C 100
● *East Slatedale Sta.*, LehighE ×
East Smethport, McKean... N ×
East Smithfield, Bradford... N 600
East Springfield, Erie.... NW 500
East Spring Mills, M't'g'y..SE ×
● East Stroudsburgh, M'roe.E 1,819
● *East Sunbury*, Northumb'dC ×
East Texas, Lehigh..........E 225
● East Titusville, Crawf'd.NW 65
East Troy, Bradford........ N 275
● East Tyrone, Blair........ C 435
East Vincent, (see Sp'g City). ×
● *East Warren*, Warren. NW ×
East Waterford, Juniata.... C 175
● *Eastwick*, Philadelphia..SE ×
Eaton, Wyoming..........NE 200
Eau Claire, Butler..........W 300
Ebenezer, Indiana..........W 50
● **Ebensburgh**, Cambria.C 1,202
Ebenton, Tioga............N 250
Eberly's Mill, Cumberland.. S 200
● Ebervale, Luzerne........ E 567
Eby's, Lancaster........... SE 50
Echo, Armstrong........... W 40
● Eckley, Luzerne.......... E 1,241
● *Eckley Junction*, Luzerne E ×
Eckville, (see Albany)........ ×
● *Eclipse*, Washington....SW 200
● Economy, Beaver........ W 413
○ Eddington, Bucks......... SE 200
● Eddystone, Delaware.... SE ×
Eddyville, Armstrong.......W 100
Edella, Lackawanna...... NE 125
● Edelman, Northampton.. E 140
Eden, Bucks...............SE 100
○ *Eden*, Chester........... SE ×
Eden, (see Binkley's Bridge). ×
● *Edenburg*, Lawrence..... W 750
Edenburg, (see Knox) .... ×
● *Edenburg*, Lawrence.... W 300
Edenville, Franklin......... S 55
Edgar, Elk................. N 500
Edgegrove, Adams.......... S ×
● Edge Hill, Montgomery..SE 400
Edgely, Bucks.............. SE ×
Edgemont, Delaware...... SE 152
Edgewood, (see Crete)......... ×
Edgewood Park, Allegheny SW 616
● *Edgeworth*, Allegheny..SW 65
● Edgwood, Bucks .... SE 65
Edie, Somerset............ SW 250
Edinborough, Erie........NW 1,107
Edinburgh, Lawrence......W 390
● *Edinburgh Sta.*, Lawr'ce W ×
Edison, Bucks............ SE 100
Edkins, Lycoming .... N ×
Edmon, Armstrong........ W ×
Edri, Indiana..............W 65
Edsallville, Bradford....... N 67
● *Edson's*, Columbia........C ×
Edvilla, Washington...... SW ×
Edwardsdale, Luzerne...... E 3,284
● Edwin, Lancaster........SE 100
Effort, Monroe.............E 250
Egypt, Lehigh...............E 190
● *Egypt*, Fayette..........SW ×
Egypt Mills, Pike...........NE 60
● Ehrenfeld, Cambria.......C 567
Eichelberger, Bedford.......S 30
Eighteenth and Chestnut Sta., **Philadelphia.......... SE** ×
● Eighty Four, Washing'n.SW 50
Ekastown, Butler.......... W ×
Elam, Delaware .... SE 186
● *Elbo*, Allegheny..........SW ×
Elbon, Armstrong.......... W ×
● Elbel, Jefferson.......... W ×
Elbinsville, Bedford.........S 125
Elbridge, Tioga............ N 79
● Elco, Washington ...... SW ×
Elder's Ridge, Indiana..... W 25
Eldersville, Washington.. SW 132
Elderton, Armstrong........W 243
● *Eldora*, Lancaster....... SE 100

● El Dorado, Blair.......... C 100
● Eldred, McKean.......... N 1,050
Eldredsville, Sullivan....... N 26
Eleanor, Jefferson.......... W ×
Eleven Mile, Potter .... N 50
● *Eleven Mile Siding*, C'b'l'd S ×
● *Elfinwild*, Allegheny....SW ×
● Elgin, Erie............. NW 169
Elimsport, Lycoming....... N 150
● Elizabeth, Allegheny....SW 1,804
● *Elizabeth Furnace*, Blair.C ×
● Elizabethtown, Lanc's'r. SE 1,218
● Elizabethville, Dauphin... C 676
● Elk City, Clarion......... W 75
Elk Creek, Erie..........NW 150
● *Elk Creek Sid.*, Erie...NW ×
Elk Dale, (see Elk View)..... ×
Elkdale, Susquehanna.....NE 190
Elk Grove, Columbia....... C 115
● Elkhorn, Allegheny.... SW 25
Elkin, Indiana............ W ×
Elk Lake, Susquehanna....NE 200
● Elkland, Tioga........... N 1,006
Elk Lick, Somerset....... SW 500
Elk Mills, Chester.......... SE 75
Elk Run, Tioga............ N 125
● Elkview, Chester......... SE 60
Ella, Jefferson.............W ×
Ellangowan, Schuylkill.... E ×
● *Ellendale Forge*, DauphinC 175
Ellenton, Lycoming.........N 57
● *Elliott*, Cumberland...... S ×
Elliottsburgh, Perry......... C 280
Elliott's Mills,(seeFarmingt'n) ×
Elliottsville, Fayette...... SW 50
Ellisburgh, Potter.......... N 100
● Ellmont, Elk............ N 180
● *Ellrod*, Allegheny.......SW 134
Ellwerth, Lancaster....... SE ×
● *Ellwood*, Lawrence...... W 200
● Ellwood, Schuylkill.......E 100
Ellwood City, Lawrence....W 400
● *Ellwood Junc.*, Beaver.. W ×
Elm, Fayette..............SW 200
● *Elm*, Montgomery...... SE ×
● Elmer, Potter............. N ×
● Elmhurst, Lackawanna. NE 200
● *Elmwood*, McKean.......N ×
● *Elmwood*, Philadelphia. SE ×
Elora, Butler...............W 25
Elrod's Station,(see Chase) .. ×
Elroy, Montgomery........SE 75
Elstie, Cambria............ C ×
Elstonville, Lancaster......SE 30
Elton, Cambria...............C 25
Elulalia, Forest............NW 150
Elvilla, Washington.......SW ×
Elwell, Bradford............N 28
● *Elwood*, Washington... SW ×
● Elwyn, Delaware........ SE 500
Elysburgh, NorthumberlandC 200
● Emaus, Lehigh............E 883
● *Emaus Junction*, Lehigh.E ×
Emblem, Allegheny........SW ×
Embreeville, Chester.......SE 100
Emerald, Lehigh............E 75
Emerickville, Jefferson.... W 100
● Emigsville, York..........S 400
Emilie, Bucks..............SE 150
● Emlenton, Venango....NW 1,126
Emmaville, Fulton..........S 30
● Emmet, Elk.............N 150
Emmens, (see New Stanton). ×
● Empire, Elk..............N ×
● *Empire*, Luzerne.......... E ×
● **Emporium**, Cameron..N 2,147
● *Emporium Jc.*, Cameron. N ×
● Emsworth, Allegheny...SW 400
Emsworth Sta.,(seeEmsworth) ×
Enders, Dauphin...........C 200
● *Engelside*, Philadelphia.SE ×
England, Washington.....SW 50
Englesville, (see Boyerstown) ×
English Centre, Lycoming..N 400
English Mills, Lycoming....N 32
Enid. Fulton............... S 25
● *Enlow*, Allegheny...... SW ×
Ennisville, Huntingdon..... C 100
Eno, Greene............. SW ×
● *Enola*, Dauphin.......... C ×
Enon, (see Simpson's Store). ×
● Enon Valley, Lawrence.. W 600
● *Enos*, Somerset.........SW 20
Enterline, Dauphin.........C 175
Enterprise, Bradford.......N ×
Enterprise,(see Bird-in-Hand) ×
Enterprise, Warren.......NW 200

Pennsylvania

Enterprise, NorthumberlandC ×
● Entriken, Huntingdon....C 650
Enyeart, Huntingdon.......C ×
● Ephrata, Lancaster......SE 950
● Epton, Allegheny.......SW ×
Equinunk, Wayne.........NE 400
● *Erb*, Blair................ C ×
Ercildoun, Chester......... SE 150
● Erdice, Jefferson..........W 40
● **Erie**, Erie..........NW 40,634
Ermine, Allegheny........SW ×
Erney's, York..............S ×
Erwinna, Bucks........... SE 250
● Eshback, Berks..........SE 150
Eshcol, Perry...............C 100
Esington, Delaware....... SE ×
● Espy, Columbia.......... C 54?
● *Espy Ferry*, Columbia... C ×
● *Espy Run*, Luzerne...... E ×
Espyville, Crawford.......NW 150
● Espyville Sta., Crawford NW 195
● Essen, Allegheney.......SW 19[illegible]
● *Essington*, Philadelphia.SE ×
Estella, Sullivan............N 2[illegible]
● Ethel Landing, Beaver....W 390
● Etna, Allegheny..........SW 3,767
● Etters, York............. S 500
● Euclid, Butler............W 50
Eunice, Susquehanna..... NE ×
Eureka, Montgomery......SE 100
● *Eureka*, Westmoreland.SW ×
Eutaw, Washington.......SW ×
● *Evan's*, Fayette........SW ×
Evansburg, (see Evans City). ×
● Evansburgh, Crawford. NW 291
● *Evansburgh*, Crawford. NW 40
Evansburg, (see Lower Providence)............ ×
● Evans City, Butler....... W 637
Evans Falls, Wyoming....NE 65
● *Evansville*, Berks.......SE ×
Evansville, Columbia........C 50
Evendale, Juniata...........C 36
● Everett, Bedford..........S 1,679
Evergreen, Bradford........N 20
● *Evergreen*, Allegheny...SW ×
● Everhart, Chester..........SE 30
● Everson, Fayette.........SW 905
Ewing, Armstrong........ W [illegible]
● Ewing's Mills, AlleghenySW 15
Ewing's Mills,(seeWashingt'n) ×
● Excelsior, NorthumberlandC 300
Exchange, Montour..........C 75
● Exeter, Luzerne.......... E 790
● *Exeter Street*, Berks.....SE ×
● Exeter Station, Berks... SE 50
● *Exmoor*, Schuylkill........E ×
Experiment Mills, Monroe..E 200
● Exton, Chester.......... SE 250
● Eyer's Grove, Columbia...C 100
● Factoryville, Wyoming. NE 577
Fades Creek, Luzerne.......E 260
Fagg's Manor, Chester.....SE 100
Fagleysville, Montgomery .SE 235
Fagundus, Warren.........NW 150
Fairbanks, (see Saltsburg)... ×
Fairbrook, Centre...........C ×
● *Fairbrook*, Centre........ C ×
● Fairchance, Fayette.... SW 1,092
Fairdale, Susquehanna....NE 400
Fairfield, Adams........... S 500
● *Fairfield*, Lycoming.......N ×
● *Fairfield*, WestmorelandSW ×
Fairfield Centre, Lycoming.N 135
● *Fair Grounds*, Potter......N ×
● Fairhaven, Allegheny...SW 50
Fair Hill Sta., Philadelphia.SE ×
● Fairhope, Somerset.......SW 550
Fairland, Lancaster........SE 75
● *Fairmount*, Butler.......W ×
Fairmount, Lancaster..... SE 30
Fairmount Ave.,PhiladelphiaSE ×
● Fairmount City, Clarion. W 599
Fairmount Locks,Philade'aSE ×
Fairmount Springs,Luzerne.E 50
● *Fair Oaks*, Beaver.........W ×
Fairplay, Adams........... S 50
Fairview, (see Brady's Bend) ×
Fairview, (see Ohioville)..... ×
Fairview, Butler...........W 308
Fairview,(seeEastConemaugh) ×
Fairview, (see Dunkard)..... ×
Fairview, (see Manor) .... ×
● Fairview, Erie..........NW [illegible],200
● *Fairview*, Cumberland....S ×
● *Fairview*, Delaware......SE ×
● *Fairview*, Luzerne........E ×

Pennsylvania

● *Fairview Mine*, SomersetSW ×
● *Fairview Station*, Erie. NW 305
Fairview Vill'e, Montgom'ySE 100
● Fairville, Chester........SE 100
Fairville, (see Terre Hill)..... ×
● Fall Brook, Tioga........ N 825
● Fallen Timber, Cambria.. C 100
Falling Springs, Perry.......C 250
Fallowfield, Washington.. SW 20
● Falls, Wyoming.........NE 100
Falls City, (see Ohiopyle) .... ×
● *Falls*, Philadelphia......SE ×
● *Falls Creek*, Jefferson... W ×
● Falls Creek, Clearfield....C ×
Fallsington, Bucks......... SE 400
● Fallof Schuylkill, Philad'aSE ×
● Fallston, Beaver......... W 541
● Falmouth, Lancaster.... SE 200
Fannettsburgh, Franklin....S 700
Farleys, Bucks........... SE ×
● *Farmdale*, Lancaster....SE ×
Farmers, York.............S 400
Farmers Mills, Centre...... C 250
● Farmers Valley, McKean. N 250
Farmersville, (see Scalp Level) ×
Farmersville, Lancaster... SE 350
Farmington, (see Eau Claire) ×
Farmington, Fayette .....SW 100
● *Farmington*, Lehigh..... E ×
Farmington Centre, Tioga..N 100
Farmington Centre, War'n NW ×
Farmington Hill, Nioga ....N 33
Farno, Wayne............ NE ×
● *Farnsworth*, Warren.. NW 195
Farnsworth, Northumbbel'dC ×
Farragut, Lycoming........N ×
● Farrandsville, Clinton....N 475
● *Fairview*, Wayne.......NE ×
● Fassett, Bradford..........N 25
Fauncetown, Crawford .....C ×
Faust, (see Obelisk).......... ×
Fawn Grove, York..........S 199
Fay, Lawrence ....W 100
● *Fayette*, Fayette...... SW ×
Fayette City, Fayette .....SW 931
Fayette Springs, Fayette..SW 25
Fayetteville, (see Shirland) .. ×
● Fayetteville, Franklin.... S 600
Fayetteville, (see Fay) .... ×
Fearnot, Schuylkill.........E ×
Feasterville, Bucks.........SE 200
Federal, Allegheny.......SW 700
Fee, Venango............NW ×
Felix, Somerset............SW 25
Felix Dam, Berks......... SE ×
Fell, (see Carbondale)........ ×
● *Felton*, Delaware........SE 25
● Felton, York...............S 200
Fenelton, Butler.............W ×
● *Fenmore*, York.............S ×
Fenwick, (see Marysville).... ×
Ferdinand, Erie............NW ×
Feree, Westmoreland.....SW ×
Ferguson, Perry............ C 25
● *Ferguson's*, Fayette....SW ×
● Fermoy, Wayne.........NE 32
Fern, Clarion...............W 200
Fern City, Clarion ....W ×
● *Ferndale*, Cambria.......C ×
● *Ferndale*, Chester........SE ×
● Ferndale, Lehigh......... E 676
● *Ferndale*, Schuylkill..... E ×
● *Ferney*, Clinton..........N ×
Fernglen, Lancaster ....SE 140
● *Fern Glen*, Luzerne ......E ×
● *Fern Hill*, Chester ....SE ×
● Fern Rock, PhiladelphiaSE ×
● Fernwood, Delaware.... SE 619
● *Ferrona*, Mercer........ W ×
Fertigs, Venango.........NW 75
Fertility, Lancaster........SE 100
Fetterman, Allegheny ....SW 100
● *Fetterman*, Beaver ......W ×
Fibre, (see Markleton)........ ×
Fiedler, Centre.............C 75
● *Fields*, Lycoming........N ×
● Field's Station, Lycoming N 400
● Figart, Cambria...........C 50
● *Filer*, Mercer.............W ×
Fillmore, Centre............C 350
Finland, Bucks.............SE 25
● Finleyville, Washington SW 300
● *Finneydale*, WashingtonSW ×
First Fork, Cameron........N 40
Fishback, Schuylkill. ......E ×
● *Fishbasket*, Potter.......N ×
Fisher, Clarion.............W 150

Place	Pop.
● *Fisher's*, Philadelphia....SE	×
● Fisher's Ferry, N'th'm'l'd C	85
● *Fisher's Summit*, Hunt'd'nC	×
Fishertown, Bedford........S	200
Fisherville, (see Downingt'n)	×
Fisherville, Dauphin........ C	200
Fishing Creek, Columbia ...C	125
● *Fishing Creek*, LancasterSE	×
Fishing Creek Mills, (see Marysville)	×
Fiske, Cambria.............C	20
● *Fites Eddy*, Lancaster.. SE	×
● *Fittler*, Philadelphia.... SE	×
● FitzHenry, Westmorel'd SW	700
Fitzwatertown, M'tgom'ry.SE	150
Five Forks, Franklin........S	100
● *Five Locks*, Berks..... .SE	×
Five Points, Mercer........W	40
● *Five Points*, Clearfield... C	×
● Flagstone, Pike.........NE	175
Flatwoods, Fayette....... SW	107
● Fleeger, Butler..........W	25
Fleetown, (see Uniontown)..	×
Fleetville, Lackawanna... NE	[illegible]
● Fleetwood, Burks....... SE	[illegible]
● Fleming, Centre...........C	400
● *Fleming Park*, Allegh'nySW	×
● Flemington, Clinton......N	912
Flick, Butler..............W	20
● Flicksville, Northampton.E	100
● Flinton, Cambria...... ...C	50
● *Flog Hill Mine*, SomersetSW	×
Flora, Indiana..............W	75
Flora Dale, Adams...........S	125
Florence, Washington.... SW	300
● Florin, Lancaster.........SE	350
● *Florinal*, Lancaster..... SE	×
Floss, Bradford ....N	×
● Flourtown, MontgomerySE	350
● *Flowing Spring*, Blair....C	100
Floyd, Venango...........NW	×
Flynn, Susquehanna...... NE	×
● *Flynn City*, Cambria......C	50
Fogelsville, Lehigh..........E	400
● *Folcroft*, Delaware......SE	×
● *Foley*, Somerset........SW	×
● Folsom, Deleware.......SE	150
Foltz, Franklin ....S	100
Fombell, Beaver............W	10
Font, Chester..............SE	50
● *Fontaine*, Chester.......SE	×
Fontana, Lebanon ....SE	260
○ *Foot of Mountain*, Schylk'lE	×
Foot of Plane, Bradford....N	50
Forcht, Butler............. W	×
○ Ford City, Armstrong....W	[illegible],255
Fordyce, Greene..........SW	50
● *Forest*, McKean..........N	×
● Forest City, SusquehannaNE	2,319
Forest Grove, Bucks.......SE	150
Forest Hill, Union C	100
● Forest House, Potter.....N	75
Forest Lake, SusquehannaNE	100
○ *Forest Siding*, Columbia. C	×
Forestville, Butler.........W	200
Forestville, Schuylkill......E	×
Forestville Sta. (see Carrier).	×
● *Forge Bridge*, Somerset. W	×
● Forks, Columbia..........C	65
● *Forks*, Centre............ C	×
Forks, Monroe..............E	200
Forkston, Wyoming...... NE	200
Forksville, Sullivan.........N	191
● *Forrest*, Chester....... SE	×
● Fort Hill, Somerset.....SW	25
● Fort Hunter, Dauphin....C	300
Fort Littleton, Fulton.......S	100
● Fort Loudon, Franklin....S	200
Fort Mifflin, Delaware....SE	×
Fortney, York ....S	75
Fort Palmer, Westmorel'dSW	25
FortPittSta.(seeWalker's Ms.)	×
● *Fortuna*, Montgomery..SE	×
● Fort Washington, Mont'gSE	400
Forty Fort, Luzerne........E	1,031
Forward, Somerset....... SW	100
● *Fossilville*, Bedford.......S	115
● *Foster*, Susquehanna... NE	450
● Foster Brook, McKean...N	300
● *Foster Brook*, McKean...N	×
Foster's Mills, Armstrong..W	40
● *Fosterville*, Westmorel'dSW	×
● Fostoria, Blair............ C	100
● *Foundryville*, Luzerne....E	×
● *Fountain*, Centre..........C	×
Fountain, Schuylkill........ E	65
Fountain Dale, Adams...... S	150
Fountain Mills, (seeScottdale)	×
Fountain Springs, SchuylkillE	400
Fountainville, Bucks....... SE	100
● *Four Mile Run*, Tioga....N	×
○ *Foustwell*, Somerset....SW	×
● *Fowler*, Centre........... C	×
● Fowlerville, Columbia.... C	50
● Foxburgh, Clarion....... W	640
● Fox Chase, Philadelphia.SE	1,354
● *Fox Hill*, Chester........SE	×
● *Foxtown*, WestmorelandSW	×
● Frackville, Schuylkill.... E	2,520
● *Fraleys*, McKean.........N	×
Frampton, Clarion......... W	75
Francis, Erie............ NW	×
Franconia, Montgomery...SE	150
FranconiaSquare, Montg'ySE	×
Frank, Allegheny.........SW	600
○ Frankford, Philadelphia SE	18,600
● *Frankford Jc.*, Philad'laSE	×
Frankfort, (see Frankfort Sprs)	×
Frankfort Springs, Beaver. W	180
● *Frankhurst*, Clearfield... C	×
Franklin, Cambria..........C	662
● **Franklin**, Venango..NW	6,221
Franklin Corners, Erie...NW	350
Franklindale, Bradford.....N	300
● *Franklin Forge*, Blair....C	200
Franklin Forks, Susque'naNE	150
● *Franklin Junc.*, Luzerne.E	×
Franklin Mills, Fulton.......S	40
● *Franklin Quarries*, LehighE	×
Franklintown, York......... S	232
Franklinville, Huntingdon..C	125
Franklinville, (see Philadelphia).....................	×
● Frankstown, Blair.........C	200
● *Frantz*, Allegheny......SW	×
● Frazer, Chester..........SE	150
Frederick, Montgomery...SE	400
Fredericksburg, (see Clover Creek)..................	×
Fredericksburgh, Lebanon.SE	612
Fredericksville, Berks.....SE	70
Fredericktown, Wash'ton.SW	150
Fredonia, Mercer...........W	429
Freeburgh, Snyder..........C	540
● Freedom, Beaver.......... W	704
Freehold, Warren........ NW	150
● Freeland, Luzerne.......E	1,730
● *Freeman*, McKean.......N	×
● Freemansburgh, N'rth'mpE	615
● *Freemansburgh Station*, Northampton...........E	×
● Freeport, Armstrong.....W	1,687
Freestone, Franklin.........S	50
Fremont, Ghester...........SE	70
● *French Creek Jc.*, ChesterSE	×
French Mills, (see Wells)....	×
Frenchtown, Crawford...NW	40
Frenchville, Clearfield...... C	150
Freys, (see York)............	×
Freystown, (see Crosskill Mills)....................	×
Freytown, Lackawanna...NE	×
Fribley, Lycoming..........N	250
Fricks, Bucks........... . SE	200
● *Frick's*, Fayette........ SW	×
● Frick's Lock, Chester... SE	×
● *Friday*, Fayette.........SW	×
● Fr edens, Somerset.......SW	100
Friedensburgh, (see Oley)....	×
Friedensburgh, Schuylkill.. E	250
Friedensville, Lehigh........ E	514
Friendsville, Susquehanna..E	139
● *Frisbie*, Schuylkill.........E	×
Frisco, Beaver.............W	150
● *Fritz*, Union..............C	×
● Fritztown, Berks........SE	100
Frogtown, (see Johnstown)..	×
Frogtown, Clarion.........W	100
● *Frost*, Fayette..........SW	150
Frostburgh, Jefferson...... W	100
● *Frost's*, Forest......... NW	150
● Frugality, Cambria..........C	[illegible]
Fruitville, Montgomery... SE	[illegible]
● *Frush Valley*, Berks....SE	×
Frutchey's, Monroe.........E	×
Fryburg, Clarion...........W	300
● Frymire, Berks..........SE	×
Frystown, (see Freys)........	×
Frysville, (see Hinkletown)..	×
● *Fuller*, Fayette.......... SW	×
● Fuller Jefferson..........W	25
● *Fullerton*, Lehigh........E	×
● *Fullmor*, Montgomery..SE	×
● *Fulton*, Northumberland.C	×
Fulton, (see Blackburg)......	×
● Fulton House, Lancaster.SE	275
Funkstown, (see Mt. Alto)...	×
Furlong, Bucks............SE	50
● *Furnace Road*, Hunt'don.C	150
Furniss, Lancaster.........SE	40
Fyan, Bedford..............S	50
Gaines, Tioga.............. N	400
Gale, Washington......... SW	10
● Galeton, Potter..........N	400
Galilee, Wayne............NE	100
Gallagher, McKean..........N	×
● *Gallagherville*, Chester..SE	×
● Gallitzin, Cambria........C	2,392
Gallows, Bucks............SE	215
Gamble's, Allegheny......SW	×
● Ganister, Blair............C	200
Ganoga, (see Maple Run)....	×
● Gap, Lancaster..........SE	500
● *Gap Junction*, Lehigh.... E	×
● *Gap Road*, Franklin......S	×
Gapsville, Bedford.......... S	150
Gardeau, McKean...........N	200
○ *Gardener*, Lehigh.........E	×
● *Gardens*, Chester.........SE	×
Gardenville, Bucks..........SE	60
● *Gardner*, Blair............C	×
Gardners, Adams...........S	×
● *Gardner's Switch*, Luzer'eE	×
Garfield, Berks............. SE	75
Garfield, (see Borard)........	×
● *Garfield*, Warren...... NW	×
○ Garland, Warren.........NW	300
Garlock Hollow, McKean.. N	×
Garman's Mills, Cambria... C	20
Garrard Ford, (see Whitely).	×
● Garrett, Somerset.........SW	450
Garrettford, Delaware.....SE	100
Garrison, Greene...........SW	×
Garver's Ferry, Westmoreland.................SW	45
○ *Garvin's*, Mercer..........W	×
Garwood, Washington.... SW	50
● Gastonville, WashingtonSW	400
Gatchellville, York...........S	200
Gatesburgh, Centre......... C	50
● *Gawango*, Warren..... NW	×
Gaysport, Blair.............C	867
● Gazzam, Clearfield........C	×
Gearhartsville, Clearfield....C	400
Geary, Westmoreland.....SW	30
Gebhart's Somerset....... SW	500
○ *Gehman*, Berks......... SE	×
Gehman, Montgomery....SE	40
● Gehrton, Crawford.....NW	32
● *Geiger's*, Somerset......SW	×
● Geiger's Mills, Berks.....SE	100
● *Geiger's Point*, Dauphin...C	×
Geistown, Cambria...........C	50
Gelatt, Susquehanna.......NE	150
Gem, Fulton.................S	30
Genesee Fork, Potter.......N	100
● Geneva, Crawford......NW	293
Geneva, (see New Geneva).....	×
● George's Sta., Westm'l'dSW	50
● Georgetown, Beaver..... W	274
Georgetown, (see Sheakleyville)..................	×
Georgetown, (see Doylestown)	×
Georgetown, (see Bart).......	×
● *Georgetown*, Wayne......NE	×
● *Georgetown*, North'mb'l'dC	400
Georgeville, Indiana........W	100
● *Gerhards*, Carbon........E	×
Germania, Potter............N	250
● *German's*, Schuylkill.....E	×
● Germansville, Lehigh.....E	150
● Germantown, Philadel'a.SE	22,000
● *Germantown Junc.*, PhilaSE	×
Germany, Warren........NW	25
Geryville, Bucks...... .....SE	25
● **Gettysburgh**, Adams...S	3,221
Gettysburgh, (see Hillsdale)..	×
Gettysburgh National Cemetery, Adams..........S	×
Gettysburgh Springs, AdamsS	×
Ghent, Bradford..... ...... N	23
Gibbon Glade, Fayette.... SW	25
Gibb Station, Beaver.......W	×
● Gibraltar, Berks.........SE	200
Gibson, (see McKee's Rocks).	×
Gibson, Susquehanna..... NE	300
● *Gibson*, Fayette.........SW	×
● Gibsonia, Allegheny.... SW	100
● *Gibson's Point*, Phila'la.SE	×
● Gibsonton, Westm'land.SW	300
Gideon, Somerset.........SW	×

● Gifford, McKean..........N 20
Gilbert, McKean..........N ×
Gilbert, Monroe..........E 120
● Gilberton, Schuylkill......E 3,687
Gilbertsville, Montgomery.SE 450
● Gilfoyle, Forest.........NW 100
● *Gilkeson*, Washington...SW ×
● Gillett, Bradford..........N 200
Gill Hall, Allegheny........SW 300
Gillingham, Clearfield......C ×
● *Gillintown*, Centre........C ×
● *Gillmor*, McKean.........N 600
Gilmore's Landing, (see Webster).................. ×
Gilpin, Indiana..........W 50
● *Gilson*, Warren.........NW ×
Ginger Hill, (see Baldland)... ×
Ginther, (see Tamanend)..... ×
Gipsey, Indiana............W ×
● Girard, Erie...........NW 626
● *Girard*, York...........S ×
● *Girard*, Erie..........NW 400
● *Girard Junction*, Erie...NW ×
Girard Mammoth, Sch'lkill.E ×
● Girard Manor, Schuylkill.E 200
Girard's Fort, (see Whitely). ×
● Girardville, Schuylkill....E 3,584
Girdland, Wayne..........NE 200
Girty, Armstrong.......... W 40
● *Gist*, Fayette...........SW ×
● *Gitt's Run*, York.........S ×
Gladdens, Somerset.......SW 50
Glade, Somerset.......... SW 150
Glade Mills, Butler.........W 50
● *Glade Run*, Somerset...SW ×
● Glade Run, Warren.....NW ×
● Gladwyne, Montgomery.SE 610
Glasgow, Beaver........... W 218
● Glasgow, Cambria......... C 170
● *Glasgow*, Montgomery..SE ×
● *Glass Works*, Fayette.. SW ×
● Glatfelters, York..........S 75
Gleason, Tioga..............N 25
● Glenburn, Lackawanna. NE 290
● Glen Campbell, Indiana..W ×
● *GlenCampbellJunc.*,Indiana W ×
● Glen Carbon, Schuylkill.. E 131
● Glen City, Columbia...... C 200
● Glencoe, Somerset...... SW 56
Glendale, (see Joint)......... ×
Glendale, (see Flinton)....... ×
● *Glendon*, Northampton...E 907
● *Glen Dower*, Schuylkill....E ×
Glen Emery, Blair.........C ×
● Glen Eyre, Pike.........NE 200
● Glenfield, Allegheny....SW 718
● Glen Fisher, Elk......... N ×
● Glen Hall, Chester.......SE 50
● Glen Hazel, Elk.......... N 500
Glen Hope, Clearfield....... C 286
Gleniron, Union.............C 100
● *Glenlake*, Bucks.........SE ×
● Glenloch, Chester....... SE 400
● Glenlyon, Luzerne........E 2,255
● *Glen Manor*, Lancaster. SE ×
● *Glen Mawr*, Lycoming... N ×
● Glenn Mills, Delaware...SE 200
● Glen Moore, Chester.... SE 300
Glenn, McKean..............N 40
Glenola, Lancaster........ S ×
● Glen Olden, Delaware... SE 250
● *Glen Onoko*, Carbon..... E ×
Glenora, Butler............ W 50
Glen Richey, Clearfield......C 527
● Glen Riddle, Delaware. SE 800
● Glen Rock, York..........S 687
● Glen Roy, Chester.......SE 50
Glen Savage, Somerset....SW 20
● Glenshaw, Allegheny.... SW 500
● Glenside, Montgomery.. SE 150
Glen Summit, Luzerne.......E 47
● *Glen Summit*, Huntingdon C ×
● Glen Union, Clinton......N 150
● Glenville, York........... S 150
● Glen White, Blair.........C ×
○ *Glen Willow*, Philadelphia SE ×
● *Glenwood*, Allegheny... SW ×
Glenwood, Susquehanna.. NE 100
● *Glenwood*, York.......... S ×
● *Glenworth*, Schuylkill.... E ×
Glessner, Somerset........SW 40
● *Glidewell*, Sullivan.......N ×
Globe, Fayette............ SW ×
● Globe Mills, Snyder.......C 375
● *Globe Run*, Huntingdon.. C ×
Glyde, Washington..........SW ×
● Glyndon, Crawford.... NW ×

● *Goat Hill*, Fayette......SW ×
Gockley, Lancaster........SE 50
● Goddard, Erie..........NW ×
● *Goehring*, Beaver........ W ×
Goff, Westmoreland.......SW 25
Goheenville, Armstrong.... W 25
Gold, Potter.............. N 50
Golden Hill, Wyoming.... NE 60
Golden Rod, Lycoming.....N ×
Goldenville, Adams..........S 25
● *Gold Mine*, Lebanon.... SE ×
Goldsboro, York............ S 345
Gold Station, Allegheny..SW ×
Golias, McKean............ N ×
Golinza, Forest............NW 80
● Gomersal, Butler........ W 200
● Goodell, McKean...........N 200
Good Hope, Cumberland.... S 50
Good Intent, Washington. SW 70
● Good Spring, Schuylkill.. E ×
Goohring, Beaver.......... W ×
Goodville, Lancaster.......SE 200
Goodville Hill, Warren...NW ×
Goodyear, Cameron........ N ×
● *Gooseberry*, Bedford...... S ×
Goram, York................ S ×
● Gordon, Schuylkill........E 1,194
● Gordonville, Lancaster.. SE 225
● *Gorgas*, Philadelphia....SE ×
Gorsuch, Huntingdon.......C 50
● *Gorton*, Centre............C ×
● Gosford, Armstrong......W 200
Goshen, Lancaster..........SE 200
Goshenville, Chester........N 100
● *Goshorn*, Huntingdon.... C 150
● *Goss Run Junc.*,Clearfield C ×
Gouglersville, Berks.........SE 100
Gouldsboro, Lackawanna. NE 141
● Gouldsboro Sta.,W'ne.. NE 750
● *Governor Dick Mountain*, Lebanon..............SE ×
● Gowen, Luzerne.......... E 300
Gowen City, Northumber'd.C 65
● *Graceton*, Indiana....... W ×
Graceton, Indiana......... W ×
Graceville, Bedford......... S 25
Gracey, Fulton.............S ×
Gradyville, Delaware......SE 150
Graefenburgh, Adams...... S 25
● Grafton, Huntingdon..... C 200
● *Graham*, Clearfield.......C ×
● *Grahams*, Lawrence..... W ×
Grahamton, Clearfield...... C 50
Grahamville, York..........S 200
Grampian, Clearfield........C 175
● Grand Tunnel, Luzerne...E 25
● Grand Valley, Warren..NW 500
Grange, Jefferson.......... W 25
● Granite Hill, Adams...... S 175
Grant, Indiana............. W 420
● *Grant*, Elk................ N ×
Grant City, Lawrence...... W 40
Grant Farm, (see Parker City) ×
Grantham, Cumberland.....S ×
● *Grantley*, York............S ×
Grantville, Dauphin.........C 300
● Granville, Mifflin......... C 200
Granville Centre, Bradford. N 200
● Granville Summit, Brad'd N 100
● Grapeville, Westmorel'd SW 400
Grassflat, Clearfield........C ×
● *Grassy Run Junc.*, Somerset............ SW ×
● Grater's Ford, Montg'ry SE 250
Gratz, Dauphin............. C 490
Gravellick, Clarion.........W ×
● *Gravel Place*, Monroe.... E ×
● *Graver's*, Philadelphia.. SE ×
Gravity, Wayne........... NE 100
Gray, Westmoreland..... SW ×
● *Graybill*, York........... S ×
Graydon, York...............S 10
● *Gray's Ferry*, Phil'del'pa SE ×
Gray's Landing, Greene...SW 25
● *Gray's Mills*, Crawford NW ×
Gray's Mills, Allegheny.. SW 30
Gray's Run, Lycoming......N ×
Graysville, (see Harvey's).... ×
Graysville, Huntingdon.... C 150
● *Grazierville*, Blair.........C ×
● Greason, Cumberland.....S 100
● Great Belt, Butler.........W 100
● Great Bend, S'queh'nna NE 1,002
● *Great Bend Station*, Susquehanna................ NE ×
Greble, Lebanon...........SE 20
Greece City, Butler.........W 25

● *Greenawald*, Berks......SE ×
● *Greenback*, N'rth'mb'rl'nd C ×
Greenbank, Lancaster..... SE 30
Greenbrier, Northumb'rl'nd C 15
Greenburr, Clinton..........N 60
● Greencastle, Franklin.....S 1,525
Greendale, Armstrong......W 20
● *Greendale*, McKean.......N ×
Greene, Lancaster......... SE 300
● *Greene Hill*, Chester....SE ×
Greene's Landing, Bradford N 61
Greenfield, Erie.......... NW 100
Greenfield, (see Cole Centre). ×
● *Greenfield*, Lancaster....SE ×
Green Garden, Beaver......W ×
Green Grove, Lackaw'nna NE 75
Greenland, Lancaster.......SE 35
● Green Lane, Montgomery SE 237
● *Green Lawn*, Chester.... SE ×
● *Green Lick*, W's'm'rl'n'd SW ×
○ *Greenlick Jc.*, West'm'l'd SW ×
Green Mount, Adams....... S 175
● *Greenmount*, Philadelphia SE ×
Green Oak, (see Atwood) .... ×
● Greenock, Allegheny...SW 400
Green Park, Perry..........C 200
● *Green Point*, Lebanon...SE ×
● *Green Ridge*, York........S 100
● *Green Ridge*, Lack'wan'a NE ×
● *Green Ridge*, Northumb'ld C ×
Greensborough, Greene...SW 427
Greensburg, Fayette......SW ×
● **Greensburgh**, Westmoreland.................SW 4,202
Green's Land., (see Athens).. ×
Green Spring, Cumberland..S 100
● *Green Springs*, Alleg'ny.SW ×
Greentown, Pike...........NE 150
Green Tree, Allegheny....SW 685
● *Green Tree*, Chester.....SE 175
● Green Village, Franklin.. S 200
Greenville, (see Buckingham) ×
Greenville, (see Penn Run)... ×
Greenville, (see Ephrata) .... ×
● Greenville, Mercer.......W 3,674
Greenwich, (see Klinesville). ×
Greenwich, Philadelphia ..SE ×
Greenwood, Bradford.......N ×
Greenwood, Columbia...... C 150
Greenwood, (see Black's Gap) ×
Greenwood Fur., Huntingd'n C 250
Greer, Butler.............. W 125
Greer's Cors., (see Dublin) .. ×
● *Greer's*, Washington....SW 50
● *Gregg*, Centre.............C ×
Gregory, Luzerne........... E 50
● Grenoble, Bucks........ SE ×
Gresham, Crawford....... NW 100
Greshville, Berks..........SE 150
Gretna, Washington...... SW ×
Grey's Eddy, (see Mahoning) ×
○ *Greythorne*, Lehigh....... E 280
Gridley's, McKean......... N ×
Grier City, Schuylkill.......E ×
Grier's Point, Perry.........C 25
Griesemersville, Berks.... SE 76
● Griffin, Somerset........SW 20
● *Griffin*, Westmoreland.. SW ×
● *Griffiths*, McKean.........N ×
Grill, Berks................ SE ×
Grimville, Berks.......... SE 200
● Grindstone, Fayette.... SW ×
Grip, Indiana.............. W ×
Grisemore, Indiana........ W 25
Grissinger, Cumberland.....S 150
● Groffdale, Lancaster.....SE ×
Groff's Store, Lancaster....SE 150
● Grovania, Montour........C 15
● *Grove*, Cameron..........N ×
Grove, Allegheny......... SW ×
● Grove City, Mercer...... W 1,160
● Grover, Bradford..........N 100
● Grove Summit, Jefferson W ×
● Groveton, Allegheny....SW ×
Guava, Columbia............C 30
Guernsey, Adams............S 50
● *Guffey*, Westmoreland..SW 200
Guffey, McKean.............N 138
Guffy's Sta., Westmorel'nd SW 200
● Guilford Springs, Franklin S 25
Guitonville, Forest.......NW 30
● *Guldens*, Adams......... S ×
Gulf Mills, Montgomery...SE 500
Gump, Greene............SW 10
● *Gum Stump*, Centre...... C ×
● Gum Tree, Chester...... SE 75
Gundaker, (see Gibsonia).... ×

Pennsylvania
Pennsylvania

● Gurnee, Tioga ... N 15
● *Gurnee Junction*, Tioga .. N ×
Guthrie, Indiana ... W ×
Guthriesville, Chester ... SE 100
● Guth's Station, Lehigh ... E 60
Guthsville, Lehigh ... E 175
● *Guyasuta*, Allegheny ... SW ×
Guyer, Centre ... C 25
Guy's Mills, Crawford ... NW 227
● *Guy's Mills*, Allegheny. SW ×
Gwendolin, Delaware ... SE ×
● Gwynedd, Montgomery. SE 150
● *Haaks*, Schuylkill ... E ×
Haas, Schuylkill ... E 50
Hackney's, Washington ... SW 10
Haddenville, Fayette ... SW 10
Haddington, (see Philadelphia) N ×
● Hadley, Mercer ... W 500
Haffey, Allegheny ... SE ×
Hagersville, Bucks ... SE 300
● *Haggerty's Quarry*, Wash. SW ×
● *Hahn's*, Somerset ... SW ×
Hahntown, Lancaster ... SE 50
Hahnstown, Westmoreland SW 621
● *Haines*, Lehigh ... E ×
● *Haines*, Lancaster ... SE ×
Haines, Wayne ... NE ×
Haley's Sta., (see Marysville) ×
Half-Way-H'se, (see Maiden Cr.) ×
● Halifax, Dauphin ... C 515
Hall, York ... S 150
● *Hallenback's*, Lackaw'na NE ×
● *Hallman's*, Montgomery SE ×
● *Halls*, Lycoming ... N 25
● *Hall's*, Potter ... N ×
Hallstead, Susquehanna ... NE 1,167
● *Hallston*, Butler ... W ×
Hallton, Elk ... N 25
● Hamburgh, Berks ... SE 2,127
● *Hamburgh*, Berks ... SE ×
Hametown, York ... S 250
Hamill, Indiana ... W 20
Hamilton, Jefferson ... W 100
● *Hamilton No. 1*, Somerset SW 200
Hamlin, Lebanon ... SE 75
● *Hamlin*, McKean ... N ×
Hamlinton, Wayne ... SE 200
Hammersley's Fork, Clinton N 100
Hammett, Erie ... NW ×
● *Hammon*, Schuylkill ... E 100
● *Hammond*, Potter ... N ×
● Hammond, Tioga ... N 30
● *Hammond Siding*, Tioga. N ×
Hamorton, Chester ... SE 175
Hampden, Cumberland ... S 25
Hampton, Berks ... SE 300
● *Hampton*, Berks ... SE ×
● Hance, Delaware ... SE 25
● *Hancock*, Berks ... SE ×
Hancock, Lancaster ... SE 150
Haneyville, Clinton ... N 95
● *Hanger*, Somerset ... SW ×
● Hamlin Sta., Washington SW 50
● *Hannah*, Centre ... C ×
Hannahstown, (see Saxonb'g) ×
Hanover, (see Harshaville) ... ×
● *Hanover*, Luzerne ... E ×
● Hanover, York ... S 3,746
● Hanover Junction, York .. S 150
Hanoverville, Northampton. E 100
● *Harbison*, Butler ... W ×
● *Harbor Bridge*, Lawrence W ×
● Harbor Mills, Lycoming .. N 53
● Harbour Creek, Erie ... NW 150
● *Harden*, Allegheny ... SW ×
Harding, Luzerne ... E 75
Hardpan, Luzerne ... E ×
Hare's Valley, Huntington .. C 25
Harford, Susquehanna ... NE 300
Harlansburg, Lawrence ... W 250
● Harleigh, Luzerne ... E 250
Harlem, Berks ... SE ×
Harleysville, Montgomery. SE 400
● Harmarville, Allegheny SE 250
● Harmonsb'gh, Crawford NW 200
● *Harmonsburgh Station*, Crawford ... NW ×
● Harmon's Creek, Wash'n SW 20
● Harmony, Butler ... W 585
Harnedsville, Somerset ... SW 100
● *Harnish*, Lancaster ... SE ×
Harpers, Northampton ... E ×
● *Harpers*, Philadelphia .. SE ×
● *Harris*, Lycoming ... N 53
● **HARRISBURG**, Dauphin ... C 39,385
Harrison City, Westmorel'd SW 700

● Harrison Valley, Potter .. N 300
Harrisonville, Fulton ... S 75
Harristown, (see Kinzers) ... ×
● Harrisville, Butler ... W 450
Harrity, Carbon ... E 75
Harrold, Elk ... N 500
● *Harrowgate*, Philadelphia SE ×
Harshaville, Beaver ... W 50
Hartford, Tioga ... N ×
Harthegig, Mercer ... W 85
● *Hartinam's*, Clinton ... N ×
Hartleton, Union ... C 261
● *Hartley*, Bedford ... S ×
Hartley, York ... S 200
● Hartley Hall, Lycoming .. N 25
Hartman, Elk ... N ×
● *Hartman*, Lancaster ... SE ×
● *Hartranft*, Montgomery. SE 130
● Hartstown, Crawford ... NW 160
● Hartsville, Bucks ... SE 150
● *Hartzell*, Lehigh ... E ×
Harvey's, Greene ... SW 175
● *Harvey's Lake*, Luzerne .. E ×
● *Harvey's Run*, Jefferson. W ×
● *Harveyville*, Chester ... SE 43
Harveyville, Luzerne ... E 200
Harwood, Luzerne ... E ×
● Haskell, Clarion ... W 10
Haskin, Potter ... N ×
Hastings, Cambria ... C 1,070
● *Hastings*, Allegheny ... SW ×
● Hatborough, Montgomery SE 781
Hatch Hollow, Erie ... NW 30
● Hatfield, Montgomery ... SE 300
Hatton, Cumberland ... S 200
● *Hauck's*, Schuylkill ... E ×
● Hauto, Carbon ... E 75
Havelock, (see McDonald's) .. ×
Haverford, (see Manoa) ... ×
● Haverford, Montgomery. SE 100
Hawes, Bradford ... N ×
● *Hawkeye*, Westmorela'd SW 30
● *Hawkins*, Allegheny ... SW ×
● *Hawk Run*, Clearfield ... C ×
● Hawley, Wayne ... NE 1,968
Hay, (see Hamilton) ... ×
Haycock Run, Bucks ... SE 75
Haydentown, Fayette ... SW 75
● *Hayes*, Centre ... C ×
Hayesville, (see Townsend) .. ×
Hayfield, Crawford ... NW 150
Haymaker, McKean ... N 125
Haynie, Clarion ... W 25
● *Hays*, Allegheny ... SW ×
● *Hays*, Somerset ... SW 10
● Hay's Grove, Cumberland. S 25
Hay's Mill, Somerset ... SW 44
● *Hays Siding*, Allegheny SW ×
Hay's Station, (see Homestead) ×
● Haysville, Allegheny ... SW ×
Haysville, (see Baldwin) ... ×
Hayville, Delaware ... SE ×
● *Hazard*, Carbon ... E ×
Hazardville, Chester ... SE ×
Hazeldell, Lawrence ... W ×
● *Hazeltine Sid'g*, Allegh'y SW ×
● *Hazelwood*, McKean ... N ×
Hazen, Jefferson ... W 100
● Hazlebrook, Luzerne ... E 150
● *Hazle Creek Junc.*, Carbon E ×
● Hazleton, Luzerne ... E 11,872
● *Hazelton Junc.*, Luzerne .. C ×
Hazlewood, (see Pittsburg) Allegheny ... SW ×
Hazzard, Mercer ... W ×
● *Head of Grade*, Schuylkill. E ×
Heart Lake, Susquehanna NE ×
● Hearthville, Jefferson ... W 50
● *Heaton*, Montgomery ... SE ×
Hebe, Northumberland ... C 65
Heberlig, Cumberland ... S 25
Hebron, Potter ... N ×
● *Hecks*, Dauphin ... C ×
● Heckscherville, Schuylkill E 100
● Hectown, Northampton ... C 170
● Hecla, Schuylkill ... E 610
Hecla, Westmoreland ... SW ×
Hecton Mills, Dauphin ... C ×
Hector, Potter ... N 32
Hegarty's Cr. Rds., Clearfield C ×
Hegins, Schuylkill ... E 175
● *Heidleberg*, Luzerne ... E ×
Heidlersburgh, Adams ... S 150
● Hellmandale, Lebanon ... SE 100
● *Heinley*, Lehigh ... E ×
Heistersburgh, Fayette ... SW 25
Helena, (see Salina) ... ×

Helen Furnace, Clarion ... W 50
● Helfenstein, Schuylkill ... E 500
Helixville, Bedford ... S 10
● Hellam, York ... S 300
● *Hellen Mills*, Elk ... N ×
Heller, York ... S 25
● *Heller's Church*, Lancaster SE ×
● Hellertown, Northampton. E 708
Helvetia, Clearfield ... C ×
Helvetia Mines, Clearfield ... C ×
Hemlock, Cambria ... C ×
● *Hemlock*, Warren ... NW ×
Hemlock Hollow, Wayne. NW 116
● *Hempfield*, Lancaster ... SE ×
Henderson, Mercer ... W 50
● *Henderson*, Montgomery. SE 100
● Hendricks, Montgomery. SE 100
● Henrietta, Blair ... C 250
● *Henry Clay*, Cumberland. S ×
● *Henry's Bend*, Venango NW ×
● *Henryville*, Monroe ... E 100
Hensel, Lancaster ... SE 100
Hensingersville, Lehigh ... E 175
Hepburn, Lycoming ... N ×
Hepler, Schuylkill ... E 100
Hereford, Berks ... SE 150
Herefordsville, Berks ... SE ×
● Herman, Butler ... W 50
● Hermitage, Mercer ... W 160
● Herndon, Northumberland C 400
● *Herr*, Allegheny ... SW ×
Herrick, Bradford ... N 210
● Herrick Centre, Susq'h'a NE 200
Herrickville, Bradford ... N 50
Herriotsville, (see Boyce Sta.) ×
Herron, Allegheny ... SW 150
Herrville, Lancaster ... SE 25
Heshbon, Indiana ... W 40
● Hess, Lancaster ... SE 300
Hestonville, Columbia ... C ×
● *Hess Mill*, McKean ... N ×
Hestonville, Philadelphia .. SE 3,000
Hetlerville, Columbia ... C 150
● *Heverly*, Clearfield ... C ×
Hibbardtown, (see New Albany) ×
Hickernell, Crawford ... NW ×
Hickman, Allegheny ... SW ×
● *Hickman Run Jc.*, Fayette SW ×
Hickory, Washington ... SW 200
● *Hickory*, Forest ... NW 250
Hickory Cors., Northumber'd C 175
● Hickory Grove, Susq'h'a NE 65
Hickory Hill, Chester ... SE 100
● Hickory Run, Carbon ... E 100
● *Hick's Ferry*, Luzerne ... E ×
● *Hiestand*, York ... S ×
Hiester's Mill, Berks ... SE 37
Higbee, Greene ... SW ×
High Bridge, Allegheny .. SW ×
High House, Fayette ... SW 25
High Lake, Wayne ... NE 200
● *Highland*, Beaver ... W ×
Highland, Bradford ... N 741
Highland, Dauphin ... C 845
● *Highland*, Philadelphia. SE ×
● *Highland Jc.*, Luzerne ... E 657
Highland Lake, Lycoming .. N ×
● *High Rock*, York ... S ×
● High Spire, Dauphin ... C 971
Highville, Lancaster ... SE 150
Hilborn, Lycoming ... N 32
Hill, Mercer ... W 100
Hillagesville, (see Red Hill) .. ×
Hill Church, Berks ... SW 270
Hill City, Venango ... NW ×
● *Hilldale*, Washington ... SW ×
● Hillegass, Montgomery .. SE 100
● Hilliard's, Butler ... W 300
● *Hillman Summit*, Indiana W ×
● *Hills*, Allegheny ... SW ×
Hillsborough, Somerset ... SW 50
Hillsborough, (see Scenery Hill) ×
● *Hillsdale*, Allegheny ... SW ×
● *Hillsdale*, Dauphin ... C ×
Hillsdale, Indiana ... W 200
Hillsdale Sta., (see Shire Oaks) ×
Hill's Grove, Sullivan ... N 563
● *Hillside*, Montgomery ... SE ×
● Hillside, Westmoreland. SW 40
Hill's Sta., (see Lawrence) ... ×
Hillsvale's Mills, (see North Hope) ×
Hill's View, Westmoreland SW 20
● Hillsville, Lawrence ... W 200
● *Hilltop*, Bucks ... SE ×
Hilltown, Bucks ... SE 50
● *Hilltown*, Lawrence ... W 400
Hinds, Indiana ... W ×

● Hine's Corners, Wayne..NE 50
Hinkletown, Lancaster.... SE 400
Hinkson's Cors., (see Media) ×
● Hites, Allegheny........SW 500
Hitner, (see Vincent)........ ×
● Hoadley's, Wayne.......NE 150
Hoagland, Mercer..........W ×
Hobbie, Lucerne............E 75
Hoblet, Bradford...........N ×
Hoblitzell, Bedford..........S 25
● Hoboken, Allegheny.... SW 450
Hockersville, (seeSwataraSta.) ×
● *Hocking Junc.*,SomersetSW ×
● *Hocking Mine*, Somerset. SW ×
Hoernerstown,(seeHummelst'n) ×
Hoffer, Snyder..............C 200
Hoffman, Lehigh............E ×
● *Hoffman*, Perry...........C ×
Hogestown, Cumberland....S 150
Hoggs, Westmoreland.... SW 25
● *Hogsett*, Fayette........SW ×
● Hokendauqua, Lehigh.... E 953
● Hokes, York..............S 50
Holbrook, Greene.........SW 10
● *Holderbaum*, Bedford.....S ×
Holicong, Bucks...........SE 125
Holland, Bucks............SE 150
● *Holland*, Bucks......... SE ×
Hollenback, Bradford...... N ×
● *Holliday*, Tioga.......... N ×
● **Hollidaysburgh**, Blair C 2,975
Hollisterville, Wayne...... NE 500
● Hollsopple, Somerset... SW 75
Hollywood, Luzerne......... E 598
Holman's, Chester..........C ×
● Holmes, Delaware.........SE 125
● Holmesburgh,Phil'd'lp'a SE 1,300
● *Holmesburgh Junc.*Phila SE ×
Holt, Beaver...............W 15
Holtz, York................S 30
Home, Indiana.............W 125
● Homer City, Indiana..... W 505
● *Homer Siding*, Indiana.. W ×
Homer Sta.,(see Homer City). ×
● Homestead, Allegheny.. SW 7,911
● *Homesville*, Schuylkill.... E ×
● *Homestown*, Schuylkill.... E ×
● Homet's Ferry, Bradford. N 115
● *Homewood*, Allegheny..SW ×
● Homewood, Beaver........ W 250
● *Hommers*, Cambria....... C 50
Honeoye, Potter.............. N 50
● **Honesdale**, Wayne... NE 2,816
● Honey Brook, Chester.... C 614
● *Honey Creek*, Mifflin......C ×
Honey Grove, Juniata........C 200
Honnerstown, Cambria.......C 1,014
Hook Creek, (see Linw'd Sta.) ×
Hooker, Butler.............W 100
Hookstown, Beaver........ W 297
● *Hoover*, Blair.............. C ×
Hoover's Run, Greene.... SW 50
● Hooversville, Somerset. SW 400
● Hooverton, Montgomery SE 130
● Hop Bottom,Susqueha'a NE 299
Hope, Greene............ SW 10
● *Hope*, Northampton....... E ×
Hope Church, Allegheny..SW 800
● *Hope Church Sta.*,A'gh'ySW ×
● *Hope Mills*, Mercer....... W ×
Hope Furnace, (see Rose Pt.) ×
Hopeville, Luzerne..........E ×
● Hopewell, Bedford......... S 213
Hopewell, Chester........... SE 213
Hopewell, (see Douglassville). ×
Hopewell Centre, York...... S 200
● Hopewell Cotton Works, Chester.................. SE 264
Hopkins' Mills, (see Swarts) ×
Hoppenville, Montgomery.S 200
Hopwood, Fayette........ SW 550
● Horatio, Jefferson........W 800
● *Horn*, Warren..........NW ×
Hornbrook, Bradford ...... N 25
Hornby, Erie............ NW ×
Hornerstown,(see Johnstown) ×
● *Horningford*, Mifflin.......C ×
● *Horn's Springs*,North'ton E ×
Horse Creek, Venango... NW ×
Horsham, Montgomery.... SE 100
Horton City, (see Cartwright) ×
Horton's, Indiana.......... W 100
● **Hosensack, Lehigh**........E 600
Host, Berks..............SE 150
Hostetter, Westmoreland.SW ×
● *Hostler*, Huntingdon......C ×
Houser Mill, Monroe........ E 70
Houserville, Centre......... C 75
Houston, (see Hoboken)..... ×
● Houstonville, Wash'g'n.SW 300
Houston Sta.,(see Houston'le) ×
Housum, Franklin......... S 50
● Houtzdale, Clearfield..... C 2,231
● *Hovers*, Warren........ NW ×
● *Howard*, Allegheny.....SW ×
● *Howard*, Cameron.........N 500
● Howard, Centre...........C 554
● *Howard Junc.*, McKean..N ×
Howe, Jefferson............W ×
Howe, McKean............ N ×
● *Howell's*, Northampton... E ×
● *Howellville*, Chester...... S 200
Howellville, (see Gradyville).. ×
Howers's Branch,Northa'on E ×
Hoyt, Montgomery......... SE 100
● Hoytville, Tioga........... N 560
Hubelsville. Huntingdon.... C 50
Hubers, Lancaster......... SE 50
Hublersburgh, Centre ...... C 150
Hudson, Jefferson.......... W ×
Hudson, Luzerne............ E 2,000
● Hudsondale, Carbon...... E 150
Huff, Indiana............... W ×
● *Huff*, Westmoreland.... SW ×
● *Huffnagle*, Bucks....... SE ×
Huff's Church, Berks...... SE 250
Hugginsville,(see Reg't'r City) ×
● *Hughestown*, Luzerne.... E 1,454
Hughesville, (see St. John's). ×
● Hughesville, Lycoming... N 1,358
Hulmeville, Bucks .... SE 418
● Hulton, Allegheny...... SW 1,500
● *Hulton Ferry*, Allegheny SW ×
Hummel's Wharf, Snyder...C 6
Hummel's Store, Berks....SE ×
● Hummelstown, Dauphin..C 1,486
● Hunker's, Westmorel'd. SW 25
● Humlock Creek, Luzerne. E 75
Humlock's, Luzerne.........E ×
● *Hunter*, Forest...........NW ×
● *Hunter*, Northumberland C 10
● *Hunter*, Susquehanna...NE ×
Hunter's, McKean .... N ×
Hunter's Cave, Greene....SW ×
Hunter's Lake, (see M'cy Val.) ×
Hunter's Run, Cumberland. S 140
Hunterstown, Adams.........S 640
Huntersville, Lycoming .... N 100
● **Huntingdon**,Hunting'nC 5,729
● Huntingdon Valley,M't'y SE 400
Huntington Mills, Luzerne..E 200
● *Huntley*, Cameron....... N ×
● Huntsdale, Cumberland... S 250
Huntsville, Luzerne.........E 150
Husband, Somerset....... SW 10
● *Huston Run*, Wash'g'n. SW ×
Hustontown, Fulton .... S 100
● *Hutchins* McKean........ N ×
● *Hutchinson*, Fayette....SW ×
Huttonville, Cumberland....S 100
Hyde Park, (see Scranton)... ×
● Hydetown, Crawford... NW 247
● Hyndman, Bedford....... S 1,056
Hynemansville, Lehigh......E 100
● Hyner, Clinton............ N 250
Ickesburgh, Perry.......... C 200
● *Ice Siding*, Somerset....SW ×
Idaville, Adams............. S 175
Ide, Luzerne............... E ×
Idetown, Luzerne............E ×
● Idlepark, Westmoreland SW 50
● Idlewood, Allegheny....SW 250
Imlertown, Bedford .... S 100
Imler Valley, Bedford .... S 25
● Imperial, Allegheny..... SW 200
● *Imperial*, Venango .... NW ×
Independence, Washing'n SW 200
● **Indiana**, Indiana....... W 1,963
Indian Creek, McKean..... N 300
● *Indian Creek*, Fayette..SW ×
● *Indian Creek Sid.*,Faye'teSW ×
Indian Head, Fayette..... SW 50
Indian Orchard, Wayne... NE ×
Indian Ridge, Schuylkill... E ×
Indian Run, Mercer........ W 75
Indiantown, (see Highville).. ×
● Industry, Beaver......... W 660
Inez, Potter................ N 42
● *Ingleby*, Centre........... C ×
● *Inglenook*, Dauphin....... C ×
Ingleside, Westmoreland..SW 40
● *Ingleside*, Cambria........C ×
Ingomar, Allegheny...... SW ×
● Ingram, Allegheny..... SW ×
Inkerman, Luzerne......... E ×
● *Ink Works*, Allegheny..SW ×
● *Instanter*, Elk .... N ×
Intercourse, Lancaster .... SE 775
● *Intersection*, Franklin.... S ×
● *Intersection*, York........ S ×
● *Inwood*, Lebanon........SE ×
Iola, Columbia.............. C 80
Iona, Lebanon............. SE 50
Irish Lane, Luzerne......... E 100
● Irish Ripple, Lawrence... W 200
Irishtown, Adams .... S ×
Irishtown, (see Bird-in Hand) ×
Ironbridge, Montgomery.. SE 300
● *Iron Bridge*, Westm'ld. SW ×
● *Iron City*, Westm'l'nd..SW ×
● *Irondale*, Columbia...... C ×
● Ironore, York .... S 50
Iron Ridge, (see Ironore) .... ×
● *Ironsides*, Montgomery..SE ×
Iron Springs, Adams........ S ×
● *Iron Stone*, Berks.......SE ×
Ironton, Lehigh............ E 274
Ironville, (see Cordelia) ..... ×
● *Iroquois*, Perry...........C ×
● Irvine, Warren......... NW 250
Irvineton, (see Irvine)........ ×
● *Irving*, Shuylkill..........E ×
● *Irvins Siding*, Clearfield..C ×
● Irvona, Clearfield......... C 1,000
● Irwin, Westmoreland... SW 2,428
● Isabella, Chester ....SE 200
Island, Clinton .... N 100
● *Island Grove*, Northamp'n E ×
Island Pond, Wayne...... NE 50
Island Run, (see Smith's Ferry) ×
● *Island Run*, Elk......... N ×
Isle, Butler..................W 10
Ithan, Delaware........... SE 200
Itley, Erie...............NW ×
Iva, Lancaster............ SE 30
Ivarea, Erie.............. NW ×
Ivison, Cambria............ C ×
● Ivyland, Bucks...........SE 130
Ivy Mills, Delaware........SE 50
● *Ivy Rock*, Montgomery..SE ×
Jacks Mountain, Adams..... S ×
● *Jack's Mountain*, Butler W ×
Jackson, Susquehanna.... NE 300
● *Jackson*, Erie........... NW ×
● *Jackson*, Warren...... NW ×
● *Jackson Branch*, Mercer W 500
● Jackson Centre, Mercer. W 232
Jacksons Mills, Bedford.... S 5
● *Jackson Mines*, Fayette SW ×
● Jackson Summit, Tioga.. N 50
Jackson Valley, Susqueh'a NE 175
● **Jacksonville Lehigh**......E 280
Jacksonville, Indiana.......W 83
Jacksonville, (see Gap)....... ×
Jacksonville, (see Irwin's Sta.) ×
● *Jacksonville*, Cumberland S 250
Jacksonville, (see Enders).... ×
Jacksonville, (see Winn Bridge) ×
Jacksonwald, Berks......... SE 59
● *Jack's Run*, Allegheny. SW ×
Jacksville, Butler.......... W 50
● Jacob's Creek,Westm'l'dSW 300
● Jacob's Mills, York....... S 40
Jacobus, York...............S 250
Jacobus Sta., Allegheny..SW ×
● *James*, Somerset........ SW ×
● James Creek, HuntingdonC 500
● *James Mill*, Forest.... NW ×
● Jamestown, Mercer......W 822
Jamison, Bucks...........SE 50
● Jamison City, Columbia.. C ×
● *Jamison*, Forest....... NW ×
● *Jamisonville*, Butler..... W 25
● *Janeway's Siding*,F'y'teSW ×
● *Janney*, Bucks..........SE ×
Jarrettown, MontgomeryNSE 200
● Jeannette, Westmorel'd SW 3,296
● Jeanesville, Luzerne......E 1,300
● Jeddo, Luzerne........... E 358
Jefferson, (see Wilmore) ..... ×
Jefferson, Greene.........SW 327
● *Jefferson*, Schuylkill......E 30
Jefferson, Clarion.......... W 50
● *Jefferson*, York........... S 374
Jefferson Centre, Butler... W ×
Jefferson Fur,(seeBlair'sCorners) ×
● *JeffersonJunc.*,SusquehannaNE ×
Jefferson Line, Clearfield....C 110
Jeffersonville, Montgomery SE 200
● *Jeffreystown*, AlleghenySW ×
Jeffries, Clearfield...........C 20

Place	Section	Population
● *Jenkins*, Luzerne	E	×
● Jenkinstown, Montgomery	SE	1,609
Jenner's Cross Roads, Somerset	SW	50
Jennerstown, Somerset	SW	95
Jennersville, Chester	SE	100
Jenningsville, Wyoming	NE	200
● Jermyn, Lackawanna	NE	2,650
Jerry, Cameron	N	×
● Jersey Mills, Lycoming	N	54
Jersey Mines, Luzerne	E	×
● Jersey Shore, Lycoming	N	1,853
Jersey Shore Junc., Lyc'ng.	N	×
● *JerseyShoreSta.*, Lycoming	N	×
● Jerseytown, Columbia	C	300
Jewel, Crawford	NW	×
● *Jim Run*, Fayette	SW	×
● *Jimtown*, Fayette	SW	×
● Joanne, Berks	SE	210
● *Joanna Height*, Berks	SE	×
Job's Corners, Tioga	N	50
Johnsburgh, Somerset	SW	75
● *Johnson Brook*, Tioga	N	×
● Johnsonburgh, Elk	N	1,280
● *Johnsons Crossing*, W'n	NW	×
● Johnsonville, Northamp'n	E	180
Johnston's Lnd'g., (see Fayette City)		×
Johnstown, (see Orwin)		×
● Johnstown, Cambria	C	21,805
Johnsville, Bucks	SE	100
● *Johnsville*, Bucks	SE	200
Joint, Allegheny	SW	×
● *Jo Jo Junction*, McKean	N	×
● Joliett, Schuylkill	E	25
Jollytown, Greene	SW	100
Jones' Mills, Westmorel'd	SW	75
● Jones' Station, Allegheny	SW	×
● Jonestown, Lebanon	SE	643
Jonestown, (see Bentleyville)		×
Jordan, Lehigh	E	350
● *Jordan*, Bucks	SE	×
● *Jordan Bridge*, Lehigh	E	×
Joville, McKean	N	×
● *Joyce's Quarry*, Fayette	SW	×
Jubilee, Wayne	NE	×
● Julian, Centre	C	200
Jumonville, Fayette	SW	130
Junction, Huntingdon	C	×
● Junction, Lancaster	SE	500
● *Junction*, Warren	NW	×
● *Junction*, York	S	×
Junction City, (see W. Newton)		×
● *Junction Number 1*, Allegheny	SW	×
● *Junction Number 2*, Allegheny)	SW	×
● *Junction Switch*, Mont'ry	SE	×
● *June Bug*, Westmorel'd	SW	×
Juniata, Perry	C	250
● *Juniata Bridge*, Perry	C	250
Juniataville, Fayette	SW	×
Justus, Lackawanna	NE	84
Juva, Erie	NW	47
Kaiser, (see Elk City)		×
Kalmia, (see Orwin)		×
● *Kalina*, Dauphin	C	×
Kammerer, Washington	SW	200
● Kane, McKean	N	2,944
Kane City, Venango	NW	175
● *Kane Junction*, McKean	N	×
● Kanesholm, McKean	N	×
● *Kantners*, Somerset	SW	×
Kantz, Snyder	C	100
Kaolin, Chester	SE	100
● *Kapps*, Northumberland	C	×
● *Karn's*, Allegheny	SW	×
● Karns City, Butler	W	427
● Karthaus, Clearfield	C	250
Kashner, Mercer	W	×
Kasota, Bradford	N	50
Kasson, McKean	N	40
Kasson Brook, Wyoming	NE	×
Kastors Corners, Crawford	NW	×
Katan, Erie	NW	×
● Katellen, Northampton	E	150
● *Kaufman Run*, Cambria	C	×
● Kauffman, Franklin	S	175
Kaylor, Armstrong	W	66
● *Kaylor*, Cambria	C	×
Kearney, Bedford	S	25
Kearsarge, Erie	NW	200
● Keating, Clinton	N	97
● *Keating*, Allegheny	SW	×
● *Keating*, Pottet	N	200
● *Keating Summit*, Potter	N	×
Kecksburg, Westmorel'd	SW	100
Keech, Potter	N	20
● *Keefer*, Northumberland	C	×
Keefers, Franklin	S	50
Keelersburgh, Wyoming	NE	83
Keelersville, Bradford	N	40
Keeneyville, Tioga	N	150
● *Keens*, Wayne	NE	×
Keepville, Erie	NW	32
Keertown, Crawford	NW	×
Keewaydin, Clearfield	C	150
Keffer, Westmoreland	SW	30
● *Keffers*, Schuylkill	E	25
Kegg, Bedford	S	25
Kehler, Schuylkill	SW	400
Keim, Somerset	SW	10
● Keister's, Butler	W	50
Keister's, Somerset	SW	×
Kelayres, Schuylkill	E	×
Kellam, Wayne	NE	×
Kellersburgh, Armstrong	W	100
Keller's Church, Bucks	SE	350
Kellersville, Monroe	E	×
Kellettville, Forest	NW	200
Kellyburg, (see Home)		×
Kellyburgh, Lycoming	N	65
Kelly Cross Roads, Union	C	57
Kelly Point, Union	C	133
● Kelly's Station, Armstr'g.	W	100
Kelly Station, (see Tunnelt'n)		×
Kellyville, Delaware	SE	×
● Kelton, Chester	SE	100
Kemble Furnace, (see Riddlesburg		×
Kemblesville, Chester	SE	200
● Kempton, Berks	SE	32
Kendall, Beaver	W	20
● Kendall Creek, McKean	N	1,937
● *Kendrick*, Clearfield	C	×
Kenilworth, Chester	SE	300
● Kennard, Mercer	W	100
● *Kennedy*, Allegheny	SW	×
Kennedy, Tioga	N	20
● *Kennedy Siding*, Cambria	C	×
Kennedy Sta., (see Hites)		×
Kennerdell, Venango	NW	250
● *Kennerdell*, Venango	NW	75
Kennerdell Mills, Butler	W	×
Kenneth, Fayette	SW	×
● Kennett Square, Chester	SE	1,326
● *Kenney*, Allegheny	SW	×
● *Kenneys*, Berks	SE	×
● *Kensington*, Phil'delphia	SE	×
Kensington, (see New K'n'gt'n)		×
Kent, Indiana	W	160
Kenwood, Indiana	W	90
● *Kenwood*, Beaver	W	×
Keown, Allegheny	SW	200
Kephart, Clearfield	C	×
● *Kepler's Mill*, Rorth'pt'n.	E	×
● Kepner, Schuylkill	E	50
● *Kerby Siding*, Mercer	W	×
● *Kermoor*, Clearfield	C	×
● *Kerr*, Allegheny	SW	×
● *Kerr's* Washington	SW	15
● Kerrsville, Cumberland	S	25
● Kerrtown, Crawford	NW	577
Kersey's Elk	N	700
Kersting, Butler	W	×
Keshaqua, McKean	N	×
Ketcham, Luzerne	E	32
● *Ketner*, Elk	N	×
Kettle Creek, Potter	N	100
Keys, York	S	150
● *Keystone*, Fayette	SW	×
Keystone, Perry	C	100
● Keystone Junc. Somerset	SW	200
Khedive, Greene	S	20
● *Kiester*, Butler	W	50
Kile, Mercer	W	×
Kilgore, Mercer	W	20
Killinger, Dauphin	C	100
Kilmer, Juriata	C	10
Kimberly, Bradford	C	×
● Kimberton, Chester	SE	150
● Kimble, Pike	NE	230
● *Kimbrae*, Jefferson	W	×
Kimmel, Indiana	W	80
King, Bedford	S	150
● King of Prussia, Montg'y	SE	150
King's Bridge, Lancaster	SE	100
● Kingsdale, Adams	S	100
● Kingsley, Susquehanna	NE	×
King's Mill, Perry	C	×
● *Kingsport*, Cambria	C	1,000
● Kingston, Luzerne	E	2,381
Kingston, Westmoreland	SW	×
Kingsville, Clarion	W	25
Kingwood, Somerset	SW	300
Kinseyville, (see Kirk's Mills)		×
Kintersburg, (see Gilpin)		×
Kintnersville, Bucks	SE	100
● Kinzer's Lancaster	SE	325
● Kinzua, Warren	NW	1,000
● *Kinzua Viaduct*, McKean	N	×
● *Kinzua Junc.*, McKean	N	×
● Kipple, Blair	C	1,000
● *Kipp's Run*, Northum'l'd	C	×
Kirby, Greene	SW	100
Kirbyville, Berks	SE	35
● *Kirkland*, Chester	SE	×
Kirkland, Bucks	SE	×
Kirkland, Westmoreland	SW	×
Kirkman, Jefferson	W	×
Kirk's Mills, Lancaster	SE	400
Kirkwood, Lancaster	SE	100
Kirtland, Westmoreland	SW	×
Kishacoquillas, Mifflin	C	300
Kissel Hill, Lancaster	SE	50
● *Kissinger*, Berks	SE	×
Kistler, Perry	C	60
Kitches Corner, Mercer	W	30
● **Kittanning**, Armstr'g.	W	3,095
● *Kittanning Point*, Blair	C	299
KittaningRoad, (see Sharpsburg)		×
● *Kittatinny*, Carbon	E	×
Kizer's, Lackawanna	NE	25
● *Kladder*, Blair	C	×
● *Klapperthal*, Berks	SE	×
Klecknerville, Northampton	E	260
Kleinfeltersville, Lebanon	SE	210
Kleins, (see Spring Mount)		×
Kline's Cor. (see Schweyers)		×
● *Kline's Corner*, Lehigh	E	×
● Kline's Grove, N'thuml'd.	C	10
Klinesville, Berks	SE	50
Klingerstown, Schuylkill	E	100
Knapp, Tioga	N	300
Knauer's, Berks	SE	100
● *Kneass*, Northumberland	C	×
● *Kneedler*, Montgomery	SE	×
● *Knepper*, Franklin	S	×
Knights, Westmoreland	SW	×
Knob, Beaver	W	50
Knobbsville, Fulton	S	90
Knousetown, Juniata	C	400
● Knowlton, Delaware	SE	200
● *Knowlton*, Potter	N	×
● Knox, Clarion	W	800
Knox City, McKean	N	×
Knox Dale, Jefferson	W	100
Knoxville, Allegheny	SW	1,723
● Knoxville, Tioga	N	679
● *Kohinoor Junc.* Sch'ylkill	E	×
Koonsville, Luzerne	E	×
Koontzville, Bedford	S	×
Kossuth, Clarion	W	25
● *Kratz*, Montgomery	SE	×
Kratzerville, Snyder	C	125
Kready, Lancaster	SE	×
● Kreamer, Snyder	C	50
● *Krebs*, Schuylkill	E	×
Kregar, Westmoreland	SW	×
Kreidersville, Northampton	E	275
● Kremis, Mercer	W	30
Kresgeville, Monroe	E	180
Krick's Mill, Berks	SE	30
● Krider, Huntingdon	C	150
● *Kring's* Cambria	C	×
Krumsville, Berks	SE	50
Kuhn, Somerset	SW	25
● *Kulps*, Northumberland	C	×
Kulpsville, Montgomery	SE	350
Kunckle, Luzerne	E	150
Kunkletown, Monroe	E	120
Kushequa, McKean	N	×
● Kutztown, Berks	SE	1,595
● *Kylers*, Clearfield	C	×
● *Kyler's Corners*, Elk	N	×
Kylertown, Clearfield	C	250
Kylesville, (see WalnutBott'm)		×
Kyttle, Luzerne	E	×
Laanna, Pike	NE	100
Labaratory, Washington	SW	×
La Bott, York	S	30
● Laceyville, Wyoming	NE	500
Lack, Juniata	C	32
● *Lackawanna*, Lackaw'a	NE	×
● *Lackawannock & Bloomsburg Junction*, Luzerne	E	×
● *LackawannockJunc.* Me'r	W	×
● Lackawaxen, Pike	NE	350
● *La Colle*, Westmoreland	SW	×
● Laddsburgh, Bradford	N	60
● Ladona, Potter	N	200

Place	Pop.
La Fayette, McKean........N	50
● *Lafayette*, McKean.......N	×
● *La Fayette*, MontgomerySE	×
Lafayette Hill, MontgomerySE	450
● *Lafferty*, McKean.......N	×
● Laflin, Luzerne..........E	231
● *Laflin*, Lackawanna.... NE	×
Lagonda, Washington.....SW	4
● *La Grange*, Wyoming.. NE	×
● Lahaska, Bucks..........SE	320
Laidig, Fulton..............S	30
Lairdsville, Lycoming...... N	125
● La Jose, Clearfield........ C	105
Lake, Luzerne ....E	100
Lake, Westmoreland......SW	×
● Lake Cary, Wyoming...NE	130
● *Lake Ariel*, Wayne......NE	×
Lake Como, Wayne.........NE	200
● *LakeConewago*, LebanonSE	×
Lake Pleasant, Erie...... NW	100
Lake Run, Sullivan.........N	50
Laketon, Luzerne...........E	×
Lake View, Susquehanna. NE	25
● *Lakeville*, Crawford....NW	×
Lake Winola, Wyoming...NE	×
● Lakin, Wayne..........NE	32
Lamar, Clinton............ N	125
Lamartine, Clarion.........W	200
Lambertsville, Somerset.. SW	150
Lambs, Venango.........NW	125
● Lamb's Creek, Tioga .....N	175
Lamoka, Bradford......... N	×
● *Lamokin*, Delaware......N	×
Lamont Station, (see Uniontown)........................	×
La Mott, Montgomery..... SE	30
Lampeter, Lancaster.......SE	250
Lampeter Square, (see Lampeter)........................	×
Lanark, Lehigh................E	40
● **Lancaster**, Lancaster..SE	32,011
● *Lancaster Junc.*, Lancas'rSE	×
● *Lancaster Switch*, North'dC	×
● Lancelot, Allegheny.....SW	×
● Landenburgh, Chester...SE	6?0
Lander, Warren...........NW	200
● Landingville, Schuylkill...E	316
Landisburgh, Perry...........C	318
Landis' Store, Berks........SE	450
Landis Valley, Lancaster...SE	200
● Landisville, Lancaster....SE	350
● Landrus, Tioga.......... ..N	25
● *Lane*, Armstrong............W	×
● Lanesborough, Susque'a NE	876
● Lane's Mills, Jefferson....W	160
● Langdon, Lycoming.........N	150
○ *Langdon*, Erie...........NW	×
Langdondale, Bedford.......S	×
● Langhorne, Bucks....... SE	727
Langville, Jefferson.........W	159
● Lansdale, Montgomery...SE	1,858
● Lansdowne, Delaware....SE	875
● Lansford, Carbon..........E	4,004
● Lansing, Tioga.............N	50
Lantz, McKean.............. N	×
● La Plume, Lackawanna. NE	253
Laporte, Sullivan.........N	375
Lapp's Lancaster...........SE	20
● Larabee, McKean..........N	250
Larden's Mills, Butler......W	×
● Larimer, Westmoreland.SW	500
Larksville, Luzerne......... E	25
● *Laros*, Lehigh..............E	×
● Larry's Creek, Lycoming. N	898
● Larue, York.................S	50
Lash, Westmoreland...... SW	×
Lashall, (see Vanceport).......	×
Lathrop, Susquehanna.....NE	60
● *Lathrop*, Tioga... ....N	×
Lattimore, Adams...........S	100
● *Latimore*, Allegheny....SW	×
● Latrobe, Westmoreland.SW	3,589
Latshaw, Northumberland..C	×
Latta Grove, Huntingdon....C	26
Lattimer Mines, Luzerne....E	1,051
● *Laubachs*, Columbia......C	×
● *Laughlin*, Allegheny....SW	×
Laughlintown, Westm'nd. SW	125
● *Laurel*, Allegheny......SW	×
● Laurel, York................S	150
● *Laurel*, Cumberland......S	×
● *Laurel*, Chester......... SE	×
● *Laurel Dale*, Berks......SE	×
LaurelHill, Fayette.......SW	65
Laurel Hill, (seeNew Holland)	×
● *Laurel Run*, Luzerne..... E	606
Laurelton, Union............C	311

Place	Pop.
Laurelville, WestmorelandSW	100
● Laury's Station, Lehigh...E	200
Lavansville, Somerset.....SW	175
Lavelle, Schuylkill..........E	400
Lavery, Erie...............NW	×
● Lawn, Lebanon..........SE	×
Lawndale, Bucks.......... SE	125
● *Lawndale*, Montgomery.SE	×
● *Lawnton*, Philadelphia..SE	×
● Lawrence, Washington..SW	50
Lawrenceburg, (see Parker's Landing)................	×
● *Lawrence Junc.*, Lawr'e..W	×
● Lawrenceville, Tioga......N	441
Lawrenceville, (see Setzler's Store)................	×
● *Lawrenceville*, AlleghenySW	×
Lawsonham, Clarion........W	100
Lawsville Centre, Susqu'a. NE	75
Layfield, Montgomery......SE	100
● Layton's Station, FayetteSW	50
Leachburgh, Allegheny...SW	75
Leacock, Lancaster.........SE	250
Lead Works, Allegheny...SW	×
League Island Navy Yard, Philadelphia...............SE	×
● Leaman Place, LancasterSE	210
Leasdale, Allegheny.......SW	200
Leasuresville, Butler....... W	65
Leatherwood, Clarion....... W	175
● **Lebanon**, Lebanon.... SE	14,664
Lebo, Perry...................C	200
● Leboeuf, Erie.............NW	168
Leck Hill, Northumberland.C	75
Leconte's Mills, Clearfield...C	200
Lederachsville, Montgom'ySE	150
Ledgedale, Wayne..........NE	100
Ledger, Lancaster..........SE	100
Lee, Luzerne.................E	×
Leechburgh, Armstrong.... W	1,921
● *Leechburgh Sta.*, West'ldSW	×
● Leech's Corners, Mercer..W	100
● *Leemine*, Luzerne.........E	×
Leeper, Clarion.............W	130
● *Lee's*, Chester............SE	×
Leesburg, (see Lee's Cross Roads)...................	×
Leesburg, (see Martinsville)..	×
Leesburgh, Mercer.......... W	100
● *Leesburgh Sta.*, Mercer.. W	×
● Lee's Cross Roads, Cumb'dS	225
● *Leesport*, Berks..........SE	×
● Leesport, Berks.......... SE	950
Leetonia, Tioga..............N	300
● Leetsdale, Allegheny....SW	400
● *Leferre*, Adams.......... S	×
● Legionville, Beaver...... W	×
● *Lehigh*, Lackawanna....NE	×
● Lehigh Gap, Carbon.......E	350
● Lehigh Tannery, Carbon..E	260
● Lehighton, Carbon.........E	2,95?
Lehman, Luzerne.............E	200
● *Lehman Station*, Luzerne.E	×
Lehnenburgh, Bucks.........SE	200
Leib, Schuylkill..............E	100
Leibysville, Schuylkill........E	75
● *Leidighs*, Cumberland.....S	×
Leidy, Clinton................N	×
Leinbach's, Berks...........SE	127
● *Leiper Switch*, Delaware.SE	×
● *Leiper and Lewis Landing*, Delaware..............SE	×
● Leisenring, Fayette..... SW	835
● *Leith*, Fayette...........SW	×
Leithsville, Northampton... E	150
Leize's Dam, Berks........ SE	×
● Lemasters, Franklin...... S	175
● Lemon, Wyoming.........NE	100
● Lemont, Centre....... C	150
● *Lemont*, Fayette........SW	×
● Lemont Furnace, Fay'teSW	1,500
● Lenape, Chester......... SE	25
● Lenhartsville, Berks.....SE	152
● *Lenkers*, Dauphin..........C	×
Lenni, (see Lenni Mills)........	×
● Lenni Mills, Delaware... SE	500
● Lenover, Chester......... SE	35
Lenox, Susquehanna...... NE	75
Lenoxville, Susquehanna..NE	75
Leona, Bradford............ N	100
Leonard, Chester...........SE	25
● *Leonard*, Clearfield.......C	×
Leonardsville, Wayne.......NE	25
Leonardsville, Greene.....SW	25
Leopard, Chester...........SE	110
Leota, Butler.................W	×
Le Raysville, Bradford......N	371

Place	Pop.
Le Roy, Bradford...........N	300
● *Leslie Run*, Carbon....... E	×
Letort, Lancaster..........SE	40
Letterkenny, Franklin...... S	23
● *Leuffer*, Westmoreland..SW	×
● *Level Corners*, Lycoming..N	×
● *Lewiston*, Carbon......... E	×
Lewis, Allegheny..........SW	125
Lewisberry, York........... S	170
● **Lewisburgh**, Union... C	3,248
● *Lewis Mills*, Chester.....SE	×
● Lewis Run, McKean.......N	200
● **Lewistown**, Mifflin.....C	3,273
Lewistown, (see Tuscarora)...	×
● *Lewistown Junc.*, Mifflin..C	×
Lewisville, Chester..........SE	459
Lexington, Lancaster...... SE	175
Liberty, Tioga................N	1,000
● *Liberty*, McKean..........N	×
Liberty Corners, Bradford.. N	30
Liberty Square, Lancaster..SE	200
Libonia, Franklin...........S	×
Library, Allegheny.........SW	100
● *Lichly*, Berks............SE	150
● *Lichtys*, Somerset...... SW	×
● Lickdale, Lebanon.........SE	400
Lickingville, Clarion.......W	110
Lick Run, Allegheny..... SW	×
Lick Run Mills, Clearfield ..C	80
● *Liddonfield*, PhiladelphiaSE	×
● Light Street, Columbia....C	600
● Ligonier, WestmorelandSW	782
Lillie, Beaver..............W	10
Lilly, Cambria...............C	915
Lillyville, Beaver...........W	100
Lima, Delaware........... SE	507
Lime Hill, Bradford......... N	32
Limekiln, Berks............SE	65
● *Limekilns*, Somerset....SW	×
Limeport, Lehigh.......... E	60
Limeport, (see Centre Bridge)	×
Limerick, Montgomery....SE	300
Limerick Square, (see Limerick)	×
Limerick Sta., (see Linfield)..	×
● Lime Ridge, Columbia....C	200
Lime Rock, Lancaster..... SE	150
Limestone, Clarion...........W	300
● *Limestone Sid'g*, LawrenceW	×
Limestoneville, Montour....C	100
Limetown, (see Coal Bluff)...	×
Lime Valley, Lancaster....SE	90
Limeville, (see Gap)..........	×
Lincoln, Lancaster..........SE	425
● *Lincoln*, Chester........ SE	×
● *Lincoln Colliery*, Schuy'kl E	×
Lincoln Falls, Sullivan......N	35
Lincoln University, ChesterSE	500
Lincolnville, Crawford...NW	150
● *Lindale*, McKean...........N	×
● *Linden*, Allegheny.......SW	×
● Linden, Lycoming.........N	225
● Linden Hall, Centre...... C	50
Lindley, Philadelphia..... SE	×
● Lindley's Mills, Wash'tnSW	56
● Lindsey, Jefferson ....W	1,006
Line Lexington, Bucks ....SE	500
Line Mountain, Northum'landC	20
● Linesville, Crawford....NW	552
Linfield, Montgomery......SE	500
Linglestown, Dauphin.......C	300
Links, Tioga.................N	×
● *Linmore*, Beaver.........W	×
● *Linn*, Fayett..............SW	×
● Linwood Sta., Delaware.SE	1,200
● Lionville, Chester.........SE	150
Lippen, Delaware...........SE	×
Lippincott, Greene.........SW	44
Lisbon, Cumberland..........S	200
Listonburgh, Somerset....SW	120
Litchfield, Bradford......... N	210
● Lititz, Lancaster..........SE	1,494
Little Britain, Lancaster...SE	150
Littlle Cooley, Crawford. NW	200
Little Elk, Erie.............NW	×
Little Equinunk, Wayne..NE	×
Little Gap, Carbon...........E	240
Little Junction City, (see West Newton)................	×
Little Marsh, Tioga.........N	180
Little Meadows, Susqehan'aNE	223
Little Narrows, Pike.....NE	×
● Little Oley, Berks.........S	250
Little Cor's., (see Hayfield)...	×
● Littlestown, Adams.........S	991
● *Little Tobey*, Clarion.....W	×
Little Washington, (seeWash.)	×
● Litzenberg, Lehigh.......E	270

Place	Pop.
● Livermore, Westmorel'd SW	211
Liverpool, Perry C	821
● *Liverpool Station*, Perry C	×
Livonia, Centre C	×
Lix, Bradford N	×
● *Lizard Creek Junc.*, Car'n. E	×
● Lizette, Bucks SE	200
● Llanwellyn, Delaware SE	×
● Llewellyn, Schuylkill E	350
● *Llewellyn Cross*, Schuylk'l E	×
● Lloyd, Tioga E	200
● Lloydville, Cambria C	50
Loag, Chester SE	47
Lobachsville, Berks SE	400
Lobeck, Wyoming NE	×
● *Lochiel*, Dauphin C	×
● Lochiel, Union C	50
● *Lockland*, Lehigh E	×
Locke Valley, Huntingdon C	×
● **Lock Haven**, Clinton N	7,358
● *Lock Haven Sta.*, Clinton N	×
● *Loch Lomond*, Clearfield C	×
● Lock Number Four, Washington SW	200
● Lock Number Three, Allegheny SW	×
● *Lockport*, Northampton E	×
Lockport, York S	×
● *Lockport*, Erie W	240
● Lockport Sta., Westm'l'd SW	100
● *Lock Ridge*, Lehigh E	×
● *Lock's Camp*, Elk N	×
● *Locksley*, Delaware SE	×
Lockville, Wyoming NE	75
● Locust Dale, Schuylkill E	600
● Locust Gap, Northumberl'd C	1,655
● *Locust Gap Jc.*, North'l'nd C	×
Locust Grove, (see West View)	×
Locust Grove, Fulton S	25
Locust Grove, (see Patterson)	×
Locust Grove, (see Bainbridge)	×
Locust Grove, York S	×
Locust Hill, (see McConnell's Mills)	×
Locust Lane, Indiana W	36
● *Locust Summit*, North'm'ld C	×
Locust Valley, Lehigh E	130
● *Locust Wood*, Montgomery SE	×
Lodi, Bucks SE	×
● Lofty, Schuylkill E	397
● *Logan*, Mifflin C	×
● Logan, Philadelphia SE	×
● Logania, Perry C	20
Logan Mills, Clinton N	150
● *Logan's*, Beaver W	×
● Logan's Ferry, Allegh'ny SW	200
● Logansport, Armstrong W	20
Loganton, Clinton N	385
Loganville, York S	296
Logue, Potter N	×
London, Mercer W	100
Londonderry, Chester SE	250
Londonderry, Lebanon SE	×
London Grove, Chester SE	150
Lone Pine, Washington SW	225
Lone Star, Greene SW	25
Lone Tree, (see Lone Star)	×
● *Longacre*, Schuylkill E	×
● *Long Bridge*, Westm'la'd SW	×
● *Long Brook*, Sullivan N	×
● *Longfellow*, Mifflin C	×
Long Level, York S	300
Long Pond, Monroe E	50
● *Long Run*, Allegheny SW	×
Long Run, Armstrong W	130
● Longsdorff, Cumberland S	×
● *Long Siding*, Lycoming N	×
● *Long Siding*, Huntingdon C	×
Long Siding, Northampton E	×
● *Long Siding*, Luzerne E	×
● *Long Siding*, Mercer W	×
Long's Stand, Crawford NW	×
● *Long's Station*, Franklin S	×
Long Swamp, Berks SE	480
Long Valley, Bradford N	260
● *Long Valley Jc.*, Bradford N	×
Longwood, Chester SE	100
Lookout, Wayne NE	×
● *Look Out*, Luzerne E	×
● *Loop*, Blair C	×
Loop, Indiana W	×
● *Loop Junction*, Lehigh E	×
● Lopez, Sullivan N	1,000
Lorah, Berks SE	260
● *Lorberry*, Schuylkill E	×
● *Lorberry Jc.*, Schuylkill E	×
Lord's Valley, Pike NE	65
Lorenton, Tioga N	×
Loretto, Cambria C	236
Lose, Westmoreland SW	50
● *Losh's Run*, Perry C	130
● Lost Creek, Schuylkill E	150
● *Lost Creek*, Schuylkill E	×
● *Lostock*, Allegheny SW	×
Lottsville, Warren NW	225
Louck's Mills, Potter N	×
● *Loudon*, Franklin S	×
Louella, (see Radnor)	×
● Lovell's Station, Erie NW	19
Lovelton, Wyoming NE	100
Lovely, Bedford S	25
Lover, Washington SW	×
● *Love's*, Mercer W	×
Lovett, Cambria C	×
Loveville, Centre C	50
● *Loveville*, Centre C	×
Lovi, Beaver W	×
Lowell, Snyder C	×
● *Lower Catasauqua*, Leh'h E	×
Lower Chanceford, (see Airv'e)	×
Lower Chichester, (see Linwood)	×
Lower Darby, (see Darby)	×
● *Lower Fullerton*, Lehigh E	×
Lower Heidelberg, Berks SE	140
Lower Mahantango, (see Val. View)	×
Lower Provid'e, Montgom'y SE	300
● *Lower Saint Clair*, Schuylkill E	×
Lower Saucon, Northampton E	120
Lower Two Licks, Indiana W	100
Lowhill, Lehigh E	250
Lowland Farm, Washington SW	×
Lowville, Erie NW	150
● Loyalhanna, Westmorel'd SW	×
Loyalsock, Lycoming N	111
● *Loyalsock*, Lycoming N	×
Loyalton, Dauphin C	50
Loyalville, Luzerne E	25
Loysburg, Bedford S	300
Loysville, Perry C	380
● Lucesco, Westmoreland SW	100
● Lucinda, Clarion W	50
● *Luckett*, Cambria C	×
Lucky, York S	25
Lucon, Montgomery SE	130
● *Lucy Furnace*, Northmb'n E	×
● *Lucyville*, Washington SW	×
● Ludlow, McKean N	500
Ludwig, Westmoreland SW	891
● *Lueilen*, Washington SW	×
Lukens Sta., (see West Point)	×
Luling, Butler W	25
Lull, Somerset SW	×
Lulu, Tioga N	10
Lumber City, Clearfield C	266
Lumberton, Bucks S	×
Lumberville, Bucks SE	800
● *Lumber Yard*, Luzerne E	×
Lundy's Lane, Erie NW	×
Lurgan, Franklin S	50
Luthersburgh, Clearfield C	450
Luther's Mills, Bradford N	200
Lutton, Mercer W	33
● Lutzville, Bedford S	40
● Luzerne, Luzerne E	2,898
Lycippus, Westmoreland SW	50
Lycoming, Lycoming N	×
Lycoming Furnace, Lyc'm'g N	×
● Lykens, Dauphin C	2,450
Lykenstown, (see Lykens)	×
● *Lyle*, Lawrence W	×
Lyles, Lancaster SE	100
● Lyndell, Chester SE	50
● **Lynn, Susquehanna NE**	60
● Lynnport, Lehigh E	240
Lynnville, Lehigh E	240
Lyona, Crawford NW	500
● *Lyon Mill*, Lycoming N	×
● Lyon's Station, Berks SE	500
Lyon Valley, Lehigh E	60
McAlevy's Fort, Huntingdon C	160
McAllisterville, Juniata C	400
● *McAlpine*, Luzerne E	×
● *McAuley*, Columbia C	×
McBride, Butler W	20
● *McCalls Ferry*, Lancaster SE	×
McCall's Ferry, York S	200
● *McCalmont*, Butler W	×
● *McCalmont*, Warren NW	×
● *McCalmont*, McKean N	×
McCance, Westmoreland SW	×
McCandless, Butler W	100
McCann's Ferry, Greene SW	×
McCaslin, Lawrence W	×
● *McCauley*, Clearfield C	×
McClarran, Westmoreland SW	×
McCleary, Beaver W	30
McClellandtown, Fayette SW	125
● *McClintock*, Venango NW	×
● McClure, Snyder C	20
● *McClure*, Westmoreland SW	300
McConnellsburgh, F'lt'n S	594
McConnell's Mill, Washin'n SW	100
● McConnellstown, Hunt'd'n C	309
McCoysville, Juniata C	150
McCracken, Greene SW	×
● *McCracken*, Washington SW	×
McCulloch's Mills, Juniata C	50
McDermott, York S	×
● McDonald, Washington SW	1,698
● McElhattan, Clinton N	100
● McEwensville, Nort'mb'l'd C	262
McFord, York S	25
● *McGarvey*, Blair C	×
● McGee's Mills, Clearfield C	×
McGhee's, (see Sandy Valley)	×
McGinnett, Crawford NW	×
McGinty, Carbon E	300
● McGovern, Washington SW	100
McGraw, Warren NW	250
● *McGrews*, Westmoreland SW	×
McHaddon, Armstrong W	28
McHenry's Mills, (see Shirland)	×
McIlhaney, Monroe E	120
McKean, Erie NW	300
● McKeansburgh, Schuylkill E	350
McKean's Old Stand, (see West Bethany)	×
● McKee's Gap, Blair C	150
McKee's Half Falls, Snyder C	20
● McKeesport, Allegheny SW	20,741
McKee's Rocks, Allegheny SW	1,687
McKeever Station, Butler W	×
● *McKelvey's*, Somerset SW	×
● *McKinms*, Beaver W	×
McKinney, Cumberland S	25
● McKnightstown, Adams S	180
● McKune's Depot, Wy'm'g NE	32
McLallen Corners, Erie NW	130
McLane, Erie NW	150
● *McLaughlin*, Allegheny SW	×
McLaughlinstown, (see Merwin)	×
● *McLean's*, Montgomery SE	×
● *McMahon*, Westmorel'd SW	×
McMichael's, Monroe E	120
● McMinn, Allegheney SW	43
McMurray, Washington SW	50
● *McMinn Sum't*, Jefferson W	×
● McNeal, Huntingdon C	150
McPherron, Clearfield C	47
● *McSherry*, Adams S	×
McSherry's L'n'dg, (see Airville)	×
McSherrystown, Adams S	1,020
McSherryville, (see Airville)	×
McSparran, Lancaster SE	50
McVeytown, Mifflin C	599
● *McVeytown Sta.*, Mifflin C	×
McVill, Armstrong W	100
McWilliams, Armstrong W	25
Mabel, Schuylkill E	150
Macbeth, Westmoreland SW	×
Macedonia, Bradford N	260
Mackeyville, Clinton N	160
● *Macks*, Susquehanna NE	×
Mackville, Armstrong W	50
● Macungie, Lehigh E	614
Maddensville, Huntingdon C	125
● Madera, Clearfield C	400
● *Madera Junc.*, Clearfield C	×
Madison, Westmoreland SW	201
Madisonburgh, Centre C	250
Madisonville, Lackawan'a NE	50
● *Madley*, Bedford S	×
● *Magees*, Warren NW	×
Maker's Sta., (see Beech Tree)	×
Magic, Butler W	50
● Mahaffey, Clearfield C	627
Mahanoy, Northumberland C	40
● *Mahanoy*, Perry C	×
● Mahanoy City, Schuylkill E	11,286
Mahanoy Jc., (see Barnesville)	×
Mahanoy Plane, Sch'ylkill E	1,300
● *Mahanoy Tunnel*, S'ylk'l E	×
● *Mahantango*, Dauphin C	×
Mahantango, Juniata C	50
Maharg, Butler W	25
Mahoning, Armstrong W	160
Mahoning Fur., (see Deanville)	×
● *Mahoning*, Carbon E	×
● Mahoningtown, Lawre'ce W	800
● Maiden Creek, Berks SE	150

 Pennsylvania Pennsylvania

Munderf, Jefferson.........W 25
● Munhall, Allegheny.... SW 2,000
Munntown, (see Thomas).... ×
Murray, Lebanon..........SE ×
● Munson Station, ClearfieldC ×
● Munster, Cambria......... C 50
Murdock Cross Road, (see Fordyce) .... ×
● *Murdock's*, Somerset... SW ×
● Murdocksville, Wash'n .SW 75
Murphy City, Warren....NW ×
● Murray, Clearfield........ C 40
Murray, Lebanon.........SE ×
Murrell, Lancaster.........SE ×
Murrinsville, Butler........W 50
Murrysville, WestmorelandSW 150
● *Musser*, Center.......... C ×
Mutual, Westmoreland.... SW 300
Myersburg, Bradford....... S 100
● Myerstown, Lebanon.....SE 1,880
● Myoma, Butler...........W 40
Myra, Cambria..............C 300
Myrtle McKean............ N 75
Mystic, Erie...............NW ×
● *M. Y. Tower*, WashingtonSW ×
Nadine, Allegheny........SW ×
● *Naginey*, Mifflin......... C ×
Nancy, Huntingdon........ C ×
● Nanticoke, Luzerne....... E 10,044
● *Nanticoke*. Luzerne...... E 400
Nantmeal Village, Chester. SE 200
● Napier, Bedford.......... S 20
Napierville, (see Reamstown) ×
● Narberth, Montgomery..SE 100
Narcissa, Montgomery.... SE ×
● *Narrows*, Mifflin.........C ×
● *Narrows*, Clearfield...... C ×
Narrowsville, (see Kintnersville) ×
Narvon, Lancaster..........SE 30
Nasby, Erie.............. NW ×
Nashes, Forest............NW 60
Nashau, Lawrence.........W 12
Nashville, (see Decker's Pt.). ×
Natalie, Northumberlaud.. C ×
● Natrona, Allegheny.....SW 1,500
Nauvoo, Tioga..............N 200
● Nayaug, Lackawanna...NE ×
● Nazareth, Northampton.. E 1,318
● *Nazareth Jc.*, Northamp'nE ×
Neale, Armstrong...........W 50
Neath, Bradford............N 25
Nebraska, Forest .... NW 150
Nectarine, Venango......NW 300
Needmore, Fulton.......... S 100
● *Neels*, Beaver........... W ×
Neelyton, Huntingdon...... C 25
Neff's, Lehigh............ E 480
Neff's Mills, Huntingdon... C 125
Neffsville, Lancaster.......SE 400
Negley, Allegheny......... SW 50
Neiffer, Montgomery...... SE 50
● *Neilly's*, McKean........N ×
Neiman, York............. S ×
Nekoda, Perry.............. C 250
● Nelson, Tioga............N 540
Nelson, Tioga..............N 600
Nelson City, (see Gir'd Manor) ×
Neola, Monroe............. E 75
Nervine, Juniata........... C 25
● Nescopeck, Luzerne...... E 698
Neshaminy, Bucks.........SE 150
● *Neshaminy Falls*, BucksSE ×
● Neshannock, Mercer.....W 400
● Neshannock Falls, La'ce W 75
● Nesquehoning, Carbon... E 1,655
● *Nesquehoning Junc.*, Car'nE ×
Nether Providence, Del're.SE 50
Nettle Hill, Greene........SW 20
● *Neversink*, Berks.........SE ×
● *Neville*, Allegheny......SW ×
● New Albany, Bradford... N 287
New Alexandria, West'l'd.SW 338
New Athens, Clarion ..... W 25
New Baltimore, Somerset.SW 183
New Bedford, Lawrence.... W 300
New Berlin, (see Akron)..... ×
New Berlin, Union......... C 617
● New Berlinville, Berks.. SE 400
● Newberry, Lycoming.... N 8,000
● *Newberry Junc.*, Lyco'g. N ×
Newberrytown, York....... S 250
● New Bethlehem, Clarion. W 1,026
New Bloomfield, Perry..C 800
● **New Boston**, Schuylkill.. E 600
● *New Boston Junc.*, Sch'll E ×
New Bridge, Franklin...... S 70
New Bridgeport, (see Hynd'n) ×

New Bridgeville, York......S 300
● New Brighton, Beaver... W 5,616
● New Britain, Bucks..... SE 150
New Buena Vista, Bedford..S 225
New Buffalo, Perry......... C 220
Newburg, Clearfield........ C 354
Newburg, (see Enon Valley). ×
Newburgh, Cumberland.... S 376
New Castle, (see Br'd M't'n). ×
● **New Castle**, Lawrence W 11,600
● *New Castle Junc.*, Law'e. W ×
● New Centreville, Chester SE 150
New Centreville, Somerset SW 104
New Chester, Adams....... S 250
● New Columbia, Union...... C 300
New Columbus, Luzerne.... E 214
● New Cumberland, Cum'l'd S 754
New Danville, Lancaster...SE 100
New Derry, Westmorel'd. SW 300
● New Eagle, Washington SW 300
Newell, Sullivan............ N 300
New England, Allegheny. SW ×
New Enterprise, Bedford....S 200
New Era, Bradford......... N 110
Newerf, McKean........... N 114
Newfield, Potter............N 50
● New Florence, West'l'd. SW 683
Newfoundland, Wayne.....NE 400
● New Franklin, Franklin.. S 250
● New Freedom, York...... S 364
New Freeport, Greene.....SW 100
● New Galilee, Beaver..... W 820
● New Garden, Chester....SE 50
New Geneva, Fayette..... SW 313
New Germantown, Perry... C 200
New Grenada, Fulton....... S 100
New Hamburgh, Mercer... W 160
New Hanover, (see Hanover) ×
New Hanover, Montgo'ery SE 240
Newhard, Lehigh........... E 75
● New Haven, Fayette....SW 1,221
New Haven, (see Kissel Hill). ×
● New Holland, Lancaster.SE 1,060
New Holland, (see Mt. Wolf). ×
● New Hope, Bucks....... SE 1,142
New Hope, (see Borard)...... ×
New Jerusalem, Berks.... SE 100
New Kensington, Westm'd SW 200
● New Kingstown, Cum'la'd S 400
● *Newkirk*, Schuylkill...... E ×
New Laceyville, Susqueh'a NE ×
New Lebanon, Mercer......W 263
New Lexington, Somerset.SW 500
Newlin, Columbia .... C 32
● *Newlin*, Chester......... SE ×
Newlin, Northampton...... E ×
New London, Chester ..... SE 300
Newlonsburg, (see Manordale) ×
New Mahoning, Carbon.....E 200
Newman's Mills, (see Cherry Tree) .... ×
Newmanstown, Lebanon.. SE 612
Newmansville, Clarion.... W 75
● New Mayville, Clarion... W 200
● New Milford, Susqueh'a. NE 763
● New Millport, Clearfield..C 225
New Milltown, (see Buyerst'n) ×
● New Oxford, Adams...... S 585
New Paradise, (see Jacobus). ×
New Paris, Bedford......... S 196
New Park, York............. S 200
New Petersburg, (see Timlin) ×
● *New Philadelphia*, Sch'll E 562
New Pleasant Grove, (see Grafton) .... ×
● Newport, Perry .... C 1,417
● *Newport*, Luzerne......... E ×
● *Newport*, Lawrence......W 200
Newportville, Bucks....... SE 500
● New Providence, Lanc'r. SE 150
New Providence, (see New Wilmington)............... ×
New Richmond, Crawford NW 100
● New Ringgold, Schuylkill.E 240
● Newry, Blair...............C 335
New Salem, (see McKnight'n) ×
New Salem, Fayette...... SW 150
New Salem, (see Detmont) ... ×
New Salem, (see Pierce) ..... ×
New Salem, York.............S 231
New Scottsville, Beaver.... W 175
New Sewickly, (see Wall Rose) ×
New Sheffield, Beaver...... W 200
● New Sinsheim, York......S 30
● New Stanton, West'la'd SW 200
New Texas, Allegheny.... SW 100
New Texas, (see Oakland) ... ×

● *New Texas*, (see Lyles) .... ×
Newton, (see Swatara)........ ×
● *Newton*, Warren ×
● Newton Hamilton, MifflinC. 333
● Newtown, Bucks........SE 1,213
Newtown, (see Newtown Sq're) ×
Newtown, (see Kirby)....... ×
Newtown Mills, Forest...NW 200
Newton Square, Delaware..SE 300
New Tripoli, Lehigh........ E 180
New Vernon, Mercer........W 150
Newville, (see Creek Side).... ×
Newville, (see Elizabethtown) ×
● Newville, Cumberland....S 1,562
New Washington, Clearfield.C 178
● New Wilmington, Law'e. W 684
New York Quarry, North'n E 521
● Ney, Lebanon........... SE ×
Niagara, Wayne .... NE 50
Niantic, Montgomery ..... SE 500
● Nicetown, Philadelphia..SE ×
● Nicholson, Wyoming....NE 734
Nickel Mines, Lancaster... SE 250
Nickelville, Venango.....NW 100
Nicktown, Cambria.......... C ×
Nicolay, Fayette ....SW ×
Nihil, Westmoreland.......SW 10
Niles, Venango...........NW ×
● Niles Valley, Tioga........ N 200
Nimble, Wyoming......... NE ×
● *Nimick*, Allegheny......SW ×
Nine Points, Lancaster.... SE 100
Nineveh, Greene...........SW 200
● *Nineveh*, Westmoreland SW 200
Nippenose, Lycoming ...... N 700
Nippono, Lycoming.........N ×
● *Nippono Park*, Lycoming N ×
● Nisbet, Lycoming........ N 100
● *Niskey*, Northampton..... E ×
Nittany, Centre .... C 75
Niven, Susquehanna...... NE 25
● *Noble*, Montgomery...... SE ×
● *Noble's*, Crawford......NW ×
● Noblestown, Allegheny.SW 100
Nobleville, (see Christiana)... ×
Nockamixon, Bucks....... SE 100
● *Noel*, Cambria............ C ×
Nolo, Indiana................W 25
Nora, (see Moselem)........... ×
● Nordmont, Sullivan.......N 24
Normal Square, Carbon.....E 200
Normalville, Fayette......SW 200
Norrace, Huntingdon....... C 25
● *Norris Sidnig*, Lycoming.. N ×
● **Norristown**, Montg'y SE 19,791
Norrisville, Crawford.... NW 75
Norritonville, Montgomery SE 240
North Bangor, NorthamptonE 75
● *North Barree*, HuntingdonC ×
North Belle Vernon, Fay'eNW 435
● North Bend, Clinton......N 560
North Bingham, Potter.....N 100
● *North Branch*, McKean.. N ×
North Branch, Susquehan'aNE 32
North Brockport, Elk.......N 200
● Northbrook, Chester.... SE 200
North Buffalo, Armstrong.. W 60
North Cedar Hill, Philade'aSE ×
North Clarendon, WarrenNW 1,000
● *North Cornwall*, LebanonSE ×
● North East, Erie........ NW 1,538
● *North Essington*, Phila'aSE ×
North Fork. Potter.........N 75
● *North Franklin*, Nort'm'dC ×
North Freedom, ArmstrongW 100
North Heidelberg, Berks.. SE 900
North Hope, Butler........ W 200
North Jackson, Susqueha'aNE 75
● *North Liberty*, McKean.. N ×
North Liberty Mercer..... W 100
● *North Mansfield*, Alleg'ySW ×
North Mehoopany, Wyom'gNE ×
North Mountain, Lycoming. N 67
North Oakland, Butler.....W 50
North Orwell, Bradford.... N 100
North Penn, Schuylkill..... E 50
● *North Pennsylvania Junction*, Philadelphia......SE ×
North Pine Grove, Clarion. W 100
● *North Pine Grove*, SchulkillE ×
North Point, Clinton.......N ×
North Point, Indiana.......W 75
● *North Reading*, Berks.. SE ×
North Rome, Bradford..... N 200
North Salem, (see Kennard).. ×
North Sandy, Mercer.......W ×

● North Sewickly, Beaver..W 100
North's Mills, Mercer...... W 60
NorthSmithfield, (seeE.Smithf'd) ×
● North Springfield, Erie. NW 150
North Star, Allegheny.... SW 50
North Summit, Indiana.... W ×
North Towanda, Bradford.. N 75
● Northumberland, North'dC 2,744
● Northville, Erie........ NW 158
● North Wales, Montgom'ySE 1,060
North Warren, Warren...NW 615
North Washington, (seeN.Hope) ×
North Washington, West'dSW 50
● *North Webster*, Westm'dSW ×
● *North West*, Westmor'dSW ×
● *North WilkesBarre*, LuzerneE ×
● Norway, Chester........ SE 175
Norwich, McKean.......... E ×
● *Norwood*, Delaware.....SE ×
Norwood Station, DelawareSE 100
Nossville, Huntingdon...... C 400
● Nottingham, Chester.... SE 50
● *Nottingham*, Washingt'nSW ×
Nottingham Colliery, Luze'eE ×
Nowrytown, Indiana....... W ×
Noxen, Wyoming......... NE ×
● *Number Sixteen*, WayneNE ×
● *Number TenSiding*, Carb'nE ×
Numidia, Columbia......... C 100
● *Nunnery*, Franklin.......S ×
Nuremberg, Schuylkill ..... E 500
Oak, Allegheny.......... SW ×
● Oakbourne, Chester..... SE 30
● *Oak Dale*, Daupin.........C ×
Oakdale, Delaware.........SE 20
● *Oakdale*, Fayette........SW ×
● *Oakdale*, Luzerne.........E ×
● Oakdale Sta., Allegheny SW 1,000
● *Oakeola*, Delaware.......SE ×
● Oakford, Bucks......... SE 500
Oak Forest, Greene.......SW 90
Oak Grove, Washington...SW ×
● *Oak Grove*, Clinton....... N ×
OakGroveFur..(seeLandisburg) ×
Oak Grove Fur., (see Ligonier) ×
● Oak Hall Station, Centre..C ×
Oak Hill, Lancaster.........SE 300
Oakland, (see Pittsburgh)... ×
Oakland, Armstrong....... W 200
● *Oakland*, Chester........SE ×
● *Oakland*, Mercer.......... W ×
Oakland, Susquehanna....NE 955
Oakland Cr. Rds., Westm'dSW 20
Oakland Mills, Juniata..... C 55
● Oak Lane, Philadelphia..SE ×
Oakley, Susquehanna..... NE 60
Oakmont, Allegheny......SW 1,678
● Oak Ridge Sta., Armstr'gW ×
● Oaks, Montgomery...... SE 500
Oak Shade, (see Six Roads) ..
Oak Station, Allegheney.. SW ×
● Oakville, Cumberland.... S 150
● *Oakville*, Westmoreland SW ×
● *Oakwood*, Beaver........ W ×
Obelisk, Montgomery......SE 100
Oberlin, Dauphin...........C 100
Obolk, Berks............. SE 375
Octoraro, Lancaster........SE 100
Odell, Washington....... SW 20
● *Odenwalder*, NorthamptonE ×
Odessa, Clearfield........... C ×
Odin, Potter.............. E 42
● *Ogden*, Delaware........SE 25
Ogdensburgh, Tioga........ N 400
Ogdonia, Sullivan..........N ×
Ogle, Butler...............W 50
● Ogontz, Montgomery....SE 300
Ogontz School, MontgomerySE ×
● Ohiopyle, Fayette.......SW 450
Ohioville, Beaver..........W 200
Ohl, Jefferson............. W ×
● Oil City, Venango...... NW 10,932
Oildom, Butler........... W ×
Okeson, Juniata.............C ×
Okete, York.................S 200
Okiola, (see Boothwyn) ...... ×
Okome, Lycoming...........N ×
● Olanta, Clearfield.........C 300
● *Olcopolis*, Venango.....NW ×
Old Brighton, (seeBeaverFalls) ×
Old Concord, Washington.SW 25
● Old Forge, Lackawanna.NE 200
Old Frame, Fayette.......SW 10
● *Old Junction*, Somerset.SW ×
Old Line, Lancaster........SE 50
● *Old Station*, Tioga........N ×
Old Zionsville, Lehigh...... E 200

Oleona, Potter............. N 100
● *Oleopolis*, Venango.....NW ×
Oley, Berks..................SE 400
Oliphant Furnace, FayetteSW 4,075
Oliveburgh, Jefferson...... W 25
● *Oliver*, Allegheny.......SW ×
● *Oliver's*, Somerset....... SW ×
● Oliver's Mills, Luzerne....E 195
Olivet, Armstrong..........W 37
● Olivia, Blair...............C 300
● *Olmsted*, Potter...........N ×
Olmsville, Tioga............ N 46
● Olney, Philadelphia......SE 720
● Olyphant, Lackawanna. NE 4,083
Onberg, Indiana............W 20
● *Oneida*, Butler.......... W ×
Oneida, Schuylkill..........E ×
Oneida, Schuylkill..........E ×
● Oneil, Allegheny........ SW ×
Ono, Lebanon..............SE 140
● *Onoko*, Carbon.............E ×
Onset, Lebanon............ SE ×
● *Ontelaunee*, Berks........SE ×
Opp, Lycoming.............. N ×
Oppelsville, Juniata.........C 25
Oppenheimer, Bedford......S 10
Opposition, Bradford........N 25
● *Opp's Crossing*, LycomingN ×
Option, Allegheny.........SW ×
Orange, Luzerne........... E 200
● Orangeville, Columbia.... C 500
Orbisonia, Huntingdon......C 963
Ord, Indiana................W 28
● Orefield, Lehigh...........E 200
Oregon, Lancaster......... SE 200
Oregon Hill, Lycoming.......N 100
● Ore Hill, Blair............ C 250
Oreland, Montgomery..... SE ×
● *Oreminea*, Blair...........C 400
Oriental, Juniata............C 250
Oriole, Lycoming............N 100
Ormond, Fayette............SW 25
● *Ormond's*, Schuylkill.....E ×
● *Ormsby*, Allegheny..... SW ×
● *Ormsby Junc*., McKean...N ×
● Orr Glen, Adams...........S 30
Orrstown, Franklin......... S 262
Orrsville, (see Mahoning) .... ×
● *Orrtanna*, Adams..........S ×
● *Orstrander*, McKean.......N ×
● Orvilla, Montgomery....SE ×
Orwell, Bradford........... N 100
● Orwigsburgh, Schuylkill..E 1,290
Orwin, Schuylkill...........E 400
Osborn, Mercer............W ×
● *Osborne*, Allegheny.....SW 221
Osborne, Westmoreland.. SW ×
Osburn, Allegheny........SW 221
Oscar, (see Echo)............ ×
● *Osceola*, Allegheny......SW 100
● *Osceola*, Clearfield.........C ×
● Osceola, Tioga............ N 838
● *Osceola Junction*, Centre. C ×
Osceola Mills, Clearfield.....C 1,730
● *Osgood*, Mercer.......... W ×
● Oshanter, Clearfield...... C ×
● Ostend, Clearfield..........C 65
Osterburgh, Bedford......... S 147
Osterhout, Wyoming...... NE 150
● *Ostrander*, McKean....... N ×
Oswayo, Potter.............. N 500
Otella, Huntingdon..........C 50
Ottawa, Montour.............C ×
● OtterCreek, Mercer.......W ×
Otttown, Bedford.......... S 50
● *Otto*, Northumberland.... C ×
● Otto Glen, Elk...........N ×
● *Otts*, Warren............NW ×
Ottsville, Bucks............SE 300
● *Outlet*, Luzerne...........E 32
Oval, Lycoming..............E ×
Overbrook, (see Park's Mills). ×
● Overbrook, Montgomery.SE 400
● *Overlook*, Lebanon...... SE ×
Overshot, Bradford..........N ×
Overton, Bradford..........N 350
● *Overton*, Westmoreland.SW ×
Ovid, Erie................NW 100
● *Owensdale*, Fayette..... SW 200
Owl Creek, Fulton.......... S ×
● Oxford, Chester..........SE 1,711
Oxford Church, PhiladelphiaSE 1,024
● Oxford Valley, Bucks.. SE 350
Oyster, Elk.................N ×
● Packerton, Carbon........E 400
● *Paddy Mountain*, Mifflin.C ×
Page, Huntingdon...........C 50

● *Paint Creek*, Cambria.... C ×
● *Painter*, Westmoreland.SW ×
Painter Run, Tioga.......... N 32
Painter's Bridge, (see Pocopson) ×
Painter's Run, (see Federal) ×
● Paintersville, Mifflin......C 150
Paintersville, (see New Stanton) ×
● *Paint Mills*, Clarion..... W ×
Paisley, Greene............SW ×
● *Palens Switch*, McKean.. N ×
Pallas, Snyder...............E 15
● Palm, Montgomery.......SE 500
● *Palmer*, Warren........ NW ×
Palmersville, (see Remington) ×
Palmyra, Lebanon......... SE 768
● *Palo Alto*, Schuylkill..... E 1,424
Pan Cake, (see Martinsburg) ×
● Pancoast, Jefferson...... W 10
Panic, Jefferson............W 25
Pansy, Jefferson............W 20
● *Panther Run*, Centre.....C 57
● Paoli, Chester............SE 200
● *Paoli Road*, Chester.....SE 200
● *Paper Mill*, Columbia.....C ×
● *Paper Mill*, Lawrence... W ×
Paper Mill, Montgomery..SE ×
Papertown, (seeMountHollySprs) ×
Paradise, Lancaster........SE 400
ParadiseSettlement, (seeBigRun) ×
● *Paradise*, Monroe........ E ×
Paradise Valley, Monroe....E 175
● *Pardee*, Snyder...... ...... ×
● Pardoe, Mercer..........SW 500
Paris, Washington........ SW 150
Paris RoadSta., (seeHarmon's Creek)............. ×
Park, Philadelphia........SE ×
Park Creek, (see Rome) ..... ×
Parkdale, Butler...........W ×
● Parke, York.............. S 25
● *Parke*, Allegheny.......SW ×
● *Parker*, Armstrong...... W 1,317
● Parker Ford, Chester....SE 600
● *Parker Long Siding*, Armstrong.................. W ×
● Parker's Glen, Pike.....NE 300
Parker'sLanding, ArmstrongW 1,500
Parkersville, Chester.......SE 200
● Parkesburgh, Chester... SE 1,514
● *Park Junc*., PhiladelphiaSE ×
Parkland, Bucks............SE ×
● Park Place, Schuylkill....E 700
Park Quarries, Beaver..... W 600
Park's Creek, Bradford.... N ×
● Parkside, Monroe......... E 100
Park's Mills, (see Mars) ..... ×
● *Park Siding*, Schuylkill.. E ×
Parkwood, Indiana..........W 50
● Parnassus, Westmorel'd SW 516
Parrish, Forest...........NW ×
● Parryville, Carbon........ E 605
● Parsons, Luzerne.........E 2,412
● Parthenia, Warren.....NW ×
Parvin, Clinton.............N ×
● *Paschall*, Philadelphia.. SE ×
Passer, Bucks..............SE 50
Passyunk, Philadelphia....SE ×
Patchinsville, Clearfield.......C 40
Patience, Bedford...........S 10
Patricksburgh, Northumb'l'dC 100
● *Patterson*, Allegheny...SW ×
● Patterson, Juniata.........C 826
Patterson's Mills, Washin'nSW 50
Patterson's Sta., (see Rosston) ×
Patton, Cambria.............C 50
● Patton's Sta., Jefferson... W 32
Paul Brook, Montgomery.SE ×
Paulton, Westmoreland...SW 320
Paupac, Pike.............NE 200
● *Paupack*, Wayne....... NE ×
Pavia, Bedford..............S 100
● Pawling, Chester....... SE 300
● *Pawling*, Snyder..........C ×
● Paxinos, Northumberland C 60
● *Paxinos Sta*., Northumb'dC ×
● *Paxtang*, Dauphin.........C ×
● Paxton, Dauphin...........C 100
Paxton's Cor., (see Aquetong) ×
● Paxtonville, Snyder.......E 166
● *Peach Bottom*, LancasterSE 250
● Peach Bottom, York.......S 150
Peachville, Butler..........W ×
Peale, Clearfield........... C 500
● *Peale Sta*., Centre....... C ×
Pearl, Venango...........NW ×
Pearl's Eddy, (seeBrattonv'e) ×
● *Pebble Dell*, Forest.....NW ×

● *Peck's*, Blair..............C ×
● Peckville, Lackawanna. NE 2,000
Peely, Luzerne..............E 620
Peetona, Wayne..........NE ×
● *Pelton*, Somerset....... SW ×
● *Pelton*, Clearfield.........C ×
● Pen Argyl, Northampton. E 2,108
Penbrook, Dauphin.........C ×
● *Penbryn*, Lycoming......N 25
● Pencoyd, Montgomery.. SE 300
Pendleton, Cambria.........C 10
● Penfield, Clearfield.........C 603
● Penllyn, Montgomery...SE 100
Penylln Sta., (see Pennlyn).. ×
● Pen Mar, Franklin.......S 50
Penn, Lancaster........... SE 175
Pennbrook, Montgomery..SE ×
Penn Hall, Centre...........C 200
Penn Haven, Carbon....... E ×
● *Penn HavenJunc.*, CarbonE ×
Penn Hill, (see Wakefield) ... ×
● *Pennington*, Huntingdon.C ×
Penningtonville, (see Atglen). ×
Penn Line, Crawford......NW 250
Penn Run, Indiana.........W 300
● Pennsburgt., Montgom'rySE 627
● *Penn's Cave*, Centre.......C ×
Penn's Creek, Snyder.......C 275
● Pennsdale, Lycoming.....N 121
● Pennside, Erie......... NW ×
Penn's Manor, (seeMorrisv'e) ×
Penn's Park, Bucks........ SE 150
Penn's Sta., (see Kelton) .... ×
● Penn's Sta., Westmorel'dSW 931
● Pennsville, Fayette...... SW 225
Pennsylvania Furnace, Huntingdon.................. C 120
● *Pennsylvania House*, Warren .... NW ×
● Penn Valley, Bucks..... SE 100
Pennville, Clearfield........ C 219
Pennville, (see Penn) .... ×
● *Pennypack*, Pennsylva'a SE ×
● *Penobscot*, Luzerne.......E ×
● *Penokee*, Forest........NW ×
Penryn, Lancaster.......... SE 50
● *Penryn*, Lebanon........SE ×
Pensyl, Columbia........... C 20
Pentecost, (see Forest City)... ×
● *Pentland*, York............S ×
Pequea, Lancaster.......... SE 400
● *Pequea*, Lancaster.......SE ×
● *Percy*, Fayette..........SW ×
● *Perdix*, Perry............. C 41
● Perkasie, Bucks.........SE 458
● *Perkiomen*, MontgomerySE ×
● *PerkiomenJunc.*, ChesterSE 300
● Perkiomenville, Mont'erySE 200
Perrine, Mercer............W ×
Perry, Forest.............NW 150
● Perryopolis, Fayette.... SW 300
Perrysville, Allegheny.... SW 100
Perryville, (see Hamilton).... ×
Perryville, (see Port Royal).. ×
● *Per Se*, Centre............C ×
Peru Mills, Juniata..........C 100
Petersburg, (seeYork Springs) ×
● Petersburgh, Huntingdon.C 555
● *Petersburgh*, Lancaster..SE 476
● *Peters Creek*, Allegheny.SW ×
● Peter's Creek, Lancaster.SE 250
● *Peter's Crossing*, Lehigh..E ×
● *Peterson*, Allegheny.... SW ×
Petersville, (see Connoquenessing)..................... ×
Petersville, (see Slackwater).. ×
Petersville, Northampton...E 150
● Petroleum Centre, Venango....................NW 200
● Petrolia, Butler......... W 546
Pettis, Crawford..........NW 32
Pfouts' Valley, Perry........C 150
Phelp's Mills, Clinton....... N 25
● **PHILADELPHIA**, Philadelphia...........SE 1,046,964
● Philipsburg, Centre.......C 3,245
● Philipston, Clarion.......W 100
Philipsville, Erie..........NW 100
● *Phillippi*, Somerset ....SW ×
Phillips City, (see Luling).... ×
● *Phillipsburgh*, Beaver...W 1,494
● *Phillip's*, Potter..........N ×
● *Phillips*, Cambria.........C ×
Phillips Mills, (see Homer City)........................ ×
● Phillips Station, Tioga....N 25
● *Philmont*, Montgomery.SE ×
● Philson, Somerset.......SW 25
● *Philson's Mine*, Som'setSW ×
Phoenix, Armstrong....... W 50
● *Phoenix Junction*, Tioga.N ×
Phoenix Park, Schuylkill..E ×
● Phoenixville, Chester... SE 9,514
Platt, Sullivan.............. N 20
● Pickering, Chester.........SE 80
● Picture Rocks, Lycoming.N 510
Pierce, Armstrong......... W 200
Pierceville, Greene.........SW 100
Pierceville, Wyoming..... NE 75
● *Pierson's*, Philadelphia..SE ×
● Pigeon, Forest..........NW 150
● *Pikeland*, Chester........SE ×
Pike Run, (see Coal Centre).. ×
Pike's Creek, Luzerne...... E 50
Pike Station, Lycoming....N ×
Pikes Peak, (see Mechanics Grove)...................... ×
Pikes Peak, Indiana.........W 32
Pikesville, (see Browzersville) ×
Pikesville, Berks.......... SE 75
Pillow, Dauphin.............C 1,000
Pinafore, (see Myoma)....... ×
Pindleton, Cambria..........C 24
Pine, Berks.................SE ×
Pine Bank, Greene..........SW 25
● *Pine Creek*, Allegheny..SW ×
● *Pine Creek Intersection*, Allegheny ....SW ×
● *Pine Creek Junction*, Potter.....................N ×
Pinedale, Schuylkill.........E 150
Pine Flats, Indiana..........W 100
Pine Glen, Centre............C 100
Pine Grove, (see Pine Grove Furnace).................. ×
Pine Grove, (see Oak Hill)..... ×
● Pine Grove, Schuylkill.....E 1,103
● *Pine Grove*, Somerset...SW ×
● Pine Grove Furnace, Cumberland.....................S 300
Pine Grove Mills, Centre....C 300
Pine Hill, (see Brunnerville). ×
Pine Hill, Somerset........ SW 750
● *PineHillStation*, Som'setSW ×
Pine Iron Works, Berks...SE 60
● *Pine Junction*, Schuylkill.E ×
Pine Ridge, Bedford......... S 10
Pine Run (see Coal Valley).. ×
● Pine Station, Clinton.....N 100
Pine Summit, Columbia.....C 150
Pineville, Bucks........... SE 350
Piney Clarion................W 50
Piney Creek, Bedford.......S 25
Pin Hook, (see Lone Pine)... ×
Pink, Wayne.................NE ×
● *Pink Ash Junction*, Luze'eE ×
● *Pinkerton*, Somerset.....SW ×
Pinney's Corners, Crawf'dNW ×
Piollett, Clarion.. ....W ×
● *Pioneer*, Venango.......NW 97
Pipersville, Bucks.......... SE 40
Pit Hole City, Venango...NW 21
Pitman, Schuylkill...........E 500
● **PITTSBURGH**, Allegheny........................SW 238,617
Pittsburgh and Lake Erie Junction, Lawrence.... W ×
● Pittsfield, Warren....... NW 500
● Pittston, Luzerne........ E 10,302
● *Pittston Station*, LuzerneE ×
● *Pittston Summit*, LuzerneE ×
Pittsville, Venango.........NW 17
Pittville, Philadelphia.....SE 97
Plainfield, Cumberland......S 450
Plain Grove, Lawrence.....W 25
Plains, Luzerne..............E 2,000
● Plainsville, Luzerne.......E 500
Plainview, Adams...........S 50
Platea, Erie.................NW 300
Platt, Cambria..............C 25
Pleasant Corners, Carbon...E 125
● Pleasant Gap, Centre.....C 200
Pleasant Grove, Lancaster.SE 150
Pleasant Grove, (see England) ×
Pleasant Grove, (see Ligonier) ×
Pleasant Hall, Franklin.....S 64
Pleasant Hill, Lawrence.... W 10
Pleasant Mount, Wayne...NE 500
Pleasant Ridge, Fulton......S 25
Pleasant Run, MontgomerySE 75
Pleasant Unity, Westm'la'dSW 561
Pleasant Valley, (see Allegheny City)............. ×
Pleasant Valley, (see Hinkletown)...................... ×
Pleasant Valley, (see Avoca) ×
Pleasant Valley, (see Lone Pine)................... ×
Pleasant Valley, Bucks.... SE 100
Pleasant Valley, Erie....NW ×
Pleasant View, Juniata......C 100
Pleasant View, see Hinkletown)...................... ×
Pleasantville, Bedford......S 257
Pleasantville, (see Oley)...... ×
Pleasantville, Venango... NW 928
Plover, Lehigh..............E 75
Plum, Venango............NW 40
Plumer, Venango........ NW 150
Plum Run, Fulton............S 25
Plumsteadville, Bucks.....SE 350
Plumville, Indiana..........W 200
● Plymouth, Luzerne.......E 9,344
● *Plymouth Ferry*, LuzerneE ×
● *Plymouth Junc.*, LuzerneE ×
● Plymouth Meeting, Montgomery.................. SE 350
Pocahontas, Somerset.....SW 150
● Pocono, Monroe.......... E 180
● Pocopson, Chester.......SE 50
Poe, Beaver................ W 20
● Poe Mills, Centre.........C 133
Point, Bedford.............. S 193
● *Point Bridge*, AlleghenySW ×
Pointersville, Westmorel'dSW ×
Point Lookout, Chester....SE ×
Point Marion, Fayette.... SW 250
● *Point Phillipp*, Northampton.......................E ×
Point Pleasant, Bucks..... SE 300
● *Point View*, Blair....... C ×
Poke Hollow, Luzerne.......E ×
● Polk, Venango.......... NW 150
● Pollock, Clarion..........W 50
● *Pollock*, Allegheny...... SW ×
● Pomeroy, Chester....... SE 250
● *Pomeroy Bridge*, Potter..N ×
● *Pond Bank*, Franklin.....S ×
● *Pond Creek Junc.*, Luz'neE 350
● *Pond Eddy*, Pike.......NE 175
Pond Hill, Luzerne..........E ×
● Pond Hill Station, LuzerneE ×
Pont, Erie.................NW ×
● *Poplar Neck*, Berks.....SE ×
● *Poplar Neck Siding*, Berks...................SE ×
Poplar Run, Blair...........C 100
Poet, Luzerne...............E ×
● Portage, Cambria......... C 564
● Portage Creek, McKean.. N 690
● Port Allegheny, McKean. N 690
Port Barnett, Jefferson.....W ×
● Port Blanchard, Luzerne..E 500
Port Bowkley, Luzerne.....E ×
● Port Carbon, Schuylkill...E 1,976
● Port Clinton, Schuylkill...E 606
● *Port ClintonStation*, Schuylkill........................E ×
Porter, Jefferson............W 25
Porterfield, Venango.....NW 50
● *Porter Hill*, Fayette....SW ×
Portersburgh, Clearfield....C ×
● *Porters*, Clearfield........C ×
Porter's Lake, Pike.......NE 150
● Porters Sideling, York....S 25
Portersville, Butler ....W 190
● *Port Griffith*, Luzerne ....E ×
● *Port Indian*, Montgom'ySE ×
● Port Kennedy, M'tgomy SE 500
● Portland, Northampton .. E 676
Portland, (see Lawnsdale) ... ×
● *Portland*, Lehigh...........E ×
● Portland Mills, Elk ...... N ×
● Port Matilda, Centre......C 300
● Port Perry, Allegheny..SW 1,031
● Port Providence, M'nt'gySE 150
Port Richmond, Phil'a ....SE ×
Port Royal, Dauphin.......C 896
● Port Royal, Juniata ....C 519
● *Port Royals*, Westm'l'd SW 43
Port Trevorton, Snyder..... C 440
Potosi, York.................S 25
● Potter Brook, Tioga......N 200
● Pottersdale, Clearfield.... C 26
Pottter's Mills, Centre......C 150
Potterville, Bradford.......N 165
● *Potts*, Montgomery.......SE ×
● Pott's Grove, N'th'mb'rl'ndC 175
● Pottstown, Montgomery SE 13,285
● **Pottsville**, Schuylkill..E 14,117

Place	Pop.
Pottstown Landing, Ch'st'r SE	175
● Powder Valley, Lehigh...E	125
Powell, Bradford..........N	200
● Powelton, Centre.........C	195
● *Power's Run*, Allegheny SW	×
Powl's Valley, Dauphin....C	300
● *Powys*, Lycoming........N	×
Poyntell, Wayne..........NE	×
Prattville, Bradford.........N	130
● *Prentice*, Venango.....NW	×
● Prentice Vale, McKean...N	100
● Prescott, Lebanon.......SE	107
Prescottville, Jefferson.....W	×
President, Venango......NW	200
President Station, Ven'go NW	×
Preston, Schuylkill........C	×
Preston, Wayne..........NE	100
● *Preston*, McKean........N	×
● *Preston Station*, Wayne NE	×
Preston Park, Wayne.....NE	426
● Priceburgh, Lackwan'a NE	32
Pricetown, Berks.........SE	450
Priceville, (see Priceburgh)	×
Prichard, Luzerne..........E	150
● Primos, Delaware.......SE	×
● Primrose, Washington SW	200
Primrose Sta., (see McDonald)	×
Prince, Carbon............E	170
Princeton, Lawrence......W	300
● *Pritchard*, Tioga.........N	×
Proctor, Lycoming.........N	425
Progress, Dauphin..........C	250
● Frompton, Wayne.....NE	269
Prospect, Butler...........W	343
Prospect, (see East Prospect)	×
● *Prospect Rock*, Luzerne E	×
Prospectville, Montgom'ry SE	150
Prosperity, Washington..SW	100
● *Providence*, Lackwan'a NE	×
Providence Square, M'tg'y SE	75
Pruth, York..............S	25
● *Puckerty*, Jefferson.....W	×
Pugh, Somerset..........SW	75
Pughtown, Chester.........SE	225
● Pulaski, Lawrence......W	350
Pump, Butler............W	×
● Punxsutawney, Jefferson W	2,792
Purcell, Bedford...........S	25
Purchase Line, Indiana....W	30
Puritan, Cambria..........C	×
Pusey's Mills, (see Mechanic's Grove)............	×
Puseyville, (see Mechanic's Grove)............	×
Putnam, Allegheny......SW	65
Putneyville, Armstrong....W	175
Puzzletown, (see Poplar Run)	×
● *Pymatuning*, Mercer....W	×
● Quakake, Schuylkill.....E	×
● Quakertown, Bucks.....SE	2,169
● *Quakertown*, Lawrence..W	×
● *Quaker Valley*, Allegh'y SW	×
● *Quarry*, Somerset......SW	×
● *Quarry*, Warren.......NW	×
Quarrey Glenn, Bradford...N	×
● Quarryville, Lancaster..SE	500
Queen, Bedford.............S	100
● *Queen Lane*, Philadelp'a SE	×
● *Queen's Run*, Clinton....N	×
Queenstown, Armstrong...W	123
Quemahoning, Somerset..SW	40
● Quincy, Franklin.........S	300
Quincyville, (see Mount Clair)	×
Quintinau, Montour.........C	×
Quinton, McKean..........N	×
Race, York...............S	×
● Raccoon, Washington...SW	10
Racine, Washington......SW	×
● *Radebaugh*, Westm'r'l'd SW	×
● Radnor, Delaware......SE	250
● *Rhan's*, Montgomery...SE	300
● Rail Road, York..........S	201
Rainsburg, Bedford.........S	241
● Raker, Northumberland..C	10
● Ralston, Lycoming........N	700
● Ramey, Clearfield........C	350
● *RameyJunction*, Clearfield C	×
● *Ramona*, Lebanon......SE	×
Ramsey, (see Federal).......	×
● Ramseyville, Lycoming..N	×
Rand, Union...............C	×
Randolph, Crawford......NW	40
● Rankin Station, Alleg'y SW	1,000
● *Rankin*, Washington...SW	×
● Ransom, Lackawanna..NE	75
● *Rappahannock*, Schuylk'l E	549
● *Raricks*, Schuylkill.......E	300

Place	Pop.
● Rasselas, Elk............N	400
● Rathbun, Elk............N	50
● Rathmel, Jefferson.......W	200
Rattigan, Butler...........W	5
● *Rattling Run*, Dauphin...C	×
● *Raub's* Luzerne..........E	×
● *Raub's Mill*, Snyder......C	×
Raubsville, Northampton...E	250
Rauchtown, Clinton........N	150
Raughts, Elk..............N	20
● Rausch's, Schuylkill......E	250
Rausch's Creek, Schuylkill E	250
Rauch's Gap, Lebanon....SE	×
● Raven Creek, Columbia..C	130
● Raven Run, Schuylkill....E	650
● Ravine, Schuylkill........E	300
Rawlinsville, Lancaster....SE	200
● Raymilton, Venango...NW	50
Raymond's Potter..........N	100
Ray's Hill, Bedford.........S	250
● **READING**, Berks....SE	58,661
Reagenstown, (see Stoners)..	×
Reamstown, Lancaster....SE	539
Reamstown Sta., (see Stevens)	×
● *Reason Run*, Fayette...SW	×
Rebecca Furnace, (see Clover Creek..............	×
Rebersburgh Centre........C	500
Rebuck's, Northumberland.C	26
Red Bank, York...........S	×
● Red Bank Furnace, Clar'n W	100
Redclyffe, Forest.........NW	200
● Red Hill, Montgomery..SE	200
● Redington, Northampton.E	200
Red Land, Adams...........S	140
● *Red Lion*, Berks.........SE	×
● Red Lion, York...........S	524
Red Lion X Roads, (see Redstone.)...................	×
Redman Mills, Allegheny SW	×
Red Rock, Luzerne..........E	30
● *Red Rock*, McKean......N	×
Red Run, Lancaster.......SE	150
Redstone, Fayette........SW	40
● *Redstone*, Fayette.......SW	×
● *RedstoneJunction*, Fay'e SW	×
Red Valley, Venango....NW	×
Red Wells, (see Salisbury)....	×
● Reed, Dauphin............C	60
● *Reed*, Indiana...........W	×
● *Reed*, Mercer............W	×
● *Reed*, Northumberland...C	×
Reeder's, Monroe...........E	75
● *Reeder*, Bucks...........SE	×
● *Reeds*, Huntingdon........C	×
Reed's Gap, Juniata.........C	250
● *Reed's Road*, Chester...SE	×
● Reedsville, Mifflin........C	800
● *Reese*, Blair..............C	×
Reesville, (see Berwyn).......	×
● Reeves, Lawrence.........W	150
● *Reevesdale*, Schuylkill....E	×
Reflectorville, Allegheny..SW	×
● Refton, Lancaster.......SE	100
Register, Luzerne...........E	170
Register City, (see Sandy Point)	×
Rehrersburgh, Berks......SE	400
● Reibold, Butler...........W	40
Reidenback's Store, L'cas'r SE	150
Reidsburgh, Clarion........W	175
● *Reiley's*, Allegheny.....SW	×
● *Reiley*, Erie..............Nw	×
Reimertown, (see Rimertown)	×
● *Reimersburg*, Clarion....W	500
ReimoldSta., (see Stewartstown)	×
Reiner City, Schuylkill.....E	×
Reinert, Berk..............SE	850
● Reinhold's Sta., L'ca'r..SE	100
***Reinholdsville*, (see Blainesp't**	×
Reissing, Washington....SW	×
Reistville, Lebanon.......SW	100
Reitz, Somerset...........SW	25
Relay, York...............S	200
● *Remington*, Beaver......W	×
Remington, Allegheny....SW	30
Rendham, Lackawanna...NE	×
● *Rene Mont*, Schuylkill...E	×
● Renfrew, Butler..........W	×
● *Rennyson*, Chester......SE	×
● Reno, Venango.........NW	350
● Renovo, Clinton..........N	4,154
● *Republic*, Westmorel'd.SW	×
● *Reservoir*, Blair..........C	×
Resler, Northumberland....C	×
● *Re ort*, Centre..........C	×
● *Retreat*, Luzerne.........E	×
Retta, Susquehanna......NE	32

Place	Pop.
Revere, Bucks..............SE	50
○ Rew, McKean............N	250
Reward, Perry..............C	100
Rexmont, Lebanon........SE	×
Reyburn, Luzerne..........E	25
● Reynolds, Schuylkill.....E	125
● Reynoldston, Allegheny.SW	1,379
● Reynoldsville, Jefferson..W	2,786
● *Rheems*, Lancaster......SE	×
● *Rhoads*, Centre..........C	×
Rhone, Luzerne.............E	×
● *Ribold's*, Butler..........W	40
Rice's Landing, Greene...SW	300
● Riceville, Crawford....NW	245
Richardsville, Jefferson....W	100
Richborough, Bucks.......SE	525
Richfield, Juniata..........C	350
Rich Hill, Bucks..........SE	160
Richland Centre, Bucks..SE	650
● Richland Sta., Lebanon. SE	600
Richlandtown, Bucks......SE	400
● *Richmond*, Clarion......W	60
Richmond, Indiana.........W	×
Richmond, Northampton..E	230
RichmondCentre, (see Moselem)	×
● Richmond Furnace, Fr'k'n S	200
● Richmond Hill, Susqu'a.NE	32
Richvale, Huntingdon,.......C	×
● *Rickenback*, Berks......SE	×
Ricketts, Wyoming.......NE	400
Riddlesburgh, Bedford......S	150
Riddle's Cross Roads, Butler W	50
● *Riderville*, Mckean.......N	×
● *Ridge*, Clearfield..........C	×
Ridge, Bucks..............SE	60
Ridgebury, Bradford.........N	36
● *Ridge Junction*, Schuylkill E	×
● *Ridge Road*, M'tgomery.SE	×
Ridgeview, (see Kecksburg)	×
● *Ridge Wood*, Berks......SE	×
Ridgewood, Luzerne.......E	×
● **Ridgway**, Elk..........N	1,903
● *Ridgway Station*, Elk....N	×
● Ridley Park, Delaware..SE	500
Riegelsville, Bucks.........SE	600
Rienzi, Bradford...........N	22
Rife, Dauphin..............C	×
Riggs, Bradford...........N	25
Rileyville, Wayne.........NE	150
● Rillton, Westmoreland.SW	×
● Rimer, Armstrong........W	200
● Rimersburgh, Clarion...W	360
Rinely, York...............S	50
Ringgold, Jefferson........W	150
Ringgold, (see New Ringgold)	×
● Ringtown, Schuylkill.....E	600
Ringville, Sullivan..........N	25
Ripple, Luzerne.............E	×
● *Risher*, Allegheny......SW	×
Rising, Tioga..............N	25
● *Rising Springs*, Centre...C	150
Rising Sun, (see Philadelphia)	×
Rising Sun, Lehigh.........E	×
● *Rist*, Fayette............SW	×
● *Rita*, Luzerne............E	×
● *Ritchie*, Clinton..........N	×
Rittenhouse, Luzerne.......E	×
● *Rittenhouse Gap*, Berks.SE	×
● *Ritter*, Northampton.....E	×
● Rittersville, Lehigh.......E	150
● *Ritts*, Clarion.............W	×
● *Riverside*, Allegheny....SW	×
● *Riverside*, Beaver........W	×
● Riverside, Northumbl'd..C	394
● *Riverton*, Allegheny....SW	×
● *Riverview*, Armstrong...W	×
● *Riverview*, Clearfield.....C	×
● Rixford, McKean..........N	506
● *Roache*, Warren.......NW	×
● *Roads*, Allegheny......SW	×
Roadside, Franklin..........S	20
● Roaring Branch, Lycom'g N	500
Roaring Brook (see Pritchard)	×
Roaring Creek, Columbia...C	150
● *Roaring Creek*, Montour...C	150
● *Roaring Run*, W'm'la'd SW	×
● Roaring Spring, Blair.....C	920
● *Robbins*, Allegheny....SW	×
● Robbins Sta., Westm'l'd SW	300
Robella, (see Bellevue).......	×
Robbins & Jenkins Landing, Allegheny..............SW	100
Roberts, Chester...........SE	30
● *Roberts*, Somerset......SW	×
● Robertsdale, Huntingdon E	651
● *Robeson*, Berks.........SE	350
● Robesonia, Berks........SE	350

● *Robinson*, Clinton...... N ×
Robinsonville, Bedford..... S 100
● Rochester, Beaver....... W 3,649
Rochester Mills, Indiana.... W 200
● Rock, Schuylkill.......... E 120
Rock Creek, Susquehanna NE ×
● *Rock Cut*, McKean....... N ×
● *Rockdale*, Franklin....... S ×
● *Rockdale*, Delaware..... SE ×
● Rockdale, Lehigh......... E 300
Rockdale Mills, Jefferson.. W 150
Rockey, York............... S 50
● Rock Glen, Luzerne....... E 300
Rock Glen Junc., Luzerne.. E ×
Rock Hill, Lancaster...... SE 50
● *Rockhill*, Bucks.......... SE ×
● Rockhill Furnace, H't'g'n C 657
Rock Lake, Wayne....... NE 32
Rockland, Venango...... NW 200
● *Rockledge*, Philadelphia SE ×
● Rock Point, Beaver...... W 500
● *Rock Point*, Lawrence... W ×
● Rockport, Carbon......... S 200
● *Rock Run*, (see Coal Valley) ×
● *Rock Run*, Centre........ C ×
● *Rock Run*, Clarion....... W ×
Rock Spring, Centre........ C 200
Rockton, Clearfield......... C 130
Rocktown, (see Lavelle)......
● Rockville, Chester....... SE 125
● *Rockville*, Dauphin....... C 300
Rockville, Northampton... E ×
● Rockwood, Somerset... SW 553
● *Rockwood*, Venago.... NW ×
Rocky Hill, Chester....... SE ×
● Rocky Hollow, Cambria.. C ×
● *Roddy*, Somerset....... SW 553
● *Roddy*, Perry............ C ×
Rodi, Allegheny.......... SW ×
● *Rodman*, Blair........... C ×
● *Rogers*, Fayette......... SW ×
Rogersville, Greene....... SW 100
● Rohrerstown, Lanc'ter.. SE 550
Rohrsburgh, Columbia...... C 175
● Roland Centre........... C 500
Roler, York............... S 25
● Rolfe, Elk............... N 400
● *Romonia*, Somerset.... SW ×
Romansville, Chester...... SE 50
Rome, Bradford............ N 226
Romola, Centre............ C 20
● Ronks, Lancaster....... SE 150
● *Roots*, Blair............ C ×
Rootville, Crawford...... NW ×
● *Rosas*, Pike............ NE ×
● Roscoe, Washington.... SW 500
● Rose Bud, Clearfield...... C 800
● *Roseburg*, Allegheny... SW ×
Roseburgh, Perry.......... C 300
Rosecrans, Clinton......... N 32
Rosedale, Greene......... SW 25
● *Rosedale*, Chester....... SE 175
● *Roseglen*, Montgomery.. SE 200
Roseland, (see Fiske) .... ×
● Rosemont, Montgomery SE 400
Rosenberry, Franklin....... S 65
● *Rosensteel*, Somerset.... SW ×
Rosenvick, Chester........ SE 50
Rose Point, Lawrence...... W 150
● *Rose's*, Forest.......... NW ×
Rose's Valley, Lycoming... N 137
Rosevale, Allegheny...... SW ×
Roseville, Tioga........... N 211
Roseville, (see Landis' Valley) ×
Ross, Allegheny.......... SW ×
● *Ross*, Allegheny........ SW ×
● *Ross Common*, Monroe... E ×
Rossland, Monroe........... E 100
● Rosston, Armstrong...... W 100
Rossville, York............. S 250
Rostraver, Westmoreland S. W 10
Rote, Clinton............... N 69
● *Rothruck*, Fayette...... SW ×
● Rothsville, Lancaster.... SE 350
Rough and Ready, Schuylkill E 110
Roughrun, Butler.......... W ×
● Roulette, Potter.......... N 600
● *Round Bottom*, Fayette SW 65
Round Hill, Adams......... S 200
● *Round Island*, Clinton... N ×
● Round Top, Tioga........ N 100
● *Round Top*, Adams....... S ×
● *Round Top Jc.*, Hunterdon C ×
● *Roup*, Allegheny....... SW ×
● Rouseville, Venango... NW 503
Rowe, Beaver............ W ×
● Rowenna, Somerset...... SW ×
○ Rowland, Pike.......... NE 125
● *Rowlands*, Philadelphia. SE ×
Rowles, Clearfield.......... C 40
Rowzersville, Franklin...... S 300
● *Roxborough*, Philadelphia SE ×
Roxbury, Northampton..... E ×
Roxbury, Franklin.......... S 300
Roxbury, (see Stony Creek).. ×
Roxton, Bucks........... SE ×
● *Roy*, Butler............ W 100
Roy, York.................. S 100
Royal, Susquehanna...... NE 150
Royalton, Dauphin.......... C ×
● Royer, Blair.............. C 10
● *Royers*, Perry........... C ×
● Royer's Ford, M'tg'm'ry. SE 1,815
● *Roystone*, Warren...... NW ×
● *Rubicum*, Montgomery.. SE ×
Ruble, Fayette............ SW 50
Ruchsville, Lehigh.......... E 100
● Rudy, Montgomery...... SE 50
Ruff Creek, Greene....... SW 75
Ruff's Dale, Westmoreland SW 300
Ruggles, Luzerne........... E 100
● *Rugh*, Indiana........... W ×
● *Rumbaugh*, Westmo'l'd SW ×
Rummel, Somerset....... SW 30
Rummerfield, (see Rummerf'd Cr.) ×
● Rummerfield Cr., Bradford N 30
● *Run*, Venango.......... NW ×
Rundell's, Crawford....... NW 75
● Rupert, Columbia......... C 225
Rural Ridge, Allegheny... SW 50
Rural Valley, Armstrong... W 200
Rush, Susquehanna....... NE 100
Rushes, Somerset......... SW ×
Rush Four Corners, Susquehanna............ NE 25
● *Rushland*, Chester....... SE ×
Rushtown, Northumberland. C 0
Rush Valley, Bucks....... SE 50
Rushville, Susquehanna... NE 150
● Russell, Warren........ NW 300
Russell Hill, Wyoming.... NE 150
Russellville, Chester....... SE 300
Rutan, Greene............ SW 50
● *Rutherford*, Dauphin...... C ×
Rutland, Tioga............ N 300
Rutledge, Delaware........ SE 269
Rutty, (see North Towanda).. ×
● Rydall, Montgomery..... SE ×
● *Ryde*, Mifflin............ C ×
● *Ryder's*, Franklin........ S ×
● *Rye*, Armstrong......... W ×
Rye, York................. S ×
● *Ryer's*, Montgomery.... SE ×
Ryersons Station, Greene.. SW 60
● *Rynd Farm*, Venango.. NW 250
Sabbath Rest, Blair.......... C 150
● Sabinsville, Tioga......... N 450
● Sabula, Clearfield......... C 50
Sackett, Elk............... N ×
Saco, Bradford............ N 30
Sacramento, Schuylkill..... E 200
● Sadsburyville, Chester... SE 325
● *Saeger's*, Lycoming....... N ×
● Saegerstown, Crawford NW 745
● Saegersville, Lehigh...... E 180
● Safe Harbor, Lancaster.. SE 613
Sagon, Northumberland.... C ×
Saint Augustine, Cambria... C 75
Saint Bonifacius, Cambria.. C 50
● *Saint Charles*, Clarion... W ×
Saint Clair, Beaver........ W 411
● Saint Clair, Schuylkill.... E 3,680
Saint Clair's Sta., (see Bradenv'e) ×
Saint Clairsville, Bedford... S 134
Saint Cloud, Washington.. SW 10
Saint Davids, Delaware.... SE ×
● *Saint Davids*, Delaware.. SE ×
● *Saint George*, Venango. NW ×
Saint Joe, Butler.......... W 100
● Saint Joe Station, Butler. W ×
Saint John's, Luzerne....... E 250
Saint Joseph, Susquehanna NE ×
Saint Lawrence, Cambria... C 75
● *Saint Lu*, Clearfield...... C ×
● Saint Mary's, Elk......... N 1,745
Saint Nicholas, Cambria.... C 250
● Saint Nicholas, Schuylkill. E 823
● Saint Peter's, Chester.... SE 140
● Saint Petersburgh, Clarion W 655
Saint Thomas, Franklin..... S 700
Saint Thomas, Montgomery SE ×
Saint Vincent, (see Pleasant Unity) ×
● *Salem*, Mercer........... W 100
Salem, Westmoreland..... SW 311
Salem, Snyder............... 40
Salem Church, Cumberland. 150
Salemville, Bedford......... S 50
● *Salford*, Montgomery.... SE 50
Salfordville, Montgomery.. SE 450
● Salina, Westmoreland... SW 50
Salisbury, Lancaster....... SE 150
● *Salisbury Jc.*, Somerset NW 689
Salix, Cambria............. C 40
Salladasburgh, Lycoming... N 374
Salona, Clinton............ N 500
Salter, Huntingdon.......... C 104
● Saltillo, Huntingdon...... C 254
Salt Lick, Clearfield......... C 120
● Saltsburgh, Indiana...... W 1,088
● *Saltsburgh*, Allegheny.. SW ×
● *Salt Spring Bottom*, Fay'e SW ×
● Salunga, Lancaster...... SE 300
Saluvia, Fulton............. S 50
● Sampsonville, Erie..... NW ×
● Sanatoga, Montgomery.. SE 358
● *Sancanac*, Chester...... SE ×
Sandbeach, Dauphin........ C ×
Sand Cut, (see Gouldsboro Sta.) ×
Sanders, Potter............ N ×
Sandiford, Philadelphia... SE ×
● Sand Patch, Somerset... SW 100
Sand Rock, Greene........ SW 10
● *Sand Siding*, Somerset. SW ×
Sandt's Eddy, Northampton E 100
● *Sandy Creek*, Allegheny SW ×
Sandy Hill, Perry........... C 100
● Sandy Lake, Mercer...... W 721
● *Sandy Lick*, Butler...... W ×
Sandy Point, Butler........ W 130
● Sandy Ridge, Centre...... C 250
Sandy Rock, Greene...... SW ×
● Sandy Run, Luzerne...... E 596
Sandy Run, (see Flourtown) ×
● *Sandy Run Junc.*, Luzerne E ×
Sandy Valley, Jefferson.... W 50
Sanford, Warren......... NW ×
● *Sandford Junc.*, Clearfield C ×
● *Sang Hollow*, Cambria... C ×
● *Sanner*, Somerset........ W ×
● Santee, Northampton..... E 75
Sarah, Huntingdon.......... C 25
● *Sarah Furnace*, Clarion. W 150
Sardis, Westmoreland..... SW 50
Sartwell, (see Burtville) ..... ×
Sargent, McKean........... N 32
● Sartwell, McKean......... N ×
Sarvers Sta., (see Sarversv'e) ×
● Sarversville, Butler...... W 40
Sassamansville, Montgom'y SE 250
● *Saucon*, Lehigh........... E ×
Saulsburgh, Huntingdon.... C 100
Savage, Somerset......... SW 10
Saville, Perry.............. C 25
Savoy, Potter.............. N ×
● Sawyer City, McKean.... N 200
● Saxonburgh, Butler...... W 250
Saxonburg Sta., (see Carbon Bl'k) ×
● Saxton, Bedford........... S 712
● Saybrook, Warren....... NW ×
● Saylorsburgh, Monroe.... E 400
● *Saylorsburgh Junction*, Northampton.......... E ×
● Sayre, Bradford.......... N 3,200
● *Scahonda*, Elk.......... N ×
● *Scales*, Clinton.......... N ×
● *Scale Siding*, Luzerne.... E ×
Scalp Level, Cambria........ C 225
Scandia, Warren.......... NW ×
Scarlet's Mill, Berks....... SE 96
Scenery Hill, Washington. SW 200
Schadts, Lehigh............ E 75
Schaefferstown, Lebanon.. SE 530
Scheidy, Lehigh............ E ×
Schellsburg, Bedford........ S 281
● *Schenck's*, Bucks........ SE 75
● Schenly Station, Armst'g. W 25
Schlichter, Bucks.......... SE 25
Schnadersville, (see Ephrata). ×
Schnecksville, Lehigh....... E 575
● *Schock's Mills*, Lancaster SE 75
Schoeneck, Lancaster...... SE 300
Schofer, Berks............. SE 250
Schoffner's Corners, Jeffer'n W 25
○ *School House*, Centre...... C ×
● *School House*, Crawford NW ×
● *School Lane*, Philadelp'a SE ×
Schubert, Berks........... SE 66
Schultzville, Lackawanna. NE 200
● *Schur's*, Philadelphia.... SE ×
● Schuyler, Northumberla'd C ×
Schuylkill, Chester........ SE 150

○ Schuylkill Haven, Schuy'l.E 3,088
● *Schuylkill Haven Junction*, Schuylkill..........E ×
○ *Schweibinz*, Somerset...SW ×
Schweibinzville, Somerset.SW 130
● Schwenkville, Montgo'rySE 700
Schweyers, Berks..........SE 79
Scioto, Monroe.............E 175
Sciotoville, Bradford........N ×
Scotch Hill, Clarion........ W 75
Scotch Hill, NorthumberlandC 560
● *Scotch Valley Station*, Columbia..........C ×
● *Scotia*, Centre.............C 200
● Scotland, Franklin........S 300
Scott, Lackawanna..........NE 75
Scott Center, Wayne.......NE 390
● Scottdale, Westmorel'ndSW 2,693
● Scott Haven, Westm'l'ndSW 525
Scottsville, Wyoming......NE 62
○ **Scranton**, LackawannaNE 75,215
Scrubgrass, (see Goheensville) ×
● Scrubgrass, Venango...NW 75
Scrubridge, Clarion........ W ×
Scullhill, Berks...........SE ×
Scullton, Somerset.........SW 100
● *Scully's Spring*, Allegh'ySW ×
Scyoc, Perry............... C ×
Seal, Chester..............SE 75
Seamans, Tioga............ N ×
Seanor, Somerset..........SW ×
Searight s, Fayette........SW 55
Sebring, Tioga............. N 10
● Secane, Delaware........SE 100
Sedan, Northumberland.....C 100
Sedgwick, Adams........... S 50
● *Sedgwick*, Fayette......SW ×
Sedgwick Mills, Butler.....W 25
● *Sedwick Mills*, Butler....W 25
Seek, Schuylkill............E 658
Seelyville, Wayne..........NE 460
Seemsville, Northampton...E 75
Seiberlingville, Lehigh......E 100
Seibert's Landing, (see Brady's Bend).......... ×
Seidersville, Northampton.. E 175
● Seigfried's Bridge, Northampton..............E 890
● Seiples, Lehigh............E 50
Seip's, Northampton........E 50
Seipstown, Lehigh......... E 115
Seisholtzville, Berks.......SE 175
Seitzville, (see Hanover Junc.) ×
● Seitzland, York...........S 200
Selea, Huntingdon.......... C 50
● Selin's Grove, Snyder.....C 1,315
● *Selin's Grove Junction*, Northumberland........C ×
● Selkirk, Warren........NW ×
● *Sellers*, Lancaster........SE ×
● Sellersville, Bucks.......SE 794
Sellersville, (see North Point). ×
● Sell's Station, Adams......S 200
Seminole, (see Rothsville).... ×
● *Semples*, Allegheny..... SW ×
Seneca, Venango......... NW 400
Sensenig, Lancaster.......SE ×
Sereno, Columbia........... C 100
● *Sergeant*, McKean.......N 150
Service, Beaver............W 150
Setzler's Store, (see Parker Ford).................. ×
Seven Points, Northumberl'dC 110
● Seven Stars, Adams.......S 25
Seven Stars, (see Schuylkill Haven).................. ×
Seventy-Six, Beaver........W 50
● Seven Valleys, York.......S 300
● Seward, Westmoreland. SW 350
● Sewickley, Allegheny...SW 2,776
● *Sewickley*, Westmorel'd.SW ×
● *Seyfert*, Berks...........SE ×
Shadagse, (see Knoxdale).... ×
Shade Gap, Huntingdon.....C 209
● Shadeland, Crawford...NW ×
Shade Valley, Huntingdon..C 25
Shadle, Snyder.............C ×
Shady Grove, Franklin......S 400
Shady Plain, Armstrong....W 50
● *Shady Side*, Allegheny..SW ×
● *Shady Side*, Mercer......W ×
Shaefferstown, Lebanon.... SE 800
Shafer's, Beaver.............W ×
Shafersville, (see Water Street) ×
● *Shaffer's Mill*, McKean....N ×
Shaff's Bridge, (see Mineral Point)................... ×

Shaft, Schuylkill...........E 200
● *Shaft Number Two*, Westmoreland.............SW ×
● *Shafton*, Westmoreland.SW 450
● *Shaintine's*, MontgomerySE ×
Shamburgh, Venango.... NW 150
● Shamokin, Northumberl'dC 14,403
Shamokin Dam, Snyder.....C 100
Shamrock, Greene.........SW 75
● *Shamrock*, Somerset....SW 80
● Shamrock Station, BerksSE 165
● *Shaner Mine Number Two*, Westmoreland........SW ×
● *Shaner's*, WestmorelandSW 50
Shanesville, Berks..........SE 100
● Shank's Run, Mifflin.....C 50
Shanksville, Somerset.....SW 900
● *Shannon*, Erie.........NW ×
● *Shannon*, Clarion........W ×
Shannondale, Clarion.......W 120
Shannonville, MontgomerySE 300
● *Shannopins*, Beaver..... W 300
Sharon, (see West Bridgewater)..................... ×
● Sharon, Mercer..........W 7,459
Sharon Centre, Potter.......N 80
● Sharon Hill, Delaware...SE 500
● Sharpsburgh, AlleghenySW 4,898
● Sharpsville, Mercer...... W 2,330
Shartlesville, Berks........SE 500
Shavertown, Luzerne....... E ×
Shaver's Creek, (see Petersb'g) ×
● *Shawmont*, PhiladelphiaSE ×
Shawmut, Clearfield........C 40
Shawnee, Monroe........... E 90
● *Shaw Run*, Blair..........C ×
● *Shaw's*, Crawford.......NW ×
● Shaw's Landing, Crawf'dNW ×
Shawsville, Clearfield....... C 40
Sheakleyville, Mercer..... W 191
Shearer's Cross Roads, Westmoreland.............SW 50
Shearsburg, (see Shearer's Cross Roads)........... ×
Sheeder, Chester...........SE 25
● *Sheffer*, York..............S 30
Sheffield, (see New Sheffield). ×
● Sheffield, Warren...... NW 1,295
● *SheffieldJunction*, ForestNW 82
● *Shehawken*, Wayne.....NE ×
Sheldon, Susquehanna.... NE 75
● *Sheldon*, Luzerne.........E ×
● Shelly, Bucks............SE 100
Shelmadine Springs, Crawford................. NW ×
● *Shelmire*, Chester........SE ×
Shelocta, Indiana...........W 82
● Shenandoah, Schuylkill...E 15,944
● *Shenandoah Junc.*, Schuylkill..................E ×
Shenango, Lawrence........W 20
● *Shenango*, Mercer........W 160
Shenkel, Chester............SE 75
● *Shenk's Ferry*, LancasterSE ×
Shenks Ferry, York......... S ×
Shenly Station, Armstrong W ×
Shepherdstown, CumberlandS 200
Sheppton, Schuylkill.........E ×
● *Sheridan*, Allegheny....SW ×
● *Sheridan*, Cambria....... C ×
● Sheridan, Lebanon.......... 440
Sheridanville, Allegheny.. SW 400
Sherman, Wayne..........NE 200
● *Sherman Run*, Fayette.SW ×
Sherman's Dale, Perry......C 700
● *Shermansville*, CrawfordNW 6,049
Sherrett, Armstrong.......W 100
● *Sherrick*, Fayette.......SW ×
Sheshequin, Bradford.......N 350
● Shickshinny, Luzerne.....E 1,448
● *ShickshinnySta.* Luzerne.E ×
● Shields, Allegheny......SW ×
Shields' Mills, (seeFoster'sMills) ×
Shillington, Berks..........SE 600
Shiloh, Clearfield...........C 275
● *Shimer*, Northampton....E 75
Shimerville, Lehigh.........E 240
● *Shindle*, Mifflin...........C ×
Shiner, Beaver.............W ×
Shinglehouse, Potter........N 300
Shingleton, Centre..........C ×
● Shintown, Clinton.........N ×
● Shippensburgh, Cumber'dS 2,188
● Shippen Station, CameronN 75
● Shippensville, Clarion.... W 336
Shippingport, Beaver.......W 50
● *Ship Road*, Chester......SE ×

Shira, Butler...............W 30
● Shiremanstown, Cumb'la'dS 432
● Shireoaks, Washington..SW 750
Shirland, Allegheny.......SW 10
Shirley, Crawford.........NW 40
● Shirleysburgh, Hunting'n.C 325
● *Shober*, Somerset.......SW ×
Shoch's Mills, Lancaster...SE 75
Shoemaker's, Monroe.......E 80
● *Shoemaker's*, Schuylkill..E ×
Shoemakerstown, (seeChester) ×
● Shoemakersville, Berks.SE 502
Shoemakersville, (see Chester) ×
● *Shoenberger*, Huntingdon.C ×
Shoenersville, Lehigh.......E 180
● Shohola, Pike...........NE 150
Shohola Falls, Pike........NE 60
● *Shohola Glen*, AlleghenySW ×
Short Line, York...........S 400
Short Mountain, Dauphin..C 120
Short Run, Potter..........N 90
● *Short's Mill*, Elk.........N ×
● *Shoup*, Westmoreland..SW ×
● Shoustown, Allegheney.SW 400
● *Shreimer*, Lancaster.....SE ×
● Shrewsbury, York.........S 562
● *Shrewsburg Sta.*, York....S 350
Shultzville, (see Colebrookdale).................. ×
● *Shuman's*, Columbia......C ×
● Shunk, Sullivan..........N 100
● Shy Beaver, Huntingdon..C 250
Siddonsburg, York...........S 220
Sideling Hill, Fulton........S 50
● *Siding No. 7*, Luzerne.. E ×
Sidney, Indiana............W 10
Siegersville, Lehigh.........E ×
● *Siegfried*, Northampton..E 400
Sigel, Jefferson.............W 110
Siglerville, Mifflin..........C 125
Sigmund, Lehigh............E 50
Siko, Wayne...............NE 38
Silbaugh, Somerset........SW 10
Silkworth, Luzerne..........E 27
● *Sills*, Bedford.............S ×
Silvara, Bradford...........N 100
● Silver Brook, Schuylkill..E ×
● *Silver Brook Junc.* Sch'killE ×
● Silver Creek, Schuylkill...E 237
Silver Hill, NorthumberlandC 593
Silver Lake, Susquehanna. NE 100
● Silver Spring, Lancaster.SE 800
● *Silverton*, Schuylkill......E ×
Simmonstown (see Gap)...... ×
Simon, Wayne............NE 25
● *Simon Station*, Wayne..NE ×
● *Simpson*, McKean.......N ×
Simpson's Store, Wash'tonSW 30
● *Singersville*, Lehigh......E ×
● Sinking Spring, Berks...SE 700
Sinking Valley, Blair.......C 25
● Sinnamahoning, CameronN 400
● *Siousca*, Chester.........SE ×
Sipe's Mill, Fulton...........S 160
Sipesville, Somerset.......SW 75
● *Sirwell*, Armstrong......W 50
Sis, (see Waterfall)........... ×
● Sitka, Fayette.............SW 200
Sittler, Schuylkill............E 50
Siverly, Venango..........NW 833
Six Mile Fy, (seeHopeChurch) ×
Six Mile Run, Bedford......S 300
Six Points, Butler...........W 30
Six Roads, Bedford.........S 100
Sizerville, Cameron.........N 120
● Skinner's Eddy, Wy'ing.NE 100
Skippack, Montgomery....SE 800
Slab, York....................S 100
Slack Water, Lancaster....SE 50
● *Slate Belt*, Adams.........S ×
Slatedale, Lehigh...........E 525
Slateford, Northampton....E 300
● Slate Hill, York.............S 150
Slate Lick, Armstrong.....W 150
● Slate Run, Lycoming......N 500
Slate Valley, Northampton.E ×
● Slatington, Lehigh.........E 2,716
Slaymakersville, (see Gap)... ×
● *Sligo*, Allegheny........SW ×
● Sligo, Clarion............W 495
Slippery Rock, Butler......W 500
Sloan, Westmoreland......SW 10
Slocum, Luzerne............E 30
● *Slocum*, Luzerne..........E ×
Slonaker, Chester..........SE 610
Smathers, Indiana..........W 5
Smedley, Chester..........SE 200

● Smethport, Mc Kean...N 1,150
Smicksburgh, Indiana.....W 229
● Smithfield, Fayette.....SW 500
Smithfield, (see E. Smithfield) ×
Smithport, (see Horton's)..W ×
Smith's Junc., Mc Kean....N ×
● *Smith's*, Tioga............N ×
● Smith's Ferry, Beaver....W 300
Smith's Mills, Clearfield.....C 200
● *Smith's Run*, Mc Kean...N ×
● Smiths Station, York.....S 60
● *Smithsville*, WashingtonSW 50
● Smithton, Westmorel'd.SW 800
Smithville, (see Grimville)... ×
Smithville, Lancaster......SE 250
Smithville, (see Eighty-Four) ×
Smitten, (see Trade City)..... ×
● Smock, Fayette..........SW 30
Smokers, Lancaster..........SE 50
● Smoke Run, Clearfield....C ×
Smoketown, (see Bird in Hand)........................ ×
Smyrna, Lancaster..........SE 125
● *Smyser*, York.............S 300
● Snedekerville, Bradford..N 60
Snarletown, (see Souderton). ×
● *Snowden*, Allegheny....SW ×
● Snow Shoe, Centre........C 1,000
● *Snow Shoe Intersection*, Centre.....................C ×
● *Snyder*, Indiana..........W ×
● *Snyder*, Northampton....E ×
● *Snyder*, Mercer..........W ×
● *Snyder's*, Somerset.....SW 20
● *Snyder's*, York...........S ×
● Snydersburgh, Clarion....W 30
Snydersville, Monroe........E 160
● Snydertown, N'th'mb'rl'dC 242
● Sober, Centre.............C 15
● Sobieski, Clearfield.......C 200
● *Social Hall*, Indiana.....W ×
Sodom, (see Upper St. Clair) ×
● *Soho*, Allegheny.........SW ×
● *Soisson*, Fayette........SW ×
○ *Soldiers* Jefferson..W ×
Solebury, Bucks...........SE 100
○ *Solomon Gap*, Luzerne...E ×
Somerfield, Somerset.....SW 100
Somerfield Sta., SomersetSW ×
● Somerset, Somerset..SW 1,713
● Somer's Lane, Tioga......N 100
● Somerton, Philadelphia. SE 400
Somerville, (see Philadelphia) ×
● *Somerville*, Tioga.........N 100
● Sonestown, Sullivan.......N 300
● *Song Bird*, Mc Kean.....N 400
● Sonman, Cambria..........C ×
Sonora, Butler..............W 25
● Soradoville, Mifflin.........C 25
Sondersburgh, Lancaster..SE 300
● Souderton, M'tgomery...SE 579
● Southampton, Bucks....SE 300
● *Southampton*, Franklin..S ×
● *Southampton*, SomersetSW ×
Southard, Mc Kean...........N 75
South Auburn, Susq'ha'a..NE 75
South Bend, Armstrong....W 150
South Bethlehem, Arm'st'ngW 111
● South Bethlehem, N'h't'nE 10,302
● *South Birdsboro*, Berks. SE ×
South Branch, Bradford.... N 25
● *South Branch*, McKean.. N ×
● *South Branch*, York....... S 30
South Bridge, Clearfield.... C ×
South Burgettstown, Wash.SW 876
South Canaan, Wayne...... NE 250
South Chester, Delaware....SE 7,076
● *South Cornwall*, LebanonSE ×
South Corydon, Warren.. NW ×
● *South Delta*, York.......... S ×
● *South Easton*, N'th'mptonE ×
● South Eaton, Wyoming. NE 5,616
● South Evansville, Berks.SE 150
● South Fork, Cambria..... C 1,295
South Gibson, Susqueha'a.NE 250
South Herberton, Luzerne.. E 1,000
South Hermitage, Lanc'ter.SE 100
South Hill, Bradford........N 50
South Montrose, Susq'h'a. NE 75
● *South Mountain Summit Siding*, Adams.......... S ×
● South Oil City, Venango NW
● *South Pennsylvania Junc.*, Franklin.................. S ×
South Pittsburg, (see Pitts'g) ×
South Renovo, Clinton..... N 135
South Side, Allegheny.....SW ×
● *South Side*, York.......... S ×
South Sterling, Wayne.... NE 200
South Strabane, Wash't'n.. SW 25
South Towanda, (see Towanda) ×
South Warren, Bradford.... N 71
South Waverly, Bradford.. N 1,082
Southwest, Westmorel'd.. SW 200
● South Whitehall, Lehigh..E 124
● *South Wilkesbarre*, L'zer'eE ×
● South Williamsport, L'c'ngN 2,900
● *South Wilmer Junction*, Clearfield.................C ×
Spangler, Lawrence..........W ×
Spang's Mills, (see RoaringSpr.) ×
Spangsville, Berks.......... SE 40
Sparta, Washington......... SW 41
● Spartansburgh, Cr'wf'd. NW 516
● *Spauldings*, McKean..... N ×
● Speelman, Bedford .... S 56
Speelman's Landing, (see Dravosburg).................. ×
Speers, Washington....... SW 200
Spiketown, (see Carrick)..... ×
Spinnerstown, Bucks...... SE 100
Sporting Hill, Lancaster... SE 200
Spragg's, Greene.......... SW 25
● *Spragueville*, Monroe..... E 150
Sprankle's Mills, Jefferson.. W 90
Springboro, Crawford.... NW 490
● *Springboro Sta.*, C'wfo'dNW ×
Spring Brook, Lackawa'a. NE 25
Spring Church, Armstrong. W 150
● Spring City, Chester..... SE 1,797
● *Spring Creek*, Elk..........N ×
● *Spring Creek*, Lehigh..... E ×
● Spring Creek, Warren. NW 200
● Springdale, Allegheny.. SW 1,200
Springdale, (see Butler)...... ×
Springfield, (see Flourtown). ×
Springet, York ....S ×
Springfield, (see Normalville) ×
Springfield, Bradford....... N 75
● *Springfield*, Chester......SE 210
● *Springfield*, Erie........ NW 150
● *Springfield Junc.*, Blair.. C ×
● Spring Forge, York....... S 600
Spring Garden, Allegheny SW 720
Spring Garden, (see Floria).. ×
● *Spring Garden*, Schuylkill E ×
Spring Garden Sta., Philad'aSE ×
● *Spring Garden Junction*, Schuylkill .... E ×
Spring Grove, Lancaster...SE 150
● *Spring Grove*, York ...... S 576
Spring Hill, Bradford.........N 25
Spring Hill, (see Dimpsey) .. ×
Spring Hope, Bedford.......S 150
Spring House, M'tgomery. SE 200
Spring Meadow, Bedford... S 18
● *Spring Mill*, Lehigh....... E ×
● *Spring Mill*, Montgom'y SE 959
● Spring Mills, Centre...... C 200
● Spring Mount, M'tgom'y SE 100
● *Spring Mt. Siding*, Sc'lk'l.. E ×
Spring Run, Franklin....... S 200
● *Springton*, Chester...... SE ×
Springtown, Bucks.......... SE 400
● Sringvale, York .... S 50
Springville, (see Spring City).. ×
Springville, (see Salisbury) ... ×
● Springville, Susqueh'a.. NE 300
Spruce, Indiana........... W 25
● Spruce Creek, Huntingdon C 400
Spruce Grove, Lancaster.. SE 75
Spruce Hill, Juniata........ C 100
Spry, York.................. S 100
Square Corner, (see Bonneauville)......................... ×
Squaretop, Wyoming......NE 39
Stackstown, (see Bainbridge) ×
Stahlstown, Westmorel'd..SW 100
Stains, Cambria............. C ×
Staley, York .... S 30
● *Stambaugh*, Fayette....SW ×
● *Standard*, Westmorel'd SW ×
● Standing Stone, Bradford. N 225
● *Stanfield*, Blair.......... SE ×
● *Stanhope*, Schuylkill..... E ×
● Stanley, Clearfield......... C ×
● Stanton, Jefferson....... W 100
Stanton's Mill, Somerset.. SW 200
● Starlight, Wayne........NE ×
● *Starners*, Adams.......... S ×
Starr, Huntingdon.......... C ×
Starr, Forest............. NW 50
● Starrucca, Wayne....... NE 431
Star View, York .... S 100
● State College, Centre......C 200
● *State Line*, Bradford......N ×
● *State Line*, Erie........ NW ×
● *State Line*, Franklin...... S 50
State Line, Franklin........ S 300
● *State Line*, McKean...... N ×
● State Line Mills, McKean. N 500
● *Statler Mine*, Somerset SW ×
● Stauffer, Westmoreland SW 1,000
Steamburgh, Crawford... NW 200
● *Steam Pump*, Crawford NW ×
Steam Valley, Lycoming....N 25
● Steelton, Dauphin .... C 9,250
Steelville, Chester..........SE 140
● *Steiner's*, Centre...........C ×
Steinsburgh, Bucks.........SE 400
Steinsville, Lehigh.......... E 430
Stembersville, Carbon.......E 150
Stemton, Northampton... E 743
Stenger, Franklin........... S ×
● *Sterling*, Clearfield....... C ×
Sterling, Wayne............NE 150
● Sterling Run, Cameron... N 300
Sterner, York.............. S 50
Sterrettania, Erie......... NW 300
Sterrett's Gap, Perry........C 150
● *Stetlers*, Lehigh............E ×
Stetlersville, Lehigh........ E 130
Steuben, Lycoming.......... N ×
Steuben, Northampton..... E ×
● Stevens, Lancaster ...... SE 200
Stevenson's Mills, Wayne. NE 75
● Stevens Point, Susqueh'a NE 300
Stevensville, Bradford...... N 500
● Stewarton, Fayette..... SW ×
● *Stewarts*, Carbon.......... E ×
● *Stewarts*, Erie..........NW ×
● *Stewarts*, Cumberland.... S ×
Stewart's Run, Forest.... NW 75
● Stewart's Sta., W'tm'rel'd SW 120
Stewartstown, (see Etna)..... ×
● Stewartstown, York .. ... S 441
Stewartsville, (see Parkwood) ×
Stewartsville, W'tmorel'd..SW ×
Stickney, McKean........ N ×
● *Stiffler*, Blair .... C ×
● Stillwater, Columbia....... C 150
● *Stillwater*, Susqueh'a... NE ×
Stiltz, York.................. S 25
Stine's Corner, Lehigh...... E 100
● *Stockdale*, Washington..SW ×
Stockertown, Northampton E 250
● Stockton, Luzerne........ E 1,200
Stoddardsville, Luzerne.....E 200
● Stokesdale, Tioga .... N 75
● *Stokesdale Junction*, TiogaN ×
● Stoneboro, Mercer........ W 1,394
● *Stone Bridge*, Franklin... S ×
Stone Church, Northampton E 250
● *Stone Glen*, Dauphin......C ×
● Stoneham, Warren..... NW 200
Stonehouse, (see Martinsburg) ×
Stonehouse, (see Nolo) .... ×
● *Stone Mill*, Tioga .... N ×
Stone Quarry, Erie ...... NW ×
● *Stoner*, York................S ×
● *Stoners*, Westmoreland. SW 600
Stoner's Siding, (see Hellam). ×
Stonerstown, (see Saxton).... ×
Stonersville, Berks.......... SE 200
● *Stone Siding*, Schuylkill.. E ×
Stoney Hollow, (see Coaltown) ×
Stonington, Northumberl'd. C ×
● Stony Brook, York........S 100
● *Stony Creek*, Berks...... SE ×
● *Stony Creek*, Cambria..... C C
● *Stony Creek*, Carbon......E ×
Stony Creek, Somerset.....SW 100
● *Stony Creek*, Schuylkill.. E ×
Stony Creek Mills, Berks.. SE 150
Stony Fork, Tioga.......... N 150
Stony Point, (see Bursonville) ×
● Stony Point, Crawford. NW 40
Stony Run, Berks..........SE 130
● *Stonytown Ferry*, ColumbiaC ×
Stoops, Allegheny..........SW 20
Stoops Ferry, Allegheny..SW ×
Stormstown, Centre.........C 100
Stormville, Monroe.......... E 100
● *Stottsville*, Chester ......SE 50
Stouchsburgh, Berks...... SE 375
Stoughstown, Cumberland.. S 125
Stouts, Northampton....... E 150
● *Stover*, Huntingdon.......C ×
● *Stoverdale*, Dauphin...... C ×
● Stowe, Montgomery.......SE ×
● Stoyestown, Somerset...SW 291

Strabane, (see South Strabane) ×
● Strafford, Chester........SE 200
● *Straight*, Elk............N ×
● Strasburgh, Lancaster...SE 918
Strattonville, Clarion.......W 831
Strausstown, Berks........SE 500
Strawberry Ridge, Montour.C ×
● Strawbridge, Lycoming.. N ×
● *Stremmels*, Adams........S ×
Strickersville, Chester.....SE 200
● *Strickhauser*, York....... S ×
● *Strickler*, York.......... S ×
Strinestown, York.......... S 300
Strobleton, Clarion.........W ×
Strode's Mills, Mifflin........C 200
● Strong, Northumberland. C ×
Strongstown, Indiana...... W 125
● **Stroudsburgh**, MonroeE 2,419
● *Stroudsburgh*, Monroe... E ×
StroudsburghJunc.,North'mE ×
Strouptown, Snyder.........C 250
Stull, Wyoming........... NE ×
Stump Creek, (see Big Run).. ×
Stumptown, (see Groff's Store) ×
● Sturgeon, Allegheny....SW 27
Sturgis, Crawford........ NW ×
Sturmersville, Luzerne......E ×
● Suedberg, Schuylkill......E 250
Sugar Creek, (see Adams).... ×
● Sugar Creek, Venango. NW 43
Sugar Grove, Mercer.......W 100
Sugar Grove, Warren.....NW 500
Sugar Hill, Jefferson....... W 75
Sugar Lake, Crawford....NW 40
● Sugarloaf, Luzerne...... ..E 53
● *Sugar Loaf*, Columbia.... C ×
● *Sugar Loaf*, Luzerne..... E ×
● Sugar Notch, Luzerne.... E 2,586
Sugar Run, Bradford....... N 300
● *Sugar Run*, Warren... NW ×
● *SugarRunJunc.*,McKean N ×
Sugartown, Chester........SE 50
Sugar Valley, Clinton......N 500
Sullivan, Tioga..............N 50
● *Sulphur Spring*, Bedford.S 100
Sulphur Spring, Perry......C ×
● *Sumac*, Lehigh........... E ×
● Summer Hill, Cambria....C 608
● Summerville; Jefferson.. W 330
Summit, Bradford.......... N ×
Summit, Cambria...........C 100
● *Summit*, Centre.......... C ×
● *Summit*, Clearfield....... C ×
● *Summit*, Clearfield........C ×
Summit, Clinton............N ×
● *Summit*, Erie.......... NW ×
● *Summit*, Fayette........SW ×
● *Summit*, Crawford.....NW ×
● *Summit*, Northampton... E ×
● *Summit*, Mercer..........W 100
● *Summit*, Franklin........ S ×
● *Summit*, Tioga............N ×
● *Summit*, Tioga............N ×
● *Summit*, York............. S 50
● Summit City, McKean....N 75
Summit Cut, (see Homewood) ×
● Summit Hill, Carbon..... E 2,816
Summit Mills, Somerset.. SW 200
● Summit Mines, Fayette.SW 200
● *Summit Siding*,Cumberl'dS ×
Summit Station, (see Greer) . ×
● SummitStation,Schuylkill E 100
● *Summit Switch*, Luzerne..E ×
Summitville, (see Remington) ×
● *Sumner*, Allegheny.....SW ×
Sumneytown,Montgomery.SE 350
● **Sunbury**, Northumb'rldC 5,930
Sunbury, Butler............W 238
Suncliff, Indiana........... W 25
Sunderlinville, Potter...... N 300
Sunflower, (sec Kinzer's).... ×
Sunnyburn, York........... S 25
● *Sunny Side*, Adams.......S 125
SunnySideSta.,(see Valencia) ×
● Sunny Side, Allegheny..SW 200
● *Sunset*, Butler........... W ×
Sunset, Huntingdon.........C ×
● Sunset, Washington.... SW 44
● Sunshine, Wayne....... NE 28
Sunville, Venango........NW 106
● *Superior*, Allegheny.... SW ×
● Suplee, Chester..........SE 30
Surgeon's Hall, Allegheny SW 50
● *Susquehanna*, LancasterSE ×
● Susquehanna,Susqehan'. NE 3,872
● *SusquehannaBridge*,Clear'C ×
Suters, (see Sutersville)...... ×

● Sutersville,Westmore'd. SW 812
Suttee, Wyoming.........NE ×
Sutton's Cor's, (see Geneva) . ×
Sutton's Station,(see Geneva) ×
Sutton's Creek, Luzerne....E ×
Swales, Juniata............. C ×
Swan, York..................S ×
● Swanville, Erie.........NW 98
● Swarthmore, Delaware..SE 150
● Swart's, Greene.........SW 20
Swartzville, Lancaster.....SE 25
Swatara, Dauphin..........C ×
● Swatara, Schuylkill.......E 800
● Swatara Station, Dauphin.C 300
● Swedeland, Montgomery SE 250
Sweden, Potter.............N 25
● Sweden Valley, Potter....N ×
● *SwedesfordRoad*,ChesterSE ×
Sweet Valley, Luzerne...... E 100
● Swengel, Union...........C 50
Swiftwater, Monroe........ E 70
Swineford, Snyder.......... C ×
● Swissvale, Allegheny... SW ×
● *Switch Back*, Schuylkill.. E ×
Switzer, Lehigh.............E ×
Sybertsville, Luzerne....... E 100
● Sycamore, Greene...... SW 15
● Sykesville, Jefferson..... W 300
Syliman, Schuylkill........ E 60
Sylvan, Franklin............S 250
Sylvania, Bradford.........N 241
Sylvester, Tioga........... N 25
Sylvis, Clearfield.......... C 32
Syner, Lebanon............SE 75
● Table Rock, Adams.......S 50
Tablet, Chester......... .. SE 30
● *Tabor*, Philadelphia.....SE ×
TaborJunc.,Montgomery . SE ×
● Tacony, Philadelphia.... SE 1,200
Tafton, Pike............. NE 150
● *Taggart*, Potter..........N ×
Taintor Mills, McKean..... N ×
Talcose, Chester...........SE 50
Talley Cavey, Allegheny..SW 50
Tally Ho, McKean.........N ×
Talmanville, Wayne.......NE 47
● Tamanend, Schuylkill.... E 250
● Tamaqua, Schuylkill..... E 6,054
● Tamarac, Crawford.... NW 125
Tank, Luzerne..............E ×
Tank Siding, Luzerne......E ×
Tannehills, Somerset.....SW ×
Tanner's Falls, Wayne.... NE 125
Tannersville, Monroe....... E 450
● *Tannery*, Carbon.........E 260
Tannery, Indiana...........W ×
● *Tannery*, Luzerne........E ×
● *Tannery*, Potter..........N ×
Tanoma, Indiana........... W 30
Tanquy, Chester...........SE 25
● Tarrentum, Allegheny..SW 4,627
Target, Westmoreland.... SW 50
● *Tarport*, McKean........ N ×
● Tarrs, Westmoreland... SW 350
Tatamy, Northampton......E 150
● Tatesville, Bedford........S 150
Taurus, Columbia...........C ×
Tazville, York..............S ×
Tayloria, Lancaster........SE 30
Taylor's Stand, Cr'wf'd..NW 20
Taylorstown, (see Dunkard) ×
● Taylorstown, W'sh't'n..SW 400
Taylorsville, Bucks........SE 100
Taylorsville, (see Utah)...... ×
● *Taylorsville*, L'ckaw'na NE ×
Taylorsville, (see Barry)..... ×
Tecumseh, (see Everett)..... ×
Teepleville, Crawford....NW 20
● Telford, Montgomery...SE 125
Telfordville, (see Telford)... ×
Tell, Huntingdon...........C 32
● *Temperanceville*, Al'h'yTW ×
Temple, Berks............SE 200
Temple, Berks............SE ×
● Templeton, Armstroug...W 50
Templeton Sta., (see Myoma) ×
Ten Mile, Washington ... SW 75
Ten Mile Bottom, V'n'go. NW 50
Terminal Junction, L'gh...E ×
Terre Hill, Lancaster......SE 891
Terrytown, Bradford.......N 200
Terwood, Montgomery ....SE 50
Texas, (see New Texas)...... ×
Texas, (see Oakland)........ ×
Texas, Lycoming............. ×
Thatcher, Bucks..........SE ×

● *Thirty-Eight Mile Siding*, Cumberland.............C ×
Thisbe, Huntingdon .... C 25
● Thomas, Washington...SW 6
● *Thomas Mine*, SomersetSW ×
Thomas' Store, (see Talley Cavey)..................
● *Thomaston*, Schuylkill...E ×
Thomaston Colliery, Sc'ylk'lE ×
Thomasville, York..........S 600
● *Thompson*, Beaver....... W ×
● *Thompson*, Forest.....NW ×
● Thompson, Susquehanna SE 302
● *Thompson*, Warren.... NW ×
Thompsontown, Juniata ....C 291
● *Thompsontown Station*, Juniata ....C ×
Thompsonville, W'sh't'n..SW 39
● *Thomson*, Allegheny... SW ×
Thornbury, Chester........SE 300
● Thorndale Iron Works, Chester ....SE 20
Thornhill, Allegheny......S.W 500
Thornton, Delaware........SE 100
● *Thornton Junction*,ErieNW 502
● *Three Runs*, Clearfield....C 26
● Three Springs, H't'g'd'n..C 192
Three Tuns, Montgomery..SE 200
Throop, Lackawanna......NE 105
● Thurlow, Delaware......SE 7,000
Tiadagton, Tioga............N 50
Tidal, Armstrong...........N 25
● Tidioute, Warren.......NW 1,328
● Tie, Columbia ....C ×
● *Tiffany's*, Susquehanna NE ×
Tilden, York................S 100
Tillie, Adams ....S ×
Tillotson Crawford......NW ×
Timblin, Jefferson ....W ×
Time, Green...............SW 20
Timicula, Chester..........SE 40
● *Tin Bridge* Bradford.....N 20
Tinicum, Bucks...........SE ×
Tinker Run, (see Circleville) ×
● *Tinstman*, Fayette......SW 200
● *Tioga*, Philadelphia..... SE ×
● Tioga, Tioga..............N 557
● *Tioga Junction*, Tioga....N 25
Tioga Valley, (see Athens)... ×
● Tiona, Warren.........NW 50
● *Tiona*, Warren.........NW 50
Tionesta, Forest....... NW 677
Tionesta Creek, Forest...NW 150
● *Tionesta Station*,ForestNW ×
● Tippecanoe, Fayette,....SW 75
● Tipton, Blair..............C 150
● *Tip Top*, Fayette.......SW ×
Tirzah, Susquehanna......NE ×
● Titusville, Crawford....NW 8,073
● Tivoli, Lycoming.........N 127
Tob Junction, PhiladelphiaSE ×
Toboyne, Perry............C 50
Toby, Clarion...............W 40
● Tobyhanna Mills, Monroe E 500
● *Toby Mines*, Elk .... N ×
Todd, Huntingdon ....C 100
Tohickon, Buck............SE 200
Toledo, Washington.......SW 20
Toll Gate, (see Carrollton)... ×
● Tolna, York...............S 30
● Tomb's Run, Lycoming..N 39
Tome's McKean............N ×
Tomhicken, Luzerne........E ×
● *Tompkins*, Tioga.........N ×
● *Tompkins Breaker*, L'z'e E ×
Tompkinsville, L'kaw'na..NE 200
Tom's Run, (see Federal).... ×
Tom's Run,(seeHoover'sRun) ×
Tom's Run, Washington SW ×
Top, Armstrong............W 10
Topsail, Washington,..... SW 10
● Topton, Berks...........SE 500
● Torpedo, Warren.......NW 300
● *Torrens*, Allegheny .... SW ×
● Torresdale, Philadelphia.SE 390
Torrey, Wayne...........NE ×
● Tougkenamon, Chester. :SE 300
● **Towanda**, Bradford....N 4,169
● **Tower City**, Schuylkill....E 2,633
Town Hill, Luzerne......... E 150
Town Line, Luzerne.........E 50
Townsend, Chester.........SE 25
● *Townsend*, Westmorel'dSW ×
● *Township Line*, Northampton.......................E ×
Townville, Crawford......NW 358

Pennsylvania

Place	Pop.
Traction, Adams....S	10
Tracy, Erie....NW	40
Trade City, Indiana....W	75
Trader's Cross Roads, (see Woodside)....	×
Tradesville, Bucks....SE	25
● Trainer, Delaware....SE	700
Tranger, Westmoreland...SW	30
● Transfer, Mercer....W	200
Trappe, Montgomery....SE	200
● *Trauger*, Westmoreland SW	×
● *Traut Creek Sta.*, Lehigh. E	×
Treddyffrin, Chester....SE	30
● *Tree Forest*, Somerset..SW	×
● Treichler's, Northampton. E	150
Treichlersville, Lehigh....E	×
● Tremont, Schuylkill....E	2,064
● Trent, Somerset....SW	50
Tresckow, Carbon....E	300
Tressler's Siding, Wayne..NE	×
Trevillian, (see Friedensburg)	×
● Trevorton, Northumberl'd C	1,100
● Trevose, Bucks....SE	110
● Trexler, Berks....SE	50
● Trexlertown, Lehigh....E	400
● Trindle Spring, Cumberl'd S	×
Trinket, Bradford....N	×
● *Tripoli*, Lehigh....E	180
Triumph, (see Tidioute)....	×
● *Trotter*, Fayette....SW	×
Trough Creek, Huntingdon..C	200
Troutman, (see Magic)....	×
● Trout Run, Lycoming....N	320
Troutville, Clearfield....C	300
● Trowbridge, Tioga....N	20
Troxelville, Snyder....C	50
● Troy, Bradford....N	1,307
Troy, (see Summerville)....	×
Troy Centre, Crawford....NW	250
Truce, Lancaster....SE	50
● Trucksville, Luzerne....E	75
Truittsburgh, Clarion....W	100
● *Truman*, Cameron....N	100
Trumbauersville, Bucks....SE	300
● Trunkeyville, Forest...NW	72
Trust, Adams....S	60
● Tryonville, Crawford...NW	300
● *Trythall*, Chester....SE	25
Tub, Somerset....SW	25
● *Tucker Siding*, Erie....NW	×
● Tuckerton, Berks....SE	150
Tuckertown, (see Searights)..	×
● *Tucquan*, Lancaster....SE	×
● Tullytown, Bucks....SE	400
Tulpehocken, Berks....SE	200
● *Tulpehocken*, Phil'd'lphia SE	×
Tumbling Run, (see Middleport)....	×
● Tuna Creek, McKean....N	150
● **Tunkhannock**, Wyoming....NE	1,253
● *Tunnel*, Luzerne....E	×
● *Tunnel*, Somerset....SW	×
● *Tunnel*, Wyoming....NE	×
Tunnel Hill, Cambria....C	730
● *Tunnel Number Two*, Washington....SW	×
● *Tunnel Siding*, Wash'ton SW	×
● Tunnelton, Indiana....W	25
Tunnelville, Armstrong....S	10
● Turbotville, Northumberl'd C	441
● Turkey City, Clarion....W	100
Turkey Foot, Somerset....SW	50
Turkey Run, Schuylkill....E	×
Turnbach, Luzerne....E	75
Turner, Tioga....N	×
● *Turner's*, Mercer....W	×
Turner's Store, (see Pine Hill)	×
● Turnersville, Crawford. NW	100
Turnip Hole, Clarion....W	×
Turnpike, York....S	×
● Turtle Creek, Allegheny SW	3,000
● Turtle Point, McKean....N	300
● *Tuscarora*, Juniata....C	×
● Tuscarora, Schuylkill....E	290
Tusseyville, Centre....C	50
● Tweedale, Chester....SE	50
● *Twenty Seven Mile Siding*, Cumberland....S	×
● Twin Oaks, Delaware....SE	25
● Two Licks, Indiana....W	×
Two Taverns, Adams....S	100
● Tyler, Clearfield....C	200
● *Tyler*, Susquehanna....NE	×
Tyler Hill, Wayne....NE	150
● Tylersburgh, Clarion....W	250
Tyler's Port, Montgomery. SE	680

Pennsylvania

Place	Pop.
Tylersville, Clinton....N	300
● Tyrone, Blair....C	4,705
● *Tyrone*, Fayette....SW	×
● *Tyrone Forges*, Hunter'on C	×
Tyrone Mines, (see Broad Ford)	×
Uber, Mercer....W	×
Uhlerstown, Bucks....SE	100
Uhlersville, Northampton..E	×
● Ulster, Bradford....N	400
Ulysses, Potter....N	700
● *Underwood*, Warren...NW	×
Unicorn, Lancaster....SE	150
Union, (see Union City)....	×
Union, (see Colerain)....	×
Union, (see Brogueville)....	×
Union Church, Huntingdon. C	25
● Union City, Erie....NW	2,261
Union Corner, Northumber'd C	25
● Union Dale, Susquehan'a NE	360
Union Deposit, Dauphin....C	400
Union Forge, (see Lickdale)..	×
● *Union Furnace*, Hunting'n C	200
Union L'd'g, (see Coal Bluff).	×
Union Square, (see Old Lion)	×
● **Uniontown**, Fayette..SW	6,359
Uniontown, Dauphin....C	333
● *Unionville*, Centre....C	348
Unionville, (see Brush Creek)	×
Unionville, (see Kintnersville)	×
Unionville, (see McCandless).	×
Unionville, (see Fleming)....	×
Unionville, (see Penn)....	×
Unionville, Chester....SE	348
Union Water Works, (see Annville)....	×
● United, Westmoreland..SW	300
● *Unity*, Allegheny....SW	300
Unity Station, Allegheny..SW	×
Unityville, Lycoming....N	50
Uno, York....S	50
● Upland, Delaware....SE	2,275
Upper Bern, Berks....SE	50
Upper Black Eddy, Bucks. SE	100
Upper Darby, Delaware....SE	300
Upper Dublin, (see Ambler)..	×
Upper Hanover, (see Red Hill)	×
● *Upper Hibernia*, Chester. SE	×
● Upper Lehigh, Luzerne...E	1,000
● *Upper Lehigh Junc.*, Luz'ne E	×
Upper Mauch Chunk, Carb'n E	×
Upper Merion, (see King of Prussia)....	×
● Upper Middlet'wn, F'yte. SW	100
● *Upper Mill*, Cumberland.S	×
Upper Providence, D'law're SE	150
Upper Saint Clair, Allegh'y SW	1,300
Upper Strasburgh, Franklin. S	450
Upper Talley Cavey, (see Talley Cavey)....	×
● *Upsal*, Philadelphia....SE	×
Upsonville Susquehanna. NE	150
● *Upton*, Delaware....SE	×
Upton, Franklin....S	200
Urban, Northumberland....C	100
Urey, Indiana....W	×
● Uriah, Cumberland....S	200
● Ursina, Somerset....SW	405
● *Ursina Branch*, Somers't SW	×
Useful, Clearfield....C	×
Uswick, Wayne....NE	×
Utah, Indiana....W	50
● Utahville, Clearfield....C	300
● *Utceter*, Lycoming....N	390
● Utica, Venango....NW	221
● Uwchland, Chester....SE	250
Vail, Blair....C	10
● Valencia, Butler....W	100
Valier, Jefferson....W	100
Valley, Clarion....W	75
● *Valley*, Chester....SE	×
● *Valley Camp*, W'stm'rel'd SW	×
● *Valley Falls*, M'tg'mery SE	×
● Valley Forge, Chester... SE	200
Valley Inn, (see Monongahela City)....	×
● *Valley Junc.*, L'ck'aw'na NE	32
● *Valley Junc.*, York....S	10
Valley Mill, Bedford....S	×
● *Valley Mines*, Fayette..SW	×
Valley Point, Huntingdon..C	25
● *Valley Store*, Chester....SE	50
Valley View, Schuylkill....E	300
● *Valley Works*, Fayette.SW	×
Vallonia, Crawford....NW	548
Van Buren, Washington..SW	40
Van Camp, Columbia....C	100
● *Vance*, Washington....SW	×

Pennsylvania

Place	Pop.
Vancefort, (see Coraopolis)..	×
Vance Mills, Fayette....SW	×
● *Vance Mills Jc.*, Fayette SW	×
Vanceville, Washington..SW	50
● Vanderbilt, Fayette....SW	1,500
● *Vandegrift*, Warren...NW	×
● Van Dyke, Juniata....C	100
● *Van Emman*, Wash'ton. SW	×
● *Vankirk*, Allegheny....SW	×
● *Vankirk*, Washington..SW	×
● Van Ormer, Cambria....C	20
● Vanport, Beaver....W	300
Vanscoyoc, Blair....C	×
Vantassel, Jefferson....W	×
Van Wert, Juniata....C	450
Varden, Wayne....NE	×
Varnersville, (see Hulton)...	×
● *Vastine*, Northumb'land. C	×
Vawter, Bradford....N	40
Velarde, Bradford....N	30
● Venango, Crawford....NW	278
● Venetia, Washington....SW	200
Venice, Washington....SW	100
Ventland, Clearfield....C	×
Venus, Venango....NW	100
● Vera Cruz, Lehigh....E	350
Vera Cruz, (see Reinhd'sSta.)	×
Verdilla, Snyder....C	15
● *Verner*, Allegheny....SW	×
Vernon, Wyoming....NE	100
Verona, (see Seward)....	×
Verona Station, (see Verona)	×
● Verona, Allegheny....SW	1,477
Verree's Mills, Philadel'ia. SE	×
Versailles, Allegheny....SW	×
Vesta, (see Marietta)....	×
Vetera, Cambria....C	25
● Viaduct, Clearfield....C	×
Vicary, Beaver....W	×
● Vicksburgh, Union....C	175
● Victor, Clearfield....C	195
Video, Greene....SW	×
● *Vienna*, Washington....SW	50
Village Green, Delaware...SE	250
● *Village Green*, Delaware SE	×
Villa Maria, Lawrence....W	×
● Villanova, Delaware....SE	50
Vincent, Chester....SE	50
Vinco, Cambria....C	59
● Vinemont, Berks....SE	65
● *Vineyard Run*, Jefferson W	×
● *Vineyard*, Mifflin....C	×
Vintage, Lancaster....SE	200
Vira, Mifflin....C	20
● *Virginia Junc.*, Wash'n SW	×
● Virginia Mills, Adams....S	×
● Virginville, Berks....SE	75
Virsoix, Allegheny....SW	×
Virtus, Bradford....N	×
Vogansville, Lancaster....SE	200
● Volant, Lawrence....W	150
● *Volcano*, Fayette....SW	×
Voltair, York....S	25
Vosburg, Wyoming....NE	150
Vose, Wyoming....NE	140
● Vowinckel, Clarion....W	75
Vrooman, Crawford....NW	32
Wade, Schuylkill....E	428
● *Wade Siding*, Wash'ton SW	×
● Wagner, Mifflin....C	100
● Wagontown, Chester....SE	50
Wakefield, Lancaster....SE	250
● *Walbert*, Lehigh....E	150
Walkchalk, Armstrong....W	60
Walker, Centre....C	200
● *Walker*, Fayette....SW	×
● *Walker's*, Tioga....N	×
● Walker's Mills, Alleg'y..SW	300
● Wall, Allegheny....SW	600
● *Wallace*, Allegheny....SW	×
● *Wallace*, Allegheny....SW	×
Wallace, Chester....SE	50
● *Wallace Junction*, Erie NW	×
● Wallaceton, Clearfield....C	250
Wallaceville, Venango....NW	75
Waller, Columbia....C	83
● Wallingford, Delaware..SE	200
Wallis Run, Lycoming....N	25
● *Wallner*, Lehigh....E	×
Wall Rose, Beaver....W	100
Wallsville, Lackawanna..NE	100
Walnut, Juniata....C	100
Walnut Bend, Venango...NW	×
● Walnut Bottom, Cumb'l'd S	250
Walnut Grove, Cambria....C	535
● *Walnut Hill*, M'tgom'ry SE	×
● *Walnut Lane*, Philad'la SE	×

● Walnutport, Northam'n..E	350
● *Walnut Town*, Berks...SE	×
Walsall, Cambria.........C	×
● Walston, Jefferson.........W	2,000
Walters, Northampton.......E	×
● Waltersburgh, Fayette..SW	30
Walter's Mill, Northampt'n E	×
Walter's Park, Berks......SE	×
● *Walton*, Allegheny......SW	×
● *Walton*, Bucks..........SE	×
Waltonville, Dauphin.......C	×
Walt's Mill, W'moreland..SW	30
Walurba, Allegheny......SW	×
● Wampum, Lawrence.....W	766
● *Wampum Junc.*, Law'ce.W	×
● Wanamakers, Lehigh.....E	75
● Wanamie, Luzerne.......E	500
Wapasening, Bradford......N	×
● Wapwallopen, Luzerne....E	200
● *Wapwallopen*, Luzerne...E	×
Warble, Juanita............C	25
Ward, Delaware...........SE	150
Wardville, Perry...........C	25
Warfordsburgh, Fulton.....S	150
● Warminster, Bucks......SE	200
● **Warren**, Warren......NW	4,332
Warren Centre, Bradford...N	160
Warrenham, Bradford.......N	58
Warren Point, Franklin.....S	10
Warrensville, Lycoming....N	200
● Warren Tavern, Chester.SE	50
Warrington, Bucks........SE	125
● *Warrior Run*, N'mberl'd.C	×
● *Warrior Run*, Luzerne...E	×
● Warrior's Mark, Hunt'on.C	550
Warsaw, Jefferson.........W	163
● *Warwick*, Bucks........SE	×
● Warwick, Chester........SE	50
Warwick, (see Lititz)........	×
Warwick Furnace, Ches'r SE	×
Washington, (see Sherrett)..	×
Washington, (see Armagh)..	×
● *Washington*, Lancaster..SE	562
● **Washington**, Wash'nSW	7,063
Washington Borough, Lancaster.....................SE	562
● *Washington Mines* Fa'teSW	×
● Washingtonville, Mont'r..C	171
Watch, (see Lancaster).......	×
● Water Cure, Beaver......W	1,200
Waterfall, Fulton...........S	64
● Waterford, Erie..........NW	838
Waterford, (see East W't'rf'd)	×
Waterford (see O'k Gr've Fur)	×
● *Water Gap*, Monroe.......E	400
Waterloo, Juniata...........C	300
Waterside, Bedford..........S	88
● *Water Station*, N'h'm'l'nd C	×
● Water Street, Huntingt'n..C	75
● *Water Street*, Crawford NW	×
Watersville, (see Wolf's Run)	×
Waterton, Luzerne..........E	50
● Waterville, Lycoming.....N	55
Waterville, Delaware......SE	×
● *Watrous*, Tioga...........N	25
● *Watson*, Allegheny......SW	×
● *Watson*, Warren.......NW	×
Watson Run, Crawford...NW	×
● *Watson Run*, Crawford NW	×
● *Watson's* Forest.......NW	×
● Watsontown, N'h'm'land.C	2,157
● *Watsontown*, Allegheny SW	×
Watsontown Station, (see Hope Church)............	×
● *Watsontown Junc.* N'la'd C	×
● Watsonville, McKean.....N	2,200
Watterson's Ferry, (see Phillipsburgh)...........	×
Wattersonville, Armstrong W	100
● *Watts*, Fayette..........SW	×
● *Watts*, Lancaster.......SE	×
Wattsburgh, Erie.........NW	382
● *Watt's Mill*, Beaver......W	×
Wauekna, Westmoreland SW	/
Waukesha, Clearfield.......C	×
● Waverly, Lackawanna..NE	292
Waverly Heights, (see Edge Hill)...................	×
● Wawa, Delaware.........SE	100
● Wawaset, Chester........SE	30
Waydesville, (see St. Clair)...	×
Wayland, Crawford.......NW	24
● Waymart, Wayne.........NE	438
● Wayne, Delaware........SE	997
Wayne, (see Ovid).......NW	×
● *Wayne*, Clinton..........N	100
● *Wayne Junc.* Philadel'a.SE	×

● Waynesborough, Franklin S	3,811
● **Waynesburgh**, Gre'eSW	2,101
● *Waynesburgh Junc.* Ch'rSE	×
Waynesville, Dauphin.......C	41
● Weatherly, Carbon........E	2,961
Weaverland, Lancaster....SE	×
● *Weaver's* Perry..........C	×
Weaver's Mills, (see Spring Grove).............	×
Weaver's Mills. (see Bottsville)	×
● *Weaver's Old Stand*, Westmoreland.............	50
Weaver...n, (see Bird in Hand)...................	×
Weaversville, Northampton E	200
● Webster, WestmorelandSW	600
● *Webster*, Washington...SW	×
Webster Mills, Fulton.......S	180
● *Weedsport*, McKean......N	×
● Weedville, Elk............N	85
Wehr, Schuylkill...........E	50
Weidasville, Lehigh.........E	150
Weigelstown, York..........S	200
● *Weigh Scales*, North'rland C	195
● Weikert, Union..........C	80
Weintz, Luzerne............E	×
Weisenburgh, Lehigh.......E	150
Weisenhample, Schuylkill..E	50
● Weissport, Carbon........E	456
● *Welch*, Somerset........SW	×
Weldon, Montgomery.....SE	300
● *Weld's*, Somerset.......SW	×
Wellersburg, Somerset....SW	183
● *Wellington*, Lehigh.......E	×
Welliversville, Columbia....C	260
Wells, Bradford..............N	300
● **Wellsborough**, Tioga.N	2,961
Wellsburg, Erie..........NW	500
Wells' Tannery, Fulton.....S	82
Wellsville, York.............S	200
● *Welshdale*, Clearfield.....C	×
● *Welshdale Mines*, Cl'rfieldC	×
Welsh Hill, Luzerne........E	×
Welsh Run, Franklin.........S	100
● *Welshtown Branch Junc.*, Lehigh...................E	×
Welty, Westmoreland.....SW	38
Wenks, Adams..............S	100
Wenksville, Adams..........S	100
Wennersville, Lehigh.......E	×
Werley's Corner, Lehigh.....E	50
● Wernersville, Berks.....SE	1,000
● *Wertz*, Blair..............C	×
Wertzville, Cumberland.....S	×
● Wesco, Washington.......SW	25
Wescosville, Lehigh.........E	200
Wesley, Venango..........NW	113
● Wesleyville, Erie.......NW	500
West, Berks..............SE	×
● West Alexandria, Wa'n.SW	444
● *West Amity*, Wash'ton S W	×
West Auburn, Susqueh'na. NE	300
West Bangor, York.........S	400
● *West Bangor*, Northam'n.E	×
West Bellevue, Allegheny..SW	804
West Bethany, Westmoreland.................. SW	200
West Bethlehem, Lehigh....E	2,759
West Bingham, Potter..... N	30
West Branch, Potter........N	16
● West Bridgewater, B'ver. W	1,200
Westbrook, Lancaster......SD	×
West Brooklyn, Susqueh'a NE	46
● West Brownsville, Wa'n.SW	735
● *West Brownsville Junction*, Washington.............SW	×
West Burlington, Bradford. N	300
● *West Carbondale*, Lackawanna..................NE	×
● *West Chartiers*, Alle'ny.SW	×
● **West Chester**, Chester SE	8,028
West Clearfield, Clearfield...C	621
West Colang, Pike.........NE	150
● *Westcolang Park*, Pike NE	×
● *West Columbia*, West'l'dSW	×
● West Conshohocken, Montgomery..................SE	1,666
West Covington, Tioga......N	25
● *West Creek*, Cameron.....N	×
West Dale, (see Oakdale).....	×
West Damascus, Wayne...NE	25
● West Decatur, Clearfield...C	50
West Dublin, Fulton..........S	50
West Earl, Lancaster......SE	940
● West Elizabeth, Alle'ny..SW	719
West End, Bedford..........S	225
West End, Allegheny......SW	×

● *West End*, Schuylkill.....E	×
● *West Eureka No. Three*, Jefferson .... W	×
West Fairfield, W'tmorel'dSW	100
● West Fairview, Cumberla'dS	1,137
● *West Falls*, PhiladelphiaSE	×
● Westfield, Tioga.......... N	1,128
West Finley, Washington. SW	150
● Westford, Crawford....NW	×
West Franklin, Bradford...N	100
West Freedom, Clarion.....W	500
West Greene, Erie.........NW	100
West Greenville, (see Greenv'e)	×
West Greenwood, Craw'f'rdNW	65
● West Grove, Chester.....SE	900
West Hanover, Dauphin.....C	250
● *West Hawley*, Wayne... NE	×
West Haverford, (see Bryn Mawr)	×
West Hazleton, Luzerne.... E	931
● West Hickory, Forest.. NW	550
West Indiana, Indiana..... W	×
West Kane, (see Kane)......	×
West Kittanning, (see Kittann'g)	×
West Latrobe, Westmor'ndSW	591
● *West Laurel Hill*, Philad'aSE	×
West Lebanon, Indiana......W	175
● *West Lebanon*, Lebanon.SE	×
● West Leesport, Berks... SE	1,000
West Leisenring, Fayette. SW	700
West Lemon, Wyoming..NE	×
West Lenox, Susquehanna. NE	25
West LeRoy, Bradford......N	25
West Liberty, Allegheny..SW	863
West Liberty, Butler....... W	100
West Mahoning, (see Smicksb'g)	×
● *West Manayunk*, Phil'iaSE	300
West Manchester, York.......S	75
● *West Meyersdale*, SomersetSW	×
● West Middlesex, Mercer. W	966
West Middletown, Washi'nSW	235
● West Mill Creek, Erie..NW	44
● West Millville, Clarion... W	376
● West Milton, Union....... C	100
● *Westmont*, Lebanon.....SE	×
● West Monterey, Clarion..W	250
● *West Moreland*, Philade'aSE	×
West Moshannon, (see Houtzd'e)	×
● West Nanticoke, Luzerne. E	400
● *West New Castle*, Lawr'ceW	1,761
● West Newton, Westmla'dSW	2,285
● *West Newton Mines*, Westmoreland............ SW	×
West Nicholson, WyomingNE	40
Weston, Luzerne............E	150
Weston, Bradford...........N	260
● Westover's, Clearfield.....C	75
● West Overton, Westmo'dSW	150
● *West Penn*, Schuylkill....E	×
● *West Pennsylvania Junc.*, Westmoreland........ SW	100
West Philadelphia, Philad'aSE	×
West Pike, Potter..........N	50
West Pikeland, Chester....SE	75
West Pike Run, Washing'nSW	26
West Pittsburg, (see Pittsburg)	×
● *West Pittson*, Luzerne....E	3,906
● West Point, MontgomerySE	350
● Westport, Clinton.........N	374
● *West Rochester*, Beaver..W	×
● *West Salisbury*, Somers'tSW	×
West Shamokin, Northum'dC	×
West Shenandoah, Schuyl'llE	×
West Spring Creek, Was'nNW	200
West Springfield, Erie....NW	200
● *West Spring Mill*, Phila'aSE	×
West Sunbury, Butler......W	450
West Terry, Bradford.......N	×
● Westtown, Chester...... SE	60
West Union, (see Leasurev'e)	×
● West Union, Greene.... SW	32
● *West Union*, Crawford. NW	×
West Union, Washington.SW	25
West Valley, Armstrong... W	×
● *West Vernon*, CrawfordNW	×
West View, Allegheny.... SW	260
Westville, Jefferson.......W	×
West Vincent, Chester.....SE	75
West Warren, Bradford.......N	115
● West Whiteland, Chester SE	1,500
● West Willow, Lancaster..SE	300
● *Westwood*, Schuylkill....E	×
● *Westwood Jc.*, Schuylkill..E	×
● *West York*, York......... S	×
● *West Yough*, Fayette....SE	×
● Westmore, McKean...... N	300
Wetonia, Bradford...........N	50
● *Wetzel*, Berks............SE	×

Wexford, Allegheny...... SW 150
Wharton, Potter........... N 150
Wheatland, (see Jefferson Fur.) ×
● Wheatland, Mercer.......W 575
● Wheatland Mills, Lancas'r SE 110
● *Wheat Sheaf*, Bucks.... SE ×
● *Wheedale*, Warren.....NW ×
Wheeler, Mercer........... W 150
● *Wheeler*, Fayette.........SE ×
Wheelock, Erie...........NW 32
● *Whetham*, Clinton........N 25
Whig Hill, Forest........ NW 150
● Whistletown, Elk........ N 65
● *Whitaker*, Lancaster....SE ×
White, Fayette............SW 10
● *White*, Indiana.........W ×
● White Ash, Allegheny.. SW 200
● *White Bear*, Berks......SE ×
White Bridge, Blair........ C ×
White Cottage, Greene.....SW 25
● *White Deer*, Union........C 217
● White Deer Mills, Union..C 165
● White Gravel, McKean...N ×
White Hall, Montour........C 195
● *Whitehall*, Lehigh........E 350
Whitehall, (see Carrick)..... ×
White Hall, (see Camp Hill).. ×
Whitehall, (see Bart)......... ×
Whitehall, (see Bryn Mawr). ×
● *Whitehall*, Allegheny...SW ×
Whitehall, (see Philadelphia) ×
Whitehallville, (see Chalfant) ×
● White Haven, Luzerne....E 1,634
● *White Hill*, Cumberland..S ×
White Horse, Chester......SE 200
● *White Horse*, Chester....SE ×
● *White Horse*, Dauphin....C ×
● *Whiteland*, Chester......SE 1,506
Whiteley, Greene......... SW 100
● *White Marsh*, Montg'ry SE 126
White Mills, (see Shire Oaks) ×
● White Mills, Wayne....NE 600
● White Oak, Lancaster... SE 50
White Pine, Lycoming......N 500
● White Rock, Lancaster..SE 100
White Rock Station, (see Connellsville)................ ×
Whitesburgh, Armstrong...W 60
White's Corners, Potter.......N 31
● *White Spring*, Dauphin...C 30
White's Tannery, Bedford...S 100
Whitestown, Butler........W 100
● White's Valley, Wayne..NE 150
Whitesville, (see Hamilton)... ×
● Whitford, Chester......... SE 75
Whitney, Westmoreland..SW ×
● Whitsett, Fayette.......SW ×
● Wick, Butler..............W 25
Wickizer, Bradford......... N ×
● Wiconisco, Dauphin....... C 800
Widnoon, Armstrong ......W 25
● *Wiggan*, Schuylkill.......E ×
Wigton, Clearfield.......... C ×
Wilawana, Bradford........N 500
Wilber, Potter..............N 26
Wilbur, McKean........... N ×
● Wilcox, Elk.............. N 1,037
● *Wilcox*, Bradford.........N ×
Wildbrier, Chester.........SE 50
Wilburton, Columbia.........C ×
● *Wild Cat Falls*, Lanc'ster SE ×
Wildwood, Allegheny...... SW 300
● Wildwood Springs, Cambria C 25
Wiley Greene,............. SW 15
Wilkes-Barre, Luzerne...E 37,718
● Wilkinsburgh, Alleghe'y SW 4,662
Willet, Indiana............. W 20
● William Penn, Montg'ry SE 800
William Penn, (see Shaft)... ×
● Williams, Somerset.....SW 100
● *Williams*, Forest...... NW ×
● *Williams*, Montgomery..SE ×
Williamsburg, (see Kittanning).............. ×
Williamsburg, Clarion..... W 50
● Williamsburgh, Blair...... C 888
● *Williamsburgh Junc.*, Bl'r C ×
● Williams Corner, Chester SE 30
● Williams Grove, Clearfield. C 200
● Williams Mill, Cumberland S 100
● *William's Mills*, McKean. N ×
● *Williams Mine*, Somerset SW ×
● Williamson, Franklin......S 20
● Williamson School, Delaware...............SE ×
● **Williamsport**, Lyco'g. N 27,132
Williamstown, (see Kinzer's) ×

● Williamstown, Dauphin...C 2,324
Williamstown, Lehigh......E ×
Willowanna, Bradford......N 500
Williston, Potter............N 32
Willistown Inn, Chester... SE 150
● Willock, Allegheny.......SW ×
Willowdale, Chester....... SE 50
● *Willow Grove*, Columbia..C ×
● Willow Grove, M'tgom'y SE 300
● *Willow Grove*, Allegh'y, SW ×
● *Willow Grove*, Allegh'y. SW ×
Willow Hill, Franklin.......S 20
● Willow Springs, Columbia C 40
Willow Street, Lancaster...SE 400
Willow Tree, Greene..... SW ×
● *Will's Creek*, Bedford.....S ×
● Wilmerding, Allegheny. SW 419
● *Wilmington Junc.*, Lawr'e W ×
Wilmington, (see New Wilmington)............... ×
● Wilmore, Cambria..........C 350
Wilmot, Bradford..........N 100
Wilna, Washington........SW ×
● *Wilson*, Allegheny.......SW ×
● *Wilson*, Allegheny......SW ×
Wilson's Mills, Crawf'd..NW ×
Wilton, Lackawanna......NE 1,797
● Wimmer's, Lackawanna NE 300
● Winburne, Clearfield......C 500
● *Windfall*, McKean.......N ×
Windfall, Bradford..........N ×
● Wind Gap, Northampton..E 200
● *Wind Gap Summit*, Northampton.............E ×
Windham, Bradford........N 210
Windham Centre, Bradford. N 160
Windham Summit, Bradf'd. N 25
Windom, Lancaster.........SE 50
Wind Ridge, Greene......SW 200
● *Windsor*, York...........S ×
Windsor, York.............S 125
Windsor Castle, Berks.....SE 80
● Winfield, Union...........C 300
Wingate, Centre............C ×
● *Wingert*, Cumberland.....S ×
Wingerton, Franklin........S 200
● *Wingohocking*, Phila....SE ×
● Winslow, Jefferson........W 90
● *Winslow Station*, Jeffers'n W ×
Winsted, Fayette..........SW ×
● Winterburn, Clearfield....C 200
Winterdale, Wayne........NE 159
Winterstown, York......... E 200
Wintersville, Berks.........SE 20
● Winton, Lackawanna...NE 1,797
Wiota, York................S 25
Wismer, Bucks.............SE 200
● *Wissahickon*, Phila......SE ×
● *Wissahickon H'ghts*, Phil. SE ×
● *Wissinoming*, Phil.......SE ×
● *Wistar*, Clinton..........N 57
● *Wister*, Philadelphia ....SE ×
● *Wister Junction*, Clearf'd. C ×
● *Wister Mine*, Clearfield...C ×
● Witmer, Lancaster.........SE 200
Wittenberg, Somerset......SW 100
● *Wittmer*, Allegheney...SW ×
Wolfenden, Delaware...... SE 260
● *Wolfersberger*, Somerset SW ×
● Wolfsburgh, Bedford......S 150
Wolf Run, Lycoming.......N 121
Wolf's Run, Fayette......SW ×
● *Wolf's Siding*, Somerset SW ×
Wolf's Store, Centre........C 50
● *Wolverton*, Northumber'd. C ×
● Womelsdorf, Berks......SE 1,141
● Woodbine, York..........S 250
● *Woodbine*, Chester......SE ×
● Woodbourne, Bucks......SE 25
Woodbury, Bedford.........S 260
Woodcock, Crawford.....NW 140
Wooddale, Fayette.........SW ×
Woodglen, Fayette.........SW 20
● *Woodhill*, Venango....NW ×
● Woodland, Clearfield......C 650
● *Woodland*, McKean......N ×
Woodland Sta. (see Concordville)............ ×
● Woodlawn, Beaver.........W 150
Woodley, Northampton.....E 150
Woodlyn, Delaware........SE ×
Woodrow, Washington....SW 20
Woodruff, Greene..........SW ×
● *Woods*, Somerset.......SW ×
Woodside, Fayette.........SW 30
● *Woodside*, Montgomery. SE ×
● *Woodside*, Luzerne.......E ×

● *Woodside*, Dauphin.......C ×
● *Wood's Mill*, Warren..NW ×
Wood's Run, Washington. SW 100
Wood's Run, (see Allegheny City).................. ×
Woodstock, Franklin.......S ×
Woodvale, (see Johnstown).. ×
● *Woodvale*, McKean.......N ×
● Woodville, Allegheny...SW 800
Woodward, Centre..........C 100
Woolrich, Clinton ....N ×
Wopsononock, Blair........C ×
Worcester, Montgomery...SE 100
Worman, Berks ....SE ×
● Wormleysburgh, Cum'l'd. S 555
Worth, Mercer............W 150
Worthington, Armstrong...W 246
Worthville, Jefferson.......W 176
● *Worthman Run*, Fay'e. SW ×
Woxall, Montgomery......SE 100
● *Wright's*, McKean.......N 100
Wrightsdale, Lancaster....SE 100
Wrightstown, Bucks.......SE 50
● Wrightsville, York..........S 1,912
● Wurtemberg, Lawrence..W 200
● Wyalusing, Bradford.....N 438
Wyattville, Venango .....NW ×
● Wyebrook, Chester......SE ×
● Wylandville, Wash'ton. SW 15
● *Wylie*, Allegheny.......SW ×
Wymps Gap, Fayette......SW 50
Wyncote, Montgomery....SE ×
● *Wyndmoor*, Philadelphia SE ×
● Wynnewood, M'tgomery SE ×
Wyola, Delaware..........SE ×
Wyoming, (see Greece City) ×
● Wyoming, Luzerne.......E 1,794
● *Wyside*, Cameron.......N ×
● Wysox, Bradford.........N 310
● Yardley, Bucks..........SE 813
Yates, Luzerne............E ×
● *Yatesville*, Luzerne.......E 414
● *Yatesville*, Schuylkill.....E 750
Yawdim, Lebanon.........SE 26
Yeadon, Delaware.........SE ×
● Yeagertown, Mifflin ......C 400
● *Yeatman*, Chester...... SE ×
Yellow Creek, Bedford.....S 65
Yellow House, Berks......SE 90
● *Yellow Run*, Cambria....C ×
Yellow Spring, Blair........C 75
● *Yellow Spring*, Lebanon SE ×
● Yerkes, Montgomery....SE 25
Yocum Hill, Potter..........N ×
Yokumtown, York..........S 300
● *Yoder*, Somerset........SW ×
Yoe, York..................S 225
● Yohogany, Westm'rland SW 50
Yordy, Northumberland.... C 75
● **York**, York..............S 20,793
Yorkana, York.............S 500
● *York Farm Junction*, Schuylkill...............E ×
York Furnace, York........S 100
● *York Furnace*, Lancaster SE ×
● York Haven, York.........S 200
York New Salem, York.....S 450
York Springs, Adams.......S 340
York Sulphur Springs, York S ×
Yorkville, Schuylkill........E 916
Yortysville, (see Odell)....... ×
Yostville, Lackawana.....NE 130
● *Yough*, Fayette...........SW ×
● *Yough Slope*, W'stm'rl'd SW ×
● *Youngstown*, Fayette.. SW ×
Youngstown, Westm'rl'd SW 486
● *Youngstown Junction*, Fayette,..............SW ×
● Youngsville, Warren... NW 667
Youngtown, (see Manor).... ×
● *Young Women's Creek*, Clinton ....N ×
● Youngwood, W'stm'rl'd SW 60
● *Younts*, Bedford..........S ×
● *Zaner's*, Columbia........ C ×
● *Zanmore*, Clinton....... N ×
● *Zediker*, Washington... SW ×
● Zehner, Luzerne..........E 350
● *Zehner's*, Schuylkill.....E ×
● Zelienople, Butler........W 639
Zella, Perry..............C ×
Zeller, Beaver.............W ×
Zeno, Butler...............W ×
● *Zerly*, Centre...........C ×
● Zermatt, Chester........SE 30
● Zieglerville, Montgomery SE 410
Zimmermantown, (see Pitman) ×

Town, County	Index	Pop.
Zion, Centre	C	100
Zion Hill, Bucks	SE	150
● *Zion's Church*, C'mbrl'd	S	×
● Zion's Grove, Schuylkill	E	300
Zion's View, York	S	75
● Zionsville, Lehigh	E	150
Zollarsville, Washington	SW	50
Zucksville, Northampton	E	×
Zullinger, Franklin	S	50

RHODE ISLAND.

COUNTIES.	INDEX.	POP.
Bristol	E	11,428
Kent	C	26,754
Newport	SE	28,552
Providence	N	255,123
Washington	S	23,649
Total		345,506

*In many of the towns of the state the population given embraces the township.

TOWN. COUNTY.	INDEX.	POP.
● Abbott Run, Providence	N	×
Adamsville, Newport	SE	400
● Albion, Providence	N	800
● *Alice Avenue*, Providence	N	×
● *Allendale*, Providence	N	100
Allenton, Washington	S	500
● Anthony, Kent	C	1,000
● Apponaug, Kent	C	700
Arcadia, Washington	S	75
● Arctic, Kent	C	800
● *Arkwright*, Kent	N	300
● *Arlington*, Providence	N	×
● Arnold Mills, Providence	N	×
● Ashaway, Washington	S	500
Ashland, Providence	N	×
● Ashton, Providence	N	1,200
● Auburn, Providence	N	500
Barrington, Bristol	E	1,461
● Barrington Centre, Bristol	E	×
● *Bay Side*, Kent	C	×
● *Bellefont*, Providence	N	×
● *Bellville*, Washington	S	×
● *Berkeley*, Providence	N	×
Block Island, Newport	SE	×
● *Boston Switch*, Providence	N	×
● *BraytonStreet*, Providence	N	×
● **Bristol**, Bristol	E	5,478
● Bristol Ferry, Newport	SE	50
● Buttonwoods, Kent	C	×
Canonchet, Washington	S	×
● Carolina, Washington	S	400
● Central Falls, Providence	N	9,000
● Centerdale, Providence	N	200
Centreville, Kent	C	1,500
● *Centreville Station*, Kent	C	×
Charlestown, Washington	S	915
Chepachet, Providence	N	900
● *Chepiwanoxet*, Kent	C	×
Chopmist, Providence	N	×
Clayville, Providence	N	300
● *Clyde*, Kent	C	×
● *Coal Mines*, Newport	SE	×
● *Cole's*, Bristol	E	×
● *Coles*, Kent	C	×
● *Conimicut*, Kent	C	×
● Coventry, Kent	C	5,068
Coventry Centre, Kent	C	300
● Cowesett, Kent	C	40
● Cranston Print Works, Providence	N	8,099
● *CranstonStreet*, Pr'v'd'nce	N	×
Crompton, Kent	C	1,000
Cross Mills, (see Charlestown)		×
Cumberland, Providence	N	8,090
Cumberland Hill, Pr'vidence	N	600
● Davisville, Washington	S	236
● Diamond Hill, Providence	N	200
● Drownville, Bristol	E	90
● *Dyerville*, Providence	N	×
● **East Greenwich**, Kent	C	3,127
● East Providence, Pr'vid'ce	N	8,422
East Providence Centre, Providence	N	293
Elmhurst, Washington	S	×
● *Elmwood*, Providence	N	×
● Enfield, Providence	N	500
Escoheag, Kent	C	40
Exeter, Washington	S	964
● *Field's Station*, Pr'vid'nce	N	×
Fiskeville, Providence	N	150
Forestdale, Providence	N	×
Fort Adams, Newport	SE	×
Foster, Providence	N	1,252
Foster Centre, Providence	N	200
Fox Point, Providence	N	×
● Georgiaville, Providence	N	600
Glendale, Providence	N	300
Gloucester, Providence	N	2,095
● Gould, Washington	S	×
Graniteville, (see Providence)		×
Graniteville, (see Centredale)		×
● *Grant's*, Kent	C	×
● *Graystone*, Providence	N	×
● Greene, Kent	C	400
Green Hill, Washington	S	×
Greenville, Providence	N	800
● *Greenwich*, Kent	C	3,050
● Greenwood, Kent	C	×
Greystone, Providence	N	×
Hamilton, Washington	S	×
● Hamlet, Providence	N	×
Harmony, Providence	N	150
● *Harris*, Kent	C	×
● Harrisville, Providence	N	5,492
● Hills Grove, Kent	C	300
● Hope, Providence	N	700
● Hope Valley, Washington	S	1,100
Hopkinton, Washington	S	2,864
● Howard, Providence	N	30
● *Hoxsie*, Providence	N	×
Hughesdale, Providence	N	×
● *India Point*, Providence	N	×
Inmanville, (see Pascoag)		×
● *Jackson*, Providence	N	×
Jamestown, Newport	SE	707
Johnston, Providence	N	9,778
Kent, Providence	N	×
● Kenyon, Washington	S	×
Kingston, Washington	S	200
● *Kingston Station*, Wash'n	S	155
Knightsville, Providence	N	200
● LaFayette, Washington	S	1,000
Lakewood, Kent	C	300
Laurel Hill, Providence	N	50
Liberty, Washington	S	×
Lime Rock, Providence	N	500
Lincoln, Providence	N	20,355
Little Compton, Newport	SE	1,128
Lock Bridge, Providence	N	×
Locustville, Washington	S	×
● Lonsdale, Providence	N	3,700
● Lymonsville, Providence	N	×
● Manton, Providence	N	600
● Manville, Providence	N	1,900
● Mapleville, Providence	N	1,000
Matunuck, Washington	S	100
Middleton, Newport	SE	1,154
Mineral Spring, Providence	N	×
Mohegan, Providence	N	400
Moosup Valley, Providence	N	350
Morgan Mills, Providence	N	30
Narragansett, Washington	S	1,408
● Narragansett Pier, Wash.	S	700
Nasonville, Providence	N	200
● Natick, Kent	C	3,500
● Nayatt Point, Bristol	E	200
● **NEWPORT**, Newport	SE	19,457
New Shoreham, Newport	SE	1,320
● Niantic, Washington	S	400
● *Nipmuc*, Kent	C	×
Nooseneck Hill, Kent	C	300
North Kingston, Washington	S	4,193
North Providence, P'vidence	N	2,084
North Sicuate, Providence	N	700
NorthSmithfield, Providence	N	3,173
North Tiverton, Newport	SE	×
● Norwood, Kent	C	50
● *Oakland*, Providence	N	400
Oakland Beach, Kent	C	×
● Oak Lawn, Providence	N	158
Ocean View, Washington	S	50
● Olneyville, Providence	N	5,500
● Pascoag, Providence	N	2,600
● Pawtucket, Providence	N	27,633
Pawtuxet, Providence	N	300
● Peace Dale, Washington	S	1,000
Perrysville, Washington	S	100
● Phenix, Kent	C	2,500
Pine Hill, Washington	S	350
Plainville, Washington	S	100
● *Pocasset*, Providence	N	×
Point Judith, Washington	S	×
Ponaganset, Providence	N	×
● Pontiac, Kent	C	1,200
Portsmouth, Newport	SE	1,949
● *Portsmouth Grove*, N'p'rt	SE	×
● Potowomut, Kent	C	×
Potter Hill, Washington	S	650
● *Primrose*, Providence	N	×
● **PROVIDENCE**, Providence	N	132,146
● *Quidnick*, Kent	C	200
Quonochontaug, Washington	S	130
Rice City, Kent	C	×
Richmond, (see South Sicuate)		×
Richmond, Washington	S	1,669
Richmond Switch, Wash'ton	S	300
● River Point, Kent	C	1,400
Riverside, Providence	N	94
● *RiversideSwitch*, Pr'vid'ce	N	×
● *River View*, Kent	C	×
Rockland, Providence	N	500
Rockville, Washington	S	250
● Rocky Brook, Washington	S	475
● *Rocky Point*, Kent	C	×
● *Roger William's Park*, K'nt	C	×
● Rumford, Providence	N	360
Saylesville, Providence	N	500
Sicuate, Providence	N	×
● Shannock, Washington	S	200
Shannock Mills, Washington	S	500
● *Showomet Beach*, Kent	C	×
● *Silver Hook*, Providence	N	×
● *Silver Spring*, Providence	N	×
Slatersville, Providence	N	1,850
● *Slocum's*, Washington	S	×
● Slocumville, Washington	S	280
● Smithfield, Providence	N	2,500
● *Sockanosset*, Providence	N	×
South Foster, Providence	N	100
South Kingston, Washington	S	4,823
SouthPier, (see N'rag'sett Pier)		×
South Portsmouth, Newp't	SE	145
South Sicuate, Providence	N	350
Spragueville, Providence	N	200
● *Spring Green*, Kent	C	×
Spring Lake, (see Coventry)		×
Stillmanville, (see Westerly)		×
● Stillwater, Providence	N	350
● Summit, Kent	C	300
● Tarklin, Providence	N	×
Thornton, Providence	N	400
● Tiverton, Newport	SE	2,837
Tiverton Four Corners, Newport	SE	225
Usquepaugh, Washington	S	140
● Valley Falls, Providence	N	3,750
Vernon, Providence	N	×
● Wakefield, Washington	S	1,000
● Warren, Bristol	E	4,489
● *Warren Avenue*, Pr'vid'nce	N	×
● Warwick, Kent	C	17,761
Warwick Neck, Kent	C	300
● Washington, Kent	C	600
Watchemoket, Providence	N	×
Watch Hill, Washington	S	120
● *Wescott*, Kent	C	×
● Westerly Washington	S	6,813
West Gloucester, Providence	N	150
West Greenwich, Kent	C	798
West GreenwichCentre, Kent	C	50
West Island, Newport	SE	×
● West Kingston, Wash'ton	S	155
● *Wharf Junction*, Pr'vid'ce	N	×
● *Whipple*, Providence	N	×
White Rock, Washington	S	525
● Wickford, Washington	S	1,500
● *Wickford, Junc.*, Wash'ton	S	1,000
● *WickfordLanding*, Wash'n	S	×
● *Woodlawn*, Providence	N	×
● Wood River Junc., Wash'n	S	×
● Woodville, Washington	S	300
● **WOONSOCKET**, Prov	N	20,830
Wyoming, Washington	S	450

South Carolina.

COUNTIES.	INDEX.	POP.
Abbeville	W	46,854
Aiken	W	31,822
Anderson	NW	43,696
Barnwell	S	44,613
Beaufort	S	34,119
Berkeley	S	55,428

South Carolina South Carolina

County	Index	Pop.
Charleston	E	59,903
Chester	N	26,660
Chesterfield	NE	18,468
Clarendon	C	23,233
Colleton	S	40,293
Darlington	NE	29,134
Edgefield	W	49,259
Fairfield	N	28,599
Florence	E	25,027
Georgetown	E	20,857
Greenville	NW	44,310
Hampton	S	20,544
Horry	NE	19,256
Kershaw	N	22,361
Lancaster	N	20,761
Laurens	NW	31,610
Lexington	C	22,181
Marion	NE	29,976
Marlborough	NE	23,500
Newberry	W	26,434
Oconee	NW	18,687
Orangeburgh	C	49,393
Pickens	NW	16,389
Richland	C	36,821
Spartanburgh	NW	55,385
Sumter	C	43,605
Union	N	25,363
Williamsburgh	E	27,777
York	N	38,831
Total		1,151,149

TOWN. COUNTY.	INDEX.	POP.
●**Abbeville C. H.**, Abbeville	W	1,696
Abney, Kershaw	N	×
●Acton, Richland	C	100
●*Ada*, Union	N	×
●*Adam's Crossing*, A'd'n	NW	×
Adam's Hill, Richland	C	×
Adams Run, Colleton	S	350
●*Adams Run Sta.*, Colleton	S	×
Adamsville, Marlborough	NE	36
Addie, Lexington	C	×
●*Adger's*, Fairfield	N	×
●Adrian, Horry	NE	×
Advance, Orangeburgh	C	×
Aerial, Marion	NE	×
●**Aiken**, Aiken	W	2,362
●*Aiken Junc.*, Aiken	W	×
Alba, Greenville	NW	30
Albion, Fairfield	N	24
Albriton, Marion	NE	150
Alcolu, Clarendon	C	×
●*Aldrich*, Orangeburgh	C	×
Alexander, Pickens	NW	×
Algood, Spartanburgh	NW	30
Alice, Anderson	NW	×
●Allendale, Barnwell	S	800
Alliance, Fairfield	N	×
Alma, Laurens	NW	48
Alma, Sumter	C	×
●Almeda, Hampton	S	60
Alpine, Anderson	NW	×
●Alston, Fairfield	N	114
Altamont, Greenville	NW	×
●*Altman's*, Hampton	S	×
Alvin Berkeley	S	×
Ambler, Pickens	NW	×
●**Anderson, C. H.**, Anderson	NW	3,018
●Anderson's Mills, P'k's	NW	30
Andersonville, Anderson	NW	60
Andover, Spartanburgh	SW	×
Andrews Mills, Darlingt'n	NE	48
Annandale, Georgetown	E	×
●Anneville, Berkeley	S	25
Annie, Anderson	NW	×
Ansel, Greenville	NW	×
Antioch, Kershaw	N	×
Antreville, Abbeville	W	25
●Appleton, Barnwell	S	358
Archdale L'nd'g, Berkeley	S	×
Arden, Greenville	NW	×
Arlington, Spartanburgh	NW	×
Armenia, Chester	N	×
Arnold's Mill, Pickens	NW	×
●*Arthur's*, Lexington	C	×
Asbury, Union	N	24
●Ashepoo, Colleton	S	102
Asheworth, Spartanburgh	NW	12
Ashland, Darlington	NE	×
●*Ashley*, Barnwell	S	×
●*Ashley Junc.*, Berkeley	S	×
●Ashley Phosphate, Berkeley	S	×
Ashton, Sumter	C	×
●Atkins, Sumter	C	×
Aurantia, Georgetown	E	×
●**Autun**, Anderson	NW	400
Awendaw, Berkeley	S	×
Babbs, Laurens	NW	×
Babbtown, Greenville	NW	43
Bagdad, York	N	×
●*Baghams*, Fairfield	N	×
Bakers, Horry	NE	×
●Baldock, Barnwell	S	96
Ballentine, Lexington	C	×
●*Ballentynes Mill*, Lex'gt'n	C	×
Balloon, York	N	×
●Bamberg, Barnwell	S	696
Bandana, York	N	×
Banks, Lexington	C	×
Bannockburn, Georgetown	E	×
Barberville, Lancaster	N	×
●Barksdale, Laurens	NW	36
●*Barnes*, Anderson	W	×
Barnes, Horry	NE	×
Barnett's, Greenville	NW	×
●**Barnwell C. H.**, Barnwell	S	937
●Barr's Landing, Lexington	C	26
Barton's Creek, Oconee	NW	36
●Bascomville, Chester	N	60
●Batesburgh, Lexington	C	528
Batesville, Greenville	NW	180
●Bath, Aiken	W	120
Baton Rouge, Chester	N	78
Batson, Greenville	NW	×
Battle Creek, Oconee	NW	12
Bayboro, Horry	NE	40
●*Bayboro Station*, Horry	NE	×
Bay Spring, Chesterfield	NE	30
Beach Branch, Hampton	S	×
Bear Creek, Fairfield	N	×
●**Beaufort**, Beaufort	S	3,587
Beaver Dam, Aiken	W	×
Beaver Dam, Union	W	×
Beaver Pond, Lexington	C	×
●Becca, Spartanburgh	NW	×
Beckett, Berkeley	S	30
Bee, Williamsburgh	E	×
●Beech Island, Aiken	W	15
Beekhamville, Chester	N	×
Bee Tree, Kershaw	N	×
Belair, Lancaster	N	60
●*Beldoc*, Barnwell	S	×
Belfast, Laurens	NW	×
Bellevue, Greenville	NW	15
Bellfield, Kershaw	N	×
Bells, Colleton	S	12
Bell Swamp, Lexington	C	×
Bellwood, Orangeburgh	C	×
Belmont, York	N	30
●Belton, Anderson	NW	494
●*Belvidere*, Berkeley	S	×
Benbow, Clarendon	C	×
●*Ben Cleveland*, Oconee	NW	40
●**Bennetsville**, M'rlb'g	NE	978
Benson, Williamsburgh	E	×
●Berkeley, Berkeley	S	×
Bermuda, Marion	NE	12
Berry, Spartanburg	NW	×
Bethany, York	N	30
Betchcar, Aiken	W	×
Bethel, York	N	42
●*Bethel*, Georgetown	E	×
Bethera, Berkeley	S	×
Bethlehem, Florence	E	36
Bettie, Greenville	NW	×
Beulah, Aiken	W	40
●*Beykirs*, Sumter	C	×
Big Creek, Edgefield	W	48
Birches, Florence	E	×
●Bishopville, Sumter	C	422
Black Mingo, Williamsb'gh	E	75
●Blacksburg, York	N	1,245
●Black Stocks, Chester	N	150
●Blackville, Barnwell	S	962
Blackwood, Spartanburgh	NW	×
Blaine, Anderson	NW	×
●Blairs, Fairfield	N	30
Blairsville, York	N	500
Blanche, Horry	NE	×
●*Blake's Switch*, Colleton	S	×
Blenheim, Marlborough	NE	275
Blooming Vale, Williamsb'h	E	30
Blossom, Florence	E	×
Bluffton, Beaufort	S	421
●Blythewood, Fairfield	N	100
Board Landing, Horry	NE	114
Boiling Springs, Sp'rt'nb'h	NW	×
Boleman, Anderson	W	×
Bolton Mines, Berkeley	S	×
●*Bonham*, Union	N	×
●Bonneau's Depot, Berkeley	S	350
Bonnet, Hampton	S	60
●Bookman, Richland	C	30
●Bordeaux, Abbeville	W	30
Bossard, Sumter	C	30
Bostick, Florence	E	200
Bouknight's Ferry, Edgef'd	W	24
Bounty Land, Oconee	NW	×
Bowers, Hampton	S	×
Bowling Green, York	N	60
Bowlingsville, Union	N	30
Bowman, Orangeburgh	C	×
Boyce's, Laurens	NW	×
●Boykin, Kershaw	N	90
Boykin's Mill, Kershaw	N	×
Bradhams, Hampton	S	×
●Bradley, Abbeville	W	200
●Branchville, Orangeburgh	C	732
Brandywine, Edgefield	W	×
Brannon's, Spartanburgh	NW	×
Brewer Mine, Chesterfield	NE	×
Brewerton, Laurens	NW	48
Brick House, Berkeley	S	36
Briggs, Pickens	NW	60
Brighton, Hampton	S	180
Brightsville, Marlboro'gh	NE	35
Britton's Neck, Marion	NE	72
●Brogdon's, Sumter	C	×
Brook Green, Georgetown	E	33
Brooklyn, Spartanburgh	NW	×
Brown, Williamsburgh	E	12
Brown Creek, Marion	NE	×
Browning, Hampton	S	31
Brownsville, Marlborough	NE	×
Broyles, Anderson	NW	42
Bruce, Lancaster	N	36
Bruno, Anderson	NW	×
●Brunson, Hampton	S	470
Brushy Creek, Anderson	NW	36
Bruton's, Greenville	NW	×
Buck Head, Fairfield	N	24
Bucksport, Horry	NE	×
Bucksville, Horry	NE	400
Buckswamp, Marion	NE	22
Buddenville, Barnwell	S	×
Buford's Bridge, Barnwell	S	60
Bullock Creek, York	N	120
Bull's Bay, Berkeley	S	×
Bulls, Orangeburgh	C	×
Bulows, Colleton	S	×
Burnt Factory, Spart'nb'h	NW	×
Butler's, Edgefield	W	48
Butlersville, Anderson	NW	×
●Byrd's, Colleton	S	48
Cabal, Chester	N	×
Cabins, Abbeville	W	×
●*Cade*, Williamsburgh	E	78
Caesars Head, Greenville	NW	30
Cainesville, Horry	NE	×
Cainhoy, Berkeley	S	200
Caldwell, Newberry	W	×
●*Calhoun*, Pickens	NW	×
●*Calhoun Falls*, Abbeville	W	×
Calhoun's Mills, Abbeville	W	65
Calla, Lexington	C	×
Callison, Edgefield	W	×
Calvert, Abbeville	W	×
Cambridge, Abbeyville	W	×
●**Camden**, Kershaw	N	3,533
●*Camden Junction*, Sumter	C	×
Campbell, Fairfield	N	×
Campbell's Bridge, Marion	NE	72
●*Campbelton*, Barnwell	S	211
●Campobello, Spartanb'h	NW	150
●Camp Ridge, Williamsb'h	E	50
●Campton, Spartanburgh	NW	25
●*Cana*, Abbeville	W	×
●*Can Savannah*, Sumter	C	×
Cantey, Kershaw	N	×
●Carlisle, Union	N	48
Carlyle, Hampton	S	×
Carmel, Union	N	×
Carrington, Marlborough	NE	×
Caro, Anderson	NW	×
Carolina, Marion	NE	24
Carp, York	N	×
Carter, Colleton	S	24
●Cartersville, Florence	E	314
Carvers Bay, Georgetown	E	×
●Cash's Depot, Chesterfi'd	NE	60
Cashville, Spartanburgh	NW	42
●*Caskeys*, Lancaster	N	×
Cason, Anderson	NW	×
Cassidy, Chesterfield	NE	×
Catarrh, Chesterfield	NE	30
Catawba, York	N	×

● *Catawba Junction*, York N ×
● *Catawba River*, York.....N ×
● *Catawba River*, Chester..N ×
Catchall, Sumter.....C 30
● Cathwood, Aiken.....W 24
Caughman's, Edgefield.....W ×
Cavins, Spartanburgh.....NW ×
Cedar, Spartanburgh.....NW 42
Cedar Bluff, (see Union)..... ×
Cedar Creek, Richland.....C ×
Cedar Grove, Laurens.....NW 20
Cedar Shoals, Chester.....N ×
● CedarSpring, Sp'rtenb'hNW 180
Celestia, Edgefield.....W 48
Centenary, Marion.....NE ×
● Central, Pickens.....NW 396
Centre Hill, Orangeburgh...C 18
Centreville, Colleton.....S ×
Centreville, Laurens.....NW 30
Chalkville, Chester.....N ×
Chandler, Greenville.....NW ×
Chandler's, Newberry.....W ×
● Chapin, Lexington.....C ×
● *Chappels*, Newberry.....W 65
● **CHARLESTON**, Charleston.....E 54,995
Cheohee, Oconee.....NW ×
● Cheraw, Chesterfield....NE 976
Cherokee, Spartansburgh. NW ×
Cherokee Heights, AbbevilleW ×
Cherokee Pond, Aiken.....W ×
Cherry, Oconee.....NW ×
● **Chester**, Chester.....N 2,703
Chesterfield, C. H., Chesterfield.....NE 350
Chick's Springs, Gre'nvilleNW 100
● *Childs*, Richland.....C ×
Chitty, Barnwell.....S 25
Choppee, Georgetown.....E 24
Chrisholm, Beaufort.....S ×
Church, Williamsburgh.....E 60
● Claremont, Sumter.....C 36
Clarence, Spartanburgh..NW ×
Clark's Fork, York.....N 20
● Clark's Hill, Edgefield...W 150
Clark's Mills, Lexington....C ×
Claussen, Florence.....E ×
Clay Hill, York.....N 120
Clayton's, Pickens.....NW 40
Clayton, Spartanburgh....NW ×
Clearspring, Greenville...NW ×
Cleora, Edgefield.....W ×
● *Cleveland*, Oconee.....NW 75
● Clifton, Spartanburgh..NW 2,639
● Clinton, Laurens.....NW 1,021
● Clintonward, Edgefield..W 250
Clio, Marlborough.....NE 300
Clouds Creek, Edgefield...W ×
● Clover, York.....N 287
Clyde, Darlington.....NE 24
Coker's, Darlington.....NE ×
● Cokesbury, Abbeville....W 355
Cold Spring, Edgefield.....W 24
Cold Well, Union.....N ×
Coleman's, Edgefield.....W 24
Colerain, Union.....N 18
Colliers, Edgefield.....W ×
Colston, Barnwell.....S 30
● **Columbia**, Richland....C 15 353
● *Columbia Junc.*, Richl'd.C ×
Coneross, Oconee.....NW ×
● *Congaree*, Orangeburgh..C ×
● Congaree, Richland.....C 12
● *Conner*, Berkeley.....S ×
● Connor's, Orangeburgh...C ×
Converse, Spartanburgh..NW ×
● **Conway**, Horry.....NE 677
Conyers, Barnwell.....S ×
Cook, Aiken.....W ×
● *Cook*, Anderson.....NW ×
Cookham, Fairfield.....N ×
Cool Spring, Horry.....NE 24
Cooper, Williamsburgh.....E 12
Coosaw, Beaufort.....S 170
● Coosawhatchie, Beaufort..S 150
● *Coosaw Sta.*, Beaufort....S ×
● Cornwell, Chester.....N 100
● Coronaca, Abbeville.....W 36
Cottageville, Colleton.....S 108
Cotton, York.....N ×
Countsville, Lexington.....C 72
Covington, Marlborough..NE ×
● *Coward's*, Floence.....E 50
Coward's, Florence.....E ×
● Cowpens, SpartanburghNW 349
Cox, Williamsburgh.....E ×
Craigsville, Lancaster.....N 24

● *Cranes*, Sumter.....C ×
Cranesville, Marion.....NE 36
Crawfordsville, (see Fairmont) ×
Crayton, Anderson.....NW 18
Crim, Spartanburgh.....NW ×
Crocketville, Hampton.....S ×
● *Crafts*, Aiken.....W ×
Cromer, Newberry.....W ×
Crosbyville, Fairfield.....N 75
Cross Anchor, Spar'burghNW 300
● Cross Hill, Laurens.....NW 216
Cross Keys, Union.....N 126
Cross Mills, Berkeley.....S ×
● Crotwell, Greenville....NW ×
Crow Creek, Pickens.....NW 36
● Cummings, Hampton.....S ×
Cureton's Store, Lancaster..N 40
Cypress, Darlington.....NE 36
Dacusville, Pickens.....NW 90
Daisy, Horry.....NE 99
Dale, Beaufort.....S ×
Dallas, Spartanburgh....NW ×
Dallas Store, Edgefield....W ×
Dalton, Pickens.....NW ×
Dameilon, Hampton.....S ×
Danford, Kershaw.....N ×
Daniel, Edgefield.....W ×
Dansfuski, Beaufort.....S ×
Dantzler, Orangeburgh.....C 80
Dargan, Marlborough....NE ×
● **Darlington, C. H.**, Darlington.....NE 2,389
● *Darraugh*, Abbeville....W ×
Darwin, York.....N ×
Davidson, Hampton.....S ×
Davis' Bridge, Aiken.....W 30
Davis Landing, Berkeley...S ×
● Davis Station, Clarendon..C ×
● Dawkins, Fairfield.....N 20
Dead Fall, Abbeville.....W ×
Dead Fall, Aiken.....W ×
● Dean, Anderson.....NW ×
Deervana, Aiken.....W ×
● *DeKalb*, Kersaw.....N ×
Delemars, Colleton.....S ×
Delphi, Edgefield.....W ×
● Delta, Union.....N ×
● Denmark, Barnwell.....S 366
Denny, Edgefield.....W 36
● Denver, Anderson.....NW ×
De Witt's Bluff, Laurens....E ×
District Line, Chester.....N ×
Dibble, Orangeburgh.....C ×
Dickson, Spartanburgh..NW ×
● Dillon, Marion.....NE 200
Dixie, Lancaster.....N ×
● *Dixie*, Sumter.....C ×
[D]ock, Williamsburgh.....E ×
[D]ominick, Newberry.....W ×
● Donalds, Abbeville.....W [illegible]16
Dongola, Horry.....NE ×
Donoho, Marion.....NE 72
Dorchester Cros., Berkeley.S ×
Dorn's Mills, (see Celestia).. ×
Dornsville, Edgefield.....W 15
Dorroh, Laurens.....NW ×
Dover, Abbeville.....W 32
● *Dover*, Laurens.....NW ×
● *Dover Junc.*, Laurens..NW ×
● Dovesville, Darlington....NE 150
Downers Institute, Aiken..W ×
Drake, Marlborough.....NE 60
● Drawdy's, Colleton.....S ×
Drayton, Berkeley.....S ×
Draytonville, Union.....N ×
Drew, Hampton.....S ×
Drummondville, Spart'ghNW 30
Dry Creek, Lancaster.....N ×
Dry Grove, Abbeville.....W ×
Dry Weir, Laurens.....NW ×
Duck Branch, Hampton.....S ×
Dudley, Chesterfield.....NE ×
Due West, Abbeville.....W 644
Dunbarton, Barnwell.....S 120
● Duncans, SpartanburghNW 200
Duncanville, Barnwell.....S ×
Dunklin, Greenville.....NW ×
Duo, Oconee.....NW ×
Dupler, Edgefield.....W ×
Durhamville, Aiken.....W 30
Dutchman, SpartinburghNW ×
D[illegible]onsville, Edgefield.....W ×
Dwight, Lancaster.....N ×
Dyers Hill, Marlborough.NE ×
● Dyson, Edgefield.....W 32
Eadytown, Berkeley.....S ×
● Easle's, Williamsburgh...E ×

Earlsville, Spartanburgh.NW ×
● Early Branch, Hampton...S 256
Early's X Roads, Darl'tonNE ×
Easley, Pickens.....NW 421
Eastatoe, Pickens.....NW ×
Easterling's Ms., Marlborough.....NE ×
● Eastover, Richland.....C 71
● Ebenezer, Florence.....E 39
Eden, Laurens.....NW 30
Edey Town, Berkeley.....S ×
● **Edgefield, C. H.** Edg'dW 1,168
● Edgmoor, Chester.....N ×
● *Edgemoor*, York.....N ×
● *Edisto*, Barnwell.....S ×
Edisto Island, Berkeley.....S 175
Edisto Mills, Aiken.....W ×
Edward, Oconee.....NW ×
● Effingham, Florence.....E 148
Ehrhardt, Barnwell.....S 32
● *Eight Mile Turn Out*, Br'lyS ×
Eighteen Mile, Pickens...NW 30
Ekom, Laurens.....NW ×
● Elko, Barnwell.....S 200
Ella, Lexington.....C ×
● Ellenton, Aiken.....W 147
● Elliott, Sumter.....C ×
Elloree, Orangeburgh.....C 311
Elm Grove, Spartanburg.NW ×
Elmore, Barnwell.....S ×
Elmwood, Edgefield.....W 90
Energy, York.....N ×
● Enoree, Spartanburgh..NW ×
Enquirer, York.....N ×
Enterprise, Berkely.....S 120
Epps, Williamsburgh.....E ×
Equality, Anderson.....NW 36
Ernest, Florence.....E ×
Erwinton, Barnwell.....S 24
Estill, Hampton.....S ×
Etheridge, Edgefield.....W 48
Etta Jane, Union.....N 30
Eulala, Edgefield.....W 100
Eulonia, Marion.....NE 12
Eureka, Aiken.....W ×
● Eutawville, Berkeley.....S 224
Evatt, Oconee.....NW ×
Evergreen, Orangeburgh....C ×
Evinsville, Spartanburgh..NW 48
Exchange, Berkeley.....S ×
Ezell, Spartanburgh.....NW ×
Factory, Chester.....N 42
Fairbanks, Lexington.....C ×
Fairdeal, Anderson.....NW 30
● Fairfax, Barnwell.....S 21
● Fair Forest, Sp'rt'nb'ghNW 36
Fairmont, Spartanburgh.NW 150
Fair Play, Oconee.....NW 90
Fairview, Greenville.....NW 90
Falfa, Edgefield.....W 30
Fant, Anderson.....NW 30
Farley, Spartanburgh.....NW ×
Farmer, Horry.....NE ×
Farr's, Pickens.....NW 25
Feasterville, Fairfield.....N 120
● Felderville, Orangeburgh.C 24
Fenwick Island, Colleton...S ×
● *Ferebeeville*, Hampton....S 42
● Ferguson, Berkeley.....S ×
● Fiddle Pond, Barnwell....S 30
Field, Pickens.....NW 130
● *Fifty-Eight*, Orangeburgh.C 78
Filbert, York.....N ×
Fingerville, Spartanburgh NW 78
Finklea, Horry.....NE ×
Fish Dam, (see Carlisle)..... ×
Flat Creek, Lancaster.....N 36
Flat Rock, Kershaw.....N 400
Flat Shoals, Oconee.....NW ×
Flint Hill, Fairfield.....N 12
Flint Ridge, Lancaster.....N ×
● **Florence**, Florence.....E 3,395
● *Floyds*, Darlington.....NE ×
Floyd's X Roads, Horry..NE ×
Fodder, York.....N ×
Fogle, Orangeburgh.....C ×
Folk's Store, Colleton.....S 51
● Foreston, Clarendon.....C 282
Forestville, Florence.....E 200
Fork, Marion.....NE 20
Fork Shoals, Greenville..NW 125
Forks of Edisto, Orangeb'rghC 30
Forney, Horry.....NE ×
Fort George, Oconee.....NW ×
Fort Hill, Pickens.....NW 25
● Fort Lawn, Chester.....N 00
● Fort Madison, Oconee..NW 40

● Pelzer, Anderson......NW 1,878
● Pendelton, Anderson..NW 476
Peniel, Florence..........E ×
● Perry, Aiken............W ×
Petersfield, Georgetown....E 36
Petra, Edgefield..........W ×
Pettigru, Abbeville.........W ×
Phifers, Newberry.........W 30
● Philadelphia, Darl'gton.NE 12
Phillips, Orangeburgh......C ×
Phoenix, Abbeville.........W 90
Pickens C. H., PickensNW 283
Pickens, Oconee.........NW ×
● Piedmont, Greenville..NW 2,436
Piercetown, Anderson...NW 36
Pindor, Pickens..........NW ×
Pine Grove, Union..........N 60
Pine Land, Berkeley........S ×
Pine Plains, Lexington.......C 48
Pine Ridge, Lexington......C 24
Pine Tree, Chesterfied.....NE 24
Pineville, Berkely...........S 60
● Pinewood, Clarendon.....C ×
Pinkney, Union............N 24
Pisgah, Sumter............C ×
Plantersville, Georgetown..E 173
Plateau, Aiken............W ×
Platt, Lexington...........C ×
Pleasant, Richland.........C ×
Pleasant Cross, Edgefield..N 30
● Pleasant Hill, Lancaster..N 96
Pleasant Lane, Edgefield...N 72
Pleasant Valley, Lancaster..N 36
Pliny, Greenville.........NW 30
● Plum Branch, Edgefield.W 24
Plylers, Lancaster..........N 24
Pocotaligo, Beaufort........S ×
Point, York...............N ×
● Pomaria, Newberry.......W 50
Pon Pon, Colleton...........S ×
Pools, Spartanburgh.....NW ×
Poorton, Edgefield.........W ×
Poplar, Horry............NE ×
Poplar Grove, Newberry..W ×
Poplar Spring, Fairfield....N 17
Poplar Swamp, Oranged'h..C ×
Port Harrelson, Horry....NE 300
● Port Royal, Beaufort......S 524
Poverty Hill, Edgefield.....W 36
Powellville, Horry........NE 300
Power; Laurens..........NW 50
Powers Shop, Laurens....NW 50
Prater, Pickens..........NW 12
● Pregnalls, Colleton........S ×
Prescott's, Edgefield.......W ×
Preston, Horry...........NE ×
Price's, Pickens..........NW ×
Priceville, Lexington.......C ×
Primus, Lancaster..........N 36
Pringle's Ferry, GeorgetownE ×
Pritchardville, Beaufort.....S ×
● *Privateer*, Sumter.........C ×
● Privetts, Horry..........NE ×
Prospect, Williamsburgh...E 100
● Prosperity, Newberry....W 565
Providence, Sumter.........C 114
Puckett's Ferry, LaurensNW ×
Pulaski, Oconee..........NW ×
Pumpkintown, GreenvilleNW ×
Purysburg, Hampton... ...S ×
Quarry, Abbeville..........W ×
Queensdale, Marlborough.NE ×
Quick, Marlborough......NE ×
Quinby Bridge, Berkeley...S ×
Quincy, Orangeburgh.......C ×
Rabb, Fairfield............N 30
Ramsey, Sumter............C 120
● Rantowles, Colleton..... .S 72
● Ravenels, Colleton.........S 24
Ravenna, Spartanburgh..NW ×
Raymond, Orangeburgh.....C ×
Ray's Barnwell.............S ×
Red Bank, Edgefield.......W ×
Red Hill, (see Cold Spring).. ×
Red Hill, Marlborough....NE 12
Red Hill, Kersaw...........N ×
Redish, Colleton.............S ×
Redmond, Pickens.......NW 36
Red Top, Berkeley.........S ×
Reeder's Store, Lexington...C 24
Reedy Creek, Marion.....NE 12
Reedy River Factory, Greenville.........NW 180
● Reevesville, Colleton......S 200
Rehoboth, Edgefield........W 24
● Reid, Greenville.........NW 36
Reidville, Spartanburgh..EW 266

Rembert, Sumter...........C 36
● Renno, Laurens........NW ×
Retreat, Oconee..........NW 72
Reuben, Newberry........NW ×
● *Reynolds*, Barnwell.......S ×
Rhems, Williamsburgh.....E ×
Rice's Pickens...........NW 30
Richardsonville, Edgefield W 24
Richardsville, Union.......N ×
● Richburg, Chester........N 200
● Rich Hill, SpartanburghNW 45
● Richland, Oconee...... NW 26
Ridell, Colleton............S 1[illegible]5
Ridgeland, Hampton........S 75
● *Ridgeland Station*, Beauf'tS ×
● Ridge Spring, Edgefield..W 390
● Ridgeville, Colleton.......S 212
● Ridgeway, Fairfield.......N 249
Rightwell, Lexington....... C ×
● Riley's Abbeville.........W ×
● Rimini, Clarendon........C ×
Rion, Fairfield..............W 24
Rish's Store, Lexington......C 60
Rishton, Lexington..........C 24
Ritter's Colleton............S ×
Riverdale, Darlington......NE ×
River's Bridge, Barnwell....S ×
Riverside, Oconee........NW 17
● *Riverside*, Lancaster.......N ×
River View, Greenville..NW 15
Roadville, Berkley...........S 24
Roanoke, Pickens........NW ×
● Robbins, Barnwell.........S 100
Robbins Neck, Darlington NE ×
Roberts, Anderson.......NW 30
Robertsville, Hampton.......S 85
Robeson, Chesterfield.....NE ×
Robinia, York..............N ×
● *Robins Neck* Marlboro' NE ×
Rock, Pickens............NW ×
Rock City, Fairfield........N ×
Rockford, Spartanburg...NW 12
● Rock Hill York..........N 2,744
Rock Mills, Anderson.....NW 30
● Rockton, Fairfield........N ×
Rockville, Berkly............S 80
Rockwell, Oconee......... NW ×
Rocky Mount, Chester......N ×
Rocky Well, Lexington..... C ×
● Roddeys, York............N ×
● Rodman, Chester..........N ×
Rogan, Union..............N ×
Rogersville, Anderson....NW ×
Roland, Kershaw...........N ×
Rollins, Willimsburgh ......E 18
Rome, Williamsburgh.......E 60
Ropers, Edgefield...........W ×
Rosa, Edgefield.............W ×
Roseborough, Laurens....NW 48
Rosebud, Hampton..........S ×
Roseland, Aiken...........W ×
● Ross Station, Colleton.....S 105
Rossville, Chester..........N 25
Round, Colleton............S 58
● Rowesville, Orangeburgh C 115
Ruby, Chesterfield........NE ×
Ruddell, Hampton..........S ×
Runs, Aiken..............W ×
Ruple, Orangeburgh........C ×
Russell Place, Kershaw.....N 35
Ruth, Horry..............NE ×
Saddler's Creek, AndersonNE 30
Saint Albans, Greenville..NW 45
● Saint Charles, Sumter,....C ×
● Saint George's, Colleton...S 629
Saint Helena Island, B'uf't S ×
Saint Luke, Newberry......W ×
● *Saint Lukes*, Lancaster...N ×
● Saint Mathew's, Orange'h C 524
● Saint Paul, Clarendon.....C ×
● Saint Steven's Depot, Ber'y S 230
Salem, Oconee............NW 30
● Salkehatchie, Colleton.....S 120
● Salley, Aiken............W 252
● Salter's Depot, Williams'h S 200
Salubrity, Pickens.......NW ×
Saluca, Abbeville..........W ×
● *Saluda*, Greenville.....NW ×
● Saluda Oldtown, Newb'y W 120
Samaria, Lexington.........C ×
Sampit, Georgetown.........E 108
● *Sampit Sta.*, Georgetown.E ×
Sanders, (see Fairfax)....... ×
Sanders Turnout, Sumpter C 50
Sandover, Abbeville........W 30
Sand Ridge, Berkley........S 24
Sandy Flat, Greenville....NW 60

Sandy Grove, Clarendon ....C 30
● *Sandy River*, Chester.....N ×
Sandy Run, Lexington......C ×
● Sanford, Horry ....NE ×
Santee, Clarendon ....C ×
● *Santee River*, Berkley.....S ×
● Santuck, Union...........N 200
Sardinia, Clarendon.........C 48
Sardis, Florence ....E ×
Savage, Florence............E 30
Savilla, Lexington...........C ×
Sawyerdale, Orangeburgh...C 24
● *Saxon*, Berkley...........S ×
Scarboro, Sumter...........C ×
Scotia, Hampton ....S ×
Scott, Edgefield...........W ×
● Scranton, Williamsburgh E 200
Scuffletown, Laurens.....NW 24
● Seabrook, Beaufort.......S ×
Seaysville, Lexington.......C ×
Sedilia, Union..............N 30
● Seigler, Edgefield.......W ×
● Selvern, Aiken..........W ×
Self, Edgefield........... W ×
Selkirk, Marion...........NE ×
● Sellers, Marion..........NE 60
Seloc, Clarendon...........C ×
Selwood, Lexington.........C ×
Seminole, Hampton ....S 30
● Seneca, Oconee.........NW 600
Senn, Lexington............C ×
● *Seven Mile*, Berkley ......S ×
Shadtown, Barnwell........S ×
Shannon, Colleton ....S ×
● Sharon, York..............N ×
● *Sharp's*, Richland.........C ×
Shell, Greenville.........NW ×
● Sheldon, Beaufort.........S 50
● Shelton, Fairfield.........N 130
Sheridan, Colleton ....S ×
Shiloh, Sumpter...........C 150
Shirley, Hampton............S 10
Shoally, Spartanburgh....SW 30
Shop Spring, Newberry....W ×
Shuler, Orangeburgh ....C ×
Sieglingville, Barnwell......S ×
● Silver, Clarendon..........C ×
Silver Glade, Anderson,..NW ×
Silver Hill, Colleton.........S ×
● Silver Street, Newberry..W 60
● *Simm's* Richland ....C ×
● *Simpson's*, Fairfield.......N ×
Simpson's Mills, Laurens NW 30
● Simpsonville, GreenvilleNW ×
Sincerity, Lancaster........N 24
Sinclair, Lexington..........C 24
Single, Williamsburgh.......E 32
● *Singleton's*, Orangeburgh C 30
Singley, Newberry ....W ×
Sineath's, Berkley ....S ×
Six Mile, Pickens ....NW ×
● *Sixty-Six*, Orangeburgh..C ×
Skull Shoals, Union.........N 36
Sligh's, Newberry..........W ×
● *Sligh's*, Lexington.........C ×
● *Smith's*, York..............N ×
Smith's Ford, Union ....N 72
Smith's Mills, Williamsburg'E 36
Smith's Turn Out, York....N 64
Smithville, Sumter..........C 25
Smoaks, Colleton............S 150
Smyrna, York................N ×
Smyrna, Barnwell..........S ×
Smyrna CampGrove, Kers'wN ×
Snelling, Barnwell...........S 30
● *Snell's* Orangeburgh......C ×
Snipes, Marion...........NE ×
Snider's, Colleton..........S ×
Socastee, Horry...........NE 75
● Society Hill, Darlington NE 501
Sondley's, Newberry.......W ×
Sonoma, Greenville ......NW ×
Sophia, Edgefield ....W ×
● **Spartanburgh**, Spartanburgh................NW 5,544
● *Spartanburgh Junction*, Spartangurgh ....NW ×
Spier's Still, Charlestown...E ×
● *Springdell*, Lancaster ....N ×
● Springfield, Orangeburgh C 221
Spring Grove, Laurens...NW ×
Springhill, Lexington....... C 24
Stafford, Hampton......... S 72
Stantonville, Anderson...NW ×
Star Farm, Union......... N 24
● Starr, Anderson.........NW ×
Statesburgh, Sumter........ C 700

Place, County	Index	Pop.
State Line, Spartanburgh	NW	60
Steer's Bottom, Hampton	S	×
Stella, Orangeburgh	C	×
● Sterling Grove, Gr'nv'le	NW	24
Stewart, Pickens	NW	21
● *Stilton*, Orangeburgh	C	×
Stockman, Newberry	W	×
● *Stockton*, Kershaw	N	×
Stokes Bridge, Darlington	NE	60
Stono, Berkeley	S	360
Stony Battery, Newberry	W	×
Stony Point, Anderson	NW	30
Storeville, Anderson	NW	60
● *Strawberry*, Berkeley	S	×
Street, Abbeville	W	×
Stribling, Spartanburgh	NW	×
● Strother, Fairfield	N	120
Stroup's, York	N	×
Sucbelle, Hampton	S	54
Sugar Loaf, Chesterfield	NE	×
● Summerton, Clarendon	C	200
● Summerville, Berkeley	S	2,219
Summerville, Colleton	S	757
● Summit, Lexington	C	77
● **Sumter C. H.**, Sumter	C	3,865
Sunny Dale, Pickens	NW	24
Sunny Plains, Orangeburgh	C	×
Sunnyside, Union	N	×
Sunny Side, Aiken	W	×
Sunshine, Newberry	W	24
Suttons, Williamsburgh	E	×
Swain, Spartanburgh	NW	30
● Switzer, Spartanburgh	NW	×
Switzer's Mill, Laurens	NW	×
● *Swygert's Mill*, Richland	C	×
● Syracuse, Darlington	NE	×
Tabernacle, Marion	NE	×
Table Mountain, Pickens	NW	38
Tabo, Greenville	NW	×
Talatha, Aiken	W	×
Talley, Oconee	NW	×
Tangier, Colleton	S	×
Tank, Lancaster	N	×
Tanney's, Newberry	W	×
Tarboro, Hampton	S	60
Tasso, Chesterfield	NE	×
● Tatum Station, M'rlb'ro	NE	×
Taxahaw, Lancaster	N	142
Taxaway, Oconee	NW	×
Taylor, Sumter	C	×
● *Taylor's*, Greenville	NW	60
● *Taylor's*, Richland	C	×
Temperance, Marion	NE	×
Temple of Health, Abbeyv'le	W	×
● Ten Mile Hill, Berkeley	S	24
● *Terzah*, York	N	×
● Thickety, Sp'rtanburgh	NW	75
Thickety Fork, Union	N	×
Thomas, Barnwell	S	×
Thompson, Fairfield	N	×
Thompson's, Sp'rtanburgh	NW	×
Thrifty, Oconee	NW	×
Tigersville, Greenville	NW	24
Tiller's Ferry, Kershaw	N	62
Tillman, Hampton	S	48
Tiluray, Greenville	NW	×
Timmerman, Edgefield	W	×
● Timmonsville, Florence	E	516
Timrod, Kershaw	N	×
● Tindal, Sumter	C	60
Tinker's Creek, Barnwell	S	×
Tippin, Spartanburgh	NW	×
Tip Top, Laurens	NW	×
● Tirza, York	N	60
Toby Bluff, Colleton	S	×
Toby's Creek, Marion	NE	120
Todd, Marion	NE	×
Toddville, Horry	NE	×
Tokeena, Oconee	NW	60
Tolness, Orangeburgh	C	×
● Tomotley, Beaufort	S	72
Toney Creek, Anderson	NW	20
Torbit, Chester	N	18
Townville, Anderson	NW	150
Toxaway, Oconee	N	×
Tradesville, Lancaster	N	64
Travellers' Rest, Gr'nville	NW	48
● Trenton, Edgefield	W	302
Trial, Berkeley	S	36
Trinity, Laurens	NW	×
● Trio, Williamsburgh	E	36
Trough, Spartanburgh	NW	×
● Troy, Abbeville	W	311
Tugaloo, Oconee	NW	30
Tular, Spartanburgh	NW	×
Tumbling Shoals, Laurens	NW	300
Turner, Aiken	W	×
Tuten, Barnwell	S	×
Tyger, Greenville	NW	×
Tylersville, Laurens	NW	48
Ulmer, Barnwell	S	30
Una, Darlington	NE	×
● **Union**, Union	N	1,609
Upwell, Newberry	W	×
Utopia, Newberry	W	30
Valdora, York	N	×
Valley Falls, (see Lolo)		×
● Vance, Orangeburgh	C	×
● Van Wyck, Lancaster	N	×
Vardelle, Horry	NE	×
Varennes, Anderson	NW	30
Varn, Barnwell	S	×
Varn's Store, Colleton	S	50
● Varnville, Hampton	S	553
● Vaucluse, Aiken	W	580
Vaughnsville, Newberry	W	24
Vaught, Horry	NE	×
● Verdrey, Abbeville	W	120
Vernon, Edgefield	W	48
Victor, Spartanburgh	NW	×
Viola, Colleton	S	×
Virgil, Richland	C	×
Waco, Anderson	NW	×
Vox, Williamsburgh	E	×
Waccamaw, Georgetown	E	36
Wadley, Barnwell	S	×
Wadmelaw, Berkeley	S	×
● Wagener, Aiken	W	200
Wagon Branch, Hampton	S	×
● **Walhalla**, Oconee	NW	820
Walker, Spartanburgh	NW	×
● *Walker's*, Barnwell	S	×
Walkersville, Greenville	NW	37
● Wallaceville, Fairfield	N	72
● Walnut Grove, Sp't'nb'g	NW	30
● **Waterborough**, C'llet'n	S	1,171
Walton, Newberry	W	24
Wampee, Horry	NE	24
Wanamaker, Horry	NE	×
Wando, Berkeley	S	200
● *Wards*, Edgefield	W	×
● *Warren*, York	N	×
Warren's Turn-Out, York	N	×
Warthen, Greenville	NW	×
● Wateree, Richland	C	24
● Waterloo, Laurens	NW	291
Wattacoo, Pickens	NW	120
Watts, Abbeville	W	50
Waverly Mills, Georgetown	E	30
Waxhaw, Lancaster	N	50
Weathersbee, Barnwell	S	30
Weaverton, Abbeville	W	×
Webster, Union	N	×
● Wedgefield, Sumter	C	197
Weeks, Aiken	W	×
Weimer, Colleton	S	×
● Welford, Spartanburgh	NW	302
Wellridge, Chester	N	30
Wells, Orangeburgh	C	32
Welsh's Mill, Kershaw	N	30
Wessinger's, Lexington	C	×
● West Chester, Chester	N	×
● Westminster, Oconee	NW	532
Weston, Richland	C	×
● *West's*, Berkeley	S	×
West Springs, Union	N	42
● West Union, Oconee	NW	235
● Westville, Kershaw	N	×
● Whaley, Barnwell	S	×
● *Wharton's*, Colleton	S	×
Whetstone, Oconee	NW	×
Whippy Swamp, Hampton	S	×
White Bluff, Lancaster	N	×
● White Hall, Colleton	NW	310
White Horse, Greenville	NW	24
● White Oak, Fairfield	N	100
White Plains, Chesterfield	NE	15
● White Pond, Aiken	W	200
White Rock, Lexington	C	×
● *White Rock*, Lexington	C	×
Whitfield, Spartanburgh	NW	×
● *Whitmire*, Union	N	×
Whitmire's, Newberry	W	30
Whitney, Spartanburgh	NW	836
Whitney Mills, Sp'rtanb'h	NW	×
Wideawake, Colleton	S	×
Wideman's, Abbeyville	W	20
Wild Cat, Lancaster	N	×
Wilkinsville, Union	N	48
Wilksburg, Chester	N	×
● Williamston, Anderson	NW	935
Willie, Spartanburgh	NW	×
● Willington, Abbeville	W	100
Willington Depot, Abbeville	W	×
● Williston, Barnwell	S	503
● *Willoughby*, Florence	E	×
Willow Swamp, Or'geburgh	C	×
● Wilson's Clarendon	C	×
Wilson's Creek, Abbeville	W	×
● Windsor, Aiken	W	148
Wingo, Spartanburgh	NW	×
● **Winnsborough**, Fair'd	N	1,738
Winterseat, Edgefield	W	30
● Wisacky, Sumter	C	×
Wise, Chester	N	×
Withers, Horry	NE	×
Witt's Mills, Lexington	C	×
Wolling, Fairfield	N	×
Woodford, Orangeburgh	C	×
● Woodlawn, Edgefield	W	90
Woodlawn, (see BrookGreen)		×
● Woodruff, Spartanburgh	NW	380
● *Woodstock*, Berkeley	S	25
Woodville, Greenville	NW	42
● Woodward, Fairfield	N	396
Wren, Berkeley	S	48
Wright, Spartanburgh	NW	×
Wyatt, Spartanburgh	NW	×
Wylie's Mill, Chester	N	30
Wyse's Ferry, Edgefield	W	×
Yauhannah, Georgetown	E	30
● Yemassee, Hampton	S	100
● **Yorkville**, York	N	1,533
● Young's Island, Colleton	S	×
Young's Store, Laurens	NW	30
Zadok, York	N	×
● *Zemp*, Sumter	C	×
Zeno, York	N	36
Zion, Marion	NE	12
Zoan, Horry	NE	×

SOUTH DAKOTA.

COUNTIES.	INDEX.	POP.
Aurora	S	5,045
Beadle	E	9,586
Bon Homme	SE	9,057
Boreman	N	×
Brookings	E	10,132
Brown	NE	16,855
Brule	S	6,737
Buffalo	S	993
Butte	W	1,037
Campbell	N	3,510
Charles Mix	S	4,178
Choteau	NW	8
Clark	E	6,728
Clay	SE	7,509
Codington	E	7,037
Custer	SW	4,891
Davison	SE	5,449
Day	NE	9,168
Delano	W	40
Deuel	E	4,574
Dewey	N	×
Douglas	S	4,600
Edmunds	N	4,399
Ewing	NW	16
Fall River	SW	4,478
Faulk	C	4,062
Grant	NE	6,814
Gregory	S	295
Hamlin	E	4,625
Hand	C	6,546
Hanson	SE	4,267
Harding	NW	167
Hughes	C	5,044
Hutchinson	SE	10,469
Hyde	C	1,860
Jackson	C	30
Jerauld	C	3,605
Kingsbury	E	8,562
Lake	E	7,508
Lawrence	W	11,673
Lincoln	SE	9,413
Lugenbeel	S	×
Lyman	C	233
McCook	SE	6,448
McPherson	N	5,940
Marshall	NE	4,544
Martin	NW	7
Meade	W	4,640
Meyer	S	×
Miner	E	5,165
Minnehaha	E	21,879

County	Index	Pop.
Moody	E	5,941
Nowlin	C	149
Pennington	W	6,540
Potter	N	2,910
Pratt	S	23
Presho	S	181
Pyatt	C	34
Rhinehart	NW	×
Roberts	NE	1,997
Sanborn	SE	4,610
Schnasse	NW	×
Scobey	W	32
Shannon	SW	×
Spink	NE	10,581
Stanley	C	1,028
Sterling	C	96
Sully	C	2,412
Todd	S	188
Tripp	S	×
Turner	SE	10,256
Union	SE	9,130
Wagner	NW	×
Walworth	N	2,153
Washabaugh	SW	×
Washington	SW	40
Yankton	SE	10,444
Ziebach	SW	510
Total		328,808

TOWN. COUNTY.	INDEX.	POP.
● **Aberdeen,** Brown	NE	3,182
Ada, Jerauld	C	×
Adelia, Turner	SE	×
Afton, Hyde	C	×
● Albee, Grant	NE	29
Albion, Edmunds	N	×
● Alcester, Union	SE	100
● **Alexandria,** Hanson	SE	500
● Alpena, Jerauld	C	150
Alpha, McPherson	N	×
Allen, Clay	SE	40
● Altamont, Deuel	E	150
● Alto, Codington	E	×
Alwilda, Sanborn	SE	×
Amboy, Sanborn	SE	32
Ames, Hand	C	×
Amherst, Marshall	NE	65
● Andover, Day	NE	232
Andrus, Bon Homme	SE	×
Anthony's, Lawrence	W	×
Antioch, Lincoln	SE	×
● *Appleby*, Codington	E	×
Applegate, Campbell	N	26
Appomattox, Potter	N	20
● Ardmore, Fall River	SW	×
Arena, McPherson	N	26
Argo, Brookings	E	40
● *Argyle*, Custer	SW	×
● Arlington, Kingsbury	E	270
Armadale, Spink	NE	150
● Armour, Douglas	S	482
● Artesian, Sanborn	SE	256
Ashcroft, Harding	NW	×
● Ashton, Spink	NE	359
Athelwold, Brookings	E	×
● Athol, Spink	NE	250
Atlantis, (see Webster)		×
● *Aubrey*, Minnehaha	E	×
Augusta, Sully	C	×
● Aurora, Brookings	E	200
Avon, Bon Homme	SE	75
Badus, Lake	E	32
Bailey, Hand	C	15
Bakerville, Custer	SW	5
Bald Mountain Mines, L'ce	W	×
● Baltic, Minnehaha	E	50
● Bancroft, Kingsbury	E	150
Bangor, Walworth	N	100
Banner, Lincoln	SE	×
Bard, Hanson	SE	25
Bartholdi, Charles Mix	S	30
Bartram, Kingsbury	E	×
Bates, Hand	C	×
● Bath, Brown	NE	125
Battle Creek, Lake	E	×
Battle River, (see Hermosa)		×
Bear Gulch, Lawrence	W	10
Beatrice, Beadle	E	×
Beaver, Miner	E	×
Belford, Aurora	S	×
● Belle Fourche, Butte	W	×
● Benclare, Minnehaha	E	×
Bend, Meade	W	×
Beotia, Spink	NE	×

South Dakota

TOWN. COUNTY.	INDEX.	POP.
● Beresford, Union	SE	404
● *Berne*, Custer	SW	×
Berton, Miner	E	25
Beulah, Douglas	S	×
Big Bend, Pennington	W	×
Big Bottom, Meade	W	19
Big Springs, Union	**SE**	**×**
● Big Stone City, Grant	NE	471
Bijou Hills, Brule	S	200
Black Jackson	C	×
● Black Hawk, Meade	W	150
Blenden, Davison	SE	×
Blinsmon, Moody	E	×
Bloomingdale, Clay	SE	25
Bloomington, Charles Mix	S	25
Blueblanket, Walworth	N	32
Blue Lake, (see Waubay)		×
Bluevale, Pennington	W	18
Bluff Centre, Clay	SE	26
● Blunt, Hughes	C	353
Bolton, Clay	SE	18
Bon Homme, Bon Homme	SE	25
● Bonilla, Beadle	E	30
Bonner, Lincoln	SE	×
● Booge, Minnehaha	E	×
Bovine, Pratt	S	×
● Bowdle, Edmunds	N	400
Bowlder, Lawrence	W	×
Boz, Spink	NE	32
● Bradley, Clark	E	60
Brainard, Brown	NE	20
● Bramhall, Hyde	C	25
● Brandon, Minnehaha	E	30
● Brandt, Deuel	E	×
Brant Lake, Lake	E	×
Brayton, Sully	C	24
● *Brennan*, Pennington	W	×
Bridgeport, Custer	SW	×
● Bridgewater, McCook	SE	410
● Bright, Spink	NE	15
Brisbine, Sanborn	SE	13
● Bristol, Day	NE	199
● **Britton,** Marshall	NE	514
● Broadland, Beadle	E	50
● **Brookings,** Brookings	E	[illegible],518
Brooklyn, Lincoln	SE	32
Brownsville, Lawrence	W	26
● Bruce, Brookings	E	100
Brule, Union	SE	×
● Bryant, Hamlin	E	172
● *Buena Vista*, Fall River	SW	×
Buffalo Centre, Buffalo	S	18
● Buffalo Gap, Custer	SW	501
● Burbank, Clay	SE	150
● Burch, Marshall	NE	60
Burdette, Hand	C	20
● Burkmere, Faulk	C	18
Burnside, Charles Mix	S	×
● *Burton*, Hanson	SE	×
● Bushnell, Brookings	E	50
Bussard, Hughes	C	32
● Butler, Day	NE	30
Butte, Butte	W	57
Callihan, Sanborn	SE	23
Campbell, Campbell	N	35
Camp Crook, Harding	NW	200
● Canastota, McCook	SE	75
● Canning, Hughes	C	75
● Canova, Miner	E	200
● **Canton,** Lincoln	SE	1,101
Canty, Aurora	S	45
Carbonate, Lawrence	W	100
Carlton, Clark	E	×
Carr, Hutchinson	SE	×
Carson, Sully	C	×
● Carthage, Miner	E	200
Cascade Springs, Fall River	SW	200
Casey, Ziebach	SW	×
Castalia, Charles Mix	S	150
● **Castlewood,** Hamlin	E	400
Cave Hills, Ewing	NW	×
Cavour, Beadle	E	300
Cedar, Hand	C	×
Cedar Creek, (see Friesland)		×
Celton, Minnehaha	E	×
Centennial Park, Lawrence	W	26
Central City, Lawrence	W	1,000
Centre Point, Turner	SE	×
● Centreville, Turner	SE	723
C[illegible]ain, Faulk	C	×
● **Chamberlain,** Brule	S	939
Chandler, Charles Mix	S	×
Chapelle, Hyde	C	20
Chautauqua, Day	NE	×
Chatham, Brown	NE	×
● Chedl, Brown	NE	×
Chester, Lake	E	×

South Dakota

TOWN. COUNTY.	INDEX.	POP.
Cheyenne Agency, Dewey	N	×
Cheyenne Falls, Fall River	SW	×
Chyenne River Agency, (see Fort Bennett)		×
Childstown, Turner	SE	32
● *Chilson*, Fall River	SW	×
Choteau Creek, Bon Homme	SE	×
● Claremont, Brown	NE	121
● **Clark,** Clark	E	592
Clarkson, Turner	SE	×
Clay Point, Clay	SE	32
● Clear Lake, Deuel	E	147
Clifton, Sully	C	50
Clyde, Hand	C	×
● Colman, Moody	E	100
● Columbia, Brown	NE	400
Colvin, Charles Mix	S	40
Como, Hand	C	32
● Conde, Spink	NE	200
Copp, Potter	N	26
● *Coral*, Spink	NE	200
Cornelion, Potter	N	26
Cornell, Sanborn	SE	20
Coreyo, Walworth	N	20
● Corona, Roberts	NE	36
● *Corson*, Minnehaha	E	×
● Cortlandt, Edmunds	N	15
Coulson, (see Fort Pierre)		×
Coyle, Brule	S	32
● Crandon, Spink	NE	200
Cresbard, Faulk	C	×
Creston, Pennington	W	32
Crook City, Lawrence	W	25
Crow Creek, Buffalo	S	50
Crow Lake, Jerauld	C	70
● **Custer,** Custer	SW	1,500
Dakota City, Pennington	W	32
Dalesberg, Clay	SE	×
Dalystown, Bon Homme	SE	×
Danforth, Hand	C	26
Danville, Turner	SE	15
Darien, Clark	E	×
Davidson, Potter	N	×
● **DEADWOOD,** L'r'nce	W	6,000
Dean, Hand	C	65
Degbert, Clark	E	×
De Grey, Hughes	C	×
Delhi, McPherson	N	26
● Dell Rapids, Minnehaha	E	993
Delmage, Lake	E	×
● Delmont, Douglas	S	150
● Dempster, Hamlin	E	50
Denis, Pennington	W	×
Denver, (see Arlington)		×
● **De Smet,** Kingsbury	E	541
Detroit, Brown	NE	32
Deuel, Deuel	E	×
De Voe, Faulk	C	25
Dexter, Codington	E	×
Dexter, Day	NE	20
Dixon, Hamlin	E	×
Dodge, Brown	NE	45
● Doland, Spink	NE	216
● *Dolton*, Turner	SE	×
Dover, McCook	SE	32
Doyles, Meade	W	×
Drakola, Kingsbury	E	25
● Dudley, Fall River	SW	×
● Dumont, Lawrence	**W**	**×**
Duncan, Buffalo	S	25
Dunlap, Brule	S	32
Dunsmore, Faulk	C	×
● *Duxbury*, Spink	NE	×
Eagle, Brule	S	×
Eagle, Hand	C	40
Earling, Presho	S	×
Earlville, Beadle	E	×
● East Pierre, Hughes	C	×
● East Sioux Falls, Minnehaha	E	577
Eckard, Fall River	SW	×
● *Eden*, Lincoln	SE	202
● *Edgemont*, Fall River	SW	1,200
Edgerton, Charles Mix	S	75
Edwin, Hyde	C	×
● Egan, Moody	E	399
Egge, Lake	E	26
Eldorado, Buffalo	S	26
Elizabeth, Hand	C	15
Elk Creek, Lawrence	W	10
● **Elk Point,** Union	SE	1,300
● Elkton, Brookings	E	331
● *Ellis*, Minnehaha	E	×
Ellisville, Faulk	C	×
Ellsworth, Clark	E	26
Elmira, Grant	NE	×
● Elrod, Clark	E	26
Embden, (see Joubert)		×

● Emery, Hanson.........SE 200
Emmett, Union.........SE ×
Empire, Butte.........W ×
Emsley, Davison.........SE 10
● *Englewood*, Lawrence.....W ×
● *Erskine*, Fall River.....SW ×
● Erwin, Kingsbury.........E 150
● Esmond, Kingsbury.......E 30
● Estelline, Hamlin.........E 210
Esterly, Codington.........E 12
Estherdale, Buffalo.........S ×
● Ethan, Davison.........SE 25
Etta Mine, Pennington.....W 32
● Eureka, McPherson.......N 552
Evans Quarry, Fall River.SW ×
● *Evans Siding*, FallRiverSW ×
Evelyn, Brule.........S ×
Fairbank, Sully.........C 50
● Fairburn, Custer.........SW 25
Fairview, Lincoln.........SE 25
Faris, Edmunds.........N ×
Farmer, Hanson.........SE ×
Farmingdale, Pennington..W ×
Farnsworth, Sanborn.......SE 20
Farwell, Sanborn.........SE 26
● **Faulkton**, Faulk.........C 462
Fauston, Jerauld.........C ×
● Ferney, Brown.........NE 38
Fielder, Hughes.........C ×
Firesteel, Aurora.........S ×
● **Flandreau**, Moody.....E 569
Fleetwood, Minnehaha.......E 45
Flensburg, Douglas.........S 32
Flora, Charles Mix.........S 26
Florence, Hand.........C 13
Flynn, Aurora.........S ×
Folsom, Custer.........SW ×
Forestburg, Sanborn.......SE 200
Forest City, Potter.........N 150
Forest City South, Potter..N ×
● *Forestville*, Codington....E ×
Fort Bennett, Stanley.......C 245
Fort Meade, Meade.........W 576
Fort Pierre, Stanley.........C 360
Fort Randall, Todd.......S 250
Fort Sisseton, Marshall....NE 150
Fort Sully, Sully.........C 136
Fort Thompson, Buffalo....S ×
Fort Ya es, Boreman.......N 125
Frank, Marshall.........NE ×
● Frankfort, Spink.........NE 186
Franklin, Lake.........E ×
● Frederick, Brown.........NE 281
● Freeman, Hutchinson......SE 500
Freya, Turner.........SE ×
Fridhem, Charles Mix.......S ×
● Fulton, Hanson.........SE 100
Gale, Campbell.........N 32
Galena, Lawrence.........W 252
Galena Junction, LawrenceW ×
Galla, Moody.........E ×
Gann Valley, Buffalo.....S 20
● Garden City, Clark.........E 150
● *Gardner*, Codington.......E ×
Garland, Union.........SE ×
● Garretson, Minnehaha....E 341
● **Gary**, Deuel.........E 277
● Gayville, Yankton.........SE 130
Gem Brown.........NE ×
Geneva, Roberts.........NE 20
● **Gettysburgh**, Potter..N 500
Giddings, Hughes.........C 32
Gilbert, Aurora.........S 10
Gilman, Lake.........E 32
Glendale, Hand.........C 32
Glenwood, Clay.........SE ×
Goddard, Sully.........C 19
Golden, Clark.........E ×
Goodle, Beadle.........E 32
Goodwill, Roberts.........NE ×
● Goodwin, Deuel.........E 100
Gordon, Jerauld.........C ×
Gothland, Union.........SE ×
Goudyville, Hyde.........C [illegible]
Grand Crossing, Walworth.N ×
Grand Meadow, Minnehaha.E 25
Grand View, Douglas.....S 50
Grant, Brookings.........E ×
Grashull, Meade.........W 40
Greenfield, Clay.........SE ×
Greenwood, Charles Mix....S 60
Gregory, Lawrence.........W ×
Grindstone, Nowlin.........C ×
Grobe, Spink.........NE 26
Gros, Day.........NE 20
● Groton, Brown.........NE 681
● Grover, Codington.........E 12

Groveland, Moody.........E ×
Halse, Codington.........E ×
Hanchett, Miner.........E ×
Hand, Hand.........C 32
Haram, Lincoln.........SE 19
Harney, Pennington.......W ×
Harrington, (see Burkmere). ×
● *Harrisburg*, Lincoln....SE ×
Harrison, Douglas.........S 150
● Harrold, Hughes.........C 250
Hartford, Minnehaha.........E 75
● Hat Creek, Fall River..SW ×
Hawlejek, Bon Homme....SE ×
Hawley, Hyde.........C 26
Hayti, Hamlin.........E ×
Hayward, Pennington......W 64
● Hazel, Hamlin.........E 45
Hazleton, Hanson.........SE ×
● Hecla, Brown.........NE 200
Hein, Campbell.........N ×
Helgen, Codington.........E ×
Helmick, Hand.........C 32
● Henry, Codington.........E 194
● Hermosa, Custer.........SW 172
● Hetland, Kingsbury.......E 200
Highland, Minnehaha.........E 25
● **Highmore**, Hyde.......C 435
Hilda, (see Underwood)..... ×
● Hill City, Pennington....W 1,000
Hillside, Douglas.........S ×
● Hillsview, McPherson....N 25
● Hitchcock, Beadle.........E 450
● Holabird, Hyde.........C 80
Home, Turner.........SE 40
Hopeland, Hand.........C ×
Horsehead, Fall River....SW ×
Horseshoe Grove, LawrenceW ×
● Hosmer, Edmunds.........N 56
Hotch City, Presho.........S ×
Hot Creek, Fall River.....SW ×
● **HotSprings**,FallRiverSW 3,000
● Houghton, Brown.........NE 25
Hoven, Potter.........N 20
● **Howard**, Miner.........E 700
Howell, Hand.........C 40
● Hudson, Lincoln.........SE [illegible]
● Hufton, Brown.........NE 5
● Humboldt, Minnehaha....E ×
● Hurley, Turner.........SE 344
● **Huron**, Beadle.........E 3,038
Huston, Gregory.........S ×
Ida, Hyde.........C 32
Idylwilde, Turner.........SE 19
Ilion, Faulk.........C ×
● **Ipswich**, Edmunds.....N 539
● Iroquois, Kingsbury.......E 183
Irving, Spink.........NE 26
● Ivanhoe, Custer.........SW ×
Jackson, (see March)........ ×
● *James*, Brown.........NE ×
Jamesville, Yankton.......SE 25
Jamesville, Hand.........C ×
● *James ValleyJunc*.Beadle E ×
Jasper, Charles Mix.........S 20
● Jefferson, Union.........SE 229
Jones, Meade.........W ×
● *Johnstown*, Codington....E ×
Joubert, Douglas.........S ×
Julian, Clark.........E ×
● Kampeska, Codington....E 75
Kaspar, Sully.........C ×
Kellerton, Hamlin.........C ×
Kellie, (see Bowdle)........ ×
● *Kent*, Hamlin.........E ×
Kidder, Marshall.........NE 20
Kila, Moody.........E ×
Kilborn, Grant.........NE 66
● Kimball, Brule.........S 593
● *Kirk*, Lawrence.........W ×
Kirkwood, Brule.........S ×
Kolda, Hand.........C ×
Komstad, Clay.........SE 10
Koto, McPherson.........N ×
● Kranzburg, Codington....E 125
La Belle Ranche, Lake......E ×
● *La Bolt*, Grant.........NE ×
La Delle, Spink.........NE ×
La Foon, Faulk.........C ×
La Grace, Campbell.........N 100
● Lake City, Minnehaha....E ×
Lake Henry, Kingsbury.....E 32
Lakeport, Yankton.........SE 20
● Lake Preston, Kingsbury.E 337
Lakeside, Beadle.........E 25
Laketon, Brookings.........E ×
● Langford, Marshall,......NE 198
Lannsburg, Clark.........E 20

Latona, Lyman.........C ×
Laurel, Sully.........C ×
Laverne, Pennington.......W ×
Lawrence, Beadle.........E 12
Lead, Lawrence.........W 6,000
● Lebanon, Potter.........N 200
Le Beau, Walworth.........N 65
● Lennox, Lincoln.........SE 363
Leola, McPherson.........N 200
Leon, Stanley.........C ×
Leslie, Sterling.........C ×
● Lesterville, Yankton.....SE 151
● Letcher, Sanborn.........SE 150
Lewiston, Sully.........C 19
Lily, Day.........NE 15
Lincoln, Clay.........SE ×
Linden, Lincoln.........SE ×
Little Bend, Sully.........C ×
Lodge, Jackson.........C ×
Lodi, Clay.........SE 32
Lone Tree Lake, Deuel......E ×
Long Creek, Lincoln.......SE 19
Long Lake, McPherson.......N 40
Longland, Jerauld.........C ×
Longmont, Pennington....W ×
Lookout, Pennington.......W 57
Loretta, Bon Homme......SE ×
● *Loring*, Custer.........SW ×
Lounsberry, Day.........NE 32
Lower Brule, Lyman.........C 25
● Loyalton, Edmunds.......N 125
Lyman, Lyman.........C ×
Lynn, Day.........NE ×
Lyons, Minnehaha.........E ×
Lyonville, Brule.........S 32
McCamley, Sully.........C 32
● *McCook*, Union.........SE 15
McGrawville, Faulk.........C 26
Mable, Hutchinson.........SE ×
Macy, Butte.........W 45
● **Madison**, Lake.........E 1,736
Maitland, Douglas.........S ×
Maitland, Fall River.......SW ×
● Manchester, Kingsbury...E 60
Manderson, Shannon.....SW ×
Mann, Potter.........N ×
● Mansfield, Brown.........NE 30
Maple Grove, Lincoln......SE ×
March, Charles Mix.........S 10
● *Marietta*, Fall River......SW ×
Marindahl, Yankton......SE ×
Marine, Faulk.........C 18
● Marion, Turner.........SE 350
Marshalltown, Clay.........SE ×
Marston, Sully.........C 32
Martin Valley, Custer.....SW ×
● Marvin, Grant.........NE 100
Maverick, Pennington......W 19
Maxwell, Hutchinson......SE 20
Mayfield, Yankton.........SE 26
● *Mayo*, Custer.........SW ×
● Meckling, Clay.........SE 40
Medas, Sanborn.........SE 25
Melbourne, Hand.........C 32
● Mellette, Spink.........NE 241
Melvin, Custer.........SW ×
● Menno, Hutchinson......SE 413
Merritt, Pennington.......W ×
Merton, Clark.........E ×
Midland, Nowlin.........C ×
Midway, Moody.........E 19
Milford, Sully.........C ×
● Millard, Faulk.........C 30
● **Millbank**, Grant......NE 1,207
● **Miller**, Hand.........C 536
Millers, Meade.........W ×
Milltown, Hutchinson......SE 85
● *Mina*, Edmunds.........N 15
Miner, Miner.........E ×
● Minnekahata, Fall RiverSW ×
Minnesela, Butte.........W 175
Miranda Faulk.........C 20
Mission Hill, Yankton.....SE ×
● **Mitchell**, Davison.....SE 2,217
Moe, Lincoln.........SE ×
Monroe, Turner.........SE ×
Montgomery, Brown.......NE 11
● Montrose, McCook.......SE 300
Moody, Brown.........NE ×
Moore, Presho.........S ×
Morrill, Potter.........N ×
Moss City, Custer.........SW ×
Moulton, Pennington,......W ×
Mound City, Campbell...N 800
● Mount Vernon, Davison..SE 127
***Mowatts*, Lawrence**.........W ×
Murray, Brown.........NE ×

South Dakota	
Myron, Faulk C	20
Myrtle, Bon Homme SE	32
● *Mystic*, Pennington W	×
● *Nahant*, Lawrence W	×
● Naples, Clark E	100
Nasby, Lawrence W	×
Nashville, Harding NW	65
Nemo, Lawrence W	×
Neptune, Kingsbury E	18
● Newark, Marshall NE	250
New Ashton (see Ashton)	×
New Holland, Douglas S	40
New Hope, Minnehaha E	×
Ney, Sully C	×
Nora, Union SE	×
Norden, Deuel E	×
Norden, Hamlin E	×
Nordland, (see Arlington)	×
Norfolk, Sully C	25
● Northville, Spink NE	200
Norway, Yankton SE	×
Nowlin, Nowlin C	×
Nurey, Lincoln SE	×
Nutley, Day NE	82
Oacoma, Lyman C	×
Oahe, Hughes C	86
Oak Hollow, Hutchinson SE	×
Oakwood, Brookings E	83
Odell City, Fall River SW	×
Odessa, Hand C	×
● Oelrichs, Fall River SW	803
Okobojo, Sully C	50
Ola, Brule S	32
Old Fort James, Hanson SE	×
● Oldham, Kingsbury E	200
Olivet, Hutchinson SE	150
Onida, Sully C	80
Opdahl, Hamlin E	×
● Ordway, Brown NE	200
● *Oreville*, Pennington W	×
● Orient, Faulk C	100
Orland, Lake E	×
Orleans, Faulk C	×
Orono, Edmunds N	32
Osceola, Kingsbury E	60
Otis, Custer SW	×
Otto, Hamlin E	10
Pactola, Pennington W	31
Palisade, Minnehaha E	100
● Palmer, Deuel E	18
● **Parker**, Turner SE	728
● Parkston, Hutchinson SE	262
Parsons, Jerauld C	×
Pearl, Beadle E	15
Pembroke, Potter N	20
Pennington, Minnehaha E	25
Perry, Lawrence W	10
Philip, Nowlin C	×
Phinney, Custer SW	×
● Piedmont, Meade W	400
● Pierpoint, Day NE	200
● **PIERRE**, Hughes C	3,235
● *PierreCreek Tank* Hanson SE	×
Pine Ridge Agency, Shan'n SW	100
Pitrodie, Clark E	20
Plainfield, Brule S	26
Plainview, Douglas S	×
● Plana, Brown NE	17
● **Plankinton**, Aurora S	604
Platte, Charles Mix N	10
Ployd, Brule S	83
● *Pluma*, Lawrence W	×
Poinsett, Hamlin E	×
Polo, Hand C	18
Porcupine Creek, Shannon SW	10
PortugueseSiding, Lawr'nce W	×
Potter, Potter N	×
Powell, Edmunds N	20
Prairie Farm, Brookings E	×
Prairie Queen, Lake E	×
Prairie Siding, (see Goodwin)	×
Presho, Presho S	×
● *Pringle*, Custer SW	×
Prior, (see Corona)	×
● Pukwana, Brule S	400
● Putney, Brown NE	15
● *Ramona*, Lake E	250
Ramsey, McCook SE	×
● **Rapid City**, Pennington W	5,000
Ravenna, Sanborn SE	×
● Rawville, Codington E	11
● Raymond, Clark E	100
● *Redfern*, Pennington W	×
● **Redfield**, Spink NE	796
Red Lake, Brule S	32
Red Stone, Hanson SE	×
● Ree Heights, Hand C	70

South Dakota	
Republican, Minnehaha E	×
● Revillo, Grant NE	150
Richards, Buffalo S	10
Richland, Union SE	95
Ridge, Spink NE	32
Riverside, Clay SE	10
Rives, Brule S	×
Roanoke, Faulk C	28
Robey, Aurora S	4
● Rochford, Pennington W	32
Rockerville, Pennington W	10
● Rockham, Faulk C	25
Rockport, Hanson SE	50
Rockton, Miner E	×
Rocks, Custer SW	×
● Romona, Lake E	65
Rondell, Brown NE	26
● Roscoe, Edmunds N	114
Rose, Spink NE	20
Rosebud, Meyer S	100
Rosebud Landing, Lyman C	×
Rosedale, Hanson SE	×
Roslyn, Day NE	33
● Roswell, Miner E	100
● Rousseau, Hughes C	50
● Rowena, Minnehaha E	126
Ruby Basin, Lawrence W	×
● Rudolph, Brown NE	50
Runkel, Meade W	×
● RunningWater, BonH'me SE	100
● *Sacoro*, Meade W	×
Saddle Creek, Lincoln SE	×
Saint Herbert, Edmunds N	32
Saint Joseph, Grant NE	×
● Saint Lawrence, Hand C	320
● Saint Mary's, Miner E	32
● Saint Onge, Lawrence W	19
● **Salem**, McCook SE	429
● *Sand Cut*, Roberts NE	×
Sandstone, (see Odell)	×
Santa Clara, Brown NE	12
Saybrook, Clay SE	×
Scandinavia, Deuel E	×
Scatterwood, Faulk C	32
Schatzville, Douglas S	×
● Scotland, Bon Homme SE	1,083
● *Scotland Junc.*, BonH'me SE	×
Scotts Mill, Pennington W	×
Scranton, Walworth N	75
Sedgwick, Hyde C	25
Selma, Lincoln SE	19
● Seneca, Faulk C	100
Seth, Day NE	32
Seward, Hamlin E	20
Shank, Turner SE	19
● *Sheffield*, Beadle E	×
Sheridan, Pennington W	40
Sherman, Lyman C	×
● Sherman, Minnehaha E	18
Sherwood, Clark E	19
Shiloh, Hughes C	×
● Shindler, Lincoln SE	×
● *Siding No. 3*, Fall River SW	×
● *Siding No. 5*, Fall River SW	×
● *Siding No. 6*, Fall River SW	×
● *Siding No. 6*, Deuel E	×
● *Siding No. 9*, Custer SW	×
Sigel, Yankton SE	×
Silex, Hand C	19
Silver City, Pennington W	25
Sinai, Brookings E	×
● **Sioux Falls**, Minnehaha E	10,177
● *Sioux Falls Junc.* Moody E	×
● *Sioux ValleyJunc.* Br'k'gs E	×
Sisseton Agency, Roberts NE	40
Skjold, Deuel E	×
Smalley, Walworth N	×
Smithville, Meade W	20
● Smithwicks, Fall River SW	20
Smyth, Moody E	×
Snoma, Butte W	×
Soldiers' Home, Fall River SW	×
● South Shore, Codington E	100
South Sioux Falls, Min'haha E	×
● Spain, Marshall NE	8
Spauldings, (see Dempster)	×
● Spearfish, Lawrence W	2,000
● Spencer, McCook SE	150
Spink, Union SE	40
Spokane, Custer SW	×
● *Spottswood*, Spink NE	130
● Springdale, Lincoln SE	40
Springfield, Bon Homme SE	302
● *SpringfieldSta.* B'nH'me SE	×
Spring Lake, Kingsbury E	×
Springs, Potter N	×

South Dakota	
Spring Valley, Turner SE	×
Stanley, Stanley C	×
Starkey, Jerauld C	×
Starr, Hutchinson SE	×
Stavely, Roberts NE	×
Stearns, Jackson C	×
Stena, Roberts NE	×
Stephan, Hyde C	130
Stock, Jerauld C	19
Stockholm, Grant NE	×
Stover, Davison SE	×
Strandburg, Grant NE	×
Strater, (see Battle River)	×
Straud, Day NE	×
● Sturgis, Meade W	2,000
Success, Clark E	32
Sullivan, Jerauld C	×
Sully, Sully C	×
Sumner, Spink NE	×
● Summit, Roberts NE	×
Sunset, Ewing NW	×
Sutley, Campbell N	32
Sverdrup, Minnehaha E	32
Swan Lake, Turner SE	32
Sweetland, Hand C	19
Tabor, Bon Homme SE	100
Talcott, Clark E	×
Taopi, Minnehaha E	400
Templeton, Jerauld C	×
Tennis, Hyde C	×
Terraville, Lawrence W	696
Te-ton-ka, Spink NE	34
Theodore, Walworth N	32
Thinney, Custer SW	×
Thorson, Day NE	32
Thule, Campbell N	×
Tigerville, Pennington W	×
● Tilford, Meade W	100
Tielo, Campbell N	×
Togstad, Deuel E	19
● Toronto, Deuel E	148
Towles, Lake E	×
Travare, Roberts NE	50
● Trent, Moody E	57
● Tripp, Hutchinson SE	226
● Troy, Grant NE	50
● Tulare, Spink NE	150
Turley, Sully C	×
Turner, Turner SE	×
● Turton, Spink NE	50
● *Tuscan*, Hutchinson SE	×
● Twin Brooks, Grant NE	150
● **Tyndall**, Bon Homme SE	509
● *Utica*, Yankton SE	×
Vale, Butte W	25
● Valley Springs, Minne'ha E	308
Vanderbilt, Campbell N	25
Vandervoort, Clark E	32
Vedette, Campbell N	×
Vega, Brule S	×
● Verdon, Brown NE	94
● **Vermillion**, Clay SE	1,496
● *Vermont City*, Edmunds N	125
Victor, Davison SE	19
● Vienna, Clark E	58
Viewfield, Meade W	50
● Vilas, Miner E	100
● Virgil, Beadle E	20
● Volga, Brookings E	298
● Volin, Yankton SE	32
Volney, Hand C	25
Volunteer, Meade W	×
● Wakonda, Clay SE	200
Walrath, Grant NE	25
Walshton, Yankton SE	×
Walworth, Walworth N	14
Wanari, Bon Homme SE	×
● Ward, Moody E	10
Warnecke, Sully C	32
● Warner, Brown NE	500
Warrington, Turner SE	25
Waterbury, Jerauld C	120
Waterford, Sully C	26
● **Watertown**, Codington E	2,672
● *Watertown Junc.* B'kings. E	×
● Waubay, Day NE	175
Waunetta, Potter N	12
● Waverly, Codington E	58
● **Webster**, Day NE	610
Welland, Potter N	15
Wellington, Minnehaha E	40
● Wentworth, Lake E	607
Wesley, Faulk C	20
● Wessington, Beadle E	150
WessingtonSprings, Jild C	150
Westerville, Clay SE	×
Westford, Hutchinson SE	90

Westover, Pratt	S	×
West Point, Minnehaha	E	45
● West Port, Brown	NE	90
Wheeler, Charles Mix	S	45
● White, Brookings	E	137
● White Lake, Aurora	S	366
● White Rock, Roberts	NE	40
White Swan, Charles Mix	S	10
Whitetail Crossing, L'w'nce	W	×
Whitetail Summit, L'w'ence	W	×
● Whitewood, Lawrence	W	443
Whitfield, Jackson	C	×
Wicklow, Lake	E	60
Willoughby, Deuel	E	×
Willow Creek, Stanley	C	×
● Willow Lake, Clark	E	240
● **Wilmot**, Roberts	NE	300
● Wilson, Grant	NE	14
● Winfred, Lake	E	350
● *Winship*, Brown	NE	×
Winthrop, Beadle	E	22
Wittenberg, Hutchinson	SE	×
Wolf Creek, Hutchinson	SE	150
● Wolsey, Beadle	E	200
Wood River Centre, (see Fort Thompson)		×
Woodville, Lawrence	W	×
● **Woonsocket**, Sanborn	SE	687
Worms, Bon Hamme	SE	×
● Worthing, Lincoln	SE	80
Wounded Knee, Shannon	SW	29
Wyatt, Aurora	S	×
● Yale, Beadle	E	25
● **Yankton**, Yankton	SE	3,670
Yankton Agency, Chas. Mix	S	60
Yellow Bank, Grant	NE	×
● Zell, Faulk	C	80
Ziskov, Yankton	SE	×

TENNESSEE.

COUNTIES.	INDEX.	POP.
Anderson	NE	15,128
Bedford	C	24,739
Benton	NW	11,230
Bledsoe	E	6,134
Blount	E	17,589
Bradley	SE	13,607
Campbell	NE	13,486
Cannon	C	12,197
Carroll	W	23,630
Carter	NE	13,389
Cheatham	N	8,845
Chester	SE	9,069
Claiborne	NE	15,103
Clay	N	7,260
Cocke	E	16,523
Coffee	C	13,827
Crockett	W	15,146
Cumberland	E	5,376
Davidson	N	108,174
Decatur	W	8,995
DeKalb	C	15,650
Dickson	N	13,645
Dyer	W	19,878
Fayette	SW	28,878
Fentress	N	5,226
Franklin	S	18,929
Gibson	W	35,859
Giles	S	34,957
Grainger	NE	13,196
Greene	NE	26,614
Grundy	C	6,345
Hamblen	NE	11,418
Hamilton	SE	53,482
Hancock	NE	10,342
Hardeman	SW	21,029
Hardin	SW	17,698
Hawkins	NE	22,246
Haywood	W	23,558
Henderson	W	16,336
Henry	NW	21,070
Hickman	C	14,499
Houston	N	5,390
Humphreys	C	11,720
Jackson	N	13,325
James	SE	4,903
Jefferson	E	16,478
Johnson	NE	8,858
Knox	E	59,557
Lake	NW	5,304
Lauderdale	W	18,756
Lawrence	S	12,286
Lewis	C	2,555
Lincoln	S	27,382
Loudon	E	9,273
McMinn	SE	17,890
McNairy	SW	15,510
Macon	N	10,878
Madison	W	30,497
Marion	SE	15,411
Marshall	C	18,906
Maury	C	38,112
Meigs	SE	6,930
Monroe	SE	15,329
Montgomery	N	29,697
Moore	S	5,975
Morgan	NE	7,639
Obion	NW	27,273
Overton	N	12,039
Perry	C	7,785
Pickett	N	4,736
Polk	SE	8,361
Putnam	N	13,683
Rhea	E	12,647
Roane	E	17,418
Robertson	N	20,078
Rutherford	C	35,097
Scott	NE	9,794
Sequatchie	SE	3,027
Sevier	E	18,761
Shelby	SW	112,740
Smith	N	18,404
Stewart	N	12,193
Sullivan	NE	20,879
Sumner	N	23,668
Tipton	W	24,271
Trousdale	N	5,850
Unicoi	NE	4,619
Union	NE	11,459
Van Buren	C	2,863
Warren	C	14,413
Washington	NE	20,354
Wayne	S	11,471
Weakley	NW	28,955
White	C	12,348
Williamson	C	26,321
Wilson	N	27,148
Total		1,767,518

TOWN. COUNTY.	INDEX.	POP.
Abbott, Campbell	NE	150
A. B. C., Sumner	N	21
Abernathy, Lauderdale	W	35
Abiff, Dickson	N	16
Abner, Lawrence	S	×
Accident, Jackson	N	×
Acorn, Monroe	SE	×
Acting, Loudon	E	×
Acuff, Union	NE	14
Ada, (see Farmville)		×
Adair's Creek, (see Knoxville)		×
● Adams Station, Robertson	N	234
Adamsville, McNairy	SW	459
Adenburgh, Dickson	N	×
Adolphus, London	E	24
● Aetna, Hickman	C	12
Afton, Sullivan	NE	×
Agee, Campbell	NE	9
Agreeable, Grainger	NE	×
● Al, Putnam	N	33
Alamo, Crockett	W	340
Alanthus Hill, Hancock	NE	49
Albany, Greene	NE	40
● *Albany*, Henry	NW	×
Alberton, Henderson	W	10
Albion View, Hamilton	SE	×
● *Alcorn Siding*, Putnam	N	×
Alcot, Grainger	NE	29
Aldon, Perry	C	×
Alena, Jefferson	E	30
Alex, Davidson	N	×
Alexander's Mills, Hender'n	W	×
Alexandria, DeKalb	C	800
Alfred, Washington	NE	×
Alice, Benton	NW	120
Allardt, Fentress	N	30
Alleghany Springs, Blount	E	80
Allendale, Claiborne	NE	×
Allen's Bridge, Greene	NE	×
Allens Creek, Wayne	S	11
Allensville, Sevier	E	35
Allenton, (see Germantown)		×
● Allentown, Carter	NE	300
Alley, Sequatchie	SE	×
Allisonia, Williamson	C	75
Allred, Overton	N	6
● *Alma*, Hardeman	SW	×
Almaville, Rutherford	C	59
Almeda, Greene	NE	×
Almy, Scott	NE	100
● Alpha, Hamblen	NE	24
Alpine Institute, Overton	N	×
● *Alta*, Shelby	SW	×
Altamont, Grundy	C	67
Alto, Franklin	S	25
Alton Hill, Macon	N	25
Alum Well, Hawkins	NE	28
Amanda, White	C	9
Ambro, Grainger	NE	14
Amis, Hawkins	NE	100
Amonett, Pickett	N	12
● Anderson, Franklin	S	84
Andersonville, Anderson	NE	100
Anderson's Cr. Rd., Camden	E	×
Andrew Chapel, Madison	W	30
Andrews, Maury	C	12
Andy Perry	C	×
● Annadel, Morgan	NE	15
● Antioch, Davidson	N	100
● Apison, James	SE	100
Appleton, Lawrence	S	50
● *Arcadia*, Shelby	SW	×
Arcadia, Sullivan	NE	75
Archer, Marshall	C	14
Arcot, Clay	N	12
Ardee, Montgomery	N	30
Ariadne, Benton	NW	11
Ark, Meigs	SE	×
● Arlington, Shelby	SW	343
Arlington Mills, Giles	S	15
Armathwaite, Fentress	N	8
Armstrong, Montgomery	N	×
Arno, Williamson	C	×
Arrington, Williamson	C	25
Arrow, Hickman	C	×
● Arthur, Claiborne	NE	22
Arthur, Sevier	E	25
Asaton, Chester	SE	24
Asaville, (see Buchanan)		×
Asbury, Knox	E	50
Ashland, Wayne	S	×
Ashland City, Cheatham	N	358
Ashport, Lauderdale	W	25
● Ashwood, Maury	C	25
● *Askins and Dirks*, Obion	NW	×
● Aspen Hill, Giles	S	60
Aster, Bradley	SE	×
● **Athens**, McMinn	SE	2,224
Atkins, Henderson	W	36
● Atoka, Tipton	W	150
● Atwood, Carroll	W	125
Auburn, Cannon	C	100
● Augustus, Hardeman	SW	×
Aunt, Hawkins	NE	×
Austin, Wilson	N	50
● Austin's Mills, Hawkins	NE	30
Austin's Springs, Washin'on	NE	50
Autry, Henderson	W	×
Avoton, Putnam	N	6
Awalt, Franklin	S	100
Ayers, Dyer	W	10
Aymett, Shelby	SW	×
Bacchus, Claiborne	NE	6
Backwoods, Carter	NE	×
Bagdad, Smith	N	15
Baggettsville, Robertson	N	50
● Bailey, Shelby	SW	50
Baileyton, Greene	NE	25
Baird's Mills, Wilson	N	56
● Baker, Davidson	N	75
● *Baker*, Davidson	N	×
Baker's Cross Roads, White	C	10
Baker's Gap, Johnson	NE	14
Bakerville, Humphreys	C	157
Bald Hornet, Montgomery	N	14
Ball Camp, Knox	E	260
Ball Play, Monroe	SE	29
Ball Point, Grainger	NE	50
Balta, Rhea	E	16
Bank, Blount	E	50
Banner, Sevier	E	×
Banner Springs, Fentress	N	20
Baptist, Rhea	E	30
Barcheers, Giles	S	78
Barefield, Rutherford	C	×
Barefoot, Macon	N	×
Bargerton, Henderson	W	29
Barnardsville, Roane	E	19
Barnett, Perry	C	6
Barnville, Lawrence	S	×
Barren Plain, Robertson	N	75
Barretville, Shelby	SW	×
Bartheny, Union	NE	30
● Bartlett, Shelby	SW	800
Bashor's Mill, Washington	NE	30

Place	Div.	Pop.
Basin Spring, Williamson	C	27
Bass, Giles	S	15
Bass Landing, Lake	NW	18
Bassam's Stand, Jackson	N	×
Bateville, Clay	N	72
Bath Springs, Decatur	W	10
Batson's Store, Dickson	N	25
Baucom, Lauderdale	W	×
Baulkom, Decatur	W	×
● *Baxter*, Davidson	N	×
Bayless, Knox	E	30
Bayne, Henry	NW	50
Beachville, Williamson	C	5
● Beacon, Decatur	W	×
Beale, Hickman	C	×
● Bean's Creek, Franklin	S	15
Bean's Station, Grainger	NE	40
Bear, Roane	E	×
Bear Branch, De Kalb	C	29
● Bearden, Knox	E	50
Beardstown, Perry	C	50
Beasley, Marshall	C	25
Beaver Hill, Overton	N	35
Beaver Ridge, Knox	E	75
● Beckwith, Wilson	N	12
Bedford, Bedford	C	16
Bee, Lincoln	S	12
Beech Bluff, Madison	W	60
Beech Creek Island, Perry	C	×
Beech Grove, Coffee	C	300
Beech Hill, Jackson	N	×
Beech Point, Obion	NW	60
Beefrange, Dickson	N	10
Beersheba Springs, Grundy	C	100
Beidleman's, Sullivan	NE	×
● Belfast, Marshall	C	50
Bellamy, Montgomery	N	14
Bellboro, Rutherford	C	×
● Bellbuckle, Bedford	C	715
Belle Eagle, Haywood	W	×
● Belleview, Davidson	N	98
● *Bellevue*, Shelby	SW	×
Bellevue Furnace, Dickson	N	×
Bell's, Crockett	W	550
Bellsburgh, Dickson	N	5
● Bell's Depot, Crockett	W	690
Belltown, Monroe	SE	35
Bellville, Lincoln	S	100
Bellwood, Wilson	N	25
Bellwood Furnace, Stewart	N	60
Belmont, Coffee	C	6
● **Belvidere, Franklin**	S	105
Ben, Maury	C	10
Benjes, Shelby	SW	33
Benton, Polk	SE	165
Bentonville, Marshall	C	×
● *Berclair*, Shelby	SW	×
Berlin, Marshall	C	15
Bermuda, Knox	E	41
Bessie, Lake	NW	×
Beta, Meigs	SE	8
Bethany, Giles	S	93
Bethel, Giles	S	161
Bethel, (see Bethel Springs)		×
● Bethel Springs, McNairy	SW	369
Bethesda, Williamson	C	84
Bethpage, Sumner	N	10
Betsystown, Dickson	N	×
Beulah, Greene	NE	5
● Beverly, Knox	E	20
Bible Hill, Decatur	W	50
Big Barren, Claiborne	NE	29
Big Bottom, Humphreys	C	31
Bigbyville, Maury	C	60
Big Creek Gap, Campbell	NE	10
Big Gully, Blount	E	×
Big Lick, Cumberland	E	15
Big Mountain, Morgan	NE	300
Big Rock, Stewart	N	128
● Big Sandy, Benton	NW	273
Big Spring, Meigs	SE	51
Big West Fork, Montgom'y	N	25
Bilbrey, Carroll	W	10
Billingsly, Bledsoe	E	21
Bingham, Williamson	C	10
Binkley's Mill, Cheatham	N	15
Birchwood, James	SE	100
Bird's Bridge, Greene	NE	28
Birdsong, Benton	NW	×
Birdsville, Cocke	E	30
Bison, Cocke	E	50
Bivens, Giles	S	×
Black Fox, Bradley	SE	×
Black Jack, Robertson	N	160
● *Black Oak Summit*, Knox	E	30
Black's Cross Roads, Rutherford	C	×

Place	Div.	Pop.
Black Water, Hancock	NE	20
Blaine, Grainger	NE	×
Blair's Gap, Sullivan	NE	20
Blake's Mills, Lawrence	S	25
Blakeville, Lincoln	S	12
Blanche, Lincoln	S	250
Blanking, Hawkins	NE	×
Blanton's, Bedford	C	×
Bledsoe, Sumner	N	15
● *Blevins*, Carter	NE	×
Blevins, Hawkins	NE	15
Blizzard, Washington	NE	11
Blockhouse, Blount	E	×
Bloomingdale, Sullivan	NE	19
Bloomington, Putnam	N	48
Blossom, Hawkins	NE	×
Blountville, Sullivan	NE	224
Blue Creek, Stewart	N	25
Blue Grass, (see Hale's Point)		×
● Blue Spring Sta., Bradley	SE	60
● *Bluff*, Henderson	W	×
● Bluff City, Sullivan	NE	662
● Bluff Creek, Smith	N	12
Bluff Mills, Wilson	N	25
Bluff Point, Hickman	C	×
Bluff Springs, Hickman	C	×
Blyth Ferry, James	SE	×
Boatland, Fentress	N	30
Boo, Decatur	W	25
Bobwhite, Robertson	N	14
Bodenham, Giles	S	50
Bogota, Dyer	W	×
Boiling, Fentress	N	25
Bokerwins Landing, Hardeman	SW	×
Bold Spring, Humphreys	C	16
Boler, Clay	N	14
● **Bolivar**, Hardeman	SW	1,100
● Boma, Putnam	N	12
● Bon Air Coal Mine, White	C	100
● Bon-aqua, Hickman	C	50
Bonbrook, Williamson	C	×
● Bond, Shelby	SW	5
Bone Cave, Van Buren	C	10
Bonham, Meigs	SE	30
Booneville, Lincoln	S	64
Boon's Creek, Washington	NE	50
Boonshill, Lincoln	S	25
Booth's Point, Dyer	W	60
Booth's Point, (see Middle Fork)		×
Bordeaux, Davidson	N	×
Boring, Sullivan	NE	24
Boston, Williamson	C	31
Botts, Scott	NE	×
Bowen, Grainger	NE	×
Bowl, Scott	NE	10
Bowmantown, Washington	NE	30
● Box, Humphrey	C	30
Boy, Campbell	NE	30
● *Boyce*, Hamilton	SE	200
● *Boyd*, Knox	E	×
Boyd's Creek, Sevier	E	25
Boyd's Landing, Hardin	SW	×
Boyett, (see Kenton)		×
Boylesville, (see Obion)		×
Bozarth, DeKalb	C	10
Brace, Lawrence	S	15
Brackentown, Sumner	N	15
● Bradens, Fayette	SW	150
● Bradford, Gibson	W	222
Bradon's Knobs, Bledsoe	E	×
Bradshaw, Giles	S	50
Bradys, Putnam	N	×
Bradyville, Cannon	C	105
Bragg's Gap, Maury	C	×
Brakebill, Monroe	SE	15
Bramley, Carroll	W	×
Branchville, Bedford	C	20
Bransford, Sumner	N	50
Braxton, Cannon	C	75
Brays, Hancock	NE	10
Brayton, Bledsoe	E	11
Brazil, Gibson	W	50
Breedenton, Meigs	SE	10
● Brentwood, Williamson	C	142
Briceville, Anderson	NE	1,354
Brick Church, Giles	S	60
Brick Mill, Blount	E	30
Bride, Tipton	W	20
● Bridgeport, Cocke	E	50
Bridges, Smith	N	11
Brier, Sevier	E	×
● *Briggs*, Humphreys	C	×
Briggs, Unicoi	NE	×
Bright, Hamblen	NE	×
Bright Hope, Greene	NE	×
● *Brighton*, Lincoln	S	×

Place	Div.	Pop.
● Brighton, Tipton	W	214
● Brinkley, Fayette	SW	10
Brinley, Chester	SE	×
● Bristol, Sullivan	NE	8,324
Bristow, Benton	NW	×
Britton, Maury	C	×
Britt's Landing, Perry	C	30
Brittsville, Meigs	SE	8
Broad, Cocke	E	×
Broadview, Maury	C	12
Broadway, Knox	E	×
Brock, Sequatchie	SE	×
Brodie's Landing, Decatur	W	20
Brooklin, Davidson	N	10
Brown, Cannon	C	×
● ***Brown*, Hickman**	C	×
Brownlow, Unicoi	NE	6
Brown Mills, Putnam	N	25
Brownsboro, Washington	NE	75
Brownsport Furnace, (see Decaturville)		×
Brownsport Landing, Dec'r	W	×
Brown's Chapel, Hamilton	SE	×
● **Brownsville**, Haywood	W	2,516
Broylesville, Washington	NE	×
Bruce's, Knox	E	×
● Brunswick, Shelby	SW	150
● Brush Creek, Smith	N	6
Bryantburgh, Hardeman	SW	30
● Bryant Station, Maury	C	14
Bryson, Giles	S	15
Buchanan, Henry	NW	50
● Buckeye, Campbell	NE	14
Bucklick, Morgan	NE	×
● Buck Lodge, Sumner	N	15
Bucksnort, Lincoln	S	12
Bud, Anderson	NE	25
Beuna Vista, Carroll	W	89
Buffalo, Humphreys	C	25
● *Buffalo*, Hickman	C	×
● *Buffalo*, Lawrence	S	×
Buffalo Ridge, Washington	NE	18
● Buffalo Valley, Putnam	N	150
● Buford, Giles	S	15
Buhler, Wilson	N	12
● Bull Run, Knox	E	100
● Bull's Gap, Hawkins	NE	150
Bumpus Mills, Stewart	N	90
Bunch, Hamilton	SE	180
Bunker Hill, Giles	S	87
● Buntyn, Shelby	SW	30
Burbank, Carter	NE	36
Burem's Store, Hawkins	NE	150
Burgen, Cannon	C	6
Burke, Cumberland	E	8
Burlison, Tipton	W	10
● Burns, Dickson	N	300
Burns Mill, Roane	E	35
Burt, Cannon	C	10
Burton, Putnam	N	300
Burville, Morgan	NE	20
● *Busby*, Lawrence	S	×
Bushing, Overton	N	×
Butchers Springs, (see Arthur)		×
Butler, Johnson	NE	200
Butler's Landing, Clay	N	40
Butterfly, Sullivan	NE	×
Buxter, Carroll	W	×
Bybee, Cocke	E	50
Byrdstown, Fentress	N	10
Byrdstown, Pickett	N	50
Byrne, Putnam	N	42
Byron, Dickson	N	×
Cabinet, Macon	N	×
Cactus, London	E	×
Cabinet, Macon	N	×
Cactus, Davidson	N	31
Cade's Cove, Blount	E	13
● *Cade's Mill*, Gibson	W	×
Caffey, McNairy	SW	87
Cagle, Sequatchie	SE	×
Cainsville, Wilson	N	50
Cairo, Crockett	W	10
Cairo, Sumner	N	8
Calf Killer, Putnam	W	78
Calhoun, McMinn	SE	222
Calista, Robertson	N	×
● *Callendar*, Williamson	C	×
Camargo, Lincoln	S	30
● **Camden**, Benton	NW	830
Camden, McNairy	SW	×
Cameron, White	C	×
Camilla, Hancock	NE	24
Campbell, Knox	E	75
● *Campbell's*, Maury	C	120
Campbellsville, Giles	S	83
Camp Creek, Greene	NE	26

Name	Section	Pop.
Camp Ground, White	C	×
Canaan, Maury	C	6
Canadaville, Fayette	SW	18
Cane Ridge, Van Buren	C	20
Caney Branch, Greene	NE	170
Caney Spring, Marshall	C	50
● *Cantrell*, Hickman	C	23
● Capleville, Shelby	SW	100
Capling, DeKalb	C	10
Capp's Ford, Claiborne	NE	60
Capuchin, Scott	NE	20
● Cardiff, Roane	E	430
● *Careyville*, Campbell	NE	×
Caringer, Monroe	SE	60
Carl, Williamson	C	10
Carlisle, Stewart	N	×
Carlock, McMinn	SE	19
Carlocksville, Rutherford	C	82
Carmel, Montgomery	N	15
● *Carnegie*, Washington	NE	×
Carnsville, Carroll	W	18
Carolina, Haywood	W	30
Carp, Rhea	E	21
Carpenter's, Williamson	C	15
● *Carpenter*, Lawrence	S	×
● Carroll, Madison	W	50
Carrollton, Campbell	NE	×
Carrollville, Wayne	S	×
Carrville, Washington	NE	18
Carson Springs, Cocke	E	×
● Carter's Creek, Maury	C	200
Carter's Depot, (see South Watauga)		×
● Carter's Furnace, Carter	NE	32
Carter's Landing, (see Dyersburg)		×
● **Carthage**, Smith	N	478
Caruthers, Wilson	N	8
● Caryville, Campbell	NE	115
Casey, Macon	N	×
Caseyville, Macon	N	15
Cashon, Weakley	NW	×
Cash Point, Lincoln	S	28
Ceson, Cannon	C	10
Casper, Johnson	NE	×
Casie, Washington	NE	×
Cassville, White	C	15
Castalian Springs, Sumner	N	75
Castoria, Tipton	W	×
● Caswell's Station, Knox	E	×
Catalpa, Madison	W	10
● *Catamount*, Wilson	N	×
Cate's Cross Roads, Sevier	E	10
Cateston, Cannon	C	37
Catlen's Mills, DeKalb	C	34
Catlettsburgh, Sevier	E	90
Cave, White	C	83
Cave Creek, Roane	E	15
Cave Mills, Dickson	N	15
Cave Springs, (see Milligan)		×
Cave Springs, Hamilton	SE	36
Cawthon, Carroll	W	32
Ceulton, Bradley	SE	×
Cedar Bluff, Smith	N	×
Cedar Chapel, Hardeman	SW	100
Cedar Creek, Greene	NE	26
Cedar Creek Furnace, Perry	C	×
Cedar Creek Landing, Perry	C	20
Cedar Ford, Knox	E	×
Cedar Fork, Claiborne	NE	31
Cedar Grove, Carroll	W	25
● Cedar Hill, Robertson	N	40
Cedar Lane, Greene	NE	34
Cedar Point, Tipton	W	×
Cedar Springs, Marion	SE	15
Celina, Clay	N	[illegible]
Cemetery, Shelby	SW	×
Centre, (see Bride)		×
Centre Grove, Bedford	C	[illegible]
Centre Point, Chester	SE	50
Centre Star, Maury	C	×
● **Centreville**, Hickman	C	498
Cerro Gordo, Hardin	SW	40
Chable, Polk	SE	30
Chadbourne, Cumberland	E	×
Chalk Bluffs, Hardin	SW	×
Chalmers, Sullivan	NE	×
Chandler, Blount	E	×
Chalybeate, Van Buren	C	30
● Chancy, Robertson	N	6
Chanute, Pickett	N	5
Chapel Hill, Marshall	C	140
Chapple Hill, Henderson	W	30
Charger, Moore	S	25
Charity, Moore	S	25
● Charleston, Bradley	SE	391
Charlotte, Dickson	N	427
Chaseville, Benton	NW	40

Tennessee

Name	Section	Pop.
Chatata, Bradley	SE	90
● **CHATTANOOGA**, Hamilton	SE	29 100
Cheap Hill, Cheatham	N	29
● *Cheatham*, Shelby	SW	×
Chelsea, Shelby	SW	×
Cherokee, Lauderdale	W	×
Cherry, Montgomery	N	×
Cherry Creek, White	C	10
Cherry Mount, Robertson	N	×
● Cherry Valley, Wilson	N	30
Chester, Henry	NW	×
● Chesterfield, Henderson	W	×
Chestna, McMinn	SE	×
Chestnut Bloom, Hamblen	NE	20
Chestnut Bluff, Crockett	W	100
Chestnut Grove, Haywood	W	×
Chestnut Hill, Jefferson	E	26
Chestnut Mound, Smith	N	100
Chestnut Ridge, Lincoln	S	50
Chestuee Mills, Polk	SE	15
● Chewalla, McNairy	SW	60
● Chickamauga, Hamilton	SE	55
Childress, Sullivan	NE	15
Chilhowee, Blount	E	19
Chimney Top, Hawkins	NE	×
Chipman, Sumner	N	×
Chisem, Lawrence	S	8
Choice, Humphreys	C	×
Choptack, Hawkins	NE	40
Christie, Washington	NE	16
● *Christiana*, Rutherford	C	62
Christmasville, Carroll	W	19
Chuckaluck, McMinn	SE	29
● Chuckey City, Greene	NE	140
Chucky Valley, Washingtn	NE	25
Chumlea, Knox	E	×
Church Grove, Knox	E	30
Church Hill, Hawkins	NE	30
Citico, Monroe	SE	×
● *Citico Junc.*, Hamilton	SE	×
Clairfield, Claiborne	NE	15
Clara, Washington	NE	14
Clardyville, Lincoln	S	23
Clarkrange, Fentress	N	20
Clarksburgh, Carroll	W	226
Clarkson, Washington	NE	×
Clarkstown, White	C	×
● **Clarksville**, M't'gmery	N	7,924
Claronation, Bradley	SE	10
Clay, Shelby	SW	×
Clay Brook, Madison	W	95
Clayton, Obion	NW	30
Clear Branch, Unicoi	NE	50
Clear Fork, Cannon	C	14
Clearmont, Warren	C	8
Clear Springs, Grainger	NE	42
● *Cleburne*, Maury	C	×
Clementsville, Clay	N	19
Clenny, Jackson	N	×
Cleo, Bradley	SE	29
● **Cleveland**, Bradley	SE	2,863
Cliff, Blount	E	×
Cliff Springs, Overton	N	×
Clifton, Wayne	S	529
Clifton, McNairy	SW	×
Clifts, Hamilton	SE	×
Climer, Bradley	SE	48
Clinch, Hancock	NE	25
Clinch River, Anderson	NE	36
● *Clinch River*, Claiborne	NE	×
● **Clinton**, Anderson	NE	1,198
Clinton, Hickman	C	×
Close, DeKalb	C	12
Clover Bottom, Sullivan	NE	57
Clovercroft, Williamson	C	×
Cloverdale, Dickson	N	30
Clover Hill, Blount	E	60
Cloverport, Hardeman	SW	30
Cloyd's Creek, Blount	E	30
Clydeton, Humphrey	C	5
Coahulla, Bradley	SE	31
● Coal Creek, Anderson	NE	1,685
Coalfield, Morgan	NE	30
Cochran, Marshall	C	25
Coffee, McNairy	SW	×
Coffee Landing, Hardin	SW	18
Cog Hill, McMinn	SE	102
Coker Creek, Monroe	SE	8
Colby, Sullivan	NE	75
Coldwater, Lincoln	S	8
Coldwell, Bedford	C	15
Colesman's Mills, Perry	C	×
● Colesburg, Dickson	N	22
● College, Bledsoe	E	60
● *College Farm*, Knox	E	×
College Grove, Williamson	C	400

Tennessee

Name	Section	Pop.
Collier's Store, Wilson	N	13
● Colliersville, Shelby	SW	696
● **Columbia**, Maury	C	5,370
Columbus, Jackson	N	×
Columbus, Polk	SE	×
Comfort, Marion	SE	×
Commerce, Wilson	N	55
Como, Henry	NW	200
Compensation, Claiborne	NE	25
Compton, Rutherford	C	8
Conasauga, Polk	SE	40
● Concord, Knox	E	271
● *Condon*, Polk	SE	×
Condry, Grainger	NE	×
Conkling, Washington	NE	11
Conway, Giles	S	8
Conyersville, Henry	NW	100
● **Cookeville**, Putnam	N	469
Coopertown, Robertson	N	75
Copeland, (see Old Fort)		×
● Corbandale, Montgomery	N	75
Corinth, (see Minott)		×
Corletts Cross Roads, Marsh'l	C	19
Corn, Blount	E	28
Cornersville, Marshall	C	300
Corning, Lake	NW	×
Corona, Tipton	W	15
● Corrytown, Knox	E	×
● Cortner, Bedford	C	5
Corums, Wilson	N	×
Cosby, Cocke	E	38
Costner, Cocke	E	19
Cottage Grove, Henry	NW	250
Cottage Home, Wilson	N	32
Cotton Port, Meigs	SE	29
Cottontown, Sumner	N	35
Couchville, Davidson	N	50
● Coulterville, Hamilton	SE	108
County Line, Moore	S	64
County Poor House, Maury	C	×
● **Covington**, Tipton	W	1,067
● **Cowan**, Franklin	S	624
Cowards, Knox	E	×
Cox, Sevier	E	10
Coxburgh, Benton	NW	50
Coytee, Loudon	E	15
Crab Orchard, Cumberland	E	8
Crab Orchard, Fentress	N	×
Crab Orchard, Carter	NE	×
Craggie Hope, Cheatham	N	50
Cranesville, Hardeman	SW	100
● *Cravens*, Hamilton	SE	×
Cravens Landing, Hardin	SW	20
Crawfords, Overton	N	10
Crawfordton, DeKalb	C	480
Creevy, Madison	W	15
Crescent, Rutherford	C	16
Creston, Cumberland	E	×
Crestview, Lawrence	S	12
Crider, Carroll	W	10
Crisp, Warren	C	28
● Crockett, Obion	NW	25
Crockett Mills, Crockett	W	100
Crooked Fork, Morgan	NE	25
Crookshanks, Washington	NE	30
Cross Anchor, Greene	NE	21
Cross Plains, Robertson	N	100
Cross Roads, Warren	C	14
Cross Roads, Bedford	C	×
Crossville, Cumberland	E	266
Croton, Coffee	C	30
Crowell, Humphreys	C	18
Crowson, Lawrence	S	10
Crucifer, Henderson	W	×
Crumps Island, Hardin	SW	5
Crump's Landing, Hardin	SW	×
Crunk, Robertson	N	33
● *Crusher*, Smith	N	×
Crystal, Obion	NW	75
Cuba, Shelby	SW	25
Cuba Landing, Humphreys	C	15
Cullen, Weakley	NW	×
Culleoka, Maury	C	334
Culp, Perry	C	12
Culpepper, Cannon	C	40
Cumberland, Sumner	N	×
● Cumberland City, Stewart	N	244
● Cumberland Furnace, D'k'n	N	600
● Cumberland Gap, Claib'e	NE	1,000
Cummingsville, Van Buren	C	10
Cundall's Mills, Smith	N	22
● Curve, Lauderdale	W	150
Cusick, Sevier	E	31
Custer, Anderson	NE	24
Cute, Meigs	SE	18
Cynthiana, Jefferson	E	5
● Cypress, McNairy	SW	×

Post Office, County	Dir.	Pop.
Cypress Inn, Wayne	S	25
Cyruston, Lincoln	S	50
Dabbs, Perry	C	×
● Daisy, Hamilton	SE	370
Daiseydell, Grainger	NE	36
Dancing Branch, Monroe	SE	5
Dancyville, Haywood	W	150
Dandridge, Jefferson	E	451
Danielsville, Dickson	N	6
● Dante, Knox	E	80
● Danville, Houston	N	107
● Darden, Henderson	W	×
Dare, Bradley	SE	×
Darius, Rhea	E	102
Darkey Springs, White	C	18
● Dark's Mill, Maury	C	10
● D'Armend, Roane	E	×
Darnall, Lake	NW	×
Darwin, (see Evansville)		×
Datura, Hancock	NE	18
● *Daws*, Sequatchie	SE	10
Daws, Madison	W	10
Daylight, Warren	C	19
● Dayton, Rhea	E	2,719
Dean, Bedford	C	×
Deanburgh, Chester	SE	50
Deane, Cheatham	N	×
● *Deans*, Hickman	C	×
● *De Armond*, Roane	E	8
Decatur, Meigs	SE	192
Decaturville, Decatur	W	350
● Decherd, Franklin	S	725
Deep Spring, Cheatham	N	×
Deer Lodge, Morgan	NE	88
Dearmont, Morgan	NE	×
Deersville, Robertson	N	×
Defeated, Smith	N	50
DeKalb, DeKalb	C	13
Delia, Jefferson	E	×
Delina, Marshall	C	15
Dellmonell, Hawkins	NE	18
Dellrose, Lincoln	S	19
Delphi, Sequatchie	SE	10
● Del Rio, Cocke	E	65
Demoss' Store, Davidson	N	20
● Denmark, Madison	W	300
Denning, Sumner	N	×
Denson's Landing, Perry	C	20
● Deptford, Marion	SE	100
De Ray, Giles	S	10
Derby, Greene	NE	×
Detroit, Tipton	W	30
Devenport, Warren	C	8
Devider, Benton	NW	19
Dew Drop, Humphreys	C	×
● Dexter, Shelby	SW	×
Diamond Hill, Henderson	W	30
Diana, Giles	S	12
Dibrell, Warren	C	16
● Dickson, Dickson	N	938
Difficult, Smith	N	50
Dildays, Stewart	N	36
Dilltown, Rutherford	N	10
● *Dilwin Springs*, Claib'ne	NE	60
Dinning, Sumner	N	7
Disco, Blount	E	18
Ditty, Putnam	N	16
Dixie Mills, Decatur	W	25
Dixieville, Decatur	W	25
Dixons Springs, Smith	N	300
Doctors, Scott	NE	10
Dodge, Cheatham	N	×
Doduburg, Wilson	N	20
Dodson, White	C	11
Doeville, Johnson	NE	15
Dollar, Carroll	W	14
Donelson, Davidson	N	240
Donnell's Chapel, Ruther'd	C	85
Donoho, Smith	N	12
● *Donovan*, Anderson	NE	×
Dorris, Hardeman	SW	×
● Dorsetts, Anderson	NE	×
Dotsonville, Montgomery	N	19
Double Bridges, Lauderdale	W	75
● Double Springs, Putnam	N	15
Doudy's Store, Fayette	SW	×
Doughertyville, Hawkins	NE	×
Douglass Shed, Wash'ton	NE	10
Dove, Marion	SE	26
Dover, Stewart	N	400
Dover Dale L'nd'g, Hu'p'ey	C	×
Dover Furnace, Stewart	N	×
● Dove's Mill, Washington	NE	×
Dowelltown, DeKalb	C	233
Doyal, Grainger	NE	×
● Doyle's Station, White	C	28
Dozier, Davidson	N	25

Post Office, County	Dir.	Pop.
● **Dresden**, Weakly	NW	420
Drift, Cocke	E	×
Driskill, Cocke	E	17
Drop, White	C	8
Drummonds, Tipton	W	10
Dry Creek, Carter	NE	24
***Dry Fork*, Sumner**	N	29
Dry Hill, Lauderdale	W	10
Dry Valley, Putnam	N	37
Duck River, Hickman	C	42
● Ducktown, Polk	SE	221
● *Dudleys*, Montgomery	N	×
Duersville, Robertson	N	8
Dug Hill, Putnam	N	6
Duke, Union	NE	×
Dukedom, Weakly	NW	100
● Dull, Dickson	N	5
● *Dummy Junc.*, Shelby	SW	×
Dumplin, Jefferson	E	15
Dunbar, Decatur	W	30
● **Dunlap**, Sequatchie	SE	332
Duo, Claiborne	NE	24
Duplex, Williamson	C	6
Durhamville, Lauderdale	W	50
Dustin, Lawrence	W	12
Dutch, Granger	NE	×
Dutch Valley, Anderson	NE	20
● Dyer, Gibson	W	606
● **Dyersburgh**, Dyer	W	2,009
Dyer's Ferry, Grainger	NE	75
Dyke's, Roane	E	×
Eads, Shelby	SW	×
● *Eagle*, Lawrence	S	×
Eagle Creek, Overton	N	25
Eagle Furnace, Roane	E	15
Eagle Tannery, Wayne	S	×
Eagleville, Rutherford	C	275
Earnest, Bradley	SE	10
Easley, Sullivan	NE	×
Eason, Macon	N	×
Eastbrook Springs, Frank'n	S	×
● East Chattanooga, Ham'n	SE	1,000
East Cumberland Gap, Claiborne	NE	32
East End, Hamilton	SE	1,000
East Fork, Sevier	E	360
Eastlake, Hamilton	SE	×
● *East Nashville*, Davidson	N	×
● *Easton*, Davidson	N	×
Eastport, Pickett	N	12
● *East Sparta*, White	C	×
● *East Troy*, Obion	W	120
Eaton, Gibson	W	25
Eaton's Cross Roads, L'don	E	48
● Ebenezer, Knox	N	21
Ebenezer, (see Mason)		×
Echo, Mason	N	62
Eclipse Furnace, Stewart	N	×
Economy, Hardin	SW	30
Eden's Ridge, Sullivan	NE	25
● Edgefield, Davidson	N	×
● Edgefield Junc., Davidson	N	250
Edgewood, Dickson	N	6
Edgeworth, Sullivan	NE	25
Edith, Lauderdale	W	20
Edmunds, Gibson	W	×
Edna, Jefferson	E	×
● *Edna*, Fayette	SW	×
Edom, Johnson	NE	×
Edwina, Cocke	E	120
Effie, Union	NE	18
Ego, Lincoln	S	8
Eggville, Benton	NW	12
Edison, Hawkins	NE	20
Eight Mile Furnace, Wayne	S	×
Elba, Fayette	SW	×
Elbridge, Obion	NW	20
Eldorado Springs, Rob'tson	N	21
Elgin, Scott	NE	15
Eli, Decatur	W	×
Elijah, White	C	×
Elizabethtown, Carter	NE	734
Elk, Decatur	W	×
Elkhorn, Henry	NW	60
Elk Mills, Carter	NE	×
Elkmont, Giles	S	×
Elkmont Springs, Giles	S	×
Elk River, Franklin	S	30
Elkton, Giles	S	165
● Elk Valley, Campbell	NE	150
Ellejoy, Blount	E	25
● *Elliotts*, Montgomery	N	×
Ellis, Stewart	N	×
Ellison, Claiborne	NE	×
Ellsworth, Blount	E	×
● *Elmers*, Decatur	W	×
Elmerville, Trousdale	N	12

Post Office, County	Dir.	Pop.
Elm Tree, Weakley	NW	10
Elmwood, Smith	N	50
Elmwood, Sumner	N	×
Elmwood Cemetery, Shelby	SW	×
● Elora, Lincoln	S	22
● Elverton, Roane	E	14
● Embreeville, Washington	NE	×
Emerts Cove, Sevier	E	29
Emory, Morgan	NE	10
● Emory Gap, Roane	E	386
English, Cocke	E	×
Enigma, Smith	N	10
Enloe, Benton	NW	×
Enoch, Smith	N	20
Enon College, Trousdale	N	45
Ensley, Shelby	SW	35
● *Ensley Station*, Shelby	SW	×
Enterprise, Maury	C	10
● *Eola*, Fayette	SW	×
Epperson, Monroe	SE	24
Epperson Springs, Macon	N	20
Equator, Wayne	S	×
Erasmus, Cumberland	E	×
Erie, Loudon	E	5
● **Erin**, Houston	N	789
Ernestville, Unicoi	NE	×
Erwin, Unicoi	NE	150
Esco, Union	NE	×
Essary Springs, Hardeman	SW	×
Estamauler, Haywood	W	×
● Estill Springs, Franklin	S	50
Ethel, Roane	N	81
● Ethridge, Lawrence	S	×
● *Etna*, Hickman	C	12
Etnaville, Benton	NW	14
Etnaville, Decatur	W	×
Etolla, Bradley	SE	11
Ettaton, Maury	C	38
Etter, Pickett	N	×
● *Etters*, Shelby	SW	×
Euchee, Meigs	SE	25
Eulia, Macon	N	46
Eurekaton, Haywood	W	39
Eusebia, Blount	E	×
● Eva, Benton	NW	50
Evanston, Warren	C	12
Eve Mills, Monroe	SE	52
● Evensville, Rhea	E	22
Everglade, Rutherford	C	9
● *Ewell*, Maury	C	32
Ewing, Blount	E	×
Exeda, Clay	N	36
Exum, DeKalb	C	×
Fairfield, Bedford	C	75
Fair Garden, Sevier	E	35
Fair Grounds, Wayne	S	×
Fairmount, Hamilton	SE	69
Fairview, Anderson	NE	51
● Falcon, McNairy	SW	275
Fall Branch, Washington	NE	80
Fall Creek, Bedford	C	100
Falling Water, Hamilton	SE	×
Fall Mills, Franklin	S	25
Fall River, Lawrence	S	60
Family, Carroll	W	19
Fancher's Mills, White	C	16
Farmers Exchange, Hickman	C	20
Farmers Valley, Perry	C	20
Farmingdale, Bledsoe	E	26
Farmington, Marshall	C	90
Farmville, Henderson	W	×
Farner, Polk	SE	×
Farris Creek, Moore	S	15
● Faxon, Benton	NW	50
Fayette Corners, Fayette	SW	50
● **Fayetteville**, Lincoln	S	2,410
Fayville, Dyer	W	×
Febuary, Washington	NE	18
Fedora, Stewart	N	×
Felker, Bradley	SE	29
Fenton, Hancock	NE	×
Fernvale, Williamson	C	20
Fernvale Springs, Willi'mson	C	×
Fetzerton, Polk	SE	34
Fews, Jefferson	E	×
● *Fifes*, Sumner	N	×
Fiketon, McMinn	SE	4
Fillmore, Sequatchie	SE	×
Fincastle, Campbell	NE	72
Finley, Dyer	W	10
Fishdam, Sullivan	NE	×
Fisher's Creek, Hawkins	NE	6
● *Fisherville*, Shelby	SW	×
Fish Spring, Carter	NE	×
Fits, Fentress	N	33
Flag Pond, Unicoi	NE	30
Flat Creek, Bedford	C	150

Place	Section	Population
Flat Gap, Jefferson	N	42
Flat Rock, Smith	N	25
Flat Rock, Davidson	N	38
Flat Woods, Wayne	S	80
● Flenniken, Knox	E	120
● Flintville, Lincoln	S	250
● Flippin, Lauderdale	W	25
Floraton, Rutherford	C	20
● Florence Sta., Rutherford	C	35
Floursville, Washington	NE	15
Flowers, Benton	NW	30
● *Floyds*, Knox	E	×
Floyedville, (see McBride)		×
Fly, Maury	C	×
Flynn's Lick, Jackson	N	44
● *Fogg Street*, Davidson	N	×
Folger, McMinn	SE	×
Foot, Putnam	N	×
Foot Island, (see Randolph)		×
Ford, Knox	E	×
Fordtown, Sullivan	NE	21
Forest, Warren	C	×
Forest Hill, Shelby	NW	45
Forest Home, Williamson	C	19
Forked Deer, Haywood	W	×
Forks of Pike, DeKalb	C	14
Forkvale, Campbell	NE	20
Fort Donelson, Stewart	N	×
Fort Henry, Stewart	N	8
Fort Pickering, Shelby	SW	×
Fort Pillow, Lauderdale	NW	60
● *Forts*, Robertson	N	×
Fort Wright, Tipton	W	×
Forty-Eight, Wayne	S	150
● *Forty-Five Mile Siding*, Fayette	SW	×
Fossil, Roane	E	8
● *Fosters*, Henderson	W	×
● Fosterville, Rutherford	C	100
Fountain City, Knox	E	×
● Fountain Creek, Maury	C	24
Fountain Head, Knox	E	×
● Fountain Head, Sumner	N	250
Four Mile Branch, Monroe	SE	28
Foutch, DeKalb	C	×
● Fowlkes, Dyer	W	50
Fox, Sevier	E	6
Fox Spring, Clay	N	20
France, Overton	N	29
Frank, Humphreys	C	15
Frankfort, Morgan	NE	8
● **Franklin**, Williamson	C	2,250
Frayser, Shelby	SW	10
Fredonia, Montgomery	N	15
Free Hill, Washington	NE	200
Freeland's Mill, (see Buchanan)		×
Freeman, (see Maury City)		×
Fremont, Obion	NW	20
● French, Knox	E	16
Friendship, Crockett	W	255
Friends Station, Jefferson	E	×
● Friendsville, Blount	E	300
Frierson, Maury	C	10
Frost, Anderson	NE	18
● Fruitland, Gibson	W	15
Fruit Valley, Bedford	C	20
Fry, Hawkins	NE	24
Fuga, Moore	S	×
● *Fulens*, Greene	NE	×
Fulton, Lauderdale	W	134
Fulton Station, Obion	NW	623
Furnace, Johnson	NE	60
Furnace Landing, Perry	C	×
Gabbatha, Jackson	N	10
Gabe, Union	NE	×
● Gadsden, Crockett	W	267
Gainesborough, Jack'n	N	462
Gainsville, Tipton	W	×
Galaville, Hickman	C	×
Galbraith's Springs, Hak's	NE	27
● **Gallatin**, Sumner	N	2,078
Gallatin Landing, Sumner	N	×
● Gallaway, Fayette	SW	81
Gamble's Store, Blount	E	50
Gann, Gibson	W	×
Gap Creek, Knox	E	27
Gap Run, Carter	NE	48
● Garber's Mills, Wash'ton	NE	36
● Gardner, Weakley	NW	253
Garfield, Benton	NW	19
Garland, Tipton	W	25
Garrott, Overton	N	×
Gas, Giles	S	×
Gassaway, Cannon	C	123
● Gates, Lauderdale	W	204
Gath, Warren	C	12
Gatlinburgh, Sevier	E	31
Gault, Hawkins	NE	×
Gayfield Mills, Houston	N	×
Ged, Haywood	W	5
Genesis, Cumberland	E	45
George, Claiborne	NE	100
Georgetown, Meigs	SE	92
● Germantown, Shelby	SE	268
Gibbs, Hardin	SW	×
Gibb's Cross Roads, Macon	N	50
● Gibson, Gibson	W	100
Gibson Wells, Gibson	W	20
Gilbertsborough, Giles	S	×
Giles, Carroll	W	×
Gillentine, Van Buren	C	82
Gillenwater, Hawkins	NE	18
Gillie, Henry	NW	×
Gillise's Mills, Hardin	SW	9
Gilt Edge, Tipton	W	10
Girlton, Campbell	NE	24
Givens, Cocke	E	15
Gizzard, Marion	SE	×
Gladdico, Jackson	N	×
Glade Creek, Bledsoe	E	×
Gladeland, Carter	NE	×
Glades, Morgan	NE	39
Gladeville, Wilson	N	200
Glascow, Rhea	E	959
Glass, Obion	NW	360
● Gleeson Station, Wek'y	NW	324
● Glen Alice, Roane	E	98
● Glen Cliff, Davidson	N	59
● Glenellen, Montgomery	N	50
Glenloch, Monroe	SE	15
● Glenmary, Scott	NE	200
Glenn's Store, Maury	C	15
Glimp, Lauderdale	W	75
Globe, Marshall	C	×
Godfrey, Knox	E	×
● Godwin, Maury	C	150
Goffton, Putnam	N	10
Goin, Claiborne	NE	16
Golddust, Lauderdale	W	100
Gold Point, Hamilton	SE	×
Gollins Landing, Shelby	SW	×
Goodbars, Warren	C	15
Goodfield, Meigs	SE	×
● Goodlettsville, Davidson	N	529
● Goodrich, Hickman	C	358
Good Spring, Giles	S	10
● Gordonsville, Smith	N	150
Gore, Bradford	SE	8
Gorman, Humphreys	C	15
Goshen, Lincoln	S	15
Gossburgh, Coffee	C	15
Goulds, Coffee	C	12
Grace, White	C	35
Grady, Madison	W	×
● Graham, Hickman	C	25
Granberry, Shelby	SW	×
● Grand Junc., Hardeman	SW	450
Grand Rapids, Carter	NE	×
● Grandview, Rhea	E	58
Grandview Landing, H'dn.	SW	10
Grant, Smith	N	100
Grantville, Montgomery	N	15
Granville, Jackson	N	227
Grapeton, Sevier	E	30
Grapevine, Bledsoe	E	32
Grassland, Williamson	C	10
Grassy Cove, Cumberland	E	47
Gravel Hill, McNairy	SW	25
● *Gravel Pit*, Houston	N	×
Graveston, Knox	E	54
Graysburgh, Franklin	S	×
Gray's Hill, Roane	E	120
● Graysville, Rhea	E	389
Graytown, Hickman	C	19
Greenawalt, Coffee	C	30
Greenback, Loudon	E	30
● Green Brier, Robertson	N	425
● **Greeneville**, Greene	NE	1,779
● Greenfield, Weakley	NW	801
● Green Hill, Wilson	N	25
Green Pond, Hamilton	SE	×
Green Tree, White	C	10
Greenvale, Wilson	N	30
● Greenwood, Wilson	N	12
Grey, Overton	N	×
Grief, Bradley	SE	15
Griffiths, Loudon	E	7
● *Grinders*, Hickman	C	×
Gromley, Monroe	SE	×
Gross, Sullivan	NE	11
Groveland, Maury	C	5
● *Grover*, Madison	W	×
Grovewood, Carroll	W	32
Gruetli, Grundy	C	50
● Gudger, Monroe	SE	19
Guenther, Roane	E	×
Gumfork, Scott	NE	60
● Guy's, McNairy	SW	×
● *Gwin's*, Carroll	W	36
Gypsy, Carroll	W	33
Hade's Gap, Maury	C	×
Haglerville, Henry	NW	×
Hale's Point, Lauderdale	W	20
Hale's Point, Lauderdale	W	×
Hale's Springs, Hawkins	NE	60
Haleville, DeKalb	C	10
● Hayley, Bedford	C	70
Half Moon Island, Roane	E	25
Halfpone, Chatham	N	×
Halfway, Cumberland	E	29
● *Halls*, Lauderdale	W	75
Hall's Cross Roads, Knox	E	32
Hall's Hill, Rutherford	C	20
Hamburgh, Hardin	SW	111
Hamilton Landing, Clay	N	×
● Hamilton Springs, Cl'b'e	NE	200
Hampshire, Maury	C	50
● *Hampshire Crossing*, Ma'y	C	×
Hampton, Carter	NE	35
● Hampton Sta., Montgo'ry	N	29
Handleyton, Robertson	N	30
Hanging Limb, Overton	N	×
Hanlan, Warren	C	12
Hanley, Haywood	W	×
● Hansford, Lauderdale	W	441
Happy Valley, Carter	NE	42
Harbour, Sullivan	NE	×
● *Harding*, Davidson	N	×
Hardin Valley, Knox	E	150
Hardison's Mills, Maury	C	90
Hargus, Grainger	NE	48
Harmony, Washington	NE	5
Harms, Lincoln	S	×
Harpeth, Williamson	C	14
Harriman, Roane	E	716
● *Harriman Junc.*, Mor'n	NE	×
● Harris, Obion	NW	31
Harrisburgh, Sevier	E	50
Harrisburg, (see Malesus)		×
Harrison's Landing, (see Corona)		×
Harrison, James	SE	60
Harrogate, Claiborne	NE	500
Hart, Bledsoe	E	×
Hartranft, Clairbone	NE	×
● **Hartsville**, Trousdale	N	654
● *Harwell*, Giles	S	×
Hascue, Greene	NE	×
Hastings, Henry	NW	×
Hatch, Roane	E	121
● Hatchie, Madison	W	85
Hatchee Landing, Lauder'e	W	×
Hathaway, Lake	NW	50
Hatmaker, Campbell	NE	14
Hattonville, Wilson	N	8
Haven, Bedford	C	10
Hawes Cross Roads, Washington	N	21
Hawks, Robinson	N	6
Haworth, Scott	NE	×
Hawthorne, Bedford	C	25
Haydenburgh, Jackson	N	10
Haynes, Union	NE	20
Haysville, Macon	N	13
Hazel Ridge, Dickson	N	24
Head of Barren, Claiborne	NE	16
Head of Laurel, Johnson	NE	48
Heads, White	C	8
Heartwood, Bedford	C	×
Heath, Dickson	N	×
Heaton Creek, Carter	NE	×
Hebbertsburgh, Cumberland	E	23
Hebronville, Blount	E	×
● *Heishell's*, Knox	E	×
Helen, Henry	NW	×
● Helenwood, Scott	NE	299
Heliotrope, Polk	SE	69
Help, Cocke	E	60
Heltonville, Grainger	NE	×
● *Hematite*, Montgomery	N	×
Hemlock, Sullivan	NE	×
Henard, Overton	N	10
● **Henderson**, Chester	SE	1,069
● *Henderson*, Rutherford	C	×
Henderson's Cross Roads, Wilson	N	20
Henderson's Springs, Sevier	E	19
● Hendersonville, Sumner	N	215
Hendrix, Dyer	W	30
● **Henning**, Lauderdale	W	420
Henrietta, Cheatham	N	19

Post office	Section	Pop.
● Henry, Henry	NW	300
Henry's Cross Roads, Sevier	E	40
Henryville, Lawrence	S	75
Henshaw, Greene	NE	13
Hercules, Knox	E	50
● Hermitage, Davidson	N	25
Heron, Giles	S	12
Hester Mills, Meigs	SE	25
● *Hiawassee*, Polk	SE	×
Hibbard, Franklin	S	×
Hickerson, Coffee	C	8
● Hickman, Smith	N	229
Hickman's Gap, Maury	C	×
Hickory Corner, Fentress	N	×
Hickory Ridge, Jefferson	E	19
● Hickory Valley, Harde'n	SW	157
Hickory Withe, Fayette	SW	100
● *Hickory Withe Station*, Fayette	SW	×
Hicks, DeKalb	C	×
Hicks, Sullivan	NE	×
● *Hico*, Carroll	W	30
Higdon, Polk	SE	×
Higgins, Scott	NE	×
High Health, Johnson	NE	×
High House, Campbell	NE	14
Highland, Jackson	N	30
Highland Park, Hamilton	SE	×
High Point, Knox	E	90
Hilham, Overton	N	30
● *Hill*, Maury	C	×
Hill City, Hamilton	SE	[illegible],763
Hillis, Warren	C	12
Hillsboro, Williamson	C	×
Hillsborough, Coffee	C	50
Hillsdale, Macon	N	40
● *Hill-Side*, Weakley	NW	×
Hillsville, Haywood	W	×
Hilton's, Sullivan	NE	250
● *Hinchs*, Bradley	SE	×
Hind's Creek, Anderson	NE	51
● *Hinson Spring*, Henderson	W	×
Hiram, Bedford	C	×
Hix, Clay	N	×
● Hixon, Hamilton	SE	15
Ho, Monroe	SE	5
● Hodges, Jefferson	E	50
Hoffasville, Cheatham	N	20
Hohenwald, Lewis	C	28
● *Holder*, White	C	×
Holladay, Benton	NW	200
Hollandsworth, DeKalb	C	8
Holloway, Wilson	N	15
● Hollow Rock, Carroll	W	281
Hollow Springs, Cannon	C	25
Holly, Coffee	C	600
Holmansville, Robertson	N	12
Holmes, Carroll	W	30
Holmes Creek, DeKalb	C	25
● *Holmes Gap*, DeKalb	C	×
Holston Valley, Sullivan	NE	36
Holt's Corner, Marshall	C	27
● Home, Greene	NE	50
● *Homer*, Madison	W	×
Hood Landing, Roane	E	25
Hoop, Claiborne	NE	19
Hoover, Rutherford	C	30
Hopewell Springs, Monroe	SE	20
Hopson, Carter	NE	30
Horace, Sullivan	NE	120
Hornbeak, Obion	NW	300
Horner, Perry	C	×
Hornet, Sevier	E	×
Horn Lake Landing, Shelby	SW	×
Hornville, Hamilton	SE	10
Horse Creek, Greene	NE	25
Horse Shoe Falls, Warren	C	×
Horville, Hamilton	SE	6
Houk, Blount	E	24
House Mountain, Knox	E	16
Houston, Wayne	S	27
Howard Springs, Cumberland	E	16
Howardville, James	SE	21
● Howell, Lincoln	S	13
Hubertville, Robertson	N	20
Hudgens, Putnam	N	12
● *Huffman's*, Morgan	NE	×
Huffstetler's Store, Blount	E	24
Hughes, Macon	M	12
Hughett, Scott	NE	15
Hughey, Lincoln	S	×
Huling, Monroe	SE	150
Hull, Pickett	N	10
● Humboldt, Gibson	W	1,837
● Hunnicutt, Morgan	NE	175

Tennessee

Post office	Section	Pop.
● *Hunsacker*, Dyer	W	30
Huntersville, (see Andrew Chapel)		×
● **Huntingdon**, Carroll	W	707
● Huntland, Franklin	S	250
Huntsville, Scott	NE	132
Hurley, Hardin	SW	18
● Huron, Henderson	W	×
Hurricane Branch, Union	NE	12
Hurricane Creek, Humphreys	C	42
Hurricane Mills, Humphreys	C	40
Hurricane Springs, Coffee	C	×
● Hurricane Switch, Maury	C	135
Hurst, McNairy	SW	30
Hustburgh, Humphreys	C	15
● *Hutton*, Marion	SE	×
Hygeia Springs, Robertson	N	100
Hypatia, Claiborne	NE	24
Ibex, Claiborne	NE	30
Idaville, Tipton	W	10
● Idlewild, Gibson	W	10
Idlewild, Obion	NW	×
Igou's Ferry, Hamilton	SE	36
Ina, Fayette	SW	×
Increase, Warren	C	24
India, Henry	NW	×
Indian Creek, Unicoi	NE	13
Indian Creek, DeKalb	C	6
Indian Mound, Stewart	N	80
Indian Ridge, Grainger	NE	14
Indian Springs, Sullivan	NE	×
Ingalls, Cannon	C	×
● Inman, Marion	SE	520
Inskip, Knox	E	×
Ipe, Monroe	SE	38
Irby, Putnam	N	6
● Iron City, Lawrence	S	425
Iron Divide, Roane	E	×
● *Iron Hill*, Dickson	N	50
Iron Mountain, Stewart	N	29
Ironville, Johnson	NE	×
Irving College, Warren	C	30
Isbel, Chester	SE	×
● Isham, Scott	NE	10
Island Ford, Morgan	NE	24
Island Mills, Sullivan	NE	17
Island Twenty-Six, Lauderdale	W	30
Isom's Store, Maury	C	50
● *Ivy*, Anderson	NE	×
Ivy Mills, Hickman	C	×
Jacksboro, Campbell	NE	374
Jacksboro, Warren	C	×
Jack's Creek, Chester	SE	100
● **Jackson**, Madison	W	10,039
Jackson Mound Park, Shelby	SW	×
Jackson Furnace, Dickson	N	×
Jacksonville, (see Fulton, Ky.)		×
Jake, Unicoi	NE	×
Jalapa, Monroe	SE	25
Jamestown, Fentress	N	84
Jared, Putnam	N	×
Jarmine, Grainger	NE	30
Jarnagin, Hamblen	NE	13
● **Jasper**, Marion	SE	902
Jeannette, Decatur	W	50
Jearoldstown, Greene	NE	59
Jeffers, Scott	NE	13
Jefferson, Rutherford	C	100
● Jellico, Campbell	NE	758
Jenkins, Loudon	E	×
Jennings, Wilson	N	15
Jennings Bluff, Perry	C	12
Jeremiah, Putnam	N	14
● Jersey, Hamilton	SE	8
Jessie, Warren	C	12
Jester, Chester	SE	32
Jewett, Cumberland	E	30
Jim Town, Rutherford	C	21
Jingo, Williamson	C	10
Jobe, Anderson	NE	×
Jockey, Greene	NE	20
Joe, Monroe	SE	120
Joelton, Davidson	N	75
John, Trousdale	N	12
Johnson City, Wash'ton	NE	4,161
Johnson's Grove, Crockett	W	40
Johnson's Landing, (see Ashport)		×
● *Johnson's Siding*, Law'ce	S	×
● Johnsonville, Humphreys	C	250
Johnston's Stand, Cumberl'd	E	×
Johnsonville, Obion	NW	×
● Jones, Haywood	W	10
● **Jonesborough**, Wash'n	NE	937
Jones' Cove, Sevier	E	16

Tennessee

Post office	Section	Pop.
Jones' Mills, De Kalb	C	19
Jonestown, Cocke	E	25
Jones' Valley, Hickman	C	60
● Jordan's Springs, Montg'y	N	35
Jordan's Station, (see Jordon, Ky.)		×
● Jordan's Valley, Rutherf'd	C	12
Jordonia, Davidson	N	80
Joshua, Mc Minn	SC	11
● *Junction*, Dickson	N	×
● *Junction*, Smith	N	×
Junkston, Cheatham	N	10
Juno, Henderson	W	25
Kangaroo, Knox	E	×
Kansas, Jefferson	E	25
Kate, Union	NE	×
Kathleen, Sevier	E	×
● *Keathley*, Morgan	NE	10
Keck's Chapel, Claiborne	NE	×
Kedron, Maury	C	50
Keebler's Cross Ro'ds, W'sh	NE	80
Keeling, Haywood	W	10
Keenburgh, Carter	NE	16
Keese, Fentress	N	8
Kellers, Bedford	C	×
Kelly's Ferry, Marion	SE	211
Kellers, Bedford	C	×
● Kelsoe, Lincoln	S	75
Kelsoe, Hickman	C	×
Keltonburgh, De Kalb	C	10
Kempville, Smith	N	5
Ken, Perry	C	×
Kendrick's Creek, Sullivan	NE	20
Kennedy, Knox	E	30
● Kenton, Obion	NW	395
● Kerrville, Shelby	SW	150
Ketchall, Marion	SE	33
Kettle Mills, Maury	C	28
Key, White	C	12
Key Corner, Lauderdale	W	36
Key Station, Johnson	NE	15
● *Kidds*, Blount	E	×
Kilbridge, Henry	NW	×
● Kimball, Marion	SE	25
Kimberlin Heigths, Knox	E	×
● *Kimbro*, Davidson	N	×
Kimbrough's St're, McMinn	SE	30
● Kimmins, Lewis	C	12
Kimsey, Polk	SE	×
● Kincaid, Monroe	S	×
Kincholoe, (see New Hope)		×
Kinderhook, Maury	C	×
● *King's Bridge*, Hamilton	SE	×
King's Creek, Roane	E	51
● Kings Point, Hamilton	SE	100
Kingsport, Sullivan	NE	100
Kingston, Roane	E	1,000
● Kingston Springs, Ch'th'm	N	50
Kinka, Rhea	E	10
● *Kinney*, Robertson	N	30
● *Kiser's*, Blount	E	×
● Kismet, Morgan	NE	100
● *Kismet*, Dyer	W	×
Kittrell, Rutherford	C	25
Kittrell's Landing, Perry	C	×
Kittyton, Unicoi	NE	×
Kiuka, Rhea	E	×
Kline, Franklin	S	×
Knob Creek, Lawrence	S	×
Knobton, Smith	N	12
Knott, Meigs	SE	200
● **KNOXVILLE**, Knox	E	22,535
Kodak, Sevier	E	×
Koko, Haywood	W	×
Kries, Roane	E	10
Kyle's Ford, Hancock	NE	25
Laden, Hardin	SW	×
La Fayette, Macon	N	256
● La Grange, Fayette	SW	500
Laguardo, Wilson	N	75
● *Lakeside*, Hamilton	SE	15
Lakewood, Shelby	SW	30
Lamar, Rutherford	C	15
Lambert, Fayette	SW	20
Lamb's Store, (see Arlington)		×
Lamontville, Mc Minn	SE	44
● Lancaster, Smith	N	50
● *Lancing*, Morgan	NE	×
Lane, Dyer	W	20
Lane's Store, Rutherford	C	×
● Lagdonia, Greene	NE	40
Lankford, Carroll	W	×
Lantana, Cumberland	E	8
Lark, Perry	C	×
Larkeyton, Grainger	NE	7
● Larkins, Dickson	N	5
Lascassas, Rutherford	C	29

Tennessee Tennessee

Lasea, Maury................C 24
Latham, Weakley........NW 10
● *Laurel*, Anderson......NE ×
Laurel Bloomey, Johnson. NE 17
Laurel Bluff, Roane........E ×
Laurelburgh, Van Buren....C 6
Laurel Hill, De Kalb........C 24
Laurel Hill, Lawrence.......S 180
Lavender, Morgan.........NE 14
● La Verge, Rutherford.....C 130
Lavinia, Carroll...........W 25
Law, Henderson............W ×
Lawrence, Mc Nairy......SW ×
● **Lawrenceburgh**, L'w'.S 618
Lawson, Sullivan..........NE ×
Lay, Knox....................E ×
Laynesville, Sequatchie.....SE 74
Leach, Carroll..............W 24
● Leadvale, Jefferson.........E 25
Leapyear, Wayne.............S 20
Leas Springs, Grainger....NE 15
● **Lebanon**, Wilson.......N 1,883
● *Lebanon Junc.*, Davidson. N ×
Lechnet Landing, (see Marr's Landing)................ ×
Ledletter, Benton........NW ×
Leedom, Anderson........NE ×
Leeds, Warren...............C ×
Le Duke Landing, Lake..NW ×
● *Lees*, Bledsoe............ E ×
Leesburg, (see Capleville).... ×
Leesburgh, Washington...NE 50
Lee Valley, Hawkins.......NE 150
● Leeville, Wilson..........N 50
Leftwich, Maury............C 6
Legate, Stewart.............N 10
Leickhart, Moore...........S 12
Leigh Chapel, Tipton.......W 30
Leiper's Fork, Williamson..C 100
Lelia, Sullivan............NE 30
Lela May, Cheatham......N 10
Lemon's Gap, Cocke........E ×
● Lenoir City, Loudon...... E 98
● Lenow, Shelby.........SW ×
Lenox, (see Dyersburg)...... ×
Leo, Union...............NE ×
Leoni, Cannon..............C 14
Leonidas, Jefferson.........E ×
Lesbia, Stewart.............N ×
● Lester's, Giles..............S 25
● *Lewis*, Lewis................C ×
Let, Bledsoe.................E ×
● **Lewisburgh**, Marshall.C 631
Lexie, Franklin...............S 10
● **Lexington**, Henderson W 715
Liberty, DeKalb............C 350
Liberty Hill, Grainger.....NE 36
Lick Creek, Hickman.......C 15
Lickton, Davidson..........N 10
● Life, Henderson..........W ×
Light, Wayne................S 14
Lightfoot, Lauderdale......W 32
Ligias, Anderson...........NE 30
Lillamay, Cheatham.......NW 10
Lillard's Mills, Marshall.....C 25
Limbs, Weakley............NW ×
● Limestone, Washington. NE 250
Limestone Cove, Unicoi...NE 25
Limestone Springs, Greene NE 16
Lime Works, Davidson.....N 27
Linaria, Cumberland........E ×
Lincoln, Lincoln.............S 55
Linden, Perry..............C 330
Lindsay's Mill, Campbell..NE ×
Lineback, Carter...........NE ×
Line Spring, Sevier..........E 84
Link, Rutherford............C ×
Linton, Davidson............N ×
Linwood, Wilson............N ×
Linwood Landing, Dyer....W ×
● *Lipe*, Benton...........NW ×
Lipscomb, Mauray...........C 40
Little Barren, Union......NE 29
Little Chucky, Greene......NE 15
Little Crab, Fentress.......N 15
Little Doe, Johnson.......NE 8
Little Lot, Hickman.........C 29
● *Little Rivers*, Blount.......E ×
Little Rock Mills, Hickman. C 20
● *Little Tennessee River*, Me SE ×
Little War Gap, Hawki's..NE ×
Litton, Bledsoe..............D 25
Live Oak, Henry...........NW 20
Live Wells, Anderson.....NE 50
Livingston, Overton.....N 320
● *Livingston*, Polk.........SE ×
Lloyd's Mills, Bledsoe......E 8

Lobelville, Perry...........C 171
Lockertsville, Cheatham....N 10
Lockport, Wilson..... .....N 15
Loco, Maury...............C 40
Locust Mount, Wash'ton..NE 40
Locust Spring, Greene....NE 50
Lodebar, Maury.............C 15
Loganton, Unicoi.........NE 30
Lohman, Sumner...........N ×
Lone Elm, Henderson......W 60
Lonely, Humphreys.........C ×
Lone Mountain, Claiborne NE 15
● *Lone Mountain Sta.*, Cl'reNE 60
Long, Henderson............W 29
Long Branch, Montgomery. N 20
Long Creek, Macon.........N 18
Long Hollow, Union.......NE 14
Long Savannah, James....SE 30
Long's Mills, McMinn......SE 38
Longview, Bedford..........C 12
Lonoke, Gibson ....W ×
Loo, Union.................NE ×
Lookout, Hamilton,........SE ×
Lookout Mountain, H'tn...SE 1,000
Looney's Creek, Marion....SE 10
Loosahatchie, (see Arlington) ×
● Lorenaton, Union.......NE 7
● Loretto, Lawrence.........S 35
● Lorraine, Rhea.............E 14
Lost Creek, Union........NE 26
Lost Mountain, Greene....NE 9
● **Loudon**, Loudon........E 942
● *Louise*, Montgomery..... N ×
● Louisville, Blount.........E 314
Lovejoy, Overton...........N 12
Lovelace, Greene...........NE ×
Loversleep, Marion.........SE 24
Love's Landing, (see Ayers).. ×
Loveville, Knox...............E ×
Lowe, Rutherford...........C 6
Lower Elkton, Giles.........S ×
Lowland, Hamblen.........NE 18
Lowryville, Hardin.........SW 35
Low's Sulphur Springs, A'nNE 21
Loyd, Bledsoe................E 360
Loy's Cross Roads, Union. NE 15
Lucas, Hawkins.............NE ×
Lucas Gin, (see Spain)....... ×
Lucilla, Jefferson.............E 5
Lucky, Warren...............C 8
Lucknow, Rhea..............E 36
● Lucy, Shelby..............SW 75
Lulaville, Grainger..........NE 30
Lunn's Store, Marshall......C 10
Lupton, Anderson.........NE 18
● Lurray, Henderson.......W ×
Luskville, McMinn.........SE 8
Luterton, Benton.........NW 45
Luther, Hancock...........NE 15
● Luttrell, Union............NE 150
Lutts, Wayne.................S 25
● Lyles, Hickman.............C 50
Lynchburgh, Moore.....S 500
Lynnville, Giles..............S 243
● *Lynnville Station*, Giles...S ×
Lyons, Monroe............SE ×
Lyonton, Knox...............E 200
Mc Allister's Cross Roads, Montgomery........... N 15
McBride, Crockett.........W 60
McBurg, Lincoln,............S 15
McCally's Ferry Landing, James.........................SE ×
McCaulin's Bluff, (seeC'xb'rg) ×
McCauley's Mill, Montgm'y N 13
● McCay's, Polk...........SE 10
● McConnell, Obion.......NW 100
McCulley, McMinn........SE 70
McCulloch, Wilson..........N 5
McDearman, Jackson......N ×
● McDonald, Bradley.......SE 45
McElroy, Van Buren.......C ×
● *McElvee*, Roane..........E ×
● McEwen, Humphreys.....C 213
● *McFarland*, Polk....... SE ×
McGhee, Monroe...........SE ×
McGhee's McMinn.........SE ×
McGill, Hamilton............SE ×
McIlaney, Henderson.......W 30
McIllwain, Benton....... NW 19
McKay, Polk..................SE ×
● McKenzie, Carroll.........W 1,166
McKinley, Blount..........E 100
● McKinnon, Houston.......N 12
McLemoresville, Carroll....W 150
● McMillan, Knox..........E 39
● **McMinnville**, Warren..C 1,677

● McNairy, McNairy......SW 200
McNebb Mine, Marion..... SE ×
McPherson, Bradley.......SE 12
McPherson, Roane.........E ×
Mable, Knox.................E ×
Macedonia, Maury..........C 808
Mack, Lauderdale..........W 10
Macon, Fayette...........SW 200
Maddox, Hardin...........SW ×
● Madison, Davidson.......N 78
Madison Heights, Shelby.SW ×
● **Madisonville**, MonroeSE 313
Mae, Cocke.................E ×
Magellen, McMinn.........SE 8
Maggart, Smith..............N 10
Magness Mills, DeKalb......C 20
Magnolia, Houston.......... N ×
● *Magnolia*, Shelby.......SW ×
Mahone, Wilson.............N 8
● Malesus, Madison.........W 30
Mallard, Maury...............C 15
Mallock, Lincoln.............S ×
● *Mallory's*, Williamson....C ×
Maloney, Meigs............SE 29
Maloneyville, Knox.........E ×
Maltsberger, Greene......NE ×
Mammy, Cumberland........E 14
● **Manchester**, Coffee....C 621
Mangum, Warren............C 30
Manire, Rutherford........C ×
Manlysville, Henry.......NW 40
Mannie, Wayne..............S ×
Mansfield, Henry.........NW 25
Maple Creek, Carroll.......W 34
Maples, Grainger..........NE 48
● Maplewood, Davidson....N ×
Marble Hill, Moore.........S 50
Marble Switch, Bradley...SE ×
Marbleton, Unicoi........NE ×
Marian, Montgomery.......N ×
Marr's Landing, Lake...NW ×
Marbut's, Giles..............S 40
Marcella Falls, Lawrence...S 50
March Bank, Putnam......N ×
Marengo, Jackson...........N 12
Margaret, Hawkins........NE 25
Marion, Henry............NW ×
Marlow, Anderson.........NE ×
Marrowbone, Cheatham....N 25
Marr's Landing, (see Darnall) ×
Marshall's Ferry, Grainger. NE 19
Marsh Creek, Perry........ C 12
● Martin, Weakley.......NW 2,000
Martin's Mills, Wayne.......S 49
Marvin, Greene............NE ×
Maryville, Blount........E 1,686
Masada, Smith...............N ×
● Mascot, Knox.............E 48
● Mason, Tipton............. W 252
Mason Hall, Obion....... NW 30
Mason's Grove, (see Gadsden) ×
Masseyville, Chester....... SE 20
Matlock, White.............. C ×
Matney, Johnson...........NE 75
Matuta, Washington...... NE ×
Maury City, Crockett.......W 150
● Maxwell, Franklin.........S 38
Mayday, Washington..... NE ×
Mayella, Rutherford....... C 25
Mayfield, Jackson.......... N 10
Maynardville, Union..NE 144
Mayo, Knox................. E 48
May Spring, Grainger.....NE 40
Mayston, Hamilton....... SE ×
Mayview, Davidson.........N 25
Meade, Van Buren...........C ×
Meadorville, Macon......... N ×
Meadow, Loudon............E ×
Meadow Brook, WashingtonNE 15
Meadowfield, Hancock....NE 18
Meagsville, Jackson........ N 25
Mecca, McMinn............SE 28
Mechanicsville, Cannon....C 24
● Medina, Gibson.......... W 273
● Medon, Madison.......... W 150
Meigs, Meigs................ SE 21
Meigsville, Jackson..........N 25
● *Methorn*, Morgan...... NE ×
● *Melrose*, Tipton........... W 30
Meltabarger, Union.......NE 60
● *Melton Hill*, Roane.......E ×
Melvine, Bledsoe............E 39
● *Melville*, Hamilton.......SE ×
● **MEMPHIS**, Shelby.. SW 64,495
Mentor, Blount..............E ×
● Mercer, Madison........ W 30
Merritt, Giles...................S 30

Place	Pop.
Messenger, Stewart.........N	24
Metcalf, Houston...........N	30
Methodist, White...........C	×
● *Meyers*, Cocke...........E	×
Middle Brook, (see Knoxville)	×
Michie, McNairy...........SW	30
● Middleburg, Hardeman.SW	50
Middleburg, (see Long)......	×
Middle Creek, Sevier.......E	×
Middle Fork, Henderson...W	50
● Middleton, Hardeman..SW	191
Midland, Rutherford........C	55
● Midway, Greene........NE	100
Mifflin, Chester............SE	100
● Milan, Gibson............W	1,546
Milburnton, Greene.......NE	19
Miles Cross Roads, Clay....N	×
Mill Brook, Washington..NE	26
Mill Creek, Morgan.........NE	13
Milledgeville, McNairy...SW	50
● *Millers*, Washington....NE	×
Millersburgh, Rutherford...C	18
Millers Cove, Blount........E	30
Millersville, Sumner.......N	×
Millican, Sevier.............E	50
Milligan, Carter............NE	20
● Millington, Shelby.......SW	400
Mill Point, Sullivan.......NE	24
Mill Spring, Jefferson.......E	24
Millview, Williamson.......C	12
Millville, Lincoln............S	50
Millville, Williamson........C	10
Millwood, Shelby.........SW	×
Milton, Rutherford...........C	50
● *Mine Lick*, Putnam.......N	33
Mingo Mountain, Claiborne NE	×
Minkton, Claiborne.........NE	9
Minnie Mines, Wayne.......S	×
Minnick's, (see Obion).......	×
Minnowford, Giles...........S	5
Minor Hill, Giles.............S	10
Mint, Blount..................E	×
Miranda, Overton............N	×
Miser, Blount.................S	18
Mission Ridge, Hamilton..SE	×
Mit, Johnson..............NE	×
Mitchburgh, Hancock.....NE	×
Mitchell, Robertson..........N	161
Mitchells Landing, Dyer...W	×
● Mitchellville, Sumner....N	100
Mixie, Carroll...............W	80
Mockeson, Lawrence........S	8
Model, Stuart.................N	6
● *Moffat*, Obion..........NW	×
● Mohawk, Greene........NE	17
Mole, Hawkins............NE	×
Molino, Lincoln...............S	65
Moltke, Stewart..............N	15
Monitor, (see Bible Hill).....	×
Monoville, Smith............N	30
Monroe, Overton............N	100
● Mont Eagle, Grundy......C	200
Montezuma, Chester.......SE	100
Monticello, Hardin........SW	×
Montgomery, Morgan.....NE	10
Montvale, Blount.............E	49
Moodyville, Fentress........N	10
Moon, Wayne.................S	24
● *Moore*, Hickman...........C	×
Mooresburgh, Hawkins...NE	60
Moore's Hill, Henderson...W	15
Mooresville, Marshall.......C	40
Moro, Chester..............SE	30
Morell's Mills, Sullivan....NE	21
Morelock, Greene..........NE	×
Morena, Weakley..........NW	72
Morgan, Henderson.........W	30
Morgan Springs, Rhea.......E	×
Morganton, Loudon..........E	75
Morning Star, Washington NE	15
Morning Sun, (see Bartlett).	×
Morny, Davidson............N	12
Morris Chapel, Hardin....SW	15
Morris Gap, Roane..........E	24
Morris Mills, Giles..........S	8
● Morrison, Warren.........C	75
● **Morristown**, Hamblen NE	1,999
● Mortimer, McMinn......SE	29
● Moscow, Fayette........SW	201
● Mosheim, Greene.......NE	32
Moss, Clay....................N	16
● Mossy Creek, Jefferson....E	800
Mount Aetna Furnace, Hic'nC	×
Mountain City, Johnson NE	249
Mountain Junc., Hamilton SE	×
Mountainville, Monroe.....SE	13

Tennessee

Place	Pop.
● Mount Airy, Sequatchie. SE	15
Mount Gilead, Cumberland. E	20
Mount Horeb, Jefferson.....E	341
● Mount Juliet, Wilson.....N	30
Mount Pelia, Weakley....NW	50
● Mount Pleasant, Maury...C	466
Mount Sterling, De Kalb....C	8
Mount Verd, McMinn.....SE	120
● Mount Vernon, Monroe.SE	19
Mount Vernon Furnace, Montgomery............N	×
● *Mount View*, Davidson..N	×
Mount Vista, Henry.......NW	10
Mount Zion, (see Atoka).....	×
● Mouse Creek, McMinn..SE	150
Mouse Tail, Perry............C	80
Mouth of Doe, Johnson...NE	60
Mouth of Wolf, Clay........N	25
Mowd, Maury.................C	8
Moxie, Wilson.................N	×
Muddy Creek, Loudon......E	20
Mud Log, Lauderdale......W	×
Mud Tavern, Davidson.....N	6
Mulberry, Lincoln.............S	206
Mulberry Gap, Hancock..NE	100
● Mullin's, Shelby........SW	×
Mulloy's, Robertson........N	26
● Munch, Tipton............W	30
Munford, Tipton.............W	25
● **Murfreesborough**, Rutherford.............C	3,739
Music, Cumberland..........E	×
● Myers, Greene...........NE	60
Mynatt, Knox.................E	10
Naillon, Cocke.................E	6
Nameless, Jackson...........N	30
Nance's Ferry, Jefferson...E	×
Nancy, Lewis..................C	24
Nankipoo, Lauderdale.....W	30
Naola, Coffee..................C	12
Naomi, Hickman..............C	10
Napier, Lewis..................C	25
● **NASHVILLE**, David'n N	76,168
Nast, Knox.....................E	×
● *National Cemetery*, Sh'y SW	×
Nathan, Perry.................C	×
Nave Hill, Union...........NE	25
Neal, Pickett...................N	×
Neapolis, Maury.............C	50
Nebo, Gibson.................W	×
Nebraska Landing, Laude W	×
● *Needmore*, Montgomery N	×
● Neeley's, Madison........W	×
Nellie, Washington.......NE	×
Nelson Hill, Wilson.........W	8
● Nemo, Morgan...........NE	25
Neptune, Cheatham.........N	15
Nero, Madison................W	10
Netherland, Overton.........N	7
Netio, Perry...................C	×
Nettle Carrier, Overton.....N	25
Neverfail, Cumberland......E	30
New, Warren...................C	12
Newark, White...............C	17
● Newbern, Dyer.............W	1,236
Newburg, Lewis...........C	50
New Boston, Henry......NW	×
New Canton, Hawkins....NE	40
Newcastle, Hardeman....SW	50
● Newcomb, Campbell....NE	284
New Era, Perry...............C	31
New Flat Creek, Union...NE	50
New Hope, Hawkins.......NE	15
New Kent, Fayette.........SW	×
New Knob Creek, Sevier...E	20
Newmansville, Greene....NE	15
● New Market, Jefferson...E	600
New Middleton, Smith.....N	200
● **Newport**, Cocke...........E	658
New Portland, Houston....N	×
New Prospect, Union.....NE	40
New Providence, Montg'y..N	700
● New River, Scott.......NE	170
New Sedalia, Hancock....NE	25
● Newsom's Station Davi'n N	25
New Tazewell, Claiborne..NE	300
Newton, Cumberland.......E	×
New York, Montgomery...N	×
Nichols, Blount...............E	×
Nina, Jefferson................E	×
Nine Mile, Bledsoe..........E	×
Nixon, Hardin...............SW	14
Noah, Coffee..................C	85
Noeton, Grainger...........NE	6
Nola Chucky, Washington NE	100
Nolan's Landing, Lake..NW	×
Nolensville, Williamson.....C	150

Tennessee

Place	Pop.
Nonaburgh, McMinn......SE	31
Norma, Scott...............NE	30
● Normandy, Bedford......C	125
Norman's Store, James....SE	21
● *Norment*, Madison.......W	×
Norris, Johnson............NE	×
Norris Creek, Lincoln.......S	100
Northford, Decatur.........W	90
North Fork Henry.......NW	18
North Knoxville, Knox.....E	2,297
North Springs, Jackson.....N	26
Northville, Cumberland ....E	16
● Norwood, Madison.......W	×
Notchy, Monroe...........SE	24
Notime, Blount...............E	12
Nough, Cocke.................E	150
Number One, Sumner.......N	5
● **Nunnelly, Hickman.......C**	28
Nutbush, Haywood.........W	50
Nutt, Lewis....................C	60
Oakdale, Campbell........NE	×
● *Oakdale*, Morgan........NE	×
● *Oakfield*, Madison........W	×
Oak Grove, (see Decaturville)	×
Oak Grove, Jefferson.......E	15
Oak Hill, Overton............N	25
Oakhill Seminery, Coffee...C	×
Oak Hills, Hamilton.......SE	×
● Oakland, Fayette ....SW	50
Oakley, Overton ....N	25
Oak Point, Wilson..........N	×
Oakview, Decatur.........W	×
● Oakville, Shelby.........SW	30
Oakwood, Montgomery.....N	75
Oasis, Warren................C	×
Oates Island, Marion......SE	×
● Obion, Obion...........NW	660
Ocoee, Polk..................SE	6
O'Conner's, White...........C	×
Odd Fellows Hall, Giles.....S	15
Odum, Wilson................N	×
● Offutt, Anderson.........NE	10
Ogden, Rhea...................E	20
Oglesby, Davidson...........N	12
Ogles Cross Roads, Sevier...E	200
Oguin, Humphreys...........C	×
O. K. Furnace, Montgom'y N	×
Okolona, Carter.............NE	15
Olcott, Grainger............NE	29
Old Fort, Polk...............SE	50
Old Fosterville, Rutherford C	×
Old Hickory, Davidson.....N	10
Old Lynnville, Giles.........S	168
Olds, Wayne ....S	×
Oldtown, Claiborne.......NE	28
Olga, Overton.................N	×
Olinton, Hickman............C	30
Ollo, Van Buren C	30
Olive Hill, Hardin.........SW	15
● Oliver Springs, Anderson NE	642
Olla, Anderson.............NE	×
Olympus, Pickett.............N	12
Omar, Montgomery ....N	15
Omega, Houston..............N	30
● Oneida, Scott ....NE	109
Oneyville, Davidson.........N	20
Only, Hickman................C	14
Onward, White...............C	10
● *Ooltewah Junc.*, James SE	300
● **Ooltewah**, James..... SE	233
Opher, McMinn ....SE	×
Oppossum, Hawkins......NE	9
Ora, Bradley.................SE	×
Oral, Roane....................E	31
Orchard Knob, Hamilton SE	250
Ore Bank, Sullivan ....NE	75
Oregon, Lincoln...............S	80
Orgain's Cross Roads, M'tg'y N	20
Orias, DeKalb C	×
Orlinda, Robertson..........N	100
Orysa, Lauderdale..........W	78
Osage, Henry.............NW	×
Osborn, Johnson..........NE	30
Ostella, Marshall.............C	10
● Otes, Hawkins ....NE	14
Othello, Roane...............E	15
Ottinger, Cocke...............E	30
Otto, Pickett...................N	6
Ottway, Greene ....NE	25
Ovand, Sullivan............NE	×
Overall, Rutherford.........C	16
● *Overtons*, Davidson.......N	×
Overton's Store, (see Greenfield)	×
Owen, Polk....................SE	×
Owen's Branch, Claiborne NE	×
Owen's Cross Roads, Wil'ms'n C	16
Owlhollow, Franklin........S	15

Tennessee		
Pace, Henry	NW	×
Pactolus, Sullivan	NE	×
Padget, Loudon	E	×
● *Paducah Junc.*, Obion	NW	30
Page's Store, Montgomery	N	90
● Pailo, Bledsoe	E	30
Painter, Greene	NE	100
● *Paint Rock*, Cocke	F	×
Paint Rock, Roane	E	35
Paintville, Van Buren	C	×
Palestine, Lewis	C	8
Palestine, (see Obion)		×
Pall Mall, Fentress	N	25
Palmersville, Weakley	NW	200
Palmetto, Bedford	C	96
● Palmyra, Montgomery	N	100
Pandora, Johnson	NE	75
Paperville, Sullivan	NE	60
Paradise Hill, Cheatham	N	×
Paragon Mills, Davidson	N	50
Parch Corn, Scott	NE	30
Pardee Point, Carter	NE	×
Parham, Sumner	N	12
● **Paris**, Henry	NW	1,917
Paris Landing, Henry	NW	100
Parker, Decatur	W	10
● Park's Station, Maury	C	10
Parksville, Polk	SE	50
Parkville, (see Darnell)		×
Parrottsville, Cocke	E	75
● *Parsons*, Decatur	W	×
Partinville, Decatur	W	×
Partlow, Wilson	N	10
Pasquo, Davidson	N	×
Pate, Fayette	SW	×
Pate's Hill, Greene	NE	×
Pate's Landing, Dyer	W	×
Patriot Landing, Perry	C	×
Patriot Landing, Wayne	S	×
Patterson's, Rutherford	C	15
Patterson, Scott	NE	×
Pattie's Gap, Roane	E	16
Patton, Bledsoe	E	24
Patty, Polk	SE	12
Paul, Lawrence	S	×
Paulett, Union	NE	×
Paulks, Hardin	SW	8
Paw Paw Ford, Roane	E	12
Payne's Cove, Grundy	C	×
Peacher's Mills, Montgom'y	N	25
Peak, Anderson	NE	×
Peanut, Cocke	E	18
Pearley, Shelby	SW	30
Pearson, Bledsoe	E	72
Peck, Weakley	NW	×
Pedigo, Knox	E	10
Peeled Chestnut, White	C	14
● Pegram, Cheatham	N	25
Pekin, Putnam	N	49
Pelham, Grundy	C	159
Peltier, Sullivan	N	9
Percyville, Scott	NE	25
Perdue, Sumner	N	25
Pertilla, White	C	10
Permelia, Pickett	N	32
● *Perry*, Madison	W	×
Perryville, Decatur	W	50
● Persia, Hawkins	NE	200
● Peryear, Henry	NW	×
● Peterburgh, Lincoln	S	290
Peter's Landing, Perry	C	25
Petway, Cheatham	N	×
Peytons Creek, Smith	N	35
Peytonsville, Williamson	C	30
Phebe, Union	NE	9
Phelan, Tipton	W	×
● Philadelphia, Loudon	E	250
Phillips, Cocke	E	×
Phoenix, Franklin	S	×
***Phoebe*, Union**	NE	9
Pickettsville, Gibson	W	120
Pickney, Lawrence	S	25
Pickwick, Hardin	SW	25
Piedmont, Jefferson	E	29
● Pierce Station, Obion	NW	10
Pigeon Forge, Sevier	E	9
● **Pikeville**, Bledsoe	E	150
Pill Jerk, (see Covington)		×
Pillowville, Weakley	NW	×
Pilot Hill, Washington	NE	29
Pilot Knob, Greene	NE	×
● *Pilot Knob*, Sumner	N	×
● Pilot Mountain, Morgan	NE	15
Pincher, Stewart	N	12
Pine Bluff, Warren	C	30
Pine Fork, Putnam	N	20
Pinegar, DeKalb	C	12

Tennessee		
Pine Land, Meigs	SE	×
Pine Mountain, Campbell	NE	10
Pine Ridge, McMinn	SE	×
Pine Top, Hardeman	SW	×
Pine Wood, Hickman	C	304
Piney, Loudon	E	10
● Piney Flats, Sullivan	NE	75
Pinhook, White	C	×
Pinhook Landing, Meigs	SE	38
Pinkard, Rutherford	C	8
Pinkney, Lawrence	S	25
Pinnacle, Cheatham	N	15
● Pinson, Madison	W	264
● Pioneer, Campbell	NE	225
● *Pioneer Sta.*, Campbell	NE	×
Piperton, Fayette	SW	×
Pipkin, Henderson	W	×
Pisgah, Giles	S	25
Pittsburgh Landing, Hard.	SW	29
Pitt's Cross Roads, Bledsoe	E	24
Plant, Humphreys	C	10
Plato, Carter	NE	×
Pleasant, Claiborne	NE	44
Pleasant Grove, Bedford	C	×
Pleasant Grove, Lawrence	S	×
● *Pleasant Grove*, Maury	C	×
Pleasant Hill, Cumberland	E	37
Pleasant Mound, M'tgom'y	N	36
Pleasant Plains, Lincoln	S	×
Pleasant Point, Lawrence	S	75
Pleasant Shade, Smith	N	20
Pleasant Valley, Wayne	S	×
Pleasant View, Cheatham	N	400
Pleasantville, Hickman	C	15
Plummer's Chapel, Hardin	SW	30
Plum Point, Lauderdale	W	28
● Pocahontas, Hardeman	SW	274
Podopholine, Anderson	NE	25
Poeville, Hamilton	SE	250
Point Mason Landing, Benton	NW	14
Point Park, Hamilton	SE	×
Point Pleasant, Decatur	W	25
Pokeberry, Sevier	E	×
Polk's Landing, Hardin	SW	×
● Polk's Station, Obion	NW	×
Pollard, White	C	17
Pomona, Cumberland	E	25
● *Pomona*, Dickson	N	×
● *Pond*, Dickson	N	×
Pond Creek, Cheatham	N	10
Pondville, Sumner	N	27
Pope, Perry	C	12
Poplar Furnace, Stewart	N	×
Poplar Spring, Henderson	W	20
Poplar Spring Furnace, Montgomery	N	×
Poplin's Cross Roads, Bed'd	C	77
Porinth, Knox	E	×
Porterfield, Cannon	C	6
● *Porters*, Henry	NW	×
● Portland, Sumner	N	100
Port Royal, Montgomery	N	300
Possible, Overton	N	36
Post, Carroll	W	×
Post Oak Springs, Roane	E	50
Poteet, Overton	N	15
Potts, Madison	W	28
Povo, Monroe	SE	19
● Powder Spring Gap, Grainger	NE	16
Powell, Union	NE	×
● *Powell River*, Claiborne	NE	×
Powell's River, Campbell	NE	60
● Powell's Station, Knox	E	117
Prairie Plains, Coffee	C	25
Prater, Cannon	C	16
Preston, Knox	E	50
● *Price*, White	C	10
Prigmore, McMinn	SE	18
● *Princeton Junc.*, M't'm'y	N	×
Profit, Carroll	W	24
Progressive, Knox	E	×
Prosise, Anderson	NE	8
● Prospect Station, Giles	S	65
Protemus, Obion	NW	10
Providence, James	SE	×
Pruxton, Scott	NE	×
Pryor, Macon	N	×
Pughville, Carroll	W	×
● **Pulaski**, Giles	S	2,274
Pullum, Hawkins	NE	×
Pulstown, Lake	NW	×
Puncheon, Grainger	NE	×
Purdy, McNairy	SW	255
● *Puryear*, Henry	NW	×
Push, Hawkins	NE	×

Tennessee		
Putt, Claiborne	NE	30
Pyburn's Bluff, Hardin	SW	×
Qualls, Overton	N	61
Quarter, Claiborne	NE	17
● Quebeck, White	C	75
Quito, Tipton	W	10
Quiz, Jackson	N	30
Quiz, Putnam	N	14
Raccoon Valley, Union	NE	31
● *Race Track*, Shelby	SW	×
● *Radors*, Greene	NE	60
Rafter, Monroe	SE	×
Raht, Bradley	SE	39
Rainbow, Sevier	E	×
Raleigh, Shelby	SW	139
Rally Hill, Maury	C	10
● Ralston's Sta., Weakley	NW	200
● Ramer, McNairy	SW	150
Ramsey, Shelby	SW	×
Randolph, Tipton	W	100
Randolph Forge, Stewart	N	×
Ranger, Madison	W	×
Rankin Ferry, Marion	SE	×
● Rankin's Depot, Cocke	E	35
Rasar, Blount	E	×
● *Rathburn*, Hamilton	SE	229
Ray, Coffee	C	10
Ray, Union	NE	×
Readyville, Rutherford	C	100
Reagan, Henderson	W	32
● *Reagans*, McMinn	SE	×
Rebecca, Franklin	S	10
Red Bank, Hamilton	SE	10
Red Boiling Springs, Macon	N	120
Reddick, Sumner	N	×
Redell, Giles	S	10
Red Hill, Grainger	NE	10
Red House Forge, Dickson	N	×
Red Mound, Henderson	W	×
Red Sulphur Sprs., Hend'n	SW	×
Reed's Store, Williamson	C	19
Reelfoot, Lake	NW	50
Reelfoot Landing, Lake	NW	×
Regret, McMinn	SE	19
Rein, Haywood	W	×
Reliance, Polk	SE	10
Reliance Coal Mine, Claibo'e	NE	×
Renegar, Lincoln	S	12
Republican, Sevier	E	×
Rest, Cheatham	N	×
● Retro, Hamilton	SE	62
Reverie, Tipton	W	×
● *Reynold*, Giles	S	20
Reynoldsburgh, Humphreys	C	×
Rhea's Forge, Johnson	NE	30
Rhea Springs, Rhea	E	300
Rheatown, Greene	NE	100
Rhodelia, Union	NE	7
● Rialto, Tipton	W	10
● Riceville, McMinn	SE	379
Richardson, Laud., Tipton	W	50
Rich Creek, Marshall	C	45
Richison Cove, Sevier	E	40
Richland, Giles	S	×
Richland, Knox	E	×
Richmond, Bedford	C	84
Riddleton, Smith	N	150
Ridgedale, Hamilton	SE	1,254
Ridgely, Lake	NW	×
Ridge Post, Davidson	N	100
● *Ridgetop*, Robertson	N	19
Ridgeville, Moore	S	25
Riggins, Montgomery	N	15
Riley's L'd'g, (see Tiptonville)		×
Rinehart, Henry	NW	×
Ringgold, Montgomery	N	50
Rio, Chester	SE	×
● **Ripley**, Lauderdale	W	682
Rip Shin, Carter	NE	180
Rita, Knox	E	×
Ritchie, Claiborne	NE	10
Riverdale, Knox	E	175
River Hill, White	C	12
● Rives, Obion	NW	377
Roan Mountain, Carter	NE	40
Roaring, Greene	NE	×
Roaring Spring, Claiborne	NE	×
● Robbins, Scott	NE	300
Robo's Cross Roads, Coffee	C	×
Roberson Fork, Marshall	C	13
Robertsonville, (see Crockett's Ms.)		×
Robertsville, Anderson	NE	24
Robinson, Bledsoe	E	×
Rockbridge, Sumner	N	×
Rock City, Smith	N	20
Rock Creek, McMinn	SE	30
● Rockdale, Maury	C	28

Place	Index	Pop.
● Wauhatchie, Hamilton	SE	25
● **Waverly**, Humphreys	C	700
WaverlyLanding, Humph'ys	C	×
Way, Benton	NW	23
● Wayland Springs, L'wr'ce.	S	35
● *Wayne*, Lawrence	S	×
Waynesborough, Wayne	S	239
Wayside, Rutherford	C	10
Weakly, Giles	S	41
Wear's Valley, Sevier	E	10
Weatherford, Wayne	S	10
Weaver's Store, Stewart	N	40
Weaw, Humphreys	C	×
Webb, Perry	C	25
Webster, Roane	E	20
Welker Mines, Roane	E	50
Wells Landing, Hardin	SW	×
Well Spring, Campbell	NE	400
Wellwood, Haywood	W	50
Wesley, Claiborne	NE	×
West, Gibson	W	×
Westernia, Cheatham	N	6
Westerville, Grainger	NE	×
West Fork, Overton	N	19
West Gibson, Gibson,	W	×
● West Harpeth, Willi'mson	C	20
West Knoxville, Knox	E	2,114
Westmoreland, Sumner	N	173
West Mouse Tail Landing, (see Mouse Tail)		×
West Nashville, Davidson	N	1,047
○ West Point, Lawrence	S	50
Wheat, Roane	E	14
Wheatley, Benton	NW	35
Wheel, Bedford	C	8
Wheeling, (see Hornbeak)		×
Whetstone, Morgan	NE	10
Whig, Greene	NE	11
● White, Shelby	SW	50
○ White Bluffs, Dickson	N	152
WhiteCliff Springs, Monroe	SE	60
WhiteCreek Springs, D'v'd'n	N	×
White Fern, Henderson	W	×
○ White Haven, Shelby	SW	75
White Hill, Robertson	N	25
● White Horn, Hawkins	NE	18
White House, Robertson	N	16
White Oak, Humphreys	C	14
White Oak, Williamson	C	14
● White Pine, Jefferson	E	500
White Rock, Carter	NE	×
White's Bend, Davidson	N	20
○ Whitesburgh, Hamblen	NE	143
White'sCreek, Davidson	N	30
● Whiteside, Marion	SE	533
Whites Landing, Decatur	W	×
Whites Plains, Putnam	N	×
Whitesides, Lewis	C	350
White's Store, Sullivan	NE	35
White Sulphur Springs, Hardin	SW	×
● Whiteville, Hardeman	SW	209
Whitefield, Hickman	C	19
Whitleyville, Jackson	N	20
Whitlock, Henry	NW	×
● *Whitlows*, Madison	W	×
Whitman, Campbell	NE	15
Whitten's Stand, Wayne	S	×
Whitthorne, Carroll	W	12
Whitton, Hardin	SW	25
○ Whitwell, Marion	SE	906
Whize, Campbell	NE	×
Wildersville, Henderson	W	50
Wild Goose, Chester	SE	100
Wilcox Furnace, Stewart	K	30
Wiley's Landing, Humphr'ys	C	×
Wilford, Wilson	N	32
Wilhoite, Marshall	C	12
● Wilkerson, Davidson	N	10
Wilkinsville, Tipton	W	×
Willard, Trousdale	N	×
Willette, Macon	N	8
● Williamsburgh, McMinn	SE	10
Williams Creek, Knox	A	×
Williams' Factory, Lawrence	S	×
Williams' Land'g, Hamilt'n	SE	×
Williamsport, Maury	C	72
Williamsville, Dickson	N	×
○ Williston, Fayette	SW	150
Willow Grove, Clay	N	12
Wills, Lawrence	S	×
Wilson's, Anderson	NE	10
● *Wilson's*, Monroe	SE	×
Wilsonville, (see Hornbeak)		×
Wilton Springs, Cocke	E	18
● **Winchester**, Franklin	S	1,313
WinchesterSprings, Franklin	S	×

Place	Index	Pop.
Windle, Overton	N	22
Window Cliffs, Putnam	N	20
Windrock, Anderson	NE	×
Winsett Mills, Henry	NW	60
Winesap, Cumberland	E	25
● Winfield, Scott	NE	200
Wingo, Henderson	W	×
● *Winsted*, Rutherford	C	×
Winston, Weakley	NW	×
Wirmingham, Overton	N	×
● *Wisdom Spur*, Lawrence	S	×
Wisener, Bedford	C	10
● Witt'sFoundry, Hamblen	NE	200
● Wolf Creek, Cocke	E	20
Womack, Bedford	C	×
Woodard, Robertson	N	8
Woodbury, Cannon	C	576
Wooddale, Knox	E	×
Woodford, Montgomery	N	48
● Woodland Mills, Obion	NW	200
Woodlawn, Montgomery	N	20
Woodlee, Marion	SE	×
Woods Hill, Carroll	W	30
● Woodstock, Shelby	SW	50
Wood's Valley, Dickson	N	5
Woodville, Haywood	W	175
Woody, Cumberland	E	10
Woolsey's College, Greene	NE	30
Woolworth, Humphreys	C	20
● *Worley*, Dickson	N	12
Wormack Sta., Lawrence	S	12
Worsham, Sumner	N	19
Wrencoe, Davidson	N	19
Wright's Store, Tipton	W	×
Wyatt, Cumberland	E	×
Wynn, Stewart	N	21
Xenophone, Hancock	NE	15
Xerxes, Hancock	NE	13
Yager, Warren	C	12
Yankee Bar, Lauderdale	W	×
Yankeetown, White	S	8
Yateston, White	C	6
Yell, Marshall	C	8
Yellow Creek, Houston	N	15
Yellow Springs, Claiborne	NE	28
Yellow Store, Hawkins	NE	10
Yellow Sulphur, Blount	E	60
Yokely, Giles	S	13
Yorkville, Gibson	W	500
Young, Giles	S	10
Youngblood, DeKalb	C	×
Young Store, Carroll	W	29
Yum Yum, Fayette	SW	×
Y. Z., Granger	NE	6
Zach, Benton	NW	×
Zeb, (see East Cumberland Gap)		×
Zep, Union	NE	×
Zephaniah, Fayette	SW	×
Zieglers, McMinn	SE	10
Zincite, Claiborne	NE	×

TEXAS.

COUNTIES.	INDEX.	POP.
Anderson	E	20,923
Andrews	NW	24
Angelina	E	6,306
Aransas	S	1,824
Archer	N	2,101
Armstrong	SW	944
Atascosa	S	6,459
Austin	SE	17,859
Bailey	N	×
Bandera	C	3,795
Bastrop	C	20,736
Baylor	N	2,595
Bee	S	3,720
Bell	C	33,377
Bexar	S	49,266
Blanco	C	4,649
Borden	NW	222
Bosque	C	14,224
Bowie	NE	20,267
Brazoria	SE	11,506
Brazos	C	16,650
Brewster	W	710
Briscoe	SW	×
Brown	C	11,421
Buchel	W	307
Burleson	C	13,001
Burnet	C	10,747
Caldwell	C	15,769

County	Index	Pop.
Calhoun	S	815
Callahan	N	5,457
Cameron	S	14,424
Camp	NE	6,624
Carson	SW	356
Cass	NE	22,554
Castro	SW	9
Chambers	SE	2,241
Cherokee	E	22,975
Childress	SW	1,175
Clay	N	7,503
Cochran	NW	×
Coke	C	2,059
Coleman	C	6,112
Collin	NE	36,736
Collingsworth	SW	357
Colorado	SE	19,512
Comal	C	6,398
Comanche	C	15,608
Concho	C	1,065
Cooke	N	24,696
Coryell	C	16,873
Cottle	NW	240
Crane	W	15
Crockett	W	194
Crosby	NW	346
Dallam	SW	112
Dallas	NE	67,042
Dawson	NW	29
Deaf Smith	SW	179
Delta	NE	9,117
Denton	N	21,289
De Witt	S	14,307
Dickens	NW	295
Dimmit	S	1,049
Donley	SW	1,056
Duval	S	7,598
Eastland	N	10,373
Ector	W	224
Edwards	C	1,970
Ellis	NE	31,774
El Paso	W	15,678
Encinal	S	2,744
Erath	N	21,594
Falls	C	20,706
Fannin	NE	38,709
Fayette	C	31,481
Fisher	NW	2,996
Floyd	NW	529
Foard	NW	×
Foley	S	16
Fort Bend	SE	10,586
Franklin	NE	6,481
Freestone	E	15,987
Frio	S	3,112
Gaines	NW	68
Galveston	SE	31,476
Garza	NW	14
Gillespi	C	7,056
Glasscock	NW	208
Goliad	S	5,910
Gonzales	S	18,016
Gray	SW	203
Grayson	NE	53,211
Gregg	NE	9,402
Grimes	E	21,312
Guadalupe	S	15,217
Hale	NW	721
Hall	SW	703
Hamilton	C	9,313
Hansford	SW	133
Hardeman	NW	3,904
Hardin	E	3,956
Harris	SE	37,249
Harrison	NE	26,721
Hartley	SW	252
Haskell	NW	1,665
Hays	C	11,352
Hemphill	SW	519
Henderson	NE	12,285
Hidalgo	S	6,534
Hill	C	27,583
Hockley	NW	×
Hood	N	7,614
Hopkins	NE	20,572
Houston	E	19,360
Howard	NW	1,210
Hunt	NE	31,885
Hutchinson	SW	58
Irion	W	870
Jack	N	9,740
Jackson	S	3,281
Jasper	E	[illegible],592
Jeff Davis	W	1,394
Jefferson	SE	5,857
Johnson	N	22,313
Jones	NW	3,797

Texas

Texas

Karnes	S	3,637
Kaufman	NE	21,598
Kendall	C	3,826
Kent	NW	324
Kerr	C	4,462
Kimble	C	2,243
King	NW	173
Kinney	S	3,781
Knox	NW	1,134
Lamar	NE	37,302
Lamb	NW	4
Lampasas	C	7,584
LaSalle	S	2,139
Lavaca	S	21,887
Lee	C	11,952
Leon	E	13,841
Liberty	E	4,230
Limestone	C	21,678
Lipscomb	SW	632
Live Oak	S	2,055
Llano	C	6,772
Loving	NW	3
Lubbock	NW	33
Lynn	NW	24
McCulloch	C	3,217
McLennan	C	39,204
McMullen	S	1,038
Madison	E	8,512
Marion	NE	10,862
Martin	NW	264
Mason	E	5,18[illegible]
Matagorda	SE	3,985
Maverick	S	3,698
Medina	S	5,730
Menard	C	1,215
Midland	NW	1,033
Milam	C	24,773
Mills	E	5,493
Mitchell	NW	2,059
Montague	N	18,863
Montgomery	E	11,765
Moore	SW	15
Morris	NE	6,580
Motley	NW	139
Nacogdoches	E	15,984
Navarro	NE	26,373
Newton	E	4,650
Nolan	NW	1,573
Nueces	S	8,093
Ochiltree	SW	198
Oldham	SW	270
Orange	E	4,770
Palo Pinto	N	8,320
Panola	NE	14,328
Parker	N	21,682
Parmer	SW	7
Pecos	W	1,326
Polk	E	10,332
Potter	SW	849
Presidio	W	1,698
Rains	NE	3,909
Randall	SW	187
Red River	NE	21,452
Reeves	W	1,247
Refugio	S	1,239
Roberts	SW	326
Robertson	C	26,506
Rockwall	NE	5,972
Runnels	C	3,193
Rusk	NE	18,559
Sabine	C	4,969
San Augustine	E	6,688
San Jacinto	E	7,360
San Patricio	SE	1,312
San Saba	C	6,641
Schleicher	C	155
Scurry	NW	1,415
Shackelford	N	2,012
Shelby	E	14,365
Sherman	SW	34
Smith	NE	28,324
Somervell	N	3,419
Starr	S	10,749
Stephens	N	4,926
Sterling	W	×
Stonewall	NW	1,024
Sutton	C	658
Swisher	SW	100
Tarrant	N	41,142
Taylor	NW	6,957
Terry	NW	21
Throckmorton	N	902
Titus	NE	8,190
Tom Green	W	5,152
Travis	C	36,322
Trinity	E	7,648
Tyler	E	10,877
Upshur	NE	12,695
Upton	W	52
Uvalde	S	3,804
Val Verde	SW	2,874
Van Zandt	NE	16,225
Victoria	S	8,737
Walker	E	12,874
Waller	SE	10,888
Ward	W	77
Washington	C	29,161
Webb	S	14,842
Wharton	SE	7,584
Wheeler	SW	778
Wichita	N	4,831
Wilbarger	N	7,092
Williamson	C	25,909
Wilson	S	10,655
Winkler	N	18
Wise	NE	24,134
Wood	NE	23,932
Yoakum	NW	4
Young	N	5,049
Zapata	S	3,562
Zavalla	S	1,097
Total		2,235,523

TOWN.	COUNTY.	INDEX.	POP.
● Abbott	Hill	C	50
Aberdeen	Collingsworth	SW	7
Aberfoyle	Hunt	NE	60
● **Abilene**	Taylor	NW	3,194
Abner	Kaufman	NE	50
● *Abneys*	Harrison	NE	×
Acme	Van Zandt	NE	×
● Acrey	Erath	N	20
Acton	Hood	N	150
Adair	Swisher	SW	×
● *Adams*	Bexar	S	×
Adamsville	Lampasas	C	×
Addicks	Harris	SE	25
Addran	Hopkins	NE	×
Adell	Parker	N	20
Ad Hall	Milam	C	20
Adieu	Jack	N	32
Adobe Walls	Hutchinson	SW	16
● *Ady*	Oldham	SW	×
Agnes	Parker	N	15
● *Aqua Dulce*	Nueces	S	×
● *Aquilares*	Encinal	S	×
● *Aikens Junction*	Hood	N	×
Aken	Shelby	E	×
Alamito	Presidio	W	×
● Alamo Mills	Cass	NE	25
Alamore	El Paso	W	100
Alamositas	Oldham	SW	×
● *Alazan*	Bexar	S	×
● Alba	Wood	NE	100
Albade	Caldwell	C	130
Albany	Shackelford	N	857
Albion	Red River	NE	32
Alcott	Falls	C	×
Alder Branch	Anderson	E	35
Aldine	Uvalde	S	32
● *Aldine*	Harris	SE	×
● Aledo	Parker	N	120
● Alexander	Erath	N	381
● *Alfalfa*	El Paso	W	×
Algereta	San Saba	C	×
● Alice	Nueces	S	100
● Allamoore	El Paso	W	×
● Allen	Collin	NE	200
Allendale	Wichita	N	×
● *Allenfarm*	Brazos	SE	25
● Alleyton	Colorado	SE	351
Alliance	Hunt	NE	100
● *Alma*	Clay	N	×
● Alma	Ellis	NE	25
Almedes	Anderson	E	×
Almira	Cass	NE	25
● *Aloe*	Victoria	S	×
Alpha	Coke	C	×
● **Alpine**	Brewster	W	600
Alsobrooks	Tyler	E	10
● Altair	Colorado	SE	20
● Alto	Cherokee	E	210
Altoga	Collin	NE	10
● *Altuda*	Brewster	W	×
Alum Creek	Bastrop	C	50
● Alvarado	Johnson	N	1,543
● Alvin	Brazoria	SE	261
● Alvord	Wise	NE	560
● *Amanda*	Kinney	S	×
Amargosa Ranch	(see Penitas)		×
● **Amarillo**	Potter	SW	482
● Ambia	Lamar	NE	25
● Amelia	Jefferson	SE	10
● *Ames*	Liberty	E	×
Amicus	Marion	NE	40
Ammannsville	Fayette	C	25
Amphion	Atascosa	S	25
Ample	Haskell	NW	×
● *Anacacho*	Kinney	S	77
Anahuac	Chambers	SE	×
Anaqua	Victoria	S	20
Ancohrage	Atascosa	S	10
Anderson	Grimes	E	600
● *Andrews*	Caldwell	C	×
Andrews	Wood	NE	×
● *Angelina*	Angelina	E	×
Angleton	Brazoria	SE	×
● Angus	Navarro	NE	10
Anhalt	Comal	C	20
● Anna	Collin	NE	250
● Anneta	Parker	N	35
Anneville	Wise	NE	20
● Annona	Red River	NE	267
Anson	Jones	NW	495
Antelope	Jack	N	150
● Antelope Gap	Mills	E	10
Anthony	Nueces	S	×
Anti	Cass	NE	×
Antioch	Houston	E	50
Apolonia	Grimes	E	×
Appleby	Nacogdoches	E	×
Apple Springs	Trinity	E	50
Aquilares	Encinal	S	20
● Aquilla	Hill	C	50
● *Aragon*	Presidio	W	×
● *Aranama*	Goliad	S	×
Aransas	Bee	S	130
Aransas City	(see Fulton)		×
● Aransas Harbor	San Patricio	SE	×
● *Aransas Pass*	Aransas	S	1,069
● Arcadia	Galveston	SE	×
Archer City	Archer	N	200
● *Arcola*	Fort Bend	SE	60
● *Arcola Junc.*	Fort Bend	SE	×
Arden	Irion	W	×
● *Argo*	Bowie	NE	×
Argo	Titus	NE	65
● Argyle	Denton	N	60
● *Arispe*	El Paso	W	×
Arkada	Fannin	NE	75
Arleston	Panola	NE	30
Arlie	Childress	SW	11
● Arlington	Tarrant	N	664
Armour	Limestone	C	25
Armstrong	Elath	N	32
Arneckville	De Witt	S	150
● *Arno*	El Paso	W	×
● *Arno*	Reeves	W	×
● *Aroya*	Ward	W	×
Arroyo	Cameron	S	10
● Arthur City	Lamar	NE	50
Asa	Fannin	NE	×
Ash	Houston	E	×
Ashby	Matagorda	SE	×
● *Ashcraft*	Smith	NE	×
Ashworth	Kaufman	NE	×
● *Asia*	Polk	E	19
Aspermont	Stonewall	NW	205
Astonia	Ellis	NE	25
Atascosa	Bexar	S	75
● **Athens**	Henderson	NE	1,035
● Atlanta	Cass	NE	1,764
Atlas	Lamar	NE	10
Atoka	Coleman	C	32
● Aubrey	Denton	N	160
Auburn	Ellis	NE	100
Audubon	Wise	NE	50
Augusta	Houston	E	150
Aurora	Wise	NE	372
● **AUSTIN**	Travis	C	14,575
● *Austin Junc.*	Lavaca	S	×
Authon	Parker	N	25
Avalon	Ellis	NE	100
Avant	(see Dew)		×
Avaton	Harrison	NE	32
● Avinger	Cass	NE	100
Avondale	Tarrant	N	×
● Axtell	McLennan	C	25
Ayr	Deaf Smith	SW	×
● *Ayres*	Montgomery	E	650
Azle	Tarrant	N	26
Baby Head	Llano	C	10
● Bagwell	Red River	NE	100
Bailey	Fannin	NE	75
● *Bailey*	Fannin	NE	×
Bailey's Prairie	Brazoria	SE	×
Baileyville	Milam	C	15
● **Baird**	Callahan	N	850

Place		Pop.
● Baker, Angelina	E	×
Baker, Cooke	N	130
Bald Prairie, Robertson	C	25
Baldridge, Ellis	NE	×
● *Baldwin's*, Duval	S	×
● **Ballinger**, Runnels	C	1,500
Balm, Cooke	N	75
Bandera, Bandera	C	372
● Bangs, Brown	C	25
Banks, (see McGregor)		×
● Banquete, Nueces	S	65
Barber's Mill, (seeSchulenburg)		×
Barclay, Falls	C	100
Barela Spring, Jeff Davis	W	×
Barksdale, Edwards	C	200
Barlow, Cooke	N	×
Barlow's Ferry, (see Dinero)		×
Barnesville, (see Rancho)		×
Barnesville, Johnson	N	15
● Barnum, Polk	E	200
● *Barrett*, Titus	NE	10
● Barry, Navarro	NE	5
Barstow, Ward	W	×
● Bartlett, Williamson	C	206
Bartonville, Denton	N	40
Basin Springs, Grayson	NE	30
Bass, Smith	NE	25
● Bassett, Bowie	NE	100
● **Bastrop**, Bastrop	C	1,634
Batesville, Zavalla	S	150
Bath, Walker	E	10
Battle, McLennan	C	11
Baulch, (see Weatherford)		×
Baurs, Harris	SE	×
Baurs, Lavaca	S	12
Bay, Matagorda	SE	10
Bay View, Harris	SE	26
Bazette, Navarro	NE	80
Bear Creek, Tarrant	N	130
Beaukiss, Williamson	C	50
● **Beaumont**, Jefferson	SE	3,296
● Beaver, Wichita	N	30
Beaver Creek, Clay	N	32
Becker, Kaufman	NE	×
Beckton, Dickens	NW	×
Beckville Panola	NE	30
Bedford, Tarrant	N	200
Bedias, Grimes	E	200
Bee Caves, Travis	C	30
Beech, Shelby	E	×
Beech Grove, Jasper	E	×
Bee Creek, Ellis,	NE	×
Bee House, Coryell	C	25
● *Beeler's*, Harris	SE	×
● **Beeville**, Bee	S	1,131
● Belcherville, Montague	N	516
Belen, El Paso	**W**	<
● *Belden*, Morris	NE	×
Bellfalls, Bell	C	×
Belgrade, Newton	E	10
Belknap, Young	N	75
Belle Plain, Callahan	N	150
● Bellevue, Clay	N	250
● Bells, Grayson	NE	429
Bell's Ferry, Jasper	E	×
● **Bellville**, Austin	SE	807
Belmont, Gonzales	S	600
Belott, Houston	E	×
● **Belton**, Bell	C	3,000
● *Ben Arnold*, Milam	C	×
● Benavides, Duval	S	800
○ Benbrook, Tarrant	N	50
● Benchley, Robertson	C	20
Bend, San Saba	C	50
● Ben Franklin, Delta	NE	200
Benina, San Augustine	E	300
Benjamin, Knox	NW	350
Benton, Atascosa	S	502
Benvanue, Clay	N	25
Ben Wheeler, VanZandt	NE	50
● Berclair, Goliad	S	×
● *Bery's Mills*, Bexar	S	×
Berlin, Erath	N	10
Bermuda, Shelby	E	30
Bernardo Prairie, Colorado	SE	50
Bernice, Andrews	NW	×
● *Berry*, Bowie	NE	×
Berry Creek, Kaufman	NE	×
Berryville, Henderson	NE	65
● Bertram, Burnett	C	150
Bethany, Fayette	C	30
Bethel, Anderson	E	15
● *Bethel*, Tarrant	N	×
Bethelder, Brazoria	SE	×
● *Bethesda*, Titus	NE	×
● Bettie, Upshur	NE	284
Beverly, Coryell	C	50

Texas

Place		Pop.
Bevilport, Jasper	E	20
Bexar, Bexar	S	20
Biardstown, Lamar	NE	100
Bibb, Comanche	C	10
Biegel, Fayette	C	50
● Big Cypress, Camp	NE	×
Bigfoot, Frio	S	10
Biggs, Panola	NE	25
Big Rock, VanZandt	NE	50
● Big Sandy, Upshur	NE	323
● **Big Spring**, Howard	NW	1,158
Big Valley, Mills	E	240
Billington, Limestone	C	×
● *Billum*, Tyler	E	×
Birch, Burleson	C	×
● *Birds*, Tarrant	N	×
Birdston, Navarro	NE	25
Birdville, Tarrant	N	100
Birthright, Hopkins	NE	50
Bisco, Howard	NW	×
● *Bissell*, Trinity	E	×
● Bivens, Cass	NE	302
Black, Titus	NE	×
Blackfoot, Anderson	E	×
Black Jack, (see Chireno)		×
● Black Jack Grove, H'p's	NE	676
Black Jack Springs, Fay'te	C	25
Blackland, Rockwall	NE	75
Black Oak, Hopkins	NE	30
Blackville, (see Ingleside)		×
Blaine, Falls	C	×
Blair, Childress	SW	×
● *Blanchette*, Jefferson	SE	×
Blanco, Blanco	C	269
Blanconia, Bee	S	10
● Blanket, Brown	C	25
Blanton, Hill	C	20
Bleakwood, Newton	E	50
Bleiberville, Austin	SE	×
Blevins, Falls	C	50
Block Creek, Kendall	C	19
Blocker, Harrison	NE	40
Bloomfield, Cooke	N	35
● Blooming Grove, Nav'ro,	NE	175
● Blossom, Lamar	NE	695
Blowout, Blanco	C	35
Blue Branch, Lee	C	32
Blue Grove, Clay	N	10
Blue Ridge, Collin	NE	200
Blue RidgeStore, (seeStafford)		×
Bluff, Fayette	C	80
● Bluff Dale, Erath	N	500
Bluff Springs, Travis	C	50
Bluffton, Llano	C	50
● Blum, Hill	C	250
Board, Navarro	NE	40
Boaz, Coryell	C	5
Bobbin, Montgomery	E	50
● *Bodan*, Angelina	E	×
● **Boerne**, Kendall	C	433
● *Boescher's*, Colorado	SE	×
Bogata, Red River	NE	100
Boggy, Leon	E	10
● *Boggy Tank*, Colorado	SE	×
Bolivar, Denton	N	200
● *Bolton*, VanZandt	NE	×
● *Bonded Warehouse*, Webb	S	×
Bonham's Store, (see Edna)		×
● **Bonham**, Fannin	NE	3,361
● Bonita, Montague	N	100
Bonner, Freestone	E	75
● Bonney, Brazoria	SE	×
Bono, Johnson	N	25
Bookman's Store, (see Prairie Plains)		×
Boon, Blanco	C	×
Boonsville, Wise	NE	75
● *Boracho*, ElPaso	W	×
● Borden, Colorado	SE	10
Boren's Mills, San Augus'ne	E	40
Bosqueville, McLennan	C	50
Boston, Bowie	NE	500
Bourland, Floyd	NW	×
Borine, Lavaca	S	90
● Bowers, Polk	E	200
● Bowie, Montague	N	1,486
Bowman, Archer	N	13
Bowser Bend, San Saba	C	×
Box, Lamar	NE	260
Box Elder, Red River	NE	5
● Boyce, Ellis	NE	10
Boydston, Donley	SW	×
Boynton, Panola	NE	×
Boz, Ellis	NE	×
● Bracken, Comal	C	15
● *Brackenbridge*, Wilson	S	18
Brackett's Spring, Foley	S	×

Texas

Place		Pop.
Brackettville, Kinney	S	1,649
Bradford, Anderson	E	15
Bradley, Sherman	SW	×
● *Bradshaw*, Cherokee	E	32
● *Bradshaw*, Rusk	NE	×
Brady, McCulloch	C	560
Branchville, Milan	C	20
● Brandon, Hill	C	75
Brannon's Store, (seeMillSap)		×
● Bransford, Tarrant	N	50
● *Brant*, Reeves	W	×
● Brantley, Montgomery	E	310
Brazoria, Brazoria	SE	432
● Brazos, Palo Pinto	N	25
Brazos Bridge, (see Marlin)		×
Brazos Point, Bosque	C	18
Breckenridge, (see Skiles)		×
Breckenridge, Stephens	N	462
● Bremond, Robertson	SW	387
● **Brenham**, Washington	C	5,209
Breslau, Lavaca	S	50
● *Brennans*, Webb	S	×
Brewer, Freestone	E	50
● *Brewster*, Austin,	SE	×
Briar, Wise	NE	303
Bridgeport, Wise	NE	198
Bristol, Ellis	NE	303
Broadway, Lamar	NE	×
Brock, Parker	N	25
Brodie, Lamar	NE	×
Bronte, Coke	C	50
Brookeland, Sabine	C	100
Brookhaven, Bell	C	10
● Brookston, Lamar	NE	237
Brownings, Smith	NE	15
● Brownsborough, Hen'r'n	NE	10
Brown's Ferry, (seeGainesv'e)		×
Brownsville, Cameron	S	6,134
● **Brownwood**, Brown	C	2,176
Broxson, Houston	E	×
Bruce, Johnson	N	33
● Bruceville, McLennan	C	250
Bruin, Montgomery	E	10
Brumlow, Wise	NE	25
Brushy Creek, Anderson	E	15
● **Bryan**, Brazos	C	2,979
Bryan's Mill, Cass	NE	200
Bryan's L'd'g, (seePerry'sL'd'g)		×
Bryson, Jack	N	100
● Buchanan, Bowie	NE	274
● Buckholts, Milan	C	64
Buckhorn, Austin	SE	100
Buckner, Parker	N	50
● Buda, Hays	C	100
Buel, Johnson	N	10
Buena Vista, (see Timpson)		×
Buena Vista Ranch, LaSalle	S	10
● Buffalo, Leon	E	200
Buffalo Gap, Taylor	NW	200
Buffalo Sprs., (see Bellevue)		×
Bulcher, Cooke	N	50
● Bullard, Smith	NE	250
Bullard Mills, Denton	N	50
Bull Head, (see Vance)		×
Bulverde, Bexar	S	20
Buncomb, Panola	NE	×
Bunn's Bluff, Orange	E	25
Bunyan, Erath	N	×
● *Burdett*, Caldwell	C	×
● Burke, Angelina	E	50
Burkett, Coleman	C	10
Burkeville, Newton	E	300
● Burleson, Johnson	N	250
● *Burlingame*, Smith	NE	×
Burlington, Milam	C	×
Burlington, (see Spanish Fort)		×
● **Burnet**, Burnet	C	1,454
Burns, Cooke	N	65
● *Burns*, Rusk	NE	×
● *Burns*, De Witt	S	×
● *Burro*, La Salle	S	×
● *Burroughs*, Au tin	SE	×
● Burton, Washington	C	384
Bush's Store, (see Parvin)		×
Butler, Freestone	E	75
Buttercup, Williamson	C	10
Bynum, Hill	C	×
Byrd's Store, Brown	C	57
● *Byron*, Anderson	E	3,000
● Cactus, Webb	S	57
Caddell, San Augustine	E	×
Caddo, Stephens	N	100
● Caddo Mills, Hunt	NE	234
Caddo Peak, Callahan	N	50
Cade, Navarro	NE	25
Cains, Harrison	NE	×
Cairo, Jasper	E	300

Texas	
● Calaveras, Wilson.........S	369
● **Caldwell**, Burleson.....C	1,250
Caldwell's Store, Bastrop....C	25
Caledonia, Rush...........NE	20
● *Calef*, Tarrant...........N	45
Calhoun, Dallas..........NE	10
Callis, Collin.............NE	×
Callisburgh, Cooke..........N	50
Calloway, Upshur.........NE	50
● Calvert, Robertson........C	2,632
Camden, Comanche.........C	390
● **Cameron**, Milam........C	1,608
Camila, (see Cold Springs)....	×
● Campbell, Hunt.........NE	472
Campbellton, Atascosa......S	40
Camp Charlotte, Irion.....W	×
Camp Colorado, Coleman....C	100
Camp Rice, (see FortHancock)	×
● *Camps*, Gregg..........NE	×
Camp San Saba, McCulloch. C	50
Camp Verde, (seeCentre Point)	×
● *Canaan*, Limestone.......C	×
● **Canadian**, Hemphill..SW	400
Caney, Matagorda..........SE	75
● *Cannon*, Camp..........NE	×
Cannon, Grayson..........NE	20
Canton, Van Zandt......NE	421
● *Canutillo*, El Paso.....W	×
● *Canyon*, Stephens........N	×
Canyon, Randall.........SW	50
● Carbon, Eastland.........N	100
Carbon City, Webb..........S	×
Carbondale, Young.........N	×
● *Carey*, Childress........SW	×
Carey Station, Childress...SW	×
● *Carl*, Navarro...........NE	10
Carl, Travis................C	×
Carlos Ranch, (see Anaqua)..	×
Carlisle, Rusk............NE	×
Carlton, Hamilton...........C	75
● *Carlyle*, Clay...........N	×
● Cameron, Fayette.........C	25
Carmel, Bexar...............S	×
● *Carmona*, Polk...........E	200
Carr, Titus...............NE	47
Carrizo, Zapata............S	243
Carrizo Springs, DimmitS	289
Carrol, Smith.............NE	×
● *Carroll's*, Tyler...........E	×
● Carroll's Prairie, HopkinsNE	3,038
Carroll's Store, (seeThurman)	×
● Carrollton, Dallas........NE	50
Carter, Parker...............N	40
Cartersville, Parker........N	57
Carthage, Panola.......NE	554
● *Carruth*, Dallas.........NE	×
● Cason, Morris............NE	300
Castell, Llano..............C	10
Castroville, Medina.......S	679
Caswell, Potter..........SW	×
Cataline, Hemphill........SW	25
Catfish, Henderson........NE	×
Cathron's Store, Lamar....NE	500
Catonville, Red River.....NE	×
Cat Spring, Austin.........SE	1,000
Causey, Gaines..........NW	×
Cavender, Dimmit...........S	×
Cawthon, Grimes...........E	×
Cayote, Bosque..............C	30
Cedar, Fayette...............C	50
● *Cedar*, Kausman.......NE	×
Cedar Bayou, Harris.......SE	50
Cedar Creek, Bastrop.......C	125
Cedar Grove, Brazoria.....SE	×
● Cedar Hill, Dallas.......NE	242
Cedar Mills, Grayson.......NE	100
● Cedar Park, Williamson.. C	10
Cedar Springs, (see Viesca)..	×
Cedarton, Brown..........C	800
Cedar Valley, Travis.........C	50
● Celeste, Hunt...........NE	250
Celina, Collin.............NE	75
Celtic, Briscoe............SW	×
Centenary, Titus..........NE	26
Centennial, Panola........NE	35
Center, Shelby............E	1,500
Centralia, Trinity...........E	150
Centre City, Mills...........E	50
Centre Mill, Hood...........N	10
Centre Point, Kerr..........C	543
Centreville, Leon.........E	288
Cestohowa, Karnes...........S	100
Chalk Mountain, Erath......N	10
Chambers Mill, (see Jake)...	×
Chanata Mines, (seeFortDavis)	×
Chances Prairie, Brazoria SE	×
Chancey, Bowie...........NE	×

Texas	
● Chandler, Henderson... NE	200
Chaney, Panola..........NE	×
● *Chaney Junction*, HarrisSE	609
Channing, Hartley........SW	25
● Chapel Hill, Washington..C	800
● *Chapin*, Hood............N	×
Charco, Goliad...............S	100
Charleston, Delta.........NE	50
Charlie, Clay................N	50
Chatfield, Navarro.........NE	50
● *Chatfield*, Uvalde.........S	×
Cheapside, Gonzales.........S	100
● *Cheetham*, Colorado.....SE	10
● Chenango, Brazoria......SE	75
Cherokee, Rusk..........NE	×
Cherokee, San Saba.........C	100
Cherry Spring, Gillespie....C	10
● Chester, Tyler..............E	50
● *Cheyenne*, Oldham......SW	×
Chicago, Dawson.........NW	×
Chico, Wise...............NE	323
Chicota, Lamar...........NE	321
● **Childress**, Childress..SW	400
● Chillicothe, Hardeman. NW	150
● Chilton, Falls.............C	58
● *China*, Jefferson..........SE	×
China Spring, McLennen....C	150
Chink, (see Seven Oaks)......	×
Chinquapin, San Jacinto....E	10
Chireno, Nacogdoches......E	276
Chisholm, Rockwall.......NE	×
● *Chispa*, Jeff Davis.......W	×
● Choctaw, Grayson.......NE	×
Chriesman, Burleson........C	25
Christian, Palo Pinto.......N	25
Christoval, Tom Green.....W	150
● Cibolo, Guadalupe........S	25
Cincinnati, Walker.........E	25
● Circleville, Williamson....C	50
● Cisco, Eastland...........N	1,063
Cistern Fayette.............C	50
Clara, Wichita..............N	10
● **Clarendon**, Donley...SW	949
● *Clark's*, Calhoun..........S	×
Clark's Ferry, (see Homer)..	×
Clarkson, Milam............C	×
● **Clarksville**, RedRiverNE	1,588
Clarksville, Cameron.........S	×
Clarksville, Travis..........C	446
● **Claude**, Armstrong...SW	285
Clawson, Angelina..........E	×
● *Clawson's Mill*, Angelina. E	&
● Clay, Burleson.............C	25
Clayton, Panola...........NE	75
Claytonville, Fisher......NW	×
● Clear Creek, Galveston..SE	10
Clear Fork, Caldwell.......C	×
Clear Lake, (see Wylie)......	×
Clear Lake, (see Duke)......	×
Clear Spring, Guadalupe....N	15
● **Cleburne**, Johnson.....N	3,278
Clements, Cass...........NE	×
● *Clemons*, Waller.........SE	×
Cleon, Shelby................E	×
Cleveland, (see Foster).......	×
● Cleveland, Liberty.........E	100
● *Cleveland*, Williamson....C	×
Click, Llano.................C	10
Clifford, Collingsworth...SW	×
● Clifton, Bosque...........C	204
● Cline, Uvalde..............S	×
● Clint, El Paso..............W	×
Clinton, Harris............SE	×
● Clinton, Hunt............NE	10
Clio, Brown..................C	50
Clisbee, Hale.............NW	×
● *Clodine*, Fort Bend......SE	×
Cloris Ranch, (see Concepcion)	×
● Clyde, Callahan............N	25
Coahoma, Howard.......NW	×
● *Coalcamp*, Cherokee......E	X
● *Coal Mine*, Palo Pinto...N	×
Coalville, (see Gordon).......	×
● *Cobb's*, Kaufman.......NE	×
Cochran, Austin...........SE	25
● *Codman*, Roberts.......SW	×
Coesfield, Cooke............N	25
Coffeeville, Upshur........NE	150
Coke, Wood...............NE	24
Cold Hill, Hopkins........NE	100
Cold Spring, San Jacinto. E	439
Coldwater, Sherman......SW	×
Coleman, Coleman........C	906
● *Coleman Junction*, Cole'nC	×
Colfax, Van Zandt.........NE	30
Colita, Polk.................E	100
● College Station, Brazos....C	300
Collingsworth, Coll'sw'th..SW	×

Texas	
● *Collins*, Nueces............S	200
● Collinsville, Grayson....NE	332
● Colmesneil, Tyler..........E	1,500
Colony, Fayette.............C	10
● **Colorado**, Mitchell...NW	1,582
● *Colorado Bridge*, Travis..C	×
Coltharp's Houston..........E	×
● Columbia, Bazoria......SE	515
● **Columbus**, Colorado.SE	2,199
● **Comanche**, Comanche.C	1,226
● *Comer*, Cherokee.........E	×
Comet, Marion............NE	×
● Comfort, Kendall.........C	307
● Commerce, Hunt.........NE	810
● Como, Bastrop............C	25
● *Como*, Hopkins..........NE	×
● Comstock, Val Verde...SW	×
Concan, Uvalde..............S	×
Concepcion, Duval............	200
● *Concord*, Hardin..........E	×
Concord, Leon...............E	12
Concrete, De Witt...........S	890
● *Cone*, Milam..............C	10
● *Conley*, Johnson..........N	×
Connor, Madison............E	×
● **Conroe**, Montgomery....E	200
Content, Runnels...........C	300
● Converse, Bexar...........S	20
Cooke's Point, Burleson.....C	20
● Cooks Springs, GraysonNE	×
Cooksville, (see Kickapoo)...	×
● Cookville, Titus.........NE	210
Cooper, Delta...........NE	629
● Coperas Cove, Coryell.....C	200
● Copeville, Collin.........NE	100
● *Coppell*, Dallas..........NE	×
● *Corbyn*, Comal............C	×
Corine, Cherokee............E	×
Corinth, Denton.............N	10
● Corley, Bowie.............NE	30
Cornelia, Armstrong......SW	×
Cornett, Marion............NE	25
Corn Hill, Williamson.......C	250
● **Corpus Christi**, Nue's.S	4,387
● Corrigan, Polk.............E	289
● **Corsicana**, Navarro..NE	6,285
Corwin, Burnet..............C	25
Coryell, **Coryell**.............C	100
Cottle, Cottle..............NW	×
Cottondale, Wise..........NE	100
Cotton Gin, Freestone......E	400
Cottonwood, Callahan......N	400
● **Cotulla**, La Salle........S	672
● Coupland, Williamson....C	×
● *Courchesne*, El Paso.....W	×
● Courtney, Grimes.........E	300
Covington, Hill..............C	25
Cowan, Erath...............N	×
Cowboy, McCulloch.........C	×
● *Cowen*, Wise.............NE	×
Cox, (see Emberson)..........	×
Coxville, Bastrop............C	×
Crab Apple, Gillespie........C	×
● *Crabb*, Fort Bend.......SE	×
Craft, Cherokee..............E	×
Crafton, Wise..............NE	300
Craig, Rusk................NE	×
● Crandall, Kaufman......NE	251
Crane's Mill, Comal.........C	32
Cranfill's Gap, Bosque......C	100
● Crawford, McLennan.....C	400
Creamlevel, Van Zandt...NE	×
Creedmoor, Travis..........C	25
Creek, Houston..............E	10
Crescent, Titus.............NE	45
Cresco, (see Santo)...........	×
● Cresson, Johnson..........N	100
Cresswell, Orchiltree......SW	15
Crim, Rusk.................NE	25
Crisp, Ellis.................NE	×
● **Crockett**, Houston......E	1,445
Crockettville, (see Carthage)..	×
● *Cronin*, Anderson........E	×
● Crosby, Harris...........SE	32
Cross Cut, Brown...........C	65
Crossland, Gray...........SW	×
Cross Plains, Callahan......N	100
Cross Roads, (see Frost).....	×
● *Cross Timbers*, Harris...SE	×
Cross Timbers, Johnson.....N	65
Crowell, Foard..........NW	16
● Crowley, Tarrant..........N	75
Crozier, Young..............N	×
Crutchfield, Fannin........NE	×
Cryer Creek, Navarro.....NE	25
Crystal Falls, Stephens......N	200
Cuba, Johnson..............N	15

Texas
Texas

● Cuero, De Witt.........S 1,142
Culbertson, Cass..........NE 50
Culver, Matagorda.........SE 10
● *Cummings*, Williamson..C ×
Cummins, Sterling.........W 17
Cundiff, Jack..............N 12
Curlew, Floyd............NW ×
Currie, Travis..............C ×
Curry's Creek, Kendall......C 825
Curtis, Eastland............N 10
Curtright, Cass............NE ×
Cushman, Wilbarger....... N ×
Cusseta, Cass..............NE 50
Custer, Brazoria...........SE ×
Custer City, Cooke.........N 25
Cuthand, Red River.......NE 25
Cuthbert, Mitchell.........NW ×
Cuthfield, Fannin..........NE 25
Cutler, Grayson............NE ×
Cutoff, Gaudalupe...........S 82
Cyclone, Bell...............C 10
Cypress Mill, Blanco........C 50
Cypress Creek, (see Woodville) ×
● Cypress Top Harris.....SE 35
Cyrus, Bosque..............C ×
Dacus, Montgomery.........E 25
● *Duffau* Travis..............C ×
Daileyville, (see Kenedy)..... ×
● **Daingerfield**, Morris, NE 553
Daisy, Rains...............NE ×
● *Dalberg*, El Paso..........W ×
Dalby Springs, Bowie.....NE 100
Dale, Caldwell...............C 400
● *Dallam*, Dallam.........SW ×
Dallardsville, Polk..........E ×
● **Dallas**, Dallas.........NE 38,067
● *Dallas Junc.*, Dallas....NE ×
Dalton, (see Marietta)........ ×
Daly's, Houston.............E 50
Damond's Mound, Brazoria SE ×
Dan, Wise.................NE ×
Daniel, Houston.............E ×
Dankworth, (see Gatesvile).. ×
Danville, Comal..............C 100
Darby, Grimes...............E 65
Darden Springs, Lee........C ×
Dargan, Panola............NE 25
● *Darling*, Maverick.........S ×
● *Darlington*, Frio...........S 26
● Daugherty, Kauffman...NE 25
Davenport, Red River.....NE 50
● *Davenport*, Comal........C 25
Davidson's, Burleson........C ×
Davilla, Milam...............C 241
● Davis, Lamar............NE 25
Dawn, Deaf Smith.........SW ×
● Dawson, Nevarro........NE 365
Day, Wichita................N ×
● *Days*, Lamar.............NE ×
● Dayton, Liberty............E 200
Deadwood, Panola.........NE 13
Dean, Deaf Smith.........SW ×
● *Dean*, Leon................E ×
Deanville, Burleson..........C 25
● *Deaver*, Grayson.........NE ×
De Berry, Panola..........NE 75
● **Decatur**, Wise.........NE 1,746
Dee, Randall...............SW ×
De Grass, Jack..............N 10
● De Kalb, Bowie..........NE 420
● *Delaware*, Brown..........C ×
Delba, Fannin.............NE 50
● De Leon, Commanche....C 364
Delhi, Caldwell..............C 32
Della Plain, Floyd.........NW ×
Delma, Newton..............E 10
● *Delmar*, Eastland.........N ×
Delray, Panola.............NE 10
● **Del Rio**, Val Verde...SW 2,500
Delvale, Travis...............C 25
Deming's Bridge, M'tg'rda SE 50
Dempsey, Cass.............NE 25
● Denison, Grayson.......NE 10,958
Denman, Van Zandt......NE ×
Denning, San Augustine....E ×
● *Densons* Upshur........NE ×
● **Denton**, Denton........N 2,558
Denver, Montague...........N 75
Deport, Lamar.............NE 274
● Derby, Frio.................S 260
Derden, Hill..................C 20
Desdimonia, Eastland......N 400
Desoto, Dallas.............NE 10
Dessau, Travis..............C 10
● Detroit, Red River......NE 604
● *Dever's*, Liberty...........E 150
● Dever, Liberty.............E 150

● *Devil's River*, Val Verde SW ×
● Devine, Medina...........S 200
Dew, Freestone.............E 75
Dexter, Cooke...............N 226
● D'Hannis, Medina.........S 266
Dial, Fannin................NE 32
● *Dial*, Cherokee............E ×
Diana, Upshur..............NE 50
● *Diana*, Orange.............E 65
Dicey, Parker................N ×
Dickens, Dickens..........NW ×
● **Dickinson, Galveston....SE** 65
Dido, Tarrant..................N 65
Dietz, Guadalupe............S ×
Dike, Hopkins..............NE ×
● Dilley, Frio.................S 10
● *Dilworth*, Gonzales........S ×
Dime Box, Lee...............C 25
Dimmitt, Castro............SW ×
Dinero, Live Oak............S 10
Dingler, Commanche.......C 25
Direct, Lamar..............NE ×
Ditto, Atascosa...............S 20
Divide, Hopkins............NE 65
Dixie, Lamar...............NE ×
● Dixon, Hunt..............NE 150
Doan's, Wilbarger...........N 100
Dockums, Dickens.......NW 61
● Dodd, Fannin............NE 333
● Dodge, Walker.............N 200
Dodson, Houston............E ×
Dollman, Stonewall.....NE ×
Donahoe, Bell...............C ×
Donelton, Hunt............NE 100
Dora, Nolan................NW ×
Dorotin, Lavaca.............S 20
● Doss, Clay.................N 10
Double Bayou, Chambers. SE 200
Double Horn, Burnet........C 25
Double Mountain, Stone'all NW ×
Double Springs, Tarrant....N 100
● *Douglas*, Red River.....NE 12
Douglas, Nacogdoches.......E 200
Douglassville, Cass........NE 300
● *Dourc*, Ector..............W ×
Dowlin, Lamar.............NE 65
Downing, Comanche.........C 18
● *Downs*, McLennan.........C ×
Downsville, McLennan......C ×
Draco, Williamson............C 10
Drane, Navarro............NE 40
Dresden, Navarro.........NE 50
Driftwood, Hays..............C ×
Dripping Springs, Grayson NE ×
Dripping Springs, Hays.....C 200
● Driscoll, Nueces............S ×
Drop, Denton................N 25
Drury, San Jacinto..........E ×
● Dryden, Pecos.............W ×
Dubina, Fayette.............B 10
● Dublin, Erath..............N 2,025
Duffau, Erath................N 200
Duffau Wells, (see Duffau).. ×
● Duke, Fort Bend.........SE 25
● Dull's Ranch, LaSalle......S 20
Dumas, Moore.............SW ×
● *Dumont*, Harris..........SE ×
Dump, Limestone...........C ×
● *Duncan*, Hartley........SW ×
● Duncanville, Dallas.....NE 200
● Dundee, Archer.............N ×
Dunlap, Travis...............C ×
● *Dunlay*, Medina............S 100
Dunn, Scurry...............NW ×
Duplex, Fannin............NE ×
Durango, Falls...............C 250
Durham, Borden...........NW ×
● *Durham*, Harrison......NE ×
● *Duroc*, Eastland...........N ×
Duster, Comanche...........C ×
● Duval, Travis...............C 25
● *Duval*, Duval...............S ×
Duxbury, (see Bonita)....... ×
Dye, Montague...............N 25
● *Dyer*, Fort Bend..........SE ×
Eagle Branch, Bastrop......C ×
Eagle Cove, Callahan........N 12
● *Eagle Flat*, El Paso.......W ×
● Eagle Ford, Dallas......NE 75
● Eagle Lake, Colorado....SE 769
● **Eagle Pass**, Maverick..S 3,000
Eagle Point, Montague.....N 83
Eagle Springs, Coryell......C 75
Earle, Bexar..................S ×
Early, Cooke.................N ×
● *Earl's*, Parker..............N ×
Easom, Polk..................E 25

● East Bernard, Wharton SE 25
● *East Dallas*, Dallas.....NE ×
Easterling, Wilson...........S 10
East El Paso, El Paso.....W ×
East Hamilton, Shelby......E 50
● **Eastland**, Eastland.....N 400
East Meridian, (see Meridian) ×
Easton, Rusk..............NE 50
● *East River*, Montgomery. E ×
● *East Waco*, Mc Lennan...C ×
● *East Yard*, Bexar..........S ×
Ebony, Mills..................E ×
● Echo, Bell...................C 65
● Ector, Fannin............NE 150
● Eddy, McLennan...........C 300
Eden, Concho................C 100
● *Eden*, Frio...................S ×
Ederville, Tarrant............N ×
● *Edey*, Comanche...........C ×
● Edgar, DeWitt...............S 25
● Edgewood, Van Zandt.. NE 75
Edinburgh, Cameron....... S ×
Edith, Coke.................. C ×
Edna, Jackson...............S 537
Edom, Van Zandt.........NE 300
● *Edy*, Comanche.............C ×
Ettie, Wilbarger............ N ×
● Egan, Johnson.............N 100
● *Egypt*, Kaufman.........NE 97
● Elam Station, Dallas....NE 260
Elbert, Polk...................E ×
● El Campo, Wharton.....SE ×
El Cuerbo, Webb............ S ×
Elderville, Gregg..........NE 50
Eldridge, Gray..............SW 12
● *Eldridge*, Pecos...........W ×
● Elgin, Bastrop.............C 800
Eliasville, Young.............N 85
Elizabeth, (see Roanoke).... ×
● Elkhart, Anderson........E 100
Elkhorn, Red River.......NE 325
● Ella, Brazos.................C 25
● Ellinger, Fayette...........C 300
● *Elliott*, Robertson.........C ×
Elliott's, Matagorda....... SE 75
Elliott's Mills, (see Omaha).. ×
Ellis, Edwards.............. C ×
● *Elmdale*, Taylor.........NW 12
● Elmendorf, Bexar......... S ×
Elm Grove, (see Taylorsville) ×
● *Elm Grove*, Brazoria.... SE ×
● Elm Mott, McLennan..... C 50
● Elmo, Kaufman..........NE 500
Elmont, Grayson..........NE 35
Elmore, Hall...............SW ×
Elmview, Grayson.........NE 10
● **El Paso**, El Paso.......W 10,338
El Sauz, Cameron........... S ×
El Sordo, Zapata............. S ×
● *El Toro*, Jackson........... S ×
● *El Vista*, Jefferson......SE ×
Elwood, Fannin............NE 32
Elysian Fields, Harrison..NE 250
Emberson, Lamar.........NE 25
Embree, (see Garland)....... ×
Emerald, Crockett...........W ×
● *Emerson*, Pecos............W ×
Emilee, Tyler..................E 10
Emma, Crosby............NW 7
Emmet, Navarro...........NE ×
● **Emory**, Rains.............NE 353
● Encinal, LaSalle............S 562
Endora, Angelina.............E 25
● **Engle, Fayette............ C** 10
Engleman, Collin......... NE 50
Englewood, (see Franklin)... ×
English, Red River........NE ×
Enless, Tarrant...............N 32
● Ennis, Ellis...............NE 2,171
Enon, Tarrant................N 25
● Enterprise, Medina....... S ×
Entry, Montgomery........ E ×
Eolian, Stephens.............N 25
Ephraim, Hall..............SW ×
Equality, Harrison.........NE 25
Equestria, Johnson.......... N 19
Era, Cooke....................N 50
● *Erath*, Callahan............N ×
Erin, Jasper................. E 15
● *Erin*, Harris................SE ×
Erna, Mason................. E 20
Ernest, Travis.............. E ×
Erskine, Concho............ C 14
Escarbada, Deaf Smith.. SW ×
● Eskota, Fisher......... NW ×
Esperaza, Starr..............S ×
Espuela, Dickens.........NW 9

Essex, Upshur............NE ×
Estacado, Crosby......NW 238
Estelle, Dallas............NE 97
Estelline, Hall............SW ×
Ethel, Grayson............NE 300
● *Etholen*, El Paso.........W ×
Etna, (see Bullard)........... ×
Etoile, Nacogdoches........E 30
Ettowa, Gonzales..........S ×
Eudora, Angelina...........E 32
Eules, Tarrant............N 25
Eulogy, Bosque............C 100
Eureka, Navarro............NE 25
● *Eureka*, Harris..........SE ×
● *Evans*, Hardeman.....NW ×
Evans Point, Hopkins.....NE 50
Evant, Coryell..............C 50
Evergreen, San Jacinto.....E 100
● *Evergreen*, Lee...........C ×
Everitt, San Jacinto........E ×
Ewell, Upshur.............NE 25
Exile, Edwards.............C 32
⊙ Eylau, Bowie............NE 200
Ezzell, Lavaca..............S 30
● *Fabens*, El Paso..........W ×
Fairfield, Freestone......E 499
● Fairland, Burnet..........C 10
● *Fairlee*, Hunt...........NE ×
Fairmount, Sabine..........C 50
● *Fair Plains*, Cooke......N ×
Fair Play, Panola.........NE 25
● *Fairview*, Burnet.........C ×
Fair View, Wilson...........S 100
Fairy, Hamilton.............C 60
Falcon, Crosby...........NW ×
● *Faker*, Camp............NE ×
● Fannin, Goliad.............S 100
Fant, Polk..................E 50
Farmer, Young...............N 125
● Farmers Branch, Dallas NE 100
● Farmersville, Collin.... NE 1,093
Farmington, Grayson......NE 100
Farrar, Limestone..........C 10
Farrar, Leon...............E 10
Farrell, Cass..............NE ×
● *Farrells*, Encinal.........S ×
Farrsville, Newton..........E 25
Farwell, Hansford........SW ×
● Farwell Park, Dallam..NE ×
● Fate, Rockwall...........NE 100
● *Faulkner*, Ellis..........EE ×
● *Fauna*, Harris...........SE ×
Fay, El Paso...............W ×
Fayburgh, Collin..........NE 75
● Fayetteville, Fayette.......C 269
Fedor, Lee..................C 25
● *Feely*, Val Verde.......SW ×
Felder, Washington.........C ×
● *Felicia*, Liberty...........E ×
● *Feodora*, Pecos..........W ×
Ferguson, Grayson........NE 10
● *Fern*, Liberty..............E ×
Ferns, Harrison............NE 25
● Ferris, Ellis...............NE 311
● *Ficklin*, Austin...........SE ×
● *Field*, Potter.............SW ×
Field Creek, Llano..........C 200
Field's Store, Waller......SE 25
Files, Hill..................C 15
Fincastle, Henderson.......NE 100
● *Finlay*, El Paso..........W ×
● *Finley*, Bowie..........NE ×
Finis, Jack..................N 75
Fischer's Store, Comal......C 100
● *Fisher*, Dallas...........NE ×
Fisher, Fisher.............NW 125
Fisherburgh, Cooke.........N ×
Fiskville, Travis.............C 25
● *Fitze*, Nacogdoches........E ×
Fitzgerald, Anderson.......E ×
Flanagan, Rusk...........NE ×
● *Flanders*, Val Verde....SW ×
● Flatonia, Fayette.........C 1,304
Fleetwood, Stephens........N ×
Fleming, Comanche..........C 12
● *Flemmings*, Tyler.........E ×
● Flint, Smith.............NE ×
Flo, Leon...................E 65
Florence, Williamson.......C 263
⊙ **Floresville**, Wilson.....S 913
● Floyd, Hunt..............NE 300
Floydada, Floyd.......NW ×
Flygap, Mason...............E 100
Fontana, Harrison.........NE ×
● *Foote's*, Gregg..........NE 325
Ford, Van Zandt...........NE ×
● *Ford*, Harrison..........NE ×

● Forest, Cherokee.........E 18
● *Forest*, Cass............NE ×
Forestburgh, Montague.... N 200
Forest Home, (see Springdale) ×
● Forney, Kaufman..... .NE 811
● Forreston, Ellis..........N 50
Fort Brown, Cameron......S ×
Fort Chadbourne, Coke.....C 15
Fort Clark, Kinney.........S 821
Fort Concho, (see San Angelo) ×
Fort Davis, Jeff Davis...W 1,500
Fort Duncan, Maverick....S ×
Fort Elliott, Wheeler.....SW 300
Fort Ewell, LaSalle.........S 65
● *Fort Gates*, Coryell.......C ×
Fort Graham, Hill...........C 25
Fort Griffin, Shackelford...N 400
● Fort Hancock, El Paso...W 200
Fort Leaton, Presidio......W ×
Fort McIntosh, Webb.......S ×
Fort McKavett, Menard.... C 500
Fort Richardson, Jack.....N ×
Fort Spunky, Hood..........N ×
Fort Stockton, Pecos... W 300
● **Fort Worth**, Tarrant.. N 23,076
Foster, Fort Bend.........SE 40
Fosterville, Anderson.......E 40
● Fowler, Bosque............C 25
Fowler's Mills, Polk........E 10
Fox, Gonzales..............N ×
Franco, Parker.............N ×
Frankford, Collin.........NE 130
● **Franklin**, Robertson...C 665
Frazer, Hopkins..........NE 75
Fred, Tyler.................E 25
Fredricksburgh, Gilles'eC 1,532
Fredonia, Mason.............E 273
Freehand, Johnson...........N 25
Freeman, **Panola**.........NE ×
Freeman's Mill, (see Forestburg.................. ×
Frelsburgh, Colorado......SE 300
Fremont, Parker...........N ×
French, Navarro..........NE ×
● *French's*, Cass..........NE ×
Frenstat, Burleson..........E ×
FresnayCity, (seeSweetWater) ×
Fresno, Collingsworth....SW ×
Freyburg, Fayette...........C ×
Friendship, Harrison..... NE 9
Frio Town, Frio..............S 100
Frio Water Hole, Bandera. C ×
Frosa, Limestone...........C 30
● Frost, Navarro...........NE 75
Fryer, McLennan............C ×
Fulbright, Red River..... NE 150
Fulp, Fannin...............NE ×
● Fulshear, Fort Bend.... SE ×
Fulton, Aransas.............S 200
Gablon, Galveston.........SE 390
Gabriel Mills, Williamson...C 10
⊙ *Gabriel River*, Williamson. C ×
Gadsden, Lamar...........NE ×
Gagne, Shelby..............E 75
Gail, Borden...............NW 14
● **Gainesville**, Cooke..N.. 6,594
● *Gall*, Polk.................E 50
Gallagher's Ranch, Medina..S ×
● *Gallaway*, Cass..........NE 10
Gallinas, Atascosa...........S 10
● **Galveston**, Galveston. SE 29,084
Galvez, Nueces.............S ×
Gamble, Ellis..............NE ×
Gamma, Sterling............W ×
● Ganado, Jackson...........S 50
● Ganahl, Kerr..............C 10
Gano, Williamson...........C ×
Gap, Comanche..............C 7
Garden City, Glasscock...NW 20
● Gardentown, Harris......SE ×
Garden Valley, Smith.....NE 300
Gardner, Milam.............C ×
Garfield, Travis.............C 2?
● Garland, Dallas.........NE 47?
Garner, Parker..............N ×
● *Garret*, Ellis.............NE 130
Garret's, Lamar...........NE 50
● Garrison, Nacogdoches...E 252
Gartenverine, Galveston...SE ×
Garth, Cherokee.............E ×
Garvin, Wise.................N 200
● Garza, Denton.............N 60
● **Gatesville**, Coryell.....C 1,375
● Gause, Milam..............C 100
Gavette, (see Omaha).......... ×
● Gay Hill, Washington.....C 50
⊙ *Geneva*, McLennan........C 50

Geneva, Sabine...............C 100
● *Genoa*, Harris...........SE ×
Gent, Cherokee.............E 100
Gentry's Mill, Hamilton.... C 20
George's Creek, Somervell..N 50
● **Georgetown**, William'nC 2,447
⊙ *Gerald*, Denton..........N ×
Gerald, McLennan..........C ×
⊙ *Germania*, Midland.... NW 26
Germantown, Goliad........S ×
Geronimo, Guadalupe.......S ×
Gertrudes, Jack.............N 25
Gholson, McLennan.........C 26
⊙ Gibbs, Dallas............NE 12
Gibson, Lamar............NE 35
Gibtown, Jack...............N 200
● **Giddings**, Lee...........C 1,203
Gilaloo, Ochiltree.........SW ×
● *Gilbert*, Palo Pinto....... N ×
Gilbert, Wichita............N ×
● Giles, Donley............SW 10
● *Gilmans*, Montgomery....E ×
⊙ **Gilmer**, Upsher.......NE 591
Gipsom Store, (see Hermitage)...................... ×
Givens, Lamar............NE ×
Glade, Polk.................E ×
⊙ Gladewater, Gregg......NE 250
Gladish, Waller..............E 32
Gladstone, Walker...........E ×
Cladys, Montague..........N ×
Glasgow, Wise............NE 50
Glass, Bastrop...............C ×
● *Glazier*, Hemphill.......SW ×
Gleam, Lee.................C ×
Gleckler, Lavaca............S 25
Glen Cove, Coleman.........C 50
Glenfawn, Rusk............NE 100
Glen Rose, Somervell....N 400
Glenwood, Upshur.........NE 15
● Glidden, Colorado.......SE 200
Glory, Lamar..............NE 25
Gober, Fannin.............NE 200
● Godley, Johnson..........N 11
Goforth, Hays...............C ×
Golden, Cass.............NE ×
● Golden, Wood............NE 100
● **Goldthwaite**, Mills.... E 1,000
● **Goliad**, Goliad..........S 2,000
Golindo, McLennan..........C 50
Golson Springs, (see Estacado) ×
● *Gomez*, Reeves...........W ×
● **Gonzales**, Gonzales.....S 1,641
Good Luck, Uvalde.........S 45
Goodman, Bastrop...........C ×
● Goodnight, Armstrong.SW ×
● *Goodnight*, Navarro.....NE ×
● Goodrich, Polk.............E 25
Goodrich Park, Clay........N ×
Goodsonville, Anderson.....E ×
● Goodwin, Comal............C ×
Goolesboro, Titus.........NE 10
Gorbit, Dallas.............NE ×
● Gordon, Palo Pinto.......N 378
Gordonville, Grayson.....NE 182
Goree, Knox..............NW 15
● Gorman, Eastland.........N 50
Goshen, Henderson.......NE 200
Gough, Delta..............NE 30
Gould, Rusk...............NE 20
Graball, Washington.........C 30
Grady, Fisher.............NW 60
Graham, Young...........N 667
● **Granbury**, Hood.......N 1,164
Granda, Mason..............E 10
● *Grand Lake*, MontgomeryE 162
● Grand Prairie, Dallas...NE 50
● Grand Saline, VanZandtNE 50
Grand View, Johnson ......N 257
Grangeno, Hildago..........S 10
● Granger, Williamson.......C 261
● Granite Mountain, Burnet C ×
Grant, Marion.............NE 15
● *Grant*, Bowie............NE ×
● Grapeland, Houston......E 300
Grapetown, Gillispie........C 130
● Grape Vine, Tarrant.......N 442
Grassbur, DeWitt...........S ×
Grasslands, Lynn..........NW ×
● *Gravel Pit*, Bowie....... NE ×
● *Gravel Pit*, Dallas...... NE ×
Gray, Eastland..............N ×
Graybill, Collin............NE 50
Gray Rock, Franklin.......NE 150
● *Grayton*, El Paso........ W 32
● *Green*, Webb..............S ×
Green Hill, Titus..........NE 32

Place, County	Loc.	Pop.
Greenock, Bosque	C	10
● *Green's*, Harris	SE	10
● **Greenville**, Hunt	NE	4,330
Greenvine, Washington	C	100
Greenwood, (see Penn)		×
Greenwood, Wise	N	300
● Gregg, Travis	C	×
● Gregory, San Patricio	SE	20
Gribble Springs, Denton	N	30
Grice, Upshur	NE	×
Griffin, Cherokee	E	50
Grigsby's Bluff, Jefferson	ES	0
Grimes, Tyler	E	×
● *Grindstaff Quarry*, Gra'n	NE	×
● **Groesbeck**, Limestone	C	663
Grove, Lamar	NE	100
Grove Ranch, Williamson	C	×
Groveland, Jack	N	10
● **Groveton**, Trinity	E	1,076
Grundyville, Lampasas	C	×
● *Guadalupe*, El Paso	W	×
● *Guadalupe*, Victoria	S	26
Guadulupe, (see Schiller)		×
● Guide, Ellis	NE	200
Guion, Taylor	NW	19
Gulf Prairie, Brazoria	SE	12
Gum, Wise	N	10
● *Gum Island*, Harris	SE	×
Gunsight, Stephens	N	255
Gurley, Falls	C	×
● *Gurley*, McLennan	C	16
Gussettville, Live Oak	S	30
Gustine, Comanche	C	×
Guthrie, King	NW	×
Guy's Store, Leon	E	25
Gwynn, Schleicher	C	×
● Gypsum, Hardeman	NW	×
Hackberry, Lavaca	S	75
Hackney, Polk	E	×
Hagansport, Franklin	NE	100
● *Hagerman*, Grayson	NE	×
Hagerville, Houston	E	×
Hale City, Hale	NW	100
Halesborough, Red River	NE	60
● *Hale Station*, Dallas	NE	×
Halfway, Shelby	E	×
Half Way, (see Rienzi)		×
● **Hallettsville**, Lavaca	S	1,011
● Hallsville, Harrison	NE	250
Hamilton, Hamilton	C	726
● Hammond, Robertson	C	50
Hamon, Gonzales	S	10
Hancock, Limestone	C	10
● *Hancock's*, Travis	C	×
Handleys, Polk	E	25
● Handley, Tarrant	N	50
Hannibal, Erath	N	20
Hanover, Milam	C	×
Hansford, Hansford	SW	×
Hanover Hill, Hill	C	33
Hanson, Fort Bend	SE	×
Happy, Swisher	SW	×
● Harbin, Erath	N	65
Hardeman, Matagorda	SE	100
Harden's Store, Leon	E	25
Hardin, Hardin	E	50
Hardy, Montague	N	100
Hargrove, Somervell	N	×
Harlem, Fort Bend	SE	10
Harmony Hill, Rusk	NE	50
Harper, Gillespie	C	32
Harper's Mill, (see Alexander)		×
Harris, Edwards	C	×
● Harrisburgh, Harris	SE	250
● *Harris Creek*, McLennan	C	×
Harris Ferry, Red River	NE	25
● Harrison, McLennan	C	20
● Harrold, Wilbarger	N	100
● Hartley, Hartley	SW	300
Hartville, Callahan	N	13
● *Hartz*, Maverick	S	×
Harvester, Waller	SE	×
Harvey, Brazos	C	25
● Harwood, Gonzales	S	200
Haskell, Haskell	NW	745
○ Haslet, Tarrant	N	40
Hastings, Kendall	C	×
Hatti, Cooke	N	×
Hatton, Polk	E	32
Hatton, Van Zandt	NE	10
Haught's Store, Dallas	NE	100
Havana, Hidalgo	S	10
Haw Creek, Fayette	C	25
Hawkeye, Denton	N	×
● Hawkins, Wood	NE	300
Hawkinsville, Matagorda	SE	65
Hayden, Van Zandt	NE	×

Place, County	Loc.	Pop.
Hayes, Robertson	C	20
● Haymond, Buchel	W	20
Hayrick, Coke	C	75
Haysland, Panola	NE	25
Haywards, Harrison	NE	×
● *Hazle*, Clay	N	×
Hazle Dell, Comanche	C	50
Headsville, Robertson	C	75
Headwigs Hill, Travis	C	×
● *Healey*, Cherokee	E	×
Heard, Uvalde	S	×
● Hearne, Robertson	C	1,600
Heath, Rockwall	NE	25
Hebron, Denton	N	×
Hedwig's Hill, Mason	E	100
● Heidenheimer, Bell	C	50
Helena, Karnes	S	300
Helinora, Fort Bend	SE	50
Helleman's, Bexar	S	×
Helotes, Bexar	S	720
Hembrie, Crockett	W	×
Hemphill, Sabine	C	300
● **Hempstead**, Waller	SE	1,671
● **Henderson**, Rusk	NE	1,536
Hendricks, Rusk	NE	10
Henly, Hays	C	20
● **Henrietta**, Clay	N	2,100
Henry, Bastrop	C	×
● *Hensley*, Parker	N	×
● *Heritage*, Hill	C	×
● *Herman*, Wise	N	×
Hermitage, Cass	NE	15
Herrsville, Smith	NE	26
● *Hermosa*, Reeves	W	×
Hester, Navarro	NE	×
Heugh, Johnson	N	80
● Hewitt, McLennan	C	10
Heynville, Harrison	NE	×
Hiawatha, Newton	E	×
Hickory Creek, Hunt	NE	10
Hickory Hill, Cass	NE	12
● *Hicks*, Shackelford	N	70
● Hico, Hamilton	C	649
Hidalgo, Hidalgo	S	389
● Higgins, Lipscomb	SW	100
High, Galvaston	SE	×
High, Lamar	NE	×
High Hill, Fayette	C	100
Highland, Erath	N	×
● *Highland*, Galveston	SE	×
Highland Pond, Montgom'y	E	65
High Prairie, Madison	E	×
Hilda, Guadalupe	S	×
Hillcoat, Kinney	S	×
Hill Creek, Bosque	C	32
Hillendahl, Harris	SE	×
● Hillister, Tyler	E	130
● **Hillsboro**, Hill	C	2,541
● *Hillsboro Junction*, Hill	C	×
Hillside, McLennan	C	×
● Hills Prairie, Bastrop	C	50
Hills Store, (see Maynard)		×
● *Hinckley*, Lamar	NE	×
Hinckley, Hunt	NE	50
Hinde, Crockett	W	×
Hiner, Parker	N	×
Hinkie's Ferry, Brazoria	SE	10
● Hitchcock, Galveston	SE	10
Hitson, Fisher	NW	×
Hobbs, Fisher	NW	×
Hochheim, De Witt	S	200
● Hockley, Harris	SE	296
● *Hodge*, Tarrant	N	398
Holland, Bell	C	363
Holliday, Archer	N	25
Hollis, Madison	E	50
Hollister, (see Hillister)		×
● *Holly*, Smith	NE	×
Holly, Houston	E	50
Holly Springs, Jasper	E	32
Holly Springs, Newton	E	25
Holman, Fayette	C	×
Holmes, Panola	NE	10
Holshausen, Polk	E	3!
Homer, Angelina	E	800
Hondo Canon, Bandera	C	65
● Hondo City, Medina	S	300
● Honey Grove, Fannin	NE	1,828
● *Honey Springs*, Dallas	NE	×
Hood, Cooke	N	×
Hookerville, Burleson	C	66
Hooks, Bowie	NE	50
Hook's Switch, Hardin	E	10
● *Hooper*, Travis	C	×
Hoover Gin, Hunt	NE	×
Hoover's, Burnet	C	32
Hope, Lavaca	S	25

Place, County	Loc.	Pop.
Horace, Upshur	NE	5
Hornhill, Limestone	C	50
Hornsby, Travis	C	30
Horsehead Tank, Foley	S	×
Horse Shoe, Erath	N	×
Hortense, Polk	E	×
● *Hortense*, Tom Green	W	×
Horton Town, (see New Braunfels)		×
Hot Springs, El Paso	W	×
● *House*, Fort Bend	SE	×
Housley, Dallas	NE	50
● **Houston**, Harris	SE	27,557
Howard, Bell	C	65
Howard, Archer	N	×
Howard Valley, Jack	N	90
● Howe, Grayson	NE	284
Howell, Jasper	E	×
● Howth Station, Waller	SE	50
● Hubbard, Hill	C	894
Huber, Shelby	E	32
Huckabay, Erath	N	50
Hudson, Red River	NE	×
Huelster, Jeff Davis	W	×
Huffins, Cass	NE	130
Huffman, Harris	SE	10
Hugh, Johnson	N	12
● Hughes Spring, Cass	NE	296
Hulltown, (see Hicks)		×
● Humble, Harris	SE	50
● Hungerford, Wharton	SE	50
Hunt, Hunt	NE	25
● Hunter, Comal	C	100
Hunter's Retreat, Motgomery	E	50
● **Huntsville**, Walker	E	1,509
Hurnville, Clay	N	×
Hurst, Coryell	C	30
● Hutchins, Dallas	NE	150
● Hutto, Williamson	C	200
● Hyatt, Tyler	E	429
Hydesport, Brown	C	10
Hye, Blanco	C	50
Hylton, Nolan	NW	25
Hynes' Bay, Refugio	S	×
● Iatan, Mitchell	NW	200
Ida, Grayson	NE	10
Idalia, Newton	E	12
● Idlewild, Bexar	S	×
Ilah, Polk	E	10
● *Ilka*, Guadalupe	S	×
Illinois Bend, Montague	N	10
● *Immermere*, Erath	N	×
Independence, Washington	C	373
● *Independence*, Cherokee	E	×
India, Ellis	NE	×
Indian Creek, Brown	C	15
● *Indian Crosssing*, Karnes	S	×
Indian Gap, Hamilton	C	25
Indianola, Calhoun	S	20
Indio, Maverick	S	19
Industry, Austin	SE	300
● Inez, Victoria	S	100
● Ingersol, Bowie	NE	215
Ingleside, Panola	NE	25
Ingram, Kerr	C	10
Inwood, San Patrico	SE	×
Iola, Grimes	E	200
● *Iona*, Parker	N	×
Ioni, Anderson	E	25
● Iowa Park, Wichita	N	424
Ira, Red River	NE	×
● *Ira*, Goliad	S	×
● Iredell, Bosque	C	251
Irene, Hill	C	60
Iron Bridge, (see Elderville)		×
Iron Mountain, Rusk	NE	32
Ironosa, San Augustine	E	15
Ironwood, Liberty	E	75
Isabel, Cameron	S	100
● Isaca, Red River	NE	10
● *Iser*, El Paso	W	×
Islana, Madison	E	×
● Italy, Ellis	NE	370
● Itasa, Hill	C	548
Iuka, Atascosa	S	×
Ivanhoe, Fannin	NE	25
Ivy, Angelina	E	×
Izoro, Coryell	C	9
Jacinto, Rusk	NE	×
Jack Camp, Polk	E	×
Jacksboro, Jack	N	751
Jackson, Van Zandt	NE	×
● Jacksonville, Cherokee	E	970
Jacobia, Hunt	NE	100
Jakin, Shelby	E	×
James, Houston	E	65
Jameson, Grayson	NE	25
Jamestown, Smith	NE	65
Japonica, Kerr	C	×

Place	Section	Pop.
Jardin, Hunt	NE	130
● *Jarvis*, Smith	NE	×
Jasper, Jasper	E	500
Jayton, Kent	NW	×
● *Jeanetta*, Harris	SE	×
Jeannette, Jack	N	32
Jeddo, Bastrop	C	559
● **Jefferson**, Marion	NE	3,072
● *Jeffries*, Ellis	NE	20
Jennings, Lamar	NE	25
Jewell, Eastland	N	100
● Jewett, Leon	E	363
Jimned, Wise	NE	10
Jim Town, Dallas	NE	50
● Joaquin, Shelby	E	100
Johnson City, Blanco	C	100
Johnson's Station, Tarrant	N	100
Johnsonville, (see Griffin)		×
● *Johnstone*, Val Verde	SW	×
● *Joiner*, Fayette	C	×
Jolly, Clay	N	10
Jonah, Williamson	C	25
Jonesboro, Coryell	C	207
Jones City, (see Anson)		×
Jones' Prairie, Milam	C	15
● Jonesville, Harrison	NE	75
Joplin, Jack	N	10
Joppa, Burnet	C	×
Jordan Spring, Foley	S	×
● **Josephine, Collin**	NE	×
● Joshua, Johnson	N	354
● Josserand, Trinity	E	461
Juan Saen's Ranch, Nueces	S	×
● *Judd*, Palo Pinto	N	×
Judson, Gregg	NE	×
● *Julia*, Victoria	S	×
Julian, Houston	E	46
Julietta, Floyd	NW	×
Juliff, Fort Bend	SE	×
Jumbo, Panola	NE	10
● *Junction*, Navarro	NE	×
● *Junction*, Travis	C	×
Junction City, Kimble	C	449
Juno, Val Verde	SW	75
● Justin, Denton	N	20
Ka, Dallas	NE	16
Kanawha, Red River	NE	10
● Karnes City, Karnes	S	×
Karney, Lavaca	S	260
Kasoga, Knox	NW	25
Katemcy, Mason	E	100
● **Kaufman**, Kaufman	NE	1,282
● *Keechie*, Leon	E	10
Keegan's Settlem't, Harris	NE	×
● *Keeran*, Victoria	S	×
Keeter, Wise	N	100
Keith, Grimes	E	50
● Keller, Tarrant	N	175
Kellogg, Hunt	NE	×
Kellum's Bend, (see Waco)		×
● *Kelly's*, Walker	SE	×
● Kellyville, Marion	NE	279
Keltys, Angelina	E	×
Kemp, Kaufman	NE	335
Kemper City, Victoria	S	×
● Kempner, Lampasas	C	300
Kendalia, Kendall	C	100
● Kendleton, Fort Bend	SE	5
● Kenedy, Karnes	S	150
● Kennedale, Tarrant	N	20
● Kenney, Austin	SE	150
Keno, Liberty	E	100
● *Kent*, El Paso	W	×
● KentuckyTown, Grayson	NE	100
● Kerens, Navarro	NE	400
● **Kerrville**, Kerr	C	1,044
Key West, Montague	N	25
Kicaster, Wilson	S	×
Kickapoo, Anderson	E	100
Kickapoo Springs, T'mGr'n	W	12
● Kildare, Cass	NE	366
● Kilgore, Gregg	NE	248
● Killeen, Bell	C	285
Kimball, Bosque	C	200
Kincaid, Clay	N	12
King, Coryell	C	100
King, Nueces	S	×
● Kingsbury, Guadalupe	S	600
● King's Farm, Cass	NE	25
● Kingston, Hunt	NE	338
King's Store, (ses Dougl'sv'le)		×
Kinkler, Lavaca	S	25
● *Kinney*, Kinney	S	×
Kiomatia, Red River	NE	32
● *Kirk*, Bexar	S	×
Kirk, Limestone	C	15

Texas

Place	Section	Pop.
Kirkham, Liberty	E	×
● Kirkland, Childress	SW	20
Kirkwood, (seeD'ble Springs)		×
Kleberg, (see Alice)		×
● Kleburg, Dallas	NE	50
○ *Kleiber*, Harris	SE	×
Klein, Harris	SE	22
Knapp, Scurry	NW	×
Knickerbocker, Tom Green	W	25
Knight, Polk	E	×
Knittel, Burleson	C	×
Knob, Parker	N	×
Knob, San Saba	C	×
Knockville, (see Mason)		×
Knox, Hamilton	C	×
Koerths, Lavaca	S	195
Koockville, Mason	E	90
● *Kokernot*, Gonzales	S	×
Kolbs, Milam	C	×
● Kopperl, Bosque	C	250
Korville, Harris	SE	×
● Kosse, Limestone	C	647
● *Kouns*, Travis	C	×
● **Kountze**, Hardin	E	295
● Krum, Denton	N	30
Kurten, Brazos	C	×
● *Kurth*, Polk	E	×
Kutach Store, Lavaca	E	32
● Kyle, Hays	C	779
LaBahia, Washington	C	40
La Baronina, (see Benavideo)		×
● *Labatt*, Wilson	S	×
LaBelle, Jefferson	SE	×
Lacasa, Stephens	N	×
● *Lacoste*, Bexar	S	×
Lacy, Burnett	C	50
● Ladonia, Fannin	NE	765
LaFayette, Upshur	NE	200
Lafitte, Galveston	SE	×
Lafruita, San Patrico	SE	×
Lagarto, Live Oak	S	150
● **La Grange**, Fayette	C	1,626
La Grulla, Star	S	520
Laguna, Uvalde	S	×
Lahai, Burnet	C	×
Lake, Galveston	SE	×
● Lake Robertson	C	×
Lake Charlotte, Chambers	SE	×
Lake City, Milam	C	32
Lake Creek, Delta	NE	15
Lake Mills, Collin	NE	32
● *Lake Fork*, Wood	NE	×
Lakeview, Hall	SW	×
Lamar, Aransas	S	50
● Lamarque, Galveston	SE	×
Lamasco, Fannin	NE	75
● Lambert, Parker	N	×
Lampkin, Comanche	C	50
● **Lampasas**, Lampasas	C	2,408
La Nana, Nacogdoches	E	×
● *Lanark*, Cass	NE	×
● Lancaster, Dallas	NE	'41
Lancing, Hamilton	C	×
Landrum, Falls	C	40
Lane, Hunt	NE	20
Laneport, Williamson	C	×
Laneville, Rusk	NE	25
● Langtry, ValVerde	SW	×
Langtry's Store, Pecos	W	10
Lanham, Hamilton	C	50
Lanier Cass	NE	50
Lannius, Fannin	NE	×
● *Lansing*, Harrison	NE	×
Lapara, Live Oak	S	×
La Plata, Deaf Smith	SW	8
La Porte, Harris	SE	×
Larch, (see Laurel)		×
● **Laredo**, Webb	S	11,339
Larissa, Cherokee	E	100
● Lasater, Marion	NE	100
Las Rucias, Cameron	S	×
Latium, Washington	C	40
Latona, Childress	SW	10
Laurel, Newton	E	×
Lavernia, Wilson	S	301
Lavon, Collin	NE	25
Lawndale, Kaufman	NE	200
● Lawrence, Kaufman	NE	50
Laws, Franklin	NE	90
Lawsonville, Rusk	NE	38
● *Lazarus*, Cooke	E	×
Leake's, Ellis	NE	12
Leakey, Edwards	C	300
● Leander, Williamson	C	300
Lebanon, Collin	NE	300
● Ledbetter, Fayette	C	300
Lee, Childress	SW	×

Texas

Place	Section	Pop.
● Leesburgh, Camp	NE	200
Lees Mill, Newton	E	10
Leesville, Gonzales	S	1,000
Legarto, Live Oak	S	266
● Leggett, Polk	E	150
Le Gress, Jack	N	×
Lelan, Montague	N	×
● *Lelia*, Donley	SW	×
● *Lem*, Eastland	N	×
● *Lemley*, Parker	N	×
● *Lenoir*, Lamar	NE	×
Lenore, Jones	NW	13
● *Lenox*, Buchel	W	×
● *Leon*, Bexar	S	×
Leona, Leon	E	75
● Leonard, Fannin	NE	392
● Leon Junction, Coryell	C	12
● Leon Springs, Bexar	S	50
● Leslie, Waller	SE	50
Leslie Mills, Montgomery	E	35
● Letot, Dallas	NE	50
Levita, Coryell	C	35
Le Walt, Stephens	N	65
● *Lewis*, Milam	C	×
Lewis Ferry, Jasper	E	65
● Lewisville, Denton	N	498
● Lexington, Lee	C	400
● **Liberty**, Liberty	E	700
● Liberty Hill, Williamson	C	309
Lieu, Collin	NE	×
Light, Howard	NW	×
Lilac, Milam	C	50
Lilla, Lavaca	S	12
● *Lime City*, Coryell	C	×
● Lincoln, Lee	C	10
● Lindale, Smith	NE	500
Linden, Cass	NE	444
● Lindsay, Cooke	N	×
Lingleville, Erath	N	100
Linksville, Jones	NW	×
Linn Flat, Nacogdoches	E	100
● *Linwood*, Cherokee	E	×
Lipan, Hood	N	250
Lipscomb, Lipscomb	SW	200
Lisbon, Dallas	NE	5
● Littig, Travis	C	×
Little Blanco, (seeTwinSisters)		×
Little Elm, Denton	S	60
● Little River, Bell	C	10
Liverpool, Brazoria	SE	65
● **Livingston**, Polk	E	1,000
Livonia, Newton	E	12
Llano, Llano	C	900
Lloyd, Denton	N	20
Lockett, Marion	NE	×
● **Lockhart**, Caldwell	C	1,233
Lockney, Floyd	NW	×
● Lodi, Marion	NE	150
● *Logan's Gap*, Comanche	C	×
● *Lola*, Nacogdoches	E	×
Lodwick, Marion	NE	30
Lohn, McCulloch	C	7
● Lometa, Lampasas	C	250
London, Kimble	C	20
Lone Grove, Llano	C	60
● Lone Oak, Hunt	NE	443
Lone Star, Cherokee	E	100
Long Branch, Panola	NE	25
● Longfellow, Pecos	W	×
● *Long Lake*, Anderson	E	×
Long Leaf, San Augustine	E	40
Long Mott, Calhoun	S	165
Longorio, Jones	NW	12
Long Point, Washington	C	50
● *Long's*, Hardin	E	×
Longstreet, Montgomery	E	50
Longview, Gregg	NE	2,034
● *Longview Junc.*, Gregg	NE	×
Looneyville, Nacogdoches	E	×
Loop, Clay	N	×
Lopena, Zapata	S	77
● Loraine, Mitchell	NW	×
● Lorena, McLennan	C	225
● *Lorine*, Colorado	SE	×
Loring, Cooke	N	×
● *Los Angeles*, Encinal	S	×
Los Encinos, (see Realitos)	S	×
Los Ojuelos, Encinal	S	×
Los Olmos Nueces	S	×
Losoya, Bexar	S	50
Lott, Falls	C	300
● *Lott*, Goliad	S	×
● *Lotus*, Harris	SE	×
● Louise, Wharton	SE	×
● Lovelady, Houston	E	500
● *Lowe*, Upshur	NE	4
● *Lowe*, Upshur	NE	×

Lower Caney, (see Hawkinsville)… ×
Lower Indianola, (see Ind'ola) ×
Lowood Landing, Brazoria SE ×
Lowry, Panola… NE 10
Loyal Valley, Mason… E 119
● *Lozier*, Pecos… W ×
Lubbock, Lubbock… NW 25
Lucas, Collin… NE 5
Lucas Springs, (see San Antonio)… ×
Lucerne, Reeves… W ×
Luckenback, Gillespie… C 345
● *Lucy*, Victoria… S ×
Luella, Grayson… NE ×
● Lufkin, Angelina… E 529
● Luling, Caldwell… C 1,792
Luma Vista, Zavalla… S 75
Lumber, Marion… NE 12
Luna, Freestone… E 75
Lunette, Eastland… N 11
Lusk, McLennan… C ×
Lutes, Henderson… NE ×
Luther, Briscoe… SW ×
● *Luther*, Harrison… NE ×
Lydia, Red River… NE 32
Lyles, Reeves… W 100
Lynchburgh, Harris… SE 25
Lynn, King… NW ×
Lynnwell, Sterling… W ×
Lynnville, (see Caney)… ×
● Lyons, Burleson… C 200
● Lytle, Atascosa… S 120
Lytton Springs, Caldwell… C 70
McAdams, Walker… E ×
McAfee's Store, Tarrant… N 325
McAnelly's Bend, Lampasas C ×
McClanahan, Falls… C 25
McCormick, Archer… N ×
McCoy, Kaufman… NE 200
McCraven, Washington… C 10
McCreaville, Lampasas… C 15
McCulloch, Red River… NE ×
● McDade, Bastrop… C 200
McDonald's Store, (see Bast'p) ×
McDuff, Bastrop… C 25
● *McDuffies*, Trinity… E ×
McGinnis, Bowie… NE 24
McGirk, Hamilton… C ×
● McGregor, McLennan… C 744
McKavitt, Tom Green… W ×
● *McKee's*, Val Verde… SW ×
● **McKinney**, Collin… NE 2,489
McLainsboro, (see Hubb'd City) ×
McLendons, Rockwall… NE 50
McLeod's Mills, (see Personv'e) ×
McNairy, Dallas… NE ×
● McNeil, Travis… C ×
McRae, Montgomery… E ×
Mable, Lipscomb… SW ×
● Macdona, Bexar… S ×
Mack, Wilbarger… N ×
● *Machay*, Wharton… SE ×
● *Mackeys*, Nueces… S ×
Macklesville, Caldwell… C ×
● *Mack's*, Wood… NE ×
Macomb, Grayson… NE 25
Macon, Franklin… NE ×
Macune, San Augustine… E ×
Macy, Brazos… SE 25
● *Madden*, El Paso… W ×
Madisonville, Madison… E 418
Madras, Red River… NE 20
● Maginnis, Bowie… NE 10
Magnolia, Brazoria… SE ×
Magnolia Springs, Jasper… E 100
Mahomet, Burnet… C 25
Mahon, Panola… NE 10
Mainzer, Dallas… NE ×
Maize, Scurry… NW ×
● Malakoff, Henderson… NE 250
Mallory, Cameron… S 22
● *Malone*, El Paso… W ×
Malony, Ellis… NE 15
● *Malta*, Bowie… NE ×
Mammoth, Lipscomb… SW ×
● *Manahuilla*, Goliad… S ×
● Manchaca, Travis… C 70
Manchester, Red River… NE 50
Manchester Mills, Tarrant… N ×
Manestee, Tom Green… W ×
● Manor, Travis… C 405
● Mansfield, Tarrant… N 415
● *Manthe*, Panola… NE ×
Mantua, Collin… NE 12
Maple, Collin… NE 5

Texas

● Marathon, Buchel… W 50
● Marble Falls, Burnet… C 587
● Marcelena, Wilson… S 10
● *Marcelina*, Wilson… S ×
● **Marfa**, Presido… W 600
Margaret, Foard… NW 100
Marianna, Polk… E 200
● *Marienfeld*, Martin… NW ×
Marietta, Cass… NE 50
● Marion, Guadalupe… S 150
● *Mark Belt*, Brazoria… SE ×
Markley, Young… N 30
● **Marlin**, Falls… C 2,058
● Marquez, Leon… E 200
● **Marshall**, Harrison… NE 7,207
Mart, McLennan… C 75
Martin, Panola… NE ×
Martin City, Nacogdoches… E 57
Martindale, Caldwell… C 50
Martin's Mills, VanZandt… NE 25
Martin Springs, Grayson… NE 25
Martinsville, Nacogdoches… E 50
Marystown, Johnson… N 100
Marysville, Cooke… N 200
Mason, Mason… E 600
Masey, Hill… C 25
● *Masterson*, Brazoria… SE ×
Masterville, Mc Lennan… C 75
Matador, Motley… NW 100
Matagorda, Matagorda… SE 399
● Mathis, Patricio… SE ×
● *Matlock*, Dallam… SW ×
Maverick, Runnels… C 50
Maxdale, Bell… C 10
Maxey, Lamar… NE 40
● Maxwell, Caldwell… C 10
● *Maxon*, Pecos… W ×
● *Maxwell*, Collin… NE ×
May, Brown… C 10
Maynard, San Jacinto… E 50
Maysfield, Milam… C 124
Meade Springs, Fannin… NE 10
Medina, Banderia… C 100
● *Medina*, Bexar… S ×
● *Medio*, Bee… S ×
● *Medley*, Montgomery… E 150
● Melissa, Collin… NE 250
Melrose, Nacogdoches… E 200
Memphis, Hall… NW 200
Menardville, Menard… C 185
Mendietie, Duval… S 65
Mendoza, Caldwell… C ×
● *Mendota*, Roberts… SW ×
Mentz, Colorado… SE 20
Mercer's Gap, Comanche… C 50
● **Meridian**, Bosque… C 1,000
● *Meredith*, Johnson… N ×
Merit, Hunt… NE 100
● Merkel, Taylor… NW 853
Merle, Burleson… C 25
Merrilltown, Travis… C 32
Merrivale, Bosque… C 8
● Mertens, Hill… C 75
Merv, Henderson… NE ×
Mesa, Randall… SW ×
● *Mesquital*, San Partrico… SE 97
● *Mesquit*, Duval… S 195
● Mesquite, Dallas… NE 135
Meteor, Floyd… NW ×
Mettina, Falls… C 6
● *Metz*, Ector… W ×
● Mezia, Limestone… C 1,674
Meyersville, DeWitt… S 300
● *Miami*, Angelina… E 25
● Miami, Roberts… SW 300
Middle Bayou, Harris… SE ×
Middleton, Leon… E 25
Middletown, (see Weesatche) ×
Midland, Midland… NW 722
● Midlothian, Ellis… NE 297
Midway, Madison… E 100
Midyett, Panola… NE ×
Miguel, Frio… S 20
Milam, Sabine… C 200
● Milano, Milam… C 400
Milburn, McCulloch… C 50
● Miles Station, Runnells… C 25
● Milford, Ellis… NE 353
Mill Creek, Guadalupe… S ×
● *Mill Creek*, Washington… C ×
● *Miller*, Dallas… NE ×
Miller, Bastrop… C 12
Miller Grove, Hopkins… NE 100
Millerton, Milam… C ×
● Millett, LaSalle… S 20
● *Millheim*, Austin… SE ×

Texas

Millheim, Austin… SE 100
● Millican, Brazos… C 700
Mills, Freestone… E 50
● Millsap, Parker… N 400
Millseat, Hays… C 10
Millwood, Collin… NE 100
Milner, Cass… NE 10
Milton, Lamar… NE 10
Minden, Rusk… NE 200
● Mineola, Wood… NE 1,333
Mineral City, Bee… S 75
● *Mineral Springs*, Panola NE ×
Mineral Wells, Palo Pinto… N 577
● *Minerva*, Milam… C ×
Minerva, Webb… S ×
● *Mingo*, Denton… N ×
Mink, Montgomery… E 10
● *Minor*, Mills… E 10
Minnis, Wilbarger… N ×
Minter, Lamar… NE 75
Mirage, Deaf Smith… SW ×
Mission Valley, Victoria… S 195
Mitchell, Lipscomb… SW ×
Mixon, Cherokee… E ×
Mixon's Creek, (see Hallettsville)… ×
Mobeetie, Wheeler… SW 400
● Mobile, Tyler… E 10
Moffat, Bell… C 100
● Monahans, Ward… W 50
Monaville, Waller… SE ×
● *Monday's*, Cass… NE ×
Monkstown, Fannin… NE 100
Monroe, Rusk… NE 30
Montague, Montague… N 795
Montalba, Anderson… E 25
Mont Belvieu, Chambers… SE ×
Montell, Uvalde… S 10
Monterey, Hockley… NW ×
● Montgomery, Montgomery E 500
Montgomery Mill, Colorado SE 32
Monticello, Titus… NE 30
● *Montoya*, El Paso… W ×
MontvaleSprings, Harrison NE ×
● Moody, McLennan… C 432
● Moore Station, Frio… S 250
Mooresville, Falls… C 100
Morales, Jackson… S 50
● Moran, Shackelford… N ×
Moravia, Lavaca… S 100
Moreland, Navarro… NE ×
● Morgan, Bosque… C 426
Morgan Mill, Erath… N 20
● *Morita*, Howard… NW ×
Mormon Grove, Grayson… NE 12
Morris, (see Omaha)… ×
Morriss' Ferry, Jasper… E 65
Morrisville, Montgomery… E 50
● Moscow, Polk… E 400
Mosel, Gillespie… C ×
Mosely, Red River… NE 15
Mosheim, Bosque… C 18
Moss Bluff, Liberty… E 400
Mossville, Cooke… N 65
Motley, Rusk… NE 65
Mott, Angelina… E 32
● Moulton, Lavaca… S 231
Moulton, Institute, Lavaca… S 140
Mound, Coryell… C 10
Mound, Dickens… NW ×
Mound Prairie, Anderson… E 12
Mountain City, Hays… C 25
Mountain Home, Kerr… C ×
Mountain Peak, Ellis… NE 100
Mountain Spring, Cooke… N 36
Mountain Tank, Buchel… W ×
Mount Blanco, Crosby… NW 53
● Mount Calm, Hill… C 200
Mount Carmel, Smith… NE 40
Mount Enterprise, Rusk… NE 80
Mount Hope, San Jacinto… E 12
Mount Joy, Delta… NE 15
Mount Moro, Taylor… NW 97
● **MountPleasant**, Tit's NE 963
● Mount Selman, Cherokee… E 100
Mount Sylvan, Smith… NE 150
● **Mount Vernon**, Fra'n NE 589
Mud, Travis… C 15
Mudville, Brazos… C 130
Muela, Maverick… S ×
● Muenster, Cooke… N 100
Mulberry, Fannin… NE 50
● Muldoon, Fayette… C 100
● Mullin, Mills… E 200
● *Mulvey*, Polk… E ×
Mumford, Robertson… C 150

Entry	Pop.
● Murchison, Henderson..NE	100
Murphy, Collin...NE	×
Murray, Young...N	200
Musquetz, Jeff Davis...W	×
● *Mustang*, Brazoria... SE	50
Mustang, Denton...N	×
Myers, Burleson...C	×
● *Myra*, Cooke...N	25
Myrtle, Clay...N	10
Myrtle Springs, Van Zandt NE	10
● **Nacogdoches**, Nacogd'sE	1,138
Nadine, (see Rockwall)...	×
Nailer, Fannin...NE	20
Naruna, Burnet...C	32
Nash, Ellis...NE	200
Nassau, Fayette...C	32
Nathan, Johnson...N	9
● *Natili*, Fort Bend...SE	×
● Navasota, Grimes...E	2,997
Navarro Mills, Navarro..NE	25
Navidad, Jackson...S	32
Navo, Denton...N	7
● *Neals*, Upshur...NE	24
Nebo, Cherokee...E	32
Nechanitz, Fayette...C	25
Neches, Anderson...E	100
Need, Lamar...NE	×
Needmore, Delta...NE	50
Neinda, Jones...NW	×
Neill's Prairie, Bastrop...C	×
Nelsonville, Austin...SE	100
Nelta, Hopkins...NE	100
Neola, Hunt...NE	×
Neri, Hood...N	×
Nesbitt, Robertson...C	218
● Nevada, Collins...NE	247
Neville, Gonzales...S	×
● New Baden, Robertson...C	10
New Berlin, Guadalupe...S	40
● NewBirmingham,Che'kee E	668
● New Boston, Bowie...NE	382
● **New Braunfels**,Comal C	1,608
Newburg, Comanche...C	25
● New Caney, Montgomery.E	30
New Columbia, Newton...E	12
New Fountain, Medina...S	150
New Hope, Dallas...NE	25
New Hope, Jack...N	165
● Newlin, Hall...SW	10
Newman, Fisher...NW	48
● *New Philadelphia*,Wh'n SE	130
Newport, Clay...N	75
New Prague, Fayette...C	97
New Salem, Rusk...NE	200
New Sweeden, Travis...C	10
Newton, Newton...E	150
New Ulm, Austin...SE	150
New Warren, Fannin...NE	32
● New Waverly, Walker...E	200
New York, Henderson...NE	15
● Neylandville, Hunt...NE	25
● *Nichols*, Karnes...S	×
Nickel, Gonzales...S	25
Nickelsville, (see Wylie)...	×
Nigh, Colorado...SE	×
Nile, Milam...C	×
Nimrod, Eastland...N	×
Nix, Lampasas...C	20
Noah, Upshur...NE	4
Nobility, Fannin...NE	25
Noble, Lamar...NE	×
Nockenut, Wilson...S	100
● Nocona, Montague...N	381
Nolan, Nolan...NW	×
● Nolanville, Bell...C	100
● Nona, Hardin...E	125
● *Noonan*, Medina...S	×
Noonday, Smith...NE	35
● *Nopal*, Presidio...W	×
Norris, Val Verde...SW	×
Norse, Bosque...C	50
● *Norton*, Grayson...NE	12
Norway Hills, (see Norse)...	×
● *Norwood*, Runnels...C	×
● *Nottawa*, Wharton...SE	×
Novice, Coleman...C	12
Noxville, Kimble...C	20
Nubia, Taylor...NW	×
● *Nueces*, Uvalde...S	50
Nueces, Nueces...S	50
Nunn, Wilbarger...N	×
● Nursery, Victoria...S	50
Oak, Ellis...NE	×
Oakalla, Burnet...C	25
● Oak Cliff, Dallas...NE	2,470
Oak Forest, Gonzalez...S	×
● *Oak Grove*, Bowie...NE	×

Entry	Pop.
Oak Grove, Tarrant...N	50
Oak Hill, Travis...C	50
Oakland, Colorado...SE	250
Oak Point, Milam...C	32
Oak Valley, (see Aquilla)...	×
Oakville, Live Oak...S	329
Oakwood, Leon...E	231
Oakwood, Limestone...C	30
Oasis, Dallas...NE	×
Ochiltree, Ochiltree...SW	25
● *Ochoa*, Encinal...S	×
Ocker, Bell...C	10
O'Daniel, Guadalupe...S	×
● Odessa, Ector...W	200
Oenaville, Bell...C	150
O'Farrell, Cass...NE	25
● *Ogles*, Lampasas...C	×
● Oglesby, Coryell...C	20
Ohio, Hamilton...C	30
Okalla, Burnet...C	×
Oklahoma, Cooke...N	97
● Oklaunion, Wilbarger...N	×
Olden, Eastland...N	125
Oldenburg, Fayette...C	100
Old Monterey, Marion...NE	40
● *Old Round Rock*, Will'sonC	300
Oletha, Limestone...C	100
● Olive, Hardin...E	383
Oliver, Denton...N	195
● *Olmos*, Maverick...S	×
Olmos, Guadalupe...S	10
Olney, Young...N	×
● Omaha, Morris...NE	219
Omega, Upshur...NE	10
Omen, Smith...NE	505
Oneta, Leon...E	×
Opah, Red River...NE	25
Ophelia, Caldwell...C	×
O'Quinn, Fayette...C	10
Ora, Angelina...E	65
Oran, Palo Pinto...N	×
Orange, Orange...E	3,170
Orangeville, Fannin...NE	130
Orlena, Cooke...N	25
Oro, (see Rancho)...	×
● Orphans Home, Dallas..NE	20
● *Orphans Home*, NavarroNE	20
● *Orr's*, Marion...NE	×
● *Orris Switch*, Marion...NE	×
Orrville, Marion...NE	40
Osage, Coryell...C	25
Osborne, Wilbarger...N	×
Osceola, Hill...C	100
● *Osman*, Pecos...W	×
Otis, Red River...NE	32
Otta, (see Margaret)...	×
Ottillie, Armstrong...SW	×
● *Otto*, Gonzales...S	×
Otto, Hardin...E	×
● Overton, Rusk...NE	401
Ovid, Jack...N	×
Ovilla, Ellis...NE	150
Owlet Green, Van Zandt..NE	50
Oxford, Llano...C	40
● Oyster Creek, Brazoria..SE	10
Ozona, Crockett...W	×
Pace's Ferry, Jasper...E	×
Pack Saddle, Llano...C	50
Padre Island, Nueces...S	65
Paclo, Delta...NE	×
Paducah, Cottle...NW	×
● Paige, Bastrop...C	400
● *Painted Cave*, Val VerdeSW	×
Paint Rock, Concho...C	323
Paisano, Starr...S	35
● *Paisano*, Brewster...W	×
Palace, Van Zandt...NE	40
● **Palestine**, Anderson...E	5 838
● Palmer, Ellis...NE	250
Paladuro, Armstrong...SW	65
● *Paloma*, Maverick...S	×
Palomas, San Patricio...SE	×
Palo Pinto, Palo Pinto...N	500
Paluxy, Hood...N	100
Pancake, (see Jonesboro)...	×
● **Panhandle**, Carson...SW	300
Pankey, Grimes...E	50
Panna Maria, Karnes...S	100
Panter, Hood...N	×
● Papalote, Bee...S	25
Paradise, Wise...N	300
● **Paris**, Lamar...NE	8,254
● Park, Bowie...NE	10
Parkdale, Bell...C	×
Parker, Collin...NE	6
Parnella, Coryell...C	10
Parnell, Roberts...SW	×

Entry	Pop.
Parrsville, Galveston...SE	32
● Parsons, Parker...N	×
Parvin, Denton...N	30
● *Paso*, Houston...E	×
Patrick, McLennan...C	50
Patroon, Shelby...E	100
● Patterson, Waller...SE	200
● *Patterson's*, Travis...C	×
Patton, McLennan...C	120
Patton Point, Brazoria...SE	×
Pattonville, Lamar...NE	100
● *Paulie*, Montgomery...E	×
Pauline, (see Frankford)...	×
Pauline, Ochiltree...SW	×
Paul's Store, Shelby...E	20
Payne, Brown...C	32
Payne, Mills...E	×
Payne'sSprings, HendersonNE	×
Payne's Store, Hunt...NE	50
Peach Creek, (see Wharton)..	×
Peach Tree, Jasper...E	40
Pearl, Coryell...C	20
Pearl, Orange...E	10
● **Pearsall**, Frio...S	766
Pease, Foard...NW	×
Peaster, Parker...N	×
● Pecan Gap, Delta...NE	100
Pecan Grove, Coryell...C	10
Peck's Spring, Midland..NW	×
● **Pecos**, Reeves...W	893
Peede, Kaufman...NE	50
Peerless, Hopkins...NE	75
Pella, Wise...N	100
Pena Colorado, Presidio...W	12
● Pena Station, Duval...S	100
Pendleton, Sabine...C	15
● Pendletonville, Bell...C	50
Penitas, Hidalgo...S	×
Penn, Hopkins...NE	25
Pennington, Trinity...E	150
Peoria, Hill...C	349
Percheron, Lynn...NW	×
Percilla, Houston...E	×
● Perry, Falls...C	50
Perryman, Liberty...E	×
Perry's Landing, Brazoria.SE	30
Personville, Limestone...C	100
Peru, La Salle...S	12
● *Pescadita*, Encinal...S	×
Pesch, Washington...C	32
● Peters, Austin...SE	×
Petersburg, Floyd...NW	×
Petteway, Robertson...C	×
● Pettus City, Bee...S	50
● Petty, Lamar...NE	200
Phair, Brazoria...SE	17
Phantom Hill, Jones...NW	50
● Phelps, Walker...E	30
● Phillipsburg, Washington. C	106
Phoenix, Polk...E	32
● Pickton, Hopkins...NE	82
Pidcock Ranch, Coryell...C	10
● *Pierce Junction*, Harris.SE	×
● Pierce Station, Wharton.SE	10
● *Pierson*, Gonzales...S	×
Pike, Collin...NE	50
Pilgrim's Lake, Gonzales...S	100
Pilot Grove, Grayson...NE	100
● Pilot Point, Denton...N	1,090
Pinckney, Polk...E	×
Pine Forest, Hopkins...NE	×
Pine Grove, Henderson...NE	5
Pine Grove, Grimes...E	390
Pine Hill, Rusk...NE	150
● *Pine Island*, Jefferson..SE	×
Pine Mills, Wood...NE	50
Pine Town, Cherokee...E	15
● *Piney Point*, Harris...SE	×
Pink Hill, Grayson...NE	10
Pin Oak, Fayette...C	130
Pioneer, Eastland...N	19
Pipe Creek, Bandera...C	25
Pirtle, Rusk...NE	60
Pisgah, Navarro...NE	×
Pitt Bridge, Burleson...C	25
● **Pittsburgh**, Camp...NE	1 203
Pittsville, Fort Bend...SE	100
● *Placedo*, Victoria...S	×
Plainview, Hale...NW	500
● Plank, Hardin...E	150
● Plano, Collin...NE	842
● Plantersville, Grimes...E	200
● *Plateau*, El Paso...W	×
Pleasant Grove, Houston...E	×
Pleasant Grove, Wood...NE	×
Pleasant Hill, Washington..C	390

Place	Dir.	Pop.
Pleasanton, Atascosa	S	367
Pleasant Point, Johnson	N	75
Pleasant Valley, Dallas	NE	50
Pledger, Matagorda	SE	25
Plehweville, Mason	E	100
Plemons, Randall	SW	×
● Plum, Fayette	C	25
Plunkett, Madison	E	×
Poe, Blanco	C	×
● *Poesta*, Bee	S	×
Poetry, Kaufman	NE	150
● Point, Rains	NE	50
Point Isabel, Cameron	S	479
Pointblank, San Jacinto	E	100
Polito Blanco, Nueces	S	×
● *Polk*, Bowie	NE	×
Pollitt, Tyler	E	×
● Pollok, Angelina	E	50
Polly, Bandera	C	100
Pomona, Burnet	C	×
Pontotoc, Mason	E	274
Poolville, Parker	N	200
● *Pooleville*, Galveston	SE	×
Poor, Leon	E	10
Popalote, Bee	S	400
● *Pope*, Cherokee	E	×
Popher, Angelina	E	×
Portersville, Montgomery	E	250
Porter's Springs, Houston	E	50
● *Portland*, Aransas	S	×
Portland, San Patricio	SE	×
● **Port Lavaca**, Calhoun	S	365
Port Sullivan, Milam	C	40
Post Oak Grove, Lavaca	S	32
Post Oak, Jack	N	300
● *Posts*, Panola	NE	×
Poteet, Atascosa	S	×
Potterville, (see Oletha)		×
● Pottsborough, Grayson	NE	286
Pottsville, Hamilton	C	250
Powder Horn, (see Indianola)		×
Powderly, Lamar	NE	×
● Powell, Navarro	NE	×
Powell Dale, Bosque	C	65
Powellton, (see Waskom)		×
Power, Parker	N	×
Praha, Fayette	C	75
Prairie Grove, Limestone	C	25
Prairie Hill, Limestone	C	15
Prairie Lea, Caldwell	C	150
Prairie Plains, Grimes	E	200
Prairie Valley, Dallas	NE	32
Prairie View, Waller	SE	×
Prairieville, Delta	NE	20
Presidio, Presidio	W	200
● *Presswood*, Montgomery	E	30
Preston, Grayson	NE	25
Prewitt, Van Zandt	NE	9
● *Price's*, Cherokee	E	×
● *Prichitt*, Upshur	NE	×
Priddy, Mills	E	×
● *Primrose*, Tarrant	N	×
● Princeton, Collin	NE	200
Prindle, Wise	NE	30
Prismoid, Montgomery	C	32
● Proctor, Comanche	C	15
Providence, Van Zandt	NE	×
Pruitt, Van Zandt	NE	×
Pueblo, Baylor	N	×
● *Pullman*, Potter	SW	×
● Purdon, Navarro	NE	50
Purgatory Springs, Hays	C	×
Purley, Franklin	NE	100
Purmela, Coryell	C	26
Pursley, Navarro	NE	40
● Putnam, Callahan	N	300
● *Pyote*, Ward	W	×
Qualls, Clay	N	45
● **Quanah**, Hardeman	NW	1,477
● Quarry, Washington	C	64
● *Quebec*, Presidio	W	×
● Queen City, Cass	NE	672
Queen Peak, Montague	N	97
Quihi, Medina	S	260
Quincy, Bee	S	×
Quinan, Wharton	SE	50
Quinn, Fayette	C	×
Quintana, Brazoria	SE	475
Quitaque, Briscoe	SW	40
Quitman, Wood	NE	300
● *Quito*, Ward	W	×
Rabb's Creek, Fayette	C	19
Race Track, Delta	NE	×
Ragsdale, Fannin	NE	60
Rainbow, Newton	E	40
Rainsville, Shelby	E	×
Raleigh, Navarro	NE	65

Texas

Place	Dir.	Pop.
Ralls, Randall	SW	×
Ramirena, Live Oak	S	5
● *Ramsey*, Colorado	SE	×
Rancho Grande, Matagorda	SE	65
Rancho, Gonzales	S	400
Rancho Santa Gertrude, Nueces	S	×
Rancho Los Portraneous, Starr	S	×
Randado, Zapata	S	390
Randal's Store, Palo Pinto	N	×
Randol, Tarrant	N	×
● Randolph, Fannin	NE	25
● *Randon*, Fort Bend	SE	×
Raney, Fannin	NE	31
Raney, Hunt	NE	×
● Ranger, Eastland	N	400
Ransom, San Augustine	E	50
Ratan, (see Duval)		×
Ratcliff, Houston	E	10
Ravenna, Fannin	NE	237
Rawlins, Dallas	NE	×
Ray, Ellis	NE	10
● *Ray*, Grayson	NE	×
Rayland, Foard	NW	×
Raymond, Leon	E	10
Rayner, Stonewall	NW	284
Rayville, Parker	N	25
Re, Navarro	NE	10
Read's Spring, Buchel	W	×
● Reagan, Falls	C	298
● Realitos, Duval	S	200
Rector, Denton	N	×
Red Bluff, Harris	SE	25
Red Branch, Grayson	NE	×
● *Red Branch*, Trinity	E	×
● *Redfield*, Nacogdoches	E	×
Red Gap, (see Cisco)		×
Red Hill, Cass	NE	50
Red Horse, Polk	E	×
Red Oak, Ellis	NE	200
● *Red Oak Sta.*, Ellis	NE	×
Red River Sta., Montague	N	97
● Red Rock, Bastrop	C	100
● *Red Rock*, Upshur	NE	×
Red Top, (see Prairie Plain)		×
Reed, Cooke	N	×
● *Reeds*, Rusk	NE	×
● Reedville, Caldwell	C	×
Reev, Frio	S	×
Reeve's Store, Victoria	S	80
Refugio, Refugio	S	200
Regency, Mills	E	50
Reilly Springs, Hopkins	NE	50
● Reinhardt, Dallas	NE	37
Rendon, Tarrant	N	×
● Renner, Collin	NE	50
● *Reno*, Lamar	NE	×
Reno, Parker	N	50
Retreat, Grimes	E	100
● *Reynolds*, Cherokee	E	12
Rhea Mills, Collin	NE	25
Rhodes, Brazoria	SE	×
● Rhome, Wise	N	350
● Rice, Navarro	NE	75
Rice's Crossing, Williamson	C	25
Richard, San Saba	C	×
● Richardson, Dallas	NE	50
● Richland, Navarro	NE	50
Richland Springs, San Saba	C	200
● **Richmond**, Fort Bend	SE	993
● *Ricker*, Brown	C	×
Riddleville, Karnes	S	100
● Ridgeway, Hopkins	NE	75
Rienzi, Hill	C	20
Riesel, McLennan	C	20
Rincon, Nueces	S	×
Ringgold Barricks (see Rio Grande City)		×
Rio Frio, Bandera	C	30
Rio Grande City, Starr	S	1,968
● *Rio Grande*, El Paso	W	×
● Riovista, Johnson	N	9
Ripley, Titus	NE	50
Rising Star, Eastland	N	300
Rising Sun, Shackelford	N	32
● *Ritchie*, McLennan	C	×
● *Rivera*, El Paso	W	×
Riverland, Clay	N	26
● *Rivers*, Hartley	SW	×
● Riverside, Walker	E	100
Riverton, Reeves	W	×
Rives, Fisher	NW	×
Roach Prairie (see Bellville)		×
Roane, Navarro	NE	×
● Roanoke, Denton	N	292
Roan's Prairie, Grimes	E	500

Texas

Place	Dir.	Pop.
● *Robard's*, Bexar	S	×
Robert Lee, Coke	C	200
● Roberts, Hunt	NE	200
Robinson, McLennan	C	100
Robinsville, Red River	NE	32
Roby, Fisher	NW	575
Rochelle, McCulloch	C	40
Rock Creek, Parker	N	×
● Rockdale, Milam	C	1,505
Rocker Springs, Kimble	C	40
Rock Hill, Collin	NE	32
Rock House, Fayette	C	75
Rockhouse, Austin	SE	75
Rockeyville, San Jacinto	E	24
Rockford, Lamar	NE	×
Rockland, Tyler	E	405
● *Rockport*, Aransas	S	1,069
Rock Springs, Edwards	C	×
● **Rockwall**, Rockwall	NE	643
Rockwood, Coleman	C	×
Rocky Branch, Morris	NE	25
Roddy, Van Zandt	NE	12
● Rodgers, Bell	C	100
Rodney, Navarro	NE	×
Rogers, Nueces	S	×
Rogers Prairie, Leon	E	100
Roland, Collin	NE	8
Roma, Starr	S	1,000
● *Rome*, Milam	C	×
Romney, Eastland	N	×
Ronda, Wilbarger	N	×
Ropesville, Nueces	S	10
Rosalie, Red River	NE	100
● Roscoe, Nolan	NW	20
Rosebud, Falls	C	20
● *Rosebud Station*, Falls	C	×
Rosedale, Jefferson	SE	×
Rose Hill, Harris	SE	250
Roseland, Collin	NE	25
● Rosenberg, Fort Bend	SE	260
● *Rosenfeld*, Pecos	W	×
Rosenthal, McLennan	C	75
Roseville (see Noonday)		×
● Ross, McLennan	C	50
Rosser, Kaufman	NE	×
Rosston, Cooke	N	175
Rossville, Atascosa	S	750
Rough Creek (see Eagle Cove)		×
Roughrock, Blanco	C	33
Round Mott, Wharton	SE	×
Round Mountain, Blanco	C	100
Round Prairie, San Jacinto	E	97
● Round Rock, Williamson	C	1,500
Round Timber, Baylor	N	60
Round Top, Fayette	C	238
● Rowe, Donley	SW	×
● *Rowena*, Runnels	C	×
Roweville, Brazoria	SE	×
● Rowlett, Dallas	NE	25
● Roxton, Lamar	NE	226
Royal, Lipscomb	SW	5
● Royse City, Rockwall	NE	299
● Runge, Karnes	S	350
Runnels, Runnels	C	400
Running Water, Hale	NW	×
Rupee, Falls	C	25
Rural Shade, Navarro	NE	15
● **Rusk**, Cherokee	E	1,383
Russell, Leon	E	32
Rutersville, Fayette	C	250
Ruth, Coryell	C	80
● *Ruthford*, Wichita	N	×
Ryan, McLennan	C	5
● *Ryan*, Presidio	W	×
Ryan, Navarro	NE	32
● Rylie, Dallas	NE	25
● Sabinal, Uvalde	S	100
● *Sabine*, Smith	NE	×
● Sabine Pass, Jefferson	SE	800
● **Sachse, Dallas**	NE	12
● *Sadler*, Grayson	NE	×
Sage, Burnet	NE	32
● Saginaw, Tarrant	N	20
Saint Elmo, Travis	C	50
Saint Hedwig, Bexar	S	400
● Saint Jo, Montague	N	710
Saint Mary's, Refugio	S	50
Saint Paul, Collin	NE	50
Saint Thomas, Lavaca	S	24
Saint Ysabel, Webb	S	×
Salado, Bell	C	400
Salem, Montague	N	19
Salem, Newton	E	22
Salesville, Palo Pinto	N	210
● Salisbury, Hall	SW	25
Salona, Montague	N	×

Texas	
●Saltillo, Hopkins NE	10
Sam, Parker N	×
Samuel, Washington C	×
●*Samuels*, Pecos W	×
●**San Angelo**, Tom Gr'n W	2,615
●**San Antonio**, Bexar S	37,673
San Antonio Viega (see Roma)	×
San Augustine, San Ag'e. E	744
San Bartolo (see Carrizo)	×
●*Sanborn*, Potter SW	×
●*Sanchez*, Webb S	×
Sanco, Coke C	7
Sanders, Trinity E	×
●Sanderson, Pecos W	100
Sandersville, Jones NW	9
Sand Hill, Comanche C	×
●*Sand Hills*, Winkler N	×
●**San Diego**, Duval S	1,877
●*Sand Pit*, Guadalupe S	×
Sand Rock, Foard NW	20
Sandusky, Grayson NE	25
Sandy, Blanco C	325
Sandy Creek, Sabine C	25
●*Sandy Fork*, Gonzales S	×
Sandy Mountain, Llano C	50
●Sandy Point, Brazoria SE	200
●*San Elizario*, El Paso W	×
San Elizario, El Paso W	1,397
●San Felipe, Austin SE	117
San Gabriel, Milam C	50
●Sanger, Denton N	40
●*San Jacinto*, Harris SE	×
●**San Marcos**, Hays C	2,335
●*San Martine*, Reeves W	×
San Miguel, Frio S	10
San Patricio, San Patricio SE	315
San Pedro, Houston E	20
San Pedro, Webb S	×
San Saba, San Saba C	697
San Seville, Webb E	×
Sanson, Uvalde S	×
●Santa Anna, Coleman C	468
Santa Cruz, Duval S	×
Santa Lucia, Pecos W	×
Santa Maria, Cameron S	100
Santarita, Hidalgo S	×
●Santo, Palo Pinto N	150
Santo Tomas, Webb E	×
San Ygnacio, Zapata S	1,000
Sapp's Store, Shelby E	×
Saralvo, Ellis NE	×
Saratoga, Hardin E	25
Sardis, Cass NE	5
●*Sardis*, Ellis NE	×
●*Saron*, Trinity E	×
●Sartartia, Fort Bend SE	75
Sattler, Comal C	32
●*Saunders*, Travis C	×
●*Saunders*, Trinity E	×
Saunders Store, (see Cummingsville)	×
Savage, Fannin NE	×
Savannah, (see Jefferson)	×
Savilla, Foard NW	×
●Savoy, Fannin NE	344
●*Saxie*, Dallas NE	25
Sayers, Bexar S	25
●Sayersville, Bastrop C	15
●*Schenck*, Grayson NE	×
Schiller, Kendall C	50
Schoofley, Brazos C	×
School, Guadalupe S	×
●Schulenburg, Fayette C	816
Schultzville, Montague N	32
Science Hall, Hays C	×
Scotland, Harrison NE	×
Scott, Lamar NE	19
Scott's Store, Burleson C	19
●Scottsville, Harrison NE	20
Scranton, Eastland N	×
Scroggins, Franklin NE	×
●*Scroggin's*, Wood NE	195
●*Scullyville*, Tarrant N	×
●Scurry, Kaufman NE	100
Scyene, Dallas NE	30
Seadrift, Calhoun S	×
●Seagoville, Dallas NE	25
Seale, Robertson C	25
●Sealy, Austin SE	837
Searcy, Madison E	×
Seaton, Bell C	×
Seaview, Galveston SE	×
Seclusion, Lavaca S	25
●*Seco*, Medina S	×
Sedalia, Collin NE	25
Sedan, Gonzales S	10
Seglar, Bexar S	×

Texas	
●**Seguin**, Guadalupe S	1,716
●*Selby*, McLennan C	×
Selden, Erath N	30
Selfs, Fannin NE	10
Seltzer, Collin NE	×
Selma, Bexar S	35
Seltzer, Tarrant N	×
Sempronius, Austin SE	×
●*Seneca*, Tyler E	31
Senior, Bexar S	30
Senterfeilt, Travis C	×
●Serbin, Lee C	75
Seven Oaks, Wheeler SW	×
Seven Oaks, Polk E	250
Sexton, Sabine C	50
Seymour, Baylor N	1,125
Shady Grove, Upshur NE	10
Shaeffer, Duval SW	50
Shafter, Presidio W	800
●*Shannon*, Montgomery E	×
●*Sharon*, Hardin E	×
Sharpsburgh, S'n P't'cio SE	371
Shavano, Bexar S	26
Shaw, Bowie NE	×
Shawneetown Ferry, Red River NE	12
Shea, Encinal S	×
Shelby, Austin SE	150
Shelbyville, Shelby E	200
Shell Bank, (see Orange)	×
●Sheldon, Harris SE	×
●*Shell Siding*, Galveston SE	×
●Shepherd, San Jacinto E	200
Sheridan, Houston E	×
Sherley, Hopkins NE	×
●**Sherman**, Grayson NE	7,335
Sherwood, Irion W	264
Shiloh, Denton N	25
●Shiner, Lavaca S	340
●*Shingle Mill*, Cherokee E	×
Shinoak, (see Gorman)	×
Shive, Hamilton C	25
Shoal Point, Galveston SE	8
Short, Shelby E	50
Shovel Mount, Burnet C	×
●*Shumla*, Val Verde SW	×
Sidney, Comanche C	20
●Sierra Blanca, El Paso W	100
●*Signal Mount*, Howard NW	×
Silver, Coke NW	×
●Silver Lake, Van Zandt NE	7
Silver Valley, Coleman C	×
Silverton, Briscoe SW	25
Silvom, Comanche C	690
Simms, Bowie NE	×
●Simonds, Dallas NE	60
Simpsonville, Coryell C	130
Simpsonville, Upshur NE	100
Singleville, Erath N	32
●Sinton, San Patricio SE	×
Sion, Walker E	10
Sipe Springs, Comanche C	300
●*Siren*, Goliad S	×
Sisterdale, Kendall C	25
Sivell's Bend, Cooke N	25
●Skidmore, Bee S	50
●*Skidway*, Tyler E	×
Skiles, Karnes S	50
Skipper's Gap, Erath N	×
Slate Shoals, Lamar NE	×
Slay, Ellis NE	×
●Slayden, Gonzales S	×
Slidell, Wise N	50
●*Sloans*, Trinity E	×
Slover, Parker N	×
Smiley, Gonzales S	25
Smithfield, Tarrant N	100
●*Smith Junc*, Colorado SE	×
Smithland, Marion NE	50
Smith Point, Chambers SE	50
●*Smith's*, San Jacinto E	×
Smith Ferry, Tyler E	10
●*Smiths Mill*, Upshur NE	10
Smith Point, Chambers SE	50
Smithson's Valley, Comal C	25
●Smithville, Bastrop C	616
Smithwick, Burnet C	25
●*Smyrl*, Cherokee E	×
Snell's, Newton E	65
Snow, Leon E	10
Snow Hill, San Jacinto E	12
Snyder, Scurry NW	200
Socorro, El Paso W	300
●*Somerville*, Burleson C	10
Sonora, Sutton C	×
Sorgo, Bandera C	×
●*Sour Lake*, Jefferson SE	130

Texas	
Sour Lake, Hardin E	100
●*Southard*, Armstrong SW	×
South Bend, Young N	25
●South Bosque, McLennan C	20
South Gray Ceeek, Kendall C	50
●*South Harrold*, Wilbarger N	×
●Southmayd, Grayson NE	35
South Prairie, Stephens N	40
South Sulphur, Hunt NE	75
Sowers, Dallas NE	50
Spanish Camp, Wharton SE	2,000
Spanish Fort, Montague N	300
Sparta, Bell C	10
Sparta, (see Santo)	×
Speakville, (see Boxville)	×
Speegleville, McLennan C	40
Speer, Wood NE	×
●*Speer*, Leon E	×
Spivey, Shelby E	×
●Spofford, Kinney S	200
●Spring, Harris SE	100
Spring Branch, Comal C	25
Spring Creek, Throckm'ton N	25
●*Spring Creek*, Tyler E	10
●Springdale, Cass NE	100
Spring Hill, Navarro NE	50
Springer's Ranch, H'phill SW	×
Spring Lake, Lamb NW	×
Springtown, Parker N	657
Sprinkle, Travis C	10
Spurger, Tyler E	50
●Stafford, Fort Bend SE	25
Stafford's Ranch, Colorado SE	40
Stall's, Marion NE	×
●Standart, Kinney S	10
Stanley, Taylor NW	×
●*Stanley's*, Burnet C	×
●**Stanton**, Martin NW	300
Staples, Guadalupe S	100
Star, Hamilton C	30
●*Stark*, Houston E	30
Starkey, Floyd NW	×
Starrville, Smith NE	150
●*State Line*, El Paso W	×
●Station Belden, Morris NE	309
●Steedman, Grayson NE	32
Steelboro, Anderson E	×
Steele's Store, Brazos C	100
●*Stella*, Harris SE	×
Stellar, Fayette C	×
●*Stephens*, Cherokee E	×
Stephensville, (see Dodd)	×
●**Stephenville**, Erath N	909
Sterling, Sterling W	15
Sterling City, Sterling W	×
●*Sterne*, Nacogdoches E	30
●Sterrett, Ellis NE	8
Steubner, Harris SE	×
Stevens, Rusk NE	65
●*Stevenson*, Van Zandt NE	×
Stewart's Creek, Denton N	32
Steward's Mill, Freestone E	50
Stockdale, Wilson S	300
●Stoneham, Grimes E	25
Stone Point, Van Zandt NE	15
Stone Prairie, Bastrop C	×
Stone's Mill, Panola NE	×
Stonewall, Gillespie C	268
Stony, Denton N	25
Stormville, Wood NE	32
Stout, Wood NE	5
Stovall, Johnson N	32
Stoverville, Denton N	×
Stranger, Falls C	10
Stratton, DeWitt S	10
●Strawn, Palo Pinto N	514
Straw's Mill, Coryell C	10
Streeter, Mason E	100
Strickling, Burnett C	10
Stringfellow, Galveston SE	×
String Prairie, Bastrop C	×
●*Strobel*, Brewster W	×
●*Strumberg*, Bexar S	×
●Stryker, Polk E	100
Stubblefield, Johnson N	×
Stubbs, Kaufman NE	50
Stuebner, Harris SE	15
Stump, Henderson NE	×
●Sublime, Lavaca S	25
Sugar Hill, Panola NE	10
Sugar Land, Fort Bend SE	1,000
Sugar Loaf, Coryell C	30
●*Sullivan*, Guadalupe S	×
Sulphur Bluff, Hopkins NE	200
●**Sulphur Springs**, Hopkins NE	3,038
●Sulphur Station, Bowie NE	246

Place	Region	Pop.
Summer's Mills, Bell	C	50
● *Summit*, Upshur	NE	57
● Summit, Tyler	E	×
● *Summit*, Milam	C	32
● *Summit*, Milam	C	×
Sumner, Lamar	NE	×
Sumner, Lamar	NE	25
Sunbeam, Grayson	NE	×
Sunny Lane, Burnet	C	10
Sunny Point, Harrison	NE	×
Sunny Side, Waller	SE	10
● Sunset, Montague	N	376
Surveyville, Newton	E	×
Sutherland Springs, Wilson	S	150
● Sutton, Robertson	C	60
Sutton, Gray	SW	×
● Swan, Smith	NE	9
Swannville, San Augustine	E	10
● *Sweden*, Duval	S	10
● Swedonia, Fisher	NW	×
● Sweet Home, Lavaca	S	150
● **Sweet Water**, Nolan	NW	614
Swift, Nacogdoches	E	25
Swiss Alp, Fayette	C	10
Sylvan, Lamar	NE	100
● *Tabor*, Pecos	W	×
Tabor, Brazos	C	×
Tacitus, Haskell	NW	×
Tadmor, Houston	E	10
Tait, Wharton	SE	×
Talley, Grayson	NE	×
● *Tally*, Harrison	NE	×
Talmage, Wilbarger	N	×
● Talpa, Coleman	C	30
Tanglewood, Lee	C	15
Tanks, Cottle	NW	×
Taopi, Fisher	NW	6
Tarkington Prairie, Liberty	E	200
● **Tascosa**, Oldham	SW	100
Tate, Travis	C	×
● Tatum, Rusk	NE	30
● Taylor, Williamson	C	2,584
Taylor's Bayou, Jefferson	SE	60
● Taylor's Gin, Burnet	C	10
Taylor's Ranche, (see Wharton)		×
Taylorsville, Caldwell	C	50
● *Teague*, Upshur	NE	×
● Tebo, Sabine	C	×
Tecumseh, Callahan	N	200
Teepee City, Motley	NW	50
Tehuacana, Limestone	C	200
Telephone, Fannin	NE	25
● Temple, Bell	C	4,047
● Tenaha, Shelby	E	800
Tennessee Colony, Anderson	E	150
● Terrell, Kaufman	NE	2,988
● Terry, Orange	E	10
Terryville, DeWitt	S	200
● *Tewena*, Harris	SE	×
Texana, Jackson	S	260
● Texarcana, Bowie	NE	2,852
● Texline, Dallam	SW	150
Thalia, Foard	NW	×
Tharp, Montgomery	E	214
● *Tharp's Mill*, Montgomery	E	×
The Grove, Coryell	C	100
Theodore, Grayson	NE	×
Theon, Williamson	C	×
Thomas, Panola	NE	25
● Thomaston, DeWitt	S	494
Thompson, Austin	SE	195
● *Thompson*, Collin	NE	×
● Thompson's, Fort Bend	SE	×
● *Thompson's*, Harris	SE	×
Thornberry, Clay	N	×
● Thorndale, Milam	C	47
● *Thorne*, Bowie	NE	×
Thornhill, (see New Braunfels)		×
● Thornton, Limestone	C	466
Thorp's Spring, Hood	N	485
Thrifty, Brown	C	100
Thockmorton, T'kmorton	N	210
Thurber, Erath	N	978
Thurman, Shelby	E	10
● *Thurston*, Pecos	W	10
● *Tiffin*, Eastland	N	×
Tiger Mill, Burnet	C	131
Tigertown, (see Cothran's Store)		×
Tilden, McMullen	S	506
● Tilmon, Caldwell	C	×
Timms City, Lipscomb	SW	25
● Timpson, Shelby	E	518
Tio, Frio	S	×
● Tioga, Grayson	NE	300
Tivy, Kerr	C	×
Todd, Grayson	NE	×
Todd's Mill, (see Timpson)		×
Toksana, Wichita	N	65
● Tolar, Hood	N	20
Tolbert, Wilbarger	N	×
Toledo, Newton	E	×
Toliver, Nacogdoches	E	20
Tolosa, Kaufman	NE	50
● Tom Bean, Grayson	NE	×
Tomday, Shelby	E	×
Tommie, Lavaca	S	×
Tompkin's Mills, Tyler	E	25
Topaz, Erath	N	×
● *Torbert*, El Paso	W	×
Tordilla, Atascosa	S	12
Toro, Callahan	N	×
● *Toronto*, Brewster	W	×
Tours, McLennan	C	×
Towash, (see Whitney)		×
Town Bluff, Tyler	E	50
● *Towne*, El Paso	W	×
Towson, Red River	NE	50
● Toyah, Reeves	W	300
Trail Crossing, (see Doan's)		×
Tram, Jasper	E	×
● *Trans-Continental Junction*, Bowie	NE	×
Travis, Austin	SE	50
Travis, Falls	C	15
Travis Peak, Travis	C	32
● Trent, Taylor	NW	20
● Trenton, Fannin	NE	200
Tres Palacios, Matagorda	SE	32
Tres Palacios River, M't'g'a	SE	×
Trial Farm, Cass	NE	40
● *Trice*, Bowie	NE	×
Trickham, Coleman	C	60
● Trinidad, Henderson	NE	×
● Trinity, Trinity	E	856
● Trinity Mills, Dallas	NE	65
● Troup, Smith	NE	465
● Troy, Bell	C	219
● *Trueloves*, Johnson	N	×
Truehart (see Monahans)		×
Truscott, Knox	NW	×
● Tryon, Hardin	E	50
● Tucker, Anderson	E	30
● *Tulane*, Orange	E	×
● *Tuna*, La Salle	S	×
Tulia, Swisher	SW	25
Tulip, Fannin	NE	25
Tunis, Burleson	C	100
Turnersville, Coryell	C	50
Turtle Bayou, Chambers	SE	150
Twin Sisters, Blanco	C	25
● *Twist*, Hartley	SW	×
● Twohig, La Salle	S	200
● **Tyler**, Smith	NE	6,908
Tyron, (see Plank)		×
Tyson, Hill	C	×
Udston, Houston	E	×
Ula, Foard	NW	×
Una, Robertson	C	25
Union, Wilson	S	100
Union, Grayson	NE	12
Unitia, Delta	NE	50
Unity, Colorado	SE	×
Upson, Maverick	S	130
● *Upton*, Bastrop	C	×
Utica, Smith	NE	×
Utley, Bastrop	C	×
Utopia, Uvalde	S	200
Uval, Upshur	NE	10
Uvalde, Uvalde	S	1,265
Uz, Montague	E	[illegible]
Valda, Polk	E	5
Valdasta, Collin	NE	15
Vale, Runnels	C	20
● Valentine, Presidio	W	250
Valenzuela, Webb	S	×
● *Valera*, Coleman	C	×
Valley, Guadalupe	S	50
Valley Creek, Fannin	NE	200
● Valley Mills, Bosque	C	300
Valley Spring, Llano	C	250
● Valley View, Cooke	N	200
● Van Alstyne, Grayson	NE	737
Vance, Edwards	C	130
Vance Mills, Jack	N	30
Vanderpool, Bandera	C	×
● Van Horn, El Paso	W	×
● Van Raub, Bexar	S	×
Vansickle's, Hunt	NE	32
Vaughan, Hill	C	10
Veal's Station, Parker	N	250
● *Velasco*, Brazoria	SE	700
Velasco, Brazoria	SE	1,500
Venice (see Wonders)		×
● Venus, Johnson	N	×
Vera, Knox	NW	×
Verdi, Atascosa	S	×
Vernon, Wilbarger	N	2,857
Verona, Collin	NE	10
Vesta, Sabine	C	×
● *Vesta*, Shackelford	N	×
Vickery (see Baird)		700
Vicksburgh, Caldwell	C	×
Victor, Erath	N	25
Victor, Fannin	NE	×
Victoria, Victoria	S	3,040
Vienna, Lavaca	S	10
Viesca, Falls	C	25
● *Vigo*, Callahan	N	×
Vigo, Concho	C	14
Vilas, Bell	C	10
● Village Mills, Hardin	E	300
Vilott, Cooke	N	57
Vina, Clay	N	×
Vineland, Collin	NE	23
Viney, Collin	NE	×
Vineyard, Jack	N	150
Vinson, Howard	NW	×
Viola, Cass	NE	32
Virgile, Johnson	N	×
● *Virginia Point*, G'lves'n	SE	×
Vivian, Foard	NW	×
Voca, McCulloch	C	50
Volente, Travis	C	×
Vollmer, Harris	SE	×
Volney, Delta	NE	×
Von Ormy, Bexar	S	×
Voxpopuli, Colorado	SE	15
Waco, McLennan	C	14,445
Wade, Guadalupe	S	×
● *Wades*, Nueces	S	×
Wadeville (see Kerens)		×
● Waelder, Gonzales	S	388
Waesser, Goliad	S	50
Wagner, Hunt	NE	×
Wakefield, Howard	NW	×
Waketon, Denton	N	20
Walburg, Williamson	C	10
Waldeck, Fayette	C	25
● *Waldo*, Kinney	S	×
Waldrip, McCulloch	C	50
Walhalla, Fayette	S	10
Walk, Lampasas	C	20
● *Walker*, Fort Bend	SE	195
Walker Station (see Annona)		×
● Waller, Waller	SE	10
● Wallis Station, Austin	SE	200
Wallisville, Chambers	SE	250
● Walnut, Bosque	C	682
Walnut Grove, Red River	NE	25
● *Walter*, Williamson	C	×
Walthall (see Runnels)		×
● *Walton*, Bee	S	25
Walton, Van Zandt	NE	25
Warda, Fayette	C	100
Waresville (see Utopia)		×
● *Warfield*, Midland	NW	32
● Waring, Kendall	C	20
● *Warner*, Grayson	NE	×
Warner's Mill (see Big Sandy)		×
● Warren, Tyler	E	833
Warren, Bell	C	19
Warren's Mill (see Swinkville)		×
Warrenton, Fayette	C	150
● *Warwick*, Buchel	W	×
● Washburn, Armstrong	SW	300
Washington, Washington	C	100
● Waskom, Harrison	NE	100
● *Wassons*, Trinity	E	×
● Watauga, Tarrant	N	77
● *Waterford*, Milam	C	×
Water Valley, Tom Green	W	12
● *Waters*, Navarro	NE	×
● *Watkins*, Pecos	W	×
Watson, Red River	NE	50
Watson, Milam	C	32
● Watters, Travis	C	×
Watterson, Bastrop	C	25
Waugh's Rancho, La Salle	S	19
Waverlan, Hansford	SW	×
● *Waverly*, Walker	E	100
Waverly, Walker	E	×
● **Waxahachie**, Ellis	NE	3,076
Way, Hall	SW	×
Wayland (see Rosalie)		×
Wayland, Stephens	N	25
Wayne, Cass	NE	50
● **Weatherford**, Parker	N	3,369
● Weaver, Hopkins	NE	×
● *Webb*, Webb	S	×
Webberville, Travis	C	350
● *Websterville*, Harris	SE	19

Town, County	Index	Pop.
Weches, Houston	E	×
Weesatche, Goliad	S	100
● Weimar, Colorado	SE	1,443
● *Weiss*, Hardin	E	×
Welcome, Austin	C	50
● *Welden*, DeWitt	S	150
Weldon, Houston	E	150
● Welfare, Kendall	C	10
● Wellborn, Brazos	C	90
Wellersburg, Lavaca	S	12
Wellington, Collingsworth	SW	24
● Wells, Cherokee	E	50
● *Wells Creek*, Anderson	E	×
● *Wendell*, Jeff Davis	W	×
Wentworth, Sutton	C	×
Weser, Goliad	S	×
Wesley, Washington	C	370
● West, McLennan	C	50
West Bevilport, Jasper	E	×
Westbrook, Blanco	C	97
● *Westbrook*, Mitchell	NW	40
West Columbia, Brazoria	SE	30
● *West Dallas*, Dallas	NE	474
● Westfield, Harris	SE	50
● *Westheimer*, Galveston	SE	×
● *Westhoff*, DeWitt	S	×
West Mountain, Upshur	NE	10
Weston, Collin	NE	300
Westphalia, Falls	C	×
● West Point, Fayette	C	250
● Wetmore, Bexar	S	×
● *Whaley's*, Bowie	NE	×
● **Wharton**, Wharton	SE	1,000
Wheat, Scurry	NW	×
● Wheatland, Dallas	NE	50
Wheeler, Potter	SW	25
Wheelock, Robertson	C	25
Whistler, Kinney	S	×
● White Deer, Carson	SW	×
White Hall, Grimes	E	200
● *Whitehead*, Cherokee	E	25
● Whitehouse, Smith	NE	25
White Mound, Grayson	NE	55
White Oak, Hopkins	NE	32
White Rock, Hunt	NE	100
● *White Rock*, Trinity	E	×
● Whitesborough, Grayson	NE	170
● *Whites*, Fort Bend	SW	×
● *White's Switch*, Brazos	C	×
● Whitewright, Grayson	NE	850
Whitman, Washington	C	25
Whitman's Ferry, (see Orange)		×
● Whitney, Hill	C	1,000
Whitson, Coryell	C	×
Whitt, Parker	N	278
Whittaker, Burleson	C	×
Whittville, Comanche	C	25
● **Wichita Falls**, Wichita	N	1,987
Wied, Lavaca	S	×
Wieland, Hunt	NE	50
Wiess Bluff, Jasper	E	200
Wildcat, Henderson	NE	65
Wilderville, Falls	C	75
● *Wild Horse*, El Paso	W	×
Wilford, Stonewall	NW	×
● *Wilkin's*, Upshur	NE	45
Wilkinson, Titus	NE	×
● *Willard*, Polk	E	×
Willard, Trinity	E	50
William Penn, Washington	C	25
Williamsburgh, Lavaca	S	60
Williams Ranch, Mills	C	325
● Willis, Montgomery	E	800
Willow City, Gillespie	C	50
Willow Grove, (see Tomday)		×
Willow Hole, Madison	E	50
Willow Point, Wise	N	195
● *Willow Springs*, Gregg	NE	×
● Will's Point, Van Zandt	NE	1,025
● Wilmer, Dallas	NE	16
Wilson, Comanche	C	12
Wimberly, Hays	C	100
● *Wimberly*, Harris	SE	×
● Winchester, Fayette	C	200
Windale, (see Burton)		×
● Windom, Fannin	NE	25
Windsor, Kendall	C	65
Windthorst, Archer	N	×
Winfree, Chambers	SE	10
Wingate, Runnels	C	×
Winkler, Navarro	NE	50
● Winnsborough, Wood	NE	388
● Winona, Smith	NE	150
Winters, Runnels	C	6
● *Wise*, Hopkins	NE	×
Wise, Van Zandt	NE	×

Town, County	Index	Pop.
● *Wither's*, Bexar	S	×
Witting, Lavaca	S	65
Woden, Nacogdoches	E	×
● Wolfe City, Hunt	NE	867
Wolf's Crossing, Burnet	C	196
● *Womack*, Victoria	S	×
Womack, Bosque	C	32
Wonders, Nacogdoches	E	×
● Woodbine, Cooke	N	30
Woodbury, Hill	NW	100
Woodland, Red River	NE	75
Woodland, Williamson	C	×
● Woodlawn, Harrison	NE	50
Wood's, Panola	NE	100
Woodstock, Bowie	NE	10
● **Woodville**, Tyler	E	518
Woodworth Mills, Cass	NE	267
Woolverton, (see Stone Point)		×
● Wootan Wells, Robertson	C	268
● Wortham, Freestone	E	401
Wren, (see Early Wine)		×
Wright, Swisher	SW	×
Wrightsborough, Gonzales	S	75
● Wyatt, Ellis	NE	×
● Wylie, Collin	NE	239
Yampareka, Hardman	NW	×
Yandell, Tom Greene	W	32
Yantis, Wood	NE	25
● Yarborough, Grimes	E	50
Yarrelton, Milam	C	58
Yegua, Burleson	C	28
Yell, Hays	C	×
Yellow House, Lamb	NW	×
● *Yellow Prairie*, Burleson	C	25
● Yoakum, De Witt	S	767
York Creek, Gaudalupe	S	50
York Creek, Comal	C	10
● Yorktown, De Witt	S	522
Young, Freestone	E	50
Youngsport, Bell	C	75
Ysleta, El Paso	W	1,528
Zana, San Augustine	E	×
Zapp, Fayette	C	25
● Zephyr, Brown	C	150
● *Zimbi*, Harris	SE	×
Zorn, Guadalupe	S	×
Zulch's Store, Madison	E	65
Zulu, Hansford	SW	75

UTAH.

COUNTIES.	INDEX.	POP.
Beaver	SW	3,340
Box Elder	NW	7,642
Cache	N	15,509
Davis	N	6,751
Emery	E	5,076
Garfield	S	2,457
Grand	E	541
Iron	SW	2,683
Juab	C	5,582
Kane	SW	1,685
Millard	W	4,033
Morgan	N	1,780
Pi Ute	S	2,842
Rich	N	1,527
Salt Lake	C	58,457
San Juan	SE	365
San Pete	C	13,146
Sevier	C	6,199
Summit	N	7,733
Tooele	W	3,700
Uintah	E	2,762
Utah	C	23,768
Wasatch	E	3,595
Washington	SW	4,009
Weber	N	22,723
Total		207,905

TOWN. COUNTY.	INDEX.	POP.
Adamsville, Beaver	SW	100
● *Agate*, Uintah	E	×
Alma, Weber	N	195
Alpine City, Utah	C	466
● Alta, Salt Lake	C	300
Altus, Summit	N	×
● American Fork, Utah	C	2,000
Annabella, Sevier	C	620
Antimony, Garfield	S	26
Argenta, Salt Lake	C	150
Asays, Garfield	S	100
Ashley, Uintah	E	800
Asphalt, Utah	C	×
● *Atkinson*, Summit	N	40
Aurora, Sevier	C	32
Axtel Station, Sevier	C	×
● *Balfour*, Box Elder	NW	×
Barclay, Salt Lake	C	×
● *Battle Creek*, Utah	C	×
Bear River City, Box Elder	NW	321
Beaver, Beaver	SW	1,800
● *Benjamin*, Utah	C	500
Benson, Cache	N	65
Big Cottonwood, (see Brinton)		×
● Bingham Canyon, S'lt L'k	C	1,000
● *Bingham Junc*, Salt Lake	C	×
● Black Rock, Millard	W	×
Blaine, Davis	N	×
● Blake, Emery	E	200
Bloomington, Washington	SW	×
● *Blue Creek*, Box Elder	NW	×
Bluff, San Juan	SE	100
● *Bolter Summit*, Tooele	W	×
● *Bonnerville*, Box Elder	NW	2,200
Bountiful, Davis	N	2,200
● *Bovine*, Box Elder	NW	×
● **Box Elder**, Box Elder	NW	2,139
Bradshaw, Beaver	SW	34
● *Brigham*, Box Elder	NW	2,139
Brighton, Salt Lake	C	×
Brinton, Salt Lake	C	604
Brock, Emery	E	×
Brown's Park, (see Ashley)		×
● *Buena Vista*, Salt Lake	C	×
Bullion City, Pi Ute	S	×
Bullionville, (see Marysvale)		×
Burbank, Millard	W	26
● *Burnt Corral*, Millard	W	×
● *Burriston*, Juab	C	×
Burrville, Sevier	C	65
Butlerville, Salt Lake	C	390
● Cache Junc., Cache	N	×
● *Cachill*, Cache	N	×
Caineville, Pi Ute	S	×
Call's Fort (see Brigham)		
Camp Douglas, Salt Lake	C	×
Canda, Salt Lake	C	×
Cannon, Cache	N	×
Cannon, (see Centre)		×
Cannonville, Garfield	S	250
● *Castilla Springs*, Utah	C	×
Castle Dale, Emery	E	303
● Castle Gate, Emery	E	×
● *Castle Rock*, Morgan	N	×
● *Cedar*, Emery	E	×
Cedar City, Iron	SW	967
● *Cedar Fort*, Utah	C	×
● Cedar Valley, Utah	C	100
Central, Sevier	C	×
● Centerville, Davis	N	600
Centre, Tooele	W	20
● *Chambers*, Salt Lake	C	×
Charleston, Wasatch	E	200
Chester, San Pete	C	300
Circleville, Pi Ute	S	200
● Cisco, Grand	E	×
Clarkston, Cache	N	400
● *Clear Creek*, Utah	C	×
Clear Lake, Millard	W	×
Cleveland, Emery	E	×
● *Cliff*, Emery	E	×
Clover Flat, Pi Ute	S	12
● *Coal Mine*, Emery	E	×
Coal Mines, Summit	N	×
● **Coalville**, Summit	N	1,116
● Collinston, Box Elder	NW	100
● Colton, Utah	C	300
Cooper's, Davis	N	×
● Corrine, Box Elder	NW	400
Corn Creek, (see Kanosh)		×
● *Cottonwood*, Salt Lake	C	×
● *Cottonwood*, Uintah	E	×
Cove, Cache	N	×
Cove Creek, Millard	W	×
Coyoto, Garfield	S	250
Craighead, Box Elder	NW	×
● *Crescent*, Garfield	S	×
Crossmans Springs, Millard	W	×
● *Croydon*, Morgan	N	150
Cub Hill, Cache	N	300
Dale, Pi Ute	S	×
Dale, Uintah	E	×
Davenport, Salt Lake	C	×
Davis, Summit	N	×
Deckers, Salt Lake	C	×

● East Highgate, Franklin NW 150
East Hubbardton, Rutland. W ×
● East Jamaica, Windham SE ×
East Middlebury, Addison.. W 500
East Monkton, Addison.... W 300
● East Montpelier, Wash'ton C 953
East Orange, Orange........E 75
East Peacham, Caledonia.. NE ×
East Pitttsford, Rutland.... W ×
East Poultney, Rutland..... W 310
● East Putney, Windham.. SE ×
East Randolph, Orange......E 197
● East Richford, Franklin NW 200
East Roxbury, Washington. C ×
East Rupert, Bennington. SW 100
East Ryegate, Caledonia... NE ×
● *East Saint Johnsbury*, Caledonia..........NE ×
East Sheldon, Franklin... NW ×
● East Shoreham, Addison. W 150
● East Swanton, Franklin NW ×
● East Thetford, Orange....E 54
● East Wallingford, Rutland W 600
East Warren, Washington... C ×
East Wilmington, Wi'dham SE ×
Eden, Lamoille............ N 851
Eden Mills, Lamoille........N ×
Elmore, Lamoille...........N 593
● *Ely*, Orange...............E 754
Enosburgh, Franklin...... NW 2,299
● Enosburgh Falls, Fr'klin NW 900
● Essex, Chittenden.......NW 2,013
● Essex Junc. Chittenden NW 800
Evansville, Orleans....... N 90
● *Fairbanks*, Caledonia... NE ×
Fairfax, Franklin......... NW 1,523
Fairfield, Franklin.........NW 1,825
● *Fairfield Sta.* Franklin NW ×
Fair Haven, Rutland....... W 2,791
● *Fair Haven Sta.* Rutland W ×
● Fairlee, Orange...........E 398
Fay's Corner, Chittenden. NW ×
Fayston, Washington.......C 533
Felchville, Windsor.........E ×
Ferdinand, Essex..........NE 73
● Ferrisburgh, Addison.... W 1,501
Fletcher, Franklin.........NW 793
● *Fletcher Station*, Fr'klin NW ×
● Florence, Rutland.........W 250
Forest Dale, Rutland.......W 500
Franklin, Franklin..........NW 1,300
● Gallups Mills, Essex .... NE ×
Garfield, Lamoille...........N ×
● *Gassett's*, Windsor.......E 75
Gaysville, Windsor...........E 372
Georgia, Franklin.........NW 1,282
Georgia Plain, Franklin.. NW 40
● *Georgia Station*, Frankl'n NW ×
● *Glastenbury*, Benningt'n SW 181
Glover, Orleans..............N 970
Goshen, Addison............W 311
Gouldsville, Washington....C 375
Grafton, Windham........SE 817
Granby, Essex..............NE 361
Grand Isle, Grand Isle....NW 793
Graniteville, Washington....C ×
Granville, Addison.........W 637
● *Gravel Pit*, Washington...C ×
● *Gravel Pit*, Washington...C ×
● *Greens Corners Sta.*, Fr. NW ×
Green River, Windham....SE ×
Greensboro, Orleans.........N 918
● Greensborough Bend, Orls. N 100
Greensboro Four Corn'rs, Or. N ×
Griffith, Rutland...........W 250
● Groton, Caledonia.......NE 1,040
● Groton Pond, Caledonia NE ×
Grove, Windham...........SE ×
Guildhall, Essex.......NE 511
Guilford, Windham.........SE 890
Guilford Centre, Windham SE 30
Halifax, Windham..........SE 702
Hancock, Addison...........W 283
● Hardwick, Caledonia ... NE 1,547
Harris, Washington.........C 15
● Hartford, Windsor.........E 3,740
● Hartland, Windsor.........E 1,393
Hartland Four Corn'rs, W'sr. E 75
Harvey's Hollow, 'Calednia NE ×
● *Hazen*, Essex............NE ×
● *Hazen's Junction*, Essex NE ×
● Healdville, Rutland...... W ×
Heartwellville, B'n'ingt'n SW 166
Highgate, Franklin........NW 1,853
● Highgate Centre, Frankl. NW 250
● Highgate Springs, Frank. NW 100
Hinesburgh, Chittenden.. NW 1,205

Holland, Orleans............N 878
Hortonville, Rutland....... W 100
Houghtonville, Windham.. SE ×
Hubbardton, Rutland.......W 506
Huntington, Chittenden... NW 723
Huntington Centre, Chit'. NW 200
● **Hyde Park**, Lamoille.. N 1,633
● Hydeville, Rutland.......W 800
Ira, Rutland..................W 421
Irasburgh, Orleans......N 999
● Island Pond, Essex..... NE 360
Isle La Motte, Grand Isle. NW 551
Jacksonville, Windham....SE 272
● Jamaica, Windham......SE 1,074
Jay, Orleans.................N 641
● Jeffersonville, Lamoille... N 225
● Jericho, Chittenden .... NW 1,461
Jericho Centre, Chittenden NW 100
● Johnson, Lamoille.........N 1,462
● Jonesville, Chittenden. NW 250
Keeler's Bay, Grand Isle. NW ×
● *Kinney's*, Washington.... C ×
Kirby, Caledonia..........NE 355
La Grange, Grand Isle....NW 800
● *Lake*, Essex..............NE ×
Lake View House, Frankl' NW ×
Landgrove, Bennington...SW 220
● Lanesboro, Washington...C ×
Langdon, Orange...........E ×
● Larrabee's Point, Addison W ×
Leicester, Addison ....W 532
● Leicester Junction, Addis' W 200
Lemington, Essex.........NE 227
Lincoln, Addison...........W 1,255
Londonderry, Windham...SE 1,010
Lowell, Orleans..............N 1,178
Lower Cabot, Washington... C 126
Lower Waterford, Caled'ia. NE ×
● Ludlow, Windsor...........E 1,081
Lunenburgh, Essex.......NE 1,019
● *Lunenburg*, Essex......NE ×
● Lyndon, Caledonia......NE 2,619
Lyndon Centre, Caledonia. NE 196
● Lyndonville, Caledonia. NE 606
● McIndoe's Falls, Caled'ia NE 375
Maidstone, Essex..........NE 198
Mallet Bay, Chittenden... NW 30
● **Manchester**, Ben'gt'n SW 1,907
Manchester Centre, B'gt'n. SW 500
Manchester Depot, B'gton. SW 200
● *Maquam*, Franklin.... NW ×
Marlborough, Windham... SE 495
Marshfield, Washington.....C 1,121
● *Marshfield Station*, Wash'n C ×
Mechanicsville, Rutland.... W 200
Mendon, Rutland............W 570
● **Middlebury**, Addison. W 1,762
● Middlesex, Washington... C 889
Middletown Springs, Rutl'd. W 786
Miles Pond, Essex..........NE 185
● *Miles Pond Station*, Essex NE ×
● Milton, Chittenden ..... NW 1,585
Miltonborough, Chitt'den. NW ×
Milton Centre, Chittenden NW ×
Monkton, Addison ....W 847
Monkton Ridge, Addison... W 49
Montgomery, Franklin... NW 1,734
Montgomery Centre, Frn. NW 100
● **MONTPELIER**, Wshn C 3,617
● *Montpelier Junction*, Wsh. C ×
Moretown, Washington .....C 952
Morgan, Orleans...............N 520
Morgan Centre, Orleans ....N 110
● *Morrills*, Essex ....NE 321
Morristown, Lamoille ......N 2,411
● Morrisville, Lamoille .....N 1,200
Morses Line, Franklin... NW ×
Moscow, Lamoille ....N 200
● Mount Holly, Rutland.... W 1,214
Mount Tabor, Rutland.....W 436
Nashville, Chittenden .... NW 100
Newark, Caledonia.........NE 536
● Newbury, Orange.........E 2,080
Newbury Centre, Orange ... E ×
● **Newfane**, Windham... SE 952
● New Haven, Addison.... W 1,224
New Haven Mills, Addison. W 175
● Newport, Orleans..........N 1,730
● Newport Centre, Orleans. N 490
● North Bennington, B'g'n. SW 1,000
North Calais, Washington... C 90
North Cambridge, Lamoille. N ×
North Chester, Windsor..... E 206
● North Clarendon, Rutland W 175
● North Concord, Essex.. NE 120
North Craftsbury, Orleans. N 195
North Danville, Caledonia. NE 108

● North Derby, Orleans .... N ×
● North Dorset, Benn'gt'n. SW 150
North Duxbury, Wash'nton. C ×
● North Enosburgh, Fr'n. NW ×
North Fairfax, Franklin. NW ×
North Fayston, Washington. C ×
North Ferrisburgh, Add'n.. W 500
● *North Ferrisburgh Station*, Addison...........W ×
● Northfield, Washington... C 1,222
● *North Georgia*, Franklin NW ×
● North Hartland, Windsor.. E 247
North Hero, Grand Isle NW 550
North Hyde Park, Lamoille N 266
North Londonderry, W'm. SE ×
North Montpelier, Wash'n.. C 103
● North Orwell, Addison... W 1,300
North Peacham, Caledonia NE ×
North Pomfret, Windsor.... E ×
● North Pownal, Benn'n.. SW 900
North Randolph, Orange.... E 65
North Rupert, Bennington SW ×
● North Sheldon, Fr'klin NW 35
North Sherburne, Rutland. W ×
North Shrewsbury, Rutl'd. W ×
North Springfield, Windsor. E ×
● North Thetford, Orange .. E ×
● North Troy, Orleans...... N 600
North Tunbridge, Orange... E 107
● North Underhill, Chit'n. NW ×
North Walden, Caledonia. NE ×
● North Williston, Chitt'n NW 400
North Windham, W'dham. SE ×
North Wolcott, Lamoille.... N ×
Norton, Essex..............NE 306
● Norton Mills, Essex..... NE 280
● Norwich, Windsor........ E 1,304
● Olcott, Windsor .... E ×
Orange, Orange.............E 589
● *Orwell*, Addison..........W ×
Orwell, Addison............W 1,265
Panton, Addison ....W 382
● Passumpsic, Caledonia.. NE 110
Pawlet, Rutland............W 1,745
● *Peabody's*, Caledonia... NE ×
Peacham, Caledonia.......NE 892
Peacham Hollow, Calad'a NE ×
Pearle, Grand Isle........NW 250
Perkinsville, Windsor...... E ×
Peru, Bennington.........SW 445
● *Piermont*, Orange....... E ×
Pittsfield, Rutland..........W 468
● Pittsford, Rutland........ W 1,175
Pittsford Mills, Rutland.... W 450
● Plainfield, Washington.... C 745
Pleasant Val., Chittenden. NW 75
Plymouth, Windsor.........E 755
Plymouth Union, Windsor.. E 275
Pomfret, Windsor.......... E 865
● Pompanoosuc, Windsor.. E ×
Post Mill Village, Orange... E 282
● Poultney, Rutland....... W 3,031
● Pownal, Bennington.... SW 1,919
Pownal Centre, Benningt'n SW 100
● Proctor, Rutland.........W 1,758
● Proctorsville, Windsor.... E ×
● *Pumpkin Hill*, Caledonia NE ×
Putnamville, Washington... C ×
● Putney, Windham.......SE 1,075
Quarries, Rutland.......... W ×
Quarries, Rutland.......... W ×
● Quechee, Windsor.........E ×
Randolph, Orange.......... E 3,232
● *Randolph*, Orange.........E 1,664
Raponda, Windham.......SE ×
Rawsonville, Windham.... SE 101
Reading, Windsor............E 749
Readsboro, Bennington... SW 910
Readsborough Falls, B'ngt'n SW 50
● Richford, Franklin..... NW 1,162
● Richmond, Chittenden. NW 1,115
Richville, Addison.......... W 160
● *Ricker's*, Caledonia..... NE ×
Ripton, Addison.............W 568
Rochester, Windsor......... E 1,257
● Rockingham, Windham. SE 4,579
● **Roxbury**, Washington.... C 768
● Royalton, Windsor.........E 1,433
● Rupert, Bennington.... SW 861
● **Rutland**, Rutland.... W 8,239
● Ryegate, Caledonia..... NE 1,125
Sadawga, Windham........SE ×
● **Saint Albans**, Fr'klin NW 7,771
Saint Albans Bay, Fr'klin. NW 300
Saint Albans Hill, Fraklin NW ×
Saint George, Chittenden. NW 106
● **Saint Johnsbury**, Caledonia..................NE 3,857

Place	Index	Pop.
●Saint Johnsbury Centre, Caledonia	NE	×
●Saint Johnsbury East, Caledonia	NE	×
Salisbury, Addison	W	740
●*Salisbury Sta.*, Addison	W	×
Sandgate, Bennington	SW	587
Saxton's River, Windham	SE	625
Searsburgh, Bennington	SW	173
Shaftsbury, Bennington	SW	1,652
○*Shaftsbury Station*, Bennington	SW	×
●Sharon, Windsor	E	737
Sheffield, Caledonia	NE	750
●Shelburne, Chittenden	NW	1,300
●Sheldon, Franklin	NW	1,365
Sheldon Junc., Franklin	NW	×
●Sheldon Springs, Frank.	NW	×
Sherburne, Rutland	W	451
Sherman, Windham	SE	×
Shoreham, Addison	W	1,240
●*Shoreham Sta.*, Addison	W	×
Shrewsbury, Rutland	W	974
Simonsville, Windsor	E	30
Slab Hollow, Windham	SE	×
Somerset, Windham	SE	61
South Albany, Orleans	N	127
South Barre, Washington	C	145
●South Barton, Orleans	N	175
South Burlington, Chit'nd	NW	845
South Cabot, Washington	C	60
South Corinth, Orange	E	×
South Danville, Caledonia	NE	120
South Dorset, Bennington	SW	150
South Elmore, Lamoille	N	×
●South Fairlee, Orange	E	820
●South Franklin, Frank.	NW	×
South Halifax, Windham	SE	×
South Hero, Grand Isle	NW	559
South Lincoln, Addison	W	×
●South Londonderry, Windham	SE	800
●South Lunenburgh, Essex	NE	×
●South Newbury, Orange	E	×
South Newfane, Windham	SE	×
South Northfield, Washingt'n	C	100
South Peacham, Caledonia	NE	×
South Pomfret, Windsor	E	×
South Poultney, Rutland	W	385
South Randolph, Orange	E	10[illegible]
South Reading, Windsor	E	×
●South Royalton, Windsor	E	325
●South Ryegate, Caledonia	NE	×
●South Shaftsbury, Bennington	SW	50[illegible]
South Starksborough, Ad'n	W	×
South Stafford, Orange	E	×
South Tunbridge, Orange	E	5[illegible]
●*South Vernon*, Windham	SE	×
South Victory, (see Victory)		×
South Walden, Caledonia	NE	×
●South Wallingford, Rutl'd	W	50[illegible]
South Wardsborough, Windham	SE	×
South Washington, Orange	E	×
South Wheelock, Caledonia	N	×
South Whittingham, Wind'm	SE	×
South Windham, Windham	SE	3[illegible]
South Woodbury, Wash'gton	C	×
South Woodstock, Windsor	E	12[illegible]
●*Spafford*, Windsor	E	7[illegible]
Springfield, Windsor	E	1,512
Stamford, Bennington	SW	645
Stannard, Caledonia	NE	239
Starksborough, Addison	W	1,070
●*Stevens*, Essex	NE	×
Steven's Mills, Franklin	NW	200
Stockbridge, Windsor	E	894
Stowe, Lamoille	N	1,886
Strafford, Orange	E	932
Stratton, Windham	SE	222
Sudbury, Rutland	W	502
Summerville, Caledonia	NE	×
●*Summit*, Caledonia	NE	×
●*Summit*, Caledonia	NE	×
●*Summit*, Essex	NE	×
●*Summit*, Rutland	W	×
●*Summit Siding*, Orleans	N	×
●Sunderland, Bennington	SW	633
Sutton, Caledonia	NE	746
●*Sutton Sta.*, Caledonia	NE	×
●Swanton, Franklin	NW	3,231
●Swanton Junc., Franklin	NW	185
●Taftsville, Windsor	E	195
Thetford, Orange	E	1,287
●*Thetford*, Orange	E	×
Thetford Centre, Orange	E	×

Place	Index	Pop.
Thetford Hill, Orange	E	×
Tinmouth, Rutland	W	435
Topsham, Orange	E	1,187
Townline, Addison	W	×
●Townshend, Windham	SE	865
Troy, Orleans	N	1,673
Tunbridge, Orange	E	1,011
Tyson, Windsor	E	×
●Underhill, Chittenden	NW	1,301
Underhill Centre, Chitten.	NW	200
Union Village, Orange	E	75
●Vergennes, Addison	W	1,773
●*Vermont*, Bennington	SW	×
●Vernon, Windham	SE	567
Vershire, Orange	E	754
●Victory, Essex	NE	564
Waitsfield, Washington	C	815
Wait's River, Orange	E	×
Walden, Caledonia	NE	810
●*Walden Sta.*, Caledonia	NE	×
●Wallingford, Rutland	W	1,733
Wallis Pond, Essex	NE	×
Waltham, Addison	W	255
Wardsborough, Windham	SE	704
●*Wardsboro*, Windham	SE	×
Warren, Washington	C	866
Washington, Orange	E	820
●Waterbury, Washington	C	955
Waterbury Centre, Wash'n	C	304
Waterford, Caledonia	NE	734
●*Water Mill*, Essex	NE	×
Waterville, Lamoille	N	577
Weathersfield, Windsor	E	1,174
Weathersfield Centre, W'ds'r	E	237
●*Weeds*, Essex	NE	×
Wells, Rutland	W	621
Wells Lannon, Orange	E	×
●Wells River, Orange	E	526
●*Wenlock*, Essex	NE	×
West Addison, Addison	W	×
West Albany, Orleans	N	×
●*West Alburgh*, Gr'd Isle	NW	×
West Arlington, Ben'gton	SW	300
West Barnet, Caledonia	NE	110
West Berkshire, Franklin	NW	100
West Berlin, Washington	C	×
West Bolton, Chittenden	NW	150
●West Braintree, Orange	E	17[illegible]
West Brattleborough, Windham	SE	409
West Bridgewater, Windsor	E	200
West Bridport, Addison	W	×
West Brookfield, Orange	E	×
●West Burke, Caledonia	NE	350
West Castleton, Rutland	W	200
West Charleston, Orleans	N	345
West Charlotte, Chitt'den	NW	×
●West Concord, Essex	NE	425
West Corinth, Orange	E	110
West Cornwall, Addison	W	50
●West Danville, Caledo'la	NE	100
West Derby, Orleans	N	×
West Dover, Windham	SE	×
West Dummerston, W'dh'm	SE	×
●*West Dummerston Station*, Windham	SE	×
West Enosburgh, Fra'kl'n	NW	300
West Fairlee, Orange	E	561
Westfield, Orleans	N	763
Westford, Chittenden	NW	1,033
West Georgia, Franklin	NW	100
West Glover, Orleans	N	75
West Halifax, Windham	SE	105
●West Hartford, Windsor	E	×
West Haven, Rutland	W	412
West Holland, Orleans	N	483
West Lincoln, Addison	W	×
West Marlborough, Windham	SE	×
West Milton, Chittenden	NW	100
●Westminster, Windham	SE	1,265
Westminster Sta. Windham	SE	×
Westminster West, W'dh'm	SE	90
Westmore, Orleans	N	395
West Newbury, Orange	E	×
West Norwich, Windsor	C	×
Weston, Windsor	E	861
●West Pawlet, Rutland	W	850
●West Randolph, Orange	E	1,573
West Rupert, Bennington	SW	350
●West Rutland, Rutland	W	3,680
●West Salisbury, Addison	W	500
●*West Swanton*, Fr'klin	NW	×
West Topsham, Orleans	N	195
●West Townshend, W'h'm	SE	×
West Wardsborough, W'h'm	SE	×

Place	Index	Pop.
West Waterford, Caledonia	NE	×
West Windsor, Windsor	E	570
West Woodstock, Windsor	E	×
Weybridge, Addison	W	543
Wheelock, Calidonia	NE	596
●*White Creek*, Be'ington	SW	×
●White River Junc. W'nds'r	E	495
●Whiting, Addison	W	355
Whitingham, Windham	SE	1,191
●Williamstown, Orange	E	1,188
●Williamsville, Windham	SE	×
Williston, Chittenden	NW	1,161
●*Williston*, Chittenden	NW	×
Willoughby, Orleans	N	×
Wilmington, Windham	SE	1,106
Windham, Windham	SE	379
●Windsor, Windsor	E	1,381
●*Winhall*, Windham	SE	523
●Winooski, Chittenden	NW	3,659
●*Winooski Sta.* Chitt'd'n	NW	×
●Wolcott, Lamoille	N	1,158
Woodbury, Washington	C	810
Woodford, Bennington	SW	353
●**Woodstock**, Windsor	E	1,218
●*Woodstock*, Windsor	E	×
Worcester, Washington	SW	725

VIRGINIA.

COUNTIES.	INDEX.	POP.
Accomack	E	27,277
Albemarle	C	32,379
Alexandria	N	18,597
Alleghany	W	9,283
Amelia	C	9,068
Amherst	C	17,551
Appomattox	C	9,589
Augusta	W	37,00[illegible]
Bath	W	4,587
Bedford	C	31,213
Bland	SW	5,129
Botetourt	W	14,854
Brunswick	S	17,245
Buchanan	SW	5,867
Buckingham	C	13,383
Campbell	C	41,087
Caroline	C	16,681
Carroll	SW	15,497
Charles City	E	5,066
Charlotte	S	15,077
Chesterfield	C	26,211
Clarke	N	8,071
Craig	W	3,835
Culpeper	N	13,233
Cumberland	E	9,482
Dickenson	SW	5,077
Dinwiddie	S	13,515
Elizabeth City	E	16,168
Essex	E	10,047
Fairfax	N	16,655
Fauquier	N	22,590
Floyd	SW	14,405
Fluvanna	C	9,508
Franklin	S	24,985
Frederick	N	17,880
Giles	SW	9,090
Gloucester	E	11,653
Goochland	C	9,958
Grayson	SW	14,394
Greene	C	5,622
Greensville	S	8,230
Halifax	S	34,424
Hanover	C	17,402
Henrico	C	103,394
Henry	S	18,208
Highland	W	5,352
Isle of Wight	SE	11,313
James City	E	5,643
King & Queen	E	9,669
King George	E	6,641
King William	E	9,605
Lancaster	E	7,191
Lee	SW	18,216
Loudoun	N	23,274
Louisa	C	16 997
Lunenburgh	S	11,372
Madison	N	10,225
Mathews	E	7,584
Mecklenburg	S	25,359
Middlesex	E	7,458
Montgomery	SW	17,742
Nansemond	SE	19,692

County	Index	Pop.
Nelson	C	15,336
New Kent	E	5,511
Norfolk	SE	77,038
Northampton	E	10,313
Northumberland	E	7,885
Nottoway	S	11,582
Orange	C	12,814
Page	N	13,092
Patrick	S	14,147
Petersburg City	S	22,680
Pittsylvania	S	59,941
Powhatan	C	6,791
Prince Edward	C	14,694
Prince George	SE	7,872
Princess Anne	SE	9,510
Prince William	N	9,805
Pulaski	**SW**	**12,790**
Rappahannock	N	8,678
Richmond	E	7,146
Roanoke	SW	30,101
Rockbridge	W	23,062
Rockingham	N	31,299
Russell	SW	16,126
Scott	SW	21,694
Shenandoah	N	19,671
Smyth	SW	13,360
Southampton	SE	20,078
Spotsylvania	C	14,233
Stafford	N	7,362
Surry	SE	8,256
Sussex	SE	11,100
Tazewell	SW	19,899
Warren	N	8,280
Warwick	E	6,650
Washington	SW	29,020
Westmoreland	E	8,399
Wise	SW	9,345
Wythe	SW	18,019
York	E	7,596
Total		1,655,980

TOWN. COUNTY.	INDEX.	POP.
Aaron, Carroll	SW	12
Abbott, Craig	W	18
Abb's Valley, (see Pocahontas)		×
Abbyville, Mecklenburg	S	50
Abell, Charlotte	S	×
Abert, Bedford	C	×
● **Abingdon**, Wash'ton	SW	1,674
Abraham, Floyd	SW	×
● Abrams Falls, Wash'ton	SW	×
● *Acca*, Henrico	C	×
Accomack C. H., Ac'm'k	E	350
Accotink, Fairfax	N	150
● *Accotink Station*, Fairfax	N	×
Achilles, Gloucester	E	×
Acorn Hill, (see Whitacre)		×
Acteon, Prince Edward	C	×
● Adams Grove, So'th'm'n	SE	60
Aden, Prince William	N	×
Adner, Gloucester	E	×
Adriance, Cumberland	E	×
Advance Mills, Albemarle	C	35
Adwolf, Smyth	SW	×
● Afton, Nelson	C	100
Agnesville, Prince William	N	×
Aguste, Isle of Wight	SE	×
Ah Sid, Rockbridge	W	×
● *Aikin Summit*, Pittsylv'a	S	35
Aily, Dickenson	SW	×
Airfield, Southampton	SE	50
Air Point, Roanoke	SW	25
Alvland, Sussex	SE	×
Akers, Floyd	SW	12
Alanthus, Culpeper	N	×
Alberene, Albemarle	C	×
Alchie, Halifax	S	20
Alden, King George	E	30
Aldie, Loudoun	N	150
Alexander's Mills, Campb'l	C	8
● **Alexandria**, Alex'dria	N	14,339
Alfred, Albemarle	C	×
Algoma, Franklin	S	×
Alhambra, Nelson	C	×
Allegheny Spring, M'tg'y	SW	30
● Alleghany Sta., Allegh'y	W	75
● Allen's Creek, Amherst	C	10
Allenslevel, Buckingham	C	×
Allen's Siding, Henrico	C	×
All[illegible], Scott	SW	12
Alliance, Surry	SE	×
● Allisonia, Pulaski	SW	125
Allmondsville, Gloucester	E	×
Allwood, Amherst	C	15
Alma, Page	N	100
Almond, Rockingham	N	12
Alone, Rockbridge	W	18
Alonzaville, Shenandoah	N	42
Alpha, Buckingham	C	×
Alphin, Rockbridge	W	24
● *Alpine*, Botetourt	W	×
Alps, Brunswick	S	10
Alrich's Crossing, Sp'sylv'ia	C	12
Altamaha, Pulaski	SW	30
Alto, (see Hop Yard)		×
● Alton, Halifax	S	50
Altoona Mines, Pulaski	SW	×
Alumine, Henry	S	×
Alum Ridge, Floyd	SW	12
Alum Springs, (see Rockb'ge Alum Springs)		×
Alum Wells, Washington	SW	48
Alvah, Henry	S	×
Ambar, King George	E	×
Amberly, Rockingham	N	50
Amburg, Middlesex	E	×
● **Amelia C. H.**, Amelia	C	50
● **Amherst C. H.**, Amh'st	C	590
Amicus, Greene	C	×
Amissville, Rappahannock	N	150
Amorita, Grayson	SW	×
Amos, Floyd	SW	12
Amsterdam, Botetourt	W	80
Amy, Amherst	C	×
Ancella, Grayson	SW	96
Anchor, Surry	SE	20
● *Anderson*, Goochland	C	×
Andersonville, Buckingham	C	30
Andrews, Spotsylvania	C	8
Angola, Cumberland	E	10
Annandale, Fairfax	N	10
Annex, Augusta	W	24
Ante, Brunswick	S	×
● *Antioch*, Cumberland	E	×
Antioch, Fluvanna	C	30
Antlers, Mecklenburgh	S	×
Apple Grove, Louisa	C	6
● *Appold's*, Rockbridge	W	×
Appomattox, Ap'mattox	C	150
● *Appomattox*, Appomattox	C	75
● Aqua, Rockbridge	W	×
Aral, Carroll	SW	12
Ararat, Patrick	S	30
Arbor Hill, Augusta	W	51
Arbutus, Grayson	SW	×
● *Arcadia*, Botetourt	W	×
Arcanum, Buckingham	C	×
Archie, Culpepper	N	×
Arch Mills, Botetourt	W	×
Arco, Warren	N	×
Arcola, Loudoun	N	20
Ark, Gloucester	E	×
Arkton, (see Oakwood)		×
Arlington, Alexandria	N	500
● *Arlington*, Alexandria	N	×
● *Armistead*, Norfolk	SE	×
Armstrong, Bath	W	×
Arringdale, Sussex	SE	×
● Arrington, Nelson	C	208
Arritt's, Alleghany	W	12
Artrip, Russell	SW	×
Arvon, (see Arvonia)		×
● Arvonia, Buckingham	C	×
Asberry's, Tazewell	SW	12
Ashby, Cumberland	E	25
● *Ashby*, Warren	N	24
● Ashcake, Hanover	C	×
Ash Grove, Fairfax	N	48
● Ashland, Hanover	C	948
Aspen Wall, Charlotte	S	75
Assamoosick, Southamp'n	SE	10
Assawoman, Accomack	E	×
Athos, Orange	C	×
● ***Atkins Junc.***, Mecklenb'gh	S	25
● Atkin's Tank, Smyth	SW	25
Atlantic, Accomack	E	80
Atlantic City, (see Norfolk)		×
Atlas, Pittsylvania	S	×
● Atlee, Hanover	C	50
Auburn, Fauquier	N	120
Auburn Mills, Hanover	C	30
● *Augusta Springs*, Aug'sta	W	20
● Austinville, Wythe	SW	×
Ava, Dickenson	SW	12
Avalon, Northumberland	E	×
Averett, Mecklenburgh	S	12
Avis, Augusta	W	18
Avon, Nelson	C	18
Axtell, Buckingham	C	×
● Axton, Henry	S	50
Ayres, Scott	SW	×
Aylett's, King William	E	150
Bachelors Hall, Pittsylvania	S	40
● Backbone, Alleghany	W	30
● *Back Creek*, Roanoke	SW	×
Back Creek, (see Gore)		×
Bacon's Castle, Surry	SE	30
Bagby, Caroline	C	×
Bagley's Mills, Lunenburgh	S	×
● *Bailey*, Lee	SW	6
● *Baileys*, Tazewell	SW	×
Bailey'sCrossRoads, Fairfax	N	106
Baileyville, Charlotte	S	×
Baker's Mills, Rockingham	N	×
Baker Mines, Carroll	SW	×
Bakersville, Mecklenburg	S	×
● Balcony Falls, Rockbri'e	W	200
Baldwin Sta., Botetourt	W	×
Ballard, Patrick	S	×
● *Balls Siding*, Montg'ery	SW	×
Ballston, Alexandria	N	200
● Ballsville, Powhattan	C	75
Balty, Caroline	C	×
Bandana, Hanover	C	×
Bane, Giles	SW	12
Bangs, (see Cambria)	SW	×
Banks, Essex	E	×
Banister, Pittsylvania	S	6
Banner, Wise	SW	×
Baptist Valley, Tazewell	TW	40
Barbee's Cross Roads (see Hume)		×
● Barboursville, Orange	C	200
Barhamsville, New Kent	E	25
● *Barksdale's*, Halifax	S	25
Barley, Greensville	S	20
Barnesville, Charlotte	S	30
Barnett, Russell	SW	×
● Barren Springs, Wythe	SW	×
Barrow's Mill, Henry	S	25
Barrow's Store, Brunswick	S	50
Bartee, Norfolk	SE	×
Barterbrook, Augusta	W	×
● *Bartonville*, Frederick	N	×
Basham, Floyd	SW	8
● *Basic*, Augusta	W	×
● Basic City, Augusta	W	1,000
● Baskerville, Mecklenburg	S	×
Basses, Halifax	S	12
● *Basset*, Henry	S	×
Bateman, Patrick	S	19
Batesville, Albemarle	E	150
Bath Alum, Bath	W	24
Batten, Isle of Wight	SE	×
Battery, Essex	E	×
Battery, Mathews	E	×
Battle Hill, Roanoke	SW	×
● Bayard, Warren	N	24
Bayford, Northampton	E	×
Baylor, Augusta	W	×
● *Baylor*, Caroline	C	×
Baynesville, Westmoreland	E	30
Bay Port, Middlesex	E	25
Bay Side, Princess Anne	S	×
Bay View, Northampton	E	50
● Beach, Chesterfield	C	×
Beale's Wharf, Westm'rl'nd	E	×
● *Bealeton*, Fauquier	N	75
● Beamon, Nansemond	SE	×
Bear Lithia Springs, Rockingham	N	×
Bear Wallow, Buchanan	SW	18
Beauford, Floyd	SW	×
● Beaver Dam Depot, Hav'r	C	100
Beaver Dam Mills, Hanover	C	×
Beaver Pond, Amelia	C	25
Bedford Alum Springs, Bedford	C	×
● Bedford City, Bedford	C	2,897
Bedford Springs, Campbell	C	25
Bee, Dickinson	SW	100
Beech Springs, Lee	SW	30
Beesville, Buckingham	C	7
Belfast Mills, Russell	SW	25
● Belfield, Greensville	S	493
Belgrade, Shenandoah	N	×
Belinda, Accomack	E	30
Belle Hampton, Pulaski	SW	25
Belle Haven, Accomack	E	200
● *Belle Isle*, Chesterfield	C	×
Belle Roi, Gloucester	E	20
Belleville, Nansemond	SE	50
● Bellevue, Bedford	C	30
● *Bellews*, Shenandoah	N	×
Belfair Mills, Stafford	N	18
Bells, Bedford	C	×
Bell's Cross Roads, Louisa	C	25
● Bell's Valley, Rockbridge	W	30
Bellwood Mills, Lancaster	E	30

Post Office	Pop.
Belmont, Spotsylvania......C	18
● *Belmont Park*, Loudoun..N	×
● Belona, Powhatan........C	10
Belsches, Sussex...........SE	×
● *Belspring*, Pulaski......SW	×
Ben, Allegheny.............W	12
Benefit, Norfolk.......... SE	×
Benhams, Washington....SW	10
● *Benham*, Washington..SW	×
Bennett's Creek, Na'se'md.SE	15
Bennett's Mill, Mo'tgo'erySW	24
Bent Creek, Appomattox... C	75
● *Bentiroglio*, Warren......C	24
Bent Mountain, Roanoke.SW	10
● Bentonville, Warren......N	200
Beraer, Stafford............N	×
Berger's Store, (see Toshen)..	×
● Berkley, Norfolk........SE	3,899
● *Berkley Junc.*, Norfolk.SE	×
Berlin, Southampton......SE	50
● Bermuda Hundred, Chr'ldC	15
Berry's, Clarke.............N	×
● **Berryville**, Clarke....N	1,500
● Bertha, Wythe..........SW	×
Berton, Giles............ SW	×
Bess, Allegheny...........W	12
Bessemer, Botetourt.......W	×
Bestland, Essex.............E	400
Bethel, (see Proffitt).........	×
● *Bethel*, Bedford...........C	×
Bethel Academy, Fauquier.N	55
● *Betty Baker*, Carroll....SW	×
Beulahville, King William..E	20
Bibb, Louisa............... C	×
● Bickley's Mills, Russell.SW	75
Big Branch, Scott........ SW	12
● Big Cut, Scott............SW	×
● Big Island, Bedford.......C	100
Big Rock, Buchanan......SW	×
BigSpring Depot, (see Elliston)	×
● Big Stone Gap, Wise....SW	350
● Big Tunnel, Montgom'rySW	×
Binford's Brunswick........S	×
Binn's Church, (see Candy Island	×
Binn's Hall, Charles City....E	×
Binwell, Henrico............C	×
Birch, Dickenson..........SW	×
● Birdsnest, Northampton..E	50
Blackberry, Henry..........S	30
BlackBranch, (seeKemysv'le)	×
Black Heath, Chesterfield..C	15
Black Lick, Wythe........SW	30
Black Rock Springs, Aug'taW	×
Black Round, (seeMachodoc)	×
Blacksburgh, Mo'tgomery SW	700
Black's Ridge, Mecklenburg.S	5
● Blackstone, Nottoway.... S	580
● Black Walnut, Halifax....S	50
● *Black Water*, Franklin... S	×
Black Water, Lee.........SW	25
Black Water, (see Land of Promise)................	×
Blackwells, NorthumberlandE	×
● *Blair's Park*, Albemarle..C	×
Blakes, Matthews...........E	×
Bland, C. H. Bland.....SW	00
Blandford, (see Petersburg).	×
Blanton's, Caroline..........C	24
● *Blanton*, Hanover........C	×
● *Blanton's* Cumberland...E	×
Blenheim, Albemarle.......C	×
Bliss, (see Cliff Mills)..........	×
Bloomfield, Loudoun........N	75
Bloomfield, (see Slate Mills)..	×
Bloomsburgh, (see South Boston)	×
● *Bloom's Grove* PrinceWmN	×
● Bloomtown, Accomack...E	×
Blossom Hill, PrincessAnne SE	25
● Bloxom, Accomack.......E	100
Bluegrass, Russell..........SW	60
● *Blue Ridge*, Augusta..... W	×
● Blue Ridge Springs, B'et'tW	300
Blue Spring Run, Allegha'y. W	12
Blue Stone, Tazewell......SW	30
Blue Stone Junction, Tazewell...................SW	×
● Bluff City, Giles........ SW	×
● *Bluff Siding*, Augusta... W	×
Bobs, Isle of Wight........SE	×
Bocock, Campbell...........C	8
Body Camp, Bedford........C	30
Boggs Wharf, Accomack....E	15
Bohannon, Mathews........E	×
Bolar, Bath.................W	12
Bolington, Loudoun........N	30

Virginia

Post Office	Pop.
● *Bolling Hall*, Goochland..C	×
Bolt, Carroll...............SW	12
Bolton, Rusell............ SW	15
● *Bolton*, Nelson.......... C	×
● Bon Air, Chesterfield..... C	250
Bonbrook, Franklin........ S	25
● Bonsack's Roanoke.....SW	80
Booker, Sussex.............SE	×
● Boone Mill, Franklin.....S	30
Booneville, Albemarle...... C	×
Boonsborough, Bedford.....C	×
Boon's Path, Lee..........SW	10
Borden, Shenandoah.......N	×
Borneo, Greene.............C	×
Borthwick, Dinwiddie...... S	×
● *Boscobel*, Goochland......C	30
Boston, Culpeper...........N	30
● *Boston*, Halifax...........S	1,789
Bostwick, Dinwiddie........S	×
Boswell's Cumberland......E	5
Boswell, Hanover..........C	5
● *Boswell Station*, FluvannaC	10
Botetourt, Botetourt.......W	×
Botetourt Springs, (see Hollins).......................	×
● Bothwell, Hanover........C	×
Boulevard, New Kent.......E	×
● *Boulton*, Henrico.........C	×
Bowden, Halifax............S	×
Bowers, Southampton.....SE	50
● Bowers Hill, Norfolk....SE	50
Bowler's Wharf, Essex......E	40
Bowlesville, Albemarle......C	25
Bowling Green, CarolineC	511
● *Bowlings*, Augusta.......W	×
Bowling's Landing, (see Payne's)................	×
Bowman's Shenandoah..... N	×
Boxwood, Floyd.......... SW	×
● Boyce, Clark..............N	250
Boyd's Tavern, Albemarle.. C	45
● **Boydton**, Mecklenburg.S	400
Boyer's Ferry, Grayson...SW	×
● Boykins, Southampton.. SE	250
Bradley's Store, Charles CityE	12
Bradshaw, Roanoke.......SW	30
Bradshaw's Mills, Southampton....................SE	×
● *Brambleton*, P'nc's An'e.SE	×
● Branchville, Southamp'nSE	65
● *Brand*, Augusta..........W	×
Brand, Page.................N	×
Brandon, Prince George...SE	50
Brandy, Culpeper..........N	×
● Brandy Station, Culpeper.N	200
Brandywine, Caroline.......C	10
Brays, Essex................E	×
Brayton, Greene............C	×
Breckenridge, (seeEagle Rock)	×
● Bremo Bluff, Fluvanna...C	25
Brentsville, Prince Wil'mN	100
Brewster, Russell......... SW	12
Brian, Louisa...............C	×
Brick Haven, Alexandria...N	×
Brick Store, Lee..........SW	10
● *Bridgeport*, Buckingham.C	×
Bridgetown, Northampton..E	75
Bridgewater, Rockingham..N	1,000
Bridle Creek, Grayson....SW	40
Brierfield, Bedford..........C	×
Briery, Prince Edward......C	12
Briggs, Clark...............N	30
Brighton, Northampton.....E	30
Brights, Pittsylvania........S	10
Brink, Greensville..........S	30
Brio, Carroll..............SW	×
Brinkley's, Nansemond... SE	×
Bristersburgh, Fauquier....N	25
● Bristoe, Prince William..N	60
● Bristol, Washington.... SW	2,902
Brittain, Loudoun..........N	×
Broadford, Smyth.........SW	60
● Broad Run Station Fauq'rN	75
Broad Shoals, Floyd...... SW	24
Broadwater, Northampton..E	30
● Broadway, Rockingham..N	497
● Brockroad, Spotsylvania..C	16
Brock's Gap, (see Coote's Store)......................	×
● Brodnax, Brunswick..... S	×
Brokenburgh, Spotsylvania. C	12
Brompton, Spotsylvania.... C	×
● Brooke, Stafford..........N	18
Brookewood, Augusta......W	×
Brook Hill, Henrico.........C	×
Brookings, Goochland...... C	×
Brooklyn, Halifax...........S	30
● Brook Neal, Campbell....C	40

Virginia

Post Office	Pop.
Brosville, Pittsylvania.......S	50
Brow, Pittsylvania..........S	×
● *Brown's*, Albemarle...... C	30
Brownburg, (see Mechum's River)......................	×
Brownsburgh, Rockbridge. W	237
Brown's Cove, Albemarle... C	×
Brown's Store, Northumb'l'dE	49
Browntown, Warren........N	400
● *Bruce*, Norfolk..........SE	×
Bruce, Rockingham........N	×
Brucetown, Frederick......N	300
Brugh's Mill, Botetourt.... W	42
Bruington, King & Queen...E	15
Bruiton, York............. E	50
Brumfield, Russell........SW	×
Brumley Gap, WashingtonSW	12
Brutus, Pittsylvania.........S	×
Bryant, Nelson.............C	×
● Buchanan, Botetourt.....W	802
● *Buchanan Station*, Bote'tW	×
Buckeye, Highland.........W	×
Buckhall, Prince William.. N	30
● Buckhorn, Nansemond..SE	100
Buckingham, C. H., Buckingham.................C	300
Buckland, Prince William..N	60
● Buckner's Station, Louisa.C	20
● Buckton, Warren.........N	25
Bucu, Dickenson..........SW	18
● Buena Vista, RockbridgeW	1,044
● Buffalo Forge, RockbridgeW	40
● Buffalo Gap, Augusta.....W	60
● Buffalo Junction, M'kl'n'gS	×
● Buffalo Lithia Spr'gs, Mecklenburg..................S	25
Buffalo Mills, Rockbridge..W	132
Buffalo Ridge, Patrick......S	40
Buffalo RidgeSpr'gs, Amh'stC	30
● Buffalo Station, Nelson...C	30
Buford, Belford............C	×
● *Buford*, Pittsylvania.....S	×
Bufordville, Bedford........C	40
Bula, Goochland............C	25
Bull Run, Fairfax..........N	5
● Bumpass, Louisa.........C	40
Bundick, Northumberland..E	×
Bunker Hill, Bedford.......C	30
● *Bunting*, Norfolk....... SE	×
Burcham, Carroll......... SW	35
● *Burfords*, Pittsylvania.... S	10
● *Burgess*, Chesterfield.....C	×
Burgess, Dinwiddie..........S	12
Burgess Store, N'th'mberl'dE	50
● *Burke*, Botetourt.........W	×
Burke's Garden, Tazewell.SW	960
Burke's Mills, Augusta.....W	50
● Burke's Station, Fairfax..N	25
● Burksville, Nottoway..... S	401
Burk's Fork, Floyd....... SW	15
● Burnleys, Albemarle.....C	×
Burnsville, Bath............W	25
● *Burnt Chimney*, Henry... S	20
Burr Hill, Orange...........C	10
Burrowsville, PrinceGe'rge SE	60
Burton's Creek, Campbell...C	24
Burts, Sussex..............SE	×
Burwell's Bay, Isle of W'htSE	20
Burwellville, Pittsylvania... C	10
Bush Park, Cumberland.... E	18
Bushy, Middlesex........... E	25
Butler's Hole, (see Westland)	×
Bybee, Fluvanna............C	30
Byrdville, Pittsylvania...... S	120
Byron, Bland..............SW	5
Cabbage Farm, MecklenburgS	5
Cabell, Carroll............SW	×
Cabin Hill, Shenandoah.....N	50
Cabin Point, Surry.........SE	20
Caddo, Pittsylvania..........S	10
● *Cady*, Hanover............C	×
Caha, Carroll............ SW	15
Ca Ira, Cumberland.........E	30
Caledonia, Goochland.......C	20
Calico Rock, Franklin......S	×
California, Rockbridge.... W	×
● Callaghan's, Allegheny...W	75
Callands, Pittsylvania........S	60
Callaville, Brunswick........S	5
Callaway's, Franklin........ S	40
Callison, Bath.............. W	×
Calvary, Shenandoah........N	12
● Calverton, Fauquier......N	×
Cambed, Campbell..........C	×
Cambria, Montgomery....SW	200
Cameron, Scott...........SW	×
● *Cameron*, Fairfax........ S	×

Camm, Buckingham........C ×
Camp, Smyth.............SW 12
●Campbell, Albemarle.....C ×
Camp Creek, Floyd.......SW 8
Cana, Carroll.............SW ×
Canon Carroll.............SW ×
Canova, Prince William.... N ×
Canterburg, Frederick..... N ×
Cany Hollow, Lee.........SW ×
Cape Henry, Princess AnneSE ×
●Cape Charles, Northampt'nE 700
Capeville, Northampton.... E 50
Cap, Carroll.............SW ×
●CaponRoadDepot, Sh'n'd'h N 40
Cappahosic, Gloucester......E 100
●Capron, Southampton... SE ×
Captain, Craig.............W ×
Cardwell, Goochland........C ×
●Carlins, Alexandria.......N ×
Carlton's Store, King&QueenE 25
Carmel, Shenandoah........N ×
●*Carnegie City*, M't'g'm'rySW 65
Carolina, (see Glen Wilton).. ×
Carrollton, Isle of Wight...SE 25
●Carrsville, Isle of Wight.SE 50
Carsley, Surry.............SE 10
Carson, Prince George.....SE ×
Carsonville, Grayson......SW 6
Carter's Bridge, Albemarle..C 24
Carter's Creek, (see Irvington) ×
Carter's Island, Bedford.... C ×
Carter's Mills, Patrick..... S 18
Cartersville, Cumberland... E 175
Cartersville, Powhattan......C 10
Carter's Wharf, Richmond. N 30
Carterton, Russell........ SW ×
Cartwright's Wharf, Nansemond.................SE 25
Cary's, Southampton......SE 5
Carysbrook, Fluvanna...... C 24
●Casanova, Fauquier....... N 20
●Cascade, Pittsylvania......S 125
●*Cascade Junc.*, Pittsyvania S ×
●*Casey's*, Campbell........ C ×
Cashville, Accomack ....E 21
Castle Craig, Campbell...... C 10
Castleman's Ferry, Clarke..N 45
Castleton, Rappahannock...N 12
●*Castlewood*, Russell.... SW ×
Cassell, (see Rocky Mount) .. ×
Castor, Pittsylvania........ S ×
Catawba, (see Barksdale).... ×
Catawba, Roanoke........ SW 24
●*Catawba*, Botetour........ W ×
Catharpin, Prince William..N 12
●Catlett, Fauquier.........N 100
Catron, Wythe........... SW ×
Cavatts, Tazewell.........SW ×
Cave Spring, Roanoke.... SW 80
●*Cave Station*, Augusta... W 200
Cavoona, Westmoreland....E ×
●Cedar Bluff, Tazewell... SW 75
CedarCreek, (seeHealing Sprs) ×
●*Cedar Creek*, Frederick.. N 30
Cedar Creek, Shenandoah...N 25
Cedar Forest, Pittsylvania...S 15
Cedar Fork, (seeRuther Glen) ×
Cedar Grove, Frederick..... N 10
Cedar Grove Ms, (see Rockbridge Baths)............. ×
●**Cedar Hill, Pittsylvania...S** 12
●Cedar Point, Page........N 56
Cedar Point, Goochland.... C [illegible]
Cedar Springs, Wythe.....SW 46
Cedar View, Sussex........SE [illegible]
●Cedarville, Warren...... . N 80
Centenary, Buckingham.... C 30
Center Mills, Montgomery SW 48
Central Depot, (see Radford). ×
●Centralia, Chesterfield.... C 20
Central Plains, Fluvanna....C 45
Central Point, Caroline......C 20
Centre Cross, Essex..........E 75
Centreville, (see Bedford City) ×
Centreville, Fairfax..........N 60
Centreville, King & Queen.. E 40
●*Centreville*, Norfolk..... SE 30
Centreville, (see Emmerton).. ×
Centreville, (see Oak Grove).. ×
Ceres, Bland..............SW 55
Chalk Level, Pittsylvania.....S 25
Chalybeate Springs, Scott SW ×
Chambersville, Frederick...N 24
Chamblissburgh, Bedford... C 25
Chandler, Lee..............SW 72
Chaney's, Pittsylvania.......S ×
Chantilly, Fairfax.......... N 30
Chap, Appomattox.........C 24
●*Chapin*, Augusta......... W ×
Chappahosie, Gloucester... E ×
Charity, Patrick.............S 12
Charity Neck, (see Pleasant Ridge)................... ×
Charlemont, Bedford....... C 30
Charles City, Charles City E 100
Charlie Hope, Brunswick... S 15
●**Charlottesville**, Albemarle..........C 5,591
●Chase City, Mecklenburg..S 618
Chase's Wharf, Lancaster... E 12
●*Chatham*, Princess Anne SE ×
●**Chatham**, Pittsylvania..S 757
Chatham, Stafford..........N ×
Chatham Hill, Smyth..... SW 25
Cheapside, Northampton....E 50
Check, Floyd..............SW 30
Cherokee, Henry............S ×
●Cherriton, Northampton..E 50
Cherry Grove, Rockingham N 30
●*Cherry Hill*, Pr'ce Will'm N 10
Cherrystone, Northampton. E 40
Chesapeake, Lancaster......E ×
Chesapeake, Northampton..E ×
Chesapeake City, (seePhœbus) ×
Chesconnessex, Accomack E 15
●Chester, Chesterfield....... C 10
Chesterfield, Chesterfield C 60
Chestnut, Amherst..........C ×
Chestnut Fork, Bedford.... C 150
Chestnut Grove, (see Whitmel) ×
Chestnut Level, Pittsylvania S 10
Childress, Montgomery... SW 25
Chilesburgh, Caroline....... C 25
●Chilhowie, Smyth.......SW 150
Chiltons, Westmoreland.... E 30
Chincoteague Island, Ac'ack E 210
Chrisman, Rockingham.... N 55
●*Christian's*, Augusta..... W ×
●**Christianburgh**, Montgomery..............SW 900
●*Christians Mills*, Pr. An.SE 150
Christie, Halifax............ S ×
Chuckatuck, Nansemond..SE 100
●Chula Depot, Amelia.......C 45
●Churchland, Norfolk.... SE 250
●Church Road, Dinwiddie..S 15
Church View, Middlesex....E 40
Churchville, Augusta.......W 80
Churchwood, Pulaski..... SW 346
Cifax, Bedford..............C ×
●City Point, PrinceGeorge SE 409
●Claremont, Surry........SE 400
●*Claremont Wharf*, SurrySE ×
Claresville, Greensville.......S 50
●Clarks, Wythe.......... SW ×
●*Clark's*, Henrico......... C ×
●Clark's Gap, Loudoun.... N 20
Clarkson, Culpeper........ N ×
●Clarksville, Mecklenburg. S 656
●Clarkton, Halifax......... S 10
●*Clay*, Bedford............ C ×
Clay Bank, Gloucester...... E 40
Clay's Mills, Halifax.........S 30
●Clear Brook, Frederick.. N ×
Clear Fork, Bland......... SW 20
Cleek's Mills, Bath.......... W 12
Clem's Branch, Grayson.. SW 30
Cleopus, Nansemond.... .SE 50
●Cleveland, Russell......SW ×
Clevilas, Bedford.......... C ×
Clifford, Amherst..........C 210
Cliff Mills, Fauquier.........N ×
Clifton, Mecklenburg........S ×
Clifton, Russell..........SW ×
●Clifton Forge, Alleghany. W 1,792
●Clifton Station, Fairfax.. N 150
Clinch, Scott..............SW 30
●Clinchport, Scott....... SW ×
Clinch River, Scott........SW 30
●*Clinch ValleyJunc.*, Taz'lSW ×
Clinton, Cumberland........E 24
Clintwood, Dickenson..SW 150
Clip, Washington..........SW ×
Clito, Grayson.............SW ×
Clover Creek, Highland.... W 15
●Cloverdale, Botetourt.... W 40
●*Cloverdale*, Pittsylvania...S ×
●Clover Depot, Halifax.....S 422
Clover Hill, Rockingham.... N 99
Clover Hill, Chesterfield.....C 97
Clung, Carroll..............SW ×
Coakley's, Stafford..........N 24
●*Coalboro*, Chesterfield....C ×
Coal Creek, Carroll..... . SW 30
●*Coalfield*, Chesterfield.....C 240
Coal Hill, Henrico..........C 12
Coan Wharf, NorthumberlandE ×
Coates, Louisa.......... C ×
●*Cobbs*, Northampton.......E ×
Cobb's Creek, Mathews..... E 55
●*CobbsCrossing*, Pittsylvania S ×
Cob's Island, Northampton E ×
●Cobham, Albemarle.......C 35
Cocks Mills, (see Marysville). ×
Coddyshore, Sussex.......SE ×
●Coeburn, Wise..........SW 30
Cody, Halifax.............. S 30
Coffee, Bedford............ C 35
●Cohoke, King William.... E 15
Colburn, (see Guest's Station) ×
Cold Harbor, Hanover...... C ×
Cold Spring, Carroll.......SW 10
●Coleman's Falls, Bedford. C 36
Colemansville, (seeCumberl'dCH) ×
Cole's, (see Horton's Store) ×
Cole's Bluff, Westmoreland E ×
Cole's Ferry, Charlotte..... S 40
Cole's Point, Westmoreland E ×
Colesville, Patrick...........S 12
Colina, Dinwiddie...........S ×
Colleen, Nelson............ C ×
Colley, Dickenson..........SW 54
Collierstown, Rockbridge.. W 500
Collingwood Beach, (see Mt. Vernon) .... ×
Collins' Mill, Grayson......SW 8
Collinsville, Frederick......N 12
ColonialBeach, WestmorelandE 30
●Columbia, Fluvanna...... C 238
Columbia Furnace, Shen'ah N [illegible]
Columbian Grove, Lun'urgh. S 45
Colvin Run, Fairfax........N 12
Coman's Well, Sussex.......SE 15
Comer's Rock, Grayson...SW 8
Comet, Isle of Wight...... SE ×
Comorn, King George...... E 20
Compton, Page.......... N ×
●Concord Depot, Campbell.C 150
Conklin, Loudoun.......... N ×
Conrad's Mills, Middlesex...E 10
Consent, Patrick............S ×
Constoel, Pittsylvania....... S 8
Contra, King & Queen......E ×
Cook, Carroll..............SW ×
●*Cool Spring*, Spotsylvania. C ×
●Cool Well, Amherst.......C 15
Coonseye, Wise.............SW ×
Coonsville, Bedford........ C 24
Cooper, Middlesex......... E ×
Cooper Hill, Floyd........SW ×
Coote's Store, Rockingham.N 30
●Copeland, Nansemond...SE ×
●*Copeland*, Bath.......... W ×
Copper Hill, Floyd.........SW 25
Copper Valley, Floyd..... SW 12
Corbin, Caroline.......... C ×
Cordova, Culpeper..........N ×
Corinth, Lee.............. SW ×
Corleyville, Roanoke......SW ×
Cornland, Norfolk.........SE ×
Cornsville, Scott.......... SW 30
Costenbader's Mills, (see Potomac Mills).............. ×
●Cornwall, Rockbridge... W ×
Cotman, Henrico............C ×
Cotopaxi, Augusta......... W ×
Cottontown, (see Adriance).. ×
Coulson, Carroll.......... SW ×
Counts, Russell........... SW ×
CountyLineCr.Rds., CharlotteS 36
CountyLine Mills, (seeCascade) ×
●**Courtland**, Southamp'nSE 200
Cove Creek, Tazewell......SW 38
●Covesville, Albemarle......C 60
●**Covington**, Allegheny. W 704
●Cowan's Depot, Rocking'm N 7
Cowan's Mills, MontgomerySW 30
Cowardin, Bath.......... W ×
Cowart, Northumberland.. W ×
●*Cowherd*, Orange......... C ×
Cox, Lee.................. SW ×
Coynee, Botetort..........SW ×
Coyner's Springs, BotetourtW 20
Crabbottom, Highland......W ×
Crab Neck, York..........E 10
Crab Orchard, Lee..........SW 12
Craddockville, Accomack...E 20
Craft, Scott..............SW ×
Craig City, Craig.......... W ×
Craig's Creek, Craig........W 18
Craig's Mills, Washington.SW 12

●Craigsville, Augusta...W 75
●*Crane*, Bath...W ×
Crane's Nest, Dickenson..SW ×
Cranks, Louisa...C ×
Crawford, Franklin...S ×
Creeds, Princess Anne...SE ×
Cremona, Cumberland...E ×
Creola, Grayson...SW ×
Crest, Stafford...N ×
Creswell, Russell...SW 30
●Crewe, Nottoway...S 887
Crichton, Brunswick...S ×
Crickett Hill, Mathews...E 500
Crider's, Rockingham... N 80
Criglersville, Madison...N 60
●Crimora Station, Augusta W ×
Cripple Creek, Wythe...SW 500
●*CrippleCreekJunc.*, P'l'kiSW ×
Cristle, Halifax...S ×
Crittenden's, Nansemond..SE 20
●Critz, Patrick...S ×
●Crockett Depot, Wythe...S 100
Crooked Run, Culpeper...N 30
Crosby, Campbell...C 30
●*Crossing*, Fairfax... N ×
Cross Junction, Frederick..N 25
Cross Keys, Rockingham... N 55
Cross Roads, Halifax... S 24
Cross Roads, (see Keezletown) ×
Crouch, King & Queen...E ×
Crowder, (see Cornwall) ... ×
Crowder's, Goochland... C ×
Crow Spring, Chesterfield...C 24
Croxton, Caroline...C ×
●Crozet, Albemarle... C 18
Cruey, Smyth...SW ×
Cruise, Patrick...S 12
Cruzen, Loudoun... N 30
Crystal, Bedford...C ×
●Crystal Hill, Halifax... S 12
Crystal Springs, Roanoke SW ×
Cub Creek, Charlotte...S 30
Cuckoo, Louisa...C 15
●**Culpeper**, Culpeper... N 1,620
●**Cumberland C. H.**, Cumberland...E 100
Cumbow, Lee... SW 12
Cumnor, King & Queen...E ×
Curdsville, Buckingham... C 100
Curtis, Bedford... C ×
●Curve, Giles...SW 24
Cuscowilla, Mecklenburg...S 30
Cynthia, Lee... SW ×
●Cypress Chapel, N'sem'nd SE 10
Dabney's, Louisa...C 8
Daggers, Botetourt... W 12
Dalby's, Northampton... E 20
Dale Enterprise, Rockl'gh'm N 60
Daleville, Botetourt...W 45
Dalzell, Campbell...C ×
Damascus, Washington... SW 30
Damon, Albemarle...C 54
Dan, Franklin...S 30
Daniel, Campbell... C 838
Daniel, Orange...C 838
●*Dan River*, Pittsylvania...S ×
Danton, Orange... C 2
●Danville, Pittsylvania...S 10,305
●*Danville and New River Junction*, Pittsylvania...S 24
Darlington Heights, Pr'ceEd.C ×
Darvill's, Dinwiddie...S 10
Darwin, Dickenson... SW ×
Daugherty, Accomack... E 30
●*Daughry*, Nansemond...SE ×
Davenport, Buchanan...SW ×
●Davis, Rockbridge... W ×
Davis Mills, Bedford... C 30
Davis Wharf, Accomack...E 30
Dawn, Caroline...C ×
●*Dawson*, Hanover... C 20
Dawsonville, Greene... C 30
Daysville, Loudoun... N ×
Dayton, Rockingham...N 350
Deane, (see Brayton)... ×
Deane's, Nansemond...SE ×
Deatonsville, Amelia...C 100
●*Decatur*, Rockbridge... W ×
Deep Creek, Norfolk... SE 300
Deerfield, Augusta... W 20
Dehaven, Frederick... N ×
●Delaplane, Fauquier...N 125
●Delaware's, Southampton SE 15
Della, Halifax... S 30
Dell, Grayson...SW ×
Delos, Caroline...C ×
Delphi, Lee...SW 12

Virginia

●Delton, Pulaski...SW ×
Denaro, Amelia...C ×
Denbigh, Warwick...E 150
Dendron, Surry...SE ×
Denmark, Rockbridge...N 25
●Denniston Junc., Halifax. S ×
Derby, Prince George... SE ×
Design, Pittsylvania...S 15
●*Deyerle*, Roanoke...SW ×
Diamond Grove, Brunswick.S ×
Diana Mills, Buckingham... C 15
●Diascond, James City...E 8
Dickensonville, Russell... SW 35
Dickinson's, Franklin...S 30
Dickson's Mill, Nottoway...S ×
Dido, King George...E ×
Diggs, Mathews...E ×
Dilbeck, Shenandoah... N ×
Dillards Wharf, Surry... SE ×
●*Dillon*, Botetourt... W ×
Dillon's Mills, Franklin... S 75
Dillwyn, Buckingham...C 12
Dingley, Northampton...E 30
Dinwiddie C.H., D'nwi'le S 40
●*Dispatch*, New Kent...E 5
●Disputanta, Prince Geo..SE 75
Diston, Dinwiddie...S 18
●*Ditchley*, Fairfax...N ×
Dix, Warren...N ×
Dobyn's, Patrick...S ×
Dodd's, Stafford...N ×
Dodson, Patrick...S ×
Doe Hill, Highland... W 100
Dooms, Augusta...W 12
Dora, Dickenson...SW ×
Dorado, Russell... SW 48
●Doran, Tazewell... SW ×
Dorcas, Augusta...W ×
Dorset, Powhatan... C 19
Double Bridge, Linnenburgh S ×
Douglas, Lee... SW 24
Dover, Loudoun...N 24
●Dover Mines, Goochland..C 100
Dovesville, Rockingham...N 15
Downing, Warren...N ×
Downing's, Richmond...E 20
Doylesville, Albemarle...C ×
DragonOrdinary, Gloucester E 5
Dragonville, King & Queen.E 30
●Drake's Branch, Charlotte S 150
Dranesville, Fairfax...N 18
●Draper's Valley, Pulaski SW 15
Drapersville, Mecklenburgh.S 25
Drauckers, Nottoway...S ×
Dreka, Accomack...E 30
Drenn, Carroll...SW ×
●Drewry's Bluff, Chester'd.C 10
●Drewyville, Southam'n..SE 20
●Driver, Nanemond... SE 10
Drumgoole's Store, Brunsw'k S 10
●*Drummond*, Nansemond SE ×
●*Dry Branch*, Pulaski. ×SW ×
Dry Bridge, Chesterfield...C ×
Dryburgh, Halifax...S 30
●Dryden, Lee...SW ×
●Dry Fork Depot, Pittsy'a..S 10
●Dublin, Pulaski...SW 410
Duck Race, (see White Hall). ×
Ducksville, Isle of Wight..SE ×
●Duffield, Scott...SW ×
Dug Spur, Carroll...SW 25
Dulany, Floyd...SW ×
Dulinsville, Madison...N 35
Dumbarton, Henrico...C ×
Dumfries, King William...E 100
Dump's Creek, Russell...SW 12
●*Duncan*, Norfolk...SE ×
Duncan's Floyd...SW 10
Duncan's Mills, Scott...SW 10
Dundee, Bedford...C 24
Dungannon, Scott...SW 50
●*Dunlop*, Alleghany...W 75
Dunn Loring, Fairfax...N ×
Dunnsville, Essex...E 100
Dumprees, Charlotte...S 18
●*Durand*, Greenville...S ×
●Durmid, Campbell...C 10
●Dutch Creek, Nelson...C 20
Duty, Dickenson...SW ×
Dwina, Wise...SW 24
Dyer's Store, Henry...S 70
Eagle Furnace, Wythe...SW ×
●Eagle Rock, Botetourt...W 223
Eakin, Craig...W ×
Eanes' Cross Roads, Br'w'k.S 10
Earls, Amelia...C ×
Early Grove, Scott...SW 24

Virginia

Early, Albemarle...C ×
Earlysville, Albemarle...C 75
●*East BigStoneGap*, Wise SW ×
Eastern Branch, Norfolk.SE ×
East End, Alexandria...N ×
Eastham, Albemarle...C 24
●*East Lexington*, Rock'h'm N ×
East Lynchburgh, Campbell C ×
●East Radford, Mo'gom'y SW 2,060
East Richmond, Henrico...C ×
East Stone Gap, Wise...SW ×
East View, Floyd...SW 12
●**Eastville**, Northampton E 350
Eastville Sta., Northampton.E ×
Ebony, Brunswick...S 5
Eckington, Culpeper...N ×
Eddy, Franklin...S ×
●Edenburgh, Shenandoah..N 512
Edge Hill, King George...E 30
●Edgerton, Brunswick...S ×
Edgewater, Grayson...SW 24
Edith, Shenandoah...N 24
Edmund's Store, Brunswick S 25
Edom, Rockingham...N 40
●*Edsalls*, Fairfax...N ×
Edville, (see Ore Bank)...C ×
Edvine, Henrico...C ×
Edwards, Carroll...SW ×
Edwardsville, (see Taylor's Store)... ×
Effna, Bland...SW ×
Eggbornsville, Culpeper...N 24
●Eggleston, Giles...SW 60
Ego, Floyd...SW ×
Eheart, Orange...C ×
●*Eighty-Seven Mile Siding*, Dinwiddie...S ×
Ela, Scott...SW 21
Elamsville, Patrick...S 50
●*Elba*, Henrico...C ×
●Elba, Pittsylvania...S 250
Elbo, Powhatan...C 60
Elcomb, Lunenburgh...S ×
Eldridge's Mills, Buckingham C 10
Elect, Pittsylvania...S ×
●*Elgin*, Page...N 75
Elijah, Patrick...S ×
●*ElizabethP'rk*, Prin.An'e SE ×
Elk Creek, Grayson...SW 55
Elk Garden, Russell...SW 200
●Elk Hill, Goochland...C 50
Elk Island, Goochland...C 50
●Elko, Henrico...C 18
Elk Run, Faquier...N 50
Elk Spur, Carroll...SW ×
●Elkton, Rockingham... N 800
Ellendale, Smythe...SW 15
●Ellerson, Hanover...C 5
Ellett, Montgomery...SW 500
●Elliston, Montgomery...SW 65
Ellisville, Louisa...C 10
Elmeria, Rockbridge...W 18
●*Elmington*, Nelson...C 20
Elmo, Halifax...S ×
Elmont, Hanover...C ×
Elon, Amherst...C 18
●Elwood, Nansemond...SE ×
Ely, Lee...SW ×
Emaus, Bedford...C 25
Embrey, (see Liberty Mills).. ×
Emma, Campbell...C ×
Emerton, Richmond...E 15
Emmetts, Hanover...C ×
●Emory, Washington...SW 150
●**Emporia**, Greensville...S 595
Emporia, Washington...SW ×
Endicott, Franklin...S ×
Enfield, King William...E 70
Engleman, Rockbridge... W ×
Enoch, Middlesex...E 24
Enon, Goochland...C ×
Enonville, Buckingham...C 36
Enterprise, Southampton..SE 18
●*Eppes*, Chesterfield...C ×
●Eppes Falls, Chesterfield..C ×
Era, Dinwiddie...S 33
Erin Shades, Henrico...C 8
Ervinton, Dickenson...SW ×
Esmont, Albemarle...C 25
●*Estillville*, Scott... SW 500
Estonoa, Wise...SW ×
Etna Mills, King William...E 15
Etter, Wythe...SW ×
Ettricks, Chesterfield...C 991
Eubanks, Lancaster... ×
Eubank's Warf, (see Kil'no'k) ×
Eubor, Lunenburgh...S ×

● *Ironville*, Botetourt...... W ×
Ironside, Henry............ S 60
Irvington, Lancaster........ E 400
● Irwin, Goochland......... C 11
● *Isaacs*, Southampton ... SE 24
Isaac, Southampton....... SE ×
● Island, Goochland......... C 50
● *Island Yard*, Campbell...C ×
Isle of Wight, Isle of W.SE 10
Issequena, Goochland...... C 5
Itata, Surry................ SE ×
● *Ivanhoe*, Wythe........ SW ×
Ivanhoe, Wythe...........SW 150
Ivondale, Richmond........ E ×
Ivor, Southampton..........SE 80
● Ivy Depot, Albemarle.....C 40
Ivy Hill, Campbell.......... C 10
Jack's Mill, Floyd........ SW 12
Jackson, Louisa............. C 5
Jackson City, (see Alexandria ×
Jacksondale, Princess AnneSE ×
Jackson River Depot, (see Selma) .... ×
● *Jackson's*, Pr'cess Anne.SE ×
Jackson's Ferry, Wythe..SW 90
Jacksontown, Campbell .... C 10
Jacksonville, (see Floyd C. H.)
Jacksonville, (see Danville) .. ×
Jacobsville, Pittsylvania.....S ×
Jadwyn, Shenandoah........ N ×
Jamaica, Middlesex.........E 20
James River, Amherst.......C ×
● *James River Siding*, C'm'l C ×
● JamesRiverJc., GreensvilleS ×
James Store, Gloucester.... E 5
Jamestown, James City...... E 24
Jamesville, Northampton... E 25
Jane, Dickenson.......... SW ×
Jap, Lee.................. SW ×
● Jarratt's, Sussex .... SE 55
Jefferson, Powhattan........C 25
Jeffersonton, Culpeper.......N 200
Jeffersonville, Tazewell.... SW ×
● Jeffress, Mecklenburg.... S ×
Jeffress' Store, Nottaway....S 10
Jenkins' Bridge, Accomack E 25
Jennings Creek, Botetourt. W ×
Jennings Gap, Augusta..... W 24
● Jennings' Ordinary, Not'y S 25
Jerome, Shenandoah........ N ×
● *Jerrys*, Alleghany........W ×
Jessee's Mills, Russell .... SW 10
● Jetersville, Amelia.........C 150
● *John's*, Powhattan........C ×
John, Russells............ SW ×
Johnson, Scott............ SW ×
John's Creek, (see Simms'lle) ×
Johnson's Creek, Patrick... S 12
Johnson's Crossing, Nansemond..................... SE 12
Johnson's Springs, Goochl'd C 90
Johnsontown, Northampton E 40
Joliet's, Page.............. N ×
Jones Wharf, Surry....... SE ×
Jonesborough, Brunswick.. S 25
Jones' Point, Essex......... E 5
Jonesville, Lee .... SW 400
Joplin, Wise............. SW ×
Joppa, Bedford.............. C ×
Jordan Springs, (see Steph'n) ×
Jordan's Store, Powhattan.. C 36
Jorgenson, Lunenburgh .....S 10
Josephine City, (see Berryv'e) ×
Joshua Falls, Amherst..... C ×
Joyceville, Mecklenburg.....S 15
Judd, Brunswick.............S ×
● *Jude's Ferry*, Goochland. C ×
Judge, Dickenson..........SW ×
Jumbo, Loudoun............ N ×
Jump, Rockbridge.......... W ×
● *Junction*, Alexandria..... N ×
● *Junction*, Pittsylvania.... S ×
Junta, Franklin..............S ×
Justisville, Accomack.......E 30
Karicofe, (see Hinton) .... ×
Karl, Appomattox..........C ×
Kasey's, Bedford............C 15
● *Kayoulah*, Wythe.......SW ×
Keats, Mecklenburg..........S ×
Keeling, Pittsylvania........ S 10
Keezletown, Rockingham... N 70
● Keller, Accomack..........E 100
● *Kelley's*, Campbell........C ×
Kelleys Ford, Culpeper..... N 24
Kelly, Tazewell............ SW 250
Kelly's Mills, (seeRappah'kSta.) ×
Kelly's Store, Hanover......C 10

Kellyview, Wise...........SW ×
● *Kelton*, James City....... E ×
Kemper's Shop, (see Shade).. ×
● Kempsville, Pri'ces AnneSE 120
● *Kendall Grove*, Northa't'nE ×
Kenmore, Fairfax.......... N 10
Kennett, Franklin.......... S 30
● *Kent*, Wythe..............SW ×
Kent's Store, Fluvanna..... C 30
Kentuck, Pittsylvania.......S 15
Kerfoot, Fauquier........... N 20
● Kernstown, Frederick....N 100
Kerr's Creek, Rockbridge..W 45
● Keswick, Albemarle...... C 50
Ketron, Washington....... SW ×
Kew, Campbell..............C 8
Keysville, Charlotte......... S 300
Kidd, (see Clinchport)........ ×
Kidd's Store, Fluvanna......C ×
● *Kilby*, Hanover...........C ×
Kildee, Westmoreland...... E ×
Kilmarnock, Lancaster......E 125
● Kimball, Page............ N 75
Kimballton, Giles.........SW 12
Kimberling, Bland..........SW ×
● *King*, Augusta...........W ×
King & Queen, C. H., King & Queen........... E 25
King George, King Ge'geE 200
King's Mill, Washington.. SW 60
King William, King William .... E 45
Kinsale, Westmoreland..... E 100
Kiracofe, Augusta..........W ×
● *Kirby*, Nansemond......SE ×
Kirkland, Richmond........ E ×
Kite, Page.................. N ×
Knightly, Augusta......... W ×
Knob, Tazewell........... SW 75
Knolls, Campbell............C 36
Knox Creek, Buchanan...SW ×
Koiner's Store, Augusta....W 45
● *Korah*, Henrico.......... C ×
Koskoo, Southampton.....SE ×
Kountz, Page............... N ×
Kunath, Lunenburgh........S ×
Kyle, Botetourt............ W ×
Laban, Mathews............ E 18
Lacey Spring, Rockingham. N 75
Lackey, Henry............. S 36
Laconia, Charlotte .... S ×
● La Crosse, Mecklenburg...S 5
Ladd, Augusta.............. W ×
● *Lafayette*, Orange......... C 12
La Fayette, Montgomery..SW 100
La Cross, King William .... E 5
La Grange, King George....E ×
● *La Grange*, Augusta...... W ×
Lahore, Orange............. C 200
Laird, Dinwiddie............ S ×
Laird, (see Friford)........... ×
Lake Drummond, (see Wallaceton.......................... ×
Lake Spring, Roanoke.... SW ×
Lake View, Clarke......... N 12
Lambert, Mecklenburg......S 24
Lambsburgh, Carroll...... SW 91
Lamberts Point, (see Norfolk) ×
Lamont, Smyth............ SW ×
Lancaster C. H., Lan't'r.E 125
Lance, Stafford............ N ×
Landmark, Fauquier....... N 50
Land of Promise, Princess Anne...................... SE 10
Land's End, Warwick...... E 0
Lansdown, Prince William. N ×
Lanesville, King William... E 20
● Lanexa, New Kent........ E 20
Langley, Fairfax............N 10
Lantz Mills, Shenandoah.... N 30
Larkin's Factory, (see Madison C. H.) .... ×
Latona, Rockingham....... N ×
● *Laurel*, Henrico...........C ×
Laurel Fork, Carroll...... SW 10
Laurel Grove, Pittsylvania...S 60
Laurel Hill, Augusta....... W 30
Laurel Hill, Lunenburg.....S 5
Laurel Mills Rappaha'ock..N 50
Lawford, Buckingham......C ×
● **Lawrenceville**, Br'w'kS 305
● Lawyers, Campbell........C 40
Layman, Craig............ W 12
Layton's, Essex.............E 10
Leach, Floyd...............SW ×
Leaksville, Page............N 50
Leander, Rockingham......N ×

● Leatherwood, Henry...... S 125
Leavens, Spotsylvania...... N 18
Lebanon, Russell.......SW 310
Lebanon Church, Shenan'h. N 44
Leda, Halifax.............. S 30
● Lee, Goochland.......... C ×
Leedstown, Westmoreland..E 30
● Lee Hall, Warwick........E 12
Leeland, Stafford............N ×
Lee Mont, Accomack........ E 150
● *Lee Park*, Chesterfield....C ×
● **Leesburgh**, Loudoun.. N 1,650
● *Lee's Mills*, Nansemond.SE ×
Lee's Mills, Washington...SW 24
Leesville, Campbell..........C 40
Legg, Wise..................SW ×
Leighs, Fairfax..............N ×
Lenah, Loudoun............ N ×
● Lennig, Halifax............S ×
Leon, Madison................N 42
Leplo, Washington........SW 36
Leroy, Rockingham......... N 25
Leslie, Roanoke.......... SW 12
● LesterManor, KingWilliamE 116
Lesters, Montgomery..... SW ×
Letcher, Bath............... W 18
Level Run, Pittsylvania..... S 10
Lewinsville, Fairfax.......... N 120
Lewisetta, Northumberland E ×
Lewiston, Spotsylvania......C 24
Lewisville, (see Osso) .... ×
● **Lexington**, RockbridgeW 3,059
Liberty, (see Bedford City)... ×
LibertyFurnace, ShenandoahN ×
Liberty Hill, (see Return).... ×
Liberty Mills, Orange....... C 37
Licking, Goochland.......... C 50
● Lick Run, Botetourt..... W 24
● Lightfoot, James City.....E ×
Lignum, Culpeper.......... N 60
Lilburn, Powhatan..........C ×
Lillian, Northumberland....E ×
Lilly, Rockingham...........N 24
Limeton, Warren............N ×
Limstrong, Prince William.N ×
Lincoln, Loudoun...........N 150
Lincolnia, Fairfax........... N ×
Lincolnsville, Norfolk......SE ×
● *Lindale*, Nansemond.... SE ×
Lindell, Washington....... SW 60
● Linden, Warren........... N 100
● Lindsay, Albemarle.......C 24
Lindward, Charlotte.........S ×
● Linville, Rockingham....N 15
Lipps, Wise................SW ×
● Lipscomb, Augusta........W 50
● *Lipscomb*, Campbell......C ×
Lisbon, Bedford..............C 150
● Lithia, Botetourt..........W 50
Little Georgetown, (see Broad Run Station)............... ×
Little Plymouth, K'n & Q'n.E 75
Little River, Floyd........SW 36
Little Stoney Cr., (see Liberty Fur.)........................ ×
Littleton, Sussex...........SE 15
Litwalton, Lancaster........E 40
Lively Oak, (see Bellwood Ms) ×
Lloyds, Essex................E 75
● *Loch Laid*, Rockbridge..W ×
Lochleven, Lunenburgh......S 50
Loco, Sussex...............SE ×
Locust Creek, Louisa........C ×
Locust Dale, Madison.......N 30
Locust Grove, (see Simpson's) ×
Locust Hill, Middlesex.......E 12
Locust Lane, Scott..........SW 24
Locust Mount, Accomack....E 150
Locustville, Accomack......E 100
Lodebar, Nelson.............C 5
Lodge, Northumberland....E 25
Lodi, Washington.........SW 18
Lodore, Amelia..............C 8
Loftis, Halifax................S ×
● Lofton, Augusta......... W ×
Lola, Pittsylvania.......... S 7
LombardyGrove, Mecklenb'h S 90
Lomond, Carroll...........SW 30
● London Bridge, Pr'sAnneSE 25
Lone Cedar, Patrick.........S 12
Lone Fountain, Augusta....W ×
Lone Gum, Bedford..........C 12
● *Lone Jack*, Campbell.....C ×
● Loneoak, Henry............S 35
Lone Pine, Bedford..........C ×
Long, Page...................N ×
Long Creek, Louisa..........C 5

Post Office	
● Long Dale, Allegheny.... W	810
Longfield, Lee............SW	30
Long Glade, Augusta....... W	120
Long Hollow, Smyth......SW	24
Long Mountain, Amherst...C	×
Long's Gap, Grayson......SW	×
Long'sShop, Montgomery.SW	30
Long's Spur, Bland.......SW	×
Longview, Isle of Wight...SE	×
Longwood, Rockbridge..... W	36
Longwood, (see Oak Grove)..	×
Looney, Craig............. W	30
Loretto, Essex............E	50
● Lorraine, Henrico.........C	5
● Lorton Valley, Fairfax....N	24
Lot, Middlesex.............E	×
Lottie, Rappahannock....... N	50
Lottsburgh, Northumb'd... E	35
Loudoun, (see Sterling)......	×
● **Louisa**, Louisa.......... C	500
Lovely Mount, (see Radford)	×
Love's Mills, Washington. SW	12
Lovettsville, Loudoun.......N	125
Loving Creek, Bedford......C	30
Lovingston, Nelson......C	300
Lovingston, Nelson......... C	85
Lowesville, Amherse.........C	75
Lowland, Washington.....SW	×
● Lowmoor, Allegheny..... W	989
● Lowry, Bedford...........C	20
● *Lucado*, Campbell........C	×
Lucians, Floyd........... SW	×
Lucile, Scott.............SW	×
Lucket's, Loudoun..........N	×
Lucretia, Pulaska.........SW	50
Lucyville, Cumberland......E	×
Lukes, Brunswick...........S	×
Lula, Charlotte............ S	23
Luma, Smyth....... ..... SW	×
● Lumberton, Sussex......SE	×
Lundy, Grayson............SW	×
Lunenburgh, C. H., Lunenburgh...................S	95
● **Luray**, Page............N	2,809
● *Lurich* Giles............SW	×
Lyells, Richmond........... E	43
● **Lynchburgh, Campbell**....C	19,709
● Lynch Station, Campbell..C	213
● Lyndhurst, Augusta......W	30
Lynhams, Northumberland.E	×
● Lynnhaven, Princ'ssAnneSE	×
● Lynnwood, Rockingham..N	12
Lyells, Richmond........... E	×
McClelland, Isle of Wight. SE	×
McConnell, Scott...........SW	12
McDonald's Mill, Montg'rySW	10
● *McDowell*, Allegheny.....S	×
McDowell, Highland......... W	218
McFarland's, Lunenburgh...S	50
McGaheysville, RockinghamN	350
McGehee's, Louisa.......... C	×
● *McGuffin*, Franklin.......S	×
● *McIvor's*, Amherst....... C	15
McMullen, Greene..........C	×
● McRae's, Cumberland.... E	25
Mableton, Hanover..........C	25
Mace's Spring, Scott...... SW	×
● Machipongo, NorthamptonE	25
Machodoc, Westmoreland....E	10
Mack, Carroll.............SW	×
Mack's Gap Patrick........S	12
● Macon, Powhatan..........C	15
● *Madison*, Orange......... C	30
Madison, C. H., Madison N	353
Madison Mills, Madison.....N	24
● Madison Run, Orange.....C	30
Madison's, (see Lippo's).......	×
Madisonville, Charlotte......S	48
Madrid, Augusta............W	×
● *Maggodee Creek*, FranklinS	×
Maggie, Craig.............. W	×
Magnet, Isle of Wight..... SE	×
● Magnolia, Nansemond...SE	50
Mahone, Giles.............SW	×
● Maidens, Goochland.......C	50
● *Major*, Bedford...........C	×
Major, Grayson............SW	12
Malaria, Mecklenburg......S	×
Mallory, Louisa............C	12
● Mallow, Alleghany........ W	30
● *Mallow*, Fairfax.........N	×
Malmaison, Pittsylvania.....S	15
Malvern Hill, Henrico.......C	×
● *Manakin*, Goochland..... C	×
Manard, Warren...........N	×
● Manassas, Prince William N	530
● Manchester, Chesterfield..C	9,246

Post Office	
Maness, Scott............ SW	12
Mangohick, King William.. E	50
Mannborough, Amelia......C	40
● *Manning*, Nansemond..SE	×
Manokin Roads, Westm'l'd E	×
● *Manor*, Warren..........N	×
Manquin, King William.....E	30
Mansfield, Louisa.......... C	10
Mansion, Campbell..........C	10
Mantapike, King & Queen..E	5
● Manteo, Buckingham.....C	×
Manteo, Nelson............ C	×
● *Mantico*, Hanover........C	×
Maple Grove, WestmorelandE	30
Maple Shade Inn, Pulaski SW	×
Maple Valley, (see Occoquan)	×
Mapleton, Princess Anne..SE	×
● Mappsburg, Accomack... E	30
Mappsville, Accomack......E	125
● *Marble Quarries*, Scott.SW	×
Marble Valley, Augusta.... W	30
Marengo, Mecklenburg......S	5
● **Marion**, Smyth........SW	1,651
Marionville, Northampton..E	40
● Markham, Fauquier......N	100
● Marksville, Page......... N	100
Marlborough, Frederick.... N	10
Marmora, Dinwiddie.........S	×
Marrowbone, Henry........S	×
● Marshall, Fauquier.......N	200
Marsh Market, Accomack..E	55
● Martin's Store, Halifax....S	10
● **Martinsville**, Henry...S	2,500
● *Marvin*, Wythe.........SW	×
Marye, Spotsylvania........C	×
Marysville, Campbell........C	25
Mascott, King & Queen.....E	12
● *Mason's*, Accomack.......E	×
● *Mason's Depot*, Sussex..SE	×
Mason's Store, Russell....SW	×
● *Mason's Tunnel*, Bath..W	×
Masonville, Accomack..... E	5
Massanetta Spring, R'k'g'mN	30
Massanutton, Page..........N	44
Massaponax, Spotsylvania...C	12
Massey, Accomack..........E	30
Massie's Mills, Nelson.......C	50
Massley's Junc., Powhatan.C	×
Masters, Alleghany.........W	×
Mathias Point, King George.E	12
Matilda, Bedford............C	×
Matoaca, Chesterfield........C	545
Mathews C. H., MathewsE	250
● Mattapony, Spotsylvania..C	25
● Mattoax, Amelia..........C	25
Mattox Creek, (see OakGrove)	×
● Maurertown, ShenandoahN	150
Mauzy, Rockingham........N	12
● Max Meadows, Wythe..SW	150
● Maxwell, Tazewell......SW	×
Mayberry Creek, Patrick....S	12
Maybrook, Giles..........SW	×
Mayfield, (see Norfolk)......	×
Mayland, Rockingham...... N	10
● Mayo, Halifax.............S	10
Mayo Forge, Patrick.........S	25
Meadow Creek, Grayson..SW	24
Meadow Dale, Highland.... W	10
Meadow Mills, Frederick...N	30
Meadows of Dan, Patrick....S	25
● Meadow Station, Henrico. C	×
● Meadow View, Washin'nSW	120
Meadowville, Chesterfield...C	×
Meadville, Halifax.........S	100
Mearsville, Accomack........E	22
Mechanicsburgh, Bland....SW	100
Mechanicsville, (see Bent'glio)	×
Mechanicsville, Chesterfield.C	300
Mechanicsville, Loudoun...N	234
● Mechum River, Albem'e..C	75
Medina, Washington......SW	×
Medlock, Louise C	×
● *Meems*, Shenandoah......N	×
Menla, Pittsylvania......... S	×
● Meetze, Fauquier.........E	×
● Meherrin, Lunenburgh....S	20
Meherrin Depot, Pr'e Edw'd C	300
● *Melfa*, Accomack.........E	×
● *Mellen*, Warwick.........E	×
Melrose, Rockingham....... N	30
Melrose Sta., (see Casanova) .	×
● Melton's, Louisa.......... C	12
Menchville, Warwick.........E	×
● Mendota, Washington...SW	400
Menla, Pittsylvania..........S	×
Meredithville, Brunswick...S	25
Meridian, Dinwiddie........ S	×

Post Office	
Mero, Fairfax............. N	×
Merrifield, Fairfax......... N	×
Merry Point, Lancaster....: E	15
Messick, York..............E	×
Messongo, Accomack.......E	45
Metompkin, Accomack.....E	30
MeyerhoeffersStore, R'kh'm N	45
Miami, Lancaster........... E	×
Michaux, Powhatan.........C	5
Middlebrook, Augusta..... W	222
Middleburgh, Loudoun..... N	429
● ***Middleton*, Fluvanna**..... C	5
● Middletown, Frederick...N	410
● Midland, Fauquier.........N	40
Midlothian, Chesterfield.... C	150
● Midvale, Rockbridge.....W	12
Midway, Halifax.............S	15
● Midway Mills, Nelson.....C	20
Mikado, (see Forestville).....	×
Mila, Northumberland...... E	5
● Millboro Depot, Bath.... W	300
Millbank, (see Mt. Herman) .	×
Millborough Springs, Bath. W	50
● *Mill Brook*, Augusta.....W	×
Mill Creek Wharf, Middl'sexE	×
Milldale, Warren............N	60
● Millford, Caroline.........C	100
Millenbeck, Lancaster...... E	75
● *Miller*, Rockbridge...... W	×
Miller's, Essex............E	40
Miller's Tavern, Essex......E	48
Mill Gap, Highland..........W	×
Millington, Albemarle...... C	×
Mill's Store, Brunswick.....S	5
Millwood, Clarke.......... N	400
Milnes, (see Shenandoah)....	×
Milnesville, Augusta........W	30
Mills Store, Brunswick..... S	×
Milton's Wharf, Richmond.E	60
Millville, (see Alden).........	×
Mineral, Amherst.......... C	×
Mineral, Appomattox........C	10
● Mineral City, Louisa...... C	40
● *Mine Road*, Spotsylvani..C	×
● Mine Run, Orange..........C	14
Mine Run Furnace, (see Seven Fountains)..........	×
Minerva, Carroll.......... SW	×
Mingo, Franklin............ S	×
● *Minneapolis*, Russell... SW	×
Minneola, Pittsylvania.......S	20
Minnieville, Prince William. N	36
Minor, Essex...............E	×
● Mint Spring, Augusta.... W	24
Mira Fork, Floyd......... SW	12
● *Mitchell's*, Henrico...... C	×
● Mitchell'sStation, CulpeperN	85
Moab, Washington........SW	×
● *Mocassin Gap*, Scott... SW	×
Modest Town, Accomack... E	75
Moffatt's Creek, Augusta...W	100
Moler's, Augusta............W	×
Molusk, Lancaster.......... E	×
Monarat, Carroll..........SW	×
Monaskon, Lancaster....... E	100
Monday, Floyd.............SW	×
Moneta, Bedford.............C	×
Monmouth, Rockbridge....W	25
Monroe'sCreek, (seeOakGr've)	×
Monrovia, Westmoreland..E	×
Mons, Bedford...............C	×
Montague, Essex............E	50
Montebello, Nelson.........C	48
Monteithville, Stafford......N	12
Monterat, Carroll.........SW	×
Monterey, Highland..... W	200
Montevideo, Rockingham.. N	40
● *Montgomery*, M'tgom'rySW	×
● Montgomery, Wash'gt'n.SW	20
● Montgomery Springs, Montgomery................SW	24
Montpelier, Hanover........C	25
Montpelier, Orange.........C	×
● Montreal, Nelson.......... C	85
● Montvale, Bedford........C	40
Montross, Westmoreland.E	200
Moomaw, Roanoke........SW	26
● *Moores*, Albemarle....... C	×
Mooreland, (see Marshall)...	×
● *Moore's Creek*, AlbemarleC	×
Moore's Mill, Henry..........S	12
Moore's Store, Shenandoah..N	40
Moorings, Surrey..........SE	×
Moorman, Roanoke.......SW	×
Moorman'sRiver, Albemarle C	150
● *Morey's*, Warwick........E	×

Morgan, Scott............SW ×
Morgan's Cross Roads, H'lf'x S 25
● Morotock, Pittsylvania....S ×
Morris Church, Campbell...C 12
Morris Hill, (see Covington). ×
● Morrison, Warwick......E 15
Morrisonville, Loudoun.....N 40
Morrisville, Fauquier.......N 35
Morven, Amelie...........C 30
Moscow, Augusta...........W 30
Moseley, Buckingham.......C 36
● Mosley's Junc., Powhattan C ×
● Mossing Ford, Charlotte..S 100
● *Moss Run*, Alleghany....W ×
Moss Neck, Caroline.........C 24
Mossy Creek, Augusta.......W 15
● Motley's, Pittsylvania.....S 50
Mount, Scott..............SW ×
Mountain Falls, Frederick..N 10
Mountain Gap, Loudoun....N ×
Mountain Grove, Bath......W 30
Mountain Hill, Pittsylvania.S 15
Mountain Lake, Giles.....SW 12
Mountain Road, Halifax.....S 30
Mountain Valley, Henry.....S 15
Mountain View, Stafford.....N ×
Mount Airy, Pittsylvania....S 25
● Mount Athos, Campbell...C 36
Mount Calvary (see W'dst'k) ×
Mount Carmel, Halifax......S 30
● Mountcastle, New Kent...E ×
Mount Clifton, Shenandoah. N 60
Mount Clinton, Rockingham N 100
● Mount Crawford, Rock'm N 500
Mount Crawford Station, (see North River)............. ×
Mount Cross, Pittsylvania...S 20
Mount Gilead, Loudoun....N 65
Mount Herman, Rocking'm N ×
Mount Holly, Westmoreland E 24
● Mount Jackson, Shenand'h N 500
Mount Landing, Essex......E 20
Mount Laurel, Halifax.......S 100
Mount Meridan, Augusta...W 40
Mount Oliver, Shenandoah..N 100
Mount Pleasant, Spt'sylvania. C ×
Mount Rock, (see Chrisman) ×
● Mount Sidney, Augusta..W 304
Mount Solon, Augusta......W 100
Mount Vernon on the Potomac, Fairfax...........N 18
Mountville, Loudoun........N 27
Mount Vinco, Buckingham. C 30
Mount Williams, Frederick. N 30
Mount Zion, Campbell...... C 55
Mouth of Wilson, Grayson. SW 200
Muckross, Mecklenburg.....S 36
Muddy Creek Mill, (see Cartersville)........... ×
Muddy Run, (see Dulinsville)
Mugler, (see Orange C. H.)... ×
● *Mullin*, Tazewell....... SW ×
Mullinsville, Henry......... S 18
Mundy Point, Northumb'ld. E ×
Mundy's Mill, Amherst..... C ×
Munford, Botetourt.........W ×
Murat, Rockbridge..........W 24
Murtleville, Stafford........N 6
Muses Fork, (see Montross). ×
Museville, Pittsylvania......S 60
Mushet, Augusta........... W 30
Musselman, Stafford........N 18
Myra Fork, Floyd.........SW ×
● Myrtle, Nansemond....... SE 50
● *Nace*, Botetourt......... W ×
Naff's, Franklin.............S 41
Nain, Frederick.............N ×
Nameless, Campbell.......... C ×
Namozine, Amelia..........C 10
● *Nance*, Charles City......C ×
Nance's Shop, Charles City. E 15
Nandua, Accomack..........E 12
Narcott, Floyd...........SW 12
● *Narrows*, Giles..........SW 35
Narrows Beach, (see Hague) ×
● Naruna, Campbell......... C 30
● *Nash*, Chesterfield........C ×
Nash, Nelson...............C ×
● Nason's, Orange.......... C 7
● Nassawadox, Northamp'n E 6
● Nathalie, Halifax......... S ×
National Soldiers Home, Elizabeth City..............E 1,200
● Natural Bridge, Rockbridge W 30
● *Natural Tunnel*, Scott. SW ×
Nauck, Alexandria.........N ×
Naylor's, Richmond........ E 25

Neabsco Mills, Prince William N 25
Nebletts, Lunenburgh.......S ×
● Nebraska, Appomattox...C 75
Neersville, Loudoun........ N 30
Negro Foot, Hanover....... C 10
Nelly's Ford, Nelson........C 10
● *Nelson*, Mecklenburg.....S ×
Nelsonia, Accomack........ E 30
Nester, Carroll............SW ×
Nethers, Madison...........N 18
Nettle Ridge, Patrick.......S 10
Neva, Pittsylvania...........S 12
New Baltimore, Fauquier.. N 100
Newbern, Pulaski...... SW 300
Newberry Mills, Wythe...SW ×
● New Canton, Buckingham C 250
● **New Castle**, Craig..... W 214
New Castle, Hanover....... C 10
● New Church, Accomack..E 75
New Design, Pittsylvania....S 15
● New Glasgow Depot, Amherst C 50
New Hampden, Highland.. W 100
New Hope, Augusta.........W 300
● *New Hope*, Augusta......W 50
Newington, Fairfax......... N ×
New Kent, New Kent....E 100
Newland, Richmond.........E 10
New London, Bedford...... C 25
New London, Campbell.....C 125
New London, Caroline......C 125
Newman's Hanover.........C ×
New Market, Middlesex....E 30
● New Market, Shenandoah N 697
New Plymouth, Lunenburgh S 24
New Point, Mathews.........E 25
Newport, Giles.............SW 200
● **Newport News**, Warw'k E 4,449
● New River Depot, P'laski SW 685
New River White Sulphur, Giles...............SW ×
● News Ferry, Halifax......S 45
● Newsom's Southampton SE. 160
New Store, Buckingham.....C 150
Newtown, (see Stephens City) ×
Newtown, King & Queen....E 20
Newtown, (See Portsmouth). ×
New Upton, Gloucester..... E 10
Newville, Prince George...SE 309
Niblett's Mill, Sussex......SE 30
● *Nicholas*, Fluvanna.......C ×
Nickelsville, Scott.........SW 100
Nimmo, Princess Anne....SE ×
Nimrod Hall, Bath..........W ×
Ninde's Store, King George. E ×
Nineveh, Warren...........N 30
Nininger, Bedford..........C ×
Noble, Wythe..............SW ×
● Noel, Hanover............C 30
● Nokesville, Prince Will'm. N 60
Nola, Franklin...............S ×
Nominy Ferry, (see Mt. Holly) ×
Nominy Grove Westmorel'd. E 15
Non Intercention, Lunenb'gh S 12
Nono, Lunenburgh..........S ×
Norcott, Floyd............SW ×
● Norfolk, Norfolk........SE 34,871
Norman, Culpeper..........N ×
North, Mathews.............E 36
North Branch, Grayson...SW 24
● North Danville, P'sylvania S 3,799
Noth Fork, Loudoun.........N 30
● North Garden, Albemarle. C 40
● *North Mountain*, Augusta W ×
North River, Rockingham...N ×
North View, Mecklenburg.. S 30
● Northwest, Norfolk..... SE 20
● Norton, Wise.............SW ×
Nortonsville, Greene........C 50
Norwood, Nelson........... C 150
● *Nottingham*, Scott......SW ×
Nottoway C.H., Nottoway S 173
● *Nottoway*, Sussex....... SE ×
Nowlin's Mills, Franklin.... S 20
Nunn's Store, (see Bateman) ×
Nurneysville, Nansemond. SE 30
Nutbush, Lunenburgh.......S 10
Oak, New Kent.............E 24
Oakdale, Rockbridge.......W 25
Oak Forest, Cumberland....E 12
Oak Grove, Washington...SW ×
Oak Grove, Westmoreland..E 40
● Oak Hall, Accomack.......E 15
● *Oak Hill*, Pittsylvania.....S 12
Oakland, Louisa.............C 30
Oak Level, (see Vernon Hill). ×
Oak Level, Henry.......... S 50
Oakley, Mecklenburg....... S 15

Oak Park, Madison......... N 100
Oak Shade, Culpeper....... N 12
Oakton, Fairfax............ N 30
Oak Tree, York.............E ×
Oakville, Appomattox.......C 25
Oakwood, Rockingham.....N ×
Oatlands, Loudon...........N 20
Obenshain, (see Arch Mills)... ×
Occoquan, Prince William..N 297
Occupacia, Essex............E ×
● Oceana, Princess Anne..SE ×
● *Ocean Shore Park*, Princess Anne...................SE ×
● Ocean View, Norfolk....SE 5
● Ochre, Chesterfield........C 36
Ocinito, Princess Anne....SE ×
Ocran, Dinwiddie............S ×
Octagon, Brunswick.........S 10
Offley, Hanover.............C ×
Oilville, Goochland..........C 20
Oklahoma, Carroll.........SW ×
Old Church, Hanover........C 100
● *Old Dominion*, Warwick..E ×
Oldenplace, Dinwiddie......S 12
Oldfield, Charles City....... E ×
Oldham's, Westmoreland... E 30
Old Hickory, Botetourt.....W 100
Old Pilot, Appomattox.......C ×
● *Old Point*, Elizabeth City..E 500
● *Old Point Junc.*, Warwick. E ×
Old Town, Grayson.......SW 150
Olesko, Cumberland ....E ×
● Olinger, Lee.............SW 6
Olive, Culpeper.............N 24
Oliver, Hanover.............C ×
Oliveville, Nottoway........ S ×
Olo, Lunenburg.............. S 5
Olympia, Smyth...........SW 10
Oma, Culpepper............. N ×
Omega, Halifax............S 30
Onan, Nelson............... C 36
Onancock, Accomack........E 1,500
O'Neal, Floyd..............SW ×
● *One Hundred and Ninety-four Mile Siding*, C'pbell C ×
● Onley, Accomack..........E 40
● Ontario, Charlotte.........S ×
Onville, Stafford...........N ×
Opal, Fauquier..............N ×
● Opequan, Frederick.......N 18
Ophelia, Northumberland..E ×
Opie, Mecklenburg..........S ×
Opie (see Green Bay).........C ×
Ora, Washington...........SW ×
Oral Oaks, Lunenburgh.....S 10
Oranda, Shenandoah.......N ×
● **Orange**, Orange........C 571
Orbit, Isle of Wight.......SE ×
Orchid, Louisa..............C ×
Ordinary, Gloucester.......E ×
Ordsburgh, Brunswick.......S 18
Ore Bank, Buckingham.....C ×
Oreville, Rockbridge........W 60
Orgainsville, Mecklenburg..S 5
● *Oriano*, Warwick.........E ×
Orkney Springs,, Shen'doah N 25
Orlando, Prince William....N ×
Orlean, Fauquier............N 100
● *Orleans Street*, Henrico...C ×
Oronoco, Amherst.......... C 25
Osage, Patrick.............. S ×
Osborn's Ford, (see Dugan'n) ×
Osborn's Gap, Dickenson. SW ×
Osceola, Washington......SW 40
Oslins, Buckingham........C ×
Osso, King George..........E 24
● *Otterburn*, Amelia........C ×
Otterdale, Chesterfield..... C ×
Otter Hill, Bedford..........C 30
● Otter River, Campbell....C 10
Otter View, Bedford........C ×
Otterville, Bedford..........C 20
Ottobine, Rockingham..... N 12
Ottoman, Lancaster.........E ×
Otway, Nelson...............C ×
Oty, Montgomery.........SW ×
● Overalls, Page............N 60
Overland, Mecklenburg.....S ×
Overly, Prince Edward..... C ×
Overton, Albemarle......... C 25
Owens, King George........E 12
Owenton, King & Queen....E 30
Owl Run, (see Calverton).... ×
Oysterman's Home, King & Queen...............E 5
Ozeana, Essex..............E 12
● Paces, Halifax.............S 12

Paddy's Mills, (see Zepp).... ×
Paige, Caroline..........C 12
Painesville, Amelia..........C 30
Paint Bank, Craig..........W ×
Painter, Accomack..........E 40
Paint Lick, Tazewell......SW 25
Palls, King William..........E 12
Palmer's Springs, Mecklenburg..........S 75
Palmetto, Patrick..........S ×
Palmyra, Fluvanna..........C 200
Palo Alto, Highland..........W ×
● Pamplin City, Appomatox C 294
● *Panther*, Bath..........W ×
Parham's Store, Sussex....SE 30
Paris, Fauquier..........N 150
Parishville, Frederick..........N 30
● *Parker*, Spotsylvania..... C 25
Parkers, (see Dendron)...... ×
Park Forest, Mecklenburg..S ×
Parkin's Mills, (see Winch'r) ×
● Parksley, Accomack ..... E 50
Parnassus, Augusta........ W 15
Parrotts, Albemarle........ C ×
Partlow's, Spotsylvania..... C ×
Passapatanzy, King George. E 48
Pastoria, Accomack..........E 30
● Patrick Springs, Patrick..S ×
Pat Store, Russell..........SW ×
● *Patterson Junc.*, Wythe SW ×
Pattie, Franklin .... S ×
Pattonsville, Scott........ SW 60
Paulington, Rockingham... N ×
Paul's Cross Roads, Essex...E 15
Pax, Floyd..........SW 18
Paxson, Loudoun.......... N 18
● Payne's, Fluvanna...... C ×
Peach Bottom, Grayson...SW 10
Peach Grove, (see Lewinsville) ×
Peach Grove, Rockingham. N 25
● Peake's Turnout, Hanover C 30
● *Peak's*, Norfolk..........SE ×
Peaksville, Bedford.......... C 35
Peanut, Sussex.......... SE ×
Pearch, Bedford.......... C ×
Pearisburgh, Giles.... SW 341
● *Pearisburgh Sta.*, Giles. SW ×
Peatross, Pittsylvania....... S ×
● *Pedlar's*, Bedford..........C 30
Pedlar Mills, Amherst...... C 150
Pedro's, Essex.......... E ×
Peers, Goochland.......... C 5
Pegram, Surry..........SE 10
● Pemberton, Goochland... C 15
● Pembroke, Giles..........SW 20
● *Pembroke*, Princess Anne SW 20
Pender, Fairfax.......... N ×
● Pendleton's, Louisa....... C 20
● Penhook, Franklin.......... S 30
Penicks, Bedford.......... C ×
Pennington Gap, Lee......SW 12
● Penola, Caroline.......... C 75
Penrith, Cumberland..........E ×
Peola Mills, Madison..........N 60
● *Perdue*, Chesterfield......C ×
Perkinsville, Goochland.... C 12
Pernello, Franklin.......... S 50
Perrows, Campbell.......... C ×
Perrowville, Bedford..........C 36
Pet, Brunswick.......... S ×
● Petersburgh, Petersburg City S 22,680
Peters Creek, Patrick....... S 12
Peytonsburgh, Pittsylvania..S 15
● *Phaup*, Powhatan.......... C ×
Phillips, Floyd.......... SW 30
● *Phillip's Switch*, Washington SW ×
Philomont, Loudoun.......... N 70
● Phœbus, Elizabeth City...E 1,000
Pickawry, Pittsylvania..........S 25
Pickett's, Henrico..........C 25
Piggs, Pittsylvania.......... S 15
Pig River, Franklin.......... S ×
● *Pig River Sta.*, Franklin..S ×
Pilkinton, Powhatan..........C ×
Pilot, Montgomery..........SW 12
Pinckney, Highland.......... W ×
Pine, Pulaski.......... SW 24
Pine Apple, Spotsylvania...C ×
Pine Top, Orange..........C ×
Pine View, Fauquier..........N 30
Pineville, Powhatan..........C. ×
Piney Fork, (see Litte River) ×
Piney Grove Sta., (see Charlottesville) ×
Pinnacle, Patrick..........S ×
● *Pinner's Point*, Norfolk SE ×
Pinopolis, Southampton...SE ×

Virginia

Piper's Gap, Carroll..........SW 8
Piscataway, Essex..........E 10
● **Pisgah**, Tazewell..........SW ×
Pittston, Pittsylvania..........S 10
● **Pittsville, Pittsylvania**..........S 100
Pizarro, Floyd..........SW ×
● *Plains*, Fauquier..........N ×
Plain View, King & Queen..E 35
Plain View, (see Baynesville) ×
Plantersville, Lunenburgh...S 12
Plasterburgh, Smyth......SW 30
Pleasant Gap, Pittsylvania.... ×
Pleasant Grove, L'nenburgh.S 40
Pleasant Hill, Tazewell....SW 12
Pleasant Oaks, Greenville..S ×
Pleasant Ridge, Pr'ces A'e.SE 25
● Pleasant Shade, Gr'nsv'le.S 25
● *Pleasant Valley*, R'k'gh'm N 120
Pleasant Valley, Fairfax....N 25
Pleasant View, Amherst....C 12
Plum Branch, Campbell....C 5
Plum Point, New Kent.....E ×
Plunkettsville, Augusta....W ×
Poage's Mill, Roanoke....SW 50
● Pocahontas, Tazewell...SW 2,953
● *Pohick*, Fairfax..........N 30
Poindexter's Store, Louisa..C 25
Point Eastern, Caroline.....C 18
Point Pleasant, Bland....SW ×
Point Truth, Russell......SW 24
Point Valley, (see Heathsville) ×
Pole Green, Hanover..........C 15
Pomona, Shenandoah..........N ×
Pomona, Westmoreland....E ×
● Pond Gap, Augusta...... W 20
Poole, Brunswick..........S ×
● Pope, Southampton..... SE ×
Poplar, Nelson..........C 12
Poplar Grove, (see Corleyville) ×
Poplar Hill, Giles.......... SW 183
Poplar Mount, Greensville...S 30
Poquoson, York.......... E 50
Port Conway, King George. E 50
Port Haywood, Mathews....E 40
Port Mi on, Essex..........E 5
Port Republic, Rockingham N 100
Port Royal, Caroline.......... C 236
● **Portsmouth**, Norfolk SE 13,268
● Port Walthall, Chesterfi'd.C 30
Posey, Floyd..........SW 12
Post Oak, Spotsylvania......C 12
Potato, Grayson..........SW 24
● Potomac, Prince William N 100
Potomac Mills, W'stmorel'd E 15
● *Potomac Run*, Stafford...N ×
● *Pottomoi*, Hanover..........C ×
Pott's Creek, Alleghany....W 30
Pound, Wise..........SW 12
● Pounding Mill, Tazewell SW ×
Poverty, Highland..........W ×
Powcan, King & Queen......E 12
● *Powells*, Charlotte..........S ×
Powellton, Brunswick......S 40
Powers, Clarke..........N ×
● **Powhatan C. H.**, Powhatan..........C 70
● *Powhatan*, Amelia..........C ×
Pratts, Madison..........N 14
Prease, Bedford..........C ×
● Preston, Henry..........S 30
● *Prettyman's*, Powhatan.. C 30
● *Prices Bluff*, Botetourt..W ×
Price's Forks, M'tgomery.SW 20
● Priddy's, Albemarle...... C 20
Pride, Dinwiddie..........S ×
● Pridemore, Lee..........SW 24
Prillaman's, Franklin..........S 24
Prince George C. H., Prince George..........SE 80
Princess Anne C. H., Princess Anne..........SE 100
● *Princess Anne*, Norfolk SE 100
● *Princeton*, Carroll..........SW ×
Printz Mill, Page.......... N ×
● Profitt, Albemarle.......... C 24
Progress, Franklin..........S ×
● Prospect, Prince Edward. C 300
Prospect Dale, Giles...... SW ×
Prospect Hill, Fairfax...... N 12
● Providence Forge, New K't E 30
Prunty's, Henry..........S ×
Pugh's Run, Shenandoah... N ×
● Pulaski City, Pulaski... SW 2,112
Pullen's, Pittsylvania..........S 10
Pungo, Princess Anne..... SE 200
Pungo Ferry, (see Blossom Hill) ×
Pungoteague, Accomack....E 200

Virginia

● Purcellville, Loudoun.....N 60
Purchase, Scott.......... SW 24
Purgatong, Botetourt...... W ×
● *Purvis*, Nansemond..... SE 100
● Push, Mecklenburgh......S ×
Putney's, Prince Edward....C ×
Quaker, Carroll.......... SW 12
● *Quantico*, Prince William N 100
Quick, King & Queen.......... E ×
● Quicksburgh, Shenandoah N 75
Quinque, Green..........C ×
● Quinton, New Kent..........E 15
Quolt, Floyd.......... SW ×
Rabbit, Halifax..........S 12
Raccoon Ford, Culpeper....N 30
Raccoon Ford, Orange......C ×
Racket, Lunenburg..........S ×
● *Radford*, Montgomery..SW 2,060
Radford Furnace, Pulaski.SW 120
Rain, Frederick.......... N 30
● Raines, Cumberland...... E 20
Rainswood, Northumberland E ×
Rakes, Floyd..........SW ×
Ramsey, Franklin..........S ×
● Randolph, Charlotte...... S 80
Rangeley, Patrick.......... S 30
Raphine, Rockbridge...... W 35
● Rapidan, Culpeper..........N 150
Rappahannock Academy, Caroline.......... C 3
● *Rappahannock Sta.*, Fau'r N 100
Rapp's Mills, Rockbridge...W 25
Ravencliff Furnace, Wythe SW ×
Ravens Nest, Washington.SW 25
● *Ravensworth*, Fairfax....N ×
Rawley Springs, Rock'ham.N 30
Ray, Pittsylvania..........S 43
● Raymond, Surry.......... SE ×
Raynor, Isle of Wight.....SE ×
Read's Wharf, Northampton E 75
● Ream's Station, Dinwiddie S 12
Reamy's Fork, (see Newland) ×
Reba, Bedford..........C 42
● Rectortown, Fauquier....N 125
Red Bank, Halifax.......... S 25
Red Bluff, Wythe.......... SW 12
● Red Hill, Albemarle.......... C 25
Red House, Charlotte..........S 45
Rediviva, Rappahannock.....N ×
Redman, Grayson.......... SW ×
Red Oak Grove, Charlotte.. S 50
Red Plains, Franklin....... S 12
● Redwood, Franklin.......... S ×
Red Creek, Henry.......... S ×
● Reed Island, Pulaski... SW 25
● *Reed Island Junc.*, Pula'i SW ×
Reed's Wharf, (see Fairport). ×
Reedville, Northumberland..E 40
Reedy, Lunenburgh.......... S 50
Reedy Springs, Appomattox C ×
Reese's, Charlotte.......... S 30
Rehoboth, Lunenburgh......S 30
Rehoboth Church, North'nd. E 30
Reliance, Warren..........N ×
Relief, Frederick .... N ×
● Remington, Fauquier.... N 100
Rens, Accomack.......... E 30
Repass, Bland.......... SW ×
Repton, Nelson.......... C 36
Republican Grove, Halifax..S 50
Rescue, Isle of Wight......SE ×
Residence, Halifax..........S ×
Rest, Frederick..........N 12
Retreat, Franklin..........S 30
Return, Caroline..........C ×
● Reusens, Campbell..........C 361
Reverie, Franklin.......... S ×
Rexburgh, Essex..........E 15
Reynold's Store, Frederick.N ×
● *Reynolds*, Orange..........C 12
● Rhoadesville, Orange..... C 12
● Rice Depot, Prince Edw'd C 100
Riceville, Pittsylvania..........S 70
● *Richards*, Henrico..........C ×
Richardsville, Culpeper.....N 15
Richland, (see Widewater)... ×
● Richlands, Tazewell.... SW 300
● **RICHMOND**, Henrico.C 81,388
Rich Patch, Alleghany..... W 18
Rich Valley, Smyth......SW ×
Ridge Church, Henrico..... C ×
● Ridgeway, Henry.......... C 236
Rieley, Nelson.......... C ×
● *Riggan*, Surry..........SE 30
Riggan, Mecklenburgh..... S ×
Rigna, Bedford..........C 12

● *Rileyville*, Page..........N 50
Riner, Montgomery..........SW 240
● Ringgold, Pittsylvania.... S 55
Rinkerton, Shenandoah.... N 24
● Rio, Albemarle........ C 36
Rio Mills, (see Rio).......... ×
● Rio Vista, Henrico........C 25
Riley's Mills, Craig..........SW 50
● Ripplemead, Giles........S 18
Ritchieville, Dinwiddie......C 12
Rival, Buckingham.........C ×
Rivanna, Albemarle........W 5
Rivanna, Fluvanna......... C 50
● Riverside, Rockbridge....C 24
● *Riversville*, Amherst......N 10
● Riverton, Warren........ N 200
River View, (see Chesapeake) ×
Rives, Prince George......SE 20
Rixeyville, Culpeper........N 10
Roane's, Gloucester.........E ×
● Roanoke, Roanoke......SW 16,159
Roanoke Red Sulphur, Roanoke.................SW ×
Roaring Run, Botetourt.... W 30
Roark, Rockingham........N 60
Roberta, Franklin............S 30
Robertson's, Bedford.........C 36
● *Robey's*, Spotsylvania.....C ×
Robinett, Russell..........SW ×
● Robious, Chesterfield...... C 19
Rocco, Rockbridge.........W ×
Rochele, Madison...........N 35
Rockbridge Alum Springs, Rockbridge............ W ×
Rockbridge Baths, Rock'ge W 70
● Rockcastle, Goochland....C 24
Rockdell, Russell.........SW ×
Rock Enon Springs, Fred'k. N 25
● Rockfish Depot, Nelson...C 75
Rockford, Stafford...........N 12
Rock House, Russell......SW 12
● Rockingham, RockinghamN 120
Rockingham Springs, Rockingham................. N ×
Rock Island, Buckingham.. C 12
Rock Mills, (see New Store) . ×
Rock Springs, (see Cripz)..... ×
Rock Spring, WestmorelandE ×
Rockville, Hanover......... C 5
Rocky Gap, Bland........ SW 20
Rocky Glen, Shenandoah...N ×
Rocky Mills, Lunenburg....S ×
● **Rocky Mount**, FranklinS 628
Rocky Point, Botetourt.... W ×
Rocky Run, Orange.........C ×
Rocky Station, Lee........SW 15
● Rodes, Bedford...........C ×
Rodden, Halifax............ S ×
Rodney, Bedford............C ×
Rodophil, Amelia........... C 10
● *Rogers*, Southampton....SE ×
● Rolla, Augusta........... W 45
Rolling Hill, Charlotte...... S 30
Rolling Mill, Campbell..... C ×
Rollins Fork, King George..E 15
Rollpone, Russell.........SW ×
Roman, Augusta........... W ×
● *Romancoke*, King WilliamE ×
Ronald, (see Bangs).......... ×
Roney, Spottsylvania....... C ×
Roper, Wythe...............SW ×
Rorrer, Patrick............. S ×
● *Rorerin*, Roanoke.........SW ×
Rose Bower, Appomattox.. C ×
Rosedale, Russell......... SW 50
Rose Hill, Lee..............SW 25
Roseland, Nelson........... C 10
Rose Mills, Nelson.......... C 15
Rosenberger, Frederick....N ×
Roseville, Stafford..........N 30
Rosney City, Buckingham.. C ×
● *Ross*, Henry.............. S ×
Rosslyn, Alexandria........N 300
Rough Creek, Charlotte.....S 30
● Round Hill, Loudoun.....N 207
Routts, Fauquier............N 25
Rover, Patrick.............. S ×
● Rowanta, Dinwiddie...... S 15
Roxton, Lunenburgh........S ×
Royalton Mills, Amelia.....C 10
Rubermont, Lunenburgh... S 7
Rucker's Cross Roads, (see Hurt's Store)............. ×
Ruckersville, Greene........C 20
Rugby, Grayson.............SW 12
Rumford Academy, King William.....................E 10
Rumford, King William.... E ×
Rural Bower, Greensville...S 10
Rural Home, Grayson.....SW 12
● Rural Retreat, Wythe...SW 300
Rushville, Rockingham.....N 37
Russell Creek, Patrick...... S 12
● **Rustburgh**, Campbell..C 352
● Ruther Glen, Caroline.... E 70
Ruthville, Charles City......E ×
Rux, Brunswick............ S ×
Ryan, Loudoun.............N ×
Rye Cove, Scott...........SW 90
Rye Valley, Smyth..........SW 30
Ryland, Culpeper...........N ×
Sabbat Island, Goochland..C 100
Sabot Island, Goochland.... C 15
Saddle, Granson...........SW 12
Sadler's Neck, Gloucester. E 25
● *Saffer's*, Augusta........ W ×
Saffolds, Mecklenburg......S ×
Sago, Pennysivania..........S 10
Saint Bridges, Norfolk.... SE ×
● *Saint Clair*, Tazewell.. SW ×
Saint Clair's Bottom, S'ythS W 10
Saint David's Church, Shen'hN ×
● Saint Just, Orange........ C 12
Saint Lukes, Shenandoah...N 12
● Saint Paul, Wise........SW ×
Saint Stephen's, King&QueenE 60
Saint Stephen's Church, King & Queen.............. E 60
Saint Tammany's, Meckl'nb'gS 70
● **Salem**, Roanoke.......SW 3,279
Salemville, Gloucester...... E ×
Salisbury Furnace, Bote'rt. W 60
Salt Creek, Amherst........ C 8
● *Saltpetre*, Botetourt..... W ×
● Saltpetre Cave, Botetourt. W 50
● Saltville, Washington...SW 250
Saluda, Middlesex.........E 150
Samos, Middlesex...........E ×
Sampson, Augusta..........W 12
Sampson's Wharf, Nor'landE ×
Sandidge's, Amherst........ C 20
Sand Lick, Dickenson.... SW 50
Sands, (see Stanleyton) ...... ×
Sandy, Rappahannock.......N ×
Sandy Bottom, Middlesex...E 10
Sandy Ford, Bedford........C ×
Sandy Hook, Goochland.....C 10
Sandy Level, Pittsylvania...S 10
Sandy River, Pittsylvania...S 100
Sanford, Accomack..........E 30
Sangerville, Augusta.........W 30
San Marino, Dinwiddie......S 27
● Sansom, Carroll.........SW 18
Santos, Floyd............. SW ×
Sassafras, Gloucester....... E 180
Sassin, Pulaski............SW 60
Saumsville, Shenandoah....N 200
● Saunders, Nansemond...SE ×
Savage Crossing, Nanse'nd SE ×
Savageville, Accomack...... E 22
Savannah, Alleghany.......W 30
● Savedge, Surry........... SE 50
● *Savernake*, Rockbridge . W ×
● Saxe, Charlotte........... S ×
Sayers' Furnace, Wythe..SW ×
Sayersville, Tazewell......SW 12
● *Schooler*, Montgomery..SW ×
Schuyler, Nelson............C ×
● Scotland, Surry...........SE ×
● Scottsburgh, Hallifax.....S 297
Scott's Creek, (seePortsmouth) ×
Scott's Cross Roads, Meck'g. S 12
Scottsford, Rockingham....N 30
● Scottsville, Albemarle... C 362
Scottsville, (see Portsmouth). ×
● *Screamerville*, Spots'vania. C ×
Scruggs, Franklin .... S 24
Seaview, Northampton..... E ×
Seay, Lunenburgh..........S 5
Sebonay, Tazewell........ SW ×
Seaysville, (see Dawn)....... ×
Sebrell, Southampton......SE 18
Sedalia, Bedford........... C 30
● *Seldon*, Goochland.........C ×
Selma, Alleghany.......... W 40
Selone, Fauquier.......... N ×
Sentinel, Warren...........N ×
Septa, Isle of Wight......... SE ×
Seven Fountains, Shen'doah. N 50
● Seven Islands, Fluvanna..C 30
● Seven Mile Ford, Smyth. SW 75
Seven Pines, Henrico....... C 10
● *Seventeen Mile Siding*, Nansemond.............SE ×
● *Seventy Five Mile Siding*, Prince George.........SE ×
Severn, Gloucester..........E 30
Seville, Madison.............N 15
Sewell's Point, Norfolk...SE ×
Shacklefords, King & Queen E 100
Shack Mills, Buchanan....SW 15
Shade, Fauquier.............N 24
● Shadwell, Albemarle......C 40
Shady Grove, Franklin......S 60
Shady Grove, (see Horner's). ×
Shadyside, Northampton....E 20
Shamrock, Grayson.......SW 73
Shanghai, King & Queen....E ×
Shanklin, Bath............W ×
Shannon Hill, Goochland....C 50
Sharp's Wharf, Richmond.. E 150
Sharon Spring, Bland.... SW 400
Shaw's Store, Mecklenburg. S 10
● Shawsville, MontgomerySW 50
Shawyer's Mills, Tazewell.SW 12
Sheets, (see Breckenridge)... ×
Shelburne, Montgomery..SW ×
Shelton, Nelson.............C 30
Shelton's Mills, Louisa......C 6
● Shenandoah, Page.........N 751
Shenandoah Alum Springs, Shenandoah.............N 50
● *Shenandoah Valley Junction*, Warren........... N ×
Shenandoah Valley Junction, Rockbridge............ W ×
● Shendun, Rockingham... N 709
Sheppards, Buckingham....C ×
Sheppton, Rockingham.... N ×
Sherando, Augusta.........W 25
Sherwood, Rockbridge.......W 120
Sheva, Pittsylvania..........S 10
Shield's Wharf, Accomack..E 12
Shiloh, King George......... E 30
Shipneck, Northumberland.E ×
Shirley, Charles City........E ×
Shockeysville, Frederick...N 24
Shockoe, Pittsylvania....... S 50
Shooting Creek, Franklin...S ×
● Shores, Fluvanna....... C 5
Short's Creek, Carroll.....SW ×
Shortsville, Washington...SW 36
● *Shoulder Hill*, Norfolk..SE ×
Showalter, Floyd............SW 30
Shraders, Tazewell.........SW ×
Shuff, Patrick...............S 36
Shuler, Page...............N ×
Shumansville, Caroline..... C ×
Siddons, Mecklenburg...... S ×
Sideburn, Fairfax..........N ×
Sidon, (see Whitmell)........ ×
Signitz, Northampton.......E ×
Silcott Springs, Loudoun....N 60
Silent Dell, Botetourt......W ×
Silver, Frederick............N ×
Silver Creek, Campbell..... C 10
Silver Leaf, Floyd..........SW ×
Silverton, Southampton.... SE ×
Simeon, Albemarle......... C 30
Simmonsville, Craig.........W 50
● *Simpson*, Campbell....... C ×
Simpson, Floyd........... SW 20
Singer, Roanoke...........SW 24
Singer's Glen, Rockingham. N 50
Sinking Creek, Craig..... .W 30
Sinnickson, Accomack.......E 30
Sirocco, Accomack...........E 50
Sitlington, Bath...........W ×
● Skinquarter, Chesterfield. C 30
● Skippers, Greensville..... S 30
● Skipwith, Mecklenburg...S 50
Slabe, Goochland........... C ×
Slate Mills, Rappahannock. N 100
Slate River Mills, Buck'ham. C 10
Slatesville, Pittsylvania.... S 5
Slate Works, Albemarle.....C ×
Slaughter, Nelson...........C 15
Slemp, Lee...............SW 12
Smithfield, Isle of Wight. SE 891
Smithland, Albemarle...... C 50
Smith's Creek, WashingtonSW 18
Smith's Cross Roads, Meck'bgS 15
● *Smith's Lock*, Campbell..C ×
Smithville, Charlotte ....S 500
Smithville (see Poquoson)..... ×
Smoky Ordinary, BrunswickS 40
Smoots, Caroline............C 15
Smyrna, Bedford............C 12
Smythers, Carroll.........SW ×
Snake Creek, Carroll......SW 10
Snake Run, Alleghany.....W ×

Snapp's, Tazewell.........SW 24
Snell, Spotsylvania..........C ×
Snickersville, Loudoun .....N 200
Snow Creek, Franklin ......S 60
Snowden, Amherst..........C 36
● *Snowden Station*, BedfordC ×
Snowflake, Scott...........SW ×
Snowville, Pulaski........SW 150
Snyder, Augusta............W ×
Solomon's, Henrico ....C ×
Somer, Chesterfield.........C ×
● Somerset, Orange.........C
Somerton, Nansemond....SE 50
Somerville, Fauquier.........N 30
Sonans, Pittsylvania..........S 24
Sontag, Franklin..............S 12
● Soudan, Mecklenburg.....S ×
● *South Anna*, Hanover....C ×
● South Boston, Halifax........S 1,789
South Clifton Forge, Alleghany ....W ×
● South Hill, Mecklenburg..S 40
South Norfolk (see Berkley). ×
South Quay, Nansemond.. SE 20
● South River, Rockbridge. W 150
Spainsville (see Wellsville) .. ×
Spanish Oaks, Appomattox..C 15
Sparta, Caroline..............C 40
Speedwell, Wythe.........SW 60
● Speer's Ferry, Scott ....SW 45
● Spencer, Henry ....S 20
Sperryville, Rappahannock..N 350
Spotcash, Brunswick........S ×
Spottsville, Surry............SE 15
● Spottswood, Augusta.....W 24
● *Spottswood*, Orange.........C ×
Spotsylvania, Spotsylva'aC 60
● Spout Spring, Appamattox C 25
Spring Creek, Rockingham. N 150
● *Springfield*, Fairfax ......N ×
Spring Garden, Pittsylvania. S 50
● Spring Grove, Surry.....SE 75
Spring Hill, Mecklenburg...S 24
● Springman, Fairfax ....N 30
Spring Mills, Appamattox...C 20
Spring Vale, Fairfax.........N 25
Spring Valley, Grayson ...SW 25
Springville, Tazewell......SW 30
● Springwood, Botetourt...W 100
Stafford C. H. Stafford....N 100
Stafford Store, Stafford .....N 24
Staffordsville, Giles.........SW 30
Stage Junction, Fluvianna..C ×
● *Stanard*, Goochland........C 100
Stanardsville, Greene ...C 330
● *Stanley*, Page...............N 100
Stanleyton, Page.............N 125
Stanly, Henry ....S ×
Stapleton Mills, Amherst....C 5
Star, Carroll ....SW ×
Starkey, Patrick ....S ×
● *Starkey*, Roanoke ....SW ×
Star Lick, Rockingham.....N ×
Star Tannery, Frederick....N 30
State Works, Albemarle ....C ×
● **Staunton**, Augusta.....W 6,975
● *Staunton River*, Pittsylv'a S 15
Stebbins, Halifax............S ×
● *Steele*, Alleghany ....W ×
Steeleburgh, Tazewell ....SW 8
Steele's Tavern, Augusta...W 108
Steeleville, Southampton..SE ×
● Stella, Patrick ....S 12
● *Stephens*, Spotsylvania....C ×
● Stephens City, Frederick. N 443
● Stephenson, Frederick....E 30
● Sterling, Loudoun........N 150
● *Sterrett*, Rockbridge.....W ×
Stevensburgh, Culpepper ...N 250
Stevens Creek, Grayson...SW 15
Stevensville, King & Queen. E 75
● *Stevers*, Nansemond.....SE 50
Stewartsville, Bedford......E 150
Stewart's Wharf, Northa'tonE ×
Stickleyville, Lee..........SW 40
Stillman, Fluvanna.........C 30
● Stockton, Henry ....S 20
Stoddert, Cumberland ....E ×
● Stokes, Goochland ....C 30
● Stokesland, Pittsylvania.. S 24
Stone Bridge, Clark..........N 20
Stoneleigh, Fairfax..........N ×
Stone Mountain, Carroll...SW 20
Stonewall, Augusta..........W 60
● Stony Creek, Sussex.....SE 195
Stony Cross, Mecklenburg...S 25
Stony Man, Page............N 100

Virginia

Stony Point, Albemarle......C 100
Stony Point Mills, Cumb'rl'dE 20
Stormont, Middlesex........E ×
● Story's, Southampton ...SE ×
Stovall, Halifax..............S 12
Stover's Shops, Augusta....W ×26
Stowersville, Bland.......SW ×
Straightstone, Pittsylvania...S 10
Strait Creek, Highland.....W 24
● Strasburgh, Shenandoah..N 646
● *StrasburghJunc.*Sh'n'd'ahN ×
Stratford, Westmoreland....E 12
Stratton, Dickenson........SW ×
● *Strawberry Hill*, Henrico C ×
Streets, Middlesex...........E ×
Stribling Springs, Augusta..W 35
Strom, Botetourt............W 12
● **Stuart**, Patrick ....S 332
● Stuart's Draft, Augusta ..W 50
Stubbs, Spottsylvania ....C ×
Studley, Hanover...........C 8
Stump, Washington.........SW 12
Sturgeon Point, Charles City E 50
Sturgeonville, Brunswick...S 519
Sublett's, Powhatan ....C 200
Success, Warren.............N 12
Sudley Mills (see Catharpin) . ×
Sudley Springs, Prince William ....N 12
● **Suffolk**, Nansemond...SE 3,354
Sugar Grove, Smyth.......SW 50
Sugarland (see Morrisville).. ×
Sulphur Mines, Louisa ......C 30
Sumerduck, Fauquier ....N 36
Summerdean, Augusta .....W 50
Summerfield, Grayson.... SW 30
Summers, Rockbridge.........W 25
● Summit, Spotsylvania.....C 18
● *Summit*, Chesterfield.....C ×
● *Summit*, Dinwiddie ....S ×
Summit Station, New Kent. E 15
Sunnybank, Northumberl'd E ×
● Sunny Side, Cumberland..E 30
Sun Rise, Bath ....W 12
Surry C. H. Surry ....SE 75
Sussex C. H., Sussex ....SE 15
Suter's, Rockingham ....N ×
Sutherland, Dinwiddie ......S 80
● Sutherlin, Pittsylvania....S 30
Swansboro, Chesterfield ....C ×
Swansonville, Pittsylvania...S 40
Sweet Chalybeate, Allegh'y W 70
Sweet Hall, King William .. E 5
Swepson, Mecklenburg.......S 60
● *Swift Creek*, Chesterfield..C ×
Swift Run, Rockingham....N 24
● Swoope, Augusta..........W 25
● Sword's Creek, Russell .SW ×
***Sycamore* (see Manteo)......** ×
● SycamoreStation, Pitts'v'a. S 45
Sycoline, Loudoun..........N ×
Sydnorsville, Franklin....... S 30
Sykes, Accomack ....E 30
Sylvatus, Carroll...........SW 12
Tabor, Washington..........SW ×
Tabscott, Goochland ....C ×
Tackett's Mills, Stafford ....N 15
● Tacoma, Wise...............SW 25
Talleysville, New Kent......E 15
Tally, Cumberland ....E 12
Talmash, Giles..............SW ×
Talpa, Prince George......SE ×
Tampico, York ....E ×
Tangier, Accomack ....E 100
● Tanner's Creek, Norfolk SE 150
Tannersville, Tazewell.... SW 12
Tan Yard, Henry..............S 18
Tappahannock, Essex...E 452
Tarkiln, Patrick..............S 12
Tarpon, Dickenson..........SW 12
Tarry's Mill, Mecklenburg.. S 20
● Tasley, Accomack..........E 20
Tasso, Wise.................SW ×
● *Tates Switch*, Scott.....SW ×
Tatum, Orange...............C ×
● *Taylor*, Orange............C ×
Taylor's Mill, (see Warsaw).. ×
Taylorsburg, Henry......... S ×
Taylor's Store, Franklin.....S 20
Taylorstown, Loudoun......N 40
● Taylorsville, Hanover.....C 25
Tazewell C. H., T'zew'llSW 700
Teck, King William.........E 18
Temperanceville, AccomackE 75
● *Temples*, Chesterfield.....C ×
Templeman's Cross Roads, Westmoreland........ E 45

Virginia

Templeton, Prince George.SE 25
Tenth Legion, Rockingham. N 4
Terrell, (see Bells)............ ×
Terry's Fork, Floyd.......SW 12
Terryville, Charlotte..........S ×
Tettington, Charles City.....E 12
Thalia, Princess Anne .... SE ×
● Thaxton, Bedford.........C 40
The Falls, Nottoway.........C 12
The Grottoes, (see Shendun) . ×
The Hollow, Patrick ....S 12
Theological Seminary, F'rf'xN 240
● The Plains, Fauquier.....N 100
Thessalia, Giles............SW 30
● *Thirty-Nine Mile Siding*, Isle of Wight........ SE ×
Thistle, Henrico............ C ×
Thomasburgh, Brunswick...S 33
● *Thompson*, Rockbridge..W ×
Thompson'sCrossRds. LouisaC 15
Thompson's Mill, Fauquier. N 15
Thompson's Valley, Taz'll. SW 30
Thornburgh, Spotsylvania .. C ×
● *Thorn Creek*, Goochland..C ×
Thornhill, Orange...........C 75
Thoroughfare, Prince Will'mN 25
Three Corners, Louisa.......C 5
Three Square, Goochland...C ×
Tide, Lee...................SW 18
Tight Squeeze, (see Chatham) ×
Tilson's Mill, Bland. ......SW 36
Tim, Patrick..................S ×
● Timber Ridge, RockbridgeW 25
● Timberville, Rockingham N 100
Timore, Pittsylvania.........S ×
Timothy, Craig..............W ×
Tim's Wharf, (see Fairport). ×
● *Tinder*, Orange.............C 14
● *Tinker Creek*, Roanoke.SW ×
Tinker Knob, Botetourt....W ×
Tinkling, Lunenburgh...... S ×
Tipton, Carroll............SW ×
● Tip Top, Tazewell...... SW ×
● Toano, James City........ E 80
● Tobaccoville, Powhatan .. C ×
Tobax, Patrick............. N ×
Toga, Buckingham...........C 12
Tolersville, Louisa.......... C 40
Topfaro, Brunswick.......... S ×
● *Tomahawk Church*, Chesterfield........................ C 10
● Tom's Brook, ShenandoahN 200
Topeco, Floyd...... ....SW ×
Topnot, Shenandoah........N ×
● *Torrison*, Alexandria.... N ×
Toshes, Pittsylvania..........S ×
Totaro, Brunswick.......... S 10
Totusky Bridge.(see Warsaw) ×
Tower Hill, Appomattox....C 15
Town House, (see Chilhowie) ×
Trammel Creek, DickensonSW 12
Trapp, Loudoun..............N 43
Traylorsville, Henry..........S 40
Treakles, Lancaster..........E ×
Tredway, Prince Edward....C 12
Trelow, Pittsylvania..........S ×
Trenholm, Powhatan..........C ×
Trenton Mills, Cumberland. E 15
● Trevillian's, Louisa.........C 60
● *Trice*, Albemarle...........C ×
Triford, Rockbridge.........W 200
Trigg, Giles..................SW ×
Trinity, Botetourt...........W ×
● *Triplett's*, Shenandoah...N ×
Trout Dale, Grayson........ SW 24
● Troutville, Botetourt.....W 100
Trower, Accomack.......... E 30
Trueblue, Orange........... C ×
Truhart, King & Queen..... E ×
Tuckahoe Pitts, Henrico....C 10
Tucker, Buckingham.......C ×
● *Tucker*, Norfolk..........SE ×
Tucker's Hill, WestmorelandE 15
● *Tuggle*, Prince Edward...C ×
Tuggle's Gap, Patrick.......N 12
Tula, Charlotte............. S ×
● *Tunis*, Princess Anne...SE ×
● Tunstall's, New Kent..... E 30
Turbeville, Halifax............S 60
Turkey Cove, Lee..........SW ×
Turman, Floyd..............SW 30
Turnbull, (seeFauquierSpr's) ×
Turner, Brunswick...........S ×
● *Turner*, Greensville.......S 30
● *Turner's*, Henrico.........C ×
Turtle Creek, Franklin.......S ×
Turtle Rock, Floyd....... SW 20

Virginia

Tweedy's, Campbell..........C 8
Twyman's Mill, Madison.....N 18
Twyman's Store, Spotsylva'aC 240
● Tye River Depot, Nelson..C 45
● Tyler's, Hanover..........C 20
● *Tyree*, Campbell..........C ×
Tyro, Nelson................C 24
Uggal, Southampton........SE ×
Ula, Franklin................S 30
● *Una*, Rockbridge........ W 60
● Union Hall, Franklin.......S 64
● Union Level, MecklenburghS 25
Union Mills, Fluvanna...... C 30
Union Village, (see Lottsburg) ×
● Unionville, Orange..........C 60
Unison, Loudoun.............N 120
University of Virginia, (see Charlottesville)......... ×
Upperville, Fauquier........N 400
Upper Zion, Caroline........C ×
Upright, Essex...............E 30
Uptonburg, King George....E ×
Urbanna, Middlesex.........E 400
● **Vaiden, James City.......E** ×
Vaiden's Cross Roads, Charles City.........................E 5
Vale, Fairfax.................N 18
Vallena, Fluvanna............C 49
Valentines, Brunswick.......S ×
Valley Centre, Highland.....W 12
Valley Creek, Scott....... SW 12
Valley Mills, (see Winchester) ×
Valley Mills, Augusta........ W 12
Valley View, Smyth.........SW 30
Valley View Springs, Shenandoah..............N ×
Van, Lee....................SW 36
Van Buren Furnace, Shenandoah.....................N 30
Vance, Pittsylvania.......... S 10
Vanderpool, Highland.......W ×
Vandola, Pittsylvania........S ×
Vanlear, Augusta............W 30
● *Variety*, Augusta..........W ×
Variety Mills, Nelson.........C 50
Variety Shade, Buckingham C ×
Varina Grove, Henrico.......C 5
● Vaucluse, Frederick.......N ×
Vaucluse Station, FrederickN ×
Vaughn, Floyd..............SW ×
Vawter's Store, Louisa.......C ×
Venner, Prince Edward.....C ×
Venus, Warren..............N 30
Verbena, Page...............N 49
● Verdierville, Orange.......C 80
● Verdon, Hanover.......... C 10
Vernon Hill, Halifax..........S 40
Vernon Mills, Fauquier......N 40
● *Verona*, Augusta.........W 45
Vesta, Patrick................S ×
● Vesuvius, Rockbridge....W 60
● Vicar's Switch, Montg'ySW ×
Vicksville, Southampton..SE 25
Victoria, Rockbridge........W ×
Victoria Mines, Rockbridge. W 60
● Vienna, Fairfax...........N 300
Viewtown, Rappahannook.N ×
Vigor, Louisa................C 30
Villa, Franklin...............S 26
Village, Northumberland....E 12
Vincent Store, Charlotte.....S ×
Vine, Princess Anne.......SE ×
● Vinitaville, Goochland....C 30
● Vinton, Roanoke.........SW 1,057
Viola, Pittsylvania...........S 15
Violetta, Halifax..............S ×
● Virgilina, Halifax...........S ×
Virginia Arsenic, Bromine and Lithia Springs, Montgomery.................SW ×
● Virginia Beach, Pr's AnneSE 20
Virginia City, Wise ....SW ×
● *Virginia Midland Junction*, Albemarle..........C ×
Volens, Halifax..............S ×
Voy, Prince William.........N 12
Vulcan, Orange..............C ×
Wabash, Giles..............SW 30
Wachapreague, Accomack...E 150
Waco, Orange...............C 10
Wade's, Bedford.............C 30
● Wadesville, Clark.........N 60
● *Wagners*, Nansemond ..SE ×
Wagram, Accomack.........E 60
● Waidsboro, Franklin.......S ×
● *Waids Summit*, Franklin.S ×
Wakefield, Surry...........SE 60

Virginia

● Wakefield Station, Sussex SE 85
Wakema, King William .....E ×
Walcot, Floyd ....SW ×
Waldemar, Dinwiddie........S ×
Waldens, King & Queen ....E ×
Waldrop, Louisa ....C ×
● *Walkers*, New Kent.......E ×
Walker Ford, Amherst.......C 12
● *Walker's Mount'n*, Wash.SW ×
Walkerton, King and Queen.E 70
● Wallace's Switch, Wash.SW 407
Wallaceton, Norfolk.......SE 30
● Wallers, Henry.............S ×
Wall's Bridge, Surry.......SE 5
● Walnut Hill, Lee.........SW ×
Walter's Ford (see Martinsville)...................... ×
● *Walthall*, Chesterfield....C 30
Walthall's Store Brunswick .S 15
Walton Furnace, Wythe..SW ×
Walton's Mills (see Flanigan's Mills)............... ×
Waltons Store, Louisa........C ×
Waltz, Carroll..............SW ×
Waqua, Brunswick............S 10
Wardsfork Mills, Charlotte..S 12
Ward's Gap, Carroll.......SW ×
● *Ward's Mill*, Lee.........SW ×
Ward's Mill, Carroll ....SW ×
Ward's Springs (see Elba).. ×
Wardtown, Northampton...E 40
Ware Neck, Gloucester......E 50
Ware's Wharf, Essex.........E 25
● *Warminster*, Nelson......C 5
Warm Springs, Bath... W 160
● Warren, Albemarle.........C 150
Warren Springs (see Buckton) ×
● **Warrenton**, Fauquier..N 1,346
Warrenton Junction (see Calverton)...................... ×
Warsaw, Richmond ....E 170
Warwick (see Denbigh)...... ×
Washington, R'pp'h'n'k.N 252
Washington, Rockbridge..W ×
Washington Springs, Washington......................SW ×
Waskey Mills, Botetourt... W 12
Waterfall, Prince William..N 30
Waterford, Loudoun.........N 385
● Waterlick, Warren.........N 25
Waterloo, Alexandria.......N 75
Waterloo, Culpeper ....N 16
Water View, Middlesex.....E 40
Watkins (see Orange C. H.).. ×
Watson, Loudoun.............N ×
Wattsborough, Lunenburgh.S 20
Wattsville, Accomack........E 15
● *Waugh*, Bedford.........C ×
Waverly (see Elkton) .... ×
● Waverly Station, Sussex.SE 150
Waxpool, Loudoun...........N ×
Way, Amherst...............C ×
Wayland, Scott..............SW 10
Waylandsburgh, Culpeper ..N 12
● Waynesborough, Augusta. W 646
● *Waynesboro Junction*, Augusta........................W ×
Wayside, Pittsylvania.......S 20
Weel, Pittsylvania............S 10
Webb, Carroll................SW ×
Weddle, Floyd..............SW ×
Weedonville, King George..E ×
Weems, Lancaster..........E 100
Welbourne, Loudoun.........N ×
Welchburgh, Scott..........SW 12
Welch's, Caroline ....C 24
Welcome, King George .....E ×
Wellford, Richmond..........E ×
● Wellington, Prince Will'mN ×
Wells Bridge, Surry.......SE ×
● *Welltown Pike*, FrederickN ×
Welltown, Frederick ....N 24
● Wellville, Nottoway........S 25
Well Water, Buckingham...C 35
● Wenonda, Pittsylvania ....S 10
Wert, Appomattox..........C ×
● *Wertz Summit*, Franklin..S ×
West Augusta, Augusta.... W 80
Westboro, Dinwiddie..........S ×
West End, Augusta ....W 283
● *West End*, Rockbridge ..W ×
● West End, Fairfax ....N ×
● *Westham*, Henrico.........C 24
Westland, Lancaster ....E 60
West Lynchburg, Campbell.C ×
● *West Miller's*, RockbridgeW ×
● West Norfolk, Norfolk..SE ×

Virginia

Westonville, Charlotte.......S 24
Westover, Charles City.....E 30
● West Point, King WilliamE 2,018
● *West Radford*, Montgo'ySW ×
● *West Roanoke*, RoanokeSW ×
West View, Goochland......C 30
Westwood, Hanover.........C ×
Wetsels, Green ....C ×
Weyanoke, Charles City.... E 12
● Weyer's Cave, Augusta... W 200
● *Whaley*, Nansemond....SE 290
● Whaleyville, NansemondSE 290
Wheatfield, Shenandoah....N ×
Wheatland, Loudoun.........N 15
Whitacre, Frederick..........N ×
Whiteforge, Scott...........SW 30
White Gate, Giles...........SW 50
Whitehall (see Mechum's Riv.) ×
White Marsh, Gloucester....E 40
White Marsh Roads, Nansemond............................ ×
● *White Oak*, Henrico........C ×
White Plains, Brunswick....S 90
● White Post, Clark.........N 150
White Ridge (see Morrisville) ×
White Rock, Bedford ....C 20
White Rock, Franklin........S 20
White's, Caroline.............C 18
● *White's*, Spotsylvania.....C ×
White Shoals, Lee..........SW 30
White Stone, Lancaster...SW 100
Whitesville, Halifax..........S 25
White Top, Grayson.......SW 24
● Whitlock, Halifax...........S 25
Whitmell, Pittsylvania......S 50
● Whittle's Depot, Pittsylv'aS 100
Whittle's Mills, Lunenburgh S 15
● *Wickham*, Hanover.......C ×
Wickliffe, Clarke ....N 30
Wicomico Church, Northumberland......................E 45
● Widewater, Stafford......N 50
● Wiehle, Fairfax ....N ×
● *Wierwood*, Northampton .E ×
Wightman, Mecklenburg ...S ×
Wilburn, Lunenburgh.......S ×
Wilcox's Wharf, Charles City..........................E 15
Wild Cat Summit, Wise ..SW ×
Wilderness, Orange..........C 15
Wildway, Appomattox......C ×
Wilkes, Bedford ....C 24
Wilkerson's, Westmoreland E ×
Willard, Fairfax.............N ×
Wilcox Wharf, Charles City.E 150
● *Williams*, Norfolk ......SE ×
● **Williamsburgh**, James City..........................E 1,831
Williams Mills, Lunenburgh.S 10
Williamsville, Bath.........W 30
Williams Wharf, Mathews ..E 10
Williesburg, Charlotte ....S ×
Willis, Cumberland,.......E ×
Willow, Amherst.............C 12
Willow Grove, MontgomerySW ×
● Willow Grove, Shenando'h N 24
Willow Spring, Russell....SW 24
● *Wilmer*, Campbell........C ×
Wilmer, Pittsylvania..........S ×
Wilmington, Fluvanna.......C 20
● Wilson's, Dinwiddie.......S 45
Wilsonville, Highland ..... W 25
Wilton, Middlesex ....E 20
Wilton Mines (see Glen Wilton) ×
● **Winchester**, FrederickN 5,196
Winder, Henrico.............C ×
● Windsor Sta., Isle of W't.SE 200
● *Windsor*, Fairfax.........N 12
● *Windsor*, New Kent.......E ×
Windsor Shades, New KentE 15
● Winfall, Campbell........ C 15
● Wingiula, Nelson.......... C 20
Winnie, Nottoway...........S ×
● Winston, Culpeper........ N ×
Winterpock, Chesterfield... C 20
Wise C. H., Wise........SW ×
● *Wiseley's*, Lee.......... SW ×
Wiseville, (see Paulington)... ×
Witten's Mills, Tazewell.. SW ×
Wittspur, Patrick...........S ×
Wolf Glade, Carroll.......SW 12
Wolftown, Madison........ N 100
● Wolf Trap, Halifax....... S 48
Woltz, Carroll...............SW 12
Wood, Scott..................SW 12
● Wood Bridge, Prince W'm N 35
Woodburn, Loudoun........N 12

Virginia

Town, County	Index	Pop.
● Woodford, Caroline	C	20
Wood Grove, (see Round Hill)		×
● Wood Lawn, Carroll	SW	10
Woodridge, Albemarle	C	25
Wood's Cross Roads, Glo'ster	E	30
● *Woods*, Albemarle	C	×
● **Woodstock**, Shenand'ah	N	1,068
Woodview, Brunswick	S	×
Woodville, Rappahannock	N	300
● *Woody*, Henry	S	×
Woolwine, Patrick	S	12
Worlds, Pittsylvania	S	10
Worrell's, Southampton	SE	10
Worsham, Prince Edward	C	40
Wyatt, Franklin	S	×
Wylliesburgh, Charlotte	S	50
● **Wytheville**, Wythe	SW	2,570
● Yale, Sussex	SE	×
Yancy, Rockingham	N	24
Yancey's Mills, Albemarle	C	10
Yanceyville, Louisa	C	25
Yanther Gap, Bath	W	×
Yards, Tazewell	SW	×
Yellow Branch, Campbell	C	29
Yellow Sulphur Springs, Montgomery	SW	12
Yokum Station, Lee	SW	24
Yorktown, York	E	221
Yost, Bath	W	×
Young's Store, Fanklin	S	24
● *Young's Summit*, Franklin	S	×
Yuma, Scott	SW	×
Zack, Rockbridge	W	×
Zamuth, Lancaster	E	×
Zepp, Shenandoah	N	24
Zion, Louisa	C	10
Zion's Hill, Botetourt	W	10
Zion's Mills, Lee	SW	150
Zollman, Rockbridge	W	×
Zulla, Fauquier	N	×
● Zuni, Isle of Wight	SE	50

WASHINGTON.

COUNTIES.	INDEX.	POP.
Adams	SE	2,098
Asotin	S	1,580
Chehalis	W	9,249
Clallam	NW	2,771
Clarke	SW	11,709
Columbia	SW	6,709
Cowlitz	SW	5,917
Douglas	C	3,161
Franklin	SE	696
Garfield	SE	3,897
Island	NW	1,787
Jefferson	W	8,368
King	C	63,989
Kitsap	W	4,624
Kittitass	S	8,777
Klickitat	S	5,167
Lewis	SW	11,499
Lincoln	E	9,312
Mason	W	2,826
Okanogan	C	1,467
Pacific	SW	4,358
Pierce	C	50,940
San Juan	NW	2,072
Skagit	NW	8,747
Skamania	S	774
Snohomish	NW	8,514
Spokane	E	37,487
Stevens	W	4,341
Thurston	W	9,675
Wahkiakum	SW	2,526
Walla Walla	SE	12,224
Whatcom	NW	18,591
Whitman	SE	19,109
Yakima	C	4,429
Total		349,390

TOWN. COUNTY.	INDEX.	POP.
Abel, Snohomish	NW	×
Abel's Landing, Chehalis	W	×
● Aberdeen, Chehalis	W	1,638
Acme, Whatcom	NW	50
Addy, Stevens	W	10
● Adelaide, King	C	35
Agate, Lewis	SW	×
Ahtanum, Yakima	C	×
● Ainslie, Lewis	SW	100
● Alderton, Pierce	C	50
● *Aldrich*, Walla Walla	SE	×
Alki, Whitman	SE	×
● *Allen's Siding*, Stevens	W	×
Allyn, Mason	W	75
Alma, Okanogan	C	20
● Almira, Lincoln	E	150
Almota, Whitman	SE	40
Alpha, Lewis	SW	×
Alpowa, Garfield	SE	25
● *Alta Vista*, Spokane	E	×
● Alto, Columbia	SW	14
Amboy, Clarke	SW	×
● *American Lake*, Pierce	C	×
Amoca, Pierce	C	×
● Anacortes, Skagit	NW	1,131
Anatone, Asotin	SE	200
Anderson, Kitsap	W	×
Appletree, Kitsap	W	×
Arden, Stevens	W	×
Argyle, San Juan	NW	×
● Arlington, Snohomish	NW	100
Artic, Chehalis	W	30
Artondale, Pierce	C	60
Asotin, Asotin	SE	200
Atahram, Yakima	C	×
Atlanta (see Samish)		×
Avon, Skagit	NW	250
Axford, Chehalis	W	×
Badger, Douglas	C	×
● *Badger*, Yakima	C	×
Baker River (see Minnehaha)		×
Balch, Pierce	C	×
● Ballard, King	C	×
● *Ballard Junction*, King	C	1,173
Bangor, Kitsap	W	×
Banyan, Lewis	SE	×
● *Barnes*, Yakima	C	×
Barry, Douglas	C	×
Battle Ground, Clarke	SW	60
Bay Centre, Pacific	SW	225
Bay View, Skagit	NW	150
Bay View, Wahkiakum	SW	×
Beach, Whatcom	NW	10
Beaver, Clallam	NW	×
Belfast, Skagit	NW	×
Bellevue, King	C	×
Bellingham (see Fairhaven)		×
● Belmont, Whitman	SE	25
● *Belmore*, Thurston	W	×
Bemis, Adams	SE	×
● *Bender*, Yakima	C	×
Benson, Lincoln	E	×
Bergen, Mason	W	×
● Berryman, Walla Walla	SE	30
Bessemer (see Birdsview)		×
Bickleton, Klickitat	S	35
Big Creek, Kittitass	C	×
● Birch, King	C	×
Birch Bay, Whatcom	NW	50
Birdsview, Skagit	NW	30
Bismarck, Pierce	C	×
● Black Diamond, King	C	561
● *Blackmans*, Snohomish	NW	×
● *Blackmans Mill*, Sno'h.	NW	×
● Black River, King	C	×
● Blaine, Whatcom	NW	1,563
Blakely, (see Port Blakely)		×
Blanchard, Skagit	NW	200
Block House, Klickitat	S	12
● *Bluff Siding*, Walla Walla	SE	×
Blyn, Clallam	NW	×
Boise, King	C	150
● *Boise Creek*, King	C	×
Boisfort, Lewis	SW	150
● *Bolles Junc.*, Walla Walla	SE	×
Bonanza, Stevens	W	×
Bossburg, Stevens	W	×
Boston, Clallam	NW	×
● Bothell, King	C	400
● Boulevard, King	C	×
Bremer, Lewis	SW	×
Brents, Lincoln	E	25
Brice, King	C	×
Brinnon, Jefferson	W	×
Brookfield, Wahkiakum	SW	75
Brooklyn, Pacific	SW	×
Brown, Yakima	C	29
Brownsville, Kitsap	W	×
Bruceport, Pacific	SW	30
Brush Prairie, Clarke	SW	30
Brush Prairie, Thurston	W	×
● *Bryant*, Snohomish	NW	×
● *Buckeye*, Spokane	E	48
● Buckley, Pierce	C	1,000
● Bucoda, Thurston	W	945
Buenna, King	C	×
Burge, Kittitass	C	50
Burlington, Skagit	NW	×
● Burnett, Pierce	C	×
Butler, Kitsap	W	×
● *Byron*, Yakima	C	×
Calispell, Stevens	W	×
Calverton, Lincoln	E	×
● *Canon*, Kittitass	C	×
● *Canton*, King	C	×
Canyon, Klickitat	S	×
Cape Horn, Skamania	S	×
Caples, Cowlitz	SW	×
● Carbanado, Pierce	C	705
● *Cardmoor*, King	C	×
Carlston, (see Bangor)		×
● Carrollton, Cowlitz	SW	50
● *Cascade Junc.*, Pierce	C	×
Cascades, Skamania	S	164
● Castle Rock, Cowlitz	SW	681
● *Cathcart*, Snohomish	NW	×
Cathlamet, Wahkiakum	SW	75
Cedarholm, Snohomish	NW	×
● Cedar Mountain, King	C	×
Cedarville, Chehalis	W	54
Center, Jefferson	W	150
Centerville, Klickitat	S	120
Central, (see Chimacum)		×
Central Ferry, Garfield	SE	×
● Centralia, Lewis	SW	2,026
● Chard, Garfield	SE	×
Charleston, Kitsap	W	×
● Chattaroy, Spokane	E	25
Chautauqua, King	C	×
● **Chehalis**, Lewis	SW	1,309
Chelan, Okanogan	C	150
Chelan Falls, Okanogan	C	×
● Cheney, Spokane	E	647
Chenowith, Skamania	S	100
Cherry Valley, King	C	70
● Chester, Spokane	E	×
● Che-we-lah, Stevens	W	75
Chico, Kitsap	W	25
Chimacum, Jefferson	W	35
Chinook, Pacific	SW	×
● Christopher, King	C	×
Chuckanut, Whatcom	NW	×
Cinebar, Lewis	SW	×
Clallam Bay, Clallam	NW	200
● Claquato, Lewis	SW	50
Clay, Lewis	SW	×
Clearbrook, Whatcom	NW	10
Clear Lake, Skagit	NW	×
● Cle Elum, Kittitass	C	243
● *Cle Elum Iron Mines*, Kittitass	C	×
Clenton, Whitman	SE	5
Cleveland, Klickitat	S	33
Clifton, Mason	W	100
● *Climax*, Walla Walla	SE	×
Clinton, (see Phinney)		×
Clover, Okanogan	C	×
Cloverdale, Yakima	C	×
● *Clyde*, Walla Walla	SE	×
Coats Creek, Asotin	S	×
Coin, Whitman	SE	50
● Colnmo, Thurston	W	×
Colby, Kitsap	W	25
● *Cole*, King	C	×
● **Colfax**, Whitman	SE	1,649
Collins Landing, Skamania	S	×
● *Collis*, Walla Walla	SE	×
● Colton, Whitman	SE	150
Columbia City, King	C	×
Columbus, Klickitat	S	100
● **Colville**, Stevens	W	539
Commercial Mills, (see Dayton)		×
Conconully, Okanogan	C	232
● *Connell*, Franklin	SE	×
Copalis, Chehalis	W	×
● *Coppei*, Walla Walla	SE	×
Cora, Lewis	SW	×
Corbin, Stevens	W	×
● Cosmopolis, Chehalis	W	287
● Coulee City, Douglas	C	35
Coupeville, Island	NW	513
Cove, Whitman	SE	×
Covello, Columbia	SW	75
Covington, King	C	×
Cowiche, Yakima	C	96
Cowlitz, Lewis	SW	375
Crab Creek, Lincoln	E	12
Crescent, Lincoln	E	31
Crescent Bay, (see Pt. Crescent)		×
● *Crest*, Whitman	SE	×
● Creston, Lincoln	E	25
Crimea, Klickitat	S	×
● *Crocker*, Pierce	C	×

● *Cross*, Pierce ... C ×
Crystal Springs, Kitsap ... W ×
Curlew, Spokane ... E 60
Custer, Whatcom ... NW 25
Cypress, Skagit ... NW ×
Daisy, Stevens ... W ×
Damon, Chehalis ... W ×
Darrington, Snohomish ... NW ×
● Davenport, Lincoln ... E 396
Davisine, (see Elmira) ... ×
● *Days*, King ... C ×
● **Dayton**, Columbia ... SW 1,880
Dean, Snohomish ... NW 50
Decatur, San Juan ... NW ×
Deception, Skagit ... NW 297
● Deep Creek Falls, Spokane E 100
Deep River, Wahkiakum ... SW ×
● Deer Park, Spokane ... E 30
● *Delaney*, Columbia ... SW ×
Delano, Pierce ... C ×
Delight, Adams ... SE ×
De Lions, Jefferson ... W ×
Delta, Whatcom ... NW 29
● Deming, Whatcom ... NW 25
● *Dennys*, Lincoln ... E ×
● Derby, King ... C ×
● *Derringer*, Pierce ... C ×
● Des Moines, King ... C 212
Dewatto, Mason ... W ×
● Diamond, Whitman ... SE 20
● *Divide*, Walla Walla ... SE ×
● Dixie, Walla Walla ... SE 150
Dixon's, Garfield ... SE ×
Doe Bay, San Juan ... NW 100
Dot, Klickitat ... S ×
Douglas, Douglas ... C 100
● *Douty*, Pierce ... C ×
● Dragoon, Spokane ... E 25
● *Dry Creek*, Walla Walla SE ×
● *Dubuque*, Snohomish ... NW ×
Duckabush, Jefferson ... W ×
● *Dudley*, Klickitat ... S ×
Dudley, Walla Walla ... SE ×
Dungeness, Clallam ... NW 75
Dunlor, Whitman ... SE ×
● Durham, King ... C ×
Dwamish, King ... C 300
Eadonia, Lewis ... SW 60
Eagle Cliff, Wahkiakum ... SW 25
● Eagle Gorge, King ... C ×
Eagle Harbor, Kitsap ... W ×
Eagleton, Lewis ... SW ×
Earl, Lincoln ... E 30
East Anacortes, (see Fidalgo) ×
East Clallam, Clallam ... NW ×
● Easton, Kittitass ... C ×
East Seattle, King ... C ×
East Sound, San Juan ... NW ×
● East Spokane, Spokane ... E ×
East Toledo, (see Eadonia) ... ×
Eatonville, Pierce ... C 32
Ebey's L'nd'g, Island ... NW ×
Echo, Stevens ... W ×
Eddyville, King ... C ×
● *Eden*, Whitman ... SE ×
● Edgewater, King ... C 191
Edison, Skagit ... NW 100
● *Edison*, Pierce ... C ×
● Edmonds, Snohomish ... NW 300
Egypt, Lincoln ... E 25
● Elberton, Whitman ... SE 100
Eliza Island, Whatcom ... NW ×
Elk, Spokane ... E ×
● **Ellensburgh**, Kittitass C 2,768
Elliott's L'nd'g, (see Brookfield) ×
● Elma, Chehalis ... W 345
Elokomin, (see Cathlamet)) ... ×
● *Eltopia*, Franklin ... SE ×
● Elwood, Walla Walla ... SE ×
● Endicott, Whitman ... SE 185
Enterprise, Whatcom ... NW ×
● Enumclaw, King ... C 200
Ethel, Lewis ... SW ×
Etna, Clarke ... SW 60
Eureka, Walla Walla ... SE 22
Eureka, Wahkiakum ... SW ×
● *EurekaJunc.* W'llaWalla SE ×
● *Evans*, Walla Walla ... SE ×
● Everett, Snohomish ... NW ×
Everson, Whatcom ... NW ×
Ewartsville, Whitman ... SE ×
Excelsior, Pierce ... C ×
● Fairfield, Spokane ... E 150
● *Fairfield*, Walla Walla ... SE ×
● Fairhaven, Whatcom ... NW 4,076
Fairview, Lincoln ... E 20
● *Fallows*, Whitman ... SE ×

Washington

● Falls City, King ... C 300
● Farmington, Whitman ... SE 418
● Fayette, Lewis ... SW ×
Felida, Clarke ... SW ×
● *Fellows*, Lincoln ... E ×
Ferndale, (see W. Ferndale) ×
● Fern Hill, Pierce ... C ×
Fern Prairie, Clarke ... SW 110
Ferry, Lewis ... SW 35
Fidalgo, Skagit ... NW 297
Fidalgo City, Skagit ... NW 144
Fir, Skagit ... NW 280
Fisher's, Clarke ... SW 96
● *Fisk*, Pierce ... C ×
Fletcher, Adams ... SE ×
● *Fletcher*, Whitman ... SE 32
● Florence, Snohomish ... NW 60
Forks, Clallam ... NW ×
Forreston, Spokane ... E ×
Fort Canby, Pacific ... SW 60
Fort Colville, (see Colville) ... ×
Fort Simcoe, Yakima ... C 30
Fort Spokane, (see Miles) ... ×
Fort Steilacoom, Pierce ... C 360
Fort Townsend, Jefferson ... W 240
● *Fort Walla Walla*, Walla Walla ... SE ×
Fox Island, Pierce ... C ×
Frankfort, Pacific ... SW 30
● Franklin, King ... C 647
Fredonia, Skagit ... NW ×
● *Freedom*, Spokane ... E ×
Freeport, Cowlitz ... SW 200
Freeport, (see Milton) ... ×
● Fremont, King ... C 802
Friday Harbor, S.J'nN. W 150
Fruitland, Stevens ... W ×
Fulda, Klickitat ... S 32
Fulton, Lewis ... SW ×
Galena, Snohomish ... NW ×
● Garfield, Whitman ... SE 317
● *Garrison*, Whitman ... SE ×
● Gate City, Thurston ... W 100
Gault, Skagit ... NW ×
Geer, Lincoln ... E ×
Geneva, Whatcom ... NW 40
Gera, Whatcom ... NW ×
Getchell, Snohomish ... NW ×
Gettysburgh, Clallam ... NW 25
Gibraltar, Skagit ... NW ×
Gig Harbor, Pierce ... C 321
● *Gilliam*, Walla Walla ... SE ×
● *Gilman*, King ... C 600
Gilmer, Klickitat ... S 33
Gilmore, Thurston ... W ×
● *Glade*, Franklin ... SE ×
Gleneden, Lewis ... SW 48
Glenwood, Klickitat ... S 36
● *Glenwood*, Whitman ... SE ×
Goble, Cowlitz ... SW ×
Golden, Okanogan ... C ×
Goldendale, Klickitat ... S 702
● Goodwin, Stevens ... W ×
Goshen, Whatcom ... NW ×
Gould City, Garfield ... SE ×
● *Govan*, Lincoln ... E ×
● *Grace*, Snohomish ... NW ×
Grand Coulee, Lincoln ... E 10
Grand Forks, Chehalis ... W ×
Grand Mound, Thurston ... W 96
● *Grand Mound Sta.* Thurston ... W ..
● *Grange City*, Columbia SW ×
Granite, Snohomish ... NW ×
Granite Falls, Snohomish NW ×
Granite Lake, Spokane ... E ×
Granville, Chehalis ... W ×
● Gravelless, Lincoln ... E 5
● Gray's Harbor, Chehalis. W 523
Gray's Harbor City, Chehalis W ×
Gray's River, Wahkiakum SW 38
Green River, King ... C 30
● *Greenwood*, Spokane ... E ×
Griffith, Adams ... SE 7
Griswold, San Juan ... NW ×
Grove, Mason ... W ×
Guemes, Skagit ... NW 70
Gull Harbor, Thurston ... W ×
● Guy, Whitman ... SE 75
● *Hadley*, Walla Walla ... SE ×
Hadlock, Jefferson ... W 237
Haller City, Snohomish ... NW 100
Hamilton, Skagit ... NW 203
Hanson Ferry, Asotin ... S ×
Hardan, Whatcom ... NW ×
Harlow Junc. (see Gate City) ×
Harmony, Lewis ... SW ×

Washington

Harrington, Lincoln ... E 30
Harrison, Mason ... W ×
● *Harriston*, Adams ... SE 24
● Hartford, Snohomish ... NW 50
Hartland, Klickitat ... S ×
● Hartline, Douglas ... C 12
Harts, Pierce ... C ×
Harvey, Stevens ... W ×
● Hatton, Adams ... SE 70
● *Hay*, Whitman ... SE ×
Hayes, Clarke ... SW ×
Haynie, Whatcom ... NW 10
Hazard, Spokane ... E 50
Heffron, Skagit ... NW ×
Hellgate, Lincoln ... E 25
Helmer, Mason ... W ×
Hesseltine, Lincoln ... E 10
● *Highland*, Walla Walla SE ×
● Hillhurst, Pierce ... C 35
Hillsdale, Whatcom ... NW 26
● *Hite*, Spokane ... E ×
Hockinson, Clarke ... SW 120
Homestead, Douglas ... C ×
Hoodsport, Mason ... W 100
● Hooper, Whitman ... SE ×
Hopewell, Clarke ... SW ×
● Hoquiam, Chehalis ... W 1,302
● Hot Springs, King ... C ×
Houghton, King ... C 200
Humptulips, Chehalis ... W 15
Hunters, Stevens ... W 33
● *Hunts*, Walla Walla ... SE ×
● *Hunt's Junc.* Walla Walla SE ×
● Huntsville, Columbia ... SW 150
Icicle, Okanogan ... C ×
Ilia, Garfield ... SE 25
Ilwaco, Pacific ... SW 517
Independence, Lewis ... SW 30
Index, Snohomish ... NW ×
● Inglewood, King ... C 9
● *Iona*, Adams ... SE ×
Irondale, **Jefferson ... W 25**
Jackson, Cowlitz ... SW ×
● Jamieson, Spokane ... E ×
● *Jarman Prairie*, Skagit NW ×
● Johnson, Whitman ... SE 50
● *Jones*, Thurston ... W ×
Juanita, King ... C ×
Junction City, Jefferson ... W 25
Juno, Chehalis ... W ×
● *Kahlotus*, Franklin ... SE ×
● **Kalama**, Cowlitz ... SW 325
Kamiac, Whitman ... SE ×
Kamilche, Mason ... W 250
Kamilche, Mason ... W 195
● Kangley, King ... C ×
Kapousen, Pierce ... C ×
Keese, Whatcom ... NW ×
● *Keith*, King ... C ×
Kelly, Lincoln ... E 72
● Kelso, Cowlitz ... SW 354
● Kennewick, Yakima ... C 30
● Kent, King ... C 853
Kerns, Cowlitz ... SW 100
Kettle Falls, Stevens ... W 525
Kettle Falls Sta. Stevens ... W ×
Kingston, Kitsap ... W 26
Kinney, (see Prosser) ... ×
● Kiona, Yakima ... C ×
● Kirkland, King ... C 1,000
Kittitass, Kittitass ... C ×
Klickitat Landing, (see Lyle) ×
● *Kline*, Lincoln ... E ×
Knab, Lewis ... SW ×
Knapp's Landing, Clarke SW ×
Knappton, Pacific ... SW 250
Konewock, Yakima ... C 30
La Camas, Clarke ... SW 417
Lacey, Thurston ... W ×
La Center, Clarke ... SW 125
La Conner, Skagit ... NW 398
● *La Cross Junc.* Whitman SE ×
Ladew, Lewis ... SW 18
La Fayette, Skagit ... NW 8
Laidlaw, Chehalis ... W 31
Lake, Asotin ... SE 120
● *Lake*, Franklin ... SE ×
Lake Bay, Pierce ... C 45
Lake Chelan, (see Chelan) ... ×
Lake City, Pierce ... C 100
Lake Hooker, Jefferson ... W ×
Lake Park, Pierce ... C ×
Lake Tapps, Pierce ... C ×
Lake Union, (see Seattle) ... ×
● Lake View, Pierce ... C 256
Langley, Island ... NW ×
Lapush, Clallam ... NW 325

Place	Population
Larene, Lincoln ... E	10
● Latah, Spokane ... E	232
● Latona, King ... C	×
Laurel, Whatcom ... NW	×
Layton, Lincoln ... E	×
Layton's Prairie, Lewis ... SW	×
Leahy, Douglas ... C	×
Lebam, Pacific ... SW	×
Leber, Pierce ... C	30
● *Lee*, Walla Walla ... SE	×
Leland, Jefferson ... W	×
Lemars, Lincoln ... E	×
● Lester, King ... C	×
Lewisville, Clarke ... NW	20
Lexington, Cowlitz ... SW	×
Licking, Whatcom ... NW	×
Lilliwaup Falls, Mason ... W	×
Lime Kiln (see McMillan) ...	×
Lime Kiln, San Juan ... NW	25
Lincoln, Douglas ... C	120
● Lind, Adams ... SE	25
● Little Dalles, Stevens ... W	10
● Little Falls, Lewis ... SW	50
● Little Rock, Thurston ... W	×
● *Little Spokane*, Spokane ... E	×
Little White Salmon (see Chenowith)	×
Lockwood, Spokane ... E	×
● Logan, Spokane ... E	10
Lone Pine, Whitman ... SE	30
Long Beach, Pacific ... SW	50
Long Branch, Pierce ... C	×
● *Long's*, Columbia ... SW	×
Lookout, Skagit ... NW	×
Loomis, Okanogan ... C	150
● Loon Lake, Stevens ... W	×
Loop Loop, Okanogan ... C	100
Lopez Island, San Juan ... NW	50
Lowell, Snohomish ... NW	63
Lower Cascades (see Cascades)	×
Lower Montesano (see Wynoochee) ...	×
Lummi, Whatcom ... NW	150
Lummi Island (see Beach) ...	×
Luna (see Pleasant) ...	×
Lyle, Klickitat ... S	×
Lyman, Skagit ... NW	50
Lynden, Whatcom ... NW	560
McBryde, Mason ... W	100
McCallum, Kittitass ... C	29
McCallum, Yakima ... C	×
McCord's Landing (see Swalwell's Landing) ...	×
● *McIntosh*, Thurston ... W	×
● McMillan, Pierce ... C	100
● McMurray, Skagit ... NW	×
● *Mabton*, Yakima ... C	×
● Machias, Snohomish ... NW	×
Macintee (see Coulee City) ...	×
Madrone, Kitsap ... W	×
Malott, Okanogan ... C	×
Mansford, Skagit ... NW	×
Maple, San Juan ... NW	×
● *Maple Leaf*, King ... C	×
● Maple Valley, King ... C	10
Marblemount, Skagit ... NW	×
● Marcus, Stevens ... W	311
Marengo, Columbia ... SW	40
Marion, Pierce ... C	×
● Markham, Chehalis ... W	25
● Marshall, Spokane ... E	47
● *Martin*, Kittitass ... C	×
Martin's Bluff, Cowlitz ... SW	×
● Marysville, Snohomish ... NW	262
Marysville, Cowlitz ... SW	×
Mason, Mason ... W	×
Matlock, Mason ... W	×
Maury, King ... C	×
● *Maxfield*, Thurston ... W	×
May View, Garfield ... SE	×
● *Maywood*, King ... C	×
● Mead, Spokane ... E	×
Meadow, Thurston ... W	×
Media (see Roy) ...	×
● Medical Lake, Spokane ... E	617
Medina, Skagit ... NW	×
● *Meeker*, Pierce ... C	×
● *Meeker*, Whitman ... SE	×
Melbourne, Chehalis ... W	120
Melrose (see South Prairie) ..	×
● *Menoken*, Columbia ... SW	×
Meridian, Pierce ... C	×
Methow, Okanogan ... C	×
Meyers Falls, Stevens ... W	×
Mica, Spokane ... E	×
Midland, Pierce ... C	×
Miles, Lincoln ... E	350
Mill Plain, Clarke ... SW	×
● *Mill Switch*, Lewis ... SW	100
Milton (see West Seattle) ...	×
Mineral City, Snohomish ... NW	×
Mineral Park, Skagit ... NW	×
Minnie Falls, Lincoln ... E	×
Minter, Pierce ... C	**50**
Mission, Kittitass ... C	×
Mitchell (see Lowell) ...	×
● *Mockonema*, Whitman .. SE	×
Mondovi, Lincoln ... E	26
● *Mondovi Station*, Lincoln ... E	×
● Monohan, King ... C	20
Monroe, Snohomish ... NW	×
Montborne, Skagit ... NW	×
Monte Cristo (see Orient) ...	×
● **Montesano**, Chehalis .. W	1,6[illegible]
Montesano Wharf, Chehalis W	×
Morris, Chehalis ... W	×
Morton, Lewis ... SW	×
Moses Coulee, Douglas ... C	×
Mossy Rock, Lewis ... SW	25
Mountain View, Whatcom .. C	×
Mount Baker, Sakgit ... NW	36
Mount Coffin, Cowlitz ... SW	13
Mount Hope, Spokane ... E	×
Mount Pleasant, Skamania .. S	50
● **Mount Vernon**, Ska'it NW	770
Moxee, Yakima ... C	50
Muck, Pierce ... C	60
● Mukilteo, Snohomish .. NW	50
Mullen (see Eureka) ...	×
● *Murray*, Pierce ... C	×
● Napavine, Lewis ... SW	50
Nasel, Pacific ... SW	50
Natchez, Yakima ... C	×
Neah Bay, Clallam ... NW	20
● *Nelson*, Kittitass ... C	×
Nelson, Skamania ... S	×
Nespilem (see Grand Coulee)	×
● Newaukum, Lewis ... SW	300
● New Castle, King ... C	600
Newhall, San Juan ... NW	75
New Kamilche, Mason ... W	×
● **New Whatcom**, Whatcom ... NW	6,776
Nibbeville, Kitsap ... W	32
● *Niblock*, King ... C	×
● *Nisqually City*, Pierce ... C	×
Nooksachk, Whatcom ... NW	50
Noocksachk Crossing, Whatcom ... NW	75
Norman, Snohomish ... NW	50
North Avon (see Avon) ...	×
● North Bend, King ... C	75
North Cove, Pacific ... SW	55
North River, Pacific ... SW	×
North Yakima, Yakima ... C	1,535
Norwood, Pierce ... C	60
Novelty, King ... C	60
● Oakesdale, Whitman ... SE	528
Oak Harbor, Island ... NW	25
Oak Point, Cowlitz ... SW	120
● Oakville, Chehalis ... W	100
● O'Brien, King ... C	2[illegible]
Ocean, San Juan ... NW	×
Ocean Park, Pacific ... SW	×
Ocosta, Chehalis ... W	40[illegible]
Olalla, Kitsap ... W	31
Old Tacoma, (see Tacoma) ..	×
● Olequa, Cowlitz ... SW	100
Olga, San Juan ... NW	×
● Olney, King ... C	100
● **OLYMPIA**, Thurston ... W	4,698
● *Omans*, Lincoln ... E	×
Ontario, Whitman ... SE	×
Ophir, Okanogan ... C	×
Orcas Island, San Juan ... NW	30
Oren, (see Thorp) ...	×
Orient, Snohomish ... NW	×
● Orillia, King ... C	×
Orondo, Douglas ... C	50
● Orting, Pierce ... C	623
Ortrand, Snohomish ... NW	×
Osborn, Lewis ... SW	×
Osceola, King ... C	80
Oso, Snohomish ... NW	×
● *Otis*, Spokane ... E	×
Oto, Klickitat ... S	×
Oyster Bay, Mason ... W	×
Oysterville, Pacific ... SW	197
Ozette, Clallam ... NW	×
Pacific Park, Pacific ... SW	×
Padilla, Skagit ... NW	40
● Paha, Adams ... SE	50
● Palmer, King ... C	40
● Palouse, Whitman ... SE	1,119
● Pampa, Whitman ... SE	12
Paradise, Spokane ... NW	×
Park, Whatcom ... NW	27
● *Parker*, Yakima ... C	×
Parkland, Pierce ... C	×
Park Place, (see Monroe) ...	×
Parnell, (see Hartline) ...	×
Parrott, Lincoln ... E	×
● **Pasco**, Franklin ... SE	400
Pataha City, Garfield ... SE	250
Pearson, Kitsap ... W	×
Pee Ell, Lewis ... SW	×
Pekin, Cowlitz ... SW	18
Penawawa, Whitman ... SE	40
Peola, Garfield ... SE	48
Peone, Spokane ... E	50
● *Peone Station*, Spokane .. E	×
Perry, Columbia ... SW	×
Peshastin, Kittitass ... C	×
● *Peterson's*, King ... C	×
Phinney, Island ... NW	20
● Pialschie, King ... C	×
Pickerings, Mason ... W	×
Pilchuck, Snohomish ... NW	×
Pillar Rock, Wahkiakum SW	×
Pine City, Whitman ... SE	26
Ping, Garfield ... SE	×
Pioneer, Clarke ... SW	120
● *Pittsburg*, Pierce ... C	×
● Plaza, Spokane ... E	15
Pleasant, Klickitat ... S	3
Pleasant Grove, Kittitass ... C	×
Pleasant Grove, (see Oren) ...	×
Pleasant Harbor, Jeff'rs'n .. W	×
● *Pleasant View*, WallaW'la SE	×
Plumbs, Thurston ... W	120
Point Agate, Kitsap ... W	×
Point-no-Point, Kitsap ... W	×
Poisoned Spring, Kittitass .. C	×
● **Pomeroy**, Garfield ... SE	661
Pomona, Snohomish ... NW	×
● Pontiac, King ... C	×
Port Angeles, Clallam ... NW	1,500
Port Blakely, Kitsap ... W	643
● Port Columbia, Douglas .. C	×
Port Crescent, Clallam ... NW	364
Port Discovery, Jefferson .. W	150
● Porter, Chehalis ... W	300
Port Gamble, Kitsap ... W	420
Port Gardiner, (see Everett)	×
Port Ludlow, Jefferson ... W	236
Port Madison, Kitsap ... W	269
Port Townsend, Jeff'son W	4,558
Port Williams, Clallam ... NW	×
Poulsbo, Kitsap ... W	×
Prairie, Skagit ... NW	60
Pratt, Spokane ... E	×
● *Prescott*, Pierce ... C	×
● Prescott, Walla Walla ... SE	31[illegible]
● *Preston*, King ... C	×
Proebstel, Clarke ... SW	×
● Prosser, Yakima ... C	100
● *Providence*, Adams ... SE	×
Puget City, Thurston ... W	100
● Pullman, Whitman ... SE	868
● *Pullman Junc.*, Whitman SE	×
Pumphrey's L'nd'g, (see Olequa)	×
Purdy, Pierce ... C	50
● **Puyallup, Pierce ... C**	**1,732**
● *Puyallup River*, Pierce ... C	×
Pysht, Clallam ... NW	42
Quartermaster, King ... C	×
Quilcene, Jefferson ... W	100
Quilayute, Clallam ... NW	×
Quiniault, Chehalis ... W	×
● Ranier, Thurston ... W	100
Rankin, Lewis ... SW	×
● Ravenna, King ... C	×
● *Raymo*, Walla Walla ... SE	×
● Reardon, Lincoln ... E	60
● Redmond, King ... C	100
● *Relief*, Columbia ... SW	×
● *Relief*, Yakima ... C	×
Rena, Clallam ... NW	×
● Renton, King ... C	406
● *Reservation*, Pierce ... C	×
Richardson, San Juan ... NW	6
● Richmond, King ... C	×
Ridgefield, Clarke ... SW	150
Rigney, Pierce ... C	150
● Riparia, Columbia ... SW	25
● **Ritzville**, Adams ... SE	300
Riverside, Pacific ... SW	×
● *Riverside*, Walla Walla .. SE	×
● *Riverside*, Whitman .. SE	×
Roche Harbor, San Juan ... NW	247
● Rochester, Thurston ... W	150

Washington

Place	Loc.	Pop.
Rock Creek, Spokane	E	×
Rockdale, Lincoln	E	×
● Rockford, Spokane	E	644
Rock Island, Kittitass	C	×
Rockland, Klickitat	S	30
● *Rocklyn*, Lincoln	E	×
Rocky Canon, Lincoln	E	10
Roeder, Whatcom	NW	×
Ronald, Kittitass	C	600
● Rosalia, Whitman	SE	248
Rosario, Skagit	NW	×
Rosedale, Pierce	C	×
● Roslyn, Kittitass	C	1,484
● Ross, King	C	218
● Roy, Pierce	C	150
● *Roza*, Kittitass	C	×
Ruby, Okanogan	C	350
● *Rulo*, Walla Walla	SE	×
Saint Andrews, Douglas	C	×
● Saint John, Whitman	SE	100
Salal, Lewis	SW	×
Salkum, Lewis	SW	×
● *Sallal Prairie*, King	C	×
Salmon, Clarke	SW	×
Samamish Lake, King	C	×
Samish, Skagit	NW	150
● *Samish Lake*, Whatcom	NW	×
San de Fuca, Island	NW	249
Sand Pit, Whatcom	NW	×
Sand Point, Island	NW	×
San Juan, San Juan	NW	60
San Poell, Lincoln	E	10
Sara, Clarke	SW	60
Sassin, Lincoln	E	31
Satsop, Chehalis	W	×
Satsop, Mason	W	×
● *Satsop Sta.*, Chehalis	W	×
● *Satus*, Yakima	C	×
Sauk, Skagit	NW	25
Saxon, Whatcom	NW	×
● *Scott*, Adams	SE	×
Scott, Klickitat	S	×
Scott's Landing, Clarke	SW	×
Seabeck, Kitsap	W	100
Seabold, Kitsap	W	40
Sea Haven, Pacific	SW	32
Sealand, Pacific	SW	150
Seatco, (see Bucoda)	C	×
● **SEATTLE**, King	C	42,837
● *Seattle Junction*, King	C	×
Sea View, Pacific	SW	300
Sedalia, Lincoln	E	19
● Sedro, Skagit	NW	300
Seguin, Clallam	NW	×
● *Sehome*, Whatcom	NW	2,700
● *Selah*, Yakima	C	×
● *Setice*, Whitman	SE	×
Semiahmoo, Whatcom	NW	75
Sequim, Clallam	NW	25
Sharon, Chehalis	W	80
● *Shawnee*, Whitman	SE	×
Shelton, Mason	W	648
Sherlock, Thurston	W	×
Sherman, Lincoln	E	20
● *Sherwood*, Stevens	W	×
Sidney, Kitsap	W	226
Sightly, Cowlitz	SW	18
Silcott, Asotin	SE	40
Silico, Douglas	C	×
Silver, Okanogan	C	×
Silver Beach, Whatcom	NW	60
Silver City, (see Mineral City)		×
Silver Creek, Lewis	SW	19
Silverdale, Kitsap	W	25
Silver Lake, Cowlitz	SW	30
Silver Lake Sta., (see Castle R'k)		×
Silverton, Snohomish	NW	×
● *Simco*, Yakima	C	×
Skagit, Skagit	NW	25
● *Skagit Stat'n*, Skagit	NW	×
Skamokawa, Wahkiakum	SW	300
Skokomish, (see Union City)		×
Skookum Chuck, (see Centralia)		×
Skye, Skamania	S	36
● Slaughter, King	C	740
Sloman, (see Haller City)		×
Smith's Cove, King	C	×
● **Snohomish**, Snoh'ish	NW	1,993
● *Snohomish Junct'n*, King	C	30
● Snoqualmie, King	C	500
● *Snoqualmie Falls*, King	C	×
Solduck, Clallam	NW	×
Sooyoos, Okanogan	E	×
● *Sopenah*, Lewis	SW	10
● *South Ainsworth*, Walla W.	SE	×
● South Bend, Pacific	SW	1,000
● *South Harbor City*, Chehalis	W	×

Washington

Place	Loc.	Pop.
● South Prairie, Pierce	C	215
South Seattle, King	C	×
South Union, Thurston	W	×
● Spangle, Spokane	E	303
Sparta, (see West Kittitass)		×
● **SPOKANE**, Spokane	E	19,922
Spokane Bridge, Spokane	E	16
● **Sprague**, Lincoln	E	1,689
Spring Creek, Walla Walla	SE	×
● Springdale, Stevens	W	300
Springfield, Pierce	W	×
Squack, (see Gilman)		×
Stackpole Harbor, Pacific	SW	×
Squire City, (see Springdale)		×
● Staley, Whitman	SE	100
● *Stampede*, King	C	×
Stanley, Pacific	SW	×
● Stanwood, Snohomish	NW	300
● Starbuck, Columbia	SW	120
Stark's Point, Wahkiakum	SW	240
Steen Landing, (see Toledo)		×
● **Steilacoom City**, Pierce	C	270
Stella, Cowlitz	SW	×
Steptoe, Whitman	SE	24
Sterling, Skagit	NW	50
Stevens, (see Tyler)		×
● Stillaguamish, Sn'hom'h	NW	38
● *Stockport*, Cowlitz	SW	×
● Stuck, King	C	×
Suez, Clallam	NW	×
● *Sulphur*, Franklin	SE	×
Sulphur Springs, Lewis	SW	×
Sultan City, Snohomish	NW	200
● Sumas City, Whatcom	NW	50
Summit, Chehalis	W	×
● *Summit*, Walla Walla	SE	×
● Sumner, Pierce	C	580
Sunnydale, King	C	×
● Sunset, Whitman	SE	20
Sunshine, Pacific	SW	80
● *Sunshine*, Whitman	SE	×
● *Sutton*, Whitman	SE	28
Suwah, Clallam	NW	×
Swalwell's L'd'g, Snoh'm'h	NW	×
Swofford, Lewis	SW	●
Sylvan, Pierce	C	×
● **TACOMA**, Pierce	C	36,006
Tampico, Yakima	C	28
Tatoosh, Clallam	NW	×
Tauwax, Pierce	C	×
Taxsas, Whitman	SE	50
● Teanaway, Kittitass	C	60
● Tekoa, Whitman	SE	301
● Tenino, Thurston	W	339
● *Terrence*, Snohomish	NW	×
Texas Ferry, (see Taxsas)		×
Thatcher, San Juan	NW	×
Theon, Asotin	SE	20
Thetis, (see Valley)		×
● *Thomas*, King	C	×
Thompson, Okanogan	C	×
● Thornton, Whitman	SE	10
● Thorp, Kittitass	C	28
● *Thrall*, Kittitass	C	28
Tildon, Lewis	SW	81
● *Tilma*, Whitman	SE	×
Tioke Point, Pacific	SW	×
Titusville, (see Kent)		×
Toata Coula, (see Loomis)		×
Toledo, Lewis	SW	276
Tolt, King	C	108
● Toppenish, Yakima	C	×
● Touchet, Walla Walla	SE	50
Toutle, Cowlitz	SW	10
Tower, Cowlitz	SW	×
Tracyton, Kitsap	W	100
Trafton, Snohomish	NW	35
● Trent, Spokane	C	5
Trout Lake, Klickitat	S	×
Tualco, Snohomish	NW	84
Tucker, Cowlitz	SW	100
Tukannon, Columbia	SW	38
Tulalip, Snohomish	NW	17
Tumwater, Thurston	W	410
Tuxedo, Whatcom	NW	20
Twin, Callam	NW	×
● Tyler, Spokane	E	75
Union City, Mason	W	250
Union Ridge, (see Ridgefield)		×
Uniontown, Whitman	SE	279
Unity, (see Ilwaco)		×
● *Untanum*, Kittitass	C	×
Useless, Island	NW	29
Utsaladdy, Island	NW	207
Valatta, Snohomish	NW	×
● Valley, Stephens	W	×

Washington

Place	Loc.	Pop.
● Valley Grove, Walla Wal'a	SE	×
● *Van Assets*, King	C	×
Van, (see White River)		×
Van Buren, Whatcom	NW	×
Vance, Lewis	SW	×
● **Vancouver**, Clarke	SW	3,545
Vancouver Barracks, Cl'rk	SW	×
Van Wyck, Whatcom	NW	×
Van Zandt, Whatcom	NW	×
Vashon, King	C	60
Vaughn, Pierce	C	50
● Veazie, King	C	×
Vega, Pierce	C	×
Verndale, Lewis	SW	×
Vernon, Garfield	SE	50
Victor, Mason	W	×
● Viora, Thurston	W	×
Voorhees, Douglas	C	×
Wahl, Whatcom	NW	×
● Waitsburgh, Walla Walla	SE	817
Waldron, San Juan	NW	48
Walker's Prairie, Stevens	W	×
Wallace, Snohomish	NW	100
● **Walla Walla**, Walla Walla	SE	4,709
Wallula, Walla Walla	SE	518
● *Wallula Junction*, Walla Walla	SE	240
Wana, Snohomish	NW	×
Wannacut Lake, (see Golden City)		×
Wapato, Pierce	SW	×
Warde, Lewis	SW	×
Washington Har., Callam	NW	×
Washougal, Clarke	SW	65
● Washtucna, Adams	SE	30
Waterford, Wahkiakum	SW	10
● *Waterloo*, Walla Walla	SE	×
Waterville, Douglas	C	293
Waverly, Spokane	E	50
Wawawai, Whitman	SE	5
● *Wayne*, King	C	×
Wayne, Snohomish	NW	×
Wayside, Spokane	E	×
Webb, Yakima	C	×
Welch, Spokane	E	50
Welcome, Whatcom	NW	16
Wenas, Yakima	C	50
● *Wenas Station*, Yakima	C	×
Wenatchee, Kittitass	C	100
Wenomah, Callam	NW	×
Werner, San Juan	NW	×
West Branch, Spokane	E	×
West Ferndale, Whatcom	SE	75
Westfield, Douglas	C	×
● *Weston*, King	C	×
Westport, Chehalis	W	×
● West Seattle, King	C	1,000
West Sound, San Juan	NW	×
● *Whatcom*, Whatcom	NW	6,776
● *Wheatdale*, Lincoln	E	×
● Whelan, Whitman	NW	10
White, King	C	×
White's L'd'ng, (see Anacortes)		×
White River, (see O'Brien)		×
White River Sid., (see Buckley)		×
White Salmon, Klickitat	S	120
● *Whitman*, Walla Walla	SE	×
Whitney, Skagit	NW	×
Whittakers, Thurston	W	×
Wickersham, Whatcom	NW	50
● Wilbur, Lincoln	E	410
Wildwood, Lewis	SW	×
● Wilkeson, Pierce	C	400
● *Willada*, Whitman	SE	×
● Willapa, Pacific	SW	200
Willis, Adams	SE	×
Wilson, Lewis	SW	×
Windom, Lewis	SW	×
Winlock, Lewis	SW	1,110
● Winona, Whitman	NW	×
Winsor, King	C	×
Winthrop, Okanogan	C	×
Wiser, Whatcom	NW	×
Wollochet, Pierce	C	×
Woodard's Landing, (see Willapa)		×
● Woodinville, King	C	50
● Woodland, Cowlitz	SW	125
● *Woodland*, Thurston	W	×
Woodlawn, Whatcom	NW	×
Woodson, Lincoln	E	×
● *Woolley*, Skagit	NW	300
Wynooche, Chehalis	W	125
Yager, Whatcom	NW	20
● **Yakima**, Yakima	C	196
● Yelm, Thurston	W	24

Town, County	Index	Pop.
● Yesler, King	C	×
● *Yesler Junction*, King	C	×
● Yew, Snohomish	NW	×
● *York*, King	C	×
● *Zumwalt*, Garfield	SE	×

WEST VIRGINIA.

COUNTIES.	INDEX.	POP.
Barbour	N	12,702
Berkeley	NE	18,702
Boone	SW	6,885
Braxton	C	13,928
Brooke	N	6,660
Cabell	W	23,595
Calhoun	C	8,155
Clay	C	4,659
Doddridge	N	12,183
Fayette	S	20,542
Gilmer	C	9,746
Grant	NE	6,802
Greenbrier	S	18,034
Hampshire	NE	11,419
Hancock	N	6,414
Hardy	NE	7,567
Harrison	N	21,919
Jackson	W	19,021
Jefferson	NE	15,553
Kanawha	W	42,756
Lewis	C	15,895
Lincoln	SW	11,246
Logan	SW	11,101
McDowell	SW	7,300
Marion	N	20,721
Marshall	N	20,735
Mason	W	22,863
Mercer	S	16,002
Mineral	NE	12,085
Monongalia	N	15,705
Monroe	S	12,429
Morgan	NE	6,744
Nicholas	C	9,309
Ohio	N	41,557
Pendleton	NE	8,711
Pleasants	NW	7,539
Pocahontas	C	6,814
Preston	N	20,355
Putnam	W	14,342
Raleigh	S	9,597
Randolph	C	11,633
Ritchie	NW	16,621
Roane	W	15,303
Summers	S	13,117
Taylor	N	12,147
Tucker	N	6,459
Tyler	NW	11,962
Upshur	C	12,714
Wayne	SW	18,652
Webster	C	4,783
Wetzel	N	16,841
Wirt	NW	9,411
Wood	NW	28,612
Wyoming	SW	6,247
Total		762,794

TOWN. COUNTY.	INDEX.	POP.
Aarons, Kanawha	W	×
● Abbs Valley, Mercer	S	24
Aberdeen, Lewis	C	×
Abney, (see Pemberton		×
Academy, Pocahontas	C	135
Acme, Kanawha	W	×
● Ada, Mercer	S	75
Adaline, Marshall	N	25
Adamston, Harrison	N	25
Adamsville, Harrison	N	36
Adamsville (see Flat Fork)		
Addison, Webster	C	200
Adkins Mills, (see East Lynn)		
Adlai, Pleasants	NW	6
Adolph, Randolph	C	×
Adonis, Tyler	NW	10
Adrian, Upshur	C	×
● *Alaska*, Fayette	S	×
Alaska, Mineral	NE	10
Albion, Nicholas	C	×
Albright, Preston	N	50
● Alderson, Monroe	S	663
● *Aldridge*, Jefferson	NE	×
● Alexander Upshur	C	×
Alfred, Lincoln	SW	×
Algeria, Pleasants	NW	×
● Algoma, McDowell	SW	
Alice, Gilmer	C	×
Allensville, Berkeley	NE	×
Alma, Tyler	NW	417
Alkire's Mills, Lewis	C	×
Alonzo, Logan	SW	×
Alpena, Randolph	C	25
Alpha, Doddridge	N	15
Alta, Greenbrier	S	5
Altizer, Calhoun	C	20
● Alton, Upshur	C	25
Alum Bridge, Lewis	C	25
Alum Hill, (see Black Fork)		×
Alvon, Greenbrier	S	15
Amanda, Grant	NE	25
● Amblersburg, Preston	N	50
Amboy, Preston	N	57
Ambrosia, Mason	W	275
Amma, Roane	W	×
Amos, Marion	N	275
Anderson, Hancock	N	218
● *Anderson's*, Preston	N	×
Andy, Wetzel	N	×
● Angerona, Jackson	W	41
Anita, Marion	N	×
Ansted, Fayette	S	500
Anthem, Wetzel	N	30
Antioch, Mineral	NE	25
Apgah, Kanawha	W	10
● Apple Grove, Mason	W	30
● Arbuckle, Mason	W	25
Arbutus, Kanawha	W	×
Arches, Wetzel	N	×
● Arden, Barbour	N	8
Argo, Greenbrier	S	×
Arlee, Mason	W	×
Arlington, Upshur	C	16
Armstrong, Fayette	S	×
Armstrong's Landing, (see Frazier's Bottom)		×
Arnettsville, Monongalia	N	50
● Arnold, Lewis	C	×
Arnoldsburg, Calhoun	C	40
Arthur, Grant	NE	30
Asbury, Greenbrier	S	10
Ashton, Mason	W	25
Aspinwall, Lewis	C	15
Assurance, Monroe	S	×
Astor, Taylor	N	100
Athey, Wood	NW	×
Atkinson, Braxton	C	×
Atlantic, Mineral	NE	×
Auburn, Ritchie	NW	150
Augusta, Hampshire	NE	35
Aurora, Preston	N	15
● Austen, Preston	N	269
Auvil, Tucker	N	20
Avon, Doddridge	N	10
Aylmer, (see Huntersville)		×
Baden, Mason	W	×
Baileysville, Wyoming	SW	16
● *Baker's*, Jackson	W	×
Baker's Landing, (see Long Reach)		×
Baker's Run, Hardy	NE	12
Bakerton, Jefferson	NE	×
Bald Knob, Boone	SW	10
Ballard, Monroe	S	×
Ballgap, Cabel	W	×
Ball's, Marshall	N	25
Ball's Landing, (see Frazier's Bottom)		×
● *Bancroft*, Putnam	W	100
Bannen, Marshall	N	×
● **Barboursville**, Cabell	W	500
● *Baresville*, Wetzel	N	×
Barger's Springs, Summers	S	×
Barkville, Mineral	NE	×
Barn, Mercer	S	×
Barnes' Mills, Hampshire	NE	95
● *Barnesville*, Marion	N	×
Barney, Marion	N	×
● Barnum, Mineral	NE	75
● Barrackville, Marion	N	200
● *Barritt*, Grant	NE	×
● *Bartlett*, Harrison	N	×
Bartlett, Roane	W	6
Bartley, Wyoming	SW	50
Bartram, Wayne	SW	10
Basin Spring, Wyoming	SW	×
Basnett, Marion	N	50
Baughman, Webster	C	10
Baxter, Berkeley	NE	×
● Bayard, Grant	NE	300
Bays, Fayette	S	15
● *Beachmont*, Fayette	S	×
Beachwood, Monongalia	N	25
Beall's Mills, Lewis	C	15
Bear Branch, (see Jesse)		×
Bearsville, Tyler	NW	30
Beatysville, Jackson	W	×
Beauty, Fayette	S	×
Beaver Mills, Nicholas	C	20
Beckley's (see Raleigh C. H.)		
● *Beckwith*, Jefferson	NE	×
Beckwith, Fayette	S	12
● Bedington, Berkeley	NE	60
Bee, Putnam	W	25
Beech, Calhoun	C	16
● *Beech Bottom*, Brooke	N	×
Beech Bottom, Webster	C	5
Beech Creek, Logan	SW	60
Beech Fork, (see Adkinsville)		
Beechgrove, Ritchie	NW	×
● Beech Hill, Mason	W	20
Beechwood (see Claremont)		
● *Beechwood*, Grant	NE	×
● Beechwood, Monongalia	N	×
Beeler's Station, Marshall	N	25
Beets, Fayette	S	×
Belcher, McDowell	SW	×
Belfont, Braxton	C	×
Belgrove, Jackson	W	20
Belington, Barbour	N	300
● Belleville, Wood	NW	208
● Bellton, Marshall	N	100
● *Belmont*, Kanawha	W	×
Belmont, Pleasants	NW	600
● *Belmont*, Ohio	N	×
Belva, Fayette	S	×
Belva, Nicholas	C	
● Ben Lemond, Mason	W	×
Bennett, Gilmer	C	×
Benson, Harrison	N	15
● *Ben's Run*, Pleasants	NW	×
● Benton's Ferry, Marion	N	15
● Benwood, Marshall	N	2,934
Berea, Ritchie	NW	50
Bergoo, Webster	C	×
● *Berkeley*, Berkeley	NE	×
● **Berkeley Springs**, Morgan	NE	1,000
Berlin, Lewis	C	50
Bernard's Town, Webster	C	×
● *Berry's Siding*, Braxton	C	×
Bert, Tyler	NW	×
Bertha, Logan	SW	×
Bethany, Brooke	N	325
Bethel, Mercer	S	90
Beury, Fayette	S	×
Beverly, Randolph	C	343
Bias, Boone	SW	×
● *Bier*, Mineral	NE	×
Bifid, Nicholas	C	16
Big Bend, Calhoun	C	30
● *Big Bend*, Summers	S	×
Big Buffalo, Harrison	N	10
Big Clear Creek, (see Rupert)		×
Big Isaac, Doddridge	N	30
Big Otter, Clay	C	50
Big Run, (see Circleville)		×
Big Sandy Creek, Roane	W	6
Big Skin Creek, Lewis	C	120
Big Springs, Calhoun	C	10
Bigsteen, Mason	W	×
Bingamon, Marion	N	30
Birch Grove, (see Unger Store)		×
Birch River, Nicholas	C	35
Bird, Tyler	NW	×
Bismark, Grant	NE	×
Black Band, (see Spring Hill)		×
Black Fork, (see Alum Hill)		×
Black Hawk, (see Kanawha)		×
● *Blacksburg*, Kanawha	W	500
Black Rock, (see Greenland)		×
Blacksville, Monongolia	N	100
Blackwater Creek, Tucker	N	×
● Blaine, Mineral	NE	200
Blair, Hancock	N	15
Blake, Wetzel	N	×
Blaker Mills, Greenbrier	S	×
Blanche, Hancock	N	×
Blandville, Doddridge	N	15
Blankenship, Wyoming	SW	×
Blennerhassett, Wood	NW	×
Bliss, Braxton	C	×
Blockston, (see Colegate)		×
Bloomery, Hampshire	NE	150
● Bluefield, Mercer	S	1,775
Bluefield Inn, Mercer	S	×
Blue Spring, Randolph	C	×
● *Blue Stone Junc.*, Mercer	S	24
● *Blue Sulphur Sprs*, Cabell	W	×

Blue Sulphur Springs, Greenbrier..... S 75
Bluff, Summers..... S ×
Blundon, Kanawha..... W ×
Bly, Gilmer..... C ×
● Board Tree, Marshall..... N 50
● Boaz, Wood..... NW 10
Bobtown, (see Eldora)..... ×
Boggs, Webster..... C ×
● *Boggs Run*, Ohio..... N ×
Bohon, Tucker..... N 35
Bolivar, Jefferson..... NE 804
Bond's Creek, (see Highlands) ×
● *Bond Summit*, Harrison.. N ×
Bone Creek, (see Auburn).... ×
Booker's Mills, Tyler..... NW 20
Booten, Wayne..... SW ×
Booth, Mercer..... S ×
Boothsville, Marion..... N 175
Boreman, Wood..... NW ×
Borland, Pleasants..... NW ×
Botten Creek, (see Totten)..... ×
Bowen, Wayne..... SW ×
Bowenmaster's Mills, (see Rockville)..... ×
Bowlby, Monongalia..... N 25
Boyds, Fayette..... S 20
Boyd, Upshur..... C ×
Bradens, Ritchie..... NW ×
Bradshaw, McDowell..... SW ×
Bradys, Mineral..... NE ×
● Bramwell, Mercer..... S 499
Brandonville, Preston..... N 82
● *Brandy Gap*, Harrison... N ×
Brandywine, Pendleton... NE 20
Brant, Marion..... N 10
Braxton, C. H., (see Sutton). ×
● Bretz, Tucker..... N 20
● *Brick Church*, Harrison.. N ×
Briartown, (see Monongah).. ×
● Bridgeport, Harrison..... N 455
Brier, Wyoming..... SW 12
● Brighton, Mason..... W 100
Brillian, Putnam..... W 50
Brink, Marion..... N 10
● Briscoe, Wood..... NW 10
Brittain, Taylor..... N 15
Brooklin, Raleigh..... S 150
Brooklyn, Hancock..... N 25
Brooklyn, Wetzel..... N 255
● Brooks, Summers..... S 75
Brookside, Preston..... N 35
Brook's Mills, Hampshire NE ×
Brookville, (see Big Bend)... ×
Broomfield, Marion..... N ×
● *Brown's*, Lewis..... C ×
● *Brown's*, Mason..... W ×
Brown's Creek, (see Mt. Clair) ×
Brown's Mill, Harrison..... N 100
● Brownstown, Kanawha.. W 307
Brownsville, Lewis..... C ×
Bruceton Mills, Preston..... N 100
Bruin, Calhoun..... C ×
Brush Creek, (see Cashmere.) ×
Brushy Run, Pendleton.. NE 30
● *Bryan*, Marion..... N 20
Bryan, Mason..... W 20
Buck, Summers..... S 20
Buckeye, Pocahontas..... C 20
● **Buckhannon**, Upshur. C 1,403
Buena Vista, Cabell..... W ×
● Buffalo, Putnam..... W 238
Buffalo Creek, Brooke..... N ×
Buffalo Fork, (see Cleveland) ×
Buffalo Lick, Roane..... W 10
Buffalo Shoals, (see Shoals).. ×
Buffington, Wood..... NW ×
Bula, Monongalia..... N ×
Bull Creek, (see Waverly).... ×
Bulltown, Braxton..... C 15
Bunger's, Greenbrier..... S ×
● Bunker Hill, Berkeley.. NE 850
Bunner's, Marion..... N 15
Burch, Logan..... SW 25
Burdett, Putnam..... W ×
Burlington, Mineral..... NE 300
Burnersville, Barbour..... N 100
Burning Springs, Wirt.... NW 542
● Burnsville, Braxton..... C 135
Burnt Church, (see Flatwoods) ×
Burnt House, Ritchie..... NW 25
● Burton, Wetzel..... N 150
Bush's, Taylor..... N ×
Bush Run, (see Rush Run)... ×
Butler, Mason..... W ×
Byrnside, Putnam..... W ×
Cabell, (see Barboursville).... ×

Cabin Creek, (see Coalburg).. ×
● *Cades*, Putnam..... W ×
● Cairo, Ritchie..... NW 150
Calcutta, Pleasants..... NW ×
● Caldwell, Greenbrier..... S ×
Calf Creek, (see Nolan)..... ×
Calhoun, Barbour..... N 30
Calis, Marshall..... N 25
Calm, Wetzel..... N ×
Camden, Lewis..... C 40
● *Camden*, Mason..... W ×
Camdenburg, (see Clarkson) ×
● Cameron, Marshall..... N 700
Camp, Doddridge..... N ×
Camp Creek, Mercer..... S ×
Canaan, (see Courtland).... ×
Canaan, Upshur..... C ×
Canebrake, (see Percyville).. ×
Canfield, Braxton..... C ×
Cannelton, Kanawha..... W 500
Canton, Marion..... N 20
Cantwell's, Ritchie..... NW 5
Capehart, Mason..... W ×
● Caperton, Fayette..... S 562
Capon Bridge, Hampsh're. NE 160
Capon Iron Works, Hardy. NE 30
Capon Springs, Hampshire NE 100
Carbondale, (see Brownstown) ×
Caress, Braxton..... C ×
Carkin, Kanawha..... W ×
Carlisle, Braxton..... C ×
Carmel, Preston..... N 50
Carney, Kanawha..... W ×
Carter, Fayette..... S ×
Cashmere, Monroe..... S ×
Cassity, Randolph..... C ×
Cassville, Monongalia..... N 100
Cassville, Wayne..... SW 266
Casto, Roane..... W ×
● Catawba, Marion..... N 25
Cave, Pendleton..... NE ×
● Cecil, Taylor..... N 20
Cedar Grove, Kanawha..... W 120
Cedar Valley, (see Georgetw'n) ×
Cedarville, Gilmer..... C ×
Centennial, Monroe..... S ×
Center, Monongalia..... N ×
Center Point, Doddridge.... N 40
● *Central*, Fayette..... S ×
Central City, Cabell..... W ×
Centralia, Braxton..... C ×
● *Central Mines*, Marion... N ×
● Central Station, Doddridge N 150
Centreville, Tyler..... NW ×
Centreville, (see Indian Cr.).. ×
Centreville, Wayne..... SW 50
● Ceredo, Wayne..... SW 923
● *Chaffee*, Mineral..... NE 10
Chap, Boone..... SW ×
Chapel, Braxton..... C 10
Chapmanville, Logan..... SW 50
Charity, (see Sheridan)..... ×
● **CHARLESTON**, Kan'a W 6,742
● **Charlestown**, Jeffer'n NE 2,287
Charlotte, Monongalia..... N ×
Chase, Jackson..... W ×
Cheat Bridge, Randolph..... C 50
● Cherry Camp, Harrison... N 100
● Cherry Run, Morgan.... NE 5
Chester, Hancock..... N 100
Chesterville, Wood..... NW 50
Chestnut, Mercer..... S ×
Chestnut, (see Bason Sprs.).. ×
● *Chestnut Hill*, Marshall.. N ×
● *Child*, Tucker..... N ×
Childs, Wetzel..... W ×
Chilton, Kanawha..... W ×
Christian, Logan..... SW 10
Churchville, Lewis..... C 40
Cicerone, Roane..... NW 6
Circleville, Pendleton..... NE 100
Cirtsville, Raleigh..... S /
Cisko, Ritchie..... NW 6
● Claremont, Fayette..... S 250
Clarence, Roane..... NW ×
● *Clarington*, Marshall..... N 35
● Clark, Harrison..... N ×
● **Clarksburgh**, Harrison N 3,008
Clay, C. H., Clay..... C 75
Claysville, (see Davisville)... ×
Claysville, Mineral..... NE 40
Clayton, Summers..... S 16
Clear Creek, Raleigh..... S ×
Clements, Barbour..... N 50
● *Clements*, Monongalia.... N ×
Clemtown, Barbour..... N ×
Clendenin, Kanawha..... W 50

Cleveland, Webster..... C 20
Cliff Top, Fayette..... S ×
● Clifton, Mason..... W 673
Clifton Mills, Preston..... N 40
Clifty, Fayette..... S 60
Cline, Wyoming..... SW ×
Clinton, Ohio..... N ×
Clinton Furnace, Mong'a... N ×
Clintonville, Greenbrier..... S 30
Clio, Roane..... W ×
Cloverdale, Monroe..... S ×
Clover Lick, Pocahontas.... C ×
Cluster, Pleasants..... NW ×
Clyde, Wetzel..... 30
Coal Bank Run, (see Volcano) ×
● Coalburgh, Kanawha..... W 700
Coaldale, Mercer..... S ×
Coalgate, Raleigh..... S ×
Coalmont, (see Winifrede)... ×
Coal River Marshes, Raleigh S. 100
Coal's Mouth, (see St. Albans) ×
Coco, Kanawha..... W ×
Coffman, Greenbrier..... S ×
● *Cogers*, Braxton..... C ×
Coggins, Greenbrier..... S ×
● *Cogley's*, Marshall..... N 8
● Coit, Fayette..... S 500
Cokeley's, Ritchie..... NW 5
● Coketon, Tucker..... N 500
Cold Stream, Hampshire.. NE 12
Cold Water, Doddridge..... N 15
Cole, Raleigh..... S ×
Colebank, Preston..... N ×
Coleman's L'nd'g, (see Muse's Bottom)..... ×
● Colfax, Marion..... N 30
● Colliers, Brooke..... N 50
Cologne, (see Leon)..... ×
Columbia Sulphur Springs, Greenbrier..... S 10
Comfort, Boone..... SW ×
Conaway, Tyler..... NW 10
Concord, Hampshire..... NE ×
Concord Church, Mercer.... S 150
Confidence, Putnam..... W 15
● *Confluence*, Braxton..... C ×
Confluence, Lewis..... C ×
Congo, Hancock..... N 25
Conings, Gilmer..... C 15
● *Consolidated*, Kanawha.. W ×
Cony, Summers..... S 16
Coon's Mills, Boone..... SW ×
Coopers, Mercer..... S 600
Copen, Braxton..... C ×
Copenhaver's Mills, K'n'w'a W 30
Copleyville, Wayne..... SW ×
Corcoran, Randolph..... C ×
Corda, Jackson..... W ×
Cork, Tyler..... NW ×
Corinth, Preston..... N ×
Corley, Braxton..... C 25
Corn, Mason..... W ×
● Cornwallis, Ritchie..... NW 75
Cortland, Tucker..... N 10
Cos, Upshur..... C ×
Cottageville, Jackson..... W 150
● Cotton Hill, Fayette..... S 100
Cottontown, (see Burton Sta.) ×
Couch, Mason..... W ×
Countsville, Roane..... W 10
Courtney, (see Fellowsville).. ×
Cove Creek, Wayne..... SW ×
Cove Gap, Wayne..... SW 10
Cove Run, (see Moatsville)... ×
Cow Creek, (see Rogland).... ×
Cow Creek, (see Willow Isl.). ×
● Cox's Landing, Cabell.... W 12
Cox's Mills, Gilmer..... C ×
Crab Orchard, (see Willey).. ×
Craigmoor, Harrison..... N 20
Craigsville, Nicholas..... C ×
Cranesville, Preston..... N 50
Crany, Wyoming..... SW ×
Crawford, Lewis..... C 75
● Cresap, Marshall..... N 10
Crescent, Fayette..... S 10
Creston, Wirt..... NW 30
Crickard, Randolph..... C 10
Crickmer, Fayette..... S ×
Crims, Harrison..... N ×
Crimson Springs, Monroe.... S 30
Crislip, Roane..... W 10
Crist, (see Leander)..... ×
CrittendenFur., (see Charl't'n) ×
Crook, Boone..... SW ×
Crosier, Monroe..... S ×
Cross, (see Shaw)..... ×

West Virginia

Place	
Cross Lanes, (see Kesler's Cross Lanes)...	×
● *Cross Creek*, Brooke...N	×
Cross Roads, Monongalia...N	21
Crow, Raleigh...S	5
● *Crown City Ferry*, Cabell W	×
● Crown Hill, Kanawha...W	240
Crump's Bottom, Summers. S	16
● Culloden, Cabell...W	100
Currence's M's, (see Alum Hill)	×
Cutlips, Braxton...C	15
Cuzzart, Preston...N	×
Cyclone, Logan...SW	×
Cyprus, Roane...W	×
Daisy, Wood...NW	×
Dale, Tyler...NW	×
Dallas, Marshall...N	125
Dallison, Wood...NW	50
● *Dana Crossing*, Kanawha W	×
Daniels, Raleigh...S	30
Danville, Boone...SW	7
● Darkesville, Berkeley...NE	250
● Davis, Tucker...N	918
● *Davis Creek*, Kanawha...W	×
● Davisville, Wood...NW	100
Dawson, Greenbrier...S	×
Day's Mills, Randolph...C	55
Dayton, Harrison...N	×
Dean, Wetzel...N	10
● *Deanville*, Lewis...C	×
Deaver, Wirt...NW	×
Debby, Mason...W	×
Decker's Creek, (see Morgantown)...	×
Decota, Kanawha...W	×
Deep Run, (see Shaw)...	×
Deepvalley, Tyler...NW	×
● Deep Water, Fayette...S	20
Deer Lick, Mason...W	20
Deer Run, Pendleton...NE	200
Deer Walk, Wood...NW	×
Deever, Wirt...NW	×
● Dego, Kanawha...W	×
Deitz, Fayette...S	×
De Kalb, Gilmer...C	10
Dell, Upshur...C	×
Dellslow, Monongalia...N	×
Delong, Pleasants...NW	10
Delphi, Nicholas...C	×
Delray, Hampshire...NE	×
Delta, Braxton...C	×
Dempsey, Fayette...S	4
***Denning*, (see Aylmer)...**	×
Dennis, Greenbrier...S	10
Denton, Marion...N	×
● *Despard Mines*, Harrison N	×
Dexter, Roane...W	×
Dial Rock, (see Stansill)...	×
● *Diamond*, Fayette...S	25
Diamond, Marion...N	25
Diana, Webster...C	15
Dickson, Wayne...SW	25
Dilley's Mill, Pocahontis...C	×
Dillon's Run, Hampshire. NE	60
● *Dimmock*, Fayette...S	×
Dingess, Logan...SW	30
Dismal, Kanawha...W	×
Dixie, Fayette...S	×
Dixie, Nicholas...C	200
● Dobbin, Grant...NE	250
Doctorsville, Braxton...C	×
Dodd, Roane...W	×
● *Doe Gully*, Morgan...NE	×
Dola, Harrison...N	10
● *Dolan's Mines*, Harrison. N	×
Doman, Hardy...NE	12
Dombey, Wood...NW	10
● *Don*, Summers...S	×
Donahoe, Ritchie...NW	5
● *Donaldson*, Hampshire. NE	×
Dority, Preston...N	×
Dorr, Webster...C	×
● Douglass, Jackson...W	15
● *Downs*, Marion...N	×
Drag, Wayne...SW	×
Drexel, Roane...W	×
Driftwood, Pocahontas...C	8
Driscol, Pocahontas...C	×
Dry Branch, Kanawha...W	×
Dry Creek, (see White Sulphur Springs)...	×
Dry Creek, Raleigh...S	30
Dryfork, Randolph...C	×
Dryland, Morgan...NE	×
Dry Run, Pendleton...NE	35
● *Ducksworth*, Doddridge..N	×
Dudley, Cabell...W	×

West Virginia

Place	
● Duffield's, Jefferson...NE	150
Duffy, Lewis...C	×
● Duhring, Mercer...S	100
Duke, Monongalia...N	×
Duin, Wirt...NW	10
Duncan, Jackson...W	×
● Dunleith, Wayne...SW	75
Dunlow, Wayne...SW	40
Dunmore, Pocahontas...C	75
Dunn's, Mercer...S	×
Duo, Greenbriar...S	20
Dutchtown, (see Swann)...	×
● Eagle, Fayette...S	175
Eagle Mills, Doddridge...N	15
Earl, Nicholas...C	×
Earnshaw, Wetzel...N	40
Eastbank, Kanawha...W	200
● *East Bank*, Kanawha...W	×
East Lynn, Wayne...SW	30
Easton, Monongalia...N	75
● *Easton's*, Marshall...N	×
East River, Mercer...S	×
● *East Sewell*, Fayette...S	×
● *Eatons*, Wood...NW	20
● *Echo*, Fayette...S	×
● Echo, Wayne...SW	×
Edgar, Jackson...W	×
● Edgewater, Fayette...S	50
Edgington, Brooke...N	×
Edmiston, Lewis...C	×
Edmond, Fayette...S	×
Edmundsburg (see Locust Knob)...	×
Edray, Pocahontas...C	75
● *Edwards*, Cabell...W	×
Effie, Wayne...SW	×
Effler, McDowell...SW	×
Egeria, Raleigh...S	×
Eglon, Preston...N	50
Egypt, Wayne...SW	×
Eldora, Marion...N	50
Elgood, Mercer...S	×
Eli, Wood...NW	10
Elizabeth, Wirt...NW	710
Elk City, Barbour...N	20
● *Elk City*, Kanawha...W	1,500
Elk Fork, Jackson...W	30
● Elk Garden, Mineral...NE	723
● Elkhorn, McDowell...SW	×
Elkins, Grant...NE	300
● Elkins, Randolph...C	737
Elkwater, Randolph...C	25
Elia, Marshall...N	×
● Ellenboro, Ritchie...NW	152
Elliot, Fayette...S	×
Ellis, Gilmer...C	10
Ellison, Summers...S	30
● Elm Grove, Ohio...N	594
Elmira, Braxton...C	×
● Elmo, Fayette...S	×
Elmwood, Mason...W	×
Elm Station (see Beury's)...	×
● Elsinore, Putnam...W	100
Elton, Summers...S	×
Elwell, Mason...W	30
Elyria, Berkeley...NE	×
Emma, Jackson...W	×
● Emory, Mineral...NE	40
Empire, Wayne...SW	×
● *Empire*, Mineral...NE	26
Endicott, Wetzel...N	×
● *Engles*, Jefferson...NE	×
● Ennis, McDowell...SW	×
Enon, Nicholas...C	×
● Enterprise, Harrison...N	50
Ernshaw, (see Burton Sta.)	×
Etam, Preston...N	×
Etna, Lewis...C	30
Eugene, Logan...SW	×
● Eureka, Pleasants...NW	400
Evans, Jackson...W	×
Evansville, Preston...N	125
Evelyn, Wirt...NW	130
Evergreen, Upshur...C	×
Everson, Marion...N	×
Extra, Putnam...W	×
Eye, Nicholas...C	×
Fabius, Hardy...NE	×
Fairfax, Logan...SW	30
● *Fairfax*, Tucker...N	×
Fairfax Stone, Preston...N	10
Fairfield, Kanawha...W	×
● **Fairmont**, Marion...N	1,023
Fairmont Depot, Marion...N	×
● *Fairmont, Morgantown and Pittsburgh Junction*, Marion N	×
Fair Plain, Jackson...W	6

West Virginia

Place	
Fairview, Hancock...N	226
Fairview, Marion...N	235
Fairview, Marshall...N	25
Fairview, Wayne...SW	36
Falling Spring, Greenbrier..S	45
● Falling Waters, Berkeley NE	80
Fallsmill, Braxton...C	25
Falls Mills, Tyler...NW	40
Falls of Kanawha (see Kanawha Falls)...	×
Falls of Twelve Pole (see Dickson)...	
Falls of Wyandotte River (see Falls Mills)...	×
Fanlight, Wetzel...N	×
● *Farland's Mines*, Harrison N	×
● Farm, Kanawha...W	×
● Farmington, Marion...N	250
Faulkner, Randolph...C	×
● Fayette Station, Fayette...S	20
Fayetteville, Fayette...S	125
Fellowsville, Preston...N	94
● Ferguson, Wayne...SW	×
Ferrell, Logan...SW	×
Festus, Marion...N	
● Fetterman, Taylor...N	557
Finch, Ritchie...NW	10
● Fire Creek, Fayette...S	400
Fish Creek, (see Woodlands).	×
● *Fisher's Summit*, Lewis...C	×
Five Mile, Mason...W	25
● *Flagg s*, Berkeley...NE	×
Flat Fork, Roane...W	15
Flat Rock, Mason...W	50
Flatrun, Marion...N	×
Flat Top, Mercer...S	40
● Flat Woods, Braxton...C	50
Fleek, Mineral...NE	30
Fleming, Wayne...SW	
● Flemington, Taylor...N	200
● *Flesher's*, Lewis...C	×
Flickersville, Monongalia..N	×
Flinn, Jackson...W	×
Flint, Doddridge...N	20
Flint Town, Roane...W	10
● *Flipping*, Mercer...S	200
Floding Springs (see Ona)...	×
Flora, Barbour...N	6
● Florence, Randolph...C	×
Floyd (see Leading Creek)...	×
● *Floyd's Siding*, Wetzel...N	×
Folsom, Wetzel...N	×
Foltz, Berkeley...NE	10
Fontaine, Logan...SW	×
Foote, Mineral...NE	×
Ford, Wood...NW	16
● *Fordyce*, Ohio...N	×
● *Foreman's*, Taylor...N	20
Forest Hill, Summers...S	10
Fork, Wood...NW	10
Forksburgh, Marion...N	×
Forks of Capon, H'mphire NE	15
Forks of Fishing Creek, Wetzel...N	100
Forks of Coal (see St. Albans)...	×
Forks of Little Sandy, Kanawha...W	×
Forks of Proctor (see Proctor)...	×
Forsyth (see William)...	×
Fort Gay, Wayne...SW	400
Fort Seybert, Pendleton...NE	25
● Fort Spring, Greenbrier...S	140
Foss, Summers...S	20
Foster, Boone...SW	×
● *Fosters*, Taylor...N	×
Fountain Spring, Wood..NW	20
Fourteen, Lincoln...SW	25
Fowler's, Brooke...N	50
Fowler's Knobs, Nicholas...C	×
Frametown, Braxton...C	30
Frankford, Greenbrier...S	250
● *Franklin*, Marshall...N	×
Franklin, Pendleton...NE	300
Frazier's Bottom, Putnam. W	50
Freed, Calhoun...C	10
Freeman's, Mercer...S	100
Freemansburgh, Lewis...C	100
Freeman's Landing (see Anderson)...	×
Freeport, Wirt...NW	20
French Creek, Upshur...C	100
● *French's*, Hampshire...NE	11
Frenchton, Upshur...C	25
● *Frenchville*, Mercer...S	82
Frew, Tyler...NW	10

Friar's Hill, Greenbrier......S ×
● Friendly, Tyler.........NW 100
Frisco, Marion..........N ×
● *Frost*, Mineral..........NE ×
Frost, Pocahontas..........C 50
Frozen Camp, Jackson.....W 25
Fry, Kanawha..............W ×
Fry, Wayne..............SW ×
Fudge's Creek, Cabell......W ×
Fullen, Monroe............S ×
Fulton, Ohio..............N ×
Gad, Nicholas..............C ×
Gaines, Upshur..............C ×
● *Gallahue's*, Marion........N ×
Gallatin, Marion...........N 30
● *Gallipolis Ferry*, Mason..W ×
Gandeeville, Roane.........W 60
Ganley, Nicholas...........C ×
Ganotown, Berkeley......NE 50
Gap Mills, Monroe..........S 75
Garfield, Jackson...........W 10
Garland, Barbour...........N ×
Garrett's Bend, Lincoln..SW ×
● Gaston, Lewis..............C 50
● *Gaston*, Marion............N ×
Gaston's Mills(see ValleyGr.) ×
● *Gaston Mines Junction*, Marion..........N
Gatewood, Fayette..........S ×
Gath, Marion..............N 10
● Gauley Bridge, Fayette....S 75
Gay, Jackson...............W 6
● *Gaymont*, Fayette.........S ×
Gazil, Kanawha............W ×
Gee Lick, Lewis............C 40
Gem, Braxton...............C ×
Genoah, Wayne.............SW ×
Georgetown, Monongalia...N 30
German, Braxton............C 10
Gerrardstown, Berkeley.. NE 350
Glatto, Mercer..............S ×
Gibson, Pleasants.........NW 15
Gilbert, Logan.............SW ×
Gilboa, Nicholas............C ×
Gil Gal, (see Ferguson)........ ×
Gilkerson, Wayne.........SW ×
Gillespie, Pocahontas....... C ×
● *Gilman*, Randolph.........C ×
Gin, Logan.................SW ×
Given, Jackson.............W ×
Glace, Monroe..............S 30
● *Glade*, Fayette............S ×
Glade Farms, Preston...... N 12
Gladesville, Preston.........N 50
Glady, Randolph............C ×
Glean Jean, Fayette.........S ×
Glebe, Hampshire..........NE 30
● Glen Dale, Marshall.......N ×
● Glen Easton, Marshall....N 350
● Glen Elk, Kanawha......W 500
● *Glen Falls*, Harrison.....N ×
Glengary, Berkeley....... NE 30
● *Glenn's Run*, Ohio.........N ×
Glenville, Gilmer.........C 329
● Glenwood, Mason......... W 100
Globe, Hancock..............N ×
Glomera, Raleigh............S ×
● Glover's Gap, Marion.....N 50
Goff's, Ritchie.............NW 10
Gold Hill, Grant.......... NE 25
Goldtown, Jackson.........W ×
Good Hope, Harrison....... N 60
● Goodwill, Mercer...........S 200
Goose Creek, Ritchie.....NW 25
Goose Neck, Ritchie......NW ×
● *Gorby's*, Marshall.........N ×
Gordon, Boone.............SW ×
● *Gordon's*, Kanawha......W ×
● **Germania, Grant.........NE** 400
Gould, Clay.................C ×
● *Grace*, Hampshire........NE ×
Grady, Wood..............NW ×
● **Grafton**, Taylor.........N 3,159
Graham Mines, Kanawha.. W 50
● Graham Station, Mason.. W 25
● *Gramms*, Taylor...........N ×
Grandview, Raleigh..........S ×
Grandville, Monongalia.....N 100
Grangeville, Harrison........N 20
Grangeville, Marion......... N 20
Grant, Hancock............. N 25
Grantsville, Calhoun.... C 300
● Grape Island, Pleasant. NW 10
Grapevine, Summers.........S ×
Grassland, Harrison......... N 10
Grass Lick, Jackson.........W 20
Grass Run, (see Marshville).. ×

Grassy Meadows, Greenbrier S ×
Gray's Flat, Marion......... N ×
Graysville, Marshall......... N 50
● Great Cacapon, Morgan. NE 40
Green Bank, Pocahontas....C 130
● Green Bottom, Cabell....W ×
Green Bottom Land'g, Mason W ×
Greenbrier Bridge, (see Caldwell)........................ ×
Green Hill, Wetzel...........N 8
Greenland, Grant........... NE 40
Green Shoals, (see Hart)..... ×
● GreenSpring, Hampshire NE 20
Green Sulphur Springs, Summers..........................S 30
Greenville, Monroe...........S 40
● Greenwood Doddridge...N 30
Greggs, Ohio................N ×
Griffithsville, Lincoln.....SW 25
Grimmett, Summers..........S ×
● Grimm's Landing, Mason W 20
Grove, Doddridge...........N 15
Gunnville, Mason.......... W ×
Guseman, Preston...........N ×
● Guyandotte, Cabell........W 1,502
● *Gypsy Grove*, Harrison...N ×
Hacker Valley, Webster.... C 20
Hackersville, (see Phillippi).. ×
Haddix, Tucker..............N ×
Hagans, Monongalia.........N ×
Hager, Boone.............SW ×
Hainesville, Hampshire... NE 10
● *Half Way*, Greenbrier....S ×
Halidon, Summers.......... S 25
Hall, Barbour................N 75
Halleck, Monongalia.........N 20
Hall's Mills, Wetzel..........N 20
Hallsville, McDowell......SW ×
● Halltown, Jefferson..... NE 600
Halo, Webster...............C ×
● Hambleton, Grant...... NE 100
Hamilton, (see Randall)...... ×
Hamilton Mills, (see Nickell's Mills).......................... ×
Hamlin, Lincoln........ SW 300
Hampton, Kanawha.........W 500
Hampton, Raleigh.......... S ×
● *Hampton*, Upshur.........C ×
● *Hancock*, Morgan....... NE ×
● Handley, Kanawha........W 100
● Hanging Rock, Hamp're NE 10
Hanging Rock Mills, Hardy NE 30
Hanley's Landing, (see Ashton)...........................
Hannahsville, Tucker.......N ×
Hanover, Wyoming........SW ×
Hardman, (see Glenville).... ×
Harman, Randolph.......... C 100
● *Harpers*, Jackson.........W ×
● Harper's Ferry, Jeffer'n NE 958
● *Harper's Ferry*, Wood. NW 20
Harpers Mills, Pendleton. NE 18
Harper's Mills, (see Salt Lick Bridge)........................ ×
● *Harris Ferry*, Wood... NW 25
Harrisville, Ritchie...... NW 361
● *Harrison*, Mineral......NE ×
Harrison, Clay.............. C ×
● *Harrison County Mines*, Harrison.........................N ×
Hart, Lincoln............SW 25
● Hartford City, Mason..... W 446
Hartley's, Ritchie.........NW ×
Hartmonsville, Mineral.... NE 60
● *Harts Run*, Greenbrier...S ×
Harvey, Raleigh..............S 25
Haven, Doddridge............N ×
Hawk's Nest, Fayette.........S 200
Hawkings, Mason...........W ×
Hawthorn, Logan............SW ×
Hayman's Landing, Mason W 10
● *Hays*, Tyler...............NW ×
Hazel, Wetzel................N ×
Hazelgreen, Ritchie.......NW 5
Hazelton, Preston............N 10
Headsville, Mineral.........NE 12
● Heater, Braxton............C ×
Hebron, Pleasants..........NW 150
Hedgesville, Berkeley.....NE 448
Heldreth, Doddridge.........N ×
Helvetia, Randolph..........C 200
Hemlock, Upshur.............C 20
● Henderson, Mason........W 200
● *Henderson*, Wood.......NW ×
● Hendricks, Tucker....... N 100
Henrietta, Calhoun..........C ×
Henry, Preston............. N ×

Hereford, Jackson.........W 15
● *Hern*, Putnam.............W ×
Herr, Calhoun...............C 5
Herold, Braxton..............C ×
Hessville, Harrison.........N 15
Hettie, Braxton..............C ×
Hewett, Boone...............SW ×
Hezron, Grant...............NE ×
Hickory, Mason..............W ×
Higby, Roane.................W ×
Higginsville, Hampshire.. NE 10
Highland, Ritchie..........NW 15
Hill, Boone..................SW ×
Hill, Ritchie................NW ×
● *Hilldale*, Summers.........S ×
Hillsboro, Pocahontas.......C 166
Hillsdale, Monroe.............S 10
Hinch, Logan................SW 30
Hinkle's Mills, Upshur......C 10
Hinkleville, Upshur..........C 60
● **Hinton**, Summers.......S 2,570
Hoard's Rocks, (see Stewartstown)........................
● *Hobbs*, Jefferson........NE ×
Hodam, (see Millard)......... ×
Hodges, Cabell............. W ×
Hogg, Jackson.............. W ×
Hogsett, Mason............. W ×
Holbrook, Ritchie.........NW 15
Holliday, Greenbrier..........S ×
● Holliday's Cove, Hancock N 200
Holly Grove, Upshur.........C 30
Holly Meadows, (see Saint George)....................... ×
Holly River, Braxton....... C 10
Hollywood, Monroe......... S ×
Holman, Monongalia....... N ×
Holmer, Lewis..............C ×
● *Holmes Water Station*, Preston....................N ×
Holton, Morgan.............NE ×
Home, Braxton.............. C ×
Hominy Falls, Nicholas.....C ×
Hoodsville, Marion......... N 10
Hookersville, Nicholas......C 25
Hook's Mills, Hampshire.. NE ×
Hope, Braxton...............C ×
Hopeville, Grant...........NE 15
Horner, Lewis............... C ×
Horseneck, Pleasants.....NW 20
Horsepen, McDowell......SW 800
Horse Shoe Run, Preston...N ×
● Hoult, Marion..............N ×
Houltown, (see Diamond)...... ×
Howard, Marshall.......... N 25
● *Howard*, Greenbrier.......S ×
Howard's Lick, Hardy.... NE 30
Howell, Cabell............... W 35
Howesville, Preston......... N 24
Hubbardstown, Wayne....SW 20
Hubb's Landing, (see W'd'ds). ×
Hudson, Preston..............N 5
Huff, Randolph.............. C ×
Huffman, Barbour............N 20
Hughart, Greenbrier..........S ×
Hugo, Putnam................W ×
Hulderman, Barbour........N ×
● Hulings, Tucker.............N 20
● Hundred, Wetzel............N 10
Hunter's Springs, Monroe...S ×
Huntersville, Pocahont's C 120
● Huntington, Cabell........W 10,108
Huntsville, Jackson.........W ×
Hur, Calhoun..................C 5
Hurdman, Gilmer.......... C 10
● Hurricane, Putnam........W 207
Huttonsville, Randolph..... C 50
Hyer, Braxton.................C ×
Iaeger, McDowell...........SW ×
Ice's Ferry, (see Laurel Iron Works)........................ ×
● Independence, Preston... N 273
● Indian Camp, Upshur.... C ×
Indian Creek, (see Greenville) ×
Indian Mills, Summers.......S 25
Industry, Calhoun........... C ×
● Ingleside, Mercer...........S 50
Inkerman, Hardy............NE ×
● Inwood, Berkeley..........NE ×
Ira, Clay.................... C ×
Ireland, Lewis................C 40
Iron, Summers...............S ×
Irondale, (see Independence) ×
● Irontown, Taylor............N 50
Island Branch, Kanawha....W 35
● *Island Park*, Jefferson. NE ×
Iuka, Tyler.................NW ×

Ivanhoe, Upshur............C ×
Ive's Branch, (see Chestnut). ×
Ivy, Upshur...............C ×
● **Jackson, C.H.**, Jackson W 417
● *Jackson*, Wood........ NW ×
Jacksonville, Lewis......... C 60
Jacox, Pocahontas ....C ×
Jake's Run, Monongalia.... N 40
● Janelew, Lewis........... C 228
Jarrett, Kanawha.......... W 41
Jarrold's Valley, Raleigh....S 30
Jarvisville, Harrison........N 50
Jefferson, Lincoln........ SW ×
Jenks, Lincoln............SW ×
Jennie's Creek, (see Spauld'g) ×
Jericho, (see Highview, Va.). ×
Jerry's Run, Wood....... NW 10
Jesse, Wyoming.......... SW ×
Jetsville, Greenbrier........S ×
Jimtown, (see Upton)........ ×
Jimtown, Harrison..........N ×
Jimtown, (see Randall)...... ×
Job, Randolph..............C 15
Joe's Branch, Wyoming..SW ×
Johnson, Barbour..........N 10
Johnson's Landing, (see Long Reach) .... ×
Johnson's Cross Roads, M'n'e S 60
Johnstown, Harrison....... N 50
Jones' Landing, (see Beach H'l) ×
Jones' Springs, Berkeley..NE 58
Jordan, Kanawha.......... W 10
Jordan's Run, Grant........NE 25
Joseph's Mills, Tyler......NW 15
Josiah, Pleasants.........NW ×
Jumbo, Webster............C 10
Jumping Branch, Summers..S 41
Junction, Hampshire......NE 10
● *Junction*, Mineral......NE ×
Junction Palace, Kanawha. W 10
Kabletown, Jefferson.....NE 700
Kalamazoo, Barbour.........N 6
Kanawha, Wood.........NW ×
● Kanawha City, Kanawha. W ×
● Kanawha Falls, Fayette...S 200
Kanawha Head, Upshur.....C ×
Kanawha Saline, (see Mald'n) ×
● Kanawha Sta., Woods...NW 20
Karn, Monroe..............S ×
Kasson, Barbour............N 25
Kausooth, Marshall.........N ×
● Kearneysville, Jefferson. NE 100
Kedron, Upshur............ C ×
Keenan, Monroe............ S ×
● *Keeney's Creek*, Fayette...S ×
● Keller, Jefferson........ NE 25
● Kellogg, Wayne.........SW ×
Kemperville, Lewis.........C ×
● Kendalia, Kanawha......W 100
Kenna, Jackson............ W 10
● Kenova, Wayne.........SW ×
Kenton, Doddridge......... N 10
Kenton Fur, (see Charlest'n). ×
Kentuck, Jackson.........W 15
● Kerens, Randolph........C 150
Kesler's Cross Lanes, Nic'as.C 25
Kester, Roane............. W ×
Kester's Mills, Putnam.... W 15
Ketterman, Grant........ NE ×
Kettle, Roane, ...W ×
● **Keyser**, Mineral.......NE 2,165
Kiahsville, Wayne.........SW ×
Kidwell, Tyler............NW 10
Kincaid, Fayette ....S ×
Kinchelo, Harrison.........N 25
Kingsbury, Wood.........NW ×
King's Landing, Mason....W 15
Kingsville, Randolph.........C 6
Kingwood, Preston......N 600
Kirby, Hampshire........ NE ×
Kirt, Barbour..............N ×
● *Kirtley*, Putnam.........W ×
Kline, Pendleton..........NE ×
Knawl's Creek, Braxton....C 10
Knight, Doddridge..........N 15
Knobley, Mineral.........NE ×
Knobs, Monroe..............S ×
Knottsville, Taylor..........N 50
Knoxville, Marshall.........N 15
Koontz Mills, (see Easton)... ×
● *Krout's Creek*, Wayne..SW ×
Kyger, Roane..............W ×
Kyle, McDowell.......... SW ×
Lafollettsville, H'mpshire.NE 12
Laformer's Store, (see Burnsville) .... ×
Lahmansville, Grant......NE 50

West Virginia

Lake, Logan.............. SW 25
Lamont, Marshall.......... N ×
Lanckport, Wood..........NW ×
Landgraff, McDowell.....S W ×
Lane's Bottom, Webster.... C 17
Lansing, Fayette........... S 4
Lashmeet, Mercer.......... S ×
Launa, Raleigh..............S 150
Laurel Branch, Monroe.....S 30
Laurel Creek, (see Cotton Hill) ×
Laural Dale, Mineral......NE 17
Laurel Fork Junc., (see Volcano Jc.) ×
Laurel Iron Works, Mon'l'a N 40
Laurel Point, Monongalia...N 50
Laurel Station, (see Cotton H'l) ×
Lavalette, Wayne.........SW ×
Lawford, Ritchie.........NW ×
Lawn, Greenbrier...........S ×
Lawson, Raleigh ....S ×
Layhigh, Grant........... NE 25
● Lazearville, Brooke...... N 317
Leachtown, Wood........NW 40
Leading Creek, Gilmer......C 25
Lead Mine, Tucker..........N 15
● *Leadsville*, Randolph..... C 60
League, Ritchie...........NW 5
Leander, Fayette........... S 60
Leatherwood, (see Wheeling) ×
Leatherwood, Webster..... C 6
Lee, Wirt................NW ×
Lee Bell, Randolph..........C ×
Leetown, Jefferson........NE 100
Left Hand, Roane...........W 6
Legg, Kanawha............ W ×
Lehew, Hampshire........NE ×
Leivasy, Nicholas.......... C ×
Lenox, Preston............ N 12
● Leon, Mason.............W 242
Leonard, Greenbrier........S ×
Leopold, Doddridge.........N 10
Le Roy, Kanawha.......... W ×
● Le Roy, Jackson.......... W 12
● *Lesage's*, Cabell.........W ×
Lester, Raleigh..............S 12
● Letart, Mason.............W 150
Letter Gap, Gilmer..........C 15
Levels, Hampshire........NE ×
Leviasy, Nicholas...........C ×
● *Lewis*, Putnam...........W ×
Lewisburgh, Greenbrier. S 1,016
Lewiston, Kanawha........W 100
Lewistown, (see Glover's Gap) ×
Liberty, Putnam............W 50
Lick, Randolph..............C 10
Lightburn, Lewis............C ×
Lile, Greenbrier.............S ×
Lillydale, Monroe........... S ×
Lima, Tyler...............NW 10
Limestone, Marshall.........N 100
Limestone Hill, Wood.... NW 15
Limestone Ridge, (see Gr'n Hill) ×
Lincoln, Wyoming..........SW ×
Lincoln, C. H., (see Hamlin). ×
Linden, Roane.............W 50
Lindside, Monroe............S 10
Link, Braxton............. C ×
Little Birch, Braxton.........C ×
● *Little Cacapon*, Hamps'e NE ×
● Little Falls, Monongalia.. N 20
Little Georgetown, Berkeley NE 50
Little Guyan, Mason....... W 6
Little Otter, Braxton........C 50
Little Sandy, Jackson.......W 15
Littlesburgh, Mercer........ S ×
Little Sewell Mountain, Greenbrier......S 50
Little's Mills, Tyler...... NW 50
● Littleton, Wetzel.......... N 250
Little Wild Cat, Lewis.......C 10
Liverpool, Jackson......... W ×
Livesay's Mills, (see Richlands) ×
Lizemore's, Clay........... C ×
Lloydsville, Braxton........ C ×
Lobelia, Pocahontas.........C ×
● *Lock Eight*, Putnam...... W 25
Lockhart's, Jackson........ W 50
Lockhart's Run, Wood... NW 30
Lockney, Calhoun.......... C ×
Lock No. 4, Kanawha...... W ×
● Lock Seven, Kanawha... W ×
Locust, Pocahontas......... C ×
Locust Knob, (see Little Guyan) ×
Logan, Logan.......... SW 200
Logansport, Marion.........N 50
Logville, Wetzel........... N ×
● Lone Cedar, Jackson..... W ×

West Virginia

Lone Tree, Tyler..........NW 8
Long, Randolph.............C ×
● *Long Falls*, (see Ada)....... ×
○ *Long Bottom*, Summers...S ×
● Long Reach, Tyler..... NW 200
● Long Run, Doddridge.... N 100
Long's Landing, (see Arbuckle) ×
Lookout, Fayette............S 4
Looneyville, Roane.........W 6
● Lorentz, Upshur..........C ×
Lorraine, Putnam..........W ×
● Lost Creek, Harrison.....N 100
Lost River, Hardy.........NE 100
Lot, Wetzel.................N ×
● Loudenville, Marshall.... N 50
● *Loup Creek*, Fayette...... S 80
Louther, Jackson.......... W ×
Love, Cabell...............W 12
Lovells, (see Paint Creek) .... ×
Loveridge, Greenbrier...... S ×
Lowdell, Wood........... NW 10
● Lowell, Summers.......... S 25
Lowell Station, (see Peterstown) ×
● *Lower Ferry*, Brooke..... N ×
Lowman, Wetzel........... N 10
Lowry's Mill, Greenbrier....S 14
Lowsville, Monongalia...... W 50
Lubeck, Wood............NW 200
Lucile, Wirt.............. NW 20
Lumberport, (see Burnsville.) ×
● Lumberport, Harrison... N 100
Lurd, Kanawha............ W ×
Lydia, Clay.................C ×
● *Lynche's Mines*, Harrison N ×
Lynch's Mills, (see Trubada). ×
Lynn Camp, Marshall........N 25
Lyon, Doddridge........... N ×
Lytton, Pleasants.........NW 10
McClains, Wirt...........NW ×
McClellan, Marion..........N 10
McCurdiesville, Monongalia W 50
McCurdy, Cabell.......... W 12
● *McDougall*, Ritchie....NW 10
McElroy, (see Centre Point). ×
McGee, Taylor.............N ×
McGill, Putnam............W 100
McGraw's, Wyoming......SW 25
● *McKendree*, Fayette......S 12
McKim, Tyler............ NW 25
McLain, Wirt.............NW 10
● McMechen, Marshall..... N 427
● *McNutts*, Braxton........C ×
McWhorter, Kanawha......W ×
Machirville, Mason.........W 10
● *Mackers*, Mason.........W ×
Macksville, Pendleton.... NE 25
Macomber, Preston.........N 60
Madison, Boone........ SW 100
Madlin, Lewis............. C ×
Maganese, Wood.........NW ×
Magazine, Kanawha........W ×
Maggie, Mason............ W 15
Magnolia, Morgan.........NE 10
● *Mahan's*, Brooke......... N ×
Maidsville, Monongalia..... N 50
Majorsville, Marshall........N 25
● Malden, Kanawha.........W 355
Malta, Barbour..............N 5
Man, Logan...............SW 10
Manchester, Ohio.......... N ×
● **Mannington, Marion**..... N 908
Maple, Monongalia.......... N ×
Mapledale, Greenbrier...... S 30
Marion, Wetzel..............N 10
Market, Doddridge.......... N 20
Marlinton, Pocahontas.......C 25
Marlow, Berkeley..........NE ×
Marquess, Preston..........N 30
Marshall, Jackson.........W 8
Marshes of Coal, (see Coal River Marshes)........... ×
Marshville, Harrison........N 20
Martin, Grant..............NE 15
● **Martinsburgh**, B'rl'y NE 7,226
● Mason, Mason............W 1,029
Mason Town, Preston......N 100
Masonville, Grant.........NE 30
Mathias, Hardy............NE ×
Mattie, Roane............. W 50
Matville, Raleigh............S ×
Maud, Wetzel..............N ×
● *Maulsby*, Harrison........N ×
Maupins, Mason...........W 10
● *Maupins*, Mason.........W 25
Maxwell, Pleasants.......NW 6
May, Doddridge............ N ×
● Maybeury, McDowell... SW 200

Maysville, Grant.......... NE 150
Mayton, Webster...........C ×
Maywood, Fayette..........S ×
Meadland, Taylor..........N 50
Meadow Bluff, Greenbrier.. S 25
● MeadowCreekSta.,SummersS 75
Meadow Dale, Jackson.....W ×
Meadow Valley,(see McKim) ×
Meadowville, Barbour......N 175
Meadville, Tyler..........NW 20
Medley, Grant............NE 100
Meeker, Tyler............NW ×
Meighen, Marshall..........N ×
● *Meldahls*, Wood.......NW ×
Mentor, Jackson...........W ×
● Mercer's Bottom, Mason.W 25
Mercer's Salt Works, S'm'rs S 35
MercersLanding,(see Ashton) ×
● Metz, Marion.............N 25
Middlebourne, Tyler. NW 250
● *Middle Ferry*, Brooke... N ×
Middle Fork, Randolph.....C ×
MiddleIslandJunc.,(seeSmithton) ×
Middleway, Jefferson..... NE 400
● Midway, Putnam.........W 25
Miletus, Doddridge.........N 15
● *Milford Road*, Harrison..N ×
Millard, Roane............W 10
Mill Brook, Hampshire... NE ×
Mill Creek, (see Coopers)...... ×
Mill Creek, Berkeley......NE 150
● *Mill Creek Junc.*, Mercer. S ×
● *Millars*, Lewis............C ×
● *Millers*, Morgan........NE ×
Miller's Camp Branch,Ra'l'h S 125
● *Millersport Ferry*,Cabell W ×
● *Milleson's*, Hampshire..NE ×
Mill Hill, Greenbrier........S 25
Milliard, Roane...........W 10
Mill Point, Pocahontas......C 45
Mill Pond, (see Dial Stansill) ×
Millsborough, Marshall..... N 17
● Millville, Jefferson......NE 20
Millwood, Jackson..........W 10
● *Millwood Junc.*, Jackson W 15
Milo, Roane...............W ×
Milo, (see Littleton)......... ×
Milroy, Braxton........... C ×
● Milton, Cabell...........W 548
Mineral Point, Harrison.... N 25
Mineral Wells, Wood.....NW 50
Mineville, (see Atlantic)...... ×
Mingo Flat, Randolph.......C 50
Mink, Kanawha...........W ×
Minnie, Wetzel............ N ×
Minnora, Calhoun...........C 30
Miracle Run, Monongalia...N 10
Moatsville, (see Nicklow).... ×
● *Mohler*, Summers........S ×
Mole Hill, Ritchie.........NW 15
Molers, Jefferson..........NE 12
Monitor, Monroe...........S ×
● Monongah, Marion.......N 300
● *Monongahelia Junction*, Harrison..........N ×
MonroeDraft.(seeOgdenCave) ×
● *Montana*, Marion........N ×
Montana Mines, Marion....N ×
Monterville, Randolph......C ×
● Montgomery, Fayette.....S 2,000
Montrado, Fayette.........S ×
● Montrose, Randolph......C 50
Moody, Gilmer.............C ×
● *Moore*, Tucker..........N ×
Moorefield, Hardy......NE 495
Mooreland, Tucker..........N ×
Moore's Tyler...........NW 30
Moore's Mill, (see Cottagev'e) ×
Mooresville, Monongalia....N 30
Morgan s Glade, Preston....N 20
● *Morgan'sGrove*,Jeffe's'nNE ×
● Morgansville, Doddridge.N 20
● **Morgantown**, Mn'galiaN 1,011
Morgantown Depot, Mo'g'laN ×
Morgan Valley, Wyoming SW ×
Morley, Braxton...........C ×
Morris, Wirt.............NW 100
Morton Grove, Morgan....NE 30
Moscow, Hancock....... ..N ×
Moses Fork, Wayne.......SW ×
Mossy, Fayette............S ×
● Mound, Kanawha.........W ×
● **Moundsville** MarshallN 2,688
Mountain Cove, Fayette.....S 5
Mountain Creek, (see Dunn's) ×
Mountain Home (see Masonville)............ ×

Mount Alto (see School House Run)........... ×
● Mount Carbon, Fayette...S 562
● Mount Clare, Harrison....N 25
● *Mount De Choutaul*, OhioN ×
Mount Freedom (see Circleville)................. ×
Mount Harmony, Marion..N ×
Mount Hope, Fayette.......S 30
Mount Ida, Fayette........S ×
Mount Lookout, Nicholas...C ×
Mount Nebo, Nicholas.......C 30
Mount Olive, Mason.........W 30
Mount Storm, Grant......NE 15
Mount Zion, Calhoun........C ×
Mouth of Big Heart (see Green Shoals)........
Mouth of Birch, Braxton...C 20
Mouth of Buffalo (see Man).. ×
Mouth of Davie (see Stansill) ×
Mouth of Holly, Braxton...C ×
Mouth of Island Cr. (see Tornado) .... ×
Mouth of Little Sandy, (see Little Sandy) .... ×
Mouth of Mate, (see Sidney). ×
Mouth of Panther Creek, (see Perryville) .... ×
Mouth of Poca, (see Poca)... ×
Mouth of Salt Lick Creek,(see Burnsville) .... ×
Mouth of Short Creek, (see Racine)............. ×
Mouth of Scary, Putnam..W 50
Mouth of Seneca, P'dletonNE 10
Mouth of Sycamore,LoganSW 60
Mouth of Sugar Creek, (see Sugar Valley)............ ×
Mouth of Thirteen Mile Creek, (see Leon)............ ×
Mouth of West Fork, (see Gordon)................ ×
Mouth of White Creek, (see White Creek)........... ×
Mud, Lincoln.............SW ×
Muddlety, Nicholas.........C ×
Mulvane, Fayette..........S ×
Munday, Wirt............NW 10
Murphytown, Wood......NW 200
● Murraysville, Jackson....W 125
● Muse's Bottom, Jackson..W 8
Mutton Run, Hampshire..NE ×
Myra, Lincoln............SW ×
Myrtle, Logan............SW ×
Naoma, Fayette............S ×
Napier, Braxton.............C ×
Nease, Mason.............W ×
Needmore, Hardy.........NE ×
Neel, Marion...............N ×
Nelson, Boone............SW 20
Neponset, Summers.........S ×
Neptune, Jackson........NE 6
Nero Barbour..............N 10
Nesselroad, Jackson......NE 6
Nestorville, Barbour.......N 90
Nettie, Wayne...........SW ×
New, Raleigh...............S ×
Newark, Wirt............NW 200
Newberne, Gilmer..........C 20
NewBrownsville(seePentress) ×
● Newburgh, Preston.......N 778
New CastleL'nd'g(seeClifton) ×
● **New Cumberland** Hancock...............N 2,305
● *New Cumberland Junction*, Hancock............N ×
New Dale, Wetzel..........N 78
New England, Wood.......NW 50
New Flat Fork (seeHarrison) ×
Newfound, Wyoming.....SW ×
New Geneva, Jackson......W 6
● New Haven, Mason......W 595
New Hope, Mercer..........S 35
● *Newlon*, Upshur..........C ×
New Manchester (see Fairview)............. ×
● **New Martinsville**, Wetzel...........N 692
New Milton, Doddridge.....N 100
Newport (see Madison)....... ×
Newport, Wood..........NW 120
● New Richmond, SummersS 80
New Salem (see Salem)...... ×
Newton, Roane.............W 100
Newville, Braxton...........C 40
New Washington, Marshall.N 20
Next, Tyler..............NW 30

Nicholas C. H., Nicholas.C 250
Nickell's Mills, Monroe......S 35
● Nicklow, Barbour........N 25
● *Nicoles*, Lewis...........C ×
Noah, Kanawha...........W 30
Nobe, Calhoun.............C 10
● *Noble*, Cabell...........W ×
Nolan, Logan.............SW 25
Nollsville (see Martinsburgh) ×
Normantown, Gilmer........C 67
North Anderson, Greenb'r..S 100
● North Mountain, B'ke'yNE 65
North River Mills, H'ms'eNE 35
North Spring, Wyoming..SW 10
Null, Ritchie.............NW ×
● *Number 12 Water Station*, Morgan...............NE ×
● Nuttallburgh, Fayette.....S 342
Nutter Farm, Ritchie....NW ×
Nutterville, Greenbrier......S 50
● Nuzums, Marion..........N 30
Nye, Putnam..............W ×
Oak Flat, Pendleton.......NE 17
Oak Hill, Fayette........... S 100
Oakland, Mason............W ×
Oakton, Berkeley..........NE 15
● Oakvale, Mercer..........S 82
Oakville, Roane............ W ×
Oak Wharf (see Flat Fork).. ×
Oceana, Wyoming.......SW 200
● *Ocean Mines*, Harrison...W ×
Odaville, Jackson..........W 6
Odd, Raleigh...............S ×
Odell, Kanawha............W ×
Ogdin, Wood.............NW 10
Oil Creek (see Burnsville).... ×
Oilville, Logan...........SW ×
Oka, Calhoun...............C ×
● Okonoka, Hampshire...NE 15
Oldaker, Putnam..........W ×
Old Fields, Hardy.........NE 35
Oldtown, Mason...........W ×
Oley, Raleigh...............S ×
Olive, Harrison............N 15
Omps, Morgan............NE ×
● Ona, Cabell...............W 100
● Opekiska, Monongalia....N ×
● *Opequon*, Berkeley......NE ×
Ophelia, Nicholas...........C 200
Oral, Harrison.............N ×
Orange, Boone............SW ×
Oreide, Taylor..............N 25
Orem, Wood..............NW ×
Orange Cave, Greenbrier...S ×
● Orleans Cross Roads, Morgan.................NE 300
Orlena, Randolph...........C 25
Orpha, Barbour............N ×
● *Orr's*, Preston...........N ×
Osborne's Mills, Roane.....W 15
Oscar, Doddridge..........N ×
Osceola, Randolph..........C ×
Osgood, Monongalia.........N ×
Otia, Mason...............W ×
Overfield, Barbour..........N 30
Overhill, Upshur............C 10
Ox Bow, Ritchie.........NW ×
Oxford, Doddridge..........N 20
Pack's Ferry, Summers......S 12
● Paden's Valley, Wetzel...N 10
● Paint Creek, Kanawha...W 300
Palace Valley, Upshur......C ×
Palatine, Marion...........N 860
● *Palatine Mines*, Marion..N ×
Palestine (see Reedy Ripple) ×
Palestine, Greenbrier........S ×
Pan Handle (see Collier)...... ×
Pansy, Grant.............NE 15
Paradise, Putnam..........W 70
Parchment Valley, JacksonW 10
Parkers, Doddridge.........N 10
● **Parkersburgh**, Wo'dNW 8,408
Parkersville (see St. Mary's) ×
● *Parsons*, Hampshire....NE ×
● Parsons, Tucker..........N 400
Pasco, Roane.............W ×
Patrick, Kanawha..........W ×
● Patterson's Depot, Mn'alNE 50
Patton, Monroe............NE ×
● Paw Paw, Morgan......NE 772
Peabody, Kanawha.........W ×
● *Peacher's Mill*, Jeff'rson.NE 25
Peachtree, Raleigh..........S ×
Peck's Run, Upshur ....C 50
Pedlar's Run, Monongalia...N 5
Peel Tree, Barbour.........N 100
● Peerless, Kanawha.......W ×

Peeryville, McDowell..SW 50
Peewee, Wirt............NW 30
Pemberton, Raleigh.........S ×
● *Pendleton*, Tucker........N 75
Peniel, Roane.............W 15
● *Penrith*, Hancock.........N ×
● Pennsborough, Ritchie.NW 570
Pentress, Monongalia.......N 40
Pepper, Barbour............N 12
Perkin's Mills (see Gillespie's Mills)..................... ×
Perry, Hardy.............NE ×
Persinger, Nicholas........C 30
Peru, Hardy..............NE 20
Petersburgh, Grant...NE 300
Peters Creek (see Winston) .. ×
● *Peterson's Siding*, Lewis..C ×
Peterstown, Monroe.........S 200
● Petroleum, Ritchie.....NW 100
Pettit, Randolph...........C ×
Pewee, Wirt.............NW 25
Peytona, Boone...........SW 100
● **Phillippi,** Barbour.....N 378
Philoah, Putnam............W ×
Phoenixville, (see Omps)..... ×
Pickaway, Monroe...........S 100
Pickens, Randolph..........C ×
● Piedmont, Mineral......NE 3,500
Pigeon, Roane..............W ×
Pike City, (see Buffalo)....... ×
Pine Bluffs, Harrison.......N 25
Pine Grove, Wetzel.........N 100
Pineville, Wyoming.......SW 12
Pink, Calhoun..............C 10
Pinnacle, Wyoming.......SW ×
● *Pinnickinick Mines*, Harrison.....................N ×
Pinoak, Mercer.............S ×
Pioneer, Marshall..........N 25
Pipestem, Summers.........S ×
Pisgah, Preston.............N 10
Pleasant Creek, Barbour....N 20
Pleasant Dale, Hampshire.NE 15
Pleasant Hill, Preston...... N 6
Pleasant Retreat, Clay...... C ×
Pleasant Run, Tucker.......N 10
Pleasant Valley, Marshall...N 8
Pleasant Valley, (see Sugar Valley).................... ×
● Pleasant View, Jackson..W 15
Pleasantville, Marion...... N ×
Pliny, Putnam............. W ×
● Plymouth, Putnam...... W 200
● Poca, Putnam............W 284
Pocotaligo, Kanawha........W 10
● *Point Mills*, Ohio.........N 30
Point Mountain, Randolph..C ×
● **Point Pleasant,** Mason W 1,853
Polandale, Wood.........NW ×
Pond Creek, Wood.........W 75
Pond Gap, Kanawha....... W ×
Pool, Nicholas............. C ×
Poplar, Logan.............SW 40
Poppa, Wayne............ SW 40
● *Porter*, Tucker...........N ×
Porter's Falls, Wetzel...... N 0
Porter's Mills, (see Hamlin). ×
Portersville, Lincoln.......SW 12
● *Portland*, Jackson.......W ×
● Potomac, Ohio............N 20
Potter, Tucker.............N ×
Powell's, Marion...........N ×
● Powellton, Fayette........S 491
● Powhatan, McDowell...SW 35
● *Powhatan*, Marshall..... N ×
Powntown, (see Jake's Run). ×
Pratt, Roane............... W ×
Prince, Fayette............ S 24
Princeton, Mercer........S 320
Procious, Clay..............C ×
● Proctor, Wetzel..........N 100
Progress, Braxton...........C ×
Prospect Valley, Harrison..N 25
Prosperity, Raleigh.........S 20
Providence, Jackson.......W ×
Pruntytown, Taylor.........N 300
Pugh, Webster..............C ×
Pughtown, (see Fairview)... ×
Pullman, Ritchie.........NW 20
Purgitsville, Hampshire...NE ×
Pursley, Tyler............NW 35
Putnam, C. H.,(see Winfield) ×
● Queen City, Putnam..... W ×
Queens, Upshur.............C 46
Queen Shoals, Kanawha....W 20
Queen's Mills, (see Cove Cr.). ×
Queen's Ridge, Wayne....SW ×

Quiet Dell, Harrison........N 50
● Quinnimont, Fayette......S 300
Racine, Boone............SW 150
Radcliffe, Putnam..........W ×
Ragland, Logan............SW ×
Raleigh, C. H., Raleigh.. S 158
Ralph, Webster.............C ×
Randall, Monongalia........N 50
Rathbone, Preston.........N ×
Rathbone, (see Burning Sprs.)
● Raven Rock, Pleasants.NW 75
Raven's Eye, Fayette........S 50
● Ravenswood, Jackson....W 817
● *Rawlings Sta.* Mineral.NE ×
● *Rawn*, Kanawha..........W ×
● Raymond City, Putnam..W 200
Reader, Wetzel............. N 10
Redbird, Raleigh............S ×
Red Creek, Tucker......... N 20
Red Hill, Wood........... NW ×
● Red House Shoals, P't'am W 150
Red Knob, Roane.......... W 30
Redmud, Mason............W ×
Red Oak Ridge, Mercer..... S ×
Red Sulphur Springs, Monroe S 60
Reedsville, Preston......... N 50
● Reedy, Roane........... W 75
Reedy Ripple, Wirt.......NW 80
Redyville, Roane...........W 20
Reese's Mill, Mineral.....NE 30
Rees Tannery, Mineral....NE 40
Removal, Webster...........C ×
Rena, Putnam..............W ×
Renick's Valley, Greenbrier.S 24
Renius, Wood............ NW 6
Replete, Webster............C ×
Respect, Harrison.......... N ×
Retreat, Monroe............ S ×
Reynolds, (see Malden)....... ×
Reynold's Store, (see Graham's Mines)................... ×
Reynoldsville, Harrison.....N 60
Rice, Wayne..............SW ×
Richardson, Calhoun........C 35
Richardsville, (see Oak Hill). ×
Rich Creek, Logan........SW 30
Rich Creek, (see Fry)........ ×
Richmond Falls, (see New Richmond)............... ×
Richlands, Greenbrier.......S 12
Rich Mountain, Randolph...C 45
Richwood, Nicholas.........C ×
Ridersville, Morgan.......NE 75
Ridge, Morgan............NE 12
Ridgeville, Mineral........NE 15
● Ridgeway, Berkeley.... NE ×
● *Ridgley*, Mineral........NE ×
Rieresville, Marion........ N 150
● *Riffe*, Summers...........S ×
Riggs, Preston..............N ×
Riley, Clay.................C ×
Rilla, Calhoun...............C 10
Rio, Hampshire........... NE 45
Ripley's, (see Centreville)...... ×
● *Ripleys Landing*, Jackson W 25
● Rippon, Jefferson........NE 200
● **Ritchie, C. H.,** Ritchie NW 400
● *Riverside*, Ohio...........N ×
● *Riverside*, Putnam....... W 30
Riverside, (see Duhring) ..... ×
● River View Fayette...... S 20
● *River View*, Marshall.....N ×
● Rivesville, Marion.......N 165
● Roanoke, Lewis............C 40
Roaring Creek, Randolph...C 20
Roberts, Doddridge......... N ×
Robinson's Mill, Wetzel.... N 15
Rock Camp, Monroe.........S ×
Rock Castle, Mason........ W ×
● *Rock Castle*, Mason...... W 15
Rock Castle, (see Rock View) ×
Rock Cave, Upshur........ C 150
Rockford, Harrison.........N 125
Rock Gap, Morgan........NE ×
Rock Lick, Marshall.........N 36
● *Rockland*, Greenbrier.... S ×
Rockland, Hardy..........NE ×
Rockoak, Hardy.......... NE ×
Rockport, Wood..........NW 150
Rocksdale, Calhoun..........C ×
Rock View, Wyoming.... SW 24
Rockville, Preston...........N 15
● *Rockwell's Run*, Morgan NE ×
Rocky Fork, Kanawha..... W ×
● Rodamers, Preston.........N 35
● *Rohrboughs Siding*, Lewis C ×
Rollins, Mason............ W ×

● Rollyson, Braxton........ C ×
Romantic, Greenbrier.......S ×
Rome, Kanawha........... W ×
Romine's Mills, Harrison...N 100
● **Romney,** Hampshire..NE 451
● Ronceverte, Greenbrier...S 481
● Roney's Point, Ohio......N 30
● Rosby's Rock, Marshall.. N 75
Rosedale, Gilmer............C 6
Roseville, Fayette............S 30
Ross, Wetzel................N ×
● *Round Bottom*, Marshall. N ×
Round Bottom, Wayne....SW 50
Round Knob, Putnam......W ×
● *Round Top*, Morgan....NE ×
● Rowlesburgh, Preston....N 560
Rowton, Barbour.. ....N ×
Roxalana, Roane...........W ×
Roxie, Raleigh...............S ×
Roy, Roane................. W ×
Ruckman, Hampshire.... NE ×
Ruddle, Pendleton......... NE 30
Ruhl, Harrison.............. N ×
Rupert, Greenbrier......... S ×
Rural Dale, Upshur......... C 40
Rush Run, Fayette...........S ×
Rushville, Lewis............ C 30
Rusk, Ritchie..............NW 15
Russellville, Fayette........ S 50
Russett, Hardy............NE ×
Ryan, Roane................W ×
Rymer, Marion..............W 50
● Sago, Upshur...............C 24
● St. Albans Kanawha....W 1,500
St. Clara, Doddridge........N 50
St. Cloud, Monongalia.......N 25
St. George, Tucker.........N 316
St. Joseph, Marshall.........N ×
St. Leo, Monongalia..........N ×
● **St. Mary's,** Pleasants.NW 520
Salama, Pleasants........NW 15
● Salem, Harrison...........N 310
Salt Lick Bridge, Braxton...C 30
Salt Rock, (see Ousley's Gap) ×
Salt Sulphur Springs, Monroe S ×
Samaria, Marion............N ×
Sancho, Tyler.............NW ×
● *Sand Cut*, Harrison......N ×
Sand Fork, Gilmer..........C 25
Sand Hill, Marshall..........N 25
Sand Hill, (see Volcano)..... ×
Sand Run, Upshur...........C 30
● *Sand Stone*, Summers.....S 80
● Sandyville, Jackson...... W 100
Santifee, Summers..........S 20
Sarah, Cabell...............W ×
● Sardis, Harrison...........N 100
Sassafras, Mason...........W ×
● Sattes, Kanawha..........W 30
Saulsbury, Wood.........NW ×
Saulsville, Wyoming.......SW 24
Savagetown, (see Strange C'k) ×
● Scary, Putnam.............W ×
● *Scaryville*, Putnam......W ×
● Schell, Mineral..........NE 50
Schilling, Roane............W ×
● School House, Jackson....W 50
Schultz, Pleasants........NW 35
Scotia, Summers...........S ×
Scott, Wood..............NW ×
Scottdale, Marion...........N ×
● Scott's Depot, Putnam...W 50
Seaflat, Mason..............W ×
Seaman, Roane..............W 6
Seatonville, (see Wolf Run).. ×
Second Creek, Greenbrier...S 100
Sedalia, Doddridge..........N 10
Sedan, Hampshire.........NE 20
Seemly, Grant.............NE 17
● Selbyville, Upshur........ C 10
Selden, Wood.............NW ×
Selection, Pleasants......NW ×
Sell, Preston................N ×
Sellars, Upshur..............C ×
Seng, Logan...............SW ×
Servia, Braxton............. C ×
Seven Pines, Marion.........N ×
● Sewell Depot, Fayette.....S 500
● *Seymour*, Lewis............C ×
● *Seymour*, Mineral......NE ×
Seymoursville, Grant.....NE 35
Shady Spring, Raleigh.......S 12
● *Shaffers*, Preston.........N ×
Shambling's Mills, Roane..W ×
Shanghai, Berkeley.......NE 48
Shannon, Ohio..............N ×
Sharon, Webster............C ×

Shaversville, (see Flat Woods) ×
● Shaw, Mineral.........NE 75
Shawnee, Pleasants........NW ×
● *Shenandoah*, Jefferson..NE ×
● Shenandoah Junction Jefferson.................NE 40
● Sheperdstown, Jeffe'sn. NE 1,515
Sheridan, Lincoln .....SW ×
● Sherman, Jackson.......W ×
Sherrard, Marshall.........N 50
Shiloh, Braxton............C 25
Shiloh, Tyler............NW 35
● Shinnston, Harrison......N 403
Shirley, Tyler............NW 50
● Shoals, Wayne..........SW ×
Shock, Braxton..............C ×
● *Shoo Fly*, Fayette........S ×
Shops, Putnam.............W ×
Short Creek, (see Racine).... ×
● Short Creek, Brooke.....N ×
Shreves, Pendleton.........NE 17
Shrewsbury, Kanawha......W 25
Siberia, Mercer..............S ×
● Sidney, Logan..........SW ×
Sigman, Putnam...........W ×
Siloam, Mason..............W ×
Silver Hill, Wetzel...........N 50
● *Silver Run*, Ritchie.....NW 8
● Silverton, Jackson.......W 20
Simmons, (see Bramwell).... ×
● *Simmon's Junc.*, Mercer..S ×
● *Simms* Putnam..........W ×
● Simpson, Taylor..........N 250
Sincerity, Wetzel...........N 10
Sinclair, Preston............N 20
Sink, Raleigh................S 24
Sinks Grove, Monroe.........S 150
Sinnett's Mills, Ritchie..NW 10
Sioto, Lincoln.............SW ×
● Sir John's Run, MorganNE 50
Sissonville, Kanawha........W 80
● Sistersville, Tyler.......NW 469
Skaggs, Monroe..............S ×
● *Skidmore's*, Harrison....N ×
Skull Run, Jackson........W ×
Slanesville, Hampshire....NE 50
Slate, Wood...............NW 6
● *Slater's*, Fayette.......... S ×
● Sleepy Creek Bridge, Morgan....................NE 50
Sleith Braxton.............C 10
Sloan, Wood..............NW ×
Smithfield, (see Middle Way). ×
● *Smith's*, Lewis.............C ×
● *Smith's Mines*, Harrison. N ×
● Smithton, Doddridge.....N 50
Smithtown, (see White Day). ×
Smithville, Ritchie........NW 150
Smithville, (see Willowton).. ×
● *Smoot's*, Preston..........N ×
Snake Root, McDowell....SW ×
● *Snowflake*, Greennbrier...S ×
Snow Hill, Nicholas........C 25
Snyder's Mills, Jefferson..NE 60
Soak Creek, Raleigh.........S ×
Soho, Berkeley............NE ×
Solon, (see Glenville)........ ×
● South Branch Depot, Hampshire....................NE 11
South Charleston, (see Charleston).................... ×
South Mill Creek, P'dlet'n. NE 24
South Morgantown, Mon'g'aN 285
● *South Ruffner*, Kanawha. W ×
Southside, Mason............W 10
South Wheeling, (see Wh'll'g) ×
Spangler, Kanawha........W ×
Spanishburgh, Mercer......S 25
Spaulding, Logan.........SW 60
Speed, Roane..............W 20
● **Spencer**, Roane........W 431
● *Spencer's*, Preston........N ×
Spilman, Mason............W ×
Split Rock, Pocahontas.....C ×
Spring Dale, Fayette........S 5
● Springfield, Hampshire. NE 175
Spring Gap, Hampshire..NE ×
Spring Garden, Roane.....W ×
● Spring Hill, Kanawha....W 275
Spring Mills, Berkeley....NE ×
● *Spring Run*, Pleasants. NW ×
Spruce, Upshur..............C 8
Spurlockville, Lincoln....SW ×
Squirejim, McDowell.....SW ×
Stafford, Wirt.......... NW 10
Stanley, Ritchie.... ....NW ×
Star, Randolph..............C ×

Staten, Calhoun............C ×
Statler Run, Monongalia....N 25
Statt's Mills, Jackson.......W 15
Stella, Wirt................NW 10
Stenders, Wetzel...........N 25
Sterling, Wetzel...........N ×
Stevens, Mason.............W 6
Stevens Mine, Boone....SW ×
Stewartstown, Monongalia. N 50
Stilner, Webster...........C ×
Stillman, Upshur...........C ×
Stinson, Calhoun............C ×
Stock, Braxton..............C ×
● Stockyard, Summers......S ×
● Stone Cliff, Fayette.......S 800
Stonecoal, Wayne.........SW 85
Stony, Fayette...............S ×
Stotler's CrossRoads, M'g'nNE 10
Stout's Mills, Gilmer.......C 35
Strange Creek, Braxton.....C 30
Strouds, Webster............C ×
Stumptown, Gilmer.........C 45
Sturm's Mill, Marion........N ×
Sue, Greenbrier..............S ×
Sugar Grove, Pendleton...NE 50
Sugar Valley, Pleasants...NW 24
Sulphur Springs, Greenb'er. S ×
Summers' Store, (seeTollGate) ×
Summersville, (see Ni'olasCH) ×
● Summit Point, JeffersonNE 75
Sunflower, Raleigh..........S ×
Sun Hill, Wyoming....... SW ×
● *Sunnyside*, Fayette.......S ×
Sunset, Pocahontas.........C ×
Suter, Hancock.............N ×
Sutton, (see Coon's Mills).... ×
● Sutton, Braxton.......... C 276
Swamp Run, Upshur.......C 40
Swamp, Cabell .... W ×
Swampond, Berkeley..... NE ×
Sweedlin Hill, Pendleton. NE ×
Sweeny's Mills, (seeCenterv'le) ×
Sweetland, Lincoln.........SW ×
Sweet Springs, Monroe......S 50
● *Switch Back*, Mineral...NE ×
Switzer, Barbour.............N 15
Sycamore, Calhoun..........C 15
Sycamore Dale, Harrison... N 10
Sylva, Roane................ W ×
Sylvan Mills, (see St. Mary's) ×
● Tabler, Berkeley........NE 9
Table Rock, Raleigh.........S 10
● *Tabbs*, Berkeley........NE ×
Tacy, Barbour...............N 30
Talbott's, Barbour...........N 10
Tattle Run, (see Petroleum). ×
● Talcott, Summers..........S 288
Tallmansville, Upshur.......C 30
Tallyho, Wood.............NW 25
Tanner's, Gilmer............C 50
Tannery, Preston............N 10
Tappan, Taylor..............N ×
Tariff, Roane.................W ×
Tate Creek, Braxton........C ×
Taylor, (see Purgettsville)... ×
Taylor, Logan..............SW ×
Teays, Putnam..............W 30
Ten Mile, (see Fourteen) .... ×
● *Ten Mile*, Upshur.........C ×
● Terra Alta, Preston...... N 443
Texas, (see Colfax)........... ×
Texas, Tucker...............N 10
The Rock, Mercer............S 50
Thoburn, Marion............N ×
● Thomas, Tucker..........N 269
● Thompson, Marshall......N ×
Thorndike, (see Ona) .... ×
● Thornton, Taylor........ N 100
Three Churches, H'pshire. NE 32
● *Three Forks*, Roane..... W 50
● Thurmond, Fayette....... S ×
Tick Ridge, Wayne....... SW ×
Tipton, Nicholas........... C ×
Toledo, Nicholas........... C ×
● Toll Gate, Ritchie......NW 50
Tomahawk Springs, B'ley. NE 10
Toney's Fork, Wyoming. SW 24
Tooley, Wayne..............SW ×
Tophet, Summers............ S ×
Topin's Grove, Jackson.... W 10
● *Top Mill*, Ohio............N ×
Top of Allegheny, Poc'ontasC ×
Tornado, Kanawha.........W ×
Toson, Cabell...............W ×
Totten, McDowell..........SW 100
Townsend Mills, Gilmer....C 20
Trace, Putnam.............W 10

Trace Fork, Wayne.......SW ×
Track, (see Pleasant Point).. ×
Tracy, Barbour............ N ×
Traveller's Repose, Poc'ntasC ×
● Triadelphia, Ohio.........N 515
Triplett, Roane..............W ×
Trout's Hill, (see WayneC.H.) ×
Trout Valley, Greenbrier....S ×
Troy, Gilmer................C 250
True, Summers..............S 24
Truebada, Gilmer.......... C 50
Try's Mills, (see Fabius)..... ×
● *Tuckahoe*, Greenbrier.... S 30
Tucker, Wirt..............NW ×
● *Tug Creek*, Summers..... S ×
Tug River, McDowell..... SW 10
Tulip, Wayne............ SW 25
● Tunnelton, Preston.......N 160
Tuppers Creek Bridge (see Sissonville)............... ×
Turkey Run, (see Viola)..... ×
Twiggs, Pleasants........ NW 20
Twistville, Braxton......... C ×
Tyler's Creek, Cabell....... W ×
Tyner, Wood...............NW 50
● Tyrconnell Mines, Taylor. N 60
● Uffington, Monongalia....N 30
Uneva, Monongalia.........N ×
Unger's Store, Morgan....NE 10
Union, Monroe.............S 348
Union Mills, Pleasants....NW 25
Union Mills, (see N.Mount'n) ×
Union Mines, Kanawha.... W ×
Union Ridge, Cabell........ W 25
Uniontown, Wetzel.........N 100
Unionville, (see Duffield)..... ×
Upland, Mason............W 5
Upper Creek, Kanawha....W ×
Upper Falls of Coal, (see St. Albans).................. ×
Upper Glade, Webster...... C 10
Upper Tract, Pendleton...NE 25
● *Upton's*, Kanawha...... W ×
Upton, Marion...............N ×
Uvilla, Jefferson..........NE ×
Vadis, Lewis............... C 15
Valley, Gilmer............... C 10
Valley Bend, Randolph..... C ×
● Valley Falls, Marion......N 30
Valley Fork, Clay........... C ×
Valley Furnace, Barbour...N 25
● Valley Grove, Ohio....... N 50
Valley Head, Randolph......C 25
Valley Mills, Wood....... NW 50
Valley Point, Preston.......N 10
Van, Boone............... SW 13
Van Camp, Wetzel...........N 25
● *Vances*, Hampshire.... NE ×
Vanceville, Logan..........SW ×
● Van Clevesville, Berkley NE 25
Vandalia, Lewis..............C ×
Vandalia, Summers........ S 120
Vanderville, Logan.........SW ×
Vannoy's Mill, Barbour......N 12
● *Vaucluse*, Pleasants... NW ×
Veranda, Mason............W 40
Vernon, Wetzel............ N ×
Victor, Fayette.............. S 25
● Vienna, Wood............NW 10
View, Greenbrier...........S ×
Vincen, Wetzel..............N ×
Vinson, Wayne...........SW ×
Vintroux Landing, (see Frazier's Bottom)............ ×
Viola, Marshall...............N 50
● *Virginia*, Mineral...... NE ×
Vista, Raleigh................S 25
Vivian, McDowell.......... SW ×
● Volcano, Wood.........NW 200
● Volcano Junc., Ritchie. NW 15
Wacoma, Kanawha...... W 240
Wadeville, Wood .... NW 150
Wadestown, Monongalia....N 100
● *Waggener*, Mason....... W ×
Waiteville, Monroe..........S ×
Waldo, Putnam........... W ×
● Walker, Wood............NW 30
Walker's L'nd'g, (see Poca) . ×
Walkersville, Lewis.........C 70
Wallace Harrison........... N 50
Walnut Grove, Roane......W ×
Walton, Cabell............. W ×
Walton, Roane............. W 50
Wappocomo, Hampshire..NE ×
Wardensville, Hardy......NE 106
Warford, Summers......... S ×
Warren, Lincoln..........SW ×

● *Warnocks*, Mineral ... NE ×
Washburn, Ritchie ... NW ×
● Washington, Wood ... NW 15
● *Washington's*, Hamp'e. NE ×
Wasp, Pleasants ... NW 20
Watson, Marion ... N ×
Wattsville, Clay ... C 30
● Waverly, Wood ... NW 100
Wayne, Wayne ... SW 500
Wayside, Monroe ... S ×
Webb's Mills, (see Smithv'le) ×
● Webster, Taylor ... N 25
Webster, (see Addison C. H.) ×
Welch, McDowell ... SW ×
Welch Glade, Webster ... C 15
● Welcome, Marshall ... N 35
Welford, Kanawha ... W ×
Wells, Marshall ... N ×
● **Wellsburg**, Brooke ... N 2,235
Wesley, Wood ... NW 30
West, Wetzel ... N 10
● *West Clarksburgh*, Har'n N ×
● West Columbia, Mason ... W 250
● *West End*, Preston ... N ×
● West Grafton, Taylor ... N 810
West Liberty, Ohio ... N 300
West Milford, Harrison ... N 210
West Morgantown, (see Morgantown) ... ×
● **Weston**, Lewis ... C 2,143
● **West Union**, Doddridge N 312
● *West Virginia Central Junc.* Mineral ... NE ×
West Warren, (see Wadest'n) 6
● Wheatland, Jefferson ... NE 30
● **WHEELING**, Ohio ... N 34,522
● *Wheeling Junc.* Brooke .. N ×
● *Whitcomb*, Greenbrier ... S ×
White, Preston ... N 6
White Creek, Wayne ... SW 50
White Day, Monongalia ... N 150
White Oak, Ritchie ... NW 10
White Pine, Calhoun ... C 60
White's, Preston ... N 6
White's Creek, Wayne ... SW 50
White's Mills, Logan ... SW 16
● White Sulphur Springs, Grenbrier ... S 500
Whitfield, Ohio ... N ×
● *Whyte*, Randolph ... C ×
Wick, Tyler ... NW 50
Wiggins, Summers ... S ×
Wilbur, Tyler ... NW ×
Wilding, Jackson ... W 10
Willey, Preston ... N 25
Wileyville, Wetzel ... N 75
● *William*, Tucker ... N 30
Williamsburgh, Greenbrier .. S 100
Williamson's, (see Mouth of Sycamore) ×
Williamson Land., (see Willow Gr.) ×
Williamsport, Grant ... NE 45
● *Williams River*, Webster .. C ×
● Williamstown, Wood ... NW 376
Willow Bend, Monroe ... S 6
Willowdale, Jackson ... W 6
Willow Grove, Jackson ... W 15
● *Willow Grove*, Mason ... W ×
● Willow Island, Pleasa's. NW 75
● Willowton, Mercer ... S ×
Willow Tree, Mason ... W 10
Wilmoth's, Barbour ... N 10
● *Wilson*, Brooke ... N ×
● *Wilson*, Cabell ... W ×
● Wilsonburgh, Harrison ... N 200
● Wilsonia, Grant ... NE 100
● *Wilson's*, Lewis ... C ×
Wilson's Mills, Grant ... NE 20
● Windom, Mineral ... NE ×
Windy, Wirt ... NW ×
Winfield, Putnam ... W 302
● Winifrede, Kanawha ... W 100
Winifrede Jc., Kanawha ... W ×
Winston, Nicholas ... C 35
Wirt C. H., (see Elizabeth) ... ×
Wise, Monongalia ... N 75
Wiseburgh, Jackson ... W 10
Wolf Creek, Monroe ... S 10
● *Wolf Creek*, Summers ... S ×
● *Wolf Mills*, Preston ... N 15
Wolf Run, Marshall ... N 25
● Wolf Summit, Harrison .. N 30
Wolf's Store, Gilmer ... C 10
Wood, Fayette ... S ×
● Woodlands, Marshall ... N 30
● *Woods*, Putnam ... W ×
Woodyard, Roane ... W ×
Woodzell, Webster ... C ×
Wootens, Logan ... SW ×
Worley, Monongalia ... N ×
Worthington, Marion ... N 100
● *Worthington Sta.*, Marion N ×
Wyatt, Harrison ... N 50
Wyoma, Mason ... W 6
Yankee Dam, Clay ... C ×
Yards, Mercer ... S ×
Yeater's Mill, (see Center Pt.) ×
Yellow Spring, Hampshire NE 16
Yorkville, Wayne ... SW ×
Young's Mills, Kanawha ... W 15
Zackville, Wirt ... NW ×
Zela, Nicholas ... C ×
Zenith, Monroe ... S ×
Zinnia, Doddridge ... N 6
Zona, Roane ... W ×

WISCONSIN.

COUNTY.	INDEX.	POP.
Adams	C	6,889
Ashland	NW	20,063
Barron	NW	15,416
Bayfield	NW	7,390
Brown	E	39,164
Buffalo	W	15,997
Burnett	NW	4,393
Calumet	E	16,639
Chippewa	NW	25,143
Clark	NW	17,708
Columbia	C	28,[illegible]56
Crawford	SW	15,987
Dane	S	59,578
Dodge	E	44,984
Door	NE	15,682
Douglas	NW	13,468
Dunn	NW	22,664
Eau Claire	NW	30,673
Florence	NE	2,604
Fond du Lac	E	44,088
Forest	N	1,012
Grant	SW	36,651
Green	S	22,732
Green Lake	C	15,165
Iowa	SW	22,117
Jackson	W	15,797
Jefferson	SE	33,530
Juneau	C	17,121
Kenosha	SE	15,581
Kewaunee	E	16,153
La Crosse	W	38,801
La Fayette	SW	20,265
Langlade	NE	9,465
Lincoln	C	12,008
Manitowoc	E	37,831
Marathon	N	30,369
Marinette	NE	20,304
Marquette	C	9,676
Milwaukee	SE	236,101
Monroe	W	23,211
Oconto	NE	15,009
Oneida	N	5,010
Outagamie	E	38,690
Ozaukee	E	14,943
Pepin	W	6,932
Pierce	W	20,385
Polk	NW	12,968
Portage	C	24,798
Price	N	5,258
Racine	SE	36,268
Richland	SW	19,121
Rock	S	43,220
St. Croix	NW	23,139
Sauk	C	30,575
Sawyer	NW	1,977
Shawano	NE	19,236
Sheboygan	E	42,489
Taylor	NW	6,731
Trempealeau	W	18,920
Vernon	W	25,111
Walworth	SE	27,860
Washburn	NW	2,926
Washington	E	22,751
Waukesha	SE	33,270
Waupaca	C	26,794
Waushara	C	13,507
Winnebago	E	50,097
Wood	C	18,127
Total		1,686,880

TOWN. COUNTY.	INDEX.	POP
● Abbotsford, Clark	NW	260
● Abelman, Sauk	C	332
● Abrams, Oconto	NE	195
● Ackerville, Washington	E	90
Acorn, Dane	S	32
Ada, Sheboygan	E	32
Adams, Walworth	SE	300
Adams Centre, Adams	C	×
Adamsville, Iowa	SW	100
Addison, Washington	E	250
● Adell, Sheboygan	E	100
Adsit, Dane	S	32
● Alton, Rock	S	1,150
Agenda, Ashland	NW	81
● *Agnew*, Ashland	NW	×
Aknapee, Kewaunee	E	1,01[illegible]
Alabama, Polk	NW	50
Alaska, Kewaunee	E	300
● *Alaska*, Waukesha	SE	×
Alban, Portage	C	650
Albanville, Monroe	W	×
● Albany, Greene	S	698
Albertville, Chippewa	NW	×
Albion, Dane	S	846
Alden, Polk	NW	20
● *Alder*, Ashland	NW	×
Alderly, Dodge	E	100
● *Aleta*, Polk	NW	×
Algona, Winnebago	E	×
Alhambra, Trempealeau	W	×
● Allen's Grove, Walworth	SE	300
● Allenton, Washington	E	97
● Allenville, Winnebago	E	32
Alexandria, Chippewa	NW	×
Alloa, Columbia	C	19
● **Alma**, Buffalo	W	1,428
● Alma Centre, Jackson	W	300
● Almena, Barron	NW	25
Almond, Portage	C	200
Alstad, Burnett	NW	15
● *Altamont*, Bayfield	NW	×
Altdorf, Wood	C	32
Alto, Fond du Lac	E	97
● Altoona, Eau Claire	NW	805
● *Alva*, Jackson	W	×
Alverno, Manitowoc	E	170
● Amberg, Marinette	NE	400
● Amery, Polk	NW	451
Ame's Station, Washburn	NW	28
● Amherst, Portage	C	433
● Amherst Junc. Portage	C	100
● *Amnicon*, Douglass	NW	×
Amy, Dunn	NW	32
Anchorage, Buffalo	W	32
● Anderson, Grant	W	×
● *Anderson*, Shawano	NE	×
Andrus, Polk	NW	×
Angelica, Shawano	NE	100
Angelo, Monroe	W	×
● Aniwa, Shawano	NE	500
Annaton, Grant	SW	100
Annsburgh, Dunn	NW	×
Anthony, Eau Claire	NW	×
● **Antigo**, Langlade	NE	4,424
Apple Creek, Outagamie	E	26
Apple River, Polk	NW	25
● **Appleton**, Outagamie	E	11,869
● *Appleton Junc.* Outagamie	E	×
● *Arcade Siding*, Fond du Lac	E	×
● Arcadia, Trempealeau	W	659
● Arena, Iowa	SW	354
● Argyle, LaFayette	SW	411
Arkansaw, Pepin	W	250
Arkdale, Adams	C	40
Arlington, Columbia	C	815
Armenia, Juneau	C	185
Armstrong, Fond du Lac	E	32
● Armstrong Creek, Forest	N	×
● Arnott, Portage	C	40
Arpin, Wood	C	×
Arthur, Grant	SW	107
Ashford, Fond du Lac	E	125
Ashippun, Dodge	E	10
● **Ashland**, Ashland	NW	9,956
● Ashland Junc. Bayfield	NW	×
Ash Ridge, Richland	SW	26
Ashton, Dane	S	57
● Askeaton, Brown	E	175
● Athens, Marathon	N	130
● *Atkins*, Forest	N	×
● *Atlantic Junc.* Douglas	NW	×
Attica, Green	S	100
● Atwater, Dodge	E	50
● Auburndale, Wood	C	253
Audorf, Wood	C	×

Place		
● Augusta, Eau Claire	NW	1,187
Aurora, Washington	E	50
Aurorahville, Waushara	C	130
Avalanche, Vernon	W	100
● Avoca, Iowa	SW	278
Avon, Rock	S	150
Aztalan, Jefferson	SW	130
● Babcock, Wood	E	250
Bacon, (see Millston)		×
Badger, Portage	C	52
● Badger Mills, Chippewa	NW	150
Bad River, (see Morse)		×
● Bagley, Grant	SW	179
Bailey's Harbor, Door	NE	175
Bakerville, Wood	C	50
● Baldwin, St. Croix	NW	482
Baldwin's Mills, Waupaca	C	260
Balmoral, Richland	SW	×
Balsam Lake, Polk	NW	75
● Bancroft, Portage	C	130
● Bangor, La Crosse	W	499
Banner, Fond du Lac	E	40
● **Baraboo**, Sauk	C	4,605
Barber, Iowa	SW	38
● *Bare Bluff*, Jackson	W	×
● *Barker*, Dunn	NW	×
● *Barker's Spur*, Wood	C	×
● Barneveld, Iowa	SW	3 0
Barre Mills, LaCrosse	W	57
● **Barron**, Barron	NW	829
● Barronett, Barron	NW	250
● *Barrow*, Ashland	NW	900
● Bartel Station, Ozaukee	E	×
Barton, Washington	E	200
Basco, Dane	S	×
Bashaw, Burnett	NW	195
● *Bashaw*, Washburn	NW	×
● Bassett, Kenosha	SE	50
Bass Wood, Richland	SW	45
Batavia, Crawford	SW	×
● *Bateman*, Chippewa	NW	×
● Bay City, Pierce	W	100
● **Bayfield**, Bayfield	NW	1,373
Bay Settlement, Brown	E	200
● *Bay View*, Door	E	386
● Bay View, Milwaukee	SE	195
Beans Eddy, Marathon	N	×
Bear Creek, Barron	NW	×
● Bear Creek, Outagamie	E	65
● Bears, Wood	C	×
● *Bear Skin*, Oneida	N	×
Bear Valley, Richland	SW	65
Beaver, Marinette	NE	260
Beaver Creek, Jackson	W	40
● Beaver Dam, Dodge	E	4,222
● *Beaver Dam Junc.* Dodge	E	×
● Becker, Outagamie	E	45
Beechwood, Sheboygan	E	10
● *Beef Slough*, Buffalo	W	×
Beet, Waushara	C	×
Beetown, Grant	SW	400
● Beldenville, Pierce	W	125
● Belgium, Ozaukee	E	400
Bell Center, Crawford	SW	40
Bellefountain, Columbia	C	12
● Belle Plaine, Shawano	NE	150
Belleville, Dane	S	319
Bellevue, Shawano	NE	26
● Bellmont, LaFayette	SW	378
● Beloit, Rock	S	6,315
● *Beloit Junction*, Rock	S	×
Bern, Green	S	35
● Bennetts Siding, D'glass	NW	×
● *Benoit*, Bayfield	NW	×
● Benton, La Fayette	SW	414
● Berlin, Green Lake	C	4,149
Bernhard, Jefferson	SE	×
● Berryville, Kenosha	SE	58
Bessemer, (see North Freedom)		×
Big Bend, Chippewa	NW	27
Big Bend, Waukesha	SE	65
Big Falls, Waupaca	C	×
Big Flats, Adams	C	239
Big Patch, Grant	SW	175
Big River, Pierce	W	25
Big Spring, Adams	C	200
● *Big Suamico*, Brown	E	×
● Big Wausaukee, Marin't	NE	200
Bing, Fond du Lac	E	×
Binghampton, Outagamie	E	390
● *Birch*, Ashland	NW	×
Birch, Chippewa	NW	40
● Birnamwood, Shawano	NE	500
Bismarck, Lincoln	C	65
Black Brook, Polk	NW	32
● Black Creek, Outagamie	E	300
Black Creek Falls, (see Athens)		×

Place		
● Black Earth, Dane	S	355
Black Hawk, Sauk	C	100
● **Black River Falls**, Jackson	W	2,261
Blaine, Portage	C	41
● Blair, Trempealeau	W	169
Blairmoor, Dunn	NW	×
Blake, Jackson	W	×
● Blanchardville, LaFyet	SW	450
Blanding, Burnett	NW	32
● Blenker, Wood	C	65
Blodgett, Waukesha	SE	52
Bloom City, Richland	SW	130
● Bloomer, Chippewa	NW	631
Bloomingdale, Vernon	W	125
Bloomington, Grant	SW	587
Bloomville, Lincoln	C	260
● *Blueberry*, Douglas	NW	×
● Blue Mounds, Dane	S	200
● Blue River, Grant	SW	300
Bluff (see Klevenville)		×
● *Bluff Siding*, Buffalo	W	×
● Boardman, St. Croix	NW	100
Boaz, Richland	SW	300
Bob Creek, Chippewa	NW	40
Bohemia, LaCrosse	W	×
Bohri, Buffalo	W	×
Bolt, Kewaunee	E	×
● *Bolton*, Oneida	N	×
Boltonville, Washington	E	150
Bon, Richland	SW	×
Bonduel, Shawano	NE	80
Borth, Waushara	C	×
● Boscobel, Grant	SW	1,570
Bovee, Portage	C	×
Bowen's Mill, Richland	SW	26
● *Bowen's Spur*, Oneida	N	×
Bowers, Walworth	SE	×
● Boyceville, Dunn	NW	200
● Boyd, Chippewa	NW	545
Boydtown, Crawford	SW	×
● *Boylston*, Douglas	NW	×
Boyington, Portage	C	40
● *Boyton*, Wood	C	×
Brackett, Eau Claire	NW	×
Bracy, Burnett	NW	12
Bradley, Marathon	N	×
● *Bradley*, Lincoln	C	32
Bradtville, Grant	SW	300
Brady's, Richland	SW	32
● Branch, Manitowoc	E	200
● Brandon, Fond du Lac	E	660
Brant, Calumet	E	100
Brantwood, Price	N	×
Brasington, Pierce	W	200
Breed, Oconto	NE	40
Briarton, Shawano	NE	40
● Bridgeport, Crawford	SW	150
Briggsville, Marquette	C	150
Brighton, Kenosha	SE	30
● Brillion, Calumet	E	582
Brinkman, Vernon	W	×
● Bristol, Kenosha	SE	80
Bristow, Vernon	W	30
British Hollow, Grant	SW	200
● Brodhead, Green	S	1,461
● Brookfield, Waukesha	SE	200
● Brooklyn, Green	S	1,273
Brookside, Oconto	NE	×
● *Brookside Station* Oc'nto	NE	×
Brookville, St. Croix	NW	150
Brothertown, Calumet	E	100
Brown Deer, Milwaukee	SE	77
● Brownsville, Dodge	E	750
● Browntown, Green	S	175
● Bruce, Chippewa	NW	500
● Brule, Douglas	NW	75
Brushville, Waushara	C	65
Brussells, Door	NE	25
● *Bryant*, Langlade	NE	100
● Buckbee, Waupaca	C	40
Buck Creek, Richland	SW	33
● *Buckhorn*, Milwaukee	SE	×
Buena Vista, Portage	C	97
Buffalo, Buffalo	W	223
● Buncombe, La Fayette	SW	165
Bungert, Outagamie	E	32
Bunyan, Polk	NW	×
● Burke, Dane	S	25
● Burkhardt, St. Croix	NW	75
● Burlington, Racine	SE	2,043
● Burnett, Dodge	E	35
● Burnett Junction, Dodge	E	140
Burns, LaCrosse	W	32
Burr, Vernon	W	40
Burr Oak, LaCrosse	W	65
Burton, Grant	SW	15

Place		
● *Burt's Siding*, Clark	NW	×
Bushman's Marathon	N	×
Busseyville (see Sumner)		×
Butler, Milwaukee	SE	150
Butte des Morts, Winnebago	E	110
● Butternut, Ashland	NE	400
Byrd's Creek, Richland	SW	×
● Byron, Fon du Lac	E	50
● Cable, Bayfield	NW	65
Cadiz, Green	S	100
● Cadott, Chippewa	NW	889
Cady Mills, St. Croix	NW	150
● Cainville, Rock	S	×
● Calamine, Rock	S	300
Caldwell, Racine	SE	200
● Caledonia, Racine	SE	97
● *Caledonia Mine*, Ash'l'd	NW	×
● Calhoun, Waukesha	SE	130
Calhoun, Chippewa	NW	×
● *Callon*, Marathon	N	×
Calumet Harbor, Fond du Lac	E	176
Calumetville, Fond du Lac	E	×
● *Calumet Siding*, Manito'oc	E	×
● Calvary, Fond du Lac	E	83
● *Calvert*, La Crosse	W	×
● Cambria, Columbia	C	524
Cambridge, Dane	S	452
● Cameron, Barron	NW	300
● Campbellsport, Fond du Lac	E	313
● Camp Douglas, Juneau	C	225
● *Camp Fire*, Wood	C	×
● *Camp Ground*, Fond du Lac	E	×
● Camp Lake, Kenosha	SE	×
● *Camp No. 4*, Oneida	N	×
● Canton, Barron	NW	48
Carlton, Kewaunee	E	100
Carnot, Door	NE	×
Caroline, Shawano	NE	50
Carrie, Washburn	NW	×
● *Carrollton*, Dunn	NW	32
● ***Carson*, Ashland**	**NW**	×
● Cartwright, Chippewa	NW	400
● *Cary*, Wood	C	×
● *Cary Siding*, St. Croix	NW	×
● Caryville, Dunn	NW	80
Cascade, Sheboygan	E	250
Casco, Kewaunee	E	100
Casco Pier, Kewaunee	E	×
● Cashton, Monroe	W	122
Casimir, Portage	C	×
Cassel, Sauk	C	130
● Cassville, Grant	SW	886
Castle Rock, Grant	SW	300
Cataract, Monroe	W	109
● *Catawba*, Price	N	×
● Cato, Manitowoc	E	150
● *Cavoit*, Marinette	C	×
● Cavour, Forest	N	33
Cazenovia, Richland	SW	176
● Cecil, Shawano	NE	130
● Cedar, Ashland	NW	×
● Cedarburgh, Ozaukee	E	1,361
● Cedar Creek, Washington	E	50
● Cedar Falls, Dunn	NW	400
● Cedar Grove, Sheboygan	E	650
● *Cedarhurst*, Clark	NW	×
Cedar Lake, Waushara	C	40
● *Cedar Lake*, Washington	E	×
Cedar Rapids, Waupaca	C	×
● *Cedarville*, Marinette	NE	×
Cementville, (see Lindwerm)		×
Center, Rock	S	65
● *Centerville*, Manitowoc	E	390
● Centralia, Wood	C	1,435
● *Central Junc.*, Chippewa	NW	×
● Centreville, Trempealeau	W	65
Chamberlin, Waukesha	SE	×
Champagne, Lincoln	C	×
● *Chandler*, Washburn	NW	×
● *Chapin*, Marinette	NE	×
● *Chapman*, Saint Croix	S	×
Charlesburg, Calumet	E	100
Chase, Oconto	NE	×
Chaseburgh, Vernon	W	200
● *Charme*, Crawford	SW	×
Chat, Lincoln	C	195
Cheeseville, Door	NE	100
● Chelsea, Taylor	NW	300
● *Cheney*, Columbia	C	×
Cherokee, Marathan	N	×
● Chester, Dodge	E	32
● Chetek, Barrow	NW	406
Chicago Junc. Washburn	NW	25
Chili, Clark	NW	×

 Wisconsin Wisconsin

● **Chilton**, Calumet	E	1,424
Chimney Rock, Tempealeau	W	40
Chippewa City, Chippewa	NW	139
● **Chippewa Falls**, C'w	NW	8,670
Chippewa Landing, Chi'pea	NW	×
Christiana, Dane	S	×
Christie, Clark	NW	40
● City Point, Jackson	W	32
Clam Falls, Polk	NW	50
● *Clarendon*, Saint Croix	NW	×
Clark's Mills, Manitowoc	E	120
Clarkson, Dane	L	×
● Clarno, Greene	S	77
Clay Banks, Door	E	75
Clayfield, Pierce	W	×
● Clayton, Polk	NW	250
● Clear Lake, Polk	NW	500
Clemansville, Winnebago	E	1,500
Cleveland, Manitowoc	E	×
Clifton, Monroe	W	10
Clifton, Calumet	E	×
Clifton Mills, Pierce	W	×
● *Cliff House*, Sauk	C	×
● Clinton, Rock	S	856
● Clintonville, Waupaca	C	1,466
Clontarf, Dane	S	×
● *Cloverdale*, Juneau	C	×
Clyde, Iowa	SW	32
Clyde, Kewaunee	E	32
● Clyman, Dodge	E	1,283
● Cobb, Iowa	SW	200
● *Cobbs*, Rock	S	265
● Cochrane, Buffalo	W	40
● Colby, Clark	NW	600
Cold Spring, Jefferson	SE	82
Colebrook, Waushara	C	×
● Coleman, Marinette	NE	250
● Colfax, Dunn	NW	350
● Colgate, Waukesha	SE	×
Collins, (see South Wayne)...		×
● *Collins*, Marinette	NE	×
Coloma, Waushara	C	75
● Coloma Station, Waushara	C	200
● Columbus, Columbia	C	1,977
● *Combined Locks*, Outag'e	E	×
● *Combs*, Lincoln	C	×
● Commonwealth, Flor'e	NE	550
Como Bay, Fond du Lac	E	×
● Comstock, Barron	NW	100
Concord, Jefferson	SE	200
Conners, (see West Superior)		×
Connersville, Dunn	NW	20
● *Conover*, Onedia	N	×
Cooksville, Rock	S	100
Cook Valley, Chippewa	NW	100
● *Coolidge*, Price	N	77
● *Coombs*, Lincoln	C	×
Coomer, Burnett	NW	×
Coon Valley, Vernon	W	48
Cooperstown, Manitowoc	E	250
● *Cornier*, Brown	E	×
Corning, Lincoln	C	65
● *Corning*, Columbia	C	×
Cortlandt, Trempealeau	W	×
Coryville, Kewaunee	E	×
Cosgrove, Barron	NW	10
● Cottage Grove, Dane	S	50
● *Cottonwood*, Price	N	×
● *County Line*, Milwaukee	SE	×
Cousins, (see Fall Creek)		×
Cox, Chippewa	NW	57
● *Cranberry Centre*, Juneau	C	×
Craft, Chippewa	NW	130
● Cranberry Center, Juneau	C	97
Crandon, Forest	N	×
Cream, Buffalo	W	×
● Crete, Winnebago	E	12
Crivitz, Marinette	NE	100
Crocker's Landing, Portage	C	32
Cronk, Brown	E	×
● Cross Plains, Dane	S	500
Crystal Lake, Waupaca	C	27
● Cuba City, Grant	SW	450
● Cumberland, Barron	NW	1,219
Curran, Kewaunee	E	×
Curry, Ashland	NW	×
● Curtiss, Clark	NW	200
Cushing, Polk	NW	×
● Custer, Portage	C	64
● *Cutter*, Douglas	NW	×
● Cylon, St. Croix	NW	75
Cypress, Kenosha	SE	×
Dacada, Sheboygan	E	20
Dakota, Waushara	C	40
● Dale, Outagamie	E	100
Dallas, Barron	NW	75
● Daly, Wood	C	×

Danby's Spur, Bayfield	NW	×
● Dancy, Marathon	N	97
● Dane, Dane	S	225
Danville, Dodge	E	250
Darbellary, Kewaunee	E	×
Darboy, Calumet	E	32
● Darien, Walworth	SE	354
● **Darlington**, LaFay'e	SW	1,589
Darrow, Jackson	W	69
● **Dartford**, Green Lake	C	204
● *Darwin*, Dane	S	×
● *Dauby*, Bayfield	NW	×
Davis, Dunn	NW	26
Davis Corners, Adams	C	×
Day, Clark	NW	40
Dayton, Greene	S	250
● Deansville, Dane	S	100
Debello, Vernon	W	32
● *Decker's*, Ozaukee	E	×
Decora Prairie, Trempeal'u	W	260
Dedham, Douglas	NW	×
● Deerbrook, Langlade	NE	65
● Deerfield, Dane	S	338
● Deer Park, St. Croix	NW	100
● *Deer Tail*, Chippewa	NW	×
● DeForest, Dane	S	150
Dekorra, Columbia	C	25
Delafield, Waukesha	SE	200
● Delavan, Walworth	SE	2,038
Delavan Lake, Walworth	SE	×
Delhi, Winnebago	E	×
Dell, Vernon	W	32
Dells Dam, La Crosse	W	×
● *Dell's Mill*, Eau Claire	NW	×
Dell Prairie, Adams	C	45
Delton, Sauk	C	200
Denmark, Brown	E	100
Denny, Marathon	N	×
Denzer, Sauk	N	×
● DePere, Brown	E	3,625
● Deronda, Polk	NW	50
DeSoto, Vernon	W	355
● *Dessert Junction*, Marathon	N	×
Detroit Harbor, Door	NE	×
Deuster, Juneau	C	97
Devies Lake, Sauk	C	×
Dexter Corners, Kenosha	SE	×
● Dexterville, Wood	C	354
● Diamond Bluff, Pierce	W	100
Dickeysville, Grant	SW	68
● Dillman, Milwaukee	SE	×
Disco, Jackson	W	×
Dixon, Richland	SW	×
Dobbston, Langlade	NE	260
● Dodge, Trempealeau	W	500
Dodge's Corners, Wauke'a	SE	45
● **Dodgeville**, Iowa	SW	1,722
Doelle, Buffalo	W	×
Dogwood, (see Saxon)		×
Door Creek, Dane	S	65
● Dorchester, Clark	NW	350
Doty, Fond du Lac	E	×
Dotyville, Fond du Lac	E	97
Douglas Centre, Marquette	C	97
● Dousman, Waukesha	SE	100
● Dover, Racine	SE	77
● Downing, Dunn	NW	425
● Downsville, Dunn	NW	400
● Doylestown, Columbia	C	125
● Dresser Juncton, Polk	NW	50
● *Drexel*, Langslade	NE	×
● Druecker, Ozaukee	E	325
● Drummond, Bayfield	E	50
Dry Bone, Iowa	SW	40
Drywood, Chippewa	NW	50
● Duck Creek, Brown	E	2,500
● *Duck Creek*, Brown	E	×
Dudley, Lincoln	C	65
● Dunbar, Marinette	NE	57
● Dunbarton, LaFayette	SW	16
● Dundas, Calumet	E	75
Dundee, Fond du Lac	E	125
● Dunnville, Dunn	NW	100
● *Dunsmore*, Marinette	NE	×
● Duplainville, Waukesha	SE	25
Dupont, Waupaca	C	60
● **Durand**, Pepin	W	1,154
Durham, Waukesha	SE	100
Duvall, Kewaunee	E	1,600
Dyckesville, Kewaunee	E	40
● Eagle, Waukesha	SE	500
Eagle Corners, Richland	SW	67
Eagle Creek, (see Alma)		×
● Eagle Point, Chippewa	NW	35
● Eagle River, Oneida	N	1,154
Eagleton, Chippewa	NW	350
East Bristol, Dane	S	40

● *EastCady Mills*, St.Cro'x	NW	×
East Delavan, Walworth	SE	13
East Farmington, Polk	NW	250
East Gibson, Manitowoc	E	×
● East Lincoln, Polk	NW	150
● *East Madison*, Dane	S	×
Eastman, Crawford	SW	75
East Marinette, (see Marinette)		×
East Middleton, Dane	S	85
Easton, Adams	C	100
East Pepin, Pepin	W	×
● *East Rio*, Columbia	C	×
● East Superior, Douglas	NW	100
East Troy, Walworth	SE	402
● *East Winona*, Buffalo	W	×
East Wrightstown, Brown	E	32
Eaton, Manitowoc	E	150
● **EAU CLAIRE**, Eau Claire	NW	17,415
● *Eau Claire Junction*, Eau Claire	NW	×
● *Eau Claire River*, Clark	NW	×
Eau Galle, Dunn	NW	250
Ebelsville, Fon du Lac	E	×
● Eden, Fon du Lac	E	100
● *Edgar*, Marathon	N	×
Edgar, Marathon	N	×
● Edgerton, Rock	S	1,595
● Edmund, Iowa	SW	50
Edson, Chippewa	NW	300
Edwards, Sheboygan	E	35
Egg Harbor, Door	NE	100
Eidsvold, Clark	NW	32
Ekdall, Burnett	NW	×
● Eland, Shawano	NE	189
● *Elba*, Dodge	E	×
● Elcho, Langlade	NE	×
Elderon, Marathon	E	×
● El Dorado, Fon du Lac	E	200
● Eleva, Trempealeau	W	85
● *Eliot*, Bayfield	NW	×
Elk Creek, Trempealeau	W	40
Elk Grove, La Fayette	SW	100
● Elkhart, Sheboygan	E	115
● **Elkhorn**, Walworth	SE	1,447
● Elk Mound, Dunn	NW	125
Ella, Peppin	W	27
Ellenborough, Grant	SW	200
Ellis, Portage	C	100
● *Ellis Junc.*, Marinette	NE	130
Ellison Bay, Door	NE	97
Ellison Pier, Door	NE	65
Ellisville, Kewaunee	E	25
● **Ellsworth**, Pierce	W	670
Elmdale, Grant	SW	45
● Elm Grove, Waukesha	SE	100
● Elmhurst, Langlade	NE	45
● *Elm Lake*, Wood	C	×
● Elmo, Grant	SW	45
Elmore, Fon du Lac	E	32
Elmwood, Pierce	W	50
Elo, Winnebago	E	25
El Paso, Pierce	W	30
● Elroy, Juneau	C	1,413
El Salem, Polk	NW	32
Elton, Langlade	NE	45
Elvers, Dane	S	50
● Embarrass, Waupaca	C	125
● Emerald, St. Croix	NW	100
Emerald Grove, Rock	S	100
Emmerich, Marathon	N	×
Emmonsville, Marathon	N	×
Endeavor, Marquette	C	×
Ephraim, Door	NE	122
Erfurt, Jefferson	SE	50
Erin, St. Croix	NW	16
ErinCorners, (see Jewett's M's)		×
Esdaile, Pierce	W	300
Esofea, Vernon	W	57
Estella, Chippewa	NW	175
Etna, La Fayette	SW	250
Ettrick, Trempealeau	W	100
Eureka, Winnebago	E	375
Euren, Kewaunee	E	50
● Evansville, Rock	S	1,523
Evanswood, Waupaca	C	
Evergreen, Door	NE	325
Exeter, Green	S	×
Excelsior Richland	SW	200
Exile, Pierce	W	×
Fagerwick, Door	NE	×
● Fairchild, Eau Claire	NW	645
Fairfield, Rock	S	40
Fair Play, Grant	SW	200
Fairview, Grant	SW	×
● Fair Water, Fon du Lac	E	175
Fall City, Dunn	NW	60

Place	Pop.
● Fall Creek, Eau Claire NW	500
Falls of St. Croix, (see St. Croix Falls)	×
● Fall River, Columbia C	283
Fancher, Portage C	×
Fancy Creek, Richland SW	650
Fargo, Vernon W	×
Farmers Grove, Green S	13
Farmhill, Pierce W	×
Farmington, Jefferson SE	60
Farmington Cen., (see Osceola Mills)	×
Farr's Corners, Columbia C	13
Faucher, Portage C	×
Fayette, La Fayette SW	57
● Fayetteville, Walworth SE	50
● Fellows, Rock S	57
● Fennimore, Grant SW	616
Fenton, Ashland NW	×
● Fenwood, Marathon N	×
● Ferryville, Crawford SW	65
Fetzer, Door NE	40
● Fifield, Price W	646
Fillmore, Washington E	97
Fish Creek, Door NE	200
● Fisk, Winnebago E	227
● Fitchburgh, Dane S	×
● *Fitzgerald*, Winnebago E	×
Five Points, Richland SW	×
Flambeau, Chippewa NW	100
Flanner, Marathon N	×
Flintville, Brown E	100
Flora, Grant SW	×
● **Florence**, Florence NE	444
Folsom, Vernon W	40
● **Fond du Lac**, F'd duL'c E	12,024
Fontana, Walworth SE	65
Fontenoy, Brown E	19
● Footville, Rock S	300
● *Forest City*, Bayfield NW	×
● *Forest House*, Waukesha SE	×
● Forest Junction, Calumet E	100
Forestville, Door NE	325
● Fort Atkinson, Jefferson SE	2,283
Fort Howard, Brown E	4,754
● *Fort Howard Junction*, Brown E	×
Forward, Dane S	×
Foscoro, Kewaunee E	150
Foster, Barron NW	×
● *Foster's Spur*, Barron NW	×
● Fountain City, Buffalo W	972
● *Fountain Park*, Milw'k'e SE	260
Fountain Spring House, Waukesha NE	×
Fourmile, Fond du Lac E	32
● Fox Lake, Dodge E	814
● *Fox Lake Junction*, Dodge E	×
● Fox River, Kenosha SE	65
Francis Creek, Manitowoc E	100
Frank, Washington E	×
Franklin, Sheboygan E	110
● Franksville, Racine N	150
Frazer, Shawano NE	520
Fredonia, Ozaukee E	400
● Fredonia Station, Ozaukee E	97
Freeman, Crawford SW	32
Freistadt, Ozaukee E	100
Fremont, Waupaca C	270
● *Fremont*, Waupaca C	390
● *Fremont Station*, Waupaca C	990
Frenchville, Trempealeau W	32
Freya, Burnett NW	×
Friendship, Adams C	550
Frydenland, Forest N	×
Fulton, Rock S	154
Fussville, Waukesha SE	26
Gad, Taylor NW	×
● Gagen, Forest N	45
Galesburgh, Shawano NE	250
● Galesville, Trempealeau W	537
● *Gardner*, Oconto NE	×
Gardner, Door NE	×
Garfield, Portage C	26
● Garth, Oneida N	×
● *Gatliff*, Racine SE	×
Genesee, Waukesha SE	165
● Genesee Depot, Wauk'k'a SE	125
● Genoa, Vernon W	350
● Genoa Junction, Walw'th SE	400
Georgetown, Grant SW	125
Germania, Marquette C	150
Germantown, Juneau C	125
● *Germantown*, Washington E	×
Gibbsville, Sheboygan E	25
● *Gibson*, Milwaukee SE	×
Giffords, Waukesha SE	×

Place	Pop.
● *Gilbert*, Lincoln C	×
● Gile, Ashland NW	×
● Gillett, Oconto NE	59
● *Gillett*, Ashland NW	×
Gillingham, Richland SW	26
● *Gills Landing*, Waupaca C	×
Gilman, Pierce W	50
Gilmantown, Buffalo W	70
Glasgow, Trempealean W	45
● Glenbeulah, Sheboygan E	500
Glencoe, Buffalo W	65
● Glendale, Monroe W	15
● Glen Flora, Chippewa NW	85
● Glen Haven, Grant SW	185
Glenmore, Brown E	32
Glenmont, (see River Falls)	×
● Glenwood, St. Croix NW	1,500
● Glidden, Ashland NW	300
Globe, Clark NW	×
Glover, Sawyer NW	×
● Glover's, Saint Croix NW	×
Golden Lake, Waukesha SE	5
● Good Hope, Milwaukee SE	260
● *Goodnow*, Oneida N	×
● Goodyear, Jackson W	×
● Gordon, Douglas NW	300
● *Gotham*, Richland SW	×
● Grafton, Ozaukee E	431
Grain, Chippewa NW	×
● *GrandCrossing*, LaCrosse W	×
Grand Marsh, Adams C	32
Grandom, (see Maple Works)	×
Grand Prairie, Green Lake C	×
● **Grand Rapids**, Wood C	1,702
● *Granite Lake*, Barron NW	20
● ***Granite***, Wood C	24
● GraniteHeights, Marathon N	×
● *Granton*, Clark NW	×
● **Grantsburgh**, Burn't NW	410
● Granville, Milwaukee SE	65
● Granville Centre, M'lw'e SE	260
● Gratiot, LaFayette SW	275
Grattan, Barron NW	×
● *Gravel Island*, Chip'wa NW	×
● *Gravel Pit*, Fond du Lac E	×
Gravesville, Calumet E	300
Graytown, Dunn NW	×
● **Green Bay**, Brown E	18,290
Greenbush, Sheboygan E	175
Green Grove, Clark NW	65
Green Lake, Green Lake C	32
● *Green Lake*, Green Lake C	×
● Greenleaf, Brown E	300
Greenstreet, Manitowoc E	390
Greenville, Chippewa NW	×
Greenville, Outagamie E	100
● *GreenvilleStation*, Outa'mie E	×
● Greenwood, Clark NW	656
● *Gregory*, Polk NW	25
Gresham, Shawano NE	46
● *Grigg's Siding*, Barron NW	×
● Grimm's, Manitowoc E	25
Grover, Marquette C	×
Guile, Ashland NW	421
Gurnoe, Sawyer NW	40
● *Hadfield's*, Waukesha SE	×
Hadleyville, Eau Claire NW	65
● Hager City, Pierce W	75
Halder, Marathon N	26
Hale, Trempealeau W	×
Hale's Corners, Milwaukee SE	150
Half Way, LaCrosse W	×
Halfway, Taylor NW	×
Hamburgh, Marathon N	32
Hamilton, Waushara C	30
Hamlin, Trempealeau W	103
● Hammond, Saint Croix S	388
● Hancock, Waushara C	50
Hanerville, Dane S	32
Haney, Crawford SW	×
● Hanover, Rock S	200
● Hansen, Wood C	350
Hardwood, Oconto NE	×
Harmony, Vernon W	×
Harper, Polk NW	20
● Harrison, Lincoln C	430
Harrisville, Marquette C	50
Harshaw, Oneida N	×
● Hartford, Washington E	1,296
● Hartland, Waukesha SE	486
● Hartman, Columbia C	32
● *Harts*, Oconto NE	×
Harvey, Jefferson SE	65
Hatchville, Dunn NW	×
● *Hatfield*, Jackson W	40
Hathorne, Douglas NW	27
● Hatley, Marathon N	57

Place	Pop.
Hatton, Waupaca C	45
● Haugen, Barron NW	×
● Hawkins, Chippewa NW	40
● Hawthorne, Douglas NW	27
Hayes, Oconto NE	97
● Hayton, Calumet E	200
● **Hayward**, Sawyer NW	1,319
Hazel Green, Grant SW	426
● Hazelhurst, Oneida N	×
Hazelton, Grant SW	32
● *HeaffordJunction*, Oneida N	×
Heart Prairie, Walworth SE	57
Heath, Clark NW	×
Hebron, Jefferson SE	300
Hedge Hog, Door NE	×
Hegg, Trempealeau W	80
● *Heights*, Marathon N	×
Hein, Clark NW	×
● Helena, Iowa SW	50
● Helenville, Jefferson SE	300
Heller, Lincoln C	×
Helvetia, Waupaca C	×
Hemlock, Clark NW	77
● *Hematite*, Florence NE	×
Hempel, Saint Croix NW	26
Henrietta, Richland SW	×
Henrysville, Brown E	40
Herbert, Pierce W	45
Herman, Dodge E	175
Herold, Buffalo W	×
● Hersey, Saint Croix NW	300
● *Herseyville*, Monroe W	×
Heth, Clark NW	×
Hewittsville, Clark NW	13
● Hewitt, Wood C	260
Hickory, Oconto NE	×
High Banks, Chippewa NW	×
● High Bridge, Ashland NW	325
High Hill, Vernon W	×
Highland, Iowa SW	751
Hika, Manitowoc E	300
● Hilbert, Calumet E	300
Hillsborough, Vernon W	461
Hillsdale, Barron NW	15
● *Hillside*, Florence NE	×
Hillside, Barron NW	×
Hillside, Iowa SW	×
Hingham, Sheboygan E	120
● *Hixon*, Oneida N	×
● Hixton, Jackson W	75
Hoard, Sheboygan E	×
Hofa Park, Shawano NE	32
● *Hogan's Spur*, Wood C	×
Hogarty, Marathon N	65
Holland, Brown NW	32
● *Holland*, Crown NW	×
● Hollandale, Iowa SW	×
● *Holliday's*, Fond du Lac E	×
Hollingshead, Price N	×
Holmen, La Crosse W	90
Holy Cross, Ozaukee E	200
Homer, Grant SW	×
Homewood, Monroe W	40
● *Homewood*, Milwaukee SE	×
● Honey Creek, Walworth SE	100
Hope, Dane S	×
● *Hopkins*, Bayfield NW	×
● Horicon, Dodge E	1,250
Horn's Corners, Ozaukee E	40
Horn's Pier, Door NE	×
Horse Shoe Bay, Door NE	×
● Hortonville, Outagamie E	440
Hotchkiss, Chippewa NW	10
● Houghton, Bayfield NW	×
Houlton, Saint Croix NW	400
● *Howard*, Chippewa NW	×
Howard Grove, Sheboygan E	150
Howard's Prairie, Milwau'e SE	26
Howe, Brown E	×
Howe's Corner, Waushara C	×
● *Hoyt*, Ashland NW	×
Hubbard, Sawyer NW	21
● *Hubbard*, Columbia C	×
● Hubbleton, Jefferson SE	50
Hub City, Richland SW	77
● **Hudson**, Saint Croix NW	2,885
Hullsburgh, Dodge E	50
Hull, Portage C	130
● *Hull's Crossing*, Sheb'gan E	×
● Humbird, Clark NW	288
Humboldt, Milwaukee SE	65
● Hunting, Shawano NE	77
Huntington (see Star Prairie)	×
Hurlbut, Crawford SW	26
● Hurley, Ashland NW	2,267
● *Hurley Junction*, Ashland NW	×
Huron, Chippewa NW	×
Hurricane, Grant SW	90

Husher, Racine..............SE ×
Hustisford, Dodge...........E 513
Hustler, Juneau.............C ×
Hutchins, Shawano.......NE 520
Hyde's Mills, Iowa........SW 130
Hyer's Corners, Dane.......S 32
● *Ilo*, Polk.................N W ×
● Independence, Tremp'u... W 382
Indian Ford, Rock..........S 164
● Ingram, Chippewa.....N W 75
Inlet, Saint Croix...........N W ×
● *Ino*, Bayfield...........N W ×
Interwald, Taylor.........N W 27
Iola, Waupaca...............C 200
● Ipswich, LaFayette......SW 25
● Irma, Lincoln.............C 19
● Iron Belt, Ashland.......N W 57
● Iron Mountain, Dodge....E 200
● Iron Ridge, Dodge........E 200
● Iron River, Bayfield....N W ×
Iron River Junc. Bayfield N W ×
Ironton, Sauk...............C 300
Ironwood, Barron........N W 200
● *Irvine*, Chippewa.......N W ×
Irving, Jackson.............W 45
Isaacson, Pierce............W ×
Isabella, (see Esdaile)........ ×
Island Lake, Chippewa...N W 12
● *Itasca*, Richland........SW ×
Ithaca, Richland...........SW 150
Ives' Grove, Racine.......SE 23
● *Ives' Station*, Racine....SE ×
● Ixonia, Jefferson........SE 300
Jackson, Washington.......E 65
● *Jackson*, Washington.....E ×
Jacksonport, Door........NE 300
Jacksonville, Monroe......W ×
Jamestown, Grant.........SW 97
● **Janesville**, Rock.......S 10,836
Jeddo, Marquette...........C ×
● **Jefferson**, Jefferson...SE 2,287
● Jefferson Junction, Jeff'n SE ×
Jeffris, Lincoln.............C ×
Jenny (see Merrill).......... ×
Jericho, Calumet.............E ×
Jewell Town (see Jewett Mills) ×
● Jewett Mills, Saint Croix. N W 150
● *Joel*, Polk...............N W ×
Johnsburgh, Fon du Lac....E 13
● Johnson's Creek, Jeffer'n. SE 176
Johnsonville, Sheboygan....E 97
Johnstown, Rock............S 100
Johnstown Centre, Rock....S 150
● Jonesdale, Iowa.........SW 45
Jordan, Green..............S 122
● Juda, Green...............S 330
● *Junction*, Dane...........S ×
● Junction, Portage.........C 100
● *Junction*, Columbia.......C ×
● **Juneau**, Dodge.........E 701
● Kansasville, Racine......SE 75
Kasson, Manitowoc.........E 60
● Kaukauna, Outagamie....E 4,667
● *Kaukauna*, Outagamie..E ×
Kayes Park, Walworth...SE ×
Kearns, Taylor............N W ×
Keegan, Oconto...........NE ×
Keene, Portage.............C 100
Kekoskee, Dodge...........E 200
● Kelley, Marathon..........N 250
Kelley Brook, Oconto.....NE ×
Kellnersville, Manitowoc....E 77
● *Kempster*, Langlade.....NE ×
● *Kempton*, Eau Claire...N W ×
● Kendall, Monroe.........W 304
● Kennan, Price.............N ×
● **Kenosha**, Kenosha....SE 6,532
Kent, Langlade............NE ×
Keshena, Shawano.........NE 65
● Ketcham, Fond du Lac....E 50
● Kewaskum, Washington..E 557
Kewaunee, Kewaunee.....E 1,216
Keyeser, Columbia.........C 17
Keyesville, Richland......SW 40
Keystone, Chippewa......N W ×
Kickapoo, Vernon..........W 40
Kickbush, Lincoln..........C ×
● Kiel, Manitowoc..........E 497
Kieler, Grant..............SW 100
● Kilbourn City, Columbia.C 961
Kilbournville, Racine......SE ×
Kildare (see Lyndon Station) ×
● Kimball, Ashland.......N W 100
● Kimberly, Outagamie....E ×
King's Bridge, Manitowoc..E 32
King's Corners, Sauk........C 65
Kingston, Green Lake......C 300

Kinnickinnick, Milwaukee SE ×
Kinnickinnick, St. Croix. N W ×
● *Kipp's Spur*, Clark.....N W ×
Kirby, Monroe.............W 40
Kirby, Monroe..............W ×
Kirchhayn, Washington.....E 77
● *Kirkland*, Sauk..........C ×
Kirkwood, Fond du Lac....E 45
● *Kirkwood*, Sauk..........C ×
● *Kirton*, Marinette.......NE ×
● Klevenville, Dane.........S 50
● Knapp, Dunn............N W 480
Knapp's Creek, Crawford. SW 400
Kneeland, Racine..........SE ×
● Knowles, Dodge...........E 45
● Knowlton, Marathon......N 100
● *Knox*, Price..............N ×
Knox Mills, Price...........N ×
Koepenick, Langlade......NE ×
Kohler, Ozaukee............E ×
Kohlsville, Washington.....E 100
Kolb, Brown.................E 27
Konetz, Marathon..........N ×
● *Korem*, Barron..........N W ×
Koro, Winnebago............E 32
● Koshkonong, Jefferson..SE 25
Kripe, Chippewa..........N W 25
Krok, Kewaunee............E 32
● Lac du Flambeau, Oneida. N ×
● **LA CROSSE**, LaCrosse W 25,090
Ladoga, Fond du Lac........E 25
La Farge, Vernon...........W 19
● *La Fayette*, Monroe.......W ×
● *La Fayette Mills*, EauC'e N W ×
La Grange, Walworth......SE 30
● *Lake*, Milwaukee........SE ×
Lake Five, Washington.....E 32
● Lake Geneva, Walworth. SE 2,297
● *Lake George*, Columbia....C ×
Lakeland (see Comstock)...... ×
Lake Marai, Green Lake....C 160
● Lake Mills, Jefferson....SE 1,053
● *Lake Park*, Calumet......E ×
● *Lake Shore Junction*, Milwaukee.......SE ×
Lakeside, Adams.............C ×
● *Lakeside*, Washburn....N W ×
Lake View, Dane............S 57
Lakeville, Chippewa......N W ×
Lamartine, Fond du Lac....E 200
Lamberton, Racine........SE 65
Lamont, La Fayette.......SW 45
Lanark, Portage.............C 19
● **Lancaster**, Grant.....SW 1,543
● *Lancaster Junction*, G'tSW ×
Landstad, Shawano.......NE ×
Laney, Shawano...........NE 10
Langlade, Langlade.......NE 32
Lannon, Waukesha........SE 1,200
Lannon Springs, Waukesha SE 65
● *Lapham Junction*, Jac'on W ×
La Pointe Ashland.......N W 250
● *Larkspur*, Forest.........N ×
Larrabee, Manitowoc.......I 40
● *Larsen*, Winnebago.......N ×
Lauderdale, Walworth.....SE 60
● Lavalle Sauk..............C 335
La Vass, Vernon............W ×
Lawrence, Marquette.......C 130
Lawrenceville, Outagamie..E ×
● *Layton Park*, Milwaukee SE ×
Leadmine, La Fayette.....SW 32
Lebanon, Dodge............E 32
Leccia, Door...............NE ×
● Ledgeville, Brown.........E 195
Ledyard, (see Kaukauna) .... ×
Leeds, Columbia............C 40
Leeds Centre, Columbia.....C 65
Leeman, Outagamie.........E 130
Lehigh, Barron...........N W ×
● *Lehigh* Chippewa.......N W ×
Leighton, Oconto.........NE 130
Leland, Sauk................C 19
● *Lemonwier*, Juneau.......C 57
Lena, Oconto..............NE 60
Leola, Adams...............C 40
● Leon, Monroe.............W 50
Lepolis, Shawano.........NE 100
Le Roy, Dodge..............E ×
● Leslie, La Fayette.......SW 60
Levee, Columbia............C 33
Levis, Jackson..............W 60
Lewiston, Columbia.........C 82
● *Lewiston Station*, Colu'bia C ×
● Leyden, Rock..............S 60
Liberty, Vernon............W ×

● Liberty Bluff, Marquette..C ×
Liberty Pole, Vernon.......W 41
● Liberty Ridge, Grant... SW 13
Lightning City, Barron...N W 25
Lily, Langlade.............NE 15
Lily Bay, Door............NE 69
● Lima Centre, Rock........S 200
● *Lime Kilns*, Ozaukee.....E ×
● *Lime Kiln Spur*, Dunn. N W ×
Lime Ridge, Sauk...........C 100
Lincoln, Kewaunee.........E 130
Lincoln Centre, Polk.....N W 130
Lind, Waupaca..............C 40
Linden, Iowa..............SW 462
● *Linderman's*, Trempeal'u W ×
● Lindsey, Wood............C 380
● Lindwerm, Milwaukee.. SE ×
Linwood, Oconto..........NE 40
● Little Black, Taylor.... N W 19
● Little Chute, Outagamie.. E 380
Little Falls, Monroe........W 97
Little Falls, Polk.........N W 50
Little Grant, Grant.......SW ×
● *Little Kaukauna*, Brown. E ×
Little Lake, Adams..........C 23
Little Prairie, Walworth...SE 50
● Little Rapids, Brown......E 200
Little Sturgeon, Door......NE 40
● Little Suamico, Oconto..NE 200
Little Wolf, Waupaca....... C 130
● Livingston, Grant.......SW 200
Lochiel, Dunn............N W 15
● Lodi, Columbia........... C 736
Logan, Oconto............ NE ×
Loganville, Sauk............C 200
● *Lombard*, Clark.........N W ×
● Lomira, Dodge.............E 200
● London, Dane..............S 200
Lone Pine, Portage..........C 40
● Lone Rock, Richland...SW 342
Longwood, Clark.........N W 250
Lookout, Buffalo............W 19
Loraine, Polk.............N W ×
Lorettoburgh, Sauk.........C ×
Lost Creek, Pierce......... W 25
Lost Lake, Dodge...........E 32
Louisburgh, Grant........ SW 65
Louis' Corners, Manitowoc..E 40
Louisville, Dunn..........N W 32
Lovass, Vernon............. W ×
Lowell, Dodge............. E 304
● *Lower Town*, Crawford SW ×
Lowville, Columbia.......SW ×
● Loyal, Clark............N W 100
Loyd, Richland........... SW 100
Lucas, Dunn..............N W 40
Lucas Place, Green Lake...C ×
Luck, Polk............... N W 50
Luddington, Eau Claire.. N W ×
Lumberman, Clark...... N W ×
Lumberville, Iowa....... SW ×
Lund, Pierce............... W 30
Luxembourg, Kewaunee.....E 97
● Lyndon Station, Juneau...C 136
● Lynn, Clark............ N W 150
● Lynxville, Crawford.... SW 243
● Lyons, Walworth........ SE 200
● *Lytle*, LaCross............W ×
● *Lytles*, Trempealeau..... W ×
● *McCartney*, Grant......SW ×
● *McCord*, Lincoln..........C ×
● McDill, Portage............C 100
● McKenna, Jackson...... W ×
● *McMannus Spur*, Barron N W ×
McMillan, Marathon.........N 83
● McNaughton, Oneida.....N ×
● Macfarland, Dane.........S 166
Mackford, Green Lake..... C ×
Mackville, Outagamie......E 40
Madely, Portage.............C 69
● **MADISON**, Dane.........S 13,426
● *Magenta*, Eau Claire...N W ×
● Magnolia, Rock...... .... S 125
● *Magnolia*, Rock.......... S 260
● Maiden Rock, Pierce.....W 343
Malakoff, Door........... NE ×
● *Malcolm*, Langlade..... NE ×
● Malone, Fond du Lac.... E 32
● *Malvern*, Oneida......... N ×
● Manawa, Waupaca.......C 350
Manchester, Green Lake.... C 1,052
Mandova, Pepin............W 32
Manhattan, Crawford....SW ×
● Manitowish, Oneida......N ×
Manitowoc, Manitowoc .E 7,710
Manitowoc Rapids, M'n'w'c C 135
Manning, Vernon........ . W ×

● Mannville, Marathon.. ..N 150
● *Manson*, Oneida.........N ×
Manwaring, Sawyer.... NW ×
● Maple, Douglas....... NW ×
Maple Grove, Manitowoc...E 100
Maple Grove, (see Cameron). ×
Maple Springs, Dunn....NW ×
Mapleton, Waukesha. ....SE 100
Maple Valley, Oconto.... NE 1,340
● *Maple Valley*, Oconto..NE ×
Maplewood, Door.........NE 75
● Maple Works, Clark....NW 150
● Marathon, Marathon.....N 258
Marble, Waupaca..........C 195
Marblehead, Fond du Lac...E 130
Marble Ridge, Sauk.........C ×
Marcellon, Columbia........C 40
March, Marathon...........N ×
Marcy, Waukesha..........SE 175
● Marengo, Ashland......NW ×
● *Marietta*, Lincoln..........C ×
● **Marinette**, Marinette...E 11,523
Marion, Waupaca..........C 470
● Markesan, Green Lake... C 475
Marengo, Jackson.........SE ×
Marquette, Green Lake.....C 814
● **Marshall**, Dane........... S 282
● Marshfield, Wood.........C 3,450
Marshfield Junction, Wood. C ×
Marsh Lake, (see Clayton)... ×
Marshland, Buffalo.........W 40
Martell, Pierce.............W 160
Martinville, Grant........SW ×
● Martintown, Green........S 275
Marxville, Dane............S 32
Marytown, Fond du Lac....E 100
● Mason, Bayfield.........NW 500
Mason Junction, Bayfield NW ×
● Mather's Juneau.......... C 100
Matt, Monroe.............. W ×
● **Mauston**, Juneau.......C 1,343
● *Maxwell*, Buffalo..........W ×
Mayfield, Washington.......E 140
May, Outagamie............E ×
● Mayhew, Walworth......SE 26
● Mayville, Dodge.........E 1,051
● Mazo Manie, Dane......... S 1,034
● Meadow Valley, Juneau...C 107
Meadry, LaCrosse...........W ×
● **Medford**, Taylor......NW 1,193
● Medina, Outagamie........E 200
● *Medina Junction*, W'n'b'oE ×
● Meechan, Portage..........C 40
Meeker, Washington........E 65
Meeker's Grove, La Fa'tte SW 195
Meeme, Manitowoc.........E 150
Meggers, Manitowoc.........E 32
Melancthon, Richland.....SW ×
● Mellen, Ashland........NW 200
Melnik, Manitowoc..........E ×
Melnick, Langlade........ NE ×
Melrose, Jackson............W 200
● Melvina, Melrose..........W 59
● Menasha, Winnebago......E 4,581
● Mendota, Dane............S 627
Menekaunee, Marinette....NE 1,800
● Menomonee Falls, W'sha SE 422
● **Menomonie**, Dunn.. NW 5,491
● *Menominee Junct'n*, D'nNW ×
● Mequon, Ozaukee..........E 60
● *Mercer*, Oneida...........N ×
● Meridian, Dunn........NW 100
● **Merrill**, Lincoln..........C 6,809
● Merrillon, Jackson.......W 639
● *Merrill Park*, MilwaukeeSE ×
● Merrimack, Sauk.........C 250
● *Merritt's Landing*, Marquette..................C ×
Merton, Waukesha........SE 200
● Metomen, Fond du Lac...E 32
Middlebury, Iowa..........SW 12
● Middle Inlet, Marinette. NE ×
Middle Ridge, La Crosse....W 19
● Middleton, Dane.......... S 500
Midland, Marquette.........C 19
● *Midland*, Douglas......NW ×
● Midway, La Crosse....... W 250
● *Midway*, Brown............E ×
Mifflin, Iowa............... SW 255
Milford, Jefferson........... SE 128
● Milladore, Wood............C 390
Millard, Walworth.........SE 100
Millburg, (see Brasington).. ×
Mill Creek, Richland.......SW 57
Mill r's Siding, ChippewaNW 25
● *Miller's Spur*, Barron..NW ×
Millersville, Sheboygan..... E 15

Millett, Crawford..........SW 40
Millhome, Manitowoc.......E 50
Mills, Jackson............ W ×
● Mills, Washburn....... NW 30
Mills Centre, Brown........ E 200
Mill Siding, Chippewa....NW 25
● Millston, Jackson........W 300
Millville, Grant..........SW 75
● Milton, Rock.............S 685
● Milton Junction, Rock....S 681
● **MILWAUKEE**, Milwaukee.... ....SE 204,468
Mindoro, La Crosse........W 260
Minehaune, Marinette....NE ×
Mineral Lake, Ashland...NW ×
● Mineral Point, Iowa....SW 2,694
Miner, Wood..............C ×
● *Minerva*, Milwaukee.....SE ×
● Minnesota Junc., Dodge...E 200
Minnewoc, Waukesha.....SE ×
● Minocqua, Oneida.........N 500
Minong, Washburn.......NW ×
Misha Mokwa, Buffalo.....W 50
Mishicot, Manitowoc.......E 150
Mitchell, Fond du Lac......E 38
● *Mitchells*, Portage.........C ×
Modena, Buffalo............W 43
Moeville, Pierce............W 11
Monches, Waukesha........SE 100
● Mondovi, Buffalo.........W 503
● Monico, Forest............N 128
● **Monroe**, Green...........S 3,768
Monroe Centre, Adams.....C 195
Moose Ear, Barron......NW ×
Montana, Buffalo...........W 12
● **Montello**, Marquette....C 761
Monterey, Waukesha......SE 150
● Montfort, Grant........SW 467
● *Montfort Junc.*, Iowa...SW ×
● Monticello, Green.........S 407
Montreal, Ashland.......NW 67
Montrose, Dane.............S 50
● *Montrose*, Mantowoc.....E ×
Moon, Marathon............N ×
Mooney's Mills, Barron..NW 43
● *Moquah*, Bayfield......NW ×
Morgan, Oconto...........NE ×
Morley, Langlade..........NE 32
Morleys, Barron.........NW ×
● *Morris*, Chippewa......NW ×
Morris, Shawano...........NE ×
Morrison, Brown............E 100
● *Morrison*, Price...........N ×
● Morrisonville, Dane.......S 130
● Morse, Ashland........ NW 331
Moscow, Iowa..............SW 50
● Mosel, Sheboygan.........E 32
Mosinee, Marathon.........N 427
● *MosineeStation*, MarathonN ×
Moskonegon, Oneida.........N ×
● Moundville, Marquette... C ×
Mountain, Oconto.........NE ×
Mount Calvary, Fond du Lac E 200
Mount Hope, Grant.......SW 122
● Mount Horeb, Dane.......S 275
Mount Ida, Grant......... SW 100
Mount Morris, Waushara... C 50
Mount Pisgah, (see Cashton) ×
Mount Sterling, Crawford. SW 150
Mount Tabor, Vernon......W 42
Mount Vernon, Dane.........S 150
Mount Zion, Juneau........C ×
● Mukwonago, Waukesha. SE 356
Muller's Lake, (seeSylvanLake) ×
Muncie, Vernon.............W ×
Murry, Chippewa.......... SW ×
● Muscoda, Grant.........SW 605
● *Muskeg*, Bayfield...... NW ×
Muskego, Waukesha........SE 97
Murrays, Chippewa......NW ×
Myra, Washington........... E 50
● Namekagon, Washburn NW ×
Namur, Door..............NE 130
● Nashotah, Waukesha.... SE 20
Nasonville, Wood..........C 300
● NationalHome, MilwaukeeSE 1,800
Naugart, Marathon.........N 950
Navan, Jefferson...........SE 41
Navarino, Shawano........NE ×
● Necedah, Juneau..........C 1,708
● *Necedah Junc.*, Monroe..W ×
● Neenah, Winnebago......E 5,083
● **Neillsville**, Clark....NW 1,936
Nekimi, Winnebago....... E 41
Nekoosta, Wood............C ×
● Nelson, Buffalo.......... W 79
● *Nelson's Siding*, Portage. C ×

Nelsonville, Portage........C 200
Nenno, Washington.........E 130
Neosha, Dodge..............E 200
Neptune, Richland........SW 26
Nero, Manitowoc............E 200
Neshkoro, Marquette....... C 100
Neshonoc, La Crosse........W ×
Neshoto, Manitowoc........E 64
Neury, (see Westby)......... ×
Nevins, Clark.............NW 45
New Amsterdam, La CrosseW 134
Newark, Rock............. S ×
Newberg's Corners, LaC'se.. W 41
New Berlin, Waukesha....SE 390
● *Newbold*, Oneida..........N ×
Newburgh, Washington.......E 289
New Bristol, Douglas.....NW ×
New Cassel, Fond du Lac...E 400
● *New Cassel*, Fond du Lac. E 650
New Centreville, St. CroixNW 100
New Chester, Adams........C 150
New Chicago, (see Eleva).... ×
New Coeln, Milwaukee.... SE 70
New Denmark, (seeDenmark) ×
New Diggings, LaFayette..SW 350
Newfane, Fond du Lac.....L 100
New Franken, Brown...... E 200
● New Glarus, Green.......S 356
● *New Grade*, Clark......EW ×
New Haven, Adams........ C ×
● New Holstein, Calumet...E 426
New Hope, Portage.........C 65
New Knapp, Washburn..NW ×
● New Lisbon, Juneau......C 990
● *New London Junc.*, Waupaca........................C ×
● New London, Waupaca... C 2,050
● *NewLondon Junction*, Outagamie.....................E ×
New Munster, Kenosha....SE 96
Newport, Door............NE 125
New Prospect, Fond du LacE 150
● New Richmond, St. Cr'xNW 1,408
New Rome, Adams..........C 70
Newry, Vernon............ W 32
● *Newton*, Manitowoc...... E ×
Newton, Vernon............ W 140
Newtonburgh, Manitowoc.. E 16
● *Newtown*, Wood...........C ×
Newville, Vernon..........W ×
Nicholson, Waupaca........ C 10
Nickel, Marathon....... ..N ×
Niebull, Adams............. C 28
Niles, Manitowoc...........E 200
Nixcorner, Eau Claire....NW 34
Nobleton, Washburn.....NW ×
Nora, Dane..................S ×
Norden, Buffalo.............W ×
Norman, Kewaunee....... . E 50
● Norrie, Marathon..........N 260
Norseville, Eau Claire....NW 46
North Anover, Grant.....SW 35
North Avenue, Milwaukee SE ×
North Bay, Door..........NE ×
North Bend, Jackson.......W 75
North Branch, Jackson.....W ×
● *North Branch Siding*, Oconto.............. NE ×
North Bristol, Dane..........S 166
North Cameron, Barron..NW 26
North Cape, Racine........SE 50
North Clayton, Crawford..SW 45
● *North Crandon*, Forest...N ×
North Division, Clark .... NW ×
North Eau Claire, (see Eau Clare) ×
Northeim, Manitowoc.......E 50
● Northern Junc, Mil'kee..SE ×
● *Northern Wisconsin Junc.* St. Croix.......... NW ×
Northfield, Jackson.........W 60
● North Freedom, Sauk.....C 316
● North Greenfield, Mil'keeSE 57
North Hudson, St. Croix..NW 26
NorthKaukauna, OutagamieE ×
● *North LaCrosse*, LaCrosseW 26
North Lake, Waukesha....SE 125
Northland, Waupaca........C ×
North Leeds, Columbia......C 50
North Menomonee, Dunn NW ×
● *North Milwaukee*, Milwaukee................... SE ×
North Pepin, (see Pepin).. ×
● Northport, Waupaca...... C 200
North Prairie, Waukesha..SE 200
North Star, Crawford......SW 26
North Valley, Polk........NW ×
North West, Milwaukee...SE ×

● *North West Union Junc.*, Fond du Lac... ....E ×
● Norwalk, Monroe..........W 308
Norway Grove, Dane..........S 32
Norway Ridge, Monroe.....W 13
● *Norwegian*, Winnebago..E ×
Norwell, Waupaca............C ×
Norwood, Langlade.........NE 325
Noys Station, Eau Claire. NW ×
Nutterville, Marathon.......N ×
● *Nye*, Polk..................NW ×
● *Oak*, Price....................N 55
● Oak Centre, Fond du Lac..E 50
● *Oak Creek*, Milwaukee...SE 300
● Oakdale, Monroe.........W 60
Oakes, Sauk....................C ×
● Oakfield, Fond du Lac....E 385
Oak Grove, Dodge.............E 100
● *Oak Grove*, Pierce.........N 55
Oak Hill, Jefferson..........SE 40
Oakland, Jefferson..........SE ×
Oakley, Green..................S 50
Oak Ridge, Pierce...........W 32
● Oakwood, Milwaukee....SE 75
Oasis, Waushara..............C 60
● Oconomowoc, Waukesha SE 2,729
● **Oconto**, Oconto.........NE 5,219
● Oconto Falls, Oconto....NE 79
● *Oconto Junc.* Oconto....NE ×
● Odanah, Ashland..........NW 25
● Ogdensburgh, Waupaca...C 350
● Ogema, Price.................N 250
Oil City, Monroe..............W 71
● Okauchee, Waukesha....SE ×
● Okee, Columbia.............C 200
Olin, Adams.....................C 40
● *Olive*, Chippewa..........NW ×
Olivet, Pierce..................W 200
● Omro, Winnebago..........E 1,232
● Onalaska, LaCrosse......W 1,587
● Oneida, Brown.............E ×
Ono, Pierce......................W 50
Ontario, Vernon...............W 250
● Oostburgh, Sheboygan....E 100
Orange, Burnett............NW 100
● *Orange*, Juneau............C 32
● *Ore Dock Yards*, Ashland NW ×
● Oregon, Dane.................S 595
● Orfordville, Rock...........S 400
Orihula, Winnebago.........E 65
Orion, Richland..............SW 50
● *Ormes*, Saint Croix......NW ×
● **Osceola Mills**, Polk. NW 384
● **OSKOSH**, Winnebago..E 22,836
Oslo, Manitowoc.............E ×
Osman, Manitowoc..........E 32
● Osseo, Trempealeau......W 300
● Ostrander, Waupaca......C 260
Otsego, Columbia............C 100
Ottawa, Waukesha...........C 50
Otter Creek, Eau Claire.. NW 65
Otter Vale, Vernon............N 390
Ottman, Pierce...............W 11
Ourtown, Sheboygan........E 32
Owen, Marinette.............NE ×
Ox Bow, Jackson.............W 32
Oxford, Marquette...........C 100
Pacific, Columbia.............C 97
● Packwaukee, Marquette..C 200
● *Packwaukee Junction*, Marquette..................C ×
● Palmyra, Jefferson.......SE 567
● Paoli, Dane...................S 100
Paradise, Waupaca...........C ×
● Pardeeville, Columbia.....C 292
Parfrayville, Waupaca......C 83
Paris, Kenosha................SE 25
● Park Falls, Price...........N ×
Parnell, Sheboygan...........E ×
● *Parrish*, Lincoln............C 97
Parrish, Langlade...........NE ×
● *Parrish Junc.*, Oneida....N ×
● Paskin, Barron............NW ×
Patch Grove, Grant.........SW 115
Patterson, Polk..............NW 75
Paynesville, Milwaukee....SE ×
● *Pearson*, Bayfield.........NW ×
● Peck, Bayfield..............NW ×
● *Peck's Station*, Walworth SE ×
Pedee, Green....................S 32
● Peebles, Fond du Lac.....E 32
● *Pelican*, Oneida.............N ×
● Pelican Lake, Forest.......N .65
Pella, Shawano...............NE 97
● Pembine, Marinette.....NE 65
● Pence, Ashland...........NW 409
● Pennington, Oneida......N ×

Wisconsin

● Penokee, Ashland.....NW ×
● Pensaukee, Oconto.....NE 40
Peot, Kewaunee...........E ×
● Pepin, Pepin...............W 369
Perkinstown, Taylor.....NW ×
● Perley, Barron.........NW 200
Perry, Dane....................S 50
Peru, Portage..................C 32
● Peshtigo, Marinette.....NE 1,719
● *Peshtigo Harbor*, Marinette....................NE 719
Petersburgh, Crawford....SW ×
● *Peterson's Spur*, Bayfi'd NW ×
● Pewaukee, Waukesha....SE 680
Pheasant Branch, Dane......S 60
● **Phillips**, Price.........N 800
● *Phipps*, Sawyer.........NW ×
Phlox, Langlade...........NE ×
● Pickett, Winnebago.......E ×
Picketts, Green..............S ×
● *Pickett*, Green..............S ×
Pierceville, Dane.............S ×
Pigeon Creek Centre, J'cks'n W ×
Pigeon Falls, Trempealeau. W 45
Pike, (see Amber)........... ×
Pike Lake, Marathon....... N ×
● *Pike River*, Bayfield....NW ×
● *Pikes Quarry*, Bayfield. NW ×
Pilot Knobs, Adams.........C ×
Pilsen, Kewaunee...........E 97
● Pine Bluff, Dane............S 50
● *Pine Creek*, Trempealeau. W ×
Pine Grove, Brown...........E 250
● *Pine G ove*, Manitowoc...E ×
Pine Hill, Jackson............W ×
Pine Knob, Iowa............SW 65
Pine River, Waushara.......C 100
● *Pine River*, Lincoln.......C ×
● Pineville, Polk............NW 50
Pipersville, Jefferson......SE 49
● Pittsville, Wood............C 653
Pittsville Junction, Wood...C ×
Pius, Sheboygan..............E 21
Plain, Sauk......................C 50
● Plainfield, Waushara......C 459
Plainville, Adams.............C ×
● Platteville, Grant...........C 2,740
Pleasant Hill, Crawford..SW ×
● Pleasant Prairie, Keno'h SE 130
● Pleasant Ridge, Clark..NW 21
Pleasant Valley, St. Croix. NW 16
Plier, Shawano.............NE ×
● Plover, Portage..............C 319
Plum City, Pierce.............W 250
● *Plumers*, Buffalo........ W ×
● Plummer, Ashland.....NW ×
● Plymouth, Sheboygan....E 1,503
Point Bluff, Adams...........C 26
● *Pokegama*, Douglas....NW ×
Poland, Brown.................E ×
Polar, Langlade.......... NE ×
Polk, Green......................S ×
Polonia, Portage...............C 165
Poniatowisky, Marathon.....N 97
● Poplar, Douglas..........NW 35
● *Poplar*, Chippewa.......NW ×
Popple, Clark.................NW ×
Porcupine, Pepin.............W 200
● **Portage**, Columbia.......C 5,143
Port Andrew, (see Westport) ×
Port Bass, Wood..............C ×
● Port Edwards, Wood......C 720
● Porterfield, Marinette..NE 97
● Porter's Mills, EauClaire NW 1,195
● *Porters*, Rock............... S ×
Portersville, Eau Claire...NW 60
Port Hope, Columbia.........C 26
Portland, Monroe............ W 20
Portland, Dodge..............E 325
● **Port Washington**, Ozaukee..........................E 1,659
Postville, Green...............S 43
● *Poskin Lake*, Barron...NW ×
● *Potato River Junc.* A'ld NW ×
Potosi, Grant..................SW 600
● *Potosi Station*, Grant..SW ×
Potter, Calumet...............E 150
● Pound, Marinette.......NE 300
● *Powell*, Oneida.............N ×
Poygan, Winnebago..........E 48
● Poynette, Columbia.......C 517
Poy Sippi, Waushara.........C 103
● **Prairie du Chien**, Crawford...........................SW 3,131
● Prairie du Sac, Sauk......C 562
Prairie Farm, Barron.....NW 150
● Pratt, Bayfield.........NW 55

Wisconsin

● Pratt Junction, Forest....N 40
● Pray, Jackson...............W 65
● Prentice, Price...............N 365
● *Prentice Junction*, Price. N ×
● Prescott, Pierce............W 911
● *Prescott Road*, St. Croix NW ×
● Preston, Grant.............SW ×
● Price, Jackson..............W 21
Primrose, Dane................S 10
● Princeton, Green Lake....C 986
Prion, Fond du Lac.........E ×
Prospect, Waukesha.......SE 130
Pulaski, Shawano...........NE ×
● Pulcifer, Shawano.......NE 150
● *Pulp*, Florence...........NE ×
Purdy, Vernon.................W 32
Quincy, Adams.................C 35
Quinney, Calumet...........E 32
● **Racine**, Racine..... .. SE 21,014
Racine Junction, Racine..SE ×
Rainbow, Oneida..............N ×
Randall, Burnett..........NW 13
● Randolph, Dodge..........E 405
Randolph Centre, Columbia. C 26
● Random Lake, Sheboygan E 250
Rangeline, Manitowoc......E 33
Rankin, Kewaunee...........E 27
● Ranney, Kenosha.........SE 32
Rantoul, Calumet.............E ×
Rapp, Monroe..................W 27
Rathbun, Sheboygan..........E 41
Rawlinsville, Marinette...NE ×
Raymond, Racine............SE 75
Readfield, Waupaca..........C 50
Readstown, Vernon...........W 101
● Red Cedar, Dunn.......NW 200
● *Red Cedar Junc.* Dunn. NW 15
● *Red Cliff*, Bayfield......NW ×
Red Mound, Vernon..........W ×
Red River, Kewaunee.......E 200
Reed, Chippewa..............NW ×
● Reedsburgh, Sauk...........C 1,737
● *Reeds Corners*, Fo'd du L'c. E ×
● Reedsville, Manitowoc....E 200
Reeseville, Dodge..............E 329
Regina, Shawano..............NE 33
Reserve, Sawyer.............NW 400
Rest, Vernon...................W ×
Retreat, Vernon...............W 57
● Rewey, Iowa...............SW 90
Reynolds, Oneida.............N ×
Rhine, Sheboygan.............E 25
● **Rhinelander**, Oneida..N 2,658
Rib Falls, Marathon.........N 97
● Rib Lake, Taylor.......NW 368
● Rice Lake, Barron.......NW 2,130
Riceville (see Jackson)....... ×
● Richardson, Polk,......NW 250
Riche's Sauk.....................C ×
● Richfield, Washington.....E 500
Richford, Waushara.........C 100
● **Richland Centre**. R'd SW 1,819
● Richland City, R'chla'd. SW 80
Richmond (see New Richm'd) ×
Richmond, Walworth.......SE 260
● Richwood, Dodge..........E 200
Ridge, Sauk......................C ×
Ridgeville, Monroe...........W ×
● Ridgeway, Iowa..........SW 100
● Riley, Dane.....................S 69
Ring, Winnebago...............E 20
● Ringle, Marathon............N ×
● Rio, Columbia.................C 339
Rio Creek, Kewaunee.........E ×
● Ripon, Fond du Lac.......E 3,358
● *Ripon Junc.* Fon du Lac..E ×
Rising Sun, Crawford.....SW 50
● *Riton*, Rock....................S ×
Ritz Mills, Waupaca..........C 130
● River Falls, Pierce.........W 1,783
River Head, Jackson..........W ×
Riverside, La Fayette......SW 40
Riverside, Shawano.........NE ×
● *River Siding*, Florence. NE ×
Roaring Creek, Jackson....W 40
● Roberts, St. Croix........NW 135
Robinson, Brown..............E ×
Roche-a-Cri, Adams.........C ×
Rochester, Racine...........SE 400
Rockbridge, Richland...SW 100
● *Rock Cut*, Monroe.........W ×
Rockdale, Dane.................S 329
Rock Elm, Pierce..............W 140
Rock Falls, Dunn..........NW 150
● Rockfield, Washington...E ×
● *Rock Junction*, Milwaukee SE ×

Place	Pop.
● Rockland, LaCrosse......W	32
Rock Prairie, Rock.........S	47
Rockton, Vernon...........W	65
Rockville, Grant..........SW	139
Rocky Run, Columbia...... C	×
Rode's Corner, Pierce......W	×
● *Roddy's*, Jackson........W	×
Rodney, Waushara..........C	×
RollingGround, Crawford. SW	×
● Rolling Prairie, Dodge....E	250
Romance, Vernon..........W	65
Rome, Jefferson..........SE	240
Romeo, Marathon........ N	×
● *Romeo*, Marathon........ N	×
● *Romulus*, Oneida......... N	×
Root Creek, Milwaukee... SE	129
Rosecrans, Manitowoc...... E	57
Rosedale, Eau Claire..... NW	200
Rose Lawn, Shawano......NE	×
● Rosendale, Fond du Lac..E	200
Rosiere, Kewanee..........E	×
Roslin, Marquette..........C	41
Ross, Vernon..............W	×
● *Round Bluff*, Juneau.....C	×
Round Hill, (see Arkansaw)..	×
Round Lake, Sawyer.....NW	×
● *Rouse*, Ashland........ NW	×
Rowleys Bay, Door..... .NE	250
Roxbury, Dane.............S	40
● Royalton, Waupaca...... .C	275
Rozellville, Marathon...... N	×
Rube, Manitowoc.......... E	19
● Rubicon, Dodge...........E	250
● Rudd'sMills, Monroe.....W	65
● Rudolph, Wood...........C	195
● *Rugby Junction*, Wash't'nE	×
● *Rummeles*, Oneida....... N	×
Rural, Waupaca.............C	125
● Rush Lake, Winnebago...E	57
Rush River, (see Martell).....	×
● Rusk, Dunn..............NW	50
Russell, Trempealeau...... W	32
Rutland, Dane..............S	45
● *Rutledge*, Grant.........SW	×
Ryan, Kewaunee............E	32
Sabin, Richland...........SW	32
Sager, Marathon...........N	×
Sagole, Outagamie......... E	100
Saint Anna, Sheboygan.....E	390
Saint Augustine, Washing'nE	×
● Saint Cloud, Fond du Lac.E	200
● *Saint Croix*, St. Croix..NW	×
● Saint Croix Falls, Polk.NW	745
● *Saint Croix Junction*, Chippewa..........NW	×
● Saint Francis, Milwa'k'e.SE	500
Saint George, Sheboygan....E	25
Saint John, Calumet........E	52
Saint Joseph, La Crosse.....W	65
Saint Joseph, (see Houlton)..	×
Saint Kilian, Fond du Lac..E	40
Saint Lawrence, Washingt'nE	250
● Saint Louis, Douglas....NW	200
● *Saint Marie*, Green Lake.C	×
Saint Martin's Milwaukee..SE	165
Saint Mary,s Monroe........W	16
Saint Michael's, WashingtonE	32
Saint Nathan's, (see Chase)..	×
Saint Nazianz, Manitowoc.. E	500
Saint Philip, Crawford... SW	×
Saint Wendel, Manitowoc...E	75
● Salem, Kenosha.......... SE	200
Salem, (see Maiden Rock) ...	×
Salemville, Green Lake.....C	×
Salona, Door.............NE	97
Salter, Washington.........E	×
● *Salters*, Juneau..........C	×
● Sanborn, Ashland......NW	×
Sand Creek, Dunn.........NW	125
Sanders, Oneida...........N	×
● *Sanders*, Lincoln.........C	×
● ***Sand Rock*, Ashland...NW**	×
Sandusky, Sauk............ C	100
Sandy Bay, Kewaunee...... E	45
● *Saranac*, Brown...........E	×
Saratoga, Wood.............C	×
● *Satiut*, Oneida............N	×
● Sauk City, Sauk...........C	876
● Saukville, Ozaukee........E	300
● *Sauntry*, Douglas......NW	×
● *Savory*, Pepin...........W	×
Sawyer, Door............ NE	500
Saxeville, Waushara........C	60
● Saxon, Ashland........ NW	300
● Scandinavia, Waupaca....C	100
Schiller, Brown...........E	250
Schleisingerville, WashingtonE	432

Wisconsin

Place	Pop.
● Schofield, Marathon......N	650
School Hill, Manitowoc......E	32
Schultz, Green..............S	×
● *Schwartzburgh*, Milw'keeSE	×
● *Scott*, Oneida............N	×
Scott, Sheboygan............E	200
● *Scranton*, Wood...........C	×
Scotia, Trempealeau.......W	×
Sechlerville, Jackson.......W	97
● *Sedgwick*, Ashland..... NW	×
Seneca, Crawford..........SW	618
Sentinel, Juneau...........C	×
Sevastopole, Door......... NE	32
● *Seven Mile Creek*, Sheb'n.E	×
Sextonville, Richland......SW	150
● Seymour, Outagamie.......E	733
Shamrock, Jackson.........W	62
Shantytown, Marathon......N	41
● Sharon, Walworth........SE	878
● **Shawano**, Shawano... NE	1,505
● *Shawtown*, Eau Claire..NW	×
● **SHEBOYGAN**, Sh'b'n E	16,359
● Sheboygan Falls, Sh'b'n...E	1,118
Shelby, La Crosse..........W	×
● **Shell Lake**, Washb'rn NW	100
● *Shepard's Lake*, Onedia...N	×
● *Sheppards*, Jackson......W	×
Sheridan, Waupaca..........C	350
● *Sheridan Station*, W'paca. C	×
Sherman, Portage.......... C	×
● Sherry, Wood..............C	825
● *Sherry*, Wood.............C	×
● Sherwood, Calumet........E	250
Shilo, Polk...............NW	×
● Shiocton, Outagamie.......E	250
Shopiere, Rock..............S	300
● *Shopiere*, Wood...........C	×
● Shullsburgh, La Fayette,SW	1,393
● *Siding No. 1*, Marinette. NE	×
Sigel, La Crosse............W	57
● *Silica*, Fond du Lac.......E	×
● *Siloam Siding*, Milw'kee.SE	×
Silver Creek, Sheboygan....E	500
● Silver Lake, Kenosha....SE	85
● Silver Spring, Milw'kee..SE	65
Sinsinawa, Grant..........SW	160
Sioux Creek, Barron.....NW	×
Sister Bay, Door.......... NE	×
Slabtown, Grant...........SW	40
Sladesburgh, Crawford...SW	×
Slade's Corners, Kenosha..SE	50
Slovan, Kewaunee..........E	×
Smith, Milwaukee..........SE	×
● *Smith's Spur*, Polk.... NW	×
● *Snell*, Winnebago........E	×
Sniderville, Outagamie......E	57
Snow, Clark...............NW	×
Soldier's Grove, CrawfordSW	200
Somers, Kenosha..........SE	390
Somerset, Saint Croix....NW	250
● *Somers Station*, KenoshaSE	×
South Beaver Dam, Dodge..E	×
● South Byron, Fond du LacE	32
● *South ChippewaFalls*, Chippewa ....NW	×
South Eden, Fond du Lac..E	×
Southern & Western Junction, Fond du Lac...........E	×
South Farmington, Polk.NW	×
● South Germantown, W'h'nE	.50
● *Suth Junction*, LaCrosse. W	×
● South Kaukauna, Outag'i.E	×
● *South Milwaukee*, Milw'eSE	
● South Milwaukee, Milw'eSE	300
● *South Necedah*, Juneau...C	×
South Osborn, Outagamie...E	×
● *SouthOshkosh*, WinnebagoE	×
● South Range, Douglas..NW	50
South Side, Milwaukee.....SE	×
● South Superior, Doug'sNW	100
South Wayne, LaFayette..SW	285
● **Sparta**, Monroe........W	2,795
● *Spaulding*, Jackson....W	260
● Spencer, Marathon.......N	526
● *Sperbeck*, Jackson.......W	34
● Split Rock, Shawano....NE	×
● Spokeville, Clark.......NW	22
● Spooner, Washburn.....NW	400
● Sprague, Barron....... NW	200
● *Sprague*, Juneau.........C	×
● *Spread Eagle*, FlorenceNE	×
Spring Bluff, Adams........ C	83
● *Spring Brook*, Washb'nNW	×
Spring Creek, Adams....... C	26
Spring Dale, Dane......... S	10
● Springfield, Walworth...SE	150
Springfield Corners, Dane...S	50
● Spring Green, Sauk.......C	625

Wisconsin

Place	Pop.
Spring Lake, (see Glenwood)	×
Spring Lake, Waushara..... C	100
● *Spring Meadow*, Milw'e.SE	×
Spring Prairie, Walworth..SE	100
Springvale, Fond du Lac...E	×
Spring Valley, Pierce.......W	100
Spring Valley, Rock........S	×
Springville, Vernon........ W	188
Spring Water, Waushara....C	325
Spruce, Oconto...........NE	48
● *Spur Junction*, Jackson..W	×
Staffordsville, Clark......NW	×
Standart, Iowa............SW	130
Stanfold, Barron.........NW	97
Stanford, Green Lake.......C	×
Stangelville, Kewaunee.....E	×
● Stanley, Chippewa......NW	850
● Stanton, Saint Croix....NW	60
Star, Vernon...............W	130
Stargard, Milwaukee...... SE	×
Stark, Manitowoc..........E	31
Star Prairie, Saint Croix..NW	325
● *State Hospital*, WinnebagoE	×
● State Line, Oneida........N	×
Stearns, Shawano.........NE	×
Stebbinsville, Rock.........S	77
Steinthal, Manitowoc.......E	30
● Stella, Oneida........... N	×
Stephensville, Outagamie... E	130
● Sterling, Clark..........NW	195
● Stetsonville, Taylor.....NW	75
Stettin, Marathon..........N	198
Steuben, Crawford........SW	57
Stevenson's Pier, Door....NE	×
● **Stevens' Point**, PortageC	7,896
Stevenstown, LaCrosse.....W	×
Stewart, Green ....S	100
● Stiles, Oconto...........NE	466
● *Stiles Junc.* Oconto......NE	×
● Stinnett, Washburn....NW	×
Stinson, Outagamie......... E	57
● Stitzer, Grant........... SW	130
Stockbridge, Calumet.......E	500
● Stockholm, Pepin........W	250
Stockton, Portage..........C	×
● *Stockton*, Portage........C	×
● Stoddard, Vernon.........W	150
Stokes, Door..............NE	×
Stone Bank, Waukesha....SE	110
Stoneville, Shawano.......NE	×
Stoops, Dunn.............NW	×
Story, Dane...............S	×
● Stoughton, Dane.........S	2,470
● *Stowell*, Monroe..........W	×
Strasburgh, Langlade..... NE	19
Stratford, Marathon........ N	×
● *Straw Bridge*, LaFayetteSW	×
Strong's Prairie, Adams.....C	130
● Strum, Trempealeau.....W	×
Sturgeon Bay, Door...NE	2,195
● Suamico, Brown......... E	200
Sugar Bush, Outagamie..... E	×
● *Sugar Bush*, Waupaca....C	×
Sugar Grove, Vernon.......W	260
● Sullivan, Jefferson.......SE	75
● *Summit*, Chippewa.....NW	×
● *Summit*, Dane.............S	×
● *Summit*, Florence.......NE	×
● *Summit*, Monroe.........W	×
Summit Centre, Waukesha SE	97
● Summit Lake, Langlade NE	×
● Summit Sta. Fond du Lac E	100
Sumner Barron..........NW	100
Sumner, Jefferson..........SE	73
● *Sunnyside*, Eau Claire. NW	×
● Sun Prairie, Dane.........S	704
● **Superior**, Douglas... NW	11,983
● *SuperiorJunc.* Washb'n.NW	25
Surat, Waupaca............C	45
Surrey, Portage.... C	×
● Sussex, Waukesha.......SE	100
● *Syene*, Dane.............S	×
Sylvan, Richland..........SW	26
● Sylvania, Racine.........SE	78
Sylvan Lake, Langlade....NE	×
Sylvan Spring, Barron...NW	×
Sylvester, Green..........S	×
Symco, Waupaca.............C	125
● Tabor, Racine..........SE	34
Taegesville, Marathon......N	44
Tainter, Dunn.............NW	10
Tamarac, Trempealeau....W	×
Tamarac, Jackson..........W	×
● *Tarbox Junction*, Wood..C	×
Taus, Manitowoc............E	41
● Taycheedah, Fond du Lac.E	150
● Taylor Station, Jackson.. W	90
● Templeton, Waukesha...SE	×

Ten MileHouse, MilwaukeeSE ×
Terrill, Waushara..........C 195
Terro, Clark............NW 56
Tess Corners, Waukesha...SE 97
Thaw Hill, Crawford.....SW ×
● Theresa, Dodge...........E 500
Thetis, Dodge.............E ×
● Theinsville, Ozaukee......E 300
Thirty Daems, Kewaunee...E ×
Thompson, Washington.....E 95
Thompsonville, Racine.....SE 46
● Thorp, Clark..........NW 723
● Three Lakes, Forest.......N 134
Thurman, Columbia...........C ×
Tibbetts, Walworth........SE 41
● Tiffany, Rock...............S 325
Tiffany Creek, Dunn.....NW ×
● Tigerton, Shawano......NE 259
Tilleda, Shawano...........NE ×
Tillinghast, Chippewa.... NW 30
Timme, Oconto...........NE ×
Timothy, Manitowoc.......E 25
Tindahl, Jackson...........W 32
Tirade, Walworth.........SE ×
Tisch Mills, Manitowoc......E 150
Token, Dane.................E 75
Toland, Dodge..............E 69
● Tomah, Monroe.......... W 2,199
● Tomahawk, Lincoln.........C 1,816
● *Tomahawk Lake*, Oneida. N ×
Tonet, Kewaunee............E ×
Tonnar, Dunn..............NW 10
● *Topside*, Bayfield....... NW ×
Tornado, Door.............NE 260
Tousley, Jefferson..........SE ×
Towerville, Crawford.....SW 48
Towne, Portage..............C 195
● *Town Line*, Sheboygan... E ×
Tracy, Shawano.............NE ×
Trade Lake, Burnett..... NW 100
Trade River, Burnett..... NW ×
● Tramway, Dunn........NW 800
● Trapp, Marathon.........N 57
● *Tremble*, Brown...........E ×
● Trempealeau, Trempeal'uW 614
Trenton, Pierce............. W 500
● *Trevino*, Buffalo..... .... W ×
● Trevor, Kenosha..........SE ×
Trim Belle, Pierce..........W 75
Trippville, Vernon..... .... W 88
Triumph, Crawford.........SW ×
Trostville, Milwaukee..... SE ×
Trout, Jackson..............W ×
Trout Brook, Washburn. NW ×
Troy, Walworth.............SE 100
Troy, St. Croix...........NW 20
● Troy Centre, Walworth..SE 200
● Truesdell, Kenosha.......SE ×
Truman, La Fayette.......SW 21
● *Truax*, Eau Claire..... NW ×
Truax, Dunn...............NW ×
● Tunnel City, Monroe..... W 100
● *Tunnel Side Track*, JuneauC ×
● Turtle Lake, Barron. ..NW 230
Tustin, Waushara...........C 200
● Twin Bluffs, Richland..SW 65
Twin Grove, Green..........S 20
● Twin Lakes, Kenosha... SE ×
Two Creeks, Manitowoc....E ×
● Two Rivers, Manitowoc...E 2,870
● *TwoRiversJunc*, M'n't'w'cE ×
● *Tyrone*, Dunn............NW ×
Tyrone, Green...............S ×
Ula, Green...................S ×
● *Ulao*, Ozaukee............E ×
Ulysses, Barron.......... NW N
● Underhill, Oconto...... NE ×
Union, Eau Claire........ NW ×
Union, Rock..................S 31
● Union Centre, Juneau.... C 175
Union Church, Racine.....SE 35
● Union Grove, Racine....SE 432
Union Mills, Iowa.........SW 15
Uniontown, (see Monico) .... ×
● Unity, Marathon...........N 700
● Upson, Ashland......... NW 400
Urban, Buffalo.......... W ×
Urne, Buffalo...............W ×
Urquhart, Taylor.........NW ×
Urwald, Marathon..........N 32
Utica, Dane...................S 50
Utley, Green Lake.......... C ×
Vale, Chippewa.............NW 32
Valley, Vernon.............W 25
● Valley Junction, Monroe. W 25
Valton, Sauk.................C 65
● Van Buskirk, Ashland. NW ×

Wisconsin

Vanceburgh, Dunn.......NW 50
● Van Dyne, Fond du Lac...E 75
● *Van Horne*, Marinette..NE ×
Vanville, (see Bloomer)...... ×
Vanzile, Forest.............N ×
Varner, Chippewa....... NW ×
● *Veazie*, Washburn..... NW 28
● *Vedum*, Wood..............C ×
● ***Veefkind*, Clark....... NW** ×
Velp, Brown.................E 91
● Vernon, Waukesha.......SE 150
● Vernona Junc. Chip'wa. NW 49
● Verona, Dane...............S 100
● Vesper, Wood...............C 300
● Victory, Vernon...........W 103
Vienna, Walworth..........SE 65
Viking, Pierce...............W ×
Vilas, Dane...................S 45
Vincent, Burnett...........NW ×
Vineland, Winnebago...... E ×
Viola, Richland...........SW 120
● **Viroqua**, Vernon......... W 1,270
● *Viroqua Junc.* Monroe.. W ×
Volga, Polk................ NW 30
Voseville, Door.............NE 130
Wagon Landing, Polk....NW 32
Wakefield, Outagamie...... E ×
● *Walbridge*, Douglas....NW ×
● Waldo, Sheboygan........ E 160
Waldrick, Iowa.............SW ×
● Wales, Waukesha.........SE ×
Walhain, Kewaunee........... E 32
Wall, Forest................N 66
Wallace, Sawyer............NW ×
Walworth, Walworth...... SE 250
Waneka, Dunn..............NW ×
● Warner, Chippewa..... NW 100
Warlich, Marathon..........N ×
Warren, (see Roberts) ...... ×
● Warren Mills, Monroe.... W 200
● Washburn, Bayfield.... NW 3,039
Washburn, Grant......... SW ×
Washington Harbor, Door NE 33
Washington Island, Door NE 33
● *Waterbury*, Jackson..... W ×
Waterford, Racine.........SE 448
● Waterloo, Jefferson..... SE 862
Waterman, Clark........NW 20
● Watertown, Jefferson...SE 8,755
● *Watertown Junc.* Jeff....SE ×
Waterville, (see Arkansaw)... ×
Waterville, Waukesha..... SE 150
Wattsville, Milwaukee.... SE 32
Waubeek, Dunn.............NW 55
● *Wauboo*, Price..............N ×
Waucousta, Fond du Lac....E 50
● Waudena, Oneida..........N ×
● Waukau, Winnebago..... E 350
Waukechon, Shawano.... NE ×
● **Waukesha**, WaukeshaSE 6,321
Waumandee, Buffalo........W 952
● Waunakee, Dane..........S 312
● **Waupaca**, Waupaca.....C 2,127
● Waupun, Fond du Lac.... E 2,757
● **Wausau**, Marathon.....N 9,253
● *Wausau Junc.* Marathon N ×
● *Wausaukee*, Marinette. NE ×
● Wausemon, Green.........S 19
Wautoma, Waushara.....C 300
● Wauwatosa, Milwaukee. SE 900
● Wauzeka, Crawford.....SW 350
Waverly, Pierce........... W 75
Wayne, Washington.........E 75
Wayside, Brown..............E 50
● *Webb Centre*, Clark.... NW ×
Weber, Marathon............N 35
● *Webster*, Portage..........C ×
Weedens, Sheboygan........E ×
Weil, Washington............E ×
Wein, Marathon..............N 100
Weiner, Waukesha.........SE ×
Wells, Marinette...........NE ×
Wentworth, Douglas..... NW ×
Wequiock, Brown.............E 250
● Werley, Grant.........SW ×
Werner, Juneau............C ×
● **West Bend**, Wash'ton..E 1,296
West Bloomfield, Waushara.C 20
● Westboro, Taylor....... NW 200
West Branch, Richland...SW ×
● Westby, Vernon...........W 186
West Denmark, Polk.....NW 150
● West DePere, Brown......E 2,200
● *West Eau Claire*, E Cl'eNW ×
● Western Union, Racine. SE 35
● Westfield, Marquette..... C 500
Westford, Richland.......SW ×

Wisconsin

West Granville, Milw'kee.SE 195
● *West Greenville*, Outaga'ieE ×
West Lima, Richland...... SW 150
West Merrill, (see Merrill) .. ×
West Middleton, Dane.......S ×
West Milwaukee Milw'keeSE ×
Weston, Dunn........... NW ×
Weston Rapids, Clark... NW ×
West Pansaukee, Oconto. NE ×
West Point, Columbia.......S 57
Westport, Richland.......SW 150
West Prairie, Vernon......W 26
● West Rosendale, F.duLac. E ×
● West Salem, LaCrosse.... W 542
● West Superior, DouglasNW 14,000
West Sweden, Polk........NW 300
● Weyauwega, Waupaca....C 706
● Weyerhauser, Chip'wa..NW 100
● Wheatland, Kenosha...SE ×
Wheatville, Crawford.....SW 45
● Wheeler, Dunn...........NW 100
● Whitcomb, Shawano.... NE 97
● White Birch, Douglas..NW 65
White Creek, Adams........C 650
● White Fish Bay, Milw'e, SE ×
● **Whitehall**, TrempeleauW 304
White Mound, Sauk.........C 36
White Oak, LaFayette ....SW 98
● *White River*, Ashland. .NW ×
● White Water, Walworth. SE 4,359
Whittlesey, Taylor........NW 97
Wilcox, Clark..............NW 12
● *Wilcox*, Marinette..... NE ×
● *Wilders*, Marathon.......N ×
Wild Rose, Waushara.......C 200
Wildwood, St. Croix......NW 400
● *Wiley*, Oneida...........N ×
● *Williams Bay*, Walworth. SE ×
Williamsburg, Milwaukee. SE 3,133
Wilmot, Kenosha..........SE 188
Wilson, St. Croix.........NW 393
● Wilton, Monroe..........W 243
Winchester, Winnebago.....E 100
Wind Lake, Racine........SE ×
● Windsor, Dane.............S 75
Winfield, Waukesha.......SE ×
● Winnebago, Winnebago...E ×
Winneoka, Clark.........NW ×
● Winneconne, Winnebago..E 1,086
● *Winona Junc.*, LaCrosseW ×
Winooski, Sheboygan........E 100
Wiota, LaFayette.........SW 119
● Withee, Clark..........NW 65
Withee, Jackson............W ×
● Wittenberg, Shawano...NE 726
Wolf Creek, Polk.........NW 100
● *WolfRiverJunc.*, LangladeNE ×
● Wonewoc, Juneau.........C 619
Wood, Vernon...............W ×
Woodboro, Oneida............N ×
● Woodford, La Fayette ..SW ×
● Woodhull, Fond du Lac...E 35
Wood Lake, Burnett......NW 400
● Woodland, Dodge....... .. E 100
● Woodman, Grant.........SW 150
● Woodruff, Oneida......... N ×
Wood River, Burnett.....NW 18
Woodside, (see Brookville).. ×
Woodstock, Richland..... SW 100
● Woodville, St. Croix.....NW 400
● **Woodworth, Kenosha....SE** 135
● Worcester, Price... .....N ½
● *Wright Ferry*, CrawfordSW ×
Wrightstown, Brown....... E 476
● *Wrightstown Sta.* Brown. E ×
● Wrightsville, Jackson.... W 45
Wuertsburg, Marathon...... N 47
● Wyalusing, Grant.......SW 120
Wyeville, Monroe.......... W ×
● Wyocena Columbia.......C 1,301
Wyoming, Iowa.............SW 15
Yankeetown, Crawford...SW ×
Yellow River, (see Grantsburg) ×
Yellow Stone, LaFayette..SW 32
York, Jackson.............. W ×
York Centre, Dane..........S ×
Yorkville, Racine......... SE 32
Yonng America, WashingtonE 165
Yuba, Richland........... SW 63
Zaris, Kewaunee.............E ×
● *Zedah*, Jackson......... W ×
Zion, Winnebago.............E ×
Zittan, Winnebago............E 35
Zoar, Winnebago............E 65

WYOMING.

COUNTIES.	INDEX.	POP.
Albany	SE	8,865
Big Horn	S	×
Carbon	S	6,857
Converse	E	2,738
Crook	NE	2,338
Fremont	N	2,463
Johnson	N	2,357
Laramie	SE	16,777
Nat. Park Reservation	NW	×
Natrona	C	1,094
Sheridan	N	1,972
Sweetwater	C	4,941
Uinta	W	7,881
Weston	E	2,422
Total		60,705

TOWN.	COUNTY.	INDEX.	POP.
Adaville	Uinta	W	10
Afton	Uinta	W	10
Alamo	Big Horn	S	×
● *Allen Junction*	Carbon	S	×
● Almond	Sweetwater	C	60
Almy	Uinta	W	600
● *Almy Junction*	Uinta	W	2,500
Altamont	Carbon	S	×
Altona	Big Horn	S	×
● *Altus*	Laramie	SE	×
Alva	Crook	NE	×
● Archer	Laramie	SE	×
● *Arcola*	Laramie	SE	×
Ariosa	Laramie	SE	×
Arland	Big Horn	S	40
● Aspen	Uinta	W	25
● *Atkins*	Laramie	SE	×
Atlantic City	Fremont	N	150
Auburn	Uinta	W	60
● Aurora	Carbon	S	×
Badger	Laramie	SE	×
Bagg's	Carbon	S	25
Banner	Sheridan	N	60
Barrett	Crook	NE	10
Bartlett	Laramie	SE	×
● *Baxter*	Sweetwater	C	×
Beaver	Converse	E	×
Beckton	Sheridan	N	60
● *Beckwith*	Uinta	W	38
Bennett	Carbon	S	×
Bessemer	Natrona	C	100
Beulah	Crook	NE	25
Big Horn	Sheridan	N	287
● *Big Muddy*	Natrona	C	×
Big Piney	Uinta	W	50
Big Red	Sheridan	N	×
Bingham	Sheridan	N	10
● Bitter Creek	Sweetwater	C	21
● Black Buttes	Sweetwater	C	10
Bonanza	Big Horn	S	50
● Bordeaux	Laramie	SE	25
● *Border*	Uinta	W	42
● *Borie*	Laramie	SE	×
Bothwell	Natrona	C	×
Box Elder	Converse	E	×
● *Bridger*	Uinta	W	30
Brownsville	Fremont	N	×
● Bryan	Sweetwater	C	30
● *Buckhorn*	Laramie	SE	×
Buffalo	Johnson	N	1,087
● *Buford*	Laramie	SE	×
Burlington	Weston	E	×
● *Burns*	Laramie	SE	×
Burnt Fork	Sweetwater	C	15
Cambria	Weston	E	329
Camp Brown	(see Ft. Washakie)		×
● Carbon	Carbon	S	1,140
Carlile	Crook	NE	×
● Carter	Uinta	W	20
● Casper	Natrona	C	544
Centennial	Albany	SE	60
● **CHEYENNE**	Laramie	SE	11,690
● Chug Water	Laramie	SE	80
● *Church Buttes*	Uinta	W	30
Clare	Converse	E	×
Clark	Big Horn	S	×
Cliff	Nat'l Park Res'vat'n	NW	×
● Cokeville	Uinta	W	50
● *Colin*	Laramie	SE	×
Collins	Carbon	NW	44
● *Colorado Junc.*	Laramie	SE	×
Columbia	Weston	E	×
● *Como*	Croo	NE	×
● Cooper	Albany	SE	30
Cora	Fremont	N	×
Corbett	Big Horn	S	30
Cortett	Albany	SE	×
Crazy Woman	(see Trabeing)		×
● *Creston*	Sweetwater	C	×
Crooks Gap	Carbon	S	10
Cummins	Albany	SE	240
● *Dale Creek*	Albany	SE	×
Dallas	Fremont	E	42
● Dana	Carbon	S	253
● Davis Ranch	Laramie	SE	92
Dayton	Sheridan	N	80
Denison	Laramie	SE	×
Derby	Fremont	N	×
Diamond	Laramie	SE	×
Dixon	Carbon	S	50
● Douglas	Converse	E	491
Douglas Creek	Laramie	SE	20
Dry Piney	Uinta	W	×
Dubois	Fremont	N	×
Durbin	Natrona	C	×
Eadsville	Natrona	C	×
● *Edson*	Carbon	S	×
● Eghert	Laramie	SE	10
Elk Mountain	Carbon	S	25
Embar	Big Horn	S	10
Eothen	Crook	NE	25
Ervay	Natrona	C	×
● **Evanston**	Uinta	W	1,995
Fairbank	Laramie	SE	15
Fairview	Uinta	W	×
Fenton	Big Horn	S	×
Ferris	Carbon	E	25
● Fetterman	Converse	C	×
Field City	Crook	NE	10
● *Fillmore*	Sweetwater	C	×
● *Fisher*	Converse	B	×
Fontenelle	Uinta	W	36
Forks	Crook	NE	10
Fort Bridger	Uinta	W	295
Fort Fetterman	Converse	E	150
● Fort Fred Steele	Carbon	S	320
Fort Halleck	Carbon	S	30
Fort Laramie	Laramie	SE	25
Fort McKinney	Johnson	N	291
● Fort Russell	Laramie	SE	553
● *Fort Steele*	Carbon	S	25
Fort Washakie	Fremont	N	20
● Fossil	Uinta	W	25
Francis	Weston	E	×
Freedom	Uinta	W	×
Freeland	Natrona	C	×
French	Carbon	S	×
● *Frewen*	Sweetwater	C	×
Geyser Basin	Nat. P'k Res.	NW	×
Geyser Basin Hot Springs	National Park Reser'n	NW	×
● Gilette	Crook	NE	400
● Glendo	Laramie	SE	×
● Glenrock	Converse	E	300
Gold	Carbon	S	×
Goodwin's Ranch	Laramie	SE	90
Goshen	Laramie	SE	×
● Granger	Sweetwater	C	25
● Granite Canon	Laramie	SE	60
Grant	Laramie	SE	×
Green	Carbon	S	×
● **Green River**	Sweetw'r	C	723
● *Grennville*	Carbon	S	×
Grover	Uinta	W	×
Hailey	Fremont	N	10
Hale	Sweetwater	C	44
● *Hallville*	Sweetwater	C	×
● *Hampton*	Uinta	W	×
● Ham's Fork	Uinta	W	25
● Hanna	Carbon	S	260
● *Harney*	Albany	SE	×
● *Harpers*	Albany	SE	×
Hartville	Laramie	SE	120
Hat Creek	Converse	E	10
Hatton	Albany	SE	72
Headquarters	Carbon	S	×
Hecla	Laramie	SE	×
● *Hereford*	Laramie	SE	×
● Hilliard	Uinta	W	80
● Hillsdale	Laramie	SE	25
Hopkins	Sweetwater	C	×
● *Horse Creek*	Laramie	SE	92
Hotel	Nat. Park Reservat'n	NW	×
● *Howell*	Albany	SE	×
Hubert	Laramie	SE	×
Hulett	Crook	NE	×
Huson	Sheridan	N	×
● *Huttons*	Albany	SE	×
Hyattville	Big Horn	S	50
● Inez	Converse	E	10
Inyan Kara	Crook	NE	30
● Iron Mountain	Laramie	SE	42
● *Iron Mountain Spur*	La'e	SE	×
● *Irvine*	Converse	E	×
● Islay	Laramie	SE	×
Jenks	Laramie	SE	×
● Jerome	Weston	E	×
Kearney	Johnson	N	10
● *Keeline*	Converse	E	×
● *Kelly*	Laramie	SE	×
Keystone	Albany	SE	10
La Barge	Uinta	W	×
Labonte	Converse	E	33
Lagrange	Laramie	SE	10
Lakeview	Laramie	SE	×
Lander	Fremont	N	525
Landgrove	Johnson	N	×
● **Laramie**	Albany	SE	6,388
● *Latham*	Sweetwater	C	×
● Leah	Albany	SE	60
Leo	Carbon	S	×
● *Leroy*	Uinta	W	×
Lewiston	Fremont	N	×
Linden	Crook	NE	×
Little Bear	Laramie	SE	25
Little Horse Creek	Laramie	SE	30
Little Powder	Crook	NE	×
Logan	Johnson	N	×
Lone Tree	Laramie	SE	×
Lone Tree	Uinta	W	×
● Lookout	Albany	SE	12
Lost Cabin	Fremont	N	10
Lost Soldier	Carbon	S	10
● *Lost Spring*	Converse	E	×
Lovell	Big Horn	S	×
● Lusk	Converse	E	253
Lyons	Fremont	N	180
McDonald	Big Horn	N	×
Mammoth Hot Springs	National Park Reservation	NW	100
● Manville	Converse	E	25
Marquette	Big Horn	N	×
● *Marston*	Sweetwater	C	×
Maxon	Sweetwater	C	×
Mayoworth	Johnson	N	×
● Medicine Bow	Carbon	S	25
Meeteetse	Big Horn	S	15
Meriden	Laramie	SE	×
○ *Merino*	Weston	E	×
Mikado	Crook	NE	×
Milford	Fremont	N	×
● *Millis*	Uinta	W	×
Miners' Delight	Fremont	N	150
● *Minturn*	Crook	NE	×
Miser	Albany	SE	×
● *Monell*	Sweetwater	C	×
Moorcroft	Crook	NE	50
Moran	Laramie	SE	10
● *Moss Agates*	Uinta	W	×
Mountain Home	Albany	SE	×
Mountain View	Uinta	W	×
● *Moxa*	Uinta	W	×
Myersville	Fremont	N	×
Myrtle	Johnson	N	×
● New Castle	Weston	E	1,715
Newfork	Fremont	N	60
Nine Mile Creek	Johnson	N	×
● *Node Ranch*	Converse	E	×
North Fork	Fremont	N	60
● *Nugget*	Uinta	W	×
Natal	Albany	SE	25
● *Nutria*	Uinta	W	×
Nylin	Converse	E	×
Ohlman	Sheridan	N	10
Oil City	Natrona	C	×
Ono	Johnson	N	×
● Opal	Uinta	W	10
● Orin Junction	Converse	E	×
Osage	Weston	E	×
Otto	Big Horn	S	×
Otto	Laramie	SE	×
Owen	Albany	SE	×
Paint Pots	Nat. Park Res.	NW	×
Pass	Sheridan	N	10
Patrick	Laramie	SE	×
● *Patrick*	Sweetwater	C	×
● *Pedro*	Weston	E	×
● Percy	Carbon	S	36
● *Peru*	Sweetwater	C	×
Phillips	Laramie	SE	44
● Piedmont	Uinta	W	50
● Pine Bluff	Laramie	SE	40
● *Point of Rocks*	Sweetwater	C	60
Pollock	Albany	SE	×
Powder River	Johnson	N	25
Prager	Albany	SE	×
● *Pyncheon*	Carbon	S	×

● *Ramsey*, Carbon..........S	×
Rankin, Carbon.............S	×
Raw Hide Butte, Laramie. SE	42
● **Rawlins**, Carbon........S	2,235
Red Bank, Big Horn........ S	×
● *Red Buttes*, Albany......SE	25
Red Cannon, Uinta..........W	10
● *Red Desert*, Sweetwater...C	×
Riverdale, Crook...........NE	×
Riverside, Johnson......... N	33
● Rock Creek, Albany.....SE	66
Rockdale, Carbon............S	67
● Rock Springs, SweetwaterC	3,406
Rognis, Fremont............N	15
Rose, Carbon................S	×
Roseville, Albany...........SE	×
Ross, Converse..............E	×
● *Rozel*, Crook............NE	×
● *Sage*, Uinta..............W	×
Saint Stephen's, Fremont.. N	×
Salem, Laramie............SE	×
● *Salt Wells*, Sweetwater...C	×
Sand Creek (see Ferris).....	×
● *Sanders*, Albany........ SE	×
Saratoga, Carbon............S	274
Savery, Carbon............. S	×
● *Schultz Spur.*, Laramie..SE	×
Seminoe, Carbon............S	42
● *Separation*, Carbon...... S	×
● *Shawnee*, Converse.......E	×
Shell, Big Horn............. S	×
Sheridan, Sheridan..........N	3,000
● Sherman, Albany.........SE	25
Shirley, Carbon............. S	×
Shoshone Agency, Fremont. N	100
● *Siding Number Ten*, Wes'nE	×
● *Siding Number Eleven*, Weston......................E	×
● *Siding Number Twelve*, Weston......................E	×
Sibylee, Albany........... SE	×
● *Silver Crown*, Laramie.. SE	×
Silver Crown, Laramie.....SE	36
● *Simpson*, Carbon..........S	×
Slack, Sheridan............ N	×
Slater, Carbon...............S	×
● *Soda Lakes*, Albany..... SE	×
● *Soda Works*, Albany....SE	×
● *Solon*, Carbon.............S	×
South Bend, Laramie......SE	10
South Pass City, Fremont ..N	25
Spencer, Weston........... E	×
Split Rock, Natrona........ C	×
Spring Creek, Big Horn.....S	×
Spring Hill, Albany.........SE	7
Spring of Petroleum, NatronaC	×
● *Strouds*, Natrona.........C	×
Suggs, Sheridan............ N	×
Sulphur, Carbon............ S	×
Summit, Albany............SE	×
Sundance, Crook....... NE	511
Sunshine, Big Horn....... ..N	×
Swan, Carbon................S	6
Sweetwater, Natrona........C	×
Sweetwater Bridge, Carbon. S	×
● *Table Rock*, Sweetwater..C	×
● *Tapioca*, Uinta,..........W	×
Ten Sleep, Big Horn........ S	×
● *Thayer*, Sweetwater......C	×
Thayne, Uinta..............W	×
Theresa, Converse.......... E	30
Thornton, Weston...........E	×
● Tie Siding, Albany.......SE	50
● *Tipton*, Sweetwater.... . C	×
Tolland, Converse..........E	20
Toltec, Albany.............SE	×
Torrey, Big Horn........... S	×
Torrington, Laramie..... SE	×
Trabing, Johnson...........N	10
● *Tracy*, Laramie......... SE	×
Trelona, Laramie ....SE	×
Twobar, Laramie..........SE	×
212 *Mile Post*, Sheridan.....N	×
215 *Mile Post*, Sheridan.....N	×
● Uva, Laramie............SE	10
● *Van Tassell*, Converse...E	×
Vermillion, Sweetwater.....C	×
Volente, Laramie..........SE	×
Voorhees, Converse.........E	×
Walbach, Laramie..........SE	×
● *Walcott*, Carbon.......... S	×
Walcott, Converse.......... E	×
Walters, Natrona........... C	×
● Wamsutter, Sweetwater.. C	×
Ward, Crook...............NE	10
● *Warren*, Laramie........SE	×
Warren, Big Horn..........N	×
Washam, Sweetwater....... C	×
● *Waterfall*, Uinta.........W	×
Webber, Albany.......... SE	×
Webel, Albany.............SE	×
● *Weed*, Carbon..............S	×
● *Wendover*, Laramie..... SE	15
● *Wessex*, Crook..........NE	×
● Wheatland, Laramie.....SE	×
Whitehead, Laramie.......SE	×
Whoop Up, Crook........ NE	10
● *Wilcox*, Albany..........SE	×
● *Wilkins*, Sweetwater..... C	×
● *Wolcott*, Converse........ E	×
Woods, Albany..............SE	8?
● Wyoming, Albany....... SE	87
Yellow Stone National Park, Uinta....................W	467